12th International Workshop on Semantic Evaluation (SemEval 2018)

New Orleans, Louisiana, USA
5 – 6 June 2018

Volume 1 of 2

ISBN: 978-1-5108-6353-8

NAACL HLT 2018

The International Workshop on Semantic Evaluation

Proceedings of the Twelfth Workshop

June 5–June 6, 2018
New Orleans, Louisiana

Introduction

Welcome to SemEval-2018!

The Semantic Evaluation (SemEval) series of workshops focuses on the evaluation and comparison of systems that can analyse diverse semantic phenomena in text with the aim of extending the current state of the art in semantic analysis and creating high quality annotated datasets in a range of increasingly challenging problems in natural language semantics. SemEval provides an exciting forum for researchers to propose challenging research problems in semantics and to build systems/techniques to address such research problems.

SemEval-2018 is the twelfth workshop in the series of International Workshops on Semantic Evaluation. The first three workshops, SensEval-1 (1998), SensEval-2 (2001), and SensEval-3 (2004), focused on word sense disambiguation, each time growing in the number of languages offered, in the number of tasks, and also in the number of participating teams. In 2007, the workshop was renamed to SemEval, and the subsequent SemEval workshops evolved to include semantic analysis tasks beyond word sense disambiguation. In 2012, SemEval turned into a yearly event. It currently runs every year, but on a two-year cycle, i.e., the tasks for SemEval-2018 were proposed in 2017.

SemEval-2018 was co-located with the 16th Annual Conference of the North American Chapter of the Association for Computational Linguistics: Human Language Technologies (NAACL HLT 2018) in New Orleans, Louisiana, US. It included the following 12 shared tasks organized in five tracks:

- Affect and Creative Language in Tweets
    - Task 1: Affect in Tweets
    - Task 2: Multilingual Emoji Prediction
    - Task 3: Irony Detection in English Tweets
- Coreference
    - Task 4: Character Identification on Multiparty Dialogues
    - Task 5: Counting Events and Participants within Highly Ambiguous Data covering a very long tail
- Information Extraction
    - Task 6: Parsing Time Normalizations
    - Task 7: Semantic Relation Extraction and Classification in Scientific Papers
    - Task 8: Semantic Extraction from CybersecUrity REports using Natural Language Processing (SecureNLP)
- Lexical Semantics
    - Task 9: Hypernym Discovery
    - Task 10: Capturing Discriminative Attributes
- Reading Comprehension and Reasoning
    - Task 11: Machine Comprehension using Commonsense Knowledge
    - Task 12: Argument Reasoning Comprehension Task

This volume contains both Task Description papers that describe each of the above tasks, and System Description papers that present the systems that participated in these tasks. A total of 12 task description papers and 184 system description papers are included in this volume.

We are grateful to all task organizers as well as to the large number of participants whose enthusiastic participation has made SemEval once again a successful event. We are thankful to the task organizers who also served as area chairs, and to task organizers and participants who reviewed paper submissions. These proceedings have greatly benefited from their detailed and thoughtful feedback. We also thank the NAACL HLT 2018 conference organizers for their support. Finally, we most gratefully acknowledge the support of our sponsor, the ACL Special Interest Group on the Lexicon (SIGLEX).

The SemEval-2018 organizers, Marianna Apidianaki, Saif M. Mohammad, Jonathan May, Ekaterina Shutova, Marine Carpuat, Steven Bethard

Organizers:

Marianna Apidianaki, LIMSI, CNRS, Université Paris-Saclay & University of Pennsylvania
Saif M. Mohammad, National Research Council Canada
Jonathan May, University of Southern California Information Sciences Institute
Ekaterina Shutova, University of Cambridge
Steven Bethard, University of Alabama at Birmingham
Marine Carpuat, University of Maryland

Task Selection Committee:

Eneko Agirre, University of the Basque Country
Isabelle Augenstein, University of Copenhagen
Timothy Baldwin, University of Melbourne
Paul Buitelaar, National University of Ireland
Alberto Barrón-Cedeño, Qatar Computing Research Institute
Yonatan Belinkov, MIT
Kalina Bontcheva, University of Sheffield
Georgeta Bordea, National University of Ireland
Daniel Cer, Google
Wanxiang Che, Harbin Institute of Technology
Keith Cortis, University of Passau
Danilo Croce, University of Rome Tor Vergata
Mrinal Das, University of Massachusetts Amherst
Noura Farra, Columbia University
Dimitris Galanis, ILSP, "Athena" Research Center
Christian Hempelmann, Texas A&M University-Commerce
Anders Johannsen, University of Copenhagen
Maria Liakata, University of Warwick
Montse Maritxalar, University of the Basque Country
Jonathan May, University of Southern California Information Sciences Institute
Rada Mihalcea, University of Michigan
Tristan Miller, Technische Universität Darmstadt
Hamdy Mubarak, Qatar Computing Research Institute
Haris Papageorgiou, ILSP, "Athena" Research Center
Mohammad Taher Pilehvar
Maria Pontiki, ILSP, "Athena" Research Center
Peter Potash, University of Massachusetts Lowell
Alan Ritter, The Ohio State University
Alexey Romanov, University of Massachusetts Lowell
Sara Rosenthal, IBM Watson
Nathan Schneider, University of Edinburgh
Parinaz Sobhani, University of Ottawa
Xiaodan Zhu, National Research Council Canada
Arkaitz Zubiaga, University of Warwick

Task Organizers:

Miguel Ballesteros, IBM Watson, USA
Francesco Barbieri, Universitat Pompeu Fabra, LaSTUS lab, Spain
Valerio Basile, Sapienza University, Italy
Steven Bethard, University of Arizona
Felipe Bravo-Marquez, The University of Waikato
Davide Buscaldi, LIPN, UMR CNRS, Université Paris 13
Jose Camacho-Collados, Sapienza University of Rome
Thierry Charnois, LIPN, UMR CNRS, Université Paris 13
Henry Y. Chen, Snap Inc.
Jinho D. Choi, Emory Univesrity
Claudio Delli Bovi, Sapienza University of Rome
Ahmed S. Elsayed, University of Colorado
Luis Espinoza-Anke, Universitat Pompeu Fabra, LaSTUS lab, Spain
Kata Gábor, LIPN, UMR CNRS, Université Paris 13
Iryna Gurevych, UKP TU-Darmstadt
Ivan Habernal, UKP TU-Darmstadt
Véronique Hoste, LT3, Faculty of Arts and Philosophy, Ghent University
Filip Ilievski, Vrije Universiteit Amsterdam
Svetlana Kiritchenko, National Research Council Canada
Alicia Krebs, Textkernel BV, Amsterdam, Netherlands
Egoitz Laparra, University of Arizona
Els Lefever, LT3, Faculty of Arts and Philosophy, Ghent University
Alessandro Lenci, Department of Philology, Literature, and Linguistics of the University of Pisa,
Italy
Wei Lu, Singapore University of Technology and Design
Ashutosh Modi, Saarland University
Saif M. Mohammad, National Research Council Canada
Roberto Navigli, Sapienza University of Rome
Sergio Oramas, Universitat Pompeu Fabra
Simon Ostermann, Saarland University
Martha Palmer, University of Colorado
Denis Paperno, Lorraine Laboratory of Computer Science and its Applications, CNRS, France
Tommaso Pasini, Sapienza University of Rome
Viviana Patti, University of Torino, Italy
Peter Phandi, Singapore University of Technology and Design
Manfred Pinkal, Saarland University
Marten Postma, Vrije Universiteit Amsterdam
Behrang QasemiZadeh, DFG Collaborative Research Centre 991, Heinrich-Heine University Düsseldorf
Francesco Ronzano, Universitat Pompeu Fabra, LaSTUS lab, Spain
Michael Roth, Saarland University
Horacio Saggion, Universitat Pompeu Fabra, LaSTUS lab, Spain
Mohammad Salameh, Carnegie Mellon University, Qatar
Enrico Santus, Singapore University
Anne-Kathrin Schumann, ProTechnology GmbH, Dresden, former: Department of Applied Linguistics, Translation and Interpreting, Saarland University
Vered Shwartz, Bar-Ilan University
Benno Stein, Webis, Bauhaus-Universität Weimar
Isabelle Tellier, Laboratoire Lattice, CNRS and Université Sorbonne Nouvelle
Stefan Thater, Saarland University

Cynthia Van Hee, LT3, Faculty of Arts and Philosophy, Ghent University
Piek Vossen, Vrije Universiteit Amsterdam
Henning Wachsmuth, Webis, Bauhaus-Universität Weimar
Dongfang Xu, University of Arizona
Haïfa Zargayouna, LIPN, UMR CNRS, Université Paris 13

Invited Speaker:

Ellie Pavlick, Brown University

Invited Talk: Why should we care about linguistics?

Ellie Pavlick
(Joint Invited Speaker with *SEM 2018)

Brown University

Abstract

In just the past few months, a flurry of adversarial studies have pushed back on the apparent progress of neural networks, with multiple analyses suggesting that deep models of text fail to capture even basic properties of language, such as negation, word order, and compositionality. Alongside this wave of negative results, our field has stated ambitions to move beyond task-specific models and toward "general purpose" word, sentence, and even document embeddings. This is a tall order for the field of NLP, and, I argue, marks a significant shift in the way we approach our research. I will discuss what we can learn from the field of linguistics about the challenges of codifying all of language in a "general purpose" way. Then, more importantly, I will discuss what we cannot learn from linguistics. I will argue that the state-of-the-art of NLP research is operating close to the limits of what we know about natural language semantics, both within our field and outside it. I will conclude with thoughts on why this opens opportunities for NLP to advance both technology and basic science as it relates to language, and the implications for the way we should conduct empirical research.

Biography

Ellie Pavlick is currently a Post Doc at Google Research in NY. She will join Brown University as an Assistant Professor in July. Ellie received her PhD from University of Pennsylvania under the supervision of Chris Callison-Burch. Her current research focus is on semantics, pragmatics, and building cognitively-plausible computational models of natural language inference.

Table of Contents

Workshop Program

5 June 2018

09:00–09:15   ***Welcome / Opening Remarks***

09:15–10:30   *Invited Talk: Why should we care about linguistics?*
Ellie Pavlick

10:30–11:00   ***Coffee***

11:00–12:30   **Tasks 1, 2 and 3**

11:00–11:15   *SemEval-2018 Task 1: Affect in Tweets*
Saif Mohammad, Felipe Bravo-Marquez, Mohammad Salameh and Svetlana Kiritchenko

11:15–11:30   *SeerNet at SemEval-2018 Task 1: Domain Adaptation for Affect in Tweets*
Venkatesh Duppada, Royal Jain and Sushant Hiray

11:30–11:45   *SemEval 2018 Task 2: Multilingual Emoji Prediction*
Francesco Barbieri, Jose Camacho-Collados, Francesco Ronzano, Luis Espinosa Anke, Miguel Ballesteros, Valerio Basile, Viviana Patti and Horacio Saggion

11:45–12:00   *Tübingen-Oslo at SemEval-2018 Task 2: SVMs perform better than RNNs in Emoji Prediction*
Çağrı Çöltekin and Taraka Rama

12:00–12:15   *SemEval-2018 Task 3: Irony Detection in English Tweets*
Cynthia Van Hee, Els Lefever and Veronique Hoste

12:15–12:30   *THU_NGN at SemEval-2018 Task 3: Tweet Irony Detection with Densely connected LSTM and Multi-task Learning*
Chuhan Wu, Fangzhao Wu, Sixing Wu, Junxin Liu, Zhigang Yuan and Yongfeng Huang

12:30–14:00   ***Lunch***

16:30–17:30   Poster Session

16:30–17:30   *NEUROSENT-PDI at SemEval-2018 Task 1: Leveraging a Multi-Domain Sentiment Model for Inferring Polarity in Micro-blog Text*
Mauro Dragoni

16:30–17:30   *FOI DSS at SemEval-2018 Task 1: Combining LSTM States, Embeddings, and Lexical Features for Affect Analysis*
Maja Karasalo, Mattias Nilsson, Magnus Rosell and Ulrika Wickenberg Bolin

16:30–17:30   *NLPZZX at SemEval-2018 Task 1: Using Ensemble Method for Emotion and Sentiment Intensity Determination*
Zhengxin Zhang, Qimin Zhou and Hao Wu

16:30–17:30   *LT3 at SemEval-2018 Task 1: A classifier chain to detect emotions in tweets*
Luna De Bruyne, Orphee De Clercq and Veronique Hoste

16:30–17:30   *SINAI at SemEval-2018 Task 1: Emotion Recognition in Tweets*
Flor Miriam Plaza del Arco, Salud María Jiménez-Zafra, Maite Martin and L. Alfonso Urena Lopez

16:30–17:30   *UWB at SemEval-2018 Task 1: Emotion Intensity Detection in Tweets*
Pavel Přibáň, Tomáš Hercig and Ladislav Lenc

16:30–17:30   *AttnConvnet at SemEval-2018 Task 1: Attention-based Convolutional Neural Networks for Multi-label Emotion Classification*
Yanghoon Kim, Hwanhee Lee and Kyomin Jung

16:30–17:30   *INGEOTEC at SemEval-2018 Task 1: EvoMSA and µTC for Sentiment Analysis*
Mario Graff, Sabino Miranda-Jiménez, Eric S. Tellez and Daniela Moctezuma

16:30–17:30   *Epita at SemEval-2018 Task 1: Sentiment Analysis Using Transfer Learning Approach*
Guillaume Daval-Frerot, Abdesselam Bouchekif and Anatole Moreau

16:30–17:30   *KDE-AFFECT at SemEval-2018 Task 1: Estimation of Affects in Tweet by Using Convolutional Neural Network for n-gram*
Masaki Aono and Shinnosuke Himeno

16:30–17:30   *RNN for Affects at SemEval-2018 Task 1: Formulating Affect Identification as a Binary Classification Problem*
Aysu Ezen-Can and Ethem F. Can

16:30–17:30   *UMDSub at SemEval-2018 Task 2: Multilingual Emoji Prediction Multi-channel Convolutional Neural Network on Subword Embedding*
Zhenduo Wang and Ted Pedersen

16:30–17:30   *UMDuluth-CS8761 at SemEval-2018 Task 2: Emojis: Too many Choices?*
Jonathan Beaulieu and Dennis Asamoah Owusu

16:30–17:30   *The Dabblers at SemEval-2018 Task 2: Multilingual Emoji Prediction*
Larisa Alexa, Alina Lorent, Daniela Gifu and Diana Trandabat

16:30–17:30   *THU_NGN at SemEval-2018 Task 2: Residual CNN-LSTM Network with Attention for English Emoji Prediction*
Chuhan Wu, Fangzhao Wu, Sixing Wu, Zhigang Yuan, Junxin Liu and Yongfeng Huang

16:30–17:30   *#TeamINF at SemEval-2018 Task 2: Emoji Prediction in Tweets*
Alison Ribeiro and Nádia Silva

16:30–17:30   *EICA Team at SemEval-2018 Task 2: Semantic and Metadata-based Features for Multilingual Emoji Prediction*
Yufei Xie and Qingqing Song

16:30–17:30   *EmojiIt at SemEval-2018 Task 2: An Effective Attention-Based Recurrent Neural Network Model for Emoji Prediction with Characters Gated Words*
Chen Shiyun, Wang Maoquan and He Liang

16:30–17:30   *Peperomia at SemEval-2018 Task 2: Vector Similarity Based Approach for Emoji Prediction*
Jing Chen, Dechuan Yang, Xilian Li, Wei Chen and Tengjiao Wang

16:30–17:30   *ECNU at SemEval-2018 Task 2: Leverage Traditional NLP Features and Neural Networks Methods to Address Twitter Emoji Prediction Task*
Xingwu Lu, Xin Mao, Man Lan and Yuanbin Wu

16:30–17:30   *NTUA-SLP at SemEval-2018 Task 2: Predicting Emojis using RNNs with Context-aware Attention*
Christos Baziotis, Athanasiou Nikolaos, Athanasia Kolovou, Georgios Paraskevopoulos, Nikolaos Ellinas and Alexandros Potamianos

16:30–17:30   *Hatching Chick at SemEval-2018 Task 2: Multilingual Emoji Prediction*
Joël Coster, Reinder Gerard van Dalen and Nathalie Adriënne Jacqueline Stierman

16:30–17:30   *EPUTION at SemEval-2018 Task 2: Emoji Prediction with User Adaption*
Liyuan Zhou, Qiongkai Xu, Hanna Suominen and Tom Gedeon

16:30–17:30   *PickleTeam! at SemEval-2018 Task 2: English and Spanish Emoji Prediction from Tweets*
Daphne Groot, Rémon Kruizinga, Hennie Veldthuis, Simon de Wit and Hessel Haagsma

16:30–17:30   *YNU-HPCC at SemEval-2018 Task 2: Multi-ensemble Bi-GRU Model with Attention Mechanism for Multilingual Emoji Prediction*
Nan Wang, Jin Wang and Xuejie Zhang

16:30–17:30   *DUTH at SemEval-2018 Task 2: Emoji Prediction in Tweets*
Dimitrios Effrosynidis, Georgios Peikos, Symeon Symeonidis and Avi Arampatzis

16:30–17:30   *TAJJEB at SemEval-2018 Task 2: Traditional Approaches Just Do the Job with Emoji Prediction*
Angelo Basile and Kenny W. Lino

16:30–17:30   *SyntNN at SemEval-2018 Task 2: is Syntax Useful for Emoji Prediction? Embedding Syntactic Trees in Multi Layer Perceptrons*
Fabio Massimo Zanzotto and Andrea Santilli

16:30–17:30   *Duluth UROP at SemEval-2018 Task 2: Multilingual Emoji Prediction with Ensemble Learning and Oversampling*
Shuning Jin and Ted Pedersen

16:30–17:30   *CENNLP at SemEval-2018 Task 2: Enhanced Distributed Representation of Text using Target Classes for Emoji Prediction Representation*
Naveen J R, Hariharan V, Barathi Ganesh H. B., Anand Kumar M and Soman K P

16:30–17:30   *Manchester Metropolitan at SemEval-2018 Task 2: Random Forest with an Ensemble of Features for Predicting Emoji in Tweets*
Luciano Gerber and Matthew Shardlow

16:30–17:30   *Tweety at SemEval-2018 Task 2: Predicting Emojis using Hierarchical Attention Neural Networks and Support Vector Machine*
Daniel Kopev, Atanas Atanasov, Dimitrina Zlatkova, Momchil Hardalov, Ivan Koychev, Ivelina Nikolova and Galia Angelova

16:30–17:30   *LIS at SemEval-2018 Task 2: Mixing Word Embeddings and Bag of Features for Multilingual Emoji Prediction*
Gaël Guibon, Magalie Ochs and Patrice Bellot

16:30–17:30   *ALANIS at SemEval-2018 Task 3: A Feature Engineering Approach to Irony Detection in English Tweets*
Kevin Swanberg, Madiha Mirza, Ted Pedersen and Zhenduo Wang

16:30–17:30   *NEUROSENT-PDI at SemEval-2018 Task 3: Understanding Irony in Social Networks Through a Multi-Domain Sentiment Model*
Mauro Dragoni

16:30–17:30   **Poster Session**

16:30–17:30   *LightRel at SemEval-2018 Task 7: Lightweight and Fast Relation Classification*
Tyler Renslow and Günter Neumann

16:30–17:30   *OhioState at SemEval-2018 Task 7: Exploiting Data Augmentation for Relation Classification in Scientific Papers Using Piecewise Convolutional Neural Networks*
Dushyanta Dhyani

16:30–17:30   *The UWNLP system at SemEval-2018 Task 7: Neural Relation Extraction Model with Selectively Incorporated Concept Embeddings*
Yi Luan, Mari Ostendorf and Hannaneh Hajishirzi

16:30–17:30   *UC3M-NII Team at SemEval-2018 Task 7: Semantic Relation Classification in Scientific Papers via Convolutional Neural Network*
Víctor Suárez-Paniagua, Isabel Segura-Bedmar and Akiko Aizawa

16:30–17:30   *MIT-MEDG at SemEval-2018 Task 7: Semantic Relation Classification via Convolution Neural Network*
Di Jin, Franck Dernoncourt, Elena Sergeeva, Matthew McDermott and Geeticka Chauhan

16:30–17:30   *SIRIUS-LTG-UiO at SemEval-2018 Task 7: Convolutional Neural Networks with Shortest Dependency Paths for Semantic Relation Extraction and Classification in Scientific Papers*
Farhad Nooralahzadeh, Lilja Øvrelid and Jan Tore Lønning

16:30–17:30   *IRCMS at SemEval-2018 Task 7 : Evaluating a basic CNN Method and Traditional Pipeline Method for Relation Classification*
Zhongbo Yin, Zhunchen Luo, Luo Wei, Mao Bin, Tian Changhai, Ye Yuming and Wu Shuai

16:30–17:30   *Bf3R at SemEval-2018 Task 7: Evaluating Two Relation Extraction Tools for Finding Semantic Relations in Biomedical Abstracts*
Mariana Neves, Daniel Butzke, Gilbert Schönfelder and Barbara Grune

16:30–17:30   *Texterra at SemEval-2018 Task 7: Exploiting Syntactic Information for Relation Extraction and Classification in Scientific Papers*
Andrey Sysoev and Vladimir Mayorov

16:30–17:30   *UniMa at SemEval-2018 Task 7: Semantic Relation Extraction and Classification from Scientific Publications*
Thorsten Keiper, Zhonghao Lyu, Sara Pooladzadeh, Yuan Xu, Jingyi Zhang, Anne Lauscher and Simone Paolo Ponzetto

16:30–17:30   *GU IRLAB at SemEval-2018 Task 7: Tree-LSTMs for Scientific Relation Classification*
Sean MacAvaney, Luca Soldaini, Arman Cohan and Nazli Goharian

16:30–17:30   *Apollo at SemEval-2018 Task 9: Detecting Hypernymy Relations Using Syntactic Dependencies*
Mihaela Onofrei, Ionut Hulub, Diana Trandabat and Daniela Gifu

16:30–17:30   *SJTU-NLP at SemEval-2018 Task 9: Neural Hypernym Discovery with Term Embeddings*
Zhuosheng Zhang, Jiangtong Li, Hai Zhao and Bingjie Tang

16:30–17:30   *NLP_HZ at SemEval-2018 Task 9: a Nearest Neighbor Approach*
Wei Qiu, Mosha Chen, Linlin Li and Luo Si

16:30–17:30   *UMDuluth-CS8761 at SemEval-2018 Task9: Hypernym Discovery using Hearst Patterns, Co-occurrence frequencies and Word Embeddings*
Arshia Zernab Hassan, Manikya Swathi Vallabhajosyula and Ted Pedersen

16:30–17:30   *EXPR at SemEval-2018 Task 9: A Combined Approach for Hypernym Discovery*
Ahmad Issa Alaa Aldine, Mounira Harzallah, Giuseppe Berio, Nicolas Béchet and Ahmad Faour

16:30–17:30   *ADAPT at SemEval-2018 Task 9: Skip-Gram Word Embeddings for Unsupervised Hypernym Discovery in Specialised Corpora*
Alfredo Maldonado and Filip Klubička

16:30–17:30   *300-sparsans at SemEval-2018 Task 9: Hypernymy as interaction of sparse attributes*
Gábor Berend, Márton Makrai and Péter Földiák

16:30–17:30   *UWB at SemEval-2018 Task 10: Capturing Discriminative Attributes from Word Distributions*
Tomáš Brychcín, Tomáš Hercig, Josef Steinberger and Michal Konkol

16:30–17:30   *Meaning_space at SemEval-2018 Task 10: Combining explicitly encoded knowledge with information extracted from word embeddings*
Pia Sommerauer, Antske Fokkens and Piek Vossen

16:30–17:30   *GHH at SemEval-2018 Task 10: Discovering Discriminative Attributes in Distributional Semantics*
Mohammed Attia, Younes Samih, Manaal Faruqui and Wolfgang Maier

16:30–17:30   *CitiusNLP at SemEval-2018 Task 10: The Use of Transparent Distributional Models and Salient Contexts to Discriminate Word Attributes*
Pablo Gamallo

16:30–17:30   *THU_NGN at SemEval-2018 Task 10: Capturing Discriminative Attributes with MLP-CNN model*
Chuhan Wu, Fangzhao Wu, Sixing Wu, Zhigang Yuan and Yongfeng Huang

16:30–17:30   *SNU_IDS at SemEval-2018 Task 12: Sentence Encoder with Contextualized Vectors for Argument Reasoning Comprehension*
Taeuk Kim, Jihun Choi and Sang-goo Lee

16:30–17:30   *ITNLP-ARC at SemEval-2018 Task 12: Argument Reasoning Comprehension with Attention*
Wenjie Liu, Chengjie Sun, Lei Lin and Bingquan Liu

16:30–17:30   *ECNU at SemEval-2018 Task 12: An End-to-End Attention-based Neural Network for the Argument Reasoning Comprehension Task*
Junfeng Tian, Man Lan and Yuanbin Wu

16:30–17:30   *NLITrans at SemEval-2018 Task 12: Transfer of Semantic Knowledge for Argument Comprehension*
Timothy Niven and Hung-Yu Kao

16:30–17:30   *BLCU_NLP at SemEval-2018 Task 12: An Ensemble Model for Argument Reasoning Based on Hierarchical Attention*
Meiqian Zhao, Chunhua Liu, Lu Liu, Yan Zhao and Dong Yu

16:30–17:30   *YNU-HPCC at SemEval-2018 Task 12: The Argument Reasoning Comprehension Task Using a Bi-directional LSTM with Attention Model*
Quanlei Liao, Xutao Yang, Jin Wang and Xuejie Zhang

16:30–17:30   *HHU at SemEval-2018 Task 12: Analyzing an Ensemble-based Deep Learning Approach for the Argument Mining Task of Choosing the Correct Warrant*
Matthias Liebeck, Andreas Funke and Stefan Conrad

16:30–17:30   *YNU Deep at SemEval-2018 Task 12: A BiLSTM Model with Neural Attention for Argument Reasoning Comprehension*
Peng Ding and Xiaobing Zhou

16:30–17:30   *UniMelb at SemEval-2018 Task 12: Generative Implication using LSTMs, Siamese Networks and Semantic Representations with Synonym Fuzzing*
Anirudh Joshi, Tim Baldwin, Richard O. Sinnott and Cecile Paris

16:30–17:30   *Joker at SemEval-2018 Task 12: The Argument Reasoning Comprehension with Neural Attention*
Sui Guobin, Chao Wenhan and Luo Zhunchen

16:30–17:30   *TakeLab at SemEval-2018 Task12: Argument Reasoning Comprehension with Skip-Thought Vectors*
Ana Brassard, Tin Kuculo, Filip Boltuzic and Jan Šnajder

16:30–17:30   *Lyb3b at SemEval-2018 Task 12: Ensemble-based Deep Learning Models for Argument Reasoning Comprehension Task*
Yongbin Li and Xiaobing Zhou

SemEval-2018 Task 1: Affect in Tweets

Saif M. Mohammad
National Research Council Canada
`saif.mohammad@nrc-cnrc.gc.ca`

Felipe Bravo-Marquez
The University of Waikato, New Zealand
`fbravoma@waikato.ac.nz`

Mohammad Salameh
Carnegie Mellon University in Qatar
`msalameh@qatar.cmu.edu`

Svetlana Kiritchenko
National Research Council Canada
`svetlana.kiritchenko@nrc-cnrc.gc.ca`

Abstract

We present the SemEval-2018 Task 1: Affect in Tweets, which includes an array of subtasks on inferring the affectual state of a person from their tweet. For each task, we created labeled data from English, Arabic, and Spanish tweets. The individual tasks are: 1. emotion intensity regression, 2. emotion intensity ordinal classification, 3. valence (sentiment) regression, 4. valence ordinal classification, and 5. emotion classification. Seventy-five teams (about 200 team members) participated in the shared task. We summarize the methods, resources, and tools used by the participating teams, with a focus on the techniques and resources that are particularly useful. We also analyze systems for consistent bias towards a particular race or gender. The data is made freely available to further improve our understanding of how people convey emotions through language.

1 Introduction

Emotions are central to language and thought. They are familiar and commonplace, yet they are complex and nuanced. Humans are known to perceive hundreds of different emotions. According to the *basic emotion model* (aka the *categorical model*) (Ekman, 1992; Plutchik, 1980; Parrot, 2001; Frijda, 1988), some emotions, such as joy, sadness, and fear, are more basic than others—physiologically, cognitively, and in terms of the mechanisms to express these emotions. Each of these emotions can be felt or expressed in varying intensities. For example, our utterances can convey that we are very angry, slightly sad, absolutely elated, etc. Here, *intensity* refers to the degree or amount of an emotion such as anger or sadness.[1] As per the *valence–arousal–dominance (VAD) model* (Russell, 1980, 2003), emotions are points in a

three-dimensional space of valence (positiveness–negativeness), arousal (active–passive), and dominance (dominant–submissive). We use the term *affect* to refer to various emotion-related categories such as joy, fear, valence, and arousal.

Natural language applications in commerce, public health, disaster management, and public policy can benefit from knowing the affectual states of people—both the categories and the intensities of the emotions they feel. We thus present the *SemEval-2018 Task 1: Affect in Tweets*, which includes an array of subtasks where automatic systems have to infer the affectual state of a person from their tweet.[2] We will refer to the author of a tweet as the *tweeter*. Some of the tasks are on the intensities of four basic emotions common to many proposals of basic emotions: anger, fear, joy, and sadness. Some of the tasks are on valence or sentiment intensity. Finally, we include an emotion classification task over eleven emotions commonly expressed in tweets.[3] For each task, we provide separate training, development, and test datasets for English, Arabic, and Spanish tweets. The tasks are as follows:

1. Emotion Intensity Regression (EI-reg): Given a tweet and an emotion E, determine the intensity of E that best represents the mental state of the tweeter—a real-valued score between 0 (least E) and 1 (most E);

2. Emotion Intensity Ordinal Classification (EI-oc): Given a tweet and an emotion E, classify the tweet into one of four ordinal classes of intensity of E that best represents the mental state of the tweeter;

3. Valence (Sentiment) Regression (V-reg): Given a tweet, determine the intensity of sentiment or valence (V) that best represents the mental state

---

[1] Intensity is different from *arousal*, which refers to the extent to which an emotion is calming or exciting.

[2] https://competitions.codalab.org/competitions/17751
[3] Determined through pilot annotations.

Proceedings of the 12th International Workshop on Semantic Evaluation (SemEval-2018), pages 1–17
New Orleans, Louisiana, June 5–6, 2018. ©2018 Association for Computational Linguistics

of the tweeter—a real-valued score between 0 (most negative) and 1 (most positive);

4. Valence Ordinal Classification (V-oc): Given a tweet, classify it into one of seven ordinal classes, corresponding to various levels of positive and negative sentiment intensity, that best represents the mental state of the tweeter;

5. Emotion Classification (E-c): Given a tweet, classify it as 'neutral or no emotion' or as one, or more, of eleven given emotions that best represent the mental state of the tweeter.

Here, E refers to emotion, EI refers to emotion intensity, V refers to valence, reg refers to regression, oc refers to ordinal classification, c refers to classification.

For each language, we create a large single textual dataset, subsets of which are annotated for many emotion (or affect) dimensions (from both the basic emotion model and the VAD model). For each emotion dimension, we annotate the data not just for coarse classes (such as anger or no anger) but also for fine-grained real-valued scores indicating the intensity of emotion. We use Best–Worst Scaling (BWS), a comparative annotation method, to address the limitations of traditional rating scale methods such as inter- and intra-annotator inconsistency. We show that the fine-grained intensity scores thus obtained are reliable (repeat annotations lead to similar scores). In total, about 700,000 annotations were obtained from about 22,000 English, Arabic, and Spanish tweets.

Seventy-five teams (about 200 team members) participated in the shared task, making this the largest SemEval shared task to date. In total, 319 submissions were made to the 15 task–language pairs. Each team was allowed only one official submission for each task–language pair. We summarize the methods, resources, and tools used by the participating teams, with a focus on the techniques and resources that are particularly useful. We also analyze system predictions for consistent bias towards a particular race or gender using a corpus specifically compiled for that purpose. We find that a majority of systems consistently assign higher scores to sentences involving one race or gender. We also find that the bias may change depending on the specific affective dimension being predicted. All of the tweet data (labeled and unlabeled), annotation questionnaires, evaluation scripts, and the bias evaluation corpus are made freely available on the task website.

2   Building on Past Work

There is a large body of prior work on sentiment and emotion classification (Mohammad, 2016). There is also growing work on related tasks such as stance detection (Mohammad et al., 2017) and argumentation mining (Wojatzki et al., 2018; Palau and Moens, 2009). However, there is little work on detecting the *intensity* of affect in text. Mohammad and Bravo-Marquez (2017) created the first datasets of tweets annotated for anger, fear, joy, and sadness intensities. Given a focus emotion, each tweet was annotated for intensity of the emotion felt by the speaker using a technique called *Best–Worst Scaling (BWS)* (Louviere, 1991; Kiritchenko and Mohammad, 2016, 2017).

BWS is an annotation scheme that addresses the limitations of traditional rating scale methods, such as inter- and intra-annotator inconsistency, by employing comparative annotations. Note that at its simplest, comparative annotations involve giving people pairs of items and asking which item is greater in terms of the property of interest. However, such a method requires annotations for N^2 items, which can be prohibitively large.

In BWS, annotators are given n items (an n-tuple, where $n > 1$ and commonly $n = 4$). They are asked which item is the *best* (highest in terms of the property of interest) and which is the *worst* (lowest in terms of the property of interest). When working on 4-tuples, best–worst annotations are particularly efficient because each best and worst annotation will reveal the order of five of the six item pairs. For example, for a 4-tuple with items A, B, C, and D, if A is the best, and D is the worst, then A > B, A > C, A > D, B > D, and C > D. Real-valued scores of association between the items and the property of interest can be determined using simple arithmetic on the number of times an item was chosen best and number of times it was chosen worst (as described in Section 3.4.2) (Orme, 2009; Flynn and Marley, 2014).

It has been empirically shown that annotations for $2N$ 4-tuples is sufficient for obtaining reliable scores (where N is the number of items) (Louviere, 1991; Kiritchenko and Mohammad, 2016). Kiritchenko and Mohammad (2017) showed through empirical experiments that BWS produces more reliable and more discriminating scores than those obtained using rating scales. (See (Kiritchenko and Mohammad, 2016, 2017) for further details on BWS.)

Mohammad and Bravo-Marquez (2017) collected and annotated 7,100 English tweets posted in 2016. We will refer to the tweets alone as *Tweets-2016*, and the tweets and annotations together as the *Emotion Intensity Dataset* (or, *EmoInt Dataset*). This dataset was used in the 2017 WASSA Shared Task on Emotion Intensity.[4]

We build on that earlier work by first compiling a new set of English, Arabic, and Spanish tweets posted in 2017 and annotating the new tweets for emotion intensity in a similar manner. We will refer to this new set of tweets as *Tweets-2017*. Similar to the work by Mohammad and Bravo-Marquez (2017), we create four subsets annotated for intensity of fear, joy, sadness, and anger, respectively. However, unlike the earlier work, here a common dataset of tweets is annotated for all three negative emotions: fear, anger, and sadness. This allows one to study the relationship between the three basic negative emotions.

We also annotate tweets sampled from each of the four basic emotion subsets (of both Tweets-2016 and Tweets-2017) for degree of valence. Annotations for arousal, dominance, and other basic emotions such as surprise and anticipation are left for future work.

In addition to knowing a fine-grained score indicating degree of intensity, it is also useful to qualitatively ground the information on whether the intensity is high, medium, low, etc. Thus, we manually identify ranges in intensity scores that correspond to these coarse classes. For each of the four emotions E, the 0 to 1 range is partitioned into the classes: *no E can be inferred, low E can be inferred, moderate E can be inferred,* and *high E can be inferred.* This data can be used for developing systems that predict the ordinal class of emotion intensity (*EI ordinal classification*, or *EI-oc*, systems). We partition the 0 to 1 interval of valence into: *very negative, moderately negative, slightly negative, neutral or mixed, slightly positive, moderately positive,* and *very positive mental state of the tweeter can be inferred.* This data can be used to develop systems that predict the ordinal class of valence (*valence ordinal classification*, or *V-oc*, systems).[5]

Dataset	Source of Tweets	Annotated In	
		2016	2017
E-c	Tweets-2016	-	✓
	Tweets-2017	-	✓
EI-reg, EI-oc	Tweets-2016	✓	-
	Tweets-2017	-	✓
V-reg, V-oc	Tweets-2016	-	✓
	Tweets-2017	-	✓

Table 1: The annotations of English Tweets.

Finally, the full Tweets-2016 and Tweets-2017 datasets are annotated for the presence of eleven emotions: anger, anticipation, disgust, fear, joy, love, optimism, pessimism, sadness, surprise, and trust. This data can be used for developing *multi-label emotion classification*, or *E-c*, systems. Table 1 shows the two stages in which the annotations for English tweets were done. The Arabic and Spanish tweets were all only from 2017. Together, we will refer to the joint set of tweets from Tweets-2016 and Tweets-2017 along with all the emotion-related annotations described above as the *SemEval-2018 Affect in Tweets Dataset* (or *AIT Dataset* for short).

3 The Affect in Tweets Dataset

We now present how we created the Affect in Tweets Dataset. We present only the key details here; a detailed description of the English datasets and the analysis of various affect dimensions is available in Mohammad and Kiritchenko (2018).

3.1 Compiling English Tweets

We first compiled tweets to be included in the four EI-reg datasets corresponding to anger, fear, joy, and sadness. The EI-oc datasets include the same tweets as in EI-reg, that is, the Anger EI-oc dataset has the same tweets as in the Anger EI-reg dataset, the Fear EI-oc dataset has the same tweets as in the Fear EI-reg dataset, and so on. However, the labels for EI-oc tweets are ordinal classes instead of real-valued intensity scores. The V-reg dataset includes a subset of tweets from each of the four EI-reg emotion datasets. The V-oc dataset has the same tweets as in the V-reg dataset. The E-c dataset includes all the tweets from the four EI-reg datasets. The total number of instances in the E-c, EI-reg, EI-oc, V-reg, and V-oc datasets is shown in the last column of Table 3.

3.1.1 Basic Emotion Tweets

To create a dataset of tweets rich in a particular emotion, we used the following methodology.

---

[4] http://saifmohammad.com/WebPages/EmoInt2017.html

[5] Note that valence ordinal classification is the traditional sentiment analysis task most commonly explored in NLP literature. The classes may vary from just three (positive, negative, and neutral) to five, seven, or nine finer classes.

For each emotion X, we selected 50 to 100 terms that were associated with that emotion at different intensity levels. For example, for the anger dataset, we used the terms: *angry, mad, frustrated, annoyed, peeved, irritated, miffed, fury, antagonism,* and so on. We will refer to these terms as the *query terms*. The query terms we selected included emotion words listed in the *Roget's Thesaurus*, nearest neighbors of these emotion words in a word-embeddings space, as well as commonly used emoji and emoticons. The full list of the query terms is available on the task website.

We polled the Twitter API, over the span of two months (June and July, 2017), for tweets that included the query terms. We randomly selected 1,400 tweets from the joy set for annotation of intensity of joy. For the three negative emotions, we first randomly selected 200 tweets each from their corresponding tweet collections. These 600 tweets were annotated for all three negative emotions so that we could study the relationships between fear and anger, between anger and sadness, and between sadness and fear. For each of the negative emotions, we also chose 800 additional tweets, from their corresponding tweet sets, that were annotated only for the corresponding emotion. Thus, the number of tweets annotated for each of the negative emotions was also 1,400 (the 600 included in all three negative emotions + 800 unique to the focus emotion). For each emotion, 100 tweets that had an emotion-word hashtag, emoticon, or emoji query term at the end (*trailing query term*) were randomly chosen. We removed the trailing query terms from these tweets. As a result, the dataset also included some tweets with no clear emotion-indicative terms.

Thus, the EI-reg dataset included 1,400 new tweets for each of the four emotions. These were annotated for intensity of emotion. Note that the EmoInt dataset already included 1,500 to 2,300 tweets per emotion annotated for intensity. Those tweets were not re-annotated. The EmoInt EI-reg tweets as well as the new EI-reg tweets were both annotated for ordinal classes of emotion (EI-oc) as described in Section 3.4.3

The new EI-reg tweets formed the EI-reg development (dev) and test sets in the AIT task; the number of instances in each is shown in the third and fourth columns of Table 3. The EmoInt tweets formed the training set.[6]

3.1.2 Valence Tweets

The valence dataset included tweets from the new EI-reg set and the EmoInt set. The new EI-reg tweets included were all 600 tweets common to the three negative emotion tweet sets and 600 randomly chosen joy tweets. The EmoInt tweets included were 600 randomly chosen joy tweets and 200 each, randomly chosen tweets, for anger, fear, and sadness. To study valence in sarcastic tweets, we also included 200 tweets that had hashtags *#sarcastic, #sarcasm, #irony,* or *#ironic* (tweets that are likely to be sarcastic). Thus the V-reg set included 2,600 tweets in total. The V-oc set is comprised of the same tweets as in the V-reg set.

3.1.3 Multi-Label Emotion Tweets

We selected all of the 2016 and 2017 tweets in the four EI-reg datasets to form the E-c dataset, which is annotated for presence/absence of 11 emotions.

3.2 Compiling Arabic Tweets

We compiled the Arabic tweets in a similar manner to the English dataset. We obtained the the Arabic query terms as follows:

- We translated the English query terms for the four emotions to Arabic using Google Translate.

- All words associated with the four emotions in the NRC Emotion Lexicon were translated into Arabic. (We discarded incorrect translations.)

- We trained word embeddings on a tweet corpus collected using dialectal function words as queries. We used nearest neighbors of the emotion query terms in the word-embedding space as additional query terms.

- We included the same emoji used in English for anger, fear, joy and sadness. However, most of the fear emoji were not included, as they were rarely associated with fear in Arabic tweets.

In total, we used 550 Arabic query terms and emoji to poll the Twitter API to collect around 17 million tweets between March and July 2017. For each of the four emotions, we randomly selected 1,400 tweets to form the EI-reg datasets. The same tweets were used for building the EI-oc datasets. The sets of tweets for the negative emotions included 800 tweets unique to the focus emotion and 600 tweets common to the three negative emotions.

---

[6]Manual examination of the new EI-reg tweets later revealed that it included some near-duplicate tweets. We kept only one copy of such pairs. Thus the dev. and test set numbers add up to a little lower than 1,400.

The V-reg dataset was formed by including about 900 tweets from the three negative emotions (including the 600 tweets common to the three negative emotion datasets), and about 900 tweets for joy. The same tweets were used to form the V-oc dataset. The multi-label emotion classification dataset was created by taking all the tweets in the EI-reg datasets.

3.3 Compiling Spanish Tweets

The Spanish query terms were obtained as follows:

- The English query terms were translated into Spanish using Google Translate. The translations were manually examined by a Spanish native speaker, and incorrect translations were discarded.
- The resulting set was expanded using synonyms taken from a Spanish lexicographic resource, Wordreference[7].
- We made sure that both masculine and feminine forms of the nouns and adjectives were included.
- We included the same emoji used in English for anger, sadness, and joy. The emoji for fear where not included, as tweets containing those emoji were rarely associated with fear.

We collected about 1.2 million tweets between July and September 2017. We annotated close to 2,000 tweets for each emotion. The sets of tweets for the negative emotions included $\sim$1,500 tweets unique to the focus emotion and $\sim$500 tweets common to the two remaining negative emotions. The same tweets were used for building the Spanish EI-oc dataset.

The V-reg dataset was formed by including about 1,100 tweets from the three negative emotions (including the 750 tweets common to the three negative emotion datasets), about 1,100 tweets for joy, and 268 tweets with sarcastic hashtags (*#sarcasmo, #ironia*). The same tweets were used to build the V-oc dataset. The multi-label emotion classification dataset was created by taking all the tweets in the EI-reg and V-reg datasets.

3.4 Annotating Tweets

We describe below how we annotated the English tweets. The same procedure was used for Arabic and Spanish annotations.

We annotated all of our data by crowdsourcing. The tweets and annotation questionnaires were uploaded on the crowdsourcing platform, Figure Eight (earlier called CrowdFlower).[8] All the annotation tasks described in this paper were approved by the National Research Council Canada's Institutional Review Board.

About 5% of the tweets in each task were annotated internally beforehand (by the authors of this paper). These tweets are referred to as gold tweets. The gold tweets were interspersed with other tweets. If a crowd-worker got a gold tweet question wrong, they were immediately notified of the error. If the worker's accuracy on the gold tweet questions fell below 70%, they were refused further annotation, and all of their annotations were discarded. This served as a mechanism to avoid malicious annotations.

3.4.1 Multi-Label Emotion Annotation

We presented one tweet at a time to the annotators and asked which of the following options best described the emotional state of the tweeter:

– anger (also includes annoyance, rage)

– anticipation (also includes interest, vigilance)

– disgust (also includes disinterest, dislike, loathing)

– fear (also includes apprehension, anxiety, terror)

– joy (also includes serenity, ecstasy)

– love (also includes affection)

– optimism (also includes hopefulness, confidence)

– pessimism (also includes cynicism, no confidence)

– sadness (also includes pensiveness, grief)

– surprise (also includes distraction, amazement)

– trust (also includes acceptance, liking, admiration)

– neutral or no emotion

Example tweets were provided in advance with examples of suitable responses.

On the Figure Eight task settings, we specified that we needed annotations from seven people for each tweet. However, because of the way the gold tweets were set up, they were annotated by more than seven people. The median number of annotations was still seven. In total, 303 people annotated between 10 and 4,670 tweets each. A total of 174,356 responses were obtained.

Annotation Aggregation: One of the criticisms for several natural language annotation projects has been that they keep only the instances with high agreement, and discard instances that obtain low agreements. The high agreement instances

---

[7]http://www.wordreference.com/sinonimos/

[8]https://www.figure-eight.com

	anger	antic.	disg.	fear	joy	love	optim.	pessi.	sadn.	surp.	trust	neutral
English	36.1	13.9	36.6	16.8	39.3	12.3	31.3	11.6	29.4	5.2	5.0	2.7
Arabic	39.4	9.6	19.6	17.8	26.9	25.2	24.5	22.8	37.4	2.2	5.3	0.6
Spanish	32.2	11.7	14.7	10.5	30.5	7.9	10.2	16.7	23.0	4.6	4.6	4.7

Table 2: Percentage of tweets that were labeled with a given emotion (after aggregation of votes).

tend to be simple instantiations of the classes of interest, and are easier to model by automatic systems. However, when deployed in the real world, natural language systems have to recognize and process more complex and subtle instantiations of a natural language phenomenon. Thus, discarding all but the high agreement instances does not facilitate the development of systems that are able to handle the difficult instances appropriately.

Therefore, we chose a somewhat generous aggregation criterion: if more than 25% of the responses (two out of seven people) indicated that a certain emotion applies, then that label was chosen. We will refer to this aggregation as *Ag2*. If no emotion got at least 40% of the responses (three out of seven people) and more than 50% of the responses indicated that the tweet was neutral, then the tweet was marked as neutral. In the vast majority of the cases, a tweet was labeled either as neutral or with one or more of the eleven emotion labels. 107 English tweets, 14 Arabic tweets, and 88 Spanish tweets did not receive sufficient votes to be labeled a particular emotion or to be labeled neutral. These very-low-agreement tweets were set aside. We will refer to the remaining dataset as E-c (Ag2), or simply *E-c*, data.

Class Distribution: Table 2 shows the percentage of tweets that were labeled with a given emotion using Ag2 aggregation. The numbers in these rows sum up to more than 100% because a tweet may be labeled with more than one emotion. Observe that joy, anger, disgust, sadness, and optimism get a high number of the votes. Trust and surprise are two of the lowest voted emotions.

3.4.2 Annotating Intensity with BWS

We followed the procedure described by Kiritchenko and Mohammad (2016) to obtain best–worst scaling (BWS) annotations.

Every 4-tuple was annotated by four independent annotators. The questionnaires were developed through internal discussions and pilot annotations. They are available on the SemEval-2018 AIT Task webpage.

Between 118 and 220 people residing in the United States annotated the 4-tuples for each of the four emotions and valence. In total, around 27K responses for each of the four emotions and around 50K responses for valence were obtained.[9]

Annotation Aggregation: The intensity scores were calculated from the BWS responses using a simple counting procedure (Orme, 2009; Flynn and Marley, 2014): For each item, the score is the proportion of times the item was chosen as having the most intensity minus the percentage of times the item was chosen as having the least intensity.[10] We linearly transformed the scores to lie in the 0 (lowest intensity) to 1 (highest intensity) range.

Distribution of Scores: Figure 1 shows the histogram of the V-reg tweets. The tweets are grouped into bins of scores 0–0.05, 0.05–0.1, and so on until 0.95–1. The colors for the bins correspond to their ordinal classes as determined from the manual annotation described in the next subsection. The histograms for the four emotions are shown in Figure 5 in the Appendix.

3.4.3 Identifying Ordinal Classes

For each of the EI-reg emotions, the authors of this paper independently examined the ordered list of tweets to identify suitable boundaries that partitioned the 0–1 range into four ordinal classes: *no emotion, low emotion, moderate emotion,* and *high emotion.* Similarly the V-reg tweets were examined and the 0–1 range was partitioned into seven classes: *very negative, moderately negative, slightly negative, neutral or mixed, slightly positive, moderately positive,* and *very positive mental state can be inferred.*[11]

Annotation Aggregation: The authors discussed their individual annotations to obtain consensus on the class intervals. The V-oc and EI-oc datasets were thus labeled.

Class Distribution: The legend of Figure 1 shows the intervals of V-reg scores that make up the seven V-oc classes. The intervals of EI-reg scores that make up each of the four EI-oc classes are shown in Figure 5 in the Appendix.

---

[9]Gold tweets were annotated more than four times.

[10]Code for generating tuples from items as well as for generating scores from BWS annotations: http://saifmohammad.com/WebPages/BestWorst.html

[11]Valence is a bi-polar scale; hence, more classes.

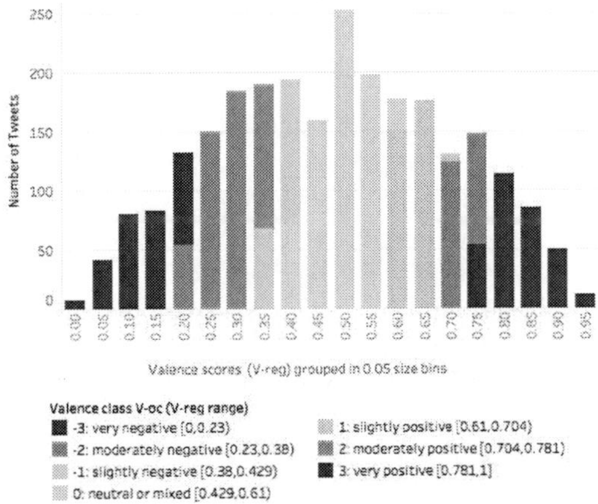

Figure 1: Valence score (V-reg), class (V-oc) distribution.

Dataset	Train	Dev	Test	Total
English				
E-c	6,838	886	3,259	10,983
EI-reg, EI-oc				
anger	1,701	388	1,002	3,091
fear	2,252	389	986	3,627
joy	1,616	290	1,105	3,011
sadness	1,533	397	975	2,905
V-reg, V-oc	1,181	449	937	2,567
Arabic				
E-c	2,278	585	1,518	4,381
EI-reg, EI-oc				
anger	877	150	373	1,400
fear	882	146	372	1,400
joy	728	224	448	1,400
sadness	889	141	370	1,400
V-reg, V-oc	932	138	730	1,800
Spanish				
E-c	3,561	679	2,854	7,094
EI-reg, EI-oc				
anger	1,166	193	627	1,986
fear	1,166	202	618	1,986
joy	1,058	202	730	1,990
sadness	1,154	196	641	1,991
V-reg, V-oc	1,566	229	648	2,443

Table 3: The number of tweets in the SemEval-2018 Affect in Tweets Dataset.

3.4.4 Annotating Arabic and Spanish Tweets

The annotations for Arabic and Spanish tweets followed the same process as the one described for English above. We manually translated the English questionnaire into Arabic and Spanish.

On Figure Eight, we used similar settings as for English. For Arabic, we set the country of annotators to fourteen Arab countries available in Crowdflower as well as the United States of America.[12] For Spanish, we set the country of annotators to USA, Mexico, and Spain.

Annotation aggregation was done the same way for Arabic and Spanish, as for English. Table 2 shows the distributions for different emotions in the E-c annotations for Arabic and Spanish (in addition to English).

3.5 Training, Development, and Test Sets

Table 14 in Appendix summarizes key details of the current set of annotations done for the *SemEval-2018 Affect in Tweets (AIT) Dataset*. AIT was partitioned into training, development, and test sets for machine learning experiments as described in Table 3. All of the English tweets that came from Tweets-2016 were part of the training sets. All of the English tweets that came from Tweets-2017 were split into development and test sets.[13] The Arabic and Spanish tweets are all from 2017 and were split into train, dev, and test sets.

---

[12] Algeria, Bahrain, Egypt, Jordan, Kuwait, Morocco, Oman, Palestine, Qatar, Saudi Arabia, Tunisia, UAE, Yemen.

[13]This split of Tweets-2017 was first done such that 20% of the tweets formed the dev. set and 80% formed the test set—independently for EI-reg, EI-oc, V-reg, V-oc, and E-c. Then we moved some tweets from the test sets to the dev. sets such that a tweet in any dev. set does not occur in any test set.

4 Agreement and Reliability of Annotations

It is challenging to obtain consistent annotations for affect due to a number of reasons, including: the subtle ways in which people can express affect, fuzzy boundaries of affect categories, and differences in human experience that impact how they perceive emotion in text. In the subsections below we analyze the AIT dataset to determine the extent of agreement and the reliability of the annotations.

4.1 E-c Annotations

Table 4 shows the inter-rater agreement and Fleiss' κ for the multi-label emotion annotations. The inter-rater agreement (IRA) is calculated as the percentage of times each pair of annotators agree. For the sake of comparison, we also show the scores obtained by randomly choosing whether a particular emotion applies or not. Observe that the scores obtained through the actual annotations are markedly higher than the scores obtained by random guessing.

4.2 EI-reg and V-reg Annotations

For real-valued score annotations, a commonly used measure of quality is reproducibility of the end result—if repeated independent manual annotations from multiple respondents result in similar

		IRA	Fleiss' κ
Random		41.67	0.00
English	avg. for all 12 classes	83.38	0.21
	avg. for 4 basic emotions	81.22	0.40
Arabic	avg. for all 12 classes	86.69	0.29
	avg. for 4 basic emotions	83.38	0.48
Spanish	avg. for all 12 classes	88.60	0.28
	avg. for 4 basic emotions	85.91	0.45

Table 4: Annotator agreement for the Multi-label Emotion Classification (E-c) Datasets.

Language	Affect Dimension	Spearman	Pearson
English	Emotion Intensity		
	anger	0.89	0.90
	fear	0.84	0.85
	joy	0.90	0.91
	sadness	0.82	0.83
	Valence	0.92	0.92
Arabic	Emotion Intensity		
	anger	0.88	0.89
	fear	0.85	0.87
	joy	0.88	0.89
	sadness	0.86	0.87
	Valence	0.94	0.94
Spanish	Emotion Intensity		
	anger	0.88	0.88
	fear	0.85	0.86
	joy	0.89	0.89
	sadness	0.86	0.86
	Valence	0.89	0.89

Table 5: Split-half reliabilities in the AIT Dataset.

intensity rankings (and scores), then one can be confident that the scores capture the true emotion intensities. To assess this reproducibility, we calculate average *split-half reliability (SHR)*, a commonly used approach to determine consistency (Kuder and Richardson, 1937; Cronbach, 1946; Mohammad and Bravo-Marquez, 2017). The intuition behind SHR is as follows. All annotations for an item (in our case, tuples) are randomly split into two halves. Two sets of scores are produced independently from the two halves. Then the correlation between the two sets of scores is calculated. The process is repeated 100 times, and the correlations are averaged. If the annotations are of good quality, then the average correlation between the two halves will be high.

Table 5 shows the split-half reliabilities for the AIT data. Observe that correlations lie between 0.82 and 0.92, indicating a high degree of reproducibility.[14]

<hr>

[14]Past work has found the SHR for sentiment intensity annotations for words, with 6 to 8 annotations per tuple to be 0.95 to 0.98 (Mohammad, 2018b; Kiritchenko and Mohammad, 2016). In contrast, here SHR is calculated from whole sentences, which is a more complex annotation task and thus the SHR is expected to be lower than 0.95.

5 Evaluation for Automatic Predictions

5.1 For EI-reg, EI-oc, V-reg, and V-oc

The official competition metric for EI-reg, EI-oc, V-reg, and V-oc was the Pearson Correlation Coefficient with the Gold ratings/labels. For EI-reg and EI-oc, the correlation scores across all four emotions were averaged (macro-average) to determine the bottom-line competition metric. Apart from the official competition metric described above, some additional metrics were also calculated for each submission. These were intended to provide a different perspective on the results. The secondary metric used for the regression tasks was:

- Pearson correlation for a subset of the test set that includes only those tweets with intensity score greater or equal to 0.5.

The secondary metrics used for the ordinal classification tasks were:

- Pearson correlation for a subset of the test set that includes only those tweets with intensity classes low X, moderate X, or high X (where X is an emotion). We will refer to this set of tweets as the some-emotion subset.

- Weighted quadratic kappa on the full test set.

- Weighted quadratic kappa on the some-emotion subset of the test set.

5.2 For E-c

The official competition metric used for E-c was multi-label accuracy (or Jaccard index). Since this is a multi-label classification task, each tweet can have one or more gold emotion labels, and one or more predicted emotion labels. Multi-label accuracy is defined as the size of the intersection of the predicted and gold label sets divided by the size of their union. This measure is calculated for each tweet t, and then is averaged over all tweets T in the dataset:

$$Accuracy = \frac{1}{|T|} \sum_{t \in T} \frac{G_t \cap P_t}{G_t \cup P_t}$$

where G_t is the set of the gold labels for tweet t, P_t is the set of the predicted labels for tweet t, and T is the set of tweets. Apart from the official competition metric (multi-label accuracy), we also calculated micro-averaged F-score and macro-averaged F-score.[15]

<hr>

[15]Formulae are provided on the task webpage.

Task	English	Arabic	Spanish	All
EI-reg	48	13	15	76
EI-oc	37	12	14	63
V-reg	37	13	13	63
V-oc	35	13	12	60
E-c	33	12	12	57
Total	190	63	66	319

Table 6: Number of teams in each task–language pair.

6 Systems

Seventy-five teams (about 200 team members) participated in the shared task, submitting to one or more of the five subtasks. The numbers of teams submitting predictions for each task–language pair are shown in Table 6. The English tasks were the most popular (33 to 48 teams for each task); however, the Arabic and Spanish tasks also got a fair amount of participation (about 13 teams for each task). Emotion intensity regression attracted the most teams.

Figure 2 shows how frequently various machine learning algorithms were used in the five tasks. Observe that SVM/SVR, LSTMs and Bi-LSTMs were some of the most widely used algorithms. Understandably, regression algorithms such as Linear Regression were more common in the regression tasks than in the classification tasks.

Figure 3 shows how frequently various features were used. Observe that word embeddings, affect lexicon features, and word n-grams were some of the most widely used features. Many teams also used sentence embeddings and affect-specific word embeddings. A number of teams also made use of distant supervision corpora (usually tweets with emoticons or hashtagged emotion words). Several teams made use of the AIT2018 Distant Supervision Corpus—a corpus of about 100M tweets containing emotion query words—that we provided. A small number of teams used training data from one task to supplement the training data for another task. (See row '*AIT-2018 train-dev (other task)*'.)

Figure 4 shows how frequently features from various affect lexicons were used. Observe that several of the NRC emotion and sentiment lexicons as well as AFINN and Bing Liu Lexicon were widely used (Mohammad and Turney, 2013; Mohammad, 2018b; Kiritchenko et al., 2014; Nielsen, 2011; Hu and Liu, 2004). Several teams used the AffectiveTweets package to obtain lexicon features (Mohammad and Bravo-Marquez, 2017).[16]

[16]https://affectivetweets.cms.waikato.ac.nz/

	#Teams				
ML algorithm	EI-reg	EI-oc	V-reg	V-oc	E-c
AdaBoost	1	1	3	1	0
Bi-LSTM	10	8	10	6	6
CNN	10	8	7	6	3
Gradient Boosting	8	3	5	4	1
Linear Regression	11	2	7	2	1
Logistic Regression	9	7	8	6	6
LSTM	13	9	10	5	4
Random Forest	8	7	5	6	6
RNN	0	0	0	0	1
SVM or SVR	15	9	8	6	6
Other	14	16	13	12	7

Figure 2: Machine learning algorithms used by teams.

	#Teams				
Features/Resources	EI-reg	EI-oc	V-reg	V-oc	E-c
affect-specific word embeddings	10	8	9	9	5
affect/sentiment lexicons	24	16	16	15	12
character ngrams	6	4	3	4	2
dependency/parse features	2	3	3	3	2
distant-supervision corpora	10	8	7	5	4
manually labeled corpora (other)	6	4	4	5	3
AIT-2018 train-dev (other task)	6	5	5	5	3
sentence embeddings	10	8	7	8	6
unlabeled corpora	6	3	5	3	0
word embeddings	32	21	25	21	20
word ngrams	19	14	12	10	9
Other	5	5	5	5	5

Figure 3: Features and resources used by teams.

6.1 Results and Discussion

Tables 7 through 11 show the results obtained by the top three teams on EI-reg, EI-oc, V-reg, V-oc, and E-c, respectively. The tables also show: (a) the results obtained by the median rank team for each task–language pair, (b) the results obtained by a baseline SVM system using just word unigrams as features, and (c) the results obtained by a system that randomly guesses the prediction—the random baseline.[17] Observe that the top teams obtained markedly higher results than the SVM unigrams baselines.

Most of the top-performing teams relied on both deep neural network representations of tweets (sentence embeddings) as well as features derived from existing sentiment and emotion lexicons. Since many of the teams used similar models when participating in different tasks, we present further details of the systems grouped by the language for which they submitted predictions.

[17]The results for each of the 75 participating teams are shown on the task website and also in the supplementary material file. (Not shown here due to space constraints.)

Test Set	Rank	Team Name	Pearson r (all instances)					Pearson r (gold in 0.5-1)				
			avg.	anger	fear	joy	sadness	avg.	anger	fear	joy	sadness
English												
	1	SeerNet	79.9	82.7	77.9	79.2	79.8	63.8	70.8	60.8	56.8	66.6
	2	NTUA-SLP	77.6	78.2	75.8	77.1	79.2	61.0	63.6	59.5	55.4	65.4
	3	PlusEmo2Vec	76.6	81.1	72.8	77.3	75.3	57.9	66.3	49.7	54.2	61.3
	23	Median Team	65.3	65.4	67.2	64.8	63.5	49.0	52.6	49.7	42.0	51.7
	37	SVM-Unigrams	52.0	52.6	52.5	57.5	45.3	39.6	45.5	30.2	47.6	35.0
	46	Random Baseline	-0.8	-1.8	2.4	-5.8	2.0	-4.8	-8.8	-1.1	-3.2	-5.9
Arabic												
	1	AffecThor	68.5	64.7	64.2	75.6	69.4	53.7	46.9	54.1	57.0	56.9
	2	EiTAKA	66.7	62.7	62.7	73.8	67.5	53.3	47.9	60.4	49.0	56.0
	3	EMA	64.3	61.5	59.3	70.9	65.6	49.0	44.4	45.7	49.7	56.2
	6	Median Team	54.2	50.1	50.1	62.8	53.7	44.6	39.1	43.0	45.4	51.0
	7	SVM-Unigrams	45.5	40.6	43.5	53.0	45.0	35.3	34.4	36.6	33.2	36.7
	13	Random Baseline	1.3	-0.6	1.6	-1.0	5.2	-0.7	0.2	0.7	1.1	-4.8
Spanish												
	1	AffecThor	73.8	67.6	77.6	75.3	74.6	58.7	54.9	60.4	59.1	60.4
	2	UG18	67.7	59.5	68.9	71.2	71.2	51.6	42.2	52.1	54.0	58.1
	3	ELiRF-UPV	64.8	59.1	63.2	66.3	70.5	44.0	41.0	37.5	45.6	51.7
	6	SVM-Unigrams	54.3	45.7	61.9	53.6	56.0	46.2	42.9	47.4	47.9	46.4
	8	Median Team	44.1	34.8	53.3	41.4	47.1	38.2	24.6	42.5	44.8	41.0
	15	Random Baseline	-1.2	-5.6	0.4	1.8	-1.4	-0.5	0.1	-4.6	1.8	0.8

Table 7: Task 1 emotion intensity regression (EI-reg): Results.

Lexicon	#Teams
AFINN	23
ANEW	9
Arabic translation of the NRC Emotion Lexicon	4
Bing Liu Lexicon	23
ElhPolar polarity lexicon for Spanish	3
LIWC	5
Mohammad et al.'s Arabic Emoticon Lexicon	5
Mohammad et al.'s Arabic Hashtag Lexicon	5
Mohammad et al.'s Arabic Hashtag Lexicon (dialectal)	2
MPQA	21
NRC Affect Intensity Lexicon	21
NRC Emoticon Lexicon (Sentiment140)	24
NRC Emotion Lexicon (EmoLex)	22
NRC Hashtag Emotion Lexicon	23
NRC Hashtag Sentiment Lexicon	25
SentiStrength	18
SentiWordNet	18
Spanish translation of the NRC Emotion Lexicon	5
No lexicons used	29

Figure 4: Lexicons used by teams.

High-Ranking English Systems: The best performing system for regression (EI-reg, V-reg) and ordinal classification (EI-oc,V-oc) sub-tasks in English was *SeerNet*. The team proposed a unified architecture for regression and ordinal classification based on the fusion of heterogeneous features and the ensemble of multiple predictive models. The following models or resources were used for feature extraction:

- *DeepMoji* (Felbo et al., 2017): a neural network for predicting emoji for tweets trained from a very large distant supervision corpus. The last two layers of the network were used as features.

- *Skip thoughts*: an unsupervised neural network for encoding sentences (Kiros et al., 2015).

- *Sentiment neurons* (Radford et al., 2017): a byte-level recurrent language model for learning sentence representations.

- Features derived from affective lexicons.

These feature vectors were used for training XG Boost and Random Forest models (using both regression and classification variants), which were later stacked using ordinal logistic regression and ridge regression models for the corresponding ordinal classification and regression tasks.

Other teams also relied on both deep neural network representations of tweets and lexicon features to learn a model with either a traditional machine learning algorithm, such as SVM/SVR (*PlusEmo2Vec*, *TCS Research*) and Logistic Regression (*PlusEmo2Vec*), or a deep neural network (*NTUA-SLP*, *psyML*). The sentence embeddings were obtained by training a neural network on the provided training data, a distant supervision corpus (e.g., AIT2018 Distant Supervision Corpus that has tweets with emotion-related query terms), sentiment-labeled tweet corpora (e.g., Semeval-2017 Task4A dataset on sentiment analysis in Twitter), or by using pre-trained models.

Test Set	Rank	Team Name	Pearson r (all classes)					Pearson r (some-emotion)				
			avg	anger	fear	joy	sadness	avg	anger	fear	joy	sadness
English												
	1	SeerNet	69.5	70.6	63.7	72.0	71.7	54.7	55.9	45.8	61.0	56.0
	2	PlusEmo2Vec	65.9	70.4	52.8	72.0	68.3	50.1	54.8	32.0	60.4	53.3
	3	psyML	65.3	67.0	58.8	68.6	66.7	50.5	51.7	46.8	57.0	46.3
	17	Median Team	53.0	53.0	47.0	55.2	56.7	41.5	40.8	31.0	49.4	44.8
	26	SVM-Unigrams	39.4	38.2	35.5	46.9	37.0	29.6	31.5	18.3	39.6	28.9
	37	Random Baseline	-1.6	-6.2	4.7	1.4	-6.1	-1.1	-3.8	-0.7	-0.2	0.1
Arabic												
	1	AffecThor	58.7	55.1	55.1	63.1	61.8	43.7	42.6	47.2	44.6	40.4
	2	EiTAKA	57.4	57.2	52.9	63.4	56.3	46.0	48.8	47.6	50.9	36.6
	3	UNCC	51.7	45.9	48.3	53.8	58.7	36.3	34.1	33.1	38.3	39.8
	6	SVM-Unigrams	31.5	28.1	28.1	39.6	30.2	23.6	25.1	25.2	24.1	20.1
	7	Median Team	30.5	30.1	24.2	36.0	31.5	24.8	24.2	17.2	28.3	29.4
	11	Random Baseline	0.6	-5.7	-1.9	0.8	9.2	1.2	0.2	-2.0	2.9	3.7
Spanish												
	1	AffecThor	66.4	60.6	70.6	66.7	67.7	54.2	47.4	58.8	53.5	57.2
	2	UG18	59.9	49.9	60.6	66.5	62.5	48.5	38.0	49.3	53.1	53.4
	3	INGEOTEC	59.6	46.8	63.4	65.5	62.8	46.3	33.0	49.8	53.3	49.2
	6	SVM-Unigrams	48.1	44.4	54.6	45.1	48.3	40.8	37.1	46.1	37.1	42.7
	8	Median Team	36.0	26.3	28.3	51.3	38.0	33.1	24.0	26.1	50.5	31.6
	15	Random Baseline	-2.2	1.1	-6.9	-0.5	-2.7	1.6	0.2	-1.8	4.4	3.6

Table 8: Task 2 emotion intensity ordinal classification (EI-oc): Results.

Rank	Team Name	r (all)	r (0.5-1)
English			
1	SeerNet	87.3	69.7
2	TCS Research	86.1	68.0
3	PlusEmo2Vec	86.0	69.1
18	Median Team	78.4	59.1
31	SVM-Unigrams	58.5	44.9
35	Random Baseline	3.1	1.2
Arabic			
1	EiTAKA	82.8	57.8
2	AffecThor	81.6	59.7
3	EMA	80.4	57.6
6	Median Team	72.0	36.2
9	SVM-Unigrams	57.1	42.3
13	Random Baseline	-5.2	2.2
Spanish			
1	AffecThor	79.5	65.9
2	Amobee	77.0	64.2
3	ELiRF-UPV	74.2	57.1
6	Median Team	60.9	50.9
9	SVM-Unigrams	57.4	51.5
13	Random Baseline	-2.3	2.3

Table 9: Task 3 valence regression (V-reg): Results.

Rank	Team Name	r (all)	r (some emo)
English			
1	SeerNet	83.6	88.4
2	PlusEmo2Vec	83.3	87.8
3	Amobee	81.3	86.5
18	Median Team	68.2	75.4
24	SVM-Unigrams	50.9	56.0
36	Random Baseline	-1.0	-1.2
Arabic			
1	EiTAKA	80.9	84.7
2	AffecThor	75.2	79.2
3	INGEOTEC	74.9	78.9
7	Median Team	55.2	59.6
8	SVM-Unigrams	47.1	50.5
14	Random Baseline	1.1	0.9
Spanish			
1	Amobee	76.5	80.4
2	AffecThor	75.6	79.2
3	ELiRF-UPV	72.9	76.5
6	Median Team	55.6	59.1
8	SVM-Unigrams	41.8	46.1
13	Random Baseline	-4.2	-4.3

Table 10: Task 4 valence ord. classifn. (V-oc): Results.

High-Ranking Arabic Systems: Top teams trained their systems using deep learning techniques, such as CNN, LSTM and Bi-LSTM (*AffecThor, EiTAKA, UNCC*). Traditional machine learning approaches, such as Logistic Regression, Ridge Regression, Random Forest and SVC/SVM, were also employed (*EMA, INGEOTEC, PARTNA, Tw-StAR*). Many teams relied on Arabic pre-processing and normalization techniques in an attempt to decrease the sparsity due to morphological complexity in the Arabic language. *EMA* applied stemming and lemmatization using MADAMIRA (a morphological analysis and disambiguation tool for Arabic), while *TwStar* and *PARTNA* used stemmer designed for handling tweets. In addition, top systems applied additional pre-processing, such as dropping punctuations, mentions, stop words, and hashtag symbols.

Many teams (e.g., *AffecThor, EiTAKA and EMA*) utilized Arabic sentiment lexicons (Mohammad et al., 2016; Badaro et al., 2014). Some teams (e.g., *EMA*) used Arabic translations of the NRC Emotion Lexicon (Mohammad and Turney, 2013). Pre-trained Arabic word embeddings (AraVec) generated from a large set of tweets were also used as additional input features by

EMA and *UNCC*. *AffecThor* collected 4.4 million Arabic tweets to train their own word embeddings. Traditional machine learning algorithms (Random Forest, SVR and Ridge regression) used by *EMA* obtained results rivaling those obtained by deep learning approaches.

High-Ranking Spanish Systems: Convolutional neural networks and recurrent neural networks with gated units such as LSTM and GRU were employed by the winning Spanish teams (*AffecThor, Amobee, ELIRF-UPV, UG18*). Word embeddings trained from Spanish tweets, such as the ones provided by Rothe et al. (2016), were used as the basis for training deep learning models. They were also employed as features for more traditional learning schemes such as SVMs (*UG18*). Spanish Affective Lexicons such as the *Spanish Emotion Lexicon* (SEL) (Sidorov et al., 2012) and *ML-SentiCon* (Cruz et al., 2014) were also used to build the feature space (*UWB, SINAI*). Translation was used in two different ways: 1) automatic translation of English affective lexicons into Spanish (*SINAI*), and 2): training set augmentation via automatic translation of English tweets (*Amobee, UG18*).

6.2 Summary

In the standard deep learning or representation learning approach, data representations (tweets in our case) are jointly trained for the task at hand via neural networks with convolution or recurrent layers (LeCun et al., 2015). The claim is that this can lead to more robust representations than relying on manually-engineered features. In contrast, here, most of the top-performing systems employed manually-engineered representations for tweets. These representations combine trained representations, models trained on distant supervision corpora, and unsupervised word and sentence embeddings, with manually-engineered features, such as features derived from affect lexicons. This shows that despite being rather powerful, representation learning can benefit from working in tandem with task-specific features. For emotion intensity tasks, lexicons such as the Affect Intensity Lexicon (Mohammad, 2018b) that provide intensity scores are particularly helpful. Similarly, tasks on valence, arousal, and dominance can benefit from lexicons such as ANEW (Bradley and Lang, 1999) and the newly created NRC Valence-Arousal-Dominance Lexicon (Mohammad, 2018a), which has entries for about 20,000 English terms.

Rank	Team Name	acc.	micro F1	macro F1
English				
1	NTUA-SLP	58.8	70.1	52.8
2	TCS Research	58.2	69.3	53.0
3	PlusEmo2Vec	57.6	69.2	49.7
17	Median Team	47.1	59.9	46.4
21	SVM-Unigrams	44.2	57.0	44.3
28	Random Baseline	18.5	30.7	28.5
Arabic				
1	EMA	48.9	61.8	46.1
2	PARTNA	48.4	60.8	47.5
3	Tw-StAR	46.5	59.7	44.6
6	SVM-Unigrams	38.0	51.6	38.4
7	Median Team	25.4	37.9	25.0
9	Random Baseline	17.7	29.4	27.5
Spanish				
1	MILAB_SNU	46.9	55.8	40.7
2	ELiRF-UPV	45.8	53.5	44.0
3	Tw-StAR	43.8	52.0	39.2
4	SVM-Unigrams	39.3	47.8	38.2
7	Median Team	16.7	27.5	18.7
8	Random Baseline	13.4	22.8	21.3

Table 11: Task 5 emotion classification (E-c): Results.

7 Examining Gender and Race Bias in Sentiment Analysis Systems

Automatic systems can benefit society by promoting equity, diversity, and fairness. Nonetheless, as machine learning systems become more human-like in their predictions, they are inadvertently accentuating and perpetuating inappropriate human biases. Examples include, loan eligibility and crime recidivism prediction systems that negatively assess people belonging to a certain pin/zip code (which may disproportionately impact people of a certain race) (Chouldechova, 2017), and resumé sorting systems that believe that men are more qualified to be programmers than women (Bolukbasi et al., 2016). Similarly, sentiment and emotion analysis systems can also perpetuate and accentuate inappropriate human biases, e.g., systems that consider utterances from one race or gender to be less positive simply because of their race or gender, or customer support systems that prioritize a call from an angry male user over a call from the equally angry female user.

Discrimination-aware data mining focuses on measuring discrimination in data (Zliobaite, 2015; Pedreshi et al., 2008; Hajian and Domingo-Ferrer, 2013). In that spirit, we carried out an analysis of the systems' outputs for biases towards certain races and genders. In particular, we wanted to test a hypothesis that a system should equally rate the intensity of the emotion expressed by two sentences that differ only in the gender/race of a person mentioned. Note that here the term *system* refers to the combination of a machine learning architecture trained on a labeled dataset, and possibly using additional language resources. The bias can originate from any or several of these parts.

We used Equity Evaluation Corpus (EEC), a recently created dataset of 8,640 English sentences carefully chosen to tease out gender and race biases (Kiritchenko and Mohammad, 2018). We used the EEC as a supplementary test set in the EI-reg and V-reg English tasks. Specifically, we compare emotion and sentiment intensity scores that the systems predict on pairs of sentences in the EEC that differ only in one word corresponding to race or gender (e.g., *'This man made me feel angry'* vs. *'This woman made me feel angry'*). Complete details on how the EEC was created, its constituent sentences, and the analysis of automatic systems for race and gender bias is available in Kiritchenko and Mohammad (2018); we summarize the key results below.

Despite the work we describe here and that proposed by others, it should be noted that mechanisms to detect bias can often be circumvented. Nonetheless, as developers of sentiment analysis systems, and NLP systems more broadly, we cannot absolve ourselves of the ethical implications of the systems we build. Thus, the Equity Evaluation Corpus is not meant to be a catch-all for all inappropriate biases, but rather just one of the several ways by which we can examine the fairness of sentiment analysis systems. The EEC corpus is freely available so that both developers and users can use it, and build on it.[18]

7.1 Methodology

The race and gender bias evaluation was carried out on the EI-reg and V-reg predictions of 219 automatic systems (by 50 teams) on the EEC sentences. The EEC sentences were created from simple templates such as '*<noun phrase> feels devastated*', where *<noun phrase>* is replaced with one of the following:

- common African American (AA) female and male first names,
- common European American (EA) female and male first names,
- noun phrases referring to females and males, such as *'my daughter'* and *'my son'*.

Notably, one can derive pairs of sentences from the EEC such that they differ only in one phrase cor-

[18]http://saifmohammad.com/WebPages/Biases-SA.html

responding to gender or race (e.g., *'My daughter feels devastated'* and *'My son feels devastated'*). For the full lists of names, noun phrases, and sentence templates see (Kiritchenko and Mohammad, 2018). In total, 1,584 pairs of scores were compared for gender and 144 pairs of scores were compared for race.

For each submission, we performed the paired two sample t-test to determine whether the mean difference between the two sets of scores (across the two races and across the two genders) is significant. We set the significance level to 0.05. However, since we performed 438 assessments (219 submissions evaluated for biases in both gender and race), we applied Bonferroni correction. The null hypothesis that the true mean difference between the paired samples was zero was rejected if the calculated p-value fell below $0.05/438$.

7.2 Results

7.2.1 Gender Bias Results

Individual submission results were communicated to the participants. Here, we present the summary results across all the teams. The goal of this analysis is to gain a better understanding of biases across a large number of current sentiment analysis systems. Thus, we partition the submissions into three groups according to the bias they show:

- $F = M$: submissions that showed no statistically significant difference in intensity scores predicted for corresponding female and male noun phrase sentences,
- $F{\uparrow}–M{\downarrow}$: submissions that consistently gave higher scores for sentences with female noun phrases than for corresponding sentences with male noun phrases,
- $F{\downarrow}–M{\uparrow}$: submissions that consistently gave lower scores for sentences with female noun phrases than for corresponding sentences with male noun phrases,

Table 12 shows the number of submissions in each group. If all the systems are unbiased, then the number of submissions for the group $F = M$ would be the maximum, and the number of submissions in all other groups would be zero.

Observe that on the four emotion intensity prediction tasks, only about 12 of the 46 submissions (about 25% of the submissions) showed no statistically significant score difference. On the valence prediction task, only 5 of the 36 submissions (14% of the submissions) showed no statistically

Task	F = M	F↑–M↓	F↓–M↑	all
EI-reg				
anger	12	21	13	46
fear	11	12	23	46
joy	12	25	8	45
sadness	12	18	16	46
V-reg	5	22	9	36

Table 12: **Analysis of gender bias:** The number of submissions in each of the three bias groups.

Task	AA = EA	AA↑–EA↓	AA↓–EA↑	All
EI-reg				
anger	11	28	7	46
fear	5	29	12	46
joy	8	7	30	45
sadness	6	35	5	46
V-reg	3	4	29	36

Table 13: **Analysis of race bias:** The number of submissions in each of the three bias groups.

significant score difference. Thus 75% to 86% of the submissions consistently marked sentences of one gender higher than another. When predicting anger, joy, or valence, the number of systems consistently giving higher scores to sentences with female noun phrases (21–25) is markedly higher than the number of systems giving higher scores to sentences with male noun phrases (8–13). (Recall that higher valence means more positive sentiment.)

In contrast, on the fear task, most submissions tended to assign higher scores to sentences with male noun phrases (23) as compared to the number of systems giving higher scores to sentences with female noun phrases (12). When predicting sadness, the number of submissions that mostly assigned higher scores to sentences with female noun phrases (18) is close to the number of submissions that mostly assigned higher scores to sentences with male noun phrases (16).

7.2.2 Race Bias Results

We did a similar analysis as for gender, for race. For each submission on each task, we calculated the difference between the average predicted score on the set of sentences with African American (AA) names and the average predicted score on the set of sentences with European American (EA) names. Then, we aggregated the results over all such sentence pairs in the EEC.

Table 13 shows the results. The table has the same form and structure as the gender result table. Observe that the number of submissions with no statistically significant score difference for sentences pertaining to the two races is about 5–11 (about 11% to 24%) for the four emotions and 3 (about 8%) for valence. These numbers are even lower than what was found for gender.

The majority of the systems assigned higher scores to sentences with African American names on the tasks of anger, fear, and sadness intensity prediction. On the joy and valence tasks, most submissions tended to assign higher scores to sentences with European American names.

We found the score differences across genders and across races to be somewhat small (< 0.03 in magnitude, which is 3% of the 0 to 1 score range). However, what impact a consistent bias, even with a magnitude $< 3\%$, might have in downstream applications merits further investigation.

8 Summary

We organized the SemEval-2018 Task 1: Affect in Tweets, which included five subtasks on inferring the affectual state of a person from their tweet. For each task, we provided training, development, and test datasets for English, Arabic, and Spanish tweets. This involved creating a new Affect in Tweets dataset of more than 22,000 tweets such that subsets are annotated for a number of emotion dimensions. For each emotion dimension, we annotated the data not just for coarse classes (such as anger or no anger) but also for fine-grained real-valued scores indicating the intensity of emotion. We used Best–Worst Scaling to obtain fine-grained real-valued intensity scores and showed that the annotations are reliable (split-half reliability scores > 0.8).

Seventy-five teams made 319 submissions to the fifteen task–language pairs. Most of the top-performing teams relied on both deep neural network representations of tweets (sentence embeddings) as well as features derived from existing sentiment and emotion lexicons. Apart from the usual evaluations for the quality of predictions, we also examined 219 EI-reg and V-reg English submissions for bias towards particular races and genders using the Equity Evaluation Corpus. We found that a majority of the systems consistently provided slightly higher scores for one race or gender. All of the data is made freely available.[19]

---

[19]https://competitions.codalab.org/competitions/17751

References

Gilbert Badaro, Ramy Baly, Hazem M. Hajj, Nizar Habash, and Wassim El-Hajj. 2014. A large scale arabic sentiment lexicon for arabic opinion mining. In *Proceedings of the EMNLP 2014 Workshop on Arabic Natural Language Processing*, pages 165–173, Doha, Qatar.

Tolga Bolukbasi, Kai-Wei Chang, James Y Zou, Venkatesh Saligrama, and Adam T Kalai. 2016. Man is to computer programmer as woman is to homemaker? debiasing word embeddings. In *Proceedings of the Annual Conference on Neural Information Processing Systems (NIPS)*, pages 4349–4357.

Margaret M Bradley and Peter J Lang. 1999. Affective norms for English words (ANEW): Instruction manual and affective ratings. Technical report, The Center for Research in Psychophysiology, University of Florida.

Alexandra Chouldechova. 2017. Fair prediction with disparate impact: A study of bias in recidivism prediction instruments. *Big data*, 5(2):153–163.

LJ Cronbach. 1946. A case study of the splithalf reliability coefficient. *Journal of educational psychology*, 37(8):473.

Fermín L Cruz, José A Troyan, Beatriz Pontes, and F Javier Ortega. 2014. Ml-senticon: Un lexicón multilingüe de polaridades semánticas a nivel de lemas. *Procesamiento del Lenguaje Natural*, (53).

Paul Ekman. 1992. An argument for basic emotions. *Cognition and Emotion*, 6(3):169–200.

Bjarke Felbo, Alan Mislove, Anders Søgaard, Iyad Rahwan, and Sune Lehmann. 2017. Using millions of emoji occurrences to learn any-domain representations for detecting sentiment, emotion and sarcasm. In *Proceedings of the 2017 Conference on Empirical Methods in Natural Language Processing, 2017, Copenhagen, Denmark, September 9-11, 2017*, pages 1615–1625.

T. N. Flynn and A. A. J. Marley. 2014. Best-worst scaling: theory and methods. In Stephane Hess and Andrew Daly, editors, *Handbook of Choice Modelling*, pages 178–201. Edward Elgar Publishing.

Nico H Frijda. 1988. The laws of emotion. *American psychologist*, 43(5):349.

Sara Hajian and Josep Domingo-Ferrer. 2013. A methodology for direct and indirect discrimination prevention in data mining. *IEEE Transactions on Knowledge and Data Engineering*, 25(7):1445–1459.

Minqing Hu and Bing Liu. 2004. Mining and summarizing customer reviews. In *Proceedings of the tenth ACM SIGKDD international conference on Knowledge discovery and data mining*, pages 168–177, New York, NY, USA. ACM.

Svetlana Kiritchenko and Saif M. Mohammad. 2016. Capturing reliable fine-grained sentiment associations by crowdsourcing and best–worst scaling. In *Proceedings of The 15th Annual Conference of the North American Chapter of the Association for Computational Linguistics: Human Language Technologies (NAACL)*, San Diego, California.

Svetlana Kiritchenko and Saif M. Mohammad. 2017. Best-worst scaling more reliable than rating scales: A case study on sentiment intensity annotation. In *Proceedings of The Annual Meeting of the Association for Computational Linguistics (ACL)*, Vancouver, Canada.

Svetlana Kiritchenko and Saif M. Mohammad. 2018. Examining gender and race bias in two hundred sentiment analysis systems. In *Proceedings of the 7th Joint Conference on Lexical and Computational Semantics (*SEM)*.

Svetlana Kiritchenko, Xiaodan Zhu, and Saif M. Mohammad. 2014. Sentiment analysis of short informal texts. *Journal of Artificial Intelligence Research*, 50:723–762.

Ryan Kiros, Yukun Zhu, Ruslan R Salakhutdinov, Richard Zemel, Raquel Urtasun, Antonio Torralba, and Sanja Fidler. 2015. Skip-thought vectors. In *Advances in neural information processing systems*, pages 3294–3302.

G Frederic Kuder and Marion W Richardson. 1937. The theory of the estimation of test reliability. *Psychometrika*, 2(3):151–160.

Yann LeCun, Yoshua Bengio, and Geoffrey Hinton. 2015. Deep learning. *Nature*, 521(7553):436.

Jordan J. Louviere. 1991. Best-worst scaling: A model for the largest difference judgments. Working Paper.

Saif Mohammad, Mohammad Salameh, and Svetlana Kiritchenko. 2016. Sentiment lexicons for arabic social media. In *Proceedings of the Tenth International Conference on Language Resources and Evaluation (LREC 2016)*, Paris, France. European Language Resources Association (ELRA).

Saif M. Mohammad. 2016. Sentiment analysis: Detecting valence, emotions, and other affectual states from text. In Herb Meiselman, editor, *Emotion Measurement*. Elsevier.

Saif M. Mohammad. 2018a. Obtaining reliable human ratings of valence, arousal, and dominance for 20,000 english words. In *Proceedings of The Annual Meeting of the Association for Computational Linguistics (ACL)*, Melbourne, Australia.

Saif M. Mohammad. 2018b. Word affect intensities. In *Proceedings of the 11th Edition of the Language Resources and Evaluation Conference (LREC-2018)*, Miyazaki, Japan.

Saif M. Mohammad and Felipe Bravo-Marquez. 2017. WASSA-2017 shared task on emotion intensity. In *Proceedings of the Workshop on Computational Approaches to Subjectivity, Sentiment and Social Media Analysis (WASSA)*, Copenhagen, Denmark.

Saif M. Mohammad and Svetlana Kiritchenko. 2018. Understanding emotions: A dataset of tweets to study interactions between affect categories. In *Proceedings of the 11th Edition of the Language Resources and Evaluation Conference (LREC-2018)*, Miyazaki, Japan.

Saif M. Mohammad, Parinaz Sobhani, and Svetlana Kiritchenko. 2017. Stance and sentiment in tweets. *Special Section of the ACM Transactions on Internet Technology on Argumentation in Social Media*, 17(3).

Saif M. Mohammad and Peter D. Turney. 2013. Crowdsourcing a word–emotion association lexicon. *Computational Intelligence*, 29(3):436–465.

Finn Årup Nielsen. 2011. A new ANEW: Evaluation of a word list for sentiment analysis in microblogs. In *Proceedings of the ESWC Workshop on 'Making Sense of Microposts': Big things come in small packages*, pages 93–98, Heraklion, Crete.

Bryan Orme. 2009. Maxdiff analysis: Simple counting, individual-level logit, and HB. Sawtooth Software, Inc.

Raquel Mochales Palau and Marie-Francine Moens. 2009. Argumentation mining: the detection, classification and structure of arguments in text. In *Proceedings of the 12th international conference on artificial intelligence and law*, pages 98–107.

W Parrot. 2001. *Emotions in Social Psychology*. Psychology Press.

Dino Pedreshi, Salvatore Ruggieri, and Franco Turini. 2008. Discrimination-aware data mining. In *Proceedings of the 14th ACM SIGKDD International Conference on Knowledge Discovery and Data Mining*, pages 560–568.

Robert Plutchik. 1980. A general psychoevolutionary theory of emotion. *Emotion: Theory, research, and experience*, 1(3):3–33.

Alec Radford, Rafal Jozefowicz, and Ilya Sutskever. 2017. Learning to generate reviews and discovering sentiment. *arXiv preprint arXiv:1704.01444*.

Sascha Rothe, Sebastian Ebert, and Hinrich Schütze. 2016. Ultradense word embeddings by orthogonal transformation. In *HLT-NAACL*.

James A Russell. 1980. A circumplex model of affect. *Journal of personality and social psychology*, 39(6):1161.

James A Russell. 2003. Core affect and the psychological construction of emotion. *Psychological review*, 110(1):145.

Grigori Sidorov, Sabino Miranda-Jiménez, Francisco Viveros-Jiménez, Alexander Gelbukh, Noé Castro-Sánchez, Francisco Velásquez, Ismael Díaz-Rangel, Sergio Suárez-Guerra, Alejandro Treviño, and Juan Gordon. 2012. Empirical study of machine learning based approach for opinion mining in tweets. In *Mexican international conference on Artificial intelligence*, pages 1–14. Springer.

Michael Wojatzki, Saif M. Mohammad, Torsten Zesch, and Svetlana Kiritchenko. 2018. Quantifying qualitative data for understanding controversial issues. In *Proceedings of the 11th Edition of the Language Resources and Evaluation Conference (LREC-2018)*, Miyazaki, Japan.

Indre Zliobaite. 2015. A survey on measuring indirect discrimination in machine learning. *arXiv preprint arXiv:1511.00148*.

Appendix

Table 14 shows the summary details of the annotations done for the SemEval-2018 Affect in Tweets dataset. Figure 5 shows the histograms of the EI-reg tweets in the anger, joy, sadness, and fear datasets. The tweets are grouped into bins of scores 0–0.05, 0.05–0.1, and so on until 0.95–1. The colors for the bins correspond to their ordinal classes: no emotion, low emotion, moderate emotion, and high emotion. The ordinal classes were determined from the EI-oc manual annotations.

Supplementary Material: The supplementary pdf associated with this paper includes longer versions of tables included in this paper. Tables 1 to 15 in the supplementary pdf show result tables that include the scores of each of the 319 systems participating in the tasks. Table 16 in the supplementary pdf shows the annotator agreement for each of the twelve classes, for each of the three languages, in the Multi-label Emotion Classification (E-c) Dataset. We observe that the Fleiss' κ scores are markedly higher for the frequently occurring four basic emotions (joy, sadness, fear, and anger), and lower for the less frequent emotions. (Frequencies for the emotions are shown in Table 2.) Also, agreement is low for the neutral class. This is not surprising because the boundary between neutral (or no emotion) and slight emotion is fuzzy. This means that often at least one or two annotators indicate that the person is feeling some joy or some sadness, even if most others indicate that the person is not feeling any emotion.

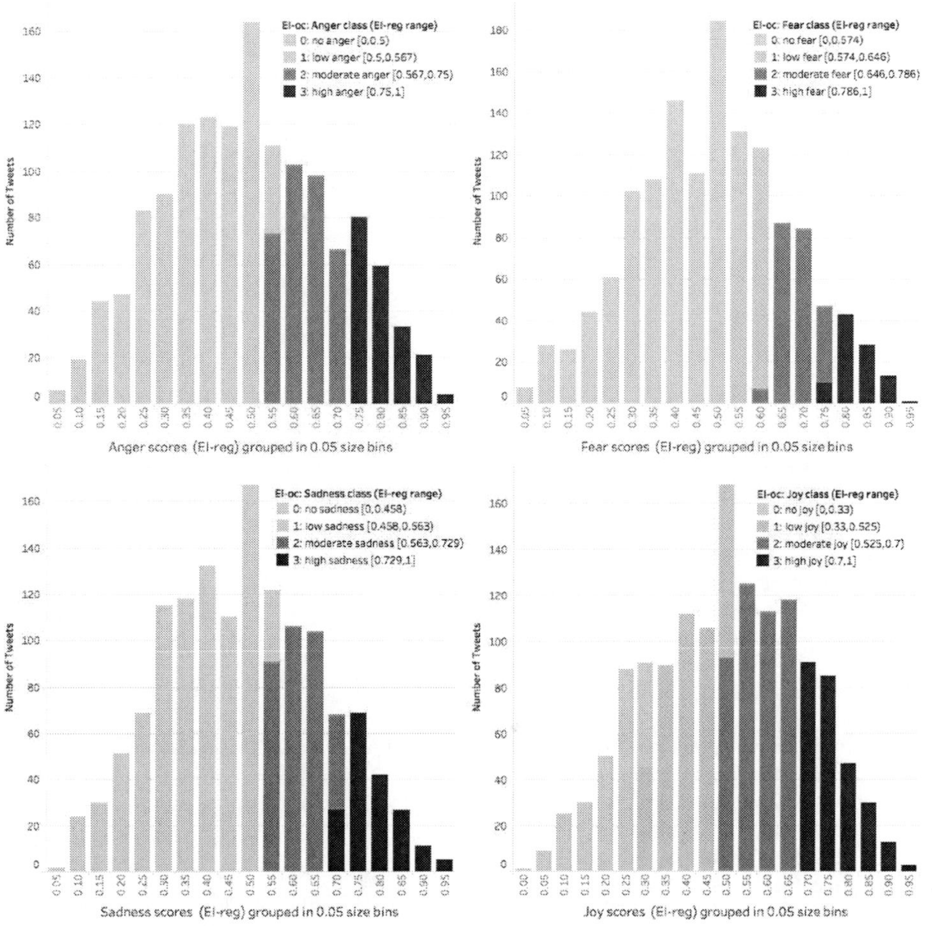

Figure 5: Emotion intensity score (EI-reg) and ordinal class (EI-oc) distributions for the four basic emotions in the SemEval-2018 AIT development and test sets combined. The distribution is similar for the training set (annotated in earlier work).

Dataset	Scheme	Location	Item	#Items	#Annotators	MAI	#Q/Item	#Annotat.
English								
E-c	categorical	World	tweet	11,090	303	7	2	174,356
EI-reg								
anger	BWS	USA	4-tuple of tweets	2,780	168	4	2	27,046
fear	BWS	USA	4-tuple of tweets	2,750	220	4	2	26,908
joy	BWS	USA	4-tuple of tweets	2,790	132	4	2	26,676
sadness	BWS	USA	4-tuple of tweets	2,744	118	4	2	26,260
V-reg	BWS	USA	4-tuple of tweets	5,134	175	4	2	49,856
Total								**331,102**
Arabic								
E-c	categorical	World	tweet	4,400	175	7	1	36,274
EI-reg								
anger	BWS	World	4-tuple of tweets	2,800	221	4	2	25,960
fear	BWS	World	4-tuple of tweets	2,800	197	4	2	25,872
joy	BWS	World	4-tuple of tweets	2,800	133	4	2	24,690
sadness	BWS	World	4-tuple of tweets	2,800	177	4	2	25,834
V-reg	BWS	World	4-tuple of tweets	3,600	239	4	2	36,824
Total								**175,454**
Spanish								
E-c	categorical	World	tweet	7,182	160	7	1	56,274
EI-reg								
anger	BWS	World	4-tuple of tweets	3,972	157	3	2	27,456
fear	BWS	World	4-tuple of tweets	3,972	388	3	2	29,530
joy	BWS	World	4-tuple of tweets	3,980	323	3	2	28,300
sadness	BWS	World	4-tuple of tweets	3,982	443	3	2	28,462
V-reg	BWS	World	4-tuple of tweets	4,886	220	3	2	38,680
Total								**208,702**

Table 14: Summary details of the current annotations done for the SemEval-2018 Affect in Tweets Dataset. MAI = Median Annotations per Item. Q = annotation questions.

SeerNet at SemEval-2018 Task 1: Domain Adaptation for Affect in Tweets

Venkatesh Duppada, Royal Jain, Sushant Hiray
Seernet Technologies, LLC
{venkatesh.duppada, royal.jain, sushant.hiray}@seernet.io

Abstract

The paper describes the best performing system for the SemEval-2018 Affect in Tweets (English) sub-tasks. The system focuses on the ordinal classification and regression sub-tasks for valence and emotion. For ordinal classification valence is classified into 7 different classes ranging from -3 to 3 whereas emotion is classified into 4 different classes 0 to 3 separately for each emotion namely anger, fear, joy and sadness. The regression sub-tasks estimate the intensity of valence and each emotion. The system performs domain adaptation of 4 different models and creates an ensemble to give the final prediction. The proposed system achieved 1st position out of 75 teams which participated in the fore-mentioned sub-tasks. We outperform the baseline model by margins ranging from 49.2% to 76.4%, thus, pushing the state-of-the-art significantly.

1 Introduction

Twitter is one of the most popular micro-blogging platforms that has attracted over 300M daily users[1] with over 500M [2] tweets sent every day. Tweet data has attracted NLP researchers because of the ease of access to large data-source of people expressing themselves online. Tweets are micro-texts comprising of emoticons, hashtags as well as location data, making them feature rich for performing various kinds of analysis. Tweets provide an interesting challenge as users tend to write grammatically incorrect and use informal and slang words.

In domain of natural language processing, emotion recognition is the task of associating words, phrases or documents with emotions from predefined using psychological models. The classification of emotions has mainly been researched from two fundamental viewpoints. (Ekman, 1992) and (Plutchik, 2001) proposed that emotions are discrete with each emotion being a distinct entity. On the contrary, (Mehrabian, 1980) and (Russell, 1980) propose that emotions can be categorized into dimensional groupings.

Affect in Tweets (Mohammad et al., 2018) - shared task in SemEval-2018 focuses on extracting affect from tweets confirming to both variants of the emotion models, extracting valence (dimensional) and emotion (discrete). Previous version of the task (Mohammad and Bravo-Marquez, 2017) focused on estimating the emotion intensity in tweets. We participated in 4 sub-tasks of Affect in Tweets, all dealing with English tweets. The sub-tasks were: EI-oc: Ordinal classification of emotion intensity of 4 different emotions (anger, joy, sadness, fear), EI-reg: to determine the intensity of emotions (anger, joy, sadness, fear) into a real-valued scale of 0-1, V-oc: Ordinal classification of valence into one of 7 ordinal classes [-3, 3], V-reg: determine the intensity of valence on the scale of 0-1.

Prior work in extracting Valence, Arousal, Dominance (VAD) from text primarily relied on using and extending lexicons (Bestgen and Vincze, 2012) (Turney et al., 2011). Recent advancements in deep learning have been applied in detecting sentiments from tweets (Tang et al., 2014), (Liu et al., 2012), (Mohammad et al., 2013).

In this work, we use various state-of-the-art machine learning models and perform domain adaptation (Pan and Yang, 2010) from their source task to the target task. We use multi-view ensemble learning technique (Kumar and Minz, 2016) to produce the optimal feature-set partitioning for the classifier. Finally, results from multiple such classifiers are stacked together to create an ensemble (Polikar, 2012).

---

[1]https://www.statista.com/statistics/282087/number-of-monthly-active-twitter-users/

[2]http://www.internetlivestats.com/twitter-statistics/

Proceedings of the 12th International Workshop on Semantic Evaluation (SemEval-2018), pages 18–23
New Orleans, Louisiana, June 5–6, 2018. ©2018 Association for Computational Linguistics

In this paper, we describe our approach and experiments to solve this problem. The rest of the paper is laid out as follows: Section 2 describes the system architecture, Section 3 reports results and inference from different experiments. Finally we conclude in Section 4 along with a discussion about future work.

2 System Description

2.1 Pipeline

Figure 1 details the System Architecture. We now describe how all the different modules are tied together. The input raw tweet is pre-processed as described in Section 2.2. The processed tweet is passed through all the feature extractors described in Section 2.3. At the end of this step, we extract 5 different feature vectors corresponding to each tweet. Each feature vector is passed through the model zoo where classifiers with different hyper parameters are tuned. The models are described in Section 2.4. For each vector, the results of top-2 performing models (based on cross-validation) are retained. At the end of this step, we've 10 different results corresponding to each tweet. All these results are ensembled together via stacking as described in Section 2.4.3. Finally, the output from the ensembler is the output returned by the system.

2.2 Pre-processing

The pre-processing step modifies the raw tweets to prepare for feature extraction. Tweets are pre-processed using **tweettokenize** [3] tool. Twitter specific keywords are replaced with tokens, namely, USERNAME, PHONENUMBER, URLs, timestamps. All characters are converted to lowercase. A contiguous sequence of emojis is first split into individual emojis. We then replace an emoji with its description. The descriptions were scraped from EmojiPedia[4].

2.3 Feature Extraction

As mentioned in Section 1, we perform transfer learning from various state-of-the-art deep learning techniques. We will go through the following sub-sections to understand these models in detail.

2.3.1 DeepMoji

DeepMoji (Felbo et al., 2017) performs distant supervision on a very large dataset (1246 million tweets) comprising of noisy labels (emojis). DeepMoji was able to obtain state-of-the-art results in various downstream tasks using transfer learning. This makes it an ideal candidate for domain adaptation into related target tasks. We extract 2 different feature sets by extracting the embeddings from the softmax and the attention layer from the pre-trained DeepMoji model. The vector from softmax layer is of dimension 64 and the vector from attention layer is of dimension 2304.

2.3.2 Skip-Thought Vectors

Skip-Thought vectors (Kiros et al., 2015) is an off-the-shelf encoder that can produce highly generic sentence representations. Since tweets are restricted by character limit, skip-thought vectors can create a good semantic representation. This representation is then passed to the classifier. The representation is of dimension 4800.

2.3.3 Unsupervised Sentiment Neuron

(Radford et al., 2017) developed an unsupervised system which learned an excellent representation of sentiment. The original model was trained to generate amazon reviews, this makes the sentiment neuron an ideal candidate for transfer learning. The representation extracted from Sentiment Neuron is of size 4096.

2.3.4 EmoInt

Apart from all the pre-trained embeddings, we choose to also include various lexical features bundled through the EmoInt package [5] (Duppada and Hiray, 2017) The lexical features include AFINN (Nielsen, 2011), NRC Affect Intensities (Mohammad, 2017), NRC-Word-Affect Emotion Lexicon (Mohammad and Turney, 2010), NRC Hashtag Sentiment Lexicon and Sentiment140 Lexicon (Mohammad et al., 2013). The final feature vector is the concatenation of all the individual features. This feature vector is of size (141, 1).

This gives us five different feature vector variants. All of these feature vectors are passed individually to the underlying models. The pipeline is explained in detail in Section 2.1

2.4 Machine Learning Models

We participated in 4 sub-tasks, namely, EI-oc, EI-reg, V-oc, V-reg. Two of the sub-tasks are ordinal classification and the remaining two are regressions. We describe our approach for building ML

---

[3]https://github.com/jaredks/tweetokenize
[4]https://emojipedia.org/

[5]https://github.com/SEERNET/EmoInt

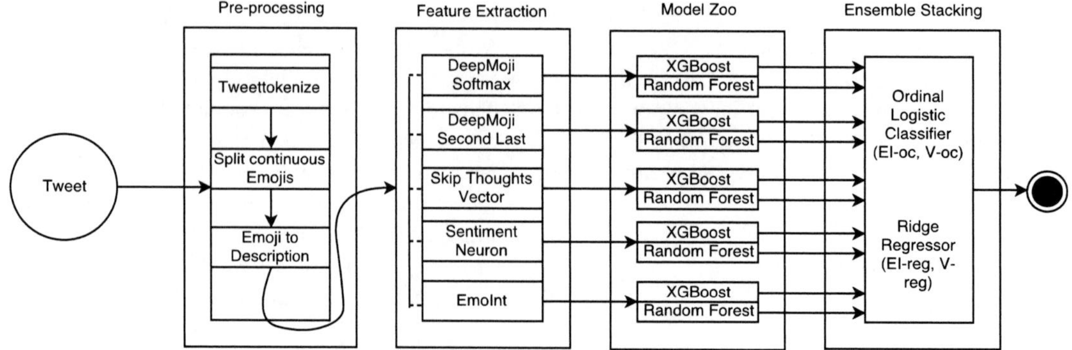

Figure 1: System Architecture.

models for both the variants in the upcoming sections.

2.4.1 Ordinal Classification

We participated in the emotion intensity ordinal classification where the task was to predict the intensity of emotions from the categories anger, fear, joy, and, sadness. Separate datasets were provided for each emotion class. The goal of the subtask of valence ordinal classification was to classify the tweet into one of 7 ordinal classes [-3, 3]. We experimented with XG Boost Classifier, Random Forest Classifier of sklearn (Pedregosa et al., 2011).

2.4.2 Regression

For the regression tasks (E-reg, V-reg), the goal was to predict the intensity on a scale of 0-1. We experimented with XG Boost Regressor, Random Forest Regressor of sklearn (Pedregosa et al., 2011).

The hyper-parameters of each model were tuned separately for each sub-task. The top-2 best models corresponding to each feature vector type were chosen after performing 7-fold cross-validation.

2.4.3 Stacking

Once we get the results from all the classifiers/regressors for a given tweet, we use stacking ensemble technique to combine the results. In this case, we pass the results from the models to a meta classifier/regressor as input. The output of this meta model is treated as the final output of the system.

We observed that using ordinal regressors gave us better performance than using classifiers which treat each output class as disjoint. Ordinal Regression is a family of statistical learning meth-

Task	Baseline	2nd best	Our Results
EI-reg	0.520	0.776	**0.799**
EI-oc	0.394	0.659	**0.695**
V-reg	0.585	0.861	**0.873**
V-oc	0.509	0.833	**0.836**

Table 1: Primary metrics across various sub-tasks.

ods where the output variable is discrete and ordered. We use the ordinal logistic classification with squared error (Rennie and Srebro, 2005) from the python library Mord. [6] (Rennie and Srebro, 2005)

In case of regression sub-tasks we observed the best cross validation results with Ridge Regression. Hence, we chose Ridge Regression as the meta regressor.

3 Results and Analysis

3.1 Task Results

The metrics used for ranking various systems are discussed in this section.

3.1.1 Primary Metrics

Pearson correlation with gold labels was used as a primary metric for ranking the systems. For EI-reg and EI-oc tasks Pearson correlation is macro-averaged (MA Pearson) over the four emotion categories.

Table 1 describes the results based on primary metrics for various sub-tasks in English language. Our system achieved the best performance in each of the four sub-tasks. We have also included the results of the baseline and second best performing system for comparison. As we can observe,

---

[6]https://github.com/fabianp/mord

Task	Pearson (SE)	Kappa	Kappa (SE)
V-oc	0.884 (1)	0.831 (1)	0.873 (1)
EI-oc	0.547 (1)	0.669 (1)	0.503 (1)

Table 2: Secondary metrics for ordinal classification sub-tasks. System rank is mentioned in the brackets.

Task	Pearson (gold in 0.5-1)
V-reg	0.697 (1)
EI-reg	0.638 (1)

Table 3: Secondary metrics for regression sub-tasks. System rank is mentioned in brackets.

our system vastly outperforms the baseline and is a significant improvement over the second best system, especially, in the emotion sub-tasks.

3.1.2 Secondary Metrics

The competition also uses some secondary metrics to provide a different perspective on the results. Pearson correlation for a subset of the test set that includes only those tweets with intensity score greater or equal to 0.5 is used as the secondary metric for the regression tasks. For ordinal classification tasks following secondary metrics were used:

- Pearson correlation for a subset of the test set that includes only those tweets with intensity classes low X, moderate X, or high X (where X is an emotion). The organizers refer to this set of tweets as the some-emotion subset (SE).

- Weighted quadratic kappa on the full test set

- Weighted quadratic kappa on the some-emotion subset of the test set

The results for secondary metrics are listed in Table 2 and 3. We have also included the ranking in brackets along with the score. We see that our system achieves the top rank according to all the secondary metrics, thus, proving its robustness.

3.2 Feature Importance

The performance of the system is highly dependent on the discriminative ability of the tweet representation generated by the featurizers. We measure the predictive power for each of the featurizer used by calculating the pearson correlation of the system using only that featurizer. We describe the results for each sub task separately in tables 4-7.

Feature Set	Pearson
Deepmoji (softmax layer)	0.808
Deepmoji (attention layer)	0.843
EmoInt	0.823
Unsupervised sentiment Neuron	0.714
Skip-Thought Vectors	0.777
Combined	**0.873**

Table 4: Pearson Correlation for V-reg task. Best results are highlighted in bold.

Feature Set	Pearson
Deepmoji (softmax layer)	0.780
Deepmoji (attention layer)	0.813
EmoInt	0.785
Unsupervised sentiment Neuron	0.685
Skip-Thought Vectors	0.748
Combined	**0.836**

Table 5: Pearson Correlation for V-oc task. Best results are highlighted in bold.

Feature Set	Pearson
Deepmoji (softmax layer)	0.703
Deepmoji (attention layer)	0.756
EmoInt	0.694
Unsupervised sentiment Neuron	0.548
Skip-Thought Vectors	0.656
Combined	**0.799**

Table 6: Macro-Averaged Pearson Correlation for EI-reg task. Best results are highlighted in bold.

Feature Set	Pearson
Deepmoji softmax layer	0.611
Deepmoji attention layer	0.664
EmoInt	0.596
Unsupervised sentiment Neuron	0.445
Skip-Thought Vectors	0.557
Combined	**0.695**

Table 7: Macro-Averaged Pearson Correlation for EI-oc task. Best results are highlighted in bold.

We observe that deepmoji featurizer is the most powerful featurizer of all the ones that we've used. Also, we can see that stacking ensembles of models trained on the outputs of multiple featurizers gives a significant improvement in performance.

3.3 System Limitations

We analyze the data points where our model's prediction is far from the ground truth. We observed some limitations of the system, such as, sometimes understanding a tweet's requires contextual knowledge about the world. Such examples can be very confusing for the model. We use deepmoji pre-trained model which uses emojis as proxy for labels, however partly due to the nature of twitter conversations same emojis can be used for multiple emotions, for example, joy emojis can be sometimes used to express joy, sometimes for sarcasm or for insulting someone. One such example is *'Your club is a laughing stock'*. Such cases are sometimes incorrectly predicted by our system.

4 Future Work & Conclusion

The paper studies the effectiveness of various representations of tweets and proposes ways to combine them to obtain state-of-the-art results. We also show that stacking ensemble of various classifiers learnt using different representations can vastly improve the robustness of the system.

Further improvements can be made in the pre-processing stage. Instead of discarding various tokens such as punctuation's, incorrectly spelled words, etc, we can utilize the information by learning their semantic representations. Also, we can improve the system performance by employing multi-task learning techniques as various emotions are not independent of each other and information about one emotion can aid in predicting the other. Furthermore, more robust techniques can be employed for distant supervision which are less prone to noisy labels to get better quality training data.

References

Yves Bestgen and Nadja Vincze. 2012. Checking and bootstrapping lexical norms by means of word similarity indexes. *Behavior research methods*, 44(4):998–1006.

Venkatesh Duppada and Sushant Hiray. 2017. Seernet at emoint-2017: Tweet emotion intensity estimator. In *Proceedings of the 8th Workshop on Computational Approaches to Subjectivity, Sentiment and Social Media Analysis*, pages 205–211.

Paul Ekman. 1992. An argument for basic emotions. *Cognition & emotion*, 6(3-4):169–200.

Bjarke Felbo, Alan Mislove, Anders Søgaard, Iyad Rahwan, and Sune Lehmann. 2017. Using millions of emoji occurrences to learn any-domain representations for detecting sentiment, emotion and sarcasm. In *Proceedings of the 2017 Conference on Empirical Methods in Natural Language Processing*, pages 1615–1625.

Ryan Kiros, Yukun Zhu, Ruslan R Salakhutdinov, Richard Zemel, Raquel Urtasun, Antonio Torralba, and Sanja Fidler. 2015. Skip-thought vectors. In *Advances in neural information processing systems*, pages 3294–3302.

Vipin Kumar and Sonajharia Minz. 2016. Multi-view ensemble learning: an optimal feature set partitioning for high-dimensional data classification. *Knowledge and Information Systems*, 49(1):1–59.

Kun-Lin Liu, Wu-Jun Li, and Minyi Guo. 2012. Emoticon smoothed language models for twitter sentiment analysis. In *Aaai*.

Albert Mehrabian. 1980. Basic dimensions for a general psychological theory implications for personality, social, environmental, and developmental studies.

Saif M Mohammad. 2017. Word affect intensities. *arXiv preprint arXiv:1704.08798*.

Saif M Mohammad and Felipe Bravo-Marquez. 2017. Wassa-2017 shared task on emotion intensity. *arXiv preprint arXiv:1708.03700*.

Saif M. Mohammad, Felipe Bravo-Marquez, Mohammad Salameh, and Svetlana Kiritchenko. 2018. Semeval-2018 Task 1: Affect in tweets. In *Proceedings of International Workshop on Semantic Evaluation (SemEval-2018)*, New Orleans, LA, USA.

Saif M Mohammad, Svetlana Kiritchenko, and Xiaodan Zhu. 2013. Nrc-canada: Building the state-of-the-art in sentiment analysis of tweets. *arXiv preprint arXiv:1308.6242*.

Saif M Mohammad and Peter D Turney. 2010. Emotions evoked by common words and phrases: Using mechanical turk to create an emotion lexicon. In *Proceedings of the NAACL HLT 2010 workshop on computational approaches to analysis and generation of emotion in text*, pages 26–34. Association for Computational Linguistics.

Finn Årup Nielsen. 2011. A new anew: Evaluation of a word list for sentiment analysis in microblogs. *arXiv preprint arXiv:1103.2903*.

Sinno Jialin Pan and Qiang Yang. 2010. A survey on transfer learning. *IEEE Transactions on knowledge and data engineering*, 22(10):1345–1359.

Fabian Pedregosa, Gaël Varoquaux, Alexandre Gramfort, Vincent Michel, Bertrand Thirion, Olivier Grisel, Mathieu Blondel, Peter Prettenhofer, Ron Weiss, Vincent Dubourg, et al. 2011. Scikit-learn: Machine learning in python. *Journal of machine learning research*, 12(Oct):2825–2830.

Robert Plutchik. 2001. The nature of emotions: Human emotions have deep evolutionary roots, a fact that may explain their complexity and provide tools for clinical practice. *American scientist*, 89(4):344–350.

Robi Polikar. 2012. Ensemble learning. In *Ensemble machine learning*, pages 1–34. Springer.

Alec Radford, Rafal Jozefowicz, and Ilya Sutskever. 2017. Learning to generate reviews and discovering sentiment. *arXiv preprint arXiv:1704.01444*.

Jason DM Rennie and Nathan Srebro. 2005. Loss functions for preference levels: Regression with discrete ordered labels. In *Proceedings of the IJCAI multidisciplinary workshop on advances in preference handling*, pages 180–186. Kluwer Norwell, MA.

James A Russell. 1980. A circumplex model of affect. *Journal of personality and social psychology*, 39(6):1161.

Duyu Tang, Furu Wei, Nan Yang, Ming Zhou, Ting Liu, and Bing Qin. 2014. Learning sentiment-specific word embedding for twitter sentiment classification. In *Proceedings of the 52nd Annual Meeting of the Association for Computational Linguistics (Volume 1: Long Papers)*, volume 1, pages 1555–1565.

Peter D Turney, Yair Neuman, Dan Assaf, and Yohai Cohen. 2011. Literal and metaphorical sense identification through concrete and abstract context. In *Proceedings of the Conference on Empirical Methods in Natural Language Processing*, pages 680–690. Association for Computational Linguistics.

SemEval 2018 Task 2: Multilingual Emoji Prediction

Francesco Barbieri[◇] Jose Camacho-Collados[♣] Francesco Ronzano[♡]
Luis Espinosa-Anke[♣] Miguel Ballesteros[♠] Valerio Basile[♥]
Viviana Patti[♥] Horacio Saggion[◇]
[◇] Large Scale Text Understanding Systems Lab, TALN. UPF. Barcelona, Spain
[♣]School of Computer Science and Informatics, Cardiff University
[♠]IBM Research, U.S
[♡] Integrative Biomedical Informatics Group, GRIB, IMIM-UPF, Barcelona, Spain
[♥]Dipartimento di Informatica, University of Turin, Italy
[◇♡]{name.surname}@upf.edu, [♠]miguel.ballesteros@ibm.com,
[♣]{espinosa-ankel,camachocolladosj}@cardiff.ac.uk,
[♥]{patti,basile}@di.unito.it

Abstract

This paper describes the results of the first shared task on Multilingual Emoji Prediction, organized as part of SemEval 2018. Given the text of a tweet, the task consists of predicting the most likely emoji to be used along such tweet. Two subtasks were proposed, one for English and one for Spanish, and participants were allowed to submit a system run to one or both subtasks. In total, 49 teams participated in the English subtask and 22 teams submitted a system run to the Spanish subtask. Evaluation was carried out *emoji-wise*, and the final ranking was based on macro F-Score. Data and further information about this task can be found at https://competitions. codalab.org/competitions/17344.

1 Introduction

Emojis are small ideograms depicting objects, people, and scenes (Cappallo et al., 2015). Emojis are one of the main components of a novel way of communication emerging from the advent of social media. They complement (usually) short text messages with a visual enhancement which is, as of now, a *de-facto* standard for online communication (Barbieri et al., 2017). Figure 1 shows an example of a social media message displaying an emoji.

Sometimes I think I wanna change the world... and I forget it just starts with changing me. ♥

Figure 1: Message from Twitter including a single red heart emoji.

Emojis[1] can be considered somehow an evolution of character-based *emoticons* (Pavalanathan and Eisenstein, 2015), and currently they represent a widespread and pervasive global communication device largely adopted by almost any social media service and instant messaging platforms.

Any system targeting the task of modeling social media communication is expected to tackle the usage of emojis. In fact, their semantic load is sufficiently rich that oversimplifying them to *sentiment carriers* or *boosters* would be to neglect the semantic richness of these ideograms, which in addition to mood (😄) include in their vocabulary references to food (🍕), sports (🏂), scenery (🏔), etc[2]. In general, however, effectively predicting the emoji associated with a piece of content may help to improve different NLP tasks (Novak et al., 2015), such as information retrieval, generation of emoji-enriched social media content, suggestion of emojis when writing text messages or sharing pictures online. Given that emojis may also mislead humans (Barbieri et al., 2017; Miller et al., 2017), the automated prediction of emojis may help to achieve better language understanding. As a consequence, by modeling the semantics of emojis, we can improve highly-subjective tasks like sentiment analysis, emotion recognition and irony detection (Felbo et al., 2017).

In this context, Barbieri et al. (2017) introduced the task of emoji prediction in Twitter by training several models based on bidirectional Long Short-Term Memory networks (LSTMs) (Graves, 2012), and showing they can outperform humans in solv-

---

[1]https://unicode.org/emoji/charts/ full-emoji-list.html
[2]https://unicode.org/emoji/charts/ emoji-ordering.html

Proceedings of the 12th International Workshop on Semantic Evaluation (SemEval-2018), pages 24–33
New Orleans, Louisiana, June 5–6, 2018. ©2018 Association for Computational Linguistics

ing the same task. These promising results motivated us to propose the first shared task on Multilingual Emoji Prediction. Following the experimental setting proposed by Barbieri et al. (2017), the task consists of predicting most likely emoji associated of a given text-only Twitter message. Only tweets with a single emoji are included in the task datasets (trial, train and test sets), so that the challenge can be cast as a single label classification problem.

In this paper, we first motivate and describe the main elements of this shared task (Section 2 and 3). Then, we cover the dataset compilation, curation and release process (Section 4). In Section 5 we detail the evaluation metrics and describe the overall results obtained by participating systems. Finally, we wrap this task description paper up with the main conclusions drawn from the organization of this challenge, as well as outlining potential avenues for future work, in Section 6.

2 Related Work

Modeling the semantics of emojis, and their applications thereof, is a relatively novel research problem with direct applications in any social media task. By explicitly modeling emojis as self-containing semantic units, the goal is to alleviate the lack of an associated grammar. This context, which makes it difficult to encode a clear and univocous single meaning for each emoji, has given rise to work considering emojis as function words or even affective markers (Na'aman et al., 2017), potentially affecting the overall semantics of longer utterances like sentences (Monti et al., 2016; Donato and Paggio, 2017).

The polysemy of emoji has been explored user-wise (Miller et al., 2017), location-wise, specifically in countries (Barbieri et al., 2016b) and cities (Barbieri et al., 2016a), gender-wise, time-wise (Barbieri et al., 2018b; Chen et al., 2017), and even device-wise, due to the fact that emojis may have different pictorial characteristics (and therefore, different interpretations), depending on the device (e.g., Iphone, Android, Samsung, etc.) or *app* (Whatsapp, Twitter, Facebook, and so forth)[3] (Tigwell and Flatla, 2016; Miller et al., 2016).

Today, modeling emoji semantics via vector representations is a well defined avenue of work. Contributions in this respect include models trained on Twitter data (Barbieri et al., 2016c), Twitter data together with the official unicode description (Eisner et al., 2016), or using text from a popular keyboard app Ai et al. (2017). In the latter contribution it is argued that emojis used in an affective context are more likely to become popular, and in general, the most important factor for an emoji to become popular is to have a clear meaning. In fact, the area of emoji vector evaluation has also experienced a significant growth as of recent. For instance, Wijeratne et al. (2017a) propose a platform for exploring emoji semantics. Further studies on evaluating emoji semantics may now be carried out by leveraging two recently introduced datasets with pairwise emoji similarity, with human annotations, namely EmoTwi50 (Barbieri et al., 2016c) and EmoSim508 (Wijeratne et al., 2017b). In the application avenue, emoji similarity has been studied for proposing efficient keyboard emoji organization, essentially for placing similar emojis close in the keyboard (Pohl et al., 2017).

An aspect related with emoji semantic modeling in which awareness is increasing dramatically is the inherent bias existing in these representations. For example, Barbieri and Camacho-Collados (2018) show that emoji modifiers can affect the semantics of emojis (they looked specifically into skin tones and gender). This recent line of research has also been explored in Robertson et al. (2018) who argue, for example, that users with darker-skinned profile photos employ skin modifiers more often than users with lighter-skinned profile photos, and that the vast majority of skin tone usage matches the color of a user's profile photo.

The application of well defined emoji representations in extrinsic tasks is, an open area of research. A natural application, however, lies in the context of sentiment analysis. This has fostered research, for example, in creating sentiment lexicons for emojis (Novak et al., 2015; Kimura and Katsurai, 2017; Rodrigues et al., 2018), or in studying how emojis may be used to retrieve tweets with specific emotional content (Wood and Ruder, 2016). Moreover, Hu et al. (2017) study how emojis affect the sentiment of a text message, and show that not all emojis have the same impact. Finally, the fact that emojis carry sentiment

---

[3]The image that represents the same emoji can vary, e.g., for the emoji U+1F40F, the following are over different renderings by platform in Unicode v11 (up to April 2018): Apple �, Google �, Twitter �, EmojiOne �, Facebook �, Samsung �, Windows �.

and emotion information is verified in the study by Felbo et al. (2017), where an emoji prediction classifier is used as pre-trained system, and then is fine-tuned for predicting sentiment, emotions and irony.

The last item to be covered in this review involves multimodality. Recently, emojis have been also studied from a prism where visual signals are incorporated, taking advantage of existing social media platforms like Instagram, with a strong focus on visual content. Recent contributions show that the usage of emojis depends on both textual and visual content, but seem to agree in that, in general, textual information is more relevant for the task of emoji prediction (Cappallo et al., 2015, 2018; Barbieri et al., 2018a).

3 Task Description

Given a text message including an emoji, the emoji prediction task consists of predicting that emoji by relying exclusively on the textual content of that message. In particular, in this task we focused on the one emoji occurring inside tweets, thus relying on Twitter data.

Figure 2: Example of tweet with an emoji at the end, considered in the emoji prediction task.

The task is divided into two subtasks respectively dealing with the prediction of the emoji associated to English and Spanish tweets. The motivation for providing a multilingual setting stems from previous findings about the idiosyncrasy of use of emojis across languages (Barbieri et al., 2016b) (see Figure 3): one emoji may be used with completely different meanings depending not only on the language of the speaker, but also on regional dialects (Barbieri et al., 2016a).

For each subtask we selected the tweets that included one of the twenty emojis that occur most frequently in the Twitter data we collected (Table 1). Therefore, the task can be viewed as a multi-label classification problem with twenty labels.

Twitter datasets were shared among participants by providing a list of tweet IDs[4] or directly the

---

Figure 3: Example of distinct use of the fire emoji across languages: the first tweet (English) comments on the torrid weather, while the second one (Spanish) exploits the same emoji to wish an happy new year ('We start the new year with enthusiasm!').

English

1	2	3	4	5	6	7	8	9	10	11	12	13	14	15	16	17	18	19	20

Spanish

1	2	3	4	5	6	7	8	9	10	11	12	13	14	15	16	17	18	19	20

Table 1: The 20 most frequent emojis of each language (due to a data processing issue we only considered 19 emojis in the Spanish task).

text of each tweet. The last approach was adopted to share the test sets (more details are provided in Section 4).

4 Task Data

The data for the task consists of a list of tweets associated with a given emoji (i.e. label). As explained in the previous section, the dataset includes tweets that contain one and only one emoji, of the 20 most frequent emojis. We split the data in trial[5], training and test data. The quantity of tweets per set is displayed in Table 2.

The tweets were retrieved with the Twitter APIs and geolocalized in United States and Spain for subtasks 1 and 2, respectively. As for the trial and training data, the tweets were gathered from October 2015 to February 2017, whereas for the test data we decided to gather the tweets corresponding to the last months until the evaluation period started (from May 2017 to Jan 2018). This would prevent participants from gathering these tweets before-hand and also would enable us to test the emoji prediction task on a more realistic setting, as the test data is subsequent to the training data.

---

[4]Participants were provided with a Java-based crawler (`https://github.com/fra82/twitter-crawler`) to ease the download of the textual

content of tweets from the ID list.

[5]Trial data was used as development by participants.

	Trial	Training	Test
English	50,000	500,000	50,000
Spanish	10,000	100,000	10,000

Table 2: Number of tweets for trial, training and test for each of the subtasks.

5 Evaluation

This section introduces the overall evaluation setting of this shared task. We first describe briefly the evaluation metrics used and then provide a succinct description of the baseline system.

5.1 Evaluation Metrics

As this was a single label classification problem, the classic *precision* (Prec.), *recall* (Recall), *f-score* (F1) and *accuracy* (Acc.) were used as official evaluation metrics. Note that because of the skewed distribution of the label set we opted for macro average over all labels.

5.2 Baseline

The baseline system for this task was a classifier based on FastText[6] (Joulin et al., 2017). Given a set of N documents, the loss that the model attempts to minimize is the negative log-likelihood over the labels (in our case, the emojis):

$$loss = -\frac{1}{N} \sum_{N}^{n=1} e_n \log(softmax(BA_{x_n}))$$

where e_n is the emoji included in the n-th Twitter post, represented as hot vector, and used as label. Hyperparameters were set as default[7].

5.3 Participant Systems

Due to the overwhelming number of participants, we cannot describe all systems.[8] We do, however,

---

[6] github.com/facebookresearch/fastText
[7] https://github.com/facebookresearch/fastText#full-documentation

[8] This is the list of systems that ranked below the baseline in either of the subtasks: #TeamINF (Ribeiro and Silva, 2018), CENNLP (J R et al., 2018), DUTH (Effrosynidis et al., 2018), ECNU (Lu et al., 2018), EICA (Xie and Song, 2018), EPUTION (Zhou et al., 2018), LIS (Guibon et al., 2018), Manchester Metropolitan (Gerber and Shardlow, 2018), Peperomia (Chen et al., 2018), PickleTeam! (Groot et al., 2018), Shi (Shiyun et al., 2018), SyntNN (Zanzotto and Santilli, 2018), TAJJEB (Basile and Lino, 2018), The Dabblers (Alexa et al., 2018), THU_NGN (Wu et al., 2018), Tweety (Kopev et al., 2018), UMDSub (Wang and Pedersen, 2018), YNU-HPCC (Wang et al., 2018). Note that some participants did not submit a final paper but they are included in the results table.

briefly mention the main features of some significant systems ranked above the baseline in either of the subtasks.

- **Tübingen-Oslo** (Çöltekin and Rama, 2018). This supervised system consists of an SVM classifier with bag-of-n-grams features (both characters and words). *Tübingen-Oslo* is the top performing system in both tasks.

- **NTUA-SLP** (Baziotis et al., 2018). This system uses a Bi-LSTM with attention, and pre-trained word2vec vectors. They used external resources for associating each tweet with information on emotions, concreteness, familiarity, and others. They only participated in the English subtask but they classified second (according to the F1 score) with the highest recall.

- **EmoNLP** (Liu, 2018). This system is based on a Gradient Boosting Regression Tree Approach combined with a Bi-LSTM on character and word ngrams. It is complemented with several lexicons as well as learning sentiment specific word embeddings.

- **UMDuluth-CS8761** (Beaulieu and Asamoah Owusu, 2018) This supervised system combines an SVM with a bag-of-words approach for extracting salient features. This is one of the most competitive systems with the highest precision in English and the third best result in Spanish.

- **Hatching Chick** (Coster et al., 2018). This system builds an SVM classifier (with gradient descent optimization) on words and character ngrams. They obtained the second best result in the Spanish subtask, but their English system performed worse than the baseline.

- **TAJJEB** (Basile and Lino, 2018). This system made use of an SVM classifier over wide variety of features such as tf-idf, part-of-speech tags and bigrams. The system was competitive on both languages, outperforming the baseline on the Spanish dataset.

- **Duluth UROP** (Jin and Pedersen, 2018). This system consists of a soft voting ensemble approach combining different machine learning algorithms (Naïve Bayes, Logistic Regression, Random Forests, etc.). Infrequent classes are oversampled using the SMOTE algorithm. As for features, they use both unigrams and bigrams.

English			Spanish		
Emo	**F1**	**%**	**Emo**	**F1**	**%**
[emoji]	87.8	21.6	[emoji]	69.6	21.4
[emoji]	37.8	9.7	[emoji]	37.3	14.1
[emoji]	47.1	9.1	[emoji]	53.4	15
[emoji]	26.9	5.2	[emoji]	8.5	3.5
[emoji]	55.5	7.4	[emoji]	14.9	5.1
[emoji]	16.2	3.2	[emoji]	26.9	4
[emoji]	22.6	4	[emoji]	39.8	3.1
[emoji]	36.2	5.5	[emoji]	16.3	4.5
[emoji]	24	3.1	[emoji]	13	1.8
[emoji]	22.2	2.4	[emoji]	49.9	4.2
[emoji]	40	2.9	[emoji]	14.7	3.4
[emoji]	64.7	3.9	[emoji]	14.2	4.1
[emoji]	63.7	2.5	[emoji]	6.8	2.4
[emoji]	17.1	2.2	[emoji]	7.7	2.7
[emoji]	13	2.6	[emoji]	5.6	0.9
[emoji]	29.2	2.5	[emoji]	20	4.2
[emoji]	14.3	2.3	[emoji]	23.7	2.1
[emoji]	73.6	3.1	[emoji]	8.6	1.3
[emoji]	38.4	4.8	[emoji]	5.1	2.1
[emoji]	9	2	-	-	-

Table 4: Best F1 measure (among all the teams) for each emoji in English (20) and Spanish (19). We also report the relative frequency percentage of each emoji in the test set.

5.4 Results

Each system was evaluated according to its capacity to perform well across all emojis under consideration. As mentioned, and due to the skewed distribution of the label set, we evaluated each participating system according to Macro F-Score (F1).

The overall results are provided in Table 3, and already several interesting conclusions can be drawn from them. For instance, it is noteworthy the fact that the best systems for both subtasks are more than 10 points apart (English better), which suggests that a *one-size-fits-all* model may be suboptimal for this task, and that indeed the

particularities of each individual language should be taken into consideration for best performance. The most precise systems were *EmoNLP* and *Tübingen-Oslo*, whereas the highest Recall was obtained by *NTUA-SLP* and again *Tübingen-Oslo* (English and Spanish respectively, in both cases). Clearly, the *Tübingen-Oslo* system shows a fine balance between precision and recall, perhaps due to its little preprocessing, fine-tuning and reliance on external libraries. It seems reasonable to assume, thus, that combining word and ngram embeddings as features, with SVMs and NN classifiers, provides a robust and high performing architecture for emoji prediction, with the added value of being resource/knowledge agnostic.

5.5 Analysis

This evaluation is finally complemented with the overall emoji-wise performance across all systems (Table 4). The lexical notion of *near synonymy* seems to clearly apply to emojis as well, as we can clearly see a worse performance on those emojis which are pictorially similar (e.g., the photo camera with and without flash, or the expected confusion between least frequent hearts and the red heart, which accounts for over 20% of the whole label set in the test data).

Finally, emojis with several interpretations and less frequent seem to be much more difficult to predict (e.g., the face [emoji] in the English and Spanish dataset, and [emoji] in the Spanish dataset). Zhou et al. (2018) showed in their system description paper how exploiting user-specific features may provide significance performance boosts.[9] This additional user-specific information may clearly help in these difficult cases which proved to be hard for all systems.

6 Conclusions

In this paper we have described the SemEval 2018 shared task in multilingual emoji prediction. The task, consisting in predicting the most likely emoji given the text of a tweet, was well received, with almost 50 system runs submitted to the English subtask and more than 20 to the Spanish subtask. One of the main conclusions that can be drawn is that the baseline we used (FastText) was highly competitive, with only 6 and 5 system runs performing better in English and Spanish.

---

[9]The use of user-specific data was not allowed by the main competition regulations and therefore none of the systems in the final ranking made use of it.

ENGLISH					SPANISH				
Team	F1	Prec.	Recall	Acc.	Team	F1	Prec.	Recall	Acc.
Tübingen-Oslo	**35.99**	36.55	36.22	47.09	Tübingen-Oslo	**22.36**	**23.49**	**22.80**	**37.27**
NTUA-SLP	35.36	34.53	**38.00**	44.74	Hatching Chick	18.73	20.66	19.16	37.23
hgsgnlp	34.02	35	33.57	45.55	UMDuluth-CS8761	18.18	19.02	18.6	34.83
EmoNLP	33.67	39.43	33.7	**47.46**	TAJJEB	17.08	18.99	20.36	25.13
ECNU	33.35	35.17	33.11	46.3	Duluth UROP	16.75	17.11	18.1	28.51
UMDuluth-CS8761	31.83	**39.80**	31.37	45.73	BASELINE	16.72	16.84	17.52	31.63
BASELINE	30.98	30.34	33	42.56	Nova	16.7	17.2	17.07	26.50
THU_NGN	30.25	31.85	29.81	42.18	ECNU	16.41	16.91	16.48	30.82
TAJJEB	30.13	29.91	33.02	38.09	MMU - Computing	16.34	17.83	16.4	28.92
EmojiIt	29.5	35.17	29.91	39.21	PickleTeam!	15.86	17.57	16.76	29.70
Reborn	29.24	33.67	28.94	42.43	ART @ Tor Vergata	14.91	15.81	15.51	30.68
freeze	29.13	31.54	29.23	37.14	CENNLP	14.68	16.32	16.2	34.85
csy	28.93	31.12	29	36.85	YNU-HPCC	14.25	17.51	15.98	31.19
Nova	27.89	28.49	28.2	34.83	Amrita_CEN_NLP1	12.13	12.46	12.41	21.64
Sheffield	27.18	28.57	26.61	37.69	erai	11.36	12.72	11.39	23.38
YNU-HPCC	26.89	26.97	29.71	32.53	Lips Eggplant	10.89	15.78	10.62	23.88
mboyanov	26.77	32.82	27.42	36.79	thelonewolf190694	10.87	11.13	12.55	27.04
kaka manData	26.59	30	26.97	36.34	The Dabblers	9.2	17.28	9.92	27.72
Duluth UROP	26.59	27.18	27.87	33.8	LIS	8.81	15.16	10.14	28.53
CENNLP	26.45	31.62	26.87	41.18	jogonba2	7.99	17.81	9.85	29.99
UMDSub	25.99	33.01	26.71	41	hjpwhu	3.9	7.46	6.81	13.81
THU_HCSI	25.83	32.38	25.9	35.34					
Peperomia	25.68	28.98	26.04	35.34					
MMU - Computing	24.98	28.94	25.04	34.59					
NoEmotionsAttached	23.3	25.27	24.47	32.76					
PickleTeam!	22.86	26.17	24.37	34.09					
Reborn	21.97	26.52	22.06	30.64					
PALM_gzy	21.97	26.52	22.06	30.64					
#TeamINF	21.5	26.21	20.84	31.59					
Hatching Chick	21.44	25.97	21.48	36.52					
CORAL	21.35	32.82	22.48	34.05					
Meisele	20.02	25.74	19.54	30.71					
erai	19.96	22.1	19.62	28.36					
SBIG	19.44	25.41	16.12	19.84					
The Dabblers	18.92	25.02	18.96	30.45					
ART @ Tor Vergata	18.39	24.49	17.25	29.45					
Amrita_CEN_NLP1	17.96	19.47	17.75	24.41					
Lips Eggplant	17.69	21.81	17.19	26.81					
XSSX	16.45	31.56	16.77	30.99					
Kno.e.sis	14.42	18.72	18.49	18.99					
thelonewolf190694	14.21	13.66	17.35	30.7					
LIS	13.53	25.58	14.14	29.42					
uaic2018	11.06	13.65	11.24	19.61					
jogonba2	8.52	24.16	9.51	25.6					
SBIG2	6.44	18.76	8.49	12.64					
alsu_wh	3.73	4.38	5.06	9.83					
Innovating world	3.09	18.47	5.73	22.74					
hjpwhu	2.04	2.63	3.22	3.92					

Table 3: Ranking of the participating systems by precision, recall, F1 and accuracy for the English track and the Spanish track. Those above the horizontal line ranked above the task baseline.

In terms of participating systems, and according to the post-participation survey the participants completed, we can see a high prevalence of neural approaches, with only 9 systems opting for more traditional linear models (6 SVMs, 3 Random Forests). Among the chosen neural architectures, LSTMs and CNNs are by far the preferred ones. It is noteworthy, however, the excellent performance of SVMs as used in the best performing system on both English and Spanish datasets.

This task has set the foundations for upcoming work on modeling emoji semantics, first, by providing a standardized testbed for emoji prediction in two languages, and second, by providing a comprehensive evaluation with a wide range of ideas, which we hope are of use for future research. Emojis, undoubtedly, are becoming increasingly important in understanding social media communication and in human-computer interaction, and thus we believe the problem of modeling emoji semantics can be further extended as follows. (1) Leveraging multimodal information (e.g., associated images (Barbieri et al., 2018a)); (2) incorporating more and more diverse languages (one step in this direction will be the re-run of this task for Italian at the Evalita 2018 evaluation campaign[10]); and (3) considering individual and communicative contexts for overall performance improvements.

Acknowledgments

We thank all the participants of the task. Francesco B. and Horacio S. acknowledge support from the TUNER project (TIN2015-65308-C5-5-R, MINECO/FEDER, UE) and the Maria de Maeztu Units of Excellence Programme (MDM-2015-0502). The work of V. Patti and V. Basile was partially funded by the IHatePrejudice project (S1618_L2_BOSC_01).

References

Wei Ai, Xuan Lu, Xuanzhe Liu, Ning Wang, Gang Huang, and Qiaozhu Mei. 2017. Untangling emoji popularity through semantic embeddings. In *ICWSM*, pages 2–11.

Larisa Alexa, Alina Lorent, Daniela Gifu, and Diana Trandabat. 2018. The dabblers at semeval-2018 task 2: Multilingual emoji prediction. In *Proceedings of The 12th International Workshop on Semantic Evaluation*, pages 402–406, New Orleans, Louisiana. Association for Computational Linguistics.

Francesco Barbieri, Miguel Ballesteros, Francesco Ronzano, and Horacio Saggion. 2018a. Multimodal emoji prediction. In *Proceedings of NAACL: Short Papers*, New Orleans, US. Association for Computational Linguistics.

Francesco Barbieri, Miguel Ballesteros, and Horacio Saggion. 2017. Are emojis predictable? In *Proceedings of the 15th Conference of the European Chapter of the Association for Computational Linguistics: Volume 2, Short Papers*, pages 105–111, Valencia, Spain. Association for Computational Linguistics.

Francesco Barbieri and Jose Camacho-Collados. 2018. How Gender and Skin Tone Modifiers Affect Emoji Semantics in Twitter. In *Proceedings of the 7th Joint Conference on Lexical and Computational Semantics (*SEM 2018)*, New Orleans, LA, United States.

Francesco Barbieri, Luis Espinosa-Anke, and Horacio Saggion. 2016a. Revealing patterns of Twitter emoji usage in Barcelona and Madrid. *Frontiers in Artificial Intelligence and Applications. 2016;(Artificial Intelligence Research and Development) 288: 239-44.*

Francesco Barbieri, German Kruszewski, Francesco Ronzano, and Horacio Saggion. 2016b. How cosmopolitan are emojis?: Exploring emojis usage and meaning over different languages with distributional semantics. In *Proceedings of the 2016 ACM on Multimedia Conference*, pages 531–535. ACM.

Francesco Barbieri, Luis Marujo, William Brendel, Pradeep Karuturim, and Horacio Saggion. 2018b. Exploring Emoji Usage and Prediction Through a Temporal Variation Lens. In *1st International Workshop on Emoji Understanding and Applications in Social Media (at ICWSM 2018)*.

Francesco Barbieri, Francesco Ronzano, and Horacio Saggion. 2016c. What does this emoji mean? a vector space skip-gram model for Twitter emojis. In *Proc. of LREC 2016*.

Angelo Basile and Kenny W. Lino. 2018. Tajjeb at semeval-2018 task 2: Traditional approaches just do the job with emoji prediction. In *Proceedings of The 12th International Workshop on Semantic Evaluation*, pages 467–473, New Orleans, Louisiana. Association for Computational Linguistics.

Christos Baziotis, Athanasiou Nikolaos, Athanasia Kolovou, Georgios Paraskevopoulos, Nikolaos Ellinas, and Alexandros Potamianos. 2018. Ntua-slp at semeval-2018 task 2: Predicting emojis using rnns with context-aware attention. In *Proceedings of The 12th International Workshop on Semantic Evaluation*, pages 435–441, New Orleans, Louisiana. Association for Computational Linguistics.

Jonathan Beaulieu and Dennis Asamoah Owusu. 2018. Umduluth-cs8761 at semeval-2018 task 2: Emojis: Too many choices? In *Proceedings of The*

---

[10]http://www.evalita.it/2018

12th International Workshop on Semantic Evaluation, pages 397–401, New Orleans, Louisiana. Association for Computational Linguistics.

Spencer Cappallo, Thomas Mensink, and Cees GM Snoek. 2015. Image2emoji: Zero-shot emoji prediction for visual media. In *Proceedings of the 23rd ACM international conference on Multimedia*, pages 1311–1314. ACM.

Spencer Cappallo, Stacey Svetlichnaya, Pierre Garrigues, Thomas Mensink, and Cees GM Snoek. 2018. The new modality: Emoji challenges in prediction, anticipation, and retrieval. *arXiv preprint arXiv:1801.10253*.

Jing Chen, Dechuan Yang, Xilian Li, Wei Chen, and Tengjiao Wang. 2018. Peperomia at semeval-2018 task 2: Vector similarity based approach for emoji prediction. In *Proceedings of The 12th International Workshop on Semantic Evaluation*, pages 425–429, New Orleans, Louisiana. Association for Computational Linguistics.

Zhenpeng Chen, Xuan Lu, Sheng Shen, Wei Ai, Xuanzhe Liu, and Qiaozhu Mei. 2017. Through a gender lens: An empirical study of emoji usage over large-scale android users. *arXiv preprint arXiv:1705.05546*.

Çağrı Çöltekin and Taraka Rama. 2018. Tübingen-oslo at semeval-2018 task 2: Svms perform better than rnns in emoji prediction. In *Proceedings of The 12th International Workshop on Semantic Evaluation*, pages 32–36, New Orleans, Louisiana. Association for Computational Linguistics.

Jol Coster, Reinder Gerard van Dalen, and Nathalie Adrinne Jacqueline Stierman. 2018. Hatching chick at semeval-2018 task 2: Multilingual emoji prediction. In *Proceedings of The 12th International Workshop on Semantic Evaluation*, pages 442–445, New Orleans, Louisiana. Association for Computational Linguistics.

Giulia Donato and Patrizia Paggio. 2017. Investigating redundancy in emoji use: Study on a Twitter based corpus. In *Proceedings of the 8th Workshop on Computational Approaches to Subjectivity, Sentiment and Social Media Analysis*, pages 118–126.

Dimitrios Effrosynidis, Georgios Peikos, Symeon Symeonidis, and Avi Arampatzis. 2018. Duth at semeval-2018 task 2: Emoji prediction in tweets. In *Proceedings of The 12th International Workshop on Semantic Evaluation*, pages 463–466, New Orleans, Louisiana. Association for Computational Linguistics.

Ben Eisner, Tim Rocktäschel, Isabelle Augenstein, Matko Bošnjak, and Sebastian Riedel. 2016. emoji2vec: Learning emoji representations from their description. *arXiv preprint arXiv:1609.08359*.

Bjarke Felbo, Alan Mislove, Anders Søgaard, Iyad Rahwan, and Sune Lehmann. 2017. Using millions of emoji occurrences to learn any-domain representations for detecting sentiment, emotion and sarcasm. *Proc. of EMNLP 2017*.

Luciano Gerber and Matthew Shardlow. 2018. Manchester metropolitan at semeval-2018 task 2: Random forest with an ensemble of features for predicting emoji in tweets. In *Proceedings of The 12th International Workshop on Semantic Evaluation*, pages 488–493, New Orleans, Louisiana. Association for Computational Linguistics.

Alex Graves. 2012. *Supervised Sequence Labelling with Recurrent Neural Networks*, volume 385 of *Studies in Computational Intelligence*. Springer.

Daphne Groot, Rémon Kruizinga, Hennie Veldthuis, Simon de Wit, and Hessel Haagsma. 2018. Pickleteam! at semeval-2018 task 2: English and spanish emoji prediction from tweets. In *Proceedings of The 12th International Workshop on Semantic Evaluation*, pages 451–455, New Orleans, Louisiana. Association for Computational Linguistics.

Gaël Guibon, Magalie Ochs, and Patrice Bellot. 2018. Lis at semeval-2018 task 2: Mixing word embeddings and bag of features for multilingual emoji prediction. In *Proceedings of The 12th International Workshop on Semantic Evaluation*, pages 499–503, New Orleans, Louisiana. Association for Computational Linguistics.

Tianran Hu, Han Guo, Hao Sun, Thuy-vy Thi Nguyen, and Jiebo Luo. 2017. Spice up Your Chat: The Intentions and Sentiment Effects of Using Emoji. *Proc. of ICWSM 2017*.

Naveen J R, Hariharan V, Barathi Ganesh H. B., Anand Kumar M, and Soman K P. 2018. Cennlp@semeval-2018 task 2: Enhanced distributed representation of text using target classes for emoji prediction representation. In *Proceedings of The 12th International Workshop on Semantic Evaluation*, pages 483–487, New Orleans, Louisiana. Association for Computational Linguistics.

Shuning Jin and Ted Pedersen. 2018. Duluth urop at semeval-2018 task 2: Multilingual emoji prediction with ensemble learning and oversampling. In *Proceedings of The 12th International Workshop on Semantic Evaluation*, pages 479–482, New Orleans, Louisiana. Association for Computational Linguistics.

Armand Joulin, Edouard Grave, Piotr Bojanowski, and Tomas Mikolov. 2017. Bag of tricks for efficient text classification. In *European Chapter of the Association for Computational Linguistics*, Valencia, Spain.

Mayu Kimura and Marie Katsurai. 2017. Automatic construction of an emoji sentiment lexicon. In *Proceedings of the 2017 IEEE/ACM International Conference on Advances in Social Networks Analysis and Mining 2017*, pages 1033–1036. ACM.

Daniel Kopev, Atanas Atanasov, Dimitrina Zlatkova, Momchil Hardalov, Ivan Koychev, Ivelina Nikolova, and Galia Angelova. 2018. Tweety at semeval-2018 task 2: Predicting emojis using hierarchical attention neural networks and support vector machine. In *Proceedings of The 12th International Workshop on Semantic Evaluation*, pages 494–498, New Orleans, Louisiana. Association for Computational Linguistics.

Man Liu. 2018. Emonlp at semeval-2018 task 2: English emoji prediction with gradient boosting regression tree method and bidirectional lstm. In *Proceedings of The 12th International Workshop on Semantic Evaluation*, pages 387–391, New Orleans, Louisiana. Association for Computational Linguistics.

Xingwu Lu, Xin Mao, Man Lan, and Yuanbin Wu. 2018. Ecnu at semeval-2018 task 2: Leverage traditional nlp features and neural networks methods to address twitter emoji prediction task. In *Proceedings of The 12th International Workshop on Semantic Evaluation*, pages 430–434, New Orleans, Louisiana. Association for Computational Linguistics.

Hannah Miller, Daniel Kluver, Jacob Thebault-Spieker, Loren Terveen, and Brent Hecht. 2017. Understanding emoji ambiguity in context: The role of text in emoji-related miscommunication. In *11th International Conference on Web and Social Media, ICWSM 2017*. AAAI Press.

Hannah Miller, Jacob Thebault-Spieker, Shuo Chang, Isaac Johnson, Loren Terveen, and Brent Hecht. 2016. "Blissfully happy" or "ready to fight": Varying interpretations of emoji. *Proc. of ICWSM16*.

Johanna Monti, Federico Sangati, Francesca Chiusaroli, Martin Benjamin, and Sina Mansour. 2016. Emojitalianobot and emojiworldbot - new online tools and digital environments for translation into emoji. In *Proceedings of Third Italian Conference on Computational Linguistics (CLiC-it 2016), Napoli, Italy, December 5-7, 2016.*, volume 1749 of *CEUR Workshop Proceedings*.

Noa Na'aman, Hannah Provenza, and Orion Montoya. 2017. Varying linguistic purposes of emoji in (Twitter) context. In *Proceedings of ACL 2017, Student Research Workshop*, pages 136–141.

Petra Kralj Novak, Jasmina Smailović, Borut Sluban, and Igor Mozetič. 2015. Sentiment of emojis. *PloS one*, 10(12):e0144296.

Umashanthi Pavalanathan and Jacob Eisenstein. 2015. Emoticons vs. emojis on Twitter: A causal inference approach. *arXiv preprint arXiv:1510.08480*.

Henning Pohl, Christian Domin, and Michael Rohs. 2017. Beyond just text: Semantic emoji similarity modeling to support expressive communication. *ACM Transactions on Computer-Human Interaction (TOCHI)*, 24(1):6.

Alison Ribeiro and Ndia Silva. 2018. #teaminf at semeval-2018 task 2: Emoji prediction in tweets. In *Proceedings of The 12th International Workshop on Semantic Evaluation*, pages 412–415, New Orleans, Louisiana. Association for Computational Linguistics.

Alexander Robertson, Walid Magdy, and Sharon Goldwater. 2018. Self-Representation on Twitter Using Emoji Skin Color Modifiers. *Proc. of ICWSM 2018*.

David Rodrigues, Marília Prada, Rui Gaspar, Margarida V Garrido, and Diniz Lopes. 2018. Lisbon emoji and emoticon database (leed): Norms for emoji and emoticons in seven evaluative dimensions. *Behavior research methods*, pages 392–405.

Chen Shiyun, Wang Maoquan, and He Liang. 2018. Shi at semeval-2018 task 2: An effective attention-based recurrent neural network model for emoji prediction with characters gated words. In *Proceedings of The 12th International Workshop on Semantic Evaluation*, pages 420–424, New Orleans, Louisiana. Association for Computational Linguistics.

Garreth W Tigwell and David R Flatla. 2016. Oh that's what you meant!: reducing emoji misunderstanding. In *Proceedings of the 18th International Conference on Human-Computer Interaction with Mobile Devices and Services Adjunct*, pages 859–866. ACM.

Nan Wang, Jin Wang, and Xuejie Zhang. 2018. Ynuhpcc at semeval-2018 task 2: Multi-ensemble bi-gru model with attention mechanism for multilingual emoji prediction. In *Proceedings of The 12th International Workshop on Semantic Evaluation*, pages 456–462, New Orleans, Louisiana. Association for Computational Linguistics.

Zhenduo Wang and Ted Pedersen. 2018. Umdsub at semeval-2018 task 2: Multilingual emoji prediction multi-channel convolutional neural network on subword embedding. In *Proceedings of The 12th International Workshop on Semantic Evaluation*, pages 392–396, New Orleans, Louisiana. Association for Computational Linguistics.

Sanjaya Wijeratne, Lakshika Balasuriya, Amit Sheth, and Derek Doran. 2017a. Emojinet: An open service and api for emoji sense discovery. *International AAAI Conference on Web and Social Media (ICWSM 2017). Montreal, Canada.*

Sanjaya Wijeratne, Lakshika Balasuriya, Amit Sheth, and Derek Doran. 2017b. A semantics-based measure of emoji similarity. *International Conference on Web Intelligence (Web Intelligence 2017). Leipzig, Germany.*

Ian Wood and Sebastian Ruder. 2016. Emoji as emotion tags for tweets. *Emotion and Sentiment Analysis Workshop, LREC.*

Chuhan Wu, Fangzhao Wu, Sixing Wu, Zhigang Yuan, Junxin Liu, and Yongfeng Huang. 2018. Thu_ngn at semeval-2018 task 2: Residual cnn-lstm network with attention for english emoji prediction. In *Proceedings of The 12th International Workshop on Semantic Evaluation*, pages 407–411, New Orleans, Louisiana. Association for Computational Linguistics.

Yufei Xie and Qingqing Song. 2018. Eica team at semeval-2018 task 2: Semantic and metadata-based features for multilingual emoji prediction. In *Proceedings of The 12th International Workshop on Semantic Evaluation*, pages 416–419, New Orleans, Louisiana. Association for Computational Linguistics.

Fabio Massimo Zanzotto and Andrea Santilli. 2018. Syntnn at semeval-2018 task 2: is syntax useful for emoji prediction? embedding syntactic trees in multi layer perceptrons. In *Proceedings of The 12th International Workshop on Semantic Evaluation*, pages 474–478, New Orleans, Louisiana. Association for Computational Linguistics.

Liyuan Zhou, Qiongkai Xu, Hanna Suominen, and Tom Gedeon. 2018. Epution at semeval-2018 task 2: Emoji prediction with user adaption. In *Proceedings of The 12th International Workshop on Semantic Evaluation*, pages 446–450, New Orleans, Louisiana. Association for Computational Linguistics.

Tübingen-Oslo at SemEval-2018 Task 2:
SVMs perform better than RNNs at Emoji Prediction

Çağrı Çöltekin
Department of Linguistics
University of Tübingen, Germany
ccoltekin@sfs.uni-tuebingen.de

Taraka Rama
Department of Informatics
University of Oslo, Norway
tarakark@ifi.uio.no

Abstract

This paper describes our participation in the SemEval-2018 task Multilingual Emoji Prediction. We participated in both English and Spanish subtasks, experimenting with support vector machines (SVMs) and recurrent neural networks. Our SVM classifier obtained the top rank in both subtasks with macro-averaged F1-measures of 35.99 % for English and 22.36 % for Spanish data sets. Similar to a few earlier attempts, the results with neural networks were not on par with linear SVMs.

1   Introduction

Emojis are graphical symbols that represent an idea or emotion. The use of emojis has become popular over the last decade, particularly in informal communication in the social media. Their popularity kindled a recent interest in investigating many aspects of emojis, including their interaction with natural language (e.g., Barbieri et al., 2016, 2017; Felbo et al., 2017; Kralj Novak et al., 2015). Although the emojis are presumably language-independent, their use typically goes together with linguistic text. In this context, the SemEval 2018 task 2, Multilingual Emoji Prediction (Barbieri et al., 2018), aims predicting the emoji from the surrounding micro-blogging (Twitter) text for English and Spanish.

The task at hand is to predict a label, an emoji, from a short text that it accompanies. This is essentially a text/document classification problem, and shares many aspects of other text classification problems such as topic classification, sentiment analysis, language identification and authorship attribution − just to name a few. Although each of these problems have some task-specific aspects, the same models can be used for all of them. In this study, we experiment with and compare two well-known methods: support vector machines

(SVMs) with bag of word/character n-gram features and recurrent neural networks (RNNs) with word and character sequences as input. The methods and implementations are similar to our earlier attempts in other text classification tasks (Çöltekin and Rama, 2016; Rama and Çöltekin, 2017; Çöltekin and Rama, 2017).[1] In the remainder of this paper, we describe our methods and experiments, present and discuss our results.

2   Experiments and Results

We participated in both subtasks using the same architectures. However, we trained and tuned the model parameters on each data set separately. The training set for the competition consisted of 500 000 tweets for English and 100 000 tweets for Spanish subtask. The data sets contained most frequent 20 emojis for English and 19 emojis for Spanish. Joining late to the party, our training set consisted of 485 151 English tweets, and 97 765 Spanish tweets, since about 3 % of the tweets were not available by the time we crawled them. As presented in Figure 1, the label distribution is similar and quite skewed for both languages. We included pre-processing steps of case normalization and discarding low-frequency features as part of our hyperparameter optimization. In all our experiments, we use only the data supplied by the organizers. We did not use any external sources (e.g., pre-trained word embeddings), nor did we perform any further linguistic processing (e.g., POS tagging, or parsing). The test size for English and Spanish is 50 000 and 10 000 respectively.

2.1   Support Vector Machines

The best results obtained in the shared task are based on multi-class (one-vs-rest) linear support

---

[1] The source code of our implementation is available at https://github.com/coltekin/emoji2018.

Proceedings of the 12th International Workshop on Semantic Evaluation (SemEval-2018), pages 34–38
New Orleans, Louisiana, June 5–6, 2018. ©2018 Association for Computational Linguistics

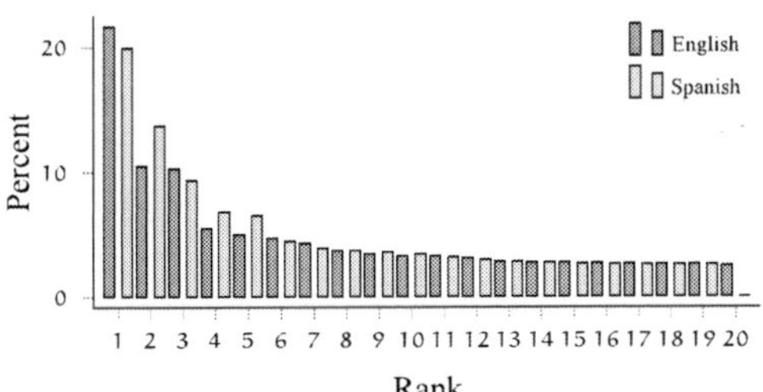

Figure 1: Label distribution in both data sets. Ratio of each label is plotted against its rank. Note that the emojis sharing the same rank are not necessarily identical in both languages.

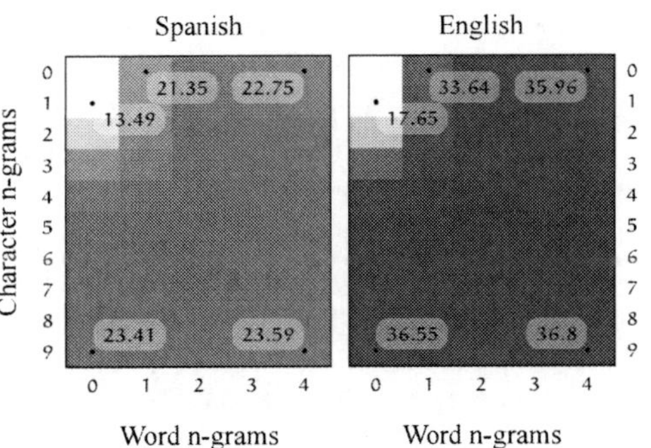

Figure 2: The effect of maximum character and word n-gram size combinations to F1-measure. Darker shades indicate higher F1-measure.

vector machines (SVM). We use 'bag of n-grams' as features, combining both character n-grams and word n-grams of different sizes, weighted by sublinear TF-IDF scaling applied globally to all n-grams (character and word n-grams with varying sizes). Although we also experimented with logistic regression and random forests using the same feature set, the results were consistently inferior to the SVMs. Therefore, we will not discuss the results of logistic regression and random forests. The models discussed in this section were implemented with scikit-learn package (Pedregosa et al., 2011) using liblinear back end (Fan et al., 2008).

We optimized the models for best macro F1-score on each language data set through a grid search using 5-fold cross validation. The hyperparameters considered during optimization were maximum character/word n-gram size, case normalization, minimum document frequency threshold for excluding low-frequency features, and SVM margin (or regularization) parameter 'C'. Although there has been other parameter settings with competitive scores, we used maximum character n-grams size of 6, maximum word n-gram size of 4, minimum document frequency threshold of 2, SVM parameter C of 0.10, and we case normalized only word (not character) n-grams. Our submitted system achieved 36.55 precision, 36.22 recall and 35.99 F1-score on the English test set, and 23.49 precision, 22.80 recall and 22.36 F1-score on the Spanish test set. These figures were about 1 % lower than the figures we obtained in 5-fold cross validation results on the training data.

Figure 2 presents the effects of character and word n-grams of different sizes. For all results presented in Figure 2, n-grams from size 1 up to the indicated number are included as features. Although both combining character and word n-grams, and

larger n-gram sizes increase the performance, the gains from higher n-gram values are rather small. The effects of other hyperparameters are smaller. In general, however, excluding features based on frequency seems to hurt the performance. Case normalization is useful if applied to word n-grams, but its effects are often negative if it is applied to both character and word n-grams. The optimum regularization parameter 'C' is stable over both languages and different training sizes.

2.2 Recurrent Neural Networks

Gaining popularity relatively recently, neural models are another common approach to text classification. Fully-connected networks are computationally impractical. However, convolutional networks (CNNs) and recurrent neural networks (RNNs) offer reasonably efficient computation, as well as better modeling of sequences. RNNs, particularly gated RNNs, have been used in many diverse natural language processing tasks successfully, and text classification is not an exception.

Our neural model includes two bidirectional RNN components: one taking a sequence of words as input and another taking a sequence of characters as input. The recurrent components of the network builds two representations for the text (one based on characters, the other based on words), the representations are concatenated and passed to a fully connected softmax layer that assigns an emoji to the document based on the RNN representations. Since the tweets are relatively short, we did not truncate the input documents. For both character and word inputs, we used embedding layers before the RNN layers. All neural network experiments were implemented with Tensorflow (Abadi et al., 2015) using Keras API (Chollet et al., 2015).

Although the history/context is not a parameter for recurrent networks, the architecture has many hyperparameters. We optimized the hyperparameters of the architecture through a random search for the embedding size of both characters and words, the hidden representation size of the RNN cells, the dropout parameter for each component of the network, frequency threshold for excluding features, RNN architecture, GRU (Cho et al., 2014) or LSTM (Hochreiter and Schmidhuber, 1997), and case normalization. For the RNN models, we used a random training–validation split (80 %–20 % for Spanish, and 90 %–10 % for English) during hyperparameter tuning. We used early stopping based on macro F1-measure, and picked the epoch with the best F1-measure for each hyperparameter setting. Besides these parameters – used for systematic random search – we also experimented with deeper architectures, both by stacking RNNs and by multiple fully-connected layers. Deeper networks, however, yielded worse results.

We obtained F1-scores of 33.02 % for English data and 17.98 % for the Spanish data on the (randomly split) development set. For both subtasks, we submitted results with the hyperparameter setting that worked best on the English data set (although it yielded a slightly lower F1-score than the best one obtained for Spanish). For both languages, the RNN results submitted used a model with embedding layers of size 32 (for characters) and 128 (for words). In the case of bidirectional GRU networks we used hidden units of sizes 32 and 128 for character and word input, respectively, minimum frequency threshold of 4 for characters and 1 for words, dropout parameter of 0.50 at the embedding layers and 0.10 at the RNN layers, and no case normalization.

2.3 Effect of training set size

The performance with different training set sizes is an important consideration in model choice. Furthermore, since the training set sizes for the two languages in present study are different, it is also be a plausible explanation for the fact that substantially lower performance of both models on the Spanish task. To shed light into these two issues, we present incremental results on (only) the English data set. In this experiment, we randomly set aside 10 % of the English training data for testing, we split the remaining 90 % into 10 splits, and train both systems by starting with one of splits, and incrementally adding another one in each iteration.

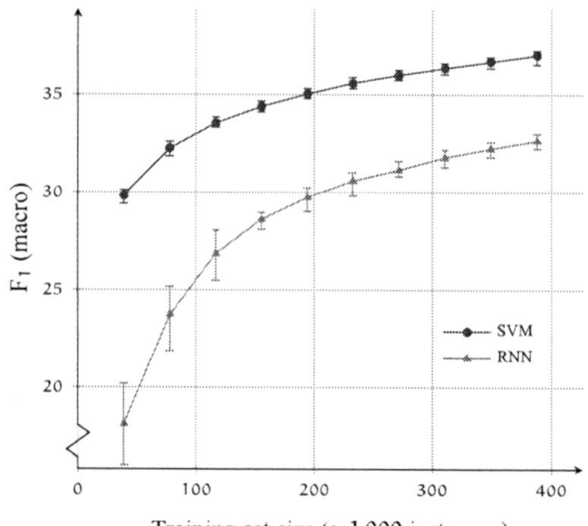

Figure 3: Learning curve for the SVM and RNN models on the English training set. The error bars indicate maximum and minimum values in 10 trials.

Figure 3 shows the F1-score against training set size, for both SVM and RNN models.

3 Discussion and conclusions

In this paper, we described our submitted systems at SemEval-2018 Task 2 on Multilingual Emoji Prediction. Besides providing details on our systems, this paper also intends to provide a comparison between two text classification methods: RNNs and linear SVMs. The comparison is motivated by the fact that, despite their popularity and argued superiority, we and others found linear models, particularly SVMs, yield better results than (deep) neural models in a series of other text classification tasks (e.g., Çöltekin and Rama, 2016; Rama and Çöltekin, 2017; Çöltekin and Rama, 2017; Medvedeva et al., 2017).

One plausible explanation is the fact that neural networks typically require more data to train. Indeed, the previous shared tasks cited above often provided modest-size training sets, mainly due to the cost of labeling. Emoji classification task has an advantage in this respect as the labeling is relatively cheap compared to many other text classification tasks. As a result, at least for English, the shared task included a rather large training set. However, our current findings also indicate that the linear SVMs still perform better than the RNN counterparts. Although the results presented in Figure 3 indicate that more data is, indeed, helpful for RNNs, the performance gap in favor of SVMs persists. Another interesting (but expected due to model complexity) observation in

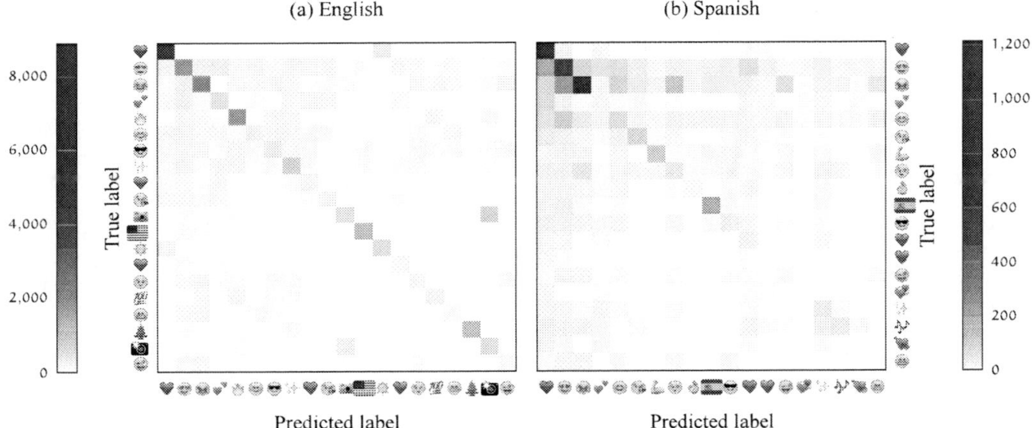

Figure 4: Confusion matrices for both data sets. The labels are sorted by frequency.

Figure 3 is that the RNNs also exhibit larger variation, especially with smaller data sizes.

Our findings seem to contradict with the majority of recent NLP literature, where RNNs are often claimed to be superior to linear models, and emoji classification is not an exception (e.g., Barbieri et al., 2017). Part of this impression comes from the fact that, in most studies, the linear baselines used in comparison are simple bag-of-words models. As words in a text are not independent, simple bag-of-words is deemed to fail. The simple addition of word n-gram features, however, circumvents this problem to a large extent, enabling the linear models to capture some local dependencies. RNNs, however, still have a potential advantage since they can, at least in theory, capture long-range dependencies as well. However, it seems either local dependencies are enough in many text classification tasks, or the data sets are (still) small for RNNs to generalize over useful long-range dependencies. Furthermore, character n-gram features are also useful, particularly for morphologically rich languages, as they also capture information present in sub-word units. Although including many overlapping character and word n-gram features result in large feature vectors, the sparse implementations of these models are computationally feasible and easy to tune – often more than corresponding deep neural network models.

A curious finding from our experiments is that despite the language-agnostic nature of our methods, both models yielded a rather large performance difference (13.63 % F1-measure on the test set) between English and Spanish. The possible explanation based on training set size is not supported by the experiments presented in Section 2.3. Figure 3 shows that, at about the training set size of Spanish data (100 000 instances), one can obtain about 32 % F1-score on the English data set, which is substantially higher than the best test and development set results we obtained using the full training data for Spanish (22.36 % and 23.59 % respectively). Hence, the difference is likely to be either due to differences between the languages, or due to some inherent confusability of the emojis in the Spanish data set. The confusion matrices in Figure 4 indicate higher majority class bias for Spanish. More experiments are needed for a better understanding of the differences.

3.1 Future directions

Past research has found that ensemble methods that combine multiple classifiers yield better performance compared to each individual classifier (Malmasi and Dras, 2015). Besides the differences in the learning algorithms, the models we compare in this work exploit rather different types of information. Hence, a combination of classifiers may result in better performance. Even though we did not experiment with ensemble methods in this work, the number of test instances that were predicted correctly by one of the models (but not by both) was 17.28 % and 19.95 % for English and the Spanish data respectively, indicating a promising upper bound for an ensemble approach.

Although we did not use any external resources in this task, another potential source of improvement is to use external information (e.g., embeddings or cluster labels) extracted from large unlabeled texts.

References

Martín Abadi, Ashish Agarwal, Paul Barham, Eugene Brevdo, Zhifeng Chen, Craig Citro, Greg S. Corrado, Andy Davis, Jeffrey Dean, Matthieu Devin, Sanjay Ghemawat, Ian Goodfellow, Andrew Harp, Geoffrey Irving, Michael Isard, Yangqing Jia, Rafal Jozefowicz, Lukasz Kaiser, Manjunath Kudlur, Josh Levenberg, Dan Mané, Rajat Monga, Sherry Moore, Derek Murray, Chris Olah, Mike Schuster, Jonathon Shlens, Benoit Steiner, Ilya Sutskever, Kunal Talwar, Paul Tucker, Vincent Vanhoucke, Vijay Vasudevan, Fernanda Viégas, Oriol Vinyals, Pete Warden, Martin Wattenberg, Martin Wicke, Yuan Yu, and Xiaoqiang Zheng. 2015. TensorFlow: Large-scale machine learning on heterogeneous systems. Software available from tensorflow.org.

Francesco Barbieri, Miguel Ballesteros, and Horacio Saggion. 2017. Are emojis predictable? In *Proceedings of the 15th Conference of the European Chapter of the Association for Computational Linguistics: Volume 2, Short Papers*, pages 105–111, Valencia, Spain. Association for Computational Linguistics.

Francesco Barbieri, Jose Camacho-Collados, Francesco Ronzano, Luis Espinosa-Anke, Miguel Ballesteros, Valerio Basile, Viviana Patti, and Horacio Saggion. 2018. SemEval-2018 Task 2: Multilingual Emoji Prediction. In *Proceedings of the 12th International Workshop on Semantic Evaluation (SemEval-2018)*, New Orleans, LA, United States. Association for Computational Linguistics.

Francesco Barbieri, Francesco Ronzano, and Horacio Saggion. 2016. What does this emoji mean? a vector space skip-gram model for twitter emojis. In *Proceedings of the Tenth International Conference on Language Resources and Evaluation (LREC 2016)*, Paris, France. European Language Resources Association (ELRA).

Kyunghyun Cho, Bart van Merrienboer, Dzmitry Bahdanau, and Yoshua Bengio. 2014. On the properties of neural machine translation: Encoder–decoder approaches. In *Proceedings of SSST-8, Eighth Workshop on Syntax, Semantics and Structure in Statistical Translation*, pages 103–111.

François Chollet et al. 2015. Keras. `https://github.com/keras-team/keras`.

Çağrı Çöltekin and Taraka Rama. 2016. Discriminating similar languages with linear SVMs and neural networks. In *Proceedings of the Third Workshop on NLP for Similar Languages, Varieties and Dialects (VarDial3)*, pages 15–24, Osaka, Japan.

Çağrı Çöltekin and Taraka Rama. 2017. Tübingen system in VarDial 2017 shared task: experiments with language identification and cross-lingual parsing. In *Proceedings of the Fourth Workshop on NLP for Similar Languages, Varieties and Dialects (VarDial)*, pages 146–155, Valencia, Spain. Association for Computational Linguistics.

Rong-En Fan, Kai-Wei Chang, Cho-Jui Hsieh, Xiang-Rui Wang, and Chih-Jen Lin. 2008. LIBLINEAR: A library for large linear classification. *Journal of Machine Learning Research*, 9:1871–1874.

Bjarke Felbo, Alan Mislove, Anders Søgaard, Iyad Rahwan, and Sune Lehmann. 2017. Using millions of emoji occurrences to learn any-domain representations for detecting sentiment, emotion and sarcasm. In *Proceedings of the 2017 Conference on Empirical Methods in Natural Language Processing*, pages 1615–1625, Copenhagen, Denmark. Association for Computational Linguistics.

Sepp Hochreiter and Jürgen Schmidhuber. 1997. Long short-term memory. *Neural computation*, 9(8):1735–1780.

Petra Kralj Novak, Jasmina Smailović, Borut Sluban, and Igor Mozetič. 2015. Sentiment of emojis. *PLOS ONE*, 10(12):1–22.

Shervin Malmasi and Mark Dras. 2015. Language identification using classifier ensembles. In *Proceedings of the Joint Workshop on Language Technology for Closely Related Languages, Varieties and Dialects*, pages 35–43.

Maria Medvedeva, Martin Kroon, and Barbara Plank. 2017. When sparse traditional models outperform dense neural networks: the curious case of discriminating between similar languages. In *Proceedings of the Fourth Workshop on NLP for Similar Languages, Varieties and Dialects (VarDial)*, pages 156–163, Valencia, Spain. Association for Computational Linguistics.

F. Pedregosa, G. Varoquaux, A. Gramfort, V. Michel, B. Thirion, O. Grisel, M. Blondel, P. Prettenhofer, R. Weiss, V. Dubourg, J. Vanderplas, A. Passos, D. Cournapeau, M. Brucher, M. Perrot, and E. Duchesnay. 2011. Scikit-learn: Machine learning in Python. *Journal of Machine Learning Research*, 12:2825–2830.

Taraka Rama and Çağrı Çöltekin. 2017. Fewer features perform well at native language identification task. In *Proceedings of the 12th Workshop on Innovative Use of NLP for Building Educational Applications*, pages 255–260, Copenhagen, Denmark. Association for Computational Linguistics.

SemEval-2018 Task 3: Irony Detection in English Tweets

Cynthia Van Hee, Els Lefever and **Véronique Hoste**
LT3 Language and Translation Technology Team
Ghent University
Groot-Brittanniëlaan 45, 9000 Ghent
`firstname.lastname@ugent.be`

Abstract

This paper presents the first shared task on irony detection: given a tweet, automatic natural language processing systems should determine whether the tweet is ironic (Task A) and which type of irony (if any) is expressed (Task B). The ironic tweets were collected using irony-related hashtags (i.e. *#irony, #sarcasm, #not*) and were subsequently manually annotated to minimise the amount of noise in the corpus. Prior to distributing the data, hashtags that were used to collect the tweets were removed from the corpus. For both tasks, a training corpus of 3,834 tweets was provided, as well as a test set containing 784 tweets. Our shared tasks received submissions from 43 teams for the binary classification Task A and from 31 teams for the multiclass Task B. The highest classification scores obtained for both subtasks are respectively $F_1 = 0.71$ and $F_1 = 0.51$ and demonstrate that fine-grained irony classification is much more challenging than binary irony detection.

1 Introduction

The development of the social web has stimulated the use of figurative and creative language, including irony, in public (Ghosh et al., 2015). From a philosophical/psychological perspective, discerning the mechanisms that underlie ironic speech improves our understanding of human reasoning and communication, and more and more, this interest in understanding irony also emerges in the machine learning community (Wallace, 2015). Although an unanimous definition of irony is still lacking in the literature, it is often identified as a trope whose actual meaning differs from what is literally enunciated. Due to its nature, irony has important implications for natural language processing (NLP) tasks, which aim to understand and produce human language. In fact, automatic irony detection has a large potential for various applications in the domain of text mining, especially those that require semantic analysis, such as author profiling, detecting online harassment, and, maybe the most well-known example, sentiment analysis.

Due to its importance in industry, sentiment analysis research is abundant and significant progress has been made in the field (e.g. in the context of SemEval (Rosenthal et al., 2017)). However, the SemEval-2014 shared task *Sentiment Analysis in Twitter* (Rosenthal et al., 2014) demonstrated the impact of irony on automatic sentiment classification by including a test set of ironic tweets. The results revealed that, while sentiment classification performance on regular tweets reached up to $F_1 = 0.71$, scores on the ironic tweets varied between $F_1 = 0.29$ and $F_1 = 0.57$. In fact, it has been demonstrated that several applications struggle to maintain high performance when applied to ironic text (e.g. Liu, 2012; Maynard and Greenwood, 2014; Ghosh and Veale, 2016). Like other types of figurative language, ironic text should not be interpreted in its literal sense; it requires a more complex understanding based on associations with the context or world knowledge. Examples 1 and 2 are sentences that regular sentiment analysis systems would probably classify as positive, whereas the intended sentiment is undeniably negative.

(1) *I feel so blessed to get ocular migraines.*

(2) *Go ahead drop me hate, I'm looking forward to it.*

For human readers, it is clear that the author of example 1 does not feel blessed at all, which can be inferred from the contrast between the positive sentiment expression "I feel so blessed", and the negative connotation associated with getting ocular migraines. Although such connotative infor-

39

Proceedings of the 12th International Workshop on Semantic Evaluation (SemEval-2018), pages 39–50
New Orleans, Louisiana, June 5–6, 2018. ©2018 Association for Computational Linguistics

mation is easily understood by most people, it is difficult to access by machines. Example 2 illustrates implicit cyberbullying; instances that typically lack explicit profane words and where the offense is often made through irony. Similarly to example 1, a contrast can be perceived between a positive statement ("I'm looking forward to") and a negative situation (i.e. experiencing hate). To be able to interpret the above examples correctly, machines need, similarly to humans, to be aware that irony is used, and that the intended sentiment is opposite to what is literally enunciated.

The irony detection task[1] we propose is formulated as follows: given a single post (i.e. a tweet), participants are challenged to automatically determine whether irony is used and which type of irony is expressed. We thus defined two subtasks:

- Task A describes a **binary irony classification task** to define, for a given tweet, whether irony is expressed.

- Task B describes a **multiclass irony classification task** to define whether it contains a specific type of irony (verbal irony by means of a polarity clash, situational irony, or another type of verbal irony, see further) or is not ironic. Concretely, participants should define which one out of four categories a tweet contains: ironic by clash, situational irony, other verbal irony or not ironic.

It is important to note that by a tweet, we understand the actual text it contains, without metadata (e.g. user id, time stamp, location). Although such metadata could help to recognise irony, the objective of this task is to learn, at message level, how irony is linguistically realised.

2 Automatic Irony Detection

As described by Joshi et al. (2017), recent approaches to irony can roughly be classified as either rule-based or (supervised and unsupervised) machine learning-based. While rule-based approaches mostly rely upon lexical information and require no training, machine learning invariably makes use of training data and exploits different types of information sources (or *features*), such as bags of words, syntactic patterns, sentiment information or semantic relatedness.

Previous work on irony detection mostly applied supervised machine learning mainly exploiting lexical features. Other features often include punctuation mark/interjection counts (e.g Davidov et al., 2010), sentiment lexicon scores (e.g. Bouazizi and Ohtsuki, 2016; Farías et al., 2016), emoji (e.g. González-Ibáñez et al., 2011), writing style, emotional scenarios, part of speech-patterns (e.g. Reyes et al., 2013), and so on. Also beneficial for this task are combinations of different feature types (e.g. Van Hee et al., 2016b), author information (e.g. Bamman and Smith, 2015), features based on (semantic or factual) oppositions (e.g Karoui et al., 2015; Gupta and Yang, 2017; Van Hee, 2017) and even eye-movement patterns of human readers (Mishra et al., 2016). While a wide range of features are and have been used extensively over the past years, deep learning techniques have recently gained increasing popularity for this task. Such systems often rely on semantic relatedness (i.e. through word and character embeddings (e.g. Amir et al., 2016; Ghosh and Veale, 2016)) deduced by the network and reduce feature engineering efforts.

Regardless of the methodology and algorithm used, irony detection often involves binary classification where irony is defined as instances that express the opposite of what is meant (e.g. Riloff et al., 2013; Joshi et al., 2017). Twitter has been a popular data genre for this task, as it is easily accessible and provides a rapid and convenient method to find (potentially) ironic messages by looking for hashtags like *#irony, #not* and *#sarcasm*. As a consequence, irony detection research often relies on automatically annotated (i.e. based on irony-related hashtags) corpora, which contain noise (Kunneman et al., 2015; Van Hee, 2017).

3 Task Description

We propose two subtasks A and B for the automatic detection of irony on Twitter, for which we provide more details below.

3.1 Task A: Binary Irony Classification

The first subtask is a two-class (or binary) classification task where submitted systems have to predict whether a tweet is ironic or not. The following examples respectively present an ironic and non-ironic tweet.

(3) *I just love when you test my patience!! #not.*

---

[1]All practical information, data download links and the final results can be consulted via the CodaLab website of our task: https://competitions.codalab.org/competitions/17468.

(4)   *Had no sleep and have got school now #not happy*

Note that the examples contain irony-related hashtags (e.g. #irony) that were removed from the corpus prior to distributing the data for the task.

3.2   Task B: Multiclass Irony Classification

The second subtask is a multiclass classification task where submitted systems have to predict one out of four labels describing i) verbal irony realised through a polarity contrast, ii) verbal irony without such a polarity contrast (i.e. other verbal irony), iii) descriptions of situational irony, and iv) non-irony. The following paragraphs present a description and a number of examples for each label.

Verbal irony by means of a polarity contrast This category applies to instances containing an evaluative expression whose polarity (positive, negative) is inverted between the literal and the intended evaluation, as shown in examples 5 and 6:

(5)   *I love waking up with migraines #not* 😖

(6)   *I really love this year's summer; weeks and weeks of awful weather*

In the above examples, the irony results from a polarity inversion between two evaluations. For instance, in example 6, the literal evaluation ("I really love this year's summer") is positive, while the intended one, which is implied by the context ("weeks and weeks of awful weather"), is negative.

Other verbal irony This category contains instances that show no polarity contrast between the literal and the intended evaluation, but are nevertheless ironic.

(7)   *@someuser Yeah keeping cricket clean, that's what he wants #Sarcasm*

(8)   *Human brains disappear every day. Some of them have never even appeared. http://t.co/Fb0Aq5Frqs #brain #human-brain #Sarcasm*

Situational irony This class label is reserved for instances describing situational irony, or situations that fail to meet some expectations. As explained by Shelley (2001), firefighters who have a fire in their kitchen while they are out to answer a fire alarm would be a typically ironic situation. Some other examples of situational irony are the following:

(9)   *Most of us didn't focus in the #ADHD lecture. #irony*

(10)   *Event technology session is having Internet problems. #irony #HSC2024*

Non-ironic This class contains instances that are clearly not ironic, or which lack context to be sure that they are ironic, as shown in the following examples:

(11)   *And then my sister should be home from college by time I get home from babysitting. And it's payday. THIS IS A GOOD FRIDAY*

(12)   *Is Obamacare Slowing Health Care Spending? #NOT*

4   Corpus Construction and Annotation

A data set of 3,000 English tweets was constructed by searching Twitter for the hashtags *#irony, #sarcasm* and *#not* (hereafter referred to as the 'hashtag corpus'), which could occur anywhere in the tweet that was finally included in the corpus. All tweets were collected between 01/12/2014 and 04/01/2015 and represent 2,676 unique users. To minimise the noise introduced by groundless irony hashtags, all tweets were manually labelled using a fine-grained annotation scheme for irony (Van Hee et al., 2016a). Prior to data annotation, the entire corpus was cleaned by removing retweets, duplicates and non-English tweets and replacing XML-escaped characters (e.g. &).

The corpus was entirely annotated by three students in linguistics and second-language speakers of English, with each student annotating one third of the whole corpus. All annotations were done using the brat rapid annotation tool (Stenetorp et al., 2012). To assess the reliability of the annotations, and whether the guidelines allowed to carry out the task consistently, an **inter-annotator agreement study** was set up in two rounds. Firstly, inter-rater agreement was calculated between the authors of the guidelines to test the guidelines for usability and to assess whether changes or additional clarifications were recommended prior annotating the entire corpus. For this purpose, a subset of 100 instances from the SemEval-2015 Task *Sentiment Analysis of Figurative Language in Twitter* (Ghosh et al., 2015) dataset were annotated. Based on the results, some clarifications and refinements were added to the annotation scheme, which are thoroughly described in Van Hee (2017). Next, a second agreement study was carried out on a subset (i.e. 100 randomly chosen instances) of the corpus. As metric, we used **Fleiss' Kappa** (Fleiss, 1971), a widespread statistical measure in the field of computational linguistics for assessing annotator agreement on categorical ratings (Carletta, 1996). The measure calculates the degree of agreement in classification over the agreement which would be expected by chance, i.e. when annotators would randomly assign class labels.

annotation	Kappa κ round 1	Kappa κ round 2
ironic / not ironic	0.65	0.72
ironic by clash / other / not ironic	0.55	0.72

Table 1: Inter-annotator agreement scores (Kappa) in two annotation rounds.

Table 1 presents the inter-rater scores for the binary irony distinction and for three-way irony classification ('other' includes both situational irony and other forms of verbal irony). We see that better inter-annotator agreement is obtained after the refinement of the annotation scheme, especially for the binary irony distinction. Given the difficulty of the task, a Kappa score of 0.72 for recognising irony can be interpreted as good reliability[2].

The distribution if the different irony types in the experimental corpus are presented in Table 2.

class label	# instances
Verbal irony by means of a polarity contrast	1,728
Other types of verbal irony	267
Situational irony	401
Non-ironic	604

Table 2: Distribution of the different irony categories in the corpus

Based on the annotations, 2,396 instances out of the 3,000 are ironic, while 604 are not. To balance the class distribution in our experimental corpus, 1,792 non-ironic tweets were added from a background corpus. The tweets in this corpus were collected from the same set of Twitter users as in the hashtag corpus, and within the same time span. It is important to note that these tweets do not contain irony-related hashtags (as opposed to the non-ironic tweets in the hashtag corpus), and were manually filtered from ironic tweets. Adding

[2]According to magnitude guidelines by Landis and Koch (1977).

these non-ironic tweets to the experimental corpus brought the total amount of data to 4,792 tweets (2,396 ironic + 2,396 non-ironic). For this shared task, the corpus was randomly split into a class-balanced training (80% or 3,833 instances) and test (20%, or 958 instances) set. In an additional cleaning step, we removed ambiguous tweets (i.e. where additional context was required to understand their ironic nature), from the test corpus, resulting in a test set containing 784 tweets (consisting of 40% ironic and 60% non-ironic tweets).

To train their systems, participants were not restricted to the provided training corpus. They were allowed to use additional training data that was collected and annotated at their own initiative. In the latter case, the submitted system was considered *unconstrained*, as opposed to *constrained* if only the distributed training data were used for training.

It is important to note that participating teams were allowed ten submissions at CodaLab, and that they could submit a constrained and unconstrained system for each subtask. However, only their last submission was considered for the official ranking (see Table 3).

5 Evaluation

For both subtasks, participating systems were evaluated using standard evaluation metrics, including accuracy, precision, recall and F_1 score, calculated as follows:

$$accuracy = \frac{true\ positives\ +\ true\ negatives}{total\ number\ of\ instances} \quad (1)$$

$$precision = \frac{true\ positives}{true\ positives\ +\ false\ positives} \quad (2)$$

$$recall = \frac{true\ positives}{true\ positives\ +\ false\ negatives} \quad (3)$$

$$F_1 = 2 \cdot \frac{precision \cdot recall}{precision\ +\ recall} \quad (4)$$

While accuracy provides insights into the system performance for all classes, the latter three measures were calculated for the positive class only (Task A) or were macro-averaged over four class labels (Task B). Macro-averaging of the F_1 score implies that all class labels have equal weight in the final score.

For both subtasks, two baselines were provided against which to compare the systems' performance. The first baseline randomly assigns irony labels and the second one is a linear SVM classifier with standard hyperparameter settings exploiting tf-idf word unigram features (implemented with scikit-learn (Pedregosa et al., 2011)). The second baseline system is made available to the task participants via GitHub[3].

6   Systems and results for Task A

In total, 43 teams competed in Task A on binary irony classification. Table 3 presents each team's performance in terms of accuracy, precision, recall and F_1 score. In all tables, the systems are ranked by the official F_1 score (shown in the fifth column). Scores from teams that are marked with an asterisk should be interpreted carefully, as the number of predictions they submitted does not correspond to the number of test instances.

As can be observed from the table, the SVM unigram baseline clearly outperforms the random class baseline and generally performs well for the task. Below we discuss the top five best-performing teams for Task A, which all built a constrained (i.e. only the provided training data were used) system. The best system yielded an F_1 score of 0.705 and was developed by THU_NGN (Wu et al., 2018). Their architecture consists of densely connected LSTMs based on (pre-trained) word embeddings, sentiment features using the AffectiveTweet package (Mohammad and Bravo-Marquez, 2017) and syntactic features (e.g. PoS-tag features + sentence embedding features). Hypothesising that the presence of a certain irony hashtag correlates with the type of irony that is used, they constructed a multi-task model able to predict simultaneously 1) the missing irony hashtag, 2) whether a tweet is ironic or not and 3) which fine-grained type of irony is used in a tweet.

Also in the top five are the teams NTUA-SLP (F_1= 0.672), WLV (F_1= 0.650), NLPRL-IITBHU (F_1= 0.648) and NIHRIO (F_1= 0.648). NTUA-SLP (Baziotis et al., 2018) built an ensemble classifier of two deep learning models: a word- and character-based (bi-directional) LSTM to capture semantic and syntactic information in tweets, respectively. As features, the team used pre-trained character and word embeddings on a corpus of 550 million tweets. Their ensem-

ble classifier applied majority voting to combine the outcomes of the two models. WLV (Rohanian et al., 2018) developed an ensemble voting classifier with logistic regression (LR) and a support vector machine (SVM) as component models. They combined (through averaging) pre-trained word and emoji embeddings with hand-crafted features, including sentiment contrasts between elements in a tweet (i.e. left vs. right sections, hashtags vs. text, emoji vs. text), sentiment intensity and word-based features like flooding and capitalisation). For Task B, they used a slightly altered (i.e. ensemble LR models and concatenated word embeddings instead of averaged) model. NLPRL-IITBHU (Rangwani et al., 2018) ranked fourth and used an XGBoost Classifier to tackle Task A. They combined pre-trained CNN activations using DeepMoji (Felbo et al., 2017) with ten types of handcrafted features. These were based on polarity contrast information, readability metrics, context incongruity, character flooding, punctuation counts, discourse markers/intensifiers/interjections/swear words counts, general token counts, WordNet similarity, polarity scores and URL counts. The fifth best system for Task A was built by NIHRIO (Vu et al., 2018) and consists of a neural-networks-based architecture (i.e. Multilayer Perceptron). The system exploited lexical (word- and character-level unigrams, bi-grams and trigrams), syntactic (PoS-tags with tf-idf values), semantic features (word embeddings using GloVe (Pennington et al., 2014), LSI features and Brown cluster features (Brown et al., 1992)) and polarity features derived from the Hu and Liu Opinion Lexicon (Hu and Liu, 2004).

As such, all teams in the top five approached the task differently, by exploiting various algorithms and features, but all of them clearly outperformed the baselines. Like most other teams, they also showed a better performance in terms of recall compared to precision.

Table 3 displays the results of each team's official submission for Task A, i.e. no distinction is made between constrained and unconstrained systems. By contrast, Tables 4 and 5 present the rankings of the **best** (i.e. not necessarily the last, and hence official submission) constrained and unconstrained submissions for Task A.

As can be deduced from Table 4, when considering all constrained submissions from each team and ranking them based on performance, we see

---

[3]https://github.com/Cyvhee/SemEval2018-Task3/

that the UCDCC team ranks first (F_1= 0.724), followed by THU_NGN, NTUA-SLP, WLV and NLPRL-IITBHU, whose approach was discussed earlier in this paper. The UCDCC-system is an LSTM model exploiting Glove word embedding features.

team	acc	precision	recall	F_1
THU_NGN	**0.735**	0.630	0.801	**0.705**
NTUA-SLP	0.732	0.654	0.691	0.672
WLV	0.643	0.532	0.836	0.650
NLPRL-IITBHU	0.661	0.551	0.788	0.648
NIHRIO	0.702	0.609	0.691	0.648
DLUTNLP-1	0.628	0.520	0.797	0.629
ELiRF-UPV	0.611	0.506	0.833	0.629
liangxh16	0.659	0.555	0.714	0.625
CJ	0.667	0.565	0.695	0.623
#NonDicevo-SulSerio	0.679	0.583	0.666	0.622
UWB	0.688	0.599	0.643	0.620
INAOE-UPV	0.651	0.546	0.714	0.618
RM@IT	0.649	0.544	0.714	0.618
DUTQS	0.601	0.498	0.794	0.612
ISP RAS	0.565	0.473	**0.849**	0.608
ValenTO	0.598	0.496	0.781	0.607
[4]binarizer	0.666	0.553	0.647	0.596
SIRIUS_LC	0.684	0.604	0.588	0.596
warnikchow	0.644	0.543	0.656	0.594
ECNU	0.596	0.494	0.743	0.593
Parallel Computing-Network Research Group	0.617	0.513	0.701	0.592
Lancaster	0.635	0.532	0.666	0.591
Unigram SVM BL	0.635	0.532	0.659	0.589
IITBHU-NLP	0.566	0.472	0.778	0.587
s1998	0.629	0.526	0.653	0.583
Random Decision - Syntax Trees	0.617	0.514	0.672	0.582
textbflyreact	0.628	0.525	0.640	0.577
UTH-SU	0.639	0.540	0.605	0.571
KLUEnicorn	0.594	0.491	0.643	0.557
ai-ku	0.643	0.555	0.502	0.527
UTMN	0.603	0.500	0.556	0.527
UCDCC	0.682	0.645	0.444	0.526
IITG	0.556	0.450	0.540	0.491
MI&T–LAB	0.614	0.514	0.463	0.487
*NEUROSENT-PDI	0.504	0.409	0.560	0.472
Lovelace	0.512	0.412	0.543	0.469
codersTeam	0.509	0.410	0.543	0.468
WHLL	0.580	0.469	0.437	0.453
DKE_UM	0.561	0.447	0.450	0.449
LDR	0.564	0.446	0.415	0.430
*YNU-HPCC	0.509	0.391	0.428	0.408
Random BL	0.503	0.373	0.373	0.373
ACMK-POZNAN	0.620	0.550	0.232	0.326
iiidyt	0.352	0.257	0.334	0.291
milkstout	0.584	0.427	0.142	0.213
INGEOTEC-IIMAS	0.628	**0.880**	0.071	0.131

Table 3: Official (CodaLab) results for Task A, ranked by F_1 score. The highest scores in each column are shown in bold and the baselines are indicated in purple.

team	acc	precision	recall	F_1
UCDCC	**0.797**	**0.788**	0.669	**0.724**
THU_NGN	0.735	0.630	0.801	0.705
NTUA-SLP	0.732	0.654	0.691	0.672
WLV	0.643	0.532	**0.836**	0.650
NLPRL-IITBHU	0.661	0.551	0.788	0.648
NCL	0.702	0.609	0.691	0.648
RM@IT	0.691	0.598	0.679	0.636
#NonDicevo-SulSerio	0.666	0.562	0.717	0.630
DLUTNLP-1	0.628	0.520	0.797	0.629
ELiRF-UPV	0.611	0.506	0.833	0.629

Table 4: Best constrained systems for Task A.

team	acc	precision	recall	F_1
#NonDicevo-SulSerio	**0.679**	0.583	0.666	**0.622**
INAOE-UPV	0.651	0.546	**0.714**	0.618
RM@IT	0.649	0.544	0.714	0.618
ValenTO	0.598	0.496	**0.781**	0.607
UTMN	0.603	0.500	0.556	0.527
IITG	0.556	0.450	0.540	0.491
LDR	0.571	0.455	0.408	0.431
milkstouts	0.584	0.427	0.142	0.213
INGEOTEC-IIMAS	0.643	**0.897**	0.113	0.200

Table 5: Best unconstrained systems for Task A.

In the top five unconstrained (i.e. using additional training data) systems for Task A are #NonDicevoSulSerio, INAOE-UPV, RM@IT, ValenTO and UTMN, with F_1 scores ranging between 0.622 and 0.527. #NonDicevoSulserio extended the training corpus with 3,500 tweets from existing irony corpora (e.g. Riloff et al. (2013); Barbieri and Saggion (2014); Ptáček et al. (2014) and built an SVM classifier exploiting structural features (e.g. hashtag count, text length), sentiment- (e.g. contrast between text and emoji sentiment), and emotion-based (i.e. emotion lexicon scores) features. INAOE-UPV combined pretrained word embeddings from the Google News corpus with word-based features (e.g. n-grams). They also extended the official training data with benchmark corpora previously used in irony research and trained their system with a total of 165,000 instances. RM@IT approached the task using an ensemble classifier based on attention-based recurrent neural networks and the Fast-

Text (Joulin et al., 2017) library for learning word representations. They enriched the provided training corpus with, on the one hand, the data sets provided for SemEval-2015 Task 11 (Ghosh et al., 2015) and, on the other hand, the sarcasm corpus composed by Ptáček et al. (2014). Altogether, this generated a training corpus of approximately 110,000 tweets. ValenTO took advantage of irony corpora previously used in irony detection that were manually annotated or through crowdsourcing (e.g. Riloff et al., 2013; Ptáček et al., 2014). In addition, they extended their corpus with an unspecified number of self-collected irony tweets using the hashtags *#irony* and *#sarcasm*. Finally, UTMN developed an SVM classifier exploiting binary bag-of-words features. They enriched the training set with 1,000 humorous tweets from SemEval-2017 Task 6 (Potash et al., 2017) and another 1,000 tweets with positive polarity from SemEval-2016 Task 4 (Nakov et al., 2016), resulting in a training corpus of 5,834 tweets.

Interestingly, when comparing the best constrained with the best unconstrained system for Task A, we see a difference of 10 points in favour of the constrained system, which indicates that adding more training data does not necessarily improve the classification performance.

7 Systems and Results for Task B

While 43 teams competed in Task A, 31 teams submitted a system for Task B on multiclass irony classification. Table 6 presents the official ranking with each team's performance in terms of accuracy, precision, recall and F_1 score. Similar to Task A, we discuss the top five systems in the overall ranking (Table 6) and then zoom in on the best performing constrained and unconstrained systems (Tables 7 and 8).

For Task B, the top five is nearly similar to the top five for Task A and includes the following teams: UCDCC (Ghosh, 2018), NTUA-SLP (Baziotis et al., 2018), THU_NGN (Wu et al., 2018), NLPRL-IITBHU (Rangwani et al., 2018) and NIHRIO (Vu et al., 2018). All of the teams tackled multiclass irony classification by applying (mostly) the same architecture as for Task A (see earlier). Inspired by siamese networks (Bromley et al., 1993) used in image classification, the UCDCC team developed a siamese architecture for irony detection in both subtasks. The neural network architecture makes use of Glove word embeddings as features and creates two identical subnetworks that are each fed with different parts of a tweet. Under the premise that ironic statements are often characterised by a form of opposition or contrast, the architecture captures this incongruity between two parts in an ironic tweet.

team	acc	precision	recall	F_1
UCDCC	**0.732**	**0.577**	0.504	**0.507**
NTUA-SLP	0.652	0.496	0.512	0.496
THU_NGN	0.605	0.486	**0.541**	0.495
NLPRL-IITBHU	0.603	0.466	0.506	0.474
NIHRIO	0.659	0.545	0.448	0.444
Random Decision Syntax Trees	0.633	0.487	0.439	0.435
ELiRF-UPV	0.633	0.412	0.440	0.421
WLV	0.671	0.431	0.415	0.415
#NonDicevo-SulSerio	0.545	0.409	0.441	0.413
INGEOTEC-IIMAS	0.644	0.502	0.385	0.406
ai-ku	0.584	0.422	0.402	0.393
warnikchow	0.598	0.412	0.410	0.393
UWB	0.626	0.440	0.406	0.390
CJ	0.603	0.412	0.409	0.384
UTH-SU	0.551	0.383	0.399	0.376
s1998	0.568	0.338	0.374	0.352
ValenTO	0.560	0.353	0.352	0.352
RM@IT	0.542	0.377	0.371	0.350
Unigram SVM BL	0.569	0.416	0.364	0.341
SSN_MLRG1	0.573	0.348	0.361	0.334
Lancaster	0.606	0.280	0.359	0.313
Parallel Computing Network Research Group	0.416	0.406	0.353	0.310
codersTeam	0.492	0.300	0.311	0.301
KLUEnicorn	0.347	0.321	0.353	0.298
DKE_UM	0.432	0.318	0.305	0.298
IITG	0.486	0.336	0.291	0.278
Lovelace	0.434	0.294	0.282	0.276
*YNU-HPCC	0.533	0.438	0.267	0.261
Random BL	0.416	0.241	0.241	0.241
LDR	0.461	0.230	0.250	0.234
ECNU	0.304	0.255	0.249	0.233
NEUROSENT-PDI	0.441	0.213	0.231	0.219
INAOE-UPV	0.594	0.217	0.261	0.215

Table 6: Official (CodaLab) results for Task B, ranked by F_1 score. The highest scores in each column are shown in bold and the baselines are indicated in purple.

NTUA-SLP, THU_NGN and NIHRIO used the same system for both subtasks. NLPRL-IITBHU also used the same architecture, but given the data skew for Task B, they used SMOTE (Chawla et al., 2002) as an oversampling technique to make sure each irony class was equally represented in the training corpus, which lead to an F_1 score increase of 5 points.

NLPRL-IITBHU built a Random Forest classifier making use of pre-trained DeepMoji embeddings, character embeddings (using Tweet2Vec) and sentiment lexicon features.

team	acc	precision	recall	F_1
UCDCC	**0.732**	**0.577**	0.504	**0.507**
NTUA-SLP	0.652	0.496	0.512	0.496
THU_NGN	0.605	0.486	**0.541**	0.495
NLPRL-IITBHU	0.603	0.466	0.506	0.474
NCL Random Decision-Syntax Trees	0.659	0.545	0.448	0.444
	0.633	0.487	0.439	0.435
ELiRF-UPV	0.633	0.412	0.440	0.421
WLV	0.671	0.431	0.415	0.415
AI-KU	0.584	0.422	0.402	0.393

Table 7: Best constrained systems for Task B. The highest scores in each column are shown in bold.

team	acc	precision	recall	F_1
#NonDicevo SulSerio	0.545	0.409	**0.441**	0.413
INGEOTEC-IIMAS	**0.647**	**0.508**	0.386	**0.407**
INAOE-UPV	0.495	0.347	0.379	0.350
IITG	0.486	0.336	0.291	0.278

Table 8: Unconstrained systems for Task B. The highest scores in each column are shown in bold.

As can be deduced from Table 7, the top five constrained systems correspond to the five best-performing systems overall (Table 6). Only four unconstrained systems were submitted for Task B. Differently from their Task A submission, #NonDicevoSulSerio applied a cascaded approach for this task, i.e. the first algorithm served an ironic/non-ironic classification, followed by a system distinguishing between ironic by clash and other forms of irony. Lastly, a third classifier distinguished between situational and other verbal irony. To account for class imbalance in step two, the team added 869 tweets of the *situational* and *other verbal irony* categories. INAOE-UPV, INGEOTEC-IIMAS and IITG also added tweets to the original training corpus, but it is not entirely clear how many were added and how these extra tweets were annotated.

Similar to Task A, the unconstrained systems do not seem to benefit from additional data, as they do not outperform the constrained submissions for the task.

team	not ironic	ironic by clash	situat. irony	other irony
UCDCC	**0.843**	**0.697**	0.376	0.114
NTUA-SLP	0.742	0.648	**0.460**	0.133
THU_NGN	0.704	0.608	0.433	**0.233**
NLPRL-IITBHU	0.689	0.636	0.387	0.185
NIHRIO Random Decision-Syntax Trees	0.763	0.607	0.317	0.087
	0.742	0.569	0.346	0.085
ELiRF-UPV	0.740	0.298	0.347	0.000
WLV	0.789	0.578	0.294	0.000
#NonDicevo SulSerio	0.683	0.533	0.315	0.121
INGEOTEC-IIMAS	0.764	0.494	0.211	0.152
ai-ku	0.699	0.529	0.258	0.087
warnikchow	0.717	0.524	0.300	0.028
UWB	0.744	0.557	0.232	0.027
CJ	0.724	0.559	0.202	0.050
*UTH-SU	0.671	0.513	0.254	0.065
s1998	0.711	0.446	0.253	0.000
emotIDM	0.713	0.456	0.165	0.074
RM@IT	0.671	0.481	0.148	0.100
SSN_MLRG1	0.704	0.499	0.105	0.027
Lancaster	0.729	0.523	0.000	0.000
Parallel Computing Network Res. Group	0.547	0.472	0.084	0.137
codersTeam	0.646	0.387	0.134	0.039
KLUEnicorn	0.423	0.384	0.200	0.186
DKE_UM	0.582	0.299	0.143	0.168
IITG	0.641	0.319	0.095	0.056
Lovelace	0.577	0.306	0.159	0.060
*YNU-HPCC	0.700	0.176	0.075	0.091
LDR	0.632	0.255	0.051	0.000
ECNU	0.444	0.259	0.118	0.110
*NEUROSENT-PDI	0.612	0.201	0.062	0.000
INAOE-UPV	0.748	0.000	0.111	0.000

Table 9: Results for Task B, reporting the F_1 score for the class labels. The highest scores in each column are shown in bold.

A closer look at the best and worst-performing systems for each subtask reveals that Task A benefits from systems that exploit a variety of handcrafted features, especially sentiment-based (e.g. sentiment lexicon values, polarity contrast), but also bags of words, semantic cluster features and PoS-based features. Other promising features for the task are word embeddings trained on large Twitter corpora (e.g. 5M tweets). The classifiers and algorithms used are (bidirectional) LSTMs, Random Forest, Multilayer Perceptron, and an optimised (i.e. using feature selection) voting classifier combining Support Vector Machines with Logistic Regression. Neural network-based systems exploiting word embeddings derived from the training dataset or generated from Wikipedia corpora perform less well for the task.

Similarly, Task B seems to benefit from (ensemble) neural-network architectures exploiting large corpus-based word embeddings and sentiment features. Oversampling and adjusting class weights are used to overcome the class imbalance of labels 2 and 3 versus 1 and 0 and tend to improve the classification performance. Ensemble classifiers outperform multi-step approaches and combined binary classifiers for this task.

Task B challenged the participants to distinguish between different types of irony. The class distributions in the training and test corpus are natural (i.e. no additional data were added after the annotation process) and imbalanced. For the evaluation of the task, F_1 scores were macro-averaged; on the one hand, this gives each label equal weight in the evaluation, but on the other hand, it does not show each class contribution to the average score. Table 9 therefore presents the participating teams' performance on each of the subtypes of irony in Task B. As can be deduced from Table 9, all teams performed best on the *non ironic* and *ironic by clash* classes, while identifying *situational irony* and *other irony* seems to be much more challenging. Although the scores for these two classes are the lowest, we observe an important difference between *situational* and *other* verbal irony. This can probably be explained by the heterogeneous nature of the *other* category, which collects diverse realisations of verbal irony. A careful and manual annotation of this class, which is currently being conducted, should provide more detailed insights into this category of ironic tweets.

8   Conclusions

The systems that were submitted for both subtasks represent a variety of neural-network-based approaches (i.e. CNNs, RNNs and (bi-)LSTMs) exploiting word- and character embeddings as well as handcrafted features. Other popular classification algorithms include Support Vector Machines, Maximum Entropy, Random Forest, and Naïve Bayes. While most approaches were based on one algorithm, some participants experimented with ensemble learners (e.g. SVM + LR, CNN + bi-LSTM, stacked LSTMs), implemented a voting system or built a cascaded architecture (for Task B) that first distinguished ironic from non-ironic tweets and subsequently differentiated between the fine-grained irony categories.

Among the most frequently used features are lexical features (e.g. n-grams, punctuation and hashtag counts, emoji presence) and sentiment- or emotion- lexicon features (e.g. based on SenticNet (Cambria et al., 2016), VADER (Hutto and Gilbert, 2014), aFinn (Nielsen, 2011)). Also important but to a lesser extent were syntactic (e.g. PoS-patterns) and semantic features, based on word, character and emoji embeddings or semantic clusters.

The best systems for Task A and Task B obtained an F_1 score of respectively 0.705 and 0.507 and clearly outperformed the baselines provided for this task. When looking at the scores per class label in Task B, we observe that high scores were obtained for the *non-ironic* and *ironic by clash* classes, and that *other irony* appears to be the most challenging irony type. Among all submissions, a wide variety of preprocessing tools, machine learning libraries and lexicons were explored.

As the provided datasets were relatively small, participants were allowed to include additional training data for both subtasks. Nevertheless, most submissions were constrained (i.e. only the provided training data were used): only nine unconstrained submissions were made for Task A, and four for Task B. When comparing constrained to unconstrained systems, it can be observed that adding more training data does not necessarily benefit the classification results. A possible explanation for this is that most unconstrained systems added training data from related irony research that were annotated differently (e.g. automatically) than the distributed corpus, which presumably limited the beneficial effect of increasing the training corpus size.

This paper provides some general insights into the main methodologies and bottlenecks for binary and multiclass irony classification. We observed that, overall, systems performed much better on Task A than Task B and the classification results for the subtypes of irony indicate that ironic by clash is most easily recognised (top $F_1 = 0.697$), while other types of verbal irony and situational irony are much harder (top F_1 scores are 0.114 and 0.376, respectively).

References

Silvio Amir, Byron C. Wallace, Hao Lyu, Paula Carvalho, and Mário J. Silva. 2016. Modelling Context with User Embeddings for Sarcasm Detection in Social Media. *CoRR*, abs/1607.00976.

David Bamman and Noah A. Smith. 2015. Contextualized Sarcasm Detection on Twitter. In *Proceedings of the Ninth International Conference on Web and Social Media (ICWSM'15)*, pages 574–577, Oxford, UK. AAAI.

Francesco Barbieri and Horacio Saggion. 2014. Modelling Irony in Twitter. In *Proceedings of the Student Research Workshop at the 14th Conference of the European Chapter of the ACL*, pages 56–64, Gothenburg, Sweden. ACL.

Christos Baziotis, Nikolaos Athanasiou, Pinelopi Papalampidi, Athanasia Kolovou, Georgios Paraskevopoulos, Nikolaos Ellinas, and Alexandros Potamianos. 2018. NTUA-SLP at SemEval-2018 Task 3: Deep Character and Word-level RNNs with Attention for Irony Detection in Twitter. In *Proceedings of the 12th International Workshop on Semantic Evaluation*, SemEval-2018, New Orleans, LA, USA. ACL.

Mondher Bouazizi and Tomoaki Ohtsuki. 2016. Sarcasm detection in twitter: "all your products are incredibly amazing!!!" - are they really? In *Global Communications Conference, GLOBECOM 2015*, pages 1–6. IEEE.

Jane Bromley, Isabelle Guyon, Yann LeCun, Eduard Säckinger, and Roopak Shah. 1993. Signature verification using a "siamese" time delay neural network. In *Proceedings of the 6th International Conference on Neural Information Processing Systems*, NIPS'93, pages 737–744, San Francisco, CA, USA. Morgan Kaufmann Publishers Inc.

Peter F. Brown, Peter V. deSouza, Robert L. Mercer, Vincent J. Della Pietra, and Jenifer C. Lai. 1992. Class-based N-gram Models of Natural Language. *Computational Linguistics*, 18(4):467–479.

Erik Cambria, Soujanya Poria, Rajiv Bajpai, and Bjoern Schuller. 2016. SenticNet 4: A Semantic Resource for Sentiment Analysis Based on Conceptual Primitives. In *Proceedings of COLING 2016, 26th International Conference on Computational Linguistics*, pages 2666–2677, Osaka, Japan. ACL.

Jean Carletta. 1996. Assessing Agreement on Classification Tasks: The Kappa Statistic. *Computational Linguistics*, 22(2):249–254.

Nitesh V. Chawla, Kevin W. Bowyer, Lawrence O. Hall, and W. Philip Kegelmeyer. 2002. SMOTE: Synthetic Minority Over-sampling Technique. *Journal of Artificial Intelligence Research*, 16(1):321–357.

Dmitry Davidov, Oren Tsur, and Ari Rappoport. 2010. Semi-supervised Recognition of Sarcastic Sentences in Twitter and Amazon. In *Proceedings of the Fourteenth Conference on Computational Natural Language Learning (CoNLL'10)*, pages 107–116, Uppsala, Sweden. ACL.

Delia Irazú Hernaǹdez Farías, Viviana Patti, and Paolo Rosso. 2016. Irony detection in twitter: The role of affective content. *ACM Transactions on Internet Technology*, 16(3):19:1–19:24.

Bjarke Felbo, Alan Mislove, Anders Søgaard, Iyad Rahwan, and Sune Lehmann. 2017. Using millions of emoji occurrences to learn any-domain representations for detecting sentiment, emotion and sarcasm. In *Proceedings of the 2017 Conference on Empirical Methods in Natural Language Processing*, pages 1615–1625, Copenhagen, Denmark. ACL.

Joseph L. Fleiss. 1971. Measuring nominal scale agreement among many raters. *Psychological Bulletin*, 76(5):378–382.

Aniruddha Ghosh. 2018. IronyMagnet at SemEval-2018 Task 3: A Siamese network for Irony detection in Social media. In *Proceedings of the 12th International Workshop on Semantic Evaluation*, SemEval-2018, New Orleans, LA, USA. ACL.

Aniruddha Ghosh, Guofu Li, Tony Veale, Paolo Rosso, Ekaterina Shutova, John Barnden, and Antonio Reyes. 2015. SemEval-2015 Task 11: Sentiment Analysis of Figurative Language in Twitter. In *Proceedings of the 9th International Workshop on Semantic Evaluation (SemEval 2015)*, pages 470–478, Denver, Colorado. ACL.

Aniruddha Ghosh and Tony Veale. 2016. Fracking Sarcasm using Neural Network. In *Proceedings of the 7th Workshop on Computational Approaches to Subjectivity, Sentiment and Social Media Analysis*, pages 161–169, San Diego, California. ACL.

Roberto González-Ibáñez, Smaranda Muresan, and Nina Wacholder. 2011. Identifying Sarcasm in Twitter: A Closer Look. In *Proceedings of the 49th Annual Meeting of the ACL: Human Language Technologies (HLT'11)*, pages 581–586, Portland, Oregon. ACL.

Raj Kumar Gupta and Yinping Yang. 2017. CrystalNest at SemEval-2017 Task 4: Using Sarcasm Detection for Enhancing Sentiment Classification and Quantification. In *Proceedings of the 11th International Workshop on Semantic Evaluation (SemEval-2017)*, pages 626–633. ACL.

Minqing Hu and Bing Liu. 2004. Mining and summarizing customer reviews. In *Proceedings of the Tenth ACM SIGKDD International Conference on Knowledge Discovery and Data Mining*, KDD '04, pages 168–177, New York, NY, USA. ACM.

Clayton J. Hutto and Eric Gilbert. 2014. VADER: A Parsimonious Rule-based Model for Sentiment Analysis of Social Media Text. In *Proceedings of the 8th International Conference on Weblogs and Social Media (ICWSM-14)*, pages 216–225. AAAI.

Aditya Joshi, Pushpak Bhattacharyya, and Mark J. Carman. 2017. Automatic Sarcasm Detection:A Survey. *ACM Computing Surveys (CSUR)*, 50(5):73:1–73:22.

Armand Joulin, Edouard Grave, Piotr Bojanowski, and Tomas Mikolov. 2017. Bag of Tricks for Efficient Text Classification. In *Proceedings of the 15th Conference of the European Chapter of the Association for Computational Linguistics: Volume 2, Short Papers*, pages 427–431, Valencia, Spain. ACL.

Jihen Karoui, Benamara Farah, Véronique MORICEAU, Nathalie Aussenac-Gilles, and Lamia Hadrich-Belguith. 2015. Towards a Contextual Pragmatic Model to Detect Irony in Tweets. In *Proceedings of the 53rd Annual Meeting of the Association for Computational Linguistics and the 7th International Joint Conference on Natural Language Processing (Volume 2: Short Papers)*, pages 644–650, Beijing, China. ACL.

Florian Kunneman, Christine Liebrecht, Margot van Mulken, and Antal van den Bosch. 2015. Signaling sarcasm: From hyperbole to hashtag. *Information Processing Management*, 51(4):500–509.

J. Richard Landis and Gary G. Koch. 1977. The measurement of observer agreement for categorical data. *Biometrics*, 33(1).

Bing Liu. 2012. *Sentiment Analysis and Opinion Mining*. Synthesis Lectures on Human Language Technologies. Morgan & Claypool Publishers.

Diana Maynard and Mark Greenwood. 2014. Who cares about Sarcastic Tweets? Investigating the Impact of Sarcasm on Sentiment Analysis. In *Proceedings of the Ninth International Conference on Language Resources and Evaluation (LREC'14)*, pages 4238–4243, Reykjavik, Iceland. European Language Resources Association.

Abhijit Mishra, Diptesh Kanojia, Seema Nagar, Kuntal Dey, and Pushpak Bhattacharyya. 2016. Harnessing Cognitive Features for Sarcasm Detection. In *Proceedings of the 54th Annual Meeting of the Association for Computational Linguistics (Volume 1: Long Papers)*, pages 1095–1104, Berlin, Germany. ACL.

Saif Mohammad and Felipe Bravo-Marquez. 2017. Emotion Intensities in Tweets. In *Proceedings of the 6th Joint Conference on Lexical and Computational Semantics, *SEM @ACM 2017*, pages 65–77.

Preslav Nakov, Alan Ritter, Sara Rosenthal, Fabrizio Sebastiani, and Veselin Stoyanov. 2016. SemEval-2016 Task 4: Sentiment Analysis in Twitter. In *Proceedings of the 10th International Workshop on Semantic Evaluation (SemEval-2016)*, pages 1–18, San Diego, California. ACL.

Finn Årup Nielsen. 2011. A new ANEW: evaluation of a word list for sentiment analysis in microblogs. In *Proceedings of the ESWC2011 Workshop on 'Making Sense of Microposts': Big things come in small packages*, volume 718, pages 93–98.

F. Pedregosa, G. Varoquaux, A. Gramfort, V. Michel, B. Thirion, O. Grisel, M. Blondel, P. Prettenhofer, R. Weiss, V. Dubourg, J. Vanderplas, A. Passos, D. Cournapeau, M. Brucher, M. Perrot, and E. Duchesnay. 2011. Scikit-learn: Machine Learning in Python. *Journal of Machine Learning Research*, 12:2825–2830.

Jeffrey Pennington, Richard Socher, and Christopher D. Manning. 2014. GloVe: Global Vectors for Word Representation. In *Proceedings of the 2014 Conference on Empirical Methods in Natural Language Processing (EMNLP)*, pages 1532–1543, Doha, Qatar. ACL.

Peter Potash, Alexey Romanov, and Anna Rumshisky. 2017. SemEval-2017 Task 6: #HashtagWars: Learning a Sense of Humor. In *Proceedings of the 11th International Workshop on Semantic Evaluation (SemEval-2017)*, pages 49–57. ACL.

Tomáš Ptáček, Ivan Habernal, and Jun Hong. 2014. Sarcasm detection on czech and english twitter. In *Proceedings of COLING 2014, the 25th International Conference on Computational Linguistics: Technical Papers*, pages 213–223, Dublin, Ireland. Dublin City University and ACL.

Harsh Rangwani, Devang Kulshreshtha, and Anil Kumar Sing. 2018. NLPRL-IITBHU at SemEval-2018 Task 3: Combining Linguistic Features and Emoji pre-trained CNN for Irony Detection in Tweets. In *Proceedings of the 12th International Workshop on Semantic Evaluation*, SemEval-2018, New Orleans, LA, USA. ACL.

Antonio Reyes, Paolo Rosso, and Tony Veale. 2013. A Multidimensional Approach for Detecting Irony in Twitter. *Language Resources and Evaluation*, 47(1):239–268.

Ellen Riloff, Ashequl Qadir, Prafulla Surve, Lalindra De Silva, Nathan Gilbert, and Ruihong Huang. 2013. Sarcasm as Contrast between a Positive Sentiment and Negative Situation. In *Proceedings of the Conference on Empirical Methods in Natural Language Processing (EMNLP'13)*, pages 704–714, Seattle, Washington, USA. ACL.

Omid Rohanian, Shiva Taslimipoor, Richard Evans, and Ruslan Mitkov. 2018. WLV at SemEval-2018 Task 3: Dissecting Tweets in Search of Irony. In *Proceedings of the 12th International Workshop on Semantic Evaluation*, SemEval-2018, New Orleans, LA, USA. ACL.

Sara Rosenthal, Noura Farra, and Preslav Nakov. 2017. SemEval-2017 Task 4: Sentiment Analysis in Twitter. In *Proceedings of the 11th International Workshop on Semantic Evaluation (SemEval-2017)*, pages 502–518, Vancouver, Canada. ACL.

Sara Rosenthal, Alan Ritter, Preslav Nakov, and Veselin Stoyanov. 2014. SemEval-2014 Task 9: Sentiment Analysis in Twitter. In *Proceedings of the*

8th International Workshop on Semantic Evaluation (SemEval 2014), pages 73–80, Dublin, Ireland. ACL and Dublin City University.

Cameron Shelley. 2001. The bicoherence theory of situational irony. *Cognitive Science*, 25(5):775–818.

Pontus Stenetorp, Sampo Pyysalo, Goran Topić, Tomoko Ohta, Sophia Ananiadou, and Jun'ichi Tsujii. 2012. BRAT: A Web-based Tool for NLP-assisted Text Annotation. In *Proceedings of the 13th Conference of the European Chapter of the ACL*, EACL'12, pages 102–107, Avignon, France. ACL.

Cynthia Van Hee. 2017. *Can machines sense irony? Exploring automatic irony detection on social media*. Ph.D. thesis, Ghent University.

Cynthia Van Hee, Els Lefever, and Véronique Hoste. 2016a. Guidelines for Annotating Irony in Social Media Text, version 2.0. Technical Report 16-01, LT3, Language and Translation Technology Team–Ghent University.

Cynthia Van Hee, Els Lefever, and Véronique Hoste. 2016b. Monday mornings are my fave #not: Exploring the Automatic Recognition of Irony in English tweets. In *Proceedings of COLING 2016, 26th International Conference on Computational Linguistics*, pages 2730–2739, Osaka, Japan.

Thanh Vu, Dat Quoc Nguyen, Xuan-Son Vu, Dai Quoc Nguyen, Michael Catt, and Michael Trenell. 2018. NIHRIO at SemEval-2018 Task 3: A Simple and Accurate Neural Network Model for Irony Detection in Twitter. In *Proceedings of the 12th International Workshop on Semantic Evaluation*, SemEval-2018, New Orleans, LA, USA. ACL.

Byron C. Wallace. 2015. Computational irony: A survey and new perspectives. *Artificial Intelligence Review*, 43(4):467–483.

Chuhan Wu, Fangzhao Wu, Sixing Wu, Junxin Liu, Zhigang Yuan, and Yongfeng Huang. 2018. THU_NGN at SemEval-2018 Task 3: Tweet Irony Detection with Densely Connected LSTM and Multi-task Learning. In *Proceedings of the 12th International Workshop on Semantic Evaluation*, SemEval-2018, New Orleans, LA, USA. ACL.

THU_NGN at SemEval-2018 Task 3: Tweet Irony Detection with Densely Connected LSTM and Multi-task Learning

Chuhan Wu[1], Fangzhao Wu[2], Sixing Wu[1], Junxin Liu[1],
Zhigang Yuan[1] and Yongfeng Huang[1]
[1]Tsinghua National Laboratory for Information Science and Technology,
Department of Electronic Engineering, Tsinghua University Beijing 100084, China
[2]Microsoft Research Asia
{wuch15,wu-sx15,ljx16,yuanzg14,yfhuang}@mails.tsinghua.edu.cn
wufangzhao@gmail.com

Abstract

Detecting irony is an important task to mine fine-grained information from social web messages. Therefore, the Semeval-2018 task 3 is aimed to detect the ironic tweets (subtask A) and their irony types (subtask B). In order to address this task, we propose a system based on a densely connected LSTM network with multi-task learning strategy. In our dense LSTM model, each layer will take all outputs from previous layers as input. The last LSTM layer will output the hidden representations of texts, and they will be used in three classification task. In addition, we incorporate several types of features to improve the model performance. Our model achieved an F-score of 70.54 (ranked 2/43) in the subtask A and 49.47 (ranked 3/29) in the subtask B. The experimental results validate the effectiveness of our system.

1 Introduction

Figurative languages such as irony are widely used in web messages such as tweets to convey different sentiment. Identifying the ironic texts can help to understand the social web better and has many applications such as sentiment analysis (Ghosh and Veale, 2016). Irony detecting techniques are important to improve the performance of sentiment analysis. For example, the tweet *"Monday mornings are my fave:)# not"* is an irony with negative sentiment, but it will be probably classified as a positive one by a standard sentiment analysis model (Van Hee et al., 2016b). Thus, capturing the ironic information in texts is useful to predict sentiment more accurately (Van Hee et al., 2016a).

However, determining whether a text is ironic is a challenging task since the the differences between ironic and non-ironic texts are usually subtle. For example, the tweet *"Love this weather #not"* is ironic, but a similar tweet *"Hate this weather #not happy"* is non-ironic. Different approaches are proposed to recognize the complex irony in texts. Existing methods to detect irony are mainly based on rules or machine learning techniques (Joshi et al., 2017). Rules based methods usually depend on lexicons to identify irony (Khattri et al., 2015; Maynard and Greenwood, 2014). However, these methods cannot utilize the contextual information from texts. Traditional machine learning based methods such as SVM (Desai and Dave, 2016) are also effective in this task, but they usually need manually feature engineering (Barbieri et al., 2014). Recently, deep learning techniques are successfully applied to this task. For example, Ghosh et al. (2016) propose to use a CNN-LSTM model to classify the ironic and non-ironic tweets. Their method can significantly improve the classification performance without heavy feature engineering. However, existing methods are aimed to detect irony in tweets with explicit irony related hashtags. For example, tweets with #irony or #sarcasm hashtags are very likely to be ironic. Therefore, models may focus on these hashtags rather than the contextual information.

To fill this gap, the SemEval-2018 task 3[1] aims to detect irony of tweets without explicit irony hashtags (Van Hee et al., 2018). The subtask A is aimed to determine whether a tweet is ironic. the subtask B is aimed to identify the irony types of tweets: Verbal irony by means of a polarity contrast, other verbal irony and situational irony. Several examples are as follows:

- **verbal irony by means of a polarity contrast**: I love waking up with migraines #not

- **other verbal irony**: @user Yeah keeping cricket clean, that's what he wants #Sarcasm

---

[1]https://competitions.codalab.org/competitions/17468

Proceedings of the 12th International Workshop on Semantic Evaluation (SemEval-2018), pages 51–56
New Orleans, Louisiana, June 5–6, 2018. ©2018 Association for Computational Linguistics

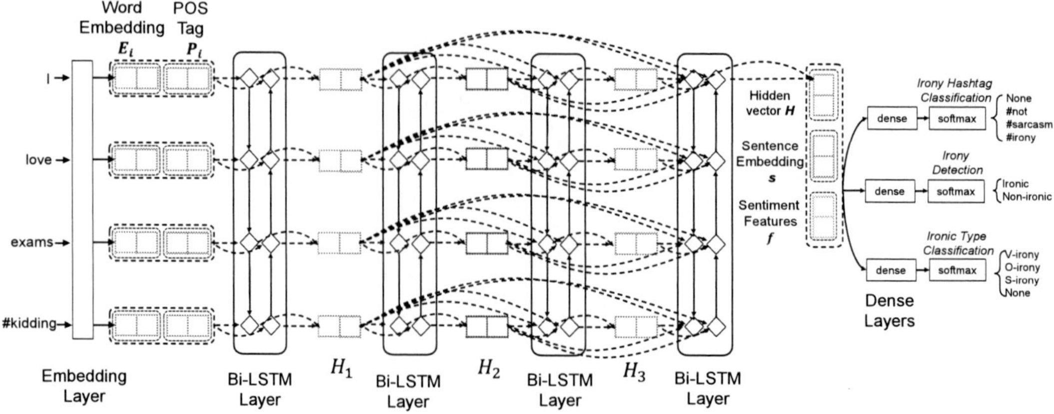

Figure 1: Architecture of our Dense-LSTM model. The V-irony, O-irony and S-irony denote the three different irony types respectively (Van Hee et al., 2018).

- **situational irony**: most of us didn't focus in the #ADHD lecture. #irony

In order to address this problem, we propose a system[2] based on a densely connected LSTM model (Wu et al., 2017) with multitask learning techniques. In our model, each LSTM layer will take all outputs of previous LSTM layers as input. Then different levels of contextual information can be learned at the same time. Our model is required to predict in three tasks simultaneously: 1) identifying the missing irony related hashtags; 2) classify ironic or non-ironic; 3) irony type classification. By using multitask learning strategy, the model can combine the information in the different tasks to improve the performance. The experimental results in both subtasks validate the effectiveness of our method.

2 Densely Connected LSTM with Multi-task Learning

The architecture of our densely connected LSTM model is shown in Figure 1. We denote this model as *Dense-LSTM*. The detailed information will be introduced in the following paragraphs.

In our model, the embedding layer is used to convert the input tweets into a sequence of dense vectors. The POS tag features P_i are one-hot encoded and concatenated with the word embedding vectors E_i. Usually the affective words and creative languages in tweets are important irony clues. Since these words usually have specific POS tags, adding these features can help our model to capture the ironic information better. We use tweetokenize[3] tool to tokenize and the Ark-Tweet-NLP[4] tool to obtain the POS tags of tweets (Owoputi et al., 2013).

The first Bi-LSTM layer takes the sequential vectors as input. For the j_{th} Bi-LSTM layer, its output H_j will input all LSTM layers after it. As shown in Figure 1, the blue dashed lines represent such over-layer connections. All inputs of an LSTM layer will be concatenated together. Thus, the input of the j_{th} ($j > 1$) layer is $[H_1; ...; H_{j-1}]$. It indicates that each layer can learn different levels of information at the same time. Since the irony information is complex, jointly using all levels of information is beneficial to predict irony more accurately. The last LSTM layer will output the hidden representation H of texts. It will be concatenated with the sentiment features and the sentence embedding features. The sentiment features can provide additional sentiment information to detect irony, such as the sentiment polarity assigned by lexicons. The sentiment features are generated via the AffectiveTweets[5] package in weka provided by Mohammad et al. (Mohammad and Bravo-Marquez, 2017). We use the TweetToLexiconFeatureVector (Bravo-Marquez et al., 2014) and TweetToSen-

[2]https://github.com/wuch15/SemEval-2018-task3-THU_NGN.git

[3]https://github.com/jaredks/tweetokenize
[4]http://www.cs.cmu.edu/ ark/TweetNLP
[5]https://github.com/felipebravom/AffectiveTweets

tiStrengthFeatureVector (Thelwall et al., 2012) filters in this package. The embedding of a sentence is obtained by taking the average of all words in this sentence using the 100-dim pre-trained embedding weights provided by Bravo et al. (Bravo-Marquez et al., 2016). By incorporating the vector representation of tweet sentence, the irony information can be easier to be captured.

Three dense layers with ReLU activation are used to predict for three different tasks including: determining the missing ironic hashtags (i.e. #not, #sarcasm, #irony or none of them) *(task1)*; identifying ironic or non-ironic *(task2)* ; identifying the irony types *(task3)*. Thus, the objective function of our model can be formulated as:

$$\mathcal{L} = \alpha_1 \mathcal{L}_1 + \alpha_2 \mathcal{L}_2 + \alpha_3 \mathcal{L}_3, \tag{1}$$

where $\mathcal{L}_i$ and α_i denote the loss function and its weight of task i. $\mathcal{L}_1$ and $\mathcal{L}_2$ are categorical and binary cross-entropy respectively. In addition, the numbers of tweets with different irony types are very unbalanced. Motivated by the cost-sensitive entropy used by Santos et al. (2009), we formulate $\mathcal{L}_3$ as follows:

$$\mathcal{L}_3 = -\sum_{i=1}^{N} w_{y_i} y_i \log(\hat{y}_i), \tag{2}$$

where N is the number of tweets, y_i is the irony type of the i_{th} tweet, $\hat{y}_i$ is the prediction score, and w_{y_i} is the loss weight of irony type label y_i. w_{y_i} is defined as $\frac{\sum_{k=1}^{C} N_k}{N_{y_i}}$, where C is the number of irony types and N_j is the number of tweets with irony type label j. Thus, the infrequent irony types will gain relatively larger loss weights. By using this multi-task learning method, our model can incorporate different information such as the irony hashtags. In addition, classifying ironic/non-ironic and the irony types are similar tasks. Therefore, the performance of both tasks can be improved by combining the information of both tasks.

In order to improve the performance of our system, we use an ensemble strategy by averaging the classification results predicted by 10 models. Each model will be trained using a random dropout rate. Therefore in this way, the classification results will be voted by different models, which can improve the model performance.

3 Experiment

3.1 Dataset and Experimental Settings

The detailed statistics of the dataset[6] in this task are shown in Table 1. V-irony, O-irony and S-irony represent the three types respectively: verbal irony by means of a polarity contrast, other types of verbal irony and situational irony (Van Hee et al., 2018). In subtask A, the performance of systems is evaluated by F-score for the positive class. In subtask B, the macro-averaged F-score over all classes is used as the metric.

Task	A		B			
Label	Ironic	Non-ironic	V-irony	O-irony	S-irony	Non-ironic
#train	1911	1923	1390	316	205	1923
#test	311	473	164	85	62	473

Table 1: The detailed statistics of the dataset.

We combine two pre-trained word embeddings: 1) the embeddings provided by Godin et al. (2015), which are trained on a corpus with 400 million tweets; 2) the embeddings provided by Barbieri et al. (2016), which are trained on 20 million tweets. The dimensions of them are 400 and 300 respectively. They are concatenated together as the embeddings of words.

In our network, the Dense-LSTM model has 4 LSTM layers with 200-dim hidden states. The hidden dimensions of dense layers are set to 300. The dropout rate of each layer is set to a random number between 0.2 to 0.4, and it will be set to a fixed value 0.3 in the comparative experiments without ensemble strategy. In subtask A, the loss weights α of the three task are set to 0.5, 1 and 0.5 respectively. In subtask B, they are 0.5, 0.5 and 1. We use RMSProp as the optimizer, and the batch size is set to 64. In addition, we use 10% training data for validation to select the hyperparameters above.

3.2 Performance Evaluation

We compare the performance of different methods including: 1) SVM, the benchmark system using SVM and BOW model; 2) CNN, using CNN with a global average pooling layer to obtain the hidden vector h, which is used to predict in the three tasks; 3) LSTM, using one Bi-LSTM layer in the network to get h; 4) 2-layer LSTM, using 2 Bi-LSTM layers; 5) Dense-LSTM, using our

---

[6]https://github.com/Cyvhee/SemEval2018-Task3/tree/master/datasets

Dense-LSTM model; 6) Dense-LSTM+ens, using our Dense-LSTM model and ensemble strategy. In addition, we apply multi-task learning technique to all models except the benchmark system based on SVM. The results are shown in Table 1. The experimental results show that our Dense-LSTM model significantly outperforms the baselines. Since the layers in our Dense-LSTM can learn from all previous outputs, our model can combine different levels of contextual information to capture the high-level irony clues. In addition, our model can predict more accurately via ensemble. Since models with random dropout can extract different information, we can take advantage of all models by voting. The ensemble strategy can reduce the noise in the dataset and make our system more stable (Xia et al., 2011).

Model	Subtask A			Subtask B
	P	R	F	Macro-F
Baseline	54.78	62.70	58.47	32.69
CNN	59.32	61.41	60.35	45.30
LSTM	57.73	67.20	62.11	45.76
2-layer LSTM	60.34	68.49	64.16	47.16
Dense-LSTM	62.78	72.69	67.36	48.28
Dense-LSTM+ens	**63.04**	**80.06**	**70.54**	**49.47**

Table 2: The performance of different methods. P, R, F represent precision, recall and F-score respectively.

3.3 Effectiveness of Multi-task Learning

The performance of our Dense-LSTM model using different combinations of training tasks is shown in Table 3. Note that we don't apply model ensemble here. Compared with the models trained in task2 or task3 only, the combination of both tasks can improve the performance. It may be because the two tasks have inherent relatedness and can share rich mutual information. Learning to predict the missing ironic hashtags (task1) can also improve the model performance. Since the ironic hashtags are often important ironic clues, identifying such clues can help our model to mine ironic information better.

3.4 Influence of Pre-trained Word Embedding

We compare the performance using different combinations of pre-trained embeddings in our model. The results are illustrated in Table 4. The results show that the pre-trained embeddings are important to capture irony information, and using the

Task Combination	Subtask A			Subtask B
	P	R	F	Macro-F
task2	60.05	71.06	65.10	-
task3	-	-	-	44.65
task2+task3	61.81	72.34	66.67	46.94
task1+task2	61.33	71.38	65.97	-
task1+task3	-	-	-	45.57
task1+task2+task3	**62.78**	**72.69**	**67.36**	**48.28**

Table 3: The performance in two subtasks using different combinations of training tasks.

combination of two different word embeddings can improve the model performance. It proves that this method can reduce the out-of-vocabulary words in the single embedding file and provide richer semantic information.

Feature	Subtask A			Subtask B
	P	R	F	Macro-F
w/o pre-trained	56.25	67.14	61.21	42.28
+emb1	60.96	69.95	65.14	47.69
+emb2	61.77	70.59	65.89	47.24
+emb1 +emb2	**62.78**	**72.69**	**67.36**	**48.28**

Table 4: Influence of pre-trained word embedding. The emb1 and emb2 denote the embeddings provided by Godin et al. (2015) and Barbieri et al. (2016) respectively.

3.5 Influence of Additional Features

The influence of different features on our model is shown in Table 5. According to this table, all features can improve the classification performance in both subtasks, and the combination of the three features can achieve better performance. The improvement brought by POS tags is most significant. Affective words are important irony clues and they are usually verbs, adjectives or hashtags. Thus, incorporating the POS tag features can help to identify these words and capture the ironic information better. The sentiment features also improve our model, which can be inferred from the results. The sentiment polarities of ironic tweets are usually negative, but these texts often contain positive sentiment words. Since our sentiment features are obtained by several different sentiment or emotion lexicons, they can be used to assign the sentiment scores of texts, which can provide rich information to detect irony. The sentence embedding can also slightly improve the performance. The sentence embedding contains information of each word in the sentence. Thus, it can help to capture the word information better, which is beneficial to identify the overall sentiment of texts. The combination of all three types of features can take advantage of them and gain significant performance improvement. It validates the effectiveness of each type of features.

Feature	Subtask A			Subtask B
	P	R	F	Macro-F
None	59.84	70.42	64.70	45.56
+*POS tags*	61.04	72.03	66.08	46.61
+*Sentiment Features*	61.16	71.38	65.88	46.37
+*Sentence Embedding*	61.39	71.06	65.87	46.24
+*All Features*	**62.78**	**72.69**	**67.36**	**48.28**

Table 5: Influence of different features on our model.

4 Conclusion

Detecting irony in web texts is an important task to mine fine-grained sentiment information. In order to address this problem, we develop a system based on a densely connected LSTM model to participate in the SemEval-2018 Task 3. In our model, every LSTM layer will take all outputs of previous layers as inputs. Thus, the different levels of information can be learned at the same time. In addition, we propose to combine three different tasks to train our model jointly, which includes identifying the missing irony hashtags, determining ironic or non-ironic and classifying the irony types. These tasks have inherent relatedness thus the performance can be improved by sharing the mutual information. Our system achieved an F-score of 70.54 and 49.47 which ranked the 2nd and 3rd place in the two subtasks. The experimental results validates the effectiveness of our method.

Acknowledgments

The authors thank the reviewers for their insightful comments and constructive suggestions on improving this work. This work was supported in part by the National Key Research and Development Program of China under Grant 2016YFB0800402 and in part by the National Natural Science Foundation of China under Grant U1705261, Grant U1536207, Grant U1536201 and U1636113.

References

Francesco Barbieri, German Kruszewski, Francesco Ronzano, and Horacio Saggion. 2016. How cosmopolitan are emojis?: Exploring emojis usage and meaning over different languages with distributional semantics. In *Proceedings of the 2016 ACM on Multimedia Conference*, pages 531–535. ACM.

Francesco Barbieri, Horacio Saggion, and Francesco Ronzano. 2014. Modelling sarcasm in twitter, a novel approach. In *Proceedings of the 5th Workshop on Computational Approaches to Subjectivity, Sentiment and Social Media Analysis*, pages 50–58.

Felipe Bravo-Marquez, Eibe Frank, Saif M Mohammad, and Bernhard Pfahringer. 2016. Determining word-emotion associations from tweets by multi-label classification. In *Web Intelligence (WI), 2016 IEEE/WIC/ACM International Conference on*, pages 536–539. IEEE.

Felipe Bravo-Marquez, Marcelo Mendoza, and Barbara Poblete. 2014. Meta-level sentiment models for big social data analysis. *Knowledge-Based Systems*, 69:86–99.

Nikita Desai and Anandkumar D Dave. 2016. Sarcasm detection in hindi sentences using support vector machine. *International Journal*, 4(7):8–15.

Aniruddha Ghosh and Tony Veale. 2016. Fracking sarcasm using neural network. In *Proceedings of the 7th Workshop on Computational Approaches to Subjectivity, Sentiment and Social Media Analysis*, pages 161–169.

Fréderic Godin, Baptist Vandersmissen, Wesley De Neve, and Rik Van de Walle. 2015. Multimedia lab @ acl wnut ner shared task: Named entity recognition for twitter microposts using distributed word representations. In *Proceedings of the Workshop on Noisy User-generated Text*, pages 146–153.

Aditya Joshi, Pushpak Bhattacharyya, and Mark J Carman. 2017. Automatic sarcasm detection: A survey. *ACM Computing Surveys (CSUR)*, 50(5):73.

Anupam Khattri, Aditya Joshi, Pushpak Bhattacharyya, and Mark Carman. 2015. Your sentiment precedes you: Using an authors historical tweets to predict sarcasm. In *Proceedings of the 6th Workshop on Computational Approaches to Subjectivity, Sentiment and Social Media Analysis*, pages 25–30.

Diana Maynard and Mark A Greenwood. 2014. Who cares about sarcastic tweets? investigating the impact of sarcasm on sentiment analysis. In *Lrec*, pages 4238–4243.

Saif M Mohammad and Felipe Bravo-Marquez. 2017. Wassa-2017 shared task on emotion intensity. *arXiv preprint arXiv:1708.03700*.

Olutobi Owoputi, Brendan O'Connor, Chris Dyer, Kevin Gimpel, Nathan Schneider, and Noah A Smith. 2013. Improved part-of-speech tagging for online conversational text with word clusters. Association for Computational Linguistics.

Raúl Santos-Rodríguez, Darío García-García, and Jesús Cid-Sueiro. 2009. Cost-sensitive classification based on bregman divergences for medical diagnosis. In *Machine Learning and Applications, 2009. ICMLA'09. International Conference on*, pages 551–556. IEEE.

Mike Thelwall, Kevan Buckley, and Georgios Paltoglou. 2012. Sentiment strength detection for the social web. *Journal of the Association for Information Science and Technology*, 63(1):163–173.

Cynthia Van Hee, Els Lefever, and Véronique Hoste. 2016a. Exploring the realization of irony in twitter data. In *LREC*.

Cynthia Van Hee, Els Lefever, and Véronique Hoste. 2016b. Monday mornings are my fave:)# not exploring the automatic recognition of irony in english tweets. In *Proceedings of COLING 2016, the 26th International Conference on Computational Linguistics: Technical Papers*, pages 2730–2739.

Cynthia Van Hee, Els Lefever, and Véronique Hoste. 2018. SemEval-2018 Task 3: Irony Detection in English Tweets. In *Proceedings of the 12th International Workshop on Semantic Evaluation*, SemEval-2018, New Orleans, LA, USA. Association for Computational Linguistics.

Chuhan Wu, Fangzhao Wu, Yongfeng Huang, Sixing Wu, and Zhigang Yuan. 2017. Thu_ngn at ijcnlp-2017 task 2: Dimensional sentiment analysis for chinese phrases with deep lstm. *Proceedings of the IJCNLP 2017, Shared Tasks*, pages 47–52.

Rui Xia, Chengqing Zong, and Shoushan Li. 2011. Ensemble of feature sets and classification algorithms for sentiment classification. *Information Sciences*, 181(6):1138–1152.

SemEval 2018 Task 4: Character Identification on Multiparty Dialogues

Jinho D. Choi
Computer Science
Emory University
Atlanta, GA 30322
`jinho.choi@emory.edu`

Henry Y. Chen
Information Security
Snap Inc.
Santa Monica, CA 90405
`henry.chen@snapchat.com`

Abstract

Character identification is a task of entity linking that finds the global entity of each personal mention in multiparty dialogue. For this task, the first two seasons of the popular TV show *Friends* are annotated, comprising a total of 448 dialogues, 15,709 mentions, and 401 entities. The personal mentions are detected from nominals referring to certain characters in the show, and the entities are collected from the list of all characters in those two seasons of the show. This task is challenging because it requires the identification of characters that are mentioned but may not be active during the conversation. Among 90+ participants, four of them submitted their system outputs and showed strengths in different aspects about the task. Thorough analyses of the distributed datasets, system outputs, and comparative studies are also provided. To facilitate the momentum, we create an open-source project for this task and publicly release a larger and cleaner dataset, hoping to support researchers for more enhanced modeling.

1 Introduction

Most of the earlier works in natural language processing (NLP) had focused on formal writing such as newswires, whereas many recent works have targeted at colloquial writing such as text messages or social media. Since the evolution of Web 2.0, the amount of user-generated contents involving colloquial writing has exceeded the one with formal writing. NLP tasks are relatively well-explored at this point for certain types of colloquial writing i.e., microblogs and reviews (Ritter et al., 2011; Kong et al., 2014; Ranganath et al., 2016; Shin et al., 2017). However, the genre of multiparty dialogue is still under-explored, even though digital contents in dialogue forms keep increasing at a faster rate than any other types of writing.[1] This inspires us

to create a new task called character identification that aims to link personal mentions (e.g, *she*, *mom*) to their global entities across multiple dialogues, where the entities indicate the specific characters referred by those mentions (e.g., *Judy*).

Due to the nature of multiparty dialogue where several speakers take turns to complete a context, character identification is a crucial step for adapting higher-end NLP tasks (e.g., summarization, question answering, machine translation) to this genre. It can also bring another level of sophistication to intelligent personal assistants or tutoring systems. This task is challenging because it needs to process through colloquialism that includes slangs, grammar mistakes, and/or rhetorical questions, as well as to handle cross-document resolution for the identification of entities that are mentioned but may not be actively participating during the conversation. Nonetheless, we believe that models produced by this task will remarkably enhance inference on dialogue contexts (e.g., business meetings, doctor-patient conversations) by providing finer-grained information about individual characters.

Section 2 illustrates the task of character identification and explains the key differences between it and other types of entity linking tasks. Section 3 describes the corpus, based on TV show transcripts, used for this task with annotation details. Section 4 gives brief overviews of the systems participated in this shared task. Section 5 explains the evaluation metrics and the results produced by those systems. Finally, Section 6 gives thorough analysis and comparative studies between these systems. This task was originally conducted at CodaLab.[2] The latest dataset and the system outputs can be found from our open source project, Emory NLP.[3]

---

[1] https://medium.com/hijiffy/10-graphs-that-show-the-immense-power-of-messaging-apps-4a41385b24d6

[2] https://competitions.codalab.org/competitions/17310

[3] https://github.com/emorynlp/semeval-2018-task4

57

Proceedings of the 12th International Workshop on Semantic Evaluation (SemEval-2018), pages 57–64
New Orleans, Louisiana, June 5–6, 2018. ©2018 Association for Computational Linguistics

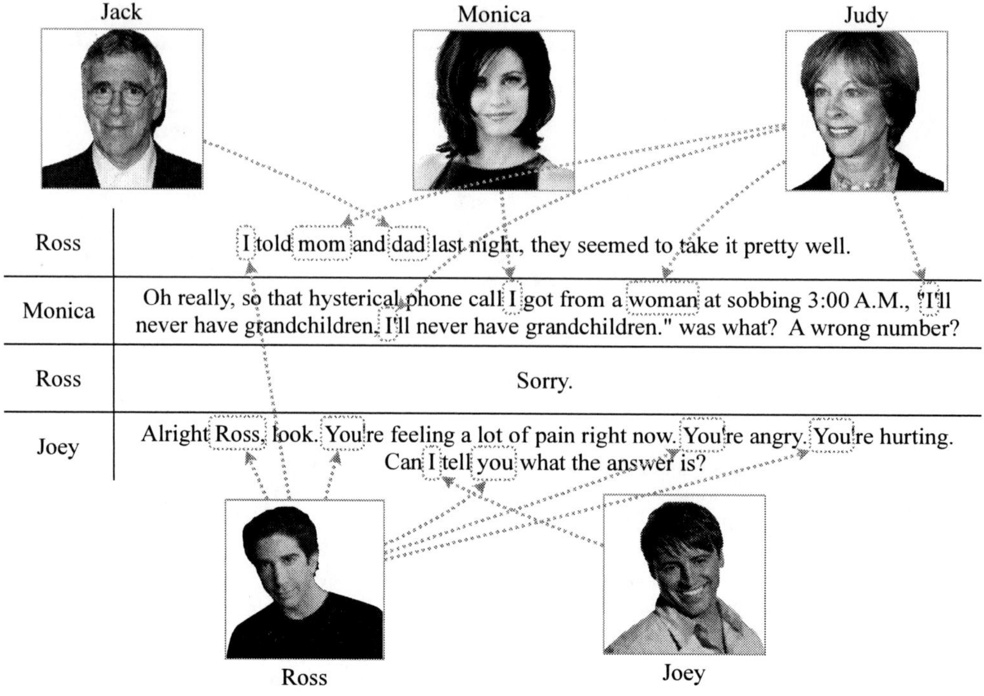

Figure 1: An example of character identification, excerpted from the Season 1 Episode 1 of *Friends*, where mentions are indicated in red boxes and entities are linked by arrows.

2 Task Description

Let a mention be a nominal that refers to a singular or a collective entity (e.g., *she*, *mom*, *Judy*), and an entity be the actual person that the mention refers to. Given a dialogue transcribed in text where all mentions are detected, the objective is to find the entity for each mention, who can be either active or passive in the dialogue. In Figure 1, entities such as *Ross*, *Monica*, and *Joey* are the active speakers of the dialogue, whereas *Jack* and *Judy* are not although they are passively mentioned as *mom* and *dad* in this context. Linking such mentions to their global entities demands inferred knowledge about the kinship from other dialogues, challenging cross-document resolution. Thus, character identification can be viewed as an entity linking task that aims for holistic understanding in multiparty dialogue.

Most of previous works on entity linking have focused on Wikification, which links named entity mentions to their relevant Wikipedia articles (Mihalcea and Csomai, 2007; Ratinov et al., 2011; Guo et al., 2013). Unlike Wikification where most entities come with structured information from knowledge bases (e.g., Infobox, Freebase, DBPedia), entities in character identification have no such precom-

piled information, which makes this task even more challenging. It is similar to coreference resolution in a sense that it groups mentions into entities, but distinguished because this task requires to identify each mention group as a known person. In Figure 1, coreference resolution would give a cluster of the four mentions, {*mom, woman, I, I*}; however, it would not identify that cluster to be the entity *Judy*, which in this case is not possible to identify without getting contexts from other dialogues.

3 Corpus

The character identification corpus was first created by collecting transcripts from the popular TV show, *Friends* (Chen and Choi, 2016). These transcripts were voluntarily provided by fans who made them publicly available.[4] Dialogues in this corpus mimic daily conversations that are more natural and various in topics than other dialogue corpora (Janin et al., 2003; Danescu-Niculescu-Mizil and Lee, 2011; Hu et al., 2013; Kim et al., 2015; Lowe et al., 2015). Although they are scripted, the interpretation of these dialogues is no easier than unscripted

---

[4]http://www.livesinabox.com/friends/
    scripts.shtml

	Episodes	Scenes	Speakers	Utterances	Sentences	Tokens
Season 1	24	229	105	4,725	8,680	66,355
Season 2	23	219	101	4,501	7,380	65,675
Total	47	448	171	9,226	16,060	132,030

Table 1: Distributions from the subset of the character identification corpus used for this shared task.

dialogues; they not only involve as much disfluency and context switching as real dialogues do, but also include more humor, sarcasm, or metaphor. Thus, models evaluated on this corpus should give a general sense about the state of character identification on multiparty dialogue.

The original transcripts collected from the fan site were formatted in HTML; we converted them into JSON so that they could be easily processed. This structured data were then manually checked for potential errors. Table 1 shows the distributions from the subset of the character identification corpus used for this shared task. The provided dataset is divided into two seasons, each season is divided into episodes, each episode is divided into scenes, each scene contains utterances, where each utterance indicates a turn of speech.

3.1 Mention Annotation

For mention annotation, a heuristic-based mention detector was developed, which utilized dependency relations (Choi and McCallum, 2013), named entity tags (Choi, 2016), and personal noun gazetteers, then automatically detected mentions for the entire corpus. In this heuristic, a noun phrase was considered a personal mention if it was either:

1. A PERSON named entity, or

2. A pronoun or a possessive pronoun excluding the pronouns *it* and *they*, or

3. One of the personal noun gazetteers that are 603 common and singular personal nouns selected from Freebase and DBPedia.

Specific mentions such as *it* and *they* were excluded because they often referred to the ambiguous entity types, *collective*, *general*, and *other* (Section 3.2). For the quality assurance, about 10% of this pseudo annotation were randomly sampled and manually evaluated, showing a precision, a recall, and the F1-score of 97.58%, 94.34%, and 95.93%, respectively. Finally, the annotation was manually checked again while it was systematically corrected for routinely produced errors. Although mention detection was

the foundational step, including it as a part of this shared task could over-complicate the evaluation. Thus, gold mentions were provided for this year's shared task such that participants could purely concentrate on the task of entity linking.

3.2 Entity Annotation

All mentions were double-annotated with their referent entities, and adjudicated upon disagreements. Annotation and adjudication tasks were conducted on Amazon Mechanical Turk. Each mention was annotated with either a primary character, that are *Ross, Chandler, Joey, Rachel, Monica,* and *Pheobe,* a secondary character (other frequently recurring characters across the show), or one of the following ambiguous types suggested by Chen et al. (2017):

- *Generic*: indicates actual characters in the show whose identities are unknown (e.g., That *waitress* is really cute, I am going to ask *her* out). Generic entities are annotated with their group names and optional numberings (e.g., `Man 1`, `Woman 1`).

- *Collective*: indicates the plural use of the pronoun *you*, which cannot be deterministically distinguished from the singular use.

- *General*: indicates mentions used in reference to a general case rather than an specific entity (e.g., The ideal *guy* you look for doesn't exist).

- *Other*: indicates all the other kinds of entities.

For this year's shared task, mentions annotated with the last three ambiguous types, *collective*, *general*, and *other*, were excluded from the dataset to reduce the high complexity of this task (Table 2).

	Primary	Secondary	Generic	Total
Season 1	5,160	2,526	178	7,864
Season 2	5,385	2,340	120	7,845
Total	10,545	4,866	298	15,709

Table 2: Distributions of the annotated entity types used for this shared task.

Speaker	Utterance
Joey	Yeah, right! ... *You$_1$* serious?
Rachel	Everything *you$_2$* need to know is in that first kiss.
Chandler	Yeah. For *us$_3$*, it's like the stand-up *comedian$_4$* *you$_5$* have to sit through before the main *dude$_6$* starts.
Ross	It's not that *we$_7$* don't like the *comedian$_8$*, it's that ... that's not why *we$_9$* bought the ticket.

$\{You_1\} \rightarrow Rachel, \{us_3, we_{7,9}\} \rightarrow Collective, \{you_{2,5}\} \rightarrow General, \{comedian_{4,8}\} \rightarrow Generic, \{dude_6\} \rightarrow Other$

Table 3: Examples of the entity annotation described in Section 3.2.

	Episodes	Scenes	Entities	Mentions	Clusters$_E$	Clusters$_S$	Singleton$_E$	Singleton$_S$
Training	47	374	372	13,280	893	2,051	209	472
Evaluation	7	74	106	2,429	304	370	54	83
Total	47	448	401	15,709	1,197	2,421	263	555

Table 4: Distributions of the training and the evaluation sets in Section 3.3.

Table 3 shows examples of these ambiguous types. About 83% were assigned to the primary and secondary characters, 1.4% were assigned to *generic*, and the rest were assigned to the other ambiguous types, *collective*, *general*, and *other*. To evaluate the annotation quality, the annotation agreement scores as well as Cohen's kappa scores were measured, showing 82.83% and 79.96%, respectively.

3.3 Data Split

The corpus was split into training and evaluation sets for this shared task (Table 4). No dedicated development set was provided; participants were encouraged to use sub-parts of the training set to create their own development sets or perform cross-validation for the optimization of statistical models. Two types of datasets are provided for both training and evaluation sets, one treating each episode as an individual dialogue and the other treating each scene as an independent dialogue.[5]

Processing a larger dialogue makes coreference resolution harder because it needs to link referential mentions that are farther apart; on the other hand, each cluster comprises a greater number of mentions which can help identifying the global entity of that cluster. The numbers of clusters grouped in each dataset are shown as Clusters$_E$ and Clusters$_S$, implying episode-level and scene-level clusters, respectively. Our corpus includes singleton mentions, which take about 22% of all mentions.

3.4 Data Format

To help participants adapting their existing coreference resolution systems to this task, the original dataset in JSON was converted into the CoNLL'12 shared task format (Pradhan et al., 2012), where each column is delimited by white spaces and represents the following:

1. Season and episode ID.

2. Document ID.

3. Token ID.

4. Word form.

5. Part-of-speech tag (auto-generated).

6. Phrase structure tag (auto-generated).

7. Lemma (auto-generated).

8. Predicate sense (not provided).

9. Word sense (not provided).

10. Speaker.

11. Named entity tag (auto-generated).

12. Entity ID.

The part-of-speech tags, lemmas, and named entity tags were automatically generated by NLP4J,[6] and the phrase structure tags were produced by the Stanford parser.[7] Table 5 shows the example of the first utterance in Figure 1 in the CoNLL'12 format.

4 System Description

This section describes the top-2 scoring systems of this shared task. The AMORE-UPF is a group of researchers from the Universitat Pompeu Fabra in Spain (Section 4.1). The KNU CI is a group of researchers from Kangwon National University in South Korea (Section 4.2).

---

[5] Each episode consists of about 10 scenes on average.

[6] https://emorynlp.github.io/nlp4j

[7] https://nlp.stanford.edu/software/lex-parser.shtml

```
s1e1u38   0    0        I    PRP   (TOP(S(S(NP*)       I   -   -   Ross          *    (7)
s1e1u38   0    1     told    VBD           (VP*    tell   -   -   Ross          *     -
s1e1u38   0    2      mom    NN            (NP*     mom   -   -   Ross          *    (9)
s1e1u38   0    3      and    CC               *     and   -   -   Ross          *     -
s1e1u38   0    4      dad    NN              *)     dad   -   -   Ross          *   (10)
s1e1u38   0    5     last    JJ        (NP-TMP*    last   -   -   Ross   (TIME*       -
s1e1u38   0    6    night    NN            *)))   night   -   -   Ross        *)       -
s1e1u38   0    7        ,    ,                *       ,   -   -   Ross          *     -
s1e1u38   0    8     they    PRP           (NP*)    they   -   -   Ross          *     -
s1e1u38   0    9   seemed    VBD           (VP*    seem   -   -   Ross          *     -
s1e1u38   0   10       to    TO         (S(VP*      to   -   -   Ross          *     -
s1e1u38   0   11     take    VB            (VP*    take   -   -   Ross          *     -
s1e1u38   0   12       it    PRP           (NP*)     it   -   -   Ross          *     -
s1e1u38   0   13   pretty    RB          (ADVP*  pretty   -   -   Ross          *     -
s1e1u38   0   14     well    RB        *)))))    well   -   -   Ross          *     -
s1e1u38   0   15        .    .              *))       .   -   -   Ross          *     -
```

Table 5: Example of the first utterance in Figure 1 annotated in the CoNLL'12 format.

4.1 AMORE-UPF System

The AMORE-UPF system approaches this task as a multi-class classification. It uses a bidirectional Long Short-Term Memory (LSTM) that processes the input dialogue and resolves mentions, by means of a comparison between the LSTM's hidden state, for each mention, to vectors in an entity library. In this model, learned representations of each entity are stored in the entity library, that is a matrix where each row represents an entity and whose values are learned during training (Figure 2).

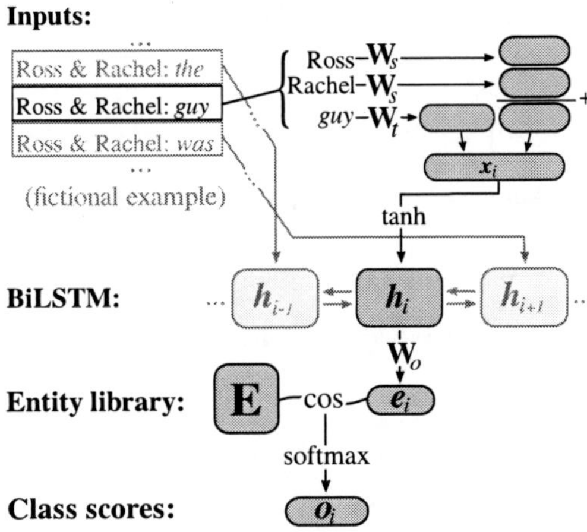

Figure 2: The overview of AMORE-UPF system.

4.2 KNU-CI System

The KNU-CI system tackles this task as a sequence-labeling problem. It uses an attention-based recurrent neural network (RNN) encoder-decoder model. The input dialogue of character identification consists of several conversations, resulting a long sequence of text. The RNN encoder-decoder model suffers from poor performance when the length of the input sequence is long. To overcome this issue, this system applies an attention, position encoding, and the self-matching network to the original RNN encoder-decoder model. As a result, the best performance is achieved by the attention-based RNN depicted in Figure 3.

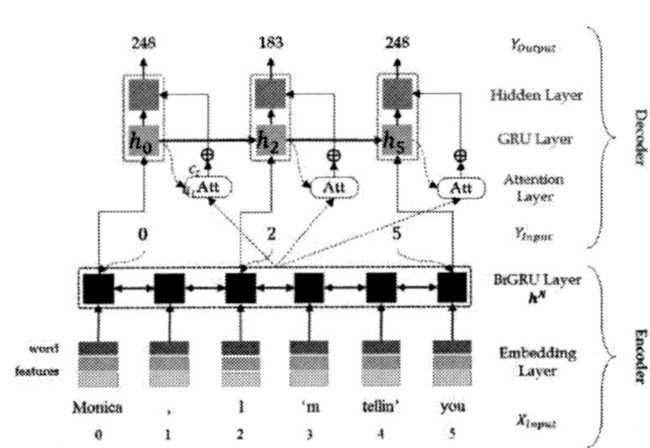

Figure 3: The overview of KNU-CI system.

5 Evaluation

Following Chen et al. (2017), the labeling accuracy (Acc) and the macro-average F1 score (F1) are used for the evaluation (C: the total number of characters, $F1_i$: the F1-score for the i'th character):

$$Acc = \frac{\text{\# of corrected identified mentions}}{\text{\# of all mentions}}$$

$$F1 = \frac{1}{C} \sum_{i=1}^{C} F1_i$$

Table 6 shows the overall scores from all submitted systems. Two types of evaluation are performed for this task. The first one is based on seven characters where six of them compose the primary characters

(Section 3.2) and every other character is grouped as one entity called `Others` (Main + Others). The other is based on 78 characters comprising all characters appeared in the dataset, except for the ones appear either in the training or the evaluation set but not both, which is grouped to the `Others` (ALL).

System	Main + Others		ALL	
	Acc	F1	Acc	F1
AMORE-UPF	77.23	79.36	**74.72**	**41.05**
KNU-CI	**85.10**	**86.00**	69.49	16.98
Kampfpudding	73.36	73.51	59.45	37.37
Zuma-AR	46.85	44.68	33.06	16.09

Table 6: Overall scores from the submitted systems.

Table 7 shows the F1 scores for the primary characters and `Others`, illustrating detailed evaluation for **Main + Others**. Table 8 gives detailed evaluation for **ALL**, showing the F1-scores for the top-12 most frequently appeared secondary characters and `Others` that appear only in the training or the evaluation set but not both. The 18 characters in these two tables comprise about 85% of all mentions.

6 Analysis

Based on the evaluation results, several interesting observations can be made for how different system architectures affect model performance on this task. The analysis in this section primarily focuses on the top-2 scoring systems, AMORE-UPF an KNU-CI, as their results vastly outperform the other two and the authors of those systems provide more detailed descriptions to the organizers.

6.1 Overall Performance

It is worth pointing out the significance of the two evaluation metrics proposed in Section 5 in terms of the model performance. The labeling accuracy indicates the raw predicative power of the model. This metric is biased towards more frequently appearing characters such as the primary characters, a total of which compose 70+% of the evaluation set. Thus, it is possible to achieve a relatively high labeling accuracy score without handling referents for the secondary characters well. On the contrary, the macro-average F1 score neutralizes the imbalance between frequently and not so frequently appearing characters. It reveals the model performance on a per-entity basis, which tends to favor transient and extra characters more because every character is treated equally in this metric.

For the overall performance, KNU-CI outperforms for **Main + Others** with the labeling accuracy of 85.10% and the macro-average F1 score of 86.00%, whereas AMORE-UPF outperforms for **ALL** with the labeling accuracy of 74.72% and the macro-average F1 of 41.05% (Table 6). All systems produce better results for **Main + Others** than **ALL**, which is expected due to the fewer number of entities to classify (7 vs 78). It is possible that KNU-CI's attention model is highly optimized for the identification of the primary characters, whereas AMORE-UPF's LSTM model distributes weights for the secondary characters more evenly, but more detailed analysis needs to be made to see the comparative strengths between these two systems.

6.2 Main + Other Identification

Table 7 depicts the strength of the KNU-CI system for the primary characters in comparisons to the others, which is attributed to its unique sequence labeling architecture and the attention mechanism. Their encoder-decoder architecture helps consolidating sequential information of the input dialogue along with the mentions. The hidden units in RNNs enable the network to aggregate character-related information and to disambiguate timeline shifts across utterances. The encoder takes the input dialogue and provides the decoder with context-rich features. Coupled with the attention mechanism, this model focuses on the primary characters; thus, it results better performance on **Main + Others**. However, this architecture is not as well-adaptive as the number of characters increases for the identification, which can be observed from the system's low macro-average F1 score for **All**.

6.3 All Character Identification

Table 8 describes the strength of the AMORE-UPF system for the secondary characters using the bidirectional LSTM model, leading it to outperform all the others for **All**. Although both AMORE-UPF and KNU-CI utilize variations of RNNs as their underlying architectures, the performance downfall is not as prominent for AMORE-UPF as the number of characters increases, thanks to its entity library. The entity library is consumed and updated as necessary given the mention embeddings. It is used to regularize training each individual character, which helps avoiding the bias towards frequently appearing characters. As the result, AMORE-UPF yields better performance for **All** while accomplishing reasonable results for **Main + Others** as well.

Character	Ross	Rachel	Chandler	Joey	Phoebe	Monica	Others
Evaluation	18.98	13.96	9.80	9.51	9.02	8.97	29.77
Training	13.93	12.37	11.43	9.43	8.79	10.61	33.44
AMORE-UPF	78.57	82.98	81.36	**79.83**	86.52	85.22	61.02
KNU-CI	**85.86**	**92.49**	**84.94**	79.67	**88.09**	**91.16**	**79.79**
Kampfpudding	73.48	70.67	79.25	63.38	79.79	73.35	74.61
Zuma-AR	38.72	43.05	43.04	36.10	42.90	46.43	51.78

Table 7: Detailed evaluation for **Main + Others** in Table 6. The Evaluation and Training rows show the percentages of individual characters appeared in the evaluation and the training set, respectively.

Character	Be	Ca	Ed	Pa	Ju	MB	Ri	Sc	Ca	Fr	Ja	OT
Evaluation	3.46	1.73	1.56	1.44	1.32	0.86	0.86	0.78	0.74	0.70	0.62	2.92
Training	1.41	1.46	1.06	0.71	1.15	0.60	1.83	0.21	0.13	0.51	0.43	13.51
AMORE-UPF	**50.00**	57.14	**80.60**	**35.56**	**72.73**	**64.52**	**80.85**	10.00	**61.54**	0.00	**42.11**	**7.89**
KNU-CI	38.46	**62.79**	73.02	15.38	42.55	0.00	66.67	**38.46**	0.00	**18.18**	16.00	0.00
Kampfpudding	31.86	33.33	68.85	33.33	60.32	50.00	61.22	10.00	0.00	0.00	23.53	0.00
Zuma-AR	0.00	12.24	44.44	0.00	27.91	15.38	77.78	0.00	38.46	0.00	12.50	0.00

Table 8: Detailed evaluation for **ALL** in Table 6. Be: Ben, Ca: Carol, Ed: Eddie, Pa: Paolo, Ju: Julie: MB: Mrs. Bing, Ri: Richard, Sc: Scott, Ca: Carl, Fr: Frank, Ja: Janice, OT: `Others`.

7 Conclusion

In this shared task, we propose a novel entity linking task called character identification that aims to find the global entities for all personal mentions, representing individual characters in the contexts of multiparty dialogue. Among 90+ participants signed up for this task at CodaLab, only four submitted their system outputs, which is unfortunate. However, the top-2 scoring systems depict unique strengths, allowing us to make a good analysis for this task. It would be interesting to see if the sequence labeling architecture from KNU-CI coupled with the entity library from AMORE-UPF could produce an even higher performing model for both the **Main + Other** and **All** evaluation.

To facilitate the momentum, we create an open-source project that will continuously support this task.[8] It is worth mentioning that *Character Identification* is a part of a bigger project called *Character Mining* that strives for machine comprehension on dialog.[9] Currently, this project provides more and cleaner annotation for character identification than the corpus described in Section 3, hoping to engage more researchers to this task.

References

Henry Yu-Hsin Chen and Jinho D. Choi. 2016. Character Identification on Multiparty Conversation: Identifying Mentions of Characters in TV Shows. In *Proceedings of the 17th Annual Meeting of the Special Interest Group on Discourse and Dialogue*. SIGDIAL'16, pages 90–100.

Henry Yu-Hsin Chen, Ethan Zhou, and Jinho D. Choi. 2017. Robust Coreference Resolution and Entity Linking on Dialogues: Character Identification on TV Show Transcripts. In *Proceedings of the 21st Conference on Computational Natural Language Learning*. Vancouver, Canada, CoNLL'17, pages 216–225. http://www.conll.org/2017.

Jinho D. Choi. 2016. Dynamic Feature Induction: The Last Gist to the State-of-the-Art. In *Proceedings of the Conference of the North American Chapter of the Association for Computational Linguistics: Human Language Technologies*. NAACL'16.

Jinho D. Choi and Andrew McCallum. 2013. Transition-based Dependency Parsing with Selectional Branching. In *Proceedings of the 51st Annual Meeting of the Association for Computational Linguistics*. ACL'13, pages 1052–1062.

Cristian Danescu-Niculescu-Mizil and Lillian Lee. 2011. Chameleons in Imagined Conversations: A New Approach to Understanding Coordination of Linguistic Style in Dialogs. In *Proceedings of the 2nd Workshop on Cognitive Modeling and Computational Linguistics*. CMCL'11, pages 76–87.

Stephen Guo, Ming-Wei Chang, and Emre Kiciman. 2013. To Link or Not to Link? A Study on End-to-End Tweet Entity Linking. In *Proceedings of the Conference of the North American Chapter of the*

---

[8] https://github.com/emorynlp/character-identification
[9] https://github.com/emorynlp/character-mining

Association for Computational Linguistics on Human Language Technology. NAACL, pages 1020–1030.

Zhichao Hu, Elahe Rahimtoroghi, Larissa Munishkina, Reid Swanson, and Marilyn A. Walker. 2013. Unsupervised Induction of Contingent Event Pairs from Film Scenes. In *Proceedings of the 2013 Conference on Empirical Methods in Natural Language Processing*. EMNLP'13, pages 369–379.

Adam Janin, Don Baron, Jane Edwards, Dan Ellis, David Gelbart, Nelson Morgan, Barbara Peskin, Thilo Pfau, Elizabeth Shriberg, Andreas Stolcke, and Chuck Wooters. 2003. The ICSI Meeting Corpus. In *Proceedings of IEEE International Conference on Acoustics, Speech, and Signal Processing*. ICASSP'03, pages 364–367.

Seokhwan Kim, Luis Fernando ĎHaro, Rafael E. Banchs, Jason D. Williams, and Matthew Henderson. 2015. The Fourth Dialog State Tracking Challenge. In *Proceedings of the 4th Dialog State Tracking Challenge*. DSTC4.

Lingpeng Kong, Nathan Schneider, Swabha Swayamdipta, Archna Bhatia, Chris Dyer, and Noah A. Smith. 2014. A Dependency Parser for Tweets. In *Proceedings of the 2014 Conference on Empirical Methods in Natural Language Processing*. EMNLP, pages 1001–1012.

Ryan Lowe, Nissan Pow, Iulian Serban, and Joelle Pineau. 2015. The Ubuntu Dialogue Corpus: A Large Dataset for Research in Unstructured Multi-Turn Dialogue Systems. In *Proceedings of the 16th Annual Meeting of the Special Interest Group on Discourse and Dialogue*. SIGDIAL'15, pages 285–294.

Rada Mihalcea and Andras Csomai. 2007. Wikify!: Linking Documents to Encyclopedic Knowledge. In *Proceedings of the Sixteenth ACM Conference on Conference on Information and Knowledge Management*. CIKM'07, pages 233–242.

Sameer Pradhan, Alessandro Moschitti, Nianwen Xue, Olga Uryupina, and Yuchen Zhang. 2012. CoNLL-2012 Shared Task: Modeling Multilingual Unrestricted Coreference in OntoNotes. In *Proceedings of the Sixteenth Conference on Computational Natural Language Learning: Shared Task*. CoNLL'12, pages 1–40.

Suhas Ranganath, Xia Hu, Jiliang Tang, Suhang Wang, and Huan Liu. 2016. Identifying Rhetorical Questions in Social Media. In *Proceedings of the 10th International Conference on Web and Social Media*. pages 667–670.

Lev Ratinov, Dan Roth, Doug Downey, and Mike Anderson. 2011. Local and Global Algorithms for Disambiguation to Wikipedia. In *Proceedings of the 49th Annual Meeting of the Association for Computational Linguistics: Human Language Technologies*. ACL'11, pages 1375–1384.

Alan Ritter, Sam Clark, Mausam, and Oren Etzioni. 2011. Named Entity Recognition in Tweets: An Experimental Study. In *Proceedings of the Conference on Empirical Methods in Natural Language Processing*. EMNLP, pages 1524–1534.

Bonggun Shin, Timothy Lee, and Jinho D. Choi. 2017. Lexicon Integrated CNN Models with Attention for Sentiment Analysis. In *Proceedings of the EMNLP Workshop on Computational Approaches to Subjectivity, Sentiment and Social Media Analysis*. Copenhagen, Denmark, WASSA'17, pages 149–158. http://optima.jrc.it/wassa2017/.

AMORE-UPF at SemEval-2018 Task 4: BiLSTM with Entity Library

Laura Aina[*]   **Carina Silberer**[*]   **Ionut-Teodor Sorodoc**[*]
Matthijs Westera[*]   **Gemma Boleda**

Universitat Pompeu Fabra
Barcelona, Spain
`{firstname.lastname}@upf.edu`

Abstract

This paper describes our winning contribution to SemEval 2018 Task 4: *Character Identification on Multiparty Dialogues*. It is a simple, standard model with one key innovation, an *entity library*. Our results show that this innovation greatly facilitates the identification of infrequent characters. Because of the generic nature of our model, this finding is potentially relevant to any task that requires effective learning from sparse or unbalanced data.

1 Introduction

SemEval 2018 Task 4 is an **entity linking** task on multiparty dialogue.[1] It consists in predicting the referents of nominals that refer to a person, such as *she*, *mom*, *Judy* – henceforth *mentions*. The set of possible referents is given beforehand, as well as the set of mentions to resolve. The dataset used in this task is based on Chen and Choi (2016) and Chen et al. (2017), and consists of dialogue from the TV show *Friends* in textual form.

Our main interest is whether deep learning models for tasks like entity linking can benefit from having an explicit **entity library**, i.e., a component of the neural network that stores entity representations learned during training. To that end, we add such a component to an otherwise relatively basic model – a bidirectional LSTM (long short-term memory; Hochreiter and Schmidhuber 1997), the standard neural network model for sequential data like language. Training and evaluating this

model on the task shows that the entity library is beneficial in the case of infrequent entities.[2]

2 Related Work

Previous entity linking tasks concentrate on linking mentions to Wikipedia pages (Bunescu and Paşca 2006; Mihalcea and Csomai 2007 and much subsequent work; for a recent approach see Francis-Landau et al. 2016). By contrast, in the present task (based on Chen and Choi 2016; Chen et al. 2017) only a list of entities is given, without any associated encyclopedic entries. This makes the task more similar to the way in which a human audience might watch the TV show, in that they are initially unfamiliar with the characters. What also sets the present task apart from most previous tasks is its focus on multiparty dialogue (as opposed to, typically, newswire articles).

A task that is closely related to entity linking is *coreference resolution*, i.e., the task of clustering mentions that refer to the same entity (e.g., the CoNLL shared task of Pradhan et al. 2011). Since mention clusters essentially correspond to entities (an insight central to the approaches to coreference in Haghighi and Klein 2010; Clark and Manning 2016), the present task can be regarded as a type of coreference resolution, but one where the set of referents to choose from is given beforehand.

Since our main aim is to test the benefits of having an entity library, in other respects our model is kept more basic than existing work both on entity linking and on coreference reso-

---

[*]denotes equal contribution.

[1]`https://competitions.codalab.org/competitions/17310`

[2]Source code for our model and for the training procedure is published on `https://github.com/amore-upf/semeval2018-task4.`

Proceedings of the 12th International Workshop on Semantic Evaluation (SemEval-2018), pages 65–69
New Orleans, Louisiana, June 5–6, 2018. ©2018 Association for Computational Linguistics

lution (e.g., the aforementioned approaches, as well as Wiseman et al. 2016; Lee et al. 2017, Francis-Landau et al. 2016). For instance, we avoid feature engineering, focusing instead on the model's ability to learn meaningful entity representations from the dialogue itself. Moreover, we deviate from the common strategy to entity linking of incorporating a specialized coreference resolution module (e.g., Chen et al. 2017).

3 Model Description

We approach the task of character identification as one of multi-class classification. Our model is depicted in Figure 1, with inputs in the top left and outputs at the bottom. In a nutshell, our model is a bidirectional LSTM (long short-term memory, Hochreiter and Schmidhuber 1997) that processes the dialogue text and resolves mentions, through a comparison between the LSTM's hidden state (for each mention) to vectors in a learned entity library.

The model is given chunks of dialogue, which it processes token by token. The ith token $\mathbf{t}_i$ and its speakers S_i (typically a singleton set) are represented as one-hot vectors, embedded via two distinct embedding matrices ($\mathbf{W}_t$ and $\mathbf{W}_s$, respectively) and finally concatenated to form a vector $\mathbf{x}_i$ (Eq. 1; see also Figure 1). In case $\mathbf{S}_i$ contains multiple speakers, their embeddings are summed.

$$\mathbf{x}_i = \mathbf{W}_t \, \mathbf{t}_i \parallel \sum_{s \in S_i} \mathbf{W}_s \, \mathbf{s} \qquad (1)$$

We apply an activation function f ($= \tanh$). The hidden state $\overrightarrow{\mathbf{h}}_i$ of a *uni*directional LSTM for the ith input is recursively defined as a combination of that input with the LSTM's previous hidden state $\overrightarrow{\mathbf{h}}_{i-1}$. For a *bi*directional LSTM, the hidden state $\mathbf{h}_i$ is a concatenation of the hidden states $\overrightarrow{\mathbf{h}}_i$ and $\overleftarrow{\mathbf{h}}_i$ of two unidirectional LSTMs which process the data in opposite directions (Eq. 2; see also Figure 1). In principle, this enables a bidirectional LSTM to represent the entire dialogue with a focus on the current input, including for instance its relevant dependencies on the context.

$$\mathbf{h}_i = \text{BiLSTM}(f(\mathbf{x}_i), \overrightarrow{\mathbf{h}}_{i-1}, \overleftarrow{\mathbf{h}}_{i+1}) \qquad (2)$$

In the model, learned representations of each entity are stored in the *entity library* $\mathbf{E} \in \mathbb{R}^{N \times k}$ (see Figure 1): $\mathbf{E}$ is a matrix which represents each of N entities through a k-dimensional vector, and whose values are updated (only) during training.

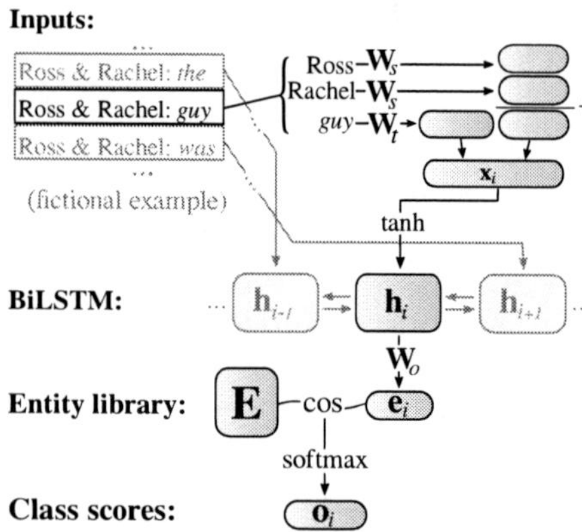

Figure 1: The AMORE-UPF model (bias not depicted).

For every token $\mathbf{t}_i$ that is tagged as a mention,[3] we map the corresponding hidden state $\mathbf{h}_i$ to a vector $\mathbf{e}_i \in \mathbb{R}^{1 \times k}$. This extracted representation is used to retrieve the (candidate) referent of the mention from the entity library: The similarity of $\mathbf{e}_i$ to each entity representation stored in $\mathbf{E}$ is computed using cosine, and softmax is then applied to the resulting similarity profile to obtain a probability distribution $\mathbf{o}_i \in [0, 1]^{1 \times N}$ over entities ('class scores' in Figure 1):

$$\mathbf{o}_i = \text{softmax}(\text{cosine}(\mathbf{E}, \underbrace{(\mathbf{W}_o \, \mathbf{h}_i + \mathbf{b})}_{\mathbf{e}_i})) \qquad (3)$$

At testing time, the model's prediction $\hat{c}_i$ for the ith token is the entity with highest probability:

$$\hat{c}_i = \text{argmax}(\mathbf{o}_i) \qquad (4)$$

We train the model with backpropagation, using negative log-likelihood as loss function. Besides the BiLSTM parameters, we optimize $\mathbf{W}_t$, $\mathbf{W}_s$, $\mathbf{W}_o$, $\mathbf{E}$ and $\mathbf{b}$. We refer to this model as **AMORE-UPF**, our team name in the SemEval competition. Note that, in order for this architecture to be successful, $\mathbf{e}_i$ needs to be as similar as possible to the entity vector of the entity to which mention t_i refers. Indeed, the mapping $\mathbf{W}_o$ should effectively specialize in "extracting" entity representations from the hidden state because of the way its output $\mathbf{e}_i$ is used in the model—to do entity retrieval. Our entity retrieval mechanism is inspired by the attention mechanism of Bahdanau et al. (2016), that has been used in previous work to interact with an external memory (Sukhbaatar et al., 2015; Boleda et al., 2017).

---

[3]For multi-word mentions this is done only for the last token in the mention.

JOEY TRIBBIANI (183):
”…see <u>Ross</u>, because <u>I</u> think <u>you</u> love <u>her</u>.”
335   183   335   306

Figure 2: Example of the data provided for the SemEval 2018 Task 4. It shows the speaker (first line) of the utterance (second line) and the ids of the entities to which the target mentions (underlined) refer (last line).

To assess the contribution of the entity library, we compare our model to a similar architecture which does not include it (**NoEntLib**). This model directly applies softmax to a linear mapping of the hidden state (Eq. 5, replacing Eq. 3 above).

$$\mathbf{o}_i = \mathrm{softmax}(\mathbf{W}_o\,\mathbf{h}_i + \mathbf{b}) \qquad (5)$$

4 Experimental Setup

Data We use the training and test data provided for SemEval 2018 Task 4, which span the first two seasons of the TV show *Friends*, divided into scenes (train: 374 scenes from 47 episodes; test: 74 scenes from 40 episodes).[4] In total, the training and test data contain 13,280 and 2,429 nominal mentions (e.g., *Ross, I*; Figure 2), respectively, which are annotated with the ID of the entity to which they refer (e.g., 335, 183). The utterances are further annotated with the name of the speaker (e.g., JOEY TRIBBIANI). Overall there are 372 entities in the training data (test data: 106). Our models do not use any of the provided automatic linguistic annotations, such as PoS or named entity tags.

We additionally used the publicly available 300-dimensional word vectors that were pre-trained on a Google News corpus with the word2vec Skip-gram model (Mikolov et al., 2013).[5]

Parameter settings Using 5-fold cross-validation on the training data, we performed a random search over the hyperparameters and chose those which yielded the best mean F1-score. Specifically, our submitted model is trained in batch mode using the Adam optimizer (Kingma and Ba, 2014) with a learning rate of 0.0005. Each batch covers 24 scenes, which are given to the model in chunks of 757 tokens. The token embeddings ($\mathbf{W}_t$) are initialized with the word2vec vectors. Dropout rates of 0.008 and 0.0013 are applied on the input $\mathbf{x}_i$ and hidden layer $\mathbf{h}_i$ of the LSTM, respectively. The size of $\mathbf{h}_i$ is set to

---

Models	all entities		main entities	
	F_1	Acc	F_1	Acc
AMORE-UPF	**41.1****	**74.7****	79.4	77.2
NoEntLib	26.4	71.6	**79.5**	**77.5**

Table 1: Results obtained for the submitted AMORE-UPF model and a variant of it that does not use an entity library (NoEntLib). Best results are in boldface. Differences with respect to the 2nd row marked by '**' are significant at the 0.001 probability level (see text).

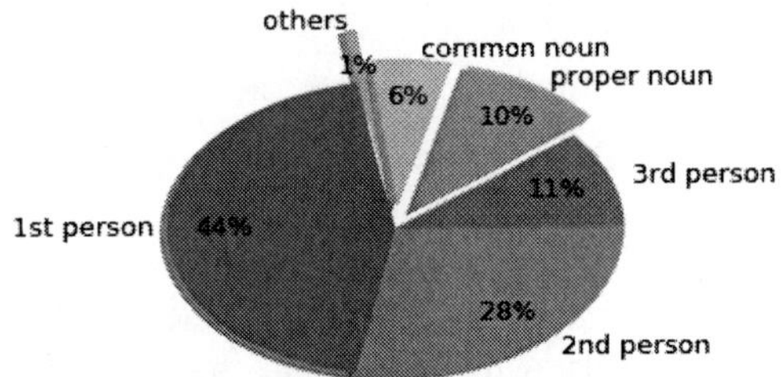

Figure 3: Distribution of all $2,429$ target mentions in the test data in terms of their part-of-speech.

459 units, the embeddings of the entity library $\mathbf{E}$ and speakers $\mathbf{W}_s$ are set to $k = 134$ dimensions.

Other configurations, including randomly initialized token embeddings, weight sharing between $\mathbf{E}$ and $\mathbf{W}_s$, self-attention (Bahdanau et al., 2016) on the input layer, a uni-directional LSTM, and rectifier or linear activation function f on the input embeddings did not improve performance.

For the final submission of the answers for the test data, we created an ensemble model by averaging the output (Eq. 3) of the five models trained on the different folds.

5 Results

Two evaluation conditions were defined by the organizers – *all entities* and *main entities* – with macro-average F_1-score and label accuracy as the official metrics, and macro-average F_1-score in the *all entities* condition applied to the leaderboard. The *all entities* evaluation has 67 classes: 66 for entities that are mentioned at least 3 times in the test set and one grouping all others. The *main entities* evaluation has 7 classes, 6 for the main characters and one for all the others. Among all four participating systems in this SemEval task our model achieved the highest score on the *all entities* evaluation, and second-highest on the *main entities* evaluation.

Table 1 gives our results in the two evaluations, comparing the models described in Section 4. While both models perform on a par on main

---

[4]The organizers also provided data divided by episodes rather than scenes, which we didn't use.

[5]The word vectors are available at `https://code.google.com/archive/p/word2vec/`.

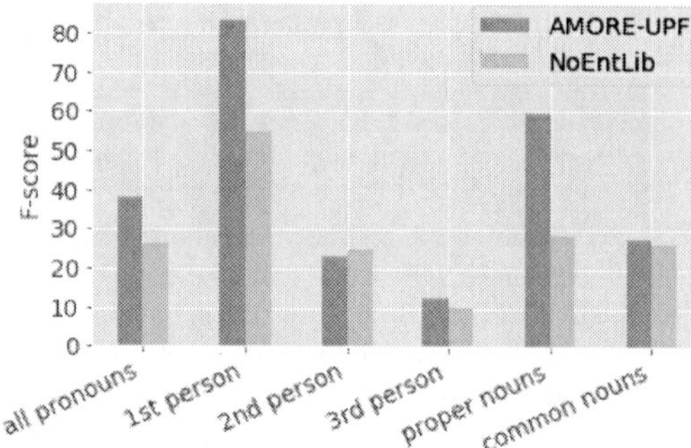

Figure 4: F_1-score of the models on *all entities* depending on the part-of-speech of the target mentions.

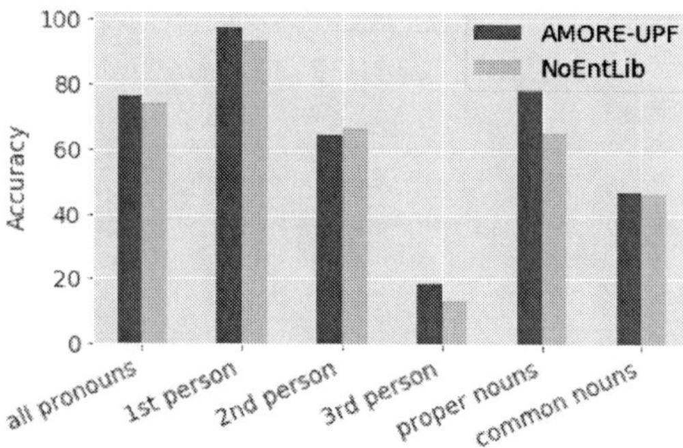

Figure 5: Aaccuracy of the models on *all entities* depending on the part-of-speech of the target mentions.

entities, AMORE-UPF outperforms NoEntLib by a substantial margin when all characters are to be predicted (+15 points in F_1-score, +3 points in accuracy; Table 1).[6] The difference between the models with/without an entity library are statistically significant based on approximate randomization tests (Noreen, 1989), with the significance level $p < 0.001$. This shows that the use of an entity library can be beneficial for the linking of rarely mentioned characters.

Figure 3 shows that most of the target mentions in the test data fall into one of five grammatical categories. The dataset contains mostly pronouns (83%), with a very high percentage of first person pronouns (44%). Figures 4 and 5 present the accuracy and F_1-score which the two models described above obtain on *all entities* for different categories of mentions. The entity library is beneficial when the mention is a first person pronoun or a proper noun (with an increase of 30 points in F_1-score for both categories; Figure 4), and closer inspection revealed that this effect was larger for rare entities.

6 Discussion

The AMORE-UPF model consists of a bidirectional LSTM linked to an entity library. Compared to an LSTM without entity library, NoEntLib, the AMORE-UPF model performs particularly well on rare entities, which explains its top score in the *all entities* condition of SemEval 2018 Task 4. This finding is encouraging, since rare entities are especially challenging for the usual approaches in NLP, due to the scarcity of information about them.

We offer the following explanation for this beneficial effect of the entity library, as a hypothesis for future work. Having an entity library requires the LSTM of our model to output some representation of the mentioned entity, as opposed to outputting class scores more or less directly as in the variant NoEntLib. Outputting a meaningful entity representation is particularly easy in the case of first person pronouns and nominal mentions (where the effect of the entity library appears to reside; Figure 4): the LSTM can learn to simply forward the speaker embedding unchanged in the case of pronoun *I*, and the token embedding in the case of nominal mentions. This strategy does not discriminate between frequent and rare entities; it works for both alike. We leave further analyses required to test this potential explanation for future work.

Future work may also reveal to what extent the induced entity representations may be useful in others, to what extent they encode entities' attributes and relations (cf. Gupta et al. 2015), and to what extent a module like our entity library can be employed elsewhere, in natural language processing and beyond.

Acknowledgments

This project has received funding from the European Research Council (ERC) under the European Unions Horizon 2020 research and innovation programme (grant agreement No 715154), and from the Spanish Ramón y Cajal programme (grant RYC-2015-18907). We are grateful to the NVIDIA Corporation for the donation of GPUs used for this research. We are also very grateful to the Pytorch developers. This paper reflects the authors' view only, and the EU is not responsible for any use that may be made of the information it contains.

---

[6]The mean difference between the single models (trained on a single fold) and the ensemble AMORE-UPF is between -1.3 points (accuracy main entities, std $= 1.3$) and -4.2 points (F_1-score all entities, std $= 1.3$).

References

Dzmitry Bahdanau, Kyunghyun Cho, and Yoshua Bengio. 2016. Neural Machine Translation by Jointly Learning to Align and Translate. *Computing Research Repository*, abs/1409.0473v7.

Gemma Boleda, Sebastian Padó, Nghia The Pham, and Marco Baroni. 2017. Living a Discrete Life in a Continuous World: Reference in Cross-modal Entity Tracking. In *IWCS 2017 — 12th International Conference on Computational Semantics — Short papers*.

Razvan Bunescu and Marius Paşca. 2006. Using Encyclopedic Knowledge for Named Entity Disambiguation. In *11th conference of the European Chapter of the Association for Computational Linguistics*.

Henry Y. Chen, Ethan Zhou, and Jinho D. Choi. 2017. Robust Coreference Resolution and Entity Linking on Dialogues: Character Identification on TV Show Transcripts. In *Proceedings of the 21st Conference on Computational Natural Language Learning (CoNLL 2017)*, pages 216–225.

Yu-Hsin Chen and Jinho D Choi. 2016. Character Identification on Multiparty Conversation: Identifying Mentions of Characters in TV Shows. In *Proceedings of the 17th Annual Meeting of the Special Interest Group on Discourse and Dialogue*, pages 90–100.

Kevin Clark and Christopher D. Manning. 2016. Improving Coreference Resolution by Learning Entity-Level Distributed Representations. In *Proceedings of the 54th Annual Meeting of the Association for Computational Linguistics (Volume 1: Long Papers)*, pages 643–653.

Matthew Francis-Landau, Greg Durrett, and Dan Klein. 2016. Capturing Semantic Similarity for Entity Linking with Convolutional Neural Networks. *Computing Research Repository*, abs/1604.00734.

Abhijeet Gupta, Gemma Boleda, Marco Baroni, and Sebastian Padó. 2015. Distributional Vectors Encode Referential Attributes. In *Proceedings of the 2015 Conference on Empirical Methods in Natural Language Processing*, pages 12–21.

Aria Haghighi and Dan Klein. 2010. Coreference Resolution in a Modular, Entity-Centered Model. In *Human Language Technologies: The 2010 Annual Conference of the North American Chapter of the Association for Computational Linguistics*, pages 385–393. Association for Computational Linguistics.

Sepp Hochreiter and Jürgen Schmidhuber. 1997. Long Short-Term Memory. *Neural Computation*, 9(8):1735–1780.

Diederik P. Kingma and Jimmy Ba. 2014. Adam: A Method for Stochastic Optimization. *Computing Research Repository*, abs/1412.6980.

Kenton Lee, Luheng He, Mike Lewis, and Luke Zettlemoyer. 2017. End-to-End Neural Coreference Resolution. *Computing Research Repository*, abs/1707.07045.

Rada Mihalcea and Andras Csomai. 2007. Wikify!: Linking Documents to Encyclopedic Knowledge. In *Proceedings of the sixteenth ACM Conference on Information and Knowledge Management*, pages 233–242.

Tomas Mikolov, Ilya Sutskever, Kai Chen, Greg Corrado, and Jeffrey Dean. 2013. Distributed Representations of Words and Phrases and Their Compositionality. In *Proceedings of the 26th International Conference on Neural Information Processing Systems - Volume 2*, pages 3111–3119.

E.W. Noreen. 1989. *Computer-Intensive Methods for Testing Hypotheses: An Introduction*. Wiley.

Sameer Pradhan, Lance Ramshaw, Mitchell Marcus, Martha Palmer, Ralph Weischedel, and Nianwen Xue. 2011. CoNLL-2011 Shared Task: Modeling Unrestricted Coreference in OntoNotes. In *Proceedings of the Fifteenth Conference on Computational Natural Language Learning: Shared Task*, pages 1–27. Association for Computational Linguistics.

Sainbayar Sukhbaatar, Arthur Szlam, Jason Weston, and Rob Fergus. 2015. End-To-End Memory Networks. *arXiv*, pages 1–11.

Sam Wiseman, Alexander M Rush, and Stuart M Shieber. 2016. Learning Global Features for Coreference Resolution. *Computing Research Repository*, abs/1604.03035.

SemEval-2018 Task 5: Counting Events and Participants in the Long Tail

Marten Postma, Filip Ilievski, Piek Vossen
Vrije Universiteit Amsterdam
The Netherlands
{m.c.postma, f.ilievski, piek.vossen}@vu.nl

Abstract

This paper discusses SemEval-2018 Task 5: a referential quantification task of counting events and participants in local, long-tail news documents with high ambiguity. The complexity of this task challenges systems to establish the meaning, reference and identity across documents. The task consists of three subtasks and spans across three domains. We detail the design of this referential quantification task, describe the participating systems, and present additional analysis to gain deeper insight into their performance.

1 Introduction

We present a "referential quantification" task that requires systems to establish the meaning, reference and identity of events[1] and participants in news articles. By "referential quantification", we mean questions concerning the number of incidents of an event type (e.g. *How many killing incidents happened in 2016 in Columbus, MS?*) or participants in roles (e.g. *How many people were killed in 2016 in Columbus, MS?*), as opposed to factoid questions for specific properties of individual events and entities (e.g. *When was 2pac murdered?*). The questions are given with certain constraints on the location, time, participants, and event types, which requires understanding of the meaning of words mentioning these properties (e.g. Word Sense Disambiguation), but also adequately establishing the identity (e.g. reference and coreference) across mentions. The task thus represents both an intrinsic and application-based evaluation, as systems are forced to resolve ambiguity of meaning and reference, as well as variation in reference in order to answer the questions.

Figure 1 shows an overview of our quantification task. We provide the participants with a set of questions and their corresponding news documents.[2] Systems are asked to distill event- and participant-based knowledge from the documents to answer the question. Systems submit both a numeric answer (*3* events in Figure 1), and the corresponding events with their mentions found in the provided texts (e.g., the leftmost incident in Figure 1 is referred to by the coreferring mentions "killed" and "assault" found in two separate documents). Systems are evaluated on both the numeric answers as well as on the sets of coreferring mentions. Mentions are represented by tokens and offsets provided by the organizers.

The incidents and their corresponding news articles are obtained from structured databases, which greatly reduces the need for annotation and mainly requires validation instead. Given this data and using a metric-driven strategy, we created a task that further maximizes ambiguity and variation of the data in relation to the questions. This ambiguity and variation includes a substantial amount of low-frequent, local events and entities, reflecting a large variety of long-tail phenomena. As such, the task is not only highly ambiguous but can also not be tackled by relying on the most frequent and popular (head) interpretations.

We see the following contributions of our task:
1. To the best of our knowledge, we propose the first task that is deliberately designed to address large ambiguity of meaning and reference over a high number of infrequent instances.
2. We introduce a methodology for creating large event-based tasks while avoiding a lot of annotation, since we base the task on structured data. The remaining annotation concerns targeted mentions given the structured data rather than full doc-

---

[1] By event, we denote a specific instance of an event, e.g. a killing incident happening at a specific location, time, and involving certain participants.

[2] Question parsing is unnecessary, as questions are provided in a structured format.

Proceedings of the 12th International Workshop on Semantic Evaluation (SemEval-2018), pages 70–80
New Orleans, Louisiana, June 5–6, 2018. ©2018 Association for Computational Linguistics

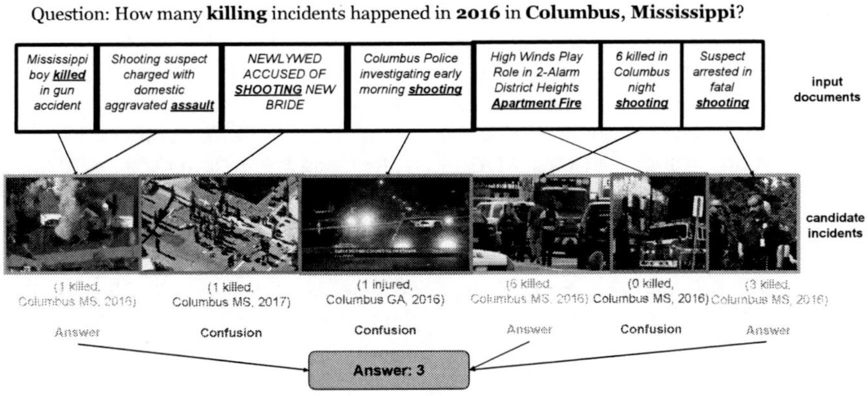

Figure 1: Task overview. Systems are provided with a question and a set of input documents. Their goal is then to find the documents that fit the question constraints and reason over them to provide an answer.

uments with open-ended interpretations.

3. We made all of our code to create the task available,[3] which may stimulate others to create more tasks and datasets that tackle long-tail phenomena for other aspects of language processing, either within or outside of the SemEval competition.

4. This task provides insights into the strengths and weaknesses of semantic processing systems with respect to various long-tail phenomena. We expect that systems need to innovate by adjusting (deep) learning techniques to capture the referential complexity and knowledge sparseness, or by explicitly modeling aspects of events and entities to establish identity and reference.

2 Motivation & Target Communities

Expressions can have many different meanings and possibly an infinite number of references. At the same time, variation in language is also large, as we can make reference to the same things in many ways. This makes the tasks of Word Sense Disambiguation, Entity Linking, and Event and Nominal Coreference extremely hard. It also makes it very difficult to create a task that represents the problem at its full scale. Any sample of text will reduce the problem to a small set of meanings and references, but also to meanings that are popular at that time excluding many unpopular ones from the distributional long tail. Given this Zipfian distribution, a task that is challenging with respect to ambiguity, reference, and variation, and that is representative for the long tail as well, needs to fit certain constraints.

Our task directly relates to the following communities in semantic processing: 1. disambiguation and reference; 2. reading comprehension and question answering.

2.1 Disambiguation & Reference

Semantic NLP tasks are often limited in terms of the range of concepts and meanings that are covered. This is a necessary consequence of the annotation effort that is needed to create such tasks. Likewise, in Ilievski et al. (2016), we observed that most well-known datasets for semantic tasks have an extremely low ambiguity and variation. Even in datasets that tried to increase the ambiguity and temporal diversity for the disambiguation and reference tasks, we still measured a notable bias with respect to ambiguity, variance, dominance, and time. Overall, tasks and their datasets show a strong semantic overfitting to the head of the distribution (the most popular part of the world) and are not representative for the diversity of the long tail.

Our task differs from existing ones in that: 1. we deliberately created a task with a high number of event instances per event, many of which with similar properties, leading to high confusability 2. we present an application-based task which requires to perform on a combination of intrinsic tasks such as reference, disambiguation, and spatial-temporal reasoning, that are usually tested separately in existing tasks.

2.2 Reading Comprehension & Question Answering

In several recent tasks, systems are asked to answer entity-based questions, typically by point-

---

[3]https://github.com/cltl/
LongTailQATask

ing to the correct segment or coreference chain in text, or by composing an answer by abstracting over multiple paragraphs/text pieces. These tasks are based on Wikipedia (SQuAD (Rajpurkar et al., 2016), WikiQA (Yang et al., 2015), QASent (Wang et al., 2007), WIKIREADING (Hewlett et al., 2016)) or on annotated individual documents (MARCO (Nguyen et al., 2016), CNN and DailyMail datasets (Hermann et al., 2015)).

Weston et al. (2015) outlined 20 skill sets, such as causality, resolving time and location, and reasoning over world knowledge, that are needed to build an intelligent QA system. These have been partially captured by the datasets MCTest (Richardson et al., 2013) and QuizBowl (Iyyer et al., 2014)), as well as the SemEval task on *Answer Selection in Community Question Answering* (Nakov et al., 2015, 2016).[4]

However, all these datasets avoid representing real-world referential ambiguity to its full extent by mainly asking questions that require knowledge about popular Wikipedia entities and/or text understanding of a single document.[5] Unlike existing work, our task deliberately addresses the referential ambiguity of the world beyond Wikipedia, by asking questions about long-tail events described in multiple documents. By doing so, we require deep processing of text and establishing identity and reference across single documents.

3 Task Requirements

Our quantification task consists of questions like *How many killing incidents happened in 2016 in Columbus, MS?* on a dataset that maximizes confusability of meaning, reference and identity. To guide the creation of such task, we defined five requirements that apply to the data for a single event type, e.g. *killing* (Postma et al., 2016).

Each event type should contain:
R1 Multiple event instances per event type, e.g. *the killing of Joe Doe* and *the killing of Joe Roe*.
R2 Multiple event mentions per event instance within the same document.
R3 Multiple documents with varying creation times that describe the same event.
R4 Event confusability by combining one or multiple confusion factors:

a) ambiguity of event mentions, e.g. *John Doe fires a gun*, and *John Doe fires a worker*.

b) variance of event mentions, e.g. *John Doe kills Joe Roe*, and *John Doe murders Joe Roe*.

c) time, e.g. *killing A that happened in January 2013*, and *killing B in October 2016*.

d) participants, e.g. *killing A committed by John Doe*, and *killing B committed by Joe Roe*.

e) location, e.g. *killing A that happened in Columbus, MS*, and *killing B in Houston, TX*.
R5 Representation of non-dominant events and entities, i.e. instances that receive little media coverage. Hence, the entities would not be restricted to celebrities and the events are not widely discussed such as general elections.

4 Data & Resources

In this Section, we present our data sources and an example document. We also discuss considerations of licensing and availability.

4.1 Structured data

The majority of the source texts in this task are sampled from structured databases that contain supportive news sources about gun violence incidents. While these texts already contain enough confusability with respect to the aspects defined in Section 3, we add confusion through leveraging structured data from two other domains: fire incidents and business.

As a direct consequence of using these databases and our exploitation strategy, we are able to satisfy all requirements we set in Section 3. These databases contain many event instances per event type (R1), multiple event mentions in the same document per event instance (R2), cover a wide spread of publishing times per event instance (R3), represent non-dominant events and entities (R5), and contain rich annotation of event properties that allows us to create high confusability (R4, see Section 5.3 for our methodology).

For a large portion of the information in the structured databases, we manually validated that this information could be found in the supportive news sources, and excluded the documents for which this was not the case. For the remaining documents, we performed automatic tests to filter out low-quality entries.

4.1.1 Gun Violence

The gun violence data is collected from the standard reports provided by the *Gun Violence Archive*

---

[4]The 2017 run can be found at `http://alt.qcri.org/semeval2017/task3/`.

[5]e.g. the Quiz Bowl dataset deliberately focuses on domains with much training data and frequent answers, thus avoiding the long tail problem in reference.

(GVA) website.[6] Each incident contains information about: 1. its **location** 2. its **time** 3. how many people were **killed** 4. how many people were **injured** 5. its **participants**. Participant information includes: (a) the **role**, i.e. victim or suspect (b) the **name** (c) the **age** 6. the **news articles** describing this incident. Table 1 provides a more detailed overview of the information available in the GVA.

Event Property	Granularity	Example value
Location	Address City State	Central Avenue Waynesboro Mississippi
Incident time	Day Month Year	14-3-2017 3-2017 2017
Participant	First name Last name Full name	John Smith John Smith

Table 1: Overview of the GVA incident properties of location, time, and participant.

To prevent systems from cheating (by using the structured data directly), the set of incidents and news articles is extended with news articles from the Signal-1M Dataset (Corney et al., 2016) and from the Web, that also stem from the gun violence domain, but are not found in the GVA.

4.1.2 Other domains

For the fire incidents domain, we make use of the *FireRescue1* reports,[7] which describe the following information about 417 incidents: 1. their **location** as a surface form 2. their **reporting time** 3. one **free text summary** describing the incidents. 4. **no** information about **participants**. Based on this information, we manually annotated the incident time and mapped the location to its representation in Wikipedia.

We further carefully selected a small amount of news articles from the business domain from The Signal-1M Dataset. Since these documents were not semantically annotated with respect to event information, we manually annotated this data with the same kind of information as the other databases: incident location, time, and information on the affected participants.

4.2 Example document

For each document, we provide its **title**, **content (tokenized)**, and **creation time**, e.g.:

Title: *$70K reward in deadly shooting near N. Philadelphia school*

Content: *A $70,000 reward is being offered for information in a quadruple shooting near a Roman Catholic school ...*

DCT: *2017-4-5*

4.3 Licensing & Availability

The news documents in our task are published on a very diverse set of (commercial) websites. Due to this diversity, there is no easy mechanism to check their licenses individually. Instead, we overcome potential licensing issues by distributing the data under the Fair Use policy.[8] [9]

During the SemEval-2018 period, but also afterwards, systems can easily test their submissions via our competition on Codalab.[10]

5 Task Design

For every incident in the task, we have fine-grained structured data with respect to its event type, location, time, and participants, and unstructured data in the form of the news sources that report on it. In this Section, we explain how we exploited this data in order to create the task. We present our three subtasks and the question template after which we outline the question creation. Finally, we explain how we divided the data into trial and test sets and provide some statistics about the data. For detailed information about the task, e.g. about the question and answer representation, we refer to the CodaLab website of the task.

5.1 Subtasks

The task contains two event-based subtasks and one entity-based subtask.

Subtask 1 (S1): Find the single event that answers the question e.g. *Which killing incident happened in Wilmington, CA in June 2014?* The main challenge is not to determine how many incidents satisfy the question, but to identify the documents that describe the single answer incident.

Subtask 2 (S2): Find all events (if any) that answer the question. This subtask differs from

---

S1 in that the system now also has to determine the number of answer incidents, which makes this subtask harder. To make it more realistic, we also include questions with zero as an answer.

Subtask 3 (S3): Find all participant-role relations that answer the question e.g. *How many people were killed in Wilmington, CA with the last name Smith?* The goal is to determine the number of entities that satisfy the question. The system not only needs to identify the relevant incidents, but also to reason over the participant roles.

5.2 Question Template

Questions in each subtask consist of an event type and two event properties.

Event type We consider four event types in this task described through their representation in WordNet (Fellbaum, 1998) and FrameNet (F. Baker et al., 1998). Each question is constrained by exactly one event type.

event type	description	meanings
killing	at least one person is killed	wn30:killing.n.02 wn30:kill.v.01 fn17:Killing
injuring	at least one person is injured	wn30:injure.v.01 wn30:injured.a.01 fn17:Cause_harm fn17:Experience-_bodily_harm
fire_burning	the event of something burning	wn30:fire.n.01 fn17:Fire_burning
job_firing	terminated employment	wn30:displace.v.03 fn17:Firing

Table 2: Description of the event types. The meanings column lists meanings that best describe the event type. It contains both FrameNet 1.7 frames (prefixed by *fn17*) and WordNet 3.0 synsets (prefixed by *wn30*).

Event properties For each event property in our task (time, location, participants), we distinguish between three levels of granularity (see Table 1). In addition, we make a distinction between the surface form and the meaning of an event property value. For example, the surface form *Wilmington* can denote several meanings: the Wilmington cities in the states of California, North Carolina, and Delaware. When composing questions, for time and location we take the semantic (meaning) level, while for participants we use the surface form of their names. This is because the vast majority of the participants in our task are long tail instances which have no semantic representation in a structured knowledge base.

5.3 Question Creation

Our question creation strategy consists of three consecutive phases: question composition, generation of answer and confusion sets, and question scoring. These steps are common for both the event-based subtasks (S1 and S2) and the entity-based subtask S3.

1. Question composition We compose questions based on the template described in Section 5.2. This entails: 1. choice of a subtask 2. choice of an event type, e.g. *killing* 3. choice of two event properties (e.g. *time and location*) with their corresponding granularities (e.g. *month and city*) and concrete values (e.g. *June 2014 and Wilmington, CA*). This step generates a vast amount of potential questions (hundreds of thousands) in a data-driven way, i.e. we select the event type and properties per question purely based on the combinations we find in our data. Example questions are:

Which killing event happened in June 2014 in Wilmington, CA? (subtask S1)

How many killing events happened in June 2014 in Wilmington, CA? (subtask S2)

How many people were killed in June 2014 in Wilmington, CA? (subtask S3)

2. Answer and confusion sets generation For each generated question, we define a set of answer and confusion incidents with their corresponding documents. **Answer** incidents are the ones which entirely fit the question parameters, e.g. *all killing incidents that occur in June 2014 and in the city of Wilmington, CA.* **Confusion** incidents fit some, but not all, values of the question parameters , i.e. they differ with respect to an event type or property (e.g. *all fire incidents in June 2014 in Wilmington, CA*; or *all killings in June 2014, but not in Wilmington, CA*; or *all killings in Wilmington, CA, but not in June 2014*).

3. Question scoring The generated questions with their corresponding answers and confusion are next scored with respect to several metrics that measure their complexity. The per-question scores allow us to detect and remove the "easy" ones, and keep those that: 1. have a high number of answer incidents (only applicable to S2 and S3) 2. have a high number of confusion incidents 3. have a high average number of answer and confusion documents, i.e. news sources describing the answer and the confusion incidents correspondingly 4. have a high temporal spread with respect to the publishing dates reporting on each incident from the answer and confusion incidents 5. have a high ambiguity with respect to the surface forms of an event property value in a granularity level (e.g. we would favor *Wilmington*, since it is a city in at least three US states in our task data).

5.4 Data Partitioning

We divided the overall task data into two partitions: **trial** and **test** data. In practice, we separated these two data partitions by reserving one year of news documents (2017) from our task for the trial data, while using all the other data as test data.

The trial data stems from the gun violence domain, whereas the test data also contains data from the fire incidents and business domain. A subset of the trial and test data has been annotated for event coreference. Table 3 presents the most important statistics of the trial and test data.

	S	#Qs	Avg answer	Avg # answer docs
trial	1	424	1.00	1.68
	2	469	4.22	7.68
	3	585	5.48	5.47
test	1	1032	1.00	1.60
	2	997	3.79	6.64
	3	2456	3.66	3.74

Table 3: General statistics about trial and test data. For each subtask (*S*), we show the number of questions (*#Qs*), the average answer (*Avg answer*), and the average number of answer documents (*Avg # answer docs*).

We made an effort to make the trial data representative for the test data with respect to the main aspects of our task: its referential complexity, high confusability, and long-tail instances. Despite the fact that the trial data contains less questions than the test data, Table 3 shows that it is similar to the test data with respect to the core properties, meaning that the trial data can be used as training data.

6 Evaluation

This Section describes the evaluation criteria in this task and the baselines we compare against.

6.1 Criteria

Evaluation is performed on three levels: incident-level, document-level, and mention-level.

The incident-level evaluation compares the numeric answer provided by the system to the gold answer for each of the questions. The comparison is done twofold: by exact matching and by Root Mean Square Error (RMSE) for difference scoring. The scores per subtask are then averaged over all questions to compute a single incident-level evaluation score.

The document-level evaluation compares the set of answer documents between the system and the gold standard, resulting in a value for the customary metrics of Precision, Recall, and F1 per question. The scores per subtask are then averaged over all questions to compute a single document-level evaluation score.

The mention-level evaluation is a cross-document event coreference evaluation. Mention-level evaluation is only done for questions with the event types *killing* or *injuring*. We apply the customary metrics to score the event coreference: BCUB (Bagga and Baldwin, 1998), BLANC (Recasens and Hovy, 2011), entity-based CEAF (CEAF_E) and mention-based CEAF (CEAF_M) (Luo, 2005), and MUC (Vilain et al., 1995). The final F1-score is the average of the F1-scores of the individual metrics. The set of mentions to annotate should conform to the schema defined in the task annotation guidelines.[11]

6.2 Baselines

To stimulate participation in general and to stimulate approaches beyond surface form or majority class strategies, we implemented one baseline to infer incidents per subtask and one baseline for mention annotation.[12]

Incident inference baseline This baseline uses surface forms based on the question components to find the answer documents. We only consider documents that contain the label of the event type or at least one of its WordNet synonyms. The labels of locations and participants are queried directly in the document (e.g. if the location requested is the *US state of Texas*, then we only consider documents that contain the surface form *Texas*, and similarly for participants such as *John*). The temporal constraint is handled differently: we only consider documents whose publishing date falls within the time requested in the question.

For subtask 1, this baseline assumes that all documents that fit the created constraints are referring

---

[11]Link to the guidelines: `https://goo.gl/8JpwCE`.
[12]The code of the baselines can be found here: `https://goo.gl/MwSqBj`.

to the same incident. If there is no such document, then the baseline does not answer the question (because S1 always has at least one supporting document). For subtask 2, we assume that none of the documents are coreferential. Hence, if 10 documents match the constraints, we infer that there are also 10 corresponding incidents. No baseline was implemented for subtask 3.

Mention annotation baseline We annotate mentions of events of type *killing* and *injuring*, when these surface forms or their synonyms in WordNet are found as tokens in a document. We assume that all mentions of the same event type within a document are coreferential, whereas all mentions found in different documents are not.

7 Participants

In this Section, we describe the systems that took part in SemEval-2018 task 5. We refer to the individual system papers for further information.

NewsReader (Vossen, 2018) consists of three steps: 1. the event mentions in the input documents are represented as Event-Centric Knowledge Graphs (ECKGs). 2. the ECKGs of all documents are compared to each other to decide which documents refer to the same incident, resulting in an incident-document index. 3. the constraints of each question (its event type, time, participant names, and location) are matched with the stored ECKGs, resulting in a number of incidents and source documents for each question.

NAI-SEA (Liu and Li, 2018) consists of three components: 1. extraction of basic information on time, location, and participants with regular expressions, named entity recognition, and term matching; 2. event classification with an SVM classifier; 3. document similarity by applying a classifier to detect similar documents. In terms of resources, NAI-SEA combines the training data with data on American cities, counties, and states.

Team **FEUP** (Abreu and Oliveira, 2018) developed an experimental system to extract entities from news articles for the sake of Question & Answering. For this main task, the team proposed a supervised learning approach to enable the recognition of two different types of entities: Locations (e.g. *Birmingham*) and Participants (e.g. *John List*). They have also studied the use of distance-based algorithms (using Levenshtein distance and Q-grams) for the detection of documents' closeness based on entities extracted.

Team **ID-DE** (Mirza et al., 2018) created KOI (Knowledge of Incidents), a system that builds a knowledge graph of incidents, given news articles as input. The required steps include: 1. Document preprocessing using various semantic NLP tasks such as Word Sense Disambiguation, Named-Entity Recognition, Temporal expression recognition, and Semantic Role Labeling. 2. Incident extraction and document clustering based on the output of step 1. 3. Ontology construction to capture the knowledge model from incidents and documents which makes it possible to run SPARQL queries on the ontology to answer the questions.

8 Results

R	Team	s2_inc_acc norm	s2_inc_acc (% of Qs answered)	s2_inc rmse
1	FEUP	**26.38**	26.38 (100.0%)	6.13
2	*NewsReader	21.87	21.87 (100.0%)	43.96
3	Baseline	18.25	18.25 (100.0%)	8.50
4	NAI-SEA	17.35	17.35 (100.0%)	20.59
5	ID-DE	13.74	20.36 (67.5%)	6.15

Table 4: For subtask 2, we report the normalized incident-level accuracy (*s2_inc_acc norm*), the accuracy on the answered questions only (*s2_inc_acc*), and the RMSE value (*s2_inc rmse*). Systems are ordered by their rank (*R*).

R	Team	s3_inc_acc norm	s3_inc_acc (% of Qs answered)	s3_inc rmse
1	FEUP	**30.42**	30.42 (100.0%)	478.71
2	*NewsReader	21.05	21.05 (100.0%)	296.45
3	NAI-SEA	20.20	20.2 (100.0%)	13.45
4	ID-DE	12.87	19.32 (66.61%)	7.87

Table 5: For subtask 3, we report the normalized incident-level accuracy (*s3_inc_acc norm*), the accuracy on the answered questions only (*s3_inc_acc*), and the RMSE value (*s3_inc rmse*). Systems are ordered by their rank (*R*).

Before we report the system results, we introduce a few clarifications regarding the result tables:

1. For the incident- and document-level evaluation, we report both the performance with respect to the subset of questions answered and a **normalized score**, which indicates the performance on all questions of a subtask. If a submission provides answers for all questions, the normalized score will be the same as the non-normalized score.

2. Contrary to the other metrics, a lower **RMSE** value indicates better system performance. In addition, the RMSE scores have not been normalized since it is not reasonable to set a default value for non-answered questions.

3. **The mention-level evaluation** was the same across all three subtasks. For this reason, results are only reported once (see Section 8.3).

4. The teams whose member **co-organized SemEval-2018 task 5** are marked explicitly with an asterisk in the results.

8.1 Incident-level evaluation

The incident-level evaluation assesses whether the system provided the right numeric answer to a question. The results of this evaluation are given in the Tables 4 and 5, for the subtasks 2 and 3 correspondingly.[13] On both subtasks, the order of the participating systems is identical, team *FEUP* having the highest score.

These tables also show the RMSE values, which measure the proximity between the system and the gold answer, punishing cases where the absolute difference between them is large. While for subtask 2 the system with the lowest error rate corresponds to the system with the highest accuracy, this is different for subtask 3. *NAI-SEA*, ranked third in terms of accuracy, has the lowest RMSE. This means that although their answers were not exactly correct, they were on average much closer to the correct answer than those of the other systems. This is more notable in subtask 3 since here the range of answers is larger than in subtask 2 (the maximum answer in subtask 3 is 171).

We performed additional analysis to compare the performance of systems per subtype and per numeric answer class. Table 6 shows that the system *FEUP* is not only superior in terms of incident-level accuracy overall, but this is also mirrored for most of the event types, especially those corresponding to the gun violence domain. On the other hand, Figure 2 shows the accuracy distribution of each system per answer class. Notably, for most systems the accuracy is highest for the questions with answer 0 or 1, and gradually declines for higher answers, forming a Zipfian-like distribution. The exception here is the team *ID-DE*, whose accuracy is almost uniformly spread across the various answer classes.

8.2 Document-level evaluation

The intent behind document-level evaluation is to assess the ability of systems to distinguish between answer and non-answer documents. The tables 9, 10, and 11 present the F1-scores for the

---

[13] Incident-level evaluation was not performed for subtask 1, because per definition, its answer is always 1.

subtasks 1, 2, and 3, respectively. Curiously, the system ranking is very different and almost opposite compared to the incident-level rankings, with the system *NAI-SEA* being the one with the highest F1-score. This can be explained by the multifaceted nature of this task, in which different systems may optimize for different goals.

Next, we investigated the F1-scores of systems per event property pair. As shown in Table 7, the best-performing system consistently has the highest performance over all pairs of event properties.

R	Team	s1_doc_f1 norm	s1_doc_f1 (% of Qs answered)
1	NAI-SEA	**78.33**	78.33 (100.0%)
2	ID-DE	36.67	82.99 (44.19%)
3	FEUP	24.65	24.65 (100.0%)
4	*NewsReader	23.82	46.2 (51.55%)
5	Baseline	11.09	67.33 (16.47%)

Table 9: For subtask 1, we report the normalized document-level F1 (*s1_doc_f1 norm*) and the accuracy on the answered questions only (*s1_doc_f1*). Systems are ordered by their rank (*R*).

R	Team	s2_doc_f1 norm	s2_doc_f1 (% of Qs answered)
1	NAI-SEA	**50.52**	50.52 (100.0%)
2	ID-DE	37.24	55.16 (67.5%)
3	*NewsReader	36.91	36.91 (100.0%)
4	FEUP	30.51	30.51 (100.0%)
5	Baseline	26.38	26.38 (100.0%)

Table 10: For subtask 2, we report the normalized document-level F1 (*s2_doc_f1 norm*) and the accuracy on the answered questions only (*s2_doc_f1*). Systems are ordered by their rank (*R*).

R	Team	s3_doc_f1 norm	s3_doc_f1 (% of Qs answered)
1	NAI-SEA	**63.59**	63.59 (100.0%)
2	ID-DE	46.33	69.56 (66.61%)
3	*NewsReader	26.84	26.84 (100.0%)
4	FEUP	26.79	26.79 (100.0%)

Table 11: For subtask 3, we report the normalized document-level F1 (*s3_doc_f1 norm*) and the accuracy on the answered questions only (*s3_doc_f1*). Systems are ordered by their rank (*R*).

8.3 Mention-level evaluation

Table 8 shows the event coreference results for the participating systems: *ID-DE* and *NewsReader*, as well as our baseline. The columns present the F1-score for the metrics BCUB, BLANC, CEAF_E. CEAF_M, and MUC. The final column indicates

Event type	Subtask	#Qs	FEUP	ID-DE	NAI-SEA	*NewsReader	Baseline
fire_burning	S2	79	40.51	-	31.65	39.24	**49.37**
	S3	0	-	-	-	-	-
injuring	S2	543	**21.92**	^13.44	14.36	21.73	17.68
	S3	1502	**30.49**	^8.39	16.78	23.17	-
job_firing	S2	4	0.0	-	25.0	25.0	**50.0**
	S3	26	**30.77**	-	26.92	15.38	-
killing	S2	371	**30.19**	^17.25	18.6	18.33	12.13
	S3	928	**30.28**	^20.47	25.54	17.78	-

Table 6: For subtask 2 (*S2*) and subtask 3 (*S3*), we report the incident-level accuracy and the number of questions (*#Qs*) per event type. The best result per event type for a subtask is marked in bold. '^' indicates that the accuracy is normalized for the number of answered questions, in cases where a system answered a subset of all questions.

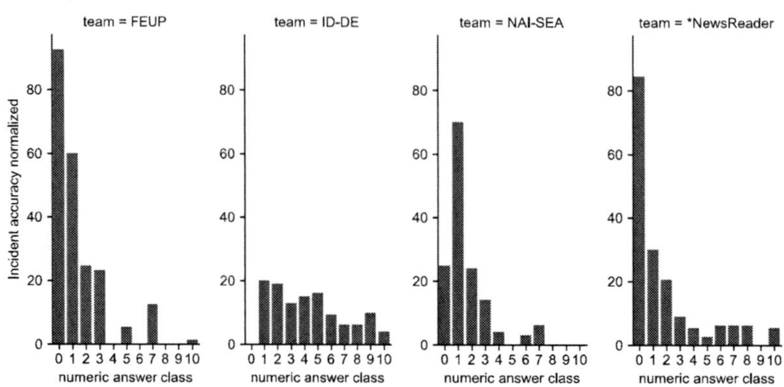

Figure 2: Incident-level accuracy of all systems per numeric answer class for subtask 2. The class *10* represents all answers of 10 or higher.

Event properties	Subtask	#Qs	FEUP	ID-DE	NAI-SEA	*NewsReader	Baseline
location&time	S1	594	23.06	^26.64	**82.91**	^26.22	^8.71
	S2	680	30.95	^41.81	**49.99**	39.22	28.61
	S3	1335	26.4	^41.55	**63.27**	36.15	-
participant&location	S1	140	13.48	^43.86	**70.22**	^11.83	^9.76
	S2	49	14.66	^21.26	**50.41**	13.53	10.02
	S3	301	14.2	^44.28	**62.38**	6.65	-
participant&time	S1	298	33.06	^53.28	**73.01**	^24.65	^16.47
	S2	268	32.27	^28.55	**51.87**	35.34	23.71
	S3	820	32.06	^54.88	**64.56**	19.09	-

Table 7: Document-level F1-score and number of questions (*#Qs*) for each subtask (*S1, S2, and S3*) and event property pair as given in the task questions. The best result per property pair for a subtask is marked in bold. '^' indicates that the F1-score is normalized for the number of answered questions, in cases where a system answered a subset of all questions.

R	Team	BCUB	BLANC	CEAF_E	CEAF_M	MUC	AVG
1	ID-DE	**44.61%**	**31.59%**	37.45%	**47.23%**	**53.12%**	**42.8%**
2	*NewsReader	37.28%	28.11%	**42.15%**	46.16%	46.29%	40.0%
3	Baseline	6.14%	0.89%	13.3%	8.45%	3.59%	6.47%

Table 8: Results for mention-level evaluation, scored with the customary event coreference metrics: BCUB (Bagga and Baldwin, 1998), BLANC (Recasens and Hovy, 2011), entity-based CEAF (CEAF_E) and mention-based CEAF (CEAF_M) (Luo, 2005), and MUC (Vilain et al., 1995). The individual scores are averaged in a single number (*AVG*), which is used to rank (*R*) the systems.

the mean F1-score over these five metrics, which is used to rank the participants. The Table shows that the system *ID-DE* has a slightly better event coreference score on average over all metrics than the second-ranked system, *NewsReader*.

9 Conclusions

In this paper we have introduced SemEval-2018 Task 5, a referential quantification task of counting events and participants in local news articles with high ambiguity. The complexity of this task challenges systems to establish the meaning, reference, and identity across documents. SemEval-2018 Task 5 consists of two subtasks of counting events, and one subtask of counting event participants in their corresponding roles. We evaluated system performance with a set of metrics, on three levels: incident-, document-, and mention-level.

We described the approaches and presented the results of four participating systems, as well as two baseline algorithms. All four teams submitted a result for all three subtasks, and two teams participated in the mention-level evaluation. We observed that the ranking of systems differs dramatically per evaluation level. Given the multifaceted nature of this task, it is not surprising that different systems optimized for different goals. Although the systems are able to retrieve many of the answer documents, the highest accuracy of counting events or participants is 30%. This suggests that further research is necessary in order to develop complete and robust models that can natively deal with the challenge of counting referential units within sparse and ambiguous textual data.

Out-of-competition participation is enabled by the Codalab platform, where this task was hosted.

References

Carla Abreu and Eugénio Oliveira. 2018. FEUP at SemEval-2018 Task 5: An Experimental Study of a Question Answering System. In *Proceedings of the 12th International Workshop on Semantic Evaluation (SemEval-2018)*. Association for Computational Linguistics.

Amit Bagga and Breck Baldwin. 1998. Algorithms for scoring coreference chains. In *The first international conference on language resources and evaluation workshop on linguistics coreference*, volume 1, pages 563–566. Granada.

David Corney, Dyaa Albakour, Miguel Martinez, and Samir Moussa. 2016. What do a million news articles look like? In *Proceedings of the First International Workshop on Recent Trends in News Information Retrieval co-located with 38th European Conference on Information Retrieval (ECIR 2016), Padua, Italy, March 20, 2016.*, pages 42–47.

Collin F. Baker, Charles J. Fillmore, and John B. Lowe. 1998. The Berkeley FrameNet Project. In *COLING 1998 Volume 1: The 17th International Conference on Computational Linguistics*.

Christiane Fellbaum, editor. 1998. *WordNet: An Electronic Lexical Database* . The MIT Press, Cambridge, MA ; London.

Karl Moritz Hermann, Tomas Kocisky, Edward Grefenstette, Lasse Espeholt, Will Kay, Mustafa Suleyman, and Phil Blunsom. 2015. Teaching machines to read and comprehend. In *Advances in Neural Information Processing Systems*, pages 1693–1701.

Daniel Hewlett, Alexandre Lacoste, Llion Jones, Illia Polosukhin, Andrew Fandrianto, Jay Han, Matthew Kelcey, and David Berthelot. 2016. WikiReading: A Novel Large-scale Language Understanding Task over Wikipedia. In *Proceedings of the 54th Annual Meeting of the Association for Computational Linguistics (Volume 1: Long Papers)*, pages 1535–1545. Association for Computational Linguistics.

Filip Ilievski, Marten Postma, and Piek Vossen. 2016. Semantic overfitting: what 'world' do we consider when evaluating disambiguation of text? In *Proceedings of COLING 2016, the 26th International Conference on Computational Linguistics: Technical Papers*, pages 1180–1191. The COLING 2016 Organizing Committee.

Mohit Iyyer, Jordan L Boyd-Graber, Leonardo Max Batista Claudino, Richard Socher, and Hal Daumé III. 2014. A Neural Network for Factoid Question Answering over Paragraphs. In *EMNLP*, pages 633–644.

Yingchi Liu and Quanzhi Li. 2018. NAI-SEA at SemEval-2018 Task 5: An Event Search System. In *Proceedings of the 12th International Workshop on Semantic Evaluation (SemEval-2018)*. Association for Computational Linguistics.

Xiaoqiang Luo. 2005. On coreference resolution performance metrics. In *Proceedings of the conference on human language technology and empirical methods in natural language processing*, pages 25–32. Association for Computational Linguistics.

Paramita Mirza, Fariz Darari, and Rahmad Mahendra. 2018. KOI at SemEval-2018 Task 5: Building Knowledge Graph of Incidents. In *Proceedings of the 12th International Workshop on Semantic Evaluation (SemEval-2018)*. Association for Computational Linguistics.

Preslav Nakov, Lluís Màrquez, Walid Magdy, Alessandro Moschitti, Jim Glass, and Bilal Randeree. 2015. Semeval-2015 task 3: Answer selection in community question answering. In *Proceedings of the 9th International Workshop on Semantic Evaluation (SemEval 2015)*, pages 269–281. Association for Computational Linguistics.

Preslav Nakov, Lluís Màrquez, Alessandro Moschitti, Walid Magdy, Hamdy Mubarak, abed Alhakim Freihat, Jim Glass, and Bilal Randeree. 2016. Semeval-2016 task 3: Community question answering. In *Proceedings of the 10th International Workshop on Semantic Evaluation (SemEval-2016)*, pages 525–545. Association for Computational Linguistics.

Tri Nguyen, Mir Rosenberg, Xia Song, Jianfeng Gao, Saurabh Tiwary, Rangan Majumder, and Li Deng. 2016. MS MARCO: A Human Generated MAchine Reading COmprehension Dataset. *CoRR*, abs/1611.09268.

Marten Postma, Filip Ilievski, Piek Vossen, and Marieke van Erp. 2016. Moving away from semantic overfitting in disambiguation datasets. In *Proceedings of the Workshop on Uphill Battles in Language Processing: Scaling Early Achievements to Robust Methods*, pages 17–21, Austin, TX. Association for Computational Linguistics.

Pranav Rajpurkar, Jian Zhang, Konstantin Lopyrev, and Percy Liang. 2016. SQuAD: 100, 000+ Questions for Machine Comprehension of Text. *CoRR*, abs/1606.05250.

Marta Recasens and Eduard Hovy. 2011. BLANC: Implementing the Rand index for coreference evaluation. *Natural Language Engineering*, 17(4):485–510.

Matthew Richardson, Christopher JC Burges, and Erin Renshaw. 2013. MCTest: A Challenge Dataset for the Open-Domain Machine Comprehension of Text. In *EMNLP*, volume 3, page 4.

Marc Vilain, John Burger, John Aberdeen, Dennis Connolly, and Lynette Hirschman. 1995. A model-theoretic coreference scoring scheme. In *Proceedings of the 6th conference on Message understanding*, pages 45–52. Association for Computational Linguistics.

Piek Vossen. 2018. NewsReader at SemEval-2018 Task 5: Counting events by reasoning over event-centric-knowledge-graphs. In *Proceedings of the 12th International Workshop on Semantic Evaluation (SemEval-2018)*. Association for Computational Linguistics.

Mengqiu Wang, Noah A Smith, and Teruko Mitamura. 2007. What is the Jeopardy Model? A Quasi-Synchronous Grammar for QA. In *EMNLP-CoNLL*, volume 7, pages 22–32.

Jason Weston, Antoine Bordes, Sumit Chopra, Alexander M Rush, Bart van Merriënboer, Armand Joulin, and Tomas Mikolov. 2015. Towards AI-complete question answering: A set of prerequisite toy tasks. *arXiv preprint arXiv:1502.05698*.

Yi Yang, Wen-tau Yih, and Christopher Meek. 2015. WikiQA: A Challenge Dataset for Open-Domain Question Answering. In *Proceedings of EMNLP*, pages 2013–2018. Citeseer.

KOI at SemEval-2018 Task 5: Building Knowledge Graph of Incidents

Paramita Mirza,[1] **Fariz Darari,**[2*] **Rahmad Mahendra**[2*]

[1] Max Planck Institute for Informatics, Germany
[2] Faculty of Computer Science, Universitas Indonesia, Indonesia
`{paramita}@mpi-inf.mpg.de`
`{fariz,rahmad.mahendra}@cs.ui.ac.id`

Abstract

We present KOI (Knowledge of Incidents), a system that given news articles as input, builds a knowledge graph (KOI-KG) of incidental events. KOI-KG can then be used to efficiently answer questions such as *"How many killing incidents happened in 2017 that involve Sean?"* The required steps in building the KG include: *(i)* document preprocessing involving word sense disambiguation, named-entity recognition, temporal expression recognition and normalization, and semantic role labeling; *(ii)* incidental event extraction and coreference resolution via document clustering; and *(iii)* KG construction and population.

1 Introduction

SemEval-2018[1] Task 5: *Counting Events and Participants in the Long Tail* (Postma et al., 2018) addresses the problem of *referential quantification* that requires a system to answer numerical questions about events such as *(i) "How many killing incidents happened in June 2016 in San Antonio, Texas?"* or *(ii) "How many people were killed in June 2016 in San Antonio, Texas?"*

Subtasks S1 and S2 For questions of type *(i)*, which are asked by the first two subtasks, participating systems must be able to identify the type (e.g., *killing, injuring*), time, location and participants of each event occurring in a given news article, and establish within- and cross-document event coreference links. Subtask S1 focuses on evaluating systems' performances on identifying *answer incidents*, i.e., events whose properties fit the constraints of the questions, by making sure that there is only *one* answer incident per question.

Subtask S3 In order to answer questions of type *(ii)*, participating systems are also required to identify participant roles in each identified answer incident (e.g., *victim, subject-suspect*), and use such information along with victim-related numerals (*"three people were killed"*) mentioned in the corresponding *answer documents*, i.e., documents that report on the answer incident, to determine the total number of victims.

Datasets The organizers released two datasets: *(i) test data*, stemming from three domains of gun violence, fire disasters and business, and *(ii) trial data*, covering only the gun violence domain. Each dataset contains *(i)* an input document (in CoNLL format) that comprises news articles, and *(ii)* a set of questions (in JSON format) to evaluate the participating systems.[2]

This paper describes the KOI (Knowledge of Incidents) system submitted to SemEval-2018 Task 5, which constructs and populates a knowledge graph of incidental events mentioned in news articles, to be used to retrieve answer incidents and answer documents given numerical questions about events. We propose a fully unsupervised approach to identify events and their properties in news texts, and to resolve within- and cross-document event coreference, which will be detailed in the following section.

2 System Description

2.1 Document Preprocessing

Given an input document in CoNLL format (one token per line), for each news article, we first split the sentences following the annotation of: *(i)* whether a token is part of the article title or content; *(ii)* sentence identifier; and *(iii)* whether a to-

---

* Both share the same amount of work.
[1] `http://alt.qcri.org/semeval2018/`

[2] `https://competitions.codalab.org/competitions/17285`

Proceedings of the 12th International Workshop on Semantic Evaluation (SemEval-2018), pages 81–87
New Orleans, Louisiana, June 5–6, 2018. ©2018 Association for Computational Linguistics

ken is a newline character. We then ran several tools on the tokenized sentences to obtain the following NLP annotations.

Word sense disambiguation (WSD) We ran Babelfy[3] (Moro et al., 2014) to get disambiguated *concepts* (excluding stop-words), which can be multi-word expressions, e.g., *gunshot wound*. Each concept is linked to a sense in BabelNet[4] (Navigli and Ponzetto, 2012), which subsequently is also linked to a WordNet sense and a DBpedia entity (if any).

Named-entity recognition (NER) We relied on spaCy[5] for a statistical entity recognition, specifically for identifying persons and geopolitical entities (countries, cities, and states).

Time expression recognition and normalization We used HeidelTime[6] (Strötgen and Gertz, 2013) for recognizing textual spans that indicate time, e.g., *this Monday*, and normalizing the time expressions according to a given document creation time, e.g., *2018-03-05*.

Semantic role labeling (SRL) Senna[7] (Collobert et al., 2011) was used to run semantic parsing on the input text, for identifying sentence-level events (i.e., predicates) and their participants.

2.2 Event Extraction and Coreference Resolution

Identifying document-level events Sentence-level events, i.e., *predicates* recognized by the SRL tool, were considered as the candidates for the document-level events. Note that predicates containing other predicates as the patient argument, e.g., *'says'* with arguments *'police'* as its agent and *'one man was shot to death'* as its patient, were not considered as candidate events.

Given a predicate, we simultaneously determined whether it is part of document-level events and also identified its type, based on the occurrence of *BabelNet concepts* that are related to four event types of interest stated in the task guidelines: *killing, injuring, fire burning* and *job firing*. A predicate is automatically labeled as a sentence-level event with one of the four types if such re-

lated concepts occur either in the predicate itself or in one of its arguments. For example, a predicate *'shot'*, with arguments *'one man'* as its patient and *'to death'* as its manner, will be considered as a *killing* event because of the occurrence of *'death'* concept.[8]

Concept relatedness was computed via path-based WordNet similarity (Hirst et al., 1998) of a given BabelNet concept, which is linked to a WordNet sense, with a predefined set of related WordNet senses for each event type (e.g., *wn30:killing.n.02* and *wn30:kill.v.01* for the killing event), setting 5.0 as the threshold. Related concepts were also annotated with the corresponding event types, to be used for the mention-level event coreference evaluation.

We then assumed all identified sentence-level events in a news article belonging to the same event type to be automatically regarded as *one* document-level event, meaning that each article may contain at most four document-level events (i.e., at most one event per event type).

Identifying document-level event participants Given a predicate as an identified event, its participants were simply extracted from the occurrence of named entities of type *person*, according to both Senna and spaCy, in the agent and patient arguments of the predicate. Furthermore, we determined the role of each participant as *victim, perpetrator* or *other*, based on its mention in the predicate. For example, if *'Randall'* is mentioned as the agent argument of the predicate *'shot'*, then he is a perpetrator. Note that a participant can have multiple roles, as is the case for a person who kills himself.

Taking into account all participants of a set of identified events (per event type) in a news article, we extracted document-level event participants by resolving name coreference. For instance, *'Randall'*, *'Randall R. Coffland'*, and *'Randall Coffland'* all refer to the same person.

Identifying document-level number of victims For each identified predicate in a given document, we extracted the first existing *numeral* in the patient argument of the predicate, e.g., *one* in *'one man'*. The normalized value of the numeral was then taken as the number of victims, as long as the predicate is not suspect-related predicates such

---

[3]http://babelfy.org/
[4]http://babelnet.org/
[5]https://spacy.io/
[6]https://github.com/HeidelTime/heideltime
[7]https://ronan.collobert.com/senna/

[8]We assume that a predicate that is labeled as a *killing* event cannot be labeled as an *injuring* event even though an injuring-related concept such as *'shot'* occurs.

as *suspected* or *charged*. The number of victims of document-level events is simply the maximum value of identified number of victims per predicate.

Identifying document-level event locations   To retrieve candidate event locations given a document, we relied on disambiguated DBpedia entities as a result of Babelfy annotation. We utilized SPARQL queries over the *DBpedia SPARQL endpoint*[9] to identify whether a DBpedia entity is a *city* or a *state*, and whether it is *part of* or *located in* a city or a state. Specifically, an entity is considered to be a city whenever it is of type `dbo:City` or its equivalent types (e.g., `schema:City`). Similarly, it is considered to be a state whenever it is either of type `yago:WikicatStatesOfTheUnitedStates`, has a senator (via the property `dbp:senators`), or has `dbc:States_of_the_United_States` as a subject.

Assuming that document-level events identified in a given news article happen at *one* certain location, we simply ranked the candidate event locations, i.e., pairs of city and state, based on their frequencies, and took the one with the highest frequency.

Identifying document-level event times   Given a document D, suppose we have dct as the document creation time and T as a list of normalized time expressions returned by HeidelTime, whose types are either `date` or `time`. We considered a time expression $t_i \in T$ as one of candidate event times $T' \subseteq T$, if $dct - t_i$ is a non-negative integer less than n days.[10] We hypothesize that the event reported in a news article may have happened several days before the news is published.

Assuming that document-level events identified in a given news article happen at *one* certain time, we determine which one is the document-level event time from the set of candidates T' by applying two heuristics: A time expression $t_j \in T'$ is considered as the event time, if *(i)* t_j is mentioned in sentences containing event-related concepts, and *(ii)* t_j is the earliest time expression in the candidate set.

Cross-document event coreference resolution
We approached cross-document event coreference by clustering similar document-level events that

Resource Type	Properties
IncidentEvent	*eventType, eventDate, location, participant, numOfVictims*
Document	*docDate, docID, event*
Participant	*fullname, firstname, lastname, role*
Location	*city, state*
Date	*value, day, month, year*

Table 1: KOI-KG ontology

are of the same type, via their *provenance*, i.e., news articles where they were mentioned. From each news article we derived TF-IDF-based vectors of *(i)* BabelNet senses and *(ii)* spaCy's persons and geopolitical entities, which are then used to compute cosine similarities among the articles.

Two news articles will be clustered together if *(i)* the computed similarity is above a certain threshold, which was optimized using the trial data, and *(ii)* the event time distance of document-level events found in the articles does not exceed a certain threshold, i.e., 3 days. All document-level events belonging to the same document cluster are assumed to be coreferring events and to have properties resulting from the aggregation of locations, times and participants of contributing events, with the exception of number of victims where the maximum value was taken instead.

2.3   Constructing, Populating and Querying the Knowledge Graph

We first built an *OWL ontology*[11] to capture the knowledge model of incidental events and documents. We rely on reification (Noy and Rector, 2006) for modeling entities, that is, incident events, documents, locations, participants and dates are all resources of their own. Each resource is described through its corresponding properties, as shown in Table 1.

An incident event can be of type *injuring*, *killing*, *fire_burning*, and *job_firing*. Documents are linked to incident events through the property *event*, and different documents may refer to the same corresponding incident event. We borrow URIs from DBpedia for values of the properties *city* and *state*. Participant roles can be either *victim*, *perpetrator* or *other*. A date has a unified literal value of the format "yyyy-mm-dd", as well as separated values for the day, month, and year.

To build the KOI knowledge graph (KOI-KG)

```
SELECT ?event ?document
WHERE {
  ?event koi:eventType koi:killing .
  ?event koi:eventDate [
    koi:year "2017" ] .
  ?event koi:participant [
    koi:firstname "Sean" ] .
  ?document koi:event ?event .
}
```

Figure 1: A SPARQL query over KOI-KG for "Which killing events happened in 2017 that involve persons with Sean as first name?"

we relied on Apache Jena,[12] a Java-based Semantic Web framework. The output of the previously explained event extraction and coreference resolution steps was imported into the Jena TDB triple store as RDF triples. This facilitates SPARQL querying, which can be done using the Jena ARQ module. The whole dump of KOI-KG is available for download at `https://koi.cs.ui.ac.id/incidents`.

Given a question in JSON format, we applied mapping rules to transform it into a SPARQL query, which was then used to retrieve corresponding *answer incidents* and *answer documents*. Constraints of questions such as event type, participant, date, and location were mapped into SPARQL join conditions (that is, triple patterns). Figure 1 shows a SPARQL representation for the question "Which killing events happened in 2017 that involve persons with Sean as first name?". The prefix *koi* is for the KOI ontology namespace (`https://koi.cs.ui.ac.id/ns#`). In the SPARQL query, the join conditions are over the event type *killing*, the date *'2017'* (as year) and the participant *'Sean'* (as firstname).

For Subtask S2, we extended the SPARQL query with counting feature to retrieve the total number of unique events. Analogously, for Subtask S3, we retrieve number of victims by counting event participants having *victim* as their roles, and by getting the value of the *numOfVictims* property (if any). The value of the *numOfVictims* property was preferred as the final value for an incident if it exists, otherwise, KOI relied on counting event participants.

We also provide a SPARQL query interface for KOI-KG at `https://koi.cs.ui.ac.id/dataset.html?tab=query&ds=/incidents`.

---

[12]`http://jena.apache.org/`

3 Results and Discussion

Evaluation results Participating systems were evaluated according to three evaluation schemes: *(i) mention-level evaluation*, for resolving cross-document coreference of event mentions, *(ii) document-level evaluation* (`doc-f1`), for identifying events and their properties given a document, and *(iii) incident-level evaluation*, for combining event extraction and within-/cross-document event coreference resolution to answer numerical questions in terms of exact matching (`inc-acc`) and Root Mean Square Error (`inc-rmse`). Furthermore, the percentage of questions in each subtask that can be answered by the systems (`%ans`) also contributes to the final ranking.

Regarding the *mention-level evaluation*, KOI achieves an average F1-score of 42.8% (36.3 percentage point increase over the baseline) from several established metrics for evaluating coreference resolution systems. For *document-level* and *incident-level evaluation* schemes, we report in Table 2 the performance of three different system runs of KOI:

v1 Submitted version of KOI during the *evaluation period*.

v2 Similar as v1, however, instead of giving no answers when we found no matching *answer incidents*, KOI simply returns *zero* as the numerical answer with an empty list of *answer documents*.

v3 Submitted version of KOI during the *post-evaluation period*, which incorporates improvement on document-level event time identification leading to enhanced cross-document event coreference.[13]

Compared to the baseline provided by the task organizers, the performance of KOI is considerably better, specifically of KOI v3 for subtask S2 with `doc-f1` and `inc-acc` around twice as much as of the baseline. Hereafter, our quantitative and qualitative analyses are based on KOI v3, and mentions of the KOI system refer to this system run.

Subtask S1 We detail in Table 3, the performance of KOI on retrieving relevant *answer documents* given questions with event constraints,

---

[13]Submission v1 and v2 did not consider heuristic *(i)* that we have discussed in Section 2.2.

system run	subtask S1		subtask S2				subtask S3			
	%ans	doc-f1	%ans	doc-f1	inc-acc	inc-rmse	%ans	doc-f1	inc-acc	inc-rmse
baseline	*16.5*	*67.3*	*100.0*	*26.4*	*18.3*	*8.5*	-	-	-	-
KOI v1*	44.2	83.0	67.5	55.2	20.4	6.2	66.6	69.6	19.3	7.9
KOI v2	44.2	83.0	100.0	51.2	25.6	5.2	100.0	49.1	24.8	7.1
KOI v3	55.1	85.7	100.0	54.8	27.4	5.3	100.0	50.9	23.0	7.7

Table 2: KOI performance results at SemEval-2018 Task 5 (in percentages) for three subtasks, *baseline* was provided by the task organizers, *) denotes the system run that we submitted during the evaluation period.

	micro-averaged			macro-averaged		
	p	r	f1	p	r	f1
Overall						
answered questions	86.6	74.0	79.8	94.2	83.6	85.7
all questions	86.6	41.6	56.2	51.7	45.9	47.1
Event type						
killing	88.5	43.2	58.1	56.8	48.6	50.3
injuring	82.8	37.4	51.5	46.4	40.1	41.4
job_firing	100.0	8.7	16.0	15.4	15.4	15.4
fire_burning	96.9	66.2	78.7	65.5	66.2	65.7
Event constraint						
participant	84.8	43.0	57.0	61.1	51.1	53.2
location	89.1	39.4	54.6	46.7	42.8	43.6
time	86.0	42.4	56.8	51.7	46.3	47.4

Table 3: KOI performance results for subtask S1, on *answer document* retrieval (p for precision, r for recall and f1 for F1-score).

	subtask S2		subtask S3	
	inc-acc	inc-rmse	inc-acc	inc-rmse
overall	27.4	5.3	23.0	7.7
zero	96.3	0.2	55.2	6.8
non-zero	18.9	5.6	11.9	8.0

Table 4: KOI performance results for subtasks S2 and S3, on answering numerical questions, i.e., number of incidents and number of victims.

in terms of *micro-averaged* and *macro-averaged* scores. Note that the official `doc-f1` scores reported in Table 2 correspond to macro-averaged F1-scores.

We first analyzed the system performance only on *answered questions*, i.e., for which KOI returns the relevant answer documents (55.1% of all questions), yielding 79.8% and 85.7% micro-averaged and macro-averaged F1-scores, respectively.

In order to have a fair comparison with systems that are able to answer *all questions*, we also report the performance of KOI that returns empty sets of answer documents for unanswered questions. In this evaluation scheme, the macro-averaged precision is significantly lower than the micro-averaged one (51.7% vs 86.6%), because systems are heavily penalized for not retrieving relevant answer documents per question, i.e., given zero precision score, which brings the average over all questions down. Meanwhile, the micro-averaged precision measures the systems' ability in returning relevant documents for all questions regardless of whether the questions were answered or not. KOI focuses on yielding high quality answer documents, which is reflected by high micro-averaged precision of above 80% in general. The following result analy-

ses are based on the *all questions* scheme.

By analyzing the document retrieval per event type, we found that KOI can identify *fire_burning* events in documents quite well, yielding the highest recall among all event types, but the contrary for *job_firing* events. With respect to event constraints, answering questions with *location* constraint results in the worst performance, meaning that our method is still lacking in identifying and/or disambiguating event locations from news documents. Specifically, questions with *city* constraint are more difficult to answer compared to the ones with *state* constraint (49.6% vs 61.5% micro-averaged F1-scores, respectively).

Subtask S2 The key differences between Subtask S1 and S2 are: *(i)* questions with *zero* as an answer are included, and *(ii)* there can be more than one *answer incidents* per question, hence, systems must be able to cluster *answer documents* into the correct number of clusters, i.e., incidents.

As shown in Table 4, KOI is able to answer questions with zero as the true answer with 96.3% accuracy. Meanwhile, for questions with non-zero number of incidents as the answers, KOI gives numerical answers with 18.9% accuracy, resulting in overall accuracy (`inc-acc`) of 27.4% and RMSE `inc-rmse`) of 5.3.

We also analyzed questions (with non-zero answer incidents) for which KOI yields perfect sets of answer documents with 100% F1-score, i.e., 7.7% of all questions. For 61.8% of such answered questions, KOI returns the perfect number of inci-

Event ID: 22409

2016-06-19

Man playing with gun while riding in a car fatally shoots, kills driver

A man was fatally shot early Sunday morning after the passenger in the car he was driving accidentally discharged the gun, according to the San Antonio Police Department. The shooting occurred about 3 a.m. when group of four men were driving out of the Iron Horse Apartments at 8800 Village Square on the Northeast Side. The passenger in the front seat was playing with a gun and allegedly shot himself in the hand, according to officers at the scene. The bullet went through his hand and struck the driver in the abdomen. The men then drove to Northeast Baptist Hospital, which was nearby, but the driver was pronounced dead at the hospital, according to investigators. Police believe the driver and passenger to be related and are still investigating the incident. The other two men in the vehicle were detained. No charges have been filed.

2016-06-19

41-year - old man killed in overnight shooting

SAN ANTONIO - A 41-year-old man is dead after a shooting police say may have been accidental. The victim died after another man drove him to Northeast Baptist Hospital for treatment of that gunshot wound. Police say they got a call at around 2:45 a.m. for the shooting in the 8800 block of Village Drive. The man told them he and the victim were in a pickup when he fired the shot, but police say it's not known why the men were in the truck. Investigators say the man told them he fired the shot accidentally and struck the victim. Police say the shooter took the victim to the emergency room at Northeast Baptist, where hospital personnel pronounced him dead. Police are questioning the man who did the shooting.

Table 5: An identified *'killing'* event by KOI for *"Which killing incidents happened in June 2016 in San Antonio, Texas?"* with two supporting documents.

dents. For the rest, KOI tends to overestimate the number of incidents, i.e., for 30.9% of the cases, KOI fails to establish cross-document event coreference links with the current document clustering method.

Subtask S3 We also show in Table 4, the KOI performance on answering numerical questions about number of victims. KOI is able to answer correctly 55.2% of questions with zero answers, and 11.9% of the ones with non-zero answers.

Analyzing the questions with zero as the true answer, for which KOI is able to answer correctly, in 41.1% of the cases KOI is able to identify the non-existence of victims when the set of answer documents is not empty. In 40.0% of the cases, the correctly predicted zero answers are actually by chance, i.e., because KOI fails to identify relevant answer documents.

Meanwhile, for questions with gold numerical answers greater than zero, KOI returns wrong answers in 88.1% of the cases. Among these answers, 66.9% of the answers are lower than the true number of victims, and 33.1% are higher. This means that KOI tends to underestimate the number of victims with 6.6 RMSE.

For 22.5% of all questions, KOI is able to identify the perfect sets of answer documents with 100% F1-score. Among these questions, 34.3% were answered correctly with the exact number of victims, for which: 52.7% of correct answers result from solely *counting participants (as victims)*, 35.3% were inferred only from *numeral mentions*, and the rest of 12.0% were answered by combining both victim counting and numeral mentions.

Qualitative Analysis Recalling the example questions mentioned in the beginning of Section 1, for the first question, KOI is able to perfectly identify 2 killing incidents with 5 supporting documents pertaining to the event-time and -location constraints. One of the identified answer incidents with two supporting documents is shown in Table 5, which shows how well the system is able to establish cross-document event coreference, given overlapping concepts and entities. However, in answering the second question, KOI returns one less number of victims since it cannot identify the killed victim in the answer incident shown in Table 5, due to the lack of numeral mentions and named event participants as victims.

4 Conclusion

We have introduced a system called KOI (Knowledge of Incidents), that is able to build a knowledge graph (KG) of incidental events by extracting relevant event information from news articles. The resulting KG can then be used to efficiently answer numerical questions about events such as *"How many people were killed in June 2016 in San Antonio, Texas?"* We have submitted KOI as a participating system at SemEval-2018 Task 5, which achieved competitive results. A live demo of our system is available at `https://koi.cs.ui.ac.id/`. Future directions of this work include the incorporation of supervised (or semi-supervised) approaches for specific steps of KOI such as the extraction of numeral information (Mirza et al., 2017), as well as the investigation of applying our approach to other domains such as disease outbreaks and natural disasters.

References

Ronan Collobert, Jason Weston, Léon Bottou, Michael Karlen, Koray Kavukcuoglu, and Pavel Kuksa. 2011. Natural language processing (almost) from scratch. *J. Mach. Learn. Res.*, 12:2493–2537.

Graeme Hirst, David St-Onge, et al. 1998. Lexical chains as representations of context for the detection and correction of malapropisms. *WordNet: An electronic lexical database*, 305:305–332.

Paramita Mirza, Simon Razniewski, Fariz Darari, and Gerhard Weikum. 2017. Cardinal virtues: Extracting relation cardinalities from text. In *Proceedings of the 55th Annual Meeting of the Association for Computational Linguistics, ACL 2017, Vancouver, Canada, July 30 - August 4, Volume 2: Short Papers*, pages 347–351.

Andrea Moro, Alessandro Raganato, and Roberto Navigli. 2014. Entity Linking meets Word Sense Disambiguation: a Unified Approach. *Transactions of the Association for Computational Linguistics (TACL)*, 2:231–244.

Roberto Navigli and Simone Paolo Ponzetto. 2012. BabelNet: The automatic construction, evaluation and application of a wide-coverage multilingual semantic network. *Artificial Intelligence*, 193:217–250.

Natasha Noy and Alan Rector, editors. 2006. *Defining N-ary Relations on the Semantic Web*. W3C Working Group Note. Retrieved Jan 10, 2017 from https://www.w3.org/TR/2006/NOTE-swbp-n-aryRelations-20060412/.

Marten Postma, Filip Ilievski, and Piek Vossen. 2018. Semeval-2018 task 5: Counting events and participants in the long tail. In *Proceedings of the 12th International Workshop on Semantic Evaluation (SemEval-2018)*. Association for Computational Linguistics.

Jannik Strötgen and Michael Gertz. 2013. Multilingual and cross-domain temporal tagging. *Language Resources and Evaluation*, 47(2):269–298.

SemEval 2018 Task 6: Parsing Time Normalizations

Egoitz Laparra
University of Arizona
Tucson, AZ 85721, USA

Dongfang Xu
University of Arizona
Tucson, AZ 85721, USA

Steven Bethard
University of Arizona
Tucson, AZ 85721, USA

laparra@email.arizona.edu dongfangxu9@email.arizona.edu bethard@email.arizona.edu

Ahmed S. Elsayed
University of Colorado Boulder
Boulder, CO 80309

ahmed.s.elsayed@colorado.edu

Martha Palmer
University of Colorado Boulder
Boulder, CO 80309

martha.palmer@colorado.edu

Abstract

This paper presents the outcomes of the Parsing Time Normalization shared task held within SemEval-2018. The aim of the task is to parse time expressions into the compositional semantic graphs of the Semantically Compositional Annotation of Time Expressions (SCATE) schema, which allows the representation of a wider variety of time expressions than previous approaches. Two tracks were included, one to evaluate the parsing of individual components of the produced graphs, in a classic information extraction way, and another one to evaluate the quality of the time intervals resulting from the interpretation of those graphs. Though 40 participants registered for the task, only one team submitted output, achieving 0.55 F1 in Track 1 (parsing) and 0.70 F1 in Track 2 (intervals).

1 Introduction

The task of extracting and normalizing time expressions (e.g., finding phrases like *two days ago* and converting them to a standardized form like 2017-07-17) is a fundamental component of any time-aware language processing system. TempEval 2010 and 2013 (Verhagen et al., 2010; UzZaman et al., 2013) included a restricted version of a time normalization task as part of their shared tasks. However, the annotation scheme used in these tasks (TimeML; (ISO, 2012)) has some significant limitations: it assumes times can be described as a prefix of YYYY-MM-DDTHH:MM:SS (so it can't represent, e.g., *the past three summers*), it is unable to represent times that are are relative to events (e.g., *three weeks postoperative*), and it fails to reflect the compositional nature of time expressions (e.g., that *following* represents a similar temporal operation in *the following day* and *the following year*). This latter issue especially has discouraged machine learning approaches to time normalization; the most accurate systems for normalizing times are still based on sets of complex, manually-constructed rules (Bethard, 2013; Lee et al., 2014; Strötgen and Gertz, 2015).

The Parsing Time Normalizations shared task is a new approach to time normalization based on the Semantically Compositional Annotation of Time Expressions (SCATE) schema (Bethard and Parker, 2016), in which times are annotated as compositional time entities. Such entities are more expressive, being able to represent many more time expressions, and are more machine-learnable, as they can naturally be viewed as a semantic parsing task. The top of Figure 1 shows an example. Each annotation in the example corresponds to a formally defined time entity. For instance, the annotation on top of *since* corresponds to a BETWEEN entity that identifies an interval starting at the most recent March 6 and ending at the document creation time. The bottom of Figure 1 shows how those time entities can be composed to identify appropriate intervals on the timeline. Here, the BETWEEN entity finds the interval on the timeline that is between the intervals of its two arguments: the LAST and the DOC-TIME. Formally, this BETWEEN operator is defined as:

$$\text{BETWEEN}([t_1, t_2] : \text{INTERVAL},$$
$$[t_3, t_4] : \text{INTERVAL}) : \text{INTERVAL}$$
$$= [t_2, t_3]$$

In the proposed task, systems need only to identify time entities in text and link them correctly to signal how they are to be composed (i.e., systems would only need to produce annotation structures like those at the top of Figure 1). The timeline intervals implied by such system output are inferred through a time entity interpreter provided to the participants by the workshop organizers.

Proceedings of the 12th International Workshop on Semantic Evaluation (SemEval-2018), pages 88–96
New Orleans, Louisiana, June 5–6, 2018. ©2018 Association for Computational Linguistics

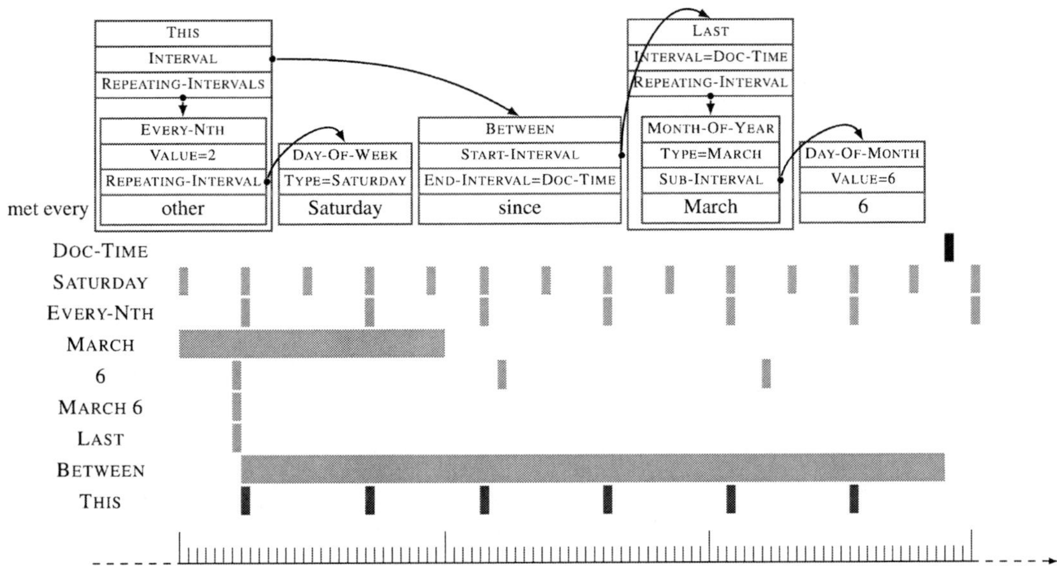

Figure 1: Example of semantically compositional time annotations and their interpretation.

The remainder of this paper is organized as follows. We describe the task goal and proposed tracks in Section 2. Section 3 contains the description of the data annotation schema and the statistics of our dataset. In Section 4, we explain the two evaluation metrics used in the task and in Section 5 the models used as baselines. We present the participant systems in Section 6 and the results obtained in Section 7. Finally, we discuss some conclusions learned in Section 8.

2 Tasks

The ultimate goal of the shared task is to interpret time expressions, identifying appropriate intervals that can be placed on a timeline. Given a document, a system must identify the **time entities** by detecting the spans of characters and labeling them with the proper SCATE type. Examples of time entities and their corresponding types in Figure 1 would be (*6*, DAY-OF-MONTH), (*Saturday*, DAY-OF-WEEK), (*March*, MONTH-OF-YEAR) or (*since*, BETWEEN). Besides the time entities explicitly expressed in the text, implicit occurrences must also be identified, like the THIS and LAST time entities in Figure 1 that do not have any explicit triggers in the text.

Once time entities have been identified, they should be linked together using the relations described in the SCATE schema. Following with the example in Figure 1, the time entity *6* should be linked as a SUB-INTERVAL of *March*, *Saturday*

should be a REPEATING-INTERVAL of the time entity *other*, and so on. Finally, all the time entities must be completed with some additional properties needed for their interpretation. For example, the time entity *other* should have a VALUE of 2, the END-INTERVAL of *since* is the Document Creation Time, etc. Once again, the properties required by each time entity type are defined by the SCATE schema.[1]

Every resulting graph, composed of a set of linked time entities, represents a **time expression** that can be semantically interpreted. For this purpose, we provide a Scala library[2] that reads the graphs in Anafora XML format (Chen and Styler, 2013) and converts them into intervals on the timeline.

An example of interpreting the time entities corresponding to the expression *every Saturday since March 6* relative to an anchor time of April 21, 2017 is given in Figure 2. In this example, the values *today* and *result* store the entities that represent the time expressions April 21, 2017 and *every Saturday since March 6* respectively. The Scala command on the right side interprets the latter and produces the corresponding time intervals.

The task includes two evaluation methods, one for the parsing step, i.e. time entity identification

---

[1] https://github.com/clulab/
anafora-annotations/blob/master/.schema/
timenorm-schema.xml

[2] https://github.com/clulab/timenorm

```
scala> val today =
     |   ThisRI(
     |     ThisRI(
     |       Year(2017),
     |       RepeatingField(MONTH_OF_YEAR, 4)),
     |     RepeatingField(DAY_OF_MONTH, 21))
scala> val result =
     |   ThisRIs(
     |     Between(
     |       LastRI(
     |         today,
     |         Intersection(Set(
     |           RepeatingField(MONTH_OF_YEAR, 3),
     |           RepeatingField(DAY_OF_MONTH, 6)))),
     |       today),
     |       RepeatingField(DAY_OF_WEEK, 6))
```

```
scala> for (Interval(start, end) <- result.intervals)
     |   println(start, end)
(2017-03-11T00:00,2017-03-12T00:00)
(2017-03-18T00:00,2017-03-19T00:00)
(2017-03-25T00:00,2017-03-26T00:00)
(2017-04-01T00:00,2017-04-02T00:00)
(2017-04-08T00:00,2017-04-09T00:00)
(2017-04-15T00:00,2017-04-16T00:00)
(2017-04-22T00:00,2017-04-23T00:00)
...
```

Figure 2: Interpretation of *every Saturday since March 6*.

and linking, and one to score the resulting time intervals. For the later, we only consider time expressions that yield a finite set of bounded intervals, for example, *last Monday*. Time expressions that refer to an infinite set of intervals, like *every month*, are not considered in the interval-based part of the evaluation.

Participants only need to produce Anafora outputs with parsed time entities; the interpretation is carried out by the evaluation system. The evaluation system is also able to obtain the intervals from timestamps in TimeML format. Thus, systems can be evaluated by both methods or just by the interval-based one, depending on the output format.

In summary, the tasks offers two tracks:

Track 1: Parse text to time entities. Systems must identify time entities in text and link them correctly to signal how they have to be composed. The output must be given in Anafora format. In this track, all time entities and relations of every time expression are evaluated.

Track 2: Produce time intervals. Systems can participate through Track 1 or by providing TimeML annotations. In both cases, the intervals are inferred by our interpreter. In this track, only bounded time intervals are scored.

3 Data

The Parsing Time Normalization corpus[3] covers two different domains: newswire and clinical notes. For the former, we have annotated a subset of Tempeval-2013 corpus (UzZaman et al., 2013), which contains a collection of news articles from

different sources, such as Wall Street Journal, New York Times, Cable News Network, Voices of America, etc. For the clinical domain, we have annotated a subset of the THYME corpus used in the Clinical TempEvals (Bethard et al., 2015, 2016, 2017), which includes a set of de-identified clinical notes and pathology reports from cancer patients at the Mayo Clinic.

The Newswire annotation was performed by linguistic students at the University of Alabama at Birmingham, and by linguistics students at the University of Arizona, funded as part of a university-sponsored undergraduate research opportunity. The clinical portion of the corpus was annotated by linguistics students at the University of Colorado, funded as part of the United States National Institutes of Health (NIH) award R01LM010090.

Documents have been annotated by two annotators and adjudicated by a third, and despite the complexity of the annotation scheme, high levels of inter-annotator agreement have been achieved: 0.917 F_1 on annotation spans and types, and 0.821 F_1 on the complete task of spans, types, and links. (We use F_1 since the κ coefficient (Cohen, 1960) converges to F_1 in cases where the number of non-annotations is much larger than the number of annotations (Hripcsak and Rothschild, 2005).)

Annotated data is stored in Anafora XML format (Chen and Styler, 2013), where, for example, the annotations from Figure 1 look like Figure 3. A more detailed explanation of the annotation guidelines can be found in Bethard and Parker (2016). Libraries for parsing this format are available to

[3]https://github.com/bethard/
anafora-annotations/releases

```
<data>                                   <entity>
 <annotations>                            <id>3@e@gold</id>
  <entity>                                <span>10,15</span><!-- "other" -->
   <id>1@e@gold</id>                      <type>Every-Nth</type>
   <span>11,19</span><!-- "Saturday" -->  <properties>
   <type>Day-Of-Week</type>                <Value>2</Value>
   <properties>                            <Repeating-Interval>1@e@gold</Repeating-Interval>
    <Type>Saturday</Type>                 </properties>
   </properties>                         </entity>
  </entity>
  <entity>
   <id>2@e@gold</id>                      ...
   <span>10,15</span><!-- "other" -->
   <type>This</type>                     </annotations>
   <properties>                        </data>
    <Interval>4@e@gold</Interval>
    <Repeating-Intervals>2@e@gold</Repeating-Intervals>
   </properties>
  </entity>
```

Figure 3: Snippet of the Anafora XML for Figure 1.

participants in both Python[4] and Scala[5].

Table 1 shows the statistics of the resulting annotation. The Newswire portion of the corpus contains 98 documents with 2,428 time entities annotated. These entities compose a total of 968 time expressions of which 564 correspond to bounded intervals. The Clinical portions of the corpus includes 408 documents. The annotation covers 27,362 time entities that compose 8,163 time expressions. From these, 4,204 yield bounded intervals.

4 Evaluation Metrics

We propose two types of scoring metrics for this task, one for the evaluation of each track. The first follows a more traditional information extraction evaluation: measure the precision and recall of finding and linking the various time entities. Specifically, we define:

$$P(S, H) = \frac{|S \cap H|}{|S|}$$

$$R(S, H) = \frac{|S \cap H|}{|H|}$$

$$F_1(S, H) = \frac{2 \cdot P(S, H) \cdot R(S, H)}{P(S, H) + R(S, H)}$$

where S is the set of items predicted by the system and H is the set of items produced by the humans. For these calculations, each item is an annotation,

[4]https://github.com/bethard/
anaforatools
[5]https://github.com/bethard/timenorm

and one annotation is considered as equal to another if it has the same character span (offsets), type, and properties (with the definition applying recursively for properties that point to other annotations).

The second scoring method evaluates the accuracy of systems with respect to the timeline in a more direct way. First, annotations, in either TimeML or SCATE format, are converted into time intervals. TimeML TIMEX3 (time expression) annotations are translated into intervals following ISO 8601 semantics of their VALUE attribute. For example, 2010-02-25 is converted to the interval [2010-02-25T00:00:00, 2018-02-26T00:00:00), that is, the 24-hour period starting at the first second of the day on 2010-02-25 and ending just before the first second of the day on 2010-02-26. SCATE annotations are converted to intervals according to the formal semantics of each entity, using the Scala library provided by Bethard and Parker (2016). For example, Next(Year(2010), SimplePeriod(YEARS, 4)), is converted to [2011-01-01T00:00, 2015-01-01T00:00), i.e., the 4 years following 2010. Note that there may be more than one interval associated with a single annotation, as in the *every Saturday since March 6* example in Figure 2. Once all annotations have been converted into intervals along the timeline, we can calculate the overlap between the intervals of different annotations.

Given two sets of intervals, we define the interval precision, P_{int}, as the total length of the intervals in common between the two sets, divided by the total length of the intervals in the first set. Interval recall, R_{int} is defined as the total length of the intervals in common between the two sets,

	Newswire			Clinical		
	Train	Dev	Test	Train	Dev	Test
Documents	64	14	20	232	35	141
SCATE entities	1,628	402	398	14,936	2,896	9,530
SCATE time exp.	636	146	186	4,469	879	2,815
SCATE bounded	391	80	93	2,303	430	1,471

Table 1: Number of documents and SCATE annotations for both sections of the corpus following the SCATE schema.

divided by the total length of the intervals in the second set. Formally:

$$I_S \bigcap I_H = \{i \cap j : i \in I_S \wedge j \in I_H\}$$

$$P_{\text{int}}(I_S, I_H) = \frac{\sum_{i \in \text{COMPACT}(I_S \cap I_H)} |i|}{\sum_{i \in I_S} |i|}$$

$$R_{\text{int}}(I_S, I_H) = \frac{\sum_{i \in \text{COMPACT}(I_S \cap I_H)} |i|}{\sum_{i \in \cup I_H} |i|}$$

where I_S and I_H are sets of intervals, $i \cap j$ is the possibly empty interval in common between the intervals i and j, $|i|$ is the length of the interval i, and COMPACT takes a set of intervals and merges any overlapping intervals.

Given two sets of annotations (e.g., one each from two time normalization systems), we define the overall precision, P, as the average of interval precisions where each annotation from the first set is paired with all annotations that textually overlap it in the second set. Overall recall is defined as the average of interval recalls where each annotation from the second set is paired with all annotations that textually overlap it in the first set. Formally:

$$\text{OI}_a(B) = \bigcup_{b \in B:\text{OVERLAPS}(a,b)} \text{INTERVALS}(b)$$

$$P(S, H) = \frac{1}{|S|} \sum_{s \in S} P_{int}(\text{INTERVALS}(s), \text{OI}_s(H))$$

$$R(S, H) = \frac{1}{|H|} \sum_{h \in H} R_{int}(\text{INTERVALS}(h), \text{OI}_h(S))$$

where S and H are sets of annotations, INTERVALS(x) gives the time intervals associated with the annotation x, and OVERLAPS(a, b) decides whether the annotations a and b share at least one character of text in common.

Note that as defined, P and R can be applied only to time expressions that yield a finite set of bounded intervals.

5 Baseline systems

Two systems were used as baselines to compare the participating systems against.

Character-based model (Laparra et al., 2018) is a novel supervised approach for time normalization that follows the SCATE schema. This model decomposes the normalization of time expressions into two modules:

time entity identification detects the spans of characters that belong to each time expression and labels them with their corresponding time entity type. This step is performed by character-based recurrent neural network with two stacked bidirectional Gated Recurrent Units.

time entity composition links relevant time entities together while respecting the entity type constraints imposed by the SCATE schema. This component is a rule-based algorithm that iterates over the time entities that are found by the previous step, linking them and filling in the required properties. The version used for the shared task includes some improvements to the sentence segmentation and Month-Of-Year normalization of Laparra et al. (2018).

These two tasks are run sequentially using the output of the former as input to the latter. Once identification and composition steps are completed, the final product, i.e. the semantic composition of the time entities, can fed to the SCATE interpreter to produce time intervals.

HEIDELTIME (Strötgen and Gertz, 2015)[6] is rule-based temporal tagger with multilingual support that includes English, German, Dutch, Vietnamese, Arabic, Spanish, Italian, French, Chinese and Russian. HeidelTime identifies temporal expressions based on language specific patterns and

---

[6] https://code.google.com/p/heideltime/

normalizes them according to TIMEX annotations (Sundheim, 1996). As the output of HeidelTime follows TimeML format, we use this system as a baseline only for Track 2.

6 Participating systems

Although 40 people registered to the the evaluation task, only 1 team submitted results. The team participated in Track 1 and, consequently, in Track 2. The team also submitted improved results just after the end of the evaluation phase. This improvement was obtained by solving a few bugs in the original system, and with no access to the test data, so we have included the fixed version in this paper as an additional run.

CHRONO (Olex et al., 2018) is a primarily rule-based system that performs time normalization by running the following three steps:

1) Temporal tokens are identified and flagged using regex expressions to identify formatted dates/times, and by parsing out specific temporal words and numeric tokens.

2) Temporal phrases are identified by searching for consecutive numeric/temporal tokens according to certain constraints.

3) Temporal phrases are parsed and normalized into the SCATE schema via detailed rule-based parsing, including the utilization of part-of-speech tags, to identify each component of an expression and link sub-intervals appropriately.

A machine learning approach is taken to disambiguate PERIODS and CALENDAR-INTERVALS after the rule-base parsing has determined it is one or the other (e.g. if it sees the word *week* it will pass it to the ML module for assignment to a PERIODS or CALENDAR-INTERVALS). The ML feature vector is a boolean vector composed of the target token's temporal status (1=temporal, 0=not temporal), the temporal context (1=at least one temporal token within a window of ±5, 0=no temporal tokens within window), the numeric context (1=a numeric token exists immediately before of after the target, 0=no numeric tokens in context), and the lexical context of all words within a 5-word window of the target (1=word is present, 0=word is not present). The group explored different supervised models like naive Bayes, decision trees, support vector machines, and neural networks. They found

Domain	Model	F_1	P	R
Newswire	Character	0.51	0.57	0.46
Newswire	Chrono	0.44	0.46	0.42
Newswire	Chrono*	0.55	0.61	0.50
Clinical	Character	0.57	0.52	0.63

Table 2: Official results in Track 1 (parsing) for the Newswire and Clinical domains.

that the best results were obtained by the neural network.

CHRONO* improves the previous version by solving three bugs in the model. First, the parsing method for various types of temporal components were supposed to be executed in a specific order. However, some of them were swapped and not analyzed in the expected order. Second, the system was supposed to assume there is only one year, one month, and one day mentioned per temporal phrase. This worked for the month and day, however, it was failing with 4-digit years. Finally, for most parsing methods the system loops through each token in the temporal phrase but it skipped the loop when identifying full numeric expressions, like "1953" or "08091998". Thus, phrases like "Last 1953" were not being counted as having any numeric values in them.

7 Evaluation Results

The official results are presented in Table 2 and Table 4. For each track we present the precision (P), recall (R) and F_1 score obtained by the metrics presented in Section 4. The only participant of the task submitted output just for the Newswire domain, thus, we only report the performance of this system in this domain. The results of the Character-based baseline have been obtained training the model with the training set of the corresponding domain (Newswire or Clinical) and a set of randomly generated dates, as explained in Laparra et al. (2018).

In Track 1 (Table 2) the original version of CHRONO do not reach the Character-based baseline, 0.44 F_1 vs 0.51 F_1. However, the fixed version of the system (CHRONO*) outperforms the baseline in terms of F_1 (0.55) as well as in terms of P (0.61) and R (0.50).

Table 3 shows a more detailed comparison between the Character-based baseline and CHRONO*. These figures represent the performances of both models for each SCATE temporal type. This includes the identification of the time entity, its prop-

SCATE-type	#	Char	Chrono*
AMPM-Of-Day	1	0.000	0.667
After	19	0.000	0.000
Before	20	0.105	0.000
Between	7	0.000	0.000
Calendar-Interval	27	0.698	0.526
Day-Of-Month	22	0.917	1.000
Day-Of-Week	16	0.812	0.903
Hour-Of-Day	2	0.000	0.667
Intersection	3	0.000	0.000
Last	40	0.500	0.333
Minute-Of-Hour	1	0.000	0.000
Month-Of-Year	36	0.824	0.917
Next	14	0.053	0.412
NthFromStart	4	0.000	0.000
Number	27	0.596	0.522
Part-Of-Day	3	0.000	1.000
Period	56	0.391	0.409
Season-Of-Year	10	0.000	0.182
Sum	1	0.000	0.000
This	37	0.429	0.552
Time-Zone	1	0.000	0.000
Two-Digit-Year	1	0.000	0.000
Year	50	0.822	0.826

Table 3: Results in Track 1 per SCATE type. Char stands for Character-based baseline. The number of gold cases per type is included (#).

Domain	Model	F_1	P	R
Newswire	HeidelTime	0.74	0.71	0.77
Newswire	Character	0.77	0.83	0.72
Newswire	Chrono	0.65	0.66	0.63
Newswire	Chrono*	0.70	0.65	0.75
Clinical	HeidelTime	0.70	0.60	0.82
Clinical	Character	0.72	0.70	0.75

Table 4: Official results in Track 2 (intervals) for the Newswire and Clinical domains.

erties and links. In general, CHRONO* performs better or similar for all the types. It is remarkable that, while the outcomes for the THIS and NEXT operators are much better, CHRONO* fails to extract properly the LAST operator.

In Track 2 (Table 4) the best system is the Character-based baseline with 0.76 F_1, followed by HEIDELTIME with 0.74 F_1. None of the versions of CHRONO performs better than the baselines, although the fixed version (CHRONO*) gets enhanced results, 0.65 F_1 vs 0.70 F_1 , following the improvement obtained in Track 1. It is re-

markable that HEIDELTIME and CHRONO*, essentially rule-based systems, obtain better R than the Character-based baseline, that relies strongly on a supervised model. Specifically, HEIDELTIME obtains the best R (0.77), but CHRONO* also outperforms the Character-based baseline in terms of R, 0.75 vs 0.71. However, the Character-based baseline obtains a much higher P (0.83) than the 0.71 of HEIDELTIME and the 0.65 of CHRONO*.

As explained in Section 4, the metric for Track 1 evaluates the individual temporal components extracted by the systems, either time entities or links between time entity pairs. On the other hand, the intervals scored by the metric for Track 2 are produced by interpreting the whole graph. Moreover, not all the time expressions yield a finite set of bounded intervals, as can be seen in Table 1. Consequently, better performances in Track 1 do not necessarily yield better results in Track 2. In particular, although CHRONO* is better than the Character-based baseline in Track 1 it produces an excessive number of time expressions yielding bounded intervals (108), which affects the P in Track 2. In contrast, the Character-based baseline is more conservative and accurate in this respect (85).

Although we didn't receive any submission for the Clinical domain, in order to set a reference for future research, we present in Table 2 and Table 4 the performances of the baseline systems in this domain.

8 Conclusion

The Parsing Time Normalization task is the first effort to extend time normalization to richer and more complex time expressions. We have provided a complete annotation for two different domains, newswire and clinical notes, and introduced two different metrics for evaluation. In particular, the interval based evaluation for Track 2 is a novelty for these kind of tasks. The performance of the systems shows that there is still room for improvement, especially for Track 1.

Although, CHRONOS included a small supervised component in its architecture, we were expecting a higher number of machine learning based approaches. However, CHRONOS shows that rule-based models can obtain competitive results. Sadly, the scarcity of participating systems does not allow us to form a further judgment.

No submissions were received for the clinical

domain, despite a wider and more complete dataset for this domain. This was almost certainly the result of a change in management at the Mayo Clinic that put on hold the data use agreement process (which is required for access to the clinical data) for several months during the practice phase. Thus, though many people showed interest in the task (more than 40 people registered) and Mayo reported several data use agreement applications, this problem de-motivated the participation.

The CodaLab competition for the Parsing Time Normalizations shared task[7] will continue to accept submissions in its Post-Evaluation phase indefinitely, so as more researchers make it through the data use agreement process, we expect we will see future participation in this task.

Acknowledgements

The work is funded by the THYME project (R01LM010090) from the National Library Of Medicine. The content is solely the responsibility of the authors and does not necessarily represent the official views of the National Library Of Medicine or the National Institutes of Health.

References

Steven Bethard. 2013. A synchronous context free grammar for time normalization. In *Proceedings of the 2013 Conference on Empirical Methods in Natural Language Processing*, pages 821–826, Seattle, Washington, USA. Association for Computational Linguistics.

Steven Bethard, Leon Derczynski, Guergana Savova, James Pustejovsky, and Marc Verhagen. 2015. Semeval-2015 task 6: Clinical tempeval. In *Proceedings of the 9th International Workshop on Semantic Evaluation (SemEval 2015)*, pages 806–814, Denver, Colorado. Association for Computational Linguistics.

Steven Bethard and Jonathan Parker. 2016. A semantically compositional annotation scheme for time normalization. In *Proceedings of the Tenth International Conference on Language Resources and Evaluation (LREC 2016)*, Paris, France. European Language Resources Association (ELRA). [Acceptance rate 60%].

Steven Bethard, Guergana Savova, Wei-Te Chen, Leon Derczynski, James Pustejovsky, and Marc Verhagen. 2016. Semeval-2016 task 12: Clinical tempeval. In *Proceedings of the 10th International Workshop on Semantic Evaluation (SemEval-2016)*, pages 1052–1062, San Diego, California. Association for Computational Linguistics.

Steven Bethard, Guergana Savova, Martha Palmer, and James Pustejovsky. 2017. Semeval-2017 task 12: Clinical tempeval. In *Proceedings of the 11th International Workshop on Semantic Evaluation (SemEval-2017)*, pages 565–572, Vancouver, Canada. Association for Computational Linguistics.

Wei-Te Chen and Will Styler. 2013. Anafora: A web-based general purpose annotation tool. In *Proceedings of the 2013 NAACL HLT Demonstration Session*, pages 14–19, Atlanta, Georgia. Association for Computational Linguistics.

Jacob Cohen. 1960. A coefficient of agreement for nominal scales. *Educational and Psychological Measurement*, 20(1):37–46.

George Hripcsak and Adam S. Rothschild. 2005. Agreement, the f-measure, and reliability in information retrieval. *Journal of the American Medical Informatics Association*, 12(3):296–298.

ISO. 2012. Language resource management – semantic annotation framework (semaf) – part 1: Time and events (semaf-time, iso-timeml). Technical report. 24617-1:2012.

Egoitz Laparra, Dongfang Xu, and Steven Bethard. 2018. From characters to time intervals: New paradigms for evaluation and neural parsing of time normalizations. *Transactions of the Association for Computational Linguistics*.

Kenton Lee, Yoav Artzi, Jesse Dodge, and Luke Zettlemoyer. 2014. Context-dependent semantic parsing for time expressions. In *Proceedings of the 52nd Annual Meeting of the Association for Computational Linguistics (Volume 1: Long Papers)*, pages 1437–1447, Baltimore, Maryland. Association for Computational Linguistics.

Amy Olex, Luke Maffey, Nicholas Morgan, and Bridget McInnes. 2018. Chrono at semeval-2018 task 6: A system for normalizing temporal expressions. In *Proceedings of the 12th International Workshop on Semantic Evaluation (SemEval-2018)*, New Orleans, Luisiana. Association for Computational Linguistics.

Jannik Strötgen and Michael Gertz. 2015. A baseline temporal tagger for all languages. In *Proceedings of the 2015 Conference on Empirical Methods in Natural Language Processing*, pages 541–547, Lisbon, Portugal. Association for Computational Linguistics.

Beth M. Sundheim. 1996. Overview of results of the muc-6 evaluation. In *Proceedings of a Workshop on Held at Vienna, Virginia: May 6-8, 1996*, TIPSTER '96, pages 423–442, Stroudsburg, PA, USA. Association for Computational Linguistics.

---

[7]`https://competitions.codalab.org/competitions/17286`

Naushad UzZaman, Hector Llorens, Leon Derczynski, James Allen, Marc Verhagen, and James Pustejovsky. 2013. Semeval-2013 task 1: Tempeval-3:
Evaluating time expressions, events, and temporal
relations. In *Second Joint Conference on Lexical
and Computational Semantics (*SEM), Volume 2:
Proceedings of the Seventh International Workshop
on Semantic Evaluation (SemEval 2013)*, pages 1–
9, Atlanta, Georgia, USA. Association for Computational Linguistics.

Marc Verhagen, Roser Sauri, Tommaso Caselli, and
James Pustejovsky. 2010. Semeval-2010 task 13:
Tempeval-2. In *Proceedings of the 5th International
Workshop on Semantic Evaluation*, pages 57–62,
Uppsala, Sweden. Association for Computational
Linguistics.

Chrono at SemEval-2018 Task 6:
A System for Normalizing Temporal Expressions

Amy L. Olex, Luke G. Maffey, Nicholas Morton, Bridget T. McInnes
Virginia Commonwealth University, Department of Computer Science
Richmond, Virginia, USA
`{alolex, maffeyl, mortonn, btmcinnes}@vcu.edu`

Abstract

Temporal information extraction is a challenging task. Here we describe Chrono, a hybrid rule-based and machine learning system that identifies temporal expressions in text and normalizes them into the SCATE schema. After minor parsing logic adjustments, Chrono has emerged as the top performing system for SemEval 2018 Task 6: Parsing Time Normalizations.

1 Introduction

Understanding and processing temporal information is vital for navigating life. The human mind processes subtle temporal expressions instantly and effortlessly; however, it is difficult for computers to do the same. Identifying, processing, and utilizing this information requires knowledge and understanding of syntax, semantics, and context to link temporal information to related events and order them on a time-line. SemEval 2018 Task 6 (Laparra et al., 2018) aims to normalize fine-grained temporal information and relationships into the Semantically Compositional Annotations for Temporal Expressions (SCATE) schema developed by (Bethard and Parker, 2016). This scheme aims to improve upon the current TIMEX3/TimeML (Pustejovsky et al., 2003) standard by representing a wide variety of temporal expressions, allowing for events to act as anchors, and using mathematical operations over a time-line to define the semantics of each annotation. To address this challenge, we developed Chrono[1], a hybrid rule-based and machine learning (ML) Python package that normalizes temporal expressions into the SCATE schema.

2 The Chrono System

Our approach to building this hybrid system includes four processing phases: 1) text pre-processing, 2) flagging numeric and temporal tokens, 3) temporal expression identification, and 4) SCATE normalization.

1) Text Pre-processing: Python's Natural Language Toolkit (NLTK) WhitespaceTokenizer and part-of-speech (POS) tagger (Bird and Loper, 2004) process raw text files to identify individual tokens, token spans, and POS tags. Punctuation is not handled at this phase as it is important for identifying correct spans.

2) Flagging Numeric and Temporal Tokens: All numeric tokens are flagged regardless of context. Subsequent phases utilize contextual information to determine if a numeric token is part of a temporal expression. Depending on the task, a rule may remove all or some punctuation, and/or convert tokens to lowercase prior to parsing. In the following, RP and LC denote **R**emoving all **P**unctuation and converting to **L**ower**C**ase, respectively.

Numeric Flagging: Tokens are flagged as numeric if either 1) the token has a POS tag of "CD" (Cardinal Number), or 2) the text can be converted to a numeric expression. Textual representations of numeric expressions are converted to numerics with the Word2Number[2] Python module. A custom method recognizes ordinals from "first" to "thirty-first" and converts them into the associated numerics 1 to 31, respectively. LC normalization is done prior to parsing textual numerics.

Temporal Flagging: Temporal tokens are flagged through rule-based parsing using lists of key words and regular expressions. This phase is more liberal in its identification of a temporal token than the SCATE normalization phase, so

---

[1] https://github.com/AmyOlex/Chrono

[2] https://github.com/akshaynagpal/w2n

Proceedings of the 12th International Workshop on Semantic Evaluation (SemEval-2018), pages 97–101
New Orleans, Louisiana, June 5–6, 2018. ©2018 Association for Computational Linguistics

it identifies a broader range of potential temporal tokens that are refined in future steps. Tokens may be numeric and temporal simultaneously. Numeric tokens with the characters '$', '#', or '%' are NOT marked as temporal. The following types of tokens are flagged as temporal:

- Formatted date patterns using '/' or '-': mm/dd/yyyy, mm/dd/yy, yyyy/mm/dd, or yy/mm/dd
- Formatted time patterns matching hh:mm:ss
- Sequence of 4 to 8 consecutive digits matching range criteria for 24-hour times or for a year, month, and/or day (e.g. 1998 or 08241998).
- Spelled out month or abbreviation, e.g. "Mar." or "March", are flagged after RP except periods as they are required to retrieve correct spans.
- Days of the week, e.g. "Sat." or "Saturday", are parsed similar to months.
- Temporal words indicating periods of time, e.g. "yesterday" or "decade", are flagged after RP and LC.
- Mentions of AM and PM in any format are flagged after RP except periods.
- The parts of a week, e.g. "weekend" and "weekends", are flagged after RP and LC.
- Seasons of the year are flagged after RP and LC.
- Various parts of a day, e.g. "noon" or "morning", are flagged after RP and LC.
- Time zones are flagged after RP.
- Other temporal words, e.g. "this", "now", "nearly", and others, are flagged after RP and LC.

3) Temporal Expression Identification: A temporal expression is represented by a *temporal phrase*, which we define as two or more consecutive temporal/numeric tokens on the same line, or an isolated temporal token, with some exceptions. If a numeric token contains a '$', '#', or '%', or the text 'million', 'billion', or 'trillion' it is not included in a temporal phrase as these generally refer to non-temporal values. Additionally, isolated numeric tokens are not considered a temporal phrase.

4) SCATE Normalization: Chrono parses each temporal phrase into zero or more SCATE entities, links sub-intervals, and disambiguates the SCATE entities "Period" and "Calendar-Interval" via a machine learning module. Chrono implements 32 types of entities with 5 parent types that have been described by (Bethard and Parker, 2016). Parsing strategies differ depending on the composition of a temporal phrase being parsed. Each temporal phrase is interrogated by all of the following parsing strategies.

Formatted Dates and Times: Formatted dates/times are parsed using regular expressions. To identify which format the date/time is in, Chrono looks for a 2-digit or 4-digit year first, then uses that position for orientation to identify the remaining elements. If a formatted date/time is identified, then the appropriate sub-intervals are linked during element parsing. 4-digit years take precedence over 2-digit years.

Numeric Dates and Times: Header and metadata for Newswire articles frequently have numeric dates listed with no punctuation (e.g. "19980218" codes for "Feb, 18 1998"), and isolated 4-digit year mentions are frequent. After formatted dates and times are parsed, any phrase containing a numeric token is interrogated for a potential date or year mention. If a numeric token is 4-digits it is tested for a year between 1500 and 2050, 6-digit tokens are parsed for 2-digit year/month/day, and 8-digit strings are parsed for a 4-digit year and 2-digit month/day. All elements must be in the proper range, otherwise the token is skipped. Appropriate sub-intervals are linked during element parsing.

24-hour Time: 24-hour times are identified by either the format $hhmmzzz$, where zzz is the time zone, or a 4-digit number that has not been classified as a year. Hour digits must be less than 24 and minutes less than 60. Sub-intervals are linked at this time if existing. Time zones are handled separately and are linked back to the hour entity during the final sub-interval linking step.

Temporal Token Search: The majority of textual temporal entities are identified by looking for specific tokens. Token categories include days of the week, months, parts of a day/week, time zones, and other temporal operators such as "early", "this", "before", etc. Prior to looking for these tokens, text is normalized by RP and LC. Exceptions to RP include searching for day/month abbreviations, such as "Sat." or "Aug.". In these cases periods are not removed because they are part of the SCATE span. Another exception to RP and LC is identifying mentions of AM or PM where periods are kept and text is not converted to lowercase in order to capture variations like "PM" or "p.m.". Non-temporal mentions of the months or seasons of the year "may", "march", "spring", and "fall" are disambiguated using POS tags, where tokens that refer to a temporal entity generally have a POS tag of "NN" or "NP". Sub-intervals are not linked during token searches.

Text Year: Another special case of parsing temporal tokens are textual representations of years such as "nineteen ninety-seven". The Word2Number Python module was modified to recognize these phrases. Previously, it would add 19 and 97 together instead of returning 1997.

Periods and Calendar-Intervals: The same temporal token can refer to either a SCATE "Period" or "Calendar-Interval". For example, in the phrases "in a week" vs "next week" the token "week" is classified differently. Due to language intricacies it is difficult to define a rule-base system to disambiguate these entities as the classification is contingent on the topic being discussed where phrasing around the entity can be different for each instance. Thus, Period/Calendar-Interval tokens are initially identified by a token search using a defined list of terms, then the identified term and its span are passed to a ML algorithm for classification.

Machine Learning Classification: Four ML algorithms are available in Chrono to differentiate between "Period" and "Calendar-Interval" entities using contextual information. Chrono implements Naive Bayes (NB), Neural Network (NN), Decision Tree (DT), and Support Vector Machine (SVM). Binary feature vectors for all implementations have the following features:

- temporal_self: If the target is flagged as temporal, this feature is set to "1".
- temporal_context: If there is at least one temporal word within a 5-word window up- or down-stream of the target this feature is set to "1".
- numeric: If there is a numeric expression either directly before or after (a 1-word window) the target, this feature is set to "1".
- context: All words within a 5-word window are identified as features and set to "1" if that word is present. Prior to identifying these features all words are normalized with RP and LC. The 5-word window includes crossing sentence boundaries before and after the target word.

We use NLTK with default parameters to implement NB and DT, NN is a simple feed-forward network with three hidden layers implemented using Python's Keras package [3] with epochs set to 5 and batch set to 10, and SVM is implemented using SciKitLearn (Pedregosa et al., 2011) with C set to 0.05 and max iterations set to 3.

Ordinals: Ordinals such as "first" or "3rd" are classified as an "NthFromStart" entity in the SCATE schema. These mentions are identified by normalizing with RP and LC before searching for the ordinal tokens representing the numbers 1-31.

Sub-Interval Linking: After all SCATE entities are identified, all temporal phrases are re-parsed to identify sub-intervals within each phrase. For example, entities in the phrase "August 1998" are parsed by two different methods leaving the sub-interval link vacant. During sub-interval linking, the year "1998" has the "August" entity added as a sub-interval. Sub-interval linking reviews entities from the smallest to the largest, adding missing sub-intervals as needed. This method assumes each temporal phrase contains zero or one of each type of SCATE entity.

Next/Last Parsing: Determining whether an entity is referring to a date in the future, "Next", or past, "Last", depends on context and the document time (doc-time). Next/Last parsing is done after all other parsing, and checks two cases: 1) if a temporal phrase contains a year, no additional annotation is made, and 2) if specific modifier words are present (e.g. "next" or "last") immediately preceding a temporal expression, the modifier is annotated with a sub-interval referencing the following temporal entity. If neither of these cases hold, the year is set as the doc-time year, and the month and day are compared to the full doc-time to determine if it occurs before or after. Note the year assumption is not always valid and more complex, content-based parsing may be required to achieve higher precision. Finally, if a day of the week (e.g. "Saturday") is mentioned, Chrono finds the first preceding verb in the sentence, and if it is past tense the temporal entity is annotated as "Last", otherwise it is annotated as "Next".

3   Results

Training and evaluation of Chrono utilizes the Newswire corpus, consisting of 81 documents, provided by the task organizers. Average preci-

---

[3]https://github.com/keras-team/keras

sion, recall, and F1-measure of 5-fold cross validation for Track 1 (parsing) are reported in Table 1 (annotations for "Event" and "Modifier" are
ignored). Scores for "100% Correct Entity" consider the entity location and all properties (like
sub-intervals), and scores for "Correct Span" only
consider the entity location.

On average, all ML algorithms perform similarly for the "100% Correct Entity". All versions
also obtain a higher F1 score when only considering correct spans versus getting all entity properties correct. This indicates that Chrono correctly
identifies the majority of temporal entities, but has
trouble parsing some of the properties.

ChronoNN processed the final evaluation
dataset, which consisted of 20 previously unseen Newswire articles, and received a F1 of .44.
The evaluation dataset contained five articles from
BBC that were not represented in the training
dataset. Chrono's low performance indicates that
it may be over-fit to the the training dataset. This
is one downfall of rule-based systems, where new
rules need to be developed for each new type of
temporal representation. Upon further review we
found the submitted version of Chrono had three
minor parsing flaws that resulted in unintentional
false positives.

1) Formatted dates such as "2013-02-22" were
being parsed twice. The first parse specifically
looked for a 4-digit year and identified all correct
entities, then the second parse looked for a formatted date with a 2-digit year, but didn't check to
see if a year had already been found, so returned a
2-digit year with the value "22". This was easily
fixed by having the 2-digit year parser check for
a 4-digit year flag before proceeding (month and
day flags were already implemented).

2) 24-hour time priority was incorrectly placed
above 4-digit year. This resulted in any isolated 4-
digit year being parsed as a 24-hour time expression rather than a year as originally intended. A
simple flip of parsing order resolved this issue.

3) Numeric temporal expressions, such as an
isolated 4-digit year, were being parsed as a whole
phrase rather than breaking out each token within
the phrase. For example, the year in the phrase
"Last 1953" was not being identified because it
was not in a phrase all by itself. To fix this the
parsing function was edited to loop through each
token in a phrase (a method that was already implemented in most other parsers and was just over-

100% Correct Entity			
	P	**R**	**F1**
Chrono NB	.686	.630	.657
Chrono NN	.684	.629	.656
Chrono DT	.687	.632	.658
Chrono SVM	.689	.630	.660
Correct Span			
Chrono NB	.823	.752	.786
Chrono NN	.820	.749	.783
Chrono DT	.822	.751	.785
Chrono SVM	.827	.755	.789
Evaluation Results			
Chrono NN	.46	.42	.44
Post-Evaluation Results			
Chrono NN	.61	.50	.55

Table 1: Chrono results on Newswire corpus for Track
1. All standard errors are $<= 0.03$, and no method
performed statistically significantly better than another.

looked here).

ChronoNN received a Post-Evaluation F1 of .55
for Track 1 after implementing these fixes, which
sets ChronoNN as the top performing system for
SemEval 2018 Task 6, Track 1.

4 Conclusions and Future Work

Chrono is currently the top performing system for
Track 1 of Task 6, but there are still many areas
that can be improved. Notably, we plan to implement "Event" and "Between" parsing, as well
as refine current strategies as new temporal expressions are identified. Utilizing sentence tokenization instead of relying on new lines could improve phrase identification; however, this did not
appear to be a major source of error in parsing the
Newswire dataset. Additionally, usability can be
improved by moving all parsing rules to separate,
customizable files. We also plan to expand ML use
to additional disambiguation tasks, and implement
an ensemble system utilizing all four ML methods.
We aim to extract the temporal phrase parser into a
stand-alone system and compare it's performance
directly to existing programs like SUTime (Chang
and Manning, 2012) and HeidelTime (Strtgen and
Gertz, 2010) as it has done a decent job of identifying temporal entities in this challenge. Finally, we will evaluate Chrono's performance on
the THYME dataset (Styler IV et al., 2014) using
the post-evaluation submission system.

References

Steven Bethard and Jonathan Parker. 2016. A semantically compositional annotation scheme for time normalization. In *Lrec*, volume 2016, pages 3779–3786.

Steven Bird and Edward Loper. 2004. Nltk: the natural language toolkit. In *Proceedings of the ACL 2004 on Interactive poster and demonstration sessions*, page 31. Association for Computational Linguistics.

Angel X. Chang and Christopher D. Manning. 2012. Sutime: A library for recognizing and normalizing time expressions. In *Lrec*, volume 2012, pages 3735–3740.

Egoitz Laparra, Dongfang Xu, Steven Bethard, Ahmed S. Elsayed, and Martha Palmer. 2018. Semeval 2018 task 6: Parsing time normalization. In *Proceedings of the 12th International Workshop on Semantic Evaluation*, SemEval '18, New Orleans, LA, USA. Association for Computational Linguistics.

F. Pedregosa, G. Varoquaux, A. Gramfort, V. Michel, B. Thirion, O. Grisel, M. Blondel, P. Prettenhofer, R. Weiss, V. Dubourg, J. Vanderplas, A. Passos, D. Cournapeau, M. Brucher, M. Perrot, and E. Duchesnay. 2011. Scikit-learn: Machine learning in Python. *Journal of Machine Learning Research*, 12:2825–2830.

James Pustejovsky, José M Castano, Robert Ingria, Roser Sauri, Robert J Gaizauskas, Andrea Setzer, Graham Katz, and Dragomir R Radev. 2003. Timeml: Robust specification of event and temporal expressions in text. *New directions in question answering*, 3:28–34.

Jannik Strtgen and Michael Gertz. 2010. Heideltime: High quality rule-based extraction and normalization of temporal expressions. In *Proceedings of the 5th International Workshop on Semantic Evaluation*, SemEval '10, pages 321–324, Stroudsburg, PA, USA. Association for Computational Linguistics.

William F. Styler IV, Steven Bethard, Sean Finan, Martha Palmer, Sameer Pradhan, Piet C. de Groen, Brad Erickson, Timothy Miller, Chen Lin, and Guergana Savova. 2014. Temporal annotation in the clinical domain. *Transactions of the Association for Computational Linguistics*, 2:143.

NEUROSENT-PDI at SemEval-2018 Task 1: Leveraging a Multi-Domain Sentiment Model for Inferring Polarity in Micro-blog Text

Mauro Dragoni

Fondazione Bruno Kessler

Via Sommarive 18

Povo, Trento, Italy

dragoni@fbk.eu

Abstract

This paper describes the NeuroSent system that participated in SemEval 2018 Task 1. Our system takes a supervised approach that builds on neural networks and word embeddings. Word embeddings were built by starting from a repository of user generated reviews. Thus, they are specific for sentiment analysis tasks. Then, tweets are converted in the corresponding vector representation and given as input to the neural network with the aim of learning the different semantics contained in each emotion taken into account by the SemEval task. The output layer has been adapted based on the characteristics of each subtask. Preliminary results obtained on the provided training set are encouraging for pursuing the investigation into this direction.

1 Introduction

Sentiment Analysis is a natural language processing (NLP) task (Dragoni et al., 2015) which aims at classifying documents according to the opinion expressed about a given subject (Federici and Dragoni, 2016a,b). Many works available in the literature address the sentiment analysis problem without distinguishing domain specific information of documents when sentiment models are built. The necessity of investigating this problem from a multi-domain perspective is led by the different influence that a term might have in different contexts. The idea of adapting terms polarity to different domains emerged only in the last decade (Blitzer et al., 2007; Dragoni and Petrucci, 2017). Multi-domain sentiment analysis approaches discussed in the literature focus on building models for transferring information between pairs of domains (Dragoni, 2015; Petrucci and Dragoni, 2015). While on the one hand such approaches allow to propagate specific domain information to others, their drawback is the neces-

sity of building new transfer models every time a new domain has to be analyzed. Thus, such approaches do not have a great generalization capability of analyzing texts, because transfer models are limited to the N domains used for building the models.

The NeuroSent tool applied in SemEval 2018 Task 1 (Mohammad et al., 2018) leverages on the following pillars: (i) the use of word embeddings for representing each word contained in raw sentences; (ii) the word embeddings are generated from an opinion-based corpus instead of a general purpose one (like news or Wikipedia); (iii) the design of a deep learning technique exploiting the generated word embeddings for training the sentiment model; and (iv) the use of multiple output layers for combining domain overlap scores with domain-specific polarity predictions.

The last point enables the exploitation of linguistic overlaps between domains, which can be considered one of the pivotal assets of our approach. This way, the overall polarity of a document is computed by aggregating, for each domain, the domain-specific polarity value multiplied by a belonging degree representing the overlap between the embedded representation of the whole document and the domain itself. Within the SemEval 2018 Task 1 challenge, we consider with the term *domain* one of the emotions that have been considered into the provided datasets.

2 Related Work

Sentiment analysis from the multi-task and multi-domain perspective is a research field which started to be explored only in the last decade. According to the nomenclature widely used in the literature (see (Blitzer et al., 2007; Dragoni and Petrucci, 2017)), we call *domain* a set of documents about similar topics, e.g. a set of reviews

Proceedings of the 12th International Workshop on Semantic Evaluation (SemEval-2018), pages 102–108

New Orleans, Louisiana, June 5–6, 2018. ©2018 Association for Computational Linguistics

about similar products like mobile phones, books, movies, etc.. The massive availability of multi-domain corpora in which similar opinions are expressed about different topics opened the scenario for new challenges. Researchers tried to train models capable to acquire knowledge from a specific domain and then to exploit such a knowledge for working on documents belonging to different ones. This strategy was called domain adaptation. The use of domain adaptation techniques demonstrated that opinion classification is highly sensitive to the domain from which the training data is extracted. The reason is that when using the same words, and even the same language constructs, we may obtain different opinions, depending on the domain. The classic scenario occurs when the same word has positive connotations in one domain and negative connotations in another one, as we showed within the examples presented in Section 1.

Several approaches related to multi-domain sentiment analysis have been proposed. Roughly speaking, all of these approaches rely on one of the following ideas: (i) the transfer of learned classifiers across different domains (Blitzer et al., 2007; Pan et al., 2010; Bollegala et al., August 2013; Xia et al., May-June 2013), and (ii) the use of propagation of labels through graph structures (Ponomareva and Thelwall, 2013; Tsai et al., March 2013; Dragoni et al., April 2015; Dragoni, 2015, 2017; Petrucci and Dragoni, 2017, 2016, 2015; Dragoni et al., 2014; Dragoni and Petrucci, 2018).

While on the one hand such approaches demonstrated their effectiveness in working in a multi-domain environment, on the other hand they suffered by the limitation of being influenced by the linguistic overlap between domains. Indeed, such an overlap leads learning algorithms to infer similar polarity values to domains that are similar from the linguistic perspective.

The adoption of evolutionary algorithms within the sentiment analysis research field is quite recent. First studies focused on the use of evolutionary solutions for modeling financial indicators by starting from investors sentiments (Yamada and Ueda, 2005; Chen and Chang, 2005; Huang et al., 2012; Yang et al., 2017; Simoes et al., 2017). Here, the evolutionary component was used for learning the trend of financial indicators with respect to the sentiment information extracted from opinions provided by the investors. With respect

to these papers, we propose an approach adopting evolutionary computation to a more fine-grained level where the evolution component affects also the polarities of opinion concepts.

Studies considering the use of evolutionary algorithms for optimizing the polarity values of opinion concepts have been proposed only recently (Ferreira et al., 2015; Onan et al., 2016, 2017). However, these works focused on learning candidate refinements of opinion concepts polarity without considering the context dimension associated with them. A variant of this problem is the use of polarity adaptation strategy in the field of social media and microblogs (Alahmadi and Zeng, 2015; Wang et al., 2014; Keshavarz and Abadeh, 2017; Hu et al., 2016; Fu et al., 2016; Gong et al., 2016).

With respect to state of the art, this work represents the first exploration of evolutionary algorithms for multi-domain sentiment analysis with the aim of learning multiple dictionaries of opinion concepts. Moreover, we differ from the literature by do not considering the propagation of polarity information across domain (i.e., we keep them completely separated) in order to avoid transfer learning drawbacks.

3   System Implementation

NeuroSent has been entirely developed in Java with the support of the Deeplearning4j library [1] and it is composed by following two main phases:

- Generation of Word vectors (Section 3.1): raw text, appropriately tokenized using the Stanford CoreNLP Toolkit, is provided as input to a 2-layers neural network implementing the skip-gram approach with the aim of generating word vectors.

- Learning of Sentiment Model (Section 3.2): word vectors are used for training a recurrent neural network with an output layer customized based on the addressed subtask. The customizations have been explained in Section 4.

In the following subsections, we describe in more detail each phase by providing also the settings used for managing our data.

3.1   Generation of Word Vectors

The generation of the word vectors has been performed by applying the skip-gram algorithm on

---

[1] https://deeplearning4j.org/

the raw natural language text extracted from the smaller version of the SNAP dataset (McAuley and Leskovec, 2013). The rationale behind the choice of this dataset focuses on three reasons:

- the dataset contains only opinion-based documents. This way, we are able to build word embeddings describing only opinion-based contexts.

- the dataset is multi-domain. Information contained into the generated word embeddings comes from specific domains, thus it is possible to evaluate how the proposed approach is general by testing the performance of the created model on test sets containing documents coming from the domains used for building the model or from other domains.

- the dataset is smaller with respect to other corpora used in the literature for building other word embeddings that are currently freely available, like the Google News ones. [2] Indeed, as introduced in Section 1, one of our goal is to demonstrate how we can leverage the use of dedicated resources for generating word embeddings, instead of corpora's size, for improving the effectiveness of classification systems.

The aspect of considering only opinion-based information for generating word embeddings is one of the peculiarity of our system. While embeddings currently available are created from big corpora of general purpose texts (like news archives or Wikipedia pages), ours are generated by using a smaller corpus containing documents strongly related to the problem that the model will be thought for. On the one hand, this aspect may be considered a limitation of the proposed solution due to the requirement of training a new model in case of problem change. However, on the other hand, the usage of dedicated resources would lead to the construction of more effective models.

Word embeddings have been generated by the Word2Vec implementation integrated into the Deeplearning4j library. The algorithm has been set up with the following parameters: the size of the vector to 64, the size of the window used as input of the skip-gram algorithm to 5, and the minimum word frequency was set to 1. The reason for

which we kept the minimum word frequency set to 1 is to avoid the loss of rare but important words that can occur in domain specific documents.

3.2 Learning of The Sentiment Model

The sentiment model is built by starting from the word embeddings generated during the previous phase.

The first step consists in converting each textual sentence contained within the dataset into the corresponding numerical matrix $\mathbf{S}$ where we have in each row the word vector representing a single word of the sentence, and in each column an embedding feature. Given a sentence s, we extract all tokens t_i, with $i \in [0, n]$, and we replace each t_i with the corresponding embedding $\mathbf{w}$. During the conversion of each word in its corresponding embedding, if such embedding is not found, the word is discarded. At the end of this step, each sentence contained in the training set is converted in a matrix $\mathbf{S} = [\mathbf{w}^{\langle 1 \rangle}, \ldots, \mathbf{w}^{\langle n \rangle}]$.

Before giving all matrices as input to the neural network, we need to include both padding and masking vectors in order to train our model correctly. Padding and masking allows us to support different training situations depending on the number of the input vectors and on the number of predictions that the network has to provide at each time step. In our scenario, we work in a many-to-one situation where our neural network has to provide one prediction (sentence polarity and domain overlap) as result of the analysis of many input vectors (word embeddings).

Padding vectors are required because we have to deal with the different length of sentences. Indeed, the neural network needs to know the number of time steps that the input layer has to import. This problem is solved by including, if necessary, into each matrix $\mathbf{S}_k$, with $k \in [0, z]$ and z the number of sentences contained in the training set, null word vectors that are used for filling empty word's slots. These null vectors are accompanied by a further vector telling to the neural network if data contained in a specific positions has to be considered as an informative embedding or not.

A final note concerns the back propagation of the error. Training recurrent neural networks can be quite computationally demanding in cases when each training instance is composed by many time steps. A possible optimization is the use of truncated back propagation through time (BPTT)

---

[2] https://github.com/mmihaltz/word2vec-GoogleNews-vectors

that was developed for reducing the computational complexity of each parameter update in a recurrent neural network. On the one hand, this strategy allows to reduce the time needed for training our model. However, on the other hand, there is the risk of not flowing backward the gradients for the full unrolled network. This prevents the full update of all network parameters. For this reason, even if we work with recurrent neural networks, we decided to do not implement a BPTT approach but to use the default backpropagation implemented into the DL4J library.

Concerning information about network structure, the input layer was composed by 64 neurons (i.e. embedding vector size), the hidden RNN layer was composed by 128 nodes, and the output layers with a different number of nodes based on the addressed subtask. The network has been trained by using the Stochastic Gradient Descent with 1000 epochs and a learning rate of 0.002.

4 The Tasks

The SemEval 2018 Task 1 is composed by a set of five subtasks aiming to attract systems able to automatically determine the intensity of emotions and the intensity of sentiment of tweets' authors. Then, organizers included also a multi-label emotion classification task for tweets. For each task, there were provide separate training and test datasets for four languages: English, Arabic, and Spanish. The proposed system implements a strategy only for the English language. Below, we provide a summary of the five subtasks including how we configured the output layer of our neural network.

Subtask #1: EI-reg   Given a tweet and an emotion E, the system has to determine the intensity of E that best represents the mental state of the tweet's author by providing a real-valued score between 0 and 1. Here, four emotions are considered: anger, fear, joy, and sadness. Separated datasets have been provided for training the system. The output layer of our neural network is composed by a single neuron implementing the SIGMOID activation function.

Subtask #2: EI-oc   Given a tweet and an emotion E, the system has to classify the tweet into one of four ordinal classes of intensity of E that best represents the mental state of the tweet's author. Also here, four emotions are considered: anger, fear, joy, and sadness. Separated datasets have been provided for training the system. The output layer of our neural network is composed by four neurons and the SOFTMAX strategy has been implemented for selecting the most candidate emotion intensity class.

Subtask #3: V-reg   Given a tweet, the system has to determine the valence of a sentiment that best represents the mental state of tweet's author by providing a real-valued score between 0 and 1. The output layer of our neural network is composed by a single neuron implementing the SIGMOID activation function.

Subtask #4: V-oc   Given a tweet, the system has to classify it into one of seven ordinal classes (from -3 to 3) corresponding to various levels of positive and negative sentiment intensity. The output layer of our neural network is composed by seven neurons and the SOFTMAX strategy has been implemented for selecting the most candidate emotion intensity class.

Subtask #5: E-c   Given a tweet, the system has to classify it as a *neutral*, or *no emotion* or as one, or more, of eleven given emotions that best represent the mental state of the tweet's author. The eleven emotions are: anger, anticipation, disgust, fear, joy, love, optimism, pessimism, sadness, surprise, and trust. The output layer of our neural network is composed by eleven neurons implementing the SIGMOID activation function. This way, each emotion has been managed separately.

The NeuroSent system has been applied to all five subtasks. In Section 5, we report the preliminary results obtained by NeuroSent on the training set compared with a set of baselines.

5 In-Vitro Evaluation

The NeuroSent approach have been preliminarily evaluated by adopting the Dranziera protocol (Dragoni et al., 2016).

The validation procedure leverages on a five-fold cross evaluation setting in order to validate the robustness of the proposed solution. The approach has been compared with four baselines: Support Vector Machine (SVM) (Chang and Lin, 2011), Naive Bayes (NB) and Maximum Entropy (ME) (McCallum, 2002), and Convolutional Neural Network (Chaturvedi et al., 2016).

In Table 1, we provide for subtasks two, four, and five the average Pearson correlation obtained

Approach	Task #1.1	Task #1.2	Task #1.3	Task #1.4	Task #1.5
Support Vector Machine	0.3189	0.4890	0.3698	0.5145	0.3498
Naive-Bayes	0.2944	0.4956	0.3544	0.5387	0.4167
Maximum Entropy	0.2765	0.5073	0.3025	0.5777	0.4178
CNN Architecture	0.2433	0.6037	0.2466	0.5895	0.5487
NeuroSent	**0.2187**	**0.6687**	**0.2079**	**0.6241**	**0.5814**

Table 1: Results obtained on the training set by NeuroSent and by the four baselines.

on the five folds in which the training set has been split. While, for subtasks one and three, we provide the average mean square error.

The obtained results demonstrated the suitability of NeuroSent with respect to the adopted baselines. We may also observed how solutions based on neural networks obtained a significant improvement with respect to the others for the Tasks #1.2 and #1.4.

Then, for Tasks #1.2, #1.4, and #1.5, we performed a detailed error analysis concerning the performance of NeuroSent. In general, we observed how our strategy tends to provide false negative predictions. An in depth analysis of some incorrect predictions highlighted that the embedded representations of some positive opinion words are very close to the space region of negative opinion words. Even if we may state that the confidence about positive predictions is very high, this scenario leads to have a predominant negative classification for borderline instances.

On the one hand, a possible action for improving the effectiveness our strategy is to increase the granularity of the embeddings (i.e. augmenting the size of the embedding vectors) in order to increase the distance between the positive and negative polarities space regions. On the other hand, by increasing the size of embedding vectors, the computational time for building, or updating, the model and for evaluating a single instance increases as well. Part of the future work, will be the analysis of more efficient neural network architectures able to manage augmented embedding vectors without negatively affecting the efficiency of the platform.

6 Conclusion

In this paper, we described the NeuroSent system presented at SemEval 2018 Task 1. Our system makes use of artificial neural networks to classify tweets by polarity or for detecting emotion levels. The results obtained on the training set

demonstrated that the adopted solution is promising and worthy of investigation. Therefore, future work will focus on improving the system by exploring the integration of sentiment knowledge bases (Dragoni et al., 2015) in order to move toward a more cognitive approach.

References

Dimah Hussain Alahmadi and Xiao-Jun Zeng. 2015. Twitter-based recommender system to address cold-start: A genetic algorithm based trust modelling and probabilistic sentiment analysis. In *27th IEEE International Conference on Tools with Artificial Intelligence, ICTAI 2015, Vietri sul Mare, Italy, November 9-11, 2015*, pages 1045–1052. IEEE Computer Society.

John Blitzer, Mark Dredze, and Fernando Pereira. 2007. Biographies, bollywood, boom-boxes and blenders: Domain adaptation for sentiment classification. In *ACL 2007, Proceedings of the 45th Annual Meeting of the Association for Computational Linguistics, June 23-30, 2007, Prague, Czech Republic*. The Association for Computational Linguistics.

Danushka Bollegala, David J. Weir, and John A. Carroll. August 2013. Cross-domain sentiment classification using a sentiment sensitive thesaurus. *IEEE Trans. Knowl. Data Eng.*, 25(8):1719–1731.

Chih-Chung Chang and Chih-Jen Lin. 2011. Libsvm: A library for support vector machines. *ACM TIST*, 2(3):27:1–27:27.

Iti Chaturvedi, Erik Cambria, and David Vilares. 2016. Lyapunov filtering of objectivity for spanish sentiment model. In *2016 International Joint Conference on Neural Networks, IJCNN 2016, Vancouver, BC, Canada, July 24-29, 2016*, pages 4474–4481. IEEE.

An-Pin Chen and Yung-Hua Chang. 2005. Using extended classifier system to forecast s&p futures based on contrary sentiment indicators. In *Proceedings of the IEEE Congress on Evolutionary Computation, CEC 2005, 2-4 September 2005, Edinburgh, UK*, pages 2084–2090. IEEE.

Mauro Dragoni. 2015. Shellfbk: An information retrieval-based system for multi-domain sentiment analysis. In *Proceedings of the 9th International Workshop on Semantic Evaluation*, SemEval '2015, pages 502–509, Denver, Colorado. Association for Computational Linguistics.

Mauro Dragoni. 2017. Extracting linguistic features from opinion data streams for multi-domain sentiment analysis. In *Proceedings of the 3rd International Workshop at ESWC on Emotions, Modality, Sentiment Analysis and the Semantic Web co-located with 14th ESWC 2017, Portroz, Slovenia, May 28, 2017.*, volume 1874 of *CEUR Workshop Proceedings*. CEUR-WS.org.

Mauro Dragoni and Giulio Petrucci. 2017. A neural word embeddings approach for multi-domain sentiment analysis. *IEEE Trans. Affective Computing*, 8(4):457–470.

Mauro Dragoni and Giulio Petrucci. 2018. A fuzzy-based strategy for multi-domain sentiment analysis. *Int. J. Approx. Reasoning*, 93:59–73.

Mauro Dragoni, Andrea Tettamanzi, and Célia da Costa Pereira. 2016. DRANZIERA: an evaluation protocol for multi-domain opinion mining. In *Proceedings of the Tenth International Conference on Language Resources and Evaluation LREC 2016, Portorož, Slovenia, May 23-28, 2016*. European Language Resources Association (ELRA).

Mauro Dragoni, Andrea G. B. Tettamanzi, and Célia da Costa Pereira. 2014. A fuzzy system for concept-level sentiment analysis. In *Semantic Web Evaluation Challenge - SemWebEval 2014 at ESWC 2014, Anissaras, Crete, Greece, May 25-29, 2014, Revised Selected Papers*, volume 475 of *Communications in Computer and Information Science*, pages 21–27. Springer.

Mauro Dragoni, Andrea G. B. Tettamanzi, and Célia da Costa Pereira. 2015. Propagating and aggregating fuzzy polarities for concept-level sentiment analysis. *Cognitive Computation*, 7(2):186–197.

Mauro Dragoni, Andrea Giovanni Battista Tettamanzi, and Célia da Costa Pereira. April 2015. Propagating and aggregating fuzzy polarities for concept-level sentiment analysis. *Cognitive Computation*, 7(2):186–197.

Marco Federici and Mauro Dragoni. 2016a. A knowledge-based approach for aspect-based opinion mining. In *Semantic Web Challenges - Third SemWebEval Challenge at ESWC 2016, Heraklion, Crete, Greece, May 29 - June 2, 2016, Revised Selected Papers*, volume 641 of *Communications in Computer and Information Science*, pages 141–152. Springer.

Marco Federici and Mauro Dragoni. 2016b. Towards unsupervised approaches for aspects extraction. In *Joint Proceedings of the 2th Workshop on Emotions, Modality, Sentiment Analysis and the Semantic Web and the 1st International Workshop on Extraction and Processing of Rich Semantics from*

Medical Texts co-located with ESWC 2016, Heraklion, Greece, May 29, 2016., volume 1613 of *CEUR Workshop Proceedings*. CEUR-WS.org.

Lohann Ferreira, Mariza Dosciatti, Júlio C. Nievola, and Emerson Cabrera Paraiso. 2015. Using a genetic algorithm approach to study the impact of imbalanced corpora in sentiment analysis. In *Proceedings of the Twenty-Eighth International Florida Artificial Intelligence Research Society Conference, FLAIRS 2015, Hollywood, Florida. May 18-20, 2015.*, pages 163–168. AAAI Press.

Peng Fu, Zheng Lin, Hailun Lin, Fengcheng Yuan, Weiping Wang, and Dan Meng. 2016. Quantifying the effect of sentiment on topic evolution in chinese microblog. In *Web Technologies and Applications - 18th Asia-Pacific Web Conference, APWeb 2016, Suzhou, China, September 23-25, 2016. Proceedings, Part I*, volume 9931 of *Lecture Notes in Computer Science*, pages 531–542. Springer.

Lin Gong, Mohammad Al Boni, and Hongning Wang. 2016. Modeling social norms evolution for personalized sentiment classification. In *Proceedings of the 54th Annual Meeting of the Association for Computational Linguistics, ACL 2016, August 7-12, 2016, Berlin, Germany, Volume 1: Long Papers*. The Association for Computer Linguistics.

Yan Hu, Xiaofei Xu, and Li Li. 2016. Analyzing topic-sentiment and topic evolution over time from social media. In *Knowledge Science, Engineering and Management - 9th International Conference, KSEM 2016, Passau, Germany, October 5-7, 2016, Proceedings*, volume 9983 of *Lecture Notes in Computer Science*, pages 97–109.

Chien-Feng Huang, Tsung-Nan Hsieh, Bao Rong Chang, and Chih-Hsiang Chang. 2012. A comparative study of regression and evolution-based stock selection models for investor sentiment. In *2012 Third International Conference on Innovations in Bio-Inspired Computing and Applications, Kaohsiung City, Taiwan, September 26-28, 2012*, pages 73–78. IEEE.

Hamidreza Keshavarz and Mohammad Saniee Abadeh. 2017. ALGA: adaptive lexicon learning using genetic algorithm for sentiment analysis of microblogs. *Knowl.-Based Syst.*, 122:1–16.

Julian J. McAuley and Jure Leskovec. 2013. Hidden factors and hidden topics: understanding rating dimensions with review text. In *Seventh ACM Conference on Recommender Systems, RecSys '13, Hong Kong, China, October 12-16, 2013*, pages 165–172. ACM.

Andrew Kachites McCallum. 2002. Mallet: A machine learning for language toolkit. `http://mallet.cs.umass.edu`.

Saif M. Mohammad, Felipe Bravo-Marquez, Mohammad Salameh, and Svetlana Kiritchenko. 2018.

Semeval-2018 Task 1: Affect in tweets. In *Proceedings of International Workshop on Semantic Evaluation (SemEval-2018)*, New Orleans, LA, USA.

Aytug Onan, Serdar Korukoglu, and Hasan Bulut. 2016. A multiobjective weighted voting ensemble classifier based on differential evolution algorithm for text sentiment classification. *Expert Syst. Appl.*, 62:1–16.

Aytug Onan, Serdar Korukoglu, and Hasan Bulut. 2017. A hybrid ensemble pruning approach based on consensus clustering and multi-objective evolutionary algorithm for sentiment classification. *Inf. Process. Manage.*, 53(4):814–833.

Sinno Jialin Pan, Xiaochuan Ni, Jian-Tao Sun, Qiang Yang, and Zheng Chen. 2010. Cross-domain sentiment classification via spectral feature alignment. In *Proceedings of the 19th International Conference on World Wide Web, WWW 2010, Raleigh, North Carolina, USA, April 26-30, 2010*, pages 751–760. ACM.

Giulio Petrucci and Mauro Dragoni. 2015. An information retrieval-based system for multi-domain sentiment analysis. In *Semantic Web Evaluation Challenges - Second SemWebEval Challenge at ESWC 2015, Portorož, Slovenia, May 31 - June 4, 2015, Revised Selected Papers*, volume 548 of *Communications in Computer and Information Science*, pages 234–243. Springer.

Giulio Petrucci and Mauro Dragoni. 2016. The IRMU-DOSA system at ESWC-2016 challenge on semantic sentiment analysis. In *Semantic Web Challenges - Third SemWebEval Challenge at ESWC 2016, Heraklion, Crete, Greece, May 29 - June 2, 2016, Revised Selected Papers*, volume 641 of *Communications in Computer and Information Science*, pages 126–140. Springer.

Giulio Petrucci and Mauro Dragoni. 2017. The IR-MUDOSA system at ESWC-2017 challenge on semantic sentiment analysis. In *Semantic Web Challenges - 4th SemWebEval Challenge at ESWC 2017, Portoroz, Slovenia, May 28 - June 1, 2017, Revised Selected Papers*, volume 769 of *Communications in Computer and Information Science*, pages 148–165. Springer.

Natalia Ponomareva and Mike Thelwall. 2013. Semi-supervised vs. cross-domain graphs for sentiment analysis. In *Recent Advances in Natural Language Processing, RANLP 2013, 9-11 September, 2013, Hissar, Bulgaria*, pages 571–578. RANLP 2013 Organising Committee/ACL.

Carlos Simoes, Rui Ferreira Neves, and Nuno Horta. 2017. Using sentiment from twitter optimized by genetic algorithms to predict the stock market. In *2017 IEEE Congress on Evolutionary Computation, CEC 2017, Donostia, San Sebastián, Spain, June 5-8, 2017*, pages 1303–1310. IEEE.

Angela Charng-Rurng Tsai, Chi-En Wu, Richard Tzong-Han Tsai, and Jane Yung jen Hsu. March 2013. Building a concept-level sentiment dictionary based on commonsense knowledge. *IEEE Int. Systems*, 28(2):22–30.

Zhitao Wang, Zhiwen Yu, Zhu Wang, and Bin Guo. 2014. Investigating sentiment impact on information propagation and its evolution in microblog. In *2014 International Conference on Behavioral, Economic, and Socio-Cultural Computing, BESC 2014, Shanghai, China, October 30 - November 1, 2014*, pages 33–39. IEEE.

Rui Xia, Chengqing Zong, Xuelei Hu, and Erik Cambria. May-June 2013. Feature ensemble plus sample selection: Domain adaptation for sentiment classification. *IEEE Int. Systems*, 28(3):10–18.

Takashi Yamada and Kazuhiro Ueda. 2005. Explanation of binarized time series using genetic learning model of investor sentiment. In *Proceedings of the IEEE Congress on Evolutionary Computation, CEC 2005, 2-4 September 2005, Edinburgh, UK*, pages 2437–2444. IEEE.

Steve Y. Yang, Sheung Yin Kevin Mo, Anqi Liu, and Andrei Kirilenko. 2017. Genetic programming optimization for a sentiment feedback strength based trading strategy. *Neurocomputing*, 264:29–41.

FOI DSS at SemEval-2018 Task 1: Combining LSTM States, Embeddings, and Lexical Features for Affect Analysis

Maja Karasalo   **Mattias Nilsson**   **Magnus Rosell**   **Ulrika Wickenberg Bolin**

FOI - Swedish Defence Research Agency

`{majkar, matnil, magros, ulrwic}@foi.se`

Abstract

This paper describes the system used and results obtained for team FOI DSS at SemEval-2018 Task 1: Affect In Tweets. The team participated in all English language subtasks, with a method utilizing transfer learning from LSTM nets trained on large sentiment datasets combined with embeddings and lexical features. For four out of five subtasks, the system performed in the range of 92-95% of the winning systems, in terms of the competition metrics. Analysis of the results suggests that improved pre-processing and addition of more lexical features may further elevate performance.

1 Introduction

In the field of automatic emotion detection, many contributions consider the issue of detecting presence of emotions (Liu, 2012). The task of detecting intensity of emotion in a given text is less studied, but is relevant to many applications in fields such as e.g., brand management, public health, politics, and disaster handling (Mohammad, 2016). When developing prediction systems, access to suitably annotated data is critical. Most annotated emotion and affect datasets are categorical, but examples of sets annotated with intensity or degree of emotional content include EmoBank (Buechel and Hahn, 2017a,b), AFINN (Nielsen, 2011), the Pietro Facebook post set (Preoţiuc-Pietro et al., 2016), and the Warriner-Kuperman set (Warriner et al., 2013). For tweets, the Tweet Emotion Intensity Dataset (Mohammad and Bravo-Marquez, 2017) has recently been published, with more than 7000 tweets annotated with emotion category and intensity.

This paper describes methods used and results achieved with the FOI DSS contribution to the five subtasks for English tweets of SemEval 2018 Task 1: Affect in Tweets (Mohammad et al., 2018).

The paper is organized as follows. A description of Task 1 is provided in Section 2. Section 3 discusses the provided datasets. Section 4 describes the methods and system used to produce predictions of scores and labels for all subtasks. In Sections 5 and 6 results are presented and analyzed, and suggestions for improvements are outlined. Finally, concluding remarks are found in Section 7.

2 Task formulation

Task 1 consisted of five subtasks, all regarding estimation of the mental state of a tweeter, based on the tweeted text. Valence[1] intensity, as well as emotion, and emotion intensity classification, were covered. The subtasks are summarized below:

1. **Emotion intensity regression (EI-reg):** For a given tweet and emotion[2], determine the intensity of the emotion as a score $\in [0, 1]$.

2. **Emotion intensity, ordinal classification (EI-oc):** For a given tweet and emotion[2], classify the tweet into one of four ordinal classes of intensity.

3. **Valence regression (V-reg):** For a given tweet, determine the intensity of valence as a score $\in [0, 1]$.

4. **Valence, ordinal classification (V-oc):** For a given tweet, classify it into one of seven ordinal classes corresponding to levels of positive and negative intensity.

5. **Multi-label emotion classification (E-c):** For a given tweet and eleven emotions[3], classify the tweet as neutral, or expressing one or more of the emotions.

---

[1]The intrinsic attractiveness (positive valence) or averseness (negative valence) of an event, object, or situation (Frijda, 1986).

[2]anger, joy, fear or sadness.

[3]anger, anticipation, disgust, fear, joy, love, optimism, pessimism, sadness, surprise and trust.

Proceedings of the 12th International Workshop on Semantic Evaluation (SemEval-2018), pages 109–115

New Orleans, Louisiana, June 5–6, 2018. ©2018 Association for Computational Linguistics

Subtask	Train	Val.	Test
EI anger	1701	388	1002
EI fear	2252	389	986
EI joy	1616	290	1105
EI sadness	1533	397	975
V	1181	449	937
E-c	6838	886	3259

Table 1: Number of tweets in the datasets for different subtasks. The sets for EI-reg and EI-oc were identical, as was also the case for V-reg and V-oc.

3 Data

The dataset made available for Task 1 was the AIT Dataset (Mohammad and Kiritchenko, 2018). For each subtask, labeled datasets for training and validation were released for the prediction system development phase. Intensity scores were roughly normally distributed, and ordinal classes were defined as intervals for the scores. Unlabeled test data was later released for the evaluation phase. Table 1 gives a brief overview of the data. Details on the data and annotation can be found in (Mohammad et al., 2018) and (Mohammad and Kiritchenko, 2018).

In addition to the test data, an unlabeled "mystery" set of 16937 short texts was provided for the regression subtasks. The task organizers asked that participants in these subtasks use their existing systems to produce predictions for the mystery set as well, and the results were used to perform a bias analysis. This is further discussed in Section 5.4.

4 Method

Initially, the team focused on Subtask 4 (V-reg). Several different approaches were explored, and evaluated using the official competition metric, the Pearson Correlation Coefficient (PCC) with gold ratings. The combination of methods found to have the best performance on the V-reg task was chosen. The approach is described in Sections 4.1 - 4.3. Contributions to Subtasks 1, 2, 3 and 5 were constructed by altering the final stage model to fit each task, and tuning the hyperparameters for best performance.

4.1 Pre-processing

We performed some rudimentary pre-processing of the tweets prior to feature extraction. Following the findings reported in (Zhao, 2015) we ex-

panded negations such as "can't" and "n't" etc., into "cannot" and "not". The hashtag character # was also removed and we replaced user names and links with "usr" and "http://url", respectively. We finally mapped unicoded emoticons into their associated emoticon text description [4].

4.2 Feature Extraction

The small amount of labeled data prevented us from automatically discovering optimal features for the different tasks. Instead, we utilized transfer learning techniques (i.e., reusing a model trained on a different but related task where more data is available) and classical natural language processing features. Three different methods were used to extract features from the tweet sets; two using variants of Long Short-Term Memory (LSTM) nets obtained by training on large sentiment datasets and extracting the internal model states, and one utilizing the Weka Affective Tweets package. The feature vectors from each of the methods described below were then concatenated to form one 5265 dimensional feature vector for each tweet.

4.2.1 Sentiment Neuron

In (Radford et al., 2017), the authors consider the problem of predicting the next character in a text given the preceding characters. More specifically, they predict next byte (each UTF-8 encoded character constitutes one to four bytes) from the previous bytes using a single layer multiplicative LSTM (Krause et al., 2016) with 4096 states. The model was trained using 82 million Amazon product reviews amounting to 38 billion bytes of training data. The authors show state-of-the-art (or close to state-of-the-art) sentiment classification performance on four different datasets when training a logistic regression classifier with the model's states as feature vector. Because of the reported strong predictive quality of the model's state we used that as one of the feature vectors for our method. We used the authors code for feature extraction available on github [5].

4.2.2 Bidirectional-LSTM

Tweets can often be quite different from typical text seen in novels, news, or product reviews.

---

[4] https://apps.timwhitlock.info/emoji/tables/unicode#block-6a-additional-emoticons

[5] https://github.com/openai/generating-reviews-discovering-sentiment

The short messages commonly contain intentional misspelling to express affects (e.g., happpppyyy), hashtags (e.g., #love), and emoticons (e.g., :-)). One option to capture the specific characteristics of tweets would be to fine-tune the sentiment neuron model described in the previous section using twitter data. We did not explore this direction in this work. Instead, in an attempt to directly capture affects, we trained (from scratch) a bidirectional LSTM on a sentiment labeled (two classes; positive and negative sentiment) twitter dataset [6]. The dataset contains 1.5 million tweets and we used 90% for training and 10% for validation. We used a bidirectional LSTM with 512 states in each direction (1024 in total). The input characters were first mapped to integers and subsequently fed to the embedding front-end (where an integer to a dense 64 dimensional embedding is learned) of the bidirectional LSTM. A dropout of 50% was used during the training for the sentiment prediction. The model achieves approximately 85% classification accuracy on the validation set. Similar to the sentiment neuron's multiplicative LSTM we use the bidirectional LSTM's state as a feature vector.

4.2.3 Weka Affective Tweets filters

A combination of tweet-level filters from the Weka Affective Tweets package (Mohammad and Bravo-Marquez, 2017) was used as the third part of the feature extraction method. These filters produce embeddings and lexical features, e.g. counts of positive and negative sentiment words, from systems such as the NRC-Canada System[7].

To evaluate contributions from different filters, the final stage model (Section 4.3) was run using their resulting feature vectors for the V-reg dataset as input. For combinations of filters, the resulting feature vectors were concatenated and run through the final stage model. Details of this evaluation can be found in Section 5.1

4.3 Final stage

For each of the different subtasks we trained a fully connected neural network with two hidden layers mapping the input feature vector (i.e., the concatenation of the feature vectors described in Sections 4.2.1 - 4.2.3) to the target value, class, or

classes. The activation function for the two hidden layers was $tanh$ and the activation functions for the output layer were set to linear, softmax, and sigmoid for the V-reg/EI-reg, V-oc/EI-oc, and E-c subtasks, respectively.

The Adam optimizer (Kingma and Ba, 2015) was used for the classification subtasks with categorical cross-entropy loss for the V-oc/EI-oc subtasks and binary cross-entropy loss for the E-c subtask. For the regression subtasks of V-reg and EI-reg we used mean squared error as loss function and the ADADELTA optimizer (Zeiler, 2012). However, the performance difference between Adam and ADADELTA was minor in our regression subtasks.

We used L2-regularization on the parameters of the hidden layers. For each subtask, the hyper-parameters (i.e., the penalty and the layer sizes) of the neural network were found by a grid search evaluating the PCC (or the Jaccard similarity score for E-c subtask) on the validation data.

The hyper-parameter search range was $[0.001, 0.05]$ for the penalty and $[5, 80]$ for the two layer sizes. Many configurations with quite different hyper-parameter values resulted in very similar scores. E.g., for the V-reg subtask the configurations[8] (0.03,10,15), (0.03,15,40), and (0.0096,70,35) all resulted in PCCs in the range 0.841-0.846.

5 Results

In this section we present a performance analysis of the set of features used, as well as results on the different subtasks.

5.1 Feature evaluation

To assess the quality of the feature vectors described in Section 4.2 we computed the PCC on the V-reg subtask using the validation data. For each set of features listed in Table 2 we performed a hyper-parameter search to find the parameters of the final stage model maximizing the PCC (cf. Section 4.3).

As seen in Table 2 the features provided by the Weka Affective Tweets package have the strongest individual predictive power. From the Weka filters, the feature combination chosen to be included in the combined method was $W_E + W_{SS} + W_L$, which produced the highest PCC during evaluation.

---

[6]http://thinknook.com/twitter-sentiment-analysis-training-corpus-dataset-2012-09-22/

[7]http://saifmohammad.com/WebPages/NRC-Canada-Sentiment.htm

[8]configuration = (penalty, layer 1 size, layer 2 size)

Features	PCC
Weka	
TweetToEmbeddings (W_E)[9]	0.665
TweetToEmbeddings 400 (W_{E400}) [10]	0.702
TweetToSentiStrength (W_{SS})	0.675
TweetToLexicon (W_L)	0.790
TweetToInputLexicon (W_{IL})	0.687
W_E + W_{SS} + W_L	**0.800**
W_E + W_{SS} + W_L + W_{IL}	0.797
W_{E400} + W_{SS} + W_L	0.795
Sentiment Neuron (SN)	0.767
Bi-LSTM	0.738
SN + Bi-LSTM	0.818
Bi-LSTM + W_E + W_{SS} + W_L	0.820
SN + W_E + W_{SS} + W_L	0.838
SN + Bi-LSTM + W_E + W_{SS} + W_L	**0.846**

Table 2: **V-reg validation set:** PCC of valence intensity score predictions with gold scores for the different feature vector combinations.

Although the sentiment neuron is not trained on Twitter specific data it still shows good performance. The bidirectional LSTM has the weakest performance but still has a positive impact on the final score.

5.2 Results on validation and test data

The official competition metric was PCC for Subtasks 1-4, but as Subtask 5 was a multi-label classification task, the metric used was multi label accuracy, or Jaccard similarity score. The PCC/Jaccard similarity score for validation and test data for the FOI DSS system is presented in Table 3. For the regression tasks, the system's performance on the test data is close to the validation data results. For the classification tasks, the gap between validation and test scores is somewhat larger, indicating that the model may be biased for the validation data.

The team's ranking in different subtasks varied from 6 (out of 46 and 35 teams, respectively) for EI-reg and V-oc, to 11 of 37 for EI-oc. For Subtasks 1,3,4, and 5 the scores of our system was in the range of 92-95 % of the winning result on each subtask. The weakest performance was observed on Subtask 2 (EI-oc), with a PCC corresponding

---

[9]The TweetToEmbeddingsFeatureVector filter using embeddings trained from the small default corpus, yielding a 100-dimensional feature vector. https://affectivetweets.cms.waikato.ac.nz. .

[10]The TweetToEmbeddingsFeatureVector filter using embeddings trained from the 10 million tweets of the Edinburgh corpus (Petrović et al., 2010), yielding a 400-dimensional feature vector.

Subtask	Validation	Test	Baseline (Test)
EI-reg	0.739	0.737	0.520
EI-oc	0.636	0.590	0.394
V-reg	0.846	0.831	0.585
V-oc	0.818	0.777	0.509
E-c	0.554	0.544	0.442

Table 3: PCC/Jaccard similarity score on validation and test data for the FOI DSS system for all English subtasks of Task 1. The performance of the organizers' SVM unigrams baseline model on the test data is provided for comparison.

to 84 % of winning PCC. Figure 1 shows results of the FOI DSS system compared to mean, median and max competition results for test data on all English subtasks.

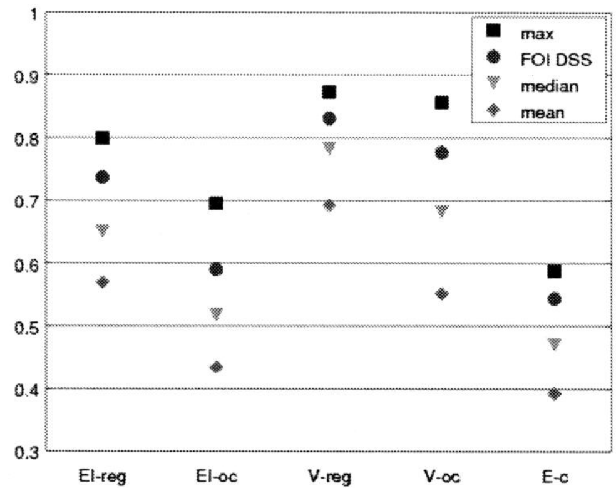

Figure 1: PCC/Jaccard similarity score of test data score and label predictions with gold scores and labels for all English subtasks. FOI DSS results compared to mean, median and max results for all participating teams.

5.3 Error analysis on the V-reg subtask

As already mentioned, our method achieved a PCC of 0.831 for the V-reg subtask on the test data. Figure 2 shows the corresponding scatter plot of the estimated and gold valence. To get some insight into potential future improvements of our system it is of interest to do analysis of tweets having poor valence estimates.

Some of the tweets from the validation and test datasets with large absolute error between the estimated and gold valence are listed in Table 4. For the first validation set tweet our method predicted a fairly low valence whereas the gold score is fairly high. A possible explanation could be that our system has problems with the constructions

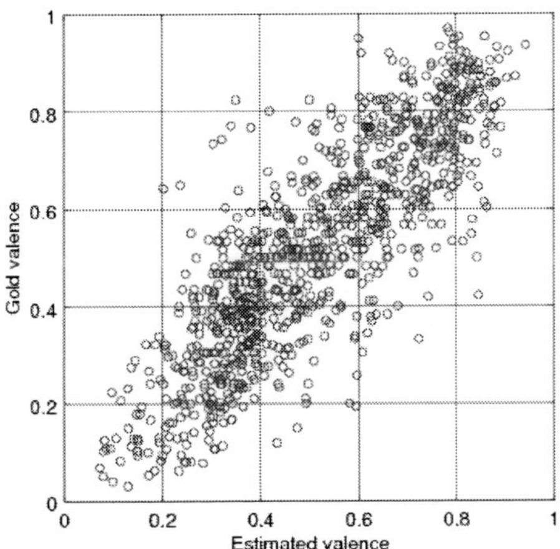

Figure 2: Scatter plot showing the estimated versus gold valence for the V-reg test dataset.

and concatenations such as B4, Thankful4all, and ImWakingUpHappyNot. Especially not properly splitting the last concatenation leaves the end of the tweet "dreading the day" which should result in a low valence.

The emoticon of the second validation tweet, \xF0\x9F\x98\xA4, is interesting. It depicts a face with steam coming out of the nostrils, which clearly signals anger, but the mapping[4] we used describes it (wrongly according to us) as "face with look of triumph". In the third tweet we failed to map the emoticon \xF0\x9F\xA4\xA3 to words. The emoticon shows some sort of laughing creature.

The top two test set tweets in Table 4 had the largest prediction errors for this set. They were both predicted to have a lower valence than the gold score. Interestingly, they both contain the hashtag #blessed and include constructions using the word *not*, where, if the negation is missed, the sentiment of the tweet would change from positive to negative. Possibly, our method has trouble correctly interpreting the negation and also has failed to award enough importance to the positive sentiment word *blessed*. Since our pre-processing involved removing hashtag character #, added intensity expressed this way will not be captured.

Finally, the third test set tweet had a high predicted valence but a low gold score. This text contains both negative words and phrases such as *nervous* and *I could puke*, but also expresses laughter. It would seem our method has deemed the latter a marker of high valence, while a human reader would probably interpret it as a nervous laughter, thus low valence, considering the context provided by the tweet as a whole.

5.4 Mystery dataset and bias analysis

An analysis for inapproperiate gender and race bias in scoring and classifications was performed by the task organizers for the "mystery" dataset (Section 3). For most teams, the bias was small (below 3%) but statistically significant, in part likely due to biases in the AIT dataset. For the FOI DSS system, the biases were below average for EI-joy, EI-sadness and valence, and 1% or less for all datasets except gender bias for EI-fear (2.3%). Biases in the datasets used to train our LSTM models as well as in the lexicons used to extract lexical features may have contributed to biases in scoring and classification.

6 Discussion

Designing high performance regression and classification algorithms using only a small amount of labeled data is always a challenge. The variability in tweets is enormous, and thus, there is a major risk of over-fitting when designing and tuning the algorithms on the the very limited labeled datasets provided for the competition. We used transfer learning and classical NLP features to alleviate the problem. We believe further improvements can be made by reducing the noise of the dataset, features, and final prediction. In the following, we discuss some of these ideas.

6.1 Pre-processing extensions

The error analysis in Section 5.3 indicates that the performance of our method could be improved by extending and refining the pre-processing. Splitting concatenations into separate words and addressing some common abbreviations would be one extension. Adjusting the emoticon lookup tables would be another.

6.2 Weka filter combinations: robustness

The combination of Weka Affective Tweets filters used in the FOI DSS system, $W_E + W_{SS} + W_L$, achieved the highest PCC during evaluation (Section 5.1). However, as results for neural networks are hard to reproduce, it should be examined what combinations of filters on average perform better. Initial findings from two such evaluations conducted after the end of the competition are reported in this section:

113

Dataset	Tweet	Pred.	Gold
Validation	B4 I couldnt get out of bed or look in mirror Thankful4all the support I have recieved here ImWakingUpHappyNot dreading theday	0.303	0.734
	3 and a half hour more \xF0\x9F\x98\xA4 #EXO	0.603	0.250
	@TheEllenShow I follow you bc your TV show keeps me laughing \xF0\x9F\xA4\xA3. When you #startle your guest sitting on that couch...booo...	0.461	0.783
Test	i'll have my own apartment and not have to sneak alcohol into my dorm room or worry about being loud #blessed	0.349	0.823
	mum got out of a rlly bad car crash completely not injured and i found a rlly sentimental piece of jewellery i thought i'd lost #blessed	0.203	0.643
	I'm so nervous I could puke + my body temp is rising ha ha ha ha ha	0.845	0.422

Table 4: Tweets with large prediction errors for the valence validation and test sets.

1. W_{E400} : When used on their own, the W_{E400} filter, which utilizes a much larger corpus[10], outperforms W_E (Table 2). Therefore it is of interest to compare performance of the two filters combined with W_{SS} and W_L.

2. W_{IL}: Using its default lexicon[11], W_{IL} produces 4-dimensional feature vectors. We wanted to investigate whether contributions from W_{IL} on average increases performance.

The different vector combinations were input to the final stage model (Section 4.3) for 486 different hyper-parameter configurations, and the resulting PCC scores were compared. For 59% of the configurations, W_E + W_{SS} +W_L still performed better than W_{E400} + W_{SS} + W_L. It would therefore seem that the loss of features captured by the larger W_{E400} vector is compensated for when combining the smaller W_E vector with W_{SS} + W_L.

However, W_E + W_{SS} +W_L +W_{IL} outperformed W_E + W_{SS} +W_L for 67% of the configurations. We may therefore conclude that including the W_{IL} filter would result in an overall more robust system.

6.3 Final stage: robustness

The purpose of the validation data is to measure generalization of the method. However, given the small dataset size there is as well an imminent risk of over-fitting against the validation data when searching for the optimal hyper-parameters. The latter might be the reason for the performance gaps between validation and test PCCs for the EI-oc and V-oc subtasks in particular. Also, even when using the same hyper-parameter settings, the

performance (in terms of PCC/Jaccard similarity score) of the final stage varies depending on the random initialization of the network parameters. Constructing an ensemble estimate, using multiple final stage models for each subtask, could perhaps be beneficial for the performance on the test set.

7 Conclusions

This paper presents the method and results for the FOI DSS contribution to SemEval-2018 Task 1. A major challenge with this task was the small amount of available labeled data. We utilized techniques such as transfer learning as well as classical NLP features. Our system used features from Weka Affective Tweets combined with two LSTM-state vectors. Fully connected neural networks with two hidden layers were used to map the features into the target outputs for each of the subtasks. For subtasks EI-reg, V-reg, V-oc, and E-c the PCC/Jaccard similarity score of our system was in the range of 92-95 % of the winning result. The weakest performance was observed on subtask EI-oc. Initial error- and robustness analysis indicates that performance might be enhanced by improved pre-processing of the tweets, and by including more lexical features. The difference between our results on validation and test data was larger for the emotion intensity classification subtasks than for the regression and emotion classification subtasks, which would be interesting to investigate further.

Acknowledgments

We would like to thank Magnus Sahlgren for valuable input on the algorithmic design.

[11]The NRC-AffectIntensity lexicon (Mohammad, 2017).

References

Sven Buechel and Udo Hahn. 2017a. Emobank: Studying the impact of annotation perspective and representation format on dimensional emotion analysis. In *Proceedings of the 15th Conference of the European Chapter of the Association for Computational Linguistics: Volume 2, Short Papers*, volume 2, pages 578–585.

Sven Buechel and Udo Hahn. 2017b. Readers vs. writers vs. texts: Coping with different perspectives of text understanding in emotion annotation. In *Proceedings of the 11th Linguistic Annotation Workshop*, pages 1–12.

Nico H Frijda. 1986. *The emotions*. Cambridge University Press.

Diederik P. Kingma and Jimmy Ba. 2015. Adam: A method for stochastic optimization. In *Proceedings of the International Conference for Learning Representations ICLR*.

Ben Krause, Iain Murray, Steve Renals, and Liang Lu. 2016. Multiplicative LSTM for sequence modelling. *arXiv preprint arXiv:1609.07959*.

Bing Liu. 2012. Sentiment analysis and opinion mining. *Synthesis lectures on human language technologies*, 5(1):1–167.

Saif M Mohammad. 2016. Sentiment analysis: detecting valence, emotions, and other affectual states from text. *Emotion Measurement*, pages 201–237.

Saif M. Mohammad. 2017. Word affect intensities. *CoRR*, abs/1704.08798.

Saif M Mohammad and Felipe Bravo-Marquez. 2017. Emotion intensities in tweets. *arXiv preprint arXiv:1708.03696*.

Saif M. Mohammad, Felipe Bravo-Marquez, Mohammad Salameh, and Svetlana Kiritchenko. 2018. Semeval-2018 Task 1: Affect in tweets. In *Proceedings of International Workshop on Semantic Evaluation (SemEval-2018)*, New Orleans, LA, USA.

Saif M. Mohammad and Svetlana Kiritchenko. 2018. Understanding emotions: A dataset of tweets to study interactions between affect categories. In *Proceedings of the 11th Edition of the Language Resources and Evaluation Conference*, Miyazaki, Japan.

Finn Årup Nielsen. 2011. A new anew: Evaluation of a word list for sentiment analysis in microblogs. *arXiv preprint arXiv:1103.2903*.

Saša Petrović, Miles Osborne, and Victor Lavrenko. 2010. The edinburgh twitter corpus. In *Proceedings of the NAACL HLT 2010 Workshop on Computational Linguistics in a World of Social Media*, pages 25–26.

Daniel Preoţiuc-Pietro, H Andrew Schwartz, Gregory Park, Johannes Eichstaedt, Margaret Kern, Lyle Ungar, and Elisabeth Shulman. 2016. Modelling valence and arousal in facebook posts. In *Proceedings of the 7th Workshop on Computational Approaches to Subjectivity, Sentiment and Social Media Analysis*, pages 9–15.

Alec Radford, Rafal Jozefowicz, and Ilya Sutskever. 2017. Learning to generate reviews and discovering sentiment. *arXiv preprint arXiv:1704.01444*.

Amy Beth Warriner, Victor Kuperman, and Marc Brysbaert. 2013. Norms of valence, arousal, and dominance for 13,915 english lemmas. *Behavior research methods*, 45(4):1191–1207.

Matthew D. Zeiler. 2012. ADADELTA: An adaptive learning rate method. *arXiv preprint arXiv:1212.5701*.

Jianqiang Zhao. 2015. Pre-processing boosting twitter sentiment analysis? In *IEEE International Conference on Smart City/SocialCom/SustainCom (SmartCity)*, pages 748–753.

NLPZZX at SemEval-2018 Task 1: Using Ensemble Method for Emotion and Sentiment Intensity Determination

Zhengxin Zhang, Qimin Zhou, Hao Wu
School of Information Science and Engineering, Yunnan University
Chenggong Campus, Kunming, P.R. China
{zzxynu, zqmynu}@gmail.com, haowu@ynu.edu.cn

Abstract

In this paper, we put forward a system that competed at SemEval-2018 Task 1: "Affect in Tweets". Our system uses a simple yet effective ensemble method which combines several neural network components. We participate in two subtasks for English tweets: EI-reg and V-reg. For two subtasks, different combinations of neural components are examined. For EI-reg, our system achieves an accuracy of 0.727 in Pearson Correlation Coefficient (all instances) and an accuracy of 0.555 in Pearson Correlation Coefficient (0.5-1). For V-reg, the achieved accuracy scores are respectively 0.835 and 0.670.

1 Introduction

Sentiment analysis is a research area in the field of natural language processing. It aims to detect the sentiment expressed by the author of some form of textual data and many deep learning approaches have been successfully exploited (Cambria, 2016). The goal of SemEval-2018 Task 1 "Affect in Tweets" is to automatically determine the intensity of emotions and intensity of sentiment of the tweeters from their tweets (Mohammad et al., 2018). All tweets fall into three languages: *English*, *Arabic* and *Spanish*. We participate in two subtasks for English tweets: EI-reg and V-reg. For EI-reg, all English tweets are separated into four emotions, anger, fear, joy and sadness. Every emotion has train, dev and test datasets. This subtask determines the intensity which is a real-valued score between 0 and 1 of emotion that represents the mental state of the tweeter. The instances with higher scores correspond to a greater degree of emotion than instances with lower scores. For V-reg, all English tweets are divided into three datasets: train, dev and test datasets. It determines the intensity of

sentiment or valence that best represents the mental state of the tweeter a real-valued score between 0 and 1. The instances with higher scores correspond to a greater degree of positive sentiment than instances with lower scores. Both the two subtasks are regression tasks.

For these two subtasks, we have adopted separate ensemble method with existing neural network components (Brueckner and Schulter, 2014; Kim, 2014; Li and Qian, 2016; Yang et al., 2017) (see Figure 1). We use BiLSTM-CNN component, BiLSTM-Attention component and Deep BiLSTM-Attention component with different embeddings for simple ensemble. In these subtasks, our final model is just an average of scores provided by what we select from these single neural network components. Every emotion or valence employs different ensemble method, so there are several distinct ensemble methods in the two subtasks. Experimental results show that our proposed ensemble methods are simple yet effective.

The remainder of the paper is structured as follows. We provide details of the proposed ensemble method in Section 2. We present the experimental result of proposed methods in Section 3. Finally, a conclusion is drawn in section 4.

2 Methodology

We propose an simple ensemble method of different neural network components. We mainly introduce the implementation details of these components, including raw tweets preprocessing, lexicon features and embedding resources we use in these components, the architecture of these components and the best parameters of different single components. The parameters that can maximize the Pearson Correlation Coefficient between the predicted values and real values are chosen to be the best parameters.

Proceedings of the 12th International Workshop on Semantic Evaluation (SemEval-2018), pages 116–122
New Orleans, Louisiana, June 5–6, 2018. ©2018 Association for Computational Linguistics

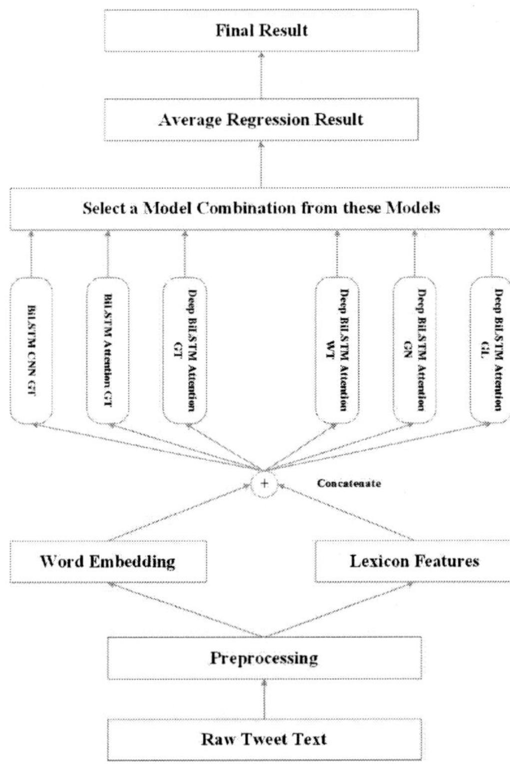

Figure 1: The architecture of our system.

2.1 Data Preprocessing

In general, tweet are not always syntactically well-structured and the language used does not always strictly adhere to grammatical rules (Barbosa and Feng, 2010). So we need to preprocess raw tweets before feature extraction. Firstly, we perform a few preprocessing steps, such as remove # and retain the word itself, remove stop words with nltk.corpus. Then the tweets are transformed into lowercase. Finally, we utilize TweetTokenizer[1] to process the tweets.

2.2 Feature Extraction

Each tweet is represented as a concatenation of two different feature vectors, one is lexicon features and another is word embedding. In our system, each tweet is divided into words, every word is represented as a $d + m$ dimension vector and thus each tweet is represented as $l(d + m)$ matrix, where d is the dimension of word embedding and m is the dimension of lexicon features. Suppose each tweet has the same length, so l is the length

[1] http://www.nltk.org/

of tweet. We utilize a variety of resources for feature extraction as follows:

1. AFINN: Calculating positive and negative sentiment scores from the lexicon (Nielsen, 2011).

2. NRC Affect Intensity Lexicon: The NRC Affect Intensity Lexicon is a list of English words and their associations with four basic emotions (anger, fear, sadness, joy) (Mohammad, 2017).

3. NRC Emotion Lexicon: The NRC Emotion Lexicon is a list of English words and their associations with eight basic emotions (anger, fear, anticipation, trust, surprise, sadness, joy, and disgust) and two sentiments (negative and positive) (Mohammad and Turney, 2010).

4. NRC Hashtag Emotion Lexicon: Association of words with eight emotions (anger, fear, anticipation, trust, surprise, sadness, joy, and disgust) generated automatically from tweets with emotion-word hashtags (Mohammad, 2012).

5. NRC Emoticon Lexicon: Association of words with positive (negative) sentiment generated automatically from tweets with emoticons (Kiritchenko et al., 2014; Mohammad et al., 2013; Zhu et al., 2014).

6. NRC Emoticon Affirmative Context Lexicon and NRC Emoticon Negated Context Lexicon: Association of words with positive (negative) sentiment in affirmative or negated contexts generated automatically from tweets with emoticons (Kiritchenko et al., 2014; Mohammad et al., 2013; Zhu et al., 2014).

7. NRC Hashtag Affirmative Context Sentiment Lexicon and NRC Hashtag Negated Context Sentiment Lexicon: Association of words with positive (negative) sentiment in affirmative or negated contexts generated automatically from tweets with sentiment-word hashtags (Kiritchenko et al., 2014; Mohammad et al., 2013; Zhu et al., 2014).

8. NRC Hashtag Sentiment Lexicon: Association of words with positive (negative) sentiment generated automatically from tweets

with sentiment-word hashtags (Kiritchenko et al., 2014; Mohammad et al., 2013; Zhu et al., 2014).

9. Emoji: This is a manual classification of the dictionary, in which each emoji has a corresponding polarity value.

10. Sentiwordnet: Sentiwordnet is a lexical resource explicitly devised for supporting sentiment classification and opinion mining applications (Baccianella et al., 2010), through the wordnet entry in the emotional classification, and marked each entry belongs to the positive and negative categories weight size.

2.3 Neural Networks

2.3.1 Embeddings

The final model combines three neural network components as *BiLSTM-CNN*, *BiLSTM-Attention*, and *Deep BiLSTM-Attention*. Towards BiLSTM-CNN and BiLSTM-Attention, we use *glove.twitter.27B.200d* which contains pre-trained word vectors with Glove algorithm (Pennington et al., 2014). For Deep BiLSTM-Attention, different pre-trained word vectors are used, such as *word2vec-twitter-model*, *GoogleNews-vectors-negative300*, *glove.twitter.27B.200d and glove.840B.300d*.

1. word2vec-twitter-model [2]: word2vec model (Mikolov et al., 2013) is a NLP tool launched by Google in 2013. It features the quantification of all words so that words can be quantified to measure the relationship between them. word2vec-twitter-model is trained on tweets and the embedding dimension used in our system is 400.

2. GoogleNews-vectors-negative300 [3]: Google-News vectors is trained on Google News corpus. It resembles word2vec-twitter-model and the embedding dimension is 300.

3. glove.840B.300d [4]: Glove is an unsupervised learning algorithm for obtaining vector representations for words. Training is conducted on aggregated co-occurrences of words from a global corpus, and the resulting representations showcase interesting linear substructures of the word vector space. The embedding dimension used in our system is 300.

4. glove.twitter.27B.200d [4]: This word embedding is trained on 2 billion tweets from twitter. It is similar to glove.840B.300d, but the embedding dimension is 200.

2.3.2 Bidirectional LSTM with CNN

The BiLSTM with CNN first transform tweets into text matrices, the BiLSTM is applied to these matrices to build new text matrices, CNN is applied to the output of the BiLSTM to obtain text vectors for the prediction of emotional intensity. The BiLSTM with CNN achieves a rather good result on the task of emotional analysis (He et al., 2017). so we choose it for our task.

Model Architecture: Embedding vectors are fed into a BiLSTM network followed by a CNN layer. The CNN layer consists of one dimensional convolutional layer and pooling layer where the number of filters is 256, the window size of the filter is 3, and the *activation function* is Relu. The input and output shape of convolutional layer are both 3D tensor. The output of the CNN layer is flattened after max-pooling operation. After the Flatten layer, two dense layers are stacked and the *activation functions* are respectively configured as Relu and Sigmoid. Also dropout (Srivastava et al., 2014) is utilized to avoid potential overfitting, it is used between two dense layers. The reason why we select Relu is to prevent the vanishing gradient problem and accelerate the calculation. Since the task is a regression problem, we put a dense projection with sigmoid activation to obtain an intensity value between 0 and 1.

Model Training: The network parameters are learned by minimizing the *mean squared error* (MSE) between the real and predicted values of emotion intensity or valence intensity. We optimize this loss function via *Adam* that is an algorithm for first-order gradient-based optimization of stochastic objective functions, based on adaptive estimates of lower-order moments (Kingma and Ba, 2014). Batch size and training *epochs* may be different for different emotions and valence. To avoid overfitting issues, we use dropout in this model. Finally, we apply these three parameters for system tuning. In addition, we try various optimization algorithms with the same param-

---

[2] http://www.spark.tc/building-a-word2vec-model-with-twitter-data/

[3] https://github.com/mmihaltz/word2vec-GoogleNews-vectors

[4] https://nlp.stanford.edu/projects/glove/

EI-reg	Anger			Fear			Joy			Sadness		
	BS	Epochs	Dp	BS	Epochs	Dp	BS	Epochs	Dp	BS	Epochs	Dp
BiLSTM CNN+GT	16	6	0.5	32	2	0.5	8	4	0.5	32	5	0.5
BiLSTM Attention+GT	32	3	0.5	32	3	0.5	8	7	0.5	32	4	0.5
Deep BiLSTM Attention	32	2	0.3	8	7	0.3	16	9	0.1	16	5	0.6

Table 1: The best parameters of EI-reg.

V-reg	Valence		
	BS	Epochs	Dp
BiLSTM CNN+GT	8	5	0.5
BiLSTM Attention+GT	8	10	0.6
Deep BiLSTM Attention+WT	16	8	0.5
Deep BiLSTM Attention+GN	32	10	0.5
Deep BiLSTM Attention+GL	8	5	0.2
Deep BiLSTM Attention+GT	16	8	0.2

Table 2: The best parameters of V-reg.

eters, such as *SGD, RMSprop, Adagrad, Adam* and *Adamax*, and find that Adam works best. So we fix the optimization algorithm with Adam (Kingma and Ba, 2014) and tune the parameters, the best configurations for EI-reg and V-reg are respectively given in Tables 2.3.1 and 2.3.1, where *BS* is batch size, *Dp* is dropout.

2.3.3 Bidirectional LSTM with Attention

Bidirectional LSTM with Attention achieves a good result on the SemEval-2017 Task 4 "Sentiment Analysis in Twitter" (Baziotis et al., 2017), so we exploit *Bidirectional LSTM with Attention model* and *Deep Bidirectional LSTM with Attention model* for our tasks.

Model Architecture: For Bidirectional LSTM with attention model, embedding vectors are fed into a BiLSTM network followed by an attention layer (Yang et al., 2017). Not all words contribute equally to the expression of sentiment in a tweet, so we use an attention layer to find the importance of each word in tweet. After the attention layer, it is consistent with Bidirectional LSTM with CNN model. The difference between the Bidirectional LSTM with attention model and its deep version is that, we use two BiLSTM layers followed by an attention layer in the deep version.

Model Training: We use the same method to learn the network parameters. In EI-reg, we use the same batch size, training *epochs* and dropout to train the Deep BiLSTM Attention model with different pre-training word embeddings in every emotion, but in V-reg, batch size, training *epochs* and dropout are different in Deep BiLSTM Attention model with different pre-training word embeddings. In these models, we also use dropout.

The best parameters of EI-reg for these models are given in Table 2.3.1 and V-reg's best parameters are given in Table 2.3.1.

2.4 Ensemble Methods

Currently, ensembling is a widely used strategy which combines multiple single components to improve overall performance, there are many ensemble methods that have been proposed, such as, Voting, Blending, Bagging, Boosting, etc [5]. In this system, due to time constraint, we choose a simple average of the scores provided by different components, as each single component can predict emotional intensity or valence intensity. It can be defined as

$$Prediction_{intensity} = \sum_{i=1}^{n} \frac{model_i}{n} \qquad (1)$$

where n is the number of neural components. Model$_i$ represents the prediction results of i-th component. Suppose three components are exploited to predict the intensity of anger, and three prediction values of a same tweet 0.76, 0.72 and 0.7 are suggested, then the final result of this tweet will be $(0.76 + 0.72 + 0.74)/3 = 0.74$.

3 Experiments

Dataset	train	dev	test	sum
anger	1,701	388	17,939	20,028
fear	2,252	389	17,923	20,564
joy	1,616	290	18,042	19,948
sadness	1,533	397	17,912	19,842
valence	1,181	449	17,874	19,504

Table 3: Statistics of the datasets.

For experiments, we use five datasets from two different subtasks, These datasets, "EI-reg-En-anger (anger)", "EI-reg-En-joy (joy)", "EI-reg-En-fear (fear)", "EI-reg-En-sadness (sadness)" and "2018-Valence-reg-En (valence)" are downloaded from SemEval-2018 Task 1 "Affect in Tweets" [6]. As for the EI-reg task dataset format, each tweet

[5]https://mlwave.com/kaggle-ensembling-guide/
[6]https://competitions.codalab.org/competitions/17751

EI-reg	Average		Anger		Fear		Joy		Sadness	
	All	0.5-1	All	0.5-1	All	0.5-1	All	0.5-1	All	0.5-1
Baseline	0.520	0.396	0.526	0.455	0.525	0.302	0.575	0.476	0.453	0.350
BiLSTM CNN+GT	-	-	-	-	0.691	0.508	0.701	0.512	0.694	0.507
BiLSTM Attention+GT	-	-	0.701	0.583	0.715	0.506	0.711	0.513	0.720	0.557
Deep BiLSTM Attention+WT	-	-	0.697	0.582	0.709	0.507	0.728	0.503	0.704	0.541
Deep BiLSTM Attention+GN	-	-	0.681	0.557	-	-	-	-	0.698	0.535
Deep BiLSTM Attention+GL	-	-	-	-	-	-	-	-	-	-
Deep BiLSTM Attention+GT	-	-	-	-	-	-	-	-	0.717	0.551
Ensemble	**0.727**	**0.555**	**0.716**	**0.607**	**0.726**	**0.519**	**0.736**	**0.529**	**0.729**	**0.565**

Table 4: Performance comparisons of models in different emotions, where the best values are marked in **bold**.

consists of the id, the tweet, the emotion of the tweet, the emotion intensity and for the V-reg task, each tweet consists of the id, the tweet, the sentiment of the tweet and the sentiment intensity. All datasets have been divided into train set, dev set and test set. Test set's gold labels are given only after the evaluation period. Statistics of the datasets are shown in Table 3.

To measure the performance of selected methods, two submetrics of Pearson Correlation Coefficient (PCC) are used. PCC (all instances) is Pearson correlation for a subset of test data that includes all tweets. The value varies between -1 and 1. PCC (0.5-1) is the Pearson correlation for a subset of test data that includes only those tweets with intensity score greater or equal to 0.5. For both metrics, a larger value indicate a better prediction accuracy.

For each dataset, we use dev set to select our ensemble methods. Firstly we run these six components on all dev datasets. Then, combine these results of different components, different combinations of components lead to different results on dev set. Finally, we select the combination with a higher score for testing.

Our system is implemented on Keras with a Tensorflow backend [7]. We present the result of PCC (all instances) and PCC (0.5-1) for each emotion and valence on the test data, shown in Tables 3 and 3. For simplicity, we denote *WT, GN, GL* and *GT* for the word vectors of *word2vec-twitter-model, GoogleNews-vectors-negative300, glove.840B.300d* and *glove.twitter.27B.200d*. We compare the results of our single components, official baseline and our ensemble system. Every emotion and valence adopts different ensemble methods, the symbol '-' means that the component is not used in the ensemble method in this emotion or valence. For example, we only use *BiLSTM Attention+GT, Deep BiLSTM Attention+WT*

---

[7] https://keras.io/

V-reg	Valence	
	All	0.5-1
Baseline	0.585	0.449
BiLSTM CNN+GT	-	-
BiLSTM Attention+GT	-	-
Deep BiLSTM Attention+WT	0.825	0.665
Deep BiLSTM Attention+GN	0.820	0.640
Deep BiLSTM Attention+GL	0.822	0.648
Deep BiLSTM Attention+GT	0.825	0.659
Ensemble	**0.835**	**0.670**

Table 5: Performance comparisons of models in valence, where the best values are marked in **bold**.

and *Deep BiLSTM Attention+GN* these three components for ensemble on anger dataset. The reason why we don't use all the six components for ensemble is that ensemble does not always have a good effect, a same component can have different effects on different datasets, either good or bad. The official result for EI-reg, our average PCC reaches 0.727 in all instances and 0.555 in 0.5-1 (both ranked 10 out of 48 participants). For V-reg, the result is 0.835 in all instances (ranked 7 out of 38) and 0.670 in 0.5-1 (ranked 6 out of 38). The average result of baseline for EI-reg is 0.520 and 0.396, for V-reg, the result is 0.585 and 0.449. These results demonstrate that the ensemble approach achieves important improvement in performance across all the emotions and valence, and gains the best performance for Anger.

4   Conclusions and Future Works

We have proposed a simple yet effective ensemble method which integrates various neural components to perform the sentiment or emotion analysis for the tweet. Experimental results reflect that our method is effective in the prediction tasks of emotional intensity and sentimental intensity. Some other useful findings can be drawn from the experimental results: a) The model of integration for each emotion is different; b) As for lexicon features and word embedding, it is important for emotion or sentiment analysis; c) ensemble is not always valid. Also, we have tried data augmentation considering insufficient training data, however the effect is not a good.

As for future works, although our ensemble method has achieved good results, we would want to examine the multi-task deep learning approach on these tasks, by which it would predict the different emotional intensity at the same time, and improve the generalization effect of the prediction model.

Acknowledgment

This work is partially supported by the National Natural Science Foundation of China (61562090) and the Graduate Research Innovation Fund Project of Yunnan University (YDY17113).

References

Stefano Baccianella, Andrea Esuli, and Fabrizio Sebastiani. 2010. Sentiwordnet 3.0: An enhanced lexical resource for sentiment analysis and opinion mining. In *International Conference on Language Resources and Evaluation, Lrec 2010, 17-23 May 2010, Valletta, Malta*, pages 83–90.

Luciano Barbosa and Junlan Feng. 2010. Robust sentiment detection on twitter from biased and noisy data. In *International Conference on Computational Linguistics: Posters*, pages 36–44.

Christos Baziotis, Nikos Pelekis, and Christos Doulkeridis. 2017. Datastories at semeval-2017 task 4: Deep LSTM with attention for message-level and topic-based sentiment analysis. In *Proceedings of the 10th International Workshop on Semantic Evaluation, SemEval@NAACL-HLT 2016, San Diego, CA, USA, June 16-17, 2016*, pages 747–754.

Raymond Brueckner and Bjorn Schulter. 2014. Social signal classification using deep blstm recurrent neural networks. In *IEEE International Conference on Acoustics, Speech and Signal Processing*, pages 4823–4827.

Erik Cambria. 2016. Affective computing and sentiment analysis. *IEEE Intelligent Systems*, 31(2):102–107.

Yuanye He, Liang-Chih Yu, K. Robert Lai, and Weiyi Liu. 2017. YZU-NLP at emoint-2017: Determining emotion intensity using a bi-directional LSTM-CNN model. In *Proceedings of the 8th Workshop on Computational Approaches to Subjectivity, Sentiment and Social Media Analysis, WASSA@EMNLP 2017, Copenhagen, Denmark, September 8, 2017*, pages 238–242.

Yoon Kim. 2014. Convolutional neural networks for sentence classification. In *Proceedings of the 2014 Conference on Empirical Methods in Natural Language Processing, EMNLP 2014, October 25-29, 2014, Doha, Qatar, A meeting of SIGDAT, a Special Interest Group of the ACL*, pages 1746–1751.

Diederik P Kingma and Jimmy Ba. 2014. Adam: A method for stochastic optimization. *arXiv preprint arXiv:1412.6980*.

Svetlana Kiritchenko, Xiaodan Zhu, and Saif M Mohammad. 2014. Sentiment analysis of short informal texts. *Journal of Artificial Intelligence Research*, 50:723–762.

Dan Li and Jiang Qian. 2016. Text sentiment analysis based on long short-term memory. In *IEEE International Conference on Computer Communication and the Internet*, pages 471–475.

Tomas Mikolov, Kai Chen, Greg Corrado, and Jeffrey Dean. 2013. Efficient estimation of word representations in vector space. *arXiv preprint arXiv:1301.3781*.

Saif Mohammad, Svetlana Kiritchenko, and Xiaodan Zhu. 2013. Nrc-canada: Building the state-of-the-art in sentiment analysis of tweets. In *Second Joint Conference on Lexical and Computational Semantics (* SEM), Volume 2: Proceedings of the Seventh International Workshop on Semantic Evaluation (SemEval 2013)*, volume 2, pages 321–327.

Saif M Mohammad. 2012. # emotional tweets. In *Proceedings of the First Joint Conference on Lexical and Computational Semantics-Volume 1: Proceedings of the main conference and the shared task, and Volume 2: Proceedings of the Sixth International Workshop on Semantic Evaluation*, pages 246–255. Association for Computational Linguistics.

Saif M Mohammad. 2017. Word affect intensities. *arXiv preprint arXiv:1704.08798*.

Saif M. Mohammad, Felipe Bravo-Marquez, Mohammad Salameh, and Svetlana Kiritchenko. 2018. Semeval-2018 Task 1: Affect in tweets. In *Proceedings of International Workshop on Semantic Evaluation (SemEval-2018)*, New Orleans, LA, USA.

Saif M. Mohammad and Peter D. Turney. 2010. Emotions evoked by common words and phrases: using mechanical turk to create an emotion lexicon. In *NAACL Hlt 2010 Workshop on Computational Approaches To Analysis and Generation of Emotion in Text*, pages 26–34.

Finn Årup Nielsen. 2011. A new anew: Evaluation of a word list for sentiment analysis in microblogs. In *Workshop on'Making Sense of Microposts: Big things come in small packages*, pages 93–98.

Jeffrey Pennington, Richard Socher, and Christopher Manning. 2014. Glove: Global vectors for word representation. In *Conference on Empirical Methods in Natural Language Processing*, pages 1532–1543.

Nitish Srivastava, Geoffrey Hinton, Alex Krizhevsky, Ilya Sutskever, and Ruslan Salakhutdinov. 2014. Dropout: a simple way to prevent neural networks from overfitting. *Journal of Machine Learning Research*, 15(1):1929–1958.

Zichao Yang, Diyi Yang, Chris Dyer, Xiaodong He, Alex Smola, and Eduard Hovy. 2017. Hierarchical attention networks for document classification. In *Conference of the North American Chapter of the Association for Computational Linguistics: Human Language Technologies*, pages 1480–1489.

Xiaodan Zhu, Svetlana Kiritchenko, and Saif Mohammad. 2014. Nrc-canada-2014: Recent improvements in the sentiment analysis of tweets. In *International Workshop on Semantic Evaluation*, pages 443–447.

LT3 at SemEval-2018 Task 1: A classifier chain to detect emotions in tweets

Luna De Bruyne, Orphée De Clercq and Véronique Hoste
LT^3, Language and Translation Technology Team, Ghent University
Groot-Brittanniëlaan 45, 9000 Ghent, Belgium
{luna.debruyne, orphee.declercq, veronique.hoste}@ugent.be

Abstract

This paper presents an emotion classification system for English tweets, submitted for the SemEval shared task on Affect in Tweets, subtask 5: Detecting Emotions. The system combines lexicon, n-gram, style, syntactic and semantic features. For this multi-class multi-label problem, we created a classifier chain. This is an ensemble of eleven binary classifiers, one for each possible emotion category, where each model gets the predictions of the preceding models as additional features. The predicted labels are combined to get a multi-label representation of the predictions. Our system was ranked eleventh among thirty five participating teams, with a Jaccard accuracy of 52.0% and macro- and micro-average F1-scores of 49.3% and 64.0%, respectively.

1 Introduction

Most research in the domain of sentiment analysis focuses on the automatic prediction of polarity or valence in text, but also the detection of emotions has attracted growing interest in the last couple of years (Mohammad and Bravo-Marquez, 2017). Although emotion detection is a rather new research focus in NLP, the study of emotions has a long history in fields like psychology and neuro-imaging. Many different frameworks exist, but the specific emotion approach, in which emotions are classified as specific discrete categories, predominates. In a lot of those approaches, some emotions are considered more basic than others, with Ekman's theory of six basic emotions (*joy, sadness, anger, fear, disgust,* and *surprise*) (Ekman, 1992) as the most well-known. Another popular theory is Plutchik's wheel of emotions (Plutchik, 1980), in which *joy, sadness, anger, fear, disgust, surprise, trust,* and *anticipation* are considered most basic.

Emotion analysis in NLP makes use of the frameworks developed by psychologists, mostly by employing categorical models of (basic) emotions. In traditional emotion classification tasks, a 'document' or sentence is classified under one or more emotion classes (or classified as neutral/no class when no emotions are present). Such emotion classification systems have been developed and tested on different kinds of data, including fairy tales (Alm et al., 2005), newspaper headlines (Strapparava and Mihalcea, 2007), chat messages (e.g. Holzman and Pottenger, 2003; Brooks et al., 2013), and tweets (e.g. Mohammad, 2012; Wang et al., 2012). The big advantage of using tweet datasets is the relative ease with which twitter data can be collected and the possibility of using hashtags as emotion labels (distant supervision approach).

For this paper, we used the data that was collected for the SemEval shared task on Affect in Tweets (Mohammad et al., 2018), a collection of tweets annotated for eleven emotions: *anger, anticipation, disgust, fear, joy, love, optimism, pessimism, sadness, surprise,* and *trust* (Mohammad and Kiritchenko, 2018). We participated in Subtask 5: Detecting Emotions (English emotion classification).

The remainder of this paper is structured as follows: in Section 2 we describe how we first analyzed the data in order to get more insight in the task. Section 3 discusses how the data was preprocessed and which information sources were extracted. Next, in Section 4 the actual experimental setup and results are discussed and we end this paper with a conclusion in Section 5.

2 Data analysis

We first analyzed the training data provided by the task organizers, which consisted of 6838 tweets. We found that *disgust, anger* and *joy* were present in the largest numbers (present in about 35 to 40%

Proceedings of the 12th International Workshop on Semantic Evaluation (SemEval-2018), pages 123–127
New Orleans, Louisiana, June 5–6, 2018. ©2018 Association for Computational Linguistics

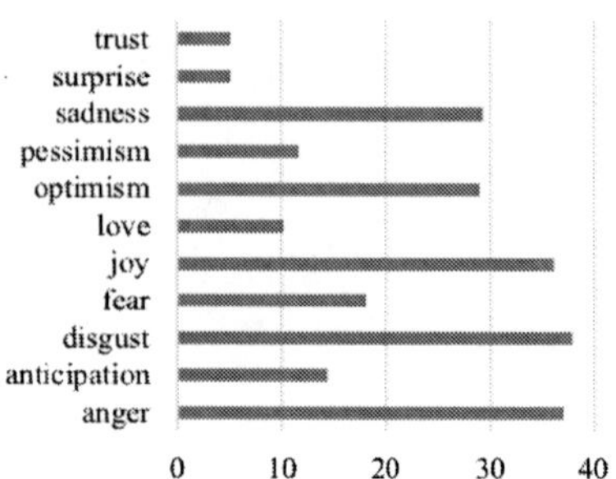

Figure 1: Proportion of training tweets in which the specified emotion is present (%).

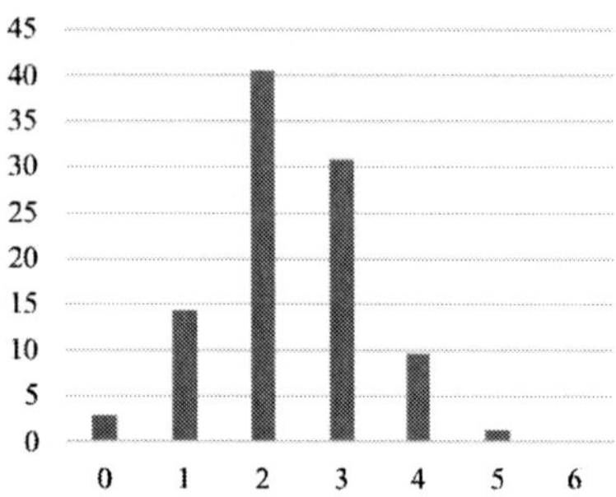

Figure 2: Proportion of training tweets in which a specific amount of emotion classes is present (%).

Pair	phi
anger - joy	-0.44
anger - optim.	-0.37
disg. - optim.	-0.41
joy - disg.	-0.46
joy - sadn.	-0.33
surpr. - pessim.	-0.40

Pair	phi
anger - disg.	0.68
joy - love	0.40
joy - optim.	0.52
sadn. - pessim.	0.30

Table 1: Phi coefficients for moderate or high negative (left) and positive (right) correlations between emotion pairs.

Emotion	Kappa	Emotion	Kappa
Anger	0.678	Optimism	0.436
Anticipation	0.259	Pessimism	0.124
Disgust	0.132	Sadness	0.537
Fear	0.399	Surprise	0.276
Joy	0.717	Trust	0.367
Love	0.470		

Table 2: IAA (Kappa) per emotion class based on 500 re-annotated instances.

of the tweets), while *surprise* and *trust* only occur in around 5% of the tweets (Figure 1). Only three percent of the tweets was annotated as neutral.

As can be derived from Figure 2, most tweets contained two or three emotions (together 70%), and in only about 1% of the tweets five or more (max six) emotions were present. We also calculated the correlations and found ten emotion pairs that were moderately or highly correlated ($\|phi\| \geq 0.30$ for moderate correlation, $\|phi\| \geq 0.50$ for high correlation, according to Cohen's conventions on effect size (Cohen, 1988)). The correlated pairs are shown in Table 1 and suggest that the classification performance can be boosted when correlations between emotion categories are implemented in the model.

In order to get more insight into the data, we re-annotated a subset of 500 tweets from the training set. In Table 2, inter-annotator agreement (IAA) scores per emotion class between the gold labels and our annotations are presented. Except for *anger* and *joy* these scores are rather low. Overall, we assigned less emotion classes to a tweet than the official annotators. We often disagreed with the gold labels and had the feeling that the anno-

tators of the official labels focused too much on lexical clues instead of keeping the context and the perspective of the writer of the tweet in mind. This leads us to presume that the threshold to assign an emotion label to a tweet when two out of seven annotators agreed (Mohammad and Kiritchenko, 2018) might have been a bit too generous.

We further noticed that some tweets appeared twice in the data set, but not completely identically: we suspect that one of them was the original tweet with emotion hashtag and the other one with the hashtag removed. An example:

(1) a. *Whatever you decide to do make sure it makes you #happy.*

   b. *Whatever you decide to do make sure it makes you .*

Since labels differed depending on the presence or absence of the emotion hashtag, we decided to keep both variants in our training set.

3 Preprocessing & Feature Extraction

3.1 Preprocessing

While we did not remove the 'almost identical' tweets from the data set, there were also some tweets in the training set that were completely identical but had been assigned other emotion labels. For those tweets, we took the majority class for each binary emotion category, and removed all other instances. This reduced our training set from 6838 to 6782 tweets. No duplicates were present in the development set, so the amount of

886 tweets was preserved. In the updated training set, as well as in the development and test set, all user names were replaced with the generic @*ID*.

All tweets were processed with Weka (Witten et al., 2016) using the Affective Tweets package (Mohammad and Bravo-Marquez, 2017), in order to extract lexicon and word embedding features. We used the default preprocessing settings for each filter. For the other features, we performed word and sentence tokenization (using NLTK), stemming (using spaCy), lowercasing, and POS-tagging (simple and detailed, corresponding to spaCy's `POS` and `Tag` function).

3.2 Feature extraction

For our supervised classification system, we employed features that measure different aspects of the tweet. These can be subsumed under five different categories: lexicon features (see Table 3 for an overview), n-gram features (binary, n equal to 3, 4 and 5 for characters and n equal to 1 or 2 for tokens), and various style, syntactic and semantic features (see Table 4).

Regarding the latter category, both features from traditional and distributional semantics were integrated. We first took the synset depth (distance to root) of all content words (calculated with WordNet (Miller, 1995)) and averaged the scores to get a mean synset depth for the tweet. Furthermore, we included two types of features from distributional semantics, namely word embeddings and word clusters. The word embeddings were extracted with Weka Affective Tweets, using pre-trained embeddings from 10 million tweets taken from the Edinburgh Twitter Corpus (Petrovic et al., 2010). For the word clusters, we downloaded a subset of around 1.5M tweets from the SemEval 2018 AIT DISC corpus (Mohammad et al., 2018). We first created word embeddings with word2vec using both skipgram and continuous bow and afterwards applied k-means clustering on the resulting word vectors. We experimented with various cluster sizes (800 of size 100, 1000 of size 100 and 800 of size 300). These clusters were implemented as binary features.

4 Experiments & Results

4.1 Baseline & Binary Experiments

We trained different models on the training set and tested them on the development set, using scikit-learn (Pedregosa et al., 2011). For the baseline ex-

Lexicon	Type
MPQA	polarity
Bing Liu	polarity
AFINN	polarity
Sentiment140	polarity
NRC Hashtag Sentiment	polarity
NRC Word-Emotion	polarity + Plutchik emotions
NRC-10 Expanded	polarity + Plutchik emotions
NRC Hashtag Emotion	Plutchik emotions
SentiWordNet	polarity
Emoticons	polarity
Sentistrength	polarity sentiment strengths
Warinner et al. 2013	valence, arousal, dominance

Table 3: Lexicons used for feature extraction.

Style	Syntax	Semantics
avg word/sent. length	POS n-grams	synset depth
# words and sents	POS freq.	embeddings
# capitals	POS 1st token	clusters
# punct. marks	presence imp.	
# non-standard words	presence fut.	
# connectives		

Table 4: Style, syntactic and semantic features.

periments, we used an SVM classifier with linear kernel (LinearSVC) and used the lexicon features from the Weka Affective Tweets package. The results for each binary classifier are shown in Table 5 (second column). Combining the predictions of these eleven binary classifiers resulted in a jaccard accuracy of 42.7%.

Before optimizing the separate classifiers, we took a more detailed look at the lexicon features and the clusters to assess whether it is beneficial to use only a part of the lexicons (e.g. only the emotion lexicons) or whether it is better to use all lexicons (even polarity lexicons). We found that the combination of all lexicons (including the valence-arousal-dominance lexicon of Warriner et al. (2013)) gave the highest performance. As regards the clusters, we tried all cluster types on each emotion category and picked the cluster that gave the highest performance on that particular category.

For every emotion category, we tested different classifiers on different combinations of features. The classifiers we used, were SVM, SGD (linear SVM with stochastic gradient descent learning), Logistic Regression, and Random Forest. Table 5 shows the F1-scores (in bold) on the positive class for the best performing classifiers and feature combinations, which are significantly higher than the baseline results. We joined the predictions of these optimized binary classifiers, and achieved a jaccard accuracy of 47.7%.

	BL		Optimized	
Emotion	F1	Classifier	Features	F1
Anger	*0.67*	SGD	all features except clusters	**0.73**
Anticip.	*0.00*	SGD	all features	**0.30**
Disgust	*0.56*	Log. R.	lexicons, embeddings, clusters	**0.67**
Fear	*0.62*	Log. R.	lexicons, embeddings, n-grams, clusters	**0.69**
Joy	*0.75*	Log. R.	lexicons, embeddings, n-grams, puncts, pos n-grams, pos frequencies, clusters	**0.80**
Love	*0.29*	Log. R.	all features	**0.55**
Optim.	*0.59*	SGD	all features	**0.68**
Pessim.	*0.04*	SGD	lexicons, embeddings, clusters	**0.20**
Sadness	*0.52*	Log. R.	all features	**0.59**
Surprise	*0.00*	SGD	all features except clusters	**0.35**
Trust	*0.00*	SGD	lexicons	**0.12**

Table 5: F1-scores on the positive class for the binary classifiers in the baseline (BL) setup (italics) and with the optimal classifier and feature sets (in bold)

4.2 Classifier Chain

Because the emotion categories are highly correlated (see Section 2), we envisaged to implement these relations in the model by using a classifier chain. We combined the best performing classifier per emotion category in a chain that passes predicted labels on to the next classifiers. We ordered the classifiers by performance on the positive class F1-score on the baseline (the emotion that is easiest to predict first, the emotion that is the most difficult to predict last). On the development set, this classifier chain approach led to a jaccard accuracy of 52.37%, which is significantly higher than the score without classifier chain (47.7%, see Section 4.1).

In our final model, the training and development data were joined, resulting in a combined training set of 7668 tweets. During the evaluation period, we achieved 52.0% jaccard accuracy, 64.0% micro-avg F1-score and 49.3% macro-avg F1-score on the held-out test set (see Table 6).

4.3 Discussion

As can be derived from Table 7 the number of false positives is rather low for all emotion classes (be-

Evaluation	jaccard	micro F1	macro F1
dev set	0.524	0.644	0.478
held-out test set	0.520	0.640	0.493

Table 6: Jaccard accuracy, micro averaged F1-score and macro averaged F1-score of the optimized model on the development and held-out test set.

		P				*P*	
	G	*0*	*1*		*G*	*0*	*1*
anger	*0*	0.72	0.28	optim.	*0*	0.65	0.35
	1	0.17	0.83		*1*	0.16	0.84
antic.	*0*	0.89	0.11	pess.	*0*	0.98	0.02
	1	0.68	0.32		*1*	0.86	0.14
disg.	*0*	0.75	0.25	sadn.	*0*	0.91	0.09
	1	0.21	0.79		*1*	0.46	0.54
fear	*0*	0.97	0.03	surpr.	*0*	>0.99	<0.01
	1	0.42	0.58		*1*	0.98	0.02
joy	*0*	0.89	0.11	trust	*0*	0.94	0.06
	1	0.20	0.80		*1*	0.82	0.18
love	*0*	0.95	0.05				
	1	0.52	0.48				

Table 7: Confusion matrices for the results on the held out test set. P = predicted labels; G = gold labels.

low 20% for most emotions). The model had most trouble with recognizing positive instances of *surprise*, *pessimism*, and *trust*, but also *love* and *anticipation* were more challenging. For these categories, the false negative rate was thus very high. We assume that these bad results are mostly due to a lack of sufficient training data for these categories.

We evaluated all features by computing the ANOVA F-values, and extracted the hundred most predictive features for each emotion category. For all emotions, the top 100 features consisted exclusively of lexical information. In none of the emotion categories, style or syntactic features occurred in this top 100. However, features regarding labels of preceding classifiers belonged to the most predictive features for all emotions except for *optimism* and *surprise*.

5 Conclusion

Our emotion classification system for English tweets achieved 52.0% jaccard accuracy on the held-out test set. We started from binary classifiers which we optimized for each emotion category separately, and combined them in a classifier chain. We proved that passing on labels from previously predicted emotions categories improves the performance significantly. For future work, it would be interesting to investigate the model's performance on other datasets than twitter data.

References

Cecilia Ovesdotter Alm, Dan Roth, and Richard Sproat. 2005. Emotions from text: machine learning for text-based emotion prediction. In *Proceedings of the conference on human language technology and empirical methods in natural language processing*, pages 579–586. Association for Computational Linguistics.

Michael Brooks, Katie Kuksenok, Megan K Torkildson, Daniel Perry, John J Robinson, Taylor J Scott, Ona Anicello, Ariana Zukowski, Paul Harris, and Cecilia R Aragon. 2013. Statistical affect detection in collaborative chat. In *Proceedings of the 2013 conference on Computer supported cooperative work*, pages 317–328. ACM.

Jacob Cohen. 1988. Statistical power analysis for the behavioral sciences . hilsdale. *NJ: Lawrence Earlbaum Associates*, 2.

Paul Ekman. 1992. An argument for basic emotions. *Cognition & emotion*, 6(3-4):169–200.

Lars E Holzman and William M Pottenger. 2003. Classification of emotions in internet chat: An application of machine learning using speech phonemes. Technical report, Leigh University.

George A Miller. 1995. Wordnet: a lexical database for english. *Communications of the ACM*, 38(11):39–41.

Saif Mohammad and Felipe Bravo-Marquez. 2017. Emotion intensities in tweets. In *Proceedings of the 6th Joint Conference on Lexical and Computational Semantics, *SEM @ACM 2017, Vancouver, Canada, August 3-4, 2017*, pages 65–77.

Saif M Mohammad. 2012. # emotional tweets. In *Proceedings of the First Joint Conference on Lexical and Computational Semantics-Volume 1: Proceedings of the main conference and the shared task, and Volume 2: Proceedings of the Sixth International Workshop on Semantic Evaluation*, pages 246–255. Association for Computational Linguistics.

Saif M. Mohammad and Felipe Bravo-Marquez. 2017. Wassa-2017 Shared Task on Emotion Intensity. In *Proceedings of the 8th Workshop on Computational Approaches to Subjectivity, Sentiment and Social Media Analysis (WASSA-2017)*, Copenhagen, Denmark.

Saif M. Mohammad, Felipe Bravo-Marquez, Mohammad Salameh, and Svetlana Kiritchenko. 2018. Semeval-2018 Task 1: Affect in tweets. In *Proceedings of International Workshop on Semantic Evaluation (SemEval-2018)*, New Orleans, LA, USA.

Saif M. Mohammad and Svetlana Kiritchenko. 2018. Understanding emotions: A dataset of tweets to study interactions between affect categories. In *Proceedings of the 11th Edition of the Language Resources and Evaluation Conference*, Miyazaki, Japan.

F. Pedregosa, G. Varoquaux, A. Gramfort, V. Michel, B. Thirion, O. Grisel, M. Blondel, P. Prettenhofer, R. Weiss, V. Dubourg, J. Vanderplas, A. Passos, D. Cournapeau, M. Brucher, M. Perrot, and E. Duchesnay. 2011. Scikit-learn: Machine learning in Python. *Journal of Machine Learning Research*, 12:2825–2830.

Sasa Petrovic, Miles Osborne, and Victor Lavrenko. 2010. The edinburgh twitter corpus. In *Proceedings of the NAACL HLT 2010 Workshop on Computational Linguistics in a World of Social Media*, pages 25–26. Association for Computational Linguistics.

Robert Plutchik. 1980. A general psychoevolutionary theory of emotion. In Robert Plutchik and Henry Kellerman, editors, *Emotion: Theory, research, and experience: Vol. 1. Theories of emotion*, pages 3–33. Academic Press, New York.

Carlo Strapparava and Rada Mihalcea. 2007. Semeval-2007 task 14: Affective text. In *Proceedings of the 4th International Workshop on Semantic Evaluations*, pages 70–74. Association for Computational Linguistics.

Wenbo Wang, Lu Chen, Krishnaprasad Thirunarayan, and Amit P Sheth. 2012. Harnessing twitter "big data" for automatic emotion identification. In *Proceedings of the 2012 ASE/IEEE international conference on social computing and 2012 ASE/IEEE international conference on privacy, security, risk and trust, SOCIALCOM-PASSAT'12*, pages 587–592, Washington, DC. IEEE Computer Society.

Amy Beth Warriner, Victor Kuperman, and Marc Brysbaert. 2013. Norms of valence, arousal, and dominance for 13,915 english lemmas. *Behavior Research Methods*, 45(4):1191–1207.

Ian H Witten, Eibe Frank, Mark A Hall, and Christopher J Pal. 2016. *Data Mining: Practical machine learning tools and techniques*. Morgan Kaufmann.

SINAI at SemEval-2018 Task 1: Emotion Recognition in Tweets

**Flor Miriam Plaza-del-Arco, Salud María Jiménez-Zafra,
M. Teresa Martín-Valdivia, L. Alfonso Ureña-López**

Department of Computer Science, Advanced Studies Center in ICT (CEATIC)
Universidad de Jaén, Campus Las Lagunillas, 23071, Jaén, Spain
{fmplaza, sjzafra, maite, laurena}@ujaen.es

Abstract

Emotion classification is a new task that combines several disciplines including Artificial Intelligence and Psychology, although Natural Language Processing is perhaps the most challenging area. In this paper, we describe our participation in SemEval-2018 Task1: Affect in Tweets. In particular, we have participated in EI-oc, EI-reg and E-c subtasks for English and Spanish languages.

1. Introduction

Emotions are playing a significant role in the effective communication of people. In fact, sometimes, emotional intelligence is more important than cognitive intelligence for successful interaction (Pantic et al., 2005). Therefore, affective computing is a key element to the advancement of Artificial Intelligence. The basic task of affective computing is emotion recognition. This task consists of identifying a set of emotions in a document.

The identification of emotions in texts has multiple benefits in different areas, such as psychology to detect some psychological disorder like depression (Cherry et al., 2012), e-learning to improve student motivation (Suero Montero and Suhonen, 2014) or business intelligence to know the preferences of consumers (Cambria, 2016).

Currently, more and more people express their emotions on social media, such as Twitter or Facebook. Therefore, the role of emotion in social media is becoming more important for the researchers in affective computing.

In this paper, we present the different systems we developed as part of our participation in SemEval-2018 Task 1: Affect in Tweets (Mohammad et al., 2018). We have participated in EI-oc, EI-reg and

E-c subtasks for English and Spanish. Below, we briefly describe these subtasks:

- **EI-oc** is an emotion intensity ordinal classification task. Given a tweet and an emotion E, it consists of classifying the tweet into one of four ordinal classes of intensity of E that best represents the mental state of the tweeter. Separate datasets are provided for anger, fear, joy, and sadness emotions.

- **EI-reg** is an emotion intensity regression task. Given a tweet and an emotion E, it consists of determining the intensity of E that best represents the mental state of the tweeter. The intensity of E is a real-valued score between 0 (least emotion) and 1 (most emotion). Separate datasets are provided for anger, fear, joy, and sadness emotions.

- **E-c** is an emotion multi-classification task. Given a tweet, it consists of classifying it as 'neutral' or 'no emotion' or as one, or more, of eleven given emotions (anger, anticipation, disgust, fear, joy, love, optimism, pessimism, sadness, surprise, trust) that best represent the mental state of the tweeter.

The rest of the paper is organized as follows. In Section 2 we explain the data used in our methods. Section 3 describes the resources used by our systems. Section 4 presents the details of the proposed systems. Section 5 displays the results and analyses them. We conclude in Section 6 with remarks on future work.

2. Data

To run our experiments, we used the datasets provided by the task organizers (Mohammad et al., 2018) as follows. During pre-evaluation period,

Proceedings of the 12th International Workshop on Semantic Evaluation (SemEval-2018), pages 128–132
New Orleans, Louisiana, June 5–6, 2018. ©2018 Association for Computational Linguistics

we trained our models on the *train* set, and evaluated our different approaches on the *dev* set. During evaluation period, we trained our models on the *train* and *dev* sets, and tested the model on the *test* set. Table 1 shows the number of tweets for each language and subtask dataset.

Subtask-language	train	dev	test	Total
EI-oc-es	4544	793	2616	7953
EI-oc-en	7102	1465	4070	12637
EI-reg-es	4544	793	2616	7953
EI-reg-en	7102	1464	71816	80382
E-c-es	7561	679	2854	11064
E-c-en	6838	886	3259	10983

Table 1: Number of tweets for each language and subtask dataset

3. Resources

For the development of the task, we used different lexicons that we explain in detail below.

- **Wordnet-Affect (WNA)** (Strapparava et al., 2004). This resource is an extension of WordNet Domains. WNA provides a set of English emotional words organized in a tree. The leaf nodes represent specific emotions that are grouped into general categories (parent nodes). For example, *anger, hate* and *dislike* belong to the overall emotion *general-dislike*. However, the emotions of WNA are not the same as the emotions of the SemEval subtasks. For this reason, each overall emotion of WNA has been mapped with SemEval subtasks emotions (see Appendix A, Table 8 and Table 9).

  In order to use this resource in Spanish, we have employed the lexical disambiguator Babelfy (Moro et al., 2014) to obtain the corresponding *BalbelNet synset id* of a term. Next, we have used the BabelNet API (Navigli and Ponzetto, 2012) to obtain a correspondence between the *BalbelNet synset id* and the *WordNet synset id*. WNA includes a subset of appropriate synsets of WordNet 1.6 to represent affective concepts. However, the *WordNet synsets id* obtained with BabelNet API corresponds to the 3.0 version of WordNet. Therefore, we have obtained the equivalent synset to the 3.0 version in the 1.6 version. With this, using the synset of the 1.6 version

of WordNet, we can map directly the associated emotion and confident value from WNA.

- **Spanish Emotion Lexicon (SEL)** (Sidorov et al., 2012). It includes 2,036 Spanish words that are associated with the measure of Probability Factor of Affective use (PFA) with respect to at least one basic emotion: joy, anger, fear, sadness, surprise, and disgust. The higher the value of the PFA, the more probable the association of the word with the emotion is.

- **NRC Affect Intensity Lexicon** (Mohammad, 2017). It has almost 6,000 entries in English. Each of them has an intensity score associated to one of the following basic emotions: anger, fear, sadness and joy. The scores range from 0 to 1, where 1 indicates that the word has a high association to the emotion and 0 that the word has a low association to the emotion. However, this resource is not in Spanish. For this reason, we have adapted it to Spanish in the following way. We have translated English terms to Spanish and we have selected the maximum value of intensity if the translation of some terms is the same.

- **NRC Word-Emotion Association Lexicon (EmoLex)** (Mohammad and Turney, 2010). This lexicon has a list of English words associated to one or more of the following emotions: anger, fear, anticipation, trust, surprise, sadness, joy. Moreover, the lexicon is also available for more than one hundred languages (including Spanish). All these versions have been generated by translating the English terms using Google Translate.

4. System description

In this section we describe the systems developed for the subtasks EI-oc, EI-reg and E-c.

In first place, we preprocessed the corpus of tweets provided for each subtask and language (English and Spanish). We applied the following preprocessing steps: the documents were tokenized using NLTK TweetTokenizer[1], stemming was performed using NLTK Snowball stemmer[2], stopwords

---

[1] http://www.nltk.org/api/nltk.tokenize.html
[2] http://www.nltk.org/_modules/nltk/

were removed (only for English), and all letters were converted to lower-case.

In relation to the resources, we have tested several combinations. However, for the final SemEval systems we have used the best systems obtained during the development phase. For EI-oc and EI-reg subtasks in Spanish, we used SEL, NRC Affect Intensity and WNA lexicons adapted to the emotions of these subtasks. On the other hand, for English, we used NRC Affect Intensity and WNA lexicons adapted to the emotions of the EI-oc and EI-reg subtasks. Regarding to subtask E-c, for Spanish, we used SEL, EmoLex Spanish version and WNA lexicons adapted to the emotions of this subtask. However, for English, we used Emolex and WNA lexicon adapted to the emotions of the E-c subtask.

Next, it is described the methodology used for each subtask:

- **Subtask EI-oc**. To perform the classification, we checked the presence of lexicon terms in the tweet and then we added the intensity value of these words grouping them by the emotional category (*anger, fear, sadness* and *joy*). The result is a vector of four values for each lexicon. Moreover, each tweet is represented as a vector of unigrams using the TF-IDF weighting scheme. The union of the lexicon vectors and the TF-IDF representation of the tweet are used as features for the classification using the SVM algorithm. We selected the SVM formulation, known as C-SVC, the value of the C parameter was 1.0 and the kernel chosen was the linear.

- **Subtask EI-reg**. In this case, we checked the presence of lexicon terms in the tweet and then we computed the sum, the average and the maximum of the intensity value of the words of the tweet grouping them by the emotional category (*anger, fear, sadness* and *joy*). The result is a vector of twelve values for each lexicon. The union of the lexicon vectors and the TF-IDF representation of the tweet are used as features for the classification using the SVM algorithm with the same configuration as that used in subtask EI-oc.

- **Subtask E-c**. In this subtask, we identified the presence of lexicon terms in the tweet and we assigned 1 as confidence value (CV).

Then, we summed the CV of the words whose emotion is the same obtaining a vector of emotions for each lexicon. The union of these vectors and the TF-IDF representation of the tweet are used as features for the classification using the Random Forest algorithm with 25 as number of trees.

5. Analysis of results

The official competition metric to evaluate the systems in EI-reg and EI-oc subtasks is the Pearson Correlation Coefficient (PCC) between semantic similarity scores of machine assigned and human judgments. In the case of the E-c subtask, systems are evaluated by calculating multi-label accuracy. Since this is a multi-label classification task, each tweet can have one or more gold emotion labels, and one or more predicted emotion labels. Multi-label accuracy is defined as the size of the intersection of the predicted and gold label sets divided by the size of their union. This measure is calculated for each tweet, and then is averaged over all the tweets in the dataset.

The results of our participation in the three subtasks and those of the teams that are in the first and the last position can be seen in Tables 2, 3, 4, 5, 6 and 7. It should be noted that the results of Spanish subtasks are lower than those obtained for English. Another important issue is that the participation in Spanish subtasks is lower than the participation in English subtasks. These facts are due to most of the works and resources for textual emotion mining are in English (Yadollahi et al., 2017).

In relation to our results, in most subtasks we obtained the lowest correlation on *anger* emotion and the best correlation on *joy* emotion. On the contrary, in WASSA-2017 Shared Task on Emotion Intensity (Mohammad and Bravo-Marquez, 2017), most of the systems performed better on *anger* emotion and worse on *fear* and *sadness* emotions. In this competition, it was found that despite using deep learning techniques, training data, and large amounts of unlabeled data, the best systems included features from affect lexicons. Given that, we plan to analyze the recall of the lexicons used in our experiments and to explore new lexicons in order to improve the classification.

On the other hand, it should be noted that we achieved higher ranking positions for Spanish subtasks. In particular, our best participation has been in the E-c subtask. An important difference found between the classification in both languages was that taking stopwords into consideration contributes to the emotion classification for Spanish while the opposite occurs for English. Therefore, we will further study this issue in order to incorporate an specific treatment to those stopwords that can modify the meaning of a sentence, such as negators, intensifiers and diminishers.

(r) Team name	Pearson				
	macro-avg	anger	fear	joy	sadness
(1) SeerNet	0.799	0.827	0.779	0.792	0.798
(39) SINAI	0.342	0.263	0.361	0.444	0.300
(48) TweetGroup	-0.016	-0.043	0.003	-0.011	-0.014

Table 2: Results of subtask EI-reg in English language

(r) Team name	Pearson				
	macro-avg	anger	fear	joy	sadness
(1) AffectThor	0.738	0.676	0.776	0.753	0.746
(10) SINAI	0.321	0.119	0.382	0.360	0.423
(16) AIT2018 Organizers	-0.012	-0.056	0.004	0.018	-0.014

Table 3: Results of subtask EI-reg in Spanish language

(r) Team name	Pearson				
	macro-avg	anger	fear	joy	sadness
(1) SeerNet	0.695	0.706	0.637	0.720	0.717
(24) SINAI	0.449	0.447	0.377	0.519	0.455
(39) TweetGroup	-0.021	0.015	-0.017	-0.029	-0.054

Table 4: Results of subtask EI-oc in English language

6. Conclusions

In this paper, we have presented the systems developed for our participation in 3 subtasks (EI-oc, EI-reg, E-c) of SemEval-2018 Task 1: Affect in Tweets. We have addressed these subtasks in two of the three available languages, English and Spanish. Overall, we have obtained better results in Spanish subtasks than in English subtasks. In future works, we plan to continue working on emotion recognition in Spanish because we have observed that the participation in this language is very low, although it is the second most spoken language. Our next study will focus on exploring more affect lexicons because in WASSA-2017 Shared Task on Emotion Intensity (Mohammad and Bravo-Marquez, 2017), it was demonstrated that using features from affect lexicons is beneficial for this task. Moreover, we will study the use of stopwords in Spanish because in the development phase it was observed that stopwords contribute to the emotion classification.

(r) Team name	Pearson				
	macro-avg	anger	fear	joy	sadness
(1) AffectThor	0.664	0.606	0.706	0.667	0.667
(7) SINAI	0.459	0.378	0.496	0.510	0.453
(16) AIT2018 Organizers	-0.022	0.011	-0.069	-0.005	-0.027

Table 5: Results of subtask EI-oc in Spanish language

(r) Team Name	accuracy
(1) NTU-SLP	0.588
(25) SINAI	0.394
(35) emotion17	0.023

Table 6: Results of subtask E-c in English Language

(r) Team Name	accuracy
(1) MILAB_SNU	0.469
(5) SINAI	0.318
(14) TeamCEN	0.050

Table 7: Results of subtask E-c in Spanish Language

Acknowledgements

This work has been partially supported by a grant from the Ministerio de Educación Cultura y Deporte (MECD - scholarship FPU014/00983), Fondo Europeo de Desarrollo Regional (FEDER) and REDES project (TIN2015-65136-C2-1-R) from the Spanish Government.

References

Erik Cambria. 2016. Affective computing and sentiment analysis. *IEEE Intelligent Systems*, 31(2):102–107.

Colin Cherry, Saif M Mohammad, and Berry De Bruijn. 2012. Binary classifiers and latent sequence models for emotion detection in suicide notes. *Biomedical informatics insights*, 5(Suppl 1):147.

Saif M Mohammad. 2017. Word affect intensities. *arXiv preprint arXiv:1704.08798*.

Saif M Mohammad and Felipe Bravo-Marquez. 2017. Wassa-2017 shared task on emotion intensity. *arXiv preprint arXiv:1708.03700*.

Saif M. Mohammad, Felipe Bravo-Marquez, Mohammad Salameh, and Svetlana Kiritchenko. 2018. Semeval-2018 Task 1: Affect in tweets. In *Proceedings of International Workshop on Semantic Evaluation (SemEval-2018)*, New Orleans, LA, USA.

Saif M Mohammad and Peter D Turney. 2010. Emotions evoked by common words and phrases: Using mechanical turk to create an emotion lexicon. In *Proceedings of the NAACL HLT 2010 workshop on computational approaches to analysis and generation of emotion in text*, pages 26–34. Association for Computational Linguistics.

Andrea Moro, Alessandro Raganato, and Roberto Navigli. 2014. Entity linking meets word sense disambiguation: a unified approach. *Transactions of the Association for Computational Linguistics*, 2:231–244.

Roberto Navigli and Simone Paolo Ponzetto. 2012. Babelnet: The automatic construction, evaluation and application of a wide-coverage multilingual semantic network. *Artificial Intelligence*, 193:217–250.

Maja Pantic, Nicu Sebe, Jeffrey F Cohn, and Thomas Huang. 2005. Affective multimodal human-computer interaction. In *Proceedings of the 13th annual ACM international conference on Multimedia*, pages 669–676. ACM.

Grigori Sidorov, Sabino Miranda-Jiménez, Francisco Viveros-Jiménez, Alexander Gelbukh, Noé Castro-Sánchez, Francisco Velásquez, Ismael Díaz-Rangel, Sergio Suárez-Guerra, Alejandro Treviño, and Juan Gordon. 2012. Empirical study of machine learning based approach for opinion mining in tweets. In *Mexican international conference on Artificial intelligence*, pages 1–14. Springer.

Carlo Strapparava, Alessandro Valitutti, et al. 2004. Wordnet affect: an affective extension of wordnet. In *Lrec*, volume 4, pages 1083–1086. Citeseer.

Calkin Suero Montero and Jarkko Suhonen. 2014. Emotion analysis meets learning analytics: online learner profiling beyond numerical data. In *Proceedings of the 14th Koli calling international conference on computing education research*, pages 165–169. ACM.

Ali Yadollahi, Ameneh Gholipour Shahraki, and Osmar R Zaiane. 2017. Current state of text sentiment analysis from opinion to emotion mining. *ACM Computing Surveys (CSUR)*, 50(2):25.

A. Mapping SemEval emotions

SemEval emotion	WNA emotion
Sadness	apathy, pensiveness, gravity, compassion, sadness, thing
Anger	despair, ingratitude, general-dislike
Fear	ambiguous-fear, ambiguous-expectation, ambiguos-agitation, positive-expectation, daze, shame, anxiety, negative-fear
Joy	humility, surprise, levity, positive-fear, neutral-unconcern, gratitude, fearlessness, affection, self-pride, enthusiasm, positive-hope, calmness, love, liking, joy

Table 8: Mapping of the general emotion of WordNet-Affect to SemEval emotion subtask EI-oc and EI-reg

SemEval emotion	WNA emotion
Sadness	pensiveness, compassion, sadness
Anger	
Fear	ambiguous-fear, gravity, daze, shame, anxiety, negative-fear
Joy	levity, positive-fear, enthusiasm, calmness, joy
Anticipation	ambiguous-expectation, positive-expectation
Disgust	neutral-unconcern, thing, ingratitude, general-dislike
Love	gratitude, affection, love, liking
Optimism	positive-hope
Pessimism	despair
Surprise	ambiguos-agitation, surprise
Trust	fearlessness, self-pride, humility

Table 9: Mapping of the general emotion of WordNet-Affect to SemEval emotion subtask E-c

UWB at SemEval-2018 Task 1: Emotion Intensity Detection in Tweets

Pavel Přibáň[1,2], **Tomáš Hercig**[1,2], and **Ladislav Lenc**[1]

[1]NTIS – New Technologies for the Information Society,
Faculty of Applied Sciences, University of West Bohemia, Czech Republic
[2]Department of Computer Science and Engineering,
Faculty of Applied Sciences, University of West Bohemia, Czech Republic
{pribanp,tigi,llenc}@kiv.zcu.cz
http://nlp.kiv.zcu.cz

Abstract

This paper describes our system created for the SemEval-2018 Task 1: Affect in Tweets (AIT-2018). We participated in both the regression and the ordinal classification subtasks for emotion intensity detection in English, Arabic, and Spanish.

For the regression subtask we use the AffectiveTweets system with added features using various word embeddings, lexicons, and LDA. For the ordinal classification we additionally use our Brainy system with features using parse tree, POS tags, and morphological features. The most beneficial features apart from word and character n-grams include word embeddings, POS count and morphological features.

1 Introduction

The task of Detecting Emotion Intensity assigns the intensity to a tweet with given emotion. The emotions include anger, fear, joy, and sadness. The intensity is either on a scale of zero to one for the regression subtask, or one of four classes (0:no, 1: low, 2: moderate, 3: high) for the classification subtask. The task was prepared in three languages: English, Arabic, and Spanish. For each language there are four training and test sets of data – one for each emotion. The data creation is described in (Mohammad and Kiritchenko, 2018) and detailed description of the task is in (Mohammad et al., 2018).

We participated in the emotion intensity regression task (**EI-reg**) and in the emotion intensity ordinal classification task (**EI-oc**) in English, Arabic and Spanish.

2 System Description

We used two separate systems for ordinal classification – AffectiveTweets (Section 3) and Brainy

(Section 4). For the regression task we just use the AffectiveTweets system. We train a separate model for each emotion. The Brainy system performed better in our pre-evaluation experiments on the development data for all emotions in Spanish and for fear and joy emotions in Arabic.

3 AffectiveTweets System

3.1 Tweets Preprocessing

Tweets often contain slang expressions, misspelled words, emoticons or abbreviations and it's needed to make some preprocessing steps before extracting features. First, every tweet was tokenized using *TweetNLP*[1](Gimpel et al., 2011). Then the AffectiveTweets[2] (Mohammad and Bravo-Marquez, 2017) package for Weka machine learning workbench (Hall et al., 2009) was used for feature extraction. The following steps were applied on tokens for every language in both tasks:

1. Tokens were converted to lowercase

2. URL links were replaced with *http://www.url.com* token

3. Twitter usernames (tokens starting with @) were replaced with *@user* token

4. Tokens containing sequences of letters occurring more than two times in a row were replaced with two occurrences of them (e.g. *huuuungry* is reduced to *huungry*, *looooove* to *loove*)

5. Common sequences of words and emojis were divided by space (e.g. token „*nice:D:D*" was divided into two tokens „*nice*" and „*:D:D*")

---

[1]http://www.cs.cmu.edu/~ark/TweetNLP/
[2]https://affectivetweets.cms.waikato.ac.nz/

133

Proceedings of the 12th International Workshop on Semantic Evaluation (SemEval-2018), pages 133–140
New Orleans, Louisiana, June 5–6, 2018. ©2018 Association for Computational Linguistics

These steps lead to reduction of feature space as shown in (Go et al., 2009). We also used some individual preprocessing for Arabic language. After the above described steps every token was also processed via *Stanford Word Segmenter*[3](Monroe et al., 2014). When using word embeddings, we transformed Arabic words from regular UTF-8 Arabic to a more ambiguous form[4]. This was done only for word embedding features.

3.2 Features

Our AffectiveTweets system used combinations of features that are described in this section. The submitted combination of features is shown in Table 1.

- **Word n-grams (WN$_i^n$):** word n-grams[5] from i to n (for $i = 1$, $n = 2$, *unigrams* and *bigrams* were used).

- **Character n-grams (ChN$_i^n$):** character n-grams[5] from i to n (for $i = 2$, $n = 3$ character *bigrams* and *trigrams* were used).

- **Word Embeddings (WE):** an average of the word embeddings of all the words in a tweet.

- **Affective Lexicons (L):** we used Affective-Tweets package to extract features from affective lexicons. In every language we also used SentiStrength **(L-se)** lexicon-based method (Thelwall et al., 2012).

- **LDA – Latent Dirichlet Allocation (D$_n$):** topic distribution of tweet, that is obtained from our pre-trained model, n indicates number of topics in model (for $n = 5$, feature vector with dimension 5 will be produced and each component of the vector refers to one topic). We used LDA features only in AffectiveTweets system.

3.2.1 English Word Embeddings:
- **Ultradense Word Embeddings (WE-ue):** Rothe et al. (2016) created embeddings in the Twitter domain.
- **Baseline Word Embeddings (WE-b):** Mohammad and Bravo-Marquez (2017) created embeddings from the Edinburgh Twitter Corpus (Petrović et al., 2010).

<hr>

[3]`https://nlp.stanford.edu/software/segmenter.shtml`

[4]Some characters were replaced, for more details see (Soliman et al., 2017).

[5]Value of each feature is set to its frequency in the tweet

3.2.2 Spanish Word Embeddings:
- **Ultradense Word Embeddings (WE-us):** Rothe et al. (2016) created embeddings from web domain.
- **FastText Word Embeddings (WE-ft):** Bojanowski et al. (2016) trained embeddings on Wikipedia.

3.2.3 Arabic Word Embeddings:
- **Zahran et al. (2015) Word Embeddings (var-SG, var-GloVe, and var-CBOW)**
- **Soliman et al. (2017) Word Embeddings (tw-SG, tw-CBOW, web-SG, web-CBOW, wiki-SG, and wiki-CBOW)**

Mentioned Arabic word embeddings were created with Global Vectors (GloVe) (Pennington et al., 2014) and Word2Vec toolkit (Mikolov et al., 2013) using skip-gram (SG) model and continuous bag-of-words (CBOW) model. These Arabic word embeddings were trained on different data domains – Twitter (tw), web pages (web), Wikipedia (wiki), and their combination (var) for more details see the cited papers.

3.2.4 English lexicons (L-en):
- We used all affective lexicons from the AffectiveTweets package.

3.2.5 Spanish lexicons (L-es):
- Translated NRC Word-Emotion Association Lexicon (Mohammad and Turney, 2013)
- Emotion Lexicon (Sidorov et al., 2012)
- Polarity lexicon (Urizar and Roncal, 2013)
- Expanded Word-Emotion Association Lexicon (Bravo-Marquez et al., 2016) (we translated this lexicon to Spanish)
- iSOL (Molina-González et al., 2013)
- ML-SentiCon (Cruz et al., 2014)
- Ultradense lexicon (Rothe et al., 2016)
- LYSA Twitter lexicon (Vilares et al., 2014)

3.2.6 Arabic lexicons (L-ar):
- Translated NRC Word-Emotion Association Lexicon
- Translation of Bing Liu's Lexicon
- Arabic Emoticon Lexicon
- Arabic Hashtag Lexicon

134

	Regression		
	English	**Arabic**	**Spanish**
anger	L-en, D_{500}	var-SG, L-ar, D_{250}, WN_1^1	L-en, L-es, WE-us, WN_1^1
fear	L-en, L-se, WE-b	var-SG, L-ar, D_{250}	L-en, L-es, L-se, WE-us, WN_1^1, D_{1000}
joy	L-en, L-se, WE-b	var-SG, L-ar D_{250}	L-es, WE-us, WN_1^2, ChN_2^3
sadness	L-en, L-se, WE-b	var-SG, L-ar	L-en, L-es, L-se, WE-us, WN_1^2, D_{1000}
	Classification		
anger	L-en, D_{250}	WN_1^1	
fear	L-en, L-se, WE-b, WN_1^2, D_{250}		
joy	L-en, L-se, WE-b, WN_1^2		
sadness	L-en, L-se, D_{250}	var-CBOW, L-ar, L-se, WN_1^1, D_{250}	

Table 1: Used features in the AffectiveTweets system

- Arabic Hashtag Lexicon (dialectal)
- Translated NRC Hashtag Sentiment Lexicon
- SemEval-2016 Arabic Twitter Lexicon

Lexicons are described in (Mohammad and Turney, 2013; Mohammad et al., 2016a; Salameh et al., 2015; Mohammad et al., 2016b).

3.3 Model Training

In our AffectiveTweets system we used an L_2-regularized L_2-loss SVM regression and classification model with the regularization parameter C set to 1, implemented in LIBLINEAR Library (Fan et al., 2008)[6].

3.4 LDA Training

To use topics created with LDA (Latent Dirichlet Allocation) (Blei et al., 2003) as features, we trained our own models for every language. Tweets used to train the Arabic and Spanish models were taken from SemEval-2018 AIT DISC corpus (Mohammad et al., 2018) and tweets for English model were taken from Sentiment140[7] training data (Go et al., 2009). We trained our LDA models with LDA implementation from MALLET[8](McCallum, 2002).

We used the same preprocessing for LDA as for regular feature extraction. Additionally we removed stopwords and following special characters [, . ! -]. Tokens from Spanish tweets were stemmed with *Snowball*[9] stemming algorithm.

4 Brainy System

We use Maximum Entropy classifier from Brainy machine learning library (Konkol, 2014) and UD-Pipe (Straka et al., 2016) for preprocessing and doesn't use any lexicons, just word embeddings. The system is based on (Hercig et al., 2016).

4.1 Preprocessing

The same preprocessing has been done for all datasets. We use UDPipe (Straka et al., 2016) with Spanish Universal Dependencies 1.2 models and Arabic Universal Dependencies 2.0 models for POS tagging and lemmatization. Tokenization has been done by TweetNLP tokenizer (Owoputi et al., 2013). We further replace all user mentions with the token "@USER" and all links with the token "$LINK".

4.2 Features

The Brainy system used the following features. The exact combination of features for each emotion and the change in performance caused by its removal is shown in Table 9.

- **Character n-grams (ChN_n):** Separate binary feature for each character n-gram in the utterance text. We do it separately for different orders $n \in \{1, 2, 3, 4, 5\}$ and remove n-grams with frequency t.

- **Bag of Words (BoW):** We used bag-of-words representation of a tweet, i.e. separate binary feature representing the occurrence of a word in the tweet.

- **Bag of Morphological features (BoM):** for all verbs in the tweet. The morphological features[10] include abbreviation, aspect, definiteness, degree of comparison, evidentiality, mood, polarity, politeness, possessive, pronominal type, tense, verb form, and voice.

---

[6] https://www.csie.ntu.edu.tw/~cjlin/liblinear/
[7] http://help.sentiment140.com/
[8] http://mallet.cs.umass.edu/
[9] http://snowballstem.org/
[10] http://universaldependencies.org/u/feat/index.html

- **Bag of POS (BoPOS):** We used bag-of-words representation of a tweet, i.e. separate binary feature representing the occurrence of a POS tag in the tweet.

- **Bag of Parse Tree Tags (BoT):** We used bag-of-words representation of a tweet, i.e. separate binary feature representing the occurrence of a parse tree tag in the tweet. We remove tags with a frequency ≤ 2.

- **Emoticons (E):** We used a list of positive and negative emoticons (Montejo-Ráez et al., 2012). The feature captures the presence of an emoticon within the text.

- **First Words (FW):** Bag of first five words with at least 2 occurrences.

- **Last Words (LW):** Bag of last five words with at least 2 occurrences.

- **Last BoM (LBoM):** Bag of last five morphological features (see BoM) with at least 2 occurrences.

- **FastText (FT):** An average of the FastText (Bojanowski et al., 2016) word embeddings of all the words in a tweet.

- **N-gram Shape (NSh):** The occurrence of word shape n-gram in the tweet. Word shape assigns words into one of 24 classes[11] similar to the function specified in (Bikel et al., 1997). We consider unigrams, bigrams, and trigrams with frequency ≤ 2.

- **POS Count Bins (POS-B):** We map the frequency of POS tags in a tweet into a one-hot vector with length three and use this vector as binary features for the classifier. The frequency belongs to one of three equal-frequency bins[12]. Each bin corresponds to a position in the vector. We remove POS tags with frequency $t \leq 5$.

- **TF-IDF:** Term frequency – inverse document frequency of a word computed from the training data for words with at least 5 occurrences and at most 50 occurrences.

Emotion intensity regression – Pearson (all instances)					
embeddings	avg	anger	fear	joy	sadness
var-SG	**0.564**	0.505	**0.569**	0.577	0.605
var-GloVe	0.523	0.489	0.520	0.529	0.557
var-CBOW	0.557	0.492	0.557	0.555	**0.622**
tw-SG	0.541	**0.513**	0.520	**0.580**	0.552
tw-CBOW	0.447	0.413	0.424	0.472	0.478
web-SG	0.492	0.419	0.465	0.559	0.526
web-CBOW	0.410	0.339	0.423	0.466	0.411
wiki-SG	0.440	0.345	0.443	0.505	0.469
wiki-CBOW	0.291	0.281	0.244	0.315	0.322
Emotion intensity classification – Pearson (all classes)					
var-SG	0.386	0.430	0.387	0.471	0.418
var-GloVe	0.318	0.410	0.383	0.430	0.385
var-CBOW	**0.397**	0.451	**0.496**	**0.536**	**0.470**
tw-SG	0.360	**0.480**	0.386	0.439	0.416
tw-CBOW	0.338	0.368	0.301	0.369	0.344
web-SG	0.325	0.426	0.424	0.375	0.388
web-CBOW	0.190	0.314	0.317	0.269	0.273
wiki-SG	0.244	0.396	0.368	0.370	0.345
wiki-CBOW	0.275	0.252	0.284	0.293	0.276

Table 2: Arabic embeddings experiments results

Emotion intensity regression – Pearson (all instances)					
embeddings	avg	anger	fear	joy	sadness
WE-us	**0.559**	**0.464**	**0.581**	**0.581**	**0.611**
WE-ft	0.510	0.369	0.577	0.528	0.565
Emotion intensity classification – Pearson (all classes)					
WE-us	**0.429**	**0.422**	0.382	0.478	0.434
WE-ft	0.407	0.256	**0.428**	**0.481**	**0.462**

Table 3: Spanish embeddings experiments results

Emotion intensity regression – Pearson (all instances)					
embeddings	avg	anger	fear	joy	sadness
WE-ue	**0.598**	**0.594**	**0.595**	**0.586**	**0.593**
WE-b	0.541	0.475	0.549	0.456	0.505
Emotion intensity classification – Pearson (all classes)					
WE-ue	**0.479**	**0.412**	**0.507**	**0.438**	**0.459**
WE-b	0.456	0.212	0.499	0.336	0.376

Table 4: English embeddings experiments results

- **Text Length Bins (TL-B):** We map the tweet length into a one-hot vector with length three and use this vector as binary features for the classifier. The length of a tweet belongs to one of three equal-frequency bins[12]. Each bin corresponds to a position in the vector.

- **Verb Bag of Words (V-BoW):** Bag of words for parent, siblings, and children of the verb from the sentence parse tree.

---

[11]We use edu.stanford.nlp.process.WordShapeClassifier with the WORDSHAPECHRIS1 setting available in Standford CoreNLP library (Manning et al., 2014).

[12]The frequencies from the training data are split into three equal-size bins according to 33% quantiles.

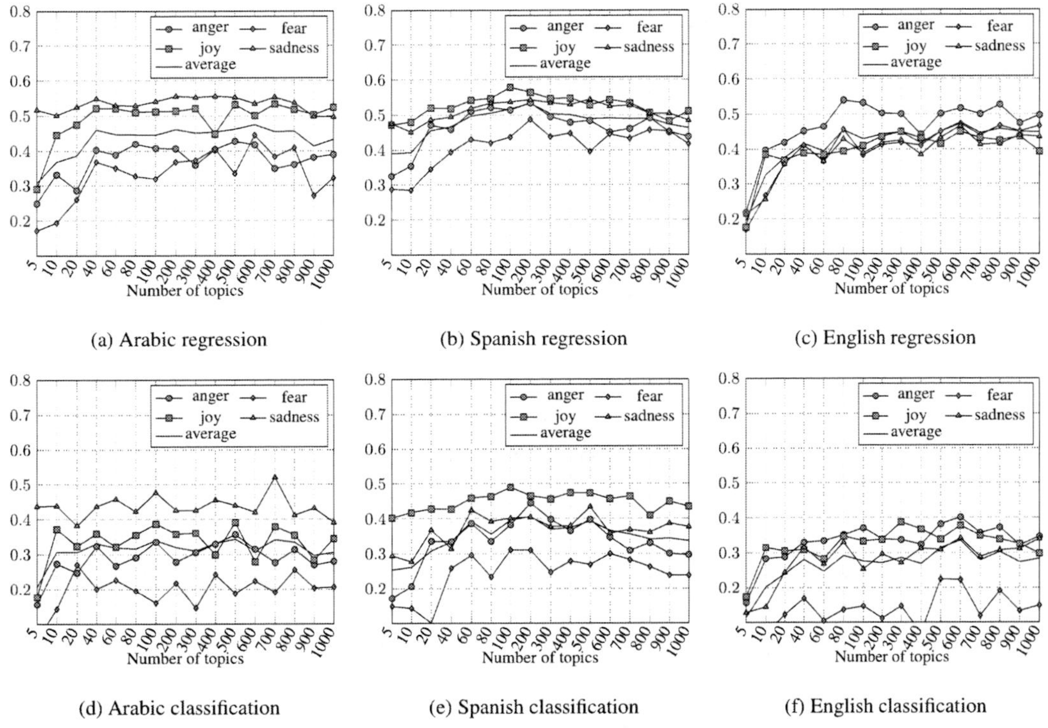

Figure 1: LDA performance based on number of topics, the y-axis denotes Pearson correlation

5 Experiments

All presented experiments are evaluated on the test data for the given task.

We performed ablation experiments to see which features are the most beneficial (see Table 9, 8, and 10). Numbers represent the performance change when the given feature is removed[13].

Word embeddings features have a great impact on system performance, so we compared several word embeddings for every language (Table 2, 3, and 4). For English was best **WE-ue** word embeddings, but for submission we used **WE-b** word embeddings, because it worked better on dev data. In Spanish tweets the **WE-us** word embeddings outperformed the **WE-ft** word embeddings in regression and **WE-us** was better for classification in anger and on average of all emotions. For classification in Arabic was **var-CBOW** best on every emotion except anger and for regression **var-SG** worked best on average and on fear.

We also experimented with only LDA features to find out how the numbers of topics in LDA model affect the performance (see Figure 1). We star-

ted with models containing 5 topics and continued up to 1000 (step was non-equidistantly increased). Our experiments suggest that the best setting is around 200-300 topics. We selected the number of topics based on the performance on the development data.

6 Results

Our results in the emotion intensity regression subtask are in Table 5 and our results in the emotion intensity ordinal classification subtask are in Table 6 and Table 7. The system settings and features for each language and emotion were selected based on our pre-evaluation experiments with evaluation on the development data.

7 Conclusion

We competed in the emotion intensity regression and ordinal classification tasks in English, Arabic and Spanish.

Our ranks are 27th out of 48 for English, 5th out of 14 for Arabic, and 5th out of 16 for Spanish for the regression task and 21st out of 39 for English, 5th out of 14 for Arabic, and 5th out of 16 for Spanish for the ordinal classification task.

---

[13]The lowest number denotes the most beneficial feature

Subtask	System	Pearson (all instances)					Pearson (gold in 0.5 − 1)				
		macro-avg	anger	fear	joy	sadness	macro-avg	anger	fear	joy	sadness
EI-reg-EN	AffectiveTweets	0.642 (27)	0.640 (27)	0.642 (27)	0.652 (24)	0.636 (23)	0.478 (25)	0.503 (29)	0.433 (27)	0.457 (23)	0.517 (23)
EI-reg-AR	AffectiveTweets	0.574 (5)	0.487 (6)	0.559 (5)	0.619 (6)	0.631 (5)	0.417 (6)	0.332 (6)	0.485 (3)	0.327 (7)	0.523 (4)
EI-reg-ES	AffectiveTweets	0.630 (5)	0.542 (5)	0.688 (3)	0.646 (5)	0.644 (4)	0.496 (3)	0.435 (2)	0.517 (3)	0.527 (3)	0.507 (4)

Table 5: Pearson correlation for the emotion intensity regression task

Subtask	System	Pearson (all classes)					Pearson (some-emotion)				
		macro-avg	anger	fear	joy	sadness	macro-avg	anger	fear	joy	sadness
EI-oc-EN	AffectiveTweets	0.506 (21)	0.477 (23)	0.470 (17)	0.555 (19)	0.522 (22)	0.346 (23)	0.308 (25)	0.273 (21)	0.452 (21)	0.350 (25)
EI-oc-AR	AT&Brainy	0.394 (5)	0.327 (5)	0.345 (5)	0.437 (5)	0.467 (5)	0.280 (5)	0.246 (6)	0.246 (6)	0.351 (5)	0.277 (7)
EI-oc-ES	Brainy	0.504 (5)	0.361 (7)	0.606 (3)	0.544 (5)	0.506 (5)	0.410 (5)	0.267 (6)	0.499 (2)	0.420 (6)	0.452 (5)

Table 6: Pearson correlation for the emotion intensity ordinal classification task

Subtask	System	Kappa (all classes)					Kappa (some-emotion)				
		macro-avg	anger	fear	joy	sadness	macro-avg	anger	fear	joy	sadness
EI-oc-EN	AffectiveTweets	0.494 (21)	0.467 (19)	0.450 (14)	0.548 (17)	0.510 (19)	0.290 (23)	0.269 (23)	0.166 (20)	0.420 (20)	0.303 (24)
EI-oc-AR	AT&Brainy	0.386 (5)	0.324 (5)	0.327 (5)	0.428 (5)	0.464 (5)	0.241 (5)	0.219 (5)	0.178 (5)	0.340 (5)	0.226 (5)
EI-oc-ES	Brainy	0.475 (5)	0.432 (5)	0.544 (6)	0.447 (8)	0.477 (6)	0.340 (6)	0.299 (5)	0.405 (5)	0.302 (8)	0.353 (6)

Table 7: Cohen's kappa for the emotion intensity ordinal classification task

Emotion intensity classification – Pearson (all classes)

Feature	Arabic		English			
	anger	sadness	anger	fear	joy	sadness
ALL*	$0.327^{\ddagger}$	0.467	0.477	0.470	$0.555^{\ddagger}$	0.522
$-D^{\dagger}_{250}$		$0.467^{\ddagger}$	$0.490^{\ddagger}$	$0.467^{\ddagger}$		$0.497^{\ddagger}$
L-en			0.000	-0.090	-0.007	-0.140
L-se		-0.019		-0.023	0.008	-0.030
WN^2_1				-0.055	-0.028	
WE-b				0.001	0.006	
WN^1_1	0.000	0.098				
L-ar		-0.038				
var-CBOW		-0.106				

* Results achieved with all used features for given emotion
† ALL without used LDA feature.
‡ Values used to calculate ablation results.

Table 8: AffectiveTweets feature ablation study

Emotion intensity classification – Pearson (all classes)

Feature	Arabic		Spanish			
	fear	joy	anger	fear	joy	sadness
BoW	-0.013	0.022	0.005	-0.041	0.018	0.003
$ChN_1\ t \leq 5$	-0.017	0.024	0.010		0.009	
$ChN_2\ t \leq 5$	0.034	-0.037	-0.009		0.018	0.014
$ChN_3\ t \leq 5$	-0.053	0.011	0.016	-0.041	0.011	0.005
$ChN_{4,5}\ t \leq 2$	-0.067	-0.036	-0.008	-0.056	-0.050	-0.011
BoM	-0.022		-0.013		0.017	-0.011
E	0.011		-0.007			
FT	-0.027	-0.008	0.006		-0.004	
BoPOS	-0.015		0.008	-0.010		-0.002
POS-B	-0.008	-0.025	-0.010	-0.013		0.013
BoT	0.017	0.006	-0.003	-0.010		0.018
TF-IDF	-0.017		-0.004		0.009	
NSh	0.010	0.006	-0.011		0.002	-0.008
FW			-0.001		0.002	0.010
LW			-0.007		-0.014	-0.003
TL-B						-0.004
LBoM	0.036		0.000			0.005
V-BoW	-0.006*		-0.005†		0,003‡	

* adverb † adverb, noun, adjective, verb, auxiliary ‡ noun

Table 9: Brainy feature ablation study

Emotion intensity regression – Pearson (all instances)

Feature	English			
	anger	fear	joy	sadness
ALL*	0.640	$0.642^{\ddagger}$	$0.652^{\ddagger}$	$0.636^{\ddagger}$
$-D^{\dagger}_{500}$	$0.634^{\ddagger}$			
L-en	0.000	-0.044	-0.031	-0.087
L-se		-0.037	-0.010	-0.013
WE-b		-0.020	-0.040	-0.017
Arabic				
ALL*	0.487	0.559	0.619	0.631
$-D^{\dagger}_{250}$	0.479	0.558	0.604	
L-ar	0.020	0.011	-0.027	-0.027
WN^1_1	0.036			
var-SG	-0.010	-0.244	-0.197	-0.196
Spanish				
ALL*	0.542	0.688	0.646	0.644
$-D^{\dagger}_{1000}$		0.688		0.639
L-en	0.008	0.006		-0.007
L-es	-0.016	0.005	-0.042	-0.009
L-se		0.002		-0.001
WE-us	-0.021	-0.027	-0.017	-0.030
WN^1_1	-0.033	-0.093		
WN^2_1			-0.050	-0.013
ChN^3_2		-0.006		

* Results achieved with all used features.
† ALL without used LDA feature.
‡ Values used to calculate ablation results

Table 10: AffectiveTweets feature ablation study.

Acknowledgments

This publication was supported by the project LO1506 of the Czech Ministry of Education, Youth and Sports under the program NPU I and by university specific research project SGS-2016-018 Data and Software Engineering for Advanced Applications.

References

Daniel M Bikel, Scott Miller, Richard Schwartz, and Ralph Weischedel. 1997. Nymble: a high-performance learning name-finder. In *Proceedings of the fifth conference on Applied natural language processing*, pages 194–201. Association for Computational Linguistics.

D. M. Blei, A. Y. Ng, M. I. Jordan, and J. Lafferty. 2003. Latent dirichlet allocation. *Journal of Machine Learning Research*, 3:2003.

Piotr Bojanowski, Edouard Grave, Armand Joulin, and Tomas Mikolov. 2016. Enriching word vectors with subword information. *arXiv preprint arXiv:1607.04606*.

Felipe Bravo-Marquez, Eibe Frank, Saif M Mohammad, and Bernhard Pfahringer. 2016. Determining word-emotion associations from tweets by multi-label classification. In *Web Intelligence (WI), 2016 IEEE/WIC/ACM International Conference on*, pages 536–539. IEEE.

Fermín L Cruz, José A Troyano, Beatriz Pontes, and F Javier Ortega. 2014. Building layered, multilingual sentiment lexicons at synset and lemma levels. *Expert Systems with Applications*, 41(13):5984–5994.

Rong-En Fan, Kai-Wei Chang, Cho-Jui Hsieh, Xiang-Rui Wang, and Chih-Jen Lin. 2008. Liblinear: A library for large linear classification. *Journal of machine learning research*, 9(Aug):1871–1874.

Kevin Gimpel, Nathan Schneider, Brendan O'Connor, Dipanjan Das, Daniel Mills, Jacob Eisenstein, Michael Heilman, Dani Yogatama, Jeffrey Flanigan, and Noah A. Smith. 2011. Part-of-speech tagging for twitter: Annotation, features, and experiments. In *Proceedings of the 49th Annual Meeting of the Association for Computational Linguistics: Human Language Technologies: Short Papers - Volume 2*, HLT '11, pages 42–47, Stroudsburg, PA, USA. Association for Computational Linguistics.

Alec Go, Richa Bhayani, and Lei Huang. 2009. Twitter sentiment classification using distant supervision. *CS224N Project Report, Stanford*, 1(12).

Mark Hall, Eibe Frank, Geoffrey Holmes, Bernhard Pfahringer, Peter Reutemann, and Ian H. Witten. 2009. The WEKA data mining software: An update. *SIGKDD Explorations*, 11(1):10–18.

Tomáš Hercig, Tomáš Brychcín, Lukáš Svoboda, and Michal Konkol. 2016. UWB at SemEval-2016 Task 5: Aspect Based Sentiment Analysis. In *Proceedings of the 10th International Workshop on Semantic Evaluation (SemEval-2016)*, pages 342–349. Association for Computational Linguistics.

Michal Konkol. 2014. Brainy: A machine learning library. In Leszek Rutkowski, Marcin Korytkowski, Rafal Scherer, Ryszard Tadeusiewicz, Lotfi Zadeh, and Jacek Zurada, editors, *Artificial Intelligence and Soft Computing*, volume 8468 of *Lecture Notes in Computer Science*, pages 490–499. Springer International Publishing.

Christopher D. Manning, Mihai Surdeanu, John Bauer, Jenny Finkel, Steven J. Bethard, and David McClosky. 2014. The Stanford CoreNLP natural language processing toolkit. In *Association for Computational Linguistics (ACL) System Demonstrations*, pages 55–60.

Andrew Kachites McCallum. 2002. Mallet: A machine learning for language toolkit. Http://mallet.cs.umass.edu.

Tomas Mikolov, Kai Chen, Greg Corrado, and Jeffrey Dean. 2013. Efficient estimation of word representations in vector space. *arXiv preprint arXiv:1301.3781*.

Saif Mohammad and Felipe Bravo-Marquez. 2017. Emotion intensities in tweets. In *Proceedings of the 6th Joint Conference on Lexical and Computational Semantics, *SEM @ACM 2017, Vancouver, Canada, August 3-4, 2017*, pages 65–77.

Saif Mohammad and Felipe Bravo-Marquez. 2017. Wassa-2017 shared task on emotion intensity. In *Proceedings of the 8th Workshop on Computational Approaches to Subjectivity, Sentiment and Social Media Analysis*, pages 34–49, Copenhagen, Denmark. Association for Computational Linguistics.

Saif Mohammad, Mohammad Salameh, and Svetlana Kiritchenko. 2016a. Sentiment lexicons for arabic social media. In *Proceedings of the Tenth International Conference on Language Resources and Evaluation (LREC 2016)*, Paris, France. European Language Resources Association (ELRA).

Saif M. Mohammad, Felipe Bravo-Marquez, Mohammad Salameh, and Svetlana Kiritchenko. 2018. Semeval-2018 Task 1: Affect in tweets. In *Proceedings of International Workshop on Semantic Evaluation (SemEval-2018)*, New Orleans, LA, USA.

Saif M. Mohammad and Svetlana Kiritchenko. 2018. Understanding emotions: A dataset of tweets to study interactions between affect categories. In *Proceedings of the 11th Edition of the Language Resources and Evaluation Conference*, Miyazaki, Japan.

Saif M Mohammad, Mohammad Salameh, and Svetlana Kiritchenko. 2016b. How translation alters sentiment. *J. Artif. Intell. Res.(JAIR)*, 55:95–130.

Saif M. Mohammad and Peter D. Turney. 2013. Crowdsourcing a word-emotion association lexicon. 29(3):436–465.

M Dolores Molina-González, Eugenio Martínez-Cámara, María-Teresa Martín-Valdivia, and José M Perea-Ortega. 2013. Semantic orientation for polarity classification in spanish reviews. *Expert Systems with Applications*, 40(18):7250–7257.

Will Monroe, Spence Green, and Christopher D Manning. 2014. Word segmentation of informal arabic with domain adaptation. In *Proceedings of the 52nd Annual Meeting of the Association for Computational Linguistics (Volume 2: Short Papers)*, volume 2, pages 206–211.

A. Montejo-Ráez, E. Martínez-Cámara, M. T. Martín-Valdivia, and L. A. Ureña López. 2012. Random walk weighting over sentiwordnet for sentiment polarity detection on twitter. In *Proceedings of the 3rd Workshop in Computational Approaches to Subjectivity and Sentiment Analysis*, WASSA '12, pages 3–10, Stroudsburg, PA, USA. Association for Computational Linguistics.

Olutobi Owoputi, Brendan O'Connor, Chris Dyer, Kevin Gimpel, Nathan Schneider, and Noah A. Smith. 2013. Improved part-of-speech tagging for online conversational text with word clusters. In *Proceedings of the 2013 Conference of the North American Chapter of the Association for Computational Linguistics: Human Language Technologies*, pages 380–390, Atlanta, Georgia. Association for Computational Linguistics.

Jeffrey Pennington, Richard Socher, and Christopher Manning. 2014. Glove: Global vectors for word representation. In *Proceedings of the 2014 Conference on Empirical Methods in Natural Language Processing (EMNLP)*, pages 1532–1543, Doha, Qatar. Association for Computational Linguistics.

Saša Petrović, Miles Osborne, and Victor Lavrenko. 2010. Streaming first story detection with application to twitter. In *Human Language Technologies: The 2010 Annual Conference of the North American Chapter of the Association for Computational Linguistics*, pages 181–189, Los Angeles, California. Association for Computational Linguistics.

Sascha Rothe, Sebastian Ebert, and Hinrich Schütze. 2016. Ultradense word embeddings by orthogonal transformation. In *Proceedings of the 2016 Conference of the North American Chapter of the Association for Computational Linguistics: Human Language Technologies*, pages 767–777, San Diego, California. Association for Computational Linguistics.

Mohammad Salameh, Saif Mohammad, and Svetlana Kiritchenko. 2015. Sentiment after translation: A case-study on arabic social media posts. In *Proceedings of the 2015 conference of the North American chapter of the association for computational linguistics: Human language technologies*, pages 767–777.

Grigori Sidorov, Sabino Miranda-Jiménez, Francisco Viveros-Jiménez, Alexander Gelbukh, Noé Castro-Sánchez, Francisco Velásquez, Ismael Díaz-Rangel, Sergio Suárez-Guerra, Alejandro Treviño, and Juan Gordon. 2012. Empirical study of machine learning based approach for opinion mining in tweets. In *Mexican international conference on Artificial intelligence*, pages 1–14. Springer.

Abu Bakr Soliman, Kareem Eissa, and Samhaa R. El-Beltagy. 2017. AraVec: A set of Arabic word embedding models for use in Arabic NLP. *Procedia Computer Science*, 117(Supplement C):256–265.

Milan Straka, Jan Hajič, and Jana Straková. 2016. UD-Pipe: trainable pipeline for processing CoNLL-U files performing tokenization, morphological analysis, pos tagging and parsing. In *Proceedings of the Tenth International Conference on Language Resources and Evaluation (LREC'16)*, Paris, France. European Language Resources Association (ELRA).

Mike Thelwall, Kevan Buckley, and Georgios Paltoglou. 2012. Sentiment strength detection for the social web. *JASIST*, 63(1):163–173.

Xabier Saralegi Urizar and Iñaki San Vicente Roncal. 2013. Elhuyar at tass 2013. In *Proceedings of the Workshop on Sentiment Analysis at SEPLN (TASS 2013)*, pages 143–150.

David Vilares, Yerai Doval, Miguel A Alonso, and Carlos Gómez-Rodrıguez. 2014. Lys at tass 2014: A prototype for extracting and analysing aspects from spanish tweets. In *Proceedings of the TASS workshop at SEPLN*.

Mohamed A Zahran, Ahmed Magooda, Ashraf Y Mahgoub, Hazem Raafat, Mohsen Rashwan, , and Amir Atyia. 2015. Word representations in vector space and their applications for arabic. In *International Conference on Intelligent Text Processing and Computational Linguistics*, pages 430–443. Springer.

AttnConvnet at SemEval-2018 Task 1: Attention-based Convolutional Neural Networks for Multi-label Emotion Classification

Yanghoon Kim[1,2], Hwanhee Lee[1] and Kyomin Jung[1,2]
[1]Seoul National University, Seoul, Korea
[2]Automation and Systems Research Institute, Seoul National University, Seoul, Korea
`{ad26kr,wanted1007,kjung}@snu.ac.kr`

Abstract

In this paper, we propose an attention-based classifier that predicts multiple emotions of a given sentence. Our model imitates human's two-step procedure of sentence understanding and it can effectively represent and classify sentences. With emoji-to-meaning preprocessing and extra lexicon utilization, we further improve the model performance. We train and evaluate our model with data provided by SemEval-2018 task 1-5, each sentence of which has several labels among 11 given emotions. Our model achieves 5th/1st rank in English/Spanish respectively.

1 Introduction

Since the revolution in deep neural networks, especially with the help of Long short-term memory(Hochreiter and Schmidhuber, 1997), it has been easy for machines to imitate human's linguistic activities, such as sentence classification(Kim, 2014), language model(Sundermeyer et al., 2010), machine translation(Bahdanau et al., 2015).

Emotion classification is a subpart of sentence classification that predicts the emotion of the given sentence by understanding the meaning of it. Multi-label emotion classification requires more powerful ability to comprehend the sentence in variety of aspects. For example, given a sentence 'For real? Look what I got for my birthday present!!', it is easy for human to figure out that the sentence not only expressing 'joy' but also 'surprise'. However, machines may require more task-specific structure to solve the same problem.

Attention mechanisms are one of the most spotlighted trends in deep learning and recently made their way into NLP. Applied to systems with neural networks, it functions as visual attention mechanisms found in humans(Denil et al., 2012) and the most effective region of features will be highlighted over time, making the system better exploit the features related to the training objective. (Bahdanau et al., 2015) is one of the most significant footprints of attention mechanism in NLP and they applied attention mechanisms to machine translation for the first time. The model generates target word under the influence of related source words. Furthermore, Vaswani et al. (2017) proposed a brand new architecture for neural machine translation. The model utilizes attention mechanisms not only as the submodule but also as the main structure, improving time complexity and performance.

Inspired by (Vaswani et al., 2017), we come up with attention-based multi-label sentence classifier that can effectively represent and classify sentences. Our system is composed of a self-attention module and multiple CNNs enabling it to imitate human's two-step procedure of analyzing sentences: comprehend and classify. Furthermore, our emoji-to-meaning preprocessing and extra lexicon utilization improve model performance on given dataset. We evaluated our system on the dataset of (Mohammad et al., 2018), where it ranked 5th/1st rank in English/Spanish respectively.

2 Model

Our system is mainly composed of two parts: self-attention module and multiple independent CNNs as depicted in Figure 1. This structure is actually imitating how human perform the same task. In general, human firstly read a sentence and try to comprehend the meaning, which corresponds to self-attention in our system. Then human categorize the sentence to each emotion separately but not all at once, and that is the reason why our system use 11 independent CNNs. In addition to main structure, we added the description of preprocessing in the model description because it makes up a large proportion in NLP tasks, especially when

Proceedings of the 12th International Workshop on Semantic Evaluation (SemEval-2018), pages 141–145
New Orleans, Louisiana, June 5–6, 2018. ©2018 Association for Computational Linguistics

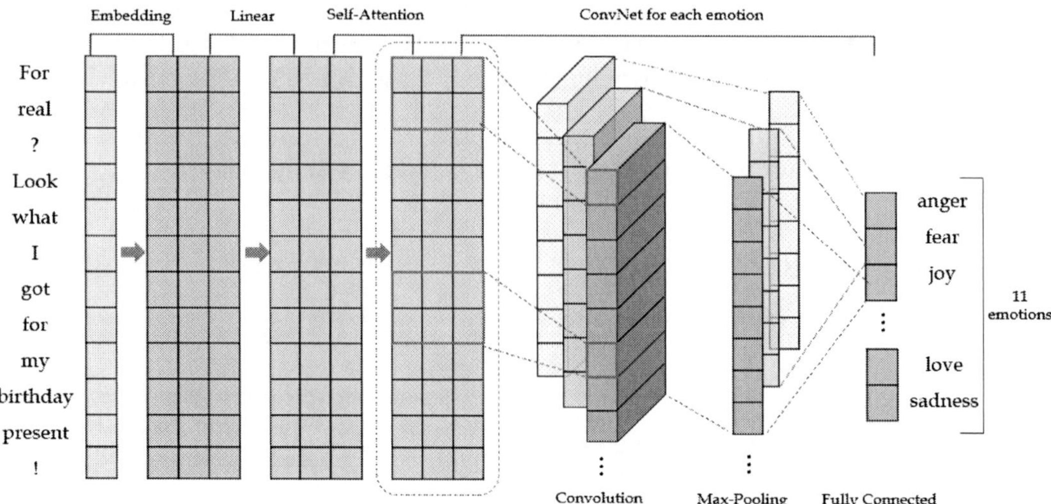

Figure 1: Overall architecture of the model. Preprocessed data goes through embedding layer, self-attention layer, Convolution layer and pooling layer step by step.

the dataset is small. Details are described in the following paragraph step by step.

Preprocessing: For raw data, we applied 3 steps of preprocessing:

(i) Our system mainly deals with limited numbers of tweet data, which is very noisy. In this case, preprocessing of data has crucial impact on model performance. Emoji may be referred to as a typical property of tweets and we found that considerable number of tweets contain emojis. Each emoji has a meaning of their own, and we converted every emoji in the data to phrase/word that represents its meaning. We call this procedure as **emoji-to-meaning** preprocessing. Some tweets have too many repetition of certain emoji that may make the sentence overbiased to certain emotions. Against expectations, removing overlapped emojis reduced performance.

(ii) Lower-case and tokenize data with **TweetTokenizer** in (Bird and Loper, 2002).

(iii) Remove all of the mentions and '#' symbols in the beginning of all topics. Unlike mentions, topics may include emotional words and hence we don't remove the topic itself.

Embedding: It is especially helpful to use pretrained word embeddings when dealing with a small dataset. Among those well-known word embeddings such as Word2Vec(Mikolov et al., 2013),

GloVe(Pennington et al., 2014) and fastText(Piotr et al., 2016), we adopt 300-dimension GloVe vectors for English ,which is trained on Common Crawl data of 840 billion tokens and 300-dimension fastText vectors for Spanish, which is trained on Wikipedia.

Self-attention: Vaswani et al. (2017) proposed a non-recurrent machine translation architecture called Transformer that is based on dot-product attention module. Usually, attention mechanisms are used as a submodule of deep learning models, calculating the importance weight of each position given a sequence. In our system, we adopt the self-attention mechanisms in (Vaswani et al., 2017) to represent sentences. The detailed structure of self-attention is shown in Figure 2. Dot-product of every embedded vector and weight matrix $W \in \mathbb{R}^{d_e \times 3d_e}$ is split through dimension as Q, K, V of the same size, where d_e is the dimensionality of embedded vectors. Then attended vector is computed as in (3).

$$E = [emb(x_1), emb(x_2), ..., emb(x_n)] \quad (1)$$

$$[Q, K, V] = [eW \; for \; e \; in \; E] \quad (2)$$

$$Attn(Q, K, V) = softmax(\frac{QK^T}{\sqrt{d_e}})V \quad (3)$$

Multi-head attention allows the model to benefit from ensemble effect only with the same amount

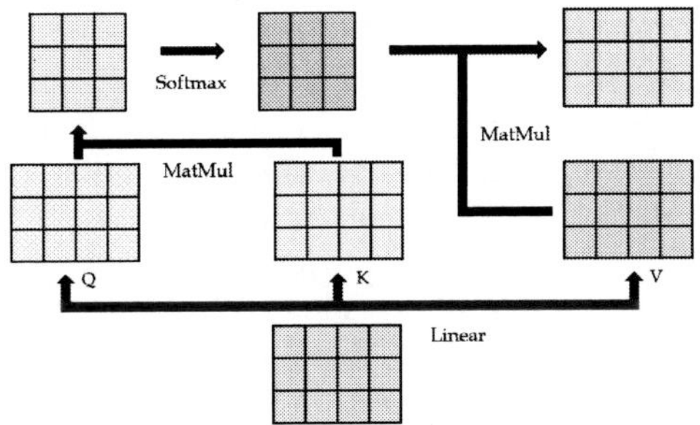

Figure 2: Inner architecture of self-attention module

of parameter.

$$Multihead(Q, K, V) = Concat(head_1, ..., head_h) \quad (4)$$

$$where\ head_i = Attn(Q_i, K_i, V_i)$$

$$Q = [Q_1, ..., Q_h],\ Q_i \in \mathbb{R}^{n \times \frac{d_e}{h}}$$

$$K = [K_1, ..., K_h],\ K_i \in \mathbb{R}^{n \times \frac{d_e}{h}}$$

$$V = [V_1, ..., V_h],\ V_i \in \mathbb{R}^{n \times \frac{d_e}{h}}$$

For each self-attention layer, there are additional position-wise feed-forward networks right after the attention submodule.

$$FFN(x) = max(0, xW_1 + b_1)W_2 + b_2 \quad (5)$$

$$where\ W_1 \in \mathbb{R}^{d_e \times d_f},\ W_2 \in \mathbb{R}^{d_f \times d_e} \quad (6)$$

In addition to these two sub-layers, there is a residual connection around each sub-layer, followed by layer normalization. Also, we can stack self-attention layers by substituting the embedding vectors in (1) with the output of the last self-attention layer.

Convolution & Pooling: Followed by self-attention layer are 11 independent 1-layer Convolution layers with max-pooling layers. Kim (2014) has proved that CNNs have lots of potential in sentence processing task and we adopt the CNNs in the same way.

Output & Loss: Each output of CNNs go through a fully-connected layer to generate a logit. Sigmoid activation is applied to calculate the probability of each emotion, and we use the sum of each class' cross-entropy as the final loss function.

3 Experiments & Results

3.1 Data

For the SemEval 2018 shared task, Mohammad et al.(2018) has provided tweet data with multiple labels among 11 pre-set emotions: 'angry', 'anticipation', 'disgust', 'fear', 'joy', 'love' 'optimism', 'pessimism', 'sadness', 'surprise' and 'trust'. We only use English and Spanish data among three different languages. The dataset consists of 6838/887/3259 tweets in English, 3561/679/2854 tweets in Spanish for train/validation/test data respectively.

3.2 Setup

We implemented a model with 3-layer self-attention and 1-layer CNN. With the restriction of fixed-size GloVe vector, we found that 300-dimension hidden state is excessive for such a small dataset that we added a position-wise linear layer between the embedding layer and self-attention layers to make $d_e = 30$. We employed $h = 2$ for multi-head attention and set $d_f = 64$. Two regularization techniques are applied to our system: Dropout with $P_{drop} = 0.1$ for self-attention, and L2 regularization for all weight matrix but not bias. We added 0.001 times regularization loss to original loss function. We optimized the loss with Gradient Descent using Adam optimization algorithm with additional learning rate decay.

3.3 Model variants

We conduct experiments with following variants of our model.

- **AC**: Self-attention + CNNs, which is our basic system.

- **AC - attn**: Basic system without self-attention module.

- **AC + nrc1**: We mainly used NRC Emotion lexicon(Mohammad and Turney, 2013) to make word-level label of each sentence, counting the occurence of each emotion in the sentence. Each of the word-level label is concatenated to the output vector of each pooling layer.

- **AC + nrc2**: At evaluation/test step, binarize the word-level label and add 0.4 times the label value to the logit.

- **AC + synth**: Inspired by (Sennrich et al., 2016), we made synthetic data using unlabeled SemEval-2018 AIT DISC data[1] with

[1]https://www.dropbox.com/s/2phcvj300lcdnpl/SemEval2018-AIT-DISC.zip?dl=0

pre-trained model, and fine-tuned the model
with synthetic data.

3.4 Experimental results

We conduct several experiments to prove the effectiveness of our model, each to verify the benefit from: (1) tweets specific preprocessing (2) self-
attention representation (3) emotional lexicon utilization. Experimental results are **mainly compared with English data.**

3.4.1 Impact of emoji-to-meaning

We firstly verify the efficiency of emoji-to-
meaning preprocessing. Table 1 shows the accuracies of the same model with different preprocessing. We found that emoji-to-meaning preprocessing can improve the model accuracy by 1%. When
a emoji is converted to its meaning, it can be represented as a combination of emotional words allowing it to not only reduce redundant vocabulary
but also further emphasize the influence of certain
emotions.

Model	Accuracy(valid)	Accuracy(test)
AC (w/o)	54.86%	54.91%
AC	55.94%	55.90%

Table 1: Experimental results with and without emoji-
to-meaning preprocessing.

3.4.2 Impact of self-attention

To examine the effectiveness of self-attention representation, we simply get rid of self-attention layers. Table 2 shows that by removing the self-
attention layers, both the validation/test accuracy
dropped over 4%. This may be attributed to the
ability of self-attention: It helps the model to better learn the long-range dependency of sentences.
Learning long-range dependencies is a key challenge in NLP tasks and self-attention module can
shorten the length of paths forward and backward
signals have to traverse in the network as described
in (Vaswani et al., 2017).

Model	Accuracy(valid)	Accuracy(test)
AC - attn	51.04%	51.60%
AC	55.94%	55.90%

Table 2: Comparison between our basic system and basic system without self-attention module.

3.4.3 Impact of extra resources

Lack of data has crucial impact on model generalization. Generalization techniques such as dropout
or L2 regularization can relieve over-fitting problem to a certain extent; however, it can't totally
substitute the effect of rich data. So we apply
some heuristic methods to exploit extra resources
as described in 3.3. Table 2 shows that model can
slightly benefit from extra lexicon if used properly. However, adding synthetic data which is
made from pre-trained model didn't help a lot, and
in some cases even reduce the accuracy of the test
result. Actually, Sennrich et al.(2016) emphasized
that they used the monolingual sentences as the
target sentences, informing that the target-side information, which corresponds to label in our task,
is not synthetic. However, we made synthetic labels with a pre-trained model and it may only
cause over-fitting problem to the original training
data.

Model	Accuracy(valid)	Accuracy(test)
AC	55.94%	55.90%
AC + nrc1	56.13%	56.02%
AC + nrc2	57.16%	56.40%
AC + synth	55.88%	55.90%
Ensemble	**59.76%**	**57.40%**

Table 3: Experimental results with extra resources and
an ensemble result

3.4.4 Ensemble

Our best results are obtained with an ensemble of 9 parameter sets of AC + nrc2 model
that differ in their random initializations. The
ensemble model achieved validation/test accuracy of 59.76%/57.40% in English data and
50.00%/46.90% in Spanish data respectively.

4 Conclusion

In this paper, we proposed an attention-based sentence classifier that can classify a sentence into
multiple emotions. Experimental results demonstrated that our system has effective structure for
sentence understanding. Our system shallowly
follows human's procedure of classifying sentences into multiple labels. However, some emotions may have some relatedness while our model
treats them independently. In our future work,
we would like to further take those latent relation
among emotions into account.

Acknowledgments

This work was supported by the National Research Foundation of Korea(NRF) funded by the Korea government(MSIT) (No. 2016M3C4A7952632), Industrial Strategic Technology Development Program(No. 10073144) funded by the Ministry of Trade, Industry & Energy(MOTIE, Korea)

References

Dzmitry Bahdanau, Kyunghyun Cho, and Yoshua Bengio. 2015. Neural machine translation by jointly learning to align and translate. *International Conference on Learning Representations Workshop*.

Steven Bird and Edward Loper. 2002. Nltk: the natural language toolkit. In *Proceedings of the ACL-02 Workshop on Effective tools and methodologies for teaching natural language processing and computational linguistics*.

Misha Denil, Loris Bazzani, Hugo Larochelle, and Nando de Freitas. 2012. Learning where to attend with deep architectures for image tracking. *Neural Computation*.

Sepp Hochreiter and Jrgen Schmidhuber. 1997. Long short-term memory. *Neural computation*, 9(8):1735–1780.

Yoon Kim. 2014. Convolutional neural networks for sentence classification. In *Proceedings of the 2014 Conference on Empirical Methods in Natural Language Processing*, pages 1746–1751. Association for Computational Linguistics.

Tomas Mikolov, Ilya Sutskever, Kai Chen, Greg Corrado, and Jeff Dean. 2013. Distributed representations of words and phrases and their compositionality. *Advances in Neural Information Processing Systems*, 26:3111–3119.

Saif Mohammad and Peter Turney. 2013. Crowdsourcing a word-emotion association lexicon. *Computational Intelligence*, 29(3):436–465.

Saif M. Mohammad, Felipe Bravo-Marquez, Mohammad Salameh, and Svetlana Kiritchenko. 2018. Semeval-2018 Task 1: Affect in tweets. In *Proceedings of International Workshop on Semantic Evaluation (SemEval-2018)*, New Orleans, LA, USA.

Jeffrey Pennington, Richard Socher, and Christopher D.Manning. 2014. Glove: Global vectors for word representation. In *Proceedings of the Conference on Empirical Methods in Natural Language Processing*.

Bojanowski Piotr, Grave Edouard, Joulin Armand, and Mikolov Tomas. 2016. Enriching word vectors with subword information. *arXiv preprint arXiv:1607.04606*.

Rico Sennrich, Barry Haddow, and Alexandra Birch. 2016. Improving neural machine translation models with monolingual data. In *Proceedings of the 54th Annual Meeting of the Association for Computational Linguistics*, volume 1, pages 86–96.

Martin Sundermeyer, Ralf Schluter, and Hermann Ney. 2010. Lstm neural networks for language modeling. *Interspeech*, pages 194–197.

Ashish Vaswani, Noam Shazeer, Niki Parmar, Jakob Uszkoreit, Llion Jones, Aidan N. Gomez, Lukasz Kaiser, and Illia Polosukhin. 2017. Attention is all you need. *Annual Conference on Neural Information Processing Systems*.

INGEOTEC at SemEval-2018 Task 1:
EvoMSA and μTC for Sentiment Analysis

Mario Graff and **Sabino Miranda-Jiménez**[*] and **Eric S. Tellez**
CONACyT - INFOTEC, Aguascalientes, México
{mario.graff, sabino.miranda, eric.tellez}@infotec.mx

Daniela Moctezuma
CONACyT - CentroGEO, Aguascalientes, México
dmoctezuma@centrogeo.edu.mx

Abstract

This paper describes our participation in Affective Tweets task for emotional intensity and sentiment intensity subtasks for English, Spanish, and Arabic languages. We used two approaches, μTC and EvoMSA. The first one is a generic text categorization and regression system; and the second one is a two-stage architecture for Sentiment Analysis. Both approaches are multilingual and domain independent.

1 Introduction

Sentiment Analysis is a research area where does a computational analysis of people's feelings or beliefs expressed in texts such as emotions, opinions, attitudes, appraisals, etc. (Liu and Zhang, 2012). People communicate not only the emotion or sentiment they are feeling, but also the intensity, that is, the degree of emotion or sentiment. In this context, SemEval is one of the forums that conducts evaluations on semantics at different levels, for instance, it proposes tasks such as sentiment analysis, the intensity of emotion or sentiment (affective tweets) (Mohammad et al., 2018), irony detection, among others (SemEval, 2017).

In this work, we present the results of our participation in Affective Tweets task for four of the five subtasks in English, Spanish, and Arabic languages and for all emotions available: anger, fear, joy, and sadness.

The subtasks are A) emotion intensity regression (EI-REG): given a tweet and an emotion, determine the intensity of the emotion that best represents the mental state of the tweeter, a real-value score between 0 and 1.

B) Emotion intensity ordinal classification (EI-OC): given a tweet and an emotion E, classify the tweet into one of four ordinal classes of intensity of emotion: anger, fear, joy, and sadness, that best represents the mental state of the tweeter.

C) A sentiment intensity regression task (V-REG): given a tweet, determine the intensity of sentiment, a real-valued score between 0 (most negative) and 1 (most positive).

D) A sentiment analysis, ordinal classification (V-OC): given a tweet, classify it into one of seven ordinal classes, corresponding to several levels of positive and negative sentiment intensity.

In this context, one crucial step is the procedure used to transform the data (i.e., tweets) into the inputs (vectors) of the supervised learning techniques used. Typically, Natural Language Processing (NLP) approaches for data representation use n-grams of words, linguistic information such as dependency relations, syntactic information, lexical units (e.g., lemmas, stems), affective lexicons, error correction, etc. However, selecting the best configuration of those characteristics could be a cumbersome task, many times disregarded in favor of some *well-known* competitive setups. (Tellez et al., 2017b) studies the dependency between the performance and the proper selection of the text model. This selection can be seen as a combinatorial optimization problem where the objective is to maximize the performance metric of the classifier being used; this approach is implemented by μTC, (Tellez et al., 2018). Due to its combinatorial nature, and the kind of parameters that compose the configuration space, the resulting classifiers are multilingual and domain independent. Therefore, with a tight dependency on the training set, it is mandatory to provide additional information about the particular task to avoid overfitting. In this sense, the use of multiple knowledge sources is essential, and combining them simply and effectively is the idea be-

---

*Corresponding author: sabino.miranda@infotec.mx

Proceedings of the 12th International Workshop on Semantic Evaluation (SemEval-2018), pages 146–150
New Orleans, Louisiana, June 5–6, 2018. ©2018 Association for Computational Linguistics

hind EvoMSA. EvoMSA (§2.2) is a stacking system based on genetic programming, and particularly on the use of semantic genetic operators, that focus on sentiment analysis. The core of our contribution is to use both μTC and EvoMSA to learn from different annotated collections and then use that diverse knowledge to tackle the SemEval 2018 Task 1 challenge.

Looking at systems that obtained the best results in previous SemEval editions, it can be concluded that it is necessary to include more datasets, see for instance BB_twtr system (Cliche, 2017) for Sentiment Analysis in the Twitter task, which uses more datasets besides the one given in the competition. Here, it was decided to follow a similar approach by including an additional human-annotated dataset publicly available for English, Spanish, and Arabic to build robust models.

2 System Description

As commented, we use two systems to evaluate the Affective Tweets task: μTC and EvoMSA. On the one hand, μTC is used mainly to evaluate two tasks for the Arabic language because in our experiments it obtained the best performance in almost all subtask in this language both for regression and classification tasks. On the other hand, EvoMSA is used to evaluate English and Spanish languages, and ordinal sentiment classification (valence) task for Arabic. In the following paragraphs, we describe these approaches.

2.1 μTC

μTC[1] is a minimalistic and wide system able to tackle text classification and regression tasks independent of domain and language a detail. For complete details of the model see (Tellez et al., 2018). Essentially, μTC creates text classifiers (or a text regressors) searching for the best models in a given configuration space. A configuration consists of instructions to enable several preprocessing functions, a combination of tokenizers among the power set of several possible ones (character q-grams, n-word grams, skip-grams, etc.), and a weighting scheme (application of frequency filters and the use of TF, TFIDF, or several distributional schemes). μTC seeks the best configurations optimizing a score which is evaluated through a classifier or a regressor; currently, it uses SVM for both tasks. In Table 1, we can see details of text

transformations used in our solution for detecting *Anger* emotion for Arabic. This set of text transformations was selected among millions of possible configurations through the combinatorial optimization process implemented in μTC. In ordinal classification tasks the model is found out based on the training dataset provided for each emotion, if this is the case.

2.2 EvoMSA

EvoMSA[2] is a Sentiment Analysis System based on B4MSA and EvoDAG. It is an architecture of two phases to solve classification or regression tasks, see Figure 1. EvoMSA improves the performance of a global classifier combining the predictions of a set of classifiers with different models on the same text to be classified. Roughly speaking, in the first stage, a set of B4MSA classifiers (see Sec. 2.2.1) are trained with two kind of datasets; datasets provided by SemEval, and large datasets annotated by humans for sentiment analysis for English and Spanish languages (Mozetič et al., 2016), called HA datasets. In the case of HA datasets, it is split into balanced small datasets that feed each B4MSA classifier which produces three real output values, one for each sentiment (negative, neutral and positive). In the case of SemEval datasets, for instance, for EI-OC, the classifier produces one of four ordinal classes of intensity of emotion (0, 1, 2, 3). It creates a decision functions space with mixtures of values coming from different views of knowledge. Finally, EvoDAG's inputs are the concatenation of all the decision functions predicted by each B4MSA system, and EvoDAG produces a final value or prediction. The following subsections describe the internal parts of EvoMSA. The precise configuration of our benchmarked system is described in Sec. 4.

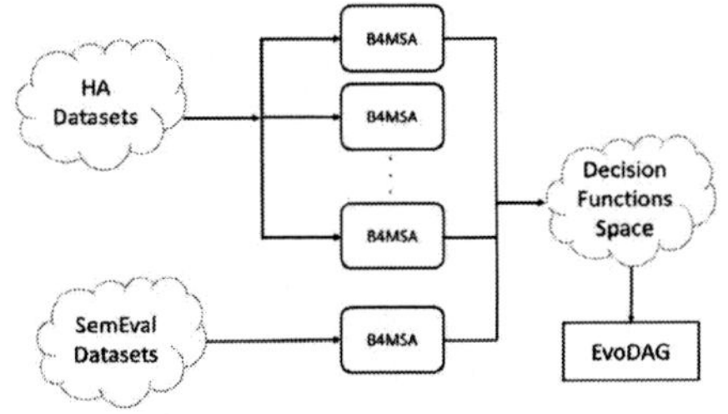

Figure 1: EvoMSA Architecture

---

[1]https://github.com/INGEOTEC/microTC

[2]https://github.com/INGEOTEC/EvoMSA

2.2.1 B4MSA

B4MSA[3] is related to μTC, but this framework is mainly focused for multilingual sentiment analysis. For complete details of the model see (Tellez et al., 2017a,b).

The core idea behind B4MSA is similar to that of μTC, i.e., it tackles the sentiment analysis problem as a model selection problem, yet using a different view of the underlying combinatorial problem. Also, contrarily to μTC, B4MSA takes advantage of several domain-specific particularities like emojis and emoticons and makes explicit handling of negation statements expressed in texts. Nonetheless, EvoMSA avoids the sophisticated use of B4MSA fixing the model for each language in favor of performing an optimization process at the level of the decision functions of several models. Table 1 shows text transformation parameters used in our system for English and Spanish languages.

2.2.2 EvoDAG

EvoDAG[4] (Graff et al., 2016, 2017) is a Genetic Programming system specifically tailored to tackle classification and regression problems on very high dimensional vector spaces and large datasets. In particular, EvoDAG uses the principles of Darwinian evolution to create models represented as a directed acyclic graph (DAG). An EvoDAG model has three distinct node's types; the inputs nodes, that as expected received the independent variables, the output node that corresponds to the label, and the inner nodes are the different numerical functions such as: sum, product, sin, cos, max, and min, among others. Due to lack of space, we refer the reader to (Graff et al., 2016) where EvoDAG is broadly described. In fact, in this research, we followed the steps explained there. In order to give an idea of the type of models being evolved, Figure 2 depicts a model evolved for the Arabic polarity classification at global message task. As can be seen, the model is represented using a DAG where direction of the edges indicates the dependency, e.g., cos depends on X_3, i.e., cosine function is applied to X_3. As commented above, there are three types of nodes; the inputs nodes are colored in red, the inner nodes are blue (the intensity is related to the distance to the height, the darker the closer), and the green node is the output node. As men-

tioned previously, EvoDAG uses as inputs the decision functions of B4MSA, then the first three inputs (i.e., X_0, X_1, and X_2) correspond to the decision functions values of the negative, neutral, and positive polarity of B4MSA model trained with SemEval Arabic dataset, and the later two (i.e., X_3 and X_4) correspond to the decision function values of two B4MSA systems each one trained with other dataset for two classes. It is important to mention that EvoDAG does not have information regarding whether input X_i comes from a particular polarity decision function, consequently from EvoDAG point of view all inputs are equivalent.

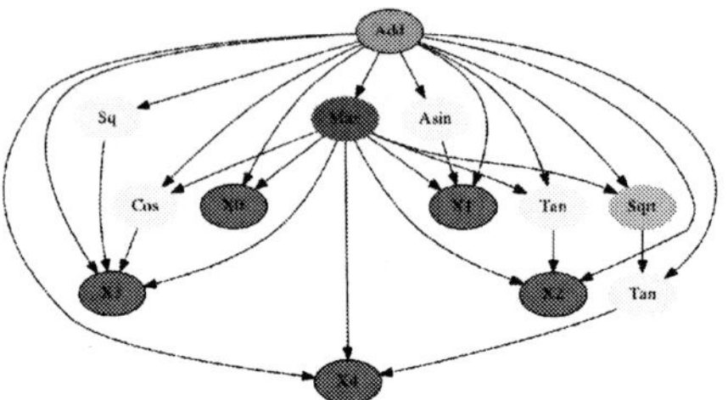

Figure 2: An evolved model for the Arabic task.

3 Experimental Settings

As we mentioned, to determine the best configuration of parameters for text modeling, μTC and B4MSA integrate a hyper-parameter optimization phase that ensures the performance of the classifier based on the training data. The text modeling parameters for B4MSA were set for all process as we show in Table 1 for English and Spanish language for classification and regression tasks. In the case of the Arabic language, the parameters were calculated by the optimization phase; an example is showed in Table 1. A text transformation feature could be binary (yes/no) or ternary (group/delete/none) option. Tokenizers denote how texts must be split after applying the process of each text transformation to texts. Tokenizers generate text chunks in a range of lengths, all tokens generated are part of the text representation. Both, B4MSA and μTC, allow selecting tokenizers based on n-words, $q-$grams, and skip-grams, in any combination. We call n-words to the well-known word n-grams; in particular, we allow to use any combination of unigrams, bigrams, and trigrams. Also, the configuration space allows selecting any combination of character q-grams (or just q-grams) for $q = 1$ to 9. Finally, we allow to

---

[3]https://github.com/INGEOTEC/b4msa
[4]https://github.com/mgraffg/EvoDAG

use $(2, 1)$ and $(3, 1)$ skip-grams (two words separated by one word, and three words separated by a gap).

Table 1 shows the final configurations for English and Spanish and an example for one emotion for Arabic. For example, *numbers* are deleted in Arabic, but it is grouped in English and Spanish. In the case of English, it is split in unigrams, bigrams, character q-grams of sizes 2, 3, and 4.

Text transformation	English	Spanish	Arabic
remove diacritics	yes	yes	yes
remove duplicates	yes	yes	yes
remove punctuation	yes	yes	yes
emoticons	group	group	group
lowercase	yes	yes	false
numbers	group	group	delete
urls	group	group	group
users	group	group	none
hashtags	none	none	none
entities	none	none	none
Term weighting			
TF-IDF	yes	yes	no
Entropy	no	no	yes
Tokenizers			
n-words	$\{1, 2\}$	$\{1, 2\}$	$\{1, 2\}$
q-grams	$\{2, 3, 4\}$	$\{2, 3, 4\}$	$\{2, 3, 7, 9\}$
skip-grams	—	—	—

Table 1: Example of set of configurations for text modeling

3.1 Datasets

SemEval provides datasets to train systems for each subtask. For instance, for emotion Anger in English, subtask emotion intensity ordinal classification, OC, the training data is distributed for four classes (class 0 = 445, class 1 = 322, class 2 = 507, class 3 = 427). The Arabic datasets for each emotion have around 800 samples each one, for English the sizes are between 1500 and 2200 samples, and for Spanish are between 1000 and 1150 samples, for more details of the data distribution and how the datasets were built we refer the reader to (Mohammad et al., 2018; Mohammad and Kiritchenko, 2018). In addition of SemEval data, we use extra datasets annotated by humans around 73 thousand tweets for English, 223 thousand for Spanish (Mozetič et al., 2016), and two thousand for Arabic (NRC, 2017). Table 2 shows the distribution of classes for datasets. Those datasets are mainly used for sentiment analysis; however, we use this extra information to improve the final decision in the approach we implemented (EvoMSA).

HA-DataSet	Positive	Neutral	Negative	Total
English	21,166	33,620	18,454	73,240
Spanish	107,252	89,782	26,272	223,306
Arabic	448	202	1,350	2,000

Table 2: Statistics of Human-Annotated training data. We used the labeled English and Spanish data from (Mozetič et al., 2016), and the Arabic data from (NRC, 2017).

4 Results

We present the results of our approaches in Table 3 and Table 4. All experiments were tested on the development dataset provided by SemEval. In the case of OC tasks, we use the macro-F1 score to measure the performance, and in the case of Reg tasks, we use the Pearson correlation coefficient. Table 3 shows the results of emotional intensity for ordinal classification (OC) and regression tasks (Reg) grouped by each emotion and language. Table 4 shows the results of sentiment analysis, ordinal classification task (V-OC) and sentiment intensity regression task (V-Reg) group by each emotion and language. We present three system configurations in Table 3 and Table 4. EvoMSA configuration uses only the training datasets provided by SemEval, and it is used as regressor or classification system. In addition of SemEval data, EvoMSA-HA uses extra information comes from sentiment analysis domain, and this information improves the performance as we can see. And μTC uses only the training data provided by the contest as the knowledge base to calculate the final class or real value. As we can see in Table 3, the best performance obtained are grouped by EvoMSA-HA configuration for both OC and Reg tasks for English and Spanish languages. For the Arabic language, μTC is quite good with OC and Reg task. According to the results we obtained, we decided to use for the evaluation phase the following configuration: EvoMSA-HA is used for OC, Reg, V-OC, and V-Reg tasks for English and Spanish; also for OC (Fear and Joy) and V-OC tasks for Arabic; and μTC is used for Arabic in OC (Anger and Sadness), Reg, and V-Reg tasks. In the table, the performance of our configuration systems, on gold standard, is labeled by subscripts; they stand for the rank in the general evaluation. For example, for Spanish in OC task, we were ranked for Anger emotion in position 4; Fear, position 2; Joy, position 3; and Sadness, position 2.

Configuration	Anger	Fear	Joy	Sadness
English				
(OC) EvoMSA	0.3938	0.3820	**0.3983**	0.4249
(OC) EvoMSA-HA	**0.4188**	**0.4187**	0.3977	**0.4389**
(OC) μTC	0.3300	0.4120	0.3167	0.3908
(Reg) EvoMSA	0.4948	0.4758	0.5371	0.5714
(Reg) EvoMSA-HA	**0.5756**	**0.5380**	**0.6249**	**0.6105**
(Reg) μTC	0.3301	0.5158	0.5042	0.5087
Performance on gold standard				
(OC) Our Approach	$0.560_{(14)}$	$0.489_{(15)}$	$0.643_{(9)}$	$0.584_{(13)}$
(Reg) Our Approach	$0.643_{(26)}$	$0.621_{(29)}$	$0.684_{(20)}$	$0.626_{(28)}$
Spanish				
(OC) EvoMSA	0.4210	**0.5013**	0.4811	0.4419
(OC) EvoMSA-HA	**0.4405**	0.5006	**0.5275**	**0.4835**
(OC) μTC	0.3741	0.4070	0.4353	0.3757
(Reg) EvoMSA	**0.5487**	**0.7338**	0.7051	**0.5965**
(Reg) EvoMSA-HA	0.4990	0.7265	**0.7129**	0.5941
(Reg) μTC	0.5241	0.6568	0.4897	0.5693
Performance on gold standard				
(OC) Our Approach	$0.468_{(4)}$	$0.634_{(2)}$	$0.655_{(3)}$	$0.628_{(2)}$
(Reg) Our Approach	$0.543_{(4)}$	$0.675_{(4)}$	$0.682_{(3)}$	$0.633_{(5)}$
Arabic				
(OC) EvoMSA	0.4062	**0.3721**	0.3688	0.4039
(OC) EvoMSA-HA	0.3805	0.3620	**0.3768**	0.3637
(OC) μTC	**0.4182**	0.3092	0.3347	**0.4689**
(Reg) EvoMSA	0.3661	0.2770	0.3782	0.5142
(Reg) EvoMSA-HA	0.2118	0.1117	**0.4279**	0.5952
(Reg) μTC	**0.4700**	**0.5011**	0.4090	**0.6191**
Performance on gold standard				
(OC) Our Approach	$0.387_{(4)}$	$0.440_{(4)}$	$0.498_{(4)}$	$0.425_{(6)}$
(Reg) Our Approach	$0.501_{(5)}$	$0.501_{(6)}$	$0.628_{(5)}$	$0.537_{(6)}$

Table 3: Results for Emotion Intensity: Ordinal Classification (OC) and Regression (Reg), in terms of macro-F1 (OC) and Pearson correlation coefficient (Reg).

Configuration	English	Spanish	Arabic
(V-OC) EvoMSA	0.3148	0.3367	**0.3304**
(V-OC) EvoMSA-HA	**0.3430**	**0.3902**	0.3251
(V-OC) μTC	0.2848	0.3418	0.2671
(V-Reg) EvoMSA	0.5993	0.6571	0.2977
(V-Reg) EvoMSA-HA	**0.6213**	**0.6693**	0.0045
(V-Reg) μTC	0.3440	0.5834	**0.6263**
Performance on gold standard			
(V-OC) Our Approach	$0.760_{(11)}$	$0.749_{(3)}$	$0.698_{(4)}$
(V-Reg) Our Approach	$0.761_{(24)}$	$0.701_{(5)}$	$0.746_{(5)}$

Table 4: Results for Valence: Ordinal Classification (OC) and Regression (Reg), in terms of macro-F1 (OC) and Pearson correlation coefficient (Reg).

5 Conclusions

In this paper was presented our solution for Affective Tweets task combining two approaches EvoMSA and μTC. Both systems are designed to be multilingual and language and domain independent as much as possible. For the training step, we use extra human annotated datasets out of any specific emotion, but related to sentiment-analysis information; our solution performs well in Spanish and Arabic languages; however, there is room for further improvements in performance for tasks in English language using another sort of knowledge such as semantic information (word embeddings) into EvoMSA architecture.

References

Mathieu Cliche. 2017. Bb_twtr at semeval-2017 task 4: Twitter sentiment analysis with cnns and lstms. In *Proceedings of the 11th International Workshop on Semantic Evaluation (SemEval-2017)*, pages 573–580.

M. Graff, E. S. Tellez, S. Miranda-Jiménez, and H. J. Escalante. 2016. Evodag: A semantic genetic programming python library. In *2016 IEEE International Autumn Meeting on Power, Electronics and Computing (ROPEC)*, pages 1–6.

Mario Graff, Eric S. Tellez, Hugo Jair Escalante, and Sabino Miranda-Jiménez. 2017. Semantic Genetic Programming for Sentiment Analysis. In Oliver Schtze, Leonardo Trujillo, Pierrick Legrand, and Yazmin Maldonado, editors, *NEO 2015*, number 663 in Studies in Computational Intelligence, pages 43–65. Springer International Publishing. DOI: 10.1007/978-3-319-44003-3_2.

Bing Liu and Lei Zhang. 2012. *A Survey of Opinion Mining and Sentiment Analysis*. Springer US, Boston, MA.

Saif M. Mohammad, Felipe Bravo-Marquez, Mohammad Salameh, and Svetlana Kiritchenko. 2018. Semeval-2018 Task 1: Affect in tweets. In *Proceedings of International Workshop on Semantic Evaluation (SemEval-2018)*, New Orleans, LA, USA.

Saif M. Mohammad and Svetlana Kiritchenko. 2018. Understanding emotions: A dataset of tweets to study interactions between affect categories. In *Proceedings of the 11th Edition of the Language Resources and Evaluation Conference*, Miyazaki, Japan.

Igor Mozetič, Miha Grčar, and Jasmina Smailović. 2016. Multilingual twitter sentiment classification: The role of human annotators. *PloS one*, 11(5):e0155036.

NRC. 2017. Syrian tweets arabic sentiment analysis dataset. http://saifmohammad.com/WebPages/ArabicSA.html. Accessed 17-Feb-2017.

SemEval. 2017. Semeval-2017: Sentiment analysis task 4. http://alt.qcri.org/semeval2017/task4/. Accessed 17-Feb-2017.

Eric S. Tellez, Sabino Miranda-Jiménez, Mario Graff, Daniela Moctezuma, Ranyart R. Suárez, and Oscar S. Siordia. 2017a. A simple approach to multilingual polarity classification in Twitter. *Pattern Recognition Letters*, 94:68–74.

Eric S. Tellez, Sabino Miranda-Jimnez, Mario Graff, Daniela Moctezuma, Oscar S. Siordia, and Elio A. Villaseor. 2017b. A case study of spanish text transformations for twitter sentiment analysis. *Expert Systems with Applications*, 81:457 – 471.

Eric S. Tellez, Daniela Moctezuma, Sabino Miranda-Jiménez, and Mario Graff. 2018. An automated text categorization framework based on hyperparameter optimization. *Knowledge-Based Systems*, 149:110–123.

Epita at SemEval-2018 Task 1: Sentiment Analysis Using Transfer Learning Approach

Guillaume Daval-Frerot   Abdessalam Bouchekif   Anatole Moreau

Graduate school of computer science, EPITA, France

`firstname.lastname@epita.fr`

Abstract

In this paper we present our system for detecting valence task. The major issue was to apply a state-of-the-art system despite the small dataset provided : the system would quickly overfit. The main idea of our proposal is to use transfer learning, which allows to avoid learning from scratch. Indeed, we start to train a first model to predict if a tweet is positive, negative or neutral. For this we use an external dataset which is larger and similar to the target dataset. Then, the pre-trained model is re-used as the starting point to train a new model that classifies a tweet into one of the seven various levels of sentiment intensity.

Our system, trained using transfer learning, achieves 0.776 and 0.763 respectively for Pearson correlation coefficient and weighted quadratic kappa metrics on the subtask evaluation dataset.

1 Introduction

The goal of detecting valence task is to classify a given tweet into one of seven classes, corresponding to various levels of positive and negative sentiment intensity, that best represents the mental state of the tweeter. This can be seen as a multiclass classification problem, in which each tweet must be classified in one of the following classes : very negative (-3), moderately negative (-2), slightly negative (-1), neutral/mixed (0), slightly positive (1), moderately positive (2) and very positive (3) (Mohammad et al., 2018).

Several companies have been interested in customer opinion for a given product or service. Sentiment analysis is one approach to automatically detect their emotions from comments posted in social networks.

With the recent advances in deep learning, the ability to analyse sentiments has considerably improved. Indeed, many experiments have used state-of-the-art systems to achieve high performance. For example, (Baziotis et al., 2017) use Bi-directional Long Short-Term Memory (B-LSTM) with attention mechanisms while (Deriu et al., 2016) use Convolutional Neural Networks (CNN). Both systems obtained the best performance at the the 2016 and 2017 SemEval 4-A task respectively.

The amount of data is argued to be the main condition to train a reliable deep neural network. However, the dataset provided to build our system is limited. To address this issue, two solutions can be considered. The first solution consists in extending our dataset by either manually labeling new data, which can be very time consuming, or by using over-sampling approaches. The second solution consists in applying a transfer learning, which allows to avoid learning the model from scratch.

In this paper, we apply a transfer learning approach, from a model trained on a similar task : we propose to pre-train a model to predict if a tweet is positive, negative or neutral. Precisely, we apply a B-LSTM on an external dataset. Then, the pre-trained model is re-used to classify a tweet according to the seven-point scale of positive and negative sentiment intensity.

The rest of the paper is organized as follows. Section 2 presents a brief definition of transfer learning. The description of our proposed system is presented in Section 3. The experimental set-up and results are described in Section 4. Finally, a conclusion is given with a discussion of future works in Section 5.

2 Transfer Learning

Transfer Learning (TL) consists in transferring the knowledge learned on one task to a second related task. In other words, the TL is about training a base network and then copy its first n layers to the first n layers of a target network (Yosinski et al., 2014). Usually the first n layers of a pre-

Proceedings of the 12th International Workshop on Semantic Evaluation (SemEval-2018), pages 151–155
New Orleans, Louisiana, June 5–6, 2018. ©2018 Association for Computational Linguistics

trained model (or source model) are frozen when training the new model. This means that weights are not changed during training on the new task. TL should not be confused with fine-tuning where the back-propagation error affects the entire neural network (including the first n layers).

For a limited number of training examples, TL allows to provide more precise predictions than the traditional supervised learning approaches. Moreover, TL significantly speeds up the learning process as training does not start from scratch. For example, (Cirean et al., 2012) use a CNN trained to recognize the Latin handwritten characters for the detection of Chinese characters. In natural language processing, TL has improved the performance of several systems from various domains such as : sentiment classification (Glorot et al., 2011), automatic translation (Zoph et al., 2016), speech recognition and document classification (Wang and Zheng, 2015).

3 Proposed System

In this section, we present the four main steps of our approach : (1) **Text processing** to filter the noise from the raw text data, (2) **Feature extraction** to represent words in tweets as vectors of length 426 by concatenating several features, (3) **Pre-training model** to predict the tweet polarity (positive, negative or neutral) based on external data and (4) **Learning** a new model where the pre-trained model is adapted to our task by removing the last layer and adding a fully-connected layer followed by an output layer.

3.1 Text processing

Tweets are processed using *ekphrasis*[1] tool which allows to perform the following tasks : tokenization, word normalization, word segmentation (for splitting hashtags) and spell correction (*i.e* replace a misspelled word with the most probable candidate word). All words are lowercase. E-mails, URLs and user handles are normalized. A detailed description of this tool is given in (Baziotis et al., 2017).

3.2 Feature extraction

Each word in each tweet is represented by a vector of 426 dimensions which are obtained by the concatenation of the following features :

— *AFINN* and *Emoji Valence*[2] are two lists of english words and emojis rated for valence scoring range from -5 (very negative) to $+5$ (very positive) (Nielsen, 2011).
— *Depeche Mood* is a lexicon of $37k$ words associated with emotion scores (afraid, amused, angry, annoyed, sad, happy, inspired and don't care) (Staiano and Guerini, 2014).
— *Emoji Sentiment Lexicon* is a lexicon of the 969 most frequent emojis. The emojis sentiment is computed from the sentiment (positive, negative or neutral) of tweets in which they occur. Each emoji is associated with a unicode, number of occurrences, position in the tweet $[0, 1]$ (0 : start of the tweet, 1 : end of the tweet), probabilities of negativity, neutrality, and positivity of the emoji (Novak et al., 2015).
— *Linguistic Inquiry and Word Count* is a dictionary containing 5,690 stems associated with 64 categories, from linguistic dimensions to psychological processes (Tausczik and Pennebaker, 2010).
— *NRC Word-Emotion Association, Hashtag Emotion/Sentiment* and *Affect Intensity Lexicons* are lists of english words and their associations with eight emotions (anger, fear, anticipation, trust, surprise, sadness, joy, and disgust) and two sentiments (positive, negative), each with specificities detailed in (Mohammad and Turney, 2013), (Mohammad and Kiritchenko, 2015) and (Mohammad, 2017). The intensity score for both emotions and sentiments takes a value between 0 and 1.
— *Opinion Lexicon English* contains around $7k$ positive and negative sentiment words for the english language (Hu and Liu, 2004).
— *Sentiment140* is a list of words and their associations with positive and negative sentiment (Mohammad et al., 2013).
— *Words embeddings* are dense vectors of real numbers capturing the semantic meanings of words. We use datastories embeddings (Baziotis et al., 2017) which were trained on 330M english twitter messages posted from 12/2012 to 07/2016. The embeddings used in this work are 300 dimensional.

---

1. `https://github.com/cbaziotis/ekphrasis`

2. `https://github.com/words/emoji-emotion`

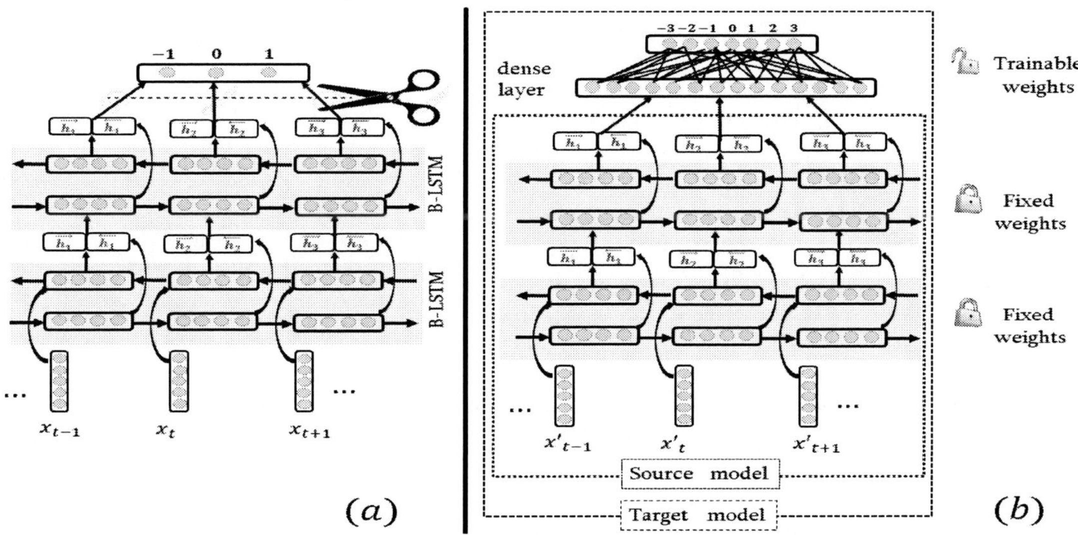

Figure 1 – Our transfer learning approach for sentiment analysis. (a) Pre-trained model learned with B-LSTM network with 2 layers of 150 neurons each to predict if a tweet is positive, negative or neutral. (b) The first layers of pre-traind model are locked and re-purposed to predict various levels of positive and negative sentiment intensity.

3.3 Pre-training model

The objective is to build a model which allows to predict the tweeter's attitude (positive, negative or neutral). Bidirectional Long Short-Term Memory networks (B-LSTM) (Schuster and Paliwal, 1997) have become a standard for sentiment analysis (Baziotis et al., 2017) (Mousa and Schuller, 2017) (Moore and Rayson, 2017). B-LSTM consists in two LSTMs in different directions running in parallel : the first forward network reads the input sequence from left to right and the second backward network reads the sequence from right to left. Each LSTM yields a hidden representation : $\vec{h}$ (left to right vector) and $\overleftarrow{h}$ (right-to-left vector) which are then combined to compute the output sequence. For our problem, capturing the context of words from both directions allows to better understand the tweet semantic. We here use a B-LSTM network with 2 layers of 150 neurons each. The architecture is shown in Figure 1 (a).

For training, we use the external dataset [3] composed of 50333 tweets (7840 negatives, 19903 positives and 22590 neutrals).

---

3. https://github.com/cbaziotis/
datastories-semeval2017-task4/tree/
master/dataset/Subtask_A/downloaded.

3.4 Learning model

Let us note that our final objective is to train a model to classify a tweet into seven classes (very negative, moderately negative, slightly negative, neutral, slightly positive, moderately positive and very positive). To train the model, we use the dataset provided for the target task (Mohammad and Kiritchenko, 2018). The training and development dataset contain respectively 1180 and 448 tweets. Since the dataset is small, fine-tuning may result in overfitting. Therefore, we propose to freeze the network layers except the final dense layer that is associated with the three classes sentiment analysis, which is removed after pre-training. Then, we add a fully-connected layer of 150 neurons followed by an output layer of 7 neurons, as illustrated on Figure 1 (b).

4 Results and Analysis

The official [4] evaluation metric is *Pearson Correlation Coefficient* (P). Submited systems are also evaluated with the weighted quadratic kappa (W). However, the pre-trained model was evaluated using classification accuracy. We implemented our system using Keras tool with the Tensorflow backend.

---

4. https://github.com/felipebravom/
SemEval_2018_Task_1_Eval

4.1 Pre-trained model evaluation

As proposed in (Baziotis et al., 2017), we used
B-LSTM with the following parameters : size of
LSTM layers is 150 (300 for B-LSTM), 2 layers of
B-LSTM, with a dropout of 0.3 and 0.5 for embedding and LSTM layers respectively. Other hyperparameters used are : Gaussian noise with σ of 0.3,
and L_2 regularization of 0.0001. We trained the B-LSTM over 18 epochs with a learning rate of 0.01
and batch size of 128 sequences.

We trained our model with external data (more
details in section 3.3) but for the evaluation we
adapted the training and development sets provided for the target task. The various levels of positive sentiments (*i.e* slightly, moderately and very
positive) were regrouped in the same class. The
same goes for the various levels of negative sentiments. Our model achieves 69.4% of accuracy.

4.2 Model evaluation

We adapted the pre-trained model described
above by removing the last fully-connected layer,
and added a dense layer of 150 neurons followed
by an output layer of 7 neurons. As a reminder,
the pre-trained layers are frozen. We used the training and development sets to train our system, and
evaluated by predicting the valence on the evaluation set. We trained our model over 8 epochs with
a learning rate of 0.01 and batch size of 50 sequences. Our model achieves 0.776 and 0.763 respectively on P and W.

4.3 Other experiments

Finally, we conducted a set of experiments to
validate our system and approach. We evaluated
more commonly used systems, with and without
transfer learning. These new systems are built by :
— using similar number of layers, parameters
  and hyper-parameters.
— replacing B-LSTM layers by LSTM, CNN
  and dense layers.
— for the DNN, computing predictions using
  the mean of each word-vector of tweets,
  since it can not use sequences as input.
— for the CNN, using multiple convolutional
  filters of sizes 3, 4 and 5.
— for the combinations of systems, averaging
  the output probabilities.

The results are presented on Table 1.

We can observe that TL approach achieves better scores, and that B-LSTM is leading the score

Approach	Systems	*Pearson*
Without TL	DNN	0.683
	CNN	0.702
	LSTM	0.721
	B-LSTM	0.735
	CNN + LSTM	**0.742**
With TL	CNN	0.741
	B-LSTM	**0.776**
	CNN + B-LSTM	0.755

Table 1 – Pearson scores on test set with different systems and combinations.

on both approaches as a single system. Moreover, combining systems enhances greatly the prediction without TL, but decreases the score with
TL : the combination of independent systems compensates a small lack of data, but becomes useless
with enough training.

5 Conclusion

In this paper, we propose to use a transfer
learning approach for sentiment analysis (SemEval2018 task 1). Using B-LSTM networks, we pretrained a model to predict the tweet polarity (positive, negative or neutral) based on an external dataset of $50k$ tweets. To avoid the overfitting, layers
(except the last one) of the pre-trained model were
frozen. A dense layer was then added followed by
a seven neurones output layer. Finally, the new network was trained on the small target dataset. The
system achieves a score of 0.776 on Pearson Correlation Coefficient.

Improvements could be made concerning the
features, and by using attention mechanisms.
However, the future work will focus on multiple
transfers, to increase the amount of data used in
the process. We will perform transfers from two
classes (positive and negative) to three classes
(adding neutral), then five classes and finally
seven classes. Numerous datasets [5] are currently
available to deploy such a system.

Acknowledgments

We thank Dr. Yassine Nair Benrekia for interesting scientific discussions.

---

5. `http://alt.qcri.org/semeval2016/task4/`

References

Christos Baziotis, Nikos Pelekis, and Christos Doulkeridis. 2017. Datastories at semeval-2017 task 6 : Siamese LSTM with attention for humorous text comparison. In *Proceedings of the 11th International Workshop on Semantic Evaluation, SemEval@ACL 2017, Vancouver, Canada*.

D. C. Cirean, U. Meier, and J. Schmidhuber. 2012. Transfer learning for latin and chinese characters with deep neural networks. In *The 2012 International Joint Conference on Neural Networks (IJCNN)*.

Jan Deriu, Maurice Gonzenbach, Fatih Uzdilli, Aurélien Lucchi, Valeria De Luca, and Martin Jaggi. 2016. Swisscheese at semeval-2016 task 4 : Sentiment classification using an ensemble of convolutional neural networks with distant supervision. In *Proceedings of the 10th International Workshop on Semantic Evaluation, SemEval@NAACL-HLT, USA*.

Xavier Glorot, Antoine Bordes, and Yoshua Bengio. 2011. Domain adaptation for large-scale sentiment classification : A deep learning approach. In *Proceedings of the 28th International Conference on Machine Learning, USA*.

Minqing Hu and Bing Liu. 2004. Mining and summarizing customer reviews. In *Proceedings of the Tenth ACM SIGKDD International Conference on Knowledge Discovery and Data Mining, Seattle, Washington, USA*, pages 168–177.

Saif Mohammad, Svetlana Kiritchenko, and Xiaodan Zhu. 2013. Nrc-canada : Building the state-of-the-art in sentiment analysis of tweets. In *Proceedings of the seventh international workshop on Semantic Evaluation Exercises (SemEval-2013)*.

Saif Mohammad and Peter D. Turney. 2013. Crowdsourcing a word-emotion association lexicon. *Computational Intelligence*, 29(3) :436–465.

Saif M. Mohammad. 2017. Word affect intensities. *CoRR*, abs/1704.08798.

Saif M. Mohammad, Felipe Bravo-Marquez, Mohammad Salameh, and Svetlana Kiritchenko. 2018. Semeval-2018 Task 1 : Affect in tweets. In *Proceedings of International Workshop on Semantic Evaluation (SemEval-2018)*, New Orleans, LA, USA.

Saif M. Mohammad and Svetlana Kiritchenko. 2015. Using hashtags to capture fine emotion categories from tweets. *Computational Intelligence*, 31(2) :301–326.

Saif M. Mohammad and Svetlana Kiritchenko. 2018. Understanding emotions : A dataset of tweets to study interactions between affect categories. In *Proceedings of the 11th Edition of the Language Resources and Evaluation Conference*, Miyazaki, Japan.

Andrew Moore and Paul Rayson. 2017. Lancaster A at semeval-2017 task 5 : Evaluation metrics matter : predicting sentiment from financial news headlines. In *Proceedings of the 11th International Workshop on Semantic Evaluation, SemEval@ACL 2017, Canada*.

Amr Mousa and Bjrn Schuller. 2017. Contextual bidirectional long short term memory recurrent neural network language models : A generative approach to sentiment analysis. In *Proceedings of the 15th Conference of the European Chapter of the Association for Computational Linguistics*.

Finn Årup Nielsen. 2011. A new evaluation of a word list for sentiment analysis in microblogs. In *Proceedings of the ESWC2011 Workshop on 'Making Sense of Microposts' : Big things come in small packages Crete, Greece*, pages 93–98.

Petra Kralj Novak, Jasmina Smailovic, Borut Sluban, and Igor Mozetic. 2015. Sentiment of emojis. *CoRR*, abs/1509.07761.

Mike Schuster and Kuldip K. Paliwal. 1997. Bidirectional recurrent neural networks. *IEEE Trans. Signal Processing*.

Jacopo Staiano and Marco Guerini. 2014. Depeche mood : a lexicon for emotion analysis from crowd annotated news. In *Proceedings of the 52nd Annual Meeting of the Association for Computational Linguistics, ACL, Baltimore, USA*, pages 427–433.

Yla R. Tausczik and James W. Pennebaker. 2010. The psychological meaning of words : Liwc and computerized text analysis methods. *Journal of Language and Social Psychology*, 29 :24–54.

Dong Wang and Thomas Fang Zheng. 2015. Transfer learning for speech and language processing. In *Asia-Pacific Signal and Information Processing Association Annual Summit and Conference*.

Jason Yosinski, Jeff Clune, Yoshua Bengio, and Hod Lipson. 2014. How transferable are features in deep neural networks ? In *Proceedings of the 27th International Conference on Neural Information Processing Systems*.

Barret Zoph, Deniz Yuret, Jonathan May, and Kevin Knight. 2016. Transfer learning for low-resource neural machine translation. In *Proceedings of the 2016 Conference on Empirical Methods in Natural Language Processing, USA*.

KDE-AFFECT at SemEval-2018 Task 1: Estimation of Affects in Tweet by Using Convolutional Neural Network for n-gram

Shinnosuke Himeno and Masaki Aono
Department of Computer Science and Engineering
Toyohashi University of Technology
`himeno@kde.cs.tut.ac.jp, aono@tut.jp`

Abstract

This paper describes our approach to SemEval-2018 Task1: Estimation of Affects in Tweet for 1a and 2a. Our team KDE-AFFECT employs several methods including one-dimensional Convolutional Neural Network for n-grams, together with word embedding and other preprocessing such as vocabulary unification and Emoji conversions into four emotional words.

1 Introduction

With the rapid spread of SNS services (e.g. Twitter, Facebook, Instagram), massive user opinions have accumulated on the Internet. Among such opinions, it has been observed that not a few SNS contents naturally entail the affects (including joy, anger, sadness, fear) within themselves. Hence, the need to accurately detect the affects is increasing year by year.

In SemEval-2018 Task 1: Estimation of Affects in Tweet, we have attempted to extend our horizon from positive, neutral, and negative polarity estimations in former SemEval sentiment analysis in tweet having been held till 2017, to multiple emotions (joy, anger, sadness, and fear) in terms of regression (Task-1 1a) and classification (Task-1 2a). In doing so, we have adopted a standard one-dimensional Convolutional Neural Network (CNN), which is believed to be effective for text polarity estimation, where the kernel window size for 1D convolution is analogous to the concept of word n-gram. In addition, as most people have noticed, a tweet has potentially many Emojis to express emotions. In the following, we first briefly survey related work on tweet sentiment analysis including emotion estimation. Then, we describe our system, followed by showing the results returned from the organizer, and finally concluding our paper.

2 Related Work

Sentiment analysis of tweets has been studied by many researchers from the standpoint of classifying a tweet into either positive or negative polarity, and classifying it into multiple emotions (Giachanou and Crestani, 2016; Silva et al., 2016). A supervised approach to polarity classification of a tweet was proposed by Go et al. (2009). They employed Naive Bayes, Maximum Entropy, Support Vector Machine, and several other machine learning methods for their supervised learning. Bravo-Marque et al. (2013) presented an approach using multiple emotion dictionaries, while Saif et al. (2016) employed co-occurrence information of words. Severyn et al. (2015) introduced a deep learning approach. Lu et al. (2013) proposed a deep learning method suited for short texts. In SemEval, since 2014, sentiment analysis tasks using Twitter have been officially conducted, where a variety of methods have been tested (Hagen et al., 2015; Giorgis et al., 2016; Deriu et al., 2016; Rouvier and Favre, 2016; Xu et al., 2016). In SemEval2017 Rosenthal et al. (2017), Cliche et al. (2017) and Hamdan et al. (2017) presented methods for combining multiple Convolutional Neural Networks (CNNs) and multiple Long Short-Term Memories (LSTMs). Mohammad (2017) published an open dictionary of emotion scores for each word. Mohammad et al. published a dataset for estimating emotion intensities (Mohammad and Bravo-Marquez, 2017).

3 Methodology

In this section, we focus on our methods and ideas employed in this task. The fundamental idea of our method is based on the observation that "n-grams" seem to have vital effects to represent the emotion of a tweet, where "n-gram" denotes n consecutive words (instead of n consecutive char-

Proceedings of the 12th International Workshop on Semantic Evaluation (SemEval-2018), pages 156–161
New Orleans, Louisiana, June 5–6, 2018. ©2018 Association for Computational Linguistics

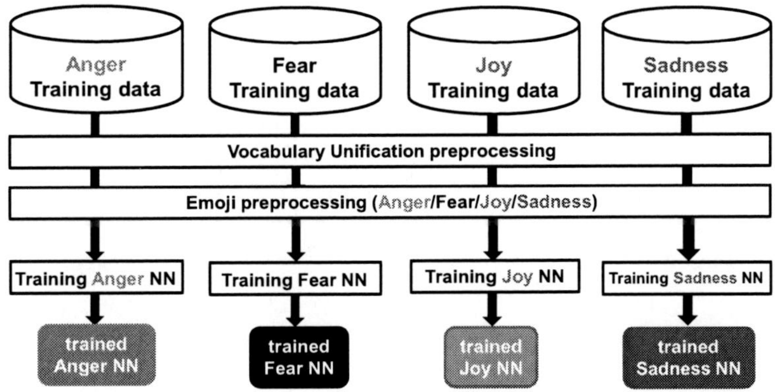

Figure 1: Overall Training Flow of KDE-AFFECT

acters). For instance, if the tweet sentence is "At last I made it.", 2-gram includes (At, last) and (made, it). Similarly, 3-gram includes (At, last, I) and (I, made, it).

We have adopted the method based on the n-gram convolution proposed by Kim (2014). Here, we prepare a matrix corresponding to a sentence representing an n-gram convolution in which this filtering process is carried out by the unit of an n-gram.

The overview of our system is as follows: First we apply preprocessing with "vocabulary unification" including lower case conversion, URL unification, two or more consecutive character squeezing, and hashtag elimination. Second, we apply Emoji conversion into four emotional words, which will be elaborated later. From Emoji conversion, we train the model independently for each emotion. Finally, we predict the emotion score for an unknown tweet by using the trained model. The overall system flow is shown in Figure 1.

3.1 Preprocessing with Vocabulary Unification

This step is applied to all emotions. It consists of the following processing:

- lower case conversion
- conversion of every instance of a URL string in a tweet to "<URL>"
- collapse of two or more consecutive letters into two
- elimination of hash sign (#)

It should be noted that by a url string we mean a regular expression starting with either "http", "https", "ftp", or "www". Any url string is converted to <URL>. For example, "I want to be happy on http://t.co/S6moxr1U" is converted to "I want to be happy on <URL>".

3.2 Preprocessing for Emoji

From our observation of real tweets, approximately more than 20% of them have some kind of Emojis. Emotions are naturally represented by many different Emojis. Hence, we introduce the conversion of possible emotions represented by an Emoji into each emotional word. Please note that Emoji preprocessing is applied to all Emoji data, regardless of emotions. For instance, each anger Emoji might appear not only in an Anger dataset, but in Fear, Joy, and Sadness datasets as well. This is why we have decided to apply the Emoji conversion despite the differences of emotions. In the following, we present Emoji for each emotion, where Emoji has been taken from a Full Emoji Web site[1]. The selection of Emoji has been made by using the labels (such as "face-positive") annotated to the above Web sites.

3.2.1 Anger Emoji

The Anger Emojis we selected are shown in Figure 2. All of them are replaced by "anger".

Figure 2: Anger Emoji

3.2.2 Fear Emoji

The Fear Emojis we selected are shown in Fig. 3. All of them are replaced by "fear".

---

[1] https://unicode.org/emoji/charts/full-emoji-list.html

Figure 3: Fear Emoji

3.2.3 Joy Emoji

The Joy Emojis we selected are shown in Fig. 4. All of them are replaced by "joy".

Figure 4: Joy Emoji

3.2.4 Sadness Emoji

The Sadness Emojis we selected are shown in Fig. 5. All of them are replaced by "sadness".

Figure 5: Sadness Emoji

3.3 Convolutional Neural Network for n-gram

Once preprocessing is done, we have a kind of rectified tweet, represented by a matrix. Figure 6 illustrates a word-by-word matrix representation of a rectified tweet. Here we take a matrix of 80 by 300, where 80 is the maximum number of words per tweet, and 300 corresponds to our embedding vector size. If a tweet has less than 80 words, zero padding is performed to fill the input matrix.

3.3.1 Embedding

In Embedding, each tweet is converted to a matrix. Specifically, we first divide a tweet into words using a whitespace, thereby treating a special character (one of ".h, ",h, "!h, and "?h) as a separate word. Second, we transform each word into its distributed representation of 300 dimensions using Word2Vec (Mikolov et al., 2013a,b). The training of Word2Vec itself is done by using approximately 470 million tweets after the processing de-

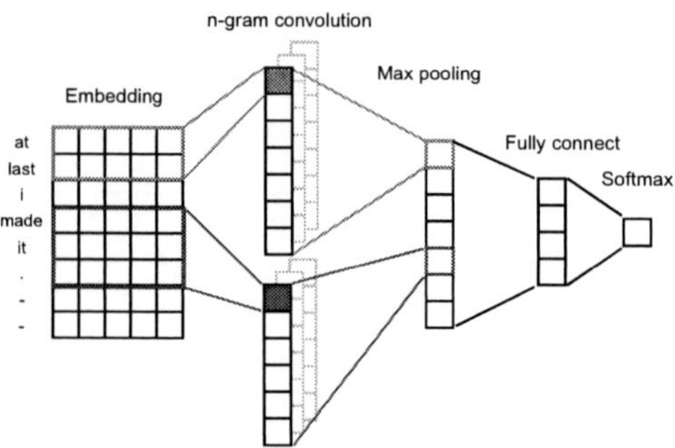

Figure 6: Our n-gram Convolution-based Approach

scribed in 3.1. We finally obtain the embedding by padding zero values to a fixed size of a 80 by 300 dimensional matrix.

3.3.2 n-gram Convolution Layer

In an n-gram convolutional layer, we perform convolution, and generate a length $m - n + 1$ vector, where m denotes the maximum word length (here 80). This is straightforward, since both ends are trimmed during the n-gram convolution stage shown in Figure 6. For instance, if 3-gram is concerned, the length in our implementation will be 80-3+1 = 78. Note that we have multiple n-gram convolutional layers for each emotion. "Joy" neural network architecture, for example, has 2-gram, 3-gram, 4-gram, and 5-gram convolutional layers, which will be discussed later in Table 3.

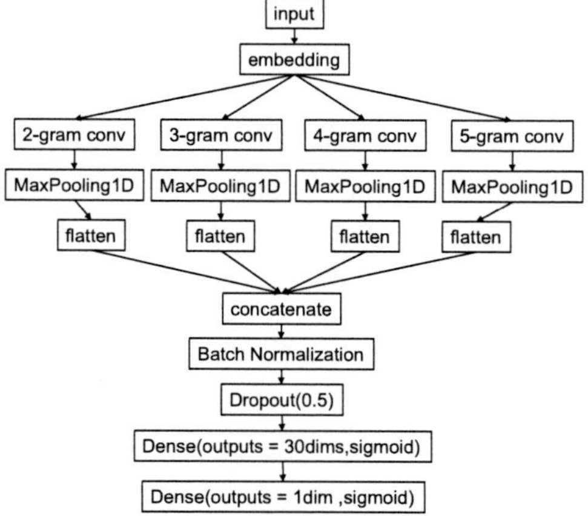

Figure 7: KDE-AFFECT system's DNN architecture

3.3.3 Max Pooling Layer

In a Max Pooling layer, from each n-gram convolutional layer, the maximum value is computed,

Intensity range	Intensity amount
$[0.0, 0.35)$	0 (no E)
$[0.35, 0.5)$	1 (low amount of E)
$[0.5, 0.65)$	2 (moderate amount of E)
$[0.65, 1.0]$	3 (high amount of E)

Table 1: Inferred Intensity Level

	Anger	Fear	Joy	Sadness
Training	1701	2252	1616	1532
Dev.	388	389	290	397
Test (1a)	17940	17924	18043	17913
Test (2a)	1002	986	1105	975

Table 2: SemEval 2018: Task 1 dataset (1a and 2a)

and a vector of the length equal to the number of filters is generated. In our system, the output of four multiple n-gram convolutional layers are flattened and concatenated in the subsequent layers. The output dimension is the number of filters multiplied by the number of n-gram convolutional layers.

3.3.4 Fully-connected Layers

In our system, we have two fully-connected layers, where the first hidden fully-connected layer accepts the input from the concatenation layer connceted from multiple max pooling layers. Empirically, we set 30 outputs for the first fully-connected layer. The second layer outputs either the estimated intensity value of an emotion (Task 1a) or the estimated intensity level (Task 2a). The way to estimate the intensity level (Task 2a) is elaborated in the next section.

3.4 Estimating Intensity Level (Task 2a)

For Task 2a, we need to estimate the intensity level. Specifically, participants are required to classify the emotional intensities into four levels; high amount, moderate amount, low amount, and nothing. Our strategy for the amount of emotional intensity amount level is simple, which is based on the inferred intensity range as shown in Table 1. In Table 1, the left column denotes the range of emotional amount that we have defined for this task. For example, $[0.0, 0.35)$ means that the left boundary 0.0 is inclusive, while the right boundary 0.35 is exclusive in the range of the amount of emotion.

4 Experiments

Here we describe the experimental environment and our evaluation results.

4.1 dataset

All participants are given SemEval 2018: Task 1 Affect in Tweets (AIT) (Mohammad et al., 2018) dataset. The details are shown in Table 2.

4.2 Evaluation Measure

Here, the evaluation measure for a model is correlation coefficient r. Given variables x and y, where x corresponds to a predicted emotion value and y to a true emotion value, and their associated sample variances S_x, S_y, and the covariance S_{xy} are represented by the following equation:

$$r = \frac{S_{xy}}{S_x S_y}$$

4.3 Experiment Environment

For our deep learning program for the task, we used the following list of hyper-parameters:

loss function: Root Mean Square Error (RMSE)
filter number: $200 \times n$
epochs: 30
dropout rate: 0.5
optimizer: Adam
batch size: 64

The framework we use is Keras with backend Tensorflow. In our Ubuntu server, it took approximately 1 second for each epoch.

4.4 Preliminary Experiments for n-gram Convolutions

For each emotion, our system attempts to find an empirical optimal combination of n-gram convolutions. Table 3 summarizes the results of preliminary experiments for this purpose. Here, $r(A)$ denotes the correlation coefficient for Anger. Similarly, $r(F)$ for Fear, $r(J)$ for Joy, and $r(S)$ for Sadness. From the table, we decided as follows: For Anger, we chose [1,2,3,4,5,6] (meaning we took the combination of 1-gram, 2-gram, 3-gram, 4-gram, 5-gram, and 6-gram convolutions). For Fear, we chose [2,3,4,5,6]. For Joy and Sadness, we chose [2,3,4,5].

4.5 Experimental Result (Task 1a)

According to the Official Leaderboard for Task 1a, our team KDE-AFFECT turned out to be 30-th. If

n	$r(A)$	$r(F)$	$r(J)$	$r(S)$
$[1, 2, 3, 4, 5, 6]$	**0.5529**	0.5919	0.5771	0.6349
$[2, 3, 4, 5, 6]$	0.5518	**0.5994**	0.5464	0.6173
$[1, 2, 3, 4, 5]$	0.5381	0.5948	0.5730	0.6078
$[2, 3, 4, 5]$	0.5309	0.5736	**0.5906**	**0.6360**

Table 3: Preliminary experiments for n-gram convolustions

Team	avg-r	$r(A)$	$r(F)$	$r(J)$	$r(S)$
KDE-AFFECT	0.620	0.630	0.621	0.598	0.630
SeerNet[1st]	0.799	0.827	0.799	0.792	0.798
NTUA-SLP[2nd]	0.776	0.782	0.758	0.771	0.792
PlusEmo2Vec[3rd]	0.766	0.811	0.728	0.773	0.753
CrystalFeel[14th]	0.717	0.740	0.700	0.708	0.720
EliRF-UPV[15th]	0.696	0.705	0.686	0.693	0.700
iit_delhi[29th]	0.621	0.633	0.645	0.618	0.588
DeepMiner[31th]	0.575	0.581	0.570	0.575	0.573
Baseline[37th]	0.520	0.526	0.525	0.575	0.453

Table 4: Our result with selected other teams for Task 1a

Team	avg-r	$r(A)$	$r(F)$	$r(J)$	$r(S)$
KDE-AFFECT	0.530	0.530	0.470	0.552	0.567
SeerNet[1st]	0.695	0.706	0.637	0.720	0.717
PlusEmo2Vec[2nd]	0.659	0.704	0.528	0.720	0.683
psyML[3rd]	0.653	0.670	0.588	0.686	0.667
UNCC[9th]	0.599	0.604	0.544	0.638	0.610
ECNU[16th]	0.531	0.565	0.441	0.581	0.536
CrystalFeel[18th]	0.530	0.576	0.466	0.540	0.538
Baseline[26th]	0.394	0.382	0.355	0.496	0.370

Table 5: Our result with selected other teams for Task 2a

we use similar notations as in Table 3, and pick up the top-3 ranked teams, as well as randomly chosen teams CrystalFeel (14-th place), ELipRF-UPV (15-th place), iit_delhi (29-th), DeepMiner (31-th), and the baseline (37-th), the result looks like Table 4.

4.6 Experimental Result (Task 2a)

According to the Official Leaderboard for Task 2a, our team KDE-AFFECT turned out to be 17-th. If we use similar notations as in Table 3, and pick up top-3 ranked teams, as well as randomly chosen teams UNCC (9-th place), ECNU (16-th place), CrystalFeel (14-th place), and the baseline (26-th), the result looks like Table 5.

5 Conclusion

This paper describes the approach we took for SemEval-2018 Task 1: Affect in Tweets (subtasks 1a and 2a). We have chosen a combination of different n-gram convolutions with preprocessing including vocabulary unification and Emoji conversion.

Acknowledgments

Part of this research is supported by MEXT KAK-ENHI, Grant-in-Aid for Scientific Research (B), Grant Number 17H01746.

References

Felipe Bravo-Marquez, Marcelo Mendoza, and Barbara Poblete. 2013. Combining strengths, emotions and polarities for boosting twitter sentiment analysis. In *Proceedings of the Second International Workshop on Issues of Sentiment Discovery and Opinion Mining*, WISDOM '13, pages 2:1–2:9, Chicago, Illinois.

Mathieu Cliche. 2017. Bb_twtr at semeval-2017 task 4: Twitter sentiment analysis with cnns and lstms. In *Proceedings of the 11th International Workshop on Semantic Evaluation (SemEval-2017)*, pages 573–580, Vancouver, Canada. Association for Computational Linguistics.

Jan Deriu, Maurice Gonzenbach, Fatih Uzdilli, Aurelien Lucchi, Valeria De Luca, and Martin Jaggi. 2016. Swisscheese at semeval-2016 task 4: Sentiment classification using an ensemble of convolutional neural networks with distant supervision. In *Proceedings of the 10th International Workshop on Semantic Evaluation (SemEval-2016)*, pages 1124–1128, San Diego, California. Association for Computational Linguistics.

Anastasia Giachanou and Fabio Crestani. 2016. Like it or not: A survey of twitter sentiment analysis methods. *ACM Computing Surveys*, 49(2):28:1–28:41.

Stavros Giorgis, Apostolos Rousas, John Pavlopoulos, Prodromos Malakasiotis, and Ion Androutsopoulos. 2016. aueb.twitter.sentiment at semeval-2016 task 4: A weighted ensemble of svms for twitter sentiment analysis. In *Proceedings of the 10th International Workshop on Semantic Evaluation (SemEval-2016)*, pages 96–99, San Diego, California. Association for Computational Linguistics.

Alec Go, Richa Bhayani, and Lei Huang. 2009. Twitter sentiment classification using distant supervision. *Processing*, pages 1–6.

Matthias Hagen, Martin Potthast, Michel Büchner, and Benno Stein. 2015. Webis: An ensemble for twitter sentiment detection. In *Proceedings of the 9th International Workshop on Semantic Evaluation (SemEval 2015)*, pages 582–589, Denver, Colorado. Association for Computational Linguistics.

Hussam Hamdan. 2017. Senti17 at semeval-2017 task 4: Ten convolutional neural network voters for tweet polarity classification. In *Proceedings of the 11th International Workshop on Semantic Evaluation (SemEval-2017)*, pages 700–703, Vancouver, Canada. Association for Computational Linguistics.

Yoon Kim. 2014. Convolutional neural networks for sentence classification. In *Proceedings of the 2014 Conference on Empirical Methods in Natural Language Processing, EMNLP 2014, October 25-29, 2014, Doha, Qatar, A meeting of SIGDAT, a Special Interest Group of the ACL*, pages 1746–1751.

Zhengdong Lu and Hang Li. 2013. A deep architecture for matching short texts. In *Advances in Neural Information Processing Systems 26*, pages 1367–1375. Curran Associates, Inc.

Tomas Mikolov, Kai Chen, Greg Corrado, and Jeffrey Dean. 2013a. Efficient estimation of word representations in vector space. *CoRR*, abs/1301.3781.

Tomas Mikolov, Ilya Sutskever, Kai Chen, Greg S Corrado, and Jeff Dean. 2013b. Distributed representations of words and phrases and their compositionality. In C. J. C. Burges, L. Bottou, M. Welling, Z. Ghahramani, and K. Q. Weinberger, editors, *Advances in Neural Information Processing Systems 26*, pages 3111–3119. Curran Associates, Inc.

Saif Mohammad and Felipe Bravo-Marquez. 2017. Emotion intensities in tweets. In *Proceedings of the 6th Joint Conference on Lexical and Computational Semantics (*SEM 2017)*, pages 65–77. Association for Computational Linguistics.

Saif M. Mohammad. 2017. Word affect intensities. *CoRR*, abs/1704.08798.

Saif M. Mohammad, Felipe Bravo-Marquez, Mohammad Salameh, and Svetlana Kiritchenko. 2018. Semeval-2018 Task 1: Affect in tweets. In *Proceedings of International Workshop on Semantic Evaluation (SemEval-2018)*, New Orleans, LA, USA.

Sara Rosenthal, Noura Farra, and Preslav Nakov. 2017. Semeval-2017 task 4: Sentiment analysis in twitter. In *Proceedings of the 11th International Workshop on Semantic Evaluation (SemEval-2017)*, pages 502–518. Association for Computational Linguistics.

Mickael Rouvier and Benoit Favre. 2016. Sensei-lif at semeval-2016 task 4: Polarity embedding fusion for robust sentiment analysis. In *Proceedings of the 10th International Workshop on Semantic Evaluation (SemEval-2016)*, pages 202–208, San Diego, California. Association for Computational Linguistics.

Hassan Saif, Yulan He, Miriam Fernandez, and Harith Alani. 2016. Contextual semantics for sentiment analysis of twitter. *Information Processing and Management*, 52(1):5–19.

Aliaksei Severyn and Alessandro Moschitti. 2015. Twitter sentiment analysis with deep convolutional neural networks. In *Proceedings of the 38th International ACM SIGIR Conference on Research and Development in Information Retrieval*, SIGIR '15, pages 959–962, Santiago, Chile. ACM.

Nadia Felix F. Da Silva, Luiz F. S. Coletta, and Eduardo R. Hruschka. 2016. A survey and comparative study of tweet sentiment analysis via semi-supervised learning. *ACM Comput. Surv.*, 49(1):15:1–15:26.

Steven Xu, HuiZhi Liang, and Timothy Baldwin. 2016. Unimelb at semeval-2016 tasks 4a and 4b: An ensemble of neural networks and a word2vec based model for sentiment classification. In *Proceedings of the 10th International Workshop on Semantic Evaluation (SemEval-2016)*, pages 183–189, San Diego, California. Association for Computational Linguistics.

RNN for Affects at SemEval-2018 Task 1: Formulating Affect Identification as a Binary Classification Problem

Aysu Ezen-Can
SAS Inst.
aysu.e.can@gmail.com

Ethem F. Can
SAS Inst.
ethfcan@gmail.com

Abstract

Written communication lacks the multimodal features such as posture, gesture and gaze that make it easy to model affective states. Especially in social media such as Twitter, due to the space constraints, the sources of information that can be mined are even more limited due to character limitations. These limitations constitute a challenge for understanding short social media posts.

In this paper, we present an approach that utilizes multiple binary classifiers that represent different affective categories to model Twitter posts (e.g., tweets). We train domain-independent recurrent neural network models without any outside information such as affect lexicons. We then use these domain-independent binary ranking models to evaluate the applicability of such deep learning models on the affect identification task. This approach allows different model architectures and parameter settings for each affect category instead of building one single multi-label classifier. The contributions of this paper are two-folds: we show that modeling tweets with a small training set is possible with the use of RNNs and we also prove that formulating affect identification as a binary classification task is highly effective.

1 Introduction

Social media platforms allow users to share information, communicate with other users, learn about new products, and get latest news. The importance of social media data is getting larger every day as social media usage grows every year (Duggan, 2015). Twitter is one such social media platform where users can write short posts as well as share links. Twitter is also used for getting news (Center, 2017).

A large body of research has been conducted using Twitter data including analyzing user intentions (Java et al., 2007), determining influence of users (Romero et al., 2011), predicting retweet counts (Can et al., 2013), classifying sentiments of tweets (Jansen et al., 2009; Agarwal et al., 2011; Neethu and Rajasree, 2013; Kontopoulos et al., 2013; Pak and Paroubek, 2010). All of these studies have one goal in common: understanding/modeling information diffuse in Twitter.

One aspect of modeling social media posts is focusing on emotional states of users. There has been plenty of efforts on determining affective states (Schwarz and Clore, 1983) and their effects to human behavior for different domains from education (Sidney et al., 2005) to health care (Lisetti et al., 2003). For Twitter, this problem is even more challenging as the information source is limited to the number of characters allowed in a single post and multimodal features (e.g., posture, gesture, and eye gaze) are not available.

In this paper, we formulate affect identification task as a binary classification problem and investigate the applicability and effectiveness of domain-independent deep learning models as well as features. Our dataset includes eleven affect categories (i.e., anger, anticipation, disgust, fear, joy, love, optimism, pessimism, sadness, surprise, and trust) for each tweet. The presence of one affect category in a tweet does not stop another category to be present (e.g., joy and optimisim can both be present in a tweet). We represent each affect category as one class and build binary classifiers for each class. Recurrent neural networks are trained for each affect category and no domain-dependent features such as affect lexicons are used. Our goal is to evaluate a generic model for different affective states.

Binary models have been successfully applied to several applications including action recognition in videos (Can and Manmatha, 2013), prediction of whether or not a tweet will be

Proceedings of the 12th International Workshop on Semantic Evaluation (SemEval-2018), pages 162–166
New Orleans, Louisiana, June 5–6, 2018. ©2018 Association for Computational Linguistics

Affect	Most frequent emoji	2nd most frequent emoji	3rd most frequent emoji
anger	(53)	(42)	(38)
anticipation	(15)	(10)	(7)
disgust	(60)	(40)	(35)
fear	(12)	(15)	(20)
joy	(138)	(39)	(28)
love	(28)	(21)	(10)
optimism	(62)	(20)	(13)
pessimism	(24)	(14)	(13)
sadness	(72)	(46)	(41)
surprise	(18)	(6)	(6)
trust	(4)	(3)	(2)

Figure 1: Most frequently used emojis and their counts for each affect category.

retweeted (Hong et al., 2011), and topic classification (Joachims, 1998). In this paper, we describe our approach for affect recognition of English tweets (Task E-c: Detecting Emotions), a subcategory of Task 1 in the SemEval 2018 challenge (Mohammad et al., 2018).

2 Corpus

In this paper, we use English tweets that have been annotated by affect categories (Mohammad et al., 2018). The dataset contains emojis, hashtags, and the textual content of tweets; however, it does not have user ids. The training, validation, and test splits are done by the task organizers. Figure 1 shows top three mostly used emojis in each class and their frequencies for the training set.

2.1 Breakdown of Emojis to Classes

Due to the importance of visual cues in predicting affective states, we pay attention to a form of visual cues: emojis. Here we present some of our findings based on different affect categories.

- *Trust*: emojis are not frequently used. Not easy to determine through emojis.

- *Sadness*: The sobbing face emoji is expectedly the most common one but interestingly laughing with joy emoji is the second most common. Weary face emoji is also very common in sadness: 56.16% of all weary face emojis are used in this class.

- *Anger* and *disgust* share the same property: the most common emoji is the laughing with joy emoji and the second most common is sobbing face emoji. The fact that a joy emoji being the most commonly used in these affective classes is quite interesting and can indicate irony. The third most common emoji in these two classes are also the same: rage emoji.

- An emoji that can be intuitively associated with love (heart eyes) actually occurs more in *joy* tweets than *love* tweets.

- An unexpected finding is on fire emoji where *joy* and *optimism* classes have a large portion of all fire emojis in the training set (46.7% and 36.7% respectively).

- The affective class that uses most emojis is *joy*.

3 Methodology

Since each tweet in the data contains eleven affect categories (i.e., anger, anticipation, disgust, fear, joy, love, optimism, pessimism, sadness, surprise, and trust), we created eleven datasets with the same tweets but with different class information. For example, the first dataset has one values (i.e., positive) for tweets that show anger and zero (i.e., negative) for those that do not have anger. Other datasets are created in the same way for the remaining affects classes. By building one model for each affect category, we formulated affect identification problem as a binary classification task. Then in testing time, we obtained predictions from every specific model and fused the results to obtain a unique result for each tweet.

3.1 Training Binary Classification Models

The advantage of using binary classification models for each affect category is that each model can be trained by itself, enabling different model architectures and parameters. For example, while one category may benefit from a deeper model, the other affect category can obtain the best results with a shallower model. In this way, the models do not have to be the same for each affect class.

3.2 Model Architecture

We built separate RNN models for each affect category, resulting with eleven classifiers. For the classifiers, we used three GRU layers, two of

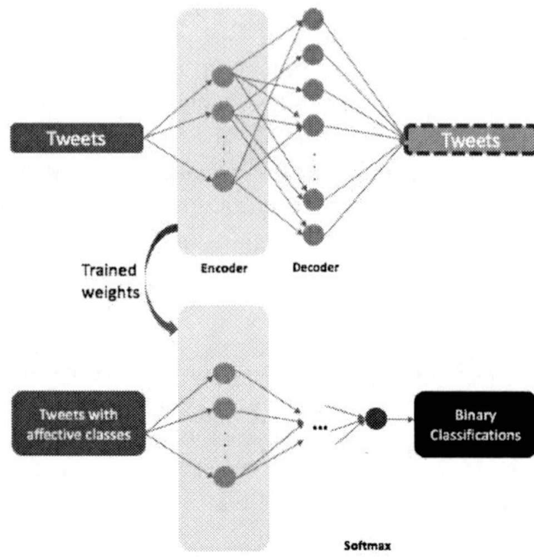

Figure 2: Using the unlabeled tweets for training an auto-encoder and using the trained weights for the affect classification process.

which are bi-directional. To be able to build a more generalized model, a dropout of 0.2 is used in each layer. Each bidirectional layer contains 100 neurons and the final encoding layer has 50 neurons.

3.3 Training Auto-Encoder

Because the dataset is not very big, we wanted the classifiers to learn as much information as possible without overfitting it. Therefore, we built an auto-encoder from the tweets' content (e.g., unlabeled tweets, no affect categories). The goal of the auto-encoder is to get weights that can be used in the classifiers. As shown in Figure 2, we used the trained weights from the auto-encoder to start building binary classifiers. To convert a text-generating auto-encoder into a classifier, we added a softmax layer.

3.4 Features

For modeling affect categories in tweets, we use only the words and emojis. No domain-dependent features, or features that are aware of task in hand (e.g., affect lexicons) are used as our goal is to determine how well a generic RNN model can perform for affect recognition task.

3.4.1 Emojis

To represent emojis as embeddings, we used the pre-trained embeddings from the emoji2vec package (Eisner et al., 2016).

3.4.2 Word Embeddings

For this study, an embedding length of 200 is used. We utilized pre-trained global vectors trained on tweets (Pennington et al., 2014)

3.4.3 Hashtags

Hashtags have a lot of semantic information about the tweets. However, most of that information is neglected if the hashtags cannot be found in the words embeddings. Therefore, we followed a greedy approach for dividing hashtags into their corresponding words.

Once the # is removed, we take the content of the hashtag and search if the content is present in the vocabulary as its entirety. If vocabulary has the hastag content, we use it. If not, more processing is done. Starting from the beggining of the word we keep a pointer, searching for a valid word that from index=0 to index=pointer. Once 0,j indices represent a substring that is a valid word, we continue the recursive search for the rest of the content (i.e., j+1 to the end of the string). The words that are found are added to the list of words that represent the hashtag. Then we use those words and represent them as embeddings.

Because this approach is greedily finding the shortest possible words contained within the hashtag, it is not guaranteed to represent the correct semantics all the time. For example, the #feelsadforyou is correctly divided to ['feel',"sad', 'for', 'you'], however, #toniteinasheville ('tonite in asheville") becomes ['tonite', 'in', 'as', 'he', 'ville'], which is not correct. Achieving perfect semantics would require human labeling, therefore, we used the greedy approach and have observed that utilizing hash tag contents significantly improves the effectiveness of the models.

3.5 Results on Validation Set

The accuracies of binary classification models for each affect category are presented in Figure 3. We compare the models' performances with majority baselines where the percentage of the class value that occurs most is taken as the majority baseline for each class.

4 Results

In this section, we report the results for the test set as well as discussion on the results.

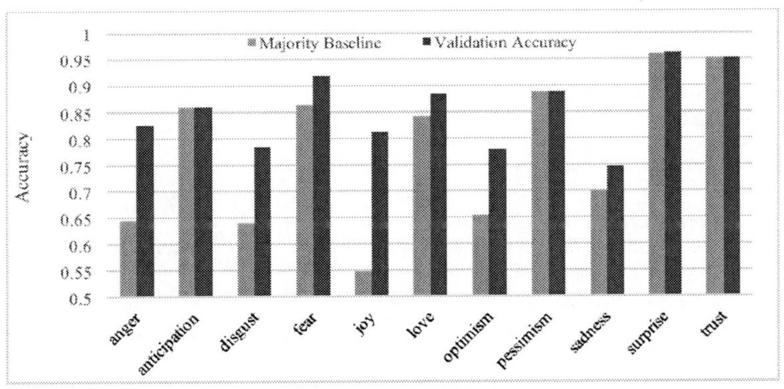

Figure 3: Accuracies per affect category. Majority baseline of each class is compared to the performance of the RNN classifier for that class.

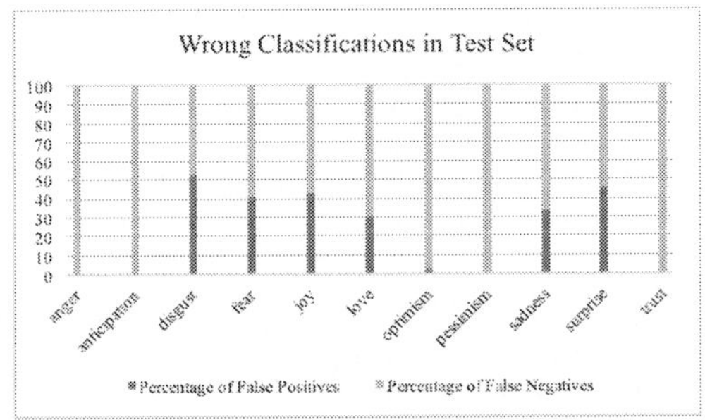

Figure 4: The distribution of false positives and false negatives for observations that are classified incorrectly in the test set.

4.1 Experimental Results

For all of our experiments, we used SAS Deep Learning Toolkit. We utilized an environment with 4 workers, with 24 threads in each worker, and mini-batch size per thread on each worker was 6. Adam optimizer is used in all experiments.

Using the test set, the proposed model achieved a 0.398 accuracy, 0.539 micro-avg F1, and 0.358 macro-avg F1. A random baseline achieves 0.185 accuracy, 0.307 micro-avg F1, and 0.285 macro-avg F1. Compared to the random baseline, the generic RNN model is quite successful at identifying affect categories.

4.2 Discussion

Some of the affect categories have very few positive examples, therefore it is very difficult for classifiers to learn nuances of those affects. For example, surprise and trust categories have 96.05% and 95.15% majority baselines respectively. In other words, only 4-5% of all training set observations have these affect categories as true.

As can be seen in Figure 4, when the number of positive observations are limited, the classifiers tend to make more false negatives. For affect categories that have a major class value that is dominant, we experimented with sampling as well where the number of positive and negative examples were equal. However, that made the dataset significantly smaller, further making it difficult for the RNN models to learn distinctions. Rather than using smaller datasets or including external data, we prefer to employ binary models. One of the main advantages of using binary models over multi-label models is to better deal with the uneven distribution of positive examples across classes.

5 Conclusion

Affect identification without visual cues is a challenging task, making the text as the only source of information that can be used for machine learning models. This problem gets more challenging as the text data gets limited by the number of characters in Twitter.

This paper presented a simple yet effective approach for classifying affect categories of Tweets. The main motivation of this paper was to evaluate how well a domain-independent RNN model can perform for classifying affects. Therefore, no domain-dependent source of information such as affective lexicons or pre-trained affect features are used. We built binary classification models per each affect category. The results showed that RNNs are powerful enough to outperform the baselines significantly, even without prior knowledge about the domain and with a relatively small dataset.

References

Apoorv Agarwal, Boyi Xie, Ilia Vovsha, Owen Rambow, and Rebecca Passonneau. 2011. Sentiment analysis of twitter data. In *Proceedings of the workshop on languages in social media*, pages 30–38. Association for Computational Linguistics.

Ethem F Can and R Manmatha. 2013. Formulating action recognition as a ranking problem. In *Computer Vision and Pattern Recognition Workshops (CVPRW), 2013 IEEE Conference on*, pages 251–256. IEEE.

Ethem F. Can, Hüseyin Oktay, and R. Manmatha. 2013. Predicting retweet count using visual cues. In *Proceedings of the 22Nd ACM International Conference on Information & Knowledge Management*, CIKM '13, pages 1481–1484, New York, NY, USA. ACM.

Pew Research Center. 2017. News use across social media platforms 2017.

Maeve Duggan. 2015. Mobile messaging and social media. Pew Research Center.

Ben Eisner, Tim Rocktäschel, Isabelle Augenstein, Matko Bošnjak, and Sebastian Riedel. 2016. emoji2vec: Learning emoji representations from their description. *arXiv preprint arXiv:1609.08359*.

Liangjie Hong, Ovidiu Dan, and Brian D. Davison. 2011. Predicting popular messages in twitter. In *Proceedings of the 20th International Conference Companion on World Wide Web*, WWW '11, pages 57–58, New York, NY, USA. ACM.

Bernard J Jansen, Mimi Zhang, Kate Sobel, and Abdur Chowdury. 2009. Twitter power: Tweets as electronic word of mouth. *Journal of the Association for Information Science and Technology*, 60(11):2169–2188.

Akshay Java, Xiaodan Song, Tim Finin, and Belle Tseng. 2007. Why we twitter: understanding microblogging usage and communities. In *Proceedings of the 9th WebKDD and 1st SNA-KDD 2007 workshop on Web mining and social network analysis*, pages 56–65. ACM.

Thorsten Joachims. 1998. Text categorization with support vector machines: Learning with many relevant features. In *European conference on machine learning*, pages 137–142. Springer.

Efstratios Kontopoulos, Christos Berberidis, Theologos Dergiades, and Nick Bassiliades. 2013. Ontology-based sentiment analysis of twitter posts. *Expert systems with applications*, 40(10):4065–4074.

Christina Lisetti, Fatma Nasoz, Cynthia LeRouge, Onur Ozyer, and Kaye Alvarez. 2003. Developing multimodal intelligent affective interfaces for tele-home health care. *International Journal of Human-Computer Studies*, 59(1-2):245–255.

Saif M. Mohammad, Felipe Bravo-Marquez, Mohammad Salameh, and Svetlana Kiritchenko. 2018. Semeval-2018 Task 1: Affect in tweets. In *Proceedings of International Workshop on Semantic Evaluation (SemEval-2018)*, New Orleans, LA, USA.

MS Neethu and R Rajasree. 2013. Sentiment analysis in twitter using machine learning techniques. In *Computing, Communications and Networking Technologies (ICCCNT), 2013 Fourth International Conference on*, pages 1–5. IEEE.

Alexander Pak and Patrick Paroubek. 2010. Twitter as a corpus for sentiment analysis and opinion mining. In *LREc*, volume 10.

Jeffrey Pennington, Richard Socher, and Christopher D. Manning. 2014. Glove: Global vectors for word representation. In *Empirical Methods in Natural Language Processing (EMNLP)*, pages 1532–1543.

Daniel M Romero, Wojciech Galuba, Sitaram Asur, and Bernardo A Huberman. 2011. Influence and passivity in social media. In *Joint European Conference on Machine Learning and Knowledge Discovery in Databases*, pages 18–33. Springer.

Norbert Schwarz and Gerald L Clore. 1983. Mood, misattribution, and judgments of well-being: Informative and directive functions of affective states. *Journal of personality and social psychology*, 45(3):513.

K Dmello Sidney, Scotty D Craig, Barry Gholson, Stan Franklin, Rosalind Picard, and Arthur C Graesser. 2005. Integrating affect sensors in an intelligent tutoring system. In *Affective Interactions: The Computer in the Affective Loop Workshop at*, pages 7–13.

Tw-StAR at SemEval-2018 Task 1: Preprocessing Impact on Multi-label Emotion Classification

Hala Mulki[1], Chedi Bechikh Ali[2], Hatem Haddad[3] and Ismail Babaoğlu[1]

[1] Department of Computer Engineering, Selcuk University, Turkey
[2] LISI laboratory, INSAT, Carthage University, Tunisia
[3] Department of Computer and Decision Engineering, Université Libre de Bruxelles, Belgium
halamulki@selcuk.edu.tr, chedi.bechikh@gmail.com
Hatem.Haddad@ulb.ac.be, ibabaoglu@selcuk.edu.tr

Abstract

In this paper, we describe our contribution in SemEval-2018 contest. We tackled task 1 "Affect in Tweets", subtask E-c "Detecting Emotions (multi-label classification)". A multi-label classification system Tw-StAR was developed to recognize the emotions embedded in Arabic, English and Spanish tweets. To handle the multi-label classification problem via traditional classifiers, we employed the binary relevance transformation strategy while a TF-IDF scheme was used to generate the tweets' features. We investigated using single and combinations of several preprocessing tasks to further improve the performance. The results showed that specific combinations of preprocessing tasks could significantly improve the evaluation measures. This has been later emphasized by the official results as our system ranked 3rd for both Arabic and Spanish datasets and 14th for the English dataset.

1 Introduction

Social media platforms and micro-blogging systems such as Twitter have recently witnessed a high rate of accessibility (Duggan et al., 2015). Tweets usually combine multiple emotions expressed by the appraisal or criticism of a specific issue. Sentiment analysis represents a coarse-grained opinion classification as it detects either the subjectivity (objective/subjective) or the polarity orientation (positive, negative or neutral) (Piryani et al., 2017).

For opinionated texts which are usually rich of several emotions, a fine-grained analysis is needed. Through such analysis, specific emotions can be recognized within a tweet which is crucial for many applications. For instance, recognizing anger emotions in the tweets representing the customers' opinions about a specific service in a hotel would definitely help to take the proper response to keep the customers satisfied (Li et al., 2016).

Existing MLC systems are conducted either by problem transformation approaches or algorithm adaptation ones. Each of which combines several methods and has different merits. While problem transformation methods are simpler and easier to implement, algorithm adaptation methods have a more accurate performance but with a high computational cost (Zhang and Zhou, 2014). Therefore, to develop a multi-label classifier that combines the simplicity of the problem transformation methods along with accurate performance remains an interesting issue to investigate.

Since preprocessing tasks have been found of positive impact on sentiment analysis of different languages (Haddi et al., 2013; Yıldırım et al., 2015; El-Beltagy et al., 2017), we hypothesize that the application of single or combinations of various preprocessing techniques on tweets before feeding them to the multi-label emotion classifier, can improve the classification performance without the need to complex methods that consider the dependencies between labels.

Here, we describe the participation of our team "Tw-StAR" (Twitter-Sentiment analysis team for ARabic) in Task 1, subtask E-c, in Arabic, English and Spanish tweets (Mohammad et al., 2018). This task requires classifying the emotions embedded in tweets into one or more of 11 emotion labels.

To accomplish this mission, we have subjected tweets to single or combinations of the following preprocessing techniques: stopwords removal, stemming, lemmatization and common emoji recognition and tagging. Manipulated tweets were then fed into a multi-label classifier built via one of the problem transformation approaches called Binary Relevance (BR) and trained with TF-IDF features using the Support Vector Machines (SVM) algorithm. Experimental study indicated the positive impact of stopwords removal, emoji tagging and lemmatization on the classification per-

167

Proceedings of the 12th International Workshop on Semantic Evaluation (SemEval-2018), pages 167–171
New Orleans, Louisiana, June 5–6, 2018. ©2018 Association for Computational Linguistics

formance. This was emphasized later through the contest's official results as Tw-StAR performed well in multi-label emotion classification of the three tackled languages where it was ranked third, for Arabic and Spanish and 14th for English.

2 Multi-Label Classification Approaches

Unlike single-label classification (binary or multi-class) which classifies an instance into one of two or more labels, each instance in MLC can be associated with a set of labels at the same time (Zhang and Zhou, 2014). MLC problems have been targeted either by algorithm adaptation or problem transformation methods.

2.1 Algorithm Adaptation Methods

Adapt traditional classification algorithms used in binary and multi-class classification to perform MLC such that multi-label outputs are obtained. Using these methods, several machine learning (ML) algorithms such as k-nearest neighbors (KNN), decision trees (DT) and neural networks were extended to address MLC (Tsoumakas et al., 2009).

2.2 Problem Transformation Methods

Rather than modifying the classification algorithm, these methods alter the MLC problem itself by converting it into one or multiple single-label classification problems that could be handled by traditional single-label classifiers (Tsoumakas et al., 2009). The most popular strategies used to conduct such transformation are:

- Label Powerset (LP): transforms an MLC problem to a multi-class classification problem where the classes represent all the possible combinations of the given training labels. After transformation, each input instance is associated with a unique single class containing a potential combination of labels. Hence, LP strategy explicitly models label correlations which leads to more accurate classification however, it usually suffers from sparsity and overfitting issues (Alali, 2016).

- Binary Relevance (BR): decomposes the MLC problem into several single-label binary classification sub-problems; each of which corresponds to one label. Thus, for each sub-problem responsible of a specific label, a separate binary classifier is trained on

the original dataset with the objective of determining the relevance of its particular label for a given instance. The predicted labels by all binary classifiers for a certain instance are then merged into one vector resulting in the multi-label class of this instance (Cherman et al., 2011). As BR is implemented in parallel and scales linearly, it forms a low cost solution to MLC problems (Read et al., 2011; Luaces et al., 2012). Several ML algorithms were used with BR approach such as KNN, DT and SVM. According to (Madjarov et al., 2012), SVM-based methods suit small datasets and perform better than DTs especially for domains with large number of features as in text classification since they exploit the information from all the features, while DTs use only a (small) subset of features and may miss some crucial information.

3 Tw-StAR Framework

To recognize the emotions embedded in the Arabic, English and Spanish datasets (Mohammad et al., 2018), Tw-StAR was applied on tweets contained in the provided datasets using the following pipeline:

3.1 Preprocessing

- Initial Preprocessing: for all datasets, a common initial preprocessing step that includes removing the non-sentimental content such as URLs, usernames, dates, digits, hashtags symbols, and punctuation was performed.

- Stopwords Removal (Stop): Stopwords are function words with high frequency of presence in texts; they usually do not carry significant semantic meaning by themselves. Therefore, it is preferable to ignore them while analyzing a textual content. In this task, Arabic was targeted by a list of 1,661 stopwords provided by the NLP group at King Abdulaziz University[1]. For English, we used a list of 1,012 words resulted from combining the list published with the Terrier package[2] and the list of snowball[3]. In Spanish, a list of 731 words from snowball [4] was used.

---

[1]https://github.com/abahanshal1/arabic-stop-words-list1
[2]https://bitbucket.org/kganes2/text-mining-resources/
[3]http://snowball.tartarus.org/algorithms/english/stop.txt
[4]http://snowball.tartarus.org/algorithms/spanish/stop.txt

- Stemming (Stem): concerns about reducing the variants of a word to their shared basic form (stem) or root. Therefore, it enables decreasing the vocabulary and increasing the recall (Darwish and Magdy, 2014). In the current study, we used ISRI stemmer (Taghva et al., 2005) for Arabic, Porter2 (Porter, 1980) for english and Snowball for Spanish[5]. ISRI stemmer does not use a root dictionary and provide a normalized form for words whose root are not found. This is done through normalizing the hamza, removing diacritics representing vowels, remove connector و if it precedes a word beginning with و, etc. The English stemmer returns the root of a word by removing suffixes related to plural, tenses, adverbs, etc. Finally, the Snowball stemmer used for Spanish translates the rules of stemming algorithms expressed in natural way to an equivalent program.

- Lemmatization (Lem): removes inflectional endings only and returns the base or dictionary form of a word. Farasa (Abdelali et al., 2016) lemmatizer was employed for Arabic while Treetagger (Schmid, 1995) was used for both English and Spanish. Farasa uses SVMrank to rank possible ways to segment words to prefixes, stems, and suffixes. On the other hand, TreeTagger[6] forms a language-independent tool for annotating text with part-of-speech and lemma information included.

- Common Emoji Recognition (Emo): we fixed a list of nine categories of the most common emoji detected in the tweets through UTF-8 encoding. Each emoji is replaced with a tag that implies the emoji's emotion. The tags included: AngryEmoj, HappyEmoj, FearEmoj, LoveEmoj, SadEmoj, SurpriseEmoj, DisgustedEmoj, OptimistEmoj and PessimismEmoj. Thus, a tweet such: "*I hung up on my manager last night* ☺" will be replaced by: "*I hung up on my manager last night SadEmoj*".

3.2 Feature Extraction

Vector space model (VSM) was used to generate the features vectors. Each tweet was represented using a vector containing all corpus words denoted by their number of occurrences in this tweet referred to as term frequency (tf). A larger value of a term frequency indicates its prominence in a given tweet, however, if this term appears in too many tweets it will be less informative such as stop words (Maas et al., 2011). Therefore, to enhance the classification and reduce the dimensionality, we focused on the most discriminative terms through applying Term Frequency-Inverse Document Frequency (TF-IDF) weighting scheme. This scheme increases the weight of a term proportionally to the number of times a term appears in the document, but is often offset by the frequency of the term in the corpus, which means how many documents it appears in (Taha and Tiun, 2016).

3.3 Emotions Classification

Having the data transformed using the BR method and the TF-IDF features generated, tweets were fed into a multi-label SVM classifier with the linear kernel. This classifier adopts one-Vs-All strategy such that each label has its own binary classifier. Consequently, a number of binary SVM classifiers equals to the number of emotion labels were trained in parallel to recognize the emotions embedded in a tweet.

4 Results and Discussion

The proposed model Tw-StAR was applied on Arabic, English and Spanish multi-labeled tweet datasets; their statistics are listed in Table 1.

Using One-Vs-All SVM classifier from Scikit-learn[7], Tw-StAR was trained to recognize the following emotions: anger, anticipation, disgust, fear, joy, love, optimism, pessimism, sadness, surprise, trust in addition to "noEmotion" label that denotes tweets that have none of the previous emotions. Within the presented framework, the preprocessing tasks listed in Section 3 were examined separately and combined. This enabled defining the preprocessing technique/combination for which the MLC performance of each language is better improved.

Tables 2, 3 and 4 list the results obtained for each language when applying several single/combinations of preprocessing tasks where accuracy, macro average f-measure and micro average f-measure are referred to as (Acc.), (Mac-F) and (Mic-F) respectively.

---

[5] http://snowball.tartarus.org/texts/introduction.html
[6] http://www.cis.uni-muenchen.de/ schmid/tools/TreeTagger/
[7] http://scikit-learn.org

Language	Train	Dev	Test
Arabic	2,278	585	1,518
English	6,838	886	3,259
Spanish	3,559	679	2,854

Table 1: Statistics of the used datasets.

Preprocessing	Acc.	Mic-F	Mac-F
Stop	0.38	0.509	0.367
Stem	0.431	0.559	0.424
Emo	0.414	0.543	0.39
Stem+Stop	0.434	0.564	0.435
Emo+Lem+Stop	0.434	0.561	0.415
Emo+ Stem+Stop	**0.449**	**0.58**	**0.444**

Table 2: Preprocessing impact on Arabic MLC.

Preprocessing	Acc.	Mic-F	Mac-F
Stop	0.446	0.577	0.429
Stem	0.449	0.58	0.443
Emo	0.459	0.588	0.434
Stem+Stop	0.462	0.593	0.458
Emo+Lem+Stop	**0.48**	**0.606**	0.461
Emo+ Stem+Stop	0.475	0.602	**0.466**

Table 3: Preprocessing impact on English MLC.

Preprocessing	Acc.	Mic-F	Mac-F
Stop	0.39	0.482	0.381
Stem	0.398	0.484	0.368
Emo	0.402	0.501	0.384
Stem+Stop	0.409	0.492	0.379
Emo+Lem+Stop	**0.431**	**0.523**	**0.413**
Emo+ Stem+Stop	0.428	0.518	0.401

Table 4: Preprocessing impact on Spanish MLC.

L.	Team(R.)	Acc.	Mic	Mac
A.	EMA(1)	**0.489**	**0.618**	**0.461**
	Tw-StAR(3)	0.465	0.597	0.446
E.	NTUA-SLP(1)	**0.588**	**0.701**	**0.528**
	Tw-StAR(14)	0.481	0.607	0.452
S.	MILAB-SNU(1)	**0.469**	**0.558**	**0.407**
	Tw-StAR(3)	0.438	0.520	0.392

Table 5: Tw-StAR official ranking.

Table 2 clearly suggests that for the Arabic tweets, stemming using ISRI stemmer improved the accuracy by 5.1% percentage points compared to that scored by stopwords removal was applied. Moreover, combining stemming with stopwords removal could further improve the micro F-measure as it increased from 55.9% to 56.4%. This is due to the fact that ISRI can handle wider range of Arabic vocabulary as it returns a normalized form of words having no stem rather than retaining them unchanged (Kreaa et al., 2014).

Unlike Arabic dataset, Table 3 and Table 4 show that stemming had a different behavior when it was applied on both English and Spanish tweets. Compared to the accuracy achieved by stopwords removal, stemming has slightly increased the accuracy by 0.3% and 0.8% in English and Spanish datasets respectively. This could be related to the insufficiency of the stemming algorithms employed by both porter2 and snowball stemmers to handle informal English and Spanish tweets. Lemmatization by Treetagger, however, was a better choice to handle English and Spanish terms as it forms a language-independent lemmatizer with implicitly POS tagger included. Thus, combining emoji tagging with lemmatization and stopwords removal could achieve the best performances with a micro average F-measure of 60.6% and 52.3% for English and Spanish respectively.

Since the provided tweets were rich of emoji, emoji tagging could effectively contribute in improving the performance in all datasets especially when it was combined with the other best-performed tasks such as stem+stop in Arabic and lem+stop in both English and Spanish. This led to the best performances as the achieved micro F-measure was 58%, 60.2% and 52% in Arabic, English and Spanish datasets respectively. Hence, these preprocessing combinations were adopted for the official submission. Table 5 lists the official results of Tw-StAR against the systems ranked first for each language where (L.), (A.), (E.), (S.), (R.) (Mic) and (Mac) refer to language, Arabic, English, Spanish, rank, micro and macro f-measure respectively.

5 Conclusion and Future Work

Here we emphasized the key role of preprocessing in emotion MLC. Stemming, lemmatization and emoji tagging were found the most effective tasks for emotion MLC. For the future work, the obtained performances would be further improved if negation detection was included to infer the negative emotions. Moreover, other ML methods could be examined with BR and deep neural models.

References

Ahmed Abdelali, Kareem Darwish, Nadir Durrani, and Hamdy Mubarak. 2016. Farasa: A fast and furious segmenter for arabic. In *Proceedings of the Demonstrations Session, NAACL HLT 2016, The 2016 Conference of the North American Chapter of the Association for Computational Linguistics: Human Language Technologies, San Diego California, USA, June 12-17, 2016*, pages 11–16.

Abdulaziz Alali. 2016. *A novel stacking method for multi-label classification*. Ph.D. thesis, University of Miami.

Everton Alvares Cherman, Maria Carolina Monard, and Jean Metz. 2011. Multi-label problem transformation methods: a case study. *CLEI Electronic Journal*, 14(1):4–4.

Kareem Darwish and Walid Magdy. 2014. Arabic information retrieval. *Foundations and Trends in Information Retrieval*, 7(4):239–342.

Maeve Duggan, Nicole B Ellison, Cliff Lampe, Amanda Lenhart, and Mary Madden. 2015. Social media update 2014. *Pew research center*, 19.

Samhaa R. El-Beltagy, Mona El kalamawy, and Abu Bakr Soliman. 2017. Niletmrg at semeval-2017 task 4: Arabic sentiment analysis. In *Proceedings of the 11th International Workshop on Semantic Evaluation (SemEval-2017)*, pages 790–795. Association for Computational Linguistics.

Emma Haddi, Xiaohui Liu, and Yong Shi. 2013. The role of text pre-processing in sentiment analysis. *Procedia Computer Science*, 17:26–32.

Abdel Hamid Kreaa, Ahmad S Ahmad, and Kassem Kabalan. 2014. Arabic words stemming approach using arabic wordnet. *International Journal of Data Mining & Knowledge Management Process*, 4(6):1.

Jun Li, Yanghui Rao, Fengmei Jin, Huijun Chen, and Xiyun Xiang. 2016. Multi-label maximum entropy model for social emotion classification over short text. *Neurocomputing*, 210:247–256.

Oscar Luaces, Jorge Díez, José Barranquero, Juan José del Coz, and Antonio Bahamonde. 2012. Binary relevance efficacy for multilabel classification. *Progress in Artificial Intelligence*, 1(4):303–313.

Andrew L Maas, Raymond E Daly, Peter T Pham, Dan Huang, Andrew Y Ng, and Christopher Potts. 2011. Learning word vectors for sentiment analysis. In *Proceedings of the 49th annual meeting of the association for computational linguistics: Human language technologies-volume 1*, pages 142–150. Association for Computational Linguistics.

Gjorgji Madjarov, Dragi Kocev, Dejan Gjorgjevikj, and Sašo Džeroski. 2012. An extensive experimental comparison of methods for multi-label learning. *Pattern recognition*, 45(9):3084–3104.

Saif M. Mohammad, Felipe Bravo-Marquez, Mohammad Salameh, and Svetlana Kiritchenko. 2018. Semeval-2018 Task 1: Affect in tweets. In *Proceedings of International Workshop on Semantic Evaluation (SemEval-2018)*, New Orleans, LA, USA.

Rajesh Piryani, D Madhavi, and Vivek Kumar Singh. 2017. Analytical mapping of opinion mining and sentiment analysis research during 2000–2015. *Information Processing & Management*, 53(1):122–150.

Martin F. Porter. 1980. An algorithm for suffix stripping. *Program*, 14(3):130–137.

Jesse Read, Bernhard Pfahringer, Geoff Holmes, and Eibe Frank. 2011. Classifier chains for multi-label classification. *Machine learning*, 85(3):333.

Helmut Schmid. 1995. Improvements in part-of-speech tagging with an application to german. In *In proceedings of the acl sigdat-workshop*. Citeseer.

Kazem Taghva, Rania Elkhoury, and Jeffrey Coombs. 2005. Arabic stemming without a root dictionary. In *Proceedings of the International Conference on Information Technology: Coding and Computing (ITCC'05) - Volume I - Volume 01*, ITCC '05, pages 152–157, Washington, DC, USA. IEEE Computer Society.

Adil Yaseen Taha and Sabrina Tiun. 2016. Binary relevance (br) method classifier of multi-label classification for arabic text. *Journal of Theoretical and Applied Information Technology*, 84(3):414.

Grigorios Tsoumakas, Ioannis Katakis, and Ioannis Vlahavas. 2009. Mining multi-label data. In *Data mining and knowledge discovery handbook*, pages 667–685. Springer.

Ezgi Yıldırım, Fatih Samet Çetin, Gülşen Eryiğit, and Tanel Temel. 2015. The impact of nlp on turkish sentiment analysis. *Türkiye Bilişim Vakfı Bilgisayar Bilimleri ve Mühendisliği Dergisi*, 7(1):43–51.

Min-Ling Zhang and Zhi-Hua Zhou. 2014. A review on multi-label learning algorithms. *IEEE transactions on knowledge and data engineering*, 26(8):1819–1837.

DL Team at SemEval-2018 Task 1: Tweet Affect Detection using Sentiment Lexicons and Embeddings

Dmitry Kravchenko
Ben-Gurion University of the Negev / Israel
to.dmitry.kravchenko@gmail.com

Lidia Pivovarova
University of Helsinki / Finland
lidia.pivovarova@cs.helsinki.fi

Abstract

The paper describes our approach for SemEval-2018 Task 1: Affect Detection in Tweets. We perform experiments with manually compelled sentiment lexicons and word embeddings. We test their performance on twitter affect detection task to determine which features produce the most informative representation of a sentence. We demonstrate that general-purpose word embeddings produces more informative sentence representation than lexicon features. However, combining lexicon features with embeddings yields higher performance than embeddings alone.

1 Introduction

The paper describes our approach for SemEval-2018 Task 1: Affect Detection in Tweets (Mohammad et al., 2018).

The research question we address in this paper is what are the best features for tweet affect detection. Our solution uses two types of features: *lexicon features* obtained from manually compiled emotion lexicons, and *word embeddings* built unsupervisedly from large corpora. We use well established lexicons, namely DepecheMood and Vader Sentiment, and most popular Word embeddings, namely GloVe and Google News. We systematically compare all features on two subtasks and demonstrate that even though lexicon features produce unsatisfactory results in isolation, they significantly improve an algorithm performance when combined with more general embeddings.

In addition, we demonstrate that special treatment of Twitter hash-tags also improves the algorithm performance.

2 Tasks and Data

The paper addresses three subtasks:

Task		Train	Dev	Test
EI-reg	all emotions	7102	1464	71816
	anger	1701	388	17939
	fear	2252	389	17923
	joy	1616	290	18042
	sadness	1533	397	17912
V-reg		1181	449	17874
E-c		6838	886	3259

Table 1: Training, development and test set split for three subtasks

- **EI-reg**—an emotion intensity regression task: Given a tweet and an emotion E, determine the intensity of E that best represents the mental state of the tweeter—a real-valued score between 0 (no E at all) and 1 (the highest magnitude of E); separate datasets are provided for fear, sadness, anger, and joy.

- **V-reg**—a sentiment intensity regression task: Given a tweet, determine the intensity of sentiment or valence (V) that best represents the mental state of the tweeter—a real-valued score between 0 (most negative) and 1 (most positive).

- **E-c**—an emotion classification task: Given a tweet, classify it as 'neutral or no emotion' or as one, or more, of eleven given emotions that best represent the mental state of the tweeter: trust, sadness, disgust, fear, optimism, love, joy, pessimism, anticipation, surprise, and anger.

We use English data for all three subtasks. The train, development and test set sizes are shown in Table 1. More details on the data can be found in the task organizers' paper (Mohammad and Kiritchenko, 2018).

Proceedings of the 12th International Workshop on Semantic Evaluation (SemEval-2018), pages 172–176
New Orleans, Louisiana, June 5–6, 2018. ©2018 Association for Computational Linguistics

3 Approach

3.1 Baseline

As a baseline we use the Text-Processing API[1]. The API uses a Naive Bayes model trained using movie reviews and NLTK. The model returns probabilities for negative, positive and neutral labels. Negative and positive probabilities sum to 1 while neutral probability stands alone.

3.2 Lexicon Features

3.2.1 DepecheMood

DepecheMood (Staiano and Guerini, 2014) is an emotion lexicon collected using crowdsourcing. The respondents annotated news articles with eight predefined emotions: afraid, amused, angry, annoyed, dont_care, happy, inspired, sad. Document annotations were then used in a dimensionality reduction algorithm to obtain word emotional scores. The lexicon contains approximately 37 thousand entry. Each entry consists of a word and eight values between 0 and 1, one value for each emotion.

3.2.2 Vader

Vader (Valence Aware Dictionary and sEntiment Reasoner) is a rule-based sentiment analysis tool and a lexicon specifically attuned to sentiments expressed in social media, such as Twitte (Hutto and Gilbert, 2014). The lexicon consists of more than 7000 term, which were compelled from other lexicons and then manualy annotated. Git repository[2] of Vader Sentiment toolkit provides function *polarity_scores* which takes as an input a text and returns 4-dimensional feature vector, which contains negative, positive, neutral and compound scores.

3.3 Embeddings

3.3.1 GloVe

GloVe (Pennington et al., 2014) is an unsupervised algorithm that constructs embeddings from large corpora. The GloVe project[3] provides a number of models trained on various collections. We use the following two models:

1. Common Crawl: 300-dimensional vectors trained on huge Internet corpus of 840 billion tokens and 2.2 million distinct words.

2. Twitter Crawl: 200-dimensional vectors trained on 2 billion tweets with 27 billion tokens and 1.2 million distinct words.

3.3.2 Google News

We use word2vecs (Mikolov et al., 2013) embedding trained on Google News collection[4], which have become almost standard embeddings since they are most frequently used in various research tasks. These embeddings are 300-dimensional vectors built using Google News dataset of 100 billion tokens and 3 million distinct words and phrases.

3.4 Method

We use various combinations of baseline, lexicon and embedding features, described above. Text-processing API and Vader return text-level features. For other sources a tweet representation is built by averaging the word vectors. Concatenation is used to combine features obtained from various sources.

We run several preliminary experiments with V-reg task to compare several algorithms, namely Gradient Boosting Regressor and Random Forest. We use sklearn implementations[5]. Gradient Boosting Regressor yields the best performance for all feature combinations (Table 2). In our official submission we apply Gradient Boosting Regressor for tasks EI-reg and V-reg, and Gradient Boosting Classifier for task E-c.

Hash-tags are special types of tokens in Twitter used to specify a topic or a context for a given message. They frequently contain emotional words. Here are several examples from the dataset:

- *@leesyatt you are a cruel, cruel man. #therewillbeblood #revenge.*

- *can't believe Achilles killed me! #angry.*

- *Worst juror ever? Michelle. You were Nicole's biggest threat. #bitter #bb18.*

- *All hell is breaking loose in Charlotte. #CharlotteProtest #anger #looting.*

- *straight people are canoodling on the quad and I'm #offended .*

Thus, we try two different setting: first, processing hash-tags similar to all other words in the text;

---

[1] http://text-processing.com/api/sentiment/
[2] https://github.com/cjhutto/vaderSentiment
[3] https://nlp.stanford.edu/projects/glove/
[4] https://code.google.com/archive/p/word2vec/
[5] http://scikit-learn.org

Feature set	Task					
	EI-reg				**V-reg**	
	anger	*fear*	*joy*	*sadness*	Boost	RF
Baseline	30.83	30.76	43.07	31.67	50.02	40.66
Lexicon						
DepecheMood	16.08	19.00	27.69	10.15	24.57	18.34
Vader	39.89	42.07	**46.58**	**34.39**	52.51	45.40
All Lexicons	**42.91**	**42.31**	45.20	33.56	**54.02**	50.43
Embeddings						
Glove Twitter	54.55	51.38	43.44	52.21	65.97	56.90
GloVe Common Crawl	46.93	53.98	43.66	56.31	66.38	59.26
Google News	51.32	54.45	42.24	54.10	64.54	54.30
Glove Twitter + #	58.15	60.32	54.60	57.20	69.92	59.19
GloVe Common Crawl + #	54.92	61.33	53.73	59.00	70.43	64.05
Google News + #	53.09	59.42	55.77	57.15	67.44	56.38
All Embeddings	**59.01**	**62.97**	**56.42**	**60.33**	**70.48**	60.38
Combined features						
Lexicons + Baseline	44.93	48.63	50.40	41.70	60.12	56.03
Lexicons + Embeddings	**65.89**	65.82	59.90	65.64	73.00	64.96
Lexicons + Embeddings + Baseline	64.09	**66.95**	**63.80**	**65.73**	**72.35**	65.93

Table 2: Experimental results for on development set for two subtasks. Pearson correlation. Gradient Boosting Regressor is used for the EI-reg subtask. Gradient Boosting Regressor (Boost) and Random Forest (RF) is used for V-reg. # means that hash-tags are used separately as additional features.

second processing hash-tags separately to preserve authors' encoding of their emotions. The second strategy consistently yields better results as can be seen from Table 2.

4 Discussion

Comparisons of feature sets and algorithms are presented in Table 2. As can be seen from the table, results are consistent: emeddings yield higher performance than lexicon features for all tasks. DepechMode, even though it has five times more entries than Vader, seems to be less suitable for tweet emotion prediction and yields performance much lower than the baseline. Moreover, using both lexicons in combination not always improves performance and in some cases works even worse than Vader alone.

There is no significant difference between different embeddings. Various embeddings achieve better performance depending on the task, though the best results obtained by using all three in combination.

It can also be seen from Table 2 that separate treatment of hash tags improves model performance. For example, for joy detection task the

difference is about 10%, which means that joy is frequently expressed explicitly in hash tags.

The best results for all tasks obtained by using all feature sets in combination (with the only exception of *angry* intensity detection subtask). This makes an improvement in 5.5% for *anger* detection subtask, 4% for *fear*, 7.5% for *joy*, 5.4% for *sadness*, and about 2% for sentiment intensity detection subtask. This means that even though lexicons cannot be used by themselves to detect emotions, they provide important features that cannot be extracted from embeddings. We hypothesize that the main reason for that is low *coverage*, meaning that many tweets have few lexicon features or no such features at all.

The coverage of the task corpora by various feature sets is presented in Table 3. It can be seen from the table that embeddings have much higher coverage than DepecheMood lexicon. Another interesting observation is that *GloVe Twitter* does not have a higher coverage than *GloVe Common Crawl* though *GloVe Twitter* has higher coverage of hash-tags.

Feature set	Task									
	EI-reg								V-reg	
	anger		fear		joy		sadness			
	$\prec$	#	$\prec$	#	$\prec$	#	$\prec$	#	$\prec$	#
DepecheMood	53.4		52.5		53.6		54.74		53.1	
GloVe Common Crawl	**86.0**	6.2	**85.1**	6.2	**85.2**	4.9	**87.4**	4.8	**85.3**	4.5
GloVe Twitter	80.1	**6.5**	80.1	**6.5**	82.0	**5.2**	82.7	**5.1**	81.7	**4.7**
Google News	74.6	5.7	74.6	5.8	75.1	4.5	76.9	4.5	75.5	4.2

Table 3: Data coverage for various feature sets, percent of word usages. Legend: # - coverage of hash tags, $\prec$ - coverage of all other words.

Baseline	3
Lexicon features	
DepecheMood	8
Vader	4
Embeddings	
GloVe Common Crawl	300
Glove Twitter	200
Google News	300

Table 4: Feature sets and their dimensionality.

5 Results

The best model, used in our officially submitted solution, exploits all six feature sets plus separate embedding vectors for hash-tags. The list of feature sets and their dimensionality is presented in Table 4.

The official results for EI-reg and V-reg tasks are presented in Table 5. We report results for all instances and for instance with highest emotion intensity. The numerical values are similar to what we obtained on the development set. The official results for E-c classification task are presented in Table 6.

6 Conclusion

In this paper we presented our approach for SemEval Affect Detection in Tweets Task. We compare manually collected lexical features with embeddings automatically extracted from huge corpora. We demonstrated that even though lexicons are less suitable for affect detection in tweets due to low coverage they can improve model performance when lexical features are used together with more general embeddings.

In addition, we demonstrated that hash tags are important features for tweet affection detection, since they frequently include emotional words.

	All instances	Gold in 0.5-1
EI-reg		
Anger	65.4 / 82.7	52.6 / 70.8
Fear	67.2 / 77.9	49.7 / 60.8
Joy	64.8 / 79.2	42.0 / 56.8
Sadness	63.5 / 79.8	51.7 / 66.6
Macro-avg	**65.3** / 79.9	**49.0** / 63.8
V-reg		
	78.2 / 87.3	**62.1** / 69.7

Table 5: Official results for EI-reg (emotion intensity regression) and V-reg (valence intensity regression). Scores are given in the format X / Y , where X is our result, and Y is the best official result on the task. Pearson correlation.

Accuracy	micro-avg F1	macro-avg F1
47.7 / 58.8	**61.0** / 70.1	**41.6** / 52.8

Table 6: Official results for E-c (emotion classification) task. Scores are given in the format X / Y , where X is our result, and Y is the best official result on the task.

In this paper we used rather simplistic methods to combine various features, i.e., vector concatenation. In the future we plan to try another approach: to build a separate classifier for each feature set and then use a meta classifier on top of their results.

Repository

Repository with the code is located on the following URL link: `https://github.com/dmikrav/SemEval2018AffectsTweets`
The web-site to this project is on the following URL link: `https://dmikrav.github.io/SemEval2018AffectsTweets/`

References

Clayton J. Hutto and Eric Gilbert. 2014. VADER: A parsimonious rule-based model for sentiment analysis of social media text. In *Proceedings of the Eighth International Conference on Weblogs and Social Media, ICWSM 2014, Ann Arbor, Michigan, USA, June 1-4, 2014*.

Tomas Mikolov, Ilya Sutskever, Kai Chen, Greg S Corrado, and Jeff Dean. 2013. Distributed representations of words and phrases and their compositionality. In *Advances in neural information processing systems*, pages 3111–3119.

Saif M. Mohammad, Felipe Bravo-Marquez, Mohammad Salameh, and Svetlana Kiritchenko. 2018. Semeval-2018 Task 1: Affect in tweets. In *Proceedings of International Workshop on Semantic Evaluation (SemEval-2018)*, New Orleans, LA, USA.

Saif M. Mohammad and Svetlana Kiritchenko. 2018. Understanding emotions: A dataset of tweets to study interactions between affect categories. In *Proceedings of the 11th Edition of the Language Resources and Evaluation Conference*, Miyazaki, Japan.

Jeffrey Pennington, Richard Socher, and Christopher D. Manning. 2014. Glove: Global vectors for word representation. In *Empirical Methods in Natural Language Processing (EMNLP)*, pages 1532–1543.

Jacopo Staiano and Marco Guerini. 2014. Depeche mood: a lexicon for emotion analysis from crowd annotated news. In *Proceedings of the 52nd Annual Meeting of the Association for Computational Linguistics (Volume 2: Short Papers)*, volume 2, pages 427–433.

EmoIntens Tracker at SemEval-2018 Task 1: Emotional Intensity Levels in #Tweets

Ramona-Andreea Turcu[1], Sandra Maria Amarandei[1],
Iuliana-Alexandra Flescan-Lovin-Arseni[1], Daniela Gifu[1,2], Diana Trandabat[1]

[1]Faculty of Computer Science, "Alexandru Ioan Cuza" University of Iasi,
[2]Institute of Computer Science, Romanian Academy - Iasi Branch

{ramona.turcu, daniela.gifu, dtrandabat}@info.uaic.ro
{maria.amarandei, flescan.alexandra}@gmail.com

Abstract

The „Affect in Tweets" task is centered on emotions categorization and evaluation matrix using multi-language tweets (English and Spanish). In this research, SemEval Affect dataset was preprocessed, categorized, and evaluated accordingly (precision, recall, and accuracy). The system described in this paper is based on the implementation of supervised machine learning (Naive Bayes, KNN and SVM), deep learning (NN Tensor Flow model), and decision trees algorithms.

1 Introduction

Emotion Analysis is still a challenging task in NLP (*Natural Language Processing*); the researchers try to recognize not only emotions "generally speaking" but also their intensity. Because the level of subjectivity is particularly high in this matter, prediction of emotions, mainly in text, demands for continuous research and improvement strategies. SemEval competition has already a tradition in developing tasks to address this subject. This year proposed an even more challenging task: emotion intensity prediction in tweets.

Within this context, this present study aims to develop a system that can not only detect emotions but also their intensities, namely emotion intensity regression and emotion intensity ordinal classification tasks for fear, joy, sadness and anger. Better results are finally provided thanks to the combination between neural network and proper decision tree algorithms.

From the four tasks, namely: EI-reg, EI-oc, VAD-reg, and VAD-oc, the system focuses on the first two of them, for both English and Spanish datasets, according to their relation with the emotion concept.

While tweets annotation, emotion intensity regression and emotion intensity ordinal classification is an active field of emotion analysis, we believe that a supervised machine learning (Naive Bayes, KNN and SVM), deep learning approach (NN Tensor Flow model), and decision trees would increase the effectiveness of this system.

2 State of the Art

Some of the most used technologies which led to considerable results and step forwards in the domain of sentiment analysis are mainly represented by machine learning algorithms which already have led to impressive results can be thoroughly analyzed in several studies such as: the work of Bac Huy Nguyen (2015); latent semantic analysis (LSA) by Andrew *et al.* (2014), support vector machines in the work of Rohini S. Rahate and Emmanuel M, (2013), grammatical dependency relations, Support Vector Regression (SVR), and Neural Networks.

Proceedings of the 12th International Workshop on Semantic Evaluation (SemEval-2018), pages 177–180
New Orleans, Louisiana, June 5–6, 2018. ©2018 Association for Computational Linguistics

An important work has been done by the tool IZU-NLP at EmoInt-2017 (Yuanye He et al., 2017), meant to determine numerical values that would represent the emotion intensity in a tweet. There are researchers who prefer to combine several methods in order to achieve better results. For instance, in the paper of Sreekanth Maunendra and Sankar Desarkar (2017) there were implemented three regression methods: (1) content-based features (ex. hashtags, emoticons); (2) training based on word and character n-grams; and finally (3) lexicons, word embeddings, word n-grams and character n-grams all together.

Best–Worst Scaling (BWS) was highly valued in the work of Saif M. Mohammad and Felipe Bravo-Marquez (2017) when producing the first datasets of tweets annotated for sentiment intensities (anger, fear, joy, and sadness).

Some existing tools and resources that enlarged the perspective and built the basis of sentiment analysis are: Emo-Int2017, NRC Emotion lexicon, Best-Worst Scaling resources; VADER-Sentiment-Analysis, SentiWordNet (Andrea Esuli *et al.*, 2010), NLTK Sentiment Analyze, and Affective Tweets. All these works prove the interest of researchers on this subject and the fast evolution of this specific domain in time.

In the context of the Semeval Competition, we developed a system for emotion intensity and ordinal classification of the subtasks already stated above.

3 Dataset and method

3.1 Data set

The SemEval affect dataset used in this work contains an annotated set multi-language tweets (English and Spanish).
For each emotion (anger, fear, sadness, joy) we had 3 sets of data (for train, developing and test).
The English data set was revised by Hardik Meisheri Dec 5, 2017 consisting of ~100 million English tweet ids and for Spanish the data set released on Dec 5, 2017 containing ~1.2 million Spanish tweet ids.

3.2 Method

This research is oriented towards the first two tasks of SemEval so it will contain two components, one for Task EI-reg and the other one for Task EI-oc. The first step was to preprocess the development data set in multiple stages as follows: basic cleaning (Ids, useless stopwords, emoticons), tokenization and parsing to make data less repetitive. Then we apply the NN Tensor Flow model, the basic one, offered by Python with 600 neurons and with a layer of 1 to 1000.

The neural network was trained separately for each language using the same configuration. Once we obtained the results, we applied a Decision Tree Algorithm in order to refine them. For all subtasks we use Neural Network Tensor Flow (NNTF): Analyzing Tweet's Sentiment with Character-Level LSTMs NN Tensor Flow - python implemented neuronal network with the same parameters for the EI-oc subtask, we improved our results by implementing also the classifiers from pattern.vector. The algorithms are based on three big approaches - they implement the Naive Bayes, KNN and SVM classifiers respectively. Even though machine learning and neural networks gave decent result, the difficulty in controlling the actual reasoning implied the necessity of adding a refining algorithm that would improve final results. An algorithm that would meet this condition is the Decision Tree Classification, a Weka J48 implementation that was improved by adding an algorithm used to generate same decision trees: check for base classification (this classification should be done by the first method described in this paper - NN Tensor Flow); for each score/class; find the normalized score; best_score will be the highest normalized score, this will be the root; create a decision node that splits on best_score; search on the sublists obtained by splitting on best_score; add those nodes as child of node.

For development and training we used the results from the first method for both English and French.

4 Results and Observations

In both sets of results we will notice that the best results were obtained in the single positive feeling dataset - the one for joy. For EI-reg, the lowest result was registered for anger (accuracy), while the highest was the recall for joy. For EI-oc the best result is in the precision of joy, the lowest result being again in accuracy, but this time for sadness.

The implementation of the Decision Tree Algorithm leads to growth and uniformization of the results in the EI-reg subtask, while it lowers those from EI-oc.

identifying manually certain patterns and indices about intensity and/or their classification.

	NNTF + Classification Algorithm							
	EI-reg				EI-oc			
	Anger	Fear	Sadness	Joy	Anger	Fear	Sadness	Joy
a	0.386667	0.595735	0.530067	0.684391	0.672700	0.66000	0.612000	0.734700
r	0.478723	0.764934	0.573668	0.873777	0.673000	0.659000	0.620100	0.735000
p	0.424373	0.449689	0.524746	0.524566	0.709000	0.68700	0.646500	0.747000

Table 1. NNTF and Classification Algoithm Results (a-accuracy, r-recall, p-precission)

This being said, it becomes clear that for ordinal classification (EI-oc) NNTF is preferred, while the additional Decision Tree Algorithm helps the improvement of intensity detection.

It would have been rather interesting to have a balance between the negative and positive emotions (the Semeval Competition providing us with three negative and only one positive emotion.) Much and interesting work is to be done as we speak about such a subjective part and manifestation of human mind - emotions.

	Decision Tree Classification							
	EI-reg				EI-oc			
	Anger	Fear	Sadness	Joy	Anger	Fear	Sadness	Joy
a	0.41986	0.502864	0.545383	0.654932	0.410097	0.438484	0.408765	0.510735
r	0.437653	0.538493	0.535273	0.669248	0.418998	0.440084	0.408763	0.510374
p	0.436753	0.527790	0.530400	0.659200	0.418843	0.430864	0.403659	0.511037

Table 2. Results obtained after implementing the Decission Tree Algorithm (a-accuracy, r-recall, p-precission)

5 Conclusions

Within our project, we succeeded to obtain relevant results as participants in Semeval-Task 1 Affect in Tweets, by implementing machine learning and decision tree algorithms.

A constant concern relates to the modalities of sentiment summarization and visualization. When the results of sentiment analysis tasks need to be presented to an end user, a corresponding level of uncertainty should be taken into account (uncertain results shown as certain may lead to incorrect conclusions). Of course it is clear that we may increase it by

Acknowledgments

This survey was published with the support by two grants of the Romanian National Authority for Scientific Research and Innovation, UEFISCDI, project number PN-III-P2-2.1-BG-2016-0390, contract 126BG/2016 and project number PN-III-P1-1.2-PCCDI-2017-0818, contract 73PCCDI/2018 within PNCDI III, and partially by the README project "Interactive and Innovative application for evaluating the readability of texts in Romanian Language and for improving users' writing styles", contract no. 114/15.09.2017, MySMIS 2014 code 119286.

References

Amir Zadeh, Rowan Zellers. 2016. *Multimodal Sentiment Intensity Analysis in Videos: Facial Gestures and Verbal Messages, - Affective Computing and Sentiment Analysis.* http://sentic.net/multimodal-sentiment-intensity-analysis-in-videos.pdf

Andrea Esuli, Fabrizio Sebastiani. 2010. *SentiWordNet: A Publicly Available Lexical Resource for Opinion Mining.* http://nmis.isti.cnr.it/sebastiani/Publications/LREC06.pdf

Andrew L. Maas, Raymond E. Daly, Peter T. Pham, Dan Huang, Andrew Y. Ng, and Christopher Potts, Learning *Word Vectors for Sentiment Analysis,* Stanford, CA 94305. http://www.aclweb.org/anthology/P11-1015

Cecilia Ovesdotter Alm, Dan Roth, Richard Sproat, *Emotions from text: machine learning for text-based emotion prediction,* https://pdfs.semanticscholar.org/4db0/80cc272c68fb45df65eccdde6317edc44c28.pdf

Carlo Strapparava, Rada Mihalcea. 2007. *SemEval-2007 Task 14 Affective Tweets,* https://pdfs.semanticscholar.org/5b19/cdfecffbcd2d82b57407863f95c42bb1f720.pdf

Hutto, C.J. & Gilbert, E.E. 2014. *VADER: A Parsimonious Rule-based Model for Sentiment Analysis of Social Media Text.* Eighth International Conference on Weblogs and Social Media (ICWSM-14). Ann Arbor, MI. https://pdfs.semanticscholar.org/a6e4/a2532510369b8f55c68f049ff11a892fefeb.pdf

Saif M. Mohammad and Felipe Bravo-Marquez, Emotion Intensities in Tweets, In Proceedings of the sixth joint conference on lexical and computational semantics (*Sem), Vancouver, Canada.

Le B., Nguyen H. 2015. *Twitter Sentiment Analysis Using Machine Learning Techniques.* In: Le Thi H., Nguyen N., Do T. (eds) Advanced Computational Methods for Knowledge Engineering. Advances in Intelligent Systems and Computing, vol 358. Springer, Cham

Saif M. Mohammad and Felipe Bravo-Marquez. 2017. *WASSA-2017 Shared Task on Emotion Intensity,* In Proceedings of the EMNLP 2017 Workshop on Computational Approaches to Subjectivity, Sentiment, and Social Media (WASSA), Copenhagen, Denmark.

Saif M. Mohammad, Felipe Bravo-Marquez, Mohammad Salameh, and Svetlana Kiritchenko. 2018. *Semeval-2018 Task 1: Affect in tweets. In Proceedings of International Workshop on Semantic Evaluation (SemEval-2018),* New Orleans, LA, USA

Sreekanth Maunendra, Sankar Desarkar. 2017. *NSEmo at EmoInt-2017. An Ensemble to Predict Emotion Intensity in Tweets,* http://www.aclweb.org/anthology/W17-5230

Vineet, John, Olga, Vechtomova. 2017. *UWat-Emote at EmoInt-2017: Emotion Intensity Detection using Affect Clues, Sentiment Polarity and Word Embeddings.* http://www.aclweb.org/anthology/W17-5235

Yuanye He, Liang-Chih Yu, K.Robert Lai, Weiyi Liu. 2017. *Determinng Emotion Intensity Using a Bi-directional LSTM-CNN Model.* http://www.aclweb.org/anthology/W17-5233

Rohini S. Rahate, Emmanuel M. 2013. *Feature Selection for Sentiment Analysis by using SVM,* International Journal of Computer Applications (0975–8887) Volume 84–No5, December

uOttawa at SemEval-2018 Task 1: Self-Attentive Hybrid GRU-Based Network

Ahmed Husseini Orabi[1], Mahmoud Husseini Orabi[1], Diana Inkpen[1], David Van Bruwaene[2]
[1]EECS, University of Ottawa, 800 King Edward Avenue, Ottawa, Canada
[2]VISR inc., 10 Dundas St E. Suite 600, Toronto, Canada
{ahuss045, mhuss092, diana.inkpen}@uottawa.ca, d@visr.co

Abstract

We propose a novel attentive hybrid GRU-based network (SAHGN), which we used at SemEval-2018 Task 1: Affect in Tweets. Our network has two main characteristics, 1) has the ability to internally optimize its feature representation using attention mechanisms, and 2) provides a hybrid representation using a character-level Convolutional Neural Network (CNN), as well as a self-attentive word-level encoder. The key advantage of our model is its ability to signify the relevant and important information that enables self-optimization. Results are reported on the valence intensity regression task.

1 Introduction

Affect analysis is one of the main topics of natural language processing (NLP). It involves many sub-tasks such as sentiment and valence analyses expressed in text. We focus on the task of determining valence intensity.

Hand-crafted features and/or sentiment lexicons are commonly used for affect analysis (Mohammad, Kiritchenko, & Zhu, 2013; Taboada, Brooke, Tofiloski, Voll, & Stede, 2011) with classifiers such as random forest and support vector machines (SVM).

Affect in tweets (AIT) is a challenging task as it requires handling an informal writing style, which typically has many grammar mistakes, slangs, and misspellings.

In this paper, we present a self-attentive hybrid GRU-based network (SAHGN) that competed at SemEval-2018 Task 1 (Mohammad, Bravo-Marquez, Salameh, & Kiritchenko, 2018; Mohammad & Kiritchenko, 2018).

Our contributions can be summarized as below.

- **The implementation of a social media text processor:** A library to help process social media text such as short-forms, emoticons, emojis, misspellings, hash tags, and slangs, as well as tokenization, word normalization, and sentence encoding.
- **The implementation of a self-attentive deep learning system:** This system can predict valence and intensity with limited corpora and vocabulary, and yet can have acceptable performance.

2 High-Level Description of Our System

Our goal is to provide a system that can predict valence and intensity for short text. Figure 1 shows a high-level description of our solution, which consists of two main components, social media text processor (Section 3) and self-attentive hybrid GRU-based network (Section 4.2).

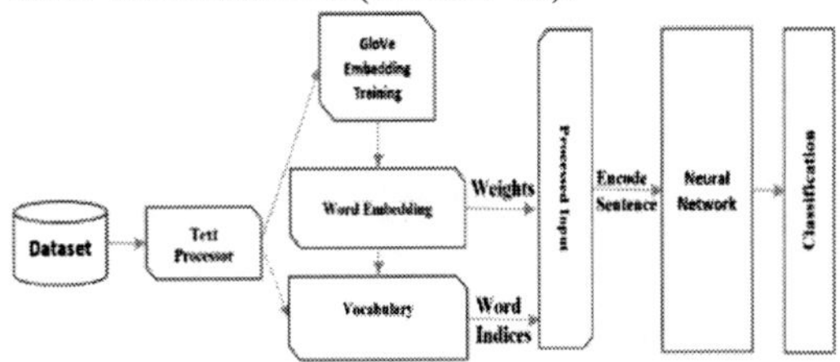

Figure 1: System architecture.

3 Social Media Text Processor

The social media text processor aims to provide a reliable and fast tokenization. It involves the following preprocessing steps:

- Use a named entity recognizer (NER) (Finkel, Grenager, & Manning, 2005) to identify entities such as persons, names, and places, and then replace them accordingly.
- Build a vocabulary using an NGram tokenizer.

Proceedings of the 12th International Workshop on Semantic Evaluation (SemEval-2018), pages 181–185
New Orleans, Louisiana, June 5–6, 2018. ©2018 Association for Computational Linguistics

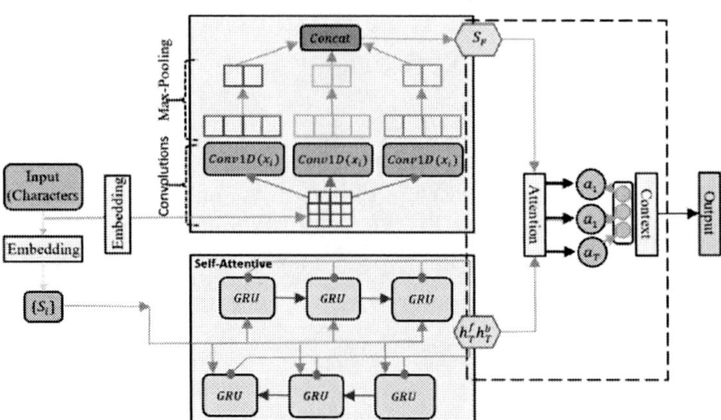

Figure 2: The architecture of Self-Attentive Hybrid GRU-Based Network.

- Tokenize sentences into a set of tokens, and then use them to encode text into a sequence of indices (Table 1), which are fed into the network.
- Clean text from accents, punctuations, and non-Latin characters.
- Identify emoticons and emojis, and then replace them with meaningful text; e.g., replace the happy face emoticon :) with <happy>.
- Recognize hashtags, URLs, and then briefly describe them; e.g. replace #depressed by <hashtag_start>depressed<hashtag_end>.
- Identify user reference mentions, and then replace them with a person entity; e.g. <person>.

Text	@name I am feeling under the weather after I met with Carl :'(#sick \\u0001F600
Processed	<SOS> <reference> I am feeling under the weather after I met with <person> <crying> <hashtag_start> sick <hashtag_end> <grinning_face> <EOS>

Table 1: Example of processed text.

4 Model Description

The overall architecture of our SAHGN model is shown in Figure 2. The main components include 1) a word sequence encoder, 2) a bidirectional GRU-based layer that applies a self-attentive mechanism on the word level, 3) a character-level CNN feature extractor, and 4) an attention with context-aware mechanism.

4.1 Word Sequence Encoder

A network input is described as a sequence (S) of tokens (such as words), where $S = [s_1, s_2, ..., s_t]$ and t denotes the timestep. S_i is a one-hot input (i) vector of a fixed length (T) of tokens. A sequence that exceeds this length is truncated.

Word encoding. We use a W word vocabulary to encode a sequence. W has fixed terms to determine the start and end of the sequence, as well as the out of vocabulary (OOV) words. We handle the variable length through padding for short sequences and truncating for long sequences.

Embedding layer. We apply a pretrained GloVe word embedding (Pennington, Socher, & Manning, 2014) on S_i. GloVe projects these words into a low-dimensional vector representation (x_i), where $x_i \in R^W$ and W is the word weight embedding matrix. W is used to initialize the word embedding layer.

We used the official training and development corpora to train the GloVe word embedding with a dimension of 100. The vocabulary size of this model is *8145* words, which is small and poses a major challenge to training, as well as to performance.

4.2 Self-attentive GRU-based Mechanism

Recurrent neural network (RNN) is commonly used for NLP problems (Yin, Kann, Yu, & Schütze, 2017; Young, Hazarika, Poria, & Cambria, 2017), as it enables remembering values over arbitrary time durations. RNN processes every element of an input embedding (x_i) sequentially, such that $h_t = \tanh(W_{x_i} + W_{h_{t-1}})$. W is the weight matrix between an input and hidden states, while h_t is the hidden state of the recurrent connection at timestep (t). The design of the RNN enables variable length processing while preserving the sequence order.

However, RNN has many limitations with long sequences, in particular the exponentially growing or decaying gradients. A common way to resolve these issues is by using gating mechanisms, such as LSTM and GRU (Gers, Schmidhuber, & Cummins, 2000; Hochreiter & Schmidhuber, 1997). We use GRU as it is faster to converge, in addition to being memory efficient.

Bidirectional GRU layer. In our model, we use bidirectional GRU layers. GRU receives a sequence of tokens as inputs, and then projects word information $H = (h_1, h_2, ..., h_T)$, where h_t denotes the hidden state of GRU at a timestep (t). It captures the temporal and abstract information of sequences in a forward (h^f) or reverse (h^b) manner. After that, we concatenate forward and backward representations; e.g. $h_t = h_t^f \| h_t^b$.

Attention mechanism. Words do not have equal valence weights in sentences. Towards that, we use an attention mechanism to signify the relatively important words.

Attention is used to compute the compatibility between a given source (x_i) and query (q). It uses an alignment function $f(x_i, q)$ to measure the level of dependency of q to x_i. This function produces an attention weight $a = f(x_i, q)_{i=1}^T$. Then, a softmax function is applied to produce a probability distribution $p(z|x, q)$ for each word (t) of an input (x). Hence, a bigger weight of x_i indicates a higher importance than other words.

The attention alignment approaches have the same implementation, but they mainly differ on how they compute weights. This can be either in an additive manner $f(x_i, q) = \tanh(W^T B(W_{x_i} + W_q))$ (Bahdanau, Cho, & Bengio, 2014), or a multiplicative manner $f(x_i, q) = \tanh((W_{x_i}.W_q))$ (Vaswani et al., 2017). In our model training, we use an additive attention mechanism, as it helped improve the prediction performance.

Self-Attention mechanism. In our model training, we have a small number of corpora, which are not sufficient to train an efficient word embedding or alleviate well-known problems such as polysemy. In an effort to overcome such limitations, we use a self-attention mechanism. This approach measures the dependency of different tokens in the same input embedding (x_i). It mainly computes attention for each word by replacing q and x_i with a set of token pairs (x_i, x_j).

4.3 Character-level CNN

The CNN encoding layer (Figure 3) takes an input of a sequence (S) of characters, where $S = [s_1, s_2, ..., s_t]$ such that t denotes the timestep. S_i is a one-hot input (i) vector of a fixed length (T) of characters.

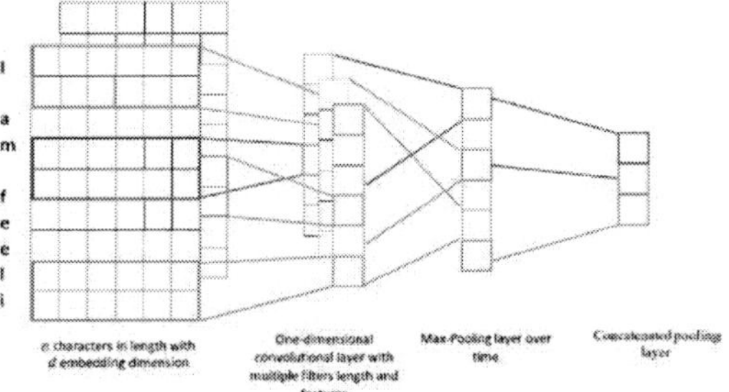

Figure 3: Character-level CNN.

CNN usually uses temporal convolutions (timestep-based) rather than spatial convolutions with text analysis.

We mainly use convolutions to extract low-level character information such as misspellings, slangs, and so on.

Character encoding. We define a charset of the size 95, including the upper and lower cases of the English alphabet, special characters, padding, and the start and end of a given input sequence. We need this charset to build a vocabulary, which is used to encode a character sequence. Similarly to the word embedding, we handle the variable length through padding and truncating (Section 4.1).

Character embedding layer. We build a character embedding of 32 dimensions. We use a uniform distribution scheme of a range (-0.5 to +0.5) to initialize its weight matrix.

We apply 3 convolutions of 100 features, as well as different filter lengths 2, 3, and 4. Each one-dimensional operation is used, where $C_i^n = Conv1d(S_i)$, and n is the filter length. After that, a max-pooling layer is applied on the feature map to extract abstract information, $\widehat{C_i^n} = \max(C_i^n)$. Then, we concatenate these feature representations into one output.

As opposed to recurrent layers (Section 4.2), convolutional operations with max-pooling are helpful to extract word features without paying attention to their sequence order (Kalchbrenner, Grefenstette, & Blunsom, 2014). These features are combined with recurrent features to improve the performance of our model.

4.4 Attention with Context

Output vectors received from previous steps are concatenated, and then fed into an attention with context.

We use a context-aware attention mechanism (Yang et al., 2016) to compute a fixed representation ($r = \sum_{i=1}^{T} a_i h_i$) of a sequence as the weighted sum of all tokens in that sequence. This representation is used as a classification feature vector to be fed to the final fully-connected sigmoid layer. This layer outputs a continuous value representing the valence of a given sentence.

4.5 Training

In our training, we use mini batch stochastic gradient of the size 32, to minimize the mean-squared error using back-propagation. We use Adam optimizer with a learning rate of 0.001 (Kingma & Ba, 2014). For training, we use 80% of the training set and 20% for validation. We test and report our results on both development and test sets.

Regularization. We use dropout to randomly drop neurons off the network, which helps preventing co-adaptation of neurons (Srivastava, Hinton, Krizhevsky, Sutskever, & Salakhutdinov, 2014). Dropout is also applied on the recurrent connection of our GRU-based layers. Additionally, we apply a weight decay approach through setting an L2 regularization penalty (Cortes, Mohri, & Rostamizadeh, 2012).

Hyperparameters. The size of the embedding layer is 200, and of the GRU layers is 150, which becomes 300 for bidirectional GRU. We apply a dropout of 0.4, and a dropout of 0.2 on the recurrent connections. Finally, an L2 regularization of 0.00001 is applied at the loss function.

5 Results

We report our results using the Pearson correlation between the prediction and gold rating sets on the test set (all instances). The other one (gold in 0.5-1 shown in Table 2) differs in including tweets only with intensity greater than or equal to 0.5.

Our model performed well on the development set scoring 0.869, while on the testing set, the performance degraded to 0.752. This degradation could be related to the size of the corpus we used to train our word embedding. We also trained only on 80% of the training set.

Dataset	**Valence task**	
	Pearson correlation (all instances)	Pearson correlation (gold in 0.5-1)
Development	0.869	0.692
Testing	0.752	0.559

Table 2: Results of valence intensity regression (English).

6 Conclusion

In this paper, we presented a self-attentive hybrid GRU-based network for predicting valence intensity for short text.

We used a hybrid approach combining low-character-level features with self-attentive word embedding. Our network uses two different attention mechanisms to signify the relevant and important words, and hence optimize feature representation.

With limited corpora and vocabulary of the size 8152, our model still managed to achieve an optimized feature representation, which achieved excellent results on the development set. However, our model failed to maintain the same performance on the testing set.

For future work, we will explore the performance of our model with larger corpora against the testing set. It would also be interesting to see if the model performs well on other long-text NLP tasks such as topic classification.

Acknowledgments

This research is funded by Natural Sciences and Engineering Research Council of Canada (NSERC), Ontario Centres of Excellence (OCE) and VISR.co.

References

Bahdanau, D., Cho, K., & Bengio, Y. (2014). Neural Machine Translation by Jointly Learning to Align and Translate. Retrieved from http://arxiv.org/abs/1409.0473

Cortes, C., Mohri, M., & Rostamizadeh, A. (2012). L2 Regularization for Learning Kernels. Retrieved from http://arxiv.org/abs/1205.2653

Finkel, J. R., Grenager, T., & Manning, C. (2005). Incorporating non-local information into information extraction systems by Gibbs sampling. In Proceedings of the 43rd Annual Meeting on Association for Computational Linguistics - ACL '05 (pp. 363–370). Morristown, NJ, USA: Association for Computational Linguistics. https://doi.org/10.3115/1219840.1219885

Gers, F. A., Schmidhuber, J., & Cummins, F. (2000). Learning to Forget: Continual Prediction with LSTM. Neural Computation, 12(10), 2451–2471. https://doi.org/10.1162/089976600300015015

Hochreiter, S., & Schmidhuber, J. (1997). Long Short-Term Memory. Neural Computation, 9(8), 1735–1780. https://doi.org/10.1162/neco.1997.9.8.1735

Kalchbrenner, N., Grefenstette, E., & Blunsom, P. (2014). A Convolutional Neural Network for Modelling Sentences. In Proceedings of the 52nd Annual Meeting of the Association for Computational Linguistics (Volume 1: Long Papers) (pp. 655–665). Stroudsburg, PA, USA: Association for Computational Linguistics. https://doi.org/10.3115/v1/P14-1062

Kingma, D. P., & Ba, J. (2014). Adam: A Method for Stochastic Optimization. Retrieved from http://arxiv.org/abs/1412.6980

Mohammad, S. M., Bravo-Marquez, F., Salameh, M., & Kiritchenko, S. (2018). Semeval-2018 Task 1: Affect in tweets. In International Workshop on Semantic Evaluation (SemEval-2018), New Orleans, LA, USA.

Mohammad, S. M., & Kiritchenko, S. (2018). Understanding Emotions: A Dataset of Tweets to Study Interactions between Affect Categories. In Proceedings of the 11th Edition of the Language Resources and Evaluation Conference (LREC-2018).

Mohammad, S. M., Kiritchenko, S., & Zhu, X. (2013). NRC-Canada: Building the State-of-the-Art in Sentiment Analysis of Tweets. Retrieved from http://arxiv.org/abs/1308.6242

Pennington, J., Socher, R., & Manning, C. (2014). Glove: Global Vectors for Word Representation. In Proceedings of the 2014 Conference on Empirical Methods in Natural Language Processing (EMNLP) (pp. 1532–1543). Stroudsburg, PA, USA: Association for Computational Linguistics. https://doi.org/10.3115/v1/D14-1162

Srivastava, N., Hinton, G., Krizhevsky, A., Sutskever, I., & Salakhutdinov, R. (2014). Dropout: a simple way to prevent neural networks from overfitting. The Journal of Machine Learning Research, 15(1), 1929–1958.

Taboada, M., Brooke, J., Tofiloski, M., Voll, K., & Stede, M. (2011). Lexicon-Based Methods for Sentiment Analysis. Computational Linguistics, 37(2), 267–307. https://doi.org/10.1162/COLI_a_00049

Vaswani, A., Shazeer, N., Parmar, N., Uszkoreit, J., Jones, L., Gomez, A. N., … Polosukhin, I. (2017). Attention is All you Need. In Advances in Neural Information Processing Systems 30 (NIPS).

Yang, Z., Yang, D., Dyer, C., He, X., Smola, A., & Hovy, E. (2016). Hierarchical Attention Networks for Document Classification. In Proceedings of the 2016 Conference of the North American Chapter of the Association for Computational Linguistics: Human Language Technologies (pp. 1480–1489). Stroudsburg, PA, USA: Association for Computational Linguistics. https://doi.org/10.18653/v1/N16-1174

Yin, W., Kann, K., Yu, M., & Schütze, H. (2017). Comparative Study of CNN and RNN for Natural Language Processing. Retrieved from http://arxiv.org/abs/1702.01923

Young, T., Hazarika, D., Poria, S., & Cambria, E. (2017). Recent Trends in Deep Learning Based Natural Language Processing. Retrieved from http://arxiv.org/abs/1708.02709

THU_NGN at SemEval-2018 Task 1: Fine-grained Tweet Sentiment Intensity Analysis with Attention CNN-LSTM

Chuhan Wu[1], Fangzhao Wu[2], Junxin Liu[1], Zhigang Yuan[1],
Sixing Wu[1] and Yongfeng Huang[1]

[1]Tsinghua National Laboratory for Information Science and Technology,
Department of Electronic Engineering, Tsinghua University Beijing 100084, China
[2]Microsoft Research Asia

`{wuch15,wu-sx15,ljx16,yuanzg14,yfhuang}@mails.tsinghua.edu.cn`
`wufangzhao@gmail.com`

Abstract

Traditional sentiment analysis approaches mainly focus on classifying the sentiment polarities or emotion categories of texts. However, they can't exploit the sentiment intensity information. Therefore, the SemEval-2018 Task 1 is aimed to automatically determine the intensity of emotions or sentiment of tweets to mine fine-grained sentiment information. In order to address this task, we propose a system based on an attention CNN-LSTM model. In our model, LSTM is used to extract the long-term contextual information from texts. We apply attention techniques to selecting this information. A CNN layer with different kernel sizes is used to extract local features. The dense layers take the pooled CNN feature maps and predict the intensity scores. Our system achieves an average Pearson correlation score of 0.722 (ranked 12/48) in the emotion intensity regression task, and 0.810 in the valence regression task (ranked 15/38). It indicates that our system can be further extended.

1 Introduction

Detecting the intensity of sentiment is an important task for fine-grained sentiment analysis (Kiritchenko et al., 2016; Mohammad and Bravo-Marquez, 2017). Intensity refers to the degree or amount of an emotion or degree of sentiment. For example, we can express our emotion by "very happy" or "a little angry". The intensity can be analysis in multiple categories (i.e. low, moderate and high) or real-valued. Identifying the intensity information of sentiment has potential to applications such as electronic business, social computing and public health (Wilson, 2008).

Twitter is a social platform which contains rich textual content. There have been many approaches to twitter sentiment analysis (Khan et al., 2015; Severyn and Moschitti, 2015; Philander et al.,

2016). However, twitter sentiment analysis is challenging because tweets usually contain non-standard languages, including emoticons, emojis, creatively spelled words, and hash tags (Mohammad and Bravo-Marquez, 2017). In order to improve the collective techniques on tweet sentiment intensity analysis, the SemEval-2018 Task 1 is aimed to identify the categorical and real-valued intensity of emotions or sentiment for English, Arabic, and Spanish (Mohammad et al., 2018).

Existing approaches to analysis the intensity of emotions or sentiment are mainly based on lexicons and supervised learning. Lexicon-based methods usually rely on lexicons to assign the intensity scores of affective words in texts (Mohammad and Bravo-Marquez, 2017). However, these method can't utilize the contextual information from texts. Supervised methods are mainly based on SVR (Madisetty and Desarkar, 2017), linear regression (John and Vechtomova, 2017) and neural networks (Goel et al., 2017; Köper et al., 2017). Usually neural network-based methods outperform SVR and linear regression-based methods siginificantly. Motivated by the successful applications of neural models in this task, we propose a system using a CNN-LSTM model with attention mechanism. Firstly, a tweet will be converted into a sequence of dense vectors by an embedding layer. Next, we use a Bi-LSTM layer to extract contextual information from them. The sequential features will be selected by an attention layer. Then we apply a CNN with different kernel sizes to extracting different local information. Thus, our model can exploit both local and long-term information by combining CNN and LSTM. Finally, two dense layers are used to predict the intensity scores. The system performance quantified by an average Pearson correlation score is 0.722 in the emotion intensity regression task (EI-reg) and 0.810 in the valence regression task (V-

Proceedings of the 12th International Workshop on Semantic Evaluation (SemEval-2018), pages 186–192
New Orleans, Louisiana, June 5–6, 2018. ©2018 Association for Computational Linguistics

reg). Our model outperforms several baseline neural networks, which proves that our model can identify the intensity of emotions and sentiment effectively.

2 Related Work

Sentiment analysis in social media such as Twitter is an important task for opinion mining (Severyn and Moschitti, 2015). Traditional Twitter sentiment analysis methods mainly focus on identifying the polarities (Da Silva et al., 2014; dos Santos and Gatti, 2014) or emotion categories (Dini and Bittar, 2016) of tweets. However, it's a difficult task to analysis the noisy tweets. They usually contain various nonstandard languages including emoticons, emojis, creatively spelled words and hash tags. In addition, these languages usually contain rich sentiment information. In order to capture such information, several lexicon-based methods are proposed. Nielsen et al. (2011) proposed to use a dictionary to incorporate emoticon information into tweet analysis models. Mohammad et al. proposed to use hash tags to identify emotion categories of tweets (2015). These lexicon-based methods are free from manual annotation, but they rely on the emotion lexicons and can't mine high-level contextual information from tweets. Supervised methods such as neural networks are also applied to tweet sentiment analysis. For example, Dos et al. (2014) propose to classify tweets using a deep convolutional neural network. Approaches based on deep neural networks need sufficient samples to train, but they usually outperforms lexicon-based methods in these tasks.

However, these approaches usually ignore the intensity of emotions and sentiment, which provides important information for fine-grained sentiment analysis. Therefore, in order to capture such information, Mohammad et al. proposed to identify the emotion and sentiment intensity (valence) of texts (2016). Different approaches have been proposed to detect the tweet emotion intensity in the EmoInt-2017 shared task (Mohammad and Bravo-Marquez, 2017). For example, Madisetty et al. (2017) proposed an ensemble model based on SVR. Goel et al. (2017) and Koper et al. (2017) applied CNN-LSTM architecture to this task. These systems reached the top ranks in the EmoInt shared task.

Motivated by the successful application of CNN-LSTM model (Zhou et al., 2015; Chen et al., 2016) and the attention mechanism for text classification (Yin et al., 2015), we propose a system using attention-based CNN-LSTM model to address this task. In our model, we first use LSTM to extract sequential information, and select features via attention layer. Then we combine CNN with different kernel sizes to learn local information. Finally the dense layers are used to predict the intensity scores. In addition, several features are incorporated into our model. The evaluation results show that our system outperform several baseline neural networks and can be further extended.

3 Attention CNN-LSTM Model

Our network architecture is shown in Figure 1. We will explain the detailed information of our system in the following subsections.

3.1 Network Architecture

As shown in Figure 1, an embedding layer is used to provide word embedding and one-hot encoded part-of-speech (POS) tags of the input tweets. The Bi-LSTM layer takes the concatenated word embedding and POS tags as input, and output each hidden states. Let h_i be the output hidden state at time step i. Then its attention weight α_i can be formulated as follows:

$$
\begin{aligned}
m_i &= tanh(h_i), \\
\hat{\alpha}_i &= w_i m_i + b_i, \\
\alpha_i &= \frac{exp(\hat{\alpha}_i)}{\sum_j exp(\hat{\alpha}_j)},
\end{aligned}
\tag{1}
$$

where $w_i m_i + b_i$ denote a linear transformation of m_i. Therefore, the output representation r_i is given by:

$$
r_i = \alpha_i h_i.
\tag{2}
$$

Based on such text representation, the sequence of features will be assigned with different attention weights. Thus, important information such as affective words can be identified more easily. The convolutional layer takes the text representation r_i as input. We use CNN with four different kernel sizes to learn local information with different contextual length. Based on this architecture, our model can combine both long-term and local information, which can help to identify sentiment information better. The output CNN feature maps are concatenated together, and will be squeezed by a global max pooling layer. They are concatenated with the lexicon features. We use two dense layers

Dense
layers

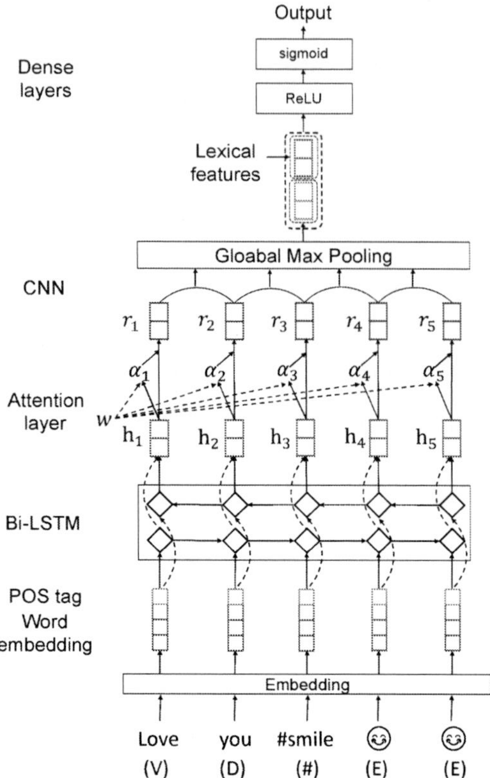

Figure 1: The architecture of our attention CNN-LSTM model.

with ReLU and sigmoid activation respectively to predict the final intensity score. In order to mitigate overfitting, we apply dropout technique at each layer to regularize our model.

3.2 Word Embedding

We use Word2Vec (Mikolov et al., 2013) as the vector representation of the words in tweets. We combine two kinds of word embeddings: The first embeddings are provided by Godin et al. (2015). They are trained on a corpus with 400 million tweets. The second embeddings are provided by Barbier et al. (2016). They are trained on 20 million geolocalized tweets. The dimensions of two embeddings are 400 and 300 respectively. We fine-tune the word embeddings during the network training.

3.3 Additional Features

We incorporate POS tags and lexicon features into our model. POS tags usually contain rich semantic information. For example, sentiment intensity can be expressed by adjectives like "very" and "slight". POS tags can help the neural model to identify such words. We use the Ark-Tweet-NLP[1] tool to obtain the POS tags of tweets (Owoputi et al., 2013). The POS tag feature of each word is concatenated with the word embedding.

Usually affective words in tweets such as specific hashtags express sentiment explicitly. Therefore, incorporating lexicon information can help our model to predict intensity more accurately. We use the AffectiveTweets[2] (Mohammad and Bravo-Marquez, 2017) package in Weka[3] to obtain the lexicon features of tweets. We use the Tweet-ToLexiconFeatureVector (Bravo-Marquez et al., 2014), TweetToSentiStrengthFeatureVector (Thelwall et al., 2012) and TweetToInputLexiconFeatureVector filters in AffectiveTweets. In our experiment, the lexicon features are 49-dim. These lexicon features are concatenated with the pooled CNN feature maps.

3.4 Model Ensemble

We use an ensemble strategy to improve the model performance. Our model is trained for 10 times by using randomly selected dropout rate. Then the final predictions on the test set are given by the average of all model predictions. In this way, the random error of our system can be reduced.

4 Experiment

4.1 Preprocess

In order to process the noisy tweet texts, we use tweetokenize[4] for tokenizing, and use Ark-Tweet-NLP tool for POS tagging. In addition, we refine the texts and POS tags using several rules: 1) all URLs will be replaced with the word "URL", and their POS tags will be set to "URL"; 2) all @users will be replaced with "USERNAME", and their POS tags will be set to @; 3) POS tags of hashtags are set to "#"; 4) POS tags of emojis and emoticons are set to "E".

---

[1] http://www.cs.cmu.edu/ ark/TweetNLP
[2] https://github.com/felipebravom/AffectiveTweets
[3] https://www.cs.waikato.ac.nz/ml/weka
[4] https://github.com/jaredks/tweetokenize

4.2 Experiment Settings

The details of English datasets[5] we use is shown in Table 1. The intensity in both task is annotated between 0 and 1. In the EI-reg task, the Pearson correlation scores across all four emotions will be averaged as the final score. In the V-reg task, the correlation score for valence is used as the competition metric.

Task	EI-reg				V-reg
Category	anger	fear	joy	sadness	valence
#train	1,701	2,252	1,616	1,533	1,174
#dev	388	389	290	397	449
#test	1,002	986	1,105	975	937

Table 1: Detailed statistics of the English datasets in our experiment

In our network, the dimension of word embeddings is $400 + 300$. The hidden states of Bi-LSTM are 2×300-dim. The kernel sizes of CNN are 3, 5, 7 and 9 respectively. The number of feature maps are 4×200. The dimension of the first dense layer is set to 200. The padding length of tweets is set to 50. The dropout rate is a random number between 0.1 and 0.3. The loss function we use is MAE, and the batch size is set to 8. We combine the training and development sets in our experiment. We use 90% for training and reserve 10% for cross validation. In our official submissions, we use the full training and development sets to train models.

4.3 Evaluation Results

We compare the performance of our model and several baselines. The models to be compared include: 1) CNN, using CNN and dense layers. 2) LSTM, using LSTM and dense layers. 3) CNN+LSTM, combing CNN with LSTM to predict. 4) CNN+LSTM+att, adding attention mechanism to CNN-LSTM model. 5) CNN+LSTM+att+ensemble, using ensemble strategy in the attention-based CNN-LSTM model. The results in the EI-reg and V-reg tasks are shown in Table 2. In comparison, we also present the cross validation results. Our system reaches average Pearson correlation score of 0.722 in the EI-reg task and 0.810 in the V-reg task. The results indicate that our CNN-LSTM model outperforms the CNN and LSTM baselines. It proves that CNN-LSTM model can combine

the long-term information and local information in texts. The attention mechanism can also improve the model performance. Since the attention layer can select important information, our model can focus on important words in texts (e.g. affective words) to predict the intensity of emotions and sentiment more accurately. Although our system still needs to be improved compared with the top systems, our model outperforms the common baseline models, which validates the effectiveness of our model.

4.4 Influence of Pre-trained Word Embedding

We compare the performance using different pre-trained embeddings in the EI-reg task. The results are shown in Table 3. The results show that the pre-trained embeddings are important, and combining different word embedding can improve the model performance. It may be because the combination of embedding can cover more out-of-vocabulary words and provide rich semantic information.

4.5 Influence of Additional Features

The influence of the POS tag features and lexicon features is shown in Table 4. The results show that POS tags can improve the model performance significantly. Affective words, emojis and hashtags usually contain rich sentiment information. POS tags can be used to identify such words. Therefore, incorporating the POS information into our neural model can help to identify these words in tweets better. The lexicon features can also improve our model. The lexicon features are obtained by the sentiment words in tweets. Thus, incorporating these features into neural networks can improve the performance of our system.

4.6 Analysis of Inappropriate Biases

In the EI-reg and V-reg tasks, an automatically generated mystery set is used for testing the inappropriate biases in NLP systems, such as gender and race (i.e. African American and European American names). For example, the pairs of sentences "She is happy." and "He is happy."; "Jamel feels angry." and "Harry feels angry." should be assigned wit the same intensity by an unbiased NLP system. The score differences are calculated for such sentence pairs. The average score difference, the p-value, and whether the score differences are statistically significant are shown in Ta-

[5] http://www.saifmohammad.com/WebDocs/AIT-2018/AIT2018-DATA

Model	EI-reg										V-reg	
	macro-avg		anger		fear		joy		sadness		valence	
	val	test	val	test	val	test	val	test	val	test	val	test
CNN	0.743	0.710	0.700	0.726	0.759	0.701	0.771	0.727	0.742	0.686	0.809	0.790
LSTM	0.741	0.706	0.701	0.720	0.751	0.694	0.766	0.726	0.746	0.683	0.802	0.785
CNN+LSTM	0.743	0.713	0.705	0.730	0.758	0.701	0.770	0.735	0.740	0.687	0.815	0.796
CNN+LSTM+att	0.749	0.718	0.706	0.731	0.760	0.706	0.774	0.739	0.756	0.695	0.828	0.801
CNN+LSTM+att+ensemble	**0.758**	**0.722**	**0.720**	**0.734**	**0.771**	**0.710**	**0.782**	**0.743**	**0.760**	**0.700**	**0.845**	**0.810**

Table 2: Evaluation and cross validation performance of our model ande baselines.

Embedding	avg	anger	fear	joy	sadness
w/o pre-trained	0.669	0.678	0.672	0.682	0.645
+emb1	0.717	0.728	0.706	0.737	0.695
+emb2	0.709	0.716	0.702	0.728	0.691
+emb1+emb2	**0.722**	**0.734**	**0.710**	**0.743**	**0.700**

Table 3: Influence of using different combinations of pre-trained word embeddings. The emb1 and emb2 denote the embeddings provided by Godin et al. (2015) and Barbieri et al. (2016) respectively.

Feature	avg	anger	fear	joy	sadness
None	0.704	0.715	0.698	0.722	0.679
+POS	0.715	0.729	0.705	0.737	0.690
+Lexicon	0.708	0.721	0.700	0.726	0.684
+POS+Lexicon	**0.722**	**0.734**	**0.710**	**0.743**	**0.700**

Table 4: Influence of POS tags and lexicon features.

ble 5. Although the average differences are small, but they are statistical significant in most tasks. Our system is based on word embedding, and we fine-tune the weights during the network training. Thus, our system will be influenced by the distribution of training data, which may lead to these biases.

Task	Gender			Race		
	Avg-D	p	Sig	Avg-D	p-value	Sig
Anger	-0.002	0.00003	√	0.002	0.01553	×
Fear	-0.023	0	√	0.023	0	√
Joy	0.02	0	√	-0.04	0	√
Sadness	-0.001	0.09654	×	0.011	0	√
Valence	0.001	0.00382	×	-0.021	0	√

Table 5: The average differences, p-value and statistical significance of predictions on the mystery set in each task. We denote them as Avg-D, p and Sig respectively.

4.7 Visualization of Attention Mechanism

Attention mechanism can encourage the neural model to focus on important words in texts. In order to prove its effectiveness of the attention layer, we present several examples in Table 6. The green color represents low attention, while red color represents high attention. We can see that the affec-

tive words (e.g. Happy) and hashtags (e.g. #funny) have high attention weights. It indicates that our attention-based model can capture important sentiment information to predict the intensity of tweets better.

5 Conclusion

Identifying the intensity of emotions or sentiment is important for fine-grained sentiment analysis. Thus, the Semeval-2018 task 1 is aimed to analyze the affective intensity of tweets. In this paper, we introduce the system participating in this task. We apply an attention-based CNN-LSTM model to predict the intensity scores of emotions and sentiment. We also use additional features to improve the performance of our system. Our system ranked 12/48 and 15/38 in the EI-reg and V-reg subtasks respectively. It indicates that our system can be further extended.

Acknowledgments

The authors thank the reviewers for their insightful comments and constructive suggestions on improving this work. This work was supported in part by the National Key Research and Development Program of China under Grant 2016YFB0800402 and in part by the National Natural Science Foundation of China under Grant U1705261, Grant U1536207, Grant U1536201 and U1636113.

References

Francesco Barbieri, German Kruszewski, Francesco Ronzano, and Horacio Saggion. 2016. How cosmopolitan are emojis?: Exploring emojis usage and meaning over different languages with distributional semantics. In *Proceedings of the 2016 ACM on Multimedia Conference*, pages 531–535. ACM.

Felipe Bravo-Marquez, Marcelo Mendoza, and Barbara Poblete. 2014. Meta-level sentiment models for big social data analysis. *Knowledge-Based Systems*, 69:86–99.

Table 6: Visualization of the attention weights of tweets. Red denotes high attention and green denotes low attention.

Xinchi Chen, Xipeng Qiu, and Xuanjing Huang. 2016. A feature-enriched neural model for joint chinese word segmentation and part-of-speech tagging. *arXiv preprint arXiv:1611.05384*.

Nadia FF Da Silva, Eduardo R Hruschka, and Estevam R Hruschka Jr. 2014. Tweet sentiment analysis with classifier ensembles. *Decision Support Systems*, 66:170–179.

Luca Dini and André Bittar. 2016. Emotion analysis on twitter: The hidden challenge. In *LREC*.

Fréderic Godin, Baptist Vandersmissen, Wesley De Neve, and Rik Van de Walle. 2015. Multimedia lab @ acl wnut ner shared task: Named entity recognition for twitter microposts using distributed word representations. In *Proceedings of the Workshop on Noisy User-generated Text*, pages 146–153.

Pranav Goel, Devang Kulshreshtha, Prayas Jain, and Kaushal Kumar Shukla. 2017. Prayas at emoint 2017: An ensemble of deep neural architectures for emotion intensity prediction in tweets. In *Proceedings of the 8th Workshop on Computational Approaches to Subjectivity, Sentiment and Social Media Analysis*, pages 58–65.

Vineet John and Olga Vechtomova. 2017. Uwat-emote at emoint-2017: Emotion intensity detection using affect clues, sentiment polarity and word embeddings. In *Proceedings of the 8th Workshop on Computational Approaches to Subjectivity, Sentiment and Social Media Analysis*, pages 249–254.

Aamera ZH Khan, Mohammad Atique, and VM Thakare. 2015. Combining lexicon-based and learning-based methods for twitter sentiment analysis. *International Journal of Electronics, Communication and Soft Computing Science & Engineering (IJECSCSE)*, page 89.

Svetlana Kiritchenko, Saif Mohammad, and Mohammad Salameh. 2016. Semeval-2016 task 7: Determining sentiment intensity of english and arabic phrases. In *Proceedings of the 10th International Workshop on Semantic Evaluation (SemEval-2016)*, pages 42–51.

Maximilian Köper, Evgeny Kim, and Roman Klinger. 2017. Ims at emoint-2017: emotion intensity prediction with affective norms, automatically extended resources and deep learning. In *Proceedings of the 8th Workshop on Computational Approaches to Subjectivity, Sentiment and Social Media Analysis*, pages 50–57.

Sreekanth Madisetty and Maunendra Sankar Desarkar. 2017. Nsemo at emoint-2017: an ensemble to predict emotion intensity in tweets. In *Proceedings of the 8th Workshop on Computational Approaches to Subjectivity, Sentiment and Social Media Analysis*, pages 219–224.

Tomas Mikolov, Kai Chen, Greg Corrado, and Jeffrey Dean. 2013. Efficient estimation of word representations in vector space. *arXiv preprint arXiv:1301.3781*.

Saif M Mohammad. 2016. Sentiment analysis: Detecting valence, emotions, and other affectual states from text. In *Emotion measurement*, pages 201–237. Elsevier.

Saif M Mohammad and Felipe Bravo-Marquez. 2017. Wassa-2017 shared task on emotion intensity. *arXiv preprint arXiv:1708.03700*.

Saif M. Mohammad, Felipe Bravo-Marquez, Mohammad Salameh, and Svetlana Kiritchenko. 2018. Semeval-2018 Task 1: Affect in tweets. In *Proceedings of International Workshop on Semantic Evaluation (SemEval-2018)*, New Orleans, LA, USA.

Saif M Mohammad and Svetlana Kiritchenko. 2015. Using hashtags to capture fine emotion categories from tweets. *Computational Intelligence*, 31(2):301–326.

Finn Årup Nielsen. 2011. A new anew: Evaluation of a word list for sentiment analysis in microblogs. *arXiv preprint arXiv:1103.2903*.

Olutobi Owoputi, Brendan O'Connor, Chris Dyer, Kevin Gimpel, Nathan Schneider, and Noah A Smith. 2013. Improved part-of-speech tagging for online conversational text with word clusters. Association for Computational Linguistics.

Kahlil Philander, YunYing Zhong, et al. 2016. Twitter sentiment analysis: capturing sentiment from integrated resort tweets. *International Journal of Hospitality Management*, 55:16–24.

Cicero dos Santos and Maira Gatti. 2014. Deep convolutional neural networks for sentiment analysis of short texts. In *Proceedings of COLING 2014, the 25th International Conference on Computational Linguistics: Technical Papers*, pages 69–78.

Aliaksei Severyn and Alessandro Moschitti. 2015. Twitter sentiment analysis with deep convolutional neural networks. In *Proceedings of the 38th International ACM SIGIR Conference on Research and Development in Information Retrieval*, pages 959–962. ACM.

Mike Thelwall, Kevan Buckley, and Georgios Paltoglou. 2012. Sentiment strength detection for the social web. *Journal of the Association for Information Science and Technology*, 63(1):163–173.

Theresa Ann Wilson. 2008. *Fine-grained subjectivity and sentiment analysis: recognizing the intensity, polarity, and attitudes of private states*. University of Pittsburgh.

Wenpeng Yin, Hinrich Schütze, Bing Xiang, and Bowen Zhou. 2015. Abcnn: Attention-based convolutional neural network for modeling sentence pairs. *arXiv preprint arXiv:1512.05193*.

Chunting Zhou, Chonglin Sun, Zhiyuan Liu, and Francis Lau. 2015. A c-lstm neural network for text classification. *arXiv preprint arXiv:1511.08630*.

EiTAKA at SemEval-2018 Task 1: An Ensemble of N-Channels ConvNet and XGboost Regressors for Emotion Analysis of Tweets

Mohammed Jabreel   **Antonio Moreno**

Intelligent Technologies for Advanced Knowledge Acquisition (ITAKA),
Departament d'Enginyeria Informàtica i Matemàtiques,
Universitat Rovira i Virgili,
Av. Països Catalans, 26, 43007 Tarragona, Spain
<first_name>.<last_name>@urv.cat

Abstract

This paper describes our system that has been used in Task1 Affect in Tweets. We combine two different approaches. The first one called N-Stream ConvNets, which is a deep learning approach where the second one is XGboost regressor based on a set of embedding and lexicons based features. Our system was evaluated on the testing sets of the tasks outperforming all other approaches for the Arabic version of valence intensity regression task and valence ordinal classification task.

1   Introduction

Sentiment Analysis is the task of automatically identifying the valence or polarity of a piece of text. This piece of text can be a user review, a document, an SMS message, a tweet, etc. According to (Mohammad, 2016), the term sentiment analysis also refers to determining the attitude towards a particular target or topic. The attitude can be the polarity (positive or negative), or an emotional or effectual attitude such as joy, anger, sadness and so on.

Most of the researchers in sentiment analysis have focused on developing systems to determine the polarity of a given text. This involves designing classifiers based on a set of examples with a manually annotated sentiment polarity. Although developing systems that automatically determine the intensity (i.e. the degree or the amount) of emotions that are communicated in a text has a wide range of applications in commerce, public health, social welfare, etc., most of the work has focused on categorical classification (whether a given piece of text communicates anger, joy, sadness, etc.). This can be attributed to the lack of suitable annotated data (Mohammad and Bravo-Márquez, 2017) .

In task1: *Affect in Tweets*, the organizers provide an array of tasks where systems have to au-
tomatically determine the intensity of emotions (anger, fear, joy, and sadness) and the intensity of the sentiment (aka valence) of the tweeters from their tweets. They provide annotated datasets for each task with English, Arabic, and Spanish tweets (Mohammad et al., 2018). We define the tasks below:

EI-reg (an emotion intensity regression task): Given a tweet and an emotion E, determine the intensity of E that best represents the mental state of the tweeter with a real-valued score between 0 (least E) and 1 (most E).

EI-oc (an emotion intensity ordinal classification task): Given a tweet and an emotion E, classify the tweet into one of four ordinal classes of intensity of E that best represents the mental state of the tweeter.

V-reg (a sentiment intensity regression task): Given a tweet, determine the intensity of sentiment or valence V that best represents the mental state of the tweeter with a real-valued score between 0 (most negative) and 1 (most positive).

V-oc (a sentiment analysis, ordinal classification, task): Given a tweet, classify it into one of seven ordinal classes, corresponding to various levels of positive and negative sentiment intensity, that best represents the mental state of the tweeter.

We proposed one system to solve the intensity regression tasks (i.e. EI-reg and V-reg) and use it as a feature extractor to train Decision Trees to solve the ordinal classification tasks (i.e. EI-oc and V-oc). We developed two versions of the proposed system for the English and the Arabic language tweets.

Our system is an ensemble of two different approaches. The first one, called N-Channels ConvNet, is a deep learning approach where the second one is an XGboost regressor based on a set of embedding and lexicons-based features.

The rest of the paper is organized as follows:

Proceedings of the 12th International Workshop on Semantic Evaluation (SemEval-2018), pages 193–199
New Orleans, Louisiana, June 5–6, 2018. ©2018 Association for Computational Linguistics

Section 2 presents the tools and the resources that are used. Section 3 describes the proposed system. In Section 4 we report the experimental results, whereas in Section 5 the conclusions and the future work are presented.

2 Resources

This section explains the tools and the resources that have been used in our system.

2.1 Sentiment Lexicons

We used the following lexicons for the English version of our system:

AFINN (Nielsen, 2011), General Inquirer (Stone et al., 1968), Bing-Liu opinion lexicon (HL) (Hu and Liu, 2004), MPQA (Choi and Wiebe, 2014), NRC hashtag sentiment lexicon (Mohammad et al., 2013), NRC emotion lexicon (EmoLex), NRC affect intensity lexicon, NRC hashtag emotion lexicon and Vader lexicon. More details about each lexicon, such as how it was created, the polarity score for each term, and the statistical distribution of the lexicon, can be found in (Jabreel and Moreno, 2016).

For the Arabic version we used the following lexicons:

Arabic Hashtag lexicon, Dialectal Arabic Hashtag lexicon, Arabic Bing Liu lexicon, Arabic Sentiment140 lexicon and Arabic translation of the NRC emotion lexicon. The first two were created manually, whereas the rest were translated to Arabic from the English version using Google Translator. (Mohammad et al., 2016).

2.2 Embeddings

Word embeddings are an approach for distributional semantics which represents words as vectors of real numbers. Such representation has useful clustering properties, since the words that are semantically and syntactically related are represented by similar vectors (Mikolov et al., 2013). For example, the words "coffee" and "tea" will be very close in the created space.

We used two publicly available pre-trained embedding models in the English version of our system. The first one was used in (Rouvier and Favre, 2016). It was trained using word2vec (skipgram model) on an unannotated corpus of 20 million English tweets containing at least one emoticon. The second one was provided by (Baziotis et al., 2017). It was trained on a big dataset of 330M English Twitter messages, gathered from 12/2012 to 07/2016 and a vocabulary size of 660K words using Glove algorithm.

Additionally, we have trained two embedding models on 60M English tweets(30M contain positive emoticons, 30M negative ones). The first one was trained by applying word2vec skipgram of window size 5 and filtering words that occur less than 4 times. The dimensionality of the vector was set to 300. The second one was trained using fastText (Bojanowski et al., 2016). The dimensionality of the vector was set to 300.

Similarly, we used two publicly available pretrained embedding models in the Arabic version of our system and trained two. The first one is the model Arabic-SKIP-G300, provided by (Zahran et al., 2015). Arabic-SKIP-G300 was trained on a large corpus of Arabic text collected from different sources such as Arabic Wikipedia, Arabic Gigaword Corpus, Ksucorpus, King Saud University Corpus, Microsoft crawled Arabic Corpus, etc. It contains 300-dimensional vectors for 6M words and phrases. The second one is Twitter-SG-AraVec (Soliman et al., 2017), which was trained using word2vec skipgram algorithm on 66M Arabic tweets and 1B tokens. The dimensionality of the vector was set to 300.

Our embedding models were trained on the distant supervision corpus (about 16M Arabic tweets) provided by the organizers. We were able to find about 12M tweets. Again, similar to our English embeddings, we trained the two Arabic embedding models.

3 System Description

This section explains the proposed system, whose architecture is shown in Figure 1. First, we preprocess the tweets (Subsection 3.1). Afterwards, we pass them to the N-Channels ConvNet and the XGboost regressors (Subsections 3.2 and 3.3). Finally we ensemble the output of the two systems to get the final result as described in subsection 3.4. The proposed system is also used as feature extractor to train an ordinal Decision Tree classifier. as described in subsection 3.5.

3.1 Preprocessing

Some standard pre-processing methods were applied on the tweets:

- *Normalization*: Each tweet in English was converted to the lowercase. URLs and user-

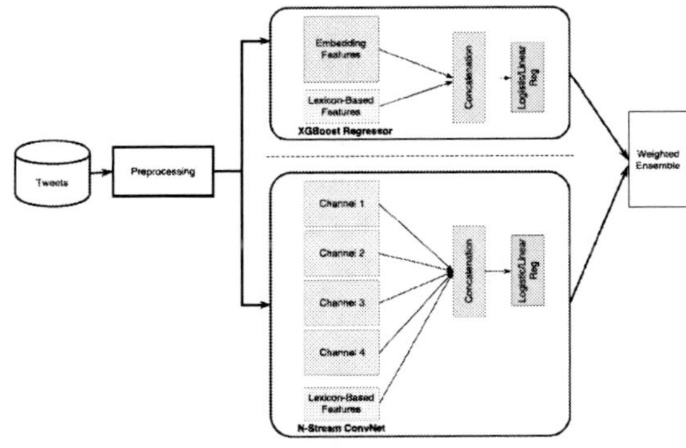

Figure 1: System Architecture.

names were omitted. Non-Arabic letters were removed from each tweet in the Arabic-language sets. Words with repeated letters (i.e. elongated) are corrected.

- *Tokenization*: All English-language tweets were tokenized using Ark Tweet NLP (Gimpel et al., 2011), while all Arabic-language tweets were tokenized using Stanford Tokenizer (Green and Manning, 2010).

3.2 N-Channels ConvNet

Convolutional Neural Networks (ConvNets) have achieved remarkable results in computer vision and speech recognition tasks in recent years. The next subsection explains the architecture of our proposed ConvNet.

3.2.1 Architecture

The N-Channels ConvNet model architecture, shown in the bottom box in figure 1, is inspired by Inception-Net (Szegedy et al., 2016) and the CNN proposed by (Kim, 2014). It is composed of multiple channels followed by a logistic regressor. Figure 2 shows the channel architecture. The input to each channel is a sequence of words $w_1, w_2, ...w_n$ where n is the number of words. We pass the input through an embedding layer to map each word w_i into a real-valued vector. Each channel has its own embedding layer which is initialized by a specific pre-trained embedding model. We use five channels with the four pre-trained embedding models described in subsection 2.2 and a character based one. The result from the embedding layer is a matrix $n \times d_c$ where d_c is the vector dimension. This matrix is passed to a projection or pre-activation layer. The projection layer is nothing but a fully-connected or dense layer whereas the

pre-activation layer can be any non-linear function such rectified linear unit (ReLU). Afterward, we feed the projected matrix to three Conv1D. Each one has a different kernel (1, 2, and 3) and 200 filters. To get more details about the architecture of this Conv1D please check (Kim, 2014). We pass the output of each Conv1D through a global max-pooling layer which produces a vector with dimensionality of 200. Finally, the three vectors are concatenated. This yields a vector with dimensionality of 600 that represents the tweet (i.e. the input sequence of words).

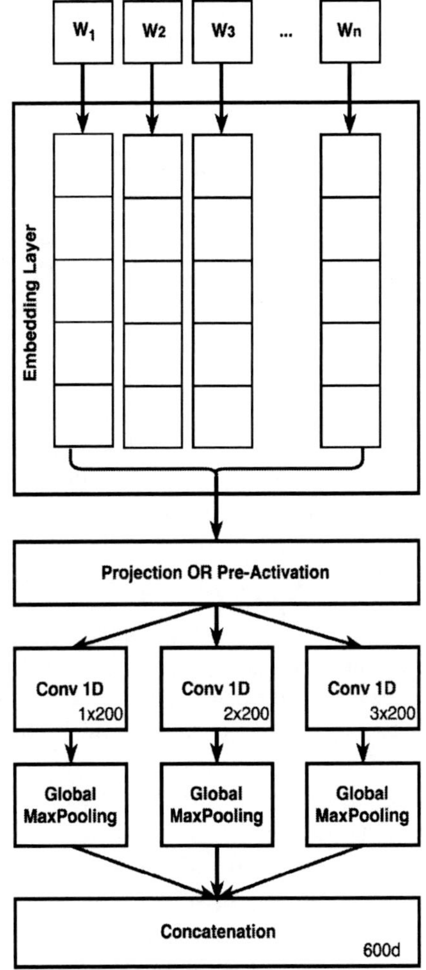

Figure 2: Channel Architecture.

Finally, the outputs of all channels are concatenated with a lexicon-based vector (see next section) and fed to a single sigmoid neuron which gives the intensity of the emotion/valence.

3.2.2 Training

The proposed model was trained by minimizing the mean squared error between the real and predicted intensities. The optimization was done by applying back-propagation through layers via minibatch gradient descent. The training parameters were the following: batch size of 32, 100 epochs and Adam optimization method with learning rate of 0.001, $\beta_1 = 0.9$ and $\beta_2 = 0.999$ and $\epsilon = 10^{-9}$. To prevent the over-fitting, we used dropout and early stopping methods.

3.3 XGBoost Regressor

XGBoost (Chen and Guestrin, 2016) has become a widely used and really popular tool among Data Scientists in industry, as it shows great performance on large-scale problems. It is a highly flexible and versatile tool that can work through most regression, classification and ranking problems as well as user-built objective functions.

We trained an XGBoost regressor to give the intensity of the emotion/valence based on the two types of features explained in the next subsection.

3.3.1 Features

Each tweet is represented with a vector by concatenating the following two feature vectors:

Lexicon Features: For each lexicon, we used the sum of the scores provided by the lexicon for each word in the tweet. Let L denote the set of lexicons and $f_i^l(w)$ the score of the word w based on the feature i in the lexicon l (note that some lexicons have only one feature like the sentiment score and some of them have multiple features like anger emotion score, positive score, etc). Then, the set of features that represent a given tweet T and a lexicon $l \in L$ can be obtained as follows:

$$V_{T,l} = \forall_{f_i^l \in F_l} \sum_{w \in T} f_i^l(w) \qquad (1)$$

Here, F_l denotes the set of features in lexicon l.

Embedding Features: We used the *sum* pooling function to obtain the tweet representation in the embedding space. More formally, let us consider an embedding matrix $E \in \mathbb{R}^{d \times |V|}$ and a tweet $T = w_1, w_2, ..., w_n$, where d is the dimension size, $|V|$ is the length of the vocabulary (i.e. the number of words in the embedding model), w_i is i-th the word in the tweet and n is the number of words. First, each word w_i is substituted by the corresponding vector v_i^j in the matrix E where j is the index of the word w_i in the vocabulary. This step ends with the matrix $W \in \mathbb{R}^{d \times n}$. The vector $V_{T,E}$ that represents the tweet T is computed by aggregating the matrix W. This aggregation is done by taking the summation over its columns. The sum spooling function is an element-wise function, and it converts texts with various lengths into a fixed-length vector allowing to capture the information throughout the entire text.

3.3.2 Training

The XGBoost regressor has some parameters that need to be tuned. Table 1 shows the values of each parameter we chose for the different emotions. All those values were chosen using the grid-search on the development sets.

	P	# Est.	S	M	O
Eng.	Anger	300	0.75	5	Logistic
	Fear	300	0.75	5	Linear
	Sadness	300	0.75	5	Logistic
	Joy	300	0.75	7	Linear
	Valence	300	0.75	5	Linear
Ara.	Anger	200	0.9	9	Logistic
	Fear	200	0.9	5	Logistic
	Sadness	200	0.9	5	Logistic
	Joy	200	0.9	5	Logistic
	Valence	200	0.9	9	Logistic

Table 1: The XGBoost regressors parameters. #Est. refers to the number of estimators, S is the subsample, M is the maximum depth and O refers to the objective function.

3.4 Ensemble

We combined the results of the two systems described above with the intention of improving the performance and increasing the generalizability of the final system. We used the weighted average method to achieve that. Let r_1 and r_2 respectively denote the output of the XGBoost regressor and the N-Channels ConvNet system. The final output r was obtained as follows:

$$r = \alpha * r_1 + (1 - \alpha) * r_2; \quad \alpha \in [0, 1] \qquad (2)$$

Table 2 shows the value of α for each individual model. All these values were obtained by grid search on the development set.

3.5 Decision Tree for Ordinal Classification Tasks

To solve the problem of ordinal classification we simply used the proposed model as feature extrac-

	Emotion	α
	Anger	0.3
	Fear	0.5
Eng.	Sadness	0.6
	Joy	0.2
	Valence	0.6
	Anger	0.5
	Fear	0.0
Ara.	Sadness	0.5
	Joy	0.4
	Valence	0.7

Table 2: The value of α for each individual model.

tor and trained a Decision Tree. The idea is to use the emotion/intensity as input feature and use rules generated from the Decision Tree to get the appropriate class. Figure 3 shows as an example the Decision Tree classifier of the *fear* emotion.

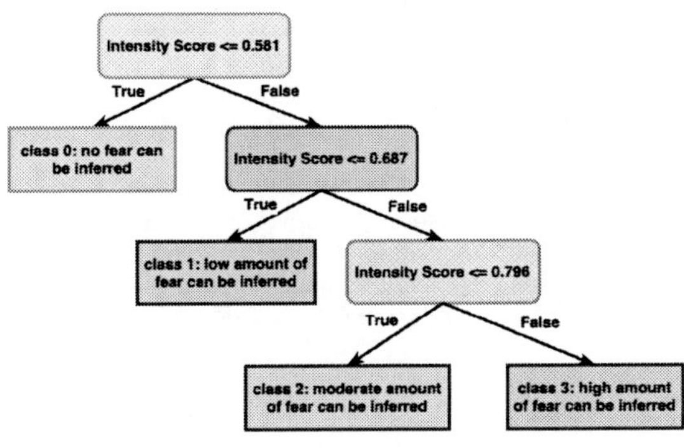

Figure 3: An example of a decision tree classifier.

4 Results

We trained and validated our models on the training and validation sets provided by the organizers. More details about the data and the evaluation metrics can be found in (Mohammad et al., 2018; Mohammad and Kiritchenko, 2018).

Tables 3 and 4 show the results of the emotion and valence intensity regression tasks of our two systems and their combination (the ensemble model). It also shows the baseline results. The evaluation metrics are the Pearson correlation for all samples and for a subset of the test set that includes only those tweets with intensity score greater or equal to 0.5. The values in the tables show the superiority of the N-Channels ConvNet over the XGBoost regressor. For instance, the results of the English version of the emotion

intensity task show that the N-Channels ConvNet outperforms the XGBoost regressor by 5.9% with respect to macro-avg measure. The performance of N-Channels Convnet is very close to the ensemble model. The improvement is only 1.2%. The improvement in the final system of the Arabic version is very small (0.3%). The results of the Pearson correlation of samples whose intensity score is greater or equal to 0.5 show that our system can be used as a classifier. This conclusion is confirmed by the results of the ordinal classification tasks, shown in Tables 5 and 6.

As we described in subsection 3.5, our approach to design a system to solve the ordinal classification tasks was to use the intensity score as input feature to train a Decision Tree. During the inference phase we used our system to produce the intensity score for the new (unseen) samples (i.e. use it as feature extractor). Thus, the performance in this phase heavily relies on the performance of the proposed system. This is clearly shown in the results reported in tables 5 and 6. For example, our system gives very good results in the valence intensity regression task for both the English and Arabic versions (the Pearson correlation is 0.828 for both). This affects positively the performance of our system for the valence ordinal classification tasks (the Pearson correlation is about 0.80 for both).

5 Conclusion

We have presented an ensemble model of two different approaches. The first one, called N-Channels ConvNet, is a deep learning approach whereas the second one is an XGBoost regressor based on a set of embedding and lexicons-based features. The ensemble technique helped to improve the performance of the final model in all subtasks. We have realized that The N-Channels ConvNet gives a performance very close to the ensemble model. This observation confirms the fact that deep learning models, and especially ConvNets, have achieved remarkable results in many fields such as computer vision, speech recognition and natural language processing. Distant Supervision is an approach of transfer learning which aims to train a model on a large amount of semi-labeled data and use it as a pre-trained model for training another model on a small amount of fully-labeled data. This approach has been shown to be very efficient. Thus, the authors are considering

		Pearson (all instances)					Pearson5 (gold in 0.5-1)				
		macro-avg	anger	fear	joy	sadness	macro-avg	anger	fear	joy	sadness
Eng.	N-Channels ConvNet	0.712	0.713	0.725	0.718	0.692	0.538	0.575	0.502	0.519	0.555
	XGBoost Regressor	0.653	0.674	0.644	0.625	0.668	0.503	0.563	0.455	0.437	0.555
	Ensemble Model	0.724	0.731	0.733	0.722	0.711	0.560	0.606	0.522	0.525	0.587
	SVM Unigrams	0.520	0.526	0.525	0.575	0.453	0.396	0.455	0.302	0.476	0.350
	Random Baseline	-0.008	-0.018	0.024	-0.058	0.020	-0.048	-0.088	-0.011	-0.032	-0.059
Ara.	N-Channels ConvNet	0,655	0.639	0.628	0.705	0.648	0,516	0.473	0.605	0.465	0.520
	XGBoost Regressor	0.596	0.494	0.540	0.713	0.637	0.464	0.376	0.492	0.449	0.540
	Ensemble Model	0.667	0.627	0.627	0.738	0.675	0.533	0.479	0.604	0.490	0.560
	SVM Unigrams	0.455	0.406	0.435	0.530	0.450	0.353	0.344	0.366	0.332	0.367
	Random Baseline	0.013	-0.006	0.016	-0.010	0.052	-0.007	0.002	0.007	0.011	-0.048

Table 3: EI-reg task results.

		Pearson	Pearson5
Eng.	N-Channels ConvNet	0.825	0.645
	XGBoost Regressor	0.768	0.598
	Ensemble Model	0.828	0.658
	SVM Unigrams	0.585	0.449
	Random Baseline	0.031	0.012
Ara.	N-Channels ConvNet	0.817	0.550
	XGBoost Regressor	0.774	0.571
	Ensemble Model	0.828	0.578
	SVM Unigrams	0.571	0.423
	Random Baseline	-0.052	0.022

Table 4: V-reg task results.

the possibility of using this technique to improve the proposed system.

Acknowledgment

This work was partially supported by URV Research Support Funds (2017PFR-URV-B2-61 and Martí i Franqués PhD grant).

References

Christos Baziotis, Nikos Pelekis, and Christos Doulkeridis. 2017. Datastories at semeval-2017 task 4: Deep lstm with attention for message-level and topic-based sentiment analysis. In *Proceedings of the 11th International Workshop on Semantic Evaluation (SemEval-2017)*, pages 747–754, Vancouver, Canada. Association for Computational Linguistics.

Piotr Bojanowski, Edouard Grave, Armand Joulin, and Tomas Mikolov. 2016. Enriching word vectors with subword information. *arXiv preprint arXiv:1607.04606*.

Tianqi Chen and Carlos Guestrin. 2016. XGBoost: A Scalable Tree Boosting System. *CoRR*, abs/1603.02754.

Yoonjung Choi and Janyce Wiebe. 2014. +/-effectwordnet: Sense-level lexicon acquisition for opinion inference. In *Proceedings of the 2014 Conference on Empirical Methods in Natural Language Processing (EMNLP)*, pages 1181–1191.

Kevin Gimpel, Nathan Schneider, Brendan O'Connor, Dipanjan Das, Daniel Mills, Jacob Eisenstein, Michael Heilman, Dani Yogatama, Jeffrey Flanigan, and Noah A. Smith. 2011. Part-of-speech Tagging for Twitter: Annotation, Features, and Experiments. In *Proceedings of the 49th Annual Meeting of the Association for Computational Linguistics: Human Language Technologies: Short Papers - Volume 2*, HLT '11, pages 42–47, Stroudsburg, PA, USA. Association for Computational Linguistics.

Spence Green and Christopher D Manning. 2010. Better arabic parsing: Baselines, evaluations, and analysis. In *Proceedings of the 23rd International Conference on Computational Linguistics*, pages 394–402. Association for Computational Linguistics.

Minqing Hu and Bing Liu. 2004. Mining and summarizing customer reviews. In *Proceedings of the tenth ACM SIGKDD international conference on Knowledge discovery and data mining*, pages 168–177. ACM.

Mohammed Jabreel and Antonio Moreno. 2016. Sentirich: Sentiment analysis of tweets based on a rich set of features. In *Artificial Intelligence Research and Development - Proceedings of the 19th International Conference of the Catalan Association for Artificial Intelligence, Barcelona, Catalonia, Spain, October 19-21, 2016*, pages 137–146.

Yoon Kim. 2014. Convolutional neural networks for sentence classification. *arXiv preprint arXiv:1408.5882*.

Tomas Mikolov, Kai Chen, Greg Corrado, and Jeffrey Dean. 2013. Efficient estimation of word representations in vector space. *arXiv preprint arXiv:1301.3781*.

Saif Mohammad, Svetlana Kiritchenko, and Xiaodan Zhu. 2013. NRC-Canada: Building the State-of-the-Art in Sentiment Analysis of Tweets. In *Proceedings of the seventh international workshop on Semantic Evaluation Exercises (SemEval-2013)*, Atlanta, Georgia, USA.

		Pearson					Kappa				
		macro-avg	anger	fear	joy	sadness	macro-avg	anger	fear	joy	sadness
Eng.	Our system	0.633 (6)	0.651 (5)	0.595 (2)	0.651 (8)	0.636 (6)	0.608 (3)	0.619 (4)	0.574 (3)	0.607 (10)	0.632 (4)
	SVM Unigrams	0.394 (26)	0.382 (27)	0.355 (26)	0.469 (26)	0.370 (29)	0.385 (26)	0.375 (26)	0.331 (25)	0.465 (25)	0.370 (28)
	Random Baseline	-0.016 (37)	-0.062 (38)	0.047 (33)	0.014 (35)	-0.061 (37)	-0.017 (38)	-0.058 (38)	0.035 (32)	0.014 (35)	-0.057 (37)
Ara.	Our system	0.574 (2)	0.572 (1)	0.529 (2)	0.634 (1)	0.563 (3)	0.542 (2)	0.547 (1)	0.516 (2)	0.588 (2)	0.518 (3)
	SVM Unigrams	0.542 (2)	0.315 (6)	0.281 (7)	0.281 (6)	0.396 (6)	0.299 (6)	0.276 (7)	0.249 (6)	0.385 (6)	0.287 (7)
	Random Baseline	0.006 (12)	-0.057 (12)	-0.019 (12)	0.008 (12)	0.092 (11)	0.006 (12)	-0.057 (14)	-0.019 (12)	0.007 (12)	0.091 (10)

Table 5: EI-oc task results.

		Pearson	Kappa
Eng.	Our system	0.796	0.791
	SVM Unigrams	0.509	0.504
	Random Baseline	-0.010	-0.010
Ara.	Ensemble Model	0.809	0.783
	SVM Unigrams	0.471	0.470
	Random Baseline	0.011	0.011

Table 6: V-oc task results.

Saif Mohammad, Mohammad Salameh, and Svetlana Kiritchenko. 2016. Sentiment lexicons for arabic social media. In *Proceedings of 10th edition of the the Language Resources and Evaluation Conference (LREC)*, Portorož, Slovenia.

Saif M. Mohammad. 2016. Sentiment analysis: Detecting valence, emotions, and other affectual states from text. In Herb Meiselman, editor, *Emotion Measurement*. Elsevier.

Saif M. Mohammad and Felipe Bravo-Márquez. 2017. WASSA-2017 shared task on emotion intensity. *CoRR*, abs/1708.03700.

Saif M. Mohammad, Felipe Bravo-Marquez, Mohammad Salameh, and Svetlana Kiritchenko. 2018. Semeval-2018 Task 1: Affect in tweets. In *Proceedings of International Workshop on Semantic Evaluation (SemEval-2018)*, New Orleans, LA, USA.

Saif M. Mohammad and Svetlana Kiritchenko. 2018. Understanding emotions: A dataset of tweets to study interactions between affect categories. In *Proceedings of the 11th Edition of the Language Resources and Evaluation Conference*, Miyazaki, Japan.

Finn rup Nielsen. 2011. A new anew: Evaluation of a word list for sentiment analysis in microblogs. *CoRR*, abs/1103.2903.

Mickael Rouvier and Benoit Favre. 2016. Sensei-lif at semeval-2016 task 4: Polarity embedding fusion for robust sentiment analysis. In *Proceedings of the 10th International Workshop on Semantic Evaluation (SemEval 2016), San Diego, US*.

Abu Bakr Soliman, Kareem Eissa, and Samhaa R. El-Beltagy. 2017. Aravec: A set of arabic word embedding models for use in arabic nlp. *Procedia Computer Science*, 117:256 – 265. Arabic Computational Linguistics.

Philip Stone, Dexter C Dunphy, Marshall S Smith, and DM Ogilvie. 1968. The general inquirer: A computer approach to content analysis. *Journal of Regional Science*, 8(1):113–116.

Christian Szegedy, Sergey Ioffe, and Vincent Vanhoucke. 2016. Inception-v4, Inception-ResNet and the Impact of Residual Connections on Learning. *CoRR*, abs/1602.07261.

Mohamed A Zahran, Ahmed Magooda, Ashraf Y Mahgoub, Hazem Raafat, Mohsen Rashwan, and Amir Atyia. 2015. Word representations in vector space and their applications for arabic. In *International Conference on Intelligent Text Processing and Computational Linguistics*, pages 430–443. Springer.

CENTEMENT at SemEval-2018 Task 1: Classification of Tweets using Multiple Thresholds with Self-correction and Weighted Conditional Probabilities

Tariq Ahmad
School of Computer Science
University of Manchester
Oxford Road, Manchester
M13 9PL, U.K.
tariq.ahmad@postgrad
.manchester.ac.uk

Allan Ramsay
School of Computer Science
University of Manchester
Oxford Road, Manchester
M13 9PL, U.K.
allan.ramsay@
manchester.ac.uk

Hanady Ahmed
CAS, Arabic Department
Qatar University
2713, Al Hala St
Doha, Qatar
hanadyma@
qu.edu.qa

Abstract

In this paper we present our contribution to SemEval-2018, a classifier for classifying multi-label emotions of Arabic and English tweets. We attempted "Affect in Tweets", specifically Task E-c: Detecting Emotions (multi-label classification). Our method is based on preprocessing the tweets and creating word vectors combined with a self correction step to remove noise. We also make use of emotion specific thresholds. The final submission was selected upon the best performance achieved, selected when using a range of thresholds. Our system was evaluated on the Arabic and English datasets provided for the task by the competition organisers, where it ranked 2nd for the Arabic dataset (out of 14 entries) and 12th for the English dataset (out of 35 entries).

1 Introduction

Social network platforms such as Facebook, LinkedIn and Twitter are now at the hub of everything we do. Twitter is one of the most popular social network platforms; as recently as 2013 an incredible 21% of the global internet population used Twitter actively on a monthly basis (globalwebindex, accessed 05/2016). Twitter is used by celebrities, movie stars, politicians, sports stars and everyday people. Every day, millions of users share their opinions about themselves, news, sports, movies and many many other topics. This makes platforms like Twitter rich sources of data for public opinion mining and sentiment analysis (Pak and Paroubek, 2010). However, although these corpora are rich, they are somewhat noisy because tweets can be informal, misspelt and contain slang, emoticons (Albogamy and Ramsay, 2015) and made-up words. Furthermore, Arabic tweets have the added complication of dialects in which the same words or expressions can have different connotations.

Multi-label classification of tweets is a classification problem where tweets are assigned to two or more classes. It is considered more complex than traditional classification tasks because the classifier has to predict several classes.

There has been much work in the areas of sentiment detection (Rosenthal et al., 2017), emotion intensity (Mohammad and Bravo-Marquez, 2017) and emotion categorisation (Hasan et al., 2014). Sentiment analysis aims to classify tweets into positive, negative, and neutral categories, emotion intensity is determining the intensity or degree of an emotion felt by the speaker and emotion categorisation is the classification of tweets based on their emotions. The most commonly used classification techniques are Naive Bayes and Support Vector Machines (SVM). Some researchers report that SVMs (Barbosa and Feng, 2010) perform better while others support Naive Bayes (Pak and Paroubek, 2010). Furthermore, sophisticated techniques such as deep neural networks have also been proposed but such techniques are rarely used by non-experts of machine learning in practice (Sarker and Gonzalez, 2017) and they also take a long time to train.

We propose a simple and effective method to classify tweets that performs reasonably well. Our system does not make use of any lexicons or stop word lists and is quick to train.

2 Methods

The SemEval Task E-c requires the classification of tweets into either a neutral emotion or one of eleven emotions (Mohammad et al., 2018). Datasets for tweets are made available in three languages; Arabic, English and Spanish. We focus firstly on Arabic and then English because this links well with our existing work. Datasets from previous SemEval tasks are also available if

Proceedings of the 12th International Workshop on Semantic Evaluation (SemEval-2018), pages 200–204
New Orleans, Louisiana, June 5–6, 2018. ©2018 Association for Computational Linguistics

required. We use the SemEval-2018 development and training data for training our system, with no external resources such as sentiment dictionaries or other corpora. We use the training set to compute scores for each of the classes in conjunction with a self correction stage and a multi-threshold stage to obtain an optimal set of scores. Apart from the preprocessing steps, notably stemming, we use exactly the same machinery for the two languages. We now briefly discuss our approach.

Preprocessing. Tweets are preprocessed by lowercasing (English tweets only), identifying and replacing emojis with emojis identifiers, tokenising and then stemming. We developed two tokenisers; one that is NLTK based and does not preserve hashtags, emoticons, punctuation and other content and one that is "tweet-friendly" because it preserves these items. Emojis cause us technical problems due to their surrogate-pair nature so we replace emojis with emoji identifiers (e.g. _45_). We also separate out contiguous emojis because we want, for example, the individual emojis in a group of repeating unhappy face emojis to be recognised, and processed, as being the same emoji as a single unhappy face emoji. We remove usernames because we believe they are noise since, by and large, they will not reappear in the test set, are not helpful to us and if not removed will compromise our ability to detect useful information. Arabic tweets are stemmed using a stemmer developed specifically for Arabic tweets by Albogamy and Ramsay (Albogamy and Ramsay, 2016). English tweets are stemmed by taking the shortest result from Morphy (Fellbaum, 1998) when tokens are stemmed as nouns, verbs, adjectives and adverbs. Although there are surprisingly few examples of these, we believe that multi-word hashtags, joined by underscore or a dash, also contain useful information so we leave the hashtag as is but also take a copy of the hashtag and split it into its constituent words. This is so that where possible we improve the quality of information in the tweet. Stop word lists are not used at any stage. We debated using stop words vs insignificant words and, as in our previous work (Ahmad and Ramsay, 2016), we prefer to let our algorithms exclude these words. We do however remove less common words on the grounds that if they do not appear very often then we are unlikely to learn anything from them. The

English training dataset contains approximately 6300 distinct words after preprocessing, we find that taking the top 2500 of these gives us the most common words and the best results.

Our approach is not to collect scores for individual emotions, instead we collect scores relative to the other emotions. Constructing scores in this manner allows us to observe that words such as "blessed" are much more significant for emotions such as "joy", "love" and "optimism" than they are for "anger" and "anticipation". Words that are insignificant will have small scores, words that are significant will have large scores and by using a varying threshold we can determine a best set.

Base set. Every tweet in the training dataset is tokenised and we count how many tweets each token in the tweet occurs in. We also remove singletons and calculate an IDF for each token. We iterate through the tokens for each tweet to create a base set of scores and obtain a count of how many times each token occurs in each of the 11 emotions as well as a count of the total number of tokens in each emotion. In a later stage we iterate over a range of thresholds, this base set is the starting point in each and is modified by the various processes as described below.

Conditional probabilities. We now use this base set to create a set of emotion probabilities for each token. One, common, way of using probabilities is in conjunction with Bayes Theorem. However, this does not seem to work very well for this task hence we perform the following steps. We calculate the probability of each token appearing in each emotion using $P(T|E)$. We do this only on the top 2500 most important tokens in the dataset, i.e. those with the highest IDF scores. We normalise these probabilities by dividing each value by the sum of all the probabilities for this token for all emotions. We get an average value for these values and subtract this from each of the scores to calculate the distance from the mean. This is, essentially, a local IDF step to ensure that if a token is equally common for all emotions then we do not allow it to contribute to any of them, and if it is below the overall average for a emotion we want it to be allowed to vote against it.

We want to assign extra weight to tokens that have very skewed distributions, hence we multiply each score by the standard deviation. This emphasises the contribution of such tokens to the emotion and allows us to remove unhelpful tokens. In this way we create a set of emotion scores for each token for every emotion.

Self-correction. We want to remove tokens that we have incorrectly assigned to emotions. We classify each tweet to determine which emotions it demonstrates and we identify the tokens that led us to these conclusions. A tweet is classified for each emotion by adding the scores for each token for each emotion. These scores are normalised and compared to a threshold t. If the value is less than t we deduce the tweet did not demonstrate the emotion, otherwise it did demonstrate the emotion. We are unsure what a good threshold is so we use a range of values for t from 0 to 1 (in steps of 0.1) to create score sets. We calculate the Jaccard for each of these and use the best one of these for classification. This approach is based on Brills (Brill, 1995) suggestion that one should attempt to learn from ones own mistakes.

As each tweet is classified we compare our prediction to the gold standard. For the ones that we predict correctly we increment a counter for each token against the correctly classified emotion. Similarly, for the ones where we failed to classify the tweet correctly we decrement the counter for each token against the incorrectly classified emotion. When all tweets have been classified we examine these counters. For each token, if we have an overall negative score for an emotion we deduce that the token is unhelpful in classifying tweets for that emotion and we downplay its significance in further calculations. Using this technique we are able to remove tokens such as "terrifying" from contributing to emotions such as "love". We have tried repeating this process multiple times, but we find that beyond one iteration the improvement is insignificant. A possible explanation for this may be because the actual numbers of tokens that are removed are quite small; 1% for Arabic and 5% for English.

Per-emotion thresholds. The raw data for each emotion is different and, hence, we find that a single fixed threshold across all emotions produces poor results. We therefore try a range of thresholds from 0 to 1 in increments of 0.1 to classify tweets, using the same mechanism described above, but this time on an emotion-by-emotion basis to generate an individual threshold for each emotion.

SemEval results. We classify the training data using our sets of scores and per-emotion thresholds. We identify the set with the best Jaccard score and use it to classify the test data to generate our eventual submission file.

2.1 Other Strategies

Increased training data. We believe that having more training data might improve our classifier. One of the obvious places to get more data is from the datasets for some of the other tasks, specifically EI-reg and EI-oc. A key problem with this data is that both of these tasks only supply datasets for anger, fear, joy and sadness. The EI-reg dataset is marked up with a per-tweet intensity value between 0-1 that represents the mental state of the tweeter. The EI-oc dataset tweets are marked up with one of four ordinal classes (0,1,2,3). To expand our training dataset we extract tweets with values of 0.5 and above from the EI-reg datasets and tweets with a value of 3 from the EI-oc dataset. The best Jaccard score we obtain with this expanded dataset is 0.417 (English). When we extract tweets with values of 0.9 or above from the EI-reg dataset we improve the quality of tweets, at the cost of decreasing the number of tweets extracted, and this slightly improves our Jaccard to 0.429.

Similarly, the competition organisers also make available a corpus of 100 million English tweet IDs. We download 10,000 of these filtered on words that we believe are representative of the emotions we are looking for e.g. "angry", "elated", "trusting". A serious weakness with this technique, however, is that the accuracy of this data is compromised, we therefore classify this data using our classifier. We then combine this data with the standard English dataset and classify it again. We do not want this data to be more relevant than the real data, so we weight down the scores from this data. The best Jaccard score we obtain with this expanded dataset is 0.430.

Latent semantic analysis (LSA). Latent Semantic Analysis (LSA) is a theory and method for extracting and representing the contextual-usage meaning of words by statistical computations applied to a large corpus of text (Landauer and

Tweet tokeniser	Split hashtags	Stem	Tune	Multi-threshold	Jaccard (AR)	Jaccard (EN)
					0.324	0.340
✓					0.318	0.340
✓	✓				0.333	0.349
✓	✓	✓			0.342	0.401
✓	✓	✓	✓		0.370	0.431
✓	✓	✓	✓	✓	**0.452**	**0.455**

Table 1: Results.

Dumais, 1997). Essentially, to improve our classifier we need to improve the quality of our tweets. We use LSA to find words in tweets that are similar to other words, e.g. "car" and "automobile". We do not have the computing power to do this on a per-tweet basis so we do this on a per-emotion basis. The concepts we find, however, are not very reliable, e.g. "blessed" and "happiness". We expand our tweets with these words but find that this does not improve our scores. A possible explanation for this might be because of the relatively small numbers of tweets in the datasets.

Duplicate tweets. We note that there are tweets in the English dataset that are semantically similar, e.g. *"You offend me, @Tansorma"* and *"@SunandBeachBum 'you people' infuriate me!"*. It may be possible to use *clustering* (Sarker and Gonzalez, 2017) to relate tweets like these as a means to removing duplicates. We further note that there are many cases of tweets that differ only by hashtags or emojis, e.g. *"@britishairways term 5 security queues at arrivals"* and *"@britishairways term 5 security queues at arrivals #shocking"*. A further study could assess the impact of using Minimum Edit Distance (Wagner and Fischer, 1974) on this later data to improve the quality of the dataset.

Emoticon weighting. Emoticons have proved crucial in the automated emotion classification of informal texts (Novak et al., 2015). To increase their significance we double their raw count values. We find that this increases the accuracy of our classifier by 0.44% for both Arabic and English.

Word frequencies. We try to use the word frequency as an extra weight to further dampen the contribution of words that are low frequency because low frequency words do not contribute very much. However, because we have earlier taken only the 2500 commonest words we find that this does not improve our scores.

2.2 Computing Resources

The system was written in Python on a MacBook Pro, 2.7 GHz Intel Core i5, 8 GB RAM. The training and classification phase takes approximately 15 minutes.

3 Results, Comments and Conclusion

We described a self-correcting, multi-threshold, classifier to solve the problem of multi-label classification of tweets.

We find that due to the nature of the data it is difficult to accurately distinguish between emotions such as "joy" and "love" because many of the words that score highly for "joy" also score highly for "love", e.g. "rejoice", "birthday" and "cheerful". Consequently when a tweet is labelled as "love" it is highly likely that it will also be labelled as "joy". We find similar issues with "anger" and "disgust", although not to the same extent, because words like "shit" and "hate" score highly for both emotions. Overall, we believe that we score much higher on emotions such as "anger", "joy", "love" and "disgust", than on "trust" "anticipation", "optimism" and "pessimism".

Our results, given in Table 1, show that although processes such as lowercasing, tokenising and stemming do contribute, the tuning stage and the introduction of multiple thresholds yield the biggest improvements. This is because removing words which are implicit in the classifier making wrong decisions and allowing each emotion to have its own threshold are obviously sensible things to do.

One unanticipated finding was that our tweet-friendly tokeniser has an adverse effect decreasing the Jaccard score when it is used. A possible explanation for this is that the simple tokeniser removes # and @ symbols, thus modifying hashtags such as "#sleep" into "sleep" and allowing them to combine with the word "sleep" in other tweets. On the other hand the tweet-friendly tokeniser preserves the "#sleep" hashtag and it therefore cannot combine with the word "sleep". We want the best of both worlds so we preserve our hashtag but also take a copy and split it into its constituent words.

Contrary to expectations, the performance improvement gained from using our Arabic stemmer is disappointingly low at just 2.67%. We believed that our Arabic stemmer would have a bigger impact than demonstrated because the stemmer is aimed at, and specifically developed for, Arabic tweets. In fact our simplistic Morphy English stemmer produced a better improvement of 14.8% for English than our carefully tuned Arabic stemmer did for Arabic.

The scores we achieved put us 2nd for the Arabic dataset and 12th for the English dataset despite the fact that we use no external resources, we simply train on the basis of the SemEval data. We will be carrying out further experiments to see whether adding external resources would give us further improvement.

Acknowledgments

This publication was made possible by the NPRP award [NPRP 7-1334-6-039 PR3] from the Qatar National Research Fund (a member of The Qatar Foundation). The statements made herein are solely the responsibility of the author[s].

References

Apoorv Agarwal, Boyi Xie, Ilia Vovsha, Owen Rambow, and Rebecca Passonneau. 2011. Sentiment analysis of twitter data. In *Proceedings of the workshop on languages in social media*, pages 30–38. Association for Computational Linguistics.

Tariq Ahmad and Allan Ramsay. 2016. Linking tweets to news: Is all news of interest? In *International Conference on Artificial Intelligence: Methodology, Systems, and Applications*, pages 151–161. Springer.

Fahad Albogamy and Allan Ramsay. 2015. POS tagging for arabic tweets. *Recent Advances in Natural Language Processing*, page 1.

Fahad Albogamy and Allan Ramsay. 2016. Unsupervised stemmer for arabic tweets. In *Proceedings of the 2nd Workshop on Noisy User-generated Text (WNUT)*, pages 78–84.

Anil Bandhakavi, Nirmalie Wiratunga, Deepak Padmanabhan, and Stewart Massie. 2017. Lexicon based feature extraction for emotion text classification. *Pattern recognition letters*, 93:133–142.

Luciano Barbosa and Junlan Feng. 2010. Robust sentiment detection on twitter from biased and noisy data. In *Proceedings of the 23rd international conference on computational linguistics: posters*, pages 36–44. Association for Computational Linguistics.

Eric Brill. 1995. Transformation-based error-driven learning and natural language processing: A case study in part-of-speech tagging. *Computational linguistics*, 21(4):543–565.

Christiane Fellbaum. 1998. *WordNet*. Wiley Online Library.

globalwebindex. accessed 05/2016. Twitter now the fastest growing social platform in the world.

Maryam Hasan, Elke Rundensteiner, and Emmanuel Agu. 2014. Emotex: Detecting emotions in twitter messages.

Thomas K Landauer and Susan T Dumais. 1997. A solution to plato's problem: The latent semantic analysis theory of acquisition, induction, and representation of knowledge. *Psychological review*, 104(2):211.

Saif M. Mohammad and Felipe Bravo-Marquez. 2017. Emotion intensities in tweets. In *Proceedings of the sixth joint conference on lexical and computational semantics (*Sem)*, Vancouver, Canada.

Saif M. Mohammad, Felipe Bravo-Marquez, Mohammad Salameh, and Svetlana Kiritchenko. 2018. Semeval-2018 Task 1: Affect in tweets. In *Proceedings of International Workshop on Semantic Evaluation (SemEval-2018)*, New Orleans, LA, USA.

Petra Kralj Novak, Jasmina Smailović, Borut Sluban, and Igor Mozetič. 2015. Sentiment of emojis. *PLOS ONE*, 10(12):1–22.

Alexander Pak and Patrick Paroubek. 2010. Twitter as a corpus for sentiment analysis and opinion mining. In *LREc*, volume 10, pages 1320–1326.

Sara Rosenthal, Noura Farra, and Preslav Nakov. 2017. Semeval-2017 task 4: Sentiment analysis in twitter. In *Proceedings of the 11th International Workshop on Semantic Evaluation (SemEval-2017)*, pages 502–518.

Abeed Sarker and Graciela Gonzalez. 2017. HLP @ UPenn at SemEval-2017 Task 4A: A simple, self-optimizing text classification system combining dense and sparse vectors. In *Proceedings of the 11th International Workshop on Semantic Evaluation (SemEval-2017)*, pages 640–643.

Robert A Wagner and Michael J Fischer. 1974. The string-to-string correction problem. *Journal of the ACM (JACM)*, 21(1):168–173.

Yuan at SemEval-2018 Task 1: Tweets Emotion Intensity Prediction using Ensemble Recurrent Neural Network

Min Wang, Xiaobing Zhou*
School of Information Science and Engineering
Yunnan University, Yunnan, P.R. China
*Corresponding author, zhouxb.cn@gmail.com

Abstract

This paper describes the performing system for SemEval-2018 Task 1 subtask 3 - Given a tweet, determine the intensity of sentiment or valence (V) that best represents the mental state of the tweeter—a real-valued score between 0 (most negative) and 1 (most positive). The proposed system gets features in tweets from the existing emotional dictionary and represents the word using word embedding, then utilizes the joint representations as the inputs of the bidirectional long short-term memory (BiLSTM) to learn and get the regression result. To boost performance we ensem- ble several BiLSTMs together. We ranked 6th in subtask 3 among all teams. Our approach achieves the Pearson(All instances) score 0.836 and Pearson(gold in 0.5-1) score 0.667, we outperform the baseline model of this task by 25.1% and 21.8% of Pearson(All instances) and Pearson(gold in 0.5-1) scores respectively.

1 Introduction

Sentiment analysis (SA) is a field of knowledge which deals with the analysis of people's opinions, sentiments, evaluations, appraisals, attitudes and emotions towards particular entities (Liu, 2012). EmoInt (Mohammad and Bravo-Marquez, 2017) is a shared task hosted by WASSA 2017, aiming to predict the emotion intensity in tweets. SemEval 2018 Task 1 subtask 3 (Mohammad et al, 2018) is similar to EmoInt, however the goal of subtask 3 is to detect valenc-e or sentiment intensity, in which scores are floating point values between 0 and 1, representing low and high intensities of the emotion being expressed, respectively. Obviously we don't know in advance whether twitter's emotional intensity is positive or negative, but in EmoInt task we can determine whether twitter emotions are positive or negative based on one of four datasets: anger, fearness, joy, sadness. This is still a challenging task and remains active areas of research. These setbacks are: extensive usage of hashtags, slang, abbreviations, and emoticons. And tweets are usually typed on mobile devices like mobile phone, laptop or iPad which can result in a substantial amount of typos.

Existing methods for modeling emotion intensity rely vastly on manually constructed lexicons, which contain information about intensity weights for each available word (Mohammad and Bravo-Marquez, 2017a; Neviarouskaya et al., 2007). The intensity for the whole tweet can be deduced by combining individual scores of words, which is easy and ignores the word order compositionality of the language. Building such lexicons is a labour-intensive procedure. We can learn from these models the skills of combining feature extraction and classification or regression stages given a sufficient amount of training data.

Some deep learning methods are used to process the same question. Deep neural archit-ectures for emotion intensity prediction in tweets (Goel et al., 2017) and character- and word-level recurrent neural models for tweet emotion intensity detection (Lakomkin et al., 2017).

205

Proceedings of the 12th International Workshop on Semantic Evaluation (SemEval-2018), pages 205–209
New Orleans, Louisiana, June 5–6, 2018. ©2018 Association for Computational Linguistics

In our work, we firstly clean tweets, then build lexical features and find optimal combinations of features to produce a final vector representation of a tweet, next train a neural network regression model and finally get the tweet's intensity scores. In addition, we adjust our models' parameters and through the ensemble models to get the best performing results.

2 Data cleaning

We use the dataset provided by the official organizers to train our system, there are 1181 labeled training tweets, 449 labeled dev tweets. Test set are unlabeled 17874 tweets and the gold labels were given only after the evaluation period. Before training model or predicting test set we firstly clean the tweets, this is imperative. We utilize the following prep- rocessing steps.

(1) **Hashtags** are crucial markers for determining sentiment. The "#" symbol is removed and the word itself is retained. Eg, a hashtag like "#the_best_one", finally we get "the best one".
(2) **Username mentions,** we replace it with "usename".
(3) **Shortening,** we transform word "don't", "I've", "I'll" et al into "do" "n't", "'ve", "'ll".
(4) **Punctuations,** only "!" and "?" are retained, others like ";" ">" ")" "," "-" are deleted.
(5) **Numerical symbols**, considering that the data in the dataset is relatively standardized and there are few numbers, so we remove the all digitals and only keep English words.
(6) Extra spaces are removed and all words become lowercase letters.

3 Feature Extraction

In order to completely extract features from tweets, we consider two characteristics which are annotated lexicons and pre-trained word embedding.

3.1 Annotated Lexicon

For extracting lexicon features, we follow the procedure as per the baseline system provided in the WASSA Emotion Intensity Task. The knowledge sources that have been used are: MPQA subjective lexicon (Wilson et al., 2005), Bing Liu lexicon (Ding et al., 2008), AFINN (Nielsen, 2011), Sentiment140 (Kiritchenko et al., 2014),

NRC Hashtag Sentiment Lexicon (Mohammad and Kiritchenko, 2015), NRC Hashtag Emotion Association Lexicon (Mohammad et al., 2013), NRC Word-Emotion Association Lexicon(, 2013), NRC-10 Expanded Lexicon (Bravo Marquez et al., 2016) and the SentiWordNet (Esuli and Sebastiani, 2007). Two more features are calculated on the basis of emoticons (obtained from AFINN (Nielsen, 2011)) and negations present in the text. We use several of the above lexicons as following:

• **Emoji Valence (EV):** This is a hand classified lexicon of Unicode emojis, rated on a scale of -5 (negative) to 5 (positive).
• **SentiWordNet (SWN):** Calculates positive and negative sentiment score using SentiWordNet, which is an opinion mining resource available through NLTK.
• **Depeche Mood (DM)** (Staiano and Guerini, 2014): This is a lexicon comprised of about 37,000 unigrams annotated with real-valued scores for the emotional states *afraid, amused, angry, annoyed, don't care, happy, inspired* and *sad*.
• **Emoticon Sentiment Lexicon:** Note that this is a sentiment lexicon drawn from emoticons, and is not an emotion lexicon.
• **NRC-Emoticon-AffLexNegLex-v1.0:** Each line of this lexicon represents a real-valued sentiment score: score = PMI(w, pos) - PMI(w, neg), where PMI stands for Point-wise Mutual Information between a term w and the positive/negative class.
• **NRC-Hashtag-Sentiment-Lexicon-v1.0** (Moh-ammad and Turney, 2013): The lexicon is an association of words with positive (negative) sentiment generated automatically from tweets with sentiment-word hashtags.
• **NRC-Hashtag-Sentiment-AffLexNegLex-1.0:** The same lexicon as Sentiment 140, but here tw- eets with only emotional hashtags are considered during training.

3.2 Word Embedding

The text can be converted into word embedding, which represents each word of the text with a d dimensional vector (Mikolov et al., 2013). Considering that we have to deal with tweets, we use GloVe word embedding trained on 2 billion tweets from twitter (Pennington et al., 2014), vectors of 100, 200 and 300 dimensions are provided as part of the pre- trained model. For this work, we use the 300 dimensional vectors of 42B tokens. We also considered GoogleNews- vectors-negative300 in our expe-riments but the effects was not as good as the GloVe word embedding.

4 Model Training

Based on the application of features extractions and word embedding, we can represent each word in a tweet as a high dimensional space vector, and the dimension of the vector is $d + l$. d represents the dimension of GloVe word embedding 300 and l stands for the length of the additional lexical dictionary. After representing the tweets, we need to train models. Since the task requires the computation of a real valued emotion intensity score for the tweets in the test set, we explore several regression methods. Our system is implemented in Keras and we finally choose the best single BiLSTM model, which contains two layers of BiLSTM following the embedding layer and, we add a dropout layer. Some parameters of our model are: dropout probability 0.25 and 0.5 respectively; units of the BiLSTM layers are 512 and 256 respectively; units of the full connection layer is 256. The complete model structure is shown below Figure 1:

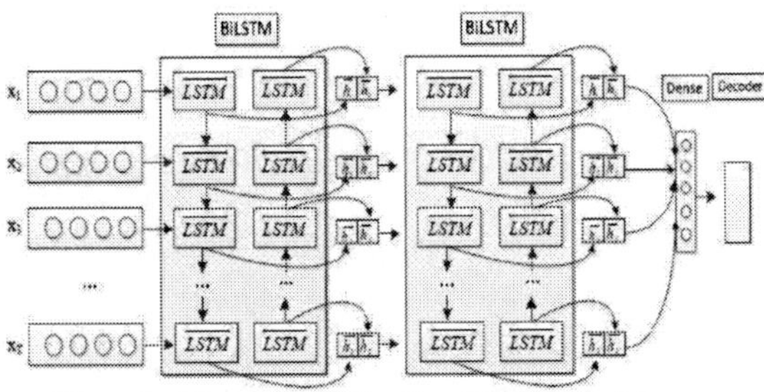

Figure 1: A two layer bidirectional LSTM model.

5 System tuning

When training model on Keras so there only some parameters need to change, we tune the parameters such as the choice of loss function, dropout probability, dimension of the BiLSTM layer. As for feature combination we use all the annotated lexicons mentioned in section 3.1 so

as to control the variables and we don't consider the impact of different dictionary combinations on the results, which may be discussed in the future work. Note that all of our tuning processes are done on the development set, each time we finished a model we record the results. Ensembling of some models is universal used method to improve the performance of the overall system by combining predictions of several classifiers. Our system ensembles ten exactly the same BiLSTMs models and average the results, it turns out that the ensemble result is better than that of a single model. That is to say when we ensemble the model, the weight of each single BiLSTM is the same.

6 Experiment and results

All our experiments have been developed using Keras deep learning library with Theano backend, and with CUDA enabled. And all our experiments are performed on a computer with Intel Core(TM) i3 @3.4GHz 16GB of RAM and GeForce GTX 1060 GPU. After testing many neural network models, we finally find the best results on LSTM and BiLSTM models. Table 1 shows the results of a single layer LSTM changing the loss function and word embedding, we can learn that MAE loss function can get the best result with Glove word embedding, in general the performance on Glove word embedding is better than word2vec embedding. Table 2 shows the results of a single BiLSTM changing the loss function and integrating ten models under different loss functions and different word embedding we can learn that MAPE loss function can get the best result with Glove word embedding, in general the performance on Glove word embedding is better than word2vec embedding. Table 3 is the result of double layers BiLSTM changing the loss function and integrating ten models under different loss functions and different word embedding we can learn that MAPE loss function can get the best result with Glove word embedding, in general the performance on Glove word embedding is better than word2vec embedding.

The system in this subtask are evaluated using the Pearson correlation coefficient, which computes a bivariate linear coefficient, and the secondary evaluation metrics, which is Pearson correlation for a subset of the test set that includes only those tweets with intensity score greater or equal to 0.5. We present the results of the system submitted to the competition leaderboard in Table 4. The score of our system is 0.836 (Pearson) and 0.667 (Pearson gold in 0.5-1). Note that the model we used on the test set is the best model on the development set, i.e., in Table 3 the third line.

Loss function	Pearson score
MSE(Glove)	0.804
MAE(Glove)	0.818
MAPE(Glove)	0.815
MSLE(Glove)	0.801
MSE(w2v)	0.801
MAE(w2v)	0.798
MAPE(w2v)	0.799
MSLE(w2v)	0.786

Table 1: Performance on development dataset. Single layer LSTM under different loss functions and different word embedding.

Loss function	Pearson score
MSE(Glove)	0.799
MAE(Glove)	0.820
MAPE(Glove)	0.822
MSLE(Glove)	0.801
MSE(w2v)	0.797
MAE(w2v)	0.810
MAPE(w2v)	0.799
MSLE(w2v)	0.784

Table 2: Performance on development dataset. Ensemble result of single layer BiLSTM under different loss functions and different word embedding.

Loss function	Pearson score
MSE(Glove)	0.805
MAE(Glove)	0.826
MAPE(Glove)	0.827
MSLE(Glove)	0.806
MSE(w2v)	0.796
MAE(w2v)	0.785
MAPE(w2v)	0.794
MSLE(w2v)	0.783

Table 3: Performance on development data-set. Ensemble result of double layers BiLSTM under different loss functions and different word embedding.

#	Team	P	P (gold 0.5-1)
1	SeerNet	0.873	0.697
2	TCS Research	0.861	0.680
3	PlusEmo2Vec	0.860	0.691
4	NTUA-SLP	0.851	0.688
5	Amobee	0.843	0.644
6	Yuan	0.836	0.667
7	nlpzzx	0.835	0.670

Table 4: Performance on test dataset. Final results in about test set on leaderboard and our system ranks 6th overall.

7 Conclusions

In this paper, we propose a deep learning framework to predict the emotion intensity in tweets. The proposed system is based on two layers BiLSTM and the last layer of model using a linear regression so that we can get the intensity score, which is a consecutive emotional value. Before training model we implement features extraction and represent the tweets by word embedding. Both single model and ensemble model are described in detail with a view of making our experiments replicable. The optimal parameters are mentioned along with our method of bringing the approaches together. Our submitted system beats the baseline system by about 25.1% on the test set. Our source code is in here https://github.com/ynuwm/SemEval-2018

Acknowledgments

This work was supported by the Natural Science Foundations of China No.61463050, No.61702443, No.61762091, the NSF of Yunn an Province No. 2015FB113, the Project of Innovative Research Team of Yunnan Province.

References

Bing Liu. 2012. Sentiment analysis and opinion mining Synthesis Lectures on Human Language Technologies. Morgan &Claypool publishers.

Saif M. Mohammad and Felipe Bravo-Marquez. 2017.WASSA-2017 shared task on emotion intensity. In Proceedings of the Workshop on Computational Approaches to Subjectivity, Sentiment and Social Media Analysis (WASSA).

Copenhagen, Denmark. Santos C D, Tan M, Xiang et al. 2016. Attentive Pooling Networks.

Alena Neviarouskaya, Helmut Prendinger, and Mitsuru Ishizuka. 2007. Textual affect sensing for sociable and expressive online comm- unication. Affective Computing and Intelligent Interaction pages 218–229.

Ozan Irsoy and Claire Cardie. 2014. Opinion mining with deep recurrent neural networks. In the Proceedings of the Conference on EMLNP. pages 720–728.

Richard Socher, Alex Perelygin, Jean Y Wu, Jason Chuang, Christopher D Manning, Andrew Y Ng, and Christopher Potts. 2013. Recursive deep models for semantic compositionality over a sentimenttreebank. In the Proceedings of the Conference on EMLNP. volume 1631, pages 1631–1642.

Theresa Wilson, Janyce Wiebe, and Paul Hoffmann.2005. Recognizing contextual polarity in phraselevel sentiment analysis. In *HLT/EMNLP 2005,Human Language Technology Conference and Conference on Empirical Methods in Natural Language Processing, Proceedings of the Conference, 6- 8 October 2005, Vancouver, British Columbia, Canada.* The Association for Computational Linguistics, pages 347–354.

Finn Arup Nielsen. 2011. A new ANEW: evaluation of a word list for sentiment analysis in microblogs. In Matthew Rowe, Milan Stankovic, Aba-SahDadzie, and Mariann Hardey, editors, *Proceedings of the ESWC2011Workshop on 'Making Sense of Microposts': Big things come in small packages, Heraklion, Crete, Greece, May 30, 2011.* CEUR-WS.org,volume 718 of *CEUR Workshop Proceedings*, pages 93–98.

Mohammad Saif and Svetlana Kiritchenko. 2015. Using hashtags to capture fine emotion categories from tweets. Computational Inte- lligence 31(2):301–326.

Saif M. Mohammad and Peter D. Turney. 2013. Crowd sourcing a word-emotion association lexicon 29(3):436–465.

Jacopo Staiano and Marco Guerini. 2014. Depeche mood: A lexicon for emotion analysis from crowd-annotated news. *arXiv preprint arXiv:1405.1605* .

Saif M Mohammad and Peter D Turney. 2013. Crowdsourcing a word–emotion association lexicon. *Computational Intelligence* 29(3):436–465.

Jeffrey Pennington, Richard Socher, and Christopher D. Manning. 2014. Glove: Global vectors for word representation. In *Empirical Methods in Natural Language Processing (EMNLP)*. Pages 1532–1543.

Saif M. Mohammad, Felipe Bravo-Marquez, Moh-ammad Salameh, and Svetlana Kiritchenko. 2018.Semeval-2018 Task 1: Affect in tweets. In Proceedings of International Workshop on S-emantic Evaluation (SemEval2018), New Orl-eans, LA, USA.

AffecThor at SemEval-2018 Task 1: A cross-linguistic approach to sentiment intensity quantification in tweets

Mostafa Abdou and **Artur Kulmizev** and **Joan Ginés i Ametllé**
{m.abdou, a.kulmizev, j.gines.i.ametlle}@student.rug.nl
CLCG, University of Groningen

Abstract

In this paper we describe our submission to SemEval-2018 Task 1: *Affects in Tweets*. The model which we present is an ensemble of various neural architectures and gradient boosted trees, and employs three different types of vectorial tweet representations. Furthermore, our system is language-independent and ranked first in 5 out of the 12 subtasks in which we participated, while achieving competitive results in the remaining ones. Comparatively remarkable performance is observed on both the Arabic and Spanish languages.

1   Introduction

The *Affects in Tweets* shared task (Mohammad et al., 2018) is the second iteration of a task which offers a new approach to Sentiment Analysis - one that concerns itself with emotion and sentiment *intensity*, rather than simple categorical classification. The shared task is divided into a set of subtasks, where the aim is to predict the emotion intensity of a predetermined emotion (fear, anger, sadness, joy) or sentiment (valence) intensity of a given set of tweets. Such predictions are either formulated as a regression problem where the output is a continuous-valued score in the interval $(0, 1)$, or as ordinal classification into a given number of classes representing intensity. Additionally, each one of the subtasks targets a particular language: English, Arabic or Spanish.

In total, we participated in 12 different subtasks and our system achieved the best performance on the test set out of all participants in 5 out of those, ranked second in 3 others, and performed compet-

itively in the rest. Moreover, our system can arguably be considered the best overall performing system for both Arabic and Spanish[1]. It should be noted, however, that the shared task includes traditional emotion classification subtasks in which we did not participate.

The system described in this paper builds upon a survey of some of the best performing systems from previous related shared tasks (Mohammad and Bravo-Marquez, 2017; Rosenthal et al., 2017). In particular, we draw inspiration from the systems described in (John and Vechtomova, 2017), which makes use of gradient boosted trees for regression; (Goel et al., 2017), which employs an ensemble of various neural models; and (Baziotis et al., 2017), which features Long Short Term Memory (LSTM) networks with an attention mechanism. Our work contributes to the aforementioned approaches by further developing a variety of neural architectures, using transfer learning via pretrained sentence encoders, testing methods of ensembling neural and non-neural models, and gauging the performance and stability of a regressor across languages.

The rest of this paper describes the pipeline of the system used for our submission, which is an ensemble of neural and non-neural models.

2   Data and features

The provided training and development data is comprised of tweets, an emotion or sentiment, and labels describing the intensity of the emotion or

---

[1] https://competitions.codalab.org/competitions/17751#results

Proceedings of the 12th International Workshop on Semantic Evaluation (SemEval-2018), pages 210–217
New Orleans, Louisiana, June 5–6, 2018. ©2018 Association for Computational Linguistics

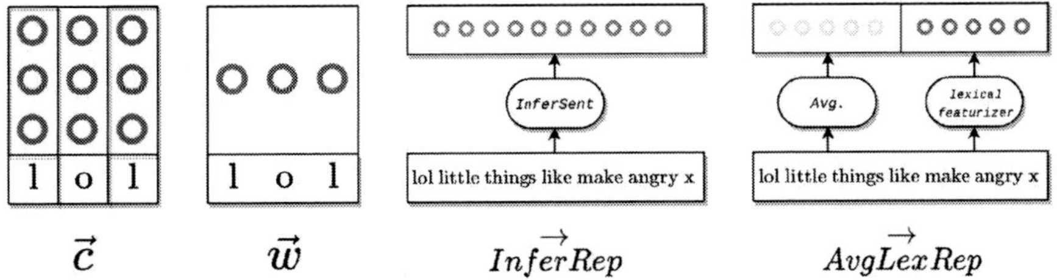

Figure 1: Graphical visualization of various feature vectors used in our ensemble model. These are from left to right: character embedding, word embedding, $\overrightarrow{InferRep}$ and $\overrightarrow{AvgLexRep}$ representations.

sentiment. We refer readers interested in an exhaustive description of the data to (Mohammad et al., 2018; Mohammad and Kiritchenko, 2018). In this work, we convert each tweet into a combination of three types of vector representations: character and word-level vectors for Arabic and Spanish; and character, word, and sentence-level vectors for English. This section describes the procedure that allows us to obtain these varied representations, which are later employed by our classification and regression models.

2.1 Preprocessing

The syntactic and orthographic form of tweets often differs substantially from text belonging to other domains (John and Vechtomova, 2017). As such, pre-processing procedures are as important as the architecture of any given model.

In pre-processing our data, we first replace all same-character sequences of length 3 or more with only 2 occurrences. We also replace all user mentions with a unique common token, as well as all control characters with whitespaces. Emojis are surrounded with spaces, enforcing that any two emojis are not consecutive characters. Finally, all text is lowercased. In the case of Spanish text, we further remove the characters ¿ and ¡, and replace accented characters with their unaccented versions, as well as ñ with n. In the case of Arabic text, we remove quotation marks as well.

Following the cleaning process, we tokenize the resulting text by applying the `twokenize` tool (Krieger and Ahn, 2010), as provided in the CMU Tweet NLP software (Owoputi et al., 2013), which is, by design, able to cope with the noise that appears in social media. Once the tokenization is completed, we filter all stopwords [2].

---

[2] We employ the stopword lists available from `https://www.ranks.nl/stopwords`

2.2 Lexicons

Lexicons are one of the resources which we employ in order to compute features. In short, a lexicon is a collection of words that are associated with a value for an arbitrary number of affective categories. In our case, given a tweet, we produce several features per lexicon which are the result of aggregating individual matching word values in each category, adding the numerical values and counting those which are nominal. We provide an overview of the lexicons used per language below, with the number of features contributed by each individual lexicon in parenthesis. In the case of English, the following lexicons and extracted values jointly produce a feature vector of dimension 43:

- MPQA lexicon (2): Number of positive and negative words (Wilson et al., 2005).

- Bing Liu lexicon (2): Number of positive and negative words (Hu and Liu, 2004).

- Emoticons (2): Positive and negative aggregated scores for emoticons (Nielsen, 2011).

- Sentiment140 lexicon (2): Positive and negative aggregated scores (Kiritchenko et al., 2014).

- NRC Word-Emotion Association Lexicon (10): Number of words matching each category (Mohammad and Turney, 2013).

- NRC Hashtag Sentiment lexicon (2): Positive and negative aggregated scores (Kiritchenko et al., 2014).

- NRC Hashtag Emotion Association Lexicon (8): Aggregated scores for each category (Mohammad and Kiritchenko, 2015).

- NRC-10-Expanded lexicon (10): Aggregated scores for each category (Bravo-Marquez et al., 2016).

- SentiWordnet (2): Positive and negative aggregated scores (Baccianella et al., 2010).

- AFINN lexicon (2): Positive and negative aggregated scores (Nielsen, 2011).

- Negations (1): Number of negative words (Mohammad and Bravo-Marquez, 2017).

In the case of Arabic we also employ the same first 6 lexicons which we listed for English, but with the content words automatically translated (Salameh et al., 2015). However, we extract 4 scores from the MPQA lexicon (on the affective categories *positive*, *negative*, *neutral* and *both*), an a single combined score from the Bing Liu and Emoticons lexicons. Furthermore, we employ 3 lexicons generated by distant supervision techniques on Arabic tweets as follows (Mohammad et al., 2016), in order to obtain a feature vector of dimension 26:

- Arabic Emoticon Lexicon (2): Number of positive and negative words.

- Arabic Hashtag Lexicon (2): Number of positive and negative words.

- Arabic dialectal Hashtag Lexicon (2): Number of positive and negative words.

Finally, the following lexicons are used in Spanish to produce a feature vector of dimension 14. In contrast to the Arabic language, the majority of the lexicons here listed are manually annotated or semi-automatically generated from Spanish data:

- Emoticons (1): Combination of positive and negative aggregated scores for emoticons (Nielsen, 2011).

- El Huyar dictionary (2): Positive and negative aggregated scores (Saralegi and San Vicente, 2013).

- ISOL lexicon (2): Number of positive and negative words (Martínez-Cámara et al., 2014).

- SDAL lexicon (3): Aggregated scores for each category (Dell' Amerlina Ríos and Gravano, 2013).

- Spanish Sentiment lexicon (2): Number of positive and negative words (Perez Rosas et al., 2012).

- ML Senticon (1): Aggregated score for polarity (Cruz et al., 2014).

- Sentwords (3): Aggregated score for each category in an automatically translated version of the lexicon described in (Beth Warriner et al., 2013).

Note that the lexicons are not directly used on tweet data, but rather that lexical features are extracted after applying the same data cleaning and tokenization process which we described for the training data to each one of the lexicons listed.

2.3 Word embeddings

Word embeddings are another popular choice for feature extraction. We employ pre-trained word embeddings for English and train our own embeddings on separated Arabic and Spanish tweet data that we manually collected. All sets of embeddings comprise 400 dimensions and are detailed below for each language:

- English: Word2vec skip-gram embeddings, trained on the Edinburgh Twitter Corpus (Petrović et al., 2010).

- Arabic: Word2vec skip-gram embeddings, trained on 4.38 million tweets[3].

- Spanish: Word2vec skip-gram embeddings, trained on 3.02 million tweets[4].

2.4 Manually-crafted representations

In the Arabic and Spanish subtasks, some model components in our ensemble use a combination of the two types of representations described so far (lexical features and word embeddings) as an input feature vector. To obtain this, we average the embeddings corresponding to each word in a given tweet up to a maximum of 25 words, and append the computed lexical features to the result. These features are extracted using the filters provided in the Affective Tweets package (Mohammad and Bravo-Marquez, 2017) available for WEKA (Hall et al., 2009). In this paper, we will refer to this combined representation as $\vec{AvgLex}Rep$.

---

[3]Available for download from `akulmizev.com/embeddings/ar_tweets.csv`.

[4]Available for download from `akulmizev.com/embeddings/es_tweets.csv`.

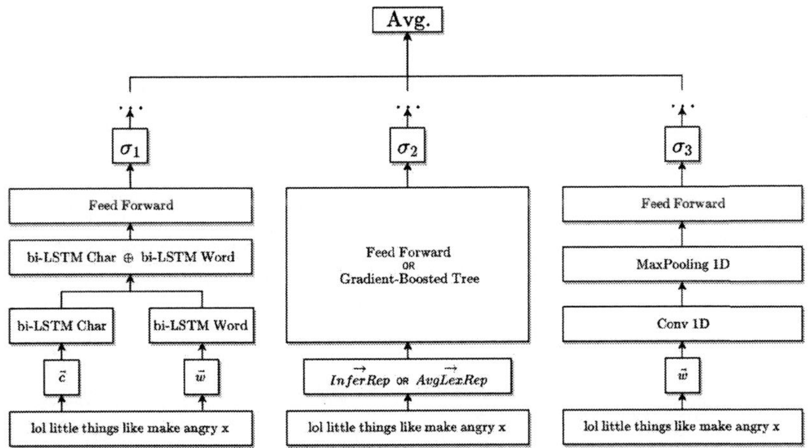

Figure 2: Diagram of our system which describes how the different models used are ensembled. The outputs of each component in the ensemble are averaged into a single score.

2.5 Learned representations

Engineering a representation of the data (such as a the one described in Section 2.4) that can support effective machine learning is a complex task, requiring human ingenuity and domain-specific knowledge. Representation learning techniques (Bengio et al., 2003) enable machine learning algorithms to automatically extract and organize discriminative features, thereby mapping raw data into forms that make it easier to extract useful information. Some model components in our ensemble employ this kind of representation, which we obtain using 2 different methods:

- Encoding a tweet using (Conneau et al., 2017)'s BiLSTM-max pooling encoder, which is pre-trained on a natural language inference dataset[5] and produces representations that perform well on a wide variety of NLP tasks. This approach in particular employs GloVe word embeddings (Pennington et al., 2014) as input and produces a vector containing 4096 dimensions, to which we will refer with the name $Inf\vec{e}rRep$. However, note that we only produce this feature vector for the English language subtasks.

- Encoding a tweet using one or a combination of three neural architectures which use skip-gram word embeddings (Mikolov et al., 2013) as input and are trained on the shared

task's training data for regression subtasks. These correspond to the CNN, Bi-LSTM and CHAR-LSTM models described in Section 3. Representations produced by the CHAR-LSTM model are of dimension 612^6, and the ones obtained via the Bi-LSTM model are of dimension 512. Representations produced by the CNN model have different dimensionality depending on the number and size of filters used. We will collectively refer to such representations with the name $Re\vec{g}Rep$.

3 System architecture

While $Re\vec{g}Rep$ is produced as part of end-to-end trainable regression and classification models, $AvgL\vec{e}xRep$ and $Inf\vec{e}rRep$ are generated independently. Thus, $AvgL\vec{e}xRep$ and $Inf\vec{e}rRep$ are fed separately into these models after being generated. The pipeline of our ensemble is represented schematically in Figure 2.

3.1 Neural models

We implement three varieties of neural network architectures which are commonly used in text classification tasks using Keras (Chollet et al., 2015) with a TensorFlow backend. In all of them, our objective function is Mean Squared Error (MSE) and dropout (Srivastava et al., 2014) is used for regularization at various levels. These architectures are listed below:

---

[5]Stanford Natural Language Inference dataset (Bowman et al., 2015). This is only available for English.

[6]512 dimensions correspond to word final hidden states and 100 dimensions to character hidden states.

- Convolutional Neural Network (CNN) with max pooling.

- Bidirectional Long-Short Term Memory (Bi-LSTM) with attention.

- Combined character and word features bi-LSTMs (CHAR-LSTM).

3.2 Regression

For *AvgLexRep* and *InferRep*, which are not part of an end-to-end trainable model, we perform regression using either a feed-forward Deep Neural Network (DNN) or Gradient Boosted Trees (GBT)[7]. The depth of the feed-forward network is determined constructively, starting with one layer and adding layers which are half the size of the previous one until performance on cross-validation stops improving.

3.3 Model selection for regression

We perform model selection using 5-fold cross-validation on the training data from the shared task. In each subtask that involves regression, the possible models are ranked according to their individual performance and ensembled through simple averaging. The ensemble itself is built constructively based on the ordering defined by the ranking, starting from a single component and adding components in order whenever the average performance on cross-validation improves.

Ensembling has long been shown to be an effective method of variance reduction for complex models (Perrone, 1993), and we indeed find in our experiments that averaging predictions leads to results better than those of any individual model[8].

Furthermore, we also find predictions obtained via simple averaging to be more accurate (on cross-validation) compared to those obtained via feeding the outputs from all model components into a sigmoid layer. Although such a finding might appear counter-intuitive, it can perhaps be explained through the fact that the training dataset is relatively small, and therefore ensembling via a non-linear function of the outputs can potentially lead to overfitting.

---

[7] We use the GBT implementation provided in scikit-learn (Pedregosa et al., 2011).

[8] We refer the reader to (Hashem and Schmeiser, 1993) for an explanation of why this is the case.

3.4 Ordinal classification

Our system for each ordinal classification subtask makes use of the ensemble model which we build for the corresponding regression subtask in the same language, and model selection is performed using the same procedure described in Section 3.3. However, instead of averaging the predictions, the best model's predictions are concatenated and fed as features to an ordinal meta-classifier (Antoniuk et al., 2013).

3.5 Hyperparameter tuning

Hyper-parameter optimization is carried out using 5-fold cross-validation. At first, a reasonable range is determined manually, and then grid-search is performed within that range. For Gradient Boosted Trees, the hyper-parameters optimized are maximum tree depth, number of estimators, and maximum leaf nodes. For neural models, the parameters optimized are batch size, number of epochs, size of the layers or filters, and whether or not dropout is used at different levels. Dropout is by default always set at 0.2. Furthermore, we use a fixed random seed to enable replicability.

4 Evaluation

System	Anger		Sadness		Joy		Fear	
	CV	Test	CV	Test	CV	Test	CV	Test
DNN (Infer.)	0.707	0.703	0.755	0.654	0.713	0.667	0.742	0.701
GBT (Infer.)	0.716	0.707	0.739	0.677	0.708	0.688	0.748	0.697
CHAR-LSTM	0.698	0.682	0.716	0.626	0.722	0.700	0.727	0.663
CNN	0.642	0.636	0.521	0.4316	0.637	0.628	0.615	0.459
Ensemble	0.756	0.749	0.770	0.699	0.758	0.740	0.773	0.726

Table 1: Comparison of Pearson correlation cross-validation (CV) and official results (Test) scores in the Emotion Intensity regression (EI-reg) English subtasks. Results are given for both the ensemble and its individual models.

Table 1 displays the scores (both 5-fold cross-validation and test scores) of the individual models and the ensemble model for the Emotion Intensity English regression subtasks. The ensemble model in this case is always for the best three models. Table 2 shows the results obtained using 5-fold cross-validation on the combined training and development data and the official test set results for each subtask. All scores are reported as the Pearson correlation coefficient between our system's predictions and the provided gold-labels (i.e. human judgments).

Task	Emotion	English		Arabic		Spanish	
		CV	Test	CV	Test	CV	Test
EI-reg	Anger	0.756	0.749	0.620	0.647	0.731	0.676
	Joy	0.758	0.740	0.690	0.756	0.712	0.753
	Fear	0.773	0.726	0.619	0.642	0.720	0.776
	Sadness	0.770	0.669	0.717	0.694	0.728	0.746
	Macro-avg.	0.764	0.728	0.662	0.685	0.723	0.738
V-reg	Valence	0.800	0.829	0.820	0.816	0.775	0.795
EI-oc	Anger	0.670	0.620	0.620	0.551	0.635	0.606
	Joy	0.701	0.686	0.610	0.631	0.668	0.667
	Fear	0.635	0.528	0.565	0.551	0.658	0.706
	Sadness	0.738	0.622	0.682	0.618	0.655	0.677
	Macro-avg.	0.691	0.616	0.619	0.587	0.654	0.664
V-oc	Valence	0.770	0.776	0.778	0.752	0.749	0.756

Table 2: Pearson correlation using cross-validation (CV) on the trainining data and official results of the shared task (Test) obtained with our system, for each one of the Emotion Intensity (EI), Valence (V), regression (reg) and ordinal classification (oc) subtasks.

5 Analysis

It can be observed in Table 2 that the test and cross-validation scores are similar, meaning that cross-validation provided an accurate estimate of the generalization error and that our system's overfitting of the different combined training and development sets is minimal. In fact, for the English valence subtasks, the Arabic Emotion Intensity regression subtask and all Spanish subtasks except the ones involving anger as the target emotion, the test scores are higher or equal than the cross-validation scores. This indicates both that our system generalizes appropriately and that the test sets are not substantially different than the training sets.

Overall performance is higher for English, likely due to the availability of better quality lexicons and word embeddings. Nonetheless, it is interesting to note that on average, cross-validation provided an optimistic estimate of the generalization error for English and a pessimistic one for Spanish and Arabic.

Furthermore, as shown in Table 1 for various English regression subtasks, it is clear that the ensemble outperforms all individual models on both cross-validation and the test set. This points towards the success of our ensembling method in reducing the variance of individual models. We omit similar results for other subtasks because the trend displayed by those is comparable.

Finally, it is interesting to note that the models using $\vec{Infer}Rep$ (DNN and GBT), which rely on tweet representations produced through transfer learning from Natural Language Inference, outperformed the models using the task-specific $\vec{Reg}Rep$ (CNN, Bi-LSTM and CHAR-LSTM) for all emotions except Sadness.

6 Conclusion and future work

In this paper we have described *AffecThor*, the system which we submitted to the SemEval-2018 *Affects in Tweets* shared task. *AffecThor* uses three different types of learned and manually-crafted representations and is an ensemble of neural and non-neural models. It is the best performing system on 5 out of 12 subtasks, and the second best performing in 3 others. Furthermore, it is arguably the best overall performer for Spanish and Arabic.

Our work explored two methods of ensembling regressors: simple averaging and using a non-linearity (sigmoid) layer on top of the different sub-models as part of an end-to-end trainable neural model, and found that simple averaging is more robust. However, we believe that ensembling using a linear combination (weighted-averaging) where the weights are learned could lead to better results, as is shown in (Perrone, 1993; Hashem and Schmeiser, 1993).

Finally, the availability of fine-grained labeled data across emotions and languages opens up the possibility of investigating multi-task and multi-lingual learning objectives. In the future, we would like to extend this work in that direction.

References

Kostiantyn Antoniuk, Vojtěch Franc, and Václav Hlaváč. 2013. Mord: Multi-class Classifier for Ordinal Regression. In *Joint European Conference on Machine Learning and Knowledge Discovery in Databases*, pages 96–111. Springer.

Stefano Baccianella, Andrea Esuli, and Fabrizio Sebastiani. 2010. Sentiwordnet 3.0: An Enhanced Lexical Resource for Sentiment Analysis and Opinion Mining. In *Proceedings of the International Conference on Language Resources and Evaluation*.

Christos Baziotis, Nikos Pelekis, and Christos Doulkeridis. 2017. Datastories at SemEval-2017 Task 4: Deep LSTM with Attention for Message-level and Topic-based Sentiment Analysis. In *Proceedings of the 11th International Workshop on Semantic Evaluation (SemEval-2017)*, pages 747–754.

Yoshua Bengio, Réjean Ducharme, Pascal Vincent, and Christian Janvin. 2003. A Neural Probabilistic Language Model. *J. Mach. Learn. Res.*, 3:1137–1155.

Amy Beth Warriner, Victor Kuperman, and Marc Brysbaert. 2013. Norms of valence, arousal, and dominance for 13,915 English lemmas. 45:1191–1207.

Samuel R Bowman, Gabor Angeli, Christopher Potts, and Christopher D Manning. 2015. A large annotated corpus for learning natural language inference. *arXiv preprint arXiv:1508.05326*.

Felipe Bravo-Marquez, Eibe Frank, Saif M. Mohammad, and Bernhard Pfahringer. 2016. Determining Word-Emotion Associations from Tweets by Multilabel Classification. In *2016 IEEE/WIC/ACM International Conference on Web Intelligence*, pages 536–539.

François Chollet et al. 2015. Keras. `https://github.com/keras-team/keras`.

Alexis Conneau, Douwe Kiela, Holger Schwenk, Loic Barrault, and Antoine Bordes. 2017. Supervised Learning of Universal Sentence Representations from Natural Language Inference Data. *arXiv preprint arXiv:1705.02364*.

Fe.L. Cruz, J.A. Troyano, Beatriz Pontes, and F. Javier Ortega. 2014. ML-SentiCon: A multilingual, lemma-level sentiment lexicon. 53:113–120.

Matías Dell' Amerlina Ríos and Agustín Gravano. 2013. Spanish DAL: A Spanish Dictionary of Affect in Language. In *Proceedings of the 4th Workshop on Computational Approaches to Subjectivity, Sentiment & Social Media Analysis (WASSA 2013)*, pages 21–28.

Pranav Goel, Devang Kulshreshtha, Prayas Jain, and Kaushal Kumar Shukla. 2017. Prayas at EmoInt 2017: An Ensemble of Deep Neural Architectures for Emotion Intensity Prediction in Tweets. In *Proceedings of the 8th Workshop on Computational Approaches to Subjectivity, Sentiment and Social Media Analysis*, pages 58–65.

Mark Hall, Eibe Frank, Geoffrey Holmes, Bernhard Pfahringer, Peter Reutemann, and Ian H. Witten. 2009. The WEKA Data Mining Software: An Update. *SIGKDD Explor. Newsl.*, 11(1):10–18.

Sherif Hashem and Bruce Schmeiser. 1993. Approximating a Function and its Derivatives Using MSE-Optimal Linear Combinations of Trained Feedforward Neural Networks. In *In Proceedings of the Joint Conference on Neural Networks*, pages 617–620.

Minqing Hu and Bing Liu. 2004. Mining and Summarizing Customer Reviews. In *Proceedings of the Tenth ACM SIGKDD International Conference on Knowledge Discovery and Data Mining*, pages 168–177.

Vineet John and Olga Vechtomova. 2017. UWat-Emote at EmoInt-2017: Emotion Intensity Detection using Affect Clues, Sentiment Polarity and Word Embeddings. In *Proceedings of the 8th Workshop on Computational Approaches to Subjectivity, Sentiment and Social Media Analysis*, pages 249–254.

Svetlana Kiritchenko, Xiaodan Zhu, and Saif M. Mohammad. 2014. Sentiment Analysis of Short Informal Texts. *Journal of Artificial Intelligence Research (JAIR)*, 50:723–762.

Michel Krieger and David Ahn. 2010. TweetMotif: Exploratory Search and Topic Summarization for Twitter. In *In Proceedings of AAAI Conference on Weblogs and Social Media*.

Eugenio Martínez-Cámara, M. Teresa Martín-Valdivia, M. Dolores Molina-González, and José M. Perea-Ortega. 2014. Integrating Spanish Lexical Resources by Meta-classifiers for Polarity Classification. *J. Inf. Sci.*, 40(4):538–554.

Tomas Mikolov, Kai Chen, Greg Corrado, and Jeffrey Dean. 2013. Efficient Estimation of Word Representations in Vector Space. *arXiv preprint arXiv:1301.3781*.

Saif M. Mohammad and Felipe Bravo-Marquez. 2017. Emotion Intensities in Tweets. In *Proceedings of the 6th Joint Conference on Lexical and Computational Semantics, *SEM @ACM 2017, Vancouver, Canada, August 3-4, 2017*, pages 65–77.

Saif M. Mohammad and Felipe Bravo-Marquez. 2017. WASSA-2017 Shared Task on Emotion Intensity. In *Proceedings of the Workshop on Computational Approaches to Subjectivity, Sentiment and Social Media Analysis (WASSA)*, Copenhagen, Denmark.

Saif M. Mohammad, Felipe Bravo-Marquez, Mohammad Salameh, and Svetlana Kiritchenko. 2018. Semeval-2018 Task 1: Affect in tweets. In *Proceedings of International Workshop on Semantic Evaluation (SemEval-2018)*, New Orleans, LA, USA.

216

Saif M. Mohammad and Svetlana Kiritchenko. 2015. Using Hashtags to Capture Fine Emotion Categories from Tweets. *Computational Intelligence*, 31(2):301–326.

Saif M. Mohammad and Svetlana Kiritchenko. 2018. Understanding Emotions: A Dataset of Tweets to Study Interactions between Affect Categories. In *Proceedings of the 11th Edition of the Language Resources and Evaluation Conference*, Miyazaki, Japan.

Saif M. Mohammad, Mohammad Salameh, and Svetlana Kiritchenko. 2016. Sentiment Lexicons for Arabic Social Media. In *Proceedings of the Tenth International Conference on Language Resources and Evaluation (LREC 2016)*. European Language Resources Association (ELRA).

Saif M. Mohammad and Peter D. Turney. 2013. Crowdsourcing a Word-Emotion Association Lexicon. 29(3):436–465.

Årup Nielsen. 2011. A New ANEW: Evaluation of a Word List for Sentiment Analysis in Microblogs. In *Proceedings of the ESWC2011 Workshop on 'Making Sense of Microposts': Big things come in small packages*, pages 93–98.

Olutobi Owoputi, Chris Dyer, Kevin Gimpel, Nathan Schneider, and Noah A. Smith. 2013. Improved Part-Of-Speech Tagging for Online Conversational Text with Word Clusters. In *In Proceedings of NAACL*.

F. Pedregosa, G. Varoquaux, A. Gramfort, V. Michel, B. Thirion, O. Grisel, M. Blondel, P. Prettenhofer, R. Weiss, V. Dubourg, J. Vanderplas, A. Passos, D. Cournapeau, M. Brucher, M. Perrot, and E. Duchesnay. 2011. Scikit-learn: Machine Learning in Python. *Journal of Machine Learning Research*, 12:2825–2830.

Jeffrey Pennington, Richard Socher, and Christopher Manning. 2014. Glove: Global Vectors for Word Representation. In *Proceedings of the 2014 conference on empirical methods in natural language processing (EMNLP)*, pages 1532–1543.

Veronica Perez Rosas, Carmen Banea, and Rada Mihalcea. 2012. Learning Sentiment Lexicons in Spanish. In *Proceedings of the international conference on Language Resources and Evaluation (LREC)*.

Michael Peter Perrone. 1993. *Improving Regression Estimation: Averaging Methods for Variance Reduction with Extensions to General Convex Measure Optimization*. Ph.D. thesis.

Saša Petrović, Miles Osborne, and Victor Lavrenko. 2010. The Edinburgh Twitter Corpus. In *Proceedings of the NAACL HLT 2010 Workshop on Computational Linguistics in a World of Social Media*, pages 25–26.

Sara Rosenthal, Noura Farra, and Preslav Nakov. 2017. SemEval-2017 Task 4: Sentiment Analysis in Twitter. In *Proceedings of the 11th International Workshop on Semantic Evaluation (SemEval-2017)*, pages 502–518.

Mohammad Salameh, Saif M. Mohammad, and Svetlana Kiritchenko. 2015. Sentiment after Translation: A Case-Study on Arabic Social Media Posts. In *HLT-NAACL*, pages 767–777. The Association for Computational Linguistics.

Xabier Saralegi and Iaki San Vicente. 2013. *Workshop on Sentiment Analysis at SEPLN (TASS2013)*.

Nitish Srivastava, Geoffrey Hinton, Alex Krizhevsky, Ilya Sutskever, and Ruslan Salakhutdinov. 2014. Dropout: A Simple Way to Prevent Neural Networks from Overfitting. *The Journal of Machine Learning Research*, 15(1):1929–1958.

Theresa Wilson, Janyce Wiebe, and Paul Hoffmann. 2005. Recognizing Contextual Polarity in Phrase-Level Sentiment Analysis. In *HLT/EMNLP 2005, Human Language Technology Conference and Conference on Empirical Methods in Natural Language Processing*, pages 347–354.

Amobee at SemEval-2018 Task 1: GRU Neural Network with a CNN Attention Mechanism for Sentiment Classification

Alon Rozental*, Daniel Fleischer*
Amobee, Tel Aviv, Israel
`alon.rozental@amobee.com`
`daniel.fleischer@amobee.com`

Abstract

This paper describes the participation of Amobee in the shared sentiment analysis task at SemEval 2018. We participated in all the English sub-tasks and the Spanish valence tasks. Our system consists of three parts: training task-specific word embeddings, training a model consisting of gated-recurrent-units (GRU) with a convolution neural network (CNN) attention mechanism and training stacking-based ensembles for each of the sub-tasks. Our algorithm reached 3rd and 1st places in the valence ordinal classification sub-tasks in English and Spanish, respectively.

1 Introduction

Sentiment analysis is a collection of methods and algorithms used to infer and measure affection expressed by a writer. The main motivation is enabling computers to better understand human language, particularly sentiment carried by the speaker. Among the popular sources of textual data for NLP is Twitter, a social network service where users communicate by posting short messages, no longer than 280 characters long—called tweets. Tweets can carry sentimental information when talking about events, public figures, brands or products. Unique linguistic features, such as the use of slang, emojis, misspelling and sarcasm, make Twitter a challenging source for NLP research, attracting the interest of both academia and the industry.

Semeval is a yearly event in which international teams of researchers work on tasks in a competition format where they tackle open research questions in the field of semantic analysis. We participated in Semeval 2018 task 1, which focuses on sentiment and emotions evaluation in tweets. There were three main problems: identifying the

presence of a given emotion in a tweet (sub-tasks EI-reg, EI-oc), identifying the general sentiment (valence) in a tweet (sub-tasks V-reg, V-oc) and identifying which emotions are expressed in a tweet (sub-task E-c). For a complete description of Semeval 2018 task 1, see the official task description (Mohammad et al., 2018).

We developed an architecture based on gated-recurrent-units (GRU, Cho et al. (2014)). We used a bi-directional GRU layer, together with a convolutional neural network (CNN) attention-mechanism, where its input is the hidden states of the GRU layer; lastly there were two fully connected layers. We will refer to this architecture as the Amobee sentiment classifier (ASC). We used ASC to train word embeddings to incorporate sentiment information and to classify sentiment using annotated tweets. We participated in all the English sub-tasks and in the valence Spanish sub-tasks, achieving competitive results.

The paper is organized as follows: section 2 describes our data sources, section 3 describes the data pre-processing pipeline. A description of the main architecture is in section 4. Section 5 describes the word embeddings generation; section 6 describes the extraction of features. In section 7 we describe the performance of our models; finally, in section 8 we review and summarize the results.

2 Data Sources

We used four sources of data:

1. Twitter Firehose: we randomly sampled 200 million tweets using the Twitter Firehose service. They were used for training word embeddings and for distant supervision learning.

2. Semeval 2017 task 4 datasets of tweets, annotated according to their general sentiment

---

*These authors contributed equally to this work.

Proceedings of the 12th International Workshop on Semantic Evaluation (SemEval-2018), pages 218–225
New Orleans, Louisiana, June 5–6, 2018. ©2018 Association for Computational Linguistics

on 3 and 5 level scales; used to train the ASC model.

3. Annotated tweets from an external source[1], annotated on a 3-level scale; used to train the ASC model.

4. Official Semeval 2018 task 1 datasets: used to train task specific models.

Datasets of Semeval 2017 and the external source were combined with compression[2]; the resulting dataset contained 88,623 tweets with the following distribution: positive: 30097 sentences (34%), neutral: 35818 (40%), negative: 22708 (26%). Description of the official Semeval 2018 task 1 datasets can be found in Mohammad et al. (2018); Mohammad and Kiritchenko (2018).

3 Preprocessing

We started by defining a cleaning pipeline that produces two cleaned version of an original text; we refer to them as "simple" and "complex" versions. Both versions share the same initial cleaning steps:

1. Word tokenization using the CoreNLP library (Manning et al., 2014).

2. Parts of speech (POS) tagging using the Tweet NLP tagger, trained on Twitter data (Owoputi et al., 2013).

3. Grouping similar emojis and replacing them with representative keywords.

4. Regex: replacing URLs with a special keyword, removing duplications, breaking #CamelCasingHashtags into individual words.

The complex version contains these additional steps:

1. Word lemmatization, using CoreNLP.

2. Named entity recognition (NER) using CoreNLP and replacing the entities with representative keywords, e.g. _date_, _number_, _brand_, etc.

3. Synonym replacement, based on a manually-created dictionary.

4. Word replacement using a Wikipedia dictionary, created by crawling and extracting lists of places, brands and names.

---

[1] https://github.com/monkeylearn/sentiment-analysis-benchmark

[2] Transformed 5 labels to 3: $\{-2, -1\} \rightarrow \{-1\}$, $\{1, 2\} \rightarrow \{1\}$, $\{0\} \rightarrow \{0\}$.

As an example, table 1 shows a fictitious tweet and the results after the simple and complex cleaning stages.

4 ASC Architecture

Our main contribution is an RNN network, based on GRU units with a CNN-based attention mechanism; we will refer to it as the Amobee sentiment classifier (ASC). It is comprised of four identical sub-models, which differ by the input data each of them receives. Sub-model inputs are composed of word embeddings and embeddings of the POS tags—see section 5 for a description of our embedding procedure. The words were embedded in a 200 or 150 dimensional vector spaces and the POS tags were embedded in a 8 dimensional vector space. We pruned the tweets to have 40 words, padding shorter sentences with a zero vector. The embeddings form the input layer.

Next we describe the sub-model architecture; the embeddings were fed to a bi-directional GRU layer of dimension 200. Inspired by the attention mechanism introduced in Bahdanau et al. (2014), we extracted the hidden states of the GRU layer; each state corresponds to a decoded word in the GRU as it reads each tweet word by word. The hidden states were arranged in a matrix of dimension 40×400 for each tweet (bi-directionality of the GRU layer contributes a factor of 2). We fed the hidden states to a CNN layer, instead of a weighted sum as in the original paper. We used 6 filter sizes $[1, 2, 3, 4, 5, 6]$, with 100 filters for each size. After a max-pooling layer we concatenated all outputs, creating a 600 dimensional vector. Next was a fully connected layer of size 30 with tanh activation, and finally a fully connected layer of size 3 with a softmax activation function.

We defined 4 such sub-models with embedding inputs of the following settings: w2v-200, w2v-150, ft-200, ft-150 (ft=FastText, w2v=Word2Vec, see discussion in the next section). We combined the four sub-models by extracting their hidden $d = 30$ layer and concatenating them. Next we added a fully connected $d = 25$ layer with tanh activation and a final fully connected layer of size 3. See figure 1 for an illustration of the entire architecture. We used the AdaGrad optimizer (Duchi et al., 2011) and a cross-entropy loss function. We used the Keras library (Chollet et al., 2015) and the TensorFlow framework (Abadi et al., 2016).

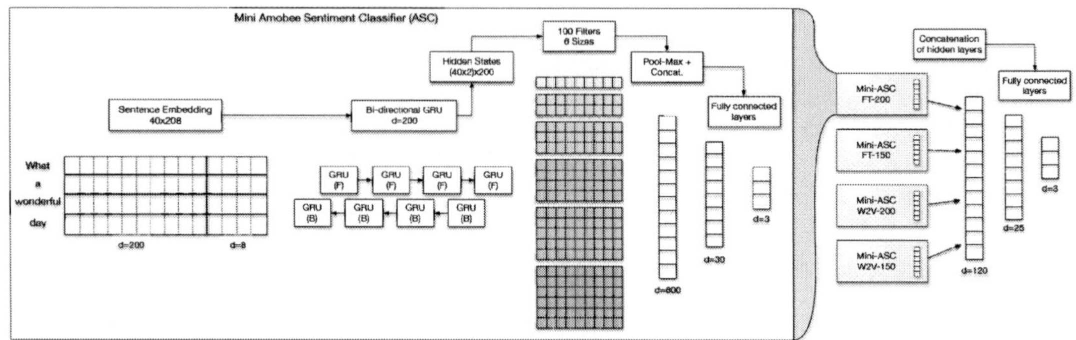

Figure 1: Architecture of the ASC nework. Each of the four sub-models on the right has the same structure as depicted in the central region.

Original	@USAIRWAYS is right :-) ! Flying in September #NiceToFly
Simple Cleaning	twitter-entity is right happy-smily ! flying in september nice to fly
Complex Cleaning	twitter-entity be right happy-smily ! fly in _date_ pleasant to fly

Table 1: An example of a tweet processing, producing two cleaned versions.

5 Embeddings Training

Word embedding is a family of techniques in which words are encoded as real-valued vectors of lower dimensionality. These word representations have been used successfully in sentiment analysis tasks in recent years. Among the popular algorithms are Word2Vec (Mikolov et al., 2013) and FastText (Bojanowski et al., 2016).

Word embeddings are useful representations of words and can uncover hidden relationships. However, one disadvantage they have is the typical lack of sentiment information. For example, the word vector "good" can be very close to the word vector "bad" in some trained, off-the-shelf word embeddings. Our goal was to train word embeddings based on Twitter data and then re-learn them so they will contain emotion-specific sentiment.

We started with our 200 million tweets dataset; we cleaned them using the pre-processing pipeline (described in section 3) and then trained generic embeddings using the Gensim package (Řehůřek and Sojka, 2010); we created four embeddings for the words and two embeddings for the POS tags: for each sentence we created a list of corresponding POS tags (there are 25 tags offered by the tagger we used); treating the tags as words, we trained $d = 8$ embeddings using the word2vec algorithm on the simple and complex cleaned datasets. The embeddings parameters are specified in table 2.

Following Tang et al. (2014); Cliche (2017),

who explored training word embeddings for sentiment classification, we employed a similar approach. We created distant supervision datasets, first, by manually compiling 4 lists of representative words for each emotion: anger, fear, joy and sadness; then, we built two datasets for each emotion: the first containing tweets with the representative words and the second does not. Each list contained about 40 words and each dataset contained roughly 2 million tweets. We used the ASC sub-model architecture (section 4) to train as following: training for one epoch with embeddings set to be untrainable (fixed). Then train for 6 epochs where the embeddings can change.

Overall we trained 16 word embeddings—4 embedding configurations for each emotion. In addition, we decided to use the trained models' final hidden layer ($d = 15$) as a feature vector in the task-specific architectures; our motivation was using them as emotion and intensity classifiers via transfer learning.

	Algorithm	Dimension	Dataset
Words	Word2Vec	200	Simple
	Word2Vec	150	Complex
	FastText	200	Simple
	FastText	150	Complex
Tags	Word2Vec	200	Simple
	Word2Vec	150	Complex

Table 2: Parameters for the word and POS tag embeddings.

6   Features Description

In addition to our ASC models, we extracted semantic and syntactic features, based on domain knowledge:

- Number of magnifier and diminisher words, e.g. "incredibly", "hardly" in each tweet.
- Logarithm of length of sentences.
- Existence of elongated words, e.g. "wowww".
- Fully capitalized words.
- The symbols #,@ appearing in the sentence.
- Predictions of external packages: Vader (part of the NLTK library, Hutto and Gilbert, 2014) and TextBlob (Loria et al., 2014).

Additionally, we compiled a list of 338 emojis and words in 16 categories of emotion, annotated with scores from the set $\{0.5, 1, 1.5, 2\}$. For each sentence, we summed up the scores in each category, up to a maximum value of 5, generating 16 features. The categories are: anger, disappointed, fear, hopeful, joy, lonely, love, negative, neutral, positive, sadness and surprise. Finally, we used the NRC Affect Intensity lexicon (Mohammad, 2017) containing 5814 entries; each entry is a word with a score between 0 and 1 for a given emotion out of the following: anger, fear, joy and sadness. We used the lexicon to produce 4 emotion features from hashtags in the tweets; each feature contained the largest score of all the hashtags in the tweet. For a summary of all features used, see table 6 in the appendix.

7   Experiments

Our general workflow for the tasks is as follows: for each sub-task, we started by cleaning the datasets, obtaining two cleaned versions. We ran a pipeline that produced all the features we designed: the ASC predictions and the features described in section 6. We removed sparse features (less than 8 samples). Next, we defined a shallow neural network with a soft-voting ensemble. We chose the best features and meta-parameters—such as learning rate, batch size and number of epochs—based on the dev dataset. Finally, we generated predictions for the regression tasks. For the classification tasks, we used a grid search method on the regression predictions

Task	Metric	Score	Ranking
V-oc-Spanish		0.765	1/14
V-reg-Spanish		0.770	2/14
V-oc	Pearson	0.813	3/37
EI-oc Average		0.646	4/39
V-reg		0.843	5/38
E-c	Jaccard	0.566	6/35
EI-reg Average	Pearson	0.721	13/48

Table 3: Summary of results.

to optimize the loss. Most model trainings were conducted on a local machine equipped with a Nvidia GTX 1080 Ti GPU. Our official results are summarized in table 3.

7.1   Valence Prediction

In the valence sub-tasks, we identified how intense a general sentiment (valence) is; the score is either in a continuous scale between 0 and 1 or classified into 7 ordinal classes $\{-3, -2, -1, 0, 1, 2, 3\}$, and is evaluated using the Pearson correlation coefficient.

We started with the regression task and defined the following model: first, we normalized the features to have zero mean and SD $= 1$. Then, we inserted 300 instances of fully connected layers of size 3, with a softmax activation and no bias term. For each copy, we applied the function $f(x) = (x_0 - x_2)/2 + 0.5$ where x_0, x_2 are the 1st and 3rd component of each hidden layer. Our aim was transforming the label predictions of the ASCs (trained on 3-label based sentiment annotation) into a regression score such that high certainty in either label (negative, neutral or positive) would produce scores close to 0, 0.5 or 1, respectively. Finally, we calculated the mean of all 300 prediction to get the final node; this is also known as a soft-voting ensemble. We used the Adam optimizer (Kingma and Ba, 2014) with default values, mean-square-error loss function, batch size of 400 and 65 epochs of training. For an illustration of the network, see figure 2. We experimented with the dev dataset, testing different subsets of the features. Finally we produced predictions for the regression sub-task V-reg.

We analyzed the relative contribution of each feature by measuring variable importance using Pratt (1987) approach. We calculated scores d_i for each feature using the following formula: $d_i = \hat{\beta}_i \hat{\rho}_i / R^2$ where $\hat{\beta}_i$ denotes the sample estimation

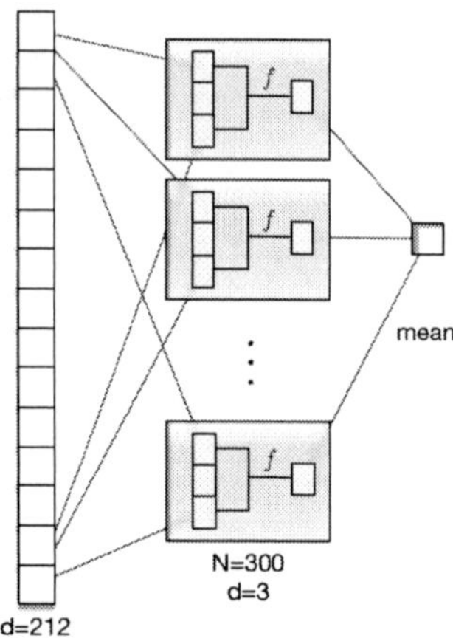

Figure 2: Architecture of the final classifier in the valence sub-tasks, where $f = (x_0 - x_2)/2 + 0.5$ and the input dimension is 212 for the V-reg sub-task.

of the feature, $\hat{\rho}_i$ is the simple correlation between the labels and the ith feature and R^2 is the coefficient of determination (see Thomas et al. 1998). We present the relative contribution of each feature in figure 3 and the top 10 features in table 4. We can see that the ASC models, both general and emotion-specific, contributed about 72% of the total contribution made by all features, in this sub-task.

For the ordinal classification task, we used the predictions of the regression task on the sentences, which were the same in both tasks. Using a grid search method, we partitioned the regression scores into 7 categories such that the Pearson correlation coefficient was maximized. We submitted the classes predictions as sub-task V-oc. Our final scores were 0.843, 0.813 in the regression and classification sub-tasks, respectively.

Name	Dim.	%
ASC_anger	25	31.38%
ASC	25	18.92%
ASC_fear	25	10.63%
ASC_joy	25	8.13%
W2V_200_sadness	15	7.10%
W2V_200_fear	15	3.82%
ASC_sadness	25	3.46%
W2V_200_joy	15	1.74%
Blob	1	1.64%
Joy	1	1.60%

Table 4: Relative contribution of features in the valence regression sub-task.

EI-reg	Anger	Fear	Joy	Sadness
Features	204	274	150	181
Learning rate	10^{-4}	10^{-5}	10^{-5}	$3 \cdot 10^{-5}$
Epochs	330	700	700	1000

Table 5: Summary of training parameters for the emotion intensity regression tasks.

7.2 Emotion Intensity

In the emotion intensity sub-tasks, we identified how intense a given emotion is in the given tweets. The four emotions were: anger, fear, joy and sadness; the score is either in a scale between 0 and 1 or classified into 4 ordinal classes $\{0, 1, 2, 3\}$. Performance was evaluated using the Pearson correlation coefficient. Our approach was similar to the valence tasks; first we generated features, then we used the same architecture as in the valence sub-tasks, depicted in figure 2. However, in these sub-tasks we used the emotion-specific embeddings for each emotion sub-task. We generated regression predictions and submitted them as the EI-reg sub-tasks; finally we carried a grid search for the best partition, maximizing the Pearson correlation and submitted the classes predictions as sub-tasks EI-oc. For a summary of the training parameters used in the regression sub-tasks, see table 5.

Our system performed as following: in the regression tasks, the scores were: 0.748, 0.670, 0.748, 0.721 for the anger, fear, joy and sadness, respectively, with a macro-average of 0.721. In the classification tasks, the scores were: 0.667, 0.536, 0.705, 0.673 for the anger, fear, joy and sadness, respectively, with a macro-average of 0.646.

7.3 Multi-label Classification

In the multi-label classification sub-task, we had to label tweets with respect to 11 emotions: anger, anticipation, disgust, fear, joy, love, optimism, pessimism, sadness, surprise and trust. The score was evaluated using the Jaccard similarity coefficient. We started with the same cleaning and feature-generation pipelines as before, creating an input layer of size 217. We added a fully connected layer of size 100 with tanh activation. Next there were 300 instances of fully connected layers of size 11 with sigmoid activation function. We calculated the mean of all $d = 11$ vectors, producing the final $d = 11$ vector. For an illustration, see figure 4 for an illustration. We used

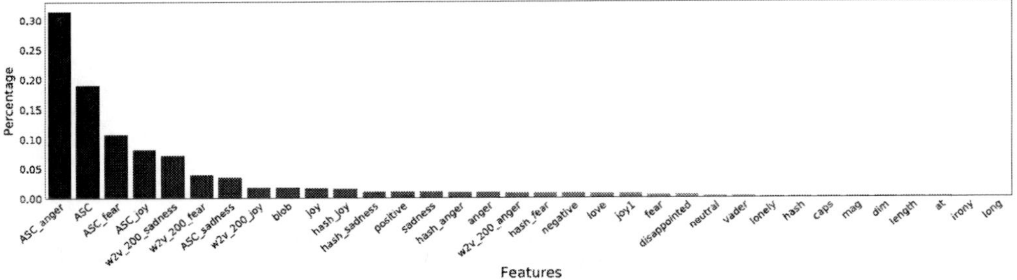

Figure 3: Relative contribution of features in the valence regression sub-task.

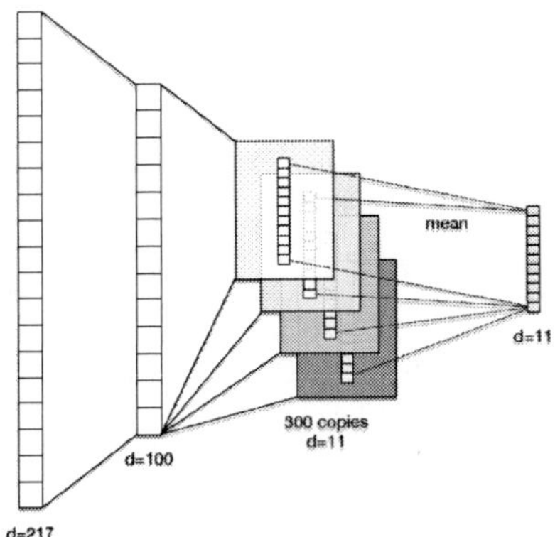

Figure 4: Architecture of the multi-label sub-task E-c.

the following loss function, based on Tanimoto distance: $L(y, \tilde{y}) = 1 - \frac{y \cdot \tilde{y}}{\|y + \tilde{y}\|_1 - y \cdot \tilde{y} + \epsilon}$, where $\| \cdot \|_1$ is an L^1 norm and $\epsilon = 10^{-7}$ is used for numerical stability. We trained with a batch size of 10, for 40 epochs with Adam optimization with default parameters. Our final score was 0.566.

7.4 Spanish Valence Tasks

We participated in the Spanish valence tasks to examine the current state of neural machine translation (NMT) algorithms. We used the Google Cloud Translation API to translate the Spanish training, development and test datasets for the two valence tasks from Spanish to English. We then treated the tasks the same way as the English valence tasks, using the same cleaning and feature extraction pipelines and the same architecture described in section 7.1 to generate regression and classification predictions. We reached 1st and 2nd places in the classification and regression sub-tasks, with scores of 0.765, 0.770, respectively.

8 Review and Conclusions

In this paper we described the system developed to participate in the Semeval 2018 task 1 workshop. We reached 3rd place in the valence ordinal classification sub-task and 5th place in the valence regression sub-task. In the Spanish valence tasks, we reached 1st and 2nd places in the classification and regression sub-tasks, respectively. In the emotions intensity sub-tasks we reached 4th and 13th places in the classification and regression sub-tasks, respectively.

Summarizing the methods used: training of word embeddings based on a Twitter corpus (200M tweets), developing and using Amobee sentiment classifier (ASC) architecture—a bi-directional GRU layer with a CNN-based attention mechanism and an additional hidden layer—used to adjust the embeddings to include emotional context, and finally a shallow feed-forward NN with a stack-based ensemble of final hidden layers from all previous classifiers we trained. This form of transfer learning proved to be important, as the hidden layers features achieved a significant contribution to minimizing the loss.

Overall, we had better performance in the valence tasks, both in English and Spanish. We posit this is due to the fact our annotated supervised training dataset (non task-specific) was based on Semeval 2017 task 4, which focused on valence classification. In addition, the annotations in Semeval 2017 were label-based, lending themselves more easily to the ordinal classification tasks. In the Spanish tasks, we used external translation (Google API) and achieved good results without the use of Spanish-specific features.

Acknowledgment

We thank Zohar Kelrich for assisting in translating the Spanish datasets to English.

References

Martín Abadi, Paul Barham, Jianmin Chen, Zhifeng Chen, Andy Davis, Jeffrey Dean, Matthieu Devin, Sanjay Ghemawat, Geoffrey Irving, Michael Isard, et al. 2016. Tensorflow: A system for large-scale machine learning. In *OSDI*, volume 16, pages 265–283.

Dzmitry Bahdanau, Kyunghyun Cho, and Yoshua Bengio. 2014. Neural machine translation by jointly learning to align and translate. *CoRR*, abs/1409.0473.

Piotr Bojanowski, Edouard Grave, Armand Joulin, and Tomas Mikolov. 2016. Enriching word vectors with subword information. *arXiv preprint arXiv:1607.04606*.

KyungHyun Cho, Bart van Merrienboer, Dzmitry Bahdanau, and Yoshua Bengio. 2014. On the properties of neural machine translation: Encoder-decoder approaches. *CoRR*, abs/1409.1259.

François Chollet et al. 2015. Keras. `https://github.com/keras-team/keras`.

Mathieu Cliche. 2017. Bb_twtr at semeval-2017 task 4: Twitter sentiment analysis with cnns and lstms. *arXiv preprint arXiv:1704.06125*.

John Duchi, Elad Hazan, and Yoram Singer. 2011. Adaptive subgradient methods for online learning and stochastic optimization. *Journal of Machine Learning Research*, 12(Jul):2121–2159.

C.J. Hutto and E.E. Gilbert. 2014. Vader: A parsimonious rule-based model for sentiment analysis of social media text. In *Eighth International Conference on Weblogs and Social Media (ICWSM-14)*, Ann Arbor, MI.

Diederik P Kingma and Jimmy Ba. 2014. Adam: A method for stochastic optimization. *arXiv preprint arXiv:1412.6980*.

Steven Loria, P Keen, M Honnibal, R Yankovsky, D Karesh, E Dempsey, et al. 2014. Textblob: simplified text processing. *Secondary TextBlob: Simplified Text Processing*.

Christopher D. Manning, Mihai Surdeanu, John Bauer, Jenny Finkel, Steven J. Bethard, and David McClosky. 2014. The Stanford CoreNLP natural language processing toolkit. In *Association for Computational Linguistics (ACL) System Demonstrations*, pages 55–60.

Tomas Mikolov, Ilya Sutskever, Kai Chen, Greg S Corrado, and Jeff Dean. 2013. Distributed representations of words and phrases and their compositionality. In C. J. C. Burges, L. Bottou, M. Welling, Z. Ghahramani, and K. Q. Weinberger, editors, *Advances in Neural Information Processing Systems 26*, pages 3111–3119. Curran Associates, Inc.

Saif M Mohammad. 2017. Word affect intensities. *arXiv preprint arXiv:1704.08798*.

Saif M. Mohammad, Felipe Bravo-Marquez, Mohammad Salameh, and Svetlana Kiritchenko. 2018. Semeval-2018 Task 1: Affect in tweets. In *Proceedings of International Workshop on Semantic Evaluation (SemEval-2018)*, New Orleans, LA, USA.

Saif M. Mohammad and Svetlana Kiritchenko. 2018. Understanding emotions: A dataset of tweets to study interactions between affect categories. In *Proceedings of the 11th Edition of the Language Resources and Evaluation Conference*, Miyazaki, Japan.

Olutobi Owoputi, Brendan O'Connor, Chris Dyer, Kevin Gimpel, Nathan Schneider, and Noah A Smith. 2013. Improved part-of-speech tagging for online conversational text with word clusters. Association for Computational Linguistics.

John W Pratt. 1987. Dividing the indivisible: Using simple symmetry to partition variance explained. In *Proceedings of the second international Tampere conference in statistics, 1987*, pages 245–260. Department of Mathematical Sciences, University of Tampere.

Radim Řehůřek and Petr Sojka. 2010. Software Framework for Topic Modelling with Large Corpora. In *Proceedings of the LREC 2010 Workshop on New Challenges for NLP Frameworks*, pages 45–50, Valletta, Malta. ELRA. `http://is.muni.cz/publication/884893/en`.

Duyu Tang, Furu Wei, Nan Yang, Ming Zhou, Ting Liu, and Bing Qin. 2014. Learning sentiment-specific word embedding for twitter sentiment classification. In *Proceedings of the 52nd Annual Meeting of the Association for Computational Linguistics (Volume 1: Long Papers)*, volume 1, pages 1555–1565.

D Roland Thomas, Edward Hughes, and Bruno D Zumbo. 1998. On variable importance in linear regression. *Social Indicators Research*, 45(1-3):253–275.

A Features List

List of features used as inputs for the task-specific models.

Name	Description	Dim.
ASC	ASC model hidden layer.	25
ASC x {anger,fear,joy,sadness}	Emotion specific ASC hidden layers.	4×25
at	'@' symbol in tweet.	1
blob	TextBlob sentiment library.	1
caps	Occurrence of all capitalized words.	1
dim	Diminisher words.	1
{ft,w2v} x {150,200} x {anger,fear,joy,sadness}	Hidden layers of models used to re-train the embeddings.	$4 \times 4 \times 15$
hash	'#' symbol in tweet.	1
hash x {anger,fear,joy,sadness}	Affection lexicon of hashtags.	4
irony	Occurrence of #irony or #sarcasm hashtags.	1
length	Logarithm of sentence length.	1
long	Elongated words, 'wowwww'.	1
mag	Magnifiers.	1
vader	Vader sentiment library.	3

Name	Description	Dim.
negative	Negative emojis.	1
neutral	Neutral emojis.	1
positive	Positive emojis.	1
anger/1		2
fear/1		2
joy/1		2
sadness/1	Detection of emojis and words related to the given emotion, taken from a manually annotated list.	2
love		1
surprise		1
disappointed		1
lonely		1
hopeful		1

Table 6: Complete list of features generated from datasets.

deepSA2018 at SemEval-2018 Task 1: Multi-task Learning of Different Label for Affect in Tweets

[1]**Zi-Yuan Gao and** [2]**Chia-Ping Chen**
Department of Computer Science and Engineering
National Sun Yat-sen University
Kaohsiung, Taiwan
[1]`m053040030@student.nsysu.edu.tw`
[2]`cpchen@cse.nsysu.edu.tw`

Abstract

This paper describes our system implementation for subtask V-oc of SemEval-2018 Task 1: affect in tweets. We use multi-task learning method to learn shared representation, then learn the features for each task. There are five classification models in the proposed multi-task learning approach. These classification models are trained sequentially to learn different features for different classification tasks. In addition to the data released for SemEval-2018, we use datasets from previous SemEvals during system construction. Our Pearson correlation score is 0.638 on the official SemEval-2018 Task 1 test set.

1 Introduction

In recent years, people began to study how to create computational systems that process and understand the human languages. Today, people share their thoughts on social networks of the Internet, e.g. Facebook, Line, Twitter and so on. Thus, if the messages in the textual contents of social networks can be extracted and summarized automatically via algorithms, it is possible to learn what people are interested in or are concerned with, and use such information to predict future market trends.

Here we continue our previous works on the task 4 of SemEval-2017: Sentiment Analysis in Twitter (Rosenthal et al., 2017). SemEval-2017 subtask 4A is similar to task 1 of SemEval-2018: Affect in Tweets (Mohammad et al., 2018). They are challenging tasks as the messages on Twitter, called tweets, are short and informal. Furthermore, in addition to noisy or incomplete texts, the emotional content of a tweet can be ambiguous and subjective.

Affect in Tweets is an expanded version of WASSA-2017 shared task (Mohammad and Bravo-Marquez, 2017). The best system in WASSA-2017 is an ensemble of three sets of approaches, including feed-forward neural network, multi-task deep learning and sequence modeling using CNNs and LSTMs (Goel et al., 2017). They attempt to use the idea of multi-task learning to explore the notion of generalized or shared learning across different emotions. In this paper, we extend the idea with different label methods.

The rest of this paper is organized as follows. In Section 2, we introduce our system. In Section 3, we describe the details of training and experimental settings. In Section 4, we present the evaluation results along with our comments.

2 System Description

2.1 Baseline System

Using RNN has become a very common technique for various NLP tasks. There are many units for RNN-based model like simple RNN, gated recurrent units (GRU) (Chung et al., 2014), and long short-term memory (LSTM) (Hochreiter and Schmidhuber, 1997). For the baseline, we use LSTM as unit for its long-range dependency.

Figure 1 shows the architecture of our baseline system. Our baseline system contains an input layer, an embedding layer, Bi-LSTM layers and an output layer. At the input layer, the words of tweet are pre-processed, and they are treated as a sequence of words $w_1, w_2, ...w_n$. Each word is represented by a one-hot vector, and the size of input layer is equal to the size of word list.

At the embedding layer, each word is converted to a word vector. We use pre-trained word vector which are stored in a matrix. Words are mapped to word vectors by the word embedding matrix. A word not in the word embedding matrix is represented by a zero vector.

A Bi-LSTM layer contains h units. We use bidirectional (Schuster and Paliwal, 1997) structure

Proceedings of the 12th International Workshop on Semantic Evaluation (SemEval-2018), pages 226–230
New Orleans, Louisiana, June 5–6, 2018. ©2018 Association for Computational Linguistics

to gather two-way contextual information at each point. The hidden states from the first word to the penultimate word in a tweet are connected to the hidden states of the next word. The state values in both directions are combined with sum. Only the last Bi-LSTM states of the last word are connected to the output layer. Finally, the network output is converted to probability by a soft-max function.

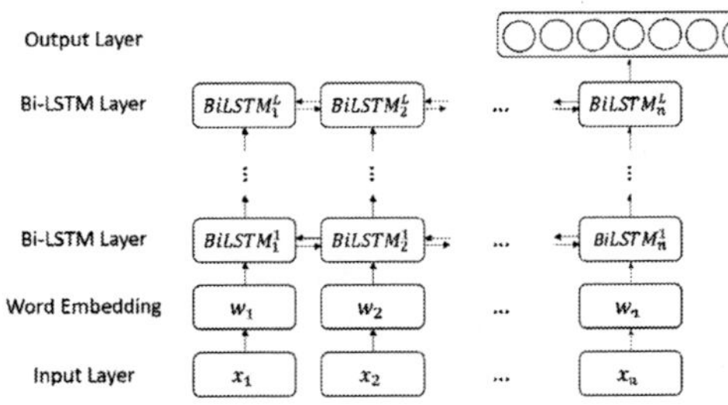

Figure 1: LSTM-RNN architecture.

2.2 Multi-task Learning

Multi-task learning has been used with success in applications of machine learning, from natural language processing (Collobert and Weston, 2008) and speech recognition (Deng et al., 2013). By sharing representations with related tasks, a model tends to generalize better on the original task (Ruder, 2017). In this work, different labels for the same data are exploited in multi-task learning.

Figure 2 shows our multi-task learning framework. The overall system is divided into five models. The Three-class model is trained first, and its trained parameters are used to initialize the parameters in other models. Then we train the Negative, Neutral, Positive class models, and their trained parameters are used to initialize the parameters of the Seven class model. The final output is obtained from the Seven class model.

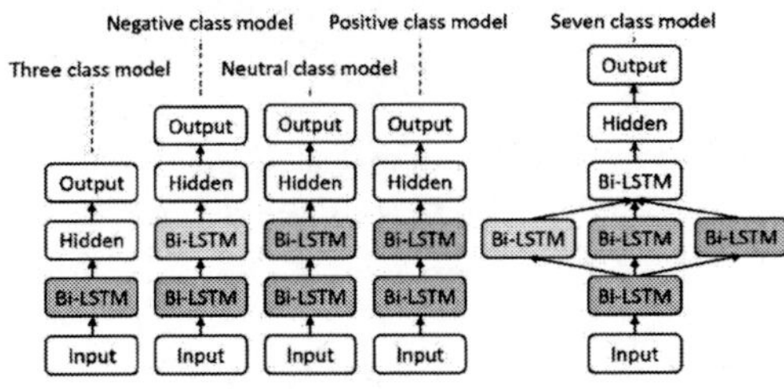

Figure 2: Multi-task learning of sentiment classification.

Three class model In Three class model, the tweets are converted to the word vector and used as the input to Bi-LSTM layer. The output layer has three units for three classes $\{-1, 0, 1\}$.

Negative class model The Negative class model has one more Bi-LSTM layer than Three class model. The output layer has four units for four classes $\{-3, -2, -1, other\}$.

Neutral class model The Neutral class model has the same architecture as the Negative class model. The output layer has two units for two classes $\{0, other\}$.

Positive class model The Positive class model has the same architecture as the Negative class model. The output layer has four units for four classes $\{other, 1, 2, 3\}$.

Seven class model The Seven class model combines the Bi-LSTM layers of the Negative class, Neutral class, and Positive class models. Further, it has one additional Bi-LSTM layer. The output layer has seven units for seven classes $\{-3, -2, -1, 0, 1, 2, 3\}$. Note that attention mechanism (Luong et al., 2015; Wang et al., 2016) is incorporated in this model.

3 Training

3.1 Data

We use the dataset provided for the SemEval-2018 shared task (Mohammad et al., 2018), which includes a new dataset and the datasets provided for SemEval-2017 (Rosenthal et al., 2017). Table 1 summarizes the statistics of these datasets.

3.2 Different Labeling

The SemEval-2017 dataset consists of three-class data, which is different from the new SemEval-2018 dataset. In order to exploit SemEval-2017 dataset, we modify the data labels. In the baseline system, we change the label to ± 1, ± 2, or ± 3. Adding a lot of data lead to imbalance problem, so we apply two methods of data balance. Method 1 is that adding data to positive and negative classes randomly such that they have same size respectively. Method 2 is that adding data to all classes randomly such that they have 3,000 tweets. Table 1 shows the numbers of data points after these different labeling methods.

dataset	labels	Negative			Neutral	Positive			total
		-3	-2	-1	0	1	2	3	
train-18	-	129	249	78	341	167	92	125	1,181
train-17	-		8,581		18,186		15,219		41,986
train-all	to ±1	129	249	8,659	18,527	15,386	92	125	43,167
train-all	to ±2	129	8,830	78	18,527	167	15,311	125	43,167
train-all	to ±3	8,710	249	78	18,527	167	92	15,344	43,167
train-all	bal-method 1	3,013	3,012	3,012	18,527	5,201	5,201	5,201	43,167
train-all	bal-method 2	3,000	3,000	3,000	3,000	3,000	3,000	3,000	21,000
dev-18	-	69	95	34	105	58	35	53	449

Table 1: Statistics of our different labeling methods and datasets. train-18 and dev-18 are from SemEval-2018 Task 1. train-17 is from SemEval-2017 task 4. train-all means the merger of the train-18 and train-17 datasets.

3.3 Pre-processing

We begin with basic pre-processing methods (Yang et al., 2017), e.g. splitting a tweet into word, replacing URLs and USERs with normalization patterns <URL> and <USER>, and converting uppercase letters to lowercase letters. As tweets are informal and complex, the basic pre-processing is too simple to convey enough important information.

Tweets often have emoticons and hashtags, which could be instrumental to sentiment analysis. Thus, we use text processing tool[1] (Baziotis et al., 2017) to improve text normalization, including sentiment-aware tokenization, spell correction, word normalization, word segmentation (for splitting hashtags). and word annotation.

3.4 Early Stopping

The early stopping method is used to prevent overfitting when the loss of a development set ceases to decrease for a few epochs. We randomly take 20% of SemEval-2018 train data as the development set for early stopping and the remaining 80% data as the train set.

3.5 Settings

The maximum length for any tweet in the used datasets is $n = 99$. The embedding is based on a publicly available set of word vectors learned from 400 million tweets for the ACL WNUT 2015 shared task (Baldwin et al., 2015).

The baseline system uses 4 hidden Bi-LSTM layers, with 300 neurons in each layer. Dropout method with probability 0.3 is used to prevent the model from overfitting (Srivastava et al., 2014).

In the multi-task learning approach, the numbers of neurons in the Bi-LSTM and hidden layers are $[200, 200]$, $[200, 150, 200]$, $[200, 150, 100]$, $[200, 150, 200]$, $[200, [150, 150, 150], 200, 200]$ for the 5 different class models, respectively.

4 Results

4.1 Baseline System

First, we compare the experiments of different labeling in baseline system to decide how to use the train-17 dataset. In baseline system, we use the basic pre-processing for text normalization. The results are shown in Table 2. The calculation of Pearson correlation coefficient (Pcc.) requires calculating the mean value of the data, which is often close to zero. From the results, labeling to more distant from zero get the higher Pcc. Therefore, we use labeling to ±3 method in the multi-task learning system.

train set	labels	Pcc.	Acc.
train-18	-	0.515	0.298
train-all	to ±1	0.572	0.261
train-all	to ±2	0.629	0.323
train-all	to ±3	**0.649**	**0.347**
train-all	bal-method 1	0.548	0.303
train-all	bal-method 2	0.553	**0.347**

Table 2: Results of different labeling. Pcc. means the pearson correlation coefficient (all classes). Acc. means the accuracy.

4.2 Multi-task Learning System

Table 3 shows the results of multi-task learning. With basic pre-processing for text normalization, the multi-task learning system is better than the

---

[1] github.com/cbaziotis/ekphrasis

model	training set	Pcc.	Pcc.(s-m)	Kappa	Kappa(s-m)	Acc.
baseline	train-18	0.515	0.567	0.499	0.534	0.298
baseline	train-all	0.649	0.712	0.628	0.700	0.347
multi-task	train-18	0.603	0.660	0.579	0.623	0.312
multi-task	train-all	0.689	0.760	0.671	0.753	0.350
multi-task*	train-18	0.622	0.667	0.616	0.653	**0.361**
multi-task*	train-all	**0.691**	0.770	0.665	0.757	0.323
multi-task*	train-all	**0.638**	0.698	0.606	0.643	-

Table 3: Results of multi-task learning. Final row is the official SemEval-2018 test set result and others are development set results. Here * means using the ekphrasis tool for pre-processing and s-m means some-emotion.

baseline system. When the basic pre-processing method is replaced by using ekphrasis tool, the performance is further improved. Finally, we submit the results from our best system for the unseen test set to SemEval-2018, getting 0.638 for Pcc. eventually. We note this is significantly lower than 0.691 on the development data.

5 Conclusion

The proposed method improves performance on SemEval-2018 over baseline systems without multi-task learning. External dataset can significantly improve the Pcc. performance, but not the Acc. performance. The possible reason is that all the labels of external dataset are marked as ± 3, resulting in data imbalance problem. In the future, we will use skewness-robust weights to solve this problem and use more resources to improve the system as sentiment lexicons.

References

Timothy Baldwin, Marie-Catherine de Marneffe, Bo Han, Young-Bum Kim, Alan Ritter, and Wei Xu. 2015. Shared tasks of the 2015 workshop on noisy user-generated text: Twitter lexical normalization and named entity recognition. In *Proceedings of the Workshop on Noisy User-generated Text*, pages 126–135.

Christos Baziotis, Nikos Pelekis, and Christos Doulkeridis. 2017. Datastories at semeval-2017 task 4: Deep lstm with attention for message-level and topic-based sentiment analysis. In *Proceedings of the 11th International Workshop on Semantic Evaluation (SemEval-2017)*, pages 747–754. Association for Computational Linguistics.

Junyoung Chung, Caglar Gulcehre, KyungHyun Cho, and Yoshua Bengio. 2014. Empirical evaluation of gated recurrent neural networks on sequence modeling. *arXiv preprint arXiv:1412.3555*.

Ronan Collobert and Jason Weston. 2008. A unified architecture for natural language processing: Deep neural networks with multitask learning. In *Proceedings of the 25th international conference on Machine learning*, pages 160–167. ACM.

Li Deng, Geoffrey Hinton, and Brian Kingsbury. 2013. New types of deep neural network learning for speech recognition and related applications: An overview. In *Acoustics, Speech and Signal Processing (ICASSP), 2013 IEEE International Conference on*, pages 8599–8603. IEEE.

Pranav Goel, Devang Kulshreshtha, Prayas Jain, and Kaushal Kumar Shukla. 2017. Prayas at emoint 2017: An ensemble of deep neural architectures for emotion intensity prediction in tweets. In *Proceedings of the 8th Workshop on Computational Approaches to Subjectivity, Sentiment and Social Media Analysis*, pages 58–65.

Sepp Hochreiter and Jürgen Schmidhuber. 1997. Long short-term memory. *Neural computation*, 9(8):1735–1780.

Minh-Thang Luong, Hieu Pham, and Christopher D Manning. 2015. Effective approaches to attention-based neural machine translation. *arXiv preprint arXiv:1508.04025*.

Saif M. Mohammad and Felipe Bravo-Marquez. 2017. WASSA-2017 shared task on emotion intensity. In *Proceedings of the Workshop on Computational Approaches to Subjectivity, Sentiment and Social Media Analysis (WASSA)*, Copenhagen, Denmark.

Saif M. Mohammad, Felipe Bravo-Marquez, Mohammad Salameh, and Svetlana Kiritchenko. 2018. Semeval-2018 Task 1: Affect in tweets. In *Proceedings of International Workshop on Semantic Evaluation (SemEval-2018)*, New Orleans, LA, USA.

Sara Rosenthal, Noura Farra, and Preslav Nakov. 2017. SemEval-2017 task 4: Sentiment analysis in Twitter. In *Proceedings of the 11th International Workshop on Semantic Evaluation*, SemEval '17, Vancouver, Canada. Association for Computational Linguistics.

Sebastian Ruder. 2017. An overview of multi-task learning in deep neural networks. *arXiv preprint arXiv:1706.05098*.

Mike Schuster and Kuldip K Paliwal. 1997. Bidirectional recurrent neural networks. *IEEE Transactions on Signal Processing*, 45(11):2673–2681.

Po-Yuan Shih. 2016. *Skewness-Robust Neural Networks with Application to Speech Emotion Recognition*. Ph.D. thesis, Masters thesis, National Sun Yat-sen University.

Nitish Srivastava, Geoffrey Hinton, Alex Krizhevsky, Ilya Sutskever, and Ruslan Salakhutdinov. 2014. Dropout: A simple way to prevent neural networks from overfitting. *The Journal of Machine Learning Research*, 15(1):1929–1958.

Yequan Wang, Minlie Huang, Li Zhao, et al. 2016. Attention-based lstm for aspect-level sentiment classification. In *Proceedings of the 2016 Conference on Empirical Methods in Natural Language Processing*, pages 606–615.

Tzu-Hsuan Yang, Tzu-Hsuan Tseng, and Chia-Ping Chen. 2017. deepsa at semeval-2017 task 4: Interpolated deep neural networks for sentiment analysis in twitter. In *Proceedings of the 11th International Workshop on Semantic Evaluation (SemEval-2017)*, pages 616–620. Association for Computational Linguistics.

Yichun Yin, Yangqiu Song, and Ming Zhang. 2017. Nnembs at semeval-2017 task 4: Neural twitter sentiment classification: a simple ensemble method with different embeddings. In *Proceedings of the 11th International Workshop on Semantic Evaluation (SemEval-2017)*, pages 621–625.

ECNU at SemEval-2018 Task 1: Emotion Intensity Prediction Using Effective Features and Machine Learning Models

Huimin Xu[1], Man Lan[1,2*] ,Yuanbin Wu[1,2]
[1]Department of Computer Science and Technology,
East China Normal University, Shanghai, P.R.China
[2]Shanghai Key Laboratory of Multidimensional Information Processing
51174506035@stu.ecnu.edu.cn, {mlan, ybwu}@cs.ecnu.edu.cn

Abstract

In this paper we describe our systems submitted to Semeval 2018 Task 1 "Affect in Tweet" (Mohammad et al., 2018). We participated in all subtasks of English tweets, including emotion intensity classification and quantification, valence intensity classification and quantification. In our systems, we extracted four types of features, including linguistic, sentiment lexicon, emotion lexicon and domain-specific features, then fed them to different regressors, finally combined the models to create an ensemble for the better performance. Officially released results showed that our system can be further extended.

1 Introduction

The Semeval 2018 Task 1 aims to automatically determine the intensity of emotions of the tweeters from their tweets, including five subtasks. That is, given a tweet and one of the four emotions (*anger, fear, joy, sadness*), the subtask 1 and 2 are to determine the intensity and classify the tweet into one of the four ordinal classes of intensity of the emotion respectively. Similarly, the subtask 3 and 4 determine the intensity and classify the tweet into one of seven ordinal classes of intensity of valance. Subtask 5 is a multi-label emotion classification task which classifies the tweets as neutral or no emotion or as one, or more, of eleven given emotions (*anger, anticipation, disgust, fear, joy, love, optimism, pessimism, sadness, surprise, trust*) that best represent the mental state of the tweeter. For each task, training and test datasets are divided into **English**, **Arabic**, and **Spanish** tweets. We participated in all subtasks of English tweets.

Traditional sentiment classification is a coarse-grained task in sentiment analysis which focuses on sentiment polarity classification of the whole sentence (*i.e.*, positive, negative, neutral, mixed).

Semeval 2018 Task 1 subtask 5 takes basic human emotion proposed by Ekman (Ekman, 1999) into consideration, including *Anger, Anticipation, Disgust, Fear, Joy, Sadness, Surprise*, and *Trust*.

The difference between these subtasks lies in the emotion granularity and classification or quantification, so in our work, the similar method is adopted for five subtasks. We extracted a rich set of elaborately designed features. In addition to linguistic features, sentiment lexicon features and emotion lexicon features, we also extracted some domain specific features. Also, we conducted a series of experiments on different machine learning algorithms and ensemble methods to obtain the better performing for each subtask. For subask 5, we adopted multiple binary classification and constructed a model for each emotion.

2 System Description

We first performed data preprocessing, then extracted several types of features from tweets and constructed supervised models for this task.

2.1 Data Preprocessing

Firstly, all words are converted to lower case, URLs are replaced by "*url*", abbreviations, s-langs and elongated words are transformed to their normal format. Then, emojis are replaced by corresponding emojis names by "Emoji Library"[1]. Finally, we use *Stanford CoreNLP tools* (Manning et al., 2014) for tokenization, POS tagging, named entity recognizing (NER) and parsing.

2.2 Feature Engineering

We extracted a set of features to construct supervised models for five subtasks, that is linguistic

---

[1]https://github.com/fvancesco/emoji/

Proceedings of the 12th International Workshop on Semantic Evaluation (SemEval-2018), pages 231–235
New Orleans, Louisiana, June 5–6, 2018. ©2018 Association for Computational Linguistics

features, sentiment lexicon features, emotion lexicon features and domain-specific features.

2.2.1 Linguistic Features

- **_Lemma unigram_** Considering there is similar emotion intensity expressed by "anger" and "angers", we choose word lemma unigram features from tweets rather than word unigram features.

- **_Negation_** Negation in a sentence often affects its sentiment orientation, and conveys its intensity of the sentiment. For example, a sentence with several negation words is more inclined to negative sentiment polarity. Following previous work (Zhang et al., 2015), we manually collected 29 negations[2] and designed two binary features. One is to indicate whether there is any negation in the tweet and the other is to record whether this tweet contains more than one negation.

- **_NER_** Given a tweet "*@JackHoward the Christmas episode genuinely had me in tears of laughter*", it has useful information like person name and festival which may convey tweeter's happiness. So we extracted 12 types of named entities (DURATION, SET, NUMBER, LOCATION, PERSON, ORGANIZATION, PERCENT, MISC, ORDINAL, TIME, DATE, MONEY) from the sentence and represented each type of named entity as a binary feature to check whether it appears in the sentence.

2.2.2 Sentiment Lexicon Features

Many tasks related to sentiment or emotion analysis depend upon affect, opinion, sentiment, sense and emotion lexicons. So we employ eight sentiment lexicons to capture the sentiment information of the given sentence. The eight sentiment lexicons are as follows: *Bing Liu lexicon*[3], *General Inquirer lexicon*[4], *IMDB*[5], *MPQA*[6], *NRC Emotion Sentiment Lexicon*[7], *AFINN*[8], *NRC Hashtag Sentiment Lexicon*[9], and *NRC Sentiment140 Lexicon*[10].

There is not a unified form among the eights lexicons. For example, Bing Liu lexicon use two values for each word to represent its sentiment scores which one for positive sentiment and the other for negative sentiment. In order to unify the form, we transformed the two scores into a one-dimensional value by subtracting negative emotion scores from positive emotion scores. Given a tweet, we calculated the following six scores:

- the ratio of positive words to all words.

- the ratio of negative words to all words.

- the maximum sentiment scores.

- the minimum sentiment scores.

- the sum of sentiment scores.

- the sentiment score of the last word in tweet.

2.2.3 Emotion Lexicon Features

Considering subtask 1, 2, 5 are related to emotion intensity prediction, subtask 3, 4 are related valence intensity prediction, three emotion lexicons and one valence lexion are adopted. That is NRC Hashtag Sentiment Lexicon (Mohammad and Kiritchenko, 2015), NRC Affect Intensity Lexicon (Mohammad, 2017), NRC Word-Emotion Association Lexicon (Bravo-Marquez et al., 2017) and ANEW-1999 Lexicon (Bradley and Lang, 1999). Given a tweet, we calculate three scores for each lexicon to construct emotion lexicon features: the maximum scores, the sum of scores, the number of words exist in lexicons.

2.2.4 Domain-specific Features

- **_Punctuation_** People often use exclamation mark(!) and question mark(?) to express surprise or emphasis. Therefore, we extract the following 6 features:

    - whether the tweet contains an exclamation mark.

    - whether the tweet contains more than one exclamation mark.

    - whether the tweet has a question mark.

---

[2]https://github.com/haierlord/resource

[3]http://www.cs.uic.edu/liub/FBS/sentiment-analysis.html#lexicon

[4]http://www.wjh.harvard.edu/inquirer/homecat.htm

[5]http://www.aclweb.org/anthology/S13-2067

[6]http://mpqa.cs.pitt.edu/

[7]http://www.saifmohammad.com/WebPages/lexicons.html

[8]http://www2.imm.dtu.dk/pubdb/views/publication details.php?id=6010

[9]http://www.umiacs.umd.edu/saif/WebDocs/NRC-Hashtag-Sentiment-Lexicon-v0.1.zip

[10]http://help.sentiment140.com/for-students/

- whether the tweet contains more than one question mark.
- whether the tweet contains both exclamation marks and question marks.
- whether the last token of this tweet is an exclamation or question mark.

- **Bag-of-Hashtags** Hashtags reflect emotion orientation of tweets directly, so we constructed a vocabulary of hashtags appearing in the training set and development set, then adopted the bag-of-hashtags method for each tweet.

- **Emoticon** We collected 67 emoticons from Internet[11], including 34 positive emoticons and 33 negative emoticons, then designed the following 4 binary features:

  - to record whether the positive and negative emoticons are present in the tweet, respectively (1 for yes, 0 for no).
  - to record whether the last token is a positive or a negative emoticon.

- **Intensity Words** Some words appeared more frequently in tweets with higher intensity, some words has higher score in emotion lexicons, these words may contain information that express strong emotion intensity. So we extracted this type words in two ways:

  - Pick up words whose emotion score is greater than threshold from emotion lexicons.
  - Calculate the probability of each word appearing at different intensity for subtask 2 and 4, then pick up words whose probability greater than threshold(*i.e.*, 0.5).

Finally, for each word in intensity words list, we use a binary feature to check whether it appears in the given tweet.

2.3 Learning Algorithms

We explore six algorithms as follows: Logistic Regression (LR) and Support Vector Regression (SVR) implemented in *Liblinear*[12], Bagging Regressor (BR), AdaBoost Regressor (ABR) and

[11]https://github.com/haierlord/resource/blob/master/Emoticon.txt

[12]https://www.csie.ntu.edu.tw/ cjlin/liblinear/

Gradient Boosting Regressor (GBR) implemented in *scikit-learn tools*[13] and XGBoost Regressor (XGB)[14]. All these algorithms are used with default parameters.

3 Experiments

3.1 Dataset

The statistics of the English datasets provided by Semeval 2018 Task 1 are shown in Table 1 and 2. How the English data created is described in (Mohammad and Kiritchenko, 2018).

Datasets		anger	fear	joy	sadness
train		1,701	2,252	1,616	1,533
dev		388	689	290	397
test	subtask 1	17,939	17,923	18,042	17,912
	subtask 2	1,002	986	1,105	975

Table 1: The statistics of data sets for subtask 1 and 2.

Subtask	train	dev	test
3	1,181	449	17,874
4	1,181	449	937
5	6,838	886	3,259

Table 2: The statistics of data sets for subtask 3, 4, 5.

3.2 Evaluation Metric

To evaluate the performance of different systems, the official evaluation measure *Pearson Correlation Coefficient* with the Gold ratings/labels is adopted for the first four subtasks. The correlation scores across all four emotions will be averaged (macro-average) to determine the final system performance.

As for the last subtask, systems are evaluated by calculating multi-label accuracy namely *Jaccard index*, the formula are follow:

$$Accuracy = \frac{1}{|T|} \sum_{t \in T} \frac{|G_t \cap P_t|}{|G_t \cup P_t|}$$

where G_t is the set of the gold labels for tweet t, P_t is the set of the predicted labels for tweet t, and T is the set of tweets.

3.3 Experiments on Training and Test Data

Firstly, we performed a series of experiments in order to explore the effectiveness of each feature type. Table 3 lists the performance contributed by

[13]http://scikit-learn.org/stable/

[14]https://github.com/dmlc/xgboost

Features	macro-avg	anger	fear	joy	sadness
Linguistic	0.393	0.398	0.402	0.485	0.286
.+SentiLexi	0.594(+20.1%)	0.606	0.532	0.634	0.603
.+EmoLexi	0.635(+4.1%)	0.689	0.632	0.612	0.606
.+domain	**0.657**(+2.2%)	**0.691**	**0.658**	**0.642**	**0.638**

Table 3: Performance of different features on development set for subtask 1. ".+" means to add current features to the previous feature set. The numbers in the brackets are the performance increments compared with the previous results.

Algorithm	macro-avg	anger	fear	joy	sadness
BR	0.602	0.609	0.618	0.584	0.597
XGBOOST	0.628	0.663	0.656	0.576	0.618
ABR	0.635	0.664	0.666	0.573	0.637
SVR	0.657	0.691	0.658	0.642	0.638
GBR	0.667	0.694	0.675	0.630	0.668
XGBOOST+ABR+SVR+GBR	**0.680**	**0.715**	**0.689**	**0.647**	**0.670**

Table 4: Performance of different learning algorithm on development set for subtask 1.

Subtask	System	macro-avg	anger	fear	joy	sadness
	rank 1	0.799 (1)	0.827 (1)	0.779 (1)	0.792 (1)	0.798 (1)
1	our system	0.695(14)	0.713(15)	0.677(18)	0.693(16)	0.697(14)
	baseline	0.520(36)	0.526(33)	0.525(34)	0.575(33)	0.453(36)
	rank 1	0.695 (1)	0.706 (1)	0.637 (1)	0.720 (2)	0.717 (1)
2	our system	0.531(16)	0.565(13)	0.441(21)	0.581(15)	0.536(20)
	baseline	0.394(26)	0.382(27)	0.355(26)	0.469(26)	0.370(29)

Table 5: Performance of our system, top-ranked system and baseline on test set for subtask 1, 2. SVM and unigrams are adopted in baseline. The numbers in the brackets are the official rankings.

System	Subtask3	Subtask4	Subtask5
rank 1	0.873 (1)	0.836 (1)	0.588 (1)
our system	0.813(14)	0.686(17)	0.501(11)
baseline	0.585(28)	0.509(24)	0.442(19)

Table 6: Performance of our system, top-ranked system and baseline on test set for subtask 3, 4, 5. SVM and unigrams are adopted in baseline. The numbers in the brackets are the official rankings.

different features on development set with Support Vector Regression algorithm for subtask 1. We find that:

(1) All feature types make contribution to the performance of emotion intensity prediction and their combination achieves the best performance.

(2) Linguistic features act as baseline and have shown poor performance for emotion intensity prediction. However, we find the system performance drops once we remove the Linguistic features.

(3) Sentiment lexicon features make a considerable contribution to the performance, which indicates that sentiment lexicon features are beneficial not only in traditional sentiment polarity analysis tasks, but also in emotion intensity prediction tasks.

(4) Beside, we find that the system performance only drops by 0.2% if we remove intensity words features. This indicates that these intensity words fail to distinguish emotion intensity. The reason may be that their function have overlap with sentiment and emotion lexicon features.

Also, we explored the performance of different learning algorithms. Table 4 shows the results of different algorithms for subtask 1 based on all features described before. From table 4, we find that GBR outperforms other single algorithm, and the ensemble model are superior to the models using single algorithm. The ensemble model use the four algorithms to build the ensemble regression models, which averages the output scores of all regression algorithm.

Therefore, the system configurations for test data are: using all features for five subtasks, ensemble model for subtask 1 and 3, Logistic Regression for subtask 2, 4 and 5.

Based on the system configurations described above, we train separate model for each subtask and evaluate them against the test set in SemEval 2018 Task 1. Table 5 and Table 6 shows the results with ranks on test set for subtask 1 to 5. Compared with the top ranked systems, there is much room for improvement in our work. First, the biggest issue is that we only used hand-craft features but ignoring deep learning method. Second, we find that our system achieves greater performance on test set compared with the development set, the possible reason might be the different data distribution held between them.

4 Conclusion

In this paper, we extracted several traditional NLP, sentiment lexicon, emotion lexicon and domain specific features from tweets, adopted supervised machine learning algorithms to perform emotion intensity prediction. The system performance ranks above average. In future work, we consider to use deep learning method to model sentence with the aid of sentiment word vectors.

Acknowledgements

This work is is supported by the Science and Technology Commission of Shanghai Municipality Grant (No. 15ZR1410700) and the open project of Shanghai Key Laboratory of Trustworthy Computing (No.07dz22304201604).

References

Margaret M. Bradley and Peter J. Lang. 1999. Affective norms for english words (anew): Instruction manual and affective ratings. *Journal Royal Microscopical Society*, 88(1):630–634.

Felipe Bravo-Marquez, Eibe Frank, Saif M. Mohammad, and Bernhard Pfahringer. 2017. Determining word-emotion associations from tweets by multilabel classification. In *Ieee/wic/acm International Conference on Web Intelligence*, pages 536–539.

Paul Ekman. 1999. Basic emotions. *Handbook of Cognition and Emotion*, 99(1):45–60.

Christopher D. Manning, Mihai Surdeanu, John Bauer, Jenny Finkel, Steven J. Bethard, and David Mcclosky. 2014. The stanford corenlp natural language processing toolkit. In *Meeting of the Association for Computational Linguistics: System Demonstrations*.

Saif M. Mohammad. 2017. Word affect intensities.

Saif M. Mohammad, Felipe Bravo-Marquez, Mohammad Salameh, and Svetlana Kiritchenko. 2018. Semeval-2018 Task 1: Affect in tweets. In *Proceedings of International Workshop on Semantic Evaluation (SemEval-2018)*, New Orleans, LA, USA.

Saif M Mohammad and Svetlana Kiritchenko. 2015. Using hashtags to capture fine emotion categories from tweets. *Computational Intelligence*, 31(2):301–326.

Saif M. Mohammad and Svetlana Kiritchenko. 2018. Understanding emotions: A dataset of tweets to study interactions between affect categories. In *Proceedings of the 11th Edition of the Language Resources and Evaluation Conference*, Miyazaki, Japan.

Zhihua Zhang, Guoshun Wu, and Man Lan. 2015. Ecnu: Multi-level sentiment analysis on twitter using traditional linguistic features and word embedding features. In *International Workshop on Semantic Evaluation*, pages 561–567.

EMA at SemEval-2018 Task 1: Emotion Mining for Arabic

Gilbert Badaro, Obeida El Jundi, Alaa Khaddaj, Alaa Maarouf, Raslan Kain
Hazem Hajj, Wassim El-Hajj[†]
Department of Electrical and Computer Engineering, American University of Beirut
[†] Department of Computer Science, American University of Beirut
Beirut, Lebanon
`{ggb05;oae15;awk11;aim20;rhk44;hh63;we07}@aub.edu.lb`

Abstract

While significant progress has been achieved for **O**pinion **M**ining in **A**rabic (**OMA**), very limited efforts have been put towards the task of Emotion mining in Arabic. In fact, businesses are interested in learning a fine-grained representation of how users are feeling towards their products or services. In this work, we describe the methods used by the team **E**motion **M**ining in **A**rabic (**EMA**), as part of the SemEval-2018 Task 1 for Affect Mining for Arabic tweets. EMA participated in all 5 subtasks. For the five tasks, several preprocessing steps were evaluated and eventually the best system included diacritics removal, elongation adjustment, replacement of emojis by the corresponding Arabic word, character normalization and light stemming. Moreover, several features were evaluated along with different classification and regression techniques. For the 5 subtasks, word embeddings feature turned out to perform best along with Ensemble technique. EMA achieved the 1st place in subtask 5, and 3rd place in subtasks 1 and 3.

1 Introduction

Emotion recognition has captured the interest of researchers for many years. Different models have been used to detect people's emotions such as human computer interaction (HCI) (Hibbeln et al., 2017; Patwardhan and Knapp, 2017; Constantine et al., 2016) and their facial expressions (Trad et al., 2012; Wegrzyn et al., 2017). Recently, with Web 2.0, the size of textual data charged with opinions and emotions on the web has tremendously increased. Thus, researchers have been looking at automatically performing sentiment and emotion analysis from textual data. In fact, learning emotions of users is critical for different applications such as shaping marketing strategies (Bougie et al., 2003), providing customers with better personalized recommendations for advertisements and products (Mohammad and Yang, 2011), improving recommendation of typical recommender systems (Badaro et al., 2013, 2014c,d), tracking emotions of users towards politicians, movies, music, products, etc, (Pang et al., 2008), or accurately predicting stock market prices (Bollen et al., 2011).

Some efforts have already been placed in developing emotion classification models from text (Shaheen et al., 2014; Houjeij et al., 2012; Abdul-Mageed and Ungar, 2017). Since sentiment lexicons helped in improving the accuracy of sentiment classification models (Liu and Zhang, 2012; Taboada et al., 2011), several researchers are working on developing emotion lexicons for different languages such as English, French, Chinese (Mohammad, 2017; Bandhakavi et al., 2017; Yang et al., 2007; Poria et al., 2012; Das et al., 2012; Mohammad et al., 2013; Abdaoui et al., 2017; Staiano and Guerini, 2014; Badaro et al., 2018a). There were also couple of attempts for developing Arabic emotion lexicons (Mohammad and Turney, 2013; Mohammad et al., 2013; El Gohary et al., 2013; Badaro et al., 2018b).

Building on our previous work on opinion mining which involved development of sentiment lexicons (ArSenL (Badaro et al., 2014a)), opinion mining models (Baly et al., 2014; Al Sallab et al., 2015; Al-Sallab et al., 2017; Baly et al., 2017b) and applications (Badaro et al., 2014b, 2015), and building on our analysis and characterization for Twitter Data (Baly et al., 2017a,c), we participate in SemEval 2018 Task 1 (Mohammad et al., 2018): Affect in Arabic Tweets. In fact, analyzing sentiment and emotions from dialectal Arabic such as text data from Twitter is of great importance given the tremendous increase of Arabic speaking users

Proceedings of the 12th International Workshop on Semantic Evaluation (SemEval-2018), pages 236–244
New Orleans, Louisiana, June 5–6, 2018. ©2018 Association for Computational Linguistics

on Twitter.[1]

In this paper, we describe our approaches to SemEval 2018 Task 1 (Mohammad et al., 2018): Affect in Arabic Tweets, along with the achieved results for each of the subtasks where we employed preprocessing steps, features and classification models based on our prior work on sentiment analysis. In section 2, we present a brief overview of related work to emotion classification for English and Arabic. In section 3, we describe the five subtasks that are part of Affect in Tweet task. In section 4, we present our proposed approach and finally, we conclude in section 5.

2   Related Work

There have been extensive efforts for extracting emotions from different modalities including HCI (Constantine et al., 2016; Hibbeln et al., 2017; Patwardhan and Knapp, 2017), facial expressions (Trad et al., 2012; Wegrzyn et al., 2017) and speech (Houjeij et al., 2012). The related work for text emotion classification can be categorized into approaches for Emotion classification in English, that are leading the advances, versus research progress in Emotion in Arabic texts.

Emotion detection task from text is usually defined as a categorical classification task, where given a text, the classifier needs to predict the emotion label corresponding to the input text. Two typical categorical representations for emotions exist: Ekman representation (Ekman, 1992) which includes anger, happiness, surprise, disgust, sadness and fear and Plutchik model (Plutchik, 1980, 1994) which includes Ekman's six emotions in addition to two labels: trust and anticipation.

2.1   English Emotion Analysis

In general, there are three different approaches for emotion classification: keyword-based detection, learning-based detection, and hybrid detection (Avetisyan et al., 2016).

Keyword-based techniques, also known as lexicon-based, depend on identifying emotional keywords in the input sentence (Strapparava et al., 2004; Mohammad and Turney, 2010, 2013). These models rely on the existence of large scale emotion lexicons and their accuracy is correlated with the accuracy of the emotion lexicon that is being utilized. On the other hand, they do not require

the existence of training data.

Learning-based approaches or feature-based approaches depend on the existence of annotated training data that are processed in order to extract several features such as syntactic, stylistic and semantic features (Ho and Cao, 2012; Bandhakavi et al., 2017). Additionally, in hybrid methods, emotions are detected by using a combination of emotional keywords and learning patterns collected from training datasets.

Due to the notable lack of resources related to emotion (annotated data and lexicons), progress on automatic affect intensity is still lagging. Mohammad and Bravo-Marquez (2017) created not only the first datasets of tweets annotated with emotion intensities, but also developed an emotion regression system with benchmark results. Abdul-Mageed and Ungar (2017) developed a large scale English dataset with fine grained emotion labels and trained deep learning models on top of it achieving an average accuracy of 87.58%.

2.2   Arabic Emotion Analysis

Emotion recognition for Arabic text has been gaining more attention recently. El Gohary et al. (2013) applied a knowledge-based approach to achieve 65% accuracy on the six basic Ekman emotions. Rabie and Sturm (2014) extracted a sample Arabic emotion lexicon and demonstrated how it enhanced the emotion detection results. Sayed et al. (2016) utilized Conditional Random Fields (CRF) and AdaBoost classifiers for classifying emotions of tweets and expression levels in which CRF achieved the best results. Alsharif et al. (2013) used Naive Bayes and SVM to classify Arabic poems into four emotion classes.

While some attempts were performed for Emotion recognition from Arabic text, there is still a lot of area for improvement as for example, developing large scale emotion lexicon for more accurate emotion recognition model, developing highly accurate emotion mining models for MSA as well as dialectal Arabic whether through the use of feature based approaches or deep learning.

3   SemEval 2018 Task 1: Affect in Arabic Tweets

We describe in this section the subtasks of SemEval 2018 task 1.

---

[1] https://weedoo.tech/twitter-arab-world-statistics-feb-2017/

3.1 Subtasks' Descriptions

SemEval 2018 Task 1 Affect in Tweets (Moham-mad et al., 2018) included five subtasks each with annotated dataset for English, Arabic and Spanish. The tasks were as follows:

1. EI-reg (Emotion Intensity Regression Task): Given a tweet and an emotion E (anger, fear, joy or sadness), determine the intensity of E that best represents the emotion intensity of the tweeter by predicting a real-valued score between 0 (least E) and 1 (most E).

2. EI-oc (Emotion Intensity Ordinal Classification): Given a tweet and an emotion E, classify the tweet into one of four ordinal classes of intensity of E, from 0 (low amount) to 3 (high amount), that best represents the mental state of the tweeter.

3. V-reg (a sentiment intensity regression task): Given a tweet, determine the valence (V) that best represents the mental state of the tweeter by predicting a real-valued score between 0 (most negative) and 1 (most positive).

4. V-oc (a sentiment analysis, ordinal classification, task): Given a tweet, classify it into one of seven ordinal classes, from -3 (very negative) to +3 (very positive), corresponding to various levels of positive and negative sentiment intensity, that best represents the sentiment of the tweeter.

5. E-c (an emotion classification task): Given a tweet, classify it as *neutral (no emotion)* or as one, or more, of eleven given emotions that best represent the tweeter.

3.2 Datasets

For each of the 5 tasks, 3 sets of datasets were released, each set corresponding to a language (English, Arabic and Spanish). For each language, 3 datasets were released (training, development and test). For subtasks 1 and 2 Arabic, each emotion of the four emotions had a training set of around 800 tweets on average and a development set of around 200 tweets. Subtasks 3 and 4 Arabic had a dataset consisting of 932 tweets for training and 138 tweets for development. For subtask 5 Arabic, 2278 tweets were used for training and 585 tweets for development.

4 Explored Models for Competition

We present a description of EMA system covering preprocessing steps, features used, machine learn-ing models employed and results achieved. An overview of the system is show in Figure 1.

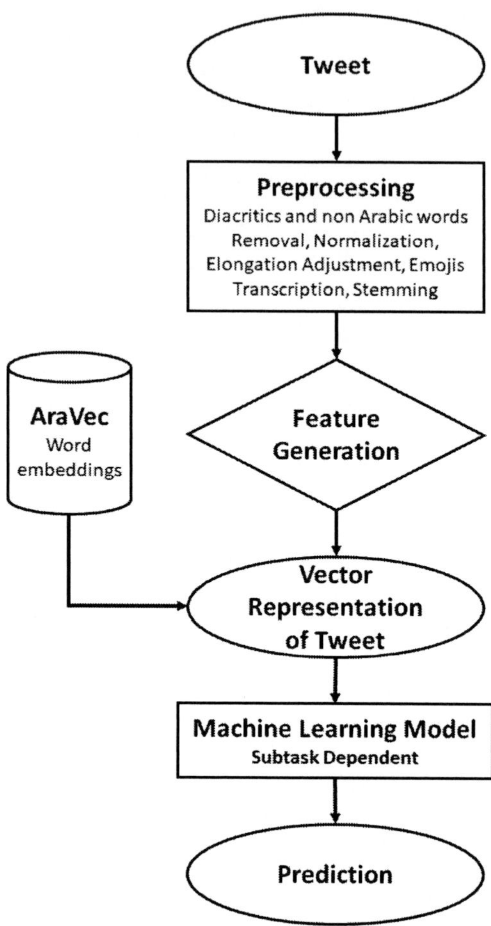

Figure 1: Overview of EMA System.

4.1 Preprocessing

The provided datasets contained raw tweets that included different properties used in Twitter such as hashtags, user mentions, urls, images, Arabizi and emojis. Thus, preprocessing steps were needed to enhance the analysis of the tweet. We experimented with different preprocessing configurations that led to mixed results. For example, using stems instead of lemmas proved to be better. One justification is that tweets are mostly in dialectal Arabic while most Arabic morphological analyzers are trained on MSA data. We present next the steps that led to the best performance.

We first applied the normalization rules followed by Shoukry and Rafea (2012): Diacritics were removed, the "hamza" on characters was

normalized in addition to normalizing some word
ending characters such as the "t marbouta" and
"ya' maqsoura". We then removed elongations
as well as non Arabic letters. We manually created a lexicon containing the most frequent emojis
in tweets and transcribed each emoji to its corresponding Arabic word. The lexicon consisted of
100 emojis. The tweets were finally stemmed using A Robust Arabic Light Stemmer (ARLSTEM)
(Abainia et al., 2017).

4.2 Features

We have tried different features separately including unigrams, bigrams, trigrams, scores from emotion lexicon, ArSEL (Badaro et al., 2018b), sentiment lexicon, ArSenL ((Badaro et al., 2014a) and
word embeddings from AraVec (Soliman et al.,
2017) and FastText by Facebook (Bojanowski
et al., 2016). AraVec was trained on three different
datasets (Wikipedia, Text data from Web and Twitter) while FastText was trained on Wikipedia. Using word embeddings from AraVec outperformed
significantly all other features including word embeddings trained on Wikipedia provided by Facebook. This is likely due to the fact that AraVec is a
large scale dataset (around 205,000 words) trained
on the same data domain (twitter), and includes
several Arabic dialects. Word embeddings overcome the problem of sparsity present with n-grams
and also reduce semantic complexity by providing
similar representations to words that can appear in
the same context. Each word was represented by a
vector of real numbers of dimension 300. The sentence embeddings were computed by taking the
average of its word embeddings. If a word did
not have a vector representation, we tried using
its stem's representation. If neither the word nor
its stem had a vector representation in AraVec, the
average of the embeddings of closest words was
utilized. By closest words, we mean words that
had the smallest minimum edit distance (Levenshtein distance) with the target term. Eventually,
each tweet was represented by a vector consisting
of 300 real valued numbers. The same feature is
used for all subtasks. For feature extraction, we
used Python with NLTK, gensim and Numpy libraries.

4.3 Classification and Regression Models

Overall, we tried different learning models including Ridge regression, support vector machines,
random forests, ensemble methods and deep neural networks such as convolutional neural networks with long short term memory layer. Deep
neural networks performed poorly compared to
other models. One possible explanation was that
the training data size was very small and deep neural networks perform best when trained on a large
scale data to ensure a well representation of the
data (Beleites et al., 2013).

For regression subtasks 1 and 3, we tried different machine learning models including Ridge,
Elastic Net, Decision Trees, random forest, xgboost and support vector regressor with (rbf kernel). The best was an Ensemble of Ridge regression (RR), Support Vector Regressor (SVR), and
Random Forests (RF). In fact, the 3 models performed reasonably well on their own. For classification subtasks 2 and 4, we also tried different
classification models including Ridge, Elastic Net,
Decision Trees, Random Forest, Support Vector
Classifier (SVC) with linear and non linear kernels
and convolutional neural nets. For subtask 2, SVC
performed best. As for subtask 4, an ensemble of
SVC and Ridge Classifier performed best. Ridge
Classifier allows defining a linear mapping without allowing weights to be large thanks to regularization effect for generalization while SVM tries
to find the best classification margins. Adding
ElasticNet did not help much since L1 and L2
errors were already covered by optimized using
the ensemble of Ridge and SVM. Moreover, Zhou
et al. (2015) shows that ElasticNet can be reduced
to SVM. Random Forest with its large number of
estimators had a better generalization than regular decision trees. Combining all these models in
an ensemble model ensured a better generalization
and accuracy on the test data.

For subtask 5, we tested SVC (with both penalties L1 and L2), RC, RF and Ensemble. SVC
with L1 performed best. While Pearson correlation measure was used for evaluating subtasks 1 to
4, Accuracy was used to evaluate subtask 5.

For all subtasks, we utilized the training data for
training the different models and the development
set was treated as unseen data in order to make
sure that comparison across the different models is
fair. The best model was selected based on its performance on the development set. Our focus was
on feature extraction and preprocessing, so most
feature-based models performed well. One main
problem faced in all problems was sparsity, since
most tweets were in Dialectical Arabic.

4.4 Experimental Results

All experiments were conducted using Python with scikit-learn and Keras libraries. A grid search mechanism was utilized to optimize the hyperparameters of the different learning models used and whose performances are reported in below tables: alpha parameter for Ridge, penalty C, kernel and gamma for Support Vectors, and, number trees, maximum tree depth and number of features per tree for Random Forests. Rows 2 to 5 in tables 1 and 2 show the results (Pearson Score) of the different regression techniques used for subtasks 1 and 3 respectively on the corresponding development sets for each of the four emotions (Joy, Sadness, Poor and Anger). Average performance is also reported in the last column. The last two rows in table 1 show the result on the test set of our Ensemble model on average and per each emotion and the performance of the best team for subtask1 respectively. The last two rows in table 2 show the performance of Ridge Regression on the test set and the performance of the best team respectively. In both subtasks, EMA ranked 3rd among participants. By examining the results of the different participants in subtask 1, we can observe that the proposed systems perform best for the Joy emotion. Tables 3 and 4 show the hyperparameters for each technique employed. For Random Forest, the number of estimators was set to 1000.

In Tables 5 and 6, we show the results of subtasks 2 and 4 respectively. SVC was the best performing model on the development set in subtask 2 and Ensemble methods performed best in subtask 4. The last column in table 5 shows the performance of SVC on the test set on average and per each of the four emotions. The last row in table 6 represents the Pearson score achieved by the Ensemble of RC and SVC on the test set. EMA was ranked 8th and 5th in subtasks 2 and 4 respectively. Tables 7 and 8 show the best hyperparameters of the classification models used.

Regression Model	Pearson Correlation
RR	**0.746**
SVR	0.744
RF	0.609
Ensemble	0.737
Ensemble on Test	**0.804**
Best (EiTAKA)	0.8284

Table 2: Subtask 3 Pearson Correlation Results on Dev and Test Sets. RR = Ridge Regression; SVR = Support Vector Regressor; RF = Random Forest.

Regression Model	Joy	Sadness	Fear	Anger
Ridge (alpha)	7.1	5.9	3.7	4.9
SVR (C)	4.4	4.7	10	4.9
RF (depth)	10	10	10	10

Table 3: Subtask 1 Regression Models' Hyperparameters.

Regression Model	Parameter Value
Ridge (alpha)	**3.9**
SVR (C)	5.6
RF (depth)	10

Table 4: Subtask 3 Regression Models' Hyperparameters.

Model	RC	SVC	Ens	SVC on Test	Best (AffecThor)
Joy	0.502	0.484	0.480	0.215	0.631
Sadness	0.587	0.594	0.589	0.535	0.618
Fear	0.373	0.431	0.390	0.242	0.551
Anger	0.472	0.518	0.497	0.077	0.551
Average	0.484	**0.507**	0.489	**0.267**	0.587

Table 5: Subtask 2 Pearson Correlation Results on Dev and Test Sets. RC = Ridge Classification; SVC = Support Vector Classifier; Ens = Ensemble.

Classification Model	Pearson Correlation
RC	0.611
SVC	0.623
Ensemble	**0.625**
Ensemble on Test	**0.643**
Best (EiTAKA)	0.809

Table 6: Subtask 4 Pearson Correlation Results on Dev and Test Sets. RC = Ridge Classification; SVC = Support Vector Classifier.

Regression Model	Joy	Sadness	Fear	Anger	Avg
RR	0.610	0.635	0.481	0.566	0.573
SVR	0.615	0.628	0.484	0.567	0.574
RF	0.578	0.547	0.413	0.458	0.499
Ensemble	0.624	0.630	0.488	0.563	**0.576**
Ensemble on Test	0.709	0.656	0.593	0.615	**0.643**
Best (Affec-Thor)	0.756	0.694	0.642	0.647	0.685

Table 1: Subtask 1 Pearson Correlation Results on Dev and Test Sets. RR = Ridge Regression; SVR = Support Vector Regressor; RF = Random Forest.

Model	RC (alpha)	SVC (C)
Joy	18.2	19.5
Sadness	3.3	29.4
Fear	20.6	17.1
Anger	15.4	19.5

Table 7: Subtask 2 Classification Models' Hyperparameters.

Finally, Table 9 shows the results of subtask 5 on the development and the test sets where for a given tweet, the tweet is classified either as neutral

Classification Model	Parameter Value
RC (alpha)	27.2
SVC (C)	10.7

Table 8: Subtask 4 Classification Models' Hyperparameters.

or as one or more of 11 emotions (anger, anticipation, disgust, fear, joy, love, optimism, pessimism, sadness, surprise, trust). Linear SVC performed best among all classifiers. EMA ranked 1st in subtask 5. Table 10 shows the best hyperparameters for each classification model used. The number of estimators for Random Forest was set to 1000.

Classification Model	Accuracy
SVC L1	**0.488**
SVC L2	0.484
RC	0.443
RF	0.370
Ensemble	0.401
SVC L1 on Test	**0.489**

Table 9: Subtask 5 Accuracy Results on Dev and Test Sets. RC = Ridge Classification; SVC = Support Vector Classifier; RF = Random Forest.

Classification Model	Parameter Value
SVC L1 (C)	1.98
SVC L2 (C)	0.3
RC (alpha)	7.9
RF (depth)	14

Table 10: Subtask 5 Classification Models' Hyperparameters.

5 Conclusion and Future Work

In this paper, we presented EMA (Emotion Mining in Arabic) at SemEval 2018 Task 1 Affect in Tweets to perform Arabic Emotion and Sentiment mining. Several methods were tested for deciding on features, regression and classification techniques. Word embeddings provided the best feature while the choice of the predictor was task dependent. EMA ranked 1st in subtask 5 and 3rd in subtasks 1 and 3. As future work, we suggest finding the best combination of the different features that were employed in separate models. Other future work includes dealing with sparsity caused by dialectal Arabic.

References

Kheireddine Abainia, Siham Ouamour, and Halim Sayoud. 2017. A novel robust arabic light stemmer. *Journal of Experimental & Theoretical Artificial Intelligence*, 29:557–573.

Amine Abdaoui, Jérôme Azé, Sandra Bringay, and Pascal Poncelet. 2017. Feel: a french expanded emotion lexicon. *Language Resources and Evaluation*, 51(3):833–855.

Muhammad Abdul-Mageed and Lyle Ungar. 2017. Emonet: Fine–grained emotion detection with gated recurrent neural networks. In *Proceedings of the 55th Annual Meeting of the Association for Computational Linguistics (Volume 1: Long Papers)*, volume 1, pages 718–728.

Ahmad Al-Sallab, Ramy Baly, Hazem Hajj, Khaled Bashir Shaban, Wassim El-Hajj, and Gilbert Badaro. 2017. Aroma: A recursive deep learning model for opinion mining in arabic as a low resource language. *ACM Transactions on Asian and Low-Resource Language Information Processing (TALLIP)*, 16(4):25.

Ahmad A Al Sallab, Ramy Baly, Gilbert Badaro, Hazem Hajj, Wassim El Hajj, and Khaled B Shaban. 2015. Deep learning models for sentiment analysis in arabic. In *ANLP Workshop*, volume 9.

Ouais Alsharif, Deema Alshamaa, and Nada Ghneim. 2013. Emotion classification in arabic poetry using machine learning. *International Journal of Computer Applications*, 65(16).

H Avetisyan, O Bruna, and J Holub. 2016. Overview of existing algorithms for emotion classification. uncertainties in evaluations of accuracies. In *Journal of Physics: Conference Series*, volume 772. IOP Publishing.

Gilbert Badaro, Ramy Baly, Rana Akel, Linda Fayad, Jeffrey Khairallah, Hazem Hajj, Khaled Shaban, and Wassim El-Hajj. 2015. A light lexicon-based mobile application for sentiment mining of arabic tweets. In *Proceedings of the Second Workshop on Arabic Natural Language Processing*, pages 18–25.

Gilbert Badaro, Ramy Baly, Hazem Hajj, Nizar Habash, and Wassim El-Hajj. 2014a. A large scale Arabic sentiment lexicon for Arabic opinion mining. *ANLP 2014*, 165.

Gilbert Badaro, Ramy Baly, Hazem Hajj, Nizar Habash, Wassim El-hajj, and Khaled Shaban. 2014b. An efficient model for sentiment classification of Arabic tweets on mobiles. In *Qatar*

Foundation Annual Research Conference, 1, page ITPP0631.

Gilbert Badaro, Hazem Hajj, Wassim El-Hajj, and Lama Nachman. 2013. A hybrid approach with collaborative filtering for recommender systems. In *Wireless Communications and Mobile Computing Conference (IWCMC), 2013 9th International*, pages 349–354. IEEE.

Gilbert Badaro, Hazem Hajj, Ali Haddad, Wassim El-Hajj, and Khaled Bashir Shaban. 2014c. A multiresolution approach to recommender systems. In *Proceedings of the 8th Workshop on Social Network Mining and Analysis*, page 9. ACM.

Gilbert Badaro, Hazem Hajj, Ali Haddad, Wassim El-Hajj, and Khaled Bashir Shaban. 2014d. Recommender systems using harmonic analysis. In *Data Mining Workshop (ICDMW), 2014 IEEE International Conference on*, pages 1004–1011. IEEE.

Gilbert Badaro, Hussein Jundi, Hazem Hajj, and Wassim El-Hajj. 2018a. Emowordnet: Automatic expansion of emotion lexicon using english wordnet. In *Proceedings of the Seventh Joint Conference on Lexical and Computational Semantics (*SEM2018) co-located with NAACL2018*.

Gilbert Badaro, Hussein Jundi, Hazem Hajj, Wassim El-Hajj, and Nizar Habash. 2018b. Arsel: A large scale arabic sentiment and emotion lexicon. In *Proceedings of the 3rd Workshop on Open-Source Arabic Corpora and Processing Tools (OSACT3) co-located with LREC2018*.

Ramy Baly, Gilbert Badaro, Georges El-Khoury, Rawan Moukalled, Rita Aoun, Hazem Hajj, Wassim El-Hajj, Nizar Habash, and Khaled Shaban. 2017a. A characterization study of arabic twitter data with a benchmarking for state-of-the-art opinion mining models. In *Proceedings of the Third Arabic Natural Language Processing Workshop*, pages 110–118.

Ramy Baly, Gilbert Badaro, Hazem Hajj, Nizar Habash, Wassim El Hajj, and Khaled Shaban. 2014. Semantic model representation for human's pre-conceived notions in arabic text with applications to sentiment mining. In *Qatar Foundation Annual Research Conference*, 1, page ITPP1075.

Ramy Baly, Gilbert Badaro, Ali Hamdi, Rawan Moukalled, Rita Aoun, Georges El-Khoury, Ahmad Al Sallab, Hazem Hajj, Nizar Habash, Khaled Shaban, et al. 2017b. Omam at semeval-2017 task 4: Evaluation of english state-of-the-art sentiment analysis models for arabic and a new topic-based model. In *Proceedings of the 11th International Workshop on Semantic Evaluation (SemEval-2017)*, pages 603–610.

Ramy Baly, Georges El-Khoury, Rawan Moukalled, Rita Aoun, Hazem Hajj, Khaled Bashir Shaban, and Wassim El-Hajj. 2017c. Comparative evaluation of sentiment analysis methods across arabic dialects. *Procedia Computer Science*, 117:266–273.

Anil Bandhakavi, Nirmalie Wiratunga, Stewart Massie, and Deepak Padmanabhan. 2017. Lexicon generation for emotion detection from text. *IEEE intelligent systems*, 32(1):102–108.

Claudia Beleites, Ute Neugebauer, Thomas Bocklitz, Christoph Krafft, and Jürgen Popp. 2013. Sample size planning for classification models. *Analytica chimica acta*, 760:25–33.

Piotr Bojanowski, Edouard Grave, Armand Joulin, and Tomas Mikolov. 2016. Enriching word vectors with subword information. *arXiv preprint arXiv:1607.04606*.

Johan Bollen, Huina Mao, and Xiaojun Zeng. 2011. Twitter mood predicts the stock market. *Journal of computational science*, 2(1):1–8.

Roger Bougie, Rik Pieters, and Marcel Zeelenberg. 2003. Angry customers don't come back, they get back: The experience and behavioral implications of anger and dissatisfaction in services. *Journal of the Academy of Marketing Science*, 31(4):377–393.

Layale Constantine, Gilbert Badaro, Hazem Hajj, Wassim El-Hajj, Lama Nachman, Mohamed BenSaleh, and Abdulfattah Obeid. 2016. A framework for emotion recognition from human computer interaction in natural setting. *22nd ACM SIGKDD Conference on Knowledge Discovery and Data Mining (KDD 2016), Workshop on Issues of Sentiment Discovery and Opinion Mining (WISDOM 2016)*.

Dipankar Das, Soujanya Poria, and Sivaji Bandyopadhyay. 2012. A classifier based approach to emotion lexicon construction. In *NLDB*, pages 320–326. Springer.

Paul Ekman. 1992. An argument for basic emotions. *Cognition & emotion*, 6(3-4):169–200.

Amira F El Gohary, Torky I Sultan, Maha A Hana, and Mohamed M El Dosoky. 2013. A computational approach for analyzing and detecting emotions in arabic text. *International Journal of Engineering Research and Applications (IJERA)*, 3:100–107.

Martin Hibbeln, Jeffrey L Jenkins, Christoph Schneider, Joseph S Valacich, and Markus Weinmann. 2017. How is your user feeling? inferring emotion through human–computer interaction devices. *MIS Quarterly*, 41(1).

Dung T Ho and Tru H Cao. 2012. A high-order hidden markov model for emotion detection from textual data. In *Pacific Rim Knowledge Acquisition Workshop*, pages 94–105. Springer.

Ali Houjeij, Layla Hamieh, Nader Mehdi, and Hazem Hajj. 2012. A novel approach for emotion classification based on fusion of text and speech. In *Telecommunications (ICT), 2012 19th International Conference on*, pages 1–6. IEEE.

Bing Liu and Lei Zhang. 2012. A survey of opinion mining and sentiment analysis. In *Mining text data*, pages 415–463. Springer.

Saif M Mohammad. 2017. Word affect intensities. *arXiv preprint arXiv:1704.08798*.

Saif M Mohammad and Felipe Bravo-Marquez. 2017. Emotion intensities in tweets. *arXiv preprint arXiv:1708.03696*.

Saif M. Mohammad, Felipe Bravo-Marquez, Mohammad Salameh, and Svetlana Kiritchenko. 2018. Semeval-2018 Task 1: Affect in tweets. In *Proceedings of International Workshop on Semantic Evaluation (SemEval-2018)*, New Orleans, LA, USA.

Saif M Mohammad, Svetlana Kiritchenko, and Xiaodan Zhu. 2013. Nrc-canada: Building the state-of-the-art in sentiment analysis of tweets. *arXiv preprint arXiv:1308.6242*.

Saif M Mohammad and Peter D Turney. 2010. Emotions evoked by common words and phrases: Using mechanical turk to create an emotion lexicon. In *Proceedings of the NAACL HLT 2010 workshop on computational approaches to analysis and generation of emotion in text*, pages 26–34. Association for Computational Linguistics.

Saif M Mohammad and Peter D Turney. 2013. Crowdsourcing a word–emotion association lexicon. *Computational Intelligence*, 29(3):436–465.

Saif M Mohammad and Tony Wenda Yang. 2011. Tracking sentiment in mail: How genders differ on emotional axes. In *Proceedings of the 2nd workshop on computational approaches to subjectivity and sentiment analysis*, pages 70–79. Association for Computational Linguistics.

Bo Pang, Lillian Lee, et al. 2008. Opinion mining and sentiment analysis. *Foundations and Trends® in Information Retrieval*, 2(1–2):1–135.

Amol S Patwardhan and Gerald M Knapp. 2017. Multimodal affect analysis for product feedback assessment. *arXiv preprint arXiv:1705.02694*.

Robert Plutchik. 1980. A general psychoevolutionary theory of emotion. *Theories of emotion*, 1(3-31):4.

Robert Plutchik. 1994. *The psychology and biology of emotion*. HarperCollins College Publishers.

Soujanya Poria, Alexander Gelbukh, Dipankar Das, and Sivaji Bandyopadhyay. 2012. Fuzzy clustering for semi-supervised learning–case study: Construction of an emotion lexicon. In *Mexican International Conference on Artificial Intelligence*, pages 73–86. Springer.

Omneya Rabie and Christian Sturm. 2014. Feel the heat: Emotion detection in arabic social media content. In *The International Conference on Data Mining, Internet Computing, and Big Data (BigData2014)*, pages 37–49. The Society of Digital Information and Wireless Communication.

Amr M Sayed, Samir AbdelRahman, Reem Bahgat, and Aly Fahmy. 2016. Time emotional analysis of arabic tweets at multiple levels. *INTERNATIONAL JOURNAL OF ADVANCED COMPUTER SCIENCE AND APPLICATIONS*, 7(10):336–342.

Shadi Shaheen, Wassim El-Hajj, Hazem Hajj, and Shady Elbassuoni. 2014. Emotion recognition from text based on automatically generated rules. In *Data Mining Workshop (ICDMW), 2014 IEEE International Conference on*, pages 383–392. IEEE.

Amira Shoukry and Ahmed Rafea. 2012. Preprocessing egyptian dialect tweets for sentiment mining. In *The Fourth Workshop on Computational Approaches to Arabic Script-based Languages*, page 47.

Abu Bakr Soliman, Kareem Eissa, and Samhaa R El-Beltagy. 2017. Aravec: A set of arabic word embedding models for use in arabic nlp. *Procedia Computer Science*, 117:256–265.

Jacopo Staiano and Marco Guerini. 2014. Depechemood: A lexicon for emotion analysis from crowd-annotated news. *arXiv preprint arXiv:1405.1605*.

Carlo Strapparava, Alessandro Valitutti, et al. 2004. Wordnet affect: an affective extension of wordnet. In *LREC*, volume 4, pages 1083–1086.

Maite Taboada, Julian Brooke, Milan Tofiloski, Kimberly Voll, and Manfred Stede. 2011. Lexicon-based methods for sentiment analysis. *Computational linguistics*, 37(2):267–307.

Chadi Trad, Hazem M Hajj, Wassim El-Hajj, and Fatima Al-Jamil. 2012. Facial action unit and emotion recognition with head pose variations. In *ADMA*, pages 383–394. Springer.

Martin Wegrzyn, Maria Vogt, Berna Kireclioglu, Julia Schneider, and Johanna Kissler. 2017. Mapping the emotional face. how individual face parts contribute to successful emotion recognition. *PloS one*, 12(5):e0177239.

Changhua Yang, Kevin Hsin-Yih Lin, and Hsin-Hsi Chen. 2007. Building emotion lexicon from weblog corpora. In *Proceedings of the 45th Annual Meeting of the ACL on Interactive Poster and Demonstration Sessions*, pages 133–136. Association for Computational Linguistics.

Quan Zhou, Wenlin Chen, Shiji Song, Jacob R Gardner, Kilian Q Weinberger, and Yixin Chen. 2015. A reduction of the elastic net to support vector machines with an application to gpu computing. In *AAAI*, pages 3210–3216.

NTUA-SLP at SemEval-2018 Task 1: Predicting Affective Content in Tweets with Deep Attentive RNNs and Transfer Learning

**Christos Baziotis[1,3], Nikos Athanasiou[1], Alexandra Chronopoulou[1],
Athanasia Kolovou[1,2], Georgios Paraskevopoulos[1,4], Nikolaos Ellinas[1]
Shrikanth Narayanan[4,5], Alexandros Potamianos[1,4,5]**

[1]School of ECE, National Technical University of Athens, Athens, Greece
[2] Department of Informatics, University of Athens, Athens, Greece
[3] Department of Informatics, Athens University of Economics and Business, Athens, Greece
[4] Behavioral Signal Technologies, Los Angeles, CA
[5] Signal Analysis and Interpretation Laboratory (SAIL), USC, Los Angeles, USA
`cbaziotis@mail.ntua.gr, el12074@central.ntua.gr`
`el12068@central.ntua.gr, akolovou@di.uoa.gr`
`geopar@central.ntua.gr, nellinas@central.ntua.gr`
`shri@sipi.usc.edu, potam@central.ntua.gr`

Abstract

In this paper we present deep-learning models that submitted to the SemEval-2018 Task 1 competition: "Affect in Tweets". We participated in all subtasks for English tweets. We propose a Bi-LSTM architecture equipped with a multi-layer self attention mechanism. The attention mechanism improves the model performance and allows us to identify salient words in tweets, as well as gain insight into the models making them more interpretable. Our model utilizes a set of word2vec word embeddings trained on a large collection of 550 million Twitter messages, augmented by a set of word affective features. Due to the limited amount of task-specific training data, we opted for a transfer learning approach by pretraining the Bi-LSTMs on the dataset of Semeval 2017, Task 4A. The proposed approach ranked 1st in Subtask E "Multi-Label Emotion Classification", 2nd in Subtask A "Emotion Intensity Regression" and achieved competitive results in other subtasks.

1 Introduction

Social media content has dominated online communication, enriching and changing language with new syntactic and semantic constructs that allow users to express facts, opinions and emotions in short amount of text. The analysis of such content has received great attention in NLP research due to the wide availability of data and the interesting language novelties. Specifically the study of affective content in Twitter has resulted in a variety of novel applications, such as tracking product perception (Chamlertwat et al., 2012), public opinion detection about political tendencies (Pla

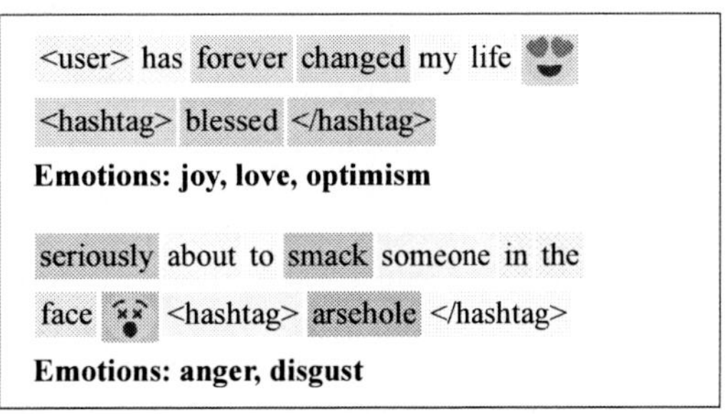

Figure 1: Attention heat-map visualization. The color intensity corresponds to the weight given to each word by the self-attention mechanism.

and Hurtado, 2014; Tumasjan et al., 2010), stock market monitoring (Si et al., 2013; Bollen et al., 2011b) etc. The wide usage of figurative language, such as emojis and special language forms like abbreviations, hashtags, slang and other social media markers, which do not align with the conventional language structure, make natural language processing in Twitter even more challenging.

In the past, sentiment analysis was tackled by extracting hand-crafted features or features from sentiment lexicons (Nielsen, 2011; Mohammad and Turney, 2010, 2013; Go et al., 2009) that were fed to classifiers such as Naive Bayes or Support Vector Machines (SVM) (Bollen et al., 2011a; Mohammad et al., 2013; Kiritchenko et al., 2014). The downside of such approaches is that they require extensive feature engineering from experts and thus they cannot keep up with rapid language evolution (Mudinas et al., 2012), especially in social media/micro-blogging context. However,

Proceedings of the 12th International Workshop on Semantic Evaluation (SemEval-2018), pages 245–255
New Orleans, Louisiana, June 5–6, 2018. ©2018 Association for Computational Linguistics

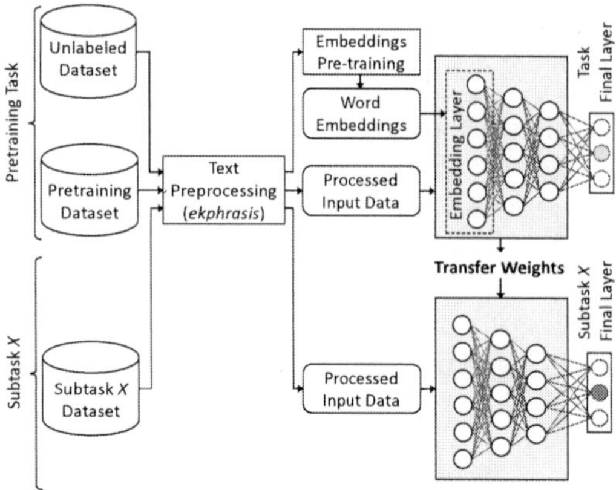

Figure 2: High-level overview of our approach

recent advances in artificial neural networks for text classification have shown to outperform conventional approaches (Deriu et al., 2016; Rouvier and Favre, 2016; Rosenthal et al., 2017a). This can be attributed to their ability to learn features directly from data and also utilize hand-crafted features where needed. Most of aforementioned works focus on sentiment analysis, but similar approaches have been applied to emotion detection (Canales and Martínez-Barco, 2014) leading to similar conclusions. SemEval 2018 Task 1: "Affect in Tweets" (Mohammad et al., 2018) focuses on exploring emotional content of tweets for both classification and regression tasks concerning the four basic emotions (joy, sadness, anger, fear) and the presence of more fine-grained emotions such as disgust or optimism.

In this paper, we present a deep-learning system that competed in SemEval 2018 Task 1: "Affect in Tweets". We explore a transfer learning approach to compensate for limited training data that uses the sentiment analysis dataset of Semeval Task 4A (Rosenthal et al., 2017b) for pretraining a model and then further fine-tune it on data for each subtask. Our model operates at the word-level and uses a Bidirectional LSTM equipped with a deep self-attention mechanism (Pavlopoulos et al., 2017). Moreover, to help interpret the inner workings of our model, we provide visualizations of tweets with annotations of the salient tokens as predicted by the attention layer.

2 Overview

Figure 2 provides a high-level overview of our approach, which consists of three main steps:

(1) the *word embeddings pretraining*, where we train word2vec and affective word embeddings on our unlabeled Twitter dataset, (2) the *transfer learning* step, where we pretrain a deep-learning model on a sentiment analysis task, (3) the *fine-tuning* step, where we fine-tune the pretrained model on each subtask.

Task definitions. Given a tweet we are asked to:
Subtask EI-reg: determine the intensity of a certain emotion (*joy, fear, sadness, anger*), as a real-valued number between in the $[0, 1]$ interval.
Subtask EI-oc: classify its intensity towards a certain emotion (*joy, fear, sadness, anger*) across a 4-point scale.
Subtask V-oc: classify its valence intensity (i.e sentiment intensity) across a 7-point scale $[-3, 3]$.
Subtask V-reg: determine its valence intensity as a real-valued number between in the $[0, 1]$ interval.
Subtask E-c: determine the existence of none, one or more out of eleven emotions: *anger, anticipation, disgust, fear, joy, love, optimism, pessimism, sadness, surprise, trust.*

2.1 Data

Unlabeled Dataset. We collected a big dataset of 550 million English tweets, from April 2014 to June 2017. This dataset is used for (1) calculating word statistics needed in our text preprocessing pipeline (Section 2.3) and (2) training word2vec and affective word embeddings (Section 2.2).

Pretraining Dataset. For transfer learning, we utilized the dataset of Semeval-2017 Task4A. The dataset consists of $61,854$ tweets with $\{positive, neutral, negative\}$ sentiment (valence) annotations. To our knowledge, this is the largest Twitter dataset with affective annotations.

2.2 Word Embeddings

Word embeddings are dense vector representations of words (Collobert and Weston, 2008; Mikolov et al., 2013), capturing their semantic and syntactic information. To this end, we train *word2vec* word embeddings, to which we add 10 affective dimensions. We use our pretrained embeddings, to initialize the first layer (embedding layer) of our neural networks.

Word2vec Embeddings. We leverage our unlabeled dataset to train Twitter-specific word embeddings. We use the *word2vec* (Mikolov et al., 2013) algorithm, with the skip-gram model, negative sampling of 5 and minimum word count of 20, utilizing Gensim's (Řehůřek and Sojka, 2010) implementation. The resulting vocabulary contains $800,000$ words.

Affective Embeddings. Starting from small manually annotated lexica, continuous norms (within the $[-1, 1]$ interval) for new words are estimated using semantic similarity and a linear model along ten affect-related dimensions, namely: valence, dominance, arousal, pleasantness, anger, sadness, fear, disgust, concreteness, familiarity. The method of generating word level norms is detailed in (Malandrakis et al., 2013) and relies on the assumption that given a similarity metric between two words, one may derive the similarity between their affective ratings. This approach uses a set of N words with known affective ratings (seed words), as a starting point. Concretely, we calculate the affective rating of a word w as follows:

$$\hat{v}(w) = \alpha_0 + \sum_{i=1}^{N} \alpha_i v(t_i) S(t_i, w), \qquad (1)$$

where $t_1...t_N$ are the seed words, $v(t_i)$ is the affective rating for seed word t_i, α_i is a trainable weight corresponding to seed t_i and $S()$ stands for the semantic similarity metric between t_i and w. The seed words t_i are selected separately for each dimension, from the words available in the original manual annotations (see 2.2). The $S()$ metric is estimated as shown in (Palogiannidi et al., 2015) using word-level contextual feature vectors and adopting a scheme based on mutual information for feature weighting.

Manually annotated norms. To generate affective norms, we need to start from some manual annotations, so we use ten dimensions from four sources. From the Affective Norms for English Words (Bradley and Lang, 1999) we use norms for valence, arousal and dominance. From the MRC Psycholinguistic database (Coltheart, 1981), we use norms for concreteness and familiarity. From the Paivio norms (Clark and Paivio, 2004) we use norms for pleasantness. Finally from (Stevenson et al., 2007) we use norms for anger, sadness, fear and disgust.

2.3 Preprocessing[1]

We utilized the *ekphrasis*[2] (Baziotis et al., 2017) tool as a tweet preprocessor. The preprocessing steps included in ekphrasis are: Twitter-specific tokenization, spell correction, word normalization, word segmentation (for splitting hashtags) and word annotation.

Tokenization. Tokenization is the first fundamental preprocessing step and since it is the basis for the other steps, it immediately affects the quality of the features learned by the network. Tokenization on Twitter is challenging, since there is large variation in the vocabulary and the expressions which are used. There are certain expressions which are better kept as one token (e.g. anti-american) and others that should be split into separate tokens. Ekphrasis recognizes Twitter markup, emoticons, emojis, dates (e.g. 07/11/2011, April 23rd), times (e.g. 4:30pm, 11:00 am), currencies (e.g. $10, 25mil, 50€), acronyms, censored words (e.g. s**t), words with emphasis (e.g. *very*) and more using an extensive list of regular expressions.

Normalization. After tokenization, we apply a series of modifications on the extracted tokens, such as spell correction, word normalization and segmentation. Specifically for word normalization we use lowercase words, normalize URLs, emails, numbers, dates, times and user handles (@user). This helps reducing the vocabulary size without losing information. For spell correction (Jurafsky and James, 2000) and word segmentation (Segaran and Hammerbacher, 2009) we use the Viterbi algorithm. The prior probabilities are obtained from word statistics from the unlabeled dataset.

The benefits of the aforementioned procedure are the reduction of the vocabulary size, without removing any words, and the preservation of information that is usually lost during tokenization. Table 1 shows an example text snippet and the resulting preprocessed tokens.

---

[1]Significant portions of the systems submitted to SemEval 2018 in Tasks 1, 2 and 3, by the NTUA-SLP team are shared, specifically the preprocessing and portions of the DNN architecture. Their description is repeated here for completeness.

[2]`github.com/cbaziotis/ekphrasis`

original	The *new* season of #TwinPeaks is coming on May 21, 2017. CANT WAIT \o/ !!! #tvseries #davidlynch :D
processed	the new <emphasis> season of <hashtag> twin peaks </hashtag> is coming on <date> . cant <allcaps> wait <allcaps> <happy> ! <repeated> <hashtag> tv series </hashtag> <hashtag> david lynch </hashtag> <laugh>

Table 1: Example of our text processor

2.4 Neural Transfer Learning for NLP

Transfer learning aims to make use of the knowledge from a source domain, to improve the performance of a model in a different, but related, target domain. It has been applied with great success in computer vision (CV) (Razavian et al., 2014; Long et al., 2014). Deep neural networks in CV are rarely trained from scratch and instead are initialized with pretrained models. Notable examples include face recognition (Taigman et al., 2014) and visual QA (Agrawal et al., 2017), where image features trained on ImageNet (Deng et al., 2009) and word embeddings estimated on large corpora via unsupervised training are combined. Although model transfer has seen widespread success in computer vision, transfer learning beyond pretrained word vectors is less pervasive in NLP.

In our system, we explore the approach of pretraining a network in a sentiment analysis task in Twitter and use it to initialize the weights of the models of each subtask. We chose the dataset of Semeval 2017 Task4A (SA2017) (Rosenthal et al., 2017b), which is a semantically similar dataset to the emotion datasets of this task. By pretraining on a dataset in a similar domain, it is more likely that the source and target dataset will have similar distributions.

To build our pretrained model, we initialize the weights of the embedding layer with the word2vec Twitter embeddings and train a bidirectional LSTM (BiLSTM) with a deep self-attention mechanism (Pavlopoulos et al., 2017) on SA2017, similar to (Baziotis et al., 2017). Afterwards, we utilize the encoding part of the network, which is the BiLSTM and the attention layer, throwing away the last layer. This pretrained model is used for all subtasks, with the addition of a subtask-specific final layer for classification/regression.

2.5 Recurrent Neural Networks

We model the Twitter messages using Recurrent Neural Networks (RNN). RNNs process their inputs sequentially, performing the same operation, $h_t = f_W(x_t, h_{t-1})$, on every element in a sequence, where h_t is the hidden state t the time step, and W the network weights. We can see that the hidden state at each time step depends on the previous hidden states, thus the order of elements (words) is important. This process also enables RNNs to handle inputs of variable length.

RNNs are difficult to train (Pascanu et al.,

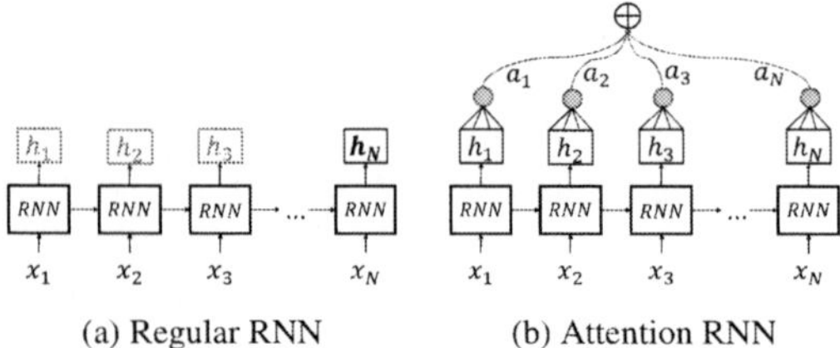

Figure 3: Comparison between regular RNN and attentive RNN.

2013), because gradients may grow or decay exponentially over long sequences (Bengio et al., 1994; Hochreiter et al., 2001). A way to overcome these problems is to use more sophisticated variants of regular RNNs, like Long Short-Term Memory (LSTM) networks (Hochreiter and Schmidhuber, 1997) or Gated Recurrent Units (GRU) (Cho et al., 2014), introducing a gating mechanism to ensure proper gradient flow through the network.

2.6 Self-Attention Mechanism

RNNs update their hidden state h_i as they process a sequence and the final hidden state holds a summary of the information in the sequence. In order to amplify the contribution of important words in the final representation, a self-attention mechanism (Bahdanau et al., 2014) is used as shown in Fig. 3. By employing an attention mechanism, the representation of the input sequence r is no longer limited to just the final state h_N, but rather it is a combination of all the hidden states h_i. This is done by computing the sequence representation, as the convex combination of all h_i. The weights a_i are learned by the network and their magnitude signifies the importance of each h_i in the final representation. Formally:

$$r = \sum_{i=1}^{N} a_i h_i \quad where \quad \sum_{i=1}^{N} a_i = 1, \quad a_i > 0$$

3 Model Description

Next, we present in detail the submitted models. For all subtasks, we adopted a transfer learning approach, by pretraining a BiLSTM network with a deep attention mechanism on SA2017 dataset. Afterwards, we replaced the last layer of the pretrained model with a task-specific layer and fine-tuned the whole network for each subtask.

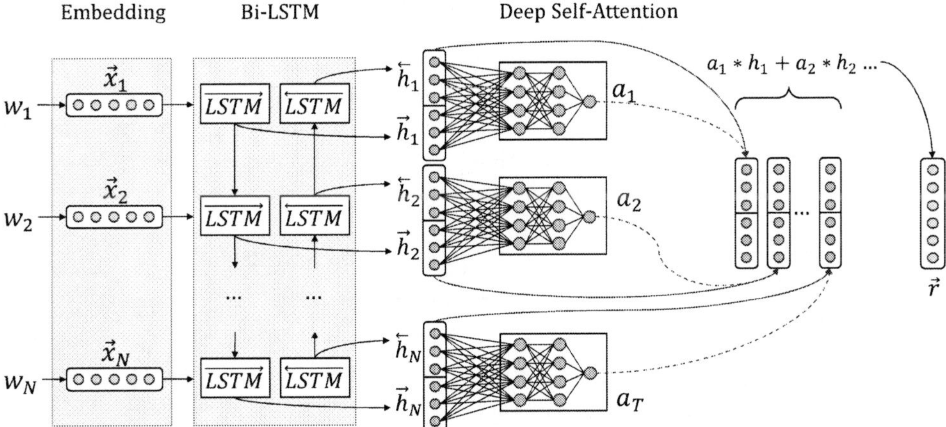

Figure 4: The proposed model, composed of a 2-layer BiLSTM with a deep self-attention mechanism.

3.1 Transfer Learning Model (TF)

Our transfer learning model is based on the sentiment analysis model in (Baziotis et al., 2017). It consists of a 2-layer bidirectional LSTM (BiLSTM) with a deep self-attention mechanism.

Embedding Layer. The input to the network is a Twitter message, treated as a sequence of words. We use an embedding layer to project the words $w_1, w_2, ..., w_N$ to a low-dimensional vector space R^W, where W is the size of the embedding layer and N the number of words in a tweet. We initialize the weights of the embedding layer with our pre-trained word embeddings (Section 2.2).

BiLSTM Layer. An LSTM takes as input a sequence of word embeddings and produces word annotations $h_1, h_2, ..., h_N$, where h_i is the hidden state of the LSTM at time-step i, summarizing all the information of the sentence up to w_i. We use bidirectional LSTMs (BiLSTM) in order to get word annotations that summarize the information from both directions. A BiLSTM consists of 2 LSTMs, a forward LSTM $\overrightarrow{f}$ that parses the sentence from w_1 to w_N and a backward LSTM $\overleftarrow{f}$ that parses the sentence from w_N to w_1. We obtain the final annotation for each word h_i, by concatenating the annotations from both directions,

$$h_i = \overrightarrow{h_i} \parallel \overleftarrow{h_i}, \quad h_i \in R^{2L} \qquad (2)$$

where $\parallel$ denotes the concatenation operation and L the size of each LSTM.

Attention Layer. To amplify the contribution of the most informative words, we augment our BiLSTM with a self-attention mechanism. We use a deep self-attention mechanism (Pavlopoulos et al., 2017), to obtain a more accurate estimation of the importance of each word. The attention weight in the simple self-attention mechanism, is replaced with a multilayer perceptron (MLP), composed of l layers with a non-linear activation function ($tanh$). The MLP learns the attention function g. The attention weights a_i are then computed as a probability distribution over the hidden states h_i. The final representation r is the convex combination of h_i with weights a_i.

$$e_i = g(h_i) \qquad (3)$$

$$a_i = \frac{exp(e_i)}{\sum_{t=1}^{N} exp(e_t)} \qquad (4)$$

$$r = \sum_{i=1}^{N} a_i h_i, \quad r \in R^{2L} \qquad (5)$$

Output Layer. We use vector r as the feature representation, which we feed to a final task-specific layer. For the regression tasks, we use a fully-connected layer with one neuron and a sigmoid activation function. For the ordinal classification tasks, we use a fully-connected layer, followed by a $softmax$ operation, which outputs a probability distribution over the classes. Finally, for the multi-label classification task, we use a fully-connected layer with 11 neurons (number of labels) and a sigmoid activation function, performing binary classification for each label.

3.2 Fine-Tuning

After training a network on the pretraining dataset (SA2017), we fine-tune it on each subtask, by replacing its final layer with a task-specific layer. We experimented with two fine-tuning schemes. The first approach is to fine-tune the whole network, that is, both the pretrained encoder (BiLSTM) and the task-specific layer. The second approach is to use the pretrained model only for weight initialization, freeze its weights during training and just fine-tune the final layer. Based on the experimental results, the first approach obtains significantly better results in all tasks.

3.3 Regularization

In both models, we add Gaussian noise to the embedding layer, which can be interpreted as a random data augmentation technique, that makes models more robust to overfitting. In addition to that, we use dropout (Srivastava et al., 2014) and we stop training after the validation loss has stopped decreasing (early-stopping).

Furthermore, we do not fine-tune the embedding layers. Words occurring in the training set, are projected in the embedding space and the classifier correlates certain regions of the embedding space to certain emotions. However, words included only in the test set, remain at their initial position which may no longer reflect their "true" emotion, leading to mis-classifications.

4 Experiments and Results

4.1 Experimental Setup

Training We use Adam algorithm (Kingma and Ba, 2014) for optimizing our networks, with mini-batches of size 32 and we clip the norm of the gradients (Pascanu et al., 2013) at 1, as an extra safety measure against exploding gradients. For developing our models we used PyTorch (Paszke et al., 2017) and Scikit-learn (Pedregosa et al., 2011).

Class Weights. In subtasks *EI-oc* and *V-oc*, some classes have more training examples than others, introducing bias in our models. To deal with this problem, we apply class weights to the loss function, penalizing more the misclassification of under-represented classes. These weights are computed as the inverse frequencies of the classes in the training set.

Hyper-parameters. In order to tune the hyper-parameter of our model, we adopt a Bayesian optimization (Bergstra et al., 2013) approach, performing a more time-efficient search in the high dimensional space of all the possible values, compared to grid or random search. We set size of the

embedding layer to 310 (300 *word2vec* + 10 affective dimensions), which we regularize by adding Gaussian noise with $\sigma = 0.2$ and dropout of 0.1. The sentence encoder is composed of 2 BiLSTM layers, each of size 250 (per direction) with a 2-layer self-attention mechanism. Finally, we apply dropout of 0.3 to the encoded representation.

4.2 Experiments

In Table 2, we compare the proposed transfer learning models against 3 strong baselines. Pearson correlation is the metric used for the first four subtasks, whereas Jaccard index is used for the *E-c* multi-label classification subtask. The first baseline is a unigram Bag-of-Words (BOW) model with TF-IDF weighting. The second baseline is a Neural Bag-of-Words (N-BOW) model, where we retrieve the *word2vec* embeddings of the words in a tweet and compute the tweet representation as the average (centroid) of the constituent *word2vec* embeddings. Finally, the third baseline is similar to the second one, but with the addition of 10-dimensional affective embeddings that model affect-related dimensions (valence, dominance, arousal, etc). Both BOW and N-BOW features are then fed to a linear SVM classifier, with tuned $C = 0.6$. In order to assess the impact of transfer learning, we evaluate the performance of each model in 3 different settings: (1) random weight initialization (LSTM-RD), (2) transfer learning with frozen weights (LSTM-TL-FR), (3) transfer learning with fine-tuning (LSTM-TL-FT). The results of our neural models in Table 2 are computed by averaging the results of 10 runs to account for model variability.

Baselines. Our first observation is that N-BOW baselines significantly outperform BOW in subtasks *EI-reg*, *EI-oc*, *V-reg* and *V-oc*, in which we have to predict the intensity of an emotion, or the tweet's valence. However, BOW achieves slightly better performance in subtask *E-c*, in which we have to recognize the emotions expressed in each tweet. This can be attributed to the fact that BOW models perform well in tasks where we the occurrence of certain words is sufficient, to accurately determine the classification result. This suggests that in subtask E-c, certain words are highly indicative of some emotions. Word embeddings, though, that encode the correlation of each word with different dimensions, enable NBOW to better predict the intensity of various emotions. Further-

	EI-reg (pearson)				EI-oc (pearson)				V-Reg	V-oc	E-c
	anger	fear	joy	sadness	anger	fear	joy	sadness	(pearson)	(pearson)	(jaccard)
BOW	0.5249	0.5227	0.5716	0.4721	0.3996	0.3491	0.4456	0.3835	0.5963	0.4954	0.4572
NBOW	0.6539	0.6318	0.6355	0.6305	0.5573	0.3796	0.5044	0.5009	0.7501	0.6527	0.4541
NBOW+A*	0.656	0.6359	0.6384	0.6341	0.5367	0.3906	0.4803	0.5005	0.7457	0.6578	0.4478
LSTM-RD	0.7568	**0.7357**	0.7313	0.7479	**0.6387**	**0.5874**	0.6226	0.6343	**0.8462**	**0.7722**	**0.5788**
LSTM-TL-FR	0.7347	0.6509	0.7321	0.7269	0.5999	0.4666	0.6264	0.6030	0.8275	0.7331	0.5243
LSTM-TL-FT	**0.7717**	0.7273	**0.7638**	**0.7665**	0.6329	0.5702	**0.6351**	**0.6400**	0.8390	0.7652	**0.5788**

Table 2: Results of our experiments across all subtasks on the official evaluation metrics. For subtasks *EI-reg, EI-oc, V-reg, V-oc*, the evaluation metric is Pearson correlation. For subtask *E-c*, the evaluation metric is multi-label accuracy (Jaccard index). BOW stands for Bag-of-Words baseline, N-BOW stands for Neural Bag-of-Words baseline and N-BOW+A indicates the inclusion of the affective word features. As for the neural models, RD stands for random initialization, TL for Transfer Learning, FR for Frozen pretrained layers (without fine-tuning) and FT for Fine-Tuning. For our deep-learning models, the results are computed by averaging 10 runs to account for the variability in training performance.

	Ave.diff. Overall	Ave.diff.	p-value
Anger	0.001	0	0.02223
Fear	-0.003	-0.003	0
Joy	0.004	0.010	0
Sadness	0.002	-0.002	0
Valence	0.005	0.005	0

Table 3: Analysis for inappropriate biases

more, regarding the affective embeddings, we can directly observe their impact by the performance gain over the NBOW baseline.

Transfer Learning. We observe that our neural models achieved better performance than all baselines by a large margin. Moreover, we can see that our transfer learning model yielded higher performance over the non-transfer model in most of the Emotion Intensity (EI) subtasks. In the Emotion multi-label classification subtask (E-c), transfer learning did not outperform the random initialization model. This can be attributed to the fact that our source dataset (SA17) was not diverse enough to boost the model performance when classifying the tweets into none, one or more of a set of 11 emotions. As for fine-tuning or freezing the pretrained layers, the overall results show that enabling the model to fine-tune always results in significant gains. This is consistent with our intuition that allowing the weights of the model to adapt to the target dataset, thus encoding task-specific information, results in performance gains. Regarding the emotion of *joy*, we observe that in EI-reg and EI-oc subtasks, LSTM-RD matches the performance of LSTM-TL-FR. We interpret this result as an indication of the semantic similarity between the source and the target task.

Mystery dataset. The submitted models were also evaluated against a mystery dataset, in order to investigate if there is statistically significant social bias in them. This is a very important experiment, especially when automated machine learning algorithms are interacting with social media content and users in the wild. The mystery dataset consists of pairs of sentences that differ only in the social context (e.g. gender or race). Submitted models are expected to predict the same affective values for both sentences in the pair. The evaluation metric is the average difference in prediction scores per class, along with the p-value score indicating if the difference is statistically significant. Results are summarized in Table 3.

4.3 Attention visualizations

Fig. 10 shows a heat-map of the attention weights on top of 8 example tweets (2 tweets per emotion). The color intensity corresponds to the weight given to each word by the self-attention mechanism and signifies the importance of this word for the final prediction. We can see that the salient words correspond to the predicted emotion (e.g. "irritated" for anger, "mourn" for sadness etc.). An interesting observation is that when emojis are present they are almost always selected as important, which indicates their function as weak annotations. Also note that the attention mechanism can hint to dependencies between words even if they far in a sentence, like the "why" and "mad" in the sadness example.

4.4 Competition Results

Our official ranking was 2/48 in subtask 1A (EI-reg), 5/39 in subtask 2A (EI-oc), 4/38 in subtask

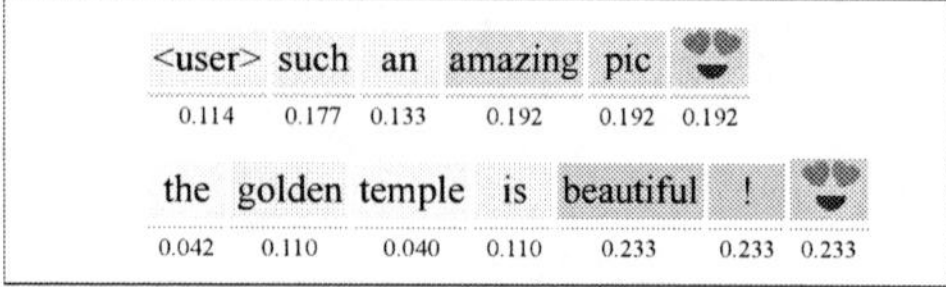

Figure 5: Examples of intensity of *joy*

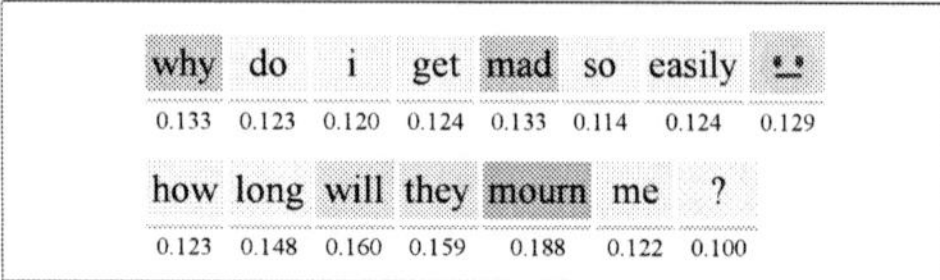

Figure 6: Examples of intensity of *sadness*

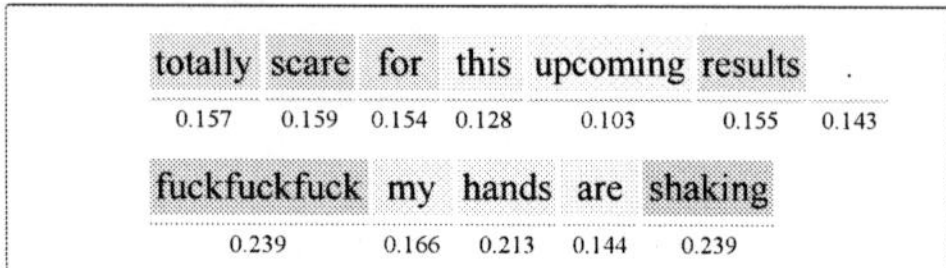

Figure 7: Examples of intensity of *fear*

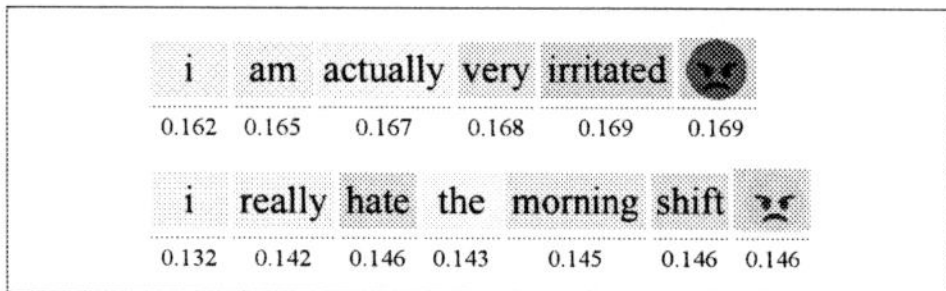

Figure 8: Examples of intensity of *anger*

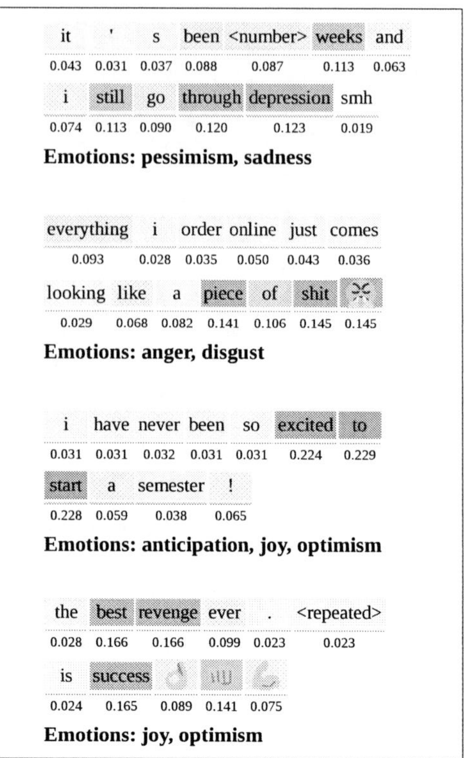

Figure 9: Examples of emotion recognition

Figure 10: Attention heat-map visualization. The color intensity of each word corresponds to its weight (importance), given by the self-attention mechanism (Section 2.6).

3A (V-reg), 8/37 (tie with 6 and 7 place) in subtask 4A (V-oc) and 1/35 in subtask 5A (E-c). All of our models achieved competitive results. We used the same transfer learning approach in all subtasks (LSTM-TL-FT), utilizing the same pretrained model.

5 Conclusion

In this paper we present a deep-learning system for short text emotion intensity, valence estimation for both regression and classification and multi-class emotion classification. We used Bidirectional LSTMs, with a deep attention mechanism and took advantage of transfer learning in order to address the problem of limited training data.

Our models achieved excellent results in single and multi-label classification tasks, but mixed results in emotion and valence intensity tasks. Future work can follow two directions. Firstly, we aim to revisit the task with different transfer learning approaches, such as (Felbo et al., 2017; Howard and Ruder, 2018; Hashimoto et al., 2016).

Secondly, we would like to introduce character-level information in our models, based on (Wieting et al., 2016; Labeau and Allauzen, 2017), in order to overcome the problem of out-of-vocabulary (OOV) words and learn syntactic and stylistic features (Peters et al., 2018), which are highly indicative of emotions and their intensity.

Finally, we make both our pretrained word embeddings and the source code of our models available to the community[3], in order to make our results easily reproducible and facilitate further experimentation in the field.

Acknowledgements. This work has been partially supported by the BabyRobot project supported by EU H2020 (grant #687831). Also, the authors would like to thank NVIDIA for supporting this work by donating a TitanX GPU.

---

[3]`github.com/cbaziotis/`
`ntua-slp-semeval2018-task1`

References

Aishwarya Agrawal, Jiasen Lu, Stanislaw Antol, Margaret Mitchell, C. Lawrence Zitnick, Devi Parikh, and Dhruv Batra. 2017. Vqa: Visual question answering. *Int. J. Comput. Vision*, 123(1):4–31.

Dzmitry Bahdanau, Kyunghyun Cho, and Yoshua Bengio. 2014. Neural machine translation by jointly learning to align and translate. *CoRR*, abs/1409.0473.

Christos Baziotis, Nikos Pelekis, and Christos Doulkeridis. 2017. Datastories at semeval-2017 task 4: Deep lstm with attention for message-level and topic-based sentiment analysis. In *Proceedings of the 11th International Workshop on Semantic Evaluation (SemEval-2017)*, pages 747–754.

Yoshua Bengio, Patrice Simard, and Paolo Frasconi. 1994. Learning long-term dependencies with gradient descent is difficult. *IEEE transactions on neural networks*, 5(2):157–166.

James Bergstra, Daniel Yamins, and David D. Cox. 2013. Making a Science of Model Search: Hyperparameter Optimization in Hundreds of Dimensions for Vision Architectures. *ICML (1)*, 28:115–123.

Johan Bollen, Huina Mao, and Alberto Pepe. 2011a. Modeling public mood and emotion: Twitter sentiment and socio-economic phenomena. *Icwsm*, 11:450–453.

Johan Bollen, Huina Mao, and Xiaojun Zeng. 2011b. Twitter mood predicts the stock market. *Journal of computational science*, 2(1):1–8.

M. Bradley and P. Lang. 1999. Affective norms for English words (ANEW): Instruction Manual and Affective Ratings. Technical report.

Lea Canales and Patricio Martínez-Barco. 2014. Emotion detection from text: A survey. In *Proceedings of the Workshop on Natural Language Processing in the 5th Information Systems Research Working Days (JISIC)*, pages 37–43.

Wilas Chamlertwat, Pattarasinee Bhattarakosol, Tippakorn Rungkasiri, and Choochart Haruechaiyasak. 2012. Discovering consumer insight from twitter via sentiment analysis. *J. UCS*, 18(8):973–992.

Kyunghyun Cho, Bart Van Merriënboer, Caglar Gulcehre, Dzmitry Bahdanau, Fethi Bougares, Holger Schwenk, and Yoshua Bengio. 2014. Learning phrase representations using RNN encoder-decoder for statistical machine translation. *arXiv preprint arXiv:1406.1078*.

J.M. Clark and A. Paivio. 2004. Extensions of the paivio, yuille, and madigan (1968) norms. *Behavior Research Methods, Instruments, & Computers*, 36(3):371–383.

Ronan Collobert and Jason Weston. 2008. A unified architecture for natural language processing: Deep neural networks with multitask learning. In *Proceedings of the 25th International Conference on Machine Learning*, pages 160–167. ACM.

M. Coltheart. 1981. The mrc psycholinguistic database. *The Quarterly Journal of Experimental Psychology Section A*, 33(4):497–505.

Jia Deng, Wei Dong, Richard Socher, Li-Jia Li, Kai Li, and Fei-Fei Li. 2009. Imagenet: a large-scale hierarchical image database.

Jan Deriu, Maurice Gonzenbach, Fatih Uzdilli, Aurelien Lucchi, Valeria De Luca, and Martin Jaggi. 2016. SwissCheese at SemEval-2016 Task 4: Sentiment classification using an ensemble of convolutional neural networks with distant supervision. *Proceedings of SemEval*, pages 1124–1128.

Bjarke Felbo, Alan Mislove, Anders Søgaard, Iyad Rahwan, and Sune Lehmann. 2017. Using millions of emoji occurrences to learn any-domain representations for detecting sentiment, emotion and sarcasm. *arXiv preprint arXiv:1708.00524*.

Alec Go, Richa Bhayani, and Lei Huang. 2009. Twitter sentiment classification using distant supervision. *CS224N Project Report, Stanford*, 1(12).

Kazuma Hashimoto, Caiming Xiong, Yoshimasa Tsuruoka, and Richard Socher. 2016. A joint many-task model: Growing a neural network for multiple nlp tasks. *arXiv preprint arXiv:1611.01587*.

Sepp Hochreiter, Yoshua Bengio, Paolo Frasconi, and Jürgen Schmidhuber. 2001. *Gradient Flow in Recurrent Nets: The Difficulty of Learning Long-Term Dependencies*. A field guide to dynamical recurrent neural networks. IEEE Press.

Sepp Hochreiter and Jürgen Schmidhuber. 1997. Long short-term memory. *Neural computation*, 9(8):1735–1780.

Jeremy Howard and Sebastian Ruder. 2018. Fine-tuned language models for text classification. *arXiv preprint arXiv:1801.06146*.

Daniel Jurafsky and H. James. 2000. Speech and language processing an introduction to natural language processing, computational linguistics, and speech.

Diederik Kingma and Jimmy Ba. 2014. Adam: A method for stochastic optimization. *arXiv preprint arXiv:1412.6980*.

Svetlana Kiritchenko, Xiaodan Zhu, and Saif M. Mohammad. 2014. Sentiment analysis of short informal texts. *Journal of Artificial Intelligence Research*, 50:723–762.

Matthieu Labeau and Alexandre Allauzen. 2017. Character and subword-based word representation for neural language modeling prediction. In *Proceedings of the First Workshop on Subword and Character Level Models in NLP*, pages 1–13.

Jonathan Long, Evan Shelhamer, and Trevor Darrell. 2014. Fully convolutional networks for semantic segmentation. *CoRR*, abs/1411.4038.

N. Malandrakis, A. Potamianos, E. Iosif, and S. Narayanan. 2013. Distributional semantic models for affective text analysis. *IEEE Transactions on Audio, Speech and Language Processing*, 21(11):2379–2392.

Tomas Mikolov, Ilya Sutskever, Kai Chen, Greg S. Corrado, and Jeff Dean. 2013. Distributed representations of words and phrases and their compositionality. In *Advances in Neural Information Processing Systems*, pages 3111–3119.

Saif M. Mohammad, Felipe Bravo-Marquez, Mohammad Salameh, and Svetlana Kiritchenko. 2018. Semeval-2018 Task 1: Affect in tweets. In *Proceedings of International Workshop on Semantic Evaluation (SemEval-2018)*, New Orleans, LA, USA.

Saif M. Mohammad, Svetlana Kiritchenko, and Xiaodan Zhu. 2013. NRC-Canada: Building the state-of-the-art in sentiment analysis of tweets. *arXiv preprint arXiv:1308.6242*.

Saif M Mohammad and Peter D Turney. 2010. Emotions evoked by common words and phrases: Using mechanical turk to create an emotion lexicon. In *Proceedings of the NAACL HLT 2010 workshop on computational approaches to analysis and generation of emotion in text*, pages 26–34. Association for Computational Linguistics.

Saif M Mohammad and Peter D Turney. 2013. Crowdsourcing a word–emotion association lexicon. *Computational Intelligence*, 29(3):436–465.

Andrius Mudinas, Dell Zhang, and Mark Levene. 2012. Combining lexicon and learning based approaches for concept-level sentiment analysis. In *Proceedings of the first international workshop on issues of sentiment discovery and opinion mining*, page 5. ACM.

Finn Årup Nielsen. 2011. A new anew: Evaluation of a word list for sentiment analysis in microblogs. *arXiv preprint arXiv:1103.2903*.

E. Palogiannidi, E. Iosif, P. Koutsakis, and A. Potamianos. 2015. Valence, Arousal and Dominance Estimation for English, German, Greek, Portuguese and Spanish Lexica using Semantic Models. In *Proc. of Interspeech*, pages 1527–1531.

Razvan Pascanu, Tomas Mikolov, and Yoshua Bengio. 2013. On the difficulty of training recurrent neural networks. *ICML (3)*, 28:1310–1318.

Adam Paszke, Sam Gross, Soumith Chintala, Gregory Chanan, Edward Yang, Zachary DeVito, Zeming Lin, Alban Desmaison, Luca Antiga, and Adam Lerer. 2017. Automatic differentiation in pytorch.

John Pavlopoulos, Prodromos Malakasiotis, and Ion Androutsopoulos. 2017. Deep learning for user comment moderation. *arXiv preprint arXiv:1705.09993*.

Fabian Pedregosa, Gaël Varoquaux, Alexandre Gramfort, Vincent Michel, Bertrand Thirion, Olivier Grisel, Mathieu Blondel, Peter Prettenhofer, Ron Weiss, Vincent Dubourg, and others. 2011. Scikit-learn: Machine learning in Python. *Journal of Machine Learning Research*, 12(Oct):2825–2830.

Matthew E Peters, Mark Neumann, Mohit Iyyer, Matt Gardner, Christopher Clark, Kenton Lee, and Luke Zettlemoyer. 2018. Deep contextualized word representations. *arXiv preprint arXiv:1802.05365*.

Ferran Pla and Lluís-F Hurtado. 2014. Political tendency identification in twitter using sentiment analysis techniques. In *Proceedings of COLING 2014, the 25th international conference on computational linguistics: Technical Papers*, pages 183–192.

Ali Sharif Razavian, Hossein Azizpour, Josephine Sullivan, and Stefan Carlsson. 2014. CNN features off-the-shelf: an astounding baseline for recognition. *CoRR*, abs/1403.6382.

Radim Řehůřek and Petr Sojka. 2010. Software Framework for Topic Modelling with Large Corpora. In *Proceedings of the LREC 2010 Workshop on New Challenges for NLP Frameworks*, pages 45–50, Valletta, Malta. ELRA. `http://is.muni.cz/publication/884893/en`.

Sara Rosenthal, Noura Farra, and Preslav Nakov. 2017a. Semeval-2017 task 4: Sentiment analysis in twitter. In *Proceedings of the 11th International Workshop on Semantic Evaluation (SemEval-2017)*, pages 502–518.

Sara Rosenthal, Noura Farra, and Preslav Nakov. 2017b. SemEval-2017 Task 4: Sentiment Analysis in Twitter. In *Proceedings of the 11th International Workshop on Semantic Evaluation*, SemEval '17, Vancouver, Canada. Association for Computational Linguistics.

Mickael Rouvier and Benoit Favre. 2016. SENSEI-LIF at SemEval-2016 Task 4: Polarity embedding fusion for robust sentiment analysis. *Proceedings of SemEval*, pages 202–208.

Toby Segaran and Jeff Hammerbacher. 2009. *Beautiful Data: The Stories Behind Elegant Data Solutions*. "O'Reilly Media, Inc.".

Jianfeng Si, Arjun Mukherjee, Bing Liu, Qing Li, Huayi Li, and Xiaotie Deng. 2013. Exploiting topic based twitter sentiment for stock prediction. In *Proceedings of the 51st Annual Meeting of the Association for Computational Linguistics (Volume 2: Short Papers)*, volume 2, pages 24–29.

Nitish Srivastava, Geoffrey E. Hinton, Alex Krizhevsky, Ilya Sutskever, and Ruslan Salakhutdinov. 2014. Dropout: A simple way to prevent neural networks from overfitting. *Journal of Machine Learning Research*, 15(1):1929–1958.

R.A. Stevenson, J.A. Mikels, and T.W. James. 2007. Characterization of the affective norms for english words by discrete emotional categories. *Behavior research methods*, 39(4):1020–1024.

Yaniv Taigman, Ming Yang, Marc'Aurelio Ranzato, and Lior Wolf. 2014. Deepface: Closing the gap to human-level performance in face verification.

Andranik Tumasjan, Timm Oliver Sprenger, Philipp G Sandner, and Isabell M Welpe. 2010. Predicting elections with twitter: What 140 characters reveal about political sentiment. *Icwsm*, 10(1):178–185.

John Wieting, Mohit Bansal, Kevin Gimpel, and Karen Livescu. 2016. Charagram: Embedding words and sentences via character n-grams. *arXiv preprint arXiv:1607.02789*.

CrystalFeel at SemEval-2018 Task 1: Understanding and Detecting Emotion Intensity using Affective Lexicons

Raj Kumar Gupta and **Yinping Yang**[*]
Institute of High Performance Computing (IHPC)
Agency for Science, Technology and Research (A*STAR), Singapore
$\{gupta\text{-}rk, yangyp\}$@ihpc.a-star.edu.sg

Abstract

While sentiment and emotion analysis has received a considerable amount of research attention, the notion of understanding and detecting the intensity of emotions is relatively less explored. This paper describes a system developed for predicting emotion intensity in tweets. Given a Twitter message, CrystalFeel uses features derived from parts-of-speech, n-grams, word embedding, and multiple affective lexicons including Opinion Lexicon, SentiStrength, AFFIN, NRC Emotion & Hash Emotion, and our in-house developed EI Lexicons to predict the degree of the intensity associated with fear, anger, sadness, and joy in the tweet. We found that including the affective lexicons-based features allowed the system to obtain strong prediction performance, while revealing interesting emotion word-level and message-level associations. On gold test data, CrystalFeel obtained Pearson correlations of .717 on average emotion intensity and of .816 on sentiment intensity.

1 Introduction

While humans experience emotions every day, the degree of one's emotions varies from one experience to another. To date, a vast majority of NLP and computational linguistics research deals with ground truth data constructed through the assignment of discrete labels to text messages by annotators. Conventionally, sentiment analysis seeks to determine the valence (positive, negative or neutral) of the feelings and opinions that annotators can recognize in a text message (Hu and Liu, 2004; Pang and Lee, 2008; Socher et al., 2013). Emotion classification, a closely related task, typically seeks to predict the presence or absence of an emotion, i.e., if there is joy or no joy, anger or no

anger, fear or no fear, in a particular message (Alm et al., 2005; Aman and Szpakowicz, 2007; Wen and Wan, 2014). The detection of emotion intensity along a continuous scale is a relatively less explored task.

One of the key reasons for the lack of work on detecting emotion intensity is plausibly attributable to the difficulty in measuring the very concept of emotion intensity. As highlighted in prior research, the question "how intense was your emotional experience on a scale of 1 to 10?" cannot generate reliable responses even for the same emotion type (Frijda et al., 1992). For example, asking people to respond to "how intense was your fear towards getting rejected" and "how intense was your fear towards receiving a medical test result" would lead to inconsistent answers across the same annotators at different times, as well as across different annotators. Because of the lack of a clear reference point, it is nearly impossible to construct ground truth datasets with adequate reliability.

To address the measurement issue, Mohammad and Bravo-Marquez (2017) used a best-worst scaling (BWS) method to create a tweet emotion intensity dataset. Annotators were asked to rank the best and worst examples of the intensity of emotions among n text examples (called n-tube, where $n > 2$ and typically $n = 4$). This reduces the reference point ambiguity issue faced by annotators with regards to which baseline they would have used to rate a text along a single scale. Upon having a target tweet annotated with 24 ranking judgements, the emotion intensity score for the tweet was computed as a real-valued score in the range of 0 to 1 (based on linear transformed value of the difference between the percentage of the number of times the tweet ranked the highest and the times ranked the lowest among all ranking judgements). In total, the dataset consists of 7,097 an-

---

[*]Both authors contributed to this research equally. Correspondence should be sent to yangyp@ihpc.a-star.edu.sg.

Proceedings of the 12th International Workshop on Semantic Evaluation (SemEval-2018), pages 256–263
New Orleans, Louisiana, June 5–6, 2018. ©2018 Association for Computational Linguistics

	Emotion intensity score in range of [0, 0.5]	Emotion intensity score in range of (0.5, 1.0]
Anger	No words Sir... Thank you for the concern.. [0.197]	Everything I order online just comes looking like a piece of shit [0.864]
Fear	They are building a shell command on a server, combining that with user input, and then executing that in a shell on the client. #shudder [0.482]	Let's hope the ct scan gives us some answers on this lump today #nervous [0.818]
Joy	'You're here to feed me. I won't die of starvation,' he said, slightly smiling. I frowned. Panira. Kainis. [0.177]	Omgsh Alexis is sooooo freaking funny on #BachelorInParadise That pizza segment! Plus I love her and Jazzy's friendship! [0.813]
Sadness	I will not fall to the dark side [0.208]	That moment when you look back and realise you've been a #selfish #horrible #judgemental person. #FeelingAshamed [0.909]

Table 1: Examples of tweets with their emotion intensity scores from the task dataset.

notated tweets across four emotions of anger, fear, joy and sadness, which formed the training dataset for the present SemEval-2018 Task 1 dataset (Mohammad et al., 2018). Table 1 provides a few examples from the dataset.

The ability to detect the degree or intensity of emotions is beneficial to many AI applications. For example, a virtual service assistant would be able to employ more appropriate response strategy when a high-intensity anger or frustration is sensed from its customer, as compared to respond monotonically in normal dialogues. Customer relationship management systems can be more targeted by engaging customers who express high degrees of joy or excitement with their products and services. Homecare robots, empowered with the ability to recognize high-intensity grief or distress, would be less likely to miss the opportunity to alert professional human care givers.

In this paper, we discuss our approach to address this emotion intensity detection task, with a focus on the use of and experiments with affective lexicons. In the following sections, we introduce our in-house developed Emotion Intensity lexicons, and compare the performance of feature sets derived from various affective lexicons as well as parts-of-speech, n-grams and word embedding with SVM-based classifier.

2 Emotion Intensity and Affective Lexicons

In its simplest form, emotion intensity refers to the degree or amount of an emotion (Mohammad and Bravo-Marquez, 2017). A basic feature of emotion intensity would be the use of quantifier words. For example, one may indicate that he or she is a *bit* annoyed, *very* pissed off, or *extremely* angry. On the other hand, one may also say that he or she feels *angry*, *livid*, or *furious*. Without quantifier

words, emotion words in itself are salient features indicating the intensity of emotions.

In 2016, we started in-house efforts to develop a multidimensional affective lexicon that computationally captures and distinguishes different psychological and linguistic meanings associated with each emotion-related word. Our initial version of Emotion Intensity (EI) Lexicon is a collection of 3,204 emotion-related English words, common emoticons and Internet slangs labelled in strength and intensity dimensions (as used in Gupta and Yang 2017). In the beginning, the rationale underlying our work centered on the fact that human emotions can be characterized using two fundamental dimensions: the dimension of evaluation *strength* in that an expression would have different levels of pleasantness or unpleasantness (Osgood et al., 1957), and the dimension of *intensity* (Shaver et al., 1987) which concerns about—and what Osgood et al. (1957) originally called as—motivational "potency" and physical "activity"[1]. By developing a lexicon that distinguishes strength and intensity, anger-based expressions (high in potency), for example, can be differentiated from equally unpleasant, sadness-based expressions (low in potency).

In EI, each lexicon item is coded with strength and intensity scores in the range of [-3, -2, -1, 0, 1, 2, 3]. For example, items such as "excited", "astonished" and "thrill" are coded as "3" (high-intensity, positive); items such as "thank", "cooperative", "concern", ":)" and ":d" are coded as "1" (low-intensity, positive); items such as "sorry", "agh" and ":/" are coded as "-2" (medium-intensity, negative); items such as "hate", "resented", "D:" are coded as "-3" (high-intensity, negative); words such as "great", "haze",

---

[1] For illustration, the feeling of depression is very negative in evaluation strength, but it may not be highly intense.

"fulfill", "sick" and "sleepy" are coded as "0" as they are related to emotions by reflecting external, bodily, physical or cognitive conditions, but are not "genuine" emotions (Ortony et al., 1987; Clore et al., 1987).

In Gupta and Yang (2017), we explored the use of the Emotion Intensity (EI) Lexicon and found it helpful in enhancing sarcasm detection and sentiment analysis. Encouraged by its effectiveness, we continue to develop and use the lexicon by adding more psychologically meaningful affective dimensions. We consider three more dimensions: the *"basic" emotion categories* (Shaver et al., 1987; Ekman, 1973) including fear, anger, sadness, joy, love and surprise, *fine-grained emotion categories* (as summarized in Robinson 2009) including finer emotions such as joy-contentment, joy-cheerfulness, joy-excitement, and *psychological conditions* including affective condition, cognitive condition, physical & bodily state and external condition (Clore et al., 1987). In addition, we also add a *levels of polarity* dimension to reflect if a word is more uni-polarized (e.g., "angry" and "careless" are *definitely* negative) or more bi-polarized (e.g., "surprised" and "sympathetic" may imply both positive and negative feelings). These new considerations contribute to forming the Enhanced Emotion Intensity (E2I) Lexicon. The following table (Table 2) presents the properties of our lexicon in the context of five affective lexicons which were shown to be useful in prior sentiment and emotion analysis research.

3   CrystalFeel System

Focusing on features design and experiments, we employed SVM as the main classifier for the CrystalFeel system. In terms of features, we considered two broad categories: affective lexicon based features, and non-affective lexicon based features.

---

[2]https://www.cs.uic.edu/~liub/FBS/sentiment-analysis.html#lexicon

[3]http://www2.imm.dtu.dk/pubdb/views/publication_details.php?id=6010

[4]http://sentistrength.wlv.ac.uk

[5]http://saifmohammad.com/WebPages/NRC-Emotion-Lexicon.htm

[6]http://saifmohammad.com/WebPages/AccessResource.htm

[7]http://www.crystalace.socialanalyticsplus.net

[8]The construction of the full Enhanced Emotion Intensity Lexicon is under development of a research manuscript. The lexicon will be released to the research community.

3.1   Affective Lexicons-Based Feature Sets

Following the discussion in Section 2, seven sets of affective lexicons based features were extracted for the experiments:

- OL (6 features): counts of positive (+ive) & negative (−ive) words (2 features), order of +ive & −ive words (1 feature), count of both +ive & −ive words (1 feature), start positions of first occurrence of +ive & −ive words (2 features)

- SS (16 features): counts of +ive & −ive words (2), order of +ive & −ive words (1), count of both +ive & −ive words (1), start positions of first occurrence of +ive & −ive words (2), count of words of different strengths of -5 to 4 (10)

- AFFIN (17 features): counts of +ive & −ive words (2), order of +ive & −ive words (1), count of both +ive & −ive words (1), start positions of first occurrence of +ive & −ive words (2), count of words of different strengths of -5 to 5 (11)

- NRC-EmoLex (14 features): counts of +ive & −ive words (2), order of +ive & −ive words (1), count of both +ive & −ive words (1), start positions of first occurrence of +ive & −ive words (2), count of words belonging to 8 emotions (8)

- NRC-Hash-Emo (14 features): counts of +ive & −ive words (2), order of +ive & −ive words (1), count of both +ive & −ive words (1), start positions of first occurrence of +ive & −ive words (2), total intensity of words belonging to 8 emotions (8)

- EI (24 features): counts of +ive & −ive words (2), order of +ive & −ive words (1), count of both +ive & −ive words (1), start positions of first occurrence of +ive & negative words (2), counts of words holding three strengths of 1 to 3 (3), count of words holding three intensities of 1 to 3 (3), counts of positive & negative words holding three strengths of 1 to 3 (6), counts of positive & negative words holding three intensities of 1 to 3 (6)

- E2I (115 features, including 24 EI features): counts of +ive & −ive words (2), order of +ive & −ive words (1), count of both +ive

		Lexicon Size	Lexical/Words Coverage	Affective Dimension Size	Affective Dimension Coverage	Construction Method
1.	Opinion Lexicon (OL)[2] (Hu and Liu, 2004)	6,789	standard English, informal English	1	sentiment/valence	Automatic
2.	AFINN[3] (Nielsen, 2011)	2,477	standard English, informal English	2	sentiment/valence, strength	Manual (Expert Annotation)
3.	SentiStrength (SS)[4] (Thelwall et al., 2012)	2,503	standard English, informal English, emoticons, idioms	2	sentiment/valence, strength	Manual (Expert Annotation)
4.	NRC Word-Emotion Association Lexicon (NRC-Emo-Lex)[5] (Mohammad and Turney, 2010, 2013)	14,182	standard English	2	sentiment/valence, emotion category (8 emotions)	Manual (Crowd-sourced Annotation)
5.	NRC Hashtag Emotion Association Lexicon (NRC-Hash-Emo)[6] (Mohammad, 2012; Mohammad and Kiritchenko, 2015)	16,862	informal English	2	emotion category (8 emotions), association (real-valued numeric score)	Automatic
6.	Emotion Intensity (EI) Lexicon[7] (Gupta and Yang, 2017)	3,204	standard English, informal English, emoticons	3	sentiment/valence, strength, intensity	Manual (Expert Annotation)
7.	Enhanced Emotion Intensity (E2I) Lexicon[8]	3,446	standard English, informal English, emoticons, idioms	7	sentiment/valence, strength, intensity, emotion category (6 basic emotions), fine-grained emotion category (31 fine emotions), psychological condition (4 conditions), polarity condition (4 conditions)	Manual (Expert Annotation)

Table 2: Affective lexicons used in our emotion intensity analysis experiments.

& −ive words (1), start positions of first occurrence of +ive & −ive words (2), counts of words holding three strengths of 1 to 3 (3), count of words holding three intensities of 1 to 3 (3), counts of words belonging to 6 emotions and unspecific words (7), counts of words belonging to 31 emotions and unspecific words (32), counts of words belonging to 4 psychological conditions (4), counts of words belonging to 4 polarity conditions (4), pairwise intersection features across all the dimensions (56)

3.2 N-grams, POS, Word Counts, and Word Embedding Feature Sets

In addition to affective lexicons, we extracted 25-dimensional Tweet part-of-speech (POS) features (Owoputi et al., 2013) for each tweet. Furthermore, as emotion intensity is likely to be associated with the total tweet length and use of capital letters, we added the word counts (WC) features set including counting of total words and counting of uppercase letters. We extracted n-grams in the same way as in our earlier work (Gupta and Yang, 2017). Lastly, we used FastText (Joulin et al., 2016) to convert the tweets into a 100-dimensional feature vectors. To train FastText model, we downloaded close to 8 million tweets using Twitter Streaming API. In summary:

- POS (25 features): Counts of proper nouns, verbs, conjunctions, adjectives, hasthags, emoticons, urls, punctuations etc. computed using TweetPOS tagger

- WC (2 features): Counts of uppercase letters, text length

- N-grams (12,650 features): uni-grams & bi-grams

- Word Embedding (100 features): word embedding features computed using FastText

3.3 Feature Experiments

Based on the setup, we use the official SemEval-2018 Task 1 training and development datasets to

	Pearson correlations (r)				
	Anger	**Fear**	**Joy**	**Sadness**	**Avg.**
Individual Affective Lexicons Feature Sets					
OL	0.364	0.426	**0.538**	0.383	0.428
SS	0.290	0.484	0.445	0.402	0.405
AFFIN	0.344	0.383	0.508	0.440	0.419
NRC-EmoLex	0.216	0.414	0.300	0.301	0.308
NRC-Hash-Emo	**0.453**	**0.492**	0.477	0.359	0.445
EI	0.195	0.378	0.368	0.375	0.329
E2I	0.362	0.475	0.458	**0.531**	**0.456**
Combined Affective Lexicon Features Sets					
OL + SS	0.300	0.508	0.545	0.457	0.453
OL + SS + AFFIN	0.358	0.497	0.587	0.525	0.492
OL + SS + AFFIN + NRC-EL	0.353	0.544	0.576	0.540	0.503
OL + SS + AFFIN + NRC-EL + NRC-H-E	0.528	0.629	**0.627**	0.585	0.592
OL + SS + AFFIN + NRC-EL + NRC-H-E + E2I	**0.544**	**0.629**	0.626	**0.622**	**0.605**
Other Individual Feature Sets					
POS	0.136	0.123	0.070	0.223	0.138
WC	-0.005	0.106	0.069	0.070	0.060
N-grams	0.378	**0.608**	0.497	0.504	0.497
Word Embedding	**0.611**	0.557	**0.585**	0.580	0.583
All Features Sets					
All Features	**0.702**	**0.689**	**0.666**	**0.689**	**0.686**

Table 3: Results of feature experiments trained and tested on SemEval-2018 training and development data (highest results in each features sets group are bolded).

train and test the performance of various individual and combined feature conditions. The results are presented in Table 3.

Among individual lexicon based feature sets, features derived from E2I alone led to highest macro-averaged Pearson correlations ($r = 0.456$). (Note that r ranges from -1 to 1 where -1 means perfect reverse correlation and 1 means perfect correlation; a random algorithm gives close to 0.) The performances of NRC-Hash-Emo and OL came closely as second ($r = 0.445$) and third ($r = 0.428$). Interestingly, on specific emotions, E2I's advantage ($r = 0.531$) on the prediction of sadness is significantly greater than the second highest prediction of sadness from AFFIN derived features ($r = 0.440$). NRC-Hash-Emo led to highest results for anger ($r = 0.453$) and fear ($r = 0.492$), and OL features led to the highest value for joy ($r = 0.538$).

For the combined affective lexicon features settings, we observed that there was a tendency for each feature set to result in additional advantage (e.g., combining OL + SS features with OL or SS features alone) on the macro-averaged scores, suggesting the complementarity across these lexicons. Combining all the lexicons resulted in a large improvement (avg. $r = 0.605$).

Among non-affective lexicons based features sets, word embedding features obtained the best result ($r = 0.583$). Except for predicting fear, in which n-grams performed better ($r = 0.608$), word embedding's advantage also held for predicting anger ($r = 0.611$), joy ($r = 0.585$) and sadness ($r = 0.580$).

Finally, we combined all the lexicon-based features (with small variations[9] from the individual experiment conditions) and non-lexicon based features. This "all-features" condition resulted in the highest performance for avg. Pearson correlation ($r = 0.684$) and individual correlations for all four emotions. The all-features setting was used for the CrystalFeel system for gold test data.

3.4 Word-level and Message-level Analysis

So to what extent are emotion words from affective lexicons indicative of emotion intensity in tweets at the message level? To explore this question, we ran correlation analysis by calculating bivariate Pearson correlation coefficients between each feature derived from the affective lexicons and the emotion intensity ground truth labels. Figure 1 shows the results.

The analysis indicated several interesting patterns related to the usefulness of lexicon dimensions. First, the sentiment/valence dimension of affective lexicons were generally useful, as the counts of +ive and −ive words (regardless the source of the lexicons) showed up in top ten fea-

---

[9]The variations are not including two features of start positions of first occurrence of +ive & −ive words (2) for NRC-EmoLex and NRC-Hash-Emo.

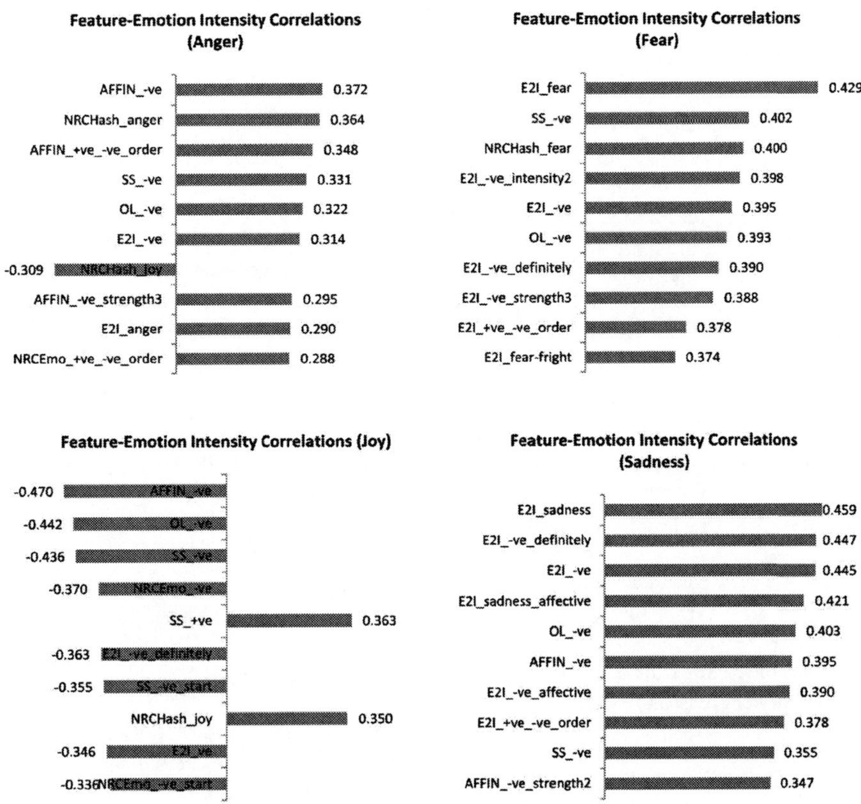

Figure 1: Top ten features with highest bivariate feature-emotion intensity correlations across the four emotion datasets.

	Pearson correlations (r)				
	Anger	Fear	Joy	Sadness	Avg.
Random_Baseline	-0.008	-0.018	-0.058	0.024	-0.008
SVM_Unigrams_Baseline	0.520	0.526	0.575	0.525	0.520
CrystalFeel	**0.740**	**0.700**	**0.708**	**0.720**	**0.717**

Table 4: Evaluation Results on subtask 1 emotion intensity regression (EI-reg).

	Pearson correlations (r)				
	Anger	Fear	Joy	Sadness	Avg.
Random_Baseline	-0.008	-0.018	0.024	-0.058	-0.008
SVM_Unigrams_Baseline	0.520	0.526	0.525	0.575	0.520
CrystalFeel	**0.576**	**0.466**	**0.540**	**0.538**	**0.530**

Table 5: Evaluation Results on subtask 2 emotion intensity ordinal classification (EI-oc).

tures for all four emotions. Second, features derived from the advanced dimensions of the affective lexicons appeared across the emotions too, suggesting the meaningfulness of lexicons distinguishing finer dimensions of psycholingusitic properties of words. Specifically, for example, on strength dimension, count of negative words with strength 3 from AFFIN lexicon (AFFIN_-ive_strength3) is positively correlated with anger intensity in tweets ($r = 0.295$). On emotion category dimension, counts of anger words from NRC-Hash-Emo (NRCHash_anger) and from E2I (E2I_anger) are positively associated with anger intensity in tweets. Third, more fine-grained dimensions from E2I are shown as top individual features correlated with anger and sadness intensities and in particular with sadness intensity. For example, count of fear-fright words from E2I (E2I_fear-fright) is highly correlated with fear intensity ($r = 0.374$) and count of sadness words as genuine emotions (E2I_sadness_affective) is highly correlated with sadness intensity ($r = 0.421$).

Furthermore, the results revealed interesting word-level and message-level feature associations across the four emotions. While the top features for intensities of anger, fear and sadness in tweets (9 or 10 out of 10 top features) are *positive* associations with the presence and higher amount of negative or emotion-specific words, the top features for intensity of joy (7 out of 10 top features) are *negative* associations with the absence and lower amount of negative words. It deserves future research to further investigate these patterns and to cross examine these patterns in other datasets.

	Pearson correlations (r)
	Valence
Random_Baseline	0.031
SVM_Unigrams_Baseline	0.585
CrystalFeel	**0.816**

Table 6: Evaluation Results on subtask 3 valence/ sentiment intensity regression (V-reg).

	Pearson	Kappa
	Valence	Valence
Random_Baseline	-0.010	-0.010
SVM_Unigrams_Baseline	0.509	0.504
CrystalFeel	**0.652**	**0.637**

Table 7: Evaluation Results on subtask 4 valence/ sentiment ordinal classification (V-oc).

	Accuracy	Micro-avg F_1	Macro-avg F_1
Random_Baseline	0.185	0.307	0.285
SVM_Unigrams_Baseline	0.442	0.570	0.443
CrystalFeel	**0.468**	**0.601**	**0.522**

Table 8: Evaluation Results on subtask 5 multi-label emotion classification (E-c).

4 Results

We evaluated the CrystalFeel system using gold test datasets provided by SemEval-2018 Task 1 (Mohammad et al., 2018). Besides testing the main task of emotion intensity, since it is our primary interest, we have also participated in all other subtasks. In all subtasks, CrystalFeel system outperformed the baseline set by the task organizer. Tables 4-8 summarize the final results.

5 Conclusion

This paper describes CrystalFeel system which is capable of predicting the intensity of emotions associated with a Twitter message. The results of the feature experiments supported the usefulness of our in-house developed EI & E2I lexicons as a new manually constructed lexicon on a relatively small number of lexicon items. In addition, the lexicon also aided us to understand the different patterns of associations between emotion-specific words and emotion-specific intensities at the tweets/messages level. Based on the current analysis, it appeared that our approach possesses a special advantage in understanding and predicting sadness-specific intensity present in tweets. For the use of classifiers, we focused on using SVM as our machine learning classifier in the present study. We plan to investigate the use of deep learning methods in future work.

Acknowledgment

This research is supported by SERC Strategic Fund from Science and Engineering Research Council (SERC), A*STAR (project no. a1718g0046). The authors thank Andrew Ortony for his valuable comments on emotions and emotion intensity and the Digital Emotions team for helpful discussions. We are grateful for the help from Nur Atiqah Othman for her proofreading and enhancement on the clarity of the paper.

References

Cecilia Ovesdotter Alm, Dan Roth, and Richard Sproat. 2005. Emotions from text: machine learning for text-based emotion prediction. *International conference on Human Language Technology and Empirical Methods in Natural Language Processing* pages 579–586.

Saima Aman and Stan Szpakowicz. 2007. Identifying expressions of emotion in text. *International Conference on Text, Speech and Dialogue* pages 196–205.

Gerald L. Clore, Andrew Ortony, and Mark A. Foss. 1987. The psychological foundations of the affective lexicon. *Journal of Personality and Social Psychology* 53(4):751–766.

Paul Ekman. 1973. cross-cultural studies of facial expression. *Darwin and facial expression: A century of research in review* .

Nico H. Frijda, Andrew Ortony, Joep Sonnemans, and Gerald Clore. 1992. The complexity of intensity: Issues concerning the structure of emotion intensity. *Personality and Social Psychology Review* 13:60–89.

Raj Kumar Gupta and Yinping Yang. 2017. CrystalNest at SemEval-2017 Task 4: Using sarcasm detection for enhancing sentiment classification and quantification. *International Workshop on Semantic Evaluation (SemEval 2017)* .

Minqing Hu and Bing Liu. 2004. Mining and summarizing customer reviews. *ACM SIGKDD* pages 168–177.

Armand Joulin, Edouard Grave, Piotr Bojanowski, and Tomas Mikolov. 2016. Bag of tricks for efficient text classification. *Proceedings of the 15th Conference of the European Chapter of the Association for Computational Linguistics* 2:427–431.

Saif M. Mohammad. 2012. #emotional tweets. *In Proceedings of the First Joint Conference on Lexical and Computational Semantics (*Sem)* .

Saif M. Mohammad and Felipe Bravo-Marquez. 2017. Emotion intensities in tweets. *In Proceedings of the Sixth Joint Conference on Lexical and Computational Semantics* .

Saif M. Mohammad, Felipe Bravo-Marquez, Mohammad Salameh, and Svetlana Kiritchenko. 2018. Semeval-2018 task 1: Affect in tweets. *SemEval* .

Saif M. Mohammad and Svetlana Kiritchenko. 2015. Using hashtags to capture fine emotion categories from tweets. *Computational Intelligence* 31(2):301–326.

Saif M. Mohammad and Peter Turney. 2010. Emotions evoked by common words and phrases: Using mechanical turk to create an emotion lexicon. *In Proceedings of the NAACL-HLT 2010 Workshop on Computational Approaches to Analysis and Generation of Emotion in Text* .

Saif M. Mohammad and Peter Turney. 2013. Crowdsourcing a word-emotion association lexicon. *Computational Intelligence* 29(3):436–465.

Finn Arup Nielsen. 2011. Afinn. *Informatics and Mathematical Modelling, Technical University of Denmark* .

Andrew Ortony, Gerald L. Clore, and Mark A. Foss. 1987. The referential structure of the affective lexiconn. *Cognitive Science* 11(3):341–364.

Charles Egerton Osgood, George J. Suci, and Percy H. Tannenbaum. 1957. The measurement of meaning. *University of Illinois Press* .

Olutobi Owoputi, Brendan O'Connor, Chris Dyer, Kevin Gimpel, Nathan Schneider, and Noah A. Smith. 2013. Improved part-of-speech tagging for online conversational text with word clusters. *NAACL: HLT* pages 380–390.

Bo Pang and Lillian Lee. 2008. Opinion ming and sentiment analysis. *New Publishers Inc* .

David L. Robinson. 2009. Brain function, emotional experience and personality. *The Netherlands Journal of Psychology* pages 152–167.

Phillip Shaver, Judith Schwartz, Donald Kirson, and Cary O'Connor. 1987. Emotion knowledge: Further exploration of a prototype approach. *Journal of Personality and Social Psychology* 52(6):1061–1086.

Richard Socher, Alex Perelygin, Jean Y. Wu, Jason Chuang, Christopher D. Manning, Andrew Y. Ng, and Christopher Potts. 2013. Recursive deep models for semantic compositionality over a sentiment treebank. *EMNLP* .

Mike Thelwall, Kevan Buckley, and Georgios Paltoglou. 2012. Sentiment strength detection for the social web. *Journal of the American Society for Information Science and Technology* 63(1):163–173.

Shiyang Wen and Xiaojun Wan. 2014. Emotion classification in microblog texts using class sequential rules. *AAAI Conference on Artificial Intelligence* pages 187–193.

PlusEmo2Vec at SemEval-2018 Task 1: Exploiting emotion knowledge from emoji and #hashtags

Ji Ho Park, Peng Xu, Pascale Fung
Centre for Artificial Intelligence Research (CAiRE)
Hong Kong University of Science and Technology
{jhpark, pxuab}@connect.ust.hk, pascale@ece.ust.hk

Abstract

This paper describes our system that has been submitted to SemEval-2018 Task 1: Affect in Tweets (AIT) to solve five subtasks. We focus on modeling both sentence and word level representations of emotion inside texts through large distantly labeled corpora with emojis and hashtags. We transfer the emotional knowledge by exploiting neural network models as feature extractors and use these representations for traditional machine learning models such as support vector regression (SVR) and logistic regression to solve the competition tasks. Our system is placed among the Top3 for all subtasks we participated.

1 Introduction

Finding a good representation of texts is very challenging since texts are sequences of words which are represented in a discrete space of the vocabulary. For this reason, many past works have investigated in finding the mapping of words (Mikolov et al., 2013; Pennington et al., 2014) or sentences (Kiros et al., 2015) to continuous spaces, so that each text can be represented by a fixed-size, real-valued N-dimensional vector. This vector representation then can be applied to machine learning models to solve problems like classification and regression. A good representation should contain essential information inside each text and be a useful input for statistical models.

Emotions in texts further deepen the complexity of modeling natural language since they not only depend on the semantics of a language but also are inherently subjective and ambiguous. Despite the difficulty, accounting for emotion is important in achieving true natural language understanding, especially in areas involving human-computer interactions such as dialogue systems (Fung, 2015).

Humans can naturally capture and express different emotions in texts, so machines should also be able to infer them. Many works (Tang et al., 2014; Felbo et al., 2017; Thelwall, 2017) explored modeling sentiment or emotion in texts in various directions. This work is highly related to these efforts.

Semeval-2018 Task 1: Affect in Tweets (AIT-2018) encourages more efforts in this area with the task of sentiment analysis, which is one of the most practical applications of modeling emotional text representations. We have participated in five subtasks regarding English tweets: emotion intensity regression, emotion intensity ordinal classification, valence (sentiment) regression, valence ordinal classification, and emotion classification (More details on the tasks in Mohammad et al. (2018)).

Although these five tasks take different formats, the most important objective is finding a good representation of the tweets regarding emotions. However, the given competition training datasets are too small to achieve our goal (Table 3). Therefore, we explore utilizing larger datasets that are distantly supervised by emojis and hashtags to learn a robust representation and transfer the knowledge of each dataset to the competition datasets to solve the tasks. We aim to minimize the use of lexicons and linguistic features by replacing them with continuous vector representations.

2 Emoji sentence representations

Thanks to the endless stream of social media such as Twitter and Facebook, researchers nowadays are lucky enough to have access to almost an unlimited number of texts generated every day. Nevertheless, annotating these texts with explicit emotion or sentiment human labels is very expensive and difficult. For this reason, many works naturally focused on finding direct or indirect evidence of emotion inside each text, such as hash-

Proceedings of the 12th International Workshop on Semantic Evaluation (SemEval-2018), pages 264–272
New Orleans, Louisiana, June 5–6, 2018. ©2018 Association for Computational Linguistics

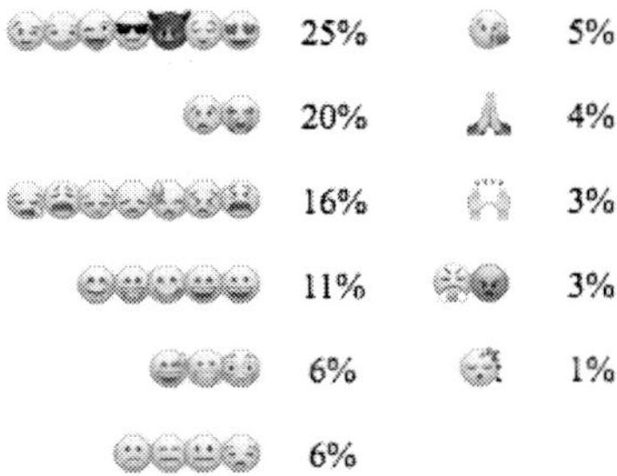

Figure 1: 11 clusters of emojis used as categorical labels and their distributions in the training set. Because some emojis appear much less frequently than others, we group the 34 emojis into 11 clusters according to the distance on the correlation matrix of the hierarchical clustering from Felbo et al. (2017) and use them as categorical labels

tags and emoticons (Suttles and Ide, 2013; Wang et al., 2012), and found them useful to distantly label an emotion of each text. Furthermore, the recent popular culture of using emojis (Wood and Ruder, 2016) inside social media posts and messages provides us even richer evidence of different emotions, and they have been proven to be very effective in learning rich representations for various affect-related tasks (Felbo et al., 2017).

2.1 Methodology & Emoji Dataset

In this paper, we compare two models using two different emoji dataset to transform the competition data into robust sentence representations.

First model is the pre-trained DeepMoji model (Felbo et al., 2017), which is trained through emoji predictions on a dataset of 1.2 billion tweets with 64 common emoji labels. We use the pretrained deep learning network, which consists of Bidirectional Long Short Term Memory (Bi-LSTM) with attention, except the last softmax layer, as a feature extractor of the original competition datasets. As a result, each sample is transformed into a 2304-dimensional vector from the model.

The second model is our proposed emoji cluster model. We crawled 8.1 million tweets with each of which has 34 different facial and hand emojis, assuming these kinds of emojis are more relevant to emotions. Since some emojis appear much less frequently than others, we cluster the 34 emojis into 11 clusters (Figure 1) according to the distance on the correlation matrix of the hierarchical clustering from Felbo et al. (2017). Sam-

ples with emojis in the same cluster are assigned the same categorical label for prediction. Samples with multiple emojis are duplicated in the training set, whereas in the dev and test set we only use samples with one emoji to avoid confusion. We then train a one-layer Bi-LSTM classifier with 512 hidden units to predict the emoji cluster of each sample. We take part of the dataset to construct a balanced dev set with 15,000 samples per class (total 165,000) for hyperparameter tuning and early stopping. We use 200 dimension Glove vectors pre-trained on a much larger Twitter corpus to initialize the embedding layer.

The motivation for exploring two different models is that, firstly, we want to replicate the effectiveness of using emoji for representing emotions from the previous work (Felbo et al., 2017) with a smaller dataset and a simpler model. Note that the dataset size of the emoji cluster model is less than 1% of that of the first model, whereas DeepMoji uses more than 1 billion training samples. Moreover, the first model implements a two-layer Bi-LSTM with self-attention, which has much more parameters than the second model's simple one-layer Bi-LSTM does. Secondly, we want to verify that ensembling both emoji representations trained from different datasets to boost our performance. We will present the result of the comparisons and the ensembles in Section 5.2.

One thing i dislike is laggers man
I hate inconsistency
The paper is irritating me
As of right now i hate dre
im sick of crying im tired of trying
why body pain why
uuugh i really have nothing to do right now
i dont wanna go back to mex
looking forward to holiday
well today am on lake garda enjoying the life
perfect time to read book
im feeling great enjoying my holiday

Table 1: Test samples from the Emoji Cluster model and their top-3 nearest sentences according to the learned representations. It shows that emotionally similar sentences are clustered together

2.2 Evaluation

As a result, the model can achieve 29.8% top-1 accuracy and 61.0% top-3 accuracy on the emoji cluster prediction task. Since the objective of this model is not to predict the cluster label but to find a good sentence representation, we visualize the test set samples to discover that samples with similar semantics and emotions are grouped together (Table 1). Finally, similar to the first model, we use this model as a feature extractor on the competition datasets. Each text sample in the competition datasets is transformed into a 512-dimensional vector through the model except the last class predicting softmax layer.

In conclusion, we trained two deep learning models with two different emoji datasets to extract emoji representations of the competition datasets. They are transformed into high dimensional, real-valued, and continuous vectors, which can be used as features for the classification and regression tasks.

From now on, we will call the vectors from the first model, *DeepMoji representations*, and those from the second, *Emoji Cluster representations*.

3 Emotional word vectors (EVEC)

We also explore word-level representations, along with emoji sentence representations. Although sentence-level representations already build up from word representations (in particular we use pretrained Glove vectors (Pennington et al., 2014)), they may not be enough to attend to the valence that each word contains. Previous works (Tang et al., 2014) examine the significance of using sentiment-specific word embedding for related tasks. For this reason, we train emotional word vectors that not only cluster together direct emotion words such as anger and joy, but also capture emotions inside indirect emotion words, such as anger inside headache and joy inside beach. We learn these vectors by training a Convolutional Neural Network (CNN) from another separate Twitter corpus distantly labeled with hashtags.

3.1 Methodology

Our intuition to learn effective emotion word vectors is that given a document labeled with emotion there exists one or more emotionally significant words inside. Nevertheless, we do not know which ones are more important. We assume that a deep learning model, which learns the representations of the data with different level of abstractions (LeCun et al., 2015) will be able to capture those words and encode the information in its word embedding layer while classifying the documents label.

For the model structure, we use CNN since it is proven to be effective in text classification tasks by looking at the documents n-gram features and its gradient can be directly back-propagated to the word embedding, whereas Recurrent Neural Network (RNN) models are updated sequentially. We use a similar structure used by (Kim, 2014), which includes a max-pooling layer to force the network to find the most relevant feature for predicting the emotion class correctly.

After the CNN network learns how to classify the documents into different emotion categories, we extract emotional word vectors from the network's embedding layer and use them as same as how other word embeddings, such as word2vec (Mikolov et al., 2013) or Glove, are used, treating them as features for other classification or regression models.

3.2 Hashtag Dataset

To accumulate a large corpus of emotion-labeled texts, we use a distant supervision method by using hashtags of tweets to automatically annotate emotions. Such method has proven to provide relevant emotion labels by previous works (Wang et al., 2012). Their source of the emotion words came from emotion words list made from Shaver et al. (1987), where the authors organize emotions into a hierarchy in which the first layer contains six basic emotions and each emotion has a list of emotion words. Wang et al. (2012) again expanded the list by including their lexical variants and also introduced some filtering heuristics, such as only using tweets with emotional hashtags at the end of tweets to make the distant supervision more relevant to human annotation. We combine their dataset, another public dataset [1], which used the same method, and our own extracted tweets between January and October 2017 using the Twitter Firehose API.

For the emotion labels, we focus on four emotion categories: joy, sadness, anger, and fear, since the competition tasks are only limited to those categories. In total, our hashtag dataset consists of 1.9 million tweets (Table 2).

3.3 Evaluation

For every sample in the SemEval competition dataset, we extract all emotional word vectors of the words in the sentence and simply average them

---

[1] http://hci.epfl.ch/sharing-emotion-lexicons-and-data#emo-hash-data

Emotion Label	%	Samples
Joy	36.5%	It's been such a great week **#happy**
Sadness	33.8%	I think I miss my boyfriend **#lonely**
Anger	23.5%	Ignoring me isn't going to make our problems go away. **#annoyed**
Fear	6%	What to wear for this job orientation.. **#nervous**

Table 2: Description of the Twitter hashtag corpus. Hashtags at the end were removed from the document and used as labels. It is hard to construct a well-balanced dataset for all four classes since Twitter users tend to use more hashtags related to happy and sad emotions.

into one vector. For words out of vocabulary of the hashtag corpus, we add zero vectors with the same dimension. As a result, every sentence is transformed into a 300-dimension vector to be used as features for the competition tasks. We expect these emotional word vectors can replace sentiment or emotion lexicons, since they are continuous representations learned from a large corpus, which can be more robust and rich in information about emotions inside words.

4 System Description

4.1 Features

These are the three features that are used as input for our system to solve SemEval-2018 Task 1.

Emoji Sentence Representations: Two models will be compared - *DeepMoji representations* (2304 dimensions) and *Emoji cluster representations* (512 dimensions). See Section 2.

Emotional Word Vectors (EVEC): Average of emotional word vectors learned from hashtag corpus (300 dimensions). See Section 3.

Tweet-specific features: We employ Tweet-specific features to capture information that two previous representations cannot. Inspired from the previous SemEval papers (Zhou et al., 2016; Balikas and Amini, 2016), we choose five features, (1) number of words in uppercase, (2) number of positive and negative emoticons, (3) Sum of emoji valence score [2], (4) number of elongated words, and (5) number of exclamation & question marks. Note that we do not use any linguistic features or sentiment/emotion lexicons for our system.

4.2 Preprocessing

Tweets in the competition datasets are tokenized after all non-alphanumeric characters are removed, except for extracting tweet-specific features. Some words, especially for hashtags, are merged together (e.g. #iloveyou), so unknown

words in the vocabulary is put into a wordsegment library [3] to preserve the right segment (e.g. i, love, you). Then, the tokens are transformed into emoji sentence representations (2304 or 512 dimensions) and emotional word vectors (300 dimensions), according to the vocabulary of the emoji and hashtag dataset. These datasets respectively have 262,975 and 48,929 words in their vocabularies.

4.3 Regression and Ordinal Classification

Due to the fact that the datasets of regression tasks (EI-reg & V-reg) and ordinal classification tasks (EI-oc & V-oc) have the same sample sentences, we assume that regression labels are more informative than the ordinals, since they tell us the rank among the samples within the same ordinal class. Therefore, we first train a regression model and then use it to predict ordinals, rather than training a separate classifier. We later prove that this trick yields a better result in ordinal classification.

For regression, since our features are extracted from deep learning models, we find Support Vector Regression (SVR) and Kernel-Ridge Regression methods, which are effective for nonlinear features, perform better than linear methods. We tune the hyper-parameters with the given development (dev) set and later merge both train and dev set to train the final model with the best hyper-parameter found. Also, we try ensembles by averaging the final regression predictions of different methods or feature combinations to boost performance. The best groups of models are selected by the development set results of many combinations.

Another important finding is that the mapping between the regression labels and ordinal labels are very different among emotion categories. For example in Figure 2, Class 0 for fear is distributed in [0,0.6], whereas class 0 for joy is distributed in [0, 0.4]. Therefore, we try to find the mapping from the regression values (continuous) to ordinal

---

[2]https://github.com/words/emoji-emotion

[3]http://www.grantjenks.com/docs/wordsegment/

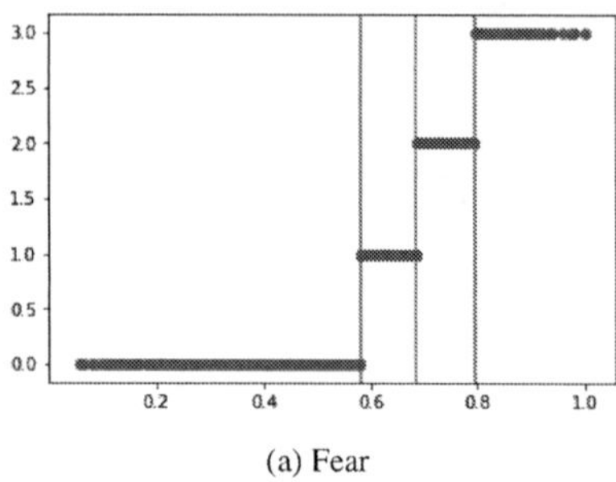

(a) Fear

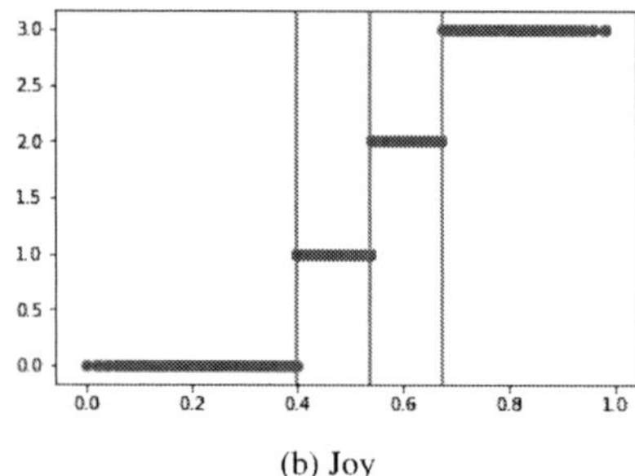

(b) Joy

Figure 2: Distribution of regression labels (x-axis) and ordinal labels (y-axis) on the training dataset of Task 1a & 2a. Class 0 for fear is distributed in [0,0.6], whereas class 0 for joy is distributed in [0, 0.4]. Vertical lines are boundaries between ordinal classes, which are used for scope mapping method

values (discrete) from the training dataset. We experiment with three different mapping:

1. *naive mapping*: divides [0,1] into same size segments according to the number of ordinals

2. *scope mapping*: finds the boundary of each segment in the training dataset (vertical lines on Figure 2)

3. *polynomial mapping*: fits a polynomial regression function from the training data and finds the closest ordinal label.

4.4 Multi-label Classification

This task of multi-label classification is different from previous tasks in that the model needs to predict the binary label for each of the 11 classes given a tweet. The task is difficult in terms of three aspects. Firstly, some of the classes have opposite emotions (such as optimism and pessimism) but may have been labeled both as true. Secondly, it is not trivial to distinguish similar emotions such as joy, love, and optimism, which will include a lot of noise in the labels and make it hard to perform classification during training. Lastly, most of the tweets are labeled with no more than 3 categories out of 11 classes, which make the labels very sparse and imbalanced (Table 4).

We propose to train two models to tackle this problem: regularized linear regression and logistic regression classifier chain (Read et al., 2009). Both models aim to exploit labels' correlation to perform multi-label classification.

4.4.1 Regularized linear regression model

We formulate the multi-label classification problem as a linear regression with label distance as the regularization term. We denote the features for i-th tweet as $x_i \in R^N$ where N is the number of features and the number of categories as C. Our prediction is $y_i' = W * x_i$ where $W \in R^{M*C}$ is the weight of the linear regression model. We take the following formula as loss function to minimize. The loss consists of two parts. First part aims to minimize the mean square loss between our prediction y_i' and ground truth label y_i. The second part is the regularization term to capture relationship among different emotion labels. To model the correlations among emotions, we implicitly treat each emotion category as a vertice in an undirected graph g and use Laplacian matrix of g for regularization (Grone et al., 1990; Shahid et al., 2016) .

$$loss = \frac{1}{M}\sum_i^M (y' - y)^2 + \lambda y_i'^T L y_i'$$

$$L = D - A$$

where M is the number of samples, $L \in R^{C*C}$ is the Laplacian matrix, $A \in R^{C*C}$ is the Euclidean matrix, $D \in R^{C*C}$ is the Degree matrix. To derive L, we first compute the co-occurrence matrix $O \in R^{C*C}$ among the emotion labels and take each row/column $O_i \in R^C$ as the representation of each emotion. Then we compute the distance matrix A by taking the Euclidean distance of different labels. That is $A_{ij} = (O_i - O_j)^2$. Here, A can be regarded as the adjacency matrix of the graph g. Afterwards, we calculate the degree matrix D by summing up each row/column and making it a diagonal matrix.

Subtasks	1a&2a	3a&4a	5a
Train	7,102	1,181	6,838
Dev	1,464	449	886
Test	4,068	937	3,259

Table 3: Statistics of the competition dataset for all 5 subtasks

# of labels	0	1	2	3	4	5	6
%	2.9	14.3	40.6	30.9	9.6	1.4	0.2

Table 4: Number of multi-labels. Most samples have from 1-3 labels, but can have no labels or up to 6 labels. (subtask 5a)

4.4.2 Logistic regression classifier chain

Classifier chain is another method to capture the correlation of emotion labels. It treats the multi-label problem as a sequence of binary classification problem while taking the prediction of the previous classifier as extra input. For example, when training the i-th emotion category, we take both the features of input tweet and also the 1st, 2nd, $\cdots$, (i-1)-th prediction as the input of our logistic regression classifier to predict the i-th emotion label of input tweet. We further ensemble 10 logistic regression chains by shuffling the sequence of 11 emotion labels to achieve better generalization ability.

5 Experiments & Results

Most of our system experiments were implemented by using PyTorch (Paszke et al., 2017) and Scikit-learn (Pedregosa et al., 2011).

5.1 Competition dataset

SemEval-2018 Affect in Tweets (AIT) is created by human annotators through crowd-sourcing methods (Mohammad and Kiritchenko, 2018). Total three datasets are given: emotion intensity (with four emotion categories; Subtask 1a & 2a), sentiment intensity (subtask 3a & 4a), and multi-label emotion classification (subtask 5a).

For emotion and sentiment intensity datasets, each tweet sample has both an *ordinal label* (coarse; {0,1,2,3} for emotion, {-3,-2,-1,0,1,2,3} for sentiment) and real-value *regression label* (fine-grained; [0,1]). For multi-label emotion classification dataset, each can have none or up to six number of multi-labels (Table 4).

We used the given development set to tune the hyper-parameters and select models. For the fi-

nal submission, we merged the train & development set together to retrain the model with the best hyper-parameter found (Table 3).

5.2 Regression: Subtask 1a & 3a

Table 5 shows the test set results on regression tasks, Subtask 1a&3a. We experimented with different features that we introduced before to analyze the effectiveness of each representation. For emoji sentence representations, *emoji cluster* worked better on sadness and sentiment, whereas *DeepMoji* outperformed in anger, fear, and joy. We presumed such difference was due to the different emoji types of the two datasets used to train each model. *Emoji cluster* only used 11 classes of emojis that were clustered together, but *DeepMoji* used 64 emoji classes. It may be possible clustering of emoji classes made it easy for regression models to predict the intensities in certain emotion categories, whereas some emotion categories needed more detailed representations.

The emotional word vectors overall did help enhance the performance of the regression model for all emotion categories. This shows that emotional word vectors can serve as additional word-level information which are helpful for solving this task.

Tweet-specific features boosted the performance, notably for sentiment, since features like capital letters, emojis, elongated words, and the number of exclamation marks, could help to figure out the subtle difference of the emotion intensities.

One thing to note is that our system's rank in the fear category (7th) is relatively lower than other emotion categories. We found out from the previous literature (Wood and Ruder, 2016) that fear emojis were the most ambiguous, having the least correlation with human-annotated emotion labels among the six emotion categories. On the other hand, joy emojis were the most highly correlated. This may explain our best performance in the joy category and worst performance in the fear category. Future systems using emojis as a dataset may need to take this shortcoming into account.

5.3 Ordinal Classification: Subtask 2a& 4a

As mentioned in Sec 4.3, we used our best regression model to also predict ordinal labels. Since each emotion category has a different distribution of regression labels and ordinal labels, we experimented three different mappings, *naive mapping*, *scope mapping*, and *polynomial mapping*. Using

Features	Regression Method	Pearson correlation (all instances)				
		1a (EI-reg)				3a(V-reg)
		Anger	Fear	Joy	Sadness	Valence
Emoji Cluster	SVR	.733	.632	.679	.693	.811
Emoji Cluster	KernelRidge	.735	.638	.675	.692	.809
DeepMoji	SVR	.772	.675	.736	.664	.798
DeepMoji	KernelRidge	.778	.672	.737	.698	.798
Emoji Cluster + EVEC	SVR	.739	.678	.701	.706	.815
Emoji Cluster + EVEC	KernelRidge	.741	.694	.709	.709	.822
DeepMoji + EVEC	SVR	.781	.694	.749	.708	.810
DeepMoji + EVEC	KernelRidge	.779	.702	.754	.710	.813
DeepMoji + feat.	SVR	.785	.680	.739	.714	.824
DeepMoji + feat.	KernelRidge	.781	.670	.691	.711	.829
Emoji Cluster + EVEC + feat.	SVR	.757	.684	.720	.725	**.844**
Emoji Cluster + EVEC + feat.	KernelRidge	.757	.698	.693	.721	.840
DeepMoji + EVEC + feat.	SVR	.792	.709	.763	.732	.837
DeepMoji + EVEC + feat.	KernelRidge	.790	**.716**	.734	**.739**	.826
Best Ensemble		**.811(2)**	**.728(7)**	**.773(2)**	**.753(5)**	**.860(3)**

Table 5: Test set results on Subtask 1a & 3a. For 1a, separate regression models were trained for each emotion category. The number next to the best result(bold & underlined) indicates our ranking of the competition. Underlined ones show the models that were selected for ensemble according to the dev set.

Task		Pearson (all instances)		
		Naive	Scope	Poly
2a (EI-oc)	Anger	.654	.664	**.704(2)**
	Fear	.498	.562	**.570(*)**
	Joy	.632	**.720(1)**	.712
	Sadness	.645	**.697(*)**	.692
4a (V-oc)	Valence	.813	.816	**.833(2)**

Table 6: Test set results on Subtask 2a & 4a. The predictions of the best regression models are mapped into ordinal predictions. The number next to the best result(bold & underlined) indicates our ranking of the competition. (*) indicates better results that we acquired after our final submission

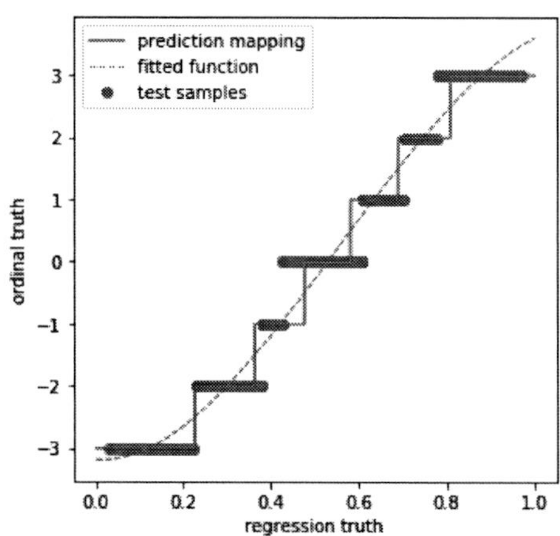

Figure 3: Plot of test labels and the mapping function derived from the training set. A polynomial function is fitted to map the regression predictions into ordinal predictions

the training set, we found the ideal mapping function to match the regression predictions and the ordinal predictions.

Test set results (Table 6) on ordinal classification show that our mapping methods are indeed much more effective. For anger, fear, and sentiment categories, polynomial mapping performed the best, whereas scope mapping outperformed for joy and sadness categories. With our method, we achieved higher ranks in ordinal classification tasks (2a & 4a), placed both in 2nd. Figure 3 shows how a cubic function is fitted to find the mapping between regression labels and ordinal labels.

Additionally, we report some results better than the final submission. The change is due to a new model selection strategy. For the final submission, we searched for the optimal pair of regression model & mapping method by looking at the ordinal classification results on the development set. However, it turned out that always using the best ensemble prediction and then searching for the optimal mapping method with respect to the development set was better.

5.4 Multi-label Classification: Subtask 5a

We found the best hyper-parameters by evaluating on our development set. We initialized the weight matrix W with a normal distribution of standard deviation of 0.1. We used gradient descent to optimize this function and set the learning rate to 1.0.

Features	CC	RLR
Emoji Cluster	.528	.545
DeepMoji	.532	.552
Emoji Cluster + EVEC	.545	.558
DeepMoji + EVEC	.544	.558
Emoji Cluster + EVEC + f	.546	.558
DeepMoji + EVEC + f	.550	.562
Best ensemble		**.576(3)**

Table 7: Test set results on Subtask 5a. The competition metric is Jaccard index.

	Gender		Race	
	Ours	Avg	**Ours**	Avg
Anger	**0.5%**	0.1%	**1%**	0.4%
Fear	**-0.9%**	-0.3%	**3.3%**	0.5%
Joy	**-1.2%**	0.4%	**-0.9%**	-0.7%
Sadness	**0%**	0.2%	**1.3%**	0.8%
Valence	**-0.6%**	0.5%	**-1%**	-0.6%

Table 8: Average differences of the system's bias. Gender difference is from female to male, and race differences is from African American names to European American names (sign of the percentage indicates the direction). "Ours" indicate the bias of our system, and "Avg" is the average of the biases of all systems from the competition.

The optimal λ we found was -0.0001.

We found that regularized linear regression model was always better than classifier chain model. The ensemble of classifier chain and regularized linear regression of both features combination(underlined elements in Table 7) achieved best performance than any single model (Table 7).

5.5 Analysis of system's gender/racial biases

In this year's competition, the organizers gave out a mystery test set that was included in the regression tasks (subtask 1a & 3a). At the end of the evaluation period, they announced that these were set of pair sentences that differ only in the subject's or object's gender or racial names (See the task paper Mohammad et al. (2018) for details). It turned out that our system also included some biases like most other systems did, but fairly small, less than 1.5% for gender bias and 3.5% for racial bias (Table 8). We believe that this is an interesting experiment and look forward to discussing more about the issue during the workshop.

6 Conclusion

In this paper, we explored a couple of different methods to find good representations of emo-

Subtask	System	Score(rank)
1a EI-reg	SeerNet	.799(1)
	NTUA-SLP	.776(2)
	PlusEmo2Vec	.766(3)
	psyML	.765(4)
2a EI-oc	SeerNet	.695(1)
	PlusEmo2Vec	.659(2)
	psyML	.653(3)
3a V-reg	SeerNet	.873(1)
	TCS Research	.861(2)
	PlusEmo2Vec	.860(3)
	NTUA-SLP	.851(4)
4a V-oc	SeerNet	.836(1)
	PlusEmo2Vec	.833(2)
	Amobee	.813(3)
5a E-c	NTUA-SLP	.588(1)
	TCS Research	.582(2)
	PlusEmo2Vec	.576(3)
	psyML	.574(4)

Table 9: Official final scoreboard on all 5 subtasks that we participated. Scores for Subtask 1-4 are macro-average of the Pearson scores of 4 emotion categories and 5 is Jaccard index. About 35 participants are in each task.

tions inside tweets for solving 5 subtasks of predicting emotion/sentiment intensity and emotion labels. We used external datasets, which were much larger than the competition dataset but distantly labeled with emojis and #hashtags, to exploit the transferred knowledge to build a more robust machine learning system to solve the task. We avoided using traditional NLP features like linguistic features and emotion/sentiment lexicons by substituting them with continuous vector representations learned from huge corpora.

We performed experiments to show that emoji sentence representations and emotional word vectors trained from neural networks can be used with tweet-specific features as input for other traditional regression models, such as SVR and Kernel Regression, to solve the task of regression and ordinal classification. We proved the effectiveness of finding the mapping of the relationship between regression and ordinal labels from the training set to perform ordinal classification. Moreover, we tried using classifier chain and regularized logistic regression to deal with multi-label classification.

As a final official result (Table 9), our system ranked among the top three in every subtask of the competition we participated. For future work, we want to work further on employing these emotion representations on other tasks, such as text generation, while we gather more data and improve the model to train the representations.

Acknowledgments

This work is partially funded by ITS/319/16FP of Innovation Technology Commission, HKUST 16214415 & 16248016 of Hong Kong Research Grants Council, and RDC 1718050-0 of EMOS.AI.

References

Georgios Balikas and Massih-Reza Amini. 2016. Twise at semeval-2016 task 4: Twitter sentiment classification. *Proceedings of the 10th International Workshop on Semantic Evaluation (SemEval-2016)*.

Bjarke Felbo, Alan Mislove, Anders Søgaard, Iyad Rahwan, and Sune Lehmann. 2017. Using millions of emoji occurrences to learn any-domain representations for detecting sentiment, emotion and sarcasm. *EMNLP 2017*.

Pascale Fung. 2015. Robots with heart. *Scientific American*, 313(5):60–63.

Robert Grone, Russell Merris, and V S‐ Sunder. 1990. The laplacian spectrum of a graph. *SIAM Journal on Matrix Analysis and Applications*, 11(2):218–238.

Yoon Kim. 2014. Convolutional neural networks for sentence classification. In *EMNLP, publisher=Citeseer,*.

Ryan Kiros, Yukun Zhu, Ruslan R Salakhutdinov, Richard Zemel, Raquel Urtasun, Antonio Torralba, and Sanja Fidler. 2015. Skip-thought vectors. In *NIPS*, pages 3294–3302.

Yann LeCun, Yoshua Bengio, and Geoffrey Hinton. 2015. Deep learning. *Nature*, 521(7553):436–444.

Tomas Mikolov, Ilya Sutskever, Kai Chen, Greg S Corrado, and Jeff Dean. 2013. Distributed representations of words and phrases and their compositionality. In *NIPS*, pages 3111–3119.

Saif M. Mohammad, Felipe Bravo-Marquez, Mohammad Salameh, and Svetlana Kiritchenko. 2018. Semeval-2018 Task 1: Affect in tweets. In *Proceedings of International Workshop on Semantic Evaluation (SemEval-2018)*, New Orleans, LA, USA.

Saif M. Mohammad and Svetlana Kiritchenko. 2018. Understanding emotions: A dataset of tweets to study interactions between affect categories. In *Proceedings of the 11th Edition of the Language Resources and Evaluation Conference*, Miyazaki, Japan.

Adam Paszke, Sam Gross, Soumith Chintala, Gregory Chanan, Edward Yang, Zachary DeVito, Zeming Lin, Alban Desmaison, Luca Antiga, and Adam Lerer. 2017. Automatic differentiation in pytorch.

Fabian Pedregosa, Gaël Varoquaux, Alexandre Gramfort, Vincent Michel, Bertrand Thirion, Olivier Grisel, Mathieu Blondel, Peter Prettenhofer, Ron Weiss, Vincent Dubourg, et al. 2011. Scikit-learn: Machine learning in python. *Journal of machine learning research*, 12(Oct):2825–2830.

Jeffrey Pennington, Richard Socher, and Christopher Manning. 2014. Glove: Global vectors for word representation. In *EMNLP2014*, pages 1532–1543.

Jesse Read, Bernhard Pfahringer, Geoff Holmes, and Eibe Frank. 2009. Classifier chains for multi-label classification. In *Joint European Conference on Machine Learning and Knowledge Discovery in Databases*, pages 254–269. Springer.

Nauman Shahid, Nathanael Perraudin, Vassilis Kalofolias, Benjamin Ricaud, and Pierre Vandergheynst. 2016. Pca using graph total variation. In *Acoustics, Speech and Signal Processing (ICASSP), 2016 IEEE International Conference on*, pages 4668–4672. Ieee.

Phillip Shaver, Judith Schwartz, Donald Kirson, and Cary O'connor. 1987. Emotion knowledge: Further exploration of a prototype approach. *Journal of personality and social psychology*, 52(6):1061.

Jared Suttles and Nancy Ide. 2013. Distant supervision for emotion classification with discrete binary values. In *International Conference on Intelligent Text Processing and Computational Linguistics*, pages 121–136. Springer.

Duyu Tang, Furu Wei, Nan Yang, Ming Zhou, Ting Liu, and Bing Qin. 2014. Learning sentiment-specific word embedding for twitter sentiment classification. In *Proceedings of the 52nd Annual Meeting of the Association for Computational Linguistics (Volume 1: Long Papers)*, volume 1, pages 1555–1565.

Mike Thelwall. 2017. The heart and soul of the web? sentiment strength detection in the social web with sentistrength. In *Cyberemotions*, pages 119–134. Springer.

Wenbo Wang, Lu Chen, Krishnaprasad Thirunarayan, and Amit P Sheth. 2012. Harnessing twitter" big data" for automatic emotion identification. In *Privacy, Security, Risk and Trust (PASSAT), 2012 International Conference on and 2012 International Confernece on Social Computing (SocialCom)*, pages 587–592. IEEE.

Ian Wood and Sebastian Ruder. 2016. Emoji as emotion tags for tweets. In *Emotion and Sentiment Analysis Workshop, at LREC2016*. LREC2016.

Yunxiao Zhou, Zhihua Zhang, and Man Lan. 2016. Ecnu at semeval-2016 task 4: An empirical investigation of traditional nlp features and word embedding features for sentence-level and topic-level sentiment analysis in twitter. In *Proceedings of the 10th International Workshop on Semantic Evaluation (SemEval-2016)*, pages 256–261.

YNU-HPCC at SemEval-2018 Task 1: BiLSTM with Attention Based Sentiment Analysis for Affect in Tweets

You Zhang, Jin Wang and **Xuejie Zhang**
School of Information Science and Engineering
Yunnan University
Kunming, P.R. China
Contact: xjzhang@ynu.edu.cn

Abstract

This paper describes the system we built as the YNU-HPCC team in the SemEval-2018 competition. As participants of Task 1, named Affect in Tweets, we implemented the sentiment system for all five subtasks in English and Spanish. All subtasks involved predicting emotion or sentiment intensity (regression and ordinal classification) and determining emotions (multi-label classification). Our system mainly applied the bidirectional long-short term memory (BiLSTM) model with an attention mechanism. We used BiLSTM in order to extract word information from both directions. The attention mechanism was used to find the contribution of each word to improving the scores. Furthermore, based on the BiLSTM with an attention mechanism, a few deep-learning algorithms were employed for different subtasks. For regression and ordinal classification tasks, we used domain adaptation and ensemble learning methods to leverage the base model, while a single base model was used for the multi-label task. Our system achieved very competitive results on the official leaderboard.

1 Introduction

Sentiment analysis is an area of natural language processing (NLP), which aims to systematically identify and study affective state, and to quantify subjective sentiment expressed in texts. Tweets in Twitter always constitute a challenging task among NLP problems because of the colorful writing styles used.

In previous work on sentiment analysis tasks, researchers usually used a variety of hand-crafted features and sentiment lexicons to generate the solution system by combining traditional methods such as naive Bayes, support vector machines (SVMs) (Mohammad et al., 2013), and decision trees (Blake, 2007). Recently, many ensemble learning models based on these traditional methods (Giorgis et al., 2016) have attracted the interest of researcher and have shown good results. These approaches require long-term studies to gather information from massive or unstructured datasets, and often result in redundant or missing features. In contrast, the novel deep learning method (Socher et al., 2013) has immediately and shown exceptionally good results in NLP.

In this paper, we primarily present a deep learning system for the SemEval-2018 shared Task 1: Affect in Tweets. We employ the bidirectional long short-term memory with an attention mechanism (BiLSTM_{ATT}) as a base model. For the regression and ordinal classification tasks, we used fine-tuning methods on the base model, combined with multi-tasking and AdaBoost algorithm. We use a simple BiLSTM with an attention mechanism for the multi-label task. Our contributions are as follows:

- We propose a base model combining the BiLSTM with an attention mechanism for the sentiment analysis problem.

- Using the base model, a domain adaptation method of fine-tuning combined with multi-tasking is used for associated tasks.

- An ensemble learning method using the AdaBoost algorithm implemented on the base model is of great use for performing the task with unevenly distributed data.

The remainder of this paper is organized as follows. In Section 2, we describe an overview of our system. The details of the model are presented in Section 3. Finally, comparative results of the experiments are discussed, and a conclusion is drawn in Sections 4 and 5, respectively.

Proceedings of the 12th International Workshop on Semantic Evaluation (SemEval-2018), pages 273–278
New Orleans, Louisiana, June 5–6, 2018. ©2018 Association for Computational Linguistics

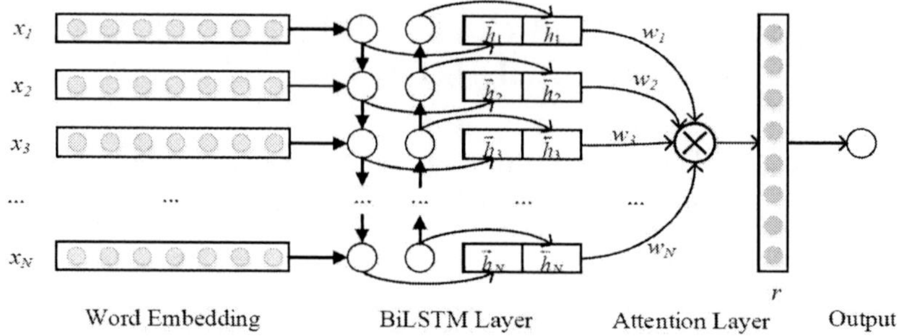

Figure 1: Architecture of the BiLSTM with Attention Mechanism.

2 Overview

This section shows an overview of our system or experiments, which consists of three steps:(1) the data processing step, in which we use some text processing tools for preparing the data as input to the deep learning models, (2) the training step, where we build and train our models, and then predict and (3) evaluate our test results.

Task description. In all five subtasks, we take participant in all subtasks for English and Spanish (Mohammad et al., 2018). Subtasks EI-reg and V-reg, which require the system to detect emotion and sentiment intensity (a real-value score between 0 and 1) from given tweets, are both treated as regression problems. The difference between them is that subtask EI-reg has four different emotion sub-datasets (anger, fear, joy and sadness). In subtasks EI-oc and V-oc, we are given the message and scores, which are ordinal values from four-level and seven-level scales corresponding to positive or negative emotion and sentiment intensity, respectively. Subtask E-c is a multi-label task that requires the system to identify the tweets as "no emotion" or as one, or more, of eleven given emotions.

2.1 Data processing

We built our text processing tools in order to utilize more information from the original text. The objectives of the tools are word-splitting, word annotation, processing of unknown word, and so on.

Text pre-processing. It is difficult to feed original tweets directly into a deep learning model. Imported from the NLTK API [1], the twitter-tokenizer shows great usefulness in fast word segmentation. The tokenizer is able to identify all the words,

most of the emoticons and emojis, and omits all useless punctuation. The English (or Spanish) dataset primarily contains English (or Spanish) text. Therefore, all non-English (or non-Spanish) letters are treated as unknown words. Moreover, we converted all words to lower case and normalized the construction of user (@user), URLs (http://ie.com), and numbers and hashtags (#hashtag).

Pre-trained word embedding. Word embedding techniques aim to use continuous low-dimension vectors representing the features of the words (Mikolov et al., 2013), captured in context. For English tasks, a pre-trained word vector with a dimension of 300, which combined word embedding from training with the GloVe algorithm (Pennington et al., 2014) with the emoji embedding (Barbieri et al., 2016), which included most of the emoticons and emojis, was used to map the tweets. For the Spanish task, we used only the word embedding training by Barbieri et al. (2016). Unknown words were added to the vocabulary, and their vectors were randomly generated from a uniform distribution of $U(-0.25, 0.25)$. The pre-trained word embeddings were used for initializing the word embedding layer (the input layer) of our deep learning models.

2.2 Deep Learning models

Recently, most advanced work in NLP employs deep learning methods.

Convolutional Neural Networks (CNNs). Although CNNs were first applied for computer vision, they also show great importance for NLP problems (Zhang and Wallace, 2015). CNNs are able to quickly extract local n-gram features, and are easy to train. However, CNNs have difficulty

---

[1] http://www.nltk.org/.

capturing long-distance dependencies.

Recurrent Neural Networks (RNNs). Another effective neural network is the RNN, which captures dynamic information in serial data by periodically connecting hidden layer nodes. RNNs can store a state of context or even a story, learn and express relevant information in any long context window, unlike CNN's fixed-input formation. An RNN is able to overcome the problem of long-distance dependency. However, it is difficult to train because gradients may explode or vanish over long sequences (Hochreiter, 1998). One way to address this problem is by employing a variant of the regular RNN, the LSTM (Graves, 2012). LSTMs have a more complex internal structure with cells replacing RNN nodes, which allows LSTMs to remember information for either a long or short time.

Attention Mechanism. Between sequences, an attention mechanism shows a considerable improvement by changing the contribution of each word to the analysis of the whole text (Rocktschel et al., 2015; Raffel and Ellis, 2015). Before the RNN model summarizes the hidden states for the output, an attention mechanism amplifies the results by aggregating the hidden states and weighting their relative importance.

Domain Adaptation. Domain adaptation enhances learning in target domains by transferring learning from source domains that may have a distribution different from the target domain. Domain adaptation not only addresses the difference between source and target domains, but also pays attention to the relevance of both domains. The method provides an elegant way to access the full resources of similar tasks for target tasks (Mou et al., 2016).

Ensemble Learning. Ensemble learning is a supervised learning algorithm that ensembles two or more weak learners to amplify system performance (Maclin and Opitz, 1999). The AdaBoost algorithm (Li et al., 2008) is one of the ensemble learning algorithms that repeats training and adjusts the weights of all weak learners continuously to take into consideration the previous iteration error prediction samples. Therefore, the AdaBoost algorithm focuses more attention on a small proportion of special samples in a dataset for better scores.

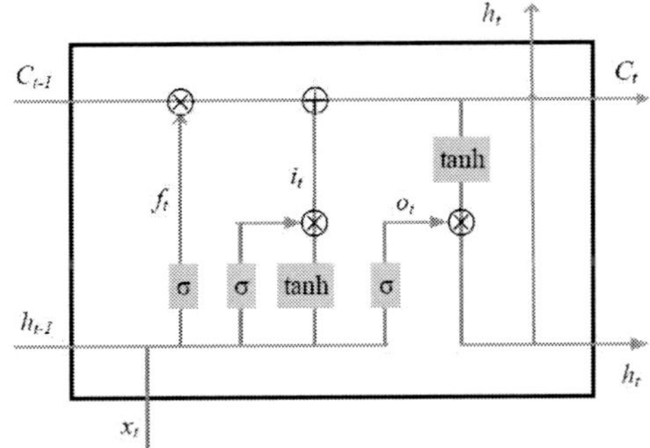

Figure 2: Architecture of cell in LSTM.

3 Model Description

We proposed the base BiLSTM model with an attention mechanism for subtask E-c (3.1). Two additional models (3.2 and 3.3) based on the BiLSTM with an attention mechanism are used for other subtasks.

4 BiLSTM with Attention Mechanism (BiLSTM$_{ATT}$)

Figure 1 shows the architecture of BiLSTM with an attention mechanism, which has four different layers as follows.

Embedding Layer. After the pre-processing of text, tweets are transformed into a sequence of words, $X = (x_1, x_2, ..., x_N), X \in R^{N \times d}$, where N is the number of a tweet, and d denotes the dimension of a word vector. The word tokens are then directly fed into the model embedding layer, which was initialized by the pre-trained word embeddings.

BiLSTM Layer. LSTM replaces the nodes of a regular RNN model with special structures (cells). The architecture of the LSTM is shown in Figure 2. It calculates the hidden state h_t at time t using the following equations:

- Gates

$$f_t = \sigma(W_f \cdot [h_{t-1}, x_t] + b_f)$$
$$i_t = \sigma(W_i \cdot [h_{t-1}, x_t] + b_i) \quad (1)$$
$$o_t = \sigma(W_o \cdot [h_{t-1}, x_t] + b_o)$$

- Transformation

$$\tilde{C}_t = \tanh(W_c \cdot [h_{t-1}, x_t] + b_c) \quad (2)$$

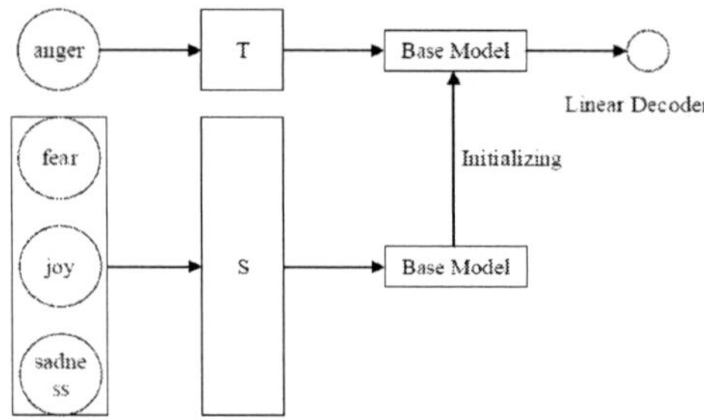

Figure 3: The Model of EIM. Here anger sub-dataset is the target domain and other three sub-datasets regarded as source domain.

- State update

$$C_t = f_t * C_{t-1} + i_t * \tilde{C}_t$$
$$h_t = o_t * \tanh(C_t) \tag{3}$$

where σ denotes the sigmoid function, x_t is the t-th word vector, C_t, f_t, i_t and o_t are all gate vectors of the cell, and W and b are cell parameters.

We use bidirectional LSTM so as to obtain word features $H = (h_1, h_2, ..., h_n)$ concatenated from both directions. A forward LSTM processes the tweet from x_1 to x_n, while a backward LSTM processes from x_n to x_1. For word x_t, a forward L-STM obtains a word feature as $\overrightarrow{h}$ and a backward LSTM obtains the feature as $\overleftarrow{h}$. Then, h is calculated as follows:

$$h_i = \overrightarrow{h_i} \oplus \overleftarrow{h_i}, h_i \in R^{2L} \tag{4}$$

Where $\oplus$ denotes the function of concatenation and L is the size of the one-directional LSTM.

Attention Layer. We add an attention layer for finding the contribution of each word to the w-hole sequence. The attention mechanism assigns a weight w_i to each word feature h_i with a focus on results. The hidden states are finally calculated to produce a hidden sentence feature vector r by a weighted sum function. Formally:

$$e_i = \tanh(W_h h_i + b_h), e_i \in [-1, 1]$$
$$w_i = \frac{\exp(e_i)}{\sum_{t=1}^{N} \exp(e_t)}, \sum_{i=1}^{N} w_i = 1 \tag{5}$$
$$r = \sum_{i=1}^{N} w_i h_i, r \in R^{2L}$$

where W_h and b_h are the weight and bias from the attention layer.

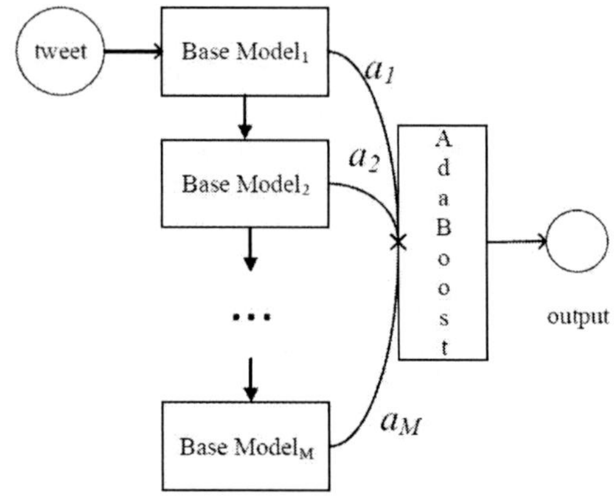

Figure 4: The Model of SIM

Output Layer. The representation r is a sentence feature vector, which we put into a fully-connected layer that outputs the results for the whole sentence. Different tasks require different forms of the output. This base model is dedicated to sub-task E-c, with eleven fully-connected sigmoid layers as the output layer.

4.1 Emotion Intensity Model (EIM)

Figure 3 shows an overview of the EIM, the model we used for task EI-reg and EI-oc with more than one sub-dataset. To train one emotion dataset as a target task (T), the other three emotion dataset-s were treated as source tasks (S). Our approach was to first train the base model on S, and then to directly initialize the base model on T using the tuned parameters. The parameters were then fine-tuned for predicting the results of S. The output layer of the EIM uses the linear decoder for regression. For ordinal classification task EI-oc, real-value scores from the EIM are translated into four-point classes with thresholds according to the training sets for EI-reg and EI-oc.

4.2 Sentiment Intensity Model (SIM)

Figure 4 shows the architecture of the SIM. Based on the base model, we use the AdaBoost algorith-m ensemble the M weak learners to a stronger learner for subtask V-reg and V-oc. Initially, each sample has the same weight. After each iteration, the algorithm weights the samples with poor predictions by the previous learner, and the weighted samples are again used to train the next learner. Finally, we use the calculated weight a_i of each

| Model | subtask EI-reg | | | | subtask V-reg |
| | p | | | | p |
	anger	fear	joy	sadness	
CNN	0.428	0.498	0.501	0.631	0.700
LSTM	0.551	0.522	0.560	0.500	0.762
CNN-LSTM	0.521	0.532	0.592	0.555	0.753
BiLSTM	0.511	0.533	0.535	0.5003	0.718
BiLSTM$_{ATT}$	0.555	0.655	0.605	0.700	0.773
EIM	**0.654**	**0.715**	**0.630**	**0.728**	-
SIM	0.558	0.659	0.621	0.713	**0.787**

Table 1: Comparable results of experiments for subtask EI-reg and V-reg.

learner for the weighted sum of scores. The output layer of the SIM is the same as the one in the task EI-reg. The results of task V-oc are obtained from the real-value scores of the SIM with thresholds according to the training sets for V-reg and V-oc.

4.3 Training and Hyper-parameters

We train the model for task E-c using the categorical cross-entropy loss function, and for other tasks using mean squared error. For all tasks, we use the Adam (Kingma and Ba, 2014) optimizer to train models, and the Relu activation function for fast calculation. An early stopping (Prechelt, 1998) strategy is used to prevent over-fitting. All models use stochastic gradient descent with mini-batches of size 32.

Hyper-parameters. The dimension of word embeddings (d) is 300; the number of each LSTM (L) is 100; the dropout ratio is 0.25 at all layers for all models. Finally, we set 30 learners from the base model to train the SIM by ensemble learning.

5 Experiment

Corpus. The datasets we used were all provided by the competition, with no other external corpus. Except for subtasks EI-reg and EI-oc, which had four sub-datasets, subtasks had only one dataset each for English and Spanish. We thank Mohammad and Kiritchenko (Mohammad et al., 2013) for contributions to the data.

Evaluation Measure. For regression and ordinal tasks (including task EI-reg, EI-oc, V-reg, and V-oc), the official competition metric was the value (p) of the Pearson Correction Coefficient. Moreover, tasks EI-oc and V-oc have a second metric, the quadratic weighted kappa (k). For the multi-label task (task E-c), apart from the official competition metric (multi-label accuracy, a), a micro-averaged F-score ($f1^{micro}$) and a macro-averaged

F-score ($f1^{macro}$) were also calculated for our submissions.

Results. On the competition leaderboard, our system placed 22/48 (9/24) for English (Spanish) in task EI-reg, 12/39 (8/16) in task EI-oc, 27/38 (7/14) in task V-reg, 14/31 (6/14) in task V-oc and 7/35 (6/14) in task E-c.

Experiments and Analysis. We trained our models on the training set and evaluated the prediction with the golden scores of the development set. In order to illustrate the good performance of our methods, we compare the results with baseline models of CNN, LSTM, CNN-LSTM (Zhang et al., 2017) and a regular BiLSTM. From the results shown in Table 1, we can see that our approach achieved a significant result. A regular LSTM tends to ignore future contextual information while processing sequences in a time series. The BiLSTM is able to use both past and future contexts by processing the text from both directions. Not all words make the same contribution to sentiment analysis in the text. The attention mechanism is able to shuffle the word annotation weights according to their importance to the meaning of sentence. We can see that the attention based BiLSTM obtained higher scores than the BiLSTM without the attention mechanism. Moreover, the SIM and the EIM showed their best performance on subtasks V-reg and EI-reg, respectively. SIM employed the AdaBoost algorithm so as to integrate 30 the models of BiLSTM$_{ATT}$. The SIM was able to adapt to the training error rate of each learner, so that the whole system was improved effectively. The EIM fine-tuned the parameters for the multi-task approach, which made full use of associated sub-datasets of the task EI-reg. Before training the target dataset, the special parameter initialization gave the target model additional knowledge from the other source datasets. In addition, for the same training tweets that were used in task EI-reg (or V-reg) and EI-oc (or V-oc), we defined the threshold for translating from real-value score to ordinal classes by referring to the training labels across the training dataset.

6 Conclusion

In this paper, we described our deep learning models for the sentiment analysis task SemEval-2018 shared Task 1: Affect in Tweets. We used the BiL-STM with an attention mechanism as a base model and built the SIM and EIM for all subtasks. The final system for submission achieved good results. We would like to further explore text sentiment analysis, and employ more interesting methods for NLP problems.

References

Francesco Barbieri, German Kruszewski, Francesco Ronzano, and Horacio Saggion. 2016. How cosmopolitan are emojis?: Exploring emojis usage and meaning over different languages with distributional semantics. In *ACM on Multimedia Conference*, pages 531–535.

Catherine Blake. 2007. The role of sentence structure in recognizing textual entailment. In *Acl-Pascal Workshop on Textual Entailment and Paraphrasing*, pages 101–106.

Stavros Giorgis, Apostolos Rousas, John Pavlopoulos, Prodromos Malakasiotis, and Ion Androutsopoulos. 2016. aueb.twitter.sentiment at semeval-2016 task 4: A weighted ensemble of svms for twitter sentiment analysis. In *International Workshop on Semantic Evaluation*, pages 96–99.

Alex Graves. 2012. *Long Short-Term Memory*. Springer Berlin Heidelberg.

Sepp Hochreiter. 1998. The vanishing gradient problem during learning recurrent neural nets and problem solutions. *International Journal of Uncertainty, Fuzziness and Knowledge-Based Systems*, 6(02):107–116.

Diederik Kingma and Jimmy Ba. 2014. Adam: A method for stochastic optimization. *Computer Science*.

Xuchun Li, Lei Wang, and Eric Sung. 2008. Adaboost with svm-based component classifiers. *Engineering Applications of Artificial Intelligence*, 21(5):785–795.

R. Maclin and D. Opitz. 1999. Popular ensemble methods: An empirical study. *Journal of Artificial Intelligence Research*, 11:169–198.

Tomas Mikolov, Kai Chen, Greg Corrado, and Jeffrey Dean. 2013. Efficient estimation of word representations in vector space. *Computer Science*.

Saif M. Mohammad, Felipe Bravo-Marquez, Mohammad Salameh, and Svetlana Kiritchenko. 2018. Semeval-2018 task 1: Affect in tweets. In *Proceedings of International Workshop on Semantic Evaluation (SemEval-2018)*, New Orleans, LA, USA.

Saif M Mohammad, Svetlana Kiritchenko, and Xiaodan Zhu. 2013. Nrc-canada: Building the state-of-the-art in sentiment analysis of tweets. *Computer Science*.

Lili Mou, Zhao Meng, Rui Yan, Ge Li, Yan Xu, Lu Zhang, and Zhi Jin. 2016. How transferable are neural networks in nlp applications?

Jeffrey Pennington, Richard Socher, and Christopher Manning. 2014. Glove: Global vectors for word representation. In *Conference on Empirical Methods in Natural Language Processing*, pages 1532–1543.

L Prechelt. 1998. Automatic early stopping using cross validation: quantifying the criteria. *Neural Networks the Official Journal of the International Neural Network Society*, 11(4):761.

Colin Raffel and Daniel P. W. Ellis. 2015. Feedforward networks with attention can solve some long-term memory problems.

Tim Rocktschel, Edward Grefenstette, Karl Moritz Hermann, TomKoisky, and Phil Blunsom. 2015. Reasoning about entailment with neural attention.

Richard Socher, Yoshua Bengio, and Christopher D. Manning. 2013. Deep learning for nlp (without magic). *Acl Tutorial*.

Ye Zhang and Byron Wallace. 2015. A sensitivity analysis of (and practitioners' guide to) convolutional neural networks for sentence classification. *Computer Science*.

You Zhang, Hang Yuan, Jin Wang, and Xuejie Zhang. 2017. Ynu-hpcc at emoint-2017: Using a cnn-lstm model for sentiment intensity prediction. In *Proceedings of the 8th Workshop on Computational Approaches to Subjectivity, Sentiment and Social Media Analysis*, pages 200–204, Copenhagen, Denmark. Association for Computational Linguistics.

UG18 at SemEval-2018 Task 1: Generating Additional Training Data for Predicting Emotion Intensity in Spanish

Marloes Kuijper
CLCG
University of Groningen
`marloes.madelon`
`@gmail.com`

Mike van Lenthe
CLCG
University of Groningen
`mikevanlenthe`
`@gmail.com`

Rik van Noord
CLCG
University of Groningen
`r.i.k.van.noord@rug.nl`

Abstract

The present study describes our submission to SemEval 2018 Task 1: Affect in Tweets. Our Spanish-only approach aimed to demonstrate that it is beneficial to automatically generate additional training data by (i) translating training data from other languages and (ii) applying a semi-supervised learning method. We find strong support for both approaches, with those models outperforming our regular models in all subtasks. However, creating a stepwise ensemble of different models as opposed to simply averaging did not result in an increase in performance. We placed second (EI-Reg), second (EI-Oc), fourth (V-Reg) and fifth (V-Oc) in the four Spanish subtasks we participated in.

1 Introduction

Understanding the emotions expressed in a text or message is of high relevance nowadays. Companies are interested in this to get an understanding of the sentiment of their current customers regarding their products and the sentiment of their potential customers to attract new ones. Moreover, changes in a product or a company may also affect the sentiment of a customer. However, the intensity of an emotion is crucial in determining the urgency and importance of that sentiment. If someone is only slightly happy about a product, is a customer willing to buy it again? Conversely, if someone is very angry about customer service, his or her complaint might be given priority over somewhat milder complaints.

Mohammad et al. (2018) present four tasks[1] in which systems have to automatically determine the intensity of emotions (EI) or the intensity of the sentiment (Valence) of tweets in the languages English, Arabic, and Spanish. The goal is to either predict a continuous regression (reg) value or

to do ordinal classification (oc) based on a number of predefined categories. The EI tasks have separate training sets for four different emotions: anger, fear, joy and sadness. Due to the large number of subtasks and the fact that this language does not have many resources readily available, we only focus on the Spanish subtasks. Our work makes the following contributions:

- We show that automatically translating English lexicons and English training data boosts performance;

- We show that employing semi-supervised learning is beneficial;

- We show that the stepwise creation of an ensemble model is not necessarily better method than simply averaging predictions.

Our submissions ranked second (EI-Reg), second (EI-Oc), fourth (V-Reg) and fifth (V-Oc), demonstrating that the proposed method is accurate in automatically determining the intensity of emotions and sentiment of Spanish tweets. This paper will first focus on the datasets, the data generation procedure, and the techniques and tools used. Then we present the results in detail, after which we perform a small error analysis on the largest mistakes our model made. We conclude with some possible ideas for future work.

2 Method

2.1 Data

For each task, the training data that was made available by the organizers is used, which is a selection of tweets with for each tweet a label describing the intensity of the emotion or sentiment (Mohammad and Kiritchenko, 2018). Links and usernames were replaced by the general tokens URL and @username, after which the tweets

---

[1] We did not participate in subtask 5 (E-c).

Proceedings of the 12th International Workshop on Semantic Evaluation (SemEval-2018), pages 279–285
New Orleans, Louisiana, June 5–6, 2018. ©2018 Association for Computational Linguistics

Task	NRC-HSL	S-140	SenStr	AFINN	EMOTICONS	Bing Liu	MPQA	NRC-10-exp	NRC-HEAL	NEGATION
EI-Reg-a	✓	✓	✗	✓	✓	✗	✓	✓	✗	✗
EI-Reg-f	✗	✗	✗	✓	✗	✓	✓	✗	✓	✓
EI-Reg-j	✓	✓	✓	✗	✗	✓	✗	✗	✗	✓
EI-Reg-s	✗	✓	✗	✗	✓	✓	✗	✓	✓	✗
EI-Oc-a	✗	✓	✗	✗	✗	✗	✓	✗	✓	✗
EI-Oc-f	✓	✗	✗	✗	✗	✗	✗	✗	✗	✓
EI-Oc-j	✗	✗	✗	✗	✗	✓	✓	✓	✗	✓
EI-Oc-s	✗	✗	✓	✓	✓	✗	✗	✓	✓	✗
V-Reg	✗	✗	✗	✗	✗	✓	✓	✓	✗	✗
V-Oc	✗	✗	✗	✗	✗	✗	✓	✗	✗	✗

Table 1: Lexicons included in our final ensemble. NRC-10 and SentiWordNet are left out of the table because they never improved the score for a task.

were tokenized by using TweetTokenizer. All text was lowercased. In a post-processing step, it was ensured that each emoji is tokenized as a single token.

2.2 Word Embeddings

To be able to train word embeddings, Spanish tweets were scraped between November 8, 2017 and January 12, 2018. We chose to create our own embeddings instead of using pre-trained embeddings, because this way the embeddings would resemble the provided data set: both are based on Twitter data. Added to this set was the Affect in Tweets Distant Supervision Corpus (DISC) made available by the organizers (Mohammad et al., 2018) and a set of 4.1 million tweets from 2015, obtained from Toral et al. (2015). After removing duplicate tweets and tweets with fewer than ten tokens, this resulted in a set of 58.7 million tweets, containing 1.1 billion tokens. The tweets were preprocessed using the method described in Section 2.1. The word embeddings were created using word2vec in the gensim library (Řehůřek and Sojka, 2010), using CBOW, a window size of 40 and a minimum count of 5.[2] The feature vectors for each tweet were then created by using the AffectiveTweets WEKA package (Mohammad and Bravo-Marquez, 2017).

2.3 Translating Lexicons

Most lexical resources for sentiment analysis are in English. To still be able to benefit from these sources, the lexicons in the AffectiveTweets package were translated to Spanish, using the machine translation platform Apertium (Forcada et al., 2011).

All lexicons from the AffectiveTweets package were translated, except for SentiStrength. Instead

of translating this lexicon, the English version was replaced by the Spanish variant made available by Bravo-Marquez et al. (2013).

For each subtask, the optimal combination of lexicons was determined. This was done by first calculating the benefits of adding each lexicon individually, after which only beneficial lexicons were added until the score did not increase anymore (e.g. after adding the best four lexicons the fifth one did not help anymore, so only four were added). The tests were performed using a default SVM model, with the set of word embeddings described in the previous section. Each subtask thus uses a different set of lexicons (see Table 1 for an overview of the lexicons used in our final ensemble). For each subtask, this resulted in a (modest) increase on the development set, between 0.01 and 0.05.

2.4 Translating Data

The training set provided by Mohammad et al. (2018) is not very large, so it was interesting to find a way to augment the training set. A possible method is to simply translate the datasets into other languages, leaving the labels intact. Since the present study focuses on Spanish tweets, all tweets from the English datasets were translated into Spanish. This new set of "Spanish" data was then added to our original training set. Again, the machine translation platform Apertium (Forcada et al., 2011) was used for the translation of the datasets.

2.5 Algorithms Used

Three types of models were used in our system, a feed-forward neural network, an LSTM network and an SVM regressor. The neural nets were inspired by the work of Prayas (Goel et al., 2017) in the previous shared task. Different regression algorithms (e.g. AdaBoost, XGBoost) were also

<hr>

[2]Embeddings available at `www.let.rug.nl/rikvannoord/embeddings/spanish/`

280

tried due to the success of SeerNet (Duppada and Hiray, 2017), but our study was not able to reproduce their results for Spanish.

For both the LSTM network and the feed-forward network, a parameter search was done for the number of layers, the number of nodes and dropout used. This was done for each subtask, i.e. different tasks can have a different number of layers. All models were implemented using Keras (Chollet et al., 2015). After the best parameter settings were found, the results of 10 system runs to produce our predictions were averaged (note that this is different from averaging our different *type* of models in Section 2.7). For the SVM (implemented in scikit-learn (Pedregosa et al., 2011)), the RBF kernel was used and a parameter search was conducted for epsilon. Detailed parameter settings for each subtask are shown in Table 2. Each parameter search was performed using 10-fold cross validation, as to not overfit on the development set.

2.6   Semi-supervised Learning

One of the aims of this study was to see if using semi-supervised learning is beneficial for emotion intensity tasks. For this purpose, the DISC (Mohammad et al., 2018) corpus was used. This corpus was created by querying certain emotion-related words, which makes it very suitable as a semi-supervised corpus. However, the specific emotion the tweet belonged to was not made public. Therefore, a method was applied to automatically assign the tweets to an emotion by comparing our scraped tweets to this new data set.

First, in an attempt to obtain the query-terms, we selected the 100 words which occurred most frequently in the DISC corpus, in comparison with their frequencies in our own scraped tweets corpus. Words that were clearly not indicators of emotion were removed. The rest was annotated per emotion or removed if it was unclear to which emotion the word belonged. This allowed us to create *silver* datasets per emotion, assigning tweets to an emotion if an annotated *emotion-word* occurred in the tweet.

Our semi-supervised approach is quite straightforward: first a model is trained on the training set and then this model is used to predict the labels of the silver data. This silver data is then simply added to our training set, after which the model is retrained. However, an extra step is applied to en-

sure that the silver data is of reasonable quality. Instead of training a single model initially, ten different models were trained which predict the labels of the silver instances. If the highest and lowest prediction do not differ more than a certain threshold the silver instance is maintained, otherwise it is discarded.

This results in two parameters that could be optimized: the threshold and the number of silver instances that would be added. This method can be applied to both the LSTM and feed-forward networks that were used. An overview of the characteristics of our data set with the final parameter settings is shown in Table 3. Usually, only a small subset of data was added to our training set, meaning that most of the silver data is not used in the experiments. Note that since only the emotions were annotated, this method is only applicable to the EI tasks.[3]

2.7   Ensembling

To boost performance, the SVM, LSTM, and feed-forward models were combined into an ensemble. For both the LSTM and feed-forward approach, three different models were trained. The first model was trained on the training data (regular), the second model was trained on both the training and translated training data (translated) and the third one was trained on both the training data and the semi-supervised data (silver). Due to the nature of the SVM algorithm, semi-supervised learning does not help, so only the regular and translated model were trained in this case. This results in 8 different models per subtask. Note that for the valence tasks no silver training data was obtained, meaning that for those tasks the semi-supervised models could not be used.

Per task, the LSTM and feed-forward model's predictions were averaged over 10 prediction runs. Subsequently, the predictions of all individual models were combined into an average. Finally, models were removed from the ensemble in a stepwise manner if the removal increased the average score. This was done based on their original scores, i.e. starting out by trying to remove the worst individual model and working our way up to the best model. We only consider it an increase in score if the difference is larger than 0.002 (i.e. the difference between 0.716 and 0.718). If at some point the score does not increase and we

---

[3]For EI-Oc, the labels were normalized between 0 and 1.

	SVM	Feed-forward		LSTM			
Task	Epsilon	Layers	Nodes	Layers	Nodes	Dropout	Dense
EI-Reg-a	0.01	2	(600, 200)	2	400	0.001	✗
EI-Reg-f	0.04	2	(700, 200)	2	400	0.01	✓
EI-Reg-j	0.05	2	(500, 500)	2	200	0.1	✗
EI-Reg-s	0.06	2	(400, 300)	2	600	0.001	✗
EI-Oc-a	0.005	2	(600, 200)	2	200	0.001	✗
EI-Oc-f	0.06	2	(700, 300)	2	200	0.001	✗
EI-Oc-j	0.04	2	(800, 200)	3	400	0.001	✓
EI-Oc-s	0.005	2	(500, 200)	3	800	0.01	✓
V-Reg	0.07	3	(400, 400, 400)	2	200	0.001	✓
V-Oc	0.09	3	(400, 400, 100)	3	600	0.01	✓

Table 2: Parameter settings for the algorithms used. For feed-forward, we show the number of nodes per layer. The *Dense* column for LSTM shows whether a dense layer was added after the LSTM layers (with half the number of nodes as is shown in the *Nodes* column). The feed-forward networks always use a dropout of 0.001 after the first layer.

	Words	Tweets	Task	Feed-forward		LSTM	
				Threshold	Tweets added	Threshold	Tweets added
Anger	23	81, 798	*EI-Reg*	0.1	2,500	0.05	2,500
			EI-Oc	0.1	1,000	0.1	2,500
Fear	17	54,113	*EI-Reg*	0.1	1,500	0.05	1,500
			EI-Oc	0.075	1,000	0.1	2,500
Joy	29	51,135	*EI-Reg*	0.125	1,500	0.15	500
			EI-Oc	0.05	500	0.05	500
Sadness	16	102,810	*EI-Reg*	0.1	5,000	0.1	2,500
			EI-Oc	0.125	2,000	0.05	2,500

Table 3: Statistics and parameter settings of the semi-supervised learning experiments.

are therefore unable to remove a model, the process is stopped and our best ensemble of models has been found. This process uses the scores on the development set of different combinations of models. Note that this means that the ensembles for different subtasks can contain different sets of models. The final model selections can be found in Table 4.

3 Results and Discussion

Table 5 shows the results on the development set of all individuals models, distinguishing the three types of training: regular (r), translated (t) and semi-supervised (s). In Tables 4 and 5, the letter behind each model (e.g. SVM-r, LSTM-r) corresponds to the type of training used. Comparing the regular and translated columns for the three algorithms, it shows that in 22 out of 30 cases, using translated instances as extra training

data resulted in an improvement. For the semi-supervised learning approach, an improvement is found in 15 out of 16 cases. Moreover, our best individual model for each subtask (bolded scores in Table 5) is always either a translated or semi-supervised model. Table 5 also shows that, in general, our feed-forward network obtained the best results, having the highest F-score for 8 out of 10 subtasks.

However, Table 6 shows that these scores can still be improved by averaging or ensembling the individual models. On the dev set, averaging our 8 individual models results in a better score for 8 out of 10 subtasks, while creating an ensemble beats all of the individual models as well as the average for each subtask. On the test set, however, only a small increase in score (if any) is found for stepwise ensembling, compared to averaging. Even though the results do not get worse, we can-

Task	SVM-r	SVM-t	LSTM-r	LSTM-t	LSTM-s	FF-r	FF-t	FF-s
EI-Reg-anger	✗	✓	✗	✓	✓	✓	✓	✓
EI-Reg-fear	✓	✓	✗	✓	✓	✗	✓	✗
EI-Reg-joy	✓	✓	✗	✓	✓	✗	✓	✓
EI-Reg-sadness	✓	✓	✓	✗	✗	✓	✓	✓
EI-Oc-anger	✓	✗	✗	✓	✓	✗	✓	✓
EI-Oc-fear	✗	✓	✓	✓	✓	✓	✓	✓
EI-Oc-joy	✗	✓	✗	✓	✓	✓	✓	✓
EI-Oc-sadness	✗	✓	✗	✓	✓	✓	✓	✓
V-Reg	✓	✗	✗	✓	✗	✓	✓	✗
V-Oc	✗	✓	✓	✓	✗	✓	✓	✗

Table 4: Models included in our final ensemble.

Task	SVMr	SVMt	LSTMr	LSTMt	LSTMs	FFr	FFt	FFs
EI-Reg-a	0.630	0.663	0.644	0.672	0.683	0.659	0.672	**0.681**
EI-Reg-f	0.683	0.700	0.666	0.702	0.682	0.675	**0.704**	0.674
EI-Reg-j	0.702	0.711	0.683	0.709	0.699	0.688	**0.720**	0.710
EI-Reg-s	0.690	0.696	0.694	0.67	0.678	0.694	0.694	**0.704**
EI-Oc-a	0.663	0.645	0.602	**0.673**	0.589	0.611	0.659	0.640
EI-Oc-f	0.621	0.579	0.610	0.603	0.615	0.596	0.598	**0.629**
EI-Oc-j	0.626	**0.674**	0.670	0.657	0.671	0.616	0.638	0.628
EI-Oc-s	0.579	0.621	0.590	0.612	0.610	0.579	**0.633**	0.595
V-Reg	0.728	0.735	0.729	0.766	-	0.751	**0.765**	-
V-Oc	0.680	0.670	0.719	0.711	-	0.724	**0.727**	-

Table 5: Scores for each individual model per subtask. Best individual score per subtask is bolded.

Task	Avg Dev	Ens Dev	Avg Test	Ens Test
EI-Reg-a	0.684	0.692	0.589	0.595
EI-Reg-f	0.709	0.718	0.687	0.689
EI-Reg-j	0.721	0.727	0.712	0.712
EI-Reg-s	0.711	0.716	0.710	0.712
EI-Oc-a	0.658	0.678	0.500	0.499
EI-Oc-f	0.643	0.666	0.592	0.606
EI-Oc-j	0.669	0.695	0.668	0.665
EI-Oc-s	0.612	0.645	0.612	0.625
V-Reg	0.728	0.744	0.686	0.682
V-Oc	0.767	0.772	0.706	0.707

Table 6: Results on the dev and test set for averaging and stepwise ensembling the individual models. The last column shows our official results.

not conclude that stepwise ensembling is a better method than simply averaging.

Our official scores (column *Ens Test* in Table 6) have placed us second (EI-Reg, EI-Oc), fourth (V-Reg) and fifth (V-Oc) on the SemEval AIT-2018 leaderboard. However, it is evident that the results obtained on the test set are not always in line with those achieved on the development set. Especially on the anger subtask for both EI-Reg and EI-Oc, the scores are considerably lower on the test set in comparison with the results on the development set. Therefore, a small error analysis was performed on the instances where our final model made the largest errors.

3.1 Error Analysis

Due to some large differences between our results on the dev and test set of this task, we performed a small error analysis in order to see what caused these differences. For *EI-Reg-anger*, the gold labels were compared to our own predictions, and we manually checked 50 instances for which our system made the largest errors.

Some examples that were indicative of the shortcomings of our system are shown in Table 7. First of all, our system did not take into account capitalization. The implications of this are shown in the first sentence, where capitalization intensi-

Example sentence	Pred.	Gold	Possible problem
QUIERES PELEA FSICA? DO YOU WANT A PHYSICAL FIGHT?	0.25	0.80	Capitalization
Ojal una precuela de Imperator Furiosa. I wish a prequel to Imperator Furiosa.	0.64	0.24	Named entity not recognized
Odio estar tan enojada y que me de risa I hate being so angry and that that makes me laugh	0.79	0.46	Reduced angriness
Yo la mejor y que te contesten as nomas me infla la vena I am the best and that they answer you like that, it just inflates my vein	0.45	0.90	Figurative speech

Table 7: Error analysis for the EI-Reg-anger subtask, with English translations.

fies the emotion used in the sentence. In the second sentence, the name *Imperator Furiosa* is not understood. Since our texts were lowercased, our system was unable to capture the named entity and thought the sentence was about an angry emperor instead. In the third sentence, our system fails to capture that when you are so angry that it makes you laugh, it results in a reduced intensity of the angriness. Finally, in the fourth sentence, it is the figurative language *me infla la vena* (it inflates my vein) that the system is not able to understand.

The first two error-categories might be solved by including smart features regarding capitalization and named entity recognition. However, the last two categories are problems of natural language understanding and will be very difficult to fix.

4   Conclusion

To conclude, the present study described our submission for the Semeval 2018 Shared Task on Affect in Tweets. We participated in four Spanish subtasks and our submissions ranked second, second, fourth and fifth place. Our study aimed to investigate whether the automatic generation of additional training data through translation and semi-supervised learning, as well as the creation of stepwise ensembles, increase the performance of our Spanish-language models. Strong support was found for the translation and semi-supervised learning approaches; our best models for all subtasks use either one of these approaches. These results suggest that both of these additional data resources are beneficial when determining emotion intensity (for Spanish). However, the creation of a stepwise ensemble from the best models did not result in better performance compared to simply averaging the models. In addition, some signs of overfitting on the dev set were found. In fu-

ture work, we would like to apply the methods (translation and semi-supervised learning) used on Spanish on other low-resource languages and potentially also on other tasks.

References

Felipe Bravo-Marquez, Marcelo Mendoza, and Barbara Poblete. 2013. Combining strengths, emotions and polarities for boosting twitter sentiment analysis. In *Proceedings of the Second International Workshop on Issues of Sentiment Discovery and Opinion Mining*, page 2. ACM.

François Chollet et al. 2015. Keras. `https:// github.com/keras-team/keras`.

Venkatesh Duppada and Sushant Hiray. 2017. Seernet at emoint-2017: Tweet emotion intensity estimator. In *Proceedings of the 8th Workshop on Computational Approaches to Subjectivity, Sentiment and Social Media Analysis*, pages 205–211, Copenhagen, Denmark. Association for Computational Linguistics.

Mikel L Forcada, Mireia Ginestí-Rosell, Jacob Nordfalk, Jim ORegan, Sergio Ortiz-Rojas, Juan Antonio Pérez-Ortiz, Felipe Sánchez-Martínez, Gema Ramírez-Sánchez, and Francis M Tyers. 2011. Apertium: a free/open-source platform for rulebased machine translation. *Machine translation*, 25(2):127–144.

Pranav Goel, Devang Kulshreshtha, Prayas Jain, and Kaushal Kumar Shukla. 2017. Prayas at emoint 2017: An ensemble of deep neural architectures for emotion intensity prediction in tweets. In *Proceedings of the 8th Workshop on Computational Approaches to Subjectivity, Sentiment and Social Media Analysis*, pages 58–65.

Saif Mohammad and Felipe Bravo-Marquez. 2017. Emotion intensities in tweets. In *Proceedings of the 6th Joint Conference on Lexical and Computational Semantics, *SEM @ACM 2017, Vancouver, Canada, August 3-4, 2017*, pages 65–77.

Saif M. Mohammad, Felipe Bravo-Marquez, Mohammad Salameh, and Svetlana Kiritchenko. 2018.

Semeval-2018 Task 1: Affect in tweets. In *Proceedings of International Workshop on Semantic Evaluation (SemEval-2018)*, New Orleans, LA, USA.

Saif M. Mohammad and Svetlana Kiritchenko. 2018. Understanding emotions: A dataset of tweets to study interactions between affect categories. In *Proceedings of the 11th Edition of the Language Resources and Evaluation Conference*, Miyazaki, Japan.

F. Pedregosa, G. Varoquaux, A. Gramfort, V. Michel, B. Thirion, O. Grisel, M. Blondel, P. Prettenhofer, R. Weiss, V. Dubourg, J. Vanderplas, A. Passos, D. Cournapeau, M. Brucher, M. Perrot, and E. Duchesnay. 2011. Scikit-learn: Machine learning in Python. *Journal of Machine Learning Research*, 12:2825–2830.

Radim Řehůřek and Petr Sojka. 2010. Software Framework for Topic Modelling with Large Corpora. In *Proceedings of the LREC 2010 Workshop on New Challenges for NLP Frameworks*, pages 45–50, Valletta, Malta. ELRA. `http://is.muni.cz/publication/884893/en`.

Antonio Toral, Xiaofeng Wu, Tommi A Pirinen, Zhengwei Qiu, Ergun Bicici, and Jinhua Du. 2015. Dublin city university at the tweetmt 2015 shared task. In *TweetMT@ SEPLN*, pages 33–39.

ISCLAB at SemEval-2018 Task 1: UIR-Miner for Affect in Tweets

Meng Li[1,2], Zhenyuan Dong[1], Zhihao Fan[1], Kongming Meng[1], Jinghua Cao[1],
Guanqi Ding[1], Yuhan Liu[1], Jiawei Shan[1], Binyang Li[1*]

[1] School of Information Science and Technology, University of International Relations
[2] University of Pittsburgh
[*] Corresponding author
mel165@pitt.edu; {byli, zydong, zhfan, kmmeng, jhcao, gqding, jwshan}@uir.edu.cn

Abstract

This paper presents a UIR-Miner system for emotion and sentiment analysis evaluation in Twitter in SemEval 2018. Our system consists of three main modules: preprocessing module, stacking module to solve the intensity prediction of emotion and sentiment, LSTM network module to solve multi-label classification, and the hierarchical attention network module for solving emotion and sentiment classification problem. According to the metrics of SemEval 2018, our system gets the final scores of 0.636, 0.531, 0.731, 0.708, and 0.408 in terms of Pearson Correlation on 5 subtasks, respectively.

1 Introduction

Recently, social media platforms are becoming more and more popular, such as Twitter microblogging, Facebook, and so on. Through these platforms, online users would like to share their opinions and emotions. Therefore, the analysis about the information on "affect" in the social media has attracted much interest from both academia and industries.

However, the short texts are usually consisted of informal expressions with much casual forms and emoticons, it brings great challenges for such research.

For this purpose, SemEval organized the evaluation of sentiment analysis on Tweet. This year comes the fifth edition that consists of new genres, including emotion intensity regression task, emotion intensity ordinal classification task, sentiment intensity regression task, sentiment degree ordinal classification task, and emotion classification task (Mohammad et al., 2018).

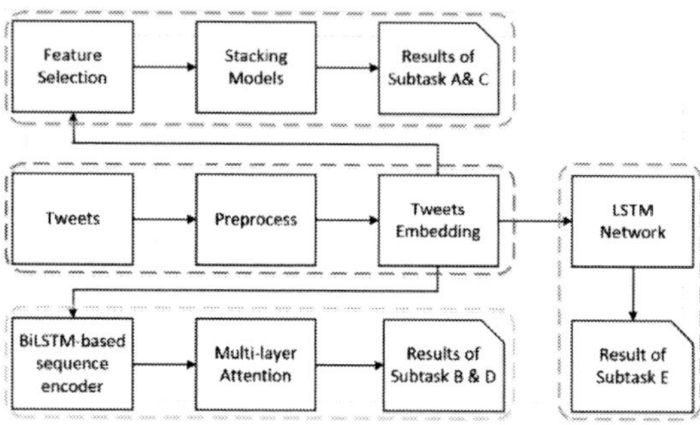

Figure 1: System architecture.

We participated in SemEval 2018 task 1 for English, i.e. Affect in Tweet. Our system considers EI-reg and V-reg (subtask A and C) as regression problems to get the emotion intensity and sentiment intensity by using regression models, while regards EI-oc and V-oc (subtask B and D) as categorization problems to classify each tweet into its corresponding emotion category and sentiment category by implementing hierarchical attention networks. Moreover, subtask E, i.e., E-c, is considered as a multi-label classification task.

This paper is organized as follows. Section 2 overviews the framework of our system. Section 3 describes the methods for subtask A and C. Section 4 describes the hierarchical attention networks for subtask B and D. Subtask E will be introduced in Section 5. Section 6 presents the evaluation results. Section 7 will conclude this paper.

2 System Overview

The architecture of UIR-Miner is shown in Figure 1. UIR-Miner system is comprised of 4 modules:
(1) Preprocessing module: involves data cleaning, topic classification, and tweets embedding.

Proceedings of the 12th International Workshop on Semantic Evaluation (SemEval-2018), pages 286–290
New Orleans, Louisiana, June 5–6, 2018. ©2018 Association for Computational Linguistics

(2) Regressor module: creates an ensemble regressor model by using different basic models simultaneously to calculate the emotion intensity and sentiment intensity, i.e. subtask A and subtask C;

(3) Classification module: constructs an LSTM network with multi-layer attention mechanism for emotion and sentiment categorization, i.e. subtask B and subtask D;

(4) Multi-label Classification module: builds a LSTM network for subtask E.

2.1 Preprocessing

Our system will firstly preprocess the Tweets data, and the main steps are as follows.

- Delete the unrelated texts, including the id, some mentions, stop words, and some meaningless punctuation combinations.
- Normalize synonymous words, like replacing "cant" and "can't" with "cannot".
- Extract emoticons from tweets through regular expressions, and then maintain the emotional ones.

2.2 Word embedding

In the preprocessing, we used the pre-trained word embedding by Glove (Penningto et. al, 2014), in which each word e_{it} will be represented by a 200-dimensional vector w_{it}, $i \in [1, L]$, $t \in [1, T]$. Here, i denotes the location of the sentence in the tweet and L is the maximum number of sentences for each tweet, t denotes the location of the word in the sentence and T is the maximum number of words for each sentence. Set $T = 140$ and $L = 5$.

3 Subtask A and C

This section will describe the methods for subtask A and C. Given a tweet and an emotion E (or a sentiment V), determine the intensity of E (or V) that best represents the mental state of the tweeter—a real-valued score between 0 and 1. We consider both of subtask A and C as a regression problem.

On the whole, we use a stacking framework to enhance the accuracy of final prediction. The original features are selected as input into the stacking model, including hashtags, emoticons, and *n-gram* features. Then, the stacking model is divided into two layer, the base layer and the stacking layer. In the base layer, we choose four basic regressors due to their excellent performance. In the stacking layer, we still use SVM model, especially, the NuSVR model, which can control its error rate. Finally, we get the final result of intensity value.

3.1 Feature Selection

Since there are many irregular expressions in tweet, we combine the features, including emoticon, hashtag, and special punctuations. In our system, we mainly select the following features:

- Hashtags: the number of hashtags in one tweet;
- Ill format: the presence of ill format with some characters replacing by *;
- Punctuation: the number of contiguous sequences of exclamation marks, question marks, and both exclamation and question marks; whether the last token contains an exclamation or question mark;
- Emoticons: the presence of positive and negative emoticons at any position in the tweet; whether the last token is an emoticon;
- OOV: the ratio of words out of vocabulary;
- Elongated words: the presence of sentiment words with one character repeated more than two times, for example, 'cooool';
- URL: whether the tweet contains a URL.
- Reply or Retweet: is the current tweet a reply/retweet tweet.

3.2 Stacking Model

To avoid overfitting, we test 6 basic models to construct our stacking model.

- B: Bayesian Ridge (Hsiang, T.C 1975)
- G: Gradient Boosting Regressor (Jerome H. Friedman, 2001)
- K: Kernel Ridge (Zhang Y et. al, 2013)
- L: Lasso Regressor (Tibshirani et al., 1996)
- M: MLP Regression (Pal and Mitra, 1992)
- R: Random Forest Regressor (Ho, 1995)
- S: SVR (Vapnik 1995)

To achieve the best performance, we also compare different combinations of our basic models with the metrics of Mean Squired Error (MSE) in the stacking method, and the experimental result is shown in Table 1.

- Baseline: we use SVR as the Baseline;
- Stacking1: B+K+S;
- Stacking2: M+K+R;
- Stacking3: B+K+R+S;
- Stacking4: B+G+K+M;
- Stacking5: G+K+L+ S;
- Stacking6: B+G+K+S.

Since Stacking 6 achieves the best performance, we use the same setting in our system.

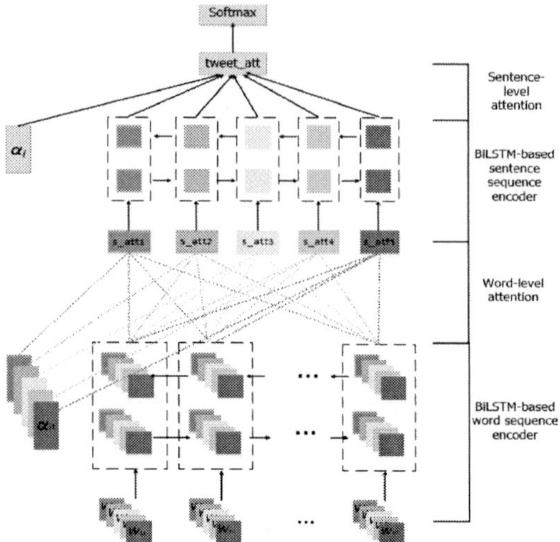

Figure 2: BiLSTM network with multi-layer attention mechanism.

Table 1: Evaluation on different combinations in stacking method.

Method	Metrics				
	Ang	Fear	Joy	Sad	Ave
Baseline	9.774	8.390	9.055	9.086	9.076
Stacking1	9.404	7.926	8.352	8.629	8.578
Stacking2	9.596	7.849	8.192	8.520	8.539
Stacking3	9.351	7.900	8.206	8.536	8.500
Stacking4	9.557	7.715	8.045	8.454	8.443
Stacking5	9.381	7.790	8.170	8.387	8.432
Stacking6	**9.300**	**7.766**	**7.794**	**8.334**	**8.298**

4 Hierarchical Attention Networks for Subtask B and D

This section will introduce our hierarchical attention model for subtask B and D. Given a tweet and an emotion category E (or a sentiment category V), classify the tweet into one of the ordinal classes of intensity of E (or V) that best represents the mental state of the tweeter. Note that, the number of category of E is 4, while that of V is 7. In our system, we consider both of subtask B and D as a classification problem.

Each tweet contains several sentences that are comprised by several words. In order to better represent the semantics of emotion or sentiment, we utilize the hierarchical structure of a tweet to capture the contextual information of both intra and inter-tweet. The architecture is shown as Figure 2.

We build a hierarchical model which contains two layers, word layer and sentence layer. Since words and sentences are highly sensitive to the con-

texts, recurrent neural networks based on bidirectional long short-term memory (BiLSTM) (Hochreiter and Schmidhuber, 1997) are implemented on both layers to get tweets' representations. Furthermore, since the words in one sentence or different sentences in a given tweet can indicate different emotion intensity or sentiment intensity. To better represent the semantics, attention mechanisms are added to both layers respectively (Xu et. al., 2015). We then use softmax as the activation

4.1 BiLSTM-based Word Encoder

A word level BiLSTM (Hochreiter and Schmidhuber, 1997) is used to represent each word. The BiLSTM consists of the forward LSTM and the backward LSTM. Forward LSTM reads the sentence s_i from e_{i1} to e_{iT} and represents the word e_{it} as $\overrightarrow{LSTM}(w_{it}), t \in [1, T]$. Backward LSTM reads the sentence s_i from e_{iT} to e_{i1} and represents the word e_{it} as $\overleftarrow{LSTM}(w_{it}), t \in [T, 1]$. Then word e_{it} can be annotated by combining both forward information and backward information, $h_{it} = [\overrightarrow{LSTM}(w_{it}), \overleftarrow{LSTM}(w_{it})]$. The equations are listed as follows:

$$i_t = \sigma(W_i w_{it} + U_i h_{t-1} + b_i) \qquad (1)$$

$$f_t = \sigma(W_f w_{ft} + U_f h_{t-1} + b_f) \qquad (2)$$

$$o_t = \sigma(W_o w_{ot} + U_o h_{t-1} + b_o) \qquad (3)$$

$$u_t = \tanh(W_u w_{ut} + U_u h_{t-1} + b_u) \qquad (4)$$

$$c_t = i_t \odot u_t + f_t \odot c_{t-1} \qquad (5)$$

$$h_t = o_t \odot \tanh(c_t) \qquad (6)$$

where i_t, f_t and o_t are the input gate, forget gate and output gate, σ is the logistic sigmoid function, $\odot$ denotes elementwise multiplication, $tanh$ is the network output activation function, and $softmax$ is used for categorization. To better support Twitter, we input the word embedding with 200 dimensions, and the max number of words in a sentence as 140.

4.2 Word Layer Attention

Different weights α_{it} are given to different words. Attention mechanism (Xu et. al., 2015) is added to the word layer and the sentence s_i can be represented as s_att_i.

$$u_{it} = \tanh(W_w h_{it} + b_w) \qquad (7)$$

$$\alpha_{it} = \frac{\exp(u_{it}^T u_w)}{\sum_t \exp(u_{it}^T u_w)} \qquad (8)$$

$$s\_att_i = \sum_t \alpha_{it} h_{it} \qquad (9)$$

More specifically, after putting h_{it} into a fully-connected layer, we get u_{it}. Then calculate weight α_{it} with a word level context u_w. Finally, we can get the sentence vector through an attention layer by calculating the sum of $\alpha_{it} h_{it}$.

4.3 Sentence Layer Attention

Similarly, a sentence level BiLSTM (Hochreiter and Schmidhuber, 1997) can be used to represent sentence s_i by adding sentence level context information,

$$h_i = [\overrightarrow{LSTM}(s_{att_{it}}), \overleftarrow{LSTM}(s_{att_{it}})].$$

We then add weights to different sentence. Take x_i as input and get $tweet\_att$ to represent each tweet through an attention layer.

$$u_i = \tanh(W_s h_i + b_s)$$

$$\alpha_i = \frac{\exp(u_i^T u_s)}{\sum_i \exp(u_i^T u_s)}$$

$$tweet\_att = \sum_i \alpha_i h_i$$

More specifically, after putting h_i into a fully-connected layer, we get u_i. Then calculate weight α_i with a sentence level context u_s. Finally, we can get the tweet vector through an attention layer by calculating the sum of $\alpha_i h_i$.

5 Subtask E

This section will introduce neural network model for subtask E. Given a tweet, classify the tweet as "neutral or no emotion" or as one, or more, of eleven given emotions that best represent the mental state of the tweeter.

Each tweet will be classified with different numbers of labels. Since there exists eleven labels each of which may be suitable, considering one of these labels every time is reasonable. Our system will calculate a score for each of the eleven labels for each tweet, and select the top-3 as the final results.

We also used a LSTM network for this task, and get the classification result by using *softmax*. The other settings of this model is quite similar to that in Section 4 except for multi-label classification.

6 Experiment

In this section, we will report our evaluation results in SemEval 2018 based on the given dataset as well as the metrics. The statistics of the dataset is shown in Table 2.

Note that any other extra external resources, such as sentiment lexicon, emoticons, and annotated corpus, are not used in the evaluation except for the training dataset provided by the organization.

Table 2: Statistics of the dataset.

	Training set	Dev set	Test set
EI-reg	anger: 1701 fear: 2252 joy: 1616 sadness: 1533	anger: 388 fear: 389 joy: 290 sadness: 397	anger: 17939 fear: 17923 joy: 18042 sadness: 17912
EI-oc	anger: 1701 fear: 2252 joy: 1616 sadness: 1533	anger: 388 fear: 389 joy: 290 sadness: 397	anger: 1002 fear: 986 joy: 1105 sadness: 975
V-reg	1181	449	17874
V-oc	1181	449	937
E-c	6838	886	3259

Table 3 shows the results of our UIR-Miner for all the subtasks on both Dev set and Test set, and the final ranking.

Table 3: The results on different datasets.

	Score in Dev	Score in Test	Ranking
EI-reg	0.576	0.636	28/48
EI-oc	0.495	0.531	15/39
V-reg	0.729	0.781	21/38
V-oc	0.694	0.708	16/37
E-c	0.421	0.407	23/35

7 Conclusion

In this paper, we present a framework for SemEval 2018 Affect in Tweet task. After the preprocessing, we firstly propose an ensembling method to calculate the intensity score of emotion and sentiment. Then a LSTM network model with multi-layer attention mechanism is constructed for emotion and sentiment classification. According to SemEval 2018's metrics, our model runs got final scores of 0.636, 0.531, 0.731, 0.708, and 0.408 in terms of Pearson Correlation on 5 subtasks, respectively.

Acknowledgements

This paper is funded by the National Natural Foundation of China 61502115, 61602326, U1636103, U1536207, 61572043, 61672361, 61632011, the Hong Kong Applied Science and Technology Research Institute Project 7050854, and the Fundamental Research Fund for the Central Universityies 3262015T70, 3262017T12.

References

Alex J. Smola, Bernhard Schölkopf. 2004. A tutorial on support vector regression. In *2004 Kluwer Academic Publishers*, pages 199-222

Hsiang, T.C. 1975.A Bayesian View on Ridge Regression. In *Journal of the Royal Statistical Society*, page 267-268.

Zhang Y, Duchi J, Wainwright M. 2013. Divide and conquer kernel ridge regression. In *Conference on Learning Theory*, pages 592-617.

Jerome H. Friedman. 2001. Greedy function approximation: a gradient boosting machine. In Annals of Statistics, pages 1189–1232

Sepp Hochreiter and Jürgen Schmidhuber. 1997. Long short-term memory. In Neural computation, 9(8): 1735-1780.

Saif M. Mohammad, Felipe Bravo-Marquez, Mohammad Salameh, and Svetlana Kiritchenko. 2018. SemEval-2018 Task1: Affect in tweets. In *Proceedings of International Workshop on Semantic Evaluation (SemEval-2018)*.

Saif M. Mohammad and Svetlana Kiritchenko. 2018. Understanding emotions: A dataset of tweets to study interactions between affect categories. In *Proceedings of the 11th Edition of the Language Resources and Evaluation Conference*.

Jeffrey Pennington, Richard Socher, and Christopher D. Manning. 2014. Glove: Global vectors for word representation. In *Empirical Methods in Natural Language Processing*, pages 1532-1543.

Kelvin Xu, Jimmy Ba, Ryan Kiros, Kyunghyun Cho, Aaron Courville, Ruslan Salakhudinov, Richard Zemel, and Yoshua Bengio. 2015. Show, attend and tell: Neural image caption generation with visual attention. In *International Conference on Machine Learning*, pages 2048-2057.

Zichao Yang, Diyi Yang, Chris Dyer, Xiaodong He, Alex Smola, and Eduard Hovy. 2016. Hierachical attention networks for document classification. In *Proceedings of the 2016 Conference of the North American Chapter of the Association for Computational Linguistics: Human Language Technologies*, pages 1480-1489.

Tibshirani R, Bickel P, Ritov Y, et al. Least absolute shrinkage and selection operator[J]. 1996.

Ho T K. Random decision forests[C]//Document analysis and recognition, 1995, proceedings of the third international conference on. IEEE, 1995, 1: 278-282.

Pal S K, Mitra S. Multilayer perceptron, fuzzy sets, and classification[J]. IEEE Transactions on neural networks, 1992, 3(5): 683-697.

TCS Research at SemEval-2018 Task 1: Learning Robust Representations using Multi-Attention Architecture

Hardik Meisheri
TCS Research
New Delhi, India
`hardik.meisheri@tcs.com`

Lipika Dey
TCS Research
New Delhi, India
`lipika.dey@tcs.com`

Abstract

This paper presents system description of our submission to the SemEval-2018 task-1: Affect in tweets for the English language. We combine three different features generated using deep learning models and traditional methods in support vector machines to create a unified ensemble system. A robust representation of a tweet is learned using a multi-attention based architecture which uses a mixture of different pre-trained embeddings. In addition, analysis of different features is also presented. Our system ranked 2nd, 5th, and 7th in different subtasks among 75 teams.

1 Introduction

In Natural Language processing, Sentiment analysis refers to the degree of positiveness or negativeness of the information presented in the text. Traditionally sentiment analysis is treated as either a binary classification task (positive, negative) or a multi-class classification task (very negative, negative, neutral, positive, very positive). Affect analysis on the other hand refers to detecting discrete sets of emotions present in the text such as anger, joy, sadness etc (Dalgleish and Power, 2000; Plutchik, 2001). Predicting intensities of these emotions to fine granularity can help us better understand the sentiment and emotions of the writer.

Detecting sentiments or affect from text have a number of useful applications. For example, the degree of disgust or anger expressed in customer complaints or reviews can help us decide the priorities of issues to look at, or the joy or optimism expressed in customer feedbacks can be a major factor in deciding the marketing strategy for a company.

Sentiment or affect analysis for social media text is a challenging task due to the extensive use of slang, frequent spelling mistakes, innovative and unpredictable use of hashtags and extensive use of emojis and smileys.

SemEval-2018 Task 1: Affect in tweets, provides data for 3 languages: English, Arabic, and Spanish. For each language, there are 5 subtasks that are presented, 2 Regression tasks, 2 classification tasks and 1 Multi-Label task. Further details of tasks are presented in section 3. This task was similar to the WASSA shared task (Mohammad and Bravo-Marquez, 2017) and dataset presented here is the extension of the data presented for WASSA shared task.

In this paper, we present our approach to solving these tasks for English language tweets. We have proposed a system which uses various pre-trained embeddings to handle out-of-vocabulary words and emoji present in the text along with cleaning of raw text. In addition, to create a better representation of the text, we use two sets of embeddings learnt over two different corpus which results in parallel attention mechanism - one set from the twitter space and another from a common crawl corpus. Finally, we combine features generated from the deep learning model with other features to generate an ensemble system.

Major contributions of this paper are:

1. Generating word vector representation of a tweet from three different set of pre-trained embeddings which can handle emoji/smileys and the out of vocabulary words in the dataset.

2. Deep neural network architecture which generates robust representation of the text with the help of parallel attention mechanism.

Rest of the paper is organized as follows, Section 2 presents the preprocessing step to generate mixed set of embeddings and the model architecture. It also presents the different sets of features that are used for final ensemble system. In section 3, data, training and experimentation setup is described for different subtasks. Section 4 states

Proceedings of the 12th International Workshop on Semantic Evaluation (SemEval-2018), pages 291–299
New Orleans, Louisiana, June 5–6, 2018. ©2018 Association for Computational Linguistics

the results of the proposed system and detailed discussion of the feature over development and test data. Finally, section 5 concludes the paper with summary of the approach presented.

2 Proposed Approach

Figure 1 describes the overall system architecture used for regression and classification subtasks. We have extracted different types of features from the raw text, which fall under three different categories. Deep learning features are the ones which are generated from the model that is trained and proposed in this paper. Lexicon-based features are generated from training sets. In addition, features from pre-trained models are used. These models were trained over large corpus.

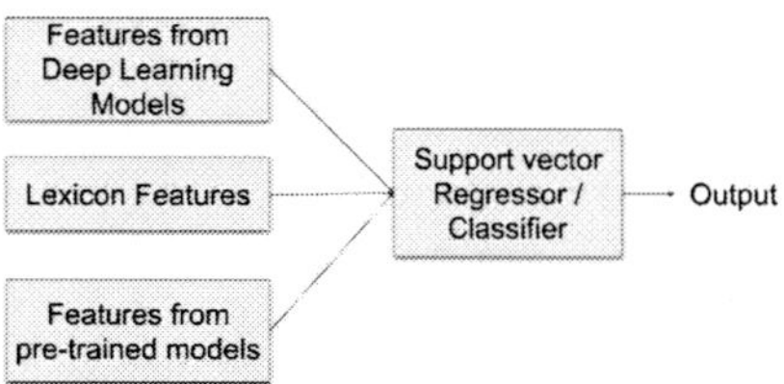

Figure 1: System Diagram.

Attention mechanism has been successful in sequence to sequence learning problems specifically for neural machine translation (NMT) (Bahdanau et al., 2014). These mechanism helps model to focus more on the task in hand. The proposed architecture uses two parallel processing towers which use attention as a means of focusing on sentiment specific words. Figure 2 presents a snapshot of the random sample for sadness emotion, first row denotes the output of the attention mechanism and row 2 denotes the output of the model. We observe that the attention mechanism helps in focusing on words which are relevant to the sentiment task in hand, such as crying, dying etc. which further helps in improving the performance of the model. The multi-attention mechanism is inspired from (Lin et al., 2017) where, they have used more multi-attention over the same embedding space to focus on more than one word. In contrast, we use limit our attention to at max 2 words as the tweet is much more compact in nature as well as we do it over different embedding space to encapsulate much more information.

For generating features as mentioned above, we employ pre-processing steps to normalize the text with respect to sentiment specific words and its usage.

2.1 Preprocessing

As mentioned earlier, tweets in the raw form are noisy and prone to many distortions in terms of syntactic and semantic structure. These pre-processing steps are common to all the features generated. Deep learning features require additional steps which are explained in respective section.

1. All the characters in the text are converted to lower case.

2. Twitter contains lot of words with more than 2 repeating characters such as happpyyyyyyy, we limited occurrence of each character to maximum of 2 successive times.

3. To handle hashtags, # symbol is removed from all the words.

4. Extra spaces and new line character is deleted from the tweet to ensure the compactness of the tweets.

2.2 Deep Learning Features

Figure 3 shows the model which was used to generate deep learning features. In this model, we have used different embeddings to enhance the representations of raw text. There are two parallel architectures which take the same raw input but generate the representation from a different embedding space. This helps in encapsulating the word and its usage in twitter space as well as keeping a general semantic and syntactic structure of word intact.

For tower one in the figure 3, text is preprocessed using steps mentioned earlier. In addition, following pre-processing steps are performed:

1. *Usernames* in twitter which starts with @ is replaced by **mention** token.

2. Punctuations are removed except *[,], [?], [!], [.]*

3. Words that are most probably used as slangs in twitter are replaced with its corresponding expanded versions such as *"y'all"* is replace by *"you all"*.

Embedding matrix is generated from the pre-processed text using combination of three pre-trained embeddings: Glove (Pennington et al.,

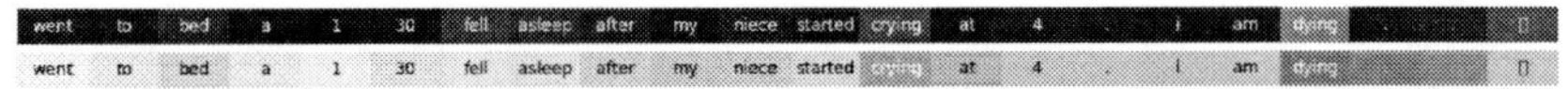

Figure 2: Attention Example.

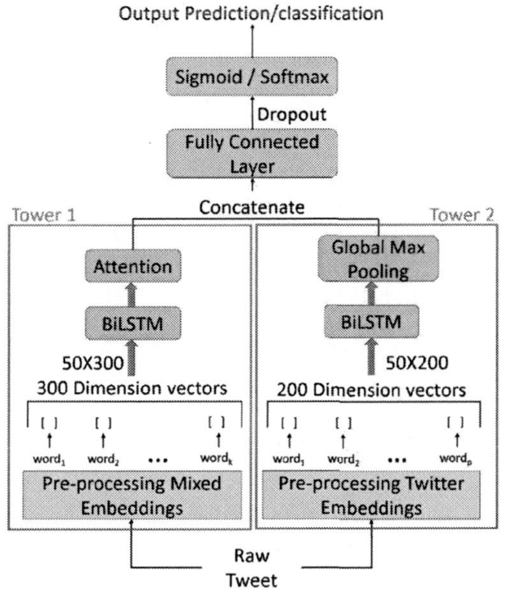

Figure 3: Model Diagram.

2014) trained over common crawl corpus with 300 dimension vector, Character[1] level embeddings trained over common crawl glove corpus providing 300 dimensional vectors for each character and emoji2vec (Eisner et al., 2016) which provides 300 dimension vectors for most commonly used emojis in twitter platform. Procedure to generate a representation of a text using all these embeddings is presented in Algorithm 1, where *get_vector* is a function of token and embedding type and returns the corresponding vector for the token from the pre-trained embedding specified.

Embedding vectors that are generated for each tweet are then converted to into matrix, with a number of rows being the size of maximum sequence, rest is zero padded. This matrix then forms the input to the Bidirectional LSTM(BiLSTM) layer (Graves and Schmidhuber, 2005), which helps in generating representations by taking all the words in sequence into account.

---

[1]https://github.com/minimaxir/char-embeddings

word_token = Tokenize tweet
for *each word in word_token* **do**
    if *word is in EmojiEmbb* **then**
        word_vector =
        get_vector(EmojiEmbb,
        word_vector)
    else if *word is in Glove* **then**
        word_vector = get_vector(Glove,
        word_vector)
    else if *word is in CharEmbb* **then**
        word_vector = get_vector(charEmbb,
        word_vector)
    else
        chars = tokeinze word_token into
        character
        n = length(chars) word_vector =
        $\sum_1^n get\_vector(charEmbb, chars)$
    end
end

Algorithm 1: Embedding Matrix generation

The output of each time-step is then fed to Attention Mechanism (Bahdanau et al., 2014). The core concept behind the attention mechanism forces the model to focus on important words that are related to the task.

Tower 2 in the Figure 3 uses pre-processed mechanism where, all the punctuations are removed, usernames are removed without any replacement with tokens and, special characters including smiley and emojis are removed. Embedding matrix is generated using pre-trained glove embeddings trained over twitter corpus and provides 200-dimensional vectors for each word. These are zero padded as mentioned earlier and is fed into another BiLSTM layer. Maxpooling is applied over the output of BiLSTM to extract the most prominent vector from the rest over the temporal dimension which act as a attention over word sequences. Maximum sequence length for the embedding space is kept at 50, as twitter has a character limit of 140 characters.

The output of tower 1 and 2 are then concatenated and then fed into the fully connected network with 2 layers. Final layer contains a different number of neurons and activation functions depending on the subtasks which are stated in the experiments section 4. To handle overfitting we have used L2 regularization dropout in layers and batch size is kept at 512.

2.3 Traditional Features

We defined features that are used in most of the traditional sentiment analysis techniques are termed as traditional features. As per the baseline system provided in the WASSA Emotion Intensity Task we define baseline features. The knowledge sources that have been used to generate baseline feature are: MPQA subjective lexicon (Wilson et al., 2005), Bing Liu lexicon (Ding et al., 2008), AFINN (Nielsen, 2011), Sentiment140 (Kiritchenko et al., 2014), NRC Hashtag Sentiment Lexicon (Mohammad and Kiritchenko, 2015), NRC Hashtag Emotion Association Lexicon (Mohammad et al., 2013), NRC Word-Emotion Association Lexicon (Mohammad and Turney, 2013), NRC-10 Expanded Lexicon (Bravo-Marquez et al., 2016) and the SentiWordNet (Esuli and Sebastiani, 2007). Two more features are calculated on the basis of emoticons (obtained from AFINN (Nielsen, 2011)) and negations present in the text. This amounts to 45 features for each tweet.

In addition to this, we have used Vader Sentiment Lexicons (Gilbert, 2014), which provides the positive, negative, neutral and compound score for the text. These lexicons are specifically designed for social media texts.

2.4 Features from pre-trained models

We use **SentiNeuron** feature (Radford et al., 2017) from a model which is trained over 82 million Amazon review dataset. The aim of the model was to predict the next word in the review. They have used LSTM with 4096 units. The 2389th neuron was found to be specifically focusing on the sentiment for a given sentence. We use output of this 2389th as a feature. Further more, we have normalized it between *0-1* which helps in performance improvement.

3 Data and Experiments

We participated in all the subtasks of English language, namely: EI-reg (intensity score prediction of 4 emotions), EI-oc (intensity ordinal classification task of 4 emotions), V-reg (intensity score prediction of valence), V-oc (intensity ordinal classifi-

Table 1: Data Distribution.

	Train	Dev	Test
Anger	1701	388	1002
Fear	2252	389	986
Joy	1616	290	1105
Sadness	1533	397	975
Valence	1181	449	937
Multi-Label	6838	886	3259

cation task for valence) and E-c (Multi-label classification task over 11 emotions). Detailed analysis and distribution of the dataset are presented in the task paper (Mohammad et al., 2018).

For each subtask, deep learning model is same as mentioned earlier, although there is a variation in the feature being used for ensemble approach. Data distribution across train, dev and test dataset is given table 1.

3.1 EI-reg and V-reg: Regression

In this task, given a tweet and its corresponding emotion, we need to predict the intensity of the given emotion in *0-1* range. For this task, Deep learning models with *sigmoid* as activation function and number of hidden unit in last layer as one is used. Official evaluation metric for this is a pearson correlation, so we define a new loss function to train deep learning models.

$$Loss = 0.7 \times (1 - pearson) + 0.3 \times MSE \quad (1)$$

This is a slightly modified version than used by (Meisheri et al., 2017; Goel et al., 2017) for WASSA dataset, where they use the negative of pearson correlation as the loss function. We observe that using weighted sum of negation of pearson correlation and mean square error improved the performance.

Training data was split into 10 different folds, by using stratified splits which were achieved by generating 10 bins over the continuous bins. Ten different models were generated with permutations of 9 out of 10 folds as training and remaining 1 as validation dataset. Finally, dev dataset is passed over all the models and mean of all the models were considered as output. This can be seen as a variation of weak learners concept in decision trees.

For the testing dataset as mentioned earlier, we combine training and development set and then generate 10 folds to create 10 models with *80-20* split for validation. Parameters used for models are stated in table 2. In addition, we have used Adam optimizer with *0.0001* as learning rate.

Table 2: Parameters for Regression Task.

Layers	Units	Activation	Regularization	Dropout
BiLSTM - Tower 1	70	Tanh	L2 - 0.05	0.35
BiLSTM - Tower 2	70	Tanh	L2 - 0.05	0.35
Attention	-	-	L2 - 0.01	-
Max Pooling	-	-	-	-
Fully Connected Layer 1	100	Selu	L2 - 0.001	0.5
Fully Connected Layer 2	50	Selu	L2 - 0.001	0.3
Output Layer	1	Sigmoid	-	-

The output of deep learning models is considered as a feature for our ensemble method, where we combine other features as mentioned in section 2.3 and section 2.4. In addition to this, the output of other emotion is also used as a feature for the ensemble model which provides an additional context for the prediction task. So, for each emotion in a task, we get additional features from deep learning model which we define as a cross emotion features.

All this features are then passed on to the support vector regression, whose parameters C and *Kernel* are tuned using 10 fold cross validation over training set.

3.2 EI-oc and V-oc: Classification

Objective of this task was to classify tweet into one of the ordinal classes, given a tweet and its corresponding emotion. Number of classes for EI-oc were four and for V-oc it was seven. Official evaluation metric for this task was provided as pearson correlation. Output layer in the deep learning model contained four and seven neurons for EI-oc and V-oc respectively with softmax as the activation function. Loss function used for classification task was *categorical crossentropy*. Similar settings of 10-fold as mentioned in regression task earlier was carried out resulting in 10 different models for each emotion and valence. Layer parameters for this task are summarized in table 3. Stochastic gradient descent with nesterov momentum and learning rate *0.01* was used as optimizer for this task.

Similar to regression task, for classification we create ensemble model by combining output of deep learning models with other features. In addition, we also consider output of regression models as additional features for classification. Support vector classifier is used as a final classifier,

Table 3: Parameters for Classification Task.

Layers	Units	Activation	Regularization	Dropout
BiLSTM - Tower 1	50	Tanh	L2 - 0.05	0.4
BiLSTM - Tower 2	50	Tanh	L2 - 0.05	0.4
Attention	-	-	L2 - 0.001	-
Max Pooling	-	-	-	-
Fully Connected Layer 1	50	Selu	L2 - 0.01	0.4
Fully Connected Layer 2	20	Selu	L2 - 0.01	0.4
Output Layer	5/7	Softmax	-	-

Table 4: Parameters for Multi-Label Classification Task.

Layers	Units	Activation	Regularization	Dropout
BiLSTM - Tower 1	120	Tanh	0	0.3
BiLSTM - Tower 2	120	Tanh	0	0.3
Attention	-	-	0	-
Max Pooling	-	-	-	-
Fully Connected Layer 1	100	relu	L2 - 0.01	0.3
Fully Connected Layer 2	50	relu	L2 - 0.01	0.2
Output Layer	11	Softmax	-	-

with C and *Kernel* being tuned using 10-fold cross validation. Final submission is done with model being trained by combining training and development dataset and then taking 80-20 split for training and validation.

3.3 E-c: Multilabel Classification

In this task, we were provided with tweet and its corresponding labels among 11 emotion: *anger, anticipation, disgust, fear, joy, love, optimism, pessimism, sadness, surprise and trust*. For this task, output layer of our deep learning model contains 11 neurons and sigmoid as a activation function. *Binary cross entropy* is used as a loss function with *Stochastic gradient descent* with Nesterov momentum, *0.01* learning rate and 10^{-6} learning rate decay as optimizer. Parameters for other layers are presented in table 4.

Official evaluation metric for this task was Jaccard similarity score. The output of the deep learning model gives values between *0-1* for each emotion. Since the task was to predict the presence or absence of any emotion continuous value must be converted to binary number. Threshold was applied which was learned from training and development set. For training set we found the threshold to be *0.35*, whereas for development set it was found to be *0.30*. For testing set, we take the mean of both the values as threshold.

4 Results and Discussion

In total *75* teams participated in the task, our system was ranked 2nd for V-reg task, 5th for EI-reg task and 7th for both V-oc and EI-oc task. For

Table 5: Comparison of proposed deep Learning model and ensemble model over train and development set for regression task.

	Development Set				Test Set			
	Original Split		80-20 Split		Original Split		80-20 Split	
	Ensemble System	Deep Learning Model	Ensemble System	Deep Learning Model	Ensemble System	Deep Learning Model	Ensemble System	Deep Learning Model
Fear	0.751	0.707	0.791	0.791	0.745	0.725	0.736	0.74
Anger	0.79	0.718	0.747	0.744	0.775	0.721	0.776	0.749
Sadness	0.735	0.689	0.77	0.767	0.764	0.723	0.776	0.741
Joy	0.723	0.675	0.812	0.775	0.767	0.724	0.77	0.731
Average	0.75	0.697	0.78	0.769	0.763	0.723	0.764	0.74
Valence	0.857	0.804	0.85	0.788	0.858	0.832	0.861	0.84

Table 6: Results of Regression and Classification task over test set.

	Reg		OC	
	Orginal Split	80-20 Split	Orginal Split	80-20 Split
Fear	0.745	0.735	0.595	0.561
Anger	0.775	0.775	0.626	0.641
Sadness	0.764	0.776	0.618	0.621
joy	0.767	0.77	0.65	0.655
Average	0.76275	0.764	0.62225	0.6195
Valence	0.858	0.861	0.727	0.777

Table 7: Regression Task Results over model different architectures over test set:80-20 Split.

	Anger	Fear	Sadness	Joy	Average	Valence
Proposed Model	0.749	0.74	0.741	0.731	0.74	0.84
Tower-1	0.727	0.727	0.704	0.709	0.717	0.825
Tower-2	0.714	0.719	0.673	0.70	0.705	0.792
Tower-1 without Attention	0.721	0.709	0.69	0.704	0.711	0.783
Tower-2 without Attention	0.693	0.692	0.673	0.682	0.685	0.766

Table 8: Results of Individual Features in combination with Deep learning features over development set.

Features	Anger	Fear	Sadness	Joy	Valence
dl	0.744	0.791	0.767	0.775	0.788
dl+baselines	0.747	0.792	0.773	0.778	0.789
dl+vader	0.747	0.792	0.772	0.775	0.785
dl+sentineuron	0.748	0.79	0.773	0.778	0.79
dl+valence	0.751	0.792	0.77	0.785	-
dl+cross emotion	0.75	0.794	0.773	0.778	0.809

Multi-Label classification, our system achieved 2nd rank among the teams, with Jaccard similarity score of *0.582*.

Table 6 shows the result for EI-reg, V-reg, EI-oc and V-oc task on official evaluation metric i.e. pearson correlation. We also compare the results over the original split and *80-20* split generated after combining training and development dataset. It can be seen that both of these gives similar results while, for classification original split is better, for regression it is other way. Table 5 shows comparison of Ensemble model and Deep learning model for EI-reg and V-reg. We observe improvement in ensemble model over development dataset in both sets of splits. On the contrary, there is relatively less difference in the test set.

Table 7 contains results of different deep learning architecture for EI-reg and V-reg task. For both of these task, we can observe what is impact of attention over both the towers. We also present the results for each single tower which helps in understanding the need for two towers. Although adding attention over Tower-1 gives little improvement for EL-reg task it provides significant improvement for V-reg task. It is worthwhile to note that *sadness* emotion shows no improvement by adding attention over tower-2.

In table 8 and table 9, results on regression task for *80-20* split for each feature when combined with deep learning feature over development and test set respectively. We observe that adding lexicon features marginally increases the performance of the system. We can conclude from this that deep learning model that we presented can encapsulate most of the information regarding the sentiment which was present in traditional features. Including cross-emotion feature shows considerable increase in the performance.

Inter-feature correlation is presented in figure 4, where we can observe that apart from anger and valence baseline features are weak negatively correlated with other features. Furthermore, vader and sentineuron are less correlated except for valence and yet they provide similar improvement when combined individually with DL features. Although, when both these features are combined together they provide a significant boost.

Table 9: Results of Individual Features in combination with Deep learning features over test set.

Features	Anger	Fear	Sadness	Joy	Valence
dl	0.749	0.74	0.741	0.731	0.84
dl+baselines	0.755	0.739	0.742	0.731	0.84
dl+vader	0.753	0.744	0.746	0.731	0.841
dl+sentineuron	0.753	0.739	0.752	0.734	0.842
dl+valence	0.756	0.743	0.745	0.74	-
dl+cross emotion	0.759	0.744	0.753	0.738	0.849

Table 10: Multi-label Error across Emotions.

Emotion	Error	Presence total	Ratio
Anger	521	1101	0.473
Anticipation	469	425	1.103
Disgust	646	1099	0.588
Fear	251	485	0.518
Joy	477	1442	0.331
Love	405	516	0.785
Optimism	704	1143	0.616
Pessimism	398	375	1.061
Sadness	539	960	0.561
Surprise	167	170	0.982
Trust	161	153	1.052

For classification task across four emotion and valence we observed that, using threshold values obtained by comparing continuous values from regression task provides a better result in pearson correlation. Possible reason for this might be the loss function that we trained for classification model was categorical cross entropy.

4.1 Error analysis

We observe that high difference between the predicted value/class and truth value/class are present at the extreme end of the spectrum. One of the possible reason might be that the distribution of the data shows a Gaussian distribution and there are few samples at the extreme end as described in (Mohammad and Kiritchenko, 2018). In addition, we manually inspect some cases where our model failed, for example for sadness *You are MINE, my baby, my headache, my love, my smile, my frown, my wrong, my right, my pain, my happiness, my everything.* has truth value of *0.140* and our system predicted *0.568* which is way higher than what the writer is trying to convey. The model is predicting slightly above neutral sentiment. Possible reasons include the presence of both positive and negative words present in the alternate sequence. This kind of discourse and irony detection can help in better prediction if incorporated into the models.

In joy emotion, *when will i ever be happy with myself?* has a truth value of *0.109* and predicted value is *0.491*. These kind of rhetorical questions is hard to understand even for humans, for model to understand we need to put in some explicit context. By observing more such samples, we find that adding more context about the different physiological and linguistic phenomenon into the model with appropriate bias can greatly increase the accuracies of the models present.

Table 10 shows the error across different emotions in multi-label task. We observe that there is a high error rate in *anticipation, pessimism, surprise and trust*, possible reasons might be that there are already fewer samples available and the ratio of percentage votes received to the percentage of tweets labeled is also high for this emotion as compared to other emotions (Mohammad and Kiritchenko, 2018). In addition, we observe that there are around *2%* of the tweets contained no emotion in test set, where our model predicted atleast one emotion.

5 Conclusion

In this paper, we describe our approach to SemEval-2018 Task-1 for English tweet. We present ensemble system which is capable of handling noisy sentiment dataset over regression, classification as well as multi-label dataset. Use of the mixture of embedding in parallel makes this system unique in terms of generating better representations with respect to sentiment. Our system achieved 2nd, 5th and 7th in different subtasks. Analyzing different feature combinations from individual results and inter-feature correlation over test data reveals that our deep learning model is able to capture most of the information that is provided by lexicon feature. Multi-label classification has proved to be a challenging task among all the subtask that has been provided as the evaluation score of all the team participating has been low.

We have also presented some examples where our model has performed poorly and conclude that including context feature for sarcasm, irony and rhetoric question can improve the performance further over all the subtasks presented in SemEval for English language.

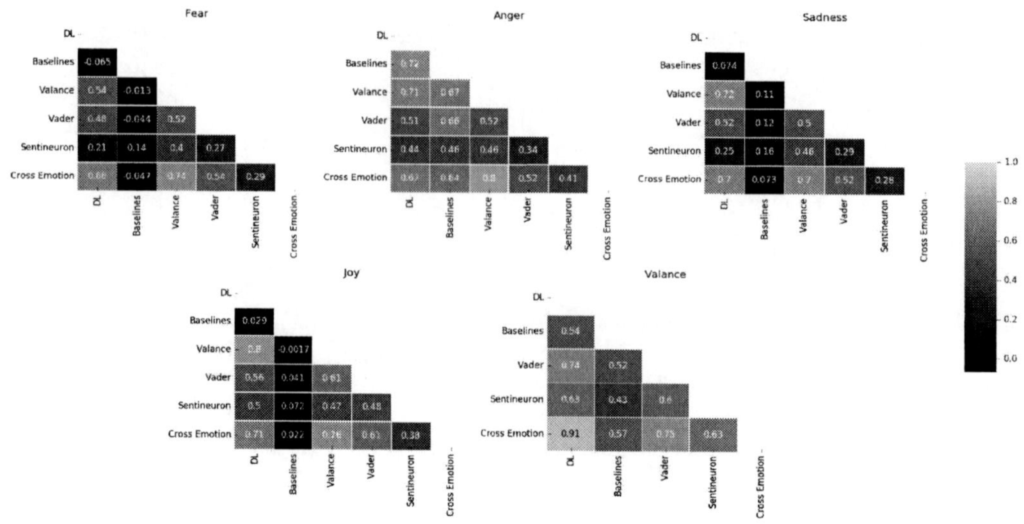

Figure 4: Correlation among various features for test set.

References

Dzmitry Bahdanau, Kyunghyun Cho, and Yoshua Bengio. 2014. Neural machine translation by jointly learning to align and translate. *arXiv preprint arXiv:1409.0473*.

Felipe Bravo-Marquez, Eibe Frank, Saif M Mohammad, and Bernhard Pfahringer. 2016. Determining word–emotion associations from tweets by multi-label classification. In *WI'16*, pages 536–539. IEEE Computer Society.

Tim Dalgleish and Mick Power. 2000. *Handbook of cognition and emotion*. John Wiley & Sons.

Xiaowen Ding, Bing Liu, and Philip S Yu. 2008. A holistic lexicon-based approach to opinion mining. In *Proceedings of the 2008 international conference on web search and data mining*, pages 231–240. ACM.

Ben Eisner, Tim Rocktäschel, Isabelle Augenstein, Matko Bosnjak, and Sebastian Riedel. 2016. emoji2vec: Learning emoji representations from their description.

Andrea Esuli and Fabrizio Sebastiani. 2007. Sentiwordnet: A high-coverage lexical resource for opinion mining. *Evaluation*, pages 1–26.

CJ Hutto Eric Gilbert. 2014. Vader: A parsimonious rule-based model for sentiment analysis of social media text. In *Eighth International Conference on Weblogs and Social Media (ICWSM-14)*. Available at (20/04/16) http://comp. social. gatech. edu/papers/icwsm14. vader. hutto. pdf.

Pranav Goel, Devang Kulshreshtha, Prayas Jain, and Kaushal Kumar Shukla. 2017. Prayas at emoint 2017: An ensemble of deep neural architectures for emotion intensity prediction in tweets. In *Proceedings of the 8th Workshop on Computational Approaches to Subjectivity, Sentiment and Social Media Analysis*, pages 58–65.

Alex Graves and Jürgen Schmidhuber. 2005. Framewise phoneme classification with bidirectional lstm and other neural network architectures. *Neural Networks*, 18(5):602–610.

Svetlana Kiritchenko, Xiaodan Zhu, and Saif M Mohammad. 2014. Sentiment analysis of short informal texts. *Journal of Artificial Intelligence Research*, 50:723–762.

Zhouhan Lin, Minwei Feng, Cicero Nogueira dos Santos, Mo Yu, Bing Xiang, Bowen Zhou, and Yoshua Bengio. 2017. A structured self-attentive sentence embedding. *arXiv preprint arXiv:1703.03130*.

Hardik Meisheri, Kunal Ranjan, and Lipika Dey. 2017. Sentiment extraction from consumer-generated noisy short texts. In *Proceedings of IEEE International Conference on Data Mining Workshops (ICDMW)*, New Orleans, USA.

Saif M. Mohammad and Felipe Bravo-Marquez. 2017. Wassa-2017 shared task on emotion intensity. In *Proceedings of the EMNLP 2017 Workshop on Computational Approaches to Subjectivity, Sentiment, and Social Media (WASSA), September 2017, Copenhagen, Denmark*.

Saif M. Mohammad, Felipe Bravo-Marquez, Mohammad Salameh, and Svetlana Kiritchenko. 2018. Semeval-2018 Task 1: Affect in tweets. In *Proceedings of International Workshop on Semantic Evaluation (SemEval-2018)*, New Orleans, LA, USA.

Saif M Mohammad and Svetlana Kiritchenko. 2015.
Using hashtags to capture fine emotion categories from tweets. *Computational Intelligence*,
31(2):301–326.

Saif M. Mohammad and Svetlana Kiritchenko. 2018.
Understanding emotions: A dataset of tweets to
study interactions between affect categories. In
*Proceedings of the 11th Edition of the Language
Resources and Evaluation Conference*, Miyazaki,
Japan.

Saif M Mohammad, Svetlana Kiritchenko, and Xiaodan Zhu. 2013. Nrc-canada: Building the state-
of-the-art in sentiment analysis of tweets. *arXiv
preprint arXiv:1308.6242*.

Saif M Mohammad and Peter D Turney. 2013. Crowdsourcing a word–emotion association lexicon. *Computational Intelligence*, 29(3):436–465.

Finn Årup Nielsen. 2011. A new anew: Evaluation of a
word list for sentiment analysis in microblogs. *arXiv
preprint arXiv:1103.2903*.

Jeffrey Pennington, Richard Socher, and Christopher D. Manning. 2014. Glove: Global vectors for
word representation. In *Empirical Methods in Natural Language Processing (EMNLP)*, pages 1532–
1543.

Robert Plutchik. 2001. The nature of emotions: Human emotions have deep evolutionary roots, a fact
that may explain their complexity and provide tools
for clinical practice. *American scientist*, 89(4):344–
350.

A. Radford, R. Jozefowicz, and I. Sutskever. 2017.
Learning to Generate Reviews and Discovering Sentiment. *ArXiv e-prints*.

Theresa Wilson, Janyce Wiebe, and Paul Hoffmann.
2005. Recognizing contextual polarity in phrase-
level sentiment analysis. In *Proceedings of the conference on human language technology and empirical methods in natural language processing*, pages
347–354. Association for Computational Linguistics.

DMCB at SemEval-2018 Task 1: Transfer Learning of Sentiment Classification Using Group LSTM for Emotion Intensity prediction

Youngmin Kim, Hyunju Lee
Gwangju Institute of Science and Technology,
Data mining and Computational Biology Lab, Gwangju, Korea
{minok00, hyunjulee}@gist.ac.kr

Abstract

This paper describes a system attended in the SemEval-2018 Task 1 "Affect in tweets" that predicts emotional intensities. We use Group LSTM with an attention model and transfer learning with sentiment classification data as a source data (SemEval 2017 Task 4a). A transfer model structure consists of a source domain and a target domain. Additionally, we try a new dropout that is applied to LSTMs in the Group LSTM. Our system ranked 8th at the subtask 1a (emotion intensity regression). We also show various results with different architectures in the source, target and transfer models.

1 Introduction

Sentiment analysis is one of the most famous Natural Language Process (NLP) task. In this study, we perform a task that predicts emotional intensities of anger, joy, fear and sadness with tweet messages, where intensity values range from 0 to 1. This task is competed at SemEval-2018 Task 1 (Mohammad et al., 2018). In previous studies, neural networks with word embedding and affective lexicons were widely used (Goel et al., 2017; He et al., 2017). Also, many studies employed support vector regression (Duppada and Hiray, 2017; Akhtar et al., 2017).

Transfer learning was recently proposed as an effecive approach to have higher performance, when data is not abundant. Using a pre-trained deep-learning model with an abundant data set has been popular and shows good results in various tasks (Donahue et al., 2014; Conneau et al., 2017). Especially in a medical image task, it is very efficient because of lacks of medical data (Tajbakhsh et al., 2016). Just as humans can learn new things better with their past knowledge, neural networks can also be trained on target domains by transferring knowledge from the source domain.

We make a transfer model that can be divided into a source model and a target model. The source model is constructed based on the paper (Baziotis et al., 2017). The model of this paper uses LSTM with attention. However, we introduce Group LSTM (GLSTM) (Kuchaiev and Ginsburg, 2017) with a new dropout. After then, we make the target model with LSTM.

In the result section, we provide comparison of LSTM and GLSTM in the source model, and results of various pre-trained word embeddings with target model. Finally, we discuss about the result of the transfer model that is a combined model with the source and target models.

2 System Description

2.1 Data and Label

For transfer learning, we use a source data provided by SemEval 2017 Task4 (a) (Rosenthal et al., 2017). The task of the source domain is to classify sentences to positive, negative and neutral sentences. Training data is 44,613 sentences (10% are used as a development set), and test data is 12,284 sentences for the source model evaluation. For transfer learning in this study, all training and test data are used as training data.

For the target domain, training data is about 2,000 sentences for each emotion. Although the main task is regression prediction, we change it as distribution prediction (Tai et al., 2015). In this way, we deal it as a classification problem. Intensity scores y are changed to labels t satisfying:

$$t_i = \begin{cases} y' - \lfloor y' \rfloor & \text{if } i = \lfloor y' \rfloor + 1 \\ \lfloor y' \rfloor - y' + 1 & \text{if } i = \lfloor y' \rfloor \\ 0 & \text{otherwise} \end{cases}$$

where $i = [1, 2, 3, 4, 5]$ and $y' = 4y$

Size of the final output is 5. For example, if an intensity score y is 0.7, label t is [0, 0, 0.2, 0.8, 0].

Proceedings of the 12th International Workshop on Semantic Evaluation (SemEval-2018), pages 300–304
New Orleans, Louisiana, June 5–6, 2018. ©2018 Association for Computational Linguistics

With given $\mathbf{r} = [0, 0.25, 0.5, 0.75, 1]$, label y can be obtained again by dot product with $\mathbf{t}$ and $\mathbf{r}$ (0.7 = 0.2*0.5 + 0.8*0.75).

2.2 Text preprocessing

To normalize words and remove noise in sentences, we use ekphrasis library (Baziotis et al., 2017). It helps to apply social tokenizer, spell correction, word segmentation and various preprocessing. We normalize time and number, and omit URL, email and user tag. Annotations are added on hashtags, emphasized and repeated words. We annotate them as a group because hashtags are gathered in many cases (see Table 1). Lastly, emoticons are changed to words that represent emoticons.

#letsdance #dancinginthemoonlight #singing
$\Rightarrow$ $\langle hashtag \rangle$ lets dance dancing in the moonlight singing $\langle /hashtag \rangle$

Table 1: Example of preprocessing hashtag

2.3 Word embedding

We try five pre-trained word embeddings to choose the best one for the target model. Two are trained with GloVe (Pennington et al., 2014) using different data sets: one[1] is trained with very large data in Common crawl, and the other[2] is made with tweets (Baziotis et al., 2017). Other word embedding methods are fastText[3] (Bojanowski et al., 2016), word2vec[4] (Mikolov et al., 2013) and LexVec[5] (Salle et al., 2016). LexVec is the mixed version of GloVe and word2vec. Dimensions of them are all 300. Among them, GloVe with tweet is used for the source and transfer models.

Emoji can be good features but most of emoji ideograms are not contained in embedding vocabulary. Hence, we change a emoji to a phrase with python 'emoji' library. For example, 😄 is decoded to "Smiling Face with Open Mouth and Smiling Eyes". Because it is quite long, embedding vectors of emoji are changed to mean of vectors of each decoded words. In this way, we reduce Out-Of-Vocabulary and prevent the sentence from lengthening.

2.4 LSTM and GLSTM

Recurrent Neural Network (RNN) works well in a sequence model like language by addressing its arbitrary length (Tai et al., 2015). However, RNN is difficult to be optimized because of a gradient vanishing problem. To solve it, LSTM suggested a cell state and gates as bridges to control the flow of error (Hochreiter and Schmidhuber, 1997).

GLSTM is just a group of several LSTMs, where outputs of LSTMs are concatenated. The idea is that LSTM can be divided into several sub-LSTMs (Kuchaiev and Ginsburg, 2017). This model has some advantages compared to the original LSTM. The number of parameters is reduced with a preserving feature size. Also, it can be parallelized and computation times are reduced because the computation of each sub-LSTM is independent.

2.5 Dropout

To avoid overfitting and achieve generality, we use three types of dropout. One is normal dropout between layers (Srivastava et al., 2014). If a shape of the layer is sequential, dropout mask is shared on sequential axis. Another dropout is inside cells of LSTM. In the each LSTM cell, the same dropout mask is applied on hidden values that come from the previous cell (Zaremba et al., 2014). Applying different dropout masks for each cell can mislead memory and information. With the same dropout mask, however, LSTM cell can dropout nodes consistently so that the model can forget or memorize information stably. The last one is dropout between sub-LSTMs. To get more generality, we dropped several LSTMs in GLSTM. For example, if GLSTM consist of five sub-LSTMs, we dropped two LSTMs and only use the rest three LSTMs.

3 Model structure

3.1 Source model

For the source model, Glove with tweets is used as input vectors of the embedding layer. After embedding layer, two GLSTM layers are stacked. GLSTM is made of 5 LSTMs with 40 feature size. Additionally, we concatenate forward and backward GLSTM to be bidirectional. So hidden size of each recurrent layer is 400 ($= 5 \times 40 \times 2$).

Next is an attention layer, which calculates importance of each time step. Attention mechanism shows good performance on sequential tasks like

---

[1] https://nlp.stanford.edu/projects/glove/
[2] https://github.com/cbaziotis/datastories-semeval2017-task4
[3] https://github.com/facebookresearch/fastText
[4] https://code.google.com/archive/p/word2vec/
[5] https://github.com/alexandres/lexvec

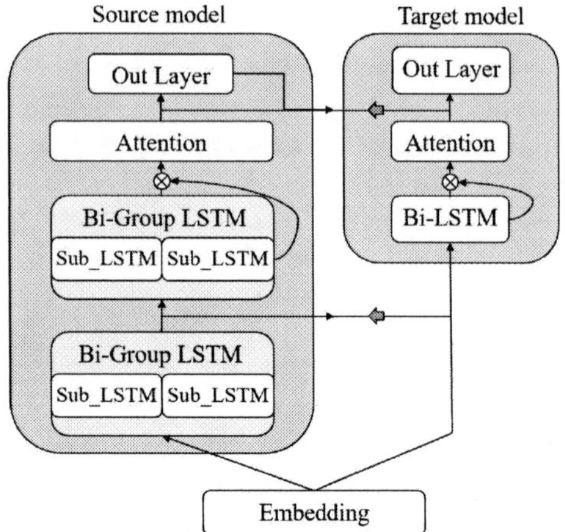

Figure 1: Structure of models. For the transfer model, connections between source and target models are used. Large arrows are paths of reduced gradient flow during backpropagation.

machine translation (Bahdanau et al., 2014) and sentiment analysis (Baziotis et al., 2017). It helps to concentrate position related to emotion. Attention values are calculated:

$$e_t = W_h h_t + b_t$$

$$a_t = \frac{exp(e_t)}{\sum_i^l exp(e_i)}, \quad \sum a_t = 1$$

Calculated attention values are multiplied by each current hidden state and they are all added up.

Passing through the attention layer, the output becomes non-sequential representation vectors. It enters a fully connected softmax layer as a final classification layer, where the size of the layer is 3.

3.2 Target model

Unlike the source model, a normal bi-LSTM is used with 100 feature size. After then, attention and output layers are stacked. The size of output layer is 5.

For transfer learning, outputs of several layers on the source model are used as additional features. The LSTM layer on the target model takes as input the concatenation of the embedding layer and the first LSTM layer output of the source model. After the attention layer, in a similar way, outputs of the attention and the final layers on the source model are concatenated and entered into the final layer as input.

3.3 Regularization

At the embedding layer, Gaussian noise is applied with sigma = 0.2. It helps models to be robust by avoiding overfitting on specific features of words. Dropouts are used everywhere between layers with probability p = 0.3 except before the final layer. Before the final layer, p = 0.5 dropout is applied. Additionally, LSTM dropout was applied on every LSTM layers with p = 0.3. The probability of dropout at GLSTM on the source model is 0.3. Also, we use L2 normalization. It prevents weights to be large values by adding weight penalty to loss. We set up it with 0.001 for the source model and 0.0001 for the target model.

3.4 Training

For the source and target models, categorical cross-entropy is used as a loss function. For updating weights, we apply the Adam (Kingma and Ba, 2014) optimizer with a learning rate of 0.001. During training the transfer model, since we want to preserve target model weight parameters with a little updating, we decrease gradient flow of backpropagation from the source model to the target model by 0.05 times (see large arrows on Figure 1). Because there are many parameters on the final model, we take that constraint to prevent overfitting.

4 Result and discussion

4.1 GLSTM

Figure 2 shows the result of GLSTM and normal LSTM on the source model for Sentiment Classification (SemEval 2017 Task 1a). We tried various feature sizes. The number of sub-LSTM in GLSTM is fixed to 5 and the feature size of each sub-LSTM is changed. As the sizes of features increase, the performances of GLSTM increase. On the other hand, although the performances of LSTM gradually improve with larger feature sizes, it starts to decrease rapidly after 100. Thus, we infer that GLSTM with dropout is more effective on overfitting than LSTM with larger feature size. Based on this result, we use GLSTM for the source model.

4.2 Various Embedding

We tested five different word embedding vectors using the target model to choose the best embedding. To compare the performances of embeddings, the embedding layers was not trained

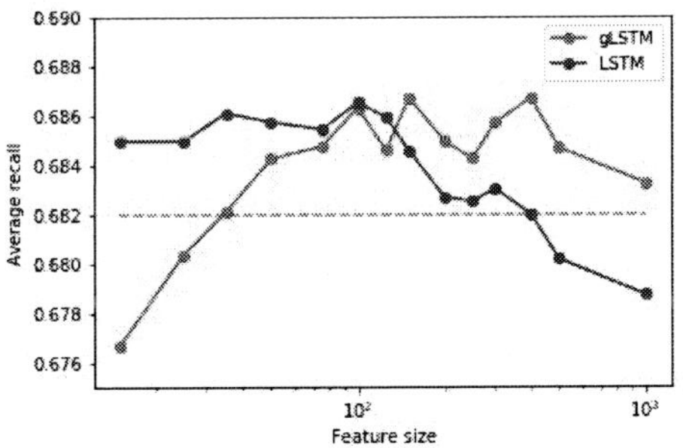

Figure 2: Performance comparison between GLSTM and LSTM on the source model for sentiment classification. A dotted line is the result of (Baziotis et al., 2017).

Embedding	Avg	Anger	Fear	Joy	Sadness
Tweet GloVe	**.690**	**.730**	**.670**	**.675**	.684
Common GloVe	.667	.690	.624	.656	**.698**
Fast Text	.639	.667	.586	.638	.665
Word2vec	.654	.704	.599	.631	.681
Lex vec	.648	.656	.630	.646	.659

Table 2: Pearsons correlation of Dev set on the target model for SemEval-2018 Task1(a).

(static). Note that we did not use transfer learning in this experiment. Table 2 shows Pearson correlation between the given emotion intensities and predicted intensities by the models on the development set. Tweet GloVe had the best score and Common GloVe showed the second best score. Hence, we decided to do transfer learning with Tweet GloVe and Common GloVe.

4.3 Transfer

Our main task results are described in Table 3. There are four models. Tweet Glove and Common GloVe were picked from the conclusion of 4.2, and we performed two approaches: training the embedding layer or not (non-static or static) (Kim, 2014). Tweet GloVe with static showed the best performance as a single model and it is almost same to non-static. However, the non-static method had a higher score than the static for Common GloVe embedding. In addition, the ensemble model by averaging all single models showed better performance than the single models. We also found that compared to the scores without trans-

fer learning on dev set (Table 2), there were significant performance improvements when transfer learning used in Table 3.

5 Conclusion

This paper described the system submitted to SemEval-2018 Task 1: Affect in tweets and analysis of various models. Various embedding vectors were tried and we chose Tweet GloVe with static. The main method is LSTM with attention and transfer learning that uses sentiment classification as source domain. In future work, we will perform transfer learning with labeled data sets such as SNLI or SST data sets. Also, training tagging or tree parsing can be used for transfer learning.

Acknowledgments

This research was supported by the Bio-Synergy Research Project (NRF-2016M3A9C4939665) of the Ministry of Science, ICT and Future Planning through the National Research Foundation.

References

Md Shad Akhtar, Palaash Sawant, Asif Ekbal, Jyoti Pawar, and Pushpak Bhattacharyya. 2017. Iitp at emoint-2017: Measuring intensity of emotions using sentence embeddings and optimized features. In *Proceedings of the 8th Workshop on Computational Approaches to Subjectivity, Sentiment and Social Media Analysis*, pages 212–218.

Dzmitry Bahdanau, Kyunghyun Cho, and Yoshua Bengio. 2014. Neural machine translation by jointly learning to align and translate. *arXiv preprint arXiv:1409.0473*.

Christos Baziotis, Nikos Pelekis, and Christos Doulkeridis. 2017. Datastories at semeval-2017 task 4: Deep lstm with attention for message-level and topic-based sentiment analysis. In *Proceedings of the 11th International Workshop on Semantic Evaluation (SemEval-2017)*, pages 747–754, Vancouver, Canada. Association for Computational Linguistics.

Piotr Bojanowski, Edouard Grave, Armand Joulin, and Tomas Mikolov. 2016. Enriching word vectors with subword information. *arXiv preprint arXiv:1607.04606*.

Alexis Conneau, Douwe Kiela, Holger Schwenk, Loic Barrault, and Antoine Bordes. 2017. Supervised learning of universal sentence representations from natural language inference data. *arXiv preprint arXiv:1705.02364*.

Embeding	Avg		Anger		Fear		Joy		Sadness	
	Test	Dev	Test	Dev	Test	Dev	Test	Dev	Test	Dev
Tweet GloVe static	**.731**	.732	.755	.774	**.731**	**.698**	.713	.728	.726	.727
Tweet GloVe Non -static	.730	**.733**	**.760**	**.777**	.708	.686	**.720**	**.736**	**.732**	**.734**
Common GloVe static	.689	.695	.707	.702	.704	.677	.680	.688	.665	.712
Common GloVe Non -static	.700	.721	.718	.738	.700	.684	.681	.725	.700	.735
Ensemble	.753	.755	.773	.786	.753	.720	.729	.744	.758	.768

Table 3: Experiment results of the transfer model on SemEval-2018 Task 1(a) Emotional Intensity regression. The submitted system to the task is Tweet GloVe with static.

Jeff Donahue, Yangqing Jia, Oriol Vinyals, Judy Hoffman, Ning Zhang, Eric Tzeng, and Trevor Darrell. 2014. Decaf: A deep convolutional activation feature for generic visual recognition. In *International conference on machine learning*, pages 647–655.

Venkatesh Duppada and Sushant Hiray. 2017. Seernet at emoint-2017: Tweet emotion intensity estimator. *arXiv preprint arXiv:1708.06185*.

Pranav Goel, Devang Kulshreshtha, Prayas Jain, and Kaushal Kumar Shukla. 2017. Prayas at emoint 2017: An ensemble of deep neural architectures for emotion intensity prediction in tweets. In *Proceedings of the 8th Workshop on Computational Approaches to Subjectivity, Sentiment and Social Media Analysis*, pages 58–65.

Yuanye He, Liang-Chih Yu, K Robert Lai, and Weiyi Liu. 2017. Yzu-nlp at emoint-2017: Determining emotion intensity using a bi-directional lstm-cnn model. In *Proceedings of the 8th Workshop on Computational Approaches to Subjectivity, Sentiment and Social Media Analysis*, pages 238–242.

Sepp Hochreiter and Jürgen Schmidhuber. 1997. Long short-term memory. *Neural computation*, 9(8):1735–1780.

Yoon Kim. 2014. Convolutional neural networks for sentence classification. *arXiv preprint arXiv:1408.5882*.

Diederik P Kingma and Jimmy Ba. 2014. Adam: A method for stochastic optimization. *arXiv preprint arXiv:1412.6980*.

Oleksii Kuchaiev and Boris Ginsburg. 2017. Factorization tricks for lstm networks. *arXiv preprint arXiv:1703.10722*.

Tomas Mikolov, Kai Chen, Greg Corrado, and Jeffrey Dean. 2013. Efficient estimation of word representations in vector space. *arXiv preprint arXiv:1301.3781*.

Saif M. Mohammad, Felipe Bravo-Marquez, Mohammad Salameh, and Svetlana Kiritchenko. 2018. Semeval-2018 Task 1: Affect in tweets. In *Proceedings of International Workshop on Semantic Evaluation (SemEval-2018)*, New Orleans, LA, USA.

Jeffrey Pennington, Richard Socher, and Christopher Manning. 2014. Glove: Global vectors for word representation. In *Proceedings of the 2014 conference on empirical methods in natural language processing (EMNLP)*, pages 1532–1543.

Sara Rosenthal, Noura Farra, and Preslav Nakov. 2017. Semeval-2017 task 4: Sentiment analysis in twitter. In *Proceedings of the 11th International Workshop on Semantic Evaluation (SemEval-2017)*, pages 502–518.

Alexandre Salle, Marco Idiart, and Aline Villavicencio. 2016. Matrix factorization using window sampling and negative sampling for improved word representations. *arXiv preprint arXiv:1606.00819*.

Nitish Srivastava, Geoffrey Hinton, Alex Krizhevsky, Ilya Sutskever, and Ruslan Salakhutdinov. 2014. Dropout: A simple way to prevent neural networks from overfitting. *The Journal of Machine Learning Research*, 15(1):1929–1958.

Kai Sheng Tai, Richard Socher, and Christopher D Manning. 2015. Improved semantic representations from tree-structured long short-term memory networks. *arXiv preprint arXiv:1503.00075*.

Nima Tajbakhsh, Jae Y Shin, Suryakanth R Gurudu, R Todd Hurst, Christopher B Kendall, Michael B Gotway, and Jianming Liang. 2016. Convolutional neural networks for medical image analysis: Full training or fine tuning? *IEEE transactions on medical imaging*, 35(5):1299–1312.

Wojciech Zaremba, Ilya Sutskever, and Oriol Vinyals. 2014. Recurrent neural network regularization. *arXiv preprint arXiv:1409.2329*.

DeepMiner at SemEval-2018 Task 1: Emotion Intensity Recognition Using Deep Representation Learning

Habibeh Naderi
Dalhousie University, Canada
habibeh.naderi@dal.ca

Behrouz H. Soleimani
Dalhousie University, Canada
behrouz.hajisoleimani@dal.ca

Svetlana Kiritchenko, Saif M. Mohammad
National Research Council Canada
{svetlana.kiritchenko, saif.mohammad}@nrc-cnrc.gc.ca

Stan Matwin
Dalhousie University, Canada
stan@cs.dal.ca

Abstract

In this paper, we propose a regression system to infer the emotion intensity of a tweet. We develop a multi-aspect feature learning mechanism to capture the most discriminative semantic features of a tweet as well as the emotion information conveyed by each word in it. We combine six types of feature groups: (1) a tweet representation learned by an LSTM deep neural network on the training data, (2) a tweet representation learned by an LSTM network on a large corpus of tweets that contain emotion words (a distant supervision corpus), (3) word embeddings trained on the distant supervision corpus and averaged over all words in a tweet, (4) word and character n-grams, (5) features derived from various sentiment and emotion lexicons, and (6) other hand-crafted features. As part of the word embedding training, we also learn the distributed representations of multi-word expressions (MWEs) and negated forms of words. An SVR regressor is then trained over the full set of features. We evaluate the effectiveness of our ensemble feature sets on the SemEval-2018 Task 1 datasets and achieve a Pearson correlation of 72% on the task of tweet emotion intensity prediction.

1 Introduction

The widespread use of micro-blogging and social networking websites such as Twitter for conveying information, sharing opinions, and expressing feelings, makes the sentiment analysis of tweets an attractive area of research. However, sentiment analysis is challenging because people often convey their emotions indirectly and creatively, rather than explicitly stating how they feel. Sentiment analysis of tweets is additionally challenging because of the frequent occurrences of nonstandard language and poor grammatical structure. Tweets also often contain misspellings, abbreviations, hashtags, and emoticons.

Various machine learning approaches have been developed for Twitter sentiment classification. Most of these algorithms train a classifier over tweets with manually annotated sentiment intensity labels and learn the most discriminative features. Hence, designing an effective feature engineering algorithm can improve classification performance, greatly. Mohammad et al. (2013; 2014) used many different sentiment lexicons (manually created and automatically generated), as well as a variety of hand-crafted features to build the top-ranked system for Twitter sentiment classification tasks in SemEval-2013 and SemEval-2014. Sentiment lexicons, either hand-crafted or algorithmically generated, consist of words and their associated polarity scores. However, since feature engineering is labour intensive and usually needs domain-specific knowledge, sentiment classification algorithms with less dependency on feature engineering are attracting considerable interest.

Socher et al. (2013) proposed a feature learning algorithm to discover explanatory factors in sentiment classification. They consider the representation of a sentence (or document) as a composition of the representations of its constituent words or phrases. This way, the sentiment classification problem reduces to learning an effective word representation (or word embedding) that not only models the syntactic context of words but also captures sentiment information of the sentence. Tang et al. (2014) extended the traditional word embedding methods (Mikolov et al., 2013b; Collobert et al., 2011) by encoding sentiment information into the existing continuous representation of words. They built sentiment-specific word embedding (SSWE) by developing three neural networks wherein the sentiment polarity of the tweet is incorporated in the neural networks' loss functions. Teng et al. (2016) proposed a context-sensitive lexicon-based method using recurrent and simple

Proceedings of the 12th International Workshop on Semantic Evaluation (SemEval-2018), pages 305–312
New Orleans, Louisiana, June 5–6, 2018. ©2018 Association for Computational Linguistics

Emotion	Train	Dev.	Test	Total
anger	1,701	388	1,002	3,091
fear	2,252	389	986	3,627
joy	1,616	290	1,105	3,011
sadness	1,533	397	975	2,905
Total	7,102	1,464	4,068	12,634

Table 1: Number of instances provided in the Tweet Emotion Intensity dataset (SemEval-2018 Task 1, EI-reg English). The data was divided into train, development, and test sets.

feed-forward neural networks to extract sentiment lexicons and produce a new polarity weight, respectively.

Unlike lexicon-based sentiment analysis, deep learning approaches are effective in exploring both linguistic and semantic relations between words (Liu et al., 2015). However, due to the limited amount of high-quality labeled data, it is difficult to train deep models with a large number of hyper-parameters for sentiment analysis tasks. Additionally, manual labeling of data is costly and requires domain expert knowledge, which is not always available.

In this paper, we describe two systems: System I, our official submission to the competition, and System II, our best model. In both systems, we combine deep learning and lexicon-based approaches to extract the most informative semantic and emotion representations of tweets. We train two LSTM models, one on the provided training data and another one on a large corpus of tweets that contain emotion words, to obtain emotion-specific tweet representations. We augment this feature space with word and character n-grams, features derived from several sentiment and emotion lexicons as well as other hand-crafted features. Our best model achieves an average Pearson correlation of 71.96% on the official EI-reg test dataset.

2 Data

The English training, development, and test datasets used in our experiments were provided as part of the SemEval-2018 Task 1, EI-reg subtask (Mohammad et al., 2018).[1] The data files include tweet id, tweet text, emotion of the tweet, and the emotion intensity. An overview of the data is provided in Table 1.

2.1 Data preparation

The following pre-processing steps were applied to each of the training and test tweets:

- Remove URLs and usernames.

- Lower-case all the tweet text.

- Substitute abbreviated phrases such as *I've, don't, I'd, etc.* with their long forms.

- Replace tweet-specific acronyms such as *gr8, lol, rotfl, etc.* with their expanded forms.

- Substitute the elongated words with the same words but keeping at most two consecutive occurrences of repeated letters.

- Standardize all the emojis in data to their explanatory phrases using emoji Python package[2].

- Remove all the HTML character codes.

- Replace all occurrences of a multi-word expression (MWE) by a unique identifier. We use WikiMWE (Hartmann et al., 2012), which contains all multi-word expressions from Wikipedia.

- Generate the negated form of all the tokens that occur between any of the negation words, such as *no, not, never, etc.*, and a punctuation mark.

- Remove special characters, numbers, non-English words or phrases.

- Normalize all adjectives and adverbs in test data that do not exist in train or development data sets with adjective or adverb in the training data which shares the most common Synsets of WordNet with it (if we find more than one candidate, we replace the adjective with the most frequent one in the training data).

- Applying WordNet lemmatizer to have the simple singular form of tokens with part-of-speech tags of adjective, adverb, verb or noun.

The tweets are now fed to the system.

---

[1] A detailed description of the English datasets and the analysis of various affect dimensions is available in Mohammad and Kiritchenko (2018).

[2] https://pypi.org/project/emoji/

3   System Description

We created two models: System I, our official submission to the competition, and System II, our best model. Both models address the task of emotion intensity prediction (EI-reg): given a tweet T and an emotion e, predict a real-valued intensity score (in the range $[0, 1]$) of e that represents the emotional state of the author of the tweet T.

3.1   System I

Our first model takes advantage of both embedding-based and lexicon-based features. In particular, the following feature sets are generated:

- Embedding-based features:

    - Average word embedding vector;
    - Representation of a tweet learned by an LSTM neural network on the provided training data;

- Lexicon-based and n-gram features:

    - Word and character n-gram features;
    - Vector of 43 lexicon-derived features, compiled using the AffectiveTweets package (Mohammad and Bravo-Marquez, 2017).[3] The lexicons used include those created by Nielsen (2011); Mohammad and Turney (2013); Kiritchenko et al. (2014); Hu and Liu (2004); Bravo-Marquez et al. (2016); Thelwall et al. (2012); Wilson et al. (2005).

We use bag-of-word (BOW) (Pang et al., 2002) and term frequency-inverse document frequency (tf-idf) methods to extract different word and character n-grams. We train word embeddings on a large corpus of tweets that contain emotion words. Then, we refine our learned word embeddings to build emotion-specific word embeddings for every emotion. Specifically, we assign emotion-specific weights to every word in our learned word embeddings and multiply each word vector by weights. These emotion-specific weights are obtained by calculating the Pearson correlation between the extracted unigram features and intensity labels of the training and development datasets of each emotion.

[3] https://affectivetweets.cms.waikato.ac.nz/

We concatenate two learned embedding-based tweet representations, word and character n-grams, and the lexicon features in a multimodal feature layer. We train a Random Forest (RF) over this heterogeneous multimodal feature layer to predict emotion intensity of a tweet.

This approach was evaluated on the datasets of SemEval-2018 Task 1, EI-reg (an emotion intensity regression task) and EI-oc (an emotion intensity ordinal classification task), for which it obtained Pearson correlations of 57.5% and 48.5% on the test sets, respectively.

Further investigation revealed that our system I was overfitted to the training data and lost its generalization ability over new unseen data. The cause of this problem was the use of development dataset labels in our feature engineering algorithm. So, we modify our model to overcome overfitting and propose system II.

3.2   System II

Similarly to System I, our second model incorporates both embedding-based representations and linguistic knowledge in a unified architecture (see Figure 1). We train a Support Vector Regressor (SVR) over the following two categories of features:

- Embedding-based features:

    - Average word embedding vector;
    - Representation of a tweet learned by an LSTM neural network on the provided training data;
    - Emotion-polarized representation of a tweet learned by an LSTM neural network on a distant supervision corpus;

- Lexicon-based and hand-crafted features:

    - Word and character n-gram features;
    - Vector of 43 lexicon-derived features, compiled using the AffectiveTweets package (Mohammad and Bravo-Marquez, 2017);
    - Hand-crafted features based on either word similarities in learned word embeddings or emotion intensity similarities in accordance to train and development labels.

Below, different components of the two systems are explained in detail.

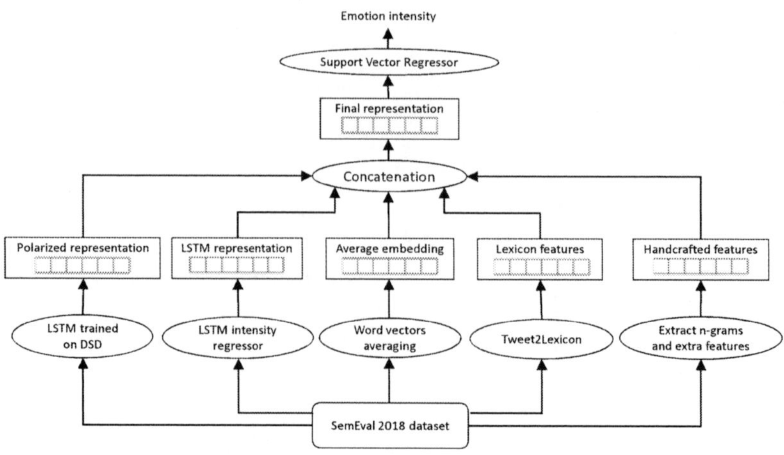

Figure 1: The architecture of our model (System II).

3.3 Word embedding layer

Since the input of our model is a sequence of tokens $\{w_1, w_2, ..., w_n\}$, it is crucial to learn an effective word representation for automatic emotion analysis. A word embedding is a dense, low-dimensional and real-valued vector associated with each word w_i. We used word2vec (Mikolov et al., 2013a) and SVD-NS (Soleimani and Matwin, 2018) to learn word embeddings and trained it on an unlabeled corpus of 21M tweets provided as part of the SemEval-2018 Affect in Tweets DIstant Supervision Corpus (SemEval-2018 AIT DISC) (Mohammad et al., 2018). SVD-NS works better for word and sentence similarity tasks and is much faster than word2vec. Such distributed word representations learned from massive text data make feature engineering less dependent on the task. However, unsupervised learning of word embeddings cannot thoroughly capture finer context-based semantic information of a specific task. Hence, to incorporate linguistic structure of tweets, we use the following two techniques to improve the word vectors:

1. Our model learns a unique distributed representation for every Multi-Word Expression (MWE). MWEs occur frequently in tweets, and their meanings are often not derivable from the meanings of the constituent words.

2. Additionally, our model learns an embedding vector to represent the negated form of every word occurring between a negation word (e.g., *no, shouldn't*) and the following punc-

tuation mark. Due to the significant impact of negation words in changing the sentiment polarity of a sentence, we treat the negated tokens differently (Zhu et al., 2014; Kiritchenko et al., 2014). By adding a 'NEG' prefix to them, we consider the negated tokens as different entities and learn separate word representations for them.

To learn word embeddings, we applied two methods: the continuous skip-gram model (Mikolov et al., 2013a) with the window size of 5, and SVD-NS (Soleimani and Matwin, 2018) with the PMI threshold of $\alpha = -2.5$. The vector dimensionality was set to $d = 100$. We also filter words that occur less than 3 times in the corpus.

3.4 Average embedding layer

To capture the global context of a tweet, we build a tweet embedding by vertically concatenating embedding vectors of its n words. This yields a tweet embedding matrix $X \in R^{n \times d}$. Then, we take the mean of these word embeddings across the tweet length. Therefore, an average embedding will add d features (equal to the number of our word embedding dimensions) to our multimodal feature layer.

3.5 Tweet embedding vector learned by LSTM layer

To learn a semantic representation of a tweet, we use an LSTM neural network, which we found effective in detecting salient words of a sentence while automatically attenuating unimportant words. The LSTM model sequentially takes each word in a sentence, extracts its information, and embeds it into a semantic vector. Due to its ability to capture long-term memory, LSTM accumulates increasingly richer information as it goes through the sentence, and when it reaches the last word, the hidden layer of the network provides a semantic representation of the whole sentence (Palangi et al., 2016). To be able to train sequential neural networks in batches, we normalize tweet length by zero padding and then feed the zero-padded tweet embedding matrix to an LSTM layer. We apply dropout (Srivastava et al., 2014) on the LSTM layer to prevent network parameters from overfitting and control the co-adaptation of features. Our LSTM layer is then followed by two fully connected hidden layers, and one output layer. Each of these layers computes the transformation $f(W_i * x_i + b_i)$ for $i = \{1, 2, 3\}$, where W is the weight matrix, b is the bias vector and f is a *Relu* non-linear activation function for hidden layers and a *Sigmoid* neuron for output layer. The full network is trained on the provided training data to predict the intensity score of the input tweet. We consider the representation obtained from the first hidden layer as a sentence embedding vector of an input tweet.

The network parameters are learned by minimizing the mean squared error (MSE) between the actual and predicted values of emotion intensity on the training data. We optimize this loss function by back-propagating through layers via mini-batch gradient descent, with batch size of 32, 40 training epochs, and Adam optimization algorithm (Kingma and Ba, 2014) with learning rate of $\alpha = 0.001$. We use one LSTM layer with 64 neurons, followed by a dropout of 0.2, and two hidden layers of sizes 32 and 16, respectively. We use the same network parameters for an LSTM model trained on the distant supervision data (see Section 3.6).

3.6 Emotion-polarized tweet representation learned by LSTM

We leverage large amount of Twitter data with distant supervision to polarize our word embeddings for each emotion. Hence, we use SemEval-2018 AIT DISC distant supervision corpus of tweets released by the competition organizers, which includes around 100M English tweet ids associated with tweets that contain emotion-related query terms such as '*#angry*', '*annoyed*', '*panic*', '*happy*', etc. We collected 21M tweets by polling the Twitter API with these tweet ids. Based on the query terms, one or more emotion labels of {'anger', 'fear', 'joy', 'sadness'} have been assigned to every tweet in this dataset. For each emotion, we randomly select $200,000$ tweets labeled with that emotion (e.g., 'anger') and $200,000$ tweets labeled with other emotions ('not anger') to build the emotion-specific word embeddings. Since the four basic emotions are not independent and may be correlated, we build these emotion-polarized word embeddings in two ways: *(i)* one against all strategy: for example, 'not anger' tweets are selected from tweets labeled with any of the other three emotions, i.e., 'fear', 'joy', or 'sadness'; *(ii)* considering emotions with similar valence as one group of labels: tweets labeled with 'anger', 'fear', and 'sadness' are treated as they have the same label. So, here 'not anger' tweets are selected from tweets that are labeled only as 'joy'. Then, we train an LSTM neural network using these emotion-specific word embeddings to build emotion-specific representations of tweets. Our final emotion-specific tweet representation obtained by concatenating two hidden state layers learned by the same LSTM neural network trained twice on the same data but with different emotion labeling according to the above two labeling strategies.

3.7 Hand-Crafted Features

In addition to the two kinds of tweet representations described above, we use bag-of-word (BOW) representation to extract most and least frequent word n-grams (unigrams, bigrams, and trigrams) as well as character n-grams (three, four, and five consecutive characters) from the training, development, and test datasets. BOW represents each word as a one-hot vector which has the same length as the size of the vocabulary, and only one dimension is 1, with all others being 0. However, the one-hot word representation cannot sufficiently capture the complex linguistic characteristics of words. We augment our feature space by generating additional hand-crafted features. We define a set of binary features by adding n adjectives with highest and lowest intensities for each emotion according to the emotion's training data. The intensity of a word (unigram) is obtained as an average emotion intensity of tweets in the train-

	Experiment	Anger	Fear	Joy	Sadness	Average
System I (EI-reg)	WE + TE + lex	58.15	57.06	57.51	57.36	57.54
System I (EI-oc)	WE + TE + lex	49.07	41.09	55.62	48.45	48.56
System II (EI-reg)	WE	62.37	60.07	56.46	60.69	60.12
	WE + MWEs	63.26	61.55	57.91	61.89	61.15
	WE + MWEs + negation	62.80	62.66	58.21	63.32	61.75
	ngram	48.30	52.65	52.44	52.01	51.35
	polTE	30.12	36.81	33.95	48.86	37.44
	TE	68.91	68.93	69.21	70.14	69.30
	WE + lex	67.74	68.74	66.20	67.21	67.48
	WE + ngram	63.70	66.38	60.87	64.55	63.87
	WE + ngram + lex	66.99	70.27	67.46	67.67	68.10
	WE + lex + handcrafted	68.82	71.63	67.74	69.27	69.37
	WE + ngram + TE	69.69	69.54	68.49	69.66	69.35
	WE + ngram + TE + lex	69.98	**73.44**	69.14	**73.33**	71.47
	all features	**72.30**	70.46	**71.55**	73.13	**71.96**

Table 2: Pearson correlation (r) % obtained on the test sets. The highest score in each emotion is shown in bold. System I indicates the results of our first overfitted model and System II shows the results of our modified model. In every experiment on system II, we train SVR regressor with linear kernel to predict emotion intensity of a tweet while in system I experiments, we use RF regressor and SVM classifier for SemEval-2018 Task 1 and 2, respectively. The all-features experiment represents the model built on concatenation of all six groups of features including WE, ngram, TE, polTE, lex, and handcrft.

ing data that contain that unigram. We also add the weighted average intensity of all extracted unigrams and the intensity of their k nearest neighbors in learned word embeddings (sorted based on cosine similarity) to our feature set.

4 Results

We train the SVR regressor on the combined set of tweets in the training and development sets and apply the model on the test set. The Pearson correlation between the predictions and the gold labels was used by the competition organizers as the official evaluation measure. The percentage of Pearson correlation scores obtained by all of our individual and combined models on the test set are shown in Table 2. To make the result table easier to understand, we shortened the feature groups' names as follows: 1) average word embedding vectors → WE, 2) tweet embedding vectors learned by LSTM → TE, 3) emotion-polarized tweet embeddings learned by LSTM → polTE, 4) word and character n-gram features → ngram, 5) AffectiveTweets lexicon features → lex, 6) hand-crafted features based on word similarities in emotion intensity → handcrft. All the results reported in the table use word embeddings that are obtained by SVD-NS (Soleimani and Matwin, 2018) method which was slightly better than word2vec (Mikolov et al., 2013b).

The 'all-features' row shows the results obtained by the model that concatenates all six groups of features including WE, ngram, TE,

polTE, lex, and handcrft. This model achieves the highest Pearson correlation score among all of our proposed models. The tweet representation learned by LSTM is the best learned unimodal feature. Considering MWEs as independent semantic units improves the average embedding model's performance by 1.03 percentage points. Learning independent embedding vectors for negated form of words further improves the score by 0.6 percentage points.

5 Conclusion

We described a deep learning framework to predict emotion intensity in tweets. We implemented an ensemble of embedding-based feature representations and sentiment lexicon-based feature learning approaches. Our best model obtained a Pearson correlation of 71.96% on Task 1 of SemEval-2018 competition (EI-reg: an emotion intensity regression task). The tweet representation feature vector learned by LSTM was the most effective feature group amongst those that we used. Various sentiment and emotion lexicon features, our hand-crafted features and word n-grams features also helped improve prediction quality.

Acknowledgments

We thank Xiang Jiang for helping us build attentive deep neural networks and fruitful discussions.

References

Felipe Bravo-Marquez, Eibe Frank, Saif M Mohammad, and Bernhard Pfahringer. 2016. Determining word-emotion associations from tweets by multi-label classification. In *Web Intelligence (WI), 2016 IEEE/WIC/ACM International Conference on*, pages 536–539. IEEE.

Ronan Collobert, Jason Weston, Léon Bottou, Michael Karlen, Koray Kavukcuoglu, and Pavel Kuksa. 2011. Natural language processing (almost) from scratch. *Journal of Machine Learning Research*, 12(Aug):2493–2537.

Silvana Hartmann, György Szarvas, and Iryna Gurevych. 2012. Mining multiword terms from wikipedia. In *Semi-Automatic Ontology Development: Processes and Resources*, pages 226–258. IGI Global.

Minqing Hu and Bing Liu. 2004. Mining and summarizing customer reviews. In *Proceedings of the tenth ACM SIGKDD international conference on Knowledge discovery and data mining*, pages 168–177. ACM.

Diederik P Kingma and Jimmy Ba. 2014. Adam: A method for stochastic optimization. In *International Conference on Learning Representations*.

Svetlana Kiritchenko, Xiaodan Zhu, and Saif M Mohammad. 2014. Sentiment analysis of short informal texts. *Journal of Artificial Intelligence Research*, 50:723–762.

Pengfei Liu, Shafiq Joty, and Helen Meng. 2015. Fine-grained opinion mining with recurrent neural networks and word embeddings. In *Proceedings of the 2015 Conference on Empirical Methods in Natural Language Processing*, pages 1433–1443.

Tomas Mikolov, Kai Chen, Greg Corrado, and Jeffrey Dean. 2013a. Efficient estimation of word representations in vector space. *arXiv preprint arXiv:1301.3781*.

Tomas Mikolov, Ilya Sutskever, Kai Chen, Greg S Corrado, and Jeff Dean. 2013b. Distributed representations of words and phrases and their compositionality. In *Advances in neural information processing systems*, pages 3111–3119.

Saif M. Mohammad and Felipe Bravo-Marquez. 2017. Emotion intensities in tweets. In *Proceedings of the sixth joint conference on lexical and computational semantics (*Sem)*, Vancouver, Canada.

Saif M. Mohammad, Felipe Bravo-Marquez, Mohammad Salameh, and Svetlana Kiritchenko. 2018. Semeval-2018 Task 1: Affect in tweets. In *Proceedings of International Workshop on Semantic Evaluation (SemEval-2018)*, New Orleans, LA, USA.

Saif M. Mohammad and Svetlana Kiritchenko. 2018. Understanding emotions: A dataset of tweets to study interactions between affect categories. In *Proceedings of the 11th Edition of the Language Resources and Evaluation Conference (LREC-2018)*, Miyazaki, Japan.

Saif M. Mohammad, Svetlana Kiritchenko, and Xiaodan Zhu. 2013. NRC-Canada: Building the state-of-the-art in sentiment analysis of tweets. In *Proceedings of the International Workshop on Semantic Evaluation*, Atlanta, GA, USA.

Saif M Mohammad and Peter D Turney. 2013. Crowdsourcing a word–emotion association lexicon. *Computational Intelligence*, 29(3):436–465.

Finn Årup Nielsen. 2011. A new anew: Evaluation of a word list for sentiment analysis in microblogs. In *Workshop on 'Making Sense of Microposts: Big things come in small packages*, pages 93–98.

Hamid Palangi, Li Deng, Yelong Shen, Jianfeng Gao, Xiaodong He, Jianshu Chen, Xinying Song, and Rabab Ward. 2016. Deep sentence embedding using long short-term memory networks: Analysis and application to information retrieval. *IEEE/ACM Transactions on Audio, Speech and Language Processing (TASLP)*, 24(4):694–707.

Bo Pang, Lillian Lee, and Shivakumar Vaithyanathan. 2002. Thumbs up?: sentiment classification using machine learning techniques. In *Proceedings of the ACL-02 conference on Empirical methods in natural language processing-Volume 10*, pages 79–86. Association for Computational Linguistics.

Richard Socher, Alex Perelygin, Jean Wu, Jason Chuang, Christopher D Manning, Andrew Ng, and Christopher Potts. 2013. Recursive deep models for semantic compositionality over a sentiment treebank. In *Proceedings of the 2013 conference on empirical methods in natural language processing*, pages 1631–1642.

Behrouz H Soleimani and Stan Matwin. 2018. Spectral word embedding with negative sampling. In *Proceedings of the Thirty-Second AAAI Conference on Artificial Intelligence*.

Nitish Srivastava, Geoffrey Hinton, Alex Krizhevsky, Ilya Sutskever, and Ruslan Salakhutdinov. 2014. Dropout: A simple way to prevent neural networks from overfitting. *The Journal of Machine Learning Research*, 15(1):1929–1958.

Duyu Tang, Furu Wei, Nan Yang, Ming Zhou, Ting Liu, and Bing Qin. 2014. Learning sentiment-specific word embedding for twitter sentiment classification. In *Proceedings of the 52nd Annual Meeting of the Association for Computational Linguistics (Volume 1: Long Papers)*, volume 1, pages 1555–1565.

Zhiyang Teng, Duy Tin Vo, and Yue Zhang. 2016. Context-sensitive lexicon features for neural sentiment analysis. In *Proceedings of the 2016 Conference on Empirical Methods in Natural Language Processing*, pages 1629–1638.

Mike Thelwall, Kevan Buckley, and Georgios Paltoglou. 2012. Sentiment strength detection for the social web. *Journal of the Association for Information Science and Technology*, 63(1):163–173.

Theresa Wilson, Janyce Wiebe, and Paul Hoffmann. 2005. Recognizing contextual polarity in phrase-level sentiment analysis. In *Proceedings of the conference on human language technology and empirical methods in natural language processing*, pages 347–354.

Xiaodan Zhu, Hongyu Guo, Saif Mohammad, and Svetlana Kiritchenko. 2014. An empirical study on the effect of negation words on sentiment. In *Proceedings of the 52nd Annual Meeting of the Association for Computational Linguistics (Volume 1: Long Papers)*, volume 1, pages 304–313.

Zewen at SemEval-2018 Task 1: An Ensemble Model for Affect Prediction in Tweets

Zewen Chi, Heyan Huang, Jiangui Chen, Hao Wu, Ran Wei

School of Computer Science, Beijing Institute of Technology, Beijing, China

`czwin32768@gmail.com, hhy63@bit.edu.cn, chenjiangui@outlook.com,`
`wuhao123@bit.edu.cn, weiranbit@163.com`

Abstract

This paper presents a method for Affect in Tweets, which is the task to automatically determine the intensity of emotions and intensity of sentiment of tweets. The term affect refers to emotion-related categories such as anger, fear, etc. Intensity of emotions need to be quantified into a real valued score in [0, 1]. We propose an ensemble system including four different deep learning methods which are CNN, Bidirectional LSTM (BLSTM), LSTM-CNN and a CNN-based Attention model (CA). Our system gets an average Pearson correlation score of 0.682 in the subtask EI-reg and an average Pearson correlation score of 0.784 in subtask V-reg, which ranks 19th among 48 systems in EI-reg and 17th among 38 systems in V-reg.

1 Introduction

Affect determination is a significant part of nature language processing. Especially, affect in tweets becomes a focus in recent years. Sentiment Analysis in Twitter, which is a task of SemEval, was firstly proposed in 2013 and not replaced until 2018. In SemEval 2018, the task Affect in Tweets (AIT) (Mohammad et al., 2018) was proposed and the objective is to automatically determine the intensity of emotions (E) and intensity of sentiment (aka valence V) of tweets. In this paper, we focus on two subtasks:

- EI-reg (emotion intensity regression) – Given a tweet and an emotion E, determine the intensity of E that best represents the mental state of the tweeter – a real-valued score between 0 (least E) and 1 (most E)

- V-reg (sentiment intensity regression) – Given a tweet, determine the intensity of sentiment or valence (V) that best represents the mental state of the tweeter – a real-valued score between 0 (most negative) and 1 (most positive)

Before 2016, most systems use Support Vector Machine (SVM), Naive Bayes, maximum entropy and linear regression (Nakov et al., 2013; Rosenthal et al., 2014, 2015). In SemEval 2014, deep learning methods started to appear and a team using them won the second place. Since 2015, more and more teams who were rank at the top used deep learning methods and now deep learning methods including CNN and LSTM networks become really popular (Nakov et al., 2016; Rosenthal et al., 2017).

The system described in this paper is an ensemble of four different DNN methods including CNN, Bidirectional LSTM (Bi-LSTM), LSTM-CNN and a CNN-based Attention model (CA). In these methods, words in tweets are firstly mapped to word vectors. After intensity scores are calculated by these models, we use a logistic regression and finally give the scores.

The rest of the paper is organized as follows. Section 2 describes the four various methods and the ensemble method used in our system. Section 3 and Section 4 give the implementation and training details of our system for subtask EI-reg and V-reg. Section 5 states the results and discussion in the evaluation period. Finally, Section 6 makes a conclusion on this work.

2 System Description

2.1 CNN

Inspired by Kim's work on sentence classification (Kim, 2014), the architecture of the CNN model used in our system is almost identical to his model. As it is shown in Figure 1, tweets are first fed into the embedding layer, which converts words into word vectors. Then the tweet is mapped into a matrix M of size $n \times d$. In order to reduce the number

313

Proceedings of the 12th International Workshop on Semantic Evaluation (SemEval-2018), pages 313–318
New Orleans, Louisiana, June 5–6, 2018. ©2018 Association for Computational Linguistics

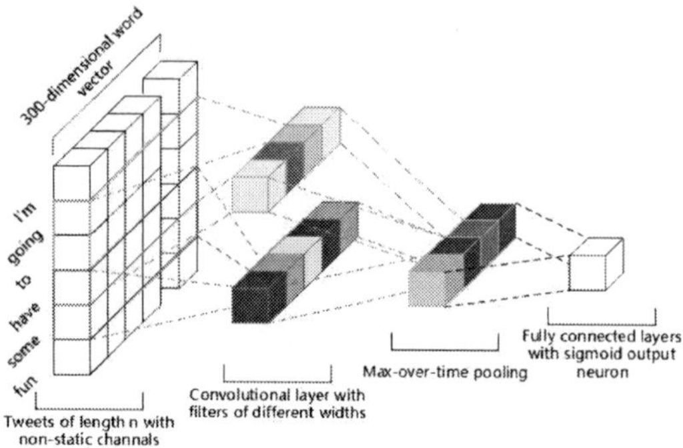

Figure 1: The architecture of our CNN model

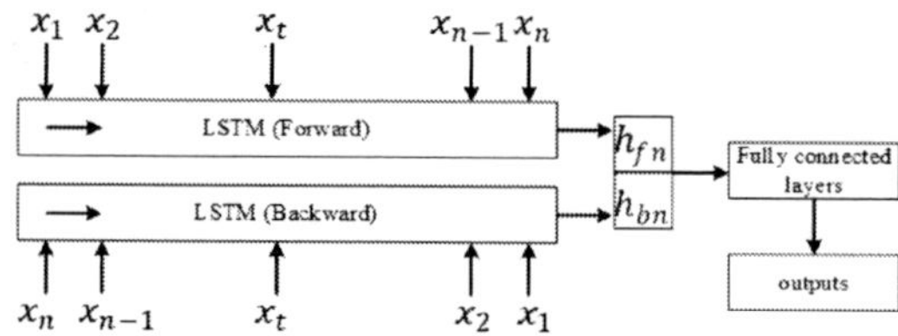

Figure 2: The architecture of our bidirectional LSTM model, where h_fn and h_bn represent the last hidden state of the forward and backward LSTM respectively.

of parameters in the neural network, we just use the single channel non-static model, which sets pre-trained word vectors in the embedding layer and can be modified in the training period. In the convolution layer, convolution operations are applied on the submatrixes of M. The convolution operation here is defined as:

$$c_k = f_k(\sum_i \sum_j \omega_{ij} x_{[i:i+h-1]} + b)$$

where $b \in \mathbb{R}$ is a bias term and f is a non-linear function such as ReLU (Jarrett et al., 2009), which is used in our approach. Filters are applied with different size of windows and in each window of size h, feature matrix $c \in \mathbb{R}^{(n-h+1)\times m}$ is produced corresponding to the filters:

$$c = [c_1, c_2, ..., c_k, ..., c_m]$$

where m is the number of filters and $c_k \in \mathbb{R}^{n-h+1}$ represents the features extracted from a word sequence. In the pooling layer, we apply a max-over-time pooling operation (Collobert et al., 2011) over feature matrix and take the maximum in each column to preserve the most important features. These maximums are concatenated and then fed into a fully-connected network (L1, L2). L2 is followed by a single sigmoid neuron node to generate the prediction of the affect on the interval $[0, 1]$.

2.2 Bidirectional LSTM

The LSTM architecture used in our system is a kind of modern Recurrent Neural Networks (RNN). Comparing to CNN, the way RNN work is more similar to that how humans read sentences. A word vector sequence x, which is converted from a tweet, will be fed to the RNN in order.

$$h_t = \sigma(W_{hx}x_t + W_{hh}h_{t-1} + b_h)$$
$$y^t = softmax(W_{yh}h_t + b_y)$$

At time t, the RNN takes the input from the cur-

rent word x_t and also from the previous hidden state h_{t-1} to calculate the hidden state h_t and the output $\hat{y}_t$, which means $\hat{y}_t$ at time t is in the influence of all previous input words $x_1, ..., x_{t-1}$. However, this regular RNN suffers from the exploding and vanishing gradient problem when using the backpropagation algorithm (Hochreiter, 1998), which makes RNN hard to train. Therefore, we use the Long short-term memory (LSTM) network (Hochreiter and Schmidhuber, 1997) to overcome this problem. Each ordinary node of hidden layer in LSTMs is replaced by a memory cell and the following equations describe the LSTM:

$$g_t = \phi(W_{gx}x_t + W_{gh}h_{t-1} + b_g)$$
$$i_t = \sigma(W_{ix}x_t + W_{ih}h_{t-1} + b_i)$$
$$f_t = \sigma(W_{fx}x_t + W_{fh}h_{t-1} + b_f)$$
$$o_t = \sigma(W_{ox}x_t + W_{oh}h_{t-1} + b_o)$$
$$s_t = g_t \odot i_t + s_{t-1} \odot f_t$$
$$h_t = \phi(s_t) \odot o_t$$

The vector h_t is the value of hidden layer of LSTM at time t, g_t is the input node, i_t is the input gate, f_t is the forget gate, o_t is the output gate and s_t is the internal state where $\odot$ is pointwise multiplication. According to Zaremba and Sutskever (2014), the function ϕ used here is the tanh function.

For every point in a given sequence, Graves et al. (2005) shows that a bidirectional LSTM can preserve more sequential information about all sequential points before and after it. As the Figure 2 shows, we concatenate the hidden states of two separate LSTMs after they process the word sequence in opposite direction and get the concatenated state $h^{'} \in \mathbb{R}^{2m}$, which is fed to fully connected layers and finally give the result with a single sigmoid neuron node.

2.3 LSTM-CNN

The architecture of LSTM-CNN is a combination of previous two model. Instead of feeding the out-

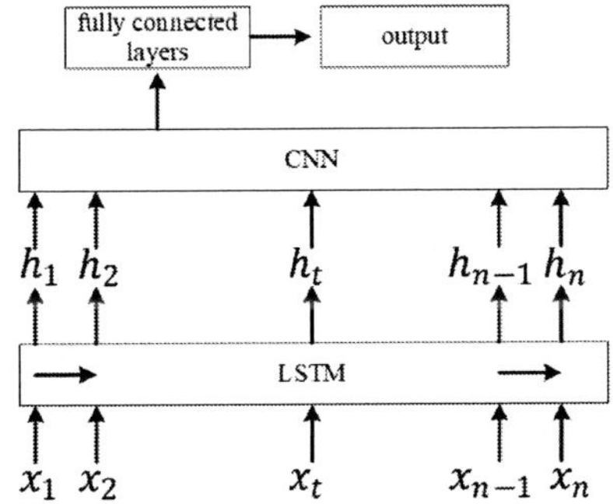

Figure 3: The architecture of our LSTM-CNN model.

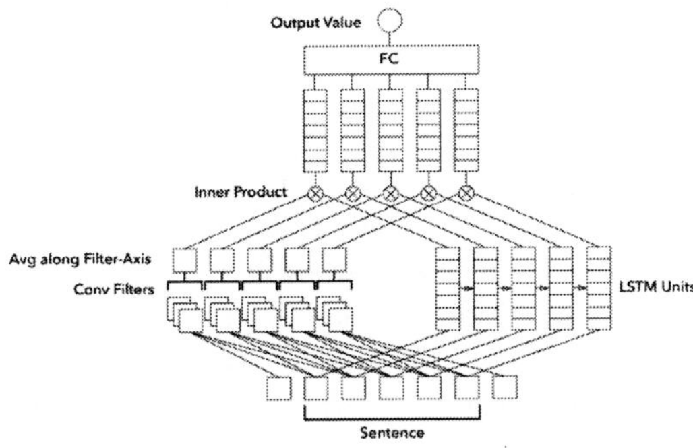

Figure 4: The architecture of CNN-based Attention Model (CA)

put of LSTM to the fully connected layers, the output of LSTM h_t at each time t are regarded as the input of CNN and Figure 3 shows the architecture.

2.4 A CNN-based Attention Model (CA)

Since attention mechanism has achieved significant improvements in many NLP tasks, including machine translation (Bahdanau et al., 2014), caption generation (Xu et al., 2015) and text summarization (Rush et al., 2015), it becomes an integral part of compelling sequence modeling and transduction models in various tasks. Motivated by Du's work on sentence classification (Du et al., 2017), the architecture of our CNN-based attention model resembles his model. We first use a CNN-based network to model the attention signal in sentences. The convolution operation here is same as that described in Section 2.1. The attention signal of original text is represented by the output of convolutional filter. In order to reduce the noise, multiple filters with same size of windows are applied. After that, we get the corresponding attention similarity:

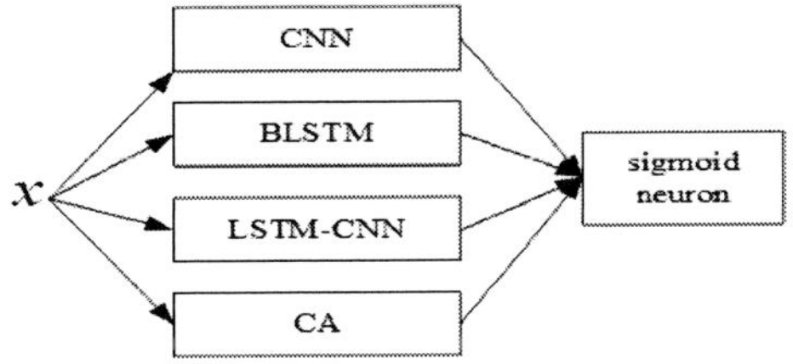

Figure 5: The architecture of the ensemble model

$[c_1, c_2, ..., c_k, ..., c_m]$. Then we obtain the attention signal of each element which represents the importance of the corresponding word by averaging the attention similarities along the filter-axis:

$$c = \frac{1}{m} \sum_{i=1}^{m} c_i$$

An RNN with LSTM units is used to encode the sentence. According to the equation in Section 2.2, the hidden state $h_t \in \mathbb{R}^d$ (where d is the dimension of the RNN) at time t is $h_t = \phi(s_t) \odot o_t$.

So far, we have obtained attention signal c_t and the corresponding hidden state vector of RNN h_t. The representation of the whole sentence can be computed by

$$s = \frac{1}{T} \sum_{t=0}^{T-1} c_t h_t$$

And then $s \in \mathbb{R}^d$ is fed into a fully-connected network (L1, L2). L2 is followed by a single sigmoid neuron node to generate the prediction of the affect on the interval [0, 1]. The architecture of this model is shown in Figure 4.

2.5 Ensemble Model

According to the results of SemEval-2017 task 4, the use of ensembles stood out clearly. Therefore, we use a mix of deep learning methods to make our system obtain better predictive performance. Inspired by the boosting algorithms, we use a logistic regression to improve the accuracy of these four methods and the architecture is shown in Figure 5. In order to make the model simple, it only takes the output of the four methods as input rather than training data.

3 Implementation

We implemented our system with PyTorch (Paszke et al., 2017) in Python 3.

Preprocessing: For making tweets string clean, we apply a preprocessing procedure on the input tweets which removes the abbreviations like 's, 've and make them lowercased.

Word Embeddings: We utilize pre-trained 300-dimensional word embeddings of Stanford's

Methods	L1	L2
CNN	300	150
BLSTM	30	Nil
LSTM-CNN	256	100
CA	150	75

Table 1: Fully connected layers hyper-parameters, the numbers represent the size of outputs of liner layers.

Methods	p	CNN	LSTM
CNN	0.2	[2, 3, 4], 256	Nil
BLSTM	0.5	Nil	300
LSTM-CNN	0.5	[3], 200	300
CA	0.5	[3], 50	150

Table 2: Network hyper-parameters for the filters of CNN and hidden size of LSTM, and p is the dropout rate. For example, [2, 3, 4], 256 means the filter height is set to 2, 3 and 4, and the number of filters is set to 256 for different sizes of filters.

GloVe (Pennington et al., 2014) trained by Common Crawl.

Model Hyper-parameters: Table 1 and Table 2 show the hyper-parameters we use in our system.

For fully connected layers, no more than two fully-connected layers are used in the four methods and all fully-connected layers are followed by ReLU. Before the outputs of pooling layers and LSTMs are fed to the fully connected layers, a dropout is applied and the details are described in Table 2.

4 Training

The dataset used in our system is provided by the AIT task and no external datasets are used in training period. For the subtask EI-reg and subtask V-reg, they are trained with the same model hyper-parameters which are listed in Table 1 and Table 2. Also, the four methods use the same word embeddings, which is a pre-trained 300-dimensional word vectors with common crawl by GloVe algorithm. For different emotions, we train the models for 10 epochs respectively. The network parameters are learned by minimizing the Mean Absolute Error (MAE) between the gold labels and predictions and the four methods used in our system are trained separately. We optimize the loss function by back-propagating algorithm via Mini-batch Gradient descent with batch size of 8 for the 4 deep learning models and full batch learning for the ensemble model, as well as the Adam opti-

mization algorithm (Kingma and Ba, 2014) for all models with initial leaning rate of 0.001 and 0.01 for the four deep learning models and the ensemble model, respectively.

5 Result and Discussion

We compare the results of the four methods used in our system, the ensemble system, the SVM_Unigrams_Baseline provided from the AIT task and the best-performing system – SeerNet in Table 3. The metric for evaluating performance is Pearson Correlation.

Its remarkable that, comparing to the individual models, our ensemble model has an improvement of at least 2% on EI-reg subtask and 1.1% on V-reg subtask. However, it's obvious that there is a gap between our models and the best-performance system. The rough preprocessing method of our system is one of the reason for the low score. Because of some words in tweets are misspelled or in a special format like 'yaaaaay!', some of the information is lost in this process. So we added an experiment on the V-reg task to study the effect of preprocessing method. We replace the text preprocessing method with the *ekphrasis*[1] for the tokenization, word normalization, word segmentation (for splitting hashtags) and spell correction and the keep the other parameters unchanged. As it is shown in Table 4, the four methods as well as the ensemble model all get an improvement on the results. Actually, some expressions like dates, urls, hashtags and emoticons are converted into the special tokens like <date> , <url>, <hashtag> and <joy>, but these tokens are not in the dictionary of pre-trained word vectors, which means the information of these tokens is still wasted in the embedding process.

There is much room for the improvement of our method:

1. In our system, a single pre-trained word embedding is used, which lack experimental evidence. For future work, combining more kinds of word embeddings should be taken into consideration.

2. We adjust the hyper-parameters by doing evaluation on dev dataset. For future work, we can apply a more advanced strategy like Cross Validation.

---

[1] `github.com/cbaziotis/ekphrasis`

Methods	Average(EI-reg)	Anger	Fear	Joy	Sadness	V-reg
CNN	0.668	0.673	0.684	0.670	0.644	0.773
BLSTM	0.625	0.619	0.645	0.630	0.604	0.731
LSTM-CNN	0.641	0.620	0.680	0.627	0.636	0.759
CA	0.640	0.606	0.662	0.670	0.624	0.761
Ensemble	0.682	0.673	0.700	0.690	0.665	0.784
SeerNet	**0.799**	**0.827**	**0.779**	**0.792**	**0.798**	**0.873**
Baseline	0.520	0.526	0.525	0.575	0.453	0.585

Table 3: Results on Subtask EI-reg and V-reg.

Methods	Rough method	ekphrasis
CNN	0.773	**0.788**
BLSTM	0.731	**0.733**
LSTM-CNN	0.759	**0.767**
CA	0.761	**0.773**
Ensemble	0.784	**0.793**

Table 4: Results of different text preprocessing method on V-reg task when the other parameters are kept unchanged.

3. For the input features, we only use the word vectors. We are supposed to experiment with more features like lexicons.

4. In our system, we just use a simple logistic regression but achieve an impressive result on the two subtasks. There is an interesting idea that we can do more work on finding a better ensemble model.

6 Conclusion

In this paper, we propose a model on the sub-task EI-reg and V-reg of SemEval-2018 Task 1: Affect on Tweets. The submitted system is an ensemble model based on CNN, Bidirectional LSTM (BLSTM), LSTM-CNN and a CNN-based Attention model (CA). All methods are described in detail to make our work replicable.

For future work, it would be significant to make an improvement on preprocessing of tweets, doing more experiment on word embeddings and feature selection, model validation and ensemble method.

References

Dzmitry Bahdanau, Kyunghyun Cho, and Yoshua Bengio. 2014. Neural machine translation by jointly learning to align and translate. *arXiv preprint arXiv:1409.0473*.

Christos Baziotis, Nikos Pelekis, and Christos Doulkeridis. 2017. Datastories at semeval-2017 task 4: Deep lstm with attention for message-level and topic-based sentiment analysis. In *Proceedings of the 11th International Workshop on Semantic Evaluation (SemEval-2017)*, pages 747–754, Vancouver, Canada. Association for Computational Linguistics.

Mathieu Cliche. 2017. Bb_twtr at semeval-2017 task 4: Twitter sentiment analysis with cnns and lstms. *arXiv preprint arXiv:1704.06125*.

Ronan Collobert, Jason Weston, Léon Bottou, Michael Karlen, Koray Kavukcuoglu, and Pavel Kuksa. 2011. Natural language processing (almost) from scratch. *Journal of Machine Learning Research*, 12(Aug):2493–2537.

Jiachen Du, Lin Gui, Ruifeng Xu, and Yulan He. 2017. A convolutional attention model for text classification. In *National CCF Conference on Natural Language Processing and Chinese Computing*, pages 183–195. Springer.

Pranav Goel, Devang Kulshreshtha, Prayas Jain, and Kaushal Kumar Shukla. 2017. Prayas at emoint 2017: An ensemble of deep neural architectures for emotion intensity prediction in tweets. In *Proceedings of the 8th Workshop on Computational Approaches to Subjectivity, Sentiment and Social Media Analysis*, pages 58–65.

Alex Graves and Jürgen Schmidhuber. 2005. Framewise phoneme classification with bidirectional lstm and other neural network architectures. *Neural Networks*, 18(5-6):602–610.

Hussam Hamdan. 2017. Senti17 at semeval-2017 task 4: Ten convolutional neural network voters for tweet polarity classification. *arXiv preprint arXiv:1705.02023*.

Sepp Hochreiter. 1998. The vanishing gradient problem during learning recurrent neural nets and problem solutions. *International Journal of Uncertainty, Fuzziness and Knowledge-Based Systems*, 6(02):107–116.

Sepp Hochreiter and Jürgen Schmidhuber. 1997. Long short-term memory. *Neural computation*, 9(8):1735–1780.

Kevin Jarrett, Koray Kavukcuoglu, Yann LeCun, et al. 2009. What is the best multi-stage architecture for object recognition? In *Computer Vision, 2009 IEEE 12th International Conference on*, pages 2146–2153. IEEE.

Yoon Kim. 2014. Convolutional neural networks for sentence classification. *arXiv preprint arXiv:1408.5882*.

Diederik P Kingma and Jimmy Ba. 2014. Adam: A method for stochastic optimization. *arXiv preprint arXiv:1412.6980*.

Saif M. Mohammad, Felipe Bravo-Marquez, Mohammad Salameh, and Svetlana Kiritchenko. 2018. Semeval-2018 Task 1: Affect in tweets. In *Proceedings of International Workshop on Semantic Evaluation (SemEval-2018)*, New Orleans, LA, USA.

Preslav Nakov, Zornitsa Kozareva, Alan Ritter, Sara Rosenthal, and Veselin Stoyanov Theresa Wilson. 2013. Semeval-2013 task 2: Sentiment analysis in twitter. volume 2.

Preslav Nakov, Alan Ritter, Sara Rosenthal, Fabrizio Sebastiani, and Veselin Stoyanov. 2016. Semeval-2016 task 4: Sentiment analysis in twitter. In *Proceedings of the 10th International Workshop on Semantic Evaluation (SemEval-2016)*, pages 1–18.

Adam Paszke, Sam Gross, Soumith Chintala, Gregory Chanan, Edward Yang, Zachary DeVito, Zeming Lin, Alban Desmaison, Luca Antiga, and Adam Lerer. 2017. Automatic differentiation in pytorch.

Jeffrey Pennington, Richard Socher, and Christopher Manning. 2014. Glove: Global vectors for word representation. In *Proceedings of the 2014 conference on empirical methods in natural language processing (EMNLP)*, pages 1532–1543.

Sara Rosenthal, Noura Farra, and Preslav Nakov. 2017. Semeval-2017 task 4: Sentiment analysis in twitter. In *Proceedings of the 11th International Workshop on Semantic Evaluation (SemEval-2017)*, pages 502–518.

Sara Rosenthal, Preslav Nakov, Svetlana Kiritchenko, Saif Mohammad, Alan Ritter, and Veselin Stoyanov. 2015. Semeval-2015 task 10: Sentiment analysis in twitter. In *Proceedings of the 9th international workshop on semantic evaluation (SemEval 2015)*, pages 451–463.

Sara Rosenthal, Alan Ritter, Preslav Nakov, and Veselin Stoyanov. 2014. Semeval-2014 task 9: Sentiment analysis in twitter. In *Proceedings of the 8th International Workshop on Semantic Evaluation (SemEval 2014)*, pages 73–80, Dublin, Ireland. Association for Computational Linguistics and Dublin City University.

Mickael Rouvier. 2017. Lia at semeval-2017 task 4: An ensemble of neural networks for sentiment classification. In *Proceedings of the 11th International Workshop on Semantic Evaluation (SemEval-2017)*, pages 760–765.

Alexander M Rush, Sumit Chopra, and Jason Weston. 2015. A neural attention model for abstractive sentence summarization. *arXiv preprint arXiv:1509.00685*.

Ilya Sutskever, Oriol Vinyals, and Quoc V Le. 2014. Sequence to sequence learning with neural networks. In *Advances in neural information processing systems*, pages 3104–3112.

Kelvin Xu, Jimmy Ba, Ryan Kiros, Kyunghyun Cho, Aaron Courville, Ruslan Salakhudinov, Rich Zemel, and Yoshua Bengio. 2015. Show, attend and tell: Neural image caption generation with visual attention. In *International Conference on Machine Learning*, pages 2048–2057.

Wojciech Zaremba, Ilya Sutskever, and Oriol Vinyals. 2014. Recurrent neural network regularization. *arXiv preprint arXiv:1409.2329*.

Amrita_student at SemEval-2018 Task 1: Distributed Representation of Social Media Text for Affects in Tweets

Nidhin A Unnithan, Shalini K., Barathi Ganesh H. B., M. Anand Kumar, K. P. Soman
Center for Computational Engineering and Networking (CEN)
Amrita School of Engineering, Coimbatore
Amrita Vishwa Vidyapeetham, India
nidhinkittu5470@gmail.com, shalinikholla@gmail.com,
bharathiganesh.hb@gmail.com, m_anandkumar@cb.amrita.edu,
kp_soman@amrita.edu

Abstract

In this paper we did an analysis of "Affects in Tweets" which was one of the task conducted by SemEval 2018. Task was to build a model which is able to do regression and classification of different emotions from the given tweets data set. We developed a base model for all the subtasks using distributed representation (Doc2Vec) and applied machine learning techniques for classification and regression. Distributed representation is an unsupervised algorithm which is capable of learning fixed length feature representation from variable length texts. Machine learning techniques used for regression is 'Linear Regression' while 'Random Forest Tree' is used for classification purpose. Empirical results obtained for all the subtasks by our model are shown in this paper.

1 Introduction

Most basic form of communication between humans is through language. Thus it can act as a medium of how we are feeling at any particular instance. For example, if we are angry at someone rather than just hitting him first we would express our feeling through our words. Thus from a conversion we can make out the different emotions a person is going through at that time. Apart from this social media texts can be used for determining the class of a person as described in (Ganesh H. B. et al., 2016b). In this work we are doing 2 ordinal classification, 1 classification and 2 regression of different emotions that people exhibits through tweets obtained from twitter (Mohammad and Kiritchenko, 2018; Bravo-Marquez et al., 2014; Mohammad et al., 2013) for three different languages namely Arabic, English and Spanish. The data set given has tweets from all the three languages for each subtask (Mohammad et al., 2018; Mohammad and Kiritchenko, 2018). There is a total of

five subtask an emotion intensity regression task, an emotion intensity ordinal classification task, a sentiment intensity regression task, a sentiment analysis ordinal classification task and an emotion classification task.

We used distributed representation (Le and Mikolov, 2014; Ganesh H. B. et al., 2016a) to create feature vector which can be feed as input to machine learning algorithms for classification and regression. Bag-of-words is one of the most common method used to create fixed length feature vectors but the ordering and semantics of the words are ignored in this method. By using Doc2Vec, an unsupervised learning algorithm, we can create fixed length features from variable length data. Thus by using Doc2Vec we can preserve the ordering as well as the semantics of data. Another method for word representation is distributional representation (Ganesh H. B. et al., 2018) which is an extension of co-occurrence based representation and have the same disadvantages as co-occurrence based methods.

Once the feature vector is created it is pushed into machine learning algorithm for classification and regression. We have used Random Forest Tree for classification which is an ensemble learning method that creates a number of decision trees during training and gives an output class which appears most often. For regression we used Linear Regression which tries to fit a line between the actual and predicted values by minimizing the error sum of squares between them. The final model is obtained after doing hyper parameter tuning for Doc2Vec $size$ and $n\_estimator$, max_depth for Random Forest Tree which are fixed through a grid search method before pushing to machine learning algorithms.

Section 2 of this paper gives a brief introduction to corpus. Section 3 describes the theory of different methods used. Section 4 describes the method-

Proceedings of the 12th International Workshop on Semantic Evaluation (SemEval-2018), pages 319–323
New Orleans, Louisiana, June 5–6, 2018. ©2018 Association for Computational Linguistics

ology used. Section 5 covers result and discussion. Section 6 talks about our conclusion.

2 Corpus

The given corpus consists of tweets from three different languages for all five subtasks. The languages are English, Arabic and Spanish. Each language have training, development and test data set (Mohammad et al., 2018; Mohammad and Kiritchenko, 2018).

While building the model training data set was splitted into 80% for training and 20% for testing. Training and development data set consist of tweet id, tweet, affect dimension and intensity score while test data set has entries as none at intensity scores.

3 Methodology

3.1 Distributed Representation

Doc2Vec is an unsupervised learning algorithm which gives a fixed length vector representation of a variable length text. The text can be a sentence, paragraph or document. It is an extension of Word2Vec in which a vector representation of words are given inorder to predict a word given the vector representation of context words are given. Word2Vec is inspired because it can be used to predict the next word in a sentence given the context word vectors thus capturing the semantics of the sentence even though the word vectors are randomly initialized. Instead of word vector we will use document vector to predict next word given context from a document in Doc2Vec. In document vector every document is represented by a column of unique vector called document matrix and words are represented by unique vectors called word matrix. Next word in a context is predicted by the concatenation or averaging of document and word vectors.

In Doc2Vec the document vector is same for all context generated from same document but differs across documents. However word vector matrix is same for different document, i.e., the vector representation of same word across different document have the same vector representation.

3.2 Linear Regression

For regression tasks Linear Regression was used. Linear Regression tries to fit a line between the actual and predicted values by minimizing the error sum of squares between them. In a Linear Regression problem there will be one dependent variable and an independent variable. A regression tries to verify two objective, firstly whether a satisfactory prediction can be made by a set of predictor variables and secondly which all variables play an important role in predicting the outcome variable. The estimated regression outputs are used to explain the connection between independent and dependent variables.

3.3 Random Forest Tree

For classification problem we used Random Forest Tree. It is an ensemble learning method that creates a number of decision trees during training and gives an output class which appears most often. Advantage of Random Forest Tree is its ability to control over-fitting by taking an average of all the decision trees for prediction. If more than one algorithm of same or different kind are combined to classify an object such an algorithm is called ensemble algorithm. For example it may run a prediction on SVM, Naive Bayes and Decision Tree before taking the vote for classification of test object.

3.4 Experiment

The corpus was obtained from SemEval2018 website. Once the data was obtained the first process was to extract tweets from the data for all the languages. Once every thing was extracted from the document next step was to build a Doc2Vec model from the extracted tweets which will produce feature vectors which can be used as inputs for our machine learning techniques for regression and classification tasks. Gensim library was used to build the Doc2Vec model. Sklearn library was used for Random Forest Tree and Linear Regression.

Before fixing the Doc2Vec base model we did hyper parameter tuning for all subtasks in all languages. The parameters tuned for regression tasks was Doc2Vec $size$ and for classification were Doc2Vec $size$ and $n\_estimator$, max_depth for Random Forest Tree. $size$ of Doc2Vec means the dimensionality of the feature vector, i.e., in which dimension each document in a corpus is represented as. $n\_estimator$ of Random Forest Tree means the number of decision trees used in the forest, i.e., before taking vote of a class how many different algorithms are to be run. max_depth of Random Forest Tree gives the maximum depth of

Tasks	size	n_estimator	max_depth
Task 1	140	-	-
Task 2	250	40	17
Task 3	280	-	-
Task 4	820	30	12
Task 5	150	10	8

Table 1: Tuned parameters for English.

Tasks	size	n_estimator	max_depth
Task 1	20	-	-
Task 2	50	90	19
Task 3	110	-	-
Task 4	90	140	17
Task 5	80	1	18

Table 2: Tuned parameters for Arabic.

Tasks	size	n_estimator	max_depth
Task 1	190	-	-
Task 2	160	40	18
Task 3	120	-	-
Task 4	320	140	16
Task 5	180	10	11

Table 3: Tuned parameters for Spanish.

the tree in algorithm. We did a grid search method to find out the optimum parameter values for each subtasks.

For emotion intensity regression task (Task 1) and sentiment intensity regression task (Task 3) Doc2Vec $size$ was varied from 10 to 1000 with an increment of 10 in each iteration. For emotion intensity ordinal classification task (Task 2), sentiment analysis ordinal classification task (Task 4) and emotion classification task (Task 5) Doc2Vec $size$ was varied from 10 to 1000 with an increment of 10 in each iteration, $n\_estimator$ of Random Forest Tree was varied from 10 to 150 with an increment of 10 in each iteration and max_depth of Random Forest Tree was varied from 2 to 20 with an increment of 1 in each iteration. Variables used to estimate the ideal parameters for regression tasks were mean square error (MSE) and variance of Linear Regression algorithm. We selected those parameters that gave the least MSE value ans large variance value. Variables used to estimate the ideal parameters for classification tasks was accuracy of the Random Forest Tree algorithm. Once the parameters were fixed we build the model for each subtask and used it to predict the values for test data. Development data was used for hyper-parameter tuning while training data was used for building Doc2Vec model.

The ideal parameters obtained after hyper-parameter tuning for each subtask for English is consolidated in Table 1, Arabic is consolidated in Table 2 and Spanish is consolidated in Table 3. The control parameter values obtained for the optimum parameters which in turn are used to build the model is consolidated in Table 4 for task 1 Table 5 for task 3 Table 6 for task 2 Table 7 for task 4 Table 8 for task 5

4   Results and Discussion

The output of test data obtained by our model was compared with golden label available with SemEval2018 and the following results were ob-

Variable	English	Arabic	Spanish
MSE	0.03	0.03	0.04
Variance	0.03	0.03	0.08

Table 4: Control variable value for optimum parameters for Task 1.

Variable	English	Arabic	Spanish
Accuracy	0.4883	0.4039	0.4047

Table 5: Control variable value for optimum parameters for Task 2.

Variable	English	Arabic	Spanish
MSE	0.03	0.04	0.05
Variance	0.06	0.06	0.02

Table 6: Control variable value for optimum parameters for Task 3.

Variable	English	Arabic	Spanish
Accuracy	0.28	0.27	0.28

Table 7: Control variable value for optimum parameters for Task 4.

Variable	English	Arabic	Spanish
Accuracy	0.9525	0.9550	0.9401

Table 8: Control variable value for optimum parameters for Task 5.

tained. The metric used for evaluation is macro average F-Score and Pearson correlation coefficient. In macro average method precision and recall on different sets of system is averaged. The harmonic mean of precision and recall will give us the F-Score. Such an obtained value is called macro F-Score. In Pearson correlation coefficient the linear correlation between two variables $X1$ and $X2$ is calculated. For emotion intensity regression task, emotion intensity ordinal classification task, sentiment intensity regression task and sentiment analysis ordinal classification task Pearson correlation coefficient is used as metric while for emotion classification task macro average F-Score is used as metric.

For emotion intensity regression task on English tweets our model obtained an accuracy of 20.0% when compared with the golden label under Pearson correlation coefficient. When compared for individual emotions we got an accuracy of 21.6%, 21.0%, 11.2%, 26.2% for anger, fear, joy and sadness respectively. On Arabic tweets our model obtained an accuracy of 22.1% when compared with the golden label under Pearson correlation coefficient. When compared for individual emotions we got an accuracy of -0.3%, 17.9%, 31.5%, 39.3% for anger, fear, joy and sadness respectively. On Spanish tweets our model obtained an accuracy of 21.8% when compared with the golden label under Pearson correlation coefficient. When compared for individual emotions we got an accuracy of 24.1%, 21.4%, 14.2%, 27.3% for anger, fear, joy and sadness respectively.

For emotion intensity ordinal classification task on English tweets our model obtained an accuracy of 3.7% when compared with the golden label under Pearson correlation coefficient. When compared for individual emotions we got an accuracy of 2.6%, -0.2%, 6.7%, 5.5% for anger, fear, joy and sadness respectively. On Arabic tweets our model obtained an accuracy of 13.8% when compared with the golden label under Pearson correlation coefficient. When compared for individual emotions we got an accuracy of -6.2%, 5.0%, 28.7%, 27.5% for anger, fear, joy and sadness respectively. On Spanish tweets our model obtained an accuracy of 2.5% when compared with the golden label under Pearson correlation coefficient. When compared for individual emotions we got an accuracy of 2.0%, -5.2%, 6.3%, 6.8% for anger, fear, joy and sadness respectively.

For sentiment intensity regression task on English tweets our model obtained an accuracy of 28.1% when compared with the golden label under Pearson correlation coefficient. On Arabic tweets our model obtained an accuracy of 47.0% when compared with the golden label under Pearson correlation coefficient. On Spanish tweets our model obtained an accuracy of 19.3% when compared with the golden label under Pearson correlation coefficient.

For sentiment analysis ordinal classification task on English tweets our model obtained an accuracy of 12.5% when compared with the golden label under Pearson correlation coefficient. On Arabic tweets our model obtained an accuracy of 38.3% when compared with the golden label under Pearson correlation coefficient. On Spanish tweets our model obtained an accuracy of 12.7% when compared with the golden label under Pearson correlation coefficient.

For emotion classification task on English tweets our model obtained an accuracy of 14.8% when compared with the golden label under macro average F-Score. On Arabic tweets our model obtained an accuracy of 25.0% when compared with the golden label under macro average F-Score. On Spanish tweets our model obtained an accuracy of 6.0% when compared with the golden label under macro average F-Score.

5 Conclusion

The task was to analyze the 'Affects of Tweets' from tweets comprising of different emotions from three different languages. We used distributed representation (Doc2Vec) for creating feature vector which was passed as the input to machine learning algorithm such as Linear Regression for regression tasks and Random Forest Tree for classification tasks. The model was fixed after doing hyperparameter tuning and the results obtained using the model on test data was evaluated using golden label by SemEval2018. The results obtained with the model after comparing with the golden label using some evaluation metric have been discussed in the paper.

References

Felipe Bravo-Marquez, Marcelo Mendoza, and Barbara Poblete. 2014. Meta-level sentiment models for big social data analysis. *Knowledge-Based Systems*, 69:86–99.

Barathi Ganesh H. B., M. Anand Kumar, and K. P. Soman. 2016a. Amrita_CEN at SemEval-2016 Task 1: Semantic relation from word embeddings in higher dimension. In *Proceedings of the 10th International Workshop on Semantic Evaluation (SemEval-2016)*, pages 706–711.

Barathi Ganesh H. B., M. Anand Kumar, and K. P. Soman. 2016b. Statistical semantics in context space : Amrita_CEN@Author Profiling. In *CEUR Workshop Proceedings, 1609*, pages 881–889.

Barathi Ganesh H. B., M. Anand Kumar, and K. P. Soman. 2018. From vector space models to vector space models of semantics. In *Lecture Notes in Computer Science (including subseries Lecture Notes in Artificial Intelligence and Lecture Notes in Bioinformatics), 10478 LNCS*, pages 50–60. Springer.

Quoc Le and Tomas Mikolov. 2014. Distributed representations of sentences and documents. In *International Conference on Machine Learning*, pages 1188–1196.

Saif M. Mohammad, Felipe Bravo-Marquez, Mohammad Salameh, and Svetlana Kiritchenko. 2018. SemEval-2018 Task 1: Affect in tweets. In *Proceedings of International Workshop on Semantic Evaluation (SemEval-2018)*, New Orleans, LA, USA.

Saif M. Mohammad and Svetlana Kiritchenko. 2018. Understanding emotions: A dataset of tweets to study interactions between affect categories. In *Proceedings of the 11th Edition of the Language Resources and Evaluation Conference (LREC-2018)*, Miyazaki, Japan.

Saif M Mohammad, Svetlana Kiritchenko, and Xiaodan Zhu. 2013. Nrc-canada: Building the state-of-the-art in sentiment analysis of tweets. *arXiv preprint arXiv:1308.6242*.

SSN MLRG1 at SemEval-2018 Task 1: Emotion and Sentiment Intensity Detection Using Rule Based Feature Selection

Angel Deborah S, Rajalakshmi S, S Milton Rajendram, Mirnalinee T T
SSN College of Engineering
Chennai 603 110, Tamil Nadu, India
`angeldeborahs@ssn.edu.in, rajalakshmis@ssn.edu.in,`
`miltonrs@ssn.edu.in, mirnalineett@ssn.edu.in`

Abstract

The system developed by the SSN MLRG1 team for Semeval-2018 task 1 on affect in tweets uses rule based feature selection and one-hot encoding to generate the input feature vector. Multilayer Perceptron was used to build the model for emotion intensity ordinal classification, sentiment analysis ordinal classification and emotion classfication subtasks. Support Vector Regression was used to build the model for emotion intensity regression and sentiment intensity regression subtasks.

1 Introduction

Twitter is a huge microblogging service with more than 500 million tweets per day from different locations of the world and in different languages (Saif and Felipe, 2017). Tweets are often used to convey ones emotions, opinions towards products, and stance over issues (Nabil et al., 2016). Automatically detecting emotion intensities in tweets has several applications, including commerce (Jansen et al., 2009), crisis management (Verma et al., 2011), tracking brand and product perception, tracking support for issues and policies, and tracking public health and well-being (Chew and Eysenbach, 2010). The task is challenging because of the informal writing style, the semantic diversity of content as well as the "unconventional" grammar. These challenges in building a classification model and regression model can be handled by using proper approaches to feature generation and machine learning.

There are several machine learning techniques that can be used for sentiment intensity prediction or emotion intensity prediction. Some of the approaches inlclude Artificial Neural Network (ANN) (Sudipta et al., 2017), Random Forests, Support Vector Machine (SVM), Naive Bayes (NB) (Tabari et al., 2017), Multi-Kernel Gaussian

Process (MKGP) (Angel Deborah et al., 2017a,b), AdaBoost Regressor (ABR), Bagging Regressor (BR)(Jiang et al., 2017) and Deep Learning (DL)(Pivovarova et al., 2017).

2 Multi-Layer Perceptron

A Multilayer Perceptron (MLP) as shown in Figure 1 is a feed-forward Neural Network model that maps input data sets onto appropriate output sets. An MLP has many layers of nodes in a directed graph, with each layer connected to the next layer. A neuron is a processing element with activation

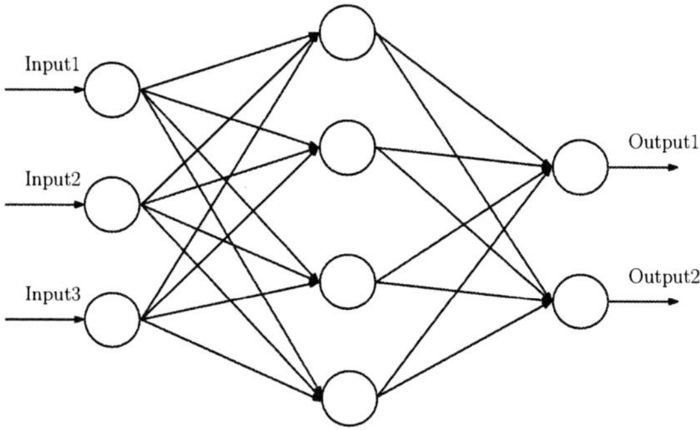

Figure 1: Multi-Layer Perceptron.

function (in the input layer the activation function is not applied). The output layer has as many nuerons as the number of class labels in the problem. Each connection has a weight assigned to it. Output of each neuron is calculated by applying the activation function on the weighted sum of the inputs. Linear, sigmoid, tanh, elu, softplus, softmax and relu are some of the commonly used activation functions. The supervised learning problem of the MLP can be solved with the backpropagation algorithm (Haykin, 1998). The algorithm consists of two steps. In the forward pass, the predicted outputs are calculated for the given inputs . In the backward pass, partial derivatives

Proceedings of the 12th International Workshop on Semantic Evaluation (SemEval-2018), pages 324–328
New Orleans, Louisiana, June 5–6, 2018. ©2018 Association for Computational Linguistics

of the cost function with respect to the weight parameters are propagated back through the network. The chain rule of differentiation gives very similar computational rules for the backward pass as the ones for the forward pass. The network weights can then be adapted using any gradient-based optimisation algorithm.

MLP was used in implementing for the following subtasks:

1. **EI-oc** (an emotion intensity ordinal classification task): Given a tweet and an emotion E, classify the tweet into one of four ordinal intensity classes of E that best represents the mental state of the tweeter.

2. **V-oc** (a sentiment analysis, ordinal classification task): Given a tweet, classify it into one of seven ordinal classes, corresponding to various levels of positive and negative sentiment intensity, that best represents the mental state of the tweeter.

3. **E-c** (an emotion classification task): Given a tweet, classify it as neutral or no emotion or as one, or more, of eleven given emotions that best represent the mental state of the tweeter.

3   Support Vector Regression

Support Vector Machines (SVM) are characterized by usage of kernels, absence of local minima, sparseness of the solution and capacity control obtained by acting on the margin or on number of support vectors, etc. As in classification, support vector regression (SVR) is characterized by the use of kernels, sparse solution, and Vapnik-Chervonenkis control of the margin and the number of support vectors. Although less popular than SVM, SVR has been proven to be an effective tool in real-value function estimation (Awad and Khanna, 2015). The idea of SVR is based on the computation of a linear regression function in a high dimensional feature space where the input data are mapped via a non-linear function. It contains all the main features that characterize maximum margin algorithm: a non-linear function is learned by a linear learning machine mapping into high dimensional kernel-induced feature space. The capacity of the system is controlled by parameters that do not depend on the dimensionality of feature space. Instead of minimizing the observed training error, Support Vector Regression (SVR) attempts to minimize the generalization error bound so as to achieve generalization performance.

SVR was used in implementing for the following subtasks:

1. **EI-reg** (an emotion intensity regression task): Given a tweet and an emotion E, determine the intensity of E that best represents the mental state of the tweeter, a real-valued score between 0 (least E) and 1 (most E).

2. **V-reg** (a sentiment intensity regression task): Given a tweet, determine the intensity of sentiment or valence (V) that best represents the mental state of the tweeter, a real-valued score between 0 (most negative) and 1 (most positive).

4   System Overview

The system consists of the following modules: data extraction, preprocessing, rule based feature selection, feature vector generation and building the model – Multilayer Perceptron model for clasification subtasks and Support Vector Regression for regression subtasks. The algorithm for preprocessing of the data is outlined below:

Algorithm: Data extraction and Preprocessing.
Input: Input dataset.
Output: Tokenized words and their parts of speech.
begin

1. Separate labels and sentences
2. Perform tokenization using `word_tokenize`, the function for tokenizing in the NLTK toolkit.
3. Perform Parts of Speech tagging using `pos_tag` function from the NLTK toolkit.
4. Return the tokenized words and their parts of speech as inputs to rule based feature selection.

end

The algorithm for rule based feature selection and feature vector generation is outlined below:
Algorithm: Rule based feature selection and feature vector generation.
Input: Tokenized words and their parts of speech.
Output: Feature vector.
begin

For each of the tokenized words, falling under one of the categories listed in Table 1, do the following steps.

1. Lemmatize the word using `WordNet Lemmatizer` from the NLTK toolkit.
2. Insert the lemmatized word into the dictio-

nary.

3. Represent each sentence as a feature vector using one-hot encoding by looking up the dictionary.

4. Return the feature vector generated as the input to build the model.

end

Abbreviation	Parts of Speech
VB	verb, base form
VBZ	verb, 3rd person sing. present
VBP	verb, non 3rd sing. present
VBD	verb, past tense
VBG	verb, gerund/present participle
VBN	verb, past participle
JJ	adjective
JJR	adjective, comparative
JJS	adjective, superlative
RB	adverb, very
RBR	adverb, comparative
RBS	adverb, superlative
NN	noun, singular
NNP	proper noun, singular
NNS	noun, plural
NNPS	proper noun, plural

Table 1: Parts of speech categories.

The Multi-Layer Perceptron (MLP) model is built by the following algorithm.

Algorithm: Build a Multi-Layer Perceptron model.

Input: Feature vectors and actual output labels.

Output: Learned MLP model.

begin

1. Represent feature vectors as `XTrain` and actual output label as `YTrain`.

2. Build the initial classification model with two hidden layers and the output layer, using `relu` and `softmax` activation functions, respectively.

3. Optimize the classification model using `nadam` optimizer of `keras` package

4. Return the learned model.

end

The Support Vector Regression(SVR) model is bulit with the following algorithm.

Algorithm: Build a SVR model.

Input: Feature vectors and actual output labels.

Output: Learned SVR model.

begin

1. Represent feature vectors as `XTrain` and ac-

tual output label as `YTrain`.

2. Build the initial classification model using appropriate kernel function.

3. Optimize the model parameters using a heuristic approach.

4. Return the learned model.

end

5 Performance Evaluation

We evaluated the system only for English language. The results obtained using MLP and SVR for the subtasks are tabulated in Table 2 to Table 6. From Table 2 which shows the Pearson scores obtained for SVR, we can infer that SVR predicts joy better compared to anger, fear and sadness. Similarly, from Table 3 which shows the Pearson scores obtained for MLP, we observe that MLP model predicts joy better compared to anger, fear and sadness. The Pearson score for valence intensity regression and sentiment intensity ordinal classification are given in Table 4 and 5 respectively.

anger	fear	joy	sadness	macro averaged
0.490	0.490	0.502	0.461	0.486

Table 2: Pearson score for EI-reg (emotion intensity regression) using SVR.

anger	fear	joy	sadness	macro averaged
0.365	0.363	0.390	0.383	0.375

Table 3: Pearson score for EI-oc (emotion intensity ordinal classification) using MLP.

Pearson (all instances)	Pearson (gold in 0.5-1)
0.582	0.424

Table 4: Pearson score for V-reg (valence intensity regression) using SVR.

Pearson (all classes)	Pearson (some-emotion)
0.427	0.479

Table 5: Pearson score for V-oc (Sentiment intensity ordinal classification) using MLP.

The Pearson score r is calculated using the Equation 1.

$$r = \frac{\sum_{i=1}^{n}(Y_i - \bar{Y})(y_i - \bar{y})}{\sqrt{\sum_{i=1}^{n}(Y_i - \bar{Y})^2}\sqrt{\sum_{i=1}^{n}(y_i - \bar{y})^2}} \quad (1)$$

Accuracy	Micro-avg F1	Macro-avg F1
0.468	0.595	0.476

Table 6: Pearson score for E-c (multi-label emotion class) using MLP.

where Y is actual output and y is predicted output. The accuracy, micro-averaged F score and macro-avearged F score for emotion classification are given in Table 6. The metrics are defined from Equations 2 to 5.

$$\text{Accuracy} = \frac{1}{|T|} \sum_{t \in T} \frac{|G_t \cap P_t|}{|G_t \cup P_t|} \quad (2)$$

where G_t is the set of the gold labels for tweet t, P_t is the set of the predicted labels for tweet t, and T is the set of tweets.

$$\text{Micro-avearge } F = \frac{2 \times \text{micro-}P \times \text{micro-}R}{\text{micro-}P \times \text{micro-}R} \quad (3)$$

where micro-P is micro-averaged precision and micro-R is micro-averaged recall

$$F = \frac{2 \times P_e \times R_e}{P_e \times R_e} \quad (4)$$

$$\text{Macro-average } F = \frac{1}{|E|} \sum_{e \in E} F_e \quad (5)$$

where P_e is precision, R_e is recall and E is the given set of eleven emotions.

6 Conclusion

We have presented the results of using MultiLayer Perceptron for emotion intensity ordinal classification, sentiment analysis ordinal classification and emotion classification. We built a basic MLP, which has an input layer, two hidden layers with 128 and 64 neurons, and an output layer with as many neurons as the number of class labels. We have used nadam optimizer with learning rate as 0.01. We have also presented the results of using Support Vector Regression for emotion intenisty and sentiment intensity regression. It is observed that both MLP and SVR predict joy more accurately when compared to anger, fear and sadness. We analyzed the feature vectors generated for various emotions. Feature vectors generated for joy helps to achieve better results than for other emotions. We used rule based feature selection and one-hot encoding to generate input feature vectors for buliding the models. The results obtained can be enhanced by using different feature selection approaches and incorporating sentiment lexicons.

References

S Angel Deborah, S Milton Rajendram, and T T Mirnalinee. 2017a. Ssn mlrg1 at semeval-2017 task 4: Sentiment analysis in twitter using multi-kernel gaussian process classifier. In *Proceedings the 11th International Workshop on Semantic Evaluation (SemEval-2017)*, pages 709–712. ACL,Vancouver, Canada.

S Angel Deborah, S Milton Rajendram, and T T Mirnalinee. 2017b. Ssn mlrg1 at semeval-2017 task 5: Fine-grained sentiment analysis using multiple kernel gaussian process regression model. In *Proceedings the 11th International Workshop on Semantic Evaluation (SemEval-2017)*, pages 823–826. ACL,Vancouver, Canada.

M Awad and R Khanna. 2015. *Support Vector Regression. In: Efficient Learning Machines.* Apress, Berkeley, CA.

C. Chew and G. Eysenbach. 2010. Pandemics in the age of twitter: content analysis of tweets during the 2009 h1n1 outbreak. *PloS ONE*, 5(11):1–13.

Simon Haykin. 1998. *Neural Networks – A Comprehensive Foundation.* Second Edition, Prentice-Hall, Englewood Cliffs, NJ.

B. J. Jansen, K. Sobel M. Zhang, and A. Chowdury. 2009. Twitter power: Tweets as electronic word of mouth. *Journal of the American Society for Information Science and Technology*, 60(11):2169–2188.

Mengxiao Jiang, Man Lan1, and Yuanbin Wu. 2017. Ecnu at semeval-2017 task 5: An ensemble of regression algorithms with effective features for fine-grained sentiment analysis in financial domain. In *Proceedings the 11th International Workshop on Semantic Evaluation (SemEval-2017)*, pages 888–893. ACL,Vancouver, Canada.

Mahmoud Nabil, Mohamed Aly, and Amir F. Atiya. 2016. Cufe at semeval-2016 task 4: A gated recurrent model for sentiment classification. In *Proceedings of SemEval-2016.ACL, Vancouver, Canada.*, pages 52–57.

Lidia Pivovarova, Llorenc Escoter, Arto Klami, and Roman Yangarber. 2017. Hcs at semeval-2017 task 5: Sentiment detection in business news using convolutional neural networks. In *Proceedings the 11th International Workshop on Semantic Evaluation (SemEval-2017)*, pages 842–846. ACL,Vancouver, Canada.

M. Mohammad Saif and Bravo-Marquez Felipe. 2017. Emotion intensities in tweets. In *Proceedings of sixth joint conference on lexical and computational semantics (*Sem). Vancouver, Canada.*, pages 65–77.

Kar Sudipta, Suraj Maharjan, and Thamar Solorio. 2017. Ritual-uh at semeval-2017 task 5: Sentiment analysis on financial data using neural networks. In *Proceedings the 11th International Workshop on Semantic Evaluation (SemEval-2017)*, pages 877–882. ACL,Vancouver, Canada.

Narges Tabari, Armin Seyeditabari, and Wlodek Zadrozny. 2017. Sentiheros at semeval-2017 task 5: An application of sentiment analysis on financial tweets. In *Proceedings the 11th International Workshop on Semantic Evaluation (SemEval-2017)*, pages 857–860. ACL,Vancouver, Canada.

S. Verma, S. Vieweg, W. J. Corvey, L. Palen, J. H. Martin, M. Palmer, A. Schram, and K. M. Anderson. 2011. Natural language processing to the rescue extracting situational awareness tweets during mass emergency. In *Proceedings of 5th International Conference on Web and Social Media*.

CENNLP at SemEval-2018 Task 1: Constrained Vector Space Model in Affects in Tweets

Naveen J R, Barathi Ganesh H. B., Anand Kumar M, Soman K P
Center for Computational Engineering and Networking (CEN)
Amrita School of Engineering, Coimbatore
Amrita Vishwa Vidyapeetham, India
`cb.en.p2cen16011@cb.students.amrita.edu,`
`barathiganesh.hb@gmail.com, m_anandkumar@cb.amrita.edu`

Abstract

This paper discusses on task 1, "Affect in Tweets" sharedtask, conducted in SemEval-2018. This task comprises of various sub-tasks, which required participants to analyse over different emotions and sentiments based on the provided tweet data and also measure the intensity of these emotions for subsequent subtasks. Our approach is to come up with a model for all the subtasks on count based representation and use machine learning techniques for regression and classification related tasks. In this work, we use bag of words technique for supervised text classification and regression. . Further, fine tuning on various parameters for the bag of word, representation model we acquired better scores over various other baseline models (Vinayan et al.) participated in the sharedtask.

1 Introduction

A huge portion of analysis in natural language processing try to find better understand and process various kinds of info in text. Day by day the development of social websites, blogging and the consummation of technologies gives vast amount text data on the internet, which opened a space to study peoples feeling, reviews, and emotion from their own written languages, called sentimental analysis. Sentimental analysis has so many attractions and has done so many research (Zhu et al., 2014) in this area.

Sentiment analysis remains a sequence of techniques, approaches, and tools about sensing and mining subjective info (such as opinion and attitudes) from language (Bravo-Marquez et al., 2014). Traditional approaches (Kiritchenko et al., 2014; Mohammad et al., 2013) are finding out the polarity of the positive, negative, neutral classification problem (Mohammad, 2018; Bravo-Marquez et al., 2015). Recent research in sentimental analysis (Mohammad and Kiritchenko, 2018) are done on the data-driven algorithm view point. But at the same time combination of good linguistic awareness data can increase the performance and insights about the task. We used machine learning techniques to build the model. Linear regression, random forest methods are used respectively for prediction and classification tasks. A mathematical system or an algorithm need some form of numeric representation to work with. The naive way of representing a word in vector form is one hot representation but it is a very ineffective way for representing a large corpus. In a more effective way, we need some semantic similarities (Soman et al., 2016) to nearby points, thus creating the representation bring beneficial info about the word actual meaning, called word embedding models that are categorized based on count and predictive word embedding models. Both embedding models at least some way share sematic meaning. We used here count based word embedding methods for inputting the word. In more specific, Feature representation is done based on the term-document matrix (TDM) and term frequency-inverse frequency (TFIDF) matrix. The optimum value of n-gram range, depth of classifier, mindf are obtained by hyper parameter tuning.

2 Corpus

Dataset provided by shared task was sourced from Twitter API by focusing emotion-correlated words. The tweets were annotated separately for 4 emotions namely anger, joy, fear and sadness. The data provided were annotated with best-worst scaling technique (Kiritchenko and Mohammad, 2016) that gave better annotation consistency and emotion intensity scores for tweets. There were 5 subtasks in task1 (Mohammad et al., 2018). For each sub-tasks, separate training and testing data

Proceedings of the 12th International Workshop on Semantic Evaluation (SemEval-2018), pages 329–333
New Orleans, Louisiana, June 5–6, 2018. ©2018 Association for Computational Linguistics

sets are given for Spanish, English, and Arabic. Subtasks 1 and 3 focused on emotion intensity and sentiment intensity tasks respectively which were categorized into regression tasks (EI-reg and V-reg). In that emotion intensity and sentimental intensity is a real-valued scale between 0 and 1, where 0 represents least and 1 represents the most intensity of the tweeters from written tweets. Rest of the subtasks EI-oc, V-oc, E-c were multi-class classifications problems that are emotion intensity ordinal classification, sentiment analysis ordinal classification, emotion classification subtasks respectively. For subtask 2(EI-oc) distinct training and testing, dataset are provided for anger, fear, joy, and sadness. Subtask 4(V-oc) gives 7 ordinal classes, according to different levels of positive and negative valence state of the tweeter. Table 1-2 shows various vocabulary sizes based on the different count and n-gram parameters, for 3 different languages.

(min,n-gram)	vocabulary size		
	English	Arabic	Spanish
(1,1)	23359	25144	15400
(2,1)	10677	9281	6022
(3,1)	6738	7067	4453
(1,2)	119782	83498	64306
(2,2)	41557	20143	18324
(3,2)	22669	16333	13405
(1,3)	250233	141916	126712
(2,3)	76696	29223	28581
(3,3)	40550	24810	21417
(1,4)	378870	196365	186213
(2,4)	109838	37527	36876
(3,4)	57970	32682	28418

Table 1: EI-reg vocabulary size with variation of parameters.

3 Background

3.1 TDM

TD is the most basic method of representation of a text used in NLP. In this technique, for every individual document present in a corpus, we take the raw count of the words present in that document over all the unique words present in the entire corpus as its representation (Larson, 2010). That is to say, a vocabulary is created using all the word in the entire corpus and for a single document representation, the count of the words are incremented in view of their occurrence only for that docu-

(min,n-gram)	vocabulary size		
	english	Arabic	Spanish
(1,1)	9019	12581	15400
(2,1)	2830	2928	2204
(3,1)	1761	1536	1291
(1,2)	38795	37013	29299
(2,2)	7157	3764	4626
(3,2)	4099	1754	2320
(1,3)	78139	60856	53978
(2,3)	10915	3922	5262
(3,3)	5670	1782	2454
(1,4)	117210	83021	186213
(2,4)	13209	4011	36876
(3,4)	6955	1799	28418

Table 2: V-reg vocabulary size with variation of parameters.

ment. The drawback of this method is that this creates a very spares matrix where only a few of the columns are accumulated with numbers whereas, the rest of the columns are all zeros, thus bringing to the term frequency method.

3.2 TF-IDF

One of the problems that occur due to the term document representation is that, it takes a raw count of all the words present in the document where most frequently occurring words like conjunction, preposition appear very often across most of the articles, thus not adding any significant importance to the individual article. On the other hand, seldom occurring words, like proper nouns give a more individual identification to the article. Thus, coming to a method where we take in the frequency of the words over the entire corpus, this method is termed as term-frequency(tf). In language processing technique a collection of commonly appearing words with apparently less significance to a document are called as 'stop words', these can be removed at pre-processing level. Whereas, more often than not a list of stop words is not a sophisticated approach to adjusting term frequency for commonly used words. Inverse document frequency (idf) is a technique (Ramos et al., 2003) wherein, less weight age is given to more commonly occurring words (not restricted to only stop words) and vice-verse for seldomly used words across the entire corpus.

$$idf_t = ln\left(\frac{N_{tot\ docs}}{n_{docs\ containing\ t}}\right)$$

Combining the two ideologies (*tf-idf*) brings, the rarity of the term intended to measure how important a word can be to the document in a collection (or corpus) of documents. it can be considered as a heuristic quantity. The term inverse document frequency for any given term is defined as

$$tf\text{-}idf_{t,d} = tf_{t,d} * idf_t$$

3.3 Linear Regression

Linear regression is a commonly used supervised learning approach for prediction. The key goal is to fit a best fit line between a dependent and independent variable so as to minimize the error sum of squares between the actual and predicted value using the model. The model for linear regression is usually fitted using least square approach, or by minimizing the error sum of squares between the actual and predicted value. In certain cases, the model can also be framed by adding a regularization term. The regularization term is added to avoid overfitting (François and Miltsakaki, 2012).

3.4 Random Forest

Random forest, an ensemble decision tree based classifier which averages various combination of trees created on arbitrary samples from the data set. A decision tree breakdown the data into minor sub-classes while instantaneously construe a tree using decision and leaf nodes. The category is embodied by leafs nodes. A decision node takes two or extra divisions with choices or leafs. Every tree in the RF is made on an arbitrary decent subclass of features present (Liaw et al., 2002) on the entire data. The RF algorithm medians trees to generate a system with short variance and insignificant trees are canceled out, left trees produce the output.

4 Methodology

The model will be effective based on how it is extracting meaningful information from raw text. The system is created with the help of scikit-learn library [1] which is a python based library very much useful for classification, regression, clustering, data preparation, dimensionality reduction etc.

[1] http://scikit-learn.org/stable/

The training, development and test data set are taken from SemEval18 website.

1. Importing training and cross-validation from the given data set

2. Removes all the stop words from data that are insignificant.

3. Create a bag of words model which is a simple numeric representation of piece of text that is easy to classify. We just count the frequency of each word in the piece of text and created a dictionary of them which is called tokenization process in NLP which is then passed to countvectorize object in scikit learn package to create a set of maximum features. We use fit transform method to model (Ganesh et al., 2016) the bag of words feature vector which are stored in an array.

4. Same tools and methods are followed for creating TDM matrix as mentioned in step 3

5. We created a classifier or prediction with the help of machine learning model. Here we used random forest classifiers consisting of one hundred trees. RF is a set of decision trees graphs that model all possibility of certain outcomes.

lang	Rep	min_df	n-gram	MSE	Var
Sp	TDM	1	3	0.04	0.19
Sp	TFIDF	1	2	**0.04**	**0.19**
Ara	TDM	1	3	0.03	0.04
Ara	TFIDF	1	2	**0.03**	**0.04**
En	TDM	1	3	0.04	-0.02
En	TFIDF	1	3	**0.03**	**0.09**

Table 3: EI-reg cross validation results.

lang	Rep	min_df	n-gram	depth of tree	acc
Sp	TDM	1	3	18	41.74
Sp	TFIDF	1	2	19	**42.62**
En	TDM	1	8	18	46.51
En	TFIDF	1	12	19	**46.58**
Ara	TDM	3	6	18	**35.09**
Ara	TFIDF	3	14	15	33.73

Table 4: EI-oc cross validation results.

Table 1-5 show the representation we adopted for making our model in each sub-tasks. Same

lang	Rep	min_df	n-gram	MSE	Var
Sp	TDM	1	2	0.03	0.33
Sp	TFIDF	1	2	0.03	**0.34**
English	TDM	1	3	0.04	0.25
En	TFIDF	1	2	0.04	**0.25**
Ara	TDM	1	2	0.03	**0.22**
Ara	TFIDF	2	3	0.03	0.21

Table 5: V-reg cross validation results.

lang	Rep	min_df	n-gram	depth	acc
Sp	TDM	3	9	17	30
SP	TFIDF	2	10	13	**31.4**
En	TDM	2	13	18	29.4
En	TFIDF	1	9	17	**29.4**
Ara	TDM	1	14	16	**26**
Ara	TFIDF	2	9	15	25.36

Table 6: V-oc cross validation results.

model is created 3 different languages, Spanish, English and Arabic. Both TDM and TFID feature matrix are tuned on the basis of accuracy and Fscore values. Accuracy shown in bold letter are used for making prediction and classification task model.

5   Result

The group of tasks is particularly focusing on automatic detection of the intensity of emotion (EI-reg) and sentiment (V-reg) of the tweeter. In this task, they have presented with the problem of classifying multi-classed emotion of tweets, such as EI-oc, V-oc, E-c . We have approached these tasks with a count based representation model, where every individual tweet is represented based on varied vocabulary size, and how these will perform for different category of subtasks over three different language dataset namely English, Spanish and Arabic. We base the model, considering in mind

lang	Rep	min_df	n-gram	depth of tree	accur
Sp	TDM	3	11	12	95.58
Sp	TFIDF	1	9	17	**95.58**
En	TDM	2	5	15	95.25
En	TFIDF	2	7	15	95.25
Ara	TDM	1	1	2	93.81
Ara	TFIDF	2	10	10	94.41

Table 7: E-c cross validation results.

that an algorithm should not be narrowed down to a certain problem. That is it should not be biased towards a particular problem overall, this inference is made on the fact that all subtasks under task1 are focused on understanding the effect of tweets from the same corpora. As all the subtasks under task1 follow a generic grid search models, which are varied over min-df, n-gram parameters. The EI-reg task was tuned on mean square error and varience for all 3 languages. EI-reg gave comparatively better accuracy in TF-IDF matrix than TDM matrix.so we used TF-IDF for creating feature matrix. This regression task gave macroavg between 32-44 percentage. English tweets gave least macro-avg value (32) and Spanish data gave high macro-avg value, among them angry got unwavering values in 3 languages.

Pearson (all instances)					
	macro -avg	anger	fear	joy	sadness
english	0.328	0.315	0.415	0.178	0.404
arabic	0.399	0.267	0.392	0.487	0.447
spanish	0.441	0.348	0.533	0.414	0.471

Table 8: EI-reg result.

V-reg is a regression task where sentiment intensity was predicted. Spanish and English used TF-IDF and Arabic corpora used term document matrix for feature input matrix. These feature are found out by grid search method. Arabic and Spanish data give 58 % prediction and English data give slight high result which is 62

	Pearson (all instances) Valence
English	0.622
Arabic	0.583
Spanish	0.580

Table 9: V-reg result.

Subtasks 2,4,5 are multi-label classification problems whose models are also generated by bag of words method. But the classification which was done by random forest did not yield expected result comparing to regression tasks.

6   Conclusion

Affect in tweets has been found out by the bag of words representation and classical machine learning algorithms. Random Forest and linear regression were used as machine learning tasks for predicting classification tasks and regression tasks respectively in which regression task gave fairly good results while classification task yield not so favorable results. TF-IDF seems to give better results for English and Spanish languages whereas TDM gave better results for the Arabic language. Emotion intensity and valence were captured by our model for the validation given data. Algorithms performed nearly same with TF-IDF and TDM but with slightly better results while using TF-IDF.

References

Felipe Bravo-Marquez, Eibe Frank, and Bernhard Pfahringer. 2015. Positive, negative, or neutral: Learning an expanded opinion lexicon from emoticon-annotated tweets. In *IJCAI*, pages 1229–1235.

Felipe Bravo-Marquez, Marcelo Mendoza, and Barbara Poblete. 2014. Meta-level sentiment models for big social data analysis. *Knowledge-Based Systems*, 69:86–99.

Thomas François and Eleni Miltsakaki. 2012. Do nlp and machine learning improve traditional readability formulas? In *Proceedings of the First Workshop on Predicting and Improving Text Readability for target reader populations*, pages 49–57. Association for Computational Linguistics.

HB Barathi Ganesh, M Anand Kumar, and KP Soman. 2016. From vector space models to vector space models of semantics. In *Forum for Information Retrieval Evaluation*, pages 50–60. Springer.

Svetlana Kiritchenko and Saif M Mohammad. 2016. Sentiment composition of words with opposing polarities. In *Proceedings of the 2016 Conference of the North American Chapter of the Association for Computational Linguistics: Human Language Technologies*, pages 1102–1108.

Svetlana Kiritchenko, Xiaodan Zhu, and Saif M Mohammad. 2014. Sentiment analysis of short informal texts. *Journal of Artificial Intelligence Research*, 50:723–762.

Ray R Larson. 2010. Introduction to information retrieval.

Andy Liaw, Matthew Wiener, et al. 2002. Classification and regression by randomforest. *R news*, 2(3):18–22.

Saif M. Mohammad. 2018. Word affect intensities. In *Proceedings of the 11th Edition of the Language Resources and Evaluation Conference (LREC-2018)*, Miyazaki, Japan.

Saif M. Mohammad, Felipe Bravo-Marquez, Mohammad Salameh, and Svetlana Kiritchenko. 2018. Semeval-2018 Task 1: Affect in tweets. In *Proceedings of International Workshop on Semantic Evaluation (SemEval-2018)*, New Orleans, LA, USA.

Saif M. Mohammad and Svetlana Kiritchenko. 2018. Understanding emotions: A dataset of tweets to study interactions between affect categories. In *Proceedings of the 11th Edition of the Language Resources and Evaluation Conference (LREC-2018)*, Miyazaki, Japan.

Saif M Mohammad, Svetlana Kiritchenko, and Xiaodan Zhu. 2013. Nrc-canada: Building the state-of-the-art in sentiment analysis of tweets. *arXiv preprint arXiv:1308.6242*.

Juan Ramos et al. 2003. Using tf-idf to determine word relevance in document queries. In *Proceedings of the first instructional conference on machine learning*, volume 242, pages 133–142.

KP Soman et al. 2016. Amrita_cen at semeval-2016 task 1: Semantic relation from word embeddings in higher dimension. In *Proceedings of the 10th International Workshop on Semantic Evaluation (SemEval-2016)*, pages 706–711.

Vivek Vinayan, JR Naveen, NB Harikrishnan, M Anand Kumar, and KP Soman. Amritanlp@ panrusprofiling: Author profiling using machine learning techniques.

Xiaodan Zhu, Svetlana Kiritchenko, and Saif Mohammad. 2014. Nrc-canada-2014: Recent improvements in the sentiment analysis of tweets. In *Proceedings of the 8th international workshop on semantic evaluation (SemEval 2014)*, pages 443–447.

TeamCEN at SemEval-2018 Task 1: Global Vectors Representation in Emotion Detection

Anon George, Barathi Ganesh HB, Anand Kumar M and Soman KP
Center for Computational Engineering and Networking (CEN)
Amrita School of Engineering, Coimbatore
Amrita Vishwa Vidyapeetham, India
anongeorge007@gmail.com, barathiganesh.hb@gmail.com

Abstract

Emotions are a way of expressing human sentiments. In the modern era, social media is a platform where we convey our emotions. These emotions can be joy, anger, sadness and fear. Understanding the emotions from the written sentences is an interesting part in knowing about the writer. In the amount of digital language shared through social media, a considerable amount of data reflects the sentiment or emotion towards some product, person and organization. Since these texts are from users with diverse social aspects, these texts can be used to enrich the application related to the business intelligence. More than the sentiment, identification of intensity of the sentiment will enrich the performance of the end application. In this paper we experimented the intensity prediction as a text classification problem that evaluates the distributed representation text using aggregated sum and dimensionality reduction of the glove vectors of the words present in the respective texts.

1 Introduction

Emotion detection from text has been an important task in recent years since the development of Natural Language Processing. Finding the affect in tweet enlarges the business intelligence towards the consumer behaviour analysis, peoples likeness towards the person, organization and policies of the government.

Intensity of the sentiment present in the text can be predicted by performing a text classification by taking texts as the observations and their intensity classes or scores as a target labels. Representation is a key part in any text classification task which can affect the further feature extractions and predictions (Ganesh et al., 2016; Soman et al., 2016; B. et al., 2016). A bad representation of the word vector can make the further

predictions fruitless. Hence we use a meaningful representation of words, that is, global vectors (Glove) for the representation of words into vectors of a tweet. This paper explains the use of global vectors representation for representing the words in a tweet and their further processing using machine learning techniques for classification and regression tasks. SemEval-2018 Task 1 provided the twitter corpus for classification and regression tasks for the emotion detection.

After representing the words in the tweets, the vector for tweets is obtained by computing the aggregated sum and dimensionality reduction. The final tweet vectors are used for further classification and regression.

2 Global Vectors

Global Vectors (GloVe) creates word vectors and it is an unsupervised machine learning technique(Pennington et al., 2014). Unlike word2vec representations like skip-gram and continuous bag of words (CBOW), word-word co occurrence statics is taken for the vector representation. It also retains the relations between words and gives a better feature extraction. The vectors represented in space gives more meanings than the traditional methods. global matrix factorization methods and local context window methods, such as the skip-gram model (Mikolov et al., 2013) is the main two types of vector representations. The word-word co occurrence count on the whole set of words are used for training and hence it captures more information.

3 Datasets

Dataset consists of tweets from three languages that are English, Spanish and Arabic. These are mainly focused on the emotions contained in it. These are annotated for the different emotions

Proceedings of the 12th International Workshop on Semantic Evaluation (SemEval-2018), pages 334–338
New Orleans, Louisiana, June 5–6, 2018. ©2018 Association for Computational Linguistics

such as joy, fear, anger and sadness. Separate datasets are provided for each emotions. The classification tasks consists of annotations marked as different intensity values for each emotion. They also contains the value corresponding to how much emotion value can be inferred from the tweets. For the regression tasks, the values between 0 and 1 are provided along with it. The value 0 means no information can be inferred and 1 means maximum information can be inferred. Sub-tasks EI-oc, V-oc, E-c are multi-class classification problems. EI-reg and V-reg are regression problems.EI-reg and EI-oc are emotion intensity tasks and V-reg is a sentiment intensity task. V-oc is a sentimental analysis task and E-c is a emotion classification task. (Mohammad and Kiritchenko, 2018)

4 Methodology

Pre-trained model of GloVe with 100 dimensions computed from 27 billion tokens and 2 billion tweets from the twitter is used in this experiment [1]. From the tweet datasets, the words are taken and checked if it is present in the downloaded GloVe model. If it is present then the vector representation corresponding to that word is taken and added to the model. After obtaining the vector representation for all the words in a tweet, the vector representation for each tweet is made after pre-processing steps like unimportant symbols and space removal. The representation for a tweet is made by writing the word vector as columns of a matrix concatenated till the tweet ends. This matrix is reduced into a single vector by two methods:

- SUM: Taking the sum of each rows and making it a new vector. This is an easy method which has less computation but the disadvantage includes the loss of word order in a tweet.

- SVD: Singular Value Decomposition is a decomposition method widely used for reducing the dimension of matrices. Here the sentence matrix is reduced to a rank one matrix by taking only the most important singular value. This is then used to take the important vector from the matrix which can be the most information containing (Golub and Reinsch, 1970). The tweet matrix is decomposed 3

parts using SVD. The most important singular value occurs in the first value of the diagonal matrix. A new vector is formed by using only one singular value from the SVD. Reducing the dimension using SVD preserves the important spread of data rather than simple summing operations of columns.

$$A = U \sum V^T \tag{1}$$

These vectors are used as the input for the different machine learning techniques. A part of the training data is split into training and validation data and is given to learning methods like Random Forest and Support Vector Machine (SVM). These methods will learn and give predictions about the classification or regression task that is assigned. Experiments are done to find out which hyper parameters give the better value for the validation accuracy. These are stored and used for predicting the new unseen data from the test set.

4.1 Random Forest

Random Forest is a powerful and popular machine learning algorithm capable of performing both regression and classification tasks. This algorithm creates a number of decision trees. When the number of these decision trees are more , the predictions will have more robustness and accuracy. Random Forest consists of multiple trees to classify a new object based on attributes. A classification is given by each tree and the tree votes for that class are saved. Choice is made for the classification by taking the most votes for consideration. It can handle the missing values and can maintain accuracy for the missing data. It can also work on large datasets which are high dimensional. It is not that good at regression like it does for the classification tasks. The control over the model is less as there are less parameters to tune.

Test features are passed through the rules of each randomly created trees for the predictions. Each tree will be predicting an output and the voting is done for the prediction to get the highest vote for a particular class of prediction. This is called majority voting. It is called ensemble machine learning algorithm. Divide and conquer approach is used for the improvement of performance. Each classifier in this group may be weak learner, but when they come together, it acts as a strong learner (Liaw et al., 2002).

---

[1]https://nlp.stanford.edu/projects/glove/

4.2 Support Vector Machine (SVM)

SVM is used to classify different classes in a dataset. It draws a decision boundary after looking at the extreme data points in a dataset. This boundary is called the hyper-plane which has one dimension less than the dimension of the data points. It is drawn near the extreme points of the dataset. SVM is a popular algorithm which segregates the different classes of data points in a dataset. If the decision boundary is drawn without making it optimized, then the further classifications will have less accuracy on new data. Support Vectors are the data points that are closer to the other classes and they are the ones pushing the boundary farther to make better predictions. This algorithm says that only those support vectors or the margins are needed for the further classifications and the other data points are ignored. This is because the margin is drawn by considering the extreme case in a class and all the other points can easily be classified with that prior knowledge.

SVMs can also be used in higher dimensional datasets and the data points will be called as vectors and they will have their coordinates lying inside the space of data. For the cases in which our function is not linearly separable, our data should be transformed in to a higher dimension using a function. Data points in higher dimensions are computationally complex for predictions. Kernel trick can be used to reduce this computational cost. A kernel function or a kernel trick is a function that takes the input vectors from the original vector space and returns the dot product of the vectors in the features in the feature space. To map every point into a higher dimensional space, dot product between two vectors can be applied using some transformation. Transformation on non-linear space into linear space is possible using that (Suykens and Vandewalle, 1999). Common kernel types are,

1. Linear Kernel

2. Polynomial Kernel

3. Radial Basis Function (RBF) Kernel

Table 1 shows the kernel functions of different kernel. Here x and y are the data points and the kernel function is found using the equations corresponding to it. d is the dimension of the space and γ is a hyper parameter. To get better performance using any kernel, parameter tuning is required. SVMs

Kernel Name	Kernel Function
Linear Kernel	$k(x,y) = x \times y$
Polynomial Kernel	$k(x,y) = (x \times y + 1)^d$
RBF Kernel	$k(x,y) = e^{-\gamma \|x-y\|^2}$

Table 1: Kenel Functions

are effective in higher dimensions and it is possible to add custom kernels to it making it adaptive. It performs poor when the number of features are greater than the number of samples.

We have reported the observations made using the linear and RBF kernel.

5 Results and Observation

Mean Squared Error (MSE) is noted for all the regression tasks and accuracy is noted for all the classification tasks. MSE near the value 0 is always better and accuracy value can be a maximum of 100%. Accuracy measures are in percentage. Validation scores for the test data provided is measured and reported for observations.

Using the SVD method always gave slightly better result compared to the SUM method. From this we can understand that the the reduction of a matrix in to vector should be done with SVD instead of SUM method. Scores for the language English gave better results compared to Spanish and Arabic. This can be due to the use of pretrained GloVe vectors which was trained on more English data.

Table 2 has MSE for validation set in EI-reg (emotion intensity regression). For English, Random Forest gave slightly better results than the other two SVM methods. Random Forest and SVM with RBF kernel were performing nearly same for the Spanish and Arabic datasets.

Table 3 has Accuracy of validation set in EI-oc (emotion intensity ord.class.). Random Forest Classifier was performing better than the other two classifiers for all the three languages. English language showed better accuracy than the other two languages and Arabic showed least accuracy.

Table 4 has MSE for validation set in V-reg (valence intensity regression). All the three regressors were performing in a similar way for English wereas Random Forest and the SVM with RBF kernel performed better for the other languages.

Table 5 contains Accuracy for validation set in V-oc (valence ord.class.). Random Forest was performing better for all the classification tasks

	Random Forest		SVM (Linear)		SVM (RBF)	
	SUM	SVD	SUM	SVD	SUM	SVD
English	0.03	0.02	0.03	0.03	0.04	0.03
Spanish	0.04	0.03	0.05	0.05	0.04	0.03
Arabic	0.03	0.02	0.03	0.03	0.03	0.02

Table 2: Mean Squared Error for validation set in EI-reg (emotion intensity regression)

	Random Forest		SVM (Linear)		SVM (RBF)	
	SUM	SVD	SUM	SVD	SUM	SVD
English	45.42	47.31	43.36	45.28	42.55	44.45
Spanish	40.35	42.20	39.72	42.12	38.58	40.56
Arabic	28.74	31.05	26.34	28.03	25.06	26.98

Table 3: Accuracy for validation set in EI-oc (emotion intensity ord.class.)

	Random Forest		SVM (Linear)		SVM (RBF)	
	SUM	SVD	SUM	SVD	SUM	SVD
English	0.05	0.04	0.05	0.04	0.05	0.04
Spanish	0.04	0.03	0.04	0.04	0.04	0.03
Arabic	0.05	0.05	0.06	0.05	0.06	0.05

Table 4: Mean Squared Error for validation set in V-reg (valence intensity regression)

	Random Forest		SVM (Linear)		SVM (RBF)	
	SUM	SVD	SUM	SVD	SUM	SVD
English	26.05	28.66	22.49	25.04	22.01	23.54
Spanish	23.58	24.05	19.65	20.12	18.05	19.57
Arabic	20.28	22.34	13.04	13.64	12.50	13.62

Table 5: Accuracy for validation set in V-oc (valence ord.class.)

	Random Forest		SVM (Linear)		SVM (RBF)	
	SUM	SVD	SUM	SVD	SUM	SVD
English	95.43	95.56	95.14	95.68	94.56	94.66
Spanish	95.14	95.41	95.43	95.54	95.01	95.34
Arabic	93.84	93.91	93.84	94.02	92.12	92.31

Table 6: Accuracy for validation set in E-c (multi-label emotion class.)

	Pearson (all instances)				
	macro-avg	anger	fear	joy	sadness
English	0.077 (44)	0.062 (44)	0.076 (44)	0.079 (43)	0.090 (44)
Arabic	0.230 (10)	0.213 (10)	0.230 (10)	0.207 (11)	0.269 (11)
Spanish	0.131 (12)	0.184 (11)	0.117 (12)	0.143 (11)	0.078 (12)

Table 7: Published Results score for EI-reg where the number in brackets is the ranking

given. Accuracy for Arabic stayed down and English stayed up. Table 6 contains Accuracy for validation set in E-c (multi-label emotion class.). All the classifiers for all languages were performing nearly same for this task. English still remained on top where as SVD always gave a slight boost in accuracy like the previous cases.

The published results for all these are also tabulated. The algorithm did not give the score and accuracy that was giving on the validation sets.

Table 7 contains published Results score for EI-reg where the number in brackets is the ranking. The minimum value is 0 and maximum value is 1. Our algorithm has lower score but comparatively the sentiment "sadness" has slightly better score. Score of published results for EI-oc was not satisfactory and the score values were less. In published results score for V-reg, Valence score for Arabic language (0.319) was better than the other 2 languages and English had the lowest. For the published results score for V-oc, algorithm's performance was not satisfactory but the arabic language had better valence (0.163) than the other 2 languages. In the published results score for E-c, the accuracy for Spanish was slightly better compared to the English and Arabic languages.

6 Conclusion

Five different tasks with common framework is experimented to find out the affect in tweets in 3 different languages. From the scores and accuracy obtained from the validation data we can conclude that the Global Vector Representation gives good results for the sentiment analysis tasks. Using a pre-trained model for the GloVe made the task simpler and easy to use for vector representation. Reducing the tweet matrix into vector using SVD always gave better results than taking the column wise sum of the matrices. This shows the importance of the word order. Random Forest algorithms gave better results for the classification tasks were as the SVD algorithm with RBF kernel performed nearly well in the regression tasks. English language showed better scores in the validation data compared to other languages. From these observations, it can be noted that this approach performed satisfactorily better in the validation step and was able to get the semantic features from the tweets. Hence the future work will be focused more on the performance of the experimented methods.

References

Barathi Ganesh H. B., M. Anand Kumar, and K. P. Soman. 2016. Statistical semantics in context space : Amrita_cen@author profiling. In *CLEF*.

HB Barathi Ganesh, M Anand Kumar, and KP Soman. 2016. From vector space models to vector space models of semantics. In *Forum for Information Retrieval Evaluation*, pages 50–60. Springer.

Gene H Golub and Christian Reinsch. 1970. Singular value decomposition and least squares solutions. *Numerische mathematik*, 14(5):403–420.

Andy Liaw, Matthew Wiener, et al. 2002. Classification and regression by randomforest. *R news*, 2(3):18–22.

Tomas Mikolov, Ilya Sutskever, Kai Chen, Greg S Corrado, and Jeff Dean. 2013. Distributed representations of words and phrases and their compositionality. In *Advances in neural information processing systems*, pages 3111–3119.

Saif M. Mohammad and Svetlana Kiritchenko. 2018. Understanding emotions: A dataset of tweets to study interactions between affect categories. In *Proceedings of the 11th Edition of the Language Resources and Evaluation Conference*, Miyazaki, Japan.

Jeffrey Pennington, Richard Socher, and Christopher Manning. 2014. Glove: Global vectors for word representation. In *Proceedings of the 2014 conference on empirical methods in natural language processing (EMNLP)*, pages 1532–1543.

KP Soman et al. 2016. Amrita_cen at semeval-2016 task 1: Semantic relation from word embeddings in higher dimension. In *Proceedings of the 10th International Workshop on Semantic Evaluation (SemEval-2016)*, pages 706–711.

Johan AK Suykens and Joos Vandewalle. 1999. Least squares support vector machine classifiers. *Neural processing letters*, 9(3):293–300.

IIT Delhi at SemEval-2018 Task 1 : Emotion Intensity Prediction

Bhaskar Kotakonda
Undegraduate
IIT Delhi
ee1140448@iitd.ac.in

Prashanth Gowda
Undergraduate
IIT Delhi
ee1140470@iitd.ac.in

Brejesh Lall
Associate Professor
IIT Delhi
brejesh@ee.iitd.ac.in

Abstract

This paper discusses the experiments performed for predicting the emotion intensity in tweets using a generalized supervised learning approach. We extract 3 kind of features from each of the tweets - one denoting the sentiment and emotion metrics obtained from different sentiment lexicons, one denoting the semantic representation of the word using dense representations like Glove, Word2vec and finally the syntactic information through POS N-grams, Word clusters, etc. We provide a comparative analysis of the significance of each of these features individually and in combination tested over standard regressors available in scikit-learn. We apply an ensemble of these models to choose the best combination over cross validation.

Our resources and the details of implementation are publicly available at :

https://github.com/prashanth470/
affect-in-tweets

1 Introduction

In Natural Language Understanding, the field of sentiment analysis deals with the process of determining the polarity of a given text, such as positive, negative, neutral and mixed. In extension to this analysis, we have the emotion recognition task which deals with associating the text with predefined set of emotions like anger, fear, joy, etc. A general method of performing the emotion recognition task is to employ weak supervision models like emojis, hashtags and emoticons to mine emotion. Instead of using this discreet approach to emotion, continuous models that map text to an n - dimensional space with valence, arousal and dominance can be used.

Another interesting problem in the NLP space is the abundance of social media texts, especially twitter. Twitter is a micro-blogging site where people express themselves and react to content in real-time. An estimated 500 million tweets are generated on a daily basis. The peculiar nature of such micro-blogging sites is the form of expression through hashtags, emojis, slang and informal words etc. But analyzing this abundant information would help us to realize several insights about an event, person or organization.

It is with this motivation that the SemEval shared task on Emotion Intensity was conducted.(Mohammad et al., 2018) Given a tweet and an emotion (anger, fear, sadness, joy) the aim is to determine the intensity score that can be seen as an approximation to the intensity felt by the reader or expressed by the author. The paper is divided into 3 sections hereon - the second section talks about the system description, the third section on a comparative analysis of results and finally a discussion on the future scope.

2 System Description

The datasets for anger, joy, fear and sadness were created using a technique called the Best Worst Scaling.(Mohammad and Kiritchenko, 2016) These annotations lead to reliable fine grained intensity scores which can be used to imply the intensity or the degree of an emotion expressed. The detailed data collection information can be found in Mohammad et al.(Mohammad and Turney)

2.1 Pre Processing

This step includes modifying the raw tweets to a form that can be easier to process for the further steps. It has already been asserted that the nature of the text in question is peculiar as it is mined from social media. In addition to regular usage of words emoticons, user ids and URLs are common in social media. It is very important to note that

Proceedings of the 12th International Workshop on Semantic Evaluation (SemEval-2018), pages 339–344
New Orleans, Louisiana, June 5–6, 2018. ©2018 Association for Computational Linguistics

while the tweet is tokenized into words, the process is twitter-aware, or the splitting is done keeping in mind the utility of User IDs and URLs as separate entities.

We tried 2 kinds of tokenizers : tweetokenize and regular expressions using the regex expression matching in python. We demonstrate below the difference in tokenizing for each of these and why we chose tweetokenize as it was more tweet aware.

The sentence used is :
What are some good #funny #entertaining #interesting accounts I should follow ? My twitter is dry

1. **Regex Python**
   'what', 'are', 'some', 'good', 'funny', 'entertaining', 'interesting', 'accounts', 'i', 'should', 'follow', '?', 'my', 'twitter', 'is', 'dry'

2. **Tweetokenize**
   'What', 'are', 'some', 'good', '#funny', '#entertaining', '#interesting', 'accounts', 'I', 'should', 'follow', '?', 'My', 'twitter', 'is', 'dry'

2.2 Feature Extraction

The baseline feature made available is the **Affective Tweets** package, which includes a number of lexicon based and syntactic feature extraction modules. After a thorough analysis of various systems of NLP competitions from Kaggle, KD Nuggets and various other conferences, we narrowed down to 3 type of important features.

1. **Lexicon Based**
   Many of the tasks related to sentiment and emotion are using these features extensively (Mohammad and Kiritchenko, 2018). A lexicon is a dictionary of words with labels specifying their sentiments and scores to identify the intensity of text. Table 1 shows the different lexicons used, the scores they contribute and the size of the corpus. Using the above features selectively leads to a 135 dimensional feature vector, which as we observe is still relatively sparse with only a few non zero values.

2. **Semantic Based**
   To overcome limitations of using the sparse lexicon based features and to add the semantic meaning of the words, compactly represented low dimesional dense vector encodings called word embeddings are also included. Glove embeddings, which are 200 dimensional vectors trained on 2 billion corpus are integrated. Although these vectors accurately represent the significance of a word in a context, the sentence embeddings or the representation in a sequential manner is not focused on in this section. The sentence embedding is considered to be the average of the individual word embeddings of the sentence. The final represented sentence embedding is a 25 dimensional vector.

3. **Syntactic Based**
   Although the meaning of the individual words have been taken into account in the semantic based vectors, it is essential to encode certain other aspects of the word, like part of speech tags, brown clusters and word n grams.

The final feature vector is chosen based on the significance of each of the individual features, when input to regressors to maximize the pearson coefficient.

2.3 Regressors

Each of the above features have very little correlation between each other as they represent different aspects of the text. Hence the regressors such as Support Vectors Regression, AdaBoost, Random Forest Regressor and Bagging regressor, etc can be used effectively. The feature vectors are used without any kind of normalization.

2.4 Hyper Tuning

The sci-kit package enables an extensive grid search mechanism to find the optimum value of the various hyper parameters of a regressor. Figure 1 shows the different values of C and gamma taken by the regressor to maximize the cost function of pearson coefficient using 10 fold cross validation. It shows anger, fear, joy and sadness metrics in a clockwise manner. Table 2 also shows the parameter values of the SVR for different emotions.

The best combination of hyper parameters are denoted by the grey spot in the grid search for each of the emotions.

Affect Lexicon	Description	Corpus Details
NRC Hashtag Emotion	Positive and negative variables by aggregating the positive and negative word scores provided by this lexicon created with tweet annotated with emotional hashtags	**emotions**: anger, anticipation fear, joy, sadness, surprise, trust **size** : 16,862 unigrams **score** : 0 to infinite
Sentiment140	Aggregating positive and negative scores	**emotions** : anger, fear **size** : 45,255 unigrams **score** : -inf to +inf
NRC 10	Adds the emotion associations of the words matching the Twitter Specific expansion	**emotions** : +ve, -ve **size** : 62,468 unigrams **score** : -inf to +inf
SentiStrength	Weighted average of the sentiment distributions of the synsets for word occurring in multiple synsets	**emotions** : anger, anticipation, fear, joy, sadness, surprise, trust **size** : 14,000 words **score** : 0 to 1
NRC Emotion	Calculates a positive and a negative score by aggregating the word associations provided by a list of emoticons	**size** : 76,400 terms **score** : count

Table 1: Lexicons used for feature extraction.

Emotion	C	Gamma
Anger	100	1e-05
Fear	1.0	1e-04
Joy	1.0	1e-04
Sadness	10	1e-05

Table 2: Final Parameters for Support Vector System.

3   Results

Only the semantic and lexicon based features are seen to be having a positive affect on the pearson coefficient while the syntactic feaatures show almost no improvement. Hence, they are discarded from further analysis. The 10 fold cross validation shows best performance in the case of employing all the different lexicons available in concatenation with the average word embedding.

3.1   Experimental Results

Table 4 shows the performance of this feature vector when trained across various regressors. The gradient boosting with XGBOOST ensemble regressor is observed to give the best results. The spearman coefficient has been skipped in the analysis as it had the same insights offered by the pearson coefficient.

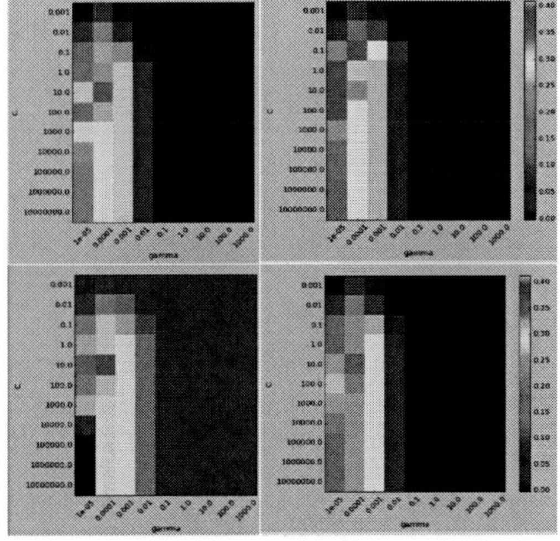

Figure 1: Hypertuning of SVR.

Emotion	Tweet	Predicted	Gold
Anger	'Pope fuming after police broke up drug-fuelled Vatican priest gay orgy' some headline.	0.539	0.545
	Lugubrious face, crestfallen eyes, forlorn heart and an agitated soul seeking serenity.	0.418	0.437
	I talked to an Asian yesterday.	0.374	0.000
	You are MINE, my baby, my headache, my love, my smile, my frown, my wrong, my right, my pain, my happiness, my everything.	0.433	0.172
Fear	i'm nervous	0.777	0.741
	The moment I joined BTS, I was nervous and amp; felt lost. I still have those feelings but whenever I do, the people who bring me back are you guys	0.713	0.732
	Considering I am 101% fine with getting tattoos, blood tests terrify me and I AM HAVING TO GET ONE AAAAAHHHH	0.435	0.845
	Every time I fart my dog jumps in fear hahahaha lol	0.610	0.242
Joy	Streetlights coming on. We can see stars! #amazing #SolarEclipse2017	0.681	0.672
	@SteveConteNYC lovely! :)	0.661	0.672
	My dads big day is only less than 2 weeks away!	0.456	0.844
	What do you call a camel with no humps? Humphrey! #joke #writerslife #WednesdayWisdom	0.286	0.6
Sadness	Do not linger too long near the howff or you risk the displeasure of a chuhaister with pubes more underwhelming than those of an aurochs.	0.427	0.417
	@rohandes Lets see how this goes. We falter in SL and this goes downhill. :(	0.377	0.385
	I wonder how many Lexas and Alexandrias there will be in 10 tears.	0.653	0.321
	Me at Start of Semester Expecting = A+ After Mids = B+ After Finals = Passing Marks. Thinking to quit	0.343	0.696

Table 3: Analysis of sample predictions in each emotion.

3.2 Limitations

The features that were chosen to represent the sentences, although having limitations in terms of missing context, perform significantly well in estimating the emotion. Table 3 analyzes the system's predictions in cases were the gold labels were close to the final value as well as the erroneous cases.

In cases where there are multiple instances of displaying emotion the model is very successful as seen in the first samples of every emotion. We also observe that the emoticons and punctuation are very well accounted for, like *@SteveConteNYC lovely! :)* and *@rohandes Lets see how this goes. We falter in SL and this goes downhill. :(.* It can also be said that the model is twitter aware as it often attributes an intensity based on the relative importance of the hashtag and emoticon.

There are broadly three cases where the system has trouble - one where there is very little context to decide an emotion, which is problematic even for the manual annotation, like *I talked to an Asian yesterday*. This should not be misunderstood with racial bias but merely a lack of training data. The second case is Sarcasm, like *Every time I fart my dog jumps in fear hahahaha lol*. While the lexicon based features attribute high intensity of fear due to direct usage of the word *fear*, it has to be understood that words such as *hahahaha, lol* have a diminishing effect on this sentiment. Finally, we

Regressor	**Emotion**	**Pearson**	**Pearson** (> 0.5)	**Spearman** (> 0.5)
SVR rbf	Anger	0.607	0.349	0.346
(gamma=0.001)	Fear	0.627	0.441	0.412
(C=1e-4)	Joy	0.415	0.328	0.331
	Sadness	**0.622**	0.483	0.493
Random forest	Anger	0.614	0.501	0.505
	Fear	0.556	0.411	0.389
	Joy	0.569	0.359	0.358
	Sadness	0.541	0.435	0.429
Adaboost	Anger	0.585	0.385	0.389
	Fear	0.612	0.502	0.483
	Joy	**0.638**	0.408	0.433
	Sadness	0.579	0.423	0.437
Gradient Boosting	Anger	**0.660**	0.506	0.516
	Fear	**0.677**	0.500	0.480
	Joy	0.622	0.380	0.393
	Sadness	0.606	0.497	0.506
Bagging	Anger	0.576	0.421	0.425
	Fear	0.590	0.459	0.429
	Joy	0.546	0.353	0.337
	Sadness	0.570	0.444	0.446

Table 4: Results over different regressors.

also see that in cases where there is no direct usage of the words from lexicon but merely the context of the preceding sentences that decide the emotion, like *Me at Start of Semester Expecting = A+ After Mids = B+ After Finals = Passing Marks. Thinking to quit MS.* This is quite expected due to the choice of features we employed.

4 Future Work

The main limitation of this approach is overlooking the importance of context and compositionality of the sentence, in addition to the semantic and syntactic attributes. This can be taken into account by using bi-directional LSTMs - long short term memory approach. LSTMs allow for learning sentence representations that account for context to be stored in memory over a longer distance through a mechanism of forgetting and memory at each stage, thus tackling the problem of vanishing gradient.(Olah)

Although Convolution Neural Networks have been discovered for image recognition tasks, recent research of (Kim, 2014) show exceptionally high accuracy of CNNs when trained on word embedding for language understanding tasks. The CNNs effectively appply filters of different sizes to images which can be understood as considering

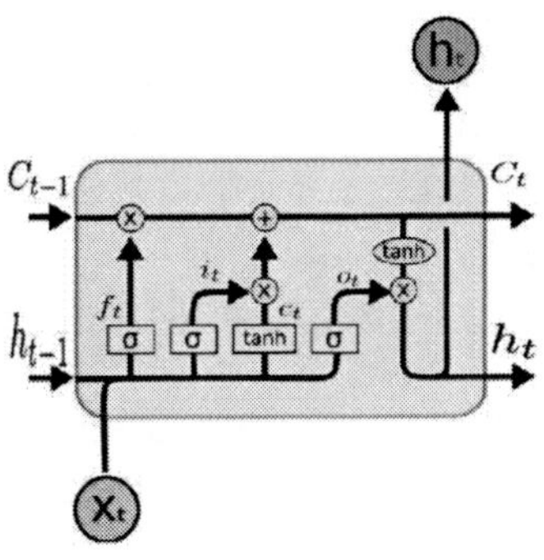

Figure 2: LSTM Model.

a n-gram featurizer and deciding on the most effective n-gram that contributes to the meaning of the tweet.

Acknowledgments

We thank our supervisor Dr.Brejesh Lall for guiding us through the process and the organizers of SemEval 2018 for providing us the opportunity to work on this task and creating datasets.

References

Yoon Kim. 2014. Convolutional neural networks for sentence classification. *CoRR*, abs/1408.5882.

Saif M. Mohammad, Felipe Bravo-Marquez, Mohammad Salameh, and Svetlana Kiritchenko. 2018. Semeval-2018 Task 1: Affect in tweets. In *Proceedings of International Workshop on Semantic Evaluation (SemEval-2018)*, New Orleans, LA, USA.

Saif M. Mohammad and Svetlana Kiritchenko. 2016. Capturing reliable fine-grained sentiment associations by crowdsourcing and bestworst scaling.

Saif M. Mohammad and Svetlana Kiritchenko. 2018. Understanding emotions: A dataset of tweets to study interactions between affect categories. In *Proceedings of the 11th Edition of the Language Resources and Evaluation Conference*, Miyazaki, Japan.

Saif M. Mohammad and Peter D. Turney. Crowdsourcing a word-emotion association lexicon. New Orleans, LA, USA.

Christopher Olah. Understanding lstm networks.

Mutux at SemEval-2018 Task 1: Exploring Impacts of Context Information On Emotion Detection

Pan Du
DIRO, University of Montreal
pandu@iro.umontreal.ca

Jian-Yun Nie
DIRO, University of Montreal
nie@iro.umontreal.ca

Abstract

This paper describes MuTuX, our system that is designed for task 1-5a, emotion classification analysis of tweets on SemEval2018[1]. The system aims at exploring the potential of context information of terms for emotion analysis. A Recurrent Neural Network is adopted to capture the context information of terms in tweets. Only term features and the sequential relations are used in our system. The result submitted ranks 16th out of 35 systems on the task of emotion detection in English-language tweets.

1 Introduction

Emotion analysis on social media is attracting more and more reserach interests (Strapparava and Mihalcea, 2008; Balahur et al., 2011; Agrawal and An, 2012; Wang et al., 2012; Hasan et al., 2014a; Canales and Martínez-Barco, 2014) from industry and academia. Commercial applications such as product recommendation, online retailing, and marketing are turning their interests from traditional sentiment analysis to emotion analysis as well. Emotion analysis is generally taken as a multi-lable classification problem. Given a piece of text, such as a tweet, it assigns several lables such as depressed, sad, angry and so on to it (Mohammad et al., 2018) based on the meaning contained in the text.

Techniques related to emotion detection can be divided into lexicon-based approaches (Valitutti, 2004; Strapparava and Mihalcea, 2008; Balahur et al., 2011) and machine learning approaches (Hasan et al., 2014b; Wang et al., 2012; Roberts et al., 2012; Suttles and Ide, 2013). Lexicon-based approaches leverage lexical resources to detect emotions, the resources can be keywords (Hasan et al., 2014a), WordNet-Affect (Valitutti,

---

[1] https://competitions.codalab.org/competitions/17751

2004), ontologies (Balahur et al., 2011) and so on. Machine learning based approaches (Balabantaray et al., 2012) generally take emotion detection as a classification problem using SVM, neural network (Abdul-Mageed and Ungar, 2017; Bravo-Marquez et al., 2016), naieve bayes, Decision Tree, KNN and so on, or using certain unsupervised techniques such as LSA (Deerwester et al., 1990; Wang and Zheng, 2013; Gill et al., 2008), pLSA, NMF to transform the feature space into a more reasonable one before conducting classification. The main challenges of emotion analysis of tweets are the following:

1. Informal languages used on social media are not always obeying formal grammar, which makes traditional grammatical features less reliable for detecting emotions on social media.

2. New words are frequently created on social media, making it difficult to understand their emotional meaning even for a human being.

To address the challenges above, we use recurrent neural network to make use of terms, sequential information, and contextual information simultaneously for emotion detection. We believe that contextual information can partly solve the new-term problem and grammar-breach problem. To use recurrent neural network, a pre-trained embedding is used as our initial input of each term.

2 External Resource

We only used one external resource in our analysis, which is a pre-trained word embedding (Mikolov et al., 2013) word2vec provided by Google. It is trained on a part of the Google News dataset (about 100 billion words) and it contains 300-dimensional vectors for 3 million words and phrases.

Proceedings of the 12th International Workshop on Semantic Evaluation (SemEval-2018), pages 345–349
New Orleans, Louisiana, June 5–6, 2018. ©2018 Association for Computational Linguistics

3 System Description

To explore the limit of term features with RNN for emotion detection, we did not use various features other than term embedding. The system could be improved by using features like emojis or emoticons. We will conduct further analysis afterwards by addressing problems in combining different feature space.

As for the system used for SemEval18 task 1, the main steps, features used in the model are described in this section.

3.1 Preprocessing

Since the method heavily depends on terms appear in the text, the corpus is carefully pre-processed as described below.

- **Normalization** Each word in each tweet is converted into lowercase. Non-linguistic content such as URLs, emojis, emoticons, user names are removed (some important features such as emojis and emoticons will be explored in the future).

- **Tokenization** Each tweet is split into a word sequence. No stemming is applied since some special word forms may convey more apparent emotions than its original form.

- **Stop-words Removing** NLTK[2] toolkits is leveraged to remove stop words from tweets. Some other meaningless terms such as single characters, digits, their compositions and so on, are also eliminated.

3.2 Embedding Usage

Word embeddings are a widely used semantic presentation of words for almost any neural network based text analysis approach. A vector of real numbers is used for a single word to represent its distributional semantics in the embedding space. Since the space is generated by the language model, words that are functional similar in certain language are close with each other in the embedding space, for example, "cat" and "dog" could be similar in the space.

In this system, a tweet is represented by concatenating embeddings of the words in it.

3.3 Our Approach

The system submitted is based on a recurrent neural network approache, GRU, to be specific.

[2]https://www.nltk.org/

3.3.1 The Basic Idea

Lexicons play the key role in lexicon-based approaches and bag-of-feature based machine learning approaches for emotion analysis. However, in addition to the emotion lexicons, we believe that linguistic characteristics may also contribute a lot to emotion analysis. For example, the context of the emotion lexicon such as negation could revert the emotion of the utterence if it is neglected. The sequence of the sentence terms also play an important role for understanding its meaning, hence important for uncovering the true emotions. Lack of newly created terms in vocabulary or grammatically incorrect utterances can also lead to poor performance of traditional emotion analysis approaches. By modeling long-term dependencies of terms inside a tweet, fusing the semantics of the terms and their contexts together with GRU, a recurrent neural network, we hope that above problems can be alleviated in the new space.

3.3.2 Problem Statement

We take emotion analysis as a multi-label classification problem in our system as usual. A tweet is represented as a sequence of terms

$$x_i = \{w_i^0, w_i^1, \cdots, w_i^M\} \tag{1}$$

where M is the length of the tweet x_i. Given a tweet x_i, the task aims at prediting the labels of it as y_i, where y_i is a d-dimensional Boolean vector $y_i \in B^d$, $d = 11$ in this case. Each dimension of vector y_{ij} indicates an emotion label of the 11 labels space *anger, anticipation, disgust, fear, joy, love, optimism, pessimism, sadness, suprise*, and *trust* respectively. For example $y_{i0} = 1$ means emotion of *anger* is detected in the tweet x_i, $y_{i9} = 0$ means emotion of *sadness* does not appear in the tweet.

3.3.3 The model architecture

The architecture of the model is shown in Figure 1. The model is composed of 3 layers. The input of the network is the pre-trained embedding of each term occurs in a tweet. The sequential term embeddings are then turned into a tweet level representation by a classical GRU, the output of GRU is directly inputed into a linear perceptron layer, and maps the tweet representation into class representation directly by this layer. The output of the linear perceptrons are then processed by a sigmoid function to get the final predictions.

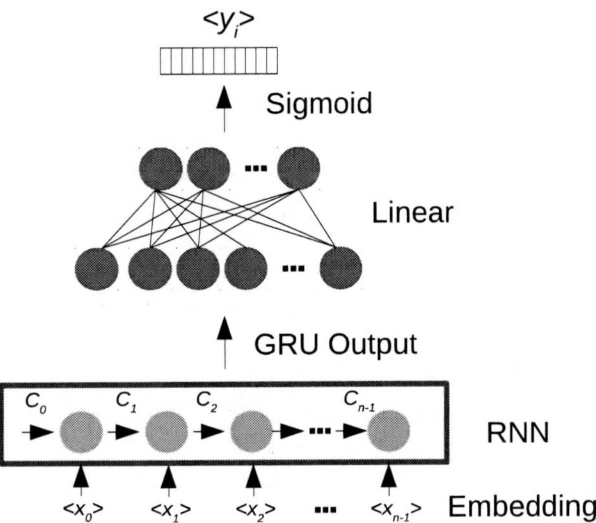

Figure 1: Overview of the architecture

3.3.4 The GRU Layer

The input of the GRU layer is the sequence of term embeddings of the tweet. We denote by $H = h_1, \ldots, h_n$ the input sequence of length n, where $h_i \in R^d$ is the term representation for the i-th token w_i. The new representation of the whole tweet r_i is then obtained from h_i via a GRU network:

$$r_i = (1 - z_i) \odot r_{i-1} + z_i \odot \tilde{r}_i \quad (2)$$

where,

$$
\begin{aligned}
g_i &= \sigma(W_g r_{i-1} + U_g h_i) \\
z_i &= \sigma(W_z r_{i-1} + U_z h_i) \\
\tilde{r}_i &= \tanh(W_r (g_i \odot r_{i-1}) + U_r h_i).
\end{aligned}
\quad (3)
$$

Here, g_i and z_i are reset and update gates respectively that control the information flow from the previous timestamp. W_g, U_g, W_z, U_z, W_r, and U_r are weight matrices to be learned for transforming r_{i-1} and h_i to gate units. By applying GRU on h_i, the tweet representation $r_i \in R^K$ encodes the context information and historical information simultaneously.

3.3.5 The Perceptron Layer

With the output of GRU, a vector $r_j \in R^K$ representing the overall information of a tweet, we use a perceptron layer together with a sigmoid activation function to map the tweet from feature space to label space $y_j \in R^L$, where L is dimension of the label space.

$$
\begin{aligned}
\hat{y}_j &= \sigma(W_p r_j) \\
\sigma(x) &= \frac{1}{1 + e^{-x}}
\end{aligned}
\quad (4)
$$

The predicted label vector $\hat{y}_j$ of each tweet t_j is then compared with the true label vector y_j on training data to guide the training process with an appropriate loss function.

3.3.6 The Loss Function

Binary cross entropy loss can be used for multi-label classification problems, it is computed as the formula below:

$$
\begin{aligned}
loss(p, q) \\
= -\frac{1}{N} \sum_{i=1}^{N} H(p_n, q_n) \\
= -\frac{1}{N} \sum_{i=1}^{N} [y_i \log \hat{y}_i + (1 - y_i) \log(1 - \hat{y}_i)]
\end{aligned}
\quad (5)
$$

where y_i is the true label vector of the tweet x_i, and $\hat{y}_i$ is its predicted label vector.

4 Training

To train these models, we use the training data provided by SemEval18 task 1, which includes $6,839$

human labeled english tweets for Subtask 1. A data set of 887 labeled english tweets for development is also avaible, we leverage this set for validation. The trained model is then applied on the testing set with 3260 unlabeled tweets in it. A vocabulary is generated by extracting terms from all the training set, validating set and testing set to ensure its coverage.

The parameter configuration for the best system performance on validation set is defined as follows:

- **Hidden Dimension** The initial embedding of each term is 300 as we adopt the pre-trained word embedding trained on part of the Google News dataset[3]. The hidden dimension of GRU is set to 200 when we get the best validation result.

- **Maximum Tweet Length** The length of each tweet is different, we regularize the length with a maximum limit of 30 meaningful terms after preprocessing steps. A tweet that is longer than that is trimmed, and shorter than that is populated with zero paddings.

- **Learning Rate** We adopt an Adam optimizer to train the model for the submitted system. The learning rate for the optimizer is set to 0.0001 when we get the best system performance on validation set.

- **Dropout Rate** Dropout operation is reported to have similar effects of boosting approches in neural network based models. A dropout operation is executed on the linear perceptron layer with a dropout rate of 0.4 when achieving the optimum.

- **Batch Size** The batch size settings also affact the performance of the proposed system. The optimum is obtained with a setting of 20 as the batch size.

The number of epochs is used for terminating the training process when optimum is obtained. Terminating condition depends on not only the values of the loss function, but also its transient performance on the validating dataset. Some random factors, such as the initial state of various random variables also show their impacts on it. In our experiments, the optimum is achieved at the 3-rd

---

[3]https://code.google.com/archive/p/word2vec/

epoch, it may vary with different intial states of other parameters.

Using the model parameters above, which produced the best performance on validating dataset, we predicted the labels of each tweet in the testing dataset. The evaluation results provided by SemEVal18 is described in the next section.

5 Results

Among all the 35 systems which participated in the task of emotion classification subtask of task 1 (Mohammad et al., 2018), our only submission is ranked 16-th on the evaluation metric of Accuracy, and 19-th on both metrics of micro-avg F1 and macro-avg F1, as is shown in Table 1. Our

Rank	System	Acc.	mi-F1	Ma-F1
1	cbaziotis	0.588	0.701	0.528
15	**mutux**	**0.473**	**0.591**	**0.446**
21	SVM	0.442	0.570	0.443
28	Random	0.185	0.307	0.285

Table 1: System Evaluation Results

model structure and feature space are designed as simple as possible intentionally, so that it can test the idea without distractive factors. As shown in above table, the system outperforms SVM-based approach consistently on all three different evaulation metrics.

6 Conclusion

We have presented a GRU-based multi-lable classifier to leverage context information and historical information for emotion analysis. It outperforms the unigram SVM model consistently on three evaluation metrics, even though only term features and a pre-trained word embedding are used. Some key factors such emojis, emoticons, emotion lexicons and multi-layer neural structures will be explored in the futrue for further analysis.

Acknowledgments

This work is partly supported by an NSERC discovery grant, as well as a donated GPU by NVIDIA.

References

Muhammad Abdul-Mageed and Lyle Ungar. 2017. Emonet: Fine-grained emotion detection with gated recurrent neural networks. In *Proceedings of the 55th Annual Meeting of the Association for Computational Linguistics (Volume 1: Long Papers)*, volume 1, pages 718–728.

Ameeta Agrawal and Aijun An. 2012. Unsupervised emotion detection from text using semantic and syntactic relations. In *Proceedings of the The 2012 IEEE/WIC/ACM International Joint Conferences on Web Intelligence and Intelligent Agent Technology-Volume 01*, pages 346–353. IEEE Computer Society.

Rakesh C Balabantaray, Mudasir Mohammad, and Nibha Sharma. 2012. Multi-class twitter emotion classification: A new approach. *International Journal of Applied Information Systems*, 4(1):48–53.

Alexandra Balahur, Jesús M. Hermida, and Andrés Montoyo. 2011. Detecting implicit expressions of sentiment in text based on commonsense knowledge. In *Proceedings of the 2Nd Workshop on Computational Approaches to Subjectivity and Sentiment Analysis*, WASSA '11, pages 53–60, Stroudsburg, PA, USA. Association for Computational Linguistics.

F. Bravo-Marquez, E. Frank, S. M. Mohammad, and B. Pfahringer. 2016. Determining word-emotion associations from tweets by multi-label classification. In *2016 IEEE/WIC/ACM International Conference on Web Intelligence (WI)*, pages 536–539.

Lea Canales and Patricio Martínez-Barco. 2014. Emotion detection from text: A survey. In *Proceedings of the Workshop on Natural Language Processing in the 5th Information Systems Research Working Days (JISIC)*, pages 37–43.

Scott Deerwester, Susan T. Dumais, George W. Furnas, Thomas K. Landauer, and Richard Harshman. 1990. Indexing by latent semantic analysis. *JOURNAL OF THE AMERICAN SOCIETY FOR INFORMATION SCIENCE*, 41(6):391–407.

Alastair J Gill, Robert M French, Darren Gergle, and Jon Oberlander. 2008. Identifying emotional characteristics from short blog texts. In *Proc. 30th Ann. Conf. Cognitive Science Soc., BC Love, K. McRae, and VM Sloutsky, eds*, pages 2237–2242.

Maryam Hasan, Emmanuel Agu, and Elke Rundensteiner. 2014a. Using hashtags as labels for supervised learning of emotions in twitter messages. In *ACM SIGKDD Workshop on Health Informatics, New York, USA*.

Maryam Hasan, Elke Rundensteiner, and Emmanuel Agu. 2014b. Emotex: Detecting emotions in twitter messages.

Tomas Mikolov, Kai Chen, Greg Corrado, and Jeffrey Dean. 2013. Efficient estimation of word representations in vector space. *CoRR*, abs/1301.3781.

Saif M. Mohammad, Felipe Bravo-Marquez, Mohammad Salameh, and Svetlana Kiritchenko. 2018. Semeval-2018 Task 1: Affect in tweets. In *Proceedings of International Workshop on Semantic Evaluation (SemEval-2018)*, New Orleans, LA, USA.

Kirk Roberts, Michael A Roach, Joseph Johnson, Josh Guthrie, and Sanda M Harabagiu. 2012. Empatweet: Annotating and detecting emotions on twitter. In *LREC*, volume 12, pages 3806–3813. Citeseer.

Carlo Strapparava and Rada Mihalcea. 2008. Learning to identify emotions in text. In *Proceedings of the 2008 ACM Symposium on Applied Computing*, SAC '08, pages 1556–1560, New York, NY, USA. ACM.

Jared Suttles and Nancy Ide. 2013. Distant supervision for emotion classification with discrete binary values. In *International Conference on Intelligent Text Processing and Computational Linguistics*, pages 121–136. Springer.

Ro Valitutti. 2004. Wordnet-affect: an affective extension of wordnet. In *In Proceedings of the 4th International Conference on Language Resources and Evaluation*, pages 1083–1086.

Wenbo Wang, Lu Chen, Krishnaprasad Thirunarayan, and Amit P Sheth. 2012. Harnessing twitter" big data" for automatic emotion identification. In *Privacy, Security, Risk and Trust (PASSAT), 2012 International Conference on and 2012 International Confernece on Social Computing (SocialCom)*, pages 587–592. IEEE.

Xuren Wang and Qiuhui Zheng. 2013. Text emotion classification research based on improved latent semantic analysis algorithm. In *Proceedings of the 2nd International Conference on Computer Science and Electronics Engineering (ICCSEE 2013)*, pages 210–213.

TeamUNCC at SemEval-2018 Task 1: Emotion Detection in English and Arabic Tweets using Deep Learning

Malak Abdullah   **Samira Shaikh**
College of Computing and Informatics
University of North Carolina at Charlotte
North Carolina, U.S
mabdull5, sshaikh2@uncc.edu

Abstract

Task 1 in the International Workshop SemEval 2018, Affect in Tweets, introduces five subtasks (El-reg, El-oc, V-reg, V-oc, and E-c) to detect the intensity of emotions in English, Arabic, and Spanish tweets. This paper describes TeamUNCC's system to detect emotions in English and Arabic tweets. Our approach is novel in that we present the same architecture for all the five subtasks in both English and Arabic. The main input to the system is a combination of word2vec and doc2vec embeddings and a set of psycholinguistic features (e.g. from AffectiveTweets Weka-package). We apply a fully connected neural network architecture and obtain performance results that show substantial improvements in Spearman correlation scores over the baseline models provided by Task 1 organizers, (ranging from 0.03 to 0.23). TeamUNCC's system ranks third in subtask El-oc and fourth in other subtasks for Arabic tweets.

1 Introduction

The rise and diversity of social microblogging channels encourage people to express their feelings and opinions on a daily basis. Consequently, sentiment analysis and emotion detection have gained the interest of researchers in natural language processing and other fields that include political science, marketing, communication, social sciences, and psychology (Mohammad and Bravo-Marquez, 2017; Agarwal et al., 2011; Chin et al., 2016). Sentiment analysis refers to classifying a subjective text as positive, neutral, or negative; emotion detection recognizes types of feelings through the expression of texts, such as anger, joy, fear, and sadness (Agarwal et al., 2011; Ekman, 1993).

SemEval is the International Workshop on Semantic Evaluation that has evolved from SensE-

val. The purpose of this workshop is to evaluate semantic analysis systems, the SemEval-2018 being the 12th workshop on semantic evaluation. Task 1 (Mohammad et al., 2018) in this workshop presents five subtasks with annotated datasets for English, Arabic, and Spanish tweets. The task for participating teams is to determine the intensity of emotions in text. Further details about Task 1 and the datasets appear in Section 3.

Our system covers five subtasks for both English and Arabic. The input to the system are word embedding vectors (Mikolov et al., 2013a), which are applied to fully connected neural network architecture to obtain the results. In addition, all subtasks except the last one, use document-level embeddings doc2vec (Le and Mikolov, 2014) that are concatenated with different feature vectors. The models built for detecting emotions related to Arabic tweets ranked third in subtask El-oc and fourth in the other subtasks. We use both the original Arabic tweets as well as translated tweets (to English) as input. The performance of the system for all subtasks in both languages shows substantial improvements in Spearman correlation scores over the baseline models provided by Task 1 organizers, ranging from 0.03 to 0.23.

The remainder of this research paper is organized as follows: Section 2 gives a brief overview of existing work on social media emotion and sentiment analyses, including for English and Arabic languages. Section 3 presents the requirements of SemEval Task1 and the provided datasets. Section 4 examines the TeamUNCC's system to determine the presence and intensity of emotion in text. Section 5 summarizes the key findings of the study and the evaluations. Section 6 concludes with future directions for this research.

Proceedings of the 12th International Workshop on Semantic Evaluation (SemEval-2018), pages 350–357
New Orleans, Louisiana, June 5–6, 2018. ©2018 Association for Computational Linguistics

2   Related work

Sentiment and Emotion Analysis: Sentiment analysis was first explored in 2003 by Nasukawa and Yi (Nasukawa and Yi, 2003). An interest in studying and building models for sentiment analysis and emotion detection for social microblogging platforms has increased significantly in recent years (Kouloumpis et al., 2011; Pak and Paroubek, 2010; Oscar et al., 2017; Jimenez-Zafra et al., 2017). Going beyond the task of mainly classifying tweets as positive or negative, several approaches to detect emotions were presented in previous research papers (Mohammad and Kiritchenko, 2015; Tromp and Pechenizkiy, 2014; Mohammad, 2012). Researchers (Mohammad and Bravo-Marquez, 2017) introduced the WASSA-2017 shared task of detecting the intensity of emotion felt by the speaker of a tweet. The state-of-the-art system in that competition (Goel et al., 2017) used an approach of ensembling three different deep neural network-based models, representing tweets as word2vec embedding vectors. In our system, we add doc2vec embedding vectors and classify tweets to ordinal classes of emotions as well as multi-class labeling of emotions.

Arabic Emotion Analysis: The growth of the Arabic language on social microblogging platforms, especially on Twitter, and the significant role of the Arab region in international politics and in the global economy have led researchers to investigate the area of mining and analyzing sentiments and emotions of Arabic tweets (Abdullah and Hadzikadic, 2017; El-Beltagy et al., 2017; Assiri et al., 2016). The challenges that face researchers in this area can be classified under two main areas: a lack of annotated resources and the challenges of the Arabic language's complex morphology relative to other languages (Assiri et al., 2015). Although recent research has been dedicated to detect emotions for English content, to our knowledge, there are few studies for Arabic content. Researchers (Rabie and Sturm, 2014) collected and annotated data and applied different preprocessing steps related to the Arabic language. They also used a simplification of the SVM (known as SMO) and the NaiveBayes classifiers. Another two related works (Kiritchenko et al., 2016; Rosenthal et al., 2017) shared different tasks to identify the overall sentiments of the tweets or phrases taken from tweets in both English and Arabic. Our work uses the state-of-the-

art approaches of deep learning and word/doc embedding.

3   Task Description and Datasets

SemEval-2018 Task 1, Affect in Tweets, presents five subtasks (El-reg, El-oc, V-reg, V-oc, and E-c.) The subtasks provide training and testing for Twitter datasets in the English, Arabic, and Spanish languages (Mohammad and Kiritchenko, 2018). Task 1 asks the participants to predict the intensity of emotions and sentiments in the testing datasets. It also includes multi-label emotion classification subtask for tweets. This paper focuses on determining emotions in English and Arabic tweets. Figure 1 shows the number of tweets for both training and testing datasets for individual subtasks. We note that subtasks *El-reg* and *El-oc* share the same datasets with different annotations, and the same for subtasks *V-reg* and *V-oc*.

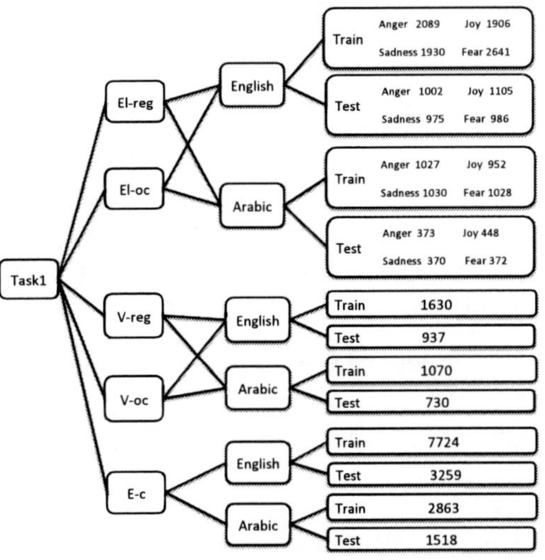

Figure 1: Datasets of SemEval-2018 Task 1.

The description of each subtask is:

EI-reg: Determine the intensity of an emotion in a tweet as a real-valued score between 0 (least emotion intensity) and 1 (most emotion intensity).

EI-oc: Classify the intensity of emotion (anger, joy, fear, or sadness) in the tweet into one of four ordinal classes (0: no emotion, 1, 2, and 3 high emotion).

V-reg: Determine the intensity of sentiment or valence (V) in a tweet as a real-valued score between 0 (most negative) and 1 (most positive).

V-oc: Classify the sentiment intensity of a tweet into one of seven ordinal classes, corresponding to various levels of positive and negative sentiment intensity (3: very positive mental state can be inferred, 2, 1, 0, -1, -2, and -3: very negative mental state can be inferred)

E-c: Classify the tweet as 'neutral or no emotion' or as one, or more, of eleven given emotions (anger, anticipation, disgust, fear,joy, love, optimism, pessimism, sadness, surprise, and trust).

4   The TeamUNCC System

Our team, TeamUNCC, is the only team that participated in all subtasks of Task 1 of SemEval-2018 for both English and Arabic tweets. Subtasks *El-reg* and *V-reg* are considered similar because they determine the intensity of an emotion or a sentiment (respectively) in a tweet as a real-valued score. While subtasks *El-oc* and *V-oc* classify the intensity of the emotion or the sentiment (respectively) to ordinal classes. Our system, designed for these subtasks, shares most features and components; however, the fifth subtask, *E-c*, uses fewer of these elements. Figure 2 shows the general structure of our system. More details for the system's components are shown in the following subsections: Section 4.1 describes the system's input and prepocessing. Section 4.2 lists the feature vectors, and Section 4.3 details the architecture of neural network. Section 4.4 discusses the output details.

4.1   Input and Preprocessing

EngTweets: The original English tweets in training and testing datasets have been tokenized by converting the sentences into words, and all uppercase letters have been converted to lowercase. The preprocessing step also includes stemming the words and removal of extraneous white spaces. Punctuation have been treated as individual words ("., ?!:;()[]#@'), while contractions (wasn't, aren't) were left untreated.

ArTweets: The original Arabic tweets in training and testing datasets have been tokenized, white spaces have been removed, and the punctuation marks have been treated as individual words ("., ?!:;()[]#@').

TraTweets: The Arabic tweets have been translated using a powerful translation tool written in python (translate 3.5.0)[1]. Next, the preprocessing steps that are applied to EngTweets are also applied on TraTweets.

---

[1] https://pypi.python.org/pypi/translate

4.2   Feature Vectors

AffectTweets-145: Each tweet, in either EngTweets or TraTweets, is represented as 145 dimensional vectors by concatenating three vectors obtained from the AffectiveTweets Weka-package (Mohammad and Bravo-Marquez, 2017; Bravo-Marquez et al., 2014), 43 features have been extracted using the TweetToLexiconFeatureVector attribute that calculates attributes for a tweet using a variety of lexical resources; two-dimensional vector using the Sentiment strength feature from the same package, and the final 100 dimensional vector is obtained by vectorizing the tweets to embeddings attribute also from the same package.

Doc2Vec-300: Each tweet is represented as a 300 dimensional vector by concatenating two vectors of 150 dimensions each, using the document-level embeddings ('doc2vec') (Le and Mikolov, 2014; Lau and Baldwin, 2016). The vector for each word in the tweet has been averaged to attain a 150 dimensional representation of the tweet.

Word2Vec-300: Each tweet is represented as a 300 dimensional vector using the pretrained word2vec embedding model that is trained on Google News (Mikolov et al., 2013b), and for Arabic tweets, we use the pretrained embedding model that is trained on Arabic tweets (Twt-SG) (Soliman et al., 2017).

PaddingWord2Vec-300: Each word in a tweet is represented as a 300 dimensional vector. The same pretraind word2vec embedding models that are used in Word2Vec-300 are also used in this feature vector. Each tweet is represented as a vector with a fixed number of rows that equals the maximum length of dataset tweets and a standard 300 columns using padding of zero vectors.

4.3   Network Architecture

Dense-Network: The input 445 dimensional vector feeds into a fully connected neural network with three dense hidden layers. The activation function for each layer is RELU (Maas et al., 2013), with 256, 256, and 80 neurons for each layer, respectively. The output layer consists of one sigmoid neuron, which predicts the intensity of the emotion or the sentiment between 0 and 1. Two dropouts are used in this network (0.3, 0.5) after the first and second layers, respectively. For optimization, we use SGD (Stochastic Gradient Descent) optimizer (lr=0.01, decay=1×10^{-6},

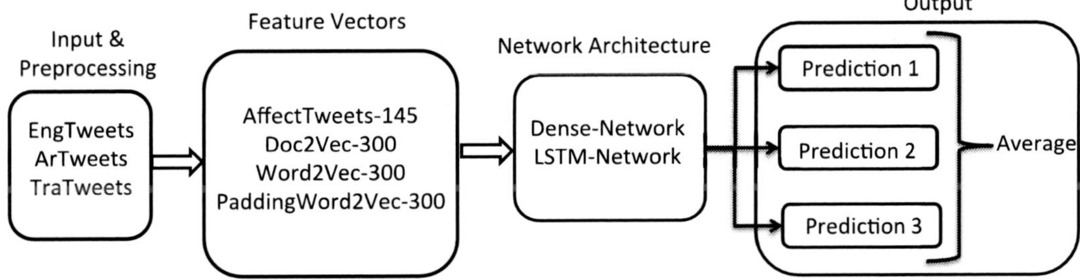

Figure 2: The structure for our system.

and momentum=0.9) [2], optimizing for 'mse' loss function and 'accuracy' metrics. Early stopping is also applied to obtain best results.

LSTM-Network: The input vector feeds an LSTM of 256 neurons that passes the vector to a fully connected neural network of two hidden layers and two dropouts (0.3, 0.5). The first hidden layer has 256 neurons, while the second layer has 80 neurons. Both layers use the RELU activation function. The output layer consists of one sigmoid neuron, which predicts the intensity of the emotion or the sentiment between 0 and 1. For optimization, we use SGD optimizer (lr=0.01, decay=1×10^{-6}, and momentum=0.9), optimizing for 'mse' loss function and 'accuracy' metrics as well as early stopping to obtain the best results.

4.4 Output

Subtasks El-reg, El-oc, V-reg, and V-oc: These four subtasks for each language (English and Arabic) share the same structure as shown in Figure 2, the only difference is in the output stage. Each subtask passes the tweets to three different models that produces three predictions. See Table 1 and Table 2 for more comprehensive details on how each prediction with English and Arabic language is produced, respectively. The average of the predictions for each tweet is a real-valued number between 0 and 1. This output is considered the final output for both subtasks *El-reg* and *V-reg*, while subtasks *El-oc* and *V-oc* classify this real-valued number to one of the ordinal classes that are shown in Section 3. We note that *El-reg* and *El-oc* shares the same datasets. We also noticed that V-reg and V-oc shares the same dataset. Therefore, we found the ranges of values for each ordinal class by comparing the datasets. Table 3 shows the range of

---
[2]https://keras.io/optimizers/

values to obtain the ordinal classes for *El-oc* subtask in English, Table 4 shows the same for *El-oc* subtask in Arabic, and Table 5 shows the for *V-oc* in both English and Arabic.

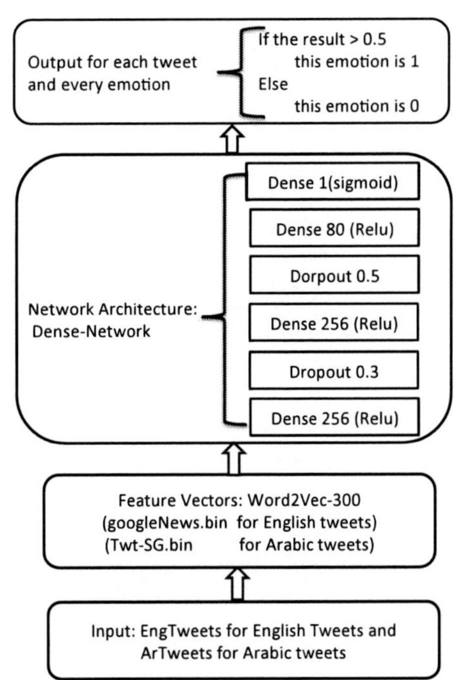

Figure 3: The detailed structure for our system related to subtask E-c.

Subtask E-c: In this subtask, our system makes only one prediction. See Figure3 for more details on the process of predicting the results. The input is *EngTweets* for English language and ArTweets for Arabic language. We use *Word2Vec-300* as the feature vector with *GoogleNews* for English tweets and *Twt-SG* for Arabic tweets. The network architecture is Dense-Network. This process is applied for each emotion of the eleven emotions:

-	**Prediction 1**	**Prediction2**	**Prediction3**
Input	EngTweets	EngTweets	EngTweets
Feature Vectors	AffectTweets-145 Doc2Vec-300	AffectTweets-145 Word2Vec-300	PaddingWord2Vec-300
Neural Network	Dense-Network	Dense-Network	LSTM-Network

Table 1: The Architecture details for English subtasks El-reg, El-oc, V-reg, and V-oc.

-	**Prediction 1**	**Prediction2**	**Prediction3**
Input	TraTweets	ArTweets TraTweets	ArTweets
Feature Vectors	AffectTweets-145 Doc2Vec-300	AffectTweets-145 Word2Vec-300	PaddingWord2Vec-300
Neural Network	Dense-Network	Dense-Network	LSTM-Network

Table 2: The Architecture details for Arabic subtasks El-reg, El-oc, V-reg, and V-oc.

Output class	Angry	Joy	Fear	Sadness
0: no emotion can be inferred	0-0.42	0-0.36	0-0.57	0-0.44
1: low amount of emotion can be inferred	0.42-0.52	0.36-0.53	0.57-0.69	0.44-0.54
2: moderate amount of emotion can be inferred	0.52-0.7	0.53-0.69	0.66-0.79	0.54-0.7
3: high amount of emotion can be inferred	0.7-1	0.69-1	0.79-1	0.7-1

Table 3: Classify the output to ordinal classes for English El-oc.

Output class	Angry	Joy	Fear	Sadness
0: no emotion can be inferred	0-0.40	0-0.31	0-0.45	0-0.47
1: low amount of emotion can be inferred	0.40-0.55	0.31-0.51	0.45-0.56	0.47-0.54
2: moderate amount of emotion can be inferred	0.55-0.64	0.51-0.75	0.56-0.76	0.54-0.67
3: high amount of emotion can be inferred	0.64-1	0.75-1	0.76-1	0.67-1

Table 4: Classify the output to ordinal classes for Arabic El-oc.

Output class	English Sentiment	Arabic Sentiment
-3: very negative emotional state can be inferred	0-0.23	0-0.20
-2: moderately negative emotional state can be inferred	0.23-0.38	0.20-0.37
-1: slightly negative emotional state can be inferred	0.38-0.43	0.37-0.43
0: neutral or mixed emotional state can be inferred	0.43-0.61	0.43-0.56
1: slightly positive emotional state can be inferred	0.61-0.70	0.56-0.69
2: moderately positive emotional state can be inferred	0.70-0.78	0.69-0.81
3: very positive emotional state can be inferred	0.78-1	0.81-1

Table 5: Classify the output to ordinal classes for English and Arabic V-oc.

anger, anticipation, disgust, fear, joy, love, optimism, pessimism, sadness, surprise, and trust. The output of each individual tweet is a real-valued number between 0 and 1. This output is normalized to either 1 (contains an emotion) if it is greater than 0.5 or 0 (no emotion) if it is less than 0.5.

5 Evaluations and Results

Each participating system in the subtasks *El-reg*, *El-oc*, *V-reg*, and *V-oc*, has been scored by using Spearman correlation score. The subtask *E-c* has been scored by using accuracy metric. Table 6 shows the performance of our system in *E-reg* and *El-oc* with each emotion and the average score for both English and Arabic. Table 7 shows the results for subtasks *V-reg*, *V-oc*, and *E-c*. The performance of our system beats the baseline model's performance, which is provided by the Task's organizers, see Figure 4 to capture the difference between the two performances. Our system ranks third in the subtask *El-oc* for Arabic language, and Fourth in the subtasks *El-reg*, *V-reg*, *V-oc*, and *E-*

Task	Angry	Joy	Fear	Sadness	Average
El-reg (English)	0.722	0.698	0.692	0.666	**0.695**
El-reg (Arabic)	0.524	0.657	0.576	0.631	**0.597**
El-oc (English)	0.604	0.638	0.544	0.610	**0.599**
El-oc (Arabic)	0.459	0.538	0.483	0.587	**0.517**

Table 6: The Spearman correlation scores for subtasks El-reg and El-oc.

Task	Spearman score
V-reg (English)	**0.787**
V-reg (Arabic)	**0.773**
V-oc (English)	**0.736**
V-oc (Arabic)	**0.748**

Task	Accuracy score
E-c (English)	**0.471**
E-c (Arabic)	**0.446**

Table 7: The results for subtasks V-reg, V-oc, and E-c.

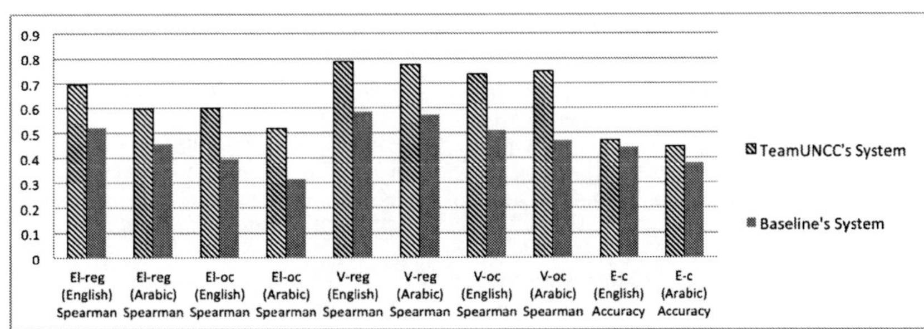

Figure 4: Comparing performances of the TeamUNCC and the baseline systems.

c for Arabic language too. It is worth mentioning that these results have been obtained by using the task datasets without using any external data.

6 Conclusion

In this paper, we have presented our system that participated in Task 1 of Semeval-2018. Our system is unique in that we use the same underlying architecture for all subtasks for both languages - English and Arabic to detect the intensity of emotions and sentiments in tweets. The performance of the system for each subtask beats the performance of the baseline's model, indicating that our approach is promising. The system ranked third in El-oc for Arabic language and fourth in the other subtasks for Arabic language too.

In this system, we used word2vec and doc2vec embedding models with feature vectors extracted from the tweets by using the AffectTweets Weka-package, these vectors feed the deep neural network layers to obtain the predictions.

In future work, we will add emotion and valence detection in Spanish language to our system by ap-

plying the same approaches that have been used with Arabic. We also want to investigate the Arabic feature attributes in order to enhance the performance in this language.

References

Malak Abdullah and Mirsad Hadzikadic. 2017. Sentiment analysis on arabic tweets: Challenges to dissecting the language. In *International Conference on Social Computing and Social Media*, pages 191–202. Springer.

Apoorv Agarwal, Boyi Xie, Ilia Vovsha, Owen Rambow, and Rebecca Passonneau. 2011. Sentiment analysis of twitter data. In *Proceedings of the workshop on languages in social media*, pages 30–38. Association for Computational Linguistics.

Adel Assiri, Ahmed Emam, and Hmood Al-Dossari. 2016. Saudi twitter corpus for sentiment analysis. *World Academy of Science, Engineering and Technology, International Journal of Computer, Electrical, Automation, Control and Information Engineering*, 10(2):272–275.

Adel Assiri, Ahmed Emam, and Hmood Aldossari. 2015. Arabic sentiment analysis: a survey. *Interna-*

tional Journal of Advanced Computer Science and Applications, 6(12):75–85.

Felipe Bravo-Marquez, Marcelo Mendoza, and Barbara Poblete. 2014. Meta-level sentiment models for big social data analysis. *Knowledge-Based Systems*, 69:86–99.

Delenn Chin, Anna Zappone, and Jessica Zhao. 2016. Analyzing twitter sentiment of the 2016 presidential candidates. *News & Publications: Stanford University*.

Paul Ekman. 1993. Facial expression and emotion. *American psychologist*, 48(4):384.

Samhaa R El-Beltagy, Talaat Khalil, Amal Halaby, and Muhammad Hammad. 2017. Combining lexical features and a supervised learning approach for arabic sentiment analysis. *arXiv preprint arXiv:1710.08451*.

Pranav Goel, Devang Kulshreshtha, Prayas Jain, and Kaushal Kumar Shukla. 2017. Prayas at emoint 2017: An ensemble of deep neural architectures for emotion intensity prediction in tweets. In *Proceedings of the 8th Workshop on Computational Approaches to Subjectivity, Sentiment and Social Media Analysis*, pages 58–65.

Salud Maria Jimenez-Zafra, M Teresa Martin Valdivia, Eugenio Martinez Camara, and Luis Alfonso Urena-Lopez. 2017. Studying the scope of negation for spanish sentiment analysis on twitter. *IEEE Transactions on Affective Computing*.

Svetlana Kiritchenko, Saif Mohammad, and Mohammad Salameh. 2016. Semeval-2016 task 7: Determining sentiment intensity of english and arabic phrases. In *Proceedings of the 10th International Workshop on Semantic Evaluation (SemEval-2016)*, pages 42–51.

Efthymios Kouloumpis, Theresa Wilson, and Johanna D Moore. 2011. Twitter sentiment analysis: The good the bad and the omg! *Icwsm*, 11(538-541):164.

Jey Han Lau and Timothy Baldwin. 2016. An empirical evaluation of doc2vec with practical insights into document embedding generation. *arXiv preprint arXiv:1607.05368*.

Quoc Le and Tomas Mikolov. 2014. Distributed representations of sentences and documents. In *International Conference on Machine Learning*, pages 1188–1196.

Andrew L Maas, Awni Y Hannun, and Andrew Y Ng. 2013. Rectifier nonlinearities improve neural network acoustic models. In *Proc. icml*, volume 30, page 3.

Tomas Mikolov, Kai Chen, Greg Corrado, and Jeffrey Dean. 2013a. Efficient estimation of word representations in vector space. *arXiv preprint arXiv:1301.3781*.

Tomas Mikolov, Ilya Sutskever, Kai Chen, Greg S Corrado, and Jeff Dean. 2013b. Distributed representations of words and phrases and their compositionality. In *Advances in neural information processing systems*, pages 3111–3119.

Saif M Mohammad. 2012. # emotional tweets. In *Proceedings of the First Joint Conference on Lexical and Computational Semantics-Volume 1: Proceedings of the main conference and the shared task, and Volume 2: Proceedings of the Sixth International Workshop on Semantic Evaluation*, pages 246–255. Association for Computational Linguistics.

Saif M Mohammad and Felipe Bravo-Marquez. 2017. Wassa-2017 shared task on emotion intensity. *arXiv preprint arXiv:1708.03700*.

Saif M. Mohammad, Felipe Bravo-Marquez, Mohammad Salameh, and Svetlana Kiritchenko. 2018. Semeval-2018 Task 1: Affect in tweets. In *Proceedings of International Workshop on Semantic Evaluation (SemEval-2018)*, New Orleans, LA, USA.

Saif M Mohammad and Svetlana Kiritchenko. 2015. Using hashtags to capture fine emotion categories from tweets. *Computational Intelligence*, 31(2):301–326.

Saif M. Mohammad and Svetlana Kiritchenko. 2018. Understanding emotions: A dataset of tweets to study interactions between affect categories. In *Proceedings of the 11th Edition of the Language Resources and Evaluation Conference*, Miyazaki, Japan.

Tetsuya Nasukawa and Jeonghee Yi. 2003. Sentiment analysis: Capturing favorability using natural language processing. In *Proceedings of the 2nd international conference on Knowledge capture*, pages 70–77. ACM.

Nels Oscar, Pamela A Fox, Racheal Croucher, Riana Wernick, Jessica Keune, and Karen Hooker. 2017. Machine learning, sentiment analysis, and tweets: an examination of alzheimers disease stigma on twitter. *Journals of Gerontology Series B: Psychological Sciences and Social Sciences*, 72(5):742–751.

Alexander Pak and Patrick Paroubek. 2010. Twitter as a corpus for sentiment analysis and opinion mining. In *LREc*, volume 10.

Omneya Rabie and Christian Sturm. 2014. Feel the heat: Emotion detection in arabic social media content. In *The International Conference on Data Mining, Internet Computing, and Big Data (Big-Data2014)*, pages 37–49. The Society of Digital Information and Wireless Communication.

Sara Rosenthal, Noura Farra, and Preslav Nakov. 2017. Semeval-2017 task 4: Sentiment analysis in twitter. In *Proceedings of the 11th International Workshop on Semantic Evaluation (SemEval-2017)*, pages 502–518.

Abu Bakr Soliman, Kareem Eissa, and Samhaa R El-
Beltagy. 2017. Aravec: A set of arabic word embedding models for use in arabic nlp. *Procedia Computer Science*, 117:256–265.

Erik Tromp and Mykola Pechenizkiy. 2014. Rule-
based emotion detection on social media: putting
tweets on plutchik's wheel. *arXiv preprint
arXiv:1412.4682*.

RIDDL at SemEval-2018 Task 1: Rage Intensity Detection with Deep Learning

Venkatesh Elango, Karan Uppal
Bloomberg
New York, NY, USA
{velango,kuppal8}@bloomberg.net

Abstract

We present our methods and results for affect analysis in Twitter developed as a part of SemEval-2018 Task 1, where the sub-tasks involve predicting the intensity of emotion, the intensity of sentiment, and valence for tweets. For modeling, though we use a traditional LSTM network, we combine our model with several state-of-the-art techniques to improve its performance in a low-resource setting. For example, we use an encoder-decoder network to initialize the LSTM weights. Without any task specific optimization we achieve competitive results (macro-average Pearson correlation coefficient 0.696) in the EI-reg task. In this paper, we describe our development strategy in detail along with an exposition of our results.

1 Introduction

Sentiment analysis is a technique to classify documents based on the polarity of opinion expressed by the author of the document (Pang et al., 2002). Traditionally this involved extracting coarse sentiment (positive, negative, or neutral) from documents such as news articles, product or movie reviews (Wiebe et al., 2005; Hu and Liu, 2004). In order to get a fine grained view of the opinion, sentiment analysis was applied at the sentence and phrase level (Yu and Hatzivassiloglou, 2003; Wilson et al., 2005). With the advent of social media, Twitter in particular, sentiment towards a wide range of topics could be extracted at a much larger scale than before. This however came with its own set of problems, viz., a lack of proper grammatical structure, prevalence of slang, acronyms, and misspellings (Jansen et al., 2009; Barbosa and Feng, 2010).

SemEval tasks have provided a curated testing environment for analysis on Twitter data with tasks to quantify sentiment on two-point, three-point, and five-point scales (Nakov et al., 2016; Rosenthal et al., 2017). While a finer gradation in polarity of the text could be inferred by introducing more nuanced categories, it faces the problem of needing to collect more labeled data as the number of classes increase. Therefore, this approach requires that the intensity of the sentiment expressed be measured on a continuous scale rather than through discrete categories. SemEval 2018 Task 1 takes a novel step in this direction by introducing tasks for predicting intensity of emotion, or sentiment expressed (Mohammad et al., 2018).

We participated in SemEval-2018 Task-1 (EI-Reg, V-reg, V-oc) and our contributions through this paper are as follows:

- We present an LSTM network combined with known state-of-the-art techniques to improve performance on low-resource setting tasks.

- The proposed model requires no task specific hyper-parameter tuning.

- We perform error analysis of our model to obtain a better understanding of strengths and weaknesses of a deep learning-based approach for these tasks and propose improvements.

2 Methods

2.1 Datasets

For each subtask, the organizers provide training and development datasets for model training and hyperparameter selection. The details on how much data and how it was labeled can be found here (Mohammad and Kiritchenko, 2018). We concatenate the training and development datasets and sample 10% of this combined dataset, to use as validation data. Our model training involves an

Proceedings of the 12th International Workshop on Semantic Evaluation (SemEval-2018), pages 358–363
New Orleans, Louisiana, June 5–6, 2018. ©2018 Association for Computational Linguistics

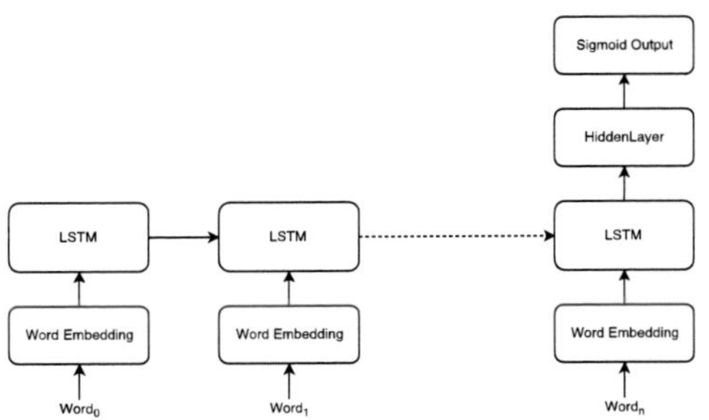

Figure 1: Network architecture.

unsupervised phase and a supervised phase, which is described in detail in Section 2.3. For the unsupervised learning phase, we use the concatenated training data from all the tasks, and for the supervised learning phase, we use the task specific training data.

2.2 Model

We start by pre-processing and tokenizing the tweets by adapting the pre-processing used in training GloVe word embeddings for Twitter (Pennington et al., 2014). Following the pre-processing techniques used in GloVe, we retain punctuations, normalize mentions, numbers, URLs, smileys (happy, neutral, and sad separately), and include tags for hashtags, repeating, and all upper case characters. In addition, we also pre-process emojis by replacing them with their Unicode text description[1].

After a tweet is broken down into a sequence of tokens, it is then converted to a sequence of vectors using the 200-dimensional GloVe word embeddings for Twitter which was trained on 2 billion tweets with a vocabulary of size 1.2 million (Pennington et al., 2014).

This sequence of word vectors is next input to an LSTM network (Hochreiter and Schmidhuber, 1997), with h_1 hidden units. The output from the last time step of the LSTM cell is passed through a layer of h_2 hidden units with ReLU activation. A final sigmoid layer then produces the output. Since all of the tasks, including the ordinal classification task, have an innate sense of ordering, we cast them as regression problems. The network architecture is shown in Figure 1.

---

[1] http://unicode.org/emoji/charts/emoji-list.html

2.3 Training

We tried two different training strategies. The results submitted before the official deadline used the first strategy. Since then, we identified a few key areas of improvement and used the second training strategy to get much better results. Both strategies are described below and the results are discussed in Section 3.

2.3.1 Strategy 1

We divide the training of our model into two phases, an unsupervised phase and a supervised phase.

Unsupervised Phase

Since the amount of training data is small (approximately 2000 labeled samples on average across all tasks) in comparison to the number of parameters (approximately 500,000) of the model, the training of the model could be unstable and prone to over-fitting. To counter this problem, the weights of the LSTM are initialized using a modified sequence auto-encoder (Dai and Le, 2015). This modified sequence auto-encoder uses separate encoder and decoder networks, attempting to reconstruct the input to the encoder at the output of the decoder by minimizing the mean squared error between them (Elango et al., 2017; Srivastava et al., 2015). For this unsupervised learning phase, we pool the training data from all the tasks and use 10% of it as a validation set. The validation set is used to tune the number of epochs. The validation loss is minimized for 5 epochs. Then, we fine-tune these weights with task specific training + validation data and this fine-tuning is run for another 10 epochs.

The unsupervised learning procedure is crucial for the good initialization of weights in the supervised task. As the model optimizes its weights for reconstruction of the sequence, it is able to learn the structure of the data.

Supervised Phase

For the supervised phase, the weights from the encoder network are used as initialization. To learn a generalizable model, instead of optimizing the hyper-parameters for each task separately, we optimize the hyper-parameters only for the anger intensity regression sub-task (EI-reg anger) which was picked arbitrarily. For tuning the hyper-parameters we combine the training and development set provided for the task and randomly sam-

Hyperparameter	Value
h_1	256
h_2	32
n_{mb}	32
e	5
p_{do}	0.5

Table 1: Hyperparameters used for network training.

ple 10% of the data from this task as a validation set. The set of hyper-parameters optimized are the number of hidden units (h_1, h_2), mini-batch size (n_{mb}), number of epochs to train the network (e) and dropout probability (p_{do}). For all the other tasks, the same optimized set of hyper-parameter values are used in training the model with all of the task specific training data.

Also, per recommendation from (Gers et al., 2000; Jozefowicz et al., 2015), to enable gradient flow, the bias term in the forget gate of the LSTM is initialized to 1. We apply dropout to the recurrent states (Gal and Ghahramani, 2016) and the hidden nodes with a probability of p_{do}, to prevent over-fitting to the training data. The model optimization is carried out by back-propagation using Adam optimizer (Kingma and Ba, 2014).

Using the above approach, the set of hyper-parameters that provide the best performance are reported in Table 1.

2.3.2 Strategy 2

After observing the results for all the subtasks we noticed that variance is fairly high in the predicted intensities. This is also visible in the scatter plots of true and predicted intensity, shown in Figures 2 and 3. We also noticed during the hyper parameter optimization on the anger task that the gap between the validation loss and training loss was high.

Simpler Model and Regularization

The above observations led us to believe that we might be over-fitting to the training data. Hence we tried the following steps to reduce over-fitting:

1. Reduced number of parameters: Number of hidden units of LSTM was reduced to 100.

2. Increased dropout rate: Increased the dropout in the hidden layer to 0.75.

Additional Unlabeled Data

Furthermore, we believed that the unsupervised phase of our training could benefit from more un-

labeled data. So we pooled in all the development and test data across all the tasks along with the training data, and used it in the unsupervised learning of weights of the LSTM. To tune the number of epochs, we set aside 10% of the combined training, development, and test as validation set. It is important to note that at no point were gold labels of test data used in any phase of training. This was simply an inexpensive way to get more data for trainining the unsupervised phase.

Ensemble

To further improve the prediction performance, we take an ensemble of 5 versions of our model and also optimize the number of epochs of training for each task for each of the 5 models. All the other hyper-parameters are kept the same across all tasks. For each of the 5 models, a random validation set with 10% of the labeled data is set aside to tune the number of epochs. Therefore, each model of the ensemble is being trained 90% of randomly sampled data. The supervised phase is trained, with random initialization for the dense layer, for 15 epochs, and the model state is saved at the end of every epoch. Finally the model corresponding to the epoch with the lowest validation loss is picked. All 5 models are used to predict on the test set, and the average of the 5 predictions is used as the final prediction of the ensemble.

3 Results

Models trained with both strategies are evaluated using Pearson correlation as the metric. We compare our performance with an unigram SVM baseline, as well as the best submission for each subtask. The official submitted results using Strategy 1 are reported in Tables 2 and 3 for subtask EI-reg and in Tables 4 and 5 for subtasks V-reg and V-oc respectively. The improved results using strategy 2 are reported in Table 6. The results in table 6 are averaged over 5 runs and report the standard deviation over the runs as well. We find that strategy 2 improves the macro-average Pearson correlation from 0.666 to 0.696.

To further analyze the results for the regression tasks, we created scatter plots shown in Figures 2 and 3. We plot the predicted intensity score against the gold label intensity score and also show the line of best fit.

Analyzing the scatter plots, we note that our model consistently overestimates the intensity

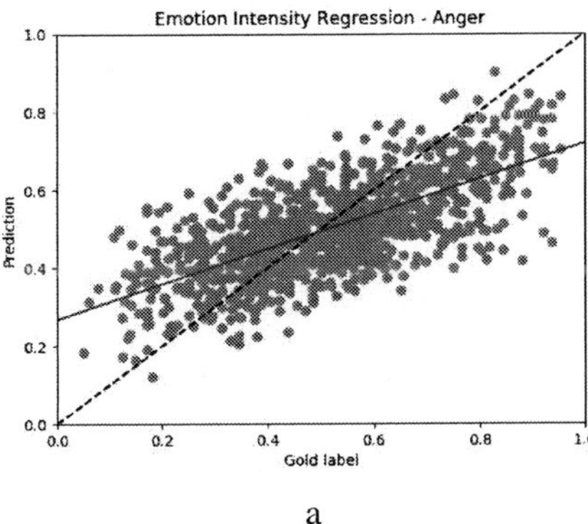

a

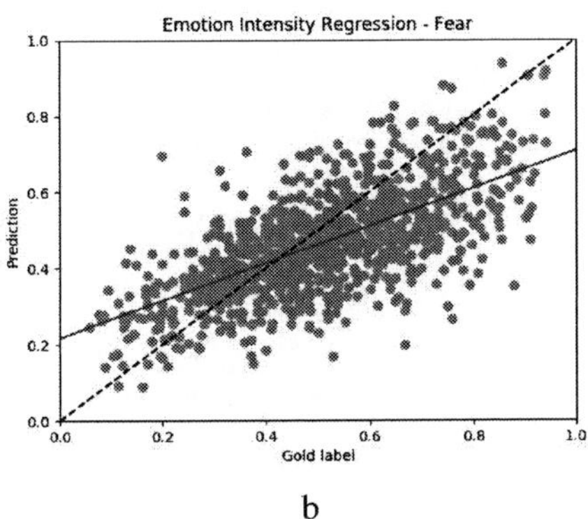

b

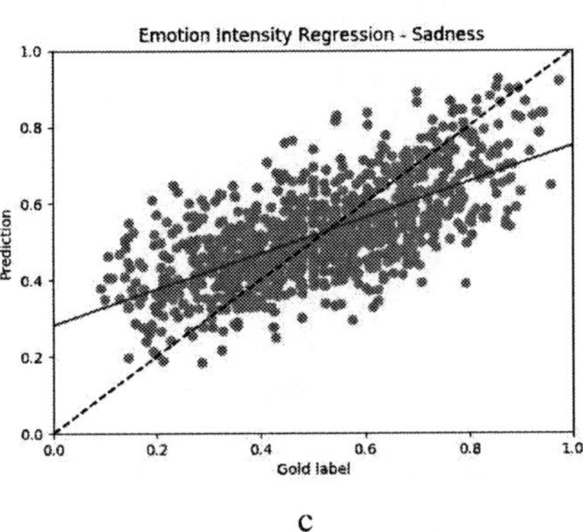

c

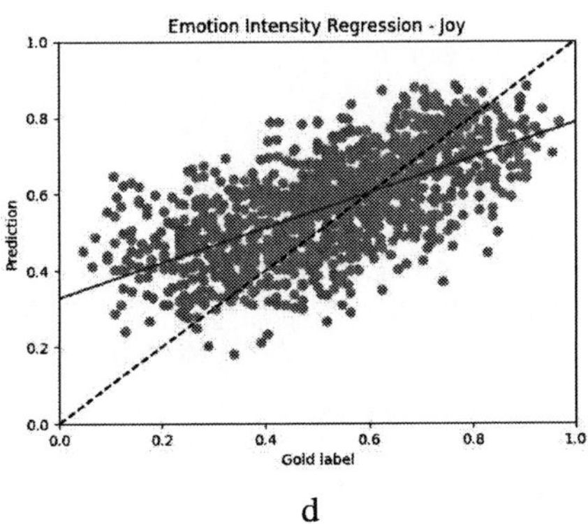

d

Figure 2: Plot of predicted against gold intensity score for emotion intensity regression using Strategy 1.

| | Emotion | | | |
Model	Anger	Fear	Joy	Sadness
Baseline	0.526	0.525	0.575	0.453
Ours	0.695	0.659	0.638	0.672
Best	0.827	0.779	0.792	0.798

Table 2: Pearson correlation on emotion intensity regression task (EI-reg) in English for each emotion using Strategy 1.

Model	Macro-average
Baseline	0.520
Ours	0.666
Best	0.799

Table 3: Macro average of Pearson correlation on emotion intensity regression task (EI-reg) in English using Strategy 1.

Model	Valence
Baseline	0.585
Ours	0.782
Best	0.873

Table 4: Pearson correlation on valence intensity regression task (V-reg) in English using Strategy 1.

Model	Valence
Baseline	0.509
Ours	0.593
Best	0.836

Table 5: Pearson correlation on valence ordinal classification task (V-oc) in English using Strategy 1.

| | Pearson Correlation | |
Emotion	Average	Std Dev
Anger	0.717	0.0021
Fear	0.695	0.0020
Joy	0.688	0.0054
Sadness	0.685	0.0020
Macro-average	0.696	0.0054

Table 6: Pearson correlation (average and standard deviation of 5 runs) on emotion intensity regression task (EI-reg) in English using Strategy 2.

when the gold label score is low and underestimates the intensity when the gold label score is high. The overestimation of low gold label score is most pronounced in the case of emotion intensity regression for *joy* and this is reflected in its low Pearson correlation in Table 2. Emotion intensity regression for *fear* has larger variance in predicted intensities for high gold label scores and

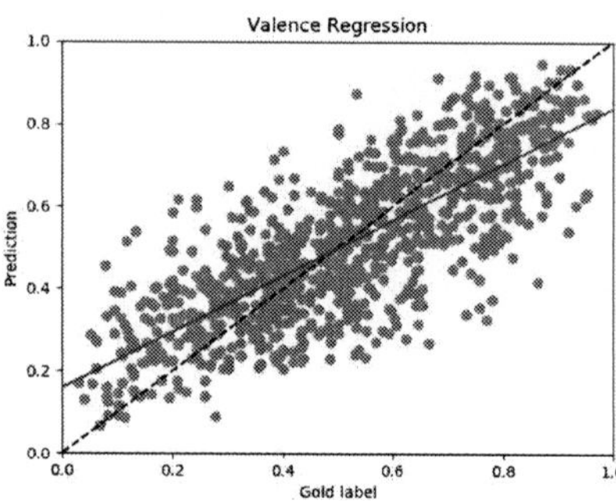

Figure 3: Plot of predicted against gold intensity score for valence regression using Strategy 1.

this too can be seen in the relatively low Pearson correlation reported in Table 2. While *anger* and *sadness* emotions also make under estimation error for high gold label scores, the line of best fit as well as the Pearson correlation are better than the corresponding ones for *joy* and *fear*.

The performance of the model in the valence regression task is markedly better in comparison to the performance in the emotion intensity regression tasks, as seen from the Pearson correlation, in Table 3, as well as the line of best fit, in Figure 3.

4   Conclusion

We presented an LSTM based approach for affect and emotion intensity regression and described our training strategy which did not involve any task specific hyper-parameter optimization. We did not employ any task specific hyper-parameter optimization to demonstrate that the training procedure is robust and that the model can be trained to achieve reasonable performance without being highly sensitive to values of hyper-parameters. We also show how the traditional LSTM network can be combined with known state-of-the-art techniques to get improvements in low resource settings. We use an encoder-decoder network to initialize the LSTM weights and use ensembles of our network to further improve performance. On the other hand, when the goal is to maximize performance, task specific hyper-parameter optimization could be employed, which is shown in strategy 2 where tuning the number of epochs on a per task basis helps the performance.

References

Luciano Barbosa and Junlan Feng. 2010. Robust sentiment detection on twitter from biased and noisy data. In *Proceedings of the 23rd international conference on computational linguistics: posters*, pages 36–44. Association for Computational Linguistics.

Andrew M Dai and Quoc V Le. 2015. Semi-supervised sequence learning. In *Advances in Neural Information Processing Systems*, pages 3079–3087.

Venkatesh Elango, Aashish N Patel, Kai J Miller, and Vikash Gilja. 2017. Sequence transfer learning for neural decoding. *bioRxiv*, page 210732.

Yarin Gal and Zoubin Ghahramani. 2016. A theoretically grounded application of dropout in recurrent neural networks. In *Advances in Neural Information Processing Systems*, pages 1019–1027.

Felix A Gers, Jürgen Schmidhuber, and Fred Cummins. 2000. Learning to forget: Continual prediction with lstm. *Neural computation*, 12(10):2451–2471.

Sepp Hochreiter and Jürgen Schmidhuber. 1997. Long short-term memory. *Neural computation*, 9(8):1735–1780.

Minqing Hu and Bing Liu. 2004. Mining and summarizing customer reviews. In *Proceedings of the tenth ACM SIGKDD international conference on Knowledge discovery and data mining*, pages 168–177. ACM.

Bernard J Jansen, Mimi Zhang, Kate Sobel, and Abdur Chowdury. 2009. Twitter power: Tweets as electronic word of mouth. *Journal of the Association for Information Science and Technology*, 60(11):2169–2188.

Rafal Jozefowicz, Wojciech Zaremba, and Ilya Sutskever. 2015. An empirical exploration of recurrent network architectures. In *Proceedings of the 32nd International Conference on Machine Learning (ICML-15)*, pages 2342–2350.

Diederik Kingma and Jimmy Ba. 2014. Adam: A method for stochastic optimization. *arXiv preprint arXiv:1412.6980*.

Saif M. Mohammad, Felipe Bravo-Marquez, Mohammad Salameh, and Svetlana Kiritchenko. 2018. Semeval-2018 Task 1: Affect in tweets. In *Proceedings of International Workshop on Semantic Evaluation (SemEval-2018)*, New Orleans, LA, USA.

Saif M. Mohammad and Svetlana Kiritchenko. 2018. Understanding emotions: A dataset of tweets to study interactions between affect categories. In *Proceedings of the 11th Edition of the Language Resources and Evaluation Conference*, Miyazaki, Japan.

Preslav Nakov, Alan Ritter, Sara Rosenthal, Fabrizio Sebastiani, and Veselin Stoyanov. 2016. Semeval-2016 task 4: Sentiment analysis in twitter. In *Proceedings of the 10th International Workshop on Semantic Evaluation (SemEval-2016)*, pages 1–18.

Bo Pang, Lillian Lee, and Shivakumar Vaithyanathan. 2002. Thumbs up?: sentiment classification using machine learning techniques. In *Proceedings of the ACL-02 conference on Empirical methods in natural language processing-Volume 10*, pages 79–86. Association for Computational Linguistics.

Jeffrey Pennington, Richard Socher, and Christopher Manning. 2014. Glove: Global vectors for word representation. In *Proceedings of the 2014 conference on empirical methods in natural language processing (EMNLP)*, pages 1532–1543.

Sara Rosenthal, Noura Farra, and Preslav Nakov. 2017. Semeval-2017 task 4: Sentiment analysis in twitter. In *Proceedings of the 11th International Workshop on Semantic Evaluation (SemEval-2017)*, pages 502–518.

Nitish Srivastava, Elman Mansimov, and Ruslan Salakhudinov. 2015. Unsupervised learning of video representations using lstms. In *International Conference on Machine Learning*, pages 843–852.

Janyce Wiebe, Theresa Wilson, and Claire Cardie. 2005. Annotating expressions of opinions and emotions in language. *Language resources and evaluation*, 39(2-3):165–210.

Theresa Wilson, Janyce Wiebe, and Paul Hoffmann. 2005. Recognizing contextual polarity in phrase-level sentiment analysis. In *Proceedings of the conference on human language technology and empirical methods in natural language processing*, pages 347–354. Association for Computational Linguistics.

Hong Yu and Vasileios Hatzivassiloglou. 2003. Towards answering opinion questions: Separating facts from opinions and identifying the polarity of opinion sentences. In *Proceedings of the 2003 conference on Empirical methods in natural language processing*, pages 129–136. Association for Computational Linguistics.

ARB-SEN at SemEval-2018 Task1: A New Set of Features for Enhancing the Sentiment Intensity Prediction in Arabic Tweets

El Moatez Billah Nagoudi

Laboratoire d'Informatique et de Mathématiques LIM, Laghouat, Algeria
Echahid Hamma Lakhdar University, El Oued, Algeria
`e.nagoudi@lagh-univ.dz`

Abstract

This article describes our proposed Arabic Sentiment Analysis system named *ARB-SEN*. This system is designed for the International Workshop on Semantic Evaluation 2018 (SemEval-2018), Task1: Affect in Tweets. *ARB-SEN* proposes two supervised models to estimate the sentiment intensity in Arabic tweets. Both models use a set of features including sentiment lexicon, negation, word embedding and emotion symbols features. Our system combines these features to assist the sentiment analysis task. *ARB-SEN* system achieves a correlation score of 0.720, ranking $6th$ among all participants in the valence intensity regression (V-reg) for the Arabic sub-task organized within the SemEval 2018 evaluation campaign.

1 Introduction and Related Work

According to Mohammad (2016) the Sentiment Analysis (SA) task is used to refer to the *"task of automatically determining the valence or polarity of a piece of text, whether it is positive, negative, or neutral"*.

Nowadays, social media platforms like Twitter, Facebook, LinkedIn, and Quora are widely used (Lenze, 2017). For instance, Ranginwala and Towbin (2017) estimate that Twitter has 320 million active monthly users. These social media platforms allow people to communicate not only the sentiment they are feeling (positive or negative) but also the intensity of this sentiment. For example, from the tweet of your friend, you can estimate that: he is very happy (most positive), slightly angry (slightly negative), absolutely sad (most negative) or neutral (Mohammad et al., 2017).

Automatically determining the sentiment intensity is an important task in several application fields, such as public health, intelligence gathering, commerce and social welfare (Mohammad and Bravo-Marquez, 2017).

In the Semantic Evaluation (SemEval), sentiment analysis in Twitter task has been proposed for the first time in *SemEval-2013* by (Nakov et al., 2013). Since *SemEval-2013*, this task has become a principal task in SemEval : *SemEval-2014* (Rosenthal et al., 2014), *SemEval-2015* (Rosenthal et al., 2015), *SemEval-2016*, (Nakov et al., 2016) and *SemEval-2017* (Rosenthal et al., 2017).

In the Arab world, Salem (2017) estimates that the number of monthly active Arabic users was 11.1 million in March 2017, which makes Arabic an emergent language for sentiment analysis in Twitter (Rosenthal et al., 2017). Sentiment analysis task in Arabic is particularly a challenging research task (Rosenthal et al., 2017) due to its complex morphological and syntactic structure (Habash, 2010).

Many Arabic sentiment analysis tools and studies have been proposed in order to overcome this challenge. For example in Arabic newswire, the most relevant works are: (Abdul-Mageed et al., 2011), (Elarnaoty et al., 2012). In Arabic reviews we find (Elhawary and Elfeky, 2010), (Elnagar, 2016), (Altowayan and Elnagar, 2017). In Arabic Twitter many researches are focused on the sentiment analysis task such as (Mourad and Darwish, 2013), (Abdul-Mageed et al., 2014), (Refaee and Rieser, 2014), , (Salameh et al., 2015) and (Aldayel and Azmi, 2016).

In this article we present our *ARB-SEN system* devoted to enhancing the detection of sentiment intensity in Arabic tweets. *ARB-SEN system* proposes two methods to measure this valence. Our best submitted method achieves a correlation of 0.720, ranking $6th$ in the Arabic Detecting Sen-

Proceedings of the 12th International Workshop on Semantic Evaluation (SemEval-2018), pages 364–368
New Orleans, Louisiana, June 5–6, 2018. ©2018 Association for Computational Linguistics

timent Intensity shared task (Mohammad et al., 2018a), SemEval-2018.

2 System Description

The sentiment intensity detection in ARB-SEN system relies on a set of features. In what follows we describe the considered features:

2.1 Sentiment Lexicon Features (SLF)

We employed the following four sentiment lexicons to extract the SLF features:

Arabic Sentiment (Valence) Lexicons

Created as part of *SemEval-2016* by Kiritchenko et al. (2016), this Arabic sentiment lexicon is a list of 1,168 single words and 198 simple phrases and their associations with positive and negative sentiment. The lexicon include both standard and dialectal Arabic terms.

Arabic Sentiment (Valence) Lexicons

This is a annotated Arabic sentiment lexicon that is created by (Saif M. Mohammad and Kiritchenko, 2016). These lexicons were created by measuring the extent to which the words in a tweets corpus co-occurred with a set of seed positive and seed negative terms. This lexicon includes about 43k entries (23k positive and 20k negative).

ArabSenti sentiment lexicon

ArabSent is a manually annotated Arabic sentiment lexicon of 14k words that was created and by Abdul-Mageed et al. (2011). Each word in *Arab-Senti* is associated with a positive/negative sentiment label.

Dialectal sentiment lexicon

This is a freely available Arabic sentiment lexicon with more than 480 dialectal Arabic words. The lexicon is proposed by Refaee and Rieser (2014) and it is manually annotated by native Arabic speakers. Using these sentiment lexicons, we extract for each tweet four features:

    1) Sum Score The sum of sentiment scores of all the words in the tweet.

    2) Average Score This feature computes the average of sentiment scores of all the words in the tweet.

    3,4) Min and Max Score Represent the minimum and maximum sentiment score of words in the tweet.

For each of these features, if one word in the tweet does not exist in a sentiment lexicon, its corresponding sentiment score is not considered.

2.2 Negation Feature (NF)

Negation refers to words that reverse the sentiment of the word/phrase coming after them. For example: انا لست سعيد (I'm not happy), in this example the word سعيد (happy) has a *positive* sentiment, however, due to the negation word لست (I'm not) the sentiment of expression becomes *negative*. This feature is used by *ENCU* system (Wang et al., 2016) the best system in SemEval-2016 (Sentiment Intensity Task). Wang et al. (2016) they showed that the sentiment of the phrase can be reversed by adding a negation. Thus, for this binary feature, we have used a list of five main negation word in the Modern Standard Arabic (MAS) { ليس , ما , لن , لا , لم } proposed by (Abdulla et al., 2013). If the tweet contains at least one negation, this feature is set to 1, else 0.

2.3 Word Embedding Feature (WEF)

One of the main advantages of word embedding model is the fact that it allows for the retrieval of a list of words that are used in the same contexts with respect to a given word (Mikolov et al., 2013). In fact , we use the Arabic CBOW model (Zahran et al., 2015) to construct a list of 5-*closet* words for each word in the tweet as described in (Nagoudi et al., 2017). Then, we extract for each tweet the same features described in the section 2.1, with the difference that we compute the sentiment score for each word based on their 5-*closet* in word embedding:

    1) Sum Score The sum of the average sentiment scores of all the 5-*closet* words in tweet.

    2) Average Score This feature computes the average of sentiment scores of the 5-*closet* words in the tweet.

    3,4) Min and Max Score Represent the minimum and maximum average sentiment score of the 5-*closet* words in tweet.

To compute these features, we have used the same sentiment lexicons presented in the section 2.1.

2.4 Emoticons and Emojis Features (EEF)

The emoticons and emojis are already used in the sentiment analysis task in twitter (Read, 2005)

Positive	
Emoticons	**Emojis**
:-) :) :D :o) =]	😆 😇 😊 😋 😌
:] :3 :c) 8) :-]	😍 😎 😏 😀 😃
Negative	
Emoticons	**Emojis**
:[:-(:(:-c :c	😕 😖 😗 😘 😙
:-C :C :-[:[:{	😚 😛 😜 😝 😞
Neutral	
Emoticons	**Emojis**
:/ :-/ :-. :/ :t :s	😐 😑 😒 😓 😔
=/ =I :L =L :Z	😶 😷 😴 😵 😶

Table 1: A sample of the positive, negative and neutral emoticons and emojis.

and (Wolny, 2016). Therefore, we have used the Emoticons and Emojis as an indicator to predict the sentiment intensity of the tweet. We have used 3 set of emoticon and emoji positive, negative and neutral. Table 2 shows a sample of the positive, negative and neutral of emoticons and emojis.

2.5 Models Construction

The previously described features are fed into two different regression classifiers : Linear Regression (*LR*) and Support Vector Regression (*SVR*). We have used the python-based machine learning *scikit-learn* library[1] to trained these classifiers on the training and development data set of SemEval 2018 (Mohammad et al., 2018b), along with the previously discussed features to predict the sentiment intensity score for each tweet. Figure 1 illustrates an overview of the *ARB-SEN* system.

3 Experiments And Results

3.1 Training Data

The organisers of SemEval 2018 provided a training and development data set, which contained 933 and 139 Arabic tweets respectively. Thus, the trial and development are used as training data for our supervised models.

3.2 Data Pre-processing

In order normalize tweets, many pre-processing techniques have been proposed in the literature, such as:(Agarwal et al., 2011), (Ahmed et al.,

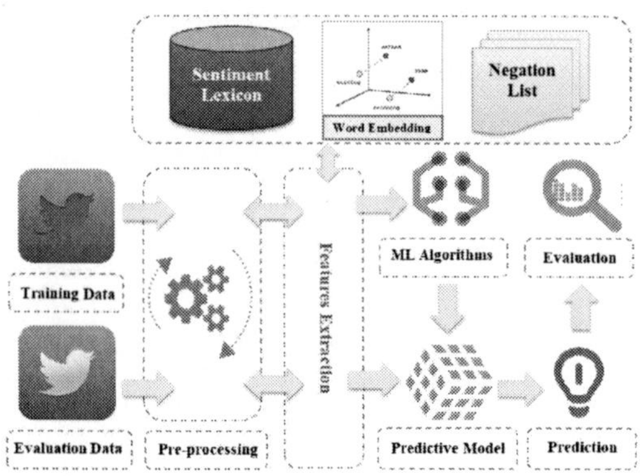

Figure 1: Architecture of the *ARB-SEN* system.

2013), and (Rosenthal et al., 2014). Therefore, we normalize our tweets using the following pre-processing steps:

1. Removing @*user_names*, *RTs*, and *URLs*;

2. Removing diacritics and non-alphanumeric characters;

3. Tokenizing the *#hashtags* of each tweet by breaking them into words, e.g: *#very_nice_day* becomes *very*, *nice* and *day*;

4. Normalizing the exchangeable Arabic letters as described in (Darwish et al., 2012), e.g: normalizing أ إ آ to ا and replacing final ى followed by ء with ئ.

3.3 Tests and Results

To evaluate the performance of our system, our two supervised models were assessed based on their accuracy on the 731 tweets in the Arabic Sentiment Intensity Evaluation Set[2]. In addition, we studied the impact of sentiment lexicon, negation, word embedding and emotion symbols features on the prediction efficiency.

We calculate the Pearson correlation between our assigned Sentiment Intensity scores and the gold labels. The results are presented in Table 2.

These results demonstrate that *SVR* classifier with all features succeed in predict the sentiment intensity in Arabic tweets with a Pearson correlation score of 0.720. However, the *LR* classifier with all features achieves a correlation score of 0.617. Thus, we can easily observe that *SVR* classifier with all features outperforms the *LR* classi-

---

[1] http://scikit-learn.org

[2] http://saifmohammad.com/WebDocs/
AIT-2018/AIT2018-DATA

Methods	Features	Correlation
	SLF	0.523
LR	SLF+NF	0.524
	SLF+NF+WEF	0.561
	SLF+NF+WEF+EEF	0.617
	SLF	0.647
SVR	SLF+NF	0.649
	SLF+NF+WEF	0.683
	SLF+NF+WEF+EEF	**0.720**
Baseline	-	-0.052

Table 2: Correlation results

fier with a gain of $+11\%$. Regarding the impact of the extracted features, all of them improve the results of the sentiment intensity prediction. Interestingly, we notice that the word embedding and emotion symbols features play a key role in improving the performance of the prediction accuracy in both classifiers with a mean of $+3.5\%$ and $+4.7\%$ respectively.

4   Conclusion and Future Work

In this article, we have presented two supervised models to predicate the sentiment intensity in Arabic tweets. Both classifiers are trained along with a set of Arabic tweets characterised by a set of features including: sentiment lexicon, negation, word embedding and emotion symbols features. The performance of our proposed system was confirmed through the Pearson correlation between our assigned sentiment scores and the golden labels. As future work, we are going to extend our features by using an Arabic Combined-Sentiment Word Embedding model. We would also like to further investigate the Arabic sentiment analysis task with more recent classifiers, namely Neural Deep learning.

References

Muhammad Abdul-Mageed, Mona T Diab, and Mohammed Korayem. 2011. Subjectivity and sentiment analysis of modern standard arabic. In *Proceedings of the 49th Annual Meeting of the Association for Computational Linguistics: Human Language Technologies: short papers-Volume 2*, pages 587–591. Association for Computational Linguistics.

Muhammad Abdul-Mageed, Mona Diab, and Sandra Kübler. 2014. Samar: Subjectivity and sentiment analysis for arabic social media. *Computer Speech & Language*, 28(1):20–37.

Nawaf A Abdulla, Nizar A Ahmed, Mohammed A Shehab, and Mahmoud Al-Ayyoub. 2013. Arabic sentiment analysis: Lexicon-based and corpus-based. In *Applied Electrical Engineering and Computing Technologies (AEECT), 2013 IEEE Jordan Conference on*, pages 1–6. IEEE.

Apoorv Agarwal, Boyi Xie, Ilia Vovsha, Owen Rambow, and Rebecca Passonneau. 2011. Sentiment analysis of twitter data. In *Proceedings of the workshop on languages in social media*, pages 30–38. Association for Computational Linguistics.

Soha Ahmed, Michel Pasquier, and Ghassan Qadah. 2013. Key issues in conducting sentiment analysis on arabic social media text. In *Innovations in Information Technology (IIT), 2013 9th International Conference on*, pages 72–77. IEEE.

Haifa K Aldayel and Aqil M Azmi. 2016. Arabic tweets sentiment analysis–a hybrid scheme. *Journal of Information Science*, 42(6):782–797.

A Aziz Altowayan and Ashraf Elnagar. 2017. Improving arabic sentiment analysis with sentiment-specific embeddings. In *Big Data (Big Data), 2017 IEEE International Conference on*, pages 4314–4320. IEEE.

Kareem Darwish, Walid Magdy, and Ahmed Mourad. 2012. Language processing for arabic microblog retrieval. In *Proceedings of the 21st ACM international conference on Information and knowledge management*, pages 2427–2430. ACM.

Mohamed Elarnaoty, Samir AbdelRahman, and Aly Fahmy. 2012. A machine learning approach for opinion holder extraction in arabic language. *arXiv preprint arXiv:1206.1011*.

Mohamed Elhawary and Mohamed Elfeky. 2010. Mining arabic business reviews. In *Data Mining Workshops (ICDMW), 2010 IEEE International Conference on*, pages 1108–1113. IEEE.

Ashraf Elnagar. 2016. Investigation on sentiment analysis for arabic reviews. In *Computer Systems and Applications (AICCSA), 2016 IEEE/ACS 13th International Conference of*, pages 1–7. IEEE.

Nizar Y Habash. 2010. Introduction to arabic natural language processing. *Synthesis Lectures on Human Language Technologies*, 3(1):1–187.

Svetlana Kiritchenko, Saif M. Mohammad, and Mohammad Salameh. 2016. Semeval-2016 task 7: Determining sentiment intensity of english and arabic phrases. In *Proceedings of the International Workshop on Semantic Evaluation*, SemEval '16, San Diego, California, June.

Nele Lenze. 2017. Social media in the arab world: Communication and public opinion in the gulf states. *European Journal of Communication*, 32(1):77–79.

Tomas Mikolov, Wen-tau Yih, and Geoffrey Zweig. 2013. Linguistic regularities in continuous space word representations. In *Hlt-naacl*, volume 13, pages 746–751.

Saif M Mohammad and Felipe Bravo-Marquez. 2017. Wassa-2017 shared task on emotion intensity. *arXiv preprint arXiv:1708.03700*.

Saif M Mohammad, Parinaz Sobhani, and Svetlana Kiritchenko. 2017. Stance and sentiment in tweets. *ACM Transactions on Internet Technology (TOIT)*, 17(3):26.

Saif M Mohammad, Felipe Bravo-Marquez, Mohammad Salameh, and Svetlana Kiritchenko. 2018a. Semeval-2018 task 1: Affect in tweets. In *Proceedings of International Workshop on Semantic Evaluation (SemEval-2018), New Orleans, LA, USA*.

Saif M. Mohammad, Felipe Bravo-Marquez, Mohammad Salameh, and Svetlana Kiritchenko. 2018b. Semeval-2018 Task 1: Affect in tweets. In *Proceedings of International Workshop on Semantic Evaluation (SemEval-2018)*, New Orleans, LA, USA.

Saif M Mohammad. 2016. Sentiment analysis: Detecting valence, emotions, and other affectual states from text. In *Emotion measurement*, pages 201–237. Elsevier.

Ahmed Mourad and Kareem Darwish. 2013. Subjectivity and sentiment analysis of modern standard arabic and arabic microblogs. In *Proceedings of the 4th workshop on computational approaches to subjectivity, sentiment and social media analysis*, pages 55–64.

El Moatez Billah Nagoudi, Jérémy Ferrero, Didier Schwab, and Hadda Cherroun. 2017. Word embedding-based approaches for measuring semantic similarity of arabic-english sentences. In *The 6th International Conference on Arabic Language Processing*, pages 19–33. Springer.

Preslav Nakov, Zornitsa Kozareva, Alan Ritter, Sara Rosenthal, Veselin Stoyanov, and Theresa Wilson. 2013. Semeval-2013 task 2: Sentiment analysis in twitter.

Preslav Nakov, Alan Ritter, Sara Rosenthal, Fabrizio Sebastiani, and Veselin Stoyanov. 2016. Semeval-2016 task 4: Sentiment analysis in twitter. In *Proceedings of the 10th International Workshop on Semantic Evaluation (SemEval-2016)*, pages 1–18.

Saad Ranginwala and Alexander J Towbin. 2017. The power of promotion: using social media to promote a radiology department. *Academic Radiology*, 24(4):488–496.

Jonathon Read. 2005. Using emoticons to reduce dependency in machine learning techniques for sentiment classification. In *Proceedings of the ACL student research workshop*, pages 43–48. Association for Computational Linguistics.

Eshrag Refaee and Verena Rieser. 2014. An arabic twitter corpus for subjectivity and sentiment analysis. In *LREC*, pages 2268–2273.

Sara Rosenthal, Alan Ritter, Preslav Nakov, and Veselin Stoyanov. 2014. Semeval-2014 task 9: Sentiment analysis in twitter. In *Proceedings of the 8th International Workshop on Semantic Evaluation (SemEval 2014)*, pages 73–80, Dublin, Ireland, August. Association for Computational Linguistics and Dublin City University.

Sara Rosenthal, Preslav Nakov, Svetlana Kiritchenko, Saif Mohammad, Alan Ritter, and Veselin Stoyanov. 2015. Semeval-2015 task 10: Sentiment analysis in twitter. In *Proceedings of the 9th international workshop on semantic evaluation (SemEval 2015)*, pages 451–463.

Sara Rosenthal, Noura Farra, and Preslav Nakov. 2017. SemEval-2017 task 4: Sentiment analysis in Twitter. In *Proceedings of the 11th International Workshop on Semantic Evaluation*, SemEval '17, Vancouver, Canada, August. Association for Computational Linguistics.

Mohammad Salameh Saif M. Mohammad and Svetlana Kiritchenko. 2016. Sentiment lexicons for arabic social media. In *Proceedings of 10th edition of the the Language Resources and Evaluation Conference (LREC)*, Portorož, Slovenia.

Mohammad Salameh, Saif Mohammad, and Svetlana Kiritchenko. 2015. Sentiment after translation: A case-study on arabic social media posts. In *Proceedings of the 2015 conference of the North American chapter of the association for computational linguistics: Human language technologies*, pages 767–777.

F. Salem. 2017. The arab social media report 2017: Social media and the internet of things: Towards data-driven policymaking in the arab world. Vol. 7.

Feixiang Wang, Zhihua Zhang, and Man Lan. 2016. Ecnu at semeval-2016 task 7: An enhanced supervised learning method for lexicon sentiment intensity ranking. In *Proceedings of the 10th International Workshop on Semantic Evaluation (SemEval-2016)*, pages 491–496.

Wiesław Wolny. 2016. Sentiment analysis of twitter data using emoticons and emoji ideograms. *Studia Ekonomiczne*, 296:163–171.

Mohamed A Zahran, Ahmed Magooda, Ashraf Y Mahgoub, Hazem Raafat, Mohsen Rashwan, and Amir Atyia. 2015. Word representations in vector space and their applications for arabic. In *International Conference on Intelligent Text Processing and Computational Linguistics*, pages 430–443. Springer.

psyML at SemEval-2018 Task 1: Transfer Learning for Sentiment and Emotion Analysis

Grace Gee, Eugene Wang

psyML, Inc.

`grace.eugene@psyml.co`

Abstract

In this paper, we describe the first attempt to perform transfer learning from sentiment to emotions. Our system employs Long Short-Term Memory (LSTM) networks, including bidirectional LSTM (biLSTM) and LSTM with attention mechanism. We perform transfer learning by first pre-training the LSTM networks on sentiment data before concatenating the penultimate layers of these networks into a single vector as input to new dense layers. For the E-c subtask, we utilize a novel approach to train models for correlated emotion classes. Our system performs 4/48, 3/39, 8/38, 4/37, 4/35 on all English subtasks EI-reg, EI-oc, V-reg, V-oc, E-c of SemEval 2018 Task 1: Affect in Tweets.

1 Introduction

SemEval-2018 Task 1: Affect in Tweets (Mohammad et al., 2018) is a shared task expanding on previous SemEval sentiment tasks and the WASSA-2017 Shared Task on Emotion Intensity (Mohammad and Bravo-Marquez, 2017). It presents 5 tasks:

1. Emotion intensity regression (EI-reg): given tweet and emotion (fear, anger, joy or sadness), predict real-valued emotion intensity from 0 to 1.

2. Emotion intensity ordinal classification (EI-oc): given tweet and emotion (fear, anger, joy or sadness), predict emotion intensity ordinal class from 0 (no emotion) to 3 (high emotion).

3. Sentiment intensity regression (V-reg): given tweet, predict real-valued sentiment intensity from 0 (no sentiment) to 1 (high sentiment). In this subtask, the directionality of the tweet sentiment is ignored. A negative tweet will be given the same score as a positive tweet with the same valence.

4. Sentiment intensity ordinal classification (V-oc): given tweet, predict sentiment ordinal intensity class from -3 (very negative) to 3 (very positive).

5. Emotion classification (E-c): given tweet, predict for each one of 11 emotions (anger, anticipation, disgust, fear, joy, love, optimism, pessimism, sadness, surprise, trust) whether the emotion is neutral (0) or present (1).

The task is particularly challenging since E-c and EI-oc are completely new subtasks. Thus, no prior data or working models are available for comparison. The leaderboard is also not public during the competition. As shown in Table 1, taken from (Mohammad and Kiritchenko, 2018), the development sets are particularly small compared to the test sets, and the test sets are comparable in size to the training sets, so the model must generalize.

For EI-oc and EI-reg, the development and test sets are also annotated separately from the training sets. This impacts performance as our system would have placed 1st with average pearson score 0.755 on the WASSA 2017 task, in which the EI-reg train, development, and test data are annotated in the same format. Furthermore, tweets are difficult to analyze due to the unstructuredness of its language (hashtags, emoticons, slang, misspellings, poor grammar).

Previously submitted systems in SemEval sentiment analysis use deep learning models such as CNN, RNN and LSTMs (Baziotis et al., 2017; Cliche, 2017; Rouvier, 2017). In a previous run of EI-reg in WASSA-2017 Shared Task on Emotion Intensity, top performing teams use deep learning models (Goel et al., 2017; Köper et al., 2017) and

Proceedings of the 12th International Workshop on Semantic Evaluation (SemEval-2018), pages 369–376
New Orleans, Louisiana, June 5–6, 2018. ©2018 Association for Computational Linguistics

Dataset	train	dev	test	Total
EI-reg, EI-oc				
anger	1,701	388	1,002	3,091
fear	2,252	389	986	3,627
joy	1,616	290	1,105	3,011
sadness	1,533	397	975	2,905
V-reg, V-oc	1,181	449	937	2,567
E-c	6,838	886	3,259	10,983

Table 1: Number of tweets in SemEval-2018: Affect in Tweets Dataset.

classifiers such as Support Vector Regressors or Random Forest Regressors (Duppada and Hiray, 2017; Köper et al., 2017). In both tasks, some participants use an ensemble approach (Goel et al., 2017; Duppada and Hiray, 2017; Rouvier, 2017).

To extract linguistic features, some systems employ pre-trained word embeddings (Baziotis et al., 2017; Cliche, 2017) or a combination of manually created features and/or lexicons (Köper et al., 2017; Duppada and Hiray, 2017). However, exclusively relying on hand-crafted features for EI-reg may result in a model that fails to encompass unforeseen linguistic relationships. Similarly, relying exclusively on deep learning models without lexicon inputs can lead to simple misclassifications due to the small training data.

To combine the best of both worlds, previous systems collapse high-dimensional word embeddings into a single dimension arithmetically, before combining it with hand-crafted features (usually one-dimensional). Goel et al. for instance averaged the word embeddings for each word in a tweet in order to concatenate it with a 43-dimensional vector. Duppada and Hiray simply averaged the two top performing model outputs.

In this paper, we present a deep learning system whose variants competed competitively in all English subtasks in SemEval-2018 Task 1: Affect in Tweets, specifically EI-reg, EI-oc, V-reg, V-oc, and E-c. We make the following contributions:

- A deep learning system that can take in a combination of one-dimensional hand-crafted and multi-dimensional word embedding inputs.

- A deep learning system that uses transfer learning from sentiment tasks to overcome the lack of training data compared to test data. To the best of our knowledge, this is the

first instance of transferring knowledge from sentiment to emotion.

- Specifically for Task E-c, procedures for training correlated target classes.

2 Overview

Fig 1 shows an overview of our system, which consists of three steps: (1) preprocessing input using a text processor and the Weka AffectiveTweets package[1] (Mohammad and Bravo-Marquez, 2017) (2) pre-training Components A to C using sentiment data (3) training the entire system, including Components A, B, C, E, using subtask-specific dataset.

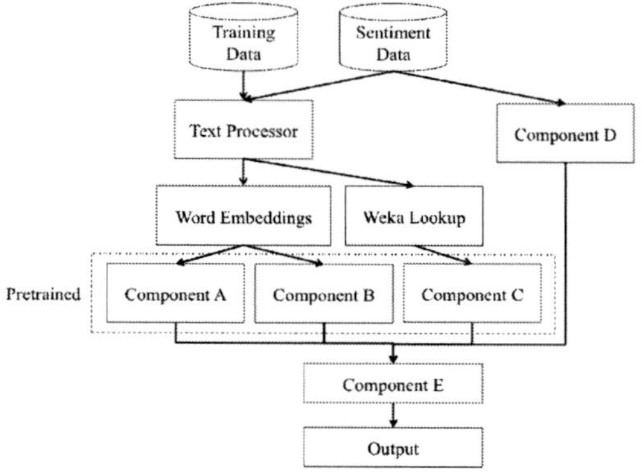

Figure 1: System Overview.

2.1 Preprocessing

We use the ekphrasis text processor[2] and word embeddings[3] built by Baziotis et al. Ekphrasis corrects for spelling, emoticons, emojis, splits hashtags and recognizes emphasized words. Its 300-dimension word embeddings are trained on 330M Twitter messages using GloVe. Other embeddings such as Stanford's GloVe (Pennington et al., 2014) do not incorporate newer popular unicode emojis. To build the Weka Lookup, we pass all 658,114 tokens in Baziotis et al. embedding dictionary into the TweetToLexiconFeatureVector filter in the Weka AffectiveTweets package. Of the 658,114, only 59,235 tokens returned nonzero

---

[1] https://github.com/felipebravom/AffectiveTweets

[2] https://github.com/cbaziotis/ekphrasis

[3] https://github.com/cbaziotis/datastories-semeval2017-task4

vectors. The TweetToLexiconFeatureVector returns a 43-dimension feature vector using sentiment and emotion lexicons such as Bing-Liu, AFINN, Sentiment140, and NRC-10 Expanded.

2.2 Transfer Learning

Transfer learning is the process of using knowledge from solving a source task to help performance in a target task. In particular, transfer learning is useful when the target task training set is small.

Another common way to deal with small data is distant supervision (Mintz et al., 2009), a process for generating labelled data from an unlabelled set according to a set of rules. For instance, for a sentiment analysis task, distant supervision can involve labelling tweets with smileys as positive and those with sad emojis as negative (Read, 2005).

Transfer learning has historically performed well on computer vision problems (Yosinski et al., 2014; Razavian et al., 2014). Traditionally, the CNN layer weights are frozen, its output treated as a feature vector input to a fully-connected layer, which will learn the new target task. Intuitively, the CNN will learn low-level image features on the source task while the dense layers will use these low-level features to predict a new target task.

Another strategy is to unfreeze the later layers weights of the pre-trained network and instead backpropagate all the way to the pre-trained network. In this case, the later layers of the pre-trained network can be fine-tuned. We choose to leave all weights from the pre-trained network unfrozen.

Transfer learning in natural language processing applications has been largely successful only within the same task such as POS tagging or sentiment (Blitzer et al., 2006, 2007). For different domains, good results are only achieved in semantically equivalent transfer (in which a source task and target task have the same objective but different data) but not for semantically different transfer (in which a source and target task have different objectives) (Mou et al., 2016).

For all subtasks, we will use transfer learning to pre-train our models on sentiment data. The source task objective is to predict sentiment categorical classes ('positive', 'negative', or 'neutral') given a tweet. Since the source task is not equivalent to any of the target tasks, we'd expect lower performance than those experiments on domain adaptation.

There are two main ways to perform transfer learning, the parameter initialization approach, in which a model is trained on a source task and the weights are transferred to a target task, and multitask learning, in which a model is trained to learn multiple tasks simultaneously. We choose to implement the parameter initialization approach as Mou et al. has shown both approaches to be comparable.

2.3 Neural Network

The Recurrent Neural Network (RNN) is an extension of the traditional neural network that allows sequential data. Fig 2 shows the architecture of a standard RNN which takes in a sequence of word embeddings $x_1, x_2, \ldots, x_N$ and outputs hidden states $h_1, h_2, \ldots, h_N$, where N is the length of the tweet.[4]

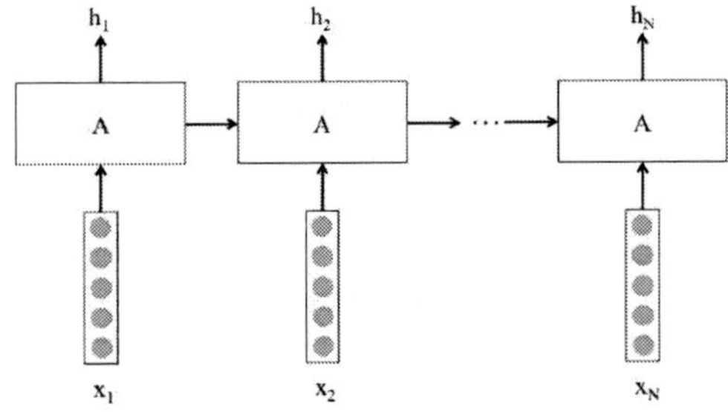

Figure 2: RNN basic structure.

In its simplest form, the hidden state $h_t \in \mathbb{R}^d$ (where d is the size of the RNN at time step t) is a function f of the current word embedding x_t, the past hidden state h_{t-1}, and the learned θ parameters.

$$h_t = f(x_t, h_{t-1}; \theta) \qquad (1)$$

Long Short-Term Memory (LSTM) (Hochreiter and Schmidhuber, 1997) is a special form of RNN with a memory cell and input, forget, and output gates that allow it to take into account long-term dependencies. It is more widely used than RNN since it overcomes the vanishing or exploding gradient problem common in RNNs. The architecture of a standard LSTM will be the same as that of an

---

[4]Figure recreated from `http://colah.github.io/posts/2015-08-Understanding-LSTMs/`

RNN as shown in Fig 2, but with a different repeating A module. Formally, each LSTM cell is computed as follows:

$$X = \begin{bmatrix} h_{t-1} \\ x_t \end{bmatrix} \tag{2}$$

$$f_t = \sigma(W_f \cdot X + b_f) \tag{3}$$

$$i_t = \sigma(W_i \cdot X + b_i) \tag{4}$$

$$o_t = \sigma(W_o \cdot X + b_o) \tag{5}$$

$$c_t = f_t \odot c_{t-1} + i_t \odot tanh(W_c \cdot X + b_c) \tag{6}$$

$$h_t = \sigma_t \odot tanh(c_t) \tag{7}$$

where f_t is the forget gate, i_t the input gate, c_t the cell state, h_t the hidden state, σ the sigmoid function and $\odot$ element-wise multiplication.

We use bidirectional LSTM (biLSTM) to incorporate both past and future context. A biLSTM employs two LSTMs, one reading forward, $\overrightarrow{LSTM}$, on the input sequence and another backward, $\overleftarrow{LSTM}$.

Whereas in a traditional LSTM, output h_i only incorporates information up till time step i, or $x_1, x_2, \ldots, x_i$, a bidirectional LSTM would incorporate information from both past input $x_1, x_2, \ldots, x_i$ and future input $x_i, x_{i+1}, \ldots, x_N$. Fig 3 shows the architecture of a standard biLSTM.

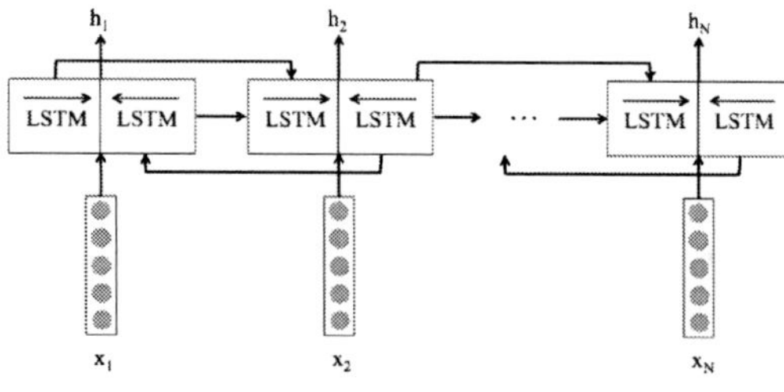

Figure 3: Bidirectional LSTM.

We use an attention mechanism (Rocktäschel et al., 2015) to learn which words in a tweet contribute more to a target task. Fig 4 shows the architecture of a standard LSTM with attention mechanism.

The attention layer is usually a 1 or 2-layer neural net that takes the output of an LSTM or RNN as input. It assigns "attention weight" α_i to each hidden state h_i and outputs a weighted representation r of the hidden states.

$$e_i = tanh(W_h h_i + b_h) \tag{8}$$

$$\alpha_i = softmax(e_i) \tag{9}$$

$$r = \sum_N \alpha_i h_i \tag{10}$$

where α is an attention weight vector, r is a weighted representation of the hidden states, and W_h and b_h are learned during backpropagation.

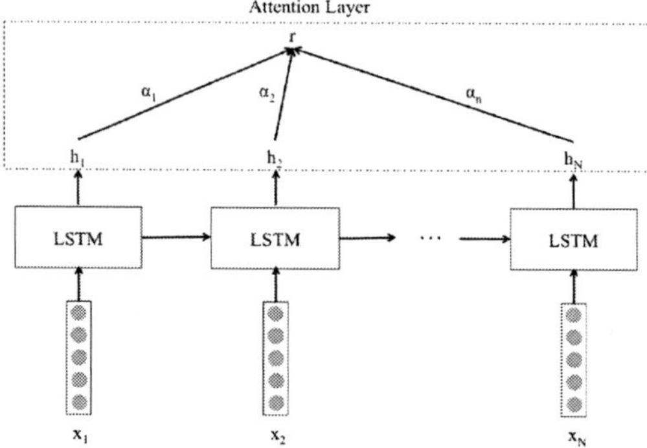

Figure 4: LSTM with Attention.

Components A and C are bidirectional LSTMs. Component B is a LSTM with attention mechanism.

3 Data

We used the dataset provided by the SemEval challenge.

For transfer learning, we pre-train Components A to C using train, development and test data from 2013 to 2017 SemEval Task 4A sentiment analysis classification tasks[5]. In total, this provided 7,723 negative, 22,195 neutral and 19,652 positive tweets.

4 Model

Component A is a 1-layer biLSTM. The input is a matrix $A \in \mathbb{R}^{n \times d}$, where n is the number of words in the tweet and d is the dimension of the word embedding. Component B is an LSTM with attention and takes in the same input as Component A. The attention layer is a 1 unit dense layer. Component C is also a 1-layer biLSTM like Component A, except the input is a matrix

---

[5]http://alt.qcri.org/semeval2017/task4/

$C \in \mathbb{R}^{n \times 43}$, since Weka's TweetToLexiconFeatureVector returns a 43-dimension vector and C is just a concatenated sequence of 43-dimension vectors of words passed into the TweetToLexiconFeatureVector. The tweet input for Components A through C are all zero padded. Component D just takes in an entire tweet and returns the 43-dimension TweetToLexiconFeatureVector vector. Component E is a 5-layer fully-connected neural net.

4.1 Regularization

In Components A through C, we apply dropout to both input and recurrent connections. Dropout (Srivastava et al., 2014) is a technique that involves randomly dropping units during training to prevent overfitting and co-adaptation of neurons. By randomly dropping units, neighboring neurons make up for the dropped units and learn representations for the target, resulting in a more robust network.

In Components A and C we apply global max pooling for the final layer.

We incorporate mini-batch gradient descent in all our models. Mini-batch gradient descent is calculated over small batches of data instead of the entire dataset as in traditional gradient descent. Compared to stochastic gradient descent, where gradient descent is calculated after every example, it is not as computationally intensive.

In the E-c dataset and sentiment classification dataset, some classes are overrepresented. This class imbalance can lead to bias in model output. To overcome this, for E-c we apply class weight to the loss function to boost recall of the minority class.

4.2 Hyper-parameters

We train all our models using mini-batches of size 8, and Adam (Kingma and Ba, 2014) optimization. For the E-c subtask, we minimize binary cross entropy loss. For EI-oc, EI-reg, V-oc and V-reg, we minimize mean squared error.

Models Components A through C all have dropout of 0.2 for their input layer and recurrent connections.

Components A and C are both biLSTM with 256 units. Component A takes in $A \in \mathbb{R}^{50 \times 300}$, while Component C takes in $C \in \mathbb{R}^{50 \times 43}$. We chose 50 since none of the tweets are longer than 50 words. Finally, we add a global max pooling layer.

Component B is a LSTM of 256 units, and takes in $B \in \mathbb{R}^{50 \times 300}$.

For source task learning, we apply a dense layer of 3 hidden units with sigmoid activation function to Components A through C.

Component E is 5 dense layers with 300, 125, 50, 25, and 1 hidden units. We use Rectified linear unit (ReLU) as the activation function for the former four layers.

4.3 Training

Source Task Learning During source task learning, we train each of Components A through C individually on the sentiment dataset with 10% hold out validation. The source task objective is to predict sentiment categorical class ('positive', 'negative', or 'neutral'). For each of the models, we train it for 1, 2, 3, 4, and 5 epochs and save the best performing one.

We experimented with RNN, CNN, LSTM, and biLSTM before settling on biLSTM and LSTM with attention.

Target Task Learning During target task learning, the final dense layers in Components A through C are removed and the penultimate layers are concatenated together with the output from Component D into a single vector as input to Component E. None of the weights are frozen and the entire system (Components A through E) is trained for between 5 to 10 epochs for subtasks EI-oc, EI-reg, V-oc, and V-reg. We choose the best performing model based on performance on the development set.

The final layer in Component E uses sigmoid as an activation function for EI-reg, EI-oc, V-reg, E-c and hyperbolic tangent for V-oc. The following functions are used to transform the ordinal classes of EI-oc, $d_{EI-oc} \in \{0, 1, 2, 3\}$, and V-oc, $d_{V-oc} \in \{-3, -2, -1, 0, 1, 2, 3\}$, to the output space of [0, 1] and [-1, 1] respectively.

$$d'_{EI-oc} = d_{EI-oc} * 0.25 + 0.125 \qquad (11)$$

$$d'_{V-oc} = d_{V-oc} * 2/7 \qquad (12)$$

For E-c, we notice the emotion classes are intercorrelated. The following Figure 5 is a dendrogram generated from E-c training data. The emotions are hierarchically clustered based on their correlations. The horizontal axis labels correspond to the 11 classes. The shorter the length of the sideways n-shape, the more correlated the two classes.

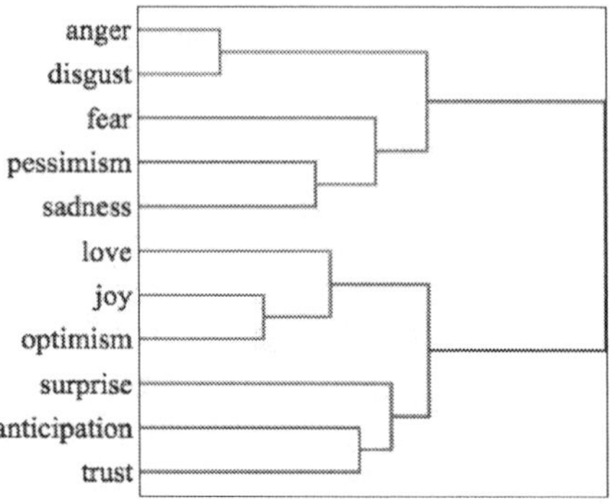

Figure 5: Dendrogram of 11 emotions, clustered using correlation and hierarchical clustering.

For E-c, we obtain the following emotion clusters from the dendrogram: [anger, disgust], [sadness, pessimism, fear], [joy, optimism, love], [anticipation, surprise, trust]. For each of the clusters, we obtain a fresh copy of the entire pretrained system and train it for 2 epochs consecutively for each target class in the aforementioned order within the emotion cluster. The pseudocode is as follows. We call this method "cluster training":

Algorithm 1 Cluster training

1: **for** *emotionCluster* in *emotionClusters* **do**
2:     $S \leftarrow$ System from Fig 1
3:     **for** *emotion* in *emotionCluster* **do**
4:         Train S for 2 epochs on *emotion* training
5:         Predict *emotion* test with S

4.4 Experimental Setup

We build all the models with the Keras library and train them on Google Datalab. The dendrogram diagram is built with Plotly.

5 Evaluation & Results

SemEval Results Our model ranks 4/48 in EI-reg, 3/39 in EI-oc, 8/38 in V-reg, 4/37 in V-oc, 4/35 in E-c (Mohammad et al., 2018). Our performance for V-reg is less than satisfactory because V-reg measures sentiment intensity without regards for directionality, whereas our source task takes into account directionality. This supports findings by

Mou et al. that pre-training is less useful in a semantically different transfer.

System To evaluate our system, we assess the performance of each Component and various combinations of them. Table 2 shows the development set performance. In particular, we note that Component A+B performs better than Component A or Component B separately, as with Component C+D. Furthermore, Component A+B+C+D perform better overall compared to Component A+B and Component C+D.

Cluster training Subtask E-c classes are imbalanced, with 95% of "Trust" and "Surprise" training examples being negative. Table 3 shows the breakdown of negative and positive training examples for each of the E-c classes.

To assess our cluster training procedure, we evaluate the performance of independently training each of the E-c emotion classes (using a fresh copy of the pre-trained system for each of the 11 emotions) as well as with various class weighing schemes. Table 4 shows our experiment results.

Within independent training experiments, squared inverse weights performed best as measured by accuracy and micro-avg F1. Using squared inverse weights, cluster training performs better than independent training, attesting to the utility of cluster training.

6 Conclusion

In this paper, we present the first attempt to perform transfer learning from sentiment to emotions. Model weights are pre-trained with past SemEval sentiment categorization tasks and the penultimate layers of the models are concatenated into a single vector as input to new dense layers. The entire system is then trained for each subtask with the weights unfrozen.

Our deep learning system combines multi-dimensional word embeddings with single dimensional lexicon-based features. Specifically we combine features of $X \in \mathbb{R}^{50 \times 300}, \mathbb{R}^{50 \times 43}, \mathbb{R}^{1 \times 43}$, which results in better performance than systems using just one of the features.

For the E-c subtask, we utilize hierarchical clustering to group correlated emotions together and train the same model incrementally for emotions within the same cluster. This novel method outperforms a system which trains on each emotion independently.

Experiment	Anger	Sadness	Fear	Joy
Component A	0.729	0.706	0.677	0.719
Component B	0.710	0.719	0.646	0.689
Component C	0.584	0.561	0.567	0.564
Component D	0.602	0.597	0.546	0.585
Component A+B	0.722	0.714	0.701	0.732
Component C+D	0.659	0.619	0.631	0.601
Component A+B+C+D	**0.761**	**0.720**	**0.723**	**0.745**

Table 2: Results on development set comparing Component experiments.

Emotion	Percentage negative	Percentage positive
Anger	63%	37%
Disgust	62%	38%
Sadness	71%	29%
Pessimism	88%	12%
Fear	82%	18%
Joy	64%	36%
Optimism	71%	29%
Love	90%	10%
Anticipation	86%	14%
Surprise	95%	5%
Trust	95%	5%

Table 3: E-c training set, breakdown of percentage of positive and negative examples.

Experiment	Accuracy	Micro-avg F1	Macro-avg F1
Cluster training, squared inverse weights	**0.576**	**0.695**	0.522
Independent training, equal weights	0.513	0.639	0.439
Independent training, inverse weights	0.447	0.586	**0.545**
Independent training, squared inverse weights	0.558	0.684	0.527

Table 4: E-c experiment results on development set.

We participated in all of the English subtasks of SemEval 2018 Task 1: Affect in Tweets and obtained top 4 in 4 out of the 5 subtasks, testifying to our model robustness.

For future work, we would like to experiment with other training methods such as multi-task learning and distant supervision, as well as tune the hyper-parameters of our model to augment its performance across all subtasks (Mohammad and Kiritchenko, 2018).

Acknowledgments

This project was kindly financed by psyML Inc., a company co-founded by Galen Buckwalter and Dave Herman to bring psychology and AI together to solve real world problems. We thank Sebastian Ruder for his paper suggestions and the task organizers of SemEval 2018 Task 1 for the data and gracious support.

References

Christos Baziotis, Nikos Pelekis, and Christos Doulkeridis. 2017. Datastories at semeval-2017 task 4: Deep lstm with attention for message-level and topic-based sentiment analysis. In *Proceedings of the 11th International Workshop on Semantic Evaluation (SemEval-2017)*, pages 747–754. Association for Computational Linguistics.

John Blitzer, Mark Dredze, and Fernando Pereira. 2007. Biographies, bollywood, boom-boxes and blenders: Domain adaptation for sentiment classification. In *Proceedings of the 45th Annual Meeting of the Association of Computational Linguistics*, pages 440–447. Association for Computational Linguistics.

John Blitzer, Ryan McDonald, and Fernando Pereira. 2006. Domain adaptation with structural correspondence learning. In *Proceedings of the 2006 Conference on Empirical Methods in Natural Language Processing*, pages 120–128. Association for Computational Linguistics.

Mathieu Cliche. 2017. Bb_twtr at semeval-2017 task 4: Twitter sentiment analysis with cnns and lstms. In *Proceedings of the 11th International Workshop on Semantic Evaluation (SemEval-2017)*, pages 573–580. Association for Computational Linguistics.

Venkatesh Duppada and Sushant Hiray. 2017. Seernet at emoint-2017: Tweet emotion intensity estimator. In *Proceedings of the 8th Workshop on Computational Approaches to Subjectivity, Sentiment and Social Media Analysis*, pages 205–211. Association for Computational Linguistics.

Pranav Goel, Devang Kulshreshtha, Prayas Jain, and Kaushal Kumar Shukla. 2017. Prayas at emoint 2017: An ensemble of deep neural architectures for emotion intensity prediction in tweets. In *Proceedings of the 8th Workshop on Computational Approaches to Subjectivity, Sentiment and Social Media Analysis*, pages 58–65. Association for Computational Linguistics.

Sepp Hochreiter and Jurgen Schmidhuber. 1997. Long short-term memory. *Neural computation*, 9(8):1735–1780.

Diederik Kingma and Jimmy Ba. 2014. Adam: A method for stochastic optimization. arXiv:1412.6980. ArXiv preprint.

Maximilian Köper, Evgeny Kim, and Roman Klinger. 2017. Ims at emoint-2017: Emotion intensity prediction with affective norms, automatically extended resources and deep learning. In *Proceedings of the 8th Workshop on Computational Approaches to Subjectivity, Sentiment and Social Media Analysis*, pages 50–57. Association for Computational Linguistics.

Mike Mintz, Steven Bills, Rion Snow, and Daniel Jurafsky. 2009. Distant supervision for relation extraction without labeled data. In *Proceedings of the Joint Conference of the 47th Annual Meeting of the ACL and the 4th International Joint Conference on Natural Language Processing of the AFNLP*, pages 1003–1011. Association for Computational Linguistics.

Saif Mohammad and Felipe Bravo-Marquez. 2017. Wassa-2017 shared task on emotion intensity. In *Proceedings of the 8th Workshop on Computational Approaches to Subjectivity, Sentiment and Social Media Analysis*, pages 34–49. Association for Computational Linguistics.

Saif M. Mohammad, Felipe Bravo-Marquez, Mohammad Salameh, and Svetlana Kiritchenko. 2018. Semeval-2018 Task 1: Affect in tweets. In *Proceedings of International Workshop on Semantic Evaluation (SemEval-2018)*.

Saif M. Mohammad and Svetlana Kiritchenko. 2018. Understanding emotions: A dataset of tweets to study interactions between affect categories. In *Proceedings of the 11th Edition of the Language Resources and Evaluation Conference (LREC-2018)*.

Lili Mou, Zhao Meng, Rui Yan, Ge Li, Yan Xu, Lu Zhang, and Zhi Jin. 2016. How transferable are neural networks in nlp applications? In *Proceedings of the 2016 Conference on Empirical Methods in Natural Language Processing*, pages 479–489. Association for Computational Linguistics.

Jeffrey Pennington, Richard Socher, and Christopher Manning. 2014. Glove: Global vectors for word representation. In *Proceedings of the 2014 Conference on Empirical Methods in Natural Language Processing (EMNLP)*, pages 1532–1543. Association for Computational Linguistics.

Ali Sharif Razavian, Hossein Azizpour, Josephine Sullivan, and Stefan Carlsson. 2014. Cnn features off-the-shelf: an astounding baseline for recognition. In *Proceedings of the IEEE Conference on Computer Vision and Pattern Recognition Workshops*, pages 806–813.

Jonathon Read. 2005. Using emoticons to reduce dependency in machine learning techniques for sentiment classification. In *Proceedings of the ACL Student Research Workshop*, pages 43–48. Association for Computational Linguistics.

Tim Rocktäschel, Edward Grefenstette, Karl Moritz Hermann, Tomáš Kočiský, and Phil Blunsom. 2015. Reasoning about entailment with neural attention. arXiv:1509.06664. ArXiv preprint.

Mickael Rouvier. 2017. Lia at semeval-2017 task 4: An ensemble of neural networks for sentiment classification. In *Proceedings of the 11th International Workshop on Semantic Evaluation (SemEval-2017)*, pages 760–765. Association for Computational Linguistics.

Nitish Srivastava, Geoffrey Hinton, Alex Krizhevsky, Ilya Sutskever, and Ruslan Salakhutdinov. 2014. Dropout: A simple way to prevent neural networks from overfitting. *The Journal of Machine Learning Research*, 15(1):1929–1958.

Jason Yosinski, Jeff Clune, Yoshua Bengio, and Hod Lipson. 2014. How transferable are features in deep neural networks? *Advances in Neural Information Processing Systems*, 27:3320–3328.

UIUC at SemEval-2018 Task 1: Recognizing Affect with Ensemble Models

Abhishek Narwekar
Department of Computer Science
University of Illinois, Urbana Champaign
USA 61820
abhisheknkar@gmail.com

Roxana Girju
Linguistics Department,
Computer Science Department,
Beckman Research Institute,
University of Illinois, Urbana Champaign
USA 61820
girju@illinois.edu

Abstract

Our submission to the SemEval-2018 Task1: *Affect in Tweets* shared task competition is a supervised learning model relying on standard lexicon features coupled with word embedding features. We used an ensemble of diverse models, including random forests, gradient boosted trees, and linear models, corrected for training-development set mismatch. We submitted the system's output for subtasks 1 (emotion intensity prediction), 2 (emotion ordinal classification), 3 (valence intensity regression) and 4 (valence ordinal classification), for English tweets. We placed $25^{th}, 19^{th}, 24^{th}$ and 15th in the four subtasks respectively. The baseline considered was an SVM (Support Vector Machines) model with linear kernel on the lexicon and embedding based features. Our system's final performance measured in Pearson correlation scores outperformed the baseline by a margin of 2.2% to 14.6% across all tasks.

1 Introduction

Affective computing deals with the recognition, interpretation, processing, and simulation of human affects. It is a highly interdisciplinary field at the heart of a broad range of technological applications in health care, media & advertisement, automotive, and others.

Although emotions are a fundamental feature of human experience, they have been long ignored by technology development mainly due to their complex and subjective nature, as well as the lack of learning capabilities to detect them. Current affective computing systems focus mainly on facial expressions, body language, speech (tone of voice, rhythm, etc.), keystroke as well as physiological input (e.g., heart rate, body temperature) to capture and process changes in a user's emotional state. However, in environments such as social media and Internet forums, most often the only signal is written language. And since language per se is the smallest portion of human communication (Mehrabian, 1981), emotions are not easy to detect.

Although emotion detection is directly related to the more popular task of sentiment analysis, they differ in many respects. Sentiment Analysis aims to detect the positive, neutral, or negative orientation of the text, while emotion detection focuses on recognizing and classifying text snippets into a set of predefined, more or less universal emotions. Various such classification models have been proposed, two famous ones being Ekman's (Ekman, 1997) six basic emotions (anger, happiness, surprise, disgust, sadness, and fear) and Plutchik's wheel of eight emotions (Plutchik, 2001), where each primary emotion has a polar opposite (joy, trust, fear, surprise, sadness, anticipation, anger, and disgust).

To date, there are many freely available tools for sentiment polarity classification of input text, yet not so many exist for emotion detection. Major challenges are: (1) the difficulty in establishing ground truth for various emotions, (2) the high variability, vagueness, ambiguity, and implicitness of language that can make the detection very problematic, (3) the scarcity of non-verbal clues in written communication, as well as (4) the challenge of getting access to and being able to process the right type of context. This can be explained by the "7% Rule" (Mehrabian, 1981): only 7% of human communication is verbal while over 90% is comprised of tone of voice (38%) and body language (55%).

This year, SemEval 2018 hosts Task1: *Affect in Tweets* (Mohammad et al., 2018) - a shared task competition aiming to predict emotions and sentiment in tweets. There are five sub-tasks (Table 1). The participating systems have to automati-

Proceedings of the 12th International Workshop on Semantic Evaluation (SemEval-2018), pages 377–384
New Orleans, Louisiana, June 5–6, 2018. ©2018 Association for Computational Linguistics

cally determine the intensity of emotions (E) and intensity of sentiment (i.e., valence V) from a collection of tweets, as experienced by the authors of these tweets. The organizers also include a multi-label emotion classification task for tweets. For each task, separate training and test data sets for each language considered are provided to the participants.

ID	Task Label	Input	Output
1	EI-reg	Tweet (t), Emotion (e)	Intensity(e, t) $\in$ (0, 1)
2	EI-oc	Tweet (t), Emotion (e)	$0 \leq$ Intensity(e, t) ≤ 3, Intensity(e, t) $\in \mathbf{N}$
3	V-reg	Tweet (t), Sentiment (s)	Intensity(s, t) $\in$ (0, 1)
4	V-oc	Tweet (t), Sentiment (s)	$-3 \leq$ Intensity(s, t) ≤ 3, Intensity(s, t) $\in \mathbf{N}$
5	E-c	Tweet (t), Emotions (s)	Class: neutral/ no emotion/ multiple emotions

Table 1: Description of the five sub-tasks of Task1: Affect in Tweets at SemEval 2018.

The contributions of the UIUC system are as follows: (1) In this competition, we demonstrate the use of a system that uses lexicon- and embedding-based features in an ensemble model of diverse approaches such as random forests, gradient boosted trees, and linear classifiers. We demonstrate how their combination in the final ensemble outperforms each of the individual methods. (2) We account for the train-development mismatch in the dataset by training a separate model to learn this mismatch. (3) We analyze the UIUC system and several variants of it, some of which improve on its performance. (4) We also perform an error analysis of "difficult" tweets, and explore areas for improvement of the model.

2   Related Work

Word-Emotion Lexicons: Word-emotion lexicons are a mapping between the words in the vocabulary to an emotion rating. Some lexicons map words to discrete emotions, such as General Inquirer (Stone et al., 1962), Wordnet Affect (Strapparava et al., 2004) and the NRC-10 Emotion Lexicon (Mohammad and Turney, 2013). Others, such as Affective Norms for English Words (ANEW) (Bradley and Lang, 1999) and WKB Corpus (Warriner et al., 2013), map them to dimensions such as valence, arousal and dominance.

Sentence-Level Labeled Corpora: Large scale corpora annotated with sentence-level emotion labels are uncommon in the literature. Affective Text (Strapparava and Mihalcea, 2007), created for SemEval 2007, contains emotion annotations headlines of news articles. Alm et al. annotated about 185 children's stories with the Ekman labels. Aman and Szpakowicz created annotated 5,000 sentences with additional labels for intensity and emotion bearing phrases. Preotiuc-Pietro et al. annotated 3,000 social media posts for valence and arousal, making this one of the few datasets that contains annotations based on the VAD model.

Approaches: *Rule-based approaches* incorporate domain knowledge. This can include term-based n-gram features, distance between certain terms or pre-specified POS patterns. Early work in this area focused mainly on linguistic heuristics (Hatzivassiloglou and McKeown, 1997). However, a major drawback of these rule-based approaches is that they are unable to detect novel expression of sentiment. *Keyword based approaches* classify text based on the detection of unambiguous words in language. They depend on large scale lexicons with affective labels for words, such NRC (Mohammad and Turney, 2013). *Knowledge-based approaches* use web ontologies or semantic networks. A major advantage of such systems is that they enable the system to use conceptual ideas derived from world knowledge (Cambria and Hussain, 2012). Recently, *distributed approaches* have been proposed that leverage word embeddings and train deep neural networks on the embedding space (Mohammad and Bravo-Marquez, 2017a).

Shared evaluations have encouraged the community to create benchmarks over shared tasks, and have been organized frequently. The Affective Text task at SemEval 2007 (Strapparava and Mihalcea, 2007) asked its participants to predict emotion labels for headlines of news articles. More recently, the Shared Task on Emotion Intensity (EmoInt) at WASSA 2017 (Mohammad and Bravo-Marquez, 2017a), had 22 participating teams who were given a corpus of 3,960 English tweets annotated with a continuous intensity score for each of four of Ekman's basic emotions: anger, fear, joy and sadness.

3   Dataset

Tasks 1 and 2 share the same training and development data sets: a total of 7,500 sentences in training and about 1,600 sentences in development across the four emotions: anger, fear, joy, sadness. It is interesting to note that the training data sets for the emotions of fear, anger and sadness overlap significantly: all pairs have a Jaccard similarity of over 0.5. This means that over 67% of the data sets across these emotions contain the same tweets.

Tasks 3 and 4 share the same data sets as well, for a total of 1,200 tweets in training and 450 tweets in development across the four emotions.

Another interesting overlap is between the tweet collections for Tasks 5 and 1 (and therefore Task 2): The data set for Task 5 appears to be made up largely of the tweets for Task 1, for both the training and development sets. These overlaps of the training and development data sets across all emotions gave us the idea to tackle all tasks using a common set of features. For instance, Tasks 2 and 4 may be solved by simply transforming the output of Tasks 1 and 3, respectively. Task 5 involves a multi-label classification and thus, needs more thought.

In the test set, with the exception of the first 1,000 or so sentences, nearly 95% of the total sentences for Tasks 1A and 3A (i.e., for English) are the so called "mystery" sentences – meaning, essentially neutral sentences without any emotional content. The scores reported by the organizers are for the non-mystery sentences only (i.e., non-neutral).

4 The UIUC System

Our system takes as input features from affective lexicons and word embeddings trained on affective Twitter corpora. We then train an ensemble of diverse models over these features. Given that the training and development labels are not directly comparable, we also model the mismatch between the two sets. Moreover, we also describe additional models that we constructed after the competition deadline (section 4.4). We report results for tasks 1A, 2A, 3A and 4A (where 'A' identifies the target language: English).

4.1 Feature Space

We have used the *AffectiveTweets* (Mohammad and Bravo-Marquez, 2017b), a package in Weka (Hall et al., 2009) for extracting certain features from a tweet. The features extracted are: MPQA (Wilson et al., 2005), BingLiu (Bauman et al., 2017), AFINN (Nielsen, 2011), Sentiment-140 Emoticon (Kiritchenko et al.,

2014), NRC Hashtag Emotion Lexicon (Mohammad and Kiritchenko, 2015), NRC emotion lexicon (wordlevel) (Mohammad and Turney, 2013), SentiWordNet (Baccianella et al., 2010), NegatingWordList(Mohammad and Bravo-Marquez, 2017b). We call these *lexicon features*. In addition, we also extract *Embedding based features* (Twitter Edinburgh 100D / 400D corpus) using the AffectiveTweets package.

4.2 Models

The UIUC system contains an ensemble constructed using stacking of several base learners. A schematic of this ensemble is shown in figure 1. We obtained out-of-fold predictions for each of these three models using 5-fold cross validation on layer 1. These predictions were concatenated and provided as input to layer 2. Parameters of the models in this ensemble are detailed below:

Layer 1
Random Forests:
n_estimators=100, max_features=$\sqrt{F}$ (F=total features), max_depth=5, min_samples_leaf=2
XGB[1]: max_depth=5, min_child_weight=150, gamma=0, n_estimators=150, reg_alpha=0.01, reg_lambda=0.87, learning_rate=0.1
SVM:kernel=linear, C=0.1

Layer 2
XGB: max_depth=3, min_child_weight=1, gamma=0, n_estimators=100, reg_alpha=0.1, reg_lambda=1, learning_rate=0.1, random_state=0

4.3 Modeling the Mismatch Between the Training and Development Sets

According to the organizers, the training set for the task was created from an annotation effort in 2016 (Mohammad and Bravo-Marquez, 2017a). The development and test sets were created from a common 2017 annotation effort. As a result, the scores for tweets across the training and development sets or across the training and test sets are not directly comparable. We therefore devise a model that can predict and eliminate the mismatch between the two sets of labels. As a means to model the mismatch in the distributions of the two label sets, we train a linear model that, for the labels in the development set, learns a function between the predictions made for the development set and

---

[1]Note: XGB stands for the XGBoost implementation of gradient boosted decision trees. SVM was implmented using sklearn (http://scikit-learn.org/stable/).

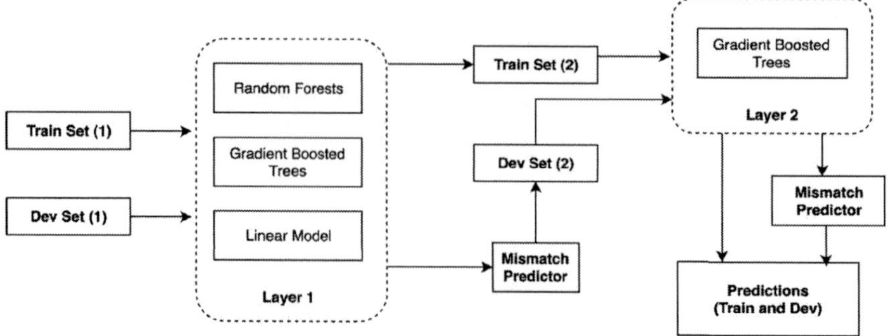

Figure 1: Ensemble used in the UIUC system.

the ground truth. This learner does not affect the training in any way, but is a way to transform the predictions made for the development set so that they are comparable to the ground truth labels.

4.4 Additional Models

After the competition deadline, we built and evaluated additional models. The overall model was an ensemble with the same structure as the official submission. Additions include implementation of neural models of computation. In particular, we implement feed-forward neural networks (using the average word embeddings as input), LSTM-CNN (using individual word embeddings) and character level LSTM (using the character stream). The neural networks were implemented in Keras (Chollet et al., 2015) with the Tensorflow (Abadi et al., 2016) backend. Details about these additional models are shown below.

Layer 1:
SVM (layer 1): C=0.1, kernel=RBF
XGB: max_depth=5, reg_lambda=0.87, min_child_weight=150, n_estimators=150
FFNN (feed forward neural network): Dense (256, sigmoid), Dropout (0.2, sigmoid), Dense (64, sigmoid), Dense (32, sigmoid), Dense (1, relu)
LSTM-CNN: Conv1D (300, 3, relu), Dropout (0.2), LSTM (150), Dropout (0.2), Dense (32, sigmoid), Dense (1, relu)
Character level language model (Char): LSTM (150), Dropout (0.2), Dense (64, sigmoid), Dense (1, relu)

Layer 2:
SVM: C=1, kernel=RBF

5 Results

In this section, we describe the results of our official submission to SemEval 2018 (subsection 5.1) as well as the results of experiments on additional models constructed after the competition deadline (section 5.2).

5.1 Performance of the UIUC system

Tables 2 and 3 show the performance of our model for Tasks 1A, 2A, 3A and 4A, respectively. We have shown the results by comparing our model against the baseline, which has been trained using an SVM with linear kernel on the lexicon and embedding based features. Our submission outperforms the baseline in nearly all the task-emotion pairs.

In particular, we observe that the results for the prediction of data points in the 0.5 − 1 range are poorer than in the overall range. The reason for this is that the finer prediction is a harder task than the overall prediction, and exactly predicting the emotion intensity given that it is high has significant variance. Scores for Task 2A are worse than those for Task 1A in spite of the similarity of the tasks. This is because in Task 2A, we essentially discretize the output, thereby either increasing or decreasing the absolute error between the intensity predicted and the actual intensity, depending on whether the discretized output is correct or not. On the whole, evidently, the correlation drops as the effect of the latter case (increase in the absolute error) dominates over the former.

Tasks 3 and 4 follow similar trends as Tasks 1 and 2 respectively, but we see a higher correlation for these tasks as compared to Tasks 1 and 2, respectively. This leads to the conclusion that predicting the sentiment is an easier task than pre-

Subtask	Submission	Pearson (all instances)					Alternate evaluation				
		macro-avg	anger	fear	joy	sadness	macro-avg	anger	fear	joy	sadness
1	UIUC System	0.647	0.663	0.646	0.649	0.628	0.463	0.514	0.431	0.422	0.485
	Baseline	0.630	0.652	0.625	0.632	0.610	0.462	0.523	0.418	0.424	0.481
2	UIUC System	0.518	0.514	0.449	0.576	0.533	0.463	0.414	0.392	0.562	0.484
	Baseline	0.448	0.512	0.258	0.527	0.493	0.334	0.335	0.219	0.415	0.366

Table 2: Results of the UIUC system for subtasks 1a (emotion intensity regression) and 2a (emotion ordinal classification) and comparison with baseline. The alternate evaluation is Pearson correlation for tweets with scores between 0.5 and 1 for subtask 1 and the Cohen Kappa (Cohen, 1960) for subtask 2.

Subtask	Model	Pearson	Alternate evaluation
3	UIUC system	0.762	0.582
	Baseline	0.746	0.565
4	UIUC system	0.724	0.694
	Baseline	0.688	0.673

Table 3: Results of the UIUC system for tasks 3a (valence intensity regression) and 4a (valence ordinal classification) and comparison with baseline. The alternate evaluation was Pearson correlation for tweets with score 0.5-1 for subtask 3a and Cohen's Kappa for subtask 4a.

dicting the intensity of a given emotion.

5.2 Performance of Additional Models

Ablation Study for Task 1: Given the multiple subsections of data, it is difficult to optimize the architecture and parameters for all emotions for all subtasks. Therefore, we focus on optimizing the architecture and parameters for only the first subtask (emotion intensity prediction) for the emotion *anger*. Given the many models developed and presented here, it is interesting to see how they perform individually on this subtask. Table 4 shows the performance of various feature-model combinations. Note that **L** and **E** in the *Features* column indicate lexicon-based and embedding-based features respectively.

Feature	Model	CV	Dev	Test
L	SVM	0.646	0.616	0.654
	XGB	0.648	0.646	0.634
	FFNN	0.699	0.674	0.664
	SVM+XGB	0.662	0.651	0.663
	SVM+XGB+FFNN [M1]	0.695	0.674	0.673
E	SVM	0.564	0.553	0.555
	LSTM	0.640	0.635	0.633
	LSTM-CNN	0.641	0.639	0.635
	LSTM-CNN (Att) [M2]	0.651	0.642	0.644
L+E	M1+M2	0.733	**0.713**	0.701
	M1+M2+Char	**0.735**	0.711	**0.704**

Table 4: An ablation study of various features and models for subtask 1: emotion intensity prediction for the specific case of the emotion *anger*.

We use the SVM trained on lexical features as the baseline. We can see that the SVM+XGB+FFNN (referred to as M1) performs

better than the SVM alone. LSTM-CNN with attention (referred to as M2) performs similarly to the SVM baseline. However, when combined together, the model M1+M2+Char performs better than each of the individual models on the test set. This means that the different models capture complementary information about the input, and work better in unison, thus demonstrating the efficacy of the idea of ensembling.

Henceforth, we use **M1** to refer to the SVM + XGBoost + Feedforward Neural Network architecture trained on lexical features, **M2** to refer to the LSTM-CNN architecture with attention trained on the embedding features and **Char** to refer to the character level LSTM model trained on the individual characters.

Task	Features	Model	Pearson Correlation Coefficient			
			Anger	Fear	Joy	Sadness
1	L	SVM	0.654	0.646	0.649	0.628
	L	M1	0.673	0.668	0.698	0.642
	E	M2	0.644	0.659	0.685	0.644
	L+E	M1+M2+Char	**0.704**	**0.688**	**0.713**	**0.652**
2	L	SVM	0.514	0.449	0.576	0.533
	L	M1	0.549	**0.462**	0.58	0.557
	E	M2	0.544	0.455	0.571	0.542
	L+E	M1+M2+Char	**0.558**	0.461	**0.601**	**0.566**

Table 5: Evaluation for subtask 1 (emotion intensity prediction) and subtask 2 (emotion ordinal classification) for all emotions with various features and models.

Tasks 1 and 2 with with Additional Models: Table 5 shows the performance of the models described above to the first two subtasks: emotion intensity prediction and emotion ordinal classification. We have shown the results for all the four emotions. As we can see, here too, the model combination M1+M2+Char combination performs the best for all emotions in subtask 1. The performance of the model is the best for the emotion *joy*, and the worst for the emotion *fear*.

Tasks 3 and 4 with with Additional Models: Coming to subtasks 3 and 4 (valence intensity prediction and valence ordinal classification respectively), Table 6 shows the performance of the var-

Task	Features	Model	Alternate Evaluation
3	L	SVM	0.762
	L	M1	0.78
	E	M2	0.764
	L+E	M1+M2+Char	**0.784**
4	L	SVM	0.724
	L	M1	0.733
	E	M2	0.745
	L+E	M1+M2+Char	**0.75**

Table 6: Evaluation for subtask 3 (emotion valence regression) and subtask 4 (valence ordinal classification) for various features and models. The alternate evaluation is the Pearson correlation for tweets with scores 0.5 - 1 for subtask 3 and the Cohen's Kappa for subtask 4.

ious models on these tasks. Consistent with the results of subtasks 1 and 2, the combined model M1+M2+Char performs the best for both tasks.

In general, we note that the correlation is significantly higher on valence prediction tasks as compared to the emotion intensity tasks. This is likely because the emotion intensity prediction is a fine grained task, requiring the model to observe patterns specific to an emotion. Valence is more of an "aggregated" effect of all the emotions.

Had the best model in additional experiments for all subtasks been submitted to SemEval with all other factors constant, its rank based on the macro-average for the first four subtasks would have been 15th, 15th, 18th and 13th respectively.

6 Discussion

In order to identify areas where the model can improve, it is necessary to study cases where it performs poorly. To do so, we select 5 sentences where the baseline SVM model performs very poorly while predicting anger intensity (based on absolute error) and 1 sentence where it performs well. We have restricted the number of sentences to 6 for brevity. In particular, for sentences 1 and 2, the model significantly overestimates the intensity, for sentence 3, the model predicts the intensity accurately. For sentences 4, 5 and 6, the model significantly underestimates the intensity. Table 7 shows the sentences considered and the true value of emotion intensity for the emotion anger.

We then compare the absolute error between the true value and model prediction for various models. This comparison is shown in Table 8. Given that 5 of the 6 sentences are "difficult" for the models, we observe that there is no clear

#	Tweet	Intensity
1	never had a dull moment with u guys	0.078
2	Fast and furious marathon soon!	0.118
3	They cancelled Chewing Gum. #devastated	0.625
4	Its taking apart my lawn! GET OFF MY LAWN!	0.797
5	I need a beer #irritated	0.806
6	Working with alergies is the most miserable shit in the world #miserable #alergies	0.856

Table 7: Test Examples for Error Analysis with intensity annotations for anger.

winner over these sentences. However, we observe that for sentences 1 and 2, the model M1 performs relatively well. For sentences 4, 5 and 6, the models involving M2 perform relatively well. This suggests that M1 is better at predicting the lower intensities, while M2 is better at the higher intensities. This may explain why though the overall scores for the two models was similar, the ensembled model outperformed the individual models. Another interesting observation is that for sentence 4, the presence of the capital letters is the reason for the high intensity. The model M1+M2+Char is able to identify this well, and contributes to reducing the error significantly as compared to all the other models.

Features	Model	Sentence-wise error					
		1	2	3	4	5	6
L	SVM	0.310	0.308	**0.004**	-0.377	-0.326	-0.327
L	M1	**0.305**	**0.287**	-0.067	-0.391	-0.286	-0.245
E	M2	0.344	0.366	0.051	-0.265	**-0.241**	**-0.199**
L+E	M1+M2+Char	0.339	0.373	0.071	**-0.213**	-0.242	-0.203

Table 8: Absolute error values for various features and models for subtask 1: emotion intensity prediction for emotion *anger*.

7 Conclusion

In this paper we presented the UIUC system that performs regression and ordinal classification of the emotion and sentiment present in English tweets. Our system comprised an ensemble trained on lexicon based and embedding based features. We also provided an account for the training and development mismatch in a given data set by training an adaptive model between the model predictions and the final test predictions. We finally perform an error analysis over the various models to identify potential sources of improvement to the model.

References

Martín Abadi, Paul Barham, Jianmin Chen, Zhifeng Chen, Andy Davis, Jeffrey Dean, Matthieu Devin, Sanjay Ghemawat, Geoffrey Irving, Michael Isard, et al. 2016. Tensorflow: A system for large-scale machine learning. In *OSDI*, volume 16, pages 265–283.

Cecilia Ovesdotter Alm, Dan Roth, and Richard Sproat. 2005. Emotions from text: machine learning for text-based emotion prediction. In *Proceedings of the conference on human language technology and empirical methods in natural language processing*, pages 579–586. Association for Computational Linguistics.

Saima Aman and Stan Szpakowicz. 2007. Identifying expressions of emotion in text. In *International Conference on Text, Speech and Dialogue*, pages 196–205. Springer.

Stefano Baccianella, Andrea Esuli, and Fabrizio Sebastiani. 2010. Sentiwordnet 3.0: An enhanced lexical resource for sentiment analysis and opinion mining. In *LREC*. European Language Resources Association.

Konstantin Bauman, Bing Liu, and Alexander Tuzhilin. 2017. Aspect based recommendations: Recommending items with the most valuable aspects based on user reviews. In *Proceedings of the 23rd ACM SIGKDD*, pages 717–725. ACM.

Margaret M Bradley and Peter J Lang. 1999. Affective norms for English words (ANEW): Instruction manual and affective ratings. Technical report, Technical report C-1, the center for research in psychophysiology, University of Florida.

Erik Cambria and Amir Hussain. 2012. *Sentic computing: Techniques, tools, and applications*, volume 2. Springer Science & Business Media.

François Chollet et al. 2015. Keras.

Jacob Cohen. 1960. A coefficient of agreement for nominal scales. *Journal of Educational and Psychological Measurement*, 20(1):37.

Paul Ekman. 1997. *Basic Emotions*. Handbook of Cognition and Emotion, John Wiley & SOns, Sussex, UK.

Mark Hall, Eibe Frank, Geoffrey Holmes, Bernhard Pfahringer, Peter Reutemann, and Ian H Witten. 2009. The weka data mining software: an update. *ACM SIGKDD explorations newsletter*, 11(1):10–18.

Vasileios Hatzivassiloglou and Kathleen R McKeown. 1997. Predicting the semantic orientation of adjectives. In *Proceedings of the 35th annual meeting of the association for computational linguistics and eighth conference of the european chapter of the association for computational linguistics*, pages 174–181. Association for Computational Linguistics.

Svetlana Kiritchenko, Xiaodan Zhu, and Saif M Mohammad. 2014. Sentiment analysis of short informal texts. *Journal of Artificial Intelligence Research*, 50:723–762.

Albert Mehrabian. 1981. *Silent messages: Implicit communication of emotions and attitudes (2nd ed)*. Wadsworth Pub. Co., Belmont, California.

Saif Mohammad and Felipe Bravo-Marquez. 2017a. Wassa shared task on emotion intensity. In *Proceedings of the 8th Workshop on Computational Approaches to Subjectivity, Sentiment and Social Media Analysis (WASSA)*, pages 34–49.

Saif M Mohammad and Felipe Bravo-Marquez. 2017b. Emotion intensities in tweets. *arXiv preprint arXiv:1708.03696*.

Saif M. Mohammad, Felipe Bravo-Marquez, Mohammad Salameh, and Svetlana Kiritchenko. 2018. Semeval-2018 Task 1: Affect in tweets. In *Proceedings of International Workshop on Semantic Evaluation (SemEval)*, New Orleans, LA, USA.

Saif M Mohammad and Svetlana Kiritchenko. 2015. Using hashtags to capture fine emotion categories from tweets. *Computational Intelligence*, 31(2):301–326.

Saif M Mohammad and Peter D Turney. 2013. Crowdsourcing a word–emotion association lexicon. *Computational Intelligence*, 29(3):436–465.

Finn Årup Nielsen. 2011. A new ANEW: Evaluation of a word list for sentiment analysis in microblogs. *arXiv preprint arXiv:1103.2903*.

Robert Plutchik. 2001. The nature of emotions. *American Scientist*, 89.

Daniel Preotiuc-Pietro, H Andrew Schwartz, Gregory Park, Johannes C Eichstaedt, Margaret Kern, Lyle Ungar, and Elizabeth P Shulman. 2016. Modelling valence and arousal in facebook posts. In *Proceedings of NAACL-HLT*, pages 9–15.

Philip J Stone, Robert F Bales, J Zvi Namenwirth, and Daniel M Ogilvie. 1962. The general inquirer: A computer system for content analysis and retrieval based on the sentence as a unit of information. *Behavioral Science*, 7(4):484–498.

Carlo Strapparava and Rada Mihalcea. 2007. Semeval-2007 task 14: Affective text. In *Proceedings of the 4th International Workshop on Semantic Evaluations*, pages 70–74. Association for Computational Linguistics.

Carlo Strapparava, Alessandro Valitutti, et al. 2004. Wordnet affect: an affective extension of wordnet. In *LREC*, volume 4, pages 1083–1086. Citeseer.

Amy Beth Warriner, Victor Kuperman, and Marc Brysbaert. 2013. Norms of valence, arousal, and dominance for 13,915 english lemmas. *Behavior research methods*, 45(4):1191–1207.

Theresa Wilson, Janyce Wiebe, and Paul Hoffmann. 2005. Recognizing contextual polarity in phrase-level sentiment analysis. In *Proceedings of HLT/EMNLP*, pages 347–354. Association for Computational Linguistics.

KU-MTL at SemEval-2018 Task 1:
Multi-task Identification of Affect in Tweets

Thomas Nyegaard-Signori, Casper Veistrup Helms,
Johannes Bjerva, Isabelle Augenstein
Department of Computer Science
University of Copenhagen
{sfq340,wqx727}@alumni.ku.dk, {bjerva,augenstein}@di.ku.dk

Abstract

We take a multi-task learning approach to the
shared Task 1 at SemEval-2018. The general
idea concerning the model structure is to use
as little external data as possible in order to
preserve the task relatedness and reduce complexity. We employ multi-task learning with
hard parameter sharing to exploit the relatedness between sub-tasks. As a base model, we
use a standard recurrent neural network for
both the classification and regression subtasks.
Our system ranks 32nd out of 48 participants
with a Pearson score of 0.557 in the first subtask, and 20th out of 35 in the fifth subtask
with an accuracy score of 0.464.

1 Introduction

We consider the task of identifying affect in
tweets, as described in Mohammad et al. (2018).
Given a tweet, the task is to predict the emotions and their corresponding intensities which the
tweet portrays. Previous approaches to this task
are outlined in Mohammad and Bravo-Marquez
(2017). The winning team of the SemEval EmoInt
2017, presented in Goel et al. (2017), tackled a
similar task as the regression task presented in
this year's SemEval Task 1. The winning system utilised an ensemble approach consisting of 5
sub-models and using a weighted average of these
models to come up with the final result. This
model is utilising most of the different approaches
mentioned in the literature and combining them
into one and with great success.

Our work bears resemblance to the runner up
in the SemEval EmoInt 2017, Köper et al. (2017),
who used a comparatively simple model consisting of a CNN-LSTM neural network. The difference between the models presented in this paper
and the IMS system is the utilisation of lexicons,
and that we take a multi-task learning approach.

We focus on two subtasks of this shared task,
namely *emotion intensity regression* and *emotion
classification* (Sub-tasks 1 and 5). These were
chosen because of the overlap in tweets but differing truth labels value and types. Furthermore, we
only consider the English versions of the subtasks.

2 System Description

Our system is a standard RNN, with the exception
that we approach the task using multi-task learning
via hard parameter sharing (Caruana, 1993). We
will now present the details of our implementation.

2.1 Preprocessing of Text and Textual Representation

We use embedded word representations as input to
our system, initialised to the weights from a large
set of pre-trained embeddings which have been
trained on Twitter data (∼400 million tweets).
These embeddings were obtained from Godin
et al. (2015). Words which are out-of-vocabulary
are replaced with UNK. Furthermore, user mentions and numbers get mapped to a place-holder
instead of their actual values.

Since the model used both word and character
representations, the characters are read in separately, although the same basic principle is followed. Every character is represented by an embedded representation, which is initialised randomly prior to training.

2.2 Augmentation of Data

Since the tweets have different formats of truth
labels, one is a singular value (regression) and
one is a multi-label list (classification), reading in
the labels has to be augmented. Since the tweets
are reused in the two tasks, some of the regression tweets can be augmented with their respective
classification label, although, if no classification
label is present, the truth labels are set to -1, which

Proceedings of the 12th International Workshop on Semantic Evaluation (SemEval-2018), pages 385–389
New Orleans, Louisiana, June 5–6, 2018. ©2018 Association for Computational Linguistics

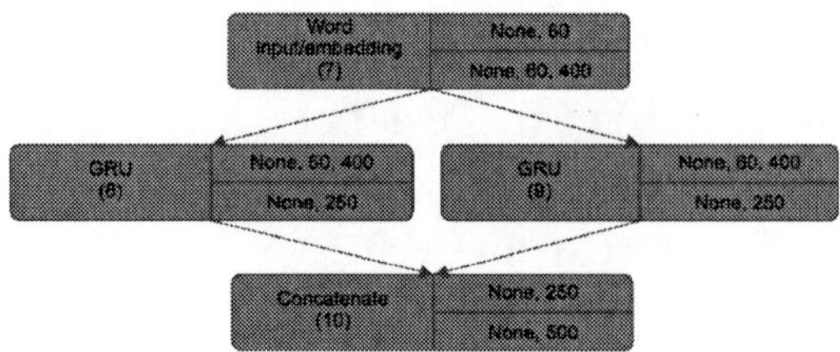

Figure 1: The word input part of the full model.

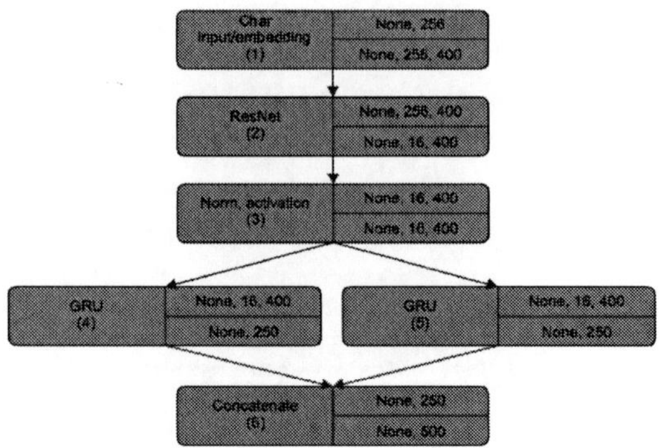

Figure 2: The character input part of the full model.

then acts as a mask. Since there are more regression tweets than classification, the augmentation is done this way around. All the tweets are padded differently based on whether or not the tweet is being read as a word representation or character representation, and tweets longer than the specified padding values are cut down to size.

2.3 Word Input Model

The word input to the model is $60 \cdot 400$ dimensional vectors that have been passed through the preprocessing and augmentation specified in section 2.1 and 2.2 ((7) in Figure 1). These vectors are then passed into two 250-dimensional, bidirectional GRUs which traverse the tweet front to back and vice versa, and the outputs of the two GRU layers are then concatenated ((8) and (9) in Figure 1). This output is then batch normalised and dropout is applied ((10) in Figure 1). This output of the word submodel is then concatenated later with the character submodel.

2.4 Character Input Model

The character input to the model is $256 \cdot 400$ dimensional vectors that have been through the same preprocessing and augmentation as the word inputs ((1) in Figure 2). These vectors then get passed into a residual neural network which works as a loop of batch normalisations, dropout applications and one-dimensional convolutions ((2) in Figure 2). Each loop ends with an addition of the values at the start of the loop and the current result and then a max pooling. These vectors are then passed into two GRU layers similar to the word input ((4) and (5) in Figure 2) which are then concatenated and passed along to be connected with the word input part ((6) in Figure 2).

2.5 Full Model

The combined model consists of four submodels, one for each regression emotion. The combined

embeddings are used to generate classification labels. A high level overview can be seen in Figure 3.

2.6 Loss Functions

Since the model is a multitask model, more than one loss function was needed. The model solves two tasks which can not share loss functions because of the inherent nature of the problem, one being a regression problem and the other a classification problem.

Regression loss function For the regression output of the model, mean squared error was chosen as a way to optimise the model with regards to Pearson-score. Since mean squared error seeks to minimise the difference between the prediction and the gold score, a low mean squared error will bring the Pearson score closer to one.

Classification loss function The loss function for the classification is a bit more convoluted since all regression tweets have regression labels, but not all regression tweets have classification labels. This is handled by way of a mask and the augmentation specified in section 2.2. Since the model has eleven output layers, there is a loss function for each of the eleven emotions/layers. The loss function ensures that tweets with no classification labels do not impact the updating of the weights of the model by giving the predicted values a loss of zero. The binary cross entropy loss function was modified to include a weighting parameter because of the uneven distribution of ones and zeros. The objective of the model is to identify the emotions indicated by a tweet, and as such a value of one is assigned a higher value.

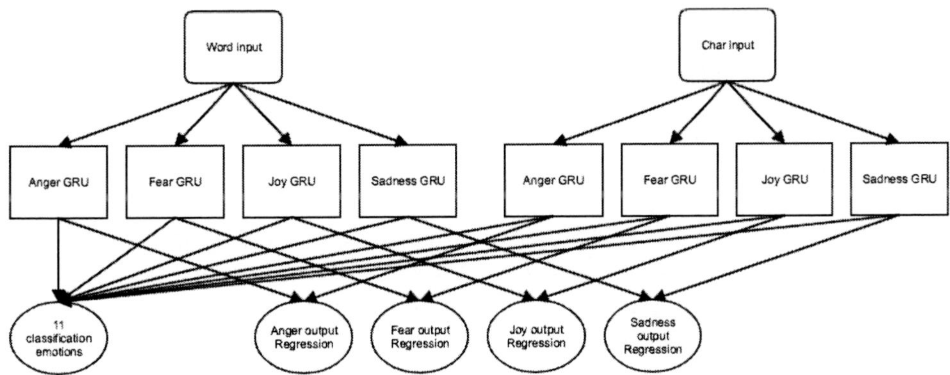

Figure 3: The character input part of the full model.

3 Error Analysis

3.1 Regression Scores

Since there is a considerable overlap in tweets, some tweets are reused in multiple emotions from Task 1 which then in turn can be reused a single time in Task 5. The actual numbers of unique and "duplicate" tweets are hard to resolve and presented a challenge in the first iterations of the model. Gold and predicted scores for an example instance are shown in Table 1 and 2.

Anger score	Fear score	Joy score	Sadness score
Gold : 0.517	Gold : 0.800	Gold : 0.197	Gold : 0.707
Pred : 0.449	Pred : 0.953	Pred : 0.139	Pred : 0.756

Table 1: Good prediction for regression task with the following tweet:
"we need to do something. something must be done!!!!!' your anxiety is amusing. nothing will be done. despair.".

Anger score	Fear score	Joy score	Sadness score
Gold : 0.953	Gold : 0.621	Gold : —	Gold : 0.680
Pred : 0.620	Pred : 0.346	Pred : 0.430	Pred : 0.326

Table 2: Bad prediction for regression task with the following tweet:
"Don't fucking tag me in pictures as 'family first' when you cut me out 5 years ago. You're no one to me.".

It is noticeable from the scoring shown in Table 1 and 2 that keywords such as *'familiy'*, *'anxiety'* and *'fucking'*, for example, have a very large effect on the values predicted. These keyword cor-

relations might have been better handled with the use of external data, such as emotive lexicons and the likes.

3.2 Classification Scores

Keeping in mind that the classification labels represent the emotions *anger, anticipation, disgust, fear, joy, love, optimism, pessimism, sadness, surprise* and *trust*, exemplary classification predictions are presented in Table 3 and Table 4.

Predictions	Hit percentage
Gold : 0 0 1 0 0 0 0 0 1 0 0 Pred : 0 1 1 0 0 0 0 0 0 0 0	82%

Table 3: Scores for classification task with the following tweet:
"Not sure tequila shots at my family birthday meal is up there with the best ideas I've ever had #grim".

Predictions	Hit percentage
Gold : 0 1 0 0 1 1 1 0 0 0 1 Pred : 1 0 1 0 0 0 0 0 0 0 0	36%

Table 4: Bad prediction scores for classification task with the following tweet:
"SheenKL I assume the manga is #good?".

There are certain structures that are prevalent in the correct and incorrect predictions. When looking at the amount of labels that are set in the datasets, it is evident just from the small amount of *surprise* or *trust* labels that have been set that these emotions will be harder to predict, since there are so few points of reference. Furthermore, when both *anger* and *disgust* labels are present in a tweet the model predicts better. This can be explained by the fact that there are a significant amount of tweets with these two labels.

Average score	Anger	Fear	Joy	Sadness	Classification
0.551	0.521	0.606	0.538	0.563	0.464

Table 5: Overall scoring of the model, both regression and classification (Task 1 and 5).

Table 5 describes the overall scores from the model run on the test set in the evaluation period of the shared task.

4 Related Work

Multi-task Learning Neural networks make multi-task learning via (hard) parameter sharing particularly easy (Caruana, 1993) and has shown to be successful for a variety of NLP tasks, such as machine translation (Dong et al., 2015; Luong et al., 2016), keyphrase boundary classification (Augenstein and Søgaard, 2018), tagging (Martínez Alonso and Plank, 2017; Bjerva et al., 2016), complex word identification (Bingel and Bjerva, 2018), and natural language understanding (Augenstein et al., 2017). For sequence labelling, many combinations of tasks have been explored, e.g., by Martínez Alonso and Plank (2017); Bjerva (2017a,b). An analysis of different task combinations was performed by Søgaard and Goldberg (2016); Bingel and Søgaard (2017). Ruder et al. (2017) presented a more flexible architecture, which learned what to share between the main and auxiliary tasks, and might require further investigation in future work. Augenstein et al. (2017) combine multi-task learning with semi-supervised learning for strongly related tasks with different output spaces. For this shared task, we opt for a simple hard parameter sharing strategy, though we would expect to see improvements with more involved architectures.

5 Conclusion

In this paper, we present our system for SemEval-2018 Task 1. We employed a simple multi-task architecture with hard parameter sharing to model Subtasks 1 and 5 jointly. The model achieved an average performance compared to the rest of the participants. We argue this is due to our not using external data or performing extensive additional engineering.

Acknowledgments

Isabelle Augenstein is supported by Eurostars grant Number E10138. We further gratefully acknowledge the support of NVIDIA Corporation with the donation of the Titan Xp GPU used for this research.

References

Isabelle Augenstein, Sebastian Ruder, and Anders Søgaard. 2017. Multi-task learning of keyphrase boundary detection. In *Proceedings of ACL*.

Isabelle Augenstein and Anders Søgaard. 2018. Multi-task learning of pairwise sequence classification tasks over disparate label spaces. In *Proceedings of NAACL, to appear*.

Joachim Bingel and Johannes Bjerva. 2018. Cross-lingual complex word identification with multitask learning. In *Proceedings of Shared Task on CWI at BEA18*.

Joachim Bingel and Anders Søgaard. 2017. Identifying beneficial task relations for multi-task learning in deep neural networks. In *EACL*. pages 164–169.

Johannes Bjerva. 2017a. *One Model to Rule them all – Multitask and Multilingual Modelling for Lexical Analysis*. Ph.D. thesis, University of Groningen.

Johannes Bjerva. 2017b. Will my auxiliary tagging task help? Estimating Auxiliary Tasks Effectivity in Multi-Task Learning. In *Proceedings of NoDaLiDa*. Linköping University Electronic Press, 131, pages 216–220.

Johannes Bjerva, Barbara Plank, and Johan Bos. 2016. Semantic tagging with deep residual networks. In *Proceedings of COLING 2016*. pages 3531–3541.

Richard A Caruana. 1993. Multitask connectionist learning. In *In Proceedings of the 1993 Connectionist Models Summer School*.

Daxiang Dong, Hua Wu, Wei He, Dianhai Yu, and Haifeng Wang. 2015. Multi-Task Learning for Multiple Language Translation. In *Proceedings of ACL*.

Fréderic Godin, Baptist Vandersmissen, Wesley De Neve, and Rik Van de Walle. 2015. Multimedia Lab @ ACL W-NUT NER Shared Task: Named Entity Recognition for Twitter Microposts using Distributed Word Representations .

Pranav Goel, Devang Kulshreshtha, Prayas Jain, and K.K. Shukla. 2017. Prayas at emoint 2017: An ensemble of deep neural architectures for emotion intensity prediction in tweets .

Maximilian Köper, Evgeny Kim, and Roman Klinger. 2017. Ims at emoint-2017: Emotion intensity prediction with affective norms, automatically extended resources and deep learning .

Minh-Thang Luong, Quoc V. Le, Ilya Sutskever, Oriol Vinyals, and Lukasz Kaiser. 2016. Multi-task Sequence to Sequence Learning. In *Proceedings of ICLR*.

Héctor Martínez Alonso and Barbara Plank. 2017. When is multitask learning effective? Semantic sequence prediction under varying data conditions. In *EACL*. pages 44–53.

Saif M. Mohammad and Felipe Bravo-Marquez. 2017. Wassa-2017 shared task on emotion intensity .

Saif M. Mohammad, Felipe Bravo-Marquez, Mohammad Salameh, and Svetlana Kiritchenko. 2018. Semeval-2018 Task 1: Affect in tweets. In *Proceedings of International Workshop on Semantic Evaluation (SemEval-2018)*. New Orleans, LA, USA.

Sebastian Ruder, Joachim Bingel, Isabelle Augenstein, and Anders Søgaard. 2017. Sluice networks: Learning what to share between loosely related tasks. *arXiv preprint arXiv:1705.08142* .

Anders Søgaard and Yoav Goldberg. 2016. Deep multi-task learning with low level tasks supervised at lower layers. In *ACL*. volume 2, pages 231–235.

EmoNLP at SemEval-2018 Task 2: English Emoji Prediction with Gradient Boosting Regression Tree Method and Bidirectional LSTM

Man Liu

liumanlalala@gmail.com

Abstract

This paper describes our system used in the English Emoji Prediction Task 2 (Barbieri et al., 2018) at the SemEval-2018. Our system is based on two supervised machine learning algorithms: Gradient Boosting Regression Tree Method (GBM) and Bidirectional Long Short-term Memory Network (BLSTM). Besides the common features, we extract various lexicon and syntactic features from external resources. After comparing the results of two algorithms, GBM is chosen for the final evaluation.

1 Introduction

Short text messages from social media websites such as Twitter and Facebook have become an important communication channel in our daily life. Although the writing styles of such short text messages are extremely diverse, the usage of emojis are generally shared. Emojis are ideograms and smiles that can be electronic expressions of natural emotions. Genres of emojis vary from facial expression, places, types of weather to animals. Emojis are used every day, rapidly changing the communication way in the social network. Due to the importance of emojis, investigations about emojis have been performed in recent years. For example, the previous work (Barbieri et al., 2017) has shown that there are relations between words and emojis, in other words, emojis are predictable given its surrounding words. Task 2 of SemEval 2018 provides a platform for the further prediction of emojis on tweets.

Our system addresses the first subtask: English emoji prediction. Note that all the emojis in the training data are removed. We models this problem as a multiclass classification problem. Specifically, we leverage on semantic and syntactic resources to extract varieties of features. After feature engineering, two models are adopted: gradient boosting regression tree method (GBM) and bi-directional long short-term memory network (BLSTM). After comparing results of these two models, GBM is selected for the final evaluation.

The reminder of this paper is structured as follows. In section 2, we describe our system in detail, including the feature description and approaches. In section 3, results of 5-fold experiments and feature ablation are presented. Finally, section 4 summarizes our work.

2 System Description

In this section, we present the details of our English emoji prediction system. In the dataset, each tweet corresponds to one label indicating one type of emojis. There are 20 types of emojis, most of which are emotions.

We treat the problem as a multiclass prediction task and extract a variety of features. For the model GBM, besides the common features such as word *n-gram* features, we utilize extensive external resources to build diverse word clusters, lexicon and syntactic features. For the model BLSTM, we adopt the pre-trained word embedding GloVe (Pennington et al., 2014).

2.1 Preprocessing

As the first step, we perform preprocessing for tweets tokenization and normalization. The tokenization of all tweets are performed using **tweetokenize**[1]. In addition, we normalize tweets by replacing all the URLs (*e.g. https://t.co/bihPimeeV9*) with "*_url_*" and all the mentions (*e.g. @Preston Hall*) with "*@mention*".

---

[1] https://github.com/jaredks/tweetokenize

Proceedings of the 12th International Workshop on Semantic Evaluation (SemEval-2018), pages 390–394
New Orleans, Louisiana, June 5–6, 2018. ©2018 Association for Computational Linguistics

2.2 Features

This section briefly describes features employed in our two models. GBM takes advantage of all the features shown in this section while BLSTM only utilizes pre-trained GloVe as the word embedding. For GBM, each tweet is represented as a feature vector consisting of all the following features. Since most of the target emojis are related to emotions, we employ diversiform lexicon features as well as emotional word (e.g. ":)") features to exploit the sentimental information in the sentence.

Character ngram: This feature represents the presence or absence of contiguous sequence of 3, 4 and 5 characters to capture the morphological information hidden in the words.

POS: The POS tag presents the information about the lexical type of the word. We part-of-speech tag the tweets with the Carnegie Mellon University (CMU) tool (Gimpel et al., 2011). This tool is designed specifically for tweets pos tagging with the capability to deal with the non-standard words. For example, it can tag "ikr" ("I know, right?") as an interjection.

Cluster: This feature is induced from CMU pos-tagging tool which provides the word cluster using the Brown clustering algorithm. These pre-trained 1,000 clusters serve as alternative representations of each tweet. This feature illustrates the presence and absence of tokens from the 1,000 clusters.

Negation: This negation feature is generated followed by Mohammad's work (Mohammad et al., 2013), where a negated context is defined from a negation word (e.g. no, none) to one of the punctuation marks:",", ".", ":", ";", "!", "?". Each word in the negated context is added with the suffix "_NEG".

Word ngram: The word ngram (*n=1, 2, 3, 4*) features are captured after negation processing and can explore additional context information.

Counting feature: This feature is inspired by Mohammad's work (Mohammad et al., 2013) and developed by combining all the number of special symbols (e.g. mentions) in each tweet.

- the number of hashtags;

- the number of words with all characters in upper case;

- the number of contiguous sequences of question marks, exclamation marks, and both of them;

- whether the last token contains an question mark or exclamation;

- the number of mentions;

- the number of URLs;

- the number of words which have repeated characters (e.g. "coooool");

- presence or absence of positive or negative emoticons in the tweet. The positive and negative emoticons are defined in (Mohammad et al., 2013).

SSWE feature: SSWE (sentiment-specific word embedding) are learned on 10 million tweets using customized neural network (Tang et al., 2014). SSWE features can capture the sentiment information of sentences as well as the syntactic context of words.

Lexicon feature: This feature is created following the method produced by (Mohammad et al., 2013). We investigate the number of sentiment words, the total sentiment score, the score of last sentiment words and the maximal sentiment score for each lexicon. Taking advantage of extensive external lexicons [2], this feature can interpret the sentimental information in tweets comprehensively.

2.3 Model

Two models are used in our system: GBM and BLSTM. We compare performances of these two models and finally use the GBM result for final evaluation.

GBM: We construct GBM model by using all the features mentioned in section 2.2. For each tweet, the concatenated feature vector can be used as the model input. Outputs of the model are the multiclassification results. The gradient boosting regression tree method generates base models sequentially and at each step updates the base model by minimizing the loss function value. The base model is a single regression tree which fits a set of features by partitioning the feature space into

---

[2] NRC Emotion Lexicon; NRC Hashtag Sentiment Lexicon; MaxDiff Twitter Lexicon; MPQA Effect Lexicon; MPQA Subjectivity Lexicon; Harvard Inquirer Lexicon; Bing Liu Lexicon; Loughran McDonald Lexicon; Amazon Laptop Review Lexicon; Sentiment140 Lexicon.

different regions. With additional regression trees added to the model, the fitted model may achieve a small training error. In other words, the gradient boosting method sequentially fits the training data by correcting base models at each step to strategically yield the best combination of trees. Therefore, the gradient boosting method is potential to produce more accurate predictions results (Zhang and Haghani, 2015). The tool we used to build GBM model is lightGBM[3]. We tune the hyperparameters on the training set by grid search. Because of the time constraints, it is impossible to tune all the hyperparameters in the GBM model. We choose two hyperparameters to tune and we set learning rate to 0.1 and minimal number of data in one leaf to 20. Table 1 summarizes the final settings and the search space of hyperparameters.

Parameters	Setting	Search space
number of leaves per tree	64	16, 32, 64, 128
number of trees	300	100, 300, 700, 1000

Table 1: Tuned hyperparameter values and search space for GBM.

BLSTM: We experiment BLSTM with published word embedding, namely Stanford's GloVe embedding[4] trained on 6 billion words from Google and Web text. Instead of a traditional feedforward network, we use the bi-directional long-short term memory network. LSTM (Hochreiter and Schmidhuber, 1997) is a powerful connectionist model that can capture time dynamics and it has special capability to cope with these gradient vanishing problems compared with the traditional recurrent neural network (RNN). However, LSTM only has access to process one directional information in the sequence which is contradictory with most of the practical situations where the bi-directional information is both beneficial. BLSTM is designed to deal with this problem with the basic idea to process the sequence backward and forward and feed the output into two separate hidden states to catch the past and future information (Ma and Hovy, 2016).

We exploit this BLSTM transforming word embedding into classification results. Figure 1 shows the network in detail. We also tuned the hyperpa-

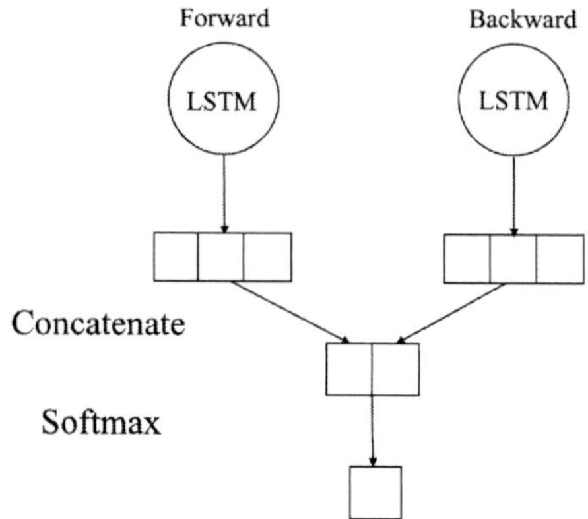

Figure 1: Architecture of BLSTM. The word embeddings of each word are fed into forward LSTMs and backward LSTMs. The outputs of each network are concatenated and decoded by a softmax function into probability for each category.

Parameters	Setting
LSTM units	64
LSTM dropout	0.2
Recurrent_dropout	0.2
Optimizer	rmsprop
Loss function	categorical_crossentropy

Table 2: Tuned hyperparameter values for BLSTM.

rameters in BLSTM to achieve the best result. The tuned parameter values used are illustrated in table 2.

2.4 Results

Our system is trained on two models. With the fine-tuned hyperparameters exhibited in table 1 and 2, we train the two separate models to determine the final classifier for evaluation.

To find out the optimum settings, we explore all the training data and conduct 5-fold cross-validation experiments. Table 3 shows the 5-fold cross-validation performances on the two models. Comparing the 5-fold cross-validation results, we observe that there is no significant difference across these 5 experiments.

By comparing results of the two models, GBM outperforms in the official macro F1 score. We finally submit the evaluation result of GBM. The precision, recall and macro F1 score of the final evaluation are 39.426, 33.695 and 33.665 respec-

---

[3] https://lightgbm.readthedocs.io/en/latest/
[4] https://nlp.stanford.edu/projects/glove/

	Micro F1	Macro F1
GBM	47.16 ± 0.157	33.90 ± 0.119
BLSTM	21.73 ± 0.114	1.78 ± 0.007

Table 3: 5-fold cross-validation results of GBM and BLSTM.

Emo	P	R	F1	%
❤	90.55	84.14	87.23	21.6
😍	27.43	56.02	36.83	9.66
😂	34.24	62.51	44.24	9.07
💕	26.88	26.91	26.89	5.21
🔥	56.31	51.99	54.06	7.43
😊	14.5	12.9	13.65	3.23
😎	26.64	16.93	20.7	3.99
✨	40.01	24.99	30.77	5.5
💙	35.51	14.72	20.81	3.1
😘	22.61	17.11	19.48	2.35
📷	28.61	51.61	36.81	2.86
🇺🇸	67.46	62.24	64.75	3.9
☀	74.35	54.07	62.61	2.53
💜	47.85	7.0	12.22	2.23
😉	18.62	4.98	7.85	2.61
💯	37.56	20.5	26.52	2.49
😁	16.58	2.69	4.63	2.31
🎄	67.31	81.17	73.59	3.09
📸	40.49	19.65	26.46	4.83
😜	15.0	1.78	3.19	2.02

Table 4: Precision, Recall, F-measure and percentage of occurrences in the test set of each emoji.

tively. Our system achieves the best accuracy in this task. In addition, the precision, recall, F1 and percentage of occurrences in the test set of each emoji are shown in table 4.

2.5 Further Analysis of Feature Engineering

Table 5 shows the F1 score and loss on the test set resulting from training with each group of feature removed. The experiment performance reveals that all features except SSWE in our system are helpful. The performance drops after adding SSWE features. This observation is probably caused by overfitting on the training set because of the curse of dimension.

Feature	F1 loss	F1 score
Character ngram	1.161	32.74
POS	0.167	33.73
Cluster	0.15	33.75
Word ngram	0.503	33.40
Counting	0.176	33.72
SSWE	-0.235	34.14
Lexicon	0.094	33.81

Table 5: Feature ablation study using the GBM model. The quantity is the F1 loss and score resulting from the removal of each feature group.

3 Conclusion

In this paper, we present the systems used in SemEval 2018 task 2 for English emoji prediction. Our effort focuses on putting forward two models to improve the multi emojis classification. By leveraging on general features (i.e. word ngram feature, character ngram feature and counting features), external resources (i.e. a variety of manual constructed lexicons, CMU brown cluster), feature selection and hyperparameters fine-tuning, GBM achieves better performance than BLSTM. This observation is attributed to the extensive usage of sentimental and syntactic features. Due to most of the target emojis are related emotions, these sentimental features can reveal the relation from words with the emotional emojis. In future, we hope to improve our BLSTM model by taking advantage of more features and incorporating more effective architecture.

References

Francesco Barbieri, Miguel Ballesteros, and Horacio Saggion. 2017. Are emojis predictable? In *Lapata M, Blunsom P, Koller A, editors. 15th Conference of the European Chapter of the Association for Computational Linguistics; 2017 Apr 3-7; Valencia, Spain. Stroudsburg (PA): ACL; 2017. p. 105-11..* ACL (Association for Computational Linguistics).

Francesco Barbieri, Jose Camacho-Collados, Francesco Ronzano, Luis Espinosa-Anke, Miguel Ballesteros, Valerio Basile, Viviana Patti, and Horacio Saggion. 2018. SemEval-2018 Task 2: Multilingual Emoji Prediction. In *Proceedings of the 12th International Workshop on Semantic Evaluation (SemEval-2018).* Association for Computational Linguistics, New Orleans, LA, United States.

Kevin Gimpel, Nathan Schneider, Brendan O'Connor, Dipanjan Das, Daniel Mills, Jacob Eisenstein,

Michael Heilman, Dani Yogatama, Jeffrey Flanigan, and Noah A Smith. 2011. Part-of-speech tagging for twitter: Annotation, features, and experiments. In *Proceedings of the 49th Annual Meeting of the Association for Computational Linguistics: Human Language Technologies: short papers-Volume 2*. Association for Computational Linguistics, pages 42–47.

Sepp Hochreiter and Jürgen Schmidhuber. 1997. Long short-term memory. *Neural computation* 9(8):1735–1780.

Xuezhe Ma and Eduard Hovy. 2016. End-to-end sequence labeling via bi-directional lstm-cnns-crf. In *Proceedings of the 54th Annual Meeting of the Association for Computational Linguistics (Volume 1: Long Papers)*. volume 1, pages 1064–1074.

Saif Mohammad, Svetlana Kiritchenko, and Xiaodan Zhu. 2013. Nrc-canada: Building the state-of-the-art in sentiment analysis of tweets. In *Second Joint Conference on Lexical and Computational Semantics (* SEM), Volume 2: Proceedings of the Seventh International Workshop on Semantic Evaluation (SemEval 2013)*. volume 2, pages 321–327.

Jeffrey Pennington, Richard Socher, and Christopher Manning. 2014. Glove: Global vectors for word representation. In *Proceedings of the 2014 conference on empirical methods in natural language processing (EMNLP)*. pages 1532–1543.

Duyu Tang, Furu Wei, Bing Qin, Ting Liu, and Ming Zhou. 2014. Coooolll: A deep learning system for twitter sentiment classification. In *Proceedings of the 8th International Workshop on Semantic Evaluation (SemEval 2014)*. pages 208–212.

Yanru Zhang and Ali Haghani. 2015. A gradient boosting method to improve travel time prediction. *Transportation Research Part C: Emerging Technologies* 58:308–324.

UMDSub at SemEval-2018 Task 2: Multilingual Emoji Prediction
Multi-channel Convolutional Neural Network on Subword Embedding

Zhenduo Wang and **Ted Pedersen**
Department of Computer Science
University of Minnesota
Duluth, MN 55812, USA
{wang7211,tpederse}@d.umn.edu

Abstract

This paper describes the UMDSub system that participated in Task 2 of SemEval-2018. We developed a system that predicts an emoji given the raw text in a English tweet. The system is a Multi-channel Convolutional Neural Network based on subword embeddings for the representation of tweets. This model improves on character or word based methods by about 2%. Our system placed 21st of 48 participating systems in the official evaluation.

1 Introduction

People use emojis on social media with text in order to express their emotions or reveal meanings hidden by figurative language. However, understanding the semantic relationship between texts and emojis is a challenging task because emojis often have different interpretations that depend on the reader. (Barbieri et al., 2018) shows that a carefully designed machine learning system can perform better than humans on an emoji prediction task. The system which gives the best predictions in that paper is a long short term memory (LSTM) network with pre-trained character embeddings as the text representation method.

(Barbieri et al., 2018) provides a new task in the context of Twitter and describes several powerful models in text sequence modeling and classification. Our work explores other possible configurations for the system, including subword embedding as a text representation method and multi-channel Convolutional Neural Networks as a feature extraction method. We conduct experiments on the Semeval-2018 Task 2 Multilingual Emoji Prediction data set and compare our results with other methods. Our results show that subword embedding based Convolutional Neural Network system is effective. It improves on character embedding by 2.1% and word embedding by 1.8%.

2 Task Description

SemEval–2018 Task 2 has two subtasks which are similar but in different languages. Subtask A is emoji prediction on English tweets, while subtask B is on Spanish. Both tasks are to predict 1 out of 20 emojis (19 in Spanish subtask) given only the text of a tweet. There are ∼500K tweets in the English training set and ∼100K tweets in the Spanish training set. The organizers use the macro F-score to evaluate the performance of the systems.

This is by definition a text classification task. It is more challenging than tasks such as sentiment analysis or authorship identification because it is on Twitter data which is extremely large and changes frequently. We build UMDSub for the English subtask and conduct several experiments with different settings.

3 System Description

UMDSub is a multi-channel Convolutional Neural Network based on subword embedding as the text representation. We use byte-pair-encoding for subword segmentation.

3.1 Word Segmentation

The goal of the word segmentation step is to break the words into subwords in order to have better representations for tweet texts.

Existing text representation methods mostly work on whole word level (Mikolov et al., 2013)(Pennington et al., 2014) or character level (Zhang et al., 2015) (Xiao and Cho, 2016). In these works, character embedding as the basis for feature extraction were shown to be more effective on text classification tasks. Also there are works such as (Bojanowski et al., 2016) which try to enrich word representations with subword information and improve upon the original word embedding methods. We believe that subword is a in-

Proceedings of the 12th International Workshop on Semantic Evaluation (SemEval-2018), pages 395–399
New Orleans, Louisiana, June 5–6, 2018. ©2018 Association for Computational Linguistics

triguing level for text representation. However, the method used to generate subwords in (Bojanowski et al., 2016) is to divide words into fixed length n-grams, which fails to use knowledge of word morphology. We believe that *Language is never, ever, ever, random* (Kilgarriff, 2005). Subwords as character n-grams could be detected by measuring their frequencies.

We detect subwords with the byte-pair-encoding (BPE) algorithm (Shibata et al., 1999), which is a frequency based text compression algorithm. The original algorithm first splits the text into bytes (characters). Then it ranks all the byte pairs (which are simply bigrams) according to their frequencies. The most frequent byte pair is then joined together and encoded by a single byte. By repeating this simple process, the original text will be compressed. In our system, we use BPE as a word segmentation algorithm. We join characters together by frequency but do not replace them with new symbols. This method was also shown to be successful in (Sennrich et al., 2015).

For example, suppose the text to be segmented is

$$S_0 = workers\ work\ in\ workshop.$$

First, we split S_0 into character sequence.

$$S_1 = w\ o\ r\ k\ e\ r\ s\ w\ o\ r\ k\ i\ n\ w\ o\ r\ k\ s\ h\ o\ p.$$

Then in the first iteration, we choose the most frequent bigram *wo* and join them together.

$$S_2 = \underline{wo}\ r\ k\ e\ r\ s\ \underline{wo}\ r\ k\ i\ n\ \underline{wo}\ r\ k\ s\ h\ o\ p.$$

In the second iteration, we choose the most frequent bigram $\underline{wor}$ and join them together.

$$S_3 = \underline{wor}\ k\ e\ r\ s\ \underline{wor}\ k\ i\ n\ \underline{wor}\ k\ s\ h\ o\ p.$$

Similarly, the next bigram should be $\underline{work}$.

$$S_4 = \underline{work}\ e\ r\ s\ \underline{work}\ i\ n\ \underline{work}\ s\ h\ o\ p.$$

The text is represented by a subword sequence after the algorithm finishes in N iterations, and will look like this :

$$S_N = \underline{work}\ \underline{er}\ s\ \underline{work}\ \underline{in}\ \underline{work}\ \underline{shop}.$$

3.2 Subword Embedding Layer

Embeddings can be categorized into two types based on how they are trained, saved (or static) and reused (or dynamic). Static embeddings are separately trained from large open corpus (such as Wikipedia) and saved for reuse. Word2vec and GloVe models are two such examples. Dynamic embeddings are jointly trained with other parts of specific systems. The Twitter corpus is not like a standard corpus, since it is extremely large and it changes frequently. We choose to use a dynamic embedding strategy since it may fit better for our system.

After word segmentation the text is made up of subword sequences. In order to use subword embedding to represent the text, we first represent each subword type with a one-hot vector. The one-hot vector for the ith subword in vocabulary is a sparse binary vector o_i which has 1 as the ith element and 0 for all others. This step results in a representation similar to a vector space model. We put all the subwords in the subword one-hot hyperspace where each unique subword type owns one dimension. The one-hot embedding is so sparse and it suffers from the Dimension Disaster. Hence we project it to a smaller hyperspace by multiplying the one-hot embedding with a projection weighting matrix $W \in \mathbb{R}^{d \times |V|}$, where d is the dimension for the target embedding hyperspace and $|V|$ is the subword vocabulary size. Now each subword is represented by a dense vector $s_i = W o_i$, and the tweet text T with length of L is represented by a sequence of subword embedding vectors $T = (s_1, s_2, ..., s_L)$.

3.3 Multi-channel Convolutional Layer

As we mentioned in Section 2, this is a text classification task. A key step in any classification system which uses the feature-classifier scheme is to choose indicative features. In NLP tasks, n-grams are commonly used features because they capture word collocations as found in text. But this may not be effective if we have no sense of what kind(s) of n-grams could be useful for a certain problem. Recently, a trend (Zhang et al., 2015) (Xiao and Cho, 2016) for solving text classification tasks is to break the text into the smallest units and build a representation for them. Then this approach can use a complex neural network such as Convolutional Neural Network (CNN) or recurrent neural network (RNN) to find abstract features upon the representations. This system configuration takes advantage of the ability of complex neural networks to extract features. (Kim et al., 2016) tries to explain the mechanism of character-entry-CNN by showing that the features extracted by CNN are specific n-grams. We believe this scheme could be very useful for finding features for classification when we have little knowledge of the corpus, as is often the case for Twitter.

In our system, we use a multi-channel CNN layer for feature extraction. Since tweets are generally short, higher-level features for classification may not exist. Instead of adding depth to our network, we add diversity to the kernel sizes in order to keep as much n-gram information as possible. A similar model is used in (Ruder et al., 2016) (Shrestha et al., 2017).

The multi-channel convolution layer consists of three parallel convolution units. They have a similar structure but different convolutional kernel sizes. Each convolution unit consists of two steps, the convolution and pooling. The convolution step is to calculate the convolutions of the resulting vector sequence from the subword embedding vector sequence $T = (s_1, s_2, ..., s_L)$ and convolution kernels $k_{1:M} \in \mathbb{R}^{d,M \times r}$, where M is the kernel number, r is the kernel size. The kernel size represents the context window of feature extraction and the kernel number represents the number of patterns.

$$f_{l=1:L}^{m'} = \sigma(k_m * [s_{l-r/2+1}, ..., s_l, .., s_{l+r/2}])$$

where σ is the activation function.

Then the pooling step is to trim the resulting sequence F' by leaving only the maximum in every r consecutive f'_ls.

$$f_{q=1:L/r}^{m} = \max\{f_{l=(q-1)\times r+1}^{m'}, ..., f_{l=q\times r}^{m'}\}$$

Then the convolution unit outputs features extracted by each kernel. The output of can be seen as all the features extracted within a certain size of context window.

$$F = [f_1^1, ..., f_1^M]$$

Each CNN unit works as above. We concatenate all the three feature maps and flatten the resulting matrix to one single vector. This single vector is later used for classification.

3.4 Classification Layer

We make two assumptions of how texts affect the usage of emojis, and how emojis are chosen to express emotions as an auxiliary symbol for the text.

1. Emojis are chosen and used to indicate the emotion of the whole tweet or the emotion of the tweeter at the moment, independent of position.

2. Emojis are tied to its context only, enhancing or revealing the true underlying meaning. This can vary depending on the position or content of the tweet.

In case 2, a "verbose" tweet which contains several sentences may map to different emojis at different positions. Given this nature of how emojis are used in tweets, the task could have been very different from traditional text classification since only a part of the text decides the classification output. Fortunately, most the tweets are chosen so that they contain only one sentence and the dataset does not provide the position information of the removed emoji, which makes the task easier. Hence we assume all the emojis are used as in case 1 and we will use the whole tweet to do prediction.

From the convolutional layer we get output of the features extracted from the whole tweet. We first reshape the features matrix into a single vector, then we feed it to a logistic regression layer for the final classification. The layer consists of a fully connected network layer and a softmax function as activation function. It takes the the one dimensional feature vector generated from convolutional layer as input and outputs a distribution over the 20 emojis denoting their probabilities of being used in the original tweet. Hence this layer can be represented by:

$$P[y = k|\vec{X}] = \frac{\exp(W_k^\top \vec{X} + b_k)}{\sum_{i=1}^{20} \exp(W_i^\top \vec{X} + b_i)}$$

Figure 1 is a summary of our system.

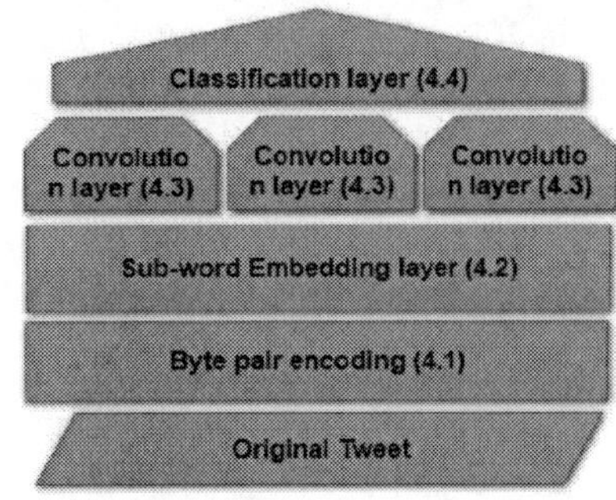

Figure 1: Diagram of UMDSub.

4 Parameter Settings

We use the training and test tweets collectively for the byte pair encoding algorithm with 2,000

Embedding	$|V|$	d	M	r	#param
Word	10K	256			4.16M
subword	2K	64	128	3, 4, 5	0.63M
Character	200	16			0.13M

Table 1: Network parameter settings.

System config	F1	Precision	Recall
sub-CNN (E)	.260	.330	.267
Word-CNN (P)	.283	.355	.285
sub-CNN (P)	**.301**	.352	**.302**
Char-CNN (P)	.289	**.382**	.291
BOW	.29	.32	.34
Word-LSTM	.33	.35	.36
Word-LSTM + P	.32	.34	.36
Char-LSTM	.32	.36	.37
Char-LSTM + P	**.34**	**.42**	**.39**

Table 2: Experimental results (both evaluation (E) and post-evaluation (P) phase). -LSTM refers to the models used in (Barbieri et al., 2018), with results from this paper. +P refers to pre-trained embeddings.

iteration. Each iteration of BPE algorithm generates a new character n-gram, resulting in a vocabulary size around 2,000. Then we embed each subword with a vector with dimension $d = 64$. In our concatenated Convolutional Neural Network, each unit has $M = 128$ filters with filter sizes and max pooling size $r = \{3, 4, 5\}$. For comparison, we also build character based system containing not only the ascii characters with vocabulary size $|V| = 200$ and embedding dimension $d = 16$ and word based system with vocabulary size $|V| = 10,000$ and embedding dimension $d = 256$. We use the same network structure for all different text representation methods. We train the network for 50 epochs. Table 1 summarizes the parameter settings used.

5 Experimental Results

Table 2 shows our experimental results and reveals that our methods have a preference towards precision. In the task evaluation, UMDSub attained precision of .330 which was 9th of 48 systems, and recall of .267 which was 20th. The overall F-score was .260 and placed 21st. This emphasis on precision can be seen in that our system was particularly accurate in predicting the most frequent emoji in the training and test data (the red heart), achieving an accuracy of .854 which was 4th among the 48 participating systems.

Our submission for the evaluation phase (sub-CNN (E)) was produced by a 4-layer single channel Convolutional Neural Network. After we changed it to the post-evaluation version of our multi-channel network (sub-CNN (P)), we saw a significant improvement where the F-score rose to .301 which would have placed 10th in the evaluation. The reasons for this success have to do with the nature of tweets, which are difficult to represent in a deep network given their very limited content. A Multi-channel CNN captures more information using various kernels in a single layer and so the content of short and somewhat noisy tweets is well represented.

6 Conclusion

Our work shows that subword embedding is an effective method of text representation for the emoji prediction task. Under the multi-channel CNN framework, it improves word embedding by 1.8% and character embedding by 2.1% while maintaining a modest computational cost.

We try to explain the reason of our results with the success of byte pair encoding (BPE) segmentation. We check the segmented text after byte pair encoding algorithm and we find a very representative example:

Before BPE: Playing the drums on RockBand made it look much easier than it is.

After BPE: Pl ay ing the dr um s on Rock B and made it look much ea si er than it is.

We observe that some of the segmentations correspond with word morphology, others not. This is because the segmentation is based on frequency and not a knowledge of morphology. Based on these observations, we consider the BPE algorithm a method that dynamically decides which n-grams are most frequent in a corpus and thus deserving of a unique representation that is included in the vocabulary. The vocabulary generated by BPE is a mixture of characters, roots, affixes, whole words and even random n-grams, chosen as such to make the representation of text statistically efficient. The advantage of such a system is that it does not consider Twitter language as a compound made of characters or atomic words. Therefore it does not limit text representation on only one single level, making the later feature extraction more efficient.

References

Francesco Barbieri, Jose Camacho-Collados, Francesco Ronzano, Luis Espinosa-Anke, Miguel Ballesteros, Valerio Basile, Viviana Patti, and Horacio Saggion. 2018. SemEval-2018 Task 2: Multilingual Emoji Prediction. In *Proceedings of the 12th International Workshop on Semantic Evaluation (SemEval-2018)*. Association for Computational Linguistics, New Orleans, LA, United States.

Piotr Bojanowski, Edouard Grave, Armand Joulin, and Tomas Mikolov. 2016. Enriching word vectors with subword information. *arXiv preprint arXiv:1607.04606* .

Adam Kilgarriff. 2005. Language is never, ever, ever, random. *Corpus linguistics and linguistic theory* 1(2):263–276.

Yoon Kim, Yacine Jernite, David Sontag, and Alexander M Rush. 2016. Character-aware neural language models. In *AAAI*. pages 2741–2749.

Tomas Mikolov, Ilya Sutskever, Kai Chen, Greg S Corrado, and Jeff Dean. 2013. Distributed representations of words and phrases and their compositionality. In *Advances in neural information processing systems*. pages 3111–3119.

Jeffrey Pennington, Richard Socher, and Christopher Manning. 2014. Glove: Global vectors for word representation. In *Proceedings of the 2014 conference on empirical methods in natural language processing (EMNLP)*. pages 1532–1543.

Sebastian Ruder, Parsa Ghaffari, and John G. Breslin. 2016. Character-level and multi-channel convolutional neural networks for large-scale authorship attribution. *CoRR* abs/1609.06686. http://arxiv.org/abs/1609.06686.

Rico Sennrich, Barry Haddow, and Alexandra Birch. 2015. Neural machine translation of rare words with subword units. *arXiv preprint arXiv:1508.07909* .

Yusuxke Shibata, Takuya Kida, Shuichi Fukamachi, Masayuki Takeda, Ayumi Shinohara, Takeshi Shinohara, and Setsuo Arikawa. 1999. Byte pair encoding: A text compression scheme that accelerates pattern matching. Technical report, Technical Report DOI-TR-161, Department of Informatics, Kyushu University.

Prasha Shrestha, Sebastian Sierra, Fabio Gonzalez, Manuel Montes, Paolo Rosso, and Thamar Solorio. 2017. Convolutional neural networks for authorship attribution of short texts. In *Proceedings of the 15th Conference of the European Chapter of the Association for Computational Linguistics: Volume 2, Short Papers*. volume 2, pages 669–674.

Yijun Xiao and Kyunghyun Cho. 2016. Efficient character-level document classification by combining convolution and recurrent layers. *arXiv preprint arXiv:1602.00367* .

Xiang Zhang, Junbo Zhao, and Yann LeCun. 2015. Character-level convolutional networks for text classification. In *Advances in neural information processing systems*. pages 649–657.

UMDuluth-CS8761 at SemEval-2018 Task 2: Emojis: Too many Choices? ☺

Dennis Asamoah Owusu & Jonathan Beaulieu
Department of Computer Science
University of Minnesota Duluth
Duluth, MN 55812 USA
{asamo012,beau0307}@d.umn.edu
https://github.com/derpferd/semeval-2018-task2/

Abstract

In this paper, we present our system for assigning an emoji to a tweet based on the text. Each tweet was originally posted with an emoji which the task providers removed. Our task was to decide out of 20 emojis, which originally came with the tweet. Two datasets were provided - one in English and the other in Spanish. We treated the task as a standard classification task with the emojis as our classes and the tweets as our documents. Our best performing system used a Bag of Words model with a Linear Support Vector Machine as its' classifier. We achieved a macro F1 score of 32.73% for the English data and 17.98% for the Spanish data.

1 Introduction

An AI system that can associate text with appropriate emojis could be useful for generating content that is sparkled with emojis among other uses (Barbieri et al., 2017). Given only the text from a tweet in English or Spanish, the SemEval (Barbieri et al., 2018) task was to determine the emoji that was in the original tweet. To learn how users associate emojis with text, a dataset comprised of 489,609 tweets in English and 98,289 tweets in Spanish was provided. Each tweet had a corresponding label representing the emoji that was in the tweet. The labels were assigned based on the frequency of the emoji, 0 being assigned to the most frequent emoji. The total number of labels was 20 for the English data and 19 for the Spanish data. We classified the tweets, our documents, by their emojis, our classes. We viewed the emojis as approximations of the sentiment expressed in the text.

For our baseline, we implemented a Bag of Words model using a Bernoulli Naive Bayes classifier. We analyzed the results and used the insights to implement our final system, which used a Linear Support Vector machine for classification and also used a Bag of Words model to represent each document. This system performed better than our baseline by ~3.5 percentage points for our English data and ~1.5 percentage points for our Spanish data. It also performed better than several neural network models we experimented with. Our macro F1 score were 32.73% and 17.98% for our English data and Spanish data respectively.

2 Baseline

For our Baseline, we used a Bag of Words model (BOW) with a Bernoulli Naive Bayes Classifier. We also implemented a Most Frequent Class Model (MFC) and a Random Model (RAND) to help draw insights from our baseline. The results of these models for the English and Spanish data are shown in Table 1 and Table 2 respectively. The tables show mean and standard deviation over the folds using 10-fold cross-validation. We reserved 10% of the data for testing and trained on the remaining 90% for each fold. We followed the same approach in all our experiments. The Micro F1 scores are heavily influenced by the performance of the dominant classes. Since ~21% of the tweets belong to label 0 (❤) for English, the micro F1 score was ~21% for the MFC model. Macro F1 scores, on the other hand, give equal weight to each class, since they average the F1 scores of each class.

We chose Bernoulli style Naive Bayes because it generally works better for short texts (e.g. Tweets) than its Multinomial counterpart (Manning et al., 2008). We empirically verified this with our task and data. To implement this model, we used the NLTK library for preprocessing and the scikit-learn framework for the model training (Bird et al., 2009; Pedregosa et al., 2011).

Our data pipeline consisted of four steps: Tok-

400

Proceedings of the 12th International Workshop on Semantic Evaluation (SemEval-2018), pages 400–404
New Orleans, Louisiana, June 5–6, 2018. ©2018 Association for Computational Linguistics

	Macro F1		Micro F1	
	Mean	**S-Dev**	**Mean**	**S-Dev**
BOW	29.1	0.2	42.1	0.3
MFC	1.8	0.0	21.7	0.2
RAND	4.5	0.1	5.0	0.1

Table 1: Baseline results for English

	Macro F1		Micro F1	
	Mean	**S-Dev**	**Mean**	**S-Dev**
BOW	16.5	0.4	29.6	0.4
MFC	1.7	0.0	20.0	0.4
RAND	4.8	0.2	5.5	0.2

Table 2: Baseline results for Spanish

enization, Bagination, Tf-idf transform and Training. For tokenization we used NLTK's Tweet-Tokenizer function. We configured it to convert all text to lowercase, crop repeating characters to a max of 3 and remove tweeter handles. We created the BOW by making a set of the tokens which appeared per the document. The next step was to normalize the frequency data into term-frequency times inverse document-frequency(tf-idf) representation. Finally, we trained a Bernoulli Naive Bayes classifier on this data.

2.1 Insights from BOW English Results

For the English tweets, the difference between the macro and micro F-scores for our Bernoulli model lies in the fact that the distribution of classes is very unbalanced. This is demonstrated from the results shown in Table 1.

Table 3 shows a confusion matrix for some labels of our BOW results for the English data. A mapping of select labels to emojis and their descriptions is shown in Table 4. The matrix illustrates the struggles of the BOW model. Generally many tweets are misclassified as ☻ and ☺ . Take ☻ for instance. While only 332 tweets were correctly labeled, 558 tweets and 385 tweets that should have been labeled ☻ were labeled ☻ and ☺ respectively. This misclassification of ☻ as ☻ and ☺ is not only the case for the selected classes represented in the matrix but also for most of the classes. Emojis ☺ and ☻ illustrate another pattern we observed. 653 out of 2312 tweets that should have been classified as ☺ were misclassified as ☻ . Since ☺ is a smiling face with smiling eyes and ☻ is smiling face with heart eyes, we inferred that the model might have trouble discriminating between classes with similar semantics.

That inference is supported by the fact that the model also struggles to discriminate between ▦ , a camera, and ▦ , a camera with flash. 458 tweets out of 1344 tweets (34%) that should have been labeled as ▦ where incorrectly labeled as ▦ . This is more significant when one notes that only 148 of ▦ tweets (11%) where labeled correctly.

	♥	☻	☺	☺	☻	Total
♥	8637	618				10752
☻		2358	832			5145
☺		1022	2718			5114
☺		653	437	251	139	2313
☻		558	385		332	2092

Table 3: BOW Confusion Matrix for English. We have choose to leave some numbers out to prevent distraction from the patterns we are trying to show. All left out numbers are negligible.

To measure the impact of these semantically similar classes on our model, we collapsed classes that were semantically similar and reran the BOW model. All of the "heart" emojis were put into a single class; the "smiling" emojis (except the hearty eyes one) were put into another class; the "camera" emojis were collapsed into one class; and each remaining emoji had its own class. In the end, we had 13 classes after merging.

After running the model on these new set of classes, the macro F1 score improved by 6 percent points suggesting that the semantic similarity between emojis, such as ▦ and ▦ , has an effect although the effect was not nearly as significant as we had expected. It is worth noting that after collapsing the semantically similar classes, plenty of tweets were misclassified as the most frequent class. Thus, it may be that the semantic similarity of the classes does really matter but the gain in performance from collapsing the classes was offset by the fact that we had a class that was relatively much larger than the largest class before.

The BOW performed relatively well for labels 0, 1, 2, 4 and 17 (♥ , ☻ , ☺ , ♦ and ♠ respectively) for the English data.

2.2 Insights from BOW Spanish Results

The Spanish results were much worse than the English results. Table 5 illustrates the major trend we noticed with the BOW model's performance on the Spanish data. Count is the number of tweets that correctly belong to a class. %C is what per-

Label	Emoji	Description
0	❤️	Red heart
1	😍	Smiley face with heart eyes
2	😂	Face with tears of joy
4	🔥	Fire
5	😊	Smiling face with smiling eyes
6	😎	Smiling face with sunglasses
13	💜	Purple Heart
10	📷	Camera
17	🎄	Christmas Tree
18	📸	Camera with Flash

Table 4: Some English Emojis

Label	Emoji	Description
0	❤️	Red heart
1	😍	Smiley with heart eyes
2	😂	Face with tears of joy
3	💕	Two hearts
4	😊	Smiley with smiling eyes
5	😘	Face blowing a kiss
9	🇪🇸	Spain
10	😎	Smiling face with sunglasses
16	🎶	Musical notes

Table 6: Some Spanish Emojis

	%C	%❤️	%😍	%😂	Count
❤️	62	-	14	0	1882
😍	43	16	-	14	1338
😂	46	0	25	-	908
💕	15	32	24	0	641
😊	9	14	32	17	647
😘	11	22	29	11	438
🇪🇸	63	5	17	4	331
😎	7	12	30	20	332
🎶	24	13	19	27	283

Table 5: BOW Spanish results. %C refers to the percent correctly labeled and %*emoji* refers to the percent mislabeled as *emoji*.

centage of tweets were correctly labeled. %❤️ , %😍 and %😂 are the percentages of tweets that our model misclassified as labels 0, 1 and 2 respectively. Thus for ❤️ , there were 1882 tweets in the test data; 62% of these were labeled correctly while 14% was incorrectly as 😍 . As the table shows, a significant percentage of tweets were either misclassified as ❤️ , 😍 or 😂 . The exception to this is 🇪🇸 - the Spanish flag. Table 6 shows the emojis corresponding to the numerical labels.

2.3 Neural Network

Upon reading about how neural models achieved high scores on similar tasks, we decided to try out methods based on (Barbieri et al., 2017) and (dos Santos and Gatti, 2014). The task this paper tries to solve is based on Barbieri et al.'s work where they do the same task. Their best performing model was a character based Bi-directional Long

Short-term Memory Network (char-BLSTM). We also took inspiration from dos Santos and Gatti's work. They were able to achieve very good results using a Convolutional Neural Network (CNN) to do sentiment analysis. We tested four different types of neural network models: LSTM, BLSTM, CNN-LSTM and CNN-BLSTM. For the LSTM based models, we used a network size of 128. The only difference between our LSTM and our BLSTM is that we added a layer to train each input bidirectionally. Our CNN's convolution layer had an output dimension of 64 and a kernel size of 5. For it's pooling layer we chose a pool size of 4. When training each of the neural network models we used a development set which was 10% of the training set to select the best parameters and to know how many epochs to train for. We settled on these specific parameters after trying out different parameters on the development set. None of our neural network models performed significantly better than our baseline.

2.4 Linear SVM

Realizing that our neural network models did not perform any better than our BOW baseline, we decided to try a BOW model with other classifiers which were not neural networks. We settled on a Linear Support Vector Machine. To enable multi-class classification we used a one-vs-rest approach.

2.5 Sampling

Roughly 20% of the tweets in the English data belong to label 0. The performance of classifiers such as Naive Bayes degrades when there is such a

	English		**Spanish**	
	Mean	**S-Dev**	**Mean**	**S-Dev**
Base	29.10	0.20	16.49	0.42
C+L	29.30	0.36	-	-
C+L(f)	29.35	0.44	-	-
LSVM	32.73	0.24	17.98	0.31

Table 7: Macro F1 scores. Base is baseline, L is LSTM, C is CNN, (f) means each class was equally represented.

dominant class (Rennie et al., 2003). This data imbalance exists in the Spanish data as well. To improve the performance of our classifiers, we perform a sampling of the data so that we train on a data set where the classes are roughly equally represented. We performed a simple under sampling by randomly selecting an equal number of tweets from each class even though a more sophisticated re-sampling method will likely improve the results (Estabrooks et al., 2004).

3 Results

The neural network models that we tested ended up achieving around the same score as our BOW baseline. The BOW model with a Linear Support Vector Machine for classification provided the best results. Table 7 shows the results of the LSVM along with the results of our baseline and our best performing neural network models for comparison. The effect of sampling the dataset to balance the frequency of each class was negligible as shown in Table 7. The improvement to employing sampling was 0.05 percentage points for our CNN combined with LSTM model. The F1 score of our LSVM model on the test data from the task organizers was 31.834 which is within one percent of the 32.73 from our 10-fold cross-validation. Precision on the test data was 39.803, recall was 31.365 and accuracy was 45.732. [1]

4 Discussion

The first important trend we observe with our system (BOW model with LSVM classifier) is the most frequently seen emojis ♥ , 😂 and 😊 perform well in terms of true positives - ~83% for ♥ (8848/10622), ~57% for 😂 (2903/5077) and ~63% for 😊 (3171/5067) while at the same time being false positives for many classes. Take 😊 (label 5) for instance. 327 tweets are correctly classified as belonging to 😊 . However, 732 tweets that should have been classified as 😊 are misclassified as 😂 . The trend of misclassifying more tweets as 😂 was seen for labels 6, 7, 8, 13, 14, 15, 16 and 19 as well. This trend carried through from our baseline; the final system performs better only because of marginal improvements in the classification itself.

Below are some tweets for 📷 that the LSVM succeed in classifying that the Bernoulli Naive Bayes could not find. We choose 📷 because the percentage difference in performance (in favor of the LSVM) is the greatest here.

> Different angles to the same goal. by @user @ New

> When iris.apfel speaks...knowledge and wisdom is all you hear so listen up... :@drummondphotog

Our supposition is that the Linear Support Vector Machine is able to make associations that the Bernoulli Naive Bayes is unable to make. "Angles", we suspect, correlates with camera than the other emojis and the LSVM finds that association. The second tweet is interesting because it would seem that the LSVM is able to connect the "photog" in "@drummondphotog" despite our use of a Bag of Words Model unless the prediction was based on some other less obvious word in the tweet.

Acknowledgments

This project was carried out as a part of CS 8761, Natural Language Processing, offered in Fall 2017 at the University of Minnesota, Duluth by Dr. Ted Pedersen. We are grateful to Dr. Ted Pedersen for his support and guidance in this project. Authors are listed in alphabetical order.

References

Francesco Barbieri, Miguel Ballesteros, and Horacio Saggion. 2017. Are emojis predictable? In *Proceedings of the 15th Conference of the European Chapter of the Association for Computational Linguistics: Volume 2, Short Papers*, pages 105–111. Association for Computational Linguistics.

Francesco Barbieri, Jose Camacho-Collados, Francesco Ronzano, Luis Espinosa-Anke, Miguel

---

[1] Task Scoreboard `https://docs.google.com/spreadsheets/d/1on1Oj53EFcE4n-yO_sJc1JEo6x8hcUh5hsWTkTYdc_o/edit#gid=885431079`. We submitted under theteam name: Hopper.

Ballesteros, Valerio Basile, Viviana Patti, and Horacio Saggion. 2018. SemEval-2018 Task 2: Multilingual Emoji Prediction. In *Proceedings of the 12th International Workshop on Semantic Evaluation (SemEval-2018)*, New Orleans, LA, United States. Association for Computational Linguistics.

Steven Bird, Ewan Klein, and Edward Loper. 2009. *Natural Language Processing with Python*. O'Reilly Media.

Andrew Estabrooks, Taeho Jo, and Nathalie Japkowicz. 2004. A multiple resampling method for learning from imbalanced data sets. *Computational Intelligence*, 20(1):18–36.

Christopher D. Manning, Prabhakar Raghavan, and Hinrich Schuetze. 2008. *Introduction to Information Retrieval*. Cambridge University Press. Pg. 268.

F. Pedregosa, G. Varoquaux, A. Gramfort, V. Michel, B. Thirion, O. Grisel, M. Blondel, P. Prettenhofer, R. Weiss, V. Dubourg, J. Vanderplas, A. Passos, D. Cournapeau, M. Brucher, M. Perrot, and E. Duchesnay. 2011. Scikit-learn: Machine learning in Python. *Journal of Machine Learning Research*, 12:2825–2830.

Jason D. M. Rennie, Lawrence Shih, Jaime Teevan, and David R. Karger. 2003. Tackling the poor assumptions of naive bayes text classifiers. In *In Proceedings of the Twentieth International Conference on Machine Learning*, pages 616–623.

Cicero dos Santos and Maira Gatti. 2014. Deep convolutional neural networks for sentiment analysis of short texts. In *Proceedings of COLING 2014, the 25th International Conference on Computational Linguistics: Technical Papers*, pages 69–78, Dublin, Ireland. Dublin City University and Association for Computational Linguistics.

The Dabblers at SemEval-2018 Task 2: Multilingual Emoji Prediction

Larisa Alexa, Alina Lorenţ,
Daniela Gîfu, Diana Trandabăţ

Faculty of Computer Science, "Alexandru Ioan Cuza" University of Iasi
Institute of Computer Science, Romanian Academy - Iasi Branch
Cognos Business Consulting S.R.L., 32 Bd. Regina Maria, Bucharest, Romania
{larisa.alexa04, alina.lorent}@gmail.com, {daniela.gifu, dtrandabat}@info.uaic.ro

Abstract

The "Multilingual Emoji Prediction" task focuses on the ability of predicting the correspondent emoji for a certain tweet. In this paper, we investigate the relation between words and emojis. In order to do that, we used supervised machine learning (Naive Bayes) and deep learning (Recursive Neural Network).

Keywords

Virtual, emojis, human sentiment, understanding of emojis.

1. Introduction

In the last few years, Social Media has evolved very fast, becoming at the moment a very important part of our daily life. There are several social networking platforms such as Twitter, Facebook, Instagram, WhatsApp, which were created in order to allow us to communicate with each other, to share our feelings or opinions related to different topics. Despite their differences or their purposes, each of these platforms shares one aspect: the use of emojis. From facial expressions to animals, objects or places, they are all used to communicate simple things or to enhance feelings and emotions. Due to the fact that their meaning is not always the same, processing emojis remains a challenge for the NLP researchers. From a language to another, for different cultures or depending on the user's sentiments, emojis meaning can vary a lot. Understanding their meaning depending on the context of use has a huge relevance in multiple fields, like: human computer interaction, multimedia retrieval, etc.

Twitter Emojis are pictures usually combined with text in order to emphasize the meaning of that text. Although these pictures are the same all over the world, they can be interpreted and used in different ways, depending on culture differences. Despite their widely usage in social media, their underlying semantics have received little attention from a Natural Language Processing standpoint.

2. Related work

Over the past few years, there has been an increased public and enterprise interest in social media. Therefore, analyzing emojis has become an important aspect for NLP researchers, because their meaning has remained for the time unexplored.

Go et al. [9] and Castellucci *et al.* [6] used in their papers distant supervision over emotion-labeled textual contents in order to train a sentiment classier and to build a polarity lexicon. Aoki *et al.* [1] described in his research a methodology to represent each emoticon as a vector of emotions, while Jiang [10] proposed a sentiment and emotion classier based on semantic spaces of emojis in the Chinese Website Sina Weibo. In his research, Cappallo *et al.* [5] proposed a multimodal approach for generating emoji labels for images (Image2Emoji). Boia *et al.* (2013) [4] analyzed sentiment lexicons generated by considering emoticons, showing that in many cases they do

Proceedings of the 12th International Workshop on Semantic Evaluation (SemEval-2018), pages 405–409
New Orleans, Louisiana, June 5–6, 2018. ©2018 Association for Computational Linguistics

not outperform lexicons created only with textual features.

Barbieri et al. [2] tried to predict the most likely emoji a Twitter message evokes. They used a model based on Bidirectional Long Short-term Memory Networks (BLSTMs) with standard lookup, word representations and character-based representation of tokens. For the word representations they replaced each word that occurred only once in the training data with a fixed representation (out- of-vocabulary words vector) (similar to the treatment of word embeddings by Dyer et al. (2015)). For the character-based representations, they computed character- based continuous-space vector embeddings (Ling et al., 2015b; Ballesteros et al., 2015) of the tokens in each tweet, using bidirectional LSTMs.

3. Data Set and Methods

In this Section, we present the data set format and the architecture we used to predict emojis. We implemented two main modules: first one is based on a Recurrent Neural Network (3.3.1) and the second one implements Naïve Bayes algorithm (**Error! Reference source not found.**).

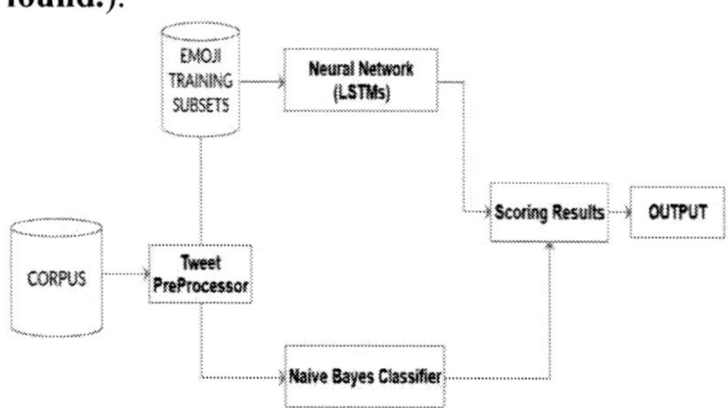
Figure 1. Architectural Diagram

3.1 Data Set

The corpus is formed from 500k tweets in English and 100K tweets in Spanish. The tweets were retrieved with the Twitter APIs, from October 2015 to February 2017, from United States and Spain. The dataset includes tweets that contain one and only one emoji from the 20 most frequent emojis. Data was split into Training Data (80%), Trial Data (10%) and Test Data (10%).

Data set is related to the 20 most frequent emoji of each language.

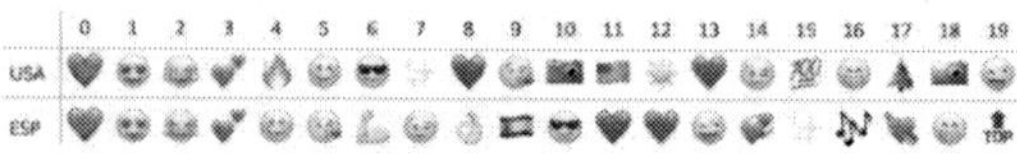
Figure 2. Emoji labels distribution

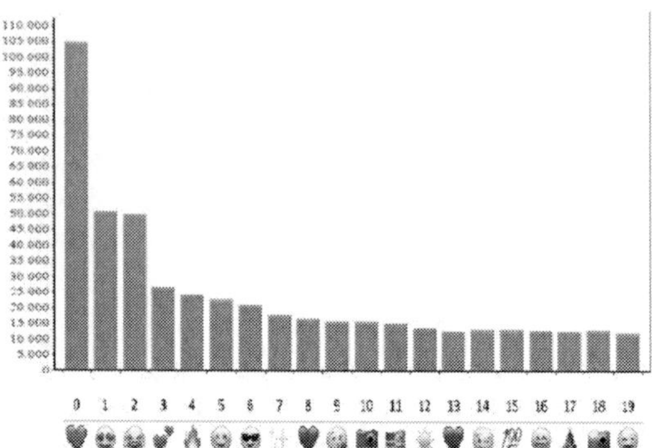
Figure 3. Label frequency in training dataset

In order to generate the training data, we used the tools given by organizers: a crawler for extracting the tweets and an emoji extractor.

For each language, data is represented through two files: one file containing one tweet per line and the other file containing the corresponded emoji label.

```
1   Plaza de Oriente , Madrid .......#madrid #city #plazadeorien
2   Por ser la columna de mi templo, por ser lo mejor que tengo.
3   Me gustan las motos! #cheste2016 #nicoabad #elañoquevienemás
4   Sevilla tiene un color especial, Sevilla tiene un color
5   Que (la) Chipi no se caiga .Cuánto os quiero chavales!!
6   Haciendo el tonto la vida se vive mucho mejor @ Pantano San
7   DANI MARTÍN Más de 7 horas de cola merecieron la pena!!…
8   Tras una semana de locura, se acaba el Arenal Sound pero nos
9   Todo más que dicho anilota, disfruta mucho ya queda menos pa
10  Cerrando el Ayuntamiento (@ Ayuntamiento de San Sebastián
```

Figure 4. Corpus-tweets file

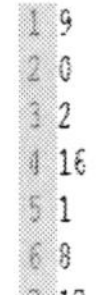

```
1  9
2  0
3  2
4  16
5  1
6  8
7  17
```

Figure 5. Corpus-labels file

3.2 Tweet Pre-Processor

The first step from the preprocessor module consists in cleaning up the data set (punctuation, stop words) in order to avoid noise in the implemented algorithms.

This step consists in removing punctuation marks and links. We identify them by using the regular expression:

((|-\"'/_%$&*+<>^•()=|¡ • ;:.,!?@#~|+)|([0-9]+))

We removed stop words and user mentions, but we decided not to eliminate the hashtag word because many tweets were made only by this kind of words. We removed instead the Hashtag sign and passed the words to the next step of preprocessing.

For the last step, we used Stanford Tokenizer in order to obtain the list of tokens for each tweet. Then we replaced each word with the correspondent lemma using WordNet Dictionary. The words that didn't have a lemma were considered noise and we choose to eliminate them.

prediction on it, by traversing a given structure in topological order.

Given the proven effectiveness and the impact of recurrent neural networks in different topics (sentiment analysis, etc.), we intend to build an emoji prediction model based on a Long Short-Term Memory Network (LSTM).

For each subtask, we divided the train data set into twenty smaller train sets, one for each emoji label. Each train subset contains tweets with only two labels (classes). For instance, the train set for label "0" contains tweets with classified with 0 or !0. We then created a model for every emoji label a trained it with the correspondent train dataset.

In order to unify the models output, we run the test dataset on each one of these model. Then, based on the probabilities of each classified label, we chose the emoji with the highest score.

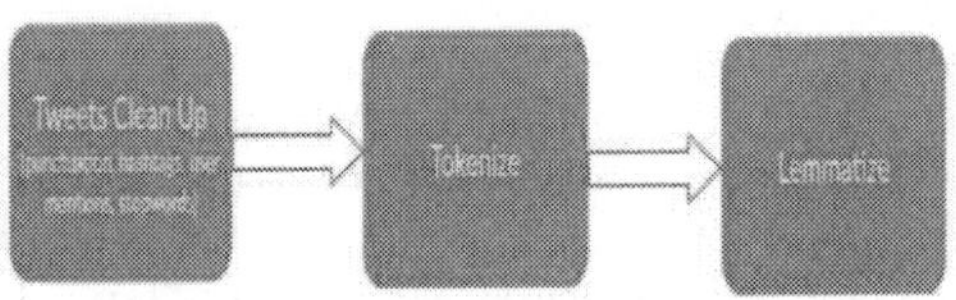

Figure 6. Preprocessing architecture

```
public String findWordLemmaWithWordNet(String word) {
    if (!this.isInitialized)
        return word;
    if (word == null)
        return null;
    if (this.morphProcessor == null)
        this.morphProcessor = this.dictionary.getMorphologicalProcessor();

    IndexWord baseForm;
    try {
        baseForm = this.morphProcessor.lookupBaseForm(POS.NOUN, word);
        if (baseForm != null)
            return baseForm.getLemma().toString();
        baseForm = this.morphProcessor.lookupBaseForm(POS.VERB, word);
        if (baseForm != null)
            return baseForm.getLemma().toString();
        baseForm = this.morphProcessor.lookupBaseForm(POS.ADJECTIVE, word);
        if (baseForm != null)
            return baseForm.getLemma().toString();
        baseForm = this.morphProcessor.lookupBaseForm(POS.ADVERB, word);
        if (baseForm != null)
            return baseForm.getLemma().toString();
    } catch (JWNLException e) {
    }
    return null;
}
```

Figure 7. Code sample for finding word lemma using WordNet Dictionary

3.3 Deep Learning Models

3.3.1 Recursive Neural Networks

Recursive neural network (RvNN) is a kind of deep neural network created by applying the same set of weights recursively over a structure, in order to produce a structured prediction over variable-size input structures, or a scalar

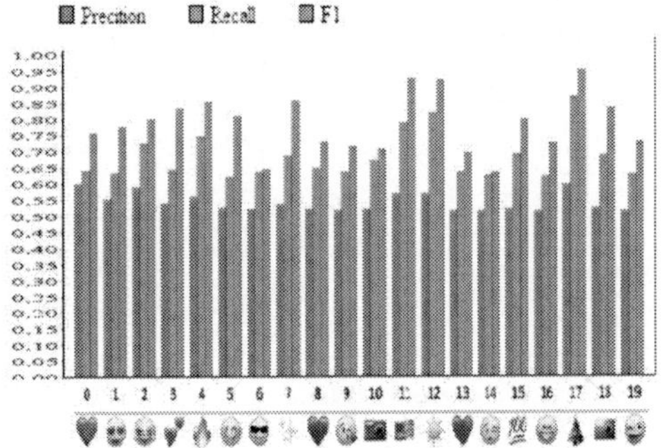

Figure 8. Evaluation for English models

3.3.2 Naïve Bayes Classifier

Naïve Bayes it's a classification technique based on Bayes' Theorem with an assumption of independence among predictors. In simple terms, a Naive Bayes classifier assumes that the presence of a particular feature in a class is unrelated to the presence of any other feature.

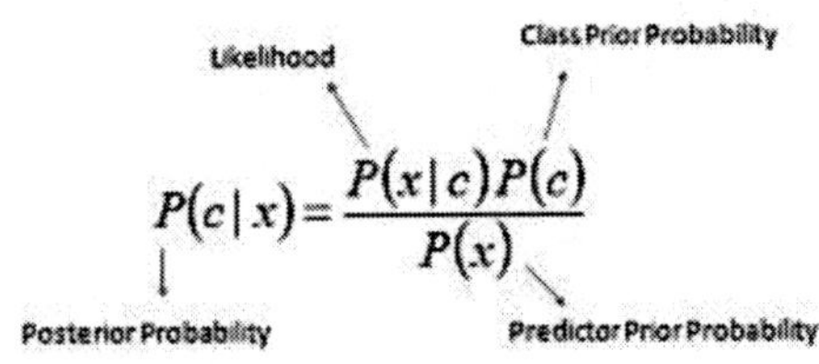

$$P(c \mid x) = \frac{P(x \mid c)P(c)}{P(x)}$$

$$P(c \mid X) = P(x_1 \mid c) \times P(x_2 \mid c) \times \cdots \times P(x_n \mid c) \times P(c)$$

- $P(c|x)$ is the posterior probability of class (c, target) given predictor (x, attributes).
- $P(c)$ is the prior probability of class.
- $P(x|c)$ is the likelihood which is the probability of predictor given class.
- $P(x)$ is the prior probability of predictor.

Naïve Bayes Classifier is written in JavaScript. We used several libraries, applications already made to make the best and smarter module. Train data receives as input ex: "en_train.txt" and "en_train.labels", after the files are read, it reads files line by line, makes a tweet array, then it assigns to each tweet from the array a number from the label file, then it calls the Naïve Bayes algorithm implementation. Finally, the test data is entered and the values are generated for them. It represents an interface that easily generates a label according to the introduced text. Moreover, it does not change values if the same tweet is entered multiple times. The output format is txt and a label is generated for each line from test data.

```
1   en pelham parkway  1
2   calm hall  0
3   witness great solar eclipse tampa florida  12
4   lady week pregnant today excite baby cam springfield  2
5   great road trip view pennsylvania  0
6   christmas deal buy small pomade receive collector tin comb  17
7   mad real night  2
8   starting love shooting dark york york  0
9   sun shine foot  12
10  bitch trill fiend mustard connecticut  15
11  line day dance scripps  0
12  sunrise miami south beach florida  12
13  york time square york city  11
14  tuesday awkward richmond virginia  2
15  rock going night national orange event center  0
```

Figure 9. Short example of US result

```
1   dias valencia comunidad valenciana spain  0
2   anoche preferia prima evazappos juan empezamos sur  0
3   porfavor llevarlas reciclar necesitamos más papel imprimir más propaganda  3
4   vecino roquero passwordlearn  0
5   placer contar profesionales sector talla gracias  1
6   podido pasar vida gracias amigos villahermosa  0
7   dedeu está limpie plaza  0
8   magia personas imposible teatro rialto  0
9   año más confidenciasconmamé tequiero playadelaalmadrava benicassim familia  0
10  sidrra sidrería zamorano  1
11  kimonos sandra más modelos marió calle san lorenzo santa eulalia marió ibiza  0
12  león visitado preciosidad niña martina lapequenaangela  1
13  good vibes sanlúcar barrameda spain  0
14  ojalá salamanca spain  0
15  amor tia prima feria málaga  0
```

Figure 10. Short example of ES result

4. Discussions

Based on the things observed during the project implementation, we think that a possible improvement consists in trying to minimize the tweets noise. For instance, many words from tweets have duplicated letters (e.g. "aaaaand"). Eliminating those duplicated letters till the word has a correspondent lemma could significantly reduce the noise.

5. Conclusions

Emojis are very used on social sites, but not much is known about their use and semantics. However, it has been noticed that emojis are used in different communities. In this paper, we tried to predict the correspondent emoji for a given tweet using a deep learning module based on a Recurrent Neural Network and a Naïve Bayes module. The results for the Naïve Bayes implementation were better than those from the network module.

Acknowledgments

This survey was published with the support by two grants of the Romanian National Authority for Scientific Research and Innovation, UEFISCDI, project number PN-III-P2-2.1-BG-2016-0390, contract 126BG/2016 and project number PN-III-P1-1.2-PCCDI-2017-0818, contract 73PCCDI/2018 within PNCDI III, and partially by the README project "Interactive and Innovative application for evaluating the readability of texts in Romanian Language and for improving users' writing styles", contract no. 114/15.09.2017, MySMIS 2014 code 119286.

References

[1] Aoki, S. and Uchida, O. 2011. *A method for automatically generating the emotional vectors of emoticons using weblog articles.* In Proceedings of 10th WSEAS Int. Conf. On Applied Computer and Applied Computational Science, Stevens Point, Wisconsin, USA, pages 132{136, 2011.

[2] Barbieri, F., Ballesteros, M., Saggion, H., 2017. *Are Emojis Predictable?* in Large Scale Text Understanding Systems Lab, TALN Group Universitat Pompeu Fabra, Barcelona, Spain IBM T.J Watson Research Center, U.S

[3] Barbieri, Francesco and Camacho-Collados, Jose and Ronzano, Francesco and Espinosa-Anke, Luis and Ballesteros, Miguel and Basile, Valerio and Patti, Viviana and Saggion, Horacio, 2018. *SemEval-2018 Task 2: Multilingual Emoji Prediction.* In Proceedings of the 12th International Workshop on Semantic Evaluation (SemEval-2018), New Orleans, LA, United States. Association for Computational Linguistics.

[4] Boia, M., Faltings, B., Musat, C.-C., and Pu, P., 2013. *A:) is worth a thousand words: How people attach sentiment to emoticons and words in tweets.* In Social Computing (SocialCom), 2013

International Conference on, pages 345–350. IEEE.

[5] Cappallo, S., Mensink, T. and Snoek, C. G. M., 2015. *Image2emoji: Zero-shot emoji predictionfor visual media.* In Proceedings of the 23rd Annual ACM Conference on Multimedia Conference, pp.1311–1314. ACM, (2015).

[6] Castellucci, G. , Croce, D. and Basili R. 2015. *Acquiring a large scale polarity lexicon through unsupervised distributional methods.* In Natural Language Processing and Information Systems, pages 73{86. Springer, 2015.

[7] Dzmitry, B., Kyunghyun, C. and Yoshua, B., 2014. *Neural machine translation by jointly learning to align and translate.* In Proceeding of the third International Conference on Learning Representations, Toulon, France, May.

[8] Eisner, B., Rocktäschel, T., Augenstein, I., Bošnjak, M. and Riedel, S., 2016. *Emoji2vec: Learning emoji representations from their description.* In Proceedings of The Fourth International Workshop on Natural Language Processing for Social Media, pages 48–54, Austin, TX, USA, November. Association for Computational Linguistics.

[9] Go, A. , Bhayani, R. and Huang, L. 2009. *Twitter sentiment classication using distant upervision.* CS224N Project Report, Stanford, 1:12, 2009

[10] Jiang, F., Liu, Y.-Q., Luan, H.-B., Sun, J.-S., Zhu, X., Zhang, M. and Ma, S.-P., 2015. *Microblog sentiment analysis with emoticon space model.* Journal of Computer Science and Technology, 30(5):1120{1129, 2015.

THU_NGN at SemEval-2018 Task 2: Residual CNN-LSTM Network with Attention for English Emoji Prediction

Chuhan Wu[1], Fangzhao Wu[2], Sixing Wu[1], Zhigang Yuan[1], Junxin Liu[1] and Yongfeng Huang[1]

[1]Tsinghua National Laboratory for Information Science and Technology, Department of Electronic Engineering, Tsinghua University Beijing 100084, China

[2]Microsoft Research Asia

{wuch15,wu-sx15,yuanzg14,ljx16,yfhuang}@mails.tsinghua.edu.cn

wufangzhao@gmail.com

Abstract

Emojis are widely used by social media and social network users when posting their messages. It is important to study the relationships between messages and emojis. Thus, in SemEval-2018 Task 2 an interesting and challenging task is proposed, i.e., predicting which emojis are evoked by text-based tweets. We propose a residual CNN-LSTM with attention (**RCLA**) model for this task. Our model combines CNN and LSTM layers to capture both local and long-range contextual information for tweet representation. In addition, attention mechanism is used to select important components. Besides, residual connection is applied to CNN layers to facilitate the training of neural networks. We also incorporated additional features such as POS tags and sentiment features extracted from lexicons. Our model achieved 30.25% macro-averaged F-score in the first subtask (i.e., emoji prediction in English), ranking 7_{th} out of 48 participants.

1 Introduction

Emojis such as ♥ and 😀 are widely used in social media and social network messages such as tweets. They are frequently combined with plain texts to visually complement the meaning of a message and convey various opinions and emotions (Novak et al., 2015; Barbieri et al., 2017). Social media platforms such as Twitter has accumulated a large number of emoji-incorporated messages. Analyzing the relationships between the textual message and emojis has many potential applications, such as emoji recommendation, automatic emoji-enriched message generation, and accurate sentiment analysis of social media messages (Barbieri et al., 2017).

However, the research on the relationships between textual message and emojis is limited. Existing studies on emojis mainly focus on analyzing the semantics, usage or sentiment of emojis (Aoki and Uchida, 2011; Barbieri et al., 2016a,b,c; Ljubešić and Fišer, 2016; Novak et al., 2015). For example, Barbieri et al. (2016b) explored the meaning and usage of emojis across different languages. Wijeratneet al. (2017) proposed to utilize the emoji sense definitions to improve the performance of emoji embedding model. However, these approaches cannot reveal the interplay between plain texts and emojis. In order to fill this gap, Barbieri et al. (2017) proposed a novel task to predict which emojis are evoked by text-based tweets. For example, given a tweet message *"Love my coworkers ! @user"*, a system is required to predict that emoji ♥ is associated with this tweet.

As an extension, the SemEval-2018 Task 2[1] aims to predict emojis for English and Spanish tweets (Barbieri et al., 2018). Given a plain tweet message without emoji, systems are required to predict which emoji is evoked by this message. We proposed a residual CNN-LSTM with attention model (**RCLA**) for this task.[2] Our model combines LSTM and multi-level CNN layers to capture both long-range and local information to learn tweet representation. In addition, attention mechanism (Yang et al., 2016) is incorporated into our approach to select important components. Besides, we applied residual connection technique (He et al., 2016) to CNN layers in our model to facilitate the training of neural networks. We also incorporated additional features such as POS tags and sentiment features extracted from sentiment lexicons. Our model achieved 30.25% macro-averaged F-score on the test data of the first subtask (i.e., emoji prediction in English), and ranked 7_{th} out of 48 participants.

---

[1]https://competitions.codalab.org/competitions/17344

[2]The codes of our **RCLA** model are publicly available at https://github.com/wuch15/SemEval-2018-task2-THU_NGN

Proceedings of the 12th International Workshop on Semantic Evaluation (SemEval-2018), pages 410–414
New Orleans, Louisiana, June 5–6, 2018. ©2018 Association for Computational Linguistics

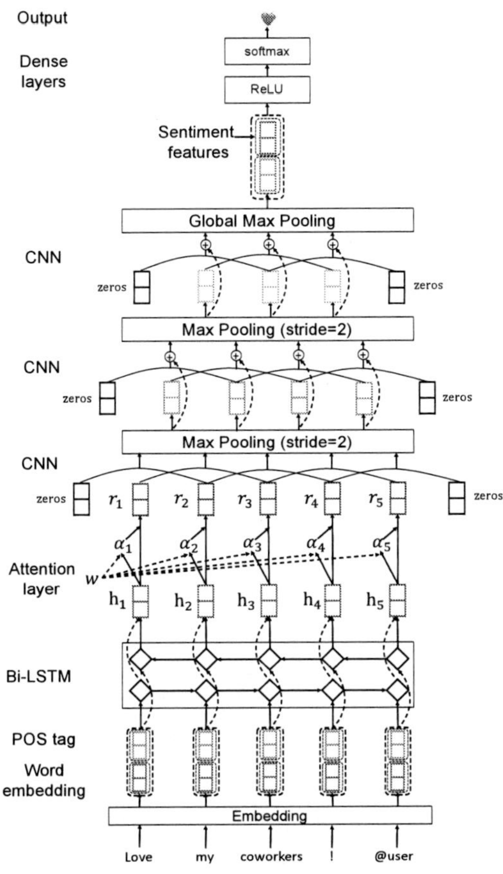

Figure 1: The architecture of our model. The dashed lines in CNN layers represent residual connections.

2 Residual CNN-LSTM with Attention

The framework of our residual CNN-LSTM with attention model (**RCLA**) is illustrated in Figure 1. Next, we will introduce each layer in our model from bottom to top in detail.

The first layer in our model is the embedding layer. This layer is used to convert a sentence from a sequence of words into a sequence of dense vectors. An embedding lookup table is used in this layer, whose parameters are obtained from pre-trained word embeddings and fine-tuned during training. POS tags have proven useful for many natural language processing tasks such as dimensional sentiment analysis (Wu et al., 2017). Motivated by existing studies, we also incorporate POS tags as additional features in our approach, and combining them with the word embeddings to form the final word features as the input of next

layer. We use the Ark-Tweet-NLP[3] tool to obtain the POS tags of tweets.

The second layer in our model is bidirectional long short-term memory (Bi-LSTM) layer. This layer is used to capture long-range contextual information from tweets. At time step i, a hidden state $\mathbf{h}_i$ is generated which contains both previous and future context information. Since different words and phrases have different importance for emoji prediction, we incorporate an attention layer after the Bi-LSTM layer to help our model focus on important words and contexts. The input of the attention layer is the hidden state vector $\mathbf{h}_i$ at each time step. The attention weight α_i for this time step can be computed as:

$$
\begin{aligned}
\mathbf{m}_i &= \tanh(\mathbf{h}_i), \\
\hat{\alpha}_i &= \mathbf{w}^T \mathbf{m}_i + b, \\
\alpha_i &= \frac{\exp(\hat{\alpha}_i)}{\sum_j \exp(\hat{\alpha}_j)},
\end{aligned}
\tag{1}
$$

where $\mathbf{w}$ and b are the parameters of the attention layer. The output of attention layer at the i_{th} time step is formulated as follows:

$$
\mathbf{r}_i = \alpha \mathbf{h}_i.
\tag{2}
$$

The third layer in our model is a 3-layer convolutional neural networks (CNN) to capture local context information. Each CNN layer has multiple kernels with different window sizes. In addition, we apply residual connections (He et al., 2016) to the CNN layers as shown in Figure 1, which have shown effectiveness in facilitating the training of deep neural networks. Max pooling is applied to the output of the last CNN layer to obtain the hidden representation of tweets.

Tweets with specific emojis such as ♥ usually convey strong sentiment information. Thus, sentiment information is helpful for emoji prediction. We incorporate sentiment features into our model to enhance its performance. These sentiment features are extracted using AffectiveTweets[4] (Mohammad and Bravo-Marquez, 2017) package in Weka[5]. Two filters are involved, i.e., TweetToLexiconFeatureVector (Bravo-Marquez et al., 2014) and TweetToSentiStrengthFeatureVector (Thelwall et al., 2012). These sentiment features are combined with the hidden tweet representations

---

[3] http://www.cs.cmu.edu/ ark/TweetNLP
[4] https://github.com/felipebravom/AffectiveTweets
[5] https://www.cs.waikato.ac.nz/ml/weka

generate by neural networks to form the final feature representation of tweets. Finally, a softmax layer is used to predict the emoji label.

The tweets with different emojis in the training set are very imbalanced. For example, the ratio of ♥ is higher than 20%, while the ratio of 😜 is only 2.4%. Motivated by the cost-sensitive cross-entropy method (Santos-Rodríguez et al., 2009), the objective function of our model is defined as:

$$\mathcal{L} = -\sum_{i=1}^{N} w_{y_i} y_i \log(\hat{y}_i), \qquad (3)$$

where N is the number of tweets, y_i is the emoji label of the i_{th} tweet, $\hat{y}_i$ is the prediction score, and w_{y_i} is the loss weight of emoji label y_i. w_{y_i} is defined as $\frac{\sum_{k=1}^{C} \sqrt{N_k}}{\sqrt{N_{y_i}}}$, where C is the number of emoji labels and N_j is the number of tweets with emoji label j. Thus, the infrequent emojis have relatively larger loss weights.

3 Experiment

3.1 Dataset and Experimental Settings

The dataset[6] for this task is collected from Twitter. There are 20 emojis in total. 489,277 tweets are used for model training. The number of tweets in the trial and test sets are both 50,000. We used the pre-trained word embeddings provided by Barbieri et al. (2016b). They were trained on 20 million geo-localized tweets and their dimension is 300. These word embedding were fine-tuned during model training.

The hyperparameters in our model were selected via cross-validation on the trail set. More specifically, the dimension of Bi-LSTM hidden states is 300, the window sizes of CNN filters are 2, 3, 4 respectively. The number of CNN filters is 200 and the number of sentiment features is 45. The dimension of dense layer is 300, and the dropout rate is 0.2 for each layer. The batch size is 500, and the maximal training epoch is set to 100. We use RMSProp as the optimizer for network training. The performance is evaluated by macro-averaged F-score.

3.2 Performance Evaluation

The performance of our model on the test set is shown in Table 1. According to Table 1, our model can achieve good performance on predicting frequent emojis, since their training data is sufficient.

---

[6]https://competitions.codalab.org/competitions/17344

In addition, the performance of our approach on some infrequent emojis is also satisfactory. For example, the F-score on emoji 🎄 is high. This is probably because specific words such as "Christmas" are frequently associated with this emoji, making it relatively easy to predict.

Emo	P	R	F1	%
♥	82.9	79.55	81.19	21.6
😂	27.52	41.61	33.13	9.66
😍	33.69	52.43	41.02	9.07
💕	20.94	20.54	20.74	5.21
🔥	51.74	45.67	48.51	7.43
😊	10.38	11.59	10.95	3.23
😎	16.16	18.44	17.22	3.99
✨	35.51	23.54	28.31	5.5
💙	22.73	14.4	17.63	3.1
😘	14.93	15.23	15.08	2.35
📷	22.0	25.63	23.68	2.86
🇺🇸	64.0	60.03	61.95	3.9
☀	64.04	53.36	58.21	2.53
💜	20.6	9.78	13.27	2.23
😉	9.99	6.89	8.16	2.61
💯	26.58	22.03	24.09	2.49
😁	8.16	6.24	7.08	2.31
🎄	66.22	67.12	66.67	3.09
📸	31.84	18.58	23.46	4.83
😜	7.1	3.47	4.66	2.02

Table 1: Precision, Recall, F-score and percentage of occurrences of each emoji in the test set.

The visualization of the confusion matrix of our model is shown in Figure 2. From this figure, we find two pairs of emojis which are difficult for our model to discriminate between them. The emoji ♥ is often wrongly identified as ✨. This is probably because these two emojis are often used to express similar meaning and feelings. For example, they both can be used in tweets which convey happy emotion. Another pair of emojis is 📷 and 📸. These two emojis look quite similar, and discriminating them is quite difficult.

In order to further validate the effectiveness of our model, we compare the performance of our model with several baseline methods. The methods to be compared include: 1) LSTM, using Bi-LSTM for tweet presentation; 2) CNN, 3-layer CNN without residual connections; 3) CNN-LSTM (denoted as *CL*), using the combination of LSTM and CNN; 4) Residual CNN-LSTM (denoted as *RCL*), CNN-LSTM with residual connections; 5) Residual CNN-LSTM with attention (denoted as *RCLA*). The results are shown in Table 2. According to Table 2, the combination of

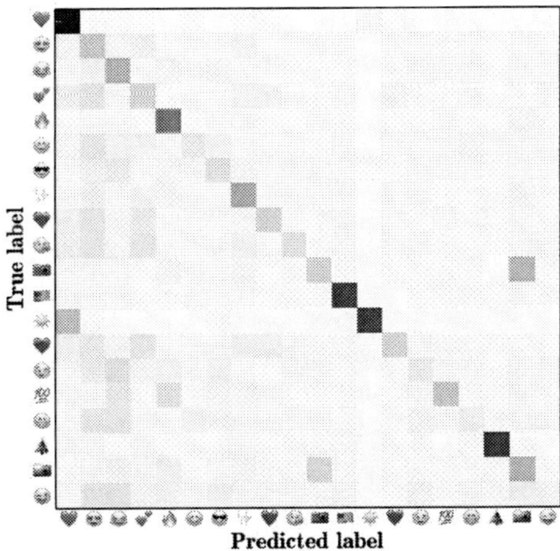

Figure 2: The confusion matrix of our model.

Emo	LSTM	CNN	CL	RCL	RCLA
❤	79.61	81.24	81.26	**82.79**	81.19
😍	28.81	31.39	30.73	32.72	**33.13**
😂	37.34	**41.16**	38.35	38.72	41.02
💕	**20.88**	16.55	18.16	17.53	20.74
🔥	45.03	47.57	46.34	44.92	**48.51**
😊	9.71	9.59	7.99	10.03	**10.95**
😎	15.49	**18.43**	14.28	17.77	17.22
✨	**28.40**	27.43	27.62	27.72	28.31
💙	**18.24**	16.82	17.70	17.21	17.63
😘	12.13	14.83	**15.87**	13.86	15.08
📷	21.34	22.06	21.35	21.31	**23.68**
🇺🇸	58.14	52.76	59.36	59.58	**61.95**
☀	56.37	57.50	**59.03**	58.65	58.21
💜	11.75	10.06	11.95	**14.89**	13.27
😉	9.17	4.00	**10.43**	8.72	8.16
💯	20.61	22.13	21.34	21.76	**24.09**
😁	6.50	6.83	**8.73**	6.26	7.08
🎄	63.88	64.73	64.65	64.50	**66.67**
📸	24.62	25.38	25.80	**27.21**	23.46
😜	6.31	**6.77**	6.11	5.97	4.66
Avg.	28.72	28.86	29.35	29.61	**30.25**

Table 2: The F-score of each emoji and the macro-F of different methods.

Feature	Macro-F
None	29.08
+POS	29.76
+Sentiment	29.55
+POS+Sentiment	**30.25**

Table 3: Influence of POS tags and sentiment features.

LSTM and CNN (*CL*) usually outperforms the single CNN and LSTM. It indicates that combining CNN and LSTM to capture both local and long-range context information is beneficial for tweet emoji prediction. In addition, by comparing *RCL* with *CL*, we find that the residual connections can improve the performance of *CL* model. It shows that the residual connections can facilitate the training of neural networks. Besides, the attention mechanism can also significantly improve the performance. It validates that employing attention mechanism to capture the important contexts for emoji prediction is useful.

3.3 Influence of Additional Features

The influence of the POS tags and sentiment features is illustrated in Table 3. The results show that both POS tags and sentiment features can help improve the performance of tweet emoji prediction. It indicates that POS tags contain useful information for predicting emojis, since important emoji clues such as hashtags, emoticons and sentiment words usually have specific POS tags. Thus, incorporating POS tag features is beneficial. Incorporating sentiment features is also useful. This is because the sentiment features we extracted from sentiment lexicons can identify both formal and information sentiment signals such as hashtags and emoticons, and these sentiment signals usually have strong associations with specific emojis. Thus, incorporating the sentiment features is also beneficial to predict emojis.

4 Conclusion

In this paper, we introduce our residual CNN-LSTM model with attention model (**RCLA**) for SemEval-2018 Task 2, i.e., emoji prediction for tweets. Our model combines CNN and LSTM layers to capture both local and long-range context information for tweet representation, and incorporates an attention layer to select important information. Besides, we applied residual connections to CNN layers to facilitate the training of our model. In addition, we incorporated additional features such as POS tags and sentiment features to further improve the performance. The experimental results validate the effectiveness of our model on emoji prediction for English tweets.

Acknowledgments

The authors thank the reviewers for their insightful comments and constructive suggestions on improving this work. This work was supported in part by the National Key Research and Development Program of China under Grant

2016YFB0800402 and in part by the National Natural Science Foundation of China under Grant U1705261, Grant U1536207, Grant U1536201 and U1636113.

References

Sho Aoki and Osamu Uchida. 2011. A method for automatically generating the emotional vectors of emoticons using weblog articles. In *Proc. 10th WSEAS Int. Conf. on Applied Computer and Applied Computational Science, Stevens Point, Wisconsin, USA*, pages 132–136.

Francesco Barbieri, Luis Espinosa Anke, and Horacio Saggion. 2016a. Revealing patterns of twitter emoji usage in barcelona and madrid. In *CCIA*, pages 239–244.

Francesco Barbieri, Miguel Ballesteros, and Horacio Saggion. 2017. Are emojis predictable? In *Proceedings of the 15th Conference of the European Chapter of the Association for Computational Linguistics: Volume 2, Short Papers*, pages 105–111. Association for Computational Linguistics.

Francesco Barbieri, Jose Camacho-Collados, Francesco Ronzano, Luis Espinosa-Anke, Miguel Ballesteros, Valerio Basile, Viviana Patti, and Horacio Saggion. 2018. SemEval-2018 Task 2: Multilingual Emoji Prediction. In *Proceedings of the 12th International Workshop on Semantic Evaluation (SemEval-2018)*, New Orleans, LA, United States. Association for Computational Linguistics.

Francesco Barbieri, German Kruszewski, Francesco Ronzano, and Horacio Saggion. 2016b. How cosmopolitan are emojis?: Exploring emojis usage and meaning over different languages with distributional semantics. In *Proceedings of the 2016 ACM on Multimedia Conference*, pages 531–535. ACM.

Francesco Barbieri, Francesco Ronzano, and Horacio Saggion. 2016c. What does this emoji mean? a vector space skip-gram model for twitter emojis. In *LREC*.

Felipe Bravo-Marquez, Marcelo Mendoza, and Barbara Poblete. 2014. Meta-level sentiment models for big social data analysis. *Knowledge-Based Systems*, 69:86–99.

Kaiming He, Xiangyu Zhang, Shaoqing Ren, and Jian Sun. 2016. Deep residual learning for image recognition. In *Proceedings of the IEEE conference on computer vision and pattern recognition*, pages 770–778.

Nikola Ljubešić and Darja Fišer. 2016. A global analysis of emoji usage. In *Proceedings of the 10th Web as Corpus Workshop*, pages 82–89.

Saif Mohammad and Felipe Bravo-Marquez. 2017. Wassa-2017 shared task on emotion intensity. In *Proceedings of the 8th Workshop on Computational Approaches to Subjectivity, Sentiment and Social Media Analysis*, pages 34–49, Copenhagen, Denmark. Association for Computational Linguistics.

Petra Kralj Novak, Jasmina Smailovic, Borut Sluban, and Igor Mozetic. 2015. Sentiment of emojis. *PLOS ONE*, 10(12).

Raúl Santos-Rodríguez, Darío García-García, and Jesús Cid-Sueiro. 2009. Cost-sensitive classification based on bregman divergences for medical diagnosis. In *Machine Learning and Applications, 2009. ICMLA'09. International Conference on*, pages 551–556. IEEE.

Mike Thelwall, Kevan Buckley, and Georgios Paltoglou. 2012. Sentiment strength detection for the social web. *Journal of the Association for Information Science and Technology*, 63(1):163–173.

Sanjaya Wijeratne, Lakshika Balasuriya, Amit Sheth, and Derek Doran. 2017. A semantics-based measure of emoji similarity. In *2017 IEEE/WIC/ACM International Conference on Web Intelligence (WI)*, Leipzig, Germany. ACM, ACM.

Chuhan Wu, Fangzhao Wu, Yongfeng Huang, Sixing Wu, and Zhigang Yuan. 2017. Thu_ngn at ijcnlp-2017 task 2: Dimensional sentiment analysis for chinese phrases with deep lstm. *Proceedings of the IJCNLP 2017, Shared Tasks*, pages 47–52.

Zichao Yang, Diyi Yang, Chris Dyer, Xiaodong He, Alex Smola, and Eduard Hovy. 2016. Hierarchical attention networks for document classification. In *Proceedings of the 2016 Conference of the North American Chapter of the Association for Computational Linguistics: Human Language Technologies*, pages 1480–1489.

#TeamINF at SemEval-2018 Task 2: Emoji Prediction in Tweets

Alison P. Ribeiro
Institute of Informatics
Federal University of Goiás
Goiânia – Goiás – Brasil
alisonrib17@gmail.com

Nádia F. F. da Silva
Institute of Informatics
Federal University of Goiás
Goiânia – Goiás – Brasil
nadia@inf.ufg.br

Abstract

In this paper, we describe a methodology to predict emoji in tweets. Our approach is based on the classic bag-of-words model in conjunction with word embeddings. The used classification algorithm was Logistic Regression. This architecture was used and evaluated in the context of the SemEval 2018 challenge (task 2, subtask 1).

1 Introduction

Over the years, technology has significantly changed the way people communicate. It was changed especially due to social media like Twitter[1], Facebook[2], WhatsApp[3], among others. Such media provide users with the ability to express their opinions/emotions not only with words, but through images, the so-called *emojis*.

However, within the context of the sentiment analysis, little research has been dedicated to explore the semantics of *emoji* (Barbieri et al., 2016), thus becoming an interesting challenge to investigate.

Understanding the meaning of *emojis* in relation to their context of use is important for indexing multimedia information, retrieval, or content extraction systems. In addition, *emoji* can complement the meaning of a message, that is, an *emoji* can determine the feeling of a text, however, such emotive figures may become fragile in the ironic/sarcastic context.

In this paper, we developed a methodology to predict *emoji* in tweets, especially our method is based on the bag-of-words model in conjunction with word embeddings (GloVe[4] pre-trained) and n-grams[5], applying a classification algorithm.

[1] https://twitter.com/

[2] https://www.facebook.com

[3] https://www.whatsapp.com/

[4] https://nlp.stanford.edu/projects/glove/

[5] terms composed by n words.

This configuration was employed and evaluated in the SemEval 2018 challenge (task 2, subtask 1), in which the goal is to predict the *emoji* of a tweet (Barbieri et al., 2018).

This work is organized as follows: section 2 explains some related works, section 3 describes the data set, section 4 addresses the methodology applied in the task, section 5 presents the results, and finally section 6 final considerations as well as future work.

2 Related Works

Emojis can express diverse types of contents in a visual way, adapting to the informal style of communication in social networks. The meaning expressed by emoticons has been explored to allow or improve various tasks related to the sentiment analysis, as in (Hogenboom et al., 2013, 2015).

Emojis can also be used to label excerpts of texts where they occur, thus making it possible to construct sentiment lexical. In this context, in (Go et al., 2009) and (Castellucci et al., 2015) use a distant supervision over the emotionally marked textual contents to form a sentiment classifier and construct a lexicon of polarity. While Novak et al. 2015 constructed lexicons and drew a map of sentiments of the 751 most used *emoji*.

In the work of Barbieri et al. 2017, the authors investigated the relationship between words and *emojis*, studying the new task of predicting which *emoji* are evoked by text-based tweet messages. The authors trained several models based on Long Memory Short-Term networks (LSTMs).

In (Barbieri et al., 2016) the authors explore the meaning and use of *emojis* in four languages: American English, British English, Peninsular Spanish and Italian. By performing several experiments the researchers were able to compare

415

Proceedings of the 12th International Workshop on Semantic Evaluation (SemEval-2018), pages 415–418
New Orleans, Louisiana, June 5–6, 2018. ©2018 Association for Computational Linguistics

how the semantics of *emoji* vary according to the languages. In a first experiment, they investigated whether the meaning of a single *emoji* is preserved in all variations of language. In the second experiment, they compared the general semantic models of the 150 most frequent *emoji* in all languages. In this study it was possible to find out that the general semantics of the most frequent *emoji* is similiar.

Finally, given the context of the challenge of Semeval 2018 (task 2, subtask 1), we propose a model capable of predicting *emoji* corresponding to the tweets.

3 Dataset and Task

Dataset. The data for the task consists of 500k tweets in English for training, 50k for trial and 50k for test. The tweets were retrieved with the Twitter APIs, from October 2015 to February 2017, and geolocalized in United States. The dataset includes tweets that contain one and only one *emoji*, of the 20 most frequent *emojis*. The amount of tweets for dataset can be seen in Figure 1.

Task details. Because of the importance of visual icons with the ability to provide additional meaning for social messaging and Twitter's key role as one of the most important communication platforms, the Semeval 2018 team invites participants to predict the *emoji* associated with a tweet in English (Barbieri et al., 2018).

Emojis	Train	Trial	Test
	105663	10760	10798
	51015	5279	4830
	50028	5241	4534
	26852	2885	2605
	24316	2517	3716
	22957	2317	1613
	20982	2049	1996
	18043	1894	2749
	16695	1796	1549
	15861	1671	1175
	15870	1544	1432
	15067	1528	1949
	13617	1462	1265
	12712	1346	1114
	13255	1377	1306
	13180	1249	1244
	12873	1306	1153
	12621	1279	1545
	13065	1286	2417
	12106	1214	1010

Figure 1: Number of labels per classes.

4 Methodology

The methodology applied in this task consists of two phases, one based on the bag-of-words model and another based on the word embeddings (GloVe) model, in the end both are concatenated, as shown in Figure 2.

4.1 Preprocessing

This step consists in eliminating noises and terms that have no semantic significance in the sentiment prediction. For this, we perform the removal of links, removal of numbers, removal of special characters, removal of *stop words* (words with low discriminative power, for example, "is", "that" etc.). The standardization of tweets in lowercase was also applied, and finally, *stemming*. The purpose of stemming is to reduce words to their radical, for example, the word "*belivies*" will be transformed into "*believ*" (Perkins, 2014).

4.2 Bag-of-words

We apply bag-of-words as baseline, since it has been successfully employed in various classification tasks (Da Silva et al., 2014; Barbieri et al., 2017; Pak and Paroubek, 2010; Kouloumpis et al., 2011; Socher et al., 2013). We represent each message with a vector of tokens, selected using term frequency-inverse document frequency (TF-IDF) with quadrigrams, and $min\_df = 1$, $max\_features = 3500$, and $ngram\_range = (1,4)$. In the Logistic Regression it was considered $C = 10.0$, while in the Support Vector Machine and Random Forest the hyperparameters were used by default.

4.3 Word embeddings

Word Embeddings (Bengio et al., 2003) is a supervised statistical language model trained using deep neural networks. The purpose of this model is to predict the next word, given the previous context in the sentence, so similar words tend to be always close. The vector presentation of words was a great advance in relation to the strategies based on bag-of-words. For the proposed task we apply the GloVe model (with 200 dimensions) by (Pennington et al., 2014), GloVe is based on a counting model, in which the vectors are derived from an array of co-occurrences used to extract statistical information about the corpus. With this model an array was generated through the simple arithmetic mean of the word vectors.

4.3.1 Challenges

Because of the need for high computational power to perform the task and the high dimensionality of the table, both in terms of number of attributes and number of rows, only a sampling of 10% of training data was used, this sampling reflects the distribution of real classes.

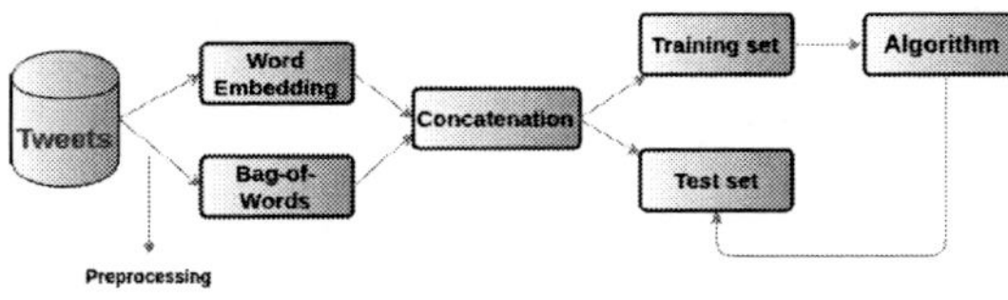

Figure 2: Model used in competition.

5 Results

In this section, we report the obtained results by our model according to the metric evaluation of the challenge, macro f1, precision and recall, accuracy, and f1 for all the *emojis* (Barbieri et al., 2018). Results are reported for five diverse configurations: (i) the system based on word embeddings and baf-of-words with Logistic Regression (LR); (ii) the system based on word embeddings and baf-of-words with Support Vector Machine (SVM); (iii) the bag-of-words system with Logistic Regression (LR); (iv) the bag-of-words system with Support Vector Machine (SVM); and (v) the bag-of-words system with Random Forest (RF). In Table 1 we show model's performances and in Figure 3 we present the predicted score for one of the 20 *emojis*.

Model	F1	P	R	Acc
WE+BoW-LR	**21.497**	**26.208**	**20.843**	**31.588**
WE+BoW-SVM	21.023	27.034	21.403	32.570
BoW-LR	20.351	24.923	19.824	30.830
BoW-SVM	20.194	26.659	20.518	31.966
BoW-RF	15.793	19.890	15.310	25.842

Table 1: Result Semeval-2018.

The obtained results on the testing data indicate that word embedding together with bag-of-word produces the best F1, on the other hand the three configurations represented only by bag-of-word obtained their results close to the central work model (Word Embedding + Bag-of- Words). It is important to remember that only 10% of training data was used, such choice directly influenced the final result.

	F1			F1
	43.287			24.111
	24.74			47.977
	36.694			33.384
	7.363			6.108
	43.543			4.348
	6.452			18.648
	13.118			5.439
	19.2			60.131
	8.763			18.306
	5.684			2.651

Figure 3: F1 per classes.

6 Conclusion

In this paper, we propose several configurations based on word embeddings and bag-of-words for the Semeval 2018 task 2, subtask 1. As base classifiers we use Logistic Regression (LR), Support Vector Machine (SVM) and Random Forest (RF) to predict *emojis* in tweets. Our best model got F1 of 21.497.

As future works we intend to explore the semantics of *emojis* more, as well as apply new word embeddings templates, such as Word2Vec (Mikolov et al., 2013), FastText (Joulin et al., 2016) and Doc2Vec (Le and Mikolov, 2014) with more computational resources.

References

Francesco Barbieri, Miguel Ballesteros, and Horacio Saggion. 2017. Are emojis predictable? *arXiv preprint arXiv:1702.07285*.

Francesco Barbieri, Jose Camacho-Collados, Francesco Ronzano, Luis Espinosa-Anke, Miguel Ballesteros, Valerio Basile, Viviana Patti, and Horacio Saggion. 2018. SemEval-2018 Task 2: Multilingual Emoji Prediction. In *Proceedings of the 12th International Workshop on Semantic Evaluation (SemEval-2018)*, New Orleans, LA, United States. Association for Computational Linguistics.

Francesco Barbieri, German Kruszewski, Francesco Ronzano, and Horacio Saggion. 2016. How cosmopolitan are emojis?: Exploring emojis usage and meaning over different languages with distributional semantics. In *Proceedings of the 2016 ACM on Multimedia Conference*, pages 531–535. ACM.

Yoshua Bengio, Réjean Ducharme, Pascal Vincent, and Christian Jauvin. 2003. A neural probabilistic language model. *Journal of machine learning research*, 3(Feb):1137–1155.

Giuseppe Castellucci, Danilo Croce, and Roberto Basili. 2015. Acquiring a large scale polarity lexicon through unsupervised distributional methods. In

International Conference on Applications of Natural Language to Information Systems, pages 73–86. Springer.

Nadia FF Da Silva, Eduardo R Hruschka, and Estevam R Hruschka Jr. 2014. Tweet sentiment analysis with classifier ensembles. *Decision Support Systems*, 66:170–179.

Alec Go, Richa Bhayani, and Lei Huang. 2009. Twitter sentiment classification using distant supervision. *CS224N Project Report, Stanford*, 1(12).

Alexander Hogenboom, Daniella Bal, Flavius Frasincar, Malissa Bal, Franciska De Jong, and Uzay Kaymak. 2015. Exploiting emoticons in polarity classification of text. *J. Web Eng.*, 14(1&2):22–40.

Alexander Hogenboom, Daniella Bal, Flavius Frasincar, Malissa Bal, Franciska de Jong, and Uzay Kaymak. 2013. Exploiting emoticons in sentiment analysis. In *Proceedings of the 28th Annual ACM Symposium on Applied Computing*, pages 703–710. ACM.

Armand Joulin, Edouard Grave, Piotr Bojanowski, and Tomas Mikolov. 2016. Bag of tricks for efficient text classification. *CoRR*, abs/1607.01759.

Efthymios Kouloumpis, Theresa Wilson, and Johanna D Moore. 2011. Twitter sentiment analysis: The good the bad and the omg! *Icwsm*, 11(538-541):164.

Quoc Le and Tomas Mikolov. 2014. Distributed representations of sentences and documents. In *International Conference on Machine Learning*, pages 1188–1196.

Tomas Mikolov, Kai Chen, Greg Corrado, and Jeffrey Dean. 2013. Efficient estimation of word representations in vector space. *arXiv preprint arXiv:1301.3781*.

Petra Kralj Novak, Jasmina Smailović, Borut Sluban, and Igor Mozetič. 2015. Sentiment of emojis. *PloS one*, 10(12):e0144296.

Alexander Pak and Patrick Paroubek. 2010. Twitter as a corpus for sentiment analysis and opinion mining. In *LREc*, volume 10.

Jeffrey Pennington, Richard Socher, and Christopher D. Manning. 2014. Glove: Global vectors for word representation. In *Empirical Methods in Natural Language Processing (EMNLP)*, pages 1532–1543.

Jacob Perkins. 2014. *Python 3 Text Processing with NLTK 3 Cookbook*. Packt Publishing Ltd.

Richard Socher, Alex Perelygin, Jean Wu, Jason Chuang, Christopher D Manning, Andrew Ng, and Christopher Potts. 2013. Recursive deep models for semantic compositionality over a sentiment treebank. In *Proceedings of the 2013 conference on empirical methods in natural language processing*, pages 1631–1642.

EICA Team at SemEval-2018 Task 2: Semantic and Metadata-based Features for Multilingual Emoji Prediction

Yufei Xie, Qingqing Song

East China Normal University, Shanghai, P.R.China

yufeixie@ica.stc.sh.cn

Abstract

The advent of social media has brought along a novel way of communication where meaning is composed by combining short text messages and visual enhancements, the so-called emojis. We describe our system for participating in SemEval-2018 Task 2 on Multilingual Emoji Prediction. Our approach relies on combining a rich set of various types of features: semantic and metadata. The most important types turned out to be the metadata feature. In subtask 1: Emoji Prediction in English, our primary submission obtain a MAP of 16.45, Precision of 31.557, Recall of 16.771 and Accuracy of 30.992.

1 Introduction

Emojis are ideograms which are naturally combined with plain text to visually complement or condense the meaning of a message (Barbieri et al., 2017). Despite being widely used in social media, their underlying semantics have received little attention from a Natural Language Processing standpoint. Barbieri et al. (2016) compare the meaning and usage of emojis across two Spanish cities: Barcelona and Madrid. Ljubešić et al. (2017) present a set of experiments and analyses on predicting the gender of Twitter users based on languageindependent features extracted either from the text or the metadata of users tweets.

Miller et al. (2016) performed an evaluation asking human annotators the meaning of emojis, and the sentiment they evoke. People do not always have the same understanding of emojis, indeed, there seems to exist multiple interpretations of their meaning beyond their designers intent or the physical object they evoke1. Their main conclusion was that emojis can lead to misunderstandings. The ambiguity of emojis raises an interesting question in human-computer interaction: how

can we teach an artificial agent to correctly interpret and recognise emojis use in spontaneous conversation? The main motivation of our research is that an artificial intelligence system that is able to predict emojis could contribute to better natural language understanding (Novak et al., 2015) and thus to different natural language processing tasks such as generating emoji-enriched social media content, enhance emotion/sentiment analysis systems, and improve retrieval of social network material.

2 Our Approach

2.1 Features

We use several semantic features and metadata features to represent the twitter.

2.1.1 Semantic Features

Semantic features represent the basic conceptual components of meaning for any lexical item (Fromkin et al., 2018). An individual semantic feature constitutes one component of a word's intension, which is the inherent sense or concept evoked (O'Grady et al., 1997).

Semantic Word Embeddings. We use semantic word embeddings obtained from Word2vec models for GoogleNews. For each twitter, we construct the centroid vector from the vectors of all words in that text.

$$centroid(w_{1..n}) = \frac{\sum_{i=1}^{n} w_i}{n} \quad (1)$$

TF-IDF. In information retrieval, tfidf or TFIDF, short for term frequencyinverse document frequency, is a numerical statistic that is intended to reflect how important a word is to a document in a collection or corpus (Leskovec et al., 2014). It is often used as a weighting factor in searches of information retrieval, text mining, and user modeling. The tf-idf value increases proportionally to

Proceedings of the 12th International Workshop on Semantic Evaluation (SemEval-2018), pages 419–422

New Orleans, Louisiana, June 5–6, 2018. ©2018 Association for Computational Linguistics

the number of times a word appears in the document, but is often offset by the frequency of the word in the corpus, which helps to adjust for the fact that some words appear more frequently in general. Nowadays, tf-idf is one of the most popular term-weighting schemes; 83% of text-based recommender systems in the domain of digital libraries use tf-idf (Beel et al., 2016).

$$tf(t, d) = 0.5 + 0.5 * \frac{f_{t,d}}{max\{f_{t',d} : t' \in d\}} \quad (2)$$

t represents the term, d represents the document (Luhn, 1957).

$$idf(t, d) = \log \frac{N}{|\{d \in D : t \in d\}|} \quad (3)$$

N is total number of documents in the corpus $N = |D|$, $|\{d \in D : t \in d\}|$ is the number of documents where the term t appears. If the term is not in the corpus, this will lead to a division-by-zero (Robertson, 2004). It is therefore common to adjust the denominator to $1 + |\{d \in D : t \in d\}|$.

2.1.2 Metadata Features

Metadata-based features provide clues about the social aspects of the twitter. Thus, except for the semantic features described above, we also used some common sense metadata features:

Twitter containing a question mark. We think if the twitter has a question mark, it may be a question, which might indicate a negative emotions (Castillo et al., 2011).

The presence and the number of links in the twitter. We count both inbound and outbound links. Our hypothesis is that the presence of a reference to another resource is indicative of a positive emotions (Adamic and Huberman, 2000).

Twitter length. The assumption here is that longer twitter could bring more useful detail (Ogasawara, 2009).

2.2 Classifier

For each twitter, we firstly extract the features described above. Then we concatenate the extracted features in a bag of features vector and have them normalized. After the normalization, the value are mapped to interval [-1,1]. At last, we input them into the classifier. In our experiments, we use L2-regularized logistic regression classifier (Buitinck et al., 2013) and SVM classifier (Zweigenbaum

and Lavergne, 2016) respectively. For the logistic regression classifier, we tune the classifier with different values of the C (cost) parameter (Aono et al., 2016), and we take the one that yield the best accuracy on 10-fold cross-validation on the training set. For the SVM classifier, we choose different kernels (Moreno et al., 2004) and achieve the best results with RBF kernel. We only show the better results of above two classifiers in the next section.

3 Experiments and Evalution

3.1 Dataset

3.1.1 Training and Evaluation Data

The data for the task will consist of 500k tweets in English and 100K tweets in Spanish (Barbieri et al., 2018). The tweets were retrieved with the Twitter APIs, from October 2015 to February 2017, and geolocalized in United States and Spain. The dataset includes tweets that contain one and only one emoji, of the 20 most frequent emojis. Data will be split into trial, training and test.

3.1.2 Label set

As labels we will use the 20 most frequent emojis of each language. They are different across the English and Spanish corpora. In the following we show the distribution of the emojis for each language (numbers refer to the percentage of occurrence of each emoji)

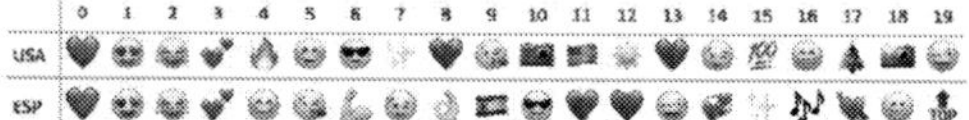

3.2 Evaluation Criteria

For evaluation, the classic Precision and Recall metrics over each emoji are used. The official results will be based on Macro F-score, as the fundamental idea of this task is to encourage systems to perform well overall, which would inherently mean a better sensitivity to the use of emojis in general, rather than for instance overfitting a model to do well in the three or four most common emojis of the test data. Macro F-score can be defined as simply the average of the individual label-wise F-scores. The official will also report Micro F-score for informative purposes.

3.3 Subtask 1 Result

We can see the results in Table 1. The cagri team obtains the best F1 value. The derpferd team gets

Table 1
Experimental Results on the SemEval-2018 Task 2

Team	F1	P	R	Acc
cagri(Top 1)	35.991	36.551	36.222	47.094
cbaziotis(Top2)	35.361	34.534	37.996	44.744
hgsgnlp(Top 3)	34.018	34.997	33.572	45.548
liu_man(Top 4)	33.665	39.426	33.695	47.464
lanman(Top 5)	33.354	35.168	33.108	46.296
derpferd(Top 6)	31.834	39.803	31.365	45.732
ChuhanWu(Top 7)	30.25	31.852	29.806	42.182
kennywlino(Top 8)	30.125	29.905	33.016	38.09
Shi(Top 9)	29.502	35.17	29.91	39.214
anbasile(Top 10)	29.426	30.637	29.583	40.928
EICA	16.45	31.557	16.771	30.992

the best Precision. The cbaziotis obtains the best Recall and the liu_man obtains the best Accuracy. The F1 value of our team is 16.45.

4 Conclusion

We have described our system for SemEval-2018, Task 2 Multilingual Emoji Prediction. Our approach rely on semantic and metadata-based features. Our primary submission obtain a F1 of 16.45 and accuracy of 30.992.

In future work, we plan to use our best feature combinations in a deep learning architecture, as in the Qius system (Qiu and Huang, 2015), which outperforms the other methods on two matching tasks. We also want to use information from entire threads (Joty et al., 2015) to make better predictions. How to combine them efficiently in the system is an interesting research question

5 Acknowledgments

This research was supported in part by Science and Technology Commission of Shanghai Municipality (No.16511102702).

References

Lada A Adamic and Bernardo A Huberman. 2000. Power-law distribution of the world wide web. *science*, 287(5461):2115–2115.

Yoshinori Aono, Takuya Hayashi, Le Trieu Phong, and Lihua Wang. 2016. Scalable and secure logistic regression via homomorphic encryption. In *Proceedings of the Sixth ACM Conference on Data and Application Security and Privacy*, pages 142–144. ACM.

Francesco Barbieri, Luis Espinosa Anke, and Horacio Saggion. 2016. Revealing patterns of twitter emoji usage in barcelona and madrid. In *CCIA*, pages 239–244.

Francesco Barbieri, Miguel Ballesteros, and Horacio Saggion. 2017. Are emojis predictable? In *Proceedings of the 15th Conference of the European Chapter of the Association for Computational Linguistics: Volume 2, Short Papers*, pages 105–111. Association for Computational Linguistics.

Francesco Barbieri, Jose Camacho-Collados, Francesco Ronzano, Luis Espinosa-Anke, Miguel Ballesteros, Valerio Basile, Viviana Patti, and Horacio Saggion. 2018. SemEval-2018 Task 2: Multilingual Emoji Prediction. In *Proceedings of the 12th International Workshop on Semantic Evaluation (SemEval-2018)*, New Orleans, LA, United States. Association for Computational Linguistics.

Joeran Beel, Bela Gipp, Stefan Langer, and Corinna Breitinger. 2016. paper recommender systems: a literature survey. *International Journal on Digital Libraries*, 17(4):305–338.

Lars Buitinck, Gilles Louppe, Mathieu Blondel, Fabian Pedregosa, Andreas Mueller, Olivier Grisel, Vlad Niculae, Peter Prettenhofer, Alexandre Gramfort, Jaques Grobler, et al. 2013. Api design for machine learning software: experiences from the scikit-learn project. *arXiv preprint arXiv:1309.0238*.

Carlos Castillo, Marcelo Mendoza, and Barbara Poblete. 2011. Information credibility on twitter. In *Proceedings of the 20th international conference on World wide web*, pages 675–684. ACM.

Victoria Fromkin, Robert Rodman, and Nina Hyams. 2018. *An introduction to language*. Cengage Learning.

Shafiq Joty, Alberto Barrón-Cedeno, Giovanni Da San Martino, Simone Filice, Lluís Màrquez, Alessandro Moschitti, and Preslav Nakov. 2015. Global thread-level inference for comment classification in community question answering. In *Proceedings of the 2015 Conference on Empirical Methods in Natural Language Processing*, pages 573–578.

Jure Leskovec, Anand Rajaraman, and Jeffrey David Ullman. 2014. *Mining of massive datasets*. Cambridge university press.

Nikola Ljubešić, Darja Fišer, and Tomaž Erjavec. 2017. Language-independent gender prediction on twitter. In *Proceedings of the Second Workshop on NLP and Computational Social Science*, pages 1–6.

Hans Peter Luhn. 1957. A statistical approach to mechanized encoding and searching of literary information. *IBM Journal of research and development*, 1(4):309–317.

Hannah Miller, Jacob Thebault-Spieker, Shuo Chang, Isaac Johnson, Loren Terveen, and Brent Hecht. 2016. Blissfully happy or ready to fight: Varying interpretations of emoji. *Proceedings of ICWSM*, 2016.

Pedro J Moreno, Purdy P Ho, and Nuno Vasconcelos.
2004. A kullback-leibler divergence based kernel
for svm classification in multimedia applications. In
Advances in neural information processing systems,
pages 1385–1392.

Petra Kralj Novak, Jasmina Smailović, Borut Sluban,
and Igor Mozetič. 2015. Sentiment of emojis. *PloS
one*, 10(12):e0144296.

Todd Ogasawara. 2009. The reason for the 160 character text message and 140 character twitter length
limits. *SocialTimes. com.*

William O'Grady, Michael Dobrovolsky, and Francis
Katamba. 1997. *Contemporary linguistics*. St. Martin's.

Xipeng Qiu and Xuanjing Huang. 2015. Convolutional
neural tensor network architecture for community-
based question answering. In *IJCAI*, pages 1305–
1311.

Stephen Robertson. 2004. Understanding inverse document frequency: on theoretical arguments for idf.
Journal of documentation, 60(5):503–520.

Pierre Zweigenbaum and Thomas Lavergne. 2016. Hybrid methods for icd-10 coding of death certificates.
In *Proceedings of the Seventh International Workshop on Health Text Mining and Information Analysis*, pages 96–105.

EmojiIt at SemEval-2018 Task 2: An Effective Attention-Based Recurrent Neural Network Model for Emoji Prediction with Characters Gated Words

Shiyun Chen, Maoquan Wang, Liang He

Department of Computer Science and Technology

East China Normal University

Shanghai, P.R.China 200241

51174506002@stu.ecnu.edu.cn, maoquanwang@ica.stc.sh.cn, lhe@cs.ecnu.edu.cn

Abstract

This paper presents our single model to Subtask 1 of SemEval 2018 Task 2: Emoji Prediction in English. In order to predict the emoji that may be contained in a tweet, the basic model we use is an attention-based recurrent neural network which has achieved satisfactory performs in Natural Language processing. Considering the text comes from social media, it contains many discrepant abbreviations and online terms, we also combine word-level and character-level word vector embedding to better handling the words not appear in the vocabulary. Our single model[1] achieved 29.50% Macro F-score in test data and ranks 9th among 48 teams.

1 Introduction

SemEval-2018 shared task 2 (Barbieri et al., 2018) provides a platform for us to explore the relationship between text and emoji in Twitter. The participants are expected to predict, given a tweet in English or Spanish, its most likely associated emoji. As the number of frequently-used emojis up to 20, this is also a multi-category classification task. Overall, both the prediction of emoji and the multi-category classification have undoubtedly increased the difficulty of task 2.

Before choosing a suitable model, we first analyze the data characteristics in detail. For each emoji, we count the total number of all tweets words under this emoji and enumerate the top 10 meaningful words with the highest frequency. And we can explore the following observations from the statistics:

- In almost all emojis, the first three words that appear frequently include "@user" suggesting that Twitter is a highly interactive social networking site (all the person names unified as "users" during the data preprocessing). Such a tweet should include an unwritten but important context information.

- Because people do not always have the same understanding of emojis, some words can evoke more than one emoji. The greater the repetition of high-frequency words among different emojis, the harder it is to distinguish among these tweets.

- There are also some easily recognizable words. They are just common words under a certain emoji, almost do not appear under others, such as "lit" and "fire" under 🔥; "photo" under 📷; "usa", "america" and "vote" under 🇺🇸; "beach" and "summer" under ☀.

- When glancing over the data, we find that tweets have the following characteristics: a) Non-standard language, some discrepant shorthand or Internet jargon causes the model to get confused about the word; b) Misspelled words, although the human can easily realize the correct words, but if the model takes word-level as the processing unit, it cannot process them correctly. All of these can affect the ability of text representation seriously.

Taking all of these factors into consideration, we explore solutions form three perspectives:

- The second observation indicates that traditional statistical-based model may not achieve good performance, so we decide to adopt a neural network.

- Considering that the importance of each word is different in one tweet although text is very

---

[1] https://github.com/wwmmqq/SemEval-2018-Task-2-Multilingual-Emoji-Prediction

Proceedings of the 12th International Workshop on Semantic Evaluation (SemEval-2018), pages 423–427

New Orleans, Louisiana, June 5–6, 2018. ©2018 Association for Computational Linguistics

short no more than 140 words, we introduce an attention mechanism to extract the key words in tweets.

- As the last observation can generate some tokens do not appear in the vocabulary (OOV), we utilizes both word-level and character-level word vector embedding.

In a word, our single model is an attention-based neural network with word-level and character-level sentence embedding.

2 System Description

Our model architecture is depicted in Fig. 1 and it consists of the following three subparts: word embedding layer, BiLSTM layer and attention layer.

2.1 Word Embedding Layer

Assuming there are n words in a giving sentence x, we denote it as $x = \langle w_1, w_2, \cdots, w_n \rangle$. At each time step t, both the word lookup table and a bidirectional LSTM take the same word w_t as an input.

Word-level embedding The word-level input is projected into a high-dimensional space by a word lookup table $\mathbf{E} \in \mathbb{R}^{|V| \times d}$, which you can get from publicly available *word2vector* [2] tool, where $|V|$ is the vocabulary size and d is the dimension of a word vector. Then we refer to the obtained vector as $x_{w_t}^{word}$.

Character-level embedding The character-level input is converted into a vector by using a recurrent neural network. In order to better capture the interaction between adjacent characters, we use a bidirectional LSTM (BiLSTM) (Graves, 2005) to model the words. BiLSTM contains a forward LSTM processing the input from the first char to the last char, and a backward LSTM performing the opposite action. The last hidden states of the forward and the backward recurrent networks are linearly combined to $x_{w_t}^{char}$.

Combine word-level and character-level embedding We generate the final vector representation of a word by combining two distinct representations of the word:

$$x_{w_t} = g_{word} x_{w_t}^{word} \oplus g_{char} x_{w_t}^{char} \qquad (1)$$

where $\oplus$ is a concatenation operator, g_{word} and g_{char} are weights which can be calculated as:

$$g_{word} = \sigma(\mathbf{W}_1 x_{w_t}^{word} + b_1) \qquad (2)$$

^{2}https://https://code.google.com/p/word2vec

$$g_{char} = \sigma(\mathbf{W}_2 x_{w_t}^{char} + b_2) \qquad (3)$$

here $\mathbf{W}_1$, $\mathbf{W}_2$, b_1 and b_2 are trainable parameters, $\sigma(\cdot)$ is a sigmoid function.

2.2 BiLSTM Layer

Recurrent Neural Network (RNN) (Elman, 1990) (Mikolov et al., 2010) (Chung et al., 2014) is proposed for modeling long-distance dependence in a sequence, but it tends to suffer from the gradient vanishing and exploding problems. RNN with Long Short-Time Memory Network unit (Hochreiter and Schmidhuber, 1997) solves such problems by introducing a memory cell and gates into the network. In order to better model the tweets, we use a bidirectional LSTM(BiLSTM) (Graves et al., 2014) (Graves, 2005) to process the inputs.

Each single LSTM ($LSTM_{forward}$ and $LSTM_{backward}$) can be formalized as shown in (Gers and Schraudolph, 2003):

Then we use $\oplus$ to obtain the hidden layer representation as below:

$$\overrightarrow{h}_{w_t} = LSTM_{forward}(x_{w_t}, \overrightarrow{h_{w_{t-1}}}) \qquad (4)$$

$$\overleftarrow{h}_{w_t} = LSTM_{backward}(x_{w_t}, \overleftarrow{h_{w_{t-1}}}) \qquad (5)$$

$$h_t = \overrightarrow{h}_{w_t} \oplus \overleftarrow{h}_{w_t} \qquad (6)$$

here $\overrightarrow{h}_t$, $\overleftarrow{h}_t$ are the hidden layer states for single word w_t, which generate from the combination of the current word information x_{w_t} and previous state information $\overrightarrow{h_{t-1}}(\overleftarrow{h_{t-1}})$. For simplicity, we note all the n h_t as $H = (h_1, h_2, \cdots, h_n)$.

2.3 Attention Layer

In our model we introduce an attention mechanism to focus on certain part of the tweet (Santos et al., 2016) (Yang et al., 2017). The motivation mainly comes from the following two observations: a) although tweet is short, it always introduces much noise; b) the emoji decided by a relative small part of tweet content itself. The attention layer produces a weight vector applied to hidden states of BiLSTM.

The attention mechanism takes the whole hidden states H as input, and outputs a vector of weights a:

$$a = softmax(\mathbf{W}_3 tanh(\mathbf{W}_4 H^T)) \qquad (7)$$

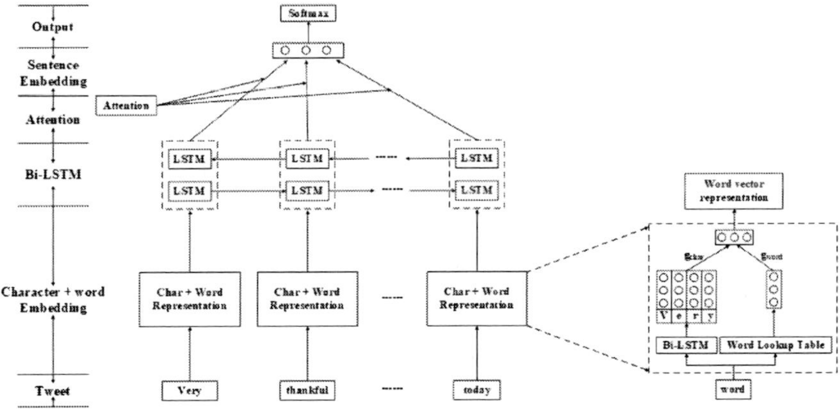

Figure 1: Our model architecture

here $\boldsymbol{W}_3$ and $\boldsymbol{W}_4$ are trainable parameters, the $softmax()$ ensures all computed weights sum up to 1.

Then we sum up the BiLSTM hidden states H according to the weight provided by a to get the input representation $\boldsymbol{r}$:

$$r = aH \qquad (8)$$

2.4 Output

At the output layer, we need to predict the emoji evoked by the tweet. We use the $softmax$ function to predict the probability distribution over all emojis:

$$p(\hat{y}|r) = softmax(\boldsymbol{W_5}r + \boldsymbol{b}_5) \qquad (9)$$

where $\boldsymbol{W}_5$ and $\boldsymbol{b}_5$ are the parameters of $softmax$ function.

The training loss based on cross-entropy is defined as follow:

$$J(\theta) = -\frac{1}{N} \sum_{t=1}^{N} \mathscr{H}(y_i, \hat{y}_i) + \beta \|\theta\|^2 \qquad (10)$$

where θ is the whole trainable parameters of the model, and β is the weight for the regularization term. $\mathscr{H}$ is the cross-entropy function for instance i between the gold category y_i and predict category $\hat{y}_i$. N is the number of training instance.

3 Experiment

3.1 Dataset

SemEval-2018 provided 500k tweets in English and 100k in Spanish for task 2, while our model is only for English. Dateset is split into trial, training and test sets. However, it was unable to download all the training set because some tweets were deleted or not available due to modified authorization status, and we finally collected $471, 455$ training tweets.

3.2 Data Pre-processing

All of the tweets before feeding to any model are pre-processed as follows: all tweets are lowercased; URLs are replaced by $< url >$ token; USERNAMEs are replaced by @user token; NLTK3 is employed to tokenize input tweets.

3.3 Training

We use the 200-dimensional vectors (Barbieri et al., 2016) to initialize our words matrix E, and set max length of one word to 10, max length of one sentence to 30. All of the models are trained for 10 epochs, and the final model is selected by trial dataset. Adam optimizer (Kingma and Ba, 2014) with initial learning rate of 0.001 is used to minimized cross-entropy loss. The learning rate is reduced by a factor of 10 for the first 3 epoch. The models were implemented in TensorFlow and experiments were run on an Intel(R) Core(TM) i7-4790 CPU.

3.4 Baselines

We compare our model with the following baselines: FastText (Joulin et al., 2016), NBOW, Convolutional Neural Networks (CNN) (Kim, 2014) (Kalchbrenner et al., 2014), Recurrent Convolutional Neural Networks (RCNN) (Sentences are first separately embedded with CNN, and then joined up with RNN) (Kalchbrenner and Blunsom,

Model		Representation	F1	P	R	Acc
Basic	FastText	Word Only	25.19	30.07	24.60	34.74
	NBOW		24.62	28.19	24.28	32.98
	CNN		20.34	22.54	23.00	34.73
	RCNN		26.89	26.97	29.62	32.53
	BiLSTM		20.36	22.41	23.00	34.74
	BiLSTM+ATT		24.95	34.87	26.34	36.44
Basic	C2W2S+ATT	Char Only	27.77	28.39	28.01	34.56
Our Submit	C2W2S+ATT	Char+Word	**29.50**	**35.17**	**29.91**	**39.21**
Rank 1: cagri		-	35.99	36.55	36.22	47.09

Table 1: Experimental results on test data and result of rank 1 system

2013), BiLSTM (Graves et al., 2014) and BiLSTM+ATT (Graves et al., 2014).

3.5 Results and Discussion on Training Data

A series of comparison experiments on training set have been performed to explore the performance of our model in macro F-score(F1), precision(P), recall(R) and accuracy(Acc). The experimental results are shown in Table 1 in percentage. For the first part, we choose some basic models which only use the word-level word vector embedding as input; for the second part, we present ablation experiments showing usefulness of word-level and character-level embedding.

Statistics show the following three conclusions: 1) among the basic model, the best performance according to different evaluation metrics achieved by RCNN (F1), BiLSTM+ATT (Precision), RCNN (Recall) and BiLSTM+ATT (Accuracy) respectively; 2) when compare the two model (Word Only and Char Only) about BiLSTM+ATT, word-level model and character-level model complement each other on the four measurements. So we consider combining the two to obtain Char+Word BiLSTM model; 3) as the ablation experiments show, our model can get best result when combine word-level input with character-level input.

4 Results on Test Data

Detailed official results of our model are shown in Table 2. And we focus on analyzing performance of our model under each emoji combined with the characteristics of tweets summarized in section 1.

On the one hand, our model achieved promising results in the following emojis: 🌲 (F1: 69.06), 🇺🇸 (F1: 64.01), and 🔥 (F1: 55.46). As for the reason, section 1 gives us inspiration: the common words evoke these emojis are easily recognizable, in oth-

Emo	P	R	F1	%
❤️	40.3	64.38	49.57	21.6
😍	30.82	32.96	31.86	9.66
😂	38.6	55.56	45.55	9.07
💕	31.23	4.57	7.97	5.21
🔥	57.83	53.28	55.46	7.43
😊	13.39	8.56	10.44	3.23
😎	22.11	17.94	19.81	3.99
✨	33.41	26.26	29.41	5.5
💙	36.05	10.26	15.98	3.1
📷	20.81	7.83	11.38	2.35
📸	31.9	53.7	40.02	2.86
🇺🇸	64.94	63.11	64.01	3.9
☀️	36.24	50.59	42.23	2.53
💜	56.49	7.81	13.72	2.23
😉	16.33	9.19	11.76	2.61
💯	32.18	26.13	28.84	2.49
😁	20.39	6.42	9.76	2.31
🌲	64.12	74.82	69.06	3.09
🏞️	43.31	23.05	30.08	4.83
😜	12.95	1.78	3.13	2.02

Table 2: Precision, Recall, F-measure and percentage of occurrences in the test set of each emoji.

er words, the word "christmas" evoking emoji 🌲 is barely used in emoji 📸.

On the other hand, for those emojis that are easily confused, our model does not perform well, such as 😊, 💕 and 😁. So we analyze data and find that these three emojis have the highest rate of repetition of common words with other emojis. For example, the common words under emoji 💕 include "love" (top2) and "happi" (top5), but the two words also evoke ❤️ and 😍 frequently.

Overall, the Macro F-score of our model ranks 9th in the subtask 1.

References

Francesco Barbieri, Jose Camacho-Collados, Francesco Ronzano, Luis Espinosa-Anke, Miguel Ballesteros, Valerio Basile, Viviana Patti, and Horacio Saggion. 2018. SemEval-2018 Task 2: Multilingual Emoji Prediction. In *Proceedings of the 12th International Workshop on Semantic Evaluation (SemEval-2018)*, New Orleans, LA, United States. Association for Computational Linguistics.

Francesco Barbieri, German Kruszewski, Francesco Ronzano, and Horacio Saggion. 2016. How cosmopolitan are emojis?: Exploring emojis usage and meaning over different languages with distributional semantics. In *Proceedings of the 2016 ACM on Multimedia Conference*, pages 531–535. ACM.

Junyoung Chung, Caglar Gulcehre, Kyung Hyun Cho, and Yoshua Bengio. 2014. Empirical evaluation of gated recurrent neural networks on sequence modeling. *Eprint Arxiv*.

Jeffrey L. Elman. 1990. Finding structure in time. *Cognitive Science*, 14(2):179–211.

Felix A. Gers and Nicol N. Schraudolph. 2003. *Learning precise timing with lstm recurrent networks*. JMLR.org.

Alex Graves. 2005. *2005 Special Issue: Framewise phoneme classification with bidirectional LSTM and other neural network architectures*. Elsevier Science Ltd.

Alex Graves, Navdeep Jaitly, and Abdel Rahman Mohamed. 2014. Hybrid speech recognition with deep bidirectional lstm. In *Automatic Speech Recognition and Understanding*, pages 273–278.

Seppu Hochreiter and Jrgen Schmidhuber. 1997. *Long short-term memory*. Springer Berlin Heidelberg.

Armand Joulin, Edouard Grave, Piotr Bojanowski, and Tomas Mikolov. 2016. Bag of tricks for efficient text classification. *arXiv preprint arXiv:1607.01759*.

Nal Kalchbrenner and Phil Blunsom. 2013. Recurrent convolutional neural networks for discourse compositionality. *Computer Science*.

Nal Kalchbrenner, Edward Grefenstette, and Phil Blunsom. 2014. A convolutional neural network for modelling sentences. *Eprint Arxiv*, 1.

Yoon Kim. 2014. Convolutional neural networks for sentence classification. *Eprint Arxiv*.

Tomas Mikolov, Martin Karafit, Lukas Burget, Jan Cernock, and Sanjeev Khudanpur. 2010. Recurrent neural network based language model. In *INTERSPEECH 2010, Conference of the International Speech Communication Association, Makuhari, Chiba, Japan, September*, pages 1045–1048.

Cicero Dos Santos, Ming Tan, Bing Xiang, and Bowen Zhou. 2016. Attentive pooling networks.

Zichao Yang, Diyi Yang, Chris Dyer, Xiaodong He, Alex Smola, and Eduard Hovy. 2017. Hierarchical attention networks for document classification. In *Conference of the North American Chapter of the Association for Computational Linguistics: Human Language Technologies*, pages 1480–1489.

Peperomia at SemEval-2018 Task 2: Vector Similarity Based Approach for Emoji Prediction

Jing Chen , **Dechuan Yang** , **Xilian Li** , **Wei Chen** * and **Tengjiao Wang**

Key Lab of High Confidence Software Technologies (MOE), School of EECS,
Peking University, Beijing, 100871, China
{chenjing.amy, yangdechuan, xilianli, pekingchenwei, tjwang}@pku.edu.cn

Abstract

This paper describes our participation in SemEval 2018 Task 2: Multilingual Emoji Prediction, in which participants are asked to predict a tweet's most associated emoji from 20 emojis. Instead of regarding it as a 20-class classification problem we regard it as a text similarity problem. We propose a vector similarity based approach for this task. First the distributed representation (tweet vector) for each tweet is generated, then the similarity between this tweet vector and each emoji's embedding is evaluated. The most similar emoji is chosen as the predicted label. Experimental results show that our approach performs comparably with the classification approach and shows its advantage in classifying emojis with similar semantic meaning.

1 Introduction

Participants for SemEval 2018 Task 2 (Barbieri et al.) are asked to predict the most likely associated emoji given the tweet. For simplicity purposes, each tweet contains one and only one emoji, which belongs to the 20 most frequent emojis. We participate in its subtask 1: Emoji Prediction in English.

With the wide-spread use on many social platforms, emoji has attracted more and more attention of researchers recently. Miller et al. (2016) explored whether emoji renderings or differences across platforms gave rise to diverse interpretations of emoji. For the same emoji, the sender and the receiver may have different interpretations of its meaning. This misinterpretation occurs when *joint perceptual experience* of sender and receiver lacks or the platforms' rendering style differs. Some efforts have been devoted to studying emoji through its distributed representation.

Barbieri et al. (2016a,b) trained emoji embeddings with a skip-gram model through millions of tweets, and explored the similarity and relatedness among these embeddings in various languages. Their results suggested that the overall semantic of emoji was preserved across languages, but some emojis were interpreted differently due to users' socio-geographical differences. Eisner et al. (2016) trained emoji embeddings with their short descriptions and demonstrated that emoji embeddings trained through this way were beneficial to sentiment analysis task.

We believe that the key to better classify emojis is understanding their meaning, since people intend a particular meaning when they send an emoji. People view the same characters during the exchange of plain text. Unlike plain text, emoji is not definite enough and doesn't have a general acknowledgement of how we should use it. It is common for different readers to have different interpretations of the same emoji, which naturally results in different ways of using emoji. Na'aman et al. (2017) investigated a wide range of emoji usage and showed that emojis served at least two very different purposes: content and function words or multimodal affective markers.

Word embeddings (Bengio et al., 2003; Mikolov et al., 2013a,b) are continuous distributed representations of words, with two good properties: 1. take word's semantic meaning into account, 2. distances between words are interpretable and can be measured using cosine distance. Based on such previous work, we proposed our *vector similarity based approach* for emoji prediction: first the neural network model is trained to generate a 300-d[1] vector, which is considered as the overall sentence vector of the tweet. Then this tweet vector's semantic similarity with

---

* Corresponding author.

[1] The embedding dimension is 300 in this paper.

Proceedings of the 12th International Workshop on Semantic Evaluation (SemEval-2018), pages 428–432
New Orleans, Louisiana, June 5–6, 2018. ©2018 Association for Computational Linguistics

each emoji's pre-trained embedding is evaluated. The predicted label is the one with the highest similarity.

2 Approach Description

This section describes our approach in detail. It consists of two parts, one is tweet representation, the other is similarity computation between tweet vector and emoji embedding. Whether tweet vector or emoji embedding is text representation. Thus we start by discussing previous researches about text representation.

Many efforts have been made to generate vectors for variable-length texts such as phrases, sentences, paragraphs or documents (Mitchell and Lapata, 2010; Larochelle and Lauly, 2012; Mikolov et al., 2013b; Le and Mikolov, 2014). The generated vectors are of fixed-size, which can be used as input features for many machine learning methods.

Word embeddings are distributed word representations trained using word2vec models such as CBOW and skip-gram, which can be interpreted as the probability distribution of the context the word exists in. If we take emoji as a normal token and train it together with its context words using word2vec models, then its embedding represents the context this emoji may exists in. We associate a tweet with its related emoji using tweet's vector and emoji's embedding.

Formally, our vector similarity based approach can be described as follows: first the tweet's vector $\hat{y}$ is generated using the neural network model, then its most similar emoji p is decided by calculating the cosine similarity(1) between $\hat{y}$ and each emoji's embedding y_i[2] in the candidate emoji set E whose size is 20.

$$cosine(\hat{y}, y_i) = \frac{\hat{y} \cdot y_i}{||\hat{y}|| \cdot ||y_i||} \quad (1)$$

$$p = \underset{i}{\operatorname{argmax}} \; cosine(\hat{y}, y_i) \quad (2)$$

where $|| \cdot ||$ is L2 norm and p is the predicted emoji label.

During training, we use the opposite of cosine similarity as the loss function, which aims to make the generated tweet vector $\hat{y}$ closer to the target emoji's embedding y.

$$loss_1 = -\sum \left(\frac{y}{||y||} \cdot \frac{\hat{y}}{||\hat{y}||} \right) \quad (3)$$

---

[2] y_i can be found in pre-trained embeddings.

We also tried another loss function which has similar idea with SVM. That is, minimize the cosine distance(4) between $\hat{y}$ and target emoji embedding y, meanwhile maximize the minimum cosine distance between $\hat{y}$ and non-target emoji embedding $\tilde{y}$. We hope to make y more distinctive when similar emojis exist.

$$d(a, b) = 1 - cosine(a, b) \quad (4)$$

$$loss_2 = \alpha d(\hat{y}, y) - (1 - \alpha) \min_{\tilde{y} \in F} d(\hat{y}, \tilde{y}) \quad (5)$$

where α is a parameter to control the proportion of each part, F is the set which consists of 19 non-target emojis' pretrained embeddings for this tweet.

3 Models

This section describes the two models we used for generating tweet vector. Barbieri et al. (2017)'s previous work showed that LSTM neural networks performed well in emoji prediction. Inspired by their research, we implement two LSTM based models: a 2-layered LSTM model and a BiLSTM model.

3.1 2-layered LSTM

Our first model is a 2-layered LSTM model. This model consists of one trainable embedding layer for mapping words into vector representations, two stacked LSTM layers for processing and extracting useful information from the tweet, and one dense layer outputs the tweet vector.

Our experiments show that 2-layered LSTM works better than single layer LSTM. When stacked LSTM layer num gets larger than 2, the system performance doesn't increase much. Besides, deeper network structure costs more time to train and more parameters make it easy to overfit.

Long Short-Term Memory network, or LSTM (Hochreiter and Schmidhuber, 1997) is an enhanced version of basic recurrent neural network (RNN), which uses purpose-built memory cells to store information selectively (Graves et al., 2013). LSTM model can better exploit long range context, and is widely used in natural language processing tasks.

3.2 BiLSTM

Our second model is a bidirectional LSTM (BiLSTM) model (Schuster and Paliwal, 1997). This model consists of one trainable embedding layer, one bidirectional LSTM layer, and one dense output layer.

BiLSTM splits the neuron of a regular LSTM into two directions, one for positive time direction (forward states), 5and another for negative time direction (backward states). Output state o_i can be the concatenation or summation of the forward and backward state fw_i and bw_i:

$$o_i = fw_i \odot bw_i \qquad (6)$$

where $\odot$ operator can be concatenate, element-wise add, etc.

4 Experiments

Our system is implemented using Keras[3] and the code is available on github[4]. We use the official evaluation metric *macro f1*, which evaluates both precision and recall of each class regardless of its sample num.

Three groups of experiments are achieved to evaluate our approach and models. To compare the vector similarity based approach with the classification approach, we implement the above 2-layered LSTM model and BiLSTM model with the same experiment settings for both approaches. To figure out which model structure is better, we compare the 2-layered LSTM model and BiLSTM model's performance on both approaches. We also test the loss functions $loss_1$ and $loss_2$'s effects on 2-layered LSTM model. Next, we will describe the key experiment settings. More detailed model settings can be found in Table 1.

Text Preprocessing: The whole tweet is lowercased. We split it into token sequence using Keras' default tokenizer, which split a sentence by spaces and following punctuations: ! " # $ % & ( ) * + , - . / : ; <=>?@ [\ ] ^ _ ` ~ \t \n { | }. Long sequences are truncated and short ones are padded with 0s from the head to meet fixed length 20.

Embedding Layer: The embedding layer is set to be trainable. It is initialized by looking up from a pre-trained twitter embedding matrix (Barbieri et al., 2016a), <UNK> is initialized as **0**.

Output Layer: For classification approach, the output layer's unit num is 20 (same with the num

[3] https://keras.io/
[4] https://github.com/MonkandMonkey/
   amyjing_emoji_predict.git

Item	Value	Description
data_set	466,233	train set size
optimizer	Adam	train optimizer
batch_size	128	batch size
max_len	20	fixed sequence len
num_words	58,205	vocab size
2-layered LSTM model		
lstm1_size	300	lstm1 output size
lstm2_size	300	lstm2 output size
BiLSTM model		
lstm_size	300	lstm output size
bilstm_size	300	bilstm output size
merge_mode	sum	bilstm merge mode

Table 1: Experiment settings.

Model		Valid	Test
CL	2-LSTM	27.119	**25.678***
	BiLSTM	26.492	25.166*
VS	2-LSTM($loss_1$)	**27.188**	25.444
	2-LSTM($loss_2$)	27.089	25.496
	BiLSTM($loss_1$)	26.441	25.281

Table 2: Experiment Results. CL for classification approach, VS for vector similarity based approach, 2-lstm for 2-layered LSTM model. The results marked with asterisk (*) are our submissions for final evaluation.

of emoji classes). For vector similarity based approach, the output layer's unit num is 300 (same with the size of the pre-trained emoji embedding). **Training Loss:** For our vector similarity approach, $loss_1$ and $loss_2$ described in section 2 are tested separately. For classification approach, *categorial_cross_entropy* is used.

5 Discussion

As is shown in Table 2, the vector similarity based approach's performance is comparable with the classification approach on both validation set and test set.

For both our vector similarity based and classification approaches, the 2-layered LSTM model outperforms the BiLSTM model, which shows that a deeper network structure contributes to capturing higher level features. Our 2-layered LSTM model consists of two stacked LSTM cells which are combined vertically. The first LSTM layer learns the shallower representation of the tweet, the second LSTM layer learns more abstract representation. Our BiLSTM layer also consists of two

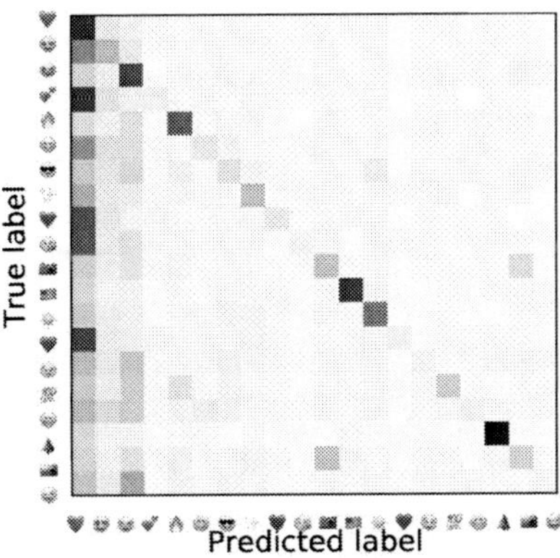

Figure 1: classification BiLSTM: confusion matrix

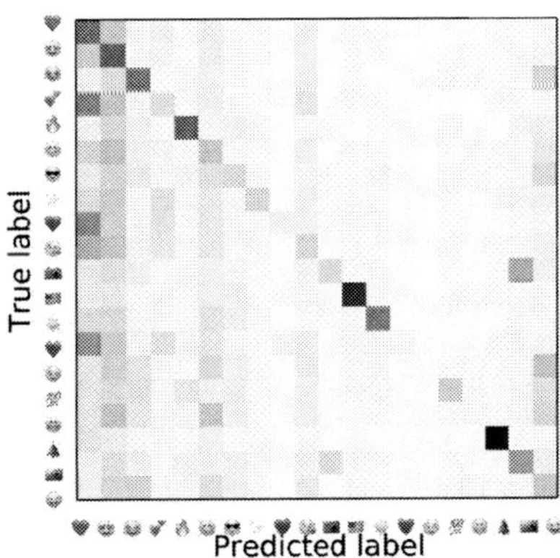

Figure 2: vector similarity BiLSTM: confusion matrix

LSTM cells, but are combined in a horizontal way. With the same number of parameters, the deeper structure (2-layered LSTM) works better than the wider structure (BiLSTM).

Experiments show that the $loss_1$ is slightly better than the $loss_2$ function. They are different in that $loss_1$ only considers the most similar emoji's distance, whereas $loss_2$ considers both most similar emoji's distance and the second most similar emoji's distance. We tested several α values in $loss_2$ from 0.8 to 0.99, and 0.9 gives the best performance, which is also dominated by the most similar emoji's distance.

Figure 1 and Figure 2 plot the confusion matrix of BiLSTM model's predictions for classification and our vector similarity approach. The ❤ (red heart) column in Figure 1 shows that the classification approach tends to misclassify other classes into the most frequent emoji ❤. And for emojis with similar semantics, it is more likely to confuse them. Like the 😘 (face-throwing-a-kiss) row, the classification approach misclassified most 😘 to 💜, whereas the vector similarity based approach only misclassified a smaller part of them, and its correctly predict num is relatively higher. In short, the classification approach is good at distinguishing emojis with concrete meanings, such as 🔥, 🇺🇸, and 🎄, but poor at distinguishing emojis with similar semantic meanings. The vector similarity based approach can make a trade-off between both situations.

Besides, for both our proposed approach and classification approach, the performance on *test set* is relatively lower than that on *validation set*. Thus dataset will also make an influence, espe-cially for tweet, which is time-sensitive text. If the test set contains many words that unseen during the training stage or its class distribution differs from the training set, the performance will be influenced.

6 Future Work and Conclusion

The pre-trained embeddings we used are trained with a skip-gram model, which treats emojis and words equally, whereas for this task we need to concentrate more on emoji's semantic, instead of its syntactic. Thus we suppose that treating emoji in a different way from word during the training stage will do a favor. That is, whether the emoji is in the head, center or tail of the tweet, its relative part can be used to train the emoji's embedding, despite it is outside the context window. Another attempt worth trying is to use a Logistic Regression or Linear SVM classifier to find tweet's most appropriate emoji, instead of cosine similarity.

In this paper, we present our work for SemEval-2018 task 2: Multilingual Emoji Prediction. We propose a vector similarity based approach which generates a vector for tweet and then use cosine similarity to find its most appropriate emoji. Through which we hope to explore the relationship between words and emojis. Experimental results show that the vector similarity based approach performs comparably with the classification approach. It provides an innovative thinking for solving the emoji prediction problem.

References

Francesco Barbieri, Miguel Ballesteros, and Horacio Saggion. 2017. Are emojis predictable? In *Proceedings of the 15th Conference of the European Chapter of the Association for Computational Linguistics: Volume 2, Short Papers*, pages 105–111. Association for Computational Linguistics.

Francesco Barbieri, Jose Camacho-Collados, Francesco Ronzano, Luis Espinosa-Anke, Miguel Ballesteros, Valerio Basile, Viviana Patti, and Horacio Saggion. SemEval-2018 Task 2: Multilingual Emoji Prediction. In *Proceedings of the 12th International Workshop on Semantic Evaluation (SemEval-2018)*.

Francesco Barbieri, German Kruszewski, Francesco Ronzano, and Horacio Saggion. 2016a. How cosmopolitan are emojis?: Exploring emojis usage and meaning over different languages with distributional semantics. In *Proceedings of the 2016 ACM on Multimedia Conference*, pages 531–535. ACM.

Francesco Barbieri, Francesco Ronzano, and Horacio Saggion. 2016b. What does this emoji mean? a vector space skip-gram model for twitter emojis. In *LREC*.

Yoshua Bengio, Réjean Ducharme, Pascal Vincent, and Christian Jauvin. 2003. A neural probabilistic language model. *Journal of machine learning research*, 3(Feb):1137–1155.

Ben Eisner, Tim Rocktäschel, Isabelle Augenstein, Matko Bošnjak, and Sebastian Riedel. 2016. emoji2vec: Learning emoji representations from their description. *arXiv preprint arXiv:1609.08359*.

Alex Graves, Abdel-rahman Mohamed, and Geoffrey Hinton. 2013. Speech recognition with deep recurrent neural networks. In *Acoustics, speech and signal processing (icassp), 2013 ieee international conference on*, pages 6645–6649. IEEE.

Sepp Hochreiter and Jürgen Schmidhuber. 1997. Long short-term memory. *Neural computation*, 9(8):1735–1780.

Hugo Larochelle and Stanislas Lauly. 2012. A neural autoregressive topic model. In *Advances in Neural Information Processing Systems*, pages 2708–2716.

Quoc Le and Tomas Mikolov. 2014. Distributed representations of sentences and documents. In *International Conference on Machine Learning*, pages 1188–1196.

Tomas Mikolov, Kai Chen, Greg Corrado, and Jeffrey Dean. 2013a. Efficient estimation of word representations in vector space. *arXiv preprint arXiv:1301.3781*.

Tomas Mikolov, Ilya Sutskever, Kai Chen, Greg S Corrado, and Jeff Dean. 2013b. Distributed representations of words and phrases and their compositionality. In *Advances in neural information processing systems*, pages 3111–3119.

Hannah Miller, Jacob Thebault-Spieker, Shuo Chang, Isaac Johnson, Loren Terveen, and Brent Hecht. 2016. Blissfully happy" or "ready to fight": Varying interpretations of emoji. *Proceedings of ICWSM, 2016*.

Jeff Mitchell and Mirella Lapata. 2010. Composition in distributional models of semantics. *Cognitive science*, 34(8):1388–1429.

Noa Na'aman, Hannah Provenza, and Orion Montoya. 2017. Varying linguistic purposes of emoji in (twitter) context. In *Proceedings of ACL 2017, Student Research Workshop*, pages 136–141.

Mike Schuster and Kuldip K Paliwal. 1997. Bidirectional recurrent neural networks. *IEEE Transactions on Signal Processing*, 45(11):2673–2681.

ECNU at SemEval-2018 Task 2: Leverage Traditional NLP Features and Neural Networks Methods to Address Twitter Emoji Prediction Task

Xingwu Lu[1], Xin Mao[1], Man Lan[1,2*], Yuanbin Wu[1,2]
[1]Department of Computer Science and Technology,
East China Normal University, Shanghai, P.R.China
[2]Shanghai Key Laboratory of Multidimensional Information Processing
{51174506023, 10131530334}@stu.ecnu.edu.cn
{mlan, ybwu}@cs.ecnu.edu.cn

Abstract

This paper describes our submissions to Task 2 in SemEval 2018, i.e., Multilingual Emoji Prediction. We first investigate several traditional Natural Language Processing (NLP) features, and then design several deep learning models. For subtask 1: Emoji Prediction in English, we combine two different methods to represent tweet, i.e., supervised model using traditional features and deep learning model. For subtask 2: Emoji Prediction in Spanish, we only use deep learning model.

1 Introduction

Visual icons play a crucial role in providing information about the extra level of social media information. SemEval 2018 shared task for researchers to predict, given a tweet in English or Spanish, its most likely associated emoji (Barbieri et al., 2018, 2017) (Task 2, Multilingual Emoji Prediction), which is organized into two optional subtask (subtask 1 and subtask 2) respectively in English and Spanish.

For subtask 1, we adopt a combination model to predict emojis, which consists of traditional Natural Language Processing (NLP) methods and deep learning methods. The results returned by the classifier with traditional NLP features, by the neural network model and by the combination model are voted to get the final result. For subtask 2, we only use deep learning model.

2 System Description

For subtask 1, we explore three different methods i.e., using traditional NLP features to learn a supervised machine learning-based classifier, learning a deep learning model to make prediction and combine features captured by neural networks with traditional NLP features to train a supervised machine learning-based classifier. For subtask 2,

we simply implement deep learning method to make prediction.

2.1 Traditional NLP Features

In this task, we extract the following three types of features to capture effective information from the given tweets, i.e., linguistic features, sentiment lexicon features and tweet specific features.

2.1.1 Linguistic Features

- *N-grams:* We extract 3 types of Bag-of-Words features as *N-grams* features, where N = 1,2,3 (i.e., *unigram*, *bigram*, and *trigram* features).

- *POS:* Generally, the sentences carrying subjective emotions are inclined to contain more adjectives and adverbs while the sentences without sentiment orientation would contain more nouns. Thus, we extract POS tag from the sentence as features with the Bag-of-Words form.

- *Correlation Degree:* For each word appear in training data, the ratio of the number of occurrences under each class and the total occurrences is counted as the correlation degree of the word to a certain class. When the feature is created, the sum of the correlation degree of words in tweet is counted as the correlation degree of the tweet to a certain class:

$$CorrDeg(s, l) = \sum_{t=1}^{|s|} \frac{O(w_t, c_l)}{\sum_i^N O(w_t, c_i)}$$

Where $|s|$ is the length of tweet and N is the number of classes, w_t means t^{th} word in tweet and c_i means i^{th} class, $O(w_t, c_i)$ denotes the number of tweets of c_i that contain w_t. The dimension of this feature is equal to the number of classes, value is correlation

Proceedings of the 12th International Workshop on Semantic Evaluation (SemEval-2018), pages 433–437
New Orleans, Louisiana, June 5–6, 2018. ©2018 Association for Computational Linguistics

degree of the tweet to each class, i.e., *CorrDeg(s,l)*.

2.1.2 Sentiment Lexicon Features (SentiLexi)

We also extract sentiment lexicon features (SentiLexi) to capture the sentiment information of the given sentence. Given a tweet, we first convert all words into lowercase. Then on each sentiment lexicon, we calculate the following six scores for one message: (1) the ratio of positive words to all words, (2) the ratio of negative words to all words, (3) the maximum sentiment score, (4) the minimum sentiment score, (5) the sum of sentiment scores, (6) the sentiment score of the last word in tweet. If the word does not exist in one sentiment lexicon, its corresponding score is set to 0. The following 8 sentiment lexicons are adopted in our systems: *Bing Liu lexicon*[1], *General Inquirer lexicon*[2], *IMDB*[3], *MPQA*[4], *NRC Emotion Sentiment Lexicon*[5], *AFINN*[6], *NRC Hashtag Sentiment Lexicon*[7], and *NRC Sentiment140 Lexicon*[8].

2.1.3 Tweet Specific Features

- *Punctuation:* Considering that users often use exclamation marks and question marks to express strongly surprised and questioned feelings, we extract 7-dimensions punctuation features by recording rules of punctuation marks in the tweets.

- *All-caps:* One binary feature is to check whether this tweet has words in uppercase.

- *Bag-of-Hashtags:* We construct a vocabulary of hashtags appearing in the training data and then adopt the bag-of-hashtags method for each tweet.

2.2 Deep Learning Modules

In addition to manually constructing features, we build deep neural models to capture the semantics of the text. Figure 1 shows the network structure of our model. The input of the network is a tweet, which is a sequence of words. The output of the network contains class elements.

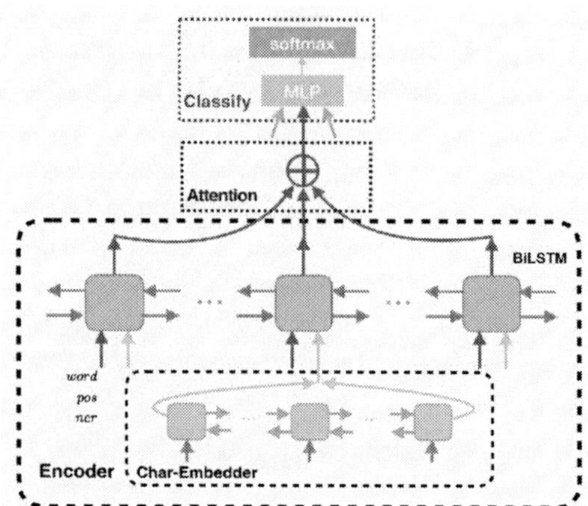

Figure 1: Deep learning model architecture.

2.2.1 Word-Level Representations

We use pre-trained word embedding concatenated with char embedding, POS embedding and NER embedding obtaining a final representation for each word type, which are learned together with the updates to the model.

- *Word Embedding:* Word embedding is a continuous-valued vector representation for each word, which can capture meaningful syntactic and semantic regularities. In this task, we use the 300-dimensional word vectors pre-trained on Twitter provided by SemEval task organizers, available in *SWM*[9]

- *Char Embedding:* We randomly initialize the representation of the character and compute character-based continuous-space vector embeddings of the words in tweets by bidirectional LSTM. The dimension of char embedding is 50.

- *POS Embedding:* We randomly initialize the representation of the POS tag in tweet with a vector size of 50.

- *NER Embedding:* We also randomly initialize the representation of the NER tag in tweet with a vector size of 50.

2.2.2 Sentence-Level Representations

- *Bi-Directional LSTM:* We apply a recurrent structure to capture contextual information as far as possible when learning word representations, to model the tweet with both of the

---

[1] http://www.cs.uic.edu/liub/FBS/sentiment-analysis.html
[2] http://www.wjh.harvard.edu/inquirer/homecat.htm
[3] http://www.aclweb.org/anthology/S13-2067
[4] http://mpqa.cs.pitt.edu/
[5] http://www.saifmohammad.com/WebPages/lexicons.html
[6] http://www2.imm.dtu.dk/pubdb/views/publication details.php?id=6010
[7] http://www.umiacs.umd.edu/saif/WebDocs/NRC-Hashtag-Sentiment-Lexicon-v0.1.zip
[8] http://help.sentiment140.com/for-students/
[9] https://github.com/fvancesco/acmmm2016

preceeding and following contexts, we apply a Bi-directional Long Short-term Memory Networks (BiLSTM, Graves et al. (2005)) architecture as shown in Figure 1.

- *Attention Mechanism:* Considering not all words contribute equally to the representation of the sentence meaning, we introduce attention mechanism (Bahdanau et al., 2014) to extract such words that are important to the meaning of the sentence and aggregate the representation of those informative words to form a sentence vector.

We first use BiLSTM and Attention Mechanism to obtain sentence-level representations and then concatenate it with several effective NLP features. At last, we use a Multi-layer Perceptron (MLP) and output the probability of emoji label based on a softmax function. The BiLSTM has a hidden size of 512. The MLP have 1 hidden layer of size 200 and *relu* non-linearity.

To learn model parameters, we minimize the KL-divergence between the outputs and gold labels. We adopt Adam (Kingma and Ba, 2014) as optimization method and set learning rate of 0.01.

3 Experimental Settings

3.1 Datasets

For training sets, the organizers provide only the list of tweet ID and a script for all participants to collect tweets. However, since not all tweets are available when downloading, participants may collect slightly different numbers of tweets for training sets. In addition, we find that the crawled training sets and the trial sets provided by the organizers have 37.26% overlap in English and 71.16% in Spanish. So we remove the duplicate data and combine train and trial sets to perform a 3-fold cross-validation. Table 1 shows the statistics of the tweets we collect in our experiments. In subtask 1, the number of class 0 is the largest, accounting for 22.28%, followed by class 1 and class 2, respectively, 10.37% and 10.20%, and the other 17 classes distribute between 2.46% and 5.51%. Subtask 2 has a similar data distribution.

3.2 Data Preprocessing

Firstly, we convert unicode encoding into corresponding characters, punctuation, emoticons. Then we use slangs[10] to transform the informal

Dataset label	Subtask 1	Subtask 2
0	116693 (22.28%)	20495 (20.41%)
1	54313 (10.37%)	13688 (13.63%)
2	53432 (10.20%)	9342 (9.30%)
3	28855 (5.51%)	6859 (6.83%)
4	25778 (4.92%)	6535 (6.51%)
5	24475 (4.67%)	4765 (4.43%)
6	22301 (4.26%)	4444 (4.42%)
7	19236 (3.67%)	3868 (3.85%)
8	17908 (3.42%)	3687 (3.67%)
9	16996 (3.25%)	3544 (3.53%)
10	16755 (3.20%)	3399 (3.16%)
11	16052 (3.07%)	2943 (2.93%)
12	15167 (2.90%)	2826 (2.81%)
13	13650 (2.61%)	2727 (2.72%)
14	14136 (2.70%)	2629 (2.62%)
15	13963 (2.67%)	2564 (2.55%)
16	13702 (2.62%)	2618 (2.61%)
17	13474 (2.57%)	2551 (2.54%)
18	13867 (2.65%)	2552 (2.54%)
19	12900 (2.46%)	–
total	523653	100440

Table 1: The statistics of data sets in combination of training sets and trial sets which we used to perform a 3-fold cross-validation. The numbers in brackets are the percentages of different classes in each data set.

writing to regular forms, e.g., *"LOL"* replaced by *"laugh out loud"*. And we recover the elongated words to their original forms, e.g., *"soooooo"* to *"so"*. Finally, we implement tokenization, POS tagging, named entity recognizing(NER) with the aid of Stanford CoreNLP tools (Manning et al., 2014).

3.3 Learning Algorithm

Considering the large dimension of the features designed by traditional NLP methods, we use learning algorithms of Logistic Regression(LR) to build classification models, which is supplied in *Liblinear*[11].

3.4 Evaluation Metrics

The official evaluation measure is Macro F-score, which would inherently mean a better sensitivity to the use of emojis in general, rather than for instance overfitting a model to do well in the three or four most common emojis of the test data. Macro F-score can be defined as simply the average of the individual label-wise F-scores.

---

[10]https://github.com/haierlord/resource/blob/master/slangs

[11]https://www.csie.ntu.edu.tw/ cjlin/liblinear/

4 Experiments on Training Data

4.1 Comparison of NLP Features

Table 2 lists the comparison of different contributions made by different features on cross-validation with Logistic Regression algorithm. From the results in Table 2, we observe the following findings:

(1) The combination of Uigram, Bigram, Correlation Degree, POS and SentiLexi achieves the best performance (i.e., 34.63).

(2) Correlation Degree feature makes more contributes than other features, as it reflects the degree of relevance between tweets and emoji label.

(3) Bigram feature makes contribution and is more effective than unigram feature. The reason may be that bigram feature can capture more contextual information and word orders.

(4) SentiLexi feature also makes contribution, which indicates that SentiLexi features are beneficial not only in traditional sentiment analysis tasks, but also in predicting the emoji in tweet.

Features	F_{macro}	change
Best Features	34.63	-
-Correlation Degree	30.59	-4.04
-Bigram	33.38	-1.25
-SentiLexi	33.63	-1.00
-POS	33.91	-0.72
-Uigram	34.22	-0.41

Table 2: Performance of different features on subtask 1. - means to exclude some features.

4.2 Comparison of Deep Learning Modules

Table 3 shows the results of different deep learning models described before. From Table 3, we observe the findings as follows:

(1) We explore the performance of three different deep learning model: Neural Bag-of-Words(NBOW, Iyyer et al. (2015)), Convolutional Neural Network (CNN, Collobert et al. (2011)) and Bi-directional Long Short-term Memory Networks (LSTM, Hochreiter and Schmidhuber (1997)). All models used only pre-trained word embedding to compare. Clearly, BiLSTM outperformed other models in this task, and our deep learning model is based on BiLSTM.

(2) POS embedding makes more contribution than other word-level representations. Since POS embedding can learn emotional tendencies, it is beneficial for tweet emojis prediction.

(3) The last two rows results shows that combine both SentiLexi and Punctuation features with sentence representations to train the deep learning model can make contribution.

Models	Subtask 1	Subtask 2
NBOW	23.73	18.67
CNN	23.64	18.91
BiLSTM	25.64	19.32
.+Char	25.66 (+0.02)	19.56
.+NER	26.57 (+0.91)	–
.+POS	30.55 (+3.98)	–
.+Attention	30.74 (+0.19)	–
.+Punctuation	32.10 (+1.36)	–
.+SentiLexi	32.59 (+0.49)	–

Table 3: Performance of different deep learning models on subtask 1 and subtask 2. .+ means to add current module to the previous model. The numbers in the brackets are the performance increments compared with the previous results.

4.3 Combination and Ensemble

For subtask 1, we also use the trained neural networks described in 4.2 to capture the features of tweets and combine it with traditional NLP features to train a Logistic Regression classifier, named *Combination Model*.

Table 4 shows the results of different methods. We find that combination model improved the performance and the ensemble of 3 methods achieve the best result. It suggests that the traditional NLP methods and the deep learning models are complementary to each other and their combination achieves the best performance.

Methods	F_{macro}
Traditional NLP Features	34.63
Deep Learning Model	32.59
Combination Model	35.21
Ensemble Model	35.57

Table 4: Performance of different methods on subtask 1.

4.4 System Configuration

Based on above experimental analysis, the two system configurations on test data sets are listed as followings:

(1) subtask 1: Logistic Regression with best NLP feature sets is used as model 1. Deep learn-

ing model is used as model 2. Logistic Regression with NLP features and the feature captured by deep learning model is used as model 3. Ensemble of three models is used as final submission.

(2) subtask 2: Deep learning model with word embedding and char embedding is used as submission.

5 Results on Test Data

	Subtask 1	Subtask 2
Our system	33.35 (5)	16.41 (7)
Rank 1	35.99 (1)	22.36 (1)
Rank 2	35.36 (2)	18.73 (2)
Rank 3	34.02 (3)	18.18 (3)

Table 5: Performance of our systems and the top-ranked systems for two subtasks on test datasets. The numbers in the brackets are the official rankings.

Table 5 shows the results on test datasets. From Table 5, we find that our system achieves almost the same performance as the cross-validation. The low performance of this task illustrates the difficulty of the task itself, especially the Spanish task.

6 Conclusion

In this paper, we extract several effective traditional NLP features, design different deep learning models and build a model in combination of traditional NLP features and deep learning method together. The extensive experimental results show that this combination improves the performance.

For the future work, we consider to focus on developing a neural networks model to handle unbalanced data and improve the performance of confusing labels.

Acknowledgements

This work is is supported by the Science and Technology Commission of Shanghai Municipality Grant (No. 15ZR1410700) and the open project of Shanghai Key Laboratory of Trustworthy Computing (No.07dz22304201604).

References

Dzmitry Bahdanau, Kyunghyun Cho, and Yoshua Bengio. 2014. Neural machine translation by jointly learning to align and translate. *arXiv preprint arXiv:1409.0473*.

Francesco Barbieri, Miguel Ballesteros, and Horacio Saggion. 2017. Are emojis predictable? In *Proceedings of the 15th Conference of the European Chapter of the Association for Computational Linguistics: Volume 2, Short Papers*, pages 105–111. Association for Computational Linguistics.

Francesco Barbieri, Jose Camacho-Collados, Francesco Ronzano, Luis Espinosa-Anke, Miguel Ballesteros, Valerio Basile, Viviana Patti, and Horacio Saggion. 2018. SemEval-2018 Task 2: Multilingual Emoji Prediction. In *Proceedings of the 12th International Workshop on Semantic Evaluation (SemEval-2018)*, New Orleans, LA, United States. Association for Computational Linguistics.

Ronan Collobert, Jason Weston, Léon Bottou, Michael Karlen, Koray Kavukcuoglu, and Pavel Kuksa. 2011. Natural language processing (almost) from scratch. *Journal of Machine Learning Research*, 12(Aug):2493–2537.

Alex Graves, Santiago Fernández, and Jürgen Schmidhuber. 2005. Bidirectional lstm networks for improved phoneme classification and recognition. In *International Conference on Artificial Neural Networks*, pages 799–804. Springer.

Sepp Hochreiter and Jürgen Schmidhuber. 1997. Long short-term memory. *Neural computation*, 9(8):1735–1780.

Mohit Iyyer, Varun Manjunatha, Jordan Boyd-Graber, and Hal Daumé III. 2015. Deep unordered composition rivals syntactic methods for text classification. In *Proceedings of ACL 2015*.

Diederik P Kingma and Jimmy Ba. 2014. Adam: A method for stochastic optimization. *arXiv preprint arXiv:1412.6980*.

Christopher D. Manning, Mihai Surdeanu, John Bauer, Jenny Finkel, Steven J. Bethard, and David McClosky. 2014. The Stanford CoreNLP natural language processing toolkit. In *Proceedings of 52nd Annual Meeting of the Association for Computational Linguistics: System Demonstrations*, pages 55–60.

NTUA-SLP at SemEval-2018 Task 2: Predicting Emojis using RNNs with Context-aware Attention

Christos Baziotis[1,3]**, Nikos Athanasiou**[1]
Georgios Paraskevopoulos[1,4]**, Nikolaos Ellinas**[1]
Athanasia Kolovou[1,2]**, Alexandros Potamianos**[1,4]

[1]School of ECE, National Technical University of Athens, Athens, Greece
[2] Department of Informatics, University of Athens, Athens, Greece
[3] Department of Informatics, Athens University of Economics and Business, Athens, Greece
[4] Behavioral Signal Technologies, Los Angeles, CA
`cbaziotis@mail.ntua.gr, el12074@central.ntua.gr`
`geopar@central.ntua.gr, nellinas@central.ntua.gr`
`akolovou@di.uoa.gr, potam@central.ntua.gr`

Abstract

In this paper we present a deep-learning model that competed at SemEval-2018 Task 2 "Multilingual Emoji Prediction". We participated in subtask A, in which we are called to predict the most likely associated emoji in English tweets. The proposed architecture relies on a Long Short-Term Memory network, augmented with an attention mechanism, that conditions the weight of each word, on a "context vector" which is taken as the aggregation of a tweet's meaning. Moreover, we initialize the embedding layer of our model, with word2vec word embeddings, pretrained on a dataset of 550 million English tweets. Finally, our model does not rely on hand-crafted features or lexicons and is trained end-to-end with back-propagation. We ranked 2nd out of 48 teams.

1 Introduction

Emojis play an important role in textual communication, as they function as a substitute for non-verbal cues, that are taken for granted in face-to-face communication, thus allowing users to convey emotions by means other than words. Despite their large appeal in text, they haven't received much attention until recently. Former works, mostly consider their semantics (Aoki and Uchida, 2011; Espinosa-Anke et al., 2016; Barbieri et al., 2016b,a; Ljubešić and Fišer, 2016; Eisner et al., 2016) and only recently their role in social media was explored (Barbieri et al., 2017; Cappallo et al., 2018). In SemEval-2018 Task 2: "Multilingual Emoji Prediction" (Barbieri et al., 2018), given a tweet, we are asked to predict its most likely associated emoji.

Figure 1: Attention heat-map visualization. The color intensity corresponds to the weight given to each word by the self-attention mechanism.

In this work, we present a near state of the art approach for predicting emojis in tweets, which outperforms the best present work (Barbieri et al., 2017). For this purpose, we employ an LSTM network augmented with a context-aware self-attention mechanism, producing a feature representation used for classification. Moreover, the attention mechanism helps us make our model's behavior more interpretable, by examining the distribution of the attention weights for a given tweet. To this end, we provide visualizations with the distributions of the attention weights.

2 Overview

Figure 3 provides a high-level overview of our approach that consists of three main steps: (1) The *text preprocessing step*, which is common both for unlabeled data and the task's dataset, (2) the *word embeddings pre-training step*, where we train custom word embeddings on a big collection of unlabeled Twitter messages and (3) the *model training step* where we train the deep learning model.

Proceedings of the 12th International Workshop on Semantic Evaluation (SemEval-2018), pages 438–444
New Orleans, Louisiana, June 5–6, 2018. ©2018 Association for Computational Linguistics

Task definition. In subtask A, given an English tweet, we are called to predict the most likely associated emoji, from the 20 most frequent emojis in English tweets according to (Barbieri et al., 2017). The training dataset consists of 500k tweets, retrieved from October 2015 to February 2017 and geolocalized in the United States. Fig. 2 shows the classes (emojis) and their distribution.

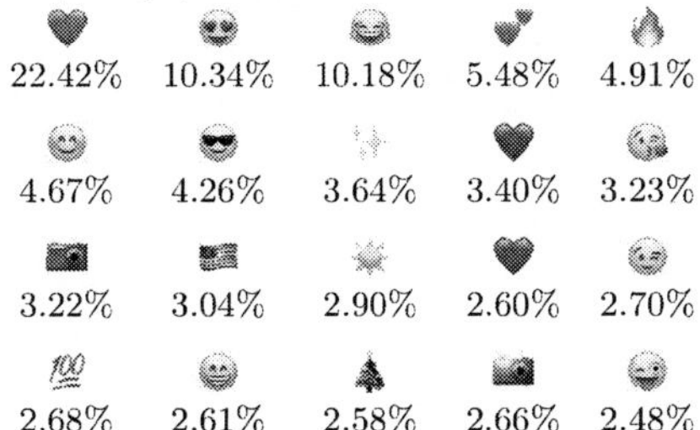

22.42%	10.34%	10.18%	5.48%	4.91%
4.67%	4.26%	3.64%	3.40%	3.23%
3.22%	3.04%	2.90%	2.60%	2.70%
2.68%	2.61%	2.58%	2.66%	2.48%

Figure 2: Distribution of emoji (class) labels.

2.1 Data

Unlabeled Dataset. We collected a dataset of 550 million archived English Twitter messages, from Apr. 2014 to Jun. 2017. This dataset is used for (1) calculating word statistics needed in our text preprocessing pipeline (Section 2.2) and (2) training word2vec word embeddings.

Word Embeddings. We leverage our unlabeled dataset to train Twitter-specific word embeddings. We use the *word2vec* (Mikolov et al., 2013) algorithm, with the skip-gram model, negative sampling of 5 and minimum word count of 20, utilizing the Gensim's (Řehůřek and Sojka, 2010) implementation. The resulting vocabulary contains $800,000$ words. The pre-trained word embeddings are used for initializing the first layer (embedding layer) of our neural networks.

2.2 Preprocessing[1]

We utilized the *ekphrasis*[2] tool (Baziotis et al., 2017) as a tweet preprocessor. The preprocessing

---

[1] Significant portions of the systems submitted to SemEval 2018 in Tasks 1, 2 and 3, by the NTUA-SLP team are shared, specifically the preprocessing and portions of the DNN architecture. Their description is repeated here for completeness.

[2] github.com/cbaziotis/ekphrasis

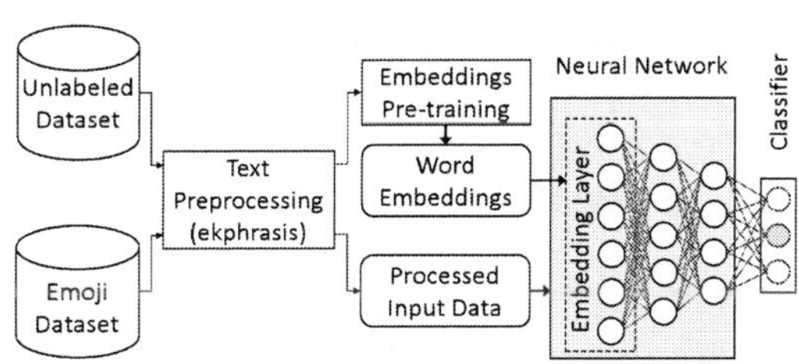

Figure 3: High-level overview of our approach

steps included in ekphrasis are: Twitter-specific tokenization, spell correction, word normalization, word segmentation (for splitting hashtags) and word annotation.

Tokenization. Tokenization is the first fundamental preprocessing step and since it is the basis for the other steps, it immediately affects the quality of the features learned by the network. Tokenization on Twitter is challenging, since there is large variation in the vocabulary and the expressions which are used. There are certain expressions which are better kept as one token (e.g. anti-american) and others that should be split into separate tokens. Ekphraris recognizes Twitter markup, emoticons, emojis, dates (e.g. 07/11/2011, April 23rd), times (e.g. 4:30pm, 11:00 am), currencies (e.g. $10, 25mil, 50€), acronyms, censored words (e.g. s**t), words with emphasis (e.g. *very*) and more using an extensive list of regular expressions.

Normalization. After tokenization we apply a series of modifications on extracted tokens, such as spell correction, word normalization and segmentation. Specifically for word normalization we lowercase words, normalize URLs, emails, numbers, dates, times and user handles (@user). This helps reducing the vocabulary size without losing information. For spell correction (Jurafsky and James, 2000) and word segmentation (Segaran and Hammerbacher, 2009) we use the Viterbi algorithm. The prior probabilities are initialized using uni/bi-gram word statistics from the unlabeled dataset. Table 1 shows an example text snippet and the resulting preprocessed tokens.

original	The *new* season of #TwinPeaks is coming on May 21, 2017. CANT WAIT \o/ !!! #tvseries #davidlynch :D
processed	the new <emphasis> season of <hashtag> twin peaks </hashtag> is coming on <date> . cant <allcaps> wait <allcaps> <happy> ! <repeated> <hashtag> tv series </hashtag> <hashtag> david lynch </hashtag> <laugh>

Table 1: Example of our text processor

2.3 Recurrent Neural Networks

We model the Twitter messages using Recurrent Neural Networks (RNN). RNNs process their inputs sequentially, performing the same operation, $h_t = f_W(x_t, h_{t-1})$, on every element in a sequence, where h_t is the hidden state t the time step, and W the network weights. We can see that hidden state at each time step depends on previous hidden states, thus the order of elements (words) is important. This process also enables RNNs to handle inputs of variable length.

RNNs are difficult to train (Pascanu et al., 2013), because gradients may grow or decay exponentially over long sequences (Bengio et al., 1994; Hochreiter et al., 2001). A way to overcome these problems is to use more sophisticated variants of regular RNNs, like Long Short-Term Memory (LSTM) networks (Hochreiter and Schmidhuber, 1997) or Gated Recurrent Units (GRU) (Cho et al., 2014), which ensure better gradient flow through the network.

Self-Attention Mechanism. RNNs update their hidden state h_i as they process a sequence and the final hidden state holds a summary of the information in the sequence. In order to amplify the contribution of important words in the final representation, a self-attention mechanism (Bahdanau et al., 2014) can be used (Fig. 4). In normal RNNs, we use as representation r of the input sequence its final state h_N. However, using an attention mechanism, we compute r as the convex combination of all h_i, with weights a_i, which signify the importance of each hidden state. Formally: $r = \sum_{i=1}^{N} a_i h_i$, where $\sum_{i=1}^{N} a_i = 1$, and $a_i > 0$.

3 Model Description

We use a word-level BiLSTM architecture to model semantic information in tweets. We also propose an attention mechanism, which conditions the weight of h_i on a "context vector" that is taken

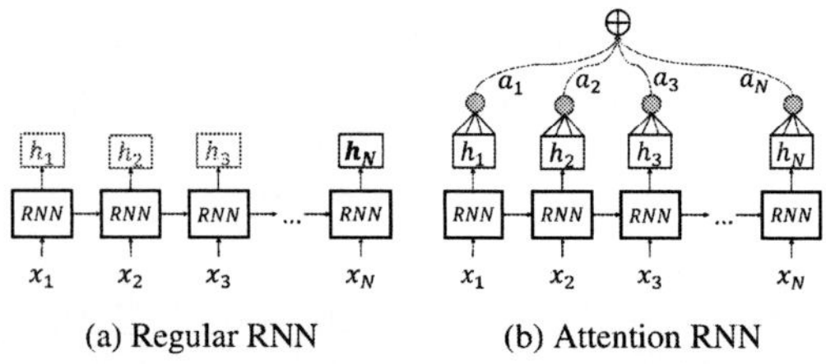

(a) Regular RNN   (b) Attention RNN

Figure 4: Comparison between the regular RNN and the RNN with attention.

as the aggregation of the tweet meaning.

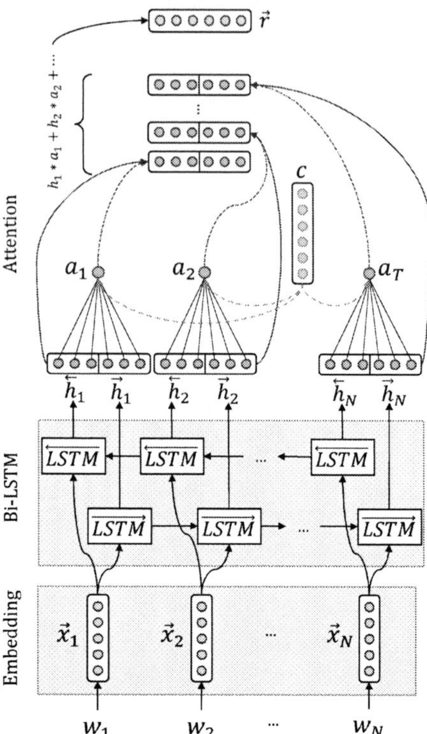

Figure 5: Architecture of the proposed model.

Embedding Layer. The input to the network is a Twitter message, treated as a sequence of words. We use an embedding layer to project the words $w_1, w_2, ..., w_N$ to a low-dimensional vector space R^W, where W the size of the embedding layer and N the number of words in a tweet. We initialize the weights of the embedding layer with our pre-trained word embeddings.

BiLSTM Layer. A LSTM takes as input the words of a tweet and produces the word annotations $h_1, h_2, ..., h_N$, where h_i is the hidden state of the LSTM at time-step i, summarizing all the information of the sentence up to w_i. We use bidirectional LSTM (BiLSTM) in order to get word annotations that summarize the information from both directions. A BiLSTM consists of a forward LSTM $\overrightarrow{f}$ that reads the sentence from w_1 to w_N and a backward LSTM $\overleftarrow{f}$ that reads the sentence from w_N to w_1. We obtain the final annotation for each word, by concatenating the annotations from both directions, $h_i = \overrightarrow{h_i} \parallel \overleftarrow{h_i}, \quad h_i \in R^{2L}$ where $\parallel$ denotes the concatenation operation and L the size of each LSTM.

Context-aware Self-Attention Layer. Even

though the hidden state h_i of the LSTM captures the local context up to word i, in order to better estimate the importance of each word given the context of the tweet we condition hidden state on a context vector. The context vector is taken as the average of h_i: $c = \frac{1}{N}\sum_1^N h_i$. The context-aware annotations u_i are obtained as the concatenation of c and h_i: $u_i = h_i \parallel c$. The attention weights a_i are computed as the softmax of the attention layer outputs e_i. W and b are the trainable weights and biases of the attention layer:

$$e_i = tanh(Wu_i + b) \qquad (1)$$

$$a_i = \frac{exp(e_i)}{\sum_{t=1}^N exp(e_t)} \qquad (2)$$

The final representation r is again taken as the convex combination of the hidden states.

$$r = \sum_{i=1}^N a_i h_i, \quad r \in R^{2L} \qquad (3)$$

Output Layer. We use the representation r as feature vector for classification and we feed it to a fully-connected softmax layer with L neurons, which outputs a probability distribution over all classes p_c as described in Eq. 4:

$$p_c = \frac{e^{Wr+b}}{\sum_{i\in[1,L]}(e^{W_i r + b_i})} \qquad (4)$$

where W and b are the layer's weights and biases.

3.1 Regularization

In both models we add Gaussian noise to the embedding layer, which can be interpreted as a random data augmentation technique, that makes models more robust to overfitting. In addition to that we use dropout (Srivastava et al., 2014) and we stop training after the validation loss has stopped decreasing (early-stopping).

4 Experiments and Results

4.1 Experimental Setup

Class Weights. In order to deal with class imbalances, we apply class weights to the loss function of our models, penalizing more the misclassification of underrepresented classes. We weight each class by its inverse frequency in the training set.
Training We use Adam algorithm (Kingma and Ba, 2014) for optimizing our networks, with minibatches of size 32 and we clip the norm of the gradients (Pascanu et al., 2013) at 1, as an extra safety

measure against exploding gradients. For developing our models we used PyTorch (Paszke et al., 2017) and Scikit-learn (Pedregosa et al., 2011).

Hyper-parameters. In order to find good hyper-parameter values in a relative short time (compared to grid or random search), we adopt the Bayesian optimization (Bergstra et al., 2013) approach, performing a time-efficient search in the space of all hyper-parameter values. The size of the embedding layer is 300, and the LSTM layers 300 (600 for BiLSTM). We add Gaussian noise with $\sigma = 0.05$ and dropout of 0.1 at the embedding layer and dropout of 0.3 at the LSTM layer.

Results. The dataset for Task 2 was introduced in (Saggion et al., 2017), where the authors propose a character level model with pretrained word vectors that achieves an F1 score of 34%. Our ranking as shown in Table 2 was 2/49, with an F1 score of 35.361%, which was the official evaluation metric, while team TueOslo achieved the first position with an F1 score of 35.991%. It should be noted that only the first 2 teams managed to surpass the baseline model presented in (Saggion et al., 2017).

In Table 3 we compare the proposed Context-Attention LSTM (CA-LSTM) model against 2 baselines: (1) a Bag-of-Words (BOW) model with TF-IDF weighting and (2) a Neural Bag-of-Words (N-BOW) model, where we retrieve the word2vec representations of the words in a tweet and compute the tweet representation as the centroid of the constituent word2vec representations. Both BOW and N-BOW features are then fed to a linear SVM classifier, with tuned $C = 0.6$. The CA-LSTM results in Table 3 are computed by averaging the results of 10 runs to account for model variability. Table 3 shows that BOW model outperforms N-BOW by a large margin, which may indicate that there exist words, which are very correlated with specific classes and their occurrence can determine the classification result. Finally, we observe that CA-LSTM significantly outperforms both baselines.

Fig. 6 shows the confusion matrix for the 20

#	Team Name	Acc	Prec	Rec	F1
1	TueOslo	47.094	36.551	36.222	35.991
2	**NTUA-SLP**	44.744	34.534	37.996	35.361
3	*Unknown*	45.548	34.997	33.572	34.018
4	Liu Man	47.464	39.426	33.695	33.665

Table 2: Official Results for Subtask A

	f1	accuracy	recall	precision
BOW	0.3370	0.4468	0.3321	0.3525
N-BOW	0.2904	0.4120	0.2849	0.3150
CA-LSTM	**0.3564**	**0.4482**	**0.3885**	**0.3531**

Table 3: Comparison against baselines

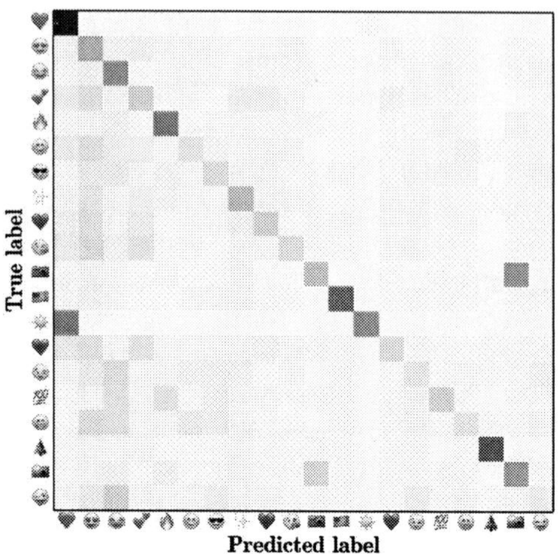

Figure 6: Confusion matrix

emojis. Observe that our model is more likely to misclassify a rare class as an instance of one of the 4 more frequent classes, even after the inclusion of class weights in the loss function (Section 4.1). Furthermore, we observe that heart or face emojis, which are more ambiguous, are easily confusable with each other. However, as expected this in not the case for emojis like the US flag or the Christmas tree, as they are tied with specific expressions. **Attention Visualization**. The attention mechanism not only improves the performance of the model, but also makes it interpretable. By using the attention scores assigned to each word annotation, we can investigate the behavior of the model. Figure 7 shows how the attention mechanism focuses on each word in order to estimate the most suitable emoji label.

5 Conclusion

In this paper, we present a deep learning system based on a word-level BiLSTM architecture and augment it with contextual attention for SemEval Task 2: "Multilingual Emoji Prediciction" (Barbieri et al., 2018). Our work achieved excellent results, reaching the 2nd place in the competition and outperforming the state-of-the-art reported in

Figure 7: Attention Visualizations

the bibliography (Barbieri et al., 2017). The performance of our model could be further boosted, by utilizing transfer learning methods from larger, weakly annotated, datasets. Moreover, the joint training of word- and character-level models can be tested for further performance improvement.

Finally, we make both our pretrained word embeddings and the source code of our models available to the community[3], in order to make our results easily reproducible and facilitate further experimentation in the field.

Acknowledgements. This work has been partially supported by the BabyRobot project supported by EU H2020 (grant #687831). Also, the authors would like to thank NVIDIA for supporting this work by donating a TitanX GPU.

---

[3]`github.com/cbaziotis/`
`ntua-slp-semeval2018-task2`

References

Sho Aoki and Osamu Uchida. 2011. A method for automatically generating the emotional vectors of emoticons using weblog articles. In *Proc. 10th WSEAS Int. Conf. on Applied Computer and Applied Computational Science, Stevens Point, Wisconsin, USA*, pages 132–136.

Dzmitry Bahdanau, Kyunghyun Cho, and Yoshua Bengio. 2014. Neural machine translation by jointly learning to align and translate. *CoRR*, abs/1409.0473.

Francesco Barbieri, Miguel Ballesteros, and Horacio Saggion. 2017. Are emojis predictable? In *Proceedings of the 15th Conference of the European Chapter of the Association for Computational Linguistics: Volume 2, Short Papers*, pages 105–111. Association for Computational Linguistics.

Francesco Barbieri, Jose Camacho-Collados, Francesco Ronzano, Luis Espinosa-Anke, Miguel Ballesteros, Valerio Basile, Viviana Patti, and Horacio Saggion. 2018. SemEval-2018 Task 2: Multilingual Emoji Prediction. In *Proceedings of the 12th International Workshop on Semantic Evaluation (SemEval-2018)*, New Orleans, LA, United States. Association for Computational Linguistics.

Francesco Barbieri, German Kruszewski, Francesco Ronzano, and Horacio Saggion. 2016a. How cosmopolitan are emojis?: Exploring emojis usage and meaning over different languages with distributional semantics. In *Proceedings of the 2016 ACM on Multimedia Conference*, pages 531–535. ACM.

Francesco Barbieri, Francesco Ronzano, and Horacio Saggion. 2016b. What does this emoji mean? a vector space skip-gram model for twitter emojis. In *LREC*.

Christos Baziotis, Nikos Pelekis, and Christos Doulkeridis. 2017. Datastories at semeval-2017 task 4: Deep lstm with attention for message-level and topic-based sentiment analysis. In *Proceedings of the 11th International Workshop on Semantic Evaluation (SemEval-2017)*, pages 747–754.

Yoshua Bengio, Patrice Simard, and Paolo Frasconi. 1994. Learning long-term dependencies with gradient descent is difficult. *IEEE transactions on neural networks*, 5(2):157–166.

James Bergstra, Daniel Yamins, and David D. Cox. 2013. Making a Science of Model Search: Hyperparameter Optimization in Hundreds of Dimensions for Vision Architectures. *ICML (1)*, 28:115–123.

Spencer Cappallo, Stacey Svetlichnaya, Pierre Garrigues, Thomas Mensink, and Cees GM Snoek. 2018. The new modality: Emoji challenges in prediction, anticipation, and retrieval. *arXiv preprint arXiv:1801.10253*.

Kyunghyun Cho, Bart Van Merriënboer, Caglar Gulcehre, Dzmitry Bahdanau, Fethi Bougares, Holger Schwenk, and Yoshua Bengio. 2014. Learning phrase representations using RNN encoder-decoder for statistical machine translation. *arXiv preprint arXiv:1406.1078*.

Ben Eisner, Tim Rocktäschel, Isabelle Augenstein, Matko Bošnjak, and Sebastian Riedel. 2016. emoji2vec: Learning emoji representations from their description. *arXiv preprint arXiv:1609.08359*.

Luis Espinosa-Anke, Horacio Saggion, and Francesco Barbieri. 2016. Revealing patterns of twitter emoji usage in barcelona and madrid. *Frontiers in Artificial Intelligence and Applications. 2016;(Artificial Intelligence Research and Development) 288: 239-44*.

Sepp Hochreiter, Yoshua Bengio, Paolo Frasconi, and Jürgen Schmidhuber. 2001. *Gradient Flow in Recurrent Nets: The Difficulty of Learning Long-Term Dependencies*. A field guide to dynamical recurrent neural networks. IEEE Press.

Sepp Hochreiter and Jürgen Schmidhuber. 1997. Long short-term memory. *Neural computation*, 9(8):1735–1780.

Daniel Jurafsky and H. James. 2000. Speech and language processing an introduction to natural language processing, computational linguistics, and speech.

Diederik Kingma and Jimmy Ba. 2014. Adam: A method for stochastic optimization. *arXiv preprint arXiv:1412.6980*.

Nikola Ljubešić and Darja Fišer. 2016. A global analysis of emoji usage. In *Proceedings of the 10th Web as Corpus Workshop*, pages 82–89.

Tomas Mikolov, Ilya Sutskever, Kai Chen, Greg S. Corrado, and Jeff Dean. 2013. Distributed representations of words and phrases and their compositionality. In *Advances in Neural Information Processing Systems*, pages 3111–3119.

Razvan Pascanu, Tomas Mikolov, and Yoshua Bengio. 2013. On the difficulty of training recurrent neural networks. *ICML (3)*, 28:1310–1318.

Adam Paszke, Sam Gross, Soumith Chintala, Gregory Chanan, Edward Yang, Zachary DeVito, Zeming Lin, Alban Desmaison, Luca Antiga, and Adam Lerer. 2017. Automatic differentiation in pytorch.

Fabian Pedregosa, Gaël Varoquaux, Alexandre Gramfort, Vincent Michel, Bertrand Thirion, Olivier Grisel, Mathieu Blondel, Peter Prettenhofer, Ron Weiss, Vincent Dubourg, and others. 2011. Scikit-learn: Machine learning in Python. *Journal of Machine Learning Research*, 12(Oct):2825–2830.

Radim Řehůřek and Petr Sojka. 2010. Software Framework for Topic Modelling with Large Corpora. In *Proceedings of the LREC 2010 Workshop on New*

Challenges for NLP Frameworks, pages 45–50, Valletta, Malta. ELRA. http://is.muni.cz/publication/884893/en.

Horacio Saggion, Miguel Ballesteros, and Francesco Barbieri. 2017. Are emojis predictable? In *EACL*.

Toby Segaran and Jeff Hammerbacher. 2009. *Beautiful Data: The Stories Behind Elegant Data Solutions*. "O'Reilly Media, Inc.".

Nitish Srivastava, Geoffrey E. Hinton, Alex Krizhevsky, Ilya Sutskever, and Ruslan Salakhutdinov. 2014. Dropout: A simple way to prevent neural networks from overfitting. *Journal of Machine Learning Research*, 15(1):1929–1958.

Hatching Chick at SemEval-2018 Task 2: Multilingual Emoji Prediction

J. Coster, R.G. van Dalen, and **N.A.J. Stierman**
Department of Information Science
University of Groningen
{j.coster.2, r.g.van.dalen, n.a.j.stierman}@student.rug.nl

Abstract

As part of a SemEval 2018 shared task an attempt was made to build a system capable of predicting the occurence of a language's most frequently used emoji in Tweets. Specifically, models for English and Spanish data were created and trained on 500.000 and 100.000 tweets respectively. In order to create these models, first a logistic regressor, a sequential LSTM, a random forest regressor and a SVM were tested. The latter was found to perform best and therefore optimized individually for both languages. During developmet f1-scores of 61 and 82 were obtained for English and Spanish data respectively, in comparison, f1-scores on the official evaluation data were 21 and 18. The significant decrease in performance during evaluation might be explained by overfitting during development and might therefore have partially be prevented by using cross-validation. Over all, emoji which occur in a very specific context such as a Christmas tree were found to be most predictable.

1 Introduction

It is said that a picture is worth a thousand words; inherently then, visual icons can provide additional meaning to text. One common example of this is the use of emoticons (emoji) accompanying primarily short, informal texts such as text messages and tweets. The role of these is interesting as they can be used in a variety of manners such as to complement text (e.g., 😊 to indicate happiness) and to replace text (e.g., *I* ❤ *you* instead of *I love you*).

This research is concerned with the development of a system for predicting the occurrence of these emoji on the basis of Twitter data and is conducted as part of a *SemEval 2018* shared task (Barbieri et al., 2018). More specifically, given the text of an English or Spanish tweet, the system will attempt to predict the emoji originally found

in that tweet. The set of emoji used is limited to the twenty most frequent emoji for each language respectively.

2 Previous Work

A similar research on predicting emoji occurring in tweets was conducted by Barbieri et al. (2017). In this study a Bidirectional Long Short-Term Memory (BLSTM) network with standard look-up word representations and character-based representations of tokens was used. While it was found that profoundly dissimilar emoji could be predicted, this method did not succeed to accurately differentiate between twenty emoji classes.

Na'aman et al. (2017) meanwhile conducted a study to further explore the linguistic varieties of the purposes of emoji on Twitter. It was found that emoji can be an integral part of the content. One common example of this is a part of a phrase being replaced by an emoji, much like the '*I* ❤ *you*' example from the previous section. The notion of these word-emoji combinations is also mentioned by Dimson (2015). These findings inherently strongly support the idea that text could to some extent be used to predict emoji, given that fixed co-occurrences do exist.

3 Data

Since this study was conducted as part of a shared task, data was made available by the organization (Barbieri et al., 2018). For the English language, data consisted of a trial set containing 50.000 and a training set containing 500.000 tweets geolocated in the United States. For Spanish, a trial set of 10.000 and a training set of 100.000 tweets geolocated in Spain were available. For both languages, the trial portion of the data was used as a development set. Evaluation then was ultimately conducted on a held out data set sized similarly to the

Proceedings of the 12th International Workshop on Semantic Evaluation (SemEval-2018), pages 445–448
New Orleans, Louisiana, June 5–6, 2018. ©2018 Association for Computational Linguistics

	English			Spanish	
	Train	**Test**		**Train**	**Test**
❤️	118425	10798	❤️	21854	2028
😍	57167	4830	😍	14962	1363
😂	56199	4534	😂	10299	970
💕	30360	2605	💕	7526	705
🔥	27137	3716	😊	7137	645
😊	25614	1613	😘	4834	415
😎	23362	1996	👌	4220	367
✨	20259	2749	😁	4053	386
💙	18817	1549	👏	3857	320
📷	17828	1175	📷	3776	369
🇺🇸	17586	1423	😎	3420	267
🇺🇸	16876	1949	💜	3198	271
☀️	15333	1265	💙	3112	313
💜	14323	1114	😉	2993	281
😉	14842	1306	💚	2908	282
💯	14655	1244	✨	2806	244
😘	14394	1153	🎶	2861	262
🎄	14122	1545	💋	2785	260
📸	14534	2417	😄	2807	252
😁	13516	1010	-	-	-

Table 1: The distribution of training and test data as used during evaluation

trial set for both languages respectively.

Analysis of the supplied data showed the tweets originated from the period between October 2015 and February 2017 with a natural distribution to the extent that slightly more tweets originated from months with a large number of public holidays such as December. All of these tweets contain one of the twenty most used emoji for their respective language, although due to an error in the data ultimately only the top nineteen had to be predicted for Spanish. The distribution of the emoji over the tweets can be seen in Table 1. Note that in this table counts for the trial and training data have been merged as a data set combining these was used during final evaluation.

4 Method

In order to build capable models for predicting emoji in English and Spanish tweets, a two step procedure was followed. First, various forms of preprocessing and multiple machine learning algorithms were tested in order to identify what type of model would most likely be successful. Then,

a system built on these results was optimized for English and Spanish tweets separately in order to create a model for each language.

4.1 Initial Model Selection

In order to determine which type of model to use, four different classification methods were tested. Specifically, a *Logistic Regression* classifier was tested using word unigrams, word bigrams and a combination of both. Next, a sequential LSTM with maximum sentence length embeddings as features was tested. This model used 40 neurons and a *softmax* activation function. The model was compiled by implementing *Categorical Crossentropy* and the *Adagrad* optimizer. Then, a *Random Forest Regressor* was implemented using the same features as the initial *Logistic Regression* model. Finally, a *linear SVM* model was built using the SKLearn *SGDClassifier* with a hinge loss function.

For all models, four preprocessing steps were tested. Namely replacing URLs occurring in the data with a general identifier, replacing mentions occurring in the data with a general identifier, tokenizing the tweets using the *NLTK TweetTokenizer* and stemming the tweets using the *Snowball* stemmer.

After all tests had been executed it was found that the linear SVM using the SGDClassifier yielded the best results. Therefore this model was selected as a basis for the per language models.

4.2 English

4.2.1 Preprocessing

For the optimized English model, most of the preprocessing steps from the previous subsection; tokenization, URL replacement and mention replacement, were used. Use of the snowball stemmer was omitted as it did not appear to improve performance. Additionally, punctuation was removed as this seemed to yield better results on trial data.

4.2.2 Optimized Model

As set out in the *Initial Model Selection* subsection the SKLearn *SGDClassifier* was used as the basis for this model. The settings used for this classifier can be seen in Table 2 and are shared with the model for Spanish. The input for this classifier then was a tf-idf vector created from the preprocessed data, which was first converted to lowercase as this was found to improve performance.

The SKLearn *FeatureUnion* function was used in order to experiment with both word and character ngram ranges simultaneously. Ultimately it was found that using only word ngrams with a range of two to four yielded the best results. However, despite not using character ngrams in the optimized model, the *Featurenion* was kept as the 0.5 weight it applied to all features improved results by approximately two percent point. This effect is most likely caused by the reduction of the absolute differences between the predictiveness of features. After these optimizations, testing on the trial set resulted in an average f1-score of 61.

4.3 Spanish

4.3.1 Preprocessing

For the final model, the Spanish optimized model used the same preprocessing procedure as the English optimized model, as described in section 4.2.1 as this procedure was found to perform best on Spanish data as well. During the development of this model however the use of a lemmatizer at the preprocessing stage was also tested as a replacement of the Snowball stemmer. While neither were included in the final model as they did not yield a significant improvement, it is interesting to note that the model with lemmatizer scored better when its language was set to English as opposed to Spanish, despite the language of the data primarily being the latter.

4.3.2 Optimized Model

Much like the English optimized model, the final model for Spanish data used the SKLearn SGD-Classifier with the same parameter settings, as seen in Table 2. The only difference then is that for Spanish data using a ngram range of one to seven instead of two to four was found to yield the best results. When tested against the trial data this model yielded an average f1-score of 82.

5 Results

Once parameter optimization on both the English and Spanish models had been completed, the models were prepared for official evaluation on previously unseen data as explained in section 3. To this end, a merged data set containing both training and trial data was created for each language respectively as during development it was found that system performance would scale with the amount of

Parameter	Value
loss	hinge
penalty	l2
alpha	1e-3
random_state	42
max_iter	20
tol	None
class_weight	dict(*1 for each class*)

Table 2: Parameters used for the *SGDClassifier*

English		Spanish	
Emoji	**F1-score**	**Emoji**	**F1-score**
❤️	57.29	❤️	64.725
😂	26.796	😂	34.635
😆	37.755	😆	51.356
💕	7.931	💕	6.847
👑	41.762	😊	10.506
😍	7.11	😜	20.755
😎	12.034	💪	32.701
✨	16.7	😌	9.339
💜	9.122	👌	10.631
📷	5.9	📷	44.649
📸	14.359	😎	11.268
🇺🇸	52.366	💚	6.391
☀	33.295	💙	1.439
💙	5.459	😄	4
😊	5.472	😘	4.651
💯	12.513	✨	13.843
😁	3.254	🎶	21.277
🌲	57.807	📸	6.03
🏔	19.568	😁	0.806
😉	2.26	-	-
Average	**21.438**	**Average**	**18.729**

Table 3: F1-scores achieved during evaluation

training data used[1]. The models were then trained on these merged data sets and tasked with predicting the corresponding emoji for the tweets in the evaluation data. These predictions were submitted to and consecutively evaluated by the task's organization. Results from this evaluation are detailed in the following subsections.

5.1 English Model

On average, the English optimized classifier achieved a f1-score of 21.438 with a precision of 25.965, a recall of 21.483 and an accuracy of 36.522. An overview of per class performance in the form of f1-scores can be seen in Table 3. Overall, the system performed best when predicting emoji which are likely to only occur in a specific context. ♥ For example is likely to occur in tweets about love, 🇺🇸 is predominantly used in the context of independence day and 🎄 is used mainly in tweets concerning Christmas. On these emoji the system achieved f1-scores of over 50. Meanwhile, the system performed worst on emoji such as 😊 and 😉, which are likely to be used in a plethora of different contexts. These findings are in line with trends seen when testing on trial data during development.

5.2 Spanish Model

Contrary to scores seen when testing on trial data, the Spanish optimized classifier performed slightly worse than the English optimized system. When tested on evaluation data, this model achieved a f1-score of 18.729 with a precision of 20.662, a recall of 19.163 and an accuracy of 37.23. Compared to English, a similar trend of weaker performance on more generic emoji is seen. Furthermore, ♥ ranked among the most accurately predicted emoji for Spanish as well. However due to lack of knowledge of the Spanish language no qualitative analysis of why other emoji such as 😎 and 📷 could be predicted relatively well was conducted.

6 Discussion

Although compared to other systems participating in the task the models did not do exceptionally bad, a significant drop in performance is seen when compared to results obtained during development. In fact, the English model saw a 40 per-

cent point drop and the Spanish model a 64 percent point drop. This decrease could partially be explained by differences in the distribution of certain emoji, as can be seen in Table 1. More importantly however, it is likely that the models were overfitted on the trial data as all testing during development was done on this portion of the data. In hindsight then, cross-validation might have been the better approach for evaluation during development.

Acknowledgments

Our contribution to this shared task was conducted as part of a course of the Information Science Master's degree programme at the University of Groningen. As such we would like to thank H. Haagsma for his insightful feedback during progress meetings.

References

Francesco Barbieri, Miguel Ballesteros, and Horacio Saggion. 2017. Are emojis predictable? *arXiv preprint arXiv:1702.07285*.

Francesco Barbieri, Jose Camacho-Collados, Francesco Ronzano, Luis Espinosa-Anke, Miguel Ballesteros, Valerio Basile, Viviana Patti, and Horacio Saggion. 2018. SemEval-2018 Task 2: Multilingual Emoji Prediction. In *Proceedings of the 12th International Workshop on Semantic Evaluation (SemEval-2018)*, New Orleans, LA, United States. Association for Computational Linguistics.

Thomas Dimson. 2015. Emojineering part 1: Machine learning for emoji trends. *Instagram Engineering Blog*, 30.

Noa Na'aman, Hannah Provenza, and Orion Montoya. 2017. Varying linguistic purposes of emoji in (twitter) context. In *Proceedings of ACL 2017, Student Research Workshop*, pages 136–141.

---

[1]Debugging was often conducted using a portion of the training data in order to reduce execution time

EPUTION at SemEval-2018 Task 2: Emoji Prediction with User Adaption

Liyuan Zhou[1,2]   **Qiongkai Xu**[1,2]   **Hanna Suominen**[1,2,3,4]   **Tom Gedeon**[1]

[1] The Australian National University, Canberra, ACT, Australia
[2] Data61, CSIRO, Canberra, ACT, Australia
[3] University of Canberra, Canberra, ACT, Australia
[4] University of Turku, Turku, Finland
{Liyuan.Zhou, Qiongkai.Xu, Hanna.Suominen, Tom.Gedeon}@anu.edu.au

Abstract

This paper describes our approach, called *EPUTION*, for the open trial of the SemEval-2018 Task 2, Multilingual Emoji Prediction. The task relates to using social media — more precisely, Twitter — with its aim to predict the most likely associated emoji of a tweet. Our solution for this text classification problem explores the idea of transfer learning for adapting the classifier based on users' tweeting history. Our experiments show that our user-adaption method improves classification results by more than 6 per cent on the macro-averaged F1. Thus, our paper provides evidence for the rationality of enriching the original corpus longitudinally with user behaviors and transferring the lessons learned from corresponding users to specific instances.

1 Introduction

Twitter sentiment analysis is an essential problem for companies and organizations to computationally measure customers' perceptions which attracts attention from fields of both social media analytics and natural language processing (Rosenthal et al., 2017; Felbo et al., 2017; Mac Kim et al., 2017). A Twitter message, called a *tweet*, is generally composed of text, *emojis*, links, and mentioned users, known as *tweeters*. An emoji is a small picture or symbol of a standardized set to represent a feeling or another concept (Dictionary.com, 2018), contributing to the sentiment of its sender (Barbieri et al., 2017). Consequently, techniques for *emoji classification* are relevant and can be used to transfer information to subsequent tasks of sentiment, emotion, and sarcasm analysis (Felbo et al., 2017).

The SemEval-2018 Task 2 challenges its participants to perform multilingual *emoji prediction* in *English* and *Spanish*. The top-20 most frequent emojis of each language are annotated as tweets'

class labels. To encourage systems with better performance on less frequent emojis, the *macro-averaged F_1 score* (Macro-F) (Suominen et al., 2008) is used as the official evaluation measure.

Emoji prediction is widely formalized as a text classification problem in which the state-of-the-art systems fail to perform satisfactory (Barbieri et al., 2018). Because individual users enjoy diverse preferences in their emoji usage, it is hard to train a generalized classifier to tackle emoji prediction. As demonstrated in Table 1, with two examples of simple tweets with various annotations from the training set, even with exactly the same tweet texts, different tweeters have various choices of emojis, such as **i)** a user can select one of the emojis express the same emotion and **ii)** a user can have different attitudes towards the same objects or topics.

Tweet	Emoji
@user happy birthday	😄 😊 🖤
@ new york, new york	😛 📷 😛

Table 1: The diversity emojis by different users.

In light of such observations, we propose to utilize a user adaption method to capture the specific preference for each individual user. We propose *Emoji Prediction with User Adaption* (*EPUTION*). It trains user-adapted classification models by applying tweeters' tweeting history to personalize a basic model trained by the benchmark training data. We implement the method on SemEval-2018 Task2 in English, where the basic model is competitive to the state-of-the-art systems, while the user-adaptation model further improves the classification results.

2 System Description

In this section, we describe the text classification method and user adaption approach.

Proceedings of the 12th International Workshop on Semantic Evaluation (SemEval-2018), pages 449–453
New Orleans, Louisiana, June 5–6, 2018. ©2018 Association for Computational Linguistics

2.1 Text Classification

The text classification component of our system is based on *FastText*[1] (Joulin et al., 2017), which can achieve results comparable to those by the state-of-the-art deep learning methods but with many orders of magnitude less running time. FastText feeds a linear classifier with averaged word representations as follows:

$$P(y|x_n) = \text{Softmax}(BAx_n) \qquad (1)$$

where y refers to the *class label* of a given document, x_n is the respective *normalized bag of features vector* of the document, and A and B are the *weight matrices*. The *cross entropy loss* is updated to optimized for parameter learning. The model is trained using hte *stochastic gradient descent* algorithm with a linearly decaying learning rate.

To optimize the computing time, *Hierarchical Softmax* based on the *Huffman tree* (Mikolov et al., 2013) is used to estimate label distribution. The probability of the label node n_y in the Huffman tree, with parents $n_1, \cdots, n_p$, is calculated as

$$P(n_y|x) = \prod_{i=1}^{p} P(n_i|x). \qquad (2)$$

In order to capture the word order information in the text, bag of n-grams are used as features.

2.2 User Adaption Framework

Our *User Adaption* (UA) framework is composed of the following two main components (Figure 1): a *pre-training process* and an *adaption process*.

During the pre-training process, we train a basic classification model M_b using the training set of the benchmark corpus C_b through FastText. During the adaption process, for each user u_i, we adapt the basic classification model M_b to a user-adapted model M_i. Namely, we initialize the parameters B_i and A_i of M_i with pre-trained parameters from M_b, and train M_i for 5 epochs using the retrospective tweet collection C_i of u_i. Out-of-vocabulary words in C_i are randomly initialized in our experiments.

3 Experimental Setup

In this section, we will describe our supplementary data collection process, model, and test settings.

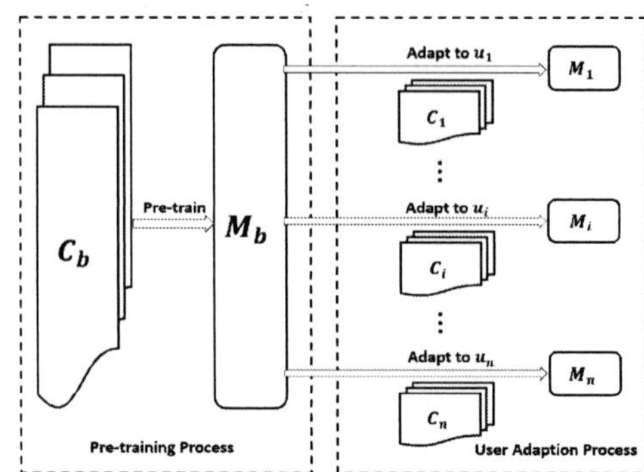

Figure 1: An overview of the user adaption framework.

3.1 Supplementary Data Collection

To implement our user adapted classification system, supplementary tweets are collected for each user. First, for each tweet of the emoji prediction task, the original tweeter who posted the tweet is retrieved by using the Twitter *Application Programming Interfaces*[2] (API). In order to map a tweet to its tweeter, we use the content of the tweet as a query to search for a match in Twitter. If precisely one result is retrieved and its content is precisely the same as the query text, the user who posted the retrieved tweet is assigned as the tweeter. Otherwise, no specific tweeter is assigned. Second, for each retrieved user, a retrospective collection of tweets is crawled from the most recent to the maximum number of $3,200$ tweets[3]. The current tweet used to retrieve the additional tweeter data is excluded from the user's tweet collection[4].

After enriching the task corpus by these user-specific collections, text content of the tweets is extracted using official scripts (Barbieri et al., 2017), removing hyperlinks while keeping texts and emojis. The tweets with only one emoji are selected, where the emoji is considered as the class label of the tweet. To ensure no overlapping instances exist between the test set and additional data that is collected for the user adaptation model (i.e., the collection of users' historical tweets), we remove the instances in the retrieved dataset that match the test tweets. More over, drawing from the use of the inverse document frequency in information retrieval as a way to scale down words

---

[1] https://fasttext.cc/

[2] https://developer.twitter.com/
[3] This number is determined by the Twitter API limitation.
[4] The crawling was performed for our SemEval-2018 Task 2 submission on 2nd February, 2018.

that only appear in few documents as too specific, all tweets that occur only in a single user's tweet collection are filtered out. This post-processing eliminates accidentally collected test cases where a user name cannot be retrieved, but keeps general cases that commonly appears in a tweet message such as *Happy Birthday* and *Good Morning*.

To summarize the dataset setting, there are $487,088$[5] and $50,000$ samples in the benchmark training and test sets, respectively. From all the tweets in the test set, $22,642$ of them matched a tweeter, from $20,594$ unique tweeters[6]. The final supplementary tweet collection contains $2,565,459$ tweets, with user IDs. This is about five times the size of the benchmark training set.

3.2 Model and Test Settings

Because the number of retrospective tweets from a single user is limited[7], the performance of training one model for each user is unsatisfactory in our preliminary experiments. Therefore, we apply a pre-training model to the benchmark training data of the task as a way to achieve properly initialized model parameters.

We implement the following three models:

- **FastText** is the baseline text classification model trained on the benchmark training set.

- **Data Augment** (DA) is the adapted model that used all tweeters' tweets grouped as a whole.

- **Individual User Adaption** (IUA) model is the adapted model that tailored the model to each individual tweeter's tweets.

After grid searching for the parameters on the benchmark development set, the *initial learning rate* α is set to be 0.01. The baseline model uses 100 dimensions of word vectors and 5 words in the context. It is trained over 50 epochs. The UA model has $\alpha = 0.05$ and is trained over 5 epochs. As the key point of this paper is the user adaption model, we explore the basic text classification features of *unigrams*, *bigrams*, and *trigrams* in our primary experiments. Trigram features achieve the best results. Thus, we follow such settings in all UA models while leaving room for further

---

[5]We retrieved $487,088$ samples among the $500,000$ tweet IDs provided by the task organizers.

[6]Some users have more than one instance in the test set.

[7]to approximately 23 tweets in the case of this paper

Model	Test-F	Test-R	Test-N
FastText	31.45	30.98	**31.24**
DA	33.17	34.94	30.81
IUA	**37.54**	**43.25**	$31.24^{\dagger}$

$\dagger$: We reuse M_b for tweets without the retrieved retrospective tweets for a given user.

Table 2: Macro-F [%] for the models on the test sets

improvements of our system performance by introducing the features implemented in other leading systems.

To demonstrate the influence of retrieved user information, we compare our approaches on the test sets with the following settings:

- **Test-F** (*Full* set of $50,000$ tweets) is the whole test set provided by the organizers of the SemEval2018 Task 2.

- **Test-R** (*Retrieved* set) is the subset of Test-F where the tweets are used to retrieve users' retrospective tweets, containing $22,642$ tweets.

- **Test-N** (*Non-retrieved* set) is the subtraction of Test-F and Test-R, where a user was not retrieved with this tweet or the retrieved user's retrospective tweets were not available, containing $27,358$ tweets.

4 Experimental Results

With additional retrospective data from the users, our model achieves more than 6 per cent better Macro-F than FastText. Consequently, it outperforms leading results from this competition.

Both DA and IUA achieve higher performance on the retrieved part of test set, Test-R, and thus improve the Macro-F on the full test set, Test-F (Table 4). This demonstrates the effectiveness of introducing the users' retrospective tweets.

IUA out performs DA, with a margin of more than 8 per cent on Test-R, indicating the necessity of training individual user adaptive models for the emoji prediction task. Compared with the best results in the task, on Test-F, — namely, 35.99 percent for *cagri* and 35.36 per cent for *cbaziotis* (Barbieri et al., 2018) — IUA achieves better results, even without an intensive feature engineering process.

5 Discussion

This section discusses and analyzes the success of our method in terms of its advantage on easily con-

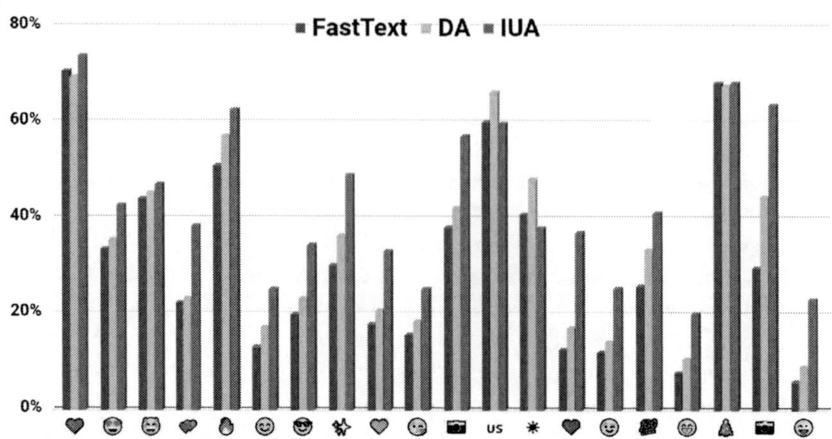

Figure 2: Class-specific results of the FastText, DA, and IUA models in emoji prediction on the Test-R data. We provide emoji labels on the x-axis and their respective label-specific F_1 score on the y-axis.

fused labels, and on users with certain amounts of historical tweets, over FastText.

We analyze the performance of IUA on different classes, by illustrating the Macro-F results of each emoji on Test-R in Figure 2. For the emojis, "Two Hearts", "Blue Heart", and "Purple Heart", they carry similar meanings but different users have diverse preference when expressing their emotions. Both "Camera With Flash" and "Camera" without flash can be chosen under the same circumstances. Compared with DA, IUA achieves a marginal improvement on distinguishing the user preferences of those emojis. For other emojis such as "United States", "Sun", and "Christmas Tree", IUA is competitive, as these emojis are aligned with single entities. These result show that our adaptive model is capable of learning user preferences in emojis with similar meanings, that is, the Case 1 of Section 1.

To demonstrate that IUA is also able to tackle the Case 2 of Section 1, we demonstrate some sample tweets that provide different emoji predictions using different user adapted models. For example, when the test tweet is *University life*, users have different attitudes towards "Red Heart", "Two Hearts", "Smiling Face With Smiling Eyes", "Face With Tears of Joy", "Hundred Points", and other emojis Meanwhile, FastText is only able to predict "Two Hearts" for all users. IUA manages to capture the attitudes of individual users towards the same tweets, while FastText and DA tend to provide common attitudes of the tweets.

Both IUA and DA outperform FastText under different scale settings of retrieved tweets, as illustrated in Figure 3. With more retrieved samples, the performance of DA increases. IUA reaches its peak performance on tweets with 64 retrieved historical tweets. More retrieved tweets do not further improve the results in our experiments. We have not observed much improvement for FastText for users with more retrieved tweets.

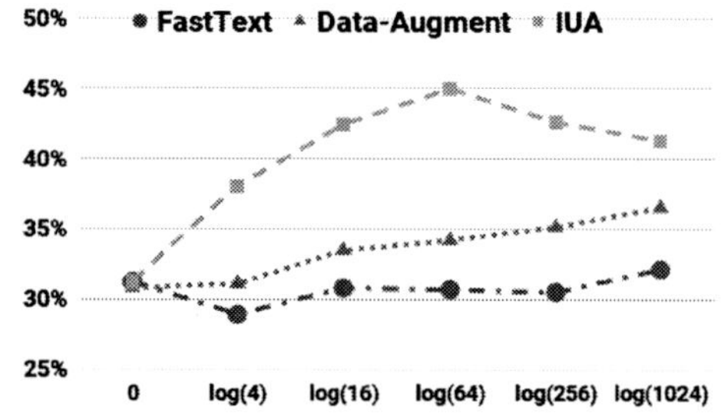

Figure 3: Macro-F of IUA, DA, and FastText on Test-R as numbers of tweets in each user collection increases.

6 Conclusion

This paper provides evidence for the rationality of enriching the original corpus longitudinally with user behaviors and transferring the lessons learned as user-adapted models to supervised machine learning tasks, such as the SemEval-2018 Task 2 on English emoji prediction. Our system achieves better performance than systems, which use all training data as a whole, even without much feature engineering. We believe this model can provide insight for introducing user-specific information for subsequent tasks of emoji prediction.

References

Francesco Barbieri, Miguel Ballesteros, and Horacio Saggion. 2017. Are Emojis Predictable? In *Proceedings of the 15th European Chapter of the Association for Computational Linguistics (EACL)*.

Francesco Barbieri, Jose Camacho-Collados, Francesco Ronzano, Luis Espinosa-Anke, Miguel Ballesteros, Valerio Basile, Viviana Patti, and Horacio Saggion. 2018. SemEval-2018 Task 2: Multilingual Emoji Prediction. In *Proceedings of the 12th International Workshop on Semantic Evaluation (SemEval)*.

Dictionary.com. 2018. Define Emoji at Dictionary. *http://www.dictionary.com/browse/emoji*, Accessed: 2018-03-05.

Bjarke Felbo, Alan Mislove, Anders Søgaard, Iyad Rahwan, and Sune Lehmann. 2017. Using Millions of Emoji Occurrences to Learn Any-domain Representations for Detecting Sentiment, Emotion and Sarcasm. In *Proceedings of the 2017 Conference on Empirical Methods in Natural Language Processing (EMNLP)*.

Armand Joulin, Edouard Grave, Piotr Bojanowski, and Tomas Mikolov. 2017. Bag of Tricks for Efficient Text Classification. In *Proceedings of the 15th European Chapter of the Association for Computational Linguistics (EACL)*.

Sunghwan Mac Kim, Qiongkai Xu, Lizhen Qu, Stephen Wan, and Cécile Paris. 2017. Demographic Inference on Twitter using Recursive Neural Networks. In *Proceedings of the 55th Annual Meeting of the Association for Computational Linguistics (ACL)*, volume 2, pages 471–477.

Tomas Mikolov, Kai Chen, Gregory S. Corrado, and Jeffrey Dean. 2013. Efficient Estimation of Word Representations in Vector Space. *Computing Research Repository (CoRR)*, abs/1301.3781.

Sara Rosenthal, Noura Farra, and Preslav Nakov. 2017. SemEval-2017 Task 4: Sentiment Analysis in Twitter. In *Proceedings of the 11th International Workshop on Semantic Evaluation (SemEval-2017)*, pages 502–518.

Hanna Suominen, Tapio Pahikkala, and Tapio Salakoski. 2008. Critical Points in Assessing Learning Performance via Cross-validation. In *Proceedings of the 2nd International and Interdisciplinary Conference on Adaptive Knowledge Representation and Reasoning (AKRR)*, pages 9–22.

PickleTeam! at SemEval-2018 Task 2:
English and Spanish Emoji Prediction from Tweets

Daphne Groot
University of Groningen
`d.groot.2@student.rug.nl`

Rémon Kruizinga
University of Groningen
`r.kruizinga.2@student.rug.nl`

Hennie Veldthuis
University of Groningen
`h.veldthuis@student.rug.nl`

Simon de Wit
University of Groningen
`s.de.wit.2@student.rug.nl`

Hessel Haagsma
University of Groningen
`hessel.haagsma@rug.nl`

Abstract

We present a system for emoji prediction
on English and Spanish tweets, prepared for
the SemEval-2018 task on Multilingual Emoji
Prediction. We compared the performance of
an SVM, LSTM and an ensemble of these two.
We found the SVM performed best on our
development set with an accuracy of 61.3%
for English and 83% for Spanish. The features used for the SVM are lowercased word
n-grams in the range of 1 to 20, tokenised by
a TweetTokenizer and stripped of stop words.
On the test set, our model achieved an accuracy of 34% on English, with a slightly lower
score of 29.7% accuracy on Spanish.

1 Introduction

The way people communicate with each other has
changed since the rise of social media. Many people use visual icons, so-called emojis, to complement their social media messages. Emojis are
frequently used on online platforms like Twitter,
Facebook, Instagram and WhatsApp. The wide
use of emojis in social media means that processing these emojis can be relevant for NLP applications dealing with social media data.

Social media text has been studied in the field
of author profiling, but only recently the interest
in the research on emojis started growing. Author
profiling is used in different fields such as marketing, forensics, psychological research and medical
diagnosis. Author profiling focuses on stylomet-
ric features, and since this new popular way of
expressing meaning by using emojis has become
mainstream, its important to research if and how
this data can be used in addition to the textual data.
It could be possible that emojis reveal a great deal

about the author's gender, location, age or other
characteristics.

We describe our approach to SemEval-2018
Task 2 on Multilingual Emoji Prediction (Barbieri et al., 2018) in this paper. We will discuss the
features, the machine learning methods we used
and analyse the performance of our best method.

2 Related Work

Author profiling tasks are focusing more and more
on social media. Oftentimes, the data that is provided is data obtained from social media platforms
Rangel et al. (2017). However, research on emojis
is more scarce. Some research on emojis is done
by Barbieri et al. (2017). They investigated the relation between words and emojis, and found that
neural models outperform baseline bag-of-words
models as well as humans when predicting which
emojis are used in tweets.

Xie et al. (2016) researched automatic emoji
recommendation using neural networks. Emojis can express more delicate feelings beyond
plain text, and suggesting valid emojis to users
of messaging systems can enhance user experience. They approached this problem with neural
networks, and they found an Hierarchical-LSTM
system significantly outperformed all other LSTM
approaches.

Zhao and Zeng (2017) also looked at emoji
prediction. The task described in this paper is
very similar to the SemEval task. They achieved
an accuracy of 40% using a CNN. As features they used the Twitter GloVe embeddings[1].
Since they worked with a noisy dataset they constructed themselves and we are provided with a

---

[1] http://nlp.stanford.edu/projects/glove/

454

Proceedings of the 12th International Workshop on Semantic Evaluation (SemEval-2018), pages 454–458
New Orleans, Louisiana, June 5–6, 2018. ©2018 Association for Computational Linguistics

clean dataset, a similar approach might yield high scores.

Author profiling on tweets is not new. At PAN 2017 (Rangel et al., 2017), Basile et al. (2017) were able to achieve a score of 82% on gender prediction of English tweets. They approached the task with an SVM using combinations of character and tf-idf word n-grams. This yields good results for predicting gender, and can provide a good basis for an emoji prediction system.

In the light of this task, sentiment analysis might be helpful. The sentiment of a tweet might point the classifier in the right direction. Mohammad et al. (2013), Han et al. (2013) and Da Silva et al. (2014) all looked into sentiment classification of tweets using machine learning algorithms. Da Silva et al. (2014) achieved an accuracy of 84.85% on predicting sentiment on a Tweet dataset using an ensemble where SVM, Random Forest and Multinomial Naive Bayes were combined using majority voting. It might be fruitful to try some features and methods used in these papers to see if sentiment can be a distinctive feature for emoji prediction. Unfortunately, we did not manage to experiment with these features.

3 Data

The dataset used for this task was provided by the organizers of the SemEval task, and is derived from Twitter and only includes Spanish and English tweets from respectively Spain and the United States. An overview of the emojis in the dataset is shown in Tables 1 and 2.

4 Method

For the task of emoji prediction, we explored a neural network approach and an SVM approach. We established a basic machine learning model per approach and improved on these models for both Spanish and English development dataset. With this approach, we aim to develop a robust model that is able to predict the emojis for both the Spanish and the English dataset accurately.

Architectures we tried for the neural network approach ranged from a simplistic sequential model with a few hidden layers to a stacked LSTM model with word embeddings.

The highest results for our neural network approach were achieved by a sequential neural network model. Our first layer was a 200-dimensional embedding layer, using the GloVe Twitter embeddings (Pennington et al., 2014). Secondly, we used an LSTM layer. After the LSTM layer, our model included a Dropout of 0.2 (Srivastava et al., 2014). The output layer was a dense layer with the sigmoid activation function. Our model used a categorical cross-entropy loss and was optimized by the Adam optimizer (Kingma and Ba, 2014). We used zero masking, 20 epochs and a batch size of 128. Other parameters were left to the Keras defaults.

By establishing a basic SVM system, we tried to improve the system with divergent features. Our basic model consisted of word and character n-gram features. Improvements on this model were applied by using different kinds of preprocessing, tokenization, stemming and POS-tagging methods. We tried tokenization with the NLTK Word Tokenizer and the NLTK Tweet Tokenizer For stemming, we tried the Porter and Snowball stemmer, also from NLTK. Both of them did slightly decrease the accuracy of our system. The POS tagger we tried was NLTK's default POS tagger.

After trying several setups for both systems on the development dataset, we concluded that our SVM approach was the most accurate for both the English and Spanish tweets.

For our best SVM system, we found that some special characters and punctuation had to be removed. Besides, we replaced the Twitter URLs with the placeholder 'URL' and we substituted '. . .', which was a reference to Instagram, with the placeholder 'INSTAGRAM'. Lastly, we applied a method to reduce each character sequence to a maximum sequence of three characters. E.g., if a user uses the word 'wooooooooooow', we normalize it to 'wooow', so the textual input to the system is less sparse.

The SVM system which yielded the best results on the development set, used the NLTK Tweet tokenizer and merely one feature, namely a tf-idf word vectorizer with a word n-gram range of (1,15), no lowercasing, removing of English stopwords for both the English and Spanish dataset (unconventional, but improved the scores) and a minimum document frequency of one. Our model was trained with sklearn's SGDClassifier[2] with a hinge loss and a maximum number of 50 iterations. All other parameters were left to the sklearn defaults.

---

[2]http://scikit-learn.org/stable/modules/generated /sklearn.linear_model.SGDClassifier.html

Emoji										
SVM	45.35	26.58	40.65	8.22	46.93	7.98	14.14	23.79	11.64	6.14
Ensemble	43.67	25.82	38.82	7.45	39.92	7.67	13.79	21.04	9.79	5.53
Emoji										
SVM	17.85	56.48	34.86	9.50	3.61	19.51	6.13	60.27	15.77	1.70
Ensemble	17.15	40.26	30.88	7.49	3.55	15.77	5.70	48.60	13.34	1.63

Table 1: Macro F1-score per emoji on test-set for English.

Emoji										
Spanish	38.79	29.12	49.89	4.25	10.32	17.34	32.01	7.85	12.96	41.68
Ensemble	38.57	28.18	47.06	4.61	10.29	16.40	27.08	6.34	13.65	41.93
Emoji									
Spanish	10.64	3.56	0.71	2.33	1.56	12.84	20.58	3.30	1.52
Ensemble	9.48	3.95	0.71	2.34	2.72	12.22	16.19	3.02	1.49

Table 2: Macro F1-score per emoji on test-set for Spanish.

In addition to the SVM and LSTM, we tried an ensemble approach that combined both. Our assumption was that both systems performed slightly better or worse in different aspects. By combining our best SVM and LSTM, we tried to achieve a higher accuracy. When the LSTM system is 95% certain about a label prediction, our ensemble system takes this label as the predicted label. When the LSTM is less certain, the ensemble system takes the label predicted by our SVM system as the predicted label. This threshold was chosen after a short trial of different thresholds, where the 0.95 provided the best results. Yet, it turned out that combining both systems yielded a slightly worse accuracy than our best SVM system alone.

5 Results

The baseline results, obtained by always predicting the most frequent label from the training set, are presented in Tables 4 and 5

The results obtained on the development set are presented in Table 3, with the highest scores, i.e. those achieved by the best systems, are printed in bold.

The results of the final SVM model that we submitted on the test set are presented in Tables 4 and 5, for English and Spanish, respectively. The scores on individual classes (==emojis) are pre-

sented in Tables 1 and 2.

Our final system achieves a macro F1-score of 22.86% for English and 15.86%.In order to provide additional insights into the system's performance, the confusion matrices for English and Spanish on the test set, are presented in Figure 1 and Figure 2.

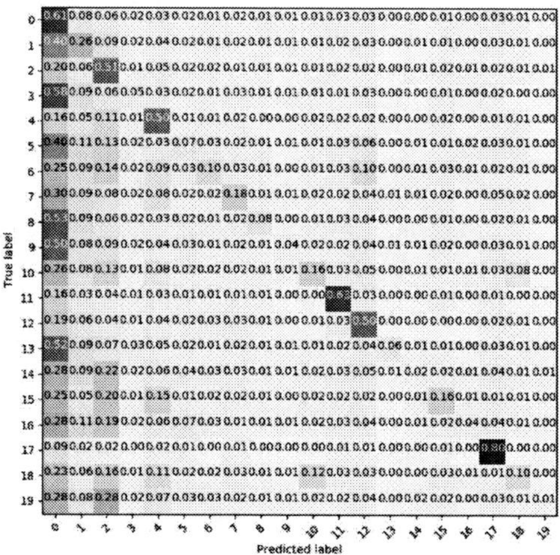

Figure 1: Confusion matrix for predicted and gold labels on the English test set.

Model	Setup	F1 (EN)	F1 (ES)
SVM	Word 1-grams	0.443	0.652
	Word 1- to 3-grams + Character 3- to 5-grams	0.519	0.790
	Word and PoS-tag 1- to 3-grams + Character 3- to 5-grams	0.556	0.804
	Word 1- to 10-grams	0.583	0.821
	Word 1- to 15-grams, no punctuation	**0.613**	**0.830**
	Word 1- to 15-grams, no punctuation + tweet length	0.525	–
LSTM	Dropout of 0.2 before LSTM, 6 epochs	0.427	–
	Dropout of 0.2 before LSTM, 20 epochs	0.529	–
	No Dropout before LSTM, 10 epochs	0.525	0.728
	No Dropout before LSTM, 20 epochs	**0.553**	**0.790**

Table 3: Macro F1-score for various system setups on the development sets for English and Spanish.

	F1	Precision	Recall	Acc.
Baseline	1.78	1.08	5.00	21.60
SVM	22.86	26.17	24.37	34.09
Ensemble	19.89	21.97	20.89	30.57

Table 4: Macro-averaged F1, Precision & Recall and Accuracy for English on the test-set.

	F1	Precision	Recall	Acc.
Baseline	1.86	1.13	5.26	21.41
SVM	15.86	17.57	16.76	29.70
Ensemble	15.06	16.38	15.90	28.17

Table 5: Macro-averaged F1, Precision & Recall and Accuracy for Spanish on the test-set.

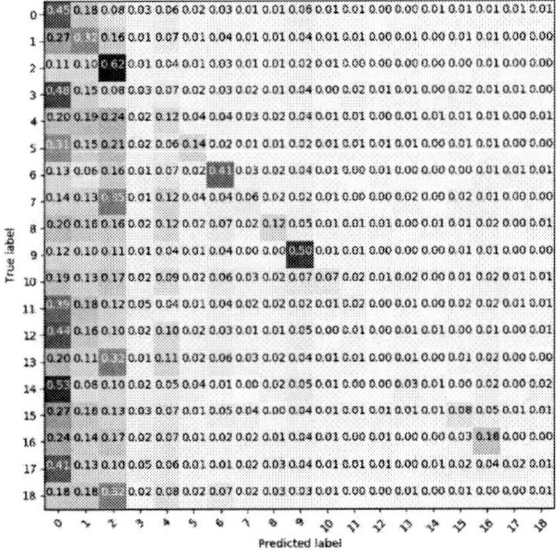

Figure 2: Confusion matrix for predicted and gold labels on the Spanish test set.

6 Discussion & Conclusion

In the confusion matrices, the diagonal lines of correct predictions can be seen. However, as also reported in the paper of Zhao and Zeng (2017), there is also a bias towards predicting the most frequent emojis. For the English tweets, the Christmas tree emoji was predicted most accurately. This is understandable, since this is an emoji that is mostly used in very distinct circumstances. For emojis 3, 8, 9 and 13 this is not the case. They were often incorrectly predicted as emoji 0 (a red heart), which is explainable by the fact that all these emojis relate to love and hearts. For the Spanish tweets, the same issues can be seen with similar emojis.

In this paper, we explored two approaches (an LSTM and an SVM) and a combination of both for predicting emojis of English and Spanish Tweets. Ultimately, the SVM classifier achieved the high-est results: F1-score of 22.86 for English and 15.86 for Spanish. Compared the other participating groups, the results were in the mid-range. These results showed that our system ranks 26th out of 49 for English and 10th out of 22 for Spanish. The results on the test set were lower than what we achieved on the development set. This is possibly due to the fact that there seemed to be an overlap between the training set and the development set. This would cause the classifier to be able to make more correct predictions, because it has seen the exact same tweets before.

References

Francesco Barbieri, Miguel Ballesteros, and Horacio Saggion. 2017. Are emojis predictable? In *Lapata*

M, Blunsom P, Koller A, editors. 15th Conference of the European Chapter of the Association for Computational Linguistics; 2017 Apr 3-7; Valencia, Spain. Stroudsburg (PA): ACL; 2017. p. 105-11. ACL (Association for Computational Linguistics).

Francesco Barbieri, Jose Camacho-Collados, Francesco Ronzano, Luis Espinosa-Anke, Miguel Ballesteros, Valerio Basile, Viviana Patti, and Horacio Saggion. 2018. SemEval-2018 Task 2: Multilingual Emoji Prediction. In *Proceedings of the 12th International Workshop on Semantic Evaluation (SemEval-2018)*, New Orleans, LA, United States. Association for Computational Linguistics.

Angelo Basile, Gareth Dwyer, Maria Medvedeva, Josine Rawee, Hessel Haagsma, and Malvina Nissim. 2017. N-GrAM: New Groningen Author-profiling Model. *arXiv preprint arXiv:1707.03764*.

Nadia FF Da Silva, Eduardo R Hruschka, and Estevam R Hruschka Jr. 2014. Tweet sentiment analysis with classifier ensembles. *Decision Support Systems*, 66:170–179.

Qi Han, Junfei Guo, and Hinrich Schütze. 2013. Codex: Combining an SVM classifier and character n-gram language models for sentiment analysis on Twitter text. In *Second Joint Conference on Lexical and Computational Semantics (* SEM), Volume 2: Proceedings of the Seventh International Workshop on Semantic Evaluation (SemEval 2013)*, volume 2, pages 520–524.

Diederik P Kingma and Jimmy Ba. 2014. Adam: A method for stochastic optimization. *arXiv preprint arXiv:1412.6980*.

Saif M Mohammad, Svetlana Kiritchenko, and Xiaodan Zhu. 2013. NRC-Canada: Building the state-of-the-art in sentiment analysis of tweets. *arXiv preprint arXiv:1308.6242*.

Jeffrey Pennington, Richard Socher, and Christopher D. Manning. 2014. GloVe: Global vectors for word representation. In *Proceedings of EMNLP 2014*, pages 1532–1543.

Francisco Rangel, Paolo Rosso, Martin Potthast, and Benno Stein. 2017. Overview of the 5th author profiling task at PAN 2017: Gender and language variety identification in Twitter. *Working Notes of CLEF 2017 - Conference and Labs of the Evaluation Forum*.

Nitish Srivastava, Geoffrey Hinton, Alex Krizhevsky, Ilya Sutskever, and Ruslan Salakhutdinov. 2014. Dropout: A simple way to prevent neural networks from overfitting. *The Journal of Machine Learning Research*, 15(1):1929–1958.

Ruobing Xie, Zhiyuan Liu, Rui Yan, and Maosong Sun. 2016. Neural emoji recommendation in dialogue systems. *arXiv preprint arXiv:1612.04609*.

Luda Zhao and Connie Zeng. 2017. Using neural networks to predict emoji usage from Twitter data.

YNU-HPCC at SemEval-2018 Task 2: Multi-ensemble Bi-GRU Model with Attention Mechanism for Multilingual Emoji Prediction

Nan Wang, Jin Wang and **Xuejie Zhang**
School of Information Science and Engineering
Yunnan University
Kunming, P.R. China
Contact:xjzhang@ynu.edu.cn

Abstract

This paper describes our approach to SemEval-2018 Task 2, which aims to predict the most likely associated emoji, given a tweet in English or Spanish. We normalized text-based tweets during preprocessing, following which we utilized a bi-directional gated recurrent unit with an attention mechanism to build our base model. Multi-models with or without class weights were trained for the ensemble methods. We boosted models without class weights, and only strong boost classifiers were identified. In our system, not only was a boosting method used, but we also took advantage of the voting ensemble method to enhance our final system result. Our method demonstrated an obvious improvement of approximately 3% of the macro F1 score in English and 2% in Spanish.

1 Introduction

As a novel means of enhancing the visual effect and meaning of short text messages, emojis are almost indispensable to each social platform, such as Facebook, Twitter, and Instagram. These graphic facial expressions and other object symbols enrich the emotion the user wishes to express in a text-based message. Although they are significant as part of social messages, emojis have scarcely attracted attention from a natural language processing (NLP) standpoint. Notable exceptions include studies focused on emoji semantics and usages (Barbieri et al., 2017). However, the interplay between text-based messages and emojis remains virtually unexplored. The aim of SemEval-2018 task 2 (Barbieri et al., 2018) is to fill this gap by providing all participants with a large set of text-based tweets and their related emojis, which were extracted from original tweet messages, in order to determine the connection between text words and emojis.

In recent years, an increasing amount of research work has been conducted on the sentiment analysis of tweets. Emojis have always played an important role in the sentiment polarity of tweets. Novak et al. (2015) proposed a sentiment map of the 751 most frequently used emojis, by computing the sentiment emoji from the sentiment of tweets in which they occurred, and they determined a significant difference in the sentiment distribution of tweets with and without emojis. As opposed to sentiment polarity prediction of tweets, we further investigated potential tweet emojis in this task, evoked by the text part.

Neural networks involving attention mechanisms have been studied extensively in the image processing and NLP fields, and have demonstrated remarkable results, particularly convolutional neural networks (CNNs) (Collobert et al., 2011) and long short-term memories (LSTMs) (Hochreiter and Schmidhuber, 1997). Cliche (2017) assembled several CNNs and LSTMs and achieved first ranking in all of five English subtasks. Raffel and Ellis (2015) proposed a feed-forward network model with attention, which selects the most important element from each time step using learnable weights, depending on the target. As a variant of LSTM, the gated recurrent units (GRUs) (Cho et al., 2014) use gating units directly in order to modulate the data flow inside the unit, rather than consisting of separate memory cells. For this task, we firstly utilized bi-directional GRUs and the attention mechanism to train the base model, following which we boosted the base model with different sample weights. In order to achieve optimum performance, soft and hard voting ensemble methods were also used in our system.

The remainder of paper is structured as follows. Section 2 provides an overview of task 2. In

459

Proceedings of the 12th International Workshop on Semantic Evaluation (SemEval-2018), pages 459–465
New Orleans, Louisiana, June 5–6, 2018. ©2018 Association for Computational Linguistics

section 3, we describe the architecture of our base model, particularly the attention mechanism, as well as the multi-ensemble methods used in our submission. Section 4 describes our experiment, which consists of system parameters, evaluation metrics, and experimental results for the two subtasks. Finally, in section 5, we list several possible improvement points, and in section 6, we outline our main conclusions.

2 Task Overview

This multilingual emoji prediction task consisted of multi-labeled emoji classification of short tweet texts, and was divided into two subtasks based on the text language: subtask 1 in English and subtask 2 in Spanish. The most frequently used emojis in English and Spanish were employed as labels, so the two task labels differed.

Subtask-1: Emoji Prediction in English

Given a text of tweets in English, its potential emojis are predicted from 20 emoji labels, as follows:

Subtask-2: Emoji Prediction in Spanish

Given a text of tweets in Spanish, its potential emojis are predicted from 19 emoji labels, as follows:

2.1 Datasets

The organizers provided a huge amount of training data, including 500K tweets in English and 100K tweets in Spanish[1]. We crawled almost the entire set of tweets with Twitter APIs[2], as parts of the training tweets were no longer available. Table 1 provides a detailed distribution of the datasets for subtasks 1 and 2.

Furthermore, all of the used emoji labels extracted from the tweets are the 20 or 19 most frequently used emojis in the languages themselves. Data samples for these classes are gradually decreasing; thus, datasets of the two

	Subtask-1	Subtask-2
Train	489660	98506
Develop	50000	10000
Test	50000	10000

Table 1: Datasets of Task2.

subtasks are both imbalanced. In subtask 1, the greatest majority class ♥ includes 106352 (21.7%) samples, nearly ten times that of the lowest minority class 😎, which includes only 12190 (2.5%) samples. For subtask 2, similar to subtask 1, the greatest majority class ♥ includes 19640 (19.9%) samples, while the lowest minority class 😎 includes 2525 (2.6%) samples.

Pre-trained Twitter embeddings for English and Spanish were offered in the task. We validated these by using another pre-trained embedding from GloVe[3] (Pennington et al., 2014), and the English embedding offered in the task presented approximately the same performance in our test.

3 System Description

As these two subtasks were rather similar, with the exception of different emoji labels, we used exactly the same thought to train every system of the respective languages. In order to choose the best one as our base model, several models were tested(such as CNN, CNN+LSTM), and superior performance was achieved by using the multi-ensemble methods as the following subsection 3.2.

3.1 Base Model

We created our base model with Bi-GRU (Bahdanau et al., 2014) rather than Bi-LSTM, owing to its faster, efficient, and superior performance. Furthermore, the bi-directional model can concatenate the sentence matrix vector forward and backward at each time step to obtain full sentence information (Irsoy and Cardie, 2014). The attention mechanism was also involved in our model, the model architecture of which is illustrated in Fig. 1, where h_t denotes the hidden vector at each time step, and t means the time step in the input sequence. Vectors in hidden state sequence h_t are fed into the learnable function to produce attention weight α_t. A single vector is computed as the weighted average of h_t.

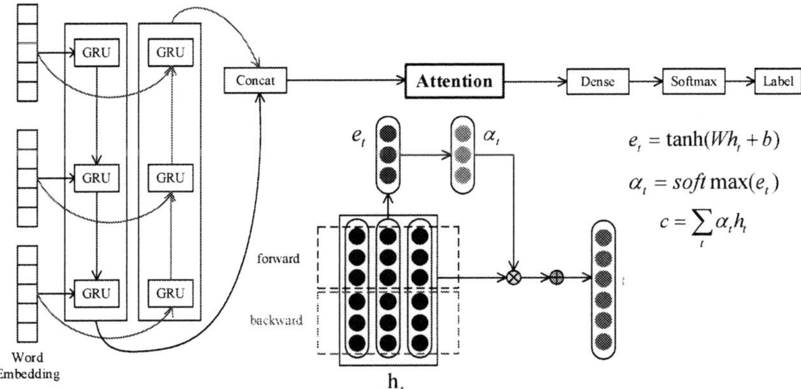

Figure 1: Architecture of Bi-GRU Model with Attention Mechanism.

The characteristic advantage of the attention mechanism over other reduction operations is that it takes an auxiliary context vector as input. The context vector is crucial because it indicates which information to discard, and a summary vector is therefore tailored to the network using it.

3.2 Ensemble

The ensemble classifier is a type of algorithm in which multiple learners are used to improve the individual classification performance by combining hypotheses. In this task, the multiple ensemble methods of boosting and voting were used to achieve the optimal result.

3.2.1 Boosting

The concept of boosting involves iteratively training the base classifier with the re-weighting method, which assigns a new list of sample weights to each round of training data samples. The weight distribution of each sample round depends on the results of the previous round classifier. Simple weights to instances are based on how arduous they are to the classification; thus, the boost classifier provides additional weights to those mis-classified instances following a round of classification in order to boost the following classifier result. Finally, the sequence-based linear weighting method was used to combine the classifiers. Although boosting is not intended for class imbalance problems, owing to this characteristic, it has become an ideal method for class imbalance problems.

3.2.2 Voting

The voting classifier can take a series of machine learning classification algorithms (possibly conceptually different) and average them to obtain final predictions. Two voting methods are available:

Soft voting: Each model outputs a probability vector for all classes, and the voting model is average-weighted to obtain a final probability vector for classification.

Hard voting: Each model outputs what it believes to be the most likely category, from which the voting model selects the category with the largest number of voting models as the final classification.

In several tasks, soft voting may obtain superior results over hard voting. In this case, both voting methods were used. We assembled our strong boosting classifier and weighted Bi-GRUATT by means of soft voting.

4 Experiment and Results

4.1 Pre-processing

Twitter messages include a great deal of irrelevant information that is useless for capturing text message features. Prior to building our model, we utilized a series of operations to normalize tweet messages, divided into the following steps.

Lowercase. We integrated all text words by converting them to lowercase.

Replace Emoticons. We began by pre-processing tweet messages with emoticon replacement. Typographic emoticon symbols that appear sideways, resembling facial expressions, such as :), :-), and (: all mean "smiley face", while :-(, :(, and):

mean "frowny face". In spite of the fact that these emoticons could barely be recognized in the pre-embedding vocabulary, they visibly advanced or changed the text message interpretation. We identified these emoticons and replaced them with the words "smile" or "sad" in the English task, and "sonreír" and "triste" in the Spanish task.

Remove marks. With Twitter as a large social communication platform, we detected user operations in order to remove them:

- remove URL link;

- do nothing with "@" and "@user";

- remove hashtag mark and retweet mark, such as "#", "rt", "&";

- remove numbers and other irrelevant punctuation marks, such as question mark "?", exclamatory mark "!", and quotation.

Revise elongated words. Incorrect words remained in the training samples,, elongated with a single letter, such as "Helloooooo". We searched for words containing repeated letters consecutively more than three times, and revised the number of letter replications to one.

Abbreviation. People are likely to use abbreviations of certain phrase to create Twitter message, and we changed these abbreviations back into original phrases in the English task. Above 60 common abbreviations of twitter were replaced in the pre-processing. For example, "thx" was changed back to "thanks" and "ASAP" to "as soon as possible". We determined to skip this step in the Spanish task because we were not familiar with Spanish or its abbreviations.

4.2 Implementation

Following preprocessing, we used a multi-language tokenizer tool, Unitok[4], for tokenization of each task, and then calculated the token number of the longest sentences in the training datasets. All tokens that could be recognized in the provided word embedding were converted into a 300-dimension vector, which would be filled in with zero if it was still unrecognized with the prefix "#". All training samples were padded out to the same length L, which is 40 in English and 38 in Spanish.

We implemented our model using the Python Keras library with a TensorFlow backend. The

____
[4]`http://corpus.tools/wiki/Unitok`

properties of our Bi-GRUATT model were as follows.

1. The GRU dropout was set to 0.2, which was the same as the dropout layer following the attention layer.

2. The active function of the dense layer was $tanh$ with a length of 100, and $softmax$ was used to output the prediction label.

3. Instead of using $Sequential.fit$ to train the model, the $Sequential.fit\_generator$ was used for huge training samples in order to solve the memory problem.

4. The optimizer $Adam$ and loss function cross entropy were used to deal with this multi-labeled task.

5. The training epoch was dependent on the early stopping monitor. If the training loss had not improved in the latest 10 epochs, the training process stopped. Both training processes in task 2 exhibited extremely slow improvement in every epoch. In English, the training epoch was approximately 180 to 230, and 280 to 400 in Spanish.

As the ratio of the majority to minority classes could be as high as 10:1, a simple means of enhancing the minority class performance is a cost-sensitive method that applies different costs for mis-classification errors to each class. Usually, there is a high cost for the minority class and a low cost for the majority class. We balanced the training samples with various class weights, and used these to train the cost-sensitive models in the English and Spanish tasks.

Boosting and voting were implemented using the AdaBoosting and Voting classifiers of scikit-learn (Pedregosa et al., 2011) in Python. During the boosting processing, we applied the Bi-GRUATT model with an equal sample weight of $1/N$ (where N is the total number of training samples) as the base estimator, and then iteratively trained a stronger classifier by paying more attention to mis-classified samples. The boosting learning rate was set to 0.001 and the number of estimators was dependent on the result of macro F1. The boosting model would be stopped if it already had three weak classifiers. Only the strong classifier in the boosting process would be used in the voting ensemble, and weak classifiers were ignored.

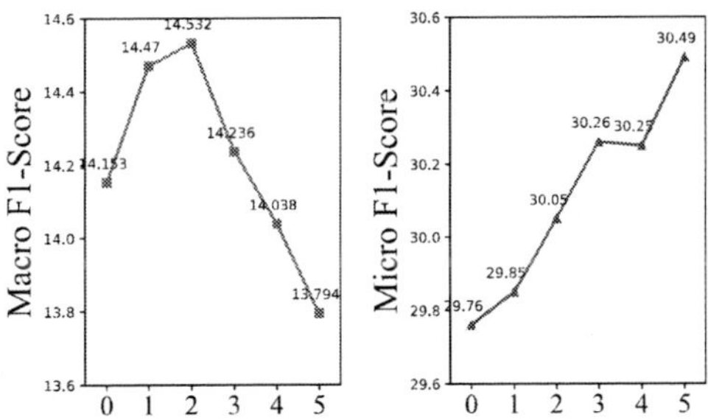

Figure 2: Macro F1 and Micro F1 of boosting classifiers in Spanish. (X-axis means the number of boosting iteration, and number '0' refers to the initial model which was trained with equal sample weight.)

4.3 Evaluation

For evaluation purposes, the official results were based on the macro F1 score for the two tasks. The F1 score was calculated as follows:

$$F_i = \frac{2\pi_i \rho_i}{\pi_i + \rho_i} \tag{1}$$

$$F_{macro} = \frac{\sum_{i=0}^{M} F_i}{M} \tag{2}$$

where F_i is the F1 score of the i-th class, and π_i and ρ_i denote the precision and recall of the i-th class, respectively. The macro average provides an equal weight to all the classes, regardless of how many samples belong to it. The micro average provides equal weights to all the samples, thereby favoring the performance of the majority classes. The macro F1 as well as micro F1 score were utilized to evaluate the performance of every model in our system.

4.4 Results

As the English datasets are fivefold the Spanish ones, we adjusted the system model and its parameters with the Spanish datasets in order to save time. We handled the two subtasks in the same manner; however, the results indicated that not all methods were appropriate for both the English and Spanish tasks.

Subtask-2: Spanish Emoji Prediction

Boosting had generated only six strong or weak classifiers, and the variation tendencies of the macro and micro F1 scores are displayed in Fig. 2.

Subtask-2	Macro F1	Micro F1
Boost_0	14.153	29.76
Boost_1	14.47	29.85
Boost_2	14.532	30.05
Soft Voting	**15.016**	**31.55**
Bi-GRUATT_1	13.768	18.93
Bi-GRUATT_2	14.144	18.86
Hard Voting	**16.015**	**30.22**

Table 2: Results of each model and voting ensemble in Spanish.

38.03	29.39	52.69	0	14.93
24.72	35.11	13.68	8.86	28.43
12.99	1.87	0	2.43	0
14.19	19.77	2.82	4.38	

Table 3: Macro F1 of each emoji label in Spanish.

It was found that, as the iteration times increased, the micro F1 score (accuracy) of the boosting system continuously increased, while the macro F1 score was increased in the first three iterations and then decreased in the following iterations. As the macro F1 score provides the official evaluation index, we identified the first three strong boost classifiers for the further ensemble. In the voting ensemble part, the three strong boost classifiers were used to achieve stronger classification by means of soft voting, and eventually, we integrated the soft voting result and the results of the two basic Bi-GRUATT models trained with a balanced class weight (same model but trained twice). The results of these models can be seen in Table 2. Soft voting achieved a 0.9% improvement in the macro F1 score, while the hard voting achieved 1% compared to the soft voting results.

Furthermore, hard voting, which provided the final result, demonstrated a 2% improvement in the weighted Bi-GRUATT model. Table 3 displays the macro F1 for each emoji label.

Subtask-1: English Emoji Prediction

Similar to the process of subtask 2, we obtained four boosting classifiers, the variation tendencies of which are illustrated in Fig. 3. The macro F1

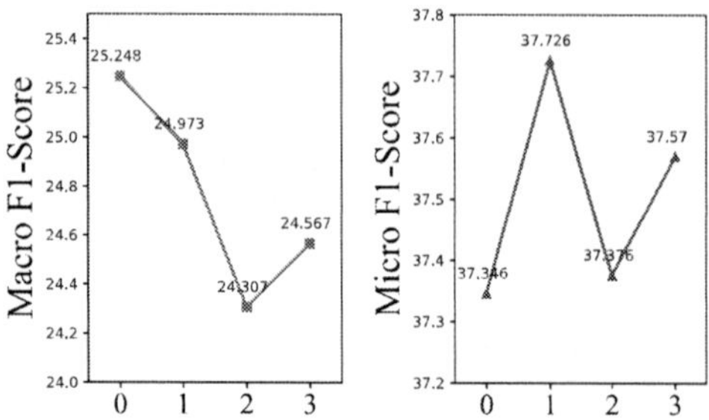

Figure 3: Macro F1 and Micro F1 of boosting classifiers in English. (X-axis means the number of boosting iteration, and number '0' refers to the initial model which was trained with equal sample weight.)

Subtask-1	Macro F1	Micro F1
Boost_0	25.248	37.346
Bi-GRUATT_1	25.656	27.556
Bi-GRUATT_2	25.552	27.28
Hard Voting	**28.112**	**35.196**

Table 4: Results of each model and voting ensemble in English.

score was decreased following each iteration. We could not conduct soft voting with only one strong classifier, but carried out the hard voting directly. Table 4 presents the results of the weighted Bi-GRUATT and hard voting. The hard voting in the English task demonstrated a 2.5% improvement in the weighted Bi-GRUATT and 2.9% improvement in the Bi-GRUATT without class weights. The macro F1 for each emoji label is displayed in Table 5.

All above-mentioned results were obtained following the competition, and we changed the learning rate from 0.01 to 0.001 for increased boost classifiers. The competition submission only used two boost classifiers for ensemble in Spanish and one was utilized in English. We ranked 16th among 48 teams in the English task and 13th among 21 teams in the Spanish task[5].

As indicated in Tables 4 and 5, predictions of similar smiley face emojis (😍😂😎😊😄 in Spanish and 😂😊😂😍 in English) exhibited unstratified results. There were not many characteristics to distinguish these from one another, as they all meant a happy feeling, and people had a different

[5]Results of all teams can be found in https://goo.gl/P515KW

❤️	😍	😂	💕	🔥
44.53	30.6	43.98	15.79	54.17
😊	😎	✨	💜	😘
10.84	17.96	31.46	17.53	16.95
📷	🇺🇸	☀️	💙	😜
28.09	55.64	37.7	11.59	12.1
💯	😂	🎄	📸	😉
25.22	11.68	66.86	24.97	4.59

Table 5: Macro F1 of each emoji label in English.

understanding and favorite emojis, which could cause certain confusion problems. Compared to the confused smiley face emojis, the label 🎄 demonstrated the best result, although it was a minority class. It was easy to predict, owing to the label 🎄 having an obvious feature to recognize, such as "tree", "Christmas Tree" or everything relevant to Christmas.

Another confused set of emojis were series of heart emojis, particularly 💕❤️💜💙❤️, and in subtask 2, some of these labels even obtained a zero result. This illustrates that the model preferred to predict the highest majority class of the same series, such as ❤️ rather than its actual emoji 💕, 💜 or other heart.

5 Discussion

In this section, we briefly discuss several points that may enhance our system results. For time reasons, we have not validated these yet.

Pre-processing

1. We simply removed hashtag mark "#", however, there were numerous unrecognized hashtag words, such as "Iamhappy", "I_am_happy" or "I-Am-Happy". A preferable method is decomposing the hashtag to invert it into a sequence of words that would enrich the information of the sentence samples (Billal et al., 2016).

2. We did not deal with the mis-spelled words, and changed all elongated words into the without repeated letters that would create mistake words, like "foooood".

Model

1. As the official evaluation index is the macro F1 score, we should set the initial sample weight to be the same as the balanced class weight in the boosting process.

2. We only trained less than 10 estimators in the boosting, which may be too small to determine the boost variation tendency in this task.

3. We only used one base model to ensemble. Assembling with different model types may achieve improved results, such as CNN, a combination of CNN and LSTM, and random forest.

6   Conclusion

In this brief paper, we have presented the system we used to compete in the SemEval-2018 task 2: Emoji Prediction in English and Spanish. Our submission system was based on a Bi-GRU model with an attention mechanism, and we aimed to ensemble the base model with multi-method boosting and voting in order to achieve superior performance. In our work, multi-ensemble exhibited a 2 to 3% improvement in the task results.

In the future, we plan to validate the points in the Discussion section in order to verify their influence of them, and add useful points to our system to implement an improved model for emoji prediction.

Acknowledgments

This work was supported by the National Natural Science Foundation of China (NSFC) under Grant No.61702443 and No.61762091, and in part by Educational Commission of Yunnan Province of China under Grant No.2017ZZX030. We would like to thank task organisers and the anonymous reviewers for their helping and constructive comments.

References

Dzmitry Bahdanau, Kyunghyun Cho, and Yoshua Bengio. 2014. Neural machine translation by jointly learning to align and translate. *CoRR*, abs/1409.0473.

Francesco Barbieri, Miguel Ballesteros, and Horacio Saggion. 2017. Are emojis predictable? *CoRR*, abs/1702.07285.

Francesco Barbieri, Jose Camacho-Collados, Francesco Ronzano, Luis Espinosa-Anke, Miguel Ballesteros, Valerio Basile, Viviana Patti, and Horacio Saggion. 2018. SemEval-2018 Task 2: Multilingual Emoji Prediction. In *Proceedings of the 12th International Workshop on Semantic Evaluation (SemEval-2018)*, New Orleans, LA, United States. Association for Computational Linguistics.

Belainine Billal, Alexsandro Fonseca, and Fatiha Sadat. 2016. Named entity recognition and hashtag decomposition to improve the classification of tweets. In *Proceedings of COLING*, pages 102–111.

KyungHyun Cho, Bart van Merrienboer, Dzmitry Bahdanau, and Yoshua Bengio. 2014. On the properties of neural machine translation: Encoder-decoder approaches. *CoRR*, abs/1409.1259.

Mathieu Cliche. 2017. Bb_twtr at semeval-2017 task 4: Twitter sentiment analysis with cnns and lstms. In *Proceedings of SemEval*, pages 573–580.

Ronan Collobert, Jason Weston, Lon Bottou, Michael Karlen, Koray Kavukcuoglu, and Pavel P. Kuksa. 2011. Natural language processing (almost) from scratch. *Journal of Machine Learning Research*, 12:2493–2537.

Sepp Hochreiter and Jürgen Schmidhuber. 1997. Long short-term memory. *Neural computation*, 9(8):1735–1780.

Ozan Irsoy and Claire Cardie. 2014. Opinion mining with deep recurrent neural networks. In *Proceedings of the Conference on Empirical Methods in Natural Language Processing(EMNLP)*, pages 720–728.

Petra Kralj Novak, Jasmina Smailović, Borut Sluban, and Igor Mozetič. 2015. Sentiment of emojis. *CoRR*, abs/1509.07761.

Fabian Pedregosa, Gaël Varoquaux, Alexandre Gramfort, Vincent Michel, Bertrand Thirion, Olivier Grisel, Mathieu Blondel, Peter Prettenhofer, Ron Weiss, and Vincent Dubourg. 2011. Scikit-learn: Machine learning in python. *Journal of Machine Learning Research*, 12(Oct):2825–2830.

Jeffrey Pennington, Richard Socher, and Christopher D Manning. 2014. Glove: Global vectors for word representation. In *Proceedings of the Conference on Empirical Methods in Natural Language Processing(EMNLP)*, volume 14, pages 1532–1543.

Colin Raffel and Daniel P. W. Ellis. 2015. Feedforward networks with attention can solve some long-term memory problems. *CoRR*, abs/1512.08756.

DUTH at SemEval-2018 Task 2: Emoji Prediction in Tweets

Dimitrios Effrosynidis **Georgios Peikos** **Symeon Symeonidis** **Avi Arampatzis**

Database & Information Retrieval research unit,
Department of Electrical & Computer Engineering,
Democritus University of Thrace, Xanthi 67100, Greece
`{deffrosy,georpeik,ssymeoni,avi}@ee.duth.gr`

Abstract

This paper describes the approach that was developed for SemEval 2018 Task 2 (Multilingual Emoji Prediction) by the DUTH Team. First, we employed a combination of preprocessing techniques to reduce the noise of tweets and produce a number of features. Then, we built several N-grams, to represent the combination of word and emojis. Finally, we trained our system with a tuned LinearSVC classifier. Our approach in the leaderboard ranked 18th amongst 48 teams.

1 Introduction

Emojis are used in everyday life to express words or feelings of microblogging users. They are commonly placed at the end of a sentence or alone. In this paper, we show how our emoji prediction framework was applied to SemEval-2018 Task 2 (Multilingual Emoji Prediction) (Barbieri et al., 2018), specifically on Subtask 1 (Emoji Prediction in English).

In the last few years, many studies concentrated on emoji prediction and analysis. The prediction of emojis, the connection of emojis and words, and their separation from content-based tweet messages, based on Long ShortTerm Memory networks (LSTMs), was examined by Barbieri et al. (2017). The combination of emojis and sentiment was investigated by Novak et al. (2015), who developed the first emoji sentiment lexicon and created a sentiment map of the 751 most frequently used emojis. The study of Barbieri et al. (2016) tested several skip-gram word embedding models to measure the difference in performance between machine-learning models and human annotation. Na'aman et al. (2017) analyzed the viability of a trained classifier to differentiate between those emojis utilized as semantic substance words and those utilized as paralinguistic or emotional multimodal markers. Miller et al. (2017) investigated the hypothesis of previous works that emojis in their regular textual contexts would generously reduce and lead to miscommunication, but they found no such evidence; the potential for miscommunication appeared to be the same.

The rest of this paper is organized as follows. Section 2 describes the architecture of our system and the dataset. In Section 3, we discuss the various parameters that were used to fine-tune the system, and present the performance of our framework. In Section 4, we lay out our main conclusions and research issues for further investigation.

2 System Description

The principal goal of SemEval-2018 Task 2 - Subtask 1 was emoji prediction in English. The framework we utilized consists of a bag of-words representation and N-gram extraction. We used the popular machine learning tool for Python, called Scikit-Learn (Pedregosa et al., 2011).

2.1 Preprocessing

For the preprocessing of tweets, we were guided by the results of our previous research (Effrosynidis et al., 2017). We used the effective combination of the following techniques:

- Replace URLs and User Mentions to the tags 'URL' and 'AT USER', as the majority of tweets on Twitter contain a URL and mentions which are considered noise.

- Replace Contractions, as it reduces the dimensionality of the problem and improves speed and accuracy according to the above-mentioned paper.

- Remove Numbers, because they do not contain any sentiment.

Proceedings of the 12th International Workshop on Semantic Evaluation (SemEval-2018), pages 466–469
New Orleans, Louisiana, June 5–6, 2018. ©2018 Association for Computational Linguistics

Label	Sentences	Unique Words	Words/Sentence	Tweets	User tags	Hashtags	Unique Hashtags
0	160220	110305	7.191	107669	20471	110655	55287
1	75706	70430	7.351	51923	11097	57839	32922
2	75879	69280	7.881	50988	13884	45182	28984
3	37068	36928	8.113	27517	4284	17984	12128
4	35327	45940	7.693	24625	10164	28940	19140
5	35347	37710	7.598	23318	5204	20811	13802
6	30406	38420	7.418	21323	4097	24013	15842
7	24859	31386	8.196	18388	3316	15783	10215
8	23623	28479	7.585	17024	2508	14594	10157
9	24983	28742	7.125	16167	4405	13862	9496
10	25705	35760	6.895	16045	11186	19929	12237
11	22136	25142	6.930	15365	2012	24937	10192
12	18482	20883	7.441	13882	1282	12848	7478
13	18538	24496	7.524	12981	2382	11317	8158
14	21060	28277	7.900	13472	3023	13113	9831
15	18353	26909	7.835	13408	3210	12886	9206
16	20531	27494	7.360	13094	3084	13044	9582
17	18631	20292	7.032	12853	1477	11607	6338
18	20164	29989	7.116	13255	8918	15628	10065
19	18900	27230	7.622	12307	2421	12653	9359
SUM	725918	764092	7.490	495604	118425	497625	300419

Table 1: Statistics per emoji.

- Replace Repetitions of Punctuation, which merges in the same feature the intensity of emotions. For example, if we find more than two consecutive exclamation, question or stop marks, we replace them with a single one.

2.2 Dataset

The training and testing datasets were provided by the organizers. The training set contained approximately $500,000$ tweets, where each tweet contained a single emoji, before they removed it and set it as class label. That emoji is used as the class label for the particular tweet.

We extracted various statistics for the dataset as it can be seen in Table 1. Some class labels contain more sentences per tweet, like label 10 (■) and 0 (♥). We also observe that the emoji ✔ has on average much fewer hashtags per tweet, while the emoji ■ has much more. All the other emojis range within reasonable limits. The emojis with labels 7 (☀) and 3 (✔) are expressed using more words on average, while the emojis 10 (■) and 11 (■) are expressed with fewer words.

All the above observations are important to understand the dataset and how people are using each emoji. One can use these statistics in order to create more features and test them to see the changes in classification accuracy. For example, one can count the words of each new sentence for classification, and compare them with the ones derived from the training dataset.

In our study, we compared several machine learning algorithms (Ridge, Logistic Regression, Passive-Aggressive, and Linear SVC), and three different word to vector representations (tf-idf Vectorizer, count Vectorizer, and hashing Vectorizer). The macro F-measure score was computed for 10-folds cross-validation on the training set and on the trial set while using the training set for training. We employed word n-grams and character n-grams (n ranging from 1 to 4), with the latter ones performing poorly.

3 Experimental Results

In this section, we describe the different classifiers and vectorizers used and present our results.

	Macro-averaged F-measure			
Vectorizer	**Ridge**	**Logistic Regression**	**Passive-Aggressive**	**LinearSVC**
tfidfVectorizer	26.2	25.1	24.0	26.6
countVectorizer	25.9	26.7	20.9	25.5
hashingVectorizer	24.6	23.0	23.6	25.9

Table 2: Results per classifier and vectorizer using 10-fold unigrams.

3.1 Classifiers

In order to gain a better perspective on the problem, we trained four different classification algorithms. We test each classifier comparing their macro F-measure score. We choose LinearSVC, because of the stability we noticed in the results it returned. Below we discuss every classifier:

- Ridge: an algorithm belonging to the Generalized Linear Models family. Text classification problems tend to be quite high dimensional, and high dimensional problems are likely to be linearly separable; this is one reason why Ridge performs quite well.

- Logistic Regression: despite its name, it is used for classification and fits a linear model as well. In the multiclass case, the training algorithm uses the one-vs-rest (OvR) scheme.

- Passive-Aggressive: belongs to a family of algorithms for large-scale learning, which does not require a learning rate and includes a regularization parameter C. On the one hand, the aggressive mode of the algorithm means that if an incorrect classification occurs, the model updates to adjust to this misclassified example. On the other hand, the model stays unchanged in every correct classification and this is the passive behavior of the algorithm (Crammer et al., 2006).

- Linear SVC: the purpose of this algorithm is to fit the data by finding a set of hyperplanes that separate space into areas representing classes. The most efficient way is considered to be the max distance between data points and the hyperplane.

3.2 Vectorizers

Nowadays, one can find many vectorizers to use in order to extract features. We used the following three vectorizers provided by Python's Scikit-Learn library (Pedregosa et al., 2011), in order to transform tweets into vectors of features.

- tf-idf Vectorizer: a vectorizer which scales the term frequency counts in each tweet by penalising terms that appear more frequently across the dataset.

- count Vectorizer: converts the collection of tweets to a matrix of token counts.

- hashing Vectorizer: a vectorizer which applies a hashing function to term frequency counts in each document. This vectorizer leads to a sparse matrix holding token occurrence counts (or binary occurrence information).

Each vectorizer we used is efficient under certain circumstances. In addition, we noticed that the combination of the vectorizer and classification algorithm is crucial for our problem. In our work, as we can see in Table 2, the combination of countVectorizer and Logistic Regression leads to the best result. However, the tfidfVectorizer achieves greater results than the countVectorizer and the hashingVectorizer in the majority of the algorithms; for this reason, we proceeded with the tfidfVectorizer.

3.3 Evaluation Results

We evaluate the performance of our system with the macro F-measure score. The macro F-measure score gives equal weight to each emoji category, regardless of its class size. The F-measure per emoji class is the harmonic mean of the precision and recall of the class:

$$\text{F-measure} = \frac{2(\text{Precision} \times \text{Recall})}{\text{Precision} + \text{Recall}} .$$

The macro-average F-measure score is obtained by taking the average of F-measure values across emoji classes:

$$\text{macro F-measure} = \frac{1}{M} \sum_{n=1}^{M} \text{F-score(n)} ,$$

where M is the total number of classes.

In Table 3 we present the macro F-measure score of tfidfVectorizer combined with LinearSVC classification algorithm. In the first column, the results of 10-folds cross validation on the training set are presented. In the second column we present the results when training with the training data and testing with the trial data. As it can be seen, four-grams performance on trial data has the highest value, but trigrams perform better on 10-folds cross-validation. This is the reason we used trigrams to train our model for the submitted runs.

	10-folds Training	Trial
word-unigrams	26.6	46.8
word-bigrams	29.3	61.4
word-trigrams	29.4	63.7
word-fourgrams	29.2	64.4

Table 3: F-measure results for word N-grams.

4 Conclusions

In this paper, we presented the framework we used to participate in the SemEval-2018 emoji prediction competition. We used a tfidfVectorizer combined with a LinearSVC classification algorithm, employing word tri-grams, to train our model. Our team ranked in the 18th place among 48 teams.

For future work, it would be interesting to test Neural Network approaches, to use emoji sentiment lexica (Novak et al., 2015), or additionally include more features. Furthermore, it would likewise be intriguing to investigate the miscommunication of emojis in their natural textual contexts.

References

Francesco Barbieri, Miguel Ballesteros, and Horacio Saggion. 2017. Are emojis predictable? In *Proceedings of the 15th Conference of the European Chapter of the Association for Computational Linguistics: Volume 2, Short Papers*, pages 105–111. Association for Computational Linguistics.

Francesco Barbieri, Jose Camacho-Collados, Francesco Ronzano, Luis Espinosa-Anke, Miguel Ballesteros, Valerio Basile, Viviana Patti, and Horacio Saggion. 2018. SemEval-2018 Task 2: Multilingual Emoji Prediction. In *Proceedings of the 12th International Workshop on Semantic Evaluation (SemEval-2018)*, New Orleans, LA, United States. Association for Computational Linguistics.

Francesco Barbieri, Francesco Ronzano, and Horacio Saggion. 2016. What does this emoji mean? A vector space skip-gram model for twitter emojis. In *Proceedings of the Tenth International Conference on Language Resources and Evaluation LREC 2016, Portorož, Slovenia, May 23-28, 2016.* European Language Resources Association (ELRA).

Koby Crammer, Ofer Dekel, Joseph Keshet, Shai Shalev-Shwartz, and Yoram Singer. 2006. Online passive-aggressive algorithms. *Journal of Machine Learning Research*, 7:551–585.

Dimitrios Effrosynidis, Symeon Symeonidis, and Avi Arampatzis. 2017. A comparison of pre-processing techniques for twitter sentiment analysis. In *Research and Advanced Technology for Digital Libraries - 21st International Conference on Theory and Practice of Digital Libraries, TPDL 2017, Thessaloniki, Greece, September 18-21, 2017, Proceedings*, volume 10450 of *Lecture Notes in Computer Science*, pages 394–406. Springer.

Hannah Jean Miller, Daniel Kluver, Jacob Thebault-Spieker, Loren G. Terveen, and Brent J. Hecht. 2017. Understanding emoji ambiguity in context: The role of text in emoji-related miscommunication. In *Proceedings of the Eleventh International Conference on Web and Social Media, ICWSM 2017, Montréal, Québec, Canada, May 15-18, 2017.*, pages 152–161. AAAI Press.

Noa Na'aman, Hannah Provenza, and Orion Montoya. 2017. Varying linguistic purposes of emoji in (twitter) context. In *Proceedings of the 55th Annual Meeting of the Association for Computational Linguistics, ACL 2017, Vancouver, Canada, July 30 - August 4, Student Research Workshop*, pages 136–141. Association for Computational Linguistics.

Petra Kralj Novak, Jasmina Smailovic, Borut Sluban, and Igor Mozetic. 2015. Sentiment of emojis. *CoRR*, abs/1509.07761.

F. Pedregosa, G. Varoquaux, A. Gramfort, V. Michel, B. Thirion, O. Grisel, M. Blondel, P. Prettenhofer, R. Weiss, V. Dubourg, J. Vanderplas, A. Passos, D. Cournapeau, M. Brucher, M. Perrot, and E. Duchesnay. 2011. Scikit-learn: Machine learning in Python. *Journal of Machine Learning Research*, 12:2825–2830.

TAJJEB at SemEval-2018 Task 2: Traditional Approaches Just Do the Job with Emoji Prediction

Angelo Basile
University of Groningen / The Netherlands
University of Malta / Msida, Malta
`angelo.basile.17@um.edu.mt`

Kenny W. Lino
University of the Basque Country /
San Sebastián, Spain
University of Malta / Msida, Malta
`kenny.lino.17@um.edu.mt`

Abstract

Emojis are widely used on social media; thus understanding their meaning is important for both practical purposes (e.g. opinion mining, sentiment detection) and theoretical purposes (e.g. How do different L1 speakers use them?, Do they have specific syntax?). This paper presents a set of models that predict an emoji given a tweet as a part of the SemEval-2018 Task 2: Multilingual Emoji Prediction. We built different models and we found that the test results were very different from the validation results.

1 Introduction

To some extent, Twitter can be considered a huge corpus and researchers exploit it in many different ways to get a proxy for various types of annotations. Purver and Battersby (2012) use distant supervision on tweets to build an emotion detection system; Bollen et al. (2011) show that it is possible to use Twitter data to predict the stock market; Mohammad et al. (2016) build a corpus from tweets for modelling stance.

Social media in general are very popular for building corpora for sentiment-related tasks since the users make a wide use of emojis. Pool and Nissim (2016) show that it is possible to achieve state-of-the-art performance in sentiment classification using only automatically gathered data.

The wide use of emojis on the web calls for systems that can automatically process them. When performing opinion mining tasks, for instance, it can be the case that all we have is just an emoji. For example, a single emoji could be used as a reply to an advertisement of a certain product; thus, being able to get the meaning of that emoji is important. Felbo et al. (2017) shows that given a text, it is possible to successfully automatically suggest the most appropriate emoji that can accompany that text.

In this paper we describe our participation in the SemEval-2018 Task 2: Multilingual Emoji Prediction (Barbieri et al., 2018), a challenge that originates from the work of (Barbieri et al., 2017). The task is structured as follows: given a tweet that originally contained one and only one emoji, predict that emoji; the emoji is removed and given as a training label.

We experimented using three different approaches: first we use a shallow feature representation with two different algorithms (Naïve-Bayes and Support Vector Machine); then we experimented with a dense feature representation (i.e. word embeddings) and a deep neural classifier; lastly, we modeled the problem as a translation problem (i.e. treating English and Spanish as the source language and 'Emoji' as the target language) using a state-of-the-art neural translation system to predict the labels as translated sentences.

To summarize, our main contributions presented in this paper are three machine learning models that predict an emoji given some text. We confirm a fact that is well known in the literature, i.e. that neural models can give good results but hyper-parameter tuning is a hard task and if it is not successful, then a good linear classifier with a bag-of-words representation can easily outperform the neural model. Our best English system was ranked 8th in SemEval Shared Task and our best Spanish system was ranked 4th[1].

2 Data

Both the training and testing data are tweet collections: overall, there are 500k English tweets and 100k Spanish tweets, provided as two distinct datasets. These tweets are accompanied by two

---

[1] We submitted on January 10, 2018. Our submission was made under the name 'The Fabulous EM-LCT Team from Malta'.

Proceedings of the 12th International Workshop on Semantic Evaluation (SemEval-2018), pages 470–476
New Orleans, Louisiana, June 5–6, 2018. ©2018 Association for Computational Linguistics

sets of labels — one per language — and these labels are the emojis that were originally in the tweet and later removed.

The English label set consists of 20 emojis, while the Spanish label set consists of 19 emojis.

We manually inspected some portions of the datasets and found that the English set contains some Spanish tweets and *vice versa*: this is due to the fact that the tweets were collected automatically using geographical information associated with the account of the user who wrote the tweet. We decided to ignore this fact and assume that the actual test set will also contain some noise. We did not perform any systematic language identification experiment since after the manual inspection it seemed to us that this would not be a problem.

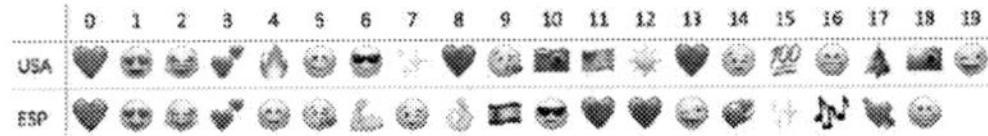

Figure 1: The label set for both English (USA) and Spanish (SPA).

The distribution of the labels is highly skewed for both English and Spanish: Figure 2 shows that the most frequent label (i.e. the red heart) is much more frequent than the others.

We decided to conduct experiments with both the original skewed dataset and a balanced version of it. To balance the dataset, we randomly sample from all classes a number of tweets which is equal to the size of the smallest class.

2.1 Normalization

We decided not to perform any sort of normalization on the dataset. The reason for this is that we think that the information that is located at the sub-token level would probably get lost with normalization (e.g. 'amaaaaazing' vs 'amazing'). Character-level differences can be important in helping deciding which emoji is the most appropriate one. For instance, we can imagine that someone who writes 'amaaaaaazing' is more prone to choose a more sophisticated and less common emoji (e.g. a purple heart), while someone who writes in a more sober style would probably pick only the most common emojis.

Furthermore, considering the domain (i.e. Twitter), it is very hard to properly normalize text.

3 Experiments

We performed two groups of experiments: for one group we used a shallow feature representation (i.e. bag-of-words), and for the other we used a dense feature representation (i.e. word embeddings). In the following sections we present these two groups of experiments.

3.1 General Experimental Set-up

In order to facilitate our work, we utilized Python 3.6.3 and set up a Python working environment using `pipenv` to make our experiments easily reproducible; for the same reason we are releasing several Jupyter notebooks containing all the code that we wrote[2]. To train our models, we utilized the standard machine learning package, `scikit-learn` (Pedregosa et al., 2011) for the models using a shallow feature representation. The neural models were built using Keras (Chollet et al., 2015). We used OpenNMT (Klein et al., 2017) to model the problem as a translation problem.

3.2 Traditional BoW Modelling

For our first set of experiments, we chose two different algorithms for text classification and common bag-of-words features.

Algorithms For our algorithms, we worked with Naïve-Bayes and Support Vector Machines. We chose these algorithms in particular because of their success in previous work such as in Wang and Manning (2012).

Features For our features, we worked with the raw counts of each word as well as the tf-idf scores, and n-grams. We used tf-idf to give more weight to the more prominent words within the tweets, and less weight to the more common words, while we used n-grams to capture sequences of words.

3.2.1 Baseline

We established our baseline by using a bag-of-words approach and the Naïve-Bayes classifier with five-fold cross validation. We chose this as our baseline as we felt that this was the most simple — but still reasonably strong — approach.

3.2.2 Dimensionality Reduction

As a test, we also looked at the effects of dimensionality reduction using truncated singular value

---

[2]They can be found here at: https://github.com/anbasile/emojiprediction

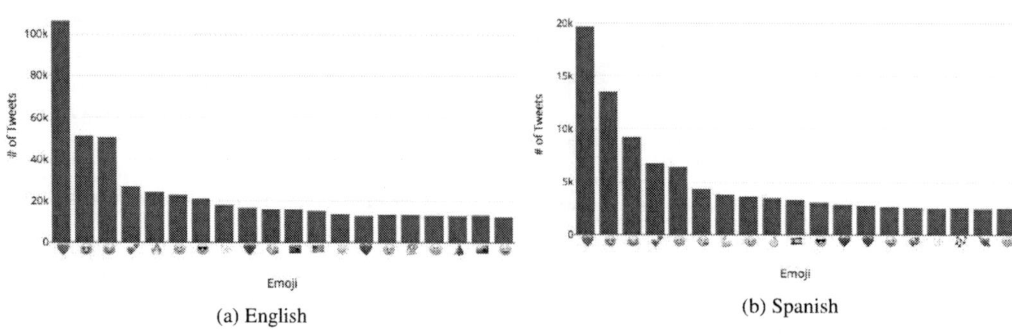

(a) English   (b) Spanish

Figure 2: Distribution of emojis in the English and the Spanish datasets.

decomposition (SVD) (also referred to as latent semantic analysis (LSA) when used on textual data) on our best support vector machine model. This was only done with the support vector machine model as it was not possible to do it with the Naïve-Bayes classifier.

We hypothesized that SVD could potentially be useful as it would be able to model topics within the data. If we could model topics within the text, then it would be likely that certain topics would align with certain emojis.

To run the test, we used 10% of our data with dimensions of $n = 100$ and $n = 500$ on our best unbalanced model — the support vector machine model with tf-idf, bi-grams, and POS-tagging. We chose to only use 10% of the data as the runtime of utilizing SVD on the whole English dataset was particularly long.

3.3 Neural Models

In order to take advantage of the large dataset, we decided to try to model the problem using a neural network, which usually requires many instances to be trained properly.

We performed two sets of experiments: first, we trained a simple recurrent neural network. From there, we moved to a more complex recurrent network using bidirectional long short term memory (LSTM) layers in order to account for context from both the right and the left side of words; we then used an already optimized sequence-2-sequence model to model the problem as a translation problem and effectively treating emoji as a language.

The main advantage of using neural networks for processing text is that the feature extraction process and the classification (or structured prediction process) can be optimized at the same time, possibly resulting in better performance.

Embeddings Word embeddings — one of the possible ways to extract feature from text — turned out to be very helpful in NLP and some of its properties (dense, high dimensional format) make it suitable to be used with neural networks. Baroni et al. (2014) have shown that word embeddings almost always perform better when compared to systems using the traditional bag-of-words approach.

To create the embeddings for our experiments, we used the Embedding layer provided in the Keras framework. This method does not make use of the most recent advancements in the field — as those described in Mikolov et al. (2013) — but it has the advantage of being fast and easily understandable.

3.3.1 Predicting Emojis with a Neural Classifier

Using Keras, we set up a network with the structure represented in Figure 3. One way to interpret this kind of modelling is to consider it as a list of matrices. The first layer is the embedding layer, where every node is a word, which is represented as an embedding; the 2 hidden layers are what makes the model able to discover eventual non-linear relationships; the last layer consists of a softmax function that gives in output a vector of probabilities: choosing the most probable class allows to get the most probable emoji.

By making the second hidden layer smaller in length than the external layers, the model implicitly performs a process of dimensionality reduction which allows it to eventually learn latent information (e.g. topic, style, etc.) present in the data.

Furthermore, following the work of Srivastava et al. (2014), we apply to our network a drop-out layer in order to avoid over-fitting and improve the capability of the network to generalize the results.

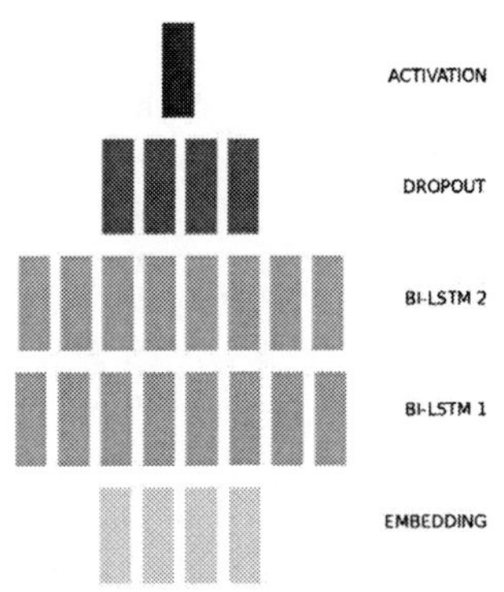

Figure 3: The structure of the neural network.

3.3.2 Seq2Seq Modelling

To some extent, we can say that emojis compress — or tend to compress — all the meaning of the English or Spanish texts that accompanies them. This suggests that the problem can be modelled as a translation problem, where the source language is either English or Spanish and the target language is the emoji language.

We use a state-of-the-art machine translation system and consider our emoji-annotated text as a parallel corpus, having English or Spanish as the source language, and the emojis as the target language.

We use the default network from the OpenNMT framework. This network consists of 2 LSTM layers with 500 hidden units each; furthermore, this implementation includes an attention layer that weights the importance of the different words in translating to the target language[3].

We trained the same network for both English and Spanish — building one model for each language — and we got similar results, even though the English dataset is considerably larger than the

Spanish one. Surprisingly, the network learned for both languages that the syntax of the emoji language — so to say — specify that only one token can be used for each sentence.

4 Evaluation

4.1 Metrics

In order to quantify our results for the shallow representation models, we chose to use F-score as our main metric, as F-score is fairly standard and gives us a more unbiased view of the results.

With the dense representation and translation models, we utilized accuracy and perplexity as we could not extract precision and recall for these models for time constraints and technical issues. For the neural networks we did not perform cross-validation since it would have been too costly to perform; however, we use a development set during training and we tested on a blind test set when we finished training.

4.2 Results

Investigating the results of the experiments, we were able to confirm some of our linguistic intuitions.

First, it is evident that the best model for both the English and Spanish dataset based on macro F1 score was the most complex SVM model using tf-idf normalization, part-of-speech tagging and bi-grams. We see that POS-tagging added a substantial increase when comparing the SVM+tfidf model to the SVM + tfidf + 2grams model with an increase of 11% and 5% in the English and Spanish dataset respectively. This suggests that POS-tagging provides key information that helps the classifiers (at least SVMs).

However, dimensionality reduction — with $n = 100$ and $n = 500$ — did not prove to be as successful as we had hypothesized. Instead, we found that it had negative effects on the models as seen in Table 1. This is likely because we remove too much information that distinguishes the individual classes.

Table 1 and Table 2 describe the results for English and Spanish respectively. The models were trained and five-fold cross-validated with various configurations[4]. Models with * were with the bal-

---

[3]We use the PyTorch implementation: see `https://github.com/OpenNMT/OpenNMT-py`

[4]The naming of each model is built in the following way: classifier, feature extraction method, n-grams and potential extra features. The following are the acronyms of the configurations– NB: Naive-Bayes; SVM: Support Vector Ma-

anced dataset. The model submitted to the challenge has also been bolded for easy viewing.

Considering the neural models, we found out that the best model using an SVM and bag-of-words outperformed the more sophisticated neural classifier that we built. We believe that this is due to either the hyper-parameters not being optimized. Our networks (emoji-nn-dp) has a structure that is very similar to the one implemented in OpenNMT (except for the attention layer). About OpenNMT: since we got development results that are much higher that test results, we believe to have over-fitted the model. For the OpenNMT network we also report on perplexity since it is a machine translation system and that metric is reported by default. Table 3 highlights the results of the NN. The systems were tested on 100k tweets: we tested our network on the English dataset only because of time constraints. We managed to test the OpenNMT system on both English and Spanish[5].

One of the most exciting things that we observed from our experiments was the impact of the skewed data on the models. In order to see what effect the skewedness had on the data, we tested the best unbalanced model by using a balanced dataset for both languages using the the number of tweets of the least frequent class.

This proved to be a huge success, as observed in the confusion matrix in Figure 4c. As we can see, there is a well-defined diagonal in the confusion matrix as compared to the best unbalanced model in Figure 4b, which shows that the balanced model is more capable of classifying tweets for *all* classes.

If we take a closer look at the matrix, we see that some categories are not retrieved at all. Of particular interest are the heart emojis, represented in categories 0, 3, 8 and 13 for the English dataset. In the best unbalanced model, categories 8 and 13 (blue heart and purple heart) are completely missing while these are actually retrieved by the balanced model. More interestingly, we see that there is a bit of confusion between these four hearts in the balanced model: we think that this is because the distribution of words that co-occur with all of the heart emojis overlap.

---

chines; tfidf: term-frequency inverse document frequency; POS: part-of-speech tagged data; 2grams: bi-grams; SVD: singular value decomposition.

[5]We are releasing both the OpenNMT systems and an hf5 version of our network with the model and the weights: this will make it easy to reproduce the results without having to train the network again.

In contrast, perhaps the most interesting observation in the balanced model is its success with certain categories. For example, if we take another closer look, we observe that the balanced model performs well at classifying tweets with the fire emoji, American flag, Christmas tree and camera emojis. This is likely due to the fact that these emojis, especially the American flag and the Christmas tree, have very predictable distributions. For example, the tweet 'Things got a little festive at the office #christmas2016 @ RedRock...' may be easy to classify because of the word 'festive' or because of the hashtag.

model	accuracy	precision	recall	macro F1
baseline (NB + bow)	0.30	0.39	0.30	0.21
NB + tfidf + POS + 2grams	0.24	0.57	0.24	0.13
SVM + bow	0.31	0.28	0.31	0.29
SVM + tfidf	0.33	0.30	0.33	0.30
SVM + tfidf + POS	0.43	0.41	0.43	0.41
SVM+ tfidf + 2grams	0.35	0.31	0.35	0.32
SVM+ tfidf + POS + 2grams	0.45	0.43	0.45	0.43
SVM + tfidf + POS + 2grams + SVD	0.31	0.23	0.31	0.23
NB + tfidf + POS + 2grams*	0.33	0.32	0.33	0.32
SVM + tfidf + POS + 2grams*	**0.35**	**0.34**	**0.35**	**0.34**

Table 1: Results of English Models.

model	accuracy	precision	recall	macro F1
baseline (NB + bow)	0.26	0.32	0.26	0.17
NB + tfidf + POS + 2grams	0.22	0.37	0.22	0.10
SVM + bow	0.23	0.21	0.23	0.21
SVM + tfidf	0.25	0.22	0.25	0.23
SVM + tfidf + POS	0.30	0.27	0.30	0.28
SVM + tfidf + 2grams	0.26	0.23	0.26	0.24
SVM + tfidf + POS + 2grams	0.31	0.28	0.31	0.29
NB + tfidf + POS + 2grams*	0.22	0.21	0.22	0.20
SVM + tfidf + POS + 2grams*	**0.21**	**0.20**	**0.21**	**0.21**

Table 2: Results of Spanish Models.

model	accuracy	perplexity
emoji-nn	38.71	-
emoji-nn-dp	34.23	-
OpenNMT-en	65.11	3.29
OpenNMT-es	71.02	3.28

Table 3: The Result of Neural Network Models.

4.3 Test Results

All the previous discussion about the results is based solely on cross-validation (for the NB and SVM based models) and validation data (for the neural models). The results based on the test set show that we ended up over-fitting the neural models and that the high-scores obtained during validation do not hold for the test set: the model that looked like to be the best during validation (i.e.

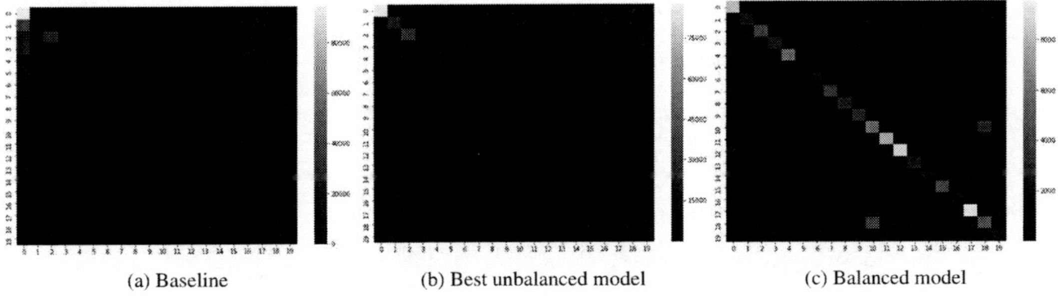

(a) Baseline   (b) Best unbalanced model   (c) Balanced model

Figure 4: Confusion matrices of select English models.

OpenNMT-es, 71.02% accuracy) saw its performance dropping by over 50%. From investigation of the test set results, it seems that the loss in performance may also be due to the fact that the translation model is conflating the different variation of hearts with the more 'plain' red heart, as we observe this in the Spanish results.

5 Conclusions

To summarize, we performed several machine learning experiments on an automatically created corpus: we experimented with both traditional bow models and with recent neural models. We conclude that when optimized properly, the neural models can outperform linear classifiers; also, we have to note that training neural models requires a significant amount of computational power, which is not always available. When a big amount of data is available, neural networks usually tend to perform better than other models.

Due to time constraints, we did not perform a systematic optimization of the hyper-parameters of the models and instead we only tried some options that are know in the literature to work well (e.g. using a linear kernel for the SVM, since text data are usually linearly separable). Furthermore, we did not try using pre-trained embeddings with neither models: in the future we plan to use the Glove (Pennington et al., 2014) embeddings trained on Twitter. In particular, the next major experiment that we will try will be the following: modelling the problem as an image description problem. Considering the nature of the labels — emoji — it is easy to see that they cannot be treated as discrete indistinct labels, but instead they share many features that are easy to represent visually: as an example, we can clearly imagine that a camera with flash and no flash or a purple and a red heart are much more similar than, for instance, a

red heart and a smile. We had this idea during the last stage of conducting our experiments and for time reasons again we could not test this idea.

Acknowledgments

We are thankful to Amazon for providing us the AWS Educate Grant that allowed us to conduct all our experiments. Furthermore, this paper originates from an assignment for an exam at the University of Malta, where we are both enrolled as students. We are thankful to our supervisors J.P. Ebejer and Claudia Borg for their suggestions and feedback. We also would like to thank our reviewers for their detailed suggestions.

As an aside, we really wanted to find a name for our system that would link our experiences in Malta to this project and landed on *tajjeb*. *Tajjeb* is Maltese for 'good', which we think accurately depicts our work here. If you've notice, 'prediction' begins with a 'P' and not a 'B', but we chose it as it was the most appropriate word for the acronym and because Maltese has word-final obstruent devoicing (thus reflecting how it actually sounds!)

References

Francesco Barbieri, Miguel Ballesteros, and Horacio Saggion. 2017. Are emojis predictable? In *Proceedings of the 15th Conference of the European Chapter of the Association for Computational Linguistics: Volume 2, Short Papers*, pages 105–111. Association for Computational Linguistics.

Francesco Barbieri, Jose Camacho-Collados, Francesco Ronzano, Luis Espinosa-Anke, Miguel Ballesteros, Valerio Basile, Viviana Patti, and Horacio Saggion. 2018. SemEval-2018 Task 2: Multilingual Emoji Prediction. In *Proceedings of the 12th International Workshop on Semantic Evaluation (SemEval-2018)*, New Orleans, LA, United States. Association for Computational Linguistics.

Marco Baroni, Georgiana Dinu, and Germán Kruszewski. 2014. Don't count, predict! a systematic comparison of context-counting vs. context-predicting semantic vectors. In *Proceedings of the 52nd Annual Meeting of the Association for Computational Linguistics (Volume 1: Long Papers)*, volume 1, pages 238–247.

Johan Bollen, Alberto Pepe, and Huina Mao. 2011. Modeling public mood and emotion: Twitter sentiment and socio-economic phenomena. *CoRR*, abs/0911.1583.

François Chollet et al. 2015. Keras. `https://github.com/keras-team/keras`.

Bjarke Felbo, Alan Mislove, Anders Søgaard, Iyad Rahwan, and Sune Lehmann. 2017. Using millions of emoji occurrences to learn any-domain representations for detecting sentiment, emotion and sarcasm. *arXiv preprint arXiv:1708.00524*.

G. Klein, Y. Kim, Y. Deng, J. Senellart, and A. M. Rush. 2017. OpenNMT: Open-Source Toolkit for Neural Machine Translation. *ArXiv e-prints*.

Tomas Mikolov, Ilya Sutskever, Kai Chen, Gregory S. Corrado, and Jeffrey Dean. 2013. Distributed representations of words and phrases and their compositionality. In *NIPS*.

Saif Mohammad, Svetlana Kiritchenko, Parinaz Sobhani, Xiao-Dan Zhu, and Colin Cherry. 2016. A dataset for detecting stance in tweets. In *LREC*.

F. Pedregosa, G. Varoquaux, A. Gramfort, V. Michel, B. Thirion, O. Grisel, M. Blondel, P. Prettenhofer, R. Weiss, V. Dubourg, J. Vanderplas, A. Passos, D. Cournapeau, M. Brucher, M. Perrot, and E. Duchesnay. 2011. Scikit-learn: Machine learning in Python. *Journal of Machine Learning Research*, 12:2825–2830.

Jeffrey Pennington, Richard Socher, and Christopher Manning. 2014. Glove: Global vectors for word representation. In *Proceedings of the 2014 conference on empirical methods in natural language processing (EMNLP)*, pages 1532–1543.

Chris Pool and Malvina Nissim. 2016. Distant supervision for emotion detection using facebook reactions. *CoRR*, abs/1611.02988.

Matthew Purver and Stuart Adam Battersby. 2012. Experimenting with distant supervision for emotion classification. In *EACL*.

Nitish Srivastava, Geoffrey E. Hinton, Alex Krizhevsky, Ilya Sutskever, and Ruslan Salakhutdinov. 2014. Dropout: a simple way to prevent neural networks from overfitting. *Journal of Machine Learning Research*, 15:1929–1958.

Sida Wang and Christopher D Manning. 2012. Baselines and bigrams: Simple, good sentiment and topic classification. In *Proceedings of the 50th Annual Meeting of the Association for Computational Linguistics: Short Papers-Volume 2*, pages 90–94. Association for Computational Linguistics.

SyntNN at SemEval-2018 Task 2: is Syntax Useful for Emoji Prediction? Embedding Syntactic Trees in Multi Layer Perceptrons

Andrea Santilli
Department of Enterprise Engineering
University of Rome Tor Vergata
Italy
andrea.santilli@live.it

Fabio Massimo Zanzotto
Department of Enterprise Engineering
University of Rome Tor Vergata
Italy
fabio.massimo.zanzotto@uniroma2.it

Abstract

In this paper, we present *SyntNN* as a way to include traditional syntactic models in multilayer neural networks used in the task of Semeval Task 2 of emoji prediction (Barbieri et al., 2018). The model builds on the distributed tree embedder also known as distributed tree kernel (Zanzotto and Dell'Arciprete, 2012). Initial results are extremely encouraging but additional analysis is needed to overcome the problem of overfitting.

1 Introduction

Syntactic models of language have always played a crucial role in many natural language processing tasks but, in recent years, it has been marginalized by the advent of neural networks and in particular long-short term memory (LSTM). These latter networks have had a tremendous impact on how linguistic tasks are modeled and, sometimes, solved.

In this paper, we want to explore the use of "traditional" syntactic information within a neural network framework in the task of Semeval Task 2 of emoji prediction (Barbieri et al., 2018, 2017). We propose *SyntNN* as a way to include traditional syntactic models in multilayer neural networks. The model builds on the distributed tree embedder also known as distributed tree kernel (Zanzotto and Dell'Arciprete, 2012; Ferrone and Zanzotto, 2014; Zanzotto et al., 2015) that is a way to transpose syntactic information in small vectors. Initial results are extremely encouraging: *SyntNN* outperforms syntax-unaware neural networks on the trial set. Unfortunately, these promising results are not confirmed on the test set. Hence, we analyzed these results to try to understand why this has happened.

2 SyntNN: a Syntax-aware Multilayer Perceptron

SyntNN is a simple, non-recurrent neural network that aims to exploit traditional syntactic interpretations of tweets in classification tasks. This network wants to explore two questions: first, investigating whether "traditional" syntactic interpretation can be used within neural networks and, second, understanding if syntactic information is useful in modeling tweets for the specific task of emoji prediction.

The architecture of *SyntNN* is then organized around two sub-networks (see Fig. 1): (1) a syntactic sub-network and (2) a semantic sub-network. These two sub-networks are then merged to obtain the final classification layer.

The rest of the section describes the two sub-networks and the merging layer.

2.1 Syntactic Subnetwork with a Distributed Tree Embedding Layer

The syntactic subnetwork aims to take syntactic interpretations of tweets and make them available to a simple, non-recurrent neural network. The key point is how to obtain the transformation of the symbolic representation of syntactic trees into tensor-based representations that have meaningful properties.

The *Distributed Tree Embedding* Layer (DTE) (see Fig. 1) is the core component of the syntactic subnetwork. DTE is based on a technique to embed the structural information of syntactic tree into dense, low-dimensional vectors of real numbers (Zanzotto and Dell'Arciprete, 2012; Ferrone and Zanzotto, 2014; Zanzotto et al., 2015). This technique has been originated as a way to replace syntactic kernel functions (Collins and Duffy, 2002) in kernel machines (Cristianini and Shawe-Taylor, 2000) but it can be seen as a principled way to

477

Proceedings of the 12th International Workshop on Semantic Evaluation (SemEval-2018), pages 477–481
New Orleans, Louisiana, June 5–6, 2018. ©2018 Association for Computational Linguistics

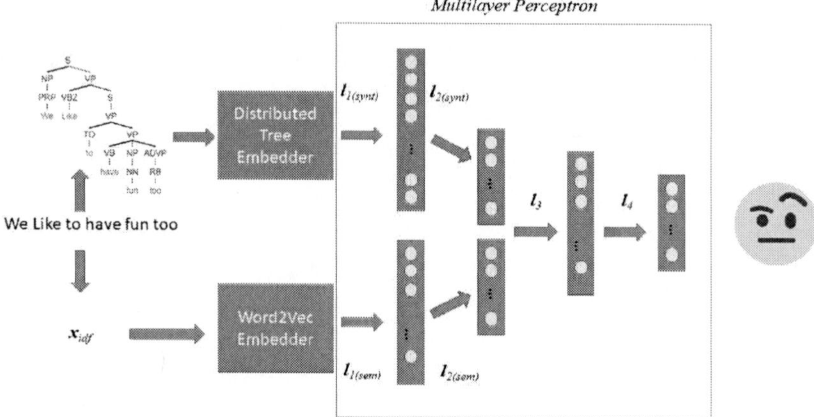

Figure 1: MultiLayer Perceptron Architecture for Syntactic and Semantic Representation of Tweets.

insert syntactic information into vectors. In this technique, tree are transformed into *distributed trees* that are low dimensional vectors. These distributed trees build on the recently revitalized research in Distributed Representations (DR) (Hinton et al., 1986; Plate, 1994; Bengio, 2009; Collobert et al., 2011; Socher et al., 2011).

DTE is a layer that maps trees into low-dimensional vectors in a space $\mathbb{R}^d$. This space is a low dimensional space that embeds the space representing trees according to their subtrees. DTE is then represented as the following embedding layer:

$$\mathbf{y} = W^{(DTE)}S(T) \qquad (1)$$

where $S(T) = \mathbf{t}$ is a onehot layer that maps trees to vectors in the space of subtrees $\mathbb{R}^n$ and $W_{d \times n}^{(DTE)}$ is a transformation matrix that embeds the huge space of subtrees $\mathbb{R}^n$ in a smaller space $\mathbb{R}^d$.

DTE is based on the Johnson-Lindenstrauss Tranform (JLT) (Johnson and Lindenstrauss, 1984; Dasgupta and Gupta, 1999) and it is not learned. Using JLT, the layer DTE maps vectors representing trees in the space of subtrees in vectors in a reduced space where similarity is approximately preserved, that is, given two syntactic trees T_1 and T_2 and given a ϵ, it is possible to find a $\mathbf{W}$ for which, if $\mathbb{R}^d$ has a specific relation with $\mathbb{R}^n$ (see (Dasgupta and Gupta, 1999)), this property holds:

$$|\mathbf{t_1} - \mathbf{t_2}| - \epsilon < |\mathbf{Wt_1} - \mathbf{Wt_2}| < |\mathbf{t_1} - \mathbf{t_2}| + \epsilon \qquad (2)$$

where $\mathbf{t_1} = S(T_1)$ and $\mathbf{t_2} = S(T_2)$. Hence, the space $\mathbb{R}^d$ embeds the space $\mathbb{R}^n$ of the subtrees.

However, directly producing a DTE with JLT is unfeasible as the space of subtrees $\mathbb{R}^n$ is huge and intractable.

Our solution is using the recursive model for computing distributed trees (Zanzotto and Dell'Arciprete, 2012; Zanzotto et al., 2015), which empirically guarantees the property in Equation 2. This model is a mapping function that encodes trees in vectors by assigning random vectors to node labels and by recursively computing vectors for subtrees by composing vectors for nodes. The mapping function has a linear complexity with respect to the size of the tree.

After the DTE, the syntactic subnetwork has two dense layers with ReLU activation functions. These dense layers should select subtrees that are relevant for the final task of emoji prediction.

As it is designed, the syntactic subnetwork should take into consideration the syntactic information of tweets and it should be a valuable model to experiment with syntactic information on the task of emoji prediction.

2.2 Semantic Subnetwork with a (Bag-of-)Word Embedding Layer

The semantic subnetwork is composed by a classic multilayer perceptron (MLP) network that takes as input tweets represented as $\mathbf{x}_{idf}$. These vectors represent tweets in the following way. Each dimension represents a word w and, if a tweet contains the word w, the dimension has the inverse document frequency (idf) value of the word w, otherwise it has a 0. Hence, the first layer of the semantic subnetwork is a word embedding layer

478

working in the following way:

$$y = E\mathbf{x}_{idf} \tag{3}$$

where E is a word embedding matrix. As word embeddings, we used the Stanford's Glove (twitter 27B, 200d) for the English task and the word embedding used in the paper *How Cosmopolitan Are Emojis?*(Barbieri et al., 2016)[1] for the Spanish task.

2.3 Merging Syntactic and Semantic Subnetworks

The merging layer of the syntactic and semantic subnetworks is composed by a concatenate layer that concatenate the syntactic vector with the semantic vector among the features axis. Then, a batch normalization layer performs the operation of batch normalization (Ioffe and Szegedy, 2015). At the end a 20 units layer compute the emoji's probability through a softmax layer.

3 Experiments and Evaluation

3.1 Experimental Setting

To ensure replicability, this section fully describes the implementation details of $SyntNN$ (Fig. 1) and the values of its metaparameters. Moreover, it introduces the networks used for comparison and the datasets used on the experiments.

For the *Syntactic Subnetwork* of SyntNN, we used the Python implementation of the Distributed Tree Encoder[2]. Tweets' parse trees are obtained by using Stanford's CoreNLP[3] probabilistic context free grammar parser. Distributed trees are represented in a space $\mathbb{R}^d$ with $d = 4000$. Then, the layer $l_{1(synt)}$ is composed of 5512 units. The layer $l_{2(synt)}$ is a cascade of two dense layers composed, respectively, of 2018 units and 1024 units. All these tree layers have dropout 0.5 and a ReLU activation function.

For the *Semantic Subnetwork* of SyntNN, we used pretrained word embeddings as Stanford's Glove[4] and the word embeddings given by the organizers of the task (Barbieri et al., 2016)[5]. The rest of the semantic subnetwork is the following. The first layer, the *input layer I*, is composed by 200/300 neurons. Each neuron take in input a dimension of the BoW vector. The number of input neuron varies according to the word embedding used: 200 if the word embedding used is Glove; 300 if the word embedding used in the other word embedding cited in the word embedding section. The second layer $l_{1(sem)}$ consists of 512 neurons, dropout 0.5 and ReLU activation function. The third layer $l_{2(sem)}$ consists of 1024 neurons, dropout 0.5 and ReLU activation function.

To understand whether SyntNN positively uses syntactic information, we compared our system with two neural networks trained in comparable conditions: (1) BOW-MLP and (2) BiLSTM. BOW-MLP is basically the Semantic Subnetwork of SyntNN without the Syntactic Subnetwork. BiLSTM is a bidirectional LSTM (Huang et al., 2015), which has been proven effective in many natural language processing tasks. For the BiLSTM, we used the same embedding layer used in SyntNN, we used a recurrent layer of 100 Bidirectional Long Short Term Memory (LSTM) neurons with activation function tanh, recurrent activation function hard sigmoid, recurrent dropout and dropout probability 0.5 and weight l2 regularizer with $\lambda = 0.01$. The output layer is composed by 20 neurons and activation function softmax.

All models are implemented using Keras library (Chollet et al., 2015) and run on tensorflow (Abadi et al., 2015) back-end on different cuda GPUs. Models are trained with Adam(Kingma and Ba, 2014) gradient descent algorithm with $lr = 0.0001, \beta_1 = 0.9, \beta_2 = 0.999$. The loss function used is the categorical crossentropy function. The BOW-MLP model and SyntNN model are trained for 140 epochs and batch size = 50, while the BiLSTM model is trained for 18 epochs and batch size = 50.

We performed our tests on the emoji prediction dataset and we used the Macro F1 Score evaluator provided by the organizers (Barbieri et al., 2018). No additional datasets have been used.

3.2 Results and Analysis

Initial experiments (Table 1), performed using the trial dataset as testing set, are extremely positive with respect to our research question: syntactic information is definitely important for both languages and SyntNN seems to be the good way to represent syntactic relations among words. In

[1]https://github.com/fvancesco/acmmm2016

[2]https://github.com/lorenzoferrone/pyDTK

[3]https://stanfordnlp.github.io/CoreNLP/

[4]https://nlp.stanford.edu/projects/glove/

[5]https://github.com/fvancesco/acmmm2016

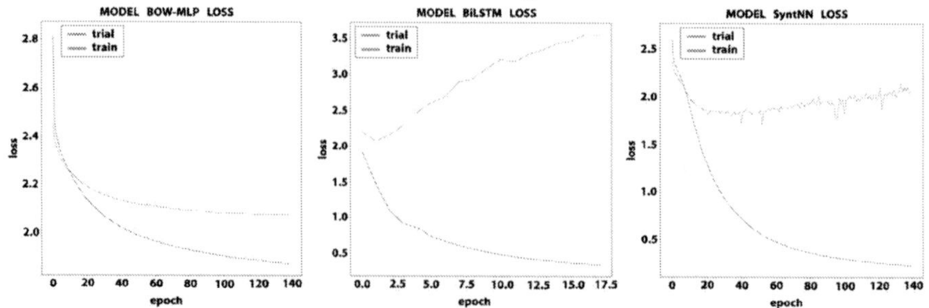

Figure 2: Loss comparison on English datasets.

Dataset	BOW-MLP	BiLSTM	SyntNN
en	30.832	47.535	**61.777**
es	74.077	72.875	**80.474**

Table 1: Macro F1 score on the Trial Set.

Dataset	BOW-MLP	BiLSTM	SyntNN
en	16.298	25.877	18.385
es	15.427	15.008	14.99

Table 2: Macro F1 score on the Test Set.

Dataset	Test	Trial
en	44.10%	19.81%
es	40.67%	7.21%

Table 3: Out-of-vocabulary words in the different datasets.

fact, SyntNN largely outperformed BOW-MLP in both languages: 61.777 vs. 30.832 for the English dataset (en) and 80.474 vs. 74.077 for the Spanish dataset (es). Moreover syntactic information captured by SyntNN seems to be totally different and more effective than the structural information exploited by recurrent neural networks as BiLSTMs. SyntNN has different results with respect to BiLSTM on both datasets with SyntNN outperforming BiLSTM (61.777 vs. 47.535 for *en* and 80.474 vs. 72.875 for *es*). These results seem to show that syntactic information is useful and distributed tree embedders are a possible, effective way to take into consideration syntactic information in multi-layer perceptrons.

Surprisingly, results on the official test set did not confirm results on the trial set (Table 2). The first observation is that Macro F1 scores on the test set are definitely lower of the results obtained with different models on the trial set. Moreover, the relative rank among the models is not fully respected. In fact, SyntNN outperforms BOW-MLP only for the *en* dataset but it is definitely worser than BiLSTM. Whereas, models are performing similarly for the *es* dataset. The question is: *Why? What happened?*

We then tried to analyze where the poor results on the test set came from. The first observation is that unknown words in the test set (Table 3) are larger than for the trial set for both datasets. The unknown words on the test set is more than double with respect to the unknown words in the trial for the English dataset and more than 4 times for the Spanish dataset. Test is definitely farer than trial with respect to the training set. This seems to be the first reason why results are poorer on the test set. The second observation is on the degree of overfitting. In fact, this seems to to be the major problem of SyntNN and of the other two models (see Fig. 2). By looking at the loss function, three models largely overfit with respect to the epochs: the loss functions on the train set and on the trial set diverge. This can partially explain poor results.

However, to have a more in-dept analysis we need to know what and how these networks are modelling symbols in general and syntactic information in particular.

4 Conclusions

In this paper we presented a way to include traditional syntactic information in neural networks and we experimented with this model within the emoji prediction task. Although results on the test set does not confirm results on the trial set, this approach is promising as it opens to an higher explainability of decisions of the neural network (Zanzotto and Ferrone, 2017).

References

Martín Abadi, Ashish Agarwal, Paul Barham, Eugene Brevdo, Zhifeng Chen, Craig Citro, Greg S. Corrado, Andy Davis, Jeffrey Dean, Matthieu Devin, Sanjay Ghemawat, Ian Goodfellow, Andrew Harp, Geoffrey Irving, Michael Isard, Yangqing Jia, Rafal Jozefowicz, Lukasz Kaiser, Manjunath Kudlur, Josh Levenberg, Dandelion Mané, Rajat Monga, Sherry Moore, Derek Murray, Chris Olah, Mike Schuster, Jonathon Shlens, Benoit Steiner, Ilya Sutskever, Kunal Talwar, Paul Tucker, Vincent Vanhoucke, Vijay Vasudevan, Fernanda Viégas, Oriol Vinyals, Pete Warden, Martin Wattenberg, Martin Wicke, Yuan Yu, and Xiaoqiang Zheng. 2015. TensorFlow: Large-scale machine learning on heterogeneous systems. Software available from tensorflow.org.

Francesco Barbieri, Miguel Ballesteros, and Horacio Saggion. 2017. Are emojis predictable? In *Proceedings of the 15th Conference of the European Chapter of the Association for Computational Linguistics: Volume 2, Short Papers*, pages 105–111. Association for Computational Linguistics.

Francesco Barbieri, Jose Camacho-Collados, Francesco Ronzano, Luis Espinosa-Anke, Miguel Ballesteros, Valerio Basile, Viviana Patti, and Horacio Saggion. 2018. SemEval-2018 Task 2: Multilingual Emoji Prediction. In *Proceedings of the 12th International Workshop on Semantic Evaluation (SemEval-2018)*, New Orleans, LA, United States. Association for Computational Linguistics.

Francesco Barbieri, German Kruszewski, Francesco Ronzano, and Horacio Saggion. 2016. How cosmopolitan are emojis?: Exploring emojis usage and meaning over different languages with distributional semantics. In *Proceedings of the 2016 ACM on Multimedia Conference*, pages 531–535. ACM.

Yoshua Bengio. 2009. Learning deep architectures for ai. *Foundations and Trends in Machine Learning*, 2(1):1–127.

François Chollet et al. 2015. Keras. https://github.com/keras-team/keras.

Michael Collins and Nigel Duffy. 2002. New ranking algorithms for parsing and tagging: Kernels over discrete structures, and the voted perceptron. In *Proceedings of the Conference of the Annual Meeting of the Association of Computational Linguistics*.

Ronan Collobert, Jason Weston, Léon Bottou, Michael Karlen, Koray Kavukcuoglu, and Pavel Kuksa. 2011. Natural language processing (almost) from scratch. *Journal of Machine Learning Research*, 12:2493–2537.

Nello Cristianini and John Shawe-Taylor. 2000. *An Introduction to Support Vector Machines and Other Kernel-based Learning Methods*. Cambridge University Press.

Sanjoy Dasgupta and Anupam Gupta. 1999. An elementary proof of the johnson-linderstrauss lemma. Technical Report TR-99-006, ICSI, Berkeley, California.

Lorenzo Ferrone and Fabio Massimo Zanzotto. 2014. Towards syntax-aware compositional distributional semantic models. In *COLING 2014, 25th International Conference on Computational Linguistics, Proceedings of the Conference: Technical Papers, August 23-29, 2014, Dublin, Ireland*, pages 721–730.

Geoffrey E. Hinton, James L. McClelland, and David E. Rumelhart. 1986. Distributed representations. In D. E. Rumelhart and J. L. McClelland, editors, *Parallel Distributed Processing: Explorations in the Microstructure of Cognition. Volume 1: Foundations*. MIT Press, Cambridge, MA.

Zhiheng Huang, Wei Xu, and Kai Yu. 2015. Bidirectional lstm-crf models for sequence tagging. *CoRR*, abs/1508.01991.

Sergey Ioffe and Christian Szegedy. 2015. Batch normalization: Accelerating deep network training by reducing internal covariate shift. *CoRR*, abs/1502.03167.

W. Johnson and J. Lindenstrauss. 1984. Extensions of lipschitz mappings into a hilbert space. *Contemp. Math.*, 26:189–206.

Diederik P. Kingma and Jimmy Ba. 2014. Adam: A method for stochastic optimization. *CoRR*, abs/1412.6980.

Tony A. Plate. 1994. *Distributed Representations and Nested Compositional Structure*. Ph.D. thesis.

Richard Socher, Eric H. Huang, Jeffrey Pennington, Andrew Y. Ng, and Christopher D. Manning. 2011. Dynamic pooling and unfolding recursive autoencoders for paraphrase detection. In *Advances in Neural Information Processing Systems 24*.

F. M. Zanzotto and L. Ferrone. 2017. Can we explain natural language inference decisions taken with neural networks? inference rules in distributed representations. In *2017 International Joint Conference on Neural Networks (IJCNN)*, pages 3680–3687.

Fabio Massimo Zanzotto and Lorenzo Dell'Arciprete. 2012. Distributed tree kernels. In *Proceedings of International Conference on Machine Learning*, pages 193–200.

Fabio Massimo Zanzotto, Lorenzo Ferrone, and Xavier Carreras. 2015. Decoding distributed tree structures. In *Statistical Language and Speech Processing*, pages 73–83, Cham. Springer International Publishing.

Duluth UROP at SemEval-2018 Task 2: Multilingual Emoji Prediction with Ensemble Learning and Oversampling

Shuning Jin and **Ted Pedersen**
Department of Computer Science
University of Minnesota
Duluth, MN 55812 USA
`{jinxx596,tpederse}@d.umn.edu`
`https://github.com/shuningjin/SemEval2018-Task2-EmojiDetection`

Abstract

This paper describes the Duluth UROP systems that participated in SemEval–2018 Task 2, Multilingual Emoji Prediction. We relied on a variety of ensembles made up of classifiers using Naive Bayes, Logistic Regression, and Random Forests. We used unigram and bigram features and tried to offset the skewness of the data through the use of oversampling. Our task evaluation results place us 19th of 48 systems in the English evaluation, and 5th of 21 in the Spanish. After the evaluation we realized that some simple changes to preprocessing could significantly improve our results. After making these changes we attained results that would have placed us sixth in the English evaluation, and second in the Spanish.

1 Introduction

Emoji prediction of tweets is an emerging problem (Barbieri et al., 2017) which combines the nuances of sentiment analysis with the noisy data characteristic of social media. SemEval–2018 Task 2 (Barbieri et al., 2018) adds to this the challenge of multilingual processing, where both Spanish and English tweets are used.

Given the relatively large amount of training data available for the task (see Section 2) we decided to approach this as a classification task, where we used relatively simple unigram and bigram features in combination with standard machine learning algorithms. We particularly focused on the use of Multinomial Naive Bayes, Logistic Regression, and Random Forests, all of which were provided to us via the scikit learn package (Pedregosa et al., 2011). Given the challenging nature of this task we decided to employ a variety of ensemble approaches, since no single classifier seemed likely to perform well in all cases.

In the sections that follow we summarize the experimental data used in the task, and then describe the methods we employed for supervised learning, ensemble building, and oversampling. We close by interpreting and discussing our results.

2 Experimental Data

The task organizers created both training and test data made up of Spanish and English tweets (separately). The training data consists of 100,000 Spanish tweets and 500,000 English tweets. The test data is made up of 10,000 Spanish tweets and 50,000 English tweets. Each instance consists of a single tweet, where 19 different emojis were observed in the Spanish data, and 20 emojis were observed in the English.

We collected the training tweets via the Twitter API on November 10–11, 2017. By that time some of the tweets selected by the organizers had been deleted or made private, but we were still able to download the vast majority of training tweets. For English we downloaded 490,272 tweets, so 9,628 were unavailable. For Spanish we obtained 98,657 tweets, so 1,343 were unavailable.

One of the most striking aspects of this data for both English and Spanish is that the number of classes (emojis) is relatively large (20 and 19 respectively), and that the distribution of these classes is skewed. In the English training data the most common emoji is ♥ which occurs 21.7% of the time. The next most frequent emoji is 😍 which occurs 10.5% of the time. The two emojis were also the most frequent in the Spanish data, occurring 19.9% and 13.7% of the time. By contrast 16 of the emojis occurred less than 5% of the time in English, and 14 occurred less than 5% in the Spanish.

The evaluation measure used to rank systems in this task is the F–measure, which rewards systems

Proceedings of the 12th International Workshop on Semantic Evaluation (SemEval-2018), pages 482–485
New Orleans, Louisiana, June 5–6, 2018. ©2018 Association for Computational Linguistics

that are able to predict instances in the low frequency classes correctly. Given that we decided to employ oversampling in order to try to improve our results on the low frequency classes which had the negative effect of degrading our performance on the more frequent classes.

3 System Description

3.1 Preprocessing

First, the text is normalized to lowercase. In preliminary experiments, we find that removing all punctuations reduces performance, thus we decided to only remove commas. In our task evaluation experiments we removed all non-ASCII characters, but then post–evaluation decided to keep most of them. Then, we tokenize the tweets with NLTK word tokenizer and identify unigrams and bigrams as potential features. To reduce noise, a document frequency cutoff of 5 is applied to sift out unigram and bigram features that occur in at least five tweets.

When applied to the English data, this process results in 166,681 features, including 35,197 unigrams and 131,484 bigrams. The Spanish data is made up of 40,420 features, including 12,356 unigrams and 28,061 bigrams. For text representation, we adopt the bag-of-words model. Each tweet is converted to a vector based on n-grams by Count Vectorizer.

3.2 Oversampling

Faced with the skewness of both the English and Spanish tweets, we introduce oversampling to adjust the class distribution to reduce bias. We use Synthetic Minority Oversampling Technique (SMOTE), where the minority classes are oversampled by creating synthetic examples using k nearest neighbors. We use imblearn in scikit-learn library for oversampling.

In our case, all classes are resampled to have equal number with the majority class ♥. As a result, the resampled Spanish data has a size of 373,825, with class size of 19,675, and English has a size of 2,130,180, with class size of 106,509.

3.3 Base Classifier

We use scikit-learn library for the base classifiers and the first-level ensemble classifier below. And the second-level ensemble is constructed with mlxtend library, which is compatible with scikit-learn.

3.3.1 Multinomial Naive Bayes (MNB):

MNB is a probabilistic classifier based on integer feature counts. It is simple yet powerful for text classification, especially for short documents (Wang and Manning, 2012). To eliminate zero counts, we use additive smoothing with a parameter value of 0.5.

3.3.2 Logistic Regression (LR):

While NB assumes strong conditional independence, LR is more robust to correlated features. We use a LR with L2 regularization to reduce overfitting. It uses the one-vs-rest (OvR) scheme for multiclass classification.

3.3.3 Random Forest (RF):

As an enhancement of decision tree, we use the RF classifier, which ensembles a multitude of decision trees. By fitting on sub-samples of the dataset, RF improves accuracy and reduces overfitting by averaging. We use 20 trees here.

3.4 Ensemble Classifier

We build an ensemble classifier to combine the strengths of a collection of base models. The ensemble method is soft voting, where the calibrated member classifiers cast weighted votes for classes based on predicted probabilities. The ensemble is also a calibrated classifier, who can either predict associated probabilities based on weighted sum, or a class with maximum probability.

$$P(c_j) = \sum_{i \in ensemble} w_i P_i(c_j) \qquad (1)$$

$$c = \underset{c_j}{\mathrm{argmax}}\, P(c_j) \qquad (2)$$

Our ensemble has two levels. On the base level, we include a diverse collection of heterogeneous classifiers: MNB, LR, RF, with weights $(1.1,1,1)$ for Spanish and $(1.5,6,1)$ for English.

On the second level, we train the base ensemble respectively on the original task data (Ensemble1) and oversampled data (Ensemble2). On the one hand, oversampling can adjust class distribution so that rare classes are well represented. On the other hand, it may exacerbate overfitting problem in the context of noisy data, and consequently harms accuracy. To seek a balance, we devise a meta-ensemble classifier (Meta) including both Ensemble1 and Ensemble2, with weights $(3,1)$ for Spanish and $(4,1)$ for English.

Method	F1	P	R	Acc.
Ensemble1	26.37	28.10	27.41	34.43
Meta	26.59	27.18	27.87	33.80

Table 1: English Task Evaluation Results

Method	F1	P	R	Acc.
Ensemble1	16.59	18.03	17.84	29.67
Meta	16.75	17.11	18.10	28.51

Table 2: Spanish Task Evaluation Results

The weights for the ensembles were set in a non-systematic fashion via trial and error. In future work, we would like to arrive at these weights in a more rigorous fashion.

3.5 Evaluation Metric

For individual classes, F_1 score is calculated as:

$$F = \frac{2 Precision \cdot Recall}{Precision + Recall}$$

The overall classification performance of the system is measured by macro-averaged F_1 score:

$$F_{macro} = \frac{1}{k} \sum_{i=1}^{k} F_i$$

where k is total number of classes.

4 Results and Discussion

4.1 Task Evaluation

For task evaluation, our two submitted systems are: Ensemble1 and Meta. The official results are shown for English in Table 1 and Spanish in Table 2. Our overall F-score was competitive in both the English (19th of 48) and Spanish tasks (5th of 21).

4.2 Post Evaluation

In post-evaluation experiments, we revised the preprocessing by including most non-ASCII characters and modified the weights assigned for ensembles. As a result, the system performance improved greatly, which was largely attributed to the changes in preprocessing.

The system was trained on the whole training data, and tested with the official test data. We show post-evaluation results for English in Table 3 and for Spanish in Table 4. The confusion matrices of Meta classifier are shown in Figure 1 and Figure 2.

Method	F1	P	R	Acc.
MNB-P	30.21	30.78	31.58	42.22
LR-P	32.73	35.05	32.08	44.79
RF-P	24.49	30.13	24.41	39.01
Ensemble1-P	33.03	34.68	33.09	45.68
Ensemble2-P	31.85	31.38	33.14	42.08
Meta-P	33.31	34.14	33.61	45.58

Table 3: English Post-Evaluation Results

Method	F1	P	R	Acc.
MNB-P	19.26	19.92	20.51	35.07
LR-P	18.43	20.98	18.28	35.23
RF-P	13.41	19.47	13.78	32.68
Ensemble1-P	19.58	21.13	20.51	37.05
Ensemble2-P	20.34	20.44	21.55	33.64
Meta-P	20.21	21.23	21.12	36.74

Table 4: Spanish Post-Evaluation Results

In the task evaluation we eliminated all non-ASCII characters during preprocessing. After the evaluation period we realized that this resulted in a significant loss of accuracy. We revised our preprocessing for our post-evaluation experiments and only removed the following non-ASCII characters (shown as Unicode value, description): (U+00B7, middle dot), (U+2019, right single quotation mark), (U+2018, left single quotation mark), (U+2022, bullet), (U+2026, horizontal ellipsis), and (U+30FB, katakana middle dot).

Preserving non-ASCIIs is important for both languages. Spanish using MNB has a F-score of 16.77 without non-ASCII and 19.08 when preserving all, and English has 25.47 without non-ASCII and 30.00 when including. While their importance for Spanish is apparent as accents are ubiquitous in Latin languages, their function for English is relatively vague. Nevertheless, they are clearly providing useful information in the tweets.

4.3 Discussion

In this section, we will discuss the results based on post-evaluation.

Ideally, we would hope an ensemble would outperform all of its components. Its performance counts on the accuracy and diversity of the members. While NB and LR are linear classifiers, RF is nonlinear. Also, the actual performance is sensitive to the assigned voting weights. Initially, we get a rough estimation based on individual per-

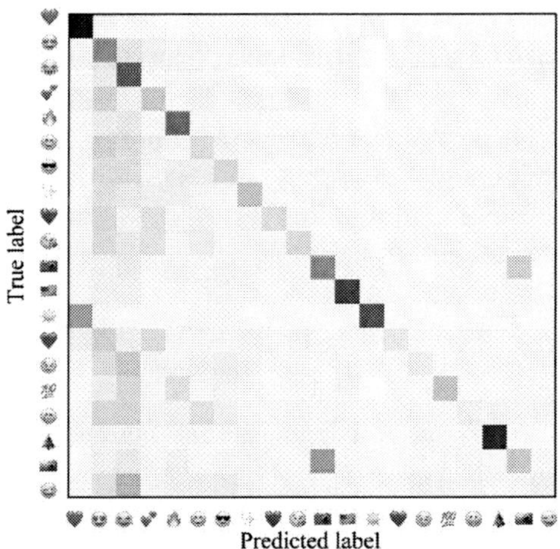

Figure 1: English Meta Confusion Matrix

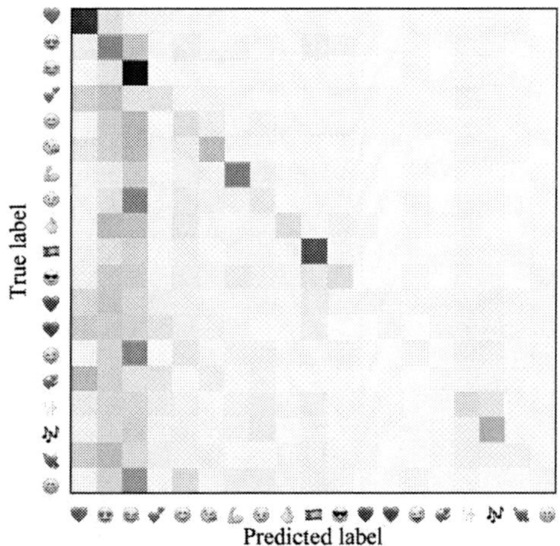

Figure 2: Spanish Meta Confusion Matrix

formances, especially accuracy. For both English and Spanish, RF has a notable inferior score, so lower weight is expected. Then we manually perform experiments to find better weights. Due to the large size of data, it is computationally expensive to perform grid search. In the future, we would like to investigate if other automated methods could find optimal hyper-parameters more efficiently.

By fitting the ensemble with oversampled data, the overall accuracy drops. However, the rare classes originally with low F-scores gain an increase. This is desirable as we attempt to maximize the overall classification performance for all classes, which is measured by macro-averaged F. In considering the weights in Meta, we perceive Ensemble1 a more reliable source as it shows notably higher accuracy. Meta tends to outperform Ensemble1 in F-score.

It is worth mentioning that the baseline classifiers like MNB and LR have robust performance compared to other more complex systems. This suggest that improvement from ensembles may be limited for this challenging problem, and new perspectives are necessary.

Additionally, there are some interesting observations from the confusion matrices. For English tweets, ☀ is frequently misclassified as ❤. And there is apparent confusion between 📷 and 📸. For Spanish tweets, 😂 has highest accuracy. Meanwhile, many other emojis are misclassified to this label, typical ones including 😅 , 😆 , and 😄 .

Acknowledgments

The first author is grateful for the support of the Undergraduate Research Opportunity Program at the University of Minnesota.

References

Francesco Barbieri, Miguel Ballesteros, and Horacio Saggion. 2017. Are emojis predictable? In *Proceedings of the 15th Conference of the European Chapter of the Association for Computational Linguistics, EACL 2017, Valencia, Spain, April 3-7, 2017, Volume 2: Short Papers*, pages 105–111.

Francesco Barbieri, Jose Camacho-Collados, Francesco Ronzano, Luis Espinosa-Anke, Miguel Ballesteros, Valerio Basile, Viviana Patti, and Horacio Saggion. 2018. SemEval-2018 Task 2: Multilingual Emoji Prediction. In *Proceedings of the 12th International Workshop on Semantic Evaluation (SemEval-2018)*, New Orleans, LA, United States. Association for Computational Linguistics.

F. Pedregosa, G. Varoquaux, A. Gramfort, V. Michel, B. Thirion, O. Grisel, M. Blondel, P. Prettenhofer, R. Weiss, V. Dubourg, J. Vanderplas, A. Passos, D. Cournapeau, M. Brucher, M. Perrot, and E. Duchesnay. 2011. Scikit-learn: Machine learning in Python. *Journal of Machine Learning Research*, 12:2825–2830.

Sida Wang and Christopher D. Manning. 2012. Baselines and bigrams: Simple, good sentiment and topic classification. In *Proceedings of the 50th Annual Meeting of the Association for Computational Linguistics: Short Papers - Volume 2*, ACL '12, pages 90–94, Stroudsburg, PA, USA. Association for Computational Linguistics.

CENNLP at SemEval-2018 Task 2: Enhanced Distributed Representation of Text using Target Classes for Emoji Prediction Representation

Hariharan V, Naveen J R, Barathi Ganesh H. B., Anand Kumar M, Soman K P
Center for Computational Engineering and Networking (CEN)
Amrita School of Engineering, Coimbatore
Amrita Vishwa Vidyapeetham, India
`cb.en.p2cen16007@cb.students.amrita.edu,`
`barathiganesh.hb@gmail.com , m_anandkumar@cb.amrita.edu`

Abstract

Emoji is one of the "fastest growing language " in pop-culture, especially in social media and it is very unlikely for its usage to decrease. These are generally used to bring an extra level of meaning to the texts, posted on social media platforms. Providing such an added info, gives more insights to the plain text, arising to hidden interpretation within the text. This paper explains our analysis on Task 2, " Multilingual Emoji Prediction" sharedtask conducted by Semeval-2018. In the task, a predicted emoji based on a piece of Twitter text are labelled under 20 different classes (most commonly used emojis) where these classes are learnt and further predicted are made for unseen Twitter text. In this work, we have experimented and analysed emojis predicted based on Twitter text, as a classification problem where the entailing emoji is considered as a label for every individual text data. We have implemented this using distributed representation of text through fastText. Also, we have made an effort to demonstrate how fastText framework can be useful in case of emoji prediction. This task is divided into two subtasks, they are based on dataset presented in two different languages English and Spanish.

1 Introduction

The consumption of technology in industry delivers potential tools for communication. Messaging has turned into a critical method of communication all through the world and is expanding at a quick rate. Adding emoji in the text convey little more information about the person's emotion, which otherwise is absent in the normal text. Emotions contents of text is better expressed by usage of emojis. Emojis are fundamentally kind of image which are logically connected with the written text. Tweets and online social media platforms are investigated to assess the emotion depth of the several issues for sentiment analysis and Opinion mining in natural language platform. In recent times, the interest in theses area received is very much increased and made several classifications which are polarity based classification such as positive, negative and neutral. In case of emojis certain remarkable studies on emoji sematic and usage find out in papers (Aoki and Uchida, 2011) Relevant study into emoji (Barbieri et al., 2018) are limited in number. The common exploration about emoji has inspired (Barbieri et al., 2017) on descriptive analysis or used them as a indication the emotional affect (Rathan et al., 2017) on social media. That is too restricted in face emojis.

2 Corpus

The shared task (Barbieri et al., 2018)provided 20 most commonly used emojis in tweets English as well as Spanish. That are distinct in nature for English and Spanish corpus (Barbieri et al., 2016). For the simplicity the corresponding emojis are labelled from 0 to 19. The data given for the task is 500k tweet ids for Spanish and 1000k tweet ids for English. Using the tweet ids, tweets are crawled from twitter using 4 different accounts. The crawled data was in JSON format, the raw data from twitter is prepocessed and the labelled data is converted into format suitable for the learning algorithm. For tuning the hyperparameters of the model 20% from the training data set is made into validation set and only the rest 80% is used for the training the model.

3 Related Works

Any mathematical system or an algorithm need some form of numeric representation to work with. One of most naive way of representing word in vector form is one hot representation but it is very ineffective way for representing words in a

Proceedings of the 12th International Workshop on Semantic Evaluation (SemEval-2018), pages 486–490
New Orleans, Louisiana, June 5–6, 2018. ©2018 Association for Computational Linguistics

large corpus since the length of one hot vector grows as the vocabulary increases, so we need a better and more effective way which captures some semantic similarities (Ganesh et al., 2016) between nearby words, thus creating the representation for words bring beneficial info about the word and its actual meaning, the methods which encodes these information about the words are called word embedding models, they are categorized into count based and predictive word embedding models. Both embedding models at least some way share syntactic meaning (Soman et al., 2016). But count based word embedding models does not preserve the word order and learn about word semantics

Predictive models attempts to calculate the word vector which captures the both syntactic and semantic meaning (Ganesh H. B. et al., 2016) of the word. This is done by calculating the softmax of the word over the context window. The word embeddings provided by the predictive model not only gives a representation for words but it is also able to learn word similarities and interesting word analogies like "king"-"man"+"woman"="queen". The wor2vec and glove models are the popular predictive models used to learn the word embeddings in many NLP pipelines.The disadvantage of above predictive models are they does not form a sentence representation and morphology of the words is not considered. These shortcomings are overcome the FastText framework which is a recent development in predictive model. (Bojanowski et al., 2016) presented the fastText embeddings, which is devolopment on the word2vec model. Since FastText is considering the char n-gram of the words it learns a good representation for words when compared to word2vec embeddings.

4 Methodology

This work explores the FastText Framework for text classification. It is a fast and lightweight implementation written in C++ to learn word embedding. FastText is a unified framework for text representation and text classification.

Generally text classification is done to categories the class of sentences or documents for task such as sentiment analysis, spam detection etc. In these tasks vector representation is assigned either to the words, sentences or documents depending upon the task. There are various methods for get-

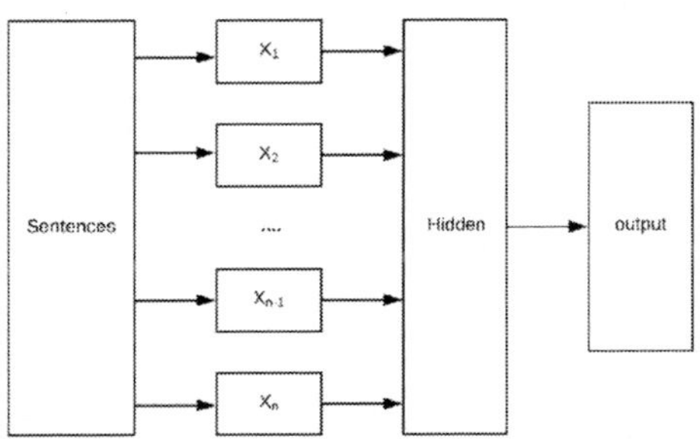

Figure 1: FastTex architecture for emoji and classification.

ting the vector representation. In this work using distributed representation, the word embedding is assigned to the words in the vocabulary over the corpora. In FastText framework for doing text classification it extends the concept of Continuous Bag Of Words (CBOW) model introduced word2vec model. Since fastText is improvised version of word2vec model so to get a good understanding the full word2vec

The word2vec model by proposed by (Mikolov et al., 2013) is shallow neural network architecture, where word embedding is learnt in an unsupervised fashion. It was proposed in the paper Distributed Representations of Words and Phrases and their Compositionality. This paper proposed two architectures for learning the word embeddings, they are continuous bag of words(CBOW) and skip-gram. In the continuous bag of words architecture given the surrounding words, the centre word is predicted, while in the skip gram model given the center word, the context word is predicted.

In a CBOW architecture, as in the figure 1. Let us consider this example sentence we built a sandcastle in the beach in this sentence every word is predicted by taking the surrounding words in the window as the input and softmax is applied over the output to predict the corresponding word (Poria et al., 2016). To reduce the computational complexity of the softmax with large vocabulary, two techniques namely negative sub sampling and hierarchical softmax are applied.

In FastText, for text classification CBOW architecture of Word2vec is slightly modified to form a representation of sentences or document. In Bag of words (BOW), instead of predicting the center word given the context words, the center word is flipped with the label which it is associated to. Then the softmax is applied over the predefined class. For N set of classes the negative log-likelyhood is given by

$$-\frac{1}{N}\sum_{n=1}^{N} y_n log(\int (BAx_n))$$

where y are the labels and x is the normalized bag of words feature. B and A are the weight matrix from the hidden layer. The BOW does not take the word order into consideration, which otherwise may increase the computation complexity of the model. The word2vec does not predict the word which it has not seen in the training time, to overcome this char N-gram is done within the word and it is given (Brown et al., 1992) to model during training along with word to overcome the unknown words at the test time. The model is trained with a decaying learning rate using stochastic gradient decent. The hierarchical softmax can come in very handy if the no of classes is very large, it basically works like a binary search tree, all the classes are arranged using the Huffmans encoding. By selecting the element in the tree, the search space for the class get reduced into half at each node, this brings the computation complexity in the order of log.

5   Result

Hyperparameter	English corpus	Spanish corpus
learning rate	0.1	0.1
dimension	200	100
window size	3	4
word n-gram	1	1
loss	softmax	softmax
neg	10	10

Table 1: Hyper parameters for english and spanish.

In this work, a classifier based on fast text framework is applied on the Sem-Eval 2018 task 2 emoji detection data set, the classifier is trained to predict the emoji on the English emoji corpus and Spanish corpus. Our team got placed in the 21th position in the English corpus and 13th position on the Spanish corpus. To make our model perform better we evaluated the classifiers hyper-parameter with various values and found the following hyper-parameter values to best performing on the English and the Spanish emoji corpus.

Emo	P	R	F1	%
[emoji]	80.56	80.24	80.4	21.6
[emoji]	24.61	48.55	32.67	9.66
[emoji]	29.1	59.86	39.16	9.07
[emoji]	23.57	24.34	23.95	5.21
[emoji]	45.29	43.97	44.62	7.43
[emoji]	11.1	12.46	11.74	3.23
[emoji]	19.88	13.18	15.85	3.99
[emoji]	29.41	19.28	23.29	5.5
[emoji]	23.71	8.59	12.61	3.1
[emoji]	17.98	12.85	14.99	2.35
[emoji]	31.19	48.67	38.01	2.86
[emoji]	43.58	38.99	41.16	3.9
[emoji]	63.2	42.77	51.01	2.53
[emoji]	35.48	0.99	1.92	2.23
[emoji]	14.75	2.45	4.2	2.61
[emoji]	22.6	11.17	14.95	2.49
[emoji]	12.04	1.13	2.06	2.31
[emoji]	65.03	59.09	61.92	3.09
[emoji]	39.31	8.9	14.51	4.83
[emoji]	0.0	0.0	0.0	2.02

Table 2: Precision, Recall, F-measure and percentage of occurrences in the test set of each emoji for english.

Emo	P	R	F1	%
[emoji]	59.47	65.58	62.37	21.41
[emoji]	24.32	49.08	32.53	14.08
[emoji]	38.07	60.37	46.7	14.99
[emoji]	10.66	5.97	7.65	3.52
[emoji]	13.22	11.67	12.4	5.14
[emoji]	25.48	13.35	17.52	3.97
[emoji]	25.07	28.01	26.46	3.07
[emoji]	10.91	1.32	2.36	4.53
[emoji]	6.58	5.56	6.02	1.8
[emoji]	26.39	41.51	32.26	4.24
[emoji]	18.75	2.65	4.65	3.39
[emoji]	0.0	0.0	0.0	4.13
[emoji]	0.0	0.0	0.0	2.35
[emoji]	0.0	0.0	0.0	2.74
[emoji]	0.0	0.0	0.0	0.93
[emoji]	35.56	7.69	12.65	4.16
[emoji]	15.69	15.09	15.38	2.12
[emoji]	0.0	0.0	0.0	1.34
[emoji]	0.0	0.0	0.0	2.09

Table 3: Precision, Recall, F-measure and percentage of occurrences in the test set of each emoji for spanish.

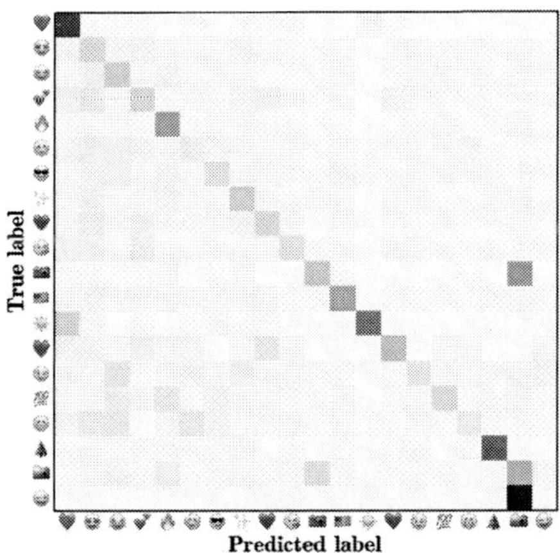

Figure 2: Confusion matrix set of each emoji for English.

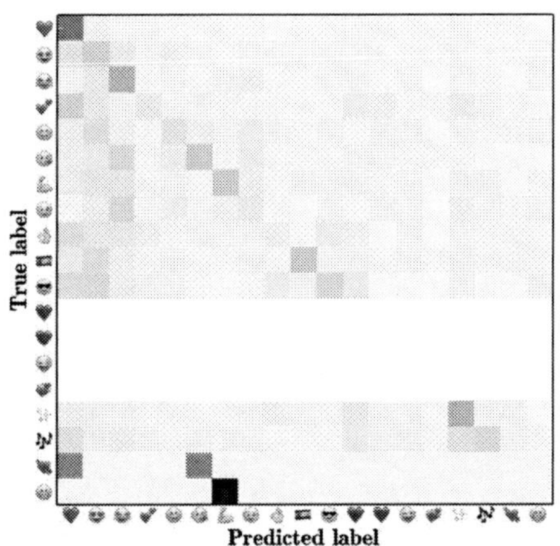

Figure 3: Confusion matrix set of each emoji for Spanish.

6 Conclusion and Future Scope

Every year we see a no of new words being added to the dictionary, most of these new words are the result of new culture trends, the same is applicable with the emojis, which expresses them visually and it is important for us to study its occurrence along with text in social media to better understand the sense of the message. A classifier trained on predicting the emoji from text is significant for understanding the interaction of emoji with the text. In this work a emoji is predicted for the sentences in English and Spanish using fastText framework which is known for being computationally efficient and the learned word representation is on par word representation learned from the standard models like Word2vec.

In this work, a single emoji is predicted for the sentence and since people usually people tend to use more the one emoji in tweets, comments and posts, so we can also extend this problem to a multi-label classification problem.

References

Sho Aoki and Osamu Uchida. 2011. A method for automatically generating the emotional vectors of emoticons using weblog articles. In *Proceedings of the 10th WSEAS International Conference on Applied Computer and Applied Computational Science*, ACACOS'11, pages 132–136, Stevens Point, Wisconsin, USA. World Scientific and Engineering Academy and Society (WSEAS).

Francesco Barbieri, Miguel Ballesteros, and Horacio Saggion. 2017. Are emojis predictable? In *Lapata M, Blunsom P, Koller A, editors. 15th Conference of the European Chapter of the Association for Computational Linguistics; 2017 Apr 3-7; Valencia, Spain. Stroudsburg (PA): ACL; 2017. p. 105-11.* ACL (Association for Computational Linguistics).

Francesco Barbieri, Jose Camacho-Collados, Francesco Ronzano, Luis Espinosa-Anke, Miguel Ballesteros, Valerio Basile, Viviana Patti, and Horacio Saggion. 2018. SemEval-2018 Task 2: Multilingual Emoji Prediction. In *Proceedings of the 12th International Workshop on Semantic Evaluation (SemEval-2018)*, New Orleans, LA, United States. Association for Computational Linguistics.

Francesco Barbieri, Luis Espinosa-Anke, and Horacio Saggion. 2016. Revealing patterns of twitter emoji usage in barcelona and madrid. *Frontiers in Artificial Intelligence and Applications. 2016;(Artificial Intelligence Research and Development) 288: 239-44.*

Piotr Bojanowski, Edouard Grave, Armand Joulin, and Tomas Mikolov. 2016. Enriching word vectors with subword information. *arXiv preprint arXiv:1607.04606.*

Peter F Brown, Peter V Desouza, Robert L Mercer, Vincent J Della Pietra, and Jenifer C Lai. 1992. Class-based n-gram models of natural language. *Computational linguistics*, 18(4):467–479.

HB Barathi Ganesh, M Anand Kumar, and KP Soman. 2016. From vector space models to vector space models of semantics. In *Forum for Information Retrieval Evaluation*, pages 50–60. Springer.

Barathi Ganesh H. B., M. Anand Kumar, and K. P. Soman. 2016. Statistical semantics in context space : Amrita_cen@author profiling. In *CLEF*.

Tomas Mikolov, Ilya Sutskever, Kai Chen, Greg S Corrado, and Jeff Dean. 2013. Distributed representations of words and phrases and their compositionality. In *Advances in neural information processing systems*, pages 3111–3119.

Soujanya Poria, Erik Cambria, and Alexander Gelbukh. 2016. Aspect extraction for opinion mining with a deep convolutional neural network. *Knowledge-Based Systems*, 108:42–49.

M Rathan, Vishwanath R Hulipalled, KR Venugopal, and LM Patnaik. 2017. Consumer insight mining: aspect based twitter opinion mining of mobile phone reviews. *Applied Soft Computing*.

KP Soman et al. 2016. Amrita_cen at semeval-2016 task 1: Semantic relation from word embeddings in higher dimension. In *Proceedings of the 10th International Workshop on Semantic Evaluation (SemEval-2016)*, pages 706–711.

Manchester Metropolitan at SemEval-2018 Task 2: Random Forest with an Ensemble of Features for Predicting Emoji in Tweets

Luciano Gerber
School of Computing, Mathematics
and Digital Technology
Manchester Metropolitan University
l.gerber@mmu.ac.uk

Matthew Shardlow
School of Computing, Mathematics
and Digital Technology
Manchester Metropolitan University
m.shardlow@mmu.ac.uk

Abstract

We present our submission to the Semeval 2018 task on emoji prediction. We used a random forest, with an ensemble of bag-of-words, sentiment and psycholinguistic features. Although we performed well on the trial dataset (attaining a macro f-score of 63.185 for English and 81.381 for Spanish), our approach did not perform as well on the test data. We describe our features and classification protocol, as well as initial experiments, concluding with a discussion of the discrepancy between our trial and test results.

1 Introduction

Written digital communication is increasingly pervaded by the use of emoji. Classic NLP systems are not well geared to handle them. Linguists are still working out how to treat them (Stark and Crawford, 2015; Danesi, 2016). Even their users may disagree on meaning (Tigwell and Flatla, 2016; Miller et al., 2016). A simple approach could be to ignore all emoji and concentrate on the words of a text, however this approach may miss valuable meaning that can be obtained by treating the emoji as semantic units.

The emoji prediction task (Barbieri et al., 2018, 2017), encourages research into the creation of text classification systems which can identify which emoji was present in a tweet. This could lead to automated suggestion systems for emoji, as well as improving the NLP communities understanding of how to deal with emoji computationally.

2 Data Acquisition + Preprocessing

The dataset was compiled between October 2015 and May 2016 (Barbieri et al., 2018). Training, trial, and test data emerge from a 80:10:10 split based on chronological order. We followed the

Emoji	top 5 words
	love heart my family ve
	obsessed wcw heaven foodporn view
	lmao funny lmfao lol hilarious
	pink breast sanfranciscoengagement lovealwaysyje strides
	lit fire mixtape heat flames
	802-3037 dickensfranklin dickensofachristmas bagsbycab 7171
	sunglasses shades cool risky coolin
	sparkle magical pixie magic getonshimmur
	royals autism bbn autismspeaks foreverroyal
	kisses kiss princessmailyana smooches smooch
	: :@ bvillain shredforaliving gdlfashion
	merica usa ivoted imwithher election2016
	sunshine sun sunny soakin beachin
	purple endalz purplerain alzheimer's relay
	mividaesunatombola multi-level silvercriketgentlemensclub azek wink
	facts rns realtalk salute t3t
	djsty cheesin braces strasberg fcpx
	christmas merry christmastree tree tis
	opus : :@ grigsby cred
	martian neh silly cray jewelrydesigner

Table 1: The top 5 words according to our class occurrence features for each emoji.

organisers instructions to obtain the training data, however we were only able to extract 491,486 tweets as some had been removed by their authors. We tokenised the tweets using the NLTK tweet tokeniser (Bird et al., 2009), but did not perform any further normalisation.

Proceedings of the 12th International Workshop on Semantic Evaluation (SemEval-2018), pages 491–496
New Orleans, Louisiana, June 5–6, 2018. ©2018 Association for Computational Linguistics

3 Features

3.1 Word-Class Occurrences

We created a set of features that describe which words occur with each emoji. We created a map describing how often each token occurred alongside each class. Let V be the vocabulary in terms of tokens. Let C be the number of total classes, where each class represents one emoji. We created a matrix M with size $|V| \times |C|$ such that each element $M_{i,j}$ indicates the number of times that token V_i occurs with class C_j. This allowed us to see whether one token occurred mostly in the context of one or two classes, or whether it occurred with similar frequency across all classes. This metric is similar to document frequency in information retrieval.

To further improve our metric, we applied a normalisation transformation to the rows (scaling each row by the total size of the row):

$$M'_{ij} = \frac{M_{ij}}{\sum\limits_{k=1}^{|C|} M_{ik}}$$

This method favoured lower frequency terms (i.e., a hashtag that occurs only a few times with one emoji), so we applied a further transformation to multiply each row by the log frequency of occurrence of the token:

$$M''_{ij} = M'_{ij} \times \sum\limits_{k=1}^{|C|} \ln M_{ik}$$

These features produced intuitive results. The top words for a few select classes are as follows (❤: love, heart, my, family; 😎: sunglasses, shades, cool; 🎄: christmas, merry, #christmastree)

These features are at the token level, however our classification labels are at the level of the sentence. To convert these features to the sentence level, we used two strategies: average and max. We calculated the average vector as the mean of all token vectors in a tweet. We calculated the max vector by taking the highest value across all tokens for each class. This led to 40 features (20 for average and 20 for max).

3.2 Sentiment

We employed Vader (Gilbert, 2014), a lexicon- and rule-based sentiment detection system to de-
rive a set of sentiment features. Vader fashions features, at sentence level, for positive, neutral, and negative polarities ranging from 0 to 1 and representing intensity. It also produces a combined sentiment score, with values between -1 (negative) and 1 (positive), where values in $[-0.5, 0.5]$ denote neutrality.

3.3 Psycholinguistic Features

We used the MRC psycholinguistic norms (imagery, concreteness, familiarity, meaningfulness, age of acquisition) (Coltheart, 1981) as token level features. These were averaged to give tweet level features in our classification scheme.

3.4 LIWC

We used the latest version of the Linguistic Inquiry Word Count (Tausczik and Pennebaker, 2010) system, LIWC2015, to produce a large set of features, at sentence level, concerning emotional, cognitive, and structural components derived from the texts. As shown in Table 2, our experiments with those features, arranged into different subsets, did not produce any significant improvement; therefore, we decided not to include those in our submissions.

4 Results

We performed subset analyses to determine the best feature grouping. In Table 2, we show our results for different feature sets when training on the training data and testing on the trial data.

We also optimised the number of trees in our random forest, finding 225 to be the best value for this parameter.

Table 3 shows the detailed classification report (precision, recall, F1, and support, by class), and Figure 1 displays the confusion heatmap for our best submission on the English test dataset. Our system ranked 24th, with a macro-averaged F1-score of **24.982** (n=48, median=23.919, min=2.038, max=35.991, Q1=18.278, Q3=28.410).On the Spanish challenge, our best submission (using only the average class-occurrence features) ranked 8th, with a macro-averaged F1-score of **16.338** (n=21, median=14.912, min=3.896, max=22.364, Q1=10.892, Q3=16.696) (see Table 4 and Figure 2 for detailed performance). For lack of space, we restrict our subsequent error analysis and findings

Features	Macro F1
Avg class occurrence, Vader, Topic-20, Avg MRC	0.6299
Avg class occurrence	0.6273
Max class occurrence	0.6266
Vader	0.1290
Topic-20	0.1126
Avg MRC	0.4922
LIWC	0.0425
Vader, Topic-20, Avg MRC	0.3530
Avg class occurrence, Topic-20, Avg MRC	0.6295
Avg class occurrence, Vader, Avg MRC	0.6319
Avg class occurrence, Vader, Topic-20	0.6287
Avg class occurrence, Vader	0.6301
Vader, Avg MRC	0.5211
Avg class occurrence, Avg MRC	0.6287
Max class occurrence, Avg class occurrence, Vader, Avg MRC	*0.6358
Max class occurrence, Avg class occurrence, Vader, Max MRC, Avg MRC	0.6352
Max class occurrence, Avg class occurrence, Vader, Max MRC	0.6355
Max class occurrence, Avg class occurrence, Vader, Avg MRC, LIWC	0.5400

Table 2: Analysis of different feature subsets. Score is reported as Macro F1 throughout. The best performing feature subset (which we used in our experiments) is marked with an asterix.

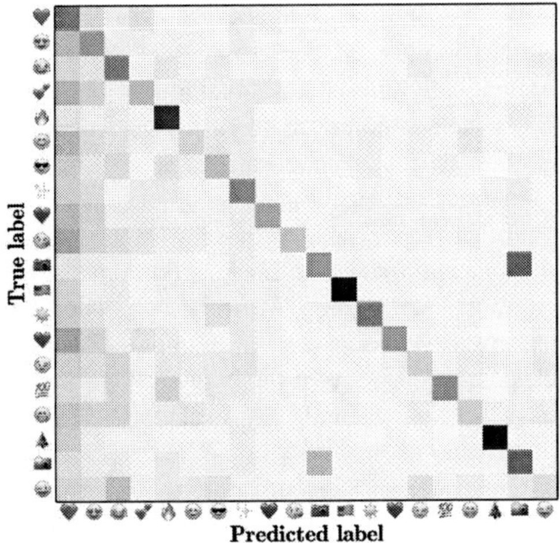

Figure 1: Confusion Heatmap For English Test Data

Emo	P	R	F1	%
	35.23	62.97	45.18	21.6
	27.9	25.51	26.65	9.66
	33.0	50.64	39.96	9.07
	20.41	4.18	6.94	5.21
	51.71	45.16	48.21	7.43
	10.36	5.7	7.36	3.23
	19.63	13.33	15.88	3.99
	30.49	17.06	21.88	5.5
	24.81	6.33	10.08	3.1
	17.45	4.09	6.62	2.35
	26.34	37.99	31.11	2.86
	60.64	52.8	56.45	3.9
	32.76	40.47	36.21	2.53
	26.28	6.46	10.37	2.23
	13.27	5.59	7.87	2.61
	28.65	20.34	23.79	2.49
	13.45	5.2	7.5	2.31
	59.81	72.43	65.52	3.09
	37.89	21.1	27.11	4.83
	8.68	3.47	4.95	2.02

Table 3: Detailed Precision, Recall, F-measure, and Support for English Test Data

to the English challenge. However, these generalise to Spanish.

The F1-score on the test data was much lower than that on the trial data (**63.185**). We hypothesise that this discrepancy might be largely due to (1) our system overfitting the training data and to (2) a test dataset whose class distribution and discriminant features differ in some measure from those of training and trial.

Figure 4 shows the class (i.e., emoji ranks) distributions on trial and test data. With respect to training (omitted here for brevity) and trial data, the shape of the distributions match al-

Emo	P	R	F1	%
❤️	32.54	48.44	38.93	21.41
😍	27.77	30.82	29.22	14.08
😂	42.11	53.77	47.23	14.99
💕	8.84	5.4	6.7	3.52
😊	11.13	11.28	11.21	5.14
😒	20.0	11.08	14.26	3.97
💪	30.93	43.32	36.09	3.07
😘	13.48	9.49	11.14	4.53
👌	11.26	9.44	10.27	1.8
🇪🇸	47.63	35.61	40.76	4.24
😎	16.26	9.73	12.18	3.39
💜	15.12	3.15	5.21	4.13
💙	3.03	0.85	1.33	2.35
😉	7.88	4.74	5.92	2.74
💋	3.51	2.15	2.67	0.93
✨	20.42	9.38	12.85	4.16
🎶	18.93	18.4	18.66	2.12
📸	1.56	0.75	1.01	1.34
😁	6.4	3.83	4.79	2.09

Table 4: Detailed Precision, Recall, F-measure, and Support for Spanish Test Data

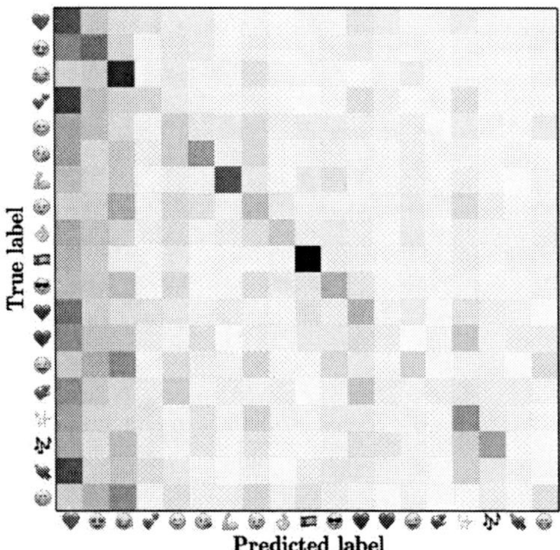

Figure 2: Confusion Heatmap For Spanish Test Data

most perfectly. Also, to a large degree, they are rank-preserving.[1] This is in contrast to the class distribution of the test data, which is not rank-preserving, particularly for those labels in the long tail (i.e., below the three most frequent).

From the classification report (Table 3) and the confusion heatmap (Figure 1) on the test data, one could infer, firstly, that our system revealed a propensity for predicting the most frequent emoji, particularly ❤️, 😍, and 😂 (accounting for about 40% of the data), which can be noticed from the consistent high values on the three left-most columns of the heatmap. Consequently, those within the surroundings of the peak of the class distribution, almost consistently, had recall significantly higher than precision.

For the majority of lower-support emoji, the system had a hard time in separating classes and quite frequently opted for higher-support ones. Secondly, it conflated classes into groups which, intuitively, could be seen as clusters of semantically-similar emoji, taking into account aspects such as emotions (e.g., joy), concepts (e.g., Christmas tree), and occasions (e.g., Christmas), to mention a few.

For instance, most of those associated with *affection*, *elation*, and other positive emotions and emotional states (e.g., 💕, 💜, 💙, 😊, 😘) presented extremely low recall and, frequently, were misclassfied as ❤️. As an example, 💕 had a recall of 4.18%, with about 64% of its tweets predicted incorrectly as ❤️.

Our system performed better at separating other seemingly distinct clusters, such as *sunny weather* (☀️, 😎), *patriotism/national holidays/travelling* (🇪🇸), *occasions/special events/holidays* (🎄), *being humorous* (😂, 😁), *photography* (📷, 📸), to name a few. For example, 📷's recall was 37.99%, with most of its misclassified instances (18%) being assigned to 📸. Conversely, 📸's recall was 21.1%, with about 32% wrongly predicted as 📷.

5 Conclusions

We presented a system for the prediction a single emoji, out of a set of the twenty most-frequent, for Twitter datasets for (1) English and (2) Spanish. Our best model was based on a random forest (n=225) employing an ensemble of (a) max-

[1]There a few discrepancies; for example, in the trial data's class distribution, contrary to the ranking in Figure 3, (14, 😂) occurs slightly more often than (13, ❤️).

Figure 3: Emoji Rankings For English (USA) and Spanish (ESP) (from (Barbieri et al., 2018))

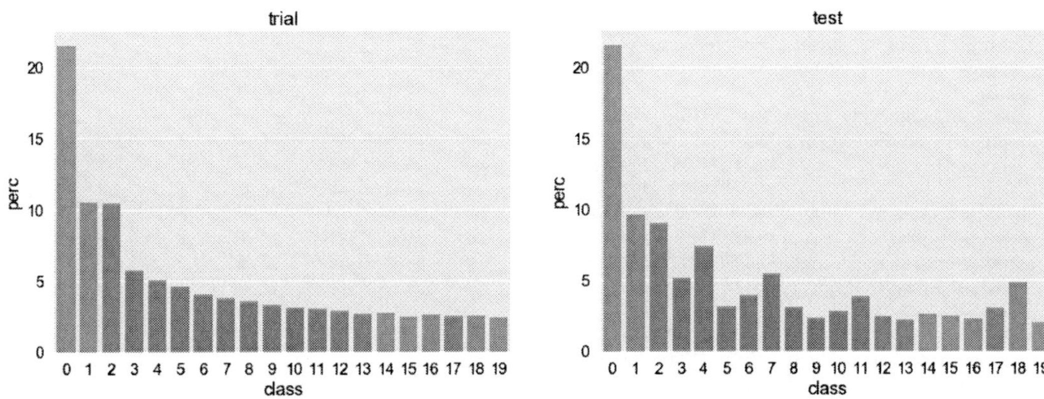

Figure 4: Class Distributions For English Trial and Test Data. The x-axis shows the classes (i.e., the emoji ranks in Figure 3), and the y-axis represents support (i.e., normalised frequencies)

and mean-aggregated normalised word-class occurrences, (b) sentiment and (c) psycho-linguistic features.

Our scores on the test data were significantly lower than those on the trial data, and we postulated that reasons for so were (1) a random forest that overfitted the training data and (2) large variance between trial and test data. It is worth investigating to which extent, and how, different periods of time explain that variance. For example, trial and test might have captured different, emerging trending topics and events; reflect drift in emoji usage; among others. It is reasonable to assume that, given the nature and the sparsity of the data, more representative samples might require much larger number of instances (say, billions of tweets) and time periods covered.

F1-scores were consistently low for all participants, which demonstrates the difficulty of the task. We are conscious that idiosyncrasies of Twitter-specific data (e.g., data sparsity, neologisms, informality, lack of grammatical structure) make it all more problematic, and some of our current research involves devising and incorporating features to address those challenges.

We believe it would be fruitful to investigate evaluation metrics that, rather than all-or-nothing (e.g., misclassification rate), reflect the semantic similarity (or distance) between labels and predicted classes.

References

Francesco Barbieri, Miguel Ballesteros, and Horacio Saggion. 2017. Are emojis predictable? In *Proceedings of the 15th Conference of the European Chapter of the Association for Computational Linguistics: Volume 2, Short Papers*, pages 105–111. Association for Computational Linguistics.

Francesco Barbieri, Jose Camacho-Collados, Francesco Ronzano, Luis Espinosa-Anke, Miguel Ballesteros, Valerio Basile, Viviana Patti, and Horacio Saggion. 2018. SemEval-2018 Task 2: Multilingual Emoji Prediction. In *Proceedings of the 12th International Workshop on Semantic Evaluation (SemEval-2018)*, New Orleans, LA, United States. Association for Computational Linguistics.

Steven Bird, Ewan Klein, and Edward Loper. 2009. *Natural language processing with Python: analyzing text with the natural language toolkit.* " O'Reilly Media, Inc.".

Max Coltheart. 1981. The mrc psycholinguistic database. *The Quarterly Journal of Experimental Psychology Section A*, 33(4):497–505.

Marcel Danesi. 2016. *The semiotics of emoji: The*

rise of visual language in the age of the internet.
Bloomsbury Publishing.

CJ Hutto Eric Gilbert. 2014. Vader: A parsimonious rule-based model for sentiment analysis of social media text. In *Eighth International Conference on Weblogs and Social Media (ICWSM-14)*.

Hannah Miller, Jacob Thebault-Spieker, Shuo Chang, Isaac Johnson, Loren Terveen, and Brent Hecht. 2016. Blissfully happy or ready to fight: Varying interpretations of emoji. *Proceedings of ICWSM*, 2016.

Luke Stark and Kate Crawford. 2015. The conservatism of emoji: Work, affect, and communication. *Social Media+ Society*, 1(2):2056305115604853.

Yla R Tausczik and James W Pennebaker. 2010. The psychological meaning of words: Liwc and computerized text analysis methods. *Journal of language and social psychology*, 29(1):24–54.

Garreth W Tigwell and David R Flatla. 2016. Oh that's what you meant!: reducing emoji misunderstanding. In *Proceedings of the 18th International Conference on Human-Computer Interaction with Mobile Devices and Services Adjunct*, pages 859–866. ACM.

Tweety at SemEval-2018 Task 2: Predicting Emojis using Hierarchical Attention Neural Networks and Support Vector Machine

Daniel Kopev, Atanas Atanasov, Dimitrina Zlatkova,
Momchil Hardalov, Ivan Koychev
FMI, Sofia University "St. Kliment Ohridski", Sofia, Bulgaria
{dkopev, amitkov, dvzlatkova}@uni-sofia.bg
{hardalov, koychev}@fmi.uni-sofia.bg

Ivelina Nikolova, Galia Angelova
IICT, Bulgarian Academy of Sciences, Sofia, Bulgaria
{iva, galia}@lml.bas.bg

Abstract

We present the system built for SemEval-2018 Task 2 on Emoji Prediction. Although Twitter messages are very short we managed to design a wide variety of features: textual, semantic, sentiment, emotion-, and color-related ones. We investigated different methods of text preprocessing including replacing text emojis with respective tokens and splitting hashtags to capture more meaning. To represent text we used word n-grams and word embeddings. We experimented with a wide range of classifiers and our best results were achieved using a SVM-based classifier and a Hierarchical Attention Neural Network.

1 Introduction

SemEval 2018 Task 2 on Emoji Prediction (Barbieri et al., 2018) is a classical task for supervised learning. Given labeled data consisting of Twitter messages and a corresponding emoji as a label, the aims is to classify new examples (tweets) into 20 categories - the most frequent emojis of two languages: English (Subtask 1) and Spanish (Subtask 2). We participated only in **Subtask 1**. The labels are presented in Figure 1:

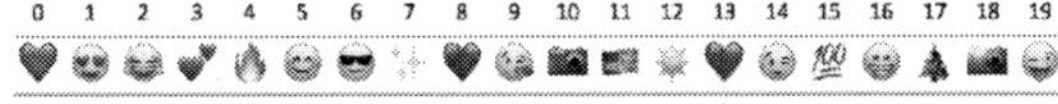

Figure 1: Labels ordered by frequency.

2 Related Work

Prior work includes using LSTM-RNN and CNN models (Zhao and Zeng) utilizing pre-trained Twitter embeddings with the latter achieving very good results. Other works (Barbieri et al., 2017) show that LSTMs have high accuracy and even outperform humans at the emoji prediction task.

In (Barbieri et al., 2016) the skip-gram neural embedding model is applied with different dimensions of the vectors and length of the windows applied to both words and emojis.

3 Data

We used the **500k training** and **50k trial** tweets provided by the organizers to train and validate our models respectively. One key mistake we made is that we did not compare those two datasets for duplicate entries. As we found out only after the submission deadline, the train and trial data had a 40% overlap, which unfortunately skewed our expected results and made them unrealistically high. The experimental results presented in Table 2 are on the data with removed duplicates.

We crawled additional 100k tweets via *Tweepy*[1] only 5k of which were compliant with the requirements to contain exactly one emoji. With this external data we aimed to improve the overall performance of our models, but since it was way too small, it did not have much effect.

Finally, when predicting on the test data, we trained our models on the combined train, trial and crawled data.

Looking at the emojis we immediately noticed two problematic groups: *1.* two emojis with a **camera** - one with flash and one without; *2.* four emojis containing a **heart** - three of them exactly the same, different only in color (red, blue, purple), and one with two pink hearts. We approach the second group with color-related features (see Section 4.2)

4 Method

4.1 Data Preprocessing

Replacing Text Emojis: Text emojis like :), :D, :o and others should in theory carry valuable

[1] http://www.tweepy.org/

497

Proceedings of the 12th International Workshop on Semantic Evaluation (SemEval-2018), pages 497–501
New Orleans, Louisiana, June 5–6, 2018. ©2018 Association for Computational Linguistics

information, thus we encode them to unique strings that will not be removed in future pre-processing steps. The encoded strings are: `_smile_` `_laughing_` `_very_happy_` `_sad_` `_cry_` and `_surprise_`.

Removing Punctuation and Artifacts: The data given by the orginizers comes with user mentions replaced by `@user` and all URLs removed. We remove `@user`, because the user mentions are taken into account in the feature engineering step, even though their position is lost. We also remove automatic location mentions in the form `@ Location`. Non-letter characters are also removed, exception is #, used to identify words in hashtags which we later attempt to split.

Hashtag Splitting: We try to break down each token starting with # to a set of words. The process iterates over the token until a word existing in a corpus is found. Then we take the rest of the token and recursively apply the same procedure until the whole original token is empty. The longest matching word is always taken first. For subtoken word identification we used the *Brown corpus*. As anticipated, adding a slang corpus seemed to worsen the splits. For simplicity we take the first found valid split, but an improvement would be to calculate and take the most probable one.

Tokenization and Lemmatization: A *WordNet* (Miller, 1995) lemmatizer is used on tokenized (*TweetTokenizer* from *NLTK*[2]) and lower-cased beforehand part-of-speech annotated tweets. High frequency words are removed.

4.2 Features

Textual Features: Since all we had was the text of the tweet without any metadata or context, we focused on extracting valuable information from the text itself. We gathered statistics like number of words, hashtags, stop-words, user mentions, mean word length and more. Some of those were specifically targeted at predicting certain emojis. For instance, we hoped counting the digits and percentage signs would help identifying 💯. Punctuation such as question marks, exclamation marks or words with all title letters could signify an intensified face emotion like 😆 or 😲.

Semantic features: Looking at the train data, we noticed that 42% of the tweets end in the following pattern: `@ LocationName`, for instance *Happy birthday Nathan!!! @ Boca Gardens*. We

Cluster Id	Words
00101111010	almost nearly practically alm0st nearlly almst
111010100010	lmao lmfao lmaoo lmaooo lool rofl loool lmfaoo
111010100011	haha hahaha hehe hahahaha hahah aha hehehe ahaha

Table 1: Twitter clusters.

figured that this was an automatically assigned location and extracted it as a separate feature.

Emotion-related features: To capture emotion, we used the *NRC Word-Emotion Association Lexicon* (Mohammad and Turney, 2013). It contains a list of English words and their associations with eight basic emotions - anger, fear, anticipation, trust, surprise, sadness, joy, and disgust.

Color-related features: Dealing with four emojis with the heart symbol in different colors, we decided to use another NRC Lexicon - on Word-Colour Associations (Mohammad, 2011). It consists of mappings for eleven colors - white, black, red, green, yellow, blue, brown, pink, purple, orange and grey, which covers the four heart colors in question.

Sentiment features: In order to capture sentiment in the tweets, we used *SentiWordNet* (Baccianella et al., 2010) to associate each token in the tweet with a positive and negative score.

Twitter clusters: Another observation we made while looking at the tweets is that there were a lot of misspelled words and words with identical meaning written with different syntax (mainly slang). To handle that we utilized *Hierarchical Twitter Word Clusters*[3]. The clusters also help identify synonymous words. Three exemplary clusters of words are shown in Table 1.

All features were used in all classification experiments, except in some of the stacking, where a subset was used.

4.3 Classifiers

Using the features above, we had represented each tweet into that vector-space. Experiments were made with classifiers from various types: Linear, Non-Linear, and Deep Learning.

Linear Classifiers: For our baseline we used Multinomial Naive Bayes, which we managed to outperform with ease. In the subsequent experiments we used linear classifiers - Logistic Regression with L-BFGS optimizer (Liu and Nocedal,

---

[2]http://www.nltk.org/

[3]http://www.cs.cmu.edu/ ark/TweetNLP

1989) and Linear SVMs with SGD optimizer (Bottou, 2010).

Non-Linear Classifiers: As we wanted to overcome the linearity of the LR and SVMs we had moved to non-linear classifiers. We had fed our feature vectors into Random Forest with 300 estimators, and AdaBoost with Decision Tree base, again with the same number of estimators.

Stacking: Another idea was to combine count-based and semantic features. For this we applied two versions of Stacking ensembles. The first includes SVM (tf-idf), AdaBoost (embeddings) and Random Forest (semantic and sentiment extracted features). The second one is composed of SVM (tf-idf), AdaBoost (embeddings) and Multi-layer Perceptrion (tf-idf). Both ensembles use hard weighted voting with coefficients 1.5 for the SVM prediction and 1.0 for the rest.

Deep Learning: We applied some of the state-of-the-art neural architectures for text-processing. Our experiments included Multi-layer Perceptrions, Recurrent NNs with LSTM (Hochreiter and Schmidhuber, 1997) and Convolutional NNs.

In the dev phase we achieved best results using *Hierarchical Attention Neural Network* (Yang et al., 2016) (HANN). The idea of HANN is to mimic the hierarchical structure of documents. It has two levels of attention mechanism: for word and for sentence. This enables them to capture and act differently on different levels of content importance. HANNs structure is build up from: word sequence encoder, word-level attention layer, sentence encoder and a sentence-level attention layer. Word Encoder gets word annotations from an embedding matrix summarizing information from both directions of the words. Word Attention (an attention mechanism), extracts the most important words, because not all words contribute equally to the sentence's meaning. Sentence Attention (another attention mechanism), is used to mark the important sentences at sentence level context.

As another experiment we used a two-layered bidirectional LSTM with a dropout rate of 0.35 and the Adam optimizer.

Another interesting approach that we adapted was to apply Convolutional Layer for text (Kim, 2014) that allows our network to learn and capture patterns for adjacent words in sentences. CNN are widely applied for image data, by using them for text classification we can learn and track correlations between close words and inputs. An advantage of CNN over RNN is that CNN are much faster than RNN architectures. CNNs allow our network to see the entire input at once and to parallelize all operations, because a convolutional kernel acts on each patch independently.

The key insight of boosting our Neural Network models was switching from ReLU to ELU as activation function. Proper Dropout Strategy (between 0.35 and 0.4) also improved our validation score.

5 Experiments and Evaluation

5.1 Experimental Setup

We transformed the training tweets into vectors using two mainstream techniques: tf-idf representation and word embeddings. While building the tf-idf weights we formed word 6-grams (without the stop words) and removed entries with DF greater than 0.5. The second approach consisted of using 200-dimensional GloVe embeddings (Pennington et al., 2014) trained on Twitter corpus with 27 billion tokens. Using the embedding of each term we concatenated the component-wise minimum and maximum vectors (De Boom et al., 2016). Some classifiers were tested using both representations when we found that appropriate.

5.2 Results

The results from those experiments on 10k train (sampled from the train dataset) and 1k test (sampled from the trial dataset) data are presented in Table 2. The experimental results are on the data with duplicates removed. The second stacking gave a better result than SVM, but we did not manage to run the model on the whole dataset in time for the submission. We placed 25th in the official ranking.

Precision, recall and Macro-F1 per class (on duplicated data) can be seen in Table 3.

The confusion matrix in Figure 2 reveals that two of the most confused classes are the ones with a camera, which was expected. Less anticipated is the strong confusion between the heart and the sun emojis. Overall, the heart emoji is confused the most with the rest of the classes, but since it's the most common one it's possible that classifiers often falsely predict it.

In terms of features, we found out that the n-gram representation of the tweets was the most important in terms of determining its label and the additional features did not have much influence.

Model	Precision	Recall	Macro-F1
Multinomial Naive Bayes	0.05	0.21	1.763
Logistic Regression with L-BFGS	0.22	0.28	13.16
Multi-Layer Perceptron 2-hidden (ReLU)	0.26	0.26	17.898
Random Forest (300 estimators)	0.20	0.26	16.167
AdaBoost with Decision Tree base (300 estimators)	0.15	0.19	7.825
SVM with tf-idf	0.23	0.27	19.554
SVM with Twitter embeddings	0.16	0.18	8.522
Stacking (SVM + AdaBoost + Random Forest)	0.25	0.24	13.764
Stacking (SVM + AdaBoost + MLP)	**0.25**	**0.28**	**20.106**
Convolutional Neural Network	0.15	0.14	12.034
Recurrent Neural Network with LSTM	0.24	0.17	13.106
HANN	0.30	0.13	15.999
SVM tf-idf	**0.30**	**0.33**	**23.3**
HANN	0.31	0.33	22.518

Table 2: Precision, Recall and F-measure of experimental classifiers on 1k tweets (top) and final classifiers on 50k tweets (bottom).

Emoji	Precision	Recall	Macro-F1	%
	36.53	54.25	43.66	21.6
	22.49	29.25	25.43	9.66
	35.72	46.52	40.41	9.07
	14.78	6.41	8.94	5.21
	46.01	48.12	47.04	7.43
	8.94	5.52	6.82	3.23
	23.07	11.97	15.77	3.99
	35.62	18.52	24.37	5.5
	20.42	10.65	14.0	3.1
	11.87	4.43	6.45	2.35
	19.26	20.11	19.68	2.86
	52.66	60.39	56.26	3.9
	31.33	45.77	37.2	2.53
	21.28	5.39	8.6	2.23
	8.03	2.91	4.27	2.61
	17.62	21.7	19.45	2.49
	13.02	4.34	6.51	2.31
	48.58	78.64	60.06	3.09
	30.14	11.83	16.99	4.83
	7.93	2.77	4.11	2.02

Table 3: Precision, Recall, F-measure and percentage of occurrences in the test set of each emoji.

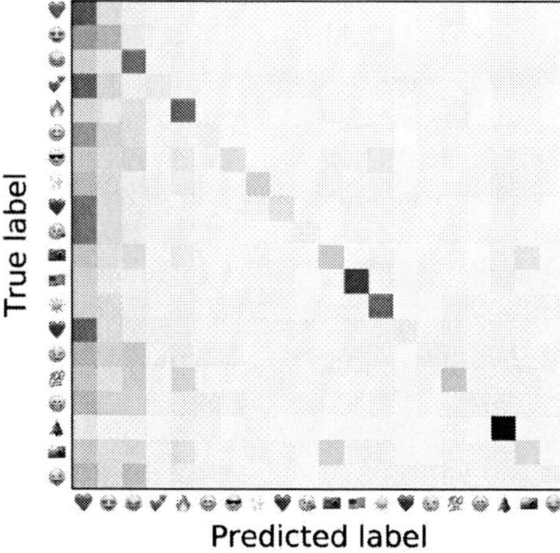

Figure 2: Confusion matrix per emoji type.

6 Conclusion

The work we did on the Emoji Prediction task seems promising, even though we could make our process better by filtering train data, retrieving more tweets and focusing more on the preprocessing of the tweets. There's a lot of room for improvement, given that the task is very challenging - tweets are short and full of slang words and ambiguous emoticons. We tried to combat those through some feature engineering, preprocessing and semantic approach for vectorization.

Improvements could be made with the semantic representation of the tweets. Because our embedding representations use coordinate-wise minimization and miximization, a lot of meaning is lost. Embedding approaches that work on a higher than word level text blocks like Skip-Thoughts vectors (Kiros et al., 2015) could decrease this loss. As future work we plan on using more sophisticated architectures like deeper CNNs and Squeeze-and-Excitation Networks for text.

Acknowledgments

This research was done by MSc students in Computer Science at the Sofia University "St Kliment Ohridski".

References

Stefano Baccianella, Andrea Esuli, and Fabrizio Sebastiani. 2010. Sentiwordnet 3.0: an enhanced lexical resource for sentiment analysis and opinion mining. In *LREC*, volume 10, pages 2200–2204.

Francesco Barbieri, Miguel Ballesteros, and Horacio Saggion. 2017. Are emojis predictable? In *Proceedings of the 15th Conference of the European Chapter of the Association for Computational Linguistics: Volume 2, Short Papers*, pages 105–111, Valencia, Spain. Association for Computational Linguistics.

Francesco Barbieri, Jose Camacho-Collados, Francesco Ronzano, Luis Espinosa-Anke, Miguel Ballesteros, Valerio Basile, Viviana Patti, and Horacio Saggion. 2018. SemEval-2018 Task 2: Multilingual Emoji Prediction. In *Proceedings of the 12th International Workshop on Semantic Evaluation (SemEval-2018)*, New Orleans, LA, United States. Association for Computational Linguistics.

Francesco Barbieri, Francesco Ronzano, and Horacio Saggion. 2016. What does this emoji mean? a vector space skip-gram model for twitter emojis. In *Language Resources and Evaluation conference, LREC*, Portoroz, Slovenia.

Léon Bottou. 2010. Large-scale machine learning with stochastic gradient descent. In *Proceedings of COMPSTAT'2010*, pages 177–186. Springer.

Cedric De Boom, Steven Van Canneyt, Thomas Demeester, and Bart Dhoedt. 2016. Representation learning for very short texts using weighted word embedding aggregation. *Pattern Recogn. Lett.*, 80(C):150–156.

Sepp Hochreiter and Jürgen Schmidhuber. 1997. Long short-term memory. *Neural computation*, 9(8):1735–1780.

Yoon Kim. 2014. Convolutional neural networks for sentence classification. In *Proceedings of the 2014 Conference on Empirical Methods in Natural Language Processing (EMNLP)*, pages 1746–1751, Doha, Qatar. Association for Computational Linguistics.

Ryan Kiros, Yukun Zhu, Ruslan Salakhutdinov, Richard S. Zemel, Antonio Torralba, Raquel Urtasun, and Sanja Fidler. 2015. Skip-thought vectors. In *Proceedings of the 28th International Conference on Neural Information Processing Systems - Volume 2*, NIPS'15, pages 3294–3302, Cambridge, MA, USA. MIT Press.

Dong C Liu and Jorge Nocedal. 1989. On the limited memory bfgs method for large scale optimization. *Mathematical programming*, 45(1-3):503–528.

George A Miller. 1995. Wordnet: a lexical database for english. *Communications of the ACM*, 38(11):39–41.

Saif Mohammad. 2011. Colourful language: Measuring word-colour associations. In *Proceedings of the 2nd Workshop on Cognitive Modeling and Computational Linguistics*, pages 97–106, Portland, Oregon, USA. Association for Computational Linguistics.

Saif M Mohammad and Peter D Turney. 2013. Crowdsourcing a word–emotion association lexicon. *Computational Intelligence*, 29(3):436–465.

Jeffrey Pennington, Richard Socher, and Christopher Manning. 2014. Glove: Global vectors for word representation. In *Proceedings of the 2014 conference on empirical methods in natural language processing (EMNLP)*, pages 1532–1543.

Zichao Yang, Diyi Yang, Chris Dyer, Xiaodong He, Alexander J. Smola, and Eduard H. Hovy. 2016. Hierarchical attention networks for document classification. In *HLT-NAACL*.

Luda Zhao and Connie Zeng. Using neural networks to predict emoji usage from twitter data.

LIS at SemEval-2018 Task 2: Mixing Word Embeddings and Bag of Features for Multilingual Emoji Prediction

Gaël Guibon
LIS UMR 7020
Aix Marseille Université
CNRS
Caléa Solutions
gael.guibon@lis-lab.fr

Magalie Ochs
LIS UMR 7020
Aix Marseille Université
CNRS
magalie.ochs@lis-lab.fr

Patrice Bellot
LIS UMR 7020
Aix Marseille Université
CNRS
patrice.bellot@lis-lab.fr

Abstract

In this paper we present the system submitted to the SemEval2018 task2 : Multilingual Emoji Prediction. Our system approaches both languages as being equal by first; considering word embeddings associated to automatically computed features of different types, then by applying bagging algorithm RandomForest to predict the emoji of a tweet.

1 Introduction

Emojis were first used to emphasize conversations before becoming representations of specific emotions, objects or ideas. They are now used in almost every social medium and conversation devices, such as messenging applications or even emails[1].

Tweets and their emoticons were used as labels to predict polarity at first (Pak and Paroubek, 2010). However, emojis are not used the same way as emoticons in messaging applications. They can convey further information, even more when combined. The advantage of emojis is that they are becoming more standardized, even though existing emojis are still growing quickly[2]. This is why emoji prediction is a relatively new task. It can be considered as a composite task mixing emotion prediction for face emojis, aspect/subject detection for object emojis, and other metadata prediction for more abstract emojis, representing ideas for instance.

This year, SemEval started the first emoji prediction task (Barbieri et al., 2018). It consists of a multiclass classification task for a total of 20 possible classes, *i.e.* emojis. This task is interesting in several ways. Firstly, it is a relatively new task that only a few studies did focus on. Secondly, it is quite important not only for research, but also for companies willing to embrace the current trend of social network and interaction analysis. Both are important topics for Natural Language Processing (NLP) and Information Retrieval (IR).

Our system obtained good results (63.65% f1-score) while using the trial dataset, and lower results (13.53% f1-score) on the test dataset. Because this pattern occurred for both English and Spanish, and for all participants, we try to explain it.

The paper is organized as follows: we first summarize the existing work related to this task and to our approach (Section 2). Then we present what we identified as the most challenging areas from this task and the dataset used (Section 3). We go on by describing our system (Section 4) and detailing the pre processing and prediction steps. Finally, we conclude by discussing the performance limits and show the benefits of our participation in this task (Section 5).

2 Related Work

Several research studies focus on emoji prediction. Most of them use word embeddings in order to do a multiclass emoji prediction. At the beginning, images were used instead of text as the source of emoji prediction (Cappallo et al., 2015). Eisner (Eisner et al., 2016) used embeddings based on emoji description in the Unicode[3] list, such as *smiling face with heart eyes*. They obtained 85% accuracy in their classification of emoji descriptions, predicting several keywords for one emoji. Xie (Xie et al., 2016) trained neural networks on Weibo[4] to predict 10 possible emojis in conversations with 65% accuracy for the 3 mostly used emojis. Barbieri (Barbieri et al., 2017) then

---

[1] http://cdn.emogi.com/docs/reports/
2015_emoji_report.pdf
[2] https://goo.gl/jbeRYW

[3] http://unicode.org/ emoji/charts/full emojilist.html
[4] http://www.weibo.com/

Proceedings of the 12th International Workshop on Semantic Evaluation (SemEval-2018), pages 502–506
New Orleans, Louisiana, June 5–6, 2018. ©2018 Association for Computational Linguistics

predicted 20 emojis in millions of tweets using LSTM (Hochreiter and Schmidhuber, 1997) and obtained 65% f1-score for the 5 most used emojis. Felbo (Felbo et al., 2017) tackled emoji prediction by LSTM with 43.8% accuracy for the top 5 emojis, while using emoji vectors to help detect sarcasm. In our recent work we considered another approach with 84.48% weighted F1-score using multi-label emoji prediction of 169 sentiment related emojis in real private messages (Guibon et al., 2018).

3   Task Specific Difficulties

Be it in English or Spanish, the proposed task has specific difficulties. Each of these difficulties represents challenges and obstacles for the classifier to make a good prediction.

First, the dataset is made of 20 classes of different types and concepts. Some are related to pure emotions ♥, facial expressions of emotions 😂, or even classes representing objects 📷 or ideas ✨. Those different classes may sometimes appear in a same context (❤ 💛, 💕, and ♥ for instance), even though the dataset was selected to only keep tweets with only one emoji.

Second, tweets are not private short messages. This means that some tweets are even difficult to understand for humans. This is the case for reaction tweets to a certain hashtag or social event. The appreciation of the event is totally dependent on the user's subjective point of view. Thus, it is also the case for the resulting emoji associated to the message. Other types of tweet-emoji associations, such as advertisements, are not even humanly predictable.

Third, the dataset is really unbalanced, which has become quite common in real applied classification. However, it still represents a challenge when associated to the two previous difficulties. Taken together, they make emoji prediction quite difficult, especially for tweets, which justifies even more the necessity for this task.

Two datasets[5] were used for emoji prediction in tweets: 500 000 tweets in training and 50 000 as trial and test for English, 100 000 tweets in training and 10 000 as trial and test for Spanish. Each dataset was made of tweets containing only one emoji between a set of 20 most frequent emojis from tweets containing only one emoji.

The emoji set only contains positive or neutral emojis, making a sentiment analysis approach less relevant, but we still kept using polarity scores in order to include the intensity of the polarity as a feature.

4   System

4.1   Preprocessing

Cleaning. To prepare the data we first cleaned tweets by removing trailing three dots, user mentions and urls. Then we used Spacy[6] to apply lemmatization and part-of-speech tagging (PoS).

Word Representation. For data representation, we compared different approaches for text vectorization. We first did a text representation using *FastText* (Bojanowski et al., 2016) but did not obtain an overall gain in the prediction in comparison to *Word2Vec* (Mikolov et al., 2013). We used *Word2Vec* in its Gensim[7] (Rehurek and Sojka, 2010) implementation with the following hyper parameters:

- Architecture: Continuous Bag-of-Words
- Batch size: 32
- Minimum count: 1
- Embedding size: 50 or 300
- Iterations: 100

The minimum count was set to 1 in order to better capture rare items from really small tweets, and the Continuous Bag of Words (CBOW) architecture was prefered after empirical tests to determine if it was useful to use it or not. The best text vectorization was obtained using live-trained embeddings, without using external pre-trained embeddings, even though we trained word embeddings and character embeddings on millions of tweets to obtain better representation, and also used existing pre-trained embeddings (Barbieri et al., 2016). This is certainly due to the overlap between the training and the trial set. Thus the local vectorization is more representative to find already known contexts. Varying the size of the embedding matrix E did not show major improvements for the following prediction, whether its dimension was $d300$ or $d50$. Thus, we chose a dimension of $d50$ to train faster. Tweets are represented as the *mean* of each word embedding vectors, allowing

[5]https://github.com/fvancesco/
Semeval2018-Task2-Emoji-Detection

[6]https://spacy.io/
[7]https://radimrehurek.com/gensim/
about.html

the same size ($d50$) for each tweet final embedding vector.

Computed Features. In addition to the embedding vectors, we computed several features represented as a feature vector F: binary features for the presence of a question or an interrogation mark, and their repetitions, another boolean feature for the usage of Title Case. Numerical counts were also added: word count, character count, average token length, number of nouns, adjectives, adverbs, interjections and verbs. Polarity prediction was also added by using SentiStrength (Thelwall et al., 2010) positive and negative scores. The advantage being that we then have polarity intensity, so it could be useful even if all 20 emojis are neutral or positive.

Finally, this feature vector F of dimension $d23$ was added to each embedding matrix E along the columns axis. The matrix is as follow: each row represents one tweet, and each column a feature. Each tweet information being represented by $E + F$. This means that before concatenation, a row (*i.e.* a tweet) has 50 columns, and after concatenation, it has 73 columns.

This pre-processing approach was used for all data separately, meaning that we based all our tests while training on the training set, and testing on the trial set. We used this approach for both English and Spanish.

4.2 Prediction

The system used was chosen after trying multiple approaches using the training set for train the model and the trial set to obtain macro F1-score. We explored multi-class RBF-SVM with gaussian distance function, LSTM network (3 LSTM layers with 64 unit cells, 0.5 dropout, then softmax layer) and decision tree based algorithms (XGBoost, decision tree, RandomForest). Decision tree based algorithms always gave us better results to take into account all classes during prediction. The number of systems were limited to 2, so we applied sightly different approaches.

In our system we used RandomForest with 700 estimators chosen empirically in order to predict emojis. To automatically find the best parameters we used a grid search with cross validation strategy for specific parameters visible in Table 1. The best parameters found were quite similar to the default one from the Scikit-Learn API except for the balanced subsample class weight. We also tried

setting the class weight manually to deal with unbalanced dataset. We gave more weight (5) to the 3 majority classes ♥😂😍 and left the other classes to 1, without improving the results. The maximum depth for each tree was then set to None because we believe a bagging approach such as Random-Forest with a number of estimators higher than the targetted classes can compensate overfitting issues coming from a higher complexity of each estimator.

Max Depths	20, 100, 200
Min Samples Splits	2, 5
Min Samples Leafs	1, 4
Max Features	sqrt, log2, None
Criterions	'gini', 'entropy'
Class Weights	None, 'balanced' 'balanced subsample'

Table 1: Grid search for RandomForest parameters.

The two submissions vary slightly, but are still the same system.

Version 1. On the one hand, data were scaled from 0 to 1 and we used a $\log_2$ parameters and χ^2 feature selection to minimize the number of features. This is based on the assumption that useful data in the word embeddings should be scaled before being concatenated with the features vector, then only embeddings and useful computed features should be used.

Version 2. On the other hand, we did not scaled any data nor limited the number of features, as suggested by the grid search.

According to feature importance scores from the classifier (Table 2), the best computed features were the average token length, the character and word counts, and the number of uppercases. The other features have minor impact even though PoS tag counts follow the top five features.

1	averageTokenLength (0.016)
2	charCount (0.015)
3	wordCount 0.012)
4	upperCharCount (0.011)
5	nounCount (0.009)
...	

Table 2: Top five computed features.

We first used only embeddings to predict, then predicted using concatenated embeddings and computed features vectors. The latter improved the overall prediction, which can also be seen by the feature importance scores.

We managed to obtain 63.65% macro f1-score on English, and 84.13% macro f1-score on Spanish while predicting on the official trial corpus. The English classification report is visible in Table 3. Also, the model obtained 61.92% accuracy on english and could be upgraded by sometimes choosing one of the best probabilities from each prediction according to the Mean Reciprocal Rank (MRR) score of 0.7126.

Emo	P	R	F1
❤️	0.42	0.92	0.58
😍	0.82	0.51	0.63
😂	0.58	0.76	0.66
💕	0.97	0.44	0.60
🔥	0.73	0.62	0.67
😊	0.97	0.44	0.61
😎	0.95	0.45	0.61
✨	0.94	0.46	0.62
💙	0.96	0.44	0.61
😘	0.97	0.43	0.60
📷	0.70	0.68	0.69
🇺🇸	0.86	0.61	0.71
☀️	0.76	0.51	0.61
💜	0.98	0.42	0.59
😉	0.99	0.48	0.64
💯	0.96	0.48	0.64
😁	0.97	0.46	0.63
🎄	0.87	0.68	0.76
📸	0.89	0.51	0.65
😜	0.99	0.45	0.62
Avg.	0.76	0.62	0.62

Table 3: Precision, Recall, F-measure for each emoji on the trial set.

However, our system obtained poor results once applied on the official test set, with only 13.528% macro f1-score on English, and 8.808% macro f1-score on Spanish.

Performance decrease in test set. An overall drastic performance decrease was shown while applying the model on the test set. We believe this is due to multiple factors. First, as we have no means to identify very difficult tweets for which even humans could not predict emoji (see Section 3), it is difficult to know to what extent the model generalized well. Of course, by comparing our approach results with other ones, we know that the model or the approach should be improved in order to better take into account all classes, as it is visible in the test set confusion matrix (Figure 1).

Another element explaining the major performance decrease is the presence of overlapping elements between the trial set and the training set

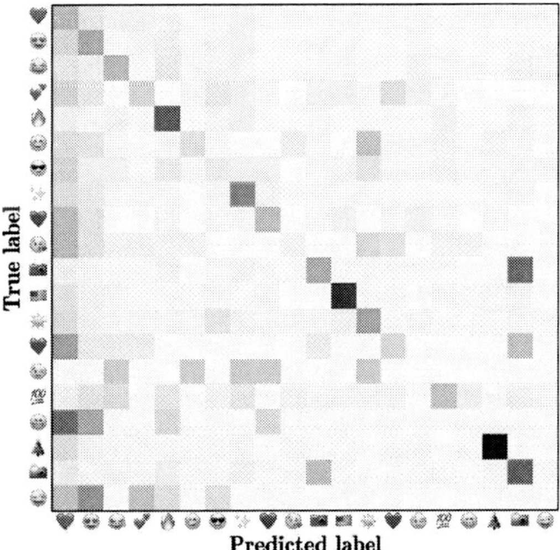

Figure 1: Confusion matrix from official test results.

that misleaded parameters tuning. Even though, we think a text representation enhancement is necessary, as this approach finally gave poor results.

5 Conclusion

In this paper we described the system we submitted to the SemEval-2018 Task 2 for Multilingual Emoji Prediction. The system presented uses text vectorization through word embeddings associated to a computed-features vector in order to represent each tweet by their polarity intensity and metrics. The classification is then done by using decision tree based algorithm for understanding, with bagging technique for better generalization to match the goal of macro F1-score metric. With this system we wanted to have a generic system for both languages without specific parameters for each language.

The system obtained good results on the trial set but the performances decreased drastically when applied to the test set. Even though this pattern was shown through all participants' systems, ours finally obtained poor results on the test set. We believe it is necessary to further process the data in order to identify recurrent difficult cases, such as really short and commons tweets. A more robust representation of each tweet is also required.

Finally, the python code used for this task is available on github[8].

---

[8] `https://github.com/ gguibon/SemEval2018-Task2- MultilingualEmojiPrediction`

References

Francesco Barbieri, Miguel Ballesteros, and Horacio Saggion. 2017. Are emojis predictable? In *Proceedings of the 15th Conference of the European Chapter of the Association for Computational Linguistics: Volume 2, Short Papers*, pages 105–111. Association for Computational Linguistics.

Francesco Barbieri, Jose Camacho-Collados, Francesco Ronzano, Luis Espinosa-Anke, Miguel Ballesteros, Valerio Basile, Viviana Patti, and Horacio Saggion. 2018. SemEval-2018 Task 2: Multilingual Emoji Prediction. In *Proceedings of the 12th International Workshop on Semantic Evaluation (SemEval-2018)*, New Orleans, LA, United States. Association for Computational Linguistics.

Francesco Barbieri, German Kruszewski, Francesco Ronzano, and Horacio Saggion. 2016. How cosmopolitan are emojis?: Exploring emojis usage and meaning over different languages with distributional semantics. In *Proceedings of the 2016 ACM on Multimedia Conference*, pages 531–535. ACM.

Piotr Bojanowski, Edouard Grave, Armand Joulin, and Tomas Mikolov. 2016. Enriching word vectors with subword information. *arXiv preprint arXiv:1607.04606*.

Spencer Cappallo, Thomas Mensink, and Cees G.M. Snoek. 2015. Image2emoji: Zero-shot emoji prediction for visual media. pages 1311–1314. ACM Press.

Ben Eisner, Tim Rocktäschel, Isabelle Augenstein, Matko Bošnjak, and Sebastian Riedel. 2016. emoji2vec: Learning emoji representations from their description. *arXiv preprint arXiv:1609.08359*.

Bjarke Felbo, Alan Mislove, Anders Søgaard, Iyad Rahwan, and Sune Lehmann. 2017. Using millions of emoji occurrences to learn any-domain representations for detecting sentiment, emotion and sarcasm. *arXiv preprint arXiv:1708.00524*.

Gaël Guibon, Magalie Ochs, and Patrice Bellot. 2018. Emoji recommendation in private instant messages. In *Proceedings of the 2018 ACM symposium on Applied computing*, pages 1810–1813. ACM.

Sepp Hochreiter and Jürgen Schmidhuber. 1997. Long short-term memory. *Neural Comput.*, 9(8):1735–1780.

Tomas Mikolov, Kai Chen, Greg Corrado, and Jeffrey Dean. 2013. Efficient estimation of word representations in vector space. *arXiv preprint arXiv:1301.3781*.

Alexander Pak and Patrick Paroubek. 2010. Twitter as a corpus for sentiment analysis and opinion mining. In *LREc*, volume 10.

Radim Rehurek and Petr Sojka. 2010. Software framework for topic modelling with large corpora. In *In Proceedings of the LREC 2010 Workshop on New Challenges for NLP Frameworks*. Citeseer.

Mike Thelwall, Kevan Buckley, Georgios Paltoglou, Di Cai, and Arvid Kappas. 2010. Sentiment strength detection in short informal text. *Journal of the American Society for Information Science and Technology*, 61(12):2544–2558.

Ruobing Xie, Zhiyuan Liu, Rui Yan, and Maosong Sun. 2016. Neural emoji recommendation in dialogue systems. *arXiv preprint arXiv:1612.04609*.

ALANIS at SemEval-2018 Task 3:
A Feature Engineering Approach to Irony Detection in English Tweets

Kevin Swanberg‡ and **Madiha Mirza†** and **Ted Pedersen†** and **Zhenduo Wang†***
‡Department of Writing Studies
†Department of Computer Science
University of Minnesota
Duluth, MN 55812, USA
{swanb034,mirz0022,tpederse,wang7211}@d.umn.edu

Abstract

This paper describes the ALANIS system that participated in Task 3 of SemEval-2018. We develop a system for detection of irony, as well as the detection of three types of irony: verbal polar irony, other verbal irony, and situational irony. The system uses a logistic regression model in subtask A and a voted classifier in subtask B, both of which rely on manually developed features to identify ironic tweets. ALANIS placed 34th of 43 systems in subtask A and 26th of 31 systems in subtask B.

1 Introduction

With the invention and growth of various social networking sites, irony and other creative linguistic devices have become increasingly prevalent in online content. Particularly when considering microblogging platforms like Twitter, which encourage users to share their thoughts and opinions on a wide variety of topics, the use of irony can be extremely common. This can have strong implications for various problems in natural language processing, which often have difficulty in processing this ironic content (e.g., (Liu, 2012; Ghosh and Veale, 2016; Maynard and Greenwood, 2014)), thus motivating the development of an accurate irony detection system.

While irony has many varying definitions, it is defined by the SemEval task organizers as a trope or figurative language whose actual meaning differs from what is literally enunciated. Our system, ALANIS (Automated Location and Naming of Ironic Sentences), uses a manually developed feature set and a logistic regression classifier for subtask A and a voted classifier for subtask B, achieving mean accuracies of .650 and .607 respectively on the training set and .512 and .434

respectively on the test set. The F1-scores are .469 and .276 on the test set.

2 Task Description

SemEval Task 3 involves two subtasks. In subtask A, a tweet simply must be identified as ironic or non-ironic. In subtask B, three types of ironic content must be individually differentiated from non-ironic content. These three types of irony are verbal polar irony, other verbal irony, and situational irony. The task organizers provided us with a training set of 3,834 tweets for both subtasks.

3 ALANIS

Our system, ALANIS, uses manually developed features indicative of ironic content, and passes a feature matrix for each tweet to a logistic regression classifier in subtask A and a voted classifier system which employs a logistic regression, SVM, and Random Forest classifier in Subtask B. It use the scores from each of these classifiers to "vote" on the correct label for a tweet.

3.1 Feature Selection

We explored two types of features, structural features and affective features. Structural features included sentence semantic similarity, irony-rich word lists, indicative parts of speech, and content features. Affective features included sentiment polarity and subjectivity. These features were used to assign scores for each tweet, creating a feature matrix.

3.2 Structural Features

Our system combines a number of structural features that are identified as indicative of ironic content by previous solutions.

Sentence Semantic Similarity is a measurement of similarity in meaning between two sentences. This is a structural feature employed in a

---

Authors are ordered alphabetically by their first name.

507

system designed by (Farías et al., 2016) with some success. Ironic tweets with multiple sentences should show a sharp change in meaning between sentences. To implement this feature we employed WordNet synsets. The similarity of the sentences is computed based on the semantic similarity of the words contained in the two sentences.

Irony-Rich Word Lists: Our system takes advantage of a number of words claimed to be indicative of irony. This involved several manually developed word lists. Most importantly, we used discourse markers, which are phrases that are indicative of discourse segments. Examples of these include *however, on the other hand*, and *in my opinion*. These have been cited as being more common in ironic content (Farías et al., 2016). Our system employs a list of 53 discourse markers. Also based on Farias et al, we measure intensifiers, like *very* and *really* that make adjectives stronger.

In addition to these, we build on our curated lists of irony-indicative words with features like swear words and top words, as well as textual markers of laughter like *lol* and *haha*, which was noted to be common in ironic content (Buschmeier et al., 2014). Another word list included interjections to detect irony. Interjections are word that express feeling rather than meaning, for example, words like *wow, gosh*, and *jeez*.

Indicative Parts of Speech: We also built features that measured the prevalence of several parts of speech thought to be indicative of ironic content. These included adjectives, adverbs, prepositions, and named entities. All of these features were identified by the NLTK[1] POS tagger in order to count their occurrence. These counts were then normalized for the length of the tweet. Adjectives and adverbs occur more frequently in ironic tweets than non-ironic according to (Kreuz and Caucci, 2007). We hypothesized that prepositions and named entities would occur more often in situational irony, due to the likely need to explain the situation.

Content Features: ALANIS also employs a number of features relevant to the content of the tweet in order to identify irony. These include Word Count, Punctuation, and URLs. According to Farias et al, ironic tweets tend to have excessive punctuation to catch the eyes of readers and to stress a point. Examples include "It is really

worth it!!!" or "Okay...". Thus, heavy punctuation sometimes implies irony. Farias et al. also identified that ironic tweets are likely to contain fewer words than non-ironic tweets, thus motivating the use of the word count feature.

URLs were also employed as a feature in our system. (Schifanella et al., 2016) found that ironic tweets often contain images and often the interpretation of the irony depends on the image. For example, a photo of a warm, sunny beach with the caption "Terrible weather we're having." However, the task data does not immediately give us images, only a link to images (which may not in fact exist online anymore), so the simplest way to identify this was to just check if a tweet had a URL.

Popular Hashtags and Keywords: Twitter hashtags and keywords are a good measure of public opinion on trending topics and current events. Through these hashtags, users express a wide variety of opinions, including irony. For example, the following hashtags were among the top Twitter hashtags for 2016: #GOPDebate, #PrayforJapan, #WomensRightsAreHumanRights. Our system finds hashtags that contain words related to global issues, sports, entertainment, and fashion using a manually created list of top hashtags.

3.3 Affective Features

While most work on irony detection (e.g., (Carvalho et al., 2009; Barbieri and Saggion, 2014; Vanin et al., 2013)) focus on the structural features, (Farías et al., 2016) show that introducing affective information can also improve state-of-the-art accuracy.

In our work, we included two commonly used sentiment features, polarity and subjectivity. Sentiment polarity reflects the general positivity of a piece of text, while subjectivity is measured against objectivity. Each of the two features is assigned a score within the range $[-1, 1]$. We used the TextBlob package in python [2] to implement the scoring functions for these features.

4 Classifiers

The classifiers we used for our system included Naive Bayes, logistic regression, Support Vector Machine (SVM) and Random Forest. We chose these because they are generally robust classifiers. As we added features to our feature list, we also

---

[1] http://www.nltk.org/

[2] http://textblob.readthedocs.io/en/dev/

kept track of the performance of the the logistic regression, Random Forest, and SVM classifiers, while Naive Bayes was only used for the bag of words baseline.

In ALANIS, all the classifiers take the tweet features matrix as input and have as output a binary label vector for the categorical result. We separate the data into a training set and a test set using cross-validation. We train the classifiers with the training set to optimize the parameters including the hyperplane and kernel. Then we evaluate the trained classifier on the test set.

Support Vector Machine: We find that SVM is relatively powerful when the feature list is short, compared with other classifiers. Also, we noticed that SVM classifier scores the highest recall, which means that it detects the most ironic tweets.

Logistic Regression Classifier: We find that logistic regression is stable in terms of total accuracy. It becomes the most accurate classifier for our long final feature list. The logistic regression classifier does not show any tendency in detecting irony or avoiding error. Because of its linear kernel, we are able to get the trained weights for each feature. This helps us know the capacities of features and select them better. We rank the importance of features according to the magnitude of their weights. See Table 3 for details.

Random Forest Classifier: This classifier does not perform well compared to the others. However, it is worth mentioning that when the feature list grows long, it retains a higher accuracy than SVM.

Voting System: We find that the confusion matrices of the classifiers are different. This means the classifiers have different specialties. Therefore, we combined them in order to get a synthesized result. We make a voting system with the classifiers discussed previously. The voting system uses majority rule.

5 Experimental Results

Our final result is that logistic regression is most accurate classifier for subtask A and the voting system is most accurate for subtask B. Table 1 shows the average cross validation scores on the training set, while Table 2 shows the scores when our system is trained on the whole training set and evaluated on the test set.

BOW+NB stands for the Bag of Words Naive Bayes baseline, while LR, RF, and Vote represent

Model	TaskA Acc	TaskB Acc
BOW+NB	0.572	0.285
LR	**0.650**	0.603
SVM	0.596	0.545
RF	0.622	0.584
Vote	0.644	**0.607**

Table 1: Performance of classifiers on training set

Model	TaskA Acc/f1	TaskB Acc/f1
LR	0.512/0.469	-
Vote	-	0.434/0.276

Table 2: Performance of classifiers on test set

logistic regression, Random Forest, and the Voting System. Based on these results, we used logistic regression or subtask A and the voting system for subtask B.

The result in Table 1 are based on 5-fold cross validation with the training data. As such we expected comparable results when we applied our classifiers to the test data. However as can be seen in Table 2 this is not the case. The results for LR decline from .65 to .51, and for Vote from .607 to .434. While some variation is to be expected, this was surprising to us. We hypothesize one of two possible explanations. First, our methods may have overfit the training data and so do not generalize well to other data. However, since we employed cross validation we are not certain how likely this explanation proves to be. The second explanation may be that the test data is in some way different from the training data, to the extent that a model learnt on the training data may not fare well on the test data. We have not yet analyzed the test data closely enough to resolve this question, but consider this to be an important step in understanding our results.

6 Discussion and Future Work

We tried to interpret the importance of the features by the magnitude of their weights in logistic regression. The weights of the features' performance in subtask A and B are shown in Table 3. In interpreting this table, the further a feature is from 0, the stronger the feature's impact is on our classifier. For instance, of our features, stop words and laughters are relative weak features. Conversely, intensifiers, discourse markers, adjective/adverbs, and prepositions are much stronger features.

In order to understand the different performance

Feature	Weight	Feature	Weight
intensifier	1.05	subjectivity	0.20
discourse	0.90	named entity	0.18
adj./adv.	0.81	swear words	0.18
preposition	0.81	URLs	0.15
polarity	0.54	word count	0.12
politcal	0.39	similarity	0.11
interjections	0.34	stopwords	0.06
celebrity	0.33	laughter	0.01
punctuation	0.32		

Table 3: Weights (in absolute) of features

of the classifiers, we made confusion matrices for all the classifiers and then also did a weight analysis for logistic regression since it employs a linear kernel. From the confusion matrices, we found that although the classifiers have their specialties, the voting system does not always work out well. We believe that this is because SVM and Random Forest are both much weaker than the logistic regression classifier (shown in Table 1) so they neutralize logistic regression's advantages.

In subtask B, we need to label a tweet with 0 (non-ironic) or 1,2,3 (three different subcategories of irony). However, the difference among these subcategories are so subtle that our features do not capture them very well. Overall these classifiers have a hard time with multi-class classification. Since all three classifiers have more similar results for task B, the voted system is more successful

We review our system and the output of our system and find several possible explanations. From the confusion matrix, we can see that class 2 (7%) and 3 (5.9%) are relatively rare. This makes the task very hard for classifiers because of lack of information to train on for class 2 and 3. However, because the majority of data in subtask B falls into class 0 and class 1 we are still able to get a high accuracy (0.6+). If the data was spread more evenly between the four classes our system would likely perform better. When analyzing individual tweets from class 1, 2 and 3, we found that their feature lists are more similar to each other than to class 0 (non-ironic). This means we miss features that are relevant for identifying different types of irony, making our feature-based classifier ill suited to this task.

To see the system's effectiveness, it is often helpful to consider some indicative examples of the system in action. Consider examples (1) and (2) below. Our system successfully classifies (1) as ironic, but fails to classify (2) as ironic.

1. Feeling like crap. And being treated horribly too. It's a great day. #iwanttogohome

2. Hey there! Nice to see you Minnesota/ND Winter Weather

Our system likely successfully classifies (1) for a number of reasons. First, the word count of the sentences is low, which seems typical of ironic tweets. It has strong sentiment polarity between the sentences. The first two sentences are negative, and the last sentence is positive. There is also a strong shift in sentence similarity between sentences.

However, (2) is classified incorrectly. This is likely because it is identified by our system as similar sentiment in both sentences. There is also very little punctuation or emojis, and there are no indicative words, like discourse markers or interjections in the tweet, causing our system to fail.

These results demonstrate that a manually-selected feature-based system, using both structural and affective features can achieve reasonable success in identifying ironic content. This system is successful even when used with non-conventional language such as that seen in Twitter data. Our mean accuracy scores of .650 and .607 on the two subtasks on the training set demonstrates both a reasonable success, and an opportunity for future work in irony detection by extending the feature set further or even applying a deep learning approach to the problem when enough data is available.

7   Acknowledgments

This project was carried out as a part of CS 8761, Natural Language Processing, a graduate level class offered in Fall 2017 at the University of Minnesota, Duluth by Dr. Ted Pedersen.

References

Francesco Barbieri and Horacio Saggion. 2014. Automatic detection of irony and humour in twitter. In *ICCC*. pages 155–162.

Konstantin Buschmeier, Philipp Cimiano, and Roman Klinger. 2014. An impact analysis of features in a classification approach to irony detection in product reviews. In *Proceedings of the 5th Workshop* on *Computational Approaches to Subjectivity, Sentiment and Social Media Analysis*. Association for Computational Linguistics, Baltimore, Maryland, pages 42–49.

Paula Carvalho, Luís Sarmento, Mário J. Silva, and Eugénio de Oliveira. 2009. Clues for detecting irony in user-generated contents: Oh...!! it's "so easy" ;-). In *Proceedings of the 1st International CIKM Workshop on Topic-sentiment Analysis for Mass Opinion*. ACM, New York, NY, USA, TSA '09, pages 53–56.

Delia Irazú Hernańdez Farías, Viviana Patti, and Paolo Rosso. 2016. Irony detection in twitter: The role of affective content. *ACM Trans. Internet Technol.* 16(3):19:1–19:24.

Aniruddha Ghosh and Tony Veale. 2016. Fracking sarcasm using neural network. In *WASSA@ NAACL-HLT*. pages 161–169.

Roger J Kreuz and Gina M Caucci. 2007. Lexical influences on the perception of sarcasm. In *Proceedings of the Workshop on computational approaches to Figurative Language*. Association for Computational Linguistics, pages 1–4.

Bing Liu. 2012. Sentiment analysis and opinion mining. *Synthesis lectures on human language technologies* 5(1):1–167.

Diana Maynard and Mark A Greenwood. 2014. Who cares about sarcastic tweets? investigating the impact of sarcasm on sentiment analysis. In *LREC*. pages 4238–4243.

Rossano Schifanella, Paloma de Juan, Joel R. Tetreault, and Liangliang Cao. 2016. Detecting sarcasm in multimodal social platforms. *CoRR* abs/1608.02289.

Aline A. Vanin, Larissa A. Freitas, Renata Vieira, and Marco Bochernitsan. 2013. Some clues on irony detection in tweets. In *Proceedings of the 22Nd International Conference on World Wide Web*. ACM, New York, NY, USA, WWW '13 Companion, pages 635–636.

NEUROSENT-PDI at SemEval-2018 Task 3: Understanding Irony in Social Networks Through a Multi-Domain Sentiment Model

Mauro Dragoni

Fondazione Bruno Kessler

Via Sommarive 18

Povo, Trento, Italy

dragoni@fbk.eu

Abstract

This paper describes the NeuroSent system that participated in SemEval 2018 Task 3. Our system takes a supervised approach that builds on neural networks and word embeddings. Word embeddings were built by starting from a repository of user generated reviews. Thus, they are specific for sentiment analysis tasks. Then, tweets are converted in the corresponding vector representation and given as input to the neural network with the aim of learning the different semantics contained in each emotion taken into account by the SemEval task. The output layer has been adapted based on the characteristics of each subtask. Preliminary results obtained on the provided training set are encouraging for pursuing the investigation into this direction.

1 Introduction

Sentiment Analysis is a natural language processing (NLP) task (Dragoni et al., 2015a) which aims at classifying documents according to the opinion expressed about a given subject (Federici and Dragoni, 2016a,b). Many works available in the literature address the sentiment analysis problem without distinguishing specific information context of documents when sentiment models are built.

The necessity of investigating this problem from a multi-domain perspective is led by the different influence that a term might have in different contexts. The idea of adapting terms polarity to different domains emerged only in the last decade (Blitzer et al., 2007; Dragoni and Petrucci, 2017). Multi-domain sentiment analysis approaches discussed in the literature focus on building models for transferring information between pairs of domains (Dragoni, 2015; Petrucci and Dragoni, 2015). While on the one hand such approaches allow to propagate specific domain in-

formation to others, their drawback is the necessity of building new transfer models every time a new domain has to be analyzed. Thus, such approaches do not have a great generalization capability of analyzing texts, because transfer models are limited to the N domains used for building the models.

The problem of detecting irony in text can be considered from a multi-domain perspective. The development of the social web has stimulated creative and figurative language use like irony. This frequent use of irony on social media has important implications for natural language processing tasks, which struggle to maintain high performance when applied to ironic text (Liu and Zhang, 2012; Maynard and Greenwood, 2014; Ghosh and Veale, 2016). Although different definitions of irony co-exist, it is often identified as a trope or figurative language use whose actual meaning differs from what is literally enunciated. As such, modeling irony has a large potential for applications in various research areas, including text mining, author profiling, detecting online harassment, and perhaps one of the most popular applications at present, sentiment analysis. As described by (Joshi et al., 2017), recent approaches to irony can roughly be classified into rule-based and machine learning-based methods. While rule-based approaches mostly rely upon lexical information and require no training, machine learning invariably makes use of training data and exploits different types of information sources, including bags of words, syntactic patterns, sentiment information or semantic relatedness. Recently, deep learning techniques gain increasing popularity for this task as they allow to integrate semantic relatedness by making use of, for instance, word embeddings.

In this paper, we discuss how the NeuroSent tool has been applied in SemEval 2018 Task 3 (Hee et al., 2018). The tool leverages on the

Proceedings of the 12th International Workshop on Semantic Evaluation (SemEval-2018), pages 512–519

New Orleans, Louisiana, June 5–6, 2018. ©2018 Association for Computational Linguistics

following pillars: (i) the use of word embeddings for representing each word contained in raw sentences; (ii) the word embeddings are generated from an opinion-based corpus instead of a general purpose one (like news or Wikipedia); (iii) the design of a deep learning technique exploiting the generated word embeddings for training the sentiment model; and (iv) the use of multiple output layers for combining domain overlap scores with domain-specific polarity predictions.

The last point enables the exploitation of linguistic overlaps between domains, which can be considered one of the pivotal assets of our approach. This way, the overall polarity of a document is computed by aggregating, for each domain, the domain-specific polarity value multiplied by a belonging degree representing the overlap between the embedded representation of the whole document and the domain itself.

2 Related Work

Sentiment analysis from the multi-task and multi-domain perspective is a research field which started to be explored only in the last decade. According to the nomenclature widely used in the literature (see (Blitzer et al., 2007; Dragoni and Petrucci, 2017)), we call *domain* a set of documents about similar topics, e.g. a set of reviews about similar products like mobile phones, books, movies, etc.. The massive availability of multi-domain corpora in which similar opinions are expressed about different topics opened the scenario for new challenges. Researchers tried to train models capable to acquire knowledge from a specific domain and then to exploit such a knowledge for working on documents belonging to different ones. This strategy was called domain adaptation. The use of domain adaptation techniques demonstrated that opinion classification is highly sensitive to the domain from which the training data is extracted. The reason is that when using the same words, and even the same language constructs, we may obtain different opinions, depending on the domain. The classic scenario occurs when the same word has positive connotations in one domain and negative connotations in another one, as we showed within the examples presented in Section 1.

Several approaches related to multi-domain sentiment analysis have been proposed. Roughly speaking, all of these approaches rely on one of the following ideas: (i) the transfer of learned classifiers across different domains (Blitzer et al., 2007; Pan et al., 2010; Bollegala et al., 2013; Xia et al., 2013), and (ii) the use of propagation of labels through graph structures (Ponomareva and Thelwall, 2013; Tsai et al., 2013; Dragoni et al., 2015b; Dragoni, 2015, 2017; Petrucci and Dragoni, 2017, 2016, 2015; Dragoni et al., 2014; Dragoni and Petrucci, 2018).

While on the one hand such approaches demonstrated their effectiveness in working in a multi-domain environment, on the other hand they suffered by the limitation of being influenced by the linguistic overlap between domains. Indeed, such an overlap leads learning algorithms to infer similar polarity values to domains that are similar from the linguistic perspective.

The adoption of evolutionary algorithms within the sentiment analysis research field is quite recent. First studies focused on the use of evolutionary solutions for modeling financial indicators by starting from investors sentiments (Yamada and Ueda, 2005; Chen and Chang, 2005; Huang et al., 2012; Yang et al., 2017; Simoes et al., 2017). Here, the evolutionary component was used for learning the trend of financial indicators with respect to the sentiment information extracted from opinions provided by the investors. With respect to these papers, we propose an approach adopting evolutionary computation to a more fine-grained level where the evolution component affects also the polarities of opinion concepts.

Studies considering the use of evolutionary algorithms for optimizing the polarity values of opinion concepts have been proposed only recently (Ferreira et al., 2015; Onan et al., 2016, 2017). However, these works focused on learning candidate refinements of opinion concepts polarity without considering the context dimension associated with them. A variant of this problem is the use of polarity adaptation strategy in the field of social media and microblogs (Alahmadi and Zeng, 2015; Wang et al., 2014; Keshavarz and Abadeh, 2017; Hu et al., 2016; Fu et al., 2016; Gong et al., 2016).

With respect to state of the art, this work represents the first exploration of evolutionary algorithms for multi-domain sentiment analysis with the aim of learning multiple dictionaries of opinion concepts. Moreover, we differ from the literature by do not considering the propagation of polarity information across domain (i.e., we keep them completely separated) in order to avoid transfer learning drawbacks.

3   System Implementation

NeuroSent has been entirely developed in Java with the support of the Deeplearning4j library [1] and it is composed by following two main phases:

- Generation of Word vectors (Section 3.1): raw text, appropriately tokenized using the Stanford CoreNLP Toolkit, is provided as input to a 2-layers neural network implementing the skip-gram approach with the aim of generating word vectors.

- Learning of Sentiment Model (Section 3.2): word vectors are used for training a recurrent neural network with an output layer customized based on the addressed subtask. The customizations have been explained in Section 4.

In the following subsections, we describe in more detail each phase by providing also the settings used for managing our data.

3.1   Generation of Word Vectors

The generation of the word vectors has been performed by applying the skip-gram algorithm on the raw natural language text extracted from the smaller version of the SNAP dataset (McAuley and Leskovec, 2013). The rationale behind the choice of this dataset focuses on three reasons:

- the dataset contains only opinion-based documents. This way, we are able to build word embeddings describing only opinion-based contexts.

- the dataset is multi-domain. Information contained into the generated word embeddings comes from specific domains, thus it is possible to evaluate how the proposed approach is general by testing the performance of the created model on test sets containing documents coming from the domains used for building the model or from other domains.

- the dataset is smaller with respect to other corpora used in the literature for building other word embeddings that are currently freely available, like the Google News ones. [2] Indeed, as introduced in Section 1, one of our goal is to demonstrate how we can leverage the use of dedicated resources for generating word embeddings, instead of corpora's size, for improving the effectiveness of classification systems.

The aspect of considering only opinion-based information for generating word embeddings is one of the peculiarity of our system. While embeddings currently available are created from big corpora of general purpose texts (like news archives or Wikipedia pages), ours are generated by using a smaller corpus containing documents strongly related to the problem that the model will be thought for. On the one hand, this aspect may be considered a limitation of the proposed solution due to the requirement of training a new model in case of problem change. However, on the other hand, the usage of dedicated resources would lead to the construction of more effective models.

Word embeddings have been generated by the Word2Vec implementation integrated into the Deeplearning4j library. The algorithm has been set up with the following parameters: the size of the vector to 64, the size of the window used as input of the skip-gram algorithm to 5, and the minimum word frequency was set to 1. The reason for which we kept the minimum word frequency set to 1 is to avoid the loss of rare but important words that can occur in domain specific documents.

3.2   Learning of The Sentiment Model

The sentiment model is built by starting from the word embeddings generated during the previous phase.

The first step consists in converting each textual sentence contained within the dataset into the corresponding numerical matrix $\mathbf{S}$ where we have in each row the word vector representing a single word of the sentence, and in each column an embedding feature. Given a sentence s, we extract all tokens t_i, with $i \in [0, n]$, and we replace each t_i with the corresponding embedding $\mathbf{w}$. During the conversion of each word in its corresponding embedding, if such embedding is not found, the word is discarded. At the end of this step, each sentence contained in the training set is converted in a matrix $\mathbf{S} = [\mathbf{w}^{\langle 1 \rangle}, \ldots, \mathbf{w}^{\langle n \rangle}]$.

---

[1] https://deeplearning4j.org/

[2] https://github.com/mmihaltz/word2vec-GoogleNews-vectors

Before giving all matrices as input to the neural network, we need to include both padding and masking vectors in order to train our model correctly. Padding and masking allows us to support different training situations depending on the number of the input vectors and on the number of predictions that the network has to provide at each time step. In our scenario, we work in a many-to-one situation where our neural network has to provide one prediction (sentence polarity and domain overlap) as result of the analysis of many input vectors (word embeddings).

Padding vectors are required because we have to deal with the different length of sentences. Indeed, the neural network needs to know the number of time steps that the input layer has to import. This problem is solved by including, if necessary, into each matrix $\mathbf{S}_k$, with $k \in [0, z]$ and z the number of sentences contained in the training set, null word vectors that are used for filling empty word's slots. These null vectors are accompanied by a further vector telling to the neural network if data contained in a specific positions has to be considered as an informative embedding or not.

A final note concerns the back propagation of the error. Training recurrent neural networks can be quite computationally demanding in cases when each training instance is composed by many time steps. A possible optimization is the use of truncated back propagation through time (BPTT) that was developed for reducing the computational complexity of each parameter update in a recurrent neural network. On the one hand, this strategy allows to reduce the time needed for training our model. However, on the other hand, there is the risk of not flowing backward the gradients for the full unrolled network. This prevents the full update of all network parameters. For this reason, even if we work with recurrent neural networks, we decided to do not implement a BPTT approach but to use the default backpropagation implemented into the DL4J library.

Concerning information about network structure, the input layer was composed by 64 neurons (i.e. embedding vector size), the hidden RNN layer was composed by 128 nodes, and the output layers with a different number of nodes based on the addressed subtask. The network has been trained by using the Stochastic Gradient Descent with 1000 epochs and a learning rate of 0.002.

4 The Tasks

The SemEval 2018 Task 3 is composed by two different subtasks for the automatic detection of irony on Twitter. For the first subtask, participants should determine whether a tweet is ironic or not by simply assigning a binary value 0 or 1. While, for the second subtask, participants have to distinguish, among the ironic tweets, one of the three classes which tweets are further split.

Subtask #1: Ironic vs. Non-ironic The first subtask is a binary classification task where the system has to predict whether a tweet is ironic or not. Example of an ironic and non-ironic tweet are presented below, respectively:

- *I just love when you test my patience!! #not*

- *Had no sleep and have got school now #not happy*

The output layer of our neural network is composed by a single neuron implementing the SIGMOID activation function.

Subtask #2: Different types of irony The second subtask is a multiclass classification task where the system has to predict one out of four labels describing:

i. verbal irony realized through a polarity contrast;

ii. verbal irony without such a polarity contrast;

iii. descriptions of situational irony; and,

iv. non-irony

i

Instances of the category *Verbal irony by means of a polarity contrast* contains an evaluative expression whose polarity (positive, negative) is inverted between the literal and the intended evaluation. An example of this category is the following: "*I really love this year's summer; weeks and weeks of awful weather.*"

Instead, instances of the category *Verbal irony without such a polarity contrast* do not show polarity contrast between the literal and the intended evaluation, but are nevertheless ironic. An example of this category is the following: "*Human brains disappear every day. Some of them have never even appeared.*"

Then, instances of the *Situational irony* category describe situations that fail to meet some expectations. An example is the following: *"Just saw a non-smoking sign in the lobby of a tobacco company."*

Finally, the *Non-ironic* category contains instances that are clearly not ironic, or which lack context to be sure that they are ironic.

The output layer of our neural network is composed by four neurons and the SOFTMAX strategy has been implemented for selecting the most candidate class.

The NeuroSent system has been applied to both subtasks. In Section 5, we report the preliminary results obtained by NeuroSent on the training set compared with a set of baselines.

5   In-Vitro Evaluation

Approach	Task #3.1	Task #3.2
Support Vector Machine	0.4294	0.4415
Naive-Bayes	0.4388	0.4378
Maximum Entropy	0.4810	0.4629
CNN Architecture	0.5420	0.4891
NeuroSent	**0.5687**	**0.5974**

Table 1: Results obtained on the training set by NeuroSent and by the four baselines.

The NeuroSent approach have been preliminarily evaluated by adopting the Dranziera protocol (Dragoni et al., 2016).

The validation procedure leverages on a five-fold cross evaluation setting in order to validate the robustness of the proposed solution. The approach has been compared with four baselines: Support Vector Machine (SVM) (Chang and Lin, 2011), Naive Bayes (NB) and Maximum Entropy (ME) (McCallum, 2002), and Convolutional Neural Network (Chaturvedi et al., 2016).

In Table 1, we provide average Pearson correlation obtained on the five folds in which the training set has been split.

The obtained results demonstrated the suitability of NeuroSent with respect to the adopted baselines. We may also observed how solutions based on neural networks obtained a significant improvement with respect to the others for both tasks.

We performed a detailed error analysis concerning the performance of NeuroSent. In general, we observed how our strategy tends to provide false negative predictions. An in depth analysis of some incorrect predictions highlighted that the embedded representations of some positive opinion words are very close to the space region of negative opinion words. Even if we may state that the confidence about positive predictions is very high, this scenario leads to have a predominant negative classification for borderline instances.

On the one hand, a possible action for improving the effectiveness our strategy is to increase the granularity of the embeddings (i.e. augmenting the size of the embedding vectors) in order to increase the distance between the positive and negative polarities space regions. On the other hand, by increasing the size of embedding vectors, the computational time for building, or updating, the model and for evaluating a single instance increases as well. Part of the future work, will be the analysis of more efficient neural network architectures able to manage augmented embedding vectors without negatively affecting the efficiency of the platform.

6   Conclusion

In this paper, we described the NeuroSent system presented at SemEval 2018 Task 3. Our system makes use of artificial neural networks to classify tweets by polarity or for detecting emotion levels. The results obtained on the training set demonstrated that the adopted solution is promising and worthy of investigation. Therefore, future work will focus on improving the system by exploring the integration of sentiment knowledge bases (Dragoni et al., 2015a) in order to move toward a more cognitive approach.

References

Dimah Hussain Alahmadi and Xiao-Jun Zeng. 2015. Twitter-based recommender system to address cold-start: A genetic algorithm based trust modelling and probabilistic sentiment analysis. In *27th IEEE International Conference on Tools with Artificial Intelligence, ICTAI 2015, Vietri sul Mare, Italy, November 9-11, 2015*, pages 1045–1052. IEEE Computer Society.

John Blitzer, Mark Dredze, and Fernando Pereira. 2007. Biographies, bollywood, boom-boxes and blenders: Domain adaptation for sentiment classification. In *ACL 2007, Proceedings of the 45th Annual Meeting of the Association for Computational Linguistics, June 23-30, 2007, Prague, Czech Republic*. The Association for Computational Linguistics.

Danushka Bollegala, David J. Weir, and John A. Carroll. 2013. Cross-domain sentiment classification using a sentiment sensitive thesaurus. *IEEE Trans. Knowl. Data Eng.*, 25(8):1719–1731.

Chih-Chung Chang and Chih-Jen Lin. 2011. Libsvm: A library for support vector machines. *ACM TIST*, 2(3):27:1–27:27.

Iti Chaturvedi, Erik Cambria, and David Vilares. 2016. Lyapunov filtering of objectivity for spanish sentiment model. In *2016 International Joint Conference on Neural Networks, IJCNN 2016, Vancouver, BC, Canada, July 24-29, 2016*, pages 4474–4481. IEEE.

An-Pin Chen and Yung-Hua Chang. 2005. Using extended classifier system to forecast s&p futures based on contrary sentiment indicators. In *Proceedings of the IEEE Congress on Evolutionary Computation, CEC 2005, 2-4 September 2005, Edinburgh, UK*, pages 2084–2090. IEEE.

Mauro Dragoni. 2015. Shellfbk: An information retrieval-based system for multi-domain sentiment analysis. In *Proceedings of the 9th International Workshop on Semantic Evaluation*, SemEval '2015, pages 502–509, Denver, Colorado. Association for Computational Linguistics.

Mauro Dragoni. 2017. Extracting linguistic features from opinion data streams for multi-domain sentiment analysis. In *Proceedings of the 3rd International Workshop at ESWC on Emotions, Modality, Sentiment Analysis and the Semantic Web co-located with 14th ESWC 2017, Portroz, Slovenia, May 28, 2017.*, volume 1874 of *CEUR Workshop Proceedings*. CEUR-WS.org.

Mauro Dragoni and Giulio Petrucci. 2017. A neural word embeddings approach for multi-domain sentiment analysis. *IEEE Trans. Affective Computing*, 8(4):457–470.

Mauro Dragoni and Giulio Petrucci. 2018. A fuzzy-based strategy for multi-domain sentiment analysis. *Int. J. Approx. Reasoning*, 93:59–73.

Mauro Dragoni, Andrea Tettamanzi, and Célia da Costa Pereira. 2016. DRANZIERA: an evaluation protocol for multi-domain opinion mining. In *Proceedings of the Tenth International Conference on Language Resources and Evaluation LREC 2016, Portorož, Slovenia, May 23-28, 2016.* European Language Resources Association (ELRA).

Mauro Dragoni, Andrea G. B. Tettamanzi, and Célia da Costa Pereira. 2014. A fuzzy system for concept-level sentiment analysis. In *Semantic Web Evaluation Challenge - SemWebEval 2014 at ESWC 2014, Anissaras, Crete, Greece, May 25-29, 2014, Revised Selected Papers*, volume 475 of *Communications in Computer and Information Science*, pages 21–27. Springer.

Mauro Dragoni, Andrea G. B. Tettamanzi, and Célia da Costa Pereira. 2015a. Propagating and aggregating fuzzy polarities for concept-level sentiment analysis. *Cognitive Computation*, 7(2):186–197.

Mauro Dragoni, Andrea Giovanni Battista Tettamanzi, and Célia da Costa Pereira. 2015b. Propagating and aggregating fuzzy polarities for concept-level sentiment analysis. *Cognitive Computation*, 7(2):186–197.

Marco Federici and Mauro Dragoni. 2016a. A knowledge-based approach for aspect-based opinion mining. In *Semantic Web Challenges - Third SemWebEval Challenge at ESWC 2016, Heraklion, Crete, Greece, May 29 - June 2, 2016, Revised Selected Papers*, volume 641 of *Communications in Computer and Information Science*, pages 141–152. Springer.

Marco Federici and Mauro Dragoni. 2016b. Towards unsupervised approaches for aspects extraction. In *Joint Proceedings of the 2th Workshop on Emotions, Modality, Sentiment Analysis and the Semantic Web and the 1st International Workshop on Extraction and Processing of Rich Semantics from Medical Texts co-located with ESWC 2016, Heraklion, Greece, May 29, 2016.*, volume 1613 of *CEUR Workshop Proceedings*. CEUR-WS.org.

Lohann Ferreira, Mariza Dosciatti, Júlio C. Nievola, and Emerson Cabrera Paraiso. 2015. Using a genetic algorithm approach to study the impact of imbalanced corpora in sentiment analysis. In *Proceedings of the Twenty-Eighth International Florida Artificial Intelligence Research Society Conference, FLAIRS 2015, Hollywood, Florida. May 18-20, 2015.*, pages 163–168. AAAI Press.

Peng Fu, Zheng Lin, Hailun Lin, Fengcheng Yuan, Weiping Wang, and Dan Meng. 2016. Quantifying the effect of sentiment on topic evolution in chinese microblog. In *Web Technologies and Applications - 18th Asia-Pacific Web Conference, APWeb 2016, Suzhou, China, September 23-25, 2016. Proceedings, Part I*, volume 9931 of *Lecture Notes in Computer Science*, pages 531–542. Springer.

Aniruddha Ghosh and Tony Veale. 2016. Fracking sarcasm using neural network. In *Proceedings of the 7th Workshop on Computational Approaches to Subjectivity, Sentiment and Social Media Analysis, WASSA@NAACL-HLT 2016, June 16, 2016, San Diego, California, USA*, pages 161–169. The Association for Computer Linguistics.

Lin Gong, Mohammad Al Boni, and Hongning Wang. 2016. Modeling social norms evolution for personalized sentiment classification. In *Proceedings of the 54th Annual Meeting of the Association for Computational Linguistics, ACL 2016, August 7-12, 2016, Berlin, Germany, Volume 1: Long Papers.* The Association for Computer Linguistics.

Cynthia Van Hee, Els Lefever, and Veronique Hoste. 2018. Semeval-2018 task 3: Irony detection in english tweets. In *Proceedings of International Workshop on Semantic Evaluation (SemEval-2018)*, New Orleans, LA, USA.

Yan Hu, Xiaofei Xu, and Li Li. 2016. Analyzing topic-sentiment and topic evolution over time from social media. In *Knowledge Science, Engineering and Management - 9th International Conference, KSEM 2016, Passau, Germany, October 5-7, 2016, Proceedings*, volume 9983 of *Lecture Notes in Computer Science*, pages 97–109.

Chien-Feng Huang, Tsung-Nan Hsieh, Bao Rong Chang, and Chih-Hsiang Chang. 2012. A comparative study of regression and evolution-based stock selection models for investor sentiment. In *2012 Third International Conference on Innovations in Bio-Inspired Computing and Applications, Kaohsiung City, Taiwan, September 26-28, 2012*, pages 73–78. IEEE.

Aditya Joshi, Pushpak Bhattacharyya, and Mark James Carman. 2017. Automatic sarcasm detection: A survey. *ACM Comput. Surv.*, 50(5):73:1–73:22.

Hamidreza Keshavarz and Mohammad Saniee Abadeh. 2017. ALGA: adaptive lexicon learning using genetic algorithm for sentiment analysis of microblogs. *Knowl.-Based Syst.*, 122:1–16.

Bing Liu and Lei Zhang. 2012. A survey of opinion mining and sentiment analysis. In C. C. Aggarwal and C. X. Zhai, editors, *Mining Text Data*, pages 415–463. Springer.

Diana Maynard and Mark A. Greenwood. 2014. Who cares about sarcastic tweets? investigating the impact of sarcasm on sentiment analysis. In *Proceedings of the Ninth International Conference on Language Resources and Evaluation, LREC 2014, Reykjavik, Iceland, May 26-31, 2014.*, pages 4238–4243. European Language Resources Association (ELRA).

Julian J. McAuley and Jure Leskovec. 2013. Hidden factors and hidden topics: understanding rating dimensions with review text. In *Seventh ACM Conference on Recommender Systems, RecSys '13, Hong Kong, China, October 12-16, 2013*, pages 165–172. ACM.

Andrew Kachites McCallum. 2002. Mallet: A machine learning for language toolkit. `http://mallet.cs.umass.edu`.

Aytug Onan, Serdar Korukoglu, and Hasan Bulut. 2016. A multiobjective weighted voting ensemble classifier based on differential evolution algorithm for text sentiment classification. *Expert Syst. Appl.*, 62:1–16.

Aytug Onan, Serdar Korukoglu, and Hasan Bulut. 2017. A hybrid ensemble pruning approach based

on consensus clustering and multi-objective evolutionary algorithm for sentiment classification. *Inf. Process. Manage.*, 53(4):814–833.

Sinno Jialin Pan, Xiaochuan Ni, Jian-Tao Sun, Qiang Yang, and Zheng Chen. 2010. Cross-domain sentiment classification via spectral feature alignment. In *Proceedings of the 19th International Conference on World Wide Web, WWW 2010, Raleigh, North Carolina, USA, April 26-30, 2010*, pages 751–760. ACM.

Giulio Petrucci and Mauro Dragoni. 2015. An information retrieval-based system for multi-domain sentiment analysis. In *Semantic Web Evaluation Challenges - Second SemWebEval Challenge at ESWC 2015, Portorož, Slovenia, May 31 - June 4, 2015, Revised Selected Papers*, volume 548 of *Communications in Computer and Information Science*, pages 234–243. Springer.

Giulio Petrucci and Mauro Dragoni. 2016. The IRMUDOSA system at ESWC-2016 challenge on semantic sentiment analysis. In *Semantic Web Challenges - Third SemWebEval Challenge at ESWC 2016, Heraklion, Crete, Greece, May 29 - June 2, 2016, Revised Selected Papers*, volume 641 of *Communications in Computer and Information Science*, pages 126–140. Springer.

Giulio Petrucci and Mauro Dragoni. 2017. The IR-MUDOSA system at ESWC-2017 challenge on semantic sentiment analysis. In *Semantic Web Challenges - 4th SemWebEval Challenge at ESWC 2017, Portoroz, Slovenia, May 28 - June 1, 2017, Revised Selected Papers*, volume 769 of *Communications in Computer and Information Science*, pages 148–165. Springer.

Natalia Ponomareva and Mike Thelwall. 2013. Semi-supervised vs. cross-domain graphs for sentiment analysis. In *Recent Advances in Natural Language Processing, RANLP 2013, 9-11 September, 2013, Hissar, Bulgaria*, pages 571–578. RANLP 2013 Organising Committee/ACL.

Carlos Simoes, Rui Ferreira Neves, and Nuno Horta. 2017. Using sentiment from twitter optimized by genetic algorithms to predict the stock market. In *2017 IEEE Congress on Evolutionary Computation, CEC 2017, Donostia, San Sebastián, Spain, June 5-8, 2017*, pages 1303–1310. IEEE.

Angela Charng-Rurng Tsai, Chi-En Wu, Richard Tzong-Han Tsai, and Jane Yung jen Hsu. 2013. Building a concept-level sentiment dictionary based on commonsense knowledge. *IEEE Int. Systems*, 28(2):22–30.

Zhitao Wang, Zhiwen Yu, Zhu Wang, and Bin Guo. 2014. Investigating sentiment impact on information propagation and its evolution in microblog. In *2014 International Conference on Behavioral, Economic, and Socio-Cultural Computing, BESC 2014, Shanghai, China, October 30 - November 1, 2014*, pages 33–39. IEEE.

Rui Xia, Chengqing Zong, Xuelei Hu, and Erik Cambria. 2013. Feature ensemble plus sample selection: Domain adaptation for sentiment classification. *IEEE Int. Systems*, 28(3):10–18.

Takashi Yamada and Kazuhiro Ueda. 2005. Explanation of binarized time series using genetic learning model of investor sentiment. In *Proceedings of the IEEE Congress on Evolutionary Computation, CEC 2005, 2-4 September 2005, Edinburgh, UK*, pages 2437–2444. IEEE.

Steve Y. Yang, Sheung Yin Kevin Mo, Anqi Liu, and Andrei Kirilenko. 2017. Genetic programming optimization for a sentiment feedback strength based trading strategy. *Neurocomputing*, 264:29–41.

UWB at SemEval-2018 Task 3: Irony detection in English tweets

Tomáš Hercig[1,2]

[1]NTIS – New Technologies for the Information Society,
Faculty of Applied Sciences, University of West Bohemia, Czech Republic
[2]Department of Computer Science and Engineering,
Faculty of Applied Sciences, University of West Bohemia, Czech Republic
`tigi@kiv.zcu.cz`
`http://nlp.kiv.zcu.cz`

Abstract

This paper describes our system created for the SemEval-2018 Task 3: Irony detection in English tweets.

Our strongly constrained system uses only the provided training data without any additional external resources. Our system is based on Maximum Entropy classifier and various features using parse tree, POS tags, and morphological features. Even without additional lexicons and word embeddings we achieved fourth place in Subtask A and seventh in Subtask B in terms of accuracy.

1 Introduction

Frequent use of creative and figurative language on social media has important implications for natural language processing tasks such as sentiment analysis. The semantics of a sentence with creative or figurative language can be quite different from the same sentence with literal meaning and misinterpreting figurative language such as irony represents a significant challenge in sentiment analysis. Hercig and Lenc (2017) explored the effect of figurative language on sentiment analysis and confirmed that figurative language affects sentiment analysis.

The issue of automatic irony and/or sarcasm[1] detection has been addressed mostly in English, however there has been some research in other languages as well (e.g. Dutch (Liebrecht et al., 2013), Italian (Bosco et al., 2013), Brazilian Portuguese (Vanin et al., 2013), and Czech (Ptáček et al., 2014)).

2 Task

The goal of SemEval-2018 Task 3 (Van Hee et al., 2018) is to detect irony in English tweets. Subtask

---

[1]There is only a weak boundary in meaning between irony, sarcasm and satire (Reyes et al., 2012)

A detects just binary score for irony and Subtask B also detects more detailed types of irony (non-ironic, ironic by clash, situational irony, and other forms of verbal irony). These subtasks correspond to their respective phases (A and B). Data for subtask B were available only after phase A was finished.

At the evaluation time the following descriptions of the submitted system labels were given:

- **Constrained:** only the provided training data were used to develop the system

- **Unconstrained:** additional training data were used

Only after the end of the phase A we learned that constrained systems can make use of additional resources like lexicons, dictionaries, embeddings, etc. Thus we introduce another system label to describe our system – strongly constrained.

- **Strongly Constrained:** using ONLY the the provided training/development data without any additional external resources (such as lexicons, embeddings, etc.)

Data statistics for Subtask A and Subtask B are shown in Table 1 and 2 respectively.

Label	Test	Train
Non-ironic	473 (60,3%)	1923 (50,2%)
Ironic	311 (39,7%)	1911 (49,8%)

Table 1: Data statistics for Subtask A.

3 System Description

For all experiments we use Maximum Entropy classifier with default settings from Brainy machine learning library (Konkol, 2014). Data preprocessing includes lower-casing and in some

Proceedings of the 12th International Workshop on Semantic Evaluation (SemEval-2018), pages 520–524
New Orleans, Louisiana, June 5–6, 2018. ©2018 Association for Computational Linguistics

Label	Test	Train
Non-ironic	473 (60,3%)	1923 (50,2%)
Ironic by clash	164 (20,9%)	1390 (36,3%)
Situational irony	85 (10,8%)	316 (8,2%)
Other irony	62 (7,9%)	205 (5,3%)

Table 2: Data statistics for Subtask B.

cases lemmatization[2]. We utilize morphological analysis, parse trees, lemmatization, and POS tags from UDPipe (Straka et al., 2016).

3.1 Features

We tried to create the best strongly constrained feature set using various features using parse tree, POS tags, and morphological features. Most features listed below are based on the work of Hercig et al. (2016).

- **Character n-grams (ChN$_n$):** Separate binary feature for each n-gram representing the n-gram presence in the text. We do it separately for different orders $n \in \{1, 2, 3, 4, 5\}$ and remove n-gram with frequency $f \leq 2$.

- **Bag of Morphological features (BoM):** We use bag-of-words representation of a tweet, i.e. separate binary feature representing the occurrence of a morphological feature for all verbs in the tweet. The morphological features[3] include abbreviation, aspect, definiteness, degree of comparison, evidentiality, mood, polarity, politeness, possessive, pronominal type, tense, verb form, and voice.

- **Bag of Parse Tree Tags (BoT):** We use bag-of-words representation of a tweet, i.e. separate binary feature representing the occurrence of a parse tree tag in the tweet. We remove tags with a frequency $f \leq 2$.

- **First Words (FW):** Bag of first five words with at least 2 occurrences.

- **Last Words (LW):** Bag of last five words with at least 2 occurrences.

- **List (List):** Binary feature representing the presence of the following words or characters (yay, yep, yes, ha, heh, um, uh, sh, so, no, !, ?, ., ', ") in tweet.

- **N-gram Shape (NSh):** The occurrence of word shape n-gram in the tweet. Word shape assigns words into one of 24 classes[4] similar to the function specified in (Bikel et al., 1997). We consider unigrams with frequency $f > 2$ and trigrams with frequency $f > 10$.

- **POS Count (POS):** We use the count of POS tags in a tweet as a feature. We remove POS tags with frequency $f \leq 10$.

- **POS Count Bins (POS-B):** We map the frequency of POS tags in a tweet into a one-hot vector with length three and use this vector as binary features for the classifier. The frequency belongs to one of three equal-frequency bins[5]. Each bin corresponds to a position in the vector. We remove POS tags with frequency ≤ 5.

- **Root Bag of Words (R-BoW):** Bag of words for parent, siblings, and children of the root from the sentence parse tree. We use only words with POS[6] matching adjective, interjection, noun, symbol, verb, and other.

- **TF-IDF:** Term frequency – inverse document frequency of a word computed from the training data for words with at least 5 occurrences and at most 50 occurrences.

- **Verb Bag of Words (V-BoW):** Bag of words for parent, siblings, and children of the verb from the sentence parse tree. We use only words with POS[6] matching adverb, noun, adjective, verb, and auxiliary.

- **Word n-grams (WN$_n$):** Separate binary feature for each word n-gram representing the n-gram presence in the text. We do it separately for different orders $n \in \{1, 2, 3\}$ and remove n-gram with frequency $f \leq 2$.

3.2 Subtask A

We use a simple binary classification approach with the Maximum Entropy classifier and the features shown in Table 5. Blank space denotes that the corresponding feature has not been used.

---

[2]Character n-grams and N-gram Shape use original words.

[3]http://universaldependencies.org/u/feat/index.html

[4]We use edu.stanford.nlp.process.WordShapeClassifier with the WORDSHAPECHRIS1 setting available in Standford CoreNLP library (Manning et al., 2014).

[5]The frequencies from the training data are split into three equal-size bins according to 33% quantiles.

[6]http://universaldependencies.org/u/pos/

Team	Accuracy	Precision	Recall	F1-score
THU_NGN	0.7347 (1)	0.6304 (4)	0.8006 (4)	0.7054 (1)
NTUA-SLP	0.7321 (2)	0.6535 (2)	0.6913 (13)	0.6719 (2)
NIHRIO, NCL	0.7015 (3)	0.6091 (5)	0.6913 (13)	0.6476 (5)
UWB best	0.7003	0.6195	0.6334	0.6264
UWB submitted	0.6875 (4)	0.5988 (7)	0.6431 (19)	0.6202 (11)

Table 3: CodaLab results for Subtask A.

Team	Accuracy	Precision	Recall	F1-score
UCDCC	0.7321 (1)	0.5768 (1)	0.5044 (4)	0.5074 (1)
WLV	0.6709 (2)	0.4311 (10)	0.4149 (9)	0.4153 (8)
NIHRIO, NCL	0.6594 (3)	0.5446 (2)	0.4475 (5)	0.4437 (5)
NTUA-SLP	0.6518 (4)	0.4959 (4)	0.5124 (2)	0.4959 (2)
INGEOTEC-IIM.	0.6441 (5)	0.5017 (3)	0.3850 (15)	0.4055 (10)
UWB best	0.6403	0.4571	0.4180	0.4080
RDST*	0.6327 (6)	0.4868 (5)	0.4388 (8)	0.4352 (6)
ELiRF-UPV	0.6327 (6)	0.4123 (12)	0.4404 (7)	0.4211 (7)
UWB submitted	0.6263 (7)	0.4404 (8)	0.4059 (12)	0.3902 (13)

* Random Decision Syntax Trees

Table 4: CodaLab results for Subtask B.

Feature	Subtask A submitted				Subtask A best			
	Accuracy	Precision	Recall	F1-score	Accuracy	Precision	Recall	F1-score
ALL*	0.6875	0.5988	0.6431	0.6202	0.7003	0.6195	0.6334	0.6264
ChN	-0.0434	-0.0586	+0.0482	-0.0137	-0.0446	-0.0636	+0.0225	-0.0246
BoM	+0.0000	+0.0000	+0.0000	+0.0000	-0.0038	-0.0044	-0.0064	-0.0054
BoT	-0.0051	-0.0037	-0.0193	-0.0110				
FW	+0.0000	+0.0006	-0.0032	-0.0012	-0.0064	-0.0089	-0.0032	-0.0061
LW List	-0.0038	-0.0042	-0.0064	-0.0052				
NSh	-0.0013	-0.0035	+0.0096	+0.0025				
POS	-0.0038	-0.0042	-0.0064	-0.0052				
POS-B					-0.0140	-0.0157	-0.0257	-0.0206
R-BoW	-0.0064	-0.0020	-0.0386	-0.0195	-0.0077	-0.0094	-0.0096	-0.0095
TF-IDF	+0.0000	+0.0000	+0.0000	+0.0000	-0.0064	-0.0068	-0.0129	-0.0098
V-BoW	+0.0051	+0.0066	+0.0032	+0.0050				
WN$_1$	+0.0013	+0.0030	-0.0064	-0.0014	-0.0089	-0.0107	-0.0129	-0.0117

* Original results achieved with all used features in the respective ablation study.

Table 5: Feature ablation study for Subtask A.

3.3 Subtask B

We classify tweets into one of four classes using the Maximum Entropy classifier and the features shown in Table 6. Blank space denotes that the corresponding feature has not been used.

4 Results and Experiments

Our results in Subtask A are in Table 3 and our results in Subtask B are in Table 4. The official evaluation metric was F1-score. The system settings and features were selected based on our pre-

Feature	Subtask B submitted				Subtask B best			
	Accuracy	Precision	Recall	F1-score	Accuracy	Precision	Recall	F1-score
ALL*	0.6263	0.4404	0.4059	0.3902	0.6403	0.4571	0.4180	0.4080
ChN	-0.0383	-0.0744	-0.0228	-0.0415	-0.0727	-0.0359	-0.0185	-0.0164
BoM	+0.0077	+0.0064	+0.0076	+0.0090	-0.0013	-0.0079	-0.0039	-0.0042
BoT								
FW	-0.0013	-0.0096	+0.0039	+0.0025	-0.0089	-0.0207	-0.0087	-0.0079
LW	+0.0089	+0.0011	+0.0091	+0.0094	+0.0000	-0.0068	+0.0000	-0.0001
List	+0.0051	+0.0001	+0.0065	+0.0066				
NSh	+0.0064	+0.0027	+0.0051	+0.0072	-0.0051	-0.0197	-0.0055	-0.0068
POS								
POS-B	+0.0051	+0.0034	+0.0069	+0.0089	-0.0102	-0.0289	-0.0145	-0.0176
R-BoW	+0.0064	+0.0062	+0.0055	+0.0097				
TF-IDF	+0.0000	-0.0042	+0.0024	+0.0035				
V-BoW	+0.0026	-0.0056	+0.0039	+0.0071				
WN_1	+0.0000	-0.0072	+0.0024	+0.0036				
$WN_{2,3}$	+0.0013	+0.0001	+0.0034	+0.0068				

* Original results achieved with all used features in the respective ablation study.

Table 6: Feature ablation study for Subtask B.

evaluation experiments using 10-fold cross validation on the training data for the team description *UWB submitted*. The team description *UWB best* represents the best settings according to the experiments on test data.

We performed ablation experiments to see which features are the most beneficial (see Table 5 and Table 6). Numbers represent the performance change when the given feature is removed.

We can see that many features in the submitted settings for both subtasks are not beneficial for the results, thus we remove them in the best settings for the given subtask. The best features apart from character n-grams include POS-B, FW, and BoM for both subtasks. In subtask A R-Bow, TF-IDF, and unigrams were also beneficial. In subtask B word shape n-grams were also helpful.

Detailed statistical analysis into the datasets and feature presence in the data would be needed in order to infer further insides.

5 Conclusion

We competed in both subtasks and ranked 4th in terms of accuracy in Subtask A and 7th in Subtask B. In terms of the F1-score measure we ranked 11th in Subtask A and 13th in Subtask B. However this comparison likely isn't fair because our system should not be be considered just constrained but strongly constrained.

Acknowledgments

This publication was supported by the project LO1506 of the Czech Ministry of Education, Youth and Sports under the program NPU I and by university specific research project SGS-2016-018 Data and Software Engineering for Advanced Applications.

References

Daniel M Bikel, Scott Miller, Richard Schwartz, and Ralph Weischedel. 1997. Nymble: a high-performance learning name-finder. In *Proceedings of the fifth conference on Applied natural language processing*, pages 194–201. Association for Computational Linguistics.

Cristina Bosco, Viviana Patti, and Andrea Bolioli. 2013. Developing corpora for sentiment analysis: The case of irony and senti-tut. *IEEE Intelligent Systems*, 28(2):55–63.

Tomáš Hercig, Tomáš Brychcín, Lukáš Svoboda, and Michal Konkol. 2016. UWB at SemEval-2016 Task 5: Aspect Based Sentiment Analysis. In *Proceedings of the 10th International Workshop on Semantic Evaluation (SemEval-2016)*, pages 342–349. Association for Computational Linguistics.

Tomáš Hercig and Ladislav Lenc. 2017. The impact of figurative language on sentiment analysis. In

Proceedings of the International Conference Recent Advances in Natural Language Processing RANLP 2017, Varna, Bulgaria. INCOMA Ltd. Shoumen, BULGARIA.

Michal Konkol. 2014. Brainy: A machine learning library. In Leszek Rutkowski, Marcin Korytkowski, Rafal Scherer, Ryszard Tadeusiewicz, Lotfi Zadeh, and Jacek Zurada, editors, *Artificial Intelligence and Soft Computing*, volume 8468 of *Lecture Notes in Computer Science*, pages 490–499. Springer International Publishing.

Christine Liebrecht, Florian Kunneman, and Antal Van den Bosch. 2013. The perfect solution for detecting sarcasm in tweets #not. In *Proceedings of the 4th Workshop on Computational Approaches to Subjectivity, Sentiment and Social Media Analysis*, pages 29–37, Atlanta, Georgia. Association for Computational Linguistics.

Christopher D. Manning, Mihai Surdeanu, John Bauer, Jenny Finkel, Steven J. Bethard, and David McClosky. 2014. The Stanford CoreNLP natural language processing toolkit. In *Association for Computational Linguistics (ACL) System Demonstrations*, pages 55–60.

Tomáš Ptáček, Ivan Habernal, and Jun Hong. 2014. Sarcasm Detection on Czech and English Twitter. In *Proceedings of COLING 2014, the 25th International Conference on Computational Linguistics: Technical Papers*, pages 213–223, Dublin, Ireland. Dublin City University and Association for Computational Linguistics.

Antonio Reyes, Paolo Rosso, and Davide Buscaldi. 2012. From humor recognition to irony detection: The figurative language of social media. *Data Knowl. Eng.*, 74:1–12.

Milan Straka, Jan Hajič, and Jana Straková. 2016. UDPipe: trainable pipeline for processing CoNLL-U files performing tokenization, morphological analysis, pos tagging and parsing. In *Proceedings of the Tenth International Conference on Language Resources and Evaluation (LREC'16)*, Paris, France. European Language Resources Association (ELRA).

Cynthia Van Hee, Els Lefever, and Véronique Hoste. 2018. SemEval-2018 Task 3: Irony Detection in English Tweets. In *Proceedings of the 12th International Workshop on Semantic Evaluation*, SemEval-2018, New Orleans, LA, USA. Association for Computational Linguistics.

Aline A Vanin, Larissa A Freitas, Renata Vieira, and Marco Bochernitsan. 2013. Some clues on irony detection in tweets. In *Proceedings of the 22nd international conference on World Wide Web companion*, pages 635–636. International World Wide Web Conferences Steering Committee.

NIHRIO at SemEval-2018 Task 3: A Simple and Accurate Neural Network Model for Irony Detection in Twitter

Thanh Vu[1], Dat Quoc Nguyen[2], Xuan-Son Vu[3], Dai Quoc Nguyen[4],
Michael Catt[1] and **Michael Trenell[1]**

[1]NIHRIO, Newcastle University, UK; [2]The University of Melbourne, Australia;
[3]Umeå University, Sweden; [4]Deakin University, Australia
`thanh.vu@io.nihr.ac.uk; dqnguyen@unimelb.edu.au;`
`sonvx@cs.umu.se; dai.nguyen@deakin.edu.au;`
`{michael.catt, michael.trenell}@io.nihr.ac.uk`

Abstract

This paper describes our NIHRIO system for SemEval-2018 Task 3 "Irony detection in English tweets." We propose to use a simple neural network architecture of Multilayer Perceptron with various types of input features including: lexical, syntactic, semantic and polarity features. Our system achieves very high performance in both subtasks of binary and multi-class irony detection in tweets. In particular, we rank <u>third</u> using the accuracy metric and <u>fifth</u> using the F_1 metric. Our code is available at: `https://github.com/NIHRIO/IronyDetectionInTwitter`.

1 Introduction

Mining Twitter data has increasingly been attracting much research attention in many NLP applications such as in sentiment analysis (Pak and Paroubek, 2010; Kouloumpis et al., 2011; Agarwal et al., 2011; Liu et al., 2012; Rosenthal et al., 2017; Cambria et al., 2018) and stock market prediction (Bollen et al., 2011; Vu et al., 2012; Bartov et al., 2015; Nofer and Hinz, 2015; Oliveira et al., 2017). Recently, Davidov et al. (2010) and Reyes et al. (2013) have shown that Twitter data includes a high volume of *"ironic"* tweets. For example, a user can use positive words in a Twitter message to her intended negative meaning (e.g., *"It is awesome to go to bed at 3 am #not"*). This especially results in a research challenge to assign correct sentiment labels for ironic tweets (Bosco et al., 2013; Ghosh et al., 2015; Farías et al., 2016; Nozza et al., 2017; Kannangara, 2018).

To handle that problem, much attention has been focused on automatic irony detection in Twitter (Davidov et al., 2010; Reyes et al., 2013; Barbieri and Saggion, 2014; Rajadesingan et al., 2015; Farías et al., 2016; Sulis et al., 2016; Karoui et al.,

2017; Joshi et al., 2017; Huang et al., 2017; Ravi and Ravi, 2017). In this paper, we propose a neural network model for irony detection in tweets. Our model obtains the fifth best performances in both binary and multi-class irony detection subtasks in terms of F_1 score (Van Hee et al., 2018). Details of the two subtasks can be found in the task description paper (Van Hee et al., 2018). We briefly describe the subtasks as follows:

Subtask 1 (A): Ironic vs non-ironic This first subtask is a binary classification problem, in which we predict whether or not a tweet is *ironic*. For example, *"I just love when you test my patience!! #not"* is ironic, but *"Had no sleep and have got school now #not happy"* is non-ironic.

Subtask 2 (B): Different types of irony This second subtask is a multi-class classification problem, where we predict the correct label of a tweet from four classes: (1) *non-irony*, (2) *verbal irony by means of a polarity contrast*, (3) *other verbal irony* and (4) *situational irony*.

The remainder of this paper is organized as follows: We describe the ironic tweet dataset provided by the SemEval-2018 Task 3 in Section 2. We then describe our system in Section 3. The experimental results and conclusion are detailed in Section 4 and Section 5, respectively.

2 Dataset

The dataset consists of 4,618 tweets (2,222 ironic + 2,396 non-ironic) that are manually labelled by three students. Some pre-processing steps were applied to the dataset, such as the emoji icons in a tweet are replaced by a describing text using the Python emoji package.[1] Additionally, all the

---

[1]`https://pypi.python.org/pypi/emoji/`

Proceedings of the 12th International Workshop on Semantic Evaluation (SemEval-2018), pages 525–530
New Orleans, Louisiana, June 5–6, 2018. ©2018 Association for Computational Linguistics

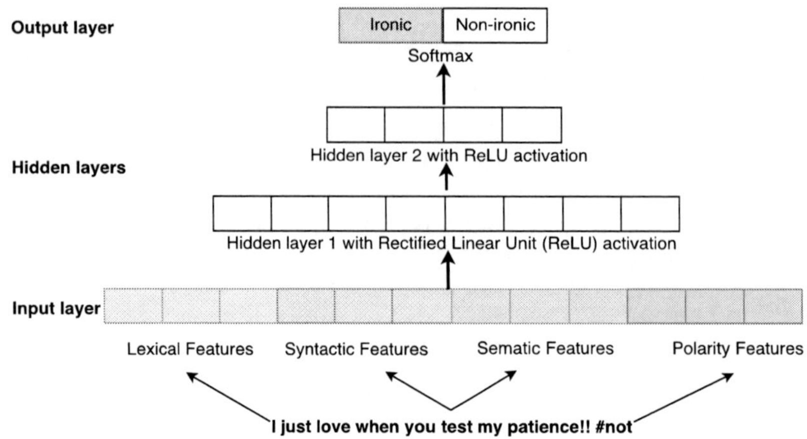

Figure 1: Overview of our model architecture for irony detection in tweets.

Statistics	Training	Test
#samples	3,834	784
#non-irony	1,923	473
#irony	1,911	311
- polarity contrast verbal	1,390	164
- other verbal	316	85
- situational	205	62

Table 1: Basic statistics of the provided dataset.

ironic hashtags, such as #not, #sarcasm, #irony, in the dataset have been removed. This makes difficult to correctly predict the label of a tweet. For example, *"@coreybking thanks for the spoiler!!!! #not"* is an ironic tweet but without #not, it probably is a non-ironic tweet. The dataset is split into the training and test sets as detailed in Table 1.

Note that there is also an extended version of the training set, which contains the ironic hashtags. However, we only use the training set which does not contain the ironic hashtags to train our model as it is in line with the test set.

Our data pre-processing step: Tweet normalization is an important pre-processing step as there are around 15% of tweets containing 50% or more out-of-vocabulary tokens (Han and Baldwin, 2011). We normalize each tweet from the dataset using a lexicon-based approach proposed by Han et al. (2012), using a manually constructed normalization dictionary (e.g., "reeeaaalll" is normalized by "real"). We then replace all tagged users and urls by specific word tokens "<USER>" and "<URL>", respectively. It is because they are likely not correlated with the ironic labels.

3 Our modeling approach

We first describe our MLP-based model for ironic tweet detection in Section 3.1. We then present the features used in our model in Section 3.2.

3.1 Neural network model

We propose to use the Multilayer Perceptron (MLP) model (Hornik et al., 1989) to handle both the ironic tweet detection subtasks. Figure 1 presents an overview of our model architecture including an input layer, two hidden layers and a softmax output layer. Given a tweet, the input layer represents the tweet by a feature vector which concatenates lexical, syntactic, semantic and polarity feature representations. The two hidden layers with ReLU activation function take the input feature vector to select the most important features which are then fed into the softmax layer for ironic detection and classification.

3.2 Features

Table 2 shows the number of lexical, syntactic, semantic and polarity features used in our model.

Lexical features: Our lexical features include 1-, 2-, and 3-grams in both word and character levels. For each type of n-grams, we utilize only the top 1,000 n-grams based on the term frequency-inverse document frequency (tf-idf) values. That is, each n-gram appearing in a tweet becomes an entry in the feature vector with the corresponding feature value tf-idf. We also use the number of characters and the number of words as features.

Name	# Features
Lexical features	2,002
Syntactic features	45
Semantic features	700
Polarity features	12
Total	**2,759**

Table 2: Number of features used in our model

Cluster	Word	Cluster	Word
110000	wife	11001000	adorable
110000	sister	11001000	excellent
110000	boyfriend	11001000	interesting
110000	daughter	11001000	blessed
110000	mum	11001000	easy
110000	son	11001000	perfect
110000	dad	11001000	cool
110000	family	11001000	funny

Table 3: Example of clusters produced by the Brown clustering algorithm.

Syntactic features: We use the NLTK toolkit to tokenize and annotate part-of-speech tags (POS tags) for all tweets in the dataset. We then use all the POS tags with their corresponding tf-idf values as our syntactic features and feature values, respectively.

Semantic features: A major challenge when dealing with the tweet data is that the lexicon used in a tweet is informal and much different from tweet to tweet. The lexical and syntactic features seem not to well-capture that property. To handle this problem, we apply three approaches to compute tweet vector representations.

Firstly, we employ 300-dimensional pre-trained word embeddings from GloVe (Pennington et al., 2014) to compute a tweet embedding as the average of the embeddings of words in the tweet.

Secondly, we apply the latent semantic indexing (Papadimitriou et al., 1998) to capture the underlying semantics of the dataset. Here, each tweet is represented as a vector of 100 dimensions.

Thirdly, we also extract tweet representation by applying the Brown clustering algorithm (Brown et al., 1992; Liang, 2005)[2]—a hierarchical clustering algorithm which groups the words with similar meaning and syntactical function together. Applying the Brown clustering algorithm, we obtain a set of clusters, where each word belongs to only

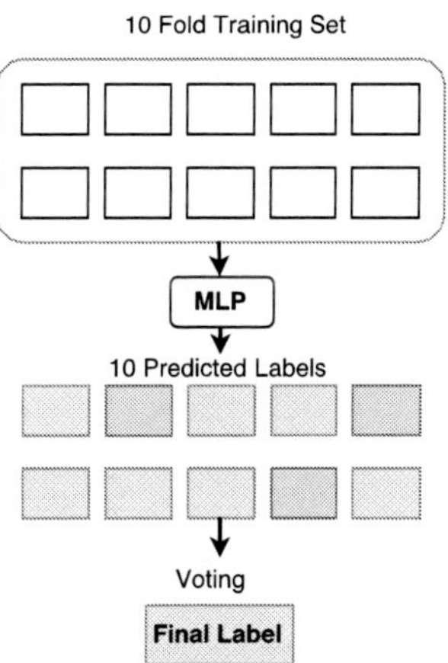

Figure 2: The training mechanism.

one cluster. For example in Table 3, words that indicate the members of a family (e.g., "mum", "dad") or positive sentiment (e.g., "interesting", "awesome") are grouped into the same cluster. We run the algorithm with different number of clustering settings (i.e., 80, 100, 120) to capture multiple semantic and syntactic aspects. For each clustering setting, we use the number of tweet words in each cluster as a feature. After that, for each tweet, we concatenate the features from all the clustering settings to form a cluster-based tweet embedding.

Polarity features: Motivated by the verbal irony by means of polarity contrast, such as *"I really love this year's summer; weeks and weeks of awful weather"*, we use the number of polarity signals appearing in a tweet as the polarity features. The signals include positive words (e.g., love), negative words (e.g., awful), positive emoji icon and negative emoji icon. We use the sentiment dictionaries provided by Hu and Liu (2004) to identify positive and negative words in a tweet. We further use boolean features that check whether or not a negation word is in a tweet (e.g., *not, n't*).

3.3 Implementation details

We use Tensorflow (Abadi et al., 2015) to implement our model. Model parameters are learned to minimize the the cross-entropy loss with L_2 regularization. Figure 2 shows our training mechanism. In particular, we follow a 10-fold cross-validation based voting strategy. First, we split the training set into 10 folds. Each time, we combine 9 folds to train a classification model and use the remaining fold to find the optimal hyperparameters.

---

[2]https://github.com/percyliang/brown-cluster

Name	1 (A)	2 (B)
Hidden layers	(800, 400)	(800, 300)
# epoch	100	100
early stop	30	30
Learning rate	10^{-4}	10^{-4}
l_2	10^{-5}	10^{-5}

Table 4: The optimal hyperparameter settings for subtasks 1 (A) and 2 (B).

Accuracy	Precision	Recall	F_1
70.15_3	60.91	69.13	64.76_5

Table 5: The performance (in %) of our model on the test set for subtask 1 (binary classification). The subscripts denote our official ranking.

Table 4 shows optimal settings for each subtask.

In total, we have 10 classification models to produce 10 predicted labels for each test tweet. Then, we use the voting technique to return the final predicted label.

4 Experiments

4.1 Metrics

The metrics used to evaluate our model include *accuracy, precision, recall* and F_1. The accuracy is calculated using all classes in both tasks. The remainders are calculated using only the positive label in subtask 1 or per class label (i.e., macro-averaged) in subtask 2. Detail description of the metrics can be found in Van Hee et al. (2018).

4.2 Results for subtask 1

Table 5 shows our official results on the test set for subtask 1 with regards to the four metrics. By using a simple MLP neural network architecture, our system achieves a high performance which is ranked **third** and **fifth** out of forty-four teams using accuracy and F_1 metrics, respectively.

4.3 Results for subtask 2

Table 6 presents our results on the test set for subtask 2. Our system also achieves a high performance which is ranked **third** and **fifth** out of thirty-two teams using accuracy and F_1 metrics, respectively. We also show in Table 7 the performance of our system on different class labels. For ironic classes, our system achieves the best performance on the verbal irony by means of a polarity contrast with F_1 of 60.73%. Note that the performance on the situational class is not high. The

Accuracy	Precision	Recall	F_1
65.94_3	54.46	44.75	44.37_5

Table 6: The performance (in %) of our model on the test set for subtask 2 (multi-class classification).

Class	Precision	Recall	F_1
Non-irony	72.97	79.92	76.29
Contrast verbal	53.21	70.73	60.73
Other verbal	48.78	23.53	31.75
Situational	42.86	4.84	8.70

Table 7: The performance (in %) of our model on the test set for each class label in subtask 2.

reason is probably that the number of situational tweets in the training set is small (205/3,834), i.e. not enough to learn a good classifier.

4.4 Discussions

Apart from the described MLP models, we have also tried other neural network models, such as Long Short-Term Memory (LSTM) (Hochreiter and Schmidhuber, 1997) and Convolutional Neural Network (CNN) for relation classification (Kim, 2014). We found that LSTM achieves much higher performance than MLP does on the extended training set containing the ironic hashtags (about 92% vs 87% with 10-fold cross-validation using F_1 on subtask 1). However, without the ironic hashtags, the performance is lower than MLP's. We also employed popular machine learning techniques, such as SVM (Hearst et al., 1998), Logistic Regression (Harrell, 2001), Ridge Regression Classifier (Le Cessie and Van Houwelingen, 1992), but none of them produces as good results as MLP does. We have also implemented ensemble models, such as voting, bagging and stacking. We found that with 10-fold cross-validation based voting strategy, our MLP models produce the best irony detection and classification results.

5 Conclusion

We have presented our NIHRIO system for participating the Semeval-2018 Task 3 on "Irony detection in English tweets". We proposed to use Multilayer Perceptron to handle the task using various features including lexical features, syntactic features, semantic features and polarity features. Our system was ranked the fifth best performing one with regards to F_1 score in both the subtasks of binary and multi-class irony detection in tweets.

Acknowledgments

This research is supported by the National Institute for Health Research (NIHR) Innovation Observatory at Newcastle University, United Kingdom.

References

Martín Abadi, Ashish Agarwal, Paul Barham, Eugene Brevdo, Zhifeng Chen, Craig Citro, Greg S. Corrado, Andy Davis, Jeffrey Dean, Matthieu Devin, Sanjay Ghemawat, Ian Goodfellow, Andrew Harp, Geoffrey Irving, Michael Isard, Yangqing Jia, Rafal Jozefowicz, Lukasz Kaiser, Manjunath Kudlur, Josh Levenberg, Dan Mané, Rajat Monga, Sherry Moore, Derek Murray, Chris Olah, Mike Schuster, Jonathon Shlens, Benoit Steiner, Ilya Sutskever, Kunal Talwar, Paul Tucker, Vincent Vanhoucke, Vijay Vasudevan, Fernanda Viégas, Oriol Vinyals, Pete Warden, Martin Wattenberg, Martin Wicke, Yuan Yu, and Xiaoqiang Zheng. 2015. TensorFlow: Large-scale machine learning on heterogeneous systems. Software available from tensorflow.org.

Apoorv Agarwal, Boyi Xie, Ilia Vovsha, Owen Rambow, and Rebecca Passonneau. 2011. Sentiment analysis of twitter data. In *Proceedings of the workshop on languages in social media*, pages 30–38.

Francesco Barbieri and Horacio Saggion. 2014. Modelling irony in twitter. In *Proceedings of the Student Research Workshop at the 14th Conference of the European Chapter of the Association for Computational Linguistics*, pages 56–64.

Eli Bartov, Lucile Faurel, and Partha Mohanram. 2015. Can twitter help predict firm-level earnings and stock returns? *The Accounting Review*.

Johan Bollen, Huina Mao, and Xiaojun Zeng. 2011. Twitter mood predicts the stock market. *Journal of computational science*, 2(1):1–8.

Cristina Bosco, Viviana Patti, and Andrea Bolioli. 2013. Developing corpora for sentiment analysis: The case of irony and senti-tut. *IEEE Intelligent Systems*, 28(2):55–63.

Peter F. Brown, Peter V. deSouza, Robert L. Mercer, Vincent J. Della Pietra, and Jenifer C. Lai. 1992. Class-based n-gram models of natural language. *Comput. Linguist.*, 18(4):467–479.

Erik Cambria, Soujanya Poria, Devamanyu Hazarika, and Kenneth Kwok. 2018. Senticnet 5: discovering conceptual primitives for sentiment analysis by means of context embeddings. In *Proceedings of the 32nd AAAI Conference on Artificial Intelligence*.

Dmitry Davidov, Oren Tsur, and Ari Rappoport. 2010. Semi-supervised recognition of sarcastic sentences in twitter and amazon. In *Proceedings of the Fourteenth Conference on Computational Natural Language Learning*, pages 107–116.

Delia Irazú Hernández Farías, Viviana Patti, and Paolo Rosso. 2016. Irony detection in twitter: The role of affective content. *ACM Trans. Internet Technol.*, 16(3):19:1–19:24.

Aniruddha Ghosh, Guofu Li, Tony Veale, Paolo Rosso, Ekaterina Shutova, John Barnden, and Antonio Reyes. 2015. Semeval-2015 task 11: Sentiment analysis of figurative language in twitter. In *Proceedings of the 9th International Workshop on Semantic Evaluation*, pages 470–478.

Bo Han and Timothy Baldwin. 2011. Lexical normalisation of short text messages: Makn sens a #twitter. In *Proceedings of the 49th Annual Meeting of the Association for Computational Linguistics: Human Language Technologies - Volume 1*, pages 368–378.

Bo Han, Paul Cook, and Timothy Baldwin. 2012. Automatically constructing a normalisation dictionary for microblogs. In *Proceedings of the 2012 Joint Conference on Empirical Methods in Natural Language Processing and Computational Natural Language Learning*, pages 421–432.

Frank E Harrell. 2001. Ordinal logistic regression. In *Regression modeling strategies*, pages 331–343.

Marti A. Hearst, Susan T Dumais, Edgar Osuna, John Platt, and Bernhard Scholkopf. 1998. Support vector machines. *IEEE Intelligent Systems and their applications*, 13(4):18–28.

Sepp Hochreiter and Jürgen Schmidhuber. 1997. Long short-term memory. *Neural Comput.*, 9(8):1735–1780.

K. Hornik, M. Stinchcombe, and H. White. 1989. Multilayer feedforward networks are universal approximators. *Neural Netw.*, 2(5):359–366.

Minqing Hu and Bing Liu. 2004. Mining and summarizing customer reviews. In *Proceedings of the tenth ACM SIGKDD international conference on Knowledge discovery and data mining*, pages 168–177.

Yu-Hsiang Huang, Hen-Hsen Huang, and Hsin-Hsi Chen. 2017. Irony detection with attentive recurrent neural networks. In *European Conference on Information Retrieval*, pages 534–540.

Aditya Joshi, Pushpak Bhattacharyya, and Mark J Carman. 2017. Automatic sarcasm detection: A survey. *ACM Computing Surveys*, 50(5):73.

Sandeepa Kannangara. 2018. Mining twitter for fine-grained political opinion polarity classification, ideology detection and sarcasm detection. In *Proceedings of the Eleventh ACM International Conference on Web Search and Data Mining*, pages 751–752.

Jihen Karoui, Benamara Farah, Véronique Moriceau, Viviana Patti, Cristina Bosco, and Nathalie Aussenac-Gilles. 2017. Exploring the impact of pragmatic phenomena on irony detection in tweets: A multilingual corpus study. In *Proceedings of the*

15th Conference of the European Chapter of the Association for Computational Linguistics (Volume 1: Long Papers), pages 262–272.

Yoon Kim. 2014. Convolutional neural networks for sentence classification. In *Proceedings of the 2014 Conference on Empirical Methods in Natural Language Processing*, pages 1746–1751.

Efthymios Kouloumpis, Theresa Wilson, and Johanna D Moore. 2011. Twitter sentiment analysis: The good the bad and the omg! *Proceedings of the 5th International Conference on Web and Social Media*, pages 538–541.

Saskia Le Cessie and Johannes C Van Houwelingen. 1992. Ridge estimators in logistic regression. *Applied statistics*, pages 191–201.

Percy Liang. 2005. *Semi-supervised learning for natural language*. Ph.D. thesis, Massachusetts Institute of Technology.

Kun-Lin Liu, Wu-Jun Li, and Minyi Guo. 2012. Emoticon smoothed language models for twitter sentiment analysis. In *Proceedings of the Twenty-Sixth AAAI Conference on Artificial Intelligence*, pages 1678–1684.

Michael Nofer and Oliver Hinz. 2015. Using twitter to predict the stock market. *Business & Information Systems Engineering*, 57(4):229–242.

Debora Nozza, Elisabetta Fersini, and Enza Messina. 2017. A multi-view sentiment corpus. In *Proceedings of the 15th Conference of the European Chapter of the Association for Computational Linguistics (Volume 1: Long Papers)*, pages 273–280.

Nuno Oliveira, Paulo Cortez, and Nelson Areal. 2017. The impact of microblogging data for stock market prediction: using twitter to predict returns, volatility, trading volume and survey sentiment indices. *Expert Systems with Applications*, 73:125–144.

Alexander Pak and Patrick Paroubek. 2010. Twitter as a corpus for sentiment analysis and opinion mining. In *Proceedings of the Seventh conference on International Language Resources and Evaluation*.

Christos H. Papadimitriou, Hisao Tamaki, Prabhakar Raghavan, and Santosh Vempala. 1998. Latent semantic indexing: A probabilistic analysis. In *Proceedings of the Seventeenth ACM SIGACT-SIGMOD-SIGART Symposium on Principles of Database Systems*, pages 159–168.

Jeffrey Pennington, Richard Socher, and Christopher Manning. 2014. Glove: Global Vectors for Word Representation. In *Proceedings of the 2014 Conference on Empirical Methods in Natural Language Processing*, pages 1532–1543.

Ashwin Rajadesingan, Reza Zafarani, and Huan Liu. 2015. Sarcasm detection on twitter: A behavioral modeling approach. In *Proceedings of the Eighth ACM International Conference on Web Search and Data Mining*, pages 97–106.

Kumar Ravi and Vadlamani Ravi. 2017. A novel automatic satire and irony detection using ensembled feature selection and data mining. *Knowledge-Based Systems*, 120:15–33.

Antonio Reyes, Paolo Rosso, and Tony Veale. 2013. A multidimensional approach for detecting irony in twitter. *Lang. Resour. Eval.*, 47(1):239–268.

Sara Rosenthal, Noura Farra, and Preslav Nakov. 2017. Semeval-2017 task 4: Sentiment analysis in twitter. In *Proceedings of the 11th International Workshop on Semantic Evaluation*, pages 502–518.

Emilio Sulis, Delia Irazú Hernández Farías, Paolo Rosso, Viviana Patti, and Giancarlo Ruffo. 2016. Figurative messages and affect in twitter: Differences between# irony,# sarcasm and# not. *Knowledge-Based Systems*, 108:132–143.

Cynthia Van Hee, Els Lefever, and Véronique Hoste. 2018. SemEval-2018 Task 3: Irony Detection in English Tweets. In *Proceedings of the 12th International Workshop on Semantic Evaluation*, page to appear.

Tien Thanh Vu, Shu Chang, Quang Thuy Ha, and Nigel Collier. 2012. An experiment in integrating sentiment features for tech stock prediction in twitter. In *The COLING Workshop on Information Extraction and Entity Analytics on Social Media Data*, pages 23–38.

LDR at SemEval-2018 Task 3:
A Low Dimensional Text Representation for Irony Detection

Bilal Ghanem
Universitat Politecnica de Valencia,
Spain
bigha@doctor.upv.es

Francisco Rangel
Universitat Politecnica de Valencia,
Spain
francisco.rangel@autoritas.es

Paolo Rosso
Universitat Politecnica de Valencia,
Spain
prosso@dsic.upv.es

Abstract

In this paper we describe our participation in
the SemEval-2018 task 3 Shared Task on Irony
Detection. We have approached the task with
our low dimensionality representation method
(LDR), which exploits low dimensional features extracted from text on the basis of the
occurrence probability of the words depending on each class. Our intuition is that words in
ironic texts have different probability of occurrence than in non-ironic ones. Our approach
obtained acceptable results in both subtasks A
and B. We have performed an error analysis
that shows the difference on correct and incorrect classified tweets.

1 Introduction

With the existence of online social networks, a
huge amount of information rapidly pervades,
which attracting the attention of researchers to investigate the linguistic phenomenon that appears.
One of these complex phenomenon is irony, where
the speaker uses words that mean the opposite of
the literal meaning and what others really think,
especially in order to be funny[1]. Moreover, irony
can be considered as a strategy intended to criticise
or to praise (Hernández-Farías et al., 2015). The
detection of irony recently is quite a hot research
topic due to its importance for efficient sentiment
analysis (Ghosh et al., 2015). Also, another figurative language device noticed recently is sarcasm,
where the writer intend to offend someone rather
than creating a humor situation. In many research
works, irony and sarcasm are often viewed as the
same language device, or they considered irony as
an umbrella term that covers also sarcasm (Wang,

2013). Several approaches have been proposed to
detect irony, where most of them have turned the
problem into a binary classification task using a
set of features. (Carvalho et al., 2009) proposed
one of the first works on irony detection. They
worked on the identification of a set of patterns
to identify ironic sentences. The adopted features
were the use of punctuation marks and emoticons.
(Reyes et al., 2013) proposed a model that employed four types of conceptual features: signatures, unexpectedness, style and emotional scenarios. (Barbieri and Saggion, 2014) proposed a
model using lexical features, such as frequency
of rare and common terms, synonyms, adjectives,
emoticons, punctuation marks, positive and negative terms. Their results showed that the most important features are structure, frequency and synonyms for detecting irony in multiple datasets.
(Karoui et al., 2015) presented a model to detect
irony using a vector composed of six main groups
of features: surface features (such as punctuation
marks), sentiment (positive and negative words),
sentiment shifter (positive and negative words in
the scope of an intensifier), shifter (presence a
negation word or reporting speech verbs), opposition (sentiment opposition or contrast between
a subjective and an objective proposition) and internal contextual (the presence of personal pronouns). (Reyes et al., 2012) also studied the effect of multiple features to distinguish ironic and
non-ironic tweets messages. The adopted features
include quantifiers of sentence complexity, mor-
phosyntactic and semantic ambiguity, polarity, unexpectedness, emotional activation, imagery, and
pleasantness of words. (Wallace et al., 2015) presented a way to approach verbal irony classification by exploits contextual features, specifically by
combining noun phrases and sentiment extracted

---

[1]As defined in the Merriam Webster Dictionary,
http://www.merriam-webster.com/dictionary/irony; accessed
on Feb. 2018.

Proceedings of the 12th International Workshop on Semantic Evaluation (SemEval-2018), pages 531–536
New Orleans, Louisiana, June 5–6, 2018. ©2018 Association for Computational Linguistics

from comments using a dataset of comments collected from reddit site which is social news aggregation. Most of these features did well in detecting ironic sentences, where in general they relied on different types of high level features that use lexical resources, sentiment analysis methods or common terms occurrence. Based on these previous works, we investigate the using of low dimensional features extracted from a given text. LDR uses terms weights to represent the probability that each Twitter message belongs to a specific class (e.g. ironic vs. non-ironic). Our intuition is that words usage in ironic texts has different probability of occurrence than in non-ironic ones, and LDR is good at capturing these differences. LDR does not need external resources, hand-crafted features, and drastically reduces the dimensionality of the representation. This allows the method to deal with big data problems. In this paper, we present the participation of LDR in the SemEval-2018 task 3 on Irony Detection (Van Hee et al., 2018). The rest of the paper is structured as follows. In Section 2, the LDR method is presented. In Section 3, we discuss the results we have achieved in both tasks and further analyse the error in Section 4. For example, to know whether the terms usage changes depending on ironic and non-ironic tweets. Finally, we draw some conclusions in Section 5 together with future work proposals.

2 Low Dimensional Representation Description

We proposed the low dimensional representation (LDR) in (Rangel et al., 2017a). LDR has been used in multiple author profiling tasks (Rangel et al., 2017b; Litvinova et al., 2017), and especially in language variety identification (Franco-Salvador et al., 2015; Fabra et al., 2015). The key aspect of the LDR is the use of weights to represent the probability of each term belonging to each one of the different language varieties. In our approach we built a vector of features from a matrix of terms weights. Starting from a set of training documents, with using Tf-Idf weighting scheme, we built a matrix of terms weights where each row represents Tf-Idf terms weights of a document (specifically this row of term weights represents a unique class C of its document), and each column corresponds to a specific term. Therefore, we obtained another matrix where each term weight was built using the ratio between the weights of

the documents belonging to a concrete language variety C and the total distribution of weights for that term t over other documents, where each column in the matrix represents a term distribution overall documents.

AVG	The average weight of a document is calculated as the sum of weights $W(t,c)$ of its terms divided by the total number of vocabulary terms of the document.
STD	The standard deviation of the weight of a document is calculated as the root square of the sum of all the weights $W(t,c)$ minus the average.
MIN	The minimum weight of a document is the lowest term weight $W(t,c)$ found in the document.
MAX	The maximum weight of a document is the highest term weight $W(t,c)$ found in the document.
PROB	The overall weight of a document is the sum of weights $W(t,c)$ of the terms of the document divided by the total number of terms of the document.
PROP	The proportion between the number of vocabulary terms of the document and the total number of terms of the document.

Table 1: LDR features for each classification class

Then, a vector of features was built where each feature was obtained in a different way, Table 1 describes the used features in LDR. In this paper, we used LDR in order to investigate its performance in irony detection classification task. LDR was proposed for different application where its discriminative statistical features proved to be efficient for classification purposes. Therefore, in this task, we investigated the LDR efficiency in irony detection, where the implicit meaning of a sentence is required to identify the correct class type.

3 Experiments and Results

During the experiments, LDR was tested using different classifiers. In the following sections we will illustrate the experiments that we carried out. For the evaluation, we used both accuracy and macro-average F-score. Moreover, the error anal-

Dataset	# of tweets	# Positive	# Negative
SemEval-2018	3,834	1,911	1,923
(Karoui et al., 2017)	540	540	-
(Ptáček et al., 2014)	67,779	18,889	48890

Table 2: Number of positive and negative tweets in the used datasets - Task A.

ysis we did allowed us to further understand the behavior of LDR in irony detection.

3.1 Data

We trained our model using the provided task 3 dataset with other two datasets collected previously by other researchers. The task A training subset consists of 3,834 tweets, where 1,911 tweets labeled as irony and 1,923 as not. While in task B, the same number of tweets was used with different type of subcategories. The tweets distribution over the categories was as follows: 1,390 irony tweets with a polarity contrast (labeled as 1), 316 as situational irony tweets (labeled as 2), 205 irony tweets without a polarity contrast (labeled as 3), and finally 1,923 non-irony tweets (labeled as 0). The second dataset that we used was provided by (Karoui et al., 2017) by collecting tweets using the Twitter API. The authors searched a set of keywords for different topics, such as politics, sport, artists, locations, Arab Spring, environment, racism, health, social media. These topics have been discussed in the French and American media during a specific period. We used the English part of the dataset which consists of 540 tweets. The last dataset was created by (Ptáček et al., 2014). The dataset approximately consists of 67,800 tweets of sarcasm linguistic phenomenon. As in the previous dataset, they used the Twitter API to collect the tweets but looking for the "sarcasm" hashtag. Table 2 summarises the statistical numbers of the datasets. We have conducted several experiments by combining the described datasets.

3.2 Task A

We have tested LDR with different classifiers using the Weka toolkit with standard parameters and conducted 10-fold cross-validation to find out the classifier that achieves the best results. LDR has achieved 64% of accuracy and 65% of F-score

with the DecisionStump classifier. To improve the results, we adopted the Majority Vote (MV) algorithm using the results that were generated by the other two datasets with the training subset, each combined with the training part of task A subset in the 10-fold cross-validation. To note, none of the datasets improves the results more than using the task A subset independently. In spite of that, combining with Karoui *et al.* dataset achieved its highest results with Multilayer Perceptron classifier, and with Ptacek *et al.* dataset with REPTree classifier. By applying MV, we improved by 0.6% in accuracy the previous results obtained only with the task A training subset. Accordingly, we submitted two different runs, constrained and not. In the constrained one, we used the DecisionStump classifier with the task A training subset independently, while in the unconstrained, we used MV combining the three described datasets.

3.3 Task B

In this task, we experimented several runs that are similar to task A experiments. Since we did not find such a dataset with the used four subcategories, no other subset involved in this task experiments. Therefore, 10-cross validation technique was used without involving any other dataset. For the accuracy, the MultiClassUpdateable classifier achieved the highest result with 60.68%, while for the macro average F-score BayesNet achieved 38%. Accordingly, we adopted the classifiers that have the highest results in F-score to apply MV where BayesNet, NaiveBayes and NaiveBayesUpdateable classifiers are involved. By applying MV, we got a value 39% of macro average F-score. Finally, when the test subset for each task was released, we submitted our runs for each task. For the task A, both constrained and unconstrained runs were submitted while for task B, only the constrained run was submitted. Upon that, LDR attained the results that are in Table 2.

Tasks	Run Type	Accuracy	F-score
Task A	Constrained	0.56	0.43
Task A	Unconstrained	-	0.43
Task B	Constrained	0.46	0.23

Table 3: LDR classification results of Task A and B using Accuracy and Macro average F-score.

The classification results for both runs in task A achieved the same score in terms of F-score mea-

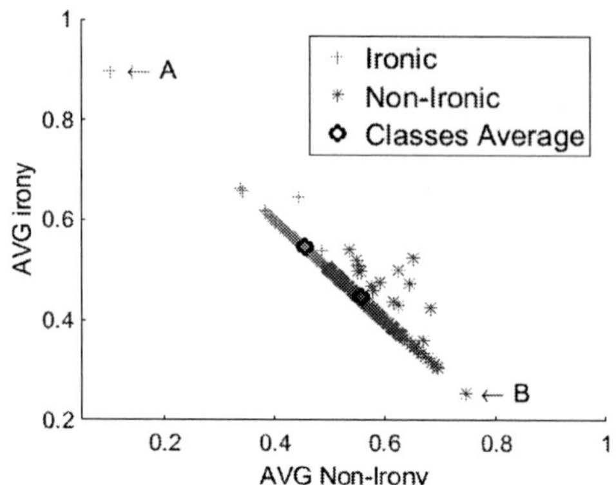

Figure 1: The distribution of **correctly classified** cases in term of AVG feature.

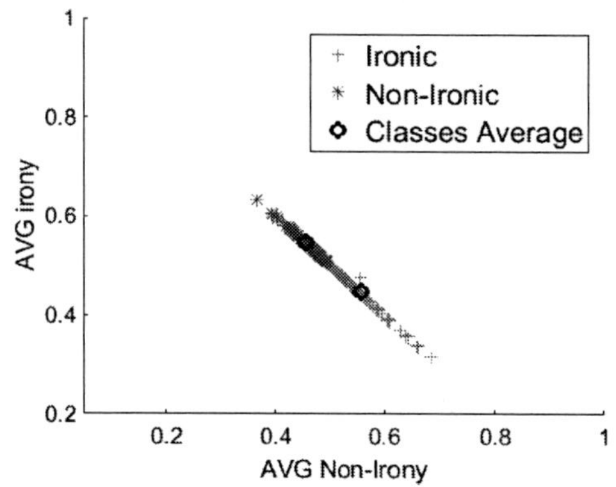

Figure 2: The distribution of **incorrectly classified** cases in term of AVG feature.

sure with some tiny progress to the unconstrained run. In the task B, LDR achieved a lower result comparing to task A. We believe that the reason is due to the number of training records for some classes in the training subset is small comparing to the other classes (unbalanced subset), where our model on these classes has a high bias (underfitting). Another possibility could be regarding to the LDR features, where maybe some of them could not be suitable for such task.

4 Error Analysis

We aim from analyzing the error of LDR to better understand the weak classification results that were obtained, especially in task B. We started with investigating the ability of LDR features to discriminate the data. So, we applied the Gain-Ratio algorithm for features selection under the Weka toolkit to evaluate and to find out how much the LDR features are relevant to the irony training subset. The GainRatio result shows that LDR features were weak in discriminating the data, where the highest ranked attribute is the AVG feature for class 1 (ironic) with a value of 10%, followed by the AVG feature of class 0 (non-ironic) with 9%, where the rest of features are lower.

In the Fig. 1 and 2, we plotted the distribution of AVG feature of both correctly classified and incorrectly classified cases in test subset of task A, to show how they are distributed. In both figures, we can figure out that there is an overlapping between ironic and the non-ironic classes. To deduce which of them is more overlapped, we calculated the Euclidean distance (Ed) between the average points (the black circles) of both classes in each figure. As a result, the Ed in the Fig.1 of the correctly classified cases is 0.143, whilst in the second figure is 0.102. Therefore, the overlapping between both classes in the Fig.1 is lower than in the second figure, which clearly shows that the AVG feature is a good feature to infer both ironic and non-ironic classes.

As we discussed before, the LDR features are built based on a weighting scheme. Therefore, the larger is the training subset used, the more classification accuracy our model produces. To infer this fact, we investigated manually the AVG weights of two cases from the Fig. 1, to show how the weights are differentiated when: 1) a correctly classified ironic and non-ironic cases are far from each other in the figure, 2) and when they are near. Therefore, in the first case, we selected the cases A and B where they are far from each other. The tweets of A and B points in the figure are:

Ironic (A)

```
Yay jury duty #sarcasm
```

We found that the term "Yay" was mentioned frequently in the ironic cases, where the writer used it as a figurative term to represent an irony situation. Meanwhile, this term was presented rarely in the non-ironic tweets. Therefore, this term made a distinctive situation for this tweet. The other two terms "jury & duty" were not used in the process of weights building of the tweets, since we excluded terms that rarely appeared in the corpus.

Classes	Classified as				Correct
	0	1	2	3	
0	270	108	59	36	57%
1	36	104	19	5	64%
2	36	16	24	9	29%
3	32	9	17	4	6%

Table 4: Confusion matrix of the 4-class classification.

Non-Ironic (B)

```
Extended cut "NICHA"
https://t.co/qdzpcuRqc1
#trailer #spoof #film #dramatic
#action #film2014 #youtube
#fightscenes
```

Similarly in this tweet, the terms have a high probability of occurrence in the non-ironic tweets while a very small probability in the ironic tweets. For the second case, we took other two tweets from the overlapping area between the ironic and non-ironic tweets. The tweets' terms weights are very similar to each other where the terms in both sentences were mentioned. This is what makes the tweets AVG features near to each in the figure.

For the task B, we built a confusion matrix to clarify the predictions of test subset cases, as in Table 3. We can conclude that: in the classes that have a low number of training records (2 and 3), our model was highly confused in detecting their original labels, where a very small number of cases was classified correctly with a detection ratio of 29% and 6% for class 2 and 3 sequentially. Moreover, the highest confusion occurs from class 0 to class 1 where 108 cases were classified incorrectly, where the lowest was from class 1 to class 3. In general, both classes 1 and 2 were correctly classified better than 2 and 3 classes. In our view, our model did not fit the training subset for the classes 2 and 3.

5 Conclusion

In this paper, we have evaluated LDR on the irony detection task to investigate its performance on irony detection. Using LDR the classification task accomplished with accepted results without using any semantic, sentiment or contextual features. Despite the fact that LDR previously showed its competitive results on language variety identification and author profiling tasks and outperformed traditional state-of-the-art representations, from the results of this shared task we can conclude that the low dimensionality features do not perform as good as other language dependent features do, and from our point of view, they are not suitable to infer of such language phenomenon as irony. As future work we will continue studying how LDR will perform on other language applications.

Acknowledgement

This research work was done in the framework of the SomEMBED TIN2015-71147-C2-1-P MINECO research project.

References

Francesco Barbieri and Horacio Saggion. 2014. Modelling irony in twitter. In *Proceedings of the Student Research Workshop at the 14th Conference of the European Chapter of the Association for Computational Linguistics*, pages 56–64.

Paula Carvalho, Luís Sarmento, Mário J Silva, and Eugénio De Oliveira. 2009. Clues for detecting irony in user-generated contents: oh...!! it's so easy;-. In *Proceedings of the 1st international CIKM workshop on Topic-sentiment analysis for mass opinion*, pages 53–56. ACM.

Raül Boluda Fabra, Francisco Rangel, and Paolo Rosso. 2015. Nlel upv autoritas participation at discrimination between similar languages (dsl) 2015 shared task. In *Proceedings of the Joint Workshop on Language Technology for Closely Related Languages, Varieties and Dialects*, pages 52–58.

Marc Franco-Salvador, Francisco Rangel, Paolo Rosso, Mariona Taulé, and M Antònia Martít. 2015. Language variety identification using distributed representations of words and documents. In *International Conference of the Cross-Language Evaluation Forum for European Languages*, pages 28–40. Springer.

Aniruddha Ghosh, Guofu Li, Tony Veale, Paolo Rosso, Ekaterina Shutova, John Barnden, and Antonio Reyes. 2015. Semeval-2015 task 11: Sentiment analysis of figurative language in twitter. In *Proceedings of the 9th International Workshop on Semantic Evaluation (SemEval 2015)*, pages 470–478.

Irazú Hernández-Farías, José-Miguel Benedí, and Paolo Rosso. 2015. Applying basic features from sentiment analysis for automatic irony detection. In *Iberian Conference on Pattern Recognition and Image Analysis*, pages 337–344. Springer.

Jihen Karoui, Farah Benamara, Véronique Moriceau, Nathalie Aussenac-Gilles, and Lamia Hadrich Belguith. 2015. Towards a contextual pragmatic model to detect irony in tweets. In *53rd Annual Meeting of the Association for Computational Linguistics (ACL 2015)*, pages PP–644.

Jihen Karoui, Benamara Farah, Véronique Moriceau, Viviana Patti, Cristina Bosco, and Nathalie Aussenac-Gilles. 2017. Exploring the impact of pragmatic phenomena on irony detection in tweets: A multilingual corpus study. In *Proceedings of the 15th Conference of the European Chapter of the Association for Computational Linguistics: Volume 1, Long Papers*, volume 1, pages 262–272.

Tatiana Litvinova, Francisco Rangel, Paolo Rosso, Pavel Seredin, and Olga Litvinova. 2017. Overview of the rusprofiling pan at fire track on cross-genre gender identification in russian. *Notebook Papers of FIRE*, pages 8–10.

Tomáš Ptáček, Ivan Habernal, and Jun Hong. 2014. Sarcasm detection on czech and english twitter. In *Proceedings of COLING 2014, the 25th International Conference on Computational Linguistics: Technical Papers*, pages 213–223.

Francisco Rangel, Marc Franco-Salvador, and Paolo Rosso. 2017a. A low dimensionality representation for language variety identification. *arXiv preprint arXiv:1705.10754*.

Francisco Rangel, Paolo Rosso, Martin Potthast, and Benno Stein. 2017b. Overview of the 5th author profiling task at pan 2017: Gender and language variety identification in twitter. In *CLEF 2017 Labs and Workshops, Notebook Papers. CEUR Workshop Proceedings*, volume 1866.

Antonio Reyes, Paolo Rosso, and Davide Buscaldi. 2012. From humor recognition to irony detection: The figurative language of social media. *Data & Knowledge Engineering*, 74:1–12.

Antonio Reyes, Paolo Rosso, and Tony Veale. 2013. A multidimensional approach for detecting irony in twitter. *Language resources and evaluation*, 47(1):239–268.

Cynthia Van Hee, Els Lefever, and Vronique Hoste. 2018. Semeval-2018 task 3: Irony detection in english tweets. In *Proceedings of the 12th International Workshop on Semantic Evaluation (SemEval-2018)*.

Byron C Wallace, Eugene Charniak, et al. 2015. Sparse, contextually informed models for irony detection: Exploiting user communities, entities and sentiment. In *Proceedings of the 53rd Annual Meeting of the Association for Computational Linguistics and the 7th International Joint Conference on Natural Language Processing (Volume 1: Long Papers)*, volume 1, pages 1035–1044.

Po-Ya Angela Wang. 2013. # irony or# sarcasma quantitative and qualitative study based on twitter. In *Proceedings of the 27th Pacific Asia Conference on Language, Information, and Computation (PACLIC 27)*, pages 349–356.

IIIDYT at SemEval-2018 Task 3: Irony detection in English tweets

Edison Marrese-Taylor[1*], Suzana Ilic[2*], Jorge A. Balazs[1*],
Helmut Prendinger[2], Yutaka Matsuo[1]
Graduate School of Engineering, The University of Tokyo, Japan[1]
emarrese,jorge,matsuo@weblab.t.u-tokyo.ac.jp
National Institute of Informatics, Tokyo, Japan[2]
suzana,helmut@nii.ac.jp
[*]Authors contributed equally to this work.

Abstract

In this paper we introduce our system for the task of Irony detection in English tweets, a part of SemEval 2018. We propose representation learning approach that relies on a multi-layered bidirectional LSTM, without using external features that provide additional semantic information. Although our model is able to outperform the baseline in the validation set, our results show limited generalization power over the test set. Given the limited size of the dataset, we think the usage of more pre-training schemes would greatly improve the obtained results.

1 Introduction

Sentiment analysis and emotion recognition, as two closely related subfields of affective computing, play a key role in the advancement of artificial intelligence (Cambria et al., 2017). However, the complexity and ambiguity of natural language constitutes a wide range of challenges for computational systems.

In the past years irony and sarcasm detection have received great traction within the machine learning and NLP community (Joshi et al., 2016), mainly due to the high frequency of sarcastic and ironic expressions in social media. Their linguistic collocation inclines to flip polarity in the context of sentiment analysis, which makes machine-based irony detection critical for sentiment analysis (Poria et al., 2016; Van Hee et al., 2015). Irony is a profoundly pragmatic and versatile linguistic phenomenon. As its foundations usually lay beyond explicit linguistic patterns in reconstructing contextual dependencies and latent meaning, such as shared knowledge or common knowledge (Joshi et al., 2016), automatically detecting it remains a challenging task in natural language processing.

In this paper, we introduce our system for the shared task of Irony detection in English tweets, a part of the 2018 SemEval (Van Hee et al., 2018). We note that computational approaches to automatically detecting irony often deploy expensive feature-engineered systems which rely on a rich body of linguistic and contextual cues (Bamman and Smith, 2015; Joshi et al., 2015). The advent of Deep Learning applied to NLP has introduced models that have succeeded in large part because they learn and use their own continuous numeric representations (Hinton, 1984) of words (Mikolov et al., 2013), offering us the dream of forgetting manually-designed features. To this extent, in this paper we propose a representation learning approach for irony detection, which relies on a bidirectional LSTM and pre-trained word embeddings.

2 Data and pre-processing

For the shared task, a balanced dataset of 2,396 ironic and 2,396 non-ironic tweets is provided. The ironic corpus was constructed by collecting self-annotated tweets with the hashtags *#irony*, *#sarcasm* and *#not*. The tweets were then cleaned and manually checked and labeled, using a fine-grained annotation scheme (Van Hee et al., 2015). The corpus comprises different types of irony:

- Verbal irony (polarity contrast): 1,728 instances

- Other types of verbal irony: 267 instances.

- Situational irony: 401 instances

Verbal irony is often referred to as an utterance that conveys the opposite meaning of what of literally expressed (Grice, 1975; Wallace, 2015), e.g. *I love annoying people*. Situational irony appears

Proceedings of the 12th International Workshop on Semantic Evaluation (SemEval-2018), pages 537–540
New Orleans, Louisiana, June 5–6, 2018. ©2018 Association for Computational Linguistics

in settings, that diverge from the expected (Lucariello, 1994), e.g. *an old man who won the lottery and died the next day*. The latter does not necessarily exhibit polarity contrast or other typical linguistic features, which makes it particularly difficult to classify correctly.

For the pre-processing we used the Natural Language Toolkit (Loper and Bird, 2002). As a first step, we removed the following words and hash-tagged words: *not, sarc, sarcasm, irony, ironic, sarcastic* and *sarcast*, in order to ascertain a clean corpus without topic-related triggers. To ease the tokenizing process with the NLTK TweetTokenizer, we replaced two spaces with one space and removed usernames and urls, as they do not generally provide any useful information for detecting irony.

We do not stem or lowercase the tokens, since some patterns within that scope might serve as an indicator for ironic tweets, for instance a word or a sequence of words, in which all letters are capitalized (Tsur et al., 2010).

3 Proposed Approach

The goal of the subtask A was to build a binary classification system that predicts if a tweet is ironic or non-ironic. In the following sections, we first describe the dataset provided for the task and our pre-processing pipeline. Later, we lay out the proposed model architecture, our experiments and results.

3.1 Word representation

Representation learning approaches usually require extensive amounts of data to derive proper results. Moreover, previous studies have shown that initializing representations using random values generally causes the performance to drop. For these reasons, we rely on pre-trained word embeddings as a means of providing the model the adequate setting. We experiment with GloVe[1] (Pennington et al., 2014) for small sizes, namely 25, 50 and 100. This is based on previous work showing that representation learning models based on convolutional neural networks perform well compared to traditional machine learning methods with a significantly smaller feature vector size, while at the same time preventing over-fitting and accelerates computation (e.g (Poria et al., 2016).

---

[1]`nlp.stanford.edu/projects/glove`

GloVe embeddings are trained on a dataset of 2B tweets, with a total vocabulary of 1.2 M tokens. However, we observed a significant overlap with the vocabulary extracted from the shared task dataset. To deal with out-of-vocabulary terms that have a frequency above a given threshold, we create a new vector which is initialized based on the space described by the infrequent words in GloVe. Concretely, we uniformly sample a vector from a sphere centered in the centroid of the 10% less frequent words in the GloVe vocabulary, whose radius is the mean distance between the centroid and all the words in the low frequency set. For the other case, we use the special *UNK* token.

To maximize the knowledge that may be recovered from the pre-trained embeddings, specially for out-of-vocabulary terms, we add several token-level and sentence-level binary features derived from simple linguistic patterns, which are concatenated to the corresponding vectors.

Word-level features

1. If the token is fully lowercased.

2. If the Token is fully uppercased.

3. If only the first letter is capitalized.

4. If the token contains digits.

Sentence-level features

1. If any token is fully lowercased.

2. If any token is fully uppercased.

3. If any token appears more than once.

3.2 Model architecture

Recurrent neural networks are powerful sequence learning models that have achieved excellent results for a variety of difficult NLP tasks (Ian Goodfellow, Yoshua Bengio, 2017). In particular, we use the last hidden state of a bidirectional LSTM architecture (Hochreiter and Urgen Schmidhuber, 1997) to obtain our tweet representations. This setting is currently regarded as the state-of-the-art (Barnes et al., 2017) for the task on other datasets. To avoid over-fitting we use Dropout (Srivastava et al., 2014) and for training we set binary cross-entropy as a loss function. For evaluation we use our own wrappers of the the official evaluation scripts provided for the shared tasks, which are based on accuracy, precision, recall and F1-score.

4 Experimental setup

Our model is implemented in PyTorch (Paszke et al., 2017), which allowed us to easily deal with the variable tweet length due to the dynamic nature of the platform. We experimented with different values for the LSTM hidden state size, as well as for the dropout probability, obtaining best results for a dropout probability of 0.1 and 150 units for the the hidden vector. We trained our models using 80% of the provided data, while the remaining 20% was used for model development. We used Adam (Kingma and Ba, 2015), with a learning rate of 0.0001 and early stopping when performance did not improve on the development set. Using embeddings of size 100 provided better results in practice. Our final best model is an ensemble of four models with the same architecture but different random initialization.

To compare our results, we use the provided baseline, which is a non-parameter optimized linear-kernel SVM that uses TF-IDF bag-of-word vectors as inputs. For pre-processing, in this case we do not preserve casing and delete English stopwords.

5 Results

To understand how our strategies to recover more information from the pre-trained word embeddings affected the results, we ran ablation studies to compare how the token-level and sentence-level features contributed to the performance. Table 1 summarizes the impact of these features in terms of F1-score on the validation set.

Feature	Yes	No
Token-level	0.6843	0.7008
Sentence-level	0.6848	0.6820

Table 1: Results of our ablation study for binary features in terms of F1-Score on the validation set.

We see that sentence-level features had a positive yet small impact, while token-level features seemed to actually hurt the performance. We think that since the task is performed at the sentence-level, probably features that capture linguistic phenomena at the same level provide useful information to the model, while the contributions of other finer granularity features seem to be too specific for the model to leverage on.

Table 2 summarizes our best single-model results on the validation set (20% of the provided data) compared to the baseline, as well as the official results of our model ensemble on the test data.

Split	Accuracy	Precision	Recall	F1-score
Baseline Valid	0.6375	0.6440	0.6096	0.6263
Ours Valid	0.6610	0.6369	0.8447	0.7262
Ours Test	0.3520	0.2568	0.3344	0.2905

Table 2: Summary of the obtained best results on the valid/test sets.

Out of 43 teams our system ranked 421st with an official F1-score of 0.2905 on the test set. Although our model outperforms the baseline in the validation set in terms of F1-score, we observe important drops for all metrics compared to the test set, showing that the architecture seems to be unable to generalize well. We think these results highlight the necessity of an ad-hoc architecture for the task as well as the relevance of additional information. The work of Felbo et al. (2017) offers interesting contributions in these two aspects, achieving good results for a range of tasks that include sarcasm detection, using an additional attention layer over a BiLSTM like ours, while also pre-training their model on an emoji-based dataset of 1246 million tweets.

Moreover, we think that due to the complexity of the problem and the size of the training data in the context of deep learning better results could be obtained with additional resources for pre-training. Concretely, we see transfer learning as one option to add knowledge from a larger, related dataset could significantly improve the results (Pan and Yang, 2010). Manually labeling and checking data is a vastly time-consuming effort. Even if noisy, collecting a considerably larger self-annotated dataset such as in Khodak et al. (2017) could potentially boost model performance.

6 Conclusion

In this paper we presented our system to SemEval-2018 shared task on irony detection in English tweets (subtask A), which leverages on a BiLSTM and pre-trained word embeddings for representation learning, without using human-engineered features. Our results showed that although the generalization capabilities of the model are limited, there are clear future directions to improve. In particular, access to more training data and the deployment of methods like transfer learning seem to be promising directions for future research in representation learning-based sarcasm detection.

References

David Bamman and Noah A Smith. 2015. Contextualized sarcasm detection on twitter. *Icwsm (International AAAI Conference on Web and Social Media)*, pages 574–577.

Jeremy Barnes, Roman Klinger, and Sabine Schulte im Walde. 2017. Assessing state-of-the-art sentiment models on state-of-the-art sentiment datasets. pages 2–12.

Erik Cambria, Dipankar Das, Sivaji Bandyopadhyay, and Antonio Feraco. 2017. *Guide to Sentiment Analysis*. Springer International Publishing AG 2017, Cham, Switzerland.

Bjarke Felbo, Alan Mislove, Anders Søgaard, Iyad Rahwan, and Sune Lehmann. 2017. Using millions of emoji occurrences to learn any-domain representations for detecting sentiment, emotion and sarcasm.

H. Paul Grice. 1975. Logic and conversation. In Peter Cole and Jerry L. Morgan, editors, *Syntax and Semantics*, volume 3, pages 41–58. Academic Press, New York.

Geoffrey E Hinton. 1984. Distributed representations.

Sepp Hochreiter and J Urgen Schmidhuber. 1997. Long short-term memory. *Neural Computation*, 9(8):1735–1780.

Aaron Courville Ian Goodfellow, Yoshua Bengio. 2017. *Deep Learning*, volume 521. MIT Press.

Aditya Joshi, Pushpak Bhattacharyya, and Mark James Carman. 2016. Automatic sarcasm detection: A survey. *ACM Computing Surveys*, V.

Aditya Joshi, Vinita Sharma, and Pushpak Bhattacharyya. 2015. Harnessing context incongruity for sarcasm detection. *Proceedings of the 53rd Annual Meeting of the Association for Computational Linguistics and the 7th International Joint Conference on Natural Language Processing (Short Papers)*, 51(4):757–762.

Mikhail Khodak, Nikunj Saunshi, and Kiran Vodrahalli. 2017. A large self-annotated corpus for sarcasm.

Diederik P. Kingma and Jimmy Ba. 2015. Adam: A method for stochastic optimization. In *Proceedings of the 3rd International Conference for Learning Representations*, San Diego.

Edward Loper and Steven Bird. 2002. Nltk: The natural language toolkit.

Joan Lucariello. 1994. Situational irony: A concept of events gone awry. *Journal of Experimental Psychology: General*, 123(2):129–145.

Tomas Mikolov, Ilya Sutskever, Kai Chen, Greg S Corrado, and Jeff Dean. 2013. Distributed Representations of Words and Phrases and their Compositionality. In C. J. C. Burges, L. Bottou, M. Welling, Z. Ghahramani, and K. Q. Weinberger, editors, *Advances in Neural Information Processing Systems 26*, pages 3111–3119. Curran Associates, Inc.

Sinno Jialin Pan and Qiang Yang. 2010. A survey on transfer learning. *IEEE Transactions on Knowledge and Data Engineering*, 22(10):1345–1359.

Adam Paszke, Gregory Chanan, Zeming Lin, Sam Gross, Edward Yang, Luca Antiga, and Zachary Devito. 2017. Automatic differentiation in pytorch. *Advances in Neural Information Processing Systems 30*, (Nips):1–4.

Jeffrey Pennington, Richard Socher, and Christopher Manning. 2014. Glove: Global vectors for word representation. *Proceedings of the 2014 Conference on Empirical Methods in Natural Language Processing (EMNLP)*, pages 1532–1543.

Soujanya Poria, Erik Cambria, Devamanyu Hazarika, and Prateek Vij. 2016. A deeper look into sarcastic tweets using deep convolutional neural networks.

Nitish Srivastava, Geoffrey Hinton, Alex Krizhevsky, Ilya Sutskever, and Ruslan Salakhutdinov. 2014. Dropout: A simple way to prevent neural networks from overfitting. *The Journal of Machine Learning Research*, 15(1):1929–1958.

Oren Tsur, Ari Rappoport, and Dmitry Davidov. 2010. Icwsm a great catchy name: Semi-supervised recognition of sarcastic sentences in online product reviews. *International AAAI Conference on Weblogs and Social Media*, (9):162–169.

Cynthia Van Hee, Els Lefever, and Veronique Hoste. 2015. Guidelines for annotating irony in social media text. *LT3 Technical Report*, 15(2).

Cynthia Van Hee, Els Lefever, and Véronique Hoste. 2018. SemEval-2018 Task 3: Irony Detection in English Tweets. In *Proceedings of the 12th International Workshop on Semantic Evaluation*, SemEval-2018, New Orleans, LA, USA. Association for Computational Linguistics.

Byron C. Wallace. 2015. Computational irony: A survey and new perspectives. *Artificial Intelligence Review*, 43(4):467–483.

PunFields at SemEval-2018 Task 3: Detecting Irony by Tools of Humor Analysis

Elena Mikhalkova, Yuri Karyakin, Dmitry Grigoriev,
Alexander Voronov, and Artem Leoznov
Tyumen State University, Tyumen, Russia
`(e.v.mikhalkova, y.e.karyakin)@utmn.ru`

Abstract

The paper describes our search for a universal algorithm of detecting intentional lexical ambiguity in different forms of creative language. At SemEval-2018 Task 3, we used PunFields, the system of automatic analysis of English puns that we introduced at SemEval-2017, to detect irony in tweets. Preliminary tests showed that it can reach the score of F1=0.596. However, at the competition, its result was F1=0.549.

1 Introduction

It requires no proof that usually language users can detect lexical ambiguity in figurative speech without classifying it into types like metaphor, pun, humor, irony, sarcasm, etc. At the same time, such terminology is necessary in studyng these phenomena as well as solving problems of automatic classification. In our opinion, programs dealing with intentional lexical ambiguity should be more like natural language users, i.e. they should have one general mechanism of its detection optimized to a certain extent to different types of creative language. In Task 3 "Irony Detection in English Tweets" of SemEval-2018 (Van Hee et al., 2018), we attempted to employ PunFields, our previously introduced classifier of English puns (Mikhalkova and Karyakin, 2017b) [1], in the task of irony classification in tweets as the constrained submission. I.e. PunFields trained only on the Gold dataset released by the Organizers.

As for the unconstrained submission, we used a bag-of-words model with an SVM classifier. The training dataset was enriched with tweets from other SemEval competitions. We will discuss it in a separate paragraph later in detail.

The results of PunFields in this competition were above the chance value (cf.: Table 1) demon-

	Ac.	Prec.	Rec.	F1 s.
Con.	0.5765	0.4753	0.6495	0.5489
Unc.	0.6033	0.5000	0.5563	0.5266
Hom.	**0.6782**	**0.7993**	**0.7337**	**0.7651**
Het.	0.5747	0.7580	0.5940	0.6661

Table 1: Results of PunFields at SemEval 2018 Task 3 and SemEval 2017 Task 7. Ac. - acuracy, Prec. - precision, Rec. - recall, F1 s. - F1 score. SemEval-2018: Con. - Constrained submission, Unc. - Unconstrained submission. SemEval-2017: Hom. - homographic puns, Het. - heterographic puns.

strating higher scores of Recall and F1 score, but lower Acuracy and Precision compared to the enriched bag-of-words (unconstrained submission). In analysis of puns, PunFields is more efficient reaching F1=0.765.

In this paper we will briefly outline the state-of-the-art system and possible reasons for its competition results.

2 Lexical Ambiguity in Irony and Puns

We will demonstrate similarity between a pun and irony by the two following examples.

> Christmas shopping on 2 hours sleep is going to be **fun**.

In this ironic tweet from the Gold dataset of the competition, the word **fun** is used simultaneously in the meaning "joy, amusement", in the context of "Christmas shopping", and in the meaning, opposite to it, "problem, trouble", in the context of "2 hours sleep." This *opposition* of meanings put into one word or phrase consitutes the essence of what many researchers call irony (Van Hee, 2017; Barbieri and Saggion, 2014).

> I could tell you a chemistry joke, but I know I wouldn't get a **reaction**.

---
[1]https://github.com/evrog/PunFields

Proceedings of the 12th International Workshop on Semantic Evaluation (SemEval-2018), pages 541–545
New Orleans, Louisiana, June 5–6, 2018. ©2018 Association for Computational Linguistics

In the pun above from the Gold dataset of SemEval2017 (Miller et al., 2017), the word **reaction** is used simultaneously in the meaning "chemical reaction", in the context of "chemistry", and in the meaning "emotional response", in the context of "joke". The only difference between the pun and irony in these examples is that in puns the opposition of meanings is more pragmatic. I.e. the two meanings of **reaction** belong to different spheres of human activity. In irony, the opposition is binary: fun=not fun.

In the both cases, the two meanings are envoked by two contexts, scripts, or themes. Therefore, if a computer program detects coexistence of two topics within an utterance, it is likely to classify correctly both pun and irony, but would be unable to tell which type it deals with. But can ordinary sentences without an intentionally ambiguous word or phrase also contain two scripts? Let us demonstrate what happens to a pun and irony if we transform them into sentences without ambiguity:

> Christmas shopping on 2 hours sleep is **not** going to be fun / is going to be a **problem**.

> I could tell you a chemistry joke, but I know I wouldn't get an **emotional** reaction / a **chemical** reaction.

When we transform these sentences, one of the scripts in a pun starts to dominate, for example the three word unity "joke + emotional reaction" would outnumber the one-word script of "chemistry", and vice versa "chemistry + chemical reaction" would outnumber the script of "joke".

However, in case of irony, this ambiguity is not so obvious. On the one hand, if we change "fun" to "problem", words "sleep", "hours" and "problem" *can* form a script. Although this script is not so easily recognizable and requires knowledge that two hours of sleep is too little (for example in the known semantic vector representations of words or documents sleep *can* be found close to lack, fatigue, and time). On the other hand, if we leave the word "fun" in the setence and just add "not" to it ("not going to be fun"), our algorithm will need to process auxiliary words and other variants of negation: never, neither, don't, etc. But these stop-words often create noise in searching for the main topics. If we ignore "not", the script "Christmas shopping + fun" would still form a union and dominate in the utterance.

In sum, intentional lexical ambiguity in irony is not easy for recognition compared to more explicit speech genres like puns. Another feature of irony that supports this statement is that otherwise there would be no need to mark irony with indicators of ambiguity like hashtags and emoji. [2]

3 PunFields

PunFields is a program that turns an utterance into a vector of length 39 based on 39 semantic classes of Roget's Thesaurus called Sections. [3] A thesaurus is a kind of dictionary that unites words into classes that build a hierarchy. Unlike WordNet, the hierarchy is designed by the author/-s of a thesaurus beforehand (top-down approach). Roget's Thesaurus places all lexemes at the lowest level on the basis of their semantic proximity. The clusters of words then unite into Sections, Sections into Divisions, Divisions into Classes. The 39 Sections of Roget's Thesaurus are in a way similar to dimensions of the word2vec algorithm (Mikolov et al., 2013), but word2vec has a fine tuning of meaning proximities.

Data Preprocessing. Before submitting data to PunFields, tweets are put into a preprocessing pipeline. The first step in the pipeline is separating symbols from words in a way that mentions (start with "@") and hashtags (start with "#") are left intact. Emoji are processed as word combiations (":ok_hand_sign:" is simply "ok hand sign"). Words in hashtags are often separated with a "_". Hence, we add a space before and after each "_". For eaxmple, the line "@kennychesney, :ok_hand_sign: #New#color#new#beginning" becomes "@kennychesney , : ok _ hand _ sign : #New #color #new #beginning".

The next step is treatment of emphatic devices in words that are not mentions and hashtags. We judge words with one letter repeated more than

---

[2]There are cases when it is impossible to recognize ambiguity without such indicators. For example, "Luv this" or "Sitting in this hall is fun" can be expressions of the real state of things unless the user adds a hashtag "#not", an emoji like "unamused face", etc. Note that these indicators quite often come at a particular place - end of the utterance. This fact also brings irony and puns together: in puns, usually the target word (the word used in the two senses) also occurs in the end.

[3]In (Mikhalkova and Karyakin, 2017a), we tried to join some of these classes together for a better performance, but it appeared that such enlargement does not improve it. And vice versa when we reach a certain number of general classes - approximately 4 - the performance starts to decrease significantly.

two times as emphasized. The words are "de-emphasized". For example, the word "everrrrrrr" becomes "ever".

We then proceed to mentions and hashtags. As there can be capitalized real names or titles, we de-capitalize them starting with the second letter and add a space before the capital letter and after the word, for example, "#ElektrikBLOOM" becomes "Elektrik Bloom ". If there are (successions of) numbers, a space is added on the both sides of the number. If there are names spelt as one word like "@WhoopiGoldberg", we add a space after every succession staring with a capital letter: "Whoopi Goldberg ".

Some mentions and hashtags are problematic to process as words are written without any indication that they should be separate, e.g. "kenny-chesney". We check in the NLTK names dictionary (Bird et al., 2009) if the glued hashtag starts with any name of length more than 5 characters. If yes, we unglue the word at the name border-line capitalizing the fisrt letters: "Kenny Chesney" (as luck would have it, most names consist of just two parts). Otherwise, we consider the word to be something other than a name. To separate words with spaces, we use Wordninja [4]. This library has problems with names and titles, so we have to check the names before using it. Words of more than two characters are also checked in a list of slang abbreviations. For example, "bbq" becomes "barbeque". [5]

Tweet to Vector. Preprocessed tweets go into the classifier. PunFields collects Section numbers for every word and collocation in a sentence, remov-ing duplicates and excluding stop words. Then, it builds a semantic vector of the sentence weighing how many of its elements belong to each Section. For example, the tweet "Christmas shopping on 2 hours sleep is going to be fun" has 7 words bel-ogning to different Sections: shopping - 33; 2 - 4; sleep - 11, 27, 14, 34; go - 11, 0, 14, 35, 7; christ-mas - 38, 5; fun - 35; hour - 5. Its vector will be as follows: $\{1, 0, 0, 0, 1, 2, 0, 1, 0, 0, 0, 2, 0, 0, 2, 0, 0, 0, 0, 0, 0, 0, 0, 0, 0, 0, 1, 0, 0, 0, 0, 0, 1, 1, 2, 0, 0, 1\}$.

Classification. When the vectors are ready, we split them into a training and test set. The classification is conducted using different Scikit-learn (Pedregosa et al., 2011) algorithms. At the present competition, we used SVM with the lin-ear kernel, because preliminary tests using the Gold dataset with a 5-fold cross validation showed that it has the highest result among the tested algorithms: Precision=0.556, Recall=0.646, F1-score=0.596 (766 samples in a training set). How-ever, when we used all the 3834 samples for train-ing during the competition, they obviously created a too noisy feature space for a good generaliza-tion. Hence, the decrease in the result. At Se-mEval2017 (Miller et al., 2017), when we tried larger datasets for training, the result grew better. Tweets generally seem to be more "noisy" than puns due to slang, contractions, glued words, etc. although there are no strict ways of calculating this "noisyness".

Instead of SVM, we also tested a deep learn-ing network with different architectures imple-mented in the Python library Keras (Chollet et al., 2015) with TensorFlow (TensorFlow Develop-ment Team, 2015) and Theano (Theano Develop-ment Team, 2016) backends, but we only managed to reach as much as 0.56 for F1-score. [6] Further-more, we tried to replace Roget's semantic classes with a vector model realization via the Gensim li-brary (Řehůřek and Sojka, 2010) summing every score in the 300 long word2vec representations similarly to what PunFields does with the 39 Sec-tions. However, it did not bring any significant result either.

All in all, PunFields appears to better classify such cases where there are two evidently differ-ent topics in one utterance that are expressed by two groups of words that outnumber other (noisy) groups. In the toy examples from the previous paragraph, the "chemistry" pun belongs to the so-called homographic puns, i.e. such puns where one word is used in two meanings. Unlike them, heterographic puns are such puns where the word used in one meaning resembles in form/sounding another word. That creates a disbalance between the two groups of words representing the two clashing topics: one of the groups gets the men-tioned word and the other one does not (as the word is only implied). For example, in the hetero-graphic pun "I relish the fact that you have mus-tard the strength to ketchup to me" the group of "mastered" and "catch up" is hidden. Similar to heterographic puns, ironic tweets have one word

---

[4] https://pypi.python.org/pypi/wordninja

[5] The pipeline is available at https://github.com/evrog/PunFields.

[6] Due to limitations in the size of papers, we will not de-scribe the architecture here. Some of the code we used for the neural network is available at our PunFields repository.

expressed in full and its opposite implied. Consequently, PunFields processes such cases worse than homographic puns.

4   Unconstrained Submission

As for the unconstrained submission, we decided to use it to test another assumption that irony is close not only to puns, but to different kinds of humor. However, as in this competition we deal with irony in Twitter, we decided to check this assumption on humorous *tweets*. We took 1,000 humorous tweets from SemEval 2017 #HashtagWars: Learning a Sense of Humor (Potash et al., 2017) and 1,000 tweets with 0 to +2 positive polarity from SemEval 2016 Task 4: Sentiment Analysis in Twitter (Nakov et al., 2016) and combined them with 2,000 tweets from the Gold dataset. For the classifier, we used Bernoulli bag-of-words SVM model with the linear kernel given as the benchmark system by the competition Organizers. After reshuffling the dataset several times, we chose that result which had a more or less equal number of items in the both classes.

The result of this test shows a decrease in the efficiency of the benchmark system. However, to our surprise it was also slightly above the chance value.

5   Conclusions

With this research, we continue to elaborate on the universal mechanism of detecting intentional lexical ambiguity in creative language. We tried to demonstrate that irony and puns share some features which can be processed by a similar algorithm. However, the results of our system, PunFields, at this competition leave much to be desired.

We are planning to replace the core of the system, the semantic scheme of 39 classes, with a more elaborate system of word2vec representations and, maybe, a deep learning classifier if it provides a better result. So far, we were unable to get the system working with these elements, but the problem was, very likely, in the technical side.

All in all, PunFields shows the result that is higher than the chance operating on the data it was not meant to process. With due elaboration, we believe, it has a greater classifying potential than what was gained at the competition.

References

Francesco Barbieri and Horacio Saggion. 2014. Modelling irony in Twitter. In *Proceedings of the Student Research Workshop at the 14th Conference of the European Chapter of the Association for Computational Linguistics*, pages 56–64.

Steven Bird, Ewan Klein, and Edward Loper. 2009. *Natural language processing with Python: analyzing text with the natural language toolkit.* " O'Reilly Media, Inc.".

François Chollet et al. 2015. Keras. https://github.com/keras-team/keras.

Elena Mikhalkova and Yuri Karyakin. 2017a. Detecting intentional lexical ambiguity in English puns. In *23rd International Conference on Computational Linguistics and Intellectual Technologies*, volume 1, pages 167–179.

Elena Mikhalkova and Yuri Karyakin. 2017b. Punfields at Semeval-2017 Task 7: Employing Roget's Thesaurus in Automatic Pun Recognition and Interpretation. In *Proceedings of the 11th International Workshop on Semantic Evaluation (SemEval-2017)*, pages 426–431.

Tomas Mikolov, Ilya Sutskever, Kai Chen, Greg S Corrado, and Jeff Dean. 2013. Distributed representations of words and phrases and their compositionality. In *Advances in neural information processing systems*, pages 3111–3119.

Tristan Miller, Christian Hempelmann, and Iryna Gurevych. 2017. Semeval-2017 task 7: Detection and interpretation of English puns. In *Proceedings of the 11th International Workshop on Semantic Evaluation (SemEval-2017)*, pages 58–68.

Preslav Nakov, Alan Ritter, Sara Rosenthal, Fabrizio Sebastiani, and Veselin Stoyanov. 2016. Semeval-2016 Task 4: Sentiment analysis in Twitter. In *Proceedings of the 10th International Workshop on Semantic Evaluation (SemEval-2016)*, pages 1–18.

F. Pedregosa, G. Varoquaux, A. Gramfort, V. Michel, B. Thirion, O. Grisel, M. Blondel, P. Prettenhofer, R. Weiss, V. Dubourg, J. Vanderplas, A. Passos, D. Cournapeau, M. Brucher, M. Perrot, and E. Duchesnay. 2011. Scikit-learn: Machine Learning in Python. *Journal of Machine Learning Research*, 12:2825–2830.

Peter Potash, Alexey Romanov, and Anna Rumshisky. 2017. Semeval-2017 Task 6:# hashtagwars: Learning a sense of humor. In *Proceedings of the 11th International Workshop on Semantic Evaluation (SemEval-2017)*, pages 49–57.

Radim Řehůřek and Petr Sojka. 2010. Software Framework for Topic Modelling with Large Corpora. In *Proceedings of the LREC 2010 Workshop on New Challenges for NLP Frameworks*, pages 45–50, Valletta, Malta. ELRA. http://is.muni.cz/publication/884893/en.

TensorFlow Development Team. 2015. TensorFlow: Large-Scale Machine Learning on Heterogeneous Systems. Software available from tensorflow.org.

Theano Development Team. 2016. Theano: A Python framework for fast computation of mathematical expressions. *arXiv e-prints*, abs/1605.02688.

Cynthia Van Hee. 2017. *Can machines sense irony? : exploring automatic irony detection on social media.* Ph.D. thesis, Ghent University.

Cynthia Van Hee, Els Lefever, and Véronique Hoste. 2018. SemEval-2018 Task 3: Irony Detection in English Tweets. In *Proceedings of the 12th International Workshop on Semantic Evaluation*, SemEval-2018, New Orleans, LA, USA. Association for Computational Linguistics.

HashCount at SemEval-2018 Task 3:
Concatenative Featurization of Tweet and Hashtags for Irony Detection

Won Ik Cho, Woo Hyun Kang, Nam Soo Kim
Department of Electrical and Computer Engineering and INMC,
Seoul National University, 1 Gwanak-ro, Gwanak-gu, Seoul, Korea, 08826
{wicho, whkang}@hi.snu.ac.kr, nkim@snu.ac.kr

Abstract

This paper proposes a novel feature extraction process for SemEval task 3: *Irony detection in English tweets*. The proposed system incorporates a concatenative featurization of tweet and hashtags, which helps distinguishing between the irony-related and the other components. The system embeds tweets into a vector sequence with widely used pretrained word vectors, partially using a character embedding for the words that are out of vocabulary. Identification was performed with BiLSTM and CNN classifiers, achieving F1 score of 0.5939 (23/42) and 0.3925 (10/28) each for the binary and the multi-class case, respectively. The reliability of the proposed scheme was verified by analyzing the Gold test data, which demonstrates how hashtags can be taken into account when identifying various types of irony.

1 Introduction

Nowadays, opinion mining from social media has become an important issue in natural language processing (NLP). Since tweets are globally used social media text that can influence the worldwide readers with just a short arrangement of words, the analysis on tweets has been widely studied in the semantic aspects such as sentiment classification (Rosenthal et al., 2017), hate speech detection (Waseem and Hovy, 2016), and irony detection (Karoui et al., 2015; Liebrecht et al., 2013). Especially, the automatic detection of ironic tweets can help the readers who are having difficulty recognizing sarcasm to notice such figurative instances from excessive amount of text data.

Despite the potential usage of the tasks, irony and sarcasm are difficult to grasp simply by analyzing word distribution. They require understandings on the language and social context, which are dependent on time and space; this implies that the study should accompany constant updates on the database used for the analysis. Also, it is important to construct a concrete criteria set to distinguish between ironic and non-ironic tweets.

In this paper, we incorporate a classification on manually labeled irony tweet corpus. The corpus contains 2,396 English tweets for ironic/non-ironic each (4,792 total), which were annotated under the scheme suggested in Van Hee et al. (2016). For the competition, the corpus was split into a training (80%, or 3,834 instances) and test (20%, or 958 instances) set. A training procedure for the system was all performed with the former (constrained).

2 Task Description

Two tasks were proposed for ironic English tweet analysis. Task A deals with the binary classification involving ironic tweets and non-ironic ones, and in Task B the ironic ones are categorized into three types (i.e. *verbal irony by means of a polarity contrast, other types of verbal irony*, and *situational irony*) (Van Hee et al., 2018). The original corpus contains 1,728/267/401 instances for each type.

3 System Description

3.1 Feature Engineering

For feature extraction, significant user behaviors were taken into account. We observed several tendencies in tweets: a large portion of irony-relevant information is conveyed by hashtags, and the hashtagged words are usually out-of-vocabulary (OOV) or non-segmented; at the same time drawing attention of the readers and emphasizing the user's point.

While extracting the features, the importance of hashtagged information was reflected in the coextensive placement of the original tweet and hashtags. This connotes the idea that the hashtagged

Proceedings of the 12th International Workshop on Semantic Evaluation (SemEval-2018), pages 546–552
New Orleans, Louisiana, June 5–6, 2018. ©2018 Association for Computational Linguistics

About once a yr I get a little nutty and reach for the orange marmalade. #livingontheedge #sarcasm

Figure 1: The capture of tweet number 63 in training set: *About once a yr I get a little nutty and reach for the orange marmalade. #livingontheedge http://t.co/sF9o6OWE1v* (ironic)

component is the metadata which needs highlighting.

3.1.1 Metadata handling

There are mainly three kinds of metadata observed in the tweets: ID tags (e.g. @someone), uniform resource locators (URLs, e.g. http://hyperlink), and hashtags (e.g. #something). The example sentences in this section are from the training set, not the Gold test data, thus they don't contain any irony hashtags, namely *#not*, *#irony*, and *#sarcasm*.

ID tags: In an empirical point of view, the ID tag of a tweet mainly delivered information on whether the user intends to notify someone the content (1a). This was not considered supportive information for irony detection, since sarcasm was observed to be conveyed in both a human-directive and non-human-directive way (1b,c) and that the presence of an ID tag ('@') could not be a crucial evidence in detecting irony.

(1) a. *@mrjamieeast I think it was the hotel owners...* (non-ironic)

b. *@LifeCheating doesn't lucky and fortunate mean the same thing?* (ironic)

c. *3 hours sleep yay loving life* (ironic)

URLs: The URLs are usually used as a hyperlink of the photo (Figure 1). However, as shown in the example, presence of photo doesn't necessarily affect the ironic nature of a tweet; we cannot infer the semantics of a photo just given an URL. Based on this observation, the URLs were not specially addressed; they were omitted in the word embedding process.

Hashtags: We paid attention to hashtagged words which were expected to contain information that can actually influence the nuance of the tweet (Chang, 2010). Thus, we created a placeholder for the vector embeddings of the hashtags (hashtag vector placeholder, HVP) and augmented it to the word vector sequence of the original tweet (Figure 2). This may cause a repetition on words in both the dictionary and the hashtags (e.g. *keep* of Figure 2), but it was assumed that the repetition would not degrade the performance. The reason for this assumption is because such words were expected to have a strong influence on the content, in that the user would have left it as a single word to notify its significance.

Firstly, a tweet was investigated whether it contains a hashtags. If not, the tweet would be compared to others based on the semantics of the original message. If any hashtag exists, the array of hashtagged words is embedded to the HVP to provide an useful evidence for the comparison with other tweets with hashtags. The numericalization of hashtags is demonstrated in the following passage.

3.1.2 Hashtag embedding

Given the nature of hashtags that does not allow spaces, most of the hashtagged words came under a category of either a single word (2a), concatenation of words with/without capital letters (2b,c), or an acronym (2d).

(2) a. *It will be impossible for me to be late if I start to dress up right now. #studing #university #lazy* (ironic)

b. *I picked a great week to start a new show on Netflix. #HellOnWheels* (ironic)

c. *Casper the friendly ghost on 2 levels! #thingsmichelleobamathinksareracist* (non-ironic)

d. *Another great day on the #TTC.* (ironic)

Instead of following the previous studies on hashtag segmentation (Bansal et al., 2015) that requires additional training processes, a simple guideline for hashtag embedding is proposed for such possible cases. Let *hash* be any hashtagged word, *dict* be a dictionary, $lower(w)$ be the character lowering process, and $D(w)$ be the vector

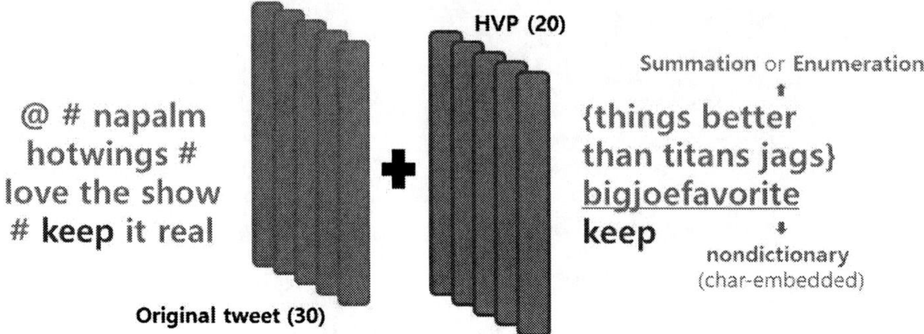

Figure 2: Feature extraction procedure for tweet number 1494. Word vector (or character-embedded vector) sequences are obtained for the original tweet and hashtags, denoted with length of 30 and 20 respectively. *keep* was colored purple since it belongs to both categories.

embedding for a word w.

- If $lower(hash)$ in *dict*: Trivial case. Compute output $O = D(lower(hash))$ and append it to the HVP.

- If $lower(hash)$ not in *dict* (OOV) and *hash* is a concatenation of words that each has a capitalized first letter:
  1) Split *hash* by the capital letters.
  2) One of the following strategies is chosen:
     a) **Summation** Compute the average $\sum_i D(lower(w_i))/W$ where w_i denotes each segmented word and W denotes the number of w_is. Assign it as an output O and append it to the HVP.
     b) **Enumeration** Append $D(lower(w_i))$ to the HVP one by one, for all w_is.

- Otherwise (character embedding): Compute $\sum_i D(lower(c_i))/C$ where c_i denotes each character in the *hash* and C denotes the number of c_is. Assign it as an output O and append it to the HVP.

The three dotted cases above can be respectively applied to the examples in Figure 2, namely *keep*, *ThingsBetterThanTitansJags*, and *bigjoefavorite*. To make it clear for the second case, for *ThingsBetterThanTitansJags*, the number of vectors appended to the HVP is 1 and 5 for the case of **Summation** and **Enumeration** respectively. Note again that only one heuristic method is chosen between those two - not being used simultaneously - in the aggregation of the word vectors from tweets.

The total size of the input feature is (*wdim*, 50), where *wdim* denotes the word vector size and 50 denotes the length of the vector sequence after the augmentation. The size was considered sufficient to cover the tokens of each tweet.

3.2 Classification

Classification was performed in a quite standard manner, utilizing both baseline sparse features and the proposed dense features. Although there have been some approaches that take into account the whole semantic relationship between terms (Kim et al., 2016; Cho et al., 2017), in this task we incorporated only the augmented feature constructed in the last section[1].

Since the sequential vectors were employed as features, descriptive models such as convolutional neural network (CNN) (Kim, 2014) and the bidirectional long short-term memory (BiLSTM) (Schuster and Paliwal, 1997) were adopted. In BiLSTM with an input size of 50 units, hidden layers had an output size of 32*2 = 64 units. In CNN, two 32*32-dim convolutional layers (for single channel) were used with a max-pooling layer between, summarized by a window of size 3. The output layer of the classifiers was fully connected

---

[1]Finding only the semantic contrasts could not cover the cases regarding situational irony.

F1 score	Task A	Task A (emoji)	Task B	Task B (emoji)
Baseline	0.6263	0.6200	0.3469	0.3455
CNN-text	0.6651	0.6425	0.3580	0.3647
CNN-enum	**0.6723**	0.6607	0.3785	0.4009
CNN-sum	0.6418	0.6543	<u>0.4084</u>	0.3517
BiLSTM-text	0.6568	0.6776	0.4022	0.3890
BiLSTM-enum	0.6701	0.6681	**0.4091**	**0.4378**
BiLSTM-sum	0.6616	**<u>0.6852</u>**	0.3843	0.3928

Table 1: 10-fold cross validation on the constrained training dataset. In task B, F1 score was obtained by macro averaging used in the scoring of competition. Bolded cases denote the best performing system for each labeled corpus. Underlined ones denote the systems that were originally submitted to the competition for each task. The score was updated according to an additional experiment.

	Accuracy	Precision	Recall	**F1 score**
Task A	0.6441	0.5426	0.6559	**0.5939**
(Best)	0.7972	0.7879	0.6688	0.7235
Task B	0.5982	0.4117	0.4096	**0.3925**
(Best)	0.7321	0.5768	0.5044	0.5074

Table 2: The submitted systems evaluated with the measurements, compared with the best scoring ones.

to the layer of 32 and then to decision layer of size 1 or 4, with either a sigmoid or a softmax activation, depending on the task.

4 Evaluation

The preprocessing was performed based on the example code[2], where the corpus was tokenized with NLTK (Bird et al., 2009). The 100dim GloVe (Pennington et al., 2014) pretrained with 27B token Twitter data[3] was employed as a dictionary for word embedding. All the training and validation procedure were carried out with Keras (TensorFlow backend) (Chollet et al., 2015). The code is provided online[4].

In this part, two main results are investigated. One deals with the comparison of performance according to classifiers and features. This is based on 10-fold cross validation using training data. In other words, the systems are trained using 3,450 instances and validated on 384 instances. In the other result, the competition score acquired using the submitted systems is inspected. Afterwards, we analyze the Gold test data, finding supportive evidences for the validity of the proposed approach regarding hashtags.

[2]https://github.com/Cyvhee/SemEval2018-Task3
[3]https://nlp.stanford.edu/projects/glove/
[4]https://github.com/warnikchow/HashCount

4.1 Result

The overall result tells that using the proposed features outperforms the baseline - term frequency-inverse document frequency (TF-IDF) on support vector machine (SVM), which was the system presented along with the train data. Table 1 shows the performance for each proposed system (*Classifier-Feature*) in each task. Here, *text* denotes the feature that includes only the original tweet (i.e. *Original tweet (30)* in Figure 2), and *enum/sum* denotes the feature that involves **Enumeration** and **Summation**, respectively.

The result suggests that employing *enum* and *sum* outperforms the vanilla case of *text* in general (Table 1). This supports our assumption in Section 3.1.1 and will be verified in Section 4.2. Although there were exceptions, employing BiLSTM outperformed the CNN-based method. This implies that the detection of irony is heavily influenced by specific terms (e.g. polarity items (Krifka, 1995)) or word sequence of the tweets. It is likely that the summarizing property of CNNs weaken the influence of such information. Also, unlike the intuition that more information will induce higher accuracy, there was no noticeable tendency regarding emoji.

4.2 Competition

The submitted systems showed F1 score of 0.5939 (ranked 23/42) and 0.3925 (ranked 10/28) in the competition, for Task A and B respectively.

Task A: The system submitted for Task A equals to the best performer of Table 1, *BiLSTM-sum* with emoji. However, it showed little an improvement compared to the CNN-based method (*CNN-enum* without emoji);%. it implies that the binary classification is less influenced by specific

Instances	Total	With @	With #	Correct	With # ($>$1)	Correct with # ($>$1)
Non-ironic	473	217 (45.8%)	255	301 (63.6%)	164 (34.6%)	125 (76.2% given #$>$1)
Ironic	311	84 (27.0%)	311	204 (65.5%)	139 (44.6%)	97 (69.7% given #$>$1)

Table 3: Analysis with the Gold test data of Task A. @ and # each denotes ID tag and hashtag.

Instances	Total	Correct	With # ($>$1)	Correct with # ($>$1)
Non-ironic	473	339 (71.6%)	164	134 (81.7%)
Polar	164	108 (65.8%)	74	51 (68.9%)
Situational	85	21 (24.7%)	40	10 (25.0%)
Other	62	1 (1.65%)	25	0 (0.0%)

Table 4: Analysis with the Gold test data of Task B.

terms or word sequence. From this, it could be inferred that the type classification of irony itself can be more difficult than just a detection.

Task B: The system submitted for task B, namely *CNN-sum* without emoji, differs from the lately-achieved best performer (*BiLSTM-enum* with emoji) which relatively outperforms the submitted model by 7.19%. The initial choice is based on overlooking the superiority of using BiLSTM, where the influence of the specific terms on nuance of the tweet has not been recognized.

There was a significant decrease in recall, compared with Task A. Since the feature is fixed, there may exist possible issues of classifier and emojis. Considering the analysis in the last subsection, it is presumed that the classifier issue is dominant over other problems. CNN seems to be a more cautious model than BiLSTM, but this is not considered a good property for the detector. In the aspect of the nature of sarcasm that at least 'sensitive' false alarms are better than generous ignorance, it is considered a reasonable decision to use a recurrent classifier model with high recall.

4.3 Gold Test Data

Further investigation regarding the Gold test data was performed for both tasks. We examined the composition of correct predictions, in terms of how the presence of hashtags positively affected the outcome.

Task A: We first figured out how ID tags and hashtags are distributed over the whole test cor-

pus. It was revealed that non-ironic tweets more frequently accompany ID tags than the ironic ones (Table 3), but we did not conclude that ID tags convey a non-ironicalness for the reasons given in 3.1.1.

For hashtags, there was an important thing to consider in counting; all ironic tweets included at least one irony hashtag, which led to 100% presence of '#' for ironic instances. Thus, only the 'effective' hashtags were taken into account in a way of identifying tweets with more than one '#'; in other words, a single default hashtag was ignored[5].

In terms of tweet ratios with effective hashtags, ironic tweets outperformed the non-ironic ones. In addition, the rate of correct prediction in instances with #$>$1 was observed to be higher than the ratio in the whole instance, for both cases (63.6% $<$ 76.2% and 65.5% $<$ 69.7% in Table 3). These validates the utility of the proposed modeling which emphasizes hashtags as indispensable metadata.

We also observed that 79, 41, and 19 instances of ironic tweets possessed one, two, and three or more effective hashtags, respectively. Except for 172 tweets with a single default hashtag, the most common case is to convey sarcasm in one word as in (3), inducing a contradiction between the literal evaluation and the intended one (Van Hee et al., 2016).

(3) *Just a @ScienceDaily article re: a robot arm you can control with your mind. Meh. Nothing huge. #sarcasm #science http://t.co/AK4bAorhBc*

Task B: We further investigated the detailed types of ironic tweets. Except for the case of *Other* where the accuracy was particularly low, hashtags performed as supportive information for correct prediction (Table 4).

Of the three irony types, *Polar* recorded the highest accuracy of correct answer prediction, also showing the most amount of enhancement given a condition of at least one effective hashtag. To be more specific than what was discussed above,

[5]This was also applied to non-ironic cases to match the proportion of instances.

Number of effective #s	0	1	2	>2
Polar	57/90 (63.3%)	27/42 (64.2%)	18/21 (85.7%)	6/11 (54.5%)
Situational	11/45 (24.4%)	6/26 (23.1%)	2/9 (22.2%)	2/5 (40.0%)
Other	1/37 (2.7%)	0/11 (0.0%)	0/11 (0.0%)	0/3 (0.0%)

Table 5: The number of effective instances for each irony types (correct/total) regarding the number of hashtags. The irony hashtags were not counted.

the number of effective hashtags was found to be most supportive in one or two cases (Table 5). This property can be effectively utilized, e.g. varying the weight given to the hashtag vector, depending on the number.

For *Situational*, the percentage was not reliable due to the shortage of the number of instances. We concluded that the case regarding the tweets only with default irony tags (11/45) is rather valid, in that the tone of the *Situational* ironic tweets appeared to be descrptive than provocative (4a). It was even more difficult to identify tendencies for the case of *Other* (4b); thus, it was assumed to resemble the case of *situational*.

(4) a. *The thirstiest of thirst buckets calling other people thirsty #irony*

b. *@BarryBlackNE I don't think the Hereditary Baronet wants to encourage a something-for-nothing culture :-$ #irony*

5   Discussion

There are a few more schemes to consider in the future implementation. First, Additional normalization of words can be done. The proposed scheme focused on the featurization of the original tweet and hashtags, and no lemmatization or stemming was carried out. This was mainly because normalization can inadvertently erase important information; but it would be tolerable if carried out just on the non-hashtagged lexical words.

It would also be effective to apply the advanced segmentation algorithm to hashtags, taking into account the improved performance of proposed systems. This does not necessarily involve an algorithm that requires additional training and a huge database. Lighter and fancy segmentation techniques that fully utilize the dictionary are expected to be introduced.

Finally, fusion of classifiers can be undertaken. This was not considered in the proposed system, since in mixed networks, it is difficult to recognize the influence of using each feature and classifier. Nonetheless, such networks can be chosen in terms of boosting performance for real-life applications.

6   Conclusion

In this paper, the feature engineering based on the coextensive placement of tweet and hashtags was presented. Two embedding schemes for hashtag vector placeholder (HVP) were employed, and concatenation of HVP and original word vector sequences was used as inputs to CNN and BiLSTM classifiers. The implementation verified that the proposed systems outperform the baseline, and the system's reliability was supported by analyzing the correlation of hashtags and prediction accuracy with the Gold test data. Future works include lemmatization that do not affect content, development of an efficient hashtag segmentation, and fusion of classifiers.

Acknowledgments

This work was supported by the Technology Innovation Program (10076583, Development of free-running speech recognition technologies for embedded robot system) funded By the Ministry of Trade, Industry & Energy (MOTIE, Korea).

References

Piyush Bansal, Romil Bansal, and Vasudeva Varma. 2015. Towards deep semantic analysis of hashtags. In *European Conference on Information Retrieval*. Springer, pages 453–464.

Steven Bird, Ewan Klein, and Edward Loper. 2009. *Natural language processing with Python: analyzing text with the natural language toolkit.* " O'Reilly Media, Inc.".

Hsia-Ching Chang. 2010. A new perspective on twitter hashtag use: Diffusion of innovation theory. *Proceedings of the Association for Information Science and Technology* 47(1):1–4.

Won Ik Cho, Woo Hyun Kang, Hyun Seung Lee, and Nam Soo Kim. 2017. Detecting oxymoron in a single statement. In *Proceedings of Conference of The Oriental Chapter of International Committee for Coordination and Standardization of Speech Databases and Assessment Techniques (O-COCOSDA)*. pages 48–52.

François Chollet et al. 2015. Keras. `https://github.com/fchollet/keras`.

Jihen Karoui, Farah Benamara, Véronique Moriceau, Nathalie Aussenac-Gilles, and Lamia Hadrich Belguith. 2015. Towards a contextual pragmatic model to detect irony in tweets. In *53rd Annual Meeting of the Association for Computational Linguistics (ACL 2015)*. pages PP–644.

Joo-Kyung Kim, Marie-Catherine de Marneffe, and Eric Fosler-Lussier. 2016. Adjusting word embeddings with semantic intensity orders. In *Proceedings of the 1st Workshop on Representation Learning for NLP*. pages 62–69.

Yoon Kim. 2014. Convolutional neural networks for sentence classification. *arXiv preprint arXiv:1408.5882* `https://arxiv.org/abs/1408.5882`.

Manfred Krifka. 1995. The semantics and pragmatics of polarity items. *Linguistic analysis* 25(3-4):209–257.

Christine Liebrecht, Florian Kunneman, and Antal van Den Bosch. 2013. The perfect solution for detecting sarcasm in tweets# not pages 29–37.

Jeffrey Pennington, Richard Socher, and Christopher Manning. 2014. Glove: Global vectors for word representation. In *Proceedings of the 2014 Conference on Empirical Methods in Natural Language Processing (EMNLP)*. pages 1532–1543.

Sara Rosenthal, Noura Farra, and Preslav Nakov. 2017. Semeval-2017 task 4: Sentiment analysis in twitter. In *Proceedings of the 11th International Workshop on Semantic Evaluation (SemEval-2017)*. pages 502–518.

Mike Schuster and Kuldip K Paliwal. 1997. Bidirectional recurrent neural networks. *IEEE Transactions on Signal Processing* 45(11):2673–2681.

Cynthia Van Hee, Els Lefever, and Veronique Hoste. 2016. Guidelines for annotating irony in social media text, ver. 2.0. *LT3 Technical Report Series* .

Cynthia Van Hee, Els Lefever, and Véronique Hoste. 2018. SemEval-2018 Task 3: Irony Detection in English Tweets. In *Proceedings of the 12th International Workshop on Semantic Evaluation*. Association for Computational Linguistics, New Orleans, LA, USA, SemEval-2018.

Zeerak Waseem and Dirk Hovy. 2016. Hateful symbols or hateful people? predictive features for hate speech detection on twitter. In *Proceedings of the NAACL student research workshop*. pages 88–93.

WLV at SemEval-2018 Task 3: Dissecting Tweets in Search of Irony

Omid Rohanian, Shiva Taslimipoor, Richard Evans and Ruslan Mitkov
Research Group in Computationa Linguistics
University of Wolverhampton
Wolverhampton, UK
`{omid.rohanian,shiva.taslimi,r.j.evans,r.mitkov}@wlv.ac.uk`

Abstract

This paper describes the systems submitted to SemEval 2018 Task 3 "Irony detection in English tweets" for both subtasks A and B. The first system leveraging a combination of sentiment, distributional semantic, and text surface features is ranked third among 44 teams according to the official leaderboard of the subtask A. The second system with slightly different representation of the features ranked ninth in subtask B. We present a method that entails decomposing tweets into separate parts. Searching for contrast within the constituents of a tweet is an integral part of our system. We embrace an extensive definition of contrast which leads to a vast coverage in detecting ironic content.

1 Introduction

In figurative language (also known as trope), there is a departure from literal use of words. In order to decode meaning, therefore, it is not enough to rely solely on the literal sense of individual words. Irony and sarcasm are two types of such language that exploit this technique in similar ways. They "both involve deliberately saying something that is incongruous or the opposite of what the speaker knows to be true" (Hanks, 2013). This is sometimes formulated as a transgression of the Gricean maxim of quality (Grice, 1975)[1].

Under this assumption it follows that the violation is only permissible thanks to shared knowledge between the speaker and the hearer. In order to achieve this goal, the speaker frames the message with some form of commentary or metamessage that signals the ironic or sarcastic nature of the message. This is usually realised through negation of the original meaning (Haiman, 1998).

Regardless of their similarities, irony and sarcasm are not technically the same as they might be employed for different purposes. It is widely accepted that sarcasm involves some degree of verbal aggression and ridicule directed at the hearer, whilst irony can simply be used for humorous or emphatic effect. It has been shown that computational processing of irony and sarcasm requires some knowledge of the context in which they appear, sometimes including paralinguistic information (Wallace et al., 2014).

Exploring ironicity has practical implications, since performance of sentiment analysis systems is directly affected by knowledge about irony and sarcasm (Pozzi et al., 2016).

As part of the 12th workshop on semantic evaluation (SemEval-2018), Shared Task 3 defines two subtasks with regards to irony detection in English tweets (Van Hee et al., 2018). Subtask A involves binary classification. The objective is to train a system that can label tweets as ironic or not. Subtask B is a multi-class classification problem with the objective to label tweets with one of the four specified labels describing the type of irony (verbal irony by means of a polarity contrast, situational irony, other verbal irony, and non-ironic).

To tackle these problems, in this paper we describe two rich feature-based systems addressing each subtask. Our systems use a combination of sentiment, distributional semantic, and text surface features. The code and data for this project is freely available[2].

The rest of this paper is organised as follows: Section 2 describes related work. Section 3 provides a comprehensive description of the overall methodology including pre-processing, feature representation, and system architecture. Sections 4 and 5 discuss experiments and results, Section 6 involves error analysis and finally Section 7 concludes the paper with some closing remarks.

---

[1]"Do not say what you believe to be false."

[2]`https://github.com/omidrohanian/irony_detection`

Proceedings of the 12th International Workshop on Semantic Evaluation (SemEval-2018), pages 553–559
New Orleans, Louisiana, June 5–6, 2018. ©2018 Association for Computational Linguistics

2 Related Work

There has been a recent surge of interest in the tasks of irony and sarcasm detection due in large part to increasing popularity of social media and the availability of data from websites like Twitter and Reddit. Some recent work focus exclusively on irony or sarcasm in isolation (Joshi et al., 2016), under the assumption that sarcasm has a stronger impact on changing the sentiment of the overall message. However in many cases, these terms are taken to be practically synonymous (Pozzi et al., 2016; Wallace et al., 2014; Ptáček et al., 2014). SemEval has a long-standing shared task on sentiment analysis that has also involved processing of figurative language including irony and sarcasm (Ghosh et al., 2015; Nakov et al., 2016). Results from recent tasks on sentiment analysis confirm that the top performing teams increasingly employ deep learning methodologies, while classical machine learning models like SVM and logistic regression remain popular (Ghosh et al., 2015; Rosenthal et al., 2017).

3 Methodology

We train our supervised systems using an ensemble soft voting classifier with logistic regression (LR) and support vector machine (SVM) as component models, and create our feature sets using a combination of sentiment, semantic, and surface features. We leverage these handcrafted features in combination with dense vector representations which differ in details between subtask A and B. The differences in feature engineering and representation between the two subtasks will be discussed in 3.2.

3.1 Pre-processing

Tweets were tokenised using NLTK's tweet tokeniser (Loper and Bird, 2002). Additional preprocessing was done to obtain a subset of the features that concerned surface orthographic features (e.g. all capitals, elongations, emoticons, etc) and pattern-based named entities (e.g. time, place, user, etc). For this we used the ekphrasis toolkit (Baziotis et al., 2017). It employs an XML-based annotation scheme that made it easy to extract this information.

For sentiment features and embeddings, however, pre-processing beyond tokenisation was deemed unnecessary as our emoji and word vectors were pre-trained on raw tweets.

3.2 Feature Representation

In our observation of the training data, we noticed that tweets often follow a fairly consistent spatial pattern. Informative words are more likely to cluster at both ends of a tweet. Hashtags, while scattered throughout the whole text, tend to occur at the end. In ironic tweets, negative sentiments are more likely to be preceded by neutral or positive ones. An example is given in (1).

(1)   What a golden morning. 😘

In order for our models to capture these spatial patterns and to provide a more rigorous representation of a tweet's structure, we propose the idea of decomposing a tweet into separate chunks and extracting features for each one separately. By concatenating these features we are able to partially preserve information about linear precedence. To this end, we simply split the sentences to two sections as represented in example (2) and (3).

(2)   8ams are just | so LOVELY .
        surface features: $time1$ | $allcaps2$

(3)   SEEING @AlpEmiel ON | SATURDAY whadddddddup #legend
        surface features: $allcaps1$, $user1$ |
        $elongated2$, $hashtag2$

In examples (2) and (3), the numbers '1' and '2' signify the first and second sections of the tweet respectively.

We use the same split structure for representation of other features, and pre-trained dense vectors.

Contrast is one of the most important properties of ironic language. One contribution of this work lies in the particular manner in which the notion of contrast is defined. Contrast is a marker of polarity shift and is usually seen as the presence of a positive sentiment referring to a negative situation, or vice versa (Riloff et al., 2013) which is sometimes referred to as "asymmetry of affect" (Clark and Gerrig, 1984).

Twitter language is non-standard and informal. Polarity shift can be realised through contrast between different elements of the tweet. The elements of a tweet are: text, hashtagged tokens, and emojis. We adopt a more inclusive stance with regards to the concept of contrast with the following scenarios:

1. Contrast between different parts of the same

element of a tweet

   a. antithetical emojis

   b. antithetical hashtagged tokens

2. Contrast between two different elements of a tweet

   c. text and hashtagged tokens

   d. text and emojis

   e. hashtagged tokens and emojis

A sizable proportion of the tweets contain multiword hashtags, such as *#NotExcitedAboutThisAtAll* or *#goodluck*, that require segmentation. For this we used ekphrasis' hashtag segmentation tool (Baziotis et al., 2017).

We separate the tweet and its segmented hashtagged tokens and run each group through the sentiment analysis tool from Stanford CoreNLP (Manning et al., 2014). CoreNLP assigns to an input any of 5 sentiment classes from very negative to very positive (0 to 4). If the resulting hashtag and text scores are on opposite sides of this spectrum, we consider this as contrast type c. as defined in 2.

For d. and e. we follow a similar procedure. To approximate the sentiments present in emoji tokens, we use Emoji Sentiment Ranking (Kralj Novak et al., 2015). This is a lexicon of 751 emojis whose sentiments are ranked based on human annotation of 70,000 tweets in 13 European languages.

The resulting contrast feature is a binary value that is set to True if any one of the aforementioned forms of contrast is present in the tweet.

Relying on sentiment information from CoreNLP, we define an additional binary feature named Intensity. It checks whether the sentiment in a segment of the tweet is sharply positive/negative. This translates to a value of 0 or 4 in the sentiment scores for that particular segment. The rationale behind definition of this feature is that too much of a positive emotion can, in certain contexts, imply a negative sentiment. To a lesser extent, the opposite is also true of an excessively negative emotion.

To track the changes of sentiment expressed throughout the whole tweet, we define sentiment patterns of Rise (R), Fall (F), and Stable (S) on a word-by-word basis and encode this information in a vector representing the number of S, R, F, RF,

and FR patterns. For these features, we rely on information from Vader sentiment lexicon (Gilbert, 2014).

For dense vectors we use word2vec embeddings pretrained on a large twitter corpus as described in Godin et al. (2015). One limitation of these embeddings is that they don't contain information on emojis. Therefore we have to complement this resource with additional embeddings specifically trained on emojis (Eisner et al., 2016).

3.3 Task-specific Selected Features

3.3.1 Subtask A

For subtask A, we found that the best way to combine embeddings is through averaging, separately for left and right parts[3]. Features we combine with these vectors are the following: Surface features, Intensity (for left and right), and Contrast.

3.3.2 Subtask B

For subtask B, concatenation of the embeddings was deemed more effective. Furthermore, we augment the combined embeddings with bigram tf-idf count vectors.

As a rhetorical trope, irony can often have subtle political and social dimensions, and is used frequently to express opinionated thoughts in general (Hutcheon, 1994). We noticed that adding topic modeling features to our system in subtask B slightly improves classification performance as these features can help the model capture more subtle forms of irony that tend to co-occur with certain topics and are not necessarily realised as polarity contrasts. Topic modeling of the tweets is done using Latent Dirichlet Allocation (LDA) and Non-negative matrix factorization (NMF).

Other features we add to the above are: Surface features (we consider these with regard to both the whole tweet and its left and right splits), Intensity (for left and right), Contrast, and Vader-based Rise and Fall sentiment patterns.

4 Experimental Settings

We use the data (text including emojis) as provided by the organisers of the shared task. We train our models on the training set using 10-fold cross-validation. Predictions were made on the held-out test data.

---

[3] word and tweet embeddings are averaged independently, and subsequently the averages are concatenated.

	ironic	non-ironic	total
train	1911 (49.84%)	1923 (50.15%)	3834
test	311 (39.66%)	473 (60.33%)	784

Table 1: Statistics of the data for subtask A

```
rightIntensity, contrast, date1,
sad1, surprise1, url1, date2,
elongated2, laugh2, sad2, shocking2,
url2, user2
```

Figure 1: The most informative features for subtask A

Train and test data in both subtasks A and B are the same and only differ in their annotation. Tables 1 and 2 present the breakdown of the classes and the number of their instances in each subtask.

The most informative features are selected using recursive feature elimination (RFE) (Guyon et al., 2002). As a result, the algorithm uses 13 features for subtask A as listed in figure 1. They are concatenated with the vectors that were derived by separately averaging the words and emoji vectors of the left and right parts of tweets.

The best features derived from RFE for subtask B did not improve the performance of the model. Therefore we use all of the 87 features which are consequently augmented with the concatenation of the word and and emoji vectors of tweets.

The baseline system provided by task organisers is an SVM classifier which uses tf-idf feature vectors. We consider this as the benchmark and report the results for 2 different settings of our system as follows:

- `setting 1`: average of word and emoji vectors of bi-sectioned tweets

- `setting 2`: concatenation of word and emoji vectors

In both settings we combine vectors with best features and feed them to the classifiers. To achieve the best system for subtask A (`best system A`) we apply a voting classifier with soft voting between LR and SVM whose model components are based on `setting 1` plus the 13 best features that were selected using RFE for subtask A.

The best system for subtask B is a voting classifier between 3 LRs with 3 different class weights as shown in Table 3. The components of the models are based on `setting 2` plus all features for subtask B.

5   Results and Discussion

Table 4 details the results for subtask A, and the results for subtask B are presented in Table 5. After cross-validation on the `TRAIN` set, the best system which is an ensemble voting classifier trained on models based on `setting 1 + best features of subtask A` achieves the highest record in F1-score and recall, but is outperformed in accuracy by its own component model. In terms of precision it also scores lower than the system based on `setting 2 + all features`.

When tested on the `TEST` data, our best system for subtask A ranked third overall on the shared tasks's official leaderboard among 44 teams with an F-score of 0.65. It has the second highest score for recall. This indicates that the coverage of the model is extensive.

For subtask B, our best system is an ensemble voting classifier comprised of three logistic regression models based on `setting 2 + all features` with the set-up indicated in Table 3.

As can be seen in Table 5, it gives the best F1-score, accuracy, and recall when cross-validated on the `TRAIN` data. On the held-out `TEST` data, the system ranked 9th in terms of F1-score, and with 0.6709 accuracy ranked second out of all participating systems in the shared task.

Table 6 shows the F1-scores for subtask B based on the system's performance on each individual label. In the case of irony by clash, our system achieves an F1-score of 0.6584. This confirms that our features are informative enough to help the model capture this type of irony fairly well, even though only 20.91% of the tweets belong to this class (Table 2).

However, in the case of situational irony the system performs much worse. There are several possible factors that collectively contribute to this poorer performance. Situational irony is less studied in the literature and designing effective features to model it is more difficult. By definition, it involves a situation that does not conform to the expectations of the speaker and elicits an emotional response (Shelley, 2001). Expectations differ among individuals and people often react differently to the same events and stimuli which further complicates the problem.

In the provided dataset, the number of instances of this type of irony is small (only 8.24% of the total in the `TRAIN` set), and there are no salient tex-

	non-ironic	clash	situational	other	total
train	1923 (50.15%)	1390 (36.25%)	316 (8.24%)	205 (5.34%)	3834
test	473 (60.33%)	164 (20.91%)	85 (10.84%)	62 (7.90%)	784

Table 2: Statistics of the data for subtask B

	non-ironic	clash	situational	other
LR1	1	1	1	1
LR2	1	1	2	2
LR3	1	1	3	3

Table 3: Weights each LR classifier assigns to the 4 classes in subtask B

tual characteristics that can signal their occurrence while distinguishing them from irony by clash.

6 Error Analysis

Vast coverage in subtask A also means that the model is quick to judge a tweet as ironic which translates to a large number of tweets getting tagged as 1. According to Table 1 the distribution of labels is slightly skewed towards non-ironic labels, but in our predictions 0.62% of the tweets are tagged as ironic (Table 4) which explains higher recall and lower precision. This can be traced back to the inclusive definition of contrast as defined in 3.2.

The gold standard provided is not without faults. As an example (4) is obviously an ironic tweet that is incorrectly labeled as 0 in the gold-standard[4]. Also in example (5) the word *tit* (altered in spelling for censorship), is being used in two ways; first in its literal sense, and the other to sarcastically refer to a politician as foolish. This was labeled as non-ironic in the dataset, which is subject to debate. Our system correctly identified both of these instances.

(4)   Corny jokes are my absolute favorite

(5)   #farage a t1t in public who doesnt agree with seeing t1ts in public #breastfeeding

Looking at the per-class performances in subtask B (Table 6), the best system is predicting non-ironic instances with a high F1-score of 0.7652. However the F1-scores for other classes remain low.

The numbers for situational is lower than irony by clash, which seems logical because in order to

effectively pinpoint a tweet as ironic by situation it is sometimes necessary to have access to information beyond the text which could involve a broader context (social, cultural, political, etc) as exemplified in the following examples that are taken from the TRAIN set:

(6)   Sure   Staff...   Now   Hiring. http://t.co/HDgfxG7elF

(7)   #mondaymorning pouring rain and i am singing 'the most wonderful time of the year' as i walk to the office

(8)   Patrick Kielty hosting Radio 2's Comedy Awards...

In (6), textual information does not provide anything of significant value. If the user clicks on the link, it seems like the image is about an employment agency that is hiring. Normally, they supply staff to clients who are recruiting but in this case, it is the agency itself which is recruiting. This goes against expectation. Realisation of this instance as situational irony requires interpretation of the image which in turn requires linking the name *Sure Staff* to an agency, and the background knowledge about the role of employment agencies.

Example (7) involves the interpretation of a rainy day on Monday morning as unpleasant, which is subjective. Example (8) implies that the comedian is not particularly known to be funny, which again requires background knowledge and is also dependent on the opinion of the annotator, as it could also read as a non-ironic sentence if the reader does not share the same impression of the comedian.

7 Conclusion

In this paper, we have described our supervised systems to identify ironic tweets and categorise them into three types. Our systems leveraging a combination of word/emoji vectors and features related to polarity contrast, intensity and text surface features achieved competitive results for bi-

---

[4]*corny* has a negative connotation, implying that the joke is unfunny, and uninteresting

		Accuracy	Precision	Recall	F1-score
TRAIN	benchmark system	0.6375	0.6440	0.6096	0.6263
	LR with setting 1	0.6643	0.6543	0.6923	0.6728
	LR with setting 2	0.6502	0.6466	0.6578	0.6521
	LR with setting 1 + best features of subtask A	**0.6808**	0.6616	0.7357	0.6967
	LR with setting 2 + all features	0.6787	**0.6726**	0.6923	0.6823
	best system A	0.6742	0.6452	**0.7698**	**0.7020**
TEST	best system A	0.6429 (15)	0.5317 (20)	0.8360 (2)	0.6500 (3)

Table 4: Results for subtask A

		Accuracy	Precision	Recall	F1-score
TRAIN	benchmark system	0.6064	0.4359	0.3540	0.3470
	LR with setting 1	0.6142	0.4952	0.3449	0.3278
	LR with setting 2	0.6239	**0.5394**	0.3796	0.3817
	LR with setting 1 + all features	0.6325	0.4867	0.3696	0.3550
	LR with setting 2 + all features	0.6450	0.5308	0.4061	0.4134
	best system B	**0.6458**	0.5280	**0.4122**	**0.4215**
TEST	best system B	0.6709 (2)	0.4311 (11)	0.4149 (10)	0.4153 (9)

Table 5: Results for subtask B

	non-ironic	clash	situational	other
TRAIN	0.7064	0.6584	0.2768	0.0444
TEST	0.7652	0.4651	0.2595	0.0299

Table 6: Per-class F1-scores for the best system in subtask B

nary classification of tweets as ironic/non-ironic. The system is ranked third out of 44 participating systems due to its high coverage in identifying ironic-tweets. For the subtask of multi-class classification, we have also used topic modeling features and features related to the distribution of polarity. The system is ranked ninth out of 32 participating systems with a very competitive accuracy.

In future, we intend to extract more sophisticated features related to situational irony. Observation of the dataset confirms that in cases where the tweet involves a URL, the contents of the external web page can play an important role in discriminating between ironic and non-ironic tweets. Therefore introduction of multimodal features is one future direction to enhance performance of such models.

References

Christos Baziotis, Nikos Pelekis, and Christos Doulkeridis. 2017. Datastories at semeval-2017 task 4: Deep lstm with attention for message-level and topic-based sentiment analysis. In *Proceedings of the 11th International Workshop on Semantic Evaluation (SemEval-2017)*, pages 747–754, Vancouver, Canada. Association for Computational Linguistics.

Herbert H Clark and Richard J Gerrig. 1984. On the pretense theory of irony. *Journal of Experimental Psychology: General.*

Ben Eisner, Tim Rocktäschel, Isabelle Augenstein, Matko Bošnjak, and Sebastian Riedel. 2016. emoji2vec: Learning emoji representations from their description. In *Proceedings of The Fourth International Workshop on Natural Language Processing for Social Media*, page 4854. Association for Computational Linguistics.

Aniruddha Ghosh, Guofu Li, Tony Veale, Paolo Rosso, Ekaterina Shutova, John Barnden, and Antonio Reyes. 2015. Semeval-2015 task 11: Sentiment analysis of figurative language in twitter. In *Proceedings of the 9th International Workshop on Semantic Evaluation (SemEval 2015)*, pages 470–478.

CJ Hutto Eric Gilbert. 2014. Vader: A parsimonious rule-based model for sentiment analysis of social media text. In *Proceedings of the Eighth International Conference on Weblogs and Social Media (ICWSM-14).*

Fréderic Godin, Baptist Vandersmissen, Wesley De Neve, and Rik Van de Walle. 2015. Multimedia lab @ acl wnut ner shared task: Named entity recognition for twitter microposts using distributed word representations. In *Proceedings of the Workshop on Noisy User-generated Text*, pages 146–153.

H. P. Grice. 1975. Logic and conversation. In Peter Cole and Jerry L. Morgan, editors, *Syntax and Se-*

mantics: Vol. 3: Speech Acts, pages 41–58. Academic Press, New York.

Isabelle Guyon, Jason Weston, Stephen Barnhill, and Vladimir Vapnik. 2002. Gene selection for cancer classification using support vector machines. *Machine learning*, 46(1-3):389–422.

John Haiman. 1998. *Talk is cheap: Sarcasm, alienation, and the evolution of language*. Oxford University Press on Demand.

Patrick Hanks. 2013. *Lexical analysis: Norms and exploitations*. MIT Press.

Linda Hutcheon. 1994. *Irony's edge: The theory and politics of irony*. Psychology Press.

Aditya Joshi, Vaibhav Tripathi, Pushpak Bhattacharyya, Mark Carman, Meghna Singh, Jaya Saraswati, and Rajita Shukla. 2016. How challenging is sarcasm versus irony classification?: A study with a dataset from English literature. In *Proceedings of the Australasian Language Technology Association Workshop 2016*, pages 123–127.

Petra Kralj Novak, Jasmina Smailović, Borut Sluban, and Igor Mozetič. 2015. Emoji sentiment ranking 1.0. Slovenian language resource repository CLARIN.SI.

Edward Loper and Steven Bird. 2002. Natural language processing toolkit. http://www.nltk.org/.

Christopher Manning, Mihai Surdeanu, John Bauer, Jenny Finkel, Steven Bethard, and David McClosky. 2014. The stanford corenlp natural language processing toolkit. In *Proceedings of 52nd annual meeting of the association for computational linguistics: system demonstrations*, pages 55–60.

Preslav Nakov, Alan Ritter, Sara Rosenthal, Fabrizio Sebastiani, and Veselin Stoyanov. 2016. Semeval-2016 task 4: Sentiment analysis in twitter. In *Proceedings of the 10th International Workshop on Semantic Evaluation (SemEval-2016)*, pages 1–18.

Federico Alberto Pozzi, Elisabetta Fersini, Enza Messina, and Bing Liu. 2016. *Sentiment analysis in social networks*. Morgan Kaufmann.

Tomáš Ptáček, Ivan Habernal, and Jun Hong. 2014. Sarcasm detection on Czech and English twitter. In *Proceedings of COLING 2014, the 25th International Conference on Computational Linguistics: Technical Papers*, pages 213–223.

Ellen Riloff, Ashequl Qadir, Prafulla Surve, Lalindra De Silva, Nathan Gilbert, and Ruihong Huang. 2013. Sarcasm as contrast between a positive sentiment and negative situation. In *Proceedings of the 2013 Conference on Empirical Methods in Natural Language Processing*, pages 704–714.

Sara Rosenthal, Noura Farra, and Preslav Nakov. 2017. Semeval-2017 task 4: Sentiment analysis in twitter. In *Proceedings of the 11th International Workshop on Semantic Evaluation (SemEval-2017)*, pages 502–518.

Cameron Shelley. 2001. The bicoherence theory of situational irony. *Cognitive Science*, 25(5):775–818.

Cynthia Van Hee, Els Lefever, and Vronique Hoste. 2018. Semeval-2018 task 3: Irony detection in English tweets. In *Proceedings of the 12th International Workshop on Semantic Evaluation (SemEval-2018)*, New Orleans, LA, USA.

Byron C Wallace, Laura Kertz, Eugene Charniak, et al. 2014. Humans require context to infer ironic intent (so computers probably do, too). In *Proceedings of the 52nd Annual Meeting of the Association for Computational Linguistics (Volume 2: Short Papers)*, volume 2, pages 512–516.

Random Decision Syntax Trees at SemEval-2018 Task 3: LSTMs and Sentiment Scores for Irony Detection

Aidan San

University of Illinois at Urbana-Champaign

asan2@illinois.edu

Abstract

We propose a Long Short Term Memory Neural Network model for irony detection in tweets in this paper. Our model is trained using word embeddings and emoji embeddings. We show that adding sentiment scores to our model improves the F1 score of our baseline LSTM by approximately .012, and therefore show that high-level features can be used to improve word embeddings in certain Natural Language Processing applications. Our model ranks 24/43 for binary classification and 5/31 for multiclass classification. We make our model easily accessible to the research community[1].

1 Introduction

Recently, irony detection has become an increasingly important problem with new applications appearing every day. In discourse analysis, it is extremely important to understand if a politician is making an ironic or a literal response, or understanding can be completely lost. In chatbots, if a chatbot misinterprets an unhappy sarcastic comment from a customer, the customer could become even more frustrated. In sentiment analysis, if irony is not taken into account, the actual sentiment could be the opposite of the prediction.

The aim of irony detection is generally a binary classfication problem: Is the piece of text ironic or literal? In SemEval2018 Task 3 (Van Hee et al., 2018), there are two subtasks. First, subtask A, is our standard binary classification problem. We are provided with a corpus of tweets annotated with 0 or 1's to specify if a tweet is ironic or literal. Second, in subtask B, we are tasked with a more challenging problem. In subtask B, participants must determine which type of irony a particular tweet contains. Is it verbal irony based on polarity,

another type of verbal irony, situational irony or not ironic at all?

Recently, research has shown that neural approaches are particularly effective in sarcasm detection (Ghosh and Veale, 2016) and similar problems such as sentiment analysis (Rosenthal et al., 2017). In this paper, we present neural network model designed to tackle the challenge of irony detection.

In subsection 2.1, we give a brief overview of the entire model. In subsection 2.2 and 2.3, we describe our neural architecture and approach. In subsection 2.5 and 2.6, we describe the embeddings and sentiment scores that are used as the input to our neural network. In section 3, we describe our results, and give quantitative evidence of the effectiveness of our features. In section 4 we conclude, and in section 5, we describe ways that our approach could be improved.

2 System Description

2.1 Overview

Our system is composed of three stages: Preprocessing, Feature Creation, and the Neural Network. Preprocessing is composed of tokenizing the input text. Feature creation is generating the word and emoji embeddings and sentiment scores and concatenating them together to form a feature vector. Finally in the third stage, the feature vector is fed into the neural network which makes a prediction. Our full model is illustrated in Figure 1.

2.2 Long Short Term Memory

In traditional Feed Forward Neural Networks, there is not a good way to represent temporal inputs. Recurrent Neural Network (RNN) cells are like traditional neural network cells, except they have the key difference of feeding their output

---

[1] github.com/Muakasan/RDST-semeval2018-task3

Proceedings of the 12th International Workshop on Semantic Evaluation (SemEval-2018), pages 560–564
New Orleans, Louisiana, June 5–6, 2018. ©2018 Association for Computational Linguistics

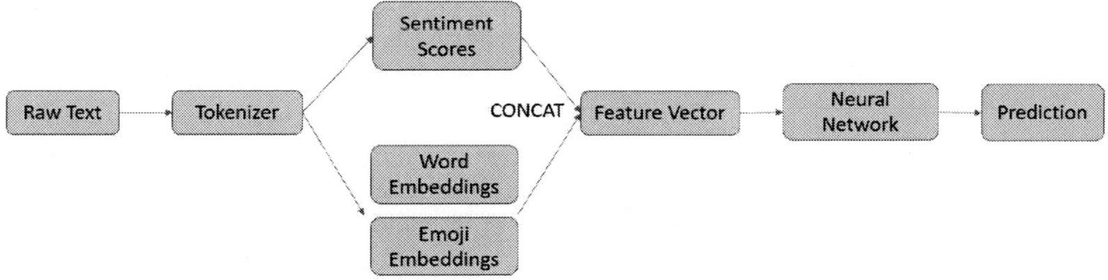

Figure 1: Overview of the entire model.

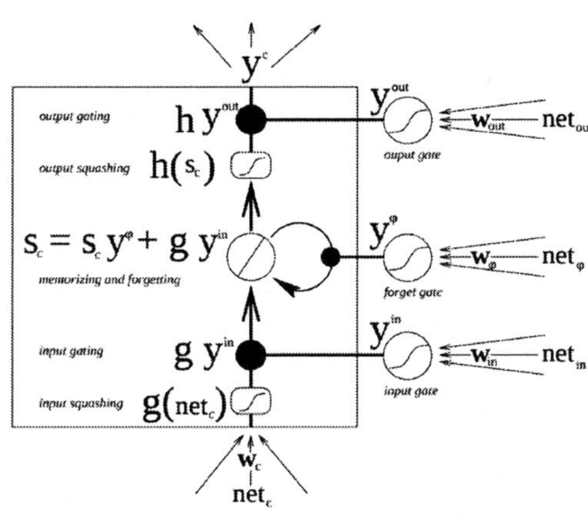

Figure 2: The various gates of the LSTM Cell and the connections between them. The data path is shown from the input $\mathbf{w_c}$ to the output $\mathbf{y^c}$. Taken from Gers et al. (1999).

back into themselves. Each time a new word representation is passed into the RNN, the RNN will take its output and pass it back into the RNN, so the RNN receives 2 inputs (the current word and the output from the previous iteration). The output of the previous iteration can be thought of as a representation of the previous words in the sentence. This is repeated until the sentence is finished. Additionally, context units can be added to the cell to imitate the idea of memory (Elman, 1990). This improves language modeling, because when reading a sentence, prior context of previous words is very important for the understanding of the current word. When we use an RNN, our model can be fed in with context from previous words.

The Long Short Term Memory Model (LSTM) improves over the naive RNN, with the addition of a memory cell and input and output gates (Hochreiter and Schmidhuber, 1997). In the naive RNN, it is easy to lose important information over many iterations of the cell. In an LSTM cell, the memory cell combats this problem. The original LSTM cell is composed of two gates. The output gate can protect other units from irrelevant information from the current iteration, and the input gate can control which information is passed into the current iteration. Additionally, Gers et al. (1999) include a forget gate which can reset memory once it is no longer relevant. Figure 2 taken from Gers et al. (1999) illustrates the architecture of the cell.

2.3 Neural Network Architecture

Our model is built with the high-level Python neural network library called Keras (Chollet et al., 2015). We use a 5 layer model. Our first layer is the input layer, where we feed integer ranks (a number representing how often a word appears in the corpus where "1" is the most common) of

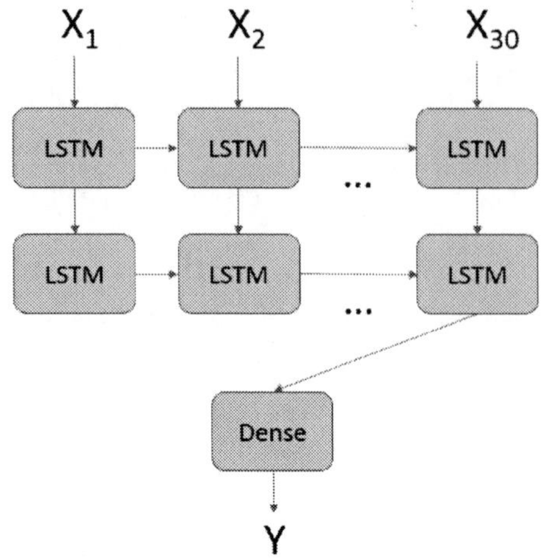

Figure 3: An unrolled Neural Network. X_1 to X_{30} represent the first 30 words in the input tweet. Y represents the irony prediction of the given tweet.

words into the layer. Then we pass the inputs into an embedding layer. This layer takes our inputs and converts them into a word or emoji embedding representation. Our third and fourth layers are both Long Short Term Memory layers. We take the outputs of the first LSTM layer and feed them into our second layer. Both LSTM layers are given a dropout of .25 (chosen by experimentation) to prevent overfitting (Srivastava et al., 2014). The output of the second LSTM is then passed into a single Dense layer. Our Dense layer has a sigmoid and softmax activation for subtask A and B respectively. We use binary cross entropy and categorical cross entropy for subtask A and B respectively. We train our model over 30 epochs (approximately when the model converged) with a batch size of 32. Our architecture is shown in Figure 3.

2.4 Preprocessing

We preprocess using Pandas (McKinney, 2010) for csv reading along with basic data processing. We then run our tweets through the Keras Tokenizer (Chollet et al., 2015). The Keras Tokenizer handles splitting, removing punctuation and lowercasing words.

2.5 Word/Emoji Embeddings

When dealing with a relatively small training set, such as a small number of tweets, pretrained word embeddings can be a very effective way of encod-

ing additional information into the model without needing additional training data. We used the Google News pretrained Word2Vec (Mikolov et al., 2013) word embeddings for our model. The word embeddings were trained using 100 billion words taken from the Google News dataset. We additionally added Emoji2Vec (Eisner et al., 2016) embeddings. As is shown by Hogenboom et al. (2013), emoticons encode a large amount of sentiment information. As the descendants of emoticons, we hypothesize emojis can encode sentiment information as well.

2.6 Sentiment Scores

We use NLTK (Bird and Loper, 2004) to get sentiment scores using the SentiWordNet (Esuli and Sebastiani, 2007) corpus. SentiWordNet is a library which uses a semi-supervised approach to give synsets (groupings of words which have the same meaning) an objective, positive, and negative sentiment score. Riloff et al. (2013) show that sentiment can be an effective way to improve sarcasm detection in tweets. For simplicity, we always use the first synset of a particular word. We take the positive and negative scores from SentiWordNet and then concatenate the results with our word/emoji embedding.

2.7 Memory Constraints

Standard practice is to pass the word embedding matrix with every word as a layer into the Neural Network. In this task, we had the additional constraint of a relatively small amount of RAM (about 8GB). To resolve this problem, instead of building our embedding matrix and then tokenizing our dataset, we tokenized first. Then, rather than building our embedding matrix with every possible entry, we could simply look through the words that we had seen during tokenization, and only put those vectors into our matrix. To put this into context, while we were storing all the embeddings in memory we were using about 6GB of RAM. After we created our much smaller embedding matrix, we were only using about 3GB of RAM.

3 Results

Task	F1	Accuracy
A (Binary)	.5822(24)	.6173(21)
B (Multiclass)	.4352(6)	.6327(6)

Table 1: Official results from the competition on the test set. The numbers between parentheses indicate ranking compared to other models.

As shown in Table 1, in the binary classification task, we achieved an F1 score of .5822 and an accuracy of .6173, and in the multiclass classification task, we achieved an F1 score of .4352 and an accuracy of .6327. This earned us a rank of 24 and 6 in tasks A, and B respectively, because teams were ranked using F1 score.

Model	F1	Accuracy
Without Emoji	.6127	**.6121**
Without Sentiment	.6093	.6097
Emoji & Sentiment	**.6210**	.6091

Table 2: Accuracy and F1 scores of various models tested on a 75%-25% split of the training data.

To test the effectiveness of the emoji embeddings feature and sentiment scores feature, we tested our binary classification model without each feature separately and compared these models to our combined model. We ran our tests over the training set with a 75%-25% split, where 75% of the training data was used to train the model and 25% of the model was designated as validation data, to verify the effectiveness of the model on unseen data. We ran 10 trials and took the average accuracy and F1 score over the 10 trials for each of the 3 models.

The task was ranked using F1 score, so we optimized for F1 score. As can be seen in Table 2, the combined model achieves an F1 score .0083 higher than not including emoji embeddings and an F1 score .0117 higher than not including sentiment scores. Interestingly, we see that the combined model actually achieves a lower accuracy score than both of the individual models. We can draw the conclusion that the combined model has more balanced predictions between the two classes, which overall creates a higher F1 score at the cost of lower accuracy in one of the classes.

4 Conclusion

In this paper, we have described our system for SemEval-2018 Task 3. We discussed LSTM-based neural models, and how we incorporate sentiment features and emoji embeddings. We show that additional high-level features such as sentiment scores can improve neural based models. We achieve rank 24/43 in subtask A and 6/31 in subtask B.

5 Future Work

Possible improvements to the model fall under two primary categories: the neural architecture and additional high-level features.

To implement our neural architecture, we experimented with other types of layers such as Bidirectional LSTMs and CNNs, but we would like to further explore these approaches in the future. We especially think Attention Layers used by models such as Baziotis et al. (2017) could be particularly effective in irony detection, because of their effectiveness in sentiment analysis. We could also try different activation functions in different layers and test out different batch sizes. Another possible direction would be to use ensemble methods which have been shown to be particularly effective by Cliche (2017) for similar tasks.

Regarding additional high-level features, we could also include sentence-level features. Goel et al. (2017) showed that high-level features could be included in a Feed Forward Neural Network which improved accuracy in an ensemble method for the task of emotion detection. Additionally, we could continue in the vein of the model we created and add other word-level features such as capitalization. To improve our sentiment features, we could also use a more advanced method of choosing the correct synset for a better fitting sentiment score.

Acknowledgments

We would like to thank the task organizers for providing the dataset and putting together the competition. We would like to thank Assma Boughoula and Julia Hockenmaier for their help in this project.

References

Christos Baziotis, Nikos Pelekis, and Christos Doulkeridis. 2017. Datastories at semeval-2017 task

4: Deep lstm with attention for message-level and topic-based sentiment analysis. In *Proceedings of the 11th International Workshop on Semantic Evaluation (SemEval-2017)*, pages 747–754.

Steven Bird and Edward Loper. 2004. Nltk: the natural language toolkit. In *Proceedings of the ACL 2004 on Interactive poster and demonstration sessions*, page 31. Association for Computational Linguistics.

François Chollet et al. 2015. Keras. `https://github.com/fchollet/keras`.

Mathieu Cliche. 2017. Bb_twtr at semeval-2017 task 4: Twitter sentiment analysis with cnns and lstms. In *Proceedings of the 11th International Workshop on Semantic Evaluation (SemEval-2017)*, pages 573–580.

Ben Eisner, Tim Rocktäschel, Isabelle Augenstein, Matko Bošnjak, and Sebastian Riedel. 2016. emoji2vec: Learning emoji representations from their description. In *Conference on Empirical Methods in Natural Language Processing*, page 48.

Jeffrey L Elman. 1990. Finding structure in time. *Cognitive science*, 14(2):179–211.

Andrea Esuli and Fabrizio Sebastiani. 2007. Sentiwordnet: a high-coverage lexical resource for opinion mining. *Evaluation*, pages 1–26.

Felix A Gers, Jürgen Schmidhuber, and Fred Cummins. 1999. Learning to forget: Continual prediction with lstm.

Aniruddha Ghosh and Tony Veale. 2016. Fracking sarcasm using neural network. In *Proceedings of the 7th Workshop on Computational Approaches to Subjectivity, Sentiment and Social Media Analysis*, pages 161–169.

Pranav Goel, Devang Kulshreshtha, Prayas Jain, and Kaushal Kumar Shukla. 2017. Prayas at emoint 2017: An ensemble of deep neural architectures for emotion intensity prediction in tweets. In *Proceedings of the 8th Workshop on Computational Approaches to Subjectivity, Sentiment and Social Media Analysis*, pages 58–65.

Sepp Hochreiter and Jürgen Schmidhuber. 1997. Lstm can solve hard long time lag problems. In *Advances in neural information processing systems*, pages 473–479.

Alexander Hogenboom, Daniella Bal, Flavius Frasincar, Malissa Bal, Franciska de Jong, and Uzay Kaymak. 2013. Exploiting emoticons in sentiment analysis. In *Proceedings of the 28th Annual ACM Symposium on Applied Computing*, pages 703–710. ACM.

Wes McKinney. 2010. Data structures for statistical computing in python. In *Proceedings of the 9th Python in Science Conference*, pages 51 – 56.

Tomas Mikolov, Ilya Sutskever, Kai Chen, Greg S Corrado, and Jeff Dean. 2013. Distributed representations of words and phrases and their compositionality. In *Advances in neural information processing systems*, pages 3111–3119.

Ellen Riloff, Ashequl Qadir, Prafulla Surve, Lalindra De Silva, Nathan Gilbert, and Ruihong Huang. 2013. Sarcasm as contrast between a positive sentiment and negative situation. In *Proceedings of the 2013 Conference on Empirical Methods in Natural Language Processing*, pages 704–714.

Sara Rosenthal, Noura Farra, and Preslav Nakov. 2017. Semeval-2017 task 4: Sentiment analysis in twitter. In *Proceedings of the 11th International Workshop on Semantic Evaluation (SemEval-2017)*, pages 502–518.

Nitish Srivastava, Geoffrey Hinton, Alex Krizhevsky, Ilya Sutskever, and Ruslan Salakhutdinov. 2014. Dropout: A simple way to prevent neural networks from overfitting. *The Journal of Machine Learning Research*, 15(1):1929–1958.

Cynthia Van Hee, Els Lefever, and Véronique Hoste. 2018. SemEval-2018 Task 3: Irony Detection in English Tweets. In *Proceedings of the 12th International Workshop on Semantic Evaluation*, SemEval-2018, New Orleans, LA, USA. Association for Computational Linguistics.

ELiRF-UPV at SemEval-2018 Tasks 1 and 3: Affect and Irony Detection in Tweets

José-Ángel González, Lluís-F. Hurtado, Ferran Pla
Departament de Sistemes Informàtics i Computació
Universitat Politècnica de València
Camí de Vera, sn
46022, València
`{jogonba2, lhurtado, fpla}@dsic.upv.es`

Abstract

This paper describes the participation of ELiRF-UPV team at tasks 1 and 3 of Semeval-2018. We present a deep learning based system that assembles Convolutional Neural Networks and Long Short-Term Memory neural networks. This system has been used with slight modifications for the two tasks addressed both for English and Spanish. Finally, the results obtained in the competition are reported and discussed.

1 Introduction

The study of figurative language and affective information expressed in texts is of great interest in sentiment analysis applications because they can change the polarity of a message. The objective of tasks 1 and 3 of Semeval 2018 is the study of these phenomena on Twitter.

Task 1 (Mohammad et al., 2018) is related to Affect in Tweets. Systems have to automatically determine the intensity of emotions and intensity of sentiment or valence of the tweeters from their tweets. The task is divided in five subtasks: emotion intensity regression (EI-Reg), emotion intensity ordinal classification (EI-Oc), sentiment intensity regression (V-Reg), sentiment analysis ordinal classification (V-Oc) and emotion classification (E-C).

Task 3 (Van Hee et al., 2018) addresses the problem of Irony detection in English Tweets. It consists of two subtasks. The first subtask is a two-class (or binary) classification task where the system has to predict whether a tweet is ironic or not. The second subtask is a multiclass classification task where the system has to predict one out of four labels describing i) verbal irony realized through a polarity contrast, ii) verbal irony without such a polarity contrast (i.e., other verbal irony), iii) descriptions of situational irony, iv) non-irony.

This paper describes the main characteristics of the developed system by the ELiRF-UPV team for tasks 1 and 3. We addressed all subtasks of task 1 both for English and Spanish, and all subtasks of task 3.

2 Data Preprocessing

In this work we have taken into account different aspects when preprocessing the tweets. First we removed the accents and converted all the text to lowercase. In general, *emoticons, web links, hashtags, numbers*, and *user mentions*, were substituted by generic tokens. For instance, "#hashtag" → "hashtag", ☺ → "Slightly Smiling Face", etc. After that, we used TweetMotif (Krieger and Ahn, 2010) as tweet tokenizer, moreover we adapted it to work with Spanish tweets.

3 Resources

On the one hand, for English, we used the following polarity/emotion lexicons: AFFIN (Nielsen, 2011), Bing Liu's Opinion Lexicon (Hu and Liu, 2004), MPQA (Wilson et al., 2005), Sentiment140 (Go et al., 2009), SentiWordnet (Baccianella et al., 2010), NRC Emotion Lexicon (Mohammad and Turney, 2013), NRC Hashtag Emotion Lexicon (Mohammad, 2012) and LIWC2007 (Pennebaker et al., 2014). We also used Word2Vec embeddings (Mikolov et al., 2013a) (Mikolov et al., 2013b) pre-trained by (Godin et al., 2015) with 400 million English tweets.

On the other hand, for Spanish, we used the following polarity/emotion lexicons: ElHPolar (Saralegi and San Vicente, 2013), ISOL (Molina-González et al., 2013), and MLSenticon (Cruz et al., 2014). In addition, we also pre-trained Word2Vec embeddings from 87 million Spanish tweets collected by our team by means of a twitter crawler. In this case, it is a skip-gram architecture

Proceedings of the 12th International Workshop on Semantic Evaluation (SemEval-2018), pages 565–569
New Orleans, Louisiana, June 5–6, 2018. ©2018 Association for Computational Linguistics

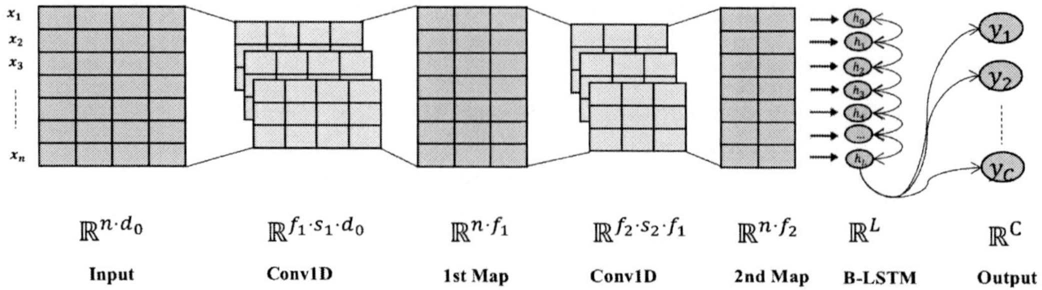

Figure 1: System architecture.

with 300 dimensions per word, negative sampling with 5 negative samples and a 5-term context on the left and right was used.

Through a tuning process on the development sets with a fixed system architecture, we selected the best lexicons for each task. For English, all the lexicons stated above for both tasks were used. For Spanish, only ElHPolar and ISOL lexicons were used.

4 System Description

In this section, we briefly describe the general characteristics of the system developed for Task 1 and Task 3 at SemEval 2018. This description includes the input representation and the system architecture.

4.1 Input representation

Regarding the representation used, in those subtasks where the input is only a tweet (V-Reg, V-Oc and E-C in task 1 and both subtasks in task 3), each tweet is represented as a matrix $M \in \mathbb{R}^{n \cdot d}$ where n is the maximum number of words per tweet and d is the embedding dimensionality. To include the information from the polarity lexicons, for each word, x, the vector of its embedding is concatenated with the vector of polarities/emotions for this word, $v(x)$. In this way, the representation matrix of a tweet finally results in $M \in \mathbb{R}^{n \cdot (d+|v|)}$.

For the EI-Reg subtask, where in addition to a tweet an emotion p is also provided, we add the representation of the word p as the last row of the M matrix. Moreover, we concatenate one column to the word embeddings to indicate if the words belong to the tweet (0) or belong to the emotion (1).

4.2 System architecture

We propose a general architecture for all subtasks. This architecture is based on a two-layer Convolutional Neural Network (CNN) (Fukushima, 1980) ensembled with a final Long Short-Term Memory (LSTM) neural network (Hochreiter and Schmidhuber, 1997) as in (González et al., 2017). We use the representation of the tweet in terms of the M matrix defined above as input to the system. Finally, a fully connected layer computes the outputs of the system. The activation function of this layer depends on the subtask.

Figure 1 shows the general architecture of the system, where d_0 is the dimensionality of the representation of each word (size of the embedding), f_i is the number of filters in the convolutional layer i, s_i the height of each filter in layer i, L is the dimensionality of the *output-state* of the LSTM network, and C is the number of outputs for a specific task.

Although the architecture was the same for all subtasks, the parameters are subtask dependent and were experimentally defined by means of a tuning phase with the development sets. The values studied for the parameters of the convolutional network are $f_i \in [64, 256]$ and $s_i = 3$. The number of neurons of the last layer depends on the subtask. We also tested a simplified version of the architecture without the convolutional network and using only the LSTM network with $L = 256$.

Moreover, we use Batch Normalization (Ioffe and Szegedy, 2015) between all convolutional layers, Dropout (Srivastava et al., 2014) after the LSTM with $p = 0.2$, ReLU activation functions (Nair and Hinton, 2010) and RMSProp (Tieleman and Hinton) as optimization algorithm.

Task 1	EI-Reg (Pearson)		V-Reg (Pearson)		E-C (Jaccard)	
	En	**Sp**	**En**	**Sp**	**En**	**Sp**
LSTM + Lexicons (MSE)	**67.57**	**68.98**	75.46	74.37	N/A	N/A
CNN-LSTM + Lexicons (MSE)	64.12	66.56	**81.13**	**80.01**	N/A	N/A
CNN-LSTM + Lexicons (CCE)	N/A	N/A	N/A	N/A	52.11	42.18
CNN-LSTM + Lexicons (Jaccard)	N/A	N/A	N/A	N/A	**55.23**	**44.59**

Table 1: Task 1 development results.

Task 3	Subtask A (F1)	Subtask B (Macro F1)
CNN-LSTM + Lexicons (CCE)	68.44	44.59
CNN-LSTM + Lexicons (F1)	**68.63**	N/A
CNN-LSTM + Lexicons (Macro F1)	N/A	**45.45**

Table 2: Task 3 development results.

Regarding the loss function, we used *Mean Squared Error* (MSE) for the regression subtasks. However, for subtask E-C and both subtasks of task 3, we used an adaptation of the evaluation metrics (*Jaccard Index*, F_1 for binary classification, and macro-average F_1) as loss functions. In future work we will define and study in more detail this kind of loss functions. In addition, we also tested Cross Entropy (CCE) to extend the comparison.

The strategy used in the ordinal classification subtasks of task 1 (EI-Oc and V-Oc) consisted in the discretization of the outputs of the equivalent regression subtasks (EI-Reg and V-Reg). The discretization process is as follows, be $\mathbb{C}$ the classes set of a ordinal classification subtask and $v_x \in \mathbb{R}$ the score assigned to sample x using a regression model. We compute $|\mathbb{C}| + 1$ thresholds by searching the minimum output for each class, according to the regression train sets. Concretely, $\{th_0, ..., th_{|\mathbb{C}|}\}$ where $th_i \in \mathbb{R}$, $th_i < th_{i+1}$, $th_0 = 0$, and $th_{|\mathbb{C}|} = 1$. Sample x is assigned to the class i such that $th_i < v_x \leq th_{i+1}$.

5 Experimental Results

We performed a tuning process with the development sets in order to select the best model for each task. We tested different ways of preprocessing the tweets, we fit the parameters of the models and we evaluated some external lexicons. Next, we summarize the best results obtained in the tuning process by considering some combinations of the tested models and configurations.

Table 3 shows the results for 3 of the subtasks in the tuning process for Task 1. For the two remaining tasks (EI-Oc and V-Oc) we do not learn specific models, in these cases we used the best models obtained for EI-Reg and V-Reg, respectively.

As it can be seen, LSTM achieved the best results for subtasks El-Reg. The rest of subtasks performed better when we combined CNN and LSTM models. In addition, when we consider the evaluation metric as loss function we improved the results (see the differences between CNN-LSTM + Lexicons (Jaccard) and CNN-LSTM + Lexicons (CCE)).

Table 3 shows the results for the two subtasks in the tuning process for Task 3. We can observe the same behavior as Task 1. The best results are obtained using a combination of CNN and LSTM models and if we consider the evaluation metric as loss function the results are improved.

Once our best system for each subtask with the development set was chosen, we tested it on the official test set and we compare it with the best results obtained by another participant. These results are shown in Table 5 for Task 1, and in Table 5 for Task 3.

Task 1	English		Spanish	
	Our	**Best**	**Our**	**Best**
EI-Reg	69.60(13/42)	79.90	64.80(3/12)	73.80
EI-Oc	59.00(10/36)	69.50	57.50(4/13)	66.40
V-Reg	80.40(15/33)	87.30	74.20(2/12)	79.50
V-Oc	75.90(12/34)	83.60	72.90(2/11)	75.60
E-C	55.20(9/35)	58.80	45.80(2/14)	46.90

Table 3: Task 1 test results.

Task 3	Our	Best
Subtask A	62.94 (7/44)	70.54
Subtask B	42.11 (8/32)	50.74

Table 4: Task 3 test results.

6 Conclusions and Future Work

We presented a deep learning based system that assembles CNN and LSTM neural networks for tasks 1 and 3 of Semeval-2018. This system has been used with slight modifications for the two tasks addressed.

We want to highlight the improvements obtained when the evaluation measures have been adapted as loss functions. In addition, we have also incorporated information extracted from different lexical resources into the models.

As future work, we will continue to study different loss functions and the incorporation of new lexical resources as well as to carry out a detailed study of the obtained results.

7 Acknowledgements

This work has been partially supported by the Spanish MINECO and FEDER founds under projects ASLP-MULAN: Audio, Speech and Language Processing for Multimedia Analytics (TIN2014-54288-C4-3-R); and AMIC: Affective Multimedia Analytics with Inclusive and Natural Communication (TIN2017-85854-C4-2-R). Work of José-Ángel González is also financed by Universitat Politècnica de València under grant PAID-01-17.

References

Stefano Baccianella, Andrea Esuli, and Fabrizio Sebastiani. 2010. Sentiwordnet 3.0: An enhanced lexical resource for sentiment analysis and opinion mining. In *in Proc. of LREC*.

Fermín L. Cruz, José A. Troyano, Beatriz Pontes, and F. Javier Ortega. 2014. Building layered, multilingual sentiment lexicons at synset and lemma levels. *Expert Systems with Applications*, 41(13):5984 – 5994.

Kunihiko Fukushima. 1980. Neocognn: A self-organizing neural network model for a mechanism of pattern recognition unaffected by shift in position. *Biological Cybernetics*, 36(4):193–202.

Alec Go, Richa Bhayani, and Lei Huang. 2009. Twitter sentiment classification using distant supervision. 150.

Fréderic Godin, Baptist Vandersmissen, Wesley De Neve, and Rik Van de Walle. 2015. Multimedia lab @ ACL W-NUT NER sharedtask: named entity recognition for Twitter microposts using distributed word representations. *ACL-IJCNLP*, 2015:146–153.

José-Àngel González, Ferran Pla, and Lluís-F. Hurtado. 2017. Elirf-upv at semeval-2017 task 4: Sentiment analysis using deep learning. In *Proceedings of the 11th International Workshop on Semantic Evaluation (SemEval-2017)*, pages 723–727. Association for Computational Linguistics.

Sepp Hochreiter and Jürgen Schmidhuber. 1997. Long Short-Term Memory. *Neural Computation*, 9(8):1735–1780.

Minqing Hu and Bing Liu. 2004. Mining and summarizing customer reviews. In *Proceedings of the Tenth ACM SIGKDD International Conference on Knowledge Discovery and Data Mining*, KDD '04, pages 168–177, New York, NY, USA. ACM.

Sergey Ioffe and Christian Szegedy. 2015. Batch normalization: Accelerating deep network training by reducing internal covariate shift. *CoRR*, abs/1502.03167.

Michel Krieger and David Ahn. 2010. Tweetmotif: exploratory search and topic summarization for twitter. In *In Proc. of AAAI Conference on Weblogs and Social*.

Tomas Mikolov, Kai Chen, Greg Corrado, and Jeffrey Dean. 2013a. Efficient estimation of word representations in vector space. *CoRR*, abs/1301.3781.

Tomas Mikolov, Ilya Sutskever, Kai Chen, Greg Corrado, and Jeffrey Dean. 2013b. Distributed representations of words and phrases and their compositionality. *CoRR*, abs/1310.4546.

Saif Mohammad. 2012. #emotional tweets. In **SEM 2012: The First Joint Conference on Lexical and Computational Semantics – Volume 1: Proceedings of the main conference and the shared task, and Volume 2: Proceedings of the Sixth International Workshop on Semantic Evaluation (SemEval 2012)*, pages 246–255, Montréal, Canada. Association for Computational Linguistics.

Saif M. Mohammad, Felipe Bravo-Marquez, Mohammad Salameh, and Svetlana Kiritchenko. 2018. Semeval-2018 Task 1: Affect in tweets. In *Proceedings of International Workshop on Semantic Evaluation (SemEval-2018)*, New Orleans, LA, USA.

Saif M. Mohammad and Peter D. Turney. 2013. Crowdsourcing a word-emotion association lexicon. 29(3):436–465.

M. Dolores Molina-González, Eugenio Martínez-Cámara, María-Teresa Martín-Valdivia, and José M. Perea-Ortega. 2013. Semantic orientation for polarity classification in spanish reviews. *Expert Systems with Applications*, 40(18):7250 – 7257.

Vinod Nair and Geoffrey E. Hinton. 2010. Rectified linear units improve restricted boltzmann machines. In *Proceedings of the 27th International Conference on International Conference on Machine Learning*, ICML'10, pages 807–814, USA. Omnipress.

F. Å. Nielsen. 2011. AFINN.

JW Pennebaker, CK Chung, M Ireland, A Gonzales, and RJ Booth. 2014. The development and psychological properties of liwc2007.

Xabier Saralegi and Inaki San Vicente. 2013. Elhuyar at tass 2013. In *XXIX Congreso de la Sociedad Espaola de Procesamiento de lenguaje natural, Workshop on Sentiment Analysis at SEPLN (TASS2013)*, pages 143–150.

Nitish Srivastava, Geoffrey Hinton, Alex Krizhevsky, Ilya Sutskever, and Ruslan Salakhutdinov. 2014. Dropout: A simple way to prevent neural networks from overfitting. *J. Mach. Learn. Res.*, 15(1):1929–1958.

T. Tieleman and G. Hinton. RMSprop Gradient Optimization.

Cynthia Van Hee, Els Lefever, and Véronique Hoste. 2018. Semeval-2018 Task 3: Irony detection in English Tweets. In *Proceedings of International Workshop on Semantic Evaluation (SemEval-2018)*, New Orleans, LA, USA.

Theresa Wilson, Janyce Wiebe, and Paul Hoffmann. 2005. Recognizing contextual polarity in phrase-level sentiment analysis. In *Proceedings of the Conference on Human Language Technology and Empirical Methods in Natural Language Processing*, HLT '05, pages 347–354, Stroudsburg, PA, USA. Association for Computational Linguistics.

Index

Association for Computational Linguistics
209 N. Eighth Street
Stroudsburg, Pennsylvania 18360

12th International Workshop on Semantic Evaluation (SemEval 2018)

New Orleans, Louisiana, USA
5 – 6 June 2018

Volume 2 of 2

12th International Workshop on Semantic Evaluation (SemEval 2018)

New Orleans, Louisiana, USA
5 – 6 June 2018

Volume 2 of 2

ISBN: 978-1-5108-6353-8

NAACL HLT 2018

The International Workshop on Semantic Evaluation

Proceedings of the Twelfth Workshop

June 5–June 6, 2018
New Orleans, Louisiana

Introduction

Welcome to SemEval-2018!

The Semantic Evaluation (SemEval) series of workshops focuses on the evaluation and comparison of systems that can analyse diverse semantic phenomena in text with the aim of extending the current state of the art in semantic analysis and creating high quality annotated datasets in a range of increasingly challenging problems in natural language semantics. SemEval provides an exciting forum for researchers to propose challenging research problems in semantics and to build systems/techniques to address such research problems.

SemEval-2018 is the twelfth workshop in the series of International Workshops on Semantic Evaluation. The first three workshops, SensEval-1 (1998), SensEval-2 (2001), and SensEval-3 (2004), focused on word sense disambiguation, each time growing in the number of languages offered, in the number of tasks, and also in the number of participating teams. In 2007, the workshop was renamed to SemEval, and the subsequent SemEval workshops evolved to include semantic analysis tasks beyond word sense disambiguation. In 2012, SemEval turned into a yearly event. It currently runs every year, but on a two-year cycle, i.e., the tasks for SemEval-2018 were proposed in 2017.

SemEval-2018 was co-located with the 16th Annual Conference of the North American Chapter of the Association for Computational Linguistics: Human Language Technologies (NAACL HLT 2018) in New Orleans, Louisiana, US. It included the following 12 shared tasks organized in five tracks:

- Affect and Creative Language in Tweets

    - Task 1: Affect in Tweets
    - Task 2: Multilingual Emoji Prediction
    - Task 3: Irony Detection in English Tweets

- Coreference

    - Task 4: Character Identification on Multiparty Dialogues
    - Task 5: Counting Events and Participants within Highly Ambiguous Data covering a very long tail

- Information Extraction

    - Task 6: Parsing Time Normalizations
    - Task 7: Semantic Relation Extraction and Classification in Scientific Papers
    - Task 8: Semantic Extraction from CybersecUrity REports using Natural Language Processing (SecureNLP)

- Lexical Semantics

    - Task 9: Hypernym Discovery
    - Task 10: Capturing Discriminative Attributes

- Reading Comprehension and Reasoning

    - Task 11: Machine Comprehension using Commonsense Knowledge
    - Task 12: Argument Reasoning Comprehension Task

This volume contains both Task Description papers that describe each of the above tasks, and System Description papers that present the systems that participated in these tasks. A total of 12 task description papers and 184 system description papers are included in this volume.

We are grateful to all task organizers as well as to the large number of participants whose enthusiastic participation has made SemEval once again a successful event. We are thankful to the task organizers who also served as area chairs, and to task organizers and participants who reviewed paper submissions. These proceedings have greatly benefited from their detailed and thoughtful feedback. We also thank the NAACL HLT 2018 conference organizers for their support. Finally, we most gratefully acknowledge the support of our sponsor, the ACL Special Interest Group on the Lexicon (SIGLEX).

The SemEval-2018 organizers, Marianna Apidianaki, Saif M. Mohammad, Jonathan May, Ekaterina Shutova, Marine Carpuat, Steven Bethard

Organizers:

Marianna Apidianaki, LIMSI, CNRS, Université Paris-Saclay & University of Pennsylvania
Saif M. Mohammad, National Research Council Canada
Jonathan May, University of Southern California Information Sciences Institute
Ekaterina Shutova, University of Cambridge
Steven Bethard, University of Alabama at Birmingham
Marine Carpuat, University of Maryland

Task Selection Committee:

Eneko Agirre, University of the Basque Country
Isabelle Augenstein, University of Copenhagen
Timothy Baldwin, University of Melbourne
Paul Buitelaar, National University of Ireland
Alberto Barrón-Cedeño, Qatar Computing Research Institute
Yonatan Belinkov, MIT
Kalina Bontcheva, University of Sheffield
Georgeta Bordea, National University of Ireland
Daniel Cer, Google
Wanxiang Che, Harbin Institute of Technology
Keith Cortis, University of Passau
Danilo Croce, University of Rome Tor Vergata
Mrinal Das, University of Massachusetts Amherst
Noura Farra, Columbia University
Dimitris Galanis, ILSP, "Athena" Research Center
Christian Hempelmann, Texas A&M University-Commerce
Anders Johannsen, University of Copenhagen
Maria Liakata, University of Warwick
Montse Maritxalar, University of the Basque Country
Jonathan May, University of Southern California Information Sciences Institute
Rada Mihalcea, University of Michigan
Tristan Miller, Technische Universität Darmstadt
Hamdy Mubarak, Qatar Computing Research Institute
Haris Papageorgiou, ILSP, "Athena" Research Center
Mohammad Taher Pilehvar
Maria Pontiki, ILSP, "Athena" Research Center
Peter Potash, University of Massachusetts Lowell
Alan Ritter, The Ohio State University
Alexey Romanov, University of Massachusetts Lowell
Sara Rosenthal, IBM Watson
Nathan Schneider, University of Edinburgh
Parinaz Sobhani, University of Ottawa
Xiaodan Zhu, National Research Council Canada
Arkaitz Zubiaga, University of Warwick

Task Organizers:

Miguel Ballesteros, IBM Watson, USA
Francesco Barbieri, Universitat Pompeu Fabra, LaSTUS lab, Spain
Valerio Basile, Sapienza University, Italy
Steven Bethard, University of Arizona
Felipe Bravo-Marquez, The University of Waikato
Davide Buscaldi, LIPN, UMR CNRS, Université Paris 13
Jose Camacho-Collados, Sapienza University of Rome
Thierry Charnois, LIPN, UMR CNRS, Université Paris 13
Henry Y. Chen, Snap Inc.
Jinho D. Choi, Emory Univesrity
Claudio Delli Bovi, Sapienza University of Rome
Ahmed S. Elsayed, University of Colorado
Luis Espinoza-Anke, Universitat Pompeu Fabra, LaSTUS lab, Spain
Kata Gábor, LIPN, UMR CNRS, Université Paris 13
Iryna Gurevych, UKP TU-Darmstadt
Ivan Habernal, UKP TU-Darmstadt
Véronique Hoste, LT3, Faculty of Arts and Philosophy, Ghent University
Filip Ilievski, Vrije Universiteit Amsterdam
Svetlana Kiritchenko, National Research Council Canada
Alicia Krebs, Textkernel BV, Amsterdam, Netherlands
Egoitz Laparra, University of Arizona
Els Lefever, LT3, Faculty of Arts and Philosophy, Ghent University
Alessandro Lenci, Department of Philology, Literature, and Linguistics of the University of Pisa,
Italy
Wei Lu, Singapore University of Technology and Design
Ashutosh Modi, Saarland University
Saif M. Mohammad, National Research Council Canada
Roberto Navigli, Sapienza University of Rome
Sergio Oramas, Universitat Pompeu Fabra
Simon Ostermann, Saarland University
Martha Palmer, University of Colorado
Denis Paperno, Lorraine Laboratory of Computer Science and its Applications, CNRS, France
Tommaso Pasini, Sapienza University of Rome
Viviana Patti, University of Torino, Italy
Peter Phandi, Singapore University of Technology and Design
Manfred Pinkal, Saarland University
Marten Postma, Vrije Universiteit Amsterdam
Behrang QasemiZadeh, DFG Collaborative Research Centre 991, Heinrich-Heine University Düsseldorf
Francesco Ronzano, Universitat Pompeu Fabra, LaSTUS lab, Spain
Michael Roth, Saarland University
Horacio Saggion, Universitat Pompeu Fabra, LaSTUS lab, Spain
Mohammad Salameh, Carnegie Mellon University, Qatar
Enrico Santus, Singapore University
Anne-Kathrin Schumann, ProTechnology GmbH, Dresden, former: Department of Applied Linguistics, Translation and Interpreting, Saarland University
Vered Shwartz, Bar-Ilan University
Benno Stein, Webis, Bauhaus-Universität Weimar
Isabelle Tellier, Laboratoire Lattice, CNRS and Université Sorbonne Nouvelle
Stefan Thater, Saarland University

Cynthia Van Hee, LT3, Faculty of Arts and Philosophy, Ghent University
Piek Vossen, Vrije Universiteit Amsterdam
Henning Wachsmuth, Webis, Bauhaus-Universität Weimar
Dongfang Xu, University of Arizona
Haïfa Zargayouna, LIPN, UMR CNRS, Université Paris 13

Invited Speaker:

Ellie Pavlick, Brown University

Invited Talk: Why should we care about linguistics?

Ellie Pavlick
(Joint Invited Speaker with *SEM 2018)

Brown University

Abstract

In just the past few months, a flurry of adversarial studies have pushed back on the apparent progress of neural networks, with multiple analyses suggesting that deep models of text fail to capture even basic properties of language, such as negation, word order, and compositionality. Alongside this wave of negative results, our field has stated ambitions to move beyond task-specific models and toward "general purpose" word, sentence, and even document embeddings. This is a tall order for the field of NLP, and, I argue, marks a significant shift in the way we approach our research. I will discuss what we can learn from the field of linguistics about the challenges of codifying all of language in a "general purpose" way. Then, more importantly, I will discuss what we cannot learn from linguistics. I will argue that the state-of-the-art of NLP research is operating close to the limits of what we know about natural language semantics, both within our field and outside it. I will conclude with thoughts on why this opens opportunities for NLP to advance both technology and basic science as it relates to language, and the implications for the way we should conduct empirical research.

Biography

Ellie Pavlick is currently a Post Doc at Google Research in NY. She will join Brown University as an Assistant Professor in July. Ellie received her PhD from University of Pennsylvania under the supervision of Chris Callison-Burch. Her current research focus is on semantics, pragmatics, and building cognitively-plausible computational models of natural language inference.

Table of Contents

Workshop Program

5 June 2018

09:00–09:15   *Welcome / Opening Remarks*

09:15–10:30   *Invited Talk: Why should we care about linguistics?*
Ellie Pavlick

10:30–11:00   *Coffee*

11:00–12:30   **Tasks 1, 2 and 3**

11:00–11:15   *SemEval-2018 Task 1: Affect in Tweets*
Saif Mohammad, Felipe Bravo-Marquez, Mohammad Salameh and Svetlana Kiritchenko

11:15–11:30   *SeerNet at SemEval-2018 Task 1: Domain Adaptation for Affect in Tweets*
Venkatesh Duppada, Royal Jain and Sushant Hiray

11:30–11:45   *SemEval 2018 Task 2: Multilingual Emoji Prediction*
Francesco Barbieri, Jose Camacho-Collados, Francesco Ronzano, Luis Espinosa Anke, Miguel Ballesteros, Valerio Basile, Viviana Patti and Horacio Saggion

11:45–12:00   *Tübingen-Oslo at SemEval-2018 Task 2: SVMs perform better than RNNs in Emoji Prediction*
Çağrı Çöltekin and Taraka Rama

12:00–12:15   *SemEval-2018 Task 3: Irony Detection in English Tweets*
Cynthia Van Hee, Els Lefever and Veronique Hoste

12:15–12:30   *THU_NGN at SemEval-2018 Task 3: Tweet Irony Detection with Densely connected LSTM and Multi-task Learning*
Chuhan Wu, Fangzhao Wu, Sixing Wu, Junxin Liu, Zhigang Yuan and Yongfeng Huang

12:30–14:00   *Lunch*

5 June 2018 (continued)

14:00–15:30   Tasks 4, 5 and 6

14:00–14:15   *SemEval 2018 Task 4: Character Identification on Multiparty Dialogues*
Jinho D. Choi and Henry Y. Chen

14:15–14:30   *AMORE-UPF at SemEval-2018 Task 4: BiLSTM with Entity Library*
Laura Aina, Carina Silberer, Ionut-Teodor Sorodoc, Matthijs Westera and Gemma
Boleda

14:30–14:45   *SemEval-2018 Task 5: Counting Events and Participants in the Long Tail*
Marten Postma, Filip Ilievski and Piek Vossen

14:45–15:00   *KOI at SemEval-2018 Task 5: Building Knowledge Graph of Incidents*
Paramita Mirza, Fariz Darari and Rahmad Mahendra

15:00–15:15   *SemEval 2018 Task 6: Parsing Time Normalizations*
Egoitz Laparra, Dongfang Xu, Ahmed Elsayed, Steven Bethard and Martha Palmer

15:15–15:30   *Chrono at SemEval-2018 Task 6: A System for Normalizing Temporal Expressions*
Amy Olex, Luke Maffey, Nicholas Morgan and Bridget McInnes

15:30–16:00   *Coffee*

16:00–16:30   *Discussion*

16:30–17:30   Poster Session

16:30–17:30   *EMA at SemEval-2018 Task 1: Emotion Mining for Arabic*
Gilbert Badaro, Obeida El Jundi, Alaa Khaddaj, Alaa Maarouf, Raslan Kain, Hazem Hajj and Wassim El-Hajj

16:30–17:30   *NTUA-SLP at SemEval-2018 Task 1: Predicting Affective Content in Tweets with Deep Attentive RNNs and Transfer Learning*
Christos Baziotis, Athanasiou Nikolaos, Alexandra Chronopoulou, Athanasia Kolovou, Georgios Paraskevopoulos, Nikolaos Ellinas, Shrikanth Narayanan and Alexandros Potamianos

16:30–17:30   *CrystalFeel at SemEval-2018 Task 1: Understanding and Detecting Emotion Intensity using Affective Lexicons*
Raj Kumar Gupta and Yinping Yang

16:30–17:30   *PlusEmo2Vec at SemEval-2018 Task 1: Exploiting emotion knowledge from emoji and #hashtags*
Ji Ho Park, Peng Xu and Pascale Fung

16:30–17:30   *YNU-HPCC at SemEval-2018 Task 1: BiLSTM with Attention based Sentiment Analysis for Affect in Tweets*
You Zhang, Jin Wang and Xuejie Zhang

16:30–17:30   *UG18 at SemEval-2018 Task 1: Generating Additional Training Data for Predicting Emotion Intensity in Spanish*
Marloes Kuijper, Mike van Lenthe and Rik van Noord

16:30–17:30   *ISCLAB at SemEval-2018 Task 1: UIR-Miner for Affect in Tweets*
Meng Li, Zhenyuan Dong, Zhihao Fan, Kongming Meng, Jinghua Cao, Guanqi Ding, Yuhan Liu, Jiawei Shan and Binyang Li

16:30–17:30   *TCS Research at SemEval-2018 Task 1: Learning Robust Representations using Multi-Attention Architecture*
Hardik Meisheri and Lipika Dey

16:30–17:30   *DMCB at SemEval-2018 Task 1: Transfer Learning of Sentiment Classification Using Group LSTM for Emotion Intensity prediction*
Youngmin Kim and Hyunju Lee

16:30–17:30   *DeepMiner at SemEval-2018 Task 1: Emotion Intensity Recognition Using Deep Representation Learning*
Habibeh Naderi, Behrouz Haji Soleimani, Saif Mohammad, Svetlana Kiritchenko and Stan Matwin

16:30–17:30   *Zewen at SemEval-2018 Task 1: An Ensemble Model for Affect Prediction in Tweets*
Zewen Chi, Heyan Huang, Jiangui Chen, Hao Wu and Ran Wei

16:30–17:30   *Amrita_student at SemEval-2018 Task 1: Distributed Representation of Social Media Text for Affects in Tweets*
Nidhin A Unnithan, Shalini K, Barathi Ganesh H. B., Anand Kumar M and Soman K P

16:30–17:30   *SSN MLRG1 at SemEval-2018 Task 1: Emotion and Sentiment Intensity Detection Using Rule Based Feature Selection*
Angel Deborah S, Rajalakshmi S, S Milton Rajendram and Mirnalinee T T

16:30–17:30   *CENNLP at SemEval-2018 Task 1: Constrained Vector Space Model in Affects in Tweets*
Naveen J R, Barathi Ganesh H. B., Anand Kumar M and Soman K P

16:30–17:30   *TeamCEN at SemEval-2018 Task 1: Global Vectors Representation in Emotion Detection*
Anon George, Barathi Ganesh H. B., Anand Kumar M and Soman K P

16:30–17:30   *IIT Delhi at SemEval-2018 Task 1 : Emotion Intensity Prediction*
Bhaskar Kotakonda, Prashanth Gowda and Brejesh Lall

16:30–17:30   *Mutux at SemEval-2018 Task 1: Exploring Impacts of Context Information On Emotion Detection*
Pan Du and Jian-Yun Nie

16:30–17:30   *TeamUNCC at SemEval-2018 Task 1: Emotion Detection in English and Arabic Tweets using Deep Learning*
Malak Abdullah and Samira Shaikh

16:30–17:30   *RIDDL at SemEval-2018 Task 1: Rage Intensity Detection with Deep Learning*
Venkatesh Elango and Karan Uppal

16:30–17:30   *ARB-SEN at SemEval-2018 Task1: A New Set of Features for Enhancing the Sentiment Intensity Prediction in Arabic Tweets*
El Moatez Billah Nagoudi

16:30–17:30   *psyML at SemEval-2018 Task 1: Transfer Learning for Sentiment and Emotion Analysis*
Grace Gee and Eugene Wang

16:30–17:30   *UIUC at SemEval-2018 Task 1: Recognizing Affect with Ensemble Models*
Abhishek Avinash Narwekar and Roxana Girju

16:30–17:30   *KU-MTL at SemEval-2018 Task 1: Multi-task Identification of Affect in Tweets*
Thomas Nyegaard-Signori, Casper Veistrup Helms, Johannes Bjerva and Isabelle Augenstein

16:30–17:30   *EmoNLP at SemEval-2018 Task 2: English Emoji Prediction with Gradient Boosting Regression Tree Method and Bidirectional LSTM*
Man Liu

16:30–17:30   Poster Session

16:30–17:30   *LightRel at SemEval-2018 Task 7: Lightweight and Fast Relation Classification*
Tyler Renslow and Günter Neumann

16:30–17:30   *OhioState at SemEval-2018 Task 7: Exploiting Data Augmentation for Relation Classification in Scientific Papers Using Piecewise Convolutional Neural Networks*
Dushyanta Dhyani

16:30–17:30   *The UWNLP system at SemEval-2018 Task 7: Neural Relation Extraction Model with Selectively Incorporated Concept Embeddings*
Yi Luan, Mari Ostendorf and Hannaneh Hajishirzi

16:30–17:30   *UC3M-NII Team at SemEval-2018 Task 7: Semantic Relation Classification in Scientific Papers via Convolutional Neural Network*
Víctor Suárez-Paniagua, Isabel Segura-Bedmar and Akiko Aizawa

16:30–17:30   *MIT-MEDG at SemEval-2018 Task 7: Semantic Relation Classification via Convolution Neural Network*
Di Jin, Franck Dernoncourt, Elena Sergeeva, Matthew McDermott and Geeticka Chauhan

16:30–17:30   *SIRIUS-LTG-UiO at SemEval-2018 Task 7: Convolutional Neural Networks with Shortest Dependency Paths for Semantic Relation Extraction and Classification in Scientific Papers*
Farhad Nooralahzadeh, Lilja Øvrelid and Jan Tore Lønning

16:30–17:30   *IRCMS at SemEval-2018 Task 7 : Evaluating a basic CNN Method and Traditional Pipeline Method for Relation Classification*
Zhongbo Yin, Zhunchen Luo, Luo Wei, Mao Bin, Tian Changhai, Ye Yuming and Wu Shuai

16:30–17:30   *Bf3R at SemEval-2018 Task 7: Evaluating Two Relation Extraction Tools for Finding Semantic Relations in Biomedical Abstracts*
Mariana Neves, Daniel Butzke, Gilbert Schönfelder and Barbara Grune

16:30–17:30   *Texterra at SemEval-2018 Task 7: Exploiting Syntactic Information for Relation Extraction and Classification in Scientific Papers*
Andrey Sysoev and Vladimir Mayorov

16:30–17:30   *UniMa at SemEval-2018 Task 7: Semantic Relation Extraction and Classification from Scientific Publications*
Thorsten Keiper, Zhonghao Lyu, Sara Pooladzadeh, Yuan Xu, Jingyi Zhang, Anne Lauscher and Simone Paolo Ponzetto

16:30–17:30   *GU IRLAB at SemEval-2018 Task 7: Tree-LSTMs for Scientific Relation Classification*
Sean MacAvaney, Luca Soldaini, Arman Cohan and Nazli Goharian

16:30–17:30   *ALB at SemEval-2018 Task 10: A System for Capturing Discriminative Attributes*
Bogdan Dumitru, Alina Maria Ciobanu and Liviu P. Dinu

16:30–17:30   *ELiRF-UPV at SemEval-2018 Task 10: Capturing Discriminative Attributes with Knowledge Graphs and Wikipedia*
José-Ángel González, Lluís-F. Hurtado, Encarna Segarra and Ferran Pla

16:30–17:30   *Wolves at SemEval-2018 Task 10: Semantic Discrimination based on Knowledge and Association*
Shiva Taslimipoor, Omid Rohanian, Le An Ha, Gloria Corpas Pastor and Ruslan Mitkov

16:30–17:30   *UNAM at SemEval-2018 Task 10: Unsupervised Semantic Discriminative Attribute Identification in Neural Word Embedding Cones*
Ignacio Arroyo-Fernández, Ivan Meza and Carlos-Francisco Meéndez-Cruz

16:30–17:30   *Luminoso at SemEval-2018 Task 10: Distinguishing Attributes Using Text Corpora and Relational Knowledge*
Robert Speer and Joanna Lowry-Duda

16:30–17:30   *BomJi at SemEval-2018 Task 10: Combining Vector-, Pattern- and Graph-based Information to Identify Discriminative Attributes*
Enrico Santus, Chris Biemann and Emmanuele Chersoni

16:30–17:30   *Igevorse at SemEval-2018 Task 10: Exploring an Impact of Word Embeddings Concatenation for Capturing Discriminative Attributes*
Maxim Grishin

16:30–17:30   *ECNU at SemEval-2018 Task 10: Evaluating Simple but Effective Features on Machine Learning Methods for Semantic Difference Detection*
Yunxiao Zhou, Man Lan and Yuanbin Wu

16:30–17:30   *AmritaNLP at SemEval-2018 Task 10: Capturing discriminative attributes using convolution neural network over global vector representation.*
Vivek Vinayan, Anand Kumar M and Soman K P

16:30–17:30   *Discriminator at SemEval-2018 Task 10: Minimally Supervised Discrimination*
Artur Kulmizev, Mostafa Abdou, Vinit Ravishankar and Malvina Nissim

16:30–17:30   *UNBNLP at SemEval-2018 Task 10: Evaluating unsupervised approaches to capturing discriminative attributes*
Milton King, Ali Hakimi Parizi and Paul Cook

16:30–17:30   *ABDN at SemEval-2018 Task 10: Recognising Discriminative Attributes using Context Embeddings and WordNet*
Rui Mao, Guanyi Chen, Ruizhe Li and Chenghua Lin

16:30–17:30   *SNU_IDS at SemEval-2018 Task 12: Sentence Encoder with Contextualized Vectors for Argument Reasoning Comprehension*
Taeuk Kim, Jihun Choi and Sang-goo Lee

16:30–17:30   *ITNLP-ARC at SemEval-2018 Task 12: Argument Reasoning Comprehension with Attention*
Wenjie Liu, Chengjie Sun, Lei Lin and Bingquan Liu

16:30–17:30   *ECNU at SemEval-2018 Task 12: An End-to-End Attention-based Neural Network for the Argument Reasoning Comprehension Task*
Junfeng Tian, Man Lan and Yuanbin Wu

16:30–17:30   *NLITrans at SemEval-2018 Task 12: Transfer of Semantic Knowledge for Argument Comprehension*
Timothy Niven and Hung-Yu Kao

16:30–17:30   *BLCU_NLP at SemEval-2018 Task 12: An Ensemble Model for Argument Reasoning Based on Hierarchical Attention*
Meiqian Zhao, Chunhua Liu, Lu Liu, Yan Zhao and Dong Yu

16:30–17:30   *YNU-HPCC at SemEval-2018 Task 12: The Argument Reasoning Comprehension Task Using a Bi-directional LSTM with Attention Model*
Quanlei Liao, Xutao Yang, Jin Wang and Xuejie Zhang

16:30–17:30   *HHU at SemEval-2018 Task 12: Analyzing an Ensemble-based Deep Learning Approach for the Argument Mining Task of Choosing the Correct Warrant*
Matthias Liebeck, Andreas Funke and Stefan Conrad

16:30–17:30   *YNU Deep at SemEval-2018 Task 12: A BiLSTM Model with Neural Attention for Argument Reasoning Comprehension*
Peng Ding and Xiaobing Zhou

16:30–17:30   *UniMelb at SemEval-2018 Task 12: Generative Implication using LSTMs, Siamese Networks and Semantic Representations with Synonym Fuzzing*
Anirudh Joshi, Tim Baldwin, Richard O. Sinnott and Cecile Paris

16:30–17:30   *Joker at SemEval-2018 Task 12: The Argument Reasoning Comprehension with Neural Attention*
Sui Guobin, Chao Wenhan and Luo Zhunchen

16:30–17:30   *TakeLab at SemEval-2018 Task12: Argument Reasoning Comprehension with Skip-Thought Vectors*
Ana Brassard, Tin Kuculo, Filip Boltuzic and Jan Šnajder

16:30–17:30   *Lyb3b at SemEval-2018 Task 12: Ensemble-based Deep Learning Models for Argument Reasoning Comprehension Task*
Yongbin Li and Xiaobing Zhou

IronyMagnet at SemEval-2018 Task 3: A Siamese Network for Irony Detection in Social Media

Aniruddha Ghosh
University College Dublin
Dublin, Ireland
`aniruddha.ghosh@ucdconnect.ie`

Tony Veale
University College Dublin
Dublin, Ireland
`tony.veale@ucd.ie`

Abstract

This paper describes our system, entitled IronyMagnet, for the 3rd Task of the SemEval 2018 workshop, "Irony Detection in English Tweets". In Task 1, irony classification task has been considered as a binary classification task. Now for the first time, finer categories of irony are considered as part of a shared task. In task 2, three types of irony are considered; "Irony by contrast" - ironic instances where evaluative expression portrays inverse polarity (positive, negative) of the literal proposition; "Situational irony" - ironic instances where output of a situation do not comply with its expectation; "Other verbal irony" - instances where ironic intent does not rely on polarity contrast or unexpected outcome. We proposed a Siamese neural network for irony detection, which is consisted of two subnetworks, each containing a long short term memory layer (LSTM) and an embedding layer initialized with vectors from Glove word embedding[1]. The system achieved a f-score of 0.72, and 0.50 in task 1, and task 2 respectively.

1 Introduction

Irony is one of the most prominent and pervasive figures of speech in human communication, dating back to ancient religious texts to modern microtexts. According to literary scholars (Grice, 1978; Lakoff, 1993), irony has been defined as a trope where the speaker intends to communicate a contradictory situation or the opposite meaning of what is literally said. It adopts a subtle technique where incongruity is used to suggest a distinction between reality and expectation in order to produce a humorous or emphatic effect on the listener. Irony poses an important challenge not only from a linguistic perspective but also from a cognitive one. Even without a solid understanding of irony, one can still recognize and produce ironic utterances from as early as childhood (Harris and Pexman, 2003). Such capabilities are often associated with one's ability to correctly infer others' communicative intentions and perspectives towards a given situation. Psychological theories, such as "echoic reminder theory" (Kreuz and Glucksberg, 1989), "allusion pretense theory" (Kumon-Nakamura et al., 1995), and "implicit display theory" (Utsumi, 2000), confirm that cues for understanding ironic intent are not restricted to language. Ironic intent involves several other aspects including, but not limited to, the context of an utterance, the world's perception and familiarity between the listener and the speaker, and psychological dimensions. Thus, as a purely text classification task, the irony detection task poses a significant challenge for computational linguists. Computational approaches focus on identifying the subtle incongruity between different parts of the text. Often, an ironic statement starts with an overtly positive attitude ("Yay I love") and ends up in an disappointment ("working on my birthday") or a negative attitude/statement ("another outage in less than 8 hours.") followed by an appreciation ("Keep up the good work!") or an incident ("I asked God to protect me from my enemies") resulting in a completely unexpected output ("shortly after I started losing friends").

Due to the limited scope of expression in social media such as Twitter[2], authors often end up lacing their statements with ironic cue words ('Yay') or social media specific features such as hashtags ('#irony') to make their ironic intent more obvious for the reader. Following this intuition, most of the attempts were made using probabilistic classification models which relied on textual cues such as lexical indicators like punctuation symbols (e.g., '?'), interjections (e.g., "gee" or "gosh"), and intensifiers (Kreuz and Caucci, 2007); the juxtaposition of positive sentiment and

---

[1] https://nlp.stanford.edu/projects/glove/

[2] www.Twitter.com

Proceedings of the 12th International Workshop on Semantic Evaluation (SemEval-2018), pages 570–575
New Orleans, Louisiana, June 5–6, 2018. ©2018 Association for Computational Linguistics

negative situations (Riloff et al., 2013); discriminative N-grams like 'yay!' or 'great!' or "oh really" or "yeah right" (Tsur et al., 2010; Lukin and Walker, 2013); social media markers like hashtags (Davidov et al., 2010); emoticon usage (González-Ibánez et al., 2011); and topics associated with irony (e.g. schools, dentists, church life, public transport, the weather). Carvalho et al. (2009) exploited text patterns in comments on articles of online newspapers to detect ironic statements, while Van Hee et al. (2016) developed a irony detection model using support vector machine (SVM) with a combination of lexical, syntactic, sentiment, and semantic (Word2Vec embedding) features. In recent times, multiple research attempts, founded on variants of the deep neural network built on top of word embeddings, showed a significant improvement over traditional methods over several natural language processing (NLP) tasks. A few representative works in this direction for detecting sarcasm, a demeaning variant of irony, especially in the colloquial form, are based on Convolutional Neural Networks(CNN) (Mishra et al., 2017), Recurrent Neural Networks (RNN) (Zhang et al., 2016) and a combination of CNNs and RNNs (Ghosh and Veale, 2016). Siamese networks (Bromley et al., 1994), widely used in image classification, have displayed a good performance over sentence similarity or document similarity tasks. A Siamese architecture contains two identical sub-networks, which are trained with two different inputs to distinguish the difference among them. Since in irony, different parts of a sentence can be incongruous with each other, we adopted the Siamese architecture to detect such incongruity between different sections of a sentence. In this implementation, each of the subnetworks consists of an embedding layer and a LSTM layer. We slice each input sentence into two fragments and feed them to the subnetworks. The output representations of subnetworks are then compared to distinguish if the two fragments are incongruous or not i.e. a sentence is considered as non-ironic if two fragments of a sentence are semantically non-incongruous, otherwise it is ironic.

2   Dataset Preparation & Resources

The train and test dataset consists of 3834 tweets and 784 tweets, respectively. The train dataset for Task 1 is balanced but in task 2, the prominent category was "irony by polarity contrast" (table 1).

2.1   Data Normalization

The distorted language, use of abbreviation, and high number of one-off words, prevents a model from being robust. Thus, each tweet is preprocessed, normalized, and cleaned with the following criteria.

1. To emphasize the ironic effect, an author often uses repetition of a character or a word. A set of regular expressions is used to normalize the word ("loooong" to "long") and the word is replaced with a word from Word-Net[3] which has the lowest minimum edit distance[4] between them. The repeated word sequence is split using a regular expression into multiple words("YAYYAYYAYYAYYAY" to "YAY YAY YAY YAY YAY").

2. Since this is a text based classification task, each link from the tweets is discarded.

3. The limited scope of social media incentivizes users to exploit different features of social media such as hashtags and emoticons more creatively and efficiently to express an opinion. Hashtags are often used by authors to emphasize key parts or themes in their texts or to convey their attitude or feeling towards the subject. This can provide a toehold for NLP techniques in order to infer the intended sense behind an ironic statement. Thus, each hashtag is processed and split into words. For example, "#TheReasonForThe-Season" is converted in "The Reason For The Season".

4. Emojis have played a significant role in expressing the hidden feelings of a person not evident in plain text. Each individual emoji is replaced with their official name[5].

5. The high number of one-off words increases the vocabulary size of a network. Due to the sparsity in the dataset because of one-off words, the model finds it difficult to train. Thus, all non-valid English words, according to WordNet dictionary, occurring less than twice in the entire dataset are removed.

6. Neural network models are data hungry and their success often relies on the size of the

---

[3]https://wordnet.princeton.edu/
[4]https://en.wikipedia.org/wiki/Edit_distance
[5]https://unicode.org/emoji/charts/full-emoji-list.html

train dataset. Since the train dataset is relatively small, it can not extract the distinctive, robust features for detecting irony. Thus, the dataset is extended by replacing the overtly positive and negative words with "positive" and "negative" respectively using the Sentiwordnet[6].

7. In order to capture the incongruity between topics, the dataset is further extended by replacing words with its category type extracted from WordNet.

2.2 Building Train Dataset

Since a Siamese network expects two inputs and performs a comparison between the generated weights, each tweet is split into two parts. A number of training examples are generated by splitting the tweets where each split contains a minimum r number of words. Consider as an input a tweet containing n words with label y. The tweet will be split into $(n - 2 \times r + 1)$ combinations. In this experiment, the value of r is chosen as 3. For example, "Working on Boxing Day is so fun" will produce the following combinations:

1. ("Working on Boxing", "Day is so fun")

2. ("Working on Boxing Day", "is so fun")

For training purposes, the train dataset is split with a 90%-10% split ratio.

3 Siamese Network

3.1 Input Layer

Each tweet, with length n, is converted to a vector by replacing a word with its index value in the dictionary $s \in \Re^{1 \times n}$. To resolve different lengths of input, each tweet is either padded or truncated to convert into a vector of size $s \in \Re^{1 \times l}$ where l is the maximum allowed length. The maximum allowed length for the input vector for each sub-network is set to the average length of the tweets. The input vector is fed to an embedding layer which converts each word into a distributional vector of dimension D. Thus, the input tweet matrix is converted $s \in \Re^{l \times D}$. The embedding layer is initialized with the embeddings extracted from Glove word embedding. We freeze the embedding layer to keep the general meaning of a word intact.

<hr>

[6]http://sentiwordnet.isti.cnr.it/

task	0	1	2	3
1	1923	1911	-	-
2	1923	1390	316	205

Table 1 Train Data Statistics

3.2 LSTM Layer

Among the variants of RNN networks, LSTM has demonstrated the power of semantic modelling by efficiently handling long term dependencies (Hochreiter and Schmidhuber, 1997) by defining each memory cell with a set of gates $\Re^d$, where d is the memory dimension of hidden states of LSTM. It does not suffer from a vanishing or exploding gradient problem while performing back propagation through time. There are three gates, which are functions of x_t and h_{t-1}: input gate i_t, forget gate f_t, and output gate o_t. The gates jointly decide whether the memory update mechanism will occur or not. Equation (2) and (1) denotes the amount of information to discard and what to store in memory. Equation (4) denotes the output of a cell c_t. Equation (3), (5), and (6) denotes the input activation, cell state, and output vector of a LSTM cell respectively.

$$i_t = \sigma(W_i[h_{t-1}, x_t] + b_i) \qquad (1)$$

$$f_t = \sigma(W_f[h_{t-1}, x_t] + b_f) \qquad (2)$$

$$q_t = sigmoid(W_q[h_{t-1}, x_t] + b_q) \qquad (3)$$

$$o_t = \sigma(W_o[h_{t-1}, x_t] + b_o) \qquad (4)$$

$$c_t = f_t \odot c_{t-1} + i_t \odot q_t \qquad (5)$$

$$h_t = o_t \odot sigmoid(c_t) \qquad (6)$$

Due to the small dataset size, extra attention has been paid in order to prevent the network from overfitting. A recurrent Dropout is used between each time step of an input. Each LSTM layer outputs a weight matrix $s \in \Re^{l \times m}$ (m = number of hidden memory units), which is passed to a Dropout layer.

3.3 Subtract Layer

The generated weights of each LSTM layer carries the conceptual representation of its input. Intuitively, the weight difference between the output of two LSTM layers should signify conceptual representations as either incongruous to each other or not. A subtract layer is used to calculate the weight difference between two sub networks.

The subtract layer produced an output matrix $s \in \Re^{l \times m}$, which is passed as an input to a fully connected layer.

3.4 Fully Connected Layer

The fully connected layer produces a higher order feature set, based on the weight matrix obtained from the LSTM layer, which is easily separable into different classes. At the end, a Softmax layer is added on top of the fully connected layer.

4 Experimental Setup

Success with a neural network model largely depends on the apt input and optimal hyper-parameters settings. After investigating different combinations of hyper-parameters, the optimal setting is obtained for each layer of the network. The LSTM has 32 hidden memory units with a *sigmoid* activation function and recurrent dropout ratio of 0.5. The fully-connected layer consisted of 16 hidden memory units and uses *ReLu* as the activation function. Both of the layers are initialized with *Xavier normal initializer* (Glorot and Bengio, 2010). As an optimizer function, Adam optimization is used with a learning rate set to 0.001, while categorical cross-entropy is chosen as a loss function. The code is developed using the *keras*[7] library.

5 Results

For both of the tasks, our model is compared with the state-of-the-art composite neural network model (Ghosh and Veale, 2016). Each model is trained with the same datasets. For the composite model, the entire tweet is fed as an input instead of just fragments of the tweet.

6 Output Analysis

In both tasks, the Siamese network outperforms the composite neural network model. The composite neural network model, trained with original tweets, is only able to capture certain ironic utterances where a similar pattern is encountered in the training dataset. The model responds well to obvious ironic markers such as "Ohh" in figure 2. Without the obvious ironic markers, the model mis-classifies the statement as non-ironic. Whereas the Siamese network classifies the statement correctly even without the obvious ironic

---

[7]http://keras.io/

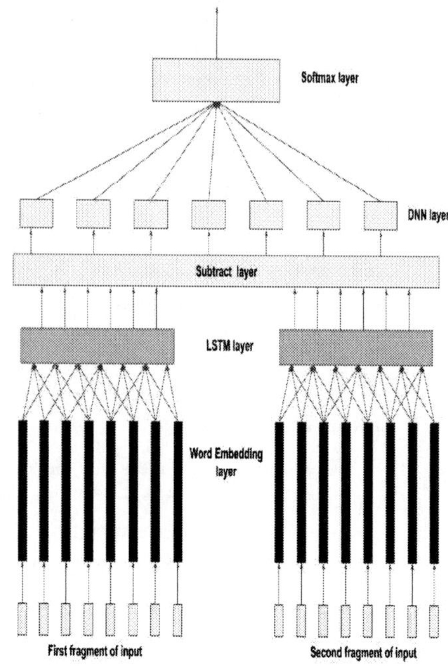

Figure 1 Siamese Neural network

Task	Model	P	R	F1
Task1	Ghosh and Veale (2016)⋆	0.6449	0.4437	0.5257
	Siamese network	0.7878	0.6688	0.7234
Task2	Ghosh and Veale (2016)	0.4099	0.4187	0.3988
	Siamese network⋆	0.5768	0.5044	0.5074

Table 2 Experiment Results; ⋆submissions considered in final standing

marker, the subtract layer captures the incongruity between two concepts in an ironic statement. However, the Siamese network fails to detect ironic statements with dropped negations. For example, the network could not figure out the ironic intent behind the following statement "Hey there! Nice to see you Minnesota/ND Winter Weather", the model has no information about "Minnesota/ND Winter Weather".

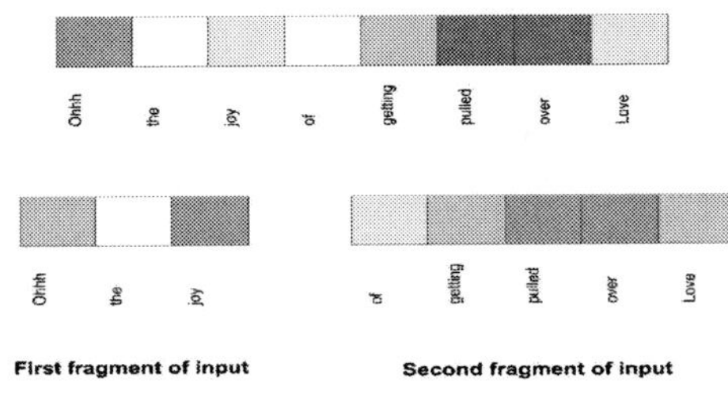

Figure 2 Output Vector of LSTM Layer

7 Conclusion and Future Works

We introduced *IronyMagnet*, a Siamese neural network model that is capable of separating ironic statements from non-ironic statements, as well as at a fine-grained level. Even with small datasets, the Siamese neural network is able to robustly capture the incongruity between two concepts. However, the system lacks the sophistication of understanding incongruity at a pragmatic level. Take, for example, "Whatever happened to the Guano Apes? Did they ever make it "Big in Japan"?". In this example, none of the models are able to establish the incongruity between "Guano Apes" and "Big in Japan". Also, it can not correctly detect if the incongruous elements are located very close to one another within the tweet. However, since the Siamese network is able to correctly classify simple cases of irony, we can therefore hypothesize that the Siamese network can be a stepping stone towards determining contrastive figurative languages. In the future, we would like to extend our model by incorporating an attention network and other psychological stimuli which pertain to Irony.

References

Jane Bromley, Isabelle Guyon, Yann LeCun, Eduard Säckinger, and Roopak Shah. 1994. Signature verification using a" siamese" time delay neural network. In *Advances in Neural Information Processing Systems*, pages 737–744.

Paula Carvalho, Luís Sarmento, Mário J Silva, and Eugénio De Oliveira. 2009. Clues for detecting irony in user-generated contents: oh...!! it's so easy;-. In *Proceedings of the 1st international CIKM workshop on Topic-sentiment analysis for mass opinion*, pages 53–56. ACM.

Dmitry Davidov, Oren Tsur, and Ari Rappoport. 2010. Semi-supervised recognition of sarcastic sentences in twitter and amazon. In *Proceedings of the Fourteenth Conference on Computational Natural Language Learning*, pages 107–116. Association for Computational Linguistics.

Aniruddha Ghosh and Tony Veale. 2016. Fracking sarcasm using neural network. In *Proceedings of the 7th Workshop on Computational Approaches to Subjectivity, Sentiment and Social Media Analysis*, pages 161–169.

Xavier Glorot and Yoshua Bengio. 2010. Understanding the difficulty of training deep feedforward neural networks. In *Proceedings of the Thirteenth International Conference on Artificial Intelligence and Statistics*, pages 249–256.

Roberto González-Ibánez, Smaranda Muresan, and Nina Wacholder. 2011. Identifying sarcasm in twitter: a closer look. In *Proceedings of the 49th Annual Meeting of the Association for Computational Linguistics: Human Language Technologies: Short Papers-Volume 2*, pages 581–586. Association for Computational Linguistics.

H Paul Grice. 1978. Further notes on logic and conversation. *1978*, 1:13–128.

Melanie Harris and Penny M Pexman. 2003. Children's perceptions of the social functions of verbal irony. *Discourse Processes*, 36(3):147–165.

Sepp Hochreiter and Jürgen Schmidhuber. 1997. Long short-term memory. *Neural computation*, 9(8):1735–1780.

Roger J. Kreuz and Gina M. Caucci. 2007. Lexical influences on the perception of sarcasm. In *Proceedings of the Workshop on Computational Approaches to Figurative Language*.

Roger J Kreuz and Sam Glucksberg. 1989. How to be sarcastic: The echoic reminder theory of verbal irony. *Journal of Experimental Psychology: General*.

Sachi Kumon-Nakamura, Sam Glucksberg, and Mary Brown. 1995. How about another piece of pie: The allusional pretense theory of discourse irony. *Journal of Experimental Psychology: General*, 124(1):3.

George Lakoff. 1993. The contemporary theory of metaphor.

Stephanie Lukin and Marilyn Walker. 2013. Really? well. apparently bootstrapping improves the performance of sarcasm and nastiness classifiers for online dialogue. In *Proceedings of the Workshop on Language Analysis in Social Media*, pages 30–40.

Abhijit Mishra, Kuntal Dey, and Pushpak Bhattacharyya. 2017. Learning cognitive features from gaze data for sentiment and sarcasm classification using convolutional neural network. In *Proceedings of the 55th Annual Meeting of the Association for Computational Linguistics (Volume 1: Long Papers)*, volume 1, pages 377–387.

Ellen Riloff, Ashequl Qadir, Prafulla Surve, Lalindra De Silva, Nathan Gilbert, and Ruihong Huang. 2013. Sarcasm as contrast between a positive sentiment and negative situation. In *EMNLP*, volume 13, pages 704–714.

Oren Tsur, Dmitry Davidov, and Ari Rappoport. 2010. Icwsm-a great catchy name: Semi-supervised recognition of sarcastic sentences in online product reviews. In *ICWSM*.

A. Utsumi. 2000. Verbal irony as implicit display of ironic environment: Distinguishing ironic utterances from nonirony. *Journal of Pragmatics*.

Cynthia Van Hee, Els Lefever, and Véronique Hoste. 2016. Monday mornings are my fave:)# not exploring the automatic recognition of irony in english tweets. In *Proceedings of COLING 2016, the 26th International Conference on Computational Linguistics: Technical Papers*, pages 2730–2739.

Meishan Zhang, Yue Zhang, and Guohong Fu. 2016. Tweet sarcasm detection using deep neural network. In *Proceedings of COLING 2016, the 26th International Conference on Computational Linguistics: Technical Papers*, pages 2449–2460.

CTSys at SemEval-2018 Task 3: Irony in Tweets

Myan Sherif

Faculty of Engineering
Alexandria University

sherif.myan@gmail.com

Sherine Mamdouh

Faculty of Engineering
Alexandria University

sherym51@gmail.com

Wegdan Ghazi

Faculty of Engineering
Alexandria University

wegdan.ghazi@gmail.com

Abstract

The objective of this paper is to provide a description for a system built as our participation in SemEval-2018 Task 3 on Irony detection in English tweets. This system classifies a tweet as either ironic or non-ironic through a supervised learning approach. Our approach is to implement three feature models, and to then improve the performance of the supervised learning classification of tweets by combining many data features and using a voting system on four different classifiers. We describe the process of pre-processing data, extracting features, and running different types of classifiers against our feature set. In the competition, our system achieved an F1-score of 0.4675, ranking 35th in subtask A, and an F1-score score of 0.3014 ranking 22th in subtask B.

1 Introduction

Irony detection in text has extended to different data forms (tweets, reviews, TV series dialogues), our domain of data in this task is a Twitter corpus provided by SemEval2018 organizers. Here, irony detection refers to computational approaches to predict if a given text is sarcastic. This problem is hard because of the nuanced ways in which irony may be expressed. The most difficult part of the problem mentioned is the process of feature engineering, because it defines the parameters and the relationships and dependencies between semantic meanings, and gives us the numerical model that the classifier would proceed to work on, thus being crucial to the soundness and efficiency of the system.

This led us to dive into deeper questions, such as the nature of tweets, and how we are dealing with a version of the English language that is not directly workable. We need to perform pre-processing to deal with annotations and hashtags. Another question is how to analyze irony in English language and derive a rule-based approach that can be implemented to better understand the semantics of ironic text.

The problem, as described by the SemEval-2018 task organizers, addresses both the binary distinction between irony and non-irony, as well as different types of irony.

1.1 Task Description

The SemEval-2018 Task 3 is divided into two subtasks:

Subtask A is a binary classification problem where we are asked to classify a tweet as ironic or not ironic, based on a given training set of labeled tweets (0 for non-ironic and 1 for ironic).

Subtask B is a multi-classification problem where we classify the tweets to which type they belong as either situational irony or verbal irony or other irony or not ironic. Each tweet in the training set is labeled as follows: (0 for non-ironic, 1 for situational irony, 2 for verbal irony, and 3 for other forms of irony).

1.2 The Dataset

The used dataset in this assignment is the one provided in SemEval-2018 task 3. It consists of 3,842 tweets in total. The tweets were collected by searching Twitter for the hashtags #irony, #sarcasm and #not.

The dataset was presented in two phases:

1- Training data: already labeled tweets used to train the classifiers. Each tweet was provided with a binary classification label and an index.

2- Testing data: unlabeled tweets to test the classifiers against. For each instance in the test

Proceedings of the 12th International Workshop on Semantic Evaluation (SemEval-2018), pages 576–580
New Orleans, Louisiana, June 5–6, 2018. ©2018 Association for Computational Linguistics

data, participants submitted a predicted label. Based on these predictions, competition scores were calculated using four metrics (F1-score, precision, recall, and accuracy).

2 Literature overview

There has been much research involving the definition of irony and the distinction between irony and sarcasm. To date, however, experts do not formally agree on the distinction between irony and sarcasm as shown by Aditya Joshi et al., (2016). Moreover, when describing how irony works, Antonio Reyes et al., (2013), distinguish between situational irony and verbal irony. Situational irony is an unexpected or incongruous quality in a situation or event, as shown by Shelley (2001). Whereas verbal irony, in contrast, is a playful use of language in which a speaker implies the opposite of what is literally said.

In his work on the Sarcasm Detector website, Mathieu Cliche collected tweets from Twitter that were labeled with the hashtag #sarcasm. His hypothesis was that sarcastic tweets carry what he calls a contrast of sentiments (e.g. start with a positive sentiment and end with a negative sentiment). He also uses features such as n-grams and topics as accompanying features then trains an SVM algorithm as a classifier. Cliche's system harbored an F1-score of 0.60, an improvement from previous work on sarcasm detection as shown in Cliche (2014).

Chun-Che Peng et al., (2015) followed up on Cliche's work to acquire improved results and stated that irony detection models are prone to suffer from high variance, which be the effect of having a high dimensional feature space, therefore making it important to reduce the dimensions of the feature space and only use the most relevant features. Their paper also suggests that using a Gaussian kernel instead of a linear kernel might be a better approach, given that the data itself is not linearly separable.

In our work, we build upon Cliche's (2014) hypothesis and try to benefit from Peng et al.'s (2015) remarks on using the most relevant features.

3 Implementation

The system is based on natural language processing where we are targeting to improve performance for classifying tweets as ironic or non-ironic by combining many data features and a voting system on many classifiers, we design pattern-based features that indicate the presence of discriminative patterns as extracted from a large irony-labeled dataset.

3.1 Text Preprocessing

To generate good results and to control the number of unneeded computations, the tweets are filtered according to certain criteria. We will briefly go through the steps of pre-processing a tweet.

3.1.1 Tokenization

The first step to handle textual data is tokenization, which is the process of splitting sentences into single words.

3.1.2 Stop Words

The second step is to filter the data and remove any insignificant and redundant words. There are known words, called stop words, as shown by Alani (2014) are always removed to enhance the performance.

For the objective of the task, irony detection in tweets, we removed some words from the **Stop Words** sets because they are significant in detecting irony, especially in the sentiment analysis model. In sentiment analysis, we removed any negating words and conjunctions, such as: ("no", "not", "until", "but"). Whereas in BoW, keeping negation was unnecessary.

3.1.3 Lemmatization

Lemmatization is the process of getting the root of a word. It takes into consideration the morphological analysis of words. A lemma is the same for variations of a word, therefore; it reduces sparsity.

3.2 Extracting Features

We here convert the tweet into a vector of dimensional attributes. While feature mapping is the hardest step in the code, the pattern of feature engineering in task A and task B is all the same, we follow the same steps of mapping and classifying to get different outputs due to different training data on the models.

We have tried three different directions in regards to extracting features from the dataset. The first being the bag of words (BoW) model, the second is rule-based sentiment analysis, and the third being word embedding.

Four classifier models were used to train and test the three feature sets implemented. Each feature set of which is tested on each classifier model. In other words, we test (feature set '1 of 3', classifier '1 of 4') pairs. Then we used a voting system to compare between the results of (feature set, classifier) pairs, and then the classification with the higher number of votes is picked as the final classification.

3.2.1   Bag of Words Feature

First, we create three arrays. The first array for the words in ironic tweets, the second array for the words in non-ironic tweets and the final array for words in all tweets. **Second**, we calculate the number of repetitions of every word in the ironic tweets array across all ironic tweets. We repeat the same step for every word in the non-ironic tweets across all non-ironic tweets. **Third**, we extract the most common words (with highest frequency) across both tweets to eliminate them from our processing to the data - since they will not be effective in determining if a tweet is ironic or not. **Fourth**, we create hash-maps for the words as 'key' attribute and their frequency value as 'value' attribute - one hash-map for words in ironic tweets, another for words in non-ironic and the last one for the common ones. **Fifth**, we sort the hash-maps for easy acquiring of the words with highest frequencies. **Finally**, we add the hash-maps as another feature for the data processing procedure.

3.2.2   Sentiment Analysis

According to Van Hee et at., (2016), verbal irony arises from a clash between two evaluation polarities. We use sentiment analysis to help detect irony in a tweet via contrasting polarity. We used the **polarity** feature of a word to determine if the feelings in the tweet changed 180 degrees. We did not apply lemmatization prior to extracting this feature because it affects polarity. We also handle **emojis** and **negation words** in the tweets since they contribute to the polarity of the sentence. Below are the steps we perform.

a. Split the tweet into two parts on a conjunction from a list created by hand. We gather all the available conjunctions in English Grammar. We handle all the conjunctions except the ones that consist of more than one word like "not only... but also"... etc.

b. Perform pre-processing on each part of the tweet individually.

c. Evaluate polarity of each word of each part of the sentence, and then define the polarity of each part given the ratios of positive, negative, and neutral words to the total length of the sentence.

d. Each part is given a tag as positive (POS), negative (NEG), or neutral (NEU).

e. We tune the parameters that define the threshold of positivity or negativity of each part of the sentence, being 0.5 in this case.

f. Compare the polarities of the sentence parts.

To sum up: The **Sentiment Analysis** method uses contrasting polarity or extra positivity and extra negativity as an indication of irony. We split the tweet into two parts, taking each part as input into the **Sentiment Intensity Analyzer**, the polarity of each word is returned by the analyzer as either positive (POS), negative (NEG) or neutral (NEU). To calculate the **overall polarity** of one part of the tweet, we search for the polarity category that has **highest** number of words and return it as the **overall** polarity. The overall polarity of both parts of a tweet is then examined and classified as ironic if contrasting polarity (e.g. POS-NEG or NEG-POS) is found.

3.2.3   Word Embedding

First, we build a model using training data to act like a dictionary for upcoming processing. The model used in this step is a Word2Vec model. **Second**, we process each tweet in the training dataset, using every word in every tweet and passing it to the model - which as a result, returns an equivalent numerical vector to the word with a fixed length, in our case; we choose a length of one hundred (100) as a moderate length value. **Third**, we add all the vectors of the words in each tweet and divide this sum by their number. Thus, we acquire a numerical representation of a fixed length for every tweet. Fourth, we append all those vectors of all tweets. Finally, we pass the resulting appended vectors of all tweets to the classifier. If the word did not exist in the dictionary we made beforehand, a vector of length 0 is returned.

3.3 Choosing a classifier

We use four models for classification and we build a voting system for them all, tune the parameters, and record the findings to enhance the performance, the classification models are selected based on the literature review. The classification algorithms used are listed below:

- Naive Bayes Classifier.
- Support Vector Machine (SVM).
- Decision Trees.
- K-Nearest Neighbor Classifier: After some tuning, k=1 generated the best results for all the features.

4 Results

Our system is divided into three classes one for each feature. Then the result of each is classified using the four different classifiers stated above. Below we present a chart of the accuracies obtained with different classification algorithms and different feature types.

	BoW	Sen-A	Word-E
NB	65	44	49
SVM	62	45	53
Trees	57	59	57
1-NN	52	60	48

Table 1: accuracy of feature-classes when tested against classifiers using the training set for task A.

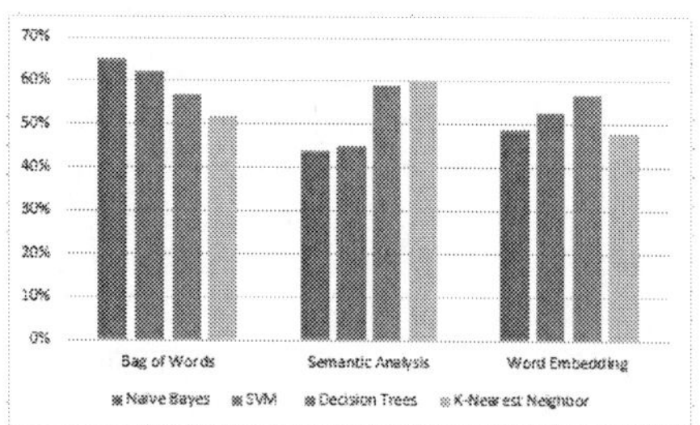

Figure 1: results obtained by two voting systems using three feature set types as shown.

4.1 Classifiers Voting System

We used a voting system to combine the predictions from the four classifiers exploiting different feature types.

4.2 Features Voting System

This voting system uses the four output results from the four classifiers voting system to get an overall result for the whole system.

The results of the system evaluation phase are as follows:

	Accuracy	Precision	Recall	F1-score
Task A	0.5089	0.4102	0.5434	0.4675
Task B	0.4923	0.2998	0.3108	0.3014

Table 2: The score obtained by the system in subtasks A and B as evaluated by SemEval.

4.3 Analysis

Looking at the results, we hypothesize that the system's performance can be improved by combining all features instead of testing them individually. It was also remarkable that the best accuracy was obtained by the bag-of-words model using the Naïve Bayes classifier.

We also believe better results can be achieved if there was a bigger dataset at hand to train upon, and if we had sufficient time to perform grammar checking on the tokens and other operations that can reduce noise.

5 Conclusion

This paper describes our irony detection system that was built in the framework of SemEval-2018 Task 3. We used the same architecture for subtask A and B and obtained F1-scores of 0.4675 and 0.3014, respectively. Our binary classification results are much better compared to multi-classification, which implies that we need to implement another feature model that could represent a whole sentence (e.g. Sentence2Vec rather than Word2Vec). In future work, we aim to enhance the performance of our classifier by combining all features. Moreover, we will add new features to solve the problem of word dependencies (by this we mean that all system features do not account for dependencies between words in the same sentence) so that the system gives more accurate results.

Acknowledgements

The authors would like to thank Prof. Ayman Khalafallah of Alexandria University for his constant guidance and support throughout the process of developing this system.

References

Harith Alani, Miriam Fernández, Yulan He and Hassan Saif. 2014. *On stopwords, filtering and data sparsity for sentiment analysis of Twitter*. In proceedings of LREC 2014, 9th International Conference on Language Resources and Evaluation:810–817.

Mathieu Cliche. 2014. *The sarcasm detector*. URL: http://www.thesarcasmdetector.com/about/.

Aditya Joshi, Mark James Carman and Pushpak Bhattacharyya. 2017. *Automatic Sarcasm Detection: A Survey*. ACM Computing Surveys 50(5) Article 73, 2017. https://doi.org/10.1145/3124420

Chun-Che Peng, Jan Wei Pan and Mohammad Lakis. 2015. *Detecting Sarcasm in Text: An Obvious Solution to a Trivial Problem*. Stanford CS 229 Machine Learning Final Project.

Antonio Reyes, Paolo Rosso and Tony Veale. 2012. *A multidimensional approach for detecting irony in Twitter*. Language Resources & Evaluation, March 2013, 47(1) :239–268.
https://doi.org/10.1007/s10579-012-9196-x

Cameron Shelley. 2001. *The bicoherence theory of situational irony*. Cognitive Science 25:775-818.
https://doi.org/10.1016/S0364-0213(01)00053-2

Cynthia Van Hee, Els Lefever and Veronique Hoste. 2016. *Guidelines for Annotating Irony in Social Media Text*. LT3, Department of Translation, Interpreting and Communication, Faculty of Arts, Humanities and Law - Ghent University, Belgium.

Irony Detector at SemEval-2018 Task 3: Irony Detection in English Tweets using Word Graph

Usman Ahmed, Lubna Zafar, Faiza Qayyum and Muhammad Arshad Islam
Parallel Computing Network,
Department of Computer Science,
Capital University of Science and Technology,
Islamabad, Pakistan.
usmanahmed189@gmail.com,
lubbnaa@gmail.com,
faizaqayyum@cust.edu.pk,
arshad.islam@cust.edu.pk.

Abstract

This paper describes the Irony detection system that participates in SemEval-2018 Task 3: Irony detection in English tweets. The system participated in the subtasks A and B. This paper discusses the results of our system in the development, evaluation and post evaluation. Each class in the dataset is represented as directed unweighted graphs. Then, the comparison is carried out with each class graph which results in a vector. This vector is used as features by machine learning algorithm. The model is evaluated on a hold on strategy. The organizers randomly split 80% (3,833 instances) training set (provided to the participant in training their system) and testing set 20% (958 instances). The test set is reserved to evaluate the performance of participants systems. During the evaluation, our system ranked 23 in the Coda Lab result of the subtask A (binary class problem). The binary class system achieves accuracy 0.6135, precision 0.5091, recall 0.7170 and F measure 0.5955. The subtask B (multi-class problem) system is ranked 22 in Coda Lab results. The multiclass model achieves the accuracy 0.4158, precision 0.4055, recall 0.3526 and f measure 0.3101.

1 Introduction

Social media are deemed as a diverse web-based network that serves as an online platform to communicate and disseminate information or ideas among individuals and fraternities. Since its advent, people all around the globe harness it as a major source to express their opinions or emotions, however, an expeditious increase in its usage has been reported in the last decade (Kelly et al., 2016; Perrin, 2015). Among the multifarious range of social media platforms, Twitter is the most popular one. It is basically a microblogging site diffuses information pertaining to what is happening around the world, and what are the current top-interest areas among the wider population (Rosenthal et al., 2017). According to a recent survey, 6000 tweets per second are sent by 320 million active monthly users, thus 500 million tweets per day (Statistics, 2014). This poses a challenge for the scientific community to accurately discern the sentiment of a tweet out of this plethora. Since certain aspects associated with sentiment analysis are quite arduous yet feasible to ascertain (such as negative, positive, a neutral aspect of the opinion) than irony.

Irony detection has its implications in sentiment analysis (Reyes et al., 2009), opinion mining (Sarmento et al., 2009) and advertising (Kreuz, 2001). For the past few years, irony-aware sentiment analysis has attained significant computational treatment due to the prevalence of irony on the web content (Farías et al., 2016). It is a broad concept, which has an association with multiple disciplines such as psychology, linguistics, etc. The irony is to efficaciously delineate a contrary aspect of the utterance (Grice, 1975). Irony cannot be detected with the simple scrutiny of words expressed in a statement, whereas, an aspect of irony is implicitly connected with the utterance. Furthermore, it could be deemed as a stance that has been expressed in an ironic or sarcastic environment (Grice, 1975; Alba-Juez and Attardo, 2014). Detection of this implicit aspect poses a strenuous computational challenge over the scientific community in terms of initiating effective models in this regard. In the stream of irony detection, the first-ever computer model was proposed by (Utsumi, 1996). Subsequently, various other models have been presented that have specifically addressed the irony detection among tweets by using different features such as, cue-words or user-generated tags (i.e., Hashtags) etc (Van Hee, 2017; Hernández-Farías et al., 2015; Reyes et al., 2013).

Proceedings of the 12th International Workshop on Semantic Evaluation (SemEval-2018), pages 581–586
New Orleans, Louisiana, June 5–6, 2018. ©2018 Association for Computational Linguistics

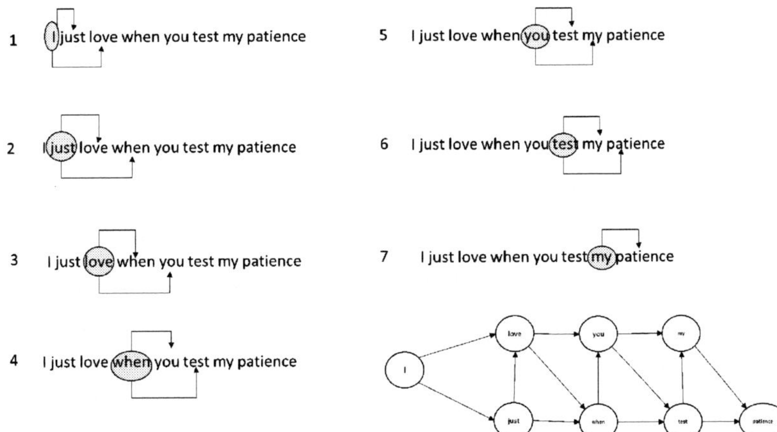

Figure 1: Graph Construction with vicinity size 2 illustrates how the vicinity size move toward the end of the tweet; in this example the frame is the two following words and for each word some edges and nodes are added to the graph.

Though, there does not exist any optimal model that could be considered as a baseline for irony detection. This paper presents a model to automatically detect sarcasm or irony from the plethora of tweets. The proposed model is used in the two subtasks. The first module assigns the binary value against tweets (i.e., 1 indicates that tweet in ironic and 0 indicates that a tweet is non-ironic). The second module performs multi-class classification: (i) verbal irony realized through a polarity contrast, ii) verbal irony without such a polarity contrast (i.e., Other verbal ironies), iii) descriptions of situational irony and iv) non-irony. For classification, data set is comprised of 4792 samples, taken from GitHub link provided by the SemEval 2018 organizers.

2 Task Overview

In SemEval-2018 (Cynthia Van Hee, 2018), task 3 contains two subtasks for the detection of Irony in English tweets. In the first task, the system has to determine whether a tweet is ironic or non- ironic, making it a binary classification problem. The second task is the multiclass classification problem where the ironic and non-ironic task is further divided into four categories as mentioned below:

1. verbal irony realized through a polarity contrast

2. verbal irony without such a polarity contrast (i.e., other verbal irony)

3. descriptions of situational irony

4. Non-irony

Systems are evaluated using standard evaluation metrics, including accuracy, precision, recall and F1-score.

3 Proposed Model

The proposed model is inspired by the previous work (Giannakopoulos et al., 2008; Maas et al., 2011), however, we used some additional features as well as a word graph similarity score. Each tweet is represented as directed unweighted word graph and the edge between each word is created based on the vicinity window size explained in 1. Each class in the dataset is represented as directed unweighted graphs. Then, the comparison is carried out with each class graph which results in a vector. This vector is used as features by machine learning algorithm. The graph is constructed based on a class assignment and then we measure the similarity of a tweet with each class graph. The similarity between two graphs (tweet graph and class graph) can be measured in multiple ways, but in this research, we used the containment similarity (non-normalized value), maximum common subgraph similarity and its variant compare graph in terms of similarity.

3.1 Graph Construction

The tweet contained a set of words. Theses word will be used to construct the word graph based on their vicinity. Each word in the tweet is represented by the labelled node. The nodes within

Class Name	Number of Coloumn
Verbal irony by means of a polarity contrast	1728
Other types of verbal irony	267
Situational Irony	401
Non-Ironic	604

Table 1: Data set Description

window size are joined by an edge. The sequence of the words is preserved by using directed edges. The size of the vicinity window can affect the accuracy of the method. In this research, we used a vicinity size of 2, as seen in 1

The graph similarity between the graph of a tweet and the graph of the irony class can define the degree of irony in the tweet. For the purposes of our study, we used the containment similarity (non-normalized value), maximum common subgraph similarity and its variant compare graph.

3.2 Dataset

The dataset is provided on the GitHub source. This corpus is constructed of 3,000 English language tweets. These tweets are searched by using hashtags #irony, #sarcasm and #not. The data were collected from the period of five months (1st December 2014 to 1st April 2015) and represent 2,676 unique users. All tweets were manually annotated using the scheme of Van el al (Van Hee et al., 2016). The organizer used the services of three students in linguistics as well as English language speakers to annotate the entire corpus. The (Stenetorp et al., 2012) tool was used as the annotation tool. The percentage agreement score (kappa scores 0.72) is also calculated for the annotation. The number of instances for each class is mentioned in Table 1.

As seen in Table, 2396 instances are ironic (1,728 + 267 + 401) while 604 are non-ironic. The organizer balances the class data by using background corpus. After balancing the total data set contain 4,792 tweets that contain 2,396 ironic and 2,396 non-ironic tweets. The SemEval-2018 competition used the hold on the strategy to check the effectiveness of each participated system. The organizers randomly split 80% (3,833 instances) training set (provided to the participant in training their system) and testing set 20% (958 instances). The test set is reserved to evaluate the performance of participants systems.

3.3 Feature Engineering

3.3.1 Containment Similarity

The containment similarity measure has been used to calculate, graph similarity (Aisopos et al., 2012). In this research, we used bigram nodes. The measure expresses the common edges between two graphs by the number of edges of the smaller graph.

$$CS(G_T, G_S) = \frac{\sum_{e=G_T} \mu(e, G_S)}{min(|G_T|, |G_S|)} \tag{1}$$

Where GT (target graph) is the word graph of a tweet, Gs (source graph) is the word graph of an irony classes. The graph size can be the number of nodes or edges that are contained. e is an edge of a word graph.

3.3.2 Maximum Common Sub graph

The maximum common sub graph similarity is based on the size of the graph. We used the three variations of the metric are described in the equation 2, 3 and 4

$$MCSNS = \frac{MCSN(|G_T|, |G_S|)}{min(|G_T|, |G_S|)} \tag{2}$$

Maximum Common Sub graph Node Similarity (MCSNS): where MCSNS (GT (target graph) — Gs (source graph)) is the total number of nodes that are contained in the MCS of that graphs..

$$MCSUES = \frac{MCSUE(|G_T|, |G_S|)}{min(|G_T|, |G_S|)} \tag{3}$$

Maximum Common Sub graph Edge Similarity (MCSNS): where MCSUE (GT (target graph) — Gs (source graph)) is the total number of the edges contained in the MCS regardless the direction of them.

$$MCSDES = \frac{MCSDE(|G_T|, |G_S|)}{min(|G_T|, |G_S|)} \tag{4}$$

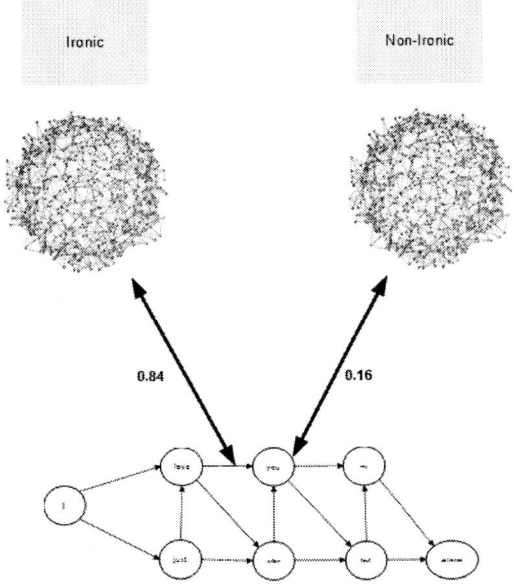

Figure 2: Graph Similarity Feature Extraction for one measure. The graph of a tweet used to compare with training data class graphs, in order to produce two numbers (depending upon the numbers of classes). These numbers will be used as a feature vector. The feature vector is provided to trained model to predict the class of the new tweet.

Maximum Common Sub graph Directed Edge Similarity (MCSNS): where MCSDES (GT (target graph) — Gs (source graph)) is the number of the edges contained in the MCS and have the same direction in the graphs.

3.3.3 Tweet Polarity and Latent Dirichlet Allocation

We used the SenticNet library to calculate the sentence polarity score as well as subjectivity score. Moreover, we also perform latent Dirichlet Allocation on the corpus and then used the trained model to calculate similarity helinger distance for each class (Blei et al., 2003; Beran, 1977).

3.4 Model Selection

In this paper, we used Tree-based Pipeline Optimization Tool (TPOT) that designs and optimizes the machine learning pipelines by using an evolutionary algorithm (Olson et al., 2016). The labelled data are provided for TPOT classification. Both TPOT classes return hyper tune model for both types of data (binary and Multiclass problem). After, data analysis, it was observed that the number of classes in the multiclass dataset is a

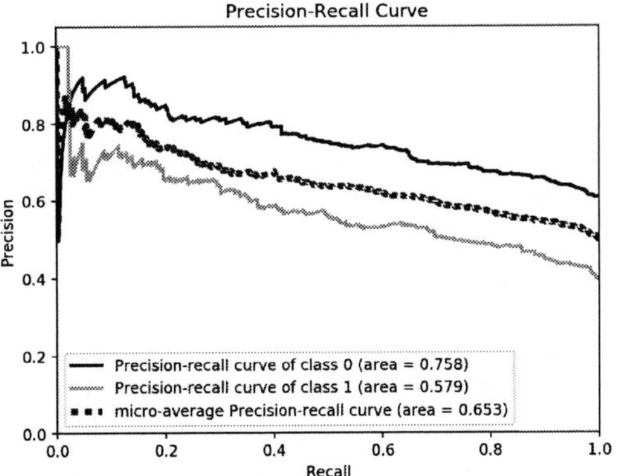

Figure 3: Precision Recall Curve of Binary Class problem

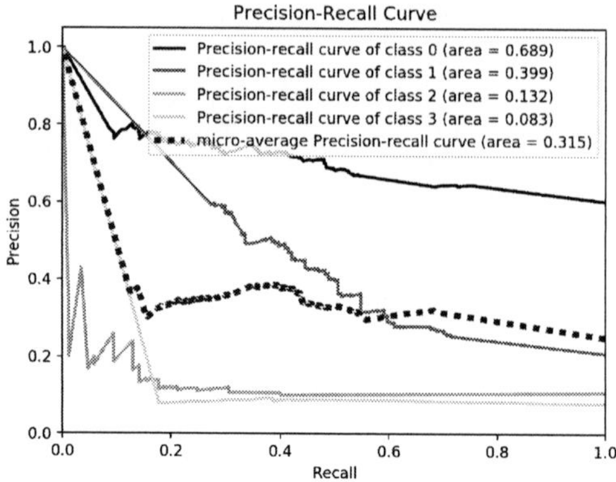

Figure 4: Precision Recall Curve of Multi Class problem

significant imbalance, which gives rise to the class imbalance problem. In order to handle this problem, we used SMOTE (Cummins et al., 2017) a Python toolbox to tackle the curse of imbalanced data. For binary classification problem, TPOT gives extreme gradient boosting classifier tune parameters. For the multiclass problem, TPOT gives stacking of extreme gradient boosting classifiers, extra trees classifier and random forest classifier.

4   Results Evaluation

For experimentation, we used efficient tool sklearn (Machine Learning Library) to train machine models mentioned above (Pedregosa et al., 2011). For both model hold on strategy was adopted. Training data contain 80% (3,833 instances) and testing sets 20% (958 instances). Our system ranked 23 in the Coda Lab result of the binary classification problem. The binary class system achieves accuracy 0.6135, precision 0.5091, recall 0.7170 and F measure 0.5955. After the release of the gold set, the model is again tuned by using TPOT library and result are evaluated as seen in Figure 3. Our system ranked 22 in the Coda Lab result of the multi-class problem. The multiclass model achieves the accuracy 0.4158, precision 0.4055, recall 0.3526 and f measure 0.3101. After the release of the gold set model was retrained and evaluated. The result of the multiclass problem is shown in Figure 4

5   Conclusion and Analysis

An innovative citation classification technique is proposed that combines the well-described structure of graphs with classification algorithm. The word graphs can seize the collection of the words that are contained in a tweet. The tweet word graph is generated and then by using several graph similarity techniques is applied to the dataset. These graph similarity metrics output is represented as a feature vector by the classification algorithm. It is concluded that word graph with different vicinity window is a good source of information to classify irony in the tweet. The model can be improved by using a large dataset. The proposed method can be enhanced by using a different graph similarity metric as features. The word graph construction method with different vicinity window size might improve results.

References

Fotis Aisopos, George Papadakis, Konstantinos Tserpes, and Theodora Varvarigou. 2012. Content vs. context for sentiment analysis: a comparative analysis over microblogs. In *Proceedings of the 23rd ACM conference on Hypertext and social media*, pages 187–196. ACM.

Laura Alba-Juez and Salvatore Attardo. 2014. The evaluative palette of verbal irony. *Evaluation in context*, 242:93.

Rudolf Beran. 1977. Minimum hellinger distance estimates for parametric models. *The annals of Statistics*, pages 445–463.

David M Blei, Andrew Y Ng, and Michael I Jordan. 2003. Latent dirichlet allocation. *Journal of machine Learning research*, 3(Jan):993–1022.

Chris Cummins, Pavlos Petoumenos, Zheng Wang, and Hugh Leather. 2017. Synthesizing benchmarks for predictive modeling. In *Code Generation and Optimization (CGO), 2017 IEEE/ACM International Symposium on*, pages 86–99. IEEE.

Veronique Hoste Cynthia Van Hee, Els Lefever. 2018. Semeval-2018 task 3: Irony detection in english tweets. in proceedings of the 12th international workshop on semantic evaluation.

Delia Irazú Hernańdez Farías, Viviana Patti, and Paolo Rosso. 2016. Irony detection in twitter: The role of affective content. *ACM Transactions on Internet Technology (TOIT)*, 16(3):19.

George Giannakopoulos, Vangelis Karkaletsis, George Vouros, and Panagiotis Stamatopoulos. 2008. Summarization system evaluation revisited: N-gram graphs. *ACM Transactions on Speech and Language Processing (TSLP)*, 5(3):5.

H Paul Grice. 1975. Logic and conversationin p. cole and j. morgan (eds.) syntax and semantics volume 3: Speech acts.

Irazú Hernández-Farías, José-Miguel Benedí, and Paolo Rosso. 2015. Applying basic features from sentiment analysis for automatic irony detection. In *Iberian Conference on Pattern Recognition and Image Analysis*, pages 337–344. Springer.

Brendan S Kelly, Ciaran E Redmond, Gregory J Nason, Gerard M Healy, Niall A Horgan, and Eric J Heffernan. 2016. The use of twitter by radiology journals: an analysis of twitter activity and impact factor. *Journal of the American College of Radiology*, 13(11):1391–1396.

R Kreuz. 2001. Using figurative language to increase advertising effectiveness. In *Office of naval research military personnel research science workshop. Memphis, TN*.

Andrew L Maas, Raymond E Daly, Peter T Pham, Dan Huang, Andrew Y Ng, and Christopher Potts. 2011. Learning word vectors for sentiment analysis. In *Proceedings of the 49th annual meeting of the association for computational linguistics: Human language technologies-volume 1*, pages 142–150. Association for Computational Linguistics.

Randal S Olson, Nathan Bartley, Ryan J Urbanowicz, and Jason H Moore. 2016. Evaluation of a tree-based pipeline optimization tool for automating data science. In *Proceedings of the Genetic and Evolutionary Computation Conference 2016*, pages 485–492. ACM.

Fabian Pedregosa, Gaël Varoquaux, Alexandre Gramfort, Vincent Michel, Bertrand Thirion, Olivier Grisel, Mathieu Blondel, Peter Prettenhofer, Ron Weiss, Vincent Dubourg, et al. 2011. Scikit-learn: Machine learning in python. *Journal of machine learning research*, 12(Oct):2825–2830.

Andrew Perrin. 2015. Social media usage: 2005-2015.

Antonio Reyes, Paolo Rosso, and Davide Buscaldi. 2009. Humor in the blogosphere: First clues for a verbal humor taxonomy. *Journal of Intelligent Systems*, 18(4):311–332.

Antonio Reyes, Paolo Rosso, and Tony Veale. 2013. A multidimensional approach for detecting irony in twitter. *Language resources and evaluation*, 47(1):239–268.

Sara Rosenthal, Noura Farra, and Preslav Nakov. 2017. Semeval-2017 task 4: Sentiment analysis in twitter. In *Proceedings of the 11th International Workshop on Semantic Evaluation (SemEval-2017)*, pages 502–518.

Luís Sarmento, Paula Carvalho, Mário J Silva, and Eugénio De Oliveira. 2009. Automatic creation of a reference corpus for political opinion mining in user-generated content. In *Proceedings of the 1st international CIKM workshop on Topic-sentiment analysis for mass opinion*, pages 29–36. ACM.

Twitter Usage Statistics. 2014. Internet live stats.

Pontus Stenetorp, Sampo Pyysalo, Goran Topić, Tomoko Ohta, Sophia Ananiadou, and Jun'ichi Tsujii. 2012. Brat: a web-based tool for nlp-assisted text annotation. In *Proceedings of the Demonstrations at the 13th Conference of the European Chapter of the Association for Computational Linguistics*, pages 102–107. Association for Computational Linguistics.

Akira Utsumi. 1996. A unified theory of irony and its computational formalization. In *Proceedings of the 16th conference on Computational linguistics-Volume 2*, pages 962–967. Association for Computational Linguistics.

Cynthia Van Hee. 2017. *Can machines sense irony?: exploring automatic irony detection on social media*. Ph.D. thesis, Ghent University.

Cynthia Van Hee, Els Lefever, and Véronique Hoste. 2016. Exploring the realization of irony in twitter data. In *LREC*.

Lancaster at SemEval-2018 Task 3: Investigating Ironic Features in English Tweets

Edward Dearden and Alistair Baron

School of Computing and Communications
Lancaster University
Lancaster, UK, LA1 4WA
`initial.surname@lancaster.ac.uk`

Abstract

This paper describes the system we submitted to SemEval-2018 Task 3. The aim of the system is to distinguish between irony and non-irony in English tweets. We create a targeted feature set and analyse how different features are useful in the task of irony detection, achieving an F_1-score of 0.5914. The analysis of individual features provides insight that may be useful in future attempts at detecting irony in tweets.

1   Introduction

With so many people using social media and microblogs such as Twitter, a huge amount of natural language data is available to be analysed. It is desirable to be able to accurately interpret what people are saying. An example of this is in the field of sentiment analysis where the aim is to determine whether the language being used by an author is positive or negative.

These kinds of tasks are made more difficult by the presence of figurative language. Figurative language is a type of language where the contents of the text are not literally true, making it difficult to ascertain the true meaning of the text purely from the content. Irony is a particular type of figurative language in which the meaning is often the opposite of what is literally said and is not always evident without context or existing knowledge. A system capable of accurately detecting irony would be a valuable addition to sentiment analysis systems, and other systems for natural language understanding which are confounded by irony.

In online discourse, examples of irony are very common. Social media platforms capture natural language which often includes sarcastic sentences. An example of a use for irony detection is in the area of online product reviews (Tsur et al., 2010)

which can contain large amounts of ironic language. An irony detection system could be used to prevent ironic negative reviews being misinterpreted as positive and highlighted in advertising.

The system described in this paper aims to identify targeted features of irony and analyse how important they are in identifying ironic tweets. The annotated twitter data we use is that provided by the event organisers. The task is described in the task description paper (Van Hee et al., 2018).

2   Related Work

The task of irony detection is an inherently difficult one. Wallace (2015) suggests that to create a good system for irony detection, one cannot rely on lexical features such as Bag of Words, and one must consider also semantic features of the text.

There have been various methods employed to detect irony. Reyes et al. (2012) created a dataset generated by searching for user-created tags and attempted to identify humour and irony. The features used to detect irony were polarity, unexpectedness, and emotional scenarios. Their classifier achieved an F_1-score of 0.54 for general tweets of various topics, rising to 0.65 when the irony features were combined with the ambiguity features used to detect humour. The score also improved when looking at domain specific tweets, suggesting domain knowledge and context can be useful for identifying irony.

More recently, Van Hee et al. (2016a) investigated annotated ironic tweet corpora and suggested that looking at contrasting evaluations within tweets could be useful for detecting irony. Van Hee et al. (2016b) also created a system to detect ironic tweets, looking beyond text-based features, using a feature set made up of lexical, syntactic, sentiment, and semantic features. They achieved an F_1-score of 0.68. They also suggested

Proceedings of the 12th International Workshop on Semantic Evaluation (SemEval-2018), pages 587–593
New Orleans, Louisiana, June 5–6, 2018. ©2018 Association for Computational Linguistics

that irony by polarity clash was more simple to detect than other forms of irony, e.g. situational irony.

A number of works have looked at detecting sarcastic tweets. Sarcasm is a type of irony in which the meaning is the opposite of what is literally said. Maynard and Greenwood (2014) used a rule based system to supplement sentiment analysis systems by flipping the predicted polarity of a tweet if it contained a mismatch of sentiment between hashtag and text. They achieved an F_1-Score of 0.91. Davidov et al. (2010) used pattern-based and punctuation-based features, achieving an F_1-Score of 0.83. González-Ibáñez et al. (2011) combined lexical and pragmatic features, aiming to distinguish between sarcastic, positive, and negative utterances. Their classifiers achieved 70% accuracy distinguishing between sarcasm and positive tweets and between sarcasm and negative tweets. Barbieri et al. (2014) looked at distinguishing sarcasm from other domains of text including irony. They achieved an F_1-score of 0.60 when differentiating between sarcasm and irony compared to 0.89 when differentiating between sarcasm and politics. These findings suggest that it is easier to distinguish sarcastic tweets over irony in general. This could link to Van Hee et al. (2016b)'s finding that situational irony and other types of irony are harder to detect than irony by polarity clash. Given much of the irony in tweets is sarcasm, looking at some of these features may be useful.

One challenge for irony detection is that the understanding of irony often relies on context. There is certain contextual information that is required for a human to parse a sentence as being ironic. For example, the sentence "I am soooo happy to be going to the dentist tomorrow" would only be noticed as being ironic if the reader understood that the word 'dentist' has certain negative associations. Rajadesingan et al. (2015) tries to address this challenge by looking at more behavioural aspects of irony including looking at positive and negative associations of certain words, achieving an accuracy of 83%.

Other approaches have aimed to capture the context in which a tweet was posted for irony detection. Bamman and Smith (2015) used author and audience features on top of tweet features. These features looked at the past tweets of authors and the people to whom the tweet is responding.

Their best performance was 85% accuracy. Wang et al. (2015) used three types of history of the tweet to try and bring in additional context: history of the conversation; history of the author; and history of the hashtag/topic. They improved the baseline F_1-Score of 0.55 to 0.60.

3　System Description

The developed system uses only the text data of the tweets provided with the task. It does not handle any contextual features as these would require gathering previous tweets and responses. The classifier we used was a standard, untuned SVM. As much of the code as possible has been made publicly available so it can be replicated[1]. There are certain parts of the system that cannot be shared, such as the USAS tagging system[2].

In the preprocessing stage the tweets were reduced to just the text, separately extracting emojis, hashtags, and user mentions, for use as features. Most of the processing of the text was performed with the python Natural Language Toolkit (NLTK) (Bird and Loper, 2004), including using the NLTK Tweet Tokeniser to tokenise the text.

For classification we used the Linear SVC implementation in the popular python machine learning package scikit-learn (Pedregosa et al., 2011). We performed no tuning of the model as we were more interested in features and their usefulness than gaining the maximum precision and we wanted to avoid overfitting. We also used a random forest classifier to compare results.

3.1　Features

The features used by this system fall into four main categories: Tweet-level features, Bag-of-X features, Sentiment features, and Complexity features. All feature values were normalised so they were between 0 and 1.

Tweet Features are the non-language features contained directly within the contents of the tweet. These features include punctuation, hashtags and emoji. These have been used in past research and found to be useful for the task. It is thought that these features are used to flag a tweet as ironic. As there were many different types of emoji used on Twitter, some very infrequently, the emojis, punctuation, and hashtags used were restricted to the

---

[1] `https://github.com/dearden/SemEval2018-Irony`
[2] `http://ucrel.lancs.ac.uk/usas/`

top 50 by frequency over the whole training set of each. Each of these top 50 were a feature and their value was 0 or 1 based on whether or not the token was present in the text. The tweets were tokenised such that repeated punctuation marks were counted as a single token. For example, "..." would be counted as a single token, not 3 instances of ".". We also count examples of repeated characters, e.g. in "Greeeeat!", and the proportion of the tweet that is capitalised. Other tweet features were: Number of links, number of mentions, number of hashtags, Tweet length, average word length, and amount of punctuation.

Bag-of-X Features is the set of features which contain the 1000 most frequent tokens of various types. The tokens used for these features were: word unigrams, word bigrams, character trigrams, POS tags, and Semantic tags. For the POS tagging, we used the NLTK POS tagger (Bird and Loper, 2004) and for Semantic tagging, the USAS semantic tagger (Rayson et al., 2004). Semantic tags put each word (or multi-word expression) into semantic categories, providing knowledge if some texts contain more emotion-based terms or more science and technology terms, for example. This should provide a higher level view of the text than achieved by bag of words. Using these techniques is like casting a wide net over the text that may find characteristics of irony not picked up by the more targeted features. They are also included to test the theory that lexical features are not useful for the task of irony detection.

For **Sentiment Features** we used a popular python package VaderSentiment (Pedregosa et al., 2011). Sentiment features may be important because if irony involves saying something positive to mean something negative, it may be that contrasts in sentiment or extreme values of sentiment are features of irony. The sentiment features gathered were: Positive sentiment score, negative sentiment score, mean score, standard deviation, range, average change of sentiment between adjacent words, number of positive to negative transitions, and emoji sentiment. When looking at changing sentiments, we modelled each sentence as a collection of words that were either positive, negative or neutral. We looked at the way the words in the sentence transitioned between positive and negative. For example, the sentence "I love how awful everything is right now", would have one transition between "love" and "awful".

Emoji Sentiments were used from the work of Kralj Novak et al. (2015) on the sentiment of emojis. We included the mean, maximum, and minimum emoji sentiment, as well as the number of positive and negative emojis.

The **Complexity features** we gathered were: negations, function words, number of syllables, Automated Readability Index, ambiguity, lexical diversity, and lexical density. These features were included to examine the difference in complexity and style between ironic and non-ironic tweets. Ambiguity was calculated as the average number of meanings for each word in the sentence according to WordNet (Kilgarriff, 2000).

3.2 Feature Sets

We tested the system with seven feature sets. The first four feature sets (Tweet, Bag-of-X, Sentiment, and Complexity) are as described above. The other three are as follows:

Submission: A combination of Tweet, Complexity, and Sentiment Features as described above containing 126 features.

Reduced: A reduced version of the submission set with the token frequency features (Emoji, Punctuation) removed. The idea of this set is to see if keeping only a focussed set of features impacts performance. This set contains 27 features.

Combined: All the features combined together to see whether performance is increased by using all the features. Contains 3,537 features.

The features representing occurrences of individual hashtags were omitted as they did not repeat very often and we did not want the model to overfit. Also, as the data was gathered using hashtags we were concerned that certain hashtags would be used in conjunction with the hashtags used to gather the data and may not be representative of irony generally. We left the Bag-of-X features out of the submission feature set because we did not want this set being too large and overfitting. With our submission set, we aimed to use targeted features as opposed to data-driven features such as bag-of-words and character n-grams. This makes the system more explainable, with the reasoning pre-defined. With data-driven features, especially character n-grams, it can be difficult to explain

Feature set	Precision	Recall	F_1 Score
Baseline	0.5296	0.5756	0.5516
Tweet	0.5209	**0.7203**	**0.6046**
Bag-of-X	0.5153	0.5949	0.5522
Sentiment	0.4691	0.5370	0.5007
Complexity	0.4350	0.6238	0.5125
Submission	0.5321	0.6656	0.5914
Reduced	0.5385	0.6527	0.5901
Combined	**0.5387**	0.6495	0.5889

Table 1: Results of Linear SVC on test set.

why features are useful for the task. For the reduced set we went further, omitting all of the data-driven features. This meant removing Emoji and punctuation features so the feature set was more likely to capture the true features of irony as well as being more explainable.

One drawback of our feature extraction is the noisiness of the text. The NLTK POS tagger and VADER Sentiment only perform well with standard text. If we had performed better normalisation on the text before extracting Bag-of-X and Sentiment features, these feature sets may have performed better.

4 Results and Discussion

We ran the classifier with a number of different feature sets to assess the power of different types of feature. Bag-of-Words using all word tokens was used as a baseline to compare the other feature sets to. The bag-of-words implementation we used was slightly different to the baseline provided with the task in so far as it does not use Scikit-learn's in-built Vectoriser. As well as the baseline bag of words, seven feature sets were evaluated, as described in Section 3.2.

The results from our system can be seen in Table 1, with a Linear SVC. The tweet feature set was more useful than expected, with the highest F_1 Score. This suggests that twitter users communicate elements of what they mean via emojis, punctuation, and the way they present their tweets. The high recall means that this feature set is causing many tweets to be flagged as ironic. However, given in most real data there are likely to be fewer ironic tweets than non-ironic, high precision may be more desirable than high recall. Another concern with relying on these features is that an irony detection implementation that is clueless if a tweet contains no emojis or hashtags is not an effective

system. This may also explain why the Tweet features did not achieve higher results. Many ironic tweets do not contain emojis or punctuation that flag their irony. The bag-of-x features and the baseline performed similarly, both getting an F_1 Score of around 0.55. The addition of Bigrams, Trigrams, POS and Semantic tags does not seem to have increased the accuracy. The performance of these feature sets is not surprising as the features were in no way targeted to irony. This supports the findings of Wallace (2015) that lexical features alone are not effective at identifying irony. The sentiment features performed the worst. This is in line with the results of Van Hee et al. (2016b), which also showed sentiment to be the weakest individual group. The reduced set performed almost as well as the submission set which is promising given it contained 99 fewer features, showing that specific targeted features are of most use.

With a random forest classifier, the results also found the Tweet feature set achieved the highest F_1 score of 0.5903 compared to the Baseline feature set score of 0.4957. The next highest was the Reduced feature set which achieved a score of 0.5657, outperforming both the Submission and Combined sets. This might be because it contains less sparse features which tree classifiers prefer, or could suggest that the emoji and punctuation features are causing the classifier to overfit. Both the Tweet and Reduced feature set achieved much higher precision than with the Linear SVC, 0.5922 and 0.5936 respectively, but lower recall, 0.5884 and 0.5401.

Next we looked at features individually, rather than looking at groups. To do this we used the coefficients for each feature in the Linear SVC model. These are the weights used by the model to decide how much each feature should weigh in on the final decision.

First we look at the features in the reduced feature set. The results are shown in Table 2. This set is interesting because it only contains the more information-dense features. Number of links, the number of mentions, and the number of hashtags are all ranked highly for identifying non-ironic tweets. This may be because tweets that have high values for these features are more focussed on sharing links, for example images, with their friends. As the focus is more on the thing they are sharing rather than in the text, these tweets may be less likely to be ironic. These features are un-

Feature	Weight	Class
Number of Links	-2.52	Non-ironic
Number of Syllables	1.89	Ironic
Number of Mentions	-1.84	Non-ironic
Punctuation Count	-1.50	Non-ironic
Repeated Characters	1.42	Ironic
Function Words	-1.20	Non-ironic
Lexical Density	-1.18	Non-ironic
Mean Sentiment	1.09	Ironic
Capitalisation	-1.04	Non-ironic
Number of Hashtags	-1.04	Non-ironic

Table 2: Top 10 LinearSVC weightings in Reduced Feature Set.

likely to be useful for identifying non-irony outside of the twitter domain. Duplicate characters are highly weighted for identifying irony. This feature is often used to signpost irony by overemphasising the emotion they are expressing ironically such as in the case of, "Loooovvveeeeeee when my phone gets wiped". Another common use is repeated punctuation to make the point clear, for example, "Gotta love being lied to....".

Looking into the rankings of individual words also provides some insights. Three of the top ranking words indicating irony for the Linear SVC with the combined feature set were "love", "great", and "fun". It is interesting that these are all positive emotional words. This could suggest that it is more common for such tweets to use positive language with a true negative meaning. A lot of tweets follow the format of "I love when...", going on to describe a negative experience. These tweets are often given a positive sentiment as the negative part of the tweet doesn't always use negative language. This highlights the effect a lack of irony detection can have on sentiment analysis. The system could be more effective if it took into account negative concepts, for example "going to the dentist", that are not explicitly negative.

Our findings suggest that social elements and structure of tweets are important for distinguishing ironic tweets from non-ironic tweets. The words that rank highly support the claim of Van Hee et al. (2016b) that irony by contrast is the easiest to detect. Irony by contrast is the most highly represented type of irony in the corpus so in most cases of irony, such features will be useful for detection. A future system would look at semantic and contextual features in more depth.

4.1 Subtask B

Subtask B involved a more complex classification task in which the system had to distinguish between different types of irony. In this task, the potential labels given by the classifier were: 0 – Non-irony, 1 – Verbal irony realised through a polarity contrast, 2 – Descriptions of situational irony, and 3 – Verbal irony without a polarity contrast. These categories are explained in detail in the task description (Van Hee et al., 2018).

We used the same feature set used for task A, aiming to test whether the same features could classify between the different types of irony. The submitted result achieved an F_1-score of 0.3130. This result was gained using a Linear SVC classifier with the submission feature set and compared to the bag-of-words baseline F_1-score of 0.3198. The random forest classifier achieved an F_1-score of 0.3465. These results suggest more complex, tailored features would be needed for this task.

Both classifiers labelled the majority of tweets as 0 – non-ironic. The next most frequent label was 1 – irony by polarity contrast. This is likely to be because the features were aimed at detecting irony from non-irony and did not take into account situational information. The results seem to support the idea that irony detection via polarity contrast is the easiest to detect. This is further supported by the fact that 76% of the examples of other irony and situational irony were classified as non-ironic.

To investigate this further, we looked at the results from subtask A and looked at how many ironic by polarity contrast tweets were correctly labelled as ironic compared to the other two forms of irony. This was to see if, when the classifier was dealing with a binary ironic/non-ironic decision, it still had the same problem of not detecting examples of irony with no polarity contrast. 82% of the ironic by polarity contrast tweets were correctly labelled as ironic by the classifier, compared to 50% of the other types. This suggests that the classifier was using the features of polarity contrast to make its decisions. This makes sense as some of the features, especially those from the sentiment set, were targeted at detecting this type of irony with features such as number of positive to negative sentiment transitions.

As a final experiment, we trained the classifier with the ironic by polarity contrast tweets removed. 164 tweets from the test set and 1,390 from the training set were removed, leaving a test set of 473 non-ironic and 147 ironic tweets and a training set of 1,923 non-ironic and 521 ironic tweets. The aim was seeing if the system could distinguish between non-irony and irony with the easiest to detect tweets removed. In this setup, the classifier only correctly labelled 4 out of the 147 ironic tweets as ironic. This suggests that it is much harder to distinguish between non-ironic text and these two forms of irony. More complex features that directly look at context may be needed for this task.

5   Conclusion

In this paper, we have described a system for the detection of irony using targetted features. The resulting F_1-score of 0.59 was an improvement over the baseline bag-of-words. The analysis of our findings provided insight into the features that are particularly useful for detecting irony. Tweet features performed well suggesting that Twitter users potentially broadcast their meaning using features such as emojis and structure. We also investigated how our system performed when distinguishing between different types of irony. Our findings suggest that deeper, more complex features will be needed to accurately identify situational irony and irony with no polarity contrast. We could improve our system by looking into contextual and semantic features. For example, we looked into sentiment of words, but not at words with positive and negative associations in certain contexts. Our analysis provides insights that may be useful for future research into irony detection.

References

David Bamman and Noah A Smith. 2015. Contextualized sarcasm detection on twitter. In *ICWSM*, pages 574–577.

Francesco Barbieri, Horacio Saggion, and Francesco Ronzano. 2014. Modelling sarcasm in twitter, a novel approach. In *Proceedings of the 5th Workshop on Computational Approaches to Subjectivity, Sentiment and Social Media Analysis*, pages 50–58.

Steven Bird and Edward Loper. 2004. Nltk: the natural language toolkit. In *Proceedings of the ACL 2004 on Interactive poster and demonstration sessions*, page 31. Association for Computational Linguistics.

Dmitry Davidov, Oren Tsur, and Ari Rappoport. 2010. Semi-supervised recognition of sarcastic sentences in twitter and amazon. In *Proceedings of the Fourteenth Conference on Computational Natural Language Learning*, CoNLL '10, pages 107–116, Stroudsburg, PA, USA. Association for Computational Linguistics.

Roberto González-Ibáñez, Smaranda Muresan, and Nina Wacholder. 2011. Identifying sarcasm in twitter: A closer look. In *Proceedings of the 49th Annual Meeting of the Association for Computational Linguistics: Human Language Technologies: Short Papers - Volume 2*, HLT '11, pages 581–586, Stroudsburg, PA, USA. Association for Computational Linguistics.

Adam Kilgarriff. 2000. Wordnet: An electronic lexical database.

Petra Kralj Novak, Jasmina Smailovi, Borut Sluban, and Igor Mozeti. 2015. Sentiment of emojis. *PLOS ONE*, 10(12):1–22.

Diana Maynard and Mark Greenwood. 2014. Who cares about sarcastic tweets? investigating the impact of sarcasm on sentiment analysis. In *Proceedings of the Ninth International Conference on Language Resources and Evaluation (LREC-2014)*. European Language Resources Association (ELRA).

Fabian Pedregosa, Gaël Varoquaux, Alexandre Gramfort, Vincent Michel, Bertrand Thirion, Olivier Grisel, Mathieu Blondel, Peter Prettenhofer, Ron Weiss, Vincent Dubourg, et al. 2011. Scikit-learn: Machine learning in python. *Journal of machine learning research*, 12(Oct):2825–2830.

Ashwin Rajadesingan, Reza Zafarani, and Huan Liu. 2015. Sarcasm detection on twitter: A behavioral modeling approach. In *Proceedings of the Eighth ACM International Conference on Web Search and Data Mining*, WSDM '15, pages 97–106, New York, NY, USA. ACM.

Paul Rayson, Dawn Archer, Scott Piao, and Anthony M McEnery. 2004. The ucrel semantic analysis system.

Antonio Reyes, Paolo Rosso, and Davide Buscaldi. 2012. From humor recognition to irony detection: The figurative language of social media. *Data Knowl. Eng.*, 74:1–12.

Oren Tsur, Dmitry Davidov, and Ari Rappoport. 2010. Icwsm-a great catchy name: Semi-supervised recognition of sarcastic sentences in online product reviews.

Cynthia Van Hee, Els Lefever, and Véronique Hoste. 2016a. Exploring the realization of irony in twitter data. In *LREC*.

Cynthia Van Hee, Els Lefever, and Veronique Hoste. 2016b. Monday mornings are my fave : #not exploring the automatic recognition of irony in english tweets. In *Proceedings of COLING 2016, 26th International Conference on Computational Linguistics*, pages 2730–2739. ACL.

Cynthia Van Hee, Els Lefever, and Véronique Hoste. 2018. SemEval-2018 Task 3: Irony Detection in English Tweets. In *Proceedings of the 12th International Workshop on Semantic Evaluation*, SemEval-2018, New Orleans, LA, USA. Association for Computational Linguistics.

Byron C. Wallace. 2015. Computational irony: A survey and new perspectives. *Artif. Intell. Rev.*, 43(4):467–483.

Zelin Wang, Zhijian Wu, Ruimin Wang, and Yafeng Ren. 2015. Twitter sarcasm detection exploiting a context-based model. In *Proceedings, Part I, of the 16th International Conference on Web Information Systems Engineering — WISE 2015 - Volume 9418*, pages 77–91, New York, NY, USA. Springer-Verlag New York, Inc.

INAOE-UPV at SemEval-2018 Task 3:
An Ensemble Approach for Irony Detection in Twitter

Delia Irazú Hernández Farías[1], Fernando Sánchez-Vega[1]
Manuel Montes-y-Gómez[1,2], and Paolo Rosso[2]
[1] Instituto Nacional de Astrofísica, Óptica y Electrónica (INAOE), Mexico
[2] PRHLT Research Center, Universitat Politècnica de València, Spain
{dirazuherfa,fer.callotl,mmontesg}@inaoep.mx
prosso@dsic.upv.es

Abstract

This paper describes an ensemble approach to the SemEval-2018 Task 3. The proposed method is composed of two renowned methods in text classification together with a novel approach for capturing ironic content by exploiting a tailored lexicon for irony detection. We experimented with different ensemble settings. The obtained results show that our method has a good performance for detecting the presence of ironic content in Twitter.

1 Introduction

Social media provide a perfect scenario for exploiting language beyond its literal sense by using figurative language devices such as, for example, irony. Correctly identifying the real intention behind user-generated content is a big challenge for different areas related to computational linguistics. For example, in Sentiment Analysis (SA), the presence of irony could undermine the performance of systems dedicated to this task (Hernández Farías and Rosso, 2016). There are several disciplines studying irony from different perspectives. The most prevalent definition is that from Grice (1975), stating that the function of irony is to effectively communicate the opposite of the literal interpretation a given utterance.

Nowadays, with the growing interest in irony detection, there are several approaches[1] for addressing such an interesting task. Probably, the most widely used is that exploiting characteristics extracted from the text (such as n-grams, punctuation marks, part-of-speech labels, among others) on its own (Riloff et al., 2013; Ptáček et al., 2014). Inherent aspects of irony such as its very subjective component have also been considered (Reyes et al., 2013; Barbieri et al., 2014; Hernández Farías

---

[1] For a more comprehensive overview of irony detection, see (Joshi et al., 2017).

et al., 2016). Other methods have opted for taking advantage of information coming from the context in which a given utterance is produced (Rajadesingan et al., 2015). There are also some approaches exploiting deep learning techniques and word embeddings (Poria et al., 2016; Ghosh and Veale, 2016; Joshi et al., 2016; Nozza et al., 2016). A less explored strategy for addressing irony detection is the use of ensemble methods. Fersini et al. (2015) and Liu et al. (2014) compared the performance of ensemble approaches against traditional classifiers; the best results were obtained by the ensemble strategy setting.

In this paper we describe our participation to the SemEval-2018 Task 3: Irony detection in English tweets (Van Hee et al., 2018). The INAOE-UPV system explores the use of an ensemble approach that considers different combinations of three methods. The main contribution of our approach lies on the use of a list of potentially ironic and non-ironic terms in order to identify irony in tweets.

2 Method Description

In order to determine the presence of ironic content in tweets, we propose an ensemble of different methods, namely, a bag-of-words and word embeddings classifiers, as well as a voting scheme based on a list of potentially ironic and non-ironic terms.

2.1 Individual classifiers
Ironic/nonironic Orientation (irO)

This approach attempts to capture the *ironic* and *non-ironic* connotation of the words in a tweet in order to identify the presence of ironic content. Building a lexicon for irony detection is not a trivial task. It has been recognized in (Nozza et al., 2016) that a lexicon for irony detection can be derived by using a huge amount of data.

Proceedings of the 12th International Workshop on Semantic Evaluation (SemEval-2018), pages 594–599
New Orleans, Louisiana, June 5–6, 2018. ©2018 Association for Computational Linguistics

To develop a lexicon for irony detection it is needed to calculate how much a word could be associated with an ironic or non-ironic sense. A widely exploited measure in SA for developing lexica is the Pointwise Mutual Information (PMI) (Church and Hanks, 1990). We decided to adopt a similar strategy to generate two lists of terms associated to ironic and non-ironic senses. As starting point we took advantage of a set of corpora from the state of the art in irony detection (henceforth *benchmark-corpora*). The datasets we used are described in (Reyes et al., 2013; Riloff et al., 2013; Barbieri et al., 2014; Ptáček et al., 2014; Mohammad et al., 2015; Ghosh et al., 2015; Sulis et al., 2016; Karoui et al., 2017). Overall, more than 165,000 tweets were used to generate the lists of words: *ironic_terms* and *nonironic_terms*. We calculate the PMI score for each term[2] in the *benchmark-corpora*. After that, we selected only those terms with a PMI score greater than zero.

In order to determine the class of an instance we assigned a vote (v) for each word (w) in a given tweet (t). First, we filter out the stopwords in each tweet. Then, we search for the most similar term in each of the lists in order to determine whether w is more related to an ironic or non-ironic sense. Mainly we compute a score that indicates the higher cosine similarity[3] among w and each of the N terms defined in our lists of words. As expected, the score for the words in t that are directly included in *ironic_terms* or *nonironic_terms* will be 1.

$$simIro(w) = \max_{j=1...N}(sim(w, ironic\_terms_j))$$

$$simNI(w) = \max_{j=1...N}(sim(w, nonironic\_terms_j))$$

After this, the vote $v(w)$ is assigned according to the following criterion:

$$v(w) = \begin{cases} simIro & \text{if } simIro > simNI \\ -simNI & \text{if } simIro < simNI \end{cases} \quad (1)$$

Finally, the class of a tweet is determined by the sum of the votes from all words in t.

$$class(t) = \begin{cases} \text{irony} & \text{if } \sum_{i=1}^{|t|} v(w \in t) \geq 0 \\ \text{non-irony} & otherwise \end{cases}$$

---

[2]We removed those terms that occurred less than five times in each class.

[3]We calculated the cosine similarity exploiting pre-trained word vectors from the Google News Corpus.

Bag-of-words based classifier (BOW)

This approach is based on a bag-of-words (Salton et al., 1975) representation of the tweets. It uses unigrams as binary features. For the classification it employs a SVM classifier[4]. From here, we will use the acronym **BOW** to refer the use of the aforementioned individual approach.

Word Embeddings based classifier (wEmb)

This approach is based on the use of word embeddings. Particularly, it employs embeddings pre-trained on the Google News corpus (Mikolov et al., 2013) using the Continuous Bag-of-Words (CBOW) model[5]. In this case, tweets are represented by the centroid of the vectors from their words. Similar to the BOW approach, the classification is done by a SVM classifier. From now on the acronym **wEmb** will be used to refer to this approach.

2.2 Ensemble approaches for irony detection

We explored the use of different techniques relying on the words content in each tweet in order to identify the presence of irony. Each of the techniques we exploited has its own advantages and limitations. The **BOW** model allows to capture the existing topics in the vocabulary as well as discursive markers used in an ironic writing style. On the other hand, **wEmb** makes possible to catch abstract semantics of the words regardless of the available data for the task. With respect to **irO**, it attempts to simulate the interpretative process carried out to understand the ironic intention. Irony comprehension at an initial stage involves getting the literal sense of words (Giora and Fein, 1999) and then recognizing the figurative intention behind them. Thus, our method quantifies how many words are likely to be used in a literal or figurative sense before deciding whether a tweet is ironic or not. By proposing an ensemble using all the methods together we attempt to encompass different aspects of the use of vocabulary when the ironic phenomenon is present. Below, we introduce some

---

[4]We employed the SVM implementation of Weka (Hall et al., 2009).

[5]We also experimented with word embeddings trained using the benchmark corpora obtaining lower results than with Google News embeddings. Therefore, in order to participate in the shared task we decided to include only the latest kinds of embeddings.

ensemble approaches[6] proposed for capturing the presence of irony in Twitter.

Coverage-based ensemble (ENS_cov)

It is composed by BOW and wEmb. In Twitter data, there are many terms such as mentions, hashtags, emoji, URL, etc., that are unlikely to have an embedding. However, such kinds of terms are indeed covered by a model like BOW. To take advantage of both methods, we decided to combine them by considering a simple criterion depending on the coverage rate of the word embeddings (cov_emb) in each single tweet. That is, if the cov_emb is greater than 75%, the tweet will be classified by the wEmb model, otherwise the decision will be made by the BOW approach.

Majority vote ensemble (ENS_vot)

In this approach, the decisions from the three individual methods (irO, BOW and wEmb) are combined following a majority vote strategy.

3 Experiments and Results

3.1 Task Description

This year, as part of SemEval-2018 the Task 3 on *Irony detection in English tweets* (Van Hee et al., 2018), was dedicated to the identification of ironic content in Twitter. The task is composed by two subtasks: ***Task A. Ironic vs. non-ironic***, the aim was to identify whether a tweet contains an ironic intention or not. The objective of the second one, ***Task B. Different types of irony***, was to classify a tweet in one out of four classes: (i) verbal irony realized through a polarity contrast, (ii) other verbal irony, (iii) situational irony, and (iv) non ironic. Participants were allowed to submit two different kinds of systems: *Constrained (C)* where only data provided for the task were used for training purposes, and *Unconstrained (U)* where additional data were exploited.

3.1.1 Task A

In order to address Task A, we applied two different ensemble approaches. Our first submission was based on the coverage-based ensemble using a constrained setting (henceforth *taskA_ENS_cov_C*).

The second submission (henceforth *taskA_ENS_vot_U*) used the majority vote ensemble built on an unconstrained setting. BOW

and wEmb models were trained by using only the training set provided by the organizers. Instead, irO involves the use of the benchmark corpora. Additionally, we collected a set of tweets containing the hashtags #irony and #sarcasm during the 2016 US Elections week[7] as well as the training data provided for the task for building the lists of ironic and non-ironic terms.

For experimental purposes, we applied a three fold cross-validation using the training data during the developing phase of the shared task. Table 1 shows the obtained results in F_1-Score.

Method	F_1-Score
BOW	0.62
wEmb	0.64
irO	0.63
taskA_ENS_cov_C	0.63
taskA_ENS_vot_U	0.65

Table 1: Results during the developing phase in Task A.

First, we evaluated each of the methods described in Section 2 individually (the first three rows in Table 1). The first two rows present the obtained results when the performance of BOW and wEmb was assessed using only the training data. Meanwhile, irO exploits both data from the task and external data. The highest result was achieved by the wEmb model. Despite being a basic method for identifying irony in tweets, our proposed approach (irO) achieves good performance even in comparison to powerful techniques such as word embeddings. Regarding the ensemble approaches, the best performance was reached by the majority vote approach.

3.1.2 Task B

In order to address the Task B, we employed two different configurations of the majority vote approach (henceforth *taskB_ENS_vot_U1* and *taskB_ENS_vot_U2*), adding an additional criterion: in both cases, when the result of irO[8] indicates the presence of irony, we assigned one of the ironic-related classes by exploiting three different lists of words (one for each class in Task B) created following the same strategy described in Section 2.1. For *taskB_ENS_vot_U1*, the BOW and wEmb models were trained using the four classes in Task B; while in *taskB_ENS_vot_U2* four binary classifiers considering the combinations between

---

[6]Due to the lack of space we are not reporting all the experiments carried out.

[7]From 8th up to 18th November 2016.

[8]In this setting we also considered the corpora of the state of the art.

ironic classes and the non-ironic class in Task B. A weighted voting strategy was adopted in both ensembles. Table 2 shows the obtained results.

Method	F_1-Score
BOW	0.48
wEmb	0.31
irO	0.41
taskB_ENS_vot_U1	0.44
taskB_ENS_vot_U2	0.46

Table 2: Results during the developing phase in Task B.

The three methods were also evaluated individually for Task B. As it can be noticed, the best performance was achieved by BOW. The irO method performs better than wEmb. This is probably due to the fact of having few data for training the classifier. Neither of the ensemble methods improves the baseline, i.e., the BOW results.

3.2 Official Results

Table 3 shows the obtained results according to the official ranking of the shared task.

Task	Method	F1-score
A	*taskA_ENS_cov_C*	**0.6265**
	taskA_ENS_vot_U	0.6184
B	*taskB_ENS_vot_U1*	0.3497
	taskB_ENS_vot_U2	0.2148

Table 3: Official results obtained by our runs at the shared task. The underlined values are those in the official ranking of the task.

Our best result was in the constrained version of Task A (we ranked in the 11th position). Regarding this, our intuition is that having data retrieved during the same time-frame the probabilities of sharing a similar vocabulary[9] (in terms of trending-topic hashtags, mentions, etc.) are higher than when using external data. Therefore, an approach exploiting only data provided in the task could perform better than one using additional data. With reference to the unconstrained setting, we observed a drop in the performance. In spite of this, we ranked in the 2nd position when only unconstrained systems were considered.

Concerning Task B, our approach showed worst performance than in Task A. The results of both submissions were quite different. Probably this is due to the amount of classifiers involved in each ensemble. Overall, all the teams participating in

the shared task had a lower performance in Task B demonstrating the difficulty of such a task. It is important to highlight that the *taskB_ENS_vot_U2* submission ranked in the 3rd position when only the unconstrained setting was considered.

4 Error Analysis

We analyze those instances that were misclassified by our submissions in Task A observing different kinds of errors:

- Tweets where the ironic sense highly depends on the context where they are produced. In the following example it is not possible to understand the ironic intention without having more information: *@LukeLPearson hmm... let me think about that*[10]
- Tweets containing terms often used in ironic instances, such as "really". This is a disadvantage of word-based methods where terms highly related to a particular class provoke misleading classifications when they appear in other classes. The following is an example of this: *I'm really excited for next semester*[11]
- Tweets containing several hashtags. Most of the time our methods predicted such instances as ironic being in reality non-ironic: *@NormanWalshUK Stunning work. #british #textiles #footwear #madeinbritain #not-a-nike-clone*

5 Conclusions

In this paper we describe our participation at SemEval-2018 Task 3. We propose an ensemble method including well-known techniques together with a novel approach based on the words in a tweet to identify the presence of irony. From the results, we observe that our approach obtained relatively good results considering its simplicity. As future work, it could be interesting to enhance the tailored lexicon by exploiting more data and other strategies for collecting words which are likely to be used for achieving an ironic sense. Moreover, considering different criteria to assign the votes in our approach is also matter of further experiments.

Acknowledgments

This research was funded by CONACYT project FC-2016/2410. The work of Paolo Rosso has been funded by the SomEMBED TIN2015-71147-C2-1-P MINECO research project.

---

[9]We found that training and test data for the task share around fifty percent of the vocabulary.

[10]Predicted class: *non-ironic*, Real class: *ironic*.

[11]Predicted class: *ironic*, Real class: *non-ironic*.

References

Francesco Barbieri, Horacio Saggion, and Francesco Ronzano. 2014. Modelling Sarcasm in Twitter, a Novel Approach. In *Proceedings of the 5th Workshop on Computational Approaches to Subjectivity, Sentiment and Social Media Analysis*, pages 50–58, Baltimore, Maryland, USA. Association for Computational Linguistics.

Kenneth Ward Church and Patrick Hanks. 1990. Word association norms, mutual information, and lexicography. *Comput. Linguist.*, 16(1):22–29.

E. Fersini, F. A. Pozzi, and E. Messina. 2015. Detecting Irony and Sarcasm in Microblogs: The Role of Expressive Signals and Ensemble Classifiers. In *2015 IEEE International Conference on Data Science and Advanced Analytics (DSAA)*, pages 1–8.

Aniruddha Ghosh, Guofu Li, Tony Veale, Paolo Rosso, Ekaterina Shutova, John Barnden, and Antonio Reyes. 2015. SemEval-2015 Task 11: Sentiment Analysis of Figurative Language in Twitter. In *Proceedings of the 9th International Workshop on Semantic Evaluation*, pages 470–478, Denver, Colorado. Association for Computational Linguistics.

Aniruddha Ghosh and Tony Veale. 2016. Fracking Sarcasm using Neural Network. In *Proceedings of the 7th Workshop on Computational Approaches to Subjectivity, Sentiment and Social Media Analysis*, pages 161–169, San Diego, California. Association for Computational Linguistics.

Rachel Giora and Ofer Fein. 1999. Irony: Context and Salience. *Metaphor and Symbol*, 14(4):241–257.

H. P. Grice. 1975. Logic and Conversation. In P. Cole and J. L. Morgan, editors, *Syntax and Semantics: Vol. 3: Speech Acts*, pages 41–58. Academic Press.

Mark Hall, Eibe Frank, Geoffrey Holmes, Bernhard Pfahringer, Peter Reutemann, and Ian H. Witten. 2009. The WEKA Data Mining Software: An Update. *SIGKDD Explor. Newsl.*, 11(1):10–18.

Delia Irazú Hernández Farías, Viviana Patti, and Paolo Rosso. 2016. Irony Detection in Twitter: The Role of Affective Content. *ACM Trans. Internet Technol.*, 16(3):19:1–19:24.

Delia Irazú Hernández Farías and Paolo Rosso. 2016. Irony, Sarcasm, and Sentiment Analysis. Chapter 7. In Federico Pozzi, Elisabetta Fersini, Enza Messina, and Bing Liu, editors, *Sentiment Analysis in Social Networks*, pages 113–127. Morgan Kaufmann.

Aditya Joshi, Pushpak Bhattacharyya, and Mark J. Carman. 2017. Automatic Sarcasm Detection: A Survey. *ACM Comput. Surv.*, 50(5):73:1–73:22.

Aditya Joshi, Vaibhav Tripathi, Kevin Patel, Pushpak Bhattacharyya, and Mark James Carman. 2016. Are Word Embedding-based Features Useful for Sarcasm Detection? In *Proceedings of the 2016 Conference on Empirical Methods in Natural Language Processing*, pages 1006–1011.

Jihen Karoui, Farah Benamara, Veronique Moriceau, Viviana Patti, Cristina Bosco, and Nathalie Aussenac-Gilles. 2017. Exploring the Impact of Pragmatic Phenomena on Irony Detection in Tweets: A Multilingual Corpus Study. In *Proceedings of the 15th Conference of the European Chapter of the Association for Computational Linguistics*, Valencia, Spain.

Peng Liu, Wei Chen, Gaoyan Ou, Tengjiao Wang, Dongqing Yang, and Kai Lei. 2014. Sarcasm Detection in Social Media Based on Imbalanced Classification. In *Proceedings of the Web-Age Information Management: 15th International Conference*, pages 459–471, Macau, China. Springer International Publishing.

Tomas Mikolov, Ilya Sutskever, Kai Chen, Greg Corrado, and Jeffrey Dean. 2013. Distributed Representations of Words and Phrases and Their Compositionality. In *Proceedings of the 26th International Conference on Neural Information Processing Systems - Volume 2*, NIPS'13, pages 3111–3119.

Saif M. Mohammad, Xiaodan Zhu, Svetlana Kiritchenko, and Joel Martin. 2015. Sentiment, Emotion, Purpose, and Style in Electoral Tweets. *Information Processing & Management*, 51(4):480–499.

Debora Nozza, Elisabetta Fersini, and Enza Messina. 2016. Unsupervised Irony Detection: A Probabilistic Model with Word Embeddings. In *Proceedings of the 8th International Joint Conference on Knowledge Discovery, Knowledge Engineering and Knowledge Management*, pages 68–76.

Soujanya Poria, Erik Cambria, Devamanyu Hazarika, and Prateek Vij. 2016. A Deeper Look into Sarcastic Tweets Using Deep Convolutional Neural Networks. *CoRR*, abs/1610.08815.

Tomáš Ptáček, Ivan Habernal, and Jun Hong. 2014. Sarcasm Detection on Czech and English Twitter. In *Proceedings of the 25th International Conference on Computational Linguistics*, pages 213–223, Dublin, Ireland. Association for Computational Linguistics.

Ashwin Rajadesingan, Reza Zafarani, and Huan Liu. 2015. Sarcasm Detection on Twitter: A Behavioral Modeling Approach. In *Proceedings of the Eighth ACM International Conference on Web Search and Data Mining*, WSDM '15, pages 97–106.

Antonio Reyes, Paolo Rosso, and Tony Veale. 2013. A Multidimensional Approach for Detecting Irony in Twitter. *Language Resources and Evaluation*, 47(1):239–268.

Ellen Riloff, Ashequl Qadir, Prafulla Surve, Lalindra De Silva, Nathan Gilbert, and Ruihong Huang. 2013. Sarcasm as Contrast between a Positive Sentiment and Negative Situation. In *Proceedings of the 2013 Conference on Empirical Methods in Natural Language Processing*, pages 704–714, Seattle, Washington, USA. Association for Computational Linguistics.

G. Salton, A. Wong, and C. S. Yang. 1975. A vector space model for automatic indexing. *Commun. ACM*, 18(11):613–620.

Emilio Sulis, Delia Irazú Hernández Farías, Paolo Rosso, Viviana Patti, and Giancarlo Ruffo. 2016. Figurative Messages and Affect in Twitter: Differences between #irony, #sarcasm and #not. *Knowledge-Based Systems*, 108:132–143.

Cynthia Van Hee, Els Lefever, and Véronique Hoste. 2018. SemEval-2018 Task 3: Irony Detection in English Tweets. In *Proceedings of the 12th International Workshop on Semantic Evaluation*, SemEval-2018, New Orleans, LA, USA. Association for Computational Linguistics.

ECNU at SemEval-2018 Task 3: Exploration on Irony Detection from Tweets via Machine Learning and Deep Learning Methods

Zhenghang Yin[1], Feixiang Wang[1], Man Lan[1,2], Wenting Wang[3]
[1]Department of Computer Science and Technology,
East China Normal University, Shanghai, P.R.China
[2]Shanghai Key Laboratory of Multidimensional Information Processing
[3]Alibaba Group
{10142130151,51151201049}@stu.ecnu.edu.cn, mlan@cs.ecnu.edu.cn,
nantiao.wwt@alibaba-inc.com

Abstract

The paper describes our submissions to task 3 in SemEval 2018. There are two subtasks: **Subtask A** is a binary classification task to determine whether a tweet is ironic, and **Subtask B** is a fine-grained classification task including four classes. To address them, we explored supervised machine learning method alone and in combination with neural networks.

1 Introduction

Irony, also known as sarcasm, refers to the use of words and sentences, whose intended meanings contrary to their literal meanings. Modeling irony has a large potential for applications in various research areas, so SemEval2018-Task3 (Hee et al.) aims to classify irony into different classes.

There are two subtasks. In subtask A, when given a tweet, the classifier should predict whether the tweet is ironic or non-ironic, and in subtask B, the ironic class is further divided into another three categories, i.e., irony by **Polarity contrast**, by **Situational** and **Other verbal** irony.

Polarity contrast irony represents the tweets containing an expression whose polarity (positive, negative) is inverted between the literal and the intended meaning. **Situational** irony stands for the ones which don't contain explicit polarity contrast. However, the events or results described in them are contrary to the desired or expected common knowledge. **Other verbal** irony tweets also don't contain any explicit polarity contrast, but they can't be classified into the **Situational irony**. Finally, **non-ironic** contains instances which are clearly not ironic, or lack adequate context to be sure that they are ironic.

In the remaining of the paper, section 2 describes our system in details. Section 3 reports datasets, experiments and results discussions. Finally, Section 4 concludes our work.

2 System Description

In both subtasks we used supervised machine learning to model the irony in datasets. Moreover, we explored neural networks in subtask A.

- In subtask A, we built a binary classification system to make predictions (see in 2.2.1). Then, we combine it with a **Bi-LSTM** neural networks(see in 2.2.2).

- In subtask B, we used two machine learning systems to train and evaluate.

  1. **4-class classification system:** We made use of classifier directly itself to make 4-class predictions.

  2. **4 binary-classification system:** We designed a two-step system as follows:
     - **Step 1** The entire problem was regarded as 4 binary-classification problems. Each tweet would be trained and evaluated within 4 classes, and 4 confidence values would be returned.
     - **Step 2** The classifier would allocate each tweet with a label gaining the highest confidence, and then made evaluation.

2.1 Feature Engineering

4 types of features were designed to extract effective information from the given tweets.

2.1.1 Linguistic-informed Features

- **Word N-grams** We extracted word n-grams features (n = 1, 2, 3) from tweets. To accomplish that, we used **TweetTokenizer** from *NLTK tools* (Bird et al., 2009). Otherwise, N-grams features with the use of **Relevant Frequency** (*RF*) (Lan et al., 2009) were also applied to this system.

Proceedings of the 12th International Workshop on Semantic Evaluation (SemEval-2018), pages 600–606
New Orleans, Louisiana, June 5–6, 2018. ©2018 Association for Computational Linguistics

- **NER** There are different types of words in tweets. NER feature can effectively express aforesaid information. The 12 types (i.e., *DURATION, SET, NUMBER, LOCATION, PERSON, ORGANIATION, PERCENT, MISC, ORDINAL, TIME, DATE, MONEY*) named entities are labeled by *Stanford CoreNLP tools* (Manning et al., 2014). We used a 12-dimensions binary feature to indicate the entities in tweets.

2.1.2 Word Embedding Features

A lot of recent studies on NLP applications were reported to have good performance through using word vectors, such as document classification (Sebastiani, 2002) and question answering (Lan et al., 2016). In our work, two widely-used word embedding features were adopted, respectively **Google Word2Vec** (Mikolov et al., 2013) and **GloVe** (Pennington et al., 2014).

For **Word2Vec**, a dictionary (Available in *Google*[1].) with 31622 words and 300 dimensions was applied. For **GloVe**, we used data from the dictionary with 2196017 words and 300 dimensions (*glove.840B.300d*, available in *GloVe*[2]).

2.1.3 Sentiment Lexicon Feature (SentiLexi)

Eight sentiment lexicons were used to extract sentiment lexicon features in our work. We adopted the following 8 sentiment features: **Bing Liu lexicon**[3], **General Inquirer lexicon**[4], **IMD-B**[5], **MPQA**[6], **NRC Emotion Sentiment Lexicon**[7], **AFINN**[8], **NRC Hashtag Sentiment Lexicon**[9], and **NRC Sentiment140 Lexicon**[10].

2.1.4 Tweet domain Features

We collected tweet related features, and used unigram to imply if a tweet contained such information.

---

[1] https://code.google.com/archive/p/word2vec
[2] https://nlp.stanford.edu/projects/glove
[3] http://www.cs.uic.edu/liub/FBS/sentiment-analysis.html#lecixon
[4] http://www.wjh.harbard.edu/inquirer/homecat.htm
[5] http://www.calweb/org/anthology/S13-2067
[6] http://mpqa.cs.pitt.edu
[7] http://www.saifmohammad.com/WebPages/lexicons.html
[8] http://www2.imm.dtu.dk/pubdb/views/publication details.php?id=6010
[9] http://www.umiacs.umd.edu/saif/WebDocs/NRC-Hashtag-Sentiment-Lexicon-v0.1.zip
[10] http://help.sentiment140.com/for-students

- **Hashtags** All the tokens begin with "#" symbol are called hashtags. We extracted all the hashtags, removed its "#" symbol and built unigram features for them.

- **Word N-grams in Hashtags** We exploited hashtags by a small tool **WordSegment**[11] to cut linked-together hashtags into a series of words, like *ilikemonday* into [*'i'*, *'like'*, *'monday'*].

- **Punctuation** Online users often use emotion symbols (i.e., ! and ?) to express strongly feelings. Hence we extracted a 7-dimension binary features by recording the following rules, they were: **1)** if exclamations (*!*) exist; **2)** if questions (*?*) exist; **3)** if multiple *!* exist (i.e. *!!!*); **4)** if multiple *?* exist (i.e. *???*); **5)** if alternative appearances of *!* and *?* exist (i.e. *!?* and *?!*); **6)** if the last token is ! and **7)** if the last token is ?.

- **Emoticon:** We collected 67 emotions labeled with positive and negative scores from the Internet[12], and used a 67-dimension binary feature to record the sentiment score of the emotion in tweets.

- **Elongated Words Feature** In the sentence *"Ahhaaaaaaa, that's sooooo funny!"*, *Ahhaa..* and *so..* are the use of elongated words. The existence of these words will lead to the overfitting in unigram features. So we designed a feature to handle them.

In our work, elongated-word feature was defined as **the word which has characters repeated for 3-11 times**. We captured and handled them by using regular expression.

2.2 Classifiers and Models

2.2.1 Machine Learning Algorithm

In both subtasks, we used following supervised machine learning algorithms to train the model:

- Logistic Regression (LR) implemented in *Liblinear* (Fan et al., 2008).

- DecisionTree, NaïveBayes, KNN, Random Forest, LR, SVM, SGD and AdaBoost all implemented in *scikit-learn tools* (Pedregosa et al., 2011).

---

[11] https://pypi.python.org/pypi/wordsegment
[12] https://github.com/haierlord/resource/blob/master/Emoticon.txt

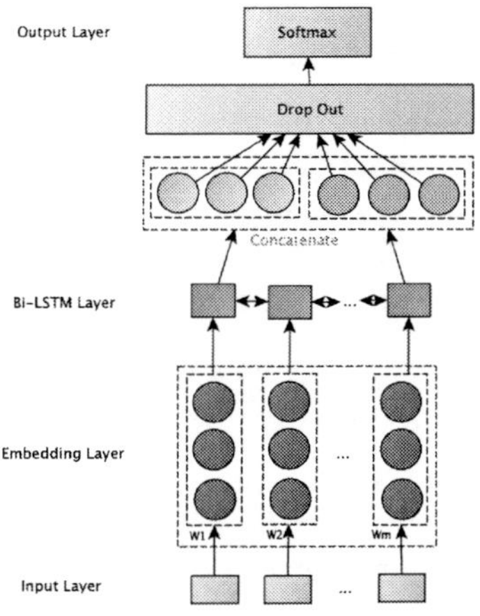

(a) Model submitted to contest

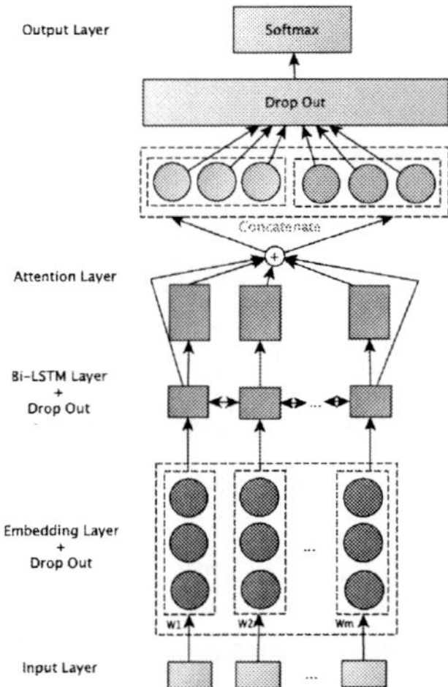

(b) Model Explored after Contest with Attention and Additional Drop Out

Figure 1: The architecture of our LSTM models. (a) The NN model submitted to Task A, which only incorporates a drop out layer after bi-lstm layer. (b) The NN model explored after contest, which adds attention layer and incorporates additional drop out at both embedding and lstm layers.

2.2.2 Deep Learning

Next, we explored neural networks in subtask A. We modeled all the tweets data through a Bi-LSTM network. The general architecture of the model was depicted in Figure 1.

- **Input and Embedding Layer:** Each tweet was preprocessed by normalizing hyper links and mentions to *someurl* and *someuser* as described in 2.1.1 and extracting word n-grams in hashtags as described in 2.1.4. Then the tweet was converted into a vector and padded to an equal length (or truncated if the tweet is longer than the pre-defined length). The input vector was fed to the embedding layer (i.e. pre-trained glove.twitter.27B vectors), which converted each word into a distributional vector.

- **Bi-LSTM Layer:** We used bi-directional L-STMs to model the input sequence. In the bidirectional architecture, two layers of hidden nodes from two LSTMs captured compositional semantics from both forward and backward directions of the word sequence.

- **Attention Layer:** We add attention layer to model the weights of input words follow (Raffel and Ellis, 2016), i.e. learning the weights of hidden states at each time stamp,

then computing the sentence representation via a weighted sum.

- **Output Layer:** The output of Bi-LSTM was passed to a fully connected (FC) layer, which produced a higher order feature set easily separable for 2 classes. Finally, a softmax layer was added on top of the fully connected layer. The network was trained by minimizing the binary cross-entropy error with ADAM (Kingma and Ba, 2015) for parameter optimization.

3 Experiments and Results

3.1 Datasets

The statistics of the datasets provided by SemEval 2018 task 3 are shown in Table 1.

Subtask A	Label 0(%)	Label 1(%)	-	-
train	1,923 (50.2%)	1,911 (49.8%)	-	-
test	473 (60.3%)	311 (39.7%)	-	-
Subtask B	Label 0(%)	Label 1(%)	Label 2(%)	Label 3(%)
train	1,923 (50.2%)	1,390 (36.3%)	316 (8.2%)	205 (5.3%)
test	473 (60.3%)	164 (20.9%)	85 (10.8%)	62 (7.9%)

Table 1: Statistics of datasets in train and test data. Label 0 stands for *non-ironic*, label 1 in subtask A is *ironic*, label 1, 2, 3 in subtask B is respectively *polarity contrast irony*, *situational irony* and *other verbal irony*.

3.2 Evaluation Metric

The official evaluation criterion is as follow:

- For **subtask A**, only F_1-score of **Ironic** class is used.

$$F = F_{pos}$$

- For **subtask B**, macro-averaged F_1-score calculated among all four classes is used.

$$F_{macro} = \frac{F_{polar\_cont} + F_{senti} + F_{other} + F_{non}}{4}$$

3.3 Experiments on training data

3.3.1 Subtask A: Irony Detection

We used a series of features and explored different machine learning algorithms, in combination with neural networks, in subtask A.

Machine Learning

The count of the train data was only 3,834 and no dev datasets were provided. To fully exploit these data, we used 10-fold cross-validation with data shuffling. The major feature selection work was done with LibLinear L2-regularized logistic regression (*LibLinear LR*).

We used the following features in Table 2 as the baseline features. Since the cross validation operations were done with data shuffling, some fluctuations in result might exist. From the table it can be observed that all these features can make contributions to the classifier.

Features	$F_{pos,macro}$
GloVe	0.6314
.+Word2Vec	0.6336 (+0.0022)
.+Punction	0.6382 (+0.0046)
.+ners	0.6406 (+0.0024)
.+Sentiment Lexicon	0.6432 (+0.0026)
.+Emoticon	0.6462 (+0.0030)
.+Elongated	0.6465 (+0.0003)

Table 2: Performance of different features on cross-validation shuffling data test. ".+" means to add current features to the previous feature set. The numbers in the parentheses are the performance increments compared with the previous results.

Then we added three other features: **Word N-grams**, **Hashtags** and **Hashtag unigrams**. Each feature had two versions, with or without **Relevant frequency** (*RF*). Simultaneously, we set different word frequency when building lexicon for these features, from frequency threshold 1 to 5. In order to choose features which can improve the performance best, we used *Hill Climbing* method.

Hill Climbing is a method which can automatically extract the best features from a set of given features. Its principle is as follows:

1. Given a **Candidate Feature** set, traverse each feature and move the feature producing the best performance into **Best Feature** set.

2. Traverse the remaining features in **Candidate Feature** set, ensemble each one with **Best Feature** set to train the model. If one feature can lead to better performance than before, move it to **Best Feature** set.

3. Repeat step 3 until that **Candidate Feature** set is empty.

4. The best feature combination can be obtained by traversing **Best Feature** set according to the insertion order of each feature.

After running *Hill Climbing* 5 times and extracted the features from each first line, we selected 7 features, as shown in Table 3.

Feature	Threshold	With *RF*
Trigram	4	Yes
Bigram	2	Yes
Hashtag	2	Yes
Hashtag	1	Yes
Hashtag unigram	1	No
Trigram	2	Yes
Unigram	2	Yes

Table 3: The results of hill climbing.

Algorithms	$F_{pos,macro}$
SkLearn NaïveBayes	0.7111
Sklearn LR	0.6953
LibLinear LR	0.6947

Table 4: Performance of three best learning algorithms.

Then we explored the performance of different learning algorithms. Table 4 lists the comparison of best three supervised learning algorithms with all above features.

Finally, we made ensemble of three algorithms in Table 4. The ensemble score was 0.6982.

Neural Networks

In our LSTM framework, the dimension of word vector was set to 100 and the hidden layers for both LSTM and FC layers were set to 256. The drop out rate was set to 0.2 for preventing overfitting. 10% of the training data were randomly selected as validation set. The best model during training was used in test evaluation stage. We implement the framework based on **Tensor-flow** (Abadi et al., 2016) and **Keras**[13].

---

[13] https://keras.io/

seed	precision	recall	f_1-score
6815_seed3	0.683908	0.639785	0.661111
6867_seed7	0.705036	0.553672	0.620253
6684_seed11	0.658654	0.709845	0.683292
6789_seed13	0.668142	0.758794	0.710588
6658_seed23	0.692308	0.574468	0.627907

Table 5: Performance of partial neural networks on subtask A on train and dev datasets.

The performance results on train datasets are listed in Table 5, and the average is about 0.66.

Ensemble of Machine Learning and Neural Networks

The average performance of machine learning and neural networks were respectively 0.69 and 0.66. We ensembled different results of neural network and of machine learning. Here we used 4 algorithms, i.e., Scikit-Learn's *NaïveBayes*, *LR*, *SVM* and LibLinear's *LR*, to avoid that label 0 and label 1 were voted same times.

During the ensemble, we also tried another strategy. Since we wanted to higher the recall value of positive labels, we ensembled only the data predicted as "label 0" by neural networks. For those "label 1" data, we remained their original labels. The results of this strategy will be discussed in 3.4.

3.3.2 Subtask B: Irony Classification

When handling subtask B, we used only machine learning. **We conducted two steps in subtask B.**

In the first step, the average f_1-*macro* score is between 0.42-0.43. Table 6 shows how much each class is graded, the f_1-scores of label 2 and 3 are much lower than that of label 0 and 1. This is caused by imbalance in data distribution.

Features	f_1-score of			
	Label 0	Label 1	Label 2	of Label 3
Other features	0.712455	0.649360	0.254167	0.066390
.+URL Unigram T1	0.710811	0.421364	0.282700	0.074074
.+URL Unigram T2	0.712627	0.655994	0.280922	0.105691
.+URL Unigram T3	0.703121	0.648396	0.241015	0.067511
.+URL Unigram T4	0.703121	0.650534	0.280922	0.074689
.+URL Unigram T5	0.709412	0.649573	0.278119	0.075630

Table 6: The f_1-scores of each label in subtask B. Here label 0 represents for *Non-ironic*, 1 for *Polarity contrast*, 2 for *Situational irony*, 3 for *Other verbal irony*.

In the second step, to solve the problem of imbalance in data distribution, we enlarged the data size of label 2 and 3. Label 2 was expanded 6 times, and label 3 was expanded to 10 times. Then we ensembled multi-algorithms. Each algorithm would perform 4 binary-classifications successive-

ly. Finally, we used Scikit-Learn LR for label 0, 1, 2, and Scikit-Learn SVM for label 3. Results are listed in Table 7.

Label	precision	recall	f_1-score
0	0.669960	0.705148	0.687104
1	0.656558	0.623022	0.639350
2	0.343333	0.325949	0.334416
3	0.167539	0.156098	0.161616
Average score			
-	0.459348	0.452554	0.455622

Table 7: The performances of using 4 binary classifications

However, when generating test files, the output results fluctuated remarkably. At last, we didn't hand in the output result generated by step 2.

3.4 Results on Test Data

Subtask	System	f_1-score (%)
Subtask A	ECNU	**0.5931 (20)**
	THU_NGN	0.7054 (1)
	NTUA-SLP	0.6719 (2)
	WLV	0.6500 (3)
Subtask B	ECNU	**0.2326 (30)**
	UCDCC	0.5074 (1)
	NTUA-SLP	0.4959 (2)
	THU_NGN	0.4947 (3)

Table 8: Performance of our systems and top-ranked teams on both two subtasks. The numbers in the parentheses are the official rankings. The evaluation metrics in mentioned in 3.2.

Table 8 shows the results of our system and the top-ranked systems provided by the official. Compared with the top ranked systems, there's so much room for improvement in our work. There are several possible reasons for this.

- First, **the overfitting problems is very serious.** The scores during Training and dev period and test period differed significantly. It will be discussed in 3.5.

- Second, **possibly the features failed to extract useful information from the test data** Unlike Word N-Grams, some features, like hashtag, the probability of the same hashtag or matching words appearing in both test files and training files is quite low.

3.5 Supplement results beside the contest

3.5.1 Ensemble of Machine Learning and Neural Networks on subtask A

This is the performance of machine learning algorithms on subtask A after the contest.

Model	seed x	precision	recall	f_1-score (%)
NN	6815 sd3	0.580282	0.662379	0.618619 (12)
NN	6867 sd7	0.626415	0.533762	0.576389 (27)
NN	6684 sd11	0.532895	0.781350	0.633638 (6)
NN	6789 sd13	0.529279	0.755627	0.622517 (10)
NN+additional dropout	6867 sd7	0.587393	0.65916	0.621212 (11)
NN+additional dropout	6684 sd11	0.525000	0.810289	0.637168 (6)
NN+additional dropout	6789 sd13	0.537079	0.768489	0.632275 (6)
NN+additional dropout+attention	6815 sd3	0.537383	0.739550	0.622463 (10)
NN+additional dropout+attention	6867 sd7	0.529870	0.655949	0.5862070 (24)
NN+additional dropout+attention	6684 sd11	0.544118	0.7138264	0.617524 (13)
NN+additional dropout+attention	6789 sd13	0.574850	0.6173633	0.595349 (19)

Table 9: Performance of pure neural networks on subtask A on test datasets. The number in parentheses is the position of this result if submitted. Performances in Group 'NN' are based on Figure 1(a); Performances in Group 'NN+more_dropout' are based on Figure 1(a) with additional drop out settings; and Performances in Group 'NN+more_dropout+attention' are based on Figure 1(b).

Ensemble	precision	recall	f_1-score (%)
TOP3	0.400000	0.553055	0.464238 (37)
4+NN, en0	0.450777	0.839228	0.586517 (24)
4+NN, en0	0.452340	0.839228	0.587838 (23)
4+NN	0.404651	0.559486	0.469636 (35)
4+NN, en0	**0.493590**	**0.742765**	**0.593068 (20)**

Table 10: Performance of ensemble on machine learning and neural networks on subtask A and test datasets. The numbers in parentheses represent positions in the official ranking if the result is submitted. The last record is the same as **ECNU**'s.

In Table 10, **TOP3** means the ensemble of 3 best algorithms on train datasets. The **4+NN** means using 4 best machine learning algorithms and ensemble them with the results of neural networks. **en0** means using the other strategy mentioned in 3.3.1. Hence, the ensemble data using the other strategy enjoys a particular high recall value. Nevertheless, the performance of these results differ greatly that on train datasets.

seed	precision	recall	f_1-score (%)
6815_sd3	0.580282	0.662379	0.618619 (12)
6867_sd7	0.626415	0.533762	0.576389 (27)
6684_sd11	0.532895	0.781350	0.633638 (6)
6789_sd13	0.529279	0.755627	0.622517 (10)
6658_sd23	0.601911	0.607717	0.604800 (17)

Table 11: Performance of pure neural networks. The numbers in parentheses represent positions in the official ranking if the result is submitted.

In Table 11, the average of f_1-scores on pure neural networks' results is about 0.61. This phenomenon indicates that in our work the training of supervised machine learning appeared to have been overfitted.

3.5.2 Neural Networks on subtask A

In Table 9 the average of f1-scores on pure neural networks' results are 0.61, 0.62 and 0.60 for three Groups respectively.

This phenomenon indicates that in our work, the training of supervised machine learning appeared to be overfitted. Moreover, turn on drop out settings in more neural network layers can further reduce overfitting.

However, our attempt of further incorporating attention layer brought negative affect on subtask A's performance. This may suggest the weighted sum of hidden states probably is not a good representation of the sentence for irony detection.

4 Conclusion

In this paper, we explored supervised machine learning algorithms and neural networks, detected whether a given tweet was ironic or not, and classified them into four more detailed categories. The result was that the machine learning classifiers overfitted, and neural networks performed better than the traditional training methods. The system performance for subtask A ranked above average, and subtask B didn't perform so well. In future work, we consider focusing more on exploring the neural networks.

Acknowledgements

This work is supported by the Science and Technology Commission of Shanghai Municipality Grant (No. 15ZR1410700) and the open project of Shanghai Key Laboratory of Trustworthy Computing (No.07dz22304201604).

References

Martín Abadi, Paul Barham, Jianmin Chen, Zhifeng Chen, Andy Davis, Jeffrey Dean, Matthieu Devin, Sanjay Ghemawat, Geoffrey Irving, Michael Isard, et al. 2016. Tensorflow: A system for large-scale machine learning. In *OSDI*, volume 16, pages 265–283.

Steven Bird, Ewan Klein, and Edward Loper. 2009. *Natural language processing with Python: analyzing text with the natural language toolkit.* " O'Reilly Media, Inc.".

Rong-En Fan, Kai-Wei Chang, Cho-Jui Hsieh, Xiang-Rui Wang, and Chih-Jen Lin. 2008. Liblinear: A library for large linear classification. *Journal of machine learning research*, 9(Aug):1871–1874.

Cynthia Van Hee, Els Lefever, and Vronique Hoste. Semeval-2018 task 3: Irony detection in english tweets. In *Proceedings of the 12th International Workshop on Semantic Evaluation (SemEval-2018).*

Diederik P Kingma and Jimmy Lei Ba. 2015. Adam: A method for stochastic optimization. *international conference on learning representations.*

Man Lan, Chew Lim Tan, Jian Su, and Yue Lu. 2009. Supervised and traditional term weighting methods for automatic text categorization. *IEEE transactions on pattern analysis and machine intelligence,* 31(4):721–735.

Man Lan, Guoshun Wu, Chunyun Xiao, Yuanbin Wu, and Ju Wu. 2016. Building mutually beneficial relationships between question retrieval and answer ranking to improve performance of community question answering. pages 832–839.

Christopher Manning, Mihai Surdeanu, John Bauer, Jenny Finkel, Steven Bethard, and David McClosky. 2014. The stanford corenlp natural language processing toolkit. In *Proceedings of 52nd annual meeting of the association for computational linguistics: system demonstrations,* pages 55–60.

Tomas Mikolov, Ilya Sutskever, Kai Chen, Gregory S Corrado, and Jeffrey Dean. 2013. Distributed representations of words and phrases and their compositionality. *neural information processing systems,* pages 3111–3119.

Fabian Pedregosa, Gaël Varoquaux, Alexandre Gramfort, Vincent Michel, Bertrand Thirion, Olivier Grisel, Mathieu Blondel, Peter Prettenhofer, Ron Weiss, Vincent Dubourg, et al. 2011. Scikit-learn: Machine learning in python. *Journal of machine learning research,* 12(Oct):2825–2830.

Jeffrey Pennington, Richard Socher, and Christopher D Manning. 2014. Glove: Global vectors for word representation. pages 1532–1543.

Colin Raffel and Daniel PW Ellis. 2016. Feed-forward networks with attention can solve some long-term memory problems. In *the workshop proceedings of ICLR 2016.*

Fabrizio Sebastiani. 2002. Machine learning in automated text categorization. *ACM Computing Surveys,* 34(1):1–47.

KLUEnicorn at SemEval-2018 Task 3: A Naïve Approach to Irony Detection

Luise Dürlich

Friedrich-Alexander Universität Erlangen-Nürnberg / Germany

`luise.duerlich@fau.de`

Abstract

This paper describes the KLUEnicorn system submitted to the SemEval-2018 task on "Irony detection in English tweets". The proposed system uses a naïve Bayes classifier to exploit rather simple lexical, pragmatic and semantic features as well as sentiment. It further takes a closer look at different adverb categories and named entities and factors in word-embedding information.

1 Introduction

Automatic irony and sarcasm detection has made great advances in recent years, evolving from considering purely lexical information (Kreuz and Caucci, 2007) to sentiment (González-Ibáñez et al., 2011) and semantics (Ghosh et al., 2015). With new approaches that are aware of the context a tweet is produced in, promising results of as much as 87% accuracy (Silvio et al., 2016) have been achieved.

In the following sections, I present a constrained contribution to the SemEval-2018 irony detection task (Van Hee et al., 2018). As useful context for the training data was rather hard to come by, a solely tweet based approach is explored. In the next section, the dataset provided by the task organizers will be discussed. Sections 3 and 4 will elaborate on data preprocessing and the types of features that were tested. Finally, sections 5, 6 and 7 will present experiments on the usefulness of different features to different classifiers, the settings used for the submitted systems and the competition results.

2 Data

To train the system, only the official training set consisting of 3,834 tweets was used. Of these tweets 1,911 were ironic and 1,923 were non-ironic. Depending on the subtask at hand, namely binary irony detection (task A) or the differentiation between different types of irony (task B), the ironic tweets were further categorized as either *verbal irony by means of polarity contrast* (class 1), *other verbal irony* (class 2) or *situational irony* (class 3). This resulted in 1,390 examples for class 1, 316 examples for class 2 and 205 examples for class 3. The tweets still contained the original URLs, that were further analyzed to get an idea of whether or not they could provide useful context information. However, only as much as 14% of the ironic sample even contained URLs and most of these just linked to images and the original tweet on Twitter. As the data did not include the names of the authors or contained any additional context information,[1] context with respect to the authors user profile was not explored further.

3 Preprocessing

As preparation for tagging, segmentation problems – especially arising around emoji and punctuation marks – were corrected, user mentions were anonymized to "*@user*" and URLs replaced by "*http://url.com*". Hashtags were stripped of the "*#*" and segmented using a simple hand-crafted hashtag tokenizer that relies on regular expressions and a dictionary consisting of the *Unix wordlist* and terms filtered from some 190,000 tweets to account for non-standard words and spelling. The tweets were then tagged using the part-of-speech tagger provided by *Ark TweetNLP* (O'Connor et al., 2013) and filtered using regular expressions. Conjunctions, determiners, existential uses of "*there*", numerals, predeterminers, prepositions, pronouns, punctuation, URLs and user mentions were discarded. Finally, some per-

---

[1] The profiles of users mentioned in the tweets were not considered.

Proceedings of the 12th International Workshop on Semantic Evaluation (SemEval-2018), pages 607–612
New Orleans, Louisiana, June 5–6, 2018. ©2018 Association for Computational Linguistics

sisting segmentation issues related to the tagging – e.g. sequences of emoji were not segmented and sometimes assigned the wrong tag – were resolved and proper nouns identified by the tagger were replaced by "`^_NNP`".

4 Features

The features described in this section were either obtained from tagged tweets, raw tweets as string or tokenized raw tweets using the tokenizer provided by *Ark TweetNLP*. For tokenization, some adaptions had to be made to ensure correct segmentation around emoji. In general, the focus was laid on quick and easy-to-extract binary or count-based tweet properties (except for embeddings and named entities). The features used to train the model, can be assigned to the following categories:

Lexical: A bag-of-words was extracted from the tagged tweets using the *TfidfVectorizer* provided by *scikit-learn* (Pedregosa et al., 2011).

As more of a structural feature, tweet length both in terms of words and in terms of characters was exploited.

Pragmatic: The amount of punctuation, quotation marks, character repetition – and as special case ellipsis (expressed by "...") – as well as uppercase words were added to the features by simply counting their occurrence. As Twitter-specific patterns, the presence and number of user mentions, urls and hashtags as well as the number of emoji in a given tweet were noted.

Sentiment: Two sentiment lexicons were used to capture the mean positive, objective and negative sentiment associated with the hashtags, emoji and normal words present in a given tweet:

1. *AFINN* (Nielsen, 2011), a list of about 2,500 entries assigned to a scale ranging from -5 to 5, that also covers some expressions common in texting and microblogging (e.g. "*lol*").

2. *SentiWordNet* (*SWN*) (Esuli and Sebastiani, 2006), a much larger resource that provides different sentiment scores for the different meanings of a word, but restricted to more standard words.

To circumvent too complex disambiguation for the senses in *SWN*, the mean sentiment scores of the possible meanings were taken and whenever an

AFINN entry existed, scores were reweighted in favor of the *AFINN* sentiment. The scores on emoji were obtained using the emoji aliases provided by the *Python emoji* package.[2]

Semantic: Inspired by the use of word embeddings to contrast a tweet's sarcastic reading with its non-sarcastic representation proposed by (Ghosh et al., 2015), separate models were trained on the ironic and non-ironic instances within the training set. The models were obtained using *word2vec* as provided by *gensim* and the model parameters were set to 100 dimensions and a window size of 5. Hierachical softmax was used for training. To obtain the literal and ironic representations of a tweet, the sums of ironic and non-ironic word embeddings were calculated and the embedding vectors were normalized to length 1 respectively.

Other: In an attempt to capture ironic tweets referring to specific numbers or amounts in a more simplified way than Kumar et al. (2017), who also take the deviation of a given number in the context of a unit of measurement with respect to the mean number encountered with that unit into account, information about the presence of certain number expressions was added to the feature vector.

To get a more fine grained representation of the adverbs used in tweets, a list of different adverb categories and corresponding adverbs was collected from *Wiktionary*[3]. The list contains 19 different categories that are illustrated in table 1. A possible advantage of this representation could be that location or temporal location adverbs – that might be informative in situational irony – can be distinguished from adverbs modifying verbs or adjectives, possibly more useful to spot verbal irony containing e.g. hyperbole.

To record references to entities, the named entity recongnizer provided by *Stanford CoreNLP* (Finkel et al., 2005) was used. After the submission for task A, some more features were added, namely the number of modals, negations and contrasting conjunctions or adverbs.

Weighting and Filtering: To account for less informative features, F-tests were performed on the features and only those that were among the 15% most significant were selected.

608

	Category	Example
1	act-related adverbs	*accidentally*
2	aspect adverbs	*still, yet*
3	conjunctive adverbs	*hence*
4	degree adverbs	*fairly*
5	demonstrative adverbs	*here*
6	focus adverbs	*especially*
7	interrogative adverbs	*why*
8	location adverbs	*there*
9	manner adverbs	*ironically*
10	pronomial adverbs	*therefore*
11	sentence adverbs	*apparently*
12	domain adverbs	*linguistically*
13	evaluative adverbs	*alarmingly*
14	speech-act adverbs	*honestly*
15	modal adverbs	*actually*
16	suppletive adverbs	*well*
17	duration adverbs	*always*
18	frequency adverbs	*constantly*
19	temporal location adverbs	*now*

Table 1: Adverb categories based on Wiktionary

Group	Features	# of Features
1	length in words, length in characters	2
2	character repetition, quotation marks, uppercase	4
3	presence and number of hashtags, URLs and user mentions, presence of emoji	7
4	number of negations, modals, comparison, adverbs contrasting conjunctions / adverbs, amounts / numbers and different types of adverbs and entities	41
5	embedding dimensions	200
6	sentiment	9
7	full feature set (group 1 - 6)	263
8	bag-of-words	A: 1,408 B: 1,455

Table 2: Feature group description

5 Feature Evaluation:

In order to gain insight on the usefulness of the features, a set of experiments[4] was performed, in which the features were assigned specific groups and a selection of classifiers was either trained on the group alone or on all features but those in the group. 10-fold cross-validation was performed on the training set comparing a Gaussian naïve Bayes classifier, support vector machines, a decision tree and a random forest classifier. The groups are reported in table 2.[5]

Results when training on the features without the bag-of-words, displayed in table 3, show that – with the exception of group 5 – most of the groups do not seem to make a big contribution to the rest of the feature set and their exclusion does not lead to substantial drops in performance. For group 5, a decrease in performance of as much as 10% can be observed for the random forest classifier compared to the performance on all features recorded in table 4.

Training on selected features from just one of the groups at a time shows that groups 3 and 5 are already very informative and can produce f-scores

Without group	NB	DT	SVM	RF
1	**69.03**	57.61	67.64	68.48
2	**69.03**	57.98	67.64	68.33
3	68.83	57.87	**69.81**	68.04
4	**68.99**	57.87	67.58	67.50
5	**65.59**	56.50	62.65	60.22
6	**69.01**	58.10	67.65	67.74

Table 3: F1-score when omitting one group at a time for binary irony detection

---

[4]Note that these experiments only focussed on task A.

[5]The bag-of-words was restricted to uni- and bigrams with a minimum document frequency of 5.

of 67.42% and 69.76% respectively. As we can see in table 4, the best score is still obtained when selecting from the entire feature set and training a random forest.

Taking a look at the importance weights assigned by the random forest classifier, it emerges that the embeddings range among the top 220 ranks and carry 91% of the importance weight. They are thus quite important for classification. Tweet length in characters is identified as the most important feature followed by positive word sentiment scores, which might indicate that the assumption by Clark and Gerrig (1984), that ironic utterances are more likely to convey negative sentiment through literally positive one, also holds for the observed tweets. Regarding adverb categories, demonstrative adverbs appear to be most informative.[6] Generally, it can be noted that every group contributes to the top 250 important features with at least one or two features.

Group	NB	DT	SVM	RF
1	48.88	51.12	50.99	**53.20**
2	50.12	47.07	**51.67**	48.66
3	67.42	67.42	67.42	67.42
4	**51.08**	41.36	43.67	42.14
5	68.76	58.22	**69.76**	67.31
6	**65.57**	53.15	47.25	54.21
7	**69.05**	56.77	67.25	68.18
8	**56.77**	51.77	53.60	54.76
all	68.61	60.52	68.18	**70.06**

Table 4: F1-score when training on one group at a time in binary irony detection

6 Submission Settings

For the submission to task A, the parameters for the *TfidfVectorizer* were set to uni-, bi- and tri-grams and a minimum document frequency of 2. The feature vectors did not account for modals, negations and contrasting conjunctions or adverbs since these were added to the feature set after the submission deadline for task A. As the two classes were balanced in training and test data, the priors of the Gaussian naïve Bayes classifier were set to 0.5 each.

For task B, the bag-of-words was based on uni-grams only with a minimum document frequency of 4. Binary features reporting the presence of hashtags, URLs and user mentions were not included. To distinguish different types of irony as well as non-irony, a two-step classification approach was adopted, first deciding whether a tweet was ironic and then labelling it as either situational or verbal irony with or without polarity change. No priors were defined for the second Gaussian naïve Bayes classifier.

7 Results

With respect to the competition results, the system did not perform very well, getting to rank 27 for task A and 23 for task B. Results compared to a benchmark system and random forest with the best settings are reported in table 5 for task A and in table 6 for task B.[7] Note that *NB* in table 6 refers to a single Gaussian naïve Bayes classifier trained on the same features as KLUEnicorn*.

The results for task A indicate that the model cannot compete with the benchmark system provided by the task organizers (a linear SVM trained on bag-of-words only). Possible reasons for that might be the restrictions imposed during preprocessing and feature extraction – a minimum document frequency of 5 might not be feasible on such a small amount of tweets and summarizing all the mentioned user names under the same token instead of at least keeping the more frequent ones as well as discarding certain parts-of-speech such as personal pronouns for example, might not be beneficial to the model. The quality of the word embeddings, trained on a relatively small amount of data, represents another issue.

System	Accuracy	Precision	Recall	F1-score
Benchmark	63.52	53.25	65.92	**58.91**
KLUEnicorn	59.44	49.14	64.31	55.71
KLUEnicorn*	65.56	57.20	52.41	54.69
RF	60.84	59.54	59.80	54.79

Table 5: Results on test data – Task A

For task B, table 6 suggests, that the submitted system still performs worse than the benchmark, yet the version taking all features into ac-

---

[6] On the full feature set, location, degree, interrogative, conjunctive, temporal location and focus adverbs rank among the top 50 most important features when ignoring word embedding dimensions.

[7] KLUEnicorn* refers to a version of the system trained on a selection of the 15% most significant out of all features including the bag-of-words.

System	Accuracy	Precision	Recall	F1-score
Benchmark	56.89	41.64	36.35	34.08
KLUEnicorn	34.69	32.14	35.39	29.82
KLUEnicorn*	49.11	42.51	48.62	**40.42**
NB	47.96	31.54	35.60	30.84
RF	51.53	40.67	33.40	30.11

Table 6: Results on test data – Task B

count shows a better performance, outperforming the benchmark by 6% in terms of f-score.

Looking at the predictions in particular, we can observe that the negative class is predicted with a rather high precision (71.55%) for task A, while in task B, non-irony is detected with a high recall of almost 80%. Apparently, the model is best at predicting non-irony. In task B, the model struggles most when predicting situational irony, achieving an f1-score of only 11%. This is not very surprising, given the small amount of examples for class 3 in the training data.

Tables 7 and 8 show examples from the test set for task A and B and the corresponding predictions made by the classifier. As we can see, short messages lacking more informative context such as the second example in table 7 or the first example in table 8 are still an issue, whereas tweets containing hashtags that oppose the initial content of the tweet text such as the third example in table 8 can correctly be assigned class 1. With "#not" not being part of the training data, this is more difficult for tweets like the fourth tweet, where only one hashtag is present.

Gold label	Pred.	Tweet
0	0	NOT GONNA WIN http://t.co/Mc9ebqjAqj
0	1	@mickymantell He is exactly that sort of person. Weirdo!
1	1	Just walked in to #Starbucks and asked for a ""'tall blonde'"" Hahahaha #irony
1	0	@LadySandersfarm: Garner protesters chant 'F*ck Fox News' despite Fox agreeing with them http://t.co/GWIS4hZAI6 #EricGarner #Irony

Table 7: Example predictions KLUEnicorn – Task A

8 Conclusion

In this paper, I described a rather simple system for irony detection based on target tweets only, considering various kinds of features from semantic information to different adverb categories. While all feature groups seem to contribute to performance, the embedded tweets were found to be most informative and to bring a performance gain of 3-10% depending on the classifier. However, the presented system does not do a very good job at detecting irony on the given data set. Both naïve Bayes and random forest cannot compete with the simple baseline when it comes to just identifying irony, but when different types of irony are to be distinguished, a two-step model trained on a selection of all features can outperform the benchmark. For better prediction, more reliable embeddings using more training data should be trained and certain filter settings for preprocessing should be revisited.

Gold label	Pred.	Tweet
0	0	@ChainAttackJay No sugar during christmas time? :(
0	1	Woke Up , showered , made a lunch and got ready for work only to realize that I have the whole weekend off. 😄
1	1	Well got the truck buried today perfect way to start a rainy Wednesday work day off #not #annoyed #pissed
1	2	Loooovvveeeeeee when my phone gets wiped -.- #not
2	2	Just walked in to #Starbucks and asked for a ""'tall blonde'"" Hahahaha #irony
2	3	and as much as I want to connect .. I like only the people who dont want to .. #Irony #Why oh why?
3	2	People complain about my backround pic and all I feel is like ""'hey don't blame me, Albert E might have spoken those words'"" #sarcasm #life
3	3	If you wanna look like a badass, have drama on social media #not

Table 8: Example predictions KLUEnicorn* – Task B

References

H. Clark and R. J. Gerrig. 1984. On the Pretense Theory of Irony. *Journal of Experimental Psychology: General*, 1:121–126.

A. Esuli and F. Sebastiani. 2006. SENTIWORDNET: A Publicly Available Lexical Resource for Opinion Mining. In *In Proceedings of the 5th Conference on Language Resources and Evaluation (LREC06*, pages 417–422.

J. R. Finkel, T. Grenager, and C. Manning. 2005. Incorporating Non-local Information into Information Extraction Systems by Gibbs Sampling. In *Proceed-*

ings of the 43nd Annual Meeting of the Association for Computational Linguistics, pages 363–370.

D. Ghosh, W. Guo, and S. Muresan. 2015. Sarcastic or Not: Word Embeddings to Predict the Literal or Sarcastic Meaning of Words. In *Proceedings of the 2015 Conference on Empirical Methods in Natural Language Processing*, pages 1003–1012. Association for Computational Linguistics.

R. González-Ibáñez, S. Muresan, and N. Wacholder. 2011. Identifying sarcasm in Twitter: a closer look. In *Proceedings of the 49th Annual Meeting of the ASsociation for Computational Linguistics: Human Language Technologies: short papers*, volume 2, pages 581–586.

R. Kreuz and G. Caucci. 2007. Lexical Influences on the Perception of Sarcasm. *Proceedings of the Workshop on Computational Approaches to Figurative Language*, pages 2–4.

L. Kumar, A. Somani, and P. Bhattacharyya. 2017. "Having 2 hours to write a paper is fun!": Detecting Sarcasm in Numerical Portions of Text. *CoRR*.

F. Å. Nielsen. 2011. *AFINN*. Informatics and Mathematical Modelling, Technical University of Denmark.

B. O'Connor, C. Dyer, K. Gimpel, N. Schneider, and N. A. Smith. 2013. Improved Part-of-Speech Tagging for Online Conversational Text with Word Clusters. In *Proceedings of NAACL*.

F. Pedregosa, G. Varoquaux, A. Gramfort, V. Michel, B. Thirion, O. Grisel, M. Blondel, P. Prettenhofer, R. Weiss, V. Dubourg, V. Vanderplas, A. Passos, D. Cournapeau, M. Brucher, M. Perrot, and E. Duchesnay. 2011. Scikit-learn: Machine learning in Python. *Journal of Machine Learning Research*, 12:2825–2830.

A. Silvio, B. C. Wallace, H. Lyu, P. Carvalho, and M. J. Silva. 2016. Modelling Context with User Embeddings for Sarcasm Detection in Social Media. In *Proceedings of the 20th SIGNLL Conference on Computational Natural Language Learning (CoNLL*, pages 167–177, Berlin, Germany.

C. Van Hee, E. Lefever, and V. Hoste. 2018. SemEval-2018 Task 3: Irony Detection in English Tweets. In *Proceedings of the 12th International Workshop on Semantic Evaluation*, SemEval-2018, New Orleans, LA, USA. Association for Computational Linguistics.

NTUA-SLP at SemEval-2018 Task 3: Tracking Ironic Tweets using Ensembles of Word and Character Level Attentive RNNs

Christos Baziotis[1,3], Nikos Athanasiou[1], Pinelopi Papalampidi[1],
Athanasia Kolovou[1,2], Georgios Paraskevopoulos[1,4], Nikolaos Ellinas[1]
Alexandros Potamianos[1,4]

[1]School of ECE, National Technical University of Athens, Athens, Greece
[2] Department of Informatics, University of Athens, Athens, Greece
[3] Department of Informatics, Athens University of Economics and Business, Athens, Greece
[4] Behavioral Signal Technologies, Los Angeles, CA
`cbaziotis@mail.ntua.gr, el12074@central.ntua.gr`
`el12003@central.ntua.gr, akolovou@di.uoa.gr`
`geopar@central.ntua.gr, nellinas@central.ntua.gr`
`potam@central.ntua.gr`

Abstract

In this paper we present two deep-learning
systems that competed at SemEval-2018 Task
3 "Irony detection in English tweets". We
design and ensemble two independent models, based on recurrent neural networks (Bi-
LSTM), which operate at the word and character level, in order to capture both the semantic
and syntactic information in tweets. Our models are augmented with a self-attention mechanism, in order to identify the most informative words. The embedding layer of our word-
level model is initialized with word2vec word
embeddings, pretrained on a collection of 550
million English tweets. We did not utilize
any handcrafted features, lexicons or external
datasets as prior information and our models
are trained end-to-end using back propagation
on constrained data. Furthermore, we provide
visualizations of tweets with annotations for
the salient tokens of the attention layer that
can help to interpret the inner workings of the
proposed models. We ranked 2nd out of 42
teams in Subtask A and 2nd out of 31 teams
in Subtask B. However, post-task-completion
enhancements of our models achieve state-of-
the-art results ranking 1st for both subtasks.

1   Introduction

Irony is a form of figurative language, considered
as "saying the opposite of what you mean", where
the opposition of literal and intended meanings is
very clear (Barbieri and Saggion, 2014; Liebrecht
et al., 2013). Traditional approaches in NLP (Tsur
et al., 2010; Barbieri and Saggion, 2014; Karoui
et al., 2015; Farías et al., 2016) model irony based
on pattern-based features, such as the contrast between high and low frequent words, the punctuation used by the author, the level of ambiguity of

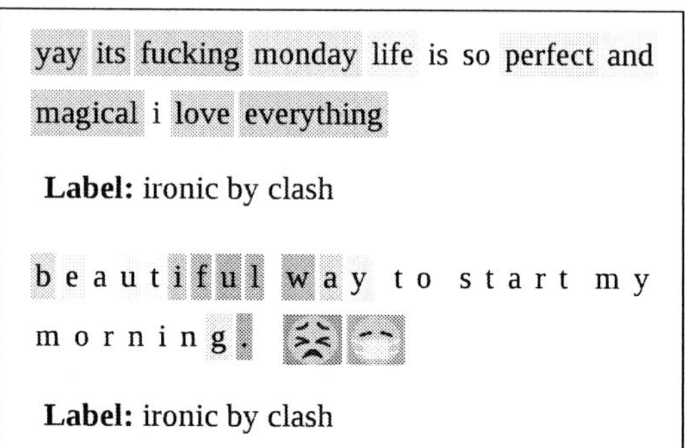

Figure 1: Attention heat-map visualization. The
color intensity of each word / character, corresponds to its weight (importance), as given by the
self-attention mechanism (Section 2.6).

the words and the contrast between the sentiments.
Also, (Joshi et al., 2016) recently added word embeddings statistics to the feature space and further
boosted the performance in irony detection.

Modeling irony, especially in Twitter, is a challenging task, since in ironic comments literal
meaning can be misguiding; irony is expressed
in "secondary" meaning and fine nuances that are
hard to model explicitly in machine learning algorithms. Tracking irony in social media posses
the additional challenge of dealing with special
language, social media markers and abbreviations.
Despite the accuracy achieved in this task by hand-
crafted features, a laborious feature-engineering
process and domain-specific knowledge are required; this type of prior knowledge must be continuously updated and investigated for each new
domain. Moreover, the difficulty in parsing tweets
(Gimpel et al., 2011) for feature extraction renders

Proceedings of the 12th International Workshop on Semantic Evaluation (SemEval-2018), pages 613–621
New Orleans, Louisiana, June 5–6, 2018. ©2018 Association for Computational Linguistics

their precise semantic representation, which is key of determining their intended gist, much harder.

In recent years, the successful utilization of deep learning architectures in NLP led to alternative approaches for tracking irony in Twitter (Joshi et al., 2017; Ghosh and Veale, 2017). (Ghosh and Veale, 2016) proposed a Convolutional Neural Network (CNN) followed by a Long Short Term Memory (LSTM) architecture, outperforming the state-of-the-art. (Dhingra et al., 2016) utilized deep learning for representing tweets as a sequence of characters, instead of words and proved that such representations reveal information about the irony concealed in tweets.

In this work, we propose the combination of word- and character-level representations in order to exploit both semantic and syntactic information of each tweet for successfully predicting irony. For this purpose, we employ a deep LSTM architecture which models words and characters separately. We predict whether a tweet is ironic or not, as well as the type of irony in the ironic ones by ensembling the two separate models (late fusion). Furthermore, we add an attention layer to both models, to better weigh the contribution of each word and character towards irony prediction, as well as better interpret the descriptive power of our models. Attention weighting also better addresses the problem of supervising learning on deep learning architectures. The suggested model was trained only on constrained data, meaning that we did not utilize any external dataset for further tuning of the network weights.

The two deep-learning models submitted to SemEval-2018 Task 3 "Irony detection in English tweets" (Van Hee et al., 2018) are described in this paper with the following structure: in Section 2 an overview of the proposed models is presented, in Section 3 the models for tracking irony are depicted in detail, in Section 4 the experimental setup alongside with the respective results are demonstrated and finally, in Section 5 we discuss the performance of the proposed models.

2 Overview

Fig. 2 provides a high-level overview of our approach, which consists of three main steps: (1) the *pre-training of word embeddings*, where we train our own word embeddings on a big collection of unlabeled Twitter messages, (2) the independent *training of our models*: word- and char-level,

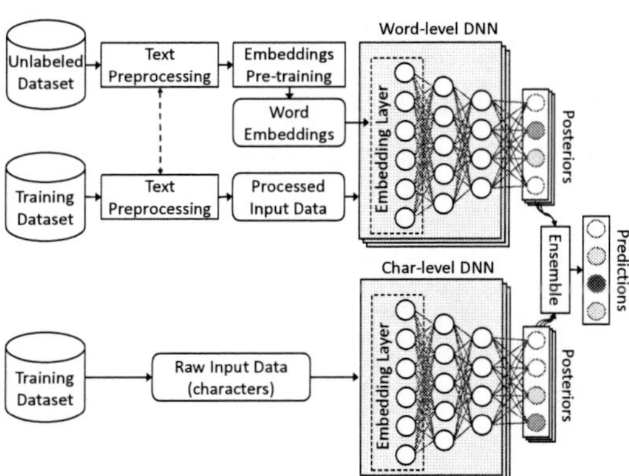

Figure 2: High-level overview of our approach

(3) the *ensembling*, where we combine the predictions of each model.

2.1 Task definitions

The goal of Subtask A is tracking irony in tweets as a binary classification problem (ironic vs. non-ironic). In Subtask B, we are also called to determine the type of irony, with three different classes of irony on top of the non-ironic one (four-class classification). The types of irony are: (1) **Verbal irony by means of a polarity contrast**, which includes messages whose polarity (positive, negative) is inverted between the literal and the intended evaluation, such as *"I really love this year's summer; weeks and weeks of awful weather"*, where the literal evaluation (*"I really love this year's summer"*) is positive, while the intended one, which is implied in the context (*"weeks and weeks of awful weather"*), is negative. (2) **Other verbal irony**, which refers to instances showing no polarity contrast, but are ironic such as *"Yeah keeping cricket clean, that's what he wants #Sarcasm"* and (3) **situational irony** which is present in messages that a present situation fails to meet some expectations, such as *"Event technology session is having Internet problems. #irony #HSC2024"* in which the expectation that a technology session should provide Internet connection is not met.

2.2 Data

Unlabeled Dataset. We collected a dataset of 550 million archived English Twitter messages, from Apr. 2014 to Jun. 2017. This dataset is used for (1) calculating word statistics needed in our text preprocessing pipeline (Section 2.4) and (2) training word2vec word embeddings (Section 2.3).

2.3 Word Embeddings

Word embeddings are dense vector representations of words (Collobert and Weston, 2008; Mikolov et al., 2013), capturing semantic their and syntactic information. We leverage our unlabeled dataset to train Twitter-specific word embeddings. We use the *word2vec* (Mikolov et al., 2013) algorithm, with the skip-gram model, negative sampling of 5 and minimum word count of 20, utilizing Gensim's (Řehůřek and Sojka, 2010) implementation. The resulting vocabulary contains $800,000$ words. The pre-trained word embeddings are used for initializing the first layer (embedding layer) of our neural networks.

2.4 Preprocessing[1]

We utilized the *ekphrasis*[2] (Baziotis et al., 2017) tool as a tweet preprocessor. The preprocessing steps included in ekphrasis are: Twitter-specific tokenization, spell correction, word normalization, word segmentation (for splitting hashtags) and word annotation.

Tokenization. Tokenization is the first fundamental preprocessing step and since it is the basis for the other steps, it immediately affects the quality of the features learned by the network. Tokenization in Twitter is especially challenging, since there is large variation in the vocabulary and the used expressions. Part of the challenge is also the decision of whether to process an entire expression (e.g. anti-american) or its respective tokens. Ekphrasis overcomes this challenge by recognizing the Twitter markup, emoticons, emojis, expressions like dates (e.g. 07/11/2011, April 23rd), times (e.g. 4:30pm, 11:00 am), currencies (e.g. $10, 25mil, 50€), acronyms, censored words (e.g. s**t) and words with emphasis (e.g. *very*).

Normalization. After the tokenization we apply a series of modifications on the extracted tokens,

such as spell correction, word normalization and segmentation. We also decide which tokens to omit, normalize and surround or replace with special tags (e.g. URLs, emails and @user). For the tasks of spell correction (Jurafsky and James, 2000) and word segmentation (Segaran and Hammerbacher, 2009) we use the Viterbi algorithm. The prior probabilities are initialized using uni/bigram word statistics from the unlabeled dataset.

The benefits of the above procedure are the reduction of the vocabulary size, without removing any words, and the preservation of information that is usually lost during tokenization. Table 1 shows an example text snippet and the resulting preprocessed tokens.

2.5 Recurrent Neural Networks

We model the Twitter messages using Recurrent Neural Networks (RNN). RNNs process their inputs sequentially, performing the same operation, $h_t = f_W(x_t, h_{t-1})$, on every element in a sequence, where h_t is the hidden state t the time step, and W the network weights. We can see that hidden state at each time step depends on previous hidden states, thus the order of elements (words) is important. This process also enables RNNs to handle inputs of variable length.

RNNs are difficult to train (Pascanu et al., 2013), because gradients may grow or decay exponentially over long sequences (Bengio et al., 1994; Hochreiter et al., 2001). A way to overcome these problems is to use more sophisticated variants of regular RNNs, like Long Short-Term Memory (LSTM) networks (Hochreiter and Schmidhuber, 1997) or Gated Recurrent Units (GRU) (Cho et al., 2014), which introduce a gating mechanism to ensure proper gradient flow through the network. In this work, we use LSTMs.

2.6 Self-Attention Mechanism

RNNs update their hidden state h_i as they process a sequence and the final hidden state holds a summary of the information in the sequence. In order to amplify the contribution of important words in the final representation, a self-attention mechanism (Bahdanau et al., 2014) can be used

---

[1] Significant portions of the systems submitted to SemEval 2018 in Tasks 1, 2 and 3, by the NTUA-SLP team are shared, specifically the preprocessing and portions of the DNN architecture. Their description is repeated here for completeness.

[2] `github.com/cbaziotis/ekphrasis`

original	The *new* season of #TwinPeaks is coming on May 21, 2017. CANT WAIT \o/ !!! #tvseries #davidlynch :D
processed	the new <emphasis> season of <hashtag> twin peaks </hashtag> is coming on <date> . cant <allcaps> wait <allcaps> <happy> ! <repeated> <hashtag> tv series </hashtag> <hashtag> david lynch </hashtag> <laugh>

Table 1: Example of our text processor

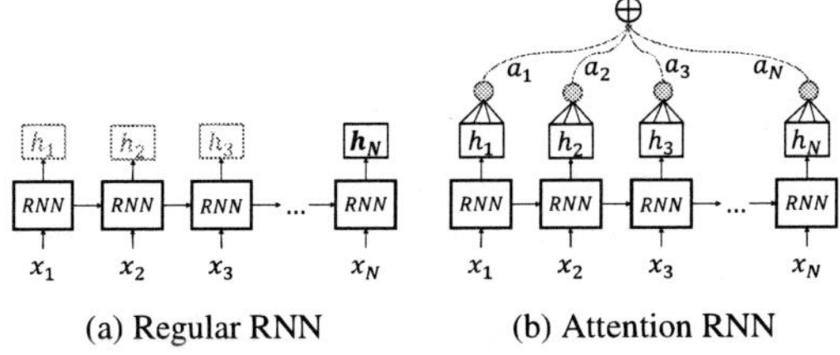

(a) Regular RNN   (b) Attention RNN

Figure 3: Comparison between the regular RNN and the RNN with attention.

(Fig. 3). In normal RNNs, we use as representation r of the input sequence its final state h_N. However, using an attention mechanism, we compute r as the convex combination of all h_i. The weights a_i are learned by the network and their magnitude signifies the importance of each hidden state in the final representation. Formally: $r = \sum_{i=1}^{N} a_i h_i$, where $\sum_{i=1}^{N} a_i = 1$, and $a_i > 0$.

3 Models Description

We have designed two independent deep-learning models, with each one capturing different aspects of the tweet. The first model operates at the word-level, capturing the semantic information of the tweet and the second model at the character-level, capturing the syntactic information. Both models share the same architecture, and the only difference is in their embedding layers. We present both models in a unified manner.

3.1 Embedding Layer

Character-level. The input to the network is a Twitter message, treated as a sequence of characters. We use a character embedding layer to project the characters $c_1, c_2, ..., c_N$ to a low-dimensional vector space R^C, where C the size of the embedding layer and N the number of characters in a tweet. We randomly initialize the weights of the embedding layer and learn the character embeddings from scratch.

Word-level. The input to the network is a Twitter message, treated as a sequence of words. We use a word embedding layer to project the words $w_1, w_2, ..., w_N$ to a low-dimensional vector space R^W, where W the size of the embedding layer and N the number of words in a tweet. We initialize the weights of the embedding layer with our pre-trained word embeddings.

3.2 BiLSTM Layers

An LSTM takes as input the words (characters) of a tweet and produces the word (character) annotations $h_1, h_2, ..., h_N$, where h_i is the hidden state of the LSTM at time-step i, summarizing all the information of the sentence up to w_i (c_i). We use bidirectional LSTM (BiLSTM) in order to get word (character) annotations that summarize the information from both directions. A bidirectional LSTM consists of a forward LSTM $\overrightarrow{f}$ that reads the sentence from w_1 to w_N and a backward LSTM $\overleftarrow{f}$ that reads the sentence from w_N to w_1. We obtain the final annotation for a given word w_i (character c_i), by concatenating the annotations from both directions, $h_i = \overrightarrow{h_i} \parallel \overleftarrow{h_i}, \quad h_i \in R^{2L}$ where $\parallel$ denotes the concatenation operation and L the size of each LSTM. We stack two layers of BiLSTMs in order to learn more high-level (abstract) features.

3.3 Attention Layer

Not all words contribute equally to the meaning that is expressed in a message. We use an attention mechanism to find the relative contribution (importance) of each word. The attention mechanism assigns a weight a_i to each word annotation h_i. We compute the fixed representation r of the whole input message. as the weighted sum of all the word annotations.

$$e_i = tanh(W_h h_i + b_h), \quad e_i \in [-1, 1] \quad (1)$$

$$a_i = \frac{exp(e_i)}{\sum_{t=1}^{T} exp(e_t)}, \quad \sum_{i=1}^{T} a_i = 1 \quad (2)$$

$$r = \sum_{i=1}^{T} a_i h_i, \quad r \in R^{2L} \quad (3)$$

where W_h and b_h are the attention layer's weights. **Character-level Interpretation**. In the case of the character-level model, the attention mechanism operates in the same way as in the word-level model. However, we can interpret the weight given to each character annotation h_i by the attention mechanism, as the importance of the information surrounding the given character.

3.4 Output Layer

We use the representation r as feature vector for classification and we feed it to a fully-connected softmax layer with L neurons, which outputs a

616

probability distribution over all classes p_c as described in Eq. 4:

$$p_c = \frac{e^{Wr+b}}{\sum_{i\in[1,L]}(e^{W_ir+b_i})} \qquad (4)$$

where W and b are the layer's weights and biases.

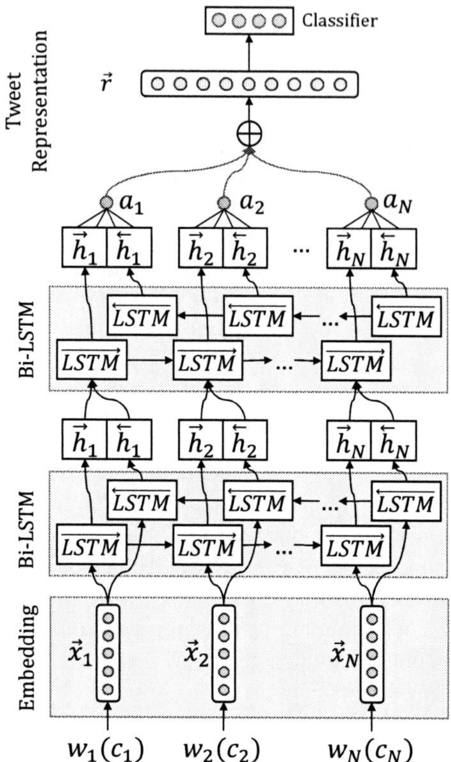

Figure 4: The word/character-level model.

3.5 Regularization

In order to prevent overfitting of both models, we add Gaussian noise to the embedding layer, which can be interpreted as a random data augmentation technique, that makes models more robust to overfitting. In addition to that, we use dropout (Srivastava et al., 2014) and early-stopping.

Finally, we do not fine-tune the embedding layers of the word-level model. Words occurring in the training set, will be moved in the embedding space and the classifier will correlate certain regions (in embedding space) to certain meanings or types of irony. However, words in the test set and not in the training set, will remain at their initial position which may no longer reflect their "true" meaning, leading to miss-classifications.

3.6 Ensemble

A key factor to good ensembles, is to utilize diverse classifiers. To this end, we combine the predictions of our word and character level models. We employed two ensemble schemes, namely unweighted average and majority voting.

Unweighted Average (UA). In this approach, the final prediction is estimated from the unweighted average of the posterior probabilities for all different models. Formally, the final prediction p for a training instance is estimated by:

$$p = \arg\max_c \frac{1}{C}\sum_{i=1}^{M}\vec{p_i}, \quad p_i \in \mathbb{R}^C \qquad (5)$$

where C is the number of classes, M is the number of different models, $c \in \{1,...,C\}$ denotes one class and $\vec{p_i}$ is the probability vector calculated by model $i \in \{1,...,M\}$ using softmax function.

Majority Voting (MV). Majority voting approach counts the votes of all different models and chooses the class with most votes. Compared to unweighted averaging, MV is affected less by single-network decisions. However, this schema does not consider any information derived from the minority models. Formally, for a task with C classes and M different models, the prediction for a specific instance is estimated as follows:

$$v_c = \sum_{i=1}^{M} F_i(c)$$
$$p = \arg\max_{c\in\{1,...,C\}} v_c \qquad (6)$$

where v_c denotes the votes for class c from all different models, F_i is the decision of the ith model, which is either 1 or 0 with respect to whether the model has classified the instance in class c or not, respectively, and p is the final prediction.

4 Experiments and Results

4.1 Experimental Setup

Class Weights. In order to deal with the problem of class imbalances in Subtask B, we apply class weights to the loss function of our models, penalizing more the misclassification of underrepresented classes. We weight each class by its inverse frequency in the training set.

Training We use Adam algorithm (Kingma and Ba, 2014) for optimizing our networks, with mini-batches of size 32 and we clip the norm of the gradients (Pascanu et al., 2013) at 1, as an extra safety measure against exploding gradients. For developing our models we used PyTorch (Paszke et al., 2017) and Scikit-learn (Pedregosa et al., 2011).

Hyper-parameters. In order to find good hyper-parameter values in a relative short time (compared to grid or random search), we adopt the Bayesian optimization (Bergstra et al., 2013) approach, performing a "smart" search in the high dimensional space of all the possible values. Table 2, shows the selected hyper-parameters.

	Word-Model	Char-Model
Embeddings	300	25
Emb. Dropout	0.1	0.0
Emb. Noise	0.05	0.0
LSTM (x2)	150	150
LSTM Dropout	0.2	0.2

Table 2: Hyper-parameters of our models.

4.2 Results and Discussion

Our official ranking is 2/43 in Subtask A and 2/29 in Subtask B as shown in Tables 3 and 4. Based on these rankings, the performance of the suggested model is competitive on both the binary and the multi-class classification problem. Except for its overall good performance, it also presents a stable behavior when moving from two to four classes.

#	Team Name	Acc	Prec	Rec	F1
1	THU_NGN	0.7347	0.6304	0.8006	0.7054
2	**NTUA-SLP**	0.7321	0.6535	0.6913	0.6719
3	WLV	0.6429	0.5317	0.8360	0.6500
4	*Unknown*	0.6607	0.5506	0.7878	0.6481
5	NIHRIO, NCL	0.7015	0.6091	0.6913	0.6476

Table 3: Competition results for Subtask A

#	Team Name	Acc	Prec	Rec	F1
1	*Unknown*	0.7321	0.5768	0.5044	0.5074
2	**NTUA-SLP**	0.6518	0.4959	0.5124	0.4959
3	THU_NGN	0.6046	0.4860	0.5414	0.4947
4	*Unknown*	0.6033	0.4660	0.5058	0.4743
5	NIHRIO, NCL	0.6594	0.5446	0.4475	0.4437

Table 4: Competition results for Subtask B

Additional experimentation following the official submission significantly improved the efficiency of our models. The results of this experimentation, tested on the same data set, are shown in Tables 5 and 6. The first baseline is a Bag of Words (BOW) model with TF-IDF weighting. The second baseline is a Neural Bag of Words (N-BOW) model where we retrieve the word2vec representations of the words in a tweet and compute

model	Acc	Prec	Rec	f1
BOW	0.6531	0.6453	0.6417	0.6426
N-BOW	0.6645	0.6543	0.6517	0.6527
LSTM-char	0.6241	0.6371	0.6342	0.6163
LSTM-word	0.7746	0.7726	0.7826	0.7698
Ens-MV	0.7462	0.7381	0.7461	0.7400
Ens-UA	**0.7883**	**0.7865**	**0.7992**	**0.7856**

Table 5: Results of our models for Subtask A

model	Acc	Prec	Rec	f1
BOW	0.5880	0.4460	0.4384	0.4371
N-BOW	0.6084	0.4649	0.4560	0.4520
LSTM-char	0.5726	0.4098	0.4102	0.3782
LSTM-word	**0.6987**	0.5394	**0.5790**	0.5315
Ens-MV	0.6888	**0.5433**	0.5442	**0.5358**
Ens-UA	0.6888	0.5361	0.4874	0.4959

Table 6: Results of our models for Subtask B

the tweet representation as the centroid of the constituent word2vec representations. Both BOW and N-BOW features are then fed to a linear SVM classifier, with tuned $C = 0.6$.

The best performance that we achieve, as shown in Tables 5 and 6 is **0.7856** and **0.5358** for Subtask A and B respectively[3][4]. In Subtask A the BOW and N-BOW models perform similarly with respect to f1 metric and word-level LSTM is the most competitive individual model. However, the best performance is achieved when the character- and the word-level LSTM models are combined via the unweighted average ensembling method, showing that the two suggested models indeed contain different types of information related to irony on tweets. Similar observations are derived for Subtask B, except that the character-level model in this case performs worse than the baseline models and contributes less to the final results.

4.3 Attention Visualizations

Our models' behavior can be interpreted by visualizing the distribution of the attention weights assigned to the words (characters) of the tweet. The weights signify the contribution of each word (character), to model's final classification decision. In Fig. 5, examples of the weights as-

---

[3]The reported performance is boosted in comparison with the results presented in Tables 3 and 4 due to the utilization of unnormalized word vectors. Specifically, after further experimentation we found that normalization of word vectors provided to the LSTM is detrimental to performance, because semantic information is encoded by both the angle and length of the embedding vectors (Wilson and Schakel, 2015).

[4]For our DNNs, the results are computed by averaging 10 runs to account for the variability in training performance.

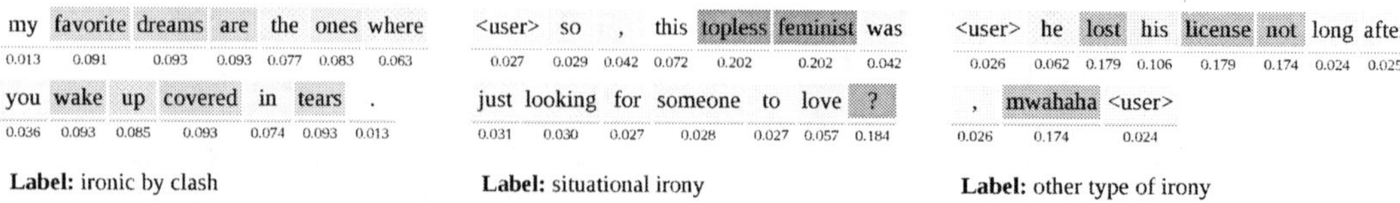

Figure 5: Examples of the attention mechanism for identification of the type of irony in each sentence.

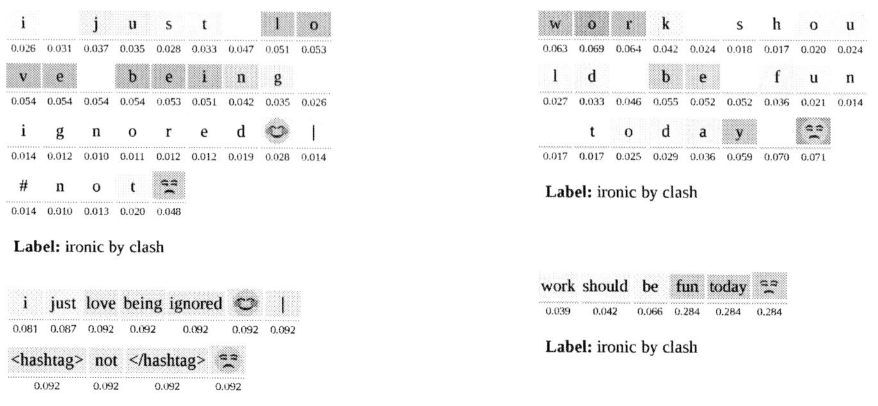

Figure 6: Comparison of the behavior of the word and character level models.

signed by the word level model to ironic tweets are presented. The salient keywords that capture the essence of irony or even polarity transitions (e.g. irony by clash) are correctly identified by the model. Moreover, in Fig. 6 we compare the behavior of the word and character models on the same tweets. In the first example, the character level model assigns larger weights to the most discriminative words whereas the weights assigned by the word level model seem uniform and insufficient in spotting the polarity transition. However, in the second example, the character level model does not attribute any weight to the words with positive polarity (e.g. "fun") compared to the word level model. Based on these observations, the two models indeed behave diversely and consequently contribute to the final outcome (see Section 3.6).

5 Conclusion

In this paper we present an ensemble of two different deep learning models: a word- and a character-level deep LSTM for capturing the semantic and syntactic information of tweets, respectively. We demonstrated that combining the predictions of the two models yields competitive results in both subtasks for irony prediction. Moreover, we proved that both types of information (semantic and syntactic) contribute to the final results with the word-level model, however, individually achieving more accurate irony prediction. Also, the best way of combining the outcomes of the separate models is by conducting majority voting over the respective posteriors. Finally, the proposed model successfully predicts the irony in tweets without exploiting any external information derived from hand-crafted features or lexicons.

The performance reported in this paper could be further boosted by utilizing transfer learning methods from larger datasets. Moreover, the joint training of word- and character-level models can be tested for further improvement of the results. Finally, we make the source code of our models and our pretrained word embeddings available to the community[5], in order to make our results easily reproducible and facilitate further experimentation.

Acknowledgements. This work has been partially supported by the BabyRobot project supported by EU H2020 (grant #687831). Also, the authors would like to thank NVIDIA for supporting this work by donating a TitanX GPU.

[5]`github.com/cbaziotis/ntua-slp-semeval2018-task3`

References

Dzmitry Bahdanau, Kyunghyun Cho, and Yoshua Bengio. 2014. Neural machine translation by jointly learning to align and translate. *CoRR*, abs/1409.0473.

Francesco Barbieri and Horacio Saggion. 2014. Automatic detection of irony and humour in twitter. In *ICCC*, pages 155–162.

Christos Baziotis, Nikos Pelekis, and Christos Doulkeridis. 2017. Datastories at semeval-2017 task 4: Deep lstm with attention for message-level and topic-based sentiment analysis. In *Proceedings of the 11th International Workshop on Semantic Evaluation (SemEval-2017)*, pages 747–754.

Yoshua Bengio, Patrice Simard, and Paolo Frasconi. 1994. Learning long-term dependencies with gradient descent is difficult. *IEEE transactions on neural networks*, 5(2):157–166.

James Bergstra, Daniel Yamins, and David D. Cox. 2013. Making a Science of Model Search: Hyperparameter Optimization in Hundreds of Dimensions for Vision Architectures. *ICML (1)*, 28:115–123.

Kyunghyun Cho, Bart Van Merriënboer, Caglar Gulcehre, Dzmitry Bahdanau, Fethi Bougares, Holger Schwenk, and Yoshua Bengio. 2014. Learning phrase representations using RNN encoder-decoder for statistical machine translation. *arXiv preprint arXiv:1406.1078*.

Ronan Collobert and Jason Weston. 2008. A unified architecture for natural language processing: Deep neural networks with multitask learning. In *Proceedings of the 25th International Conference on Machine Learning*, pages 160–167. ACM.

Bhuwan Dhingra, Zhong Zhou, Dylan Fitzpatrick, Michael Muehl, and William W Cohen. 2016. Tweet2vec: Character-based distributed representations for social media. *arXiv preprint arXiv:1605.03481*.

Delia Irazú Hernandez Farías, Viviana Patti, and Paolo Rosso. 2016. Irony detection in twitter: The role of affective content. *ACM Transactions on Internet Technology (TOIT)*, 16(3):19.

Aniruddha Ghosh and Tony Veale. 2016. Fracking sarcasm using neural network. In *Proceedings of the 7th Workshop on Computational Approaches to Subjectivity, Sentiment and Social Media Analysis*, pages 161–169.

Aniruddha Ghosh and Tony Veale. 2017. Magnets for sarcasm: Making sarcasm detection timely, contextual and very personal. In *Proceedings of the 2017 Conference on Empirical Methods in Natural Language Processing*, pages 482–491.

Kevin Gimpel, Nathan Schneider, Brendan O'Connor, Dipanjan Das, Daniel Mills, Jacob Eisenstein,

Michael Heilman, Dani Yogatama, Jeffrey Flanigan, and Noah A. Smith. 2011. Part-of-speech tagging for twitter: Annotation, features, and experiments. In *Proceedings of the 49th Annual Meeting of the Association for Computational Linguistics: Human Language Technologies: Short Papers-Volume 2*, pages 42–47. Association for Computational Linguistics.

Sepp Hochreiter, Yoshua Bengio, Paolo Frasconi, and Jürgen Schmidhuber. 2001. *Gradient Flow in Recurrent Nets: The Difficulty of Learning Long-Term Dependencies*. A field guide to dynamical recurrent neural networks. IEEE Press.

Sepp Hochreiter and Jürgen Schmidhuber. 1997. Long short-term memory. *Neural computation*, 9(8):1735–1780.

Aditya Joshi, Pushpak Bhattacharyya, and Mark J Carman. 2017. Automatic sarcasm detection: A survey. *ACM Computing Surveys (CSUR)*, 50(5):73.

Aditya Joshi, Vaibhav Tripathi, Kevin Patel, Pushpak Bhattacharyya, and Mark Carman. 2016. Are word embedding-based features useful for sarcasm detection? *arXiv preprint arXiv:1610.00883*.

Daniel Jurafsky and H. James. 2000. Speech and language processing an introduction to natural language processing, computational linguistics, and speech.

Jihen Karoui, Farah Benamara, Véronique Moriceau, Nathalie Aussenac-Gilles, and Lamia Hadrich Belguith. 2015. Towards a contextual pragmatic model to detect irony in tweets. In *53rd Annual Meeting of the Association for Computational Linguistics (ACL 2015)*, pages PP–644.

Diederik Kingma and Jimmy Ba. 2014. Adam: A method for stochastic optimization. *arXiv preprint arXiv:1412.6980*.

CC Liebrecht, FA Kunneman, and APJ van Den Bosch. 2013. The perfect solution for detecting sarcasm in tweets# not.

Tomas Mikolov, Ilya Sutskever, Kai Chen, Greg S. Corrado, and Jeff Dean. 2013. Distributed representations of words and phrases and their compositionality. In *Advances in Neural Information Processing Systems*, pages 3111–3119.

Razvan Pascanu, Tomas Mikolov, and Yoshua Bengio. 2013. On the difficulty of training recurrent neural networks. *ICML (3)*, 28:1310–1318.

Adam Paszke, Sam Gross, Soumith Chintala, Gregory Chanan, Edward Yang, Zachary DeVito, Zeming Lin, Alban Desmaison, Luca Antiga, and Adam Lerer. 2017. Automatic differentiation in pytorch.

Fabian Pedregosa, Gaël Varoquaux, Alexandre Gramfort, Vincent Michel, Bertrand Thirion, Olivier Grisel, Mathieu Blondel, Peter Prettenhofer, Ron

Weiss, Vincent Dubourg, and others. 2011. Scikit-learn: Machine learning in Python. *Journal of Machine Learning Research*, 12(Oct):2825–2830.

Radim Řehůřek and Petr Sojka. 2010. Software Framework for Topic Modelling with Large Corpora. In *Proceedings of the LREC 2010 Workshop on New Challenges for NLP Frameworks*, pages 45–50, Valletta, Malta. ELRA. `http://is.muni.cz/publication/884893/en`.

Toby Segaran and Jeff Hammerbacher. 2009. *Beautiful Data: The Stories Behind Elegant Data Solutions.* "O'Reilly Media, Inc.".

Nitish Srivastava, Geoffrey E. Hinton, Alex Krizhevsky, Ilya Sutskever, and Ruslan Salakhutdinov. 2014. Dropout: A simple way to prevent neural networks from overfitting. *Journal of Machine Learning Research*, 15(1):1929–1958.

Oren Tsur, Dmitry Davidov, and Ari Rappoport. 2010. Icwsm-a great catchy name: Semi-supervised recognition of sarcastic sentences in online product reviews. In *ICWSM*, pages 162–169.

Cynthia Van Hee, Els Lefever, and Véronique Hoste. 2018. SemEval-2018 Task 3: Irony Detection in English Tweets. In *Proceedings of the 12th International Workshop on Semantic Evaluation*, SemEval-2018, New Orleans, LA, USA. Association for Computational Linguistics.

Benjamin J Wilson and Adriaan MJ Schakel. 2015. Controlled experiments for word embeddings. *arXiv preprint arXiv:1510.02675*.

YNU-HPCC at SemEval-2018 Task 3: Ensemble Neural Network Models for Irony Detection on Twitter

Bo Peng, Jin Wang and **Xuejie Zhang**
School of Information Science and Engineering
Yunnan University
Kunming, P.R. China
Contact:xjzhang@ynu.edu.cn

Abstract

This paper describes our proposed to participate in the first year of the irony detection in English tweets competition. Previous works have demonstrated that long short-term memory models have achieved remarkable performance in natural language processing; moreover, combining multiple classifications from various individual classifiers is generally more powerful than a single classification. In order to obtain more precise irony detection classification, our system trains several individual neural network classifiers and combines their results according to the ensemble-learning algorithm.

1 Introduction

In most sentiment analysis tasks, recognition of the precise emotional polarity of a sentence forms the basis for further work. However, much of the corpus we used for analysis and training contains numerous sarcasm and irony features that will have a negative impact on the results of our analysis and training. For example, although the tweets provided by Twitter constitute a valuable and widely applicable corpus for many natural language processing tasks, Twitter users express their feelings and opinions on social networks with frequent irony (Amir et al., 2016). Therefore, such tweets may contain converse sentiments information compared their literal meaning. For example, @*someuser Yeah keeping cricket clean, that's what he wants #Sarcasm:* ignoring the hash tag, this tweet would be positive, which would miss lead an analysis system that uses these types of tweets as input.

Thus, it makes sense to discriminate whether a text is ironic, particularly for social network texts such as tweets. Further applications including tweet sentiment analysis, will benefit from automatic irony detection. The SemEval-2018 Twitter competition promotes research in this area, and is divided into two subtasks that involve binary and four-class classification.

Subtask A is a two-class (or binary) classification task whereby the system must predict whether or not a tweet is ironic. The subtask B is a multi-class classification task where the system has to predict one out of four labels describing i) verbal irony realized through a polarity contrast, ii) verbal irony without such a polarity contrast (i.e., other verbal irony), iii) descriptions of situational irony, and iv) non-irony (Cynthia Van Hee and Hoste, 2018). For a more detailed description, please see Carman et al. (2017).

In recent years, deep learning techniques have significantly outperformed traditional methods in several natural language processing (NLP) tasks (Cliche, 2017). In such task, several deep learning architecture-based methods have achieved outstanding performance in irony and sarcasm detection in social media. Silvio (Amir et al., 2016) presented a novel convolutional network-based method for learning user embeddings from their previous posts and used the user embeddings with lexical signals to recognize sarcasm. Ghosh and Veale (2016) proposed a combined convolutional neural network (CNN) model and long short-term memory (LSTM) method followed by a deep neural network (DNN), which also achieved an improvement compared to traditional machine learning approaches such as support vector machines (SVM).In this paper, we propose an ensemble of multiple deep learning models with a voting classifier in order to enhance the performance of individual neural network models for to detecting the ironic tweets. We trained six individual classifiers, including LSTMs, bi-directional LSTMs, gated recurrent units (GRUs), bi-directional GRUs, attention-based BiLSTMs and attention-based Bi-GRU. Thereafter, we use a voting mechanism to

Proceedings of the 12th International Workshop on Semantic Evaluation (SemEval-2018), pages 622–627
New Orleans, Louisiana, June 5–6, 2018. ©2018 Association for Computational Linguistics

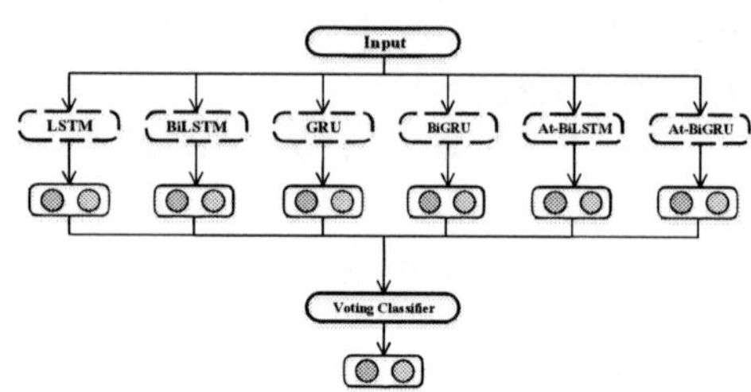

Figure 1: Ensemble voting classifier.

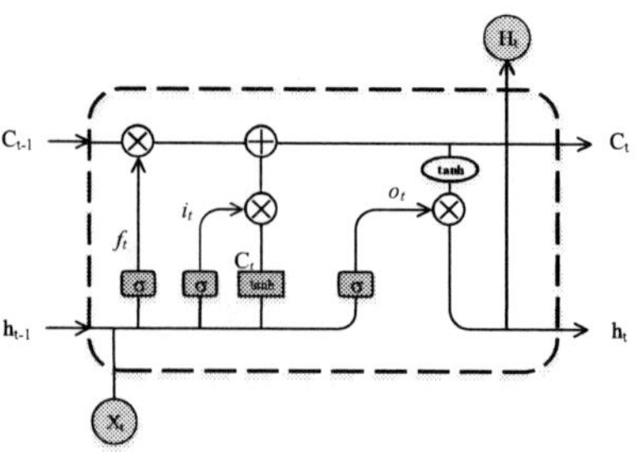

Figure 2: The LSTM memory cell

combine the results from the six classifiers in order to produce the final prediction label.

The remainder of this paper is organized as follows. In section 2, we describe the overall structure of our system and the LSTM-based models, as well as the selected individual classifiers. In section 3, we present the experimental results of our system, and conclusions are drawn in section 4.

2 System Description

2.1 Overview

Numerous previous research studies have demonstrated that the resulting classifier is generally more accurate than any of the individual classifiers making up the ensemble (Maclin and Opitz, 1999). For this reason, we decided to build our system following this strategy. Our system is based on ensemble learning and combined with various popular LSTM models. As illustrated in Figure 1, each classifier is a LSTM-based model, such as bidirectional LSTM (BiLSTM) and attention LSTM (AtLSTM). Each classifier is trained using the complete training set for that network. Following this, for each classifier, the predicted outputs of all classifiers are combined to produce the ensemble system output. As the ironic and non-ironic samples in the training set are evenly distributed (1911 irony samples; 3834 in total), and each classifier in our system is trained by the entire training set. Therefore, we selected the voting classifier as the combining scheme for our system. The principle of the voting classifier is the selection of the prediction supported by most of classifiers according certain rules. For example, if the predictions for a given sample are:

- classifier 1 - class 1

- classifier 2 - class 2

- classifier 3 - class 1

According to majority voting rules, the voting classifier would classify the sample as class 1.

Combining the output of several classifiers is useful only if disagreement exists among them. Thus, the selection of classifiers is rather important for our system.

Neural networks, particularly for recurrent neural networks (RNNs) (Mikolov et al., 2010), have achieved effective results in NLP. Owing to their circular network structure, which allows them to save previous information in a text sentence. Furthermore, conventional RNNs contain cyclic connections, making them powerful for modeling sequences. However, RNNs will face vanishing and exploding gradient problems when dealing with lengthy sequences. The LSTM, which is also a special type of RNN, was designed to address these problems. Therefore, we selected LSTM-based models as our individual classifiers.

2.2 LSTMs

The difference between the RNN and LSTM is that an LSTM (Sak et al., 2014) includes a different and more complex repeating module, as illustrated in Figure 2. This repeating module, also known as cell, provides the LSTM with the ability to discriminate whether input information is useful. A cell contains three gates, namely the input, forgotten and output gates. These gates determine the selection of information by means of the following formulae:

$$f_t = \sigma(W_f \cdot [h_{t-1}, x_t] + b_f)$$
$$i_t = \sigma(W_i \cdot [h_{t-1}, x_t] + b_i) \tag{1}$$

where f_t and i_t are the forgotten and retained features; σ denotes the sigmoid function; x_t and h_t are the t-th input and output; and W and b are cell parameters.

Following this, the cell decides which new information will be stored in the cell state according

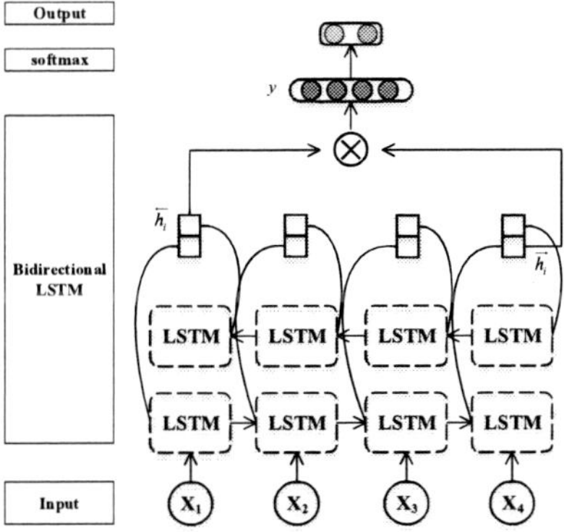

Figure 3: BiLSTM

to the next equation. Here $\tilde{C}_t$ represents the candidate values, created by a tanh gate.

$$\tilde{C}_t = \tanh(W_c \cdot [h_{t-1}, x_t] + b_C) \tag{2}$$

Finally, updating of the cell state and calculating the output of the cell are carried out according to the equations,

$$o_t = \sigma(W_o \cdot [h_{t-1}, x_t] + b_o)$$
$$C_t = f_t * C_{t-1} + i_t * \tilde{C}_t \tag{3}$$
$$h_t = o_t * \tanh(C_t)$$

For an input tweet with length t, we firstly place it into an LSTM layer and generate vector h_t; then, use this vector to calculate the possibility of whether it is ironic by means of a softmax layer.

2.3 BiLSTMs

Standard RNNs use only the previous context and ignore the future context information when dealing with sequence texts. Bidirectional RNNs process the data in both directions with two separate hidden layers which then feed forward to the same output layer (Schuster and Paliwal, 1997). BiLSTMs replace the RNN cell with an LSTM cell based on BiRNNs, as illustrated in Figure 3. BiLSTMs compute the forward hidden state $\overrightarrow{h_t}$ and back forward hidden state $\overleftarrow{h_t}$, and then output the sequence y by calculating equation (4), following which the output layer is updated.

$$y = \overrightarrow{h_t} \otimes \overleftarrow{h_t} \tag{4}$$

2.4 Attention BiLSTMs

LSTMs have promoted RNNs to a great extent in NLP, and a further significant step is the attention

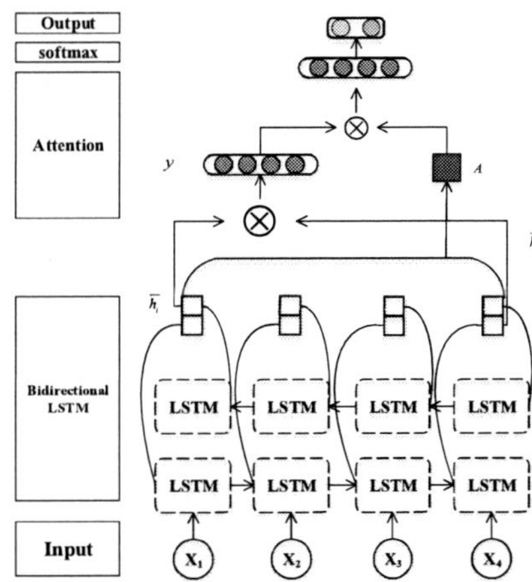

Figure 4: The LSTM memory cell

mechanism. We combined the attention mechanism (Wang et al., 2016) with the BiLSTM as illustrated in Figure 4. The attention captures the context information of an entire tweet, defined as follows:

$$e_t = \tanh(W_e h_t + b_e)$$
$$\alpha_t = softmax(e_t) \tag{5}$$

where W_e and b_e denote the weight and bias, respectively, and α_t represents the attention vector that will be combined with the internal representation generated by BiLSTM layers. The remaining steps are consistent with the BiLSTMs.

2.5 GRUs

The GRU is a variant of LSTM. GRUs reduce the gating signals to two from LSTMs to two, namely reset and update gates. Although GRUs are simpler in terms of structure and calculation compared to LSTMs, their performance and efficiency in specific tasks are not reduced (Cho et al., 2014).

Therefore, we also trained three similar models using GRU cells. In total, we trained six individual classifiers: they are LSTM, BiLSTM, GRU, BiGRU, Attention BiLSTM and attention BiGRU.

3 Experiment

3.1 Datasets

The training dataset is constructed from 3834 English tweets collected by the organizers by means of searching Twitter for the hashtags #irony, #sarcasm, and #not. The training dataset for task A consists of tweets with a binary value score (0 or 1)

Subtask A	Accuracy	F1 score (macro)	Recall (macro)	Precision (macro)
LSTM	0.64163	0.64161	0.64174	0.65364
BiLSTM	**0.64163**	0.64161	**0.64174**	**0.65364**
GRU	0.63109	0.63108	0.63111	0.64031
BiGRU	0.64295	0.64099	0.64232	0.65110
Attention BiLSTM	0.64295	0.64085	0.64230	0.64519
Attention BiGRU	0.65744	0.65506	0.65673	0.66053
Ensemble	0.66007	**0.66871**	0.61894	0.62095

Table 1: Cross-validation results for subtask A.

Subtask B	Accuracy	F1 score (macro)	Recall (macro)	Precision (macro)
LSTM	0.7148	0.4939	0.5071	0.5341
BiLSTM	0.7330	0.4885	0.4964	0.5103
GRU	0.7369	0.5150	0.5017	0.5438
BiGRU	0.7031	0.4800	0.4946	0.5319
Attention BiLSTM	0.7200	0.5129	0.5315	0.5324
Attention BiGRU	0.7278	0.5081	0.5099	0.5216
Ensemble	**0.7539**	**0.5172**	**0.5198**	**0.5385**

Table 2: Cross-validation results for subtask B.

indicating whether the tweet is ironic. The training data for subtask B includes tweets with a numeric value corresponding to one of the subcategories, namely ironic by clash, other irony, situational irony and non-ironic. For subtasks A and B, the content of the tweet is exactly the same apart from the labels. The organizers also provided a version with no emoticons or hashtags and one with emoticons or hashtags. According to people's tweeting habits, emoticons and hashtags are important tools for expressing emotions, thus, we used tweets with these features for training.

3.2 Preprocessing

Before feeding the tweets to any classifier, they are pre-processed by following procedure:

- All uppercase letters are converted to lowercase.

- URLs are replaced by <url>; instance of @someone are replaced by <user>.

- Certain emoticons and emojis expressing positive sentiments are transformed into words such as *smile, like,* and *happy*. Others that express negative emotions are all replaced by <irony>.

- For subtask A, all hashtags are replaced by <hashtag>; for subtask B: except for *#irony,* *#sarcasm* and *#not*, all other hashtags are replaced by <hashtag>, and the remainder are all converted to the word *irony*.

We did not replace #irony, #sarcasm and #not with word irony for subtask A because it is easy for overfitting to occur while training. We consider that the reason for this is that the searching and labeling of these tweets mostly dependent on their hashtags. In the four-category subtask B, this does not lead to over-fitting, but aids in improving accuracy.

3.3 Word embedding

We obtain word embeddings by training with the corpus of English articles in Wikipedia pages using Global Vector (GloVe) (Pennington et al., 2014). Compared to Word2vec (Mikolov et al., 2013), GloVe achieves superior performance in this task under the same conditions. Moreover, we set the dimension of a single word as 300. Following the above steps, we create a look-up table that allows for most of the words in the training dataset to correspond to word vectors trained in advance, with the dataset containing 9056 unique words. However, 1266 words remain that cannot be matched, with most of these be-ing numbers and certain user-created words.

	Accuracy	**F1 score (macro)**	**Recall (macro)**	**Precision (macro)**
Subtask A	0.5089	0.4086	0.4277	0.3912
Subtask B	0.466	0.3127	0.3229	0.3384

Table 3: Evaluation for Subtask A and B.

3.4 Parameters

We used earlystopping to observe the accuracy value convergence of each epoch, with patience set to 3 and min_delta set to 0.05; we found that each model stopped training with no more than 35 epochs or even less. Consequently, we set the number of epochs to 30 for the training of every classifier. Furthermore, we set the batch size to 100 and drop-out rate to 0.25 for training of each model. We selected the categorical cross-entropy as the loss function and Adagrad as the optimizer (Duchi et al., 2011).

For subtasks A and B, the individual classifiers are trained with the training dataset. Ow-ing to the lack of development dataset, we only evaluated the performance of the classifiers and prevented overfitting by cross-validation. The models were implemented in Keras using TensorFlow backend.

3.5 Results and analysis

The experimental results of the individual classifiers and ensemble are displayed in Table 1 for subtask A and Table 2 for subtask B.

As indicated in Table 1, BiLSTM and attention GRU achieved a superior performance. However, there is no significant difference among the results of each model. This may be the reason why the ensemble does not operate effectively, because a good ensemble is one in which the individual classifiers are both ac-curate and create their errors in different parts of the input space (Maclin and Opitz, 1999). Our input space is not sufficiently large and the classifiers are similar, creating their errors in the same place.

For subtask B, our preprocessing strategy aids in improving accuracy. However, the samples in the training set are not as evenly distributed as subtask A, reflecting the ensemble effect. The precision achieved by our system achieved in subtask B ranks 10th out of 32 participants. However, numerous aspects of our system require further improvement.

The evaluation results from the committee are illustrated in Table 3. Due to our negligence, we submitted a wrong result of Subtask B. After the organizing committee reminded us that we have corrected the error and re-evaluated our result for Subtask b. Table 3 shows the corrected results for Subtask B. We apologize for the inconvenience caused by our own negligence and we thanked the organizers for prompt reminders so that we could correct the results in a timely manner.

4 Conclusion and future work

In this paper, we have presented the system we used to compete in SemEval-2018 task 3 - Irony detection in English tweets. The purpose of our participation in this competition is to deepen our understanding of irony detection as a novel NLP application. Moreover, we hope to determine an effective combination approach to ensemble learning and neural networks by means of practical application.

For future work, it would be meaningful to improve the neural network by combining the characteristic that ironic sentences are often inconsistent. Moreover, the goal is to identify superior practical ensemble methods to achieve improved performance in increased NLP applications.

References

Silvio Amir, Byron C Wallace, Hao Lyu, and Paula Carvalho Mrio J Silva. 2016. Modelling context with user embeddings for sarcasm detection in social media. pages 167–177.

Mark J. Carman, Mark J. Carman, and Mark J. Carman. 2017. *Automatic Sarcasm Detection: A Survey*. ACM.

Kyunghyun Cho, Bart Van Merrienboer, Caglar Gulcehre, Dzmitry Bahdanau, Fethi Bougares, Holger Schwenk, and Yoshua Bengio. 2014. Learning phrase representations using rnn encoder-decoder for statistical machine translation. *Computer Science*.

Mathieu Cliche. 2017. BB_twtr at semeval-2017 task 4: Twitter sentiment analysis with cnns and lstms.

Els Lefever Cynthia Van Hee and Vronique Hoste. 2018. Semeval-2018 task 3: Irony detection in english tweets. In *Proceedings of the 12th International Workshop on Semantic Evaluation (SemEval-2018)*.

John Duchi, Elad Hazan, and Yoram Singer. 2011. Adaptive subgradient methods for online learning and stochastic optimization. *Journal of Machine Learning Research*, 12(7):257–269.

Aniruddha Ghosh and Tony Veale. 2016. Fracking sarcasm using neural network. In *The Workshop on Computational Approaches To Subjectivity*.

R. Maclin and D. Opitz. 1999. Popular ensemble methods: An empirical study. *Journal of Artificial Intelligence Research*, 11:169–198.

Tomas Mikolov, Martin Karafit, Lukas Burget, Jan Cernocky, and Sanjeev Khudanpur. 2010. Recurrent neural network based language model. In *INTERSPEECH 2010, Conference of the International Speech Communication Association, Makuhari, Chiba, Japan, September*, pages 1045–1048.

Tomas Mikolov, Ilya Sutskever, Kai Chen, Greg Corrado, and Jeffrey Dean. 2013. Distributed representations of words and phrases and their compositionality. 26:3111–3119.

Jeffrey Pennington, Richard Socher, and Christopher Manning. 2014. Glove: Global vectors for word representation. In *Conference on Empirical Methods in Natural Language Processing*, pages 1532–1543.

Ha?im Sak, Andrew Senior, and Fran?oise Beaufays. 2014. Long short-term memory based recurrent neural network architectures for large vocabulary speech recognition. *Computer Science*, pages 338–342.

Mike Schuster and Kuldip K Paliwal. 1997. *Bidirectional recurrent neural networks*. IEEE Press.

Binarizer at SemEval-2018 Task 3: Parsing dependency and deep learning for irony detection

Nishant Nikhil
IIT Kharagpur
Kharagpur, India
nishantnikhil@iitkgp.ac.in

Muktabh Mayank Srivastava
ParallelDots, Inc.
muktabh@paralleldots.com

Abstract

In this paper, we describe the system submitted for the SemEval 2018 Task 3 (Irony detection in English tweets) Subtask A by the team Binarizer. Irony detection is a key task for many natural language processing works. Our method treats ironical tweets to consist of smaller parts containing different emotions. We break down tweets into separate phrases using a dependency parser. We then embed those phrases using an LSTM-based neural network model which is pre-trained to predict emoticons for tweets. Finally, we train a fully-connected network to achieve classification.

1 Introduction

The micro-blogging site Twitter has created an abundance of data about opinions and sentiments regarding almost every aspect of daily life. A deeper study of the public opinion can be obtained by applying natural language processing techniques on this data. However, the performance of these NLP models is detrimentally affected by irony (Pozzi et al., 2016). As per the Oxford English Dictionary, irony is the expression of one's meaning by using language that normally signifies the opposite, typically for humorous or emphatic effect. This deviation between what is said and what is intended makes irony hard to detect. Being a platform where users are free to communicate and express themselves colloquially, Twitter generates considerable data injected with irony. Studying this would provide us with a better sentiment analysis of these tweets.

Prior work on irony detection includes the use of unigrams and emoticons (González-Ibánez et al., 2011; Carvalho et al., 2009; Barbieri et al., 2014). Maynard and Greenwood (2014) describe an unsupervised pattern mining approach where the sentiment of the hashtag in the tweet is proposed to be a key indicator of sarcasm. If the sentiment of the tweet does not match the sentiment of the hashtag, it is predicted to be sarcastic. Riloff et al. (2013) illustrates a semi-supervised approach where rule-based classifiers are used to look for negative situation phrases and positive verbs in a sentence. Tsur et al. (2010) build pattern-based features that detect the presence of discriminative patterns as extracted from a large sarcasm-labelled corpus. N-gram-based approaches have also been used (Davidov et al., 2010; Ptáček et al., 2014; Joshi et al., 2015) with sentiment features. Joshi et al. (2017) use similarity between word embeddings as feature and Poria et al. (2016) use convolutional neural networks to extract sentiment, emotion and personality features for sarcasm detection.

SemEval-2018 Task 3 (the 12th workshop on semantic evaluation) specifies two subtasks in relation to irony detection in English tweets (Van Hee et al., 2018). In subtask A the goal was to train a binary classifier that detects whether a given tweet is ironic or not. Subtask B was a multi-class classification problem where four labels were specified to describe the nature of irony (verbal irony by means of a polarity contrast, situational irony, other verbal irony, and non-ironic). The goal was to assign one of the four labels to each tweet.

We propose a new method which considers ironical tweets to be collections of smaller parts containing different emotions. We break down tweets into these collections using a dependency parser and embed them using DeepMoji (Felbo et al., 2017) which is pre-trained to predict emoticons for tweets. Finally we train a classifier to detect irony. The paper is organized as follows: We discuss our methods in section 2. Section 3 contains the details about the experiments and the training data. In Section 4 we discuss the results and Section 5 concludes the paper with closing remarks.

Proceedings of the 12th International Workshop on Semantic Evaluation (SemEval-2018), pages 628–632
New Orleans, Louisiana, June 5–6, 2018. ©2018 Association for Computational Linguistics

2 Method

In order to identify the chunks of various emotions in an ironic tweet, we split the tweets into phrases using a dependency parser. We use Tweeboparser (Kong et al., 2014), which is a dependency parser for English tweets. The parser is trained on a subset of a labelled corpus for 929 tweets (12,318 tokens) drawn from the POS-tagged tweet corpus of Owoputi et al. (2013), Tweebank. TweeboParser predicts the syntactic structure of the tweet represented by unlabelled dependencies. Tweets contain multiple sentences or fragments called "utterances" each with their own syntactic root disconnected from the others. Since a tweet often contains more than one utterance, the output of TweeboParser will often be a multi-rooted graph over the tweet. Also, many elements in tweets have no syntactic function. These include, in many cases, hashtags, URLs, and emoticons. TweeboParser attempts to exclude these tokens from the parse tree. For our purpose, we club the words arising from the same root to create a phrase. Multiple roots would create multiple phrases. As we can see from Figure 1, these phrases can convey the different sentiments attached to the different subjects of the tweet.

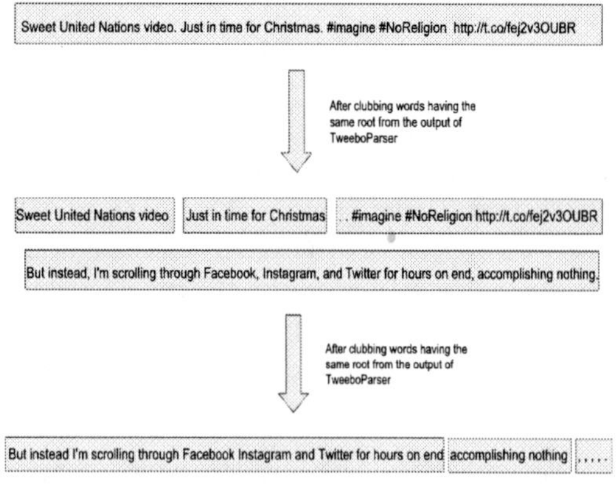

Figure 1: Parser results

After extracting a set of phrases for the sentence, we embed the phrases into vectors. We used the DeepMoji (Felbo et al., 2017) model, which is trained on 1.2 billion tweets with emojis to understand how language is used to express emotions. It encodes the provided phrase into a 2,304-dimensional feature vector. Under the hood, DeepMoji model projects each word into a 256-dimensional vector space followed by a hyperbolic

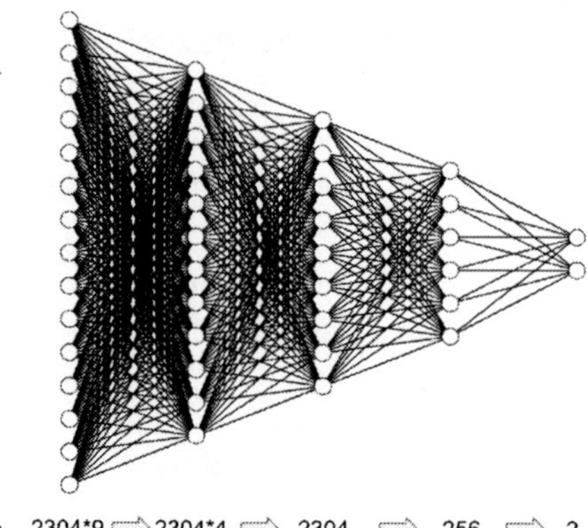

Figure 2: Neural network architecture

tangent activation function. After this, two bidirectional LSTMs with 1,024 hidden units each are used to capture the context of each word. Finally, the model uses skip connections from each layer to an attention layer and hence the attention layer outputs a 2,304 (256+1,024+1,024) dimensional vector. Now this 2,304-dimensional output is connected to a softmax layer for classification. We did not use the final softmax layer but took the 2,304-dimensional vector for each phrase. As the model was trained for prediction of emoticons, this feature vector contains information about the semantic and sentimental content of the phrases. To make the predictions we need to account for the sentiment behind every utterance. To this end, we concatenate these vectors and pass the resulting concatenated vector through a fully-connected network as described in Figure 2.

Tweets can have a varying number of roots, which implies that they split into a varying number of phrases. Our model considers a maximum of nine roots. A tweet with an excess of nine roots is truncated suitably. On the other hand, a tweet with less than nine roots is zero-padded. We have described the complete process flowchart in Figure 3.

3 Experiments

For subtask A, we were provided with a dataset consisting of tweets along with a binary class (0 or 1) which indicates whether this tweet is ironic or not (0 for non-ironic tweets and 1 for ironic tweets). The data was collected from Twitter API by querying tweets using the hashtags #irony, #sarcasm and #not, with subsequent manual an-

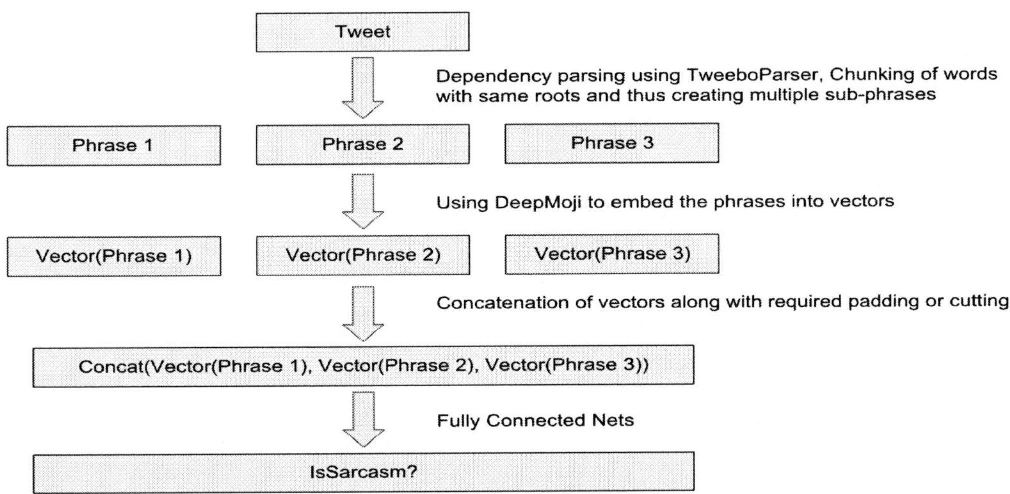

Figure 3: Process Flowchart

notation to remove noise. 3,833 tweets for training and 784 tweets for testing were provided. The evaluation was done by using accuracy, precision, recall and F1 score.

$$Accuracy : \frac{\text{number of correctly predicted instances}}{\text{total number of instances}}$$

$$Precision : \frac{\text{number of correctly predicted instances}}{\text{number of predicted labels}}$$

$$Recall : \frac{\text{number of correctly predicted instances}}{\text{number of labels in the gold standard}}$$

$$F1\ score : \frac{2 \text{ x precision x recall}}{\text{precision + recall}}$$

Method	Accuracy	Precision	Recall	F1 score
Winning team	0.7347	0.6304	0.8006	0.7054
Our System $\beta 1$	**0.6659**	**0.5527**	**0.6471**	**0.5962**
Our System $\beta 2$	0.6390	0.5198	0.6941	0.5944
Our System α	0.6951	0.6197	0.5176	0.5641

Table 1: Results
SemEval Task 3A

We used the pipeline described in Figure 3. The final step of the process used a fully connected neural network with four layers. The input layer of the FC network has a dimension of 20,736 (2,304*9), the second layer has a dimension of 9,216 (2,304*4), the third layer has a dimension of 2,304 and the fourth layer has 256 dimensions. The final layer has 2 dimensions, with one for each class. This is depicted in Figure 2. We used the hyperbolic tangent activation function in all of the layers, and stochastic gradient descent with a learning rate of 0.01 and a momentum of 0.5.

Two models were then devised. The difference in these models lies in the input supplied to the FC network. In the first model, this input is the concatenation of the vectors obtained by embedding phrases. In the second model, the input is the concatenation of the input in the first model along with a 2,304-dimensional vector representing the embedding of the tweet as a whole. The results we get from various experiments on these models are shown in Table 1.

System α is the first model. The best F1 score for this model was achieved after four epochs, as shown in Table 1. System $\beta 1$ and $\beta 2$ are the second model running for five and four epochs respectively.

4   Results and Discussions

We participated only in the shared task 3A as the team Binarizer. We came ninth as per accuracy and seventeenth as per F1 score among the forty-three participating systems. Due to a glitch on our side during submission the results are based on 446 out of 784 instances in the test data.

The models perform better than the baseline system as per the competition leaderboard. This reinforces the notion that separate phrases in a tweet carry information required for irony detection. System α has greater precision whereas System β has higher recall. So an application which demands urgent detection of ironic tweets would profit more from System β. This demonstrates that the sentiment information of the context provided from the whole tweet is also important.

5   Conclusion and Future works

We have shown how using the sentiments of different segments of tweets can enable irony detection. From the results of our experiments, we conclude that the segments have sufficient sentiment information in them for the identification of irony. In future research, we aim to improve the algorithm for parsing these chunks by replacing the dependency parser. Also, more experimentation can be performed for the last part of the pipeline. As the phrases from the tweets are sequences themselves, we can apply sequence modelling with LSTMs or CNNs.

References

Francesco Barbieri, Horacio Saggion, and Francesco Ronzano. 2014. Modelling sarcasm in twitter, a novel approach. In *Proceedings of the 5th Workshop on Computational Approaches to Subjectivity, Sentiment and Social Media Analysis*, pages 50–58.

Paula Carvalho, Luís Sarmento, Mário J Silva, and Eugénio De Oliveira. 2009. Clues for detecting irony in user-generated contents: oh...!! it's so easy;-. In *Proceedings of the 1st international CIKM workshop on Topic-sentiment analysis for mass opinion*, pages 53–56. ACM.

Dmitry Davidov, Oren Tsur, and Ari Rappoport. 2010. Semi-supervised recognition of sarcastic sentences in twitter and amazon. In *Proceedings of the fourteenth conference on computational natural language learning*, pages 107–116. Association for Computational Linguistics.

Bjarke Felbo, Alan Mislove, Anders Søgaard, Iyad Rahwan, and Sune Lehmann. 2017. Using millions of emoji occurrences to learn any-domain representations for detecting sentiment, emotion and sarcasm. In *Conference on Empirical Methods in Natural Language Processing (EMNLP)*, pages 1615–1625.

Roberto González-Ibánez, Smaranda Muresan, and Nina Wacholder. 2011. Identifying sarcasm in twitter: a closer look. In *Proceedings of the 49th Annual Meeting of the Association for Computational Linguistics: Human Language Technologies: Short Papers-Volume 2*, pages 581–586. Association for Computational Linguistics.

Aditya Joshi, Pushpak Bhattacharyya, and Mark J. Carman. 2017. Automatic sarcasm detection: A survey. *ACM Computing Surveys*, 50(5):73:1–73:22.

Aditya Joshi, Vinita Sharma, and Pushpak Bhattacharyya. 2015. Harnessing context incongruity for sarcasm detection. In *Proceedings of the 53rd Annual Meeting of the Association for Computational Linguistics and the 7th International Joint Conference on Natural Language Processing (Volume 2: Short Papers)*, volume 2, pages 757–762.

Lingpeng Kong, Nathan Schneider, Swabha Swayamdipta, Archna Bhatia, Chris Dyer, and Noah A Smith. 2014. A dependency parser for tweets. In *Proceedings of Empirical Methods in Natural Language Processing (EMNLP)*, pages 1001–1012, Doha, Qatar.

Diana Maynard and Mark Greenwood. 2014. Who cares about Sarcastic Tweets? Investigating the Impact of Sarcasm on Sentiment Analysis. In *Proceedings of the Ninth International Conference on Language Resources and Evaluation (LREC'14)*, pages 4238–4243, Reykjavik, Iceland. European Language Resources Association.

Olutobi Owoputi, Brendan O'Connor, Chris Dyer, Kevin Gimpel, Nathan Schneider, and Noah A Smith. 2013. Improved part-of-speech tagging for online conversational text with word clusters. In *The 2013 Conference of the North American Chapter of the Association for Computational Linguistics: Human Language Technologies (NAACL 2013)*, pages 380–390.

Soujanya Poria, Erik Cambria, and Alexander Gelbukh. 2016. Aspect extraction for opinion mining with a deep convolutional neural network. *Knowledge-Based Systems*, 108:42–49.

Federico Alberto Pozzi, Elisabetta Fersini, Enza Messina, and Bing Liu. 2016. *Sentiment analysis in social networks*. Morgan Kaufmann Publishers Inc., San Francisco, CA.

Tomáš Ptáček, Ivan Habernal, and Jun Hong. 2014. Sarcasm detection on czech and english twitter. In *Proceedings of COLING 2014, the 25th International Conference on Computational Linguistics: Technical Papers*, pages 213–223.

Ellen Riloff, Ashequl Qadir, Prafulla Surve, Lalindra De Silva, Nathan Gilbert, and Ruihong Huang. 2013. Sarcasm as contrast between a positive sentiment and negative situation. In *Proceedings of the 2013 Conference on Empirical Methods in Natural Language Processing*, pages 704–714.

Oren Tsur, Dmitry Davidov, and Ari Rappoport. 2010. Icwsm-a great catchy name: Semi-supervised recognition of sarcastic sentences in online product reviews. In *Proceedings of International AAAI Conference on Web and Social Media*, pages 162–169.

Cynthia Van Hee, Els Lefever, and Vronique Hoste. 2018. Semeval-2018 task 3: Irony detection in english tweets. In *Proceedings of the 12th International Workshop on Semantic Evaluation (SemEval-2018), New Orleans, LA, USA.*

SSN MLRG1 at SemEval-2018 Task 3: Irony Detection in English Tweets Using MultiLayer Perceptron

Rajalakshmi S, Angel Deborah S, S Milton Rajendram, Mirnalinee T T
SSN College of Engineering
Chennai 603 110, Tamil Nadu, India
`rajalakshmis@ssn.edu.in, angeldeborahs@ssn.edu.in`
`miltonrs@ssn.edu.in, mirnalineett@ssn.edu.in`

Abstract

Sentiment analysis plays an important role in E-commerce. Identifying ironic and sarcastic content in text plays a vital role in inferring the actual intention of the user, and is necessary to increase the accuracy of sentiment analysis. This paper describes the work on identifying the irony level in twitter texts. The system developed by the SSN MLRG1 team in SemEval-2018 for task 3 (irony detection) uses rule based approach for feature selection and MultiLayer Perceptron (MLP) technique to build the model for multiclass irony classification subtask, which classifies the given text into one of the four class labels.

1 Introduction

Humans have the natural ability to identify the sentiment or the irony intended in a review or comment. However, identifying the intention of the user is a difficult task for the machine. Detecting irony present in a text is critical to sentiment analysis since it will inverse the polarity of the sentiment inferred (Hernandez-Farias et al., 2015).

Choice of shops, books, movies, hotels and various other services and products is influenced by comments and reviews in social media to a large extent. Huge amount of data is available in the Internet about the choices people make and their reviews about it.

Irony in texts affects the polarity of the sentiment inferred from them. Since it gives the text a meaning that is just the opposite to what is actually said, it is called as a *polarity reverser* (Farias et al., 2016). Irony is studied in various disciplines such as linguistics, philosophy and psychology. Due to the frequent use of irony in social media, its detection has gained importance in natural language processing, which faces difficulty in achieving a high performance (Liu, 2012; Wallace, 2015). The potential applications of irony

detection include text mining, author profiling, detecting online harassment and sentiment analysis (Van Hee et al., June 2018). SSN MLRG1 team has already worked in sentiment analysis tasks conducted in SemEval 2017 (Angel Deborah et al., 2017a,b).

We can identify three types irony namely *verbal* irony, *situational* irony and *dramatic* irony. Subtask B in task 3 is a multiclass classification task for classifying a given tweet to one of these four classes:

1. verbal irony realized through a polarity contrast,
2. verbal irony without such a polarity contrast,
3. situational irony, and
4. non-irony.

2 Related Work

Unlike factual information, sentiment analysis and opinion mining have to deal with subjective information. Consequently, for any problem, it is important to analyze opinions collected from many people and summarize them. Social and political discussions are much harder due to complex topic and sentiment expressions, instances of sarcasm and irony (Liu, 2012). Maynard and Greenwood (2014) discusses the need for analyzing sarcasm in social media. They have developed a hashtag tokenizer for GATE (General Architecture for Text Engineering) tool and detected the sentiments and sarcasm in hashtags. Ghosh and Veale (2016) have found deep neural networks to perform better compared to Support Vector Machines (SVM) for sarcasm detection. Hernandez-Farias et al. (2015) have used MLP for automatic irony detection using the basic features from sentiment analysis and observed that MLP yields better results, compared to Naive Bayes, decision trees, maximum entropy and SVM. Barbieri and Saggion (2014) have used

633

random forest and decision tree for analyzing the irony and humour content in twitter dataset using Weka tool. They have used seven features for detecting imbalance, unexpectedness and common patterns.

3 System Overview

The system consists of the following modules: data extraction, preprocessing, rule based feature selection, feature vector generation and multilayer perceptron for classification.

3.1 Feature Engineering and Implementation

The dataset is cleaned and processed using functions from NLTK toolkit. We identified the keywords for irony detection using rule based feature selection. The selected features are formed into a Bag of Words (BoW) dictionary. For each sentence, feature vectors are generated by one-hot encoding method, using the sentence keywords and BoW dictionary. The feature vectors are given to the MLP and output class label is predicted. Error is calculated and backpropagated to update the weight vectors. Nadam (Nesterov-accelerated Adaptive Moment Estimation) algorithm is used for optimization.

The procedure for data preprocessing is outlined in Algorithm 2:

Algorithm 2: Data preprocessing.
Input: Input dataset.
Output: Tokenized words and their parts of speech.
begin

1. Separate labels and sentences.
2. Perform tokenization using `word_tokenize` function of the NLTK toolkit.
3. Perform Parts of Speech tagging using `pos_tag` function from the NLTK toolkit.
4. Return the tokenized words and their parts of speech which will be given as inputs to rule based feature selection.

end

The procedure for rule based feature selection and feature vector generation is outlined in Algorithm 3:

Algorithm 3: Rule based feature selection and feature vector generation
Input: Tokenized words and their parts of speech.
Output: BoW feature representation with labels.
begin

For each of the tokenized words, falling under one of the categories listed in Table 1, do the following steps.

1. Lemmatize the word using `WordNet Lemmatizer` from the NLTK toolkit.
2. Insert the lemmatized word into the dictionary.
3. Represent each sentence as a feature vector using one-hot encoding by looking up the dictionary.
4. Store the corresponding label in target vector using one-hot encoding.
5. Return the feature vector generated as the input to build the model.

end

Abbreviation	Parts of Speech
VB	verb, base form
VBZ	verb, 3rd person sing. present
VBP	verb, non 3rd sing. present
VBD	verb, past tense
VBG	verb, gerund/present participle
VBN	verb, past participle
JJ	adjective
JJR	adjective, comparative
JJS	adjective, superlative
RB	adverb
RBR	adverb, comparative
RBS	adverb, superlative
NN	noun, singular
NNP	proper noun, singular
NNS	noun plural
NNPS	proper noun, plural

Table 1: Parts of speech categories.

The procedure for building Multilayer Perceptron is outlined in Algorithm 4:

Algorithm 4: Build a Multilayer Perceptron model.
Input: BoW feature representation with labels.
Output: Learned model.
begin

1. Prepare the training dataset. `XTrain` contains the feature vectors and `YTrain` contains the target labels for irony class.
2. Build the classification model which comprises an input layer, two hidden layers and an output layer with `relu` activation function in the hidden layers and `softmax` activation function in the output layer.

3. Optimize the classification model using nadam optimizer of `keras` package for some n iterations.

4. Return the learned model.

end

For the test dataset, preprocessing is done and the feature vectors are generated from the training data BoW representation. The feature vectors are given as input to the learned model and the predicted output labels are stored.

3.2 MultiLayer Perceptron

MLP is a feedforward artificial neural network for supervised learning. MLP can be used for both classification and regression tasks. It consists of an input layer, one or more hidden layers and an output layer. Each neuron in one layer is fully connected to the neurons in next layer. Number of neurons in the output layer depends on the number of class labels in the given problem.

Each connection has a weight assigned to it. Output of each neuron is calculated by applying an activation function on the weighted sum of the inputs. Some of the common activation functions are linear, sigmoid, tanh, elu, softplus, softmax, relu, relu6, crelu, selu and relu_x.

Error value is calculated from the value predicted by the output layer and the actual class label. This error value is backpropagated and the weights and biases are updated. This procedure is repeated for the feature vectors of each input sentence. The whole procedure is repeated for some n iterations or until the error value converges to a value below a threshold.

Figure 1 depicts a simple MLP model, consisting of a single hidden layer. It takes four inputs and produces one output.

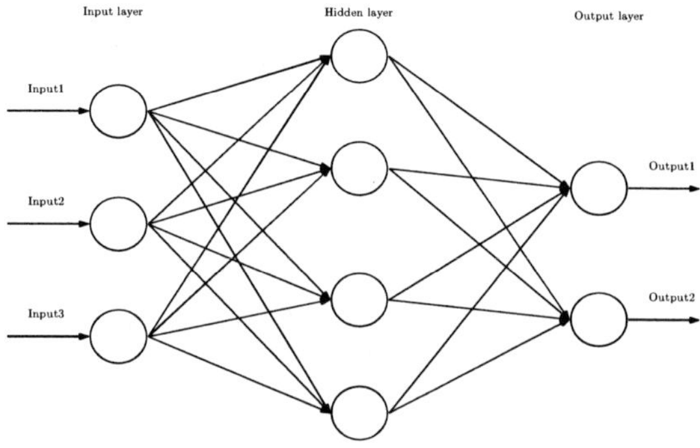

Figure 1: Multilayer Perceptron.

The working of Multilayer Perceptron model is outlined in Algorithm 1:

Algorithm 1: Multilayer Perceptron.
Input: Feature vectors and targets.
Output: Learned model.
begin

1. Initialize the weights with random values and choose a learning rate η.
2. Repeat steps 3 to 6 until the neural network is trained.
3. For each input example (feature_vector, target), do steps 4 to 6.
4. Forward Pass
   (a) For each neuron of a layer, find the weighted sum of the input vectors. Apply the activation function and pass the outputs as inputs to the next layer.
   (b) Predict the value in the output layer.
5. Backward Pass
   (a) Compute the error ∇ between the actual target and the predicted class.
   (b) Backpropagate the error and compute the error in all hidden layer neurons.
6. Update all the weights Δw_{ij} and biases b_{ij} by gradient descent technique.
7. Return the learned model.

end

4   Dataset

The dataset consists of 4792 English tweets that are collected between 01/12/2014 and 04/01/2015 from 2676 unique users. The entire corpus is split into training (80%) and test (20%) sets. The tweets are manually labeled using a fine grained annotation scheme for irony (Van Hee et al., 2016). The training dataset is further divided into training set and development test set for system building.

5   Performance Evaluation

The performance of the system is measured using accuracy, precision, recall and F1-score, using formulas shown in Equations 1 to 4.

$$\text{Accuracy (A)} = \frac{\text{TP} + \text{TN}}{\text{N}} \qquad (1)$$

$$\text{Precision (P)} = \frac{\text{TP}}{\text{TP} + \text{FP}} \qquad (2)$$

$$\text{Recall (R)} = \frac{\text{TP}}{\text{TP} + \text{FN}} \qquad (3)$$

$$F_1 \text{ score} = 2 \times \frac{\text{Precision} \times \text{Recall}}{\text{Precision} + \text{Recall}} \qquad (4)$$

where TP denotes True Positive, TN denotes True Negative, FP denotes False Positive, FN denotes False Negative and N denotes total number of tweets.

The optimization of the model was performed using different gradient descent algorithms such as SGD, adam, adaGrad, RMSProp and nadam. Adam and nadam are the widely used optimizers. Adam (Adaptive Moment Estimation) computes the adaptive learning rates using momentum and RMSProp. Momentum points the model in the best direction, while RMSProp adapts how far the model goes in that direction on parameter basis. Nadam combines Nesterov momentum with Adam which is superior to momentum. (Dozat, 2016).

We split the training set into training set (80%) and development test set (20%). The different optimization algorithms were used with the model and nadam optimizer produced better results compared to other algorithms for the development test set.

There are 32 submissions for this particular task. The model has achieved the following values for the various measures as listed in Table 2.

Measure	Value	Ranking
Accuracy	0.5727	15
Precision	0.3484	21
Recall	0.3609	19
F1-Score	0.3337	20

Table 2: Performance.

From the result, it appears as if the basic text features selected by rule based approach is not enough to detect the irony level in the given text. Additional features like emoticons and hashtags can be added to the feature set to enhance the performance.

6 Conclusion

We built a basic MLP to detect the irony level in twitter text, which has an input layer, two hidden layers with 128 and 64 neurons, and an output layer with 4 neurons for the four class labels. Relu activation function was used in both hidden layers and softmax activation function in output layer. The various optimizers such as SGD, RMSprop, adam, adagrad, and nadam were tried. Nadam optimizer performed better than others.

The text features were taken into consideration for BoW representation. Since irony renders an opposite meaning to the text, it is difficult to detect the irony from the text features alone. The system performance can be enhanced with the emoticon and hashtag information. The performance can also be improved by doing tweet normalization before the feature selection. The accuracy of system can be increased by using deep neural networks such as Convolutional Neural Network (CNN) or Recurrent Neural Network (RNN). Feature selection techniques can be enhanced with semantics and lexicon information.

References

S Angel Deborah, S Milton Rajendram, and T T Mirnalinee. 2017a. Ssn mlrg1 at semeval-2017 task 4: Sentiment analysis in twitter using multi-kernel gaussian process classifier. In *Proceedings the 11th International Workshop on Semantic Evaluation (SemEval-2017)*, pages 709–712. ACL, Vancouver, Canada.

S Angel Deborah, S Milton Rajendram, and T T Mirnalinee. 2017b. Ssn mlrg1 at semeval-2017 task 5: Fine-grained sentiment analysis using multiple kernel gaussian process regression model. In *Proceedings the 11th International Workshop on Semantic Evaluation (SemEval-2017)*, pages 823–826. ACL, Vancouver, Canada.

Francesco Barbieri and Horacio Saggion. 2014. Automatic detection of irony and humour in twitter. In *ICCC, Fifth International Conference on Computational Creativity, Ljubljana, Slovenia, 9th 13th June 2014*, pages 155–162.

Timothy Dozat. 2016. Incorporating nesterov momentum into adam. In *Workshop track - ICLR 2016*.

Delia Irazu Hernandez Farias, Viviana Patti, and Paolo Rosso. 2016. Irony detection in twitter: The role of affective content. *ACM Transactions on Internet Technology (TOIT)*, 16(3):19.

Aniruddha Ghosh and Tony Veale. 2016. Fracking sarcasm using neural network. In *Proceedings of the 7th Workshop on Computational Approaches to Subjectivity, Sentiment and Social Media Analysis*, pages 161–169.

Irazu Hernandez-Farias, Jose-Miguel Benedi, and Paolo Rosso. 2015. Applying basic features from sentiment analysis for automatic irony detection. In *Iberian Conference on Pattern Recognition and Image Analysis*, pages 337–344. Springer.

Bing Liu. 2012. Sentiment analysis and opinion mining. *Synthesis lectures on human language technologies*, 5(1):1–167.

Diana Maynard and Mark A Greenwood. 2014. Who cares about sarcastic tweets? investigating the impact of sarcasm on sentiment analysis. In *Lrec*, pages 4238–4243.

Cynthia Van Hee, Els Lefever, and Veronique Hoste. 2016. Guidelines for annotating irony in social media text. Technical report, version 2.0. Technical Report 16-01, LT3, Language and Translation Technology Team–Ghent University.

Cynthia Van Hee, Els Lefever, and Veronique Hoste. June 2018. Semeval-2018 task 3: Irony detection in english tweets. In *In Proceedings of the 12th International Workshop on Semantic Evaluation (SemEval-2018), New Orleans, LA, USA.*

Byron C Wallace. 2015. Computational irony: A survey and new perspectives. *Artificial Intelligence Review*, 43(4):467–483.

NLPRL-IITBHU at SemEval-2018 Task 3: Combining Linguistic Features and Emoji Pre-trained CNN for Irony Detection in Tweets

Harsh Rangwani, Devang Kulshreshtha and Anil Kumar Singh

Indian Institute of Technology (Banaras Hindu University) Varanasi, India
{harsh.rangwani.cse15, devang.kulshreshtha.cse14, aksingh.cse}@iitbhu.ac.in

Abstract

This paper describes our participation in Se-mEval 2018 Task 3 on Irony Detection in Tweets. We combine linguistic features with pre-trained activations of a neural network. The CNN is trained on the emoji predic-tion task. We combine the two feature sets and feed them into an XGBoost Classifier for classification. Subtask-A involves classifica-tion of tweets into ironic and non-ironic in-stances, whereas Subtask-B involves classifi-cation of tweets into *non-ironic, verbal irony, situational irony* or *other verbal irony*. It is observed that combining features from these two different feature spaces improves our sys-tem results. We leverage the SMOTE algo-rithm to handle the problem of class imbal-ance in Subtask-B. Our final model achieves an F1-score of 0.65 and 0.47 on Subtask-A and Subtask-B respectively. Our system ranks 4th on both tasks, respectively, outperforming the baseline by 6% on Subtask-A and 14% on Subtask-B.

1 Introduction

According to the Merriam-Webster dictionary[1], one of the meanings of irony is defined as 'the use of words to express something other than and es-pecially the opposite of the literal meaning' (*e.g. I love getting spam emails.*). Irony can have dif-ferent forms, such as verbal, situational, dramatic etc. Sarcasm is also categorized as a form of ver-bal irony. Various attempts have been made in the past for detection of sarcasm (Joshi et al., 2017). Sarcastic texts are characterized by the presence of humor and ridicule, which are not always present in the case of ironic texts (Kreuz and Glucksberg, 1989). The absence of these characteristics makes automatic irony detection a more difficult problem than sarcasm detection.

Irony detection is a problem that is important for the working of many Natural Language Un-derstanding Systems. For example, people often use irony to express their opinions on social media like Twitter (Buschmeier et al., 2014). Detecting irony in social texts can aid in improving opinion analysis.

The SemEval 2018 task 3 (Van Hee et al., 2018) consists of two subtasks. Subtask-A involves predicting whether a tweet is ironic or not and Subtask-B involves categorizing a tweet into Non-Ironic, Verbal Irony (by means of a polarity con-trast), Situational Irony and Other Forms of Verbal Irony. The task organizers use macro averaged F1, rather than accuracy to force systems to optimize to work well on all the four classes of tweets, as described in Section 3.1.

Systems built in the past primarily used hand-crafted linguistic features for classification of ironic texts (Buschmeier et al. 2014; Farías et al. 2016). In our system, we try to combine them with the pre-trained activations of a neural network. Our results show that both types of features com-plement each other, as the results produced by the combination of them surpass the results of using either the linguistic or the pre-trained activation features individually by a large margin. We use XGBoost Classifier (Chen and Guestrin, 2016), as it performs at par with neural networks when the provided training data is of small size.

Our results indicate that oversampling tech-niques like SMOTE (Chawla et al., 2002) can also be used to oversample the representations gen-erated using neural networks to improve perfor-mance on imbalanced datasets.

The rest of the paper is organized as follows: Section 2 gives a detailed description of how our system was built, Section 3 then describes the ex-perimental setup and the results obtained and Sec-tion 4 concludes the paper.

---

[1] https://www.merriam-webster.com/dictionary/irony

Proceedings of the 12th International Workshop on Semantic Evaluation (SemEval-2018), pages 638–642
New Orleans, Louisiana, June 5–6, 2018. ©2018 Association for Computational Linguistics

2 Proposed Approach

For modeling irony in tweets, our system makes use of a combination of features. These features can be classified into two broad groups:

- Linguistic (Structure and User Behavior)

- Pre-trained Activations of a Neural Network.

These features were concatenated and the XG-Boost classifier (Chen and Guestrin, 2016) was used to perform the classification.

For subtask B, to counter the imbalance in the dataset, which might lead classifiers to favor the majority class in classification, we used SMOTE for oversampling the data (Chawla et al., 2002). Then we used XGBoost Classifier again for classification into various classes.

The details of the classifier parameters are provided in Section 2.2. Basic preprocessing of tweets was performed before feature extraction, which involved removing hash symbols ('#'), converting contractions ('doesn't' to 'does not'), removing links and quotations and normalizing the text into lower case. We will explicitly mention those features whose extraction require the original tweets.

2.1 Feature Extraction

Our system generates a 72-dimensional hand-crafted feature vector, based on the linguistic structure and user behavior. We then combine this with a 2304 dimensional feature vector generated using activations of a pre-trained CNN. The combined features are categorized into 11 broad classes:

Contrast Based Features: Contrast of sentiments is a feature that has been observed in sarcastic and ironic texts (Rajadesingan et al., 2015), *e.g. I love being ignored #not*. For capturing contrast, we use the affect score of lemmas (Warriner et al., 2013) and the sentiment score of words based on **SentiStrength** (Thelwall et al., 2010). The final feature vector consists of:

- The difference between the highest and lowest sentiment values of the words present in the tweet. (1 feature)

- The difference between the highest and lowest affect scores of the words present in the tweet. (1 feature)

- Longest unimodal sequence size and the number of transitions of sentiment polarity. (2 features)

- Sum of sentiment scores and counts of positive and negative n-grams. (4 features)

Readability Based Features: Ironical texts are usually complex, and hence we use the total number of syllables in the tweet, along with number of words that contain polysyllables as features. According to Automated Readability Index (Senter and Smith, 1967), the standard deviation, the average and the median of the word length serve as indicators of the complexity of the text (Rajadesingan et al., 2015).

Incongruity of Context: Ironic similes are common in literature (*e.g. as clear as mud* in which both *clear* and *mud* are sentiment neutral words.). Due to this neutrality, the lexicon based methods are unable to capture the incongruity present. Therefore, maximum and minimum GloVe (Pennington et al., 2014) cosine similarity between any two words in a tweet are used as features in our system (Joshi et al., 2016).

Repetition-based Features: Users often change their writing style to depict sarcasm and irony, which is analogous to the change of tone in speech while expressing sarcasm, *e.g. Loooovvveeeeeee when my phone gets wiped*. We use the count of of words with repetitive characters and the count of 'senti words' (sentiment score ≥ 2 and sentiment score ≤ -2) with repetitive characters as our features (Rajadesingan et al., 2015).

Punctuation-based Features: Punctuation counts can sometimes serve as an indicator of ironic texts (Kreuz and Caucci, 2007). We use the counts of characters like hashtag (#), ellipsis (...), exclamation mark (!), question mark (?), colon (:), quote (") and apostrophe (') in a tweet as features.

Presence of Markers: Discourse markers are certain words that help in expressing ideas and performing specific functions (Farías et al., 2016). Our system uses a curated list of discourse markers. Similar to the list of discourse markers, we also use a list of intensifiers (*e.g. heck*), laughter words (*e.g. lmao, lol etc.*), interjections (*e.g. oops*) and swear words (*e.g. shit*) as their appearance in a tweet indicates the presence of unexpectedness, which can, in turn, serve as an indicator of irony. We use counts of these different types of words separately as features.

Word Count Features: According to (2016), ironic tweets depict their content in fewer words compared to normal tweets. Hence we use the word count of tweets as a feature. Apart from the word count, (Kreuz and Caucci, 2007) suggest that the counts of adjectives and adverbs can also be used as markers of ironic content. We also use the preposition count as a separate feature.

Semantic Similarity: Ironic tweets that span multiple lines are often found to have lines that are very much semantically dissimilar to each other (Farías et al., 2016). We use the **WordNet** based similarity function (Mihalcea et al., 2006) available online[2] to obtain a similarity score, which is used as a feature.

Polarity and Subjectivity: Ironic texts are usually subjective and often convey something negative (or positive) about the target (Wallace et al., 2015). We use the Polarity and Subjectivity Scores (Sentiment Score) generated using **TextBlob** as features in our model (Loria et al., 2014).

URL Counts: We observed in the training set that users often used irony to express their opinion about online content, e.g. blogs, images, tweets, etc. For specifying the context of a comment (tweet), they often add a URL to the original content. So we used the counts of URLs in a tweet as a feature. Our system requires raw tweets for extracting this feature.

Apart from the above features, we also experimented with Named Entity Count and occurrence of popular hashtags like (*#hypocrisy*), using a curated list, as our features (Van Hee, 2017).

2.1.1 Pre-trained CNN Features

Apart from extracting linguistic features from tweets, we leverage the activations of a Convolutional Neural Network (CNN) pre-trained on emoji prediction task. We use DeepMoji[3] (Felbo et al., 2017), a model trained on 1.2 billion tweets with emojis, and tested on eight benchmark datasets within sentiment, emotion and sarcasm detection. Since sarcasm is a form of verbal irony that expresses ridicule or contempt (Long and Graesser, 1988), we believe transferring the knowledge of CNN trained on sarcasm can improve the results of Irony Detection task.

Each tweet is converted into a 2304-dimensional feature vector by feeding into

DeepMoji-CNN and extracting activations of the last hidden layer.

2.2 Classifiers

We construct XGBoost (Chen and Guestrin, 2016) feature-based classifiers for irony detection using the above features. Based on the 10-fold cross validation performance, the best performing parameters prove to be the default parameters used by the XGBoost Classifier Package [4].

2.3 Handling Class Imbalance

The data provided for subtask-B is highly skewed. To perform well on every class of irony, we used an oversampling technique (SMOTE (Chawla et al., 2002)). In SMOTE, for generating a new synthetic sample, from the k-nearest neighbors of an instance, one is chosen at random, and a new sample is generated on the line joining the instance and the chosen neighbor. We use the SMOTE implementation available in *imblearn* (Lemaître et al., 2017) package for our system, with k-neighbors equal to 5.

3 Experiments and Evaluation

3.1 Dataset and Metrics

The annotated tweet corpus provided for training consists of 1390 instances of Verbal Irony due to polarity contrast, 205 instances of Other Types of Verbal Irony, 316 Situational Ironic instances, and 1923 Non Ironic instances. Our system only uses the training data provided by the organizers and no other annotated data is used (Constrained System).

The test dataset for Subtask-A contains 473 non-ironical tweets and 311 ironical tweets. For Subtask-B, the 311 ironical tweets are further classified into Verbal Irony by means of Polarity Contrast (164), Situational Irony (85) and Other Forms Of Verbal Irony (62).

The evaluation metric used for ranking teams in Sub-task A is the F1 score of the positive (Ironic) class whereas in Subtask-B, the organizers use macro averaged F1 (average of F1 for each class) as an evaluation metric for ranking teams.

3.2 Results and Discussion

We present the results achieved by our approaches, as well as the combination of our methods in Table 1. Our final submitted systems are: (Linguistic

---

[2]http://nlpforhackers.io/
wordnet-sentence-similarity/
[3]https://github.com/bfelbo/DeepMoji

[4]http://xgboost.readthedocs.io/en/
latest/parameter.html

<table>
<tr><td rowspan="2">Approach</td><td colspan="3">Task-A</td><td colspan="3">Task-B</td></tr>
<tr><td>Precision</td><td>Recall</td><td>F1-score</td><td>Precision</td><td>Recall</td><td>F1-score</td></tr>
<tr><td>Linguistic</td><td>0.48</td><td>0.78</td><td>0.59</td><td>0.32</td><td>0.36</td><td>0.30</td></tr>
<tr><td>Pretrained CNN</td><td>0.60</td><td>0.63</td><td>0.62</td><td>0.51</td><td>0.44</td><td>0.42</td></tr>
<tr><td>Linguistic + Pretrained CNN</td><td>0.55</td><td>0.79</td><td>0.65</td><td>0.53</td><td>0.44</td><td>0.42</td></tr>
<tr><td>Linguistic + Pretrained CNN + SMOTE</td><td>-</td><td>-</td><td>-</td><td>0.46</td><td>0.51</td><td>0.47</td></tr>
<tr><td>Baseline (Linear SVC over BoW)</td><td>0.56</td><td>0.63</td><td>0.59</td><td>0.48</td><td>0.36</td><td>0.33</td></tr>
</table>

Table 1: F1 scores in Task A and Macro F1 in Task B on test set.

+ Pretrained CNN) for Task-A and (Linguistic + Pretrained CNN + SMOTE) for Task-B. We discuss the major takeaways from the results below.

- Our submitted models achieve 4th position in public leaderboard [5] on both Task-A and Task-B and beat the task baselines by about 6% and 14%, respectively, on both tasks on the test set.

- Leveraging DeepMoji model for Irony detection domain yields a considerable improvement over purely linguistic features (0.03 and 0.12). This is because the model is trained on over a *billion* tweets on sarcasm and four other domains. As stated earlier, sarcasm is a verbal form of irony (Long and Graesser, 1988), and transfer learning works as domains are quite similar.

- Our combination of linguistic features with pre-trained CNN achieves an F-score of 0.65 and 0.42, with an improvement of at least 0.03 on Task-A and significant improvement in Task-B, compared to linguistic features. The higher accuracy points to the power of ensemble learning by combining different feature spaces, as both feature sets specialize in different types of tweets.

- The use of SMOTE oversampling technique leads to an F-score of 0.47 in Task-B, which is an improvement of 0.05 over (Linguistic + Pretrained CNN) model.

- The improvement in scores due to linguistic features are not as pronounced in Subtask-B, as compared to Subtask-A. One of the possible reasons for this is that linguistic features are not able to capture the fine grained differences between different forms of irony.

---

[5] https://competitions.codalab.org/competitions/17468#results

4   Conclusion

We reported the use of handcrafted features and pre-trained CNN activations for predicting the irony in tweets. We implemented a variety of features based on user behavior as well as the linguistic structure in a tweet. We further exploit the SMOTE oversampling technique to handle the class imbalance problem in Subtask-B, which involves categorizing a tweet into Non Ironic, Verbal Irony, Situational Irony and Other Verbal Irony. We then feed the features into XGBoost classifier for both the tasks. The benefit of using CNN models pre-trained on sarcasm, sentiment, and emotion domains can be clearly seen, yielding an improvement of 3% and 9% over task baselines. Our final submitted system stood 4th in both the subtasks in the SemEval 2018 shared task on "Irony Detection in English Tweets".

References

Konstantin Buschmeier, Philipp Cimiano, and Roman Klinger. 2014. An impact analysis of features in a classification approach to irony detection in product reviews. In *Proceedings of the 5th Workshop on Computational Approaches to Subjectivity, Sentiment and Social Media Analysis*, pages 42–49.

Nitesh V Chawla, Kevin W Bowyer, Lawrence O Hall, and W Philip Kegelmeyer. 2002. Smote: synthetic minority over-sampling technique. *Journal of artificial intelligence research*, 16:321–357.

Tianqi Chen and Carlos Guestrin. 2016. Xgboost: A scalable tree boosting system. In *Proceedings of the 22nd acm sigkdd international conference on knowledge discovery and data mining*, pages 785–794. ACM.

Delia Irazú Hernández Farías, Viviana Patti, and Paolo Rosso. 2016. Irony detection in twitter: The role of affective content. *ACM Transactions on Internet Technology (TOIT)*, 16(3):19.

Bjarke Felbo, Alan Mislove, Anders Søgaard, Iyad Rahwan, and Sune Lehmann. 2017. Using millions of emoji occurrences to learn any-domain representations for detecting sentiment, emotion and sarcasm. *arXiv preprint arXiv:1708.00524*.

Aditya Joshi, Pushpak Bhattacharyya, and Mark J Carman. 2017. Automatic sarcasm detection: A survey. *ACM Computing Surveys (CSUR)*, 50(5):73.

Aditya Joshi, Vaibhav Tripathi, Kevin Patel, Pushpak Bhattacharyya, and Mark Carman. 2016. Are word embedding-based features useful for sarcasm detection? *arXiv preprint arXiv:1610.00883*.

Roger J Kreuz and Gina M Caucci. 2007. Lexical influences on the perception of sarcasm. In *Proceedings of the Workshop on computational approaches to Figurative Language*, pages 1–4. Association for Computational Linguistics.

Roger J Kreuz and Sam Glucksberg. 1989. How to be sarcastic: The echoic reminder theory of verbal irony. *Journal of experimental psychology: General*, 118(4):374.

Guillaume Lemaître, Fernando Nogueira, and Christos K. Aridas. 2017. Imbalanced-learn: A python toolbox to tackle the curse of imbalanced datasets in machine learning. *Journal of Machine Learning Research*, 18(17):1–5.

Debra L Long and Arthur C Graesser. 1988. Wit and humor in discourse processing. *Discourse processes*, 11(1):35–60.

Steven Loria, P Keen, M Honnibal, R Yankovsky, D Karesh, E Dempsey, et al. 2014. Textblob: simplified text processing. *Secondary TextBlob: Simplified Text Processing*.

Rada Mihalcea, Courtney Corley, Carlo Strapparava, et al. 2006. Corpus-based and knowledge-based measures of text semantic similarity. In *AAAI*, volume 6, pages 775–780.

Jeffrey Pennington, Richard Socher, and Christopher Manning. 2014. Glove: Global vectors for word representation. In *Proceedings of the 2014 conference on empirical methods in natural language processing (EMNLP)*, pages 1532–1543.

Ashwin Rajadesingan, Reza Zafarani, and Huan Liu. 2015. Sarcasm detection on twitter: A behavioral modeling approach. In *Proceedings of the Eighth ACM International Conference on Web Search and Data Mining*, pages 97–106. ACM.

RJ Senter and Edgar A Smith. 1967. Automated readability index. Technical report, CINCINNATI UNIV OH.

Mike Thelwall, Kevan Buckley, Georgios Paltoglou, Di Cai, and Arvid Kappas. 2010. Sentiment strength detection in short informal text. *Journal of the Association for Information Science and Technology*, 61(12):2544–2558.

Cynthia Van Hee. 2017. *Can machines sense irony? : exploring automatic irony detection on social media*. Ph.D. thesis, Ghent University.

Cynthia Van Hee, Els Lefever, and Véronique Hoste. 2018. SemEval-2018 Task 3: Irony Detection in English Tweets. In *Proceedings of the 12th International Workshop on Semantic Evaluation*, SemEval-2018, New Orleans, LA, USA. Association for Computational Linguistics.

Byron C Wallace, Eugene Charniak, et al. 2015. Sparse, contextually informed models for irony detection: Exploiting user communities, entities and sentiment. In *Proceedings of the 53rd Annual Meeting of the Association for Computational Linguistics and the 7th International Joint Conference on Natural Language Processing (Volume 1: Long Papers)*, volume 1, pages 1035–1044.

Amy Beth Warriner, Victor Kuperman, and Marc Brysbaert. 2013. Norms of valence, arousal, and dominance for 13,915 english lemmas. *Behavior research methods*, 45(4):1191–1207.

ValenTO at SemEval-2018 Task 3: Exploring the Role of Affective Content for Detecting Irony in English Tweets

Delia Irazú Hernández Farías
Inst. Nacional de Astrofísica,
Óptica y Electrónica (INAOE)
Mexico
dirazuherfa@hotmail.com

Viviana Patti
Dip. di Informatica
University of Turin
Italy
patti@di.unito.it

Paolo Rosso
PRHLT Research Center
Universitat Politècnica de València
Spain
prosso@dsic.upv.es

Abstract

In this paper we describe the system used by the ValenTO team in the shared task on *Irony Detection in English Tweets* at SemEval 2018. The system takes as starting point emotIDM, an irony detection model that explores the use of affective features based on a wide range of lexical resources available for English, reflecting different facets of affect. We experimented with different settings, by exploiting different classifiers and features, and participated both to the binary irony detection task and to the task devoted to distinguish among different types of irony. We report on the results obtained by our system both in a constrained setting and unconstrained setting, where we explored the impact of using additional data in the training phase, such as corpora annotated for the presence of irony or sarcasm from the state of the art. Overall, the performance of our system seems to validate the important role that affective information has for identifying ironic content in Twitter.

1 Introduction

People use social media platforms as a forum to share and express themselves by using the language in creative ways and employing figurative language devices such as *irony* to achieve different communication purposes. Irony is closely associated with the indirect expression of feelings, emotions and evaluations, and detecting the presence of irony in social media texts is considered a challenge for research in computational linguistics, also for the impact on sentiment analysis, where irony detection is important to avoid misinterpreting the polarity of ironic statements.

Broadly speaking, under the umbrella term of *irony* two main concepts are covered: *verbal irony* and *situational irony*. Verbal irony is commonly defined as a figure of speech where the speaker intends to communicate the opposite of what is liter-

ally said (Sperber and Wilson, 1986). Situational irony, instead refers to a contradictory or unexpected outcome of events (Lucariello, 2014). In Twitter we can find many examples both of verbal irony and of posts where users describe aspects of an ironic situation. Most of the proposed approaches to the automatic detection of irony in social media (Riloff et al., 2013; Buschmeier et al., 2014; Ptáček et al., 2014)take advantage of lexical factors such as n-grams, punctuation marks, among others. Information related to affect has been also exploited (Reyes et al., 2013; Barbieri et al., 2014; Hernández Farías et al., 2015). Other scholars proposed methods exploiting the context surrounding an ironic utterance (Wallace et al., 2015; Karoui et al., 2015). Recently, also deep learning techniques have been applied (Nozza et al., 2016; Poria et al., 2016).

This paper describes our participation in the SemEval-2018 Task 3. The aim of this task is to identify ironic tweets. ValenTO exploited an extended version of *emotIDM* (Hernández Farías et al., 2016), an irony detection model based mainly on affective information. In particular, we experimented the use of a wide range of affect-related features for characterizing the presence of ironic content, covering different facets of affect, from sentiment to finer-grained emotions. Most theorist (Grice, 1975; Wilson and Sperber, 1992; Alba-Juez and Attardo, 2014) recognized, indeed, the important role of affective information for irony communication-comprehension.

2 The emotIDM model

Irony is a very subjective language device that involves the expression of affective contents such as emotions, attitudes, or evaluations towards a particular target. Attempting to take advantage of the emotionally-laden characteristics of ironic expressions, we relied on *emotIDM*, an irony detection

Proceedings of the 12th International Workshop on Semantic Evaluation (SemEval-2018), pages 643–648
New Orleans, Louisiana, June 5–6, 2018. ©2018 Association for Computational Linguistics

model that, taking advantage of several affective resources available for English (Nissim and Patti, 2016), exploits various facets of affective information from sentiment to finer-grained emotions for characterizing the presence of irony in Twitter (Hernández Farías et al., 2016).

In (Hernández Farías and Rosso, 2016) the robustness of *emotIDM* was assessed over different Twitter state-of-the-art corpora for irony detection (Reyes et al., 2013; Barbieri et al., 2014; Mohammad et al., 2015; Ptáček et al., 2014; Riloff et al., 2013). The obtained results outperform those in the previous works confirming the significance of affective features for irony detection. An additional aspect to be mentioned about *emotIDM* is that it was designed to identify ironic content in a general sense, i.e. considering irony as a broad term covering different types of irony in tweets.

emotIDM comprises two main groups of features that are described below:

Structural Features (Str). This group includes different markers that could help to identify ironic intention in tweets: punctuation marks (colon, exclamation, question marks), Part-Of-Speech labels (verbs, adverbs, nouns, adjectives), emoticons, uppercase characters, among others.

Affective Features. They are organized in three sub-groups representing different facets of affect:

Sentiment-Related Features *(Sent)*. Hu&Liu (Hu and Liu, 2004), General Inquirer (Stone and Hunt, 1963), EffectWordNet (Choi and Wiebe, 2014), Subjectivity lexicon (Wilson et al., 2005), and EmoLex (Mohammad and Turney, 2013), AFINN, SWN, Semantic Orientation lexicon (Taboada and Grieve, 2004), and SenticNet (SN) (Cambria et al., 2014).

Emotional Categories *(eCat)*. EmoLex, EmoSenticNet (Poria et al., 2013), SentiSense (Carrillo de Albornoz et al., 2012), and the Linguistic Inquiry and Word Count dictionary (Pennebaker et al., 2001).

Dimensional Models of Emotions *(eDim)*. ANEW (Bradley and Lang, 1999), DAL (Whissell, 2009), and SN.

3 emotIDM at SemEval-2018 Task 3: Irony Detection in English Tweets

3.1 Task Description and Datasets

In the framework of SemEval-2018 was organized the *Task 3* on *Irony detection in English tweets* (Van Hee et al., 2018). The main objective of this task is to identify the presence of irony in Twitter. It was divided in two different subtasks:

1. **Task A: Ironic vs. non-ironic**: to determine whether a tweet is ironic or not.

2. **Task B: Different types of irony**: to predict one out of four labels: 0) *non-irony (nI)*, 1) *verbal_irony_by_polarity_contrast (vI)*, 2) *other_verbal_irony (oI)*, 3) *situational_irony (sI)*.

Organizers provided datasets for training and test labeled according the objectives of each subtask. The whole dataset was collected by exploiting a set of hashtags (#irony, #sarcasm and #not). Therefore, a manual annotation process was applied in order to minimize the noise in the data. For Task A, 1,911 ironic and 1,923 non-ironic tweets where provided. While for Task B, the distribution was: 1923 for *nI*, 1393 for *vI*, 213 for *oI* and 328 for *sI*. Participants were allowed to submit systems trained under two settings: *constrained (C)*, where only the training data provided for the task should be used; *unconstrained (U)*, where the use of additional data was permitted.

3.2 Our Proposal

We decided to participate to the shared task by using *emotIDM*. By analyzing the training data, an interesting characteristic was found: 857 out of 3,834 tweets contain an URL. From these tweets, 265 were belonging to the ironic class, while 592 were labeled as non-ironic. Notice that, in (Hernández-Farías et al., 2014), the authors found a similar behavior regarding URL information in the dataset provided by the organizers of SentiPOLC-2014 (Basile et al., 2014). Furthermore, Barbieri et al. (2014) exploited a feature for alerting the existence of an URL in a tweet; such feature was ranked among the most discriminative ones according to an information gain analysis. Since, information regarding to the presence of URL in a tweet has proven to be useful for detecting irony in Twitter, we decided to enrich *emotIDM* by adding a binary feature for reflecting the presence of URL in a tweet.

Below, we describe our participation in the task.

Task A: Ironic vs. non-ironic

We addressed this task as a binary classification by taking advantage of two of the most widely applied classifiers in irony detection: Decision Tree (DT) and Support Vector Machine

(SVM)[1]. Moreover, we also included Random Forest (RF) as a classifier in our experiments[2]. We carried out a set of experiments for assessing the performance of the original version of *emotIDM* and the one including information concerning URL (*emotIDM+URL*). Besides, to investigate the contribution of the different sets of features in *emotIDM* further experiments were performed. Several classifiers were used in order to identify the most promising setting.

As mentioned before, exploiting external data was allowed in the *unconstrained* setting. We took advantage of a set of corpora previously used in the state of the art in irony detection. We exploited data from a set of corpora collected exploiting different approaches: *self-tagging* or *manual annotation or crowd-sourcing*[3]. We exploited the corpora developed by (Reyes et al., 2013), (Barbieri et al., 2014), (Mohammad et al., 2015), (Ptáček et al., 2014), (Riloff et al., 2013), (Ghosh et al., 2015), (Karoui et al., 2017), and (Sulis et al., 2016). Besides, we also take advantage of an in-house collection of tweets containing the hashtags #irony and #sarcasm[4].

Table 1 shows the obtained results during the developing phase for Task A. We experimented with different sets of features and classifiers considering a five fold-cross validation setting.

| Features | Classifiers | | | | | |
| | DT | | RF | | SVM | |
	C	U	C	U	C	U
emotIDM	0.57	0.70	0.64	0.71	0.64	0.79
emotIDM + URL	0.56	0.74	0.62	0.70	0.64	**0.81**
Str + Sent	0.59	0.69	0.60	0.70	0.63	0.78
Str+eCat+eDim	0.58	0.69	0.62	0.70	0.65	0.77
Sent+eCat+eDim	0.52	0.61	0.54	0.62	0.57	0.70

Table 1: Training phase: results for Task A with different experimental settings in *C* and *U* scenarios.

SVM emerges as the classifier with the best performance in both C and U scenarios. We noticed that, when using SVM, adding the URL feature

---

to *emotIDM* helps to improve the overall performance of our system. When we experimented by removing a set of features in *emotIDM*, a drop in the performance (in most of the cases) is observed. The results of the experiments with external data are higher than those using only the training data. The last row in Table 1 shows the obtained results when only affect-related features were used; even though there is a drop in the performance respect to the experiments using structural features, it seems that affective features on their own provide useful information for irony detection.

We participated in the subtask A by submitting two runs (constrained and unconstrained) exploiting the experimental setting with the best performance: *emotIDM+URL* with a SVM as classifier.

Task B: Different types of irony

Distinguishing between different kinds of ironic devices is still a controversial issue. In computational linguistics, only few research works have attempted to address such a difficult task (Wang, 2013; Barbieri et al., 2014; Sulis et al., 2016; Van Hee et al., 2016). We are interested in assessing the performance of *emotIDM* when it deals with different types of irony, in order to test if a wide variety of affective features can help in discriminating also in the finer-grained classification task here proposed. This could give some insights on the role of affective content among ironic devices having different communication purposes.

emotIDM+URL was trained with the dataset provided for Task B (constrained setting) to test the effectiveness of affective features in such finer-grained task. We exploited the same classifiers than in Task A attempting to evaluate their performance when different classes of irony should be classified. Overall, the best performance was achieved by SVM (see Table 2). However, when the performance of each single class was considered, the best results were those obtained with DT. For this reason, we decided to combine two classifiers with the following criterion: the *sI* and *oI* classes are assigned by the DT; while *irony* and *non-irony* are assigned by SVM or RF. Table 2 shows the obtained results of the experiments carried out over the dataset for Task B. A five fold cross-validation was applied. From the results in Table 2, it can be noticed that when two classifiers are combined the performance of our model improves. The DT + SVM was selected as the system for participating in the Task B.

---

[1] For experimental purposes we used Scikit-learn: `http://scikit-learn.org/`. The default configuration of parameters in the classifiers was applied.

[2] This was motivated by the fact that it demonstrated a competitive performance for classifying tweets with #irony, #sarcasm, and #not hashtags in (Sulis et al., 2016).

[3] Further details on the approaches for collecting corpora for irony detection can be found in (Hernández Farías and Rosso, 2016).

[4] The tweets were retrieved during the 2016 US Elections period from 8th up to 18th November 2016.

Classifier (s)	Macro F-measure
DT	0.31
RF	0.30
SVM	0.31
DT + RF	0.33
DT + SVM	**0.34**

Table 2: Training phase: obtained results for Task B.

3.3 Results

The results of ValenTO participation in the shared task are summarized in Table 3. In Task A, on the official CodaLab ranking, we ranked in the 16th position with the unconstrained version of our submission. When comparing our official result with the one obtained by the best-ranked system (0.7054), it can be noticed that the difference is lower than 0.1 in F-score terms. It is an interesting result considering that our system relies mainly on features covering different facets of affect in ironic tweets, and confirms the key role that such kind of affective information plays for detecting irony in Twitter. In addition, the organizers also provided separate rankings for constrained and unconstrained submissions. Our system ranked in the 17th position in the constrained setting, while in the unconstrained one we ranked as 4th. Moreover, the performance of our system seems to be stable in the two C and U settings. Concerning Task B, our system performed relatively well, considering that we did not apply further tuning to capture different ironic devices. We ranked in the 17th position of 31 submissions in the Official ranking at CodaLab.

Run	Accuracy	Precision	Recall	F1-score
		Task A		
C	0.6709	0.5764	0.6431	0.6079
U	0.5982	0.4959	0.7814	**0.6067**
		Task B		
C	0.5599	0.3534	0.3521	0.3520

Table 3: Official results of ValenTO team in both tasks

3.4 Discussion and Error Analysis

Data provided for the task were retrieved by exploiting hashtags #irony, #sarcasm and #not, which according to (Sulis et al., 2016) seems to label different kinds of ironic phenomena. We analyzed the gold standard labels provided by the organizers (where the ironic hashtags were also included in the tweets) in order to see the performance of our model for recognizing tweets labeled with distinct hashtags. Considering the results in Task A, we noticed that our system was able to identify all the three kinds of tweets without any kind of skew towards a particular hashtag.

It somehow confirms the robustness of emotIDM for recognizing irony in a broad sense.

Our system was able to correctly identify instances expressing an apparent positive emotional distress with an ironic intention, such as: *Sunday is such a fun day to study #ew #saywhat* and *Yay I just love this time of the month...!*. A special mention is for tweets labeled with #not. This hashtag is not always used for highlighting a figurative meaning. Our system was able to correctly identify instances containing #not when it was used for figurative meaning such as: *Yay for Fire Alarms at 3AM #not*, and also when it was used as part of the text in a tweet: *#Myanmar #men #plead #not #guilty to #murder of #British #tourists. http://t.co/flrKr3H6Kl via @reuters.*

For what concerns the performance of *emotIDM* in Task B, Table 4 [5] shows that our model performed better in identifying tweets where verbal irony was expressed by means of a polarity contrast. Moreover, it was recognizing better "situational irony" than "other irony".

	vI	oI	sI	nI	tT	Correct (%)
vI	**75**	10	14	66	166	**45**
oI	6	**4**	11	25	62	**9.2**
sI	16	9	**13**	35	85	**40**
nI	67	39	47	**347**	473	**79**

Table 4: Confusion Matrix: Task B.

Since our model relies mainly on affective information, ironic instances lacking of subjective-related content are hard to recognize, as in: *Being a hipster now is so mainstream. Oh, the irony. #hipster #irony*. Moreover, we found some tweets where context information is crucial for capturing the ironic sense, like in: *So there used to be a crossfit place here.... #irony #pizzawins http://t.co/9BDkxT9GFJ*; or where the hashtag is the only signal for ironic intention.

4 Conclusions

In this paper, we described our participation at SemEval-2018 Task 3. We exploited an enhanced version of *emotIDM*. In our experiments, SVM emerges as the classifier with the best performance. The obtained results serve to validate the usefulness of affect-related features for distinguishing ironic tweets. As future work, it could be interesting to enrich *emotIDM* with features for capturing other kinds of information such as common-knowledge and semantic incongruity.

---

[5]The column "tT" refers to the amount of tweets in the test set. The column "Correct" refers to the percentage of instances correctly classified per class.

Acknowledgments

The work of D. I. Hernández Farías was funded by CONACYT project FC-2016/2410. The work of P. Rosso has been funded by the SomEM-BED TIN2015-71147-C2-1-P MINECO project. The work of V. Patti was partially funded by the IHatePrejudice project (S1618_L2_BOSC_01).

References

Laura Alba-Juez and Salvatore Attardo. 2014. The Evaluative Palette of Verbal Irony. In Geoff Thompson and Laura Alba-Juez, editors, *Evaluation in Context*, pages 93–116. John Benjamins Publishing Company, Amsterdam/Philadelphia.

Jorge Carrillo de Albornoz, Laura Plaza, and Pablo Gervás. 2012. SentiSense: An Easily Scalable Concept-based Affective Lexicon for Sentiment Analysis. In *Proceedings of the Eight International Conference on Language Resources and Evaluation (LREC'12)*, pages 3562–3567. European Language Resources Association (ELRA).

Francesco Barbieri, Horacio Saggion, and Francesco Ronzano. 2014. Modelling Sarcasm in Twitter, a Novel Approach. In *Proceedings of the 5th Workshop on Computational Approaches to Subjectivity, Sentiment and Social Media Analysis*, pages 50–58. Association for Computational Linguistics.

Valerio Basile, Andrea Bolioli, Malvina Nissim, Viviana Patti, and Paolo Rosso. 2014. Overview of the Evalita 2014 SENTIment POLarity classification task. In *Proceedings of the Fourth Evaluation Campaign of Natural Language Processing and Speech Tools for Italian EVALITA 2014*, pages 50–57.

Margaret M Bradley and Peter J Lang. 1999. Affective Norms for English Words (ANEW): Instruction Manual and Affective Ratings. Technical report, Center for Research in Psychophysiology, University of Florida, Gainesville, Florida.

Konstantin Buschmeier, Philipp Cimiano, and Roman Klinger. 2014. An Impact Analysis of Features in a Classification Approach to Irony Detection in Product Reviews. In *Proceedings of the 5th Workshop on Computational Approaches to Subjectivity, Sentiment and Social Media Analysis*, pages 42–49.

Erik Cambria, Daniel Olsher, and Dheeraj Rajagopal. 2014. SenticNet 3: A Common and Common-Sense Knowledge Base for Cognition-Driven Sentiment Analysis. In *Proceedings of AAAI Conference on Artificial Intelligence*, pages 1515–1521. AAAI.

Yoonjung Choi and Janyce Wiebe. 2014. +/-EffectWordNet: Sense-level Lexicon Acquisition for Opinion Inference. In *Proceedings of the 2014 Conference on Empirical Methods in Natural Language Processing (EMNLP)*, pages 1181–1191.

Aniruddha Ghosh, Guofu Li, Tony Veale, Paolo Rosso, Ekaterina Shutova, John Barnden, and Antonio Reyes. 2015. SemEval-2015 Task 11: Sentiment Analysis of Figurative Language in Twitter. In *Proceedings of the 9th International Workshop on Semantic Evaluation*, pages 470–478. Association for Computational Linguistics.

H. P. Grice. 1975. Logic and Conversation. In P. Cole and J. L. Morgan, editors, *Syntax and Semantics: Vol. 3: Speech Acts*, pages 41–58. Academic Press.

Delia Irazú Hernández Farías, Viviana Patti, and Paolo Rosso. 2016. Irony Detection in Twitter: The Role of Affective Content. *ACM Trans. Internet Technol.*, 16(3):19:1–19:24.

Delia Irazú Hernández Farías and Paolo Rosso. 2016. Irony, Sarcasm, and Sentiment Analysis. Chapter 7. In Federico A. Pozzi, Elisabetta Fersini, Enza Messina, and Bing Liu, editors, *Sentiment Analysis in Social Networks*, pages 113–127. Morgan Kaufmann.

Irazú Hernández Farías, José-Miguel Benedí, and Paolo Rosso. 2015. Applying Basic Features from Sentiment Analysis for Automatic Irony Detection. In *Pattern Recognition and Image Analysis*, volume 9117 of *Lecture Notes in Computer Science*, pages 337–344. Springer International Publishing.

Irazú Hernández-Farias, Davide Buscaldi, and Belém Priego-Sánchez. 2014. IRADABE: Adapting English Lexicons to the Italian Sentiment Polarity Classification Task. In *Proceedings of the First Italian Conference on Computational Linguistics (CLiC-it 2014) & the Fourth Evaluation Campaign of Natural Language Processing and Speech Tools for Italian EVALITA 2014*, pages 75–81.

Minqing Hu and Bing Liu. 2004. Mining and Summarizing Customer Reviews. In *Proceedings of the Tenth ACM SIGKDD International Conference on Knowledge Discovery and Data Mining*, KDD '04, pages 168–177, Seattle, WA, USA. ACM.

Jihen Karoui, Farah Benamara, Véronique Moriceau, Nathalie Aussenac-Gilles, and Lamia Hadrich-Belguith. 2015. Towards a Contextual Pragmatic Model to Detect Irony in Tweets. In *Proceedings of the 53rd Annual Meeting of the Association for Computational Linguistics and the 7th International Joint Conference on Natural Language Processing (Volume 2: Short Papers)*, pages 644–650. Association for Computational Linguistics.

Jihen Karoui, Farah Benamara, Veronique Moriceau, Viviana Patti, Cristina Bosco, and Nathalie Aussenac-Gilles. 2017. . In *Proceedings of the 15th Conference of the European Chapter of the Association for Computational Linguistics: Volume 1, Long Papers*, Valencia, Spain. Association for Computational Linguistics.

Joan Lucariello. 2014. Situational Irony: A Concept of Events Gone Awry. *Journal of Experimental Psychology: General*, 123(2):129–145.

Saif M. Mohammad and Peter D. Turney. 2013. Crowdsourcing a Word–Emotion Association Lexicon. *Computational Intelligence*, 29(3):436–465.

Saif M. Mohammad, Xiaodan Zhu, Svetlana Kiritchenko, and Joel Martin. 2015. Sentiment, Emotion, Purpose, and Style in Electoral Tweets. *Information Processing & Management*, 51(4):480 – 499.

Malvina Nissim and Viviana Patti. 2016. Semantic aspects in sentiment analysis. In Fersini Elisabetta, Bing Liu, Enza Messina, and Federico Pozzi, editors, *Sentiment Analysis in Social Networks*, chapter 3, pages 31–48. Elsevier.

Debora Nozza, Elisabetta Fersini, and Enza Messina. 2016. Unsupervised Irony Detection: A Probabilistic Model with Word Embeddings. In *Proceedings of the 8th International Joint Conference on Knowledge Discovery, Knowledge Engineering and Knowledge Management*, pages 68–76.

James W. Pennebaker, Martha E. Francis, and Roger J. Booth. 2001. Linguistic Inquiry and Word Count: LIWC 2001. *Mahway: Lawrence Erlbaum Associates*, 71.

Soujanya Poria, Erik Cambria, Devamanyu Hazarika, and Prateek Vij. 2016. A Deeper Look into Sarcastic Tweets Using Deep Convolutional Neural Networks. *CoRR*, abs/1610.08815.

Soujanya Poria, Alexander Gelbukh, Amir Hussain, Newton Howard, Dipankar Das, and Sivaji Bandyopadhyay. 2013. Enhanced SenticNet with Affective Labels for Concept-Based Opinion Mining. *IEEE Intelligent Systems*, 28(2):31–38.

Tomáš Ptáček, Ivan Habernal, and Jun Hong. 2014. Sarcasm Detection on Czech and English Twitter. In *Proceedings of COLING 2014, the 25th International Conference on Computational Linguistics*, pages 213–223. Dublin City University and Association for Computational Linguistics.

Antonio Reyes, Paolo Rosso, and Tony Veale. 2013. A Multidimensional Approach for Detecting Irony in Twitter. *Language Resources and Evaluation*, 47(1):239–268.

Ellen Riloff, Ashequl Qadir, Prafulla Surve, Lalindra De Silva, Nathan Gilbert, and Ruihong Huang. 2013. Sarcasm as Contrast between a Positive Sentiment and Negative Situation. In *Proceedings of the 2013 Conference on Empirical Methods in Natural Language Processing*, pages 704–714. Association for Computational Linguistics.

Dan Sperber and Deirdre Wilson. 1986. *Relevance: Communication and Cognition*. Harvard University Press, Cambridge, MA, USA.

Philip J. Stone and Earl B. Hunt. 1963. A Computer Approach to Content Analysis: Studies Using the General Inquirer System. In *Proceedings of the May 21-23, 1963, Spring Joint Computer Conference*, AFIPS '63 (Spring), pages 241–256. ACM.

Emilio Sulis, Delia Irazú Hernández Farías, Paolo Rosso, Viviana Patti, and Giancarlo Ruffo. 2016. Figurative Messages and Affect in Twitter: Differences between #irony, #sarcasm and #not. *Knowledge-Based Systems*, 108:132–143.

Maite Taboada and Jack Grieve. 2004. Analyzing Appraisal Automatically. In *Proceedings of the AAAI Spring Symposium on Exploring Attitude and Affect in Text: Theories and Applications*, pages 158–161, Stanford, US. AAAI.

Cynthia Van Hee, Els Lefever, and Veronique Hoste. 2016. Exploring the realization of irony in Twitter data. In *Proceedings of the Tenth International Conference on Language Resources and Evaluation (LREC 2016)*. European Language Resources Association (ELRA).

Cynthia Van Hee, Els Lefever, and Véronique Hoste. 2018. SemEval-2018 Task 3: Irony Detection in English Tweets. In *Proceedings of the 12th International Workshop on Semantic Evaluation*, SemEval-2018, New Orleans, LA, USA. Association for Computational Linguistics.

Byron C. Wallace, Do Kook Choe, and Eugene Charniak. 2015. Sparse, Contextually Informed Models for Irony Detection: Exploiting User Communities, Entities and Sentiment. In *Proceedings of the 53rd Annual Meeting of the Association for Computational Linguistics and the 7th International Joint Conference on Natural Language Processing (Volume 1: Long Papers)*, pages 1035–1044. Association for Computational Linguistics.

Angela P. Wang. 2013. #irony or #sarcasm — A Quantitative and Qualitative Study Based on Twitter. In *Proceedings of the 27th Pacific Asia Conference on Language, Information, and Computation*, pages 349–356. National Chengchi University.

Cynthia Whissell. 2009. Using the Revised Dictionary of Affect in Language to Quantify the Emotional Undertones of Samples of Natural Languages. *Psychological Reports*, 2(105):509–521.

Deirdre Wilson and Dan Sperber. 1992. On Verbal Irony. *Lingua*, 87(1-2):53–76.

Theresa Wilson, Janyce Wiebe, and Paul Hoffmann. 2005. Recognizing Contextual Polarity in Phrase-level Sentiment Analysis. In *Proceedings of the Conference on Human Language Technology and Empirical Methods in Natural Language Processing*, HLT '05, pages 347–354. Association for Computational Linguistics.

#NonDicevoSulSerio at SemEval-2018 Task 3: Exploiting Emojis and Affective Content for Irony Detection in English Tweets

Endang Wahyu Pamungkas, Viviana Patti
Dipartimento di Informatica, University of Turin
`{pamungka,patti}@di.unito.it`

Abstract

This paper describes the participation of the #NonDicevoSulSerio team at SemEval2018-Task3, which focused on *Irony Detection in English Tweets* and was articulated in two tasks addressing the identification of irony at different levels of granularity. We participated in both tasks proposed: Task A is a classical binary classification task to determine whether a tweet is ironic or not, while Task B is a multi-class classification task devoted to distinguish different types of irony, where systems have to predict one out of four labels describing verbal irony by clash, other verbal irony, situational irony, and non-irony. We addressed both tasks by proposing a model built upon a well-engineered features set involving both syntactic and lexical features, and a wide range of affective-based features, covering different facets of sentiment and emotions. The use of new features for taking advantage of the affective information conveyed by emojis has been analyzed. On this line, we also tried to exploit the possible incongruity between sentiment expressed in the text and in the emojis included in a tweet. We used a Support Vector Machine classifier, and obtained promising results. We also carried on experiments in an unconstrained setting.

1 Introduction

The use of creative language and figurative language devices such as irony has been proven to be pervasive in social media (Ghosh et al., 2015). The presence of these devices makes the process of mining social media texts challenging, especially because they can influence and twist the sentiment polarity of an utterance in different ways. Glossing over differences across different theoretical accounts proposed in the context of various disciplines (Gibbs and Colston, 2007; Grice, 1975; Wilson and Sperber, 1992; Attardo, 2007; Giora,

2003), irony can be defined as an incongruity between the literal meaning of an utterance and its intended meaning (Karoui et al., 2017). The term irony covers mainly two phenomena: verbal and situational irony (Attardo, 2006). Situational irony refers to events or situations which fail to meet expectations, such as for instance "warnings the dangerous effect of smoking on the cigarette advertisement", while verbal irony occurs when the speaker intend to communicate a different meaning w.r.t what he/she is literally saying. Most of the time it involves the intention of communicating an *opposite meaning*, and this kind of opposition can be expressed by polarity contrast. However this is not the only possibility, and social media messages well reflect such variety, including different expressions of verbal irony and descriptions of situational irony (Van Hee et al., 2016a; Sulis et al., 2016). Automatic irony detection is an important task to improve sentiment analysis (Reyes et al., 2013; Maynard and Greenwood, 2014). However, detecting irony automatically from textual messages is still a challenging task for scholars (Joshi et al., 2017). The linguistic and social factors which impact on the perception of irony contribute to make the task complex.

In this paper, we will describe the irony detection systems we developed for participating in SemEval2018-Task3: *Irony Detection in English Tweets* (Van Hee et al., 2018). Our systems used a support vector classifier model by exploiting some novel and well-handcrafted features including lexical, syntactical and affective based features. We participated in 3 different scenarios (Task A constrained, Task A unconstrained, and Task B unconstrained). The official results show that our system outperformed all systems in the unconstrained setting on both tasks and was able to achieve a reasonable score in Task A constrained, ranking in the top ten out of 44 submissions.

Proceedings of the 12th International Workshop on Semantic Evaluation (SemEval-2018), pages 649–654
New Orleans, Louisiana, June 5–6, 2018. ©2018 Association for Computational Linguistics

2 The #NonDicevoSulSerio System

We performed our experiments using a support vector machine classifier, with *radial basis function* kernel. We exploited different kind of features (lexical, syntactical and affective-based), which has been proven effective in literature to identify ironic phenomena. In addition, we also investigated the use of novel features aimed at exploiting information conveyed by emojis, studying in particular sentiment incongruity between sentiment expressed in the text and in the emojis of a tweet.

2.1 Structural Features

Structural features consist of lexical and syntactical features which characterize Twitter data. Such kind of features has been proven beneficial in several tasks dealing with Twitter data, and we selected the most relevant ones for irony detection. **Hashtag Presence**: binary value 0 (if no hashtag in tweet) and 1 (if hashtag contained in tweet). **Hashtag Count**: number of hashtags contained in tweet. **Mention Count**: number of mentions contained in tweet. **Exclamation Mark Count**: number of exclamation marks contained in tweet. **Upper Case Count**: number of upper case characters in tweet. **Link Count**: number of links (http) contained in tweet. **Link Presence**: binary value 0 (if no link in tweet) and 1 (if at least one link found in tweet). **Has Quote**: binary value 0 (if quote (" " or ' ') not found in tweet) and 1 (if at least one pair of quote (" " or ' ') found in tweet). **Intensifiers & Overstatement Words Count**: number of intensifiers and words typically used in ironic overstatements [1] found in tweet. **Emoji Presence**: binary value 0 (if no emoji found in tweet) and 1 (if at least one emoji found in tweet). **Repeated Character**: binary value 0 (if there is no repeated character found in tweet) and 1 (if at least three characters repeated consequently in one word found in tweet). **Text Length**: the length of characters in each tweet. **Conjunction Count**: the number of conjunctions found in tweet. **Verb Count**: the number of verbs found in tweet. **Noun Count**: the number of nouns found in tweet. **Adjective Count**: the number of adjectives found in tweet. We use Standford PoS-Tagger [2] to get the count of conjunctions, verbs, nouns, and adjectives.

2.2 Affective-Based Features

Affective features were proven effective in prior work to detect irony in tweets (Farías et al., 2016). We exploited available affective resources to extract affective information trying to capture multiple facets of affects -sentiment polarity and emotions- by selecting a few resources developed for English, which refers to both categorical and dimensional models of emotions.

AFINN.: AFINN is a sentiment lexicon consisting of English words labeled with valence score between -5 and 5. We used the normalized version of AFINN in (Farías et al., 2016), where the valence score was already normalized to the range between 0 and 1.

Emolex. Emolex (Mohammad and Turney, 2013) was developed by using crowdsourcing. Emolex contains 14,182 words associated with eight primary emotion based on (Plutchik, 2001).

EmoSenticNet. EmoSenticNet(EmoSN) (Poria et al., 2013) is an enriched version of SenticNet, where emotion labels were added by mapping WordNet-Affect labels to the SenticNet concepts. WordNet-Affect labels refers to six Ekman's basic emotions.

Linguistic Inquiry and Word Count (LIWC). LIWC dictionary (Pennebaker et al., 2001) has 4,500 words distributed into 64 different emotional categories including positive and negative. Here we only use the positive (PosEMO) and negative emotion (NegEMO) categories.

Dictionary of Affect in Language (DAL). DAL was developed by (Whissell, 2009) and composed of 8,742 English words. These words were labeled by three scores representing the emotion dimensions *Pleasantness*, *Activation*, and *Imagery*.

Emoji Sentiment Ranking. Since we observed the presence of a lot of emojis in Twitter data, we used the emoji sentiment ranking lexicon by (Novak et al., 2015) to get the sentiment score of each emoji in the tweet. We also tried to detect *sentiment incongruity* between text and emoji in the same tweet. We used VADER (Hutto and Gilbert, 2014) to extract the polarity score of the text.

3 Experiment and Results

3.1 Task Description and Dataset

SemEval2018-Task3's organizers proposed two subtasks related to the topic of detecting irony in Twitter automatically (Van Hee et al., 2018). Sub-Task A is a binary classification task, where every

---

[1] love, really, lovely, like, great, brilliant, perfect, thank, glad.

[2] https://nlp.stanford.edu/software/tagger.shtml

SubTask A		
	Irony	**Not Irony**
Training	1911	1923
Testing	311	473

SubTask B				
	0	**1**	**2**	**3**
Training	1923	1390	316	205
Testing	473	164	85	62

Table 1: Dataset Distribution on Both Tasks.

0 : Not irony
1 : Verbal irony by polarity contrast
2 : Others irony
3 : Situational irony

SubTask A		
Amt.	**HashTag**	**Source**
500	#irony	(Barbieri et al., 2014)
400	#sarcasm	(Riloff et al., 2013)
100	#sarcasm	(Barbieri et al., 2014)
500	#not	(Sulis et al., 2016)
500	non-irony	(Mohammad et al., 2015)
500	non-irony	(Ptáček et al., 2014)
500	non-irony	(Riloff et al., 2013)

SubTask B		
Amt.	**HashTag**	**Source**
867	#irony	(Barbieri et al., 2014)

Table 2: Additional data on Unconstrained Scenario.

system should determine whether a tweet is ironic or not ironic. Meanwhile, SubTask B is defined as a multi-class classification problem, where the aim is to classify each tweet into four different categories including: verbal irony by polarity contrast, other verbal irony, situational irony, and not irony. In both tasks, organizers allowed submissions in two scenarios: constrained and unconstrained. In unconstrained settings, participants were allowed to exploit external data from other corpora annotated with irony labels in the training phase. Standard evaluation metrics were proposed for the task, including, precision, recall, accuracy, and F_1-score.

Dataset The organizers provided 3,834 training data and 784 test data for both tasks. Table 1 shows the dataset distribution. Data were collected by using three irony-related hashtags: #irony, #sarcasm, and #not. Datasets for both tasks were manually labeled by using the fine-grained annotation scheme in (Van Hee et al., 2016b). A two-layer annotation has been applied on the same tweets, one concerning the presence and absence of irony, the second one identifying different types of irony, when irony is present. As a consequence, as Table 1 shows, there is a class imbalance on SubTask B dataset in favor of non-ironic class (50%), verbal irony by polarity contrast (25%), other verbal irony (13%) and situational irony (12%). The irony-related hashtags were removed from the final dataset release.

3.2 Experimental Setup

We built our supervised systems based on available training data. In this phase performances were evaluated based on the mean of F_1-score, by using 10-fold cross validation. We chose an SVM classifier with radial basis function kernel[3]. Our system implementation is free available for research purpose in GitHub page [4]. Therefore, we lean on feature selection process to improve the system performance. We carried on an ablation test on our feature sets to get the highest F_1-score. We decided to participate in three different scenarios: SubTask A constrained, SubTask A unconstrained, and SubTask B unconstrained.

For unconstrained scenario in SubTask A, we used the available corpora from previous work. We tried to add new data with balance proportion (1500 ironic and 1500 non-ironic). We also added a balance proportion of ironic data based on different hashtag (500 #irony, 500 #sarcasm, and 500 #not) from three different corpora, with the aim of enriching the training data with ironic samples of various provenance and trying to avoid biases. The distribution and source of our additional data can be seen in Table 2.

In SubTask B, we proposed to use a pipeline approach in three-steps classification scenario. First, we classify the ironic and non-ironic (similar configuration with SubTask A). Second, we classify the ironic data from step one into two categories, *verbal_irony_by_polarity_contrast* and the rest (other_verbal_irony+situational_irony). In the second step, we add more training data on the *other_verbal_irony+situational_irony class* to

---

[3]SVM good performances for similar tasks were recognized (Joshi et al., 2017). We built our system by using scikit-learn Python Library `http://scikit-learn.org/`.

[4]`https://github.com/dadangewp/SemEval-2018-Task-3`

Structural Features	System 1	System 2	System 3	System 4
	Task A (C)	Task A (U)		
	Task B (U)-1		Task B (U)-2	Task B (U)-3
Hashtag Count	✓	✓	✓	✓
Hashtag Presence	✓	✓	✓	-
Mention Count	✓	✓	-	-
Exclamation Mark	-	-	✓	-
UpperCase Count	-	✓	-	-
Link Count	✓	✓	-	✓
Link Presence	✓	✓	-	-
Has Quote	-	-	✓	-
Intensifiers/Overstatement	✓	✓	✓	-
Emoji Presence	-	-	✓	✓
Repeated Chars	-	-	✓	✓
Text Length	✓	-	✓	✓
Conjunction Count	✓	-	✓	✓
Noun Count	✓	✓	-	✓
Adjective Count	-	-	✓	✓
Verb Count	-	-	✓	✓
Affective Features				
AFINN Score	-	-	✓	✓
DAL Pleasantness	✓	-	-	-
DAL Activation	✓	-	-	-
DAL Imagery	-	-	✓	-
Emolex Surprise	-	-	✓	-
Emolex Trust	✓	-	-	-
Emolex Positive	-	-	✓	-
Emolex Negative	✓	-	✓	-
Emolex Anticipation	-	-	✓	-
Emolex Fear	✓	✓	✓	✓
LIWC Positive	-	-	✓	-
LIWC Negative	-	-	-	✓
EmoSenticNet Disgust	✓	✓	✓	✓
EmoSenticNet Fear	-	-	-	✓
EmoSenticNet Joy	-	✓	✓	✓
EmoSenticNet Sad	-	✓	-	✓
EmoSenticNet Surprise	-	-	✓	-
Vader Sentiment Score	-	-	✓	-
Emoji Incongruity	✓	✓	-	-

Table 3: Feature Selection on each System.

overcome the imbalance issue. We decided to use only additional tweets marked with #irony hashtags, relying on the analysis in (Sulis et al., 2016) suggesting that the polarity reversal phenomenon seems to be relevant in messages marked with #sarcasm and #not, but less relevant for messages tagged with #irony. In the last step, we classify between *other_verbal irony* and *situational_irony*. Table 3 shows selected features on each submitted system based on our ablation test.

3.3 Result and Analysis

Table 4 shows our experimental results based on four different metrics including accuracy, precision, recall, and F_1-score. For experiments on the training set we used 10-fold cross validation, and we report the score for each metric. However, F_1-score has been used as the criterion to tune the configuration. Official Codalab results show that our system ranked 10th out of 44 submissions on Sub-

Task A and 9th out of 32 on SubTask B. We obtained F_1-score 0.6216 (Best system: 0.7054) on SubTask A and 0.4131 (Best system: 0.5074) on SubTask B. However, our system outperformed all systems in the unconstrained setting on both tasks.

Based on our analysis, several stylistic features were very effective in Task A (both in constrained and unconstrained settings). Especially, Twitter specific symbols such as hashtags, mentions, and URLs were very useful to discriminate non ironic tweets. In addition, we found that affective resource were very helpful in the Step 2 and Step 3 of Task B, especially Emolex (Step 2) and EmoSenticNet (Step 3). Another important finding is that additional data on Task A did not improve the classifier performance. Instead, additional tweets marked with #irony on Task B were very useful to handle the imbalance dataset in Step-2 (*verbal_irony_by_polarity_contrast* vs *other_verbal_irony+situational_irony*). Our clas-

SubTask A Constrained			
	Acc	Prec	Rec	F_1
Training	0.630	0.616	0.664	0.638
Testing	0.666	0.562	0.717	0.630
SubTask A Unconstrained			
	Acc	Prec	Rec	F_1
Training	0.617	0.615	0.646	0.630
Testing	0.679	0.583	0.666	0.622
SubTask B Unconstrained			
	Acc	Prec	Rec	F_1
Training-1	0.630	0.616	0.664	0.638
Training-2	0.702	0.671	0.779	0.720
Training-3	0.689	0.651	0.488	0.544
Testing	0.555	0.409	0.441	0.413

Table 4: Results on Training and Test sets.

sifier was able to achieve a high F_1 score on the training phase in this case. Furthermore, we also found that our new features for capturing affective information in emojis (e.g. emoji incongruity) were very helpful in classifying between ironic and not ironic data.

Table 5 shows the confusion matrix of our classification result on SubTask B. Our system performed quite well in Step 1 (*irony* vs *non-irony*) and Step 2 (*verbal_irony_by_polarity_contrast* vs *other_verbal_irony+situational_irony*). However, our system was struggling in distinguishing between *other_verbal_irony* and situational_irony (Step 3). Our system got very low precision in detecting situational irony, and this has a huge impact on macro average F-score. The difficulties to find an important feature to discriminate other verbal and situational irony was, indeed, for us the main challenge in Task B. A qualitative error analysis was conducted. We found a lot of tweets which where difficult to understand without the context), like:

(tw1)*"Produce Mobile Apps
http://t.co/3OV57ZhqcH
http://t.co/wX1DbI8W9M"*

(tw2) *"#Consensus of Absolute Hilarious -
#MichaelMann to lecture on #Professional
#Ethics for #Climate #Scientists?
http://t.co/pD0TEMq1Z0"*

The first tweet is featured by situational irony and was originally including a #not hashtag before the link. Also for humans it is very difficult to get the

	0	**1**	**2**	**3**
0	**285**	80	75	33
1	19	**96**	31	18
2	29	7	**38**	11
3	29	13	12	**8**

Table 5: Confusion Matrix SubTask B.

0 : Not irony
1 : Verbal irony by polarity contrast
2 : Others irony
3 : Situational irony

ironic intention behind the tweet when the #not hashtag is removed and without having access to the information in the URL, which was anyway inactive. The second example was labelled as *other_verbal_irony*. Although it is very difficult to resolve the context of this tweet, accessing to the URL contained was helpful in understanding the ironic intent.

4   Conclusion

This paper described the participation of the #NonDicevoSulSerio[5] team at SemEval2018-Task3: *Irony Detection of English Tweets*. We proposed to use several stylistic features and exploited several affective resources to deal with this task. Based on our evaluation and analysis, classifying irony into its several types (verbal irony by polarity contrast, other verbal irony, and situational irony) is a very challenging task. Especially, getting relevant features to discriminate between other verbal irony and situational irony will become our main focus on the future research direction. In this case, capturing semantic incongruity by exploiting word embedding semantic similarity is an issue worth to be explored (Joshi et al., 2015).

References

Salvatore Attardo. 2006. Irony. *Encyclopedia of Language & Linguistics*, 6:26–28.

Salvatore Attardo. 2007. Irony as relevant inappropriateness. In H. Colston and R. Gibbs, editors, *Irony in language and thought: A cognitive science reader*, pages 135–172. Lawrence Erlbaum.

---

[5]"Non dicevo sul serio" (Italian) means: 'I didn't mean that".

Francesco Barbieri, Horacio Saggion, and Francesco Ronzano. 2014. Modelling sarcasm in twitter, a novel approach. In *Proc. of the 5th Workshop on Computational Approaches to Subjectivity, Sentiment and Social Media Analysis*, pages 50–58.

Delia Irazú Hernańdez Farías, Viviana Patti, and Paolo Rosso. 2016. Irony detection in twitter: The role of affective content. *ACM Transactions on Internet Technology (TOIT)*, 16(3):19.

Aniruddha Ghosh, Guofu Li, Tony Veale, Paolo Rosso, Ekaterina Shutova, John Barnden, and Antonio Reyes. 2015. Semeval-2015 task 11: Sentiment analysis of figurative language in twitter. In *Proceedings of the 9th International Workshop on Semantic Evaluation (SemEval 2015)*, pages 470–478.

Raymond W. Gibbs and Herbert L. Colston, editors. 2007. *Irony in language and thought*. Routledge (Taylor and Francis), New York.

R. Giora. 2003. *On Our Mind: Salience, Context, and Figurative Language*. Oxford University Press.

H. P. Grice. 1975. Logic and Conversation. In P. Cole and J. L. Morgan, editors, *Syntax and Semantics: Vol. 3: Speech Acts*, pages 41–58. Academic Press.

Clayton J Hutto and Eric Gilbert. 2014. Vader: A parsimonious rule-based model for sentiment analysis of social media text. In *Eighth international AAAI conference on weblogs and social media*.

Aditya Joshi, Pushpak Bhattacharyya, and Mark James Carman. 2017. Automatic sarcasm detection: A survey. *ACM Comput. Surv.*, 50(5):73:1–73:22.

Aditya Joshi, Vinita Sharma, and Pushpak Bhattacharyya. 2015. Harnessing context incongruity for sarcasm detection. In *Proc. of the 53rd Annual Meeting of the ACL and the 7th Int. Joint Conference on NLP*, pages 757–762, Beijing, China. ACL.

Jihen Karoui, Benamara Farah, Véronique Moriceau, Viviana Patti, Cristina Bosco, and Nathalie Aussenac-Gilles. 2017. Exploring the impact of pragmatic phenomena on irony detection in tweets: A multilingual corpus study. In *Proc. of the 15th Conf. of the European Chapter of the Association for Computational Linguistics: Volume 1, Long Papers*, volume 1, pages 262–272.

Diana Maynard and Mark A. Greenwood. 2014. Who cares about sarcastic tweets? Investigating the impact of sarcasm on sentiment analysis. In *Proc. of the 9th Int. Conference on Language Resources and Evaluation*, pages 4238–4243. ELRA.

Saif M Mohammad and Peter D Turney. 2013. Crowdsourcing a word–emotion association lexicon. *Computational Intelligence*, 29(3):436–465.

Saif M Mohammad, Xiaodan Zhu, Svetlana Kiritchenko, and Joel Martin. 2015. Sentiment, emotion, purpose, and style in electoral tweets. *Information Processing & Management*, 51(4):480–499.

Petra Kralj Novak, Jasmina Smailović, Borut Sluban, and Igor Mozetič. 2015. Sentiment of emojis. *PloS one*, 10(12):e0144296.

James W Pennebaker, Martha E Francis, and Roger J Booth. 2001. Linguistic inquiry and word count: Liwc 2001. *Mahway: Lawrence Erlbaum Associates*, 71(2001):2001.

Robert Plutchik. 2001. The nature of emotions human emotions have deep evolutionary roots, a fact that may explain their complexity and provide tools for clinical practice. *American scientist*, 89(4):344–350.

Soujanya Poria, Alexander Gelbukh, Amir Hussain, Newton Howard, Dipankar Das, and Sivaji Bandyopadhyay. 2013. Enhanced senticnet with affective labels for concept-based opinion mining. *IEEE Intelligent Systems*, 28(2):31–38.

Tomáš Ptáček, Ivan Habernal, and Jun Hong. 2014. Sarcasm detection on Czech and English Twitter. In *Proceedings of COLING 2014*, pages 213–223.

Antonio Reyes, Paolo Rosso, and Tony Veale. 2013. A multidimensional approach for detecting irony in Twitter. *Language resources and evaluation*, 47(1):239–268.

Ellen Riloff, Ashequl Qadir, Prafulla Surve, Lalindra De Silva, Nathan Gilbert, and Ruihong Huang. 2013. Sarcasm as contrast between a positive sentiment and negative situation. In *Proc. of EMNLP 2013*, pages 704–714.

Emilio Sulis, Delia Irazú Hernández Farías, Paolo Rosso, Viviana Patti, and Giancarlo Ruffo. 2016. Figurative messages and affect in Twitter: Differences between# irony,# sarcasm and# not. *Knowledge-Based Systems*, 108:132–143.

Cynthia Van Hee, Els Lefever, and Veronique Hoste. 2016a. Exploring the realization of irony in Twitter data. In *Proc. of the 10th Int. Conference on Language Resources and Evaluation (LREC 2016)*. ELRA.

Cynthia Van Hee, Els Lefever, and Veronique Hoste. 2016b. Guidelines for annotating irony in social media text, version 2.0. *LT3 Technical Report Series*.

Cynthia Van Hee, Els Lefever, and Véronique Hoste. 2018. SemEval-2018 Task 3: Irony Detection in English Tweets. In *Proceedings of the 12th International Workshop on Semantic Evaluation*, SemEval-2018, New Orleans, LA, USA. ACL.

Cynthia Whissell. 2009. Using the revised dictionary of affect in language to quantify the emotional undertones of samples of natural language. *Psychological reports*, 105(2):509–521.

Deirdre Wilson and Dan Sperber. 1992. On Verbal Irony. *Lingua*, 87(1-2):53–76.

KNU CI System at SemEval-2018 Task4: Character Identification by Solving Sequence-Labeling Problem

Cheoneum Park[*], Heejun Song[**], Changki Lee[*]

[*]Department of Computer Science, Kangwon National University, South Korea
[**]Samsung Research, Samsung Electronics Co., Ltd., South Korea
[*]{parkce, leeck}@kangwon.ac.kr
[**]heejun7.song@samsung.com

Abstract

Character identification is an entity-linking task that finds words referring to the same person among the nouns mentioned in a conversation and turns them into one entity. In this paper, we define a sequence-labeling problem to solve character identification, and propose an attention-based recurrent neural network (RNN) encoder–decoder model. The input document for character identification on multiparty dialogues consists of several conversations, which increase the length of the input sequence. The RNN encoder–decoder model suffers from poor performance when the length of the input sequence is long. To solve this problem, we propose applying position encoding and the self-matching network to the RNN encoder–decoder model. Our experimental results demonstrate that of the four models proposed, Model 2 showed an F1 score of 86.00% and a label accuracy of 85.10% at the scene-level.

1 Introduction

In this paper, we define character identification (CI) (Chen et al., 2017) as a sequence-labeling problem and use a recurrent neural network (RNN) encoder–decoder (Enc–Dec) model (Cho et al., 2014) based on the attention mechanism (Bahdanau et al., 2015) to solve it. An Enc–Dec is an extension of the RNN model; it generates an encoding vector using an RNN in the encoder when an input sequence is given and performs decoding using the encoding vector. The attention mechanism calculates the alignment score for the two sequences and

performs the input sequence and weighted sum so that they can focus more on the position that affects the output result. The self-matching network (Wang et al., 2017) is used to calculate an attention weight for itself and a context vector by using a weighted sum, after which the weights of similar words in the RNN sequence can be applied to aid in coreference resolution. Position encoding (PE) (Sukhbaatar et al., 2015, Park and Lee, 2017, Vaswani et al., 2017) is a method of applying weights differently, according to the positions of words appearing in a sequence. Training and prediction are performed by multiplying a weight vector by a vector of positions to be identified in a given input sequence.

In an Enc–Dec model, a long input sequence results in performance degradation due to loss of information in the front portion of the input sequence when encoding is performed. In this paper, we propose four models that apply PE, attention mechanism, and self-matching network to Enc–Dec models to solve the problem of performance degradation due to long input sequences.

To summarize, the main contributions of this paper are as follows:

1. In this paper, we define CI task as sequence-labeling problem, and perform training and prediction in end-to-end model.

2. We propose four models using Enc-Dec based on attention mechanism and achieve high performance.

2 System Description

An Enc–Dec model maximizes $P(y|x)$ using an RNN. The encoder generates an encoder hidden

Proceedings of the 12th International Workshop on Semantic Evaluation (SemEval-2018), pages 655–659
New Orleans, Louisiana, June 5–6, 2018. ©2018 Association for Computational Linguistics

state by encoding the input sequence, and the decoder generates an output sequence that maximizes $P(y|x)$ using the hidden state of the decoder, which was generated until this time step, with the encoder hidden state. The attention mechanism is a method of determining which part of the target class should be focused using the hidden state of the decoder and the hidden state of the encoder when performing decoding.

2.1 Model 1: Attention-based Enc–Dec model

The first model proposed in this paper is a general attention mechanism-based Enc–Dec model, as shown in Figure 1.

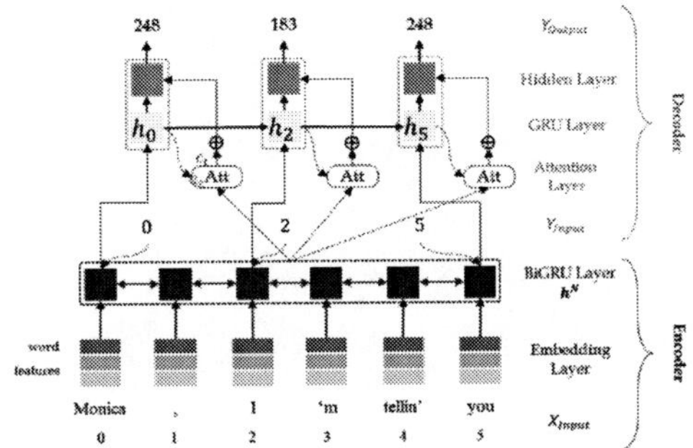

Figure 1: Attention-based Enc-Dec.

The input of the encoder is one document that contains S sentences (multiparty dialogue). Each sentence S consists of n_S words, and the input sequence X_{input} is $X_{input} = \{x_1, x_2, \dots, x_{n_S}\}$. The input to the decoder is $Y_{input} = \{yi_0, yi_1, \dots, yi_m\}$ consisting of the positions of the words given in the gold mentions, and the output sequence accordingly becomes $Y_{output} = \{yo_0, yo_1, \dots, yo_m\}$ consisting of the character number, which is corresponded with the decoder's input mentions.

We use word embedding and adopt the K-dimensional word embedding $e_i^k, k \in [1, K]$ for all input words, where i is the word index in the input sequence. We perform feature embedding for three features — speaker, named entity recognition (NER) tags, and capitalization — and concatenate them to make $\tilde{x}_i$.

- The uppercase feature is a binary feature (1 or 0) that verifies whether the uppercase is included in the word.

- 10-dimensional speaker embedding for a total of 205 different types of speakers included by "unknown".

- 19-dimensional NER embedding for a total of 19 different types of NER tags.

We use bidirectional gated recurrent unit (BiGRU) (Cho et al., 2014) for the encoder. The hidden state of the encoder for the input (word) sequence is defined as h_i^N.

$$e_i = W_e x_i \tag{1}$$

$$\tilde{x}_i = [e_i; uc_i; spk_i; NER_i] \tag{2}$$

$$h_i = biGRU(\tilde{x}_i, h_{i-1}) \tag{3}$$

where $\vec{h}_i$ and $\overleftarrow{h}_i$ are forward and backward networks, respectively, and h_i^N concatenates $\vec{h}_i$ and $\overleftarrow{h}_i$.

The decoder of our model uses the GRU as follows.

$$h_t = GRU(h_{yi_t}^N, h_{t-1}) \tag{4}$$

The input of the decoder is the hidden state h_i^N generated by the encoder corresponding to each position of Y_{input} which is the gold mention sequence. The hidden state h_t of the current decoder receives the hidden state h_i^N of the encoder corresponding to the output position of the previous decoder and the previous hidden state of the decoder.

$$\alpha_i^t = \frac{\exp\left(score_a\left(h_t, h_{yi_i}^N\right)\right)}{\sum_j \exp\left(score_a\left(h_t, h_{yi_j}^N\right)\right)} \tag{5}$$

$$score_a\left(h_t, h_{yi_i}^N\right) = v_t^T \tanh(W_a\left[h_t; h_{yi_i}^N; h_{yi_t}^N\right]) \tag{6}$$

$$y_t = \text{argmax}_i(a_i^t) \tag{7}$$

$$c_t = \begin{cases} \sum_i a_i^t h_i^N, & \text{soft attention} \\ h_{y_t}^N, & \text{hard attention} \end{cases} \tag{8}$$

At the attention layer of the decoder, we use the attention weight α_i^t to compute the alignment score for the gold mention input into the decoder and the encoder hidden state h_i^N input. The attention layer acts as a coreference resolution for each gold mention and input sequence. After calculating the attention weights, we create the context vector c_t. We use soft attention and hard attention in Eq. (8). Soft attention $c_t = \sum_i a_i^t h_i^N$ is an attention-pooling vector of the whole input sentence of the encoder (h^N). The other attention-pooling vector is hard attention $c_t = h_{y_t}^N$, which is based on the argmax function Eq. (7) for attention weight α_i^t to choose the position with high score for the decoder input as the gold mention.

$$score_z\left(h_t, c_t, h_{yi_t}^N\right) = W_{z2}^T \text{ReLU}(W_z[h_t; c_t; h_{yi_t}^N]) \tag{9}$$

$$yo_t = \text{argmax}_t \left(softmax \left(score_z(h_t, c_t, h_{yi_t}^N) \right) \right) \tag{10}$$

After calculating the context vector between the input of the encoder and the input of the decoder, we calculate $score_z$, using which the context vector c_t, decode hidden state h_t and encoder hidden state h^N are concatenated in the decoder hidden layer. Next, the softmax function is used to calculate the alignment score for $score_z$, and then the character index (Y_{output}) for the CI task corresponding to the input of the decoder is obtained using the argmax function.

2.2 Model 2: Attention–based Enc–Dec w/ model with PE

The second model is based on the first model but uses PE which is a method of applying a weight to an input sequence of an RNN according to the word order. Among the words in the coreference resolution, the antecedent has a feature that appears mainly in the preceding context. In this paper, we apply PE with a feature to the encoder input sequence, and use the weight according to the word order as the feature. As shown in Eq. (11), PE information is concatenated to Eq. (2) to produce $\tilde{x}_i$, and PE is calculated as shown in Eq. (12).

$$\tilde{x}_i = [e_i; PE_i; uc_i; spk_i; NER_i] \tag{11}$$

$$PE_i = (1 - i/n_s) - (s/k)(1 - 2i/n_s) \tag{12}$$

In PE, i is the index of the word, n_s is the total length of the input sequence, s is the position of the sentence, and k is the number of dimensions of the word expression. The weight of PE is calculated as a real value that gradually decreases between 1 and 0, and is applied to the input of the encoder to take advantage of the feature that the predecessor precedes the current mention. In Eq. (12), $(1 - 2i/n_s)$ denotes the order of words. If it is a front word, it has a higher value than the next word. (s/k) is a weight based on the sentence order, and when the sentence is different, the weight reduction rate difference is calculated to be higher than the value decreasing in the sentence. The expression for the encoder and decoder are the same as for model 1.

2.3 Model 3: Self-matching Network-based Enc-Dec model

The third model is also based on the first model, but performs encoding by using the self-matching network in the encoder without using PE, as shown in Figure 2. The self-matching network is used for calculating the alignment score for a given RNN sequence and itself, and then for performing a weighting sum with itself to create a context vector. While using the self-matching network for encoding, attention weights are weighted with high alignment scores between similar words. For example, if "Rachel's child-hood best friend" and "Monica" appear in a sentence, a high alignment score between them is calculated by the self-matching network.

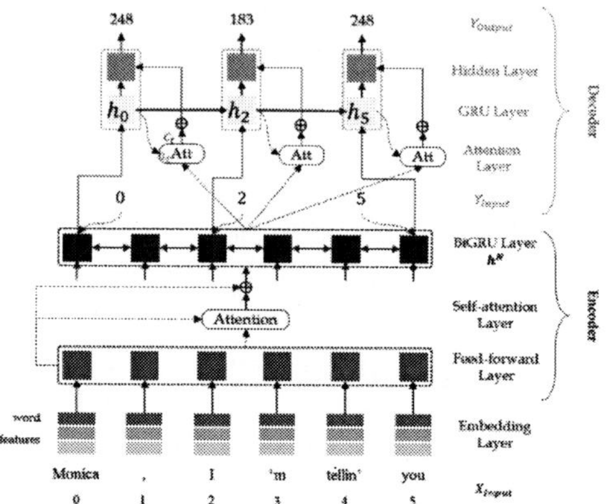

Figure 2: Self-matching–Network-based Enc–Dec.

The input sequence of the encoder becomes $\tilde{x}_i$ in Eq. (2), and a feed-forward neural network is used, as in Eq. (13). Next, we use the self-matching network to compute the attention weight for the t sequence and create a context vector c_i^{self} that reflects the self-attention (Eqs. 14–16).

$$h_i^{src} = W_{src}\tilde{x}_i + b_{src} \tag{13}$$

$$\alpha_j^i = \frac{\exp\left(score_{self}\left(h_j^{src}, h_i^{src}\right)\right)}{\sum_t \exp\left(score_{self}\left(h_t^{src}, h_i^{src}\right)\right)} \tag{14}$$

$$score_{self}\left(h_j^{src}, h_i^{src}\right) = v_i^T \tanh(W_a^{src}[h_j^{src}; h_i^{src}]) \tag{15}$$

$$c_i^{self} = \sum_j \alpha_j^i h_j^{src} \tag{16}$$

Subsequently, we construct $\left[h_i^{src}; c_i^{self}\right]$ by concatenating the context vector c_i^{self}, created using the self-matching network, and the hidden state h_i^{src}; it is then fed to the input of the hidden layer of the encoder to perform BiGRU.

We apply $\left[h_i^{src}; c_i^{self}\right]$ to the additional gate to make $\left[h_i^{src}; c_i^{self}\right]^*$, this determines whether or not the information of $\left[h_i^{src}; c_i^{self}\right]$ is transmitted to the encoder hidden layer input. The equation is as follows:

$$g_t = sigmoid(W_g[h_i^{src}; c_i^{self}]) \qquad (17)$$

$$\left[h_i^{src}; c_i^{self}\right]^* = g_t \odot [h_i^{src}; c_i^{self}] \qquad (18)$$

The decoder of model 3 performs training and prediction using a decoder such as the one used in model 1 (Eqs. 4–8) based on the hidden state where encoding is performed as above.

2.4 Model 4: Self–matching Network–based RNN Enc-Dec model with PE

Model 4 is based on model 3 using the self-matching network; it additionally uses PE, which was also used for model 2, as a feature to confirm the word order.

3 Experimental Results

We evaluate the entity linking performance of the models using label accuracy and macro-F1 (Chen et al., 2017), and the coreference resolution performance using CoNLL F1 (Rahman and Ng, 2009).

The word representation used in this paper is a data–set provided by LDC, which is learned by a neural network language model (Bengio et al., 2003, Lee et al., 2014), and is set to 50 dimensions. The experiments were performed with cross validation. The hyper parameters used in the experiment are as follows. We used tanh for the encoder and decoder, and ReLU for the attention layer. The hidden layers had 150 dimension, and the dropout of all layers was set to 0.3. The learning was done using RMSprop (Hinton et al., 2012) and the learning rate was reduced by 50% for every 5 epochs without performance improvement starting at 0.1. The decoder attention functions of the models used in the experiments are all based on hard attention, and are compared with soft attention in Table 1.

	Episode-Level		Scene-Level	
	Main F1	**All F1**	**Main F1**	**All F1**
M 1	85.57	**23.33**	83.45	21.13
M 2	82.91	23.15	85.58	22.40
M 2'	82.46	22.04	83.56	19.67
M 3	**86.30**	22.93	84.10	21.84
M 4	83.65	22.13	**87.41**	22.06
M 4'	85.48	19.46	86.23	**23.92**

Table 1: Entity-linking results on the trial set (in %). Main and All in column mean main and other characters, and all characters.

Table 1 shows a comparison between the CI performances of the models on the trial set. M 2' is a model in which PE proposed by Vaswani et al. (2017) is applied, and M 4' is a model in which soft attention is applied to M 4. At the episode-level, M 3 showed the best Main F1 performance (86.30%) and M 1 showed the best All F1 performance (23.33%). At the scene-level, M 4 showed the highest Main F1 performance (87.41%), and M 4 showed the highest All F1 performance (23.92%). In the case of M 2 and M 2', we can see that the proposed PE method resulted in a better overall performance.

At the episode-level, M 4' showed a better Main F1 performance (1.83%) than M 4, whereas M 4 showed a better All F1 performance (by 2.67%). At the scene-level, M 4 showed a better Main F1 performance (by 1.18%) than M 4', whereas M 4'

		Characters							Main + Other		All	
	Model	**Chandler**	**Joey**	**Monica**	**Phoebe**	**Rachel**	**Ross**	**Others**	**F1**	**Acc**	**F1**	**Acc**
E	M 1	81.17	76.39	86.86	84.70	87.13	81.03	72.86	81.45	80.32	15.75	67.19
	M 2	85.77	81.59	85.19	87.67	59.64	84.79	80.42	**85.01**	**84.36**	16.47	**68.42**
	M 3	82.76	82.06	86.36	84.21	88.76	81.78	77.40	83.33	82.38	**17.02**	66.65
	M 4	83.52	79.92	87.17	86.43	86.72	83.73	78.46	83.71	82.96	15.19	65.83
S	M 1	83.55	79.19	90.99	86.43	90.01	84.11	76.08	84.34	83.08	15.93	68.59
	M 2	84.94	79.67	91.16	88.09	92.49	85.86	79.79	**86.00**	**85.10**	**16.98**	**69.49**
	M 3	83.87	84.30	88.24	86.10	88.79	79.65	76.23	83.88	82.34	16.99	67.31
	M 4	78.21	83.06	84.42	84.30	89.94	79.08	90.41	85.33	84.64	15.43	67.68
Amore		-	-	-	-	-	-	-	79.36	77.23	**41.05**	**74.72**
Kamp.		-	-	-	-	-	-	-	73.51	73.36	37.37	59.45
`zuma		-	-	-	-	-	-	-	43.15	46.07	14.42	25.81

Table 2: Entity-linking results on the evaluation set (in %). The F1 score is reported for each character. E/S: episode/scene level. F1 is macro-average F1 score. Acc is character label accuracy.

showed a better All F1 performance (by 1.86%). Thus, it can be seen that the use of hard attention results in a better performance.

Table 2 presents the experimental results of the test set (episode- and scene-level) for the method proposed in this paper, and the performance comparison with other competing models, namely AMORE UPF (Amore), Kampfpudding (Kamp.), and zuma. In the Main + Other character evaluations at episode-level, M 2 showed the best performance among all models (F1 of 85.01%, Acc of 84.36%), whereas in the All character evaluations, M 3 showed the best F1 performance (17.02%) and M 2 showed the best Acc performance (68.42%). At the scene-level, M 2 showed the best performance in both the Main + Other and the All character evaluation. The proposed method showed a lower overall performance in the All character evaluation compared with other competing models, but showed a higher performance in the Main + Other character evaluations. The reason for the lower performance in the All character evaluation is that the number of data points is smaller than that of the main characters.

4   Conclusion

In this paper, we defined the entity-linking problem of SemEval-2018 Task 4 as a sequence-labeling problem and proposed four models to solve it. Experimental results showed that M 2 shows the best performance in the test set scene-level (Main + Other characters), with an F1 of 86.00% and Acc of 85.10%. In the Main entities + Others evaluation of SemEval-2018 Task 4, it ranked 1st with an F1 of 83.37% and Acc of 82.13%. In All Entities + Others, it ranked 2nd with an F1 of 13.53% and Acc of 68.55%.

In future work, we will apply character CNN to solve the unknown word problem, and we will add word expressions such as GloVe (Pennington et al., 2014) and ELMo (Peters et al., 2018). We will also enhance the performance by tightening the model with less data by adding the features used in the task 4-based model.

References

Henry Y. Chen, Ethan Zhou, and Jinho D. Choi. 2017. Robust Coreference Resolution and Entity Linking on Dialogues: Character Identification on TV Show Transcripts. *In: Proceedings of the 55th Annual Meeting of the Association for Computational Linguistics.*

Kyunghyun Cho, Bart van Merrienboer, Caglar Gulcehre, Dzmitry Bahdanau, Fethi Bougares, Holger Schwenk, and Yoshua Bengio. 2014. Learning Phrase Representations using RNN Encoder-Decoder for Statistical Machine Translation. *arXiv:1406.1078.*

Dzmitry Bahdanau, Kyunghyun Cho, and Yoshua Bengio. 2015. Neural machine translation by jointly learning to align and translate. *Proc. of ICLR' 15, arXiv:1409.0473.*

Wenhui Wang, Nan Yang, Furu Wei, Baobao Chang, and Ming Zhou. 2017. Gated Self-Matching Networks for Reading Comprehension and Question Answering, *In: Proceedings of the 55th Annual Meeting of the Association for Computational Linguistics (Volume 1: Long Papers),* pages 189-198.

Sainbayar Sukhbaatar, Arthur Szlam, Jason Weston, and Rob Fergus. 2015. End-To-End Memory Networks. *arXiv:1503.08895.*

Cheoneum Park and Changki Lee. 2017. Korean Coreference Resolution using Pointer Networks based on Position Encoding. *In: Proceedings Of the KIISE and the KBS Joint Symposium,* pages 76-78.

Ashish Vaswani, Noam Shazeer, Niki Parmar, Jakob Uszkoreit, Llion Jones, Aidan N. Gomez, Lukasz Kaiser, and Illia Polosukhin. 2017. Attention Is All You Need. *arXiv:1706.03762.*

Altaf Rahman and Vincent Ng. 2009. Supervised Models for Coreference Resolution. *In: Proceedings of the 2014 Conference on Empirical Methods in Natural Language Processing (EMNLP),* pages 968-977.

Changki Lee, Junseok Kim, and Jeonghee Kim. 2014. Korean Dependency Parsing using Deep Learning. *In: Proceedings of the KIISE for HCLT,* pages 87-37.

Yoshua Bengio, Réjean Ducharme, Pascal Vincent, and Christian Jauvin. 2003. A Neural Probabilistic Language Model. *Journal of machine learning research,* pages 1137-1155.

Geoffrey Hinton, Nitish Srivastava, and Kevin Swersky. 2012. Rmsprop: Divide the gradient by a running average of its recent magnitude. *Neural networks for machine learning, Coursera lecture 6e.*

Jeffrey Pennington, Richard Socher, and Christopher Manning. 2014. Glove: Global vectors for word representation. *Proceedings of the 2014 conference on empirical methods in natural language processing* (EMNLP), pages. 1532-1543.

Matthew E Peters, Mark Neumann, Mohit Iyyer, Matt Gardner, Christopher Clark, Kenton Lee, and Luke Zettlemoyer. 2018. Deep contextualized word prepresentations. *arXiv:1802.05365.*

NewsReader at SemEval-2018 Task 5: Counting events by reasoning over event-centric-knowledge-graphs

Piek Vossen

VU University Amsterdam / De Boelelaan 1105, 1081HV Amsterdam, Netherlands

`piek.vossen@vu.nl`

Abstract

In this paper, we describe the participation of the NewsReader system in the SemEval-2018 Task 5 on *Counting Events and Participants in the Long Tail*. NewsReader is a generic unsupervised text processing system that detects events with participants, time and place to generate Event Centric Knowledge Graphs (ECKGs). We minimally adapted these ECKGs to establish a baseline performance for the task. We first use the ECKGs to establish which documents report on the same incident and what event mentions are coreferential. Next, we aggregate ECKGs across coreferential mentions and use the aggregated knowledge to answer the questions of the task. Our participation tests the quality of News-Reader to create ECKGs, as well as the potential of ECKGs to establish event identity and reason over the result to answer the task queries.

1 Introduction

This paper describes the NewsReader system participating in the SemEval 2018 Task 5 *Counting Events and Participants in the Long Tail* (Postma et al., 2018). Task 5 requires detection of certain events (cases of gun violence, dismissal of employees, and burning fire incidents) with participants, as well as extraction of their location and time in a set of documents and reasoning over their identity, in order to answer queries over the data set. A typical query in the task is *How many people were killed in 2016 in Columbus, MS?*. Participants were given a collection of news articles in CoNLL format to distill the answer to the queries. The task consists of 3 subtasks: subtask 1 asks for all documents from the data set that report on a single incident that fits the question constraints; subtask 2 is to provide the number of incidents (zero or more) and the documents that report on these

incidents given the constraints of a query; subtask 3 asks for the number of affected (injured, dead, or fired) people in the incidents that match the query constraints, and the supporting documents for these incidents. In addition to answering the subtask queries, participants were asked to mark the (cross-document) coreferential event mentions in the CoNLL file according to a specific event schema for gun violence.

Since we also organized the task, we decided to participate out-of-competition. Our system is a version of the NewsReader system (Vossen et al., 2016) as it was delivered at the end of the project, with as little adaptation as possible to the processing of the text to answer the queries of the task. The generic NewsReader system created the semantic output by applying a deep reading approach to the text, and the tasks were addressed by loading that output and reasoning over the results.

We participated in all three subtasks by first resolving the event coreference (or identity) and next answering the questions for each task using event representations that are the results of resolving the coreference. Our approach consists of three steps: 1. the event mentions in the input documents are represented as Event-Centric Knowledge Graphs (ECKGs) using the NewsReader system as is. 2. the ECKGs of all documents are compared to each other to decide which documents refer to the same incident, resulting in an incident-document index and in cross-document event-coreference relations. 3. the constraints of each question (its event type, time, participant names, and location) are matched with the stored ECKGs, resulting in a number of incidents and source documents for each question.

Our approach is fully unsupervised and follows compositional semantic principles to 1) define the semantics of events and participants, 2) establish their identity, and 3) reason over the results.

Proceedings of the 12th International Workshop on Semantic Evaluation (SemEval-2018), pages 660–666
New Orleans, Louisiana, June 5–6, 2018. ©2018 Association for Computational Linguistics

The remainder of this paper is structured as follows. In Section 2, we briefly describe the NewsReader system and the preprocessing steps. In Section 3, we explain how we establish event identity and cross-document coreference starting from the NewsReader output. The aggregated event representations are used to answer the queries for the tasks, which we describe in Section 4.

Finally in Section 5, we discuss the results. For further details on the NewsReader system, we point to the NewsReader website and its Github repository.[1] The specific wrapper for this task that takes the Newsreader output as a starting point is available in a separate Github.[2]

2 The NewsReader system

NewsReader processes text by applying a wide range of NLP modules, among which named entity recognition, classification and disambiguation (NERCD), semantic role labeling (SRL), word sense disambiguation (WSD), and temporal expressions detection and normalization (TIMEX). The NLP modules store their output as separate layers in the Natural language processing Annotation Format (NAF) (Fokkens et al., 2014). For example, events are detected by the SRL system as PropBank predicates (Kingsbury and Palmer, 2002), while FrameNet frames (Baker, 2008) and Wordnet synsets (Fellbaum, 1998) are attached to these predicates on the basis of the WSD output. Similarly, NERCD will annotate the text with entities and entity classes and it will annotate some of them with DBpedia URIs. From these entities, we derive participant names and locations for the predicates in the SRL output, while TIMEX anchors these predicates to dates.

In a second step, NewsReader derives so-called Event-Centric-Knowledge-Graphs (ECKGs) by combining the results of the NLP module. The ECKGs follow the Simple Event Model (SEM) (Van Hage et al., 2011), which represents events as instances through URIs with relations to their participants, location, and time. The same event instance and participants can be mentioned several times throughout a text and across different documents. Identity across mentions is then modeled through the Grounded Annotation Framework (GAF) (Fokkens et al., 2013), by giving

event instances the same unique URI in SEM and pointing to the different mentions in the source text via a *denotedBy* relation to mention URIs based on their offsets. Assigning unique URIs to coreferential event mentions results in ECKGs with all the knowledge and information aggregated across mentions in the form of RDF properties for this subject URI.

Figure 1 shows two examples of ECKGs with the event URIs 094fe5921b642e30a00cd52ece7b0157#ev1 and 60ad5103290ae7aa16e39d3cd2695496#ev1. The ECKGs are derived from two mentions in two different documents. The triple representations capture the following properties for each event: subclass relations with WordNet synsets and FrameNet frames, *denotedBy* pointers to the offset positions in the original texts, the words or labels used to mention the event, PropBank roles filled by DBpedia URIs, or unresolved phrases that are not entities and finally, the date to which the events are anchored.

In this output of NewsReader, we did not apply any event coreference and we represent each mention as a separate event instance or ECKG. The WordNet synsets and FrameNet frames are associated through the WSD modules in NewsReader. We used the UKB (Agirre and Soroa, 2009) and IMS ((Zhong and Ng, 2010) to score the WordNet synsets for each predicate. Next, we take the highest scoring synsets and use the Predicate Matrix (Carreras et al., 2014) to obtain the associated FrameNet frames. The interpretation of the predicates as events for the task is thus derived from the SRL output in combination with the WSD output and the Predicate Matrix association.

We call the above output of NewsReader the **raw-ECKGs**. In the next sections, we describe how we post-process these to derive so-called **task-ECKGs** with only the information relevant for the task. We finally reason over these task-ECKGs to answer the queries. Both the raw-ECKGS and the task-ECKGs are available in the Github repository, including the scripts to extract the latter from the former.

3 Event coreference

As a first step for the task, we read the raw-ECKGs and filter out only those events that are relevant for the task: see section 3.2 for details. Next, we establish event identity across the different event

---

[1] www.newsreader-project.eu and https://github.com/newsreader

[2] https://github.com/cltl/nwr-semeval2018-5

```
094fe5921b642e30a00cd52ece7b0157#ev1
    a                   wn:eng-30-00069879-v , wn:eng-00069879-v ,
                        fn:Cause_harm , fn:Experience_bodily_harm ;
    gaf:denotedBy       094fe5921b642e30a00cd52ece7b0157#char=11,18;
    skos:prefLabel      "injure" ;
    pb:A1               dbpedia:East_Palo_Alto,_California ;
    time:inDateTime     date:20130505 .

60ad5103290ae7aa16e39d3cd2695496#ev1
    a                   wn:eng-30-00069879-v , wn:eng-30-07950786-n ,
                        wn:eng-02738701-v , wn:eng-01882814-v ,
                        fn:Cause_harm , fn:Path_shape , fn:Travel ;
    gaf:denotedBy       60ad5103290ae7aa16e39d3cd2695496#char=9,16;
    skos:prefLabel      "wound"  ;
    pb:A1               semeval2018-5:non-entities/person ;
    pb:A2               dbpedia:East_Palo_Alto,_California ;
    time:inDateTime     date:20130505 .
```

Figure 1: ECKG representation of events extracted by NewsReader for two different mentions in two different documents, showing the type of event, the mentions linked through the *denotedBy* property, the PropBank roles, the date and the actual words used to make reference. The denotedBy links are simplified to reduce space.

mentions: see subsections 3.3 and 3.4. For this, we assume that each document reports on a single incident and mentions within a document are coreferential. We carried out the following steps for this:

1. We build an index of all documents that report on the same incident as follows:

   (a) We determine the incident time for a document.

   (b) We determine the overall incident type for a document: killing, injuring, job firing, or fire burning.

   (c) We compare all documents with the same incident time and incident type to further match the locations and participants.

   (d) If there are sufficient matching locations and participants across documents, we store them relative to the same incident.

2. Iterating over the incident-document index, we determine the mentions of incidents and their subevents over all documents that report on the same incident. We establish coreference relations among these mentions:

   (a) All mentions of the incident as a whole, e.g. *accident*, *shooting*, *this*, receive the same URI that represents the incident.

   (b) All further subevents of an incident (*hit*, *injure*, *death*) are identified by their subevent type and the victims associated within and across documents related to

the same incident. Incident subevents of the same type and with the same victims become coreferential and receive the same URI.

In the next subsections, we explain these steps in more detail.

3.1 Incident time

The document-creation-time is given by the organizers for each document but it does not necessarily correspond with the date of the incident. We therefore extract the mostly mentioned year and month throughout the document and select the most frequently mentioned date for that year/month. We experimented with selecting different proportions of the text, as we assumed that the actual incident data is most likely mentioned in the beginning and other incidents from the past may be mentioned later in the text. We tested these approaches on the trial data and found that restricting the date references to the first two sentences gave the best results. If there are no time expressions in the first two sentences, we use the document-creation-time as the incident date as a fall-back.[3]

3.2 Incident type

For each document, we classify all the predicates for the event types of the task: *shooting*, *burning*, and *dismissal of employees* and count which type is most dominant. To classify the predicates, we

---

[3]We also experimented with other granularities e.g. by lumping incidents by the week of the month but these did not give better results.

collected all FrameNet frames that NewsReader assigned to the trial data and ordered the frames by frequency. We manually selected the following frames for each event type:

incident fn:Attack,fn:Catastrophe,fn:Cause_harm, fn:Destroying

kill fn:Cause_to_end,fn:Death,fn:Killing

injured fn:Cause_harm,fn:Cause_impact, fn:Experience_bodily_harm, fn:Hit_target,fn:Recovery,fn:Resurrection

hit fn:Cause_impact,fn:Hit_target

shoot fn:Shoot_projectiles,fn:Use_firearm

burn fn:Absorb_heat,fn:Apply_heat, fn:Setting_fire,fn:Fire_burning,fn:Fire_going_out

dismiss fn:Firing,fn:Quitting_a_place, fn:Quitting,fn:Get_a_job,fn:Hiring,fn:Employing, fn:Being_employed

We further noticed that some task-relevant words in the trial data were not matched with WordNet synsets or FrameNet frames by our system. After analysing the output of the trial data, we manually selected 84 predicates that were sometimes missed by the system (due to upper case, part-of-speech errors, out-of-vocabulary) to ensure higher coverage. We used this word list together with the FrameNet mappings to select only those events that are relevant for the tasks and derive the dominant event type of the document.

3.3   Incident-document index

After determining the dominant date and the type of incident, we compare documents with the same incident date and the same incident type to determine which documents report on the same incident. For this we compare the locations and the participants. If there is a sufficient degree of matching, we assume that documents report on the same incident.[4] For participants, we first check the names of the entities detected by the NERC module. If there was no match, we check all other phrases with PropBank A0 or A1 role, such as *person*, *child*, *girl* that denote persons, but are not classified as entities by NERC.[5] For locations, we assume that the entity linking software[6] found a

match to DBpedia. We directly compare the DBpedia URIs for locations across the documents to find a match. Eventually when documents match in terms of all properties: same incident date, same incident type, one participant and one location, we assume they report on the same incident and we store them together in an incident-document index.

3.4   Coreference across incident mentions

The second step in this process establishes the event coreference relations across all event mentions in all the documents related to the same incident. All references to the incident as a whole will receive a unique URI that identifies that incident. For example, if a document has *shooting* as the dominant incident type, then we consider all references to *shooting* as a mention of the incident as a whole. We consider abstract incident mentions such as *catastrophe*, *accident*, and even pronouns such as *it* and *this*, as coreferential with the incident as a whole. Next, we extract all references to subevents, e.g. *hit, injured, death* as separate event instances relative to the incident to which they are associated. Subevents are separated by their subtype in combination with the participants or victims. Each subevent receives a URI that is composed of the incident URI, the subevent type, and the participant string. An example of such a subevent URI is shown in Figure 2. It starts with a document reference[7] followed by #incident, #INJURED and the words that make up all linked participant phrases: 6-year+old+girl+child+little+girl+person +young+girl. These participant phrases are aggregated across various mentions. In the case of phrases such as this one, it is difficult to reason over the participant identity; how many participants are injured? In this approach, we assume that the URI and therefore their identity was resolved by the generic processing of NewsReader. No specific matching strategy was implemented to establish coreference across participants. We see in Figure 2 the resulting list of distinct participant URIs based on their surface forms. In case of entity names, it is more likely to match participants across mentions directly through their URIs or their first name or surname. For example in Figure 2, the second ECKG shows

---

[4]In our experiments, matching a single participant and a single location was sufficient.

[5]In NewsReader, these phrases are typed as non-entities because they can refer to generic or role instantiations, e.g. *victim, mother*

[6]mendes2011dbpedia

[7]We arbitrarily take the name of the first document used in comparison just to get a unique URI

an incident reference with the participant name *Tewalt* that needs to match a participant in another document with the same name to find a match.

3.5 Aggregating properties

Establishing coreference through the same URI, results in further aggregation of all properties that were initially expressed for separate event mentions. We also normalised the properties by lumping all PropBank A0 and A1 roles to *sem:hasActor* for participants and *sem:hasPlace* for location. Figure 2 shows two examples of **task-ECKG** resulting after aggregating data from mentions from the **raw-ECKGs**. The first ECKG shows a subevent of the type INJURED based on the raw-ECKGs shown in Figure 1. The second ECKG shows an event at the incident level, aggregated over various mentions in the same document and their corresponding properties. We also include all subevents for the incident as links. There are subevents both for being injured and for death although the participants detected are linked only to injured subevents. This has consequences for answering subtask 3 questions for number of people injured or died.

After aggregating the properties, we store these task-ECKGs to an output file named after the incident date inside a subfolder that corresponds with each incident event type: (*BURN*, *DISMISS* and *SHOOT*). For example for the test data, the software created a BURN subfolder with 6 ECKGs files in TRiG-RDF format: 20071026.trig, 20071022.trig, 20151027.trig, 20151024.trig, 20070207.trig, 20070201.trig, each representing the incident date. Each of these TRiG files contains all incidents of the same type that are associated with the same date. For SHOOT and DISMISS the number of RDF files with incidents on the same date is far larger: 1,367 and 43 respectively.

In addition to storing the task-ECKGs, we also read the CoNLL file and annotate its tokens with numeric event identifiers by taking the checksum of each URI in the ECKGs and assign the checksum to each *denotedBy* match with a token. The annotated CoNLL file is submitted for the task.

4 Counting incidents and victims

Given the ECKG representations of incident instances and their subevents, it is straightforward to answer the task questions. To achieve this, we process all the questions and match their constraints with the knowledge on the task-ECKGs: the incident type, the date, the participant name, and location (if any). This results in a number of matching incidents and their associated source documents. For subtask 3, we additionally extract the victims for the specified subevents *killing* and *injuring*.

To obtain the answers, we first check the type of event in the query (*killing*, *injuring*, *fire_burning*, and *job_firing*) and match it with the subfolders of the adapted-ECKGs. We only consider the ECKGs files for a matching type. For *shooting* events that are differentiated into *killing* and *injuring* incidents, we additionally filter the ECKGs for the occurrence of the corresponding subevents. From each subfolder, we only load the ECKGs with matching dates. If there is no date constraint, we load all ECKGs. In case of a date constraint, we check if the constraint specifies a day or only a year or month. If no specific day is specified, we check if the ECKG files start with the corresponding year and/or month. Else if a specific day is asked for, we match the full date with the incident time.

We load all ECKG files that match the above constraints and consider each incident and its properties for further matching with other constraints on location or participant names. In the case of location, we first directly match the DBpedia URI for each incident against the sem:hasPlace properties. If there is no match, we expand the location in the query to DBPedia URIs that are related using spatial properties: north, east, west, south, northeast, southeast, northwest, and southwest of the specified location. For participants, we first check all participants of the incident that are classified as an entity of type PERSON by the NERCD module. We check the beginning of the name in case of a first name constraint and the ending of the name in case of a surname constraint.

After selecting incidents that match the query constraints, we derive the answers. In the case of subtask 1, we only provide the document ids for matched incidents and the numeric answer 1 (if any document was recovered). In the case of subtask 2, we count the unique number of incidents within the selected ECKGs and the associated documents of their mentions. If there are none, the answer is zero. If there is one or more, we provide the number of incidents and the associated document identifiers for their mentions. In the case of

```
<094fe5921b642e30a00cd52ece7b0157#incident#INJURED#
  6-year+old+girl+child+little+girl+person+young+girl>
  a                 nwrontology:INJURED ;
  gaf:denotedBy     094fe5921b642e30a00cd52ece7b0157#char=11,18,
                    60ad5103290ae7aa16e39d3cd2695496#char=20,28, etc...;
  sem:hasActor      se2018-5:non-entity/6-year+old+girl ,
                    se2018-5:non-entity/person, se2018-5:non-entity/child ,
                    se2018-5:non-entity/young+girl, se2018-5:non-entity/little+girl ;
  sem:hasPlace      dbpedia:East_Palo_Alto,_California, dbpedia:Richmond,_California ;
  time:inDateTime   time:20130505 ;
  skos:prefLabel    "injury" , "injure" , "shoot" , "wound" .

<8554b200f12a9e9f6fed68f6795ada07#incident>
  a                 nwrontology:SHOOT ;
  gaf:denotedBy     8554b200f12a9e9f6fed68f6795ada07#char=2311,2318, etc. ;
  sem:hasActor      se2018-5:non-entity/kuna+man, se2018-5:entity/Tewalt ;
  sem:hasSubEvent   <8554b200f12a9e9f6fed68f6795ada07#incident#DEAD#>,
                    <#incident#INJURED#kuna+man>, <#incident#INJURED#Tewalt+kuna+man>,
                    <#incident#HIT#Tewalt>, <#incident#INJURED#Tewalt> ;
  sem:hasSubType    nwrontology:INJURED , nwrontology:DEAD , nwrontology:HIT ;
  time:inDateTime   time:20161228
  skos:prefLabel    "accident", "shooting", "incident", "gun", "start", "leave",
                    "hit", "it", "use", "discharge", "handling", "handle" .
```

Figure 2: task-ECKG representation of an *injure* event resulting from establishing event-coreference and aggregating the event properties across different mentions. The denotedBy and subevent links are adapted to save space.

subtask 3, we additionally extract all victims from the ECKGs as being *injured* or *killed*. If the victims in the ECKG are entities of the type PERSON, we count the unique list of names. If there are no entities of the type PERSON associated with the subevents, we simple count the unique strings of the non-entities associated with *injuring* or *death*. The victim count is then used to answer subtask 3 queries numerically.

5 Results and discussion

Our system answers the task queries using ECKGs in which event and participant identity is established by the unsupervised NewsReader system. Next, we reason over the properties of the ECKGs in relation to the query constraints. We did minimal adaptations for the task and the performance heavily relies on the quality of the ECKGs. The adaptations mainly involved detecting the relevant event types among all events detected by NewsReader, reasoning over the incident date and matching the location in the query with locations in the ECKGs using spatial relations from DBpedia. Furthermore, we relied on the one-document-one-incident heuristic. We expect that the system can be improved considerably by: 1) improving the incident-document index using state-of-the-art clustering techniques ((Li et al., 2005; Nicholls and Bright, 2018; Wei et al., 2018)), 2) improving the detection of predicates and the associated event type on the basis of WSD, 3) improve the detection and reasoning over locations, 4) establishing coreference relations and identity of the participants of the events.

Except for subtask 1, our system ranked 2nd in all tasks. This suggests that it is relatively stable and can be used to obtain detailed interpretations such as the victim counts for subtask 3. Also for the event coreference, our system ranks 2nd. Given the low performance on the document-incident clustering in subtask 1, where we have an F1 of 23.82, we can expect that this performance can be substantial higher if we use a state-of-the-art document-incident clustering technique. Currently, we used a very simple semantic comparison over the event properties and do not use most of the textual data in the documents. We also noticed that the NewsReader raw-ECKG output is noisy with respect to the event participants and the location detection. There is room for improvement to better associate frames to events, interpret locations in the documents and the victims and their names.

Acknowledgments

This research was funded by the Netherlands Organization for Scientific Research (NWO) via the Spinoza grant awarded to Piek Vossen in the project *Understanding Language by Machines*.

References

Eneko Agirre and Aitor Soroa. 2009. Personalizing pagerank for word sense disambiguation. In *Proceedings of the 12th Conference of the European Chapter of the Association for Computational Linguistics*, pages 33–41. Association for Computational Linguistics.

Collin Baker. 2008. Framenet, present and future. In *The First International Conference on Global Interoperability for Language Resources*, pages 12–17.

Xavier Carreras, Lluís Padró, Lei Zhang, Achim Rettinger, Zhixing Li, Esteban García-Cuesta, Željko Agić, Bozo Bekavac, Blaz Fortuna, and Tadej Štajner. 2014. Xlike project language analysis services. In *Proceedings of the Demonstrations at the 14th Conference of the European Chapter of the Association for Computational Linguistics*, pages 9–12.

Christiane Fellbaum. 1998. *WordNet*. Wiley Online Library.

Antske Fokkens, Marieke van Erp, Piek Vossen, Sara Tonelli, Willem Robert van Hage, Luciano Serafini, Rachele Sprugnoli, and Jesper Hoeksema. 2013. Gaf: A grounded annotation framework for events. In *Proceedings of the 1st workshop on Events: Definition, Detection, Coreference, and Representation, NAACL2013*, Atlanta, GA, USA.

Antske Fokkens, Aitor Soroa, Zuhaitz Beloki, German Rigau, Willem Robert van Hage, and Piek Vossen. 2014. NAF: the NLP Annotation Format. Technical report, Vrije Universiteit Amsterdam.

Paul Kingsbury and Martha Palmer. 2002. From treebank to propbank. In *LREC*, pages 1989–1993. Citeseer.

Zhiwei Li, Bin Wang, Mingjing Li, and Wei-Ying Ma. 2005. A probabilistic model for retrospective news event detection. In *Proceedings of the 28th annual international ACM SIGIR conference on Research and development in information retrieval*, pages 106–113. ACM.

Tom Nicholls and Jonathan Bright. 2018. Understanding news story chains using information retrieval and network clustering techniques. *arXiv preprint arXiv:1801.07988*.

Marten Postma, Filip Ilievski, and Piek Vossen. 2018. Semeval-2018 task 5: Counting events and participants in the long tail. In *Proceedings of the 12th International Workshop on Semantic Evaluation (SemEval-2018)*. Association for Computational Linguistics.

Willem Robert Van Hage, Véronique Malaisé, Roxane Segers, Laura Hollink, and Guus Schreiber. 2011. Design and use of the simple event model (sem). *Web Semantics: Science, Services and Agents on the World Wide Web*, 9(2):128–136.

Piek Vossen, Rodrigo Agerri, Itziar Aldabe, Agata Cybulska, Marieke van Erp, Antske Fokkens, Egoitz Laparra, Anne-Lyse Minard, Alessio Palmero Aprosio, and German Riga. 2016. Newsreader: using knowledge resources in a cross-lingual reading machine to generate more knowledge from massive streams of news. *Knowledge-Based Systems*.

Yifang Wei, Lisa Singh, David Buttler, and Brian Gallagher. 2018. Using semantic graphs to detect overlapping target events and story lines from newspaper articles. *International Journal of Data Science and Analytics*, 5(1):41–60.

Zhi Zhong and Hwee Tou Ng. 2010. It makes sense: A wide-coverage word sense disambiguation system for free text. In *Proceedings of the ACL 2010 system demonstrations*, pages 78–83. Association for Computational Linguistics.

FEUP at SemEval-2018 Task 5: An Experimental Study of a Question Answering System

Carla Abreu
Faculdade Engenharia
Universidade do Porto
ei08165@fe.up.pt

Eugénio Oliveira
Faculdade Engenharia
Universidade do Porto
LIACC
eco@fe.up.pt

Abstract

We present the approach developed at the Faculty of Engineering of the University of Porto to participate in SemEval-2018 Task 5: *Counting Events and Participants within Highly Ambiguous Data covering a very long tail.*[1] The work described here presents the experimental system developed to extract entities from news articles for the sake of Question Answering. We propose a supervised learning approach to enable the recognition of two different types of entities: *Locations* and *Participants*. We also discuss the use of distance-based algorithms (using Levenshtein distance and Q-grams) for the detection of documents' closeness based on the entities extracted. For the experiments, we also used a multi-agent system that improved the performance.

1 Introduction

Thousands of news articles are published every day on several media outlets. Representing and reasoning over all events in these articles is a challenging task. For instance, if we would like to answer questions about these articles like: *How many people died on the shootings in Philippi in 30th September, 2017?* or *How many people died last year on Birmingham?* or *How many people were killed by John List?*, a deep understanding is needed of many phenomena in the articles. For example, news story updates and duplicate news need to be considered in the answer processing. We can simplify the problem by identifying relevant elements from the news entities and create a structured representation to store these data.

Named Entity Recognition (NER) is a task that aims at identifying and classifying entity mentions in free text. Message Understanding Conference (MUC) defines the entities as belonging to three

categories:[2] 1. *Enamex*: names, such as Locations, Persons, Organizations, and others 2. *Timex*: temporal expressions 3. *Numex*: numerical elements, such as numbers and percentages.

In this paper, we present an experimental study to extract entities from news articles to answer questions. We make use of a supervised learning approach to deal with the recognition of two different kind of entities: Locations (e.g. *Philippi, Birmingham*) and Participants (e.g. *John List*). We also have studied the use of distance algorithms (Levenshtein and Q-grams) for the near document detection based on entities extracted.

The remainder of the paper is organized as follows. In Section 2, we describe SemEval-2018 Task 5, followed by an overview of the state of the art in Named Entity Recognition in Section 3. In Section 4, we present the state of the art in the Near Document Detection task, followed by the description of the system architecture in Section 5. In Section 6, we presents the approach, followed by the experimental setup in Section 7. The results are discussed in Section 8.

2 Task Description

The main goal of SemEval-2018 Task 5 (Postma et al., 2018) is to answer questions based on a set of provided news articles, e.g. *How many killing incidents happened in 2016 in Columbus, Mississippi?*. Each question has three components: an event type and two event properties. Each question contains one out of four event types: *killing, injuring, fire burning*, and *job firing*. Event Properties are all the related characteristics associated with the event. They can include *Locations* (City or State), *Participants* (First Name, Last Name, Full Name), and *Time* (Day (e.g. 1/1/2015), Month (e.g. 1/2015) or Year (e.g. 2015)). There are three

---

[1] https://competitions.codalab.org/competitions/17285

[2] http://afner.sourceforge.net/what.html

Proceedings of the 12th International Workshop on Semantic Evaluation (SemEval-2018), pages 667–673
New Orleans, Louisiana, June 5–6, 2018. ©2018 Association for Computational Linguistics

subtasks:

- Subtask 1 (S1): Find the single event that answers the question

- Subtask 2 (S2): Find all events (if any) that answer the question

- Subtask 3 (S3): Find all participant-role relations that answer the question

3 Named Entity Recognition

A wide range of approaches have been developed to tackle NER. Early systems deal with this issue by making use of handcrafted rule-based algorithms (Hearst, 1992). More recently, systems focus on machine learning techniques (supervised learning (Florian et al., 2003), semi-supervised (Collins and Singer, 1999; Mikheev et al., 1999), and unsupervised learning). However, the major drawback of supervised learning is its dependence on annotated data. In the case of unavailability of training examples, handcrafted rules remain the practical technique (Riaz, 2010).

4 Near Document Detection

In the large amount of news articles that are published every day, the same information can be repeated in many different articles. The identification of similar or near-duplicate documents is applied in: plagiarized documents detection (Hoad and Zobel, 2003), similar web pages detection (Henzinger, 2006), and similar news articles detection (Abreu et al., 2015).

Identification of similar or near-duplicate pairs of documents in a large collection is a significant problem with wide-spread applications. Kumar and Govindarajulu (2009) present approaches used to solve this issue. For those kind of problems, three main approaches are proposed: based on URLs, on lexicon and, the third and more sophisticated, on semantics (Abreu et al., 2015).

In the work presented here, we are using the semantics-based approach applied to the information previously extracted from the news articles.

5 Architecture

The system consists of the following main components:

Creating a Structured News Representation.

| Copyright 2017 by WJXT News4Jax - All rights reserved. |
| To get alerts for breaking news, grab the free NBC4 News App for iPhone or Android. |
| contact kimber laux at klaux@reviewjournal.com or 702 - 383 - 0283. |
| Contact Jessica Terrones at jterrones@reviewjournal.com or at 702-383-0381. |

Table 1: Journalistic Patterns

D	M	Y	Regular Expression
x	x	x	(Jan. [1-9]+[1-9]*, [1-2][0-9][0-9][0-9])
	x	x	(December [1-2][0-9][0-9][0-9])
		x	[1-2][0-9][0-9][0-9]

Table 2: Temporal Regular Expressions

Figure 1 presents the architecture used to parse the news article. After converting CoNLL to plain text, journalists patterns are removed as demonstrated in Table 5. Journalistic patterns could be relevant for the reader, but not for the entity recognition task. The output of this system is a structured news representation with a list of Event Types, Locations, Participants, and Temporal Expressions. Additionally, the following sources of information are also extracted: the news identifier, publication date, and news title. To result in this representation, the following four extractions are performed:

Extract list of Event Types. We use WordNet (Fellbaum, 1998) to create a list of words that can be used to describe an event type. Our approach uses the news article title and body for the event type recognition. For each one of these elements, the English Snowball Stemmer is applied. We consider a document to have a certain event type if at least one term that describes an event type is present in the news title or body.

Extract Locations and Participants. For the Locations and Participants recognition, a supervised approach is used. The approach proposed is described in Section 6.

Extract Temporal Expressions. Our approach to finding temporal information in the news article is based on the application of regular expressions. Table 2 presents some of the regular expressions used.

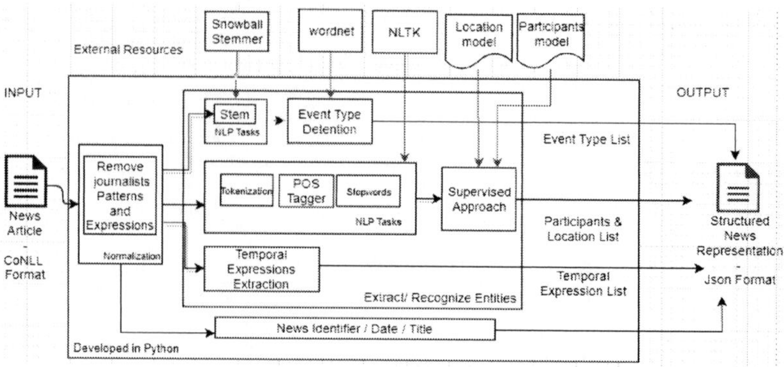

Figure 1: Create a structured news representation approach

Extract Auxiliar Information. The title, publication date, and news identifier are also extracted from the news article to create the structured news representation.

Search all the news that answer a question

When the system receives a question, an answer will be retrieved based on the structured news representation. Firstly, for each element (Event Type and Event Propreties) a list of news articles that has some relation with the element under analysis is composed. In the end, the news or set of news articles that address all the items under analysis are extracted.

Near document detection

The near document detection was done based on the set of news that answers a question. The approach is explained in Section 6.

Counting participants

Similarly to what happened in the case of previously mentioned events' extraction, this one only uses a news article or a set of news articles that answer a question. For this set of news articles, we only process the information given by the news article title. For each Event Type we manually define the variation trend (increase/ decrease/ stable) - e.g. the number of death can increase with the decrease of the number of injured - in a killing event. We started this process by normalizing and removing temporal expressions from the news article title. After, we applied the POS-tagger and split the sentence into subsentences separated by comas. We started to recognize the event type for each subsentence. When we found it, we checked if

the subsentence also includes a numerical element ('CD' - Post tagger) - this element is considered as a number of participants associated with the event type. Once extracted the number of participants associated with each news article, we connect this information with news article's date. Finally, we try to find the maximum or the minimum of participants depending on the temporal event type trend.

The system we are presenting here was developed in Python 2.7. It uses some python libraries: Natural Language Toolkit (NLTK) - Wordnet, English Snowball Stemmer, Stopwords, POSTagger; Python multi-Agent Development Environment (SPADE); Scikit-Learn - tree, RandomForestClassifier, ExtraTreesClassifier, LinearSVC; Json; and, Regular Expressions (re).

6 The proposed approach

6.1 NER Supervised Approach

In this subsection, we describe the implementation details of the proposed approach for recognizing Locations and Participants.

Natural Language Processing Tasks:

The data was preprocessed with two NLP tasks: part of speech tagging and stop word recognition.

Features

Supervised learning techniques require their input to be categorized. When extracting information from news documents, it is common to label each word with a set of features. These features allow the SL approach to recognize an entity in a given document. We extracted the following features: 1. CAP (Capitalized) indicates whether a word: contains no capital characters,

	shooting	at	a	west	Phoenix	apartment	that	left	one	man	dead
CAP	0	0	0	0	1	0	0	0	0	0	0
PT	D	NN	IN	DT	NNP	NN	WDT	VBD	CD	NN	NN
SWI	0	1	1	0	0	0	1	0	0	0	0
SWA		at	a				that				

Table 3: Categorizing each word on a sentence

	Current			Previous				Next				Loc	
Exp	Cap	SW	Pos	Cap	SW	Pos	Sw	Cap	SW	Pos	Sw	NP	P
S1	x	x	x	x	x	x	x	x	x	x	x	x	x
S2	x	x	x	x	x	x	x	x	x	x	x		
S3	x	x	x	x	x	x	x						
S4	x	x	x					x	x	x	x		

Figure 2: Features used in each scenario

has only its first letter capitalized, or all its characters are capitalized; 2. PT (POS Tagger Association)[3] identifies the part of speech tag of a word, such as noun, verb, adjective, etc.; 3. SWI (Stop–Words Identification) indicates whether a word is a stop-word; 4. SWA (Stop-Words Association) associates a corresponding stop-word; 5. NP - Paragraph records a numeric identifier of the paragraph in which the word appears.

Table 3 presents example of features computed for each word in the phrase "shooting at a west Phoenix apartment that left one man dead". For instance, the word "Phoenix" is capitalized ($CAP = 1$), corresponds to a noun ($PT = NNP$), and is not a stop-word ($SWI = 0$). Note that we aggregate all sequential capitalized words as one, e.g. "Salt Lake City" will be combined in a single word to be classified.

We believe that a simple association as illustrated in Table 3 is not enough to categorize a word for the Named Entity Recognition task. For this reason, we also consider the word context in the document, i.e., the current word (C), the previous word (P), and the next word (N). Here we indicate the word position following the feature abbreviation, e.g., "C CAP" indicates whether the current word is capitalized or not.

Data Cleaning and Transformation

Data quality is the main challenge of information management. To guarantee data quality, two processes were executed: data cleaning and data transformation. Tables 4 and 5 present the data transformation for POS tags and stop-words.

<hr>

[3](POSTagger - All Tags) - http://www.nltk.org/book/ch05.html visited on 2017, November

Stop-words have no value for SWA. To fix this, we replace an empty value by the character "X" and we encode this value as demonstrated in Table 5.

PostTagger	Rep
DT	0
NN	1
NNP	2
VBD	3
...	...

Stop-Word	Rep
X	0
a	1
that	2
and	3
...	...

Table 4: POSTtagger   Table 5: Stop Words

Classification Algorithms

Supervised learning techniques create a model that predicts the value of a target variable based on a set of input variables. One challenge is to select the most appropriate algorithm for the task of classifying Locations and Participants. We have compared the following algorithms: Support Vector Classifier (SVC); Decision Tree Classifier (Tree); Random Forest Classifier (Random); Extra Trees Classifier (Extra). As demonstrated on Table 6, different configurations were attempted for each algorithm. Implementations of these algorithms are provided by the Python library scikit-learn library[4].

6.2 Near Document Detection

The answer to a question in this SemEval task consists of the following: question identifier, set of the news articles that help to answer the question, and a numerical answer.

The numerical answer of a question is dependent on the question task. Task 2 requires a number of unique events that correspond to a question. For this purpose, it is essential to detect similar news documents within the given set. To detect similar documents, we use the structured news representation described above. Each pair of news articles is compared based on: their titles, their lists of Participants, and their lists of Locations.

7 Experimental Setup

7.1 NER Approach

Data Resources

The SemEval 5 competition provides data for the purpose at stake. The data made available in this competition is a set of English news articles. To extract locations and participants from crime

<hr>

[4]http://scikit-learn.org/stable/, visited in November 2017

Alg/ID	Configuration
SVC 1	Default scikit learn configuration
SVC 2	kernel="linear"
SVC 3	kernel="sigmoid"
Tree 1	Default scikit-learn configuration
Tree 2	criterion="gini", splitter="best", min samples split=2
Tree 3	criterion="entropy", splitter="best", min samples split=2
Tree 4	criterion="entropy", splitter="random", min samples split=2
Tree 5	criterion="gini", splitter="random", min samples split=2
Tree 6	criterion="gini", splitter="best", min samples split=4
Tree 7	criterion="entropy", splitter="best", min samples split=4
Random 1	criterion="gini", n estimators=10
Random 2	criterion="gini" n estimators=5
Random 3	criterion="gini",n estimators=20
Random 4	criterion="entropy", n estimators=10
Random 5	criterion="entropy",n estimators=5
Random 6	criterion="entropy",n estimators=20
Extra 1	criterion="gini", max features="auto"
Extra 2	criterion="entropy", max features="auto"
Extra 3	criterion="gini", max features="sqrt"
Extra 4	criterion="entropy",max features="sqrt"
Extra 5	criterion="gini", max features="log2"
Extra 6	criterion="entropy" max features="log2"
Extra 7	criterion="gini" max features=None
Extra 8	criterion="entropy", max features=None

Table 6: Classification Algorithm Configurations

news, additional annotations were done. A set of 10,580 individual words were annotated in three categories: Locations, Participants, and Others - where all the sequential capitalized words were aggregated as one, e.g., in "as she left Jackson Memorial Hospital", the annotated elements are: [as], [she], [left],[Jackson Memorial Hospital].

Evaluation

The evaluation metrics used to evaluate this approach are Precision (P), Recall (R), and F1 (F). Due to a large number of experiences and in order to correctly analyze the obtained results, we made use of a multi-agent architecture to find the best results. For this evaluation, we defined a utility function and we introduced an auction mechanism to enable some kind of negotiation. This mechanism is based on English auction, where each agent can propose their bids following the auction requirements. Our agents represent the different configuration of the classification algorithms and each bid reveals their result on a specific test scenario. We expect that in this experiment recall is the most important metric, thus it is assigned a higher weight than the other metrics. Our utility function was defined as follows:

$$U = 0.5 * R + 0.25 * P + 0.25F1$$

In order to reduce the data to be analyzed we exclude all combinations with low performance, namely all combinations where either Recall, Precision, or F1 has a mean value bellow 60% or a standard deviation above 15%.

Experiments

A supervised learning system was needed to generate a model. The classification algorithms and the scenarios (S1, S2, S3, and S4) defining values of features are those described in section 6.1.

Our experiments were done taking cross-validation with $k = 7$ into account. We divided the annotated data into partitions of training data (75%) and testing data (15%).

7.2 Near Document Detection

Data Resources

Near document detection approach was studied with the dataset provided at the end of the competition. Each intended answer includes a list of similar documents identified in the given dataset and aggregated according to the corresponding question. For each answer, we created a script to aggregate all news articles in pairs. Additionally, a label indicating whether a pair is similar or nor (pairs that are contained in the same set are similar) was added. In total, this resulted in 61,931 pairs of news articles.

Evaluation

We evaluate the performance of various thresholds on near document detection by applying the metrics: Precision, Recall, and Accuracy.

Experiments:

For each pair of news articles, we have calculated the similarity between their elements: title (T), list of participants (Part), and list of locations (Loc). For the sake of comparison, we have used two distance algorithms: Levenshtein (L) (Levenshtein, 1966) and Qgrams (Q) (Ullmann, 1977). We defined two scenarios (SS1, SS2), differing in the weights of the document elements as follows:

$$SS1 = 0.50T + 0.25Loc + 0.25Part$$

$$SS2 = 0.34T + 0.33Loc + 0.33Part$$

Exp	Alg	P	R	F	U
S3	Tree 6	66.47	70.94	68.34	69.17
S1	Extra 8	71.67	67.63	69.13	69.02
S1	Tree 2	71.28	67.53	69.08	68.85
S1	Tree 3	70.53	67.79	68.90	68.75
S2	Tree 4	70.35	67.55	68.54	68.50

Table 7: Recognizing Participants - Results

Exp	Alg	P	R	F	U
S3	Tree 3	70.32	66.68	68.13	67.95
S1	Extra 8	68.91	67.53	67.97	67.98
S1	Extra 4	68.13	67.40	67.64	67.64
S1	Extra 7	67.11	70.06	68.34	67.16
S1	Extra 2	68.28	64.84	66.41	66.09

Table 8: Recognizing Location - Results

8 Analysis and Results

8.1 NER Approach

Due to the large volume of combinations and their corresponding results, we used a multi-agent system to simplify the analysis. Tables 7 and 8 present the best 5 results achieved on extracting Participants and Locations respectively. We considered the results only from two algorithms: Decision Tree and Extra Tree Classifier. Both approaches show that context helps the recognition task.

8.2 Near Document detection

Table 9 presents the results achieved for various threshold values. Changing the threshold value causes small variations in the performance of the Qgrams algorithm, but large variation in the performance of the Levenshtein distance algorithm. The scenarios presented here are not sufficient to determine if two news articles are similar or not. These results indicate that in cases where news articles refer to the same subject, a reduced news article representations is not sufficient to distinguish different events.

Alg	Function	Threshold	P	R	A
L	SS1	75	12.24	12.86	86.56
L	SS1	80	6.97	60.86	36.22
L	SS1	85	8.26	39.98	62.22
L	SS2	75	13.46	11.96	87.64
L	SS2	80	7.97	40.79	60.30
L	SS2	85	9.37	16.05	82.21
Q	SS1	75	12.30	12.86	86.60
Q	SS1	80	13.38	10.98	88.00
Q	SS1	85	13.38	10.97	88.00
Q	SS2	75	13.61	10.70	88.21
Q	SS2	80	13.23	11.07	87.89
Q	SS2	85	13.38	10.98	88.00

Table 9: Near Document Detection Results by Threshold

8.3 SemEval Results

SemEval-2018 Task 5 contains 3 subtasks, on which we achieved F1 score of 24.65, 30.51, 26.79 respectively.

9 Conclusion and Future Work

In this work, we presented an experimental study that addresses the Question Answering challenge in SemEval-2018 task 5. We have used Named Entity Recognition approaches to identify entities such as Location, Participants, Temporal Expressions, and Event Types. We used a structured news representation to perform the required tasks: 1. to answer questions on counting events 2. to detect which distinct documents provide an answer to a question; and 3. to answer questions by counting event participants.

The use of multi-agent system was crucial in order to find the best performing algorithm. Our utility function allowed us to have a previous definition of the influence of each evaluation metric on the overall evaluation. The resulting system can be applied to other scenarios by adapting the utility function according to their requirements. In the future, our system can be improved to include multiple combinations (e.g., on the near document detection we can use a different combination of elements and algorithms).

Task 2 has been solved with extracting information. Future work for this task could include another study of a supervised learning approach that is based on the entire information available in a news article. However, such a requires a corresponding annotated corpus. Our approach to Task 3 was relatively naive, since it does not consider the relationships between entities (participants and event type). Future work should investigate a more elaborate approach.

Event type behavior should also be studied, as we believe that some events could present temporal trends. For instance, we expect to observe an increase of the number of deaths/injuries described in crime news documents over time.

References

Carla Abreu, Jorge Teixeira, and Eugénio Oliveira. 2015. Encadear: Encadeamento automático de notícias. *Oslo Studies in Language*, 7(1).

Michael Collins and Yoram Singer. 1999. Unsupervised models for named entity classification. In

1999 Joint SIGDAT Conference on Empirical Methods in Natural Language Processing and Very Large Corpora.

Christiane Fellbaum, editor. 1998. *WordNet An Electronic Lexical Database*. The MIT Press, Cambridge, MA ; London.

Radu Florian, Abe Ittycheriah, Hongyan Jing, and Tong Zhang. 2003. Named entity recognition through classifier combination. In *Proceedings of the seventh conference on Natural language learning at HLT-NAACL 2003-Volume 4*, pages 168–171. Association for Computational Linguistics.

Marti A Hearst. 1992. Automatic acquisition of hyponyms from large text corpora. In *Proceedings of the 14th conference on Computational linguistics-Volume 2*, pages 539–545. Association for Computational Linguistics.

Monika Henzinger. 2006. Finding near-duplicate web pages: a large-scale evaluation of algorithms. In *Proceedings of the 29th annual international ACM SIGIR conference on Research and development in information retrieval*, pages 284–291. ACM.

Timothy C Hoad and Justin Zobel. 2003. Methods for identifying versioned and plagiarized documents. *Journal of the Association for Information Science and Technology*, 54(3):203–215.

J Prasanna Kumar and P Govindarajulu. 2009. Duplicate and near duplicate documents detection: A review. *European Journal of Scientific Research*, 32(4):514–527.

Vladimir I Levenshtein. 1966. Binary codes capable of correcting deletions, insertions, and reversals. In *Soviet physics doklady*, volume 10, pages 707–710.

Andrei Mikheev, Marc Moens, and Claire Grover. 1999. Named entity recognition without gazetteers. In *Proceedings of the ninth conference on European chapter of the Association for Computational Linguistics*, pages 1–8. Association for Computational Linguistics.

Marten Postma, Filip Ilievski, and Piek Vossen. 2018. Semeval-2018 task 5: Counting events and participants in the long tail. In *Proceedings of the 12th International Workshop on Semantic Evaluation (SemEval-2018)*. Association for Computational Linguistics.

Kashif Riaz. 2010. Rule-based named entity recognition in urdu. In *Proceedings of the 2010 named entities workshop*, pages 126–135. Association for Computational Linguistics.

Julian R. Ullmann. 1977. A binary n-gram technique for automatic correction of substitution, deletion, insertion and reversal errors in words. *The Computer Journal*, 20(2):141–147.

NAI-SEA at SemEval-2018 Task 5: An Event Search System

Yingchi Liu, Quanzhi Li and Luo Si
Alibaba Group, Inc
Bellevue, WA 98004, USA
{yingchi.liu,quanzhi.li,luo.si}@alibaba-inc.com

Abstract

In this paper, we describe Alibaba's participating system in the semEval-2018 Task5: Counting Events and Participants in the Long Tail. We designed and implemented a pipeline system that consists of components to extract question properties and document features, document event category classifications, document retrieval and document clustering. To retrieve the majority of the relevant documents, we carefully designed our system to extract key information from each question and document pair. After retrieval, we perform further document clustering to count the number of events. The task contains 3 subtasks, on which we achieved F1 score of 78.33, 50.52, 63.59 , respectively, for document level retrieval. Our system ranks first in all the three subtasks on document level retrieval, and it also ranks first in incident-level evaluation by RSME measure in subtask 3.

1 Introduction

In this paper we present our system developed for participanting in the semEval-2018 Task5: Counting Events and Participants in the Long Tail. Given a set of questions and a corpus of documents mainly from news articles, the system needs to provide a numeric answer together with the supporting documents that directly relate to the answer (Postma et al., 2018). According to the official task rule, participants can also optionally provide the text mentions of events in the documents, but we did not participate this year. The task contains 3 subtasks. Subtask 1 is to retrieve all the relevant documents related to one single event asked in the question. Subtask 2 and subtask 3 require the system not only retrieve relevant documents, but also count the number of events or number of participants. Event detection and extraction has been intensively studied (Choubey and Huang, 2017; Nguyen et al., 2016a,b; Nguyen and Grishman, 2016; Feng et al., 2016; Ji and Grishman, 2008). Most of those research used a corpus of annotated documents for training. In this task, annotated documents were not provided, but the key factors to retrieve relevant documents are provided by the questions. Therefore, our system starts from a document retrieval system via key information extraction and matching and follows a document clustering component.

2 System Description

We developed a pipeline system for the task, including question parsing, document feature generation, document event type classifications, document retrieval and document clustering.

2.1 Question Properties

In this task, each question contains three components: the event type and two event properties. The two event properties provided are either the time, the location or the participant of the event. And specifications for these properties can vary in granularity (e.g. day/month/year, city/state, first/last/full name). Details can refer to official task description (Postma et al., 2018). In this task, we consider four event types (i.e. killing, injuring, fire_burning, job_firing). But in training data, only killing and injuring events are provided. Our system first processes each question to extract the question event type and propeties. Later each question and document will be paired (q-d pair) and assigned question properties as binary features. For instance, if a question asks for killing event(s) that happened at specific location and time, the features related to the asked event type and properties (i.e. ask_killing, ask_time, ask_location) will be 1 and others

Proceedings of the 12th International Workshop on Semantic Evaluation (SemEval-2018), pages 674–678
New Orleans, Louisiana, June 5–6, 2018. ©2018 Association for Computational Linguistics

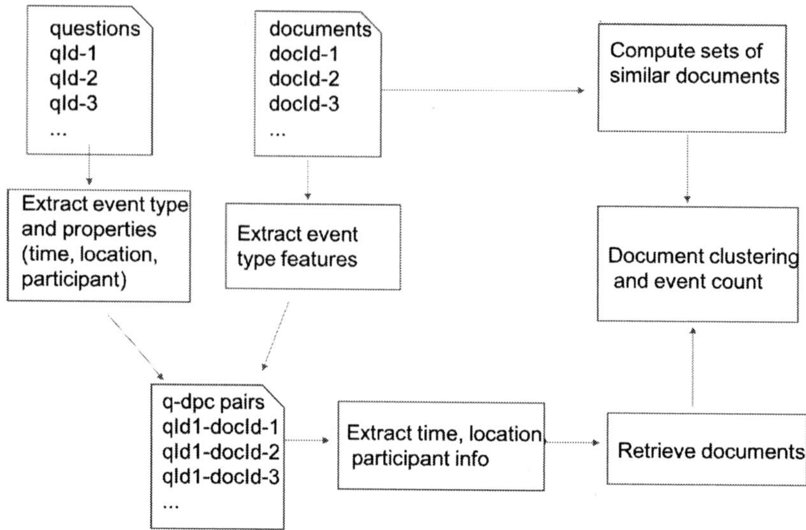

Figure 1: System Overview.

(i.e. ask_injuring, ask_fire_burning, ask_job_firing, ask_participant) will be 0.

2.2 Document Features

2.2.1 Event Type Feature

Event type is a feature which can be defined by the document itself. To decide if a document is one of the four types defined in this task, we ultized both word count feature and classification results. Given the root event trigger keywords for an event type, we first made a synonym word list by including the top similar words from word2vec, based on a cosine similarity score threshold (Mikolov et al., 2013a,b), and adding a couple of missing common words associated with the event. Then we scanned through all documents and count total number of words from the event word list in the document. These counts are then used as word count feature for each event type.

To prepare the training data for the classifier, we selected the killing and injuring documents according to the answer document in trial data. And we used a keyword list to select fire_burning ("firefighter", "fire department", "wildfire", "burn") and job_firing ("employee", "employment", "fired for") related documents. To remove confusing documents that are actually gun violence related, a short list of gun violence keywords ("gun", "shot", "bullet", "shoot") were used when selecting fire_burning and job_firing documents. Two SVM models were trained

for event classification. One for classification between gun violence and non-gun violence. Another one is to determine if an event is an injuring event (not killing-only).

2.2.2 Location Feature

If a question asks for a specific location, the system will extract a location feature from each document according to such location. For instance, if a question asks for an event that occurred in Phoenix, Arizona, it will scan each token in the document and decide if "Phoenix" and "Arizona" are in the document. Based on the granularity of the location asked, a score is assigned to the q-d pair as document location feature. As the states in the U.S. are often abbreviated, a dictionary of the U.S. states with their abbreviations [1] is used for better recall. Additionally, a database of cities in states of the U.S. [2] is used to retrieve a document in the case that a state is asked but the document only mentions the city in that state. In the current system, a partial score is assigned to such a document. And one problem raised by this method is the possibility to retrieve the false positive documents which contain the city with the same name that is in a different state. This issue has not been resolved in the current system, although

---

[1] https://en.wikipedia.org/wiki/List_of_U.S._state_abbreviations
[2] https://github.com/agalea91/city_to_state_dictionary

Feature	Description
DCT_DIFF	document creation time difference, in days
Title_Cosine	cosine similarity of title words
Title_NE_Match	number of common NE in title
Title_NE_Jaccard	Jaccard similarity of NE in title
All_Person_Cosine	cosine similarity of Person entities in the document
All_Person_1gram_Cosine	cosine similarity of 1gram of Person in the document
All_Location_Cosine	cosine similarity of Location in the document
All_Organization_Cosine	cosine similarity of Org in the document
All_NE_Cosine	cosine similarity of all NE in the document
All_NE_Jaccard	jaccard similarity of all NE in the document
All_Cosin_1gram	cosine similarity of 1-gram
All_Cosine_2gram	cosine similarity of 2-gram

Table 1: Features used for clustering documents talking about same events.

	S1	S2	S3
F1	78.33	50.52	63.59

Table 2: Document-Retrieval Performance.

attempts with using additional county information are tried.

2.2.3 Participant Feature

If a question asks for a specific participant name, the system will extract a participant feature based on the match of the name and the granularity of the name that is asked. For example, if a name "Michael Farrow" is asked in the question, it will assign a max score to this participant feature when "Michael Farrow" is found, or partial score when only first or last name is found. To avoid the case that partial name matches to a wrong entity, we used named entity recognition tool from Stanford CoreNLP [3] to extract all named entities, and if the partial name is found in the named entities other than a person, a relatively low score will be assigned as the feature. In addition, in real life a location name (e.g. a street, a mountain or a station etc.) may sometimes be named after a person (e.g. Franklin Street). The system combines these partial names with the common location words and their abbreviations (e.g. street and st.), and use regular expression to check if the documents contain such combination. If so, a relative low score is given.

---

[3]https://nlp.stanford.edu/software/CRF-NER.html

2.2.4 Time Feature

In case a question asks about a specific time, the system extracts potential times via word level matching and Stanford named entity recognition tool. And all the extracted time phrase are normlized to the format as 'DD/MM/YYYY'. Each document has a creation time, i,e. DCT. Because errors may occur during time extraction, it select a potential time only if it is before the DCT, and then such time is compared with the question's time.

2.3 Document Retrieval

To decide the event type, we considered both event keywords and classification results. For violence events (killing and injuring), whether the document contains killing keywords is the only factor to decide if it is killing event, but for injuring event the classification result is used to decide if it is an injuring incidence. For the other two events, both the keyword count and gun violence classification results are considered. With all the features prepared for each q-d pair, a threshold is set for each feature and only q-d pairs with all the feature scores above their thresholds are considered as one corret q-d pair, which means the document is considered as an correct answer for the corresponding question.

2.4 Document Clustering

In subtask 2, after we identify documents that meet the requirements of the question, we need to group the documents that talk about the same event into the same cluster. We used the features listed in Table 1 to train a classifier, to determine

	Time	Location	Participant
questions	892	734	438
non-recalled correct documents	70	86	265

Table 3: Number of questions asked for each properties and number of correct documents missing the corresponding key information.

if two documents are taking about the same event. It is a binary classifier, with two classes: Yes and No. Based on the classification result, we used 1NN for clustering. The trial data of subtask 1 and 2 are used as the training data to train the classifier. In total, there are 599 positive samples (document pairs that talk about the same event), and we randomly generated 1000 document pairs as the negative samples. The classification algorithm used is Random Forest. Based on 10-fold validation, the F measure of the classifier is 0.96. This classifier was also used in subtask 1 and 3 for expanding the root documents for improving recall.

3   Evaluation

Document retrieval performance for all the three subtasks are shown in Table 2.

To understand the loss of the recall, we counted the numbers of questions that ask for time, participant, and location, respectively, and the numbers of documents our system did not retrieve due to the property (e.g. time, participant, and location) was not found, which is shown in Table 3. We use the following two documents as examples:

1.   "Probable cause hearing being held for 3 accused in fatal shooting of 3-year-old DE-TROIT (AP MODIFIED)- Three men charged in the shooting of a 3-year-old Detroit girl were in court today for a probable cause hearing. The Wayne County prosecutor's office said the three are charged in the death of Makanzee Oldham, who died after she was shot while in a car with her father after a fight erupted and someone poured juice on a woman getting ready for prom. Thirty - year - old Cleveland Smelley is accused of firing the shot that killed Makanzee. He and two other men, Deonta Bennett and Antoine Smelley, are also charged with attempted murder because there were oth-ers in the car ", and

2.   "Suspect arrested in Detroit shooting, 2-year-old girl still in critical condition DETROIT (WXYZ)- A 2-year-old girl remains in critical condition after she was shot in the head on Detroit's east side on Wednesday One of the men is the father of the little girl , the other is the suspected shooter , Cleveland Smelley Police say Smelley pulled out a gun and fired one shot at the other man , missing him and hitting the little girl in the head She was sitting in her car seat when she was shot Police confirmed they arrested Cleveland Smelley on Thursday afternoon "

The above two documents are correct answer to this question, *"Which ['killing'] event happened in 05/2016 (month) that involve the name Deonta (first)?"*

Document 1 was created on 06/09/2016, but there is no indication in it showing that the event happened in 05/2016, though it has the correct person name "Deonta". In contrast, document 2 does not have the name "Deonta". Therefore, neither of the two documents were retrieved via our current system. The document clustering method described in Section 2.4 does help in retrieving documents missing certain question properties, but there are still documents we cannot retrieve, especially for questions that we cannot find any document containing both required properties as the root document for document expansion using the clustering method.

As shown in Table 3, missing participants information in the documents is most common. We did not participant in the coreference competition and our system cannot correctly retrieve such documents without the key information that is asked in the question. Recent works on event nuget detection and coreference have proposed nerual networks models (Nguyen et al., 2016a,b; Nguyen and Grishman, 2016; Choubey and Huang, 2017). Those works could be studied in the future, where one can elaborate the coreference information across the document to boost the recall of correct documents without key information.

References

Prafulla Kumar Choubey and Ruihong Huang. 2017. TAMU at KBP 2017: Event nugget detection and coreference resolution. *CoRR*, abs/1711.02162.

Xiaocheng Feng, Lifu Huang, Duyu Tang, Bing Qin, Heng Ji, and Ting Liu. 2016. A language-independent neural network for event detection. In *Proceedings of the 54th Annual Meeting of the Association for Computational Linguistics*, page 66. Association for Computational Linguistics.

Heng Ji and Ralph Grishman. 2008. Refining event extraction through cross-document inference. In *ACL-08: HLT - 46th Annual Meeting of the Association for Computational Linguistics: Human Language Technologies, Proceedings of the Conference*, pages 254–262.

Tomas Mikolov, Kai Chen, Greg Corrado, and Jeffrey Dean. 2013a. Efficient estimation of word representations in vector space. *CoRR*, abs/1301.3781.

Tomas Mikolov, Ilya Sutskever, Kai Chen, Greg Corrado, and Jeffrey Dean. 2013b. Distributed representations of words and phrases and their compositionality. *CoRR*, abs/1310.4546.

Thien Huu Nguyen, Kyunghyun Cho, and Ralph Grishman. 2016a. Joint event extraction via recurrent neural networks. In *2016 Conference of the North American Chapter of the Association for Computational Linguistics: Human Language Technologies, NAACL HLT 2016 - Proceedings of the Conference*, pages 300–309. Association for Computational Linguistics (ACL).

Thien Huu Nguyen and Ralph Grishman. 2016. Modeling skip-grams for event detection with convolutional neural networks. In *Proceedings of the 2016 Conference on Empirical Methods in Natural Language Processing*, page 886891. Association for Computational Linguistics.

Thien Huu Nguyen, Adam Meyers, and Ralph Grishman. 2016b. New york university 2016 system for kbp event nugget: A deep learning approach. In *Proceedings of Ninth Text Analysis Conference*.

Marten Postma, Filip Ilievski, and Piek Vossen. 2018. Semeval-2018 task 5: Counting events and participants in the long tail.

SemEval-2018 Task 7: Semantic Relation Extraction and Classification in Scientific Papers

Kata Gábor[1], Davide Buscaldi[1], Anne-Kathrin Schumann[2], Behrang QasemiZadeh[3],
Haïfa Zargayouna[1], Thierry Charnois[1]

[1] LIPN, CNRS (UMR 7030), Université Paris 13
`firstname.lastname@lipn.univ-paris13.fr`
[2] ProTechnology GmbH, Dresden
`annek_schumann@gmx.de`
[3] DFG SFB 991, Heinrich-Heine University, Dsseldorf
`zadeh@phil.uni-duesseldorf.de`

Abstract

This paper describes the first task on semantic relation extraction and classification in scientific paper abstracts at SemEval 2018. The challenge focuses on domain-specific semantic relations and includes three different subtasks. The subtasks were designed so as to compare and quantify the effect of different pre-processing steps on the relation classification results. We expect the task to be relevant for a broad range of researchers working on extracting specialized knowledge from domain corpora, for example but not limited to scientific or bio-medical information extraction. The task attracted a total of 32 participants, with 158 submissions across different scenarios.

1 Introduction

One of the emerging trends of natural language technologies is their use for the humanities and sciences. Recent works in the semantic web (Osborne and Motta, 2015; Wolfram, 2016) and natural language processing (Tsai et al., 2013; Luan et al., 2017; Augenstein and Søgaard, 2017; Kim et al., 2010) aimed to improve the access to scientific literature, and in particular to respond to information needs that are currently beyond the capabilities of standard search engines. Such queries include finding all papers that address a problem in a specific way, or discovering the roots of a certain idea. This ambition involves the identification and classification of concepts, and the relations connecting them.

The purpose of the task is to automatically identify relevant domain-specific semantic relations in a corpus of scientific publications. In particular, we search for and classify relations that provide snippets of information such as "a (new) method is proposed for a task", or "a phenomenon is found in a certain context", or "results of different experiments are compared to each other". Identifying such semantic relations between domain-specific concepts allows us to detect research papers which deal with the same problem, or to track the evolution of results on a certain task.

2 Related Work

SemEval 2010 Task 8 (Hendrickx et al., 2010) proposed a discrete classification of word pairs into 9 semantic relations, however, this task was not tailored to the needs of scientific text analysis as neither relation types nor the vocabulary were domain-specific. SemEval 2012 Task 2 (Jurgens et al., 2012) proposed a gradual notion of relational similarity: the task was to quantify the similarity between examples of relation instances. The data set was aimed at evaluating specific semantic representations for relational similarity, but does not fit our task: in this task, entity pairs were treated as static class instances; in particular, they were presented without any context. However, the relation types we deal with are contextual: e.g., a specific *machine learning method* is trained on a specific *data set* to perform an *NLP task* in the context of a given experiment reported by a paper. Finally, the most closely related to our task is SemEval 2017 Task 10 (Augenstein et al., 2017), which responds to the growing interest towards the semantic analysis of scientific corpora. This task focuses mostly on keyword extraction and categorization. The subtask concerned with relation classification proposes 3 categories of taxonomic relations (synonym, hypernym, unrelated). Our task goes a step further by proposing a more fine-grained and, thus, more informative set of semantic relations (see Table 1). The relation types were selected and annotated based on a careful corpus study and are intended to represent the major re-

Proceedings of the 12th International Workshop on Semantic Evaluation (SemEval-2018), pages 679–688
New Orleans, Louisiana, June 5–6, 2018. ©2018 Association for Computational Linguistics

lations that define the information content of the abstract of a scientific paper.

3 Task description

The task consists in identifying and classifying instances of semantic relations between concepts in a set of 6 discrete categories. The relations are specific to the science domain and their instances can frequently be found in the abstract/introduction of scientific papers. The task is split into three subtasks. This is done to provide a framework for the systematic evaluation of the steps that are necessary for full information extraction from scientific text, i. e. relation extraction and relation classification. Two of the subtasks focus solely on the *classification* of relation instances into 6 relation categories. Another subtask includes both the *extraction* of relation instances and their *classification*. The data we provide is presented as complete abstracts of scientific papers. An abstract contains about 100 words on average. Entities are annotated in both the training and the test data. Furthermore, in the classification subtasks, the relation instances (entity pairs that belong to one of the relation classes) as well as the directionality of the relation (argument1, argument2) are given in the training and test data. In the extraction subtask, relation instances are not provided in the test data. The training data for each subtask contains 350 annotated abstracts with the corresponding relation instances and their categories[1]. The test data consists of 150 abstracts[2]. Participants were allowed three submissions/subtask/team.

3.1 Relation classification scenario

Given a pair of entities in an abstract, the task consists in classifying the semantic relation between them. A pre-defined list of relations is given (see Table 1), together with training examples for each relation.

- **Subtask 1.1 : Relation classification on clean data.**
  Entity occurrences are *manually* annotated in both the training and the test data. In the training data, semantic relations are manually annotated between entities. In the test data, only

entity annotations and unlabeled relation instances are given. The task is to predict the semantic relation between the entities. The following example shows a text snippet with the information provided in the test data :

> Korean, a <entity id="H01-1041.10">verb final language</entity>with <entity id="H01-1041.11">overt case markers</entity>(...)

A relation instance is identified by the unique identifier of the entities in the pair, e.g. (H01-1041.10, H01-1041.11). The information to be predicted is the relation class label: MODEL-FEATURE(H01-1041.10, H01-1041.11).

- **Subtask 1.2 : Relation classification on noisy data.**
  Entity occurrences are *automatically* annotated in both the training and the test data. Delimitation errors may occur in the entity annotation. In the training data, semantic relations are manually annotated between the entities. In the test data, only automatic entity annotations and unlabeled relation instances are given. The task is to predict the semantic relation between the entities. The following example shows a text snippet with the information provided in the test data:

> This <entity id="L08-1203.8"> paper </entity> introduces a new <entity id="L08-1203.9">architecture</entity>(...)

The relation instance is (L08-1203.8, L08-1203.9). The information to be predicted is the relation class label: TOPIC(L08-1203.8, L08-1203.9)

3.2 Relation extraction and classification scenario

Given an abstract with annotated entities, the subtask consists in:

- identifying instances of semantic relations between entities in the same sentence,

- assigning class labels, i.e. one of six predefined relation types (see Table 1), to the relation instances.

---

[1] The training data for subtask 1.1 and subtask 2 were identical.

[2] After the end of the competition, the complete dataset was published at `https://lipn.univ-paris13.fr/~gabor/semeval2018task7/`

RELATION TYPE	Explanation	Example
USAGE	*Methods, tasks, and data are linked by usage relations.*	
used_by	ARG1: *method, system* ARG2: *other method*	approach – model
used_for_task	ARG1: *method/system* ARG2: *task*	approach – parsing
used_on_data	ARG1: *method* applied to ARG2: *data*	MT system – Japanese
task_on_data	ARG1: *task* performed on ARG2: *data*	parse – sentence
RESULT	*An entity affects or yields a result.*	
affects	ARG1: *specific property of data* ARG2: *results*	order – performance
problem	ARG1: *phenomenon* is a problem in a ARG2: *field/task*	ambiguity – sentence
yields	ARG1: *experiment/method* ARG2: *result*	parser – performance
MODEL	*An entity is a analytic characteristic or abstract model of another entity.*	
char	ARG1: *observed characteristics* of an observed ARG2: *entity*	order – constituents
model	ARG1: *abstract representation* of an ARG2: *observed entity*	interpretation – utterance
tag	ARG1: *tag/meta-information* associated to an ARG2: *entity*	categories – words
PART_WHOLE	*Entities are in a part-whole relationship.*	
composed_of	ARG2: *database/resource* ARG1: *data*	ontology – concepts
datasource	ARG1: *information* extracted from ARG2: *kind of data*	knowledge – domain
phenomenon	ARG1: *entity, a phenomenon* found in ARG2: *context*	expressions – text
TOPIC	*This category relates a scientific work with its topic.*	
propose	ARG1: *paper/author* presents ARG2: *an idea*	paper – method
study	ARG1: *analysis* of a ARG2: *phenomenon*	research – speech
COMPARISON	*An entity is compared to another entity.*	
compare	ARG1: *result, experiment* compared to ARG2: *result, experiment*	result – standard

Table 1: Semantic relation typology. The six major relation types result from a finer grained classification which was used in manual annotation.

The training data we provide contains the same information as in the classification scenario, i.e. manually annotated entities, and labeled semantic relations holding between entities. The test data contains only abstracts with annotated entities: both the entity pairs and their relation type are to be predicted.

3.3 Evaluation

Submissions are evaluated differently for the individual subtasks. A dedicated gold standard containing entity and relation annotations is used.

3.3.1 Metrics for the classification scenario (subtasks 1.1 and 1.2)

Submissions for scenario 1 are assessed by means of standard metrics:

- **Class-wise evaluation**: Precision, recall, and F1 ($\beta = 1$) for each relation type.
- **Global evaluation**:
  - Macro-average of the F1 scores obtained for every relation type.
  - Micro-average of the F1 scores obtained for every relation type.

The official ranking of submissions is performed according to the **macro-average F1 score**.

3.3.2 Metrics for the extraction and classification scenario (Subtask 2)

Evaluation of submissions for scenario 2 is carried out in two steps:

- **Evaluation of relation extraction**: Extraction evaluation assesses the quality of identified relation instances. Relation labels and directionality are ignored in this step. *Precision* is calculated as the percentage of correctly connected entity pairs. *Recall* is calculated as the percentage of gold entity pairs found by the system. The official **F1 score** is calculated as the harmonic mean of precision and recall.

- **Evaluation of relation classification**: Classification evaluation considers only correctly identified relation instances as per step 1. For these instances, the same evaluation metrics are calculated as for task 1. The official score for this task is **macro-average F1**.

4 Data Preparation

The task is carried out on abstracts from published research papers in computational linguistics. Two existing high-quality corpora were used as starting points for data creation, namely ACL RD-TEC 2.0 (QasemiZadeh and Schumann, 2016) and ACL-RelAcS (Gábor et al., 2016a). Both resources are based on the ACL Anthology Reference Corpus (Bird et al., 2008). In ACL RD-TEC 2.0 entities were annotated manually, and it was used for the "clean" subtasks (subtasks 1.1 and 2). In ACL-RelAcS, entities were annotated fully automatically, and it was used for the "noisy" subtask (1.2).

4.1 Entity annotation

Manual ("clean") entity annotations were carried out in accordance with the ACL RD-TEC annotation guidelines (Schumann and QasemiZadeh, 2015). Thus, for subtasks 1.1 and 2 (training data) termhood is defined by a combination of semantic, linguistic, and formal criteria. The formal criteria, for instance, aim at making the annotations maximally useful for real-world extraction scenarios by accounting for various contextual usage patterns of terminological units in scientific prose. Therefore, annotators are instructed to annotate maximal noun phrases, abbreviations, and their contextual variants, including variants with incorrect spelling. Still, entity annotation proves to be a non-trivial task even for human expert annotators: Qasemi-Zadeh and Schumann (2016) show that agreement scores are satisfactory (e.g., $\kappa > 0.7$) only after a thorough annotation training phase and the subsequent refinement of the annotation guidelines.

To extend the set of abstracts that were already available in ACL RD-TEC with double entity annotations, expert annotators were recruited from amongst the task organizers. Annotators were asked to read the ACL RD-TEC annotation guidelines. A training phase was carried out, during which each annotator carried out test annotations on unseen data. To facilitate annotations, abstracts were pre-annotated automatically using the automatic entity annotator of the ACL-RelAcS corpus (see below). Annotators were asked to correct the automatic annotations, in particular, to correct the boundary of the identified entity. Individual feedback was provided to novice annotators and annotation difficulties were clarified. Annotations were consistently monitored and potential causes for disagreement discussed and corrected.

The ACL RD-TEC already provided 171 double-annotated and 129 single-annotated abstracts. While double-annotations could directly be passed over to manual relation annotation, more single-pass annotations had to be performed to create a fully double-annotated training set. The remaining 150 abstracts for the test set of subtask 1.1 were single-annotated. It should be noted that, due to their origin from ACL RD-TEC, abstracts for subtask 1.1 contain not only entity annotations, but also information about the the semantic class of the annotated entity. This information was not explicitly included in the provided data, but was accessible to participants through the original ACL RD-TEC corpus.

The "noisy" subtask (1.2) was carried out on data coming from the ACL-RelAcS corpus 1.0 (Gábor et al., 2016a). The corpus consists of 4.2 million words from the abstract and introduction sections of papers in the ACL Anthology Corpus, with an automatic annotation of entities. This automatic annotation is based on a gazetteer which, in turn, was created using a combination of terminology extraction tools and ontological resources. As a domain specific resource, the domain models and topic hierarchies in the NLP domain from Saffron Knowledge Extraction Framework[3] (Bordea, 2013; Bordea et al., 2013) were included. Terminology extraction was performed with TermSuite (Daille et al., 2013) and the resulting list of terms was filtered by part of speech and looked up in BabelNet (Navigli and Ponzetto, 2012). The extracted terms that were found in BabelNet were added to the gazetteer and used for automatic annotation.

4.2 Relation annotation

The work was divided as 1) defining the typology of semantic relations, 2) validation of the typology and of the annotation guidelines and 3) annotation. A data-driven approach was adopted to identify the relation types and define a typology (Gábor et al., 2016b). Domain experts studied the abstracts with entity annotation and were instructed to read the text and indicate the semantic relations that are explicit and relevant for the understanding of the abstract. They annotated entity pairs and the text span between them which explicitly indicates the relation.

Instances of explicit relations were thus discovered and manually annotated in a sample of 100 abstracts from ACL-RelAcS. A fine-grained typology of domain-specific relations was set up. The fine-grained relation types (see Table 1) were defined very precisely and specifically, e.g. using strict constraints on which types of entities the relations take as argument. The manual annotation used this typology; the relations were then automatically converted to the 6 types used in the classification tasks.

Only explicit relations were annotated, between already annotated entities. Entity annotation itself is never modified or corrected manually during the relation annotation phase. On the textual level, a semantic relation is conceived as a text span link-

---

[3] http://saffron.insight-centre.org/

ing two annotated instances of concepts within the same sentence. On the semantic level, relation types need to be specific enough to be easily distinguished from each other by a domain expert. Annotation was carried out by one of the organizers and two NLP student annotators who were subjected to a training of three weeks during which they annotated 100 abstracts under supervision. This training material was not included in the future dataset. Weekly feedback was given and difficult instances were discussed. If the annotation quality in the 100 abstracts was judged satisfactory, the annotator was allowed to carry on, and their subsequent annotations were included in the dataset (two out of three annotator candidates passed this phase).

Inter-annotator agreement was calculated using a double annotation on a sample of 150 abstracts from subtask 1.1 by two annotators. The overall class label agreement rate on these annotations was 90.8%. We also calculated the macro-averaged F1 score across classes, taking one of the annotators as "gold standard". The result was 0.91 (the performance of the best ranking system on this task is 0.81). When comparing agreement for individual relations, it turns out that the relation with the lowest agreement (F1=0.83) is PART_WHOLE, followed by RESULT (F1=0.89).

5 Results

5.1 Baseline system

As a baseline, we created a simple memory-based k-nearest neighbor (k-nn) search (Daelemans and van den Bosch, 2005) which relies on a small set of hand-crafted features.

Given a sentence s annotated with an ordered set of $e_1 \ldots e_n$ entities appearing in it, we first pull out all tuples (e_i, e_j), in which $j - i \leq 2$. For each tuple (e_i, e_j), we encode their co-occurrence context using a set of 5 vectors of low dimensionality ($n = 100$). These vectors encode information about (a) tokens that appear before e_i in s (we use simple white-space tokenization), (b) tokens that appear between e_i and e_j, (c) tokens appearing after e_j, as well as (d) two additional vectors that capture the context of e_i and e_j occurrences in the ACL Anthology Reference Corpus (Bird et al., 2008). To encode information about these context-token occurrences into low-dimensional vectors, we use positive-only random projections (Qasemi-Zadeh and Kallmeyer, 2016). Additionally, feature vectors in each of the above-mentioned categories

are weighted using positive pointwise mutual information with respect to the collected co-occurrence information in vectors for each category for all the tuples in the training and test data (for each subtask). Finally, the weighted vectors are concatenated to form a 500 dimensional feature vector for each entity pair.

For each subtask, all the (e_i, e_j) extracted from the sentences in the training set are added to the k-nn's training instance memory T: if (e_i, e_j) is annotated with a relation, then the fetched label is assigned to it, otherwise it is marked as a negative example. Given the feature vector $\vec{v}$ for a tuple (e_x, e_y) in the test set, the similarity between $\vec{v}$ and all the training instances $t_i \in T$ is computed using the Pearson's correlation to find the k *most similar* t_i. Finally, we assign (e_x, e_y) to the relation category l_y using a majority voting.

Results obtained from this baseline system are listed in Tables 5, 7, 6, and 8 in the Appendix. We choose $k = 5$ based on the observed performances over the development dataset.

5.2 Summary of participating systems and results

The task attracted 32 participants altogether who took part in at least one subtask. The most popular subtask was the classification on clean data (subtask 1.1) with 28 participants; 19 of them also participated in the classification on noisy data (subtask 1.2). One participant chose to compete only in subtask 1.2. Subtask 2 attracted 11 teams. The scenario allowed to compete only in relation extraction, without classifying the extracted instances; only one team used this opportunity. The complete results and rankings are available in the Appendix section. Most participants opted for the use of deep learning methods, with a clear preference for Convolutional Neural Networks (CNN) which were used by 10 systems, and Long Short Term Memory (LSTM) networks, used by 5 systems. Support Vector Machines (SVM) were the preferred non-DL method, used by 5 systems. One participant (Bf3R) opted for a combination of existing tools in Subtask 2. In Figure 1 and 2 we show an overview of the number of methods chosen by participants and the average results obtained by each family of methods for each subtask. The average was calculated on all submissions. The number of systems doesn't necessarily match the number of participants (some participants tested different methods). Most par-

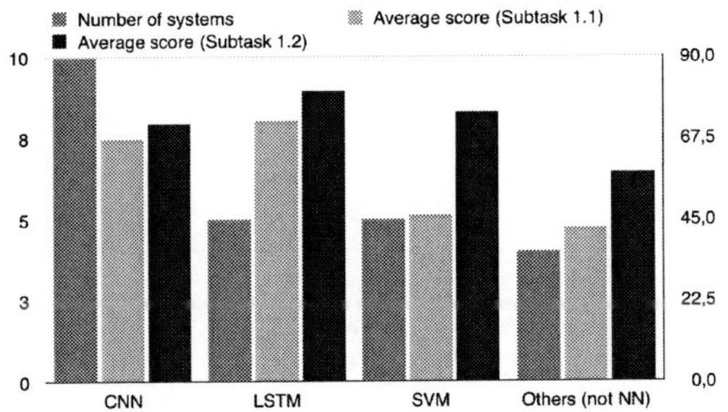

Figure 1: Popularity of methods chosen by participants (as number of systems that used the method, left) and average F1 score obtained for each method (right) in Subtask 1.1 and 1.2.

ticipants exploited the possibility of aggregating training data from subtask 1.1 and subtask 1.2.

Word embeddings were used as features by the majority of systems (13 systems). Some participants chose to calculate the embeddings on domain-specific corpora, such as ACL (4 systems) and arXiv (3 systems), sometimes in combination with pre-trained embeddings. Pre-trained embeddings alone were used by a minority of participants, with TakeLab highlighting some problems in dealing with out-of-vocabulary words. Apart from the corpora dedicated to training the embeddings, participants didn't use external resources, with the exception of one system which employed VerbNet and two systems that used WordNet synonyms and hypernyms.

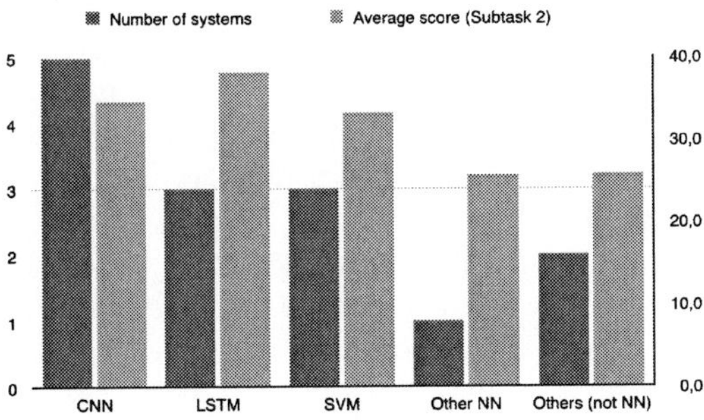

Figure 2: Popularity of methods chosen by participants (as number of systems that used the method, left) and average F1 score obtained for each method (right) in Subtask 2.

Among the chosen features, positional embeddings were quite popular (5 systems), to account for the relative position of the left and right entities.

Only three participants recurred to syntactic features, in particular dependency trees, despite their apparent relevance for the task.

SpaCy[4] and CoreNLP[5] were the most popular tools to analyze and preprocess text, with a slight preference for the first one (4 participants vs. 2).

6 Analysis of Results

6.1 Which processing step is the most difficult?

From the overall task results provided in the Appendix (Tables 5 – 8), it seems straightforward to conclude that the reliable identification of semantic relation instances is by far the most difficult step in the complete processing pipeline: Whereas systems reached an average F1 score of 47.28 in subtask 1.1 and 62.51 in subtask 1.2, performance scores drop rather sharply in scenario 2, namely to an average F1 of 30.8 for the extraction task and 20.34 for the extraction+classification task.

6.2 Which relation types are the most difficult to classify?

We examined whether there were relation types that were more difficult for the systems to classify, and whether it is possible to relate this to the semantics of the relations. For instance, the class MODEL-FEATURE is broad because it encompasses relatively different sub-classes: models, parts of models (such as a representation, a tag used for a word), or attributes (frequency of a phenomenon). To analyze this, we calculated the average recall by relation type over a sample of submissions to subtask 1.1 (70 submissions) and 1.2 (42 submissions) and the characteristic prediction error types by relation, if any (Table 2). We also calculated the average F1 score by relation type of the five top scoring systems from different participants (Tables 3 and 4).

Our analysis suggests that rather than the semantics of the relation types, it is their distribution in the data that poses difficulties. Class distribution is very imbalanced. Moreover, the distribution of classes in training and test data of subtask 1.1 and 1.2 is different. This difference is due to the nature of entities annotated automatically and those annotated manually. Because of the terminology extraction process and the resources that were used

---

[4]https://spacy.io/
[5]https://stanfordnlp.github.io/CoreNLP/

Relation	Average recall	Frequently mistaken for	Training frequency	Test frequency
Subtask 1.1				
USAGE	73%	MODEL-FEATURE	483	175
TOPIC	66%	-	18	3
MODEL-FEATURE	51%	USAGE, PART_WHOLE	326	66
PART_WHOLE	44%	USAGE, MODEL-FEATURE	234	70
COMPARE	42%	USAGE	95	21
RESULT	40%	USAGE	72	20
Subtask 1.2				
TOPIC	77%	-	243	69
USAGE	72%	PART_WHOLE	470	123
COMPARE	66%	-	41	3
RESULT	65%	USAGE	123	29
PART_WHOLE	64%	USAGE	196	56
MODEL-FEATURE	52%	USAGE, PART_WHOLE	175	75

Table 2: Relations: results and distribution.

for annotation, entities in subtask 1.2 are typically shorter terms with an intermediate level of specificity. On the other hand, entities in the clean scenario are more complex and more specific to the NLP domain. For instance, the TOPIC relation is more frequent in 1.2 than in 1.1 because entities like "paper" or "article" were annotated by the automated process, but not in the manual annotation.

Another aspect is that certain classes are lexically less varied than others and this might well affect the "difficulty" of the classification task. For instance, the TOPIC class has the lowest type-token ratio of all classes in subtask 1.2[6]. This does not seem surprising. Neither does it seem surprising that in subtask 1.2, TOPIC has gained the best average recall (2) and the highest F1 score among the top-5 systems (4). TOPIC is also much more frequent in subtask 1.2 than in subtask 1.1 and this effect is one likely cause for the difference in performance achieved over subtasks 1.1 and 1.2.

Relation	Top 5 Average F1
USAGE	0.85
RESULT	0.75
PART_WHOLE	0.73
TOPIC	0.71
MODEL-FEATURE	0.69
COMPARE	0.59

Table 3: Relations: Task 1.1 average results top 5 systems.

6.3 The effects of entity annotation

Entity annotation has a demonstrable effect on system performance. As stated earlier, annotation decisions have direct consequences for the distribution of certain types in the data and thus influence measurable system performance.

---

⁶In this analysis, a tuple of two entities pertaining to a certain relation class was counted as a "type".

Relation	Top 5 Average F1
TOPIC	0.97
RESULT	0.91
USAGE	0.87
COMPARE	0.80
PART_WHOLE	0.80
MODEL-FEATURE	0.79

Table 4: Relations: Task 1.2 average results top 5 systems.

A maybe rather surprising result of this task is the difference in system performance for subtasks 1.1 and 1.2. While "clean" entities can, with some plausibility, be considered more useful for a potential human user of the extracted information, "noisy" entity annotations seem to be more machine-friendly. The difference in the distribution of the TOPIC relation between subtasks 1.1 and 1.2 has already been pointed out as one potential cause for this effect. Moreover, the complexity of clean entities in subtask 1.1 could also have contributed to the performance gap. Manually annotated entities, in most cases, are long noun phrases, whereas automatically annotated entities in subtask 1.2 are generally shorter, partial (and therefore less specific!) entity matches. This also means that more training examples are likely to be found for automatically annotated entities. Moreover, some instances of automatic annotations in subtask 1.2 included explicit verbal relation cues. These cues sometimes explicitly state the type of the semantic relation, but they were not annotated in subtask 1.1. Verbal cues (e. g. the well-known Hearst patterns (Hearst, 1992)) have typically been used in earlier work on relation classification and, in fact, several teams participating in the task describe recurrent verbal elements between relation arguments.

The role of the specialized lexicon in relation extraction and classification is a topic that deserves further exploration for the following reasons: Firstly, highly specialized, complex terminological units are the main units of knowledge representation in specialized domains. Secondly, task results clearly show that a careful handling of lexical information improves performance: many successful systems in the task used domain-specific training data. The only system that treated complete specialized entities as semantic units, UWNLP, ranked first in the relation extraction task. None of the systems participating in subtasks 1.1 or 2 used semantic class information available for annotated entities from ACL RD-TEC, although it may be hypothesized that this feature helps to generalize lexical instance information.

7   Conclusion and Future Work

We presented the setup and results of SemEval 2018 Task 7: Semantic relation extraction and classification in scientific papers. The task is divided into three subtasks: classification on clean data, classification on noisy data, and a combined extraction and classification scenario. We also presented the dataset used for the challenge: a subset of abstracts of published papers in the ACL Anthology Reference Corpus, annotated for domain specific entities and semantic relations.

32 participants submitted to one or more subtasks. The most popular methods include Convolutional Neural Networks and Long Short Term Memory networks, with word embedding based features, often calculated on domain-specific corpora. Although it was allowed, only a minority of the participants used external knowledge resources. The results show that while good results can be obtained on the supervised multi-class classification of relation instances, the extraction of such instances remains very challenging. Moreover, the quality and type of entity annotation also plays an important role in determining relation extraction and classification results.

Knowledge extraction from a special domain poses specific challenges, such as working with a smaller corpus, dealing with specialized vocabularies, and the scarcity of annotated data and available domain-specific resources. One of the important future directions is to explore domain adaptation techniques to address these issues.

Acknowledgments

This work was generously supported by the program "Investissements d'Avenir" overseen by the French National Research Agency, ANR-10-LABX-0083 (Labex EFL). Behrang QasemiZadeh is funded by the Deutsche Forschungsgemeinschaft through the "Collaborative Research Centre 991 (CRC 991): The Structure of Representations in Language, Cognition, and Science".

References

Isabelle Augenstein, Mrinal Das, Sebastian Riedel, Lakshmi Vikraman, and Andrew McCallum. 2017. Semeval 2017 task 10: ScienceIE - extracting keyphrases and relations from scientific publications. In *Proceedings of the 11th International Workshop on Semantic Evaluation (SemEval-2017)*, pages 546–555, Vancouver, Canada. Association for Computational Linguistics.

Isabelle Augenstein and Anders Søgaard. 2017. Multi-task learning of keyphrase boundary classification. In *Proceedings of the 55th Annual Meeting of the Association for Computational Linguistics (ACL)*.

Steven Bird, Robert Dale, Bonnie Dorr, Bryan Gibson, Mark Joseph, Min-Yen Kan, Dongwon Lee, Brett Powley, Dragomir Radev, and Yee Fan Tan. 2008. The ACL Anthology Reference Corpus: A Reference Dataset for Bibliographic Research in Computational Linguistics. In *Proceedings of the 6th International Conference on Language Resources and Evaluation (LREC 2008)*. European Language Resources Association.

Georgeta Bordea. 2013. *Domain Adaptive Extraction of Topical Hierarchies for Expertise Mining*. Phd thesis, National University of Ireland, Galway.

Georgeta Bordea, Paul Buitelaar, and Tamara Polajnar. 2013. Domain-independent term extraction through domain modelling. In *10th International Conference on Terminology and Artificial Intelligence (TIA 2013)*.

Walter Daelemans and Antal van den Bosch. 2005. *Memory-Based Language Processing*. Studies in Natural Language Processing. Cambridge University Press.

Beatrice Daille, Christine Jacquin, Laura Monceaux, Emmanuel Morin, and Jerome Rocheteau. 2013. TTC TermSuite : Une chaine de traitement pour la fouille terminologique multilingue. In *Proceedings of the Traitement Automatique des Langues Naturelles Conference (TALN)*.

Kata Gábor, Hafa Zargayouna, Davide Buscaldi, Isabelle Tellier, and Thierry Charnois. 2016a. Semantic annotation of the ACL Anthology Corpus for the automatic analysis of scientific literature. In *Proceedings of the International Conference on Language Resources and Evaluation (LREC)*, pages 3694–3701.

Kata Gábor, Hafa Zargayouna, Isabelle Tellier, Davide Buscaldi, and Thierry Charnois. 2016b. A typology of semantic relations dedicated to scientific literature analysis. In *SAVE-SD Workshop at the 25th World Wide Web Conference. Lecture Notes in Computer Science 9792*, pages 26–32.

Marti Hearst. 1992. Automatic acquisition of hyponyms from large text corpora. In *COLING '92*, pages 539–545.

Iris Hendrickx, Su Nam Kim, Zornitsa Kozareva, Preslav Nakov, Diarmuid Saghdha, Sebastian Pad, Marco Pennacchiotti, Lorenza Romano, and Stan Szpakowicz. 2010. Semeval-2010 task 8: Multi-way classification of semantic relations between pairs of nominals. In *Proceedings of the Workshop on Semantic Evaluations (SemEval-2010)*.

David A. Jurgens, Peter D. Turney, Saif M. Mohammad, and Keith J. Holyoak. 2012. SemEval-2012 Task 2: Measuring degrees of relational similarity. In *Proceedings of the Workshop on Semantic Evaluations*.

Su Nam Kim, Olena Medelyan, Min-Yen Kan, and Timothy Baldwin. 2010. Semeval-2010 task 5: Automatic keyphrase extraction from scientific articles. In *Proceedings of SemEval 2010*.

Yi Luan, Mari Ostendorf, and Hannaneh Hajishirzi. 2017. Scientific information extraction with semi-supervised neural tagging. In *EMNLP 2017*.

Roberto Navigli and Simone Paolo Ponzetto. 2012. BabelNet: The automatic construction, evaluation and application of a wide-coverage multilingual semantic network. *Artificial Intelligence*, 193:217–250.

F. Osborne and E. Motta. 2015. Klink-2: Integrating multiple web sources to generate semantic topic networks. In *Proceedings of the 14th International Conference on The Semantic Web - ISWC 2015 - Volume 9366*, pages 408–424, New York, NY, USA. Springer-Verlag New York, Inc.

Behrang QasemiZadeh and Laura Kallmeyer. 2016. Random Positive-Only Projections: PPMI-enabled incremental semantic space construction. In *Proceedings of the Fifth Joint Conference on Lexical and Computational Semantics*, pages 189–198, Berlin, Germany. Association for Computational Linguistics.

Behrang QasemiZadeh and Anne-Kathrin Schumann. 2016. The ACL RD-TEC 2.0: A language resource for evaluating term extraction and entity recognition methods. In *Proceedings of the International Conference on Language Resources and Evaluation (LREC)*.

Anne-Kathrin Schumann and Behrang QasemiZadeh. 2015. The ACL RD-TEC Annotation Guideline: A Reference Dataset for the Evaluation of Automatic Term Recognition and Classification. Technical report.

Chen-Tse Tsai, Gourab Kundu, and Dan Roth. 2013. Concept-based analysis of scientific literature. In *ACM Conference on Information and Knowledge Management ACM*, pages 1733–1738.

Dietmar Wolfram. 2016. Bibliometrics, information retrieval and natural language processing: Natural synergies to support digital library research. In *Proceedings of the Joint Workshop on Bibliometric-enhanced Information Retrieval and Natural Language Processing for Digital Libraries (BIRNDL)*, pages 6–13.

Appendix: Competition Results

Rank	Participant	Macro-F1 Score
1	ETH-DS3Lab	81.7
2	UWNLP	78.9
3	SIRIUS-LTG-UiO	76.7
4	ClaiRE	74.9
5	Talla	74.2
6	MIT-MEDG	72.7
7	TakeLab	69.7
8	Texterra	64.9
9	GU IRLAB	60.9
10	sbuNLP	49.7
11	IRCMS	49.1
12	OhioState	48.1
13	NTNU	47.4
14	danish037	45.7
15	HeMu	45.2
16	UniMa	44.0
17	LaSTUS/TALN	43.2
18	LIGHTREL	39.9
19	LTRC	37.3
N/A	*Baseline*	*34.4*
20	BIT_NLP	32.9
21	likewind_1234	29.3
22	Vitk	29.0
23	hccl	28.1
24	xingwang	27.8
25	SciREL	20.3
26	UKP	19.3
27	NEUROSENT-PDI	18.0
28	angelocsc	15.0

Table 5: Results for subtask 1.1.

Rank	Participant	F1 Score
1	UWNLP	50.0
2	ETH-DS3Lab	48.8
3	SIRIUS-LTG-UiO	37.4
4	UC3M-NII	35.4
5	NTNU	33.9
6	Bf3R	33.4
7	UniMa	28.4
N/A	*Baseline*	*26.8*
8	NEUROSENT-PDI	25.6
9	Texterra	15.6
10	xingwang	15.3
11	danish037	15.0

Table 6: Results for subtask 2: Extraction.

Rank	Participant	Macro-F1 Score
1	ETH-DS3Lab	90.4
2	Talla	84.8
3	SIRIUS-LTG-UiO	83.2
4	MIT-MEDG	80.6
5	GU IRLAB	78.9
6	ClaiRE	78.4
7	TakeLab	75.7
8	OhioState	74.7
9	Texterra	74.4
10	IRCMS	71.1
11	LaSTUS/TALN	69.5
12	LIGHTREL	68.2
13	NTNU	66.0
14	LTRC	65.7
N/A	*Baseline*	*53.5*
15	likewind_1234	45.8
16	BIT_NLP	40.7
17	hccl	38.0
18	xingwang	26.7
19	NEUROSENT-PDI	21.8
20	UKP	15.3

Table 7: Results for subtask 1.2.

Rank	Participant	Macro-F1 Score
1	ETH-DS3Lab	49.3
2	UWNLP	39.1
3	SIRIUS-LTG-UiO	33.6
4	Bf3R	20.3
5	UC3M-NII	18.5
6	NTNU	17.0
N/A	*Baseline*	*12.6*
7	Texterra	9.6
8	xingwang	8.3
9	danish037	4.6
10	NEUROSENT-PDI	3.1

Table 8: Results for subtask 2: Extraction + Classification.

ETH-DS3Lab at SemEval-2018 Task 7: Effectively Combining Recurrent and Convolutional Neural Networks for Relation Classification and Extraction

Jonathan Rotsztejn[1], Nora Hollenstein[1,2], Ce Zhang[1]
[1] Systems Group, ETH Zurich
{rotsztej,noraho}@ethz.ch, ce.zhang@inf.ethz.ch
[2] IBM Research, Zurich

Abstract

Reliably detecting relevant relations between entities in unstructured text is a valuable resource for knowledge extraction, which is why it has awaken significant interest in the field of Natural Language Processing. In this paper, we present a system for relation classification and extraction based on an ensemble of convolutional and recurrent neural networks that ranked first in 3 out of the 4 subtasks at SemEval 2018 Task 7. We provide detailed explanations and grounds for the design choices behind the most relevant features and analyze their importance.

1 Introduction and related work

One of the current challenges in analyzing unstructured data is to extract valuable knowledge by detecting the relevant entities and relations between them. The focus of SemEval 2018 Task 7 is on relation classification (assigning a type of relation to an entity pair - *Subtask 1*) and relation extraction (detecting the existence of a relation between two entities and determining its type - *Subtask 2*).

Moreover, the task distinguishes between relation classification on clean data (i.e.: manually annotated entities - *Subtask 1.1*) and noisy data (automatically annotated entities - *Subtask 1.2*). It addresses semantic relations from 6 categories, all of them specific to scientific literature. Relation instances are to be classified into one of the following classes: USAGE, RESULT, MODEL-FEATURE, PART-WHOLE, TOPIC, COMPARE, where the first five are asymmetrical relations and the last is order-independent (see Gábor et al. (2018) for a more detailed description of the task). Since the training data was provided by the task organizers, we focused on supervised methods for relation classification and extraction. Similar systems in the past have been based on Support Vector Machines (Uzuner et al., 2011; Minard et al.,

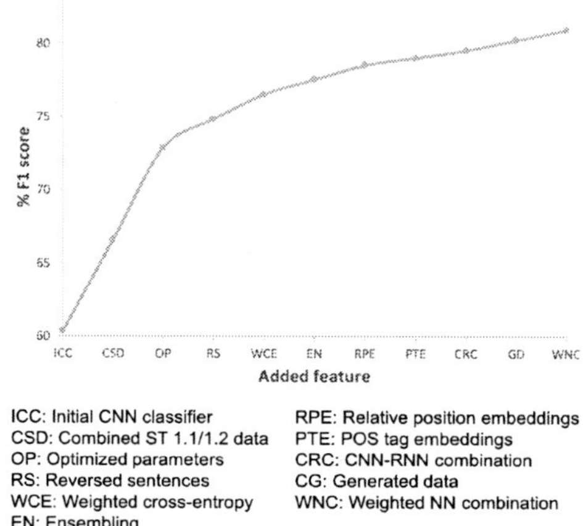

Figure 1: Feature addition study to evaluate the impact of the most relevant features on the F_1 score of the 5-fold cross-validated training set of Subtasks 1.1 and 1.2

2011), Naïve Bayes (Zayaraz et al., 2015) and Conditional Random Fields (Sutton and McCallum, 2006). More recent approaches have experimented with neural network architectures (Socher et al., 2012; Fu et al., 2017), especially convolutional neural networks (CNNs) (Nguyen and Grishman, 2015; Lee et al., 2017) and recurrent neural networks (RNNs) based on LSTMs (Zheng et al., 2017; Peng et al., 2017). The system presented in this article builds upon the latest improvements in employing neural networks for relation classification and extraction. An overview of the most relevant features is shown on Figure 1.

2 Method

2.1 Neural architecture

Figure 2 shows the full architecture of our system. Its main component is an ensemble of CNNs and RNNs. The CNN architecture follows closely on (Kim, 2014; Collobert et al., 2011). It consists of

Proceedings of the 12th International Workshop on Semantic Evaluation (SemEval-2018), pages 689–696
New Orleans, Louisiana, June 5–6, 2018. ©2018 Association for Computational Linguistics

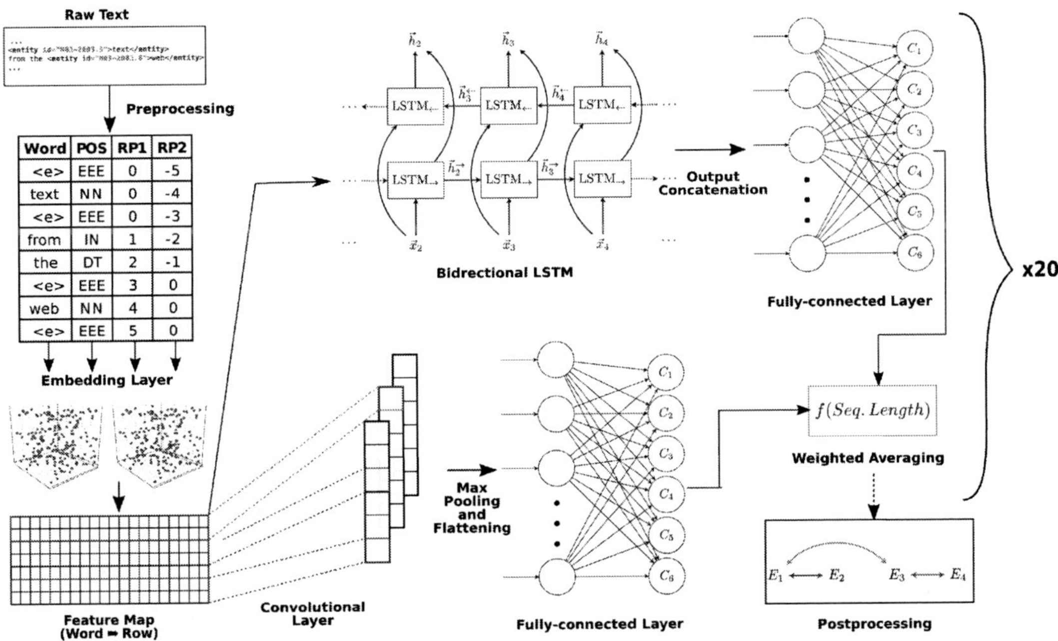

Figure 2: Full pipeline architecture

an initial embedding layer, which is followed by a convolutional layer with multiple filter widths and feature maps with a ReLU activation function, a max-pooling layer (applied over time) and a fully-connected layer, that is trained with dropout, and produces the output as logits, to which a softmax function is applied to obtain probabilities. The RNN consists of the same initial embedding layer, followed two LSTM-based sequence models (Hochreiter and Schmidhuber, 1997), one in the forward and one in the backward direction of the sequence, which are dynamic (i.e.: work seamlessly for varying sequence lengths). The output and final hidden states of the forward and backward networks are then concatenated to a single vector. Finally, a fully-connected layer, trained with dropout, connects this vector to the logit outputs, to which a softmax function is applied analogously to obtain probabilities.

The complete architecture was replicated and trained independently several times (see Table 2) using different random seeds that ensured distinct initial values, sample ordering, etc. in order to form an ensemble of classifiers, whose output probabilities were averaged to obtain the final probabilities for each class. We analyzed and tried several deeper and more complex neural architectures, such as multiple stacked LSTMs (up to 4)

and models with 2 to 4 hidden layers, but they didn't achieve any significant improvements over the simpler models. Conclusively, the strategy that produced the best results consisted of adequately combining the individual predictions of the single models (see section 4).

2.2 Domain-specific word embeddings

We collected additional domain-specific data from scientific NLP papers to train word embeddings. All *ArXiv cs.CL* abstracts since 2010 (1 million tokens) and the *ACL ARC corpus* (90 million tokens; Bird et al. (2008)) were downloaded and preprocessed. We used *gensim* (Řehůřek and Sojka, 2010) to train word2vec embeddings on these two data sources, and additionally the sentences provided as training data for the SemEval task (in total: 91,304,581 tokens). We experimented with embeddings of 100, 200 and 300 dimensions, where 200 dimensions yielded the best performance for the task as shown in Figure 3.

2.3 Preprocessing

Cropping sentences Since the most relevant portion of text to determine the relation type is generally the one contained between and including the entities (Lee et al., 2017), we solely analyzed that part of the sentences and disregarded the surrounding words. For Subtask 2, we initially con-

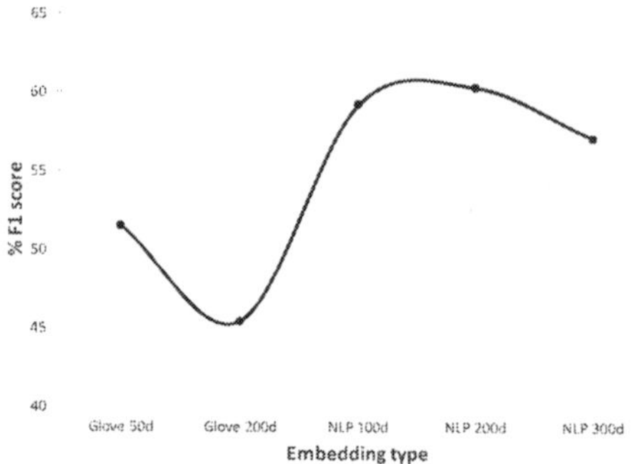

Figure 3: Effect of different word embedding types based on a simple CNN classifier for Subtask 1.1

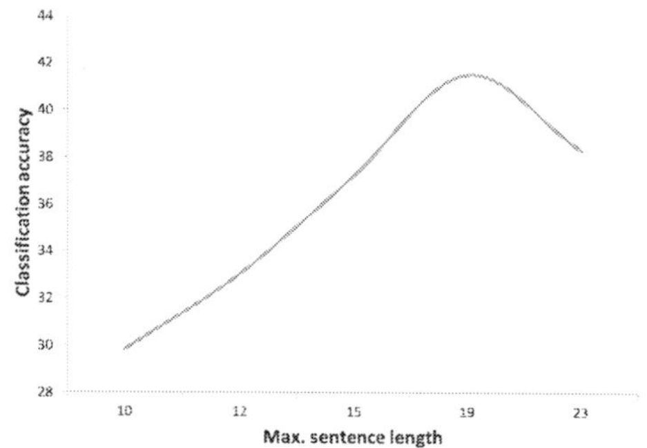

Figure 4: Effect of max. length threshold on accuracy for a preliminary RNN-based classifier

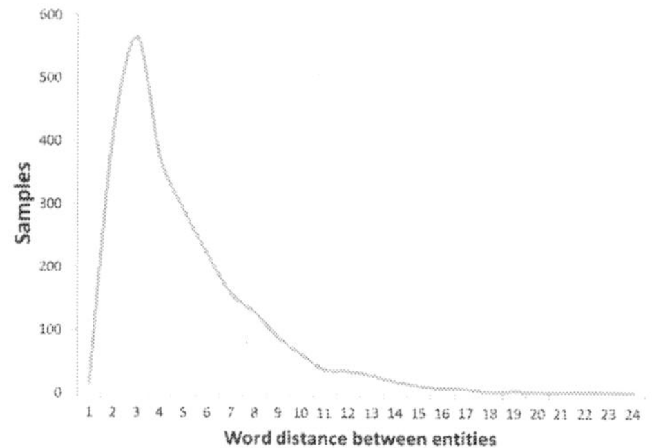

Figure 5: Word distance between entities in a relation for training data in Subtask 1.1

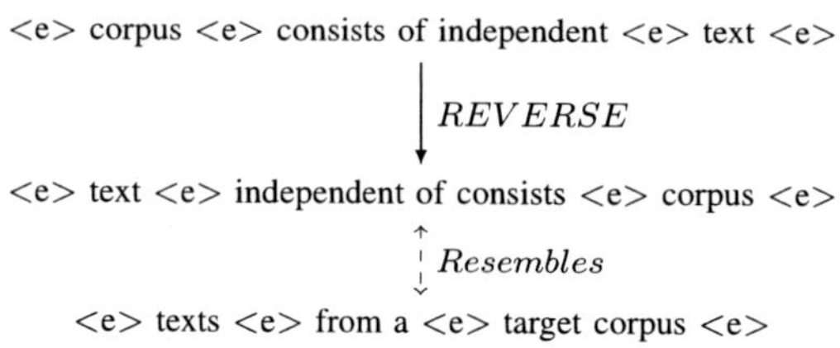

Figure 6: Example of a reversed sentence

sidered every entity pair contained within a single sentence as having a potential relation. Since the probability that a relation between two entities exists drops very rapidly with increasing word distance between them (see Figure 5), we only considered sentences that didn't exceed a maximum length threshold (see Table 2) between entities to diminish the chances of predicting false positives in long sentences.

Various experiments with different thresholds between 7 and 23 words on the training set showed that the best results on sentences from scientific papers are achieved with a threshold of 19 words, as shown in Figure 4.

Cleaning sentences Some of the automatically annotated samples contained nested entities such as *<entity id="L08-1220.16"> signal <entity id="L08-1220.17"> processing </entity></entity>*. We flattened these structures into simple entities and considered all the entities separately for each train and test instance. Moreover, all tokens between brackets [] and parentheses () were deleted, and the numbers that were not part of a proper noun replaced with a single wildcard token.

Using entity tags In order to provide the neural networks with explicit cues of where an entity started and ended, we used a single symbol, represented as an XML tag <e> before and after the entity, to indicate it (Dligach et al., 2017).

Relative order strategy & number of classes As mentioned in Section 1, 5 out of the 6 relation types are asymmetrical and the tagging is always done by using the same order for the entities as the one found in the abstracts' text/title. For that reason, it was important to carefully devise a schema that allowed generalization by exploiting the information from both ordered and reversed (words that will be treated here as antonyms) relations. Apart from using the relative position embeddings presented by Lee et al. (2017), for Subtask 1, we incorporated a full text reversal of those sentences in which a reverse relation was present, both at training and testing time. The result were instances that, although not corresponding to a valid English grammar, frequently resembled more in structure to their ordered counterparts. This has been illustrated by an example of two instances belonging to the *PART-WHOLE* class in Figure 6.

Thus, the system could operate by using only the 6 originally specified relation types and merely learn how to identify ordered relations, rather than having to handle the two different types of patterns or to add extra classes to describe both the ordered and the reversed versions of each class, which helped improve the overall accuracy of the classifier (+2.0% F_1).

For Subtask 2, since no information regarding the ordering of the arguments was available (the extraction and the ordering were part of the task), we opted for a 12-class strategy: one for each of the 5 ordered and reversed relations, plus the symmetrical relation (COMPARE) and a NONE class for the negative instances, i.e.: those that didn't contain any relation at all. An alternative 6-class approach based on presenting the sentences both ordered and reversed to the network, computing two predictions for each and afterwards consolidating both did not produce good results (-3.4% F_1).

Part-of-speech tags We used the Stanford CoreNLP tagger (Manning et al., 2014) to obtain POS tags for each word in every sentence in the dataset and trained high-dimensional embeddings for the 36 possible tags defined by the Penn Treebank Project (Marcus et al., 1993). Moreover, the XML tags to identify the entities and the number wildcard received their own corresponding artificial POS tag embedding (see Figure 2 for a detailed example).

3 Experiments

3.1 Exploiting provided data

One of the main challenges of the task was the limited size of the training set, which is a common drawback for many supervised novel machine learning tasks. To overcome it, we combined the provided datasets[1] for Subtask 1.1 and 1.2 to train the models for both Subtasks (+6.2% F_1). Furthermore, we leveraged the predictions of our system for Subtasks 1.1 and 1.2 and added them as training data for Subtask 2 (+3.6% F_1).

3.2 Generating additional data

Due to the limited number of training sentences provided, we explored the following approach to augment the data: We generated automatically-tagged artificial training samples for Subtask 1 by combining the entities that appeared in the test

---

[1] Link to forum post 1 - Link to forum post 2

data with the text between entities and relation labels of those from the training set (see Table 1). To evaluate the quality of the sentences and augment our data only with sensible instances, we estimated an NLP language model using the KenLM Language Model Toolkit (Heafield, 2011) on the corpus of NLP-related text described in Section 2.2 and evaluated the generated sentences with it. Furthermore, we set a minimum threshold of 5 words for the length of the text between entities, limited the number of sentences generated from each of them to a single instance in order to promote variety, and only kept those sentences that score a very high probability (-21 in log scale) against the language model. This process yielded 61 additional samples on the development set (+0.7% F_1).

3.3 Parameter optimization

To determine the optimal tuning for our richly parameterized models, we ran a grid search over the parameter space for those parameters that were part of our automatic pipeline. The final values and evaluated ranges are specified in Table 2.

3.4 Defining the objective

The cross-entropy loss, defined as the cross-entropy between the probability distribution outputted by the classifier and the one implied by the correct prediction is one of the most widely used objectives for training neural networks for classification problems (Janocha and Czarnecki, 2017). A shortcoming of this approach is that the cross-entropy loss usually only constitutes a conveniently decomposable proxy for what the ultimate goal of the optimization is (Eban et al., 2017): in this case, the macro-averaged F_1 score. Motivated by the fact that individual instances of infrequent classes have a bigger impact on the final F_1 score than those of more frequent ones (Manning et al., 2008), we opted for a weighted version of the cross-entropy as loss function, where each class had a weight w that was inversely proportional to their frequency in the training set:

$$w_{class\ i} = \frac{\sum_j \#_{class\ j}}{N_{classes} * \#_{class\ i}}$$

where $\#$ indicates the count for a certain class and $N_{classes}$ is the total number of classes.

The weights are scaled as to preserve the expected value of the factor k_i that accompanies the logarithm in the mathematical expression of the loss

Dev set:	*<e> predictive performance <e> of our <e> models <e>*
Train set:	*<e> methods <e> involve the use of probabilistic <e> generative models <e>*
New sample:	*<e> predictive performance <e> involve the use of probabilistic <e> models <e>*

Table 1: Generated sample

Parameter	Final value	Experiment range
Word embedding dimensionality	200	100-300
Embedding dimensionality for part-of-speech tags	30	10-50
Embedding dimensionality for relative positions	20	10-50
Number of CNN filters	192	64-384
Sizes of CNN filters	2 to 7	2-4 to 5-9
Norm regularization parameter (λ)	0.01	0.0-1.0
Number of LSTM units (RNN)	600	0-2400
Dropout probability (CNN and RNN)	0.5	0.0-0.7
Initial learning rate	0.01	0.001-0.1
Number of epochs (Subtask 1)	200	20-400
Number of epochs (Subtask 2)	10	5-40
Ensemble size	20	1-30
Training batch size	64	32-192
Upsampling ratio (only Subtask 2)	1.0	0.0-5.0
Max. sentence length (only subtask 2)	19	7-23

Table 2: Final parameter values and their explored ranges

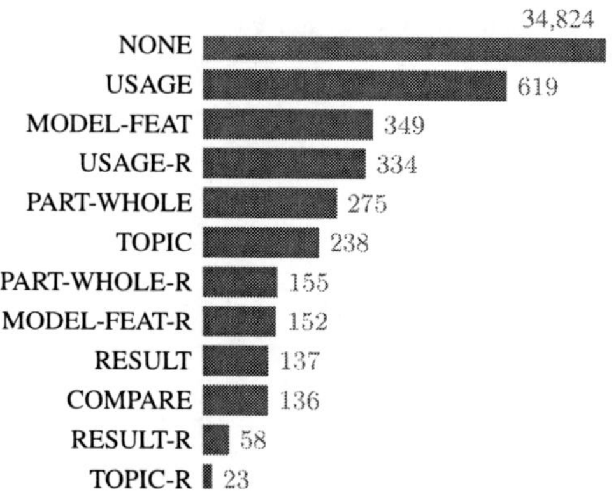

Figure 7: Class frequencies for Subtask 2

formula: $L = -\sum k_i log(y_i)$, which is equal to wy_i' for the weighted cross-entropy and y_i' for the unweighted version, where $y_i' = 1$ for the correct class and y_i is the predicted probability for that class. Illustrating this concept, it can be observed that a single instance of class *TOPIC* (support of only 6 instances) could account for up to 2.8% of the final score on the test set. This function proved to be a better surrogate for the global final score than the standard cross-entropy (+1.6% F_1).

3.5 Upsampling

One of the challenges of our approach for Subtask 2 was the existence of a large imbalance between the target classes. Namely, the NONE class constituted the clear majority (Figure 7). To overcome it, we resorted to an upsampling scheme for which we defined an arbitrary ratio of positive to negative examples to present to the networks for the combination of all positive classes (+12.2% F_1).

4 Training and validating the model

The neural networks were trained using an Adam optimizer with parameter values $\beta_2 = 0.9$, $\beta_2 = 0.999$, $\epsilon = 1e - 08$ (suggested default values in the TensorFlow library (Abadi et al., 2015)) with a step learning rate decay scheme on top of it. This consisted in halving the learning rate every 25 and 1 iterations through the whole dataset for Subtasks 1 and 2 respectively (note: the size of the upsampled dataset for Subtask 2 was about 25 times that of Subtask 1), starting from the initial value determined in Section 3.3. In order to avoid overfitting the development set of each Subtask, we evaluated the quality of our models by applying a 5-fold cross-validation on the combined training data of Subtasks 1.1 and 1.2 and on the training data of Subtask 2.

Combining predictions During the development, we observed that similar F_1 scores could be achieved by using either a convolutional neural network or a recurrent one separately, but the combination of both outperformed the individual models. Moreover, since the RNN-based architecture had a tendency to obtain better results than its CNN-based counterpart for long sequences, we combined both predictions in such a way that a higher weight was assigned to the RNN predictions for longer sentences by applying:

$$w_{rnn,i} = 0.5 + sign(s_i) \cdot s_i^2, \text{ where}$$

$$s_i = \frac{length_i - \min_j(length_j)}{\max_j(length_j) - \min_j(length_j)} - 0.5$$

and $length_i$ is the length of the i-th sentence.

Post-processing To enforce consistency with the text annotation scheme, some rules that were not built into the system had to be applied ex-post. First, predictions of reversed relations should not be of type COMPARE, since it is the only symmetrical relation. When this condition occurred, we simply predicted the class that had the 2nd highest probability. Second, each entity could only be part of one relation. To address this for Subtask 2, we run a conflict-solving algorithm that, in case of overlaps, always preferred short relations (cf. Figure 3]) and broke ties by choosing the relation with the most frequent class in the training data and at random when it persisted.

5 Results

5.1 Feature analysis

We conducted a feature addition study to evaluate the impact of the most relevant features on the F_1 score of the 5-fold cross-validated training/development set of Subtasks 1.1 and 1.2.

The results have been previously shown in Figure 1. It can be observed from the plot that substantial gains can be obtained by applying standalone data manipulation techniques that are independent of the type of classifier used, such as combining the data of subtask 1.1 and 1.2 (*CSD* in Figure 1), reversing the sentences (*RS*), generating additional data (*GD*) and the pre-processing techniques from Section 2.3. Moreover, as in most machine learning problems, appropriately tuning the model hyperparameters also has a significant impact on the final score.

Subtask	P	R	F_1
1.1	79.2	84.4	81.7
1.2	93.3	87.7	90.4
2.E	40.9	55.3	48.8
2.C	41.9	60.0	49.3

Table 3: Precision (P), recall (R) and F_1-score (F_1) in % on the test set by Subtask

Relation type	P	R	F_1
COMPARE	100.00	95.24	97.56
MODEL-FEATURE	71.01	74.24	72.59
PART-WHOLE	78.87	80.00	79.43
RESULT	87.50	70.00	77.78
TOPIC	50.00	100.00	66.67
USAGE	87.86	86.86	87.36
Micro-averaged total	82.82	82.82	82.82
Macro-averaged total	79.21	84.39	81.72

Table 4: Detailed results (Precision (P), recall (R) and F_1-score (F_1)) in % for each relation type on the test set for Subtask 1.1

5.2 Final results

After presenting and analyzing the impact of each system feature separately, we show the overall results in this section. The final results on the official test set are presented on Table 3, ranking 1st in Subtasks 1.1, 1.2 and Subtask 2.C (joint result of classification and extraction) and 2nd for 2.E (relation extraction only). Furthermore, Table 4 shows the differences in performance between relation types for Subtask 1.1.

6 Conclusion

In this article we presented the winning system of SemEval 2018 Task 7 for relation classification, which also achieved the 2nd place for the relation extraction scenario. Our system, based on an ensemble of CNNs and RNNs, ranked first on 3 out of the 4 Subtasks (relation classification on clean and noisy data, and relation extraction and classification on clean data combined). We have tested various approaches to improve the system such as generating more additional training samples and experimenting with different order strategies for asymmetrical relation types. We demonstrated the effectiveness of preprocessing the samples by taking into account their length, marking the entities with explicit tags, defining an adequate surrogate optimization objective and combining effectively the outputs of several different models.

References

Martín Abadi, Ashish Agarwal, et al. 2015. TensorFlow: Large-scale machine learning on heterogeneous systems. Software available from tensorflow.org.

Steven Bird, Robert Dale, Bonnie J Dorr, Bryan Gibson, Mark Thomas Joseph, Min-Yen Kan, Dongwon Lee, Brett Powley, Dragomir R Radev, and Yee Fan Tan. 2008. The ACL anthology reference corpus: A reference dataset for bibliographic research in computational linguistics. *EUROPEAN LANGUAGE RESOURCES ASSOC-ELRA.*

Ronan Collobert, Jason Weston, Léon Bottou, Michael Karlen, Koray Kavukcuoglu, and Pavel Kuksa. 2011. Natural language processing (almost) from scratch. *Journal of Machine Learning Research*, 12(Aug):2493–2537.

Dmitriy Dligach, Timothy Miller, Chen Lin, Steven Bethard, and Guergana Savova. 2017. Neural temporal relation extraction. *EACL 2017*, page 746.

Elad Eban, Mariano Schain, Alan Mackey, Ariel Gordon, Ryan Rifkin, and Gal Elidan. 2017. Scalable learning of non-decomposable objectives. In *Artificial Intelligence and Statistics*, pages 832–840.

Lisheng Fu, Thien Huu Nguyen, Bonan Min, and Ralph Grishman. 2017. Domain adaptation for relation extraction with domain adversarial neural network. In *Proceedings of the Eighth International Joint Conference on Natural Language Processing (Volume 2: Short Papers)*, volume 2, pages 425–429.

Kata Gábor, Davide Buscaldi, Anne-Kathrin Schumann, Behrang QasemiZadeh, Hafa Zargayouna, and Thierry Charnois. 2018. SemEval-2018 Task 7: Semantic Relation Extraction and Classification in Scientific Papers. In *Proceedings of the 12th International Workshop on Semantic Evaluation (SemEval-2018).*

Kenneth Heafield. 2011. Kenlm: Faster and smaller language model queries. In *Proceedings of the Sixth Workshop on Statistical Machine Translation*, pages 187–197. Association for Computational Linguistics.

Sepp Hochreiter and Jürgen Schmidhuber. 1997. Long short-term memory. *Neural computation*, 9(8):1735–1780.

Katarzyna Janocha and Wojciech Marian Czarnecki. 2017. On loss functions for deep neural networks in classification. *arXiv preprint arXiv:1702.05659.*

Yoon Kim. 2014. Convolutional neural networks for sentence classification. *arXiv preprint arXiv:1408.5882.*

Ji Young Lee, Franck Dernoncourt, and Peter Szolovits. 2017. MIT at SemEval-2017 Task 10: Relation Extraction with Convolutional Neural Networks. *arXiv preprint arXiv:1704.01523.*

Christopher D Manning, Prabhakar Raghavan, Hinrich Schütze, et al. 2008. *Introduction to information retrieval*, volume 1. Cambridge university press Cambridge.

Christopher D. Manning, Mihai Surdeanu, John Bauer, Jenny Finkel, Steven J. Bethard, and David McClosky. 2014. The Stanford CoreNLP natural language processing toolkit. In *Association for Computational Linguistics (ACL) System Demonstrations*, pages 55–60.

Mitchell P Marcus, Mary Ann Marcinkiewicz, and Beatrice Santorini. 1993. Building a large annotated corpus of English: The Penn Treebank. *Computational linguistics*, 19(2):313–330.

Anne-Lyse Minard, Anne-Laure Ligozat, and Brigitte Grau. 2011. Multi-class SVM for relation extraction from clinical reports. In *Proceedings of the International Conference Recent Advances in Natural Language Processing 2011*, pages 604–609.

Thien Huu Nguyen and Ralph Grishman. 2015. Relation extraction: Perspective from convolutional neural networks. In *Proceedings of the 1st Workshop on Vector Space Modeling for Natural Language Processing*, pages 39–48.

Nanyun Peng, Hoifung Poon, Chris Quirk, Kristina Toutanova, and Wen-tau Yih. 2017. Cross-sentence n-ary relation extraction with graph LSTMs. *arXiv preprint arXiv:1708.03743.*

Radim Řehůřek and Petr Sojka. 2010. Software Framework for Topic Modelling with Large Corpora. In *Proceedings of the LREC 2010 Workshop on New Challenges for NLP Frameworks*, pages 45–50, Valletta, Malta. ELRA. http://is.muni.cz/publication/884893/en.

Richard Socher, Brody Huval, Christopher D Manning, and Andrew Y Ng. 2012. Semantic compositionality through recursive matrix-vector spaces. In *Proceedings of the 2012 joint conference on empirical methods in natural language processing and computational natural language learning*, pages 1201–1211. Association for Computational Linguistics.

Charles Sutton and Andrew McCallum. 2006. *An introduction to conditional random fields for relational learning*, volume 2. Introduction to statistical relational learning. MIT Press.

Özlem Uzuner, Brett R South, Shuying Shen, and Scott L DuVall. 2011. 2010 i2b2/va challenge on concepts, assertions, and relations in clinical text. *Journal of the American Medical Informatics Association*, 18(5):552–556.

Godandapani Zayaraz et al. 2015. Concept relation extraction using naïve bayes classifier for ontology-based question answering systems. *Journal of King Saud University-Computer and Information Sciences*, 27(1):13–24.

Suncong Zheng, Yuexing Hao, Dongyuan Lu, Hongyun Bao, Jiaming Xu, Hongwei Hao, and Bo Xu. 2017. Joint entity and relation extraction based on a hybrid neural network. *Neurocomputing*, 257:59–66.

SemEval-2018 Task 8: Semantic Extraction from CybersecUrity REports using Natural Language Processing (SecureNLP)

Peter Phandi   **Amila Silva**   **Wei Lu**

8 Somapah Road, Singapore 487372
Singapore University of Technology and Design
{peter_phandi,amila_silva,wei_lu}@sutd.edu.sg

Abstract

This paper describes the SemEval 2018 shared task on semantic extraction from cybersecurity reports, which is introduced for the first time as a shared task on SemEval. This task comprises four SubTasks done incrementally to predict the characteristics of a specific malware using cybersecurity reports. To the best of our knowledge, we introduce the world's largest publicly available dataset of annotated malware reports in this task. This task received in total 18 submissions from 9 participating teams.

1 Introduction

As a result of the world getting more connected and digitized, cyber attacks become increasingly common and pose serious issues for the society. More recently in 2017, a ransomware called WannaCry, which has the capability to lock down the data files using strong encryption, spread around the world targeting public utilities and large corporations (Mohurle and Patil, 2017). Another example is the botnet known as Mirai, which used infected Internet of Things (IoT) devices to disable Internet access for millions of users in the US West Coast (US-CERT, 2016) through large-scale Distributed Denial of Service (DDoS) attacks. The impact levels of these attacks is ranging from simple ransomware on personal laptops (Andronio et al., 2015) to taking over the control of moving cars (Checkoway et al., 2011).

Along with the importance of cybersecurity in today's context, there is an increasing potential for substantial contribution in cybersecurity using natural language processing (NLP) techniques, even though this has not been significantly addressed. We introduced this task as a shared task on SemEval for the first time with the intention of motivating NLP researchers for this critical research

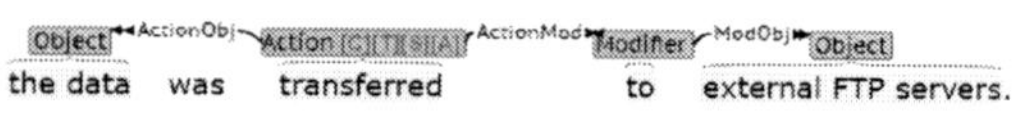


```
[C] Capability: 006:MalwareCapability-
data_exfiltration
[A] Action: 097:Network-upload_file
[S] StrategicObjectives: 020:DataExfiltration-
perform_data_exfiltration
[T] TacticalObjectives: 057:DataExfiltration-
exfiltrate_via_network
```

Figure 1: Annotated sentence and sentence fragment from MalwareTextDB. Such annotations provide semantic-level information to the text.

area. Even though there exists a large repository of malware related texts online, the sheer volume and diversity of these texts make it difficult for NLP researchers to quickly move to this research field. Another challenge is that most of the data is unannotated. Lim et al. (2017) has introduced a dataset of annotated malware reports for facilitating future NLP work in cybersecurity. In the light of that, we improved Lim's malware dataset to create, to the best of our knowledge, the world's largest publicly available dataset of annotated malware reports. The aim of our annotation is to mark the words and phrases in malware reports that describe the behaviour and capabilities of the malware and assign them to some certain categories.

Most of the machine learning efforts in the task of malware detection were based on the system calls. Rieck et al. (2011) and Alazab et al. (2010) proposed models using machine learning techniques for detecting and classifying malware through system calls. Previously, our group has proposed models to predict a malware's signatures based on the text describing the malware (Lim et al., 2017). We defined the same SubTasks mentioned in this paper and used the proposed models as the standard baselines for the shared task. This shared task is hosted on CodaLab[1].

The remainder of this paper is organized as

---

[1] https://competitions.codalab.org/competitions/17262

Proceedings of the 12th International Workshop on Semantic Evaluation (SemEval-2018), pages 697–706
New Orleans, Louisiana, June 5–6, 2018. ©2018 Association for Computational Linguistics

follows: the information regarding the annotated dataset and its statistics, together with the Sub-Tasks are described in Section 2. Information about the evaluation measures and the baselines is described in Section 3. Different approaches used by the participants are described in Section 4. The evaluation scores of the participating systems and rankings are presented and discussed in Section 5. Finally, the paper concludes with an overall assessment of the task.

2 Data description and Task Definition

In this shared task we expanded upon our previous work, MalwareTextDB (Lim et al., 2017), which was published in ACL 2017. In this paper, we initiated a framework for annotating malware reports and annotated 39 Advanced Persistent Threat (APT) reports (containing 6,819 sentences) with attribute labels from the Malware Attribute Enumeration and Characterization (MAEC) vocabulary (Kirillov et al., 2010). An example of such annotation is shown in Figure 1. During this shared task, we have further annotated 46 APT reports (6,099 sentences), bringing the total number of annotated APT reports to 85 (12,918 sentences). We continue to follow our annotation procedure from the paper, which we will describe in the following subsection.

2.1 Annotation Procedure

This subsection contains the explanation of our annotation procedure.

2.1.1 Data Collection

The APT reports in our dataset are taken from APTnotes, a GitHub repository of publicly-released reports related to APT groups (Blanda, 2016). It provides a constant source of APT reports for annotations with consistent updates. At the time this paper was written, the repository contains 488 reports. We have chosen 85 reports from year 2014 and 2015 for annotation.

We consulted the cybersecurity team from DSO National Laboratories[2] when selecting the APT reports in order to ensure that the preliminary dataset will be relevant for the cybersecurity community.

2.1.2 Preprocessing

The APT reports from APTnotes are in PDF format, hence we used the PDFMiner tool

(Shinyama, 2004) to convert the PDF files into plaintext format. We also manually removed the non-sentences, such as the cover page or document header and footer, before the annotation. Hence only complete sentences were considered for subsequent steps.

2.1.3 Annotation

The annotation was performed using the Brat Rapid Annotation Tool (Stenetorp et al., 2012) . In this annotation, our aim is to mark the words and phrases that describe malware behaviors and map them to the relevant *attribute labels*, which are the labels we extracted from the MAEC vocabulary. There are a total of 444 attribute labels, consisting of 211 *ActionName* labels, 20 *Capability* labels, 65 *StrategicObjectives* labels and 148 *TacticalObjectives* labels. The annotation was performed by a team of research assistants and student interns. The annotation work done by the student interns was further reviewed by the research assistants to ensure the quality.

The annotation was performed in three main stages:

2.1.4 Stage 1 - Token Labels

The first stage involves annotating the text with the following *token labels*, illustrated in Figure 2:

Action This refers to an event, such as *"implements"*, *"deploy"*, and *"transferred"*.

Subject This refers to the initiator of the Action such as *"Babar"* and *"they"*.

Object This refers to the recipient of the Action such as *"an obfuscation technique"*, *"the data"*, and *"privilege escalation tools"*; it also refers to word phrases that provide elaboration on the Action such as *"hide certain API names"* and *"external FTP servers"*.

Modifier This refers to the tokens that link to other word phrases that provide elaboration on the Action such as *"to"*.

This stage helps to identify word phrases that are relevant to the MAEC vocabulary.

2.1.5 Stage 2 - Relation Labels

The second stage involves annotating the text with the following *relation labels*:

SubjAction links an Action with its relevant Subject.

---

[2]https://www.dso.org.sg/

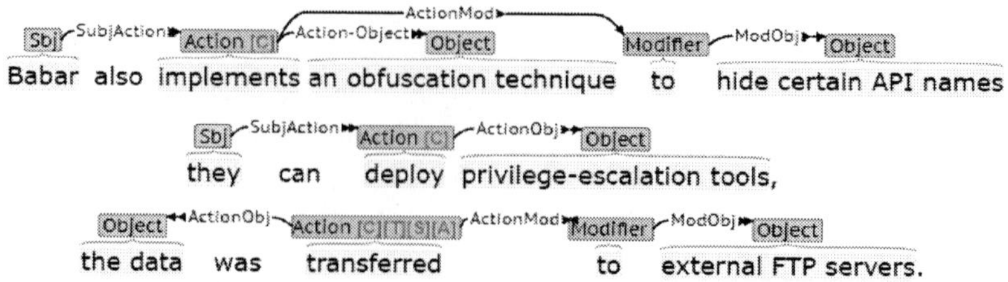

Figure 2: Examples of annotated sentences.

```
The myth of Babar has been around for a while in
the intelligence community.

The drawing of personal educated conclusions is
left as an exercise for the interested reader.
```

Figure 3: Examples of irrelevant sentences.

ActionObj links an Action with its relevant Object.

ActionMod links an Action with its relevant Modifier.

ModObj links a Modifier with the Object that provides elaboration.

This stage indicates the links between the labeled tokens. Such annotations are important in cases where an Action has more than one Subjects, Objects or Modifiers. The illustration on how the relation label links token labels is shown in Figure 2.

2.1.6 Stage 3 - Attribute Labels

The third stage involves annotating the text with the *attribute labels* extracted from the MAEC vocabulary. We decided to annotate the attribute labels onto the Action tokens tagged in the first stage. This is because Action is usually the main indicator of the malware's behaviour. This scheme requires each Action token to be annotated with at least one attribute label.

The attribute labels are categorized into four classes: ActionName, Capability, StrategicObjectives and TacticalObjectives. These classes describe different kinds of actions and capabilities of the malware.

2.1.7 Irrelevant Sentences

The document also contains sentences that provide no indication of malware action or capability. We call these sentences *irrelevant sentences* and do not annotate them. Examples of such sentences

can be seen in Figure 3.

2.1.8 Annotation Challenges

We took a portion of the dataset and calculated the agreement for the token labels annotation based on Cohen's kappa (Cohen, 1960). The agreement between annotators is quite low at 0.36, suggesting that this is a difficult task. The main challenges the annotators faced are:

Multiple ways of annotating the same sentence
There might be multiple ways of annotating the same sentence that are equally valid. An example of this is demonstrated in Figure 4. Both annotations highlight the malware ability to *conduct profiling*.

Large amount of annotation labels
There are 444 attribute labels and it is very challenging for the annotators to remember all of them. There are also some attribute labels that are very similar to each other, such as *ActionName 084: load library* and *Action-Name 119: map library into process*.

Required special domain knowledge
The annotation requires the annotator to have some cybersecurity domain knowledge. For example, given the phrase *"conduct profiling"*, the annotator must be able to classify it as *Capability 015: probing*.

2.2 SubTask Description

We focus on the evaluations for the following 4 different SubTasks, which are formulated as follows:

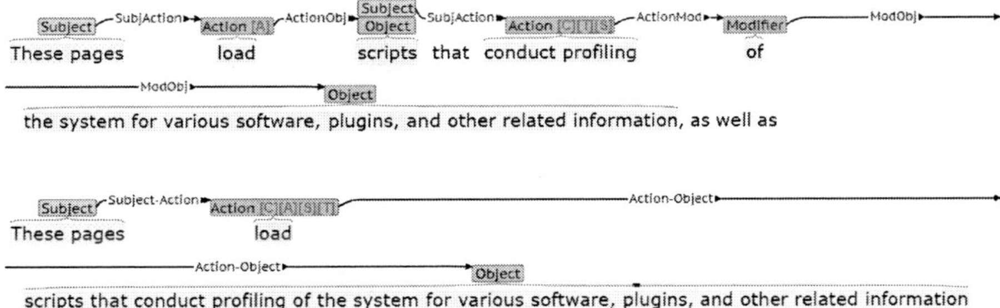

Figure 4: Two different ways of annotating an example sentence.

- SubTask 1: Classify relevant sentences for inferring malware actions and capabilities

- SubTask 2: Predict token labels for a malware related text

- SubTask 3: Predict relation labels between tokens for a malware-related text

- SubTask 4: Predict attribute labels for a malware-related text

In SubTask 1, participants were asked to solve the challenge of sifting out critical sentences from lengthy malware reports and articles. This is modeled as a binary classification task, where each sentence had to be labeled as either relevent or irrelevant. The participants are provided with a list of sentences.

In SubTask2, special tokens in a relevant sentence had to be identified and labeled with one of the following *token labels* (examples are taken from Figure 2):

- **Action** This refers to an event, such as *"implements"*, *"deploys"*, and *"transferred"*.

- **Entity** This refers to the initiator of the Action such as *"Babar"* and *"They"* or the recipient of the Action such as *"an obfuscation technique"*, *"privilege-escalation tools"*, and *"the data"*; it also refers to word phrases that provide elaboration on the Action such as *"hide certain API names"* and *"external FTP servers"*.

- **Modifier** This refers to tokens that link to other word phrases that provide elaboration on the Action such as *"to"*.

	#Documents	#Sentences
Train	65	9,424
Dev	5	1,213
SubTask1,2 test	5	618
SubTask3 test	5	668
SubTask4 test	5	995
Total	85	12,918

Table 1: Statistics of the MalwareTextDBv2.0.

The formulation is similar to the *token labels* in section 2.1.4. The only difference is the Entity label, which is a combination of the Subject and Object labels. This is to accommodate cases where a single word-phrase is annotated as both the initiator and the recipient of an Action (as seen in Figure 5). This SubTask uses the same list of sentences used in SubTask 1.

In SubTask 3, participants were asked to identify the relation between the tokens. We decided to provide the gold labels for the tokens here due to the low performance of our initial models on SubTask 2. The relation labels are as we described in section 2.1.5.

In SubTask 4, participants were asked to label each action token with the corresponding attribute label(s). In our ACL paper, we did the evaluation on token groups (a set of token labels connected by relation labels) instead of action tokens. However, we decided to evaluate on action tokens in order to encourage the participants to make use of the surrounding context, not limiting themselves just to the tokens in the token group. We also provided the gold labels for the token and relation labels here, following the same consideration as we described for SubTask 3.

In our ACL paper, we also had the experiments

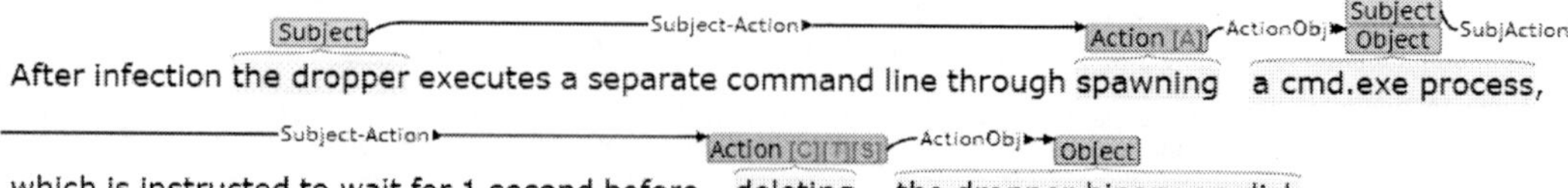

Figure 5: An example of a token (a cmd.exe process) labelled as both Subject and Object. In the first case, it is the recipient of the Action spawning, while in the latter case, it is the initiator of the Action deleting.

	#Relevant	#Irrelevant	#Sentences
Train	2,204	7,220	9,424
Dev	79	1,134	1,213
Test	90	528	618

Table 2: Data distribution of SubTask 1.

on predicting the malware signatures for each document. The list of malware signatures are taken from Cuckoo Sandbox[3]. We excluded such an evaluation at this stage as precise information like malware signatures might be easily obtained from external resources such as malware information websites.

2.3 Data Statistics

We decided to call the dataset we used for this shared task MalwareTextDBv2.0[4], which has twice the number of documents compared to MalwareTextDB. The total statistics are shown in Table 1. The training data for this shared task contains 9,424 sentences, the dev set contains 1,213 sentences, and each test set has various amount of sentences. SubTask 1 and 2 share the same test set, while SubTask 3 and 4 use different test sets. This is because the gold labels from the previous annotation stages are provided for SubTask 3 and 4.

The data distribution for SubTask 1, 2, 3, and 4 can be seen in Table 2, 3, 4, and 5 respectively.

We can see from the distribution of SubTask 1 that the dataset mostly contains *irrelevant* sentences. This shows the importance of SubTask 1 in which the participants filter out the *irrelevant* sentences. Our preliminary result in the ACL paper also shows that removing the *irrelevant* sentences can improve the score for SubTask 2.

From the distribution of SubTask 2, an interesting observation is that the number of *Entity* tokens is roughly double the number of *Action* tokens.

This is quite intuitive since *Entity* token refers to either *Subject* or *Object* token and an *Action* usually has one *Subject* and one *Object*.

In the distribution table for SubTask 3, we can observe that the number of *ActionMod* is roughly the same as the number of *ModObj*. This is in-line with our observation that a *Modifier* is usually connected to an *Action* and an *Object*.

For SubTask 4, we can see that the *Capability* attribute class has the highest count in the dataset. This is also the category that has the least amount of unique labels (with only 20 different labels). On the other hand, *ActionName* class appears the least in the dataset but has the highest number of unique labels (with 211 different labels).

3 Evaluation Measures and Baselines

Our baseline and evaluation measures follow our ACL paper (Lim et al., 2017). We used F1 score for the evaluation metric for all the Sub-Tasks. Simple baselines were utilized, such as linear support vector machines (SVM) and multinomial Naive Bayes (NB) implementation from the scikit-learn library (Pedregosa et al., 2011). For the conditional random fields (CRF) (Lafferty et al., 2001) models, we used the CRF++ implementation (Kudo, 2005). For the feature extraction, we used spaCy[5] to extract the part-of-speech (POS) features and a C++ implementation (Liang, 2005) of the Brown clustering algorithm.

For SubTask 1, our baseline models are the SVM and NB baselines with bag-of-words features. We also performed some hyper-parameter tuning based on the development set. Other simple baselines, such as random uniform and stratified, are also included as a comparison.

For SubTask 2, we used the CRF baseline with unigrams, bigrams, POS, and Brown clustering features (Brown et al., 1992). CRF model was trained only on the malware related sentences in

---

[3]https://cuckoosandbox.org/
[4]http://www.statnlp.org/research/resources
[5]https://spacy.io/

	Action	Entity	Modifier	Total
Train	3,202	6,875	2,011	12,088
Dev	122	254	79	455
Test	125	249	79	453

Table 3: Data distribution of SubTask 2.

	#Root	#ActionMod	#ActionObj	#ModObj	#SubjAction	Total
Train	3,378	1,859	2,552	1,760	2,307	11,856
Dev	111	74	110	74	82	451
Test	97	52	86	53	72	360

Table 4: Data distribution of SubTask 3.

	#ActName	#Capability	#StratObj	#TactObj	Total
Train	1,154	2,817	2,206	1,783	7,960
Dev	46	102	77	63	288
Test	34	88	70	64	256

Table 5: Data distribution of SubTask 4.

the training set. The Brown clustering features for words were trained on the 84 additional unannotated APT reports provided with the training materials.

For SubTask 3, a simple rule-based model was utilized. The rules are listed in the Appendix section of our ACL paper. They consist of simple rules, such as connecting a *Modifier* token to the nearest *Action* token with *ActionMod* relation.

Finally, for SubTask 4, we trained SVM and NB model with bag-of-words features. The features for SubTask 4 are extracted from token groups, which are the set of tokens connected via relation labels. In creating the token groups, we only traverse the direction of Action $\rightarrow$ Subj, Action $\rightarrow$ Mod, Action $\rightarrow$ Obj, and Mod $\rightarrow$ Obj. This will prevent multiple *Action* tokens from having the same token group when they are connected to a common *Subject* or *Modifier*.

4 Participants

We received 18 submissions from 9 different teams; 9 submissions to SubTask 1, 8 submissions to SubTask 2, and 1 submission to SubTask 4. Unfortunately, none of the teams submitted to Sub-Task 3. Participants generally submitted to both SubTask 1 and 2. Here is the list of the participants who submitted a system description paper together with a brief summary of the method they used:

Villani (Loyola et al., 2018) submitted only to SubTask 1. They used word-embeddings initialized using Glove vectors (Pennington et al., 2014) trained on Wikipedia text to represent the tokens. In addition to that, they also used an LSTM to get another token representation from the characters. After that, they trained a binary classifier using Bi-directional Long Short-Term Memory network (BiLSTM) (Graves et al., 2013). They made use of attention mechanism (Luong et al., 2015) to weigh the importance of the tokens.

Flytxt_NTNU (Sikdar et al., 2018) submitted to both SubTask 1 and SubTask 2. They constructed an ensemble of CRF and NB classifiers for SubTask 1. The CRF model used lexical-based and context-based features. The same CRF model was also used to predict the answers for SubTask 2. If the CRF predicts any token labels for the sentence, the sentence is considered relevant in SubTask 1. They did SubTask 2 in 2 steps. First, they detect whether a token is either an *Action*, *Entity*, or *Modifier* (Mention identification). After that, they classify the tokens into one of the three types (Token identification).

DM_NLP (Ma et al., 2018) also submitted to

SubTask 1 and 2, but focuses on SubTask 2 and just used the predicted output labels from SubTask 2 to get the predictions for SubTask 1. They model this task as a sequence labeling task and used a hybrid approach with BiLSTM-CNN-CRF following the method of Ma and Hovy (2016). The CNN layer was used to extract char-level feature representation. They then added other features, such as POS, dependency labels, chunk labels, NER labels, and brown clustering labels as the input to BiLSTM layer. They also made use of word-embeddings, pre-trained using unlabeled data. The output of the BiLSTM layer is then fed into a CRF layer that makes the entity label prediction.

HCCL (Fu et al., 2018) submitted to SubTask 1 and 2. They performed a very similar approach to team DM_NLP using the same BiLSTM-CNN-CRF architecture. The main difference is that they just used POS features, instead of the more complicated linguistic features used by team DM_NLP. They aim to build an end-to-end system that does not require any feature engineering or data preprocessing. Their output for SubTask 1 was also generated from their predictions for SubTask 2.

Digital Operatives (Brew, 2018) participated in SubTask 1 and 2. They utilized a passive aggressive classifier (Crammer et al., 2006), which has similar cost and performance with the linear SVM classifier, for SubTask 1. The features they used include POS, lemma, dependency links, and bigrams. For SubTask 2, they implemented a linear CRF approach using a window of words and POS tags surrounding the focus token as features.

TeamDL (R et al., 2018) made the submissions for SubTask 1 and 2. For SubTask 1, they built a convolutional neural network with original glove embeddings. Their model followed the work of Kim (2014). They also used a CRF for SubTask 2 with features like N-grams (N∈{1,2,..6}), POS tags, word lemmas, word shape features, etc. In order to tackle unknown malware entities, they used additional set of features taken from malware

documents from the web and the training corpus.

UMBC (Padia et al., 2018) participated in Sub-Task 1, 2 and 4. They are the only team participated in SubTask 4. They used a Multi-Layer Perceptron model for the submission of SubTask 1. After the submission deadline, they have explored other methods for Sub-Task 1 like LSTM. For SubTask 2, they used a CRF model with features similar to TeamDL. The main difference is that their model had less features compared to TeamDL's model. For SubTask 4, they mainly focused on learning better word embedding features. They developed an Annotation Word Embedding (AWE) model that is capable of incorporating domain-specific knowledge to the embeddings.

5 Results and Discussion

5.1 SubTask 1 Results

Table 6 shows the scores of the submissions to SubTask 1. We also added the precision, recall, and accuracy scores as additional metrics. All 9 participating teams submitted to SubTask 1. This might be because SubTask 1 is the simplest and can be done as a by-product of doing SubTask 2. We can see that by guessing randomly we get an F1 score of 25.06%. However, this does not mean that this SubTask is not challenging as we can see that the scores of top systems are far from perfect. We submitted the NB baseline result in the competition page since it achieved a better performance compared to the SVM baseline in the development data.

Most of the teams used neural network models to tackle this task, which were shown to perform quite well. However, approaches using classifiers such as naive Bayes are still competitive. Team Villani achieved the best F1 score of 57.14% using a neural approach and Flytxt_NTNU reached the second place with an F1 score of 56.87% using an ensemble of naive Bayes and CRF approach.

Some of the teams utilized their results from SubTask 2 to generate predictions for SubTask 1. This method seems to have performed quite well too, with 3 of the top-5 teams using it. Flytxt_NTNU is notable for combining this method with a naive Bayes approach as an ensemble system.

	Prec	Recall	F1	Acc
Our baselines				
Our SVM baseline	**49.55**	62.22	**55.17**	**80.58**
Our NB baseline	38.17	**78.89**	51.45	78.32
Random uniform baseline	16.09	56.67	25.06	50.65
Random stratified baseline	11.45	16.67	13.57	69.09
Participants Outputs				
Villani	47.76	71.11	**57.14**	84.47
Flytxt_NTNU	49.59	66.67	56.87	85.28
DM_NLP	39.43	**76.67**	52.08	79.45
HCCL	**53.57**	50.00	51.72	**86.41**
Digital Operatives	39.31	75.56	51.71	79.45
TeamDL	38.46	72.22	50.19	79.13
NLP_Foundation	36.13	**76.67**	49.11	76.86
UMBC	11.14	43.33	17.73	41.42
NanshanNLP	13.56	17.78	15.38	71.52

Table 6: SubTask 1 results sorted by F1 score, the highest score in each column from the baselines and the participants outputs are marked in **bold.**

5.2 SubTask 2 Results

The scores of the submissions for SubTask 2 are shown in Table 7. This task attracted 8 teams and 4 teams were able to outperform our baseline which is a CRF model with unigrams, bigrams, POS, and Brown clustering features. Though all participants have used the CRF model as the final layer of their models, 3 teams used neural architectures like Bi-LSTM and CNN-BiRNN architectures to generate better embeddings for the features.

Team DM_NLP achieved the best F1 score of 29.23%. In addition, we considered a relaxed scoring scheme where predictions are scored at token level instead of phrase level to give credit to the model when the span for a predicted label intersects with the span for the actual label. The model from team DM_NLP still achieved the highest F1 score of 39.18% under this scoring scheme. Team HCCL showed significant improvement in their scores for the relaxed scoring schemes for their model based on CNN-BiRNN-CRF architecture.

5.3 SubTask 3 Results

The results of our baselines for SubTask 3 can be seen in Table 8. As we mentioned in an earlier section, no participant submitted to this SubTask. From our baselines, we can see that this task cannot be done using random prediction. However, our rule-based method still works well on this new test set.

5.4 SubTask 4 Results

We summarized the results for SubTask 4 in Table 9. The main challenges to this SubTask are the data sparsity and the number of attribute labels. The only participant who submitted to this Sub-Task is from team UMBC. They used a domain-specific word embedding model trained on APT reports and their automatically generated text annotations to train an SVM classifier.

6 Conclusion and Future Work

In this work, we have presented the results of SemEval 2018 shared task on Semantic Extraction from CybersecUrity REports using Natural Language Processing (SecureNLP). This new SemEval task attracted 9 participating teams with 18 submissions. We have provided a new dataset on annotated malware report and also the evaluation criteria for the 4 SubTasks that we proposed. We also described the methods that the participants used to tackle this shared task. We hope that this shared task can spark the interest of the research community to use NLP techniques for cybersecurity purposes.

The participants have improved the state-of-the-art results for SubTask 1 and 2. They explored many interesting methods to tackle the SubTasks that we proposed. Since the post evaluation phase is still ongoing on the competition website, hopefully other people will be interested in testing their models.

	Normal Scores			Relaxed Scores		
	Prec	**Recall**	**F1**	**Prec**	**Recall**	**F1**
Our baselines						
CRF baseline	24.05	22.30	23.14	31.22	30.80	31.01
Participants Outputs						
DM_NLP	23.35	**39.07**	**29.23**	30.14	**55.98**	**39.18**
Flytxt_NTNU	25.98	29.36	27.56	32.96	40.06	36.17
NLP_Foundation	25.57	29.80	27.52	35.42	42.46	38.62
TeamDL	22.90	28.26	25.30	30.64	43.08	35.81
UMBC	18.19	28.48	22.20	24.42	46.31	31.98
HCCL	7.64	17.88	21.72	**38.39**	36.84	37.60
NanshanNLP	**26.96**	17.44	21.18	34.03	23.84	28.03
Digital Operatives	16.58	14.57	15.51	23.65	26.43	24.96

Table 7: SubTask 2 results sorted by F1 score, the highest score in each column from the baselines and the participants outputs are marked in **bold**.

	Prec	**Recall**	**F1**
Rule-based baseline	**85.60**	**85.83**	**85.71**
Random uniform baseline	3.24	14.17	5.27
Random stratified baseline	3.14	2.22	2.60

Table 8: SubTask 3 baseline results sorted by F1 score.

	Prec	**Recall**	**F1**
Our baselines			
SVM baseline	**40.30**	**31.64**	**35.45**
NB baseline	36.77	32.03	34.24
Participants Outputs			
UMBC	**15.23**	**26.17**	**19.25**

Table 9: SubTask 4 results sorted by F1 score, the highest score in each column from the baselines and the participants outputs are marked in **bold**.

Acknowledgments

We would like to thank all the teams who participated in this shared task. Special mention to Chris Brew and Arpita Roy for their valuable feedback. We also thank the authors of the ACL 2017 paper: Swee Kiat Lim, Aldrian Obaja Muis for doing the initial work, and Chen Hui Ong from DSO for her feedback during the annotation.

References

Mamoun Alazab, Sitalakshmi Venkataraman, and Paul Watters. 2010. Towards understanding malware behaviour by the extraction of api calls. In *Proc. of CTC*, pages 52–59.

Nicoló Andronio, Stefano Zanero, and Federico Maggi. 2015. Heldroid: Dissecting and detecting mobile ransomware. In *Proc. of RAID*, pages 382–404.

Kiran Blanda. 2016. APTnotes. https://github.com/aptnotes/.

Chris Brew. 2018. Digital Operatives at SemEval-2018 Task 8: Using dependency features for malware NLP. In *Proc. of SemEval*.

Peter F. Brown, Peter V. deSouza, Robert L. Mercer, Vincent J. Della Pietra, and Jenifer C. Lai. 1992. Class-based N-gram Models of Natural Language. *Comput. Linguist.*, 18:467–479.

Stephen Checkoway, Damon McCoy, Brian Kantor, Danny Anderson, Hovav Shacham, Stefan Savage, Karl Koscher, Alexei Czeskis, Franziska Roesner, Tadayoshi Kohno, et al. 2011. Comprehensive experimental analyses of automotive attack surfaces. In *Proc. of USENIX Security Symposium*. San Francisco.

Jacob Cohen. 1960. A Coefficient of Agreement for Nominal Scales. *Educational and Psychological Measurement*, 20(1):37–46.

Koby Crammer, Ofer Dekel, Joseph Keshet, Shai Shalev-Shwartz, and Yoram Singer. 2006. Online passive-aggressive algorithms. *Journal of Machine Learning Research*, 7:551–585.

Mingming Fu, Xuemin Zhao, and Yonghong Yan. 2018. HCCL at SemEval-2018 Task 8: An End-to-End System for Sequence Labeling from Cybersecurity Reports. In *Proc. of SemEval*.

Alex Graves, Abdel-rahman Mohamed, and Geoffrey Hinton. 2013. Speech recognition with deep recurrent neural networks. In *Proc. of ICASSP*, pages 6645–6649.

Yoon Kim. 2014. Convolutional neural networks for sentence classification. In *Proc. of EMNLP*.

Ivan Kirillov, Desiree Beck, Penny Chase, and Robert Martin. 2010. Malware Attribute Enumeration and Characterization. *The MITRE Corporation, Tech. Rep.*

Taku Kudo. 2005. CRF++. https://taku910. github.io/crfpp/.

John Lafferty, Andrew McCallum, and Fernando Pereira. 2001. Conditional Random Fields: Probabilistic Models for Segmenting and Labeling Sequence Data. In *Proc. of ICML*, pages 282–289.

Percy Liang. 2005. Semi-supervised learning for natural language. Master's thesis, Massachusetts Institute of Technology.

Swee Kiat Lim, Aldrian Obaja Muis, Wei Lu, and Chen Hui Ong. 2017. MalwareTextDB: A Database for Annotated Malware Articles. In *Proc. of ACL*, volume 1, pages 1557–1567.

Pablo Loyola, Kugamoorthy Gajananan, Yuji Watanabe, and Fumiko Satoh. 2018. Villani at SemEval-2018 Task 8: Semantic Extraction from Cybersecurity Reports using Natural Language Processing (SecureNLP). In *Proc. of SemEval*.

Thang Luong, Hieu Pham, and Christopher D Manning. 2015. Effective approaches to attention-based neural machine translation. In *Proc. of EMNLP*, pages 1412–1421.

Chunping Ma, Huafei Zheng, Pengjun Xie, Chen Li, Linlin Li, and Si Luo. 2018. DM_NLP at SemEval-2018 Task 8: neural sequence labeling with linguistic features. In *Proc. of SemEval*.

Xuezhe Ma and Eduard Hovy. 2016. End-to-end sequence labeling via bi-directional lstm-cnns-crf. In *Proc. of ACL*, volume 1, pages 1064–1074.

Savita Mohurle and Manisha Patil. 2017. A brief study of Wannacry Threat: Ransomware Attack 2017. *International Journal of Advanced Research in Computer Science*, 8(5).

Ankur Padia, Arpita Roy, Taneeya Satyapanich, Francis Ferraro, Shimei Pan, Anupam Joshi, and Tim Finin. 2018. UMBC at SemEval-2018 Task 8: Understanding Text about Malware. In *Proc. of SemEval*.

Fabian Pedregosa, Gaël Varoquaux, Alexandre Gramfort, Vincent Michel, Bertrand Thirion, Olivier Grisel, Mathieu Blondel, Peter Prettenhofer, Ron Weiss, Vincent Dubourg, Jake Vanderplas, Alexandre Passos, David Cournapeau, Matthieu Brucher, Matthieu Perrot, and Édouard Duchesnay. 2011. Scikit-learn: Machine Learning in Python. *Journal of Machine Learning Research*, 12:2825–2830.

Jeffrey Pennington, Richard Socher, and Christopher Manning. 2014. Glove: Global vectors for word representation. In *Proc. of EMNLP*, pages 1532–1543.

Manikandan R, Krishna Madgula, and Snehanshu Saha. 2018. TeamDL at SemEval-2018 Task 8: Cybersecurity Text Analysis using Convolutional Neural Network and Conditional Random Fields. In *Proc. of SemEval*.

Konrad Rieck, Philipp Trinius, Carsten Willems, and Thorsten Holz. 2011. Automatic analysis of malware behavior using machine learning. *Journal of Computer Security*, 19:639–668.

Yusuke Shinyama. 2004. PDFMiner. https:// euske.github.io/pdfminer/.

Utpal Kumar Sikdar, Biswanath Barik, and Björn Gambäck. 2018. Flytxt_NTNU at SemEval-2018 Task 8: Identifying and Classifying Malware Text Using Conditional Random Fields and Nave Bayes Classifiers. In *Proc. of SemEval*.

Pontus Stenetorp, Sampo Pyysalo, Goran Topić, Tomoko Ohta, Sophia Ananiadou, and Jun'ichi Tsujii. 2012. BRAT: A Web-based Tool for NLP-assisted Text Annotation. In *Proc. of EACL*, pages 102–107.

US-CERT. 2016. Heightened ddos threat posed by mirai and other botnets.

DM_NLP at SemEval-2018 Task 8:
Neural Sequence Labeling with Linguistic Features

Chunping Ma, Huafei Zheng, Pengjun Xie, Chen Li, Linlin Li, Si Luo
Alibaba Group, China
{chunping.mcp, huafei.zhf, chengchen.xpj, puji.lc, linyan.lll, luo.si}@alibaba-inc.com

Abstract

This paper describes our submissions for SemEval-2018 Task 8: Semantic Extraction from CybersecUrity REports using NLP. The DM_NLP participated in two subtasks: SubTask 1 classifies if a sentence is useful for inferring malware actions and capabilities, and SubTask 2 predicts token labels ("Action", "Entity", "Modifier" and "Others") for a given malware-related sentence. Since we leverage results of Subtask 2 directly to infer the result of Subtask 1, the paper focus on the system solving Subtask 2. By taking Subtask 2 as a sequence labeling task, our system relies on a recurrent neural network named BiLSTM-CNN-CRF with rich linguistic features, such as POS tags, dependency parsing labels, chunking labels, NER labels, Brown clustering. Our system achieved the highest F1 score in both token level and phrase level.

1 Introduction

As a growing number of mobile devices and facilities are getting connected and digitized, malware attacks become increasingly rampant and dangerous. CybersecUrity attracts more public attention but few NLP research and efforts. A large number of malware-related texts is available online, such as malware reports and relevant blogs (DiMaggio, 2015). However due to the sheer volume and diversity of these texts, NLP researchers encounter problems to obtain valuable information, such as the specific actions taken by a certain malware and the capabilities described. Therefore, automatic screening malware-related contents and labeling every token of the contents become potential applications of NLP and have drawn growing research interests.

In order to create a database in CybersecUrity domain which helps researchers to parse malware-related texts, the organizers of SemEval 2018 Task 8 (Phandi et al., 2018) (Lim et al., 2017)proposed the follow tasks:

1. **SubTask1**: Classify if a sentence is relevant for inferring malware actions and capabilities.

2. **SubTask2**: Predict token labels for a given malware-related text.

3. **SubTask3**: Predict relation labels for a given malware-related text.

4. **SubTask4**: Predict attribute labels for a given malware-related text.

However, due to lack of time, we decided to address only SubTask 1 and SubTask 2. In this paper, we describe the system that we submitted for the SemEval 2018 shared task. Our system is based on RNN network and ranked first in both token level and phrase level.

Most existing high performance sequence labeling methods are linear statistical models, such as HMM (Hidden Markov Models) (Eddy, 1996) and CRF (Conditional Random Fields) (Lafferty et al., 2001). In the past few years, neural networks have been widely used to solve NLP problems. Specially, several RNN-based neural networks have been proposed to handle sequence labeling tasks including Chinese word segmentation (Yao and Huang, 2016), POS tagging (Huang et al., 2015), NER (Chiu and Nichols, 2015) (Lample et al., 2016), which achieved outstanding performance against traditional methods.

In this paper, we simple derive the result of SubTask1 from SubTask2 and regard SubTask 2 as the preorder. Namely, our system firstly outputs sequence labels of a given sentence, and then checks whether some target labels turn out, such as Action, Entity, Modifier. Sentences which have

Proceedings of the 12th International Workshop on Semantic Evaluation (SemEval-2018), pages 707–711
New Orleans, Louisiana, June 5–6, 2018. ©2018 Association for Computational Linguistics

those target labels will be classify as malware-related one. Focusing on SubTask1, We propose a neural network architecture using a hybrid bidirectional LSTM and CNN architecture which takes character-level and word-level representations combined with rich linguistic features as input. Instead of decoding each label independently, we feed the output vectors of BiLSTM to a CRF layer. Experiments show the significant improvement of our system compared with baselines.

The remainder of this paper includes a detail description of our system in Section 2. Experiments and analysis of results are presented in Section 3. Finally, Section 4 draws a conclusion and Section 5 describes our future work.

2 System Overview

We treat Subtask 2 as a sequence labeling problem and design a neural network architecture with some hand-crafted features. Our system is mainly based on the BiLSTM-CNN-CRF model and apply model average strategy to avoid over-fitting problem.

2.1 Data Preprocessing

In order to exclude the noise from data provided by the organizers, we use a python program to correct spelling mistakes and unreadable characters. After that, in order to avoid data distribution problem, we mix the training set development set, and then shuffle and split them into five parts randomly. We take four parts as training set and the rest as development set.

2.2 Feature Extraction

Based upon many previous work on sequence labeling, our system incorporates 5 types of features: POS tags, dependency parsing, NER labels, Chunking labels and Brown clustering. All features are generated automatically. In detail, we use Stanford CoreNLP (Manning et al., 2014) [1] to annotate POS tags, dependency parsing, NER labels, and use Apache OpenNLP [2] to annotate Chunking labels. Brown clustering labels are generated by an open source implementation.

2.2.1 POS Tags

POS Tagging (part-of-speech Tagging), which attaches each word of a sentence a part of speech tag based on both its definition and its context, produces a generalization of words and is a fundamental procedure of other NLP tasks such as syntactic parsing and information extraction.

2.2.2 Dependency Labels

Dependency parsing describes the syntactic structure of a sentence in terms of the words (or lemmas) in a sentence and an associated set of directed binary grammatical relations that hold among the words. For a given word, our system takes the concatenation the dependency edge and its syntactic head as its dependency label, or 'ROOT' if the word has no syntactic head.

2.2.3 NER Labels

Named Entity Recognition (NER) labels sequences of words in a text which are the names of things, such as person and company names, or gene and protein names. We utilize NER labels as significant information to detect named token labels, such as Subject and Object.

2.2.4 Chunking Labels

Text chunking divides a text into phrases in such a way that syntactically related words become member of the same phrase. For instance, "technology organizations" is a noun phrase, our system annotates "technology" as "B-NP" and "organizations" as "I-NP".

2.2.5 Brown Clustering Labels

Similar words have similar distributions of words to their immediate left and right. Motivated by this intuition, Brown Clustering algorithm (Brown et al., 1992) gives an unsupervised class label to a word. Our system uses a C++ implementation [3] of the Brown clustering algorithm (Liang, 2005) and sets cluster number as 50. The Brown clusters was trained on a large corpus of APT reports [4] provided by the organizer.

2.3 Model Introduction

Similar to (Ma and Hovy, 2016), as shown in Figure 1, before feeding into the BiLSTM network, the model concatenates character-level representations obtained from CNN (LeCun et al., 1989), word-level representations and linguistic feature representations to acquire the final representation of the word. At the end, the model feeds the output

---

[1] https://stanfordnlp.github.io/CoreNLP/
[2] https://opennlp.apache.org/
[3] https://github.com/percyliang/brown-cluster
[4] https://www.atp.dk

vectors of BiLSTM into a CRF layer, using sentence level tag information to jointly decode sequence labels.

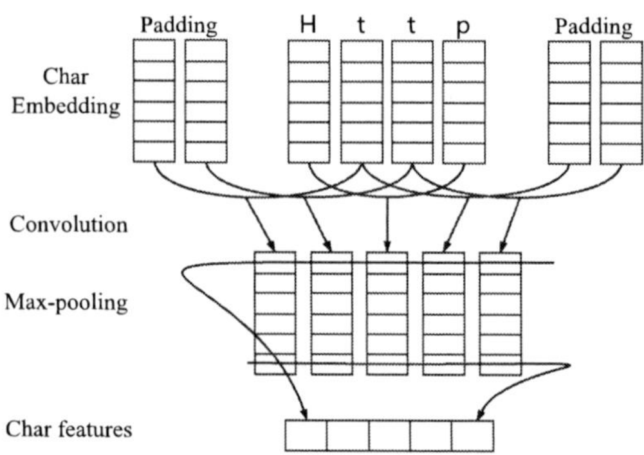

Figure 2: CNN feature extraction

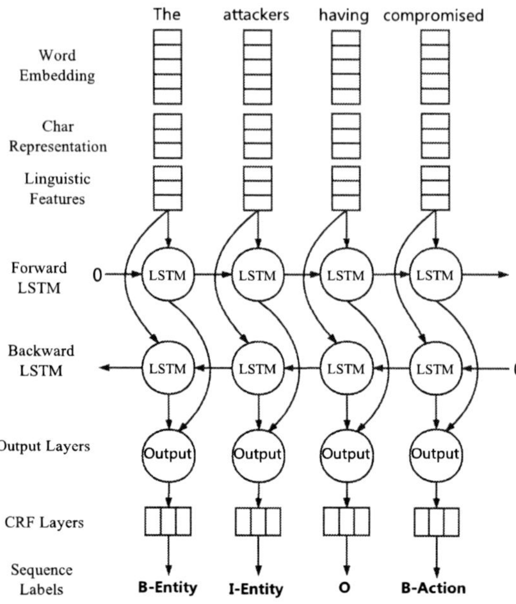

Figure 1: BiLSTM + CRF network architecture

Designing a neural network architecture with character representation as input is appealing for several reasons. First, words which have the same morphological properties(like the prefix or suffix of a word) often share the same grammatical function or meaning. Second, a character-level analysis can help to dual with the OOV (out-of-vocabulary) problem and the word starts with a capital letter may provide additional information. Previous studies (Santos and Zadrozny, 2014) (Chiu and Nichols, 2015) have shown that CNN is an effective approach to extract morphological information from characters of words, and consequently help to improve the performance of NER and POS tagging. As shown in Figure 2, we employ a max-pooling and a convolution layer to extract a new feature vector from character embeddings for each word. Then words are padded with a number of PADDING characters on both sides depending on the window size of the CNN.

2.3.1 BiLSTM for Word Representation

RNNs are well-studied solutions for a neural network to process variable length input and have

long term memory. As a variant of RNNs, the long-short term memory (LSTM) unit with three multiplicative gates allows highly non-trivial long-distance dependencies to be easily learned. For sequence labeling tasks, we use a bidirectional LSTM network proposed in (Graves et al., 2013) in order to efficiently utilize both past features (via forward states) and future features (via backward states) for a specific time frame. Furthermore, pre-trained word embeddings learned from large unlabeled data are used.

2.3.2 Neural Network with Features

Before feeding into the BiLSTM network, we concatenate the char embedding, word embedding, POS embedding, NER embedding, Chunking labels embedding, Brown Clustering labels embedding as input.

2.3.3 CRF Layer

For sequence labeling task, such as POS tagging or NER, the output labels adjacent are often strongly related(e.g. I-ORG cannot follow B-PER or I-LOC in NER task of CoNLL2003). Therefore, we model BiLSTM networks jointly using a CRF layer to decode each label.

2.3.4 Model Average

Random initialization and shuffling order of training sentences introduce randomization into model training. During experiments, we found that model predictions vary considerably even when the same pre-trained data and parameters are used. In order to utilize the power of models ensembling and avoid over-fitting problem, we use a script provided by tensor2tensor to average values

Model	Phrase Level			Token Level		
	Precision	Recall	F1-score	Precision	Recall	F1-score
CRF	0.4867	0.2374	0.3191	0.5766	0.2739	0.3714
CRF with Linguistic Features	0.4971	0.2627	0.3438	0.5839	0.2911	0.3885
BiLSTM-CRF	0.5082	0.4305	0.4661	0.6273	0.4296	0.5100
BiLSTM-CRF with Linguistic Features	0.5265	0.4410	0.4799	0.6354	0.4437	0.5225
BiLSTM-CNN-CRF	0.5289	0.4461	0.4840	0.6370	0.4456	0.5243
BiLSTM-CNN-CRF with Linguistic Features	**0.5436**	**0.4623**	**0.4997**	**0.6428**	**0.4531**	**0.5315**

Table 1: Experiment results in phrase level and token level.

of variables in a list of checkpoint files generated by BiLSTM-CNN-CRF networks[5].

3 Experiments and Analysis

3.1 Experiment Settings

We found that in the original dataset provided by organizers, the average percentage of positive samples dropped from 23% in training set to less than 6.6% in development set, which suggests that a model may be strongly biased if trained on the training set and fine-tuned on the development set without randomization. Therefore we combined the training data and development data after spelling correction and removal of unreadable characters. In order to avoid over-fitting problem, we adopted 5-fold cross validation by randomly splitting the combined data into five folds. Each time we took four folds as training data and the rest as development data.

We downloaded GloVe (Pennington et al., 2014) data as the source of pre-trained word embeddings. For char and feature embeddings, we randomly initialized them with values drawn from the standard normal distribution.

The evaluation metrics were calculated by the CoNLL2000 Perl script at token level and phrase level. For each level, precision, recall and F1-score were calculated. Based on the highest F1-score we selected the best hyper-parameters (CNN output size, LSTM State size, learning rate, dropout, etc.) for single model in 5-fold cross validation. Besides, for the submission generated by the BiLSTM-CNN-CRF, we adopted model average strategy by averaging values of variables of 5 checkpoint files from 5 independent experiments sharing the same experiment settings.

3.2 Experiment Results

Our experiments focus on improving the performance in phrase level because of two motivations: phrase level is more meaningful than token level and the model superior in phrase level also outperforms the others in token level.

The comparison of models in Table 1 shows that neural networks models significantly outperform the traditional model based on CRF. Meanwhile models including character-level features in pre-trained word embeddings show better result. Last but not least, models with additional linguistic features improve the performance in both phrase level and token level significantly.

4 Conclusion

This paper describes our system for Subtask 1 and Subtask 2 of SemEval-2018 Task 8. For Subtask 2 we design a BiLSTM-CNN-CRF model combining several hand-crafted features, such as POS tagging, NER labels, Chunking labels, etc. For Subtask 1 we simply use the output labels generated by Subtask 2 to classify where a sentence is relevant to malware. It can be observed that rich linguistic features and pre-trained word embeddings for large unlabeled data benefit the task. The system is proven valid and effective to achieve the highest F1-score in Subtask 2.

5 Future Work

The fact is our system is not good enough to help semantic extraction from CybersecUrity reports. In the future, we will design a multi-task network to solve Subtask 1 and Subtask 2 simultaneously since they are highly related. Besides, more features, e.g., stemming and lemmatization, can be utilized in predicting token labels.

Acknowledgments

We thank the task organizers for providing malware corpus and organizing the shared task 8. Furthermore, we also appreciate the peer reviewers for their helpful comments on our first draft. We are especially grateful to Li Xiaoning for his insightful advice on the understanding of CybersecUrity reports.

[5]https://github.com/tensorflow/tensor2tensor

References

Peter F Brown, Peter V Desouza, Robert L Mercer, Vincent J Della Pietra, and Jenifer C Lai. 1992. Class-based n-gram models of natural language. *Computational linguistics*, 18(4):467–479.

Jason PC Chiu and Eric Nichols. 2015. Named entity recognition with bidirectional lstm-cnns. *arXiv preprint arXiv:1511.08308*.

Jon DiMaggio. 2015. The black vine cyberespionage group. *Retrieved January*, 26:2016.

Sean R Eddy. 1996. Hidden markov models. *Current opinion in structural biology*, 6(3):361–365.

Alex Graves, Abdel-rahman Mohamed, and Geoffrey Hinton. 2013. Speech recognition with deep recurrent neural networks. In *Acoustics, speech and signal processing (icassp), 2013 ieee international conference on*, pages 6645–6649. IEEE.

Zhiheng Huang, Wei Xu, and Kai Yu. 2015. Bidirectional lstm-crf models for sequence tagging. *arXiv preprint arXiv:1508.01991*.

John Lafferty, Andrew McCallum, and Fernando CN Pereira. 2001. Conditional random fields: Probabilistic models for segmenting and labeling sequence data.

Guillaume Lample, Miguel Ballesteros, Sandeep Subramanian, Kazuya Kawakami, and Chris Dyer. 2016. Neural architectures for named entity recognition. *arXiv preprint arXiv:1603.01360*.

Yann LeCun, Bernhard Boser, John S Denker, Donnie Henderson, Richard E Howard, Wayne Hubbard, and Lawrence D Jackel. 1989. Backpropagation applied to handwritten zip code recognition. *Neural computation*, 1(4):541–551.

Percy Liang. 2005. *Semi-supervised learning for natural language*. Ph.D. thesis, Massachusetts Institute of Technology.

Swee Kiat Lim, Aldrian Obaja Muis, Wei Lu, and Chen Hui Ong. 2017. Malwaretextdb: A database for annotated malware articles. In *Proceedings of the 55th Annual Meeting of the Association for Computational Linguistics (Volume 1: Long Papers)*, volume 1, pages 1557–1567.

Xuezhe Ma and Eduard Hovy. 2016. End-to-end sequence labeling via bi-directional lstm-cnns-crf. *arXiv preprint arXiv:1603.01354*.

Christopher Manning, Mihai Surdeanu, John Bauer, Jenny Finkel, Steven Bethard, and David McClosky. 2014. The stanford corenlp natural language processing toolkit. In *Proceedings of 52nd annual meeting of the association for computational linguistics: system demonstrations*, pages 55–60.

Jeffrey Pennington, Richard Socher, and Christopher D. Manning. 2014. Glove: Global vectors for word representation. In *Empirical Methods in Natural Language Processing (EMNLP)*, pages 1532–1543.

Peter Phandi, Amila Silva, and Wei Lu. 2018. Semeval-2018 Task 8: Semantic Extraction from CybersecUrity REports using Natural Language Processing (SecureNLP). In *Proceedings of International Workshop on Semantic Evaluation (SemEval-2018)*, New Orleans, LA, USA.

Cicero D Santos and Bianca Zadrozny. 2014. Learning character-level representations for part-of-speech tagging. In *Proceedings of the 31st International Conference on Machine Learning (ICML-14)*, pages 1818–1826.

Yushi Yao and Zheng Huang. 2016. Bi-directional lstm recurrent neural network for chinese word segmentation. In *International Conference on Neural Information Processing*, pages 345–353. Springer.

SemEval-2018 Task 9: Hypernym Discovery

Jose Camacho-Collados♣   Claudio Delli Bovi♡   Luis Espinosa-Anke♣
Sergio Oramas◇   Tommaso Pasini♡   Enrico Santus♥
Vered Shwartz♠   Roberto Navigli♡   Horacio Saggion◇
♣School of Computer Science and Informatics, Cardiff University, United Kingdom
♡ Computer Science Department, Sapienza University of Rome, Italy
◇ Pompeu Fabra University, Barcelona, Spain   ♥ MIT, United States
♠ Bar-Ilan University, Ramat Gan, Israel
♣{camachocolladosj,espinosa-ankel}@cardiff.ac.uk,
♡{dellibovi,pasini,navigli}@di.uniroma1.it,
◇{name.surname}@upf.edu, ♥esantus@mit.edu, ♠vered1986@gmail.com

Abstract

This paper describes the SemEval 2018 Shared Task on Hypernym Discovery. We put forward this task as a complementary benchmark for modeling hypernymy, a problem which has traditionally been cast as a binary classification task, taking a pair of candidate words as input. Instead, our reformulated task is defined as follows: given an input term, retrieve (or discover) its suitable hypernyms from a target corpus. We proposed five different subtasks covering three languages (English, Spanish, and Italian), and two specific domains of knowledge in English (Medical and Music). Participants were allowed to compete in any or all of the subtasks. Overall, a total of 11 teams participated, with a total of 39 different systems submitted through all subtasks. Data, results and further information about the task can be found at https://competitions.codalab.org/competitions/17119.

1 Introduction

Hypernymy, i.e. the capability to relate generic terms or classes to their specific instances, lies at the core of human cognition. It is not surprising, therefore, that identifying hypernymic (*is-a*) relations has been pursued in NLP for more than two decades (Shwartz et al., 2016): indeed, successfully identifying this lexical relation substantially improves Question Answering applications (Prager et al., 2008; Yahya et al., 2013), Textual Entailment and Semantic Search systems (Hoffart et al., 2014; Roller et al., 2014; Roller and Erk, 2016). In addition, hypernymic relations are the backbone of almost every ontology, semantic network and taxonomy (Yu et al., 2015), which are in turn useful resources for downstream tasks such as web retrieval, website navigation or records management (Bordea et al., 2015).

Generally, evaluation benchmarks for modeling hypernymy have been designed such that in most cases they are reduced to binary classification (Baroni and Lenci, 2011; Snow et al., 2004; Boleda et al., 2017; Vyas and Carpuat, 2017), where a system has to decide whether a hypernymic relation holds between a given candidate pair of terms. Criticisms to this experimental setting point out that supervised systems tend to benefit from the inherent modeling of the datasets in the hypernym detection task, leading to lexical memorization phenomena (Levy et al., 2015; Santus et al., 2016a; Shwartz et al., 2017). In this respect, recent work has attempted to alleviate this issue by including a graded scale for evaluating the degree of hypernymy on a given pair (Vulić et al., 2017).

Crucially, Espinosa-Anke et al. (2016) proposed to frame the problem as *Hypernym Discovery*, i.e. given the search space of a domain's vocabulary, and given an input term, discover its best (list of) candidate hypernyms. This formulation addresses one of the main drawbacks of the evaluation criterion described above, and better frames the evaluated systems within downstream real-world applications (Camacho-Collados, 2017). In fact, lessons learned from these studies have motivated the construction of a full-fledged benchmarking dataset for the shared task we present here, which covers multiple languages and knowledge domains. The main goal of this task is that of complementing current research in hypernymy modeling with this novel discovery setting.

Proceedings of the 12th International Workshop on Semantic Evaluation (SemEval-2018), pages 712–724
New Orleans, Louisiana, June 5–6, 2018. ©2018 Association for Computational Linguistics

	Term	Hypernym(s)	Source
1A: English	sorrow	sadness, unhappiness	WordNet
1B: Italian	Nina Simone	musicista, pianista, persona	MultiWibi
1C: Spanish	guacamole	salsa para mojar, salsa, alimento	Wikidata (via BabelNet)
2A: Medical	pulmonary embolism	pulmonary artery finding, trunk arterial embolus, embolism	SnomedCT
2B: Music	Green Day	artist, rock band, band	MusicBrainz

Table 1: Some example terms and hypernyms extracted from different sources (see Section 4.1.4), for each of the subtasks and languages considered in the task.

2 Related Work

Traditionally, identifying hypernymic relations from text corpora has been addressed with two main approaches: pattern-based and distributional (Wang et al., 2017). Pattern-based (path-based) methods, which provide higher precision at the price of lower coverage, exploit the co-occurrence of a hyponym and its hypernym in a textual corpus (Hearst, 1992; Navigli and Velardi, 2010; Boella and Di Caro, 2013; Flati et al., 2016; Gupta et al., 2016; Pavlick and Pasca, 2017). Conversely, distributional models rely on a distributional representation for each observed word, and are capable of identifying hypernymic relations between concepts even when they do not co-occur explicitly in text. Earlier work on hypernym modeling was unsupervised, and leveraged various interpretations of the distributional hypothesis.[1] Most of the recent work on the subject is however supervised, and in the main based on using word embeddings as input for classification or prediction (e.g Baroni et al., 2012; Santus et al., 2014; Fu et al., 2014; Weeds et al., 2014; Espinosa-Anke et al., 2016; Sanchez Carmona and Riedel, 2017; Nguyen et al., 2017). As shown by Shwartz et al. (2016), pattern-based and distributional evidences can be effectively combined within a neural architecture. In this shared task we have actually received systems of both natures, including a combination of pattern-based and distributional cues, similar to the one mentioned above, which also proved to be highly effective (see Section 5).

3 Task Description

We define Hypernym Discovery operatively as the task of finding and extracting the appropriate hypernym(s) for a target input term. As input for the task, together with the target term,[2] a large textual corpus (*source corpus* henceforth) is provided, and participating systems are intended to exploit this large source of textual data to retrieve (i.e. "discover") as many suitable hypernyms as possible for the target term. A different source corpus, as well as the corresponding vocabulary, is specified for each subtask and language (cf. Section 4) in order to set a level playing field for competing systems, and constrain their search space.

For each input term (or *hyponym*) the expected output is a ranked list of *candidate hypernyms* (up to 15) drawn from the provided vocabulary. Some example input-output pairs (i.e. terms and corresponding hypernym lists) are shown in Table 1 for each subtask and language. Table 1 also reports the sources of hypernymy information beside each pair, which vary depending on the subtask and language, as detailed in Section 4.1.4.

The structure of our Hypernym Discovery task consists of five independent but related subtasks, split into two larger groups: *general-purpose* hypernym discovery and *domain-specific* hypernym discovery. Participants were allowed to submit systems for any individual subtask. Along with a specific source corpus and vocabulary, each subtask features its specific training and testing data, consisting of input terms and corresponding gold hypernym lists, obtained as described throughout Section 4.

General-Purpose Hypernym Discovery consists in discovering hypernyms in a large corpus of general-purpose textual data, gathered from different and heterogeneous sources. A system operating in this setting requires the flexibility to provide hypernyms for terms in a wide range of domains. In this shared task we consider three different lan-

---

[1] See Shwartz et al. (2017) for a detailed review on unsupervised distributional hypernymy detection.

[2] A valid input term is any word or multi-word expression drawn from the predefined vocabulary (cf. Section 4.1.2) up to trigrams.

guages for general-purpose hypernym discovery:

- **English (subtask 1A)**, with a gold standard of 3,000 labeled terms;

- **Italian (subtask 1B)** and **Spanish (subtask 1C)**, each with a gold standard of 2,000 labeled terms;

All the gold standards provide a balanced set of input terms, with different degrees of frequency and for different domains. The corresponding gold hypernyms have been extracted from multiple resources and manually validated (cf. Sections 4.1.4-4.1.5). Training and testing data are split evenly (50% training - 50% testing).

Domain-Specific Hypernym Discovery deals with the same problem, but constrains it to a specific domain of knowledge. As a consequence, in this case participants test their systems (which might be general or specifically tailored to the target domain) in a much more focused and reduced environment. In this shared task we focus on English and consider two different domains of knowledge:

- **Medical (subtask 2A)**, with a gold standard of 1,000 labeled terms;

- **Music (subtask 2B)**, also with a gold standard of 1,000 labeled terms;

As in the previous subtask, we provide a balanced set of terms and gold hypernyms, with different degrees of frequency and for different subdomains. Again, training and testing data are split evenly (50% training - 50% testing).

Subclass vs. Instance. Although many hypernym detection approaches tend to overlook this distinction, it is customary to consider two different varieties of the "is-a" relation: a `subclass-of` variety (e.g. a dog *is a* mammal), and an `instance-of` variety (e.g. Rome *is a* city).[3] From a practical standpoint, the former occurs between two concepts, while the latter connects a named entity with a concept. We make this distinction explicit in our shared task by hand-labeling each input term as either a concept or a

named entity. This strategy serves a double purpose: on one hand, it helps reducing lexical ambiguity, and narrowing the search space of potential hypernyms even further;[4] on the other hand, it enables participants to study and develop models specifically tailored to one of the two varieties, and possibly submit them separately. In this respect, Boleda et al. (2017) has indeed shown how systems tend to perform differently on these two kinds of hypernymy relation.

4 Task Data

In this section we present the data collection process carried out for each source corpus and gold standard featured in the task (Section 4.1). We then summarize and provide some global statistics on all these datasets (Section 4.2).

4.1 Data Collection Process

The process of collecting data for each subtask and language comprised five successive steps: compilation of the source corpus (Section 4.1.1), creation of the vocabulary (Section 4.1.2), collection and selection of the input terms (Section 4.1.3), extraction of the gold hypernyms (Section 4.1.4), and final filtering and validation of such hypernyms (Section 4.1.5).

4.1.1 Corpus Compilation

First, we selected and compiled a source corpus for each dataset, which was also considered in the vocabulary creation step (Section 4.1.2). Naturally, we considered three corpora as general and as large as possible for the general-purpose track, whereas for the domain-specific datasets we opted for more targeted and specific text collections.

General-purpose corpora. As source corpus for the English subtask (1A) we used the 3-billion-word UMBC corpus[5] (Han et al., 2013), which is a resource composed of paragraphs extracted from the web as part of the Stanford WebBase Project[6] (Hirai et al. 2000). The UMBC corpus is considerably large and contains information from many and diverse domains. This corpus presents additional challenges and different

---

[3]In fact, WordNet encodes `hypernym` and `instance` as two separate semantic relations. Instances are always leaf (terminal) nodes in their hierarchies.

[4]As an example, the term *apple* could either refer to a fruit (if labeled as concept) or to a company (if labeled as named entity).

[5]`http://ebiquity.umbc.edu/blogger/2013/05/01/umbc-webbase-corpus-of-3b-english-words/`

[6]`http://dbpubs.stanford.edu:8091/~testbed/doc2/WebBase/`

sources of information with respect to the corpora used in previous tasks, such as Wikipedia in the SemEval 2016 task on taxonomy extraction (Bordea et al., 2016). In fact, the encyclopedic nature of Wikipedia has been exploited in a wide variety of works (Ponzetto and Strube, 2007; Flati et al., 2016; Gupta et al., 2016), and differs substantially from the web-based corpus we put forward here. As source corpus for the Italian subtask (1B) we instead used the 1.3-billion-word itWac corpus[7] (Baroni et al., 2009), extracted from different sources of the web within the `.it` domain. Finally, as source corpus for the Spanish subtask (1C) we considered the 1.8-billion-word Spanish corpus[8] (Cardellino, 2016), which also contains heterogeneous documents from different sources.

Domain-specific corpora. As source corpus for the medical domain (subtask 2A) we provided a combination of texts drawn from the MEDLINE[9] (Medical Literature Analysis and Retrieval System) repository, which contains academic documents such as scientific publications and paper abstracts. This corpus contains 130 million words. As regards the music domain (subtask 2B), instead, the source corpus we compiled is a concatenation of several music-specific corpora, i.e. music biographies from `Last.fm` contained in ELMD 2.0 (Oramas et al., 2016), articles from the music branch of Wikipedia, and a corpus of album customer reviews from Amazon (Oramas et al., 2017). The resulting corpus reaches 100 million words in total.

4.1.2 Vocabulary Creation

With the aim of simplifying the task for participants by providing a unified hypernym search space, we built a series of vocabulary files including all the possible hypernyms on each dataset. Each vocabulary was constructed by considering all the words occurring at least N times across the source corpus of the corresponding subtask. We set N to five and three in the general-purpose and domain-specific subtasks, respectively. We also included bigrams and trigrams, by considering all the instances present in any of the resources that we leveraged as part of the hypernym extraction process (see Section 4.1.4), provided that they also surpassed the corresponding frequency thresholds.

In order to reduce the high granularity of some hypernymy relations (for example, *dog* is an *entity*) we created an additional blacklist of very general terms not considered in the vocabulary files. This list was obtained semi-automatically. We first extracted the most common hypernyms from the lexical sources we used for creating the datasets. Then, we filtered the resulting blacklist by removing manually a number of suitable hypernyms that, despite being general, provided useful information worthy to be taken into account (e.g. *animal*).

4.1.3 Term Collection

After compiling a source corpus and a corresponding vocabulary, we selected a suitable collection of input terms (i.e. hyponyms) to construct the gold standard for each subtask. Term selection was based on three key constraints. First, as in vocabulary creation step (Section 4.1.2), input terms were required to occur five and three times in the general-purpose and domain-specific datasets, respectively. Second, only terms up to trigrams were considered. Finally, we only allowed terms with at least one extracted hypernym (see Section 4.1.4) present in the corresponding vocabulary file.

We carried out the term collection process with a semi-automatic two-pass procedure, which we applied to the source corpus of each subtask. First, candidate terms were extracted automatically from the source corpus, taking into account frequency, type (i.e. concept and entity) and knowledge domain[10] in order to produce a list as balanced and representative as possible. After a preliminary list of input terms was obtained, we carried out an extensive validation and refinement step by manually normalizing each item (e.g. changing plurals to singulars, capitalizing named entities and lowercasing concepts), and by pruning all the terms that appeared too vague or general, as well as terms with mis-attributed domains.

4.1.4 Automatic Hypernym Extraction

Once the terms were collected we proceeded to extract a set of candidate hypernyms from a number of heterogeneous taxonomies. We drew taxonomic information from the following lexical resources: WordNet (Miller, 1995), Wikidata

---

[7]http://wacky.sslmit.unibo.it/doku.php?id=corpora

[8]http://crscardellino.me/SBWCE/

[9]https://www.nlm.nih.gov/databases/download/pubmed_medline.html

[10]We leveraged the domains from the Wikipedia featured articles pages available in BabelDomains (Camacho-Collados and Navigli, 2017).

(Vrandečić and Krötzsch, 2014), MultiWiBi (Flati et al., 2016), and Yago (Suchanek et al., 2007). In order to be able to use seamlessly all hypernymy information for languages other than English, we exploited the inter-resource mappings provided by BabelNet (Navigli and Ponzetto, 2012).[11] For the domain-specific datasets we additionally used SnomedCT (Spackman et al., 1997) and MusicBrainz (Swartz, 2002) for the medical and music datasets, respectively.

The hypernym extraction process was carried out as follows: given a term (hyponym), we first retrieved all the BabelNet synsets which included the given term as lexicalization; then, starting from that synset, we iteratively visited the father nodes across all the reference taxonomies up to five levels[12] and selected all the lexicalizations of the traversed synsets (i.e. concepts) as given by BabelNet, provided that they appeared in the corresponding vocabulary files (see Section 4.1.2).

4.1.5 Hypernym Validation

Starting from the candidate gold hypernyms extracted in the previous step, we carried out a validation step using human annotators. We leveraged crowdsourcing for the English data in subtask 1A (which featured the largest dataset), and then expert verification in all subtasks (including English).

Crowdsourcing. We validated the English gold standard (both training and test set) by using crowdsourcing workers from Amazon Mechanical Turk. To ensure the quality of workers, we required workers to have answered at least 500 prior HITs with an approval rate of at least 95%, and applied a qualification test. For each target term, we showed the workers multiple candidate hypernyms, extracted in the previous step (Section 4.1.4), and asked them to select all the correct hypernyms. We also added 20% of random false candidates to prevent bias towards a positive answer. Finally, we assigned each HIT to 3 workers and determined the gold label with majority voting. The resulting annotations yielded an inter-annotator agreement of 73%.

---

[11] Yago is the only resource which is not mapped to Babel-Net. For the mapping we simply relied on the WordNet and Wikipedia identifiers provided in Yago.

[12] We decided to consider only five levels for two reasons: first, to avoid very general hypernyms; and second, to avoid errors which would propagate to other levels and make the validation task much harder. To this aim, five levels seemed to provide a fine balance between precision and recall.

	1A	1B	1C	2A	2B
Trial	50	25	25	15	15
Training	1,500	1,000	1,000	500	500
Test	1,500	1,000	1,000	500	500

Table 2: Number of terms (hyponyms) for each dataset in trial, training and test sets.

Expert verification. Expert verification comprised two steps. First, all the extracted data was verified by an expert human annotator. In this first step, the annotator was focused on removing the incorrect hypernyms, or normalizing them if required (e.g. plural to singular). This first verification was performed in all dataset except English, which underwent the crowsourcing validation explained earlier. Then, all datasets (including the English one) were again verified by other experts. However, in this case the annotators were given different guidelines: in particular, they were asked to fix clear hypernym errors (which may have been missed in the previous step) and to add obvious hypernyms which they found to be missing.

4.2 Statistics

Table 2 shows the number of input terms in each dataset. The dataset was split equally in training and testing, while the trial data provided a fewer examples and could also be used as development set. English (subtask 1A) was the largest dataset with 1,500 terms (hyponyms) and for training and other 1,500 for testing. Then, for the Italian (subtask 1B) and Spanish (subtask 1C) datasets, 2,000 terms were given overall between training and testing. Finally, both domain-specific datasets (i.e. medical, subtask 2A, and music, subtask 2B) contained half of this quantity, with 1,000 terms each.

Note that each term may be associated with one or (in most cases) more than one hypernym. Therefore, counting all the term-hypernym pairs per dataset, as it is done in hypernymy detection datasets, would provide much larger figures. As an example, the number of term-hypernym pairs in the test gold standard is 7,048 for English, 4,770 for Italian, 6,070 for Spanish, 4,116 for the medical dataset, and 5,233 for the music dataset.

5 Evaluation

Parting ways from the classic precision-recall-F_1 metrics used so far in hypernym detection/extraction, we decided to evaluate this shared task as a soft ranking problem. Systems were evaluated over the top 15 (at most) hypernyms retrieved for each input term, which let us assess their performance through Information Retrieval metrics. Let us briefly introduce each of them.

Mean Average Precision (MAP). We use MAP as the main evaluation metric of this task. Intuitively, this metric should give a fine estimate on the capability of a system to retrieve a sizable number of hypernyms from textual data, as well as considering the precision of each of them. Formally:

$$\text{MAP} = \frac{1}{|Q|} \sum_{q \in Q} \text{AP}(q)$$

where Q is a sample of experiment runs, $\text{AP}(\cdot)$ refers to *average precision*, i.e. an average of the correctness of each individual obtained hypernym from the search space.

Mean Reciprocal Rank (MRR). MRR rewards the position of the first correct result in a ranked list of outcomes, and is defined as:

$$\text{MRR} = \frac{1}{|Q|} \sum_{i=1}^{|Q|} \frac{1}{rank_i}$$

where $rank_i$ refers to the rank position of the *first* relevant outcome for the ith run. While its main field of application is Information Retrieval, it has also been used in NLP tasks such as collocation recognition (Wu et al., 2010; Rodríguez-Fernández et al., 2016).

In addition to the above, we also provide results according to **P@k**, i.e. the number of correctly retrieved hypernyms at different cut-off thresholds, specifically $k \in \{1, 3, 5, 15\}$.[13]

5.1 Baselines

We compared the participating systems with both supervised and unsupervised baselines for each subtask, inspired by recent work on hypernym detection and discovery. In this section we briefly describe each of them.

5.1.1 Supervised Baselines

We first used a naïve *most frequent hypernym* (**MFH**) baseline, which simply returns, for each input term, the 15 most frequent hypernyms found in the training data. As a less naïve baseline, we also trained a *transformation matrix* (Mikolov et al., 2013; Fu et al., 2014), using the same optimization described by Espinosa-Anke et al. (2016). For this baseline the hypernyms in the vocabulary which are among the fifteen closest vectors by applying the transformation matrix are retrieved. However, unlike in the original implementation, in this case we did not perform any a priori domain clustering of the embeddings space, and thus used the same matrix for all input terms.[14] This second supervised baseline is referred to as **vTE** (*vanilla Taxoembed*).

5.1.2 Unsupervised Baselines

We developed an unsupervised baseline by reducing hypernymy discovery to hypernymy detection. We generated a list of candidate hypernyms for each target word, and then employed unsupervised hypernymy detection measures to decide whether a hypernymy relation holds. We used the open-source code by Shwartz et al. (2017).[15]

Our baseline starts by creating a distributional semantic model (DSM) for each domain/language (English, Spanish, Italian, Music and Medical). We used a non-directional window of size 5 as context type, and PPMI as feature weighting. Similarly to the hyponym selection step (Section 4.1.3), all the terms with frequency of at least 3 occurrences in the source corpus are considered as valid targets. For the context words, instead, we required a minimum of 100 occurrences, as in Shwartz et al. (2017). To generate candidates, we took the 50 most similar terms for each target word via cosine similarity in the DSM.

We chose the hypernym detection measures as representative algorithms from each "family" of unsupervised measures: **APSyn** (Santus et al., 2016b) as similarity measure, **balAPInc** (Kotlerman et al., 2010) as measure based on the distributional inclusion hypothesis, and **SLQS** (Santus et al., 2014) as measure based on informativeness.[16] Finally, we tuned the thresholds for the above measures by maximizing the average of the performance metrics on the training set, separately for each subtask and measure.

---

[13] Although only P@5 is displayed in the tables due to lack of space, the other thresholds were used in the official evaluation as well.

[14] We used the open-source code available at `https://bitbucket.org/luisespinosa/taxoembed`

[15] `https://github.com/vered1986/UnsupervisedHypernymy`

[16] Following the conclusions from Shwartz et al. (2017), we set the hyper-parameters to: SLQS: median, PLMI, $N = 100$ and APSyn: $N = 500$.

5.2 Participant Systems

Table 3 shows a summary of all participant systems, displaying their main features with respect to supervison and external resources used, if any.

5.3 Results

A summary of the results is provided in tables 3 to 7, respectively describing results for English, Italian, Spanish and Music and Medical domains. Almost all systems performed better than the unsupervised baselines, while the supervised ones showed to be more challenging, with few systems outperforming them. For English, Music and Medical domains, **CRIM** (Bernier-Colborne and Barriere, 2018) obtained the best results, with a large margin on the other systems and baselines. This system is based on learning a projection between hyponym-hypernym pairs in terms of their corresponding embeddings, and combines this module with an unsupervised system which uses Hearst-style patterns. Moreover, in Italian, the best system was **300-sparsans_r1** (Berend et al., 2018), a logistic regression model informed mostly with information coming from word embeddings; whereas for Spanish, the best performing team was **NLP_HZ** (Qiu et al., 2018), who approached the task with a nearest neighbors algorithm trained with the provided training data.

From the summary tables we can also appreciate the difference in performance of the systems on concepts and entities. Such difference is due to several factors, including the quantity and type of hypernyms that needed to be identified for the two subclasses. Except for the Music domain, systems tended to perform better with entities than with concepts. This is probably due to the fact that entities contain many hypernyms which appear often (e.g. *person*, *company*), which in principle favor the inherent lexical memorization (Levy et al., 2015) of supervised systems. Hence, as expected, systems performed better in the specialized domains (i.e. medical and music) than in the general-domain dataset (34.05% and 40.97% MAP performance by the best systems in the medical and music domains, respectively, compared to the 19.78% result of the best system in the English dataset).

Finally, the results also show the clear superiority of supervised systems over unsupervised approaches in all languages and domains. As far as fully unsupervised systems are concerned, they achieved a diverse degree of success. While in general they were outperformed by supervised systems, in some cases their performance came close, especially for concepts. For instance, the **ADAPT** (Maldonado and Klubika, 2018) system, which is based on a simple similarity measure applied to word embeddings, achieved a very decent 8.13 MAP percentage performance on the medical dataset, using neither supervision nor external resources. Supervised systems produced a larger gap for entities, probably due, as mentioned above, to the lower diversity of possible hypernyms.

Cross-evaluation. In addition to the normal setting on which supervised systems trained their system on the same dataset training data, we ask participants to train systems on the English general-purpose data and trained on the domain-specific datasets. This experiment could enable us to test how a system could perform on a particular dataset when training data is not available. A few teams provided results on this setting and the results showed that even though trained on general data, they are still competitive with respect to other approaches. In fact, they tend to equally outperform unsupervised systems and in the medical dataset, for example, CRIM trained on the general English corpora outperformed all remaining participant systems trained on the medical training data.

6 Analysis

Inspired by previous tasks in taxonomy learning (Bordea et al., 2015), we sampled for each system 50 incorrect hypernyms (25 entities, 25 concepts) which were retrieved as first choice, and manually assessed their correctness. This evaluation of false positives is intended to account for the inevitable scenario in which not all possible correct hypernyms according to human judgement were included in the gold standard. The results in false positives were measured by accuracy (i.e. percentage of correct false positives on the given sample) and are displayed in Tables 4-8 under *FPs*.

In general, we observe that the systems' performances in this false positives experiment are correlated with the figures they obtained with the other automatic evaluation measures. Nonetheless, according to this false positives evaluation, most systems (both supervised and unsupervised) were able to retrieve some hypernyms which were not present in the gold standard. This result is encouraging, as not only hypernym discovery sys-

	Team Name	Reference	Supervision	External Resources
	CRIM	(Bernier-Colborne and Barrière, 2018)	✓	-
	MSCG-SANITY	-	✓	Microsoft Concept Graph
	NLP_HZ	(Qiu et al., 2018)	✓	-
	300-sparsans	(Berend et al., 2018)	✓	-
	SJTU BCMI	(Zhang et al., 2018)	✓	-
Systems	UMDuluth	(Hassan et al., 2018)	✓	-
	ADAPT	(Maldonado and Klubika, 2018)		-
	Apollo	(Onofrei et al., 2018)		-
	EXPR	(Issa Alaa Aldine et al., 2018)		-
	Team 13	-		-
	Anu	-		WordNet
	vanillaTaxoEmbed	(Espinosa-Anke et al., 2016)	✓	-
	MFH	-	✓	-
Baselines	APSyn	(Shwartz et al., 2017)		-
	balAPInc	(Shwartz et al., 2017)		-
	SLQS	(Shwartz et al., 2017)		-

Table 3: Summary of participating systems and baselines, along with their main features (i.e. with or without supervision, and usage of external resources).

		1A: English										
	Concepts				**Entities**				**All**			
	MAP	MRR	P@5	FPs	MAP	MRR	P@5	FPs	MAP	MRR	P@5	FPs
CRIM_r1	**16.08**	**30.04**	**15.41**	20	**29.21**	**51.82**	**27.74**	24	**19.78**	**36.10**	**19.03**	22
CRIM_r2	15.49	29.29	14.97	24	28.63	50.55	27.65	20	19.54	35.94	18.74	22
MSCG-SANITY_r1	9.36	18.9	9.38	28	17.72	38.85	16.91	20	11.83	24.79	11.60	24
vTE*	6.99	16.05	6.55	**36**	19.22	42.39	17.92	12	10.60	23.83	9.91	24
MSCG-SANITY_r2	8.66	17.24	8.76	24	12.49	28.20	12.09	**40**	9.80	20.48	9.74	**32**
NLP_HZ	7.17	13.13	7.11	24	14.61	27.21	14.14	20	9.37	17.29	9.19	22
300-sparsans_r1	6.41	13.92	6.33	24	15.02	32.61	14.10	16	8.95	19.44	8.63	20
MFH*	4.73	12.48	4.13	0	18.42	42.65	16.59	16	8.77	21.39	7.81	8
300-sparsans_r2	5.97	12.72	5.73	20	14.78	30.62	14.21	20	8.58	18.00	8.23	20
SJTU BCMI	3.29	5.68	3.57	0	11.70	22.19	11.67	12	5.77	10.56	5.96	6
Team 13	3.70	7.92	3.66	12	0.52	1.65	0.46	20	2.77	6.07	2.72	16
Apollo_r2	2.72	6.05	2.76	16	2.60	5.91	2.51	20	2.68	6.01	2.69	18
Apollo_r1	1.36	3.28	1.34	16	1.48	4.05	1.31	16	1.40	3.51	1.33	16
APSyn*	1.73	3.69	1.74	16	0.55	1.41	0.55	4	1.38	3.02	1.39	10
balAPInc*	1.73	3.87	1.67	8	0.47	1.53	0.44	4	1.36	3.18	1.30	6
SLQS*	0.70	1.68	0.73	4	0.37	0.92	0.33	4	0.60	1.46	0.61	4
UMDuluth_C	8.13	18.93	7.53	20	-	-	-	-	-	-	-	-
EXPR_C	4.94	11.64	4.52	16	-	-	-	-	-	-	-	-
UMDuluth_E	-	-	-	-	3.79	9.99	3.66	28	-	-	-	-

Table 4: Results for the English subtask (1A). Baselines are marked with *, and those system participating only on Concepts or Entities are shown at the bottom and marked with either 'C' or 'E'.

tems can be used to speed up the hypernym discovery process, but they can also provide new hypernyms not considered beforehand.

Unsupervised distributional methods (e.g. the unsupervised baselines) seemed to perform poorly overall, as these systems tended to retrieve similar words which are not necessarily hypernyms. For example, false positives for APSyn and balAPInc are characterized by a large number of cohyponyms (e.g. *Exodus* and *Genesis*) and syntagmatically related words (e.g. *orange* and *juice*).

As regards the top performing systems, it is worth noting that they often tended to retrieve correct or near-correct hypernyms. The hypernyms that were retrieved on the gold standard were of several kinds: first, some hypernyms were present in the gold standard but normalized differently (for example, for *About.com* the gold standard contained *website* but not *web site* retrieved by CRIM_r1); second, they retrieved hy-

| 1B: Italian | | | | | | | | | | | |
| Concepts | | | | Entities | | | | All | | | |
	MAP	MRR	P@5	FPs	MAP	MRR	P@5	FPs	MAP	MRR	P@5	FPs
300-sparsans_r1	**8.94**	**18.77**	8.71	12	**22.56**	**46.34**	**21.79**	16	**12.08**	**25.14**	**11.73**	14
NLP_HZ	9.28	15.23	**9.12**	12	18.32	32.37	18.26	**28**	11.37	19.19	11.23	**20**
300-sparsans_r2	7.32	16.02	7.31	**16**	16.18	36.12	16.02	12	9.36	19.94	9.32	14
MFH*	5.07	13.30	4.31	0	16.71	39.56	15.18	8	7.76	19.37	6.82	4
vTE*	4.85	11.09	4.62	12	13.74	33.08	12.63	16	6.91	16.17	6.47	14
balAPInc*	4.84	10.71	4.84	**16**	0.72	1.96	0.77	4	3.89	8.69	3.90	10
APSyn*	4.30	9.50	4.33	12	1.00	2.06	1.00	4	3.54	7.56	3.56	8
SLQS*	2.02	4.02	2.07	4	0.26	0.75	0.17	0	1.62	3.26	1.63	2
Team 13	0.62	1.69	0.57	8	0.13	0.27	0.17	8	0.51	1.36	0.48	8

Table 5: Results for the Italian subtask (1B). Baselines are marked with *.

| 1C: Spanish | | | | | | | | | | | |
| Concepts | | | | Entities | | | | All | | | |
	MAP	MRR	P@5	FPs	MAP	MRR	P@5	FPs	MAP	MRR	P@5	FPs
NLP_HZ	**18.17**	25.17	**18.71**	12	23.19	33.48	23.21	**24**	**20.04**	28.27	**20.39**	**18**
300-sparsans_r1	13.21	**28.07**	12.80	8	**25.91**	**53.51**	**24.24**	4	17.94	**37.56**	17.06	6
300-sparsans_r2	11.10	22.90	11.07	**20**	14.92	30.87	15.14	12	12.52	25.87	12.59	16
MFH*	8.33	17.19	8.51	0	18.58	50.89	15.88	8	12.16	29.76	11.26	4
vTE*	6.08	14.32	6.01	12	8.84	20.96	9.10	4	7.11	16.80	7.16	8
balAPInc*	3.52	7.99	3.62	0	0.59	1.39	0.55	0	2.43	5.53	2.48	0
APSyn*	3.28	6.76	3.29	8	0.74	1.71	0.79	0	2.33	4.88	2.35	4
Team 13	2.57	6.08	2.06	12	0.06	0.13	0.05	4	1.63	4.31	1.65	8
SLQS*	1.21	2.27	1.14	0	0.37	0.89	0.32	0	0.90	1.75	0.83	0

Table 6: Results for the Spanish subtask (1C). Baselines are marked with *.

| 2B: Music | | | | | | | | | | | |
| Concepts | | | | Entities | | | | All | | | |
	MAP	MRR	P@5	FPs	MAP	MRR	P@5	FPs	MAP	MRR	P@5	FPs
CRIM_r1	**43.38**	**63.79**	**43.87**	24	38.42	55.54	38.76	12	**40.97**	**60.93**	41.31	16
CRIM_r2	41.98	63.07	42.32	20	34.59	51.08	35.80	8	40.88	60.18	**41.58**	16
MFH*	33.56	56.82	35.22	0	32.72	38.03	37.11	0	33.32	51.48	35.76	0
300-sparsans_r1	23.52	39.26	22.66	16	**44.71**	**64.53**	**44.48**	20	29.54	46.43	28.86	18
CRIM_CE	24.62	42.92	25.46	8	11.93	24.03	12.24	16	21.20	37.55	21.70	12
300-sparsans_r2	12.49	27.33	12.79	20	35.72	60.35	38.63	4	19.08	36.71	20.13	12
vTE*	11.53	35.78	10.28	12	16.67	48.39	17.77	20	12.99	39.36	12.41	16
Anu	10.68	27.13	10.84	**32**	3.43	7.19	3.90	8	8.62	21.47	8.87	**20**
vTE*_CE	6.31	16.54	6.81	4	13.37	33.58	14.87	4	3.51	9.79	3.62	4
SJTU BCMI	5.16	9.84	5.41	4	6.30	11.57	6.67	4	4.71	9.15	4.91	4
Team 13	4.83	14.33	4.51	12	2.82	7.92	3	8	5.62	16.87	5.11	16
ADAPT	1.88	5.34	1.89	2	0.00	0.00	0.00	0	2.63	7.46	2.64	4
balAPInc*	1.44	3.65	1.58	4	0.15	0.23	0.14	0	1.95	5.01	2.15	2
APSyn*	1.13	2.55	1.30	8	0.15	0.23	0.18	4	1.51	3.47	1.74	6
SLQS*	0.64	1.25	0.65	0	0.11	0.14		0	0.86	1.69	0.85	0

Table 7: Results for the Music subtask (2B). Baselines are marked with *.

pernyms which were either more or less fine-grained than the gold standard hypernyms (e.g. the list of gold hypernyms for *downfall* includes *natural phenomenon* but not *storm*, discovered by some supervised systems); third, some systems were able to retrieve hypernyms which correspond to another hyponym's sense not captured in the gold standard (e.g. *facultad* in Spanish can be either an educational institution or a virtue/ability, the latter not being captured by the gold standard

2A: Medical			
	MAP	MRR	P@5	FPs
CRIM_r1	**34.05**	**54.64**	**36.77**	20
CRIM_r2	31.54	46.19	35.49	12
MFH*	28.93	35.80	34.20	4
CRIM_CE	27.18	49.51	29.10	12
300-sparsans_r1	20.75	40.60	21.43	16
vTE*	18.84	41.07	20.71	12
300-sparsans_r2	14.96	32.18	15.81	12
EXPR_C	13.77	40.76	12.76	**40**
SJTU BCMI	11.69	25.95	11.69	12
vTE*_CE	11.66	23.83	12.64	32
ADAPT	8.13	20.56	8.32	20
Anu	7.05	17.51	7.29	32
Team 13	2.55	7.19	2.52	8
EXPR_C_CE	1.36	3.70	1.42	12
balAPInc*	0.91	2.10	1.08	0
APSyn*	0.65	1.43	0.72	4
SLQS*	0.29	0.66	0.33	0

Table 8: Results for the Medical subtask (2A). Baselines are marked with * and *cross evaluation* systems are followed by '_CE'.

but retrieved by the 300-sparsans_r2 system). Perhaps surprisingly, this latter case also extends to baselines such as MFH: in fact, many named entities have very skewed sense distributions, with less popular senses corresponding to people, cities, or companies often unbeknownst to most human annotators.[17] In addition to these three common patterns, there are also other correct false positives which do not clearly correspond to any of these three.

7 Conclusion

In this paper we have presented the SemEval 2018 task on *Hypernym Discovery*. We provided a large, reliable framework to evaluate hypernym discovery system in various languages (English, Italian, and Spanish) and domains (medical and music). This evaluation framework aims at going beyond the common practice of seeing hypernymy detection as a binary classification task, and provides a more challenging setting, inherently closer to how the task should be modeled within downstream applications. We hope this framework will contribute to the development of hypernym discovery systems in several languages and, more generally, to a wider understanding of hypernymy from a computational perspective.

As far as the results are concerned, this newly-proposed task proved to be challenging for all participating systems, leaving considerable room for improvement. It is clear from the figures that supervised systems perform considerably better than unsupervised systems. This might suggests that, given a well-defined downstream task, it could be more valuable to annotate hypernyms manually or semi-automatically (whenever possible) and then train a supervised system, than proposing unsupervised solutions with suboptimal performances. On the other hand, it is also noteworthy that the best system across three of the subtasks (i.e. CRIM) combined a supervised neural network architecture with the output of an unsupervised system using Hearst-style patterns (Hearst, 1992).

Acknowledgements

The authors gratefully acknowledge the economic support in the construction of the datasets from the Maria de Maeztu-UPF Grant provided to Horacio Saggion, Luis Espinosa-Anke and Sergio Oramas; Google Research through the Google Doctoral Fellowship in Natural Language Processing to Jose Camacho-Collados; and Bar-Ilan University through Vered Shwartz. This work is partially supported by the TUNER project (TIN2015-65308-C5-5-R, MINECO/FEDER, UE), Spanish Ministry of Economy and Competitiveness.

We would also like to thank the task participants who provided helpful inputs to improve the task through their comments in the Google Group.

References

Marco Baroni, Raffaella Bernardi, Ngoc-Quynh Do, and Chung-chieh Shan. 2012. Entailment above the word level in distributional semantics. In *Proceedings of EACL*, pages 23–32.

Marco Baroni, Silvia Bernardini, Adriano Ferraresi, and Eros Zanchetta. 2009. The wacky wide web: a collection of very large linguistically processed web-crawled corpora. *Language resources and evaluation*, 43(3):209–226.

Marco Baroni and Alessandro Lenci. 2011. How we blessed distributional semantic evaluation. In *Proceedings of the GEMS 2011 Workshop on GEometrical Models of Natural Language Semantics*, pages 1–10. Association for Computational Linguistics.

Gbor Berend, Mrton Makrai, and Peter Fldik. 2018. 300-sparsans at semeval-2018 task 9: Hypernymy

---

[17]As an example, *Cervantes* is universally known as the famous Spanish writer who authored '*Don Quixote*', but the word might also refer to a town in Western Australia.

as interaction of sparse attributes. In *Proceedings of The 12th International Workshop on Semantic Evaluation*, pages 925–931, New Orleans, Louisiana. Association for Computational Linguistics.

Gabriel Bernier-Colborne and Caroline Barriere. 2018. Crim at semeval-2018 task 9: A hybrid approach to hypernym discovery. In *Proceedings of The 12th International Workshop on Semantic Evaluation*, pages 722–728, New Orleans, Louisiana. Association for Computational Linguistics.

Guido Boella and Luigi Di Caro. 2013. Supervised learning of syntactic contexts for uncovering definitions and extracting hypernym relations in text databases. In *Machine learning and knowledge discovery in databases*, pages 64–79. Springer.

Gemma Boleda, Abhijeet Gupta, and Sebastian Padó. 2017. Instances and concepts in distributional space. In *Proceedings of EACL (2)*, Valencia, Spain. Association for Computational Linguistics.

Georgeta Bordea, Paul Buitelaar, Stefano Faralli, and Roberto Navigli. 2015. Semeval-2015 task 17: Taxonomy extraction evaluation (texeval). In *Proceedings of the SemEval workshop*.

Georgeta Bordea, Els Lefever, and Paul Buitelaar. 2016. Semeval-2016 task 13: Taxonomy extraction evaluation (texeval-2). In *SemEval-2016*, pages 1081–1091. Association for Computational Linguistics.

Jose Camacho-Collados. 2017. Why we have switched from building full-fledged taxonomies to simply detecting hypernymy relations. *arXiv preprint arXiv:1703.04178*.

Jose Camacho-Collados and Roberto Navigli. 2017. BabelDomains: Large-Scale Domain Labeling of Lexical Resources. In *Proceedings of EACL (2)*, Valencia, Spain.

Cristian Cardellino. 2016. Spanish Billion Words Corpus and Embeddings.

Luis Espinosa-Anke, Jose Camacho-Collados, Claudio Delli Bovi, and Horacio Saggion. 2016. Supervised distributional hypernym discovery via domain adaptation. In *Proceedings of EMNLP*, pages 424–435.

Tiziano Flati, Daniele Vannella, Tommaso Pasini, and Roberto Navigli. 2016. MultiWiBi: the Multilingual Wikipedia Bitaxonomy Project. *Artificial Intelligence*.

Ruiji Fu, Jiang Guo, Bing Qin, Wanxiang Che, Haifeng Wang, and Ting Liu. 2014. Learning semantic hierarchies via word embeddings. In *Proceedings of ACL*.

Amit Gupta, Francesco Piccinno, Mikhail Kozhevnikov, Marius Pasca, and Daniele Pighin. 2016. Revisiting taxonomy induction over wikipedia. In *Proceedings of COLING 2016, the 26th International Conference on Computational Linguistics: Technical Papers*, pages 2300–2309, Osaka, Japan.

Lushan Han, Abhay L Kashyap, Tim Finin, James Mayfield, and Jonathan Weese. 2013. Umbc_ebiquity-core: semantic textual similarity systems. In *Second Joint Conference on Lexical and Computational Semantics (* SEM), Volume 1: Proceedings of the Main Conference and the Shared Task: Semantic Textual Similarity*, volume 1, pages 44–52.

Arshia Zernab Hassan, Manikya Swathi Vallabhajosyula, and Ted Pedersen. 2018. Umduluth-cs8761 at semeval-2018 task 9: Hypernym discovery using hearst patterns, co-occurrence frequencies and word embeddings. In *Proceedings of The 12th International Workshop on Semantic Evaluation*, pages 911–915, New Orleans, Louisiana. Association for Computational Linguistics.

Marti A Hearst. 1992. Automatic acquisition of hyponyms from large text corpora. In *Proceedings of the 14th conference on Computational linguistics*, pages 539–545.

Johannes Hoffart, Dragan Milchevski, and Gerhard Weikum. 2014. Stics: searching with strings, things, and cats. In *Proceedings of the 37th international ACM SIGIR conference on Research & development in information retrieval*, pages 1247–1248. ACM.

Ahmad Issa Alaa Aldine, Mounira Harzallah, Giuseppe Berio, Nicolas Bchet, and Ahmad Faour. 2018. Expr at semeval-2018 task 9: A combined approach for hypernym discovery. In *Proceedings of The 12th International Workshop on Semantic Evaluation*, pages 916–920, New Orleans, Louisiana. Association for Computational Linguistics.

Lili Kotlerman, Ido Dagan, Idan Szpektor, and Maayan Zhitomirsky-Geffet. 2010. Directional distributional similarity for lexical inference. *Natural Language Engineering*, 16(04):359–389.

Omer Levy, Steffen Remus, Chris Biemann, Ido Dagan, and Israel Ramat-Gan. 2015. Do supervised distributional methods really learn lexical inference relations? In *Proceedings of NAACL 2015*, Denver, Colorado, USA.

Alfredo Maldonado and Filip Klubika. 2018. Adapt at semeval-2018 task 9: Skip-gram word embeddings for unsupervised hypernym discovery in specialised corpora. In *Proceedings of The 12th International Workshop on Semantic Evaluation*, pages 921–924, New Orleans, Louisiana. Association for Computational Linguistics.

Tomas Mikolov, Quoc V Le, and Ilya Sutskever. 2013. Exploiting similarities among languages for machine translation. *arXiv preprint arXiv:1309.4168*.

George A Miller. 1995. Wordnet: a lexical database for english. *Communications of the ACM*, 38(11):39–41.

Roberto Navigli and Simone Paolo Ponzetto. 2012. BabelNet: The automatic construction, evaluation and application of a wide-coverage multilingual semantic network. *Artificial Intelligence*, 193:217–250.

Roberto Navigli and Paola Velardi. 2010. Learning word-class lattices for definition and hypernym extraction. In *ACL*, pages 1318–1327.

Kim Anh Nguyen, Maximilian Köper, Sabine Schulte im Walde, and Ngoc Thang Vu. 2017. Hierarchical embeddings for hypernymy detection and directionality. In *Proceedings of the 2017 Conference on Empirical Methods in Natural Language Processing*, pages 233–243, Copenhagen, Denmark.

Mihaela Onofrei, Ionut Hulub, Diana Trandabat, and Daniela Gifu. 2018. Apollo at semeval-2018 task 9: Detecting hypernymy relations using syntactic dependencies. In *Proceedings of The 12th International Workshop on Semantic Evaluation*, pages 895–899, New Orleans, Louisiana. Association for Computational Linguistics.

Sergio Oramas, Luis Espinosa-Anke, Mohamed Sordo, Horacio Saggion, and Xavier Serra. 2016. Elmd: An automatically generated entity linking gold standard dataset in the music domain. In *Proceedings of the 10th International Conference on Language Resources and Evaluation (LREC 2016)*. European Language Resources Association.

Sergio Oramas, Oriol Nieto, Francesco Barbieri, and Xavier Serra. 2017. Multi-label music genre classification from audio, text, and images using deep features. In *Proceedings of the 18th International Society of Music Information Retrieval Conference (ISMIR 2017)*.

Ellie Pavlick and Marius Pasca. 2017. Identifying 1950s american jazz musicians: Fine-grained isa extraction via modifier composition. In *Proceedings of the 55th Annual Meeting of the Association for Computational Linguistics (Volume 1: Long Papers)*, pages 2099–2109. Association for Computational Linguistics.

Simone Paolo Ponzetto and Michael Strube. 2007. Deriving a large scale taxonomy from wikipedia. In *AAAI*, volume 7, pages 1440–1445.

John Prager, Jennifer Chu-Carroll, Eric W Brown, and Krzysztof Czuba. 2008. Question answering by predictive annotation. In *Advances in Open Domain Question Answering*, pages 307–347. Springer.

Wei Qiu, Mosha Chen, Linlin Li, and Luo Si. 2018. Nlp_hz at semeval-2018 task 9: a nearest neighbor approach. In *Proceedings of The 12th International Workshop on Semantic Evaluation*, pages 906–910, New Orleans, Louisiana. Association for Computational Linguistics.

Sara Rodríguez-Fernández, Luis Espinosa Anke, Roberto Carlini, and Leo Wanner. 2016. Semantics-driven recognition of collocations using word embeddings. In *Proceedings of the 54th Annual Meeting of the Association for Computational Linguistics (Volume 2: Short Papers)*, volume 2, pages 499–505.

Stephen Roller and Katrin Erk. 2016. Relations such as hypernymy: Identifying and exploiting hearst patterns in distributional vectors for lexical entailment. In *Proceedings of EMNLP*, pages 2163–2172, Austin, Texas.

Stephen Roller, Katrin Erk, and Gemma Boleda. 2014. Inclusive yet selective: Supervised distributional hypernymy detection. In *Proceedings of COLING 2014*, Dublin, Ireland.

V. Ivan Sanchez Carmona and Sebastian Riedel. 2017. How Well Can We Predict Hypernyms from Word Embeddings? A Dataset-Centric Analysis. In *Proceedings of EACL (short)*, pages 401–407.

Enrico Santus, Alessandro Lenci, Tin-Shing Chiu, Qin Lu, and Chu-Ren Huang. 2016a. Nine features in a random forest to learn taxonomical semantic relations. *arXiv preprint arXiv:1603.08702*.

Enrico Santus, Alessandro Lenci, Tin-Shing Chiu, Qin Lu, and Chu-Ren Huang. 2016b. Unsupervised measure of word similarity: How to outperform co-occurrence and vector cosine in vsms. In *Thirtieth AAAI Conference on Artificial Intelligence*, pages 4260–4261.

Enrico Santus, Alessandro Lenci, Qin Lu, and Sabine Schulte im Walde. 2014. Chasing hypernyms in vector spaces with entropy. In *Proceedings of the 14th Conference of the European Chapter of the Association for Computational Linguistics, volume 2: Short Papers*, pages 38–42. Association for Computational Linguistics.

Vered Shwartz, Yoav Goldberg, and Ido Dagan. 2016. Improving hypernymy detection with an integrated path-based and distributional method. In *Proceedings of ACL*, Berlin, Germany.

Vered Shwartz, Enrico Santus, and Dominik Schlechtweg. 2017. Hypernyms under siege: Linguistically-motivated artillery for hypernymy detection. In *Proceedings of EACL*, Valencia, Spain. Association for Computational Linguistics.

Rion Snow, Daniel Jurafsky, and Andrew Y Ng. 2004. Learning syntactic patterns for automatic hypernym discovery. *Advances in Neural Information Processing Systems 17*.

Kent A Spackman, Keith E Campbell, and Roger A Côté. 1997. Snomed rt: a reference terminology for health care. In *Proceedings of the AMIA annual fall symposium*, page 640. American Medical Informatics Association.

Fabian M Suchanek, Gjergji Kasneci, and Gerhard Weikum. 2007. Yago: A core of semantic knowledge. In *WWW*, pages 697–706. ACM.

Aaron Swartz. 2002. Musicbrainz: A semantic web service. *IEEE Intelligent Systems*, 17(1):76–77.

Denny Vrandečić and Markus Krötzsch. 2014. Wikidata: a free collaborative knowledgebase. *Communications of the ACM*, 57(10):78–85.

Ivan Vulić, Daniela Gerz, Douwe Kiela, Felix Hill, and Anna Korhonen. 2017. Hyperlex: A large-scale evaluation of graded lexical entailment. *Computational Linguistics*.

Yogarshi Vyas and Marine Carpuat. 2017. Detecting asymmetric semantic relations in context: A case-study on hypernymy detection. In *Proceedings of the 6th Joint Conference on Lexical and Computational Semantics (*SEM 2017)*, pages 33–43. Association for Computational Linguistics.

Chengyu Wang, Xiaofeng He, and Aoying Zhou. 2017. A short survey on taxonomy learning from text corpora: Issues, resources and recent advances. In *Proceedings of the 2017 Conference on Empirical Methods in Natural Language Processing*, pages 1190–1203.

Julie Weeds, Daoud Clarke, Jeremy Reffin, David Weir, and Bill Keller. 2014. Learning to distinguish hypernyms and co-hyponyms. In *Proceedings of COLING 2014, the 25th International Conference on Computational Linguistics: Technical Papers*, pages 2249–2259.

J.C. Wu, Y.C. Chang, T. Mitamura, and J.S. Chang. 2010. Automatic collocation suggestion in academic writing. In *Proceedings of the ACL Conference, Short paper track*, Uppsala.

Mohamed Yahya, Klaus Berberich, Shady Elbassuoni, and Gerhard Weikum. 2013. Robust question answering over the web of linked data. In *Proceedings of the 22nd ACM international conference on Conference on information & knowledge management*, pages 1107–1116. ACM.

Zheng Yu, Haixun Wang, Xuemin Lin, and Min Wang. 2015. Learning term embeddings for hypernymy identification. In *Proceedings of IJCAI*, pages 1390–1397.

Zhousheng Zhang, Jiangtong Li, Hai Zhao, and Bingjie Tang. 2018. Sjtu-nlp at semeval-2018 task 9: Neural hypernym discovery with term embeddings. In *Proceedings of The 12th International Workshop on Semantic Evaluation*, pages 900–905, New Orleans, Louisiana. Association for Computational Linguistics.

CRIM at SemEval-2018 Task 9: A Hybrid Approach to Hypernym Discovery

Gabriel Bernier-Colborne
g.b.colborne@gmail.com

Caroline Barrière
caroline_barriere@yahoo.ca

Abstract

This report describes the system developed by
the CRIM team for the hypernym discovery
task at SemEval 2018. This system exploits a
combination of supervised projection learning
and unsupervised pattern-based hypernym discovery. It was ranked first on the 3 sub-tasks
for which we submitted results.

1 Introduction

The goal of the hypernym discovery task at Sem-
Eval 2018 is to predict the hypernyms of a query
given a large vocabulary of candidate hypernyms.
A query can be either a concept (e.g. *cocktail* or
epistemology) or a named entity (e.g. *Craig Anderson* or *City of Whitehorse*). Two types of data
were provided to train the systems: a large unlabeled text corpus and a small training set of examples comprising a query and its hypernyms. More
details on this task may be found in the task description paper (Camacho-Collados et al., 2018).

The system developed by the CRIM team for
the task of hypernym discovery exploits a combination of two approaches: an unsupervised,
pattern-based approach and a supervised, projection learning approach. These two approaches are
described in Sections 2 and 3, then Section 4 describes our hybrid system and Section 5 presents
our results.

2 Pattern-Based Hypernym Discovery

Pattern-based approaches to relation extraction
have been discussed in the literature for quite some
time (see surveys by Auger and Barrière (2008)
and Nastase et al. (2013)). They can be used to discover various relations, including domain-specific
ones (Halskov and Barrière, 2008) and more general ones, such as hypernymy. The pattern-
based approach to hypernym discovery was pi-
oneered by Hearst (1992), who defined specific
textual patterns (e.g. *Y such as X*) to mine hy-
ponym/hypernym pairs from corpora.

This approach is known to suffer from low recall because it assumes that hyponym/hypernym
pairs will occur together in one of these patterns,
which is often not the case. For instance, using the
training data of sub-task 1A, we found that the majority of training pairs never co-occur within the
same paragraph in corpus 1A, let alone within a
pattern that suggests hypernymy.

To increase recall, we extend the basic pattern-
based approach to hypernym discovery in two
ways. First, we identify co-hyponyms for each
query and add the hypernyms discovered for these
terms to those found for the query. These co-
hyponyms are identified using patterns, and filtered based on distributional similarity using the
embeddings described in Section 3.3. Furthermore, we discover additional hypernyms using a
method based on the following assumptions: most
multi-word expressions are compositional, and the
prevailing head-modifier relation is hypernymy.

The co-hyponym patterns we use are limited to
enumeration patterns (e.g. X_1, X_2 *and* X_3). For
hypernyms, we use an extended set of Hearst-like
patterns which we selected empirically (e.g. *Y
such as X, Y other than X, not all Y are X, Y including X, Y especially X, Y like X, Y for example
X, Y which includes X, X are also Y, X are all Y,
not Y so much as X*).

Our pattern-based hypernym discovery algorithm can be defined as follows: given a query q,

1. Create the empty set Q, which will contain
   an extended set of queries.

2. Search for the co-hyponym patterns in the
   corpus to discover co-hyponyms of q. Add
   these to Q and store their frequency (number
   of times a given co-hyponym was found using these patterns).

Proceedings of the 12th International Workshop on Semantic Evaluation (SemEval-2018), pages 725–731
New Orleans, Louisiana, June 5–6, 2018. ©2018 Association for Computational Linguistics

3. Score each co-hyponym $q' \in Q$ by multiplying the frequency of q' by the cosine similarity of the embeddings of q and q'. Rank the co-hyponyms in Q according to this score, keep the top n,[1] and discard the rest.

4. Add the original query q to Q.

5. Create the empty set of hypernyms H_q.

6. For each query $q' \in Q$, search for the hypernym patterns in the corpus to discover hypernyms of q'. Add these to H_q.

7. Add the head of each term in H_q to this set, as well as the head of the original query q.

8. Score each candidate $c \in H_q$ by multiplying its normalized frequency[2] by the cosine similarity between the embeddings of c and q, and rank the candidates according to this score.

Although the pattern-based search for both co-hyponyms and hypernyms can find terms not included in the provided vocabulary (which could also be useful), we discarded out-of-vocabulary terms because we had not learned embeddings for them.

3 Learning Projections for Hypernym Discovery

Several supervised learning approaches based on word embeddings have recently been developed for the task of hypernym detection and the related task of hypernym discovery (Camacho-Collados, 2017). The general idea is to learn a function that takes as input the word embeddings of a query q and a candidate hypernym h and outputs the likelihood that there is a hypernymy relationship between q and h. To discover hypernyms for a given query q (rather than classify a given pair of words), we apply this decision function to all candidate hypernyms, and select the most likely candidates (or all those classified as hypernyms).

This decision function can be learned in a supervised fashion using examples of pairs of words that are related by hypernymy and pairs that are not. The supervised model can take as input a combination of the embeddings of q and h, and different ways of combining the embeddings for this purpose have been used (Baroni et al., 2012;

Roller et al., 2014; Weeds et al., 2014). In related work, models have been proposed that learn to project the embedding of q such that its projection is close to that of its hypernym h (Fu et al., 2014; Yamane et al., 2016; Espinosa-Anke et al., 2016). This has been termed *projection learning* (Ustalov et al., 2017). The decision function is then based on how close the projection of q is to a given candidate h.

Fu et al. (2014) introduced a model that learns multiple projection matrices representing different kinds of hypernymy relationships. In this model, each (q, h) pair is first assigned to a cluster based on their vector offsets, then projection matrices are learned for each cluster. Based on this work, Yamane et al. (2016) proposed a model that jointly learns the clusters and projection matrices.

We use a similar method to learn projections for hypernym discovery, but our approach differs from that of Yamane et al. (2016) in several ways: our model performs a soft clustering of query-hypernym pairs rather than a hard clustering, and we modified the training algorithm in several ways.

3.1 The Model

Given a query q and a candidate hypernym h, the model retrieves their embeddings $e_q, e_h \in \mathbb{R}^{d \times 1}$ using a lookup table. These embeddings were learned beforehand on a large unlabeled text corpus (i.e. the corpora provided for this task). The embedding e_q is then multiplied by a 3-D tensor containing k square projection matrices $\phi_i \in \mathbb{R}^{d \times d}$ for $i \in \{1, \ldots, k\}$, producing a matrix $P \in \mathbb{R}^{k \times d}$ containing the projections of e_q:

$$P_i = (\phi_i \cdot e_q)^T \tag{1}$$

The model then checks how close each of the k projections of e_q are to e_h by taking the dot product:

$$s = P \cdot e_h \tag{2}$$

The column vector $s \in \mathbb{R}^{k \times 1}$ is then fed to an affine transformation and a sigmoid activation function (in other words, a logistic regression classifier) to obtain an estimate of the likelihood that q and h are related by hypernymy:

$$y = \sigma(W \cdot s + b) \tag{3}$$

To discover the hypernyms of a given query, we compute the likelihood y for all candidates and select the top-ranked ones.

---

[1] We set $n = 5$ empirically.

[2] Frequencies were normalized in the range $[0.05, 1.0]$.

3.2 The Training Algorithm

We train the model using negative sampling: for each positive example of a (query, hypernym) pair in the training data, we generate a fixed number m of negative examples by replacing the hypernym with a word randomly drawn from the vocabulary.[3] We then train the model to output a likelihood (y) close to 1 for positive examples and close to 0 for negative examples. This is accomplished by minimizing the binary cross-entropy of the positive and negative training examples. For a particular example, this is computed as follows:

$$H(q, h, t) = t \times \log(y) + (1 - t) \times \log(1 - y)$$

where q is a query, h is a candidate hypernym, t is the target (1 for positive examples, 0 for negative), and y is the likelihood predicted by the model. If we sum H for every example in the training set D (containing both the positive and negative examples), we obtain the cost function $J = \sum_{(q,h,t) \in D} H(q, h, t)$. This function is minimized by gradient descent, using the Adam optimizer[4] (Kingma and Ba, 2014).

A few details of the setup we use for training are worth mentioning:

- We use a fixed number of projections (k) rather than the dynamic clustering algorithm of Yamane et al. (2016). For our official runs, we used $k = 24$.

- The word embeddings are normalized to unit-length before training.

- For the initialization of the projection matrices, we add random noise to an identity matrix, which means that at first, the projections of a query are simply k randomly corrupted copies of the query's embedding.

- We train the model on random mini-batches containing 32 positive examples and $32 \times m$ negative examples (m being the number of negative examples).

- Dropout is applied to the embeddings e_q and e_h and the query projections P. For regularization, we also use gradient clipping, as well as early stopping.

- We sample positive examples using a function based on the frequency of the hypernyms in the training data, such that we subsample (q, h) pairs where h occurs often in the training data. The probability of sampling (q, h) is given by:

$$P(q, h) = \sqrt{\frac{\min_{h' \in D}(\text{freq}(h'))}{\text{freq}(h)}}$$

where $\text{freq}(h)$ returns the frequency of h in the training data.[5]

- The word embeddings are optimized (or "fine-tuned") during training.

- We use a multi-task learning setup whereby we train two separate logistic regression classifiers, each with their own parameters W and b, and use one for queries that are named entities, and the other for queries that are concepts.[6] The rest of the parameters (i.e. the projection matrices ϕ) are shared.

The various hyperparameters mentioned above were tuned on the trial set (i.e. development set) provided for sub-task 1A.

3.3 The Word Embeddings

We learned term embeddings for all queries and candidates using the pre-tokenized corpora provided for sub-tasks 1A, 2A, and 2B. We preprocessed the corpora by converting all characters to lower case and replacing multi-word terms found in the vocabulary (candidates and lower-cased queries) with a single token, starting with trigrams, then bigrams.[7] We then used the skip-gram algorithm with negative sampling (Mikolov et al., 2013) to learn the embeddings.

3.4 Data Augmentation

For one of our 2 runs, we experimented with a method to add synthetic examples to the positive examples in the training set provided (D). This

---

[3]Different ways of selecting the negative examples for this purpose have been proposed. See Ustalov et al. (2017).

[4]We use $\beta_1 = \beta_2 = 0.9$.

[5]On the training data of subtask 1A, this produces a sampling probability of 0.06 for the most frequent hypernym (*person*), while the least frequent hypernyms have a sampling probability of 1.

[6]Multi-task learning was not used on subtask 2A, because all queries were concepts.

[7]It is worth noting that a small number of candidates (e.g. less than 0.1% of candidates on corpus 1A) had a frequency of 0 in this preprocessed corpus, so we could not train an embedding for these candidates. These appear to be terms that always occur within a longer candidate.

was meant to provide additional training data and avoid overfitting the embeddings of the words in the training set. We use 2 heuristics to generate these synthetic examples:

1. Given a positive example $(q, h) \in D$, add (q', h) to the positive examples, where q' is the nearest neighbour of q, based on the cosine similarity of the embeddings of all the words in the vocabulary. This was motivated by the observation that nearest neighbours were often co-hyponyms.

2. Given a query q and the set H_q containing the hypernyms of q according to the training data, compute the α nearest neighbours of each hypernym in H_q, and for each neighbour that is shared by at least 2 of the hypernyms in H_q, add that neighbour to H_q.[8]

Negative examples are generated for each of the synthetic examples, as with the actual positive examples in the training set.

4 Hybrid Hypernym Discovery

Our hybrid approach to hypernym discovery combines supervised projection learning and unsupervised pattern-based hypernym discovery (see Sections 2 and 3). To combine the outputs of the 2 systems, we take the top 100 candidates according to each,[9] normalize their scores and sum them, then rerank the candidates according to this new score. This reranking function favours candidates found by both systems, but also gives a chance to strong candidates found by a single system.

5 Experiments and Results

We submitted 2 runs on 3 of the 5 sub-tasks: 1A (general), 2A (medical), and 2B (music). The system outputs its top 15 predictions in all cases. The difference between the 2 runs is that for run 1, we used data augmentation (see Section 3.4) to train the supervised system – the same unsupervised output was used for both runs. We also submitted one run for cross-evaluation (training on 1A, but testing on 2A or 2B). First, we added the queries and candidates of 2A or 2B to those of 1A be-

fore training embeddings on the corpus of 1A.[10] These embeddings were used to train the supervised model on the 1A training data. We then combined the predictions of the supervised and unsupervised models on test set 2A/2B.[11]

A summary of our system's results is shown in Table 1. This table shows the mean average precision (MAP), mean reciprocal rank (MRR) and precision at rank 1 (P@1) of our system and those of the 2 strongest baselines which were computed by the task organizers. The first is a supervised baseline[12] and the second is based on the most frequent hypernyms in the training data. For more details, see (Camacho-Collados et al., 2018).

Our hybrid system was ranked 1st on all three sub-tasks for which we submitted runs. As shown in Table 1, the scores obtained using this system are much higher than the strongest baselines for this task. Furthermore, it is likely that we could improve our scores on 2A and 2B, since we only tuned the system on 1A.

If we compare runs 1 and 2 of our hybrid system, we see that data augmentation improved our scores slightly on 1A and 2B, and increased them by several points on 2A.

Our cross-evaluation results are better than the supervised baseline computed using the normal evaluation setup, so training our system on general-purpose data produced better results on a domain-specific test set than a strong, supervised baseline trained on the domain-specific data.

Table 1 also shows the scores we would have obtained on the test set if we had used only the unsupervised (pattern-based) or supervised (projection learning) parts of our system. Note that the unsupervised system outperformed all other unsupervised systems evaluated on this task, and even outperformed the supervised baseline on 2A.

Combining the outputs of the 2 systems improves the best score of either system on all test sets, sometimes by as much as 10 points.

Notice also that the results obtained using only the supervised system indicate that data augmentation had a positive effect on our 2A scores only (compare runs 1 and 2), although our tests on the

---

[8]We use $\alpha = 2$.

[9]Analyzing the individual and combined recall of the two systems at various ranks indicated that using more than 100 candidates would not increase recall.

[10]Several of the domain-specific queries that were added to the vocab were not found in corpus 1A. We decided to only use the output of the unsupervised system in these cases.

[11]Note that the unsupervised system used the corpora of 2A/2B, but no supervised learning was carried out on the training data of 2A/2B.

[12]This is a "vanilla" version of TaxoEmbed (Espinosa-Anke et al., 2016).

	Test set 1A			Test set 2A			Test set 2B		
	MAP	MRR	P@1	MAP	MRR	P@1	MAP	MRR	P@1
Hybrid run 1	19.78	36.10	29.67	34.05	54.64	49.20	40.97	60.93	48.20
Hybrid run 2	19.54	35.94	29.67	31.54	46.19	41.40	40.88	60.18	47.60
Supervised run 1	19.09	34.53	28.33	30.63	44.18	40.00	38.24	53.45	38.20
Supervised run 2	19.11	34.99	28.80	28.51	37.63	34.40	39.95	57.34	43.00
Unsupervised	7.36	15.44	10.73	21.74	47.85	38.60	15.86	34.98	28.60
BaselineSUP	10.60	23.83	19.73	18.84	41.07	35.40	12.99	39.36	33.20
BaselineMFH	8.77	21.39	19.80	28.93	35.80	32.60	33.32	51.48	36.20
Hybrid cross-eval	N/A	N/A	N/A	27.18	49.51	43.20	21.02	37.55	29.20
Supervised cross-eval	N/A	N/A	N/A	22.89	38.30	30.60	16.80	29.28	19.20
BaselineSUP cross-eval	N/A	N/A	N/A	11.66	23.83	17.20	6.31	16.54	9.60

Table 1: Our system's results on test sets 1A, 2A, and 2B. The runs we submitted are the hybrid runs. The supervised and unsupervised runs were produced by using our 2 sub-systems separately. BaselineSUP is a strong, supervised baseline and BaselineMFH is the most-frequent-hypernym baseline. Cross-evaluation results were obtained by training the supervised system on 1A and evaluating on 2A or 2B.

trial set suggested it would also have a positive effect on our 1A scores. Given this observation, we find it somewhat surprising that run 1 is the best on all 3 test sets when we use the hybrid system. One possible explanation is that adding the synthetic examples makes the errors of the supervised system *more different* from those of the unsupervised system, and that this in turn makes the ensemble method more beneficial, but we haven't looked into this.

5.1 Ablation Tests

To assess the influence of different aspects of the supervised system and its training algorithm, we carried out a few simple ablation tests on sub-task 1A. The baseline for these tests is our supervised projection learning system – we did not apply pattern-based hypernym discovery for any of these tests. We used the setup of run 1 (with data augmentation) and used the trial set for early stopping. We conducted the following tests (one by one, without combining any of the ablations):

1. No subsampling: we sample positive examples uniformly from the training set.

2. No MTL: instead of multi-task learning (MTL), we use a single classifier for both named entities and concepts.

3. Random init: the weights of ϕ are initialized randomly, instead of adding random noise to an identity matrix.

4. Single projection: $k = 1$ instead of 24.

5. Single neg. example: $m = 1$ instead of 10.

6. Frozen embeddings: the word embeddings are not fine-tuned during training.

The results obtained on test set 1A are shown in Table 2.[13] These results show that 2 of the techniques we used, namely subsampling and multi-task learning, actually harmed our system's performance on test set 1A, although our experiments on the trial set suggested that they would be beneficial. This may be due to the small size of the trial set (i.e. 50 queries) or some difference in the underlying distributions of the trial and test sets.

	MAP	MRR	P@1
Baseline	19.05	34.36	27.93
No subsampling	19.47	35.56	29.33
No MTL	19.22	35.09	28.67
Random init	16.54	30.60	24.93
Single projection	12.88	26.50	23.33
Single neg. example	11.58	21.75	15.20
Frozen embeddings	8.01	17.15	11.67

Table 2: Results of ablation tests on test set 1A. The baseline is our supervised system (run 1).

On the other hand, fine-tuning the word embeddings during training seems to be one of the keys to the success of this approach, as are the use of multiple projection matrices, and the sampling of

---

[13]Note that the baseline results are slightly different than those shown in Table 1 for run 1 (supervised), because we retrained the model to get the results on the trial set, and a random number generator used during training was not seeded with a fixed value.

Query	Predictions
Suzy Favor Hamilton	**athlete**, **sportsperson**, **person**, competitor, sport, olympic sport, ...
wicketkeeper	**cricketer**, **sportsperson**, **athlete**, **competitor**, footballer, **person**, ...
aquamarine	**stone**, crystal, precious stone, **pebble**, gem, **rock**, **gemstone**, ...
tenpence	monetary unit, **metal money**, **note of hand**, person, silver coin, **coin**, ...
vegetarian	dessert, dish, recipe, veggie, food product, organic food, meal, salad, ...
Local Group	voluntary association, locale, coalition, club, country, mapmaking, ...
Swarthmore	university, college, educational institution, school, student, ...
hypostasis	figure of speech, intellection, philosophy, ordinary language, ...

Table 3: Examples of predictions made by our system (run 1) on the test queries of 1A. Correct predictions are in bold. Midline separates high-accuracy examples from low-accuracy examples.

multiple negative examples for each positive example. The way we initialize ϕ also seems to have helped quite a bit.

It is important to remember that a more thorough exploration of hyperparameter space would produce results very different from those of simple ablation tests such as these.

It is worth noting that our supervised model outperforms the supervised baseline provided for this task (see Table 1) even when it exploits a single projection matrix, however the difference in scores between these 2 systems is only 2 or 3 points, depending on the evaluation metric.

We should also note that the supervised model is prone to overfitting, and we found early stopping to be particularly important.

5.2 Qualitative Analysis

We manually inspected the results of run 1 on some of the 1A test queries to get a better idea of the ability of the model to discover hypernyms, and to identify potential sources of errors. Table 3 shows a few of these test cases. Below we will outline a few of our observations, and will refer repeatedly to examples in Table 3.

The model is indeed able to discover valid hypernyms for both concepts and named entities. It seems that it can even handle very low-frequency queries in some cases (*Suzy Favor Hamilton* occurs only 5 times in the corpus), but we have not had the chance to investigate how sensitive the model is to term frequency.

Lexical memorization (Levy et al., 2015) can sometimes be observed. For example, *person* is the most frequent hypernym in the 1A training data, and the model often predicts this candidate incorrectly, even when its other top predictions are completely unrelated (e.g. *tenpence*).

The model can discover hypernyms of different senses of the same query (e.g. *aquamarine*, for which the top 15 predictions contain the valid hypernyms *spectral color* and *primary color*), and it sometimes discovers hypernyms for senses that are not represented in the gold standard (e.g. there is a college named *Swarthmore*, and *hypostasis* has senses related to linguistics and philosophy). It is likely that the senses that dominate the model's top predictions for a given query are its most frequent senses in the corpus.

The case of *vegetarian* suggests that syntactic ambiguity is a source of errors: the predicted hypernyms include some that might be considered valid for the query *vegetarian food*, where *vegetarian* is an adjective, but not for the noun *vegetarian*.

Lastly, the model sometimes confuses concepts and named entities (e.g. *Local Group*, which refers to a group of galaxies). Preserving the true case of the characters in the corpus would mitigate this issue.

6   Concluding Remarks

Our approach to hypernym discovery combines a novel supervised projection learning algorithm and an unsupervised pattern-based algorithm which exploits co-hyponyms in its search for hypernyms. This hybrid approach produced very good results on the hypernym discovery task, and was ranked first on all 3 sub-tasks for which we submitted results.

Acknowledgments

This research was conducted while both authors were affiliated with the Computer Research Institute of Montréal (CRIM), and was supported by the Natural Sciences and Engineering Research Council of Canada.

References

Alain Auger and Caroline Barrière. 2008. Pattern-based approaches to semantic relation extraction: A state-of-the-art. *Terminology, Special Issue on Pattern-based Approaches to Semantic Relation Extraction*, 14(1):1–19.

Marco Baroni, Raffaella Bernardi, Ngoc-Quynh Do, and Chung-chieh Shan. 2012. Entailment above the word level in distributional semantics. In *Proceedings of the 13th Conference of the European Chapter of the Association for Computational Linguistics*, pages 23–32. Association for Computational Linguistics.

José Camacho-Collados. 2017. Why we have switched from building full-fledged taxonomies to *simply* detecting hypernymy relations. *CoRR*, abs/1703.04178.

Jose Camacho-Collados, Claudio Delli Bovi, Luis Espinosa-Anke, Sergio Oramas, Tommaso Pasini, Enrico Santus, Vered Shwartz, Roberto Navigli, and Horacio Saggion. 2018. SemEval-2018 Task 9: Hypernym Discovery. In *Proceedings of the 12th International Workshop on Semantic Evaluation (SemEval-2018)*, New Orleans, LA, United States. Association for Computational Linguistics.

Luis Espinosa-Anke, Jose Camacho-Collados, Claudio Delli Bovi, and Horacio Saggion. 2016. Supervised distributional hypernym discovery via domain adaptation. In *Proceedings of the 2016 Conference on Empirical Methods in Natural Language Processing*, pages 424–435.

Ruiji Fu, Jiang Guo, Bing Qin, Wanxiang Che, Haifeng Wang, and Ting Liu. 2014. Learning semantic hierarchies via word embeddings. In *Proceedings of the 52nd Annual Meeting of the Association for Computational Linguistics (Volume 1: Long Papers)*, volume 1, pages 1199–1209.

Jakob Halskov and Caroline Barrière. 2008. Web-based extraction of semantic relation instances for terminology work. *Terminology*, 14(1):20–44.

Marti A. Hearst. 1992. Automatic acquisition of hyponyms from large text corpora. In *Proceedings of the 14th conference on Computational linguistics - Volume 2*, volume 2, pages 539–545. Association for Computational Linguistics.

Diederik P. Kingma and Jimmy Ba. 2014. Adam: A method for stochastic optimization. *CoRR*, abs/1412.6980.

Omer Levy, Steffen Remus, Chris Biemann, and Ido Dagan. 2015. Do supervised distributional methods really learn lexical inference relations? In *Proceedings of the 2015 Conference of the North American Chapter of the Association for Computational Linguistics: Human Language Technologies*, pages 970–976.

Tomas Mikolov, Kai Chen, Greg Corrado, and Jeffrey Dean. 2013. Efficient estimation of word representations in vector space. *CoRR*, abs/1301.3781.

Vivi Nastase, Preslav Nakov, Diarmuid Ó Séaghdha, and Stan Szpakowicz. 2013. *Semantic Relations Between Nominals*. Morgan & Claypool, Toronto.

Stephen Roller, Katrin Erk, and Gemma Boleda. 2014. Inclusive yet selective: Supervised distributional hypernymy detection. In *Proceedings of COLING 2014, the 25th International Conference on Computational Linguistics: Technical Papers*, pages 1025–1036.

Dmitry Ustalov, Nikolay Arefyev, Chris Biemann, and Alexander Panchenko. 2017. Negative sampling improves hypernymy extraction based on projection learning. In *Proceedings of the 15th Conference of the European Chapter of the Association for Computational Linguistics: Volume 2, Short Papers*, pages 543–550, Valencia, Spain. Association for Computational Linguistics.

Julie Weeds, Daoud Clarke, Jeremy Reffin, David Weir, and Bill Keller. 2014. Learning to distinguish hypernyms and co-hyponyms. In *Proceedings of COLING 2014, the 25th International Conference on Computational Linguistics: Technical Papers*, pages 2249–2259. Dublin City University and Association for Computational Linguistics.

Josuke Yamane, Tomoya Takatani, Hitoshi Yamada, Makoto Miwa, and Yutaka Sasaki. 2016. Distributional hypernym generation by jointly learning clusters and projections. In *Proceedings of COLING 2016, the 26th International Conference on Computational Linguistics: Technical Papers*, pages 1871–1879.

SemEval-2018 Task 10: Capturing Discriminative Attributes

Alicia Krebs
Textkernel
krebs@
textkernel.nl

Alessandro Lenci
University of Pisa
alessandro.lenci@
unipi.it

Denis Paperno
Loria (UMR 7503), CNRS
denis.paperno@
loria.fr

Abstract

This paper describes the SemEval 2018 Task 10 on Capturing Discriminative Attributes. Participants were asked to identify whether an attribute could help discriminate between two concepts. For example, a successful system should determine that *urine* is a discriminating feature in the word pair *kidney,bone*. The aim of the task is to better evaluate the capabilities of state of the art semantic models, beyond pure semantic similarity. The task attracted submissions from 21 teams, and the best system achieved a 0.75 F1 score.

1 Introduction

State of the art semantic models do an excellent job at detecting semantic similarity, a traditional semantic task; for example, they can tell us that cappuccino, espresso and americano are similar to each other. It is obvious, however, that no model can claim to capture semantic competence if it does not, in addition to similarity, predict semantic differences between words. If one can tell that americano is similar to cappuccino and espresso but cannot tell the difference between them, one only has a very approximate idea of the meaning of these words. As a step beyond similarity, one should at the very least recognize that americano is bigger than espresso, and that capuccino contains milk foam. In this spirit, we present Semeval 2018 Task 10 (Capturing Discriminative Attributes) as a new challenge for lexical semantic models.

1.1 Task description

A semantic model that has only been evaluated on similarity detection may very well fail to be of practical use for specific applications. For example, word sense disambiguation could benefit greatly from representations that can model complex semantic relations. This means that the evaluation of word representation models should not only be centered on semantic similarity and relatedness, and should include different, complementary tasks. To fill this gap, we proposed a novel task of semantic difference detection as Task 10 of the SemEval 2018 workshop. The goal of the systems in this case was to predict whether a word is a discriminative attribute between two other words. For example, given the words *apple* and *banana*, is the word *red* a discriminative attribute?

Semantic difference is a ternary relation between two concepts (*apple*, *banana*) and a discriminative attribute (*red*) that characterizes the first concept but not the other. By its nature, semantic difference detection is a binary classification task: given a triple *apple,banana,red*, the task is to determine whether it exemplifies a semantic difference or not.

In practice, when preparing the task, we started out with defining potential discriminative attributes as semantic features in the sense of (McRae et al., 2005): properties that people tend to think are important for a given concept. McRae et al.'s features are expressed as phrases, but these phrases can usually be reconstructed from a single word (e.g. *red* as a feature of *apple* stands for the phrase *is red*, *carpentry* as a feature of *hammer* can be used as a shorthand of *used for carpentry*, etc.) Given this general reconstructability, we have for simplicity used single words rather than phrases to represent features. The same solution was also adopted in the feature norming studies by (Vinson and Vigliocco, 2008) and (Lenci et al., 2013).

Following McRae et al., we did not define discriminative features in purely logical but rather in psychological terms. Accordingly, features are prototypical properties that subjects tend to associate to a certain concept. For example, not all apples are red and some bananas are, but *red* tends to be judged as an important feature of apples and not of bananas. We therefore fully trust human anno-

732

Proceedings of the 12th International Workshop on Semantic Evaluation (SemEval-2018), pages 732–740
New Orleans, Louisiana, June 5–6, 2018. ©2018 Association for Computational Linguistics

tators in deciding what counts as a distinguishing attribute and what does not.

1.2 Motivation

Exploring semantic differences between words can allow us to grasp subtle aspects of meaning: while it is relatively easy to train a model to recognize that *apple* and *banana* are somewhat similar, it is less straightforward to learn that, contrary to an apple, a typical banana is not red. This task is therefore more challenging than, and complementary to, the traditional similarity task, and we expect it to contribute to the progress in computational modeling of meaning.

While semantic similarity and relatedness measures have been used extensively to evaluate semantic representations, they may not be sufficient as a method for evaluating lexical semantic models (Faruqui et al., 2016; Batchkarov et al., 2016). Firstly, it has been noted that the relevant notions of similarity and relatedness can vary depending on the linguistic context, on the downstream application, etc. The difference task resolves this concern by effectively providing a context. In our example, comparison with bananas determines the relevance of the redness attribute for apples, which, out of context, might not necessarily be a salient attribute of apples.

Existing similarity and relatedness datasets have also been criticized for low inter-annotator agreement. The semantic difference detection task alleviates this issue, too. Binary choice is easier for human annotators than rating on a continuous scale, and produces more consistent patterns of answers. In our pilot study, the agreement between annotators was over 0.80. To further ensure the quality of our data, we discarded any items that caused disagreement.

1.3 Expected impact

The semantic difference task can enable further progress in the field of word representation learning. Indeed, state of art models have reached ceiling performance in the tasks of semantic similarity and relatedness (in part because the ceiling, as determined by the agreement of human subjects, is relatively low). Another commonly employed task, analogy, has its own issues (Linzen, 2016) and effectivey boils down to similarity optimization (Levy and Goldberg, 2014). A new general evaluation task for lexical semantics is long due,

and we hope that the semantic difference task is capable of filling this gap.

In the future, solving the discriminative attributes task could help in a range of applications, from conversational agents (choosing lexical items with contextually relevant differential features can help create more pragmatically appropriate, human-like dialogues), to coreference resolution (differentiating features of concepts mentioned or alluded to in text could help in reference disambiguation), to machine translation and text generation, where explicitly taking into account semantic differences between competing translation variants can improve the quality of the output.

2 Data and resources

2.1 Overview

One can express semantic differences between concepts by referring to attributes of those concepts. A difference can usually be expressed as presence or absence of a specific attribute. For instance, one of the differences between a *narwhal* and a *dolphin* is the presence of a tusk.

The task dataset includes 5062 manually verified triples of the form <word1,word2,attribute>. The set is built in such a way that the attribute in each positive example characterizes the first word of the triple. For example, in Table 1, *wings* is an attribute of *airplane*. The word pair `[airplane,helicopter]` is included in the order `[helicopter,airplane]` if *helicopter* has a feature that *airplane* does not have. We thereby assume, in contrast to the standard formalization of similarity, that semantic difference is not symmetric: the triple *apple,banana,red* is a semantic difference but *banana,apple,red* is not since *red* is not an attribute of bananas.[1]

We supplemented positive data (as described above) with negative examples. Two types of negative examples were added: examples where the attribute is shared between $word_1$ and $word_2$ (both concepts have the attribute in question), and examples where the attribute is neither an attribute of $word_1$ nor $word_2$ (both concepts lack the attribute). For that last type of attributes, since their

---

[1]This is a somewhat arbitrary choice. One could experiment with a symmetric notion of a discriminative attribute, whereby both *apple,banana,red* and *banana,apple,red* are considered examples of semantic difference, but in our opinion such an approach would only make the task more challenging.

$word_1$	$word_2$	$attribute$
airplane	helicopter	wings
bagpipe	accordion	pipes
dolphin	seal	fins
gorilla	crocodile	bananas
oak	pine	leaves
octopus	lobster	tentacles
pajamas	necklace	silk
skirt	jacket	pleats
subway	train	dirty

Table 1: Sample data: Word pairs and their distinguishing features (positive examples)

number is potentially huge, the examples were selected randomly so that the number of negative examples matches the number of positive examples. Presence of both positive and negative examples makes it possible to train a binary classifier that, for a given triple, predicts whether the attribute is a difference between $word_1$ and $word_2$.

$word_1$	$word_2$	$attribute$
tractor	scooter	wheels
crow	owl	black
squirrel	leopard	fur
pillow	jacket	white
dresser	cupboard	large
spider	elephant	legs
gloves	pants	wool
gorilla	panther	long
scarf	slippers	colours
lion	zebra	large

Table 2: Sample data: Word pairs and non-distinguishing features (negative examples)

Approximately half of the manually checked triples was given to participants as a validation set for parameter tuning of their systems, the rest was used for testing (cf. Section 2.4 for detailed statistics about the dataset composition). A larger training set of almost 18K examples (automatically constructed by the procedure described below, without manual filtering) was provided for training parameter-rich systems.

2.2 Data collection and annotation

When creating the dataset, we started from the approach that Lazaridou et al. (2016) used for visual discriminating attribute identification, followed by manual filtering for the test and validation data. Dataset creation consisted of three phases:

1. Semi-automatically created triples (section 2.2.1)

2. Manually created triples (section 2.2.2)

3. Automatically created triples (section 2.2.3)

As an initial source of data, we used the feature norms collected by McRae et al. (2005) and created a pilot dataset (Krebs and Paperno, 2016). This set was then reverified and manually extended to improve the quality and the variety of the data. Finally, a large number of triples were automatically generated for training purposes.

2.2.1 Triples from Mcrae norms

The first part of the dataset was created semi-automatically by identifying discriminative attributes of the concepts in the McRae norms, which consist of a list of features for 541 concepts (living and non-living entities), collected by asking 725 participants to produce features for each concept. Production frequencies of these attributes indicate how salient they are. Concepts that have different meanings had been disambiguated before being shown to participants. For example, there are two entries for *bow*, bow_(weapon) and bow_(ribbon).

Because our task is not intended to test word sense models, we did not differentiate between entries that have multiple senses and ignored the disambiguating phrase. In our dataset, the concept bow has the attributes of both the weapon and the ribbon. This is not problematic because we do not refer to more than one attribute at a time, so senses of a word do not mix.[2] The McRae dataset uses the brain region taxonomy (Cree and McRae, 2003) to classify attributes into different types, such as *function*, *sound* or *taxonomic*. For the construction of our dataset, we decided to only work with visual attributes, which exist for all concrete concepts, while attributes such as *sound* or *taste* are only relevant for some classes of concepts.

Any one word concept that has at least one visual attribute was considered a candidate. Each

---

[2]An anonymous reviewer points out that the presence or absence of a feature in w_1 can be influenced by the context of w_2: e.g. *tail* could be considered a distinguishing feature for the pair *mouse,cheese* but not for *mouse, keyboard*, because *keyboard* primes the device sense of the word *mouse* as opposed to the animal sense. Such strong contextualization effects could make our task even more interesting, but we believe that these cases are too rare to strongly influence the outcomes.

candidate concept was paired with another candidate concept from the list of its 100 closest neighbours in a PPMI-based distributional vector space (using the best settings from Baroni et al. (2014)). The motivation for this step is that finding non-trivial semantic differences only makes sense in the context of related words; detecting the difference between two unrelated concepts, such as a narwhal and a tractor, is rather trivial and would not constitute a very interesting task.

For each word pair, if there was an attribute in McRae feature norms that the first word has but the second doesn't, the word pair – attribute triple was added to the list of candidate positive examples. For simplicity, multi-word attributes were processed so that only the last word is taken into account (e.g. has_wings becomes wings). At this point, we had 512 unique concepts, 1645 unique attributes, 6355 unique word pairs, and 41723 triples (word pair-concept combinations). A random sample of triples was selected for manual annotation.

For candidate positive examples, two annotators agreed to keep 45.2% of items, agreed to discard 33% of items, and disagreed on 21.8% of items. A total of 54.8% of candidate positive examples were discarded. Among the negative examples, 12.5% of items were discarded. Annotators agreed to keep 87.5% of items, agreed to discard 0.8% of items, and disagreed on 11.6% of items. The examples that both annotators agreed to discard from the positive examples were added to the negative examples. Finally, the third author manually filtered the data removing dubious examples.

2.2.2 Manual triples

In the second phase, we extended the dataset by adding new concepts and attributes. Our intention was to make the dataset more diverse and more representative of the noun lexicon by including words and features that are not part of the McRae feature norms (e.g., human nouns such as *doctor* or *student*).

To select new nouns, we used SimLex-999 (Hill et al., 2015), one of the largest and most popular datasets for semantic similarity. We extracted from SimLex all the nouns with a concreteness rating above the median, and identified 204 candidate items that were not included in the McRae Norms. Each selected noun was paired with candidate concepts from the list of its 20 closest neighbours in the distributional vector space. We then filtered the neighbors by frequency, keeping the neighbors that belong to the frequency range of the original McRae and SimLex vocabulary. We also made sure at this step that candidate word pairs belong to the same WordNet supersense. This latter constraint was added because distributional models often return neighbors that are only loosely related to the target, while finding non-trivial semantic differences makes sense only for words that are taxonomically similar. We also discarded grammatical number pairs like *seed/seeds* and hypernym/hyponym pairs like *doctor/surgeon*, since by definition there is no feature that a hypernym has but its hyponym does not have.

Each of the three task organizers was given a third of the resulting 1851 candidate noun pairs to annotate, generating discriminative and non-discriminative attributes for each pair. The suggested triples were then manually filtered by the other two authors.

2.2.3 Random triples

Finally, to further ensure the diversity of examples and to alleviate any biases unintentionally introduced in the annotation pipeline, we generated 500 additional triples by randomly matching words and features produced at earlier stages. Each of the three authors annotated these random triples, which contained mainly negative (*motorbike,rifle,liquor*) and some positive examples (e.g. *maid,evening,help*). Again, only those examples for which a full consensus of the three authors existed were kept.

2.3 Training, test and validation partitions

The manually validated dataset of semantic differences consists of examples from three sources described above: combinations of nouns with McRae features, triples with manually suggested attributes, and random triples. All of these examples have been verified by the three authors and were then randomly split into a validation partition and a test partition, making sure that no feature occurs in both.

	McRae	**manual**	**random**
positive	897	1477	37
negative	634	1656	361
total	1531	3133	398

Table 3: Composition of the manually validated part of the dataset

To enable development of systems that require more training data, we also created a distinct, bigger training set that was not manually curated. The training set was derived from McRae feature norms using automatically matched examples as described in 2.1.1, but without manual validation. We have to note that this training partition is very noisy, its main advantage being its size. In fact, the best performing system in our task was trained directly on validation data.

We further filtered the training set to minimize lexical overlap between partitions, making sure that no attribute present in the test set or the validation set is also present in the training set. For example, if the attribute "red" appears in some triple in the test partition, you will not find it anywhere in the training set. This was done to ensure that models cannot rely on attribute memorization from training data but are forced to transfer lexical knowledge from other sources.

2.4 Dataset composition

The final dataset consists of 22884 items, divided into:

1. A training set of 17782 examples with 515 distinct concepts and 1292 distinct features.

2. A validation set of 2722 examples with 1283 concepts and 576 distinct features.

3. A test set of 2340 triples with 1272 distinct concepts and 577 distinct features.

The proportion of positive and negative examples is reported in Table 2.4.

	training	validation	testing
positive	6591	1364	1047
negative	11191	1358	1293
total	17782	2722	2340

Table 4: Total size of the final dataset.

All data used in this task can be accessed from the competition's github repository.[3]

3 Evaluation

3.1 Metrics

The submitted systems were evaluated on F1 measure, as is standard in binary classification tasks.

The evaluation script can be found in the competition's github repository. The competition results can be seen at the corresponding Codalab page.[4] Participants were allowed to make up to 2 submissions, resulting in 47 total submissions from 28 different teams (but only 21 teams submitted papers). Only the better of the two submissions of each team is included in final results.

3.2 Baselines

Since our task is formalized as binary classification, the random baseline has 0.50 accuracy. As our test set is not perfectly balanced, a most frequent class baseline would get 0.517 F1.

We also computed an unsupervised distributional vector cosine baseline based on the idea that a discriminative attribute is close to the word it characterizes and further away from the other member of the pair. In the cosine method, each item is classified as a semantic difference if the cosine similarity of $word_1$ and the attribute is greater than the cosine similarity of $word_2$ and the attribute. To compute the cosine baseline, we used a PPMI-based vector space with the best settings from Baroni et al. (2014).

The cosine baseline correctly classifies 0.691 of positive items and 0.539 of negative items in the test data, which corresponds to an average F1 measure of 0.607.

3.3 Human upper bound

In order to obtain a performance upper bound for our task, we measured how complex it is for expert human annotators to identify discriminative attributes. We asked three PhD and post-doc computational linguists to classify a batch of 100 items randomly sampled from the test set. The annotators received two rounds of training on the task by classifying a batch of 100 triples from the validation and test sets. The triples used at annotator training and testing stages were all distinct. Various questions and doubts about the annotation were clarified before passing to the test annotation phase. The agreement between aggregated human judgments (majority vote) and the gold standard was very high, with an accuracy of 0.9, an F1 of 0.89 for the positive class, and an F1 of 0.91 for the negative class.

---

[3]https://github.com/dpaperno/DiscriminAtt/

	correct	incorrect
positive	724	323
negative	697	596

Table 5: Number of correct and incorrect classifications for the test set using the cosine baseline.

Rank	Team	Score
1	SUNNYNLP	0.75
2	Luminoso	0.74
3	BomJi	0.73
3	NTU NLP	0.73
4	UWB	0.72
5	ELiRF-UPV	0.69
5	Meaning Space	0.69
5	Wolves	0.69
6	Discriminator	0.67
6	ECNU	0.67
5	AmritaNLP	0.66
6	GHH	0.65
7	ALB	0.63
7	CitiusNLP	0.63
7	THU NGN	0.63
8	UNBNLP	0.61
9	UNAM	0.60
10	UMD	0.60
11	ABDN	0.52
12	Igevorse	0.51
13	bicici	0.47
ceiling	human	0.90
baselines	(strong) cosine	0.607
	(weak) random	0.517

Table 6: Codalab competition results, compared to baselines and the human-based performance ceiling.

System type	Count	Average F1	Best F1
NN	4	0.66	0.73
Rule-based	7	0.63	0.69
SVM / SVC	6	0.68	0.75
XGB	2	0.70	0.73

Table 7: Average and best F1 score per system type.

4 Systems Overview

Table 6 shows the best performing system submitted by each participating team which submitted descriptions of their systems.

Many participants created custom rules to tackle the task, using for example cosine similar-

---

Resource type	Average F1
WE + KB	0.678
WE	0.638

Table 8: Average F1 score per resource type (KB = Knowledge Base, WE = Word Embeddings).

ity or co-occurrence frequency thresholds (Meaning Space, Sommerauer et al.; ELiRF-UPV, Gonzlez et al.; CitiusNLP Gamallo; UNAM Arroyo-Fernndez et al.; Discriminator, Kulmizev et al.; UNBNLP, King et al.; ABDN, Mao et al.; Igevorse, Grishin).

Some of the most successful systems employed traditional machine learning algorithms such as SVMs (SUNNYNLP, Lai et al.; ALB, Dumitru et al.; Wolves, Taslimipoor et al.; ECNU, Zhou et al.; UMD, Zhang and Carpuat), SVC (Luminoso, Speer and Lowry-Duda) and Maximum Entropy Classifiers (UWB, Brychcn et al.).

Other teams chose to build their systems using deep learning systems such as neural networks (GHH, Attia et al.; Shiue et al.), CNNs (THU NGN, Wu et al.; AmritaNLP, Vinayan et al.) and XGB classifiers (BomJi, Santus et al.; ECNU, Zhou et al.).

Participants made use of a large number of resources. Such resources can be divided into word embeddings (e.g., Word2Vec, GloVe, fastText) and knowledge base type resources (e.g., WordNet, ConceptNet, Probase). Participants' analyses of their results indicate that although using knowledge bases can yield high precision results, they cannot easily cover all cases. When employing pre-trained word embeddings, participants noted that out-of-vocabulary items become a challenge. But most importantly, a shortcoming of word embeddings with regard to our task is their inability to distinguish between different types of semantic relatedness. As noted by the GHH team (Attia et al.), *garlic* is related to *wings* not because garlic has the ability to fly but because garlic chicken wings are a popular dish choice; a shallow cooccurence-based model will fail to recognize that wings characterize chicken but not garlic.

On average, systems which combined word embeddings and knowledge bases outperformed systems that only used word embeddings (Table 8).

Subset	Accuracy	F1 pos	F1 neg
Easy	0.98	0.97	0.98
Hard	0.56	0.61	0.66
Hardest	0.38	0.35	0.39

Table 9: Results of human annotation of the Easy, Hard and Hardest subsets of the test data.

label	McRae pos	McRae neg	manual pos	manual neg	random pos	random neg
Easy	1	9	20	7	13	0
Hard	8	2	12	26	0	2

Table 10: Example label and source distribution for the Easy and Hard subsets of the test data.

5 Results analysis

We have carried out an in-depth exploration of the systems results in order to get a better insight on the relationship between their performance and the dataset structure and complexity. We ranked all the test triples by the number of systems that annotated them correctly and we selected the 50 top triples that were scored correctly by the most systems and the 50 top triples that were failed by most systems. We called these two subsets the **Easy** and the **Hard** data, respectively. Then, we focused on the results produced by the top 5 systems in Table 6, with an overall performance greater than 70%. Out of the 1340 triples that were failed by at least one of these top systems, we selected the 112 triples (8.3%) that were failed by all 5 systems. We called this subset the **Hardest** data. These datasets were annotated by the same three expert annotators used to compute the human upper bound (cf. Section 3.3). The accuracy and F1 of the aggregated human judgments (majority vote) with respect to the gold standard are reported in Table 9.

The annotation results show an interesting correlation between the system and human performances. The "easy" triples for the systems are easy for humans too, and conversely the harder a triple is for a system the harder it is for humans. The lowest annotation accuracy is on the Hardest subset, less than 40%. However, since this set contains the triples that were failed by all top systems, the human accuracy also proves that theres is still plenty of room for improvement even for the best performing models.

Table 9 shows that the F1 on the negative class is usually higher than the one on the positive class. This is again similar to systems behavior. In fact, 70% of the top 100 triples scored correctly by most systems are negative cases, while 67% of the top 100 triples failed by most systems are positive cases. The 112 triples failed by all top file systems contain 54% positive cases. This suggests that for systems and humans alike it is usually harder to

identify a discriminative attribute, rather than a non-discriminative one. Finally, out of the 1340 triples that were failed by at least one of the top 5 systems, 502 (37%) were failed by just one model. This shows that a great variance exists in the behavior and in the weaknesses of these systems, despite their very close performance.

Types of attributes seem to vary in how difficult they are to differentiate in the context of our task. For example, attributes that stand in the whole-part relation with the word, as in *door,gate,handle*, lean on the hard side (9 examples in the **Hard** sample vs. 2 in the **Easy** one). Attributes that are adjectives, as in *rods,wire,hard*, also tend to be hard (25 examples in the **Hard** sample vs. 13 in the **Easy** one), presumably because of the gradient and context-dependent meaning of adjectives; indeed, 9 of the 13 "easy" examples with adjective attributes involve colours, which are relatively context-independent (as opposed to 4 colour out of the 25 "hard" adjective examples).

Further analysis reveals an unequal distribution of positive and negative examples in the Easy and Hard subsets across different types of data, as shown in Table 10. While overall easy examples tend to be the positive ones and hard examples tend to be negative, among the examples derived from McRae feature norms the pattern is reversed.

Lastly, it is an important issue to understand the causes of the low human performance on the Hard and especially on the Hardest subset. By looking at the wrongly annotated triples in this dataset, we can identify various possible reasons. The first one are mistakes in the gold standard annotation. For instance, *peel* was marked as a discriminative attribute of *banana* from *onion*, but actually peeling is a possible action for both entities. Other cases are instead related to the inherent vagueness of the notion of prototypical attribute. For example, the feature *acts* was marked as non-discriminative of *actress* from *artist*, because any artist can in principle act. Conversely, humans annotators have identified acting as a truly specific attribute for *ac-*

tress, but not for *artist*. The former type of problems prompt for a further revision of the gold standard, while the latter type reveals the complexity of the notion of discriminative attribute and its difficult applications in some cases, which will require a deeper specification of annotation guidelines.

6   Conclusion

Discriminative attribute detection is an intuitively simple and appealing yet challenging new task for lexical semantic systems. For the SemEval competition, we created a high quality dataset of semantic differences, with estimated ceiling performance of human annotators of 0.90. While the task is far from being solved, participating systems showed promising results, most of them beating the cosine baseline.

It is clear that learning to discriminate differentiating features is not trivial and requires training, both for human annotators and for computational systems; all of the top performing systems used machine learning techniques of some kind.

While different teams employed different linguistic resources, the results of the competition do not allow us to conclude that a particular resource gives one's system an edge. On the one hand, exploiting information from knowledge base resources like WordNet does improve the performance on average. On the other hand, traditional machine learning systems that entered our competition were much more likely to make use of knowledge bases. Therefore, combining neural approaches with knowledge bases may very well lead to improved performances.

As we mentioned above, ceiling performance has already been achieved in traditional tasks such as word similarity, causing a stagnation of lexical semantic modeling. As the best systems in our competition showed very promising results, we hope to see novel semantic models demonstrate their full potential on our task.

Acknowledgements

We thank Marco Baroni, Roberto Zamparelli, and three anonymous reviewers for their helpful comments. We thank Giulia Cappelli, Patrick Jeunieaux, and Marco Senaldi for their valued support in the data analysis. This work was supported by the CNRS PEPS I3A project ReSeRVe.

References

Ignacio Arroyo-Fernndez, Carlos-Francisco Mendez-Cruz, and Ivan Meza. 2018. Unam at semeval-2018 task 10: Unsupervised semantic discriminative attribute identification in neural word embedding cones. In *Proceedings of the 12th international workshop on semantic evaluation (SemEval 2018)*.

Mohammed Attia, Younes Samih, Manaal Faruqui, and Wolfgang Maier. 2018. Ghh at semeval-2018 task 10: Discovering discriminative attributes in distributional semantics. In *Proceedings of the 12th international workshop on semantic evaluation (SemEval 2018)*.

Marco Baroni, Georgiana Dinu, and Germán Kruszewski. 2014. Don't count, predict! a systematic comparison of context-counting vs. context-predicting semantic vectors. In *ACL (1)*, pages 238–247.

Miroslav Batchkarov, Thomas Kober, Jeremy Reffin, Julie Weeds, and David Weir. 2016. A critique of word similarity as a method for evaluating distributional semantic models. In *First Workshop on Evaluating Vector Space Representations for NLP (RepEval 2016)*.

Tom Brychcn, Tom Hercig, Josef Steinberger, and Michal Konkol. 2018. Uwb at semeval-2018 task 10: Capturing discriminative attributes from word distributions. In *Proceedings of the 12th international workshop on semantic evaluation (SemEval 2018)*.

George S Cree and Ken McRae. 2003. Analyzing the factors underlying the structure and computation of the meaning of chipmunk, cherry, chisel, cheese, and cello (and many other such concrete nouns). *Journal of Experimental Psychology: General*, 132(2):163.

Bogdan Dumitru, Alina Maria Ciobanu, and P. Dinu Liviu. 2018. Alb at semeval-2018 task 10: A system for capturing discriminative attributes. In *Proceedings of the 12th international workshop on semantic evaluation (SemEval 2018)*.

Manaal Faruqui, Yulia Tsvetkov, Pushpendre Rastogi, and Chris Dyer. 2016. Problems with evaluation of word embeddings using word similarity tasks. In *First Workshop on Evaluating Vector Space Representations for NLP (RepEval 2016)*.

Pablo Gamallo. 2018. Citiusnlp at semeval-2018 task 10: The use of transparent distributional models and salient contexts to discriminate word. In *Proceedings of the 12th international workshop on semantic evaluation (SemEval 2018)*.

Jos-ngel Gonzlez, Llus-F. Hurtado, Encarna Segarra, and Ferran Pla. 2018. Elirf-upv at semeval-2018 task 10: Capturing discriminative attributes. In *Proceedings of the 12th international workshop on semantic evaluation (SemEval 2018)*.

Maxim Grishin. 2018. Igevorse at semeval-2018 task 10: Exploring an impact of word embeddings concatenation for capturing discriminative attributes. In *Proceedings of the 12th international workshop on semantic evaluation (SemEval 2018)*.

Felix Hill, Roi Reichart, and Anna Korhonen. 2015. Simlex-999: Evaluating semantic models with (genuine) similarity estimation. *Computational Linguistics*, 41(4):665–695.

Milton King, Ali Hakimi Parizi, and Paul Cook. 2018. Unbnlp at semeval-2018 task 10: Evaluating unsupervised approaches to capturing discriminative attributes. In *Proceedings of the 12th international workshop on semantic evaluation (SemEval 2018)*.

Alicia Krebs and Denis Paperno. 2016. Capturing discriminative attributes in a distributional space: Task proposal. In *Proceedings of RepEval 2016: The First Workshop on Evaluating Vector Space Representations for NLP*.

Artur Kulmizev, Mostafa Abdou, Vinit Ravishankar, and Malvina Nissim. 2018. Discriminator at semeval-2018 task ten: Zero-shot discrimination. In *Proceedings of the 12th international workshop on semantic evaluation (SemEval 2018)*.

Sunny Lai, Kwong Sak Leung, and Yee Leung. 2018. Sunnynlp at semeval-2018 task 10: A support-vector-machine-based method for detecting semantic difference using taxonomy and word embedding features. In *Proceedings of the 12th international workshop on semantic evaluation (SemEval 2018)*.

Angeliki Lazaridou, Nghia The Pham, and Marco Baroni. 2016. The red one!: On learning to refer to things based on their discriminative properties. *arXiv preprint arXiv:1603.02618*.

Alessandro Lenci, Marco Baroni, Giulia Cazzolli, and Giovanna Marotta. 2013. BLIND: a set of semantic feature norms from the congenitally blind. *Behavior Research Methods*, 45(4):1218–1233.

Omer Levy and Yoav Goldberg. 2014. Linguistic regularities in sparse and explicit word representations. In *Proceedings of the eighteenth conference on computational natural language learning*, pages 171–180.

Tal Linzen. 2016. Issues in evaluating semantic spaces using word analogies. *arXiv preprint arXiv:1606.07736*.

Rui Mao, Guanyi Chen, Ruizhe Li, and Chenghua Lin. 2018. Abdn at semeval-2018 task 10: Recognising discriminative attributes using context embeddings and wordnet. In *Proceedings of the 12th international workshop on semantic evaluation (SemEval 2018)*.

Ken McRae, George S Cree, Mark S Seidenberg, and Chris McNorgan. 2005. Semantic feature production norms for a large set of living and nonliving things. *Behavior research methods*, 37(4):547–559.

Enrico Santus, Chris Biemann, and Emmanuele Chersoni. 2018. Bomji at semeval-2018 task 10: Combining vector-, pattern- and graph-based information to identify discriminative attributes. In *Proceedings of the 12th international workshop on semantic evaluation (SemEval 2018)*.

Yow-Ting Shiue, Hen-Hsen Huang, and Hsin-Hsi Chen. 2018. Ntu nlp lab system at semeval-2018 task 10: Verifying semantic differences by integrating distributional information and expert knowledge. In *Proceedings of the 12th international workshop on semantic evaluation (SemEval 2018)*.

Pia Sommerauer, Antske Fokkens, and Piek Vossen. 2018. Meaning space at semeval-2018 task 10: Combining explicitly encoded knowledge with information extracted from word embeddings. In *Proceedings of the 12th international workshop on semantic evaluation (SemEval 2018)*.

Robert Speer and Joanna Lowry-Duda. 2018. Luminoso at semeval-2018 task 10: Distinguishing attributes using text corpora and relational knowledge. In *Proceedings of the 12th international workshop on semantic evaluation (SemEval 2018)*.

Shiva Taslimipoor, Omid Rohanian, and Le An Ha. 2018. Wolves at semeval-2018 task 10: Semantic discrimination based on knowledge and association. In *Proceedings of the 12th international workshop on semantic evaluation (SemEval 2018)*.

Vivek Vinayan, Anand Kumar, and K P Soman. 2018. Amritanlp@semeval-2018 task 10: Capturing discriminative attributes using convolution neural network over global vector representation. In *Proceedings of the 12th international workshop on semantic evaluation (SemEval 2018)*.

David P Vinson and Gabriella Vigliocco. 2008. Semantic feature production norms for a large set of objects and events. *Behavior Research Methods*, 40(1):183–190.

Chuhan Wu, Fangzhao Wu, Sixing Wu, Zhigang Yuan, and Yongfeng Huang. 2018. Thu ngn at semeval-2018 task 10: Capturing discriminative attributes with mlp-cnn model. In *Proceedings of the 12th international workshop on semantic evaluation (SemEval 2018)*.

Alexander Zhang and Marine Carpuat. 2018. Umd at semeval-2018 task 10: Can word embeddings capture discriminative attributes? In *Proceedings of the 12th international workshop on semantic evaluation (SemEval 2018)*.

Yunxiao Zhou, Man Lan, and Yuanbin Wu. 2018. Ecnu at semeval-2018 task 10: Evaluating simple but effective features on machine learning methods for semantic difference detection. In *Proceedings of the 12th international workshop on semantic evaluation (SemEval 2018)*.

SUNNYNLP at SemEval-2018 Task 10: A Support-Vector-Machine-Based Method for Detecting Semantic Difference using Taxonomy and Word Embedding Features

Sunny Lai[1,3], Kwong Sak Leung[1,3] and Yee Leung[2,3]
[1]Department of Computer Science and Engineering
[2]Department of Geography and Resource Management
[3]Institute of Future Cities
The Chinese University of Hong Kong
Shatin, N.T., Hong Kong
`{slai, ksleung}@cse.cuhk.edu.hk, yeeleung@cuhk.edu.hk`

Abstract

We present SUNNYNLP, our system for solving SemEval 2018 Task 10: "Capturing Discriminative Attributes". Our Support-Vector-Machine(SVM)-based system combines features extracted from pre-trained embeddings and statistical information from *Is-A* taxonomy to detect semantic difference of concepts pairs. Our system is demonstrated to be effective in detecting semantic difference and is ranked 1st in the competition in terms of F1 measure. The open source of our code is coined SUNNYNLP[1].

1 Introduction

Measuring semantic similarity between words has been a fundamental issue in Natural Language Processing (NLP). Semantic similarity measurements are used to improve downstream applications including paraphrase detection (Xu et al., 2014), question answering (Lin, 2007), taxonomy enrichment (Jurgens and Pilehvar, 2016) and dialogue state tracking (Mrksic et al., 2016).

Despite the current success in using semantic model to measure semantic similarity, lesser attention is paid to teaching machines to make reference (Searle, 1969; Abbott, 2010) to the real world in detecting semantic difference. The semantic difference detection problem can be formalized as a binary classification task: given a triplet (*concept1, concept2, attribute*) which comprises two concepts *(e.g. apple, banana)* and one attribute *(e.g. red)*, determine whether the attribute characterizes the former concept but not the latter. Compared to pairwise semantic similarity detection, this problem is more complex than measuring similarity in general because of its underlying asymmetric property and the extra attribute involved. The SemEval 2018 Task 10 (Krebs et al., 2018) is

therefore posed to attract attention to solving this problem.

Although the task of semantic difference detection is novel, similar tasks like referring expression generation (REG) have been studied in the literature. Resources such as ontologies, knowledge bases (Krahmer and Van Deemter, 2012) and images (Kazemzadeh et al., 2014; Lazaridou et al., 2016) are used to learn referring expressions. The major difference between the present task and referring expression is that REG systems can choose salient attributes for making successful reference to objects, while our system is required to decide whether a given attribute can be used to differentiate two similar objects.

The rest of the paper is organized as follows: Section 2 explains our motivation and approach. Section 3 describes the official and external data used. Section 4 details our system implementation. We analyze and discuss the result in Section 5 and conclude our work in Section 6.

2 General Approach

Our approach to this problem is to divide the ternary concept-concept-attribute relationship (*concept1, concept2, attribute*) into two concept-attribute relationships (*concept, attribute*)[2]. The ternary relationship will hold only when the first pair of concept-attribute relation is true and the second false. This approach allows us to use well developed pairwise similarity measurements to extract semantic information from the two concept-attribute pairs, and aggregate the features to train a support vector machine (Cortes and Vapnik, 1995) to detect semantic difference of the triplet, *i.e.* identifying whether a concept contains a specific attribute is a key task of our system.

---

[1]https://github.com/Yermouth/sunnynlp

[2]For instance, dividing the concept-concept-attribute relationship *(apple, banana, red)* into two concept-attribute relationships: *(apple, red)* and *(banana, red)*.

Proceedings of the 12th International Workshop on Semantic Evaluation (SemEval-2018), pages 741–746
New Orleans, Louisiana, June 5–6, 2018. ©2018 Association for Computational Linguistics

Concept-instance example (*Is-A*) from Probase
(*yellow* food, *lemon*)
Possible concept-attribute (*Has-A*) pairs
(yellow, food), (food, yellow), (yellow, lemon),
(*lemon, yellow*), (food, lemon), (lemon, food)
Useful concept-attribute (*Has-A*) pairs
(*lemon, yellow*)
Semantic difference triplet in official test cases
(*lemon*, cranberry, *yellow*)

Table 1: Concept-attribute pairs (*Has-A*) can be inferred from concept-instance (*Is-A*) entries in taxonomy, and used to determine whether a semantic difference relationship (*concept1, concept2, attribute*) holds in official test cases.

By observation, we draw similarities between concept-attribute relationship and meronomy *(Has-A)*. They are similar in a sense that both describe subtype relationships. Although linguistics resources constructed by human subjects including norms and priming effect data can help us detect and verify these relationships effectively, they are not allowed to be used in this SemEval Task.

This SemEval Task also limits the scope of concepts and attributes to concrete concepts and visual attributes only. As instances of the same concept are likely to share common attributes from our intuitive perspective[3], we would like to experiment on extracting meronomy (*Has-A*) information from hypernymy (*Is-A*) pairs. Taxonomies and ontologies which contain rich *Is-A* information in terms of concept-instance pairs are therefore the key external linguistic resources which we rely on to extract concept-attribute relationships.

Another intuition that guides our research direction is that modifiers such as adjectives, adverbs and noun modifiers are useful for capturing salient attribute of a specific class of objects[4]. As modifiers are used to describe the scope of concepts or specify context of instances, we can leverage on the co-occurrence probability of modifiers to analyze their dependence/independence relationships with different concepts, and hence, to determine whether a concept-attribute relationship holds.

As the SemEval Task limits the word length of the concept and attribute to be 1, we can enumerate all possible pairs of modifiers and concepts from large scale taxonomy and ontology and use them as features to train our system. Table 1 shows an *Is-A* entry in taxonomies which we find instructive for learning semantic difference relationship. For instance, verifying whether semantic difference relationship holds for the triplet *(lemon, cranberry, yellow)* would require the information of "*lemon* has the attribute *yellow*?" and "*cranberry* does not have the attribute *yellow*?". With the *Is-A* pair *(yellow food, lemon)* from Probase, we can extract possible concept-attribute pairs and their frequency to train our system, such that our system knows with high probability that *lemon* has the attribute *yellow* while *cranberry* does not.

3 Data

We use the official dataset together with two external linguistic resources, GloVe (Pennington et al., 2014) and Probase (Wu et al., 2012; Cheng et al., 2015), to train our system.

3.1 Official Dataset

Official datasets[5] are split into three parts – training, validation and testing, where the testing holds a disjoint attribute sets apart from training and validation. This further increases the difficulty of the task as it prevents *lexical memorization* (Roller et al., 2014; Levy et al., 2015; Weeds et al., 2014) and tests for generalization.

3.2 Probase

Probase is a web scale open domain taxonomy which uses Hearst patterns (Hearst, 1992) to extract *Is-A* relationship from web documents. Each *Is-A* entry in Probase is represented as a triplet form: super-concept, sub-concept and number of co-occurrence. We choose Probase for two main reasons:

1. Large number of concepts covered: The number of concepts covered in Probase (Wu et al., 2012) exceeds other publicly available

---

[3]As both apple and banana are hypernyms of fruit, i.e. apple *Is-A* fruit and banana *Is-A* fruit. If we know apple is "edible", then banana may have a higher chance of being "edible" by intuition because "edible" can be a common attribute for most fruits.

[4]When we want to differentiate one object from another, we usually use a salient and outstanding attribute to describe the object instead of using a common or similar attribute. Similar viewpoint is previously raised in (Pechmann, 1989; Dale and Haddock, 1991), which states that human beings prefer using efficient and sufficiently distinguishing description when they are constructing referring expressions.

[5]in the form of concept-concept-attribute triplet with human annotated label indicating whether semantic difference exists.

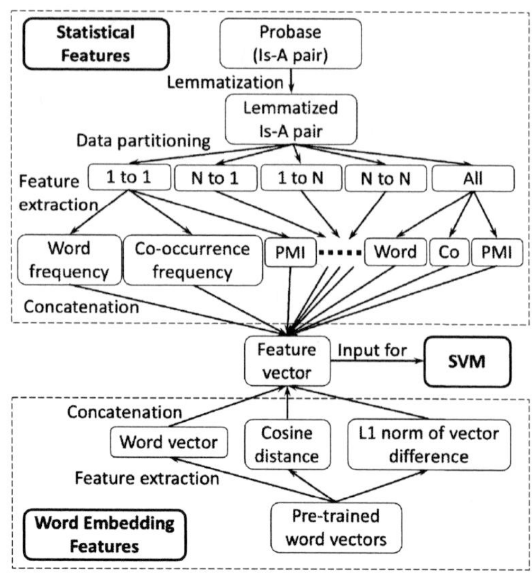

Figure 1: System architecture pipeline diagram.

Partition	Concept-Instance(*Is-A*) example	Size
1 to 1	(fruit, banana)	2.12M
N to 1	(high sugar fruit, banana)	7.91M
1 to N	(plant, banana tree)	9.32M
N to N	(dried fruit, banana chip)	14.01M
Total		33.37M

Table 2: Partitioning of dataset into 4 subsets with an example entrand partition size provided.

Frequency Type	Feature Extracted
Individual word	(dried), (fruit), (banana), (chip)
Concept-Concept	(dried, fruit)
Instance-Instance	(banana, chip)
Concept-Instance	(dried, banana), (dried, chip), (fruit, banana), (fruit, chip)

Table 3: Example of how individual word frequency (the first row) and three types of co-occurrences (the last three rows) are counted for the *Is-A* pair (dried fruit, banana chip) in Probase.

taxonomies and ontologies including Word-Net (Miller, 1995) and YAGO (Suchanek et al., 2007)[6].

2. Rich in semantic features: Probase provides *Is-A* relationship pairs with concepts of different senses and abstraction levels, which allows our system to extract rich statistical information for training. For instance, *Is-A* pairs in Table 2 are extracted from Probase.

3.3 GloVe

Pre-trained embeddings such as Word2Vec (Mikolov et al., 2013), GloVe (Pennington et al., 2014) and FastText (Bojanowski et al., 2016) encode syntactic and semantic relationships of words in low-dimension space, which is crucial to the capturing of semantic difference. We use the GloVe embedding pre-trained on both Gigaword corpus and 2014 Wikipedia dump in our final submission system.

4 System Description

Our system architecture pipeline (Figure 1) includes the process of data preprocessing, feature extraction and classifier selection.

4.1 Data Preprocessing

Preprocessing procedure is applied to Probase including:

---

[6]Probase includes 2,653,872 concepts while WordNet and YAGO contain 25,229 and 352,297, respectively.

- Lemmatization: As Probase is crawled using a rule-based system, we lemmatize the data using stanford CoreNLP (Manning et al., 2014) to reduce words of different forms and allow better matching between *Is-A* entries in taxonomy and official dataset.

- Data partitioning: To give our system additional information regarding the adjectives, adverbs and modifiers of both concepts and instances, we partition Probase into 4 sub datasets, according to the word length of the concept and instance pair. For instance, partition "1 to 1" indicates that both concept and instance are of word length 1. Partition "N to 1" indicates concepts of arbitrary word length (more than 1) and instances of word length 1. Example of each partition are given in Table 2.

4.2 Feature Extraction

4.2.1 Statistical Features

As for statistical features, we consider the statistical features of the individual words, *i.e. concept1, concept2, attribute*, and the two concept-attribute relationship pairs, *i.e.* $(concept1, attribute)$, $(concept2, attribute))$ using individual or co-occurrence frequency in Probase.

Word frequency is extracted from individual words, and the following features are extracted from the *Is-A* pairs:

- Co-occurrence frequency

Model (Features)	Valid(cv=5)	Train/Test	Train+Valid/Test	Valid/Test
SVM(GloVe, Probase)	**0.790**	**0.644**	0.714	<u>**0.754**</u>
SVM(FastText, Probase)	0.764	**0.649**	0.709	**0.757**
SVM(Word2Vec, Probase)	0.757	0.636	**0.721**	0.732
Logistic Regression(Probase)	0.698	0.602	0.644	0.717
SVM(Probase)	0.730	0.553	0.637	0.691
Logistic Regression(GloVe, Probase)	0.753	0.607	0.674	0.674
SVM(GloVe)	0.712	0.597	0.652	0.668
SVM(FastText)	0.689	0.563	0.593	0.650
SVM(Word2Vec)	0.667	0.556	0.581	0.634

Table 4: Result (F1-score) obtained by our system. The underlined value represents the score of our official submission. Best scores for each partition are denoted in boldface.

- Pointwise Mutual Information(PMI) (Fano, 1961; Church and Hanks, 1990)

- Asymmetric Pointwise Mutual Information(APMI)

There are three types of pairwise word co-occurrence frequencies, including Concept-Concept, Instance-Instance and Concept-Instance. All types of frequencies are calculated for all partitions as distinct features. Table 3 gives an example of how occurrence and co-occurrence are counted. We apply logarithm to the statistical features to reduce the scale of frequently occurring words.

4.2.2 Word Embedding Features

We use the Python package Gensim (Rehurek and Sojka, 2010) to match each word in the triplet (*concept1, concept2, attribute*) in the official dataset with their corresponding pre-trained vectors $v_{con1}, v_{con2}, v_{attr}$, each of 300 dimensions. We then divide the triplet into three pairwise relationships *i.e.* (v_{con1}, v_{con2}), (v_{con1}, v_{attr}), and (v_{con2}, v_{attr}), and calculate the cosine similarity and L1-norm of the vector difference of these pairs as features. Dot-product is considered initially but removed as it adversely affects the performance of our system.

4.3 Classifiers

Using the same set of word embedding and statistical features, we compared the performance of four off-the-shelf classifiers including SVM (Cortes and Vapnik, 1995), Logistic Regression Classifier, Decision Tree Classifier and Random Forest Classifier. SVM classifier with RBF kernel (Vert et al., 2004) is used in our system as it outperforms other classifiers in terms of precision and F1-score.

5 Results and Discussion

5.1 Results

We provide the results of our system with different combinations of features and datasets in Table 4. Column *Train+Valid/Test* represents the F1-score obtained by training our system with both the training partition and validation partition, while column *Train/Test* and *Valid/Test* are F1-score obtained by training our system on the training partition and validation partition individually. Training our SVM system with Probase and GloVe (or Fast-Text) gives the best result in terms of F1-score for official evaluation (column *Valid/Test*). Our system achieves a F1-score of 0.754 and outperforms those of the other teams.

5.2 Discussion

During the competition phase, we noticed that our system performs better when we did not use training partition together with validation partition. As the entries in the training partition are automatically generated, there may be false entries or noise which can adversely affect our system. Since the validation partition comprises manually curated examples, we evaluate our models using 5-fold cross validation on the clean validation partition only (indicated by column *Valid(cv=5)*).

6 Conclusion

In this paper, we have discussed how our simple yet effective SVM system leverages on hypernymy (*Is-A*) relationships and word embeddings to detect single word semantic difference relationship. SVM has been shown useful especially in performing semantic relationship detection tasks (Filice et al., 2016; Panchenko et al., 2016). We would like to extend our system for detecting multiple-words semantic difference relationship, and to broaden the scope of concepts and attributes from visual only to sound and taxonomic.

As our system separates a concept-concept-instance relationship into two concept-instance relationships, our system is relatively weak in capturing attributes that are comparative or fuzzy, for instance, *young* and *tall*. It would be interesting to explore how semantic difference relationship can be embedded into taxonomies, ontologies and vector representations, so that comparative attributes can be comprehensively and directly captured.

Acknowledgments

This research was supported by the Chinese University of Hong Kong - Utrecht University - University of Toronto tripartite collaboration fund of The Chinese University of Hong Kong.

References

B. Abbott. 2010. *Reference*. Oxford Surveys in Semantics & Pragmatics No.2. OUP Oxford.

Piotr Bojanowski, Edouard Grave, Armand Joulin, and Tomas Mikolov. 2016. Enriching word vectors with subword information. *arXiv preprint arXiv:1607.04606*.

Jianpeng Cheng, Zhongyuan Wang, Ji-Rong Wen, Jun Yan, and Zheng Chen. 2015. Contextual text understanding in distributional semantic space. In *Proceedings of the 24th ACM International on Conference on Information and Knowledge Management*, pages 133–142. ACM.

Kenneth Ward Church and Patrick Hanks. 1990. Word association norms, mutual information, and lexicography. *Computational linguistics*, 16(1):22–29.

Corinna Cortes and Vladimir Vapnik. 1995. Support-vector networks. *Machine learning*, 20(3):273–297.

Robert Dale and Nicholas Haddock. 1991. Content determination in the generation of referring expressions. *Computational Intelligence*, 7(4):252–265.

Robert M Fano. 1961. Transmission of information: A statistical theory of communications.

Simone Filice, Danilo Croce, Alessandro Moschitti, and Roberto Basili. 2016. Kelp at semeval-2016 task 3: Learning semantic relations between questions and answers. In *Proceedings of the 10th International Workshop on Semantic Evaluation (SemEval-2016)*, pages 1116–1123, San Diego, California. Association for Computational Linguistics.

Marti A Hearst. 1992. Automatic acquisition of hyponyms from large text corpora. In *Proceedings of the 14th conference on Computational linguistics-Volume 2*, pages 539–545. Association for Computational Linguistics.

David Jurgens and Mohammad Taher Pilehvar. 2016. Semeval-2016 task 14: Semantic taxonomy enrichment. In *Proceedings of the 10th International Workshop on Semantic Evaluation (SemEval-2016)*, pages 1092–1102.

Sahar Kazemzadeh, Vicente Ordonez, Mark Matten, and Tamara Berg. 2014. Referitgame: Referring to objects in photographs of natural scenes. In *Proceedings of the 2014 conference on empirical methods in natural language processing (EMNLP)*, pages 787–798.

Emiel Krahmer and Kees Van Deemter. 2012. Computational generation of referring expressions: A survey. *Computational Linguistics*, 38(1):173–218.

Alicia Krebs, Alessandro Lenci, and Denis Paperno. 2018. Semeval-2018 task 10: Capturing discriminative attributes. In *Proceedings of the 12th international workshop on semantic evaluation (SemEval 2018)*.

Angeliki Lazaridou, Marco Baroni, et al. 2016. The red one!: On learning to refer to things based on discriminative properties. In *Proceedings of the 54th Annual Meeting of the Association for Computational Linguistics (Volume 2: Short Papers)*, volume 2, pages 213–218.

Omer Levy, Steffen Remus, Chris Biemann, and Ido Dagan. 2015. Do supervised distributional methods really learn lexical inference relations? In *Proceedings of the 2015 Conference of the North American Chapter of the Association for Computational Linguistics: Human Language Technologies*, pages 970–976.

Jimmy Lin. 2007. An exploration of the principles underlying redundancy-based factoid question answering. *ACM Transactions on Information Systems (TOIS)*, 25(2):6.

Christopher D. Manning, Mihai Surdeanu, John Bauer, Jenny Finkel, Steven J. Bethard, and David McClosky. 2014. The Stanford CoreNLP natural language processing toolkit. In *Association for Computational Linguistics (ACL) System Demonstrations*, pages 55–60.

Tomas Mikolov, Ilya Sutskever, Kai Chen, Greg S Corrado, and Jeff Dean. 2013. Distributed representations of words and phrases and their compositionality. In *Advances in neural information processing systems*, pages 3111–3119.

George A Miller. 1995. Wordnet: a lexical database for english. *Communications of the ACM*, 38(11):39–41.

Nikola Mrksic, Diarmuid Ó Séaghdha, Tsung-Hsien Wen, Blaise Thomson, and Steve J. Young. 2016. Neural belief tracker: Data-driven dialogue state tracking. *CoRR*, abs/1606.03777.

Alexander Panchenko, Stefano Faralli, Eugen Ruppert, Steffen Remus, Hubert Naets, Cedrick Fairon, Simone Paolo Ponzetto, and Chris Biemann. 2016. Taxi at semeval-2016 task 13: a taxonomy induction method based on lexico-syntactic patterns, substrings and focused crawling. In *Proceedings of the 10th International Workshop on Semantic Evaluation (SemEval-2016)*, pages 1320–1327, San Diego, California. Association for Computational Linguistics.

Thomas Pechmann. 1989. Incremental speech production and referential overspecification. *Linguistics*, 27(1):89–110.

Jeffrey Pennington, Richard Socher, and Christopher D. Manning. 2014. Glove: Global vectors for word representation. In *Empirical Methods in Natural Language Processing (EMNLP)*, pages 1532–1543.

Radim Rehurek and Petr Sojka. 2010. Software framework for topic modelling with large corpora. In *In Proceedings of the LREC 2010 Workshop on New Challenges for NLP Frameworks*. Citeseer.

Stephen Roller, Katrin Erk, and Gemma Boleda. 2014. Inclusive yet selective: Supervised distributional hypernymy detection. In *Proceedings of COLING 2014, the 25th International Conference on Computational Linguistics: Technical Papers*, pages 1025–1036.

John R Searle. 1969. *Speech acts: An essay in the philosophy of language*, volume 626. Cambridge university press.

Fabian M Suchanek, Gjergji Kasneci, and Gerhard Weikum. 2007. Yago: a core of semantic knowledge. In *Proceedings of the 16th international conference on World Wide Web*, pages 697–706. ACM.

Jean-Philippe Vert, Koji Tsuda, and Bernhard Schölkopf. 2004. A primer on kernel methods. *Kernel methods in computational biology*, 47:35–70.

Julie Weeds, Daoud Clarke, Jeremy Reffin, David Weir, and Bill Keller. 2014. Learning to distinguish hypernyms and co-hyponyms. In *Proceedings of COLING 2014, the 25th International Conference on Computational Linguistics: Technical Papers*, pages 2249–2259. Dublin City University and Association for Computational Linguistics.

Wentao Wu, Hongsong Li, Haixun Wang, and Kenny Q Zhu. 2012. Probase: A probabilistic taxonomy for text understanding. In *Proceedings of the 2012 ACM SIGMOD International Conference on Management of Data*, pages 481–492. ACM.

Wei Xu, Alan Ritter, Chris Callison-Burch, William B Dolan, and Yangfeng Ji. 2014. Extracting lexically divergent paraphrases from twitter. *Transactions of the Association for Computational Linguistics*, 2:435–448.

SemEval-2018 Task 11: Machine Comprehension Using Commonsense Knowledge

Simon Ostermann   Michael Roth   Ashutosh Modi   Stefan Thater   Manfred Pinkal

Saarland University

Saarbrücken, Germany

`{simono|mroth|ashutosh|stth|pinkal}@coli.uni-saarland.de`

Abstract

This report summarizes the results of the SemEval 2018 task on machine comprehension using commonsense knowledge. For this machine comprehension task, we created a new corpus, *MCScript*. It contains a high number of questions that require commonsense knowledge for finding the correct answer. 11 teams from 4 different countries participated in this shared task, most of them used neural approaches. The best performing system achieves an accuracy of 83.95%, outperforming the baselines by a large margin, but still far from the human upper bound, which was found to be at 98%.

1 Introduction

Developing algorithms for understanding natural language is not trivial. Natural language comes with its own complexity and inherent ambiguities. Ambiguities can occur, for example, at the level of word meaning, syntactic structure, or semantic interpretation. Traditionally, Natural Language Understanding (NLU) systems have resolved ambiguities using information from the textual context (e.g. neighboring words and sentences), for example via distributional methods (Lenci, 2008). However, many times context may be absent or may lack sufficient information to resolve the ambiguity. In such cases, it would be beneficial to include commonsense knowledge about the world in an NLU system. For example, consider example (1).

(1)   The waitress brought Rachel's order. She ate the food with great pleasure.

Looking at the example in isolation, the person eating the food could be either Rachel or the waitress. Using commonsense knowledge, or, more specifically, script knowledge about the RESTAURANT scenario, helps to resolve the referent of the pronoun: Rachel ordered the food. The person who orders the food is the customer. So Rachel should eat the food, *she* thus refers to Rachel.

This shared task assesses how the inclusion of commonsense knowledge benefits natural language understanding systems. In particular, we focus on commonsense knowledge about everyday activities, referred to as *scripts*. Scripts are sequences of events describing stereotypical human activities (also called *scenarios*), for example baking a cake, taking a bus, etc. (Schank and Abelson, 1975). The concept of scripts has its underpinnings in cognitive psychology and has been shown to be an important component of the human cognitive system (Bower et al., 1979; Schank, 1982; Modi et al., 2017). From an application perspective, scripts have been shown to be useful for a variety of tasks, including story understanding (Schank, 1990), information extraction (Rau et al., 1989), and drawing inferences from texts (Miikkulainen, 1993).

Factual knowledge is mentioned explicitly in texts from sources such as Wikipedia and news papers. On the contrary, script knowledge is often implicit in the texts as it is assumed to be known to the comprehender. Because of this implicitness, learning script knowledge from texts is very challenging. There are few exceptions of corpora containing narrative texts that explicitly instantiate script knowledge. An example is the *InScript* (Modi et al., 2016), which contains short and simple narratives, that very explicitly mention script events and participants. The *Dinners from Hell* corpus (Rudinger et al., 2015a) is a similar dataset centered around the EATING IN A RESTAURANT scenario.

In the past, script modeling systems have been evaluated using intrinsic tasks such as event ordering (Modi and Titov, 2014), paraphrasing (Regneri et al., 2010; Wanzare et al., 2017), event prediction (namely, the narrative cloze task) (Chambers and Jurafsky, 2008, 2009; Rudinger et al., 2015b; Modi, 2016) or story completion (e.g. the story cloze task

Proceedings of the 12th International Workshop on Semantic Evaluation (SemEval-2018), pages 747–757
New Orleans, Louisiana, June 5–6, 2018. ©2018 Association for Computational Linguistics

T	It was a long day at work and I decided to stop at the gym before going home. I ran on the treadmill and lifted some weights. I decided I would also swim a few laps in the pool. Once I was done working out, I went in the locker room and stripped down and wrapped myself in a towel. I went into the sauna and turned on the heat. I let it get nice and steamy. I sat down and relaxed. I let my mind think about nothing but peaceful, happy thoughts. I stayed in there for only about ten minutes because it was so hot and steamy. When I got out, I turned the sauna off to save energy and took a cool shower. I got out of the shower and dried off. After that, I put on my extra set of clean clothes I brought with me, and got in my car and drove home.
Q1	Where did they sit inside the sauna? a. on the floor b. on a bench
Q2	How long did they stay in the sauna? a. about ten min- b. over thirty utes minutes

Figure 1: An example for a text from MCScript with 2 reading comprehension questions.

(Mostafazadeh et al., 2016)). These tasks test a system's ability to learn script knowledge from a text but they do not provide a mechanism to evaluate how useful script knowledge is in natural language understanding tasks.

Our shared task bridges this gap by directly relating commonsense knowledge and language comprehension. The task has a machine comprehension setting: A machine is given a text document and asked questions based on the text. In addition to what is mentioned in the text, answering the questions requires knowledge beyond the facts mentioned in the text. In particular, a substantial subset of questions requires inference over commonsense knowledge via scripts. For example, consider the short narrative in (1). For the first question, the correct choice for an answer requires commonsense knowledge about the activity of going to the sauna, which goes beyond what is mentioned in the text: Usually, people sit on benches inside a sauna, an

information that is not given in the text. The dataset also comprises questions that can just be answered from the text, as the second question: The information about the duration of the stay is given literally in the text.

The paper is organized as follows: In Section 2, we give an overview of other machine comprehension datasets. In Section 3, we describe the dataset used for our shared task. Section 4.2 gives details about the setup of our task. In Section 5, information about participating systems is given. Results are presented and discussed in Sections 6 and 8, respectively.

2 Related Work

Recently, a number of datasets have been proposed for machine comprehension. One example is *MCTest* (Richardson et al., 2013), a small curated dataset of 660 stories, with 4 multiple choice questions per story. The stories are crowdsourced and not limited to a domain. Answering questions in *MCTest* requires drawing inferences from multiple sentences from the text passage. In our dataset, in contrast, answering requires drawing inferences using knowledge not explicit in the text. Another recently published multiple choice dataset is RACE (Lai et al., 2017), which contains 100,000 questions on reading examination data.

Rajpurkar et al. (2016) have proposed the *Stanford Question Answering Dataset (SQuAD)*, a data set of 100,000 questions on Wikipedia articles collected via crowdsourcing. In that dataset, the answer to a question corresponds to a segment/span from the reading passage. Since Wikipedia articles mostly contain factual knowledge, *SQuAD* does not assess how in practice, language comprehension relies on implicit and underrepresented knowledge about everyday activities i.e. script knowledge.

Weston et al. (2015) have created the *BAbI* dataset. *BAbI* is a synthetic reading comprehension data set testing different types of reasoning to solve different tasks. In contrast to our dataset, the artificial texts in *BAbI* are not reflective of a typically occurring narrative text.

Two recently published datasets that also have a larger focus on commonsense reasoning are *NewsQA* and *TriviaQA*. NewsQA (Trischler et al., 2017) contains newswire texts from CNN with crowdsourced questions and answers. During the question collection, workers were only presented with the title of the text, and a short summary. This method ensures that literal repetitions of the text are avoided and the generation of non-trivial questions requiring background knowledge is supported. The NewsQA text collection differs from MCScript in domain and genre (newswire texts vs. narrative stories about everyday events). Knowledge required to answer the questions is mostly factual knowledge and script knowledge is only marginally relevant.

TriviaQA (Joshi et al., 2017) contains automatically collected question-answer pairs from 14 trivia and quiz-league websites, together with web-crawled evidence documents from *Wikipedia* and *Bing*. While a majority of questions require world knowledge for finding the correct answer, it is mostly factual knowledge.

3 Data

In 3.1, we now briefly describe the machine comprehension dataset used for the shared task, *MCScript*. Parts of the following Section are taken from Ostermann et al. (2018). For a more detailed description of the resource collection and a more thorough discussion of the dataset, we refer to the original paper. Section 3.2 gives details about script data collections that were made available to the participants.

3.1 Machine Comprehension Data - MCScript

For our shared task, we use the *MCScript* data set (Ostermann et al., 2018). It is a collection of narrative texts, questions of various types referring to these texts, and pairs of answer candidates for each question. It comprises 2,119 such texts and a total of 13,939 questions. The texts in the data set talk about everyday activities and cover 110 script scenarios of differing complexity. For the text collection, we followed Modi et al. (2016): All texts are simple and explicit in the description of script events and script participants.

The data set was crowdsourced via Amazon Mechanical turk[1]. In the crowdsourcing experiments, participants were asked to write questions independent of a concrete narrative, but only based on short descriptions of a scenario. By doing so, the collected questions were related to the scenario only and could be answered from different texts, independent of story details.

The scenario-based questions were paired randomly with texts from the same scenario. The

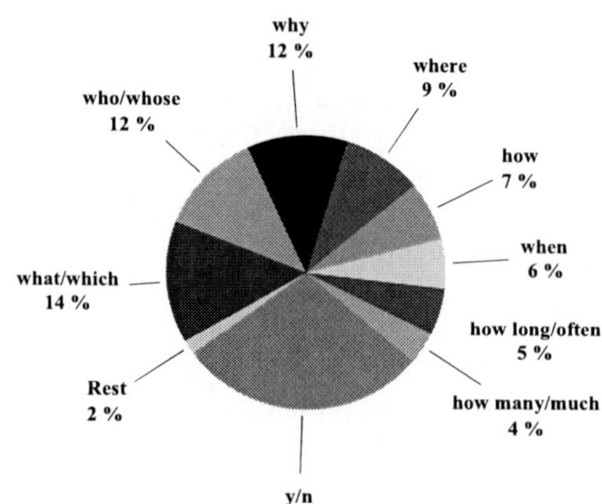

Figure 2: Distribution of question types in MCScript, from Ostermann et al. (2018).

subsequent answer collection was divided up into two steps: First, crowdsourcing workers had to annotate whether a question could be answered based on the given text. If it could be answered, they had to explicitly mark whether it could be answered from the text directly or based on commonsense knowledge. Second, they had to write a plausible correct and incorrect answer, if the question was answerable. Afterwards, all texts, questions and answers were manually validated by trained annotators, and corrected, if necessary.

Due to the design of the data acquisition process, a substantial subset of questions (27.4%) require commonsense inference about everyday activities. Figure 2 gives an overview of the distribution of question types on the data. *Yes/No* questions form the largest group, with 29%, followed by questions asking for details of a narration or scenario (*what/which* and *who*).

For the task, the corpus was split into training (9,731 questions on 1,470 texts), development (1,411 questions on 219 texts), and test set (2,797 questions on 430 texts). For 5 scenarios, all texts were held out for the test set, in order to avoid that models overfit and memorize the scenarios in the training data. Texts, questions, and answers contain on average 196.0 words, 7.8 words, and 3.6 words, respectively. There are 6.7 questions per text on average.

3.2 Script and Commonsense Knowledge Data

We also encouraged participants to make use of existing script data collections. Thus, we provided several existing collections of script data together with the machine comprehension corpus: DeScript (Wanzare et al., 2016), RKP (Regneri et al., 2010) and the OMCS stories (Singh et al., 2002). The three datasets contain sequences of short, telegraph-styled descriptions of all events that need to be conducted in a scenario (*event sequence descriptions, ESDs*). The data sets contain ESDs for different numbers of scenarios, with a total coverage of over 200 scenarios. The complexity of scenarios varies from simple activities, such as *opening a window*, to more complex ones, such as *attending a wedding*.

For 90 of the 110 scenarios in MCScript, there exist multiple ESDs per scenario in at least one of the 3 script data collections.

We also advised participants to make use of other representations for script knowledge, such as narrative chains (Chambers and Jurafsky, 2008), or event embeddings (Modi and Titov, 2014).

Some participants also made use of *ConceptNet* (Speer et al., 2017) as a resource for commonsense knowledge. ConceptNet is a large-scale knowledge graph that is built from several handcrafted and crowdsourced sources, and that encodes various types of commonsense knowledge.

4 Shared Task Setup

4.1 Evaluation Method

In our evaluation, we measured how well a system was capable of correctly answering questions that may involve commonsense knowledge. As evaluation metric, we used accuracy, calculated as the ratio between correctly answered questions and all questions in our evaluation data. We also evaluated systems with regard to specific question types and based on whether a question is directly answerable, or only inferable from the text.

4.2 Baselines

We provide results of two baseline systems as lower bounds for comparison: a rule-based baseline (*Sliding Window*) and a neural end-to-end system (*Attentive Reader*). Both baselines are described in

more detail below. For details about the tuning of hyperparameters, we refer to Ostermann et al. (2018).

Sliding Window

The sliding window baseline is a simple rule-based method that answers a question on a text by predicting the answer option with the highest similarity to the text. The intuition underlying this method is that answers similar to a text should be more plausible than answer options that are different from the text (independent of the question). In our baseline implementation, we compute similarity using a sliding window that compares each answer option to any possible "window" of w tokens of the text. For comparison, each window and each answer is represented by an average vector, computed over the components of word embeddings corresponding to the words in the window and answer, respectively. For each possible window, we compute similarity as the cosine similarity between the window and the answer representation. The answer with the higher maximum similarity (over possible windows) is predicted to be the correct answer.

Attentive Reader

The attentive reader is an established machine comprehension model that reaches good performance e.g. on the *CNN/Daily Mail* corpus (Hermann et al., 2015; Chen et al., 2016). It is a neural network-based approach, which scores answers to a question on a text by finding ("paying attention to") and scoring relevant passages in the text. The scoring and attention mechanisms are learned directly ("end-to-end") from text–question–answer triples, without the need for manual rule writing or feature engineering. As a baseline for the shared task, we use the model formulation by Chen et al. (2016) and Lai et al. (2017), who employ bilinear weight functions to compute both attention and answer-text fit. Bi-directional gated recurrent units (GRUs) are used to encode questions, texts and answers into hidden representations. For a question q and an answer a, the last state of the GRU, $\mathbf{q}$ and $\mathbf{a}$, are used as representations, while the text is encoded as a sequence of hidden states $\mathbf{t}_1...\mathbf{t}_n$. We compute an attention score s_j for each hidden state $\mathbf{t}_j$ using the question representation $\mathbf{q}$, a weight matrix $\mathbf{W}_a$, and an attention bias b. The text representation $\mathbf{t}$ is computed as a weighted average of hidden

---

[2] IUCM cluster MCScript texts and try to find answers also in other texts, that are topically similar. In that sense, MCScript itself is used to represent commonsense knowledge.

Rank	Team name	Main model	Commonsense	Other resources	Acc.
1	Yuanfudao	LSTM	ConceptNet	GloVe, Wikipedia, POS and NE tagging	0.84
2	MITRE	LSTM	–	word2vec, Twitter, stemming	0.82
3	Jiangnan	LSTM	–	GloVe, CoVe, POS and NE tagging	0.81
4	ELiRF-UPV	LSTM	ConceptNet	–	0.75
5	YNU_Deep	LSTM	–	GloVe	0.75
6	ZMU	LSTM	–	word2vec, GloVe	0.74
7	ECNU	LSTM	–	GloVe	0.73
8	YNU_AI1799	LSTM/CNN	–	word2vec, GloVe	0.72
9	YNU-HPCC	LSTM/CNN	–	word2vec	0.71
10	CSReader	LSTM	–	lemmatization, GloVe	0.63
11	IUCM	k-means	DeScript, MCScript[2]	NLTK	0.61

Table 1: Overview of techniques and resourced used by the participating systems.

representations:

$$s_j = softmax_j(\mathbf{t}_j^\top \mathbf{W}_a \mathbf{q} + b)$$
$$\mathbf{t} = \sum_j s_j \mathbf{t}_j \tag{1}$$

The probability p of answer a being correct is predicted using another bilinear weight matrix $\mathbf{W}_s$, followed by an application of the softmax function over both answer options for the question:

$$p(a|t, q) = softmax(\mathbf{t}^\top \mathbf{W}_s \mathbf{a}) \tag{2}$$

5 Participants

We ran our shared task through the CodaLab platform[3]. 24 teams submitted results during the evaluation period, out of which 11 teams provided system descriptions: 8 teams from China, and one team each from Spain, Russia and the US. The full leader board containing all 24 submissions can be found on the shared task website.

Except for one team, all participating models rely on recurrent neural network techniques to encode texts, questions and/or answers. The one team that did not apply neural methods proposed an alternative approach based on clustering techniques and scoring word overlap. Only 3 of the 11 teams made explicit use of commonsense knowledge: Two approaches used ConceptNet, either in the form of features extracted from ConceptNet relations or in the form of pretrained *Numberbatch*

embeddings (Speer et al., 2017). One participating system made use of script knowledge in the form of event sequence descriptions. Resources commonly used by participants include pretrained word embeddings such as GloVe (Pennington et al., 2014) or word2vec (Mikolov et al., 2013), and preprocessing pipelines such as NLTK[4]. In the following, we provide short summaries of the participants' systems and we give an overview of models and resources used by them (Table 1).

Non-neural methods *IUCM* (Reznikova and Derczynski, 2018) applied an unsupervised approach that assigns the correct answer to a question based on text overlap. Text overlap is computed based on the given passage and text sources of the same topic. Different clustering and topic modeling techniques are used to identify such text sources in MCScript and DeScript.

Neural-network based models Apart from *IUCM*, all participating systems are neural end-to-end models that employ recurrent and/or convolutional neural network architectures. Systems mainly differ with respect to details of the architecture and the form of how words are represented.

Yuanfudao (Liang Wang, 2018) applies a three-way attention mechanism to model interactions between the text, question and answers, on top of BiLSTMs. Each word in a text, question, and answer is represented by a vector of GloVe embeddings and additional information from part-of-speech tagging, name entity recognition, and relation extraction

[3]https://competitions.codalab.org/competitions/17184

[4]https://www.nltk.org/

Rank	Team name	Total	Commonsense	Text	Out of Domain
1	Yuanfudao	**0.84***	**0.82**	**0.85**	**0.79**
2	MITRE	0.82	0.79	0.83*	0.78
3	Jiangnan	0.81*	0.80	0.81*	0.75*
4	ELiRF-UVP	0.75	**0.82**	0.73	0.70
5	YNU_Deep	0.75	0.79	0.73	0.66
6	ZMU	0.74	0.80	0.72	0.66
7	ECNU	0.73	0.77	0.72	0.69
8	YNU_AI1799	0.72	0.76	0.71	0.67
9	YNU_HPCC	0.71*	0.78*	0.69*	0.64*
10	CSReader	0.63	0.64*	0.63	0.59
11	IUCM	0.61	0.54	0.64	0.58
–	Attentive Reader	0.72	0.75	0.71	0.69
–	Sliding Window	0.55	0.53	0.56	0.52
–	Human Performance	0.98			

Table 2: The accuracy of participating systems and the two baselines in total, on commonsense-based questions (*CS*), text-based questions (*TXT*) and on out-of-domain questions (from the 5 held-out testing scenarios). The best performance for each column is marked in **bold print**. Significant differences in results between two adjacent lines are marked by an asterisk (* $p<0.05$) in the upper line. The last line shows the human upper bound (Ostermann et al., 2018) as comparison.

(based on ConceptNet). The model is pretrained on another large machine comprehension dataset, namely the RACE corpus.

MITRE (Merkhofer et al., 2018) use a combination of 3 systems - two LSTMs with attention mechanisms, and one logistic regression model using patterns based on the vocabulary of the training set. The two neural models use different word embeddings - one trained on GoogleNews, another one trained on Twitter, which were enriched with word overlap features. Interestingly, the simple logistic regression model achieves competitive performance and would have ranked 4th as an individual system.

Jiangnan (Xia, 2018) applies a BiLSTM over GloVe and CoVe embeddings (McCann et al., 2017) with an additional attention mechanism. The attention mechanism computes soft word alignment between words in the question and the text or answer. Manual features, including part-of-speech tags, named entity types, and term frequencies, are employed to enrich word token representations.

ELiRF-UPV (José -Ángel González et al., 2018) employs a BiLSTM with attention to find similarities between texts, questions, and answers. Each word is represented based on Numberbatch embeddings, which encode information from ConceptNet.

YNU_Deep (Ding and Zhou, 2018) test different LSTMs and BiLSTMs variants to encode questions, answers and texts. A simple attention mechanism is applied between question–answer and text–answer pairs. The final submission is an ensemble of five model instances.

ZMU (Li and Zhou, 2018) consider a wide variety of neural models, ranging from CNNs, LSTMs and BiLSTMs with attention, together with pretrained Word2Vec and GloVe embeddings. They also employ data augmentation methods typically used in image processing. Their best performing model is a BiLSTM with attention mechanism and combined GloVe and Word2Vec embeddings.

ECNU (Sheng et al., 2018) use BiGRUs and BiLSTMs to encode questions, answers and texts. They implement a multi-hop attention mechanism from question to text (a Gated Attention Reader (Dhingra et al., 2017)).

YNU_AI1799 (Liu et al., 2018) submitted an ensemble of neural network models based on LSTMs, RNNs, and BiLSTM/CNN combinations, with attention mechanisms. In addition to word2vec embeddings, positional embeddings are used that are generated based on word embeddings.

Rank	Team name	y/n	what	why	who	where	when
1	Yuanfudao	**0.76**	**0.87**	**0.85**	**0.93**	**0.88**	0.81
2	MITRE	**0.76**	0.83	0.82	0.91	0.85	0.77
3	Jiangnan	0.75*	0.80*	0.80	0.88	0.84*	**0.82***
4	ELiRF-UVP	0.72	0.68	0.79	0.86	0.69	0.74
5	YNU_Deep	0.73	0.66	0.75	0.86	0.71	0.72
6	ZMU	0.73	0.65	0.77	0.81	0.72	0.75
7	ECNU	0.71	0.66	0.75	0.82	0.73	0.68
8	YNU_AI1799	0.70	0.68	0.78*	0.80	0.67	0.72
9	YNU_HPCC	0.72*	0.66*	0.71	0.83*	0.65	0.66
10	CSReader	0.54	0.59*	0.68	0.76*	0.62*	0.63
11	IUCM	0.54	0.75	0.66	0.45	0.77	0.61
–	Attentive Reader	0.67	0.66	0.75	0.84	0.73	0.71
–	Sliding Window	0.47	0.69	0.56	0.48	0.61	0.51

Table 3: Accuracy of participating systems and the baselines on the six most frequent question types. The best performance for each column is marked in **bold print**. Significant differences in results between two adjacent lines are marked by an asterisk (* p<0.05) in the upper line.

YNU-HPCC (Yuan et al., 2018) use an ensemble of neural networks with stacked CNN and LSTM layers and attention.

CSReader (Jiang and Sun, 2018) use GRUs to encode questions and texts. Answer and text are combined by using an attention mechanism that models soft word alignments, inspired by work on Natural Language Inference (Bowman et al., 2015). Two answer classifiers based on these representations are ensembled for prediction.

6 Results

Tables 2 and 3 give detailed results for all participating systems. We performed pairwise significance tests using an approximate randomization test (Yeh, 2000) over texts. At an accuracy of 84%, the best participating team Yuanfudao performed significantly better (p<0.05) than the second best system, MITRE (82%).

Except for *when* questions, Yuanfudao also achieved the best performance at each question type. However, individual differences in results over the 2nd place system were not found to be significant. The top three participating teams, Yuanfudao, MITRE and Jiangnan, all significantly outperform the remaining teams on text-based questions (>80% vs. <74%) as well as on *yes/no*, *what*, *where* and *when* questions.

In comparison to our baselines, all teams but Innopolis significantly outperform Sliding Window. Results of the Attentive Reader are in line with those of the participating systems ranked 7–9: ECNU, YNU_AI1799 and YNU_HPCC. The six top-ranked systems all significantly outperform both of our baselines. On out-of-domain questions, only the top 3 performing models significantly outperform the Attentive Reader baseline, while all models significantly outperform the Sliding Window approach.

For commonsense-based questions as well as for questions on *why* and *who*, results are considerably less consistent: while the top ranked system significantly outperforms teams ranked 7th or lower, most pairwise differences between the top teams are not statistically significant. This implies that the set of correctly answered questions considerably varies between systems, either due to randomness or because they excel at different inference problems.

We found that 19.3 % of the questions in the test set were answered correctly by each participating system. These questions mainly contain text-based questions with an answer that is literally given in the text. Also, there are many commonsense-based questions with a standardized correct answer, as shown in Example 2. Only few of the stories in MCScript cover a long timespan, so the answer to such questions is always similar.

(2) **Q:** How long did it take to pump up the tires?

    a. just a few minutes   b. a few hours

In contrast, only 1% of questions could not be answered by any of the participating models. Answering these questions mainly requires complicated inference steps, such as counting or plausibility judgements.

7 Discussion

We briefly highlight some of the findings by the shared task participants.

External knowledge sources. One of the main goals of this shared task was to provide an extrinsic evaluation framework for models of commonsense knowledge. However, only three participants actually made use of resources of commonsense knowledge.

Most prominent is the use of ConceptNet, a large-scale knowledge graph that is built from several handcrafted and crowdsourced sources. It was employed by two of the top 5 scoring models: Yuanfudao use it to learn their own ConceptNet-based relation embeddings. ELiRF-UPV make use of Numberbatch word embeddings, which are learned based on ConceptNet data. Ablation analyses conducted by Yuanfudao indicate that the addition of ConceptNet increases overall accuracy by almost 1% absolute. In contrast, only one participant used crowdsourced script data from the DeScript corpus in their final submission, IUCM. They found that the use of script data, instead of or in addition to texts, improved performance by up to 0.3% absolute.

CSReader tried to extend their neural model with script data from OMCS, but report that it did not result in an improvement.

No participant made use of narrative chains or other forms of structured/learned representations of scripts or events (such as event embeddings).

Pretraining. Most participants made use of pretraining in the form of word embeddings such as word2vec or GloVe, that were build on large data collections. Yuanfudao used the RACE dataset, which is the largest available multiple-choice machine comprehension corpus, for pretraining the complete model for several epochs. In their ablation analysis, they found pretraining to have the largest effect on model performance, with improvements in accuracy of up to 1.4% absolute. This result underlines that the comparably small size of MCScript naturally restricts how much neural approaches can learn from the data without overfitting.

Word representations. For representing tokens, most participants used word2vec embeddings, GloVe embeddings, or combinations thereof. The participating teams used different dimensionality sizes, and some of them refitted the vectors while others did not, leading to differing outcomes for both embedding types. In summary, none of both representations seems to clearly outperform the other.

In contrast, participants consistently found that extending word representations with additional features improves results: For example, Yuanfudao and Jiangnan use predicted part-of-speech tags and named entity information, as well as term frequency, and report improvements of up to 1% absolute in accuracy. Also, some participants report the use of word overlap features. Most notably, MITRE found that a logistic regression classifier based on overlap features can achieve performance competitive with neural approaches.

In general, additional features seem to be beneficial, since they provide more explicit or additional information that can be leveraged by neural networks and other classifiers.

Preprocessing. Several participants reported that lemmatizing and stop word removal further improved their results. A prominent example is the submission by MITRE, who use a stemmer to derive root forms for all words, in order to compute overlap and co-occurrence statistics between answers and text/questions.

8 Conclusions

This shared task provides an evaluation framework for commonsense knowledge in a machine comprehension setting. We create the MCScript corpus, which provides 2,119 stories and 13,939 answers for 110 everyday activities of different complexity. In contrast to previous datasets, MCScript was created in a way that results in a relatively large amount of *common sense questions,* i.e. questions which can not be answered directly from the text but require some form of common-sense knowledge about the scenario under consideration to be answered correctly.

24 teams submitted systems during the the evaluation period of the shared task, of which 11 teams submitted task description papers. The best-performing system achieves an overall accuracy of 84%, which outperforms the two baselines by a

large margin; yet, there gap to the human upper
bound (98%) is still relative large.

Although participants were explicitly encouraged to use additional common-sense knowledge
resources like DeScript of OMCS, only 3 systems
(including the best-performing system) actually
used such additional resources. The evaluation results suggest that additional common-sense knowledge is in fact beneficial for overall accuracy. However, the positive effect is relatively small, which
might be due to the fact that our dataset has been
created in a way that leads to relatively "easy" stories, and that the systems are able to learn a certain
amount of common sense knowledge directly from
the stories. In future work, it would be interesting
to see if the results of our shared task carry over
to other, presumably more complex stories like for
instance personal blog stories from the Spinn3r
corpus (Burton et al., 2011).

Acknowledgments

We thank the reviewers for their helpful comments.
Also, we thank all teams for their participation and
the effort they put into their submissions and the
discussions, making this shared task a success.

This research was funded by the German Research Foundation (DFG) as part of SFB 1102 Information Density and Linguistic Encoding and
EXC 284 Multimodal Computing and Interaction.

References

Gordon H Bower, John B Black, and Terrence J Turner.
1979. Scripts in memory for text. *Cognitive psychology*, 11(2):177–220.

Samuel R Bowman, Gabor Angeli, Christopher Potts,
and Christopher D Manning. 2015. A large annotated corpus for learning natural language inference.
In *Proceedings of the 2015 Conference on Empirical Methods in Natural Language Processing*, pages
632–642.

Kevin Burton, Niels Kasch, and Ian Soboroff. 2011.
The icwsm 2011 spinn3r dataset. In *Proceedings of
the Annual Conference on Weblogs and Social Media (ICWSM 2011)*.

Nathanael Chambers and Dan Jurafsky. 2008. Unsupervised Learning of Narrative Event Chains. In
*Proceedings of the 46th Annual Meeting of the Association for Computational Linguistics: Human
Language Technologies*, pages 789–797, Columbus,
Ohio. Association for Computational Linguistics.

Nathanael Chambers and Dan Jurafsky. 2009. Unsupervised Learning of Narrative Schemas and their Participants. In *Proceedings of the Joint Conference of
the 47th Annual Meeting of the ACL and the 4th International Joint Conference on Natural Language
Processing of the AFNLP*, pages 602–610, Singapore. Association for Computational Linguistics.

Danqi Chen, Jason Bolton, and Christopher D Manning. 2016. A Thorough Examination of the
CNN/Daily Mail Reading Comprehension Task. In
*Proceedings of the 54th Annual Meeting of the Association for Computational Linguistics (Volume 1:
Long Papers)*, volume 1, pages 2358–2367.

Bhuwan Dhingra, Hanxiao Liu, Zhilin Yang, William
Cohen, and Ruslan Salakhutdinov. 2017. Gated-attention readers for text comprehension. In *Proceedings of the 55th Annual Meeting of the Association for Computational Linguistics (Volume 1: Long
Papers)*, volume 1, pages 1832–1846.

Peng Ding and Xiaobing Zhou. 2018. YNU_Deep at
SemEval-2018 Task 11: An Ensemble of Attention-based BiLSTM Model for Machine Comprehension.
In *Proceedings of the 12th International Workshop
on Semantic Evaluations (SemEval-2018)*.

Karl Moritz Hermann, Tomas Kocisky, Edward Grefenstette, Lasse Espeholt, Will Kay, Mustafa Suleyman,
and Phil Blunsom. 2015. Teaching machines to read
and comprehend. In *Advances in Neural Information Processing Systems*, pages 1693–1701.

Zhengping Jiang and Qi Sun. 2018. CSReader at
SemEval-2018 Task 11: Multiple Choice Question
Answering as Textual Entailment. In *Proceedings of
the 12th International Workshop on Semantic Evaluations (SemEval-2018)*.

José -Ángel González, Lluís-F. Hurtado, Encarna
Segarra, and Ferran Pla. 2018. ELiRF-UPV at
SemEval-2018 Task 11: Machine Comprehension
using Commonsense Knowledge. In *Proceedings of
the 12th International Workshop on Semantic Evaluations (SemEval-2018)*.

Mandar Joshi, Eunsol Choi, Daniel S. Weld, and Luke
Zettlemoyer. 2017. TriviaQA: A Large Scale Distantly Supervised Challenge Dataset for Reading
Comprehension. In *Proceedings of the 55th Annual
Meeting of the Association for Computational Linguistics*, Vancouver, Canada. Association for Computational Linguistics.

Guokun Lai, Qizhe Xie, Hanxiao Liu, Yiming Yang,
and Eduard Hovy. 2017. Race: Large-scale reading
comprehension dataset from examinations. *arXiv
preprint arXiv:1704.04683*.

Alessandro Lenci. 2008. Distributional semantics in
linguistic and cognitive research. *Italian journal of
linguistics*, 20(1):1–31.

Yongbin Li and Xiaobing Zhou. 2018. ZMU at SemEval-2018 Task 11: Machine Comprehension Task using Deep Learning Models. In *Proceedings of the 12th International Workshop on Semantic Evaluations (SemEval-2018)*.

Liang Wang. 2018. Yuanfudao at SemEval-2018 Task 11: Three-way Attention and Relational Knowledge for Commonsense Machine Comprehension. In *Proceedings of the 12th International Workshop on Semantic Evaluations (SemEval-2018)*.

Qingxun Liu, HongDou Yao, and Xiaobing Zhou. 2018. YNU_AI1799 at SemEval-2018 Task 11: Machine Comprehension using Commonsense Knowledge of Different model ensemble. In *Proceedings of the 12th International Workshop on Semantic Evaluations (SemEval-2018)*.

Bryan McCann, James Bradbury, Caiming Xiong, and Richard Socher. 2017. Learned in translation: Contextualized word vectors. In *Advances in Neural Information Processing Systems*, pages 6297–6308.

Elizabeth M. Merkhofer, John Henderson, David Bloom, Laura Strickhart, and Guido Zarrella. 2018. MITRE at SemEval-2018 Task 11: Commonsense Reasoning without Commonsense Knowledge. In *Proceedings of the 12th International Workshop on Semantic Evaluations (SemEval-2018)*.

Risto Miikkulainen. 1993. *Subsymbolic natural language processing: An integrated model of scripts, lexicon, and memory*. MIT press.

Tomas Mikolov, Ilya Sutskever, Kai Chen, Greg S Corrado, and Jeff Dean. 2013. Distributed representations of words and phrases and their compositionality. In *Advances in neural information processing systems*, pages 3111–3119.

Ashutosh Modi. 2016. Event Embeddings for Semantic Script Modeling. In *Proceedings of The 20th SIGNLL Conference on Computational Natural Language Learning*, pages 75–83, Berlin, Germany. Association for Computational Linguistics.

Ashutosh Modi, Tatjana Anikina, Simon Ostermann, and Manfred Pinkal. 2016. InScript: Narrative texts annotated with script information. In *Proceedings of the Tenth International Conference on Language Resources and Evaluation (LREC 2016)*, Portorož, Slovenia. European Language Resources Association (ELRA).

Ashutosh Modi and Ivan Titov. 2014. Inducing Neural Models of Script Knowledge. In *Proceedings of the Conference on Computational Natural Language Learning (CoNLL)*, Baltimore, MD, USA.

Ashutosh Modi, Ivan Titov, Vera Demberg, Asad Sayeed, and Manfred Pinkal. 2017. Modeling semantic expectations: Using script knowledge for referent prediction. *Transactions of the Association for Computational Linguistics*, 5:31–44.

Nasrin Mostafazadeh, Nathanael Chambers, Xiaodong He, Devi Parikh, Dhruv Batra, Lucy Vanderwende, Pushmeet Kohli, and James Allen. 2016. A corpus and cloze evaluation for deeper understanding of commonsense stories. In *Proceedings of the 2016 Conference of the North American Chapter of the Association for Computational Linguistics: Human Language Technologies*, pages 839–849, San Diego, California. Association for Computational Linguistics.

Simon Ostermann, Ashutosh Modi, Michael Roth, Stefan Thater, and Manfred Pinkal. 2018. MCScript: A Novel Dataset for Assessing Machine Comprehension Using Script Knowledge. In *Proceedings of the 11th International Conference on Language Resources and Evaluation (LREC 2018)*, Miyazaki, Japan.

Jeffrey Pennington, Richard Socher, and Christopher D. Manning. 2014. GloVe: Global Vectors for Word Representation. In *Proceedings of the 2014 Conference on Empirical Methods in Natural Language Processing (EMNLP)*, pages 1532–1543.

Pranav Rajpurkar, Jian Zhang, Konstantin Lopyrev, and Percy Liang. 2016. SQuAD: 100,000+ Questions for Machine Comprehension of Text. In *Proceedings of the 2016 Conference on Empirical Methods in Natural Language Processing*, pages 2383–2392.

Lisa F Rau, Paul S Jacobs, and Uri Zernik. 1989. Information extraction and text summarization using linguistic knowledge acquisition. *Information Processing & Management*, 25(4):419–428.

Michaela Regneri, Alexander Koller, and Manfred Pinkal. 2010. Learning Script Knowledge with Web Experiments. In *Proceedings of the 48th Annual Meeting of the Association for Computational Linguistics*, pages 979–988, Uppsala, Sweden. Association for Computational Linguistics.

Sofia Reznikova and Leon Derczynski. 2018. IUCM at SemEval-2018 Task 11: Similar-Topic Texts as a Knowledge Source. In *Proceedings of the 12th International Workshop on Semantic Evaluations (SemEval-2018)*.

Matthew Richardson, Christopher J.C. Burges, and Erin Renshaw. 2013. MCTest: A Challenge Dataset for the Open-Domain Machine Comprehension of Text. In *Proceedings of the 2013 Conference on Empirical Methods in Natural Language Processing*, pages 193–203, Seattle, Washington, USA. Association for Computational Linguistics.

Rachel Rudinger, Vera Demberg, Ashutosh Modi, Benjamin Van Durme, and Manfred Pinkal. 2015a. Learning to predict script events from domain-specific text. *Lexical and Computational Semantics (* SEM 2015)*, page 205.

Rachel Rudinger, Pushpendre Rastogi, Francis Ferraro, and Benjamin Van Durme. 2015b. Script induction as language modeling. *Proceedings of the 2015 Conference on Empirical Methods in Natural Language Processing*, pages 1681–1686.

Roger C Schank. 1982. *Dynamic memory: A theory of learning in people and computers*. Cambridge University Press.

Roger C Schank. 1990. *Tell me a story: A new look at real and artificial memory*. Scribner New York.

Roger C Schank and Robert P Abelson. 1975. Scripts, Plans, and Knowledge. In *Proceedings of the 4th international joint conference on Artificial intelligence-Volume 1*, pages 151–157. Morgan Kaufmann Publishers Inc.

Yixuan Sheng, Man Lan, and Yuanbin Wu. 2018. ECNU at SemEval-2018 Task 11: Using Deep Learning Method to Address Machine Comprehension Task. In *Proceedings of the 12th International Workshop on Semantic Evaluations (SemEval-2018)*.

Push Singh, Thomas Lin, Erik T Mueller, Grace Lim, Travell Perkins, and Wan Li Zhu. 2002. Open Mind Common Sense: Knowledge Acquisition from the General Public. In *On the move to Meaningful Internet Systems 2002: CoopIS, DOA, and ODBASE*, pages 1223–1237. Springer.

Robert Speer, Joshua Chin, and Catherine Havasi. 2017. Conceptnet 5.5: An open multilingual graph of general knowledge. In *Proceedings of the Thirty-First AAAI Conference on Artificial Intelligence (AAAI-17)*, pages 4444–4451.

Adam Trischler, Tong Wang, Xingdi Yuan, Justin Harris, Alessandro Sordoni, Philip Bachman, and Kaheer Suleman. 2017. NewsQA: A Machine Comprehension Dataset. In *Proceedings of the 2nd Workshop on Representation Learning for NLP*, pages 191–200.

Lilian Wanzare, Alessandra Zarcone, Stefan Thater, and Manfred Pinkal. 2016. DeScript: A Crowdsourced Database for the Acquisition of High-quality Script Knowledge. In *Proceedings of the Tenth International Conference on Language Resources and Evaluation (LREC 2016)*, Portorož, Slovenia. European Language Resources Association (ELRA).

Lilian Wanzare, Alessandra Zarcone, Stefan Thater, and Manfred Pinkal. 2017. Inducing Script Structure from Crowdsourced Event Descriptions via Semi-Supervised Clustering. In *Proceedings of the 2nd Workshop on Linking Models of Lexical, Sentential and Discourse-level Semantics*, pages 1–11, Valencia, Spain. Association for Computational Linguistics.

Jason Weston, Antoine Bordes, Sumit Chopra, Alexander M Rush, Bart van Merriënboer, Armand Joulin, and Tomas Mikolov. 2015. Towards AI-complete question answering: A set of prerequisite toy tasks. *arXiv preprint arXiv:1502.05698*.

Jiangnan Xia. 2018. Jiangnan at SemEval-2018 Task 11: Attention-Based Reading Comprehension System. In *Proceedings of the 12th International Workshop on Semantic Evaluations (SemEval-2018)*.

Alexander Yeh. 2000. More accurate tests for the statistical significance of result differences. In *Proceedings of the 18th Conference on Computational Linguistics*, volume 2, pages 947–953.

Hang Yuan, Jin Wang, and Xuejie Zhang. 2018. YNU-HPCC at Semeval-2018 Task 11: Using an Attention-based CNN-LSTM for Machine Comprehension using Commonsense Knowledge. In *Proceedings of the 12th International Workshop on Semantic Evaluations (SemEval-2018)*.

Yuanfudao at SemEval-2018 Task 11: Three-way Attention and Relational Knowledge for Commonsense Machine Comprehension

Liang Wang   **Meng Sun**   **Wei Zhao**   **Kewei Shen**   **Jingming Liu**

Yuanfudao Research

Beijing, China

{wangliang01,sunmeng,zhaowei01,shenkw,liujm}@fenbi.com

Abstract

This paper describes our system for *SemEval-2018 Task 11: Machine Comprehension using Commonsense Knowledge* (Ostermann et al., 2018b). We use **Three**-way Attentive Networks (*TriAN*) to model interactions between the passage, question and answers. To incorporate commonsense knowledge, we augment the input with relation embedding from the graph of general knowledge *ConceptNet* (Speer et al., 2017). As a result, our system achieves state-of-the-art performance with 83.95% accuracy on the official test data. Code is publicly available at `https://github.com/intfloat/commonsense-rc`.

1 Introduction

It is well known that humans have a vast amount of commonsense knowledge acquired from everyday life. For machine reading comprehension, natural language inference and many other NLP tasks, commonsense reasoning is one of the major obstacles to make machines as intelligent as humans.

A large portion of previous work focus on commonsense knowledge acquisition with unsupervised learning (Chambers and Jurafsky, 2008; Tandon et al., 2017) or crowdsourcing approach (Singh et al., 2002; Wanzare et al., 2016). *ConceptNet* (Speer et al., 2017), *WebChild* (Tandon et al., 2017) and *DeScript* (Wanzare et al., 2016) etc are all publicly available knowledge resources. However, resources based on unsupervised learning tend to be noisy, while crowdsourcing approach has scalability issues. There is also some research on incorporating knowledge into NLP tasks such as reading comprehension (Lin et al., 2017; Yang and Mitchell, 2017) neural machine translation (Zhang et al., 2017a) and text classification (Zhang et al., 2017b) etc. Though experiments show performance gains over baselines, these gains are often quite marginal over the state-of-the-art system without external knowledge.

In this paper, we present **Three**-way Attentive Networks(*TriAN*) for multiple-choice commonsense reading comprehension. The given task requires modeling interactions between the passage, question and answers. Different questions need to focus on different parts of the passage, attention mechanism is a natural choice and turns out to be effective for reading comprehension. Due to the relatively small size of training data, *TriAN* use word-level attention and consists of only one layer of LSTM (Hochreiter and Schmidhuber, 1997). Deeper models result in serious overfitting and poor generalization empirically.

To explicitly model commonsense knowledge, relation embeddings based on ConceptNet (Speer et al., 2017) are used as additional features. ConceptNet is a large-scale graph of general knowledge from both crowdsourced resources and expert-created resources. It consists of over 21 million edges and 8 million nodes. ConceptNet shows state-of-the-art performance on tasks like word analogy and word relatedness.

Besides, we also find that pretraining our network on other datasets helps to improve the overall performance. There are some existing multiple-choice English reading comprehension datasets contributed by NLP community such as *MCTest* (Richardson et al., 2013) and *RACE* (Lai et al., 2017). Although those datasets don't focus specifically on commonsense comprehension, they provide a convenient way for data augmentation. Augmented data can be used to learn shared regularities of reading comprehension tasks.

Combining all of the aforementioned techniques, our system achieves competitive performance on the official test set.

758

Proceedings of the 12th International Workshop on Semantic Evaluation (SemEval-2018), pages 758–762

New Orleans, Louisiana, June 5–6, 2018. ©2018 Association for Computational Linguistics

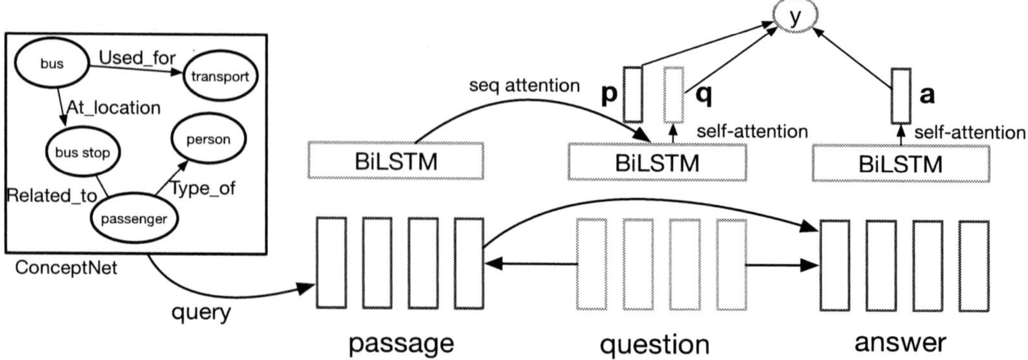

Figure 1: *TriAN* Model Architecture.

2 Model

The overall architecture of *TriAN* is shown in Figure 1. It consists of an input layer, an attention layer and an output layer.

Input Layer.   A training example consists of a passage $\{P_i\}_{i=1}^{|P|}$, a question $\{Q_i\}_{i=1}^{|Q|}$, an answer $\{A_i\}_{i=1}^{|A|}$ and a label $y^* \in \{0, 1\}$ as input. P, Q and A are all sequences of word indices. For a word P_i in the given passage, the input representation of P_i is the concatenation of several vectors:

- **GloVe embeddings.**   Pretrained 300-dimensional *GloVe* vector $\mathbf{E}_{P_i}^{glove}$.

- **Part-of-speech and named-entity embeddings.**   Randomly initialized 12-dimensional part-of-speech embedding $\mathbf{E}_{P_i}^{pos}$ and 8-dimensional named-entity embedding $\mathbf{E}_{P_i}^{ner}$.

- **Relation embeddings.**   Randomly initialized 10-dimensional relation embedding $\mathbf{E}_{P_i}^{rel}$. The relation is determined by querying ConceptNet whether there is an edge between P_i and any word in question $\{Q_i\}_{i=1}^{|Q|}$ or answer $\{A_i\}_{i=1}^{|A|}$. If there exist multiple different relations, just randomly choose one.

- **Handcrafted features.**   We also add logarithmic term frequency feature and co-occurrence feature $\mathbf{f}_{P_i}$. Term frequency is calculated based on English Wikipedia. Co-occurrence feature is a binary feature which is true if P_i appears in question $\{Q_i\}_{i=1}^{|Q|}$ or answer $\{A_i\}_{i=1}^{|A|}$.

The input representation for P_i is $\mathbf{w}_{P_i}$:

$$\mathbf{w}_{P_i} = [\mathbf{E}_{P_i}^{glove}; \mathbf{E}_{P_i}^{pos}; \mathbf{E}_{P_i}^{ner}; \mathbf{E}_{P_i}^{rel}; \mathbf{f}_{P_i}] \quad (1)$$

In a similar way, we can get input representation for question $\mathbf{w}_{Q_i}$ and answer $\mathbf{w}_{A_i}$.

Attention Layer.   We use word-level attention to model interactions between the given passage $\{P_i\}_{i=1}^{|P|}$, the question $\{Q_i\}_{i=1}^{|Q|}$ and the answer $\{A_i\}_{i=1}^{|A|}$. First, let's define a sequence attention function (Chen et al., 2017):

$$Att_{seq}(\mathbf{u},\ \{\mathbf{v}_i\}_{i=1}^{n}) = \sum_{i=1}^{n} \alpha_i \mathbf{v}_i$$
$$\alpha_i = \text{softmax}_i(f(\mathbf{W}_1\mathbf{u})^T f(\mathbf{W}_1\mathbf{v}_i)) \quad (2)$$

$\mathbf{u}$ and $\mathbf{v}_i$ are vectors and $\mathbf{W}_1$ is a matrix. f is a non-linear activation function and is set to $ReLU$.

Question-aware passage representation $\{\mathbf{w}_{P_i}^q\}_{i=1}^{|P|}$ can be calculated as: $\mathbf{w}_{P_i}^q = Att_{seq}(\mathbf{E}_{P_i}^{glove}, \{\mathbf{E}_{Q_i}^{glove}\}_{i=1}^{|Q|})$. Similarly, we can get passage-aware answer representation $\{\mathbf{w}_{A_i}^p\}_{i=1}^{|A|}$ and question-aware answer representation $\{\mathbf{w}_{A_i}^q\}_{i=1}^{|A|}$. Then three BiLSTMs are applied to the concatenation of those vectors to model the temporal dependency:

$$\mathbf{h}^q = \text{BiLSTM}(\{\mathbf{w}_{Q_i}\}_{i=1}^{|Q|})$$
$$\mathbf{h}^p = \text{BiLSTM}(\{[\mathbf{w}_{P_i}; \mathbf{w}_{P_i}^q]\}_{i=1}^{|P|}) \quad (3)$$
$$\mathbf{h}^a = \text{BiLSTM}(\{[\mathbf{w}_{A_i}; \mathbf{w}_{A_i}^p; \mathbf{w}_{A_i}^q]\}_{i=1}^{|A|})$$

$\mathbf{h}^p, \mathbf{h}^q, \mathbf{h}^a$ are the new representation vectors that incorporates more context information.

Output Layer.   Question sequence and answer sequence representation $\mathbf{h}^q, \mathbf{h}^a$ are summarized into fixed-length vectors with self-attention (Yang et al., 2016). Self-attention function is defined as follows:

$$Att_{self}(\{\mathbf{u}_i\}_{i=1}^n) = \sum_{i=1}^{n} \alpha_i \mathbf{u}_i$$

$$\alpha_i = \text{softmax}_i(\mathbf{W}_2^T \mathbf{u}_i)$$

(4)

Then we have question representation $\mathbf{q} = Att_{self}(\{\mathbf{h}_i^q\}_{i=1}^{|Q|})$, answer representation $\mathbf{a} = Att_{self}(\{\mathbf{h}_i^a\}_{i=1}^{|A|})$ and passage representation $\mathbf{p} = Att_{seq}(\mathbf{q}, \{\mathbf{h}_i^p\}_{i=1}^{|P|})$. The final output y is based on their bilinear interactions:

$$y = \sigma(\mathbf{p}^T \mathbf{W}_3 \mathbf{a} + \mathbf{q}^T \mathbf{W}_4 \mathbf{a})$$

(5)

Model Learning.　We first pretrain *TriAN* on *RACE* dataset for 10 epochs. Then our model is fine-tuned on official training data. Standard cross entropy function is used as the loss function to minimize.

3　Experiments

3.1　Setup

Data.　For data preprocessing, we use *spaCy* [1] for tokenization, part-of-speech tagging and named-entity recognition. Statistics for official dataset *MCScript* (Ostermann et al., 2018a) are shown in Table 1. *RACE* [2] dataset is used for network pretraining. English stop words are ignored when computing handcrafted features. Input word embeddings are initialized with 300-dimensional *GloVe* (Pennington et al., 2014) vectors [3].

	train	dev	test
# of examples	9731	1411	2797

Table 1: Official dataset statistics.

Hyperparameters.　Our model *TriAN* is implemented based on *PyTorch* [4]. Models are trained on a single GPU(Tesla P40) and each epoch takes about 80 seconds. Only the word embeddings of top 10 frequent words are fine-tuned during training. The dimension of both forward and backward LSTM hidden state is set to 96. Dropout rate is set to 0.4 for both input embeddings and BiL-STM outputs (Srivastava et al., 2014). For parameter optimization, we use *Adamax* (Kingma and

[1] https://github.com/explosion/spaCy
[2] http://www.cs.cmu.edu/~glai1/data/race/
[3] http://nlp.stanford.edu/data/glove.840B.300d.zip
[4] http://pytorch.org/

Ba, 2014) with an initial learning rate 2×10^{-3}. Learning rate is then halved after 10 and 15 training epochs. The model converges after 50 epochs. Gradients are clipped to have a maximum L2 norm of 10. Minibatch with batch size 32 is used. Hyperparameters are optimized by random search strategy (Bergstra and Bengio, 2012). Our model is quite robust over a wide range of hyperparameter configurations.

3.2　Main Results

The experimental results are shown in Table 2. Human performance is shared by task organizers. For *TriAN-ensemble*, we average the output probabilities of 9 models trained with the same datasets and network architecture but different random seeds. *TriAN-ensemble* is the model that we used for official submission.

model	dev	test
Random	50.00%	50.00%
TriAN-RACE	64.78%	64.28%
TriAN-single	83.84%	81.94%
TriAN-ensemble	**85.27%**	**83.95%**
HFL	–	84.13%
Human	–	98.00%

Table 2: Main results. *TriAN-RACE* only use *RACE* dataset for training; *HFL* is the 1st place team for *SemEval-2018 Task 11*. The evaluation metric is accuracy.

From Table 2, we can see that even though *RACE* dataset contains nearly $100k$ questions, *TriAN-RACE* achieves quite poor results. The accuracy on development set is only 64.78%, which is worse than most participants' systems. However, pretraining acts as a way of implicit knowledge transfer and is beneficial for overall performance, as will be seen in Section 3.3. The accuracy of our system *TriAN-ensemble* is very close to the 1st place team *HFL* with 0.18% difference. Yet there is still a large gap between machine learning models and human.

We also compared the performances of shallow and deep TriAN models. On datasets such as *SQuAD* (Rajpurkar et al., 2016), deep models typically works better than shallow ones. Notice that the attention layer in our proposed *TriAN* model can be stacked multiple times if we treat the output vectors of BiLSTMs as new input representations.

Maybe a little bit surprising, Table 3 shows that *2-layer TriAN* model performs worse than *1-layer*

model	dev	test
1-layer TriAN-single	**83.84%**	**81.94%**
2-layer TriAN-single	82.71%	80.55%

Table 3: Accuracy comparison of shallow and deep TriAN models.

TriAN. One possible explanation is that the labeled dataset is relatively small and deeper models tend to easily overfit.

3.3 Ablation Study

The input representation consists of several components: part-of-speech embedding, relation embedding and handcrafted features etc. We conduct an ablation study to investigate the effects of each component. The results are in Table 4.

model	dev	test
TriAN-single	**83.84%**	**81.94%**
w/o pretraining	82.71%	80.51%
w/o ConceptNet	82.78%	81.08%
w/o POS	82.84%	81.27%
w/o features	82.92%	81.35%
w/o NER	83.60%	81.87%

Table 4: Ablation study for input representation.

Pretraining on *RACE* dataset turns out to be the most important factor. Without pretraining, the accuracy drops by more than 1% on both development and test set. Relation embeddings based on ConceptNet make approximately 1% difference. Part-of-speech and named-entity embeddings are also helpful. In fact, combining input representations from multiple sources has been a standard practice for reading comprehension tasks.

At attention layer, our proposed *TriAN* involves applying several attention functions to model interactions between different text sequences. It would be interesting to examine the importance of each attention function, as shown in Table 5.

model	dev	test
TriAN-single	**83.84%**	81.94%
w/o passage-question attention	83.51%	**82.20%**
w/o passage-answer attention	83.07%	81.39%
w/o question-answer attention	83.23%	81.84%
w/o attention	81.93%	80.65%

Table 5: Ablation study for attention. The last one "*w/o attention*" removes all word-level attentions.

Interestingly, removing any of the three word-level sequence attentions does not seem to hurt the performance much. In fact, removing passage-question attention even results in higher accuracy on test set than *TriAN-single*. However, if we remove all word-level attentions, the performance drastically drops by 1.9% on development set and 1.3% on test set.

3.4 Discussion

Even though our system is built for commonsense reading comprehension, it doesn't have any explicit knowledge reasoning component. Relation embeddings based on ConceptNet only serve as additional input features. Methods like event calculus (Mueller, 2014) are more rigorous mathematically and resemble the way of how human brain works. The problem of event calculus is that it requires large amounts of domain-specific axioms and therefore doesn't scale well.

Another limitation is that our system relies on hard-coded commonsense knowledge bases, just like most systems for commonsense reasoning. For humans, commonsense knowledge comes from constant interactions with the real-world environment. From our point of view, it is quite hopeless to enumerate all of them.

There are a lot of reading comprehension datasets available. When the size of training data is relatively small like this *SemEval-2018 task*, transfer learning among different datasets is a useful technique. This paper shows that pretraining is a simple and effective method. However, it still remains to be seen whether there is a better alternative approach.

4 Conclusion

In this paper, we present the core ideas and design philosophy for our system *TriAN* at *SemEval-2018 Task 11: Machine Comprehension using Commonsense Knowledge*. We build upon recent progress on neural models for reading comprehension and incorporate commonsense knowledge from ConceptNet. Pretraining and handcrafted features are also proved to be helpful. As a result, our proposed model *TriAN* achieves near state-of-the-art performance.

Acknowledgements

We would like to thank SemEval 2018 task organizers and several anonymous reviewers for their helpful comments.

References

James Bergstra and Yoshua Bengio. 2012. Random search for hyper-parameter optimization. *Journal of Machine Learning Research*, 13(Feb):281–305.

Nathanael Chambers and Dan Jurafsky. 2008. Unsupervised learning of narrative event chains. *Proceedings of ACL-08: HLT*, pages 789–797.

Danqi Chen, Adam Fisch, Jason Weston, and Antoine Bordes. 2017. Reading wikipedia to answer open-domain questions. *arXiv preprint arXiv:1704.00051*.

Sepp Hochreiter and Jürgen Schmidhuber. 1997. Long short-term memory. *Neural computation*, 9(8):1735–1780.

Diederik Kingma and Jimmy Ba. 2014. Adam: A method for stochastic optimization. *arXiv preprint arXiv:1412.6980*.

Guokun Lai, Qizhe Xie, Hanxiao Liu, Yiming Yang, and Eduard Hovy. 2017. Race: Large-scale reading comprehension dataset from examinations. *arXiv preprint arXiv:1704.04683*.

Hongyu Lin, Le Sun, and Xianpei Han. 2017. Reasoning with heterogeneous knowledge for commonsense machine comprehension. In *Proceedings of the 2017 Conference on Empirical Methods in Natural Language Processing*, pages 2032–2043.

Erik T Mueller. 2014. *Commonsense reasoning: an event calculus based approach*. Morgan Kaufmann.

Simon Ostermann, Ashutosh Modi, Michael Roth, Stefan Thater, and Manfred Pinkal. 2018a. MCScript: A Novel Dataset for Assessing Machine Comprehension Using Script Knowledge. In *Proceedings of the 11th International Conference on Language Resources and Evaluation (LREC 2018)*, Miyazaki, Japan.

Simon Ostermann, Michael Roth, Ashutosh Modi, Stefan Thater, and Manfred Pinkal. 2018b. SemEval-2018 Task 11: Machine Comprehension using Commonsense Knowledge. In *Proceedings of International Workshop on Semantic Evaluation(SemEval-2018)*, New Orleans, LA, USA.

Jeffrey Pennington, Richard Socher, and Christopher Manning. 2014. Glove: Global vectors for word representation. In *Proceedings of the 2014 conference on empirical methods in natural language processing (EMNLP)*, pages 1532–1543.

Pranav Rajpurkar, Jian Zhang, Konstantin Lopyrev, and Percy Liang. 2016. Squad: 100,000+ questions for machine comprehension of text. *arXiv preprint arXiv:1606.05250*.

Matthew Richardson, Christopher JC Burges, and Erin Renshaw. 2013. Mctest: A challenge dataset for the open-domain machine comprehension of text.

In *Proceedings of the 2013 Conference on Empirical Methods in Natural Language Processing*, pages 193–203.

Push Singh, Thomas Lin, Erik T Mueller, Grace Lim, Travell Perkins, and Wan Li Zhu. 2002. Open mind common sense: Knowledge acquisition from the general public. In *OTM Confederated International Conferences" On the Move to Meaningful Internet Systems"*, pages 1223–1237. Springer.

Robert Speer, Joshua Chin, and Catherine Havasi. 2017. Conceptnet 5.5: An open multilingual graph of general knowledge. In *AAAI*, pages 4444–4451.

Nitish Srivastava, Geoffrey Hinton, Alex Krizhevsky, Ilya Sutskever, and Ruslan Salakhutdinov. 2014. Dropout: A simple way to prevent neural networks from overfitting. *The Journal of Machine Learning Research*, 15(1):1929–1958.

Niket Tandon, Gerard de Melo, and Gerhard Weikum. 2017. Webchild 2.0: fine-grained commonsense knowledge distillation. *Proceedings of ACL 2017, System Demonstrations*, pages 115–120.

Lilian DA Wanzare, Alessandra Zarcone, Stefan Thater, and Manfred Pinkal. 2016. Descript: A crowdsourced corpus for the acquisition of high-quality script knowledge. In *The International Conference on Language Resources and Evaluation*.

Bishan Yang and Tom Mitchell. 2017. Leveraging knowledge bases in lstms for improving machine reading. In *Proceedings of the 55th Annual Meeting of the Association for Computational Linguistics (Volume 1: Long Papers)*, volume 1, pages 1436–1446.

Zichao Yang, Diyi Yang, Chris Dyer, Xiaodong He, Alex Smola, and Eduard Hovy. 2016. Hierarchical attention networks for document classification. In *Proceedings of the 2016 Conference of the North American Chapter of the Association for Computational Linguistics: Human Language Technologies*, pages 1480–1489.

Jiacheng Zhang, Yang Liu, Huanbo Luan, Jingfang Xu, and Maosong Sun. 2017a. Prior knowledge integration for neural machine translation using posterior regularization. In *Proceedings of the 55th Annual Meeting of the Association for Computational Linguistics (Volume 1: Long Papers)*, volume 1, pages 1514–1523.

Ye Zhang, Matthew Lease, and Byron C Wallace. 2017b. Exploiting domain knowledge via grouped weight sharing with application to text categorization. *arXiv preprint arXiv:1702.02535*.

SemEval-2018 Task 12: The Argument Reasoning Comprehension Task

Ivan Habernal[†]   Henning Wachsmuth[‡]   Iryna Gurevych[†]   Benno Stein[‡]

[†] Ubiquitous Knowledge Processing Lab (UKP) and Research Training Group AIPHES
Department of Computer Science, Technische Universität Darmstadt, Germany
`www.ukp.tu-darmstadt.de`   `www.aiphes.tu-darmstadt.de`
[‡] Faculty of Media, Bauhaus-Universität Weimar, Germany
`<firstname>.<lastname>@uni-weimar.de`

Abstract

A natural language argument is composed of a claim as well as reasons given as premises for the claim. The *warrant* explaining the reasoning is usually left implicit, as it is clear from the context and common sense. This makes a comprehension of arguments easy for humans but hard for machines. This paper summarizes the first shared task on *argument reasoning comprehension*. Given a premise and a claim along with some topic information, the goal is to automatically identify the correct warrant among two candidates that are plausible and lexically close, but in fact imply opposite claims. We describe the dataset with 1970 instances that we built for the task, and we outline the 21 computational approaches that participated, most of which used neural networks. The results reveal the complexity of the task, with many approaches hardly improving over the random accuracy of ≈ 0.5. Still, the best observed accuracy (0.712) underlines the principle feasibility of identifying warrants. Our analysis indicates that an inclusion of external knowledge is key to reasoning comprehension.

1 Introduction

When we argue in natural language, we give reasons as premises for our claims. A fundamental pragmatic instrument in this regard is to leave those parts of an argument unstated that can be presupposed. This is particularly common for the reasoning between an argument's premises and its claim, called implicit *warrants* there (Toulmin, 1958). A warrant takes the role of an inference rule, i.e., the abstract structure of an argument is *reason* → (since) *warrant* → (therefore) *claim*. In principle, this structure applies to deductive arguments, which allows us to validate arguments properly formalized in propositional logic. However, most natural language arguments are in fact inductive (Govier, 2010) or defeasible (Walton, 2007).

Topic: Tax Break for Sports.

Additional Information: Should pro sports leagues enjoy nonprofit status?

Premise (Reason): Government is already struggling to pay for basic needs.

And since

- ✔ **Warrant 0:** the government isn't required to pay for all the country's needs
- ✗ **Warrant 1:** the government is required to pay for the country's needs

Claim: Sport leagues should not enjoy nonprofit.

Figure 1: Instance of the argument reasoning comprehension task. The correct warrant has to be classified.

Now, when we comprehend an argument, we reconstruct its warrant driven by the cognitive principle of relevance (Wilson and Sperber, 2004). What is easy for humans in many cases, however, turns out to be hard for machines, because reasoning usually depends on context and common sense. In (Habernal et al., 2018), we have thus introduced the *argument reasoning comprehension task* in order to study the construction and identification of implicit warrants for natural language arguments. It forms the basis of the shared task presented here:

Task Given an argument with a *reason* serving as a premise for a *claim*, along with the *topic* and some *additional information* of the discussion they occur in, identify the correct warrant among two opposing candidates, *warrant0* and *warrant1*.

With opposing, we here mean that the two candidate warrants actually imply contradicting claims, the correct one and its opposite. An instance of the task is shown in Figure 1. Being a binary classification task, the main evaluation measure of argument reasoning comprehension is accuracy.

To our knowledge, this is the first shared NLP task directly targeting argumentation; others tasks have only been sketched so far (Kiesel et al., 2015).

Proceedings of the 12th International Workshop on Semantic Evaluation (SemEval-2018), pages 763–772
New Orleans, Louisiana, June 5–6, 2018. ©2018 Association for Computational Linguistics

A solution to our task will represent a substantial step towards automatic warrant reconstruction, which in turn is important for the general long-term goal of automatic argument evaluation. So far, most research on computational argumentation focused on mining claims and premises from text and assessing their properties. In contrast, filling the gap between claims and premises computationally remains an open issue, due to the inherent difficulty of reconstructing the world knowledge and reasoning patterns in arguments (Feng and Hirst, 2011; Green, 2014; Boltužić and Šnajder, 2016). Previous tasks have dealt with the textual entailment of a hypothesis from a proposition (Dagan et al., 2009) or with semantic inference (Bowman et al., 2015). While understanding semantics is important in the given task, argumentation also reasoning beyond what is understood, i.e., pragmatics.

As a basis for the shared task, we built a new dataset with 1970 instances based on authentic English arguments, whose concept and construction process is detailed in Section 2. We outline the systems that participated in the task in Section 3. Most systems implement a computational approach that employs one or more neural networks (often LSTMs, often with attention) based on different pre-trained embedding models. We then present the results of all systems on the test set of the shared task in Section 4 and analyze specific cases in Section 5, before we finally conclude (Section 6).

2 Dataset

This section presents the dataset with all instances used in the shared task. We summarize the main points from its construction process, which is described in detail in (Habernal et al., 2018).

2.1 Task Instances

Let R be the reason for the claim C in a natural language argument. Then there is a warrant W that explains why R supports C, but W is left implicit. For example, if C is "It should be illegal to declaw your cat" and R is "They need to use their claws for defense and instinct", then W could be specified as 'If cat needs claws for instincts, declawing would be against nature' or similar.

The question is how to find a warrant W for a given reason R and claim C. To obtain candidate warrants systematically for our dataset, we propose a trick. In particular, we first construct an *alternative warrant AW* that explains why R may serve as

Unit	Text
Reason	Cooperating with Russia on terrorism ignores Russia's overall objectives.
Claim	Russia cannot be a partner.
Warrant0	Russia has the same objectives of the US.
Warrant1	Russia has the opposite objectives of the US.
Reason	Economic growth needs innovation.
Claim	3-D printing will change the world.
Warrant0	There is no innovation in 3-d printing since it's unsustainable.
Warrant1	There is much innovation in 3-d printing and it is sustainable.
Reason	College students have the best chance of knowing history.
Claim	College students' votes do matter in an election.
Warrant0	Knowing history doesn't mean that we will repeat it.
Warrant1	Knowing history means that we won't repeat it.

Table 1: Three example task instances from the dataset. In all cases, *warrant1* is the alternative warrant. For brevity, we omit the topic and additional information.

support for the opposite $\neg C$ of the claim C. For the example above, we invert C to "It should be *legal* to declaw your cat" ($\neg C$). $\neg C$ may be explained based on R quite plausibly with the alternative warrant "Most house cats don't face enemies" (*AW*). Analog to C and $\neg C$, we then invert *AW* to "Most house cats face enemies", which is a plausible warrant W for the original reason-claim pair (R, C).

Constructing a plausible alternative warrant is not always possible, as many reasons already convey the arguer's stance. If it is, however, W and *AW* usually capture the core of a reason's relevance and reveal the implicit presuppositions, due to the trick we performed for construction. For such as cases, we define an instance of our task as a 6-tuple:

Instance *(reason, claim, warrant0, warrant1, topic, additional information)*

The question to be answered is whether *warrant0* is W and *warrant1* is *AW*, or vice versa. As context, we provide a short *topic* specification and some *additional information* describing the topic. Figure 1 has already shown an example. Further are given in Table 1. They all result from the following process.

2.2 Data Acquisition and Annotation

To obtain a dataset with a permissive license, we decided to build a new dataset from scratch. As source data, we used user-generated web comments from the well-moderated *Room for Debate* of the New York Times, which covers arguments on a variety of contemporary controversial issues.[1]

---

[1] https://www.nytimes.com/roomfordebate

We manually selected 188 debates with polar questions in the title from a six-year span (2011–2017). We converted each question into a claim C (e.g., "It should be illegal to declaw your cat") and derived a directly opposing claim $\neg C$ ("It should be legal to declaw your cat"). Then, we crawled all comments from the debates and sampled about 11,000 high-ranked, root-level comments[2] from which 5,000 were selected randomly as a basis for the dataset construction. Each comment was split into elementary discourse units using SistaNLP (Surdeanu et al., 2015). To obtain task instances, we then performed the following eight-step crowdsourcing process using Amazon Mechanical Turk:

1. Stance Annotation. For each comment, the crowdworkers first classified what stance it takes, if it remains neutral, or if it does not take any stance.

2. Reason Span Annotation. In all 2,884 comments taking a stance, the workers then marked sequences of discourse units that give a reason for the claim.

3. Reason Gist Summarization. In this step, the workers rewrote all 5,119 marked reasons (2,026 within arguments), such that their gist remains the same but the clutter is removed. The result is a reason R for the claim C.

4. Reason Disambiguation. In order to ensure that R *implies* C really holds, the workers next decided whether C or $\neg C$ is more plausible for R, or whether both are similarly (im)plausible. We kept only those 1,955 reason-claim pairs where workers agreed that C is most plausible.

5. Alternative Warrant. This step was the trickiest. As in the example above, the workers had to specify a plausible alternative warrant AW, explaining why R implies $\neg C$, or declare that impossible.

6. Alternative Warrant Validation. Afterwards, other workers validated each of the 5,342 specified alternative warrants AW as to whether it actually relates to R, by identifying R among two alternatives: R itself and the lexically most similar reason from the same debate topic. For the 3,791 correctly validated cases, we let workers score how logical AW is (0–2) and only kept those 2,613 that had a mean score of at least 0.68. This threshold was chosen based on a manual examination of the scores.

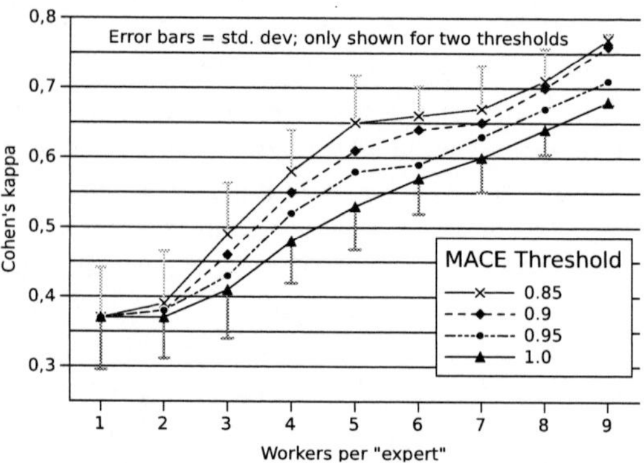

Figure 2: Cohen's κ agreement for stance annotation on 98 comments. As a trade-off between the number of kept instances and their reliability, we chose five annotators and a threshold of 0.95 for this task, which resulted in $\kappa = 0.58$ (moderate to substantial agreement).

7. Warrant For Original Claim. Given R and C, workers then should create a minimally modified version of each AW that may serve as an actual warrant W for C (as in the second half of the example above). They succeeded to do so in 2,447 cases.

8. Warrant Validation. To ensure that only W is correct for R and C, all tuples (R, C, W, AW) were validated again. Unclear cases were resolved by an expert. We obtained 1,970 instances of the argument reasoning comprehension task, so 1,970 pairs of *warrant0* and *warrant1* for a reason and a claim, along with a topic and the additional information.

2.3 Agreement

To assess quality in the crowdsourcing process, we relied on MACE (Hovy et al., 2013), which estimates gold labels for a set of workers, outperforming simple majority votes. Given the number of the different crowdsourcing tasks and their variety, here we only demonstrate the first step, namely stance annotation. We collected 18 assignments per item and split them into two groups (9+9) based on their submission time. We then considered each group as an independent experiment and estimated gold labels for each group. Having two independent "experts from the crowd" allowed us to compute standard agreement scores. We also varied the size of each group from 1 to 9 by repeated random sampling of assignments, and we tuned the MACE threshold for keeping only the most confident predictions. Figure 2 shows the Cohen's κ agreement for stance annotation with respect to the crowd size computed by our method. The decision what number of workers per task to take (five in case of

---

[2]We removed 'noisy' candidates based on several indicators, such as the absence of quotations or URLs and certain lengths. We did not check any quality criteria of arguments, though, because this was not our focus; see, for instance, (Wachsmuth et al., 2017) for argumentation quality.

stance annotation) implies a trade-off between the number of instances and their reliability. We performed similar quality measures with reasonable agreement for the other crowdsourcing steps too. Details are given in (Habernal et al., 2018).

2.4 Datasets in the Shared Task

For the shared task, we split the 1,970 instances into three sets based on the year of the debate they were taken from: 2011–2015 became the training set (1,210 instances), 2016 the development set (316 instances), and 2017 the test set (444 instances). This follows the paradigm of learning on past data and predicting on new ones. In addition, it removes much lexical and topical overlap. The same split has been used by Habernal et al. (2018).

The shared task had two phases, trial and test. In the trial phase, the training and development set were given, both with gold labels stating the correct warrant for all instances. In the test phase, all three datasets were available. Naturally, no labels were given for the test set instances. All provided data is licensed under Creative Commons-family license.

3 Approaches

This section briefly summarizes the computational approaches of the systems that participated in the shared task as well as baselines. Intuitions and detailed explanations are given in the system description papers associated to the shared task.

3.1 Participating Systems

The following 20 systems participated in the shared task, sorted alphabetically. In addition, a 21st system called *Joker* took part, but the team behind did not provide any description. For many of the systems, many more details are given in the respective SemEval-2018 system description papers.

ArcNet uses GloVe embeddings and an LSTM encoder to get the semantic representation of each input (*reason*, *claim*, and both *warrants*). Then an attention mechanism aligns the *reason* and the *warrant* so that the reason-aware warrant representation is generated. Finally, a bilinear function matches the claim with the reason-aware warrant. The network is trained to minimize margin loss. The submission was based on an ensemble model of 10 training runs with the identical architecture.

ArgEns-GRU votes a majority on an ensemble of the following three systems: First, a shared GRU network that learns one representation of the *reason*, *claim*, and both *warrants* each, initialized with 100-dimensional GloVe embeddings. Its output is concatenated and passed through a softmax layer for the final predictions. Second, an extension of the GRU with an attention on the *reason*, *claim*, and both *warrants* each. And third, another GRU model extended with negation and polarity features.

ART uses a bi-directional LSTM with an attention mechanism on top, followed by a multi-layer perceptron network.

blcu_nlp not only pays attention to the consensual part between each warrant and other information, but also to the contradictory part between two warrants. On the model's input (GloVe embeddings), *warrant0*, *claim*, *reason*, and *debate info* are concatenated in order to put attention on *warrant1*. An analog structure is used for the attention on *warrant0*. After obtaining two vectors 'attented_w0' and 'attented_w1' — referring to the ESIM model (Chen et al., 2017) — the two warrants are aligned. A similarity matrix helps to highlight the consensual and the contradictory part. The decision is then drawn after passing through feed-forward layers. A majority voting strategy is used in the final ensemble, which is based on five models performing best on the development data.

Deepfinder shares one LSTM layer for *warrant0*, *warrant1*, *claim*, and *reason*, while the *topic* part uses one LSTM alone. All of them share the same word embedding layer before LSTM layers. After that, one individual dot product is computed for the output of the *warrant0* LSTM and each of the *claim*, *reason* and *claim* (the same is done for the *warrant1* LSTM). The resulting dot products are concatenated and fed into a softmax layer.

ECNU modifies the baseline intra-warrant attention (Habernal et al., 2018) by using a CNN and an LSTM for representing each sentence (*claim*, *reason*, *debate*, *warrant0*, and *warrant1*). Different parts of *warrant0* and *warrant1* are used as an attention vector to obtain representations of the warrants. Similarly, different parts of *claim* and the opposite *claim* serve as attention for the final representation. The final decision is then given by a vote from three networks.

GIST uses pretrained word2vec embeddings as well as the ESIM model (Chen et al., 2017), trained on the SNLI (Bowman et al., 2015) and MultiNLI

(Nangia et al., 2017) datasets. The parameters have been frozen afterwards. Then, pairs of sentences are fed into the the ESIM model. For *warrant0*, for example, these pairs are *(claim, warrant0)*, *(warrant0, reason)*, and *(warrant0, warrant1)*. Also, another bi-LSTM module encoding *claim*, *warrant*, and *reason* is added. The output vectors of each pair and the bi-LSTM are concatenated after averaging and max pooling, and the final prediction is made through feed-forward layers.

HHU encodes *reason*, *claim*, and *warrants* using a bi-directional LSTM. Next, *warrant0*, *reason*, and *claim* are fed into another LSTM; similarly, *warrant1*, *reason*, and *claim* to another LSTM in parallel. Both branches are followed by a dropout and two common dense layers. Embeddings have been pre-trained in four different flavors: fasttext-embeddings trained on the entire Wikipedia corpus, two embeddings trained on the task's dataset using the word2vec skip-gram model with different dimensionalities, and another word2vec model based on the tasks vocabulary but augmented with related articles from Wikipedia. For all embeddings, different parameter combinations and seeds were used to train an ensemble of 623 models in total.

ITNLP-ARC first encodes sentences (*warrant*, *reason*, *claim*) using LSTMs. Attention is used to merge the *reason* vector with the *claim* vector. A shared weight matrix then holds the relationship between the *warrant* and the attention vector, from which the maximum is chosen as the answer. An ensemble method is used for the final vote.

lyb3b encodes sentences using word2vec or GloVe embeddings and a bi-directional LSTM. The instances are treated as positive or negative, depending on the correct training *warrant*. The network then combines the *warrant* with the *reason*, *claim*, and *additional info*. Finally, a fully-connected layer is used to decide whether the instance is correct.

mingyan performs a word-by-word attention that is fused with the original representation then. Self-attention pooling produces a single vector fed into a sigmoid function, trained with cross-entropy loss.

NLITrans attempts to leverage the transfer of semantic knowledge from a bi-directional LSTM encoder with max pooling trained on the MultiNLI corpus (Nangia et al., 2017). This yields a small performance boost on the development set. All sentences (*claim, reason, warrant0,* and *warrant1*) are

encoded with this a transferred encoder. Then, task-specific representations of two 'arguments', one for each warrant, are learned via fully-connected layers. A final linear layer generates an independent score representing the fit of each warrant to the argument. These are concatenated and passed through softmax to generate a probability distribution over the two warrants.

RW2C uses two neural networks. The first one classifies each *warrant* as true or false separately and chooses the one with higher confidence as the right one. The second model makes a decision given two warrant candidates. The final prediction is an ensemble over the previous predictions. Both models represent sentences using a CNN.

SNU_IDS decides whether a logic built on a set of given sentences (*claim*, *reason*, and *warrant*) is plausible. It accepts only one *warrant* at a time and outputs a score on the warrant's validity. The intuition is that the model can learn what has more meaningful semantics of natural language when it judges whether the logic of the given sequence is correct, instead of just selecting the more probable warrant among two candidates. The model consists of an encoding layer with GloVe embeddings (Pennington et al., 2014) and a CoVe sentence encoder (McCann et al., 2017), a 'localization' layer (a set of fully connected layers), and output layers that combine calculating several arithmetic measures over the input representation and compute a final score using a logistic layer on top.

TakeLab preprocesses sentences from the dataset, applies some arithmetic, converts them to Skip-Thought vectors, and feeds them into an SVM classifier with fine-tuned hyperparameters. The Skip-Thought vectors are sentence representation vectors whose encoder and decoder (with an identical structure to RNN encoder-decoders used for neural machine translation) are trained on a large corpus of books unbiased in domain (Kiros et al., 2015).

TRANSRW learns the semantic representation of sentences (*reason*, *warrants*, *claim*) using a convolutional neural network. The assumption behind is that a composition of the *reason* and the *warrant* is close to the representation of the *claim*.

UniMelb combines 3 stacked LSTMs, one for the *reason*, one for the *claim*, and one shared Siamese Network for the two *warrants* under investigation. It generates semantic feature vectors that

serve as input to a shared compressed feature space
by using simple vector operations and semantic
similarity classification to enforce the interrelationships between them. In doing so, the aim is to
learn a form of "generative implication" through
the semantic feature vectors. The vectors are able
to correctly encode the interrelationships between
a reason, a claim, and both the correct and incorrect
warrants. The given data is augmented by utilizing
WordNet synonym fuzzing.

YNU-HPCC uses a bi-directional LSTM with
attention whose input is divided into three parts
(*claim*, *reason*, and both *warrants*). To prevent
overfitting, dropout is added before the final layer.

YNU_Deep combines the *reason* and the *claim*
with a so-called 'story' feature. The story feature
is merged with the *warrant*. The network is a bidirectional LSTM with attention and uses GloVe
embeddings. Ensemble technology is put on top to
mitigate the small size of the data.

ztangfdu first concatenates the *claim* and the *reason* as one sentence named 'sent1', and denotes the
correct *warrant* as 'sent2' and the wrong *warrant*
as 'sent3', respectively. The output of an LSTM
layer with non-trained embeddings then represents
each of the sentences. After applying mean pooling to transform the output matrices to vectors, two
fully connected layers cater for obtaining the difference score between 'sent2' and 'sent3', whose
minimization is the core of the loss function.

3.2 Baselines

For the official task, we provided only a simple
naïve random baseline. The outcome (*warrant0* or
warrant1) is drawn from a Bernoulli distribution
($\theta = 0.5$) resulting in a theoretical accuracy of 0.5.
The reported baseline was a single random draw.

Further computational baseline approaches, such
as a language model, are evaluated in (Habernal
et al., 2018), but we did not consider them within
the official competition. There, we also report human bounds for argument reasoning comprehension based on a crowdsourcing study, where each
of 173 participants had to solve 10 instances. The
mean accuracy was 0.798, but varied depending
on the participants' prior knowledge of reasoning,
logic, and argumentation. Those with extensive
prior knowledge achieved 0.909, and 30 participants solved all instances correctly. We conclude
that the task is reasonably solvable for humans.

Rank	System	Accuracy
1	GIST	0.712
2	blcu_nlp	0.606
3	ECNU	0.604
4	NLITrans	0.590
5	Joker*	0.586
6	YNU_Deep	0.583
7	mingyan	0.581
8	ArcNet	0.577
8	UniMelb	0.577
10	TRANSRW	0.570
11	lyb3b	0.568
12	SNU_IDS	0.565
13	ArgEns-GRU	0.556
14	ITNLP-ARC	0.552
15	YNU-HPCC	0.550
16	TakeLab	0.541
17	HHU	0.534
18	**Random baseline**	0.527
19	Deepfinder	0.525
20	ART	0.518
21	RW2C	0.500
22	ztangfdu	0.464

Table 2: Final results of the competition. For the star-
denoted system, no description has been provided.

4 Results

The final accuracies of all participating systems
are ranked in Table 2. Due to the limited size of
the test set (444 instances) and the subtle accuracy
differences of many systems, we also measured
significance using the approximate randomization
test, as described in (Riezler and Maxwell, 2005).[3]
Table 3 shows p-values of all system pairs, including the random baseline. As p-values lower than
0.05 are usually considered statistically significant,
only three systems outperform the random baseline.
However, we would like to emphasize that drawing
a strong conclusion about superiority of a particular neural-based system given only one benchmark value might be misleading, as Reimers and
Gurevych (2017) showed for several NLP tasks.

We see that the winning system GIST significantly outperforms all other systems on this particular test data ($p \ll 0.05$). For future SemEval tasks,
however, we encourage task organizers to solicit
multiple submissions of the same system trained
with different random initializations, and perform a
proper Bayesian system comparison. The machine
learning community has already abandoned the
controversial p-value and replaced it with Bayesian
methods that are easily interpretable and account
well for uncertainty (Benavoli et al., 2017).

---

[3]The implementation of the complete task evaluation is available at `https://github.com/habernal/`
`semeval2018-task12-results`.

	GIST	blcu_nlp	ECNU	NLITrans	YNU_Deep	mingyan	ArcNet	UniMelb	TRANSRW	lyb3b	SNU_IDS	ArgEns-GRU	ITNLP-ARC	YNU-HPCC	TakeLab	HHU	Random bsl.	Deepfinder	ART	RW2C	ztangfdu
GIST	**.71**																				
blcu_nlp	.00	**.61**																			
ECNU	.00	1.0	**.60**																		
NLITrans	.00	.59	.67	**.59**																	
YNU_Deep	.00	.42	.47	.85	**.58**																
mingyan	.00	.39	.45	.80	1.0	**.58**															
ArcNet	.00	.25	.34	.64	.84	.90	**.58**														
UniMelb	.00	.33	.37	.69	.87	.94	1.0	**.58**													
TRANSRW	.00	.25	.29	.55	.71	.76	.88	.87	**.57**												
lyb3b	.00	.12	.17	.38	.54	.62	.74	.80	1.0	**.57**											
SNU_IDS	.00	.13	.13	.37	.50	.60	.70	.74	.94	1.0	**.57**										
ArgEns-GRU	.00	.09	.08	.23	.31	.41	.47	.52	.71	.71	.78	**.56**									
ITNLP-ARC	.00	.03	.05	.11	.15	.21	.19	.40	.58	.47	.63	.92	**.55**								
YNU-HPCC	.00	.02	.03	.12	.17	.22	.24	.35	.54	.35	.54	.86	1.0	**.55**							
TakeLab	.00	.02	.03	.09	.16	.18	.21	.28	.37	.39	.42	.63	.73	.80	**.54**						
HHU	.00	.00	.01	.03	.03	.04	.04	.12	.23	.10	.18	.41	.39	.49	.87	**.53**					
Random bsl.	.00	.03	.03	.08	.11	.13	.16	.17	.23	.25	.30	.42	.50	.54	.74	.89	**.53**				
Deepfinder	.00	.00	.00	.02	.03	.04	.04	.07	.14	.06	.09	.25	.26	.27	.64	.75	1.0	**.52**			
ART	.00	.00	.00	.00	.01	.01	.01	.03	.07	.00	.04	.15	.10	.10	.47	.44	.84	.83	**.52**		
RW2C	.00	.00	.00	.00	.01	.01	.01	.02	.01	.02	.03	.07	.07	.10	.20	.24	.47	.45	.58	**.50**	
ztangfdu	.00	.00	.00	.00	.00	.00	.00	.00	.00	.00	.00	.00	.00	.00	.01	.00	.07	.02	.02	.24	**.46**

Table 3: *p*-values obtained by running the approximate randomization test among all systems. For convenience, the diagonal (bold values) shows the accuracy of each system as in Table 2 but rounded to two decimal numbers. Only the three top systems (GIST, blcu_nlp, and ECNU) are significantly better than the random baseline (*p*-values < 0.05). The first system (GIST) also significantly outperforms the second system (blcu_nlp) (*p*-value ≪ 0.05).

5 Analysis

First, we show a quantitative analysis of the results on the test instances. Figure 3 displays the distribution of all instances over the number of systems that classified each of them correctly. The shape of this rather bi-modal distribution reveals that there are both easy and hard cases. In particular, there are 13 instances completely unsolved and about 90 instances solved by fewer than five participating systems. On the other hand, 32 instances were solved by all systems.

5.1 Easy instances

We qualitatively investigated instances that were classified correctly by all participating systems. It turned out that systems needed to learn only one single property common to all of them: *negation*. Correct warrants in these instances contain negating words ("not", "don't") or negated modals ("can't", "wouldn't"), as shown in Figure 4. This artifact originates from the process of intentionally creating the dichotomy between the alternative warrant and warrant (see Section 2) that in many cases consist of an assertion firstly created for the alternative warrant, and its negation for the correct warrant.

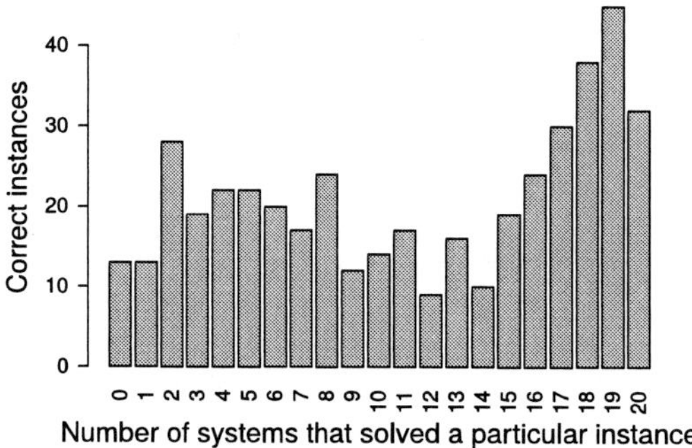

Figure 3: Despite many solvable instances (centered around the right mode), there are hard cases that most systems were not able to cope with (the left mode).

5.2 Difficult instances

A similar problem arises for the difficult instances, such as those not solved by any system. We manually analyzed them and found that the opposite of the easy instances caused misclassification here, namely *misleading negation*. In these instances, the correct warrant is a positive assertion while the alternative warrant is negated. It seems that the

Topic: Have Comment Sections Failed?

Additional Information: In recent years, many media companies have disabled them because of widespread abuse and obscenity.

Premise (Reason): Comment sections are just a propaganda device.

And since

- ✗ **Warrant 0:** propaganda is the grease of the democratic wheels
- ✔ **Warrant 1:** propaganda is not the grease of the democratic wheels

Claim: Comment sections have failed.

Topic: Does Turkey Still Belong in NATO?

Additional Information: Given President Erdogan's record on human rights and how his focus on the Kurdish minority has interfered with his fight against ISIS, is he a reliable ally?

Premise (Reason): Turkey does not have much in common with the rest of the countries in NATO.

And since

- ✔ **Warrant 0:** diversity wouldn't be good for NATO
- ✗ **Warrant 1:** diversity would be good for NATO

Claim: Turkey doesn't belong to NATO

Figure 4: Examples of "easy" instances from the test data solved by all systems, revealing that relying solely on the negation artifact in the correct warrant gives the right answer (IDs: 18247022_132_A104V8NZIQFN2F, 18068301_176_A3TKD7EJ6BM0M5).

Topic: Have Christians Created a Harmful Atmosphere for Gays?

Additional Information: Church-backed efforts to fight L.G.B.T. rights have been blamed for feeding a hateful atmosphere that accommodates attacks on gays.

Premise (Reason): The Bible is not consistent in it's treatment of sex and marriage.

And since

- ✔ **Warrant 0:** many Christians take the Bible literally
- ✗ **Warrant 1:** many Christians do not take the Bible literally

Claim: Christians have created a harmful atmosphere for gays

Topic: Is Google a Harmful Monopoly?

Additional Information: European regulators say the company's Android phone blocks rival services.

Premise (Reason): People can choose not to use Google.

And since

- ✔ **Warrant 0:** they can opt-out from being indexed by their search engine
- ✗ **Warrant 1:** they cannot opt-out from being indexed by their search engine

Claim: Google is not a harmful monopoly

Figure 5: Examples of "difficult" instances from the test data on which all systems failed. One possibly explanation is the misleading negation contained in these instances (IDs: 18865357_593_A1CF6U3GF7DZEJ, 18362833_247_A1CF6U3GF7DZEJ).

learned negation "feature" then makes the systems fall into the trap; see examples in Figure 5.

This data analysis clearly shows that it is possible to guess some answers right only given their surface or syntactic form, perhaps because such "features" are prevalent in the training data. However, they do not really help to find any underlying connections between the reasons, warrants, and claims. One solution to test for such cases would be to double the test set simply by adding to each instance another one with an opposite claim and switched warrants. From the reasoning perspective, such an instance still makes sense (which is actually a backbone principle of creating our data), but would clearly penalize systems relying on simple features, such as negation.

6   Conclusion

This paper has overviewed the first shared task on argument reasoning comprehension, one of the tasks at SemEval-2018. Being able to identify the correct warrant connecting an argument's reason to its claim automatically, which is the goal of the task, is the first step of understanding the argu-

ment's reasoning. We have outlined the dataset used in the task, the participating system, and the performance they achieved. The results have revealed how challenging the task is: Many systems improved only little over the random baseline. At the same time, the accuracy of GIST, the best system in the evaluation, suggests that it is possible in principle to identify warrants computationally.

Our analysis of the results showed that the participating systems were capable to solve cases with discriminative surface features, but failed where exactly these were misleading. The strongest systems relied on models trained on natural language inference corpora, which suggests that external knowledge may be key to argument reasoning comprehension. Still, more research needs to be done in the future to further investigate this hypothesis.

Acknowledgments

This work was supported by the German Research Foundation (DFG) within the ArguAna Project GU 798/20-1, and by the DFG-funded research training group "Adaptive Preparation of Information form Heterogeneous Sources" (AIPHES, GRK 1994/1).

References

Alessio Benavoli, Giorgio Corani, Janez Demsar, and Marco Zaffalon. 2017. Time for a Change: a Tutorial for Comparing Multiple Classifiers Through Bayesian Analysis. *Journal of Machine Learning Research*, 18:1–36.

Filip Boltužić and Jan Šnajder. 2016. Fill the Gap! Analyzing Implicit Premises between Claims from Online Debates. In *Proceedings of the Third Workshop on Argument Mining*, pages 124–133, Berlin, Germany. Association for Computational Linguistics.

Samuel R. Bowman, Gabor Angeli, Christopher Potts, and Christopher D. Manning. 2015. A large annotated corpus for learning natural language inference. In *Proceedings of the 2015 Conference on Empirical Methods in Natural Language Processing*, pages 632–642, Lisbon, Portugal. Association for Computational Linguistics.

Qian Chen, Xiaodan Zhu, Zhenhua Ling, Si Wei, Hui Jiang, and Diana Inkpen. 2017. Enhanced LSTM for Natural Language Inference. In *Proceedings of the 55th Annual Meeting of the Association for Computational Linguistics (Volume 1: Long Papers)*, pages 1657–1668, Vancouver, Canada. Association for Computational Linguistics.

Ido Dagan, Bill Dolan, Bernardo Magnini, and Dan Roth. 2009. Recognizing textual entailment: Rational, evaluation and approaches. *Natural Language Engineering*, 15(Special Issue 04):i–xvii.

Vanessa Wei Feng and Graeme Hirst. 2011. Classifying arguments by scheme. In *Proceedings of the 49th Annual Meeting of the Association for Computational Linguistics: Human Language Technologies - Volume 1*, HLT '11, pages 987–996, Portland, Oregon. Association for Computational Linguistics.

Trudy Govier. 2010. *A Practical Study of Argument*, 7th edition. Wadsworth, Cengage Learning.

Nancy L Green. 2014. Towards Creation of a Corpus for Argumentation Mining the Biomedical Genetics Research Literature. In *Proceedings of the First Workshop on Argumentation Mining*, pages 11–18, Baltimore, Maryland USA. Association for Computational Linguistics.

Ivan Habernal, Henning Wachsmuth, Iryna Gurevych, and Benno Stein. 2018. The argument reasoning comprehension task: Identification and reconstruction of implicit warrants. In *Proceedings of the 2018 Conference of the North American Chapter of the Association for Computational Linguistics: Human Language Technologies*, page (to appear), New Orleans, LA, USA. Association for Computational Linguistics.

Dirk Hovy, Taylor Berg-Kirkpatrick, Ashish Vaswani, and Eduard Hovy. 2013. Learning whom to trust with MACE. In *Proceedings of NAACL-HLT 2013*, pages 1120–1130, Atlanta, Georgia. Association for Computational Linguistics.

Johannes Kiesel, Khalid Al Khatib, Matthias Hagen, and Benno Stein. 2015. A shared task on argumentation mining in newspaper editorials. In *Proceedings of the 2nd Workshop on Argumentation Mining*, pages 35–38. Association for Computational Linguistics.

Ryan Kiros, Yukun Zhu, Ruslan R Salakhutdinov, Richard Zemel, Raquel Urtasun, Antonio Torralba, and Sanja Fidler. 2015. Skip-Thought Vectors. In *Advances in Neural Information Processing Systems 28*, pages 3276–3284, Montreal, CA. Curran Associates, Inc.

Bryan McCann, James Bradbury, Caiming Xiong, and Richard Socher. 2017. Learned in Translation: Contextualized Word Vectors. In *Advances in Neural Information Processing Systems 30*, pages 6294–6305, Long Beach, CA, USA. Curran Associates, Inc.

Nikita Nangia, Adina Williams, Angeliki Lazaridou, and Samuel Bowman. 2017. The repeval 2017 shared task: Multi-genre natural language inference with sentence representations. In *Proceedings of the 2nd Workshop on Evaluating Vector Space Representations for NLP*, pages 1–10, Copenhagen, Denmark. Association for Computational Linguistics.

Jeffrey Pennington, Richard Socher, and Christopher Manning. 2014. Glove: Global vectors for word representation. In *Proceedings of the 2014 Conference on Empirical Methods in Natural Language Processing (EMNLP)*, pages 1532–1543, Doha, Qatar. Association for Computational Linguistics.

Nils Reimers and Iryna Gurevych. 2017. Reporting Score Distributions Makes a Difference: Performance Study of LSTM-networks for Sequence Tagging. In *Proceedings of the 2017 Conference on Empirical Methods in Natural Language Processing*, pages 338–348, Copenhagen, Denmark. Association for Computational Linguistics.

Stefan Riezler and John T. Maxwell. 2005. On some pitfalls in automatic evaluation and significance testing for MT. In *Proceedings of the ACL Workshop on Intrinsic and Extrinsic Evaluation Measures for Machine Translation and/or Summarization*, pages 57–64, Ann Arbor, Michigan. Association for Computational Linguistics.

Mihai Surdeanu, Tom Hicks, and Marco Antonio Valenzuela-Escarcega. 2015. Two practical rhetorical structure theory parsers. In *Proceedings of the 2015 Conference of the North American Chapter of the Association for Computational Linguistics: Demonstrations*, pages 1–5, Denver, Colorado. Association for Computational Linguistics.

Stephen E. Toulmin. 1958. *The Uses of Argument*. Cambridge University Press.

Henning Wachsmuth, Nona Naderi, Ivan Habernal, Yufang Hou, Graeme Hirst, Iryna Gurevych, and Benno Stein. 2017. Argumentation Quality Assessment: Theory vs. Practice. In *Proceedings of the*

55th Annual Meeting of the Association for Computational Linguistics (Volume 2: Short Papers), pages 250–255, Vancouver, Canada. Association for Computational Linguistics.

Douglas Walton. 2007. *Media Argumentation: Dialect, Persuasion and Rhetoric*. Cambridge University Press.

Deirdre Wilson and Dan Sperber. 2004. Relevance Theory. In Laurence R. Horn and Gregory Ward, editors, *The Handbook of Pragmatics*, chapter 27, pages 607–632. Wiley-Blackwell, Oxford, UK.

GIST at SemEval-2018 Task 12: A network transferring inference knowledge to Argument Reasoning Comprehension task

HongSeok Choi, Hyunju Lee
Department of Electrical Engineering and Computer Science,
Gwangju Institute of Science and Technology, Gwangju, Republic of Korea
Data Mining and Computational Biology Laboratory
{hongking9,hyunjulee}@gist.ac.kr

Abstract

This paper describes our GIST team system that participated in SemEval-2018 Argument Reasoning Comprehension task (Task 12). Here, we address two challenging factors: unstated common senses and two lexically close warrants that lead to contradicting claims. A key idea for our system is full use of transfer learning from the Natural Language Inference (NLI) task to this task. We used Enhanced Sequential Inference Model (ESIM) to learn the NLI dataset. We describe how to use ESIM for transfer learning to choose correct warrant through a proposed system. We show comparable results through ablation experiments. Our system ranked 1st among 22 systems, outperforming all the systems more than 10%.

1 Introduction

Argument Reasoning Comprehension is a task that choose correct warrant from two options given a claim and a reason. The Argument Reasoning Comprehension is a very important task because *"argument comprehension requires not only language understanding and logic skills, but it also heavily depends on common sense"*, as mentioned by Habernal et al. (2018). There are two challenging factors. One is a certain part of an argument is left unstated (Habernal et al., 2018). Because of the unstated part, humans or machines need reasoning ability about that part. Human can reconstruct the unstated part depending on common knowledge. However, it has still remained difficult to machines. Another is that *"both options are plausible and lexically very close while leading to contradicting claims"*, as mentioned by Habernal et al. (2018). To address these factors, we have two assumptions. One is that similar and large datasets may help to address the unstated common sense by learning various cases. Another is that an inference model to distinguish semantic differences between two sentences may help to choose one of two lexically close warrants that lead to contradicting claims. There are two suitable datasets in the Natural Language Inference (NLI) task, Stanford NLI (SNLI) (Bowman et al., 2015) and Multi NLI (MNLI) (Williams et al., 2017) datasets. NLI is a task choosing one of relationships *(Entailment, Contradiction, Neutral)* between two sentences. Both SNLI and MNLI are very large corpus (each 0.5M sentence pairs). In addition, there is a good performance model for the task, Enhanced Sequential Inference Model (ESIM) (Chen et al., 2017). To make use of other datasets for our task, we use transfer learning. About transfer learning, Conneau et al. (2017) showed a good precedent, using SNLI dataset. By learning the NLI task, the model can obtain inference knowledge. Therefore, we propose a network transferring inference knowledge to argument reasoning comprehension task. We summarize our system with 5 main components.

1. ESIM is trained on SNLI and MNLI datasets. Then, parameters are frozen and used to transfer the inference knowledge.

2. As inputs of the ESIM, we make sentence pairs such as *(claim, warrant)*, *(warrant, reason)* and *(warrant, other warrant)*.

3. To add flexibility, we added biLSTM module encoding *claim*, *reason* and *warrant*.

4. To make a fixed length vector from variable one, we used average and max pooling.

5. Finally, all the fixed length vectors from ESIM and biLSTM are concatenated and fed into a fully-connected neural network to determine whether the warrant is correct or not.

The detail process is described in Section 2.

Proceedings of the 12th International Workshop on Semantic Evaluation (SemEval-2018), pages 773–777
New Orleans, Louisiana, June 5–6, 2018. ©2018 Association for Computational Linguistics

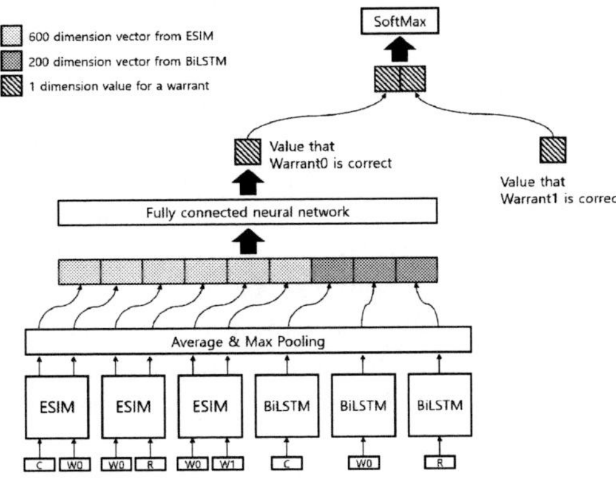

Figure 1: Overview of our system

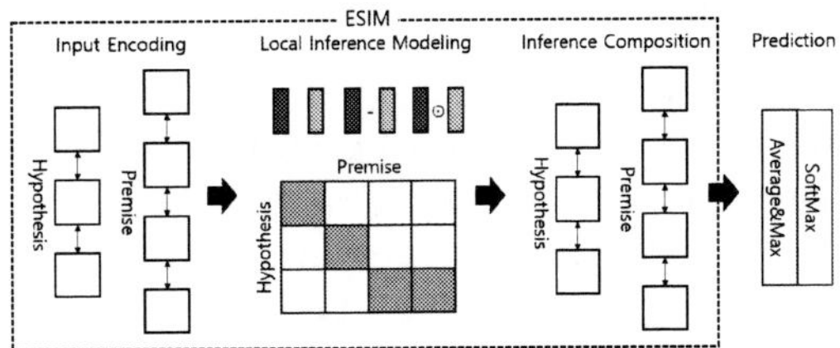

Figure 2: A high-level view of ESIM with prediction part. The prediction part is used when training on the NLI task, and two sentence vectors generated after inference composition are used in our system. This picture is taken from the author (Chen et al., 2017) with a few modifications.

2 System Description

Figure 1 shows an overview of our system. The preprocessing is described in subsection 2.1. ESIM is described in subsection 2.2. Then, to apply transfer learning, we describe how to compose the inputs of the ESIM in subsection 2.3. In the subsection 2.4, we describe a simple biLSTM module added to our model. Pooling is described in subsection 2.5. Finally, the fully-connected neural network is described in subsection 2.6 to determine whether the warrant is correct or not. We introduce our notations for following sections. A sentence is notated as $S = (w_1^S, ..., w_{len(S)}^S)$. $len(S)$ denotes the length of the sentence S. The $w_i^S \in \mathbb{R}^d$ is a d-dimensional word embeddings. Also C, R, $W0$ and $W1$ denote the sentence of *Claim, Reason, Warrant0* and *Warrant1* respectively. Our goal is to predict which warrant ($W0$ or $W1$) is more correct given a claim (C) and a reason (R).

2.1 Preprocessing

First, we initialize all words that exist in the vocabulary with pre-trained 300 dimension `word2vec` (Mikolov et al., 2013). When the word does not exist in the vocabulary, we use following several preprocessing rules.

1. All ['s] are removed. (ex. He' s, something's)

2. All words with number are split into number and word. (ex. 17th → 17, th)

3. All abbreviations are replaced with <abbreviation> token.

4. All number is replaced with <number> token.

After this preprocessing, if the preprocessed word exists in the vocabulary, we initialized it with the `word2vec` again. Otherwise, we replaced it with <unknown> token. Each token is randomly initialized.

2.2 Pre-trained ESIM on NLI dataset

Because of page limit, we briefly explain this part. Chen et al. (2017) described that ESIM is composed of the following major components: input encoding, local inference modeling, and inference composition. Figure 2 shows a high-level view of the architecture. For more details, refer to the paper (Chen et al., 2017). ESIM generates two sentence vectors after comparing two input sentences with each other. We notate it as follows.

$$\mathbf{sv}_{S_1}^{(S_1,S_2)}, \mathbf{sv}_{S_2}^{(S_1,S_2)} = ESIM(S_1, S_2) \quad (1)$$

The $\mathbf{sv}$ consists of vectors of l dimension, the number of which correspond to the length of each sentence. The $\mathbf{sv}$ is the output of the inference composition part. We implemented it as 300 dimensions. The ESIM was trained on SNLI and MNLI datasets. The training was stopped when the average of development set accuracies was maximum. Then, the parameters were frozen so as to be not updated.

2.3 Input sentence pair for transfer learning

To exploit transfer learning, the sentence pairs are composed of (C, $W0$), ($W0$, R) and ($W0$, $W1$) for Warrant0. In the case of Warrant1, the pairs are composed of (C, $W1$), ($W1$, R) and ($W1$, $W0$). Then, these sentence pairs are fed into the ESIM.

2.4 BiLSTM for Flexibility

LSTM (Hochreiter and Schmidhuber, 1997) is a building block well-suited to learn long and short information in a sequence. We employed bidirectional LSTM, where forward and backward directional LSTMs are concatenated. For more detailes, refer to the paper (Hochreiter and Schmidhuber, 1997).

$$\mathbf{sv}_S = biLSTM(S) \tag{2}$$

We add 100 dimension biLSTMs to our model. Since the ESIM is only trained on NLI dataset, it may be over-fitted to the NLI task. By adding a new module that is not trained on the NLI task, our system may have a chance to learn new knowledge about the target task. We feed *Claim*, *Warrants* and *Reason* into the biLSTM. The biLSTMs for Warrant0 and Warrant1 share the parameters.

2.5 Pooling Layer

To generate a fixed length sentence vector, we use both average and max pooling per one sentence. The equations are as follow:

$$\mathbf{sv}_{S,ave} = \frac{1}{len(S)} \sum_{i=1}^{len(S)} \mathbf{sv}_{S,i} \tag{3}$$

$$\mathbf{sv}_{S,max} = \max_{i=1}^{len(S)} (\mathbf{sv}_{S,i}) \tag{4}$$

After pooling, the vector of average pooling and max pooling are concatenated. We notate it as $\mathbf{sv}_{S,pool} = [\mathbf{sv}_{S,ave}; \mathbf{sv}_{S,max}]$.

2.6 Fully-connected neural network

To determine whether the warrant is correct or not, a fully-connected neural network (FCNN) is used. Finally, all the vectors from ESIM and biLSTM are concatenated. For Warrant0, the vectors are concatenated as follow: $[\mathbf{sv}_{C,pool}^{(C,W0)}; \mathbf{sv}_{W0,pool}^{(C,W0)}; \mathbf{sv}_{W0,pool}^{(W0,R)}; \mathbf{sv}_{R,pool}^{(W0,R)}; \mathbf{sv}_{W0,pool}^{(W0,W1)}; \mathbf{sv}_{W1,pool}^{(W0,W1)}; \mathbf{sv}_{C,pool}; \mathbf{sv}_{W0,pool}; \mathbf{sv}_{R,pool}]$. The Warrant1 is also composed as the same way. The concatenated vector is fed into FCNN. We build two layers of FCNN. The first layer has 600 dimension with the ReLu function. The second layer has only 1 dimension without any activation function. Then, the 1 dimension value for Warrant0 and Warrant1 are concatenated with the softmax function.

3 Experimental setup

Pre-training First, to learn the inference knowledge, we implemented ESIM and trained on NLI training dataset. Our implemented ESIM dimension is 300. Except for the ESIM dimension, we used the same hyperparameter values as those in Chen et al. (2017). The preprocessing process is implemented in the same way with subsection 2.1. The word embeddings are not updated during training. The training was stopped when the average of development set accuracies is maximum. We got development accuracy of 86.58%, 74.09%, 74.67% on SNLI, MNLI match, MNLI mismatch datasets, respectively.

Training We used the ADAM (Kingma and Ba, 2014) optimizer for updating weight parameters. The parameters of ADAM set to be as follow: $\beta1 = 0.9$, $\beta2 = 0.999$, $\epsilon = 10^{-8}$. The initial learning rate is 0.0002 and is decayed with 0.9 rate per one epoch. We did not use dropout but added L2 regularization on the first FCNN layer. The regularization parameter λ was set to be 5×10^{-4}. The word embeddings were not updated during training. We randomly shuffled training data during training. The minibatch size was 25. We trained 10 epochs and chose our model when the development set reached the max accuracy. We implemented our system by using lasagne (Dieleman et al., 2015) and theano (Theano Development Team, 2016) library. Our code is available at here[1].

4 Results and Discussion

To get more reliable results, all accuracies were calculated by averaging after repeating ten experiments. In this competition, the official accuracy of our system recorded 0.712 on test set. Table 1 shows accuracies of other approaches and ours on Argument Reasoning Comprehension task. Our approach showed best performance except human, outperforming all the systems more than 10%. Table 2 shows the results of ablation experiments. Model (a) is our proposed system. Model (d) indicates a model that is same as the model (a), except that the inference knowledge is not transferred. This model is directly trained on our task. Models (b) and (e) indicate that the modules including warrant pair inputs $(W0, W1)$ and $(W1, W0)$ are removed from model (a) and (d), respectively.

---

[1] https://github.com/hongking9/SemEval-2018-task12

Approach	Dev	Test
Human average	-	0.798
Human w/ training in resoning	-	0.909
Our system	**0.716** ± 0.006	**0.711** ± 0.007
Random baseline	0.473	0.491
2nd ranked system	-	0.606
Attention[†]	0.488	0.513
Attention w/ context [†]	0.502	0.512
Intra-warrant attention[†]	0.638	0.556
Intra-warrant attent. w/ context[†]	0.637	0.560

Table 1: Accuracy of each approch. The human and baseline results are taken from Habernal et al. (2018). Our approach ranked 1st among 22 systems, outperforming all the systems more than 10%. [†] indicates approaches implemented by Habernal et al. (2018). Readers can check all system results at here[2].

Model	Dev	Test
(a) Our system	0.716	**0.711**
(b) − warrants pair input	0.685	0.696
(c) − biLSTM	**0.726**	0.706
(d) No Transferring	0.652	0.599
(e) − warrants pair input	0.653	0.605
(f) − biLSTM	0.656	0.608

Table 2: Ablation experiments.

Models (c) and (f) indicate that the biLSTM module is removed from model (a) and (d), respectively.

As we mentioned above introduction section, our proposed model addresses two challenging factors. The one is about common sense and the other is about the two lexically close warrants that lead to contradicting claims.

Transfer learning First, by comparing models (a) and (d), we can observe that the inference knowledge of the NLI task is very helpful to the argument reasoning comprehension task. We may assume that machine can accommodate common sense by learning similar tasks and large corpus.

Warrants pair input Second, by comparing models (a) and (b), we can observe that the warrants pair input result in improved performance. We may infer that the model can distinguish fine difference of the two warrants well by directly feeding the warrant pair. However, in the case of model (d) and (e), there is no sufficient difference of the performance. We think this is because the model

did not learn to infer the relationship between two sentences.

Adding biLSTM Finally, by comparing (a) and (c), we can observe that adding biLSTM results in a little improved performance on the test set. Also, the performance on the test set was nearly similar with those in development set in model (a) whereas there was 2% difference in model (c). We carefully infer that the performance on the development set was more reliable and the model becomes flexible to the target task when adding nottrained module to pre-trained and frozen model. However, since the data is not large enough to prove it, we leave it as future work.

5 Conclusion

To address argument reasoning comprehension task, we proposed a network transferring inference knowledge to the Argument Reasoning Comprehension task. First, we implemented ESIM and trained it on a large NLI task corpus. We took full advantage of the model to transfer inference knowledge of NLI task, appropriately building the network. Our approach showed robustness on this task. Through ablation experiment, we showed the following effects: transfer learning, warrants pair input, and adding biLSTM. Also, we showed our system can address the factors about common sense and two lexically close warrants that lead to contradicting claims.

Acknowledgments

This research was supported by the Bio-Synergy Research Project (NRF-2016M3A9C4939665) of the Ministry of Science, ICT and Future Planning through the National Research Foundation.

References

Samuel R Bowman, Gabor Angeli, Christopher Potts, and Christopher D Manning. 2015. A large annotated corpus for learning natural language inference. *arXiv preprint arXiv:1508.05326*.

Qian Chen, Xiaodan Zhu, Zhen-Hua Ling, Si Wei, Hui Jiang, and Diana Inkpen. 2017. Enhanced lstm for natural language inference. In *Proceedings of the 55th Annual Meeting of the Association for Computational Linguistics (Volume 1: Long Papers)*, volume 1, pages 1657–1668.

Alexis Conneau, Douwe Kiela, Holger Schwenk, Loic Barrault, and Antoine Bordes. 2017. Supervised learning of universal sentence representations from

[2]https://github.com/habernal/semeval2018-task12-results

natural language inference data. *arXiv preprint arXiv:1705.02364*.

Sander Dieleman, Jan Schlter, Colin Raffel, Eben Olson, Sren Kaae Snderby, Daniel Nouri, et al. 2015. Lasagne: First release.

Ivan Habernal, Henning Wachsmuth, Iryna Gurevych, and Benno Stein. 2018. The argument reasoning comprehension task: Identification and reconstruction of implicit warrants. In *Proceedings of the 2018 Conference of the North American Chapter of the Association for Computational Linguistics: Human Language Technologies*, page (to appear), New Orleans, LA, USA. Association for Computational Linguistics.

Sepp Hochreiter and Jürgen Schmidhuber. 1997. Long short-term memory. *Neural computation*, 9(8):1735–1780.

Diederik P Kingma and Jimmy Ba. 2014. Adam: A method for stochastic optimization. *arXiv preprint arXiv:1412.6980*.

Tomas Mikolov, Ilya Sutskever, Kai Chen, Greg S Corrado, and Jeff Dean. 2013. Distributed representations of words and phrases and their compositionality. In *Advances in neural information processing systems*, pages 3111–3119.

Theano Development Team. 2016. Theano: A Python framework for fast computation of mathematical expressions. *arXiv e-prints*, abs/1605.02688.

Adina Williams, Nikita Nangia, and Samuel R Bowman. 2017. A broad-coverage challenge corpus for sentence understanding through inference. *arXiv preprint arXiv:1704.05426*.

LⒾGHTREL at SemEval-2018 Task 7: Lightweight and Fast Relation Classification

Tyler Renslow
DFKI, Saarbrücken, Germany
`tdrenslow@gmail.com`

Günter Neumann
DFKI, Saarbrücken, Germany
`neumann@dfki.de`

Abstract

We present LIGHTREL, a lightweight and fast relation classifier. Our goal is to develop a high baseline for different relation extraction tasks. By defining only very few data-internal, word-level features and external knowledge sources in the form of word clusters and word embeddings, we train a fast and simple linear classifier.

1 Introduction

The main motivation for our participation at SemEval-2018 (Gábor et al., 2018) was the ideal opportunity to test and improve our relation extraction system LIGHTREL. The system design and development was inspired by the work described in (Nguyen and Grishman, 2015). Their goal was to depart from traditional relation extraction approaches with complicated feature engineering by exploring a deep neural network that would minimize its dependence on external toolkits and resources, e.g. external word embeddings. That allowed them to design a rather lightweight relation extraction approach that would basically only require supervised training data, external word embeddings and a few hyperparameters. Their "end-to-end" relation extraction approach produced competitive results.

Since tuning hyperparameters for neural networks can be a intricate process, we considered whether it would be possible to define an even simpler system and use it as a baseline for our future research. Thus, we adopted some of the design decisions made by (Nguyen and Grishman, 2015) and combined them with a well-known, fast linear classifier, viz. LibLinear (Fan et al., 2008).

Following Nguyen and Grishman (2015), we represent a relation mention as a sequence of tokens. The core idea of our approach consists of transforming this sequence into a a vector of fixed length, such that each token (or word) is represented only by: 1) the word itself, 2) its shape (a small, fixed amount of character-based features), 3) the word's cluster id, and 4) the word's embedding of fixed size.

For this competition, we introduce a new relation-level feature, namely the ID of the word directly following and preceding entities one and two, respectively. Furthermore, we ignore all tokens to the left of the first entity and to the right of second entity. The size of the whole vector therefore hinges on the maximum number of elements between the two entities found in the training set.

These representations are then used to train a LibLinear model. Note that this reduces manual feature engineering to defining the shape features, finding an appropriate number of clusters and word embedding dimensions, and hyperparameters for LibLinear. All other information is automatically computed from the training data. In this sense, we consider our system lightweight.

We initially developed and tested our approach on the previous and widely-used SemEval-2010 Task 8 data set (Hendrickx et al., 2010), and obtained as our best result an F1 measure of 79.78% on the test-data using the standard evaluation script from SemEval-2010 (see also Sec. 3). Although this result is behind the best reported ones (the majority between 83%-85%, and the best 88.0%, cf. (Wang et al., 2016)), we think it provides a strong baseline compared to the manually-engineered, feature-heavy approaches or complex neural architectures. Thus, when the SemEval-2018 Task 7 challenge was announced, it was a natural decision to use it as an additional testing ground for LIGHTREL.

2 Approach

LIGHTREL can be divided into three major steps:

Proceedings of the 12th International Workshop on Semantic Evaluation (SemEval-2018), pages 778–782
New Orleans, Louisiana, June 5–6, 2018. ©2018 Association for Computational Linguistics

1) extracting information from the training data and external sources and storing it in an internal representation; 2) converting the internal representation into feature vectors; 3) using feature vectors to train a logistic regression classification model to predict classes.

In the first step of the system, pertinent information is extracted from the training data. Each relation instance (the two entities and the text between them) is collected. Along with the relation instance, the ID of the abstract, the IDs of the entities, the relation type and the length of the sentence are all gathered into one internal representation to facilitate vector computation later. We do not include additional data in our training set, e.g. from other tasks or subtasks, previous SemEval years, etc. For example, the following relation:

```
<entity id="E89-1006.1">French tenses
</entity> in the framework of <entity
id="E89-1006.2">Discourse
Representation Theory</entity>
```

would be represented in our system as:

```
('E89-1006', ['French_tenses', 'in',
'the', 'framework', 'of',
'Discourse_Representation_Theory'],
'E89-1006.1', 'E89-1006.2',
'MODEL-FEATURE REVERSE', 6)
```

The only processing done on the text is: 1) merging any punctuation and the word before it into a single string and 2) joining multi-word entities into a single string with an underscore. Using the words from these instances, we index a unique vocabulary and the single word immediately following or preceding entity one or entity two, respectively, provided that the word isn't the other entity. The unique relation types are also indexed later so that their unique identifiers can be used as a feature in the training vectors for LibLinear. In the case of the competition, the test data is used to expand the unique vocabulary and entity context words. Once this information is collected, it can be converted into vector representations to train a LibLinear model.

The next step involves converting our relation instances into feature vectors. In addition to the information gleaned from the training data, we use features that are independent of our training data. For instance, we include a word-shape feature, a unique vector representing certain character-level features found in a word. In particular the features are based on whether: any character is capitalized; a comma is present; the first character is capitalized and the word is the first in the relation (representing the beginning of a sentence); the first character is lower-case; there is an underscore present (representing a multi-word entity); and if quotes are present in the token. These features were left unchanged from the ones that achieved the best results on SemEval-2010 Task 8.

We also incorporate our own word embeddings into our feature vectors. Our previous system developed for the SemEval-2010 task used Numberbatch embeddings from ConceptNet (Speer et al., 2017) to yield the best results, but development was slower than desired due to the size of the embedding file. We therefore hand-pick the data used to calculate the new, smaller embeddings in order to experiment with domain-specific word embeddings better tuned to the task at hand.

We pre-compute two word embedding files: one based on the ACM-Citation-network V9 corpus of abstracts and the other on the DBLP-Citation-network V5 corpus.[1] The embeddings are calculated using the word2vec[2] tool with the following constraints: the continuous bag-of-words model, 300-dimension vectors (chosen for portability from the old system that used 300-d Numberbatch vectors) and leaving out tokens occurring fewer than five times. The DBLP corpus embedding file used for the final system was around half the size of the Numberbatch embeddings.

Cluster-membership features are also included in our feature vectors. We used the MarLin (Müller and Schuetze, 2015) clustering tool to pre-compute word clusters for the aforementioned two corpora based on their bigram context. In particular, we ran five training epochs to cluster the words into 1000 classes. MarLin was chosen over the Brown clustering algorithm (Brown et al., 1992), as these clusters produced better results for SemEval-2010 Task 8. Using all of our features, we convert our internal representation into the proper input format for training a LibLinear model. All features are binary besides the word embeddings. The test data is converted into the same format for predicting, albeit without relation IDs in the case of the competition run.

In the same way as (Nguyen and Grishman, 2015), we represent a relation mention x of length n as a sequence of tokens $x = [x_1, x_2, ..., x_n]$, where x_i is the i-th word in the mention. Further-

---

[1]Corpora available at https://aminer.org/citation.

[2]https://code.google.com/archive/p/word2vec/

more, let x_{i_1} and x_{i_2} be the head of the two entity mentions of interest. Now, we transform this into a vector of fixed length l, whose size is determined by the relation mention with highest number of tokens k between its entity head tokens, and by using L tokens left to the entity token x_{i_1}, and R tokens to the right of x_{i_2}. In all experiments described below, L and R are set to 0, which is also done by (Nguyen and Grishman, 2015). If a relation mention has fewer than k elements between entities, we add padding elements (i.e. dummy word tokens). One of the system parameters we tuned was the padding strategy employed: in the end, we got better results when padding after entity one as opposed to padding before entity two. Thus, initially, all relation mentions are represented by a fixed length vector $x' = [x'_1, x'_2, ..., x'_{k+2}]$, where $x'_1 = x_{i_1}$ and $x'_{k+2} = x_{i_2}$, with words plus the necessary number of padding elements between.

Once we have a fixed-length vector for each relation, we append the word-context feature to the vector. The motivation behind this feature is to provide some distributional information to the model regarding the syntactic contexts in which entities occur. In the case where there are no words between entities, we use no word context in our feature vector. If a single word occurs between entities, they share the same context. Otherwise, word context is represented by the word directly to the right and left of entity one and two, respectively. The context features are calculated based on the original, non-normalized sentence, so that padding elements are not involved.

The last step involves training a model to predict classes based on our vector representations of the training data. We employ LibLinear's default classifier (version 2.11), cf. also Sec. 3. Once the model is trained, it can then make predictions on the vectors that represent test relation instances. The predictions are then converted back into the format necessary for evaluating our system using the scorer script provided by SemEval.

3   Experiments

As mentioned before, our system was an adaptation to the one that produced the optimal result on SemEval-2010 Task 8. Through cross-validation, we tuned our system parameters to produce the best results on SemEval-2018 training data, bearing in mind the goal of keeping our system as lightweight as possible. It is important to note that hyperparameter tuning was only done according to system performance on task 1.1's training data; we simply used the optimal parameters from this task while participating in task 1.2 for the competition.

Through experimentation, we found a LibLinear classifier that performed better on the current task than the one that we used for the SemEval-2010 task. We also developed a novel word-context feature for the 2018 task, which modestly improved our cross-validation results (anywhere from a 1% to 3% increase in F1 score, depending on the different parameters used). We will display the parameters that produced optimal results in cross-validation, as well as the results obtained using these same parameters in the competition phase in tabular form below.

For the SemEval-2010 task, we obtained the best results using LibLinear's support vector classifier by Crammer and Singer (Crammer and Singer, 2000) with a cost of 0.1 and a stopping tolerance of 0.3. Given the fewer relation types and smaller training vectors in the SemEval-2018 task, we experimented with different classifiers. In development, we achieved the best performance in using LibLinear's default classifier, which performs dual L2-regularized L2-loss support vector classification, cf. (Fan et al., 2008). We set cost and stopping tolerance parameters equal to 0.1, using default settings for all other parameters.

The total competition data was made up of $1228 + 355 = 1583$ relation instances (#training + #test), corresponding to an approximate train-test split of $\approx 78\%$-22%. Because of this, we developed our system using 5-fold cross-validation on the training set, which entails an even 80%-20% split of data, i.e. $982 + 246 = 1228$ instances. Even though a subset of the training data was provided by the organizers for system development, we opted to split the data in accordance with the proportion of training and test instances, in order to get the best estimate of system performance in the competition phase.

We obtained the best average F1 score for tasks 1.1 and 1.2 when using all features but the shape feature (word, embeddings, clusters, entity one context, entity two context); the second best score was obtained when using all features and the third best by removing the entity two context feature from the entire feature set. These feature sets represent a modest approach to the task at hand compared to more complex systems incorporating knowledge from sources like part-of-speech tagging or dependency parsing. An exception to these feature sets was cross-validation on task 1.2's training data, where an average F1 score of 61.83% was obtained when using neither context-related feature. However, since removing a context-related feature (no e2 context) already produced the best results in development, we decided to hedge our bets in the competition with a feature set composed of all features but the shape feature, i.e. of no manually engineered features.

The results from cross-validation on task 1.1 and task 1.2 are shown in Table 1 below. Based on these results, we expected our system to perform similarly in the competition.

feature set	task 1.1	task 1.2
all features	45.4%	62.0%
w/o shape	46.4%	61.7%
w/o e2 context	45.5%	62.1%

Table 1: Average F1 scores from 5-fold cross-validation.

The actual results of the competition can be seen below in Table 2. These results placed us in 18th out of 28 groups in subtask 1.1 and 12th out of 20 in subtask 1.2.

feature set	task 1.1	task 1.2
all features	39.3%	67.5%
w/o shape	39.9%	68.2%
w/o e2 context	39.2%	67.5%

Table 2: Competition F1 scores.

The best result was obtained when using all features except the shape feature. This points to evidence that there is overlap in the information gained from the shape feature and the word feature. The same token, differing only in punctuation (e.g. the strings 'IR' and 'IR,'), is represented with both different word and different shape IDs in our system. However, for the shape feature to provide extra information to the model, the word feature would have to remain the same, since the shape feature changed.

The results on the first task were worse than the cross-validation results suggested. Since we incorporated the words from the test data into our word and context features, there was no information that the model could have missed in the competition phase. Therefore, we attribute the slight decrease in performance to the fact that more training and less test data were used in development, meaning that our models were overfitting in training.

Surprisingly, our system performed better on noisily annotated data, given no extra development in relation to the task. It is difficult to say with conviction why these results occurred, as our features do not incorporate the entity markup. Another difference in this task is the data itself; it could be that more tokens were found in the embedding and cluster features, providing more information to the model. However, this fact alone hardly explains an almost 30% increase in F1.

Finally, we assessed our system's speed. The final system which produced the best results for subtask 1.1 needed a total of 35 seconds to run on a 2012 MacBook Pro with 16GB of RAM and a 2.6 GHz quad-core Intel Core i7 processor[3]. The bottleneck occurred in the creating of vectors (80% of total time), which can be attributed to the simple way we stored and accessed the embeddings. Training lasted 5 seconds, while testing/prediction only required a fraction of a second. These results demonstrate our system's agility in relation to complex neural architectures, which typically need hours, or even days, to train.

4 Conclusion

We believe our system has established a useful baseline for relation classification. Our approach is simple in that it involves few features. These few features yield remarkable results given the amount of time required to deploy the system, allowing for quicker development and prototyping of models compared to more cumbersome neural networks. The performance on task 1.2 as opposed to task 1.1 demonstrates our system's flexibility, as we obtained fair results with no extra development. However, further research is needed to explain the jump in performance between the tasks.

Acknowledgments

This work was partially funded by the BMBF through the project DEEPLEE (01IW17001) and the European Union's Horizon 2020 grant agreement No. 731724 (iREAD).

---

[3]implementation available at `https://github.com/trenslow/LightRel`

References

Peter F. Brown, Peter V. deSouza, Robert L. Mercer, Vincent J. Della Pietra, and Jenifer C. Lai. 1992. Class-based n-gram models of natural language. *Comput. Linguist.* 18(4):467–479.

Koby Crammer and Yoram Singer. 2000. On the learnability and design of output codes for multiclass problems. In *Proceedings of the Thirteenth Annual Conference on Computational Learning Theory (COLT 2000), June 28 - July 1, 2000, Palo Alto, California.* pages 35–46.

Rong-En Fan, Kai-Wei Chang, Cho-Jui Hsieh, Xiang-Rui Wang, and Chih-Jen Lin. 2008. Liblinear: A library for large linear classification. *Journal of machine learning research* 9(Aug):1871–1874.

Kata Gábor, Davide Buscaldi, Anne-Kathrin Schumann, Behrang QasemiZadeh, Haïfa Zargayouna, and Thierry Charnois. 2018. Semeval-2018 Task 7: Semantic relation extraction and classification in scientific papers. In *Proceedings of International Workshop on Semantic Evaluation (SemEval-2018).* New Orleans, LA, USA.

Iris Hendrickx, Su Nam Kim, Zornitsa Kozareva, Preslav Nakov, Diarmuid Ó Séaghdha, Sebastian Padó, Marco Pennacchiotti, Lorenza Romano, and Stan Szpakowicz. 2010. Semeval-2010 task 8: Multi-way classification of semantic relations between pairs of nominals. In *Proceedings of the 5th International Workshop on Semantic Evaluation, SemEval@ACL 2010, Uppsala University, Uppsala, Sweden, July 15-16, 2010.* pages 33–38.

Thomas Müller and Hinrich Schuetze. 2015. Robust morphological tagging with word representations. In *Proceedings of the 2015 Conference of the North American Chapter of the Association for Computational Linguistics: Human Language Technologies.* Association for Computational Linguistics, Denver, Colorado, pages 526–536.

Thien Huu Nguyen and Ralph Grishman. 2015. Relation extraction: Perspective from convolutional neural networks. In *Proceedings of the 1st Workshop on Vector Space Modeling for Natural Language Processing, VS@NAACL-HLT 2015, June 5, 2015, Denver, Colorado, USA.* pages 39–48.

Robert Speer, Joshua Chin, and Catherine Havasi. 2017. Conceptnet 5.5: An open multilingual graph of general knowledge. In *31st AAAI Conference on Artificial Intelligence.* San Francisco, USA, pages 4444–4451.

Linlin Wang, Zhu Cao, Gerard de Melo, and Zhiyuan Liu. 2016. Relation classification via multi-level attention cnns. In *Proceedings of the 54th Annual Meeting of the Association for Computational Linguistics, ACL 2016, August 7-12, 2016, Berlin, Germany, Volume 1: Long Papers.*

OhioState at SemEval-2018 Task 7: Exploiting Data Augmentation for Relation Classification in Scientific Papers Using Piecewise Convolutional Neural Networks

Dushyanta Dhyani

The Ohio State University OH, USA

`dhyani.2@osu.edu`

Abstract

We describe our system for SemEval-2018 Shared Task on Semantic Relation Extraction and Classification in Scientific Papers where we focus on the Classification task. Our simple piecewise convolution neural network (PCNN) performs decently in an end to end manner. A simple inter-task data augmentation significantly boosts the performance of the model. Our best-performing systems stood 8th out of 20 teams on the classification task on noisy data and 12th out of 28 teams on the classification task on clean data.

1 Introduction

Relation extraction (RE) and Classification (RC) is an integral component of information extraction systems which aim to extract all the entity pairs and their relation $\langle e_1, r, e_2 \rangle$ from a given text corpora. An alternate formulation of relation extraction task focuses on identifying if a relation exists between a predefined pair of entities, and if yes classify from a given set of class relations. RE finds applications in a variety of domains, ranging from knowledge base construction to semantic parsing and question answering. However, the applicability of existing efforts in relation extraction to scientific text calls for a quantitative and qualitative analysis which is the aim of this shared task.

2 Related Work

Existing efforts for RE range from traditional strategies (Qian et al., 2008; Bunescu and Mooney, 2006, 2005; Mintz et al., 2009; Riedel et al., 2010) to more recent end to end deep learning based methods (Zeng et al., 2014, 2015; Lin et al., 2016; Wu et al., 2017) that are more suitable in situations where a lot of training data is available. While a majority of efforts in the RE community are specifically focused towards using

distantly supervised data and reduce the associated noise, their discussion is not relevant to the current scenario. The most relevant work is that of (Zeng et al., 2014) who demonstrated the efficacy of convolution neural networks for relation classification and (Zeng et al., 2015) who further enhanced the architecture by proposing the piecewise max-pooling strategy.

3 Task Description

The semantic relation extraction and classification in scientific papers task (Gábor et al., 2018) aims at identifying semantic relations expressed by entity pairs in scientific literature. The contest is further divided into three subtasks, where the first two focus on classification of varying nature of data and the third focuses on extraction task. Since our submitted systems focused only on the classification task, we would from here on discuss mostly about the classification sub-tasks.

3.1 Dataset

The data contains titles and abstracts of papers from ACL Anthology Corpus where entity mentions are either manually annotated (Subtask 1.1 and Subtask 2) or heuristically (Subtask 1.2) determined. However, the relations are manually annotated across all subtasks. For the classification scenario, we are provided with relevant entities and the directionality of their relation. There are 6 class labels: USAGE, RESULT, MODEL, PART_WHOLE, TOPIC, COMPARISON. The classes are highly imbalanced in nature as shown in Fig. 2

3.2 Evaluation

For both Task 1.1 and 1.2, given that the classes are imbalanced, macro-f1 score is used as the official evaluation metric and thus the metric we use for hyperparameter tuning. For more details, we

783

Proceedings of the 12th International Workshop on Semantic Evaluation (SemEval-2018), pages 783–787
New Orleans, Louisiana, June 5–6, 2018. ©2018 Association for Computational Linguistics

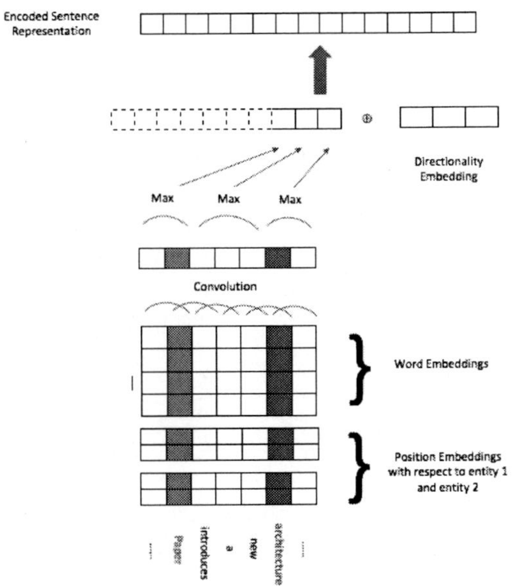

Figure 1: PCNN Encoder with Word, Position and Directionality embeddings.

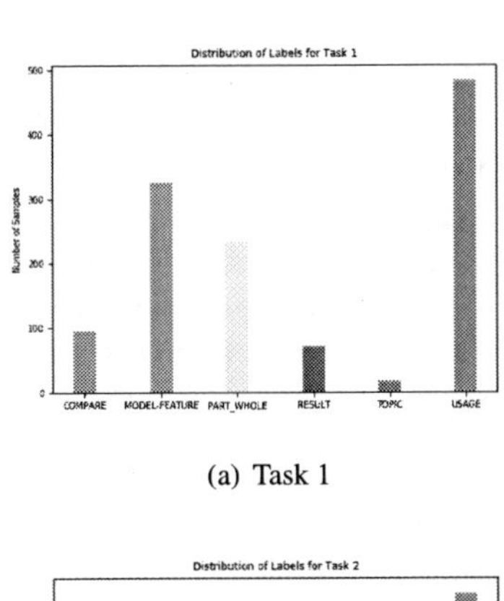

(a) Task 1

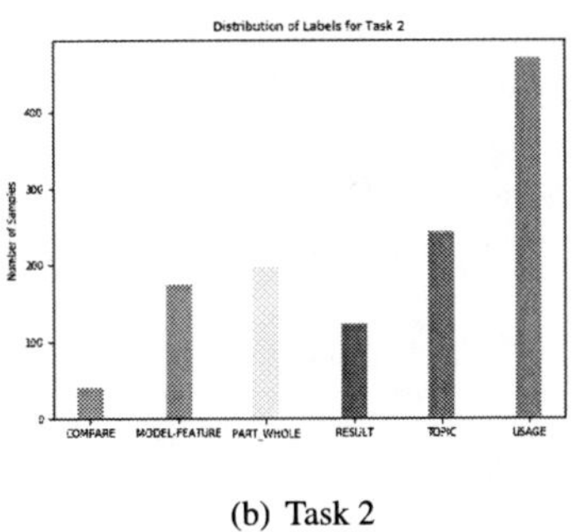

(b) Task 2

Figure 2: Class Sizes for Task 1 & Task 2.

would refer the reader to the task description paper (Gábor et al., 2018)

4 Methodology

As shown in Fig. 1, we use the piecewise convolutional encoder proposed by (Zeng et al., 2015) which encodes the sentence into an embedding space taking into account the context of text around the entities in an end to end manner. The various components of the encoder are described below

4.1 Preprocessing

Since the original training dataset provided is annotated using XML tags which can be utilized in a variety of ways, we briefly describe our preprocessing steps. Each text item contains a title of a paper and its abstract. Both the entities for a particular training/testing instance could only either be in the title or in the abstract. While it would be interesting to see the impact of incorporating the effect of paper titles on the entities in abstracts and vice versa, to simplify the architecture, we simply treat titles and abstracts as separate and independent sentences. For the representation of entities, the two most obvious options are to either combine sub-words in an entity using a special character (e.g. *word sense disambiguation* becomes *word_sense_disambiguation*) or to simply use entity head words to represent the starting position of the entity as proposed by (Nguyen and Grishman, 2015). We chose the latter approach for two reasons: 1) The amount of data is relatively small to learn word embeddings on the data itself 2) The conjoined entity representation as in the former approach would probably not exist in the pre-trained word embeddings and thus would have to be replaced by an unknown token. Finally, we used common text cleaning techniques like removing non-alphanumeric characters, replacing all numbers by a unique token, etc.

4.2 Word Representation

Each word in the input is transformed to a static, dense feature representation by looking up a pre-trained word embedding dictionary. We use dependency based word embeddings (Levy and Goldberg, 2014) which incorporate long-range dependencies between words and thus generate embeddings that are more functional in nature (than the traditional bag of words based embeddings) which is presumably more suitable to the current task as dependency based features have been shown to be useful for relation extraction (Xu et al., 2015; Bunescu and Mooney, 2005). All words that do not exist in the dictionary are replaced by *UNK* token and initialized randomly.

4.3 Position Embedding

Since convolved representations are position invariant, incorporating positional information using embeddings has been shown to be useful for a variety of task (Zeng et al., 2014; Gehring et al., 2017) when using a convolutional encoder. We evaluate the distance of each word in the sentence with respect to both *entity 1* and *entity 2* (we limit the values to a maximum distance of *position_window_size*). These position values are then projected into a relatively small embedding space using a trainable embedding layer.

4.4 Directionality Embedding

Since the relations are directional in nature, it is important to incorporate the available directionality information in the sentence representation. While this can be implicitly done when using dependency tree base input representation, to incorporate the directionality of the relation exhibited by the two entities ($< e_1, r, e_2 >$ or $< e_2, r, e_1 >$)

we also project the direction information into the embedding space by another embedding layer that is trained along with the entire network.

4.5 Convolution and Piecewise Max-Pooling

CNN's have been shown to be good at encoding sentences into vector representations for text classification tasks (Kim, 2014; Zhang et al., 2015; Hu et al., 2014; Kim et al., 2016) and at the same time also speed up the training and inference time. The word representations and position embeddings are concatenated and fed into a convolution encoder which generates features using varying width of filters. To take into account the context of text around and between the entities in consideration, we then perform a piecewise max-pooling operation as shown in Fig. 1. The input representations (word-embedding $\oplus$ position-embedding) are appropriately padded before the convolution operation to ensure that the convolved features have the same length as the input sentence in order to correctly use entity positions for piecewise max-pooling. These features generated by the PCNN are finally concatenated with the directionality embeddings discussed above to generate the sentence level representation.

4.6 Regularization, Output and Training

We use dropout (Srivastava et al., 2014) on the sentence representations with a keep probability of 0.5 as a simple regularization strategy. This is followed by a fully connected layer and a softmax operation for the classification task. We use the standard multi-class cross-entropy loss as our training objective and Adam (Kingma and Ba, 2014) for optimization.

Parameter	Values
Number of Epochs	100,200,400
Maximum Sequence Length	100,200
Batch Size	32,64
Number of Filters	32,64,128
Learning Rate	0.001, 0.0005

Table 1: Hyperparameter Values.

5 Experiments

5.1 Data Augmentation

Deep neural models require significant amount of training data to extract relevant features. While

Task	Data	Epoch	Batch Size	No. of Filters	Macro-F1 Score
1.1	1.1	200	32	64	35.3
1.1	1.1 + 1.2	200	64	32	**48.1**
1.2	1.2	200	32	64	64.4
1.2	1.1 + 1.2	100	64	128	**74.7**

Table 2: Results of our best performing systems on the official test set with/without data augmentation.

our neural model is relatively shallow, the data size for each of the subtask is also small. As a workaround, we simply mix the data from subtask 1.1 with data from subtask 1.2 which hopefully helps in improving the model's generalizability.

5.2 Experimental Settings

While the final training and prediction was performed on the entire training dataset, we use the official validation split provided by contest organizers to perform hyper-parameter tuning. For the data augmentation scenario, however, we also make use of the validation data from the other task. Given that CNN's are fast to train, we easily use grid search to find the optimal combination of a subset of parameters for each task and each data configuration (with or without augmentation) which are listed in Table 1. For the remaining parameters, we used standard values as recommended by prior literature as follows: convolution filters of width 3,4 and 5; position and directionality embeddings of size 5; windows size for relative positions from entities was set to 30.

6 Results

We report our performance on the classification tasks (Subtask 1.1 and 1.2) according to the official evaluation. While all task settings perform best for a maximum sequence length of 200 and learning rate of 0.001, the rest of the parameters and their corresponding results are listed in Table 2. Even a simple mixing of the two datasets which differ significantly in the nature of tagged entities lead to a significant improvement. Surprisingly though, adding the noisy data to the clean dataset also leads to a 36% increase in performance. This could be attributed to the fact that while heuristically annotated entities are high-level concepts thus sharing a lot of context with similar concepts, most of the manually annotated entities are full noun phrases, thus adding to the complexity of the task. These results also falsify our initial assumption/expectation of Task 1.1 to be easier.

7 Conclusion

We presented a simple end to end model that is fast to train and though does not perform competitively well, makes effective use of additional data for a significant improvement in performance. These results show the effectiveness of mixing/transferring supervision from data coming from a different distribution and thus invites further exploration in semi-supervised/supervised domain adaptation scenarios.

References

Razvan Bunescu and Raymond Mooney. 2005. A shortest path dependency kernel for relation extraction. In *Proceedings of Human Language Technology Conference and Conference on Empirical Methods in Natural Language Processing*, pages 724–731, Vancouver, British Columbia, Canada. Association for Computational Linguistics.

Razvan Bunescu and Raymond J. Mooney. 2006. Subsequence kernels for relation extraction. In *Advances in Neural Information Processing Systems, Vol. 18: Proceedings of the 2005 Conference (NIPS)*.

Kata Gábor, Davide Buscaldi, Anne-Kathrin Schumann, Behrang QasemiZadeh, Haïfa Zargayouna, and Thierry Charnois. 2018. Semeval-2018 Task 7: Semantic relation extraction and classification in scientific papers. In *Proceedings of International Workshop on Semantic Evaluation (SemEval-2018)*, New Orleans, LA, USA.

Jonas Gehring, Michael Auli, David Grangier, and Yann Dauphin. 2017. A convolutional encoder model for neural machine translation. In *Proceedings of the 55th Annual Meeting of the Association for Computational Linguistics (Volume 1: Long Papers)*, pages 123–135. Association for Computational Linguistics.

Baotian Hu, Zhengdong Lu, Hang Li, and Qingcai Chen. 2014. Convolutional neural network architectures for matching natural language sentences.

In Z. Ghahramani, M. Welling, C. Cortes, N. D. Lawrence, and K. Q. Weinberger, editors, *Advances in Neural Information Processing Systems 27*, pages 2042–2050. Curran Associates, Inc.

Yoon Kim. 2014. Convolutional neural networks for sentence classification. In *Proceedings of the 2014 Conference on Empirical Methods in Natural Language Processing (EMNLP)*, pages 1746–1751, Doha, Qatar. Association for Computational Linguistics.

Yoon Kim, Yacine Jernite, David Sontag, and Alexander M Rush. 2016. Character-aware neural language models. In *AAAI*, pages 2741–2749.

Diederik P Kingma and Jimmy Ba. 2014. Adam: A method for stochastic optimization. *arXiv preprint arXiv:1412.6980*.

Omer Levy and Yoav Goldberg. 2014. Dependency-based word embeddings. In *Proceedings of the 52nd Annual Meeting of the Association for Computational Linguistics (Volume 2: Short Papers)*, pages 302–308, Baltimore, Maryland. Association for Computational Linguistics.

Yankai Lin, Shiqi Shen, Zhiyuan Liu, Huanbo Luan, and Maosong Sun. 2016. Neural relation extraction with selective attention over instances. In *Proceedings of the 54th Annual Meeting of the Association for Computational Linguistics (Volume 1: Long Papers)*, pages 2124–2133, Berlin, Germany. Association for Computational Linguistics.

Mike Mintz, Steven Bills, Rion Snow, and Daniel Jurafsky. 2009. Distant supervision for relation extraction without labeled data. In *Proceedings of the Joint Conference of the 47th Annual Meeting of the ACL and the 4th International Joint Conference on Natural Language Processing of the AFNLP*, pages 1003–1011, Suntec, Singapore. Association for Computational Linguistics.

Thien Huu Nguyen and Ralph Grishman. 2015. Relation extraction: Perspective from convolutional neural networks. In *Proceedings of the 1st Workshop on Vector Space Modeling for Natural Language Processing*, pages 39–48.

Longhua Qian, Guodong Zhou, Fang Kong, Qiaoming Zhu, and Peide Qian. 2008. Exploiting constituent dependencies for tree kernel-based semantic relation extraction. In *Proceedings of the 22nd International Conference on Computational Linguistics (Coling 2008)*, pages 697–704, Manchester, UK. Coling 2008 Organizing Committee.

Sebastian Riedel, Limin Yao, and Andrew McCallum. 2010. Modeling relations and their mentions without labeled text. In *Proceedings of the European Conference on Machine Learning and Knowledge Discovery in Databases (ECML PKDD)*.

Nitish Srivastava, Geoffrey Hinton, Alex Krizhevsky, Ilya Sutskever, and Ruslan Salakhutdinov. 2014. Dropout: A simple way to prevent neural networks from overfitting. *Journal of Machine Learning Research*, 15:1929–1958.

Yi Wu, David Bamman, and Stuart Russell. 2017. Adversarial training for relation extraction. In *Proceedings of the 2017 Conference on Empirical Methods in Natural Language Processing*, pages 1778–1783, Copenhagen, Denmark. Association for Computational Linguistics.

Yan Xu, Lili Mou, Ge Li, Yunchuan Chen, Hao Peng, and Zhi Jin. 2015. Classifying relations via long short term memory networks along shortest dependency paths. In *Proceedings of the 2015 Conference on Empirical Methods in Natural Language Processing*, pages 1785–1794. Association for Computational Linguistics.

Daojian Zeng, Kang Liu, Yubo Chen, and Jun Zhao. 2015. Distant supervision for relation extraction via piecewise convolutional neural networks. In *Proceedings of the 2015 Conference on Empirical Methods in Natural Language Processing*, pages 1753–1762, Lisbon, Portugal. Association for Computational Linguistics.

Daojian Zeng, Kang Liu, Siwei Lai, Guangyou Zhou, and Jun Zhao. 2014. Relation classification via convolutional deep neural network. In *Proceedings of COLING 2014, the 25th International Conference on Computational Linguistics: Technical Papers*, pages 2335–2344, Dublin, Ireland. Dublin City University and Association for Computational Linguistics.

Xiang Zhang, Junbo Zhao, and Yann LeCun. 2015. Character-level convolutional networks for text classification. In C. Cortes, N. D. Lawrence, D. D. Lee, M. Sugiyama, and R. Garnett, editors, *Advances in Neural Information Processing Systems 28*, pages 649–657. Curran Associates, Inc.

The UWNLP system at SemEval-2018 Task 7: Neural Relation Extraction Model with Selectively Incorporated Concept Embeddings

Yi Luan   Mari Ostendorf   Hannaneh Hajishirzi
University of Washington
{luanyi, ostendor, hannaneh}@uw.edu

Abstract

This paper describes our submission for the SemEval 2018 Task 7 shared task on semantic relation extraction and classification in scientific papers. We extend the end-to-end relation extraction model of (Miwa and Bansal, 2016) with enhancements such as a character-level encoding attention mechanism on selecting pretrained concept candidate embeddings. Our official submission ranked the second in relation classification task (Subtask 1.1 and Subtask 2 Senerio 2), and the first in the relation extraction task (Subtask 2 Scenario 1).

1 Task Overview

The SemEval 2018 Task 7 Shared Task (Gábor et al., 2018) focuses on the task of recognizing the semantic relation that holds between scientific concepts. The task involves semantic relation extraction and classification into six categories specific to scientific literature: USAGE, RESULT, MODEL-FEATURE, PART_WHOLE, TOPIC, COMPARE. Two types of tasks are proposed: 1) identifying pairs of entities that are instances of any of the six semantic relations (extraction task), and 2) classifying instances into one of the specific relation types (classification task).

Consider the following input sentence: "[*Unsupervised training*] is first used to train a [*phone n-gram model*] for a particular domain." Given the concept pair [*Unsupervised training*] and [*phone n-gram model*], the relation extraction task is to identify whether there is a relation between the concepts, while the the relation classification task is to identity the relation as USAGE. Relation directionality is not taken into account for the evaluation of the extraction task. Directionality is taken into account when relevant for the classification task (5 out of the 6 semantic relations are asymmetrical). We will use this example throughout the paper to illustrate various parts of our system.

The SemEval 2018 Task 7 dataset contains 350 abstracts from the ACL Anthology for training and validation, and 150 abstracts for testing each subtask. Since the scale of the data is small for supervised training of neural systems, we introduce several strategies to leverage a large quantity of unlabeled scientific articles. In addition to initializing a neural system with pre-trained word embeddings, as in (Luan et al., 2017), we also try to incorporate embeddings of concepts that span multiple words. In neural models such as (Miwa and Bansal, 2016), phrases are often represented by an average (or weighted average) of the token's sequential LSTM representation. The intuition behind explicit modeling of multi-word concept embeddings is that the concept use may be different from that of its individual words. Due to the size of the dataset and the nature of scientific literature, a large number of the scientific terms in the test set have never appeared in the training set, so supervised learning of the phrase embeddings is not feasible. Therefore, we pre-trained scientific term embeddings on a large scientific corpus and provide a strategy to selectively incorporate the pre-trained embeddings into the relation extraction system.

2 System Description

2.1 Neural Architecture Model

Our system is an extension of (Luan et al., 2017) and (Miwa and Bansal, 2016) with LSTM RNNs that represent both word sequences and dependency tree structures, and perform relation extraction between concepts on top of these RNNs. As illustrated in Figure 1, it is composed of a 5 types of layers in a hierarchical neural model to encode context information. The first two layers (token, token LSTM) use the neural modeling framework in (Luan et al., 2017). The forward and backward dependency layers and the relation classification

Proceedings of the 12th International Workshop on Semantic Evaluation (SemEval-2018), pages 788–792
New Orleans, Louisiana, June 5–6, 2018. ©2018 Association for Computational Linguistics

layer are based on (Miwa and Bansal, 2016). The concept selection layer is novel, to the best of our knowledge. The different layers are described in more detail below.

Token Layer. The token layer concatenates three types of vector space embeddings. *Word embeddings* are learned for words from a fixed vocabulary (plus the unknown word token), initialized using Word2vec pre-training with large scholarly corpora. The *character-based embedding* for a token is derived from its characters as the concatenation of forward and backward representations from a bidirectional LSTM. The character look-up table is initialized at random. The advantage of building a character-based embedding layer is that it can handle out-of-vocabulary words and equations, which are frequent in this data, all of which are mapped to "UNK" tokens in the Word Embedding Layer. *Word embeddings* are learned for words from a fixed vocabulary (plus the unknown word token), initialized using Word2vec pre-training with large scholarly corpora. A *feature embedding* is learned as a mapping from features associated with capitalization (all capital, first capital, all lower, any capital but first letter) and part-of-speech tags. The embeddings are randomly initialized and trained jointly with other parameters during supervised training.

Token LSTM Layer We apply a bidirectional LSTM at the token level taking the concatenated character-word-feature embedding as input. An LSTM hidden state generated in this layer is denoted as h^S.

Forward & Backward Dependency Layers Given the concept pair (C_l, C_r), the Forward Dependency Layer (generating h^F) traces from the closest common ancestor w_a (for example the word *"used"* in Fig. 1) to the headword w_j (word *"model"*) of the right target concept C_r (*"phone n-gram model"*). The Backward Dependency Layer (generating h^B) traces from the ancestor to the headword w_i of the left concept C_l. We map the dependency relation into vector space and concatenate the resulting embedding to the embedding (h^S) of the headword of the concepts C_l or C_r for the backward and forward dependency layers, respectively. We concatenate the resulting bi-directional LSTM vector for the headwords together with the common ancestor in both Forward & Backward Dependency Layer as input to Relation Classification Layer

$$h^{DP} = [\overleftarrow{h^B_{w_i}}; \overrightarrow{h^B_{w_i}}, \overleftarrow{h^F_{w_j}}; \overrightarrow{h^F_{w_j}}; \overleftarrow{h^B_{w_a}}; \overrightarrow{h^B_{w_a}}; \overleftarrow{h^F_{w_a}}; \overrightarrow{h^F_{w_a}}] .$$

Concept Selection Layer The concepts in the task are mostly phrases rather than single words, in the SemEval Task 7. We therefore seek ways to obtain prior knowledge for those terms. We train a scientific concept extraction model using the state-of-the-art scientific neural tagging technique in (Luan et al., 2017), given the scientific concept annotation in the SemEval 2018 Task7 training data. We were able to achieve 79.8% F1 score (span level) to identify the scientific concepts. We then use the model to extract all scientific concepts in the ACL anthology and AI2 dataset (refer to Sec. 3). We keep all the concepts that occur more than 10 times in the whole corpus, which results in around 15k concepts. We treat each of the 15k concepts as an individual token and retrain word2vec embeddings v_k together with all other single words. At training time, given a scientific concept pair (C_l, C_r), we search through the 15k concepts to get all the concept candidates that have n-gram string match with C_l and C_r respectively (n is from 1 to the length of the target concept C). For example, for the concept *phone n-gram model*, the candidate concepts we get are {*phone n-gram, n-gram model, n-gram, model, phone*}. Since there may exist cases where no match could be found in the 15k concepts, we introduce a null vector $v_\varnothing$. $v_\varnothing$ is learned with other neural network parameters. Assume there are K concept candidates in the candidate list, we denote the embeddings for the concept candidates to be $V = \{v_1 \ldots v_K, v_\varnothing\}$. The attention weights are calculated by $\alpha_{lk} \propto \exp(h^S_{C_l} W_{ATT} v_k)$, where $v_k \in V$. $h^S_{C_l}$ is the concatenation of bidirectional LSTM hidden states of the first and last word in C_l.[1] W_{ATT} is a parameter matrix for the bilinear score for $h^S_{C_l}$ and v_k. The final concept embedding v_{C_l} is $v_{C_l} = \sum_{v_k \in V} \alpha_{lk} v_k$. For a target concept C, if exact match exists in the 15K concepts, we set the pre-trained concept embedding to be v_{C_l}. We concatenate the resulting embedding for both concepts in the concept pair as input to the final classification layer ($v_C = [v_{C_l}; v_{C_r}]$).

Relation Classification Layer We concatenate the output of Forward & Backward Dependency Layer h^{DP} and Concept Embedding Selection Layer v_C as input to Relation Classification Layer.

---

[1] We also tried using the weighted average of all LSTM word embeddings in the span to calculate $h^S_{C_l}$; this yields a slightly worse result.

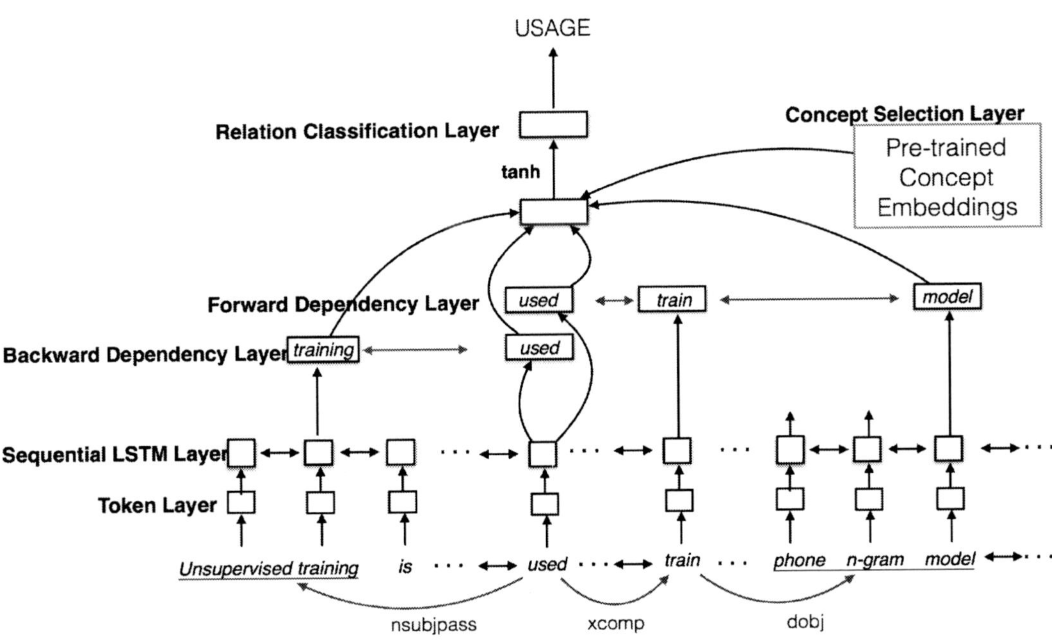

Figure 1: Neural relation extraction model with bidirectional sequential and dependency path LSTMs.

Besides, we also introduce a distance feature between the two concepts which indicates how many other concepts there are in between the target concept pairs. We concatenate the distance embedding with all the other features. The concatenated features are then projected down to a lower dimension through $tanh$ function and make the final prediction through a $softmax$ function.

3 Experimental Setup

External Data We use two external resources for pretraining word embeddings: i) the Semantic Scholar Corpus,[2] a collection of over 20 million research papers from which we extract a subset of 110k abstracts of publications in the artificial intelligence area; and ii) the ACL Anothology Reference Corpus, which contains 22k full papers published in the ACL Anothology (Bird et al., 2008).

Baseline We compare our model with a baseline that removes the Concept Selection Layer and replaces it with a weighted sum (using attention) of hidden states (from the Sequential LSTM Layer) for all words in a concept.

Implementation details All parameters are tuned based on dev set performance; the best parameters are selected and used for final evaluation.

For all experiments, we explore tuning with two different evaluation metrics: macro-F1 score and micro-F1 score.[3] We keep the pre-trained concept embedding fixed as additional input feature. The word embedding dimension is 250; the LSTM hidden dimension is 100 (for both sequential and dependency layer); the character-level hidden dimension is 25; and the optimization algorithm is SGD with a learning rate of 0.05. For Subtask 2, since 5 out of 6 relation types have directionality, we add relation label "_REVERSE" to all the 5 directional relations together with a "NONE" type, which result in 12 labels in total. For each epoch, we also randomly filter out some "NONE" samples with probability p during training, since the "NONE" type relation dominates the training set and would bias the model towards predicting "NONE" types. We tune p according to dev set, and use $p = 0.4$ for the final evaluation.

4 Experimental Results

Ablation Study Table 1 provides the results of an ablation study on the dev set showing the impact of removing different components of our system.

---

[2]http://labs.semanticscholar.org/corpus/

[3]The official evaluation is macro-F1, but since the number of instances in each class is highly unbalanced, the observed macro-F1 scores were unstable. We therefore introduce micro-F1 score for tuning and evaluation as well.

Model	Macro			Micro		
	P	R	F1	P	R	F1
Our system	49.4	36.7	**42.1**	46.2	42.2	**44.1**
-DepFeat	38.2	39.6	39.0	45.2	41.9	43.0
-DistFeat	43.4	37.8	40.4	38.7	47.8	42.7
-DepLSTM	51.5	30.0	37.9	48.6	32.6	39.0
-Concept	36.2	41.8	38.8	37.6	46.5	41.6
Baseline	40.9	32.5	36.2	41.9	38.0	39.9

Table 1: Ablation study showing the impact of neural network configurations on system performance on the dev set for the relation classification task (Subtask 2, senerio 2). -DepFeat removes the input dependency relation embeddings from the Backward & Forward Dependency Layers. -DistFeat and -Concept omit the distance and concept selection features, respectively, from the final classification layer. -DepLSTM removes the Backward & Forward Dependency Layers entirely (using the LSTM embeddings in the weighted token average).

Looking at micro F1 scores, dependency path information is very important (performance dropped 11.5% without it), and the Concept Selection Layer is also important as it gives 2.5 absolute improvement. The Dependency relation feature and the distance feature also show 1-2 points gain. It is worth noticing that removing the Concept Layer (-Concept) does better than replacing it with the weighted sequential LSTM sum (Baseline). With the small amount of training data, it is difficult for the baseline system to learn a good transformation from word to phrase.

Competition Result The results of our system is in Table 2. We submit two sets of results, one tuned with micro F1 and the other with macro F1. It turns out that even though the official evaluation metric is macro F1 score, our model tuned by micro F1 gets better results in the final competition. In Subtask 1.1 and Subtask 2 scenario 2, we were the second place team with F1 score of 78.9% and 39.1% respectively. We were the first place in Subtask 2 scenario 1 with 50.0% F1.

5 Related Work

There has been growing interest in research on automatic methods to help researchers search and extract information from scientific literature. Past research has addressed citation sentiment (Athar and Teufel, 2012b,a), citation networks (Kas, 2011; Gabor et al., 2016; Sim et al., 2012; Do et al., 2013; Jaidka et al., 2014), summarization (Abu-Jbara and

Model	T1.1	T2-E	T2-C
Our system (Micro)	78.9	**50.0**	39.1
Our system (Macro)	78.4	49.3	37.0
Team-1	**81.7**	48.8	**49.3**
Team-2	76.7	37.4	33.6

Table 2: Competition result for the top 3 teams. The official evaluation metric is macro F1 score. T1.1 means Subtask 1.1, T2-E means Subtask 2 senerio 1 (extraction task), T2-C means Subtask 2 senerio 2 (classification task).

Radev, 2011) and some analysis of research community (Vogel and Jurafsky, 2012; Anderson et al., 2012). However, due to scarce hand-annotated data resources, previous work on information extraction (IE) for scientific literature is very limited. Most previous work focuses on unsupervised methods for extracting scientific terms such as bootstrapping Gupta and Manning (2011); Tsai et al. (2013), or extracting relations (Gábor et al., 2016). Luan et al. (2017); Augenstein and Søgaard (2017) applied semi-supervised learning and multi-task learning to neural based models to leverage large unannotated scholarly datasets for a scientific term extraction task (Augenstein and Søgaard, 2017).

Although not much supervised relation extraction work has been done on scientific literature, neural network techniqueshave obtained the state of the art for general domain relation extraction. Both convolutional (Santos et al., 2015) and RNN-based architectures (Xu et al., 2016; Miwa and Bansal, 2016; Peng et al., 2017; Quirk and Poon, 2017) have been successfully applied to the task and significantly improve performance.

6 Conclusion

This paper describes the system of the UWNLP team submitted to SemEval 2018 Task 7. We extend state-of-the-art neural models for information extraction by proposing a Concept Selection module which can leverage the semantic information of concepts pre-trained from a large scholarly dataset. Our system ranked second in the relation classification task (subtask 1.1 and subtask 2 senerio 2), and first in the relation extraction task (subtask 2 scenario 1).

Acknowledgments

This research was supported by the NSF (IIS 1616112), Allen Distinguished Investigator Award, and gifts from Allen Institute of AI, Google, Amazon, Samsung, and Bloomberg. We thank the anonymous reviewers for their helpful comments

References

Amjad Abu-Jbara and Dragomir Radev. 2011. Coherent citation-based summarization of scientific papers. In *Proc. Annual Meeting of the Association for Computational Linguistics: Human Language Technologies*. volume 1, pages 500–509.

Ashton Anderson, Dan McFarland, and Dan Jurafsky. 2012. Towards a computational history of the ACL: 1980-2008. In *Proc. ACL Special Workshop on Rediscovering 50 Years of Discoveries*. pages 13–21.

Awais Athar and Simone Teufel. 2012a. Context-enhanced citation sentiment detection. In *Proc. Conf. North American Assoc. for Computational Linguistics: Human Language Technologies (NAACL-HLT)*. pages 597–601.

Awais Athar and Simone Teufel. 2012b. Detection of implicit citations for sentiment detection. In *Proc. ACL Workshop on Detecting Structure in Scholarly Discourse*. pages 18–26.

Isabelle Augenstein and Anders Søgaard. 2017. Multi-task learning of keyphrase boundary classification. In *Proc. Annu. Meeting Assoc. for Computational Linguistics (ACL)*. pages 341–346.

Steven Bird, Robert Dale, Bonnie J Dorr, Bryan R Gibson, Mark Thomas Joseph, Min-Yen Kan, Dongwon Lee, Brett Powley, Dragomir R Radev, Yee Fan Tan, et al. 2008. The ACL anthology reference corpus: A reference dataset for bibliographic research in computational linguistics. In *Proc. Language Resources and Evaluation Conference (LREC)*.

Huy Hoang Nhat Do, Muthu Kumar Chandrasekaran, Philip S Cho, and Min Yen Kan. 2013. Extracting and matching authors and affiliations in scholarly documents. In *Proc. ACM/IEEE-CS Joint Conference on Digital libraries*. pages 219–228.

Kata Gábor, Davide Buscaldi, Anne-Kathrin Schumann, Behrang QasemiZadeh, Haïfa Zargayouna, and Thierry Charnois. 2018. Semeval-2018 Task 7: Semantic relation extraction and classification in scientific papers. In *Proc. Int. Workshop on Semantic Evaluation (SemEval)*.

Kata Gabor, Haifa Zargayouna, Davide Buscaldi, Isabelle Tellier, and Thierry Charnois. 2016. Semantic annotation of the ACL anthology corpus for the automatic analysis of scientific literature. In *Proc. Language Resources and Evaluation Conference (LREC)*.

Kata Gábor, Haïfa Zargayouna, Isabelle Tellier, Davide Buscaldi, and Thierry Charnois. 2016. Unsupervised relation extraction in specialized corpora using sequence mining. In *International Symposium on Intelligent Data Analysis*. Springer, pages 237–248.

Sonal Gupta and Christopher D Manning. 2011. Analyzing the dynamics of research by extracting key aspects of scientific papers. In *Proc. IJCNLP*. pages 1–9.

Kokil Jaidka, Muthu Kumar Chandrasekaran, Beatriz Fisas Elizalde, Rahul Jha, Christopher Jones, Min-Yen Kan, Ankur Khanna, Diego Molla-Aliod, Dragomir R Radev, Francesco Ronzano, et al. 2014. The computational linguistics summarization pilot task. In *Proc. Text Analysis Conference*.

Miray Kas. 2011. Structures and statistics of citation networks. Technical report, DTIC Document.

Yi Luan, Mari Ostendorf, and Hannaneh Hajishirzi. 2017. Scientific information extraction with semi-supervised neural tagging. In *Proc. Conf. Empirical Methods Natural Language Process. (EMNLP)*.

Makoto Miwa and Mohit Bansal. 2016. End-to-end relation extraction using lstms on sequences and tree structures. In *Proc. Annu. Meeting Assoc. for Computational Linguistics (ACL)*. pages 1105–1116.

Nanyun Peng, Hoifung Poon, Chris Quirk, Kristina Toutanova, and Wen-tau Yih. 2017. Cross-sentence n-ary relation extraction with graph lstms. *Trans. Assoc. for Computational Linguistics (TACL)* 5:101–115.

Chris Quirk and Hoifung Poon. 2017. Distant supervision for relation extraction beyond the sentence boundary. In *Proc. Meeting of the European Association of Computational Linguistics*. pages 1171–1182.

Cicero Nogueira dos Santos, Bing Xiang, and Bowen Zhou. 2015. Classifying relations by ranking with convolutional neural networks. In *Proc. Annual Meeting of the Association for Computational Linguistics and the 7th International Joint Conference on Natural Language Processing*. pages 626–634.

Yanchuan Sim, Noah A Smith, and David A Smith. 2012. Discovering factions in the computational linguistics community. In *Proc. ACL Special Workshop on Rediscovering 50 Years of Discoveries*. pages 22–32.

Chen-Tse Tsai, Gourab Kundu, and Dan Roth. 2013. Concept-based analysis of scientific literature. In *Proc. ACM Int. Conference on Information & Knowledge Management*. ACM, pages 1733–1738.

Adam Vogel and Dan Jurafsky. 2012. He said, she said: Gender in the ACL anthology. In *Proc. ACL Special Workshop on Rediscovering 50 Years of Discoveries*. pages 33–41.

Yan Xu, Ran Jia, Lili Mou, Ge Li, Yunchuan Chen, Yangyang Lu, and Zhi Jin. 2016. Improved relation classification by deep recurrent neural networks with data augmentation. In *Proc. Int. Conf. Computational Linguistics (COLING)*. pages 1461–1470.

UC3M-NII Team at SemEval-2018 Task 7: Semantic Relation Classification in Scientific Papers via Convolutional Neural Network

Víctor Suárez-Paniagua, Isabel Segura-Bedmar
Computer Science Department
Universidad Carlos III de Madrid
Leganés 28911, Madrid, Spain
`vspaniag,isegura@inf.uc3m.es`

Akiko Aizawa
National Institute of Informatics
2-1-2 Hitotsubashi, Chiyoda-ku
Tokyo, Japan
`aizawa@nii.ac.jp`

Abstract

This paper reports our participation for SemEval-2018 Task 7 on extraction and classification of relationships between entities in scientific papers. Our approach is based on the use of a Convolutional Neural Network (CNN) trained on 350 abstract with manually annotated entities and relations. Our hypothesis is that this deep learning model can be applied to extract and classify relations between entities for scientific papers at the same time. We use the Part-of-Speech and the distances to the target entities as part of the embedding for each word and we blind all the entities by marker names. In addition, we use sampling techniques to overcome the imbalance issues of this dataset. Our architecture obtained an F1-score of 35.4% for the relation extraction task and 18.5% for the relation classification task with a basic configuration of the one step CNN.

1 Introduction

Nowadays, there is a high increase in the publication of scientific articles every year, which demonstrates that we are living in an emerging knowledge era. Experts cannot deal with this explosion of information and it is very hard to be up to date about the state-of-the-art techniques in a given field. This arduous task could be reduced if we automatically identify concepts from scientific articles and recognize the semantic relations between them with Natural Language Processing (NLP) techniques.

The Semantic Relation Extraction and Classification in Scientific Papers task at SemEval-2018 task 7 (Gábor et al., 2018) provides a framework for measuring the automatic annotation performance by models which are trained on scientific publications abstracts. The task defines six categories of relations between concepts and two tasks

are proposed: (1) the classification of the relations between two entities in the predefined categories, which is divided in two scenarios according to the data used: clean or noisy; and (2) the extraction of the relations given the entities from the clean data, which also could involve their subsequent classification.

In this paper, we describe our participation for SemEval-2018 Task 7 on the extraction of relationships between entities in scientific papers and also the subsequent classification in the predefined classes of this relations with one step classifier. The model is based on the Convolutional Neural Network (CNN) proposed in (Kim, 2014), which was the first work to exploit this architecture for the task of sentence classification. CNN is a robust deep-learning architecture which has exhibited good performance in others NLP tasks such as semantic clustering (Wang et al., 2016), sentiment analysis (Dos Santos and Gatti, 2014) and event detection (Nguyen and Grishman, 2015). The model uses as the input of each instance the transformation into real value vectors of the words of the sentence, the distances to the target entities of each word and the Part-of-Speech types. Furthermore, we carry out a sampling technique to alleviate the imbalance issues of the dataset equalizing the number of the instances for all the classes.

2 Dataset

An annotated corpus for training and testing the participating systems was provided in the SemEval-2018 Task 7. The dataset contains 350 and 150 abstract from scientific articles for training and testing set, respectively.

The relation instances are divided into the following classes: *USAGE, RESULT, MODEL, PART WHOLE, TOPIC* and *COMPARISON*. All of them are asymmetrical except *COMPARISON*, where

793

Proceedings of the 12th International Workshop on Semantic Evaluation (SemEval-2018), pages 793–797
New Orleans, Louisiana, June 5–6, 2018. ©2018 Association for Computational Linguistics

both entities are involved in the same bidirectional relation. A detailed description and analysis of the corpus and its methodology used to collect and process the scientific abstracts can be found in (Gábor et al., 2018).

2.1 Pre-processing phase

The relations between scientific concepts are annotated pair by pair in the abstracts. All annotated relations span within one sentence, thus, we split the paragraphs of the abstracts into sentences with NLTK tool[1] to generate all the possible instances in the corpus.

After that, each instance was tokenized, all words were converted to lower-case and special character were removed in order to clean the sentences as the approach described in (Kim, 2014). In addition, we used entity blinding for each relation to generalize the model, in which the two target entities of the relations were replaced by entity markers as "entity1" and "entity2", and "entity0" for the remaining entities. Since relations can be asymmetrical, we considered both directions. In other words, for each pair of candidates entities, we generated two different instances. For the *COMPARISON* class, which is a bidirectional relationship, we annotated both instances with the same class label. For example, the sentence: *'We suggest a method that mimics the behaviour of the oracle using a neural network or a decision tree.'* should be transformed to the relation instances showed in Table 1.

Instances after entity blinding (*entity1, entity2*)
(oracle, neural network)   *'We suggest a method that mimics the behaviour of the entity1 using a entity2 or a entity0.'*
(neural network, oracle)   *'We suggest a method that mimics the behaviour of the entity2 using a entity1 or a entity0.'*
(oracle, decision tree)   *'We suggest a method that mimics the behaviour of the entity1 using a entity0 or a entity2.'*
(decision tree, oracle)   *'We suggest a method that mimics the behaviour of the entity2 using a entity0 or a entity1.'*
(neural network, decision tree)   *'We suggest a method that mimics the behaviour of the entity0 using a entity1 or a entity2.'*
(decision tree, neural network)   *'We suggest a method that mimics the behaviour of the entity0 using a entity2 or a entity1.'*

Table 1: Instances of a sentence in the corpus after applying the pre-processing phase with entity blinding.

[1] http://www.nltk.org

Table 2 shows the number of the instances extracted in the training set per each class. The *None* class represents the number of pairs of entities that are not related (negative instances). The number of positive instances is very low compared to the negative ones, 1323 over 19210 (around 7%), mainly because most classes are unidirectional and we annotated the reverse instance as *None*.

We followed a similar sampling technique described in (Wang et al., 2017) to adjust the same numbers of instances per each class. Therefore, we randomly discard 60% of the negative instances and we duplicate the instances in each class until having the same number as the more representative class, 483 corresponding to *USAGE*. Thus, we try to solve possible issues associated with the imbalanced dataset.

Classes	Instances
COMPARE	190
MODEL-FEATURE	326
PART WHOLE	234
RESULT	72
TOPIC	18
USAGE	483
None	17887
Total	19210

Table 2: Number of instances in the dataset.

3 Method

In this section, we present a CNN model to detect and classify relationships between scientific concepts. Figure 1 shows the whole process from its input, which is a sentence with blinded entities, until the output, which is the classification of the instance into one of the relation types defined by the task.

3.1 Word table layer

Firstly, we determined n as the maximum sentence length in the training dataset. Those sentences with lengths shorter than n are padded with an auxiliary token "0". After that, we assigned a randomly initialized vector for each different word, creating thus a word embedding matrix: $\mathbf{W}_e \in \mathbb{R}^{|V| \times m_e}$ where V is the vocabulary size and m_e is the word embedding dimension. Finally, we obtained a matrix $\mathbf{x} = [x_1; x_2; ...; x_n]$ for each instance where the words are represented by their corresponding word embedding vectors.

In addition, we used the word position embedding described in (Zeng et al., 2014), which

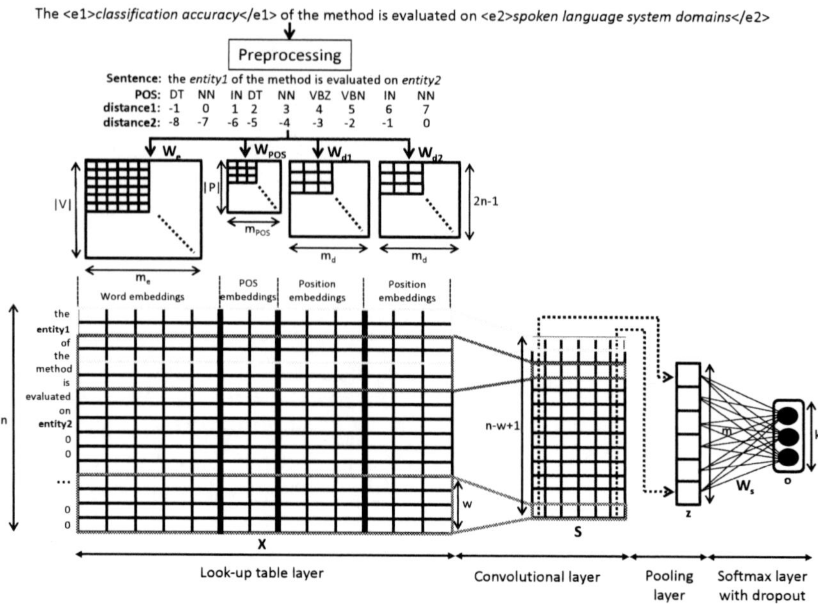

Figure 1: CNN model for the semantic relation classification in scientific papers of SemEval-2018 Task 7.

maps the distances of each word with respect to the two candidate entities into a real value vector using two position embedding matrices $\mathbf{W}_{d1} \in \mathbb{R}^{(2n-1) \times m_d}$ and $\mathbf{W}_{d2} \in \mathbb{R}^{(2n-1) \times m_d}$ where m_d is the position embedding dimension. Moreover, we extracted the Part-of-Speech (POS) feature of each word (entities are marked as common nouns) and create a POS embedding matrix as (Zhao et al., 2016) $\mathbf{W}_{POS} \in \mathbb{R}^{|P| \times m_{POS}}$ where P is the POS types vocabulary size and m_{POS} is the POS embedding dimension.

Finally, we created an input matrix $\mathbf{X} \in \mathbb{R}^{n \times (m_e + m_{POS} + 2m_d)}$ which is represented by the concatenation of the word embedding, the POS embedding and the two position embeddings for each word in the instance.

3.2 Convolutional layer

Once we obtained the input matrix, we applied the convolutional operation with a context window of size w to create higher level features. For each filter in $\mathbf{f} = [f_1; f_2; ...; f_w]$, we created a score matrix for the whole sentence as

$$s_i = g\left(\sum_{j=1}^{w} f_j x_{i+j-1}^T + b\right)$$

where b is a bias term and g is a non-linear function (such as tangent or sigmoid) of m number of filters.

3.3 Pooling layer

We extracted the most relevant features of each filter using the max function, which produces a single value in each filter as $z_f = max\{\mathbf{s}\} = max\{s_1; s_2; ...; s_{n-w+1}\}$. Thus, we created a vector $\mathbf{z} = [z_1, z_2, ..., z_m]$, whose dimension is the total number of filters m representing the relation instance. In the end, we concatenated the output values of the different filters in this layer.

3.4 Softmax layer

In this layer, we performed a dropout to prevent over-fitting obtaining a reduced vector $\mathbf{z}_d$ randomly dropping elements in $\mathbf{z}$. After that, we fed this vector into a fully connected softmax layer with weights $\mathbf{W}_s \in \mathbb{R}^{m \times k}$ to compute the output prediction values for the classification as

$$\mathbf{o} = \mathbf{z}_d \mathbf{W}_s + d$$

where d is a bias term. At test time, the vector $\mathbf{z}$ of a new instance is directly classified by the softmax layer without a dropout.

3.5 Learning

We defined the CNN parameter set to be learned in the training phase as $\theta = (\mathbf{W}_e, \mathbf{W}_{POS}, \mathbf{W}_{d1}, \mathbf{W}_{d2}, \mathbf{W}_s, \mathbf{F}_m)$, where $\mathbf{F}_m$ are all of the m filters $\mathbf{f}$. For this purpose, we used the conditional probability of a relation r obtained by the softmax operation as

$$p(r|\mathbf{x}, \theta) = \frac{\exp(\mathbf{o}_r)}{\sum_{l=1}^{k} \exp(\mathbf{o}_l)}$$

to minimize the cross-entropy function for all instances $(\mathbf{x}_i, y_i)$ in the training set T as follows

$$J(\theta) = \sum_{i=1}^{T} \log p(y_i|\mathbf{x}_i, \theta)$$

In addition, we minimized the objective function by using stochastic gradient descent over shuffled mini-batches and the Adam update rule (Kingma and Ba, 2014) to learn the parameters.

4   Results and Discussion

We define the CNN parameters for the experiments using the values described in Table 3. The number of epochs was fine-tuned in the validation set using the stopping criteria.

Parameter	Value
Maximal length in the dataset , n	152
Word embeddings dimension, M_e	300
POS embeddings dimension, M_{POS}	10
Position embeddings dimension, M_d	5
Filters for each window size, m	200
Filter sizes, w	(3, 4, 5)
Dropout rate, p	50%
Mini-batch size	50
Non-linear function, g	ReLU

Table 3: The CNN model parameters and their values used for the results.

Our CNN system obtained an F1-score of 35.4% for the relation extraction task in which only the detection of relation is taken into consideration. The official results obtained for the relation classification task are showed in Table 4. Our model reaches an F1-score in Macro-average of 18.5% with one step classifier, which means that the extraction and classification are considered at the same time. This performance was expected because we reached the similar results with a validation set created from the training set. Furthermore, we correctly predicted 147 instances with correct directionality over 367 (i.e. 40.05% in coverage).

The main problem is the high number of FP in the majority of classes, which are the *None* instances classified as a class. In some classes such as *PART WHOLE* and *USAGE* we have also a high number of FN compared to the total number of instances. We consider that the main reason is that the representation of the two directions of each relation is very similar, only the position distances and the target entity names are inverted, and the CNN cannot distinguish between them.

Classes	TP	FP	FN	P	R	F1
COMPARE	8	116	11	6.45%	42.11%	11.19%
MODEL-FEATURE	36	185	37	16.29%	49.32%	24.49%
PART WHOLE	22	66	60	25%	26.83%	25.88%
RESULT	2	21	14	8.7%	12.5%	10.26%
TOPIC	0	0	3	0%	0%	0%
USAGE	41	96	133	29.93%	23.56%	26.37%
Micro-averaged	-	-	-	18.38%	29.7%	22.71%
Macro-averaged	-	-	-	14.39%	25.72%	18.46%

Table 4: Results over the dataset using a CNN model measured by True Positives, False Positives, False Negatives, Precision, Recall and F1-measure, respectively.

5   Conclusions and Future work

A CNN model is used for the Relation Classification task of SemEval 2018 by UC3M-NII Team. Moreover, we balanced the dataset using sampling techniques, blinded the entities in the sentence and aggregated position embedding and POS embedding to the word embedding of each word to have more representation of each instance. This architecture obtained an F1-score of 35.4% and 18.5% for the relation extraction and classification task, respectively.

As future work, we proposed to use a two steps model to overcome the extraction of the relationships between two concepts and subsequently classify them in the different semantic classes. In addition, we also plan to rule out the reverse instances of each class as *None* in order to avoid having very similar representation with different labels. We plan to tackle the directionality problem with post-processing rules after the classification. Furthermore, we will train a CNN with different pre-trained word embedding models instead of using a random initialization.

Funding

This work was supported by the Research Program of the Ministry of Economy and Competitiveness - Government of Spain, (DeepEMR project TIN2017-87548-C2-1-R) and the TEAM project (Erasmus Mundus Action 2-Strand 2 Programme) funded by the European Commission.

Acknowledgments

We would like to thank the members of the Aizawa Laboratory and the HULAT research group for their fruitful discussions which were held.

References

C.N. Dos Santos and M. Gatti. 2014. Deep convolutional neural networks for sentiment analysis of short texts. In *Proceedings of the 25th International Conference on Computational Linguistics, (COLING 2014), Technical Papers*, pages 69–78.

Kata Gábor, Davide Buscaldi, Anne-Kathrin Schumann, Behrang QasemiZadeh, Haïfa Zargayouna, and Thierry Charnois. 2018. Semeval-2018 Task 7: Semantic relation extraction and classification in scientific papers. In *Proceedings of International Workshop on Semantic Evaluation (SemEval-2018)*, New Orleans, LA, USA.

Y. Kim. 2014. Convolutional neural networks for sentence classification. In *Proceedings of the 2014 Conference on Empirical Methods in Natural Language Processing (EMNLP)*, pages 1746–1751.

Diederik P. Kingma and Jimmy Ba. 2014. Adam: A method for stochastic optimization. *CoRR*, abs/1412.6980.

Thien Huu Nguyen and Ralph Grishman. 2015. Event detection and domain adaptation with convolutional neural networks. In *ACL-IJCNLP 2015 - 53rd Annual Meeting of the Association for Computational Linguistics and the 7th International Joint Conference on Natural Language Processing of the Asian Federation of Natural Language Processing, Proceedings of the Conference*, volume 2, pages 365–371. Association for Computational Linguistics (ACL).

Peng Wang, Bo Xu, Jiaming Xu, Guanhua Tian, Cheng-Lin Liu, and Hongwei Hao. 2016. Semantic expansion using word embedding clustering and convolutional neural network for improving short text classification. *Neurocomputing*, 174, Part B:806 – 814.

Wei Wang, Xi Yang, Canqun Yang, Xiaowei Guo, Xiang Zhang, and Chengkun Wu. 2017. Dependency-based long short term memory network for drug-drug interaction extraction. *BMC Bioinformatics*, 18(16):578.

Daojian Zeng, Kang Liu, Siwei Lai, Guangyou Zhou, and Jun Zhao. 2014. Relation classification via convolutional deep neural network. In *Proceedings of the 25th International Conference on Computational Linguistics (COLING 2014), Technical Papers*, pages 2335–2344, Dublin, Ireland. Dublin City University and Association for Computational Linguistics.

Zhehuan Zhao, Zhihao Yang, Ling Luo, Hongfei Lin, and Jian Wang. 2016. Drug drug interaction extraction from biomedical literature using syntax convolutional neural network. *Bioinformatics*.

MIT-MEDG at SemEval-2018 Task 7: Semantic Relation Classification via Convolution Neural Network

Di Jin
MIT CSAIL
Cambridge, MA
jindi15@mit.edu

Franck Dernoncourt
Adobe Research
San Jose, CA
dernonco@adobe.com

Elena Sergeeva
MIT CSAIL
Cambridge, MA
elenaser@mit.edu

Matthew B. A. McDermott
MIT CSAIL
Cambridge, MA
mmd@mit.edu

Geeticka Chauhan
MIT CSAIL
Cambridge, MA
geeticka@mit.edu

Abstract

SemEval 2018 Task 7 tasked participants to build a system to classify two entities within a sentence into one of the 6 possible relation types. We tested 3 classes of models: Linear classifiers, Long Short-Term Memory (LSTM) models, and Convolutional Neural Network (CNN) models. Ultimately, the CNN model class proved most performant, so we specialized to this model for our final submissions.

We improved performance beyond a vanilla CNN by including a variant of negative sampling, using custom word embeddings learned over a corpus of ACL articles, training over corpora of both tasks 1.1 and 1.2, using reversed feature, using part of context words beyond the entity pairs and using ensemble methods to improve our final predictions. We also tested attention based pooling, up-sampling, and data augmentation, but none improved performance. Our model achieved rank 6 out of 28 (macro-averaged F1-score: **72.7**) in subtask 1.1, and rank 4 out of 20 (macro F1: **80.6**) in subtask 1.2.

1 Introduction

SemEval 2018 Task 7 (Gbor et al., 2018) focuses on relation classification and extraction on a corpus of 350 scientific paper abstracts consisting of 1228 and 1248 annotated sentences for subtasks 1.1 and 1.2, respectively. There are six possible relations: *USAGE, RESULT, MODEL-FEATURE, PART_WHOLE, TOPIC*, and *COMPARE*.

Given this data, our task is to take an example sentence, as well as the left and right entities within that sentence, and an indicator as to whether the relation is reversed, and predict the relation type for that sentence. In subtasks 1.1 and 1.2, all presented sentences have a relation.

We submitted predictions based on a self-ensembled convolutional neural network (CNN) model trained with a negative sampling augmented loss using ACL-specific embeddings as input features. We achieved rank 6 out of 28 (macro-averaged F1-score: 72.7) in subtask 1.1, and rank 4 out of 20 (macro F1 80.6) in subtask 1.2.

2 Related Work

Previous SemEval challenges have explored relation identification and extraction. The 2010 SemEval Task 8 (Hendrickx et al., 2010) explored classification of natural language relations, such as *CONTENT-CONTAINER* or *ENTITY-ORIGIN*. This challenge differs from ours in its generalizability; our relations are specific to ACL papers (e.g. *MODEL-FEATURE*) whereas the 2010 relations are more general, and may necessitate more common-sense knowledge than the 2018 relations. The 2010 data has been extensively studied and has offered significant opportunity for other researchers to test their model. Rink and Harabagiu (2010) produced a strong SVM/LR model to attack this challenge. Several deep architectures have also been proposed for this task, including the work of Cai et al. (2016), which demonstrated a novel approach merging ideas from recurrent networks and convolutional networks based on shortest dependency path (SDP). Xu et al. (2015a) and Santos et al. (2015) both used convolutional architectures along with negative sampling to pursue this task. More recently, Wang et al. (2016) used two levels of attention, one for input selection and the other for output pooling, to boost the performance of their model to state of the art.

The 2017 SemEval Task 10 (Augenstein et al., 2017) also featured relation extraction within

Proceedings of the 12th International Workshop on Semantic Evaluation (SemEval-2018), pages 798–804
New Orleans, Louisiana, June 5–6, 2018. ©2018 Association for Computational Linguistics

Model	Acc. (%)
SVM	64.0 ± 5.3
LR	65.3 ± 4.3
DEEP RF	63.1 ± 4.1
LSTM	61.4 ± 5.5
CNN	$\mathbf{66.3 \pm 4.4}$

Table 1: Comparison of best performance of different model types in our initial experimentation.

scientific publications. Here, however, there were only 2 relation types, *HYPONYM-OF* and *SYNONYM-OF*. One successful model on this task utilized a convolutional network operating on word, tag, position, and part-of-speech features (Lee et al., 2017), and found that restricting network focus to only the words between the requisite entities offered a notable performance improvement.

3 Methods

3.1 Pre-processing

Data was tokenized using the SpaCy tokenizer[1]. Part of speech (POS) tags were extracted using SpaCy, while lemmas and hypernyms were extracted via WordNet (Miller et al., 1990), inspired by Rink and Harabagiu (2010).

3.2 Initial Experiments

We tested several machine learning methods on these data, including a logistic regression classifier over `tf-idf` features extracted from words, lemmas, hypernyms, and POS. Additionally, we tested deep random forests with multi-grain sequence scanning over word embeddings sequences (Zhou and Feng, 2017) and LSTM with attention (Zhou et al., 2016) over both word/lemma/hypernym embeddings, character sequence embeddings, and position indicators. Lastly, we tested a CNN model over these data, using word/lemma embeddings, position embeddings, and a variant of negative sampling. After optimizing all model configurations and doing preliminary hyperparameter optimization via automatic grid search, early comparisons between the differing model classes yielded the results in Table 1. These results were measured in accuracy over 15-fold cross validation on the 1.1 train set.

Given these initial results, we focused principally on the CNN model.

3.3 CNN Model Details

Figure 1 presents the architecture of the CNN model. The model first takes the tokenized sentence, as well as the targeted entities, and transforms it to a sequence of continuous embedding vectors (Subsection 3.3.1). Next, the model uses a convolution layer to transform the embedded sentence to a fixed-size representation of the whole sentence (Subsection 3.3.2). Finally, it computes the score for each relation class via a linear transformation (Subsection 3.3.3). The overall system is trained end-to-end via a cross entropy loss augmented with a variant of negative sampling (Subsection 3.3.4).

3.3.1 Feature Embeddings

Given a sentence $x = [x_1, \ldots, x_n]$, the tokens x_i are featurized into continuous embedding vectors via concatenated word embeddings (e^{w_i}) and word position embeddings (e^{wp_i}): $e_i = [e^{w_i}, e^{wp_i}]$.

Word Embeddings Word representations are encoded by the column vector in the embedding matrix $W^{word} \in \mathbb{R}^{d_w \times |V|}$, where V is the vocabulary of the dataset. Each column $W_i^{word} \in \mathbb{R}^{d_w}$ is the word embedding vector for the ith word in the vocabulary. This matrix is trainable during the optimization process and initialized by pre-trained embedding vectors described in Section 3.4.

Word Position Embeddings (WPEs) In general, the information needed to determine the sentence's relations mostly comes from the words close to the two entities. In addition, some information needs to be input into the model to indicate which words are entities. We use the word's relative position to either entity as a feature to fulfill the above-mentioned two functions. For instance, in the sentence "the **probabilistic model** used in the **alignment**" shown in Figure 1, the relative distance of all the words to the left entity "probabilistic model" is $-1, 0, 0, 1, 2, 3, 4$ and that to the right entity "alignment" is $-6, -5, -4, -3, -2, -1, 0$. Each relative distance is mapped into a vector of dimension d^{wp}, which is randomly initialized then updated during training. Each word w has two relative distances wp_1 and wp_2 with respect to two entities $entity_1$ and $entity_2$, and each distance is mapped to corresponding embedding vector and the position embedding e^{wp} of word w is the concatenation of these two vectors: $e^{wp} = [e^{wp_1}, e^{wp_2}]$.

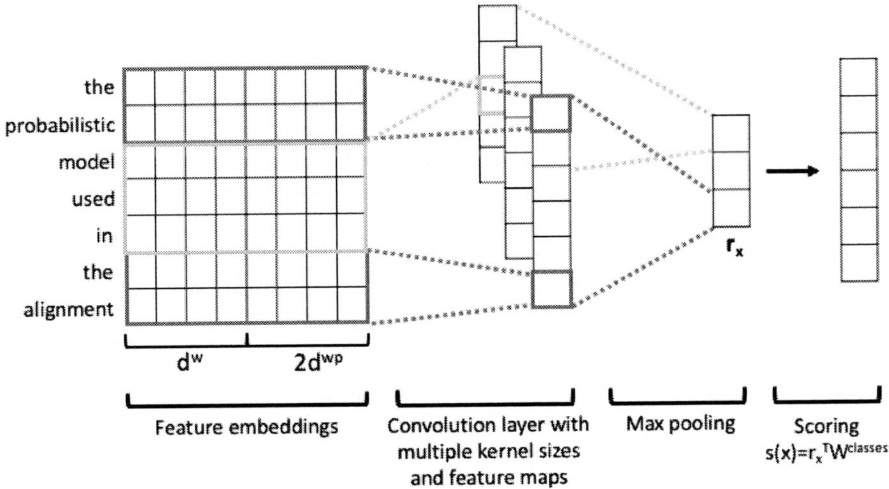

Figure 1: Illustration of CNN model architecture.

3.3.2 Sentence Representation

After featurization, a sentence x of length N is represented as $e = [e_1, e_2, ...e_N]$. We denote $e_{i:i+j}$ as the concatenation of featurized tokens: $e_{i:i+j} = [e_i, e_{i+1}, ..., e_{i+j}]$. A convolution operation involves a filter weight matrix $W \in \mathbb{R}^{(d^w+2d^{wp}) \times k}$, which is applied to a window of k words to produce a new feature c_i, as represented by:

$$c_i = \tanh(W \cdot e_{i:i+k-1} + b),$$

where $b \in \mathbb{R}$ is a bias term. This filter is applied to each possible window of words in the sentence $e_{1:h}, e_{2:h+1}, ..., e_{N-h+1:N}$ to produce a feature map vector $c = [c_1, c_2, ..., c_{N-k+1}]$. We then apply a max pooling operation to this feature map to obtain the maximum value $\hat{c} = max\{\mathbf{c}\}$ as the feature corresponding to this particular filter. This is how we extract one feature by one filter. And the model can use multiple filters with varying window sizes and filter parameters to produce multiple features. We concatenate all the obtained features to form the fixed size sentence representation r_x.

3.3.3 Inference Scoring

Given the vector representation r_x of the sentence x, class scores are computed via a linear transfor-

mation mediated by a trainable matrix $W^{classes}$:

$$s(x) = W^{classes} r_x.$$

At prediction time, the relation class is inferred by taking the index of maximum score.

3.3.4 Loss with Negative Sampling

After obtaining the score vector $s(x)$ for the sentence x, we use a loss function motivated by ideas in negative sampling as follows. Let y be the correct label for sentence x, and $I = \mathcal{Y} \setminus \{y\}$ be the set of all incorrect labels for x. Then, we compute the loss:

$$L = \log\left(1 + e^{\gamma\left(m^+ - s(x)_y\right)}\right)$$
$$+ \log\left(1 + e^{\gamma\left(m^- + \max_{y' \in I}\left(s(x)_{y'}\right)\right)}\right),$$

where m^+ and m^- are margins, γ is the penalty scale factor. Minimizing this loss function will both increase the score of the correct label and decrease that of the wrong label. We used Adam optimizer (Kingma and Ba, 2014) to minimize the loss function.

3.4 ACL Corpus Embeddings

We pretrained 50-dimensional word embeddings on the ACL anthology corpus (Radev et al., 2013) using word2vec (Mikolov et al., 2013a,b) (we

Symbol	Name	Value
d^w	Word Embed. Size	50
d^{wp}	Pos. Embed. Size	42
d^c	Convolution Units	900
k	Convolution Kernel	2,3,4
m^+	Correct Label Margin	2.2
m^-	Incorrect Label Margin	0.7
γ	Penalty Scale Factor	3.1
λ	Learning Rate	0.0008
β	L2 Regularization	0.01
d	Dropout Ratio	0.5

Table 2: CNN model final hyperparameters.

have also tried 100-dimensional word embeddings pre-trained in the same way but it performed worse in this small dataset). The corpus was derived by downloading all ACL anthology articles in PDF format, then converting them into text via some imperfect optical character recognition (OCR). The corpus contains 25,938 papers totaling 136,772,370 tokens, with 49,600 unique tokens. We used the following parameters for word2vec: skip-gram model, maximum skip length between words of 10, negative sampling with 10 negative examples, discard words that appear less than 5 times, and 5 training iterations[2].

4 Results

4.1 Model Tuning

We first optimized the CNN model hyperparameters via random search with 90 samples; final hyperparameters are shown in Table 2.

Beyond traditional hyperparameter optimization, a number of modifications with this model incurred performance gains during our final stages of experimentation, as determined by cross validation over either the 1.1 or 1.2 data. We detail the types of these changes below, then show the performance results obtained on the *test set* (not the cross validation results which motivated their use in our system) in Table 3.

Merged Training Sets Merging the 1.1 & 1.2 training datasets as a new training set had a large impact on the macro F1 score of our models. Both training datasets are relatively small, containing only approximately 1200 examples. Merging the 1.1 and 1.2 training

sets helps equalize class imbalance and expand the dataset size, at the cost of introducing a biased distribution of relation types for either class alone.

Reversal Indicator Features Each entity pair was given the information whether the relation of it is reversed or not. We added this binary feature, which proved performant.

Custom ACL Embeddings Specializing our word vector embeddings pre-training source to an ACL-specific corpus (described in section 3.4) offered notable gains.

Context words We explored using a context window of varying sizes around the entity-enclosed text within the sentence. Our pre-submission cross validation experiments suggested a context window of ± 50 words was optimal, but post-submission evaluation on the provided test set yielded better results with a ± 20 word window. Empirically, the number of context words to be included needs to be optimized on the specific dataset.

Ensembling We trained 50 copies of our network, using different random initializations and dev sets (for early stopping), then averaged their scores for prediction. This reduced variance of our predictions and improved performance.

Besides the above successful strategies, we also tested some settings that, in reality had a negative effect. We experimented with attention based pooling as suggested by (Wang et al., 2016), but it hurt performance in our cross validation experiments so we discarded that mechanism. Additionally, we also tried replacing the original words with their corresponding lemmas—this increased performance in our cross validation results, however, (post-submission evaluation revealed) harmed our results on the SemEval test set, where it yielded average macro-F1 scores of 71.48% and 77.01% for subtasks 1.1 and 1.2, respectively, after 10 runs. The potential reason for this degradation could be that the word embeddings are all trained on original words instead of lemmas so the embeddings of lemmas cannot be as well initialized as original words. Additionally, we tried data augmentation (via synonym substitution), and up-sampling (via duplication to equalize

---

[2] -cbow 0 -window 10 -negative 10 -hs 0 -sample 1e-3 -threads 15 -binary 0 -iter 5 -min-count 5 -size 50

Condition	1.1 (%)	1.2 (%)
1.1 Train Set	49.0 ± 1.2	N/A
1.2 Train Set	N/A	66.5 ± 3.2
Merged Train Sets	68.5 ± 3.8	74.4 ± 3.2
Reversed Feature	69.0 ± 1.2	78.0 ± 3.6
ACL Embeddings	71.7 ± 0.7	80.5 ± 1.5
Context Words	71.3 ± 1.0	82.5 ± 1.6
Ensemble	**72.7**	**85.0**

Table 3: CNN Improvements over a series of modifications. Each row includes the modifications of the previous rows. All numbers are macro-F1 scores on test set after 10 runs in the form of {average}±{standard deviation} (the "Ensemble" row lacks deviation numbers as it, being a variance reduction technique, does not have the same sources of variation as the other models). We report ± 20 context words here, which was found to be optimal in post-submission experimentation, but our submitted models used ± 50 context words, which was preferred under initial cross validation.

data size of each label), but all proved ineffective at the cross validation level and were not included in our final submission.

4.2 Submission Results

We entered 6 submissions in total, 3 for subtask 1.1, and 3 for subtask 1.2. Their final performances are listed in Table 4. All the submissions were based on the ensemble model listed in Table 3 except that the lemmas were used instead of original words and we used ± 50 context words. The major difference between submissions was the strategy for early stopping. Detailed settings for each submission of subtask 1.1 are:

Submission 1 We randomly extracted 10% training data as validation set and made test set predictions when the highest validation accuracy was reached.

Submission 2 We randomly extracted 10% training data as validation set with stratification (stratification is based on the proportion of labels in the train set) and made test set predictions when the highest validation accuracy was reached.

Submission 3 No validation set was used. Test set predictions were made at fixed number of training epochs, chosen by cross validation using training data.

Detailed settings for each submission of subtask 1.2 are:

Subtask	Submission	Macro-F1 (%)
	1	71.5
1.1	2	72.3
	3	**72.7**
	1	**80.6**
1.2	2	76.4
	3	79.8

Table 4: Final submission performance.

Submission 1 We randomly extracted 10% training data as validation set and made test set predictions when the highest validation accuracy was reached.

Submission 2 No validation set was used. Test set predictions were made at fixed number of training epochs, chosen by cross validation using training data.

Submission 3 Settings are the same as submission 2 except that we added the embeddings of the two entities (max pooled) to the sentence representation vector extracted by CNN model as additional features prior to scoring and inference.

In summary, early stopping made based on the validation set accuracy does not guarantee better test set performance than that using a fixed number of training epochs. Stratifying the label ratio of validation set according to the training set does help improve the test set performance. The benefit of adding embeddings of entities as extra features is not clear.

5 Future Work

Our custom ACL embeddings offered significant performance boosts over embeddings pre-trained on the corpus in the general domain such as wikipedia, but the corpus we obtained for pre-training is noisy due to the imperfect OCR. Cleaning up the input ACL dataset may result in better embeddings, offering even larger performance gains. Additionally, we could try restricting the ACL dataset to only those papers published more recently, in hopes to further specify the embedding space to a relevant subset—of course, this would also have reduced the embedding dataset size, so it may have cost more than it gained and experimentation would be warranted.

We also never explored any dependency tree-based featurizations of our data, though those were found to be helpful in prior works (Cai et al., 2016; Xu et al., 2015b).

The class imbalance of the training dataset is one of the greatest obstacles, where performance of common classes is a lot better than the rare classes. To tackle this problem, adversarial generative network (GAN) models (Goodfellow et al., 2014) could be used for data augmentation so that the data size of all labels can be equalized.

6 Conclusion

We tested linear classifiers, sequential random forests, LSTM models, and CNN models on these data. Within each model, we explored many variations, including two models of attention, negative sampling, entity embedding or sentence-only embeddings, among others. The most performant combination found was a CNN model trained over ACL-specific embeddings and a negative sampling augmented loss, without attention. We submitted self-ensembled predictions from this model both with and without early stop–ultimately early stop proved efficacious only on task 2. This model achieved rank 6 out of 28 (macro F1 72.7) in subtask 1.1, and rank 4 out of 20 (macro F1 80.6) in subtask 1.2.

Acknowledgements

This work was supported (in part) by funding grants U54-HG007963 from National Human Genome Research Institute (NHGRI) and P50-MH106933 from National Institute of Mental Health (NIMH).

References

Isabelle Augenstein, Mrinal Das, Sebastian Riedel, Lakshmi Vikraman, and Andrew McCallum. 2017. Semeval 2017 task 10: Scienceie - extracting keyphrases and relations from scientific publications. *CoRR*, abs/1704.02853.

Rui Cai, Xiaodong Zhang, and Houfeng Wang. 2016. Bidirectional recurrent convolutional neural network for relation classification. In *Proceedings of the 54th Annual Meeting of the Association for Computational Linguistics (Volume 1: Long Papers)*, volume 1, pages 756–765.

Ian Goodfellow, Jean Pouget-Abadie, Mehdi Mirza, Bing Xu, David Warde-Farley, Sherjil Ozair, Aaron Courville, and Yoshua Bengio. 2014. Generative adversarial nets. In *Advances in neural information processing systems*, pages 2672–2680.

Kata Gbor, Davide Buscaldi, Anne-Kathrin Schumann, Behrang QasemiZadeh, Hafa Zargayouna, and Thierry Charnois. 2018. Semeval-2018 task 7: Semantic relation extraction and classification in scientific papers. In *Proceedings of the 12th International Workshop on Semantic Evaluation (SemEval-2018)*, New Orleans, LA, USA, June 2018.

Iris Hendrickx, Su Nam Kim, Zornitsa Kozareva, Preslav Nakov, Diarmuid Ó Séaghdha, Sebastian Padó, Marco Pennacchiotti, Lorenza Romano, and Stan Szpakowicz. 2010. SemEval-2010 Task 8 : Multi-Way Classification of Semantic Relations Between Pairs of Nominals. *Computational Linguistics*, (June 2009):94–99.

Diederik P Kingma and Jimmy Ba. 2014. Adam: A method for stochastic optimization. *arXiv preprint arXiv:1412.6980*.

Ji Young Lee, Franck Dernoncourt, and Peter Szolovits. 2017. MIT at SemEval-2017 Task 10: Relation Extraction with Convolutional Neural Networks.

Tomas Mikolov, Kai Chen, Greg Corrado, and Jeffrey Dean. 2013a. Efficient estimation of word representations in vector space. *arXiv preprint arXiv:1301.3781*.

Tomas Mikolov, Ilya Sutskever, Kai Chen, Greg S Corrado, and Jeff Dean. 2013b. Distributed representations of words and phrases and their compositionality. In *Advances in neural information processing systems*, pages 3111–3119.

George A Miller, Richard Beckwith, Christiane Fellbaum, Derek Gross, and Katherine J Miller. 1990. Introduction to wordnet: An on-line lexical database. *International journal of lexicography*, 3(4):235–244.

DragomirR. Radev, Pradeep Muthukrishnan, Vahed Qazvinian, and Amjad Abu-Jbara. 2013. The ACL anthology network corpus. *Language Resources and Evaluation*, pages 1–26.

Bryan Rink and Sanda Harabagiu. 2010. UTD: Classifying Semantic Relations by Combining Lexical and Semantic Resources. *Proceedings of the 5th International Workshop on Semantic Evaluation*, (July):256–259.

Cicero Nogueira dos Santos, Bing Xiang, and Bowen Zhou. 2015. Classifying relations by ranking with convolutional neural networks. *arXiv preprint arXiv:1504.06580*.

Linlin Wang, Zhu Cao, Gerard de Melo, and Zhiyuan Liu. 2016. Relation Classification via Multi-Level Attention CNNs. In *Proceedings of the 54th Annual Meeting of the Association for Computational Linguistics (Volume 1: Long Papers)*.

Kun Xu, Yansong Feng, Songfang Huang, and Dongyan Zhao. 2015a. Semantic relation classification via convolutional neural networks with simple negative sampling. *CoRR*, abs/1506.07650.

Yan Xu, Lili Mou, Ge Li, Yunchuan Chen, Hao Peng, and Zhi Jin. 2015b. Classifying relations via long short term memory networks along shortest dependency paths. In *Proceedings of the 2015 Conference on Empirical Methods in Natural Language Processing*, pages 1785–1794.

Peng Zhou, Wei Shi, Jun Tian, Zhenyu Qi, Bingchen Li, Hongwei Hao, and Bo Xu. 2016. Attention-based bidirectional long short-term memory networks for relation classification. In *Proceedings of the 54th Annual Meeting of the Association for Computational Linguistics (Volume 2: Short Papers)*, volume 2, pages 207–212.

Zhi-Hua Zhou and Ji Feng. 2017. Deep forest: Towards an alternative to deep neural networks. *arXiv preprint arXiv:1702.08835*.

SIRIUS-LTG-UiO at SemEval-2018 Task 7:
Convolutional Neural Networks with Shortest Dependency Paths for Semantic Relation Extraction and Classification in Scientific Papers

Farhad Nooralahzadeh, Lilja Øvrelid, Jan Tore Lønning
Department of Informatics
University of Oslo, Norway
`{farhadno,liljao,jtl}@ifi.uio.no`

Abstract

This article presents the SIRIUS-LTG-UiO system for the SemEval 2018 Task 7 on Semantic Relation Extraction and Classification in Scientific Papers. First we extract the shortest dependency path (sdp) between two entities, then we introduce a convolutional neural network (CNN) which takes the shortest dependency path embeddings as input and performs relation classification with differing objectives for each subtask of the shared task. This approach achieved overall F1 scores of 76.7 and 83.2 for relation classification on clean and noisy data, respectively. Furthermore, for combined relation extraction and classification on clean data, it obtained F1 scores of 37.4 and 33.6 for each phase. Our system ranks 3rd in all three sub-tasks of the shared task.

1 Introduction

Relation extraction and classification can be defined as follows: given a sentence where entities are manually annotated, we aim to identify the pairs of entities that are instances of the semantic relations of interest and classify them based on a pre-defined set of relation types. A range of different approaches have been applied to solve this task in previous work. Conventional classification approaches have made use of contextual, lexical and syntactic features combined with richer linguistic and background knowledge such as WordNet and FrameNet (Hendrickx et al., 2010; Rink and Harabagiu, 2010).

Recently, the re-emergence of deep neural networks provides a way to develop highly automatic features and representations to handle complex interpretation tasks. These approaches have yielded impressive results for many different NLP tasks. The use of deep neural networks for relation classification has been investigated in several recent studies (Socher et al., 2012; Lin et al., 2016; Zhou et al., 2016). Convolutional neural networks (CNNs) have been effectively applied to extract lexical and sentence level features for relation classification (Zhang and Wang, 2015; Lee et al., 2017; Nguyen and Grishman, 2015). However, these works consider whole sentences or the context between two target entities as input for the CNN. Such representations suffer from irrelevant sub-sequences or clauses when target entities occur far from each other or there are other target entities in the same sentence. To avoid negative effects from irrelevant chunks or clauses and capture the relation between two entities, Xu et al. (2015a); Liu et al. (2015) and Xu et al. (2015b) employ a CNN to learn more robust and effective relation representations from the shortest dependency path (sdp) between two entities. The sdp between two entities in the dependency graph captures a condensed representation of the information required to assert a relationship between two entities (Bunescu and Mooney, 2005). In this work, we continue this line of work and present a system based on a CNN architecture over shortest dependency paths combined with domain-specific word embeddings to extract and classify semantic relations in scientific papers.

2 System description

In this section, we describe the various components of our system.

Text pre-processing. For each relation instance in the training data set, we assign a sentence that contains the participant entities. Sentence and token boundaries are detected using the Stanford CoreNLP tool (Manning et al., 2014). Since most of the entities are multi-word units, in order to obtain a precise dependency path between entities, we replace the entities with their codes. The example sentence in (1) below is thus transformed to

Proceedings of the 12th International Workshop on Semantic Evaluation (SemEval-2018), pages 805–810
New Orleans, Louisiana, June 5–6, 2018. ©2018 Association for Computational Linguistics

(2).

(1) Syntax-based statistical machine translation
(MT) aims at applying statistical models to
structured data .

(2) P05-1067.1 aims at applying P05-1067.2 to
P05-1067.3 .

Given an encoded sentence, we find the sdp connecting two target entities for each relation instance using a syntactic parser, see below.

For syntactic parsing we employ the parser described in Bohnet and Nivre (2012), a transition-
based parser which performs joint PoS-tagging
and parsing. We train the parser on the standard
training sections 02-21 of the Wall Street Journal (WSJ) portion of the Penn Treebank (Marcus et al., 1993). The constituency-based treebank is converted to dependencies using two different conversion tools: (i) the pennconverter software[1] (Johansson and Nugues, 2007), which produces the so-called CoNLL-style dependencies
employed in the CoNLL08 shared task on dependency parsing (Surdeanu et al., 2008)[2], and (ii) the
Stanford parser using the option to produce basic
Stanford dependencies (de Marneffe et al., 2014)[3].
The parser achieves a labeled accuracy score of
91.23 when trained on the CoNLL08 representation and 91.31 for the Stanford basic model,
when evaluated against the standard evaluation set
(section 23) of the WSJ. We also experimented
with the pre-trained parsing model for English included in the Stanford CoreNLP toolkit (Manning
et al., 2014), which outputs Universal Dependencies. However, it was clearly outperformed by our
version of the Bohnet and Nivre (2012) parser in
the initial development experiments.

Based on the dependency graphs output by the
parser, we extract the shortest dependency path
connecting two entities. The path records the direction of arc traversal using left and right arrows
(i.e. ← and →) as well as the dependency relation
of the traversed arcs and the predicates involved,
following Xu et al. (2015a). The entity codes in
the final sdp are replaced with the corresponding
word tokens at the end of the pre-processing step.

For the sentence in (1) and the two entities *statistical models* and *structured data* we thus extract the
path in (3) below.

(3) `statistical models ← OBJ ←`
    `applying → DIR → to → PMOD`
    `→ structured data`

Label encoding. The classification sub-tasks
contain five asymmetric relations (USAGE,
RESULT, MODEL-FEATURE, PART_WHOLE,
TOPIC) and one symmetric relation (COM-
PARE). The relation instance along with its
directionality are provided in both the training
and the test data sets. For these sub-tasks we
therefore use the same labels in our system. For
sub-task 2 which combines the extraction and
classification tasks, however, we construct an
extra set of relation types. First, we collect every
pair of entities within a single sentence that are
not included in the annotated relation set. To
minimize the noise, we retain only the entity
pairs which are not further away than 6 tokens.
From these entity pairs we generate negative
instances with the NONE class and extract the
corresponding sdp. Second, to preserve the
directionality in the asymmetric relations, we
add the ¬ symbol to the instances with reverse
directionality (e.g., USAGE(e1,e2,REVERSE)
becomes ¬USAGE(e1,e2)). The final label set for
sub-task 2 thus consists of 12 relations.

Word embeddings. In our system, two different sets of pre-trained word embeddings are used
for initialization. One is the 300-d pre-trained embeddings provided by the NLPL repository[4](Fares
et al., 2017), trained on English Wikipedia data
with word2vec (Mikolov et al., 2013), here dubbed
wiki-w2v. In addition, we train a second set of
domain-specific embeddings on the ACL Anthology corpus. We obtain the XML versions of
22,878 articles from ACL Anthology [5]. After extracting the raw texts, for training of the 300-d
word embeddings (acl-w2v), we exploit the available word2vec (Mikolov et al., 2013) implementation *gensim* (Řehůřek and Sojka, 2010) for training.

Classification Model Our system is based on
a Convolutional Neural Network (CNN) architecture similar to the one used for sentence classification in Kim (2014). Figure 1 provides an overview

---

[1] `http://nlp.cs.lth.se/software/`
`treebank-converter/`

[2] The pennconverter tool is run using the
`rightBranching=false` flag.

[3] The Stanford parser is run using the `-basic` flag to produce the basic version of Stanford dependencies.

[4] `http://vectors.nlpl.eu/repository/`
[5] `https://acl-arc.comp.nus.edu.sg/`

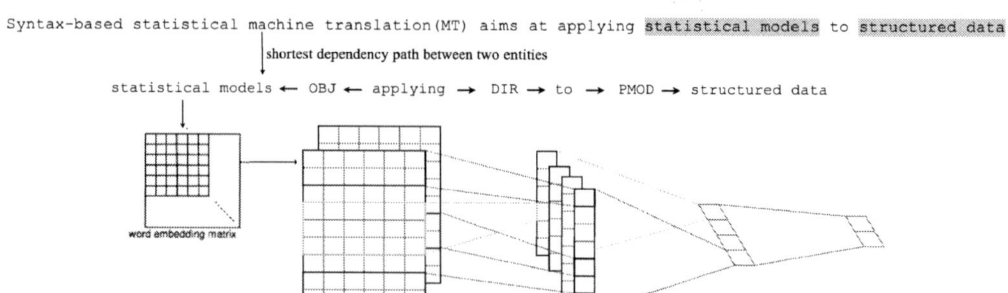

Figure 1: Model architecture with two channels for an example shortest dependency path (CNN model from Kim (2014)).

of the proposed model. It consists of 4 main layers as follows:

Look-up Table and Embedding layer: In the first step, the model takes a dependency path, as in (3) as input and transforms it into a matrix representation by looking up the pre-trained word embeddings.

Convolutional Layer: The next layer performs convolutions with the ReLU activation to the embedding layer using multiple filter sizes (*filter_sizes* $\in [3, 4, 5]$) and extracts feature maps over the tokens.

Max pooling Layer: By applying the *max* operator, the most effective local features are generated from each feature map.

Fully connected Layer: Finally, the higher level syntactic features are fed to a fully connected *softmax* layer which outputs the probability distribution over each relation.

3 Experiments

Dataset For each sub-task, the training data includes abstracts of papers from the ACL Anthology corpus with pre-annotated entities. For sub-task 1.1 and 2, the training datasets are the same. It contains entities that are manually annotated and they represent domain concepts specific to Natural Language Processing (NLP). In sub-task 1.2 the entities are automatically assigned and therefore contain a fair amount of noise (verbs, irrelevant words). The terms include high-level terms (e.g. "algorithm", "paper", "method") and are not always full NPs (Gábor et al., 2018). Since the related entity pairs and the relation types are provided for the full dataset, we extend the dataset for sub-task 1.1 and 2 by extracting the related entities and their corresponding sdp from the sub-task 1.2

	Subtask		Reverse		
Relation	1.1 & 2	1.2	False	True	**Total**
USAGE	483	464	615	332	947
MODEL-FEATURE	326	172	346	152	498
RESULT	72	121	135	58	193
TOPIC	18	240	235	23	258
PART_WHOLE	233	192	273	152	425
COMPARE	95	41	136	-	136
NONE	2315	-	2315	-	2315

Table 1: Number of instances for each relation in the final dataset.

dataset. In order to train a model for sub-task 2, we also augment the dataset by extracting NONE relation instances (see Section 2), extracted from the corresponding dataset. Table 1 shows the number of instances for each relation class. As we can see, the class distribution is clearly unbalanced.

Model settings We keep the value of hyperparameters equal to the ones that are reported in the original work (Kim, 2014), i.e., 128 filters for each window size, a dropout rate of $\rho = 0.5$ and l_2 regularization of 3. To deal with the effects of class imbalance, we weight the cost by the ratio of class instances, thus each observation receives a weight, depending on the class it belongs to. The effect of the minority class observations is thereby increased simply by a higher weight of these instances and is decreased for majority class observations. Furthermore, to guarantee that each fold in n-fold cross validation will have the proportion of same classes during training, evaluation and test, we apply the stratification technique proposed by Sechidis et al. (2011). We use the validation set to detect when overfitting starts during the training of our model; using *early stopping*, training is

			F1	
Sub-task	Model	Representation	Ext.	Class.
1.1	cnn.multi.acl-w2v.rand	Stanford Basic	-	74.16
1.2			-	77.70
2	cnn.acl-w2v	CoNLL08	74.26	60.31

Table 2: F1 (macro-average) scores for selected configurations during training.

then stopped before convergence to avoid overfitting (Prechelt, 1998). The official evaluation metric is the macro-averaged F1-score, therefore we implement early-stopping (*patience*= 20) based on macro-F1 score in the development set.

Model variants We run experiments with several variants of the model as follows: `cnn.rand`: A baseline model, where all elements in the embedding layer are randomly initialized and updated in the training process. `cnn.wiki-w2v`: The embedding layer is initialized with the pre-trained Wikipeida word embeddings and fine-tuned for the target task. `cnn.acl-w2v`: The embedding layer is initialized with the pre-trained ACL Anthology word embeddings and fine-tuned for the target task. `cnn.multi.rand`: There are two embedding layers as a 'channel' in the CNN architecture. Both channels are initialized randomly and only one of them is updated during training while the other remains static. `cnn.multi.wiki-w2v`: Same as before, but the channels are initialized with Wikipedia embedding vectors. `cnn.multi.acl-w2v`: The two channels are initialized with ACL embedding vectors. `cnn.multi.wiki-w2v.rand`: First channel is initialized with Wikipedia embeddings in static mode and the second initialized randomly with a non-static mode. `cnn.multi.acl-w2v.rand`: Same as previous setting, but the first channel makes use of ACL embeddings.

Results During development, we investigate the performance of different configurations; different dependency representations (CoNLL08 and Stanford basic) and model variants (see above); by running 5-fold cross validation (i.e. 3 folds for training, 1 fold for evaluation and 1 fold for test). The experiments show that, the multi-channel mode performs better only in the classification sub-tasks compared to the single channel setting. The results suggest that having a significant amount of

instances per relation assists the model to classify better. The use of the pre-trained embeddings helps the model in class assignment. Particularly, the domain-specific embeddings (i.e. acl-w2v) provide higher performance gains when used in the model. Table 2 presents the F1-score of the best performing model for each sub-task via 5-fold cross validation on the training data. In the evaluation period, we re-run 5-fold cross validation using selected model for each sub-task. However, in this setting we use 4 folds as training and 1 fold as development set, and we apply the output model to the evaluation dataset. We select the 1st and 2nd best performing models on the development datasets as well as the majority vote (mv) of 5 models for the final submission. The final results are shown in Table 3.

	1st		2nd		*mv*	
Sub-task	Ext.	Class.	Ext.	Class.	Ext.	Class.
1.1	-	72.1	-	74.7	-	**76.7**
1.2	-	**83.2**	-	82.9	-	80.1
2	**37.4**	**33.6**	36.5	28.8	35.6	28.3

Table 3: Official evaluation results of the submitted runs on the test set.

4 Conclusion

We present a CNN model over shortest dependency paths between entity pairs for relation extraction and classification. We examine various architectures for the proposed model. The experiments demonstrate the effectiveness of domain-specific word embeddings for all sub-tasks as well as sensitivity to the specific dependency representation employed in the input layer. Our future work includes: 1) to perform error analysis for the different sub-tasks, and 2) to investigate the effects of different dependency representations in relation extraction and classification.

References

Bernd Bohnet and Joakim Nivre. 2012. A transition-based system for joint part-of-speech tagging and labeled non-projective dependency parsing. In *Proceedings of EMNLP*, pages 1455–1465, Jeju Island, Korea. ACL.

Razvan C. Bunescu and Raymond J. Mooney. 2005. A shortest path dependency kernel for relation extraction. In *Proceedings of the Conference on Human Language Technology and Empirical Methods in Natural Language Processing*, HLT '05, pages 724–731, Stroudsburg, PA, USA. Association for Computational Linguistics.

Murhaf Fares, Andrey Kutuzov, Stephan Oepen, and Erik Velldal. 2017. Word vectors, reuse, and replicability: Towards a community repository of large-text resources. In *Proceedings of the 21st Nordic Conference on Computational Linguistics, NoDaLiDa, 22-24 May 2017, Gothenburg, Sweden*, 131, pages 271–276. Linköping University Electronic Press, Linköpings universitet.

Kata Gábor, Davide Buscaldi, Anne-Kathrin Schumann, Behrang QasemiZadeh, Haïfa Zargayouna, and Thierry Charnois. 2018. Semeval-2018 Task 7: Semantic relation extraction and classification in scientific papers. In *Proceedings of International Workshop on Semantic Evaluation (SemEval-2018)*, New Orleans, LA, USA.

Iris Hendrickx, Su Nam Kim, Zornitsa Kozareva, Preslav Nakov, Diarmuid Ó. Séaghdha, Sebastian Padó, Marco Pennacchiotti, Lorenza Romano, and Stan Szpakowicz. 2010. Semeval-2010 task 8: Multi-way classification of semantic relations between pairs of nominals. In *Proceedings of the 5th International Workshop on Semantic Evaluation*, pages 33–38. Association for Computational Linguistics.

Richard Johansson and Pierre Nugues. 2007. Extended constituent-to-dependency conversion for english. In *NODALIDA 2007 Proceedings*, pages 105–112. University of Tartu.

Yoon Kim. 2014. Convolutional neural networks for sentence classification. In *Proceedings of the 2014 Conference on Empirical Methods in Natural Language Processing*, pages 1746–1751. Association for Computational Linguistics.

Ji Young Lee, Franck Dernoncourt, and Peter Szolovits. 2017. MIT at semeval-2017 task 10: Relation extraction with convolutional neural networks. *CoRR*, abs/1704.01523.

Yankai Lin, Shiqi Shen, Zhiyuan Liu, Huanbo Luan, and Maosong Sun. 2016. Neural relation extraction with selective attention over instances. In *Proceedings of the 54th Annual Meeting of the Association for Computational Linguistics (Volume 1: Long Papers)*, pages 2124–2133. Association for Computational Linguistics.

Yang Liu, Furu Wei, Sujian Li, Heng Ji, Ming Zhou, and Houfeng Wang. 2015. A dependency-based neural network for relation classification. *CoRR*, abs/1507.04646.

Christopher D. Manning, Mihai Surdeanu, John Bauer, Jenny Finkel, Steven J. Bethard, and David Mc-Closky. 2014. The Stanford CoreNLP natural language processing toolkit. In *Association for Computational Linguistics (ACL) System Demonstrations*, pages 55–60.

Mitchell Marcus, Beatrice Santorini, and Mary Ann Marcinkiewicz. 1993. Building a large annotated corpora of English. The Penn Treebank. *Journal of Computational Linguistics*, 19:313–330.

Marie-Catherine de Marneffe, Timothy Dozat, Natalia Silveira, Katri Haverinen, Filip Ginter, Joakim Nivre, and Christopher D. Manning. 2014. Universal Stanford dependencies. A cross-linguistic typology. In *International Conference on Language Resources and Evaluation*, pages 4585–4592, Reykjavik, Iceland.

Tomas Mikolov, Kai Chen, Greg Corrado, and Jeffrey Dean. 2013. Efficient estimation of word representations in vector space. *CoRR*, abs/1301.3781.

Thien Huu Nguyen and Ralph Grishman. 2015. Relation extraction: Perspective from convolutional neural networks. In *Proceedings of the 1st Workshop on Vector Space Modeling for Natural Language Processing*, pages 39–48. Association for Computational Linguistics.

Lutz Prechelt. 1998. Early stopping-but when? In *Neural Networks: Tricks of the Trade, This Book is an Outgrowth of a 1996 NIPS Workshop*, pages 55–69, London, UK, UK. Springer-Verlag.

Radim Řehůřek and Petr Sojka. 2010. Software Framework for Topic Modelling with Large Corpora. In *Proceedings of the LREC 2010 Workshop on New Challenges for NLP Frameworks*, pages 45–50, Valletta, Malta. ELRA.

Bryan Rink and Sanda Harabagiu. 2010. Utd: Classifying semantic relations by combining lexical and semantic resources. In *Proceedings of the 5th International Workshop on Semantic Evaluation*, SemEval '10, pages 256–259, Stroudsburg, PA, USA. Association for Computational Linguistics.

Konstantinos Sechidis, Grigorios Tsoumakas, and Ioannis Vlahavas. 2011. On the stratification of multi-label data. In *Proceedings of the 2011 European Conference on Machine Learning and Knowledge Discovery in Databases - Volume Part III*, ECML PKDD'11, pages 145–158, Berlin, Heidelberg. Springer-Verlag.

Richard Socher, Brody Huval, Christopher D. Manning, and Andrew Y. Ng. 2012. Semantic compositionality through recursive matrix-vector spaces. In

Proceedings of the 2012 Joint Conference on Empirical Methods in Natural Language Processing and Computational Natural Language Learning, pages 1201–1211. Association for Computational Linguistics.

Mihai Surdeanu, Richard Johansson, Adam Meyers, Lluís Màrquez, and Joakim Nivre. 2008. The CoNLL 2008 Shared Task on Joint Parsing of Syntactic and Semantic Dependencies. In *Proceedings of the Conference on Natural Language Learning*, pages 159–177, Manchester, UK.

Kun Xu, Yansong Feng, Songfang Huang, and Dongyan Zhao. 2015a. Semantic relation classification via convolutional neural networks with simple negative sampling. *CoRR*, abs/1506.07650.

Yan Xu, Lili Mou, Ge Li, Yunchuan Chen, Hao Peng, and Zhi Jin. 2015b. Classifying relations via long short term memory networks along shortest dependency path. *CoRR*, abs/1508.03720.

Dongxu Zhang and Dong Wang. 2015. Relation classification via recurrent neural network. *CoRR*, abs/1508.01006.

Peng Zhou, Wei Shi, Jun Tian, Zhenyu Qi, Bingchen Li, Hongwei Hao, and Bo Xu. 2016. Attention-based bidirectional long short-term memory networks for relation classification. In *Proceedings of the 54th Annual Meeting of the Association for Computational Linguistics*. Association for Computational Linguistics.

IRCMS at SemEval-2018 Task 7 : Evaluating a basic CNN Method and Traditional Pipeline Method for Relation Classification

Zhongbo Yin, Zhunchen Luo, Wei Luo*, **Bin Mao, Changhai Tian, Yuming Ye, Shuai Wu**

Information Research Center of Military Science, PLA Academy of Military Science, China

zhongboyin@foxmail.com; {zhunchenluo,lwowen79}@gmail.com;
{miscy210,jamestch,yuming_ye}@163.com; wus1986@gmail.com

Abstract

This paper presents our participation for subtask1 (1.1 and 1.2) in SemEval 2018 task 7: Semantic Relation Extraction and Classification in Scientific Papers (Gábor et al., 2018). We experimented on this task with two methods: CNN method and traditional pipeline method. We use the context between two entities (included) as input information for both methods, which extremely reduce the noise effect. For the CNN method, we construct a simple convolution neural network to automatically learn features from raw texts without any manual processing. Moreover, we use the softmax function to classify the entity pair into a specific relation category. For the traditional pipeline method, we use the Hackabout method as a representation which is described in section3.5. The CNN method's result is much better than traditional pipeline method (49.1% vs. 42.3% and 71.1% vs. 54.6%).

1 Introduction

Scientific paper, as a major source of new technology, is a common way for tracing the dynamics of a research domain. With lots of papers published every year, scholars can't read all of them to extract useful aspects for our research domain. Information extraction (IE) is a main NLP aspects for analyzing scientific papers, which includes named entity recognition (NER) and relation extraction (RE). Scientific papers' information extraction is identify concepts or semantic relation between these concepts. This paper focuses on the relation classification between relative concepts in scientific paper.

Relation classification is one of the most important topics for analyzing scientific papers. Most of the traditional relation classification methods

---

*Corresponding author

are influenced by the handcrafted features or extra NLP tools to derive lexical features (Surdeanu et al., 2012; Kozareva, 2012). However, these methods are time consuming and there is a problem of error propagation. Additionally, the traditional semantic textual similarity measuring approaches are using a large number of pairwise similarity features to represent the text. It is difficult for these features to represent the syntactic information.

To address these problems, DNN methods have been proposed and made remarkable achievement (Qin et al., 2016a; Guo et al., 2016). This paper is based on the work of (Qin et al., 2016b) which uses a CNN architecture to control feature learning automatically. As a result, Qin et al. (2016b) minimize the application of external toolkits and resources, which is used for part of speech (POS) or other basic pretreatment. Additionally, Zeng et al. (2014) proposes position feature to locate the entity pair, so as to highlight its promotion for the semantic relation. Owing to this position feature is mapped to several (e.g. 5) dimension followed each word's vector (e.g. 100 dimension), which represents the relative distances of current word to first and second entity. This position feature will disappear because of the excessive training times or error propagation during the training procedure. Thus we use the Qin et al. (2016b)'s entity tag features to strengthen the entity pair information, which use the tag words ($\langle e1s \rangle$, $\langle e1e \rangle$, $\langle e2s \rangle$, $\langle e2e \rangle$) to represent start and end position features of entities. What's more, these tag features are represented as independent vector so as to avoid position feature's disappeared defect in Zeng et al. (2014).

As far as we know, most of the pervious DNN methods used entire sentence's words embedding as the input information for DNN to extracting features for relation classification such as (Xu et al.,

Proceedings of the 12th International Workshop on Semantic Evaluation (SemEval-2018), pages 811–815
New Orleans, Louisiana, June 5–6, 2018. ©2018 Association for Computational Linguistics

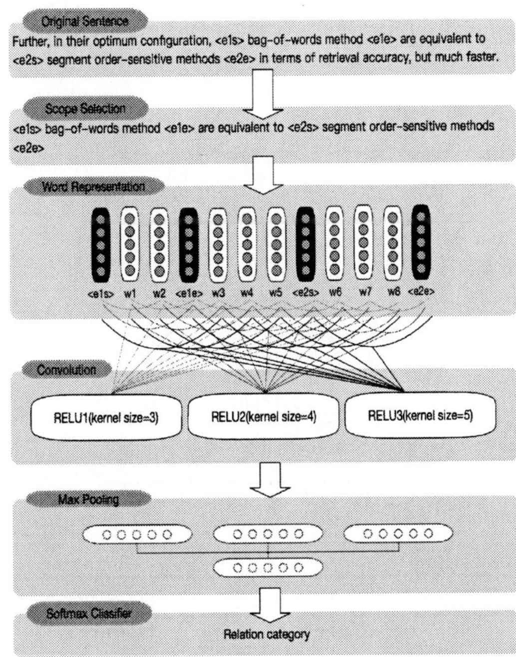

Figure 1: The architecture of CNN

2015; Liu et al., 2015). However, our goal is to achieve relation classification instead of sentence classification. Even though we use the position feature or entity tag feature to highlight the entity effect, it still suffers from that the long sentences have lots of noise words which is useless for relation classification. In pervious working, Qin et al. (2016b) just use the context between two entities, which got a remarkable performance promotion. Thus, we use Qin et al. (2016b)'s context scope as our CNN's input information.

The contributions of this paper can be summarized as follows: Firstly, we construct a simple convolution neural network architecture for relation classification without sophisticated NLP preprocessing. Secondly, we use a more effective context input for convolution neural network, which extremely reduce the useless context's noise effect. Then, we use entity tag feature to replace the entity position feature. Finally, we conduct experiments on subtasks 1.1 and 1.2 datasets, and the experiment results reveal that the proposed approaches is helpful to improve the performance.

2 Methodology

Our relation classification architecture is depicted as Figure 1. First, we select the scope of context

words and convert them to word embeddings. In the word representation step, the entity tag feature ($\langle e1s \rangle$, $\langle e1e \rangle$, $\langle e2s \rangle$, $\langle e2e \rangle$) will also be encoded into embeddings. Then, all the embeddings will be transmitted to three convolution network whose kernel size is 3, 4 and 5. Finally, these three convolution outputs are pooled into the same dimensional vector which will be concatenated as a input of a softmax classifier.

2.1 Context Scope for Convolution Neural Network

Most of the existing DNN relation classification methods use entire sentence's words embedding as context information. As the following sentence, the entity *bag-of-words method* and *segment order-sensitive methods* have a **Compare** relation. However, the sub sentence *Further, in their optimum configuration* and *in terms of retrieval accuracy, but much faster* have little relevance to the target relation category. However, the sub sentence $\langle e1s \rangle$ *bag-of-words method* $\langle e1e \rangle$ *are equivalent to* $\langle e2s \rangle$ *segment order-sensitive methods* $\langle e2e \rangle$ have more relevant information to the target relation. As a result, we extract the context between two entities for relation classification. As for the no-words between entities' condition, only two entities' names have been extracted.

Further, in their optimum configuration, $\langle e1s \rangle$ bag-of-words method $\langle e1e \rangle$ are equivalent to $\langle e2s \rangle$ segment order-sensitive methods $\langle e2e \rangle$ in terms of retrieval accuracy, but much faster.

2.2 Convolution Neural Network Architecture

As the Convolution part in Figure 1, the input embedding is delivered to three convolution neural networks whose kernel size is 3, 4 and 5 respectively. It means that all the 3-grams, 4-grams and 5-grams features will be considered. Since each input sentence has a different length, the convolution output will be pooled into the same dimensional vector space. Finally, we use the multiclass classifier softmax to classify the relation into a specific category.

3 Experiment

3.1 Dataset

We use the SemEval-2018 Task 7.1.1 & 7.1.2 datasets Gábor et al. (2018) in experiment, which is in computational linguistic domain. This task

Embedding dim	Batch size	Dropout	Learning rate	Filter num	Epoch num	Activation
300	30	0.5	1e-4	100	30	Softmax

Table 1: CNN Parameters

Description	Macro-F1	
	sub1.1	sub1.2
CNN input: all words in the sentence (scope1)	47.2	67.8
+ Zeng et al. (2014)'s position feature	47.5	67.9
+Qin et al. (2016b)'s position feature	48.1	69.1
CNN input: entity pair and words between them (scope2)	48.2	68.9
+ Zeng et al. (2014)'s position feature	48.6	69.6
+Qin et al. (2016b)'s position feature	**49.1**	**71.1**
rules filtering before CNN	48.1	69.6
traditional pipeline method	42.3	54.6

Table 2: Experiment Results

addresses 6 semantic relation categories (5 relationships with bi-directions and an undirected *Compare* class) in scientific papers. We use datasets of subtasks 1.1 and 1.2 that contain titles and abstracts of papers in computational linguistic domain where entity mentions are either manually annotated (Subtask 1.1) or automatically annotated (Subtask 1.2). The relations are manually annotated and belong to 6 semantic relation categories (5 relationships with bi-directions and an undirected *Compare* class). There are 1228/1248 training examples and 355/255 testing examples in dataset 1.1/1.2. These relation instances are classified into one of the following relations: USAGE, RESULT, MODEL, PART-WHOLE, TOPIC, COMPARISON. The official evaluation metric is macro-F1 score.

3.2 Parameter Settings

The experiment settings are listed in Table 2.2, we use the Wikipedia general English 300 dimensional embeddings which have 408 million words[1]. After testing, we find the parameters in the Table 2.2 achieve the most effective performance. As there are lots of parameters in CNN, we list some primary data in Table 2.2. For more detailed, we will share the whole project in our Github[2].

Rule	Category
"than" between entity pair	Compare
"used" between entity pair	Usage
"propose" between entity pair	Topic
"contain" between entity pair	Part-Whole
"precision" in entity name	Result
"model" in entity name	Model-Feature

Table 3: Filtering Rules.

3.3 Effect of Position Feature

As described in previous sections, position feature is helpful to promote the classification's performance. Moreover, results in table 2.2 (first 3 lines or 4th to 6th lines) proved that Qin et al. (2016b)'s position features have a better performance than Zeng et al. (2014)'s features.

3.4 Effect of New Context Scope

By comparing 1st and 4th lines' result, we could conclude that the entity names and words between them contain more accurate and cleaner semantic relation information.

By analyzing the predicted relation of the two experiments, we find that many wrong predicted long sentence instances in entire scope (scope1) experiment have been corrected in words between entity pair scope (scope2) as Table 4.

3.5 Result of Rule-based Experiment

In our early research, we explored lots of heuristic rules (as in Table 3.5) for each category by ob-

[1]https://www.cs.york.ac.uk/nlp/extvec/wiki_extvec.gz
[2]https://github.com/zhongboyin/SemEval2018_task7

Sentence	Scope	Prediction	True/False
We present an implementation of the model based on finite-state models, demonstrate the $\langle e1s \rangle$ model's $\langle e1e \rangle$ ability to significantly reduce $\langle e2s \rangle$ character and word error rate $\langle e2e \rangle$, and provide evaluation results involving extraction of translation.	scope1	Compare	False
	scope2	Result	True

Table 4: Input Scope Experiment Result Analyzing.

serving the provided training set manually. However, most of sentences' category couldn't be determined by these rules. Thus, we divided this task into two-steps method. For the first step, we use the heuristic rules to classify some sentences into a specific category. Then, for the second step, we use our CNN method to classify the remaining sentence into a specific category. Before the testing set published, the heuristic rules achieved remarkable improvement in development set. On the contrary, the heuristic rules' filtering step drops the performance in the testing set as the 7th line result in Table 2. After analyzing the result, we noticed that the rules are overfitting, since all of them are explored by training set and promoted by development set. As a result, it causes the decrease of the final evolution performance in the testing set.

3.6 Results of Comparison Experiment

To further prove the better performance of our CNN's relation classification method, we also evaluated the same dataset using a more traditional NLP method which is based on the Multinomial Naive Bayes Classifier[3]. First the data from the training text file is extracted. The labels are extracted and encoded using a LabelEncoder. All the words from e1 to e2 in a sentence are considered for training the Multinomial Naive Bayes classifier. These words are also lemmatized and stemmed for better prediction. However, traditional pipeline method not only excises the error propagation problem, but also can't detect some complicated semantic information such as hyponymy or synonymy. As a result, CNN method has a better performance than traditional method. The 8th line's result in Table 2 shows that our CNN method is better than the general NLP processing method.

4 Conclusion and Future Work

In this paper, we propose a new convolution neural network architecture for relation classification in scientific paper. We showed that the words between entity pairs are the most important for relation classification. Finally, our proposed method gets the macro-f1 value of 49.1 for subtask 1.1 and 71.1 for subtask 1.2.

For the future work, we will explore more features which are helpful for relation classification such as entity type and preposition features. Moreover, we will explore a more flexible sub-sentence scope as the context information for relation classification.

Acknowledgements

Firstly, we want to express gratitudes to the anonymous reviewers for their hard work and kind comments, which will further improve our work in the future. Additionally, this work was supported by the National Natural Science Foundation of China (No. 61602490).

References

Kata Gábor, Davide Buscaldi, Anne-Kathrin Schumann, Behrang QasemiZadeh, Haïfa Zargayouna, and Thierry Charnois. 2018. Semeval-2018 Task 7: Semantic relation extraction and classification in scientific papers. In *Proceedings of International Workshop on Semantic Evaluation (SemEval-2018)*, New Orleans, LA, USA.

Jiang Guo, Wanxiang Che, Haifeng Wang, Ting Liu, and Jun Xu. 2016. A unified architecture for semantic role labeling and relation classification. In *Proceedings of COLING 2016, the 26th International Conference on Computational Linguistics: Technical Papers*, pages 1264–1274.

Zornitsa Kozareva. 2012. Cause-effect relation learning. In *Workshop Proceedings of TextGraphs-7 on Graph-based Methods for Natural Language Processing*, pages 39–43. Association for Computational Linguistics.

---

[3] https://github.com/shouryaj98/Hackabout-2017-Round-1

Yang Liu, Furu Wei, Sujian Li, Heng Ji, Ming Zhou, and Houfeng Wang. 2015. A dependency-based neural network for relation classification. *arXiv preprint arXiv:1507.04646*.

Lianhui Qin, Zhisong Zhang, and Hai Zhao. 2016a. A stacking gated neural architecture for implicit discourse relation classification. In *Proceedings of the 2016 Conference on Empirical Methods in Natural Language Processing*, pages 2263–2270.

Pengda Qin, Weiran Xu, and Jun Guo. 2016b. An empirical convolutional neural network approach for semantic relation classification. *Neurocomputing*, 190:1–9.

Mihai Surdeanu, Julie Tibshirani, Ramesh Nallapati, and Christopher D Manning. 2012. Multi-instance multi-label learning for relation extraction. In *Proceedings of the 2012 joint conference on empirical methods in natural language processing and computational natural language learning*, pages 455–465. Association for Computational Linguistics.

Kun Xu, Yansong Feng, Songfang Huang, and Dongyan Zhao. 2015. Semantic relation classification via convolutional neural networks with simple negative sampling. *arXiv preprint arXiv:1506.07650*.

Daojian Zeng, Kang Liu, Siwei Lai, Guangyou Zhou, and Jun Zhao. 2014. Relation classification via convolutional deep neural network. In *Proceedings of COLING 2014, the 25th International Conference on Computational Linguistics: Technical Papers*, pages 2335–2344.

Bf3R at SemEval-2018 Task 7: Evaluating Two Relation Extraction Tools for Finding Semantic Relations in Biomedical Abstracts

Mariana Neves[1], Daniel Butzke[1], Gilbert Schönfelder[1,2], Barbara Grune[1]
[1] German Federal Institute for Risk Assessment (BfR)
Diedersdorfer Weg 1, 12277, Berlin, Germany
[2] Charité - Universitätsmedizin Berlin, Institute of Clinical Pharmacology and Toxicology,
Charitéplatz 1, 10117 Berlin, Germany
`mariana.lara-neves@bfr.bund.de`

Abstract

Automatic extraction of semantic relations from text can support finding relevant information from scientific publications. We describe our participation in Task 7 of SemEval-2018 for which we experimented with two relations extraction tools - jSRE and TEES - for the extraction and classification of six relation types. The results we obtained with TEES were significantly superior than those with jSRE (33.4% vs. 30.09% and 20.3% vs. 16%). Additionally, we utilized the model trained with TEES for extracting semantic relations from biomedical abstracts, for which we present a preliminary evaluation.

1 Introduction

Finding relevant publications for a certain topic is an important task daily carried out by most researchers in various domains, such as computer science or biomedicine. However, most information retrieval methods usually consider only words and terms (named entities) and do not usually profit from semantic relationships between these entities (Lu, 2011). Many approaches frequently consider words and entities as bags of words but do not take advantage from intrinsic properties of scientific texts, such as subsections (e.g., introduction, methods, results), common concepts (e.g., task, material) and relations between these concepts (e.g., model-feature, part-whole). However, extracting semantic relations from scientific text can potentially support finding relevant information for a certain topic by focusing on particular terms which participate in those relations. In addition, the relation type and the corresponding arguments provide further information regarding the role that a certain entity plays in the text.

We describe the experiments that we carried out during our participation in Subtask

2 of SemEval-2018 Task 7[1] (Gábor et al., 2018). The task consisted on the extraction of six semantic relations from scientific abstracts, namely: "USAGE", "RESULT", "MODEL", "PART_WHOLE", "TOPIC" and "COMPARISON". While the entities were given (and all belong to the general type "ENTITY"), participants of subtask 2 were required to identify the relations and classify these into one of the six types. All relations were asymmetrical (regarding their direction), except for "COMPARISON", and the identification of the direction of the relations was mandatory. The documents came from the ACL Anthology[2], thus belonged to the domain of computational linguistic, and were derived from a more comprehensive corpus which includes more relations than the ones under evaluation in the challenge (Gábor et al., 2016).

Our contribution in this work is two-fold: (a) we experimented with two available relation extraction (RE) tools in the context of the Subtask 2 of SemEval-2018 Task 7; and (b) we evaluated the models trained on the task data for the extraction of the relations mentioned above from biomedical abstracts. In the next section, we present a short overview of related work, followed by a detailed description of our methods in section 3, the results that we obtained both during the development and official evaluation phases (section 4) and the discussion of our results and the preliminary experiments with biomedical publications.

2 Related Work

Despite the importance of the task, few previous work has focused on the identification of semantic elements in publications. Document zoning is probably the task that more attention received in

---

[1] `https://competitions.codalab.org/competitions/17422`
[2] `http://aclweb.org/anthology/`

Proceedings of the 12th International Workshop on Semantic Evaluation (SemEval-2018), pages 816–820
New Orleans, Louisiana, June 5–6, 2018. ©2018 Association for Computational Linguistics

the last years and covered the identification of sections both in abstracts (Hirohata et al., 2008) and full text (Liakata et al., 2012). A more comprehensive study and comparison of different schemes for zoning was carried out in (Guo et al., 2010).

Regarding automatic extraction of scientific relations, many researchers have proposed various scheme based on either (or both) concepts or relations. For instance, (Gupta and Manning, 2011) proposed the annotation of the focus, technique and domain in scientific publications. A more comprehensive schema was proposed by (Tateisi et al., 2016), who developed an ontology of semantic structures in research articles. More recently, the ScienceIE task in SemEval-2017 (Augenstein et al., 2017) proposed the automatic extraction of both entities (Task, Process and Material) and relations from scientific abstracts. Finally, (Gábor et al., 2016) recently proposed a schema of about 20 relations, some of which are considered in the challenge.

The current task focuses on relation extraction and classification, for which many approaches have been proposed in the past years and for which some tools are readily available, including the ones we describe here. Similar to other natural language processing (NLP) tasks, recent work has shifted to the use of neural networks, as reported in (Nguyen and Grishman, 2015) and (Sorokin and Gurevych, 2017).

3 Methods

We evaluated the performance of two existing tools for relation extraction, namely, jSRE (Giuliano et al., 2006) and TEES (Björne et al., 2012). Both tools can be trained for any RE task, provided that a corpus in the appropriate format is available. The methods behind jSRE utilize kernel methods, features derived from shallow linguistic information and both global (sentence level) and local (regarding the relations) contexts (Giuliano et al., 2006). TEES trains support vector machines algorithms using a variety of features derived from the sentence, tokens and dependency chains (Björne et al., 2012).

The workflow of our experiments is shown in Figure 1. After parsing the corpus provided by the organizers, we performed standard NLP preprocessing, followed by preparing input files in the appropriate format required by the two RE tools. This included the generation of negative examples, which are necessary for the jSRE tool. After training the models with each tool and classifying the test documents, we merged predictions (only for jSRE) and printed the predicted relations in the format required by the challenge.

Corpus reader. The main corpus was provided in two files: (a) one XML file which includes the text and entities (all belonging to the general format "ENTITY"); and (b) one file in plain text format with the list of the positive relations and one of the corresponding types listed above. For reading the data, we utilized the BioC format (Comeau et al., 2013). Our model also includes the identification of the direction of the relation (which is necessary for the task).

Pre-processing. We processed all documents using the Stanford CoreNLP library[3] (Manning et al., 2014), including sentence splitting, tokenization, part-of-speech (POS) tagging, chunking, constituency parsing and dependency parsing. While jSRE is based on shallow parsing, TEES relies on both dependency and constituency parsing.

Corpus preparation. We prepared the input format required by each RE tool as specified in their documentation. For jSRE, we generated plain text files for each relation type. These included the original tokens, lemma, POS tagging, indicative of participation in the relation (T or O, otherwise) and the relation category. For multi-token entities, the corresponding tokens should be merged into one, e.g., "storage_media_and_networks" instead of the four individual tokens. The relation category were the following: -1 (unknown), 1 (positive), (2 positive reverse) and 0 (negative). For TEES, we generated a combined XML file which included complete pre-processing analysis (sentences, tokens, full parse tree, constituents and dependency parsing), as well as entities and relations (including their types). The indicative for the direction of the relation is provided as an attribute.

Negative examples generation. We automatically generated negative examples for jSRE. We produced negative examples for each pair of entities following the following guidelines: (a) the entities should belong to the same sentence (according to the sentence splitting analysis); (b) just one

---

[3] https://stanfordnlp.github.io/ CoreNLP/

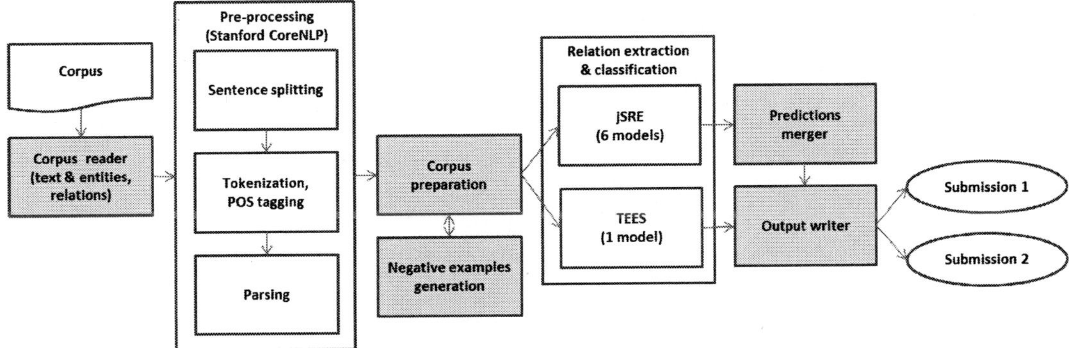

Figure 1: Workflow of the components in our approach. The components that we developed are displayed in blue.

training example (negative or positive) for each pair (always in the order that these appear in the sentence). We generated negatives examples also for sentences which contain no positive example at all. This step was not necessary for TEES, as the tool includes it in its training procedure.

Relation extraction and classification. Provided the training and development files in the format required by each tool, we trained the system according to their documentation. In the case of jSRE, we build six models, one for each relation type. Each model from jSRE calculates scores for one of the categories: 1 (positive), 2 (positive reverse) and 0 (negative). We tried the three kernels included in jSRE (LC - Local Context, GC - Global Context and SL - Shallow Linguistic), and we obtained best results with the later. In the case of TEES, we only trained one model, which performs the both the automatic extraction and classification into a category.

Predictions merger. This component is only necessary for jSRE and it consisted on reading the prediction for each of the categories (0, 1 or 2) from each of the six models and choosing the one that scored higher.

Output writer. We converted the output from both tools to the output (submission) format required by the challenge. We also checked whether a reverse relation was predicted for the "COMPARISON" type and avoided printing it, given that this is a symmetrical relation.

4 Data and Results

The training set released by the organizers consisted of 350 documents which we split in the

following datasets: 250 for training, 50 for tuning (only for TEES) and 50 for development test. The whole dataset contained the following distribution of relation types which appear in 342 (out of 350) documents: 483 for "USAGE", 326 for "MODEL", 234 for "PART_WHOLE", 95 for "COMPARE", 72 for "RESULT" and only 18 for "TOPIC". Our evaluation during the development of the system (over the development test dataset) is shown in Table 1. We did not obtain predictions for the "TOPIC" from none of the RE tools, given the low frequency of this relation in the training set. Indeed, only three instances of this relation type are present in the development set.

Regarding the official test set, the organizers released 152 documents for this aim. All our submissions were based on models trained only on the 250 documents, i.e., we did not train models based on the totality of the 350 documents. Our official results for Subtask 2 is shown in Table 2.

5 Discussion

Relation extraction and classification. We tried two available RE tools for extracting semantic relations from scientific publications. TEES performed significantly superior to jSRE and we chose to use this tool for our further experiments with biomedical publications (cf. below). However, the performance of TEES is rather low in comparison to the best results in the challenge (cf. Table 4). Finally, we did experiment with a simple union of predictions generated by both tools, but adding the predictions from jSRE only harmed the performance of TEES (cf. Table 1).

With respect to both tools, we found TEES easier to use and run, also given our previous experience with it (Thomas et al., 2013). Addition-

Tool	USAGE	RESULT	MODEL	PART_WHOLE	COMPARISON	TOPIC
TEES (t)	29.63%	38.10%	26.23%	26.32%	28.57%	0.00%
jSRE (j)	16.67%	12.50%	24.56%	6.67%	20.00%	0.00%
(t) + (j)	19.58%	28.57%	24.62%	20.00%	28.57%	0.00%

Table 1: Results for each category for the development set (50 documents).

Tool	Extraction		Classification	
	D	T	D	T
TEES (t)	44.69%	33.4%	25.45%	20.3%
jSRE (j)	22.32%	30.9%	15.03%	16.0%
(t) + (j)	37.63%	-	20.88%	-

Table 2: Results for Sub-task 2 of SemEval-2018 Task 7, for the extraction and classification tasks, for both development (D) and official test (T) sets. The highest F1 in the official test set were 50% and 49.3% for the extraction and classification tasks, respectively.

ally, we found the input format from jSRE harder to process. On the other hand, TEES requires full parsing while jSRE is based on shallow parsing. Finally, TEES is readily available for download while we needed to contact the developers of jSRE in order to get a copy of it and needed to do some changes on the code in order to run it. Changes on the code were also necessary in order to obtain scores (probabilities) for the various categories and thus, obtain the predicted relation type. TEES, on the other hand, supports both relation extraction and classification by default.

Semantic relations in biomedical abstracts. We experimented with the model trained on TEES to extract the same semantic relations from biomedical abstracts. Our aim was to evaluate whether the predicted relations is part of either the research goal or the methods in the publication. In particular, we were interested in assessing whether the relations could potentially support the automatic extraction of either an animal experiment or an alternative method to animal experiment (e.g., in vitro or in silico experiments) (Liebsch et al., 2011). This information could later support the automatic identification of abstracts which describe either of the two experiments (animal or alternative to animal).

We processed a set of 161 abstracts retrieved from PubMed[4]. We followed the same workflow showed on Figure 1 only that we performed NER on the abstracts using the Metamap tool (Aronson

and Lang, 2010). We used exactly the same model (from TEES) that we used to predict relations for the official test set of the challenge. We obtained a total of 241 relations from 108 abstracts (out of a total of 161). The number of relations detected for each type were the following: 99 for "MODEL", 87 for "USAGE", 30 for "PART_WHOLE", 22 for "RESULT", two for "COMPARISON" and one for "TOPIC".

We manually checked 28 relations detected from a sample of 13 abstracts. During these attempts, the definitions of the semantic relations as provided by the organizers gave much room for individual interpretations by the evaluating researcher. Being aware of this possible pitfall, however, we judged 9 out of 28 suggested relations as correct.

6 Conclusions

During our participation in the SemEval-2018 Task 7, we experimented with two available relation extraction tools - jSRE and TEES. As future work, we plan to run additional experiments with the current tools, such as using the totality of the training data as well as combination of the systems, as carried out in (Thomas et al., 2013). Additionally, we plan to use additional tools, such as ones based on neural networks (Nguyen and Grishman, 2015).

We applied the generated model from TEES for extraction of semantic relations from biomedical abstracts. Our manual evaluation of some of those relations shows that these have the potential to support the identification of the methods that are part of the research goal. We now plan to run a comprehensive evaluation based on a larger collection of biomedical abstracts as well as a task-specific assessment.

Acknowledgments

We would like to thank Jari Björne for support with TEES, Alberto Lavelli for providing a copy of jSRE and Roland Roller for fruitful discussions on the generation of negative examples.

---

[4]http://www.ncbi.nlm.nih.gov/pubmed/

References

Alan R Aronson and Franois-Michel Lang. 2010. An overview of metamap: historical perspective and recent advances. *Journal of the American Medical Informatics Association* 17(3):229–236.

Isabelle Augenstein, Mrinal Das, Sebastian Riedel, Lakshmi Vikraman, and Andrew McCallum. 2017. Semeval 2017 Task 10: ScienceIE - Extracting Keyphrases and Relations from Scientific Publications. In *Proceedings of the 11th International Workshop on Semantic Evaluation (SemEval-2017)*. Association for Computational Linguistics, Vancouver, Canada, pages 546–555.

Jari Björne, Filip Ginter, and Tapio Salakoski. 2012. University of Turku in the Bionlp'11 Shared Task. *BMC Bioinformatics* 13(11):S4.

Donald C. Comeau, Rezarta Islamaj Doan, Paolo Ciccarese, Kevin Bretonnel Cohen, Martin Krallinger, Florian Leitner, Zhiyong Lu, Yifan Peng, Fabio Rinaldi, Manabu Torii, Alfonso Valencia, Karin Verspoor, Thomas C. Wiegers, Cathy H. Wu, and W. John Wilbur. 2013. Bioc: a minimalist approach to interoperability for biomedical text processing. *Database* 2013:bat064.

Kata Gábor, Davide Buscaldi, Anne-Kathrin Schumann, Behrang QasemiZadeh, Haïfa Zargayouna, and Thierry Charnois. 2018. Semeval-2018 Task 7: Semantic relation extraction and classification in scientific papers. In *Proceedings of International Workshop on Semantic Evaluation (SemEval-2018)*. New Orleans, LA, USA.

Kata Gábor, Haifa Zargayouna, Davide Buscaldi, Isabelle Tellier, and Thierry Charnois. 2016. Semantic annotation of the acl anthology corpus for the automatic analysis of scientific literature. In Nicoletta Calzolari (Conference Chair), Khalid Choukri, Thierry Declerck, Sara Goggi, Marko Grobelnik, Bente Maegaard, Joseph Mariani, Helene Mazo, Asuncion Moreno, Jan Odijk, and Stelios Piperidis, editors, *Proceedings of the Tenth International Conference on Language Resources and Evaluation (LREC 2016)*. European Language Resources Association (ELRA), Paris, France.

Claudio Giuliano, Alberto Lavelli, and Lorenza Romano. 2006. Exploiting shallow linguistic information for relation extraction from biomedical literature. In *Proceedings of the 11th Conference of the European Chapter of the Association for Computational Linguistics (EACL 2006)*. Trento, Italy.

Yufan Guo, Anna Korhonen, Maria Liakata, Ilona Silins Karolinska, Lin Sun, and Ulla Stenius. 2010. Identifying the information structure of scientific abstracts: An investigation of three different schemes. In *Proceedings of the 2010 Workshop on Biomedical Natural Language Processing*. Association for Computational Linguistics, Stroudsburg, PA, USA, BioNLP '10, pages 99–107.

Sonal Gupta and Christopher D. Manning. 2011. Analyzing the dynamics of research by extracting key aspects of scientific papers. In *In Proceedings of IJCNLP*.

Kenji Hirohata, Naoaki Okazaki, Sophia Ananiadou, and Mitsuru Ishizuka. 2008. Identifying sections in scientific abstracts using conditional random fields. In *In Proc. of the IJCNLP 2008*.

Maria Liakata, Shyamasree Saha, Simon Dobnik, Colin Batchelor, and Dietrich Rebholz-Schuhmann. 2012. Automatic recognition of conceptualization zones in scientific articles and two life science applications. *Bioinformatics* 28(7):991–1000.

Manfred Liebsch, Barbara Grune, Andrea Seiler, Daniel Butzke, Michael Oelgeschläger, Ralph Pirow, Sarah Adler, Christian Riebeling, and Andreas Luch. 2011. Alternatives to animal testing: current status and future perspectives. *Archives of Toxicology* 85(8):841–858.

Zhiyong Lu. 2011. Pubmed and beyond: a survey of web tools for searching biomedical literature. *Database* 2011:baq036.

Christopher D. Manning, Mihai Surdeanu, John Bauer, Jenny Finkel, Steven J. Bethard, and David McClosky. 2014. The Stanford CoreNLP natural language processing toolkit. In *Association for Computational Linguistics (ACL) System Demonstrations*. pages 55–60.

Thien Huu Nguyen and Ralph Grishman. 2015. *Relation extraction: Perspective from convolutional neural networks*.

Daniil Sorokin and Iryna Gurevych. 2017. Context-aware representations for knowledge base relation extraction. In *Proceedings of the 2017 Conference on Empirical Methods in Natural Language Processing*. Association for Computational Linguistics, Copenhagen, Denmark, pages 1784–1789.

Yuka Tateisi, Tomoko Ohta, Sampo Pyysalo, Yusuke Miyao, and Akiko Aizawa. 2016. Typed entity and relation annotation on computer science papers. In Nicoletta Calzolari (Conference Chair), Khalid Choukri, Thierry Declerck, Sara Goggi, Marko Grobelnik, Bente Maegaard, Joseph Mariani, Helene Mazo, Asuncion Moreno, Jan Odijk, and Stelios Piperidis, editors, *Proceedings of the Tenth International Conference on Language Resources and Evaluation (LREC 2016)*. European Language Resources Association (ELRA), Paris, France.

Philippe Thomas, Mariana Neves, Tim Rocktäschel, and Ulf Leser. 2013. Wbi-ddi: Drug-drug interaction extraction using majority voting. In *Second Joint Conference on Lexical and Computational Semantics (*SEM), Volume 2: Proceedings of the Seventh International Workshop on Semantic Evaluation (SemEval 2013)*. Association for Computational Linguistics, pages 628–635.

Texterra at SemEval-2018 Task 7: Exploiting Syntactic Information for Relation Extraction and Classification in Scientific Papers

Andrey Sysoev and **Vladimir Mayorov**
Ivannikov Institute for System Programming of the Russian Academy of Sciences
25 Alexander Solzhenitsyn Street
Moscow, Russia
sysoev@ispras.ru, vmayorov@ispras.ru

Abstract

In this work we evaluate applicability of entity pair models and neural network architectures for relation extraction and classification in scientific papers at SemEval-2018. We carry out experiments with representing entity pairs through sentence tokens and through shortest path in dependency tree, comparing approaches based on convolutional and recurrent neural networks. With convolutional network applied to shortest path in dependency tree we managed to be ranked eighth in subtask 1.1 ("clean data"), ninth in 1.2 ("noisy data"). Similar model applied to separate parts of the shortest path was mounted to ninth (extraction track) and seventh (classification track) positions in subtask 2 ranking.

1 Introduction

Information extraction is an important part of natural language processing. During SemEval-2018 an evaluation devoted to extraction and classification of relations in scientific papers was held (Gábor et al., 2018). The task is described as follows: given abstracts of scientific articles with detected entities, the goal is to choose correct relations for provided $\langle source, target \rangle$ entity pairs (subtask 1 - relation classification) and to determine correct relations among all entity pairs (subtask 2 - relation extraction and classification). The target quality metric in classification is macro-average of F1-scores of every class; for extraction scenario the target metric is F1-score.

Our method is based on multinomial classification of entity pairs and their sentences with neural networks. We experiment with representing entity pairs through all sentence tokens and through tokens along the shortest path between entities in dependency tree (Bunescu and Mooney, 2005). We employ convolutional (CNN) (LeCun et al., 1989)

and bidirectional Long Short-Term Memory (biL-STM) (Hochreiter and Schmidhuber, 1997; Tan et al., 2015) neural network based approaches to encode sentences and dependency tree paths.

In this work we mainly focus on relation classification, so most of analysis and experiments are carried out for this task. Slightly modified models which achieve the best results on subtask 1 are adapted for solving relation extraction and classification problem.

The rest of the paper is organized as follows: in section 2 we describe some known approaches for relation extraction and classification. In section 3 our approach is presented in details. Section 4 outlines results of described approach evaluation on official SemEval-2018 task 7 test set. We wrap up with some final thoughts in section 5.

2 Related Work

The relation extraction and classification problem has a long history. Early approaches were based on manually constructed patterns, used to detect entities in the relation under consideration (Blaschke and Valencia, 2001). Further approaches utilized machine learning algorithms (Zelenko et al., 2003) with various hand-crafted features (GuoDong et al., 2005) - syntactic labels, part of speech tags, morphological properties and so on. A brief overview of such methods is presented in (Bach and Badaskar, 2007). Significant part of recent approaches is based on neural networks, trying to eliminate dependency on natural language processing tools: (dos Santos et al., 2015; Lin et al., 2016) use CNNs to extract and classify relations; (Zeng et al., 2014) adapts deep CNNs for the same task. (Socher et al., 2012) introduces recursive neural networks which capture information from phrases and sentences and applies it to relation classification task.

Proceedings of the 12th International Workshop on Semantic Evaluation (SemEval-2018), pages 821–825
New Orleans, Louisiana, June 5–6, 2018. ©2018 Association for Computational Linguistics

In this work we try to inject extra - syntactic - information gained from natural language processing tools into neural networks based approaches.

3 System Description

Our method is based on multinomial classification with neural networks. The decision about the relation being held is made by analysing sentence, which contains examined entities. Each sentence is represented as a sequence of tokens or as a dependency tree.

3.1 Modelling Tokens

Tokens are encoded with fasttext (Bojanowski et al., 2017). Each token embedding also contains binary indicators of its belonging to source or target entity or other part of the sentence.

3.2 Modelling Entity Pair

The basic way to model entity pair is just to take all tokens of the sentence containing these entities and to encode them with described embedding (section 3.1). Binary indicators of token belonging to entities allow us to distinguish several relations in a single sentence.

Another idea is to use path from source to target entity tokens in dependency tree. In our approach the shortest path is considered: it rises up from source entity directly to the lowest common ancestor and then immediately goes down to target entity tokens (Figure 1). Note that dependency trees are built automatically and are sometimes inconsistent with layout of entities, which may be represented differently in the tree.

When using shortest path in dependency tree, each token embedding is extended with additional information - fasttext of the parent token, syntactic label and direction indicator (whether token is on path from source or target entity to lowest common ancestor).

3.3 Neural Network Architectures

General architecture can be described as follows: some method is utilized to encode sequence of input embeddings into a vector, which is then passed through fully-connected layer L and finally fed into softmax to output predicted label. We experiment with two well-known approaches to encode sequences of input embeddings - biLSTM and CNN.

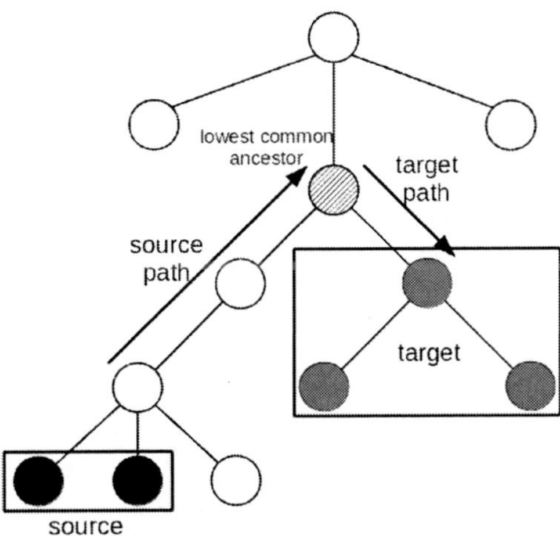

Figure 1: Modelling $\langle source, target \rangle$ entity pair in dependency tree with shortest path.

3.3.1 BiLSTM

BiLSTM-based method is hugely inspired by (Yang et al., 2016). For each sequence item w_k^0 we analyse its nearest context - two items to the left (w_k^{-2}, w_k^{-1}) and to the right (w_k^1, w_k^2). Instead of using w_k^0 directly, its "attentioned" version ω_k is used:

$$\omega_k = \sum_{i=-2}^{2} \alpha_k^i w_k^i, \quad \alpha_k^i = tanh(W w_k^i + b)^T u,$$

where w_k^i are D-dimensional embedding vectors; b and u are A-dimensional attention vectors; W is an $A \times D$-dimensional attention matrix.

Computed ω_k are further fed into biLSTM network (hidden layer size B). Its final cells output and hidden state together with attention vector (computed similarly to what has been described earlier, but on all biLSTM outputs) are concatenated to form final sequence coding vector.

3.3.2 CNN

Another method is based on CNN. All input sequences are trimmed or padded to fit the same size. Then a number of filters F are applied. Each filter application yields a vector of dimensionality $sequence\_length - filter\_height + 1$; a single maximum value is pulled from each such vector. These values are finally concatenated to form final sequence encoding.

3.3.3 Separate CNNs for Shortest Path Parts

The final method is a modification of CNN one, which is specifically designed to be used when modelling entity pairs with shortest paths. Instead of merging different parts of the path into a single sequence, we use four individual sequences by analogy with (Zeng et al., 2015) - source entity tokens, tokens on path from source to lowest common ancestor, tokens on path from lowest common ancestor to target and target entity tokens - and four separate CNNs for them (sCNN). Outputs of all networks are merged into a single final vector.

3.4 Relation Extraction

We adapt classification approach to relation extraction subtask. The first idea is to apply the same model for seven-class classification (six known relations and absence of relation). Secondly we try two-step approach with successive classifiers of the same architecture: extraction classifier detects entity pairs associated with any relation and then another classifier assigns relation labels for extracted pairs of entities.

For negative examples generation the following strategies are examined: *reflection* - reversed correct asymmetric (all except $COMPARE$) relations are supposed to be negative examples; *in-sentence* - some random portion of entity pairs which co-occur in the same sentence is treated as negative examples.

Finally an attempt to filter out excess relations is made (according to guidelines each entity is allowed to participate in not more than a single relation). We employ greedy method that chooses the most confident relation being held using classifier output weights.

4 Evaluation

We took part in both relation classification and relation extraction subtasks. All results reported in this section are gained on official SemEval-2018 task 7 test data developed by organizers and released after the evaluation phase. Official scores for corresponding submissions are specified in Tables 2 and 3 after the slash sign. The difference is explained by minor parameter variations, typically randomness in variables initialization and number of training epochs.

Relation classification (subtask 1) has two datasets - with manually annotated entities (subtask 1.1 - "clean data") and with automatically detected entities (subtask 1.2 - "noisy data"). We decided to construct a single model merging

Relation	1.1	1.2	1.1+1.2
COMPARE	95	41	136
MODEL-FEATURE	326	175	501
PART_WHOLE	234	196	430
RESULT	72	123	195
TOPIC	18	243	261
USAGE	483	470	953

Table 1: Number of relations in subtask datasets.

both datasets into one in order to increase the amount of training examples and to diminish skew in number of sample relations for different types (Table 1).

To encode tokens fasttext (skipgram; minimum length of character n-gram is 1, maximum - 5) is used. We build two separate models with different embedding dimensions - 100 and 300 - using the English Wikipedia.

Evaluation results are presented in Table 2. The target metric is F1. The first part of method name specifies whether all sentence tokens or tokens from shortest path in dependency tree are used. The second part specifies neural network architecture being utilized. We report results for the following neural network parameter values: attention size A is 400; biLSTM hidden layer size B is 1000; CNN filters F - 200 with height 3, 50 with heights 2 and 4, width matches the embedding dimensionality; size of fully-connected layer L is 1000 for biLSTM and 900 for CNN. Specified values are selected during experiments, which are out of this paper scope.

As for subtask 1.1, we conclude that: context attention tends to be beneficial (the only counterexample is sentence biLSTM with fasttext size 300); larger token embeddings are typically better (the only counterexample is sentence biLSTM); syntactic information is helpful for relation classification with neural networks.

For subtask 1.2 the results are more controversial: smaller embeddings sometimes surpass larger ones; utilizing syntactic information seems still beneficial, but the results are not as convincing as in 1.1; in contrast to subtask 1.1 context attention does not tend to improve quality of the approach. From our point of view, such strange behaviour on subtask 1.2 dataset requires further investigation.

Quality evaluations for subtask 2 solutions are presented in Table 3. Target metrics are extrac-

Method	Context attention	Fasttext size	1.1			1.2		
			P	R	F1	P	R	F1
sentence biLSTM	-	100	47.29	57.07	51.72	63.78	60.73	62.21
sentence biLSTM	-	300	52.88	52.21	52.54	73.55	74.92	74.23
sentence biLSTM	+	100	51.14	56.36	53.62	68.17	74.77	71.32
sentence biLSTM	+	300	49.45	55.37	52.24	65.25	67.11	66.17
sentence CNN	-	100	53.53	54.10	53.81	71.62	67.71	69.61
sentence CNN	-	300	57.16	54.96	56.04	73.81	**75.35**	74.57
syntax biLSTM	-	100	55.31	61.71	58.33	71.74	75.13	73.39
syntax biLSTM	-	300	62.35	61.57	61.95	73.76	74.43	74.10
syntax biLSTM	+	100	55.29	**70.97**	62.16	69.52	72.60	71.02
syntax biLSTM	+	300	58.15	70.42	**63.70** / 55.8	63.75	68.62	66.10 / 69.0
syntax CNN	-	100	50.42	61.66	55.48	62.80	65.51	64.13
syntax CNN	-	300	56.27	58.62	57.42 / 64.9	71.79	72.74	72.26 / 74.4
syntax sCNN	-	100	62.83	59.82	61.29	**86.49**	72.87	**79.10**
syntax sCNN	-	300	**64.21**	63.12	63.66 / 62.4	74.22	75.27	74.74 / 73.7

Table 2: Final quality results for subtasks 1.1 and 1.2.

Method	Negative examples	Extraction			Classification		
		P	R	F1	P	R	F1
7-class biLSTM	reflections	8.11	81.74	14.76	4.43	53.58	8.19
7-class CNN	reflections	8.37	82.83	15.21	5.26	56.31	9.63
7-class sCNN	reflections	7.94	80.11	14.44 / 15.6	6.12	66.08	11.21 / 9.6
2-step biLSTM	reflections	7.77	92.64	14.33 / 14.4	3.49	53.35	6.55 / 8.0
2-step CNN	reflections	7.98	88.56	14.63 / 13.9	4.64	52.11	8.53 / 8.2
2-step sCNN	reflections	7.97	79.84	14.50	4.81	52.03	8.80
7-class sCNN	reflections + 20%	8.20	83.65	14.94	8.05	57.71	14.13
7-class sCNN	reflections + 50%	8.55	67.85	15.19	6.22	57.78	11.23
7-class sCNN	reflections + 100%	8.43	**93.19**	15.46	5.37	**66.13**	9.94
2-step sCNN	reflections + 20%	10.36	81.47	18.38	6.47	53.24	11.55
2-step sCNN	reflections + 50%	14.67	65.94	**24.00**	9.53	41.25	15.49
2-step sCNN	reflections + 100%	11.40	81.20	19.99	6.66	52.17	11.81
7-class sCNN + filter	reflections + 20%	14.73	43.05	21.94	13.69	36.54	19.91
2-step sCNN + filter	reflections + 50%	**20.36**	28.07	23.60	**17.25**	26.47	**20.89**

Table 3: Final quality results for subtask 2.

tion and evaluation F1. All experiments are performed with the same input vector size (fasttext dimensionality equals to 300); entity pairs are modelled with shortest path in dependency tree. The second column specifies negative examples generation strategy: reflection with some portion (0-100%) of in-sentence negative examples is always used. For training purposes both subtask 1.1 and 1.2 data is utilized.

When reflection strategy for negative examples generation is used seven-class approach performs better. With utilization of both strategies two-step approach breaks forward. Post-processing improves quality for both approaches, however it is still rather low compared with the results of other participants.

5 Conclusion

In this work we tried to study how utilization of syntactic information influences the quality of relation extraction and classification in scientific papers. According to our experiments the approach based on shortest path in dependency tree yields the best results. The actual network architecture delivering the best result depends on the subtask being solved.

References

Nguyen Bach and Sameer Badaskar. 2007. A review of relation extraction. *Literature review for Language and Statistics II*, 2.

Christian Blaschke and Alfonso Valencia. 2001. Can bibliographic pointers for known biological data be found automatically? protein interactions as a case study. *Comparative and Functional Genomics*, 2(4):196–206.

Piotr Bojanowski, Edouard Grave, Armand Joulin, and Tomas Mikolov. 2017. Enriching word vectors with subword information. *Transactions of the Association for Computational Linguistics*, 5:135–146.

Razvan C Bunescu and Raymond J Mooney. 2005. A shortest path dependency kernel for relation extraction. In *Proceedings of the conference on human language technology and empirical methods in natural language processing*, pages 724–731. Association for Computational Linguistics.

Kata Gábor, Davide Buscaldi, Anne-Kathrin Schumann, Behrang QasemiZadeh, Haïfa Zargayouna, and Thierry Charnois. 2018. Semeval-2018 Task 7: Semantic relation extraction and classification in scientific papers. In *Proceedings of International Workshop on Semantic Evaluation (SemEval-2018)*, New Orleans, LA, USA.

Zhou GuoDong, Su Jian, Zhang Jie, and Zhang Min. 2005. Exploring various knowledge in relation extraction. In *Proceedings of the 43rd annual meeting on association for computational linguistics*, pages 427–434. Association for Computational Linguistics.

Sepp Hochreiter and Jürgen Schmidhuber. 1997. Long short-term memory. *Neural computation*, 9(8):1735–1780.

Yann LeCun, Bernhard Boser, John S Denker, Donnie Henderson, Richard E Howard, Wayne Hubbard, and Lawrence D Jackel. 1989. Backpropagation applied to handwritten zip code recognition. *Neural computation*, 1(4):541–551.

Yankai Lin, Shiqi Shen, Zhiyuan Liu, Huanbo Luan, and Maosong Sun. 2016. Neural relation extraction with selective attention over instances. In *Proceedings of the 54th Annual Meeting of the Association for Computational Linguistics (Volume 1: Long Papers)*, volume 1, pages 2124–2133.

Cicero dos Santos, Bing Xiang, and Bowen Zhou. 2015. Classifying relations by ranking with convolutional neural networks. In *Proceedings of the 53rd Annual Meeting of the Association for Computational Linguistics and the 7th International Joint Conference on Natural Language Processing (Volume 1: Long Papers)*, volume 1, pages 626–634.

Richard Socher, Brody Huval, Christopher D Manning, and Andrew Y Ng. 2012. Semantic compositionality through recursive matrix-vector spaces. In *Proceedings of the 2012 joint conference on empirical methods in natural language processing and computational natural language learning*, pages 1201–1211. Association for Computational Linguistics.

Ming Tan, Cicero dos Santos, Bing Xiang, and Bowen Zhou. 2015. Lstm-based deep learning models for non-factoid answer selection. *arXiv preprint arXiv:1511.04108*.

Zichao Yang, Diyi Yang, Chris Dyer, Xiaodong He, Alex Smola, and Eduard Hovy. 2016. Hierarchical attention networks for document classification. In *Proceedings of the 2016 Conference of the North American Chapter of the Association for Computational Linguistics: Human Language Technologies*, pages 1480–1489.

Dmitry Zelenko, Chinatsu Aone, and Anthony Richardella. 2003. Kernel methods for relation extraction. *Journal of machine learning research*, 3(Feb):1083–1106.

Daojian Zeng, Kang Liu, Yubo Chen, and Jun Zhao. 2015. Distant supervision for relation extraction via piecewise convolutional neural networks. In *Proceedings of the 2015 Conference on Empirical Methods in Natural Language Processing*, pages 1753–1762.

Daojian Zeng, Kang Liu, Siwei Lai, Guangyou Zhou, and Jun Zhao. 2014. Relation classification via convolutional deep neural network. In *Proceedings of COLING 2014, the 25th International Conference on Computational Linguistics: Technical Papers*, pages 2335–2344.

UniMa at SemEval-2018 Task 7: Semantic Relation Extraction and Classification from Scientific Publications

Thorsten Keiper,[1] Zhonghao Lyu,[1] Sara Pooladzadeh,[1] Yuan Xu,[1] Jingyi Zhang,[1] Anne Lauscher,[1,2] and Simone Paolo Ponzetto[1]

[1]University of Mannheim, Germany

[2]Stuttgart Media University, Germany

{tkeiper, zlyu, spooladz, yuaxu, jizhang}@mail.uni-mannheim.de

{anne, simone}@informatik.uni-mannheim.de

Abstract

Large repositories of scientific literature call for the development of robust methods to extract information from scholarly papers. This problem is addressed by the SemEval 2018 Task 7 on extracting and classifying relations found within scientific publications. In this paper, we present a feature-based and a deep learning-based approach to the task and discuss the results of the system runs that we submitted for evaluation.

1 Introduction

Nowadays, the exploding amount of scientific literature makes it ever more problematic for researchers and scholars to get focused access to the state-of-the-art in a certain field of science. Therefore, it is getting increasingly important to develop effective computational approaches for extracting information from large scholarly corpora. SemEval 2018 Task 7 (Gábor et al., 2018) addresses this problem with a shared task on extracting and classifying semantic relations in scientific papers. The task is divided into two subtasks:

1. **Relation Classification.** Given an existing relation between two entities and their context, the task is to predict the label of the relation out of the set of possible classes, namely USAGE, RESULT, MODEL-FEATURE, PART_WHOLE, TOPIC, COMPARISON. The task is decomposed into two different scenarios according to the data used, namely with either manually annotated entities (1.1) or noisy data with automatically extracted entities (1.2).

2. **Relation Extraction and Classification.** This subtask addresses the whole end-to-end pipeline of relation extraction. Given abstracts

of scientific papers annotated with entities, systems are required to extract pairs of entities in a semantic relation, as well as assign a label and directionality to the extracted relation.

We participated in the subtask 1.1, relation classification on clean data, and subtask 2 (relation extraction only). Our approach relies on supervised learning using Support Vector Machines (SVMs), k-Nearest Neighbors (kNNs), and Convolutional Neural Networks (CNNs). We were ranked 16th on task 1.1 with an F1 score 44.0% and 7th on task 2 with an F1 of 28.4%.

2 Related Work

A series of supervised systems for extracting keyphrases and relations in scientific publications was presented in the context of the SemEval task 10 in 2017 (Augenstein et al., 2017). In contrast to the present task formulation, the set of relations consisted only of two, namely hyponymy and synonymy. For this task, the best systems were those based on neural approaches.

Lee et al. (2017) obtained the highest score by employing a convolutional neural network with a specific embedding layer encoding manually crafted features such as the word, the position of the word and the part-of-speech (POS) tag. The second best system was a neural end-to-end model by Ammar et al. (2017). It predicted the relation types based on a context-sensitive representation of the keyphrases which they obtained by using a variety of information, e.g., entity type embeddings and syntactic and sequential path information generated by a bidirectional Long Short-Term Memory (LSTM) layer. As opposed to the former systems, the approach of Barik and Marsi (2017), ranked third, was based on manually crafted features and more traditional classifiers such as decision trees and SVMs.

826

Proceedings of the 12th International Workshop on Semantic Evaluation (SemEval-2018), pages 826–830

New Orleans, Louisiana, June 5–6, 2018. ©2018 Association for Computational Linguistics

Outside SemEval, Zelenko et al. (2003) proposed different kernel methods combined with the SVM and Voted Perceptron learning algorithms for extracting `person-affiliation` and `organization-location` relations. Another kernel-based approach using different sources of syntactic information was presented by Zhao and Grishman (2005).

Our neural approach is inspired by the work of Nguyen and Grishman (2015), who employ a CNN with word embedding and position embedding lookup. Embeddings are concatenated for obtaining positionally and semantically sensitive token representations and then fed into a convolutional layer, followed by a maximum pooling layer and a fully connected feed-forward network with a softmax classifier.

3 Methodology

3.1 Feature-based Approach

Feature Engineering. For our feature-based approach we explored the following pool of features.

1. **Structural Features.** We compute for each entity the distance to the last and next entity and the relative position of the entity in the sentence. Furthermore, assuming that verb phrases are a strong indicator for the specific type of relationship, we also add the distance to the next verb.

2. **Lexical features.** We include the first and last five letters of the given surface form of each entity. Furthermore, for each word we add the last and next three words in the surrounding context window and the word length. Again emphasizing the relative importance of verbs, we specifically encode the last and the next verb. Manual exploration of the training data revealed patterns such as the preposition 'of' and the verb 'use' being a strong indicator of the relations PART_WHOLE and USAGE respectively. Therefore, we add two binary features `hasOf` and `hasUse`. The last lexical feature we employ is the Tf-Idf representation of the sentence.

3. **Syntactic features.** We use the POS tag of each word as shallow syntactic feature.

4. **Semantic features.** In order to add semantic information we employ an embedding representation of the sentence by averaging the GloVe word embeddings pretrained on Wikipedia 2014 and Gigaword 5.[1]

Experimental Setup. We experimented with two classifiers, namely linear SVM and kNN. Both models were wrapped in a 5-fold cross validation in order to obtain performance estimates on the whole training set. Furthermore, we tuned the hyperparameters of the models by nesting the cross validation in a grid search, optimizing the penalty term c of the linear SVM given the search space $c \in \{0,001, 0.01, 0.1, 1, 10\}$ and weighting the penalty term either balanced according to the distribution of the classes or leaving all classes with equal penalty. In the relation classification, we also experimented with one-vs-rest and Crammer-Singer as multi-class classification strategies.

Similarly, for the kNN we optimized the number of neighbors in the search space $k \in \{3, 5, 7, 9\}$ and tried uniform weighting and weighting neighbors based on their inverse distance. All other parameters were left to the default values provided by scikit-learn,[2] which we used as implementation framework.

To find suitable subsets of our heuristically extracted pool of features, a forward feature selection was employed.

3.2 Deep Learning-based Approach

Model Architecture. We employ a CNN (LeCun and Bengio, 1998) for the relation extraction task, which was first introduced to the natural language processing community by Collobert and Weston (2008). Our CNN architecture is inspired by Nguyen and Grishman (2015) and consists of four main layers: (1) embedding layer, (2) convolutional layer, (3) maximum pooling layer, and (4) fully connected output layer.

In a first step, given a word and its relative position in the sentence, we lookup the accompanying vector representations and concatenate them in order to obtain a position-sensitive semantic representation of the token. Next, the model convolutes, i.e., slides, over the embeddings to capture the context of the token in a window of size k, which is followed by subsampling the obtained matrices using maximum pooling, e.g., preserving the N maximal values. This allows the model to recognize the most informative k-grams for the task. In a last step, the representations are fed into a fully

---

[1] `https://nlp.stanford.edu/projects/glove/`
[2] `http://scikit-learn.org/`

word	d1	d2	entity ID
word	0	-9	C08-1105.1
Semantic	0	-8	C08-1105.1
Role	0	-7	C08-1105.1
Labeling	1	-6	none
are	2	-5	none
usually	3	-4	none
limited	4	-3	none
in	5	-2	none
a	6	-1	none
syntax	7	0	C08-1105.3
subtree	8	0	C08-1105.3

Table 1: Example of how we assign relative position to training and test instances.

connected layer followed by a softmax classifier predicting the label.

Experimental Setup. As input to the model we feed pairs of candidate entities together with the textual content between them. As the CNN expects fixed-size vector representations, we pad the texts to the length of the longest sequence using a special token to which we assign a random embedding vector. We compute the relative position for each word w_i as distance vector $d_i = [d_{i1}, d_{i2}]$. Table 1 shows a example of how we assign relative distances to each word in our instances. The word embedding matrix is initialized with 300-dimensional domain-specific word embeddings from Lauscher et al. (2017), which showed during prototyping superior performance when compared with standard domain-independent ones. Finally, we obtain a position-sensitive representation of the word w_i by concatenating its embedding e_i as well as the position embedding into a single vector $v_i = [e_i, d_{i1}, d_{i2}]$.

Since the data for the relation extraction task is highly skewed towards the number of negative instances (i.e., only 1,228 out of 8,768 are positive), we decided to experiment with data balancing techniques. More specifically, we tried upsampling the positive instances applying an upsampling rate $r_u \in [1, 5]$ and similarly, downsampling the negative instances with a rate $r_d \in [0.1, 1]$.

Optimizing the hyperparameters of our model, we experimented with the numbers of CNN filters in range $f \in [50, 500]$ and with a filter size $s \in [3, 15]$. For the regularization of our model we apply dropout before the fully connected layer and experimented with a dropout keep probabil-

Class	Count	Ratio
Usage	483	39.33%
Model-Feature	326	26.55%
Part_whole	234	19.06%
Topic	95	07.74%
Result	72	05.86%
Compare	18	01.47%
Total	**1,228**	**100%**

Table 2: Class distribution in the training data.

ity of $d \in [0, 1]$. For all other hyperparameters we use the values from Nguyen and Grishman (2015). Last, in order to make our models comparable among each other, we nested the CNN in a 5-fold cross validation.

4 Evaluation

Here, we briefly give an overview of the data provided by the organizers of the shared task as well as our submitted runs. We also present and discuss the final results achieved.

Data. The training data provided by the task organizers for subtask 1.1 and subtask 2 is composed of 350 abstracts of scientific publications with manually annotated entities and relations. In total, the number of relation instances amounts to 1,228 samples. Table 2 shows the distribution of the labels for the relation classification.

For the relation extraction task, entity pairs for all semantic relations appear in the very same sentence. Therefore, we generate relation candidates by pairing all entity mentions found within the same sentence boundary. This way we end up with 8,386 candidate entity pairs among which 1,228 are positive instances.

The test data for task 1.1 and 2 was provided in the same format as training data, containing 150 abstracts and 355 relation instances (for subtask 1.1 only).

Submitted runs. We selected two models for the relation classification and three models for the relation extraction task for the final submission according to their scores on the development data using the official scoring script. The model configurations are summarized in Table 3 and Table 4, respectively.

Final Results. The official scores for the submitted models are listed in Tables 5 and 6.

Model	Hyperparameter	Choice	Features
SVM	c	1	tfidf
	multi class	one-vs-rest	isReverse
	class weight	balanced	nextEntityDist(x)
			position(y)
			POStag(x)
kNN	k	5	tfidf
	weights	distance	isReverse
			hasOf

Table 3: Submitted models for task 1.1 (relation classification). In the features listed, x represents the first entity while y represents the second entity of a candidate pair.

Model	Hyperparameter	Choice	Features
SVM	c	0.1	position(x,y)
	class weight	balanced	lastEntityDist(y)
			nextEntityDist(x)
			tokenLength(y)
			POStag(x,y)
			firstLetter(y)
kNN	k	3	relativePosition(x,y)
	weights	distance	lastEntityDist(y)
			position(y)
			avgEmbedding
			hasUse
			POStag(x,y)
CNN	dropout	0.5	word embedding
	upsampling rate	3	relative position
	number of filters	200	
	filter size	3-8	

Table 4: Submitted models for task 2 (relation extraction). In the features listed, x represents the first entity while y represents the second entity of a candidate pair.

In the relation classification task, SVM achieves better performance than kNN by a large margin, while in the relation extraction task, it is the deep learning models that perform best. Within the scope of the traditional models, SVM consistently outperforms kNN for both the classification (on every relation type, cf. Table 5), as well as the extraction task (Table 6). Furthermore, for task 1.1, SVM performed better than kNN, in every relation type. The reason could be that the vector-like features we used, such as Tf-Idf and the binary POS-tags, suit better for SVM, while kNN was not able to handle the high-dimensional dataset.

For task 2 the linear SVM model results in a relatively high recall but considerably low precision. This result could be related to the following reasons. First, since the training data is highly skewed towards negative examples as described in subsection 4, more false positive cases are predicted. Second, the data is likely to be nonlin-

Class	SVM	kNN
Usage	73.68%	63.04%
Model-Feature	51.70%	43.97%
Part_Whole	45.53%	34.90%
Topic	22.22%	00.00%
Result	37.50%	37.50%
Compare	26.32%	12.12%
Macro F1	44.00%	32.49%

Table 5: Results (F1) on relation classification (task 1.1).

	Precision	Recall	F1
SVM	15.67%	90.19%	26.70%
kNN	9.93%	11.44%	10.63%
CNN	18.84%	57.49%	28.38%

Table 6: Results on relation extraction (task 2).

early distributed. As a result, the linear SVM is not able to perform better even when increasing feature dimensionality. In addition to a better feature engineering, we explored the use of an Radial Basis Function (RBF) kernel and Gradient Boosting Tree to increase the precision without hurting the recall. Another interesting point is that the improvement of precision contributed more to the overall F1-score in this official evaluation method. This can be inferred from the results listed in Table 6, where the CNN has higher F1-score, with a higher precision but much lower recall compared to the SVM.

5 Conclusion

In this paper we have presented our approach to the SemEval 2018 Task 7 on extracting and classifying semantic relations from scientific publications. We experimented with feature-based versus neural models. For the classification task, SVM performed better than kNN, although both show problems in predicting minority classes with few examples. For the extraction task, the deep learning method outperformed SVM by a narrow margin. The overall comparable results across methods seem to indicate that, in the future, more work should turn to devising better features or architectures that are able to capture the nuances of semantic relations in the domain of scientific texts.

Acknowledgements. This work was partly funded by the German Research Foundation (DFG), project number EC 477/5-1 (LOC-DB).

References

Waleed Ammar, Matthew Peters, Chandra Bhaga-vatula, and Russell Power. 2017. The AI2 system at SemEval-2017 task 10 (ScienceIE): semi-supervised end-to-end entity and relation extraction. In *Proceedings of the 11th International Workshop on Semantic Evaluation (SemEval-2017)*. Association for Computational Linguistics, Vancouver, Canada, pages 592–596. http://www.aclweb.org/anthology/S17-2097.

Isabelle Augenstein, Mrinal Das, Sebastian Riedel, Lakshmi Vikraman, and Andrew McCallum. 2017. Semeval 2017 task 10: ScienceIE - extracting keyphrases and relations from scientific publications. In *Proceedings of the 11th International Workshop on Semantic Evaluation (SemEval-2017)*. Association for Computational Linguistics, Vancouver, Canada, pages 546–555. http://www.aclweb.org/anthology/S17-2091.

Biswanath Barik and Erwin Marsi. 2017. NTNU-2 at SemEval-2017 task 10: Identifying synonym and hyponym relations among keyphrases in scientific documents. In *Proceedings of the 11th International Workshop on Semantic Evaluation (SemEval-2017)*. Association for Computational Linguistics, Vancouver, Canada, pages 965–968. http://www.aclweb.org/anthology/S17-2168.

Ronan Collobert and Jason Weston. 2008. A unified architecture for natural language processing: deep neural networks with multitask learning. In *Machine Learning, Proceedings of the Twenty-Fifth International Conference (ICML 2008), Helsinki, Finland, June 5-9, 2008.* pages 160–167. https://doi.org/10.1145/1390156.1390177.

Kata Gábor, Davide Buscaldi, Anne-Kathrin Schumann, Behrang QasemiZadeh, Hafa Zargayouna, and Thierry Charnois. 2018. Semeval-2018 task 7: Semantic relation extraction and classification in scientific papers. In *Proceedings of the 12th International Workshop on Semantic Evaluation (SemEval-2018)*. Association for Computational Linguistics, New Orleans, LA, USA, page tba.

Anne Lauscher, Goran Glavaš, Simone Paolo Ponzetto, and Kai Eckert. 2017. Investigating convolutional networks and domain-specific embeddings for semantic classification of citations. In *Proceedings of the 6th International Workshop on Mining Scientific Publications*. ACM, New York, NY, USA, pages 24–28. https://doi.org/10.1145/3127526.3127531.

Yann LeCun and Yoshua Bengio. 1998. The handbook of brain theory and neural networks. MIT Press, Cambridge, MA, USA, chapter Convolutional Networks for Images, Speech, and Time Series, pages 255–258.

Ji Young Lee, Franck Dernoncourt, and Peter Szolovits. 2017. MIT at SemEval-2017 task 10: Relation extraction with convolutional neural networks. In *Proceedings of the 11th International Workshop on Semantic Evaluation (SemEval-2017)*. Association for Computational Linguistics, Vancouver, Canada, pages 978–984. http://www.aclweb.org/anthology/S17-2171.

Thien Huu Nguyen and Ralph Grishman. 2015. Relation extraction: Perspective from convolutional neural networks. In *Proceedings of the 1st Workshop on Vector Space Modeling for Natural Language Processing*. Association for Computational Linguistics, Denver, Colorado, pages 39–48. http://www.aclweb.org/anthology/W15-1506.

Dmitry Zelenko, Chinatsu Aone, and Anthony Richardella. 2003. Kernel methods for relation extraction. *Journal of Machine Learning Research* 3:1083–1106. http://www.jmlr.org/papers/v3/zelenko03a.html.

Shubin Zhao and Ralph Grishman. 2005. Extracting relations with integrated information using kernel methods. In *Proceedings of the 43rd Annual Meeting of the Association for Computational Linguistics (ACL'05)*. Association for Computational Linguistics, Ann Arbor, Michigan, pages 419–426. https://doi.org/10.3115/1219840.1219892.

GU IRLAB at SemEval-2018 Task 7:
Tree-LSTMs for Scientific Relation Classification

Sean MacAvaney, Luca Soldaini, Arman Cohan, and Nazli Goharian
Information Retrieval Lab
Department of Computer Science
Georgetown University
`{firstname}@ir.cs.georgetown.edu`

Abstract

SemEval 2018 Task 7 focuses on relation extraction and classification in scientific literature. In this work, we present our tree-based LSTM network for this shared task. Our approach placed 9th (of 28) for subtask 1.1 (relation classification), and 5th (of 20) for subtask 1.2 (relation classification with noisy entities). We also provide an ablation study of features included as input to the network.

1 Introduction

Information Extraction (IE) has applications in a variety of domains, including in scientific literature. Extracted entities and relations from scientific articles could be used for a variety of tasks, including abstractive summarization, identification of articles that make similar or contrastive claims, and filtering based on article topics. While ontological resources can be leveraged for entity extraction (Gábor et al., 2016), relation extraction and classification still remains a challenging task. Relations are particularly valuable because (unlike simple entity occurrences) relations between entities capture lexical semantics. SemEval 2018 Task 7 (Semantic Relation Extraction and Classification in Scientific Papers) encourages research in relation extraction in scientific literature by providing common training and evaluation datasets (Gábor et al., 2018). In this work, we describe our approach using a tree-structured recursive neural network, and provide an analysis of its performance.

There has been considerable previous work with scientific literature due to its availability and interest to the research community. A previous shared task (SemEval 2017 Task 10) investigated the extraction of both keyphrases (entities) and relations in scientific literature (Augenstein et al., 2017). However, the relation set for this shared task was limited to just synonym and hypernym relationships. The top three approaches used for relation-only extraction included convolutional neural networks (Lee et al., 2017a), bi-directional recurrent neural networks with Long Short-Term Memory (LSTM, Hochreiter and Schmidhuber, 1997) cells (Ammar et al., 2017), and conditional random fields (Lee et al., 2017b).

There are several challenges related to scientific relation extraction. One is the extraction of the entities themselves. Luan et al. (2017) produce the best published results on the 2017 ScienceIE shared task for entity extraction using a semi-supervised approach with a bidirectional LSTM and a CRF tagger. Zheng et al. (2014) provide an unsupervised technique for entity linking scientific entities in the biomedical domain to an ontology.

Contribution. Our approach employs a tree-based LSTM network using a variety of syntactic features to perform relation label classification. We rank 9th (of 28) when manual entities are used for training, and 5th (of 20) when noisy entities are used for training. Furthermore, we provide an ablation analysis of the features used by our model. Code for our model and experiments is available.[1]

2 Methodology

Syntactic information between entities plays an important role in relation extraction and classification (Mintz et al., 2009; MacAvaney et al., 2017). Similarly, sequential neural models, such as LSTM, have shown promising results on scientific literature (Ammar et al., 2017). Therefore, in our approach, we leverage both syntactic structures and neural sequential models by employing a tree-based long-short term memory cell (tree-LSTM). Tree-LSTMs, originally introduced by Tai et al. (2015), have been successfully used to

---

[1] `https://github.com/Georgetown-IR-Lab/semeval2018-task7`

Proceedings of the 12th International Workshop on Semantic Evaluation (SemEval-2018), pages 831–835
New Orleans, Louisiana, June 5–6, 2018. ©2018 Association for Computational Linguistics

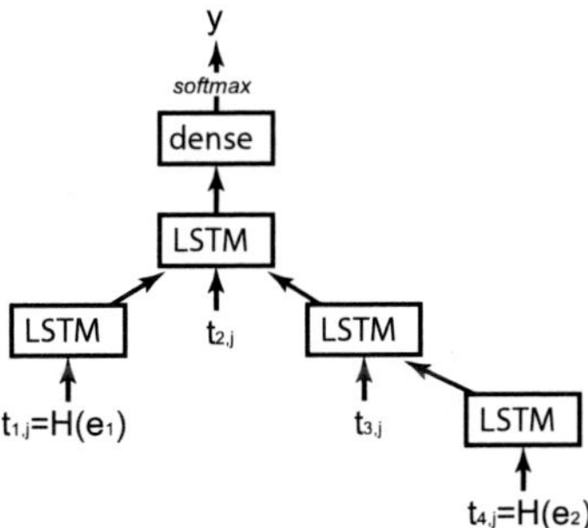

Figure 1: Our tree LSTM network.

Relation (abbr.)	Example
USAGE (U)	<u>Oral communication</u> may offer additional <u>indices</u>...
MODEL-FEATURE (M-F)	We look at the <u>intelligibility</u> of <u>MT output</u>...
PART_WHOLE (P-W)	As the <u>operational semantics</u> of <u>natural language applications</u> improve...
COMPARE (C)	<u>Bag-of-words methods</u> are shown to be equivalent to <u>segment order-sensitive methods</u> in terms of...
RESULT (R)	We find that <u>interpolation methods</u> improve the <u>performance</u>...
TOPIC (T)	A formal <u>analysis</u> for a large class of <u>words called alternative markers</u>...

Table 1: Example relations for each type. Entities are underlined, and all relations are from the first entity to the second entity (non-reversed).

capture relation information in other domains (Xu et al., 2015; Miwa and Bansal, 2016). On a high level, tree-LSTMs operate very similarly to sequential models; however, rather than processing tokens sequentially, they follow syntactic dependencies; once the model reaches the root of the tree, the output is used to compute a prediction, usually through a dense layer. We use the child-sum variant of tree-LSTM (Tai et al., 2015).

Formally, let $S_j = \{t_{1,j}, \ldots, t_{n,j}\}$ be a sentence of length n, $e_1 = \{t_i, \ldots, t_k\}$ and $e_2 = \{t_p, \ldots, t_q\}$ two entities whose relationship we intend to classify; let H(e_1), H(e_2) be the root of the syntactic subtree spanning over entities e_1 and e_2. Finally, let T(e_1, e_2) be the syntactic sub-tree spanning from H(e_1) to H(e_2). For the first example in Table 1, $e_1 = \{$'Oral', 'communication'$\}$, $e_2 = \{$'indices'$\}$, H(e_1) $= \{$'communication'$\}$, T(e_1, e_2) $= \{$'communication', 'offer', 'indices'$\}$. The proposed model uses word embeddings of terms in T(e_1, e_2) as inputs; the output of the tree-LSTM cell on the root of the syntactic tree is used to predict one of the six relation types (y) using a softmax layer. A diagram of our tree LSTM network is shown in Figure 1.

In order to overcome the limitation imposed by the small amount of training data available for this task, we modify the general architecture proposed in (Miwa and Bansal, 2016) in two crucial ways. First, rather than using the representation of entities as input, we only consider the syntactic head of each entity. This approach improves the generalizability of the model, as it prevents overfitting on very specific entities in the corpus. For example, by reducing *'Bag-of-words methods'* to *'methods'* and *'segment order-sensitive models'* to *'models'*, the model is able to recognize the COM-

PARE relation between these two entities (see Table 1). Second, we experimented with augmenting each term representation with the following features:

- Dependency labels (DEP): we append to each term embedding the label representing the dependency between the term and its parent.

- PoS tags (POS): the part-of-speech tag for each term is append to its embedding.

- Entity length (ENTLEN): we concatenate the number of tokens in e_1 and e_2 to embeddings representation of heads H(e_1) to H(e_2). For terms that are not entity heads, the entity length feature is replaced by '0'.

- Height: the height of each term in the syntactic subtree connecting two entities.

3 Experimental Setup

SemEval 2018 Task 7 focuses on relation extraction, assuming a gold set of entities. This allows participants to focus on specific issues related to relation extraction with a rich set of semantic relations. These include relations for USAGE, MODEL-FEATURE, PART_WHOLE, COMPARE, RESULT, and TOPIC. Examples of each type of relation are given in Table 1.

The shared task evaluates three separate subtasks (1.1, 1.2, and 2). We tuned and submitted

Dataset	U	M-F	P-W	C	R	T
Subtask 1.1						
Train	409	289	215	86	57	15
Valid.	74	37	19	9	15	3
Test	175	66	70	21	20	3
Subtask 1.2						
Train	363	124	162	29	94	207
Valid.	107	51	34	12	29	36
Test	123	75	56	3	29	69

Table 2: Frequency of relation labels in train, validation, and test sets. See Table 1 for relation label abbreviations. Subtask 1.1 uses manual entity labels, and subtask 1.2 uses automatic entity labels (which may be noisy).

our system for subtasks 1.1 and 1.2. In both of these subtasks, participants are given scientific abstracts with entities and candidate relation pairs, and are asked to determine the relation label of each pair. For subtask 1.1, both the entities and relations are manually annotated. For subtask 1.2, the entities are automatically generated using the procedure described in Gábor et al. (2016). This procedure introduces noise, but represents a more realistic evaluation environment than subtask 1.1. In both cases, relations and gold labels are produced by human annotators. All abstracts are from the ACL Anthology Reference Corpus (Bird et al., 2008). We randomly select 50 texts from the training datasets for validation of our system. We provide a summary of the datasets for training, validation, and testing in Table 2. Notice how the proportions of each relation label vary considerably among the datasets.

We experiment with two sets of word embeddings: Wiki News and arXiv. The Wiki News embeddings benefit from the large amount of general language, and the arXiv embeddings capture specialized domain language. The Wiki News embeddings are pretrained using fastText with a dimension of 300 (Mikolov et al., 2018). The arXiv embeddings are trained on a corpus of text from the cs section of arXiv.org[2] using a window of 8 (to capture adequate term context) and a dimension of 100 (Cohan et al., 2018). A third variation of the embeddings simply concatenates the Wiki News and arXiv embeddings, yielding a dimension of 400; for words that appear in only one of

System	F1	Rank
Subtask 1.1 (28 teams)		
Our submission	60.9	9
Median team	45.5	
Mean team	37.1	
Subtask 1.2 (20 teams)		
Our submission	78.9	5
Median team	70.3	
Mean team	54.0	

Table 3: Performance result comparison to other task participants for subtasks 1.1 and 1.2.

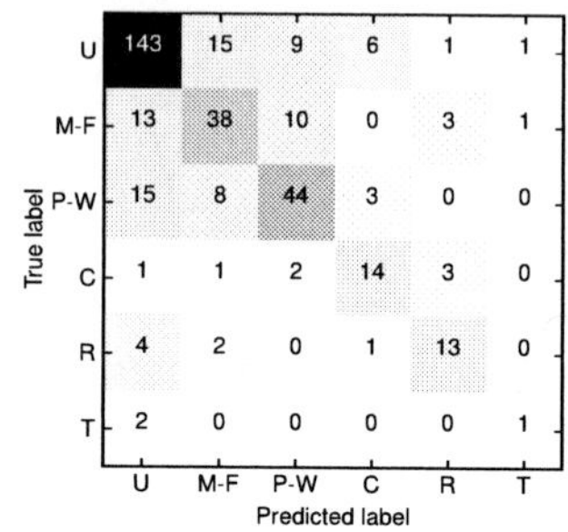

Figure 2: Confusion matrix for subtask 1.1.

the two embedding sources, the available embeddings are concatenated with a vector of appropriate size sampled from $\mathcal{N}(0, 10^{-8})$.

For our official SemEval submission, we train our model using the concatenated embeddings and one-hot encoded dependency label features. We use a hidden layer of 200 nodes, a 0.2 dropout rate, and a training batch size of 16. Syntactic trees were extracted using SpaCy[3], and the neural model was implemented using MxNet[4].

The official evaluation metric is the macro-averaged F1 score of all relation labels. For additional analysis, we use the macro precision and recall, and the F1 score for each relation label.

4 Results and Discussion

In Table 3, we provide our official SemEval results in the context of other task participants. In both subtasks, we ranked above both the median and mean team scores, treating the top-ranking approach for each team as the team's score. For Subtask 1.1, we ranked 9 out of 28, and for Subtask 1.2, we ranked 5 out of 20. This indicates

---

[2] https://github.com/acohan/long-summarization

[3] https://spacy.io/

[4] https://mxnet.incubator.apache.org/

Features	Overall			F1 by label					
	P	R	F1	U	M-F	P-W	C	R	T
Subtask 1.1									
(no features)	56.9	64.1	59.5	**81.4**	51.5	59.9	57.8	61.9	44.4
DEP	53.5	54.1	53.6	79.1	55.5	58.2	63.8	**64.9**	0.0
DEP + POS	**60.1**	59.1	59.5	79.9	57.1	58.5	**68.3**	60.0	33.3
DEP + POS + EntLen	59.4	**64.1**	**60.9**	80.0	**59.0**	56.9	58.3	61.1	**50.0**
DEP + POS + EntLen + Height	52.1	53.3	52.4	79.2	57.4	**62.2**	56.0	59.5	0.0
Subtask 1.2									
(no features)	74.2	78.9	75.4	80.0	65.6	72.6	57.1	80.0	**97.1**
DEP	76.4	78.5	76.4	79.2	67.2	73.0	**66.7**	79.4	93.1
DEP + POS	75.5	**80.3**	77.3	**82.0**	**73.9**	**73.6**	57.1	80.0	**97.1**
DEP + POS + EntLen	**78.2**	79.7	**78.0**	81.9	69.3	70.5	**66.7**	**82.5**	**97.1**
DEP + POS + EntLen + Height	73.0	78.7	74.8	79.5	70.7	70.3	57.1	74.3	**97.1**

Table 4: Feature ablation results for subtasks 1.1 and 1.2. DEP are dependency labels, POS are part of speech labels, EntLen is is the length of the input entities, and Height is the height of the entities in the dependency tree. In both subtasks 1.1 and 1.2, the combination of dependency labels, parts of speech, and entity lengths yield the best performance in terms of overall F1 score.

Embeddings	P	R	F1
Subtask 1.1			
Wiki News	59.2	57.3	57.6
arXiv	58.5	55.1	56.4
Wiki News + arXiv	**59.4**	**64.1**	**60.9**
Subtask 1.2			
Wiki News	73.1	76.2	72.7
arXiv	65.4	67.4	65.9
Wiki News + arXiv	**78.2**	**79.7**	**78.0**

Table 5: Performance comparison for subtasks 1.1 and 1.2 when using Wiki News and arXiv embeddings. The concatenated embeddings outperform the individual methods.

that our approach is generally more tolerant to the noisy entities given in Subtask 1.2 than most other approaches. Figure 2 is a confusion matrix for the official submission for subtask 1.1. The three most frequent labels in the training data (USAGE, MODEL-FEATURE, and PART_WHOLE) are also the most frequently confused relation labels. This behavior can be partially attributed to the class imbalance.

In Table 4, we examine the effects of various feature combinations on the model. Specifically, we check the macro averaged precision, recall, and F1 scores for both subtask 1.1 and 1.2 with various sets of features on the test set. Of the combinations we investigated, including the dependency labels, part of speech tags, and the token length of entities

yielded the best results in terms of overall F1 score for both subtasks. The results by individual relation label are more mixed, with the overall best combination simply yielding better performance on average, not on each label individually. Interestingly, the entity height feature reduces performance, perhaps indicating that it is easy to overfit the model using this feature.

Table 5 examines the effect of the choice of word embeddings on performance. In both subtasks, concatenating the Wiki News and arXiv embeddings yields better performance than using a single type of embedding. This suggests that the two types of embeddings are useful in different cases; perhaps Wiki News better captures the general language linking the entities, whereas the arXiv embeddings capture the specialized language of the entities themselves.

5 Conclusion

In this work, we investigated the use of a tree LSTM-based approach for relation classification in scientific literature. Our results at SemEval 2018 were encouraging, placing 9th (of 28) at subtask 1.1 (relation classification with manually-annotated entities), and 5th (of 20) at subtask 1.2 (relation classification using automatically-generated entities). Furthermore, we conducted an analysis of our system by varying the system parameters and features.

References

Waleed Ammar, Matthew E. Peters, Chandra Bhaga-vatula, and Russell Power. 2017. The AI2 system at SemEval-2017 Task 10 (ScienceIE): semi-supervised end-to-end entity and relation extraction. In *SemEval-2017*.

Isabelle Augenstein, Mrinal Das, Sebastian Riedel, Lakshmi Vikraman, and Andrew D McCallum. 2017. SemEval 2017 Task 10: ScienceIE - extracting keyphrases and relations from scientific publications. In *SemEval-2017*.

Steven Bird, Robert Dale, Bonnie J. Dorr, Bryan R. Gibson, Mark Thomas Joseph, Min-Yen Kan, Dongwon Lee, Brett Powley, Dragomir R. Radev, and Yee Fan Tan. 2008. The ACL anthology reference corpus: A reference dataset for bibliographic research in computational linguistics. In *LREC*.

Arman Cohan, Franck Dernoncourt, Doo Soon Kim, Kim Seokhwan Bui, Trung, Walter Chang, and Nazli Goharian. 2018. A discourse-aware attention model for abstractive summarization of long documents. In *NAACL-HLT*.

Kata Gábor, Davide Buscaldi, Anne-Kathrin Schumann, Behrang QasemiZadeh, Haïfa Zargayouna, and Thierry Charnois. 2018. SemEval-2018 Task 7: Semantic relation extraction and classification in scientific papers. In *SemEval-2018*.

Kata Gábor, Haïfa Zargayouna, Davide Buscaldi, Isabelle Tellier, and Thierry Charnois. 2016. Semantic annotation of the ACL anthology corpus for the automatic analysis of scientific literature. In *LREC*.

Sepp Hochreiter and Jürgen Schmidhuber. 1997. Long short-term memory. *Neural computation*, 9(8):1735–1780.

Ji Young Lee, Franck Dernoncourt, and Peter Szolovits. 2017a. MIT at SemEval-2017 Task 10: Relation extraction with convolutional neural networks. In *SemEval-2017*.

Lung-Hao Lee, Kuei-Ching Lee, and Y Jane Tseng. 2017b. The NTNU system at SemEval-2017 Task 10: Extracting keyphrases and relations from scientific publications using multiple conditional random fields. In *SemEval-2017*.

Yi Luan, Mari Ostendorf, and Hannaneh Hajishirzi. 2017. Scientific information extraction with semi-supervised neural tagging. In *EMNLP*.

Sean MacAvaney, Arman Cohan, and Nazli Goharian. 2017. GUIR at SemEval-2017 Task 12: A framework for cross-domain clinical temporal information extraction. In *SemEval-2017*.

Tomas Mikolov, Edouard Grave, Piotr Bojanowski, Christian Puhrsch, and Armand Joulin. 2018. Advances in pre-training distributed word representations. In *LREC*.

Mike Mintz, Steven Bills, Rion Snow, and Dan Jurafsky. 2009. Distant supervision for relation extraction without labeled data. In *ACL/IJCNLP*. Association for Computational Linguistics.

Makoto Miwa and Mohit Bansal. 2016. End-to-end relation extraction using lstms on sequences and tree structures. In *ACL*.

Kai Sheng Tai, Richard Socher, and Christopher D Manning. 2015. Improved semantic representations from tree-structured long short-term memory networks. *arXiv preprint arXiv:1503.00075*.

Yan Xu, Lili Mou, Ge Li, Yunchuan Chen, Hao Peng, and Zhi Jin. 2015. Classifying relations via long short term memory networks along shortest dependency paths. In *EMNLP*.

Jinguang Zheng, Daniel P Howsmon, Boliang Zhang, Juergen Hahn, Deborah L. McGuinness, James A. Hendler, and Heng Ji. 2014. Entity linking for biomedical literature. In *DTMBIO@CIKM*.

ClaiRE at SemEval-2018 Task 7: Classification of Relations using Embeddings

Lena Hettinger, Alexander Dallmann, Albin Zehe, Thomas Niebler and Andreas Hotho
DMIR Group
University of Wuerzburg
{hettinger,dallmann,zehe,niebler,hotho}
@informatik.uni-wuerzburg.de

Abstract

In this paper we describe our system for SemEval-2018 Task 7 on classification of semantic relations in scientific literature for clean (subtask 1.1) and noisy data (subtask 1.2). We compare two models for classification, a C-LSTM which utilizes only word embeddings and an SVM that also takes hand-crafted features into account. To adapt to the domain of science we train word embeddings on scientific papers collected from arXiv.org. The hand-crafted features consist of lexical features to model the semantic relations as well as the entities between which the relation holds. **Cla**ssification of **R**elations using **E**mbeddings (ClaiRE) achieved an F1 score of 74.89 % for the first subtask and 78.39 % for the second.

1 Introduction

The goal of SemEval-2018 Task 7 is to extract and classify semantic relations between entities into six categories that are specific to scientific literature (Gábor et al., 2018). In this work, we focus on the subtask of classifying relations between entities in manually (subtask 1.1) and automatically annotated and therefore noisy data (subtask 1.2). Given a pair of related entities, the task is to classify the type of their relation among the following options: `Compare`, `Model-Feature`, `Part_Whole`, `Result`, `Topic` or `Usage`. Relation types are explained in detail in the task description paper (Gábor et al., 2018). The following sentence shows an example of a `Result` relation between the two entities **combination methods** and **system performance**:

> **Combination methods** are an effective way of improving **system performance**.

This sentence is a good example for two challenges we face in this task. First, almost half of all entities consist of noun phrases which has to be considered when constructing features. Secondly, the vocabulary is domain dependent and therefore background knowledge should be adopted.

Previous approaches for semantic relation classification tasks mainly employed two strategies. Either they made use of a lot of hand-crafted features or they utilized a neural network with as few background knowledge as possible. The winning system of an earlier SemEval challenge on relation classification (Hendrickx et al., 2009) adopted the first approach and achieved an F1 score of 82.2% (Rink and Harabagiu, 2010). Later, other works outperformed this approach by using CNNs with and without hand-crafted features (Santos et al., 2015; Xu et al., 2015) as well as RNNs (Miwa and Bansal, 2016).

Approach We present two approaches that use different levels of preliminary information. Our first approach is inspired by the winning method of the SemEval-2010 challenge (Rink and Harabagiu, 2010). It models semantic relations by describing the two *entities*, between which the semantic relation holds, as well as the words between those entities. We call those in-between words the *context* of the semantic relation. We classify relations by using an SVM on lexical features, such as part-of-speech tags. Additionally we make use of semantic background knowledge and add pre-trained word embeddings to the SVM, as word embeddings have been shown to improve performance in a series of NLP tasks, such as sentiment analysis (Kim, 2014), question answering (Chen et al., 2017) or relation extraction (Dligach et al., 2017). Besides using existing word embeddings generated from a general corpus, we also train embeddings on scientific articles that better reflect scientific vocabulary.

In contrast, our second approach relies on word

Proceedings of the 12th International Workshop on Semantic Evaluation (SemEval-2018), pages 836–841
New Orleans, Louisiana, June 5–6, 2018. ©2018 Association for Computational Linguistics

embeddings only, which are fed into a convolutional long-short term memory (C-LSTM) network, a model that combines convolutional and recurrent neural networks (Zhou et al., 2015). Therefore no hand-crafted features are used. Because both CNN and RNN models have shown good performance for this task, we assume that a combination of them will positively impact classification performance compared to the individual models.

By combining lexical information and domain-adapted scientific word embeddings, our system ClaiRE achieved an F1 score of 74.89% for the first subtask with manually annotated data and 78.39% for the second subtask with automatically annotated data.

2 Features

In this section, we describe the features which are used in our two approaches. All sentences are first preprocessed before constructing boolean lexical features on the one hand and word embedding vectors on the other. Both feature groups are based on the entities of relations as well as the context in which those entities appear.

Apart from the `Compare` relation, all relation types are asymmetric, and therefore the distinction between start and end entity of a relation is important. If entities appear in reverse order, that means the end entity of a relation appears first in the sentence, this is marked by a *direction* feature which is part of the data set.

In our entrance example, **combination methods** denotes the start entity, **system performance** the end entity, and **are an effective way of improving** the context.

2.1 Preprocessing

Early experiments showed that it is beneficial to filter the vocabulary of our data and reduce noise by leaving out infrequent context words. The best setting was found to be a frequency threshold of 5 on lemmatized words. Therefore we discard a context word if its lemma appears less than 5 times in the corpus of the respective subtask.

2.2 Context features

First we will explain feature construction based on the context of a relation. Abbreviations for feature names are denoted in brackets. Context is defined as the words between two entities. Early

tests showed that using those words described the relation better than the words surrounding the relation entities.

Lexical We construct several lexical boolean features which are illustrated in Table 1. First we apply a bag of words (*bow*) approach where each lemmatized word forms one boolean feature, which for example takes 1 as value if the lemma *improve* is present and 0 if it is not. Second we determine whether the context words contain certain part-of-speech (POS) tags (*pos*), such as *VERB*. POS-tagging was done with the help of SpaCy[1] (`v.2.0.2`). To represent the structure of the context phrase we add a path of POS tags feature, which contains the order in which POS tags appear (*pospath*). The distance feature depicts whether the POS-path and therefore the context phrase has a certain length (*dist*).

Additionally we add background knowledge by extracting the top-level Levin classes of intermediary verbs from VerbNet[2] (*lc*), a verb lexicon compatible with WordNet. It contains explicitly stated syntactic and semantic information, using Levin verb classes to systematically construct lexical entries (Schuler, 2005). For example the verb *improve* belongs to class 45.4, which is described by Levin as consisting of "alternating change of state" verbs.[3]

Embeddings Aside from lexical features we also use word embedding vectors to leverage information from the context of entities (*c*). For each filtered context word we extract its word embddding from a pre-trained corpus, where out-of-vocabulary words (OOV) are represented by the zero vector. The individual word vectors are later applied to train a C-LSTM.

In contrast, for use in an SVM we found it beneficial to represent the context embedding features as the average over all context word embeddings.

2.3 Entity features

In the second set of features, we model the relation entities themselves as they may be connected to a certain relation class. For example, the token *performance* or one form of it mostly appears as an end entity of a `Result` relation, and in the rare

---

[1] `https://spacy.io/`
[2] `http://verbs.colorado.edu/~mpalmer/projects/verbnet.html`
[3] `http://www-personal.umich.edu/~jlawler/levin.verbs`

Lexical Feature Set	Exemplary Boolean Features
BagOfWords (*bow*)	an, be, effective, improve, of, way
POS tags (*pos*)	ADJ, ADP, DET, NOUN, VERB
POS path (*pospath*)	VDANAV
Distance (*dist*)	6
Levin classes (*lc*)	45
Entities without order (*ents*)	combination methods, methods, system performance, performance
Start entity (*startEnt*)	combination methods, methods
End entitiy (*endEnt*)	system performance, performance
Similarity (*sim*100)	0.43
Similarity bucket (*simb*)	q50

Example Sentence: **Combination methods** are an effective way of improving **system performance**.

Table 1: Examples for lexical context and entity features.

case when it represents a start entity, it is almost always part of a `Compare` relation. Therefore we leverage information about entity position for the creation of lexical and embedding entity features.

Lexical For the creation of boolean lexical features, we first take the lowercased string of each entity and construct up to three distinct features from it. One feature which marks its general appearance in the corpus without order (*ents*) and one each if it occurs as start (*startEnt*) or end (*endEnt*) entity of a relation, taking its direction into account. Additionally we add the head noun to the respective feature set if the entity consists of a nominal phrase to create greater overlap between instances.

Furthermore we measure the semantic similarity of the relation entities using the cosine of the corresponding word embedding vectors (*sim*100). While the cosine takes every value from [-1, 1] in theory, we cut off after two digits to reduce the feature space and get 99 boolean similarity features for our corpus. To again enable learning across instances we additionally discretize the similarity range and form another five boolean similarity features (*simb*) that capture into which of the following buckets the similarity score falls: $q0 = [-1, 0), q25 = [0, 0.25), q50 = [0.25, 0.5), q75 = [0.5, 0.75), q100 = [0.75, 1]$ (values below zero are very rare in this corpus).

Embeddings Similar to the context features we also want to add word embeddings of entities to our entity feature set. This is not straighforward as more than 44% of all entities consist of nominal phrases, while a word embedding usually corresponds to a single word. By way of comparison, the proportion of nominals in the relation classification corpus of the SemEval-2010 challenge was

only 5%. Thus we tested different strategies to obtain a word embedding for nominal phrases and found that averaging over the individual word vectors of the phrase yielded the best results for this task. These word embeddings for start (e_s) and end (e_e) entities of relations were then presented to our two classification methods, which will be described in detail in the following section.

3   Classification Methods

We utilize two different models for classifying semantic relations: an SVM which incorporates both the lexical and embedding features described in Section 2 and a Convolutional Long Short Term Memory (C-LSTM) neural network that only uses word embedding vectors

To fully exploit our hand-crafted lexical features we employ a traditional classifier. In comparison to Naive Bayes, Decision Trees and Random Forests we found a Support Vector Machine to perform best for this task. Instead of utilizing the decision function of the SVM to predict test labels we decided to make use of the probability estimates according to Wu et al. (2004) as this proved to be more successful. As mentioned before, the lexical features are fed into the SVM as boolean features whereas the word embeddings are normalized using MinMax-Scaling to the range $[0, 1]$ to make it easier for the SVM to handle both feature groups.

In contrast to SVM, neural network models do not necessarily rely on handcrafted features and are therefore faster to implement. We experiment with standard C-LSTM (Zhou et al., 2015) which extracts a sentence representation by combining one-dimensional convolution and an LSTM network and uses the representation to perform a classification.

label	subtask 1.1	subtask 1.2	total
COMPARE	95 (8%)	41 (3%)	136 (5%)
MODEL-F.	326 (27%)	174 (14%)	500 (20%)
PART_W.	234 (19%)	196 (16%)	430 (17%)
RESULT	72 (6%)	123 (10%)	195 (8%)
TOPIC	18 (1%)	243 (20%)	261 (11%)
USAGE	483 (39%)	468 (38%)	951 (38%)

Table 2: Distribution of class labels for training data as absolute and relative values.

4 Evaluation

After describing the two models we employ for relation classification, we now portray the data set we use and present results for both SVM and C-LSTM as micro-F1 and macro-F1. The latter is the official evaluation score of the SemEval Challenge. We describe the experimental setup for both models and compare different feature sets and pre-trained embeddings.

4.1 Data and Background Knowledge

We evaluate our approach on a set of scientific abstracts, D_{test}. It consists of 355 semantic relations for each subtask which are similarly distributed as its respective training data set. As training data we received 350 abstracts of scientific articles per subtask, which resulted in 1228 labeled training relations for subtask 1.1 and 1245 training instances for subtask 1.2 (c.f. Table 2). We combine data sets of both subtasks for training, resulting in 2473 training examples in total (D_{train}).

Background Knowledge In our experiments, we compare different pre-trained word embeddings as a source of background knowledge. As a baseline, we employ a publicly available set of 300-dimensional word embeddings trained with GloVe (Pennington et al., 2014) on the Common Crawl data[4] (CC). To better reflect the semantics of scientific language, we trained our own scientific embeddings using word2vec (Mikolov et al., 2013) on a large corpus of papers collected from arXiv.org[5] (*arXiv*).

In order to create the scientific embeddings, we downloaded LaTeX sources for all papers published in 2016 on arXiv.org using the provided dumps.[6] After originally trying to extract the plain text from the sources, we found that it was more feasible to first compile the sources to pdf (exclud-

data	context		+ entities	
	macro F1	micro F1	macro F1	micro F1
1.1	44.35	58.87	50.30	65.63
+1.2	47.43	61.69	64.38	69.30
CC	51.79	65.07	72.47	74.93
arXiv	52.15	65.92	**74.89**	**76.90**

Table 3: SVM results for subtask 1.1.

data	context		+ entities	
	macro F1	micro F1	macro F1	micro F1
1.2	67.25	69.75	72.48	80.39
+1.1	64.54	69.30	74.69	83.10
CC	62.64	70.70	75.87	**84.79**
arXiv	63.07	70.70	**78.39**	83.10

Table 4: SVM results for subtask 1.2.

ing all graphics etc.) and then use pdftotext[7] to convert the documents to plain text. This resulted in a dataset of about 166 000 papers. Using gensim (Řehůřek and Sojka, 2010), for each document we extracted tokens of minimum length 1 with the wikicorpus tokenizer and used word2vec to train 300-dimensional word embeddings on the data. We kept most hyper-parameters at their default values, but limited the vocabulary to words occurring at least 100 times in the dataset, reducing for example the noise introduced by artifacts from equations.

4.2 Parameters and Results

After an extensive grid search per cross validation the best parameters for the SVM were found to be a rbf-kernel with $C = 100$ and $\gamma = 0.001$ for both tasks.

Results of the SVM for subtask 1.1. are shown in Table 3. Adding entity features proves to be very beneficial compared to using only context features, as we could improve macro-F1 by 12 points on average. Results are further improved by enlarging the data set with the training samples of subtask 1.2 and by adding word embeddings to the feature set. While adding the CC embeddings enhances the micro-F1 by more than 4 points, our domain-adapted arXiv embeddings prove to perform even better and deliver the best result with a macro-F1 score of 74.89 % and a micro-F1 of 76.90 %.

Similar observations can be made for subtask 1.2., as is pictured in Table 4.

Due to space limitations we publish parameter

---

[4]http://commoncrawl.org/
[5]https://arxiv.org
[6]https://arxiv.org/help/bulk_data
[7]https://poppler.freedesktop.org

details and elaborate results for the C-LSTM on arXiv.org (Hettinger et al., 2018). In comparison to the SVM, which additionally uses hand-crafted features, the C-LSTM achieves lower scores. For arXiv embeddings it reaches a macro-F1 of 63.3 % for the first subtask and 68.0 % for the second.

5 Discussion

We briefly discuss our approach during the training phase of the SemEval-Challenge and how label distribution and evaluation measure influences our results. Ahead of the final evaluation phase where the concealed test data D_{test} was presented to the participants we were given a preliminary test partition D_{pre} as part of the training data D_{train}. To be able to estimate our performance we evaluated it on D_{pre} as well as for a 10-fold stratified cross validation setting. We chose this procedure to be sure to pick the best system for submission at the challenge.

As some classes were strongly underrepresented in the training corpus and D_{pre}, we assumed that this is also true for the final test set D_{test}. When in doubt we therefore chose to optimize according to D_{pre} as cross validation is based on a slightly more balanced data set (of train data for subtask 1.1 + 1.2). The best system we submitted for subtask 1.1 of the challenge achieved a macro-F1 of 75.05% on D_{pre} during the training phase which shows that we were able to estimate our final result pretty closely.

During training we also noticed that for heavily skewed class distributions as in this case, macro-F1 as an evaluation measure strongly depends on a good prediction of very small classes. For example, macro-F1 of subtask 1.1 increases by 5 points if we correctly predict one `Topic` instance out of three instead of none. Thus we pick a configuration that optimizes the small classes.

We also omitted some lexical feature sets from our system as performance on the temporary and final test set showed that they did not improve results. These features were hypernyms of context and entity tokens from WordNet and dependency paths between entities. Using tf-idf normalization instead of boolean for lexical features also worsened our results.

6 Conclusion

In this paper, we described our SemEval-2018 Task 7 system to classify semantic relations in sci-entific literature for clean (subtask 1.1) and noisy (subtask 1.2) data. We constructed features based on relation entities and their context by means of hand-crafted lexical features as well as word embeddings. To better adapt to the scientific domain, we trained scientific word embeddings on a large corpus of scientific papers obtained from arXiv.org. We used an SVM to classify relations and additionally contrasted these results with those obtained from training a C-LSTM model on the scientific embeddings. We were able to obtain a macro-F1 score of 74.89 % on clean data and rank 4th out of 28 and 78.39 % on noisy data, which resulted in a 6th place out of 20.

In future work, we will improve the tokenization of the scientific word embeddings and also take noun compounds into account, as they make up a large part of the scientific vocabulary. We will also investigate more complex neural network based models, that can leverage additional information, for example relation direction and POS tags. Some minor changes we applied to the feature generation during the post-evaluation phase and which further improved our results by more than 2 % are published on arXiv.org together with more detailed evaluation (Hettinger et al., 2018).

References

Danqi Chen, Adam Fisch, Jason Weston, and Antoine Bordes. 2017. Reading wikipedia to answer open-domain questions. In *ACL (1)*, pages 1870–1879. Association for Computational Linguistics.

Dmitriy Dligach, Timothy Miller, Chen Lin, Steven Bethard, and Guergana Savova. 2017. Neural temporal relation extraction. In *Proceedings of the 15th Conference of the European Chapter of the Association for Computational Linguistics: Volume 2, Short Papers*, volume 2, pages 746–751.

Kata Gábor, Davide Buscaldi, Anne-Kathrin Schumann, Behrang QasemiZadeh, Haïfa Zargayouna, and Thierry Charnois. 2018. Semeval-2018 Task 7: Semantic relation extraction and classification in scientific papers. In *Proceedings of International Workshop on Semantic Evaluation (SemEval-2018)*, New Orleans, LA, USA.

Iris Hendrickx, Su Nam Kim, Zornitsa Kozareva, Preslav Nakov, Diarmuid Ó Séaghdha, Sebastian Padó, Marco Pennacchiotti, Lorenza Romano, and Stan Szpakowicz. 2009. Semeval-2010 task 8: Multi-way classification of semantic relations between pairs of nominals. In *Proceedings of the Workshop on Semantic Evaluations: Recent Achievements and Future Directions*, pages 94–99. Association for Computational Linguistics.

Lena Hettinger, Alexander Dallmann, Albin Zehe, Thomas Niebler, and Andreas Hotho. 2018. Claire at semeval-2018 task 7 - extended version. *Computation and Language Repository*, arXiv:1804.05825.

Yoon Kim. 2014. Convolutional neural networks for sentence classification. In *Proceedings of the 2014 Conference on Empirical Methods in Natural Language Processing, EMNLP 2014, October 25-29, 2014, Doha, Qatar, A meeting of SIGDAT, a Special Interest Group of the ACL*, pages 1746–1751.

Tomas Mikolov, Ilya Sutskever, Kai Chen, Greg S Corrado, and Jeff Dean. 2013. Distributed representations of words and phrases and their compositionality. In *NIPS*, pages 3111–3119. Curran Associates, Inc.

Makoto Miwa and Mohit Bansal. 2016. End-to-end relation extraction using lstms on sequences and tree structures. Cite arxiv:1601.00770Comment: Accepted for publication at the Association for Computational Linguistics (ACL), 2016. 13 pages, 1 figure, 6 tables.

Jeffrey Pennington, Richard Socher, and Christopher D Manning. 2014. Glove: Global vectors for word representation. In *EMNLP*, volume 14, pages 1532–1543.

Radim Řehůřek and Petr Sojka. 2010. Software Framework for Topic Modelling with Large Corpora. In *Proceedings of the LREC 2010 Workshop on New Challenges for NLP Frameworks*, pages 45–50, Valletta, Malta. ELRA. `http://is.muni.cz/publication/884893/en`.

Bryan Rink and Sanda Harabagiu. 2010. Utd: Classifying semantic relations by combining lexical and semantic resources. In *Proceedings of the 5th International Workshop on Semantic Evaluation*, pages 256–259. Association for Computational Linguistics.

Cicero Nogueira dos Santos, Bing Xiang, and Bowen Zhou. 2015. Classifying relations by ranking with convolutional neural networks. *Proceedings of the 7th International Joint Conference on Natural Language Processing [IJCNLP]*.

Karin Kipper Schuler. 2005. *Verbnet: A Broad-coverage, Comprehensive Verb Lexicon*. Ph.D. thesis, University of Pennsylvania, Philadelphia, PA, USA. AAI3179808.

Ting-Fan Wu, Chih-Jen Lin, and Ruby C. Weng. 2004. Probability estimates for multi-class classification by pairwise coupling. *Journal of Machine Learning Research*, 5(Aug):975–1005.

Kun Xu, Yansong Feng, Songfang Huang, and Dongyan Zhao. 2015. Semantic relation classification via convolutional neural networks with simple negative sampling. In *Proceedings of the 2015 Conference on Empirical Methods in Natural Language Processing [EMNLP]*, pages 536–540.

Chunting Zhou, Chonglin Sun, Zhiyuan Liu, and Francis C. M. Lau. 2015. A c-lstm neural network for text classification. *CoRR*, abs/1511.08630.

TakeLab at SemEval-2018 Task 7: Combining Sparse and Dense Features for Relation Classification in Scientific Texts

Martin Gluhak, Maria Pia di Buono, Abbas Akkasi, Jan Šnajder
Text Analysis and Knowledge Engineering Lab
Faculty of Electrical Engineering and Computing
University of Zagreb
Unska 3, 10000 Zagreb, Croatia
{name.surname}@fer.hr

Abstract

We describe two systems for semantic relation classification with which we participated in the SemEval 2018 Task 7, subtask 1 on semantic relation classification: an SVM model and a CNN model. Both models combine dense pretrained word2vec features and hancrafted sparse features. For training the models, we combine the two datasets provided for the subtasks in order to balance the under-represented classes. The SVM model performed better than CNN, achieving an F1-macro score of 69.98% on subtask 1.1 and 75.69% on subtask 1.2. The system ranked 7th among 28 submissions on subtask 1.1 and 7th among 20 submissions on subtask 1.2.

1 Introduction

Relation extraction is a traditional information extraction task which aims at detecting and classifying semantic relations between entities in text (Pawar et al., 2017). The task essentially induces structure from unstructured textual information, allowing us to obtain valuable information about the way in which entities interact, thus improving human capacity to analyze (often large) quantities of textual data. Relation extraction is typically framed as a classification task: pairs of entities from a document are inspected and the type of relation is predicted by means of local linguistic cues (Culotta et al., 2006).

Relation extraction has been extensively studied in the literature; see (Konstantinova, 2014) for a comprehensive overview. Etzioni et al. (2008) group the relation extraction approaches into three classes: (1) knowledge-based methods, (2) supervised methods, and (3) self-supervised methods. Traditional approaches mostly relied on shallow machine learning models with handcrafted features (GuoDong et al., 2005) and specific kernel methods (Zelenko et al., 2003). Some systems leverage unlabeled data to improve classification and use semi-supervised or unsupervised learning (Chen et al., 2006; Hasegawa et al., 2004). The current state of the art is a deep recurrent neural network model by Xu et al. (2016). Most research on relation extraction has leveraged standard benchmark datasets from the ACE (Doddington et al.) and SemEval-2010 Task 8 (Hendrickx et al., 2009).

This paper describes the systems with which we participated in the SemEval 2018 task 7 on Semantic relation extraction and classification in scientific papers. We focused on the subtask 1 (relation classification), which featured two scenarios: 1.1 Relation classification on clean (i.e., manually annotated) data and 1.2 Relation classification on noisy (i.e., automatically annotated) data. Both scenarios start out with pre-extracted entity pairs, which makes the task simpler than relation extraction proper. On the other hand, the task remains challenging because of the choice of the domain: scientific publications abound with complex syntactic structures and rely on specialist terminology, which makes it more difficult to predict the correct relation type. We framed the problem as a supervised classification task and devised two models: a support vector machine (SVM) model, which utilizes a rich set of features combining dense pretrained word2vec features and handcrafted sparse features, and a convolutional neural network (CNN) model. The best result was achieved with the SVM model, which ranked 7th in both scenarios of subtask 1.

2 Dataset

The organizers have provided different training datasets for scenarios 1.1 and 1.2 of subtask 1, each consisting of 350 abstracts of scientific papers from the Natural Language Processing (NLP)

842

Proceedings of the 12th International Workshop on Semantic Evaluation (SemEval-2018), pages 842–847
New Orleans, Louisiana, June 5–6, 2018. ©2018 Association for Computational Linguistics

domain (Gábor et al., 2018) to be used for training the models. All entities representing domain concepts (e.g., *word sense disambiguation* and *translation*) are already annotated and listed in pairs according to one of the relations that holds between them. For example, in the sentence "High quality *translation* via *word sense disambiguation* and accurate word order generation of the target language", the entity *word sense disambiguation* is used for *translation*, hence it is annotated as an instance of the USAGE relation type. There are six distinct relation types: USAGE, TOPIC, COMPARE, MODEL-FEATURE, RESULT, PART-WHOLE. Except for COMPARE, all relations are asymmetric, which means that the direction of relation matters. For this reason, every asymmetrical relation instance has additionally been annotated with the direction of the relation using the "reverse" flag to indicate that the order of entities should be flipped.

The total number of training instances is 1228 and 1248 for subtask 1.1 and subtask 1.2 datasets, respectively. Each instance contains exactly two entities and both appear in the same sentence. The subtask 1.2 dataset uses the same annotation scheme as the first subtask, but the entities are automatically extracted rather than manually annotated, thus introducing noise.

Table 1 shows the breakdown of relation types for the two datasets. In general, the class distribution is rather imbalanced, especially the TOPIC relation, which is heavily under-represented in the dataset for subtask 1.1.

3 System Description

We devised two supervised machine learning models: an SVM with a rich set of features and a CNN model. We next describe these models in more detail.

3.1 SVM Model

Our best-performing model uses an SVM classifier with a combination of sparse and dense features.

Sparse feature encoding. To encode the sparse features, we adopt the method of Chen et al. (2006) who divide the sentence into contexts. In a nutshell, the method consists in describing the context in which the entities occur by dividing the sentence into five contexts around the entity mentions. Two of these five contexts are related to the entities involved in the relation, while the remaining three contexts represent the words before, between, and after the entity mention pair. Every feature describing a word contains the information about which context it is located in. It also additionally contains the position of the word relative to the start of that context. While this increases the total number of parameters, it also provides information about the word ordering in the context independently of the size of other contexts.

This encoding scheme is used to create features of word tokens, part-of-speech tags, and named entities. Similarly as Chen et al. (2006), who in turn followed Charniak (2000) and Zhang (2004), we experimented with additional constituency parse features describing grammatical functions and chunk tag information for all five contexts, and IOB-chains of the heads of the two entities. However, as preliminary experiments showed that these additional features do not provide any performance gains, we decided not to include them in our final models, intending to evaluate these results in future work.

Word windows. In the scientific domain sentence structures may be very complex, increasing the distance between the two entity mentions. This presents a considerable problem for sparse feature encoding of the context between two entities: as there the features are encoded for each word separately, the increase in distance yields a proportional increase in the number of parameters, which may cause overfitting. To mitigate this problem, instead of representing the contexts for the whole sentence, we use word windows that focus on the words around the entity mentions. Based on preliminary experiments, we decided to use different sizes of word windows for before, between, and after contexts: the window size for the context in between the entities is a maximum of eight words (at most four on the side of each entity; for longer distance the middle words get ignored), while the window size of the before and after contexts is at most two words to the left and right, respectively. The rationale for this is the assumption that words indicative of relation type are more likely to lie in between and close to one of the two entities.

Dependency features. Many systems from the literature make use of dependency features (Nguyen and Grishman, 2015a; Xu et al., 2016, 2015), which, intuitively, should be useful for re-

| | Subtask 1.1 | | | Subtask 1.2 | | | |
Relation type	Regular	Reversed	All	Regular	Reversed	All	Combined
USAGE	296	187	483	323	147	470	953
TOPIC	8	10	18	230	13	243	261
COMPARE	95	–	95	41	–	41	136
MODEL-FEATURE	226	100	326	123	52	175	501
RESULT	52	20	72	85	38	123	195
PART-WHOLE	158	76	234	117	79	196	430
Total	835	393	1228	919	329	1248	2476

Table 1: Class distribution in subtask 1 training datasets for scenario 1.1 (clean annotation) and scenario 1.2 (noisy annotation). Last column shows the combined counts of both datasets.

lation extraction and classification. Specifically for the relation classification task, we are interested in the connection between the two entities involved in a relation within an instance. Thus, after performing a dependency parse of the whole sentence in which the relation appears, we find the shortest dependency path between the two entities. As demonstrated by Xu et al. (2016), the shortest dependency path between two entities is advantageous over a raw word sequence or a whole parse tree, because it reduces irrelevant information and because the shortest path dependency relations focus on the action and agents in a sentence and are thus naturally suitable for relation classification. The dependency parsing was done using the SpaCy parser.[1]

Considering that the edges on the shortest dependency path also have directions, we split the path into two sub-paths based on the edge direction. Usually, the first path goes from the first entity node towards the lowest common ancestor in the dependency parse tree, while the other path goes downwards to the second entity from the ancestor node. Then, each sub-path is encoded into a series of one-hot sparse features that represent the edge dependency type and the distance of the edge from the starting point. Preliminary experiments showed that these features lead to substantial performance improvement.

Word embeddings and OOV words. To capture the semantic meaning of the words we used 300-dimensional pre-trained Google word2vec word embeddings.[2] In accordance with standard practice, which leverages the additive compositionality of word embeddings (Gittens et al., 2017), we represent each context as a sum of its word embeddings. As we divided the sentence into five context, the result is five vectors, which are subsequently concatenated into a single 1500-dimensional vector.

Using a pre-trained word2vec model combined with a scientific domain dataset led to many out-of-vocabulary (OOV) words. After some very basic word preprocessing, e.g., handling of hyphens and underscores, 1108 out of 9319 unique words from the datasets (combined datasets of subtasks 1.1. and 1.2) remained uncovered by the word2vec model. To tackle the OOV problem, we experimented with a fallback mechanism based on the context2vec (Melamud et al., 2016), an off-the-shelf lexical substitution system. Our idea was to retrieve the lexical substitutes for each OOV word[3] and retrieve their vectors instead – a technique akin to query expansion in information retrieval. We experimented with a number of variants of this method, however as none led to performance improvements, we decided not to include lexical substitution fallback in the final model.

Reversed relations. We use a boolean feature to indicate the reverse direction of a relation in an instance, as provided in the training datasets. With the addition of that feature the model can more easily differentiate between the regular and reversed instances of a class. We expand the number of classes from the initial six types of relations to include reversed relations as distinct classes, resulting in an 11-way classification model. The results obtained this way were better then using a 6-way classification model; while this appears counter-intuitive, we leave a more thorough investigation for future work. Once the predicted classes are obtained, we map regular and reversed relation types into one class, as in the original task.

Considering that COMPARE relation cannot be

---

[1]https://spacy.io/
[2]https://code.google.com/archive/p/word2vec/

[3]A lexical substitute is a meaning-preserving replacement of a word in its context.

reversed, we perform a post-prediction correction if a relation instance has an active reverse flag in the test set but the model predicted the instance to be of the COMPARE class. In this case, we change the prediction for that instance to be the second most probable class according to the predicted class probabilities.

3.2 CNN model

Motivated by the high performance that deep learning techniques have achieved in this area (Kumar, 2017), we experimented with a convolutional neural network (CNN) model. This model outperforms traditional feature-engineered approaches on relation extraction benchmarks, as shown by Nguyen and Grishman (2015b).

Architecture. The idea behind the use of a CNN model is to use the convolutional layer to capture the local content and meaning of a few consecutive words, depending on the size of the convolution kernel. Our CNN model comprises a single convolution layer connected to a max-pooling layer. As proposed by Nguyen and Grishman (2015b), pooling is followed by a dropout layer, which has been shown to work working well in fully-connected layers (Hinton et al., 2012; Wan et al., 2013; Krizhevsky et al., 2012). We use the softmax function at the output layer activation function. The model is implemented using TensorFlow.[4]

Features. The CNN model uses the same pre-trained word2vec embeddings as the SVM model. Since the training data is limited, the word embeddings are kept static and not adjusted during training. In addition to word embeddings, the model is fed as input the position of words relative to the entities. In this way, the model is provided with the information on the positions of entities and the distance of context words, which could affect their relevance for predicting the relation type (Nguyen and Grishman, 2015b). Thus, each word has two position features: (1) a relative distance to the closest word for the first entity and (2) a relative distance to the closest word for the second entity. Position embeddings are randomly initialized to 50-dimensional vectors and are shared for the two entities. Unlike with the word embeddings, the position embeddings are adjusted during training. The assumption is that this relative

distance from the entity mentions is inversely proportional to the importance of words. In line with this assumption, we capped the distance values at 15, as words at longer distances are likely not to have much effect on relation type.

Another feature that we added is the information about the shortest dependency path, as described by Nguyen and Grishman (2015a). Assuming that words from the shortest dependency path are more relevant than others, we add for each word a boolean value feature indicating whether that word belongs to the shortest dependency path. We also use an additional indicator feature to distinguish the relation instances with the REVERSE attribute, even though the CNN model has been trained as a 6-way classifier. All the features pertaining to a word are concatenated and considered as a single element when passed to the first layer of the network.

Lastly, we include word windows into the CNN model, in the same manner as we did for the SVM model, but this time increasing the window sizes of contexts around the entities, as this has less of an effect on the number of parameters than it was the case for the SVM model. Thus, we set the window size for between context to four words from each side, while the window size of before and after contexts has been set to the five words closest to the entities. For clarification, word windows simply decide the size of the sentence (not to be confused with position features, which embed previously discussed distances of each word inside the window).

4 Evaluation and Results

As subtask 1.1 and 1.2 are very similar and differ only in how the labeling was carried out (manual or automatic), we decided to combine the training sets of the two tasks in one training set. This allowed us to increase the number of instances for the TOPIC relation type, which was severely under-represented in subtask 1.1 training set (cf. Table 1).

The hyperparameters for the SVM model were selected using cross-validated grid search. The CNN model was trained using early stopping with batch size of 64. Kernel sizes of the convolution layers are 3, 4, and 5 words, each size having 32 kernels. Adam algorithm was used for the model optimization. A dropout rate of 0.5 was used during the training.

---

[4]https://www.tensorflow.org/

Test set	Model	P	R	F1
Subtask 1.1	SVM	64.64	75.57	69.68
	CNN	63.35	72.42	67.58
Subtask 1.2.	SVM	71.64	80.24	75.69
	CNN	14.78	15.81	15.28

Table 2: Relation classification results

The evaluation was performed on the test sets provided by the task organizers. Each test set is comprised of 150 scientific paper abstracts with 350 relation instances. Table 2 shows macro-averaged precision, recall, and F1 score for the two models on the two test sets.

Differently from previous findings (Nguyen and Grishman, 2015b), in our case the SVM outperformed the CNN model. This might be explained by the relatively small size size of the training set. On subtask 1.1, the CNN performs slightly worse than the SVM model, while it fails completely on the second subtask. We presume this might be due to an implementation error, but we were unable to identify the problem. In the official SemEval competition, the SVM model ranked 7th among 28 submissions on subtask 1.1 and 7th among 20 submissions on subtask 1.2.

5 Conclusion

We described two models for relation classification with which participated in the SemEval-2018 Task 7, subtasks 1.1 and 1.2 on relation classification: an SVM model and a CNN model. Our models combine sparse, handcrafted features and dense features based on word embeddings. Although deep learning models currently excels at relation extraction tasks, in our case, probably due to the small relatively small training set available, SVM outperformed the CNN model, ranking 7th in both evaluation runs. Overall, the tasks proved to be very challenging, mainly due to the peculiarities of the domain.

For future work, we intend to retrain our models on a larger dataset using distant supervision based on publicly available scientific corpora, and also experiment with training domain-specific word2vec embeddings.

Acknowledgments

This research has been partly supported by the European Regional Development Fund under the grant KK.01.1.1.01.0009 (DATACROSS).

References

Eugene Charniak. 2000. A maximum-entropy-inspired parser. In *Proceedings of the 1st North American chapter of the Association for Computational Linguistics conference*, pages 132–139. Association for Computational Linguistics.

Jinxiu Chen, Donghong Ji, Chew Lim Tan, and Zhengyu Niu. 2006. Relation extraction using label propagation based semi-supervised learning. In *Proceedings of the 21st International Conference on Computational Linguistics and the 44th annual meeting of the Association for Computational Linguistics*, pages 129–136. Association for Computational Linguistics.

Aron Culotta, Andrew McCallum, and Jonathan Betz. 2006. Integrating probabilistic extraction models and data mining to discover relations and patterns in text. In *Proceedings of the main conference on Human Language Technology Conference of the North American Chapter of the Association of Computational Linguistics*, pages 296–303. Association for Computational Linguistics.

George R Doddington, Alexis Mitchell, Mark A Przybocki, Lance A Ramshaw, Stephanie Strassel, and Ralph M Weischedel. The automatic content extraction (ACE) program-tasks, data, and evaluation.

Oren Etzioni, Michele Banko, Stephen Soderland, and Daniel S. Weld. 2008. Open information extraction from the web. *Communications of the ACM*, 51(12):68–74.

Kata Gábor, Davide Buscaldi, Anne-Kathrin Schumann, Behrang QasemiZadeh, Haïfa Zargayouna, and Thierry Charnois. 2018. Semeval-2018 Task 7: Semantic relation extraction and classification in scientific papers. In *Proceedings of International Workshop on Semantic Evaluation (SemEval-2018)*, New Orleans, LA, USA.

Alex Gittens, Dimitris Achlioptas, and Michael W. Mahoney. 2017. Skip-gram-zipf+ uniform= vector additivity. In *Proceedings of the 55th Annual Meeting of the Association for Computational Linguistics (Volume 1: Long Papers)*, volume 1, pages 69–76.

Zhou GuoDong, Su Jian, Zhang Jie, and Zhang Min. 2005. Exploring various knowledge in relation extraction. In *Proceedings of the 43rd annual meeting on association for computational linguistics*, pages 427–434. Association for Computational Linguistics.

Takaaki Hasegawa, Satoshi Sekine, and Ralph Grishman. 2004. Discovering relations among named entities from large corpora. In *Proceedings of the 42nd Annual Meeting on Association for Computational Linguistics*, page 415. Association for Computational Linguistics.

Iris Hendrickx, Su Nam Kim, Zornitsa Kozareva, Preslav Nakov, Diarmuid Ó Séaghdha, Sebastian

Padó, Marco Pennacchiotti, Lorenza Romano, and Stan Szpakowicz. 2009. SemEval-2010 Task 8: Multi-way classification of semantic relations between pairs of nominals. In *Proceedings of the Workshop on Semantic Evaluations: Recent Achievements and Future Directions*, pages 94–99. Association for Computational Linguistics.

Geoffrey E. Hinton, Nitish Srivastava, Alex Krizhevsky, Ilya Sutskever, and Ruslan R. Salakhutdinov. 2012. Improving neural networks by preventing co-adaptation of feature detectors. *arXiv preprint arXiv:1207.0580*.

Natalia Konstantinova. 2014. Review of relation extraction methods: What is new out there? In *International Conference on Analysis of Images, Social Networks and Texts_x000D_*, pages 15–28. Springer.

Alex Krizhevsky, Ilya Sutskever, and Geoffrey E. Hinton. 2012. ImageNet classification with deep convolutional neural networks. In *Advances in neural information processing systems*, pages 1097–1105.

Shantanu Kumar. 2017. A survey of deep learning methods for relation extraction. *arXiv preprint arXiv:1705.03645*.

Oren Melamud, Jacob Goldberger, and Ido Dagan. 2016. context2vec: Learning generic context embedding with bidirectional lstm. In *Proceedings of The 20th SIGNLL Conference on Computational Natural Language Learning*, pages 51–61.

Thien Huu Nguyen and Ralph Grishman. 2015a. Combining neural networks and log-linear models to improve relation extraction. *arXiv preprint arXiv:1511.05926*.

Thien Huu Nguyen and Ralph Grishman. 2015b. Relation extraction: Perspective from convolutional neural networks. In *Proceedings of the 1st Workshop on Vector Space Modeling for Natural Language Processing*, pages 39–48.

Sachin Pawar, Girish K Palshikar, and Pushpak Bhattacharyya. 2017. Relation extraction: A survey. *arXiv preprint arXiv:1712.05191*.

Li Wan, Matthew Zeiler, Sixin Zhang, Yann Le Cun, and Rob Fergus. 2013. Regularization of neural networks using dropconnect. In *International Conference on Machine Learning*, pages 1058–1066.

Yan Xu, Ran Jia, Lili Mou, Ge Li, Yunchuan Chen, Yangyang Lu, and Zhi Jin. 2016. Improved relation classification by deep recurrent neural networks with data augmentation. *arXiv preprint arXiv:1601.03651*.

Yan Xu, Lili Mou, Ge Li, Yunchuan Chen, Hao Peng, and Zhi Jin. 2015. Classifying relations via long short term memory networks along shortest dependency paths. In *Proceedings of the 2015 Conference on Empirical Methods in Natural Language Processing*, pages 1785–1794.

Dmitry Zelenko, Chinatsu Aone, and Anthony Richardella. 2003. Kernel methods for relation extraction. *Journal of machine learning research*, 3(Feb):1083–1106.

Zhu Zhang. 2004. Weakly-supervised relation classification for information extraction. In *Proceedings of the thirteenth ACM international conference on Information and knowledge management*, pages 581–588. ACM.

NEUROSENT-PDI at SemEval-2018 Task 7: Discovering Textual Relations With a Neural Network Model

Mauro Dragoni
Fondazione Bruno Kessler
Via Sommarive 18
Povo, Trento, Italy
dragoni@fbk.eu

Abstract

Discovering semantic relations within textual documents is a timely topic worthy of investigation. Natural language processing strategies are generally used for linking chunks of text in order to extract information that can be exploited by semantic search engines for performing complex queries. The scientific domain is an interesting area where these techniques can be applied. In this paper, we describe a system based on neural networks applied to the SemEval 2018 Task 7. The system relies on the use of word embeddings for composing the vectorial representation of text chunks. Such representations are used for feeding a neural network aims to learn the structure of paths connecting chunks associated with a specific relation. Preliminary results demonstrated the suitability of the proposed approach encouraging the investigation of this research direction.

1 Introduction

One of the emerging trends of natural language technologies is their application to scientific literature. There is a constant increase in the production of scientific papers and experts are faced with an explosion of information that makes it difficult to have an overview of the state of the art in a given domain. Recent works from the semantic web, scientometry, and natural language processing (NLP) communities aimed to improve the access to scientific literature, in particular to answer queries that are currently beyond the capabilities of standard search engines. Examples of such queries include finding all papers that address a given problem in a specific way, or to discover the roots of a certain idea.

The NLP tasks that underlie intelligent processing of scientific documents are those of information extraction: identifying concepts and recognizing the semantic relation that holds between them. Information extraction from corpora including relation extraction and classification normally involves a complicated multiple-step process.

In this paper, we present a neural network strategy for addressing the challenge of extracting informative entities from scientific papers and inferring their semantic relation among a set of six alternatives. This challenge is part of the SemEval 2018 Task 7 (Gábor et al., 2018). One of the pillar of the proposed approach is that the word embeddings used for representing the text within the neural network have been generated from a corpus containing only scientific papers instead of a general purpose one, like news repositories or Wikipedia.

2 System Implementation

NeuroSent has been entirely developed in Java with the support of the Deeplearning4j library [1] and it is composed by following two main phases:

- Generation of Word vectors (Section 2.1): raw text, appropriately tokenized using the Stanford CoreNLP Toolkit, is provided as input to a 2-layers neural network implementing the skip-gram approach with the aim of generating word vectors.

- Learning of Relations Model (Section 2.2): word vectors are used for training a recurrent neural network (RNN) (Gelenbe, 1993) with an output layer containing one node for each type of relation supported by the model. We decided to use RNN due to the necessity of working with input information provided through a sequence of input instances (i.e. the ordered arrays of embeddings corresponding to each word of the text to analyze).

---

[1] https://deeplearning4j.org/

Proceedings of the 12th International Workshop on Semantic Evaluation (SemEval-2018), pages 848–852
New Orleans, Louisiana, June 5–6, 2018. ©2018 Association for Computational Linguistics

In the following subsections, we describe in more detail each phase by providing also the settings used for managing our data.

2.1 Generation of Word Vectors

The generation of the word vectors has been performed by applying the skip-gram algorithm on the raw natural language text extracted from a collection of 2,459,264 scientific papers collected from proceedings of past conferences and journals. In particular, we used the text extracted from the papers contained within the ACM Digital library, IEEE Xplore and Springer LNCS website. The rationale behind the choice of this dataset focuses on two reasons:

- the dataset contains only scientific documents. This way, we are able to build word embeddings focused on the scientific context.

- the dataset is smaller with respect to other corpora used in the literature for building other word embeddings that are currently freely available, like the Google News ones. [2] Indeed, as introduced in Section 1, one of our goal is to demonstrate how we can leverage the use of dedicated resources for generating word embeddings, instead of corpora's size, for improving the effectiveness of classification systems.

These two points represent the main original contributions of this work, in particular the aspect of considering only scientific information for generating word embeddings. While embeddings currently available are created from big corpora of general purpose texts (like news archives or Wikipedia pages), ours are generated by using a smaller corpus containing documents strongly related to the problem that the model will be thought for. On the one hand, this aspect may be considered a limitation of the proposed solution due to the requirement of training a new model in case of problem change. However, on the other hand, the usage of dedicated resources would lead to the construction of more effective models.

Word embeddings have been generated by the Word2Vec implementation integrated into the Deeplearning4j library. The algorithm has been set up with the following parameters: the size of

---

[2]https://github.com/mmihaltz/word2vec-GoogleNews-vectors

the vector to 64, the size of the window used as input of the skip-gram algorithm to 5, and the minimum word frequency was set to 1. The reason for which we kept the minimum word frequency set to 1 is to avoid the loss of rare but important words that can occur in specific documents.

2.2 Learning of The Relations Model

The relations model is built by starting from the word embeddings generated during the previous phase.

The first step consists in converting each textual sentence contained within the dataset into the corresponding numerical matrix S. Given a sentence s, we extract all tokens t_i, with $i \in [0, n]$, and we replace each t_i with the corresponding embedding w. During the conversion of each word in its corresponding embedding, if such embedding is not found, the word is discarded. At the end of this step, each sentence contained in the training set is converted in a matrix $S = [w^{\langle 1 \rangle}, \ldots, w^{\langle n \rangle}]$.

Before giving all matrices as input to the neural network, we need to include both padding and masking vectors in order to train our model correctly. Padding and masking allows us to support different training situations depending on the number of the input vectors and on the number of predictions that the network has to provide at each time step. In our scenario, we work in a many-to-one situation where our neural network has to provide one prediction as result of the analysis of many input vectors (word embeddings).

Padding vectors are required because we have to deal with the different length of sentences. Indeed, the neural network needs to know the number of time steps that the input layer has to import. This problem is solved by including, if necessary, into each matrix S_k, with $k \in [0, z]$ and z the number of sentences contained in the training set, null word vectors that are used for filling empty word's slots. These null vectors are accompanied by a further vector telling to the neural network if data contained in a specific positions has to be considered as an informative embedding or not.

A final note concerns the back propagation of the error. Training recurrent neural networks can be quite computationally demanding in cases when each training instance is composed by many time steps. A possible optimization is the use of truncated back propagation through time (BPTT) (Werbos, 1990) that was developed for reducing the computational complexity of each parameter update in a recurrent neural network. On the one hand, this strategy allows to reduce the time needed for training our model. However, on the other hand, there is the risk of not flowing backward the gradients for the full unrolled network. This prevents the full update of all network parameters. For this reason, even if we work with recurrent neural networks, we decided to do not implement a BPTT approach but to use the default backpropagation implemented into the DL4J library.

Concerning information about network structure, the input layer was composed by 64 neurons (i.e. embedding vector size), the hidden RNN layer was composed by 128 nodes, and the output layer contained 6 nodes, one for each relation (described in Section 3). The network has been trained by using the Stochastic Gradient Descent with 1000 epochs and a learning rate of 0.002.

3 The Tasks

The SemEval 2018 Task 7 is composed by two different subtasks concerning the identification and classification of semantic relations. For the first subtask the participants had to identify pairs of entities that are instances of any of the six semantic relations. This was an extraction task. While for the second subtask, participants had to classify extracted instances into one of the six semantic relation types. This was a classification task.

The six semantic relations subject of this task are the following.

- **USAGE**: this is an asymmetrical relation holds between two entities X and Y, where, for example: "X is used for Y".

- **RESULT**: this is an asymmetrical relation holds between two entities X and Y, where, for example: "X gives as a result Y" (where Y is typically a measure of evaluation).

- **MODEL-FEATURE**: this is an asymmetrical relation holds between two entities X and Y, where, for example: "X is a feature/an observed characteristic of Y".

- **PART_WHOLE**: this is an asymmetrical relation holds between two entities X and Y, where, for example: "X is a part, a component of Y".

- **TOPIC**: this is an asymmetrical relation holds between two entities X and Y, where, for example: "X deals with topic Y" or "X (author, paper) puts forward Y" (an idea, an approach).

- **COMPARE**: this is a symmetrical relation holds between two entities X and Y, where "X is compared to Y" (e.g. two systems, two feature sets or two results).

Below, we briefly described the two subtasks composing the SemEval 2018 Task 7.

Subtask #1: Relation classification The subtask is decomposed into two scenarios according to the data used: classification on clean data and classification on noisy data.

For this subtask, instances with directionality are provided in both the training data and the test data and they are not to be modified or completed in the test data.

This subtask was then split in two separated activities.

1.1 *Relation classification on clean data.* The classification task is performed on data where entities were manually annotated following the ACL RD-TEC 2.0 guidelines [3]. Entities represent domain concepts specific to NLP, while high-level scientific terms (e.g. "hypothesis", "experiment") are not annotated.

1.2 *Relation classification on noisy data.* This activity is identical to the previous one with the difference is that the entities are annotated automatically and contain noise. The annotation comes from the ACL-RelAcS corpus [4] (Gábor et al., 2016) and it is based on a combination of automatic terminology extraction and external ontologies. Entities are therefore terms specific to the given corpus, and include high-level terms (e.g. "algorithm", "paper", "method"). Relations were manually annotated in the training data and in the gold standard, between automatically annotated entities.

Subtask #2: Relation extraction and classification This subtask combines the extraction task and the classification task. The training data for

---

[3]https://lipn.univ-paris13.fr/ gabor/Relacs/
[4]http://pars.ie/publications/papers/pre-prints/acl-rd-tec-guidelines-ver2.pdf

this scenario is the same that is used for the previous subtask, i.e. manually annotated entities, semantic relations with relation types between these entities. The test data contains different abstracts than the previous subtask and only entity annotations were provided. For the extraction task, participants need to identify pairs of entities in the abstracts that correspond to an instance of any of the six relations. While, for the classification task, relation labels of the extracted relations need to be predicted similarly to Subtask #1.

The NeuroSent system has been applied to both subtasks. In Section 4, we report the preliminary results obtained by NeuroSent on the training set compared with a set of baselines.

4 In-Vitro Evaluation

Approach	Task #1.1	Task #1.2
Support Vector Machine	0.4534	0.4551
Naive-Bayes	0.4788	0.4787
Maximum Entropy	0.4917	0.4892
CNN Architecture	0.5329	0.4918
NeuroSent	**0.5572**	**0.5749**

Table 1: Results obtained on the training set by NeuroSent and by the four baselines for the Task#1.

Approach	Task #2.1	Task #2.2
Support Vector Machine	0.3591	0.3498
Naive-Bayes	0.3842	0.3658
Maximum Entropy	0.3982	0.3755
CNN Architecture	0.4103	0.3814
NeuroSent	**0.4274**	**0.4009**

Table 2: Results obtained on the training set by NeuroSent and by the four baselines for the Task#2.

Approach	Task #1.1	Task #1.2
ETH-DS3Lab	0.817	0.904
NeuroSent	0.180	0.218

Table 3: Results obtained on the test set by NeuroSent and by the best system of Task#1.

The NeuroSent approach have been preliminarily evaluated by adopting the Dranziera protocol (Dragoni et al., 2016). This protocol, even if it was thought for the sentiment analysis task, can be easily adapted to any NLP task.

Approach	Task #2.1	Task #2.2
ETH-DS3Lab	0.488	0.493
UWNLP	0.500	0.391
NeuroSent	0.256	0.031

Table 4: Results obtained on the test set by NeuroSent and by the best systems of Task#2.

The validation procedure leverage on a five-fold cross evaluation setting in order to validate the robustness of the proposed solution. The approach has been compared with four baselines:

- Support Vector Machine (SVM): classification was run with a linear kernel type by using the Libsvm (Chang and Lin, 2011). Libsvm uses a sparse format so that zero values do not need to be captured for training files. This can cause training time to be longer, but keeps Libsvm flexible for sparse cases.

- Naive Bayes (NB) and Maximum Entropy (ME): the MALLET: MAchine Learning for LanguagE Toolkit (McCallum, 2002) was used for classification by using both Naive Bayes and Maximum Entropy algorithms. For the experiments conducted in our evaluation, the Maximum Entropy classification has been performed by using a Gaussian prior variance of 1.0.

- Convolutional Neural Network (Chaturvedi et al., 2016) (CNN): we compared our architecture with a classic CNN. Models have been trained with the embeddings created from the Blitzer dataset.

Tables 1 and 2 show the results obtained on Tasks #1 and #2 respectively. In each table, we provide averaged F1-Score obtained on the five folds in which the training set has been split.

We performed a detailed error analysis concerning the performance of NeuroSent. In general, we observed how our strategy tends to provide false negative predictions. Unfortunately, on the test set our approach obtained significant worse results with respect to the other systems participated to the competition (Tables 3 and 4). We are investigating about the reasons of these low performance.

On the one hand, a possible action for improving the effectiveness our strategy is to increase the granularity of the embeddings (i.e. augmenting the size of the embedding vectors) in order to increase the distance between the space regions of each kind of relation. On the other hand, by increasing the size of embedding vectors, the computational time for building, or updating, the model and for evaluating a single instance increases as well. Part of the future work, will be the analysis of more efficient neural network architectures able to manage augmented embedding vectors without negatively affecting the efficiency of the platform.

5   Conclusion

In this paper, we described the NeuroSent system presented at SemEval 2018 Task 7. Our system makes use of artificial neural networks to extract relevant text chunk from scientific documents and to label pairs of them with semantic relation tags. Obtained results demonstrated the suitability of NeuroSent with respect to the adopted baselines. We may also observed how solutions based on neural networks obtained a significant improvement with respect to the others for both tasks. Future work will focus on improving the system by exploring the integration of knowledge bases (Dragoni et al., 2015) in order to move toward a more cognitive approach.

References

Chih-Chung Chang and Chih-Jen Lin. 2011. Libsvm: A library for support vector machines. *ACM TIST*, 2(3):27:1–27:27.

Iti Chaturvedi, Erik Cambria, and David Vilares. 2016. Lyapunov filtering of objectivity for spanish sentiment model. In *2016 International Joint Conference on Neural Networks, IJCNN 2016, Vancouver, BC, Canada, July 24-29, 2016*, pages 4474–4481. IEEE.

Mauro Dragoni, Andrea Tettamanzi, and Célia da Costa Pereira. 2016. DRANZIERA: an evaluation protocol for multi-domain opinion mining. In *Proceedings of the Tenth International Conference on Language Resources and Evaluation LREC 2016, Portorož, Slovenia, May 23-28, 2016*. European Language Resources Association (ELRA).

Mauro Dragoni, Andrea G. B. Tettamanzi, and Célia da Costa Pereira. 2015. Propagating and aggregating fuzzy polarities for concept-level sentiment analysis. *Cognitive Computation*, 7(2):186–197.

Kata Gábor, Davide Buscaldi, Anne-Kathrin Schumann, Behrang QasemiZadeh, Haïfa Zargayouna, and Thierry Charnois. 2018. Semeval-2018 Task 7: Semantic relation extraction and classification in scientific papers. In *Proceedings of International Workshop on Semantic Evaluation (SemEval-2018)*, New Orleans, LA, USA.

Kata Gábor, Haïfa Zargayouna, Davide Buscaldi, Isabelle Tellier, and Thierry Charnois. 2016. Semantic annotation of the ACL anthology corpus for the automatic analysis of scientific literature. In *Proceedings of the Tenth International Conference on Language Resources and Evaluation LREC 2016, Portorož, Slovenia, May 23-28, 2016*. European Language Resources Association (ELRA).

Erol Gelenbe. 1993. Learning in the recurrent random neural network. *Neural Computation*, 5(1):154–164.

Andrew Kachites McCallum. 2002. Mallet: A machine learning for language toolkit. http://mallet.cs.umass.edu.

P. J. Werbos. 1990. Backpropagation through time: what it does and how to do it. *Proceedings of the IEEE*, 78(10):1550–1560.

SciREL at SemEval-2018 Task 7: A System for Semantic Relation Extraction and Classification

Darshini Mahendran   **Chathurika S. Wickramasinghe**   **Bridget T. McInnes**
Virginia Commonwealth University, Richmond, Virginia
{mahendrand, brahmanacsw, btmcinnes}@vcu.edu

Abstract

This paper describes our system, SciREL (Scientific abstract RELation extraction system), developed for the SemEval 2018 Task 7: Semantic Relation Extraction and Classification in Scientific Papers. We present a feature-vector based system to extract explicit semantic relation and classify them. Our system is trained in the ACL corpus (Bird et al., 2008) that contains annotated abstracts given by the task organizers. When an abstract with annotated entities is given as the input into our system, it extracts the semantic relations through a set of defined features and classifies them into one of the given six categories of relations through feature engineering and a learned model. For the best combination of features our system SciREL obtained an F-measure of 20.03 on the official test corpus in the relation classification Subtask 1.1. In this paper, we provide an in-depth error analysis of our results to prevent duplication of research efforts in the development of future systems.

1   Introduction

Automatic detection and extraction of semantic relations among the entities from unstructured text has received growing attention in the recent years (Konstantinova, 2014), (Augenstein et al., 2017), (Fundel et al., 2006), (Luo et al., 2016). Text mining is the process of automatically extracting knowledge from unstructured text documents and this idea of text mining is to link extracted information together which possibly results in new facts or hypothesis to be explored further through conventional scientific experimentations (Delen and Crossland, 2008), (Fleuren and Alkema, 2015).

SemEval 2018 Task 7 (Gábor et al., 2018) aims to extract and classify semantic relations to improve the access to scientific literature. Their tasks focus on identifying pairs of entities that are instances of six semantic relation types and classifying those instances into one of the six semantic relation types. To address this challenge, we implemented a supervised machine learning based approach in order to extract explicit semantic relations from the ACL anthology corpus (Bird et al., 2008) for Subtask 1.1.

2   Methodology

In this section, we describe our relation extraction system (SciREL) which classifies the semantic relations into one of the given six categories of relations. The main steps of our approach can be summarized as follows. First, an abstract with annotated entities is given as the input into our system and all the sentences in the abstract are segmented, preprocessed, and the entity pairs are identified. Second, a set of features are defined and are combined into a feature vector which is used to train a machine learning model. This is the most crucial part of our system, as the idea is to decrease the size of the effective vocabulary which would in turn increase the classification accuracy by eliminating the noise in the features (GuoDong et al., 2005). Relations between entities are extracted and classified into one of the six relations through this learned model. Each step of our approach is discussed in detail in the following subsections.

2.1   Preprocessing Steps

All sentences in the abstracts are preprocessed to normalize the text so that the input text is guaranteed to be consistent and feature extraction/classification is simplified. Some of the existing NLP techniques and tools are used for preprocessing. Preprocessing is performed as follows [1]:

---

[1] Natural Language Toolkit's (NLTK) Tokenizers, part-of-speech (POS) tagger and Porter Stemmer are used in text preprocessing.

Proceedings of the 12th International Workshop on Semantic Evaluation (SemEval-2018), pages 853–857
New Orleans, Louisiana, June 5–6, 2018. ©2018 Association for Computational Linguistics

1) tokenization; 2) convert text to lower case; 3) removal of special characters; and 4) lemmatization.

2.2 Feature selection

The most challenging part of our system is the feature selection and the feature vector generation (Sammons et al., 2016). After preprocessing the input text, a subset of words which contain the respective entity pair are selected from each sentences, a set of features are computed and a feature vector is created by combining the computed features.

After the initial text processing, a separate set of steps are followed where each feature is computed. Some features are extracted in two different scenarios: before removing the stop words and after removing the stop words. Stop words are the most common words of the language that do not contribute to the semantics of the documents or contain any significance but has a high frequency. Filtering out such words prevents from returning vast amount of unnecessary information.

Bigram is a sequence of words formed from two adjacent words, and bigram frequency of the word pairs between entities is calculated in some features. Collocations [2] are words that appear successively and the frequencies of such words appearing in the the context of other words are calculated in some features and the highest value of the bigram collocations is considered during the feature selection. The bag-of-words model which represents a text as the bag of its words, ignoring its grammar and word order is used in some features to group the words from the sentence for further processing (Peng et al., 2016).

Part-of-speech tagging (POS tagging) is applied on words in some features which assigns parts of speech to those words (Fundel et al., 2006). This helps in disambiguating homonyms and improving the efficiency of feature selection. Term frequency-inverse document frequency (TF-IDF) values are calculated for a set of selected words in some features to distinguish important words based on how frequently they appear across multiple documents (GuoDong et al., 2005). During the feature selection, a representative set of features is computed for each entity pair. Features used in building our system are listed below; E1 refers to

the first entity and E2 refers to the second entity.

1. Number of words before E1 with / without stop words
2. Number of words after E2 with / without stop words
3. Word before E1
4. Word after E2
5. POS of the words before E1 with / without stop words
6. POS of the words after E1 with / without stop words
7. POS of the words before E2 with / without stop words
8. POS of the words after E2 with / without stop words
9. Bigram of the first word before E1 with / without stop words
10. Bigram of the first word after E2 with / without stop words
11. Bigram of E1
12. Bigram of E2
13. Highest bigram value of words in between entities with / without stop words
14. Number of unique POS types in between the entities with / without stop words
15. Number of unique POS types before E1 with / without stop words
16. Number of unique POS types after E2 with / without stop words
17. POS type of the word with highest tf-idf score in between the entities
18. POS type of the word with highest tf-idf score in before E1
19. POS type of the word with highest tf-idf score in after E2

2.3 Multi-class classification

In the final step of our approach, a feature vector is generated for each sentence by incorporating the extracted features in the previous step. The generated feature vector is then used to train a classifier which classifies the relation into the given six categories. The following classifiers which represent three main classification algorithms are used to train and evaluate the data set in our approach: [3] Decision Trees, Naive Bayes, and Support Vector Machines (SVMs). The resulting model is then used to classify the extracted semantic relations into one of the six categories below: Usage, Result, Model-feature, Part-whole, Topic, Compare.

---

[2] Natural Language Toolkit's (NLTK) bigramcollocation-finder is used.

[3] Natural Language Toolkit's (NLTK) scikit-learn library classifiers are used.

3 Dataset

We evaluated our system on the dataset provided by the SemEval 2018 - Task 7. The dataset contains abstracts from the ACL Anthology Corpus (Bird et al., 2008) with pre-annotated entities that represent concepts. The dataset provided for the evaluation is divided into two subsets: training set and test set. The training set includes 350 abstracts containing 5259 entities and 1228 annotated types of relations between entities. The test set includes 150 abstracts containing 2246 entities and 355 annotated types of relations between entities. During the development, the training set is split into 60/40 and k-fold cross validation was used to evaluate the performance.

4 Results

Our system was evaluated on both the development corpus and the official test corpus and the set of features are extracted for each entity pair from the training corpus which was used to compute the feature vector. The feature set of our model included 37 features in total which resulted in 2^{37} combinations of features. We conducted an ablation study to determine the efficacy of the different combinations of features when run with different classifiers and selected the feature combination that resulted in high performance. Consequently, it was found that the following features produce the best performance:

1. Lexical information

   - Bigram of the first word after E1 with stop words
   - Bigram of the first word before E2 without stop words
   - Highest bigram value of words in between entities with stop words
   - Highest bigram value of words in between entities without stop words

2. Syntactic information

   - POS of the word before E2 with stop words
   - Number of unique POS types in between the entities with stop words
   - Number of unique POS types in between the entities without stop words

Validation was performed using 60/40 split evaluation. Performance of each classifier was

	Development	Test
Accuracy	48.07	
F1-measure	**29.25**	**20.03**
Precision	34.29	20.58
Recall	28.55	20.03

Table 1: Performance of our model on the development and official test corpus.

	U	MF	PW	R	C	T
USAGE (U)	119	5	24	18	2	7
MODEL-FEATURE (MF)	12	1	5	1	0	1
PART-WHOLE (PW)	29	1	17	18	0	1
RESULT (R)	48	0	13	5	0	4
COMPARE (C)	2	0	1	0	0	0
TOPIC (T)	15	1	2	0	0	3

Table 2: Confusion matrix of the model trained on the official test corpus where the predicted tags are horizontal and the actual tags are vertical.

measured by the following commonly used evaluation metrics: Accuracy, F-measure, Precision, Recall. Our model was evaluated using three classifiers and it was found that SVMs is the most suitable classifier for our approach through a set of experiments. The results for our development corpus and the official test corpus are presented in the Table 1.

From the Table 1 we can see that our system (SciREL) achieves the accuracy of 48.07 and the F-measure of 29.25 on the development corpus which includes 350 abstracts and the F-measure of 20.03 on the official test corpus which includes 150 abstracts.

5 Error analysis

The performance of our system is quite low therefore, we performed an error analysis to identify some of the mistakes from our system output and find ways to improve it. Our classification model was trained to distinguish between six semantic relations and the confusion matrix displays the results of testing the model for further inspection. Table 2 shows the confusion matrix based on the performance of our classification model trained on the test corpus. We identified three main areas which affected the performance of our system: 1) feature selection; 2) vector representation; and 3) class imbalance.

Feature Selection. We compared the effects of different features and from this analysis, we found several reasons for their poor performance. First, for the lexical information, we are only incorporating the word prior to each of the entities and a single bigram that exists between them. This misses information such as if there is only a single word in between the entities, and in the case were there are more than two words, we miss additional contextual information describing the relationship. Second the syntactic information does not contain an explicit representation of what was seen between the two entities. We focused on the number of unique types of POS tags rather than what type of tags were actually present. In conclusion, we believe that our feature set does contain enough contextual information from between the two entities.

Vector representation. Another major reason for the poor performance of our system is the way the feature vectors are representing the relationship. We generated a feature vector for each entity pair and for all the proposed features which resulted in a feature vector with only 37 features initially. Then, we selected the best set of features that gave the best performance with the model and eliminated the rest, which reduced the size of the feature vector further and we ended up with the feature vector that contained only 7 features. Each feature was represented numerically, therefore if there were more than one bigram, or POS tag sequence between the entities, we were not able to incorporate it into our representation. In addition, analysis of the test instances show that for 100 of the 355 instances, we do not have any contextual or syntactic information due to the stop word removal for three of the features. In conclusion, we believe that this feature vector representation is too compact and does not hold sufficient contextual information to identify patterns between the relationships.

Class Imbalance. From Table 2, we can see most of the instances of the USAGE class are correctly classified and most of the misclassified instances are classified under PART-WHOLE and RESULT. Most of the instances that should have been classified under PART-WHOLE are classified under USAGE and RESULT. None of the instances of the class COMPARE are classified correct and again most of them are classified under the class USAGE. A similar behavior is observed with TOPIC where almost all instances are classified under USAGE. Reason for this observation is mainly due to the imbalanced na-

	U	MF	PW	R	C	T
number of instances	175	66	70	20	21	3
F-measure	59.50	7.14	26.56	8.93	0	16.22

Table 3: Number of instances and the F-measure of the given six classes on the official test corpus where U - USAGE, MF- MODEL-FEATURE, PW- PART-WHOLE, R- RESULT, C- COMPARE, T- TOPIC.

ture of the dataset used to train our system. The number of instances belonging to the classes USAGE, MODEL-FEATURE and PART-WHOLE is approximately five times larger than the number of instances of the rest of the classes. For comparison purposes, we have provided the number of instances of each class and their individual F-measures in the Table 3. From the results, we can clearly see that USAGE which is the majority class shows high performance compared to other categories. In conclusion, we can say most of the misclassified instances belong to the category of USAGE indicating that the machine learning algorithm was unable to identify discriminating features between the classes and defaulted to the majority class.

6 Conclusions

Our goal is to design a system that identify pairs of entities that are instances of any of the given semantic relations. Our system (SciREL) is built to serve this purpose, so that when an input with annotated entities is fed into the model it identifies, extracts and classify the semantic relations. The model selects the set of features that shows the best performance with the classifier and combines the features to compute a feature vector. The classifier then classifies the instances into one of the six semantic relation types. Our system classifies the given ACL anthology corpus with the F-measure of 20.03 on the official test corpus with the SVM classifier. Due to the low results, we provide an in-depth error analysis of our results to prevent duplication of research efforts in the development of future systems. We identified three main areas which affected the performance of our system: 1) feature selection; 2) vector representation; and 3) class imbalance. In conclusion, we believe our feature set does contain enough contextual information from between the two entities and the feature vector representation is too compact to hold sufficient contextual information to discriminate between the classes.

References

Isabelle Augenstein, Mrinal Das, Sebastian Riedel, Lakshmi Vikraman, and Andrew McCallum. 2017. Semeval 2017 task 10: Scienceie-extracting keyphrases and relations from scientific publications. *arXiv preprint arXiv:1704.02853*.

Steven Bird, Robert Dale, Bonnie J Dorr, Bryan Gibson, Mark Thomas Joseph, Min-Yen Kan, Dongwon Lee, Brett Powley, Dragomir R Radev, and Yee Fan Tan. 2008. The ACL anthology reference corpus: A reference dataset for bibliographic research in computational linguistics. pages 1755–1759.

Dursun Delen and Martin D Crossland. 2008. Seeding the survey and analysis of research literature with text mining. *Expert Systems with Applications*, 34(3):1707–1720.

Wilco WM Fleuren and Wynand Alkema. 2015. Application of text mining in the biomedical domain. *Methods*, 74:97–106.

Katrin Fundel, Robert Küffner, and Ralf Zimmer. 2006. Relexrelation extraction using dependency parse trees. *Bioinformatics*, 23(3):365–371.

Kata Gábor, Davide Buscaldi, Anne-Kathrin Schumann, Behrang QasemiZadeh, Haïfa Zargayouna, and Thierry Charnois. 2018. Semeval-2018 Task 7: Semantic relation extraction and classification in scientific papers. In *Proceedings of International Workshop on Semantic Evaluation (SemEval-2018)*, New Orleans, LA, USA.

Zhou GuoDong, Su Jian, Zhang Jie, and Zhang Min. 2005. Exploring various knowledge in relation extraction. In *Proceedings of the 43rd annual meeting on association for computational linguistics*, pages 427–434. Association for Computational Linguistics.

Natalia Konstantinova. 2014. Review of relation extraction methods: What is new out there? In *International Conference on Analysis of Images, Social Networks and Texts*, pages 15–28. Springer.

Yuan Luo, Özlem Uzuner, and Peter Szolovits. 2016. Bridging semantics and syntax with graph algorithmsstate-of-the-art of extracting biomedical relations. *Briefings in bioinformatics*, 18(1):160–178.

Yifan Peng, Chih-Hsuan Wei, and Zhiyong Lu. 2016. Improving chemical disease relation extraction with rich features and weakly labeled data. *Journal of Cheminformatics*, 8(1):53.

Mark Sammons, Christos Christodoulopoulos, Parisa Kordjamshidi, Daniel Khashabi, Vivek Srikumar, and Dan Roth. 2016. Edison: Feature extraction for NLP, simplified. In *LREC*, pages 4085–4092.

NTNU at SemEval-2018 Task 7: Classifier Ensembling for Semantic Relation Identification and Classification in Scientific Papers

Biswanath Barik[1], Utpal Kumar Sikdar[2] and Björn Gambäck[1]
[1]Department of Computer Science, NTNU, Norway
[2]Flytxt, Thiruvananthapuram, India
`{biswanath.barik,gamback}@ntnu.no`
`utpal.sikdar@gmail.com`

Abstract

The paper presents NTNU's contribution to SemEval-2018 Task 7 on relation identification and classification. The class weights and parameters of five alternative supervised classifiers were optimized through grid search and cross-validation. The outputs of the classifiers were combined through voting for the final prediction. A wide variety of features were explored, with the most informative identified by feature selection. The best setting achieved F_1 scores of 47.4% and 66.0% in the relation classification subtasks 1.1 and 1.2. For relation identification and classification in subtask 2, it achieved F_1 scores of 33.9% and 17.0%,

1 Introduction

Scientific papers are valuable knowledge sources providing authentic insights about certain aspects of the research domains. With the advancement of scientific research, a massive growth of published articles are observed. As per the American Journal Experts (AJE) scholarly publishing report[1], approximately 2.2 million articles were added to the literature in 2016 only. The sheer volume of the ever increasing literature of any scientific discipline makes it hard for human capability and expertise to quickly process and identify information of interest. Therefore, there is a need to efficiently exploit automatic means of accessing this reliable unstructured knowledge repository.

Semantic relation extraction is one of the main information extraction tasks, and aims to identify a pair of arguments connected by certain predefined relation types based on a target application. The relation arguments are of different types such as Named Entities (Freitas et al., 2009), nominals (Hendrickx et al., 2009), general keyphrases

(Gábor et al., 2016; Augenstein et al., 2017), quantitative variables (Marsi et al., 2014) or events (Barik et al., 2017), and are syntactically represented by noun phrases, clauses or larger complex structures. A semantic relation may be either symmetric (undirected) or asymmetric (hierarchical).

Supervised machine learning approaches have been successfully used for identifying semantic relations encoded in texts. Broadly, three types of supervised approaches to relation extraction have been investigated: *feature-based* (Kambhatla, 2004; Jiang and Zhai, 2007), *kernel-based* (Zelenko et al., 2003), and *neural network based* (Zeng et al., 2014; Miwa and Bansal, 2016).

In this work, various relation identification and classification subtasks of SemEval 2018 Task 7 (Gábor et al., 2018) were addressed using feature-based approaches. A wide variety of features was explored, including lexical (e.g., bag-of-words, lemmata, n-grams), syntactic (e.g., part-of-speech, parsing information), semantic (e.g., dependency information, WordNet (Miller, 1995)), and other binary indicators. A χ^2-based feature selection technique was used to identify informative features. The class weights and parameters of five different classifiers—Support Vector Machines (SVM), Decision Trees (DT), Random Forests (RF), Multinomial Naïve Bayes (MNB), and k-Nearest Neighbor (kNN)—were optimized for each subtask through grid search and k-fold cross-validation. These classifiers were chosen as they are effective in identifying and classifying semantic relations in feature-based classification scenario (Barik and Marsi, 2017). The trained classifiers were ensembled using majority class labels (hard voting) for the final predictions. All classifier, feature selection and classifier ensembling modules used were implemented in the `scikit-learn` (Pedregosa et al., 2011) machine learning library.

---

[1]https://www.aje.com/en/arc/dist/docs/International-scholarly-publishing-report-2016.pdf

858

Relation Type	Data Set	Frequency/ Percentage			
		Total	(%)	Fwd %	Rev %
USAGE	D_1	483	39.33	61.28	38.72
	D_2	470	37.67	68.72	31.28
RESULT	D_1	72	5.86	72.22	27.78
	D_2	123	9.86	69.10	30.90
MODEL-FEATURE	D_1	326	26.55	69.32	30.68
	D_2	175	14.02	70.29	29.71
PART_WHOLE	D_1	234	19.05	67.52	32.48
	D_2	196	15.70	59.70	40.30
TOPIC	D_1	18	1.46	44.44	55.56
	D_2	243	19.47	94.65	5.35
COMPARE	D_1	95	7.74	100	
	D_2	41	3.28	100	
Total	D_1	1228	100	68.00	32.00
	D_2	1248	100	73.63	26.37

Table 1: Relation type statistics in datasets D_1 and D_2

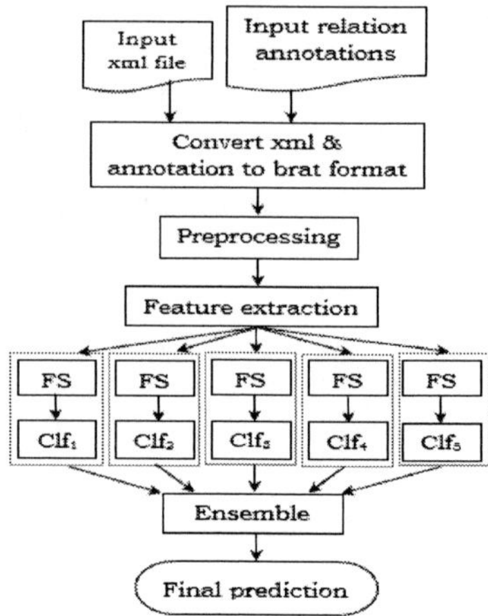

Figure 1: Relation detection and classification pipeline: 5 classifiers (Clf_n) work on extracted feature sets (FS)

The tasks and the datasets are described in Section 2, while Section 3 outlines the experimental setup, system architecture and parameter optimisation. Section 4 discusses the results of the final evaluation of SemEval 2018 Task 7, where the system achieved 47.4% and 66.0% F_1 scores on the relation classification subtasks 1.1 and 1.2. In subtask 2, the system reached 33.9% and 17.0% F_1 scores for relation identification and relation classification, respectively. These results are eloborated on in Section 5, before Section 6 concludes and points to future research.

2 Task and Dataset Description

SemEval 2018 Task 7 (Gábor et al., 2018) consisted of two main relation extraction subtasks:

(a) identifying entity mentions related with any predefined set of relation (Subtask 2), and

(b) classifying them into specific relation types (Subtasks 1.1, 1.2, and 2).

There are six relation types, among which USAGE, RESULT, MODEL-FEATURE, PART_WHOLE, and TOPIC are asymmetric, while COMPARE is the only symmetric relation. All the relations are intra-sentential and there are no referring expressions.

The training dataset consisted of two subsets:

D_1: 350 abstracts of scientific papers that have been manually annotated with entity mentions and relation labels (*clean data*), and

D_2: 350 abstracts with entity mentions automatically labelled, but with the relations labelled manually (*noisy data*).

Subtask 1.1 and subtask 2 are associated with the clean dataset D_1, while subtask 1.2 is associated with the noisy D_2 dataset. The test data consisted of 150 abstracts each for subtask 1.1, 1.2 and 2.

Table 1 shows the distribution of relation instances into different relation types, and their forward (Fwd) and reverse (Rev) directionalities in datasets D_1 and D_2. The highest number of instances are of the USAGE type in both datasets, whereas TOPIC is the least frequent relation type (1.46%) in D_1, but significant (19.47%) in D_2. The overall forward directionalities of relations are 68% in D_1 and 73.63% in D_2. The directionalities of individual relation types are similar.

The most frequent lengths of the entity mentions are two and one word(s) in D_1 and D_2, respectively, with maximum lengths of 13 and 4. The most frequent context lengths of the relation instances are two words, with a highest length of 31 words (RESULT(I05-3022.6, I05-3022.16)) in D_1 and 24 words (USAGE(E91-1004.30, E91-1004.37)) in D_2. The average number of entities in the sentences are 3 and 6 in D_1 and D_2, with highest number of entities being 17 and 29, respectively.

3 Experimental Setup

Figure 1 shows the processing pipeline common to both relation identification and classification. The processing steps are elaborated on below.

Inputs to brat annotation: The input training and test files are in `xml` format with the entity mentions marked. Each entity mention has an `ID` with two parts, abstract ID and entity number. For example, the entity ID `H91-1045.18` denotes abstract ID `H91-1045` and entity number 18. The relation labels are in a separate file with the format `TOPIC(A92-1023.7,A92-1023.8,REVERSE)`, where the first two arguments of the relation type are entity IDs and the last is the directionality of the relation. The xml and relation label files were converted into 'brat' (Stenetorp et al., 2012) format, with the text content of each abstract ID kept in a text file, and entity and relation information kept in an annotation file. Conversion to brat format helps to visualize and study the annotations of the training and test set output. Also, the text content (without entity tags) is used for preprocessing.

Text Processing: The text content of each abstract is analyzed with the Stanford CoreNLP toolkit (Manning et al., 2014) for sentence boundary detection, tokenization, lemmatization, part-of-speech (POS) tagging, and constituent and dependency parsing. Character offset-based brat entity annotations are mapped into word level indices using the tokens' character offsets. Finally, the dependency heads of entity mentions, in between context and the text window representing the relation expression are identified.

Feature Extraction: Given a sentence with more than one entity mention, all possible entity pairs are considered in left to right order. For each entity pair, the text span containing the entities and their middle context is considered as the representation of the relation instance. As word features, unigrams and bigrams of the context and entity mentions (excluding articles, adjectives, cardinals, ordinals, pronouns, brackets and punctuations) are considered. Corresponding to word features, POS, word+POS, and lemma+POS combinations are included, as well as word and POS of entity dependency heads, context dependency heads, and their combinations.

As the shortest dependency path between the entity pair contains major information for relation identification (Bunescu and Mooney, 2005), dependency path features are added for the distance from left entity head to right entity head, words belonging to the dependency path and their rela-

tions to the parent node. WordNet synonyms and hyponyms of dependency head of entities and contexts are included. Also, other binary indicators such as adjacent or overlapping entities are included.

Parameters Optimization through Cross-Validation (CV): As there was no development data available for model parameter tuning, 20% of the training data was kept as development data, and the remaining training data was used for parameters optimization with 5-fold cross-validation. For relation labeling in subtask 1.1 and 1.2, the relation type is predicted against 11 classes (five directed and one undirected relation). Relation instance identification in subtask 2 is a binary classification problem, and the class weights of positive instances are optimized through CV. In the final system, the parameters are optimized on the entire training set.

Classifiers Ensembling and Final Prediction: The optimized parameters of the classifiers and class weights are set to the classifiers. For each classifier, the χ^2-based `SelectKBest()` method selects the top k features from the input feature space, where the k for each classifier is determined through cross-validation. The predictions of the classifiers are then ensembled with (majority) voting where each participating classifier uses its own feature selection method.

4 Results

Three separate submissions were made on the test data. The first two submissions were on relation classification on clean (subtask 1.1) and noisy data (subtask 1.2). The third submission (subtask 2) consisted of relation identification followed by classification on clean data. In subtask 2, a separate system was created for the relation identification, while the relation classification system of subtask 1.1 was used for the classification.

Table 2 shows the performance (precision, recall and F_1 score) of individual classifiers, as well as their combinations in the relation classification subtask 1.1, where the scores are micro-averaged over all (11) classes. Among the individual classifiers, SVM gives the best result (56% F_1 score). Voting with the top-3 classifiers (SVM, DT & MNB) gave a slightly higher F_1 score of 58%.

Table 3 shows the scores of the relation classification subtask on noisy training data (subtask 1.2).

Classifier	#Features	P	R	F_1
SVM	13,200	0.59	0.56	**0.56**
DT	3,400	0.58	0.53	0.54
RF	6,600	0.38	0.42	0.40
MNB	2,300	0.40	0.79	0.53
kNN	7,800	0.43	0.30	0.35
Ensemble-all	–	0.56	0.42	0.48
Ensemble-best	–	0.57	0.63	**0.58**

Table 2: Precision, recall and F-scores of individual and ensemble classifiers on subtask 1.1. The scores are micro-averaged over 11 classes. Ensemble-best is SVM+DT+MNB.

Classifier	#Features	P	R	F_1
SVM	9,700	0.71	0.70	**0.69**
DT	7,200	0.72	0.66	0.65
RF	8,900	0.60	0.58	0.53
MNB	3,700	0.70	0.67	0.62
kNN	6,700	0.48	0.70	0.57
Ensemble-all	–	0.57	0.71	0.63
Ensemble-best	–	0.81	0.67	**0.73**

Table 3: Result of individual and ensemble classifiers on subtask 1.2. Scores are micro-averaged over 11 classes. Ensemble-best is SVM+RF+MNB.

As individual classifier, SVM gave the best performance with 69% F_1 score followed by Decision Trees (65%) and Multinomial Naïve Bayes (62%). The best performance of voting classifiers scored 73% using the classifiers SVM, RF and MNB.

Table 4 shows the results of the relation identification in subtask 2. Again SVM gave the best single classifier level performance.

5 Discussion

The total relation instances in the clean data and in the noisy data are almost the same (1228 and 1248, respectively). However, it is interesting to observe that the best performance in relation classification both at the single classifier level and in ensemble voting on noisy data (subtask 1.2) is significantly higher than on clean data (subtask 1.1). This behaviour is consistent also on the test data.

One explanation may be the differences in relation expressions in dataset D_1 and D_2. In the clean data (D_1), 25.66% of the entity mentions have three or more words with a maximum length of 13 words, whereas in the noisy data (D_2) only 0.96%

Classifier	#Features	P	R	F_1
SVM	18,100	0.39	0.46	**0.42**
DT	5,800	0.50	0.29	0.36
RF	6,300	0.33	0.26	0.29
MNB	4,900	0.43	0.30	0.35
KNN	8,100	0.14	0.25	0.18
Ensemble-all	–	0.31	0.26	0.28
Ensemble-best	–	0.44	0.31	**0.36**

Table 4: Performance of positive class in relation identification on clean data (subtask 2). Ensemble-best is SVM+DT+MNB.

of the mentions have more than three words. The feature-based approach with n-grams as major feature source might not be able to capture the semantics of entity mentions having very large text spans. Furthermore, the context length between entity pairs in the clean data is larger than in the noisy data. Therefore, the shortest dependency paths and context n-grams—which are the two major feature sources—generate many insignificant features. Modeling the relation instances through a neural network could be a better alternative in this scenario.

Feature selection has a positive impact on prediction both in relation identification and in classification. SVM gave the best results at the single classifier level on all subtasks, but needs a larger feature space, whereas MNB performed reasonably although needing the smallest number of features for training the classifier.

6 Conclusion

In this work, we experimented with the relation identification and classification subtasks of SemEval 2018 Task 7 using a feature-based approach. A wide variety of features are explored, including lexical, syntactic, semantic, and other binary features. Two relation classification systems are developed on clean and noisy data and the third system is developed to identify relations in clean data. Five classifiers are trained for each subtask, with the final predictions made through voting based on the corresponding predictions of the individual classifiers. Experimental results shows that the lengths of the entity mentions and the lengths of the context in-between a pair of entities have significant impact on the relation identification and relation classification.

References

Isabelle Augenstein, Mrinal Das, Sebastian Riedel, Lakshmi Vikraman, and Andrew McCallum. 2017. Semeval 2017 task 10: ScienceIE—extracting keyphrases and relations from scientific publications. In *Proceedings of the 11th International Workshop on Semantic Evaluation (SemEval-2017)*, pages 546–555, Vancouver, Canada.

Biswanath Barik and Erwin Marsi. 2017. NTNU-2 at SemEval-2017 Task 10: Identifying synonym and hyponym relations among keyphrases in scientific documents. In *Proceedings of the 11th International Workshop on Semantic Evaluation (SemEval-2017)*, pages 965–968, Vancouver, Canada.

Biswanath Barik, Erwin Marsi, and Pinar Öztürk. 2017. Extracting causal relations among complex events in natural science literature. In *International Conference on Applications of Natural Language to Information Systems*, pages 131–137, Liège, Belgium. Springer.

Razvan C. Bunescu and Raymond J. Mooney. 2005. A shortest path dependency kernel for relation extraction. In *Proceedings of the Conference on Human Language Technology and Empirical Methods in Natural Language Processing*, pages 724–731, Vancouver, Canada.

Cláudia Freitas, Diana Santos, Cristina Mota, Hugo Gonçalo Oliveira, and Paula Carvalho. 2009. Relation detection between named entities: report of a shared task. In *Proceedings of the Workshop on Semantic Evaluations: Recent Achievements and Future Directions*, pages 129–137, Boulder, Colorado. ACL.

Kata Gábor, Davide Buscaldi, Anne-Kathrin Schumann, Behrang QasemiZadeh, Haïfa Zargayouna, and Thierry Charnois. 2018. Semeval-2018 task 7: Semantic relation extraction and classification in scientific papers. In *Proceedings of International Workshop on Semantic Evaluation (SemEval-2018)*, New Orleans, Louisiana.

Kata Gábor, Haïfa Zargayouna, Davide Buscaldi, Isabelle Tellier, and Thierry Charnois. 2016. Semantic annotation of the ACL anthology corpus for the automatic analysis of scientific literature. In *LREC 2016*, pages 3694–3701, Portorož, Slovenia.

Iris Hendrickx, Su Nam Kim, Zornitsa Kozareva, Preslav Nakov, Diarmuid Ó Séaghdha, Sebastian Padó, Marco Pennacchiotti, Lorenza Romano, and Stan Szpakowicz. 2009. Semeval-2010 task 8: Multi-way classification of semantic relations between pairs of nominals. In *Proceedings of the Workshop on Semantic Evaluations: Recent Achievements and Future Directions*, pages 94–99, Boulder, Colorado. ACL.

Jing Jiang and ChengXiang Zhai. 2007. A systematic exploration of the feature space for relation extraction. In *Human Language Technologies 2007: The Conference of the North American Chapter of the Association for Computational Linguistics; Proceedings of the Main Conference*, pages 113–120, Rochester, New York.

Nanda Kambhatla. 2004. Combining lexical, syntactic, and semantic features with maximum entropy models for information extraction. In *Proceedings of the 42nd Annual Meeting of the Association for Computational Linguistics: Interactive Poster and Demonstration Sessions*, Barcelona, Spain. ACL. Paper 22.

Christopher Manning, Mihai Surdeanu, John Bauer, Jenny Finkel, Steven Bethard, and David McClosky. 2014. The Stanford CoreNLP natural language processing toolkit. In *Proceedings of 52nd Annual Meeting of the Association for Computational Linguistics: System Demonstrations*, pages 55–60, Baltimore, Maryland. ACL.

Erwin Marsi, Pinar Øzturk, Elias Aamot, Gleb Sizov, and Murat Van Ardelan. 2014. Towards text mining in climate science: Extraction of quantitative variables and their relations. In *Proceedings of Bio-Text Mining*, Reykjavik, Iceland. European Language Resources Association.

George A. Miller. 1995. WordNet: a lexical database for English. *Communications of the ACM*, 38(11):39–41.

Makoto Miwa and Mohit Bansal. 2016. End-to-end relation extraction using LSTMs on sequences and tree structures. In *Proceedings of the 54th Annual Meeting of the Association for Computational Linguistics*, pages 1105–1116, Austin, Texas.

F. Pedregosa, G. Varoquaux, A. Gramfort, V. Michel, B. Thirion, O. Grisel, M. Blondel, P. Prettenhofer, R. Weiss, V. Dubourg, J. Vanderplas, A. Passos, D. Cournapeau, M. Brucher, M. Perrot, and E. Duchesnay. 2011. Scikit-learn: Machine learning in Python. *Journal of Machine Learning Research*, 12:2825–2830.

Pontus Stenetorp, Sampo Pyysalo, Goran Topić, Tomoko Ohta, Sophia Ananiadou, and Jun'ichi Tsujii. 2012. BRAT: A web-based tool for NLP-assisted text annotation. In *Proceedings of the 13th Conference of the European Chapter of the Association for Computational Linguistics: Demonstrations*, pages 102–107, Jeju Island, Republic of Korea. ACL.

Dmitry Zelenko, Chinatsu Aone, and Anthony Richardella. 2003. Kernel methods for relation extraction. *Journal of Machine Learning Research*, 3(Feb):1083–1106.

Daojian Zeng, Kang Liu, Siwei Lai, Guangyou Zhou, and Jun Zhao. 2014. Relation classification via convolutional deep neural network. In *Proceedings of COLING 2014, the 25th International Conference on Computational Linguistics: Technical Papers*, pages 2335–2344, Dublin, Ireland.

Talla at SemEval-2018 Task 7: Hybrid Loss Optimization for Relation Classification using Convolutional Neural Networks

Bhanu Pratap, Daniel Shank, Oladipo Ositelu, Byron V. Galbraith

Talla Inc.

Boston, MA, USA

{bhanu, daniel, ladi, byron}@talla.com

Abstract

This paper describes our approach to SemEval-2018 Task 7 – given an entity-tagged text from the ACL Anthology corpus, identify and classify pairs of entities that have one of six possible semantic relationships. Our model consists of a convolutional neural network leveraging pre-trained word embeddings, unlabeled ACL-abstracts, and multiple window sizes to automatically learn useful features from entity-tagged sentences. We also experiment with a hybrid loss function, a combination of cross-entropy loss and ranking loss, to boost the separation in classification scores. Lastly, we include WordNet-based features to further improve the performance of our model. Our best model achieves an F1(macro) score of 74.2 and 84.8 on subtasks 1.1 and 1.2, respectively.

1 Introduction

Classifying the relationship between entities is an important natural language processing (NLP) task that serves as a building block for a variety of NLP applications such as knowledge base construction and question-answering tasks. SemEval-2018 Task 7 (Gábor et al., 2018) provided entity-tagged texts from the ACL Anthology corpus and asked participants to identify and classify entity pairs into one of six semantic relationships.

Our approach to this problem consisted of selecting two architectures shown to be successful (Zeng et al., 2014; Nguyen and Grishman, 2015) in this problem domain and adapting them to this particular task. We found that pre-trained word embeddings were effective for this problem, as well as a combined loss function, and using Word-Net features at a later stage of our model.

Sentence: High quality <e1>**translation**</e1> via <e2>**word sense disambiguation**</e2> and accurate word order generation of the target language .

Relation: USAGE

Figure 1:   An example of sentence-level relation Instance. Sentences marked with entity positions were the input to our model.

2 System Description

Convolutional neural networks (CNNs) have been proven to significantly outperform other methods for Relation Classification (Zeng et al., 2014; dos Santos et al., 2015; Nguyen and Grishman, 2015). Our approach was inspired by Nguyen and Grishman (2015) and dos Santos et al. (2015), both systems being minimally dependent on explicit feature engineering. While Nguyen and Grishman (2015) relied solely on their model architecture to automatically extract useful features, we also included additional features based on part-of-speech tags and WordNet hypernyms. Following dos Santos et al. (2015), we trained our model on a hybrid objective function, a combination of cross entropy loss and ranking loss. Finally, we also trained our model in two stages to utilize large amounts of unlabeled ACL corpus abstracts (Bird et al., 2008). We describe these stages in detail in section 4.1.

Each abstract is first tokenized into sentences. For each sentence, we then formed training examples by taking all combinations of pairs of entities annotated in the sentence. If a pair is annotated with a relation label, we labeled the sentence as this relation. Otherwise, we labeled the sentence as an artificial class called *OTHER* . Figure 1 shows an example of a training instance in our sentence-level dataset.

For an input sentence, each word was mapped to a word-vector to form a sentence matrix. These sentence matrices were provided as inputs to the

Proceedings of the 12th International Workshop on Semantic Evaluation (SemEval-2018), pages 863–867
New Orleans, Louisiana, June 5–6, 2018. ©2018 Association for Computational Linguistics

CNN. The output of this layer was then fed into a softmax layer to classify the relationship between two entities. Section 3 provides a detailed description of the underlying CNN.

3 Convolutional Neural Network for Relation Classification

Our model consists of a preprocessing feature generation step followed by a 2D convolutional layer with max pooling and then a fully connected layer with softmax output.

3.1 Preprocessing and Feature Generation

The input to our model was a raw sentence marked with entity positions. This raw sentence was first converted into a real-valued sentence matrix by tokenizing the sentence and then replacing each token with a corresponding word embedding. We used three different look-up tables: publicly available pre-trained word embeddings, randomly initialized word positions, and randomly initialized part-of-speech tags. Following Collobert et al. (2011), the final word embedding for each token in the sentence was a concatenation of these three embeddings.

For pre-trained word embeddings, we evaluated word2vec (Mikolov et al., 2013), GloVe (Pennington et al., 2014), and Numberbatch (Speer and Chin, 2016), ultimately choosing word2vec as the best performer for this task.

The specific process used to generate the feature vector for a given token in a sentence is as follows. Let n be the number of tokens in a sentence $x = [x_1, x_2, ..., x_n]$ with x_{i_1} and x_{i_2} being the two head words of the two entities in relationship r. Relative positions between a token x_i and two entities are given by $(i - i_1)$ and $(i - i_2)$. These positions are also mapped into real-valued vectors using a position embeddings look-up table W_p. Also, W_e, and W_t embeddings look-up tables are used to map each word and its part-of-speech tag into a real valued vector. Finally, x_i is transformed into a vector $v_i = [e_i; u_{i_1}; u_{i_2}; t_i]^T$, where v_i is the concatenation of vectors $e_i, u_{i_1}, u_{i_2}, t_i$, e_i is the word-vector mapped using the W_e look-up table, u_{i_1} and u_{i_2} are the word-position vectors mapped using the W_p look-up table, and t_i is the word-part-of-speech vector mapped using the W_t look-up table. Dimension d of the final input vector is given by $d = (d_e + 2 * d_p + d_t)$, where d_e, d_p and d_t are the dimensions of pre-trained word-embeddings, word-position embeddings and word-part-of-speech tag embeddings. As a result of these look-up operations, the raw sentence $x = [x_1, x_2, ..., x_n]$ is transformed into a real-valued sentence matrix $\mathbf{x} = [\mathbf{x_1}, \mathbf{x_2}, ..., \mathbf{x_n}]$ of size $d \times n$.

3.2 2D Convolution with Max Pooling

We used multiple window sizes to extract features corresponding to various n-grams. Let w be a window size and n_w be the number of unique window sizes, a filter $\mathbf{f} = [\mathbf{f_1}, \mathbf{f_2}, .., \mathbf{f_w}]$ is a weight matrix where $\mathbf{f_i}$ is a column vector of size $d = (d_e + 2 * d_p + d_t)$. A convolutional operation is then performed using $\mathbf{x}$ and $\mathbf{f}$ to produce a feature map $s = [s_1, s_2, ..., s_{n-w+1}]$ as:

$$s_i = g(\sum_{j=0}^{w-1} f_{j+1}^T x_{j+i}^T + b)$$

where b and g are bias and ReLU (Nair and Hinton, 2010) activation function respectively. This convolutional operation was repeated for different filters and window sizes, and then a max pooling strategy Zhang and Wallace (2017) was applied to extract only 1 feature (the one with highest activation) from each feature map. That is, for each feature map s, a max function was applied to produce a single value: $p_f = max(s)$.

3.3 Classification Layer

We took all the individually selected features from the max pooling operation and concatenated them together, producing $z = [p_1, p_2, ..., p_m]$, where m is the number of feature maps and p_i is the pooled value for i^{th} feature map. A random proportion of input vector z was set to zero for regularization purposes to produce a drop-out version z_d of input vector z. The vector z_d was then fed into a dense layer followed by a softmax operation to produce the final classification probability for a relation class r as:

$$\mathbf{o} = \mathbf{C z_d} + \mathbf{b}$$

$$p(r|\theta) = \frac{e^{o_i}}{\sum_{k=1}^{L} e^{o_k}}$$

where $\mathbf{o}$ is the output of the dense layer, $\mathbf{b}$ is a bias term, L is the number of relation categories, and $\mathbf{C}$ is a weight matrix of size $(n_w m \times L)$ with n_w being the number of unique window sizes and m being the number of filters.

3.4 Additional Features

In addition to the output of the CNN layer, we explored a variety of additional features derived from the input sentences.

Part-of-speech features, *pos* We randomly initialized embeddings for each part-of-speech tag and used these embeddings as additional input to our network. Part-of-speech tags for raw sentences were generated using *spaCy*[1].

WordNet hypernym features, *hyp* We incorporated WordNet hypernyms using the implementation[2] provided by Ciaramita and Altun (2006).

Semantic Similarity between two entities, *sim* We computed the cosine similarity between the word-embeddings of the head-words of the two entities in a relation instance.

REVERSE flag feature, *rev* We applied an indicator function on the REVERSE flag of the relationship instance.

We fed *hyp*, *sim* and *rev* features as additional inputs to the classification layer. While *pos* features were provided as input to the convolution layer.

4 Training Methods

We evaluated three different loss functions for training our model: cross-entropy loss, ranking loss (dos Santos et al., 2015), and a weighted combination of the two, where

$$L_{combined} = \alpha L_{ranking} + (1 - \alpha) L_{cross\ entropy}$$

with α as a weighting parameter. The combined loss function was determined to be the most effective.

4.1 Two-Staged Training

To make use of unlabeled data for fine-tuning word-position and word-part-of-speech embeddings, we trained our model in two-stages following Severyn and Moschitti (2015): a *distant* training stage and a *supervised* training stage.

Distant Training We first created a distantly supervised training dataset using unlabeled ACL corpus abstracts (Bird et al., 2008) based on the naive assumption that *two entities have the same relationship across all aligned sentences*. By aligned sentences, we mean all sentences which have exactly two entities. In order to create distantly supervised training data based on the above assumption, we performed the following operations:

i) All the sentences in the ACL-corpus were indexed in an IR system. Here we used *Whoosh*[3].

ii) For each relation instance in the labeled training data, the top 40 sentences which contained both the entity texts in the relation were returned from the IR system.

iii) Result sentences in which the distance (number of characters) between the two entity texts was greater than 170 were removed. This number was derived from distance statistics from given labeled datasets.

iv) The remaining sentences were labeled with the same relationship as the relation instance in (ii).

Following above steps, we created distant-datasets of around 1600 and 11000 training instances for subtasks 1.1 and 1.2, respectively. We also verified that there is no overlap between these generated distant-datasets and the provided test datasets.

Once the distantly supervised training data is created, we train our model using these datasets to fine-tune only word-position and part-of-speech tag embeddings, while keeping word-embeddings fixed.

Supervised Training In the second stage, we initialized our model with the fine-tuned embeddings trained in the distantly supervised training stage and then train our model using the provided labeled training data. In this stage we also train word-embeddings but freeze them for first 10 epochs to prevent any large updates.

5 Experiments and Results

The class labels for subtasks 1.1 and 1.2 are highly imbalanced (Table 1). To compensate for this imbalance, we trained our models for subtasks 1.1 and 1.2 jointly on a combined dataset and used class-weights to weight our loss function.

5.1 Resources and Hyperparameters

We chose all the hyperparameters based on the model performance on our validation set. All experiments below use the hyperparameters as shown in Table 2.

---

[1] spacy.io
[2] sourceforge.net/projects/supersensetag/
[3] http://Whoosh.readthedocs.io/en/latest/index.html

Class	Train 1.1	Test 1.1	Train 1.2	Test 1.2
USAGE	0.39	0.49	0.38	0.35
PART-WHOLE	0.19	0.20	0.16	0.16
MODEL-FEATURE	0.27	0.19	0.14	0.21
COMPARE	0.08	0.06	0.03	0.01
RESULT	0.06	0.06	0.10	0.08
TOPIC	0.01	0.01	0.19	0.19
n	1228	355	1249	355

Table 1: Distribution of classes within datasets. Here, n is the total number of instances in a dataset.

Parameter	Value
Window Sizes	2,3,4,5
Number of Filters	25
Word-Embeddings Size (d_e)	300
Word-Position Embeddings Size (d_p)	25
Positive Class Margin (m^+)	2.5
Negative Class Margin (m^-)	0.5
λ	1.0
α	0.1
learning rate	0.01

Table 2: Hyperparameters used in all experiments.

Our final model is a soft-voting ensemble of the best models obtained using 10-fold stratified cross-validation. All the models were implemented using *TensorFlow*[4]. We trained our models using a stochastic gradient descent optimizer with momentum (Sutskever et al., 2013). Lastly, based on our experiments, we chose the 300-dimensional word2vec pre-trained word embeddings trained on the Google News corpus.

5.2 Evaluation

Model	F1-Macro Subtask 1.1	F1-Macro Subtask 1.2
CNN	72.8	84.1
CNN+*pos*	72.1	82.8
CNN+*pos*+*hyp*	**74.4**	82.4
CNN+ *pos*+*hyp*+*sim*	73.7	**84.8**[a]
CNN+*pos*+*hyp*+*sim*+*rev*	74.2[b]	84.7
—"— (2-staged)	73.9	84.7
Overall Best(DS3Lab)	81.7	90.4

[a] *our official submission ranked second*
[b] *our official submission ranked fifth*

Table 3: Performance of our final model on Subtasks 1.1 and 1.2. Additional features are incrementally added to our plain CNN model. Here *(2-staged)* refers to the results of our experiments using 2-staged training method.

Table 3 shows the results of our ablation studies using different feature sets on subtasks 1.1 and 1.2. It shows that the simple similarity (*sim*) feature helps in case of subtask 1.2, while it degrades the performance in case of subtask 1.1. Similarly, WordNet features with part-of-speech features boosted the performance only of subtask 1.1. Fine tuning using the two-staged training approach did not yield any performance gain in either the subtasks.

We also evaluated the effect of loss function choice. Table 4 shows the results of our final

Loss Function	F1-Macro Subtask 1.1	F1-Macro Subtask 1.2
Cross Entropy Loss	72.7	83.9
Ranking Loss	70.6	81.5
Combined Loss	**74.2**	**84.7**

Table 4: Effect of Loss Functions

model trained on different loss functions. A combination of ranking loss and cross entropy loss does yield a performance boost.

While we did not provide a formal submission for subtask 2, we evaluated our approach on it given the labeled test data. Table 5 shows the re-

Model	F1-Macro Subtask 2(ANY)
CNN	35.0
CNN+*pos*	**36.6**
CNN+*pos*+*hyp*	34.7
Overall Best(UWNLP)	50.0

Table 5: Performance of our final model on Subtask 2(Relation Extraction).

sults of our experiments on subtask 2 (relation extraction). While this method did not outperform the top submissions, it still demonstrated competitive results.

6 Conclusion

Our experiments indicate that pre-training on an unlabeled corpus did not noticeably impact performance on our evaluation set. Our plain CNN model (without any external features) has comparable performance to the competition's best submission. We also observed improved performance of our model on Subtask 1.1 when using the Word-Net features as additional input to the final layer. Finally, when we combine the cross-entropy and ranking loss functions, performance of our model improved on both Subtasks 1.1 and 1.2.

[4]https://www.tensorflow.org/

References

Steven Bird, Robert Dale, Bonnie Dorr, Bryan Gibson, Mark Joseph, Min-Yen Kan, Dongwon Lee, Brett Powley, Dragomir Radev, and Yee Fan Tan. 2008. The acl anthology reference corpus: A reference dataset for bibliographic research in computational linguistics. In *Proceedings of the Sixth International Conference on Language Resources and Evaluation (LREC-08)*, Marrakech, Morocco. European Language Resources Association (ELRA). ACL Anthology Identifier: L08-1005.

Massimiliano Ciaramita and Yasemin Altun. 2006. Broad-coverage sense disambiguation and information extraction with a supersense sequence tagger. In *Proceedings of the 2006 Conference on Empirical Methods in Natural Language Processing*, EMNLP '06, pages 594–602, Stroudsburg, PA, USA. Association for Computational Linguistics.

Ronan Collobert, Jason Weston, Léon Bottou, Michael Karlen, Koray Kavukcuoglu, and Pavel Kuksa. 2011. Natural language processing (almost) from scratch. *J. Mach. Learn. Res.*, 12:2493–2537.

Kata Gábor, Davide Buscaldi, Anne-Kathrin Schumann, Behrang QasemiZadeh, Haïfa Zargayouna, and Thierry Charnois. 2018. Semeval-2018 Task 7: Semantic relation extraction and classification in scientific papers. In *Proceedings of International Workshop on Semantic Evaluation (SemEval-2018)*, New Orleans, LA, USA.

Tomas Mikolov, Ilya Sutskever, Kai Chen, Greg Corrado, and Jeffrey Dean. 2013. Distributed representations of words and phrases and their compositionality. In *Proceedings of the 26th International Conference on Neural Information Processing Systems - Volume 2*, NIPS'13, pages 3111–3119, USA. Curran Associates Inc.

Vinod Nair and Geoffrey E. Hinton. 2010. Rectified linear units improve restricted boltzmann machines. In *ICML*, pages 807–814. Omnipress.

Thien Huu Nguyen and Ralph Grishman. 2015. *Relation extraction: Perspective from convolutional neural networks*.

Jeffrey Pennington, Richard Socher, and Christopher D. Manning. 2014. Glove: Global vectors for word representation. In *Proceedings of the 2014 Conference on Empirical Methods in Natural Language Processing, EMNLP 2014, October 25-29, 2014, Doha, Qatar, A meeting of SIGDAT, a Special Interest Group of the ACL*, pages 1532–1543.

CÃcero Nogueira dos Santos, Bing Xiang, and Bowen Zhou. 2015. Classifying relations by ranking with convolutional neural networks. In *ACL (1)*, pages 626–634. The Association for Computer Linguistics.

Aliaksei Severyn and Alessandro Moschitti. 2015. Unitn: Training deep convolutional neural network for twitter sentiment classification. In *SemEval@NAACL-HLT*, pages 464–469. The Association for Computer Linguistics.

Robert Speer and Joshua Chin. 2016. An ensemble method to produce high-quality word embeddings. *CoRR*, abs/1604.01692.

Ilya Sutskever, James Martens, George Dahl, and Geoffrey Hinton. 2013. On the importance of initialization and momentum in deep learning. In *Proceedings of the 30th International Conference on International Conference on Machine Learning - Volume 28*, ICML'13, pages III–1139–III–1147. JMLR.org.

Daojian Zeng, Kang Liu, Siwei Lai, Guangyou Zhou, and Jun Zhao. 2014. Relation classification via convolutional deep neural network. In *COLING 2014, 25th International Conference on Computational Linguistics, Proceedings of the Conference: Technical Papers, August 23-29, 2014, Dublin, Ireland*, pages 2335–2344.

Ye Zhang and Byron C. Wallace. 2017. A sensitivity analysis of (and practitioners' guide to) convolutional neural networks for sentence classification. In *IJCNLP(1)*, pages 253–263. Asian Federation of Natural Language Processing.

TeamDL at SemEval-2018 Task 8: Cybersecurity Text Analysis using Convolutional Neural Network and Conditional Random Fields

Manikandan R [1]*, Krishna Madgula[2], Snehanshu Saha[1,2]
[1]CAMMS, Dept of CSE ,PESIT-Bangalore South Campus
[2]PESIT-Bangalore South Campus
`manikandan.ravikiran@gmail.com`
`krishnac.madgula@gmail.com`
`snehangshusaha@gmail.com`

Abstract

In this paper we present our participation to SemEval-2018 Task 8 subtasks 1 & 2 respectively. We developed Convolution Neural Network system for malware sentence classification (subtask 1) and Conditional Random Fields system for malware token label prediction (subtask 2). We experimented with couple of word embedding strategies, feature sets and achieved competitive performance across the two subtasks. Code is made available at `https://bitbucket.org/vishnumani2009/securenlp`

1 Introduction

Cybersecurity risks and malware threats are becoming common and increasingly dangerous requiring analysis of large repositories of malware related information in realtime to understand its capabilities and mount an effective defense. The sheer volume of data and its potential applications alone have increased traction in recent times among NLP researchers. In this line, SemEval 2018 Task-8 offers 4 subtasks addressing text classification and token, relation and attribute label prediction in cybersecurity domain using MalwareTextDB (Lim et al., 2017). While subtask 1 focuses on predicting sentences relevance to malware , subtasks 2, 3 and 4 focus on predicting token, relation and attribute labels for malware text from subtask 1. More details about the each of the subtasks can be found in Phandi et al. (2018).

Concerning subtask 1, which was inherently formulated as a text classification problem very few works are done till date in cybersecurity domain (Lim et al., 2017; Zhang et al., 2016). However, in general domain the problem of text classification is well addressed with extensive usage of deep learning approaches (Zhou et al., 2016; Liang and Zhang, 2016; Kim, 2014; Kalchbrenner et al., 2014; Zhang et al., 2015), Support vector machines, logistic regression (Genkin et al., 2007; Jiang et al., 2016) and Tree based approaches (Bouaziz et al., 2014). On the other hand, subtask 2 was formulated as sequence tagging problem which is addressed till date by CRF (Finkel et al., 2005; R. et al., 2016, 2017), deep learning approaches (Chiu and Nichols, 2016; Ma and Hovy, 2016; Lample et al., 2016) and SVM (Ekbal and Bandyopadhyay, 2012).

In this paper, we describe our system that addresses subtasks 1 and 2 involving malware sentence classification and malware token label prediction. We designed these systems by adapting various insights from previous works on text classification and sequence tagging. We submitted a Convolutional Neural Network(CNN) based system based system for subtask 1 and Conditional Random Field (CRF) based system for subtask 2.

The rest of the paper is organized as follows. In section section 2, we discuss datasets and preprocessing. In section 3, we describe the algorithms and features used in the process of model development. In section 4, we describe our results and some of our findings. Finally in section 5, we conclude with summary and possible implications on future work.

2 Dataset and Preprocessing

The MalwareTextDB corpus used for this work consists of APT reports describing malware reported information taken from APTnotes[1]. We designed an end-to-end pipeline consisting on three module which process input text across multiple stages. In stage 1, the input sentence is fed to a preprocessing module which pre-processes the

---

*Work performed during weekend part time assistantship at CAMMS

[1]https://github.com/aptnotes/

Proceedings of the 12th International Workshop on Semantic Evaluation (SemEval-2018), pages 868–873
New Orleans, Louisiana, June 5–6, 2018. ©2018 Association for Computational Linguistics

Token	Placeholder
`C:/ProgramData/Mail/`	`__PATH__`
`www.ducklink.com/`	`__URL__`
`securityblog@gdata.de`	`__EMAILID__`
`profapi.dll`	`__EXE__`
`"epsilon"`	`__SPECIAL__`

Table 1: Tokens and placeholders used in stage 1

text for stage 2 where the sentence are subject to classification and finally stage 3 sequence tags the tokens of the input sentence. We used following preprocessing steps in stage 1.

1. All the words are lower-cased.

2. All the words that can be grouped under common category were replaced by a category placeholder as shown in table 1.

We used following opensource tools 1) Stanford Core-NLP (Manning et al., 2014) 2) Keras (Chollet et al., 2015) 3) CNTK (Seide and Agarwal, 2016) 4) Gensim (Řehůřek and Sojka, 2010) 5) NLTK for preprocessing (Loper and Bird, 2002) 6) Scikit-learn (Pedregosa et al., 2011) for grid search 7) Glove (Pennington et al., 2014).

3 Model

In this section, we explain the algorithms and hyperparameters used for system development. More specifically, in section 3.1 we explain our CNN architecture for subtask 1 and in section 3.2 we show our CRF architecture for subtask 2.

3.1 Algorithm - Subtask 1

For subtask 1, we focused more towards deep learning. Previous works (Yin et al., 2017) suggests that both Convolutional Neural Network (CNN) and Recurrent Neural Network (RNN) architectures has been successfully applied for various instances of text classification analysis at various level. With most of recent works (Zhang and Wallace, 2017) showing success of CNN, we developed a CNN architecture based on work of Kim (2014). The architecture developed in this work is as shown in figure 1.

3.1.1 Convolutional Neural Network

Our CNN architecture was derived from original works of Kim (2014) by using grid search over input channel size, number of convolution layers and number of filters. We use a multichannel model architecture with five input channels for processing

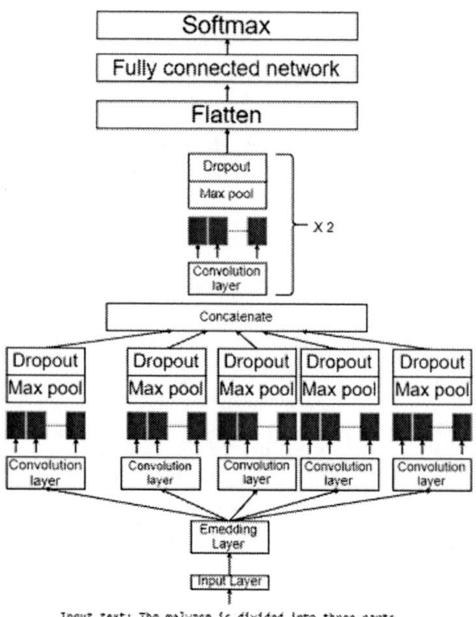

Figure 1: CNN Architecture

2-6 grams of input malware text. Each channel is comprised of the following elements:

1. Input layer that defines the length of input sequences.

2. Embedding layer set to the size of the vocabulary and 100-dimensional real-valued representations.

3. One-dimensional convolutional layer with 128 filters and a kernel size set to the number of words to read at once.

4. Channel wise Pooling layer with pool size of 5 to consolidate the output from the convolutional layer.

Following CNN, we use a Fully Connected Neural Network (FCNN) to transfer the the concatenated feature map (600 dimension) to a probability distribution over the two class labels. The number of layers in FCNN is set to be 2. The first layer uses 128 units with a tanh activation function. The second layer produces the classification probability distribution over 2 units combined with a softmax activation function.

Further to handle overfitting we use regularization via dropout (Srivastava et al., 2014) with

Feature	Value
Sentence pad length	1000
Dimensions of wordvectors	100
Number of CNN layers	8
Dimension of CNN layers	1
Number of CNN filters	128
Activation function	relu
Initialization function	Xavier
Number of FC layers	2
Dimension of 1st FC layers	128
Dimension of 2nd FC layers	2
Activation of Final layer	Softmax
Optimizer	Adam
Batch size	32
Max Epoch	10
Loss function	Cross Entropy

Table 2: Hyper parameters of CNN

	Word2vec			Glove		
	P	**R**	**F**	**P**	**R**	**F**
test17	0.47	0.77	0.58	0.48	0.78	0.47
dev18	0.18	0.32	0.23	0.35	0.80	0.18
test18	0.24	0.34	0.28	0.38	0.72	0.50

Table 3: Results of subtask 1 on native Embeddings

	Word2vec-Task			Glove-Task		
	P	**R**	**F**	**P**	**R**	**F**
test17	0.28	0.50	0.36	0.43	0.71	0.54
dev18	0.18	0.30	0.22	0.33	0.72	0.45
test18	0.20	0.30	0.24	0.38	0.67	0.48

Table 4: Results of subtask 1 on task specific embeddings

threshold of 0.25. Additionally, we also apply cost sensitive learning (Zhou and Liu, 2006) in order to balance the effect of the larger negative samples present in the training dataset. For each class, we assigned weight proportional to class frequency. We implemented the neural network model using Keras. We trained our networks using Adam optimizer (Kingma and Ba, 2014). All the hyper parameters are listed in table 2.

3.1.2 Input Embeddings

We experimented with two category of word embeddings namely native embeddings and task specific embedding using Word2vec (Le and Mikolov, 2014) and Glove (Pennington et al., 2014) algorithms. Characteristics of each of the embedding is as explained below.

1. **Native Embeddings**: All words including the unknown ones that are randomly initialized use embeddings from original Word2vec/Glove models.

2. **Task specific** : The embeddings are generated by training Word2vec/Glove algorithms on sentences from MalwareTextDB.

3.2 Algorithm - Subtask 2

For subtask 2, we developed a Conditional Random Field (CRF) system (Finkel et al., 2005) based on previous works of Lim et al.(2017).

3.2.1 Conditional Random Fields

We used Conditional Random Fields with following features that is available as part of Stanford CoreNLP ToolKit.

Common Features: N-grams of size 6, previous, next tokens and labels, features giving disjunctions of words anywhere in the left or right,

word shape features, word lemma of current, previous and next words, word-tag pair features, POS tags, prefix and suffixes. The description of the features are given in CoreNLP(2014).

Additional features: Based on analysis of corpus, to tackle unknown malware entities we used a gazette with token that describes malware entity. These tokens were taken from training corpus and internet[2].

4 Experiments and Results

In this section, we present results for each of the developed systems. The original dataset was split into **train17, test-17**[3] released at the start of competition and **dev-18, test-18** released during the competition pre-evaluation period for tuning of parameters and final evaluation respectively . We submitted CNN system for subtask 1 and CRF system for subtask 2. Tables 3-5 show the results of subtasks 1 and 2 respectively across the datasets. Our systems achieve F-score of 0.5 for subtask 1 and 0.25, 0.36 for subtask 2 over strict, relaxed runs of subtask 2.

4.1 Discussion

In previous sections we described the system developed for malware text analysis using which we achieved competitive performance for subtask 1 and subtask 2.

For subtask 1, we developed a CNN system and experimented the same with different embedding strategies as explained in section 3.1.2. Across all

---

[2]https://www.mcafee.com/threat-intelligence/malware/
[3](train/dev/test)-(17/18) is not an official naming convention , instead used here for ease of understanding

	CRF-Strict			CRF-Relaxed		
	P	**R**	**F**	**P**	**R**	**F**
test17	0.51	0.26	0.34	0.45	0.36	0.40
dev18	0.18	0.25	0.21	0.38	0.22	0.29
test18	0.29	0.23	0.25	0.42	0.30	0.36

Table 5: Results of subtask 2 on Conditional Random fields

the subset of datasets, glove embeddings consistently outperformed Word2Vec embeddings. This is in line with works of Kim (2014). We initially hypothesized that since "the context of the malware texts are different from normal English texts", task-specific embeddings would improve the results of subtask 1. However, we observe that task specific embeddings produced lower results compared to native embeddings. Observations of results revealed high false negative predictions of non-malware texts, we believe that this may attributed to limited dataset used for developing embeddings, unlike native embeddings which was created using very large corpus. This results also agrees the general observation, that the size of the training corpus has often a greater impact on results than its strict matching with the target domain(Tourille et al., 2017).

For subtask 1, we achieved an accuracy of 0.50 and were 7% behind the top performing systems. We identified three different sources of errors across the sentences in line with previous works(Lim et al., 2017) namely misclassification of i) Sentences consisting of malware related keywords without implication on actions; ii) Sentences describing attacker actions and additionally we also found iii) misclassification of sentences containing specific patterns like presence of _PATH_ and _EXE_. Further, we had initially hoped that the multichannel architecture would prevent overfitting(Kim, 2014) and thus work better than the single channel model, especially on small datasets like MalwareTextDB. The results, however, are vice versa and hence further work on regularizing the training process and simpler single channel architecture is warranted.

For subtask 2, during analysis we found that there were multiple malware names which were previously unseen and felt only orthographic features would be insufficient. Hence in addition to commonly used features, we also included gazette features with words that quantify malware entity. However, during evaluation on development set

we found high drop in precision when we used gazette features owing to its deterministic nature. Hence, we submitted CRF only with common features described in section 3.2.1 for final evaluation. With this system we achieved a result of 0.25 and 0.36 in strict and relaxed evaluation respectively. Our accuracy is 3.5% (avg) behind the top performing system across the evaluations. We identified following sources of errors i) Tagging of tokens in sentences containing only actions but not entities - these are sentences with only attackers actions in line with error from subtask 1 ii) Lack of sensitivity to context - some tokens in test document are given same label from train irrespective of context iii) Miss tagging of some of the tokens with common suffixes. For subtask 2, we experimented with simple CRF architecture with basic features, hence we believe further exploration of future engineering is needed to reduce context related errors. As far as addressing rest of the errors, we plan to explore combination of rule based and deep learning approaches.

5 Conclusion

In this work, we developed CNN and CRF systems for malware text classification and token label prediction, achieving competitive results. For subtask 1, we experimented with couple of word embedding strategies and found native glove embedding to be useful. For subtask 2, we used CRF with simple features achieving results closer to top performing system and above the official benchmark. Further, we described various sources of errors identified in the due process of analysis. In future, we plan to further improve our system to show higher performance based on the above observations.

Acknowledgments

We thank the task organizers for providing access to MalwareTextDB corpus and organizing the shared task. Further, we would like to thank various authors for open sourcing the codes of various algorithms used in this work.

References

Ameni Bouaziz, Christel Dartigues-Pallez, Célia da Costa Pereira, Frédéric Precioso, and Patrick Lloret. 2014. Short text classification using semantic random forest. In *DaWaK*.

Jason P. C. Chiu and Eric Nichols. 2016. Named entity recognition with bidirectional lstm-cnns. *TACL*, 4:357–370.

François Chollet et al. 2015. Keras. `https://github.com/fchollet/keras`.

Stanford CoreNLP. 2014. Nerfeaturefactory. `https://nlp.stanford.edu/nlp/javadoc/javanlp/edu/stanford/nlp/ie/NERFeatureFactory.html`.

Asif Ekbal and Sivaji Bandyopadhyay. 2012. Named entity recognition using support vector machine: A language independent approach.

Jenny Rose Finkel, Trond Grenager, and Christopher D. Manning. 2005. Incorporating non-local information into information extraction systems by gibbs sampling. In *ACL*.

Alexander Genkin, David D. Lewis, and David Madigan. 2007. Large-scale bayesian logistic regression for text categorization. *Technometrics*, 49:291–304.

Mingyang Jiang, Yanchun Liang, Xiaoyue Feng, Xiaojing Fan, Zhili Pei, Yu Xue, and Renchu Guan. 2016. Text classification based on deep belief network and softmax regression. *Neural Computing and Applications*, pages 1–10.

Nal Kalchbrenner, Edward Grefenstette, and Phil Blunsom. 2014. A convolutional neural network for modelling sentences. In *ACL*.

Yoon Kim. 2014. Convolutional neural networks for sentence classification. In *EMNLP*.

Diederik P. Kingma and Jimmy Ba. 2014. Adam: A method for stochastic optimization. *CoRR*, abs/1412.6980.

Guillaume Lample, Miguel Ballesteros, Sandeep Subramanian, Kazuya Kawakami, and Chris Dyer. 2016. Neural architectures for named entity recognition. In *HLT-NAACL*.

Quoc V. Le and Tomas Mikolov. 2014. Distributed representations of sentences and documents. In *ICML*.

Depeng Liang and Yongdong Zhang. 2016. Acblstm: Asymmetric convolutional bidirectional lstm networks for text classification. *CoRR*, abs/1611.01884.

Swee Kiat Lim, Aldrian Obaja Muis, Wei Lu, and Ong Chen Hui. 2017. Malwaretextdb: A database for annotated malware articles. In *ACL*.

Edward Loper and Steven B Bird. 2002. Nltk: The natural language toolkit. *CoRR*, cs.CL/0205028.

Xuezhe Ma and Eduard H. Hovy. 2016. End-to-end sequence labeling via bi-directional lstm-cnns-crf. *CoRR*, abs/1603.01354.

Christopher D. Manning, Mihai Surdeanu, John Bauer, Jenny Rose Finkel, Steven Bethard, and David McClosky. 2014. The stanford corenlp natural language processing toolkit. In *ACL*.

Fabian Pedregosa, Gaël Varoquaux, Alexandre Gramfort, Vincent Michel, Bertrand Thirion, Olivier Grisel, Mathieu Blondel, Peter Prettenhofer, Ron Weiss, Vincent Dubourg, Jacob VanderPlas, Alexandre Passos, David Cournapeau, Matthieu Brucher, Matthieu Perrot, and Edouard Duchesnay. 2011. Scikit-learn: Machine learning in python. *Journal of Machine Learning Research*, 12:2825–2830.

Jeffrey Pennington, Richard Socher, and Christopher D. Manning. 2014. Glove: Global vectors for word representation. In *EMNLP*.

Peter Phandi, Amila Silva, and Wei Lu. 2018. Semeval-2018 Task 8: Semantic Extraction from CybersecUrity REports using Natural Language Processing (SecureNLP). In *Proceedings of International Workshop on Semantic Evaluation (SemEval-2018)*, New Orleans, LA, USA.

Sarath P. R., Manikandan R, and Yoshiki Niwa. 2016. Hitachi at semeval-2016 task 12: A hybrid approach for temporal information extraction from clinical notes. In *SemEval@NAACL-HLT*.

Sarath P. R., Manikandan R, and Yoshiki Niwa. 2017. Hitachi at semeval-2017 task 12: System for temporal information extraction from clinical notes. In *SemEval@ACL*.

Radim Řehůřek and Petr Sojka. 2010. Software Framework for Topic Modelling with Large Corpora. In *Proceedings of the LREC 2010 Workshop on New Challenges for NLP Frameworks*, pages 45–50, Valletta, Malta. ELRA. `http://is.muni.cz/publication/884893/en`.

Frank Seide and Amit Agarwal. 2016. Cntk: Microsoft's open-source deep-learning toolkit. In *KDD*.

Nitish Srivastava, Geoffrey E. Hinton, Alex Krizhevsky, Ilya Sutskever, and Ruslan Salakhutdinov. 2014. Dropout: a simple way to prevent neural networks from overfitting. *Journal of Machine Learning Research*, 15:1929–1958.

Julien Tourille, Olivier Ferret, Xavier Tannier, and Aurélie Névéol. 2017. Limsi-cot at semeval-2017 task 12: Neural architecture for temporal information extraction from clinical narratives. In *SemEval@ACL*.

Wenpeng Yin, Katharina Kann, Mo Yu, and Hinrich Schütze. 2017. Comparative study of cnn and rnn for natural language processing. *CoRR*, abs/1702.01923.

Xiang Zhang, Junbo Jake Zhao, and Yann LeCun. 2015. Character-level convolutional networks for text classification. In *NIPS*.

Ye Zhang and Byron C. Wallace. 2017. A sensitivity analysis of (and practitioners' guide to) convolutional neural networks for sentence classification. In *IJCNLP*.

Yunan Zhang, Qingjia Huang, Xinjian Ma, Zeming Yang, and Jianguo Jiang. 2016. Using multifeatures and ensemble learning method for imbalanced malware classification. *2016 IEEE Trustcom/BigDataSE/ISPA*, pages 965–973.

Peng Zhou, Zhenyu Qi, Suncong Zheng, Jiaming Xu, Hongyun Bao, and Bo Xu. 2016. Text classification improved by integrating bidirectional lstm with two-dimensional max pooling. In *COLING*.

Zhi-Hua Zhou and Xu-Ying Liu. 2006. Training cost-sensitive neural networks with methods addressing the class imbalance problem. *IEEE Transactions on Knowledge and Data Engineering*, 18:63–77.

HCCL at SemEval-2018 Task 8: An End-to-End System for Sequence Labeling from Cybersecurity Reports

Mingming Fu [1,2], Xuemin Zhao [1], Yonghong Yan [1,2,3]

[1]The Key Laboratory of Speech Acoustics and Content Understanding
Institute of Acoustics, Chinese Academy of Sciences
[2]University of Chinese Academy of Sciences
[3]Xinjiang Laboratory of Minority Speech and Language Information Processing
Xinjiang Technical Institute of Physics and Chemistry, Chinese Academy of Sciences
{fumingming, zhaoxuemin, yanyonghong}@hccl.ioa.ac.cn

Abstract

This paper describes HCCL team systems that participated in SemEval 2018 Task 8: SecureNLP (Semantic Extraction from cybersecurity reports using NLP). To solve the problem, our team applied a neural network architecture that benefits from both word and character level representaions automatically, by using combination of Bi-directional LSTM, CNN and CRF (Ma and Hovy, 2016). Our system is truly end-to-end, requiring no feature engineering or data preprocessing, and we ranked 4th in the subtask 1, 7th in the subtask 2 and 3rd in the SubTask2-relaxed.

1 Introduction

Recently, cybersecurity defense has also been recognized as one of the problem areas likely to be important both for advancing AI and for its long-run impact on society. In particular, natural language processing (NLP) has the potential for substantial contribution in cybersecurity and that this is a critical research area given the urgency and risks involved (Lim et al., 2017).

In SemEval 2018 Task 8 (Phandi et al., 2018), there are four subtask:

1. SubTask1: Classify if a sentence is useful for inferring malware actions and capabilities

2. SubTask2: predict the token labels in the sentences. The output needs to be in BIO format. There are 3 types of token labels: "Action", "Entity", and "Modifier".

3. SubTask3: predict the relations between the token labels

4. SubTask4: predict the attributes for each entity token

In this evaluation, our team submitted the results of Subtask 1 and Subtask 2. To tackle this problem, we treat subtask 2 as a sequence labeling problem. Most traditional high performance sequence labeling models are linear statistical models, including Hidden Markov Models (HMM) and Conditional Random Fields (CRF) (Luo et al., 2015), which rely heavily on hand-crafted features and taskspecific resources.

Recently, many neural network based methods have been successfully applied to sequence labeling task: Named Entity Recognition (Lample et al., 2016). In this paper, we present an end-to-end System (combined CNN, LSTM and CRF) for sequence labeling that uses no complicated handcrafted features or domain knowledge. LSTM is capable of learning long-term dependencies, which is beneficial to sequence modeling tasks. And character level CNN can get character-level representation. For sequence labeling (or general structured prediction) tasks, it is beneficial to consider the correlations between labels in neighborhoods and jointly decode the best chain of labels for a given input sentence. So we model label sequence jointly using a conditional random field (CRF), instead of decoding each label independently. Therefore, the system we proposed is based on CNN, Bi-directional LSTM and CRF. And in the SubTask2-relaxed our group ranked third. As for SubTask1, we proposed a ruled based method that if any token in the sentence is labled "Action", "Entity", or "Modifier", the sentence would be considered relevant. Our team ranked 4th in the subtask 1.

2 System Description

In this section, we describe the components (layers) of our end-to-end system. We design our model with CNN-BiLSTM-CRF that combined word level representation, character level representation and POS representation as feature in-

Proceedings of the 12th International Workshop on Semantic Evaluation (SemEval-2018), pages 874–877
New Orleans, Louisiana, June 5–6, 2018. ©2018 Association for Computational Linguistics

put, and outperform than the baseline in subtask2-relaxed.

2.1 Feature Embedding

Feature representation as the meta input of neural network have received a great deal of attention, and there are many outstanding achievements. In our system, the word level embedding is trained by the Google's Word2Vec (Mikolov et al., 2013) tool. Previous studies (Santos and Guimaraes, 2015; Chiu and Nichols, 2015)have shown that CNN is an effective approach to extract morphological information (like the prefix or suffix of a word) from characters of words and encode it into neural representations. To get more diverse information, our team decided to use Part-Of-Speech(POS) as extra feature input.

Word level Embeddings: Taking into account the particularity of the cybersecurity, we use the evaluation data to train our own word embeddings. Word level embeddings are trained by Word2Vec[1], and we set embedding dim = 300.

Character level Embeddings: Character level embeddings are random initialization(trainable), and we set embedding dim = 30.

POS Embeddings: POS embeddings are random initialization(trainable), and we set embedding dim = 30.

2.2 Model

We provide a brief description of CNN, LSTM and CRF, and present a hybrid sequence labeling architecture. This architecture is similar to the ones presented by (Ma and Hovy, 2016).

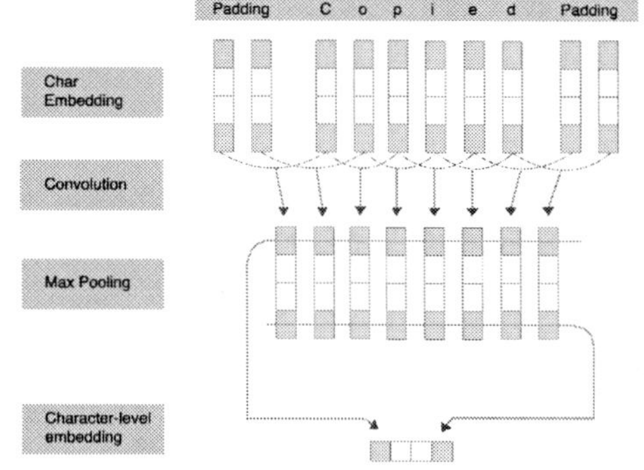

Figure 1: The CNN network for extracting character-level embedding of words.

---

[1]https://code.google.com/archive/p/word2vec/

2.2.1 CNN

Figure 1 shows the CNN we use to extract character-level representation of a given word. The CNN is similar to the (Chiu and Nichols, 2015), except that we use only character embeddings as the inputs to CNN, without character type features. A dropout layer (Srivastava et al., 2014) is applied before character embeddings are input to CNN.

2.2.2 LSTM

Recurrent neural networks (RNNs) are a family of neural networks that operate on sequential data. Although RNN can, in theory, learn long dependencies, in practice they fail to do so and tend to be biased towards their most recent inputs in the sequence (Bengio et al., 1994). Long Short-term Memory Network (LSTM) have been designed to combat this issue by incorporating a memory-cell and have been shown to capture long-range dependencies. They do so using several gates that control the proportion of the input to give to the memory cell, and the proportion from the previous state to forget (Hochreiter and Schmidhuber, 1997). We use the following implementation:

We will refer to the former as the forward LSTM and the latter as the backward LSTM. This forward and backward LSTM pair is referred to as a bidirectional LSTM (Graves and Schmidhuber, 2005; Dyer et al., 2015).The basic idea is to present each sequence forwards and backwards to two separate hidden states to capture past and future information, respectively.

2.2.3 CRF

For sequence labeling (or general structured prediction) tasks, it is beneficial to consider the correlations between labels in neighborhoods and jointly decode the best chain of labels for a given input sentence. Therefore, we model label sequence jointly using a conditional random field (CRF) (Lafferty et al., 2001), instead of decoding each label independently.

For a sequence CRF model (only interactions between two successive labels are considered), training and decoding can be solved efficiently by adopting the Viterbi algorithm.

2.2.4 CNN-BiLSTM-CRF

Finally, we construct our neural network model by feeding the output vectors of BiLSTM into a

CRF layer. Figure 2 illustrates the architecture of our network in detail. For each word, the character-level is computed by the CNN in Figure 1 with character embeddings as inputs, and we use NLTK[2] to get POS information. Then the character-level representation vector the POS representation vector are concatenated with the word embedding vector to feed into the BiLSTM network. Finally, the output vectors of BiLSTM are fed to the CRF layer to jointly decode the best label sequence. As shown in Figure 2, dropout layers are applied on both the input and output vectors of BiLSTM. Experimental results show that using dropout significantly improve the performance of our model.

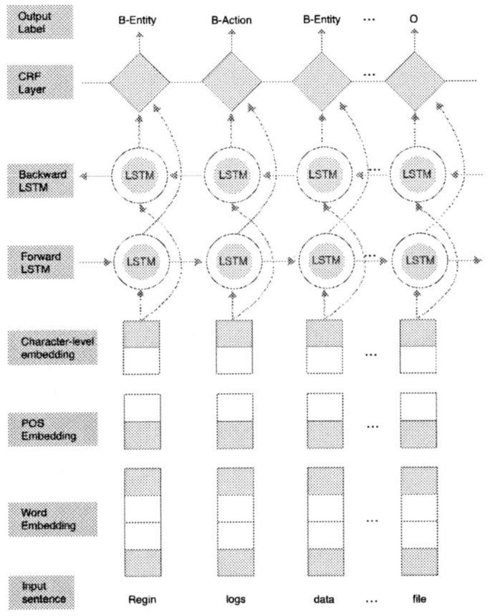

Figure 2: Main architecture of the network. Concatenated feature embeddings are given to BiLSTM.

3 Experiments and Results

3.1 Training

For model presented, we train our networks using the back-propagation algorithm updating our parameters on every training batch, using Adam with a learning rate of 0.001 and a gradient clipping of 5.0. Our CNN-BiLSTM-CRF model uses a single layer for the forward and backward LSTMs whose dimensions are set to 300. Tuning this dimension did not significantly impact model performance. We set the dropout rate to 0.5. Using

higher rates negatively impacted our results, while smaller rates led to longer training time. The models were implemented in TensorFlow[3] and experiments were run on K80 GPU.

3.2 Result

In this work, our team submitted the subtask 1 and subtask 2 results. The results of all the teams are shown in Table 2.

For subtask1, its goal is to classify if a sentence is relevant for inferring malware actions and capabilities. We make use of the result in subtask2 for this subtask and consider a sentence to be relevant as long as it has an annotated token label. Table 2 shows that our system is ranked 4th and behave better than baseline for subtask1.

For subtask2, our CNN-BiLSTM-CRF model is then trained to predict token labels from cybersecurity reports. From Table 2 we can see that in subtask2, our system is slightly worse than the baseline. However, our system has a 22.5% improvement in subtask2-relaxed than baseline.

3.3 Error Analysis

For subTask1, a lot of non-malware sentences are regarded as malware sentences. May be due to the fact that we use the subTask2 output to estimate whether the current sentence is non-malware sentence or malware sentence, so the errors of subTask2 will affect subTask1. And both non-malware sentences and malware sentences contain annotated tokens.

For subTask2, we find that many unannotated tokens are labeled as annotated tokens and annotated tokens are not labeled. By analyzing the data, we found that the same words occurring as both unannotated and annotated tokens in the sentences, which might make our system achieve a low F-score.

4 Conclusion

In this paper we presented the system we used to compete in the SemEval-2018 Semantic Extraction from cybersecurity reports using NLP competition. Our goal is to implement a deep learning based end-to-end system that can solve cross domain sequence labeling issues without complicated feature engineering.

For future work, it would be interesting to explore systems that can solve the problem of self-

---

[2]http://www.nltk.org/

[3]https://www.tensorflow.org/

Team	SubTask1	SubTask2	SubTask2-relaxed
Team 1	0.57	0.23	0.31
Team 2	0.57	0.28	0.36
Team 3	0.52	0.29	0.39
Our Team	**0.52 (4)**	**0.22 (7)**	**0.38 (3)**
Team 5	0.52	0.16	0.25
Team 6	0.50	0.25	0.36
Team 7	0.49	0.28	0.39
Team 8	0.18	0.22	0.32
Team 9	0.15	0.21	0.28
Baseline	0.51	0.23	0.31

Table 1: Results on subtask1 and subtask2.

adaptation between different domains. And transfer learning might be a way to handle the lack of labeled data.

5 Acknowledgments

This work is partially supported by the National Natural Science Foundation of China (Nos. 11590770-4, 61650202, U1536117, 61671442, 11674352, 11504406, 61601453), the National Key Research and Development Program (Nos. 2016YFB0801203, 2016YFC0800503) and the Key Science and Technology Project of the Xinjiang Uygur Autonomous Region (No. 2016A03007-1).

References

Yoshua Bengio, Patrice Y Simard, and Paolo Frasconi. 1994. Learning long-term dependencies with gradient descent is difficult. *IEEE Transactions on Neural Networks*, 5(2):157–166.

Jason P C Chiu and Eric Nichols. 2015. Named entity recognition with bidirectional lstm-cnns. *Transactions of the Association for Computational Linguistics*, 4(0):357–370.

Chris Dyer, Miguel Ballesteros, Wang Ling, Austin Matthews, and Noah A Smith. 2015. Transition-based dependency parsing with stack long short-term memory. *meeting of the association for computational linguistics*, pages 334–343.

Alex Graves and Jurgen Schmidhuber. 2005. Framewise phoneme classification with bidirectional lstm networks. 4:2047–2052.

Sepp Hochreiter and Jurgen Schmidhuber. 1997. Long short-term memory. *Neural Computation*, 9(8):1735–1780.

John D Lafferty, Andrew Mccallum, and Fernando Pereira. 2001. Conditional random fields: Probabilistic models for segmenting and labeling sequence data. pages 282–289.

Guillaume Lample, Miguel Ballesteros, Sandeep Subramanian, Kazuya Kawakami, and Chris Dyer. 2016. Neural architectures for named entity recognition. pages 260–270.

Swee Kiat Lim, Aldrian Obaja Muis, Wei Lu, and Chen Hui Ong. 2017. Malwaretextdb: A database for annotated malware articles. In *Proceedings of the 55th Annual Meeting of the Association for Computational Linguistics (Volume 1: Long Papers)*, volume 1, pages 1557–1567.

Gang Luo, Xiaojiang Huang, Chin Yew Lin, and Zaiqing Nie. 2015. Joint entity recognition and disambiguation. In *Conference on Empirical Methods in Natural Language Processing*, pages 879–888.

Xuezhe Ma and Eduard Hovy. 2016. End-to-end sequence labeling via bi-directional lstm-cnns-crf. In *Proceedings of the 54th Annual Meeting of the Association for Computational Linguistics (Volume 1: Long Papers)*, pages 1064–1074, Berlin, Germany. Association for Computational Linguistics.

Tomas Mikolov, Kai Chen, Greg Corrado, and Jeffrey Dean. 2013. Efficient estimation of word representations in vector space. *arXiv: Computation and Language*.

Peter Phandi, Amila Silva, and Wei Lu. 2018. Semeval-2018 Task 8: Semantic Extraction from CybersecUrity REports using Natural Language Processing (SecureNLP). In *Proceedings of International Workshop on Semantic Evaluation (SemEval-2018)*, New Orleans, LA, USA.

Cicero Nogueira Dos Santos and Victor Guimaraes. 2015. Boosting named entity recognition with neural character embeddings. *arXiv: Computation and Language*, pages 25–33.

Nitish Srivastava, Geoffrey E Hinton, Alex Krizhevsky, Ilya Sutskever, and Ruslan Salakhutdinov. 2014. Dropout: a simple way to prevent neural networks from overfitting. *Journal of Machine Learning Research*, 15(1):1929–1958.

UMBC at SemEval-2018 Task 8: Understanding Text about Malware

Ankur Padia[1], Arpita Roy[1], Taneeya Satyapanich[1], Francis Ferraro[1], Shimei Pan[1],
Youngja Park[2], Anupam Joshi[1], Tim Finin[1]

[1] University of Maryland, Baltimore County
Baltimore, MD, 21250 USA
{pankur1,arpita2,taneeya1,ferraro,shimei,joshi,finin}@umbc.edu
[2] IBM T. J. Watson Research Center
Yorktown Heights, New York, USA
young_park@us.ibm.com

Abstract

We describe the systems developed by the UMBC team for 2018 SemEval Task 8, SecureNLP (Semantic Extraction from CybersecUrity REports using Natural Language Processing). We participated in three of the subtasks: (1) classifying sentences as being relevant or irrelevant to malware, (2) predicting token labels for sentences, and (4) predicting attribute labels from the Malware Attribute Enumeration and Characterization vocabulary for defining malware characteristics. We achieved F1 scores of 50.34/18.0 (dev/test), 22.23 (test-data), and 31.98 (test-data) for Task1, Task2 and Task2 respectively. We also make our cybersecurity embeddings publicly available at https://bit.ly/cybr2vec.

1 Introduction

Task 8 for SemEval 2018 asked participants to work on a set of related sub-tasks involving analyzing information from text about malware drawn from the Advanced Persistent Threats Notes collection (Blanda and Westcott, 2018) using the semantic framework found in the Malware Attribute Enumeration and Characterization language (Kirillov et al., 2011; Beck et al., 2014). The task was composed of four related sub-tasks that could be part of a processing pipeline for an information extraction system for cybersecurity related text (Phandi et al., 2018).

Subtask 1 required classifying a sentence as being relevant or irrelevant for inferring malware actions and capabilities. Subtask 2 involved predicting token labels for entities, actions and modifiers in sentences. Subtask 3, which we did not undertake, expanded on subtask 2 by asking participants to label relevant relations between the entities. Subtask 4 required predicting more detailed attribute labels, including ActionName, Capability,

StrategicObjectives and TacticalObjectives, drawn from the MAEC vocabulary.

One of our aims is to better understand the differences between cybersecurity text and general, non-cybersecurity text; another is to also better understand differences and variation within cybersecurity texts. To that end, we focus on learning and extracting better representations of the input reports. Specifically, for our approaches, we focus on approaches that incorporate additional, domain-specific knowledge into our system, and we use these enhanced representations and features in well-studied classification, representation, and sequence prediction models.

2 Subtask 1

In this section we describe our approaches to classify a given sentence as relevant or irrelevant to malware. We used logistic regression (LR), multi-layer perceptron (MLP), and Long-Short Term Memory (Hochreiter and Schmidhuber, 1997, LSTM) as classifiers, and we used multiple encoding schemes to represent features for the classification task.

2.1 Models

We experimented with and evaluated three different techniques for implementing the Subtask 1 relevance classifier. Each approach used similar features; we opted for bag-of-words or bag-of-embeddings due to their simplicity and competitive performance (Wang and Manning, 2012).

- **Logistic Regression**: We used logistic regression, as a baseline classifier with an L2 penalty of 10.

- **Multi-Layer Perceptron**: We used two architectures for MLP for two different kinds of input; one was bag-of-words, the other

Proceedings of the 12th International Workshop on Semantic Evaluation (SemEval-2018), pages 878–884
New Orleans, Louisiana, June 5–6, 2018. ©2018 Association for Computational Linguistics

	LR			MLP		
	ACC	**AUC**	**F1**	**ACC**	**AUC**	**F1**
Avg. Binary BOW	**89.78**	**81.58**	**47.9**	**90.85**	**77.44**	**46.89**
Binary BOW	78.9	79.29	32.98	65.05	77.77	25.61
Avg. Count BOW	89.94	79.31	46.49	91.01	75.76	45.77
Count BOW	78.4	81.38	33.84	83.35	75.2	33.99
Wiki embeddings	93.49	50	0	93.49	50	0
Cyber embeddings	88.38	79.65	43.82	83.51	82.35	39.02

Table 1: Performance on Task 1 (dev-data) for each of the model we implemented. We used the best MLP model for SemEval submission (test-data) and had F1 score of 18. We found LR and MLP to always label majority class resulting in zero F1 score using Wiki embeddings.

was dense embeddings. When the input representation was bag-of-words, we used one hidden layer of dimension 32 followed by a classification layer. When embeddings were used we used a network of three hidden layers followed by a classification layer; we found adding up to 3 layers to the network helped improving training accuracy. We used L2 regularization (Tibshirani, 1996) of 0.1 and dropout (Srivastava et al., 2014) of 0.1 to avoid overfitting. We fixed the value of dropout and experimented with multiple values of L2 and chose one giving the best performance on the development dataset. Performance decreased gradually when L2 penalty was either increased to $\{0.2, 0.25, 0.5\}$ or decreased to $\{0.01, 0.001, 0.0001\}$. We set the size of the hidden layer to 100 when embeddings were used.

- **LSTM (for embeddings)**: We applied an LSTM network with one hidden layer of size 128. We used dense, pre-trained embeddings (§2.2) for each word in the input sentence.

2.2 Features for the models

We experimented with the following four feature sets in order to determine the best performing representation for Task 1.

- **(Average) Count Bag-Of-Words**: We created standard bag-of-words features from the training dataset. We experimented with normalizing each vector via averaging.

- **(Average) Binary Bag-Of-Words**: We also considered binary bag-of-words features, by replacing each term frequency count with binary value where positive value is set to one and a negative value to zero. We also experimented with normalizing each feature vector by averaging.

- **Cybersecurity embeddings**: The cybersecurity embeddings were generated using word2vec Skipgram model with negative samplings of 100 dimension and a window size of five (Mikolov et al., 2013b) on one million cybersecurity related documents.[1]

- **Wikipedia embeddings**: We generated 400 dimensional word2vec skip-gram embeddings from a recent Wikipedia dump. We used a window size of 5.[2]

2.3 Datasets, embeddings & hyperparameters

For Subtask 1, we used all 65 files available as part of SemEval Task 8. We tuned and tested our model on development data available as part of SemEval. For logistic regression we swept the L2 regularization coefficient ($\{100, 10, 1, 0.1, 0.01, 0.001\}$) and chose the value that gave best performance on the development dataset. For neural approaches we used stochastic gradient descent with momentum of 0.4 for LSTM and 0.9 for MLP. We tried multiple learning rates and chose one which gave best performance on the development dataset. We chose starting learning rate of 0.2 for LSTM and 0.1 for MLP. We also tried using Adam optimizer (Kingma and Ba, 2014) with the same learning rate as MLP but found the resulting model labeled all test instances with the majority class.

For our implementation we used Keras (Chollet,

---

[1]We used an embedding model produced by IBM Research trained on a collection of 1 million cybersecurity-related documents with a vocabulary size of 6.4 millions words and 100 dimensions.

[2]Reported models use the 20180220 English Wikipedia dump; we did not notice large differences in performance when using this vs. an earlier version for the competition.

	LSTM		
	ACC	**AUC**	**F1**
Wiki embeddings	80.21	82.35	35.83
Cyber embeddings	**93.98**	**72.05**	**50.34**

Table 2: LSTM Performance (dev data). We offer these as supplementary evaluations.

2015) with a Tensorflow backend to train neural network based models and Gensim (Řehůřek and Sojka, 2010) to train word embeddings. We used Scikit-learn (Pedregosa et al., 2011) for Logistic Regression. For the LSTM, we let the size of the input sequence be the maximum length of all sentences in the batch and padded shorter sentences with zero vectors.

The input was a matrix of dimension $l \times d$ where d is the size of embedding vector and l is the length of the longest sentence.

2.4 Discussion

As evident from Tables 1 and 2, the neural network based classifiers perform better compared to other methods depending on the features.

However, we find a considerable gap between the score from Table 1 and 2. As explained later, we believe that the models' low scores are related to the scope of the task. Overall, the LSTM performs better compared to the MLP due its ability to capture subtle nuances.

We note the positive impact that domain-centered cybersecurity embeddings have. Nevertheless, not all cybersecurity texts may accurately reflect other cybersecurity texts, especially ones with the task-specific annotations as considered here. We posit that the performance of all our models, in particular the LSTM, may be improved with embeddings that are learned from documents more representative of those evaluated.[3]

Comparing the results of Wikipedia embeddings and embeddings trained on cybersecurity text we found Wikipedia based embeddings to consistently perform poorly. We believe one of the reasons Wikipedia embeddings performed poorly for this task is due to less overlap between the technicality of the task and content.

Moreover the F1 score is zero sometimes as the features are rich enough to classify positive instance and predicts only negative (as evident from

---

| **False Positive**: Attackers always use this minimal effort approach in order to bypass a victim s defenses. |
| **False Negative**: Trojan.Karagany first checks for a live Internet connection by visiting Microsoft or Adobe websites. |
| **General Information**: The group has used two main malware tools: Trojan.Karagany and Backdoor.Oldrea. |

Table 3: Task 1 classification examples.

AUC). On the other hand, the cybersecurity embeddings performed better when compared with Wikipedia embeddings, due to the more focused corpus, but we believe there is scope to improve the quality of embeddings. Frequency based features tend to perform better than binary features; averaging the features improves the performance score across all classifiers.

2.5 Error analysis

Among the classifiers, the MLP makes mistakes by getting caught into to domain specific words that occur frequently, like *attack* and *attackers*, and skips less frequent but indicative words like *Trojan.Karagany*. Additionally we found the MLP incorrectly classifies general sentences as relevant. We demonstrate examples in Table 3.

Looking at the example sentences from 3, we see that whether or not a sentence is "relevant" is task-dependent. For example, the general information sentence above could be useful for identifying relationships among different malware instances or families. However, the sentence would be irrelevant in the context of action and capabilities of a particular malware mention.

3   Subtask 2

In this section we describe our approach for Task 2, which required participants to predict token labels for malware-related documents. The Task 2 system served as an automatic labeling tool using one of four labels:

- `Action`, referring to an malware-related event;

- Entities, referring to either `Subjects` or `Objects` in the malware-related sentence; or

- `Modifiers`, referring to prepositions that link between action and phrases.

---

[3]The actual collection of APT notes included about 400 documents, vs. the 1 million documents trained on broader cybersecurity texts.

Each label is represented by a tag using the inside, outside, beginning (IOB) format (Ramshaw and Marcus, 1999). The performance was measured using F1 score and the relaxed measurement by omitting the IOB tags.

3.1 Our Approach

We extended the previous work Lim et al. (2017), who trained a conditional random field (CRF) on unigram and bigram features of the surface words, part-of-speech tags and Brown clustering signatures (Brown et al., 1992). Like Lim et al. (2017), we also trained a CRF. Our features include:

- unigrams and bigrams of words in the dependency parse tree,

- unigrams and bigrams of the word lemmas,

- wordshape equivalence class analysis (Christopher, 2016), and

- Brown clustering signatures from a larger APT collection .

The word's context, which are words in the window of size three, was included. These features were extracted using Stanford CoreNLP (Manning et al., 2014). We did not use the surface word as in development we found it yielded lower performance. The dependency function will help to recognize the similar sentence by comparing similar sentence's structure. The wordshape features represent the classes of upper case, lower case, digits, and punctuations, and also groups the sequence of the same class. The wordshape features help to recognize named entities.[4]

We trained our own Brown clustering features (Liang, 2005) with our own APT corpus of 456 APT files from 2008 to 2017. We experimented with the Brown clustering hyperparameters: the Brown cluster size (1000,10000) and its prefix length (6,8,10,12,16). The best result from the experiment is the prefix of size 8 and cluster size 1000. We built our own Brown clustering for two reasons. First, we will not be able to identify Brown clustering feature when we encounter out of vocabulary word; we found the larger corpus to partially alleviate this concern. Second, we believed that the bigger size of the corpus, with an appropriate clustering size and prefix length, would yield better clustering features.

---

[4] We use the 'dan2' wordshape classes from CoreNLP (Manning et al., 2014).

	P	R	F1
Action	24.50	39.20	30.15
Entity	11.26	17.34	13.65
Modifier	29.37	46.84	36.10
Average	18.22	28.54	22.24

Table 4: Official Task 2 scores on Test set

	P	R	F1
Action	25.67	50.00	33.92
Entity	23.71	45.45	31.16
Modifier	29.92	48.10	36.89
Average	24.42	46.31	31.98

Table 5: Official Task 2 relaxed/token-level scores on Test set

3.2 Experimental Results

We used the CRF++ toolkit (Kudo, 2005) to develop our conditional random field (CRF) models. For the official evaluation, we ran our system on Test set provided by SemEval2018. The test set contains 13,080 tokens in total. The official scoring reported our F1 performance of 22 for strict scoring, and 32 for relaxed scoring. Our F1-score for subtask 2 are generally on par with the baselines (23 for the strict, and 31 for the relaxed, measures). Detailed performance analyses are shown in Tables 4 and 5.

3.3 Discussion

Table 4 demonstrates that our system performance of predicting Entity is lower than Action and Modifier. We believe this is because malware-related entities are different from other text; in particular, they can be quite long. For example, the following (gold test) entity is a long clause with complex syntactic structure: *'method of leaving the encoded file on disk and only decoding it in memories.'* This entire clause is labeled as an Entity. Despite the dependency features, our system cannot identify these long spans as an entity. Another example of this limitation is shown in Figure 1. This is a rich area for future improvement.

4 Subtask 4

In this section we describe our approach for task 4. The task is to predict attribute labels (ActionName, Capability, StrategicObjectives and TacticalObjectives) for a given malware-related text

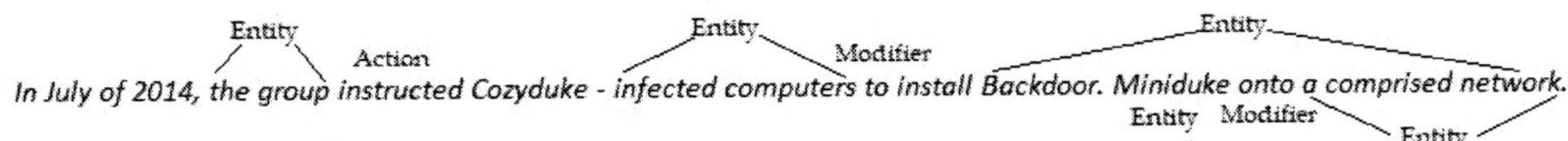

Figure 1: An example of wrong prediction of Task 2. Above the line is the gold standard annotation. Under the line is our predictions.

describing action of a malware.

4.1 Our Approach

For this task we focus on learning better quality word embedding features for a classifier, as classifier performance depends on the quality of its features. In addition to encoding semantics present in the text via embeddings, we want to encode domain specific knowledge in the embeddings. For this purpose, we developed an Annotation Word Embedding (AWE) model that is capable of incorporating diverse types of domain knowledge, such as metadata, keyword information, ontology knowledge, and manual annotation. The AWE model learns to predict this knowledge from the text, resulting in better quality embedding since domain knowledge can be incorporated in the embeddings. We then train a classifier with these high quality word embedding features to classify attribute labels.

4.1.1 Annotation Word Embedding

The AWE model's learning task is to predict annotations and context words given a target word. A sliding window on the input text generates the training samples. In each sliding window the task is to use target word to predict its own annotation as well as the context words. Formally, we maximize the log probability of context words and annotations given target word.

Given a sequence of T training words $(W_1, W_2 ... W_{t-1}, W_t, W_{t+1} ... W_T)$ and their annotations $((A_{1,1}, A_{1,2} ... A_{1,M_1}), (A_{2,1} ... A_{2,M_2}) ... (A_{T,1}, ... A_{T,M_T}))$, our objective is to maximize the average log probability shown in Equation 1:

$$\frac{1}{T} \sum_{t=1}^{T} \left(\sum_{-C \leq j \leq C, j \neq 0} \log P(W_{t+j}|W_t) + \sum_{0 \leq k \leq M_t} \log P(A_{t,k}|W_t) \right) \quad (1)$$

where C is the size of the context window, W_t is the target word, W_{t+j} is a context word, $A_{t,k}$ is the kth annotation of target word W_t. In addition to using the target word to predict context words, like Mikolov et al. (2013a)'s skipgram model, the AWE embedding model predicts annotations of target word using target word itself.

4.2 Experiments

To train the AWE model we used all 456 APT reports as text corpus. In addition we used keywords for each attribute label described in MAEC vocabulary (Kirillov et al., 2011) and gold annotation given for 65 APT reports available as part of the SemEval task to create text annotation.

To create text annotation we collected keywords from attribute label descriptions and extracted the token groups from the gold annotations. Token groups consist of the subject, action and object linked to each other via relation labels. We used these token words and keywords to create text annotation; we deleted stop words.

For example, one token group extracted from gold annotation is "these configuration issued commands to attack following domain and IPs." After deleting stop words this token group we get "configuration," "issued," "commands," "attack," "domain," and "IPs." In the gold annotation, this token group has label Capability12 in attribute category of Capability. In MAEC vocabulary (Kirillov et al., 2011) keywords given for this capability label are "machine access," "control," "execute," "terminate," and "create." All these token words and keywords will have an annotation of Capability12 in our AWE model.

After creating the text annotation we train an AWE model with 100 dimension feature vectors, window size 5 and negative sampling. After training embeddings we use these embeddings to create features for classifier. We use average embeddings of all the words in each token group to create classifier instance. We use SVM as classifier. On the test dataset we get F-score of 0.19.

4.3 Discussion

This task is one of the most challenging tasks because of data sparsity and large number of attribute labels. In fact, out of the 444 attribute labels, 185 labels do not appear in dataset. For the remaining 259 attribute labels 169 labels occur less than five times. In addition, among 3348 instances there are 2298 instances without any ActionName attribute, 642 instances without a Capability attribute, 1244 instances without a StrategicObjective attribute and 1675 instances without a TacticalObjective attribute.

To improve classifier performance future work can try training a classifier that focuses on the common classes, with non frequent classes labeled as "other." Applying other techniques like similarity score to classify infrequent classes may also be beneficial. Additionally, we noticed that in the gold annotation there are often missing relation labels. This missing relation labels result in incomplete token group as token groups are tokens linked by relation labels.

5 Conclusion

We described the systems developed by the UMBC team for 2018 SemEval Task 8, SecureNLP (Semantic Extraction from CybersecUrity REports using Natural Language Processing). We participated in three of the subtasks: (1) classifying sentences as relevant or irrelevant for further malware analysis, (2) predicting token labels for sentences about malware, and (4) adding detained attribute labels to sentences from the MAEC vocabulary for defining malware characteristics. Our cybersecurity embeddings are available at `https://bit.ly/cybr2vec`.

We plan to continue development our systems by getting additional annotations for training, exploring the application of different machine learning algorithms, making use of the knowledge in our Unified Cybersecurity Ontology (Syed et al., 2016) and associated data, and through our ongoing collaboration with colleagues at IBM as part of the AI Horizons Network.

Acknowledgments

The research described in this paper was partially supported by gifts from IBM and Northrop Grumman. We thank Agniva Banerjee, Sudip Mittal, Sandeep Narayanan, Maithilee Prabodh, Vishal Rathod, and Arya Renjan for helping with annotations.

References

Desiree Beck, Ivan Kirillov, and Penny Chase. 2014. The MAEC language. Technical report, MITRE.

Kiran Blanda and David Westcott. 2018. APTnotes.

Peter F. Brown, Peter V. deSouza, Robert L. Mercer, Vincent J. Della Pietra, and Jenifer C. Lai. 1992. Class-based n-gram models of natural language. *Comput. Linguist.*, 18(4):467–479.

Franois Chollet. 2015. keras. `https://github.com/fchollet/keras`.

M Bishop Christopher. 2016. *PATTERN RECOGNITION AND MACHINE LEARNING*. Springer-Verlag New York.

Sepp Hochreiter and Jürgen Schmidhuber. 1997. Long short-term memory. *Neural computation*, 9(8):1735–1780.

Diederik P Kingma and Jimmy Ba. 2014. Adam: A method for stochastic optimization. *arXiv preprint arXiv:1412.6980*.

Ivan Kirillov, Desiree Beck, Penny Chase, and Robert Martin. 2011. Malware attribute enumeration and characterization. Technical report, MITRE.

Taku Kudo. 2005. CRF++: Yet another CRF toolkit. `https://taku910.github.io/crfpp/`.

Percy Liang. 2005. *Semi-supervised learning for natural language*. Ph.D. thesis, Massachusetts Institute of Technology.

Swee Kiat Lim, Aldrian Obaja Muis, Wei Lu, and Chen Hui Ong. 2017. Malwaretextdb: A database for annotated malware articles. In *Proceedings of the 55th Annual Meeting of the Association for Computational Linguistics (Volume 1: Long Papers)*, pages 1557–1567. Association for Computational Linguistics.

Christopher D. Manning, Mihai Surdeanu, John Bauer, Jenny Finkel, Steven J. Bethard, and David McClosky. 2014. The Stanford CoreNLP natural language processing toolkit. In *Association for Computational Linguistics (ACL) System Demonstrations*, pages 55–60.

Tomas Mikolov, Kai Chen, Greg Corrado, and Jeffrey Dean. 2013a. Efficient estimation of word representations in vector space. *arXiv preprint arXiv:1301.3781*.

Tomas Mikolov, Ilya Sutskever, Kai Chen, Greg S Corrado, and Jeff Dean. 2013b. Distributed representations of words and phrases and their compositionality. In *Advances in neural information processing systems*, pages 3111–3119.

F. Pedregosa, G. Varoquaux, A. Gramfort, V. Michel, B. Thirion, O. Grisel, M. Blondel, P. Prettenhofer, R. Weiss, V. Dubourg, J. Vanderplas, A. Passos, D. Cournapeau, M. Brucher, M. Perrot, and E. Duchesnay. 2011. Scikit-learn: Machine learning in Python. *Journal of Machine Learning Research*, 12:2825–2830.

Peter Phandi, Amila Silva, and Wei Lu. 2018. Semeval-2018 Task 8: Semantic Extraction from CybersecUrity REports using Natural Language Processing (SecureNLP). In *Proceedings of International Workshop on Semantic Evaluation (SemEval-2018)*, New Orleans, LA, USA.

Lance A Ramshaw and Mitchell P Marcus. 1999. Text chunking using transformation-based learning. In *Natural language processing using very large corpora*, pages 157–176. Springer.

Radim Řehůřek and Petr Sojka. 2010. Software Framework for Topic Modelling with Large Corpora. In *Proceedings of the LREC 2010 Workshop on New Challenges for NLP Frameworks*, pages 45–50, Valletta, Malta. ELRA. `http://is.muni.cz/publication/884893/en`.

Nitish Srivastava, Geoffrey Hinton, Alex Krizhevsky, Ilya Sutskever, and Ruslan Salakhutdinov. 2014. Dropout: A simple way to prevent neural networks from overfitting. *The Journal of Machine Learning Research*, 15(1):1929–1958.

Zareen Syed, Ankur Padia, Tim Finin, M Lisa Mathews, and Anupam Joshi. 2016. Uco: A unified cybersecurity ontology. In *AAAI Workshop: Artificial Intelligence for Cyber Security*.

Robert Tibshirani. 1996. Regression shrinkage and selection via the lasso. *Journal of the Royal Statistical Society. Series B (Methodological)*, pages 267–288.

Sida Wang and Christopher D Manning. 2012. Baselines and bigrams: Simple, good sentiment and topic classification. In *Proceedings of the 50th Annual Meeting of the Association for Computational Linguistics: Short Papers-Volume 2*, pages 90–94. Association for Computational Linguistics.

Villani at SemEval-2018 Task 8: Semantic Extraction from Cybersecurity Reports using Representation Learning

Pablo Loyola, Kugamoorthy Gajananan, Yuji Watanabe and Fumiko Satoh

IBM Research Tokyo

Tokyo, Japan

`{e57095,gajan,muew,sfumiko}@jp.ibm.com`

Abstract

In this paper, we describe our proposal for the task of Semantic Extraction from Cybersecurity Reports. The goal is to explore if natural language processing methods can provide relevant and actionable knowledge to contribute to better understand malicious behavior. Our method consists of an attention-based Bi-LSTM which achieved competitive performance of 0.57 for the Subtask 1. In the due process we also present ablation studies across multiple embeddings and their level of representation and also report the strategies we used to mitigate the extreme imbalance between classes.

1 Introduction

Cybersecurity represents one of the most comprehensive and challenging tasks to tackle from a data-driven perspective. It is inherently technical, covering field such as networking and programming languages, but at the same time, it considers human aspects, such as intent, trust and strategy among benign and malicious agents (Buczak and Guven, 2016).

This rich mixture makes it an ideal playground for machine learning, to extract patterns and characterize the interaction between the different set of actors involved. Moreover, as we can collect large amounts of data from security related sources, such as trace logs and reports, the level of generalization that machine learning methods could achieve could increase. Nevertheless, several challenges also emerge such as noise, lack structure, unavailability of annotated sources and a characteristic class imbalance when data is labeled. Therefore, for machine learning to be considered useful in a cybersecurity context, it must provide robust and reliable results, overcoming the aforementioned issues.

In that sense, how we represent the data plays a key role, as it is known that in any machine learning setting, different feature representations yield to different results, entangling different explanatory factors of variation on the data (Bengio et al., 2013). We are interested in study the tradeoff between the use of hand crafted features the process of automatically learning feature representations.

In that sense, the present SemEval Task 8 (Phandi et al., 2018) represents a relevant scenario to test several hypotheses in the context of a controlled semantic extraction competition. The dataset, provided by Lim et al. (2017), contains over 6,800 labeled sentences from 39 malware reports. From the subtasks, we focused on the first one, as it provides compact goal to assess a proof of concept.

Our approach consists on the use of an attention based LSTM-based recurrent architecture (Hochreiter and Schmidhuber, 1997; Luong et al., 2015) which is capable of learning sentence level feature representations at both character and token level. Additionally, we prepend an embedding layer from which pretrained feature vectors can be associated to the tokens. Given the natural class imbalance of the data, we tried several techniques to alleviate generalization issues.

Our results show that out approach can outperform the baselines, reaching up to 0.57 in the competition leaderboard for the Subtask 1. Nevertheless, the actual scores show that the task is far from being solved, illustrating the difficulty of the problem and the need for more powerful methods that allow us to obtain more expressive feature representations.

2 Data Pre-processing

We tried to keep the data as natural as possible in an attempt to retain most of the characteristics and

Proceedings of the 12th International Workshop on Semantic Evaluation (SemEval-2018), pages 885–889

New Orleans, Louisiana, June 5–6, 2018. ©2018 Association for Computational Linguistics

nuances from the original reports. Therefore, we did not perform any transformation or cleaning on the tokens extracted from each sentence.

Given the configuration of the contest, where the leaderboard on the test set was kept hidden to the public, the only way to obtain a reliable estimation of the performance of the experiments were to look at the validation set. While this is not usually a problem, in our exploratory study, we found that the set of sentences on the provided validation set differed in distributional terms from the sentences on the provided testing set.

To alleviate this issue we implemented an adjustment procedure that consisted of merging all the sources of data (training, validation and test) into one set while re-labeling each sentence as *part to the test set* or not.

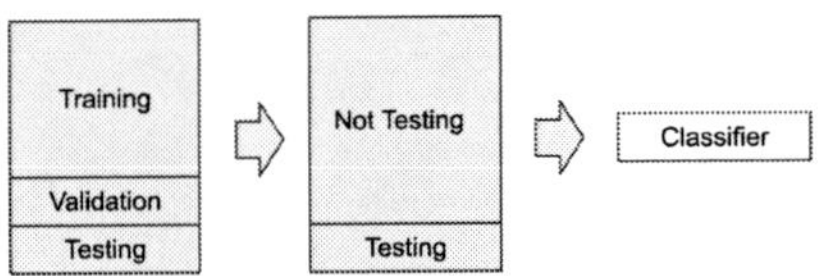

Figure 1: Data Re-classification process.

With this relabeled set, we trained a classifier to predict if a given sentence belonged to the test set or not. In this case, for feature extraction, we computed trigram based vectors for each sentence using Scikit-learn package[1], and a standard feed forward neural network was used. Figure 1 illustrates the approach.

We then considered the sentences that originally belonged to the training + validation set but that obtained the highest probability to be part of the test set by the trained model. This new set presented slightly more similar characteristics to the original test set than the original validation set, in both average sentence length and vocabulary overlap perspectives. For the empirical study, we experimented with both the original validation set and the proposed variation.

3 Proposed Approach

The problem we are trying to solve is, given a sentence from a report, estimates if it contains relevant information about malware characterization or not. Therefore, we can treat it as a binary classification.

---

[1]http://scikit-learn.org/

3.1 Use of pretrained feature vectors

The use of pretrained feature vectors has shown positive effects when initializing recurrent architectures (Le et al., 2015). In that sense, we provide three initialization sources.

The first one is the use of an external source represented by Glove vectors (Pennington et al., 2014). The decision of incorporating such source is related to the fact that given that Glove vectors are trained on a Wikipedia corpus, in theory they can provide a considerable level of coverage. On the other hand, we are aware that, as the corpus for this competition is highly focused on security topics, there is a chance that a portion of the token may not have a corresponding feature vector from Glove source. For this cases, we decided to initialize such tokens with a vector computed as the average of the top 10 % less frequent words appearing in Glove set.

In the second place, we wanted to test if pretraining with the same sources used for the competition could have a positive outcome. This is natural decision as we are building an ad-hoc feature representation that is narrowed to the security context. To achieve that, we computed a feature vector based on i) bigrams and trigrams combination and ii) learning a continuous vector representation by means of a word2vec (Mikolov et al., 2013) configuration. We experimented with these three sources isolated as well as combined.

Finally, in addition to a token-level feature representation, we implemented a character level feature learning pretraining that consists of a single LSTM that passes through each token and from which we capture the last hidden state to use as a token representation.

3.2 Model Architecture

The resulting sequence of vectors associated to a given sentence is then passed to a BiSTM module. In this step, as we need to obtain a learned representation of the entire sequence, we explored three configurations. The first one consists of just take the last hidden state and treat it as the sentence level representation. The second one consists of performing a simple averaging on all the hidden states obtained from the sequence. This average can be further complemented by means of element wise operations, such as direct sum or the dot product, following a schema similar to (Mou et al., 2015). The third configuration was the use

the kernel sends commands to each module using its module id .

the victim is then redirected to a url which in turn determines the best exploit to use based on the information collected .

here also it uses hashes to look up apis .

pipe server is a special mode of the injected dll .

it appears this method makes sending sms easy .

Table 1: Sample of false positives from the custom validation set.

the data is sent encrypted with rc4 , and base64-encoded .

the malicious content is stored inside the document in encoded form , and the shellcode decodes and writes this to disk .

it is designed as a survey tool .

its method of exfiltrating the logged keystrokes relied upon a hardcoded email address stored in the binary .

the communication between the attacker and the sockss is encoded using the rc4 key .

Table 2: Sample of false negatives from the custom validation set.

of an attention mechanism, as proposed by (Luong et al., 2015). In this case, a feedforward neural network is trained jointly with the recurrent module and it is in charge of learning the portions of the sentences that are more expressive for the classification.

The learned sentence representations are then passed to a binary classifier that estimates the likelihood of a sentence to be relevant or not by minimizing the categorical cross entropy loss. For all our experiments we use as optimizer Rmsprop (Tieleman and Hinton, 2012). For regularization, we added Dropout (Srivastava et al., 2014) both in the recurrent module as well as in the binary classifier.

4 Results and Discussion

The main results are shown on Table 3 and Table 4. From them, we can see that taking Glove as a baseline and incorporating n-grams vectors produce the best results. The addition of word2vec based vectors did not have a positive impact. We hypothesize this is due to the size of the training set used, the resulting vectors are based on a model that could not converge.

In the case of the configurations used to obtain a sentence representation, a clear improvement is obtained by using an attention mechanism, which outperforms both the selection of the last hidden state and all the averaging alternatives. These results are aligned with the current state of the art in language modeling, as attention is a robust way to prioritize the elements the conforms a sentence. The use of a character level representation learning module slightly improved the results, while at the same time increased the time consumption of the model in approximately 15%. Therefore, it is not clear if such addition is cost effective in all cases.

Name	Accuracy
Glove	0.612
Glove+Ngrams	0.683
Glove+Ngrams+ w2v	0.681

Table 3: Classification results for different initializations.

We tried regularization via Dropout, from 0.2. to 0.7 but it did not show relevant improvements. Another technique we implemented was to re-weight the labels to mitigate the imbalance problem, but such addition decreased the overall performance of the model.

We repeated the experiments using the original train-validation schema, as well as with the variation proposed. On average using the proposed variation only increased the performance in around 2% (obtained once the test set was released) by the competition organizers.

From the results showed above, we can summarize the best configuration for the proposed task as follows:

- Initialize token vectors by means of a concatenation between Glove vectors and tri-grams captured from the training set.

- The use of an BiLSTM module and an attention mechanism to efficiently weight the importance of the tokens in a sentence.

4.1 Misclassification Analysis

To obtain a better understanding of the performance of the model, we sampled a group of instances coming from both the false positive and false negative sets.

Table 1 shows a set of false positives, i.e., not relevant sentences misclassified as relevant by the

Name	Accuracy
Last hidden	0.692
Average hidden	0.694
Attention	0.822
Attention + char	0.828

Table 4: Classification results for different sentence level representation learning.

model. One of the main characteristics is the lack of specific details expressed on the sentences and the shallow descriptions of processes or tasks. On the other hand, on Table 2, the set of false negatives, i.e., relevant sentences classified as not relevant by the model, presents a denser population of specific terms, usually associated to tools or protocols used by the attackers. From this, we can hypothesize the model is not able to effectively understand the context of the token usage, especially when it is rare and probably has very low frequency. In that sense, this could represent the need for additional information the model requires treating this cases in a particular way (e.g. passing explicitly token dependencies). Further experiments are needed to find ways to operationalize such additions.

4.2 Parameter Sensibility Analysis

Given the considerable number of hyperparameters that can be configured, we decided to study how such tuning impact model performance. During training, we found that the learning rate was key factor. While it is known that a small learning rate is beneficial when working with recurrent architectures, we found that in this case, give the extreme class imbalance, it was required to search for learning rates in a considerable lower spectrum. Figure 2 and Figure 3 show different learning dynamics sampled from several learning rates configurations. Values higher than 0.0001 produce uniform increments in the validation loss, which means the model was not able to generalize (as seen on Figure 2, training loss rapidly converged in such cases, not giving the model enough space to learn efficiently). Learning rates around 0.0001 or below started providing a decreasing validation loss. This phenomenon provides some insights on the difficulty of the task and the challenges associated when trying to achieve generalization.

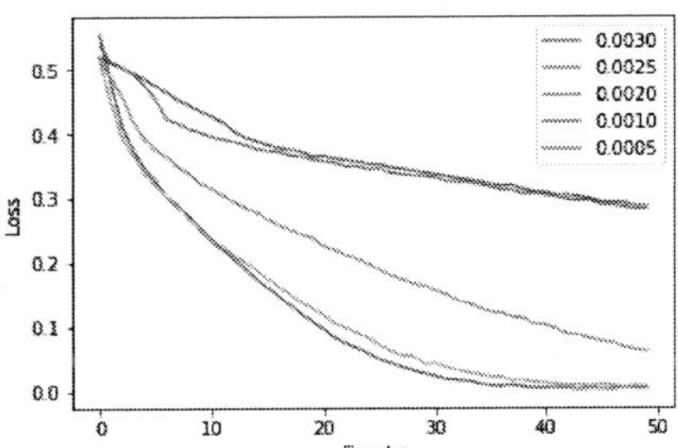

Figure 2: Impact of the learning rate on the training loss.

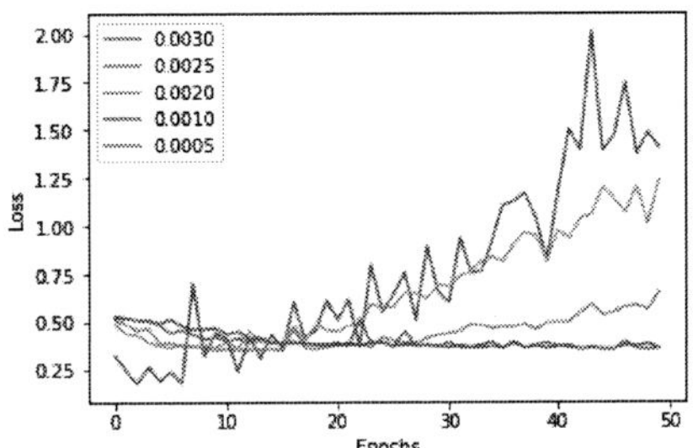

Figure 3: Impact of the learning rate on the validation loss.

5 Conclusion and Future work

In this work, we described our experience on the semantic extraction from cybersecurity reports. We were able to produce a model the generate feasible results for estimating the relevance of sentences in the context of security information. For future work, we consider that while keep improving the performance of the model is vital task, equally important is to explore ways to allow decision makers to have a clear understanding of the internals of the model to assess how much they can depend on it to support their actions. Therefore, we consider working towards incorporating an explanatory or interpretable layer in the design of a model.

References

Yoshua Bengio, Aaron Courville, and Pascal Vincent. 2013. Representation learning: A review and new perspectives. *IEEE transactions on pattern analysis and machine intelligence*, 35(8):1798–1828.

Anna L Buczak and Erhan Guven. 2016. A survey of data mining and machine learning methods for cyber security intrusion detection. *IEEE Communications Surveys & Tutorials*, 18(2):1153–1176.

Sepp Hochreiter and Jürgen Schmidhuber. 1997. Long short-term memory. *Neural computation*, 9(8):1735–1780.

Quoc V Le, Navdeep Jaitly, and Geoffrey E Hinton. 2015. A simple way to initialize recurrent networks of rectified linear units. *arXiv preprint arXiv:1504.00941*.

Swee Kiat Lim, Aldrian Obaja Muis, Wei Lu, and Chen Hui Ong. 2017. Malwaretextdb: A database for annotated malware articles. In *Proceedings of the 55th Annual Meeting of the Association for Computational Linguistics (Volume 1: Long Papers)*, volume 1, pages 1557–1567.

Minh-Thang Luong, Hieu Pham, and Christopher D Manning. 2015. Effective approaches to attention-based neural machine translation. *arXiv preprint arXiv:1508.04025*.

Tomas Mikolov, Ilya Sutskever, Kai Chen, Greg S Corrado, and Jeff Dean. 2013. Distributed representations of words and phrases and their compositionality. In *Advances in neural information processing systems*, pages 3111–3119.

Lili Mou, Hao Peng, Ge Li, Yan Xu, Lu Zhang, and Zhi Jin. 2015. Discriminative neural sentence modeling by tree-based convolution. *arXiv preprint arXiv:1504.01106*.

Jeffrey Pennington, Richard Socher, and Christopher Manning. 2014. Glove: Global vectors for word representation. In *Proceedings of the 2014 conference on empirical methods in natural language processing (EMNLP)*, pages 1532–1543.

Peter Phandi, Amila Silva, and Wei Lu. 2018. Semeval-2018 Task 8: Semantic Extraction from CybersecUrity REports using Natural Language Processing (SecureNLP). In *Proceedings of International Workshop on Semantic Evaluation (SemEval-2018)*, New Orleans, LA, USA.

Nitish Srivastava, Geoffrey Hinton, Alex Krizhevsky, Ilya Sutskever, and Ruslan Salakhutdinov. 2014. Dropout: A simple way to prevent neural networks from overfitting. *The Journal of Machine Learning Research*, 15(1):1929–1958.

Tijmen Tieleman and Geoffrey Hinton. 2012. Lecture 6.5-rmsprop: Divide the gradient by a running average of its recent magnitude. *COURSERA: Neural networks for machine learning*, 4(2):26–31.

Flytxt_NTNU at SemEval-2018 Task 8:
Identifying and Classifying Malware Text Using Conditional Random Fields and Naïve Bayes Classifiers

Utpal Kumar Sikdar[1], Biswanath Barik[2] and Björn Gambäck[2]
[1]Flytxt, Thiruvananthapuram, India
[2]Department of Computer Science, NTNU, Norway
`utpal.sikdar@gmail.com`
`{biswanath.barik,gamback}@ntnu.no`

Abstract

Cybersecurity risks such as malware threaten the personal safety of users, but to identify malware text is a major challenge. The paper proposes a supervised learning approach to identifying malware sentences given a document (subTask1 of SemEval 2018, Task 8), as well as to classifying malware tokens in the sentences (subTask2). The approach achieved good results, ranking second of twelve participants for both subtasks, with F-scores of 57% for subTask1 and 28% for subTask2.

1 Introduction

Malware is a major problem in the digital world. Recently, Lim et al. (2017) addressed the malware threat by creating a new database of malware texts. In addition, they constructed different models for identifying and classifying malware sentences, and discussed the outstanding challenges. Sutskever et al. (2016) also pointed to cybersecurity defense as a key area because of its long-term impact on society. Still, there have been very few efforts addressing the problem. Many cybersecurity agencies such as Cylance (Gross, 2016) and Symantec (DiMaggio, 2015) have collected large repositories of malware-related online texts. The diversity of those texts shows that identifying malware is quite challenging.

The organizers of SemEval 2018, Task 8 defined four subtasks for Semantic Extraction from CybersecUrity REports using NLP, SecureNLP (Phandi et al., 2018). The paper outlines a supervised approach to the first two subtasks, on malware sentence and token identification, respectively. In subTask1, given a sentence, the systems need to predict whether the sentence is relevant for inferring the malware's actions and capabilities. For this subtask, two machine learning classifiers were used, Naïve Bayes (Rish, 2001) and

Data	Total		Malware	
	Sents	**Tokens**	**Sents**	**Tokens**
Train	9,435	231,180	2,204	12,165
Dev	1,213	32,029	79	459
Test	618	13,080	90	453

Table 1: Malware dataset statistics

Conditional Random Fields (CRF, Lafferty et al., 2001), as well as a combination of the two models.

In subTask2, the systems should predict and classify malware tokens in the sentences into three different categories, namely Action, Entity, and Modifier. A CRF-based classifier was used also for the second subtask.

The paper is organized as follows: The datasets are presented in Section 2. The malware sentence identification is described in Section 3, while the token label malware identification is described in Section 4. Results are presented in Section 5, with system comparison and error analysis reported in Sections 6 and 7, respectively. Section 8 addresses future work and concludes.

2 Datasets

The SecureNLP shared task organizers provided three different datasets: training, development and test sets. The statistics of the datasets are reported in Table 1, with the total number of sentences and tokens in each set as well as the number of those sentences and tokens containing malware.

3 Malware Sentence Identification

Two classifiers, CRF and Naïve Bayes were used for malware sentence identification. When both the classifiers identified a sentence as malware, the outputs of the classifiers were combined. The system architecture is shown in Figure 1.

Proceedings of the 12th International Workshop on Semantic Evaluation (SemEval-2018), pages 890–893
New Orleans, Louisiana, June 5–6, 2018. ©2018 Association for Computational Linguistics

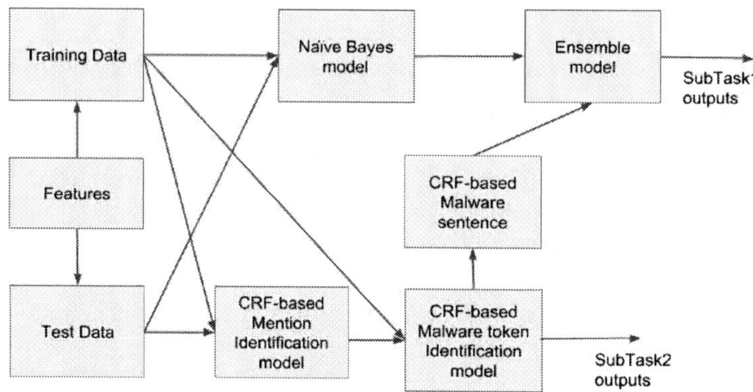

Figure 1: Overall system architecture

3.1 Conditional Random Fields

Token level malware words were identified in the texts described in Section 2. If a sentence contains malware token(s) as identified by the CRF classifier, the sentence is considered as a potential malware sentence. A range of features (further described in Section 4 below) were utilized to train the CRF classifier to predict malware tokens.

3.2 Naïve Bayes

A Naïve Bayes classifier is a probabilistic classifier based on Bayes' theorem an independence assumption between the features. As an initial step, a dictionary was created using the vocabulary found in all the sentences. In the next step, a term-document matrix was built for each sentence. Then Bayes' Theorem was applied to calculate the malware ($y = 1$) and non-malware ($y = 0$) probabilities for each sentence. Equation 1 represents the malware probability, P for each sentence.

$$P(y = 1|S) = \frac{P(S|y = 1) \times P(y = 1)}{P(S)} \quad (1)$$

Here S denotes the set of words in a particular sentence and $P(S) = P(S|y = 1) \times P(y = 1) + P(S|y = 0) \times P(y = 0)$. The non-malware probability for each sentence can be calculated in the same way. If $P(\text{malware}) > P(\text{non-malware})$, the sentence is considered to be a malware sentence, otherwise it is assumed to be non-malware.

3.3 Classifier Ensemble Prediction

An ensemble classifier was created by merging the outputs of the two classifiers described above. If both classifiers identify a sentence as malware, it is considered to be malware, otherwise non-malware. Combining the two classifiers gave better accuracy than using each classifier individually.

4 CRF-based Malware Token Identification and Classification

To identify and classify each token from unstructured text into the three categories Action, Entity and Modifier, a supervised CRF-based approach was used. The task was divided into two steps. In the first step, each token (called a mention) was identified as belonging to one of the three categories or not. In the next step, the identified tokens were classified into one of the three categories.

The CRF token label malware identification model was implemented using the C++ CRF++ package[1], which allows for fast training by utilizing L-BFGS (Liu and Nocedal, 1989), a limited memory quasi-Newton algorithm for large scale numerical optimization. The classifier was trained with L2 regularization and the following features:

- local context (with a -1 to +2 window, i.e., from one preceding to two following tokens),
- part-of-speech information (-1 to +3 tokens),
- suffix (last two or three characters)
- prefix characters (three initial characters)
- starts-with-upper-case,
- stem (-3 to +2 tokens),
- is-a-stop-word,
- is-alphanumeric,
- is-sentence-initial,
- identified mention (-3 to +3 tokens),
- bi-gram: a combination of the current token output and previous token output.

---

[1] `https://taku910.github.io/crfpp/`

System	Precision	Recall	F-score
CRF	0.30	0.80	0.43
Naïve Bayes	0.30	0.89	0.45
Ensemble	0.43	0.75	0.55

Table 2: SubTask1 Development Results

System	Precision	Recall	F-score
CRF	0.40	0.71	0.51
Naïve Bayes	0.32	0.88	0.47
Ensemble	0.49	0.67	0.57

Table 3: SubTask1 Test Results

Data	Precision	Recall	F-score
Dev	22.22	28.32	24.90
Test	26.00	29.40	28.00

Table 4: SubTask2 Results (%)

Team Name	T1	T2	T2-rel
Villani	0.57	0.23	0.31
Flytxt_NTNU	0.57	0.28	0.36
DM_NLP	0.52	0.29	0.39
HCCL	0.52	0.22	0.38
TeamDL	0.50	0.25	0.36
NLP_Found	0.49	0.28	0.39
ACL benchmark	0.51	0.23	0.31

Table 5: Top-7 results (F-score) for SubTask-1 (T1), SubTask-2 (T2), and SubTask2-relaxed (T2-rel)

To identifying the mentions, the above features (except the mention feature) were used together with the current word and a context consisting of the previous two and the next two words.

5 Results

The supervised learning approaches were applied to subTask1 and subTask2. The systems were learned from the training data and tested on the development data. Table 2 reports the precision, recall and F_1-score on the subTask1 development data for the CRF approach, the Naïve Bayes, and the combined ensemble approach. The ensemble achieved 10% better F-score than the Naïve Bayes approach, which in turned slightly out-performed the CRF classifier. Before evaluating on the unseen test data, the development set was merged with the training set to build the classifiers. The combined approach also produced the best results on unseen test data, as reported in Table 3. Note that the enlarged training set helped to increase precision on the test set for all classifiers, while recall went down in all cases.

For subTask2, token label malware identification, we applied the Conditional Random Fields classifier using the features given in Section 4. The results are shown in Table 4. When tested on the development data, the classifier and achieved an F-score of 24.90%, with slightly higher recall than precision. Again, the unseen test data results were somewhat better, with an F-score of 28%. Tentatively since also here the development data was merged with the training data when learning the classifier used for the unseen test data.

6 Comparison with Other Systems

Comparing our system ('Flytxt_NTNU') with the other systems participating in the shared task, Table 5 reports the top 7 results and shows that in subTask1 (malware sentence identification) we secured second position, while achieving the same F-score (57%) as the top-rated system (Villani). Also for token label malware identification (subTask2), our system got second position with a 28% F-score. For both subtasks, we achieved clearly better scores than the baseline system ('ACL benchmark').

7 Error Analysis and Discussion

To analyze the outputs of the development data for subTask1 and subTask2, Tables 6 and 7 draws the confusion matrices for each subtask.

For subTask1, Table 6 shows that many non-malware sentences are identified as malware sentences by both classifiers, tentatively since many common words are shared by both malware and non-malware sentences. Both classifiers generate higher recall than precision values because the classifiers try to identify as many sentences as possible as malware. Once the outputs of the two classifiers were combined (when both classifiers agreed on a sentence being potential malware), about half of the non-malware sentence classification errors were removed, and the ensemble thus produced better F-scores than the Naïve Bayes and CRF models in isolation.

	CRF		Naïve Bayes		Ensemble	
	Non-Malware	Malware	Non-Malware	Malware	Non-Malware	Malware
Non-Malware	985	149	969	165	1057	77
Malware	16	63	9	70	20	59

Table 6: Confusion Matrix for SubTask1 on the development data

	B-Entity	I-Entity	B-Action	I-Action	B-Modifier	I-Modifier	O
B-Entity	51	68	1	0	1	0	135
I-Entity	8	122	1	0	7	0	383
B-Action	2	1	57	7	0	0	57
I-Action	0	0	0	0	0	0	6
B-Modifier	0	6	0	0	28	1	44
I-Modifier	0	0	0	0	0	0	0
O	277	537	107	12	46	3	30061

Table 7: Confusion Matrix for SubTask2 on the development data

The confusion matrix for subTask2 is reported in Table 7, in the BIO (beginning, inside, outside) format for each of the three classes (entity, action, modifier). We observe that many non-malware tokens (**O**) are identified as malware and vice versa. Again, this might be due to same words occurring as both malware and non-malware tokens in the sentences, which is why the system achieved low precision and recall values. Furthermore, two of the inside mention classes (**I-Action** and **I-Modifier**) are tiny, indicating that training machine learners on them will be difficult.

8 Conclusion and Future Work

The paper has proposed Naïve Bayes and CRF based approaches to identify malware sentences (subTask1). In the future, we will incorporate other features such as tf-idf and information gain to improve system performance. Furthermore, we aim to apply deep learning-based approaches such as LSTM (Long Short-Term Memory) and CNN (Convolution Neural Network) to malware sentence classification.

For subTask2, many features were developed to identify malware tokens using Conditional Random Fields. Most of the features were extracted directly from training data, but the features could have been further optimized using grid search and evolutionary approaches. Also for this subtask, we will in the future experiment with applying other approaches, such as LSTM and CNN, to identify the types of malware tokens in the sentences.

References

Jon DiMaggio. 2015. The Black Vine cyberespionage group. Technical report, Symantec.

Jon Gross. 2016. Operation Dust Storm. Technical report, Cylance.

John Lafferty, Andrew McCallum, and Fernando C.N. Pereira. 2001. Conditional Random Fields: Probabilistic models for segmenting and labeling sequence data. In *Proceedings of the 18th International Conference on Machine Learning*, pages 282–289, Williamstown, MA, USA. IMIS.

Swee Kiat Lim, Aldrian Obaja Muis, Wei Lu, and Chen Hui Ong. 2017. MalwareTextDB: A database for annotated malware articles. In *Proceedings of the 55th Annual Meeting of the Association for Computational Linguistics*, volume 1: Long Papers, pages 1557–1567, Vancouver, Canada. ACL.

Dong C. Liu and Jorge Nocedal. 1989. On the limited memory BFGS method for large scale optimization. *Mathematical Programming*, 45(1):503–528.

Peter Phandi, Amila Silva, and Wei Lu. 2018. Semeval-2018 Task 8: Semantic Extraction from CybersecUrity REports using Natural Language Processing (SecureNLP). In *Proceedings of International Workshop on Semantic Evaluation (SemEval-2018)*, New Orleans, Louisiana.

Irina Rish. 2001. An empirical study of the Naïve Bayes classifier. In *Proceedings of the IJCAI-01 Workshop on Empirical Methods in Artificial Intelligence*, pages 41–46. AAAI.

Ilya Sutskever, Dario Amodei, and Sam Altman. 2016. Special projects. Technical report, OpenAI.

Digital Operatives at SemEval-2018 Task 8: Using dependency features for malware NLP

Chris Brew

Digital Operatives

`chris.brew@digitaloperatives.com`

Abstract

The four sub-tasks of SecureNLP build towards a capability for quickly highlighting critical information from malware reports, such as the specific actions taken by a malware sample. Digital Operatives (DO) submitted to sub-tasks 1 and 2, using standard text analysis technology (text classification for sub-task 1, and a CRF for sub-task 2). Performance is broadly competitive with other submitted systems on sub-task 1 and weak on sub-task 2. The annotation guidelines for the intermediate sub-tasks create a linkage to the final task, which is both an annotation challenge and a potentially useful feature of the task. The methods DO chose do not attempt to make use of this linkage, which may be a missed opportunity. This motivates a post-hoc error analysis. It appears that the annotation task is very hard, and that in some cases both deep conceptual knowledge and substantial surrounding context are needed in order to correctly classify sentences.

1 Introduction

The SecureNLP challenge is motivated by (Lim et al., 2017) and further described in (Phandi et al., 2018), it aims to provide automation for malware analysts who might otherwise be overwhelmed by the task of finding key data in long threat reports. The annotation guidelines used to create the task ask analysts to include actions carried out by the malware, but exclude actions carried out by the human designers of the malware. These actions are related to the MAEC cybersecurity ontology (Kirillov et al., 2010). The guidelines include one substantial caveat:

> As a general guide [for a positive annotation], the sentence should imply a particular malware action or capability, with reference to the list of attribute labels. [i.e. the MAEC labels]

Sub-task 1 calls for a determination of relevance or irrelevance to malware activity on a per-sentence basis. However a number of issues make this difficult. See detail in (Lim et al., 2017). First, it is not obvious what to do when a sentence describes malware activity but does not fit in with any MAEC category. Second, the distinction between things done by the malware and things done (or intended) by its designers is not easy to maintain.

We describe the systems that we built for tasks 1 and 2 and use them to conduct ablation studies and error analyses.

2 Digital Operatives Systems

The Digital Operatives submission used spaCy (Honnibal and Johnson, 2015). to generate features for each token, then aggregated the features from the whole sentence. To estimate performance, we used 5-fold cross-validation on the combined training and development sets.

As an example, consider the word "ago" in the sentence:

"A few days ago we detected a watering hole campaign in a website owned by one big industrial company ."

We extract:

- the word itself

- the lemmatized form provided by spaCy,

- the orthographic shape (all lower case, represented as "xxx")

- the part-of-speech ("ADV")

- the detailed part-of-speech ("RB")

- Brown cluster (6442) (Brown et al., 1992)

- the fact that it does or does not look like a URL

Proceedings of the 12th International Workshop on Semantic Evaluation (SemEval-2018), pages 894–897
New Orleans, Louisiana, June 5–6, 2018. ©2018 Association for Computational Linguistics

- the bigrams in which it participates ("days ago" and "ago we")

- similar bigrams for lemma, Brown cluster and shape.

- extract features from dependency links. Each token has a head from which it depends, and the relation that it holds to the head has a name. The head of "ago" is the verb "detected", and the relation is "advmod". We package this up into the feature detected-ADVMOD-ago.

- features of the form X-advmod-Y where X and Y are either both cluster ids or both orthographic shapes.

The result is passed to a passive aggressive classifier (Crammer et al., 2006)[1]. This learner, which is similar in cost and performance to a linear kernel SVM and to a number of other linear classifiers, seems to be close to the best choice from a large number of experiments. Grid search was used to choose the C regularization parameter for the classifier. On our 5 validation splits this method had a mean f1 of 0.60 with standard deviation 0.045. Performance on the actual test set was lower, at 0.52. This was rank 5 among the 11 submitted systems, well behind the top 2 systems and slightly ahead of the organizers' benchmark.

Our system classifies each sentence in isolation. No attempt was made to establish the referents of pronouns.

For sub-task 2 we used CRFsuite (Okazaki, 2007) to implement a linear-chain conditional random field. Per-word features were: the lowercased word and its part-of-speech tag; a two-letter prefix of the word; two- and three-letter character prefixes of the word; shape indicators for whether the word is numeric, title-case or upper-case; indicators for whether the word is beginning or end of sentence; the nltk part of speech of previous and subsequent words, if present; the shape indicators of previous and subsequent words, if present. We would have preferred to use features from spaCy, as in task 1, but did not overcome tokenization differences in time. This system was not competitive, with an F-score of 0.16 and a ranking of 9th. The best system had an F1 score of 0.39.

[1] In scikit-learn's implementation (Pedregosa et al., 2011)

	precision	recall	f1-score	sup
irrelevant	0.96	0.83	0.89	528
relevant	0.44	0.79	0.57	90
avg / total	0.88	0.83	0.84	618

Table 1: F1-scores using only lemmas and dependencies between lemmas.

2.1 Ablation study

The submitted system used all the features generated by spaCy. We augmented this with ablation studies in which only subsets of the features were used. The best performance came using only unigrams and bigrams derived from lemmas, along with dependency features derived from lemmas. Ablation actually improved performance over the submission, as shown in table 1. Presumably, these features give the sparse linear classifier an appropriate level of generality. There are 89 false positives in the complete test set and 19 false negatives. There are only 71 true positives.

3 Task analysis

MAEC labels classify malware along several dimensions. We focus on a tractable subset that can be assigned to Actions and that describe capabilities of malware. Table 2 lists these labels.

3.1 Error analysis

We carried out our own annotation of the 112 examples from the test set for which our system did not agree with the organizers annotations. To these we added a further 111 randomly chosen examples from the test set, for which our system did agree. We assessed each of these examples against the 20 categories from table 2, There were differences of judgment between our annotations and those of the organizers. Potential reasons for this include simple errors, misunderstandings, and consequences of the linkage between sub-task 1 and sub-task 4.

Table 4 shows performance when using the new annotations. There are now 72 false positives in the complete test set and 13 false negatives. True positives now slightly outnumber false positives, at 88. It is of course possible that some of our annotations are unintentionally biased in our favor. See table 3. In future work, it may be beneficial to apply the crowdsourcing methods and careful evaluation of annotation found in, for example, (Snow et al., 2008).

Number	Capability	Example	Frequency
000	anti-behavioral_analysis	avoid detection and frustrate analysis,	36
001	anti-code_analysis	XOR 0xAA applied on top of it,	36
002	anti-detection	making its open ports invisible to scanners.	240
003	anti-removal	block access to where the rootkit keeps its file	5
004	availability_violation	DDoS attacks were launched	28
005	command_and_control	C & C proxies talk to [other] proxies	580
006	data_exfiltration	exfiltrate data back to the C&C server	189
007	data_theft	extract Internet Explorer passwords	186
008	destruction	collects file names and overwrites them	63
009	fraud	smart meters could be manipulated	7
010	infection/propagation	infected via a multi-stage attack	525
011	integrity_violation	attacker can hijack the network	85
012	machine_access/control	control the keyboard and mouse.	245
013	persistence	the malware creates a registry key	57
014	privilege_escalation	achieve admin privileges	23
015	probing	malware checks if an old versn is installed	77
016	remote_machine_manipulation	the malware will access network shares	13
017	secondary_operation	The dropper installs a second file	280
018	security_degradation	bypass User Account Control (UAC)	33
019	spying	Babar is able to sniff all keystrokes	128

Table 2: Malware capability labels. Note that the frequency distribution is highly skewed. Examples are edited to fit.

Example	DO	SN	MAEC
A screenshot of the desktop is saved into the `C:\\ProgramData\\Mail\\MailAg\\scs.jpg` file .	0	1	spying?
As you can see this powershell script simply extracts another VBScript and executes it .',	0	1	
Cozyduke was used throughout these attacks to harvest and exfiltrate sensitive information to the attackers .	1	0	exfiltration
Cozyduke will periodically contact these websites to retrieve task information to be executed on the local machine .	0	1	C&C
Execute contents in unlabeled textbox1 as a SQL query and return binary data to adversary.	0	1	exfiltration
The malware hides behind numerous layers of encryption and obfuscation and is capable of quietly stealing and exfiltrating sensitive information such as email from the victim's computer	1	0	anti-detection,data_theft
To communicate with the C&C - server , the Trojan makes use of asymmetric encryption with a hardcoded pair of private and public keys .	1	0	c&c

Table 3: Sample annotation disagreements. The column labeled DO reflects our classification, SN represents that given by the SecureNLP organizers. The column labeled MAEC gives detail on the capability that DO thinks is being described. When we feel confident that one of the annotations for a sentence is clearly right, it is shown in bold. If not, neither is bold.

	P	R	F1	sup
irrelevant	0.97	0.86	0.91	517
relevant	0.55	0.87	0.67	101
avg / total	0.90	0.86	0.87	618

Table 4: Performance against DO's (possibly unintentionally biased) annotations.

4 Discussion and conclusions

We suspected that the secure NLP task is difficult (Lim et al., 2017). Results bear this out:

- Our post-hoc annotation study suggests that it is indeed difficult to distinguish between things done by attackers and things done by malware.

- Often, the system described is distributed, consisting of downloaded malware, websites and C&C servers. The MAEC classification and the SecureNLP annotation guidelines emphasize measurable properties of malware samples. This puts tension into the annotation scheme and may well be a contributor to annotation errors.

- A more extensive effort using multiple annotators and reformulated guidelines could be beneficial.

- With the technology that we used, analysts relying on the classifier's judgment as a filter will still need to read approximately double the number of sentences that actually contain relevant information, and will miss 10% to 20% of the relevant material, which the classifier regards as irrelevant.

Acknowledgments

Thanks to Nathan Landon and colleagues at Digital Operatives for resources, feedback and encouragement. Particular thanks to Jordan Bryant for detailed discussions. This work was funded, in part, by IARPA's Cyber-attack Automated Unconventional Sensor Environment (CAUSE) program. Judgments and opinions are our own. Thanks to two anonymous reviewers for thoughtful suggestions on how to improve the paper.

References

Peter F. Brown, Peter V. deSouza, Robert L. Mercer, Vincent J. Della Pietra, and Jenifer C. Lai. 1992. Class-based n-gram models of natural language. *Comput. Linguist.*, 18(4):467–479.

Koby Crammer, Ofer Dekel, Joseph Keshet, Shai Shalev-Shwartz, and Yoram Singer. 2006. Online passive-aggressive algorithms. *J. Mach. Learn. Res.*, 7:551–585.

Matthew Honnibal and Mark Johnson. 2015. An improved non-monotonic transition system for dependency parsing. In *Proceedings of the 2015 Conference on Empirical Methods in Natural Language Processing*, pages 1373–1378, Lisbon, Portugal. Association for Computational Linguistics.

Ivan Kirillov, Desiree Beck, Penny Chase, and Robert Martin. 2010. Malware attribute enumeration and characterization. Technical report, The MITRE Corporation.

Swee Kiat Lim, Aldrian Obaja Muis, Wei Lu, and Chen Hui Ong. 2017. Malwaretextdb: A database for annotated malware articles. In *Proceedings of the 55th Annual Meeting of the Association for Computational Linguistics (Volume 1: Long Papers)*, pages 1557–1567, Vancouver, Canada. Association for Computational Linguistics.

Naoaki Okazaki. 2007. Crfsuite: a fast implementation of conditional random fields (CRFs).

F. Pedregosa, G. Varoquaux, A. Gramfort, V. Michel, B. Thirion, O. Grisel, M. Blondel, P. Prettenhofer, R. Weiss, V. Dubourg, J. Vanderplas, A. Passos, D. Cournapeau, M. Brucher, M. Perrot, and E. Duchesnay. 2011. Scikit-learn: Machine learning in Python. *Journal of Machine Learning Research*, 12:2825–2830.

Peter Phandi, Amila Silva, and Wei Lu. 2018. Semeval-2018 Task 8: Semantic Extraction from CybersecUrity REports using Natural Language Processing (SecureNLP). In *Proceedings of International Workshop on Semantic Evaluation (SemEval-2018)*, New Orleans, LA, USA.

Rion Snow, Brendan O'Connor, Daniel Jurafsky, and Andrew Y. Ng. 2008. Cheap and fast—but is it good?: Evaluating non-expert annotations for natural language tasks. In *Proceedings of the Conference on Empirical Methods in Natural Language Processing*, EMNLP '08, pages 254–263, Stroudsburg, PA, USA. Association for Computational Linguistics.

Apollo at SemEval-2018 Task 9: Detecting

Hypernymy Relations Using Syntactic Dependencies

Mihaela Onofrei, Ionuț Hulub,
Diana Trandabăț, Daniela Gîfu

University Alexandru Ioan Cuza of Iași, Romania

Institute of Computer Science of the Romanian Academy, Iași Branch

Cognos Business Consulting S.R.L., 32 Bd. Regina Maria, Bucharest, Romania

{mihaela.onofrei, ionut.hulub, daniela.gifu, dtrandabat} @info.uaic.ro

Abstract

This paper presents the participation of Apollo's team in the SemEval-2018 Task 9 "Hypernym Discovery", Subtask 1: "General-Purpose Hypernym Discovery", which tries to produce a ranked list of hypernyms for a specific term. We propose a novel approach for automatic extraction of hypernymy relations from a corpus by using dependency patterns. The results show that the application of these patterns leads to a higher score than using the traditional lexical patterns.

Keywords: hypernymy relations, semantic relations, corpus, taxonomy, syntactic dependencies.

1 Introduction

This paper presents the Apollo team's system for hypernym discovery which participated in task 9 of Semeval 2018 (Camacho-Collados et al., 2018) based on unsupervised machine learning. It is a rule-based system that exploits syntactic dependency paths that generalize Hearst-style lexical patterns.

The paper is structured in 4 sections: this section presents existing approaches for automatic extraction of hypernymy relations, Section 2

contains the current system architecture. The next section presents the web interface of the project, and, finally, Section 4 briefly analyses the results and drafts some conclusions.

Since language is a "vital organ", constantly evolving and changing over time, there are many words which lose one of their meanings or attach a new meaning. For instance, when searching the word "apple" in WordNet (Miller, 1995), it appears defined as "fruit with red or yellow or green skin and sweet to tart crisp whitish flesh" and "native Eurasian tree widely cultivated in many varieties for its firm rounded edible fruits" but searching in British National Corpus[1], we will remark that the term is used more frequently as a named entity (referring to a "company").

From this point of view, we consider that developing a system for hypernym discovery that uses linguistic features from a corpus could be more useful for this task than using a manually-crafted taxonomy.

It is well known that in natural language processing (NLP), one of the biggest challenges is to understand the meaning of words. Also, detecting hypernymy relations is an important task in NLP, which has been pursued for over two decades, and it is addressed in the literature using two complementary approaches: rule-based and distributional

---

[1] https://corpus.byu.edu/bnc/

Proceedings of the 12th International Workshop on Semantic Evaluation (SemEval-2018), pages 898–902
New Orleans, Louisiana, June 5–6, 2018. ©2018 Association for Computational Linguistics

methods. Rule-based methods (Hearst, 1992; Snow et al., 2004) base the decision on the lexico-syntactic paths connecting the joint occurrences of two or more terms in a corpus. In the case of supervised distributional methods (Baroni et al., 2012; Roller et al., 2014, Weeds et al., 2014; Levy et al., 2015, Kruszewski et al., 2015), term-pair is represented using some combination of the terms' embedding vectors.

This challenge has been shown to directly help in downstream applications such automatic hypernymy detection is useful for NLP tasks such as: taxonomy creation, recognizing textual entailment, text generation, Question Answering systems, semantic search, Natural Language Inference, Coreference Resolution and many others.

Traditional procedures to evaluate taxonomies have focused on measuring the quality of the edges, i.e., assessing the quality of the *is-a* relations. This process typically consists of extracting a random sample of edges and manually labeling them by human judges. In addition to the manual effort required to perform this evaluation, this procedure is not easily replicable from taxonomy to taxonomy (which would most likely include different sets of concepts), and do not reflect the overall quality of a taxonomy. Moreover, some taxonomy learning approaches link their concepts to existing resources such as Wikipedia.

2   A new Approach to Detect Hypernymy Relation

The main purpose of this project was to identify the best (set of) candidate hypernyms for a certain term from the given corpus[2].

In our system, we considered the rule-based approach and, in order to extract the corresponding patterns, we used syntactic dependencies relations (Universal Dependencies Parser[3]).

Below, we present our method of extracting hypernyms from text:

- **Tokenization**: sentence boundaries are detected and punctuation signs are separated from words;

- **Part-of-speech tagging**: the process of assigning a part-of-speech or lexical class marker to each word in a corpus. Words in natural languages usually encode many pieces of information, such as: *what the word "means" in the real world, what categories, if any, the word belongs to, what is the function of the word in the sentence?* Many language processing applications need to extract the information encoded in the words. Parsers which analyze sentence structure need to know/check agreement between: subjects and verbs, adjectives and nouns, determiners and nouns, etc. Information retrieval systems benefit from know what the stem of a word is. Machine translation systems need to analyze words to their components and generate words with specific features in the target language.

- **Dependency parsing:** the syntactic parsing of a sentence consists of finding the correct syntactic structure of that sentence in a given formalism/grammar. Dependency parsing structure consists of lexical items, linked by binary asymmetric relations called dependencies. It is interested in grammatical relations between individual words (governing & dependent words), it does not propose a recursive structure, rather a network of relations. These relations can also have labels and the phrasal nodes are missing in the dependency structure, when compared to constituency structure.

One of the boosts for this approach was to develop new dependency patterns for identifying hypernymy relations from text that are based on dependency relations. The increased popularity and the universal inventory of categories and guidelines (which facilitate annotation across languages) of Universal Dependencies determined us to use this resource in order to automatically extract the hypernyms from the corpus.

---

[2] For this subtask, we used the 3-billion-word UMBC corpus, which consists of paragraphs extracted from the web as part of the Stanford WebBase Project. This is a very large corpus containing information from different domains.

[3] Universal Dependencies (UD) is a framework for cross-linguistically consistent grammatical annotation and an open community effort with over 200 contributors producing more than 100 treebanks in over 60 languages.

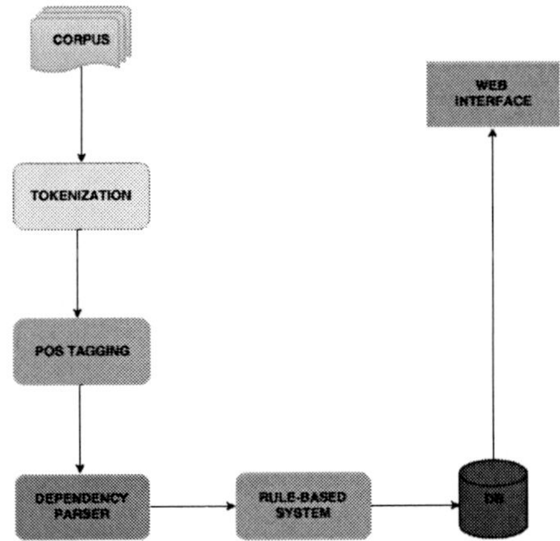

Figure 1: Project's architecture

In this manner, we managed to compress a list of 44 lexico-syntactic patterns used for the hypernyms extraction[4] in only 8 dependencies patterns. In the next lines, we present few examples of lexico-syntactic patterns that were replaced by dependencies patterns:

```
{X and other Y; X or other
Y; X and any other Y; X and
some other Y; Y other than X;
X like other Y; Y other than
X}⟶ replaced by X "amod" Y;

{X is a Y; X was a Y; X are
a Y; X are Y; X will be a Y; X
is an adj Y; X was a adj. Y; X
are a adj. Y; X was a adj. Y;
X are examples of Y; X is ex-
ample of Y; Y for example X;
examples of Y is X; examples
of Y are X; X which is named
Y; X which is called Y; Y
which are similar to X; Y
which is similar to X}    re-
placed by X "nmod" Y.
```

Because we used syntactic dependencies relations (no lexical patterns were involved), our system is language independent. Unfortunately, the limited hardware resources determined us to run our system only in English but we are looking forward to running it in both Spanish and Italian.

3   The Web Interface

The interface[5] was implemented in the form of a website. The site is backed by a Mongodb database. When a user types in a query and hits enter a post request is sent and the backend will do some processing on the query (tokenizing, lemmatizing) and then search in the database. The results are then sent back to the user where they are rendered.

Figure 2: Project's interface

4   Results

We consider that a qualitative way of analyzing our system is to look at which relations are more productive. Table 1 presents the percentages of the most representative syntactic relations which we have identified. While some relations have not been very fruitful (such as *X "obj" Y*, for insance), others, instead, have been very productive, generating tens of thousands relations.

---

[4] http://webdatacommons.org/isadb/lrec2016.pdf

[5] http://hypernymy.arlc.ro

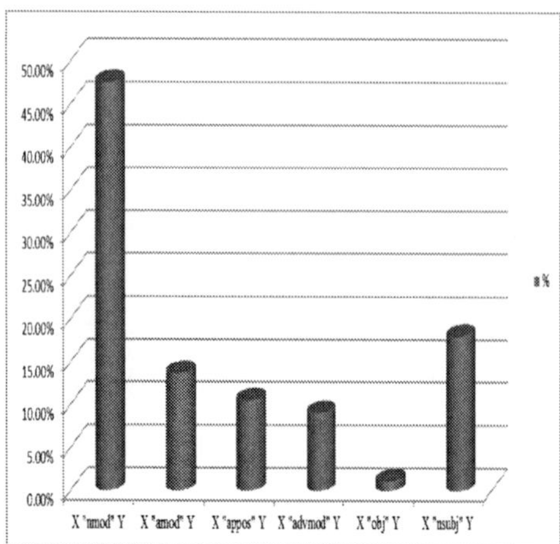

Table 1: Percentages of the identified syntactic

relations

The project's results show that we have managed to accomplish the main objective of this project, to outperform the random strategy. The lower scores have been obtained for multiword expressions, for which we plan to add dedicated modules.

An issue that we have noticed was that the given vocabulary was quite restrictive, for instance, it contains words like "above-water", "artesian water", "bath water" etc., but it doesn't contain the word "water" (we had a case when our system identified the word "water" as a hypernym and it was a correct hypernym, but due to the fact that the vocabulary doesn't contain the word "water", it cannot be evaluated) and many other examples like this.

Acknowledgements

This survey was published with the support by two grants of the Romanian National Authority for Scientific Research and Innovation, UEFISCDI, project number PN-III-P2-2.1-BG-2016-0390, contract 126BG/2016 and project number PN-III-P1-1.2-PCCDI-2017-0818, contract 73PCCDI/2018 within PNCDI III, and partially by the README project "Interactive and Innovative application for evaluating the readability of texts in Romanian Language and for improving users' writing styles", contract no. 114/15.09.2017, MySMIS 2014 code 119286.

References

Baroni, M., Lenci, A. 2011. *How we blessed distributional semantic evaluation.* In Proceedings of the GEMS 2011 Workshop on GEometrical Models of Natural Language Semantics, pages 1-10.

Bordea, G., Buitelaar, P., Faralli, S., Navigli, R. 2015. *Semeval-2015 task 17: Taxonomy extraction evaluation (Texeval).* In *Proceedings of the SemEval workshop.*

Camacho-Collados, J. 2017. Why we have switched from building full-fledged taxonomies to simply detecting hypernymy relations. *arXiv preprint arXiv:1703.04178.*

Camacho-Collados, J., Deli Bovi, C., Espinosa-Anke, L., Oramas, S., Pasini, T., Santus, E., Scwartz, V., Navigli, R., Saggion, H. 2018. *SemEval-2018 Task 9: Hypernymy Discovery.* In Proceedings of the 12th International Workshop on Semantic Evaluation (Sem-Eval2018), New Orleans, LA, United States. Association for Computational Linguistics.

Hearst, M. 1992. *Automatic acquisition of hyponyms from large text corpora.* In *ACL*, pages 539-545.

Kruszewski, G., Paperno, D., Baroni, M. 2015. *Deriving Boolean structures from distributional vectors.* Transactions of the Association for Computational Linguistics, 3:375-388.

Levy, O., Remus, S., Biemann, C., Dagan, I. Ramat-Gan, I. 2015. Do supervised distributional methods really learn lexical inference relations? *In Proceedings of NAACL, pages 970–976.*

Miller, G. 1995. *WordNet: A lexical database for English. Communications of the ACM,* 38(11): 39-41.

Roller, S., Erk, K. 2016. *Relations such as Hypernymy: Identifying and Exploiting Hearst Patterns in Distributional Vectors for Lexical Entailment.* In *Proceedings of EMNLP*, pages 2163–2172.

Roller, S., Erk, K., Boleda, G. 2014. *Inclusive yet selective: Supervised distributional hypernymy detection.* In *COLING*, pages 1025-1036.

Shwartz, V., Santus, E., Schlechtweg, D. 2017. *Hypernyms under siege: Linguistically-motivated artillery for hypernymy detection.* In *Proceedings of EACL,* pages 65–75.

Snow, R., Jurafsky, D., Y Ng, A. 2004. *Learning syntactic patterns for automatic hypernym discovery.* In *NIPS.*

Wang, Ch., He, X., Zho, A. 2017. *A Short Survey on Taxonomy Learning from Text Corpora: Issues, Resources and Recent Advances.* In *Proceedings of EMNLP,* pages 1201–1214.

Weeds, J., Clarke, D., Reffin, J., Weir, D., Keller, B.
2014. *Learning to distinguish hypernyms and co-
hyponyms.* In *COLING*, pages 2249-2259.

SJTU-NLP at SemEval-2018 Task 9:
Neural Hypernym Discovery with Term Embeddings

Zhuosheng Zhang[1,2], Jiangtong Li[3], Hai Zhao[1,2,*], Bingjie Tang[4]
[1]Department of Computer Science and Engineering, Shanghai Jiao Tong University
[2]Key Laboratory of Shanghai Education Commission for Intelligent Interaction
and Cognitive Engineering, Shanghai Jiao Tong University, Shanghai, 200240, China
[3]College of Zhiyuan, Shanghai Jiao Tong University, China
[4]School of Computer, Huazhong University of Science and Technology, China
{zhangzs, keep_moving-lee}@sjtu.edu.cn, zhaohai@cs.sjtu.edu.cn,
alexistang@foxmail.com

Abstract

This paper describes a hypernym discovery system for our participation in the SemEval-2018 Task 9, which aims to discover the best (set of) candidate hypernyms for input concepts or entities, given the search space of a pre-defined vocabulary. We introduce a neural network architecture for the concerned task and empirically study various neural network models to build the representations in latent space for words and phrases. The evaluated models include convolutional neural network, long-short term memory network, gated recurrent unit and recurrent convolutional neural network. We also explore different embedding methods, including word embedding and sense embedding for better performance.

1 Introduction

Hypernym-hyponym relationship is an *is-a* semantic relation between terms as shown in Table 1. Various natural language processing (NLP) tasks, especially those semantically intensive ones aiming for inference and reasoning with generalization capability, such as question answering (Harabagiu and Hickl, 2006; Yahya et al., 2013) and textual entailment (Dagan et al., 2013; Roller and Erk, 2016), can benefit from identifying semantic relations between words beyond synonymy.

The *hypernym discovery* task (Camacho-Collados et al., 2018) aims to discover the most appropriate hypernym(s) for input concepts or entities from a pre-defined corpus. A relevant well-known scenario is *hypernym detection*,

which is a binary task to decide whether a hypernymic relationship holds between a pair of words or not. A hypernym detection system should be capable of learning taxonomy and lexical semantics, including pattern-based methods (Boella and Caro, 2013; Espinosa-Anke et al., 2016b) and graph-based approaches (Fountain and Lapata, 2012; Velardi et al., 2013; Kang et al., 2016). However, our concerned task, hypernym discovery, is rather more challenging since it requires the systems to explore the semantic connection with all the exhausted candidates in the latent space and rank a candidate set instead of a binary classification in previous work. The other challenge is representation for terms, including words and phrases, where the phrase embedding could not be obtained by word embeddings directly. A simple method is to average the inner word embeddings to form the phrase embedding. However, this is too coarse since each word might share different weights. Current systems like (Espinosa-Anke et al., 2016a) commonly discover hypernymic relations by exploiting linear transformation matrix in embedding space, where the embedding should contain words and phrases, resulting to be parameter-exploded and hard to train. Besides, these systems might be insufficient to obtain the deep relationships between terms.

Hyponym	Hypernyms
Heming	actor, person, company
Kralendijk	town, city, provincial capital, capital
StarCraft	video game, pc game, computer game, videogaming, comic, electronic game, sci-entifiction

Table 1: Examples of hypernym-hyponym relationship.

Recently, neural network (NN) models have shown competitive or even better results than traditional linear models with handcrafted sparse fea-

---

* Corresponding author. This paper was partially supported by National Key Research and Development Program of China (No. 2017YFB0304100), National Natural Science Foundation of China (No. 61672343 and No. 61733011), Key Project of National Society Science Foundation of China (No. 15-ZDA041), The Art and Science Interdisciplinary Funds of Shanghai Jiao Tong University (No. 14JCRZ04).

Proceedings of the 12th International Workshop on Semantic Evaluation (SemEval-2018), pages 903–908
New Orleans, Louisiana, June 5–6, 2018. ©2018 Association for Computational Linguistics

tures (Qin et al., 2016b; Pang et al., 2016; Qin et al., 2016a; Wang et al., 2016c; Zhao et al., 2017a; Wang et al., 2017; Qin et al., 2017; Cai and Zhao, 2017; Zhao et al., 2017b; Li et al., 2018). In this work, we introduce a neural network architecture for the concerned task and empirically study various neural networks to model the distributed representations for words and phrases.

In our system, we leverage an unambiguous vector representation via term embedding, and we take advantage of deep neural networks to discover the hypernym relationships between terms.

The rest of the paper is organized as follows: Section 2 briefly describes our system, Section 3 shows our experiments on the hyperym discovery task including the general-purpose and domain-specific one. Section 4 concludes this paper.

2 System Overview

Our hypernym discovery system can be roughly split into two parts, *Term Embedding* and *Hypernym Relationship Learning*. We first train term embeddings, either using word embedding or sense embedding to represent each word. Then, neural networks are used to discover and rank the hypernym candidates for given terms.

2.1 Embedding

To use deep neural networks, symbolic data needs to be transformed into distributed representations(Wang et al., 2016a; Qin et al., 2016b; Cai and Zhao, 2016; Zhang et al., 2016; Wang et al., 2016b, 2015; Cai et al., 2017). We use *Glove* toolkit to train the word embeddings using *UMBC* corpus (Han et al., 2013). Moreover, in order to perform word sense induction and disambiguation, the word embedding could be transformed to sense embedding, which is induced from exhisting word embeddings via clustering of ego-networks (Pelevina et al., 2016) of related words. Thus, each input word or phrase is embedded into vector sequence, $w = \{x_1, x_2, \ldots, x_l\}$ where l denotes the sequence length. If the input term is a word, then $l = 1$ while for phrases, l means the number of words.

2.2 Hypernym Learning

Previous work like TAXOEMBED (Espinosa-Anke et al., 2016a) uses transformation matrix for hypernm relationship learning, which might be not optimal due to the lack of deeper nonlinear fea-

ture extraction. Thus, we empirically survey various neural networks to represent terms in latent space. After obtaining the representation for input term and all the candidate hypernyms, to give the ranked hypernym list, the cosine similarity between the term and the candidate hypernym is computed by,

$$cosine = \frac{\sum_{i=1}^{n}(x_i \times y_i)}{\sum_{i=1}^{n} x_i^2 \times \sum_{i=1}^{n} y_i^2}$$

where x_i and y_i denote the two concerned vectors. Our candidate neural networks include Convolutional Neural Network (CNN), Long-short Term Memory network (LSTM), Gated Recurrent Unit (GRU) and Recurrent Convolutional Neural Network (RCNN).

GRU The structure of GRU (Cho et al., 2014) used in this paper are described as follows.

$$r_t = \sigma(W_r x_t + U_r h_{t-1} + b_r),$$
$$z_t = \sigma(W_z x_t + U_z h_{t-1} + b_z),$$
$$\tilde{h}_t = \tanh(W_h x_t + U_h(rt \odot h_{t-1}) + b_h)$$
$$h_t = (1 - z_t) \odot h_{t-1} + z_t \odot \tilde{h}_t$$

where $\odot$ denotes the element-wise multiplication. r_t and z_t are the reset and update gates respectively, and $\tilde{h}_t$ the hidden states.

LSTM LSTM (Hochreiter and Schmidhuber, 1997) unit is defined as follows.

$$i_t = \sigma(W_i x_t + W_h h_{t-1} + b_i),$$
$$f_t = \sigma(W_f x_t + W_f h_{t-1} + b_f),$$
$$u_t = \sigma(W_u x_t + W_u h_{t-1} + b_u),$$
$$c_t = f_t \odot c_{t-1} + i_t \odot \tanh(W_c x_t + W_c h_{t-1} + b_c),$$
$$h_t = \tanh(c_t) \odot u_t,$$

where σ stands for the sigmoid function, $\odot$ represents element-wise multiplication and $W_i, W_f, W_u, W_c, b_i, b_f, b_u, b_c$ are model parameters. i_t, f_t, u_t, c_t, h_t are the input gates, forget gates, memory cells, output gates and the current state, respectively.

CNN Convolutional neural networks have also been successfully applied to various NLP tasks, in which the temporal convolution operation and associated filters map local chunks (windows) of the input into a feature representation.

Concretely, let n denote the filter width, filter matrices $[W_1, W_2, \ldots, W_k]$ with several variable sizes $[l_1, l_2, \ldots, l_k]$ are utilized to perform the convolution operations for input embeddings. For the sake of simplicity, we will explain the procedure for only one embedding sequence. The embedding will be transformed to sequences $c_j (j \in [1, k])$:

$$c_j = [\ldots; \tanh(W_j \cdot x_{[i:i+l_j-1]} + b_j); \ldots]$$

where $[i : i + l_j - 1]$ indexes the convolution window. Additionally, we apply wide convolution operation between embedding layer and filter matrices, because it ensures that all weights in the filters reach the entire sentence, including the words at the margins.

A *one-max-pooling* operation is adopted after convolution and the output vector s is obtained through concatenating all the mappings for those k filters.

$$s_j = max(c_j)$$
$$s = [s_1 \oplus \cdots \oplus s_j \oplus \cdots \oplus s_k]$$

In this way, the model can capture the critical features in the sentence with different filters.

RCNN Since some input terms are phrases, whose member words share different weights. In RCNN, an adaptive gated decay mechanism is used to weight the words in the convolution layer. Following (Lei et al., 2016), we introduce neural gates similar λ to LSTMs to specify when and how to average the observed signals. The resulting architecture integrates recurrent networks with non-consecutive convolutions:

$$\lambda = \sigma(W^\lambda x_t + U^\lambda h_{t-1} + b^\lambda)$$
$$c_t^1 = \lambda_t \odot c_{t-1}^1 + (1 - \lambda_t) \odot W_1 x_t$$
$$c_t^2 = \lambda_t \odot c_{t-1}^2 + (1 - \lambda_t) \odot (c_{t-1}^1 + W_2 x_t)$$
$$\cdots$$
$$c_t^n = \lambda_t \odot c_{t-1}^n + (1 - \lambda_t) \odot (c_{n-1}^1 + W_n x_t)$$
$$h_t = \tanh(c_t^n + b)$$

where $c_t^1, c_t^2, \cdots, c_t^n$ are accumulator vectors that store weighted averages of 1-gram to n-gram features.

For discriminative training, we use a max-margin framework for learning (or fine-tuning) parameters θ. Specifically, a scoring function $\varphi(\cdot, \cdot; \theta)$ is defined to measure the semantic similarity between the corresponding representations of input term and hypernym. Let $p = \{p_1, ...p_n\}$ denote the hypernym corpus and $h \in p$ is the

ground-truth hypernym to the term t_i, the optimal parameters θ are learned by minimizing the max-margin loss:

$$\max\{\varphi(t_i, p_i; \theta) - \varphi(t_i, a; \theta) + \delta(p_i, a)\}$$

where $\delta(., .)$ denotes a non-negative margin and $\delta(p_i, a)$ is a small constant when $a \neq p_i$ and 0 otherwise.

3 Experiment

In the following experiments, besides the neural networks, we also simply average the embeddings of an input phrase as our baseline to discover the relationship of terms and their corresponding hypernyms for comparison (denoted as *term embedding averaging, TEA*).

3.1 Setting

Our hypernym discovery experiments include general-purpose substask for English and domain-specific ones for medical and music. Our evaluation is based on the following information retrieval metrics: Mean Average Precision (MAP), Mean Reciprocal Rank (MRR), Precision at 1 (P@1), Precision at 3 (P@3), Precision at 5 (P@5), Precision at 15 (P@15).

For the sake of computational efficiency, we simply average the sense embedding if a word has more than one sense embedding (among various domains). Our model was implemented using the Theano[1] . The diagonal variant of Ada-Grad (Duchi et al., 2011) is used for neural network training. We tune the hyper-parameters with the following range of values: learning rate $\in \{1e - 3, 1e - 2\}$, dropout probability $\in \{0.1, 0.2\}$, CNN filter width $\in \{2, 3, 4\}$. The hidden dimension of all neural models are 200. The batch size is set to 20 and the word embedding and sense embedding sizes are set to 300. All of our models are trained on a single GPU (NVIDIA GTX 980Ti), with roughly 1.5h for general-purpose subtask for English and 0.5h domain-specific domain-specific ones for medical and music. We run all our models up to 50 epoch and select the best result in validation.

3.2 Result and analysis

Table 2 shows the result on general-domain subtask for English. All the neural models outperform term embedding averaging in terms of

---

[1]https://github.com/Theano/Theano

Embedding	Model	MAP	MRR	P@1	P@3	P@5	P 15
Word	TEA	6.10	11.13	4.00	6.00	5.40	5.14
	GRU	8.13	16.22	8.00	**8.00**	6.67	6.94
	LSTM	3.95	7.52	4.00	4.33	3.97	3.97
	CNN	7.32	13.33	**8.00**	9.00	7.80	6.94
	RCNN	**8.74**	**12.83**	6.00	**9.67**	**8.87**	**9.15**
Sense	TEA	4.42	8.71	0.00	4.04	4.19	5.31
	GRU	5.42	9.44	0.00	4.44	4.89	5.83
	LSTM	5.62	9.97	4.00	4.35	5.01	6.83
	CNN	6.41	10.92	2.00	5.01	5.67	6.29
	RCNN	5.79	9.24	0.00	4.71	5.29	6.43

Table 2: Gold standard evaluation on general-purpose subtask.

Embed	Model	medical						music					
		MAP	MRR	P@1	P@3	P@5	P 15	MAP	MRR	P@1	P@3	P@5	P 15
Word	TEA	8.91	16.77	0.00	8.79	9.41	9.39	7.11	14.32	0.00	10.01	10.77	9.21
	GRU	13.27	21.89	0.00	13.33	14.89	14.06	15.20	20.33	0.00	17.78	18.67	15.45
	LSTM	11.49	21.11	0.00	**17.78**	12.22	11.83	14.08	20.77	0.07	13.33	16.00	15.00
	CNN	**18.31**	**24.52**	0.00	15.56	**20.44**	**20.00**	**17.58**	**27.15**	0.00	**20.00**	**20.00**	**16.04**
	RCNN	16.78	23.40	0.00	13.33	13.00	14.50	13.60	21.67	0.07	13.33	14.67	13.08
Sense	TEA	2.01	4.77	0.00	2.91	2.77	3.21	2.59	5.28	0.00	2.12	3.01	2.93
	GRU	4.88	9.11	0.00	6.67	6.42	6.91	5.32	10.74	**2.00**	4.44	5.33	4.95
	LSTM	5.10	10.22	0.00	6.67	6.12	6.94	4.39	10.21	0.00	8.89	5.33	3.61
	CNN	4.15	7.84	0.00	4.44	6.09	6.42	4.75	9.61	0.00	6.67	6.67	4.43
	RCNN	4.63	9.84	0.00	6.67	6.89	6.43	4.73	8.56	0.00	4.44	6.22	4.94

Table 3: Gold standard evaluation on domain-specific subtask. "Embed" is short for "Embedding".

all the metrics. This result indicates simply averaging the embedding of words in a phrase is not an appropriate solution to represent a phrase. Convolution or recurrent gated mechanisms in either CNN-based (CNN, RCNN) or RNN (GRU, LSTM) based neural networks could essentially be helpful of modeling the semantic connections between words in a phrase, and guide the networks to discover the hypernym relationships. We also observe CNN-based network performance is better than RNN-based, which indicates local features between words could be more important than long-term dependency in this task where the term length is up to trigrams.

To investigate the performance of neural models on specific domains, we conduct experiments on medical and medicine subtask. Table 3 shows the result. All the neural models outperform *term embedding averaging* in terms of all the metrics and CNN-based network also performs better than RNN-based ones in most of the metrics using word embedding, which verifies our hypothesis in the general-purpose task. Compared with word embedding, the sense embedding shows a much poorer result though they work closely in general-purpose subtask. The reason might be the simple averaging of sense embedding of various domains for a word, which may introduce too much noise and bias the overall sense representation. This also discloses that modeling the sense embedding of specific domains could be quite important for further improvement.

4 Conclusion

In this paper, we introduce a neural network architecture for the hypernym discovery task and empirically study various neural network models to model the representations in latent space for words and phrases. Experiments on three subtasks show the neural models can yield satisfying results. We also evaluate the performance of word embedding and sense embedding, showing that in domain-specific tasks, sense embedding could be much more volatile.

References

Guido Boella and Luigi Di Caro. 2013. Supervised learning of syntactic contexts for uncovering definitions and extracting hypernym relations in text databases. *Joint European Conference on Machine Learning and Knowledge Discovery in Databases*, pages 64–79.

Deng Cai and Hai Zhao. 2016. Neural word segmentation learning for Chinese. In *Proceedings of the 54th Annual Meeting of the Association for Computational Linguistics (ACL 2016)*, pages 409–420.

Deng Cai and Hai Zhao. 2017. *Pair-Aware Neural Sentence Modeling for Implicit Discourse Relation Classification*. IEA/AIE 2017, Part II, LNAI 10351.

Deng Cai, Hai Zhao, Zhisong Zhang, Yuan Xin, Yongjian Wu, and Feiyue Huang. 2017. Fast and accurate neural word segmentation for Chinese. In *Proceedings of the 55th Annual Meeting of the Association for Computational Linguistics (ACL 2017)*, pages 608–615.

Jose Camacho-Collados, Claudio Delli Bovi, Luis Espinosa-Anke, Sergio Oramas, Tommaso Pasini, Enrico Santus, Vered Shwartz, Roberto Navigli, and Horacio Saggion. 2018. SemEval-2018 Task 9: Hypernym Discovery. In *Proceedings of the 12th International Workshop on Semantic Evaluation (SemEval-2018)*, New Orleans, LA, United States. Association for Computational Linguistics.

Kyunghyun Cho, Bart Van Merrienboer, Caglar Gulcehre, Dzmitry Bahdanau, Fethi Bougares, Holger Schwenk, and Yoshua Bengio. 2014. Learning phrase representations using rnn encoder-decoder for statistical machine translation. In *Proceedings of the 2014 Conference on Empirical Methods in Natural Language Processing (EMNLP 2014)*, pages 1724–1734.

Ido Dagan, Roth Dan, Fabio Zanzotto, and Mark Sammons. 2013. Recognizing textual entailment:models and applications. *Computational Linguistics*, 41(1):157–160.

John C. Duchi, Elad Hazan, and Yoram Singer. 2011. Adaptive subgradient methods for online learning and stochastic optimization. *Journal of Machine Learning Research*, 12(39):2121–2159.

Luis Espinosa-Anke, Jose Camacho-Collados, Claudio Delli Bovi, and Horacio Saggion. 2016a. Supervised distributional hypernym discovery via domain adaptation. In *Proceedings of the 2016 Conference on Empirical Methods in Natural Language Processing (EMNLP 2016)*, page 424435.

Luis Espinosa-Anke, Horacio Saggion, Francesco Ronzano, and Roberto Navigli. 2016b. Extasem! extending, taxonomizing and semantifying domain terminologies. In *Proceedings of the Thirtieth AAAI Conference on Artificial Intelligence (AAAI-16)*, pages 2594–2600.

Trevor Fountain and Mirella Lapata. 2012. Taxonomy induction using hierarchical random graphs. In *Conference of the North American Chapter of the Association for Computational Linguistics: Human Language Technologies*, pages 466–476.

Lushan Han, Abhay Kashyap, Tim Finin, James Mayfield, and Jonathan Weese. 2013. Umbc ebiquitycore: Semantic textual similarity systems. *Second Joint Conference on Lexical and Computational Semantics (*SEM)*, 1:4452.

Sanda Harabagiu and Andrew Hickl. 2006. Methods for using textual entailment in open-domain question answering. In *Proceedings of the 21st International Conference on Computational Linguistics and 44th Annual Meeting of the ACL (ACL 2006)*, pages 905–912.

Sepp Hochreiter and Jrgen Schmidhuber. 1997. Long short-term memory. *Neural Computation*, 9(8):1735–1780.

Yong Bin Kang, Pari Delir Haghighi, and Frada Burstein. 2016. Taxofinder: A graph-based approach for taxonomy learning. *IEEE Transactions on Knowledge & Data Engineering*, 28(2):524–536.

Tao Lei, Hrishikesh Joshi, Regina Barzilay, Tommi Jaakkola, Katerina Tymoshenko, Alessandro Moschitti, and Lluis Marquez. 2016. Semi-supervised question retrieval with gated convolutions. In *Proceedings of NAACL-HLT 2016*, pages 1279–1289.

Haonan Li, Zhisong Zhang, Yuqi Ju, and Hai Zhao. 2018. Neural character-level dependency parsing for Chinese. In *The Thirty-Second AAAI Conference on Artificial Intelligence (AAAI-18)*.

Chenxi Pang, Hai Zhao, and Zhongyi Li. 2016. I can guess what you mean: A monolingual query enhancement for machine translation. In *The Fifteenth China National Conference on Computational Linguistics (CCL 2016)*.

Maria Pelevina, Nikolay Arefiev, Chris Biemann, and Alexander Panchenko. 2016. Making sense of word embeddings. In *Proceedings of the 1st Workshop on Representation Learning for NLP*, pages 174–183.

Lianhui Qin, Zhisong Zhang, and Hai Zhao. 2016a. Shallow discourse parsing using convolutional neural network. In *Proceedings of the 54th Annual Meeting of the Association for Computational Linguistics (ACL 2016)*, pages 70–77.

Lianhui Qin, Zhisong Zhang, and Hai Zhao. 2016b. A stacking gated neural architecture for implicit discourse relation classification. In *Conference on Empirical Methods in Natural Language Processing (EMNLP 2016)*, pages 2263–2270.

Lianhui Qin, Zhisong Zhang, Hai Zhao, Zhiting Hu, and Eric P. Xing. 2017. Adversarial connective-exploiting networks for implicit discourse relation classification. In *Proceedings of the 55th Annual Meeting of the Association for Computational Linguistics (ACL 2017)*, pages 1006–1017.

Stephen Roller and Katrin Erk. 2016. Relations such as hypernymy: Identifying and exploiting hearst patterns in distributional vectors for lexical entailment. In *Proceedings of the 2016 Conference on Empirical Methods in Natural Language Processing (EMNLP 2016)*, page 21632172.

Paola Velardi, Stefano Faralli, and Roberto Navigli. 2013. Ontolearn reloaded: A graph-based algorithm for taxonomy induction. *Computational Linguistics*, 39(3):665–707.

Hao Wang, Hai Zhao, and Zhisong Zhang. 2017. A transition-based system for universal dependency parsing. In *CONLL 2017 Shared Task: Multilingual Parsing From Raw Text To Universal Dependencies (CONLL 2017)*, pages 191–197.

Peilu Wang, Yao Qian, Frank K. Soong, Lei He, and Hai Zhao. 2016a. Learning distributed word representations for bidirectional lstm recurrent neural network. In *Conference of the North American Chapter of the Association for Computational Linguistics: Human Language Technologies (NAACL 2016)*, pages 527–533.

Rui Wang, Masao Utiyama, Isao Goto, Eiichiro Sumita, Hai Zhao, and Bao Liang Lu. 2016b. Converting continuous-space language models into n-gram language models with efficient bilingual pruning for statistical machine translation. *ACM Transactions on Asian and Low-Resource Language Information Processing*, 15(3):11.

Rui Wang, Hai Zhao, Bao Liang Lu, Masao Utiyama, and Eiichiro Sumita. 2015. Bilingual continuous-space language model growing for statistical machine translation. *IEEE/ACM Transactions on Audio Speech & Language Processing*, 23(7):1209–1220.

Rui Wang, Hai Zhao, Bao Liang Lu, Masao Utiyama, and Eiichro Sumita. 2016c. Connecting phrase based statistical machine translation adaptation. In *Proceedings of COLING 2016, the 26th International Conference on Computational Linguistics: Technical Papers (COLING 2016)*, page 31353145.

Mohamed Yahya, Klaus Berberich, Shady Elbassuoni, and Gerhard Weikum. 2013. Robust question answering over the web of linked data. In *Proceedings of the 22nd ACM international conference on Conference on information & knowledge management (CIKM 2013)*, pages 1107–1116.

Zhisong Zhang, Hai Zhao, and Lianhui Qin. 2016. Probabilistic graph-based dependency parsing with convolutional neural network. In *Proceedings of the 54th Annual Meeting of the Association for Computational Linguistics (ACL 2016)*, pages 1382–1392.

Hai Zhao, Deng Cai, Changning Huang, and Chunyu Kit. 2017a. *Chinese Word Segmentation, a decade review (2007-2017)*. China Social Sciences Press, Beijing, China.

Hai Zhao, Deng Cai, Yang Xin, Yuzhu Wang, and Zhongye Jia. 2017b. A hybrid model for Chinese spelling check. *ACM Transactions on Asian Low-Resource Language Information Process*, pages 1–22.

NLP_HZ at SemEval-2018 Task 9: a Nearest Neighbor Approach

Wei Qiu
Alibaba Group, China
qiuwei.cw@alibaba-inc.com

Mosha Chen
Alibaba Group,China
chenmosha.cms@alibaba-inc.com

Linlin Li
Alibaba Group, China
linyan.lll@alibaba-inc.com

Luo Si
Alibaba Group, China
luo.si@alibaba-inc.com

Abstract

Hypernym discovery aims to discover the hypernym word sets given a hyponym word and proper corpus. This paper proposes a simple but effective method for the discovery of hypernym sets based on word embedding, which can be used to measure the contextual similarities between words. Given a test hyponym word, we get its hypernym lists by computing the similarities between the hyponym word and words in the training data, and fill the test word's hypernym lists with the hypernym list in the training set of the nearest similarity distance to the test word. In SemEval 2018 task9, our results, achieve 1st on Spanish, 2nd on Italian, 6th on English in the metric of MAP.

1 Introduction

Hypernymy relationship plays a critical role in language understanding because it enables generalization, which lies at the core of human cognition (Yu et al. (2015)). It has been widely used in various NLP applications (Espinosa Anke et al. (2016)), from word sense disambiguation (Agirre et al. (2014)) to information retrieval (Varelas et al. (2005)) , question answering (Prager (2006)) and textual entailment (Glickman et al. (2005)). To date, the hypernymy relation also plays an important role in Knowledge Base Construction task.

In the past SemEval contest (SemEval-2015 task 17[1], SemEval-2016 task 13[2]), the "Hypernym Detection" task was treated as a classfication task, i.e., given a (hyponym, hypernym) pair, deciding whether the pair is a true hypernymic relation or not. This has led to criticisms regarding its oversimplification (Levy et al., 2015). In the SemEval 2018 Task 9 (Camacho-Collados et al., 2018), the task has shifted to "Hypernym Discovery" , i.e.,

given the search space of a domain's vocabulary and an input hyponym, discover its best (set of) candidate hypernyms.

In this paper, the content is organized as follows: Section 2 gives an introduction to the related work; Section 3 describes our methods for this task, including word embedding projection learning as the baseline and the nearest-neighbour-based method as the submission result; The experimental results are presented in Section 4. We conclude the paper with Section 5.

2 Related Work

The work of identifying hypernymy relationship can be categorized from different aspects according to the learning methods and the task formulization. The earlier work (Hearst (1992)) formalized the task as an unsupervised hypernym discovery task, i.e., none hyponym-hypernyms pairs (x, y) are given as the training data. Hearst (1992) handcrafted a set of lexico-syntactic paths that connect the joint occurrences of x and y which indicate hypernymy in a large corpus. Snow et al. (2004) trained a logistic regression classifier using all dependency paths which connect a small number of known hyponym-hypernym pairs. Paths that were assigned high weights by the classifier are used to extract unseen hypernym pairs from a new corpus. Variations of Snow et al. (2004) were later used in tasks such as taxonomy construction (Snow et al. (2006); Kozareva and Hovy (2010); Carlson et al. (2010)), analogy identification (Turney (2006)), and definition extraction (Borg et al. (2009); Navigli and Velardi (2010)).

A major limitation in relying on lexico-syntactic paths is the requirement of the coocurence of the hypernym pairs. Distributional methods are developed to overcome this limitation. Lin (1998) developed symmetric similarity

---

[1]http://alt.qcri.org/semeval2015/task17/
[2]http://alt.qcri.org/semeval2016/task13/

909

Proceedings of the 12th International Workshop on Semantic Evaluation (SemEval-2018), pages 909–913
New Orleans, Louisiana, June 5–6, 2018. ©2018 Association for Computational Linguistics

measures to detect hypernym in an unsupervised manner. Weeds and Weir (2003); Kotlerman et al. (2010) employed directional measures based on the distributional inclusion hypothesis. More recent work (Santus et al. (2014); Rimell (2014)) introduces new measures, based on the distributional informativeness hypothesis. Yu et al. (2015); Tuan and Ng (2016); Nguyen et al. (2017) learn directly the word embeddings which are optimized for capturing the hypernymy relationship.

The supervised methods include Baroni and Lenci (2011); Roller et al. (2014); Weeds and Weir (2003). These methods were originally word-count-based, but can be easily adapted using word embeddings (Mikolov et al. (2013a); Pennington et al. (2014)). However, it was criticized that the supervised methods only learn prototypical hypernymy (Levy et al. (2015)).

3 Hyponym-hypernym Discovery method

3.1 Preprocessing

For the corpus and the train/gold/test data, we have two preprocessing steps: 1) Lowercase all the words; 2) Concatenate the phrases (hyponym or hypernym composed with more than one word) which occur in the training set or the test set with underline, i.e., "executive president" is replaced by "executive_president". It is quite useful for training word embedding models because we want to treat phrases as single words.

If there are multiple phrases in one sentence, we generate multiple sentences, one per phrase. For example, "executive president" and "vice executive president" both exist in the corpus sentence "Hoang Van Dung , vice executive president of the Vietnam Chamber of Commerce and Industry.". After preprocessing, two more sentences are generated and included in the training corpus for word embeddings:

- Hoang Van Dung , vice executive_president of the Vietnam Chamber of Commerce and Industry.

- Hoang Van Dung , vice_executive_president of the Vietnam Chamber of Commerce and Industry.

The size of the original corpus has increased after the preprocessing step, e.g., The English corpus has increased from $\sim$18G to $\sim$32G.

3.2 Word Embedding

We train our word embedding models using the Google word2vec (Mikolov et al. (2013a,b)) tool[3] on the preprocessed corpus. We employ the skip-gram model since the skip-gram model is shown to perform best in identifying semantic relations among words. The trained word embeddings are used in the projection learning and nearest-neighbour based method.

3.3 Method based on Projection Learning

The intuition of this method is to assume that there is a linear transformation in the embedding space which maps hyponyms to their correspondent hypernyms. We first learn a projection matrix from the training data, then apply the matrix to the test data. Our method is similar to that described in Fu et al. (2014), the main idea can be summarized as follows:

1. Give a word x and its hypernym y, assuming there exists a linear projection matrix Φ to meet $y = \Phi x$. We need to learn a approximate Φ using the following equation to minimize the MSE loss:

$$\Phi^* = \arg\min_{\Phi} \frac{1}{N} \sum_{(x,y)} \|\Phi x - y\|^2 \quad (1)$$

2. Learn the piecewise linear projection by clustering the training data into different groups according to the vector offsets. The motivation for the clustering is two-fold: firstly, the hypernym-hyponym relation is diverse, e.g., offset from "carpenter" and "laborer" is distant from the one from "gold fish" to "fish"; Secondly, if a hyponym x has many hypernyms (or hierarchical hypernyms), we can't use a single transition matrix Φ to project x to different hypernym y. So a piecewise projection learning is needed in each individual group. Thus, the optimization goal can be formalized as follows:

$$\Phi_k^* = \arg\min_{\Phi_k} \frac{1}{N_k} \sum_{(x,y \in C_k)} \|\Phi_k x - y\|^2$$

$$(2)$$

Where N_k is the number of word pairs in the kth cluster C_k.

---

[3]https://code.google.com/archive/p/word2vec/

3. Learn the threshold δ_k for each cluster, by assumming that positive (hyponmy-hypernmy) pairs can locate in radius δ while negative pairs can not:

$$d(\Phi_k x - y) = \|\Phi_k x - y\|^2 < \delta_k \quad (3)$$

Where d stands for the euclidean distance.

4. Once the piecewise projection and the threshold is learned, given a new hyponym x, all of the hypernym candidates ys from the vocabulary are paired with x. The pairs are assigned to the proper cluster by the vector offset $(y\text{-}x)$. According to the threshold δ in that group, it can be decided whether (x, y) is a reasonable hyponym-hypernym pair.

3.4 Method Based on Nearest Neighbors

We noticed that the hypernyms are often very distant from the correspondent hyponyms in the embedding space. Meanwhile, hyponyms which are close to each other often share the same hypernyms. We propose a simple yet effective approach based on this observation.

Suppose the training set H consists of a number of hyponyms and their correspondent hypernyms

$$H : \{Hypo^k : Hyper_1^k...Hyper_i^k\}$$

During the test time, for an unseen hyponym x, the top K nearest hyponyms in the training set , i.e., $Hypo_i$ are found, and their hypernyms are used as the output , i.e., the hypernyms of x. The found hypernyms are sorted according to the distance between x and $Hypo_i$. This can be formalized as follows:

$$\text{HypoN} = [\text{Hypo}_i].\text{sort\_by}(\text{distance}(\text{Hypo}_i, x))$$
$$\text{Hyper}(x) = [\text{Hyper}(w)|w \text{ in HypoN}]$$

where the *distance* function measures the similarity between $Hypo_i$ and x, HypoN is the list of words from the training set sorted according to their distances to x. Consine similarity in the embedding space is used for the distance function in our setup. According to the requirements of Task 9, only the top 15 of $Hyper(x)$ are submitted for evaluation.

4 Evaluation

4.1 Experimental Setup

Word2vec is used to produce the word embeddings. The skip-gram model (**-cbow 0**) is used with the embedding dimension set to 300 (**-size 300**). The other options are by default. We use 10-fold cross validation to evaluate both methods on the provided training data. The results are shown in Table 1 [4]

4.2 Results Based on Projection Learning

For the projection learning method, we followed experimental settings described in Fu et al. (2014).The negative (hyponym, hypernym) pairs are randomly sampled from the vocabulary. The training set consists of the negative pairs and the positive pairs in 3:1 ratio.

By using the same evaluating metrics as PRF in the cited paper, our best F-value on the validation set is 0.68 (the paper result is 0.73) when the best cluster number is 2 and the threshold is (17.7, 17.3). We apply the learned projection matrices and thresholds on the validation data, extract out the candidate hypernyms from the given vocabulary and truncate the top 15 candidates by sorting them according to the $d(\Phi_k x, y)/\delta_k$ scores. The generated results are not very promising, see Table 1 for details.

This projection learning method performs not very well on task9, we think the most probable reason is that in Fu et al. (2014), the problem is formalized as a classification problem, in which the **(hyponym, hypernym)** pairs are given. However, our task is formalized as a hypernym discovery problem given only **hyponmys**. This task might be inherently much harder than the classification task; a second reason might be related to the relative small amount of training data, i.e., $\sim$7500 training pairs in total.

4.3 Results Based on NN

The results are shown in Table 1 from row 2 to row 5. Table 2 shows the results evaluated on the test data. The performance evaluated using either cross validation or the test data is much worse than that of a typical hypernym prediction task reported by Weeds and Weir (2003). This illustrates that hypernym discovery is indeed a much harder task than the hypernym prediction task.

Although the method proposed by us is quite simple, our submissions are the 1st on Spanish, the 2nd on Italian, the 6th on English, ranked by the

---

[4]The PL based method is not evaluated on Italian or Spanish corpus due to its poor performance on English corpus. The result of PL method is not submitted for the task evaluation either.

System	Language	MAP	MRR	P@1	P@3	P@5	P@15
PL	English	2.8	7.6	7.5	3.3	2.6	2.0
NN	English	13.3	25.1	18.7	13.9	13.5	12.5
NN	Spanish	16.6	27.2	19.0	17.2	16.4	16.1
NN	Italian	19.3	32.4	25	19.8	18.6	18.6

Table 1: Cross validation results of the two methods on training set(%). PL stands for the projection-learning based system. NN stands for the nearest-neighbor based method.

Language	MAP	MRR	P@1	P@3	P@5	P@15
English	9.37	17.29	12	10.14	9.19	8.78
Spanish	20.04	28.27	21.4	20.95	20.39	19.38
Italian	11.37	19.19	13.1	12.08	11.23	10.9

Table 2: Results on the test data for our submissions(%).

metric of MAP. This proves the effectiveness of the method.

Compared with the results got by cross validation, the performance evaluated on the test data (Table 2) dropped significantly on English (MAP dropped by 4%) and Italian (MAP dropped by 8%), but increased by a margin on Spanish (MAP increased by 3.6%). We consider that it is due to the properties of provided data , i.e., the hypernyms in the test set are similar to those in the training set for Spanish, but dissimilar for English or Italian.

The performance drop for English and Italian exposes one of the main drawbacks of our method: the method can not discover the hypernyms that have never occurred in the training set. To overcome this shortcoming, using syntactic patterns to extract hyponym-hypernym with high confidence can be employed to enlarge the training set. We leave this to the future work.

5   Conclusion

In this paper we describe two methods we have tried out for the hypernym discovery task in SemEval 2018. We extended the method originally proposed for hypernym prediction by Fu et al. (2014) as a baseline system. However the performance of this method is poor. The nearest-neighbor-based method is relatively simple, yet quite effective. We analyzed the experimental results, reveal some shortcomings, and propose a potential extension to future improvement.

References

Eneko Agirre, Oier López de Lacalle, and Aitor Soroa. 2014. Random walks for knowledge-based word sense disambiguation. *Comput. Linguist.*, 40(1):57–84.

Marco Baroni and Alessandro Lenci. 2011. How we BLESSed distributional semantic evaluation. *GEMS '11 Proceedings of the GEMS 2011 Workshop on GEometrical Models of Natural Language Semantics*, pages 1–10.

Claudia Borg, Mike Rosner, and Gordon Pace. 2009. Evolutionary algorithms for definition extraction. *Proceedings of the 1st Workshop on Definition Extraction*, pages 26–32.

Jose Camacho-Collados, Claudio Delli Bovi, Luis Espinosa-Anke, Sergio Oramas, Tommaso Pasini, Enrico Santus, Vered Shwartz, Roberto Navigli, and Horacio Saggion. 2018. SemEval-2018 Task 9: Hypernym Discovery. In *Proceedings of the 12th International Workshop on Semantic Evaluation (SemEval-2018)*, New Orleans, LA, United States. Association for Computational Linguistics.

Andrew Carlson, Justin Betteridge, and Bryan Kisiel. 2010. Toward an Architecture for Never-Ending Language Learning. In *Proceedings of the Conference on Artificial Intelligence (AAAI) (2010)*, pages 1306–1313.

Luis Espinosa Anke, Jose Camacho-Collados, Claudio Delli Bovi, and Horacio Saggion. 2016. Supervised distributional hypernym discovery via domain adaptation. In *Proceedings of the 2016 Conference on Empirical Methods in Natural Language Processing*, pages 424–435. Association for Computational Linguistics.

Ruiji Fu, Jiang Guo, Bing Qin, Wanxiang Che, Haifeng Wang, and Ting Liu. 2014. Learning semantic hierarchies via word embeddings. In *Proceedings of the 52nd Annual Meeting of the Association for Computational Linguistics (Volume 1: Long Papers)*, pages

1199–1209, Baltimore, Maryland. Association for Computational Linguistics.

Oren Glickman, Ido Dagan, and Moshe Koppel. 2005. A probabilistic classification approach for lexical textual entailment. In *AAAI*, pages 1050–1055. AAAI Press / The MIT Press.

Marti A. Hearst. 1992. Automatic acquisition of hyponyms from large text corpora. *Proceedings of the 14th conference on Computational linguistics - , 2:539.

Lili Kotlerman, Ido Dagan, Idan Szpektor, and Maayan Zhitomirsky-Geffet. 2010. Directional distributional similarity for lexical inference. *Natural Language Engineering*, 16(4):359–389.

Zornitsa Kozareva and Eduard Hovy. 2010. A Semi-Supervised Method to Learn and Construct Taxonomies using the Web. *Proceedings of EMNLP, MIT, Massachusets, USA*, (October):1110–1118.

Omer Levy, Steffen Remus, Chris Biemann, and Ido Dagan. 2015. Do supervised distributional methods really learn lexical inference relations? *Proceedings of the 2015 Conference of the North American Chapter of the Association for Computational Linguistics: Human Language Technologies*, pages 970–976.

Dekang Lin. 1998. An Information-Theoretic Definition of Similarity. *Proceedings of ICML*, pages 296–304.

Tomas Mikolov, Kai Chen, Greg Corrado, and Jeffrey Dean. 2013a. Distributed Representations of Words and Phrases and Their Compositionality. *In Advances in neural information processing systems*, pages 3111–3119.

Tomas Mikolov, Ilya Sutskever, Kai Chen, Greg Corrado, and Jeffrey Dean. 2013b. Distributed representations of words and phrases and their compositionality. *CoRR*, abs/1310.4546.

Roberto Navigli and Paola Velardi. 2010. Learning Word-Class Lattices for Definition and Hypernym Extraction. *Proceedings of the 48th Annual Meeting of the Association for Computational Linguistics (ACL 2010).*, (July):1318–1327.

Kim Anh Nguyen, Maximilian Köper, Sabine Schulte im Walde, and Ngoc Thang Vu. 2017. Hierarchical Embeddings for Hypernymy Detection and Directionality. pages 233–243.

Jeffrey Pennington, Richard Socher, and Christopher Manning. 2014. Glove: Global Vectors for Word Representation. *Proceedings of the 2014 Conference on Empirical Methods in Natural Language Processing (EMNLP)*, pages 1532–1543.

John Prager. 2006. Open-domain question: Answering. *Found. Trends Inf. Retr.*, 1(2):91–231.

Laura Rimell. 2014. Distributional Lexical Entailment by Topic Coherence. *In Proceedings of the 14th Conference of the European Chapter of the Association for Computational Linguistics, Gothenburg, Sweden, April 26-30 2014*, pages 511–519.

Stephen Roller, Katrin Erk, and Gemma Boleda. 2014. Inclusive yet Selective: Supervised Distributional Hypernymy Detection. *In Proceedings of COLING 2014, the 25th International Conference on Computational Linguistics: Technical Papers, Dublin, Ireland, August 23-29 2014*, pages 1025–1036.

Enrico Santus, Alessandro Lenci, Qin Lu, and Sabine Schulte im Walde. 2014. Chasing Hypernyms in Vector Spaces with Entropy. *Proc. European Chapter of the Association for Computational Linguistics*, pages 38–42.

Rion Snow, Daniel Jurafsky, and Andrew Y Ng. 2004. Learning syntactic patterns for automatic hypernym discovery. *Advances in Neural Information Processing Systems 17*, 17:1297–1304.

Rion Snow, Daniel Jurafsky, and Andrew Y Ng. 2006. Semantic taxonomy induction from heterogenous evidence. In *Proceedings of the 21st International Conference on Computational Linguistics and the 44th annual meeting of the ACL - ACL '06*, pages 801–808.

Luu Anh Tuan and See Kiong Ng. 2016. Learning Term Embeddings for Taxonomic Relation Identification Using Dynamic Weighting Neural Network. *Proceedings of the 2016 Conference on Empirical Methods in Natural Language Processing (EMNLP-16)*, pages 403–413.

Peter D. Turney. 2006. Similarity of Semantic Relations. (March 2005):1–39.

Giannis Varelas, Epimenidis Voutsakis, Paraskevi Raftopoulou, Euripides G.M. Petrakis, and Evangelos E. Milios. 2005. Semantic similarity methods in wordnet and their application to information retrieval on the web. In *Proceedings of the 7th Annual ACM International Workshop on Web Information and Data Management*, WIDM '05, pages 10–16, New York, NY, USA. ACM.

Julie Weeds and David Weir. 2003. A general framework for distributional similarity. *Proceedings of the 2003 Conference on Empirical Methods in Natural Language Processing*, pages 81–88.

Zheng Yu, Haixun Wang, Xuemin Lin, and Min Wang. 2015. Learning term embeddings for hypernymy identification. *IJCAI International Joint Conference on Artificial Intelligence*, 2015-January(Ijcai):1390–1397.

UMDuluth-CS8761 at SemEval-2018 Task 9: Hypernym Discovery using Hearst Patterns, Co-occurrence frequencies and Word Embeddings

Arshia Z. Hassan and **Manikya S. Vallabhajosyula** and **Ted Pedersen**
Department of Computer Science
University of Minnesota
Duluth, MN 55812 USA
{hassa418,valla045,tpederse}@d.umn.edu
https://github.com/manikyaswathi/SemEval2018HypernymDiscovery

Abstract

Hypernym Discovery is the task of identifying potential hypernyms for a given term. A hypernym is a more generalized word that is super-ordinate to more specific words. This paper explores several approaches that rely on co-occurrence frequencies of word pairs, Hearst Patterns based on regular expressions, and word embeddings created from the UMBC corpus. Our system Babbage participated in Subtask 1A for English and placed 6th of 19 systems when identifying concept hypernyms, and 12th of 18 systems for entity hypernyms.

1 Introduction

Hypernym-hyponym pairs exhibit an *is-a* relationship where a hypernym is a generalization of a hyponym. The objective of SemEval–2018 Task 9 (Camacho-Collados et al., 2018) is to generate a ranked list of hypernyms when given an input hyponym and a vocabulary of candidate hypernyms. For example, the input hyponym *lemongrass* could yield the hypernyms [*grass, oil plant, herb*], where *herb* would be the best candidate. This scenario is illustrated in Figure 1, where the three leaf nodes are hyponyms and the root is a hypernym.

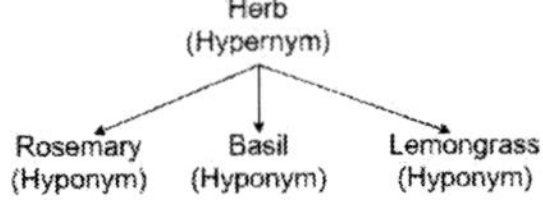

Figure 1: Hypernym-hyponym example

Note that hypernym discovery is distinct from hypernym detection, where the problem is to detect if a hyponym-hypernym relationship exists between a given pair, such as *lemongrass-grass*.

In our first module, we retrieve candidate hypernyms for an input term using a paragraph-length context-window and calculate their co-occurrence frequencies, which is later used for ranking the candidates. Our second module uses Hearst Patterns (Hearst, 1992) to extract hyponym-hypernym pairs and ranks candidate hypernyms based on co-occurrence frequency of the pairs. Our final module employs word-embeddings created using word2vec (Mikolov et al., 2013). This paper continues with a more detailed discussion of each module, and then a review of our results.

2 Implementation

Babbage begins by pre-processing (2.2.1) the UMBC Corpus (2.1) and extracting candidate hypernyms using four different strategies (2.2.2). The first and second module calculates the co-occurrence frequencies between the input term and words in context using the pre-processed UMBC Corpus and the Hearst Pattern set extracted from the UMBC Corpus. The third module uses the IS-A Hearst Pattern set extracted from UMBC Corpus to obtain hypernyms. The final module constructs a word embedding over the UMBC corpus and uses a distance measure to fetch candidate hypernyms for a given input term.

2.1 UMBC Corpus

Our training corpus is the University of Maryland, Baltimore County (UMBC) WebBase Corpus (Han et al., 2013). It contains 3 billion words from paragraphs obtained from more than 100 million web pages over various domains. We use the 28 GB tokenized version of UMBC corpus which is part-of-speech tagged and divided among 408 files. There is also a vocabulary file with 218,755 unigram, bigram and trigram hypernym terms provided by task organizers. This file defines the set of possible candidate hypernyms.

Proceedings of the 12th International Workshop on Semantic Evaluation (SemEval-2018), pages 914–918
New Orleans, Louisiana, June 5–6, 2018. ©2018 Association for Computational Linguistics

2.2 Architecture of System Babbage

The following are the steps involved in constructing our system:

1. **Pre-processing the input text corpus [2.2.1]:** Corpora obtained in this stage include:

   (a) Normalize the input corpus and store as *Normalized Corpus*

   (b) Fetch Hearst Patterns (see Figure 2) from input corpus and store as *Hearst Corpus*

   (c) Fetch IS-A Pattern from the input corpus and store as *IS-A Corpus*

   (d) Creating the word-embedding matrix *UMBC Embedding* using Normalized Corpus.

   The Hearst Corpus and the IS-A Corpus patterns are extracted from the original text corpus which has been preprocessed to eliminate punctuation, prepositions, and conjunctions. All possible combinations of bigram and trigram noun phrases are retained in the Normalized Corpus. A Word-Embedding matrix is built over this Normalized Corpus.

2. **Extracting candidate hypernyms [2.2.2]:**

   (a) **Co-occurrence frequencies from Normalized Corpus:** A co-occurrence map is built for the input terms with the words in the context of the input term and the frequency of their co-occurrence using the Normalized Corpus. Words with co-occurrence frequency higher than *5* are listed as candidate hypernyms for an input term. This is considered the first module result.

   (b) **Co-occurrence frequencies from Hearst Corpus:** A co-occurrence map similar to the previous step is built by using the Hearst Corpus. All the words which occur at least once in context of the input term in the Hearst Patterns are listed as candidate hypernyms for this term. This is considered the second module result.

   (c) **Co-occurrence frequencies from IS-A Corpus:** All the words which occur at least once in the context of the input term in the IS-A Corpus are listed as candidate hypernyms for this term. If the input term is a concept and is a bigram or trigram term, then part of it is considered as a hypernym for that term. This is considered the third module result.

   (d) **Applying word similarity to word embeddings:** A fixed distance value called *Phi* is used to extract words at this distance to the input term in the UMBC Embedding. These words are listed as the candidate hypernyms for an input term. This is considered our final module result.

3. **Merging results from various modules [2.3]:** The order of merging these results is decided by the evaluation scores from these modules for training data. The same order is applied to the test data.

2.2.1 Pre-processing

The task description states that our system should predict candidate hypernyms for an input word which is either a concept or an entity. Hence, the part-of-speech tag for all candidate hypernyms is *noun*. This restricts our search space to words with *noun* part-of-speech tag and bigram or trigram phrases with a *noun* head word. Our system focuses on concepts, so we do not have any module specific for entities. To refine the input corpus as per these specifications, the input UMBC Corpus is processed through the following modules:

Normalized Corpus: The POS tagged input corpus is processed per paragraph. Each paragraph is converted to lower-case text. Then, bigram and trigram noun phrases from each paragraph are obtained using the POS tags given for each word. It is further filtered by removing punctuation marks and words with part-of-speech tags other than *noun*, *verb*, *adverb* or *adjective*. This filtered line is modified by appending it with bigram and trigram noun phrases obtained earlier.

Hearst Corpus: The original input paragraph is searched for the Hearst Patterns (shown in Figure 2) and all the possible matches are returned in the form of *hypernym : one or more hyponyms*. Figure 2 shows the extraction of Hearst Patterns, where NP represents a noun-phrase where the head word is tagged as a *noun*, *the loved-ones* **such as** *family and friends* is a match for Hearst Patterns (from

Figure 2) with noun phrases *the loved-ones, family* and *friends*.

IS-A Corpus: A pattern which is not used in the construction of the Hearst Corpus is used here: **Hyponym Noun Phrase *is (a | an | the)* Hypernym Noun Phrase**. Here the original input paragraph is searched against this pattern and all the possible matches are returned in the form of *hyponym : hypernym*. *a fennel* **is a** *plant* is a match for this pattern with noun phrases *a fennel* and *plant*.

UMBC Embedding: A word embedding matrix is created over the Normalized Corpus using word2vec (Mikolov et al., 2013). The specifications of the model are as follows:

(a) **Model** : ***Continuous Bag of Words (CBOW)*** - a term's embedding value is determined by its context words. The order of the words in the window size does not matter.

(b) **Window Size :** *10*. The context window size for a term which determines its vector value.

(c) **Minimum Frequency Count :** *5*. If the frequency of a word is less than this value, the word does not exist in the embedding.

(d) **Embedding Dimension Size :** *300*. The number of dimensions for the embedding matrix.

2.2.2 Extracting candidate hypernyms:

Once the UMBC corpus is pre-processed and the three required corpora and an embedding matrix are derived, candidate hypernyms are acquired by applying the below processes.

Co-occurrence frequency from Normalized Corpus: With this module, we hypothesized that a hyponym and its possible hypernyms are more likely to co-occur within a context-window. The context window of a term is its own paragraph. We start by creating a map for all the input terms. If a normalized paragraph 2.2.1 contains any of the input terms, then all the words in the context are added to the map of this particular term which considers them to be hypernyms for this input hyponym term. Every time a hypernym-hyponym pair co-occurs in one line, their co-occurrence count is increased by one. Finally, the candidate hypernyms are ranked in descending order of their co-occurrence frequencies.

Co-occurrence frequency from Hearst Corpus: In the pre-processing step 2.2.1, we extracted possible hypernym-hyponym mapping data using

Hearst Patterns. Each line of the data is of the form *hypernym : hyponym-1 , hyponym-2, , hyponym-n*. In this module, we created a map where each *hyponym* is a key mapped to *hypernyms* occurring with that *hyponym* and their co-occurrence frequencies. For example, values for keys *hyponym-1, hyponym-2, and hyponym-n* are updated with *hypernym* and the frequencies are increased by 1. Finally the top 15 *hyponyms* (based on frequencies) for each key are reported as the result hypernyms.

Co-occurrence frequencies from IS-A Corpus: This module uses hypernym-hyponym pairs from the IS-A Corpus 2.2.1 which are in the form *hyponym : hypernym*. We use the same strategy as *Co-occurrence frequency from Hearst Corpus* to obtain the result.

Applying word similarity to word embeddings: We need a general distance vector which represents a hypernym-hyponym distance in the UMBC Embedding. We use training data input term (x) and the gold data hypernyms (y) to calculate this distance(Φ^*) which is calculated by:

$$\Phi^* = \underset{\Phi}{\mathrm{argmin}} \frac{1}{N} \sum_{(x,y)} \Phi \|x - y\|^2 \qquad (1)$$

Φ is used to get candidate hypernyms from the UMBC word embedding matrix for the input terms (test data).

2.3 Merging results from various modules

For this task, our system is required to report the 15 most probable hypernyms for each input term. We have four modules each reporting their top 15 candidate hypernyms. By looking at the training scores of these modules, we merge the co-occurrence frequencies from IS-A corpus that have higher ranks followed by the co-occurrence frequencies from Normalized corpus and Hearst Pattern corpus. Results from word embedding module are given the lowest ranks.

3 Experimental Results and Discussion

Output candidate hypernym lists are evaluated against gold hypernym lists using the following evaluation criteria : Mean Reciprocal Rank (MRR), Mean Average Precision (MAP) and Precision At k (P@k), where k is 1, 3, 5 and 15. We ran our model against two sets of data training data

Tagged UMBC Corpus

Hearst Patterns

1.	NP such as NP[, NP, NP.. and/or NP]	:	*<Hypernym> such as <Hyponym List>*
2.	such NP as NP[, NP, NP.. and/or NP]	:	*such <Hypernym> as <Hyponym List>*
3.	NP[, NP, NP,...NP] or other NP	:	*<Hyponym List> or other <Hypernym>*
4.	NP[, NP, NP,...NP] and other NP	:	*<Hyponym List> and other <Hypernym>*
5.	NP including NP[, NP,...,and/or NP]	:	*<Hypernym> including <Hyponym List>*
6.	NP especially NP[, NP,...,and/or NP]	:	*<Hypernym> especially <Hyponym List>*

Resulting hypernym-hyponym list

	<Hypernym>		<set of Hyponyms>
1.	theme parks	:	disney world
2.	technologies	:	internet, multimedia, assistive software
3.	Family members	:	parents
4.	Physical problems	:	significant trauma, anxiety
5.	range of areas	:	premises, accommodation, goods, services, facilities
6.	non governmental	:	organizations of disabled persons, organizations

Figure 2: Creating Hearst Corpus using 6 Hearst Patterns

	Cooc	Hearst	Phi	Is-A	Merged
MRR	.103	.020	.025	.165	.188
MAP	.050	.008	.012	.071	.080
P@1	.061	.013	.012	.140	.152
P@3	.055	.008	.012	.076	.087
P@5	.048	.008	.012	.066	.075
P@15	.047	.007	.011	.062	.070

Table 1: Test Data 1A English - Concept Scores

	Cooc	Hearst	Phi	Is-A	Merged
MRR	.000	.000	.008	.090	.099
MAP	.000	.000	.003	.036	.037
P@1	.000	.000	.004	.069	.081
P@3	.000	.000	.003	.041	.045
P@5	.000	.000	.003	.035	.036
P@15	.000	.000	.003	.031	.030

Table 2: Test Data 1A English - Entity Scores

and test data with 1500 input terms each. These results are shown in Tables 1 and 2, where it can be clearly observed that our system performs much better for concepts. However, the IS-A module seemed to fetch good candidates for both entity and concept data.

The gold data provided with the task does not always consider all possible word senses or domains of an input term. As a result, we observed numerous candidate hypernyms that seem to be plausible solutions that are not considered correct when compared to the gold data.

For example, the input concept *navigator* has gold standard hypernyms of *[military branch, explorer, military machine, travel, adventurer, seaman]*. Our system finds candidate hypernyms *[browser, web browser, website, application]*. We also noticed that due to our normalization decisions (i.e., using all lower-case characters) and the contents of the corpus, Babbage performs poorly in some cases. For example, the gold hypernyms for input entity *Hurricane* are *[video game, software program, computer program]* but our system produced *[storm, windstorm, typhoon, tornado, cyclone]*. Clearly, our system did not differentiate between the named entity *Hurricane* and the common noun *hurricane* while training the word–embedding models.

On the positive side, our system produced promising results in some cases. Hyponym *liberalism* produced *[theory, philosophy, economic policy]* which is very similar to the gold data *[economic theory, theory]*. It also correctly generated the hyponym *person* for hypernyms such as collector, moderator, director, senior, and reporter. For input *reporter* it produced *[writer, person]* which matches the gold hypernym set.

Acknowledgments

This project was carried out as a part of CS 8761, Natural Language Processing, a graduate level class offered in Fall 2017 at the University of Minnesota, Duluth by Dr. Ted Pedersen. All authors of this paper have contributed equally and are listed in alphabetical order by first name.

References

Jose Camacho-Collados, Claudio Delli Bovi, Luis Espinosa-Anke, Sergio Oramas, Tommaso Pasini, Enrico Santus, Vered Shwartz, Roberto Navigli, and Horacio Saggion. 2018. SemEval-2018 Task 9: Hypernym Discovery. In *Proceedings of the 12th International Workshop on Semantic Evaluation (SemEval-2018)*. Association for Computational Linguistics, New Orleans, LA, United States.

Lushan Han, Abhay L. Kashyap, Tim Finin, James Mayfield, and Johnathan Weese. 2013. Umbc_ebiquity-core: Semantic textual similarity systems. In *proceedings of the Second Joint Conference on Lexical and Computational Semantics*. Association for Computational Linguistics.

Marti A. Hearst. 1992. Automatic acquisition of hyponyms from large text corpora. In *Proceedings of the 14th Conference on Computational Linguistics - Volume 2*. Association for Computational Linguistics, Stroudsburg, PA, USA, COLING '92, pages 539–545. https://doi.org/10.3115/992133.992154.

Tomas Mikolov, Kai Chen, Greg Corrado, and Jeffrey Dean. 2013. Efficient estimation of word representations in vector space. *CoRR* abs/1301.3781. http://arxiv.org/abs/1301.3781.

EXPR at SemEval-2018 Task 9: A Combined Approach for Hypernym Discovery

Ahmad Issa Alaa Aldine[1,3]**, Mounira Harzallah**[2]
Berio Giuseppe[1]**, Nicolas Béchet**[1]**, Ahmad Faour**[3]
[1] IRISA - University Bretagne Sud, France
[2] LINA - University of Nantes, France, [3] Lebanese University, Lebanon
`ahmad.issa-alaa-eddine@univ-ubs.fr`
`mounira.harzallah@univ-nantes.fr, giuseppe.berio@univ-ubs.fr`
`nicolas.bechet@irisa.fr, ahmad.faour@ul.edu.lb`

Abstract

In this paper, we present our proposed system (EXPR) to participate in the hypernym discovery task of SemEval 2018. The task addresses the challenge of discovering hypernym relations from a text corpus. Our proposal is a combined approach of path-based technique and distributional technique. We use dependency parser on a corpus to extract candidate hypernyms and represent their dependency paths as a feature vector. The feature vector is concatenated with a feature vector obtained using Wikipedia pre-trained term embedding model. The concatenated feature vector fits a supervised machine learning method to learn a classifier model. This model is able to classify new candidate hypernyms as hypernym or not. Our system performs well to discover new hypernyms not defined in gold hypernyms.

1 Introduction

Hypernymy is an important lexical-semantic relation that is useful for many applications such as question answering, machine translation, information retrieval, and so on. In addition, hypernym relations are the backbone for building ontologies.

Various methods have been proposed to detect hypernym relation from text corpora. Most of these techniques are either path-based techniques or distributional techniques. In path-based methods, the detection of hypernym relations is based on the lexico-syntactic paths connecting a pair of terms in a corpus. Conversely, distributional methods are based on the distribution of term pair contexts. Most of these methods were unsupervised. Recently, focus shifted towards supervised methods.

This task inherits complexity and is far from being solved. The SemEval organizers address the same task but with a novel formulation (Camacho-Collados et al., 2018). They reformulate the task from hypernym detection into hypernym discovery. This novel formulation makes the task more realistic in terms of actual downstream application, while also enabling the benefits of information retrieval evaluation metrics. Hypernym detection focuses on deciding whether a hypernymic relation holds between a given pair of terms or not. Hypernym discovery focuses on discovering a set containing the best hypernyms for a given term from a given vocabulary search space. The task is divided into two subtasks: General-Purpose Hypernym Discovery and Domain-Specific Hypernym Discovery. The first consists of discovering hypernym in a general-purpose corpus, thus the SemEval organizers provide the participants with data for three languages: English, Italian, and Spanish. The second consists of discovering hypernym in a domain-specific corpus, thus they provide the participants with data for two specific domains: Medical and Music. The data contains a list of training terms along with gold hypernyms, a list of testing terms, and a vocabulary search space. The term is either a concept or an entity.

To tackle this task, we propose an approach that combines a path-based technique and distributional technique via concatenating two feature vectors: a feature vector constructed using dependency parser output and a feature vector obtained using term embeddings. Then, by using the concatenated vector we create a binary supervised classifier model based on support vector machine (SVM) algorithm. The model predicts if a term and its candidate hypernym are hypernym related or not.

2 Related Work

Most of the previous approaches for hypernymy detection are either path-based (patterns) or distributional based. Recently, some approaches are taking advantages of the combination of path-based and distributional techniques.

Proceedings of the 12th International Workshop on Semantic Evaluation (SemEval-2018), pages 919–923
New Orleans, Louisiana, June 5–6, 2018. ©2018 Association for Computational Linguistics

2.1 Path-Based

Path-based approaches are heuristic methods that predict hypernymy between a pair of terms if they match a particular pattern in a sentence of the corpus. These patterns are either manually identified (Hearst, 1992) or automatically extracted (Snow et al., 2005; Navigli and Velardi, 2010; Sheena et al., 2016). Approaches based on handcrafted patterns yield a good precision, but their recall is very low (Buitelaar et al., 2005). Approaches based on automatic learning of patterns achieve better performance by a small improvement in terms of precision and a considerable improvement in terms of recall, but the main limitation of these approaches is the sparsity of the feature space (Shwartz et al., 2016).

2.2 Distributional

Distributional approaches predict hypernym relations between terms based on their distributional representation, by either unsupervised or supervised models. The early unsupervised distributional models are based on symmetric measures (Lin, 1998). Later, asymmetric measures are introduced based on the Distributional Inclusion Hypothesis (DIH) (Weeds and Weir, 2003; Kotlerman et al., 2010). More recent, Santus et al. (2014); Rimell (2014) introduce new measures based on assumption that DIH is not correct for all cases. While, most of the supervised models rely on term embedding (Mikolov et al., 2013; Pennington et al., 2014) to represent the feature vector between the terms x and y. Various vector representations have been used such as concatenation $\vec{x} \oplus \vec{y}$ (Baroni et al., 2012) and difference $\vec{y} - \vec{x}$ (Roller et al., 2014; Weeds et al., 2014). More recent, Yu et al. (2015); Luu et al. (2016) suggested that models rely on term embedding are useful to indicate similarity between words, not to indicate hypernymy relations. Consequently, they learn their own term embedding models that are more relevant to indicate hypernym relations.

2.3 Combined Approaches

Combined approaches of distributional and lexico-syntactic paths are proposed based on the assumption that distributional approaches and path-based approaches have certain complementary properties. To our best knowledge, there are little works on integrating them (Mirkin et al., 2006; Kaji and Kitsuregawa, 2008). The recent work on integrat-

ing them is proposed by Shwartz et al. (2016). They use a long short-term memory (LSTM) network (Hochreiter and Schmidhuber, 1997) to encode dependency paths into a feature vector, then they concatenate the feature vector by the term embedding vectors of term x and term y.

3 System Description

As a preliminary step, we split each corpus into a training corpus and a testing corpus. Training corpus is a corpus of all sentences that contains training data terms (Concept/Entity), while testing corpus is a corpus of all sentences that contains testing data terms (Concept/Entity). Some sentences may contain training and testing data terms. These sentences will exist in both training and testing corpus.

3.1 Candidate Hypernyms

The first step in the system is to extract candidate hypernyms for the given training and testing data terms from a training corpus and a testing corpus respectively. We consider a term as a candidate hypernym if:

1. The term and its candidate occur in the same sentence.

2. The candidate exists in the vocabulary list.

3. The term and its candidate are noun phrases.

4. The term and its candidate are linked by short dependency path.

We consider a dependency path as short if it doesn't exceed two grammatical dependency relations. Using the short dependency path, we are capable representing paths similar to Hearst Patterns and other patterns. For example of short dependency paths, the dependency path between X and Y in the sentence S_1 "X such as Y" is $\{\texttt{nmod:such\_as}(X , Y)\}$ and in the sentence S_2 "X includes Y" is $\{\texttt{nsubj(includes} , X), \texttt{dobj(includes} , Y)\}$. We use Stanford dependency parser[1] (Marneffe et al., 2006) to extract dependency paths.

3.2 Feature Vector

The feature vector used to learn a model capable of predicting hypernym relations between a term

---

[1] https://stanfordnlp.github.io/CoreNLP/

and a candidate hypernym consists of the concatenation of two vectors: the first one is a vector extracted using a path-based technique while the second is extracted using a distributional technique.

The path-based vector consists of a set of features representing the short dependency path between a term y and its candidate hypernym x. The feature set is: $[Tag(x), GRel(x), HR, Freq, Tag(y), GRel(y)]$. $Tag(x)$ and $Tag(y)$ are the POS tag of x and y, $GRel(x)$ and $GRel(y)$ are the grammatical dependency relation of x and y, HR is the hypernym ratio of a dependency path and it is equal to the number of occurrences of a dependency path when indicating hypernm relation divided by the total occurrences of the same dependency path, and $Freq$ is the relative frequency of a dependency path and it is equal to the occurrence of a dependency path divided by the total occurrences of all dependency paths.

$$HR = \frac{hypernym\_DP\_occurrences}{DP\_occurrences}$$

$$Freq = \frac{DP\_occurrences}{Total\_DPs\_occurrences}$$

For a distributional based vector, We use pre-trained 300 dimensional Word2Vec[2] term embeddings, trained on Wikipedia (Mikolov et al., 2013). We apply the difference between the embedding vector of term y and the embedding vector of term x ($\vec{y} - \vec{x}$)(Roller et al., 2014; Weeds et al., 2014). The term is either a single word or a multi-word expression.

3.3 Model Learning and Hypernym Discovery

In each training corpus, we extract a set of candidate hypernyms for each training term and label them if they are hypernym related or not using the gold hypernym data. Next, we represent each term and its candidate hypernym by a concatenated feature vector. These concatenated vectors are used for training the model. The classification method we used is SVM[3] with RBF kernel ($C = 1.0$, $gamma = 1/FeatureSize$). The training dataset was unbalanced, the ratio of hypernym instances w.r.t. not hypernym is less than 0.05. To represent the two categories (hypernym and not hypernym)

---

[2]https://radimrehurek.com/gensim/

[3]We use a machine learning python library scikit-learn (http://scikit-learn.org/stable/)

in the training set, we improved this ratio to 0.2 by random elimination of not hypernym instances (20% hypernym instances and 80% not hypernym instances).

The classifier model is then used to discover hypernyms from a set of candidate hypernyms extracted from a testing corpus for each testing term by predicting if a term and its candidate hypernym are hypernym related or not. Each predicted hypernym is associated with a probability value. These values are used as ranking values to select the best fifteen hypernyms for each term (from higher to lower probability).

4   Results and Analysis

We submit our systems predictions for three corpora: English, Medical, and Music. The table 1 (a,b and c) below shows the result of our system and other supervised systems to discover hypernyms for Concept terms only. For the three corpora, our system performs better than STJU system, and it performs better than the MFH system on the English corpora. In addition, the result shows that our system performs well in discovering new hypernyms not defined in the gold hypernyms where it yields good False Positive values in the three corpora and we achieve the best False Positive value in Medical corpus (40) with a large difference to the second value (20) achieved by CRIM system.

Systems	MAP	MRR	P@1	P@3	P@5	P@15	False +
CRIM	**16.08**	**30.04**	**23.94**	**17.23**	**15.41**	**14.88**	20
MSCG	9.36	18.9	13.81	10.67	9.38	8.31	**28**
UMDuluth	8.13	18.93	15.33	8.83	7.53	7.07	20
NLP_HZ	7.17	13.13	8.99	7.69	7.11	6.71	24
Vanilla	6.99	16.05	12.3	7.69	6.55	6.18	
Begab	6.41	13.92	9.74	6.75	6.33	5.86	24
EXPR	*4.94*	*11.64*	*10.12*	*5.27*	*4.52*	*4.28*	*16*
MFH	4.73	12.48	11.92	4.84	4.13	3.93	
SJTU	3.29	5.68	0.28	3.45	3.57	3.54	0

(a) English Corpus.

Systems	MAP	MRR	P@1	P@3	P@5	P@15	False +
CRIM	**34.05**	**54.64**	**49.2**	**40.13**	**36.77**	**27.1**	20
MFH	28.93	35.8	32.6	34.27	34.2	21.39	
Begab	20.75	40.6	31.6	23.5	21.43	17.05	16
Vanilla	18.84	41.07	35.4	27.07	20.71	12.4	
EXPR	*13.77*	*40.76*	*38.2*	*17.17*	*12.76*	*9.34*	*40*
STJU	11.69	25.95	15.2	13.57	11.69	10.24	12

(b) Medical Corpus.

Systems	MAP	MRR	P@1	P@3	P@5	P@15	False +
CRIM	**43.38**	**63.79**	**52.79**	**47.16**	**43.87**	**40.14**	**24**
MFH	33.56	56.82	46.65	38.41	35.22	27.47	
Begab	23.52	39.26	24.02	23.23	22.66	23.13	16
Vanilla	11.53	35.78	31.28	13.59	10.28	8.46	
EXPR	*6.74*	*20.15*	*15.64*	*9.22*	*6.65*	*4.64*	20
SJTU	4.71	9.15	2.23	4.98	4.91	4.67	4

(c) Music Corpus.

Table 1: The evaluation results of our system and other supervised systems.

Our system result was beneath the expectation. By a short look into the output result files, we notice a lot of empty lines, meaning that our system was unable to discover any hypernym for a lot of terms and unexpectedly these terms correspond to all entity terms. In other words, our system lacks the ability to discover hypernyms for entity terms.

The table 2 (a,b and c) below shows the coverage of Wikipedia pre-trained term embedding model (TEM) and the coverage of candidate hypernym extraction (CHE) for the training and testing terms of the three corpora (English, Medical, and Music). The table shows that our system is unable to discover hypernyms for a considerable number of terms due to two main reasons. The first reason is that Wikipedia pre-trained term embedding model is limited in coverage, where many terms (Concepts/Entities) are not covered by the pre-trained embeddings, which leads to failure to discover hypernyms for these terms. For example, the term embedding (TEM) coverage of Medical Testing terms is 249 (50%), which means the system is unable to discover hypernyms for 251 (50%) terms not covered by the pre-trained term embedding. The second reason is that some conditions used to extract candidate hypernyms restrict the number of candidate hypernyms. For instance, the condition of the existence of a short dependency link between the term and its candidate causes the system to miss many candidate hypernyms if they are not linked by a short dependency path with the terms. In addition, the term and its candidate hypernym must occur as noun phrases in the sentence. This condition leads to failure to extract candidate hypernyms for some entity terms that can't be identified as noun phrases in the corpus such as "Up All Night", "Someday Came Suddenly", "Now What", etc. As shown in the table 2, the candidate hypernym extraction (CHE) coverage for English testing terms is 950 (63%), that means our system is unable to extract any candidate hypernym for 550 (37%) terms (398 entities and 152 concepts).

Furthermore, our system suffers from a major computational issue when applied to a large corpus. Parsing the corpus took to long and failed to complete before the submission deadline. Approximately, we processed 50% sentences of English corpus and 80% sentences of Music corpus, while we processed all sentences of Medical corpus. This explains why the performance of our

Terms	Training			Testing		
	Total	TEM	CHE	Total	TEM	CHE
Concept	979	824 (84%)	825 (84%)	1057	862 (81%)	905 (86%)
Entity	521	361 (69%)	49 (9%)	443	298 (67%)	45 (10%)
Total	1500	1185 (79%)	874 (58%)	1500	1160 (77%)	950 (63%)

(a) English Corpus.

Terms	Training			Testing		
	Total	TEM	CHE	Total	TEM	CHE
Concept	500	151 (30%)	414 (83%)	500	249 (50%)	427 (85%)
Entity	0			0		
Total	500	151 (30%)	414 (83%)	500	249 (50%)	427 (85%)

(b) Medical Corpus.

Terms	Training			Testing		
	Total	TEM	CHE	Total	TEM	CHE
Concept	387	227 (59%)	344 (89%)	358	228 (64%)	330 (92%)
Entity	113	57 (50%)	45 (40%)	142	82 (58%)	62 (44%)
Total	500	284 (57%)	389 (78%)	500	310 (62%)	392 (78%)

(c) Music Corpus.

Table 2: The coverage of wikipedia pre-trained term embedding model and candidate hypernym extraction.

system on Medical corpus is better than its performance on the two others corpora.

5 Conclusion

In this paper, we presented our proposed system (EXPR) that is a combination of path-based technique and distributional technique to participate in Hypernym Discovery task of SemEval 2018. In this work, two feature vectors were extracted and concatenated: the first one is obtained using dependency parser on sentences and the second vector is obtained using pre-trained term embedding. A supervised classifier model based on SVM is built using training dataset composed of concatenated vectors. This model is used to discover hypernyms for new terms. The result was good but didnt fulfill our ambition due to several issues.

Our future work is to improve our approach for hypernym discovery by solving several issues. We believe that relying on term embedding model learned from the corpus provided in this task may be a good choice. In addition, we will work on the definition of a new dependency links not only those defined in this paper. Also, we will work to propose an unsupervised approach by using sequential pattern mining technique to automatically extract frequent sequential pattern between hyponym terms and their given hypernyms from the corpus.

References

Marco Baroni, Raffaella Bernardi, Ngoc-Quynh Do, and Chung chieh Shan. 2012. Entailment above the word level in distributional semantics. *In EACL*, pages 23–32.

Paul Buitelaar, Philipp Cimiano, and Bernardo Magnini. 2005. Ontology learning from text: An overview. *In Ontology Learning from Text: Methods, Applications and Evaluation*, pages 3–12.

Jose Camacho-Collados, Claudio Delli Bovi, Luis Espinosa-Anke, Sergio Oramas, Tommaso Pasini, Enrico Santus, Vered Shwartz, Roberto Navigli, and Horacio Saggion. 2018. SemEval-2018 Task 9: Hypernym Discovery. *In Proceedings of the 12th International Workshop on Semantic Evaluation (SemEval-2018)*, New Orleans, LA, United States. Association for Computational Linguistics.

M. A. Hearst. 1992. Automatic acquisition of hyponyms from large text corpora. *In Proceedings of the 14th International Conference on Computational Linguistics*, pages 539–545.

Sepp Hochreiter and Jürgen Schmidhuber. 1997. Long short-term memory. *Neural Comput.*, 9(8):1735–1780.

Nobuhiro Kaji and Masaru Kitsuregawa. 2008. Using hidden markov random fields to combine distributional and pattern-based word clustering. *In COLING*, pages 401–408.

Lili Kotlerman, Ido Dagan, Idan Szpektor, and Maayan Zhitomirsky-Geffet. 2010. Directional distributional similarity for lexical inference. *NLE*, pages 359–389.

Dekang Lin. 1998. An information-theoretic definition of similarity. *In ICML*, pages 296–304.

Anh Tuan Luu, Yi Tay, Siu Cheung Hui, and See-Kiong Ng. 2016. Learning term embeddings for taxonomic relation identification using dynamic weighting neural network. In *Proceedings of the 2016 Conference on Empirical Methods in Natural Language Processing, EMNLP 2016, Austin, Texas, USA, November 1-4, 2016*, pages 403–413.

Marie-Catherine De Marneffe, Bill MacCartney, and Christopher D. Manning. 2006. Generating typed dependency parses from phrase structure parses. *Proceedings of the 5th International Conference on Language Resources and Evaluation (LREC 2006)*, pages 449–454.

Tomas Mikolov, Ilya Sutskever, Kai Chen, Gregory S. Corrado, and Jeffrey Dean. 2013. Distributed representations of words and phrases and their compositionality. *In NIPS*, pages 3111–3119.

Shachar Mirkin, Ido Dagan, and Maayan Geffet. 2006. Integrating pattern-based and distributional similarity methods for lexical entailment acquisition. *In COLING and ACL*, pages 579–586.

Roberto Navigli and Paola Velardi. 2010. Learning word-class lattices for definition and hypernym extraction. In *Proceedings of the 48th Annual Meeting of the Association for Computational Linguistics*, ACL '10, pages 1318–1327, Stroudsburg, PA, USA. Association for Computational Linguistics.

Jeffrey Pennington, Richard Socher, and Christopher D. Manning. 2014. Glove: Global vectors for word representation. *In EMNLP*, pages 1532–1543.

Laura Rimell. 2014. Distributional lexical entailment by topic coherence. *In EACL*, pages 511–519.

Stephen Roller, Katrin Erk, and Gemma Boleda. 2014. Inclusive yet selective: Supervised distributional hypernymy detection. *In COLING*, pages 1025–1036.

Enrico Santus, Alessandro Lenci, Qin Lu, and Sabine Schulte Im Walde. 2014. Chasing hypernyms in vector spaces with entropy. *In EACL*, pages 38–42.

N. Sheena, Smitha M. Jasmine, and Shelbi Joseph. 2016. Automatic extraction of hypernym and meronym relations in english sentences using dependency parser. *In Procedia Computer Science*, pages 539–546.

Vered Shwartz, Yoav Goldberg, and Ido Dagan. 2016. Improving hypernymy detection with an integrated path-based and distributional method. *CoRR*, abs/1603.06076.

Rion Snow, Daniel Jurafsky, and Andrew Ng. 2005. Learning syntactic patterns for automatic hypernym discovery. *MIT Press*, pages 1297–1304.

Julie Weeds, Daoud Clarke, Jeremy Reffin, David Weir, and Bill Keller. 2014. Learning to distinguish hypernyms and co-hyponyms. *In COLING*, pages 2249–2259.

Julie Weeds and David Weir. 2003. A general framework for distributional similarity. *In EMLP*, pages 81–88.

Zheng Yu, Haixun Wang, Xuemin Lin, and Min Wang. 2015. Learning term embeddings for hypernymy identification. In *Proceedings of the 24th International Conference on Artificial Intelligence*, IJCAI'15, pages 1390–1397. AAAI Press.

ADAPT at SemEval-2018 Task 9: Skip-Gram Word Embeddings for Unsupervised Hypernym Discovery in Specialised Corpora

Alfredo Maldonado
ADAPT Centre
Trinity College Dublin
Ireland

Filip Klubička
ADAPT Centre
Dublin Institute of Technology
Ireland

`firstname.lastname@adaptcentre.ie`

Abstract

This paper describes a simple but competitive unsupervised system for hypernym discovery. The system uses skip-gram word embeddings with negative sampling, trained on specialised corpora. Candidate hypernyms for an input word are predicted based on cosine similarity scores. Two sets of word embedding models were trained separately on two specialised corpora: a medical corpus and a music industry corpus. Our system scored highest in the medical domain among the competing unsupervised systems but performed poorly on the music industry domain. Our approach does not depend on any external data other than raw specialised corpora.

1 Introduction

The SemEval-2018 shared task on Hypernymy Discovery sought to study approaches for identifying words that hold a hypernymic relation (Camacho-Collados et al., 2018). Two words have a hypernymic relation if one of the words belongs to a taxonomical class that is more general than that of the other word. For example, the word *vehicle* belongs to a more general taxonomical class than *car* does, as *car* is a type of *vehicle*. Hypernymy can be seen as an *is-a* relationship. Hypernymy has been studied from different angles in the natural language processing literature as it is related to the human cognitive ability of generalisation.

This shared task differs from recent taxonomy evaluation tasks (Bordea et al., 2015, 2016) by concentrating on Hypernym Discovery: the task of predicting (discovering) n hypernym candidates for a given input word, within the vocabulary of a specific domain (Espinosa-Anke et al., 2016). This shared task provided a general language domain vocabulary and two specialised domain vocabularies in English: medical and music indus-

try. For each vocabulary, a reference corpus was also supplied. In addition to these English vocabularies, general language domain vocabularies for Spanish and Italian were also provided. The ADAPT team focused on the two specialised domain English subtasks by developing an unsupervised system that builds word embeddings from the supplied reference corpora for these domains.

Word embeddings trained on large corpora have been shown to capture semantic relations between words (Mikolov et al., 2013a,b), including hypernym-hyponym relations. The word embeddings built and used by the system presented here exploit this property. Although these word embeddings do not distinguish one semantic relation from another, we expect that true hypernyms will constitute a significant proportion of the predicted candidate hypernyms. Indeed, we show that for the medical domain subtask, our system beats the other unsupervised systems, although it still ranks behind the supervised systems.

Even though unsupervised systems tend to rank behind supervised systems in NLP tasks in general, our motivation to focus on an unsupervised approach is derived from the fact that they do not require explicit hand-annotated data, and from the expectation that they are able to generalise more easily to unseen hypernym-hyponym pairs.

The rest of this system description paper is organised as follows: Section 2 briefly surveys the relevant literature and explains the reasons for choosing to use a particular flavour of word embeddings. Section 3 describes the components of the system and its settings. Section 4 summarises the results and offers some insights behind the numbers. Section 5 concludes and proposes avenues for future work.

Proceedings of the 12th International Workshop on Semantic Evaluation (SemEval-2018), pages 924–927
New Orleans, Louisiana, June 5–6, 2018. ©2018 Association for Computational Linguistics

2   Related Work

Modern neural methods for natural language processing (NLP) use pre-trained word embeddings as fixed-sized vector representations of lexical units in running text as input data (Goldberg, 2017, ch. 10). However, as mentioned previously, word embedding vectors can be used on their own to measure semantic relations between words in an unsupervised manner by, for example, taking the cosine similarity of two word embedding vectors for which semantic similarity is to be measured.

There are several competing approaches for producing word embedding vectors. One such approach is skip-gram with negative sampling (SGNS), introduced by Mikolov et al. (2013a,b) as part of their Word2Vec software package. The skip-gram approach assumes that a focus word occurring in text depends on its context words (the words the focus word co-occurs with inside a fixed-sized window), but that those context words occur independently of each other. This conditional independence assumption in the context words makes computation more efficient and produces vectors that work well in practice. The negative sampling portion of the algorithm is a way of producing "negative" context words for the focus word by simply drawing random words from the corpus. These random words are assumed to be "bad" context words for the focus word. The positive and negative examples are used by an objective function that seeks to maximise the probability that the positive examples came from the corpus whilst the negative examples did not.

Cosine measures on word embeddings pairs (or even on other distributional lexical semantic representations) give an indication of the overall *semantic relatedness* of the word pairs they represent (Turney and Pantel, 2010), without specifying the type(s) of semantic relation(s) the two words hold. There have been endeavours to train word embeddings that emphasise one semantic relation over another. For example, Nguyen et al. (2016) modified the skip-gram objective function to train word embeddings that distinguished synonymy from antonymy. In a similar vein, Nguyen et al. (2017) developed an algorithm called Hypervec by adapting the skip-gram objective function to emphasise the non-symmetric hypernym-hyponym relations.

Our team indeed implemented a variant of the Hypervec method but failed to obtain better performance scores on the training set than those obtained by using traditional SGNS (see Section 4). Whilst it is possible that a software bug in our implementation could be the cause of this lower performance, we decided to submit the SGNS results to the official shared task due to time constraints.

3   System Description

Our system consists of two components: a **trainer** that learns word vectors using an implementation of the Skip-Gram with Negative Sampling algorithm, and a **predictor** that outputs (predicts) the top 10 hypernyms of an input word based on the trained vectors. These two components and their settings are described here.

Trainer   The trainer is a modification of PyTorch SGNS[1], a freely available implementation of the Skip-Gram with Negative Sampling algorithm. One set of vectors per specialised corpus (medicine and music industry) were trained on a vocabulary that consists of the 100,000 most frequent words in each corpus, using a word window of 5 words to the left and 5 words to the right of a sliding focus word. The windows do not cross sentence boundaries. For negative sampling, 20 words were randomly selected from the vocabulary based on their frequency[2]. All vectors had a dimensionality of 300.

Predictor   For each input word in the test file, the predictor attempts to produce 10 candidate hypernyms based on the vectors it learned during training. If there is no vector for an input word, no output for that word is given. If the input word is a multiword expression, then the learned vectors for the individual component words are retrieved and averaged together. This averaged vector is interpreted to represent the input multiword expression. After a vector is retrieved (or computed, in the case of averaged multiword expressions), pairwise cosine similarities are taken between this vector and all other vectors (i.e. the vectors corresponding to the other 99,999 most frequent words). The words represented by the 10 highest ranking cosine similarities are output as the 10 candidate hypernyms for the input word or multiword expression.

---

[1] https://github.com/theeluwin/pytorch-sgns

[2] The frequencies were smoothed by raising them to the power of 0.75 before dividing by the total.

Domain	Approach	MAP	MRR	P@1	P@3	P@5	P@15
medical	SGNS	8.13	20.56	13.20	10.80	8.32	6.33
medical	HV	4.40	13.05	10.60	5.60	4.27	3.10
music	SGNS	1.88	5.34	4.00	2.40	1.89	1.35
music	HV	1.79	5.39	5.00	2.07	1.62	1.28

Table 1: Automatic evaluation results for the submitted system (SGNS) and a Hypervec variant (HV).

As can be seen, our system is completely unsupervised as it does not require corpora with tagged examples of words holding hypernym-hyponym relations or any external linguistic or taxonomical resources.

4   Results

Table 1 shows the results for our SGNS-based approach, which was submitted to the official shared task (SGNS), and for our Hypervec variant (HV), which was not submitted.

Our official submission ranked at eleven out of eighteen on the medical domain subtask with a Mean Average Precision (MAP) of 8.13. However, it ranked first place among all the unsupervised systems on this subtask. On the music industry domain subtask, our system ranked 13th out of 16 places with a MAP of 1.88, ranking 4th among the unsupervised systems. We believe that one reason why the music industry scores are so much lower than the medical results is due to our system not producing an output for 233 of the music industry input words (45% of the total), compared to the 128 medical input words (26%) it failed to predict.

Another aspect that seems to work against our system is its simplistic way of handling multiword expressions, namely by averaging together the individual word's vectors. The total number of multiword expressions in the medical test set is 264, slightly higher than in the music test set, which contains 220 multiword expressions. Similarly, our system does not have a way of predicting multiword expressions as hypernym candidates, as it can only output the unigrams for which it has vector representations. 82% of the medical domain input words have at least one hypernym that is a multi-word expression, whilst 92% of the music industry domain input words have multi-word expression hypernyms.

5   Conclusions and Future Work

We presented a simple but competitive unsupervised system to predict hypernym candidates for input words, based on cosine similarity scores of word embedding vectors trained on specialised corpora.

Unsupervised systems in general tend to have lower performance than supervised systems as they lack explicit information to train on. So we are encouraged that our system beat other unsupervised systems on one corpus, as this gives us more avenues to explore.

One such avenue is to revisit our Hypervec implementation. We suspect that it might require more training epochs than the traditional SGNS method in order to achieve reasonable results. We also seek to experiment with refining pre-trained SGNS word embeddings with Hypervec, rather than training word embeddings from scratch using Hypervec directly.

Another avenue to explore involves incorporating taxonomical information into our word embeddings. One way to achieve this is by retrofitting pre-trained SGNS word embeddings with information derived from existing taxonomies like WordNet (Faruqui et al., 2015). Another way of incorporating taxonomical information is by generating a pseudo-corpus via a random walk over such a taxonomy and then learn SGNS word embeddings in the usual way (Goikoetxea et al., 2015).

These approaches (Hypervec, retrofitting and taxonomy random-walk) however, would relax the unsupervised constraint we followed in our implementation. So yet another avenue to explore is to instead apply different similarity functions that might be more sensitive to the one-way, general-specific nature of hypernymic relationships between words.

Acknowledgements

We thank our anonymous reviewers for their input. The ADAPT Centre for Digital Content Technology is funded under the SFI Research Centres Programme (Grant 13/RC/2106) and is co-funded under the European Regional Development Fund.

References

Georgeta Bordea, Paul Buitelaar, Stefano Faralli, and Roberto Navigli. 2015. Semeval-2015 task 17: Taxonomy extraction evaluation (texeval). In *Proceedings of the 9th International Workshop on Semantic Evaluation*. Association for Computational Linguistics.

Georgeta Bordea, Els Lefever, and Paul Buitelaar. 2016. Semeval-2016 task 13: Taxonomy extraction evaluation (texeval-2). In *Proceedings of the 10th International Workshop on Semantic Evaluation*. Association for Computational Linguistics.

Jose Camacho-Collados, Claudio Delli Bovi, Luis Espinosa-Anke, Sergio Oramas, Tommaso Pasini, Enrico Santus, Vered Shwartz, Roberto Navigli, and Horacio Saggion. 2018. SemEval-2018 Task 9: Hypernym Discovery. In *Proceedings of the 12th International Workshop on Semantic Evaluation (SemEval-2018)*, New Orleans, LA. Association for Computational Linguistics.

Luis Espinosa-Anke, Jose Camacho-Collados, Claudio Delli Bovi, and Horacio Saggion. 2016. Supervised Distributional Hypernym Discovery via Domain Adaptation. In *Proceedings of the 2016 Conference on Empirical Methods in Natural Language Processing*, pages 424–435, Austin, TX.

Manaal Faruqui, Jesse Dodge, Sujay K Jauhar, Chris Dyer, Eduard Hovy, and Noah A Smith. 2015. Retrofitting Word Vectors to Semantic Lexicons. In *Human Language Technologies: The 2015 Annual Conference of the North American Chapter of the ACL*, pages 1606–1615.

Josu Goikoetxea, Aitor Soroa, and Eneko Agirre. 2015. Random Walks and Neural Network Language Models on Knowledge Bases. In *Human Language Technologies: The 2015 Conference of the North American Chapter of the Association for Computational Linguistics*, pages 1434–1439, Denver, CO.

Yoav Goldberg. 2017. *Neural Network Methods for Natural Language Processing*. Morgan & Claypool Publishers.

Tomas Mikolov, Greg Corrado, Kai Chen, and Jeffrey Dean. 2013a. Efficient Estimation of Word Representations in Vector Space. In *Proceedings of the International Conference on Learning Representations (ICLR 2013)*, pages 1–12, Scottsdale, AZ.

Tomas Mikolov, Ilya Stutskever, Kai Chen, Greg Corrado, and Jeffrey Dean. 2013b. Distributed Representations of Words and Phrases and their Compositionality. In *Proceedings of the Twenty-Seventh Annual Conference on Neural Information Processing Systems (NIPS) In Advances in Neural Information Processing Systems 26*, pages 3111–3119, Lake Tahoe, NV.

Kim Anh Nguyen, Maximilian Köper, Sabine Schulte im Walde, and Ngoc Thang Vu. 2017. Hierarchical Embeddings for Hypernymy Detection and Directionality. In *Proceedings of the 2017 Conference on Empirical Methods in Natural Language Processing*, pages 233–243, Copenhagen.

Kim Anh Nguyen, Sabine Schulte im Walde, and Ngoc Thang Vu. 2016. Integrating Distributional Lexical Contrast into Word Embeddings for Antonym-Synonym Distinction. In *Proceedings of the 54th Annual Meeting of the Association for Computational Linguistics*, pages 454–459, Berlin.

Peter D. Turney and Patrick Pantel. 2010. From Frequency to Meaning: Vector Space Models of Semantics. *Journal of Artificial Intelligence Research*, 37:141–188.

300-sparsans at SemEval-2018 Task 9:
Hypernymy as interaction of sparse attributes

Gábor Berend
Department of Informatics
University of Szeged
Árpád tér 2, H6720 Szeged, Hungary
`berendg@inf.u-szeged.hu`

Márton Makrai
Institute for Linguistics
Hungarian Academy of Sciences
Benczúr u. 33, H1068 Budapest, Hungary
`makrai.marton@nytud.mta.hu`

Péter Földiák
Secret Sauce Partners
657 Mission Suite 410,
San Francisco CA 94105
`Peter.Foldiak@gmail.com`

Abstract

This paper describes 300-sparsans' participation in SemEval-2018 Task 9: *Hypernym Discovery*, with a system based on sparse coding and a formal concept hierarchy obtained from word embeddings. Our system took first place in subtasks *(1B) Italian (all* and *entities), (1C) Spanish entities*, and *(2B) music entities*.

1 Introduction

Natural language phenomena are extremely sparse by their nature, whereas continuous word embeddings employ dense representations of words. Turning these dense representations into a much sparser form can help in focusing on most salient parts of word representations (Faruqui et al., 2015; Berend, 2017; Subramanian et al., 2018).

Sparsity-based techniques often involve the coding of a large number of signals over the same dictionary (Rubinstein et al., 2008). Sparse, overcomplete representations have been motivated in various domains as a way to increase separability and interpretability (Olshausen and Field, 1997) and stability in the presence of noise.

Non-negativity has also been argued to be advantageous for interpretability (Faruqui et al., 2015; Fyshe et al., 2015; Arora et al., 2016). As Subramanian et al. (2018) illustrates this in the language domain, where sparse features are interpreted as lexical attributes, "to describe the city of Pittsburgh, one might talk about phenomena typical of the city, like erratic weather and large bridges. It is redundant and inefficient to list negative properties, like the absence of the Statue of Liberty". Berend (2018) utilizes non-negative sparse coding for word translation by training

sparse word vectors for the two languages such that coding bases correspond to each other.

Here we apply sparse feature pairs to hypernym extraction. The role of an attribute pair $\langle i, j \rangle \in \phi(q) \times \phi(h)$ (where q is the query word, h is the hypernym candidate, and $\phi(w)$ is the index of a non-zero component in the sparse representations of w) is similar to *interaction terms* in regression, see section 2 for details.

Sparse representation is related to hypernymy in various natural ways. One of them is through *Formal concept Analysis (FCA)*. The idea of acquiring concept hierarchies from a text corpus with the tools of Formal concept Analysis (FCA) is relatively new (Cimiano et al., 2005). Our submissions experiment with formal concept analysis tool by Endres et al. (2010). See the next section for a description of formal concept lattices, and how hypernyms can be found in them.

Another natural formulation is related to *hierarchical sparse coding* (Zhao et al., 2009), where trees describe the order in which variables "enter the model" (i.e., take non-zero values). A node may take a non-zero value only if its ancestors also do: the dimensions that correspond to top level nodes should focus on "general" meaning components that are present in most words. Yogatama et al. (2015) offer an implementation that is efficient for gigaword corpora. Exploiting the correspondence between the variable tree and the hypernym hierarchy offers itself as a natural choice.

The task (Camacho-Collados et al., 2018) evaluated systems on their ability to extract hypernyms for query words in five subtasks (three languages, English, Italian, and Spanish, and two domains,

928

Proceedings of the 12th International Workshop on Semantic Evaluation (SemEval-2018), pages 928–934
New Orleans, Louisiana, June 5–6, 2018. ©2018 Association for Computational Linguistics

medical and music). Queries have been categorized as concepts or entities. Results were reported for each category separately as well as in combined form, thus resulting in 5×3 combinations. Our system took first place in subtasks *(1B) Italian* (*all* and *entities*), *(1C) Spanish entities*, and *(2B) music entities*. Detailed results for our system appear in section 3. Our source code is available online[1].

1.1 Formal concept analysis

Formal concept Analysis (FCA) is the mathematization of *concept* and conceptual hierarchy (Ganter and Wille, 2012; Endres et al., 2010). In FCA terminology, a *context* is a set of *objects* $\mathcal{O}$, a set of *attributes* $\mathcal{A}$, and a binary incidence relation $\mathcal{I} \subseteq \mathcal{O} \times \mathcal{A}$ between members of $\mathcal{O}$ and $\mathcal{A}$. In our application, $\mathcal{I}$ associates a word $w \in \mathcal{O}$ to the indices of its non-zero sparse coding coordinates $i \in \mathcal{A}$. FCA finds formal *concepts*, pairs $\langle O, A \rangle$ of object sets and attribute sets ($O \subseteq \mathcal{O}, A \subseteq \mathcal{A}$) such that A consists of the shared attributes of objects in O (and no more), and O consists of the objects in $\mathcal{O}$ that have all the attributes in A (and no more). (There is a closure-operator related to each FCA context, for which O and A are closed sets iff $\langle O, A \rangle$ is a concept.) O is called the extent and A is the intent of the concept.

There is an order defined in the context: if $\langle A_1, B_1 \rangle$ and $\langle A_2, B_2 \rangle$ are concepts in C, $\langle A_1, B_1 \rangle$ is a *subconcept* of $\langle A_2, B_2 \rangle$ if $A_1 \subseteq A_2$ which is equivalent to $B_1 \supseteq B_2$. The concept order forms a lattice. The smallest concept whose extent contains a word is said to *introduce* the object. We expect that h will be a hypernym of q iff $n(q) \leq n(h)$ where $n(w)$ denotes the node in the concept lattice that introduces w.

The closedness of extents and intents has an important structural consequence. Adding attributes to $\mathcal{A}$ (e.g. responses of additional neurons) will very probably grow the model. However, the original concepts will be embedded as a substructure in the larger lattice, with their ordering relationships preserved.

2 Our approach

Now we describe our system that is based on sparse non-negative word representations and FCA besides more traditional features.

We use the popular skip-gram (SG) approach (Mikolov et al., 2013) to train $d = 100$ dimensional dense distributed word representations for each sub-corpus. The word embeddings are trained over the text corpora provided by the shared task organizers with the default training parameters of `word2vec` (w2v), i.e. a window size of 10 and 25 negative samples for each positive context.

We derived *multi-token units* by relying on the `word2phrase` software accompanying the w2v toolkit. An additional source for identifying multi-token units in the training corpora was the list of potential hypernyms released for each subtask by the shared task organizers.

Given the dense embedding matrix $W_x \in \mathbb{R}^{d \times |V_x|}$, for some subcorpus of the shared task $x \in \{1A, 1B, 1C, 2A, 2B\}$, where $|V_x|$ is the size of the vocabulary and d is set to 100. As a subsequent step, we turn W_x into *sparse word vectors* akin to Berend (2017) by solving for

$$\min_{D \in \mathcal{C}, \alpha \in \mathbb{R}_{\geq 0}} \|D\alpha - W_x\|_F + \lambda\|\alpha\|_1, \quad (1)$$

where $\mathcal{C}$ refers to the convex set of $\mathbb{R}^{d \times k}$ matrices consisting of d-dimensional columns vectors with norm at most 1, and α contains the sparse coefficients for the elements of the vocabulary. The only difference compared to Berend (2017) is that here we ensure a non-negativity constraint over the elements of α.

For the elements of the vocabulary we ran the *formal concept analysis* tool of Endres et al. (2010)[2]. In order to keep the size of the DAG outputted by the FCA algorithm manageable, we only included the query words and those hypernyms in the analysis which occur in the training dataset for the corpora. As we will see in the next section, this restriction turns out to be very useful.

Next, we determine a handful of features for a pair of expressions (q, h) consisting of a query q and its potential hypernym h. Table 1 provides an overview of the features employed for a pair (q, h). We denote with **q** and **h** the 100-dimensional dense vectorial representations of q and h. Additionally, we denote with Q and H the sequence of tokens constituting the query and hypernym phrases. Finally, we refer to the set of basis vectors (in the FCA terminology, attributes)

Core feature name	
cosine	$\frac{\mathbf{q}^\mathsf{T}\mathbf{h}}{\|\mathbf{q}\|_2\|\mathbf{h}\|_2}$
difference	$\|\mathbf{q} - \mathbf{h}\|_2$
normRatio	$\frac{\|\mathbf{q}\|_2}{\|\mathbf{h}\|_2}$
qureyBeginsWith	$Q[0] = h$
queryEndsWith	$Q[-1] = h$
hasCommonWord	$Q \cap H \neq \emptyset$
sameFirstWord	$Q[0] = H[0]$
sameLastWord	$Q[-1] = H[-1]$
logFrequencyRatio	$\log_{10} \frac{count(q)}{count(h)}$
isFrequentHypernym[3]	$c \in MF_{50}(q.type)$
sameConcept	$n(h) = n(q)$
parent	$n(q) \prec n(h)$
child	$n(h) \prec n(q)$
overlappingBasis	$\phi(q) \cap \phi(h) \neq \emptyset$
sparseDifference$_{q\backslash h}$	$|\phi(q) - \phi(h)|$
sparseDifference$_{h\backslash q}$	$|\phi(h) - \phi(q)|$
attributePair$_{ij}$	$\langle i, j \rangle \in \phi(q) \times \phi(h)$

Table 1: The features employed in our classifier. $MF_{50}(q.type)$ refers to the set of top-50 most frequent hypernyms for a given query type.

which are assigned non-zero weights in the reconstruction of the vectorial representation of q and h as $\phi(q)$ and $\phi(h)$. It is also considered as a feature (isFrequentHypernym) whether a particular candidate hypernym h belongs to the top-50 most frequent hypernyms for the category of q (i.e. concept or entity). Modeling the two categories separately played an important role in the success of our systems.

Three additional features are defined for incorporating the concept lattice output by FCA. With $n(w)$ denoting the concept that introduces w, i.e. the most specific location within the DAG for w, our features indicate whether $n(q)$ (1) coincides with that of h, (2) is the parent (immediate successor) for that of h, or (3) is the child (immediate predictions) for that of h. Parents, and even the inverse relation, proved to be more predictive than the conceptually motivated $q \leq h$. In Table 1, $n_1 \prec n_2$ denotes that n_1 is an immediate predecessor of n_2. We will see in post-evaluation ablation experiments, where we refer to the above three features as the *FCA* features, that they were not useful in our submissions.

The attributePair$_{ij}$s above, our most important features, are indicator features for every possible interaction term between the sparse coefficients in α. That means that for a pair of words (q, h) we defined $\phi(q) \times \phi(h)$, i.e. candidates get assigned with the Cartesian product derived from the indices of the non-zero coefficients in α. Note that this feature template induces k^2 features, with k being the number of basis vectors introduced in the dictionary matrix D according to Eq. 1.

In order to rank potential hypernym candidates over the test set we trained a *logistic regression* classifier for concepts and entities utilizing the sklearn package (Pedregosa et al., 2011)[4] with the regularization parameter defaulting to 1.0.

For each appropriate (q, h) pair of words for which h is a hypernym of q, we generated a number of *negative samples* (q, h'), such that the training data does not include h' as a valid hypernym for q. For a given query q, belonging to either of the *concept* or *entity* category, we sampled h' from those hypernyms which were included as a valid hypernym in the training data with respect to some $q' \neq q$ query phrase.

When making predictions for the hypernyms of a query, we relied on our query type sensitive logistic regression model to determine the ranking of the hypernym candidates. In our official submission we treated such phrases to rank which were included in the training data for being a proper hypernym at least once.

After the appropriate model ranked the hypernym candidates, we selected the top 15 ranked candidates and applied a *post-ranking* heuristic over them, i.e. reordered them according to their background frequency from the training corpus. Our assumption here is that more frequent words tend to refer to more general concepts and more general hypernymy relations potentially tend to be more easily detectable than more specialized ones.

3 Results

3.1 Our submissions

Our submissions were based on $k = 200$ dimensional sparse vectors computed from unit-normed 100-dimensional dense vectors with $\lambda = .3$. The sum of the two dimensions motivates our group name. For training the regression model with negative samples, 50 false hypernyms were sampled for each query q in the training dataset. One of our

---

[3]At submission time, this feature did not work properly.

[4]scikit-learn.org

		without attribute pairs						with attribute pairs					
		MAP	MRR	P@1	P@3	P@5	P@15	MAP	MRR	P@1	P@3	P@5	P@15
1A	offic	8.6	18.0	13.0	8.9	8.2	7.9	8.9	19.4	14.9	9.3	8.6	8.1
1A	reprd	9.07	18.7	13.5	9.4	8.8	8.5	9.2	19.9	14.9	9.5	8.7	8.4
1B	offic	9.4	19.9	13.2	9.5	9.3	8.8	12.1	25.1	17.6	12.9	11.7	11.2
1B	reprd	9.2	19.5	12.8	8.9	8.9	8.7	12.8	26.7	18.9	13.6	12.4	11.9
1C	offic	12.5	25.9	16.6	13.6	12.6	11.5	17.9	37.6	27.8	19.7	17.1	16.3
1C	reprd	12.9	26.0	16.2	13.9	13.0	11.9	18.3	38.4	28.5	20.2	17.4	16.6
2A	offic	15.0	32.2	24.8	17.7	15.8	11.6	20.8	40.6	31.6	23.5	21.4	17.1
2A	reprd	15.1	32.4	24.4	18.0	16.2	11.8	21.5	43.7	35.6	25.3	21.8	17.0
2B	offic	19.1	36.7	27.2	23.0	20.1	15.4	29.5	46.4	33.0	31.9	28.9	27.7
2B	reprd	21.5	40.9	29.6	25.6	22.1	18.0	30.4	46.8	33.8	31.8	29.5	28.9

Table 2: Our submissions results: `official` and those that can be `reproduced` with the code in the project repo (with the *isFrequentHypernym* feature being turned off).

	MAP	MRR	P@1	P@3	P@5	P@10
1A	9.8	22.6	19.8	10.0	9.0	8.6
1A	8.8	21.4	19.8	8.9	7.8	7.5
1B	8.9	21.2	17.1	9.1	8.3	7.9
1B	7.8	19.4	17.1	8.3	6.8	6.5
1C	16.4	33.3	24.6	17.5	16.1	14.9
1C	12.2	29.8	24.6	12.0	11.3	11.0
2A	29.0	35.9	32.6	34.3	34.2	21.7
2A	28.9	35.8	32.6	34.3	34.2	21.4
2B	40.2	58.8	50.6	44.6	40.3	35.5
2B	33.3	51.5	36.2	40.1	35.8	28.4

Table 3: Baseline results, most frequent training hypernyms. We (upper) consider the most frequent hypernym in the given query type (concept or entity). For comparison, we also show the `MFH` baseline provided by the organizers (lower) that is based on the most frequent hypernyms in general.

	Train		Test	
1A	975(4)	0.41%	1055(4)	0.38%
1B	709(1)	0.14%	767(2)	0.26%
1C	776(2)	0.26%	625(2)	0.32%
2A	442(58)	11.60%	433(67)	13.40%
2B	366(21)	5.43%	341(17)	4.75%

(a) concept

	Train		Test	
1A	379(142)	27.26%	344(99)	22.35%
1B	249(41)	14.14%	205(26)	11.26%
1C	184(38)	17.12%	328(45)	12.06%
2A	0(0)	—	0(0)	—
2B	79(34)	30.09%	102(40)	28.17%

(b) entity

Table 4: Number of in-vocabulary (and out-of-vocabulary, OOV) queries per query type. The ratio of the latter is also shown.

submissions involved attribute pairs, the other not. Both submissions used the conceptually motivated but practically harmful FCA-based features.

Table 2 shows submission results. The figures that can be reproduced with the code in the project repo (`reprd`) is slightly different from our official submissions (`offic`) for two reasons: because the implementation of `isFreqHyp` contained a bug, and because of the natural randomness in negative sampling. For reproducibility, we report result without the `isFreqHyp` feature. The randomness introduced by negative sampling is now factored out by random seeding.

3.2 Query type sensitive baselining

Our submission with attribute pairs achieved first place in categories (1B) Italian (all and entities), (1C) Spanish entities, and (2B) music entities. This is in part due to our good choice of a fallback solution in the case of OOV queries: we applied a category-sensitive baseline returning the most frequent train hypernym in the corresponding query type (concept or entity). Table 4 shows how frequently we had to rely on this fallback, and Table 3 shows the corresponding pure baseline results.

		candidate filtering off						candidate filtering on					
k	ns	MAP	MRR	P@1	P@3	P@5	P@15	MAP	MRR	P@1	P@3	P@5	P@15
200	50	6.5	14.9	13.1	7.4	6.1	5.5	12.1	25.4	18.9	12.9	11.6	10.9
200	all	6.9	15.8	14.1	7.6	6.3	5.8	13.0	27.1	19.9	14.2	12.5	11.8
300	50	6.9	15.8	13.9	7.6	6.4	5.9	12.1	25.7	19.5	13.0	11.5	11.0
300	all	8.0	17.8	15.4	8.9	7.4	6.8	13.5	28.0	21.1	14.5	12.9	12.3
1000	50	9.0	20.0	17.2	9.8	8.3	7.7	13.3	**28.1**	**21.3**	13.8	12.6	12.3
1000	all	11.6	26.1	22.5	12.5	10.8	10.0	**13.6**	27.2	19.4	**13.9**	**13.2**	**12.8**

Table 5: Post evaluation results on the 1A dataset investigating the effect of various hyperparameter choices. k and ns denotes the number of basis vectors and negative samples generated during training per each positive (q, h) pair. Best results obtained for each metric are marked as bold.

		MAP	MRR	P@1	P@3	P@5	P@15
off	off	10.3	21.3	15.0	10.6	10.1	9.6
off	on	10.1	21.1	14.9	10.5	9.9	9.5
on	off	12.1	25.4	18.9	12.9	11.6	10.9
on	on	12.1	25.3	18.7	13.0	11.6	11.0

Table 6: Ablation experiments, on the 1A dataset with $k = 200, ns = 50$ (and the implementation of `isFreqHyp` fixed). The first two columns indicate whether attributePair$_{ij}$ and FCA-derived features are utilized, respectively.

	MAP	MRR	P@1	P@3	P@5	P@15
1A	76.1	92.2	92.2	82.3	76.4	71.6
1B	71.2	93.4	93.4	78.5	70.9	65.7
1C	81.0	95.9	95.9	87.2	81.7	76.4
2A	72.6	89.6	89.6	81.0	75.3	64.1
2B	95.4	98.8	98.8	97.3	96.0	93.7

Table 7: Test results of an oracle system which uses candidate filtering.

3.3 Post-evaluation analysis

After the evaluation closed, we conducted ablation experiments the results of which are included in Table 6. In these experiments, we investigated the contribution of the features derived from sparse attribute pairs and FCA. These ablation experiments corroborate the importance of features derived from sparse attribute pairs and reveal that turning off FCA-based features does not hurt performance at all. For this reason – even though our official shared task submission included FCA-related features – we no longer employed them in our post-evaluation experiments.

Table 5 includes the detailed behavior of our model on subtask 1A with respect three distinct factors, that is

1. the number of basis vectors employed during sparse coding ($k \in \{200, 300, 1000\}$),

2. the number of negative training samples per positive sample ($ns \in \{50, all\}$),

3. candidate filtering being turned on/off.

In our original submission we generated 50 negative samples (ns) generated per query q during training. In our post evaluation experiments we investigated the effects of generating more negative samples, i.e. we regarded all the valid hypernyms over the training set – not being a proper hypernym for q – as h' upon the creation of the (q, h') negative training instances. This latter strategy is referenced as $ns = all$ in Table 5.

In our official submission we regarded only those hypernyms as potential candidates to rank during test time which occurred at least once as a correct hypernym in the training data. We call this strategy as candidate filtering. Historically, we applied this restriction to speed up the FCA algorithm because this way the size of the concept lattice could be made smaller. As there are valid hypernyms on the test set which never occurred in the training data, our official submission would not be able to obtain a perfect score even in theory. Table 7 contains the best possible metrics on the test set that we could achieve when candidate filtering is applied. In our post evaluation experiments we also investigated the effects of turning this kind of filtering step off. As Table 5 illustrates, however, our scores degrade after turning candidate filtering off.

Our post evaluation experiments in Table 5 sug-

	MAP	MRR	P@1	P@3	P@10	P@15
1A	13.3	28.1	21.3	13.8	12.6	12.3
1A	19.8	36.1	29.7	21.1	19.0	18.3
1B	12.5	24.2	14.5	13.4	12.5	12.0
1B	12.1	25.1	17.6	12.9	11.7	11.2
1C	21.8	43.8	33.7	22.9	21.4	19.9
1C	20.0	28.3	21.4	20.9	21.0	19.4
2A	21.9	39.5	34.2	25.5	22.6	18.5
2A	34.0	54.6	49.2	40.1	36.8	27.1
2B	31.5	43.6	29.8	30.3	30.3	31.5
2B	41.0	60.9	48.2	44.9	41.3	38.0

Table 8: Post evaluation results for the different subtasks using $k = 1000, ns = 50$ and hypernym candidate filtering. Upper: our system, lower: subtask winner.

gest that it is advantageous to apply sparse representation of more expressive power (i.e. a higher number of basis vectors). Generating more negative samples also provides some additional performance boost. These previous observations hold irrespective whether candidate filtering is employed or not, however, their effects are more pronounced when hypernym candidates are not filtered.

Finally, we report our post-evaluation results for all the subtasks and compare them to the official scores of the best performing systems in Table 8. It can be seen from these enhanced results for category "all" (concepts and entities mixed) that we would win (1B) Italian and (1C) Spanish. Our post-evaluation system – which only differs from our participating system that it fixes the calculation of a features, does not rely on FCA-based features and uses $k = 1000$ – would also place third in the rest of the subtasks.

4   Conclusion

In this paper we experimented with the integration of sparse word representations into the task of hypernymy discovery. We strived to utilize sparse word representations in two ways, i.e. via building concept lattices using formal concept analysis and modeling the hypernymy relation with the help of interaction terms. While our former approach for deriving formal concepts from sparse word representations was not successful, the interaction terms derived from sparse word representations proved to be highly beneficial.

Acknowledgements

We would like to thank András Kornai for useful comments on negative sampling. This research was supported by the project *Integrated program for training new generation of scientists in the fields of computer science*, no. EFOP-3.6.3-VEKOP-16-2017-0002. The project has been supported by the European Union and co-funded by the European Social Fund.

References

Sanjeev Arora, Yuanzhi Li, Yingyu Liang, Tengyu Ma, and Andrej Risteski. 2016. Linear algebraic structure of word senses, with applications to polysemy. *arXiv:1601.03764v1*.

Gábor Berend. 2017. Sparse coding of neural word embeddings for multilingual sequence labeling. *Transactions of the Association for Computational Linguistics*, 5:247–261.

Gábor Berend. 2018. Towards cross-lingual utilization of sparse word representations. In *MSZNY2018, XVI. Magyar Számítógpes Nyelvészeti Konferencia*.

Jose Camacho-Collados, Claudio Delli Bovi, Luis Espinosa-Anke, Sergio Oramas, Tommaso Pasini, Enrico Santus, Vered Shwartz, Roberto Navigli, and Horacio Saggion. 2018. SemEval-2018 Task 9: Hypernym Discovery. In *Proceedings of the 12th International Workshop on Semantic Evaluation (SemEval-2018)*, New Orleans, LA, United States. Association for Computational Linguistics.

Philipp Cimiano, Andreas Hotho, and Steffen Staab. 2005. Learning concept hierarchies from text corpora using formal concept analysis. *Journal Artificial Intelligence Research (JAIR)*, 24:305–339.

Dominik Endres, Peter Földiák, and Uta Priss. 2010. An Application of Formal Concept Analysis to Semantic Neural Decoding. *Annals of Mathematics and Artificial Intelligence*, 57(3-4):233–248. Reviewed.

Manaal Faruqui, Jesse Dodge, Sujay Jauhar, Chris Dyer, Ed Hovy, and Noah Smith. 2015. Retrofitting word vectors to semantic lexicons. In *Proceedings of NAACL 2015*. Best Student Paper Award.

Alona Fyshe, Leila Wehbe, Partha P Talukdar, Brian Murphy, and Tom M Mitchell. 2015. A compositional and interpretable semantic space. In *Proceedings of the 2015 Conference of the North American Chapter of the Association for Computational Linguistics: Human Language Technologies*, pages 32–41.

Bernhard Ganter and Rudolf Wille. 2012. *Formal concept analysis: mathematical foundations*. Springer Science & Business Media.

Tomas Mikolov, Kai Chen, Greg Corrado, and Jeffrey Dean. 2013. Efficient estimation of word representations in vector space. In *International Conference on Learning Representations (ICLR 2013)*.

Bruno A Olshausen and David J Field. 1997. Sparse coding with an overcomplete basis set: A strategy employed by v1? *Vision research*, 37(23):3311–3325.

F. Pedregosa, G. Varoquaux, A. Gramfort, V. Michel, B. Thirion, O. Grisel, M. Blondel, P. Prettenhofer, R. Weiss, V. Dubourg, J. Vanderplas, A. Passos, D. Cournapeau, M. Brucher, M. Perrot, and E. Duchesnay. 2011. Scikit-learn: Machine learning in Python. *Journal of Machine Learning Research*, 12:2825–2830.

Ron Rubinstein, Michael Zibulevsky, and Michael Elad. 2008. Efficient implementation of the k-svd algorithm and the batch-omp method. *Department of Computer Science, Technion, Israel, Tech. Rep*.

Anant Subramanian, Danish Pruthi, Harsh Jhamtani, Taylor Berg-Kirkpatrick, and Eduard Hovy. 2018. Spine: Sparse interpretable neural embeddings. *AAAI*.

Dani Yogatama, Manaal Faruqui, Chris Dyer, , and Noah A. Smith. 2015. Learning word representations with hierarchical sparse coding. In *ICML*. Previous version in NIPS Deep Learning and Representation Learning Workshop 2014.

Peng Zhao, Gulherme Rocha, and Bin Yu. 2009. The composite and absolute penalties for grouped and hierarchical variable selection. *The Annals of Statistics*, 37(6A):3468–3497.

UWB at SemEval-2018 Task 10: Capturing Discriminative Attributes from Word Distributions

Tomáš Brychcín[1], **Tomáš Hercig**[1,2], **Josef Steinberger**[2], and **Michal Konkol**[1]

[1]NTIS – New Technologies for the Information Society,
Faculty of Applied Sciences, University of West Bohemia, Czech Republic
[2]Department of Computer Science and Engineering,
Faculty of Applied Sciences, University of West Bohemia, Czech Republic
`{brychcin,tigi,jstein,konkol}@kiv.zcu.cz`
`http://nlp.kiv.zcu.cz`

Abstract

We present our UWB system for the task of capturing discriminative attributes at SemEval 2018. Given two words and an attribute, the system decides, whether this attribute is discriminative between the words or not. Assuming Distributional Hypothesis, i.e., a word meaning is related to the distribution across contexts, we introduce several approaches to compare word contextual information.

We experiment with state-of-the-art semantic spaces and with simple co-occurrence statistics. We show the word distribution in the corpus has potential for detecting discriminative attributes. Our system achieves F1 score 72.1% and is ranked #4 among 26 submitted systems.

1 Introduction

In this paper, we describe our UWB system participating in the pilot shared task on capturing discriminative attributes held at SemEval 2018. Given two words and an attribute, the goal of this task is to decide, whether the attribute is discriminative between them. For example, we can distinguish between the words *car* and *boat* by a discriminative feature (attribute) *wheels*. On the other hand, both *tennis* and *basketball* use a *ball*, so that the *ball* is not discriminative between them. By its nature, capturing discriminative attributes is a binary classification task. In general, there is no assumption on the input words and their attributes (e.g., part of speech, etc.).

While most related works focus on extracting discriminative features from images (Guo et al., 2015; Huang et al., 2016; Lazaridou et al., 2016), this shared task is oriented purely on textual level. The first experiments have been performed by Krebs and Paperno (2016) and have shown the promising potential of this task.

The fundamental assumption of our work is *Distributional Hypothesis*, i.e., two words are expected to be semantically similar if they occur in similar contexts (they are similarly distributed across the text). This hypothesis was formulated by Harris (1954) several decades ago. Today it is the basis of state-of-the-art distributional semantic models (Mikolov et al., 2013; Pennington et al., 2014; Bojanowski et al., 2017). We present several approaches, which rely on Distributional Hypothesis and employ the word contexts for statistical comparison of their meanings.

2 Proposed Approach

Given two words $w_1 \in V$, $w_2 \in V$ and the attribute $a \in V$, where V is a word vocabulary. The task is to predict, whether the attribute a is discriminative between the words w_1 and w_2, which leads to a binary classification task.

We propose several metrics, which estimate the degree to which the attribute a is important for the word w. We denote this importance as $\varphi(w, a) \in \mathbb{R}$. Clearly, if the attribute is important for one word and not for the other, it is likely to be discriminative. In general, we do not place any assumption on the importance metric $\varphi(w, a)$. We transform this score onto the binary vector $\mathbf{b}_{w,a}$ containing exactly one non-zero element (*one-hot vector*). Let $\mathcal{T} : \mathbb{R} \mapsto \{0, 1\}^b$ be the transformation function so that $\mathbf{b}_{w,a} = \mathcal{T}\big(\varphi(w, a)\big)$. In our case, we split the scores $\varphi(w, a)$ for all pairs (w, a) from training data into b bins according to $\frac{100}{b}\%$ quantiles. The bin, where the importance score belongs to, represents the value 1 in the vector $\mathbf{b}_{w,a}$.

Having the one-hot vectors $\mathbf{b}_{w_1,a}$ and $\mathbf{b}_{w_2,a}$ for the pair of words w_1 and w_2, we represent the discriminativeness of the attribute a as a conjunction matrix $\mathbf{C}_{w_1,w_2,a} = \mathbf{b}_{w_1,a}\mathbf{b}_{w_2,a}^{\top}$ (note $\mathbf{b}_{w_1,a}$ is a column vector). The matrix $\mathbf{C}_{w_1,w_2,a} \in \{0, 1\}^{b \times b}$

935

Proceedings of the 12th International Workshop on Semantic Evaluation (SemEval-2018), pages 935–939
New Orleans, Louisiana, June 5–6, 2018. ©2018 Association for Computational Linguistics

has exactly one non-zero element at the coordinates given by the bins, onto which the scores $\varphi(w_1, a)$ and $\varphi(w_2, a)$ are mapped. Values in the matrix are used as binary features for the classifier. The main motivation behind this binarization is to allow combining different importance metrics on different scale.

In the following subsections, we introduce several approaches to estimate the importance score $\varphi(w, a)$.

2.1 Semantic Spaces

Let $\mathcal{S} : \boldsymbol{V} \mapsto \mathbb{R}^n$ be a semantic space, i.e., a function which projects word w into Euclidean space with dimension n. The meaning of the word w is represented as a real-valued vector $\mathcal{S}(w)$.

We assume, the more similar is the attribute a to the word w in meaning, the more likely a represents some feature of w. We estimate this similarity as a cosine of the angle between the corresponding vectors

$$\varphi(w, a)^{[SS]} = cos\big(\mathcal{S}(w), \mathcal{S}(a)\big). \quad (1)$$

2.2 Word Co-occurrences

We follow the intuition behind the Global Vectors (GloVe) model (Pennington et al., 2014), i.e., that the co-occurrence probabilities have the ability to encode the meaning of words.

We are given the corpus $c = \{c_i\}_{i=1}^k$, i.e., a sequence of words $c_i \in \boldsymbol{V}$, where subscript i denotes the position in the corpus. Let $N(w, a)$ denote the weighted frequency of the word w in the context of the word a

$$N(w, a) = \sum_{c_i=w, c_j=a, 1 \leq |i-j| \leq d} \lambda(|i - j|), \quad (2)$$

where λ is a weighting function. We experiment with two types of weighting: a) *uniform* weighting, where $\lambda(m) = 1$ independently of the distance between words and b) *hyperbolic* weighting, where $\lambda(m) = \frac{1}{m}$. For uniform weighting the equation expresses the number of times the word w occurs in the context of word a. Hyperbolic weighting incorporates the assumption that closer words are more important for each other (the weight decreases with increasing distance).

Let $N(w) = \sum_{a \in \boldsymbol{V}} N(w, a)$ be the number of times any word occurs in the context of w. We estimate the conditional probability of an attribute a given the word w and use it as an importance metric

$$\varphi(w, a)^{[WC-a|w]} = P(a|w) = \frac{N(w, a)}{N(w)}. \quad (3)$$

The core idea is that if a often occurs in the context of w_1 and not in the context of w_2, then a is likely to be discriminative attribute between w_1 and w_2. The similar idea can also be expressed in an opposite way, i.e., to use probability of the word w given the attribute a

$$\varphi(w, a)^{[WC-w|a]} = P(w|a) = \frac{N(w, a)}{N(a)}. \quad (4)$$

2.3 ConceptNet

ConceptNet (Speer and Havasi, 2012) is a large semantic graph, which connects words and phrases with labeled edges. It is based on knowledge collected from many sources, including Wiktionary, WordNet, DBPedia, etc. When ConceptNet is combined with state-of-the-art semantic spaces (e.g., GloVe (Pennington et al., 2014) or Skip-Gram (Mikolov et al., 2013)) it provides exceptional performance in intrinsic tasks (Speer and Lowry-Duda, 2017).

In this paper, we use ConceptNet API, which enables to measure the relatedness between words[1]. It is built using an ensemble that combines data from ConceptNet, SkipGram, GloVe, and OpenSubtitles 2016, using a variation on retrofitting (Speer et al., 2016). We use the relatedness weight as an importance metric $\varphi(w, a)^{[CN]}$.

3 Experiments

In all our experiments we employ *Maximum Entropy* classifier (Berger et al., 1996) implemented in the Brainy machine learning library (Konkol, 2014). For every importance metric we use mapping onto $b = 5$ bins. This leads to $5 \times 5 = 25$ binary features describing the discriminativeness of an attribute for single importance metric.

We train the classifier on the *validation* dataset[2] proposed by the organizers of this task, containing 2722 manually annotated examples (1364 positive and 1358 negative) with total 576 distinct attributes. We do not use automatically generated data *train.txt*. For the selection of optimal feature

---

[1] An example of the relatedness between the words *bird* and *bat*: `http://api.conceptnet.io/related/c/en/bird?filter=/c/en/bat`.

[2] Available at `https://github.com/dpaperno/DiscriminAtt`.

set we perform 10-fold cross-validation. The official test data consists of 2340 examples (1047 positive and 1293 negative). F1 score is the official evaluation measure of this task. Note the majority class system achieves F1 score 50.1% and 55.3% on the validation and test data sets, respectively.

3.1 Settings

We estimate word co-occurrence probabilities (Section 2.2) using the English Wikipedia corpus. We experiment with several semantic spaces:

SkipGram is a neural-network based model (Mikolov et al., 2013). Levy and Goldberg (2014) provide pre-trained SkipGram models on English Wikipedia with two sizes of the context window (2 and 5) and their own model with dependency-based context.

GloVe is a log-bilinear model for word representations, which encodes global word co-occurences (Pennington et al., 2014). We use vectors provided by authors of the model, pre-trained on various corpus sizes (6, 42, and 840 billion words)[3].

FastText (Bojanowski et al., 2017) is a character-n-gram-based SkipGram model. We use word vectors pre-trained on English Wikipedia[4].

LexVec is based on factorization of positive point-wise mutual information matrix using proven strategies from GloVe, SkipGram, and methods based on singular value decomposition (Salle et al., 2016). We use pre-trained word vectors provided by the authors of the model[5].

Latent Semantic Analysis (LSA) (Landauer et al., 1998) first creates a word-document co-occurrence matrix and then reduces its dimension by singular value decomposition. We trained the model on English Wikipedia.

Latent Dirichlet Allocation (LDA) (Blei et al., 2003) represents the text as a topic distribution. In our case, each value in the word vector corresponds to the probability of this word conditioned by the particular topic.

3.2 Results

In Table 1 we show F1 scores for individual importance metrics including all three approaches,

---

[3]Available at https://nlp.stanford.edu/projects/glove.
[4]Available at https://fasttext.cc.
[5]Available at https://github.com/alexandres/lexvec.

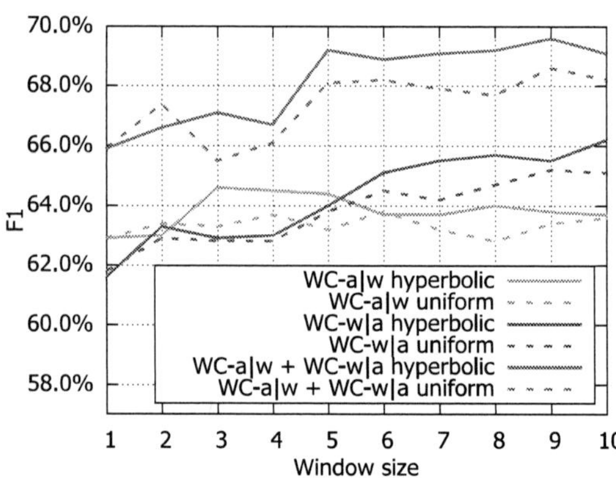

Figure 1: Results of word co-occurrence metric with different weighting and different window size d.

namely, semantic spaces (Section 2.1), word co-occurrences (Section 2.2), and ConceptNet (Section 2.3). The last two columns in the table contain F1 scores for 10-fold cross-validation on the validation dataset and F1 scores on the official test data. All three approaches provide comparable F1 scores on both datasets.

Detailed experiments with different context window sizes $1 \leq d \leq 10$ for estimating co-occurrence probabilities are shown in Figure 1. We show F1 scores achieved by 10-fold cross-validation on the validation dataset. The hyperbolic weighting performs better than uniform for both cases w|a and a|w independently on the size of the context window. Bigger context window seems to be more suitable for capturing discriminativeness. We can see that both metrics enrich each other and their combination leads to significantly better results than using standalone metrics. Based on this graph, we chose context window size $d = 9$ and use it in all further experiments.

Based on the cross-validation F1 scores, we combine different importance metrics to boost the performance (see Table 2). LexVec proved to perform best among semantic spaces. We found out that LDA enrich LexVec and improve the performance by approximately 1%. We believe this is because of the different context type (we used Wikipedia articles as documents for LDA). Significant improvements are achieved when we combine co-occurrence probabilities with semantics spaces or with ConceptNet (both cases give approximately 70% F1 score on both validation and test data). Combining all three approaches to-

	Imp. metrics	Training data	Settings	Cross-validation	Test
semantic spaces	SS-GloVe	6B, Wikipedia + Gigaword 5	$n = 300$	62.0%	62.5%
	SS-GloVe	42B, Common Crawl	$n = 300$	62.6%	62.7%
	SS-GloVe	840B, Common Crawl	$n = 300$	62.1%	62.6%
	SS-fastText	1-5B, Wikipedia	$n = 300$	60.4%	63.3%
	SS-LSA	1-5B, Wikipedia	$n = 300$	55.7%	58.3%
	SS-LDA	1-5B, Wikipedia	$n = 200$	60.5%	63.1%
	SS-LexVec	58B, Common Crawl	$n = 300$	**64.1%**	**64.9%**
	SS-LexVec	7B, Wikipedia + News Crawl	$n = 300$	59.3%	64.3%
	SS-SkipGram	1-5B, Wikipedia	$n = 300$, BoW 2	59.0%	60.6%
	SS-SkipGram	1-5B, Wikipedia	$n = 300$, BoW 5	58.0%	62.0%
	SS-SkipGram	1-5B, Wikipedia	$n = 300$, Dependencies	54.9%	56.0%
word co-oc.	WC-a|w	1-5B, Wikipedia	hyperbolic weighting, $d = 9$	63.8%	60.7%
	WC-w|a	1-5B, Wikipedia	hyperbolic weighting, $d = 9$	**65.5%**	65.5%
	WC-a|w	1-5B, Wikipedia	uniform weighting, $d = 9$	63.4%	59.9%
	WC-w|a	1-5B, Wikipedia	uniform weighting, $d = 9$	65.2%	**66.8%**
	CN			**65.1%**	**66.8%**

Table 1: Results for individual importance metrics based on semantic spaces, word co-occurrences, and ConceptNet.

Importance metric combinations	Settings	Cross-validation	Test
SS-LexVec + SS-LDA		65.6%	66.0%
WC-a|w + WC-w|a	hyperbolic weighting	69.6%	68.2%
WC-a|w + WC-w|a	uniform weighting	68.6%	67.1%
WC-a|w + WC-w|a + CN	hyperbolic weighting	70.4%	70.0%
WC-a|w + WC-w|a + SS-LexVec + SS-LDA	hyperbolic weighting	70.6%	69.8%
WC-a|w + WC-w|a + CN + SS-LexVec + SS-LDA	hyperbolic weighting	72.0%	71.3%
WC-a|w + WC-w|a + CN + SS-LexVec + SS-LDA	hyperbolic weighting, conjunction	**73.9%**	**72.1%**
Winner of SemEval 2018			75%

Table 2: Combinations of proposed importance metrics.

gether yields additional improvements (72.0% and 71.3% on validation and test data, respectively).

Our final UWB system combines all three approaches with one extra trick. We create additional binary features represented as a product of each pair of features ($x_a \times x_b$ for $a \neq b$) and add them into the classifier. We do this to better model the dependencies between single features. In the table, we denote this trick as a *conjunction*. Despite the fact that this setting leads to increasing sparseness of the feature set, it boosts F1 score on validation data by 1.9% and on test data by 0.8%.

4 Conclusion

In this paper we described our UWB system participating in SemEval 2018 shared task for capturing discriminative attributes. We explored three approaches based on word distribution in the corpus, including various semantic spaces, co-occurrence probabilities, and ConceptNet. Our best results have been achieved by Maximum Entropy classifier combining all three approaches with careful feature engineering. Our system is ranked #4 among 26 participating systems.

Acknowledgments.

This publication was supported by the project LO1506 of the Czech Ministry of Education, Youth and Sports under the program NPU I, by university specific research project SGS-2016-018 Data and Software Engineering for Advanced Applications, and by the project MediaGist, EUs FP7 People Programme (Marie Curie Actions), no. 630786.

References

Adam L. Berger, Vincent J. D. Pietra, and Stephen A. D. Pietra. 1996. A maximum entropy approach to natural language processing. *Computational Linguistics*, 22:39–71.

David M. Blei, Andrew Y. Ng, and Michael I. Jordan. 2003. Latent dirichlet allocation. *Journal of Machine Learning Research*, 3:993–1022.

Piotr Bojanowski, Edouard Grave, Armand Joulin, and Tomáš Mikolov. 2017. Enriching word vectors with subword information. *Transactions of the Association for Computational Linguistics*, 5:135–146.

Yuchen Guo, Guiguang Ding, Xiaoming Jin, and Jianmin Wang. 2015. Learning predictable and discriminative attributes for visual recognition. In *Proceedings of the Twenty-Ninth AAAI Conference on Artificial Intelligence*, AAAI'15, pages 3783–3789. AAAI Press.

Zellig Harris. 1954. Distributional structure. *Word*, 10(23):146–162.

Chen Huang, Chen C. Loy, and Xiaoou Tang. 2016. Unsupervised learning of discriminative attributes and visual representations. In *2016 IEEE Conference on Computer Vision and Pattern Recognition (CVPR)*, pages 5175–5184.

Michal Konkol. 2014. Brainy: A machine learning library. In Leszek Rutkowski, Marcin Korytkowski, Rafa Scherer, Ryszard Tadeusiewicz, Lotfi A. Zadeh, and Jacek M. Zurada, editors, *Artificial Intelligence and Soft Computing*, volume 8468 of *Lecture Notes in Computer Science*. Springer Berlin Heidelberg.

Alicia Krebs and Denis Paperno. 2016. Capturing discriminative attributes in a distributional space: Task proposal. In *Proceedings of the 1st Workshop on Evaluating Vector-Space Representations for NLP*. Association for Computational Linguistics.

Thomas K. Landauer, Peter W. Foltz, and Darrell Laham. 1998. An introduction to latent semantic analysis. *Discourse processes*, 25(2-3):259–284.

Angeliki Lazaridou, Nghia The Pham, and Marco Baroni. 2016. The red one!: On learning to refer to things based on discriminative properties. In *Proceedings of the 54th Annual Meeting of the Association for Computational Linguistics (Volume 2: Short Papers)*, pages 213–218, Berlin, Germany. Association for Computational Linguistics.

Omer Levy and Yoav Goldberg. 2014. Dependency-based word embeddings. In *Proceedings of the 52nd Annual Meeting of the Association for Computational Linguistics (Volume 2: Short Papers)*, pages 302–308, Baltimore, Maryland. Association for Computational Linguistics.

Tomáš Mikolov, Kai Chen, Greg Corrado, and Jeffrey Dean. 2013. Efficient estimation of word representations in vector space. *CoRR*, abs/1301.3781.

Jeffrey Pennington, Richard Socher, and Christopher Manning. 2014. Glove: Global vectors for word representation. In *Proceedings of the 2014 Conference on Empirical Methods in Natural Language Processing (EMNLP)*, pages 1532–1543, Doha, Qatar. Association for Computational Linguistics.

Alexandre Salle, Aline Villavicencio, and Marco Idiart. 2016. Matrix factorization using window sampling and negative sampling for improved word representations. In *Proceedings of the 54th Annual Meeting of the Association for Computational Linguistics (Volume 2: Short Papers)*, pages 419–424, Berlin, Germany. Association for Computational Linguistics.

Robert Speer, Joshua Chin, and Catherine Havasi. 2016. Conceptnet 5.5: An open multilingual graph of general knowledge. *CoRR*, abs/1612.03975.

Robert Speer and Catherine Havasi. 2012. Representing general relational knowledge in conceptnet 5. In *Proceedings of the Eight International Conference on Language Resources and Evaluation (LREC'12)*, Istanbul, Turkey. European Language Resources Association (ELRA).

Robert Speer and Joanna Lowry-Duda. 2017. Conceptnet at semeval-2017 task 2: Extending word embeddings with multilingual relational knowledge. In *Proceedings of the 11th International Workshop on Semantic Evaluation (SemEval-2017)*, pages 85–89, Vancouver, Canada. Association for Computational Linguistics.

Meaning_space at SemEval-2018 Task 10: Combining explicitly encoded knowledge with information extracted from word embeddings

Pia Sommerauer   **Antske Fokkens**   **Piek Vossen**

Computational Lexicology & Terminology Lab (CLTL)

Vrije Universiteit Amsterdam, the Netherlands

`{pia.sommerauer,antske.fokkens,piek.vossen}@vu.nl`

Abstract

This paper presents the two systems submitted by the meaning_space team in Task 10 of the SemEval competition 2018 entitled *Capturing discriminative attributes*. The systems consist of combinations of approaches exploiting explicitly encoded knowledge about concepts in WordNet and information encoded in distributional semantic vectors. Rather than aiming for high performance, we explore which kind of semantic knowledge is best captured by different methods. The results indicate that WordNet glosses on different levels of the hierarchy capture many attributes relevant for this task. In combination with exploiting word embedding similarities, this source of information yielded our best results. Our best performing system ranked 5th out of 13 final ranks. Our analysis yields insights into the different kinds of attributes represented by different sources of knowledge.

1 Introduction

SemEval Task 10 "Capturing Discriminative Attributes" (Krebs et al., 2018) provides participants with triples of words consisting of two concepts and an attribute. The task is to determine whether the attribute is a distinguishing property of the first concept compared to the second concept. This is the case in triple *shrimp, spinach, pink*, for instance, because shrimp can be pink whereas spinach is usually of a different color. When the first concept does not have a semantic relation with the attribute or both the concepts have the same semantic relation with it, the attribute is considered not to be discriminative.

In general, Task 10 can be understood as detecting whether there is a semantic relation between the concepts and the attribute. The dataset includes a wide range of variation. For instance, the attribute may be a part of the concept (e.g.

tortoise, snail, legs) or category membership (e.g. *polyurethane, polyester, material*), relations between entities and activities they engage in (e.g. *cheetah, lion, runs*) as well as rather specific relations, for instance the relation between a specialist and the phenomenon they are specialized in (e.g. *optician, dentist, eyes*).

Rather than finding specific solutions for each kind of relation, we investigate different approaches exploiting different sources of knowledge. Both of our systems comprise a component exploiting the glosses and hierarchical structure of WordNet (Fellbaum, 1998) in order to determine whether an attribute applies to a concept. Our underlying assumption is that definitions should provide the most important distinctive attributes of a concept. Since concepts are not necessarily always distinguished on the same level of concreteness, but might also be distinguished on a more abstract level (e.g. *herbs, root, green* v.s. *apse, nightgown, royal*) we exploit the entire WordNet hierarchy.

In both of our systems, the second component exploits information encoded in distributional vector representations of words. Word vectors have not only been shown to capture information about semantic similarity and relatedness but, beyond that, seem to encode information about individual components of word meaning that are necessary to solve analogy tasks such as in the famous example *man* is to *woman* as *king* is to *queen* (Mikolov et al., 2013b). This indicates that the dimensions of the distributional vector representations encode information about specific attributes of words. We experiment with two approaches: a basic approach comparing cosine similarities and an exploratory approach that deducts word vectors from one another to detect meaning differences. Best performance was obtained by the system using cosine similarity. The second approach per-

Proceedings of the 12th International Workshop on Semantic Evaluation (SemEval-2018), pages 940–946
New Orleans, Louisiana, June 5–6, 2018. ©2018 Association for Computational Linguistics

forms lower in isolation, but performance is comparable to the first system in combination with the WordNet component.

The main insights gained from our experiments are the following. First, despite the limited coverage of information on attributes in WordNet (as pointed out by Poesio and Almuhareb (2005)), the contribution of the WordNet component to the overall results indicates that definitions yield a valuable source of knowledge with respect to discriminative attributes. Second, we analyze how individual systems perform across different types of attributes. Our analysis shows that similarity performs best on general descriptive properties and WordNet definitions help most for finding specific properties. These observations indicate that more sophisticated methods of combining these components could lead to superior results in future work.

The remainder of this paper is structured as follows: After presenting background and related work (Section 2), our system designs are introduced in Section 3. Section 4 provides an overview of the results achieved by different systems and system components, including our analysis across attribution types. This is followed by a conclusion (Section 5).

2 Background and related work

Solving the task at hand requires both knowledge about lexical relations and the world. We assume that this knowledge cannot be found in one resource alone. Rather, different approaches of representing word meaning may comprise complementary information. In this exploratory work, we exploit explicitly encoded knowledge in a lexical resource and information encoded in the distribution of words in large corpora. While attributes of concepts have been studied before from a cognitive (e.g. McRae et al. (2005)) and computational (e.g. Poesio and Almuhareb (2005)) perspective, this task is, to our knowledge, the first task aiming at detecting discriminative features.

We use WordNet (Fellbaum, 1998) as a source of explicitly represented knowledge. Whereas the WordNet structure contains a vast amount of information about lexical relations (hyponymy, synonymy, meronymy), its definitions constitute a resource of world knowledge. WordNet definitions have been used successfully in approaches to word sense disambiguation (Lesk, 1986) and inferring verb frames (Green et al., 2004). The only

study requiring knowledge and reasoning about attributes we are aware of is an exploratory study examining what knowledge in definitions contributes to question-answering tasks (Clark et al., 2008).

Vector representations of word meaning based on the distribution of words in large corpora do not yield explicit information about specific relations, but implicitly encode all kinds of associations between concepts. In contrast to manually constructed resources, their coverage is much larger. More specifically, they have been shown to encode information relevant in solving analogy tasks (Mikolov et al., 2013a; Levy and Goldberg, 2014b; Gladkova et al., 2016; Gábor et al., 2017; Linzen, 2016) and inferring semantic hierarchies (Fu et al., 2014; Pocostales, 2016). This indicates that the dimensions of distributional representations encode information about attributes of concepts (Levy and Goldberg, 2014b, p.177). For instance, in order to find the fourth component in the analogy *man* is to *woman* as *king* is to *queen*, a model has to detect the relation holding between the pairs in the analogy. In this example, the relations are formed by the two features of royalty and gender. One way of solving this is to use the vector offsets resulting from *woman - man + king*. The result should be closest to the fourth component (*queen*). Thus, the first component for this calculation, B - A, should capture information about the distinguishing features between A and B, as the subtraction eliminates the identical (or very similar) dimensions in both representations, but keeps the features associated with B.

Our first system follows the basic assumption that if there is some kind of association between a concept and an attribute, this should be reflected by the vector representations. We assume that attributes occur in the linguistic contexts of the concepts they apply to and thus appear in proximity to them. In a comparative set-up such as in this task, the attribute should be closer to the concept it applies to. In our second system, we attempt to exploit the operations used for solving analogies in order to determine whether an attribute distinguishes two concepts.

3 System description

Each of our systems[1] consists of a WordNet component and a component exploiting word embed-

---

[1]Code can be found at `https://github.com/cltl/meaning_space`

ding vectors. If the WordNet component is unable to classify an example, it is passed on to the word embedding component. After presenting the WordNet component, we describe the two embedding-based systems. The word vectors used in all approaches are taken from the Word2Vec Google News model (Mikolov et al., 2013a).[2] The systems are developed using training and validation data and evaluated using test data.[3]

3.1 WordNet glosses and hierarchical structure

We design rules to exploit explicitly encoded knowledge in synset glosses and the hierarchical structure. We assume that (1) the most important discriminative attributes are mentioned in definitions and (2) concepts can be distinguished on different levels of abstraction. Essentially, we check whether the attribute is in any of the definitions of the concepts. We employ two variants of the system. The first variant simply relies on string match (definition string match), whereas the second one employs cosine similarity between the attribute and the words in the glosses (definition similarity). For both variants, we retrieve the glosses of all WordNet synsets containing the concepts and the glosses of all their hypernyms. We preprocess the definitions by tokenizing them and excluding stopwords using NLTK (Bird et al., 2009). In the two best-performing full systems, we used the definition-similarity variant.

3.1.1 Definition string match

This variant employs one rule to detect positive cases and two rules to detect negative cases:

POS The attribute matches a word in the glosses of concept 1 and no word in the glosses of concept 2.

NEG The attribute matches a word in the glosses of both concepts.

NEG The attribute matches a word in the glosses of concept 2 and no word in the glosses of concept 1.

We could also count all cases in which the attribute matches no word as negative cases, but

since only a selection of attributes is mentioned in the glosses, this would yield a high number of false negative decisions. Instead, we fall back on one of two distributional approaches in case none of the above-mentioned cases applies. If run in isolation, we label all instances for which none of the conditions apply as negative.

3.1.2 Definition similarity

In the second variant, we replace words by their vectors and measure the cosine similarity between the attribute and the words in the glosses in order to determine positive and negative cases. As a first step, we search for the word in the glosses with the highest cosine similarity to the attribute. Next, we employ an upper and a lower threshold in order to determine whether the attribute is similar or dissimilar enough to the word in the glosses. We assume this strategy allows us to extend the scope from exact pattern match to highly similar words, such as synonyms or hypernyms. The transformed rules are shown below:

POS The similarity between concept 1 and the attribute is above the upper threshold and the similarity between concept 2 and the attribute is below the lower threshold.

NEG The similarity between concept 2 and the attribute is above the upper threshold and the similarity between concept 1 and the attribute is below the lower threshold.

NEG The similarity between concept 1 and the attribute and the similarity between concept 2 and the attribute are above the upper threshold.

NEG The similarity between concept 1 and the attribute and the similarity between concept 2 and the attribute are below the lower threshold.

Here, we do include a condition for cases in which both similarities are below the threshold, as we assume a wider coverage due to the vector representations. The best performing similarity thresholds (0.75 for upper and 0.23 for lower threshold) were determined by testing several configurations on the validation data.

In addition to glosses, several other kinds of semantic relations encoded in the WordNet hierarchy can be expected to increase the performance

---

on this task. We experimented with meronymy relations, synonymy as well as the hypernyms themselves. Whereas these additions increased the performance in a set-up consisting of only the WordNet component, they harmed the performance in our overall system set-ups where we also use word embeddings.

3.2 Word embeddings

As a second component, we employ two different ways of extracting semantic knowledge from word embeddings.

3.2.1 Vector similarity

This component compares the similarities between the attribute and the concept and counts all cases in which the similarity between concept 1 and the attribute is higher than the similarity between concept 2 and the attribute as positive cases. All other cases are counted as negative. Setting even low thresholds harmed performance.

3.2.2 Vector subtraction

We subtract the vector of concept 2 from the vector of concept 1 and assume that the resulting vector representation is close to the kind of attribute that distinguishes the concepts. If this vector is close to the attribute, we assume it is discriminative. The subtraction should eliminate the shared aspects leaving information about the differences. The vector resulting from for instance *man - woman* cannot be seen as a representation of the specific word *male*, but rather reflects something like for instance 'maleness'.

Rather than setting a definitive similarity threshold, we employ a supervised classification approach in which we use the similarity between the calculated vector and the attribute vector as a sole feature. For reasons of time constraints, we only experimented with a Multi-Layer Perceptron, implemented in the SciKit learn toolkit (Buitinck et al., 2013).[4]

4 Results

Table 1 provides an overview of our different implementations on the test set. The highest performance was reached by the combination of WordNet gloss information and embedding similarity. In the overall SemEval ranking, performance

---

[4]http://scikit-learn.org/stable/index.html, best configuration on the validation set: layer size: (1,1) activation function: logistic.

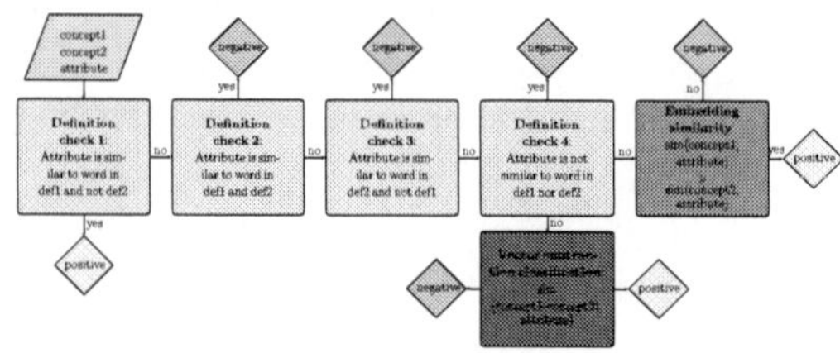

Figure 1: System overview.

System	P-pos	P-neg	R-pos	R-neg	F1-av
def-emb-sim	0.63	0.75	0.73	0.65	0.69
def-emb-sub	0.69	0.68	0.52	0.82	0.67
sim	0.58	0.73	0.75	0.56	0.64
def-sim	0.65	0.59	0.22	0.90	0.52
def	0.65	0.59	0.22	0.90	0.52
sub	0.45	0.55	0.19	0.82	0.46

Table 1: Performance overview of systems and system components on the test set.

ranges from 0.47 to 0.75. Our similarity-centered systems rank in the upper mid range (performing between 0.69 and 0.64), with the best run achieving 5th rank among 13 ranks (and 21 submitted system).

The combination of WordNet gloss information and information from subtracting word vectors performs 2 points lower than our best performing system. When comparing the two word embedding approaches in isolation, we see that the system based on subtraction performs almost 18 points lower than the system using embedding similarity. This indicates that the overlap of correct answers between the Wordnet system and the subtraction system is lower than between the WordNet system and the embedding similarity system. The following sections provide insights into the level at which properties are found in WordNet definitions and the kinds of attributes successfully recognized by the different approaches.

System	P-pos	P-neg	R-pos	R-neg	F1-av
def-emb-sim	0.66	0.69	0.71	0.63	0.67
def-emb-sub	0.74	0.62	0.51	0.82	0.65
sim	0.60	0.64	0.72	0.51	0.61
sub	0.70	0.58	0.39	0.83	0.59
def-sim	0.70	0.54	0.24	0.90	0.52
def	0.70	0.54	0.24	0.90	0.52

Table 2: Performance of the systems and system components on the validation set.

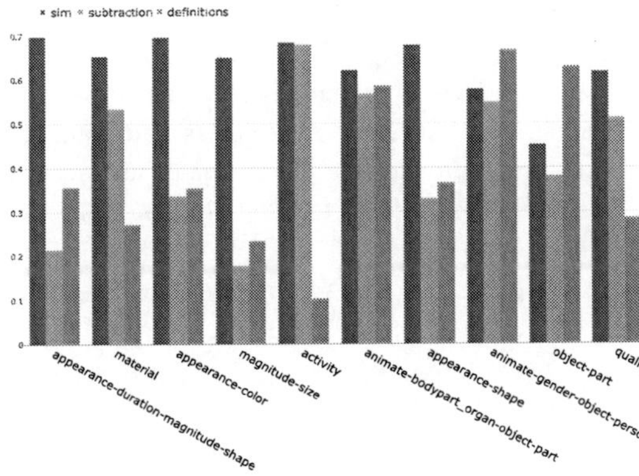

Figure 2: Comparison of f1-scores reached by the three main system components on the 10 most frequent attribute categories.

4.1 Level of distinction in the WordNet hierarchy

We hypothesized that concepts might not always be distinguished on the same level of concreteness, but could also be distinguished on a more abstract level. In order to test this, we counted how many properties are found in glosses of synsets containing the concept and how many are found in glosses of their hypernyms. Out of the total 1,098 attributes found in WordNet glosses, 699 are found on the same level as the concept (i.e. in the definitions of one of the synsets containing the concept) and 366 are found in gloss of one of the hypernyms of the synsets containing the concept.[5] In total, the definition system is able to classify 799 (out of 2,340) concept-concept-attribute triples.

4.2 Comparison of systems across attribute categories.

In this section, we aim at giving some insights into the kinds of attributes systems can detect and identify as discriminative. The attributes in the validation set were categorized by one annotator. The categories are not based on an existing framework, but were chosen intuitively. In most cases, multiple labels are used as the attributes are ambiguous. As there is no overlap between attributes from the validation set and the test set, we present the performance of the systems across the different attribute categories on the validation set. The overall

<hr>

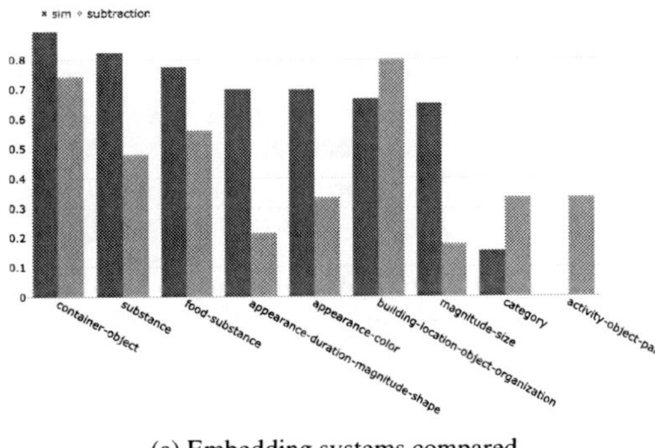

(a) Embedding systems compared.

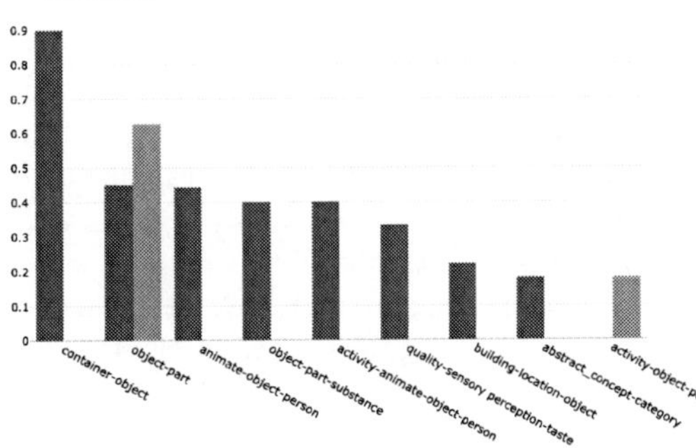

(b) WordNet definition match system compared to embedding similarity system.

Figure 3: Comparison f1-scores reached by the system components showing the categories with the highest performance differences (frequency >10).

all performance on the validation set (presented in Table 2) is similar to the test set with the exception that on the validation set, the system based on vector subtraction performed several points higher than on the test set (0.59) and ranked higher than the WordNet definition systems.

Figure 2 shows the performance of the three individual systems across the 10 most frequent categories. Overall, the vector similarity system outperforms the other system in almost all categories. Of these 10 most frequent categories, there is no category in which the subtraction system outperforms the similarity system.

One of the most striking differences between the embedding-based systems and the WordNet definition system can be seen in the 'activity' category, in which both embedding systems perform almost seven times higher than the WordNet system. This could be explained by the fact that activities associated with concepts can be expected to occur in large corpora, whereas they might not be specific or relevant enough to be mentioned in a definition. In contrast, WordNet outperforms both embedding systems in the categories 'object-part' and 'animate-object-gender-person' (usually referring to a person of a specific gender), which could be expected to consist of more specific attributes.

We expected rather generic descriptions that are not specific to a concept, but mostly relevant in comparison to the other concept to be the most difficult for any system. These kinds of attributes are not relevant enough to be included in definitions nor do we expect them to frequently co-occur with concepts in texts and thus be apparent from a distributional model. It turned out, however, that these kinds of attributes ('appearance-color', 'magnitude-size') were accurately detected as discriminative by the embedding similarity system. A possible explanation might be that they can co-occur with a wide number of concepts, leading to proximity in the vector space.

When considering the categories with the biggest performance differences and a frequency of at least 10 (presented in Figure 3) the following observations can be made: Whereas the embedding similarity system outperforms the subtraction system in most categories, the subtraction system captures about twice as many attributes that indicate a category (usually meaning that the attribute is a hypernym of one of the concepts) and performs higher on 'building-location-object-organization' attributes (Figure 3a). It could be the case that despite their polysemy, these attributes apply to a more limited range of concepts than general descriptions on which the system performs poorly. The subtraction system also correctly detects attributes that are ambiguous between 'activity', 'object' and 'part' (e.g. attributes such as *sail* and *bark*) category, which is not detected by the similarity system. Finally, we observe that a number of attribute categories that are handled correctly by the embedding-based systems are not captured by WordNet definitions at all (Figure 3b).

Overall, the differences between the approaches seem to indicate that distributional models are stronger in capturing attributes expressing related concepts than attributes expressing similar concepts (e.g. hypernyms). This is in line with the general trend observed in large-scale evaluations (Levy et al., 2015; Baroni et al., 2014) of embedding models using a bag-of-words approach (such as the Google News model). Gamallo (2017) and Levy and Goldberg (2014a) show that embedding models using dependency structures perform better on similarity than relatedness and could thus improve the results for the attributes that are similar rather than related to the concepts.

5 Conclusion

For this SemEval task, we submitted systems consisting of combinations of exploratory approaches. Our best performing systems consisted of a component exploiting knowledge in WordNet definitions and a component extracting knowledge from distributional representations. In our best performing system, the latter component consisted of comparing cosine similarities between concepts and attributes. The vector component in our second full system employs a different strategy of extracting information from vector representations than our highest ranked system. Despite its limitations, its performance is comparable to our best performing system.

As expected, WordNet definitions encode rather specific attributes that are probably most informative for distinguishing one concept from another, while they give less importance to rather general descriptions. In contrast, embedding approaches seem to perform highly on attributes that are related rather than similar to the concepts, also encompassing rather general descriptions.

The main contribution of this paper is an exploration of the different types of attributes that can be recognized by different systems. These strengths and weaknesses of the methods could be further exploited by using the information obtained by vector similarity and subtraction as input of a classifier. We plan to investigate the representation of attribute categories in the semantic space in future work.

6 Acknowledgments

This research is funded by the PhD in the Humanities Grant provided by the Netherlands Organization of Scientific Research (Nederlandse Organisatie voor Wetenschappelijk Onderzoek, NWO) PGW.17.041 awarded to Pia Sommerauer and NWO VENI grant 275-89-029 awarded to Antske Fokkens.

References

Marco Baroni, Georgiana Dinu, and Germán Kruszewski. 2014. Don't count, predict! a systematic comparison of context-counting vs. context-predicting semantic vectors. In *Proceedings of the 52nd Annual Meeting of the Association for Computational Linguistics (Volume 1: Long Papers)*, volume 1, pages 238–247.

Steven Bird, Ewan Klein, and Edward Loper. 2009. *Natural language processing with Python: analyzing text with the natural language toolkit.* " O'Reilly Media, Inc.".

Lars Buitinck, Gilles Louppe, Mathieu Blondel, Fabian Pedregosa, Andreas Mueller, Olivier Grisel, Vlad Niculae, Peter Prettenhofer, Alexandre Gramfort, Jaques Grobler, Robert Layton, Jake VanderPlas, Arnaud Joly, Brian Holt, and Gaël Varoquaux. 2013. API design for machine learning software: experiences from the scikit-learn project. In *ECML PKDD Workshop: Languages for Data Mining and Machine Learning*, pages 108–122.

Peter Clark, Christiane Fellbaum, and Jerry Hobbs. 2008. Using and extending wordnet to support question-answering. In *Proceedings of the 4th Global WordNet Conference (GWC08)*. Citeseer.

Christiane Fellbaum. 1998. *WordNet*. Wiley Online Library.

Ruiji Fu, Jiang Guo, Bing Qin, Wanxiang Che, Haifeng Wang, and Ting Liu. 2014. Learning semantic hierarchies via word embeddings. In *Proceedings of the 52nd Annual Meeting of the Association for Computational Linguistics (Volume 1: Long Papers)*, volume 1, pages 1199–1209.

Kata Gábor, Haifa Zargayouna, Isabelle Tellier, Davide Buscaldi, and Thierry Charnois. 2017. Exploring vector spaces for semantic relations. In *Proceedings of the 2017 Conference on Empirical Methods in Natural Language Processing*, pages 1815–1824, Copenhagen, Denmark. Association for Computational Linguistics.

Pablo Gamallo. 2017. Comparing explicit and predictive distributional semantic models endowed with syntactic contexts. *Language Resources and Evaluation*, 51(3):727–743.

Anna Gladkova, Aleksandr Drozd, and Satoshi Matsuoka. 2016. Analogy-based detection of morphological and semantic relations with word embeddings: what works and what doesn't. In *Proceedings of the NAACL Student Research Workshop*, pages 8–15.

Rebecca Green, Bonnie J Dorr, and Philip Resnik. 2004. Inducing frame semantic verb classes from wordnet and ldoce. In *Proceedings of the 42nd Annual Meeting on Association for Computational Linguistics*, page 375. Association for Computational Linguistics.

Alicia Krebs, Alessandro Lenci, and Denis Paperno. 2018. Semeval 2018 task 10: Capturing discriminative attributes. In *Proceedings of the 12th internations workshop on semantic evaluation (SemEval 2018)*.

Michael Lesk. 1986. Automatic sense disambiguation using machine readable dictionaries: how to tell a pine cone from an ice cream cone. In *Proceedings of the 5th annual international conference on Systems documentation*, pages 24–26. ACM.

Omer Levy, Yaov Goldberg, and Ido Dagan. 2015. Improving distributional similarity with lessons learned from word embeddings. In *Transactions of the Association for Computational Linguistics*.

Omer Levy and Yoav Goldberg. 2014a. Dependency-based word embeddings. In *Proceedings of the 52nd Annual Meeting of the Association for Computational Linguistics (Volume 2: Short Papers)*, volume 2, pages 302–308.

Omer Levy and Yoav Goldberg. 2014b. Linguistic regularities in sparse and explicit word representations. In *Proceedings of the eighteenth conference on computational natural language learning*, pages 171–180.

Tal Linzen. 2016. Issues in evaluating semantic spaces using word analogies. In *Proceedings of the 1st Workshop on Evaluating Vector-Space Representations for NLP*, pages 13–18.

Ken McRae, George S Cree, Mark S Seidenberg, and Chris McNorgan. 2005. Semantic feature production norms for a large set of living and nonliving things. *Behavior research methods*, 37(4):547–559.

Tomas Mikolov, Kai Chen, Greg Corrado, and Jeffrey Dean. 2013a. Efficient estimation of word representations in vector space. *arXiv preprint arXiv:1301.3781*.

Tomas Mikolov, Wen-tau Yih, and Geoffrey Zweig. 2013b. Linguistic regularities in continuous space word representations. In *Proceedings of the 2013 Conference of the North American Chapter of the Association for Computational Linguistics: Human Language Technologies*, pages 746–751.

Joel Pocostales. 2016. Nuig-unlp at semeval-2016 task 13: A simple word embedding-based approach for taxonomy extraction. In *Proceedings of the 10th International Workshop on Semantic Evaluation (SemEval-2016)*, pages 1298–1302.

Massimo Poesio and Abdulrahman Almuhareb. 2005. Identifying concept attributes using a classifier. In *Proceedings of the ACL-SIGLEX Workshop on Deep Lexical Acquisition*, pages 18–27. Association for Computational Linguistics.

GHH at SemEval-2018 Task 10: Discovering Discriminative Attributes in Distributional Semantics

Mohammed Attia
Google Inc.
New York City
NY, 10011
attia@google.com

Younes Samih
Dept. of Computational Linguistics
Heinrich Heine University,
Düsseldorf, Germany
samih@phil.hhu.de

Manaal Faruqui
Google Inc.
New York City
NY, 10011
mfaruqui@google.com

Wolfgang Maier
Independent Researcher
Tübingen, Germany
wolfgang.maier@gmail.com

Abstract

This paper describes our system submission to the SemEval 2018 Task 10 on Capturing Discriminative Attributes. Given two concepts and an attribute, the task is to determine whether the attribute is semantically related to one concept and not the other. In this work we assume that discriminative attributes can be detected by discovering the association (or lack of association) between a pair of words. The hypothesis we test in this contribution is whether the semantic difference between two pairs of concepts can be treated in terms of measuring the distance between words in a vector space, or can simply be obtained as a by-product of word co-occurrence counts.

1 Introduction

Equipped with their cognitive skills, encyclopedic knowledge and linguistic competence, humans generally can identify the lexical association or semantic relation between two words or concepts with relative ease. However, building a computational model for identifying fine-grained semantic relations (such as synonymy, antonymy, hyponymy, or hypernymy, meronymy, holonymy, metonymy, containment or causality) or even detecting binary relatedness has proven to be a challenging task.

Efforts to model semantic representation computationally are generally classified into statistical and knowledge-driven semantics. This classification depends on whether the assumption is that human knowledge is encapsulated in language man-ifestation or that explicit manual encoding of this knowledge is needed. The statistical approach to the encoding of semantic relations is referred to as "distributional semantics" or "distributed word representations" (Speer et al., 2017), and its theoretical appeal stems from the fact that it gives practical application to the Firthian dictum "You shall know a word by the company it keeps" (Firth, 1957) which has become commonsense wisdom in lexical semantics. Features of the statistical model are extracted from unstructured data, such as words embeddings, n-gram counts, or directly from raw data.

The basic idea with word embeddings is to formulate semantic relations in arithmetic fashion by creating a vector space in which words with similar contextual embeddings have closer vectors distance (Hinton et al., 1986; Rumelhart et al., 1986; Elman, 1990; Bengio et al., 2003; Kann and Schtze, 2008; Mikolov et al., 2013c). The public availability of word embedding training programs such as word2vec (Mikolov et al., 2013a) and GloVe (Pennington et al., 2014) allowed researchers to create models with different parameters and dimensionality sizes for different purposes including capturing semantic relations (Gladkova et al., 2016; Attia et al., 2016).

The Google n-gram corpus (Brants and Franz, 2006) is a collection of English word n-grams and their observed counts generated from 1 trillion words of texts from web pages. This corpus has been used in many different applications including estimating word-relatedness (Islam et al., 2012),

Proceedings of the 12th International Workshop on Semantic Evaluation (SemEval-2018), pages 947–952
New Orleans, Louisiana, June 5–6, 2018. ©2018 Association for Computational Linguistics

comparison of semantic similarity (Joubarne and Inkpen, 2011), information retrieval (Tandon and De Melo, 2010; Klein and Nelson, 2009), lexical disambiguation (Bergsma et al., 2009), improving general purpose NLP classifiers (Bergsma et al., 2010), and improving parsing performance (Pitler et al., 2010).

Knowledge-driven approaches to the detection of semantic relations rely on manually constructed lexical and encyclopedic resources, such as ConceptNet (Speer et al., 2017), ImageNet (Russakovsky et al., 2015), WordNet (Miller and Fellbaum, 1998), Wiktionary, Open Mind Common Sense (Singh et al., 2002) and DBpedia (Mendes et al., 2012).

In this work we follow a statistical based approach and show the strengths and weakness of the distributional semantics of the word vectors and n-gram frequency counts in capturing the different types of discriminative attributes.

2   Task and Data Description

The goal of the shared task on Capturing Discriminative Attributes (Krebs et al., 2018) is to detect semantic difference between pairs of concepts, or in other words, determine whether a semantic property differentiates between two possibly related concepts. For example both 'bear' and 'goat' are animals, but only a 'bear' has 'claws'. Therefore 'claws' is considered as a discriminative feature.

The shared task data is formatted in triples that represent a ternary relation between two concepts ($Word_1$, $Word_2$) on one hand and an attribute ($Word_3$) on the other. $Word_3$ is considered as a discriminative attribute if, and only if, it characterizes $Word_1$ but not $Word_2$. For example, in the triple (*sailboat,yacht,mast*), 'mast' is discriminative as it is found in $Word_1$, 'sailboat', but not in $Word_2$. By contrast, in the triple (*goose,duck,flies*) the event 'flies' is not discriminative as it characterizes both entities. Similarly in the triple (*pickle,lemon,round*), 'round' is not a discriminative feature, as it characterizes $Word_2$, not $Word_1$.

The size of the shared task data is described in Table 1. It is to be noted that there is no intersection between the discriminative attributes in any of the datasets. We think the purpose is to make sure that the participating systems are able to learn how to estimate the relations, regardless of the lexical items involved.

Dataset	# of triples	# of attributes
Training	17,547	1,292
Validation	2,722	576
Test	2,340	577

Table 1: Sizes of the shared task datasets.

3   System Description

In our system we use a deep neural network for the binary classification of discriminative attributes. The basic idea with deep learning is to use hidden layers of neural nets to automatically capture the underlying factors that lead from the input to the output, eliminating the need for feature engineering.

The system is trained on features extracted from two main publicly available resources that fall within the paradigm of unstructured data as no manual lexical or encyclopedic knowledge is encoded. The two resources are the Google n-gram counts and the Google News Word2Vec.

Google n-gram counts.   We use the Google 5-gram counts as provided by Google Books ngrams[1] (Michel et al., 2011; Lin et al., 2012).

Google News Word2Vec.   This is a publicly available pre-trained word vector[2], built with the word2vec architecture (Mikolov et al., 2013b) from a news corpus of 100B words (3M vocabulary entries) with 300 dimensions, negative sampling, using continuous bag of words and window size of 5.

3.1   Features Used

We describe the features used to train our DNN binary classifier to detect discriminative attributes. In this section we use the abbreviations W_1, W_2, and W_3 for $Word_1$, $Word_2$, and $Word_3$, respectively.

We use pre-trained word vectors in order to obtain similarity scores between words. This leads to the following features.

- $distW_1W_3$: Cosine distance between W_1 and W_3

- $distW_2W_3$: Cosine distance between W_2 and W_3

- $cosDiff$: Difference between $distW_1W_3$ and $distW_2W_3$

---

[1]https://books.google.com/ngrams/info
[2]https://goo.gl/tyVGqW

- *similarityCompare*: We compute the cosine similarity between two sets of words using the Gensim 'n_similarity' function. So it gives a single number for comparing the similarity between W_1 and W_3, and W_2 and W_3.

In order to capture all morphological variations of the words, we use word lemmas and then expand to all variants that share the same lemma.

- *lemmaDistW$_1$W$_3$Ex*: The average cosine distance between W_1 and all lemma expansions of W_3

- *lemmaDistW$_2$W$_3$Ex*: The average cosine distance between W_2 and all lemma expansions of W_3

We use to Google 5-gram counts to obtain the following features.

- *cntW$_1$W$_3$*: counts of W_1 and W_3 co-occurring

- *cntW$_2$W$_3$*: counts of W_2 and W_3 co-occurring

- *cntW$_1$W$_3$Ex*: counts of W_1 and the lemma expansions of W_3 co-occurring

- *cntW$_2$W$_3$Ex*: counts of W_2 and the lemma expansions of W_3 co-occurring

3.2 Machine Learning Models

We use a deep neural network model for the binary classification of attributes as either True or False (or discriminative or non-discriminative) based on the set of features described above.

We use a simple and straight-forward architecture consisting of 5 feed-forward fully-connected (or dense) layers with single dropout layer with a rate of 0.3. The network is narrow on the top and wide on the bottom. The function of the dropout layer (Hinton et al., 2012) is to mitigate overfitting and make sure that our model learns significant representations by randomly omitting a certain percentage of the neurons in the hidden layer for each presentation of the samples during training. This encourages each neuron to depend less on other neurons and to try to learn generalizations. Table 2 shows the layer configuration of the model.

4 Experiments and Results

We test our system on various combination of the features mentioned in subsection 3.1. We assume

Layer type	Output Shape	Param #
Dense$_1$	(None, 12)	132
Dropout$_1$	(None, 12)	0
Dense$_2$	(None, 12)	156
Dense$_3$	(None, 100)	1300
Dense$_4$	(None, 200)	20200
Dense$_5$	(None, 1)	201

Table 2: Neural Network Layout.

the baseline is 50% as this is what a random system would generate given that the validation set has an almost equal number of True's and False's. Table 3 shows the system results on the dev set, with the last row showing results on the test set using our best model, "all features". Surprisingly, using the cosine distance between pairs of words gives a low score (56.17%) which is slightly above the baseline, indicating the ineffectiveness of cosine distances in capturing this kind of relationships. Word counts alone were the most impactful of all the features.

5 Error Analysis

In order to be able to analyze the performance of the system and identify where it is faring well and where it is failing, we first manually classify the relations between concepts and attributes in the validation set into 8 types.

1. **Part-whole**. This is when the attribute denotes an entity that can be part or whole of *concept$_1$*, e.g. *tractor, wheels*; *moose, legs*; *cat, eyes*; *iguana, tongue*; *condos, rooms*.

2. **Container-contained**. This is when the entity attribute can be located/situated physically or temporally in *concept$_1$*, e.g. *oven, kitchen*; *fort, cannons*; *mouse, house*; *priest, parish*; *surfboard, water*.

3. **Made-of**. This is when the entity attribute is a material of which *concept$_1$* can be made, e.g. *cart, wood*; *wire, metal*; *rum, sugarcane*; *scarf, wool*; *wine, grape*; *roof, clay*.

4. **Agent-patient**. This is when the attribute is a topic or theme on which *concept$_1$* can act on, e.g. *politician, politics*; *physiotherapist, muscles*; *dermatologist, skin*; *mammals, milk*.

5. **HasAttribute**. This is when the attribute is an adjective that can be used to describe *con-*

Features	Accuracy
baseline	50.00
$distW_1W_3$, $distW_2W_3$	56.17
$distW_1W_3$, $distW_2W_3$, $lemmaDistW_1W_3Ex$, $lemmaDistW_2W_3Ex$	55.79
$cosDiff$, $similarityCompare$	59.12
$cntW_1W_3$, $cntW_2W_3$	65.27
$cntW_1W_3$, $cntW_2W_3$, $cntW_1W_3Ex$, $cntW_2W_3Ex$	65.45
all features	**66.50**
result on the test set	65.17

Table 3: System results with different feature combinations.

class	Total	%	correct	%
event	346	12.71	260	75.14
containment	228	8.38	167	73.25
made-of	158	5.80	113	71.52
relates-to	164	6.02	115	70.12
agent-patient	121	4.45	84	69.42
part-whole	524	19.25	361	68.89
hasAttribute	850	31.23	515	60.59
hyper-hypo	331	12.16	196	59.21
Total	2,722		1,811	66.53

Table 4: Discriminative classes sorted by system performance.

$cept_1$, e.g. *garlic, white*; *girl, virgin*; *alligator, long*; *tuna, large*; *honey, sweet*; *pumpkin, round*.

6. **Hyper-hypo**. That is when the attribute is a hyponym or hypernym of the concept, e.g. *rum, alcohol*; *orthodontist, profession*; *steak, meat*; *mother, female*; *lorry, vehicle*; *lavender, plant*.

7. **Event**. That is when the attribute is a verb that is associated with the concept/entity, e.g. *woman, talk*; *educator, teaches*; *knee, bend*; *tuna, swims*; *frog, jumps*; *shirt, wear*; *seabirds, fly*; *novelist, write*.

8. **Relates-to**. This is when the relationship cannot stated with any of the aforementioned types, e.g. *bus, passengers*; *knee, pads*; *lung, transplant*; *widow, death*; *brother, sister*; *uncle, nephew*.

Table 4 shows our manual classification of the discriminative attributes in the validation set. It is to be noted that the majority of relations (62.64%) are of three types: hasAttribute, part-whole and hyper-hypo.

The types of discriminative features in Table 4 are sorted by system performance, highlighting strengths and weaknesses of the system. The deep learning algorithm assumes that the attribute is discriminative for $concept_1$ if it has considerably higher n-gram counts with $concept_1$ than with $concept_2$. In the upper end n-gram counts shows strength in dealing with events and container-contained relationships, where co-occurrence statistics showed to be very helpful. The examples below shows frequency counts that indicate stronger relation between $Word_1$ and $Word_2$ than between $Word_2$ and $Word_3$. Gold answers are the numbers (0 or 1) following the triples.

(*shoulder, cheek, carry*, 1), $cntW_1W_3$: 104620, $cntW_2W_3$: 498

(*teacher, pupil, teaches*, 1), $cntW_1W_3$: 134656, $cntW_2W_3$: 0

(*albums, music, picture*, 1), $cntW_1W_3$: 3937564, $cntW_2W_3$: 374572

It is to be mentioned that in the validation set, there were 246 (9%) instances where no frequency counts were found for either concepts.

In the lower end of our system performance there were the classes of *hasAttribute*, *part-whole* and *hyper-hypo*. As these classes constitute the majority of the data, the overall system performance is compromised. We make further detailed analysis of our top losses with *hasAttribute* and *part-whole*.

Analysis of Errors with *hasAttribute*

Most of the errors in this class can be identified with one of three reasons.

- N-gram counts are not aware of the qualification scope. For example, in the tuple below, 'large' has equally high frequency with 'brick', not because a brick can be large, but

they co-occur in phrases like, "large brick house/ranch"
(*garage, brick, large*, 1), $cntW_1W_3$: 245802, $cntW_2W_3$: 193816

- Contrary to common sense knowledge, data could prove the association between a concept and attribute that might not be readily perceived. The example below shows that "green tomato" is not a rarity. This could indicate an error with manual annotation of the data.
  (*zucchini, tomato, green*, 1), $cntW_1W_3$: 29280, $cntW_2W_3$: 179646

- The collocation between the attribute and $concept_2$ could be higher than with $concept_1$.
  (*drizzle, rain, light*, 1), $cntW_1W_3$: 231348, $cntW_2W_3$: 4108548

Analysis of Errors with *part-whole*
Similarly the errors in this class can be attributed to one of three causes.

- Disproportionate frequency count, which could be tied to the disparity in the individual frequency of the concepts themselves. This might be solved by taking the n-gram count as a function of the unigram counts of the concepts themselves.
  (*car, taxi, wheels*, 0), $cntW_1W_3$: 504848, $cntW_2W_3$: 2734

- There could be an association of different kind between $concept_2$ and the attribute that yield higher frequency counts. For instance in the example below, 'garlic' and 'wings' have higher frequency, not because garlic has wings, but because they co-occur in phrases like "garlic chicken wings".
  (*pheasant, garlic, wings*, 1), $cntW_1W_3$: 500, $cntW_2W_3$: 11136

- Either of the two concepts has no n-gram co-occurrence with the given attribute leading to missing information.
  (*owl, buzzard, eyes*, 0), $cntW_1W_3$: 10088, $cntW_2W_3$: 0

6   Conclusion

In this paper we have presented our system for detecting discriminative features using distributional semantics. We have shown that, without resort to human knowledge, a great deal of encyclopedic knowledge can be captured from unstructured data. We also conducted a detailed error analysis which shows the strengths and weaknesses of the system.

In its quest to approximate the distance between words with similar contexts, the cosine distance becomes oblivious to the internal intrinsic relationship between words and their immediate neighbors, and this is why many relations that are induced from co-occurrence counts are not captured by cosine distance.

While n-gram counts from raw data can present a great wealth for mining for lexical information and inducing semantic knowledge, co-occurrence counts can suffer from considerable constraints when two or more adjacent words have different scope of predication or qualification. For example, while "wood spoon" has a high frequency due to the semantic relation of 'made-of', "wood pepper" has an even higher frequency count, not due to any semantic relationship, but because 'wood' is scoped to a subsequent word, "wood pepper mill". If syntactic information related to the head of noun compounds and scope of modification, more meaningful assumptions can be made.

References

Mohammed Attia, Suraj Maharjan, Younes Samih, Laura Kallmeyer, and Thamar Solorio. 2016. Cogalex-v shared task: Ghhh - detecting semantic relations via word embeddings. In *Proceedings of the 5th Workshop on Cognitive Aspects of the Lexicon (CogALex-V)*, pages 86–91.

Y. Bengio, R. Ducharme, and P. Vincent. 2003. A neural probabilistic language model. *Journal of Machine Learning Research*, 3:1137–1155.

Shane Bergsma, Dekang Lin, and Randy Goebel. 2009. Web-scale n-gram models for lexical disambiguation. In *IJCAI*, volume 9, pages 1507–1512.

Shane Bergsma, Emily Pitler, and Dekang Lin. 2010. Creating robust supervised classifiers via web-scale n-gram data. In *Proceedings of the 48th Annual Meeting of the Association for Computational Linguistics*, pages 865–874. Association for Computational Linguistics.

Thorsten Brants and Alex Franz. 2006. The google web 1t 5-gram corpus version 1.1. In *LDC2006T13*.

J. Elman. 1990. Finding structure in time. *Cognitive Science*, 14:179–211.

John R Firth. 1957. A synopsis of linguistic theory, 1930-1955. *Studies in Linguistic Analysis*.

Anna Gladkova, Aleksandr Drozd, and Satoshi Matsuoka. 2016. Analogy-based detection of morphological and semantic relations with word embeddings: What works and what doesn't. In *Proceedings of the NAACL Student Research Workshop*, pages 8–15.

G.E. Hinton, J.L. McClelland, and D.E. Rumelhart. 1986. Distributed representations. *In: Parallel distributed processing: Explorations in the microstructure of cognition*, 1.

Geoffrey E Hinton, Nitish Srivastava, Alex Krizhevsky, Ilya Sutskever, and Ruslan R Salakhutdinov. 2012. Improving neural networks by preventing co-adaptation of feature detectors. *arXiv preprint arXiv:1207.0580*.

Aminul Islam, Evangelos Milios, and Vlado Keselj. 2012. Comparing word relatedness measures based on google n-grams. *Proceedings of COLING 2012: Posters*, pages 495–506.

Colette Joubarne and Diana Inkpen. 2011. Comparison of semantic similarity for different languages using the google n-gram corpus and second-order co-occurrence measures. In *Canadian Conference on Artificial Intelligence*, pages 216–221. Springer.

Katharina Kann and Hinrich Schtze. 2008. A unified architecture for natural language processing: Deep neural networks with multitask learning. In *Proceedings of the 25th International Conference on Machine Learning*, pages 160–167.

Martin Klein and Michael L Nelson. 2009. Correlation of term count and document frequency for google n-grams. In *European Conference on Information Retrieval*, pages 620–627. Springer.

Alicia Krebs, Alessandro Lenci, and Denis Paperno. 2018. Semeval-2018 task 10: Capturing discriminative attributes. In *Proceedings of the 12th international workshop on semantic evaluation (SemEval 2018)*.

Yuri Lin, Jean-Baptiste Michel, Erez Lieberman Aiden, Jon Orwant, William Brockman, and Slav Petrov. 2012. Syntactic annotations for the Google Books Ngram Corpus. In *Proceedings of the 50th Annual Meeting of the Association for Computational Linguistics Volume 2: Demo Papers (ACL '12)*.

Pablo N Mendes, Max Jakob, and Christian Bizer. 2012. Dbpedia: A multilingual cross-domain knowledge base. In *LREC*, pages 1813–1817. Citeseer.

Jean-Baptiste Michel, Yuan Kui Shen, Aviva Presser Aiden, Adrian Veres, Matthew K. Gray, William Brockman, The Google Books Team, Joseph P. Pickett, Dale Hoiberg, Dan Clancy, Peter Norvig, Jon Orwant, Steven Pinker, Martin A. Nowak, and Erez Aiden Lieberman. 2011. Quantitative analysis of culture using millions of digitized books. *Science*, 331(6014):176–182.

Tomas Mikolov, Kai Chen, Greg Corrado, and Jeffrey Dean. 2013a. Efficient estimation of word representations in vector space. In *In Proceedings of International Conference on Learning Representations (ICLR) 2013. arXiv:1301.3781v3*, pages 746–751, Scottsdale, AZ.

Tomas Mikolov, Ilya Sutskever, Kai Chen, Greg Corrado, and Jeffrey Dean. 2013b. Distributed representations of words and phrases and their compositionality. *Advances in neural information processing systems*, pages 3111–3119.

Tomas Mikolov, Wen tau Yih, and Geoffrey Zweig. 2013c. Linguistic regularities in continuous space word representations. In *Proceedings of NAACL-HLT 2013*, pages 746–751, Atlanta, Georgia.

George Miller and Christiane Fellbaum. 1998. Wordnet: An electronic lexical database.

Jeffrey Pennington, Richard Socher, and Christopher D. Manning. 2014. Glove: Global vectors for word representation. In *Proceedings of the 2014 Conference on Empirical Methods in Natural Language Processing (EMNLP)*, pages 1532–1543, Doha, Qatar.

Emily Pitler, Shane Bergsma, Dekang Lin, and Kenneth Church. 2010. Using web-scale n-grams to improve base np parsing performance. In *Proceedings of the 23rd International Conference on Computational Linguistics*, pages 886–894. Association for Computational Linguistics.

D. E. Rumelhart, G. E. Hinton, and R. J. Williams. 1986. Learning internal representations by back-propagating errors. *Nature. 323:533.536*.

Olga Russakovsky, Jia Deng, Hao Su, Jonathan Krause, Sanjeev Satheesh, Sean Ma, Zhiheng Huang, Andrej Karpathy, Aditya Khosla, Michael Bernstein, et al. 2015. Imagenet large scale visual recognition challenge. *International Journal of Computer Vision*, 115(3):211–252.

Push Singh, Thomas Lin, Erik T Mueller, Grace Lim, Travell Perkins, and Wan Li Zhu. 2002. Open mind common sense: Knowledge acquisition from the general public. In *OTM Confederated International Conferences" On the Move to Meaningful Internet Systems"*, pages 1223–1237. Springer.

Robert Speer, Joshua Chin, and Catherine Havasi. 2017. Conceptnet 5.5: An open multilingual graph of general knowledge. In *AAAI*, pages 4444–4451.

Niket Tandon and Gerard De Melo. 2010. Information extraction from web-scale n-gram data. In *Web N-gram Workshop*, volume 7.

CitiusNLP at SemEval-2018 Task 10: The Use of Transparent Distributional Models and Salient Contexts to Discriminate Word Attributes

Pablo Gamallo

Centro Singular de Investigación en
Tecnoloxías da Información (CiTIUS)
Universidade de Santiago de Compostela, Galiza
`pablo.gamallo@usc.es`

Abstract

This article describes the unsupervised strategy submitted by the CitiusNLP team to SemEval 2018 Task 10, a task which consists of predicting whether a word is a discriminative attribute between two other words. The proposed strategy relies on the correspondence between discriminative attributes and relevant contexts of a word. More precisely, the method uses transparent distributional models to extract salient contexts of words which are identified as discriminative attributes. The system performance reaches about 70% accuracy when it is applied on the development dataset, but its accuracy goes down (63%) on the official test dataset.

1 Introduction

The goal of SemEval-2018 Task 10 (Paperno, Lenci and Krebs, To Appear) is to predict whether a word is a discriminative attribute between two other words. The key idea underlying this task is to capture semantic attributes of words in order to discriminate their senses. Distributional semantics is based on the assumption that two words have similar senses if they tend to appear with the same contextual words (Firth, 1957). As contextual words actually refer to the semantic attributes of a given word, I will focus on identifying the most salient word contexts. So, my method to identify discriminative attributes relies on the identification of salient contexts, since they represent the main semantic attributes of a word.

For this purpose, in this paper we will make use of distributional models built with transparent and lexico-syntactic contexts. To capture discriminative attributes, I will rank the most relevant contexts of a word by using lexical association measures between a given word and their contexts. My method is unsupervised and only requires pretrained distributional models.

This paper is organized as follows. The method is described in Section 2. Experiments, results, and a discussion on them are presented in Section 3. Finally, conclusions are addressed in Section 4.

2 The method

As mentioned in the previous section, discriminative attributes might be captured by searching for the most salient contexts of words. For this purpose, the distributional vector space I have adopted is a transparent count-based model with explicit and sparse dimensions. Sparseness reduction is performed by selecting the most salient contexts per word using a filtering strategy (Bordag, 2008; Gamallo and Bordag, 2011; Gamallo, 2017). The filtering strategy to select the most salient contexts consists of selecting, for each word, the S (salient) contexts with highest lexical association scores (e.g. loglikelihood, ppmi, etc). The top S contexts are considered to be the most *relevant* and informative for each word. S is a global, arbitrarily defined constant whose usual values range from 10 to 1000 (Biemann et al., 2013; Padró et al., 2014). In short, I keep at most the S most relevant contexts for each target word. This is an explicit and transparent distributional representation giving rise to a non-zero matrix. By contrast, methods based on dimensionality reduction, such as LSA (Landauer and Dumais, 1997) or neural-based embeddings (Mikolov et al., 2013), make the vector space more compact with dimensions that are not transparent in linguistic terms (Gamallo, 2017).

SemEval-2018 Task 10 to detect discriminative attributes consists of predicting whether a word is a discriminative attribute between two other words. For instance, given a triple <*car, table, wheels*>, the system must determine if the last word of the triple, *wheels*, represents a semantic

Proceedings of the 12th International Workshop on Semantic Evaluation (SemEval-2018), pages 953–957
New Orleans, Louisiana, June 5–6, 2018. ©2018 Association for Computational Linguistics

feature that characterizes the first word, *car*, but not the second one, *table*. The task is a binary classification task. For this particular example, the classifier must return a positive answer since cars have wheels but tables have not. By taking into account the objective of SemEval-2018 Task 10 and my concept of *salient context* introduced above, the classification method I propose is the following very simple rule:

> Given the triplet $< w1, w2, att >$, att is a discriminative attribute of $w1$ and not of $w2$ if att belongs to the most salient contexts of $w1$ and not to those of $w2$.

Concerning the type of context used to represent word distributions, there is a great number of previous studies that evaluate and compare syntactic contexts (usually dependencies) with bag-of-words techniques (Grefenstette, 1993; Seretan and Wehrli, 2006; Padó and Lapata, 2007; Peirsman et al., 2007; Gamallo, 2008, 2009; Levy and Goldberg, 2014; Gamallo, 2017). The cited papers state that syntax-based methods outperform bag-of-words techniques, in particular when the objective is to compute semantic similarity between functional equivalent words, such as detection of co-hyponym/hypernym word relations (i.e. near synonymy).

In my proposal, I use lexico-syntactic contexts to model word distributions. When contexts are defined as lexico-syntactic contexts, I consider that a word is an attribute of $w1$ if that word is the lexical element in at least one of the salient contexts of $w1$. For instance, consider the following three lexico-syntactic contexts:

$[NOUN, with, wheels]$
$[NOUN, nsubj, run]$
$[red, nmod, NOUN]$

If they are salient contexts of the word *car*, then the three lexical words of these three contexts, i.e. *wheels*, *run*, and *red*, will be considered as attributes of *car*.

The number of salient contexts considered per word will be determined experimentally.

3 Experiments

3.1 Resources

The count-based, explicit and transparent distributional model used in the exeperiments was generated from the English Wikipedia (August 2013 dump) containing almost 2 billion tokens. The description of this model is reported in Gamallo (2017), and a version with the 500 most salient contexts per word is freely available.[1] To process the corpus and create the transparent matrices, I used the multilingual PoS tagger of LinguaKit[2] (Garcia and Gamallo, 2015) and DepPattern, a rule-based and multilingual dependency parser (Gamallo, 2015) also taking part of LinguaKit. I also generated other models with different thresholds: from 10 to 2000 salient contexts per word.

As will be described in the next subsection, I will compare the transparent matrix with dense word embeddings, in particular with those reported in Levy and Goldberg (2014), which are publicly available.[3] These embeddings were generated from the same Wikipedia dump as the transparent model. Given that embeddings are opaque and, thereby, their dimensions are not easily associated to specific words, I use Cosine similarity to find discrimative attributes. A word is a discriminative attribute of $w1$ and not of $w2$, if the similarity score between the attribute and $w1$ is higher than a given threshold whereas it is lower in the case of $w2$.

3.2 Preliminary Experiments

To find the best configuration of the proposed system, I carried out several experiments on the train and validation datasets (20,510 examples). As the system is unsupervised, I am not required to separate training from validation. First, I searched for the best lexical association by comparing loglikelihood (Dunning, 1993) and positive pointwise mutual information (ppmi) (Niwa and Nitta, 1994), by using models with 400 and 500 salient contexts. As loglikelihood performed slightly better than ppmi, I chose the former measure to carry out the next experiments. Second, I searched for the best number of salient contexts. For this purpose, several evaluations were made with models from 10 to 2000 salient contexts. Figure 1 shows that the peak is quickly reached with 500 contexts (more than 0.67 accuracy), while performance is getting down slowly as more contexts are added.

---

[1] http://fegalaz.usc.es/~gamallo/resources/count-models.tar.gz
[2] https://github.com/citiususc/Linguakit
[3] https://levyomer.wordpress.com/2014/04/25/dependency-based-word-embeddings/

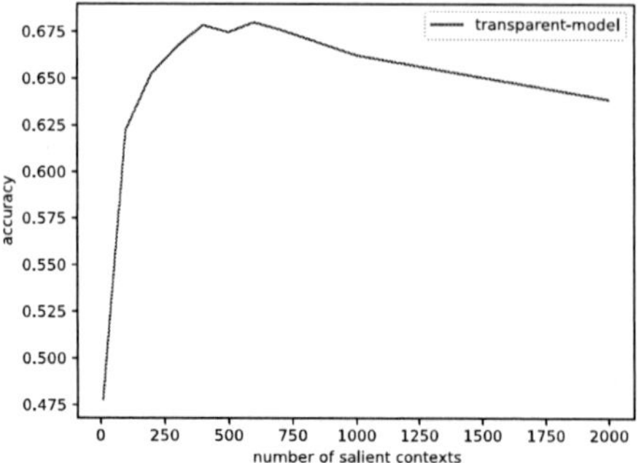

Figure 1: Accuracy of the system at different settings: from 10 to 2000 salient contexts. The experiments were carried out with the development corpus: training + validation.

models	accuracy	word-cntx pairs
wiki	0.674	36 million
wiki+bnc	0.690	38 million
wiki+bnc+reddit	0.701	45 million

Table 1: Accuracy obtained with three corpus-based models: just Wikipedia, Wikipedia and BNC, Wikipedia, BNC and Reddit. The experiments were carried out with the development dataset: training and validation. All models were built by filtering 500 contexts per word. The last column shows the size of the filtered word-context pairs.

I therefore decided to use models with 500 salient contexts per word for the next experiments.

Next, I merged the Wikipedia-based model with other models generated from two different corpora: British National Corpus (BNC),[4] and a sample with 500 million words from Reddit corpus.[5] Results are shown in Table 1. As expected, accuracy is improved as the model grows.

Given these preliminary experiments, I submitted the two best configurations to the test evaluation (2,340 examples):

syst.	meas.	saliency	corpora
run1	loglike	500 ctxs	wiki+bnc
run2	loglike	500 ctxs	wiki+bnc+reddit

In my preliminary experiment, I also used the word embeddings described in the previous subsection to capture discriminative attributes. As

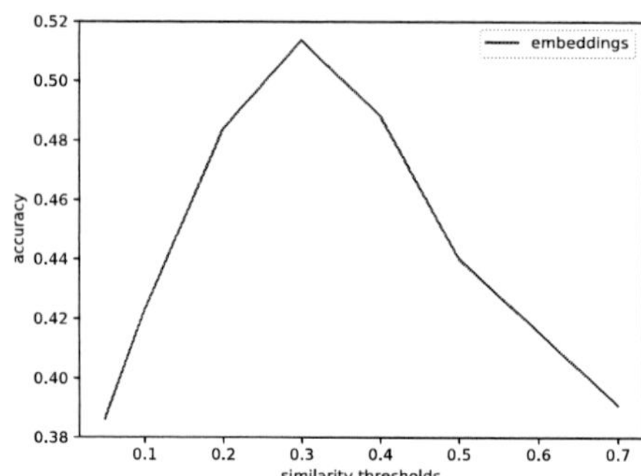

Figure 2: Accuracy of the embedding-based system at different settings: from 0.05 to 0.7 similarity values. The experiments were carried out with the development corpus: training + validation.

mentioned above, a word is considered to be an attribute of a target word if their similarity is higher than a specific threshold, otherwise it is not a discriminative attribute. Several similarity scores were set to determine whether a word is an attribute or not. Figure 2 shows that the best similarity threshold is around 0.3 (cosine value). Accuracy drops dramatically with higher threshold values. The best accuracy reached by this strategy is about 20 points below the best models based on salient contexts. Therefore, for this particular task, transparent models consistently outperform word embeddings.

3.3 Official Test

The test dataset consists of 2,340 examples. My *run1* (wiki+bnc) merely reached 0.625 accuracy while *run2* (wiki+bnc+reddit) reached 0.634. These results are very far below those obtained with the development dataset, which is nevertheless 10 times larger.

3.4 Discussion

With regard to the rest of teams at the shared task, my *run2* is just in the middle of the ranking (13 out of 26 runs). However, its performance in the development dataset (0.700 accuracy) is close to the third best system. I am not able to explain the difference between the development and the test dataset. It would require a deep error analysis to understand that significant difference. This disparity is not due to a difference in the corpus frequency of the words included in the test set. I have checked the frequency of all words (test and

---

[4]https://corpus.byu.edu/bnc/

[5]https://www.reddit.com/r/datasets/comments/3mg812/full_reddit_submission_corpus_now_available_2006/

development) and there is no important contrast at this regard. The reason could just be that the test dataset might contain more difficult triples.

The best system at the shared task achieves 0.75, leading by 12 points my *run2*. Even though the score of my system is lower, it is worth mentioning that my strategy is fully unsupervised and no tunning or specific configuration has been carried out to adapt the system to the test dataset.

4 Conclusions and Future Work

I presented a very basic unsupervised strategy to predict whether a word is a discriminative attribute between two other words. The current strategy relies on the correspondence between discriminative attribute and context saliency, and it works on transparent distributional models to extract salient contexts of words.

As I observed that accuracy improves as the corpus grows, in future work, I will compile specific text corpora for just the words of the test. This should lead to select more salient contexts (and so more discriminative attributes) per word. In addition, I will make new experiments with relational lexical resources, such as WordNet, to compare them with distributional models in this particular task.

Acknowledgments

This work has received financial support from a 2016 BBVA Foundation Grant for Researchers and Cultural Creators, TelePares (MINECO, ref:FFI2014-51978-C2-1-R), the Consellería de Cultura, Educación e Ordenación Universitaria (accreditation 2016-2019, ED431G/08) and the European Regional Development Fund (ERDF).

References

Biemann, C., and Riedl M. 2013. Text: Now in 2d! a framework for lexical expansion with contextual similarity. *Journal of Language Modelling*, 1(1):55–95.

Stefan Bordag. 2008. A Comparison of Co-occurrence and Similarity Measures as Simulations of Context. In *9th CICLing*, pages 52–63.

Ted Dunning. 1993. Accurate methods for the statistics of surprise and coincidence. *Computational Linguistics*, 19(1):61–74.

J.R. Firth. 1957. A synopsis of linguistic theory 1930-1955. *Studies in linguistic analysis*, pages 1–32.

Pablo Gamallo. 2008. Comparing window and syntax based strategies for semantic extraction. In *PROPOR-2008*, pages 41–50. Lecture Notes in Computer Science, Springer-Verlag.

Pablo Gamallo. 2009. Comparing different properties involved in word similarity extraction. In *14th Portuguese Conference on Artificial Intelligence (EPIA'09), LNCS, Vol. 5816*, pages 634–645, Aveiro, Portugal. Springer-Verlag.

Pablo Gamallo. 2015. Dependency parsing with compression rules. In *Proceedings of the 14th International Workshop on Parsing Technology (IWPT 2015)*, pages 107–117, Bilbao, Spain. Association for Computational Linguistics.

Pablo Gamallo. 2017. Comparing explicit and predictive distributional semantic models endowed with syntactic contexts. *Language Resources and Evaluation*, 51(3):727–743.

Pablo Gamallo and Stefan Bordag. 2011. Is singular value decomposition useful for word simalirity extraction. *Language Resources and Evaluation*, 45(2):95–119.

Marcos Garcia and Pablo Gamallo. 2015. Yet another suite of multilingual NLP tools. In *Languages, Applications and Technologies*, volume 563 of *Communications in Computer and Information Science*, pages 65–75, Switzerland. Springer. Revised Selected Papers of the Symposium on Languages, Applications and Technologies (SLATE 2015).

Gregory Grefenstette. 1993. Evaluation techniques for automatic semantic extraction: Comparing syntactic and window-based approaches. In *Workshop on Acquisition of Lexical Knowledge from Text SIGLEX/ACL*, Columbus, OH.

T.K. Landauer and S.T. Dumais. 1997. A solution to Plato's problem: The Latent Semantic Analysis theory of acquision, induction and representation of knowledge. *Psychological Review*, 10(2):211–240.

Omer Levy and Yoav Goldberg. 2014. Dependency-based word embeddings. In *Proceedings of the 52nd Annual Meeting of the Association for Computational Linguistics, ACL 2014, June 22-27, 2014, Baltimore, MD, USA*, pages 302–308.

Tomas Mikolov, Ilya Sutskever, Kai Chen, Gregory S. Corrado, and Jeffrey Dean. 2013. Distributed representations of words and phrases and their compositionality. In *Advances in Neural Information Processing Systems*, pages 3111–3119.

Yoshiki Niwa and Yoshihiko Nitta. 1994. Co-occurrence vectors from corpora vs. distance vectors from dictionaries. In *Proceedings of the 15th Conference on Computational Linguistics - Volume 1*, COLING '94, pages 304–309, Stroudsburg, PA, USA. Association for Computational Linguistics.

Sebastian Padó and Mirella Lapata. 2007. Dependency-Based Construction of Semantic Space Models. *Computational Linguistics*, 33(2):161–199.

Muntsa Padró, Marco Idiart, Aline Villavicencio, and Carlos Ramisch. 2014. Nothing like good old frequency: Studying context filters for distributional thesauri. In *Proceedings of the 2014 Conference on Empirical Methods in Natural Language Processing, EMNLP 2014, October 25-29, 2014, Doha, Qatar, A meeting of SIGDAT, a Special Interest Group of the ACL*, pages 419–424.

Yves Peirsman, Kris Heylen, and Dirk Speelman. 2007. Finding semantically related words in Dutch. Co-occurrences versus syntactic contexts. In *CoSMO Workshop*, pages 9–16, Roskilde, Denmark.

Violeta Seretan and Eric Wehrli. 2006. Accurate Collocation Extraction Using a Multilingual Parser. In *21st International Conference on Computational Linguistics and the 44th annual meeting of the ACL*, pages 953–960.

THU_NGN at SemEval-2018 Task 10: Capturing Discriminative Attributes with MLP-CNN model

Chuhan Wu[1], Fangzhao Wu[2], Zhigang Yuan[1], Sixing Wu[1] and Yongfeng Huang[1]
[1]Tsinghua National Laboratory for Information Science and Technology,
Department of Electronic Engineering, Tsinghua University Beijing 100084, China
[2]Microsoft Research Asia
{wuch15,yuanzg14,wu-sx15,yfhuang}@mails.tsinghua.edu.cn
wufangzhao@gmail.com

Abstract

Existing semantic models are capable of identifying the semantic similarity of words. However, it's hard for these models to discriminate between a word and another similar word. Thus, the aim of SemEval-2018 Task 10 is to predict whether a word is a discriminative attribute between two concepts. In this task, we apply a multilayer perceptron (MLP)-convolutional neural network (CNN) model to identify whether an attribute is discriminative. The CNNs are used to extract low-level features from the inputs. The MLP takes both the flatten CNN maps and inputs to predict the labels. The evaluation F-score of our system on the test set is 0.629 (ranked 15th), which indicates that our system still needs to be improved. However, the behaviours of our system in our experiments provide useful information, which can help to improve the collective understanding of this novel task.

1 Introduction

Evaluating the similarity of words is an important task in semantic modeling. There have been different approaches based on corpus statistics (Jiang and Conrath, 1997; Mihalcea et al., 2006) and ontology (Seco et al., 2004; Sánchez et al., 2012). After an effective word representation proposed by mikolov et al (2013), word similarity can be evaluated based on word embedding weights (Levy and Goldberg, 2014). Usually higher cosine similarity of word embedding vectors indicates higher semantic similarity.

However, existing semantic methods are not capable of discriminating similar words between each other without additional information. For example, it is easy for these models to tell "dog" and "puppy" is similar, but they can't tell the differences between each other. It limits the use of these models to mine such fine-grained semantic information from texts. Thus, the SemEval-2018 Task

10 is proposed to determine whether an attribute can help to discriminate between two words(Krebs et al., 2018). One can express semantic differences between concepts by referring to attributes associated with those concepts. The differences between concepts can usually be identified by the presence or absence of specific attributes. For example, the attributes "red" and "yellow" are discriminative for concepts "apple" and "banana", while "sweet" or "fruit" are not discriminative.

Capturing such discriminative attributes can be regarded as a binary classification task: given two words and an attribute, predict whether the attribute is a difference between the two words. Existing methods to capture discriminative attributes are mainly based on dictionary (Parikh and Grauman, 2011). In recent years, CNN have been successfully applied to text classification task (Kim, 2014). In order to address this task, we develop a system based on MLP-CNN model. Firstly, the input words will be converted into dense vectors using the combination of different word embeddings. Then the CNN layers are used to extract features from these vectors. Finally, a MLP classifier is used to predict binary labels based on both embedding and CNN features. The experimental results show that our model outperforms several baseline neural model, and the additional features can improve the model performance. Our system still has room for development according to the experimental analysis. The behaviours of our system in our experiments can help to further fix and extend our model.

2 MLP-CNN model with Word Feature

2.1 Network Architecture

The architecture of our MLP-CNN model is shown in Figure 1. The input of our system is a pair of words with an attribute. First, an em-

958

Proceedings of the 12th International Workshop on Semantic Evaluation (SemEval-2018), pages 958–962
New Orleans, Louisiana, June 5–6, 2018. ©2018 Association for Computational Linguistics

bedding layer is used to provide different kinds of pre-trained embedding weights ($v_1 - dim$) and the word features ($v_f - dim$) . We use three different pre-trained embedding weights and concatenate them together with the additional features of each word. Thus, the output of embedding layer is $(v_1 + v_f) - dim$.

Second, a 2-layer convolutional neural network take these vectors as input, and output the flatten feature maps. We use zeros to pad in both sides to keep the same output length. Since the length of inputs is 3, the 3 time steps of the convolutional feature maps can respectively extract the inherent relatedness of the first word with attribute, the second word with attribute and all three words. The feature map dimensions of the two CNN layers are v_2 and v_3 respectively. In order to reduce the difficulties of gradient propagation in neural networks, we use a over-layer connection between input and output of CNN. We concatenate the flatten feature maps with all word embedding and features together. Finally a MLP with ReLU and sigmoid activation function is used to predict the normalized binary label. With the help of the over-layer connection, the MLP classifier can learn from high-level word information and raw semantic information at the same time. Since the final labels are obtained from the triples of words through the embedding, CNN and dense layers, all parameters can be tuned in model training.

2.2 Word Embedding

Since there are several out-of-vocabulary words in the dataset when using single pre-trained word embedding, we use three different embedding models to cover them. The three embedding models include pre-trained word2vec embedding[1] provided by Mikolov et al. (Mikolov et al., 2013), the Glove embedding[2] provided by Pennington et al. (Pennington et al., 2014) and the fastText embedding[3] released by bojanowski et al. (Bojanowski et al., 2016). These embedding weights are all 300-dim. They are concatenated together as the representation of input words.

2.3 Word Feature

In our model, we use one-hot encoded POS tags and two binary features obtained by Word-

---

[1]https://code.google.com/archive/p/word2vec/

[2]http://nlp.stanford.edu/data/glove.840B.300d.zip

[3]https://s3-us-west-1.amazonaws.com/fasttext-vectors/wiki.en.vec

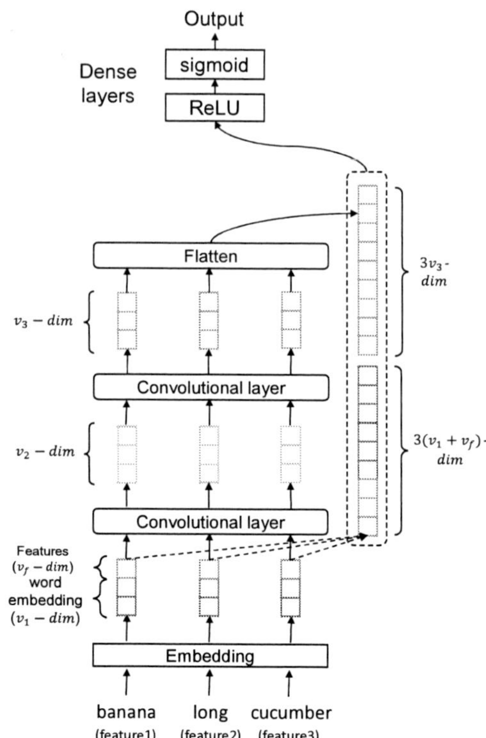

Figure 1: The architecture of our MLP-CNN model.

Net (Miller and Fellbaum, 1998). In the dataset, the words to be discriminated are nouns, but attributes are nouns, adjectives, verbs and so on. Thus, POS tags of words can help to identify the types of attributes and the relationship between them.)We use the Stanford parser tool[4] to get the POS tags of words.

The WordNet feature we use is based on synsets. Among every three input words, if one word is in the synset of another word, the corresponding feature digit will be set to 1, or it will be set to 0. In this way, a 2-dim synset feature of each word can be obtained. We use the nltk tool(Bird et al., 2009) to generate the WordNet features. The features above are concatenated with word embedding as the input of MLP-CNN model.

2.4 Model Training and Ensemble

Since the *train set* is unbalanced, we randomly select same numbers of positive (the attribute is discriminative) and negative (the attribute is not discriminative) samples from the *train set* every time. Thus, the training data we used in our experiments

---

[4]https://nlp.stanford.edu/software/lex-parser.shtml

consists of the sampled data from the *train set* and 80% data sampled from the *dev set*. The remaining 20% part in *dev set* is used for validation.

Model ensemble strategy has been proven useful to neural networks (Wu et al., 2017). Therefore, we build different training samples using the method described in the above paragraph and train our model for 10 times. The final predictions on the test set are the average of the predictions of the 10 models. In this way, the performance of neural model can be further improved.

3 Experiment

3.1 Experiment Settings

The dataset we use is constructed based on the approach proposed by Lazaridou et al. (2016) and the initial source of data is provided by McRae et al. (2005). The entire dataset contains 17,547 samples for training, 2,722 for validation and 2,340 for testing. The training set is automatically generated, while the validation and test set are manually refined. The models will be evaluated by F1-measure, as is standard in a binary classification task.

In our network, the kernel sizes of CNN are set to 3. The dimensions of feature maps v_2 and v_3 are set to 256, and the dimensions of dense layers are 300. The dropout rate of both embedding weights and CNN is set to 0.2. The training batch size is set to 50. We use Adam as the optimizer for network training, which takes 10 epochs per time. We train our model for 10 times and average their predictions on the test set.

3.2 Performance Evaluation

The experimental results on the test and validation set are shown in Table 1. For comparison, we also present several baseline models here. Our official submission is the MLP-CNN model with ensemble techniques. Our F-score is 62.9 (ranked 15th) in the evaluation phase. From the evaluation results, we can see that our model outperforms these baseline models. It shows that our network architecture can learn more semantic information from the words and attributes. However, our system needs to be improved compared with the top system (75.0 of F-score). In addition, the testing results are much lower than validation results. Some detailed information will be analysis in the next section.

Model	F-score	
	test	validation
MLP	53.5	63
CNN	57.8	66.2
MLP-CNN	61.7	71.5
MLP-CNN w/o over-layer	61.0	70.3
MLP-CNN+ensemble (ours)	**62.9**	**73.4**

Table 1: Performance evaluation of our system and several baselines.

4 Discussion

4.1 Influence of Trainable Word Embedding

The influence of different word embedding weights and fine-tuning them or not is shown in Table 2. Note that we don't apply the model ensemble technique here. From the results, we can see that the combination of different word embedding can significantly improve the model performance. It may be because that using different word embedding can provide richer semantic information. In addition, using the combinations of different word embedding can cover more words and the out-of-vocabulary words in the single embedding file can be reduced. Thus, the predictions of such words can be more accurate.

However, we find fine-tuning the pre-trained word embedding is not a good choice. The fine-tuned model performance is significantly worse than models using untrainable embedding. Since the training, validation and test sets have no feature overlap between them, fine-tuning the embedding weights will lead to serious over-fitting and poor model generalization ability. We fine-tuned the embedding of our models used in the official submission, so the results are lower than the models with untrainable embedding.

4.2 Influence of Word Features

The influence of the two types of features is shown in Table 3. The results show that additional word features can improve the performance of our neural model. Attributes with different POS tags provide different semantic information. For example, given a pair of words "boy" and "woman", the attributes "young" and "run" describe very different aspects. Therefore, POS tag features can help the model to extract different features from the input words. Another feature based on WordNet can also improve our model. It may be because if the attribute is in the synsets of a concept, it's usu-

pre-trained	F-score	
Embedding	test	validation
w/o	44.9	63.7
word2vec+tune	50.6	65.8
Glove+tune	53.5	66.7
fastText+tune	51.5	64.4
all+tune	61.7	71.5
word2vec-tune	54.9	66
Glove-tune	57.7	69.6
fastText-tune	58.3	68.9
all-tune	**65.7**	**75.5**

Table 2: Comparisons of using different pre-trained embedding.

ally an attribute of this concept. Thus, the synset information can help the model to identify the relationships between words and attibutes.

Features	F-score
w/o	59.2
+POS	61
+WordNet	60.1
+POS+WordNet	**61.7**

Table 3: Influence of word features on the test set.

4.3 Case Study

Several examples of model predictions on the test set are shown in Table 4. From the true predictions, we can see that our model can capture simple attributes of concepts such as colors. However, more complex relationships between words and attributes are difficult for our system to mine. For example, the word "mouse" can be an animal or electronic device. It's hard to identify such semantic differences without incorporating external knowledge, since the information provided by the training data is limited.

True Positive	False Positive
corn,tomato,yellow	alcohol,liquor,strong
ant,snail,black	bar,shop,sell
True Negative	**False Negative**
father,brother,family	mouse,dog,plastic
father,mother,parent	engine,vehicle,component

Table 4: Representative examples of the predictions on the test set.

5 Conclusion

Discriminating similar words between each other without additional information is difficult for existing semantic models. Therefore, the SemEval-2018 task 10 is proposed to fill this gap. In this paper, we apply a MLP-CNN model with word feature to this task. In our model, the input and output of our CNN are highway connected. They are taken by a MLP classifier for binary classification. Based on this model, the local relationships between each pair of words can be mined. Our evaluation F-score is 62.9 (ranked 15th). The detailed analysis on our system shows our system can be further improved.

Acknowledgments

The authors thank the reviewers for their insightful comments and constructive suggestions on improving this work. This work was supported in part by the National Key Research and Development Program of China under Grant 2016YFB0800402 and in part by the National Natural Science Foundation of China under Grant U1705261, Grant U1536207, Grant U1536201 and U1636113.

References

Steven Bird, Ewan Klein, and Edward Loper. 2009. *Natural language processing with Python: analyzing text with the natural language toolkit.* " O'Reilly Media, Inc.".

Piotr Bojanowski, Edouard Grave, Armand Joulin, and Tomas Mikolov. 2016. Enriching word vectors with subword information. *arXiv preprint arXiv:1607.04606.*

Jay J Jiang and David W Conrath. 1997. Semantic similarity based on corpus statistics and lexical taxonomy. *arXiv preprint cmp-lg/9709008.*

Yoon Kim. 2014. Convolutional neural networks for sentence classification. *arXiv preprint arXiv:1408.5882.*

Alicia Krebs, Alessandro Lenci, and Denis Paperno. 2018. Semeval-2018 task 10: Capturing discriminative attributes. In *Proceedings of the 12th international workshop on semantic evaluation (SemEval 2018).*

Angeliki Lazaridou, Nghia The Pham, and Marco Baroni. 2016. The red one!: On learning to refer to things based on their discriminative properties. *arXiv preprint arXiv:1603.02618.*

Omer Levy and Yoav Goldberg. 2014. Neural word embedding as implicit matrix factorization. In *Advances in neural information processing systems*, pages 2177–2185.

Ken McRae, George S Cree, Mark S Seidenberg, and Chris McNorgan. 2005. Semantic feature production norms for a large set of living and nonliving things. *Behavior research methods*, 37(4):547–559.

Rada Mihalcea, Courtney Corley, Carlo Strapparava, et al. 2006. Corpus-based and knowledge-based measures of text semantic similarity. In *AAAI*, volume 6, pages 775–780.

Tomas Mikolov, Kai Chen, Greg Corrado, and Jeffrey Dean. 2013. Efficient estimation of word representations in vector space. *arXiv preprint arXiv:1301.3781*.

George Miller and Christiane Fellbaum. 1998. Wordnet: An electronic lexical database.

Devi Parikh and Kristen Grauman. 2011. Interactively building a discriminative vocabulary of nameable attributes. In *Computer Vision and Pattern Recognition (CVPR), 2011 IEEE Conference on*, pages 1681–1688. IEEE.

Jeffrey Pennington, Richard Socher, and Christopher Manning. 2014. Glove: Global vectors for word representation. In *Proceedings of the 2014 conference on empirical methods in natural language processing (EMNLP)*, pages 1532–1543.

David Sánchez, Montserrat Batet, David Isern, and Aida Valls. 2012. Ontology-based semantic similarity: A new feature-based approach. *Expert Systems with Applications*, 39(9):7718–7728.

Nuno Seco, Tony Veale, and Jer Hayes. 2004. An intrinsic information content metric for semantic similarity in wordnet. In *ECAI*, volume 16, page 1089.

Chuhan Wu, Fangzhao Wu, Yongfeng Huang, Sixing Wu, and Zhigang Yuan. 2017. Thu_ngn at ijcnlp-2017 task 2: Dimensional sentiment analysis for chinese phrases with deep lstm. *Proceedings of the IJCNLP 2017, Shared Tasks*, pages 47–52.

ALB at SemEval-2018 Task 10:
A System for Capturing Discriminative Attributes

Bogdan Dumitru, Alina Maria Ciobanu, Liviu P. Dinu
Faculty of Mathematics and Computer Science, University of Bucharest
Human Language Technologies Research Center, University of Bucharest
bogdan27182@gmail.com,
alina.ciobanu@my.fmi.unibuc.ro, ldinu@fmi.unibuc.ro

Abstract

Semantic difference detection attempts to capture whether a word is a discriminative attribute between two other words. For example, the discriminative feature *red* characterizes the first word from the *(apple, banana)* pair, but not the second. Modeling semantic difference is essential for language understanding systems, as it provides useful information for identifying particular aspects of word senses. This paper describes our system implementation (the ALB system of the NLP@Unibuc team) for the 10th task of the Semaval 2018 workshop, "Capturing Discriminative Attributes". We propose a method for semantic difference detection that uses an SVM classifier with features based on co-occurrence counts and shallow semantic parsing, achieving 0.63 F1 score in the competition.

1 Introduction and Related Work

Semantic similarity detection is a well-studied research problem with numerous applications. State of the art models are extremely capable, determining the degree of semantic similarity between words with high accuracy.

However, looking the other way around, the semantic difference between words has received significantly less attention. As a result, one can argue that a semantic similarity model without the capability of spotting the semantic difference as well is not a complete system, and may not prove very useful in practice.

Semantic difference is a ternary relation (w_1, w_2, w_3), where w_1 and w_2 are called *concepts* and w_3 is called *discriminative feature*. The discriminative feature characterizes the first concept, w_1, but not the second one, w_2. If the discriminative feature characterizes both w_1 and w_2 or none of them, then we do not have semantic difference.

Semantic difference detection is a binary classification task where given a triplet of words, a model needs to determine if a semantic difference is present or not. As emphasized by Krebs and Paperno (2016), this non-trivial task has numerous applications, such as automatized lexicography, conversational agents or machine translation.

Most research on discriminative features is related to computer vision (Farhadi et al., 2009; Russakovsky and Fei-Fei, 2012), as these attributes proved to be very useful in interpreting visual data (Huang et al., 2016), being able to link visual features and semantic labels (Guo et al., 2015). A recent study on this topic belongs to Lazaridou et al. (2016), who proposed a method for identifying discriminative attributes when given word pairs and their visual representations.

In this paper, we describe a system for semantic difference detection that outputs a set of features for every triplet in the input data, based on preprocessed external resources (the English Wikipedia database). Further, these features are used to train an SVM for binary classification. The current feature selection allows even a direct approach such as evaluating the following inequation:

$$\sum_{i=1}^{|F_1|} f_i - \sum_{i=1}^{|F_2|} f_i > 0 \qquad (1)$$

to obtain similar results as the SVM. Here, F_1 and F_2 are values of the same features, extracted for (w_1, w_3) and (w_2, w_3), respectively.

Our model uses two different classes of features. The first class is generated using simple co-occurrence counts and the second class is generated by an arc-factored approach (McDonald et al., 2005) for semantic dependency parsing.

Semantic dependency parsing aims to provide a shallow semantic analysis of the text. As distinct

963

Proceedings of the 12th International Workshop on Semantic Evaluation (SemEval-2018), pages 963–967
New Orleans, Louisiana, June 5–6, 2018. ©2018 Association for Computational Linguistics

from deeper semantic analysis, shallow semantic parsing captures relationships between pairs of words or concepts in a sentence (Thomson et al., 2014).

2 Dataset and Preprocessing

The input data (training, validation and testing) is translated into an intermediary configuration as described below.

Each word triplet from the input data is split into two word pairs: (w_1, w_3) and (w_2, w_3). The initial part of our model extracts features for each pair, and in the last steps, where the performance is computed, a cross-reference is done with the original input database.

We use the English Wikipedia as an external data source for feature extraction. We convert the raw Wikipedia database to plain text and concatenate the sentences of all the articles in a large text corpus.

3 System Framework

In this section we present our approach and methodology for capturing discriminative attributes.

3.1 Problem Reduction

First, we transform the problem of semantic difference detection into a simpler one: detecting if a feature characterizes a concept. Every ternary relation in the input data is split into two subproblems of detecting if a feature (i.e. w_3) characterizes w_1 and w_2, respectively. Solving subproblems independently gives us more flexibility in feature extraction.

Determining the validity of the ternary relation from the outputs of the newly created binary relations is achieved with the following equation:

$$o = \neg(p \implies q) \tag{2}$$

which for convenience can be rewritten as:

$$o = p \wedge \neg q \tag{3}$$

where $p = C(w_1, w_3)$, $q = C(w_2, w_3)$, o is the triplet label and $C(w_a, w_b)$ is the model or function that decides if w_b characterizes w_a.

3.2 Features

We use two categories of features in training our system: *co-occurrence* and *POS-tag* features. Features from both categories are extracted from English Wikipedia sentences.

3.2.1 Co-occurrence

This is a measure of occurrence of two words in a text alongside each other and in a specific order. For our system, we consider the two words as an unordered pair and count accordingly. For every pair of words (w_1, w_2) we extract the following features:

- *Co-occurrence₁*: counts the number of adjacent occurrences of w_1 and w_2 disregarding the order.

- *Co-occurrence₂*: counts the number of occurrences of both w_1 and w_2 in a text window of size 2.

- *Co-occurrence₃*: counts the number of occurrences of both w_1 and w_2 in a text window of size 3.

If two words occur in the same sentence, it provides the intuition that there should be a relation between the distance $d = |w_1 - w_2|$ and their semantic relation. This is what we attempt to capture with the features described above. We drop *co-occurrence₂* and *co-occurrence₃* in our final system configuration, since they do not add any contribution to the final score, as shown in Table 2.

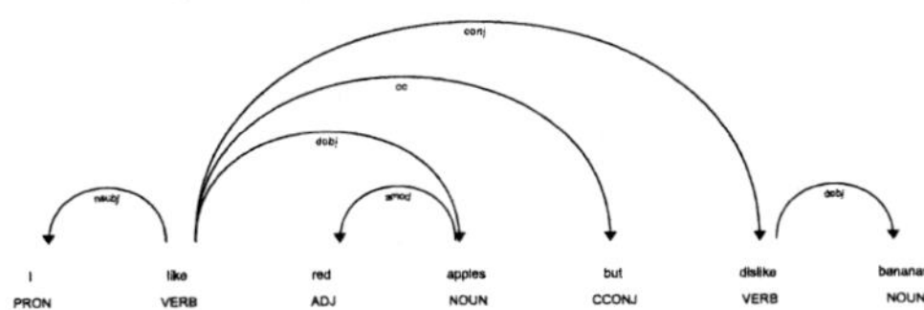

Figure 1: Syntactic dependency tree.

3.2.2 POS-tag Features

Every sentence that contains a pair of words (w_1, w_2) is parsed and tagged. Based on a statistical model, a prediction is made of which tag applies to each word. Next, a syntactic dependency tree is built as shown in Figure 1 and used to derive various rules that are used to extract POS-related features.

For every sentence containing both words of the pair, if a rule R_i hits, then we increment the total hit count H_c of that specific pair. $|R|$ represents the total number of rules to be applied and H_c is defined by the following formula:

$$H_c = \sum_{i=1}^{|R|} R_i(w_1, w_2) \qquad (4)$$

As an example, if we take the pair of words (w_1 = *moth*, w_2 = *flies*), we obtain the following values: 1,088 *co-occurrence$_1$* and a count of 763 hits of the rules on sentences containing both words. Hence the pair *(moth, flies)* has feature values (1,088, 763). Several more examples are presented in Table 1.

w_1, w_2	*co-occurrence$_1$*	H_c
desk, drawers	169	120
cod, honks	0	0
shirt, sleeves	450	1,109
tie, sleeves	16	13
lime, holes	0	3
cheese, holes	29	20

Table 1: Examples of word pairs and feature values.

3.3 Rules

We perform rules implementation in a purely heuristic manner, using methods from previous research (Kübler et al., 2009). While we keep rules composition simple, they turn out to be very powerful and we use only two of them in the final system implementation. Rules are prone to both false positives and false negatives, but provided enough input sentences, both errors tend to be minimized.

- *Rule$_1$*: if w_2 is the root of an arc in the parsing tree and w_1 is one of its children and no negation is present in the children list, then the rule will return a hit.

- *Rule$_2$*: if the child of a root noun is a verb, then recursively the children of the verb will be considered related to the noun and the pairs *(root_noun, verb_child)* will be compared with (w_1, w_2), increasing the hit count if the pairs match.

3.4 Linear SVM

For classification we use a linear SVM (Vapnik, 1995). The output of the SVM is given by the equation:

$$u = wx - b \qquad (5)$$

where w is the normal vector to the hyperplane and x represents the input data.

In the linear case, the margin is defined as the distance between the closest positive and negative example, and the hyperplane defined by the above equation (see Figure 2). Maximizing the margin can be approached as an optimization problem:

Minimize $\frac{1}{2}\|w\|^2$ subject to $y_i(wx_i - b) \geq 1, \forall i$;

where x_i is the ith training sample and y_i is the correct classification of the sample.

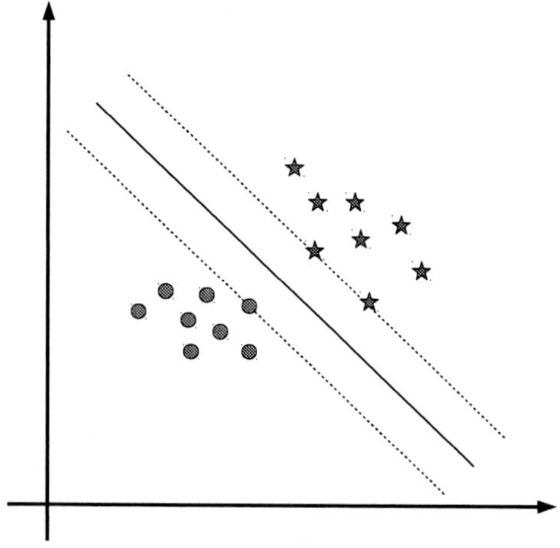

Figure 2: Linear SVM.

3.5 System Workflow

Until now we have described all the building blocks of our system. Now we chain them together.

The first step is to transform the original datasets into datasets of pairs. For all training, validation and testing data we run Algorithm 1. After this step, we end up with a dataset containing the features of all pairs, of all three datasets.

The next step is to train and validate the SVM on the datasets of triplets. The last step is to use the trained SVM to predict labels for the triplets in

```
for every dataset do
    transform data into pairs of words;
    for every pair of words do
        extract all sentences from Wikipedia
        containing $w_1$ and $w_2$;
        extract co-occurrence features;
        for every sentence do
            run active rules;
        end
        compute $H_c$ using active rules;
    end
end
```

Algorithm 1: Dataset preparation.

the test dataset. A slightly different approach that we try is to train the SVM on pairs extracted from triplets with label 1, and then apply Equation 2 to obtain the labels for the initial test dataset triplets.

In another system configuration, we eliminate the SVM and compute the final triplet score from the existing features using Equation 1. By doing so, we eliminate the training and validation steps, thus transforming our system from a learning one to a purely deterministic one. However, if the number of features is increased, such an approach may prove unfeasible and inefficient.

4 Results

We have implemented several system configurations by selecting different rules, features and learning methods. We have chosen three configurations: two of them produced the top results in our experiments on the development dataset, and the other had the peculiarity of not having a learning mechanism. The performance of these systems on the development dataset is reported in Table 2. The systems are evaluated using the F1 score.

The first system, *ALB*, uses only the first co-occurrence score, along with H_c. Even if only two features per pair of words are used, this system configuration produced the best F1 score of 0.69. This is the only system that we submitted for evaluation, obtaining 0.63 F1 score on the test dataset.

The second system, *ALB+*, uses all three co-occurrence scores as features and treats rules output as separate features. Both *ALB* and *ALB+* use the SVM trained on triplets.

The third system, *EQ1*, uses the same two features as *ALB* and replaces the SVM component

with Equation 1. This system obtained the lowest F1 score, but not too distant from the others.

It is interesting to mention that if we use only *co-occurrence$_1$* as a discriminant, the score is > 0.6. Analyzing the output of our best system, we observe that the errors it produces are not biased towards one of the labels (417 errors for label 0 and 430 for label 1).

System	F1 Score
ALB	**0.69**
ALB+	0.67
EQ1	0.62

Table 2: Results for capturing discriminative attributes on the validation dataset.

5 Conclusions

In this paper we have presented our results and system description for Task 10 of SemEval 2018, "Capturing Discriminative Attributes".

Our approach shows promising results in using the relation between words in context for semantic differences. The obtained results are competitive, although being outperformed by other approaches in the official ranking. There is enough room for improvements and at least two possible approaches are already being analyzed.

The first one is straightforward: extending the feature set with at least one order of magnitude compared with *ALB+*, and if necessary replacing the SVM with a fully connected neural network. The heavily used sequence-to-sequence model can also be applied on sentences to automatically capture relations between word pairs.

The second possible approach is to use a neural network to automatically infer rules. Next, we can apply generated rules to compute H_c and assign a semantic difference probability to every pair in our dataset. We can use a pruned version of the training dataset from this task, extract word pairs in the same manner as we did in our system implementation and feed word pairs along with sentences and labels to a convolutional neural network.

6 Acknowledgments

Research supported by UEFISCDI, project number 53BG/2016.

References

Ali Farhadi, Ian Endres, Derek Hoiem, and David A. Forsyth. 2009. Describing Objects by Their Attributes. In *Proceedings of the Conference on Computer Vision and Pattern Recognition*, pages 1778–1785.

Yuchen Guo, Guiguang Ding, Xiaoming Jin, and Jianmin Wang. 2015. Learning Predictable and Discriminative Attributes for Visual Recognition. In *Proceedings of the Twenty-Ninth AAAI Conference on Artificial Intelligence*, pages 3783–3789.

Chen Huang, Chen Change Loy, and Xiaoou Tang. 2016. Unsupervised Learning of Discriminative Attributes and Visual Representations. In *Proceedings of the Conference on Computer Vision and Pattern Recognition*, pages 5175–5184.

Alicia Krebs and Denis Paperno. 2016. Capturing Discriminative Attributes in a Distributional Space: Task Proposal. In *Proceedings of the 1st Workshop on Evaluating Vector-Space Representations for NLP*, pages 51–54.

Sandra Kübler, Ryan McDonald, and Joakim Nivre. 2009. *Dependency Parsing*. Morgan and Claypool Publishers.

Angeliki Lazaridou, Nghia The Pham, and Marco Baroni. 2016. "The red one!": On Learning to Refer to Things Based on Discriminative Properties. In *Proceedings of the 54th Annual Meeting of the Association for Computational Linguistics (Volume 2: Short Papers)*, pages 213–218.

Ryan McDonald, Koby Crammer, and Fernando Pereira. 2005. Online Large-margin Training of Dependency Parsers. In *Proceedings of the 43rd Annual Meeting on Association for Computational Linguistics*, pages 91–98.

Olga Russakovsky and Li Fei-Fei. 2012. Attribute Learning in Large-Scale Datasets. In *Trends and Topics in Computer Vision*, pages 1–14. Springer Berlin Heidelberg.

Sam Thomson, Brendan O'Connor, Jeffrey Flanigan, David Bamman, Jesse Dodge, Swabha Swayamdipta, Nathan Schneider, Chris Dyer, and Noah A Smith. 2014. CMU: Arc-Factored, Discriminative Semantic Dependency Parsing. In *Proceedings of the 8th International Workshop on Semantic Evaluation (SemEval 2014)*, pages 176–180.

Vladimir Vapnik. 1995. *The Nature of Statistical Learning Theory*. Springer-Verlag New York.

ELiRF-UPV at SemEval-2018 Task 10: Capturing Discriminative Attributes with Knowledge Graphs and Wikipedia

José-Ángel González, Lluís-F. Hurtado, Encarna Segarra, Ferran Pla
Universitat Politècnica de València
Camí de Vera sn, 46022, València
{jogonba2|lhurtado|esegarra|fpla}@dsic.upv.es

Abstract

This paper describes the participation of ELiRF-UPV team at task 10, Capturing Discriminative Attributes, of SemEval-2018. Our best approach consists of using ConceptNet, Wikipedia and NumberBatch embeddings in order to stablish relationships between concepts and attributes. Furthermore, this system achieves competitive results in the official evaluation.

1 Introduction

Capturing Discriminative Attributes, task 10 of SemEval-2018 (Krebs et al., 2018), proposes working on semantic difference detection . The goal of the task is to predict whether a word is a discriminative attribute between two other words. This problem is known as semantic difference detection, which is a binary classification task: given a triple $(apple, banana, red)$, it consists in determining whether it exemplifies a semantic difference. Regarding semantic difference, it is a ternary relation between two concepts, for instance, $(apple, banana)$ and a discriminative feature (red) that characterizes the first concept but not the other.

As task 10 is related to the semantic relations among different words, knowledge graphs seems the most appropriate resources to be used. An interesting knowledge resource that we used for this task is ConceptNet. In particular, ConceptNet (Speer et al., 2016) is a knowledge graph that connects words and phrases of natural language using labeled edges. It was designed to represent some general knowledge involved in natural language and could be used in combination with other resources. The combination of ConceptNet with distributed representations such as Word2Vec (Mikolov et al., 2013) and GloVe (Pennington et al., 2014), is known as NumberBatch embeddings (Speer et al., 2016).

Regarding the relations specified in ConceptNet, there are a total of 36 relations such as *IsA* (A banana is a dessert), *UsedFor* (A net is used for catching fish), or *FormOf* ("Leaves" is a form of the word "leaf"), intended to represent a relationship independently of the language or the source of the terms it connects.

In this work, we propose five knowledge based systems and one additional machine learning system based on Siamese networks. We used ConceptNet in order to determine if each input concept and the input attribute are related through a relation edge or path. When there is a relationship between the first concept and the attribute and there is no relationship between the second concept and the attribute, then the answer is 1, otherwise, the answer is 0. However, there are cases in which ConceptNet does not provide enough information to take a decision. In those cases, we have implemented a system that seeks the information in Wikipedia articles by using distances between NumberBatch embeddings.

2 Resources and Preprocess

As we stated in Section 1, ConceptNet 5 is used in order to find the relationships among concepts and attributes. ConceptNet 5 is freely available under the Creative Commons Attribution-ShareAlike license (CC BY SA 4.0) from `http://conceptnet.io`. Moreover, we use two additional resources next to ConceptNet.

On the one hand, in order to use more information of each concept we used the Wikipedia articles. In this way, we get the most related article for each concept, following the recommendation of the Wikipedia disambiguation system. Wikipedia articles had been preprocessed. First, we remove non relevant sections such as "See

Proceedings of the 12th International Workshop on Semantic Evaluation (SemEval-2018), pages 968–971
New Orleans, Louisiana, June 5–6, 2018. ©2018 Association for Computational Linguistics

Also", "References" and "External Links" which links to other resources. After that, we normalized tokens like numbers or urls e.g. "678.2" → "number" y "https://en.wikipedia.org" → "url" and we made a tokenization of the articles.

On the other hand, we used distributed representations of words, more specifically, we used NumberBatch embeddings (Speer et al., 2016).

3 System Description

We tested several approaches to address this task, mostly knowledge-based. Let (c_1, c_2, at) be a triple where, c_1 and c_2 are concepts and at is an attribute. The goal of the task is to define a function d to decide whether at is a discriminative feature of c_1 (value 1 for d) or not (value 0 for d). That is, if at characterizes c_1 but not c_2.

Although the training and the development sets were not very large, we wanted to test the performance of Machine Learning (ML) approaches for this task. We selected a siamese neural network (Bromley et al., 1993) because these kind of systems are suitable for similar tasks such as knowledge base completion (Yang et al., 2014). This system works as follow. First, the input to this network are the NumberBatch embeddings of c_1, c_2 and at. From this, a shared Multilayer Perceptron is applied in order to extract a complex representation of each term, $f(c_1)$, $f(c_2)$ and $f(at)$. With these representations, we compute the differences s_1 and s_2 where $s_1 = f(c_1)-f(at)$ and $s_2 = f(c_2)-f(at)$ with the aim of establishing relationships between each concept and the attribute. Finally, we concatenate s_1 and s_2 and we apply a fully-connected layer with softmax activation functions to carry out a classification i.e. $d_{Sia} = 1$ if at is discriminative for c_1 and not for c_2 or $d_{Sia} = 0$ otherwise.

The rest of the systems were knowledge-based. As first knowledge-based approach, we use the relationships between each concept and the attribute to determine if the attribute is discriminant. To do this, we use the ConceptNet relations. Note that, ConceptNet contains both positive (*IsA, FormOf, DerivedFrom, SimilarTo, ...*) and negative relations (*DistinctFrom, NotHasProperty*). In our proposals, we only consider positive edges, that is, those that denote positive relationships.

We look for positive edges between each concept and the attribute. If an edge between c_1 and at exists but there is not any edge between c_2 and

at, we assume that at is discriminant. In other words, at is discriminant if it is reachable from c_1 but not from c_2. In this way, the function d_{CN} that determines if the attribute at is discriminant for concepts c_1 and c_2 can be defined as shown in Equation 1.

$$d_{CN} = \begin{cases} 1 & : & \text{if } at \in R(c_1) \wedge at \notin R(c_2) \\ 0 & : & otherwise \end{cases}$$
(1)

where, $R(c_1)$ and $R(c_2)$ are the sets of reachable nodes from c_1 and c_2 respectively using positive edges.

The main problem of this proposal is its low coverage. In many cases, there is no edge between any of the two concepts and the attribute, and therefore, it is decided that the attribute is not discriminant. In order to increase the coverage of d_{CN}, we extend the set of reachable nodes from a concept to those nodes reachable from other concepts closely related to the original concept. We have considered as related concepts those that are linked by the *FormOf* relation in ConceptNet. Considering the extended sets of reachable nodes, we can redefine the function d_{CN} of Equation 1 as shown in Equation 2.

$$d_{CN^2} = \begin{cases} 1 & : & \text{if } at \in R^2(c_1) \wedge at \notin R^2(c_2) \\ 0 & : & otherwise \end{cases}$$
(2)

where $R^2(c)$ is the set of nodes reachable from c or from any concept closely related to c.

Nevertheless, this approach still has coverage problems. In order to mitigate this problem, we proposed two new approaches based on Wikipedia. The main idea is simple, we search for the attribute at in the Wikipedia article of concepts c_1 and c_2 ($doc(c_1)$ and $doc(c_2)$) and, we decide if at is discriminant based on the result of this search. In this way, function d_{We} can be defined as shown in Equation 3.

$$d_{We} = \begin{cases} 1 & : & \text{if } at \in doc(c_1) \wedge at \notin doc(c_2) \\ 0 & : & otherwise \end{cases}$$
(3)

Further, we can relax the exact match criterion. Concretely, if we use NumberBatch distributed representations of words (h), we can compute similarities between at and all the tokens of $doc(c_1)$ and $doc(c_2)$ in order to decide which concept is the closest to at.

We define a threshold ϵ to ensure that there is enough difference between the maximum similarity $\max\limits_{w \in doc(c_1)} cos(h(w), h(at))$ and $\max\limits_{w \in doc(c_2)} cos(h(w), h(at))$. Using the development set, the value of ϵ was fixed to 0.2. This new decision function d_{Wt} is presented in the Equation 4.

$$d_{Wt} = \begin{cases} 1 & : \text{if } \max\limits_{w \in doc(c_1)} cos(h(w), h(at)) \\ & \quad - \max\limits_{w \in doc(c_2)} cos(h(w), h(at)) \geq \epsilon \\ 0 & : otherwise \end{cases} \tag{4}$$

Finally, in order to explore the joint behavior of the knowledge-based approaches, we propose the combination of d_{CN^2} and d_{Wt}. When there is a relationship between at and any concept –it does not matter if it is c_1, c_2 or both– we decide if at is discriminant using d_{CN^2}. But if there is no relationship in ConceptNet between them, we *smooth* the decision using d_{Wt}. Thus, we only use d_{CN^2} when we really have information in ConceptNet. The definition of this new decision function d_{CN^2+Wt} is shown in Equation 5.

$$d_{CN^2+Wt} = \begin{cases} d_{CN^2} & : \text{if } at \in R^2(c_1) \\ & \quad \vee at \in R^2(c_2) \\ d_{Wt} & : otherwise \end{cases} \tag{5}$$

4   Experimental Results

In order to validate the correctness of the proposed approaches and also to select the one with the best performance for the competition, we carried out an evaluation of the approaches using the development set provided by the organizers. The results obtained are shown in Table 4.

d	Approach	Macro F_1
d_{Sia}	Siamese network	57.07
d_{CN}	ConceptNet	58.51
d_{CN^2}	ConceptNet ^{2}	61.94
d_{We}	Wiki. exact match	58.46
d_{Wt}	Wiki. threshold	60.34
d_{CN^2+Wt}	ConceptNet + Wiki.	68.20

Table 1: Results on the development set.

As can be seen in Table 4, the knowledge-based systems which use knowledge resources obtain among 1.31 and 11.13 points of macro F_1 more

than the Siamese network which uses only NumberBatch embeddings. The approaches that use only ConceptNet (d_{CN} and d_{CN^2}) achieved as good results as those based on Wikipedia (d_{We} and d_{Wt}). Note that the coverage of d_{CN} and d_{CN^2} is very low, 48.71% for d_{CN} and 56.61% for d_{CN^2}. In cases where there are no links in ConceptNet –more than fifty percent of the time for d_{CN}– it is decided that the attribute is not discriminant. Moreover, the more knowledge incorporated into the system, the better results are obtained. We achieved the best results using the combination of ConceptNet graph and Wikipedia articles (d_{CN^2+Wt}), achieving 68.20 macro F_1.

Regarding the evaluation with the test set, we used d_{CN^2+Wt} as decision function for the SemEval competition. Our system achieved competitive results (69.00 macro F_1, 6 points of macro F_1 below the best system that obtains 75.00 macro F_1). Our proposal was ranked in 5th place out of a total of 26 participating teams. Several results from the official evaluation are shown in Table 4.

Team	Macro F_1
Sunnynlp (1/26)	75.00
Esantus (2/26)	73.00
ELiRF-UPV (5/26)	69.00
...	
Amrita_student (25/26)	49.00
Luminoso (26/26)	49.00

Table 2: Official results

5   Analysis of Results

Once the evaluation is finished, we want to carry out an analysis of the behavior of our system. Our goal is to detect in which types of attribute the system works worse. This way, we could add specific knowledge resources to deal with these attributes.

Although we have not completed this analysis, a group of attributes that caught our attention were the colors. While the overall error rate of our system was about 30%, the error in samples with attributes related to colors was about 50%. More details about the behavior of our system can be seen in Table 5.

Therefore, it would be possible to improve the system behavior by treating the color attributes in a specific way. For instance, by using image resources, such as ImageNet (Deng et al., 2009), to compute the color palette of images of each concept and compare it with the color attribute.

Attributes	Errors	Occurences
Black	56	116
Brown	41	56
Yellow	11	46
Red	12	19
Blue	1	3
Color	121 (50.42%)	240
Other	586 (27.90%)	2100
Total	707	2340

Table 3: Error analysis in samples with attributes related to colors.

6 Conclusions and Future Work

In this work, we proposed a knowledge-based system for the discriminative attributes task. This system is based on the combination of two knowledge resources: a knowledge graph with semantic links such as ConceptNet and a general resource such as Wikipedia.

With this system, we achieved good results in the development set, compared to a supervised learning approach like siamese neural networks. That is, a combination of knowledge-based approaches produces significative improvements compared to the supervised approach. Regarding the evaluation with the test set, we obtained competitive results.

As future work, we propose an extension of our system based on the addition of more knowledge resources such DBpedia (Lehmann et al., 2015), Wordnet (Fellbaum, 1998) or Microsoft Concept Graph (Wang et al., 2015). Moreover, it could be interesting to consider the sections of Wikipedia with links to other resources in order to extract more information.

Finally, we propose the incorporation of knowledge resources into Deep Learning systems, beyond using only distributed representations of words. This offers us end-to-end systems capable of learning more complex decision algorithms. Concretely, the siamese neural networks seems to be promising for this work due to their good results in related fields such as knowledge-based completion (Yang et al., 2014).

7 Acknowledgements

This work has been partially supported by the Spanish MINECO and FEDER founds under projects ASLP-MULAN: Audio, Speech and Language Processing for Multimedia Analytics (TIN2014-54288-C4-3-R); and AMIC: Affective Multimedia Analytics with Inclusive and Natural Communication (TIN2017-85854-C4-2-R). Work of José-Ángel González is also financed by Universitat Politècnica de València under grant PAID-01-17.

References

Jane Bromley, Isabelle Guyon, Yann LeCun, Eduard Säckinger, and Roopak Shah. 1993. Signature verification using a "siamese" time delay neural network. In *Proceedings of the 6th International Conference on Neural Information Processing Systems*, NIPS'93, pages 737–744, San Francisco, CA, USA. Morgan Kaufmann Publishers Inc.

J. Deng, W. Dong, R. Socher, L.-J. Li, K. Li, and L. Fei-Fei. 2009. ImageNet: A Large-Scale Hierarchical Image Database. In *CVPR09*.

Christiane Fellbaum. 1998. *WordNet: An Electronic Lexical Database*. Bradford Books.

Alicia Krebs, Alessandro Lenci, and Denis Paperno. 2018. SemEval-2018 Task 10: Capturing discriminative attributes. In *Proceedings of International Workshop on Semantic Evaluation (SemEval-2018)*, New Orleans, LA, USA.

Jens Lehmann, Robert Isele, Max Jakob, Anja Jentzsch, Dimitris Kontokostas, Pablo N. Mendes, Sebastian Hellmann, Mohamed Morsey, Patrick van Kleef, Sören Auer, and Christian Bizer. 2015. DBpedia - A Large-scale, Multilingual Knowledge Base Extracted from Wikipedia. *Semantic Web Journal*, 6(2):167–195.

Tomas Mikolov, Ilya Sutskever, Kai Chen, Greg Corrado, and Jeffrey Dean. 2013. Distributed representations of words and phrases and their compositionality. *CoRR*, abs/1310.4546.

Jeffrey Pennington, Richard Socher, and Christopher D Manning. 2014. Glove: Global vectors for word representation. In *EMNLP*, volume 14, pages 1532–1543.

Robert Speer, Joshua Chin, and Catherine Havasi. 2016. Conceptnet 5.5: An open multilingual graph of general knowledge. *CoRR*, abs/1612.03975.

Zhongyuan Wang, Haixun Wang, Ji-Rong Wen, and Yanghua Xiao. 2015. An inference approach to basic level of categorization. In *Proceedings of the 24th ACM International on Conference on Information and Knowledge Management*, CIKM '15, pages 653–662, New York, NY, USA. ACM.

Bishan Yang, Wen-tau Yih, Xiaodong He, Jianfeng Gao, and Li Deng. 2014. Embedding entities and relations for learning and inference in knowledge bases. *CoRR*, abs/1412.6575.

Wolves at SemEval-2018 Task 10: Semantic Discrimination based on Knowledge and Association

Shiva Taslimipoor[1], Omid Rohanian[1], Le An Ha[1], Gloria Corpas Pastor[2] and Ruslan Mitkov[1]

[1]Research Group in Computational Linguistics, University of Wolverhampton, UK
[2]University of Malaga, Spain
{shiva.taslimi, m.rohanian, l.a.ha, r.mitkov}@wlv.ac.uk
gcorpas@uma.es

Abstract

This paper describes the system submitted to SemEval 2018 shared task 10 'Capturing Discriminative Attributes'. We use a combination of knowledge-based and co-occurrence features to capture the semantic difference between two words in relation to an attribute. We define scores based on association measures, ngram counts, word similarity, and Concept-Net relations. The system is ranked 4th (joint) on the official leaderboard of the task.

1 Introduction

When it comes to investigating semantic similarities, it is worth noting that similarity between two words can be too general to quantify. Accordingly, the discriminating power of a model is also important in limiting the scope of similarity between words.

The main idea behind distributional semantics, known as Distributional Hypothesis (DH), states that linguistic items with similar distributions have similar meanings (Blevins, 2016). Therefore these methods are biased towards finding similarities between concepts. The SemEval shared task 10 'Capturing Discriminative Attributes' poses the new problem of semantic difference detection, thus putting difference, rather than similarity at the forefront. It is about modeling semantic difference in the case of already related words. The idea is that while similarity can group words together in a generic way, understanding semantic differences sheds additional light on the meaning of each individual word.

A semantic model can potentially become more robust if it can benefit from sensitivity to differences alongside similarities in meaning. Considering difference can also help researchers assess semantic representations more rigorously. The effectiveness of a semantic similarity model can be evaluated further by quantifying its strength in finding differences between words.

In the shared task, semantic difference is operationalised as the relation between two semantically related words and a discriminative feature. This relation is realised if the feature characterises only the first word. An example is the triple *airplane, helicopter, wings*. In this formulation, semantic difference is an asymmetric relation.

In this work, we compute several scores for word pairs and triples with the aim of capturing different semantic relations. Specifically, we define scores based on a knowledge-based ontology and co-occurrence counts. For knowledge-based features we rely on ConceptNet semantic network (Speer and Havasi, 2013), and our co-occurrence based features are derived from association measures, ngrams and pre-trained embeddings. We use the scores in both supervised and unsupervised scenarios to identify triples that constitute semantic difference; i.e. the attribute (third) word is discriminative between the first two words. The code and data used for this system are freely available.[1]

The rest of this paper is organised as follows: Section 2 describes related work. Section 3 provides a description of the approach including the details of the features we use. Sections 4 and 5 discuss experiments and results. Section 6 involves error analysis and some closing remarks and finally the paper concludes with Section 7.

2 Related Work

Distributional similarity methods rely on classical DH, meaning in order to determine how similar two words are, they consider similarity of their contexts. This similarity is usually approximated by taking the cosine of the word vectors. In this

---

[1]https://github.com/shivaat/
discriminative_attribute

972

Proceedings of the 12th International Workshop on Semantic Evaluation (SemEval-2018), pages 972–976
New Orleans, Louisiana, June 5–6, 2018. ©2018 Association for Computational Linguistics

way, semantic difference can be modeled as the subtraction of vectors from semantically related words. As a classic example, subtraction of word vectors for *king* and *man* is similar to that of *queen* from *woman* (Mikolov et al., 2013).

However not all semantic differences can be adequately captured using this method. There are many cases where the difference between two words originates from the lack or presence of a feature that cannot be directly mapped to the vector difference between two related words. One such example is *dolphin* and *narwhal* that only differ in having a *horn* (Krebs and Paperno, 2016).

Therefore, combining linguistic and conceptual information would potentially strengthen a semantic model in capturing meaning of a word. To tackle this issue, some studies rely on human annotated list of different attributes related to a concept which are called feature norms (McRae et al., 2005). Despite their strength in encoding semantic knowledge, feature norms have not been widely used in practice because they are small in size and require a lot of work to assemble (Fagarasan et al., 2015). Lazaridou et al. (2016) is an earlier attempt at identification of discriminative features which focuses on visual attributes.

3   Approach

Our goal is to define a simple interpretable metric, using which we can gauge semantic difference and identify discriminative attributes. We hypothesise that for a triple in this task, a stronger relation between the first word and the attribute (in comparison with the second word and the attribute)[2] is indicative of the attribute word being discriminative between the two words.

For each triple we define a discriminative score $Disc\_Score(w1, w2, attr)$ as follows:

$$Disc\_Score(w1, w2, attr) =$$
$$Score(w1, attr) - Score(w2, attr) \quad (1)$$

where $w1$, $w2$ and $attr$ are the first, second, and third word respectively. $Score$ is a variable function of relation between two words that can be any of the scores explained in Sections 3.1, 3.2, 3.3, and 3.4.

---

[2]This stronger relation corresponds to more common semantic context and/or higher co-occurrence probability.

3.1   Association-based Score

Statistical association measures have a long history in language processing. With the availability of huge corpora, these measures can be even more effective than before in finding collocations and associations between words.

Collocational behaviour between two words is a strong signal that suggests one of the words can identify the other. As an example, in the triple $(hair, body, curly)$, the association score in $(hair, curly)$ is much more than $(body, curly)$, suggesting that *curly* is a discriminative attribute between the other two words.

For each triple in this task, collocational behaviour of the attribute word with the first two words is measured to see whether the first word can be a better collocate than the other. To this end, we use several different association measures to compute the outputs of the $Score$ function in Eq. 1.

We measure the association of two words based on their co-occurrence in the span of 5 words. We use SketchEngine (Kilgarriff et al., 2004) to extract these statistics from the huge enTenTen corpus (Jakubíček et al., 2013). Specifically, for each pair of words, we extract PMI (Church and Hanks, 1990) (known as MI in SketcEngine), MI3 (Oakes, 1998), log-likelihood (Dunning, 1993), T-score (Krenn and Evert, 2001), log-Dice (Dice, 1945), and Salience (Kilgarriff et al., 2004) all as defined in SketchEngine.

3.2   Google Ngrams

Ngrams are frequently used in computational linguistics for a variety of purposes including language modeling and association measures based on lexical co-occurrence. Google Books Ngram Dataset[3] is a collection of phrases (between 1 and 5 words long) extracted from over 8 million books printed between 1500 and 2008.

We use PhraseFinder (Trenkmann, 2016), a free web API that makes it possible to look up words or phrases from this dataset using a wildcard-supporting query language. Using this resource, we derive two different features. In the first one, we only consider bigrams, and in the other, we consider up to 5-grams. In both cases, we count the number of times that words occur near one another in a span of interest regardless of order. We follow the same formula as defined

---

[3]https://books.google.com/ngrams

in Eq. 1. In order to eliminate the bias of high/low frequency words we devide $Disc\_Score$ by $Score(w1, attr) + Score(w2, attr)$ that we compute from ngram co-occurrence counts.

3.3 Word Embedding Based Score

In distributional semantics, word embeddings are used to induce meaning representations for words. These methods are inspired by neural network language modeling and have become a basic building block for most applications in computational linguistics. The most popular word embedding method is word2vec (with the skip-gram architecture) which learns dense vector representations for words using an unsupervised model. Word2vec's training objective is based on DH, defined so that the model can learn word vectors that are good at predicting nearby words (Mikolov et al., 2013). Another popular embedding technique is GloVe, which like word2vec, preserves semantic analogies in the vector space. One major difference between the two models is that GloVe utilises corpus statistics by training on global co-occurrence counts rather than local context windows (Pennington et al., 2014).

In our system we use a concatenation of two sets of pre-trained embeddings. The first is trained on English Wikipedia using a variation of word2vec (Bojanowski et al., 2016). The other called ConceptNet Numberbatch (Speer and Lowry-Duda, 2017), is an ensemble of pre-trained Glove and word2vec vectors whose values are readjusted using a technique called retrofitting (Faruqui et al., 2014). In retrofitting, the values of the embeddings are updated using a training function that considers relational knowledge.

Using each word embedding, we compute cosine similarity between each word in a triple and the attribute word to account for the statistics $Score(w1, attr)$ and $Score(w2, attr)$ in Eq. 1.

3.4 ConceptNet Score

Co-occurrence based measures are not sufficient to account for all the various semantic relations that can exist between two words. Knowledge-based ontologies (e.g. ConceptNet, BabelNet etc) encode information about words and their relations in a structured way. This additional source of semantic information can be used to determine whether or not an attribute is discriminative. Because of its free web interface and ease of use, we use ConceptNet to empower our system with relational knowledge (Speer and Havasi, 2013).

For any given $(w1, w2, attr)$ triple, using ConceptNet's REST API we query $w1$, limiting the number of search results to $1,000$. The output is a JSON file that contains all relations between the queried word and other concepts. We traverse all the relations and count the number of times $attr$ is linked to $w1$ to compute $score(w1, attr)$. We repeat the procedure for $w2$ and compute $score(w2, attr)$ and substitute them in Eq. 1.

4 Experimental Settings

We use the data as provided by the organisers of the shared task. We train our model on the train set and find the optimised parameters based on the validations set. Predictions were made on the held-out test data.

The final feature set is the collection of $Disc\_Score$ measures based on the set of proposed scores. As a result we have 6 association-based scores, 2 google ngram based scores, 2 embedding based scores, and 1 ConceptNet score. In total, we have 11 scores as our features.

In ConceptNet, reliability of each relation is given by a weight score. We decided to ignore this information and opted for raw counts because it didn't help performance. Furthermore, binarising the scores based on raw counts (with 0 as a threshold) slightly improved the results.

We use the features in both a supervised scenario (using SVM) and an unsupervised scenario (using KMeans). In both cases all of the 11 features are exploited.

The evaluation in this shared task is in terms of the average of positive and negative F1-scores. In this paper, we report the precision, recall and F1-score for both positive and negative labels separately, along with the average F1-score.

5 Results and Discussion

Table 1 shows the results on the validation set both in the supervised (SVM) and the unsupervised scenario (KMeans).

In this table, we mainly focus on the results that we achieved with our best system after the official evaluation. We also briefly report our official result for $TEST$ as recorded on the shared task leaderboard. The only difference between our system in official evaluation and post evaluation is the setting we have used to extract measures

			Precision	Recall	F1-score	Average F1-score
Validation	SVM	pos	0.7679	0.5652	0.6512	0.6913
		neg	0.6548	0.8284	0.7315	
	KMeans	pos	0.7039	0.6833	0.6935	**0.6972**
		neg	0.6910	0.7113	0.7010	
TEST (Official Evaluation)	SVM					0.69
TEST (Post Evaluation)	SVM	pos	0.7299	0.6065	0.6625	**0.7142**
		neg	0.7197	0.8183	0.7658	
	KMeans	pos	0.6464	0.7001	0.6722	0.6930
		neg	0.7396	0.6899	0.7139	

Table 1: Results on Validation and TEST sets.

from SketchEngine. For the official evaluation, by querying SketchEngine we extracted all the collocations of an attribute word. However, the lists of resulted entries in SketchEngine are limited to a $1,000$ for each query. We later bypassed this limitation by searching for the attribute word with only a limited number of words (from the dataset) in its context. This improves the results on validation and test sets.

Surprisingly, it can be seen in the first part of Table 1 that the unsupervised model (KMeans) can cluster the validation data as well as or even better than the supervised classification approach (SVM).[4] This can be explained by the fact that the features we employ for this task are all computed using a formula that is specifically defined to represent semantic difference, and finding whether a feature is discriminative between two words closely correlates with the semantic difference between them.

It can be concluded from the results that the features are well generalised as they lead to even better performance on the held-out test data.

6 Error Analysis

A sizable portion of the train and test triples bear on genealogical and kinship relations, as in $(grandson, brother, male)$. Some require hierarchical reasoning, as in $(invertebrate, insect, shell)$. Our model captures these kinds of relations very well, as it has access to information from a knowledge base.

In order to see the effectiveness of the scores we obtain from ConceptNet, we re-train the model excluding the ConceptNet based measure and also

the vectors derived from Numberbatch embedding. As a result, the validation performance dropped to 0.6857 and the test result decreased to 0.6969 in terms of average F1-score.

A large part of the test triples require the knowledge to understand whether something is a constituent of another entity, as in $(beer, wine, foam)$. It appears that these relations are well captured using co-occurrence based metrics alone since deleting knowledge-base features leaves the results for these triples for the most part unchanged.

7 Conclusions

For this shared task we develop a classification system to determine whether an attribute word can distinguish one word from another. To model semantic difference, we define a discriminative score, and make use of a variety of different association measures derived from huge corpora, and also pre-trained distributional semantic vectors. To augment our method with structured knowledge, we utilise a knowledge-based ontology. We use the feature set in supervised and unsupervised settings. The results suggest that the defined score is capable of generating features that can help our model in capturing instances where a feature is discriminative between two words. Our system shows particular strength in recognising kinship and genealogical relations that are not consistently captured using naive distributional semantic techniques.

In the future, we intend to exploit ConceptNet in a more sophisticated way rather than limiting ourselves to number of relations. It would also be interesting to extract co-occurrence measures from various corpora including domain-specific resources in order to improve the coverage of the model.

---

[4]In order to evaluate the results from KMeans, we label the clusters in a way that best matches the truth values. These values need to be known to perform this analysis. Therefore, we used SVM for official submission since the TEST data is blind.

References

James P Blevins. 2016. *Word and paradigm morphology*. Oxford University Press.

Piotr Bojanowski, Edouard Grave, Armand Joulin, and Tomas Mikolov. 2016. Enriching word vectors with subword information. *arXiv preprint arXiv:1607.04606*.

Kenneth Ward Church and Patrick Hanks. 1990. Word association norms, mutual information, and lexicography. *Computational Linguistics*, 16(1):22–29.

Lee R. Dice. 1945. Measures of the amount of ecologic association between species. *Ecology*, 26:297–302.

Ted Dunning. 1993. Accurate methods for the statistics of surprise and coincidence. *COMPUTATIONAL LINGUISTICS*, 19(1):61–74.

Luana Fagarasan, Eva Maria Vecchi, and Stephen Clark. 2015. From distributional semantics to feature norms: grounding semantic models in human perceptual data. In *Proceedings of the 11th International Conference on Computational Semantics*, pages 52–57.

Manaal Faruqui, Jesse Dodge, Sujay K Jauhar, Chris Dyer, Eduard Hovy, and Noah A Smith. 2014. Retrofitting word vectors to semantic lexicons. *arXiv preprint arXiv:1411.4166*.

Miloš Jakubíček, Adam Kilgarriff, Vojtěch Kovář, Pavel Rychlý, and Vít Suchomel. 2013. The tenten corpus family. In *7th International Corpus Linguistics Conference CL*, pages 125–127.

Adam Kilgarriff, Pavel Rychly, Pavel Smrz, and David Tugwell. 2004. Itri-04-08 the Sketch Engine. *Information Technology*, 105:116.

Alicia Krebs and Denis Paperno. 2016. Capturing discriminative attributes in a distributional space: Task proposal. In *Proceedings of the 1st Workshop on Evaluating Vector-Space Representations for NLP*, pages 51–54.

Brigitte Krenn and Stefan Evert. 2001. Can we do better than frequency? a case study on extracting pp-verb collocations. *Proceedings of the ACL Workshop on Collocations*, pages 39–46.

Angeliki Lazaridou, Marco Baroni, et al. 2016. The red one!: On learning to refer to things based on discriminative properties. In *Proceedings of the 54th Annual Meeting of the Association for Computational Linguistics (Volume 2: Short Papers)*, volume 2, pages 213–218.

Ken McRae, George S Cree, Mark S Seidenberg, and Chris McNorgan. 2005. Semantic feature production norms for a large set of living and nonliving things. *Behavior research methods*, 37(4):547–559.

Tomas Mikolov, Ilya Sutskever, Kai Chen, Greg S Corrado, and Jeff Dean. 2013. Distributed representations of words and phrases and their compositionality. In *Advances in neural information processing systems*, pages 3111–3119.

Michael P. Oakes. 1998. *Statistics for Corpus Linguistics*. Edinburgh University Press.

Jeffrey Pennington, Richard Socher, and Christopher Manning. 2014. Glove: Global vectors for word representation. In *Proceedings of the 2014 conference on empirical methods in natural language processing (EMNLP)*, pages 1532–1543.

Robert Speer and Catherine Havasi. 2013. Conceptnet 5: A large semantic network for relational knowledge. In *The Peoples Web Meets NLP*, pages 161–176. Springer.

Robert Speer and Joanna Lowry-Duda. 2017. Conceptnet at semeval-2017 task 2: Extending word embeddings with multilingual relational knowledge. In *Proceedings of the 11th International Workshop on Semantic Evaluation (SemEval-2017)*, pages 85–89.

Martin Trenkmann. 2016. PhraseFinder – Search millions of books for language use. `http://phrasefinder.io/`. Accessed: 2018-01-30.

UNAM at SemEval-2018 Task 10: Unsupervised Semantic Discriminative Attribute Identification in Neural Word Embedding Cones

Ignacio Arroyo-Fernández
Universidad Nacional
Autónoma de México (UNAM)
`iaf@ccg.unam.mx`

Ivan Meza
Instituto de Investigaciones
en Matemáticas Aplicadas
y en Sistemas – UNAM
`ivanvladimir@turing`
`.iimas.unam.mx`

Carlos F. Méndez-Cruz
Centro de Ciencias
Genómicas – UNAM
`cmendezc@ccg.unam.mx`

Abstract

In this paper we report an unsupervised method aimed to identify whether an attribute is discriminative for two words (which are treated as concepts, in our particular case). To this end, we use geometrically inspired vector operations underlying unsupervised decision functions. These decision functions operate on state-of-the-art neural word embeddings of the attribute and the concepts. The main idea can be described as follows: if attribute q discriminates concept a from concept b, then q is excluded from the feature set shared by these two concepts: the intersection. That is, the membership $q \in (a \cap b)$ does not hold. As a, b, q are represented with neural word embeddings, we tested vector operations allowing us to measure membership, i.e. fuzzy set operations (t-norm, for fuzzy intersection, and t-conorm, for fuzzy union) and the similarity between q and the convex cone described by a and b.

1 Introduction

There exist nowadays a number of arithmetic vector operations for computing word relationships interpreted as linguistic regularities. A very popular setting is solving word analogies (Lepage, 1998), which is mainly used to evaluate the quality of word embeddings (Mikolov et al., 2013). Recently other alternatives to solve word analogies have been proposed (Linzen, 2016), including supervised methods (Drozd et al., 2016).

Solving word analogies requires three word arguments, and a fourth one is inferred. Such an inference raises from the similarity between common or similar contexts shared by the two pairs of words. Thus, given words "queen", "woman", "king", "man", the following arithmetic operation holds for their corresponding embeddings $x_{(\cdot)}$:
$$x_{king} - x_{man} + x_{woman} = x_{queen}.$$

In this work, we explore similar approaches for Discriminative Attribute Identification (DAI). This task requires tree word arguments a, b, q, and a binary label $y \in \{0, 1\}$ is inferred from them (Cree and McRae, 2003; Lazaridou et al., 2016; McRae et al., 2005). Such a label indicates whether the third word, q, is identified as a discriminative (semantic) attribute between words (concepts) a, b. We observed that the task of identifying discriminative attributes between words, represented via word embeddings, evokes that of solving word analogies.

We propose geometrically inspired vector operations on word embeddings $x_a, x_b, x_q \in \mathbb{R}^n$ of the words a, b, q, respectively. The output of each of these operations is in turn operated by a unsupervised decision function aimed to predict the label y. The decision functions are based on the reasoning given originally in (Lepage, 1998) for solving word analogies. Under this reasoning, the important thing is to look for those items shared by the objects compared, and verify whether the item of interest is included among them.

In other words, in the case of DAI, if we are asked whether x_q, the attribute embedding, discriminates x_a from x_b, then an idea is to verify whether the attribute is contained in the set shared by the two concepts in question, i.e. does the set operation $q \in (a \cap b)$ hold? Our hypothesis, is that x_q discriminates x_a from x_b if the result of such an operation is false in terms of the subspace delimited by x_a and x_b, i.e. a convex cone. Thus, a number of vector operations and decision functions were tested as different vector versions of this set operation on state-of-the-art neural word embeddings.

Proceedings of the 12th International Workshop on Semantic Evaluation (SemEval-2018), pages 977–984
New Orleans, Louisiana, June 5–6, 2018. ©2018 Association for Computational Linguistics

The proposed method does not rely on language or knowledge resources (i.e. knowledge bases and graphs, PoS or any kind of taggers, etc.). Furthermore, with the help of the geometrical insight that our method provides, we also discuss the possibilities of it for being used to study measures of how concepts can be generated from attributes in the sense of vector space modeling of natural language. Thus, this study can be considered, e.g., for designing semantically driven word embedding methods or to explore alternatives for building knowledge resource applications.

Our results showed that the proposed approach hold coherence with respect to the semantic notions proposed in the DAI task. This approach reached 0.622 of F-measure in predicting discriminative attributes.

2 Literature Review

Up to our knowledge, there is not work proposing unsupervised methods for discriminative attribute identification or extraction with a direct link to word embeddings. Most related work deals with semantic relation extraction or with labeling semantic relations in lexical semantics, e.g. given a hypernym, to perform hyponym extraction (Fu et al., 2014).

There is also work on using semantic attributes to classify images of objects in a supervised fashion (Chen et al., 2012; Lazaridou et al., 2016). In this case, dictionaries of discriminative attributes of objects are used (e.g. fruits by their *color or form*), but experiments are not performed on text data, e.g., a snippet describing the object. In more applicative cases, the use of dictionaries of object attributes has shown to be a good approach in clothing recommender systems. These systems group images of items sharing attributes the customers are usually interested in, e.g. images of jackets *with a hat* (Chen et al., 2012; Kalra et al., 2016; Zhou et al., 2016).

Other contributions provide methods for object classification by using multiple data sources, including text. In (Farhadi et al., 2009, 2010; Lampert et al., 2009) it is proposed supervised learning of semantic attributes and textual descriptions of objects. Their methods are aimed to generalize recognition and (template) textual description of unseen objects with similar and shared attributes. In the particular case of (Berg et al., 2010), a supervised algorithm learns to label object attributes by fitting multinomial associations between text segments and recognized image segments as co-occurring objects within a Web corpus (Su and Jurie, 2012). After that, the learned attributes of the objects are detected and used as features for feeding an unsupervised method for categorizing images and text. In (Deeptimahanti and Sanyal, 2011; Overmyer et al., 2001) natural language descriptions of case uses of user requirements are parsed to obtain Unified Modeling Language (UML) diagrams including object attributes. This approach is aimed to facilitate design in software engineering by semi-automatically building code objects (Yue et al., 2011).

3 A Convex Combination

Lepage (1998) proposed solving word analogies based on characters shared by words and sentences. We extrapolated such an idea for feature similarities, similarly to what (Mikolov et al., 2013) did on vectors for solving word analogies. Thus, our method attempts taking into account these two ideas in the following way. Thinking about neural word embeddings as vectors generated by axis of attributes, our approach is to observe the linear subspace A delimited by embeddings of words a and b, and to see how the embedding of q is contained in it. This linear subspace has the properties of a convex cone. Thus, in geometrical terms, to assess whether an attribute can generate a pair of concepts or not, we propose to measure the degree, λ, to which the embedding x_q is a convex combination of the embeddings x_a and x_b. This measure can be derived from the convex combination

$$\lambda x_a + (1 - \lambda)x_b = x_q, \qquad (1)$$

where $\lambda \in [0, 1]$. The embeddings $x_a, x_b, x_q \in \mathbb{R}^d$ represent nouns a and b and the query attribute q, respectively (see Figure 1). The requirement of x_a, x_b to describe a convex cone A is due to the fact that, geometrically, features shared by these embeddings would be enclosed within such cone. This can be observed by testing extreme values in Eq. (1). Assume all embeddings are normalized in magnitude. Let us making q to be, simultaneously, as far as possible from a and b while keeping the volume of A greater than zero. Also make that $\langle x_a, x_b \rangle$ to be small. In this scenario, embeddings x_a, x_b delimit a cone of less than 90 degrees. As the embedding x_q is as far as possible from the

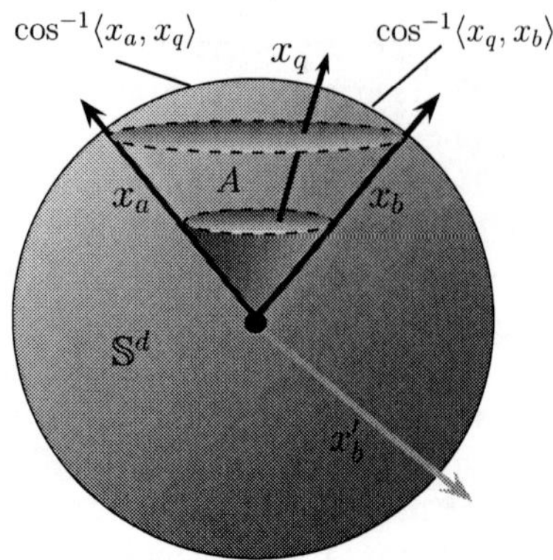

Figure 1: The $d-$dimensional vector space defined in the unitary-sphere $\mathbb{S}^d$.

x_a and x_b and it is contained in A, then it passes close to the center of the circular basis of the cone. Thus, we have

$$\|x_q - x_a\| \approx \|x_q - x_b\|.$$

This geometrical scenario indicates that q is shared equally by a and b, so it is not discriminative for them. In the case of $\langle x_a, x_b \rangle \approx -1$ it means that the set A is not convex. This is because x_a and x_b describe a unique line and have opposite directions (they are anti-parallel). This geometrical scenario prevents the pair of word embeddings from being generated by linear combinations of attributes in common to them (see x_a and x_b' in Figure 1). In the case when a, b are semantically very similar, we have that[1] $\langle x_a, x_b \rangle \to 1$. It means that both vectors are (almost) parallel, so they refer concepts sharing most of their attributes. In this case, if x_q is far away from both x_a and x_b, then determining discriminativeness has not sense (probably x_q is not an attribute of either of them).

The geometrical scenario of identifying a discriminative attribute q can occur when $\langle x_a, x_b \rangle$ is small and either $\langle x_q, x_a \rangle \to 1$ or $\langle x_q, x_b \rangle \to 1$. For example, if $\langle x_q, x_b \rangle \to 1$, it means that x_q tends to be parallel to x_b and we can see x_b as a linear combination of x_q. As $\langle x_a, x_b \rangle$ is small (x_a and x_b are almost orthogonal), then $\langle x_a, x_q \rangle$ is also small. Therefore, this analysis leads us to think that q discriminates a from b, and that q is an attribute of b rather than of a.

---

[1]The symbol '$\to$' denotes tendency ("*tends to*").

4   The Convex Cone Method

The scenarios depicted in Section 3 overall show how projections among word embeddings form convex combinations and how these projections can be exploited in DAI. Without loss of generality, these projections can be seen as distances. In this sense, the convex parameter λ in Eq. (1) indeed weighs distances involving x_a, x_b, x_q. Now, notice that Eq. (1) expresses x_q in terms of x_a and x_b. However, in DAI they are know and we would like to measure the relationship among them given they are $d-$dimensional vectors. This measure is can be given by λ, which now becomes into the unknown. In this case, λ acts as a bounded measure of how much a given pair of concepts a, b shares a given attribute q. Thus, by performing some comprehensive algebra starting from Eq. (1), we arrive at

$$\lambda(x_a - x_b) + x_b = x_q,$$

which leads to the $d-$dimensional Euclidean (*cone*) version of the convex parameter

$$\lambda = \frac{\|x_q - x_b\|}{\|x_a - x_b\|}. \tag{2}$$

Furthermore, in addition to (2), we consider an alternative distance criterion. That is, it is possible measuring distance in terms of arcs instead of doing it in terms of straight line segments. Therefore, we have the arc (*arcone*) version of the convex parameter:

$$\lambda = \frac{\cos^{-1}\langle x_q, x_b \rangle}{\cos^{-1}\langle x_a, x_b \rangle}, \tag{3}$$

where $\langle x, x' \rangle \in [-1, 1]$ given that $\|x\| = 1$ for all $x \in \mathbb{S}^d$ (the unitary sphere). Both arcs $\cos^{-1}\langle x, x' \rangle$ in the numerator and in the denominator of (3) are in the interval $[0, 2\pi]$.

The convex parameter λ measures the degree to which x_q is a convex combination of x_a and x_b. Form the point of view of the combination degree, rather than from the point of view of the absolute value of λ, some function $f(\lambda)$ must be maximum at $\lambda = 0.5$ (see Figure 2). When it occurs, x_q passes close to the axis of the cone A (so it also passes close to the center of the shaded circular area of radius $0.5\|x_a - x_b\|$ in Figure 1). Therefore, $\lambda \to 0.5$ indicates that the attribute q is highly shared by both concepts a and b.

The extreme values of λ must be interpreted contrarily by f, i.e. $\lambda \to 0$ means that, on the

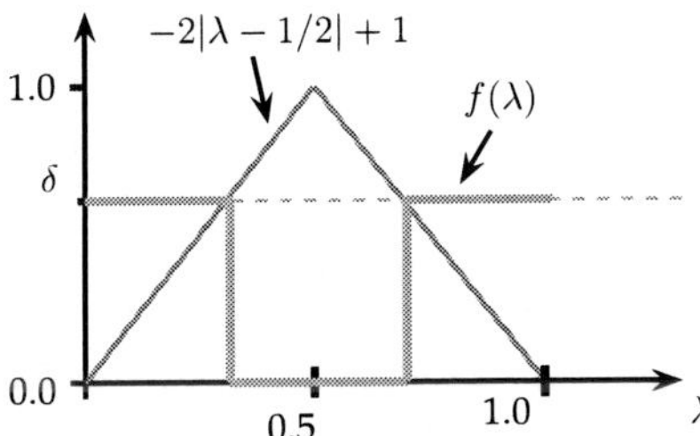

Figure 2: The decision function $f(\lambda)$.

one hand, the attribute q uniquely characterizes (or generates) the concept a, so x_a is approximately parallel to x_q. On the other hand, $\lambda \to 1$ means that the attribute q uniquely characterizes the concept b. Thus, we need that some decision function f to take advantage of extreme values of λ for making decision on whether an attribute q is discriminative of a pair of concepts a and b.

Therefore, we define our decision criterion subject to some threshold $\delta \in [0, 1]$ (say $\delta = 0.7$):

$$f(\lambda) = \begin{cases} 1 & \text{if } -2|\lambda - 1/2| + 1 < \delta \\ 0 & \text{if } -2|\lambda - 1/2| + 1 \geq \delta \end{cases} \quad (4)$$

where if upper inequality (4) holds, it means either that $\lambda \to 0$ or that $\lambda \to 1.0$, so $f(\lambda) = 1$ and therefore attribute q discriminates concepts a and b. Conversely, if lower inequality (4) holds, it means that $\lambda \to 0.5$. Therefore, $f(\lambda) = 0$ and the decision function determines that q does not discriminate a and b. See Figure 2.

5 Other Geometrical Methods

In addition to the convex cone method, we also tested mean-based, sum-based and fuzzy methods for quantifying the containment $q \in (a \cap b)$.

5.1 Similarity with Respect to the Sum and to the Mean

The sum-based method computes the resultant vector of x_a and x_b. The similarity between such a vector and the candidate attribute x_q should be smaller than some threshold δ so as to consider that q discriminates a from b, that is:

$$f(x_q; x_a, x_b) = \begin{cases} 1 & \text{if } \langle x_q, x_a + x_b \rangle < \delta \\ 0 & \text{if } \langle x_q, x_a + x_b \rangle \geq \delta \end{cases} \quad (5)$$

Unlike to the convex cone method, Eq. (5) indicates that the sum-based method measures directly the similarity between the resultant vector $x_a + x_b$

and x_q. The motivation of this operation is similar to that of the convex cone method. That is, $x_a + x_b$ is an embedding that embeddings x_a and x_b have in common. Therefore, probably such embedding is similar to x_q if this latter also is common to x_a and x_b.

The mean-based method follows exactly the same principle, but only requires multiplying $x_a + x_b$ in (5) by 0.5.

5.2 Similarity with Respect to a Fuzzy Connective

The fuzzy method computes the connective:

$$x_{\{a,b\}} = \alpha \min\{x_a, x_b\} + (1 - \alpha) \max\{x_a, x_b\}$$

between the fuzzy intersection ($\min\{\cdot\}$) and the fuzzy union ($\max\{\cdot\}$) of the embeddings x_a, x_b (Zadeh, 1965). These set operations are known as the Gödel's t-norm and t-conorm (Klement et al., 2013), respectively and they are defined elementwise for vectors. α is known as the compensation parameter and controls the mixture between union and intersection. Thus, the connective acts as a convex combination of the fuzzy union and the fuzzy intersection operators, so if $\alpha \to 0$ it causes that the intersection ($\min\{\cdot\}$) vanishes whereas the union ($\max\{\cdot\}$) survives. The contrary effect can be induced if $\alpha \to 1$.

Fuzzy set operations are conceptually more akin to the idea of observing whether the intersection set of concept attributes contains some query attribute. To contextualize word embeddings with fuzzy sets, we assume the embedding $x_a \in \mathbb{R}^d$ is given by a membership function $x_a = \mu(\mathcal{A})$. Herein, $\mathcal{A}$ is the set of items in some subset (of cardinality d) of the contexts of the word a. We also assume that the subset of contexts was statistically estimated by the word embedding method, which is in this case though as the membership function defined on the set $\mathcal{C} \supset \mathcal{A}$ of all contexts in the corpus $\mu : \mathcal{C} \to \mathbb{S}^d$.

As a first attempt to explore a relationship between fuzzy sets and word embeddings, in this paper we induced bias α to a decision function f based on the inner product between the connective $x_{\{a,b\}}$ (a biased version of $x_a + x_b$) and the query attribute x_q. In this way, the decision of DAI is made according to the threshold δ, i.e.:

$$f(x_q; \alpha; x_a, x_b) = \begin{cases} 1 & \text{if } \langle x_q, x_{\{a,b\}} \rangle < \delta \\ 0 & \text{if } \langle x_q, x_{\{a,b\}} \rangle \geq \delta \end{cases}$$

$$(6)$$

where α is the tolerance parameter of the fuzzy connective and it must be manually set.

6 Experiments and Results

For our experiments, we computed our decision functions $f(\cdot)$ on tuples of the form $\{x_a, x_b, x_q, y\}$. To this end, we used state-of-the-art word embeddings, i.e. Glove (Pennington et al., 2014), FastText (Bojanowski et al., 2016), Word2Vec (Mikolov et al., 2013) and Dependency-Based Word2Vec (DBW2V) (Levy and Goldberg, 2014). We also explored embeddings tanking into account external knowledge. This is the case of ConceptNet embeddings (Speer and Lowry-Duda, 2017). DBW2V embeddings are W2V embeddings enriched by using syntactic dependencies and Conceptnet are embeddings enriched with both syntactic dependencies and knowledge graphs (Faruqui et al., 2015). We trained W2V and FastText by using the Wikipedia dataset[2]. In the case of Glove[3], ConceptNet[4] and DBW2V[5] we downloaded pretrained embeddings from authors' websites. For Word2Vec and Fast-Text we trained models of $200, 300, 400, 500$ and 1000 dimensions. In our results we only report the dimensionality that performed best.

As our approach is unsupervised, we report experiments on the validation dataset available on the competition's repository[6]. We can see in Table 1 that the arcone operation defined in (3) provided the best results for all word embedding methods. Our general best result was obtained by using Glove embeddings of 300 dimensions. We expected a good result from these embeddings as they specifically learn from mutual information statistics of word pairs. This enables Glove to encode feature contrasts, which also allows it for being the state-of-the-art method in word analogy tasks. During the competition we submitted our best configuration as unique run (Glove $300d$ and arcone operation with $\delta = 0.4$), which gave us $F1 = 0.60$ (place 19/26).

---

[2]The 2012 English Wikipedia available at
`http://inex.mmci.uni-saarland.de/data/`
`documentcollection.html`
[3]`https://nlp.stanford.edu/projects/`
`glove`
[4]`https://github.com/commonsense/`
`conceptnet-numberbatch`
[5]`https://levyomer.wordpress.com/2014/`
`04/25/dependency-based-word-embeddings`
[6]`https://github.com/dpaperno/`
`DiscriminAtt/tree/master/training`

Regarding to the threshold δ of the decision functions $f(\cdot)$, we tested a set of values $\delta \in \{0.0, 0.1, 0.4, 0.7, 1.0\}$. Our best result was obtained when $\delta = 0.4$ for almost all embedding methods, excepting DBW2V. This means that the convex parameter λ can vary 60% around the maximum (0.5) in order to consider that an attribute q is shared by (or to generate) both concepts a, b. Thus, by evaluating δ in (4) we see either that x_q is too biased towards x_a if it holds that $\lambda < 0.4(0.5) = 0.2$, or that x_q is too biased towards x_b if it holds that $\lambda > 0.3 + 0.5 = 0.8$. In these cases we can say that q is discriminative for the concepts a, b as it is an attribute only (or mainly) of one of them.

Embedding	Dim.	$f(\cdot)$	δ	F1-score
Glove	300	arcone	0.4	**0.622**
		cone	0.4	0.615
		sum	-0.4	0.457
		fuzzy	-0.4	0.438
		mean	-0.4	0.426
ConceptNet	300	arcone	0.4	0.585
		cone	0.4	0.581
		mean	0.1	0.469
		fuzzy	-0.1	0.465
		sum	-0.4	0.451
Word2Vec	300	arcone	0.4	0.584
		cone	0.4	0.577
		fuzzy	-0.1	0.448
		mean	-0.1	0.444
		sum	-0.4	0.439
FastText	500	arcone	0.4	0.570
		cone	0.4	0.568
		fuzzy	0.4	0.451
		mean	0.4	0.450
		sum	0.7	0.437
DBW2V	300	arcone	0.7	0.541
		cone	0.7	0.536
		sum	-0.7	0.498
		fuzzy	-0.4	0.485
		mean	-0.4	0.475

Table 1: Best results for all the word embedding and vector operation methods on the validation dataset.

Given that it was needed $\delta = 0.7$ for DBW2V, we inferred that these embeddings allowed much less bias from the center of the cone and λ must be within 30% of its maximum in order to decide that an attribute is shared by two concepts. In other words, with DBW2V, it is more difficult to distinguish whether the attribute q is discriminative of a, b because it is allowed to be distant from both them even when it can be discriminative. This condition allows for much more feature overlapping and therefore the ranking on bottom of these embeddings can be explained.

Notice that the Euclidean version of the cone vector operation was the second best method for all word embedding methods. In fact, no difference was registered greater than 0.7% between cone and arcone operations.

The fuzzy approach did not show noticeable results. The variation of both, the threshold and the compensation parameter.

7 Discussion

We consider a bit surprising the difference in performance of Glove with respect to knowledge-based (ConceptNet) and Dependency-based (DBW2V) embeddings: 5.9% with respect to ConceptNet and 13.0% with respect to DBW2V. Such embeddings were expected to provide much more information about discriminative features because they are trained by taking into account semantic features explicitly by using knowledge and language resources for training.By using our arcone vector operation, W2V was ranked barely next to ConceptNet with a small difference of 0.17%. We think there are three possible motivations for this behavior. The first one is that the nature of our decision functions did not allowed to capture semantic features embedded into ConceptNet and into DBW2V. The second possibility is that semantic features are better embedded by Glove and, the third possibility, is that embedding semantic features explicitly can lead to overfitting of the resulting word representations. This latter possibility could be an additional explanation that DBW2V ended at bottom of our ranking.

In the case of FastText, these embeddings have been tested in word analogy tasks with success. However, as in the case of DBW2V, they are better than W2V or Glove mainly for syntactic analogies, which probably makes better FastText (and probably DBW2V) for NLP tasks other than DAI, e.g. sentence representation (Arroyo-Fernández et al., 2017).

Some assumptions were made for practical reasons in the case of fuzzy set operations. We are aware that this could affected drastically the results. The first assumption was that word embeddings were produced by membership functions, which take values in $[0, 1] \subset \mathbb{R}$ exclusively. This is not the case of word embeddings and they cannot directly mapped to identifiable textual items. Therefore, applying the t-norm and the t-conorm to these vectors is not completely intuitive. Nevertheless, with real-valued vectors we still had: as both embeddings tend to be in the same quadrant, the larger the magnitude of the connective embedding $x_{\{a,b\}}$. This latter embedding is somewhat oriented to the direction of the resultant $x_a + x_b$, which can be regulated by α, inducing a bias with respect to that direction. Although, this interpretation was worth exploring it did not gave us interesting results. Thus a better version of this fuzzy approach is pending.

At this moment, we have not clear what was the reason several of our results were contradictory with respect to the F-measure. Particularly for distributed representations. That is, we have balanced binary labels in the gold standard, but some scores resulted less than 50%. It is difficult to figure out how it happened analyzing directly distributed representations. Therefore, it remains an open issue proposing an alternative geometrical approach to tackle this inconsistency with respect to the main hypothesis of this paper.

8 Conclusions

The results of our experiments showed that the arcone vector operation is a simple method for quantifying discriminativeness. This operation showed to be correlated with respect to human judgments annotated in the validation dataset when Glove word embeddings were used. From the vector operations presented in this paper, the arcone operation, Eq. (3), best represents the abstract operation between sets $a \cap b = A$. Notice that the concept of cone is limited to euclidean metrics neither on $\mathbb{R}^d$ nor on $\mathbb{S}^d$. Therefore, other kind of transformations and related theories can be explored.

The effectiveness of our approach can be further explored as part of a learning algorithm aimed to obtain specialized (or enriched) word embeddings such that their geometrical structure is fitted in sets of convex volumes. An immediate experiment is using vector operations proposed in this paper as restrictions or as objectives for learning such embeddings for building knowledge resources.

Acknowledgments

Thanks to *Laboratorio Universitario de Cómputo de Alto Rendimiento* (IIMAS-UNAM); to *Sistemas Linux y SuperCómputo (Secretaría de Telecomunicaciones e Informática, IINGEN-UNAM)* to the CONACyT (grant No. 386128) and to the CS graduate program (UNAM).

References

Ignacio Arroyo-Fernández, Carlos-Francisco Méndez-Cruz, Gerardo Sierra, Juan-Manuel Torres-Moreno, and Grigori Sidorov. 2017. Unsupervised sentence representations as word information series: Revisiting TF–IDF. *arXiv preprint arXiv:1710.06524* .

Tamara L. Berg, Alexander C. Berg, and Jonathan Shih. 2010. Automatic attribute discovery and characterization from noisy web data. In Kostas Daniilidis, Petros Maragos, and Nikos Paragios, editors, *Computer Vision – ECCV 2010*. Springer Berlin Heidelberg, Berlin, Heidelberg, pages 663–676.

Piotr Bojanowski, Edouard Grave, Armand Joulin, and Tomas Mikolov. 2016. Enriching word vectors with subword information. *arXiv preprint arXiv:1607.04606* .

Huizhong Chen, Andrew Gallagher, and Bernd Girod. 2012. Describing clothing by semantic attributes. *Computer Vision–ECCV 2012* pages 609–623.

George S Cree and Ken McRae. 2003. Analyzing the factors underlying the structure and computation of the meaning of chipmunk, cherry, chisel, cheese, and cello (and many other such concrete nouns). *Journal of Experimental Psychology: General* 132(2):163.

Deva Kumar Deeptimahanti and Ratna Sanyal. 2011. Semi-automatic generation of UML models from natural language requirements. In *Proceedings of the 4th India Software Engineering Conference*. ACM, New York, NY, USA, ISEC '11, pages 165–174.

Aleksandr Drozd, Anna Gladkova, and Satoshi Matsuoka. 2016. Word embeddings, analogies, and machine learning: Beyond king-man+ woman= queen. In *COLING*. pages 3519–3530.

Ali Farhadi, Ian Endres, and Derek Hoiem. 2010. Attribute-centric recognition for cross-category generalization. *2010 IEEE Computer Society Conference on Computer Vision and Pattern Recognition* pages 2352–2359.

Ali Farhadi, Ian Endres, Derek Hoiem, and David A. Forsyth. 2009. Describing objects by their attributes. *2009 IEEE Conference on Computer Vision and Pattern Recognition* pages 1778–1785.

Manaal Faruqui, Jesse Dodge, Sujay K. Jauhar, Chris Dyer, Eduard Hovy, and Noah A. Smith. 2015. Retrofitting word vectors to semantic lexicons. In *Proceedings of NAACL*.

Ruiji Fu, Jiang Guo, Bing Qin, Wanxiang Che, Haifeng Wang, and Ting Liu. 2014. Learning semantic hierarchies via word embeddings. In *Proceedings of the 52nd Annual Meeting of the Association for Computational Linguistics (Volume 1: Long Papers)*. volume 1, pages 1199–1209.

Bhavya Kalra, Kingshuk Srivastava, and Manish Prateek. 2016. Computer vision based personalized clothing assistance system: A proposed model. In *Next Generation Computing Technologies (NGCT), 2016 2nd International Conference on*. IEEE, pages 341–346.

Erich Peter Klement, Radko Mesiar, and Endre Pap. 2013. *Triangular norms*, volume 8. Springer Science & Business Media.

C. H. Lampert, H. Nickisch, and S. Harmeling. 2009. Learning to detect unseen object classes by between-class attribute transfer. In *2009 IEEE Conference on Computer Vision and Pattern Recognition*. pages 951–958.

Angeliki Lazaridou, Nghia The Pham, and Marco Baroni. 2016. The red one!: On learning to refer to things based on their discriminative properties. *arXiv preprint arXiv:1603.02618* .

Yves Lepage. 1998. Solving analogies on words: an algorithm. In *Proceedings of the 36th Annual Meeting of the Association for Computational Linguistics and 17th International Conference on Computational Linguistics-Volume 1*. Association for Computational Linguistics, pages 728–734.

Omer Levy and Yoav Goldberg. 2014. Dependency-based word embeddings. In *ACL (2)*. pages 302–308.

Tal Linzen. 2016. Issues in evaluating semantic spaces using word analogies. In *Proceedings of the 1st Workshop on Evaluating Vector-Space Representations for NLP*. Association for Computational Linguistics, Berlin, Germany, pages 13–18.

Ken McRae, George S Cree, Mark S Seidenberg, and Chris McNorgan. 2005. Semantic feature production norms for a large set of living and nonliving things. *Behavior research methods* 37(4):547–559.

Tomas Mikolov, Ilya Sutskever, Kai Chen, Greg S Corrado, and Jeff Dean. 2013. Distributed representations of words and phrases and their compositionality. In *Advances in Neural Information Processing Systems*. pages 3111–3119.

Scott P. Overmyer, Benoit Lavoie, and Owen Rambow. 2001. Conceptual modeling through linguistic analysis using LIDA. In *Proceedings of the 23rd International Conference on Software Engineering*. IEEE

Computer Society, Washington, DC, USA, ICSE '01, pages 401–410.

Jeffrey Pennington, Richard Socher, and Christopher D. Manning. 2014. GloVe: Global vectors for word representation. In *Empirical Methods in Natural Language Processing (EMNLP)*. pages 1532–1543. http://www.aclweb.org/anthology/D14-1162.

Robert Speer and Joanna Lowry-Duda. 2017. ConceptNet at semeval-2017 task 2: Extending word embeddings with multilingual relational knowledge. In *Proceedings of the 11th International Workshop on Semantic Evaluation (SemEval-2017)*. Association for Computational Linguistics, pages 85–89.

Yu Su and Frédéric Jurie. 2012. Improving image classification using semantic attributes. *International journal of computer vision* 100(1):59–77.

Tao Yue, Lionel C. Briand, and Yvan Labiche. 2011. A systematic review of transformation approaches between user requirements and analysis models. *Requirements Engineering* 16(2):75–99.

L.A. Zadeh. 1965. Fuzzy sets. *Information and Control* 8(3):338 – 353.

Jingjin Zhou, Zhengzhong Zhou, and Liqing Zhang. 2016. Hierarchical semantic classification and attribute relations analysis with clothing region detection. In *Advanced Multimedia and Ubiquitous Engineering*, Springer, pages 429–435.

Luminoso at SemEval-2018 Task 10: Distinguishing Attributes Using Text Corpora and Relational Knowledge

Robert Speer
Luminoso Technologies, Inc.
675 Massachusetts Avenue
Cambridge, MA 02139
`rspeer@luminoso.com`

Joanna Lowry-Duda
Luminoso Technologies, Inc.
675 Massachusetts Avenue
Cambridge, MA 02139
`jlowry-duda@luminoso.com`

Abstract

Luminoso participated in the SemEval 2018 task on "Capturing Discriminative Attributes" with a system based on ConceptNet, an open knowledge graph focused on general knowledge. In this paper, we describe how we trained a linear classifier on a small number of semantically-informed features to achieve an F_1 score of 0.7368 on the task, close to the task's high score of 0.75.

1 Introduction

Word embeddings are most effective when they learn from both unstructured text and a graph of general knowledge (Speer and Lowry-Duda, 2017). ConceptNet 5 (Speer et al., 2017) is an open-data knowledge graph that is well suited for this purpose. It is accompanied by a pre-built word embedding model known as ConceptNet Numberbatch[1], which combines skip-gram embeddings learned from unstructured text with the relational knowledge in ConceptNet.

A straightforward application of the Concept-Net Numberbatch embeddings took first place in SemEval 2017 task 2, on semantic word similarity. For SemEval 2018, we built a system with these embeddings as a major component for a slightly more complex task.

The Capturing Discriminative Attributes task (Paperno et al., 2018) emphasizes the ability of a semantic model to recognize relevant differences between terms, not just their similarities. As the task description states, "If you can tell that americano is similar to capuccino and espresso but you can't tell the difference between them, you don't know what americano is."

The ConceptNet Numberbatch embeddings only measure the similarity of terms, and we hy-

pothesized that we would need to represent more specific relationships. For example, the input triple "frog, snail, legs" asks us to determine whether "legs" is an attribute that distinguishes "frog" from "snail". The answer is yes, because a frog *has* legs while a snail does not. The *has* relationship is one example of a specific relationship that is represented in ConceptNet.

To capture this kind of specific relationship, we built a model that infers relations between ConceptNet nodes, trained on the existing edges in ConceptNet and random negative examples. There are many models designed for this purpose; the one we decided on is based on Semantic Matching Energy (SME) (Bordes et al., 2014).

Our features consisted of direct similarity over ConceptNet Numberbatch embeddings, the relationships inferred over ConceptNet by SME, features that compose ConceptNet with other resources (WordNet and Wikipedia), and a purely corpus-based feature that looks up two-word phrases in the Google Books dataset.

We combined these features based on Concept-Net with features extracted from a few other resources in a LinearSVC classifier, using liblinear (Fan et al., 2008) via scikit-learn (Pedregosa et al., 2011). The classifier used only 15 features, of which 12 ended up with non-zero weights, from the five sources described. We aimed to avoid complexity in the classifier in order to prevent overfitting to the validation set; the power of the classifier should be in its features.

The classifier produced by this design (submitted late to the contest leaderboard) successfully avoided overfitting. It performed better on the test set than on the validation set, with a test F_1 score of 0.7368, whose margin of error overlaps with the evaluation's reported high score of 0.75.

At evaluation time, we accidentally submitted our results on the validation data, instead of the

---

[1] `https://github.com/commonsense/
conceptnet-numberbatch`

Proceedings of the 12th International Workshop on Semantic Evaluation (SemEval-2018), pages 985–989
New Orleans, Louisiana, June 5–6, 2018. ©2018 Association for Computational Linguistics

test data, to the SemEval leaderboard. Our code had truncated the results to the length of the test data, causing us to not notice the mismatch. This erroneous submission got a very low score, of course. This paper presents the corrected test results, which we submitted to the post-evaluation CodaLab leaderboard immediately after the results appeared. We did not change the classifier or data; the change was a one-line change to our code for outputting the classifier's predictions on the test set instead on the validation set.

2 Features

In detail, these are the five sources of features we used:

ConceptNet vector similarity. Given the triple $(term_1, term_2, att)$, we look up the ConceptNet Numberbatch embeddings for the root words of the three terms (with root words determined using ConceptNet's built-in lemmatizer). We determine the cosine similarity of $(term_1, att)$ and the cosine similarity of $(term_2, att)$. We then subtract the square roots of the similarity scores (floored at 0). If this difference is large enough, it indicates a positive example, a discriminative attribute that applies to $term_1$ and not to $term_2$.

ConceptNet relational inference. We train a Semantic Matching Energy model to represent ConceptNet nodes and relations as vectors, along with a 3-tensor of interactions between them. This model can then assign a confidence score to any triple (a relation connecting two terms). We used this model to infer values for each of 11 different ConceptNet relations. As in the case of vector similarity, each feature value is the difference between the value inferred for $rel(term_1, att)$ and $rel(term_2, att)$. This model is described in more detail in the next section.

Wikipedia lead sections. This feature expands on ConceptNet vector similarity: instead of computing the similarity between the attribute and the term, it computes the maximum of the similarity between the attribute and any word that appears in the lead section of the Wikipedia article for the term (Wikipedia, 2017). This helps to identify attributes that would be used to define the term, such as "amphibian" as an attribute for "frog".

WordNet entries. This feature is similar to the "Wikipedia lead sections" feature. It expands each term by looking up its synonyms in WordNet (Miller et al., 1998), the synonyms in synsets it is connected to, and the words in its gloss (definition), and taking the maximum similarity of the attribute to any of these terms.

Google Books 2-grams. This feature determines if $term_1$ forms a significant two-word phrase with att, more than $term_2$ does, based on the Google Books English Fiction data (Lin et al., 2012). The "significance" (s) of a two-word phrase is determined by comparing the smoothed log-likelihood of the individual unigrams to the smoothed log-likelihood of the phrase:

$$\text{s}(term, att) = 10 + \log_{10}(\#(term, att) + 1)$$
$$- \log_{10}((\#(term) + 10^5)(\#(att) + 10^5))$$

where $\#$ represents the number of occurrences of a unigram or bigram in the corpus.

The "ConceptNet relational inference" feature provides 11 entries to the feature vectors, while the other sources each provide one. In total, there are 15 features that represent each input triple.

Across multiple data sources, we use the square root of cosine similarity to measure the strength of the match between a term and an attribute. Because attributes should be at least somewhat related to the terms they describe, and because weak semantic similarity can be interpreted as relatedness, the square root helps us emphasize the important part of the scale. The difference between "somewhat related" and "not related" is more important to the task than the difference between "very similar" and "somewhat related", as a discriminative attribute should ideally be unrelated to the second term.

2.1 The Relational Inference Model

To infer truth values for ConceptNet relations, we use a variant of the Semantic Matching Energy model (Bordes et al., 2014), adapted to work well on ConceptNet's vocabulary of relations. Instead of embedding relations in the same space as the terms, this model assigns new 10-dimensional embeddings to ConceptNet relations, yielding a compact model for ConceptNet's relatively small set of relations.

The model is trained to distinguish positive examples of ConceptNet edges from negative ones. The positive examples are edges directly contained in ConceptNet, or those that are entailed by changing the relation to a more general one or switching the directionality of a symmetric relation. The negative examples come from replacing one of the terms with a random other term, the relation with a random unentailed relation, or switching the directionality of an asymmetric relation.

We trained this model for approximately 3 million iterations (about 4 days of computation on an nVidia Titan Xp) using PyTorch (Paszke et al., 2017). The code of the model is available at `https://github.com/LuminosoInsight/conceptnet-sme`.

To extract features for the discriminative attribute task, we focus on a subset of ConceptNet relations that would plausibly be used as attributes: *RelatedTo*, *IsA*, *HasA*, *PartOf*, *CapableOf*, *UsedFor*, *HasContext*, *HasProperty*, and *AtLocation*.

For most of these relations, the first argument is the term, and the second argument is the attribute. We use two additional features for *PartOf* and *AtLocation* with their arguments swapped, so that the attribute is the first argument. The generic relation *RelatedTo*, unlike the others, is intended to be symmetric, so we add its value to the value of its swapped version and use it as a single feature.

3   The Overfitting-Resistant Classifier

The classifier that we use to make a decision based on these features is scikit-learn's LinearSVC, using the default parameters in scikit-learn 0.19.1. (In Section 4, we discuss other models and parameters that we tried.) This classifier makes effective use of the features while being simple enough to avoid some amount of overfitting.

One aspect of the classifier that made a noticeable difference was the scaling of the features. We tried L_1 and L_2-normalizing the columns of the input matrix, representing the values of each feature, and decided on L_2 normalization.

We took advantage of the design of our features and the asymmetry of the task as a way to further mitigate overfitting. All of the features were designed to identify a property that $term_1$ has and $term_2$ does not, as is the case for the discriminative examples, so they should all make a non-negative contribution to a feature being discriminative. We can inspect the coefficients of the features in the SVC's decision boundary. If any feature gets a negative weight, it is likely a spurious result from overfitting to the training data. So, af-

Feature	Coefficient
ConceptNet vector similarity	13.82
SME: RelatedTo	14.01
SME: (x IsA a)	2.13
SME: (x HasA a)	0.00
SME: (x PartOf a)	0.56
SME: (x CapableOf a)	3.72
SME: (x UsedFor a)	0.92
SME: (x HasContext a)	0.88
SME: (x HasProperty a)	0.00
SME: (x AtLocation a)	0.00
SME: (a PartOf x)	3.22
SME: (a AtLocation x)	0.69
Wikipedia lead sections	12.46
WordNet relatedness	13.95
Google Ngrams	28.82

Table 1: Coefficients of each feature in our linear classifier. x represents a term and a represents the attribute.

ter training the classifier, we clip the coefficients of the decision boundary, setting all negative coefficients to zero.

If we were to remove these features and re-train, or require non-negative coefficients as a constraint on the classifier, then other features would inherently become responsible for overfitting. By neutralizing the features *after* training, we keep the features that are working well as they are, and remove a part of the model that appears to purely represent overfitting. Indeed, clipping the negative coefficients in this way increased our performance on the validation set.

Table 1 shows the coeffcients assigned to each feature based on the training data.

4   Other experiments

There are other features that we tried and later discarded. We experimented with a feature similar to the Google Books 2-grams feature, based on the AOL query logs dataset (Pass et al., 2006). It did not add to the performance, most likely because any information it could provide was also provided by Google Books 2-grams. Similiarly, we tried extending the Google Books 2-grams data to include the first and third words of a selection of 3-grams, but this, too, appeared redundant with the 2-grams.

We also experimented with a feature based on bounding box annotations available in the OpenImages dataset (Krasin et al., 2017). We hoped it would help us capture attributes such as colors, materials, and shapes. While this feature did not improve the classifier's performance on the validation set, it did slightly improve the performance on the test set.

Before deciding on scikit-learn's LinearSVC,

Dataset	F1	Error (SEM)
train	.7617	± .0032
validation	.7281	± .0085
test	.7368	± .0091

Table 2: F_1 scores by dataset. The reported F_1 score is the arithmetic mean of the F_1 scores for both classes.

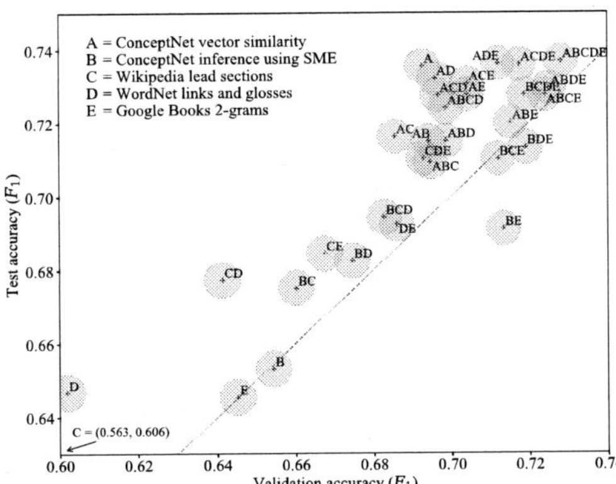

Figure 1: This ablation analysis shows the contributions of subsets of the five sources of features. Ellipses indicate standard error of the mean, assuming that the data is sampled from a larger, unseen set.

we experimented with a number of other classifiers. This included random forests, differentiable models made of multiple ReLU and sigmoid layers, and SVM with an RBF kernel or a polynomial kernel.

We also experimented with different parameters to LinearSVC, such as changing the default value of the penalty parameter C of the error term, changing the penalty from L_2 to L_1, solving the primal optimization problem instead of the dual problem, and changing the loss from squared hinge to hinge. These changes either led to lower performance or had no significant effect, so in the end we used LinearSVC with the default parameters for scikit-learn version 0.19.1.

5 Results

When trained on the training set, the classifier we describe achieved an F_1 score of 0.7617 on the training set, 0.7281 on the validation set, and 0.7368 on the test set. Table 2 shows these scores along with their standard error of the mean, supposing that these data sets were randomly sampled from larger sets.

5.1 Ablation Analysis

We performed an ablation analysis to see what the contribution of each of our five sources of features was. We evaluated classifiers that used all non-empty subsets of these sources. Figure 1 plots the results of these 31 classifiers when evaluated on the validation set and the test set.

It is likely that the classifier with all five sources (*ABCDE*) performed the best overall. It is in a statistical tie ($p > .05$) with *ABDE*, the classifier that omits Wikipedia as a source.

Most of the classifiers perfomed better on the test set than on the validation set, as shown by the dotted line. Some simple classifiers with very few features performed particularly well on the test set. One surprisingly high-performing classifier was *A* (ConceptNet vector similarity), which gets a test F_1 score of 0.7355 ± 0.0091. This is simple enough to be called a heuristic instead of a classifier, and we can express it in closed form. It is equivalent to this expression over ConceptNet Numberbatch embeddings:

$$\mathrm{sim}(term_1, att) - \mathrm{sim}(term_2, att) > 0.0961$$

where $\mathrm{sim}(a, b) = \sqrt{\max\left(\frac{a \cdot b}{||a|| \cdot ||b||}, 0\right)}$.

It is interesting to note that source *A* (ConceptNet vector similarity) appears to dominate source *B* (ConceptNet SME) on the test data. SME led to improvements on the validation set, but on the test set, any classifier containing *AB* performs equal to or worse than the same classifier with *B* removed. This may indicate that the SME features were the most prone to overfitting, or that the validation set generally required making more difficult distinctions than the test set.

6 Reproducing These Results

The code for our classifier is available on GitHub at `https://github.com/LuminosoInsight/semeval-discriminatt`, and its input data is downloadable from `https://zenodo.org/record/1183358`.

References

Antoine Bordes, Xavier Glorot, Jason Weston, and Yoshua Bengio. 2014. A semantic matching energy function for learning with multi-relational data. *Machine Learning*, 94(2):233–259.

Rong-En Fan, Kai-Wei Chang, Cho-Jui Hsieh, Xiang-Rui Wang, and Chih-Jen Lin. 2008. LIBLINEAR: A library for large linear classification. *Journal of Machine Learning Research*, 9(Aug):1871–1874.

Ivan Krasin, Tom Duerig, Neil Alldrin, Vittorio Ferrari, Sami Abu-El-Haija, Alina Kuznetsova, Hassan Rom, Jasper Uijlings, Stefan Popov, Andreas Veit, Serge Belongie, Victor Gomes, Abhinav Gupta, Chen Sun, Gal Chechik, David Cai, Zheyun Feng, Dhyanesh Narayanan, and Kevin Murphy. 2017. OpenImages: A public dataset for large-scale multi-label and multi-class image classification.

Yuri Lin, Jean-Baptiste Michel, Erez Lieberman Aiden, Jon Orwant, Will Brockman, and Slav Petrov. 2012. Syntactic annotations for the Google Books Ngram Corpus. In *Proceedings of the ACL 2012 system demonstrations*, pages 169–174. Association for Computational Linguistics.

George Miller, Christiane Fellbaum, Randee Tengi, P Wakefield, H Langone, and BR Haskell. 1998. *WordNet*. MIT Press Cambridge.

Denis Paperno, Alessandro Lenci, and Alicia Krebs. 2018. SemEval-2018 Task 10: Capturing discriminative attributes. In *Proceedings of the 12th International Workshop on Semantic Evaluation (SemEval-2018)*, New Orleans, LA, United States. Association for Computational Linguistics.

Greg Pass, Abdur Chowdhury, and Cayley Torgeson. 2006. A picture of search. In *Proceedings of the 1st International Conference on Scalable Information Systems*, InfoScale '06, New York, NY, USA. ACM.

Adam Paszke, Sam Gross, Soumith Chintala, Gregory Chanan, Edward Yang, Zachary DeVito, Zeming Lin, Alban Desmaison, Luca Antiga, and Adam Lerer. 2017. Automatic differentiation in pytorch.

Fabian Pedregosa, Gaël Varoquaux, Alexandre Gramfort, Vincent Michel, Bertrand Thirion, Olivier Grisel, Mathieu Blondel, Peter Prettenhofer, Ron Weiss, Vincent Dubourg, et al. 2011. Scikit-learn: Machine learning in Python. *Journal of machine learning research*, 12(Oct):2825–2830.

Robert Speer, Joshua Chin, and Catherine Havasi. 2017. ConceptNet 5.5: An open multilingual graph of general knowledge. In *AAAI*, San Francisco.

Robert Speer and Joanna Lowry-Duda. 2017. ConceptNet at SemEval-2017 task 2: Extending word embeddings with multilingual relational knowledge. In *Proceedings of the 11th International Workshop on Semantic Evaluation (SemEval-2017)*, pages 85–89, Vancouver, Canada. Association for Computational Linguistics.

Wikipedia. 2017. Wikipedia, the free encyclopedia — English data export. (A collaborative project with thousands of authors.) Retrieved from `https://dumps.wikimedia.org/enwiki/` on 2017-12-20.

BomJi at SemEval-2018 Task 10:
Combining Vector-, Pattern- and Graph-based Information to Identify Discriminative Attributes

Enrico Santus[1], Chris Biemann[2], Emmanuele Chersoni[3]

esantus@mit.edu,
biemann@informatik.uni-hamburg.de,
emmanuelechersoni@gmail.com

[1] Massachussetts Institute of Technology,
[2] Universität Hamburg,
[3] Aix-Marseille University

Abstract

This paper describes BomJi, a supervised system for capturing discriminative attributes in word pairs (e.g. *yellow* as discriminative for *banana* over *watermelon*). The system relies on an XGB classifier trained on carefully engineered graph-, pattern- and word embedding-based features. It participated in the SemEval-2018 Task 10 on Capturing Discriminative Attributes, achieving an F1 score of 0.73 and ranking 2nd out of 26 participant systems.

1 Introduction

The recent introduction of popular software packages for training *neural word embeddings* (Mikolov et al., 2013a,b; Levy and Goldberg, 2014) has led to an increase of the number of studies dedicated to lexical similarity and to remarkable performance improvements on related tasks (Baroni et al., 2014).

However, the validity of similarity estimation as the only benchmark for semantic representations has been questioned, for several reasons. One for all, most evaluation datasets provide human-elicited similarity scores, with the consequences that the ratings are subjective and the performance of some automated systems is already above the upper bound of the inter-annotator agreement (Batchkarov et al., 2016; Faruqui et al., 2016; Santus et al., 2016a).

Originally proposed as an alternative benchmark for Distributional Semantic Models (DSMs), the Discriminative Attributes task focuses instead on the extraction of *semantic differences* between lexical meanings (Krebs and Paperno, 2016): given two words and an *attribute* (i.e., a discrete semantic feature), a system has to predict whether the attribute describes a difference between the corresponding concepts or not (e.g. *wing* is an attribute of *plane*, but not of *helicopter*).

Since even related words may differ for some non-shared attributes (e.g. hypernyms and hyponyms), the ability of automatically recognize discriminative features would be an extremely useful addition for the creation of ontologies and other types of lexical resources and would make machine decisions interpretable, enabling human validation (Biemann et al., 2018). Moreover, one can think to applications to many other NLP domains, such as machine translation and dialogue systems (Krebs and Paperno, 2016).

In the present contribution, we describe the BomJi classification system, which we used for the identification of discriminative features between concept pairs. According to the official evaluation results provided by the organizers[1], our system ranked second out of 26 participants. Our score, $F1 = 0.73$ lags slightly behind the best score of 0.75. After the evaluation period, we run further experiments including all investigated features and found that the system can achieve up to 0.75 F1 score.

2 Capturing Discriminative Attributes

2.1 Task and Dataset Description

The task of capturing discriminative attributes between words can be described as a binary classification task, in which the system has to assign a positive label if the feature is discriminative for the first concept over the second one, and a negative label otherwise.

In the test data, the first two words correspond to the concepts being compared (they are called, respectively, the *pivot* and the *comparison* term) and the third word is the feature, which could describe a discriminative attribute or not (some examples are shown in Table 1). In the paper, we will refer

---

[1] https://competitions.codalab.org/competitions/17326#results

Proceedings of the 12th International Workshop on Semantic Evaluation (SemEval-2018), pages 990–994
New Orleans, Louisiana, June 5–6, 2018. ©2018 Association for Computational Linguistics

Pivot	Comparison	Feature	Label
belt	plate	buckles	1
orange	cherry	sections	1
razor	brush	mink	0
necklace	bracelet	clasp	0

Table 1: Examples of triples from the training dataset.

Dataset	Examples	Features	Split P-N
Training	17,782	1,292	37.06%-62.94%
Validation	2,722	576	50.1%-49.9%
Test	2,340	577	44.74%-55.26%

Table 2: Number of examples, distinctive features and Positive-Negative split for each dataset.

to the elements of the triples as $w1$, $w2$ and $feat$.

A training and validation set have been provided for system development (figures in Table 2).

2.2 Embeddings and Graphs

For the Discriminative Attributes task, we combined word embeddings, patterns and information extracted from a graph-based distributional model.

Concerning the word embeddings, we used the vectors produced by two popular frameworks for word embeddings: Word2Vec (Mikolov et al., 2013a,b) and GloVe (Pennington et al., 2014).[2] The Word2Vec Skip-Gram architecture is a single-layer neural network, based on the dot-product between word vectors, in which the vector representation is optimized to predict the context of a target word given the word itself. The context generally consists of a word window of a fixed width around the target. The other framework, GloVe, is similar to traditional count models based on matrix factorization (Turney and Pantel, 2010; Baroni et al., 2014), in the sense that vectors are trained on global word-word co-occurrence counts. In the case of GloVe, the training objective is to learn word vectors such that their dot product equals the logarithm of the probability of the word to co-occur (Pennington et al., 2014).

As for graph-based information, we used the Jo-BimText architecture introduced by Biemann and Riedl (2013). In JoBimText, lexical items are represented as the set of their p most salient contexts, where the contexts are words connected to the target by a given syntactic link or by a lexical pattern, and saliency is defined as an association measure

between target and context, such as Positive Local Mutual Information (Evert, 2004). Differently from vector models, similarity between words in JoBimText is simply based on the overlap count of their common contexts.

Regarding patterns, first we extracted sentences where words and their features co-occur from a web-scale sentence-based index of English web (Panchenko et al., 2018) and then we extracted the patterns connecting our target words.

2.3 Methodology

The predictions submitted for the evaluation of Task 10 were obtained with a system that consists of a classifier, the Extreme Gradient Boosting (or XGBoost, Chen and Guestrin (2016)), trained on vectors aggregating carefully engineered graph-, pattern- and word embedding features.

In this section, we provide an overview of each feature type, leaving the discussion of their contribution to Section 3. The total of 55,026 features we used can be divided into five major groups.

CO-OCCURRENCE. Thirteen features related to word and word-feature frequency were calculated on the basis of the information extracted from a corpus of $3.2B$ words, corresponding to about 20% of the Common Crawl. For each word-feature combination (i.e. $w1 - feat$ and $w2 - feat$), we calculated: i) the co-occurrence count; ii) word count; iii) feature count; iv) Positive Pointwise Mutual Information (PPMI (Church and Hanks, 1990)) between each word and the feature; v) Positive Local Mutual Information (PLMI (Evert, 2004)) between each word and the feature. Further, we added three features representing the subtractions between the values of i), iv) and v) for the two word-feature combinations.

JOBIMTEXT. Another set of twenty-four features comes directly from JoBimText. They were calculated after extracting information through the public accessible JoBimText API[3], which returns a JSON file containing - for every target - a sorted list of N features and their association scores (up to $N = 1,000$). As JoBimText distinguishes features according to their POS and dependency roles (i.e. features are in form WORD#POS#DEPENDENCY), a given $feat$ may appear multiple times in different POS-dependency combinations. However, we found that $feat$ rarely appears in the top N features

---

of $w1$ and $w2$, so we calculated our features not only for the given targets (i.e. w_x), but also for the first among their top 10 neighbors for which $feat$ was found (i.e. $top(neighbor(w_x) \ni feat, max = 10)$) and the first among the top 10 $feat$ neighbors for which the target was found (i.e. $top(neighbor(feat) \ni w_x, max = 10)$). This allowed us to check also whether the neighbors of the given words were associated with the candidate discriminative attributes or *vice versa*. The features are defined as follows (here they are described only with reference to the query on w_x, but this should be generalized to the other cases):

- *prediction by rank*: it is 1 if $feat$ is ranked higher for w_1 than for w_2, 0 otherwise;

- *prediction by score*: it is 1 if the total score between $w1 - feat$ is higher than for $w_2 - feat$, 0 otherwise;

- *total score*: sum of the scores of $w_1 - feat$ if prediction by score is 1, of $w_2 - feat$ otherwise;

- *top rank*: top rank of $feat$ for w_1 if prediction by score is 1, for w_2 otherwise;

- *bottom rank*: last rank of $feat$ for w_1 if prediction by score is 1, for w_2 otherwise;

- *number of occurrences*: count of how many times a feature appears among the features of w_1 if prediction by score is 1, otherwise the occurrences among the features w_2 are counted;

- *which neighbor?*: integer showing whether the query was performed on $w1/w2$ (in this case it would be initialized to 0), or on its neighbors (in this case it would be initialized with the rank of the first neighbor where $feat$ was found);

- *which feat neighbor?*: integer showing whether the query was performed on $w1/w2$ (in this case it would be initialized to 0) or on the $feat$ neighbors (in this case it would be initialized with the rank of the first $feat$ neighbor where $w1$ or $w2$ was found).

WORD EMBEDDING FEATURES. Mikolov et al. (2013a) showed how vector offsets encode semantic information. We decided to include five features computed from either the Word2Vec or the Glove vectors, in order to take advantage of the offset information.

They are computed, respectively, as: $cos((w1 - w2), feat)$, $cos((w1 - feat), (w2 - feat))$, $cos((w1 - feat), w2)$, $cos((w2 - feat), w1)$. Finally, also the cosine between the word vectors (i.e. $cos((w1, w2))$) has been included.

WORD EMBEDDING VECTORS. These features are the simple concatenation of the three vectors of $w1$, $w2$ and $feat$. Again, we have two versions of these features, one for Word2Vec and one for Glove.

PATTERNS. In order to characterize the relation between words and features, we used an index to extract patterns occurring between them, independently of the order in which they appeared, and limited the maximum number of results to 10,000 sentences.

The patterns consist of sequences of either lemmatized tokens, POS or dependency tags, which are used to abstract from the surface form, thereby increasing the recall. Since the number of extracted patterns was far too high, we decided to use only patterns with a frequency higher than 100, obtaining a set of 53,136 items, using the observed pattern frequency per word pair as a predictor.

3 Experiments

3.1 Choosing the Training Set

During the practice phase, we noticed that the training set and the validation set show very different distributions. Running 5-fold cross validation experiments on either dataset, we obtained very high scores (sometimes close to 0.95). However, such scores did not generalize to the other dataset, where they dropped to about 0.60.

This was only partially due to lexical memorization (some lexemes were present in multiple triples of the same dataset, cf. Levy et al. (2015); Santus et al. (2016b)). In fact, investigating the frequency of the words in the triples, we found that, on average, in our index, the first and the second words, $w1$ and $w2$, were about four times more frequent in the validation than in the training set (respectively $4.7M$ and $5.4M$ versus $0.9M$ and $1M$); similarly, the third word (i.e. $feat$) was almost twice more frequent in the validation than in the training set (i.e. $3.9M$ versus $2.9M$). When the test set was made available, we could verify that its frequency distribution resembled the one in the validation set, with the first and second words respectively at $3.3M$ and $2M$, and the third at about $4.5M$ occurrences.

Given these differences, we have chosen to train our system only on the validation set, tuning the hyper-parameters by means of 5-fold cross validation. Because of its small size, we decided to train our second submission on a derived training set (henceforth New Validation), consisting of the 2,722 triples from the validation set plus 2,278 triples randomly extracted from the training, for a

| | Feature Type | # Feat | Training/Test | | Validation/Test | | New Validation/Test | |
| | | | 17547 vs. 2340 | | 2722 vs 2340 | | 5000 vs 2340 | |
			F1	F1++	F1	F1++	F1	F1++
1	Co-occurrence	13	0.68	0.68	0.72	0.72	0.72	0.72
2	W2V Features	5	0.55	NA	0.66	NA	0.63	NA
3	W2V + Vectors	905	0.57	0.68 (1 & 3)	0.67	0.75 (1 & 3)	0.66	0.73 (1 & 3)
4	Glove Features	5	0.61	NA	0.66	NA	0.67	NA
5	Glove + Vectors	905	0.62	0.66 (1 & 5)	0.68	0.74 (1 & 5)	0.68	0.73 (1 & 5)
6	JoBim Features	24	0.53	0.68 (1 & 6) 0.67 (1, 3 & 6) 0.66 (1, 5 & 6)	0.62	0.74 (1 & 6) **0.75 (1, 3 & 6)** ***0.74 (1, 5 & 6)***	0.62	0.74 (1 & 6) **0.75 (1, 3 & 6)** ***0.73 (1, 5 & 6)***
7	Patterns	53176	0.56	0.67 (1, 3, 6 & 7) 0.67 (1, 5, 6 & 7) 0.68 (1, 3, 5, 6 & 7)	0.52	**0.75 (1, 3, 6 & 7)** 0.74 (1, 5, 6 & 7) 0.74 (1, 3, 5, 6 & 7)	0.51	0.71 (1, 3, 6 & 7) 0.69 (1, 5, 6 & 7) 0.69 (1, 3, 5, 6 & 7)

Table 3: Results both in absolute (F1) and in incremental terms (F1++: in brackets the features used to obtain the score) on the test set, organized by training set. In bold, we report the best results. In bold-italics, we report the submitted systems.

total of 5,000 samples. The use of different training data was the only difference between the two submissions.

3.2 Model Selection

During the practice phase, we performed experiments with several classifiers, including K-Neighbors (with $K = 3$), Decision Tree (with $max\_depth = 5$), Random Forest (with $max\_depth = 5$, $n\_estimators = 10$ and $max\_features = 1$), Multilayer Perceptron (with $alpha = 1$), AdaBoost and XGB (the latter two with default settings).

Before running the classifiers, we also used Linear Support Vector Classification (SVC) with $penalty =' l1'$ and we tested several values of C (i.e. 0.05, 0.1, 0.25, 0.5, 1) for feature selection.

In almost all settings we found that the best performing classifiers were the Random Forest, the Multilayer Perceptron and, above all others, XGB. With respect to the value of C for the feature selection, instead, we noticed that it varied in relation to the feature types, with minor influence on the performance of XGB (+/-2%). In the final submission, therefore, we opted for removing this step from the pipeline and for keeping the full vector.

Concerning feature selection, we found that the pattern features had a neutral effect on the performance during cross validation. Similarly we noticed that Glove and Word2Vec performed comparably. Thus, we opted for submitting the output of the systems without using the pattern features and only Glove features (Word2Vec had lower coverage on the dataset). As it can be noticed in Table 3, however, this decision has slightly lowered the performance of our system in the competition.

3.3 Feature Contribution

In order to measure the contribution of the features, we re-ran the experiments over the test set, after training our model on the three available sets: training, validation and new validation sets.

Results are reported in Table 3, in which it is easy to notice a few things: the performance is strongly related to the choice of the training set, with Validation being better that New Validation, which is in turn better than the original Training set; the thirteen co-occurrence features are those that provide the major contribution to the performance, reaching a F1 score of 0.72. Further useful features are the word embedding vectors (900 features), the word embedding features (5 features) and, to some extent, the information from JoBim-Text. Pattern-based features perform the worst, almost on par with random guessing.

The submitted systems do not correspond to the systems obtaining the best performance in post-evaluation experiments (see the bold and bold-italics scores in Table 3); this was due to the use of Glove instead of Word2Vec in our submitted systems, because none of the embedding models had an edge over the other in the validation process.

4 Conclusions

In this paper we have presented BomJi, a supervised system for capturing discriminative attributes in word pairs (e.g. *yellow* as discriminative for *banana* over *watermelon*). BomJi relies on an XGB classifier trained on carefully engineered graph-, pattern- and word embedding-based features. In the paper we have reported the contribution for each features, discussing the model selection and showing that a major factor affecting the performance was the choice of the training data.

In the official Task 10 evaluation, our submitted systems achieved an F1 score of 0.73, ranking 2nd out of 26 participant systems.

References

Marco Baroni, Georgiana Dinu, and Germán Kruszewski. 2014. Don't Count, Predict! A Systematic Comparison of Context-Counting vs. Context-Predicting Semantic Vectors. In *Proceedings of ACL*, pages 238–247.

Miroslav Batchkarov, Thomas Kober, Jeremy Reffin, Julie Weeds, and David Weir. 2016. A Critique of Word Similarity as a Method for Evaluating Distributional Semantic Models. In *Proceedings of the 1st Workshop on Evaluating Vector-Space Representations for NLP*, pages 7–12.

Chris Biemann, Stefano Faralli, Alexander Panchenko, and Simone Paolo Ponzetto. 2018. A Framework for Enriching Lexical Semantic Resources with Distributional Semantics. *Natural Language Engineering*, 24(2):265–312.

Chris Biemann and Martin Riedl. 2013. Text: Now in 2D! A Framework for Lexical Expansion with Contextual Similarity. *Journal of Language Modeling*, 1(1):55–95.

Tianqi Chen and Carlos Guestrin. 2016. XGBoost: A Scalable Tree Boosting System. In *Proceedings of the 22nd ACM Sigkdd International Conference on Knowledge Discovery and Data Mining*, pages 785–794.

Kenneth W. Church and Patrick Hanks. 1990. Word Association Norms, Mutual Information, and Lexicography. *Computational Linguistics*, 16(1):22–29.

Stefan Evert. 2004. *The Statistics of Word Cooccurrences: Word Pairs and Collocations*. Ph.D. thesis.

Manaal Faruqui, Yulia Tsvetkov, Pushpendre Rastogi, and Chris Dyer. 2016. Problems With Evaluation of Word Embeddings Using Word Similarity Tasks. In *Proceedings of the 1st Workshop on Evaluating Vector-Space Representations for NLP*, pages 30–35.

Alicia Krebs and Denis Paperno. 2016. Capturing Discriminative Attributes in a Distributional Space: Task Proposal. In *Proceedings of the 1st Workshop on Evaluating Vector-Space Representations for NLP*, pages 51–54.

Omer Levy and Yoav Goldberg. 2014. Neural Word Embedding as Implicit Matrix Factorization. In *Advances in Neural Information Processing Systems 27*, pages 2177–2185.

Omer Levy, Steffen Remus, Chris Biemann, and Ido Dagan. 2015. Do Supervised Distributional Methods Really Learn Lexical Inference Relations? In *Proceedings of NAACL-HLT*, pages 970–976.

Tomas Mikolov, Kai Chen, Greg Corrado, and Jeffrey Dean. 2013a. Efficient Estimation of Word Representations in Vector Space. *arXiv preprint arXiv:1301.3781*.

Tomas Mikolov, Ilya Sutskever, Kai Chen, Greg Corrado, and Jeffrey Dean. 2013b. Distributed Representations of Words and Phrases and Their Compositionality. In *Proceedings of the 26th International Conference on Neural Information Processing Systems - Volume 2*, NIPS, pages 3111–3119.

Alexander Panchenko, Eugen Ruppert, Stefano Faralli, Simone Paolo Ponzetto, and Chris Biemann. 2018. Building a Web-Scale Dependency-Parsed Corpus from Common Crawl. In *Proceedings of LREC*.

Jeffrey Pennington, Richard Socher, and Christopher Manning. 2014. Glove: Global vectors for word representation. In *Proceedings of EMNLP*, pages 1532–1543.

Enrico Santus, Emmanuele Chersoni, Alessandro Lenci, Chu-Ren Huang, and Philippe Blache. 2016a. Testing APSyn Against Vector Cosine on Similarity Estimation. In *Proceedings of PACLIC*, pages 229–238.

Enrico Santus, Alessandro Lenci, Tin-Shing Chiu, Qin Lu, and Chu-Ren Huang. 2016b. Nine Features in a Random Forest to Learn Taxonomical Semantic Relations. In *Proceedings of LREC*.

Peter D. Turney and Patrick Pantel. 2010. From Frequency to Meaning: Vector Space Models of Semantics. *Journal of Artificial Intelligence Research*, 37:141–188.

Igevorse at SemEval-2018 Task 10: Exploring an Impact of Word Embeddings Concatenation for Capturing Discriminative Attributes

Maxim Grishin

Innopois University

Innopolis, Russia

m.grishin@innopolis.ru

igevorse@gmail.com

Abstract

Semantic differences extraction is a challenging problem in Natural Language Processing and its solution is necessary for a realistic semantic representation as similarity information is not sufficient to capture individual aspects of meaning. This paper presents a comparison of several approaches for capturing discriminative attributes and considers an impact of concatenation of several word embeddings of different nature on the classification performance. A similarity-based method is proposed and compared with machine learning approaches. It is shown that this method outperforms others on all the considered word vector models and there is a performance increase when concatenated datasets are used.

1 Introduction

Detecting semantic similarity is done well by state-of-the-art models. However, if the model is only good at similarity detection, it would have a limited practical usage (Krebs et al., 2018), since the task of *understanding* the semantics of words cannot be done without capturing semantic differences.

Semantic difference is a ternary relation between two concepts $(apple, banana)$ and a discriminative feature (red) that characterizes the first concept but not the other. Semantic difference detection is a binary classification task: given a triple $(apple, banana, red)$, the task is to determine whether it exemplifies a semantic difference or not (Krebs et al., 2018). In this paper two concepts and a discriminative attribute $attr$ are represented as $(word_1, word_2, attr)$.

This research was done during the participation in "Capturing Discriminative Attributes" task of SemEval 2018 competition.

The paper is organized as follows. Section 2 describes the methods used. Section 3 shows the results and analyzes them. Section 4 mentions future directions. Section 5 concludes the paper.

2 Methods

There were several approaches considered: classical machine learning algorithms and a similarity-based model.

2.1 Data Preparation

Dataset is provided by SemEval 2018 challenge organizers.

- The train set consists of 17501 automatically generated samples of the form $(word_1, word_2, attr, y)$, where y is a binary target variable indicating whether $attr$ is a discriminative attribute for $word_1$ and $word_2$. Classes are imbalanced: there are 63.83% samples for class 0 (not a discriminative attribute) and 36.16% for class 1 (is a discriminative attribute).

- The validation set contains 2722 manually curated samples of the same form. Classes are almost balanced: 50.1% of samples have class 0, 49.9% - class 1.

- There are 2340 samples in the test set, 55.3% for class 0, 44.7% for class 1.

Each triple $(word_1, word_2, attr)$ was converted to a numeric vector using pre-trained word embeddings. These vectors form a vector space, such that words that share common contexts in the corpus are located in close proximity to one another in space.

Three word embedding models were used:

1. Google News (Mihltz, 2017) corpus word vector model (3 million 300-dimension English word vectors). The disadvantage of this

Proceedings of the 12th International Workshop on Semantic Evaluation (SemEval-2018), pages 995–998

New Orleans, Louisiana, June 5–6, 2018. ©2018 Association for Computational Linguistics

model is that despite having a lot of words, it includes misspellings and multiple cases of the same word (McCormick, 2017). Its vocabulary does not contain all words from the dataset, so 45 samples (1.27%) are missing.

2. Wikipedia 2014 + Gigaword 5 (Pennington et al., 2014) dataset has 400 thousand 300-dimension word vectors. It contains almost all words from the dataset: only 4 samples (0.11 %) are missing.

3. Concatenated word embeddings of different nature, i.e. collected on different corporas using different methods. It consists of concatenated word vectors from both Google News and Wikipedia models. Thus, each word is represented as a 600-dimensional vector.

The problem of missing words was solved by replacing them with another spelling or a synonym. For each triple $(word_1, word_2, attr)$ corresponding word vectors were concatenated, so each triple is converted to a 900-dimensional vector when using Google News or Wikipedia word vectors, and 1800-dimensional for concatenated word embeddings.

2.2 Machine Learning Approaches

There were several machine learning classification approaches chosen for comparison: logistic regression, stochastic gradient descent (SGD) classifier, k-nearest neighbors classifier and artificial neural network.

The best parameters that maximize F_1 score on the validation set:

- **Logistic regression** with L_2 regularization with regularization strength set to 10.

- **Stochastic gradient descent classifier** with perceptron loss and regularization term set to 1e-05.

- **K-nearest neighbors** with k = 1 using Manhattan distance metric and weighting points by the inverse of their distance.

- The multilayer perceptron **neural network** model was built using Keras with TensorFlow as a backend. Structure of this network is described in Table 1.

Layer	# of inputs	Activation function
Input	900	-
Dense	128	tanh
Dense	64	relu
Dense	1	sigmoid

Table 1: Structure of the neural network.

2.3 Similarity-based Approach

Another approach is to derive an interpretable algorithm based on knowledge about word semantics. The intention is to use word similarities for distinguishing discriminative attributes while keeping the model as simple as possible. Cosine similarity between words a and b is represented as the cosine between corresponding word vectors A and B.

$$sim(a, b) = cos(A, B) = \frac{A \cdot B}{\|A\|\|B\|}.$$

For each given triple $(word_1, word_2, attr)$ similarities of $attr$ with $word_1$ and $attr$ with $word_2$ are computed. Then obtained similarities are compared using a threshold t. If the gap between them is big enough, i.e.

$$sim(word_1, attr) > sim(word_2, attr) + t,$$

$attr$ is treated as a discriminative attribute of $word_1$. It means that the $attr$ word vector is much closer to $word_1$ than to $word_2$ in vector space. Thus, this model has only one tunable hyperparameter: t. Dependency of F_1 score on the threshold is shown in Figure 1.

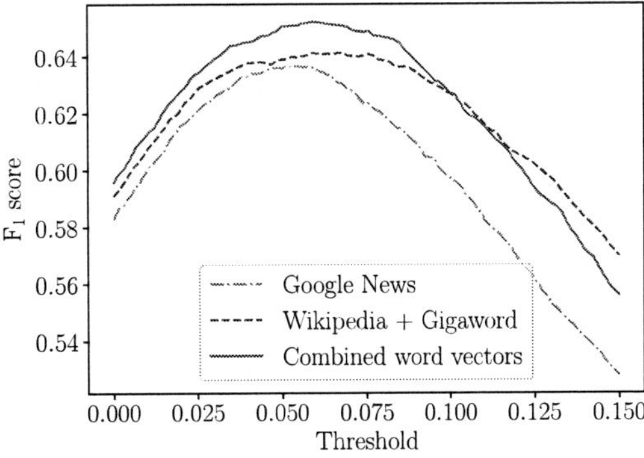

Figure 1: Dependency of F_1 score on the threshold in similarity-based model.

Embeddings Model	Google News	Wikipedia	Concatenated
K-nearest neighbors	0.4778	**0.4832**	0.4809
SGD classifier	**0.5211**	0.5036	0.5169
Logistic regression	0.4843	0.5036	**0.5120**
Neural network	0.5169	**0.5625**	0.5440
Similarity-based	0.6066	0.6126	**0.6131**

Table 2: Experimental results on the validation set (F_1 score).

3 Results and Discussions

3.1 Experimental Results

Models are evaluated on F_1 measure.

Figure 1 shows that the behavior of the similarity-based model is highly dependent on the selected word vectors model. Thresholds, learned from the train set for Google News, Wikipedia and concatenated word vectors are 0.053030, 0.066667 and 0.060606 correspondingly.

Experimental results on the validation set are presented in Table 2. K-nearest neighbors showed the worst F_1 score, while neural network is the best among machine learning methods. The proposed similarity-based method outperforms all other models on all considered word embeddings.

Word embeddings with the highest F_1 score on the validation set were chosen for the final comparison: Google News for SGD classifier, Wikipedia for k-nearest neighbors and neural network, concatenated embeddings for logistic regression and similarity-based model. The results on the test set are presented in Table 3. K-nearest neighbors has the smallest F_1 score. In contrast with the performance on the validation set, the result of neural network is noticeably worse, which means that overfitting took place. Logistic regression performed better than SGD classifier, while similarity-based method showed the highest score.

Model	Best F_1 score
K-nearest neighbors	0.502
SGD classifier	0.515
Logistic regression	0.527
Neural network	0.503
Similarity-based	**0.646**

Table 3: Experimental results on the test set.

3.2 Error Analysis

In this section error analysis of similarity-based model is provided. During the evaluation on the test set 65.5% of samples were classified correctly, while 34.5% were not. Predicted classes are imbalanced: 1436 (61.4%) samples were classified as 0 and 904 (38.6%) samples as 1.

Considering misclassified samples, 332 of them were assigned class 1 while it should have been 0, whereas 475 of them got label 0, when it should have got 1. As we can see, the model is more likely to consider attributes as non-discriminative.

108 distinct attributes (130 samples) were misclassified completely. 270 distinct attributes (480 samples) were classified 100% correctly. 70 attributes (180 samples) were classified 50% correctly.

Attributes could be divided in several categories. For example, there are attributes representing colors: 'black', 'brown', 'red', 'blue' and 'yellow'. It worth mentioning that 43.36% of samples with color attributes were misclassified, which is more than 34.5% of misclassified samples for the whole test set.

As can be seen from Table 4, other categories of attributes have 33.4% of misclassified samples.

Attribute	Misclassified	Total occurences
Color	111 (43.36%)	256
Other	696 (33.4%)	2084
Total	807 (34.5%)	2340

Table 4: Error analysis of attribute categories.

4 Future Work

It was shown that there is a performance increase of the similarity-based model when concatenated word vectors are used. Training a Word2Vec model specifically for the task instead of using pre-trained models can solve the mentioned prob-

lem of missing words and multiple cases of the
same word in word embeddings.

According to SemEval Task 10 organizers,
training set contains noisy data, which was not
verified by humans. Another potential improvement is training models only on validation dataset,
since it was created manually and should not have
noise.

It was discovered that samples with color attributes have higher misclassification rate than
other samples. There are proposed solutions
for learning discriminative properties of images
(Lazaridou et al., 2016), which could be combined
with a text-based approach to derive a multimodal
classifier.

It also worth analyzing other categories of attributes and their misclassification rate.

5 Conclusion

This paper presents several approaches for capturing discriminative attributes. The main contribution is the proposed similarity-based method,
which is interpretable and takes into account the
semantic similarity of words. This method is compared with machine learning methods, such as Logistic regression, SGD classifier, KNN and Multi-
layer perceptron neural network. Experiments on
three pre-trained word vector models show that
similarity-based method outperforms others. It
was discovered that concatenation of word embeddings of different nature leads to a quality improvement for several methods.

References

Alicia Krebs, Alessandro Lenci, and Denis Paperno.
2018. Semeval-2018 task 10: Capturing discriminative attributes. In *Proceedings of the 12th international workshop on semantic evaluation (SemEval
2018)*.

Angeliki Lazaridou, Nghia The Pham, and Marco Baroni. 2016. The red one!: On learning to refer
to things based on their discriminative properties.
CoRR, abs/1603.02618.

Chris McCormick. 2017. Google's pre-trained
word2vec model in Matlab. https://github.com/
chrisjmccormick/word2vec_matlab. [Online; accessed 15-April-2018].

Mrton Mihltz. 2017. Pre-trained Word2vec Google
News corpus. https://github.com/mmihaltz/
word2vec-GoogleNews-vectors. [Online; accessed
15-April-2018].

Jeffrey Pennington, Richard Socher, and Christopher D
Manning. 2014. GloVe: Global Vectors for Word
Representation. In *Empirical Methods in Natural
Language Processing (EMNLP)*, pages 1532–1543.

ECNU at SemEval-2018 Task 10: Evaluating Simple but Effective Features on Machine Learning Methods for Semantic Difference Detection

Yunxiao Zhou[1], Man Lan[1,2*] ,Yuanbin Wu[1,2]
[1]Department of Computer Science and Technology,
East China Normal University, Shanghai, P.R.China
[2]Shanghai Key Laboratory of Multidimensional Information Processing
51164500061@stu.ecnu.edu.cn, {mlan, ybwu}@cs.ecnu.edu.cn

Abstract

This paper describes the system we submitted to Task 10 (Capturing Discriminative Attributes) in SemEval 2018. Given a triple (*word₁, word₂, attribute*), this task is to predict whether it exemplifies a semantic difference or not. We design and investigate several word embedding features, PMI features and WordNet features together with supervised machine learning methods to address this task. Officially released results show that our system ranks above average.

1 Introduction

The Capturing Discriminative Attributes task (Paperno et al., 2018) in SemEval 2018 is to provide a standard testbed for semantic difference detection, which will benefit many other applications in Natural Language Processing (NLP), such as automatized lexicography and machine translation (Krebs and Paperno, 2016). The goal of this task is to predict whether a word is a discriminative attribute between two concepts. Specifically, given two concepts and an attribute, the task is to predict whether the first concept has this attribute but the second concept does not. For example, given the concepts *apple* and *pineapple*, participants are required to predict whether the attribute *seeds* characterizes the first concept but not the other. In other words, semantic difference detection is a binary classification task: given a triple (*apple, pineapple, seeds*), the task is to determine whether it exemplifies a semantic difference or not, i.e., *positive* or *negative*. Table 1 shows more data examples.

If $word_1$ has a specific attribute but $word_2$ does not, then the correlation of attribute and $word_1$ should be higher than that of attribute and $word_2$. The semantic similarity is in the same way. In view of the above considerations, to address this task, we explore supervised machine learn-

word₁	word₂	attribute	label
apple	pineapple	seeds	positive
candle	chandelier	melts	positive
apple	coconut	brine	negative
apple	cucumber	seeds	negative

Table 1: Examples from the training data.

ing methods which use PMI features and WordNet features. In recent years, more and more studies have focused on word embeddings as an alternative to traditional hand-crafted features (Pennington et al., 2014; Tang et al., 2014). Therefore we use word embeddings to obtain the semantic similarity as word embedding features. Besides, we perform a series of experiments to explore the effectiveness of feature types and supervised machine learning algorithms.

2 System Description

To perform semantic difference detection of given triples, we adopt supervised learning algorithms with several features that represent semantic similarity and correlation. In the next paragraphs, we will introduce feature engineering and learning algorithms.

2.1 Feature Engineering

In this task, we design three types of features: WordNet features, PMI features and word embedding features.

2.1.1 WordNet Features

WordNet (Miller et al., 1990) is an on-line lexical reference system, which is organized by semantic properties of words. Therefore, the WordNet features are designed to utilize WordNet to obtain the semantic information.

Each word may have a number of different semantics, corresponding to different senses in the

Proceedings of the 12th International Workshop on Semantic Evaluation (SemEval-2018), pages 999–1002
New Orleans, Louisiana, June 5–6, 2018. ©2018 Association for Computational Linguistics

WordNet. And the WordNet provides the definitions of the senses for each word. If a word is an attribute of the target word, the attribute word may appear in the sense definition of the target word. For example, a semantic definition of *"snow"* is *"white crystals of frozen water"* and *"white"* is the attribute of *"snow"* which appears in the above definition. Therefore, we design the following features to record the semantic information. Given the triple ($word_1$, $word_2$, *attribute*), we first load all senses definitions of $word_1$, $word_2$ and *attribute*. Then we implement four types of binary features: (1) whether *attribute* appears in the senses definitions of $word_1$, (2) whether *attribute* appears in the senses definitions of $word_2$, (3) whether $word_1$ appears in the senses definitions of *attribute* and (4) whether $word_2$ appears in the senses definitions of *attribute*. As a result, we get four features.

2.1.2 PMI Features

Pointwise mutual information (PMI) (Church and Hanks, 1990) is a measure of association between two things used in information theory and statistics. And in NLP, this metric can be used to measure the correlation between two words. The higher the PMI, the stronger the correlation between the two words. So we obtain the PMI features of the given triple ($word_1$, $word_2$, *attribute*). We record the PMI value of $word_1$ and *attribute* as well as the PMI value of $word_2$ and *attribute* as PMI features. The PMI values we used are calculated using Wikimedia dumps[1] and directly obtained from SEMILAR (Rus et al., 2013). As a result, we get four PMI features.

2.1.3 Word Embedding Features

Word embedding is a continuous-valued vector representation for each word, which usually carries syntactic and semantic information. In this work, we employ two types of word embeddings which are pre-trained word vectors downloaded from Internet with dimensionality of 300: *GoogleW2V* (Mikolov et al., 2013) and *GloVe* (Pennington et al., 2014). The former is pre-trained on News domain, available in Google[2]. And the latter is pre-trained on tweets, available in GloVe[3].

- **WE_similarity:** Given the triple ($word_1$,

$word_2$, *attribute*), if *attribute* characterizes $word_1$ rather than $word_2$, the semantic similarity score of *attribute* and $word_1$ should be higher than that of *attribute* and $word_2$. After acquiring the vectors of three words in the triple, we calculate the similarity scores of *attribute* and $word_1$ as well as *attribute* and $word_2$ using *cosine similarity* and *pearson coefficient*. Finally, we got four word embedding similarity features.

- **WE_operation:** In addition to the above similarity functions, we also explore two different ways of interaction between word vectors in order to capture the semantic information as much as possible. The operations between three vectors include *concatenation* and *subtraction*. Specifically, given the vectors V_1, V_2 and V_a of the triple ($word_1$, $word_2$, *attribute*), the concatenation operation is to concatenate three vectors as $[V_1 \oplus V_2 \oplus V_a]$, and the subtraction operation is the element-wise subtraction of *attribute* from $word_1$ and $word_2$ respectively, i.e., $[V_1 - V_a]$ and $[V_2 - V_a]$. Since we employ two types of word embeddings, finally, we get $3,000$ dimensional vectors as word embedding operation features.

2.2 Learning Algorithm

We grant this task as a binary classification task and explore six supervised machine learning algorithms: Logistic Regression (LR) and Support Vector Machine (SVM) both implemented in Liblinear toolkit (Fan et al., 2008), Stochastic Gradient Descent (SGD), RandomForest and AdaBoost all implemented in scikit-learn tools (Pedregosa et al., 2011), and XGBoost[4] provided in (Chen and Guestrin, 2016). All these algorithms are used with default parameters.

3 Experiments

3.1 Datasets

Table 2 shows the statistics and distributions of training, development, test data sets of this task provided by task organizers.

3.2 Evaluation Metric

To evaluate the system performance, the official evaluation criterion is *macro-averaged F1-score*,

---

[1] https://dumps.wikimedia.org/enwiki/20170724/
[2] https://code.google.com/archive/p/word2vec
[3] http://nlp.stanford.edu/projects/glove

[4] https://github.com/dmlc/xgboost

Dataset	Positive	Negative	Total
train	6,330 (36%)	11,171 (64%)	17,501
dev	1,364 (50%)	1,358 (50%)	2,722
test	1,293 (55%)	1,047 (45%)	2,340

Table 2: The statistics of data sets in training, development and test data. The numbers in brackets are the percentages of different classes in each data set.

which is calculated among two classes (positive and negative) as follows:

$$F_{macro} = \frac{F_{Pos} + F_{Neg}}{2}$$

3.3 Experiments on Training Data

Firstly, in order to explore the effectiveness of each feature type, we perform a series of experiments. Table 3 lists the comparison of different contributions made by different features on development data with *Logistic Regression* algorithm. We observe the following findings.

(1) The simple PMI features and word embedding similarity features are effective for semantic difference detection and it shows the effectiveness of semantic similarity and correlation for semantic difference detection.

(2) The combination of the first three features not only achieves the best performance for the overall classification but also for each class. These three types of features make contributions to semantic difference detection task. Therefore we use these features in following experiments.

(3) The result of merging the *WE_operation* features is not as good as we expected and the possible reason is that the dimensionality of *WE_operation* features is quite huger than the other three features($3, 000$ Vs. 16), which dominates the performance of classification rather than other low dimension features. And the operations of word vectors are too simple to detect the semantic difference.

(4) The WordNet features are not as effective as expected, and the reason maybe that in many cases the attribute words do not appear in the sense definitions of concepts, so we can not get nonzero features.

Secondly, we also explore the performance of different supervised machine learning algorithms. Table 4 lists the comparison of different learning algorithms with *WordNet*, *PMI* and *WE_similarity* features. We find:

Features	F_{Pos}	F_{Neg}	F_{macro}
WordNet	0.683	0.237	0.459
.+PMI	0.653	0.598	0.625 (+0.166)
.+WE_similarity	**0.684**	**0.64**	**0.662** (+0.037)
.+WE_operation	0.561	0.616	0.588 (-0.074)

Table 3: Performance of different features on development data in terms of F1-score. ".+" means to add current features to the previous feature set. The numbers in the brackets are the performance increments compared with the previous results.

(1) LR and SVM achive better results than the other supervised machine learning algorithms and Logistic Regression algorithm achieves the best performance when considering single classification algorithm.

(2) The ensemble of the top 3 machine learning algorithms (LR + SVM + XGBoost) achives higher performance than any single learning algorithm, i.e., 0.663.

Algorithms	F_{Pos}	F_{Neg}	F_{macro}
LR	**0.684**	0.64	0.662
SVM	0.681	0.64	0.661
XGBoost	0.598	0.613	0.606
SGD	0.623	0.559	0.591
AdaBoost	0.631	0.551	0.591
RandomForest	0.565	0.607	0.586
Ensemble	0.683	**0.643**	**0.663**

Table 4: Performance of different learning algorithms on development data in terms of F1-score.

Based on the above results, the system configuration of our final submission is ensemble of LR, SVM and XGBoost algorithms with WordNet, PMI and WE_similarity features. The models are trained on both training and development data sets.

3.4 Results on Test Data

Table 5 shows the results of our system and the top-ranked systems provided by organizers for this semantic difference detection task. Compared with the top ranked systems, there is much room for improvement in our work. There are several possible reasons for this performance lag. First, the features we used are simple. We only record some semantic similarity information and correlations between words. More complex interactions of word vectors could be tried. Second, we only extract features from three words that need to be classified and have not used some extended resources like the sentences returned from search engines when retrieving these words.

Team ID	F_{macro}
ECNU	0.67 (8)
SUNNYNLP	0.75 (1)
BomJi	0.73 (2)
NTU NLP Lab	0.73 (2)

Table 5: Performance of our system and the top-ranked systems. The numbers in the brackets are the official rankings.

4 Conclusion

In this paper, we extract WordNet features, PMI features and word embedding features from triples and adopt supervised machine learning algorithms to perform semantic difference detection. The system performance ranks above average. In future work, we consider to try more complex interactions of word vectors and use more web resources to capture semantic information.

Acknowledgements

This work is is supported by the Science and Technology Commission of Shanghai Municipality Grant (No. 15ZR1410700) and the open project of Shanghai Key Laboratory of Trustworthy Computing (No.07dz22304201604).

References

Tianqi Chen and Carlos Guestrin. 2016. XGBoost: A scalable tree boosting system. In *Proceedings of the 22nd acm sigkdd international conference on knowledge discovery and data mining*, pages 785–794. ACM.

Kenneth Ward Church and Patrick Hanks. 1990. Word association norms, mutual information, and lexicography. *Computational linguistics*, 16(1):22–29.

Rong-En Fan, Kai-Wei Chang, Cho-Jui Hsieh, Xiang-Rui Wang, and Chih-Jen Lin. 2008. Liblinear: A library for large linear classification. *Journal of machine learning research*, 9(Aug):1871–1874.

Alicia Krebs and Denis Paperno. 2016. Capturing discriminative attributes in a distributional space: Task proposal. In *Proceedings of the 1st Workshop on Evaluating Vector-Space Representations for NLP*, pages 51–54.

Tomas Mikolov, Ilya Sutskever, Kai Chen, Greg S Corrado, and Jeff Dean. 2013. Distributed representations of words and phrases and their compositionality. In *Advances in neural information processing systems*, pages 3111–3119.

George A Miller, Richard Beckwith, Christiane Fellbaum, Derek Gross, and Katherine J Miller. 1990. Introduction to WordNet: An on-line lexical database. *International journal of lexicography*, 3(4):235–244.

Denis Paperno, Alessandro Lenci, and Alicia Krebs. 2018. Semeval-2018 Task 10: Capturing discriminative attributes. In *Proceedings of International Workshop on Semantic Evaluation (SemEval-2018)*, New Orleans, LA, USA.

Fabian Pedregosa, Gaël Varoquaux, Alexandre Gramfort, Vincent Michel, Bertrand Thirion, Olivier Grisel, Mathieu Blondel, Peter Prettenhofer, Ron Weiss, Vincent Dubourg, et al. 2011. Scikit-learn: Machine learning in python. *Journal of machine learning research*, 12(Oct):2825–2830.

Jeffrey Pennington, Richard Socher, and Christopher Manning. 2014. GloVe: Global vectors for word representation. In *Proceedings of the 2014 conference on empirical methods in natural language processing (EMNLP)*, pages 1532–1543.

Vasile Rus, Mihai Lintean, Rajendra Banjade, Nobal Niraula, and Dan Stefanescu. 2013. Semilar: The semantic similarity toolkit. In *Proceedings of the 51st Annual Meeting of the Association for Computational Linguistics: System Demonstrations*, pages 163–168.

Duyu Tang, Furu Wei, Nan Yang, Ming Zhou, Ting Liu, and Bing Qin. 2014. Learning sentiment-specific word embedding for twitter sentiment classification. In *Proceedings of the 52nd Annual Meeting of the Association for Computational Linguistics (Volume 1: Long Papers)*, volume 1, pages 1555–1565.

AmritaNLP at SemEval-2018 Task 10: Capturing discriminative attributes using convolution neural network over global vector representation.

Vivek Vinayan, Anand Kumar M, Soman K P
Center for Computational Engineering and Networking (CEN)
Amrita School of Engineering, Coimbatore
Amrita Vishwa Vidyapeetham, India
`cb.en.p2cen16018@cb.students.amrita.edu,`
`m_anandkumar@cb.amrita.edu`

Abstract

The "Capturing Discriminative Attributes" sharedtask is the tenth task, conjoint with SemEval2018. The task is to predict if a word can capture distinguishing attributes of one word from another. We use GloVe word embedding, pre-trained on openly sourced corpus for this task. A base representation is initially established over varied dimensions. These representations are evaluated based on validation scores over two models, first on an SVM based classifier and second on a one dimension CNN model. The scores are used to further develop the representation with vector combinations, by considering various distance measures. These measures correspond to offset vectors which are concatenated as features, mainly to improve upon the F1score, with the best accuracy. The features are then further tuned on the validation scores, to achieve highest F1score. Our evaluation narrowed down to two representations, classified on CNN models, having a total dimension length of 1204 & 1203 for the final submissions. Of the two, the latter feature representation delivered our best F1score of 0.658024 (as per result[1].)

1 Introduction

As famously quoted by firth "You shall know a word by the company it keeps" that is, the semantic information embedded in a representation can only be described by the words surrounding it. This can only get you somewhere when, company itself is unambiguous and a representation goes through capturing "hypothetically" every sense of the word over a corpus. The capturing discriminative attributes sharedtask, conducted with SemEval(2018) is a task proposed by alicia kerbs and denis paperno (2016). It describes, how lexical similarity may not be enough to access qualitatively, the semantic information for a multitude of tasks. Wherein they propose that, with this task, a

system can be modelled for effectively extracting certain semantic differences in the words for understanding the sense embedded within them. This is provided as a proof of concept dataset for this sharedtask, where a certain word is used to check if it can distinguish between a pair of words. The dataset in itself seems simple where, in the training set a label information for the two classes, positive or negative are provided making this a binary classification task.

The three words that are provided in each instance are given in the order as, a pivot word followed by a compare word and ending with a attribute or feature word, that may or may not be associated with the pivot word. Based on the last word it is decided, if that attribute word actually is a distinguishing feature that is able to discriminate the pivot word from that of the compare word. *e.g (apple,banana,red)* here apple is the pivot word, banana the compare word and red, the word which decides if this is a feature that can be associate with apple to distinguish it from banana. This is a rather oversimplified example to a human, as from a very young age we are taught to distinguish objects based on visual aid, which simplifies the task for us as we have embedded subconsciously to differentiate the fruits mainly based on their color or size. This information is seldom used to describe the fruits when illustrated in written form, thus lacking that visual form of information for a machine to make this judgment call, making it that much more difficult to take an informed decision. Their work is based on a method, that was presented by Lazaridou et al. (2016) for prediction of distinguishing feature with use of image as reference for visual discrimination attribute identification task, more prominently it was related to capturing of lexical information using offset vectors.

---

[1]Results/Evaluation under the team name "AmritaNLP"

Proceedings of the 12th International Workshop on Semantic Evaluation (SemEval-2018), pages 1003–1007
New Orleans, Louisiana, June 5–6, 2018. ©2018 Association for Computational Linguistics

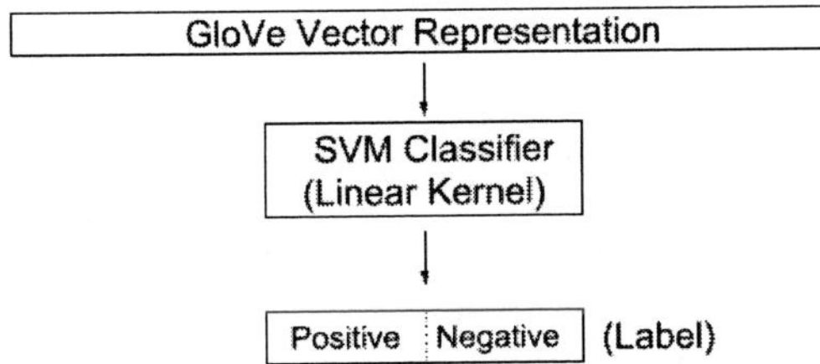

Figure 1: SVM architecture for feature representation.

2 Dataset

The dataset in the sharedtask2018 (Krebs and Paperno, 2018) is divided into three sets namely train test and validation. The training set contains automatically generated examples which are not manually curated. Whereas, the test and validation set are manually verified examples which include just over 5000 instances. The test set instances are made keeping in consideration that feature word overlap between the words in train and test are minimal. The validation set is similar to that of the test set and is used for parameter tuning of the models.

There are in total 17782 instances in the training set, 2722 in the validation set and 2340 in the test set. With the automated nature of the data, the training set is noisier in comparison to that of the validation and test set.

In the dataset, positive examples are annotated with the label '1', signifying that the attribute/feature word is a positive association only to the pivot word in the order presented and not vice verse. *e.g.* (*airplane,helicopter,wings*) here 'wings' is an attribute only associated to 'airplane', whereas (*helicopter,airplane,wings*) is an invalid entry. The combination of (*helicopter,airplane*) in this order will only be added if the concept 'helicopter' has a feature that airplane does not have in this set.

On the other hand, the negative examples are annotated with label '0' at the end. These are considered when the attribute/feature words are either similar to both pivot and the compare word or are dissimilar to them, *e.g.* (*Tractor,scooter,wheels*), (*Spider,elephant,legs*) e.t.c.

In the training dataset, there is a total of 508 unique concepts (pivot) words, of which 375 words have positive attributes and 505 of these have negative attributes, seeing the big contrast between the two labeled attributes we can infer that

not every concept word has an equal proportion of labeled instances.

W_p	Pivot word
W_c	Compare word
W_a	Attribute word
Cos_p	cosine_similarity ($W_p W_a$)
Cos_c	cosine_similarity ($W_c W_a$)
Dis_p	kulsinski($W_p W_a$)
Dis_c	kulsinski($W_c W_a$)
Min_p	minkowski($W_p W_a$p=1)
Min_c	minkowski($W_c W_a$p=1)
Coref_p	corrcoef($W_p W_a$)
Coref_c	corrcoef($W_c W_a$)
Sqeu	sqeuclidean(W, W_a)

Table 1: Nomenclature for feature representation.

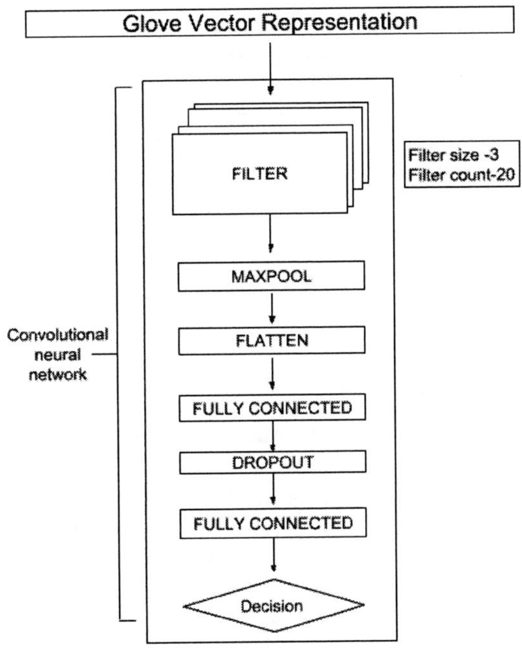

Figure 2: Convolution neural network architecture for feature representation.

3 Methodology

Here discussed are methods which are considered in our implementation. On a cursory look at the dataset, we decided to go with a pre-trained representation of the words, rather than preparing a word embedded representation of the dataset. This is devised with a notion that, word pair associated models on this dataset would not help educate the

SN	GloVe Pre-trained word Vectors	Representation	Representation Length	Validation	
				Accuracy	F1score
1	6B_50d	W_p,W_c,W_a	150	51.16	42.20
2		W_p,W_a,W_c,W_a	200	51.08	42.10
3		$W_p,W_a,W_c,W_a,$ Cos_p	201	51.48	51.10
4		$W_p,W_a,W_c,W_a,$ Cos_p, Dis_p	202	51.37	50.90
5		CR 1	200	50.28	41.90
6		CR 2,Cos	202	47.59	46.00
7		CR 2,Cos,Min_c,Min_p	204	49.61	46.80
8	6B_300d	W_p,W_c,W_a	900	52.04	45.80
9		W_p,W_a,W_c,W_a	1200	51.64	45.57
10	840B_300d	W_p,W_c,W_a	900	51.10	41.00
11		W_p,W_a,W_c,W_a	1200	51.41	40.34

Table 2: Validation accuracy for varied dimension GloVe representation using SVM.

SN	GloVe Pre-trained word Vectors	Representation	Representation Length	Validation	
				Accuracy	F1score
1	6B_300d	W_p,W_c,W_a	900	51.3	41.1
2		W_p,W_a,W_c,W_a	1200	50.9	43.8
3		CR 1	1200	50.8	42.2
4	840B_300d	W_p,W_c,W_a	900	52.0	51.0
5		W_p,W_a,W_c,W_a	1200	52.0	45.3
6		CR 1	1200	53.8	48.4

Table 3: Validation accuracy for varied dimension GloVe representation using CNN.

embedding. Further, using the pre-trained embeddings, the representation are evaluated based on validation accuracy with machine learning techniques like SVM, where we use ten fold ten cross with linear kernel for validation. This algorithm was earlier explored for sense disambiguation of a native language (Tamil), having rich feature representation presented in his work by Anand Kumar et al. (2014a), and is also implemented in his work (2014b). A simple one dimension convolution neural networks model is also illustrated upon, based on the works by Vinayakumar et al. (2017). The CNN model is fixed on an empirical method where the representation is convoluted with *twenty* filters, of size *three*, on a batch size of *sixty-four*, with activation ReLU over a wayward *ten* epochs, which are flattened and reduced to *thirty-two* and later to one at the final layer for evaluation. The architectures for the models, are as shown in Figure 1 & 2 respectively.

Moving ahead, a GloVe pre-trained word embedding (Pennington et al., 2014) of various dimensions are considered, which is learned over public data, available under the PDDL.[2] (100, 300 dimension word representation, embedded over 6B, 840B sizes common crawl corpus are considered). The focus is on using one of these representations for our base method. Upon these embedding, various distance, dissimilarity and similarity measures are considered, to provide a measure between vectors or in our case between the words.

In Table 1, provided are abbreviations that we used through out the upcoming discussion regarding the methods and the representations. With the implementation of pre-trained vectors, we refer few vector measurement technique that could be used to measure a sense of semantic similarity among them. These vector carry within them a spacial correlation between words which has be discussed in their work by (Pennington et al.,

---

[2] Public Domain Dedication and License v1.0. http://www.opendatacommons.org/licenses/pddl/1.0/.

SN	Conditional representation (CR)	
	If :	Else :
1	$W_p,(W_p + W_a),W_c,W_a$	$W_p,(W_p - W_a),W_c,(W_c - W_a)$
2	$W_p,(W_p+ W_a),W_c,W_a,(Dis\_c - Dis\_p)$	$W_p,(W_p- W_a),W_c,(W_c - W_a),(Dis\_c - Dis\_p)$

Table 4: Various feature representation taken for the classification task.

SN	GloVe Pre-trained word Vectors	Representation	Representation length	Validation	
				Accuracy	F1score
1		CR 1, Dis	1201	53.1	47.3
2		CR 1, Cos	1201	50.3	50.1
3		CR 1, Dis, Cos	1202	55.1	53.1
4		CR 1, Min, Dis_p, Dis_c	1203	50.9	51.6
5		CR 1, (Coref_p – Coref_c), Min_c, Min_p	1203	51.1	56.8
6		CR 1, Cos, Min_c, Min_p	1203	54.6	58.9
7	840B_300d	CR 2	1201	51.3	45.6
8		CR 2, (Coref_p – Coref_c), Min_c, Min_p	1204	55.7	56.4
9		CR 2, (Min_c – Min_p)	1202	61.5	55.8
10		CR 2, Cos, Min_c, Min_p	1204	**60.1**	**56.1**
11		CR 2, Min_c, Min_p	1203	**61.1**	**60.2**
12		CR 2, (Cos_p – Cos_c), Min_c, Min_p	1204	58.9	51.3
13		CR 2, Cos, Min_c, Min_p, Sqeu	1205	54.4	54.9

Table 5: Validation accuracy of 300 dimension, GloVe representations on 840B common crawl tokens using CNN.

2014).

Initially, a simple concatenation of the three words is considered as an instance, which are the pivot(W_p), compare(W_c) and attribute(W_a) words, for the entire dataset. The same representation is taken of two different dimensions lengths as mentioned earlier. Based on the model fit across training data, the validation accuracy and F1score are measured, these are as shown in Table 2. Similarly, these representations are also passed on to a convolution neural network, where their respective accuracy and F1scores are measured and shown in Table 3.

With an empirical approach, the representations are further extended by appending (W_a) to (W_p) and (W_c) sequentially and passing it to the two models(As shown by representation two in the Table 2). The SVM model did not show any significant improvement in the score, over the representations. In comparison, the CNN model observed a slight improvement in scores on the same representation. Word embedding being a vector representation in higher dimensional space, has proved (Pennington et al., 2014) to captures spatial information, that can be employed to use as features for the representation. This is exerted by using certain measures between the (W_p), (W_a) and (W_c), (W_a). These measures are cal-

culated using Scipy libraries (Jones et al., 2001) and Sklearn library (Pedregosa et al., 2011) to find the distance, similarity and dissimilarity measure between the two 1-D array words. The similarity of the two words indicates how similarly associated these words are, this measure is calculated using the cosine distance which is a scalar representation that signifies, larger the number between the two words the more similar they are. Whereas, the dissimilarity is the vice-versa of this measure. Of the various distance measures explored, we considered euclidean, chebyshev, sqeuclidean, minkowski and for dissimilarity measures jaccard, kulsinski, Hamming and these are implemented using the Scipy (Jones et al., 2001) library. Amongst the measures considered, kulsinski dissimilarity gave the nearest disambiguation between the comparison of W_p, W_a and W_c, W_a, thus we chose it as the threshold measured for differentiating the representations between a positive and a negative instances i.e if the dissimilarity of W_c, W_a is greater than that of the W_p, W_a then the W_a were added to the W_P and concatenated to form a representation. Otherwise the second representation is considered where the W_a is subtracted from both the words. This is as shown in the first conditional representation (CR) of the Table 4.

The CR based representation accuracy decreased for SVM models. Whereas, the F1score and accuracy increased for the CNN model over the initial representations shown in Table 3. Thus, the further representation where improved on the CNN model to achieve better F1score with good accuracy. Comparing the two GloVe pre-trained vectors of 300 dimension for varied corpus size shown in Table 3, the 840B_300d trained model has achieved better F1score and accuracy compared to the other, thus moving along further with word embedding.

In Table 5 we see that subsequent representations, built upon the simple representation of CR1 are concatenated with kulsinski(Dis^3) distance and Cosine similarity (Cos^3) have improved the F1score. As show in the third representation, where the F1score increased to 53.1% with a considerable accuracy over the previous iteration. Further improvisation on CR1 representation with different features like correlation coefficient have increased the F1score to 56.8% but brought down the accuracy. Representation six is the next feature representation for which the accuracy, as well as the F1score, increases to 54.6% and 58.9% respectively. After many iterations of adding features, the representation eleven is the one that gave the highest F1score with the best accuracy, and this representation based model is submitted along with the representation ten, which also had good F1score, but a lower accuracy on the validation dataset.

4 Results & Conclusion

The tenth and eleventh representation of Table 5 are the two feature set based on CNN models, which are predicted on the test set and submitted for the competition. The results published for our models showed that the first set was scored at 0.52, where as the second set was scored at 0.66 for F1score. Comparing the predicted labels of the two systems with that of the gold standard, we see that our system fit over the tenth representation predicted correctly only 399 of 1293 as negative example and 855 of 1047 as the positive example. On the eleventh representation it gave 857 of 1293 and 687 of 1047 for negative and positive example respectively. Comparing the outcomes of the sys-

tems we see that majority of negative sample are mis-classified for system ten, on the other hand, the eleventh system improved upon this classification of the negative samples which increased the F1score for the system.

References

M Anand Kumar, S Rajendran, and KP Soman. 2014a. Tamil word sense disambiguation using support vector machines with rich features. *International Journal of Applied Engineering Research*, 9(20):7609–20.

M Anand Kumar and KP Soman. 2014b. Amrita-cen@ fire-2014: Morpheme extraction and lemmatization for tamil using machine learning. In *ACM International Conference Proceeding Series*, pages 112–20.

Eric Jones, Travis Oliphant, Pearu Peterson, et al. 2001. SciPy: Open source scientific tools for Python.

Alicia Krebs and Denis Paperno. 2016. Capturing discriminative attributes in a distributional space: Task proposal. In *Proceedings of the 1st Workshop on Evaluating Vector-Space Representations for NLP*, pages 51–54.

Alicia Krebs and Denis Paperno. 2018. Semeval-2018 Task 10: Capturing discriminative attributes. In *Proceedings of International Workshop on Semantic Evaluation (SemEval-2018)*.

Angeliki Lazaridou, Nghia The Pham, and Marco Baroni. 2016. The red one!: On learning to refer to things based on their discriminative properties. *arXiv preprint arXiv:1603.02618*.

Fabian Pedregosa, Gaël Varoquaux, Alexandre Gramfort, Vincent Michel, Bertrand Thirion, Olivier Grisel, Mathieu Blondel, Peter Prettenhofer, Ron Weiss, Vincent Dubourg, et al. 2011. Scikit-learn: Machine learning in python. *Journal of machine learning research*, 12(Oct):2825–2830.

Jeffrey Pennington, Richard Socher, and Christopher Manning. 2014. Glove: Global vectors for word representation. In *Proceedings of the 2014 conference on empirical methods in natural language processing (EMNLP)*, pages 1532–1543.

R. Vinayakumar, K. P. Soman, and Prabaharan Poornachandran. 2017. Applying convolutional neural network for network intrusion detection. *2017 International Conference on Advances in Computing, Communications and Informatics (ICACCI)*, pages 1222–1228.

---

[3] These representations are same as earlier mentioned in Table 1 wherein here the pivot word based measure is taken for the 'if' condition and the compare word based on the other

Discriminator at SemEval-2018 Task 10: Minimally Supervised Discrimination

Artur Kulmizev
CLCG
University of Groningen
a.kulmizev@student.rug.nl

Mostafa Abdou
CLCG
University of Groningen
m.abdou@student.rug.nl

Vinit Ravishankar
Institute of Formal and Applied Linguistics
Charles University in Prague
vinit.ravishankar@gmail.com

Malvina Nissim
CLCG
University of Groningen
m.nissim@rug.nl

Abstract

We participated to the SemEval-2018 shared task on capturing discriminative attributes (Task 10) with a simple system that ranked 8th amongst the 26 teams that took part in the evaluation. Our final score was 0.67, which is competitive with the winning score of 0.75, particularly given that our system is a minimally supervised system that requires no training and minimal parameter optimisation. In addition to describing the submitted system, and discussing the implications of the relative success of such a system on this task, we also report on other, more complex models we experimented with.

1 Introduction and Background

Traditional evaluation tasks for semantic models have aimed to evaluate semantic relatedness (Bruni et al., 2014; Agirre et al., 2009) or similarity (Hill et al., 2014). More recently, analogy tasks (Mikolov et al., 2013; Gladkova et al., 2016; Abdou et al., 2018) have emerged in order to assess a model's ability to correctly answer questions in the form of "a is to b as c is to ?" using vector arithmetic. However, these approaches are not sufficient in evaluating the semantic competence of any given model: there are numerous flaws with similarity and analogy-based evaluation, the most pressing being the lack of correlation with downstream performance in real-world tasks (Schnabel et al., 2015). Furthermore, though analogy questions can assess how well certain semantic relations are modeled (*country : capital, country: language*), this is arguably more of a measure of context co-occurrence than it is a testament to any semantic understanding.

Capturing Discriminative Attributes is a novel semantic evaluation task which aims to assess the extent to which semantic models can capture semantic *differences* between words. Particularly, the task is concerned with identifying how well a given model represents attributes that discriminate between two related semantic concepts. For instance, given the terms *steak* and *salad*, **meat** would serve as a discriminative attribute, drawing a distinction between the former and latter as a quality that the two do not have in common.

2 Data

The data provided for this task was split between training and validation sections, with 17,500 and 2,721 samples comprising the former and latter, respectively. Every sample was composed of three terms (*pivot, comparison,* and *feature*) and their corresponding label $\in \{0, 1\}$. A sample was deemed as discriminative (label 1) if the *feature* served as an attribute that distinguished the *pivot* from the *comparison*. Otherwise, the sample was labeled as non-discriminative (0). Examples from the data are shown in Table 2. Please note that directionality is meaningful, i.e., swapping the *pivot* and *comparison* columns for the first two examples can change the label. For instance, *pink* is considered as discriminative for *pig* with regard to *sheep* (label is 1), but not the other way round (label would be 0). For a detailed description of the dataset, see (Krebs et al., 2018).

pivot	comparison	feature	label
sandwiches	breakfast	lunch	1
pig	sheep	pink	1
banana	raisin	round	0
uncle	father	male	0

Table 1: Samples of provided data. In the first two samples, the feature is discriminative (sandwiches are eaten at lunch; pigs are pink). In the last two, the feature is not discriminative (neither bananas nor raisins are round; an uncle and a father are both male).

Proceedings of the 12th International Workshop on Semantic Evaluation (SemEval-2018), pages 1008–1012
New Orleans, Louisiana, June 5–6, 2018. ©2018 Association for Computational Linguistics

It is important to note that only 5,000 instances were manually verified for consistency out of the combined training and validation datasets. Thus, whilst the entire validation set comprised of a subset of these verified samples (2,721), only 2,279 were represented in the training set (13%). Furthermore, the training set was heavily imbalanced towards negative ("non-discriminative") samples, accounting for a total 11,171 out of 17,500 (63.8%). As such, we largely focused our experiments on the validation set, since it was comprised entirely of manually curated data.

3 Models

In all models we describe, words not present in the vocabulary of a vector-space model were assigned the same 'unknown' vector drawn randomly from a normal distribution.

3.1 Baseline

The baseline we constructed was a simple support-vector machine classifier. We converted each word into a vector from a vector-space model. For every 4-tuple example, we passed the concatenation of vectors of the three words as a feature with the fourth as a label. This model failed to learn sufficiently, performing at near-chance levels on the validation set for all vector-space models.

3.2 Neural Models

Another model (**NN**) that we investigated was a feed-forward network with the concatenation of the word vector representations as an input layer, and a single binary output neuron as the output. Ultimately, we employed three hidden layers of sizes 450, 200 and 100, with ReLU as the activation function for each, and 20% dropout between each layer. Our output function was a sigmoid function. We used binary cross-entropy loss with a learning rate of 10^{-5} and Adam (Kingma and Ba, 2014) as our stochastic optimization function. This model outperformed the baseline for all vector-space models on the validation set.

Our next model (**NN-WN**) was built on the intuition that representations of more descriptive elements than just words could prove to be more helpful. We therefore converted each word into its first matching definition in WordNet (Miller, 1995), and condensed this definition into a dimension 4096 representation using Conneau et al. (2017)'s BiLSTM-max pooling encoder which is

pre-trained on the *Stanford Natural Language Inference* dataset (Bowman et al., 2015). Similar to the previous model, this representation was passed to a feed-forward network, albeit with two hidden layers of sizes 1024 and 128 and sigmoid non-linearities. We did not evaluate this model with every set of embeddings due to time constraints and disappointing initial results; evaluated on standard GloVe (840B) embeddings, the performance of this model on the validation set was slightly lower than the feed-forward network (**NN**) (when utilizing the same vector-space model).

3.3 Discriminator

Our final submitted system (**Discriminator**), unlike any of our other models, consisted of a surprisingly simple set of rules which were designed to leverage the information encoded in distributional semantic vector-space models (VSM) for the purpose of classifying an attribute as discriminative or non-discriminative. We relied on the widely-used metric of cosine similarity; we measured the cosine similarities between the vector assigned to the *pivot* (word 1), *comparison* (word 2), and *feature* (word 3) in a given VSM. Words not found in the VSM were assigned the vector for the UNK token. Our algorithm is summarized in Algorithm 1.

Algorithm 1 Classification algorithm

1: **procedure** CLASSIFY(w)
2:      $s_{12} \leftarrow$ SIM(w_1, w_2)
3:      $s_{13} \leftarrow$ SIM(w_1, w_3)
4:      $s_{23} \leftarrow$ SIM(w_2, w_3)
5:      **if** $s_{13} - s_{23} > 0.015 \,\&\, s_{12} > 0.30 \,\&\, s_{13} > 0.1 \,\&\, s_{23} < 0.54$ **then**
6:          **return** 1
7:      **else**
8:          **return** 0

These thresholds were obtained via grid-search over both the training data and validation data, per VSM. The range of evaluated thresholds was between 0 and 0.50, with strides of 0.02. Besides choice of VSM, these thresholds were the only variable parameters in our model. The VSM used in our final submission consisted of an average of three sets of embeddings: GloVe word embeddings trained on Common Crawl (840B tokens) (Pennington et al., 2014), the same GloVe embeddings post counter-fitting (Mrkšić et al., 2016) using data from the training and validation sets, and Paragram$_{sl999}$ embeddings provided by Wieting et al. (2015), also post counter-fitting. Counter-fitting is detailed in Section 4.2. The VSM obtained by averaging these three models (**AvgVSM**) outperformed each individual VSM, and was therefore submitted as our official system.

4 Model Variations

4.1 Distributional Vector-Space models

In the course of our investigation we tested a large number of vector-space models which were generated using different methods. All VSMs were evaluated with each of our models and with our final system in order to determine the model which best encodes the discriminative information required for this task. Below is a description of all VSMs we tried:

(a) Skipgram embeddings trained on the Google News Corpus (Mikolov et al., 2013).

(b) Glove embeddings trained on Common Crawl (6B and 840B tokens).

(c) LexVec embeddings trained on Common Crawl (58B tokens) (Salle et al., 2016).

(d) Paragram embeddings trained on English Wikipedia[1] and tuned on SimLex-999.

(e) Items (b) (840B), (c), and (d) counter-fitted using the training and validation sets.

(f) AvgVSM: Average of three models cf. Section 3.3.

4.2 Counter-fitting

Counter-fitting is a method of post-processing VSMs to adapt them to certain linguistic constraints such as information from semantic lexicons or ontologies. Mrkšić et al. (2016) for instance, successfully used counter-fitting with semantic lexicons to achieve a new state of the art on the SimLex-999 similarity judgment dataset.

We employed counter-fitting to move pivot and comparison vectors (from the training set)[2] closer together in the vector-space for all training and validation examples with label 1, under the rationale that pivot and comparison words should be related for a feature to be considered discriminative.

4.3 kNN Averaging

In evaluating VSMs, we experimented with words outside of the *pivot, comparison, feature* triples that occurred in the data. For all three words, we extracted the respective k-nearest neighbors ($k \in \{5, 10, 20\}$) and averaged their corresponding vectors. This was motivated by the intuition that it is not just the *pivot, comparison* pairs that determine a discriminative feature distance threshold, but also their general semantic neighborhoods. As in the main approach, we computed cosine difference thresholds via grid search for a variety of *term-neighborhood, neighborhood-neighborhood* combinations. Unfortunately, this approach brought marginal improvements (when tested on the validation set) at best under any configuration of thresholds, models, etc. and was thus discarded in favor of the much more lightweight **Discriminator** model.

4.4 Hierarchical Vector-Space models

Poincaré embeddings (Nickel and Kiela, 2017) are a new approach to learning representations for datasets with a latent hierarchal structure. By learning embeddings in hyperbolic spaces instead of euclidean vector spaces using an algorithm based on Riemannian optimization, this method has been shown to outperform Euclidean embeddings on datasets with latent hierarchies, such as HYPERLEX (Véronis, 2004), a dataset used to evaluate if semantic models can capture hyponymy-hypernymy or lexical entailment relationships. This can be seen as closely related to capturing concept attribute relationships, as is required in this task. We used two different sets:

- Size 50 embeddings, trained on the all WordNet common-noun hypernyms, provided by Nickel and Kiela (2017)[3];

- Size 50 embeddings trained on all feature norm derived concept-attribute pairs (i.e. all pivot-feature pairs when label is 1).

Since there was no overlap between the features in the training and testing sets, this method was not of immediate use for the task, as it could not account for the features in the test set. Therefore, our objective was solely to measure the embedding method's effectiveness in modeling the dataset's

---

[1]December 2, 2013 snapshot

[2]The lexicon used for counter fitting can be found at https://github.com/rutrastone/discrimemb

[3]https://github.com/TatsuyaShirakawa/poincare-embedding

VSM	NN (T)	Dsc. (T)	Dsc. (V)
Skipgram	55.00	65.42	64.62
GloVe (6B)	55.38	66.06	64.30
GloVe (840B)	58.50	65.85	64.96
GloVe-cf (840B)	57.74	64.82	63.47
LexVec	59.66	65.98	64.71
LexVec-cf	**60.94**	66.29	64.92
Paragram$_{sl999}$	58.60	66.32	62.68
Paragram$_{sl999}$-cf	57.80	57.86	62.27
Poincare (Wnet)	51.71	53.56	51.78
Poincare (FN)	57.22	62.29	56.91
AvgVSM	58.63	**67.01**	**68.21**

Table 2: Performance of different Vector-space models on the official test set (T) and the validation set (V).

concept-attribute relations. To achieve this, we trained it on attribute concept pairs extracted from the feature norms which were used to build the task's dataset (McRae et al., 2005; Krebs et al., 2018). Since the use of feature norms was not permitted in this shared task, the results from this method were not submitted.

5 Results and Discussion

We report the performance of all vector-space models for each classification system in Table 2. The **NN** model is trained on the validation set[4] and all results for both models are reported on the official test set. Validation set results are only reported for the Discriminator models as the **NN** model fails to learn when training on the training set and testing on the validation set.

5.1 Discriminator

Considering its simple architecture, our system's performance was remarkable. Using nothing but cosine similarity, it performed on a level that is well above our far more complex models, and competitive with the task's best performing systems. This is demonstrative of two things: a) the information required to classify an attribute as discriminative or not with respect to two concepts is (to different extents) present in the distributional vector-space models, and b) the concatenation of the vectors associated with each word is not a sufficient feature for our trained models to learn the simple thresholds which our final model uses. We hypothesize that this is because concatenation fails

to account for the interactions between the *pivot*, *comparison*, and *feature*. Further investigation is needed to assert this.

5.2 Vector-space models

Examining the degree to which different VSM could capture whether an attribute is discriminative was one of our main goals. Our initial intuition was that the relationship between concept and attribute is too specific to be adequately captured by distributional vector-space models which are, after all, based only on co-occurrence. Our results, however, contradict this expectation, showing that they are, to a certain extent, successful. For Discriminator, the best performing vector-space model was AvgVSM.

Furthermore, we found that counter-fitting using the training and validation sets did not prove effective, leading to a degradation in performance, with the exception of LexVec-cf when it did lead to improvements and AvgVSM when it was averaged with non-counter-fit models. Further investigation is required to determine exactly under what conditions counter-fitting works well.

Finally, we note that the WordNet-trained Poincaré hierarchical vector-space model had low coverage and performed poorly. However, the model trained on feature norms showed promise, particularly as it required far less space, training time, and data in order to model the dataset when compared to the distributional models.

6 Conclusion and Future work

In this paper we present Discriminator, our contribution to *SemEval 2018 Task 10: Capturing Discriminative Attributes*. Though this model is simple and does not require any training, our minimally supervised thresholding system achieved a score of 0.67, which was 0.08% below the top submitted system. We found the average of GloVe (840B), GloVe counter-fitted, and Paragram$_{sl999}$ counter-fitted vector-space models to achieve best performance in our system, out of a set of 8 different models. Future work will explore leveraging image-processing inspired models, given the intuition that such methods have the ability to capture attributes-concept relations. Preliminary work with a 2D convolutional architecture, where different sets of word embeddings serve as channels in the feature space, has shown promise.

---

[4]While larger, the training set is very noisy.

References

Mostafa Abdou, Artur Kulmizev, and Vinit Ravishankar. 2018. MGAD: Multilingual Generation of Analogy Datasets. In *Proceedings of the Twelfth International Conference on Language Resources and Evaluation (LREC 2018)*, Paris, France. European Language Resources Association (ELRA).

Eneko Agirre, Enrique Alfonseca, Keith Hall, Jana Kravalova, Marius Paşca, and Aitor Soroa. 2009. A study on similarity and relatedness using distributional and wordnet-based approaches. In *Proceedings of Human Language Technologies: The 2009 Annual Conference of the North American Chapter of the Association for Computational Linguistics*, pages 19–27. Association for Computational Linguistics.

Samuel R Bowman, Gabor Angeli, Christopher Potts, and Christopher D Manning. 2015. A large annotated corpus for learning natural language inference. *arXiv preprint arXiv:1508.05326*.

Elia Bruni, Nam Khanh Tran, and Marco Baroni. 2014. Multimodal distributional semantics.

Alexis Conneau, Douwe Kiela, Holger Schwenk, Loic Barrault, and Antoine Bordes. 2017. Supervised learning of universal sentence representations from natural language inference data. *arXiv preprint arXiv:1705.02364*.

Anna Gladkova, Aleksandr Drozd, and Satoshi Matsuoka. 2016. Analogy-based detection of morphological and semantic relations with word embeddings: what works and what doesn't. In *Proceedings of the NAACL Student Research Workshop*, pages 8–15.

Felix Hill, Roi Reichart, and Anna Korhonen. 2014. Simlex-999: Evaluating semantic models with (genuine) similarity estimation. *CoRR*, abs/1408.3456.

Diederik P Kingma and Jimmy Ba. 2014. Adam: A method for stochastic optimization. *arXiv preprint arXiv:1412.6980*.

Alicia Krebs, Alessandro Lenci, and Denis Paperno. 2018. Semeval-2018 task 10: Capturing discriminative attributes. In *Proceedings of the 12th international workshop on semantic evaluation (SemEval 2018)*.

Ken McRae, George S Cree, Mark S Seidenberg, and Chris McNorgan. 2005. Semantic feature production norms for a large set of living and nonliving things. *Behavior research methods*, 37(4):547–559.

Tomas Mikolov, Kai Chen, Greg Corrado, and Jeffrey Dean. 2013. Efficient estimation of word representations in vector space. *CoRR*, abs/1301.3781.

George A Miller. 1995. Wordnet: a lexical database for english. *Communications of the ACM*, 38(11):39–41.

Nikola Mrkšić, Diarmuid O Séaghdha, Blaise Thomson, Milica Gašić, Lina Rojas-Barahona, Pei-Hao Su, David Vandyke, Tsung-Hsien Wen, and Steve Young. 2016. Counter-fitting word vectors to linguistic constraints. *arXiv preprint arXiv:1603.00892*.

Maximillian Nickel and Douwe Kiela. 2017. Poincaré embeddings for learning hierarchical representations. In *Advances in Neural Information Processing Systems*, pages 6341–6350.

Jeffrey Pennington, Richard Socher, and Christopher Manning. 2014. Glove: Global vectors for word representation. In *Proceedings of the 2014 conference on empirical methods in natural language processing (EMNLP)*, pages 1532–1543.

Alexandre Salle, Marco Idiart, and Aline Villavicencio. 2016. Matrix factorization using window sampling and negative sampling for improved word representations. *arXiv preprint arXiv:1606.00819*.

Tobias Schnabel, Igor Labutov, David M Mimno, and Thorsten Joachims. 2015. Evaluation methods for unsupervised word embeddings. In *EMNLP*, pages 298–307.

Jean Véronis. 2004. Hyperlex: lexical cartography for information retrieval. *Computer Speech & Language*, 18(3):223–252.

John Wieting, Mohit Bansal, Kevin Gimpel, and Karen Livescu. 2015. Towards universal paraphrastic sentence embeddings. *arXiv preprint arXiv:1511.08198*.

UNBNLP at SemEval-2018 Task 10: Evaluating unsupervised approaches to capturing discriminative attributes

Milton King and **Ali Hakimi Parizi** and **Paul Cook**
Faculty of Computer Science, University of New Brunswick
Fredericton, NB E3B 5A3, Canada
`milton.king@unb.ca, ahakimi@unb.ca, paul.cook@unb.ca`

Abstract

In this paper we present three unsupervised models for capturing discriminative attributes based on information from word embeddings, WordNet, and sentence-level word co-occurrence frequency. We show that, of these approaches, the simple approach based on word co-occurrence performs best. We further consider supervised and unsupervised approaches to combining information from these models, but these approaches do not improve on the word co-occurrence model.

1 Introduction

In the task of capturing discriminative attributes, a system is presented with three words, and must determine whether the third word — the attribute — characterizes the first word, but not the second. For example, for the triple (*chicken,bread,legs*), *legs* is a discriminative attribute because chickens typically have legs, but bread typically does not. On the other hand, for the triple (*mother,woman,female*), *female* is not a discriminative attribute because both mothers and women are typically female. In the case of the triple (*brush,chocolate,chicken*), *chicken* is not a discriminative attribute because there is no clear relationship between chicken and brushes, or between chicken and chocolate.

In this paper we focus primarily on unsupervised approaches to the task of capturing discriminative attributes. We consider three unsupervised models drawing on information from word embeddings, WordNet (Fellbaum, 1998), and sentence-level word co-occurrence frequency. We then consider three approaches to combining information from these models: one unsupervised majority vote approach, and two supervised approaches. Somewhat surprisingly, we achieve our best F1 score of 0.61 with the remarkably simple approach

based on word co-occurrence. None of the approaches to model combination improve over this.

2 Base models

In this section, we discuss three unsupervised models for identifying discriminative attributes that incorporate information from word embeddings, WordNet, and word co-occurrences. We refer to these models as "base models". In Section 3 we describe unsupervised and supervised approaches to combining these base models. Throughout the description of our models we refer to the words in the triples in the dataset as word1, word2, and attribute, respectively.

2.1 Word2vec

If an attribute is a discriminative attribute for word1, then we hypothesize that word1 and the attribute will be more semantically similar than word2 and the attribute. We use similarity of word embeddings as a proxy for semantic similarity.

We train word2vec's skip-gram model (Mikolov et al., 2013) on a snapshot of English Wikipedia from 1 September 2015 containing roughly 2.6 billion tokens, tokenized using the tokenizer available in the Stanford CoreNLP tools (Manning et al., 2014).[1] We use a window size of $\pm$ 8 and 300 dimensions. We remove all words that occur less than 15 times in the corpus. We did not set a maximum vocabulary size. We train our model using negative sampling, and set the number of training epochs to 5.

We then calculate the cosine similarity between the word embeddings for word1 and the attribute ($\cos(\text{word1}, \text{attribute})$), and word2 and the attribute ($\cos(\text{word2}, \text{attribute})$). We label the instance as a discriminative at-

---

[1] `http://nlp.stanford.edu/software/corenlp.shtml`

1013

Proceedings of the 12th International Workshop on Semantic Evaluation (SemEval-2018), pages 1013–1016
New Orleans, Louisiana, June 5–6, 2018. ©2018 Association for Computational Linguistics

tribute if $\cos(word1, attribute)$ is greater than $\cos(word2, attribute)$.

2.2 WordNet

In this approach we again hypothesize that if an attribute is a discriminative attribute for word1, then word1 and the attribute will be more similar than word2 and the attribute. Here, however, we take an approach loosely inspired by (Lesk, 1986) and (Banerjee and Pedersen, 2002), and measure similarity based on word overlap in definitions, and information available through various lexical relations, in WordNet (Fellbaum, 1998).

For each of word1, word2, and the attribute, we represent that word by a set of words that includes, for each synset for the word, all lemmas in each synset, and all words in the definition and example sentences in each synset.[2] We then optionally also include the same information — i.e., the lemmas, and the words in the definition and example sentences — for hypernyms up to level three, and meronyms. Casefolding was applied to all words in the sets of words representing word1, word2, and the attribute.

An instance is labeled as a discriminative attribute if the size of the intersection of the set of words representing word1 and the set of words representing the attribute is greater than the intersection of the set of words representing word2 and the set of words representing the attribute.

We considered various configurations of this model, differing with respect to the level of hypernyms considered, and whether meronyms were included, for word1, word2, or the attribute. The specific configurations considered, and their average F1 score on the validation data, are shown in Table 1. In subsequent experiments we only use the configuration found to perform best in Table 1.

2.3 Word co-occurrence

We hypothesize that if an attribute is a discriminative attribute for word1, then word1 and the attribute will co-occur more frequently than word2 and the attribute. Various definitions of co-occurrence could be used to operationalize this, for example, co-occurrence within a window of $\pm n$ words, a sentence, or a document. In this preliminary work we consider co-occurrence within a sentence.

---

[2] We tokenize the definitions and example sentences using a simple regular expression-based tokenizer, and exclude stopwords.

We calculate sentence-level co-occurrences for each pair of (word1,attribute) and (word2,attribute) in the provided shared task datasets using the ukWaC (Ferraresi et al., 2008), a corpus of roughly 1.9 billion tokens automatically constructed from a web crawl of the `.uk` domain. This model then predicts that an attribute is a discriminative attribute if the number of sentences in which word1 and the attribute co-occur is greater than the number of sentences in which word2 and the attribute co-occur. Based on its performance on the validation data (see Section 4), this model was submitted as one of our two official runs.

3 Combined models

In this section, we consider one unsupervised, and two supervised, approaches to combining the individual models discussed in Section 2.

3.1 Majority vote

In this unsupervised approach we use a majority vote of the output of the word2vec, WordNet, and word co-occurrence models. We label an attribute as a discriminative attribute if at least two of the three models predict that it is. This approach was submitted as our second official run, again based on its performance over the validation data (see Section 4), and because we are particularly interested in unsupervised approaches to this task.

3.2 Supervised: output

In this supervised approach, we represent each instance as a vector of three binary features, corresponding to the output of the word2vec, WordNet, and word co-occurrence models. We then train a logistic regression classifier on these representations of the instances. Specifically, we use the logistic regression implementation available in scikit-learn (Pedregosa et al., 2011), with l2 normalization using the liblinear solver for a maximum of 100 iterations and a stopping criteria of 0.0001.

3.3 Supervised: features

In this supervised approach we use a total of 8 features that are based on the information used by the word2vec, WordNet, and word co-occurrence models. The following features are used:

1. the cosine similarity between the word embeddings for word1 and the attribute, based

Synsets	Hypernymy level 1	Hypernymy level 2	Hypernymy level 3	Meronymy	Validation average F1
w1,w2,att	w1,w2,att	w1,w2,att	w1,w2,att	w1,w2,att	0.544
w1,w2,att	w1,w2	w1,w2	w1,w2	w1,w2	0.566
w1,w2,att	w1,w2	w1,w2	w1,w2	w1	**0.567**
w1,w2,att	w1,w2			w1,w2	0.565
w1,w2,att	w1				0.553
w1,w2,att					0.553

Table 1: F1 score on the validation data for the WordNet method. Each row corresponds to a different configuration for this model, with information for word1 (w1), word2 (w2), and the attribute (att) taken from the indicated relations in WordNet. The best F1 is indicated in boldface.

on the word2vec approach (Section 2.1);

2. the cosine similarity between the word embeddings for word2 and the attribute;

3. the size of the intersection between the set of words representing word1 and the set of words representing the attribute, as formed for the WordNet approach (Section 2.2);

4. the size of the intersection between the set of words representing word2 and the set of words representing the attribute;

5. $3-4$, i.e., the difference between the previous two features;

6. the number of times word1 and the attribute co-occur, using the sentence-level approach to co-occurrence (Section 2.3);

7. the number of times word2 and the attribute co-occur;

8. $6-7$, i.e., the difference between the previous two features.

Similarly to the supervised: output approach (Section 3.2), we train a logistic regression classifier (using the same settings as for that model) on these representations of the instances.

4   Results

Table 2, shows the average F1 score for each of our models on the validation and test sets. For the test set, the supervised models (supervised: output and supervised: features) were trained on the validation data, and tested on the test set; for the validation data, results for the supervised models are for 10-fold cross-validation.[3]

Model	Average F1	
	Validation	Test
Word2vec	0.57	0.58
WordNet	0.57	0.56
✓ Word co-occurrence	**0.61**	**0.61**
✓ Majority vote	0.60	**0.61**
Supervised: output	0.59	**0.61**
Supervised: features	0.60	0.59

Table 2: Average F1 score for each of our models on the validation and test sets. Officially submitted runs are indicated with checkmarks. The highest F1 for each dataset is shown in boldface.

On the validation data, the word co-occurrence model achieved the highest F1 of the base models of 0.61, and indeed the highest F1 overall; none of the approaches to combining information from the base models (i.e., majority vote, supervised: output, or supervised: features) improved over the word co-occurrence model. The word co-occurrence model was therefore submitted as an official run. The majority vote and supervised: features models achieved the next best F1 of 0.60. Keeping with our primary interest of exploring unsupervised approaches to this task, the majority vote model was selected as our second official run.

Turning to results on the test set, the word co-occurrence, majority vote, and supervised: output models all achieved the highest F1 of 0.61. That the word-cooccurrence model outperforms the other two base models — word2vec and WordNet — shows that sentence-level word co-occurrence is more informative about discriminative attributes than the information carried by

---

³We did not use the training data, which was not constructed in the same way as the test data, for training our

supervised models. In preliminary experiments we considered models trained on the training data, and tested on the validation data, but found the performance to be relatively poor.

word embeddings and the information available in WordNet, at least as it has been incorporated in these models. That none of the combined models is able to improve on the best base model suggests that, although these models are based on very different sources of information, they are not complementary.

5 Conclusions

In this paper we evaluated three unsupervised models for capturing discriminative attributes based on information from word embeddings, WordNet, and sentence-level word co-occurrence frequency. Surprisingly we found that the simple approach based on word co-occurrence performed best. We further considered supervised and unsupervised approaches to combining information from these models, but were unable to improve on the word co-occurrence model.

In future work, because of its relatively good performance, we intend to further explore the word co-occurrence model. In this work we only considered sentence-level co-occurrence. In future work we intend to consider other definitions of co-occurrence, such as co-occurrence within a window of $\pm n$ words, and document-level co-occurrence. We also only considered raw frequency in the word co-occurrence model. As an alternative to this, we also intend to consider using various lexical association measures, such as pointwise mutual information (Church and Hanks, 1990) and log-likelihood ratio (Dunning, 1993). In a similar vein, we also intend to explore the impact of the window size and number of dimensions on the word2vec model. Finally, we intend to consider other WordNet-based measures of similarity (e.g., Resnik, 1995; Jiang and Conrath, 1997).

References

Satanjeev Banerjee and Ted Pedersen. 2002. An adapted Lesk algorithm for word sense disambiguation using WordNet. In *Proceedings of the 3rd International Conference on Intelligent Text Processing and Computational Linguistics (CICLing-2002)*, pages 136–145, Mexico City, Mexico.

Kenneth W. Church and Patrick Hanks. 1990. Word association norms, mutual information, and lexicography. *Computational Linguistics*, 16(1):22–29.

Ted Dunning. 1993. Accurate methods for the statistics of surprise and coincidence. *Computational Linguistics*, 19(1):61–74.

Christiane Fellbaum, editor. 1998. *WordNet: An Electronic Lexical Database*. MIT Press, Cambridge, MA.

Adriano Ferraresi, Eros Zanchetta, Marco Baroni, and Silvia Bernardini. 2008. Introducing and evaluating ukWaC, a very large web-derived corpus of English. In *Proceedings of the 4th Web as Corpus Workshop (WAC-4): Can we beat Google?*, pages 47–54, Marrakech, Morocco.

Jay J. Jiang and David W. Conrath. 1997. Semantic similarity based on corpus statistics and lexical taxonomy. In *Proceedings of International Conference Research on Computational Linguistics (ROCLING X)*, pages 19–33, Taipei, Taiwan.

Michael Lesk. 1986. Automatic sense disambiguation using machine readable dictionaries: How to tell a pine cone from an ice cream cone. In *Proceedings of the 1986 SIGDOC Conference*, pages 24–26, Toronto, Canada.

Christopher Manning, Mihai Surdeanu, John Bauer, Jenny Finkel, Steven Bethard, and David McClosky. 2014. The Stanford CoreNLP Natural Language Processing Toolkit. In *Proceedings of the 52nd Annual Meeting of the Association for Computational Linguistics: System Demonstrations*, pages 55–60, Baltimore, USA.

Tomas Mikolov, Kai Chen, Greg Corrado, and Jeffrey Dean. 2013. Efficient estimation of word representations in vector space. In *Proceedings of Workshop at the International Conference on Learning Representations, 2013*, Scottsdale, USA.

F. Pedregosa, G. Varoquaux, A. Gramfort, V. Michel, B. Thirion, O. Grisel, M. Blondel, P. Prettenhofer, R. Weiss, V. Dubourg, J. Vanderplas, A. Passos, D. Cournapeau, M. Brucher, M. Perrot, and E. Duchesnay. 2011. Scikit-learn: Machine learning in Python. *Journal of Machine Learning Research*, 12:2825–2830.

Philip Resnik. 1995. Using information content to evaluate semantic similarity. In *Proceedings of the 14th International Joint Conference on Artificial Intelligence*, pages 448–453, Montreal, Canada.

ABDN at SemEval-2018 Task 10: Recognising Discriminative Attributes using Context Embeddings and WordNet

Rui Mao, Guanyi Chen, Ruizhe Li and Chenghua Lin
Computing Science Department
University of Aberdeen
Aberdeen, Scotland, UK
{r03rm16, g.chen, ruizhe.li, chenghua.lin}@abdn.ac.uk

Abstract

This paper describes the system that we submitted for SemEval-2018 task 10: capturing discriminative attributes. Our system is built upon a simple idea of measuring the attribute word's similarity with each of the two semantically similar words, based on an extended word embedding method and WordNet. Instead of computing the similarities between the attribute and semantically similar words by using standard word embeddings, we propose a novel method that combines word and context embeddings which can better measure similarities. Our model is simple and effective, which achieves an average F1 score of 0.62 on the test set.

1 Introduction

Capturing discriminative attributes is a novel task, which is very different from classical semantic tasks that model similarities in semantics. The task aims to recognise semantic differences between words. Traditional semantic similarity evaluation tasks were designed for evaluating the quality of word representations based on the fact that words with similar semantics will be close to each other in vector space. Recent state-of-the-art distributed semantic models (Ling et al., 2015; Bojanowski et al., 2017) inspired by the success of word2vec (Mikolov et al., 2013) gave good performance in these similarity measure tasks. Nevertheless, how to capture discriminative attributes between semantically similar words is still a challenge for traditional word embedding methods, because these methods are designed to capture similar semantics.

We have two observations for the nature of the task and the provided data: (1) only limited data is available for model training; (2) the inputs of the model are merely isolated words themselves, which lack context information for applying complex models. Therefore, we propose a novel framework that differentiates two semantically similar words with the attribute word by using their word and context embeddings. We experimented with both Continuous Bag of Words (CBOW) and Skip-gram, demonstrating that using the combination of word and context embeddings outperforms using word embeddings alone.

The contribution of this work can be summarised as follows. We examine word and context embeddings in CBOW and Skip-gram, showing that using both word and context embeddings can better measure the co-occurrence of two words in sentences than simply using word embeddings. Hence our similarity measure can recognise the discriminative attributes of two semantically similar words more accurately.

2 System Description

Our system is trained based on word and context embedding features as well as WordNet features (Fellbaum, 1998). Before introducing our framework in detail, we first introduce the two key technical parts of our framework, i.e., context embedding and WordNet.

2.1 Context embeddings

In contrast to simply using traditional word embeddings which model semantic similarities based on contextual similarities, we consider using both word and context embeddings. Word and context embeddings are the vectors of target words and context words in CBOW and Skip-gram. Using them together can model the co-occurrence of attribute words and distinguished words in a sentence, which is useful in predicting whether the attribute word can distinguish two semantically similar words.

Take the Skip-gram model as an example. Skip-gram uses a neural network with a single hidden

Proceedings of the 12th International Workshop on Semantic Evaluation (SemEval-2018), pages 1017–1021
New Orleans, Louisiana, June 5–6, 2018. ©2018 Association for Computational Linguistics

layer of neurons. Given a target word, the objective function is to maximize the probability of predicting each context word (several words before and after the target word in a training sentence) (Rong, 2014):

$$\arg\max p(w_c|w_t) \qquad (1)$$

where w_t is a target word in a training sentence, w_c is a context word of w_t, appearing within the same sentence.

During every training epoch on each context word, the weight matrices before and after the hidden layer will be updated. A row vector in the matrix before the hidden layer is a traditional word embedding v_t, as the vector is updated when the corresponding word w_t is in the target word position. A column vector in the matrix after the hidden layer is defined as context embedding v_c, as the column vector is updated when the corresponding word w_c is in the context word position. Each word has two vectors, v_t and v_c, as each word can be a target word or a context word of other target words. Some popular toolkits, e.g., gensim word2vec (Řehůřek and Sojka, 2010), abandon Skip-gram's context embeddings v_c after training, as experimental research (Nalisnick et al., 2016) proves that simply using v_t or v_c (IN-IN or OUT-OUT in the original paper) for two function or type similar words to measure their similarity yields higher scores.

Actually, the conditional probability in the objective function in Eq. 1 can be expanded as:

$$p(w_c|w_t) = \frac{\exp\left(v_t \cdot v_c\right)}{\sum_{i \in |V|} \exp\left(v_t \cdot v_i\right)} \qquad (2)$$

where V is the vocabulary of the training set, the dot product $v_t \cdot v_c$ in numerator computes the similarity between the target word vector and the context word vector. The denominator is to normalise the similarity into a probability. Thus, given a target word, training the whole model involves updating the matrices before and after the hidden layer to maximize the probability of predicting the context word. This is similar to maximizing the similarity between the target word embeddings v_t and context word embeddings v_c. It means that if we can reuse this trained similarity measure, to compute e.g., cosine similarity, then we will get a much better result. In other words, using both the word and context embeddings of two words that frequently appeared within each other's contexts

will result in a better similarity measure, which may be incorporating the co-occurrence information of the two words.

CBOW can be considered as the reverse of Skip-gram. Given a context, the target is to maximize the probability of predicting the target word appearing in the context. Later, we will examine both CBOW and Skip-gram's word and context embeddings in our model.

2.2 Word definition in WordNet

We also introduce features based on word sense definitions in WordNet (Fellbaum, 1998), considering the differences between the definitions of two semantically similar words. The two words may be similar in semantics, but different in definitions. An eligible discriminative attribute word may have high possibility to appear within one of the two word definitions, rather than both of them. For example, *ears* can distinguish *corn* and *broccoli*, as in WordNet, *ears* occurs in the definition of *corn* as *"tall annual cereal grass bearing kernels on large ears: widely cultivated in America in many varieties; the principal cereal in Mexico and Central and South America since pre-Columbian times"*, rather than *broccoli*'s definition that *"plant with dense clusters of tight green flower buds"*. We will also capture such characters to distinguish two words.

2.3 Hypothesis and framework

Our first hypothesis is that an attribute word w_A can distinguish two semantically similar words w_1 and w_2, if the attribute word co-occurs much more frequently with one word than the other in the corpora. In vector space, the attribute word can be closer to a distinguished word than the other one. Our second hypothesis is that if w_A can distinguish w_1 and w_2, w_A may appear within one of the definitions of w_1 and w_2 in WordNet.

The framework of our model can be summarized as: (1) we firstly train word embeddings v_t and context embeddings v_c on a Wikipedia dump. (2) Given a triple (w_1, w_2, w_A), we then compute w_A's cosine similarities with w_1 and w_2, and the difference in their similarities, which are used as three input features in the following classifications. For example, given the context embeddings of w_1 and w_2 and the word embedding of w_A, we compute Feature 1: $\text{cosine}(v_c^{w_1}, v_t^{w_A})$; Feature 2: $\text{cosine}(v_c^{w_2}, v_t^{w_A})$; and Feature 3: $|\text{cosine}(v_c^{w_1}, v_t^{w_A}) - \text{cosine}(v_c^{w_2}, v_t^{w_A})|$, respec-

1	$\mathrm{cosine}(w_1, w_A)$
2	$\mathrm{cosine}(w_2, w_A)$
3	$|\mathrm{cosine}(w_1, w_A) - \mathrm{cosine}(w_2, w_A)|$
4	binary variable, indicating if w_A appears in the WordNet definitions of w_1
5	binary variable, indicating if w_A appears in the WordNet definitions of w_2

Table 1: Feature descriptions.

tively. (3) Next, we introduce two binary features to indicate whether w_A appears in any sense definitions of w_1 and w_2 in WordNet (Feature 4 and 5), respectively. (4) We train a random forest classifier with the above five features (see Table 1) to classify if the attribute word w_A can distinguish two semantically similar words w_1 and w_2.

3 Experimental Settings

Data. The data was provided by the organizers of SemEval 2018 Task 10: Capturing Discriminative Attributes[1]. There are 17,501, 2,722 and 2,340 triples (w_1, w_2, w_A) in training, validation and testing sets, respectively. All the words in the triples are nouns. Note that the discriminative attribute words w_A in the given dataset are selected, because they represent the visual attribute of one of two semantically similar words. For example, *red* can differentiate *apple* and *banana*, because visually, apple is red, while banana is yellow. The task does not consider other discriminative features, such as sound and taste. So, using image features may take advantages in this dataset, however, semantic features can also capture invisible discriminative attributes.

Word and context embedding. We first iteratively train 300 dimensional word and context embeddings based on CBOW and Skip-gram with a Wikipedia dump[2] for 3 epochs respectively, setting a context window of 5 words before and after the target word. Words with frequency less than 5 in the Wikipedia are ignored. The down sampling rate is 10^{-4}.

Based on CBOW and Skip-gram, we test all possible combinations of word and context embeddings to compute cosine similarities. The first combination is context embeddings of the two semantically similar words w_1 and w_2, and word embeddings of the attribute word w_A. In Table 2

and 4, this approach is represented as $v_c^{w1} v_c^{w2} v_t^{wA}$. The second $v_t^{w1} v_t^{w2} v_c^{wA}$ uses word embeddings of w_1 and w_2, and context embeddings of w_A. The third $v_c^{w1} v_c^{w2} v_c^{wA}$ is simply context embeddings of w_1, w_2 and w_A. The fourth $v_t^{w1} v_t^{w2} v_t^{wA}$ is simply word embeddings of w_1, w_2 and w_A.

4 Results

We cast the challenge task as a supervised classification problem. We first examine which combination of word and context embeddings and which training method (CBOW or Skip-gram) is optimal in this task. In this step, we only use Feature 1-3 (see Table 1) to classify the triple (w_1, w_2, w_A).

As can be seen in Table 2, both the CBOW based methods that use word and context embeddings yield the highest average F1 of 0.55 in the validation set. Skip-gram based models generally perform worse than CBOW based models, but using Skip-gram word embeddings of w_1 and w_2 and context embeddings of w_A also outperforms the word embedding based model in the validation set. The experiments running on the test set show similar trends that word and context embedding based models outperform word embedding based models. Such results demonstrate that using word and context embeddings together can better distinguish two semantically similar words with an attribute word, than simply using standard word embeddings. The results also support our first hypothesis that if the attribute word frequently appears in one word's context than the other one, it can distinguish the two words.

We also examine WordNet definition features individually. As shown in Table 3, simply using Feature 4-5 cannot classify the triple accurately. The F1 score of setting positive label as 1 is very low on the validation set (F1=36%). This is for the reason that an eligible discriminative attribute word cannot always associate with the definitions of one of two semantically similar words. So, simply using such features cannot identify discriminative words precisely.

Finally, we combine both similarity and WordNet features together to address this challenge. There is no significant difference between CBOW based $v_c^{w1} v_c^{w2} v_t^{wA}$ and $v_t^{w1} v_c^{w2} v_c^{wA}$ in the validation set in terms of average F1. We select $v_c^{w1} v_c^{w2} v_t^{wA}$ as the winner combination of word and context embeddings, because this approach has closer F1 scores, when setting different la-

---

[1] https://competitions.codalab.org/competitions/17326

[2] https://dumps.wikimedia.org/enwiki/20170920/

setup		positive=1			positive=0			average F1
		P	R	F1	P	R	F1	
validation	CBOW	$v_c^{w1} v_c^{w2} v_t^{wA}$	0.56	0.46	0.51	0.54	0.64	0.59	**0.55**
		$v_t^{w1} v_t^{w2} v_c^{wA}$	0.57	0.45	0.50	0.55	0.66	0.60	**0.55**
		$v_c^{w1} v_c^{w2} v_c^{wA}$	0.50	0.37	0.43	0.50	0.63	0.56	0.49
		$v_t^{w1} v_t^{w2} v_t^{wA}$	0.50	0.30	0.37	0.50	0.70	0.58	0.48
	Skip-gram	$v_c^{w1} v_c^{w2} v_t^{wA}$	0.54	0.38	0.45	0.52	0.68	0.59	0.52
		$v_t^{w1} v_t^{w2} v_c^{wA}$	0.55	0.47	0.51	0.54	0.62	0.58	**0.54**
		$v_c^{w1} v_c^{w2} v_c^{wA}$	0.52	0.33	0.40	0.51	0.70	0.59	0.49
		$v_t^{w1} v_t^{w2} v_t^{wA}$	0.53	0.41	0.46	0.52	0.64	0.57	0.52
test	CBOW	$v_c^{w1} v_c^{w2} v_t^{wA}$	0.54	0.56	0.55	0.63	0.62	0.63	**0.59**
		$v_t^{w1} v_t^{w2} v_c^{wA}$	0.54	0.53	0.53	0.62	0.63	0.63	0.58
		$v_c^{w1} v_c^{w2} v_c^{wA}$	0.50	0.47	0.49	0.59	0.62	0.61	0.55
		$v_t^{w1} v_t^{w2} v_t^{wA}$	0.49	0.39	0.44	0.58	0.67	0.62	0.53
	Skip-gram	$v_c^{w1} v_c^{w2} v_t^{wA}$	0.52	0.50	0.51	0.61	0.63	0.62	0.56
		$v_t^{w1} v_t^{w2} v_c^{wA}$	0.52	0.56	0.54	0.62	0.59	0.60	**0.57**
		$v_c^{w1} v_c^{w2} v_c^{wA}$	0.50	0.43	0.46	0.59	0.65	0.62	0.54
		$v_t^{w1} v_t^{w2} v_t^{wA}$	0.51	0.51	0.51	0.60	0.61	0.61	0.56

Table 2: Experimental results by using word and context embeddings (Feature 1-3).

setup		positive=1			positive=0			average F1
		P	R	F1	P	R	F1	
WordNet	validation	0.66	0.24	0.36	0.53	0.87	0.66	0.51
	test	0.66	0.26	0.37	0.60	0.89	0.71	0.54

Table 3: Experimental results by using WordNet definition features (Feature 4-5).

setup			positive=1			positive=0			average F1
			P	R	F1	P	R	F1	
CBOW+WordNet	validation	$v_c^{w1} v_c^{w2} v_t^{wA}$+WN	0.57	0.53	**0.55**	0.56	0.59	**0.57**	**0.56**
	test	$v_c^{w1} v_c^{w2} v_t^{wA}$+WN	0.58	0.60	**0.59**	0.66	0.65	0.65	**0.62**

Table 4: Final results by using CBOW word and context embeddings, and WordNet features (Feature 1-5).

bels (1 or 0) as the positive label. Thus, in the final submission, we use CBOW trained context embeddings of w_1 and w_2, and word embeddings of w_A to compute similarity features. We identify whether an attribute word w_A can distinguish w_1 and w_2 by using the above similarity features and WordNet definition features together. Although word and context embedding based similarity features are much more effective than WordNet features, by introducing WordNet features, the model further improves its performance, achieving 62% F1 on the test set (Table 4). WordNet definitions are also supportive features in this task.

Error analysis. We found that a significant portion of failures appear in those examples that the textual associations of the attribute words and the semantically similar words are not always discriminative. E.g., given a triple, (sons, father, young), our model failed in identifying *young* as a discriminative attribute, because *young* has been widely used to describe *sons* and *father* in the text (e.g., *young sons* and *a young father*). In this case, our word co-occurrence based method is suboptimal.

5 Conclusion

In this paper, we extended traditional word embedding methods (CBOW and Skip-gram) to distinguish two semantically similar words using an attribute word. In contrast with simply using traditional word representations, using both context and word embeddings can better model the co-occurrence between the two similar words and their discriminative attribute word. If the attribute word frequently co-occurs with one of the similar words more than another one within the same sentences, then the two semantically similar words can be distinguished by the attribute word. By using CBOW word and context embedding based similarity features and simple WordNet based word sense definition features, our model performs an average F1 of 62% on the test set.

Acknowledgments

This work is supported by the award made by the UK Engineering and Physical Sciences Research Council (Grant number: EP/P005810/1).

References

Piotr Bojanowski, Edouard Grave, Armand Joulin, and Tomas Mikolov. 2017. Enriching word vectors with subword information. *Transactions of the Association for Computational Linguistics*, 5:135–146.

Christiane Fellbaum. 1998. *WordNet: An Electronic Lexical Database*. Bradford Books.

Wang Ling, Chris Dyer, Alan Black, and Isabel Trancoso. 2015. Two/too simple adaptations of word2vec for syntax problems. In *Proceedings of the 2015 Conference of the North American Chapter of the Association for Computational Linguistics: Human Language Technologies*. Association for Computational Linguistics.

Tomas Mikolov, Kai Chen, Greg Corrado, and Jeffrey Dean. 2013. Efficient estimation of word representations in vector space. *Proceedings of International Conference on Learning Representations*.

Eric Nalisnick, Bhaskar Mitra, Nick Craswell, and Rich Caruana. 2016. Improving document ranking with dual word embeddings. In *Proceedings of the 25th International Conference Companion on World Wide Web*, pages 83–84. International World Wide Web Conferences Steering Committee.

Radim Řehůřek and Petr Sojka. 2010. Software Framework for Topic Modelling with Large Corpora. In *Proceedings of the LREC 2010 Workshop on New Challenges for NLP Frameworks*, pages 45–50, Valletta, Malta. ELRA. `http://is.muni.cz/publication/884893/en`.

Xin Rong. 2014. word2vec parameter learning explained. *arXiv preprint arXiv:1411.2738*.

UMD at SemEval-2018 Task 10:
Can Word Embeddings Capture Discriminative Attributes?

Alexander Zhang and **Marine Carpuat**
Department of Computer Science
University of Maryland
College Park, MD 20742, USA
`alexz@umd.edu, marine@cs.umd.edu`

Abstract

We describe the University of Maryland's submission to SemEval-018 Task 10, "Capturing Discriminative Attributes": given word triples (w_1, w_2, d), the goal is to determine whether d is a discriminating attribute belonging to w_1 but not w_2. Our study aims to determine whether word embeddings can address this challenging task. Our submission casts this problem as supervised binary classification using only word embedding features. Using a gaussian SVM model trained only on validation data results in an F-score of 60%. We also show that cosine similarity features are more effective, both in unsupervised systems (F-score of 65%) and supervised systems (F-score of 67%).

1 Introduction

SemEval-2018 Task 10 (Krebs et al., 2018) offers an opportunity to evaluate word embeddings on a challenging lexical semantics problem. Much prior work on word embeddings has focused on the well-established task of detecting semantic similarity (Mikolov et al., 2013a; Pennington et al., 2014; Baroni et al., 2014; Upadhyay et al., 2016). However, semantic similarity tasks alone cannot fully characterize the differences in meaning between words. For example, we would expect the word *car* to have high semantic similarity with *truck* and with *vehicle* in distributional vector spaces, while the relation between *car* and *truck* differs from the relation between *car* and *vehicle*. In addition, popular datasets for similarity tasks are small, and similarity annotations are subjective with low inter-annotator agreement (Krebs and Paperno, 2016).

Task 10 focuses instead on determining semantic difference: given a word triple (w_1, w_2, d), the task consists in predicting whether d is a discriminating attribute applicable to w_1, but not to w_2. For instance, $(w_1$ =apple, w_2 =banana, d =red) is a positive example as *red* is a typical attribute of *apple*, but not of *banana*.

This work asks to what extent word embeddings can address the challenging task of detecting discriminating attributes. On the one hand, word embeddings have proven useful for a wide range of NLP tasks, including semantic similarity (Mikolov et al., 2013a; Pennington et al., 2014; Baroni et al., 2014; Upadhyay et al., 2016) and detection of lexical semantic relations, either explicitly by detecting hypernymy, lexical entailment (Baroni et al., 2012; Roller et al., 2014; Turney and Mohammad, 2013), or implicitly using analogies (Mikolov et al., 2013b). On the other hand, detecting discriminating attributes requires making fine-grained meaning distinctions, and it is unclear to what extent they can be captured with opaque dense representations.

We start our study with unsupervised models. We propose a straightforward approach where predictions are based on a learned threshold for the cosine similarity difference between (w_1, d) and (w_2, d), representing words using Glove embeddings (Pennington et al., 2014). We use this unsupervised approach to evaluate the impact of word embedding dimensions on performance.

We then compare the best unsupervised configuration to supervised models, exploring the impact of different classifiers and training configurations. Using word embeddings as features, supervised models yield high F-scores on development data, on the final test set they perform worse than the unsupervised models. Our supervised submission yields an F-score of 60%. In later experiments, we show that using cosine similarity as features

Proceedings of the 12th International Workshop on Semantic Evaluation (SemEval-2018), pages 1022–1026
New Orleans, Louisiana, June 5–6, 2018. ©2018 Association for Computational Linguistics

is more effective than directly using word embeddings, reaching an F-score of 67%.

2 Task Data Overview

Dataset	Pos	Neg	Total	d Vocab
train	6,591	11,191	17,782	1,292
validation	1,364	1,358	2,722	576
test	1,047	1,293	2,340	577

Table 1: Dataset statistics for the training and validation set: number of positive examples (Pos), number of negative examples (Neg), total number of examples (total), size of vocabulary for discriminant words d (d Vocab)

For development purposes, we are provided with two datasets: a training set and a validation set, whose statistics are summarized in Table 1.

Word triples (w_1, w_2, d) were selected using the feature norms set from McRae et al. (2005). Only visual discriminant features were considered for d, such as *is_green*. Positive triples (w_1, w_2, d) were formed by selecting w_2 among the 100 nearest neighbors of w_1 such that a visual feature d is attributable to w_1 but not w_2. Negative triples were formed by either selecting an attribute attributable to both words, or by randomly selecting a feature not attributable to either word.

The distribution of the training and validation sets differ: the validation and test sets are balanced, while only 37% of examples are positive in the training set. In addition, the validation and test sets were manually filtered to improve quality, so the training examples are more noisy. The data split was chosen to have minimal overlap between discriminant features.

3 Unsupervised Systems

All our models rely on Glove (Pennington et al., 2014), generic word embeddings models, pretrained on large corpora: the Wikipedia and English Gigaword newswire corpora. In addition to capturing semantic similarity with distances between words, Glove aims for vector differences to capture the meaning specified by the juxtaposition of two words, which is a good fit for our task.

Because the discriminant features are distinct between train, validation and test, our systems should be able to generalize to previously unseen discriminants. This makes approaches based on word embeddings attractive, as information about word identity is not directly encoded in our model.

3.1 Baseline

We first consider the baseline approach introduced by Krebs and Paperno (2016) to detect the positive examples, where cs denotes the cosine similarity function:

$$cs(word_1, disc) > cs(word_2, disc) \qquad (1)$$

3.2 2-Step Unsupervised System

We refine this baseline with a 2-step approach. Our intuition is that d is a discriminant between w_1 and w_2 if the following two conditions hold simultaneously:

1. w_1 is more similar to d than w_2 by more than a threshold t_{thresh}:

$$cs(w_1, d) - cs(w_2, d) > t_{thresh} \qquad (2)$$

2. d is highly similar to w_1:

$$cs(w_1, d) > t_{diverge} \qquad (3)$$

The condition in Equation 2 aims at detecting negative examples that share the discriminant attribute, and the condition defined by Equation 3 targets negative examples that share a random discriminant. Thresholds t_{thresh} and $t_{diverge}$ are hyper-parameters tuned on the *train.txt*.

3.3 Results

We evaluate unsupervised systems using word embeddings of varying dimensions on the validation set, and report averaged F-scores. As can be seen in Table 2, increasing the dimension of word embeddings improves performance for both systems, and the 2-step model consistently outperforms the baseline. The best performance is obtained by the 2-step model with 300-dimensional word embeddings. We therefore select these embeddings for further experiments.

Vector Dim	50	100	200	300
baseline	.5765	.5965	.6171	.6183
2-step model	.4034	.6130	.6266	.6312

Table 2: Averaged F-Score across GloVe Dimensions between our 2-step unsupervised system and the baseline from Krebs and Paperno (2016), for word vectors of size 50, 100, 200 and 300.

4 Supervised Systems

4.1 Submitted System

During system development, we consider a range of binary classifiers that operate on feature representations derived from word embeddings $\vec{w_1}, \vec{w_2}$ and $\vec{d}$. We describe the system used for submission which was selected based on 10-fold cross-validation using the concatenation of the training and validation data.

Feature Representations We seek to capture the difference in meaning between w_1 and w_2 and its relation to the meaning of the discriminant word d. Given word embeddings for each of these words $\vec{w_1}, \vec{w_2}$ and $\vec{d}$, respectively, we therefore construct input features based on various embedding vector differences. We experimented with the concatenation of $\vec{w_1}, \vec{w_2}, \vec{d}, \vec{w_1} - \vec{d}$ and $\vec{w_1} - \vec{d}$. Based on cross-validation performance on training and validation data, we eventually settled on the concatenation of $\vec{w_1} - \vec{d}$ and $\vec{w_1} - \vec{d}$, which yields a compact representation of $2D$ features, if D is the embedding dimension.

Binary Classifier We consider a number of binary classification models found in scikit-learn: logarithmic regression (LR), decision tree (DT), naïve Bayes (NB), K nearest neighbors (KNN), and SVM with linear (SVM-L), and Gaussian (SVM-G) kernels. We compare linear combinations of word embeddings to the more complex combinations enabled by non-linear models.

Submission Our submission used the refined SVM-G trained on *validation.txt*. There were three input triplets for which one word was out of the vocabulary of the Glove embedding model: random predictions were used for these. This system achieved an F-Score of .6018. This is a substantial drop from the averaged cross-validation F-scores obtained during development which reached F-scores of 0.9318 using cross-validation on the validation and training sets together, and 0.9674 using cross-validation on the training set only. Using the released test dataset, *truth.txt*, we consider various experiments to understand the poor performance of the model.

4.2 Analysis: Embedding Selection

We first evaluate our hypothesis that word embeddings that perform well in the unsupervised setting would also, in general, perform well for classification. We vary embedding dimensions keeping the rest of the experimental set-up constant (train on *validation.txt*, evaluate on *truth.txt*).

Table 3 shows the performance of all supervised model configurations and of the 2-step unsupervised system. Increasing the word embedding dimensions improves the performance of the 2-step unsupervised system, as observed during the development phase (Section 3). However, the supervised classifier behaves differently: for several linear classifiers (e.g., LR, DT, SVM-L) the best performance is achieved with smaller word embeddings. For the non-linear SVM used for submission (SVM-G), varying the embedding dimensions has little impact on overall performance. The SVM-G classifier's performance is now on par with the linear classifiers, while it performed better on development data.

The best performance overall is achieved by the unsupervised model, and taken together, the supervised results suggest that the submitted system overfit the validation set, and was not able to generalize to make good predictions on test examples.

4.3 Analysis: Feature Variants

Motivated by the good performance of the unsupervised model based on cosine similarity, we consider four feature representations variants for the supervised classifiers,[1]:

$$V1 = [cs(w_1, w_2), cs(w_1, w_d), cs(w_2, d)]$$
$$V2 = [V1, w_1 - w_2, w_d]$$
$$V3 = [V1, w_1 - w_d, w_2]$$
$$V4 = [V1, cs(w_1 - w_2, w_d), cs(w_1 - w_d, w_2)]$$

Variant V1 based only on cosine similarity between all pairs yields competitive F-scores from both the SVM-G and LR models (Table 4), and it competitive with the best-performing unsupervised model. We thus use it as a starting point for subsequent variants. Variants V2 and V3 encode the intuition that we expect $w_1 - w_2 \approx w_d$ and $w_1 - w_d \approx w_2$ for positive examples, and therefore, it is possible that these input representations may perform better than the differences-only model. In doing so, we also risk memorizing actual input words as w_d and w_2 are encoded directly as features. These two variants performed worse than the cosine-only models, suggesting that cosine similarity captures semantic

---

[1]The KNN, SVM-L, and SVM-G used tuned hyperparameters.

Model	dim=50			dim=100			dim=200			dim=300		
	F	P	R	F	P	R	F	P	R	F	P	R
LR	.5742	.5750	.5741	.5769	.5788	.5770	.5739	.5741	.5738	.5525	.5525	.5524
DT	.5494	.5498	.5503	.5356	.5357	.5359	.5304	.5311	.5314	.5283	.5290	.5293
NB	.5618	.5674	.5634	.5873	.5999	.5903	.5885	.5904	.5884	.5908	.5972	.5918
KNN	.5640	.5746	.5677	.5677	.5715	.5720	.5738	.5737	.5740	.5537	.5575	.5579
SVM-L	.5769	.5778	.5768	.5847	.5904	.5856	.5781	.5791	.5779	.5364	.5372	.5376
SVM-G	.5901	.5909	.5919	.6098	.6099	.6097	.5924	.5923	.5924	.5995	.6002	.5993
2-step	.5937	.5938	.5947	.6042	.6041	.6044	.6278	.6278	.6290	.6484	.6481	.6490

Table 3: F-Score, Precision and Recall computed on *truth.txt* for the full range of supervised classification models across different embedding dimensions trained on *validation.txt*. The first 6 row are supervised systems, the last row shows the performance of the unsupervised 2-step system.

Vector Dim.	50	100	200	300
V1-LR	.6083	.6076	.6369	.6526
V1-KNN	.6045	.6115	.6335	.6587
V1-SVMG	.6039	.6227	.6479	.6681
V2-LR	.6398	.6475	.6463	.6490
V2-KNN	.5376	.5239	.5334	.5221
V2-SVMG	.6304	.6435	.6592	.6598
V3-LR	.6203	.6108	.6167	.6193
V3-KNN	.5356	.5182	.5116	.5308
V3-SVMG	.6099	.6233	.6269	.6309
V4-LR	.6089	.6072	.6378	.6525
V4-KNN	.6088	.6120	.6402	.6589
V4-SVMG	.6102	.6239	.6451	.6708

Table 4: F-score for well-performing models of alternative input variant representations

difference better than the high-dimensional word vectors themselves. Also interestingly, the KNN model performed significantly worse in these two variants. The best result is achieved using V4, which augments V1 with cosine features that better capture word relations through embedding differences, with an averaged F-score of .6708 using the SVM-G classifier.

4.4 Analysis: Cross-Validation Set-up

We further explore why cross-validation scores differed greatly from the final test scores. We constructed initial cross-validation sets using sequential 10% cuts of the training set. This is inconsistent with the actual experimental setup, which had distinct sets of d, the discriminating attribute, between the training and test sets. We experiment segmenting the validation dataset so that each of the cross-validation sets had distinct discriminat-

ing attributes. This yields only minor gains (Table 5), suggesting that overfitting to the identity of the discriminating attributes was not an issue.

Vector Dim.	50	100	200	300
V4-KNN	.6050	.6172	.6394	.6574
V4-SVML	.6109	.6042	.6301	.6478
V4-SVMG	.6104	.624	.6404	.6716

Table 5: F-score from well-formed cross-validation sets

5 Conclusion

This study showed the limits of directly using word embeddings as features for the challenging task of capturing discriminative attributes between words. Supervised models based on raw embedding features are highly sensitive to the nature and distribution of training examples. Our Gaussian Kernel SVM overfit the training set and performed worse than unsupervised models that threshold cosine similarity scores on the official evaluation data. Based on this finding, we explore the use of cosine similarity scores as features for supervised classifiers, to capture similarity between word pairs, and between words and word relations as represented by embedding differences. These features turn out to be more useful than directly using the word embedding themselves, yielding our best performing system (F-score of 67%).

While these results are encouraging, it remains to be seen how to best design models and features that capture nuanced meaning differences, for instance by leveraging metrics complementary to cosine and resources complementary to distributional embeddings.

References

Marco Baroni, Raffaella Bernardi, Ngoc-Quynh Do, and Chung-chieh Shan. 2012. Entailment above the word level in distributional semantics. In *Proceedings of EACL 2012*, pages 23–32.

Marco Baroni, Georgiana Dinu, and Germán Kruszewski. 2014. Don't count, predict! A systematic comparison of context-counting vs. context-predicting semantic vectors. In *ACL (1)*, pages 238–247.

Alicia Krebs, Alessandro Lenci, and Denis Paperno. 2018. Semeval-2018 task 10: Capturing discriminative attributes. In *Proceedings of SemEval-2018: International Workshop on Semantic Evaluation*.

Alicia Krebs and Denis Paperno. 2016. Capturing discriminative attributes in a distributional space: Task proposal. In *RepEval@ACL*.

Ken McRae, George S. Cree, Mark S. Seidenberg, and Chris Mcnorgan. 2005. Semantic feature production norms for a large set of living and nonliving things. *Behavior Research Methods*, 37(4):547–559.

Tomas Mikolov, Kai Chen, Greg Corrado, and Jeffrey Dean. 2013a. Efficient estimation of word representations in vector space. In *arXiv Preprint*.

Tomas Mikolov, Wen-tau Yih, and Geoffrey Zweig. 2013b. Linguistic Regularities in Continuous Space Word Representations. In *HLT-NAACL*, volume 13, pages 746–751.

Jeffrey Pennington, Richard Socher, and Christopher D. Manning. 2014. GloVe: Global Vectors for Word Representation. In *EMNLP 2014*, pages 1532–1543.

Stephen Roller, Katrin Erk, and Gemma Boleda. 2014. Inclusive yet Selective: Supervised Distributional Hypernymy Detection. *Proceedings of COLING 2014*, pages 1025–1036.

Peter Turney and Saif Mohammad. 2013. Experiments with three approaches to recognizing lexical entailment. *Natural Language Engineering*, 1(1):1–42.

Shyam Upadhyay, Manaal Faruqui, Chris Dyer, and Dan Roth. 2016. Cross-lingual Models of Word Embeddings: An Empirical Comparison. In *Proceedings of ACL*, Berlin, Germany.

NTU NLP Lab System at SemEval-2018 Task 10: Verifying Semantic Differences by Integrating Distributional Information and Expert Knowledge

Yow-Ting Shiue[1], Hen-Hsen Huang[1], and Hsin-Hsi Chen[1,2]

[1]Department of Computer Science and Information Engineering,
National Taiwan University, Taipei, Taiwan
[2]MOST Joint Research Center for AI Technology and All Vista Healthcare, Taiwan
`orinal123@gmail.com`, `hhhuang@nlg.csie.ntu.edu.tw`, `hhchen@ntu.edu.tw`

Abstract

This paper presents the NTU NLP Lab system for the SemEval-2018 Capturing Discriminative Attributes task. Word embeddings, pointwise mutual information (PMI), ConceptNet edges and shortest path lengths are utilized as input features to build binary classifiers to tell whether an attribute is discriminative for a pair of concepts. Our neural network model reaches about 73% F1 score on the test set and ranks the 3rd in the task. Though the attributes to deal with in this task are all visual, our models are not provided with any image data. The results indicate that visual information can be derived from textual data.

1 Introduction

Modern semantic models are good at capturing semantic similarity and relatedness. The widely-used distributional word representations, or word embeddings, have achieved promising performance on various semantic tasks. The word pair similarities calculated with these models are to some extent consistent with human judgments, and many downstream applications such as sentiment analysis and machine translation have benefited from word embeddings' ability to aggregate the information of lexical items with similar meaning but different surface forms.

However, the ability to *distinguish* one concept from another similar concept is also core to linguistic competence. Our knowledge about what is a "subway", for example, may contain "it is a kind of train that runs underground". Also, discriminating things is an important mechanism for teaching and learning. For example, if we would like to explain how a "plate" is different from a "bowl", we may use expressions like "a plate is flatter" or "a bowl is deeper". All these examples show that one form of semantic difference is a *discriminative at-*

tribute which applies to one of the two concepts being compared but does not apply to the other.

In the SemEval-2018 Capturing Discriminative Attributes task (Krebs et al., 2018), participants need to put forward semantic models that are aware of semantic differences. A data instance consists of a triple and a label. In this paper, we denote a triple with $< w_1, w_2, a >$, in which w_1 and w_2 are the two words (concepts) to be compared, and a is an attribute. The label is either positive (1) or negative (0). In a positive example, a is an attribute of w_1 but not an attribute of w_2. For negative examples, there are two cases: 1) both w_1 and w_2 have attribute a ; 2) neither w_1 nor w_2 has attribute a. In this task, a is limited to visual ones such as color and shape. The evaluation metric is the macro-averaged F1 score of the positive and the negative classes.

Visual attribute learning has been investigated by past researchers. Silberer et al. (2013) build a dataset of concept-level attribute annotations based on images in ImageNet (Deng et al., 2009). For each attribute, they train a classifier to predict its presence or absence in the input image. Lazaridou et al. (2016) propose a model that does not learn visual attributes explicitly, but learns discriminativeness. Their model predicts whether an attribute can be used to discriminate a referent from a context. Both the referent and the context are represented by visual instances sampled from ImageNet. This setting is similar to that of this SemEval task. However, one critical difference is that in this task, the set of attributes is open. The dataset is partitioned so that all the attributes in the test set are unseen in the training set, which makes this task more challenging.

The use of word embeddings for detecting semantic properties is studied by Rubinstein et al. (2015). They focus on a fixed set of properties and train a binary classifier for each property. Their

Proceedings of the 12th International Workshop on Semantic Evaluation (SemEval-2018), pages 1027–1033
New Orleans, Louisiana, June 5–6, 2018. ©2018 Association for Computational Linguistics

results indicate that word embeddings capture taxonomic properties (e.g. "an animal") better than attributive properties (e.g. "is fast"), possibly because attributive signal is weak in text.

In this task, most visual attributes are attributive properties. The signal of "visual" attributes can be even weaker in text since they are not mainly communicated through language in human cognition. The word "red" in "I bought a red apple" sounds more like a linguistic redundancy than that in "I bought a red jacket" does, since "red" is a typical attribute of apples. However, these visual attributes may impose constraints on valid expressions. For instance, we can say "the bananas turned yellow", but it would be extremely difficult to find some context where "the bananas turned red" makes sense. Therefore, visual attributes can be signaled in some implicit and indirect ways. By utilizing several computational approaches, we reveal to what extent visual attributes can be acquired from text.

This paper aims at capturing semantic difference by incorporating information from both corpus statistics and expert-constructed knowledge bases. We build a rule-based system and a learning-based system for the binary classification problem, i.e., to tell whether an attribute is discriminative for two concepts. The learning-based system achieved F1 score of 0.7294, which is the third best in the official evaluation period of SemEval-2018 Task 10. Our approach is purely based on textual data, without access to image instances, which indicates that it is possible to figure out substantial visual information from text.

2 Distributional Information

We utilize two kinds of computational approaches to derive information from co-occurrence statistics in large copora. The first one is word embedding, which has been shown to encode semantic information in low-dimensional vectors. The second one is pointwise mutual information (PMI), which is a commonly-used measurement of the strength of association between two words. We analyze the performance of rule-based or learning-based models with different sets of features to reflect their effectiveness.

2.1 Concatenation of Word Embeddings

A very straight-forward approach is concatenating the embedding of w_1, w_2 and a into a fea-

Embeddings			Train		Validation	
w_1	w_2	a	Acc.	Macro F1	Acc.	Macro F1
V	V	V	**0.7468**	**0.6484**	**0.5184**	0.3409
		V	0.6379	0.5216	0.5180	0.2908
V	V		0.7017	0.5040	0.4996	0.2748
V		V	0.6790	0.5938	0.4945	**0.3558**
	V	V	0.6733	0.5421	0.5029	0.3170

Table 1: Training and validation scores of MLP model with embeddings of different subsets of the triple.

ture vector to train a binary classifier. We use the pre-trained 300-dimensional Word2vec embeddings (Mikolov et al., 2013) trained on Google News[1] as input features. We construct a multi-layer perceptron (MLP) model with two hidden layers of size 1,024 to conduct preliminary experiments. The activation function is ReLU and the dropout rate is 0.5. The model is implemented with Keras (Chollet, 2015). We train for 20 epochs and report the best validation scores.

However, we find out that there is a serious issue of overfitting. As shown in Table 1, the gap between training and validation scores is large. We also experimented simpler models such as Logistic Regression and Random Forest, and got similar results. A possible cause of overffiting is that the model does not learn to extract and compare attributes, but learns the "pattern" of some combination of words in the triples.

To verify the above speculation, we train similar MLP models which only take "partial" triples as input. Theoretically, the label cannot be determined correctly with an incomplete triple. However, according to the results shown in Table 1, the models considering solely a part of every triple can still "learn" some information from the training set (majority-class baseline accuracy on the training set: 0.6383). Some models with partial information even achieve better validation scores than that with complete information. This indicates that the models overfit to the vocabulary of the training set. At the test time, all the attributes are unknown, so the model cannot make effective predictions. In fact, these results are similar to the lexical memorization phenomenon reported by Levy et al. (2015) on the hypernym detection task.

2.2 Embeddings Similarity Difference

Because "raw" word embedding features do not work, we turn to more abstract features. Let sim_1 and sim_2 be the cosine similarity of the vector of a

---

[1] https://code.google.com/archive/p/word2vec/

to the vector of w_1 and w_2 respectively. We compare the values sim_1 and sim_2. The rationale is that if a word w has an attribute a, then it tends to, though not necessarily, be more similar to a than other words without a.

The following six embedding models are experimented with. The embedding size is fixed to 300.

1. **W2V(GNews):** The standard Word2vec model as described in Section 2.1.

2. **fastText:** fastText (Bojanowski et al., 2017) is a modification of Word2vec that takes subword information into account. We adopt the pre-trained vectors trained on 6B tokens[2].

3. **Numberbatch:** Numberbatch embeddings are built upon several corpus-based word embeddings and improved by retrofitting on Concept-Net, a large semantic network containing an abundance of general knowledge (Speer et al., 2017). We use the pre-trained embeddings of English concepts[3].

4. **GloVe(Common Crawl):** The GloVe model (Pennington et al., 2014) obtains word representation according to global co-occurrence statistics. We use the pre-trained vectors trained on 840B tokens of Common Crawl[4].

5. **Sense(enwiki)-c:** Sense vectors may encode more fine-grained semantic information than word vectors do, so we also experimented with sense vectors. We perform word sense disambiguation (WSD) on the English Wikipedia corpus to get a sense-annotated corpus, using the Adapted Lesk algorithm implemented in pywsd[5]. The sense inventory is based on synsets in WordNet. We train a Word2vec Skip-gram (SG) model with this corpus to obtain sense vectors. To apply sense vectors to words and attributes in this SemEval task, we propose the following *closest* sense-selection method (denoted by -c) to choose a sense for each of w_1, w_2 and a. $S(w)$ denotes the set of synsets that a word w belongs to and $emb(s)$ denotes the vector of synset (sense) s.

$$s_1*, s_a* = \underset{\substack{s_1 \in S(w_1) \\ s_a \in S(a)}}{\operatorname{argmax}} \cos(\operatorname{emb}(s_1), \operatorname{emb}(s_a))$$

$$s_2* = \underset{s_2 \in S(w_2)}{\operatorname{argmax}} \cos(\operatorname{emb}(s_1*), \operatorname{emb}(s_2))$$

Since a might be an attribute of w_1, we choose the closest pair of senses for them. Then, we choose the sense of w_2 that is closest to s_1*, the selected sense for w_1. The reason is that a semantic difference is more likely to be meaningful for two similar concepts. Finally, we use the vector of the selected senses to compute similarities.

6. **Sense(enwiki)-f:** We use the same sense embeddings as described previously but directly select the *first* sense (predominant sense) in WordNet for w_1, w_2 and a respectively, without performing WSD. This method is denoted by *-f*.

We first use these similarities in a simple rule-based model: if $sim_1 > sim_2$ then output 1; otherwise output 0. The results are summarized in Table 2. In general, this similarity comparison rule performs better on the positive class than on the negative class. GloVe results in the highest negative F1, while Numberbatch results in the best macro-averaged F1. We show the confusion matrix for this rule with Numberbatch in Table 3. As can be seen, similarity differences are helpful for discriminating the positive examples, but they are not good indicators of negative examples.

We use $sim_1 - sim_2$ of different kinds of embeddings as features and train MLP models as described in the previous section. The results of different combinations of embeddings are shown in Table 4. However, there is only slight macro-

Embeddings	Acc.	Pos. F1	Neg. F1	Macro F1
1. W2V	0.6128	0.6512	0.5648	0.6080
2. fastText	0.6047	0.6435	0.5565	0.6000
3. Numberbatch	**0.6653**	**0.7142**	0.5964	**0.6553**
4. GloVe	0.6330	0.6594	**0.6022**	0.6308
5. Sense-*c*	0.5981	0.6609	0.5068	0.5838
6. Sense-*f*	0.5816	0.5597	0.6013	0.5805

Table 2: Performance of the $sim_1 > sim_2$ rule with different embeddings on the validation set.

True label	$sim_1 > sim_2$	otherwise
1	1138	226
0	685	673

Table 3: Confusion matrix of the $sim_1 > sim_2$ rule with Numberbatch embeddings on the validation set.

Embeddings	Acc.	Pos. F1	Neg. F1	Macro F1
[**sim x3**] $1. - 3.$	**0.6598**	**0.6640**	**0.6555**	**0.6598**
[**sim x4**] $1. - 4.$	0.6547	0.6572	0.6521	0.6546
[**sim x6**] $1. - 6.$	0.6565	0.6609	0.6520	0.6564

Table 4: Performance of MLP models with different combinations of word vector similarity differences.

---

[2]https://fasttext.cc/docs/en/english-vectors.html
[3]https://github.com/commonsense/conceptnet-numberbatch
[4]https://nlp.stanford.edu/projects/glove/
[5]https://github.com/alvations/pywsd

F1 improvement over the rule-based models. On the other hand, though including the last three embedding models does not yield better result in this setting, we find them useful when combined with other kinds of features. Therefore, they are included in one of our submitted systems.

2.3 PMI Difference

Similar to word embedding, PMI reflects the co-occurrence tendencies of words. It has been shown that the Skip-gram with Negative Sampling (SGNS) algorithm in Word2vec corresponds to implicit factorization of the PMI matrix (Levy and Goldberg, 2014). Nevertheless, PMI should be interpreted differently from word vector similarity. Since PMI is calculated in an exact matching manner, there is no propagation of similarity as in the case of word vectors. That is, suppose that both PMI("red", "yellow") and PMI("apple", "banana") are high, this does not imply that PMI("red", "banana") will be high. Thus, PMI might be less prone to confusion of similar concepts.

We calculate PMI on the English Wikipedia corpus. We first experimented with a $PMI_1 > PMI_2$ rule that is similar to the one for vector similarities. In Table 5, we report the results of PMI calculated with different sizes of context window within which a pair of words is considered to be a co-occurrence. 20-word context window yields the best performance so we show its corresponding confusion matrix in Table 6. As can be seen, PMI performs slightly better in discriminating the negative class, compared to word similarities (Table 3).

Based on the above observation, we propose a heuristic rule of combining vector similarity and PMI: if $sim_1 > sim_2$ **and** $PMI_1 > PMI_2$ then output 1. We use the Numberbatch embeddings and PMI of 20-word context. This majority-voting model is more reliable and achieves macro-F1 above 0.69. It is one of our submitted systems so the result is shown in Table 14. According to the confusion matrix in Table 7, both the positive and the negative classes can be discriminated well with the combination of distributional vectors and PMI.

We also build learning-based models with combinations of PMI of different context window sizes. Since the range of PMI can be large, we only consider the sign of the difference. The sign of zero is defined to be negative. In addition, we also combine vector similarities to train the MLP model. The results are all shown in Table 8. However, none of the results show improvement over the corresponding rule-based models.

Context window	Acc.	Pos. F1	Neg. F1	Macro F1
10 words	0.6550	0.6986	**0.5968**	0.6477
20 words	**0.6561**	**0.7013**	0.5948	**0.6481**
30 words	0.6506	0.6959	0.5896	0.6427
whole sentence	0.6447	0.6906	0.5830	0.6368

Table 5: Performance of the $PMI_1 > PMI_2$ rule with different context windows on the validation set.

True label	$PMI_1 > PMI_2$	otherwise
1	1099	265
0	671	687

Table 6: Confusion matrix of the $PMI_1 > PMI_2$ rule with context window size 20 on the validation set.

True label	$sim_1 > sim_2$ & $PMI_1 > PMI_2$	otherwise
1	964	400
0	429	929

Table 7: Confusion matrix of the $sim_1 > sim_2$ & $PMI_1 > PMI_2$ rule on the validation set.

Features	Acc.	Pos. F1	Neg. F1	Macro F1
PMI(10+20+30)	0.6492	0.7026	0.5723	0.6375
sim x6 + PMI x3	**0.6763**	**0.7039**	**0.6432**	**0.6735**

Table 8: Performance of MLP models with combinations of word vector similarity differences and sign of PMI differences.

3 Expert Knowledge from ConceptNet

3.1 Edge Connection

ConceptNet can be regarded as a directed graph of concepts (vertices) connected by different relations (edges). There are 47 relation types in ConceptNet. Some of them, such as `HasProperty` and `CapableOf`, are directly related to attributes. Other relations such as `RelatedTo` can also reflect some kinds of attributes.

We experiment with a simple rule-based model that outputs 1 if there exists a relation from w_1 to a and there is no relation from w_2 to a. Additionally, we augment the ConceptNet graph with reverse edges and apply the rule again. The results of both versions are shown in Table 9. The

Graph	Acc.	Pos. F1	Neg. F1	Macro F1
ConceptNet edges	0.5996	0.4593	0.6820	0.5707
+ reverse edges	**0.6297**	**0.5140**	**0.7009**	**0.6074**

Table 9: Performance of the $w_1 \rightarrow a$ & $w_2 \nrightarrow a$ rule with the ConceptNet graph and its extension on the validation set.

Features	Acc.	Pos. F1	Neg. F1	Macro F1
$w_1/w_2 \overset{r}{\leftrightarrow} a$ for **each** r	0.5724	0.4785	0.6376	0.5581
$w_1/w_2 \overset{r}{\leftrightarrow} a$ for **any** r	**0.5974**	**0.4931**	**0.6661**	**0.5796**

Table 10: Performance of MLP models with Concept-Net edge features on the validation set.

version with reverse edges performs competitively with the vector similarity rule (macro F1 about 0.6), but the behavior is quite different. As can be seen, the ConceptNet features help achieve better negative F1. The relatively low performance on the positive class might be due to the sparseness of the knowledge graph. Some w_1 might have attribute a but it is not directly connected to a on the graph.

To encode edge connection information for training learning-based models, we compute the following four binary features:

- Is there an edge from w_1 to a?
- Is there an edge from a to w_1?
- Is there an edge from w_2 to a?
- Is there an edge from a to w_2?

We also experimented with two versions. In the first version, each type of relations are considered separately, so the total dimensionality is 4 * 47 = 188. In the second version, we set a binary feature to 1 if there is at least one edge that satisfies its condition, so the feature dimensionality is only 4. The results are shown in Table 10. Although different types of relations have different semantics and should be treated differently, the version considering relation type does not perform better. A possible reason is that it can suffer from the data sparseness problem, since some dimensions are zero for almost all the instances.

3.2 Shortest Path Length

To include connections between words and attributes that take more than one step, we calculate the shortest path lengths. Let $dis(w_i, a)$ be the shortest path length between w_i and a on the ConceptNet graph. We first experiment with a simple rule-based model that outputs 1 when $\underline{dis(w_1, a) < dis(w_2, a)}$, that is, when w_1 is closer to a. The results are reported in Table 11. Including reverse edges slightly improves the accuracy but does not improve the macro F1 score. A confusion matrix is presented in Table 12, showing that this rule is a strong indicator for the negative class. Compared to the ones with edge connection features, however, these rule-based classifiers

Graph	Acc.	Pos. F1	Neg. F1	Macro F1
ConceptNet edges	0.6308	**0.5740**	0.6742	**0.6241**
+ reverse edges	**0.6315**	0.5622	**0.6819**	0.6220

Table 11: Performance of the $dis(w_1, a) < dis(w_2, a)$ rule with the ConceptNet graph and its extension on the validation set.

True label	$dis(w_1, a) < dis(w_2, a)$	otherwise
1	644	720
0	283	1075

Table 12: Confusion matrix of the $dis(w_1, a) < dis(w_2, a)$ rule (reverse edges considered) on the validation set.

Graph	Acc.	Pos. F1	Neg. F1	Macro F1
ConceptNet edges	0.6532	0.6629	**0.6430**	0.6529
+ reverse edges	**0.6646**	**0.6984**	0.6223	**0.6603**

Table 13: Performance of MLP models with one-hot representation of ConceptNet shortest path lengths on the validation set.

achieve slightly lower negative F1 but higher positive F1.

Since the maximum shortest path distance between a word and an attribute in the training set is 5 (when reverse edges are included), we encode $dis(w_i, a)$ into 6-dimensional discrete binary features as follows.

- No path from w_i to a
- $dis(w_i, a) = 1$
- $dis(w_i, a) = 2$
- $dis(w_i, a) = 3$
- $dis(w_i, a) = 4$
- $dis(w_i, a) \geq 5$

We build similar MLP models that take these features as input. The features for w_1 and w_2 are computed separately and then concatenated., There are clear improvements of learning-based models (Table 13) over rule-based ones (Table 11). The improvements are mostly contributed by the higher positive F1 scores. On the other hand, in general it is helpful to include a separate set of features calculated on the graph with reverse edges.

4 Submitted Systems

We submitted the predictions of a rule-based system and a learning-based system. The evaluation results are summarized in Table 14. Run 1 system is a rule-based combination of similarity differences of the Numberbatch embedding and the sign of PMI differences (window size 20). Run 2 is an MLP model with three size-2048 hidden layers that takes input features of the similarity dif-

Model	Validation				Test			
	Acc.	Pos. F1	Neg. F1	Macro F1	Acc.	Pos. F1	Neg. F1	Macro F1
[1] Rule: $sim_1 > sim_2$ & $PMI_1 > PMI_2$	0.6954	0.6993	0.6915	0.6954	0.7047	0.6944	0.7143	0.7044
[2] MLP: sim x6 + PMI(10,20,30) + ConceptNet	**0.7175**	**0.7213**	**0.7136**	**0.7174**	**0.7303**	**0.7138**	**0.7451**	**0.7294**

Table 14: Evaluation results of the two submitted systems.

ference of the six kinds of embeddings, the sign of PMI differences of three different context window sizes and the ConceptNet edge and shortest path length features.

Our run 2 system performed the third best among all 26 participants with macro-F1 0.7294, showing that the features we proposed are highly effective. On the other hand, our run 1 system got an only slightly lower macro-F1 of 0.7044 and would get a rank between 5 (0.69) and 4 (0.72) if it was considered. This again proves the complementary effect of word vector similarity and PMI.

5 Error Analysis

Since even the top system in this task did not achieve macro-F1 above 75%, we think that there might be some cases that are very difficult to handle. Based on the test ground-truth released officially, we analyze the errors of our best system. We find out that the difficulties mainly arise from the following cases.

Ambiguous concept: Word ambiguity is not considered in this task. However, this may be problematic in some cases such as the positive example <mouse, squirrel, plastic>. According to the answer, we know that the word "mouse" is interpreted as a "computer device" instead of an "animal". Therefore, sometimes the answer is dependent on which sense is selected.

Vague or ambiguous attribute: Since the attribute is expressed only with a single word in this task, sometimes it is hard to tell what the attribute means, even from a human's perspective. For example, the triple <philanthropist, lawyer, active> is labeled 0 in the gold answer. Nevertheless, a positive interpretation also makes sense: philanthropists usually engage in philanthropy actively, while lawyers usually handle matters under the authorization of someone.

Relative attribute: In some positive examples, w_1 does not necessarily have a, but only more likely to have it. In the positive example <father, brother, old>, "father" might be "old" when being compared to "brother", but not necessarily so when considered isolatedly. It is even more diffi-

cult to determine when to evaluate the absence of an attribute relatively, given that we also encounter cases such as <banker, lawyer, rich>, whose gold label is 0.

6 Conclusions

We propose several approaches to tackle the SemEval 2018 Capturing Discriminative Attributes task in this paper. We utilize information derived from both corpus distribution statistics and expert knowledge in ConceptNet to build our systems. According to the experimental results, word embedding and PMI, though both based on co-occurrence, can complement each other in a simple heuristic rule-based system. Moreover, the ConceptNet features with high sensitivity to the negative class can complement the corpus-based features, which are more sensitive to the positive class. Our best learning-based system achieved F1 score of 0.7294 and got the 3rd place in the official run. We did not adopt image features, which suggests that it is possible to learn substantially about visual attributes solely from text.

Given the limited advancement of the learning-based model over the rule-based one, it is worth studying how to design some mechanism in machine learning models that can guide them to "compare" the features of the two concepts and determine the discriminativeness.

Acknowledgements

This research was partially supported by Ministry of Science and Technology, Taiwan, under grants MOST-107-2634-F-002-011-, MOST-106-2923-E-002-012-MY3, and MOST-105-2221-E-002-154-MY3.

References

Piotr Bojanowski, Edouard Grave, Armand Joulin, and Tomas Mikolov. 2017. Enriching Word Vectors with Subword Information. *Transactions of the Association for Computational Linguistics*, 5:135–146.

François Chollet. 2015. Keras. `https://github.com/fchollet/keras`.

Jia Deng, Wei Dong, Richard Socher, Li-Jia Li, Kai Li, and Fei-Fei Li. 2009. ImageNet: A large-scale hierarchical image database. In *2009 IEEE Computer Society Conference on Computer Vision and Pattern Recognition (CVPR 2009)*, pages 248–255.

Alicia Krebs, Alessandro Lenci, and Denis Paperno. 2018. Semeval-2018 task 10: Capturing discriminative attributes. In *Proceedings of the 12th international workshop on semantic evaluation (SemEval 2018)*.

Angeliki Lazaridou, Nghia The Pham, and Marco Baroni. 2016. The red one!: On learning to refer to things based on discriminative properties. In *Proceedings of the 54th Annual Meeting of the Association for Computational Linguistics (Volume 2: Short Papers)*, pages 213–218. Association for Computational Linguistics.

Omer Levy and Yoav Goldberg. 2014. Neural word embedding as implicit matrix factorization. In *Advances in neural information processing systems*, pages 2177–2185.

Omer Levy, Steffen Remus, Chris Biemann, and Ido Dagan. 2015. Do Supervised Distributional Methods Really Learn Lexical Inference Relations? In *Proceedings of the 2015 Conference of the North American Chapter of the Association for Computational Linguistics: Human Language Technologies*, pages 970–976. Association for Computational Linguistics.

Tomas Mikolov, Kai Chen, Greg Corrado, and Jeffrey Dean. 2013. Efficient estimation of word representations in vector space. *arXiv preprint arXiv:1301.3781*.

Jeffrey Pennington, Richard Socher, and Christopher Manning. 2014. GloVe: Global Vectors for Word Representation. In *Proceedings of the 2014 Conference on Empirical Methods in Natural Language Processing (EMNLP)*, pages 1532–1543. Association for Computational Linguistics.

Dana Rubinstein, Effi Levi, Roy Schwartz, and Ari Rappoport. 2015. How Well Do Distributional Models Capture Different Types of Semantic Knowledge? In *Proceedings of the 53rd Annual Meeting of the Association for Computational Linguistics and the 7th International Joint Conference on Natural Language Processing (Volume 2: Short Papers)*, pages 726–730. Association for Computational Linguistics.

Carina Silberer, Vittorio Ferrari, and Mirella Lapata. 2013. Models of Semantic Representation with Visual Attributes. In *Proceedings of the 51st Annual Meeting of the Association for Computational Linguistics (Volume 1: Long Papers)*, pages 572–582. Association for Computational Linguistics.

Robert Speer, Joshua Chin, and Catherine Havasi. 2017. ConceptNet 5.5: An Open Multilingual Graph of General Knowledge. In *Proceedings of the 31st AAAI Conference on Artificial Intelligence*, pages 4444–4451.

ELiRF-UPV at SemEval-2018 Task 11: Machine Comprehension using Commonsense Knowledge

José-Ángel González, Lluís-F. Hurtado, Encarna Segarra, Ferran Pla
Universitat Politècnica de València
Camí de Vera sn, 46022, València
{jogonba2|lhurtado|esegarra|fpla}@dsic.upv.es

Abstract

This paper describes the participation of ELiRF-UPV team at task 11, Machine Comprehension using Commonsense Knowledge, of SemEval-2018. Our approach is based on the use of word embeddings, NumberBatch Embeddings, and a Deep Learning architecture to find the best answer for the multiple-choice questions based on the narrative text. The results obtained are in line with those obtained by the other participants and they encourage us to continue working on this problem.

1 Introduction

In the Machine Comprehension using Commonsense Knowledge task, systems must answer multiple-choice questions given narrative texts about everyday activities. In addition to what is mentioned in the text, a substantial number of questions require inference using script knowledge about different scenarios.

In order to capture some script knowledge we decided to use a word representation based not only on distributional semantics word models but also on a knowledge graph, ConceptNet (Speer et al., 2016). ConceptNet is a knowledge graph that connects words and phrases of natural language with labeled edges. It is designed to represent the general knowledge involved in understanding language. ConceptNet could be used in combination with sources of distributional semantics, particularly the word2vec Google News skip-gram embeddings (Mikolov et al., 2013)) and GloVe 1.2 (Pennington et al., 2014), to produce new embeddings, NumberBatch embeddings, with state-of-the-art performance across many word-relatedness evaluations (Speer and Lowry-Duda, 2017).

More specifically, NumberBatch is a list of semantic word vectors which contains a complex meaning of those terms, beyond containing only contextual information like other kinds of embeddings based on distributional semantics e.g. Word2Vec or Glove. These embeddings are obtained through a combination of Word2Vec and Glove embeddings with knowledge extracted from ConceptNet by means of a technique known as retrofitting (Faruqui et al., 2014).

In this work, we used word representations based on NumberBatch embeddings because these representations encode semantically rich information related to the commonsense. Moreover, in order to tackle this machine comprehension task, we used a Deep Learning architecture with new attention mechanisms. The inclusion of these new attention mechanisms allow us to better capture the similarities among the elements of the input. The attention mechanisms we introduce in this work are suggested in the work (Seo et al., 2016), that obtained very competitive results in Question Answering tasks.

2 Resources and Preprocess

As we pointed in Section 1, NumberBatch embeddings were used for the representation of words. These embedding are provided by ConceptNet 5, which was compiled by the Commonsense Computing Initiative. ConceptNet 5 is freely available under the Creative Commons Attribution-ShareAlike license (CC BY SA 4.0) from `http://conceptnet.io`.

We explored several preprocessing techniques in the development phase The best results were obtained with the following preprocess: the conversion of all text to lowercase and the elimination of the question marks "?". After this, we carried out a tokenization process.

Proceedings of the 12th International Workshop on Semantic Evaluation (SemEval-2018), pages 1034–1037
New Orleans, Louisiana, June 5–6, 2018. ©2018 Association for Computational Linguistics

3   System Description

We tested Deep Learning architectures based on similarities between d-dimensional NumberBatch embeddings of story (x), question (q) and answer (r). Specifically, our approaches learn representations of x, q and r to first compute similarities, and then make a classification decision.

These kind of systems work well in Question Answering tasks, for instance, BiDAF (Seo et al., 2016) or QA-LSTM-Story(Pal and Sharma, 2016). For this reason, with the aim of improving the accuracy of these systems for this task, we incorporated some attention mechanisms of BiDAF in the QA-LSTM-Story system. A scheme of our system is shown in Figure 1.

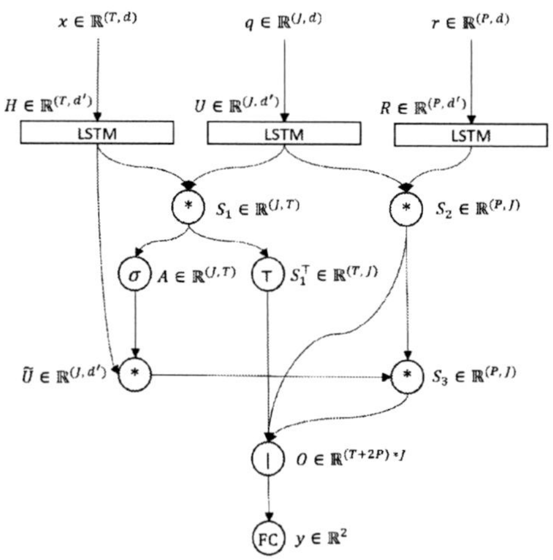

Figure 1: System architecture.

All Deep Learning systems tested in this work take first a story ($x \in \mathbb{R}^{\{T,d\}}$), a question ($q \in \mathbb{R}^{\{J,d\}}$) and an answer ($r \in \mathbb{R}^{\{P,d\}}$) as input. Specifically, each of these elements is a matrix with their word embeddings as rows. Note that the length of the representations (T, J and P) is fixed by adding zero padding at the beginning to reach the length of the longest element.

Second, x, q and r are processed by means of three non-shared Bidirectional Long Short Term Memory (BLSTM) (Hochreiter and Schmidhuber, 1997) (Schuster and Paliwal, 1997). These networks capture useful features (X, Q and R) to make decisions based on similarities among the inputs. Moreover, we used BatchNormalization (Ioffe and Szegedy, 2015) and Dropout (Srivastava et al., 2014) with $p = 0.3$, after the input layer and

after the BLSTM output to improve the generalization of the model.

After that, we compute similarities between each term of Q and each term of X ($S_1 = QX \in \mathbb{R}^{\{J,T\}}$) and similarities between each term of R and each term of Q (in a similar way, $S_2 = RQ \in \mathbb{R}^{\{P,J\}}$).

Now, if we concatenate S_1 and S_2, and we apply a fully-connected layer with softmax activation functions to classify, we reproduce exactly the QA-LSTM-Story system. However, in this work, we incorporated several attention mechanisms to this architecture in order to learn more complex relationships among the inputs.

One of these attention mechanisms is an adaptation of BiDAF. This adaptation used, in addition to Query2Context (Q2X) and Context2Query (X2Q), two additional attention mechanisms, Answer2Query (R2Q) and Query2Answer (Q2R). R2Q and Q2R are identical to X2Q and Q2X but applied to the question q and the answer r.

We have also tested many other attentions, but the best system obtained in the development phase only contains X2Q. In order to obtain this attention, we first transform the similarities S_1 by applying a softmax activation function to each row i.e. $A[i,j] = \frac{e^{S_1[i,j]}}{\sum_{t=0}^{T} e^{S_1[i,t]}}$. After this, we compute $\widetilde{Q} = AX$, to represent each row of Q as a weighted sum of the rows in X. That is, each row of Q is adapted in order to consider the most relevant rows of X.

From $\widetilde{Q}$, we can consider more explicit relationships between x and r if we compute the similarities between $\widetilde{Q}$ and R, in the same way as S_1 and S_2, to obtain S_3.

With all, we transpose the matrix S_1 to later concatenate all the similarity matrices. The result, $(S_1^\mathsf{T}, S_2, S_3) \in \mathbb{R}^{\{(T+2P),J\}}$, is flattened by concatenating all rows as columns to obtain a vector $O^{(T+2P)*J}$. Finally, we apply a softmax fully-connected layer to O to carry out the classification.

To train the system, we generated a training set consisting of all the triples of the corpus (x, q, r). Thus, for each x and q, we generate two triples, (x, q, r_1) and (x, q, r_2). Then, if r_1 is correct, $y(x,q,r_1) = 1$, else $y(x,q,r_1) = 0$. At inference time, given x, q and their two possible answers r_1 and r_2, we first build two triples (x, q, r_1) and (x, q, r_2) and, second, we obtain the network outputs y_1 and y_2, respectively. Finally, in order to decide which answer is correct, we select the one

Sys.	System Description	Acc. (%)
1	QA-LSTM-Story	79.21
2	BiDAF Adaptation	76.47
3	QA-LSTM-Story with X2Q	80.08

Table 1: Results on the development set.

Team	Acc. (%)
Yuanfudao (1/11)	83.95
Mitre (2/11)	82.27
Jiangnan (3/11)	80.91
ELiRF-UPV (4/11)	74.97
YNU_Deep (5/11)	74.72
. . .	
IUCM (11/11)	61.35

Table 2: Official results on the test set.

that maximizes the output for the correct class i.e. $y_i[1]$ (2nd component of the network output for a triple i).

4 Experimental Results

The results obtained during the development phase for the different systems above mentioned are shown in the Table 1. It can be observed that Deep Learning systems with simpler attention mechanisms worked better than those with more complex attention mechanisms (system 2 versus systems 1 and 3). If X2Q was added to compute more explicit relations between x and r, the accuracy slightly improved from 79.21% to 80.08% (system 1 versus system 3). Moreover, we tested system 3 with word2vec (Google News skip-gram) instead of NumberBatch embeddings obtaining an accuracy of 78.84%.

With these results, we chose the best system in the development phase (system 3 in Table 1).

The results obtained with this system on the test set are shown in Table 2.

5 Analysis of Results

Now, we make an analysis of the results obtained with our best system. In particular, we analyze the network confidence at intervals when deciding what is the correct answer (r_1 or r_2) given a story x and a question q. This confidence c is defined as the absolute difference between the outputs for the correct class of each answer ($y_1[1]$ and $y_2[1]$) i.e. $c = |y_1[1] - y_2[1]|$.

During this analysis, we get a maximum confidence $c_{max} = 0.999$ and a minimum confidence $c_{min} = 0.000$. Thus, there are extreme cases where the system is totally sure about what is the correct answer, or has total uncertainty. In the instance ($ix = 235$, $iq = 1$), we observe that the system is totally sure about the correct answer due to the answer has been explicitly found in the story. In a second instance ($ix = 131$, $iq = 4$), the system has total uncertainty because "$20.00" and "$15.00" do not appear in the NumberBatch embeddings. (Where ix and iq refers to the index of the story and the question in the test set).

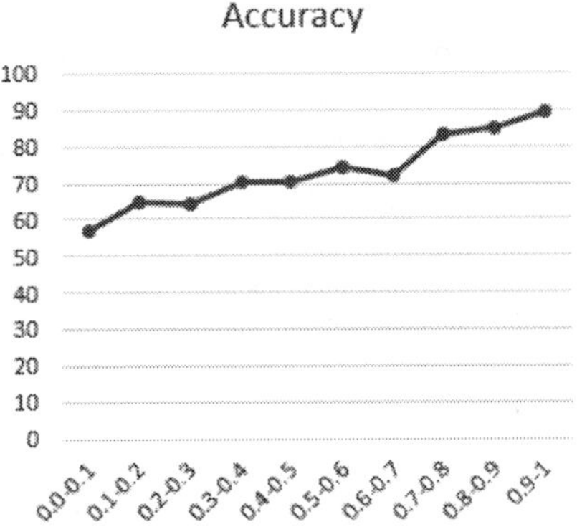

Figure 2: Accuracy in each confidence interval.

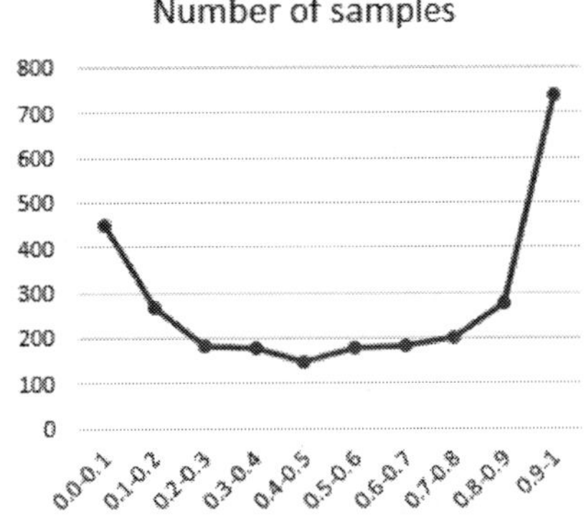

Figure 3: Number of samples in each confidence interval.

Moreover, we have also performed a study on the system accuracy and the number of samples for each confidence level between [0, 1]. The results obtained are shown in the Figures 2 and 3.

In general, as it can be observed in Figure 2,

the greater the confidence, the better results were obtained. However, in Figure 3, we observed that there are many samples with very low confidence values, e.g. 0.0-0.1. We think that in order to reduce the number of samples in this confidence interval, it would be necessary to incorporate new knowledge resources.

6 Conclusions

In this work, we presented a Deep Learning architecture with new attention mechanisms in order to learn more complex representations and similarities among input elements (story x, question q and answer r). In order to capture some script knowledge, NumberBatch embeddings were used for the representation of words. With this approach we obtained competitive results.

As future work, we propose the study and development of new attention mechanisms to learn complex features and relationships. Moreover, we also find interesting the enrichment of the Deep Learning architectures with some commonsense information beyond the use of NumberBatch embeddings, such as the script knowledge resources suggested by the competition organizers.

7 Acknowledgements

This work has been partially supported by the Spanish MINECO and FEDER founds under projects ASLP-MULAN: Audio, Speech and Language Processing for Multimedia Analytics (TIN2014-54288-C4-3-R); and AMIC: Affective Multimedia Analytics with Inclusive and Natural Communication (TIN2017-85854-C4-2-R). Work of José-Ángel González is also financed by Universitat Politècnica de València under grant PAID-01-17.

References

Manaal Faruqui, Jesse Dodge, Sujay Kumar Jauhar, Chris Dyer, Eduard H. Hovy, and Noah A. Smith. 2014. Retrofitting word vectors to semantic lexicons. *CoRR*, abs/1411.4166.

Sepp Hochreiter and Jürgen Schmidhuber. 1997. Long Short-Term Memory. *Neural Computation*, 9(8):1735–1780.

Sergey Ioffe and Christian Szegedy. 2015. Batch normalization: Accelerating deep network training by reducing internal covariate shift. *CoRR*, abs/1502.03167.

Tomas Mikolov, Ilya Sutskever, Kai Chen, Greg Corrado, and Jeffrey Dean. 2013. Distributed representations of words and phrases and their compositionality. *CoRR*, abs/1310.4546.

Sujit Pal and Abhishek Sharma. 2016. Deep learning models for question answering. Elsevier Search Guild Question Answering Workshop.

Jeffrey Pennington, Richard Socher, and Christopher D Manning. 2014. Glove: Global vectors for word representation. In *EMNLP*, volume 14, pages 1532–1543.

M. Schuster and K.K. Paliwal. 1997. Bidirectional recurrent neural networks. *Trans. Sig. Proc.*, 45(11):2673–2681.

Min Joon Seo, Aniruddha Kembhavi, Ali Farhadi, and Hannaneh Hajishirzi. 2016. Bidirectional attention flow for machine comprehension. *CoRR*, abs/1611.01603.

Robert Speer, Joshua Chin, and Catherine Havasi. 2016. Conceptnet 5.5: An open multilingual graph of general knowledge. *CoRR*, abs/1612.03975.

Robert Speer and Joanna Lowry-Duda. 2017. Conceptnet at semeval-2017 task 2: Extending word embeddings with multilingual relational knowledge. *CoRR*, abs/1704.03560.

Nitish Srivastava, Geoffrey E. Hinton, Alex Krizhevsky, Ilya Sutskever, and Ruslan Salakhutdinov. 2014. Dropout: a simple way to prevent neural networks from overfitting. *Journal of Machine Learning Research*, 15(1):1929–1958.

YNU_AI1799 at SemEval-2018 Task 11: Machine Comprehension using Commonsense Knowledge of Different model ensemble

QingXun Liu, HongDou Yao, Xiaobing Zhou*, Ge Xie
School of Information Science and Engineering
Yunnan University, Yunnan, P.R. China
*Corresponding author, zhouxb.cn@gmail.com

Abstract

In this paper, we describe a machine reading comprehension system that participated in SemEval-2018 Task 11: Machine Comprehension using commonsense knowledge. In this work, we train a series of neural network models such as multi-LSTM, BiLSTM, multi-BiLSTM-CNN and attention-based BiLSTM, etc. On top of some sub models, there are two kinds of word embedding: (a) general word embedding generated from unsupervised neural language model; and (b) position embedding generated from general word embedding. Finally, we make a hard vote on the predictions of these models and achieve relatively good result. The proposed approach achieves 8th place in Task 11 with the accuracy of 0.7213.

1 Introduction

Machine Comprehension using Commonsense Knowledge is a well-researched problem in NLP. In order to simplify the task of the process, we turn this task into text classification work and use a deep learning neural network to fulfill it. The method of deep learning models used in text analysis has achieved numerous notable advances in recently years (e.g., (Breck et al., 2007), (Yessenalina and Cardie, 2011) and (Socher et al., 2011)). However, in most previous works, the tasks are to apply a single model to a particular data set task.

The single model is a vertical stack of multiple hidden layers, which is not good for text analysis and processing. The first drawback is the need to consume more hardware resources, followed by over-fitting and loss of feature information. So the task here is to apply different structure sub models to the same train-set. We train many classic sub models with one layer on top of word embedding, like LSTM, CNN, Attention,Attention+BiLSTM, multi-BiLSTM+CNN and some other models which are slightly different from the above models with different activation functions and different layers inside the model. In each single model, we use a flag to determine which embedding tool is used or not.

Most of the deep learning involve word vectors represented by neural language models ((Morin and Bengio, 2005) , (Yih et al., 2011) and (Mikolov et al., 2013)). Using the learned word vectors for classification task will naturally increase the effect. Word vectors are expressed as a hidden-layer word vector of the specified dimension (1-of-V, here V is the vocabulary size), the training methods can be found here[1]. In our system, we introduce different word vectors: 100 billion words of Google News, Glove vectors of 100 dimensions and word vectors self-trained on the basis of official task data. Finally, a hard vote(the majority voting from result document) is made on the results of those different models. Many tasks often suffer from insufficient training data. In this work, we parse external data from CodaLab introduction data, including DeScript(**?**) data, RKP(Regneri et al., 2010) data and OMCS (Singh et al., 2002) data to trained embedding.

2 System Description

We treat this task as a classification process. First we repeat the question and answer text, making it match instance texts. The final number of samples are same as the number of answers in the data-set. After statistical analysis of the data-set, we treat Instance texts, Question texts and Answers texts as to a rational text length of words $\{w_1, w_2, \ldots, w_n\}$ in which n is the max length of a text. Here, the length of Instance is controlled as 350, and the length of Question is controlled as 14 as well as Answer. Before that, we count the frequency of

---

[1] https://radimrehurek.com/gensim/models/word2vec.html

Proceedings of the 12th International Workshop on Semantic Evaluation (SemEval-2018), pages 1038–1042
New Orleans, Louisiana, June 5–6, 2018. ©2018 Association for Computational Linguistics

occurrence of each word in the data-set, and use this word frequency to create a dictionary, then express each word in terms of frequency order of corresponding word (Kim, 2014). Next, we train word embeddding according to (Chiu et al., 2016), and at the same time download the trained embedding sets that have been trained[2].

The ensemble model architecture, shown in figure 1, is an ensemble of many single models(We call them sub models). Because each sub model is independent of each other, their weights are not shared and just use the same word embedding when training each sub model. The process of the whole ensemble model is carried out model by model. First, each model is run independently, and then the result file is saved. After running all the independent models, the result files are taken out and the final result is determined by the majority vote. In model training, we use the early stop mechanism (Sarle, 1995) to terminate the training of subsequent epoch when the overfitting is appeared. At the same time, the data is shuffled on every epoch. The core of our paper is based on classic models, adding other network layers, so that the independent models have their own structure. Next, are introduced the input structures of the sub models.

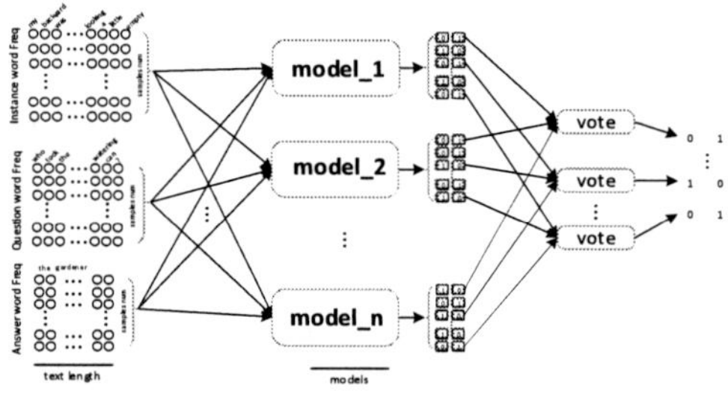

Figure 1: The architecture of the models ensemble.

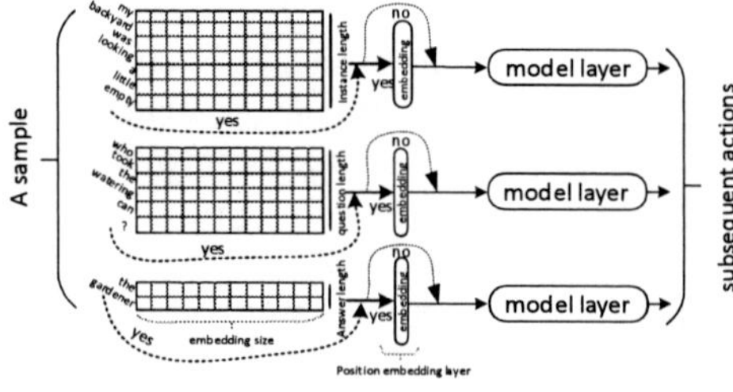

Figure 2: The input structure of the submodel

[2]https://github.com/xgli/word2vec-api

2.1 Similar input structures

Figure 2 shows the architecture of the sub models input. The input part of all sub models uses this structure. Within the structure, two flag variables are used to control the use of word embedding. One is whether to use the position embedding, and the other is to control whether or not the trained word embedding is used. From this structure, data flow to the subsequent network layer such as the classic model layer CNN, LSTM, BiLSTM and Attention.

2.2 The merge layer

In order to combine three text feature information, we have a merge layer in all of our sub models. The merge layer of these sub models is almost the same. Only the attention layer merge is different from other sub models. The merge of most sub models first combines the instance matrix data with the question in sum operation, while combining the matrix data with the answer, and finally combining the two sets of matrix data in the *dot* operation. However, in the sub model with Attention, merge layer combines the matrix data of the three texts with *dot* operation. Next, we will focus on two sub models using classical models,while the rest of the other part of each sub models are similar to the two models.

2.3 Based on multi-BiLSTM+CNN model

Long short-term memory (LSTM or BiLSTM) is applied to text classification ((Liu et al., 2016) and (Lai et al., 2015)). The Convolutional Neural Networks (CNN) is for local feature extraction (LeCun et al., 1998). CNN can achieve good results in the semantic analysis (Yih et al., 2014), and other traditional NLP tasks (Collobert et al., 2011), especially in sentiment analysis and question classification (Kim et al., 2016). It is our novelty to combine CNN with multiple layers of BiLSTM with BiLSTM in front.

Here set the *multi* = 2, of course, it can be 3 or more. Each multi-BiLSTM internal implies a dropout layer to prevent over-fitting (Srivastava et al., 2014). Multi-BiLSTM is one of the core layers in this model which takes an input sequence of word embedding. Just like (Liu et al., 2016) and (Lai et al., 2015), this layer runs on the data of word embedding. After these three branches running (Just as the three model layers in Figure 2), we make batch normalization and then merge them into CNN1D layer. Finally, we use the Softmax classifier to predict the results. Other sub models that do not use Attention are similar to the sub model structure, instead of replacing CNN1D with other structures.

2.4 Based on Attention + BiLSTM model

Attention is mostly used for document categorization (Yang et al., 2016).The model architecture is different from the multi-BiLSTM+CNN architecture of word embedding layer. The structure of this model is roughly: a word embedding input structure, followed by attention layer which include the merge layer. Next to the batch normalization layer, BiLSTM layer , Softmax layer. We do a position embedding operation before inputting the word embedding into attention layer. According to (Vaswani et al., 2017), the formula for constructing Position Embedding is as follows:

$$\begin{cases} PE_{2i(p)} = sin(p/10000^{2i/dpos}) \\ PE_{2i+1(p)} = sin(p/10000^{2i/dpos}) \end{cases} \quad (1)$$

Here is to map the position p to the position vector of $dpos$ dimension. The value of the i th element of this vector is $PE_i(p)$. Word embedding first goes through the position embedding layer which is included in the architecture of the sub model input. Then the feature data enters into attention layer. In attention layer, weights and bias are randomly added to position embedding and excess numbers are masked as zero. We do batch normalization for the data coming out of attention layer, then input them into BiLSTM. Similarly, the results are obtained after Softmax layer.

3 Data Preparation

Although official data is regular, we have done a further normalization. All data set used by each model undergoes the following preprocessing steps:

1) The texts were lowercased

2) Using NLTK to tokenize each text

3) Abbreviations:
   We're very careful about the abbreviation, as "'s" in "it's time for me to take her out." is not the same as "s" in "Tom's dad ordered pizza yesterday for the family." We treat the first "s"

examples	normalization
I'm	I am
n't	not
does't	does not
it's	it is
. . .	. . .
that's	that is
neighbor's	neighbor
wouldn't	would not
wont't	will not

Table 1: normalization patterns.

as "is," and the second, of course, is an adjective. We restore those abbreviations in Table 1 to normal forms.

4) Removing other characters:
   Removing other characters, such as "!","% ","?", "#", "'","@" Etc. Of course, not all other symbols that seem useless are removed. Like "$" are not removed.

4 Experiments and Results

In order to optimize our network, we use (Kingma and Ba, 2014) optimizer on training model. All our experiments have been developed using an open source software library of Tensorflow with CUDA enabled, and run on a computer with Intel Core(TM) i3 CPU 760 @2.8GHz, 8GB of RAM and GeForce GTX960 GPU. Due to the lack of hardware capacity, we do not run the entire system in one time. Instead, we run single model each time with different word embeddings. When we use the word embedding of Google News 300d on some sub models, the system gives memory exhausted, and we switch to a smaller glove_27B_100d to run successfully. Table 2 shows our results for various models. As it can be seen from the table, ensemble results from the more different models get better results when other conditions are similar. Here we ensemble these models: RNN, GRU, BiLSTM, multi-BiLSTM+CNN and Attention+BiLSTM, based on their high accuracy. The dropout probability is 0.6 in each model, and the initial learning rate is 0.01.

5 Conclusion

In this project, we ensemble a variety of structurally different models to tackle this task. The

model	self trained	glove_twitter_27B_100d	GoogleNews_300d.bin
RNN	—	0.6638	—
LSTM	0.7001	0.7042	0.6932
GRU	—	0.6732	—
CNN1D	0.5634	0.6324	—
CNN2D	—	0.5683	—
CNN2D+LSTM	—	0.5573	—
BiLSTM	0.6734	0.7135	—
Attention	—	0.6731	0.6863
Attention+BiLSTM	0.6653	0.6943	0.6934
multi-BiLSTM+CNN	0.6725	0.6834	—
Combine to all models	0.6550	0.7213	0.6923

Table 2: Result for various models on task data set.

performance of a single model is poorer than the ensemble model. And the bigger the difference between the models, the higher performance the ensemble model makes. Still our results are less satisfying than top teams on the leaderboard. We will adjust the model, improve the hardware configuration of the computer, collect more external data, and do more experiments to get a better result in the future.

Acknowledgments

This work was supported by the Natural Science Foundation of China No.61463050, No.61702443, No.61762091, the NSF of Yunnan Province No.2015FB113, the Project of Innovative Research Team of Yunnan Province.

References

Eric Breck, Yejin Choi, and Claire Cardie. 2007. Identifying expressions of opinion in context. In *International Joint Conference on Artificial Intelligence*, pages 2683–2688.

Billy Chiu, Gamal Crichton, Anna Korhonen, and Sampo Pyysalo. 2016. How to train good word embeddings for biomedical nlp. In *Proceedings of the 15th Workshop on Biomedical Natural Language Processing*, pages 166–174.

Ronan Collobert, Jason Weston, Léon Bottou, Michael Karlen, Koray Kavukcuoglu, and Pavel Kuksa. 2011. Natural language processing (almost) from scratch. *Journal of Machine Learning Research*, 12(Aug):2493–2537.

Yoon Kim. 2014. Convolutional neural networks for sentence classification. In *Proceedings of the 2014 Conference on Empirical Methods in Natural Language Processing (EMNLP)*, pages 1746–1751.

Yoon Kim, Yacine Jernite, David Sontag, and Alexander M Rush. 2016. Character-aware neural language models. In *AAAI*, pages 2741–2749.

Diederik P Kingma and Jimmy Ba. 2014. Adam: A method for stochastic optimization. *In International Conference on Learning Representations (ICLR)*.

Siwei Lai, Liheng Xu, Kang Liu, and Jun Zhao. 2015. Recurrent convolutional neural networks for text classification. In *AAAI*, volume 333, pages 2267–2273.

Yann LeCun, Léon Bottou, Yoshua Bengio, and Patrick Haffner. 1998. Gradient-based learning applied to document recognition. *Proceedings of the IEEE*, 86(11):2278–2324.

Pengfei Liu, Xipeng Qiu, and Xuanjing Huang. 2016. Recurrent neural network for text classification with multi-task learning. In *International Joint Conference on Artificial Intelligence*, pages 2873–2879.

Tomas Mikolov, Ilya Sutskever, Kai Chen, Greg S Corrado, and Jeff Dean. 2013. Distributed representations of words and phrases and their compositionality. In *Advances in neural information processing systems*, pages 3111–3119.

Frederic Morin and Yoshua Bengio. 2005. Hierarchical probabilistic neural network language model. In *Aistats*, volume 5, pages 246–252.

Michaela Regneri, Alexander Koller, and Manfred Pinkal. 2010. Learning script knowledge with web experiments. In *Meeting of the Association for Computational Linguistics*, pages 979–988.

Warren S. Sarle. 1995. Stopped training and other remedies for overfitting. *In Proceedings of Symposium on the Interface*, pages 352–360.

Push Singh, Thomas Lin, Erik T. Mueller, Grace Lim, Travell Perkins, and Wan Li Zhu. 2002. Open mind common sense: Knowledge acquisition from the general public. 2519(5):1223–1237.

Richard Socher, Jeffrey Pennington, Eric H Huang, Andrew Y Ng, and Christopher D Manning. 2011. Semi-supervised recursive autoencoders for predicting sentiment distributions. In *Conference on Empirical Methods in Natural Language Processing, EMNLP 2011, 27-31 July 2011, John Mcintyre Conference Centre, Edinburgh, Uk, A Meeting of Sigdat, A Special Interest Group of the ACL*, pages 151–161.

Nitish Srivastava, Geoffrey Hinton, Alex Krizhevsky, Ilya Sutskever, and Ruslan Salakhutdinov. 2014. Dropout: a simple way to prevent neural networks from overfitting. *Journal of Machine Learning Research*, 15(1):1929–1958.

Ashish Vaswani, Noam Shazeer, Niki Parmar, Jakob Uszkoreit, Llion Jones, Aidan N Gomez, Ł ukasz Kaiser, and Illia Polosukhin. 2017. Attention is all you need. In I., editor, *Advances in Neural Information Processing Systems 30*, pages 5998–6008.

Zichao Yang, Diyi Yang, Chris Dyer, Xiaodong He, Alex Smola, and Eduard Hovy. 2016. Hierarchical attention networks for document classification. In *Proceedings of the 2016 Conference of the North American Chapter of the Association for Computational Linguistics: Human Language Technologies*, pages 1480–1489.

Ainur Yessenalina and Claire Cardie. 2011. Compositional matrix-space models for sentiment analysis. In *Conference on Empirical Methods in Natural Language Processing, EMNLP 2011, 27-31 July 2011, John Mcintyre Conference Centre, Edinburgh, Uk, A Meeting of Sigdat, A Special Interest Group of the ACL*, pages 172–182.

Wen-tau Yih, Xiaodong He, and Christopher Meek. 2014. Semantic parsing for single-relation question answering. In *Proceedings of the 52nd Annual Meeting of the Association for Computational Linguistics (Volume 2: Short Papers)*, volume 2, pages 643–648.

Wen-tau Yih, Kristina Toutanova, John C Platt, and Christopher Meek. 2011. Learning discriminative projections for text similarity measures. In *Proceedings of the Fifteenth Conference on Computational Natural Language Learning*, pages 247–256.

YNU_Deep at SemEval-2018 Task 11: An Ensemble of Attention-based BiLSTM Models for Machine Comprehension

Peng Ding, Xiaobing Zhou*

School of Information Science and Engineering
Yunnan University, Yunnan, P.R. China
*Corresponding author, zhouxb.cn@gmail.com

Abstract

This paper reports our submission to task 11 (Machine Comprehension using Commonsense Knowledge) in SemEval 2018. We firstly use GloVe to learn the distributed representations automatically from the instance, question and answer triples. Then an attention-based Bidirectional LSTM (BiLSTM) model is used to encode the triples. We also perform a simple ensemble method to improve the effectiveness of our model. The system we developed obtains an encouraging result on this task. It achieves the accuracy 0.7472 on the test set. We rank 5th according to the official ranking.

1 Introduction

Machine comprehension of text is one of the ultimate goals of natural language processing. The machine comprehension problem can be formulated as follows: Given an instance i, a question q and an answer candidate pool $\{a_1, a_2, \ldots, a_s\}$, the aim is to search for the best answer candidate a_k, where $1 \leq k \leq s$. The major challenge of this task is that the words in the answer do not necessarily appear in the instance.

In recent years, deep learning models are widely used in the field of NLP, such as semantic analysis (Tang et al., 2015), machine translation (Bahdanau et al., 2014) and text summarization (Rush et al., 2015). (Bahdanau et al., 2014) also introduced the attention mechanism into NLP task for the first time. This attention-based model yielded state-of-the-art performance on the machine translation task. (Hermann et al., 2015) built a supervised reading comprehension data set, the CNN/Daily Mail data sets[1]. They also presented Attentive Reader for machine comprehension, which allows a model to focus on the aspects of an instance that

---

[1] http://www.github.com/deepmind/rc-data/

can help to answer a question, and also allows us to visualize its inference process (Hermann et al., 2015). The key point of the attention-based models is the design of attention function. Compared to Attentive Reader, Attention Sum Reader (Kadlec et al., 2016) used the dot products instead of a $tanh$ layer to compute the attention between question and contextual embeddings. Stanford Attention Reader (Chen et al., 2016) took a bilinear term as the attention function and obtained state-of-the-art results on the CNN/Daily Mail data sets.

The reasoning process was implemented in some models for machine comprehension. Memory Networks (Sukhbaatar et al., 2015) was the first model to propose reasoning process, which had important influence on other follow-up models. Compared to the traditional attention model, Memory Networks additionally uses a function t that constantly updates the representation of the instance and the question so as to realize the reasoning process. (Tseng et al., 2016) proposed an attention-based multi-hop recurrent neural network which achieved good performance on the machine listening comprehension test of TOEFL. Other reasoning models (Dhingra et al., 2017; Sordoni et al., 2016) shared the same idea as previous models, i.e., the representations of the instance and the question embedding were updated through continuous conversion of attention. Some more complex models (Hu et al., 2017; Liu et al., 2017) were proposed based on SQuAD data set (Rajpurkar et al., 2016). Their performances have been very close to or even exceeded the human performance on this dataset.

In this paper, we introduce a simple ensemble method on multiple identical attention-based BiLSTM models, only changing the dropout parameters in each model. We use each model to generate a soft prediction, and sum each result, then take the sum as the final prediction result. Experiments

Proceedings of the 12th International Workshop on Semantic Evaluation (SemEval-2018), pages 1043–1047
New Orleans, Louisiana, June 5–6, 2018. ©2018 Association for Computational Linguistics

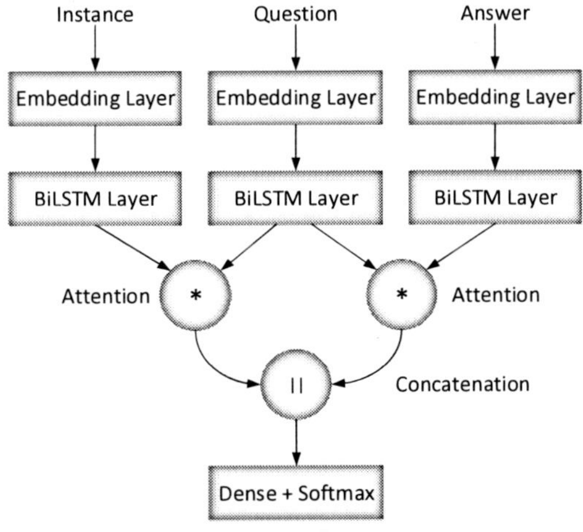

Figure 1: Our attention-based BiLSTM model for machine comprehension.

show that the ensemble model is about 2% higher than the single model in terms of accuracy on both development and test sets. Besides, we also made our code available online[2].

2 System Description

Our model is called an ensemble of attention-based BiLSTM models. Firstly, we use an embedding layer to obtain the distributed representations of the instance, question and answer triples. They are encoded by three different BiLSTM layers. The attention mechanism is implemented by *dot* products via a merge layer. Finally, we assign the same weight to each model when ensembling. The final result is the sum of the soft probabilities yielded by each single model. We keep the structure of each model the same, just fine tune the dropout parameters. The model architecture is shown in Figure 1. The attention mechanism is developed by calculating the *dot* product of the outputs from two BiLSTM layers. Then we use '||' operation to concatenate two matrices from the previous layer in the specified dimension. Finally, a *Dense* fully connected layer with activation *softmax* is used to get the predicted probabilities.

---

[2]https://github.com/Deep1994/An-Ensemble-of-Attention-based-BiLSTM-Model-for-Machine-Comprehension

2.1 BiLSTM

Single direction LSTM (Hochreiter and Schmidhuber, 1997) suffers a weakness of not using the contextual information from the future tokens. Bidirectional LSTM (BiLSTM) exploits both the previous and future context by processing the sequence on two directions and generates two independent sequences of LSTM output vectors. One processes the input sequence in the forward direction, while the other processes the input in the backward direction. The words in the instances, questions and answers are represented by the concatenation of the hidden layer outputs in both directions at each time step.

2.2 Word Embedding

Word embedding is arguably the most widely known technology in the recent history of NLP. It is well-known that using pre-trained embedding helps (Kim, 2014). We try two word embedding tools, GloVe (Pennington et al., 2014) and Word2Vec (Mikolov et al., 2013) on this task.

Tool	Size	Vocab	Dimension
GloVe	5.5G	2.2million	300
Word2Vec	3.5G	3million	300

Table 1: Summary statistics for the embedding tools: Size is the file size after decompression. Both tools have a dimension of 300. The Vocab is the number of word vectors contained in the tool.

2.3 Attention Mechanism

The LSTM model can alleviate the problem of gradient vanishing, but this problem persists in long range reading comprehension contexts. The attention mechanism breaks the constraint on fix-length vector as the context vector, enables the model to focus on those more helpful to outputs. (Luong et al., 2015) presented several attention computation ways, such as *dot*, *general*, *concat*. In our model, we adopt the *dot* mode to compute the attention. After BiLSTM layer, we implement a *dot* product operation on the output vectors produced by previous layer. It is proven effective to improve the performance of our model.

The attention mechanism in our model uses a matching function f to associate the target module with the source module, the function f is implemented as follows:

$$f(m_t, m_s) = m_t^T m_s \qquad (1)$$

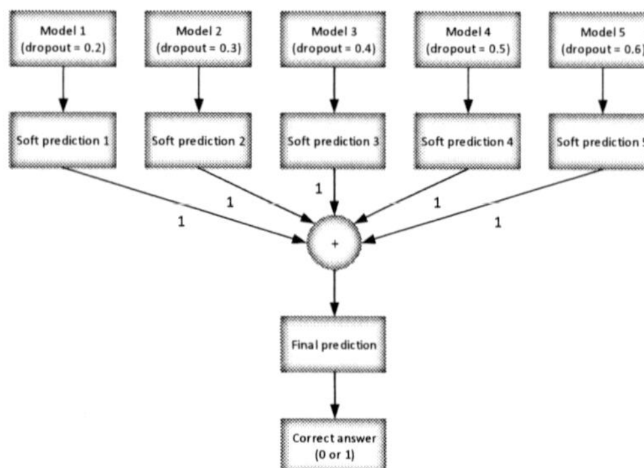

Figure 2: The ensemble method used in our model. The dropout parameters for the five models varied from 0.2 to 0.6 after the BiLSTM layer.

where m_t and m_s correspond to instance and question vectors, or answer and question vectors produced by previous BiLSTM layers, respectively.

2.4 Model Ensemble

Combining multiple models into an ensemble by averaging their predictions is a proven strategy to improve model performance. While predicting with an ensemble is expensive at test time, recent advances in distillation allow us to compress an expensive ensemble into a much smaller model (Hinton et al., 2015; Kuncoro et al., 2016; Kim and Rush, 2016).

In our model, each single model will yield a soft probability to determine if the candidate answer is correct or not. As is shown in figure 2, we train several models and sum the results produced by them. Then we use the sum of the probabilities as the final prediction. We found that the performance of the ensemble model is always better than that of a single model.

3 Experiments

We run each model 10 times, taking the average results as the final experimental results to enhance reliability. In all single models, the dropout parameter is taken as 0.3, and the ensemble model is trained through 5 BiLSTM models. Their dropout parameters are changed from 0.2 to 0.6, respectively, and then the results of the 5 models are summed as the final prediction. We set *epoch* = 6, *batch size* = 512 and *LSTM Units* = 64. Optimization is carried out using Adaptive Moment Estimation (Adam).

3.1 Data Processing

The organizers provided training, development, and test sets, containing 9837, 1417, 2797 questions, respectively. Each question corresponds two answers, only one is correct.

We firstly substitute the abbreviation characters and remove the meaningless characters. Then we combine the instance, question and answer as the supervised training set. Labels are represented by 0 (False) or 1 (True). The *TweetTokenizer*[3] in NLTK is adopted for word segmentation. Furthermore, we find the maximum length of instances is much longer than that of questions and answers, so we remove the stop words in the instances. Our experiments show that doing so not only does not harm the accuracy, but also drastically reduces the training time.

3.2 Experiments and Result Analysis

We compare two word embedding tools, Word2Vec and GloVe, and the experimental results show that GloVe almost always outperforms Word2Vec on this task. Although the vocabularies in GloVe are less than those in Word2Vec, GloVe contains more abbreviations, which are especially useful after tokenizing the instance, question and answer triples, and greatly reduce the number of unknown words in word embedding, making the context semantics better learned by the model. We make random assignments on unknown words, ranging from -0.25 to 0.25.

Tool	Ukw	Time	Dev Acc	Test Acc
GloVe	33	597s	**0.7448**	**0.7276**
Word2Vec	276	40s	0.7415	0.7087

Table 2: Comparison between Word2Vec and GloVe tools on BiLSTM models. Ukw is the number of unknown words. Time is the loading time of two tools. We can see GloVe performs better, but its loading time is much longer than that of Word2Vec.

As seen in Table 3, we compare two network architectures, LSTM and BiLSTM. The results show that the BiLSTM model performs better than the LSTM model on this task.

Based on Glove word embedding and BiLSTM architecture, we train 5 single models for ensemble. The only difference between them is the difference in dropout parameters, which increases from 0.2 to 0.6. In our experiments, we train the

---

[3]http://www.nltk.org/api/nltk.tokenize.html

Network	Tool	Dev Acc	Test Acc
LSTM	GloVe	0.7448	0.7276
BiLSTM	GloVe	**0.7508**	**0.7301**

Table 3: Comparison between LSTM and BiLSTM. BiLSTM performs better than LSTM on both datasets.

single model with the dropout in order of 0.3, 0.5, 0.4, 0.2, 0.6, then the first ensemble is the result of adding the first two models with the dropout of 0.3, 0.5 as the predictive result, the result of the second ensemble is based on the first ensemble plus the single model with dropout of 0.4, and so on. We perform a total of 4 ensemble experiments, the results show that the accuracy of each ensemble model improved on both datasets. The final ensemble model has an accuracy rate of 0.7699 on the development set and 0.7472 on the test set. However, we find that our model was slightly more accurate on the test set without the ensemble of the model with a dropout of 0.6, but the overall effect is not obvious. Ensemble makes our model perform well on this task, ranking 5th out of 11 submissions.

Dropout	Dev Acc	Test Acc
0.3	0.7476	0.7311
0.5	0.7516	0.7183
Ensemble 1	0.7608	0.7386
0.4	0.7615	0.7294
Ensemble 2	0.7692	0.7408
0.2	0.7354	0.7143
Ensemble 3	0.7664	**0.7479**
0.6	0.7410	0.7308
Ensemble 4	**0.7699**	**0.7472**

Table 4: Results on single and ensemble models. All models adopt GloVe + Attention-based BiLSTM architecture. The dropout layer is behind the BiLSTM layer.

4 Conclusion and Future Work

In this paper, we present an ensemble of attention-based BiLSTM models for machine comprehension task. We find GloVe is superior to Word2Vec on this task, a simple ensemble method can significantly enhance the overall performance.

In the future, we plan to explore more ways to compute the attention, such as a bilinear term. Future work also involves using more external knowledge and deeper network to improve model performance. We will explore the ensemble method in greater depth, trying ensemble on the models with more structural difference.

Acknowledgments

This work was supported by the Natural Science Foundations of China No.61463050, No.617-02443, No.61762091, the NSF of Yunnan Province No. 2015FB113, the Project of Innovative Research Team of Yunnan Province.

References

Dzmitry Bahdanau, Kyunghyun Cho, and Yoshua Bengio. 2014. Neural machine translation by jointly learning to align and translate. *arXiv preprint arXiv:1409.0473*.

Danqi Chen, Jason Bolton, and Christopher D Manning. 2016. A thorough examination of the cnn/daily mail reading comprehension task. In *Proceedings of the 54th Annual Meeting of the Association for Computational Linguistics (Volume 1: Long Papers)*, volume 1, pages 2358–2367.

Bhuwan Dhingra, Hanxiao Liu, Zhilin Yang, William Cohen, and Ruslan Salakhutdinov. 2017. Gated-attention readers for text comprehension. In *Proceedings of the 55th Annual Meeting of the Association for Computational Linguistics (Volume 1: Long Papers)*, volume 1, pages 1832–1846.

Karl Moritz Hermann, Tomas Kocisky, Edward Grefenstette, Lasse Espeholt, Will Kay, Mustafa Suleyman, and Phil Blunsom. 2015. Teaching machines to read and comprehend. In *Advances in Neural Information Processing Systems*, pages 1693–1701.

Geoffrey Hinton, Oriol Vinyals, and Jeff Dean. 2015. Distilling the knowledge in a neural network. *stat*, 1050:9.

Sepp Hochreiter and Jürgen Schmidhuber. 1997. Long short-term memory. *Neural computation*, 9(8):1735–1780.

Minghao Hu, Yuxing Peng, and Xipeng Qiu. 2017. Reinforced mnemonic reader for machine comprehension. *CoRR, abs/1705.02798*.

Rudolf Kadlec, Martin Schmid, Ondřej Bajgar, and Jan Kleindienst. 2016. Text understanding with the attention sum reader network. In *Proceedings of the 54th Annual Meeting of the Association for Computational Linguistics (Volume 1: Long Papers)*, volume 1, pages 908–918.

Yoon Kim. 2014. Convolutional neural networks for sentence classification. In *Proceedings of the 2014 Conference on Empirical Methods in Natural Language Processing (EMNLP)*, pages 1746–1751.

Yoon Kim and Alexander M Rush. 2016. Sequence-level knowledge distillation. In *Proceedings of the 2016 Conference on Empirical Methods in Natural Language Processing*, pages 1317–1327.

Adhiguna Kuncoro, Miguel Ballesteros, Lingpeng Kong, Chris Dyer, and Noah A Smith. 2016. Distilling an ensemble of greedy dependency parsers into one mst parser. In *Proceedings of the 2016 Conference on Empirical Methods in Natural Language Processing*, pages 1744–1753.

Xiaodong Liu, Yelong Shen, Kevin Duh, and Jianfeng Gao. 2017. Stochastic answer networks for machine reading comprehension. *arXiv preprint arXiv:1712.03556*.

Thang Luong, Hieu Pham, and Christopher D Manning. 2015. Effective approaches to attention-based neural machine translation. In *Proceedings of the 2015 Conference on Empirical Methods in Natural Language Processing*, pages 1412–1421.

Tomas Mikolov, Ilya Sutskever, Kai Chen, Greg S Corrado, and Jeff Dean. 2013. Distributed representations of words and phrases and their compositionality. In *Advances in neural information processing systems*, pages 3111–3119.

Jeffrey Pennington, Richard Socher, and Christopher Manning. 2014. Glove: Global vectors for word representation. In *Proceedings of the 2014 conference on empirical methods in natural language processing (EMNLP)*, pages 1532–1543.

Pranav Rajpurkar, Jian Zhang, Konstantin Lopyrev, and Percy Liang. 2016. Squad: 100,000+ questions for machine comprehension of text. In *Proceedings of the 2016 Conference on Empirical Methods in Natural Language Processing*, pages 2383–2392.

Alexander M Rush, Sumit Chopra, and Jason Weston. 2015. A neural attention model for abstractive sentence summarization. In *Proceedings of the 2015 Conference on Empirical Methods in Natural Language Processing*, pages 379–389.

Alessandro Sordoni, Philip Bachman, Adam Trischler, and Yoshua Bengio. 2016. Iterative alternating neural attention for machine reading. *arXiv preprint arXiv:1606.02245*.

Sainbayar Sukhbaatar, Jason Weston, Rob Fergus, et al. 2015. End-to-end memory networks. In *Advances in neural information processing systems*, pages 2440–2448.

Duyu Tang, Bing Qin, and Ting Liu. 2015. Document modeling with gated recurrent neural network for sentiment classification. In *Proceedings of the 2015 conference on empirical methods in natural language processing*, pages 1422–1432.

Bo-Hsiang Tseng, Sheng-syun Shen, Hung-Yi Lee, and Lin-Shan Lee. 2016. Towards machine comprehension of spoken content: Initial toefl listening comprehension test by machine. *Interspeech 2016*, pages 2731–2735.

ECNU at SemEval-2018 Task 11: Using Deep Learning Method to Address Machine Comprehension Task

Yixuan Sheng[1], Man Lan[1,2*], Yuanbin Wu[1,2]
[1]Department of Computer Science and Technology,
East China Normal University, Shanghai, P.R.China
[2]Shanghai Key Laboratory of Multidimensional Information Processing
51164500026@stu.ecnu.edu.cn, {mlan, ybwu}@cs.ecnu.edu.cn

Abstract

This paper describes the system we submitted to the Task 11 in SemEval 2018, i.e., Machine Comprehension using Commonsense Knowledge. Given a passage and some questions that each have two candidate answers, this task requires the participate system to select out one answer meet the meaning of original text or commonsense knowledge from the candidate answers. For this task, we use a deep learning method to obtain final predict answer by calculating relevance of choices representations and question-aware document representation.

1 Introduction

In recent years, the presentation of challenge and large-scale reading comprehension corpora has driven the development of technology for machine reading comprehension, and most of these machine comprehension datasets do not need commonsense knowledge to answer questions. The purpose of Machine Comprehension using Commonsense Knowledge task in Semeval 2018 is to provide a platform for finding a way for the machine to better understand the text and enable the machine answer questions based on the text, and encourage participants to make use any external resources (e.g., DeScript, narrative chains, Wikipedia, etc) to improve the system performance (Ostermann et al., 2018b). The task 11 is a multiple-choice machine comprehension, which requires a system read a narrative text about everyday activities (Ostermann et al., 2018a) and then answer multiple-choice questions based on this text. Some questions need to be answered according to the original text, and others can be answered by commonsense knowledge. Each question is associated with a set of two answers. Table 1 gives an example of the dataset.

To address this machine comprehension task, we utilized rule-based methods and a deep learn-

document: Early this morning I woke up to the sound of my newspaper landing on my driveway. I sat up and wrapped my pink robe around me. I slipped my feet into my slippers and looked at the clock. It was only 7:00 but it was time for me to get my newspaper and drink some coffee. I looked out the window and noticed it was raining quite a bit. I saw the newspaper at the end of my driveway, as far away as it could be. I grabbed my umbrella out of my coat closet and opened my front door enough to stick the umbrella through and open it outside. I stepped out the door and quickly covered my head with the umbrella. Then I ran to the end of my driveway, scooped up the newspaper in its plastic wrapping, and ran back to my front door. I closed my umbrella, took off my slippers, and dried off. Then, I unwrapped my newspaper and sat down to read it. **question**: Do they read the paper daily? **candidate answers**: 0. No they usually watch TV in the mornings. 1. Yes **answer**: 1

Table 1: An example from the SemEval2018 task11 dataset.

ing method. Our final submission use Gated-Attention Reader (Dhingra et al., 2016) to fuse question information into document and acquire a question-awared document representation, the degree of interaction between choices and document are regard as the probabilities of choices being returned as an answer. The above two methods do not use additional commonsense knowledge, which may lead to the poor preformance of our system. In future work, we may explore more methods to integrate common knowledge into models.

The rest of this paper is organized as follows. Section 2 describes our systems. Section 3 describes datasets, experimental setting and analyse results on datasets. Finally, Section 4 concludes this work.

Proceedings of the 12th International Workshop on Semantic Evaluation (SemEval-2018), pages 1048–1052
New Orleans, Louisiana, June 5–6, 2018. ©2018 Association for Computational Linguistics

2 System Description

2.1 Task Description

Formally, this multiple-choice machine comprehension task can be expressed as a quadruple:$<$**D, Q, A, a**$>$. Where **D** represents a narrative text about everyday activities, **Q** represents a question for the content of the narrative text, **A** is the candidate answer choice set to the question(this task contains two candidate answers choice a_0 and a_1) and **a** represents the correct answer. The system is expected to select an answer from **A** that best answers **Q** according to the evidences in document D or commonsense knowledge.

2.2 Two Rule-based Baselines

First of all, we implemented a rule-based system proposed in (Richardson et al., 2013), which used the sliding-window (SW) and word distance-based (WD) algorithms to calculate the answer scores according to the rules and return the highest-score answer. We also tried the improved SW and WD algorithms proposed in (Smith et al., 2015), and the system performance has improvement. Sliding-window and Word Distance-based algorithms are are described as follows:

Sliding-Window: Given a data sample $<$**D, Q,** a_0(or a_1), **a**$>$, firstly, we calculate the inverse word counts of each word in the document **D**. Then we set a window that slides word by word from the beginning of the document to the end. When the window slides to a position, the sum of inverse word counts of all the words that appears in the question **Q** or the candidate choice a_0 (or a_1) is the score of the window at this moment. Until the window slides to the end of the passage, we choose the highest window score as the final score of the candidate choice a_0 (or a_1). Window size is size of union of the question **Q** and the choice a_0 (or a_1), and the window slides over full passage only once. In the improved SW algorithm, the window size is 2-30, and window passes full passage window several times, and increasing the size of the window by one after each sliding over the full passage. The summing up values of all passes is served as improved sliding window score.

Word Distance-based: Given a data sample $<$**D, Q,** a_0(or a_1), **a**$>$, firstly, we define two collections, set_{dq} and set_{dc}, set_{dq} represents the intersection of the question words and the document words, and set_{dc} represents the intersection of the words in the choice and the words of the docu-

ment. If neither set_{dq} nor set_{dc} is empty set, we calculate the shortest distance between words of set_{dp} and words of set_{dc} in the document, denote the shortest distance as d_{min}, and the word distance score of the choice is $\frac{d_{min}+1}{|D|-1}$, otherwise, the word distance score of the choice is zero.

The sliding-window score minus the word distance-based score is the final score of the choice. We separately calculated the scores of the two choices for the question and then selected the choice with higher score as the answer to the question.

2.3 Deep Learning model

Both of the above unsupervised methods score the overlap that between each answer and the document by making a sliding-window passes over the document. Therefore, we roughly count the proportion of words in correct answers appear in the document[1], and we find that the proportion of correct answers whose words appear entirely in the article is not high in all correct answers. The proportion show that there is a limit to using the above method to improve system performance. Hence we used a deep learning approach to passage representations modeling. Inspired by (Lai et al., 2017), we use the state-of-art Gated-Attention Reader which performs well on several datasets. When a sample data $<$**D, Q, A, a**$>$ is given, the steps of the model processing this data sample are described below, Figure 1 shows the system.

2.3.1 Passage, Question and Choice Encoder

First, each word in **D**, **Q**, and choices (two choices in candidate answer set **A**) is mapped to d-dimensional vector. The 300-dim GloVe embedding (Pennington et al., 2014) is used. For the input word vectors of **D**, we also include a 5-dim binary feature to indicates the overlap between the ducument and the question(or choices) which inspired by (Chen et al., 2017). Each dimension of the 5-dim binary match feature represent whether the word present in the query, in the choice a_0, in the choice a_1, in both question and

---

[1]We use the following equations to estimate how many answers appear entirely in the document: if $|answer\ word \cap document\ word|/|answer\ word| = 1$, it means the answer appears entirely in the document, where $|A|$ means size of set A. Then we calculate $|ans_{ce}|/|ans_c|$, where ans_{ce} means correct answers which entirely appeared in document, and ans_c means correct answers. The percentage of the correct answers entirely appeared in document is about 24%.

choice a_0, in both question and choice a_1, respectively. Take passage as an example, we have document $\mathbf{D}$: $x_1^{\mathbf{D}}, x_2^{\mathbf{D}}, ..., x_m^{\mathbf{D}} \in R^{|D|*dim}$, and next we use bi-directional GRU to encode each document word embedding $x_i^{\mathbf{D}}$,

$$\overrightarrow{h_i^{\mathbf{D}}} = biGRU(\overrightarrow{h_{i-1}^{\mathbf{D}}}, x_1^{\mathbf{D}}), i = 1, 2, ..., m$$

$$\overleftarrow{h_i^{\mathbf{D}}} = biGRU(\overleftarrow{h_{i+1}^{\mathbf{D}}}, x_1^{\mathbf{D}}), i = m, m-1, ..., 1$$

we define $\boldsymbol{h}_i^{\mathbf{D}} \in R^{2d}$ is concatenation of the $\overrightarrow{h_i^{\mathbf{D}}}$ and $\overleftarrow{h_i^{\mathbf{D}}}$, where d is hidden size. At this time, we get the encoded document representation $\mathbf{D}^e = \{$ $\boldsymbol{h}_1^{\mathbf{D}}, \boldsymbol{h}_2^{\mathbf{D}}, ... , \boldsymbol{h}_m^{\mathbf{D}} \}$. Meanwhile, we use separate bi-directional GRU to form representation for question, we denote these representations as $\mathbf{Q}^e = \{ \boldsymbol{h}_1^{\mathbf{Q}}, \boldsymbol{h}_2^{\mathbf{Q}}, ... , \boldsymbol{h}_n^{\mathbf{Q}} \}$. As for choices, we concat $\overrightarrow{h_n^{\mathbf{C}}}$ and $\overleftarrow{h_1^{\mathbf{C}}}$ to make up a vector represent a choice, so we get $\mathbf{C}_0 \in R^{2d}$ and $\mathbf{C}_1 \in R^{2d}$.

2.3.2 Summarize Question-aware Passage Representation

The interaction layer of Gated-Attention Reader is a l-layers multi-hop architecture with gated-attention units. Each multi-hop layer contain a bi-GRU and a gated-attention unit. As shown in Figure 1, we sent $\mathbf{Q}^e \in R^{|Q|*2d}$ and $\mathbf{D}^e \in R^{|D|*2d}$ into a gated-attention unit. Gated-attention unit fuses information from question to each document tokens and generates a set of vectors $\mathbf{D}_l^{GA} = \{ \mathbf{d}_1^{(l)}, \mathbf{d}_2^{(l)}, ..., \mathbf{d}_m^{(l)} \}$, where superscript (l) denote l-th multi-hop layer. To generates $\mathbf{D}_l^{GA}$, firstly, the question soft attention to each document word to obtain attention weight α_i, and then we use α_i to calculate a weighted question representation $\overline{q}_i$ for i-th word in $\mathbf{D}$, finally, the weighted question $\overline{q}_i$ representation is element-wise multiplied by $\boldsymbol{h}_i$ makes $\mathbf{d}_i$. The specific calculation steps of a gated-attention unit are as follows.

$$\alpha_i = softmax(\mathbf{Q}^e \mathbf{h}_i) \quad (1)$$

$$\overline{q}_i = \mathbf{Q}^{eT} \alpha_i \quad (2)$$

$$\mathbf{d}_i = \mathbf{h}_i \cdot \overline{q}_i \quad (3)$$

After obtaining the current layer question-aware document representation, we put this representation into next hop layer, until after l layers multi-hops, we generate the a set of question-aware vectors $\mathbf{D}_l^{GA}$ for document. Finally, we sent $\mathbf{D}_l^{GA}$ into a layer biGRU and concat the last outputs of each direction ($\overrightarrow{h_{l+1}^{GA}}$ and $\overleftarrow{h_{l+1}^{GA}}$) to get a ultimate question-aware document representation vector $\widetilde{\mathbf{D}} \in R^{2d}$

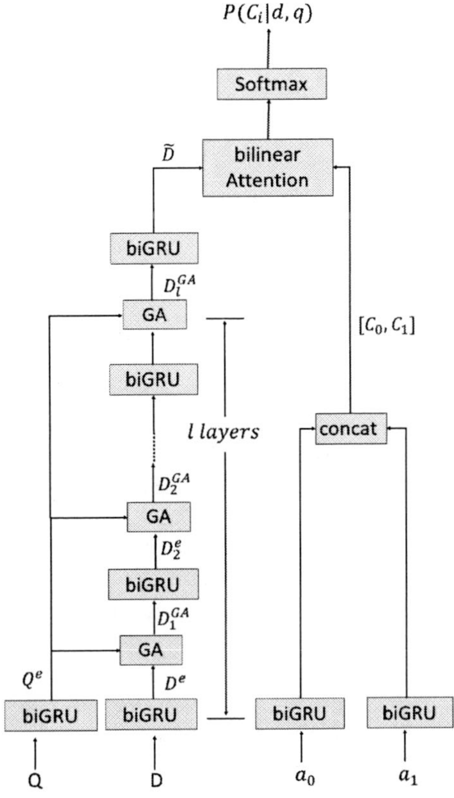

Figure 1: Architecture of our system.

2.3.3 Answer Selection

Now, we have a question-aware representation $\widetilde{\mathbf{D}}$, two choice representations $\mathbf{C}_0$ and $\mathbf{C}_1$. We estimate the probability that the choice selected as the correct answer by equation (4), and the choice with a higher-probability is returned as the predict answer.

$$[p_0, p_1] = softmax([\mathbf{C}_0, \mathbf{C}_1]W\widetilde{\mathbf{D}}) \quad (4)$$

3 Experiments

3.1 Datasets and Evaluation Metric

Table 2 shows the statistics of articles and questions in training, development, test data sets of this task. Here "#text" and "#commonsense" represent the question types, which are unknown during test and officially provided by organizors after test. Therefore, we do not use the class information of questions for system construction. Clearly, around 70% questions are from text and 30% are from commonsense. Without the aid of additional commonsense knowledge base, these questions from commonsense makes this task a huge challenge.

Dataset	Articles	Questions		
		#text	#commonsense	#total
train	1,470	7,032	2,699	9,731
dev	219	1,006	405	1,411
test	429	2,074	723	2,797

Table 2: The statistics of data sets in training, development and test data.

To evaluate the system performance, the official evaluation criterion is *accuracy*.

3.2 Preprocessing and Experimental Setting

For rule-based baselines, we first converted words into their lowercase and then performed tokenization and stemming using Stanford CoreNLP[2]. For deep learning system, we use 300-D pretrained word vectors provided by GloVe[3] as initial word embedding, which are fine-tuned during training. The encoding layer use one layer biGRU with 128-dims hidden size to encoder texts. Learning rate is 0.3, droprate is 0.5, epoch is 100, and num of multi-hops is 2. We use cross entropy and vanilla stochastic gradient descent (SGD) to train our models.

3.3 Experiments on Training Data

Table 3 shows the results of Task 11 with different methods on dev dataset, where "GA(biGRU)" denotes the final system we submit, "GA(biLSTM)" represents the experiment that we replace all biGRU units in the system with biLSTM units, "GA $-f_{match}$" represents the system without 5-dim match feature, "#text" and "#commonsens" represent the accuracy under different question types, respectively.

Methods	Accuracy		
	#text	#commonsense	#total
SW + WD	62.62%	45.92%	57.83%
improved SW+WD	65.01%	47.65%	60.02%
GA(biGRU)	77.33%	78.51%	77.63%
GA(biLSTM)	76.41%	77.53%	76.76%
GA $-f_{match}$	76.34%	78.02%	76.82%

Table 3: The results on dev.

Based on above experimental results, we find that the performance of GA system is much better than rule-based approaches, this is because the multi-hop structure merges the information of the question and the document repeatedly which is helpful to select final answer, unlike the rule-based approach that considers only word matching within a window-size distance. Furthermore, we find that the improved SW + WD algorithm is better than SW + WD algorithm, because the improved SW + WD algorithm considers the degree of word matching at different distances. From the GA system results, we find the performance of using biGRU units is better than that of biLSTM units and matching features also improves the system performance. Compare the accuracy of different types of questions under different methods, we find that the rule-based approaches considers only the word-matched features lead to lower accuracy on the commonsense type questions. GA systems perform better than rule-based systems on both types of questions, because the GA system takes into account the semantic similarity of the question-aware document and choices. Further, there are some commonsense types questions which the document content does not clearly indicate the correct answer but clearly does not meet the meaning of wrong answer. This may be the reason why we did not use external resources but the accuracy of the commonsense type question predicted by GA system is improved.

3.4 Results on Test Data

Table 4 shows the our result and official results of top-ranked teams on SemEval 2018 Task 11 test set.

Teamname	Rank	Accuracy(total)
ECNU	10	0.7311
iFLYTEK & HIT (HFL)	1	0.8413
Yuanfudao	2	0.8395
MITRE	3	0.8227

Table 4: Our result and the top three results on test sets.

The final result we submitted is generated by GA system used biGRU units, the specific configuration of which is mentioned in Section 3.2. Compared with the top ranked systems, there is much room for improvement in our work. In addition, the use of external knowledge resources by the system also have an impact on system performance because there are about 26% commonsense type questions in the dataset. This is where our system lacks.

4 Conclusion

In this paper, we implement rule-based and deep learning approaches to address Machine Comprehension Using Commonsense Knowledge task in SemEval 2018. We explored two rule-based algorithm i.e., sliding window and word distance-based algorithm. We also utilized a deep learning method which use a multi-hop architecture (Gated-attention Reader). The above two methods do not use additional commonsense knowledge, this is a point that we need to improve.

Acknowledgements

This work is is supported by the Science and Technology Commission of Shanghai Municipality Grant (No.15ZR1410700) and the open project of Shanghai Key Laboratory of Trustworthy Computing (No.07dz22304201604).

References

Danqi Chen, Adam Fisch, Jason Weston, and Antoine Bordes. 2017. Reading wikipedia to answer open-domain questions. *arXiv preprint arXiv:1704.00051*.

Bhuwan Dhingra, Hanxiao Liu, Zhilin Yang, William W Cohen, and Ruslan Salakhutdinov. 2016. Gated-attention readers for text comprehension.

Guokun Lai, Qizhe Xie, Hanxiao Liu, Yiming Yang, and Eduard Hovy. 2017. Race: Large-scale reading comprehension dataset from examinations. In *EMNLP*.

Simon Ostermann, Ashutosh Modi, Michael Roth, Stefan Thater, and Manfred Pinkal. 2018a. MCScript: A Novel Dataset for Assessing Machine Comprehension Using Script Knowledge. In *Proceedings of the 11th International Conference on Language Resources and Evaluation (LREC 2018)*, Miyazaki, Japan.

Simon Ostermann, Michael Roth, Ashutosh Modi, Stefan Thater, and Manfred Pinkal. 2018b. SemEval-2018 Task 11: Machine Comprehension using Commonsense Knowledge. In *Proceedings of International Workshop on Semantic Evaluation (SemEval-2018)*, New Orleans, LA, USA.

Jeffrey Pennington, Richard Socher, and Christopher Manning. 2014. Glove: Global vectors for word representation. In *Proceedings of the 2014 conference on empirical methods in natural language processing (EMNLP)*, pages 1532–1543.

Matthew Richardson, Christopher J. C. Burges, and Erin Renshaw. 2013. Mctest: A challenge dataset for the open-domain machine comprehension of text. In *EMNLP*, pages 193–203. ACL.

Ellery Smith, Nicola Greco, Matko Bosnjak, and Andreas Vlachos. 2015. A strong lexical matching method for the machine comprehension test. In *Proceedings of the 2015 Conference on Empirical Methods in Natural Language Processing*, pages 1693–1698, Lisbon, Portugal. Association for Computational Linguistics.

CSReader at SemEval-2018 Task 11: Multiple Choice Question Answering as Textual Entailment

Zhengping Jiang
Laboratory of Machine Perception
Peking University
`tony.jiang.zhengping@gmail.com`

Qi Sun
Laboratory of Machine Perception
Peking University
`1500012917@pku.edu.cn`

Abstract

In this document we present an end-to-end machine reading comprehension system that solves multiple choice questions with a textual entailment perspective. Since some of the knowledge required is not explicitly mentioned in the text, we try to exploit common sense knowledge by using pretrained word embeddings during contextual embeddings and by dynamically generating a weighted representation of related script knowledge. In the model two kinds of prediction structure are ensembled, and the final accuracy of our system is 10 percent higher than the naiive baseline.

1 Introduction

K. M. Arivuchelvan et al.(2017) stated that machine reading comprehension can be defined as a task that deals with the automatic understanding of texts. In their paper, it was also mentioned that machine comprehension can be evaluated by two methods, namely (1) translating the text into formal language representations and evaluating it using structured queries. (2) evaluating it through natural language questions. Recently a lot of datasets are available for evaluating machine reading comprehension systems, for example, there are SQuAD(Rajpurkar et al., 2016) and the MCTest(Richardson et al., 2013). On many of these datasets human-like performance has been achieved. However, one of the biggest challenges in machine comprehension is how to provide common sense knowledge regarding daily events to machines(Mostafazadeh et al., 2016). The SemEval2018-Task11(Ostermann et al., 2018) provides a dataset containing questions that can only be answered with the help of common sense knowledge.To address this problem, we first propose a model to solve normal reading comprehension problems and then try to modify the model to embody common sense knowledge. In section two, we give a brief in-troduction to ideas and models that might be useful to a comprehensive understanding of our work. Section three carefully describes our model implementation, and why we chose this kind of model structure. And section four briefly examines the datasets used. Section five provides a simple evaluation of our result. Finally, our conclusion can be found in section six.

2 Background Knowledge

In this section, we present some basic knowledge required for a comprehensive understanding of our model. We first give a basic introduction to RNN models and the implementation of GRU Cell, then cast a little glance upon the textual entailment problems.

2.1 Recurrent Neural Network

Lipton et al.(2015) stated that Recurrent neural networks (RNNs) are "connectionist models with the ability to selectively pass information across sequence steps, while processing sequential data one element at a time." An RNN model captures features of a sequence by updating a hidden set of variables at every input element, as illustrated in figure 1. In many language modelling tasks, the output of every RNN iteration step will simply be a prediction of the one-hot representation of the next element in the sequence. However, as we intended to train our model end-to-end, we will not care much about the output of the RNN model, but pay attention instead to the hidden state because it is likely to be a contextual representation influenced by every input element.

2.2 GRU Cell

One of the commonly used RNN hidden units is LSTM (Hochreiter and Schmidhuber, 1997). This kind of hidden unit can retain short-term memory for a long time during sequence processing, thus

Proceedings of the 12th International Workshop on Semantic Evaluation (SemEval-2018), pages 1053–1057
New Orleans, Louisiana, June 5–6, 2018. ©2018 Association for Computational Linguistics

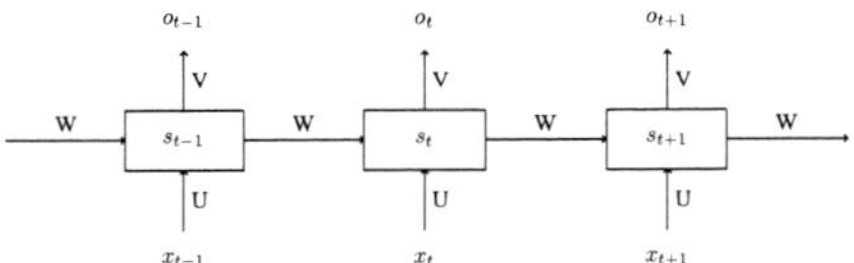

Figure 1: An illustration of unfolded RNN cells.

is able to recognize long-term dependency information. GRU Cell (Cho et al., 2014) is inspired by LSTM, and is simpler to compute. For each timestep t, two gating vector is computed, i.e., the reset gate r and the update gate z by

$$r_j = \sigma([W_r x]_j + [U_r h^{<t-1>}]_j)$$
$$z_j = \sigma([W_z x]_j + [U_z h^{<t-1>}]_j)$$

Where x is the input vector and h is the hidden-state vector, and $[\cdot]_j$ means the jth element of a given vector. $W_{(\cdot)}$ $U_{(\cdot)}$ are matrix parameters to be trained. With these variables defined, the hidden state can be updated as

$$h_j^{<t>} = z_j h_j^{<t-1>} + (1 - z_j)\tilde{h}_j^{<t>}$$

where $\tilde{h}$ is calculated as

$$\tilde{h}_j^{<t>} = \phi([Wx]_j + [U(r \odot h^{<t-1>})]_j)$$

Therefore with the interaction of these two gate the cell is able to learn a pattern whether to reset the hidden state using current input, or to retain the previous hidden state largely.

2.3 Textual Entailment Model

We try to first adapt an existing textual entailment model to this machine comprehension problem. The model is first proposed by Rocktaschel et al. (2015)., in which the premise is first contextually encoded, then a hypothesis-to-premise word by word attention is calculated. The model implicitly modify a hidden variable r_t to regulate the attention distribution at timestep t as

$$M_t = \tanh(W^y Y + (W^h h_t + W^r r_{t-1}) \otimes e_L)$$
$$\alpha_t = \mathrm{softmax}(w^T M_t)$$
$$r_t = Y\alpha_t^T + \tanh(W^t r_{t-1})$$

Here we have maintained the original symbol usage of Rocktaschel et al., where $W_{(\cdot)}$ and $U_{(\cdot)}$ are variable matrices to be trained, and Y is the matrix containing all hidden states of the premise

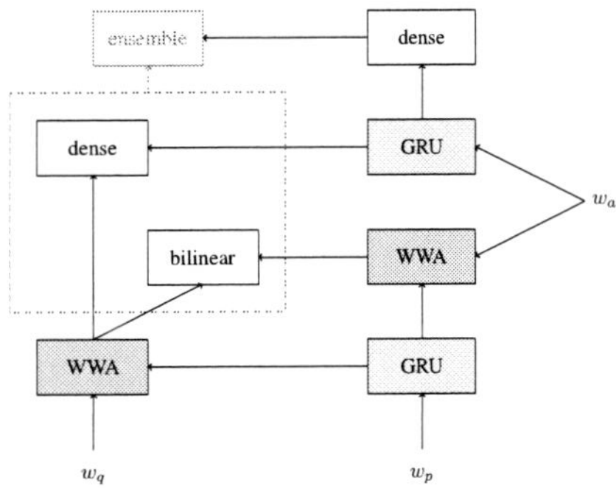

Figure 2: Our basic model, where "dense" represents fully connected layers, and WWA represents word-wise-attention structure described in section 2.3.

encoder. We generally follow the framework of this model, with modifications made to embody common sense knowledge and answer multiple choice questions.

3 Method

3.1 Bilinear Form

One of our classifiers uses the bilinear form. According to Milnor et al. (1973), a bilinear form is a function:

$$\beta : X \times X \to R$$

such that $\beta(x, y)$ is R-linear as a function of x for fixed y, and is R-linear as a function of y for fixed x. Then such a bilinear form can be called as an inner product on X. Thus this kind of inner product can intuitively be used to measure similarity between two representations of the same space, we design our bilinear classifier as follow:
Let α_1^N and α_2^N denote answer representations generated by our word-wise-attention mechanism from answers to text described in last section, and let q^N denote the question representation generated through the same process. Then we construct a trainable matrix $B^{N \times N}$. Then we can get a similarity score vector s where:

$$s_i = \alpha_i^T B q$$

Then to normalize probability representation we perform a softmax function upon s to give our classification result.

3.2 Dense Classifier

We have another fully-connected classifier that works as described below. Let α_1^N and α_2^N denote the answer representations generated with pure RNN layer with GRU cell (compare with the WWA generated representation in the bilinear classifier), and let q^N denote the attended question representation generated by word-wise-attention mechanism described in subsection 2.3. Then we concatenate these three representation as c:

$$c = [q : \alpha_1 : \alpha_2]$$

Then we use c as the input of a two layer fully-connected neural network, where the hidden layer in the middle has nodes only half the number of the input, and the output layer is a softmaxed probability distribution representing our model's final choice.

3.3   General Model

Our model answers the multiple choice question by first encoding the question and the passage combined using the aforementioned textual entailment encoding, and then using two different question answering classifier to choose one of the two choices. A weighted sum is then calculated from the two answers each represented by a binary distribution. The weight is dynamically decided by a feed-forward network taking two contextually encoded answer strings as input. First the contextual embedded answer string representations of two answer choices are calculated by RNN-encoder, then we concatenate them and put them into a feed-forward network to calculate weights for the ensemble of the two aforementioned classifier. A general illustration can be seen in figure 2. Here GRU stands for an rnn unit using GRU cell, while WWA stands for word-wise attention used in textual entailment. We can see that our model can be trained end-to-end, and most of the weights can be dynamically learnt during training.

During training, the text is tokenized and lemmatized using python NLTK (Bird and Loper, 2002), and word stemming is not performed. We have made this choice because which words should be classified as stop word is hard to decide for an RNN model that are likely to capture some of the syntactic features of a given language.

The motivation for our using two different classifier is that we want to softly provide different solutions to different kinds of problems. The bilinear classifier measures similarity between question-attended and answer-attended contextual representations, which we believe should have better result on non-TF questions (By non-TF questions

we mean those open questions which can not be answered by "Yes—True" or "No—False"), while the dense classifier should do better on TF questions according to our expectation. A detailed analysis of the model weights can be seen in next section.

3.4   Common Sense Knowledge

However some of the question in the test set cannot be answered merely with information provided in the passage. We try to embody some kinds of common sense knowledge representation into the general model, however their influence to system performance varies.

3.4.1   Word Embedding

In the general model, the embedding layer that converts the one-hot representation of an input word to its corresponding embedding vector is trainable, and is optimized during training using back-propagation(Rumelhart et al., 1986) algorithm. However, due to the relatively small database size, we have finally marked the embedding layer untrainable, and use GloVe (Pennington et al., 2014) word embeddings instead.

3.4.2   Script Knowledge

The script knowledge we have chosen is the OMCS (Singh et al., 2002) database. In the database are presented many different step by step descriptions of some daily events. To use this script knowledge, we first encode every single description as a passage using the RNN that was once used to encode our mission text. Then for every event e_i we calculate the event representation as an average of each description representation in that event category:

$$e_i = \frac{1}{M} \sum_{j=1}^{M} x_{i,j}^N$$

Where $x_{i,j}$ is the jth description representation of event i. Then let E denote the event representation matrix with its ith row representing event i, then every time context representation r_t is calculated, we calculate a similarity vector s as:

$$s = \text{softmax}(EWr_t)$$

Then if $\max_{i<M}(s_i) > t$ where t is a threshold hyper-parameter, we substitute r_t and its time series matrix with corresponding e_i and its time series matrix. But as this treatment provided little enhancement to our accuracy, we excluded

System	Accuracy
1st place	0.843
SCReader	0.631
baseline	About 0.53

Figure 3: Table comparing performance of different systems.

this structure from our final submission. Still we believe that other common sense representation might be helpful, like ConceptNet (Liu and Singh, 2004).

4 Experiment Setting and Evaluation

4.1 Overview

We Trained our model using SGD with weight decay. No minibatch grouping is used, and we trained our model on training set for 20000 time steps. When near convergence, our model can reach around 80% to 90% accuracy upon training set (The accuracy is sampled), and in last two model we trained that finally lead to our only submission, we get an accuracy result of about 68% on developing set. This accuracy is a little higher than our final accuracy on test set. Our final result compared with baseline and the first rank system is given in the form.

4.2 Preprocessing

Before inputting the raw text into out model, we first transform words into their one-hot representation without stemming and lemmatization, and tokenization is done using NLTK toolkit. Then we push the data through an embedding layer in which the GloVe 50 was used due to time concerns.

4.3 Further Discussion

Providing our scarce usage of common sense knowledge, our model performed surprisingly well on time deduction problems. Even in questions where an addition of fifteen minutes to thirty minutes to get forty-five minutes as answer is required, our model successfully chose the right answer. However, the ensemble didn't work as we intended. The bilinear classifier was unalterably providing $[0, 1]$ after softmaxing, probably due to machine floating point precision limit. And the result weight determiner always assign the GRU related classifier a far greater weight. This is

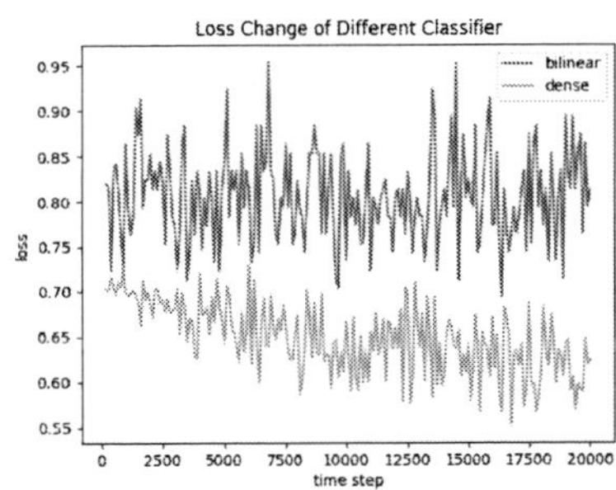

Figure 4: The loss change of our two classifier.

very counterintuitive, and we are still trying hard to find its real cause. Pre-trained word embedding boosted our accuracy for about 5% - 10% on developing set, and the training became faster and converged far more quickly. To further analyse the prediction ability of our two classification, we trained our two classifer separately by 20,000 steps, and calculated a sampled loss function according to 100 samples every 100 steps. The result is given in figure 4. We found that the bilinear classifier converges very slowly, while the dense classifier, if used separately, has a converging tendency even in 20,000 timesteps. This result corresponds with our observation that when used together, the weights assigned to these two classifiers always converge to $[0, 1]$, where little importance is given to the bilinear classifier, which is counter-intuitive.

5 Conclusions and Future Work

Our model is a machine comprehension model based on textual entailment logics, and on the basis of previous works we made several renovations to embody common sense knowledge representation. We finally reached accuracy for about 63% on test dataset, however due to time limit, we have never tried any fine-tuning techniques. Observing this model we are able to say that it is useful to have common sense knowledge data integrated to machine comprehension problems, though a proper knowledge representation should be worked out. We are currently switching to other kinds of common sense knowledge representations, and trying to devise new answer selection logics. From the competition result it is very clear that there's still much space for our accuracy improvements.

References

KM ARIVUCHELVAN and K LAKAHMI. 2017. Reading comprehension system–a review. *Indian J. Sci. Res*, 14(1):83–90.

Steven Bird and Edward Loper. 2002. Nltk: The natural language toolkit. *CoRR*, cs.CL/0205028.

Kyunghyun Cho, Bart Van Merriënboer, Caglar Gulcehre, Dzmitry Bahdanau, Fethi Bougares, Holger Schwenk, and Yoshua Bengio. 2014. Learning phrase representations using rnn encoder-decoder for statistical machine translation. *arXiv preprint arXiv:1406.1078*.

Sepp Hochreiter and Jrgen Schmidhuber. 1997. Long short-term memory. 9:1735–80.

Zachary C Lipton, John Berkowitz, and Charles Elkan. 2015. A critical review of recurrent neural networks for sequence learning. *arXiv preprint arXiv:1506.00019*.

Hugo Liu and Push Singh. 2004. Conceptneta practical commonsense reasoning tool-kit. *BT technology journal*, 22(4):211–226.

John Willard Milnor and Dale Husemoller. 1973. *Symmetric bilinear forms*, volume 60. Springer.

Nasrin Mostafazadeh, Nathanael Chambers, Xiaodong He, Devi Parikh, Dhruv Batra, Lucy Vanderwende, Pushmeet Kohli, and James Allen. 2016. A corpus and evaluation framework for deeper understanding of commonsense stories. *arXiv preprint arXiv:1604.01696*.

Simon Ostermann, Michael Roth, Ashutosh Modi, Stefan Thater, and Manfred Pinkal. 2018. Semeval2018 task 11: Machine comprehension using commonsense knowledge. In *Proceedings of International Workshop on Semantic Evaluation(SemEval2018)*.

Jeffrey Pennington, Richard Socher, and Christopher D. Manning. 2014. Glove: Global vectors for word representation. In *Empirical Methods in Natural Language Processing (EMNLP)*, pages 1532–1543.

Pranav Rajpurkar, Jian Zhang, Konstantin Lopyrev, and Percy Liang. 2016. Squad: 100,000+ questions for machine comprehension of text. *arXiv preprint arXiv:1606.05250*.

Matthew Richardson, Christopher JC Burges, and Erin Renshaw. 2013. Mctest: A challenge dataset for the open-domain machine comprehension of text. In *Proceedings of the 2013 Conference on Empirical Methods in Natural Language Processing*, pages 193–203.

Tim Rocktäschel, Edward Grefenstette, Karl Moritz Hermann, Tomáš Kočiskỳ, and Phil Blunsom. 2015. Reasoning about entailment with neural attention. *arXiv preprint arXiv:1509.06664*.

David E Rumelhart, Geoffrey E Hinton, and Ronald J Williams. 1986. Learning representations by back-propagating errors. *nature*, 323(6088):533.

Push Singh, Thomas Lin, Erik T Mueller, Grace Lim, Travell Perkins, and Wan Li Zhu. 2002. Open mind common sense: Knowledge acquisition from the general public. In *OTM Confederated International Conferences" On the Move to Meaningful Internet Systems"*, pages 1223–1237. Springer.

YNU-HPCC at SemEval-2018 Task 11: Using an Attention-based CNN-LSTM for Machine Comprehension Using Commonsense Knowledge

Hang Yuan, Jin Wang and **Xuejie Zhang**
School of Information Science and Engineering
Yunnan University
Kunming, P.R. China
Contact:xjzhang@ynu.edu.cn

Abstract

This shared task is a typical question answering (QA) task. Specially, this task must give the answer to the question based on the text provided. The essence of the problem is actually reading comprehension. For each question, there are two candidate answers, and only one of them is correct. Existing method for this task is to use convolutional neural network (CNN) and recurrent neural network (RNN) or their improved models, such as long short-term memory (LSTM). In this paper, an attention-based CNN-LSTM model is proposed for this task. By adding an attention mechanism and combining the two models, the experimental results have been significantly improved. The accuracy of our final submission is 0.7143.

1 Introduction

Question answering has long been an important research topic in the field of natural language processing. Prior to this, there have been many similar tasks, and many scholars have made very significant contributions to the research in this field. Such as the Allen AI Science Challenge on the Kaggle (Schoenick et al., 2016) and the IJCNLP-2017 shared task 5: Multi-choice Question Answering in Exams (Yuan et al., 2017).

Machine comprehension using commonsense knowledge is required to answer multiple-choice questions based on narrative texts about daily activities of human beings. The answer to many questions does not appear directly in the text, but requires simple reasoning to achieve. In terms of the nature of the problem, this task can be considered as a binary classification. That is, for each question, the candidate answers are divided into two categories: the correct answers and the wrong answers.

In recent years, many achievements have been made in machine comprehension-based question answering. Among the existing methods, the main differences are in the data processing and the application of the model. A dataset for multi-choice question answering was released by Richardson et al. (2013). Clark (2015) described how to obtain more information from the background knowledge base by introducing the use of background knowledge to build the best scene. A large cloze-style dataset using CNN and Daily Mail news articles was created by Hermann et al. (2015). Unlike previous datasets, Rajpurkar et al. (2016) released a machine comprehension-based dataset (SQuAD dataset). It contains over 1M text-question-answer triples crawled from 536 Wikipedia articles, and the questions and answers are structured primarily through crowdsourcing. It also requires people to submit up to five article-based questions and provide the correct answer that has appeared in the original text. For the open-domain QA dataset, it is even more challenging to get answers because it requires simple word matching and some simple reasoning. In SearchQA (Dunn et al., 2017), the question-answer pairs are crawled from the Jeopardy archives and are augmented with text snippets retrieved from Google search. Kundu and Ng (2018) proposed an end-to-end, problem-based, multi-factor attention network that addresses the task of answering document-based questions. This model can collect scattered evidence from multiple sentences for the generation of answers.

In this paper, we mainly propose to use an attention-based CNN-LSTM model for this task. The word-embedding model we choose is Word2Vec. Then, the word vectors are fed into the convolutional neural network (CNN) layer. After that, the results of the CNN layer are fed into the long short-term memory (LSTM) layer. Finally, an attention mechanism is added into the neu-

Proceedings of the 12th International Workshop on Semantic Evaluation (SemEval-2018), pages 1058–1062
New Orleans, Louisiana, June 5–6, 2018. ©2018 Association for Computational Linguistics

ral networks, and the prediction results are output via the softmax activation. All the data is processed into (text-question-answer) form. For each candidate answer, the system will give a correct probability (probability of a correct answer) and a wrong probability (probability of a wrong answer), and the sum of these probabilities is 1. The answer with the larger correct probability of those two candidate answers will be selected by the system as the correct answer. Furthermore, in order to exclude the experimental error caused by chance, nine such models are assembled together for training. The answers are obtained by hard voting. At the same time, we also selected a number of other models (such as the Bi-LSTM, the attention-based Bi-LSTM and the attention-based LSTM) for comparative experiments. The experimental results show that attention-based CNN-LSTM can achieve better results when using Word2Vec as the word embedding technique.

The rest of our paper is structured as follows. Section 2 introduces the CNN, LSTM and attention-based CNN-LSTM. Experiments and evaluation will be described in Section 3. The conclusions are drawn in Section 4.

2 Model

For this task, we select 10 models for comparison. Among these models, the attention-based CNN-LSTM models can get the best results. This model combines the CNN with the LSTM and incorporates the attention mechanism. The most important elements of this model are the CNN, the LSTM and the attention mechanism.

The CNN has been proven to be very effective for local feature extraction. Since the operation of the CNN layer will lose the long-distance dependency, a LSTM layer is added to handle the sequential information of the input vectors. The attention mechanism is a good solution to the information vanish problem in long sequence input situations. When dealing with machine comprehension problems, their combined use is more effective than their use individually.

2.1 Convolutional Neural Network

The convolutional neural network was originally used to process image data. In recent years, the application of the convolution neural network has gradually infiltrated into many fields, such as speech recognition and natural language process-

ing. The convolutional neural network consists of three parts. The first part is the input layer. The second part consists of a combination of n convolution layers and a pooling layer. The third part consists of a fully connected multi-layer perceptron classifier. The difference between the convolutional neural networks and ordinary neural networks is that the convolutional neural networks consist of a feature extractor made up of the convolutional layers and the sub-sampling layers. In the convolutional layers, one neuron is connected to only a few adjacent neurons.

In our experiment, the convolution layer was mainly used to extract features. The convolution matrix has m columns, and m is the maximum length of the sentence. The convolution matrix has n rows, and n refers to the number of sentences. The direct benefit of sharing weights (convolution kernels) is to reduce the number of connections between layers of the network while reducing the risk of overfitting.

2.2 Long Short-Term Memory

Traditional recursive neural networks are ineffective when dealing with very long sentences. The LSTM model is developed to solve the gradient vanishing or exploding problems in the RNN. Currently, the LSTM is mainly used in natural language processing such as speech recognition and machine translation. Compared with the traditional RNN, a LSTM unit is added to the traditional model for judging the usefulness of information. Each unit mainly contains three gates (the forget gate, the input gate, and the output gate) and a memory cell. The system will judge the usefulness of the information after the input information is fed into an LSTM. Only the information that matches the rules of the algorithm will be saved, and the other information will be discarded by the forget gate.

In our experiment, the LSTM layer is designed to ensure that important information in the front part of a long sequence can also have an impact on the processing of the latter part of the long sequence.

2.3 Attention-based CNN-LSTM

Both the CNN and LSTM models have their own advantages and disadvantages. The former performs well in local feature extraction, but easily loses the long-distance dependency of words. The latter can only solve the problem of information

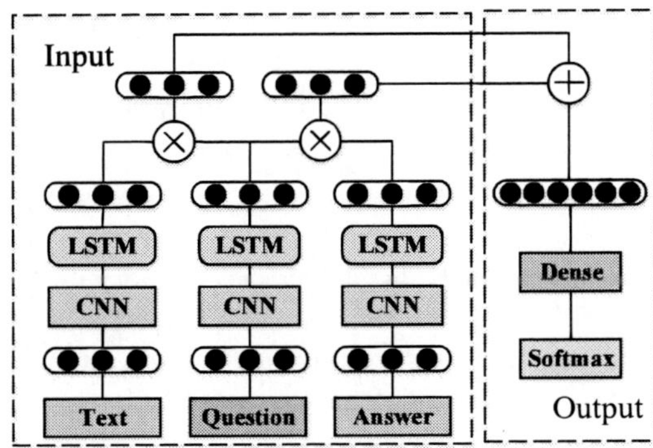

Figure 1: Architecture of a AT-CNN-LSTM.

Word2Vec	Acc
CNN	0.638
LSTM	0.651
BiLSTM	0.654
AT-BiLSTM	0.669
CNN-LSTM	0.687
AT-CNN-LSTM	0.699
AT-CNN-LSTM Ensemble	0.714
GloVe	Acc
CNN	0.629
LSTM	0.642
BiLSTM	0.649
AT-BiLSTM	0.658
CNN-LSTM	0.666
AT-CNN-LSTM	0.678
AT-CNN-LSTM Ensemble	0.692

Table 1: Comparative experiment results

vanish in long sequence input situations to a certain extent. Therefore, we combined the two models with additional attention mechanisms to form an attention-based CNN-LSTM model for this task, as shown in Fig 1.

In this model, all the texts, questions, and answers will be converted into word vectors through the word-embedding layer. These word vectors will be first fed into the CNN layer, and then the output feature vectors will be fed into the LSTM layer. Subsequently, the word vectors are expressed as hidden vectors. Next, the attention mechanism assigns a weight to each hidden vector. The attention mechanism produces an attention weight vector and a weighted hidden representation. The attention weight vector is mainly obtained by calculating the similarity. The main operation here is dot. An attention weight vector is generated by computing the question vector matrix and answer vector matrix. Another attention weight vector is generated by computing the question vector matrix and text vector matrix. Next, two attention weight vectors are connected via contact method. Then the attention weight vector is fed into the softmax layer.

The attention mechanism allows the model to retain some important hidden information when the sentences are quite long. In our task, the text, questions and answers are relatively long sentences. The use of a standard CNN or LSTM will result in the loss of hidden information. To address this possible problem, the attention-based CNN-LSTM model is used to design the machine comprehension system.

3 Experiments and Evaluation

3.1 Experiments

Data Pre-processing. The dataset provided by the organizer mainly include three parts: texts, questions, and answers. In the data pre-processing phase, texts and questions-answers pairs are divided into two separate files. The content of each piece of text data mainly includes the text id and the text content. Each question-answer pair data mainly includes the text id, the question id, and the question-answer pair content. In the final experiment, we added validation data to the training set to expand the training data. We also tried sorting the training data randomly to expand the data set, but the result was not satisfactory. All input data is converted into word vectors through the word-embedding layer, and the word-embedding model is Word2Vec. Here, all the punctuation is ignored, and all non-English characters are treated as unknown words. In the word vectors, unknown word vectors are randomly generated from a uniform distribution U(-0.25, 0.25).

Two different methods of word-embedding are used in this experiment: Word2Vec and GloVe (Pennington et al., 2014). They are used to initialize the weights of the embedding layer in building 300-dimension word vectors for all the texts and question-answer pairs. Word2Vec achieved better performance than GloVe in every model we used. Through the list of unknown words, we know that the use of Word2Vec results in fewer unknown words than GloVe.

Implementation Details. All the code involved in this experiment was written in Python 3.5.2. Keras 2.0.4 is used as the framework for the program. The backend used in this experiment is Ten-

Parameters	Optimal
Filter size	250
Kernel size	3
Dropout rate	0.3
Epoch	10
Batch size	64
Word embedding dim	300
Accuracy	0.7143

Table 2: Optimal parameters

sorFlow 1.1.0. We use the attention-based CNN-LSTM to obtain the results for the test dataset.

The first model we use is a standard CNN model. As shown in Table 1, it can achieve an accuracy of 0.638 and 0.629 when respectively using Word2Vec and GloVe as the word-embedding layer. Due to the impact of jagged sentences, the poor result obtained by the CNN model is predictable. After that, a standard LSTM model is used to complete this task. It can achieve an accuracy of 0.651 and 0.642 when respectively using Word2Vec and GloVe as the word-embedding layer. However, the results obtained by the LSTM model have been somewhat improved over the CNN model. Next, we also apply the BiLSTM model and the best result is 0.654, but there are still many points that can be improved. Combining the two models effectively seems to be the perfect choice. In this way, we achieve an accuracy of 0.687. Finally, after adding the attention mechanism, the result is raised to 0.699. Under the same experimental conditions, the attention-based CNN-LSTM model obtained a better result than other models we used in most cases (Wang et al., 2016). To exclude the experimental error caused by chance, nine such models are assembled together for training. The final accuracy can be raised to 0.714. Table 1 presents the results of a comparative experiment for all models we used.

The choice of model parameters has a significant effect on the final accuracy. The main parameters of this model are the word-embedding dimension, the batch size, the epoch, the filter size, the kernel size, the dropout and so on. To get the optimal parameters, the Sklearn grid search function (Liu et al., 2015) is used to determine the best combination of the parameters. Table 2 lists the parameters of the model when the best result is obtained.

3.2 Evaluation

Evaluation Metrics. For this experiment, it measures how well a system is capable of correctly answering questions that may involve commonsense knowledge. This problem is a typical binary classification problem. Therefore, the system is evaluated by calculating the accuracy.

Results. According to the final results provided by the organizers, a total of 199 teams enrolled in the competition. Only 24 teams eventually submitted their results. Our team ranked 13th overall among all teams. As shown in Table 1, the attention-based CNN-LSTM model can achieve the highest accuracy when using Word2Vec as the word-embedding layer. This model combines the advantages of the CNN model, the LSTM model and the attention mechanism. Furthermore, the use of Word2Vec for word-embedding is better than the GloVe word-embedding. The main difference between the two embeddings is in the training sets. The training sets of Word2Vec are practically from the news, while the training sets of GloVe are from Twitter. Therefore, the Word2Vec data source is better suited to this task.

4 Conclusion

This paper mainly focuses on our attention-based CNN-LSTM system for the task of machine comprehension using commonsense knowledge. It gives a brief introduction of the model and gives a detailed description for the experimental process and results. Compared with the attention-based LSTM model, the attention-based CNN-LSTM is better at feature extraction. The experimental results also show that the use of multiple models for ensemble training can also, to some extent, avoid the accidental results and improve the accuracy of the experiment. In the future, we will focus on methods combination and models ensemble. In addition, our team will also continue to propose a new model that can improve the existing results.

Acknowledgments

This work was supported by the National Natural Science Foundation of China (NSFC) under Grants No.61702443 and No.61762091, and in part by Educational Commission of Yunnan Province of China under Grant No.2017ZZX030. The authors would like to thank the anonymous reviewers and the area chairs for their constructive comments.

References

Peter Clark. 2015. Elementary School Science and Math Tests as a Driver for AI: Take the Aristo Challenge! In *Proceedings of the Twenty Ninth AAAI Conference on Artificial Intelligence*, pages 4019–4021.

Matthew Dunn, Levent Sagun, Mike Higgins, V. Ugur Guney, Volkan Cirik, and Kyunghyun Cho. 2017. SearchQA: A New QA Dataset Augmented with Context from a Search Engine. In *arXiv:1704.05179*.

Hermann, Kocisky, Grefenstette, Espeholt, Kay, Suleyman, and Blunsom. 2015. Teaching Machines to Read and Comprehend. In *Advances in NIPS*.

Souvik Kundu and Hwee Tou Ng. 2018. A Question-Focused Multi-Factor Attention Network for Question Answering. In *arXiv:1801.08290v1*.

Pengfei Liu, Shafiq Joty, and Helen Meng. 2015. Fine-grained Opinion Mining with Recurrent Neural Networks and Word Embeddings. In *Proceedings of the 2015 Conference on Empirical Methods in Natural Language Processing (EMNLP)*, pages 1433–1443.

Jeffrey Pennington, Richard Socher, and Christopher Manning. 2014. Glove: Global Vectors for Word Representation. In *Proceedings of the 2014 Conference on Empirical Methods in Natural Language Processing (EMNLP)*, pages 1532–1543.

Pranav Rajpurkar, Jian Zhang, Konstantin Lopyrev, and Percy Liang. 2016. SQuAD: 100,000+ Questions for Machine Comprehension of Text. In *Proceedings of the 2016 Conference on Empirical Methods in Natural Language Processing (EMNLP)*, pages 2383–2392.

Matthew Richardson, Christopher, J.C. Burges, and Erin Renshaw. 2013. MCTest: A Challenge Dataset for the Opendomain Machine Comprehension of Text. In *Proceedings of the 2013 Conference on Empirical Methods on Natural Language Processing (EMNLP)*, pages 397–401.

Carissa Schoenick, Peter Clark, Oyvind Tafjord, Peter Turney, and Oren Etzioni. 2016. Moving beyond the Turing Test with the Allen AI Science Challenge. In *arXiv:1604.04315*.

Jin Wang, Liang Chih Yu, K. Robert Lai, and Xuejie Zhang. 2016. Dimensional Sentiment Analysis Using a Regional CNN-LSTM Model. In *Proceedings of the Association for Computational Linguistics(ACL)*, pages 225–230.

Hang Yuan, You Zhang, Jin Wang, and Xuejie Zhang. 2017. YNU-HPCC at IJCNLP-2017 Task 5: Multichoice Question Answering in Exams Using an Attention-based LSTM Model. In *Proceedings of IJCNLP, Shared Tasks*, pages 208–212.

Jiangnan at SemEval-2018 Task 11: Deep Neural Network with Attention Method for Machine Comprehension Task

Jiangnan Xia
Alibaba Group
Hangzhou, China
jiangnan_xjn@alibaba-inc.com

Abstract

This paper describes our submission for the International Workshop on Semantic Evaluation (SemEval-2018) shared task 11– Machine Comprehension using Commonsense Knowledge (Ostermann et al., 2018b). We use a deep neural network model to choose the correct answer from the candidate answers pair when the document and question are given. The interactions between document, question and answers are modeled by attention mechanism and a variety of manual features are used to improve model performance. We also use CoVe (McCann et al., 2017) as an external source of knowledge which is not mentioned in the document. As a result, our system achieves 80.91% accuracy on the test data, which is on the third place of the leaderboard.

1 Introduction

In recent years, machine reading comprehension (MRC) which attempts to enable machines to answer questions when given a set of documents, has attracted great attentions. Several MRC datasets have been released such as the Stanford Question Answering Dataset (SQuAD) (Rajpurkar et al., 2016) and the Microsoft MAchine Reading COmprehension Dataset (MS-MARCO) (Nguyen et al., 2016). These datasets provide large scale of manually created data, greatly inspired the research in this field. And a series of neural network model, such as BiDAF (Seo et al., 2016), R-Net (Wang et al., 2017), have achieved promising results on these evaluation tasks. However, machine reading comprehension is still a difficult task because without knowledge, machines cannot really understand the question and make a correct answer.

As an effort to discover how machine reading comprehension systems would be benefited from commonsense knowledge, (Ostermann et al., 2018b) developed the Machine Comprehension using Commonsense Knowledge task. In this task, commonsense knowledge is given as the form of script knowledge. Script knowledge is defined as the knowledge about everyday activities which is mentioned in narrative documents. For each document, a series questions are asked and each question is associated with a pair of candidate answers. Machines have to choose which is the correct answer. To let machines make correct decisions, explicit information which can be found in the document and external commonsense knowledge are both required. Table 1 shows an example of the dataset in this task.

In this paper, we make a description about our submission system for the task. The system is based on a deep neural network model. The input of the model is a $(document, question, answer)$ triple and the output is the probability that the answer is the correct one for the given document and question. We also combine the neural network model with a variety of manual features, including word exact match features and token features such as part-of-speech (POS) ,named entity recognition (NER) and term frequency (TF). These manual features are helpful in solving the problem that the correct answer can be easily found in the given document.

Furthermore, for more complicated problem that the answer is not explicitly mentioned in the document, we try to model the interactions between document, question and answer by computing the attention score of question to document and question to answer respectively, which is described in (Lee et al., 2016). These features add soft alignments between similar but non-identical words (Chen et al., 2017). We evaluate our system on the shared task and obtain 80.91% accuracy on the test set, which is on the third place of the leaderboard.

The rest of this paper is organized as follows.

Proceedings of the 12th International Workshop on Semantic Evaluation (SemEval-2018), pages 1063–1067
New Orleans, Louisiana, June 5–6, 2018. ©2018 Association for Computational Linguistics

Document:
I went into my bedroom and flipped the light switch. Oh, I see that the ceiling lamp is not turning on. It must be that the light bulb needs replacement. I go through my closet and find a new light bulb that will fit this lamp and place it in my pocket. I also get my stepladder and place it under the lamp. I make sure the light switch is in the off position. I climb up the ladder and unscrew the old light bulb. I place the old bulb in my pocket and take out the new one. I then screw in the new bulb. I climb down the stepladder and place it back into the closet. I then throw out the old bulb into the recycling bin. I go back to my bedroom and turn on the light switch. I am happy to see that there is again light in my room.
Question1: Which room did the light go out in?
0. Kitchen. (Wrong)
1. Bedroom. (Correct)
Question2: Was the light bulb still hot?
0. yes. (Wrong)
1. No. (Correct)

Table 1: An example from the machine comprehension using commonsense knowledge task (Ostermann et al., 2018b). The first line shows the document and the following lines show question and answer pair respectively. The answer of $question1$ can be easily found in the text while answering $question2$ requires external knowledge which is not mentioned in the text.

Section 2 describes the submission system. Section 3 presents and discusses the experiment results. Section 4 makes a conclusion about our work.

2   Model

In this task, a document (D), a question (Q), and a pair of answers (A_0, A_1) are given and a machine comprehension system should choose the correct answer from the answers pair. We attempt to solve this problem by leveraging a deep neural network model which can generate the probability $p_\theta(A_i|D, Q), i = 0 \, or \, 1$ that the input answer is correct for the given document and question. The system predicts the probability for each answer in (A_0, A_1) respectively and decides which is the correct answer by comparing their probability scores. We represent the set of all trainable parameters of the neural network model as θ. The model basically consists 3 parts: an encode layer, an interaction layer and a final inference layer, which is depicted in figure 1. Below we will discuss the model in more detail.

2.1   Encode layer

We first represent all tokens of document $\{d_1, ..., d_m\}$, question $\{q_1, ..., q_n\}$ and answer $\{a_1, ..., a_l\}$ as sequences of word embeddings $\{E_1^d, ..., E_m^d\}$, $\{E_1^q, ..., E_n^q\}$ and $\{E_1^a, ..., E_l^a\}$, where m, n and l are sequence lengths of document, question and answer respectively. In this task, we use the 300-dimensional 840B Glove word embeddings (Pennington et al., 2014). We then pass each sequence through a multi-layer bidirectional long short term memory network (BiLSTM) to get the word level semantic representations of each sequence:

$$\boldsymbol{h}_j^d = BiLSTM_j(\{E_i^d\}_{i=1}^m) \tag{1}$$

$$\boldsymbol{h}_j^q = BiLSTM_j(\{E_i^q\}_{i=1}^n) \tag{2}$$

$$\boldsymbol{h}_j^a = BiLSTM_j(\{E_i^a\}_{i=1}^l) \tag{3}$$

The index j represents the jth BiLSTM layer. We concat all the output units of each BiLSTM layer and get the final word level representations: h^d, h^q and h^a. The BiLSTM layers used to encode document, question and answer sequence share same parameters in order to reduce the number of trainable parameters and make the model uneasily overfitting.

2.2   Interaction layer

This layer models the interactions between document, question and answer. We first align each word representation vectors in the question sequence to document and answer by leveraging attention mechanism and get question-aware representation $\boldsymbol{Att}^d$, $\boldsymbol{Att}^a$ for document and answer respectively:

$$Att_i^d = \Sigma_j s_{i,j}^d h_j^q \tag{4}$$

$$Att_i^a = \Sigma_j s_{i,j}^a h_j^q \tag{5}$$

The attention score $s_{i,j}^d$ captures the similarity between the word representation vector $\boldsymbol{d}_i$ and $\boldsymbol{q}_j$ in document sequence and question sequence respectively. And $s_{i,j}^a$ captures the similarity between answer vector $\boldsymbol{a}_i$ and question vector $\boldsymbol{q}_j$.

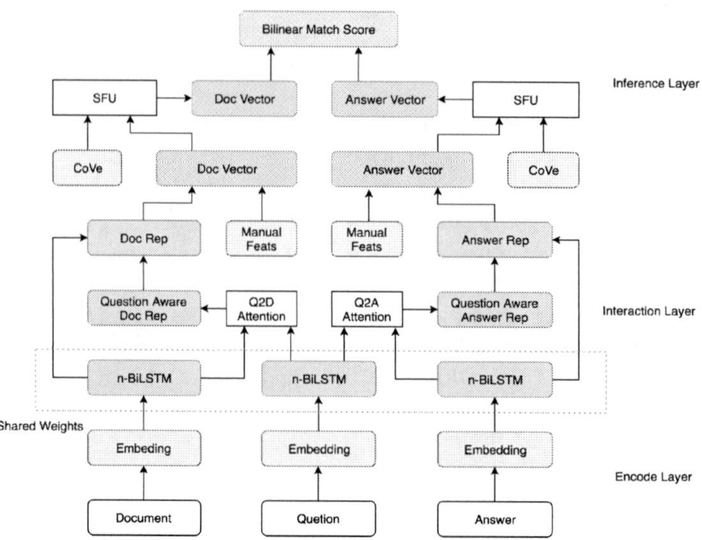

Figure 1: Neural network model architecture for the machine comprehension task

We get $s_{i,j}^d$ and $s_{i,j}^a$ by computing the dot products between the nonlinear mappings of two word representation vectors:

$$s_{i,j}^d = \frac{exp(\alpha(d_i) \cdot \alpha(q_j))}{\Sigma_{j'} exp(\alpha(d_i) \cdot \alpha(q_{j'}))} \quad (6)$$

$$s_{i,j}^a = \frac{exp(\alpha(a_i) \cdot \alpha(q_j))}{\Sigma_{j'} exp(\alpha(a_i) \cdot \alpha(q_{j'}))} \quad (7)$$

$\alpha(\cdot)$ is a single dense layer with ReLU nonlinearity. We concat Att_i^d and Att_i^a behind each h_i^d and h_i^a and get new word representation vectors $\boldsymbol{r}^d$ and $\boldsymbol{r}^a$ for document and answer.

Following (Chen et al., 2017), we combine the model with a variety of manual features, including word exact match features and token features. For exact match features, we use three binary features indicating whether a token in $\boldsymbol{d}$ and $\boldsymbol{a}$ can be exactly matched by one token in $\boldsymbol{q}$, either in its original, lowercase or lemma form. For token features, we use part-of-speech (POS), named entity recognition (NER) and term frequency (TF). For document and answer, we combine the manual features as vectors f_i^d, f_i^a and concat to r_i^d, r_i^a and get new word level representation vectors r'^d_i and r'^a_i:

$$\boldsymbol{r'^d} = \{r'^d_i\}_{i=1}^m = \{[r_i^d; f_i^d]\}_{i=1}^m \quad (8)$$

$$\boldsymbol{r'^a} = \{r'^a_i\}_{i=1}^l = \{[r_i^a; f_i^a]\}_{i=1}^l \quad (9)$$

2.3 Inference layer

In inference layer, we first convert the document and answer sequence $\boldsymbol{r'^d}$, $\boldsymbol{r'^a}$ into fixed length vectors with weighted pooling method and get sequence level representation vectors R_d and R_a:

$$R_d = \Sigma_{i=1}^m u_i^d r'^d_i \quad (10)$$

$$R_a = \Sigma_{i=1}^l u_i^a r'^a_i \quad (11)$$

$$u_i^d = \frac{exp(w^d \cdot r'^d_i)}{\Sigma_{j'=1}^m exp(w^d \cdot r'^d_{j'})} \quad (12)$$

$$u_i^a = \frac{exp(w^a \cdot r'^a_i)}{\Sigma_{j'=1}^l exp(w^a \cdot r'^a_{j'})} \quad (13)$$

The weight vector w^d and w^a are learnable parameters of the model.

As we haven't use any external source of knowledge, we attempt to use other pre-trained language model as external knowledge, in order to get more implicit information which is not mentioned in the document. Here we use CoVe (McCann et al., 2017) in document and answer sequences. The Glove embedding of each token will pass through a pre-trained BiLSTM layer. The BiLSTM layer outputs a sequence of CoVe vectors of document and answer $\boldsymbol{c}^d = \{c_i^d\}_{i=1}^m$, $\boldsymbol{c}^a = \{c_i^a\}_{i=1}^l$. We then convert the sequences into fixed length vectors C_d and C_a by using the weighted pooling method which is mentioned above.

We fuse the pooled CoVe vectors with the sequence level representation vectors with semantic fusion unit (SFU) (Hu et al., 2017) and get the final sequence level representation vectors R'_d and R'_a:

$$R'_d = SFU_d(R_d, C_d) \quad (14)$$

$$R'_a = SFU_a(R_a, C_a) \qquad (15)$$

Finally, we represent the probability that the answer is correct by computing the bilinear match score of document and answer vectors:

$$P = \sigma(R'_d W R'_a) \qquad (16)$$

W is a trainable matrix and $\sigma(\cdot)$ is the sigmoid function. In this task, we use this model to predict the probability for each answer in (A_0, A_1) and decide which is the correct one by selecting the answer with higher probability score.

3 Experiments

3.1 Datasets

The statistics of official training, development and test data are shown in Table 2.

	Training	Dev	Test
Num of examples	9,731	1,411	2,797

Table 2: Statistics of the official datasets

We remove the words occurring less than 2 times and finally get about 12000 words in the vocabulary. We keep most pre-trained word embeddings fixed during training and only fine-tune the 100 most frequent words. For manual features, we get POS and NER features by using Stanford CoreNLP[1] toolkits.

3.2 Experimental Settings

We implement our model by using PyTorch[2]. The model is trained in the given training set and we choose the model which performs best on the development set among training epochs. We train the model with mini batch size 32. We use two layers BiLSTM with 128 hidden units. A dropout rate of 0.4 is applied to word embeddings and all hidden units in BiLSTM layers. We use logistic loss as the loss function optimized by using Adamax optimizer (Kingma and Ba, 2014) with learning rate $\eta = 0.002$.

3.3 Results

The performances of our model are depicted in Table 3. The single model achieves accuracy of 85.05% on the development data and 79.03% on

[1] https://stanfordnlp.github.io/CoreNLP/
[2] http://pytorch.org/

the test data. The ensemble model which we finally submitted to the shared task achieves accuracy of 87.30% on the development data and 80.91% on the test data. From the result we can see that there is a gap between development data and test data for both single model and ensemble model. The model overfits the development data but does not perform well on the test data. Shows that the robustness of our model needs to be improved.

We conduct ablation analysis of different features used in the model on the development data. Table 4 shows the ablation analysis results from which we can see that all the features we used can contribute to model performance. Without manual features, the model accuracy is 83.70%, which is 1.3% less than the full model. and without CoVe, the accuracy drops 1.8%. The accuracy drops 6.6% when neither manual features nor CoVe are used. The results show that the model requires both explicit information which can be found in the document and external source of knowledge to make correct decisions.

Model	Acc.(Dev)	Acc.(Test)
Single Model	0.8505	0.7903
Ensemble Model	0.8730	0.8091

Table 3: Results of the single and ensemble model on development data and test data.

Features	Acc.(Dev)
Full	0.8505
w/o Manual features	0.8370
w/o CoVe	0.8320
w/o Manual features and CoVe	0.7845

Table 4: Ablation analysis of features.

4 Conclusion

In this paper, we make a description of our submitted system to the SemEval-2018 shared task 11. The system is based on a deep neural network model which will choose the correct answer from the answers pair when the document and question are given. We combine the model with a variety of manual features which are helpful in solving the problem that the correct answer can be easily found in the given document. For the problem that the answer is not explicitly mentioned in the document, we model the interactions between document, question and answers by using attention mechanism. We also attempt to use CoVe as an external source of knowledge. We conduct experiment and prove that the features we used are helpful in contributing to the model performance. Our system achieves 80.91% accuracy on the test data, which is on the third place of the leaderboard.

References

Danqi Chen, Adam Fisch, Jason Weston, and Antoine Bordes. 2017. Reading Wikipedia to answer open-domain questions. In *Association for Computational Linguistics (ACL)*.

Minghao Hu, Yuxing Peng, and Xipeng Qiu. 2017. Mnemonic reader for machine comprehension. *arXiv preprint arXiv:1705.02798*.

Diederik P Kingma and Jimmy Ba. 2014. Adam: A method for stochastic optimization. *arXiv preprint arXiv:1412.6980*.

Kenton Lee, Shimi Salant, Tom Kwiatkowski, Ankur Parikh, Dipanjan Das, and Jonathan Berant. 2016. Learning recurrent span representations for extractive question answering. *arXiv preprint arXiv:1611.01436*.

Bryan McCann, James Bradbury, Caiming Xiong, and Richard Socher. 2017. Learned in translation: Contextualized word vectors. In *Advances in Neural Information Processing Systems*, pages 6297–6308.

Tri Nguyen, Mir Rosenberg, Xia Song, Jianfeng Gao, Saurabh Tiwary, Rangan Majumder, and Li Deng. 2016. Ms marco: A human generated machine reading comprehension dataset. *arXiv preprint arXiv:1611.09268*.

Simon Ostermann, Michael Roth, Modi Ashutosh, Stefan Thater, and Manfred Pinkal. 2018b. Semeval-2018 task 11: Machine comprehension using commonsense knowledge. *In Proceedings of International Workshop on Semantic Evaluation(SemEval-2018)*.

Jeffrey Pennington, Richard Socher, and Christopher Manning. 2014. Glove: Global vectors for word representation. In *Proceedings of the 2014 conference on empirical methods in natural language processing (EMNLP)*, pages 1532–1543.

Pranav Rajpurkar, Jian Zhang, Konstantin Lopyrev, and Percy Liang. 2016. Squad: 100,000+ questions for machine comprehension of text. *arXiv preprint arXiv:1606.05250*.

Minjoon Seo, Aniruddha Kembhavi, Ali Farhadi, and Hannaneh Hajishirzi. 2016. Bidirectional attention flow for machine comprehension. *arXiv preprint arXiv:1611.01603*.

Wenhui Wang, Nan Yang, Furu Wei, Baobao Chang, and Ming Zhou. 2017. Gated self-matching networks for reading comprehension and question answering. In *Proceedings of the 55th Annual Meeting of the Association for Computational Linguistics (Volume 1: Long Papers)*, volume 1, pages 189–198.

IUCM at SemEval-2018 Task 11: Similar-Topic Texts as a Comprehension Knowledge Source

Sofia Reznikova
Innopolis University
Innopolis, Russia
s.reznikova@innopolis.ru

Leon Derczynski
IT University of Copenhagen
Denmark
leod@itu.dk

Abstract

This paper describes the IUCM entry at SemEval-2018 Task 11, on machine comprehension using commonsense knowledge. First, clustering and topic modeling are used to divide given texts into topics. Then, during the answering phase, other texts of the same topic are retrieved and used as commonsense knowledge. Finally, the answer is selected. While clustering itself shows good results, finding an answer proves to be more challenging. This paper reports the results of system evaluation and suggests potential improvements.

1 Introduction

The goal of SemEval-2018 Task 11 is to find a way to incorporate commonsense knowledge into a question-answering task (Ostermann et al., 2018b). In this case, questions are either directly or indirectly related to given English texts; some questions may be answered using the text while others require background (commonsense) knowledge. The challenge is to use this knowledge in such a way as to enhance the quality of chosen answers.

There are many approaches to question answering including using structured knowledge (Yao and Durme, 2014), knowledge databases (Yih et al., 2015), deep learning methods (Minaee and Liu, 2017) and hybrid methods (Xu et al., 2016; Das et al., 2017). The present task accepts any method or any source of background knowledge.

The training data consists of 1469 texts covering more than 100 topics. The number of questions per text varies from 1 to 14 and there are two answer options. The development data has 219 texts and the test data has 430. (Ostermann et al., 2018a)

The main idea behind the method proposed in this paper is to use the given texts as potential sources of knowledge. Texts from training and development data can be divided into topics using existing clustering algorithms (e.g. k-Means, Hierarchical, Grid-based or Density-based). The hypothesis is that texts which come from the same topic as the current question's text may contain the correct answer. A matching function with a scoring scheme is used to identify the correct combination of words for the answer.

Another potential source of knowledge is scripts (Wanzare et al., 2016) that have been used to search for an answer. The DeScript dataset includes descriptions of everyday activities such as baking, getting a haircut, going grocery shopping, and others, corresponding to topics present in the given data.

Section 2 describes the methods as well as specifics of implementation. Section 3 provide interpretation and analysis of the results. Section 4 concludes the present paper.

2 Methodology

All texts, questions and answers were tokenized, punctuation and extra symbols were removed. WordNet (Fellbaum, 1998) was used for lemmatization using its *morphy()* function. Transforming all words into their initial form resulted in an approximately 1% increase of accuracy.

The overall process of answering a question could be broadly divided into two phases: clustering texts (or searching for the most similar DeScript's topic), and finding the correct answer. The former is discussed in the following subsections, and the latter is described below.

There are minor modifications to the base *choose-answer* method across all solutions but overall the structure is as follows. First, we search for a full-length match. If one is found, then we consider it to be a correct one. If not, we remove all common words (such as articles, prepositions

Proceedings of the 12th International Workshop on Semantic Evaluation (SemEval-2018), pages 1068–1072
New Orleans, Louisiana, June 5–6, 2018. ©2018 Association for Computational Linguistics

and auxiliary verbs) from the answer, and count how many words can be found in text. Finally, we compare all answers and choose the one with the highest match count.

A modification was introduced to account for yes-no questions. If words from the question were present in the text, the "yes" answer was selected; otherwise, the "no" answer was selected. This, however, actually decreased the accuracy as it did not consider negations that occurred in the text and were tokenized separately. Therefore, the prior version of the method was used in all submissions.

The baseline solution used the method described above to find the answer in the given text only. This resulted in accuracy of around 60% for all data sets (see Section 3).

2.1 Comparison of BigARTM and KMeans

The next step was to cluster texts from training and development data into topics, in order to use them later as sources of background knowledge. BigARTM, a tool to infer topics based on additive regularization of topic models proposed in Vorontsov and Potapenko (2014), was used to model the texts as topics.

Since the language of the given texts consisted of many everyday words, it was necessary to first make sure that the data used for clustering was clear of common, uninformative words. BigARTM provides tools to make the resulting matrix of document-topic mapping sparser, however, it did not provide as good a result as simple removal of the English stopwords contained in the NLTK library (Bird and Loper, 2004).

The texts then were transformed into batches in vectorized form, the number of topics varied between 100 and 110, and the model initialized with scores for sparsity (PhiScore and ThetaScore) and perplexity. The model was then trained with 15 passes through the collection of texts (bigger numbers didn't result in better accuracy).

Topic	Probability
topic 33	0.024480
topic 90	0.021954
topic 26	0.020483
topic 37	0.017545
topic 82	0.016841

Table 1: Probability of the topic being the top choice for the text

Table 1 shows five most frequent topics and the probability of the topic being the top one for the text. Below are the top 15 tokens for three most frequent topics:

- 'pan', 'eggs', 'milk', 'heat', 'stove', 'egg', 'turn', 'make', 'pour', 'cook', 'add', 'hot', 'get', 'omelette', 'bowl'

- 'wall', 'paint', 'room', 'new', 'floor', 'look', 'decide', 'house', 'want', 'put', 'buy', 'color', 'get', 'painting', 'work'

- 'water', 'shower', 'get', 'soap', 'rinse', 'towel', 'turn', 'body', 'hot', 'take', 'bucket', 'dry', 'clean', 'start', 'warm'

Another approach to clustering was to use k-Means. First, texts were embedded in the vector space using the gensim (Řehůřek and Sojka, 2010) implementation of Doc2Vec (Le and Mikolov, 2014), and then NLTK's k-Means was applied over the result.

The Doc2Vec model was trained on the texts from all data sets and for several runs DeScript's gold standard was also added. At each step the learning rate was decreased by 0.002. Number of epochs varied from 20 to 30 and window size was also experimented with.

The top 15 tokens for three most frequent topics are as follows:

- 'wall', 'paint', 'painting', 'room', 'look', 'get', 'would', 'want', 'go', 'hang', 'decide', 'put', 'nail', 'wallpaper', 'color'

- 'bed', 'sheet', 'pillow', 'put', 'make', 'take', 'top', 'get', 'corner', 'tuck', 'fit', 'sure', 'clean', 'mattress'

- 'dish', 'put', 'dishwasher', 'dry', 'sink', 'plate', 'water', 'clean', 'rack', 'wash', 'silverware', 'one', 'start', 'top', 'take'

The top clusters for the two methods are slightly different in terms of their topics but there are obvious differences in words: k-Means clusters include more general language (e.g. verbs like 'go', 'take', 'make') and less specific language related to the topic. At the same time k-Means' distribution of classes has a larger number of texts per cluster on average. This can be seen in Figures 1 and 2. The horizontal axis is number of texts and the vertical one is the cluster ID number.

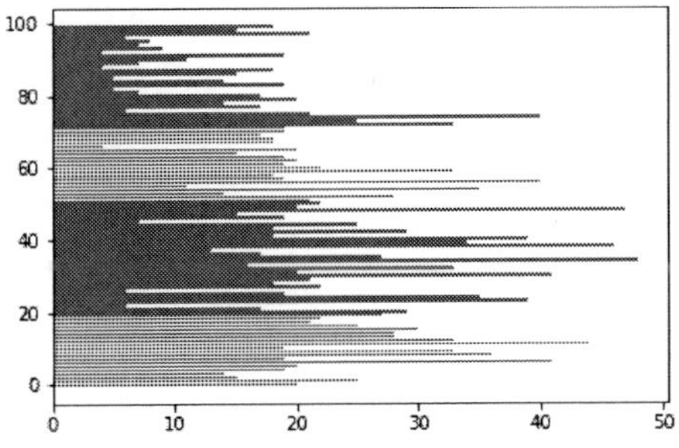

Figure 1: Distribution of texts for KMeans (*y-axis*: topic numbers, *x-axis*: number of texts belonging to the topic

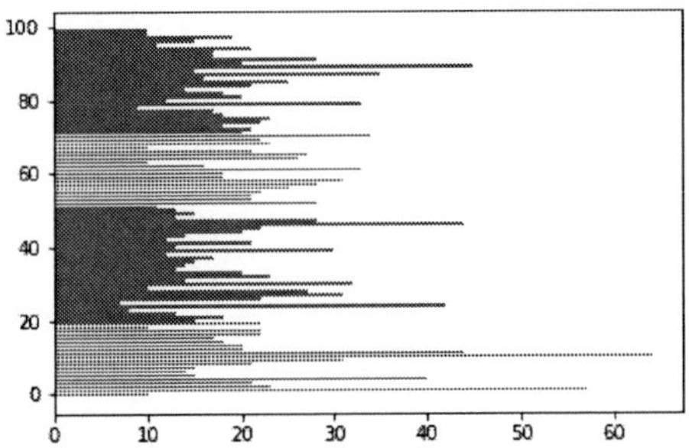

Figure 2: Distribution of texts for BigARTM (*y-axis*: topic numbers, *x-axis*: number of texts belonging to the topic

For both clustering methods, choosing the correct answer was done in two steps. The first step was the same as in the baseline, finding full answers or scoring individual words. If the answer was not found, the second step was carried out, which involved looking up other texts from the same cluster as the given text and searching for an answer in them.

2.2 Using DeScript

DeScript (Wanzare et al., 2016) sequences are divided into events which, in turn, include many different paraphrases of the same event (*check timetable, locate a train schedule, check train schedules* and other similar ones).

To simplify comparison between training data texts and DeScript sequences, all events corresponding to the same topic were combined. Then the vector for each topic was built using the 15 most frequent words from the topic as keys and

their TF-IDFs as values. The same was done for each text.

The method for choosing the answer was as described above. The difference was that instead of using texts from the same cluster as a source of commonsense knowledge, DeScript paraphrases were used. Cosine similarity between the given text and each DeScript topic was calculated based on most frequent word vectors, in order to find the most suitable events. This approach resulted in better performance than with clustering methods (Section 3).

3 Evaluation

The results for the test data are summarized in Table 2. These are the configurations that resulted in the best performance.

Model	Accuracy
Baseline	60.70
Yes/No Modification	59.52
BigARTM topics	61.38
DeScript paraphrases	61.67
Doc2Vec/KMeans	61.95

Table 2: Results

BigARTM's advantage over the baseline solution is not much, but there is an interesting trend that explains why the score is higher. Questions with no word-for-word answer in the texts were answered correctly when individual words were found within the same-topic clusters. This showed that given texts could be a useful knowledge source.

There are also cases when both answers get zero scores and in that case the first one is chosen.

Another observation is that correct answers were more often selected if they contained full sentences rather than a couple of words.

The DeScript and BigARTM methods answered 6% of questions differently. These were, for the most part, for answers that were not explicitly phrased in the text but obvious to a human (such as *evening* when the text talked about dinner, or *bedroom* when a bed was mentioned). This requires an additional logical step, so this kind of questions can be in a category of their own – neither text nor commonsense.

For k-Means the number of clusters was 100. Table 3 describes the results for Doc2Vec/k-Means method with various configurations (number of epochs, window size, whether DeScript texts were included into the training or not).

Epochs	Window	DeScript	Accuracy
20	10	No	61.70
20	12	No	61.60
20	10	Yes	61.56
30	10	No	61.74
30	12	No	61.88
30	10	Yes	61.24
30	12	Yes	61.95

Table 3: Doc2Vec/KMeans configurations and accuracy

The model with a larger window size performs better as it takes into account more words at the same time, sometimes spanning multiple sentences at once. Adding DeScript dat does not have significant impact on the results. However, as the scripts are succinct and topic-related they give a slight boost to the overall accuracy.

The k-Means-based system generally does better in questions related to timing (e.g. how much some activity takes) and in questions about text's meta-information (answers that include *author* or *narrator*). This observation could be explained by the fact that there are some activities that happen at a specific time of the day (e.g. breakfast, going out and others) and Doc2Vec could do a better embedding for numbers.

Overall, while the clustering step provided commonsense knowledge for the system and successfully mapped texts to topics, the bottleneck was the method of choosing an answer. It is based on the assumption that finding the exact answer or individual words from it leads to the correct solution. Different scoring and prioritizing methods for searching did not improve accuracy in any significant way. Therefore, a function that incorporates different approaches (e.g. comparing vector representations of questions and answers, POS-tagging for the question, deep similarity) along with simple matching might lead to better results.

4 Conclusion

This paper described the methodology behind the IUCM at SemEval-2018 Task 11 on machine comprehension using commonsense knowledge. The proposed solution is based on different techniques of unsupervised learning. The method shows above-the-baseline performance and results in clear topic division and mapping. The code for the system is available here: `https://github.com/sonyareznikova/semeval2018task11`.

References

Steven Bird and Edward Loper. 2004. NLTK: the natural language toolkit. In *Proceedings of the ACL 2004 on Interactive poster and demonstration sessions*, page 31. Association for Computational Linguistics.

Rajarshi Das, Manzil Zaheer, Siva Reddy, and Andrew McCallum. 2017. Question answering on knowledge bases and text using universal schema and memory networks. *In ACL*, arXiv:1704.08384.

Christiane Fellbaum. 1998. *WordNet: An Electronic Lexical Database*. MIT Press, Cambridge, MA.

Quoc V. Le and Tomas Mikolov. 2014. Distributed representations of sentences and documents. arXiv:1405.4053.

Shervin Minaee and Zhu Liu. 2017. *Automatic Question-Answering Using A Deep Similarity Neural Network.*, arXiv:1708.01713.

Simon Ostermann, Ashutosh Modi, Michael Roth, Stefan Thater, and Manfred Pinkal. 2018a. MCScript: A Novel Dataset for Assessing Machine Comprehension Using Script Knowledge. In *Proceedings of the 11th International Conference on Language Resources and Evaluation (LREC 2018)*, Miyazaki, Japan.

Simon Ostermann, Michael Roth, Ashutosh Modi, Stefan Thater, and Manfred Pinkal. 2018b. SemEval-2018 Task 11: Machine Comprehension using Commonsense Knowledge. In *Proceedings of International Workshop on Semantic Evaluation (SemEval-2018)*, New Orleans, LA, USA.

Radim Řehůřek and Petr Sojka. 2010. Software Framework for Topic Modelling with Large Corpora. In *Proceedings of the LREC 2010 Workshop on New Challenges for NLP Frameworks*, pages 45–50, Valletta, Malta. ELRA. `http://is.muni.cz/publication/884893/en`.

Konstantin Vorontsov and Anna Potapenko. 2014. Tutorial on probabilistic topic modeling: Additive regularization for stochastic matrix factorization. *International Conference on Analysis of Images, Social Networks and Texts*.

Lilian D. A. Wanzare, Alessandra Zarcone, Stefan Thater, and Manfred Pinkal. 2016. DeScript: A Crowdsourced Corpus for the Acquisition of High-Quality Script Knowledge.

Kun Xu, Yansong Feng, Songfang Huang, and Dongyan Zhao. 2016. Hybrid question answering over knowledge base and free text. In *COLING*.

Xuchen Yao and Benjamin Van Durme. 2014. Information extraction over structured data: Question answering with Freebase. In *ACL*.

Scott Wen-tau Yih, Ming-Wei Chang, Xiaodong He, and Jianfeng Gao. 2015. Semantic parsing via staged query graph generation: Question answering with knowledge base. ACL Association for Computational Linguistics.

ZMU at SemEval-2018 Task 11: Machine Comprehension Task using Deep Learning Models

Yongbin Li[1,2], Xiaobing Zhou[1,*]
[1]Yunnan University, Kunming, Yunnan, P.R. China
[2]Zunyi Medical University, Zunyi, Guizhou, P.R. China
* Corresponding author, zhouxb.cn@gmail.com

Abstract

Machine Comprehension of text is a typical Natural Language Processing task which remains an elusive challenge. This paper is to solve the task 11 of SemEval-2018, Machine Comprehension using Commonsense Knowledge task. We use deep learning model to solve the problem. We build distributed word embedding of text, question and answering respectively instead of manually extracting features by linguistic tools. Meanwhile, we use a series of frameworks such as CNN model, LSTM model, LSTM with attention model and biLSTM with attention model for processing word vector. Experiments demonstrate the superior performance of biLSTM with attention framework compared to other models. We also delete high frequency words and combine word vector and data augmentation methods, achieved a certain effect. The approach we proposed rank 6th in official results, with accuracy rate of 0.7437 in test dataset.

1 Introduction

Machine Comprehension of text is one of the important goals of natural language processing. The traditional approaches to machine reading and comprehension have been based on either hand engineered grammars (Riloff and Thelen, 2000), or information extraction methods of detecting predicate argument triples that can later be queried as a relational database (Poon et al., 2010). These methods show effectiveness, but they rely on feature extraction and language tools. Recently, with the advances of neural networks, there have been great interests in building neural architectures for various NLP task, including several pieces of work on machine comprehension (Hermann et al., 2015; Hill et al., 2015; Yin et al., 2016; Kadlec et al., 2016; Cui et al., 2016), which have gained significant performance in machine comprehension domain. We also adopt deep learning models to solve this task.

The goal of Machine Comprehension using Commonsense Knowledge task is to choose a correct answer in two candidates to the question based on the contents of text. This task relates to how the inclusion of commonsense knowledge in the form of script knowledge would benefit machine comprehension systems, answering the questions requires knowledge beyond the facts mentioned in the text. We do not employ extra commonsense knowledge resources in the proposed approach, we assume that word vectors have contained some commonsense knowledge information, so we only use the deep learning model to solve this problem.

In the train dataset provided by this task, there are 1432 instances, each instance contains a text and several questions, and each question is associated with a set of two answers which are short and limited to a few words. The texts used in this task cover more than 100 everyday scenarios, hence include a wide variety of human activities. Therefore, each example can be summed up as {*text, question, answer_0, answer_1, correct option*}. There are 9731, 1411, 2797 examples in train, validation, test datasets, respectively.

Being a binary classification task, we split an example into two triples, which are {*text, question, answer_0*} and {*text, question, answer_1*}, the label is true or false. In validation and test datasets, we employ the same processing mode to determine the matching degree of fit between triples, the highest will be chosen. We adopt the method of word distributed representation from (Mikolov et al., 2013) and a series of deep learning (DL) models, such as Convolutional Neural Network (CNN) from (Kim, 2014), Long Short-Term Memory (LSTM) model proposed from (Hochreiter and Schmidhuber, 1997) and improved by (Graves et al., 2013), attention mechanism from

1073

Proceedings of the 12th International Workshop on Semantic Evaluation (SemEval-2018), pages 1073–1077
New Orleans, Louisiana, June 5–6, 2018. ©2018 Association for Computational Linguistics

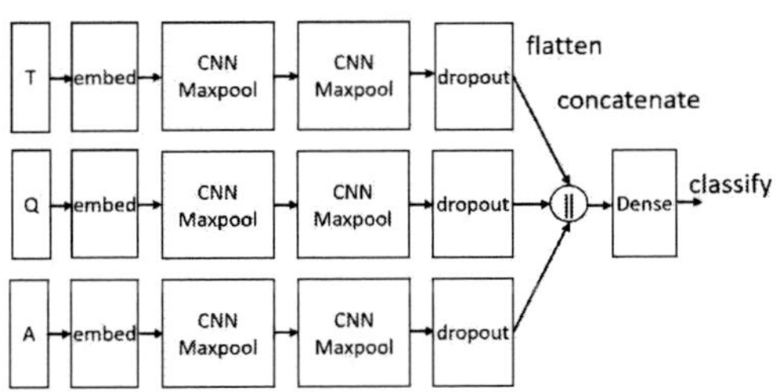

Figure 1: The architecture of CNN framework, T for text, Q for question, A for answer.

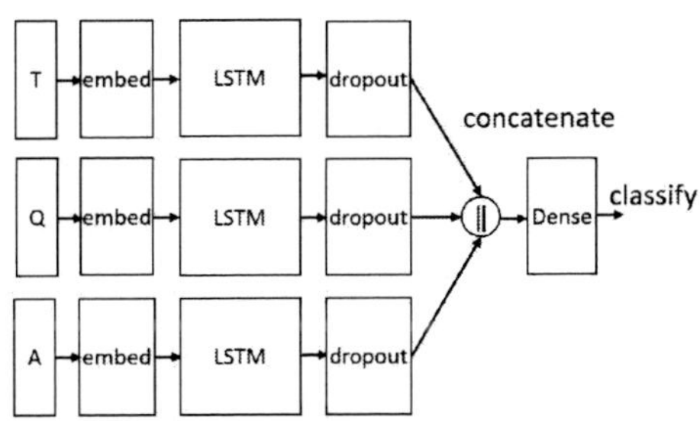

Figure 2: The architecture of LSTM framework.

(Graves and Schmidhuber, 2005). The four main frameworks we applied are as follows:

- CNN framework

- LSTM framework

- LSTM with attention framework

- biLSTM with attention framework

Above the framework, a joint feature vector is constructed, which is used to classify (Tan et al., 2015). In order to increase the accuracy of the model, we also delete high frequency word and combine word vector and data augmentation methods, thus achieve a better effect. Experiments demonstrate the superior performance of biLSTM with attention framework compared to other models, and data preprocessing is also important to improve the model accuracy.

2 Model description

In this section, we describe the four main proposed deep learning frameworks, which are shown in figures 1 to 4. The main idea of these systems is the same: learn a distributed vector representation of given text, question and answer candidates, then use a dense layer which processes the joint feature to measure the matching degree.

2.1 CNN framework

The first framework is based on CNN model. Step one is to obtain word embedding from pre-trained word distributed representation models. In preliminary experiment, there are two distributed representation models used. One is the pre-trained word2vec model which is trained by 100 billion words of Google News and has a dimensionality of 300, the other is pre-trained Glove model which is trained by Wikipedia data and has a dimensionality of 300 too. The two models are all initialized from an unsupervised neural language model. The word embedding provides the distributed representation for each token in sequence.

Text, question and answer will be transformed to a word vector matrix and be entered into CNN layer respectively. In order to get more comprehensive representation of semantic features, we adopt double layer CNN model. The numbers of filters are 64 and 32, respectively, and the filter size is set as 3. After each CNN layer, we resort to a MaxPooling layer of size 2.

Above the CNN layer, the output of text, question and answer is merged to one and performs flatten operations, through a dense layer, the final output is passed through a two-dimensional softmax layer.

2.2 LSTM framework

Its the same way of producing word vector representation in embedding layer. Because LSTM model can process variable length sequence, masking method is introduced. The main principle of masking is to skip time steps which tokens are equal to zero, thus ignoring the meaningless padding in the text.

Above the embedding layer, we introduce the LSTM layer with a unit number of 64. LSTM is a special type of RNN that has three gates (input i, forget f and output o), and a cell memory vector C, and can learn to rely on long-distance history and the immediate previous hidden vector. Its a remarkable variations of RNN to alleviate the gradient vanish problem. Through the LSTM layer, text, question and answer will be transformed to a vector respectively.

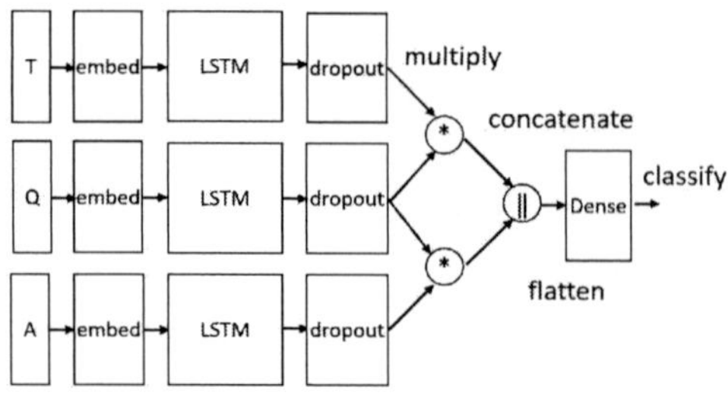

Figure 3: The architecture of LSTM with attention framework.

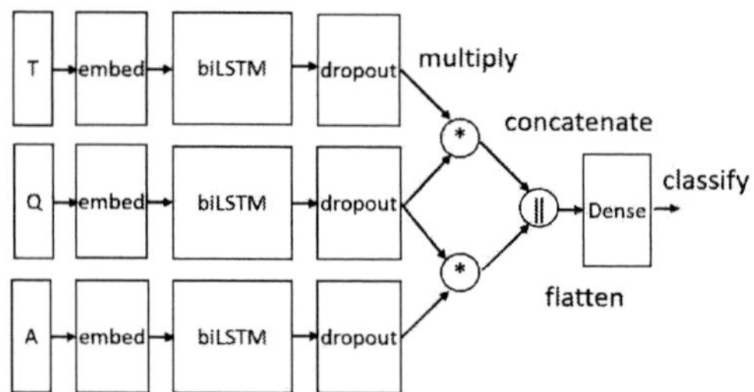

Figure 4: The architecture of biLSTM with attention framework.

2.3 LSTM with attention framework

Like the LSTM framework, the masking method is used in the embedding layer. Text, question and answer are respectively processed through the embedded layer and the LSTM layer, generating three sequences of LSTM output vectors. Unlike the LSTM framework, here returns full output sequences, instead of the final output of model.

Now, we investigate a state-of-the-art attention model for the question vector generated by text, and the answer vector generated by question, instead of generating representation respectively. If the input sentence is long, semantics are expressed by an intermediate semantic vector, and the information of the word itself has disappeared, which results in the loss of a great deal of detail information. An attention mechanism is used to alleviate the weakness by dynamically aligning the more informative parts. Specifically, attention model gives more weights on certain words, just like tf-idf for each word, while the weight is calculated by another vector. Therefore, the formula of the attention matrix f of text and question vectors is as follows:

$$f(m_t, m_q) = m_t{}^T m_q \qquad (1)$$

where m_t and m_q correspond to text and question vectors produced by previous LSTM layers, respectively. The attention matrix of answer and question is constructed in the same way.

2.4 biLSTM with attention framework

The framework is similar to the above, just changing the LSTM model into a biLSTM model. Single direction LSTMs suffer a weakness of not utilizing the contextual information from the future tokens. biLSTM utilizes both the previous and future context by processing the sequence on two directions, and generates two independent sequences of LSTM output vectors.

3 Data Preprocessing

In order to improve the accuracy of the model, we have tried a series of data preprocessing methods, such as deleting high frequency words, combining word vectors and data augmentation methods, which achieve a certain effect.

3.1 Deleting high frequency words

In a large corpus, many common words appear, such as "the", "a" and so on. Although these words have higher word frequency, few useful information can be provided. We try to delete stopwords through the NLTK tools, but the effect was not ideal. So we calculate the word frequency statistics on the words in all dataset, and delete the top 20 words in frequency, that is, the most frequently occurring 20 words. We also tried other numbers in preliminary experiment, but 20 worked best.

3.2 Combining word vectors

Pre-trained word2vec model is trained by Google News, Glove model is trained by Wikipedia data. The effect of the former is slightly better. In order to obtain more comprehensive semantic features, we try to combine two vectors of each token, so that the word vector of each token is transformed into 600 dimensions, which is better than using only one word vector model.

3.3 Data augmentation

Our idea is inspired by data augmentation in the image domain, where one can increase the amount of train data by the geometric transformation of the image. In order to enrich the train dataset of

	Framework	val	test
1	CNN	71.32	70.13
2	CNN(data augmentation)	72.86	70.65
3	LSTM	72.10	69.57
4	LSTM(data augmentation)	72.57	70.36
5	LSTM with attention	73.11	69.97
6	LSTM with attention(data augmentation)	73.99	70.15
7	biLSTM with attention	75.90	71.11
8	biLSTM with attention(data augmentation)	76.61	72.47
9	biLSTM with attention(data augmentation and combine word vector)	77.75	74.37

Table 1: Results of four main framework

images, extract image features better and generalize models (prevent models from over fitting), data augmentation is done on images data. We know that in text understanding, we can still read articles even if we disorder the order of the words. In this task, we've implemented the data augmentation by randomly disordering the word order in the sentence. The preliminary implementation proves that this method is effective.

4 Experimental setup

Our approach in this task use the accuracy on validation dataset to locate the best parameters. The final rate of accuracy is expressed in the correct proportion chosen in test dataset. **All the model parameters were adjusted by preliminary experiment, at the same time, the results are taken three times, and the average value is taken**.

In the experiment, we use the loss function of categorical cross entropy and the optimizer of adaptive moment estimation. The length of text, question and answer tokens sequence all take the maximum length, if the length is not enough, then zero is added. To prevent over fitting, we employ dropout layers which the parameter is 0.3.

For comparison, we report the performance and analysis of four framework in Table 1, which summarizes the results of our system for this task. All the experiments have deleted the high frequency words. The word embedding we employed is word2vec in Rows (1) to (8). Because in preliminary experiment, the accuracy of model using word2vec is generally better than Glove.

In Row (1) to (2), we list the results on validation dataset and test dataset respectively of CNN framework which employ filter size of 3, and filter number of 64. The difference is that Row (2) model uses the data augmentation. Row (3) to

(4) correspond to LSTM framework which uses 64 as output dimensionality parameter of LSTM unit. The framework results in similar result with the CNN framework. In Row (5) to (6), we can observe that the framework for using the attention mechanism has been significantly improved in the accuracy rate. In Row (7) to (8), the improvement from biLSTM with attention compared to LSTM with attention is remarkable, increase more than 2%, illustrating that Bi-directional LSTM can achieve more comprehensive features than unidirectional LSTM. Row (9) is the approach proposed in this paper, which combines word2vec vector and Glove vector of each tokens. The model gets a significantly result, achieving a precision of 77.75% in validation dataset and 74.37% in test dataset. Compared to single word2vec, the improvement on the test set is more significant.

5 Conclusion

In this paper, we solve the Machine Comprehension Task by employing four main frameworks and a series of Data Preprocessing methods. Although the commonsense knowledge library is not used, the results are acceptable. The experiment results demonstrate the effectiveness of the biLSTM with attention framework in dealing with this task, the Bi-directional LSTM model is more advanced than the unidirectional LSTM model, and attention mechanism allows a model to focus on the aspects of a text that it will help answering a question. For a deep learning model, the Data Preprocessing is more critical, data augmentation and combining word vectors are beneficial to improve the model ability in some task backgrounds.

Acknowledgments

This work was supported by the Natural Science Foundations of China No.61463050, No.617-02443, No.61762091, the NSF of Yunnan Province No. 2015FB113, the Project of Innovative Research Team of Yunnan Province.

References

Yiming Cui, Ting Liu, Zhipeng Chen, Shijin Wang, and Guoping Hu. 2016. Consensus attention-based neural networks for chinese reading comprehension. *arXiv preprint arXiv:1607.02250.*

Alex Graves, Abdel-rahman Mohamed, and Geoffrey Hinton. 2013. Speech recognition with deep recurrent neural networks. In *Acoustics, speech and signal processing (icassp), 2013 IEEE international conference on*, pages 6645–6649. IEEE.

Alex Graves and Jürgen Schmidhuber. 2005. Framewise phoneme classification with bidirectional lstm networks. In *Neural Networks, 2005. IJCNN'05. Proceedings. 2005 IEEE International Joint Conference on*, volume 4, pages 2047–2052. IEEE.

Karl Moritz Hermann, Tomas Kocisky, Edward Grefenstette, Lasse Espeholt, Will Kay, Mustafa Suleyman, and Phil Blunsom. 2015. Teaching machines to read and comprehend. In *Advances in Neural Information Processing Systems*, pages 1693–1701.

Felix Hill, Antoine Bordes, Sumit Chopra, and Jason Weston. 2015. The goldilocks principle: Reading children's books with explicit memory representations. *arXiv preprint arXiv:1511.02301.*

Sepp Hochreiter and Jürgen Schmidhuber. 1997. Long short-term memory. *Neural computation*, 9(8):1735–1780.

Rudolf Kadlec, Martin Schmid, Ondrej Bajgar, and Jan Kleindienst. 2016. Text understanding with the attention sum reader network. *arXiv preprint arXiv:1603.01547.*

Yoon Kim. 2014. Convolutional neural networks for sentence classification. *arXiv preprint arXiv:1408.5882.*

Tomas Mikolov, Ilya Sutskever, Kai Chen, Greg S Corrado, and Jeff Dean. 2013. Distributed representations of words and phrases and their compositionality. In *Advances in neural information processing systems*, pages 3111–3119.

Hoifung Poon, Janara Christensen, Pedro Domingos, Oren Etzioni, Raphael Hoffmann, Chloe Kiddon, Thomas Lin, Xiao Ling, Alan Ritter, Stefan Schoenmackers, et al. 2010. Machine reading at the university of washington. In *Proceedings of the NAACL HLT 2010 First International Workshop on Formalisms and Methodology for Learning by Reading*, pages 87–95. Association for Computational Linguistics.

Ellen Riloff and Michael Thelen. 2000. A rule-based question answering system for reading comprehension tests. In *Proceedings of the 2000 ANLP/NAACL Workshop on Reading comprehension tests as evaluation for computer-based language understanding sytems-Volume 6*, pages 13–19. Association for Computational Linguistics.

Ming Tan, Cicero dos Santos, Bing Xiang, and Bowen Zhou. 2015. Lstm-based deep learning models for non-factoid answer selection. *arXiv preprint arXiv:1511.04108.*

Wenpeng Yin, Sebastian Ebert, and Hinrich Schütze. 2016. Attention-based convolutional neural network for machine comprehension. *arXiv preprint arXiv:1602.04341.*

MITRE at SemEval-2018 Task 11: Commonsense Reasoning without Commonsense Knowledge

Elizabeth M. Merkhofer, John Henderson, David Bloom,
Laura Strickhart and **Guido Zarrella**
The MITRE Corporation
202 Burlington Road
Bedford, MA 01730-1420, USA
{emerkhofer, jhndrsn, dtbloom, lstrickhart, jzarrella}@mitre.org

Abstract

This paper describes MITRE's participation in
SemEval-2018 Task 11: Machine Comprehension using Commonsense Knowledge. The
techniques explored range from simple bag-of-ngrams classifiers to neural architectures
with varied attention and alignment mechanisms. Logistic regression ties the systems together into an ensemble submitted for evaluation. The resulting system answers reading
comprehension questions with 82.27% accuracy.

1 Introduction

Reading comprehension tasks measure the ability
to answer questions that require inference from a
free text story. This SemEval task, like many standardized tests (e.g., the SAT), provides multiple-choice answers. Reading comprehension may rely
on information explicitly contained in the text,
such as which actors are present, as well as elements of world knowledge, like understanding
common scripts.

Early attempts at statistical reading comprehension include fill-in-the-blank questions and combine rich question categorization, information retrieval techniques, and entity recognition with
type-specific, hand-crafted tactics (Hirschman
et al., 1999; Anand et al., 2000).

More recent neural work uses continuous, distributed semantic space rather than n-gram overlap
to find answers similar to the story. Trischler et al.
(2016) compute a version of word overlap by finding cosine similarity of word representations between sections. Yin et al. (2016) restate the question and answer and incorporate a question-type
classifier.

In this effort we explored neural distributed representations and lexicon-based machine learning
approaches, especially attention and word overlap.

2 Task, Data and Evaluation

Machine Comprehension using Commonsense
Knowledge was a shared task organized within
SemEval-2018 (Ostermann et al., 2018b).

The task organizers released a dataset of 1,689
stories and 10,872 questions (up to 14 questions
per story), split into training and development sets.
The stories were first-person, English language
narratives written by Mechanical Turk workers in
response to prompts asking them to describe a scenario, like going on a date. Stories were up to 860
words long, with 90% under 273 words and a median length of 183 words. Questions are up to 22
words long, with a median length of seven. Each
question has two possible answers. Answers vary
in length from a single word, including *yes* or *no*,
to 30 words, with a median length of three. Many
questions are repeated between multiple stories. A
sample story and questions are shown in Figure 1.
Dataset construction is detailed in Ostermann et al.
(2018a). The evaluation metric for the task is simple accuracy: the portion of correct answers.

Question types Table 1 quantifies the question
types in the development set. We created this taxonomy to better understand the dataset. It also allowed us to direct our development toward model
weaknesses.

**Common Sense Knowledge and Inference
Types** Reading comprehension relies on inference. We explored an inference taxonomy outlined in Chikalanga (1992) to better characterize
the types of questions and answers involved in this
shared task. For a subset of the training dataset,
we manually classified whether questions required
a reader to make lexical, propositional, or pragmatic inferences about the story. We found that
many questions could be answered with more than
one type of inference and some questions required
multiple inferences. We considered which infer-

Proceedings of the 12th International Workshop on Semantic Evaluation (SemEval-2018), pages 1078–1082
New Orleans, Louisiana, June 5–6, 2018. ©2018 Association for Computational Linguistics

I went to the airport to go see my friend in North Carolina. So I drove up and had to go to the gate to go park. I paid my money to go park and went to park. From there I walked up into the airport to figure out where I need to check in. After much confusion, I found the place to check in and walked up. I gave them my boarding pass and they took my bags. From there they weighed them to make sure that they were not over the weight limit for carry on items. After that I went to security. I arrived super early so that I would have plenty of time in the line. I got in line for security and just waited. After getting to the front of the line, I took off my shoes and belt and put those on an x-ray scanner and got scanned myself. I put them back on and went to my flight.

Did they check in any baggage?
✓ yes
X no
Where were they flying to?
✓ North Carolina
X South Carolina
Why did they arrive to the airport early?
X They were not early, they were late.
✓ To have enough time to wait in line
Why do they have to check in?
✓ To board their flight
X They had to check in because they were going overseas.

Figure 1: Sample story with questions.

%	description
22.8	yes/no questions – One answer began with the string *yes* and the other answer began with the string *no*
9.4	yes/no only questions – answers were entirely the word *yes* or *no*
13.0	*who* questions
12.8	*what* questions
8.9	*where* questions
5.4	*when* questions
17.6	*how* questions
12.1	*why* questions
0.4	*which* questions
23.7	all correct answer words are in the story
30.7	none of the correct answer words are in the story
13.7	all incorrect answer words are in the story
37.6	none of the incorrect answer words are in the story
15.6	none of the correct or incorrect answer words are in the story

Table 1: Question types in the development set.

ences could require knowledge and data sources external to the story, like temporal-spatial relationships or physical properties such as temperature. Our analysis determined that this was unnecessary for task completion.

3 System Overview

We created an ensemble of three systems, each of which independently predicted the correct answer. Two of the systems use a neural attention architecture, and the third is a logistic regression.

3.1 Neural Attention

A recurrent neural system uses attention to create a representation for each answer that considers the question and story. Our ensemble includes two versions of this model with word embeddings trained on different corpora.

The words of each section (story, question, and answer) are embedded using a frozen projection layer, a fully-connected layer, and a recurrent layer. Another Long Short-Term Memory (LSTM) layer operates over the words in each story sentence to represent the story as a sequence of sentence embeddings. Each embedded answer sequence attends the words of the question using a parameterized attention mechanism (described below). This output attends the story sentences using a similar attention mechanism, and an LSTM reduces the sequence. A fully-connected layer produces a prediction for each answer output, and a softmax converts these to probabilities over the two answers. All hidden layers are of size 128, 50% dropout follows on the embedding and RNN layers, and the adam optimizer is used for training.

Components of this neural system include: pretrained distributed word representations, word overlap/hard attention features, and an attention mechanism.

For one model, **NN-T**, we used `word2vec` (Mikolov et al., 2013) to learn distributed representations of words from the text of English tweets collected from 2011 to 2016. We applied `word2phrase` twice to identify phrases of up to four words, and trained a skip-gram model of size 256, using a context window of 10 words and 15 negative samples per example. Twitter embeddings were chosen because at least some of the corpus matches the informal, first-person register of the task dataset. Our other set of word vectors, used in **NN-GN**, was released by Google alongside the tool and is made up of 300-vectors trained on a billion words of Google News (GoogleCode, 2013 (accessed March 3, 2018). For both vector sets, we used only the 100,000 most frequent vocabulary items, since the shared data vocabulary was quite limited.

Word-overlap features were concatenated to the pretrained word embeddings. These consist of four channels that compare the present section (question or answer) with the story and question. The first two channels are binary overlap: whether

	$\sigma\|w\|$	w	description
1	1.99	1.2814	$\|S \cap A\|$
2	1.18	-0.5591	answer length (words)
3	0.49	0.0394	answer length (chars)
4	0.15	-0.1728	$\|Q \cap A\|$
5	0.11	-0.0005	story length (chars)
6	0.09	0.0026	story length (words)
7	0.04	0.0041	question length (chars)
8	0.03	-0.0219	$\|S \cap Q\|$
9	0.02	0.0114	question length (words)

Table 2: Length and count features in the logistic regression model, ranked by influence ($\sigma\|w\|$).

the word in this position appears in the compared section. The cosine similarity channels contain the similarity of the present word with the closest word in the other section, computed using the same set of pretrained word vectors used by the neural model.

Our model adapts the attention mechanism described in Vaswani et al. (2017). The scaled dot product attention mechanism takes a memory and a query representation, e.g., the embedded words of the question and answer, respectively. Linear transformations are used to create a key and value from the former, and a query from the latter. Compatibility is computed as the scaled dot product of the key and query. This determines the weights over each timestep in the value, for each timestep of the query. Our model did not improve using parallel multi-head memory mechanisms nor by including fully-connected layers on top of them.

3.2 Logistic Regression

A logistic regression (LR) system was developed as a baseline against which the neural approach would be compared. This system was competitive enough to be included in the final ensemble.

The vocabulary of the LR system was limited to the training set. The Porter stemmer (Porter, 1980) was used to strip the non-information bearing suffixes from all of the words. Standard stopword lists removed words like *yes* and *no* that were important to the questions and answers, so the stopword list was reduced to just {*a,an,the*}. Various lengths were included as features. Taking S, Q, and A as the sets of words in the story, question, and answer respectively, the following three counts were added to the feature set: $\|S \cap A\|$, $\|Q \cap A\|$ and $\|S \cap Q\|$. Table 2 shows the full list of length and word count features.

The rest of the features were lexicalized patterns. Table 3 shows examples. Features include

	$\sigma\|w\|$	w	story	question	answer
1	0.61	1.85			ye
2	0.50	-1.89	it		it
3	0.45	-2.22	they		they
4	0.35	1.00			they
5	0.34	-1.64	wa		wa
6	0.33	-1.42	in		in
7	0.28	-2.25	at		at
8	0.27	-1.97			friend
9	0.26	1.98			narrat
10	0.24	-1.66	for		for
11	0.22	-1.60	of		of
12	0.22	2.03	friend		friend
13	0.21	-1.39	on		on
14	0.20	-1.90	with		with
15	0.20	0.82		did	no
16	0.19	-0.57			no
17	0.19	-1.78	were		were
18	0.19	-1.88	them		them
19	0.18	1.84			author
20	0.17	1.86		who	author
21	0.16	-1.75	one		one
22	0.16	-1.85	had		had
23	0.15	-1.09			hour
24	0.14	-1.82			neighbor
25	0.14	1.12		who	narrat
26	0.13	2.10		long	not
27	0.13	-1.73	out		out
28	0.13	1.20			home
29	0.13	1.50		mani	one
30	0.13	-1.22	minut		minut
31	0.13	-1.49	after		after
32	0.13	0.57		did	it
33	0.12	1.80	morn		morn
34	0.12	1.76		who	they
35	0.12	0.74		they	their
36	0.12	2.00			speaker

Table 3: Stemmed word factors in the logistic regression model ranked by influence ($\sigma\|w\|$).

the set of words in the answer (A), the words common to the story and the answer ($S \cap A$) and the Cartesian product of the question and answer ($Q \times A$).

A bias term was added and `Liblinear` (Fan et al., 2008) was used to compute the model. L2 regularization was used to encourage generalization. The best value for the regularization parameter was the default, 1. The target variable for the LR model to predict was the distinction between a correct answer and an incorrect answer. At decode time, the answer with the higher probability of being correct was chosen. This simple logistic regression model performed surprisingly well, less than 1% off from our best neural model.

Tables 2 and 3 show each feature's influence on fitting the training set. The rank ordering is standard deviation times the magnitude of the feature weight, $\sigma\|w\|$. This figure of merit balances features with high weights that were rare and features with low weights that were common.

3.3 Ensemble

An L2-regularized logistic regression weights the predictions of the above systems. MITRE's official submission is an ensemble of the subsystems' binary class predictions. We submitted this system because it is simpler than an ensemble of continuous predictions and found it had the same accuracy on the development data, though more than 50 test set predictions were different.

4 Additional Experiments

We applied several approaches to the problem that did not generalize as well to the development data and were not included in the final ensemble.

Baselines We trained two baseline classifiers with incomplete information to gauge the difficulty of the task and to measure the relative importance of the story, question, and answers separately. Each baseline was a recurrent neural network with a layer of pretrained word embeddings and a stack of two 128-dimensional GRU layers. The *QA-only* baseline received as input only a concatenation of a question and its candidate answers, separated by special tokens. The *A-only* baseline received only a concatenation of the two candidate answers. *A-only* scored at 71.9% accuracy on the dev set, while *QA-only* was slightly higher at 73.2% accuracy. Other attempts to augment these models with attention over a lengthy story sequence frequently failed to eclipse the *QA-only* baseline, leading us to investigate hierarchical attention models and explicit overlap features.

Negative sampling We explored negative sampling to augment the training data, to improve our models' ability to exclude wrong answers. We selected the 10 nearest neighbors for each question and supplemented the original positive and negative answer with the other questions' answers. These were deduplicated after minimal preprocessing (normalizing case and punctuation), increasing the number of answers per question to between four and 20. Our nearest neighbors calculation is based on the average of word vectors for the in-vocabulary words in the questions.

Negative sampling did not improve accuracy. We tested conditions where 1) the original negative answer was sampled with equal probability or 2) always kept, and considered different values of N, where N is the total number of answers the model considered. We found no accuracy gain from using negative sampling beyond normal variance when the original negative was always included. When N was small, not necessarily in-

Component	Factored		Ablated	
	dev	test	dev	test
NN-T	81.93	80.23	81.72	79.76
NN-GN	81.01	80.12	83.06	79.51
LR	81.36	79.66	81.64	79.87
All In			**85.12**	**82.27**

Table 4: Factored and ablated system components evaluated on our dev set and the official test set.

cluding the original negative seems to hurt accuracy, suggesting that the randomly drawn negatives were not as plausible as the original negatives. For larger values of N, both conditions hurt performance.

We experimented with condition 1 and the LR model. The best value of N was 5 for this model, but accuracy was still below the model trained with the original dataset.

5 Experiment Details

The systems included in our model were trained only on the data released for this task, aside from word vector pretraining. The dev set was used to select hyperparameters for individual components and final ensemble.

6 Results

The columns of Table 4 show the accuracy of each system in isolation on the dev and test data ("Factored") and the performance of the ensemble when the individual system was removed ("Ablated"). The final line shows the overall accuracy of the submission.

7 Conclusion

An ensemble of models was used to answer multiple-choice reading comprehension questions about informal, first person narratives. The resulting official system ranked second in the shared task. Our system relies heavily on lexical and overlap features, without an explicit reasoning component or external sources of world knowledge. Word embeddings trained on larger corpora contribute a semantic space that supports some inference beyond simple word overlap.

Acknowledgments

Approved for Public Release; Distribution Unlimited. Case Number 18-1298.

References

Pranav Anand, Eric Breck, Brianne Brown, Marc Light, Gideon Mann, Ellen Riloff, Mats Rooth, and Michael Thelen. 2000. Fun with reading comprehension. In *Final report, Reading Comprehension group, Johns Hopkins Center for Language and Speech Processing Summer Workshop*.

Israel Chikalanga. 1992. A suggested taxonomy of inferences for the reading teacher. *Reading in a Foreign Language*.

Rong-En Fan, Kai-Wei Chang, Cho-Jui Hsieh, Xiang-Rui Wang, and Chih-Jen Lin. 2008. LIBLINEAR: A library for large linear classification. *Journal of Machine Learning Research*, 9:1871–1874.

GoogleCode. 2013 (accessed March 3, 2018). Word2vec. https://code.google.com/archive/p/word2vec/.

Lynette Hirschman, Marc Light, Eric Breck, and John D. Burger. 1999. Deep read: a reading comprehension system. In *Proceedings of the 37th Annual Meeting of the Association for Computational Linguistics on Computational Linguistics*, ACL '99, pages 325–332, Stroudsburg, PA, USA. Association for Computational Linguistics.

Tomas Mikolov, Ilya Sutskever, Kai Chen, Greg S Corrado, and Jeff Dean. 2013. Distributed representations of words and phrases and their compositionality. In *Advances in Neural Information Processing Systems*.

Simon Ostermann, Ashutosh Modi, Michael Roth, Stefan Thater, and Manfred Pinkal. 2018a. MCScript: A Novel Dataset for Assessing Machine Comprehension Using Script Knowledge. In *Proceedings of the 11th International Conference on Language Resources and Evaluation (LREC 2018)*, Miyazaki, Japan.

Simon Ostermann, Michael Roth, Ashutosh Modi, Stefan Thater, and Manfred Pinkal. 2018b. SemEval-2018 Task 11: Machine Comprehension using Commonsense Knowledge. In *Proceedings of International Workshop on Semantic Evaluation (SemEval-2018)*, New Orleans, LA, USA.

Martin F Porter. 1980. An algorithm for suffix stripping. *Program*, 14(3):130–137.

Adam Trischler, Zheng Ye, Xingdi Yuan, Jing He, Phillip Bachman, and Kaheer Suleman. 2016. A parallel-hierarchical model for machine comprehension on sparse data. *arXiv preprint arXiv:1603.08884*.

Ashish Vaswani, Noam Shazeer, Niki Parmar, Jakob Uszkoreit, Llion Jones, Aidan N Gomez, Łukasz Kaiser, and Illia Polosukhin. 2017. Attention is all you need. In *Advances in Neural Information Processing Systems*, pages 6000–6010.

Wenpeng Yin, Sebastian Ebert, and Hinrich Schütze. 2016. Attention-based convolutional neural network for machine comprehension. *arXiv preprint arXiv:1602.04341*.

SNU_IDS at SemEval-2018 Task 12: Sentence Encoder with Contextualized Vectors for Argument Reasoning Comprehension

Taeuk Kim, Jihun Choi and **Sang-goo Lee**
Department of Computer Science and Engineering,
Seoul National University, Seoul, Korea
{taeuk, jhchoi, sglee}@europa.snu.ac.kr

Abstract

We present a novel neural architecture for the Argument Reasoning Comprehension task of SemEval 2018. It is a simple neural network consisting of three parts, collectively judging whether the logic built on a set of given sentences (a claim, reason, and warrant) is plausible or not. The model utilizes contextualized word vectors pre-trained on large machine translation (MT) datasets as a form of transfer learning, which can help to mitigate the lack of training data. Quantitative analysis shows that simply leveraging LSTMs trained on MT datasets outperforms several baselines and non-transferred models, achieving accuracies of about 70% on the development set and about 60% on the test set.

1 Introduction

The Argument Reasoning Comprehension Task (Habernal et al., 2018) is a newly released task that tackles the core of reasoning in natural language argumentation, highlighting the importance of implicit warrants.

Even though the task could be regarded as simple binary classification, it is quite challenging in several perspectives. First, the task requires human-level reasoning to judge whether a claim supported by a reason and a warrant is logically correct. Second, common knowledge, which is not present in the input sentences themselves, is often required to solve the problem. Third, even though each instance of the data is helpful, the number of training data is relatively small to train prevailing complex neural models such as convolutional neural networks (Kim, 2014; Kalchbrenner et al., 2014) and recurrent neural networks (Hochreiter and Schmidhuber, 1997; Chung et al., 2014) with (or without) attention mechanisms (Liu et al., 2016; Lin et al., 2017).

In this paper, we propose a new architecture named **SECOVARC**[1] (Sentence Encoder with COnextualized Vectors for Argument Reasoning Comprehension) to deal with the complicated task. The main idea behind our model is that *transfer learning* can be a remedy to resolve the difficulties we face. With experimental results and analysis, we show that the simple neural model enhanced by transferred knowledge can be competitive, compared to complex models trained on the given data only.

2 Related Work

2.1 Argument Reasoning Comprehension

The argument reasoning comprehension task is a new dataset whose goal is to choose the correct implicit reasoning from two warrants, given a natural language argument with a reason and a claim. It consists of about 2K crowdsourced instances, each of which has a title and a short description of the debate from which the claim, reason, and two candidates arose. For more details, refer to Habernal et al. (2018).

2.2 Transfer Learning in NLP

Transfer learning is a classic technique in machine learning, which seeks to transfer beneficial knowledge from external resources to target models. It is well-known to be effective especially when one suffers from the lack of training data.

An important example showing the successfulness of transfer learning in natural language processing (NLP) is pre-trained word representations such as Word2Vec (Mikolov et al., 2013) and GloVe (Pennington et al., 2014), on which most of the modern models for NLP have been built.

---

[1] The implementation of our model is available at https://github.com/galsang/SemEval2018-task12

Proceedings of the 12th International Workshop on Semantic Evaluation (SemEval-2018), pages 1083–1088
New Orleans, Louisiana, June 5–6, 2018. ©2018 Association for Computational Linguistics

Furthermore, there are some recent works (Collobert et al., 2011; Mou et al., 2016; Min et al., 2017) that concentrate on pre-training more sophisticated neural modules over word embeddings, proving that transfer learning can be a key to boost the performance of NLP systems.

2.3 Unsupervised Sentence Representation

Following the success of unsupervised word representations, there arises another line of research to facilitate transfer learning in sentence-level. The idea is that a generic sentence encoder, which is pre-trained in an unsupervised way, can generate sentence representations suitable for downstream tasks.

For instance, Kiros et al. (2015) propose an approach called Skip-Thoughts vectors that abstracts the skip-gram of Word2Vec (Mikolov et al., 2013) to the sentence-level. Moreover, many other unsupervised methods (Le and Mikolov, 2014; Dai and Le, 2015; Hill et al., 2016; Gan et al., 2017; Chen, 2017) are also introduced as a way of building sentence representations.

2.4 Supervised Sentence Representation

Despite several attempts at learning sentence representations in an unsupervised manner, there has been no consensus established thus far, on which is the best method and can be adopted as a standard.

Meanwhile, sentence encoders trained on labeled datasets are proposed as an alternative, showing that they outperform the previous models even with the limited number of data. Conneau et al. (2017) suggest a method named InferSent, which uses a simple bidirectional LSTM (Long Short Term Memory, Hochreiter and Schmidhuber (1997)) with max-pooling trained on the Stanford Natural Language Inference (SNLI, Bowman et al. (2015)). And McCann et al. (2017) propose CoVe and demonstrate that the encoder part of the trained sequence-to-sequence (Sutskever et al., 2014) model for machine translation can be reused as a generic sentence encoder.

In the paper, we focus on supervised pre-training with external data as an instantiation of transfer learning.

3 Model

In this section, We describe SECOVARC (Figure 1) which takes a set of 3 sentences, i.e. a claim, reason, and warrant, as input and outputs a score between 0 and 1, indicating *how reasonable the claim is when it is based on the reason and the warrant*.

3.1 Model Design

Before jumping into the details, we explain about our motivation upon which the decisions on model design were made.

First, we let the model accept only one warrant instead of two candidates. This decision comes from the intuition that it may learn how to reason better when it *judges* whether the logic constructed on a set of a claim, reason, and warrant is plausible, instead of just *choosing* the more probable one between the two candidates.

Second, as mentioned earlier, one of the main concerns behind the model design is the lack of training data. To alleviate this problem, we decide to utilize transfer learning while maintaining the model as simple as possible (e.g. without introducing complex architectures such as attention mechanism).

3.2 Model Specification

In this part, we describe the details of the proposed model, which is composed of three layers.

3.2.1 Encoding Layer

The encoding layer is the first part of our model, which is in charge of encoding three input sentences to corresponding sentence representations. In detail, it accepts the sequence of n words $(w_1, w_2, \ldots, w_n)$ in a sentence at a time and outputs a fixed-length sentence representation $\mathbf{s}$. Note that the same generic encoder is used to encode each input sentence.

Formally, each one-hot encoded word $w_i \in \mathbb{R}^V$ of the input sentence is converted into the corresponding word vector $\mathbf{x}_i \in \mathbb{R}^{d_w}$ by a word embedding matrix $\mathbf{E} \in \mathbb{R}^{d_w \times V}$. Then, a sequence of the word vectors $\mathbf{x} = [\mathbf{x}_1, \mathbf{x}_2, \ldots, \mathbf{x}_n]$ is combined into $\mathbf{s} \in \mathbb{R}^{d_s}$ by an encoder. While a wide range of selection for the encoder is possible, in our case we utilize CoVe[2] (McCann et al., 2017) (with pooling operation), which is a two-layered Bi-LSTM pre-trained on large MT datasets, to obtain meaningful and contextualized sentence representations that would not be achieved if we train the encoder from scratch.

---

[2]Available at https://github.com/salesforce/cove

As a result, each representation for the claim ($\mathbf{s}_c$), reason ($\mathbf{s}_r$), and warrant ($\mathbf{s}_w$) is derived from $\mathbf{x}_c, \mathbf{x}_r$ and $\mathbf{x}_w$ as follows.

$$\mathbf{s}_c = \text{Pooling}(\text{CoVe}(\mathbf{x}_c))$$
$$\mathbf{s}_r = \text{Pooling}(\text{CoVe}(\mathbf{x}_r))$$
$$\mathbf{s}_w = \text{Pooling}(\text{CoVe}(\mathbf{x}_w))$$

From various options for the pooling operation, we use max-pooling, which selects the maximum value over each dimension of the output, and last-pooling that just selects the last state of the output. We call the CoVe encoder with max-pooling as SECOVARC-max and the encoder with last-pooling as SECOVARC-last.

3.2.2 Localization Layer

Although all of the input sentences (i.e. the claim, reason, and warrant) are encoded by the universal encoder, there is a need to make a difference among them so that each of the sentence representations keeps its own role. For this reason, the localization layer is introduced to project (or 'localize') each $\mathbf{s}$ onto its own semantic space.

We implement this layer simply in the form of three separate fully-connected layers, pursuing the intuition that our model should be simple. Therefore, a set of the sentence representations $\{\mathbf{s}_c, \mathbf{s}_r, \mathbf{s}_w\}$ is converted into $\{\mathbf{v}_c, \mathbf{v}_r, \mathbf{v}_w\} \in \mathbb{R}^{d_f}$ as follows.

$$\mathbf{v}_c = \tanh(\mathbf{W}_c\mathbf{s}_c + \mathbf{b}_c)$$
$$\mathbf{v}_r = \tanh(\mathbf{W}_r\mathbf{s}_r + \mathbf{b}_r)$$
$$\mathbf{v}_w = \tanh(\mathbf{W}_w\mathbf{s}_w + \mathbf{b}_w)$$

3.2.3 Output Layer

The output layer collects all features extracted from the previous layer and computes a final score between 0 and 1. To help the model make correct decisions, we introduce heuristic methods such as $|\mathbf{v}_w - \mathbf{v}_r - \mathbf{v}_c|$ and $\mathbf{v}_w \odot \mathbf{v}_r \odot \mathbf{v}_c$[3], inspired from the work of Mou et al. (2015) for the SNLI task.

In the end, a final feature $\mathbf{v}_f$ for computing a score $y \in \mathbb{R}\ (0 \leq y \leq 1)$ becomes a concatenation of the five vectors,

$$\mathbf{v}_f = \begin{bmatrix} \mathbf{v}_c \\ \mathbf{v}_r \\ \mathbf{v}_w \\ |\mathbf{v}_w - \mathbf{v}_r - \mathbf{v}_c| \\ \mathbf{v}_w \odot \mathbf{v}_r \odot \mathbf{v}_c \end{bmatrix}$$

---

[3] $\odot$: element-wise multiplication

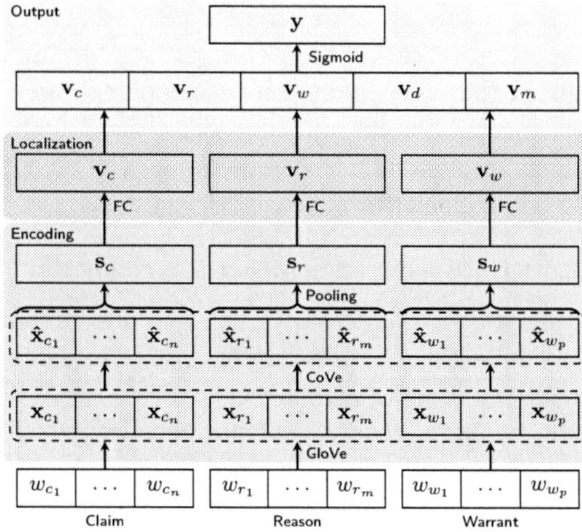

Figure 1: The architecture of SECOVARC. Dotted boxes represent the elements computed by parameter-shared modules (GloVe and CoVe) for all inputs. Note that $\mathbf{v}_d : |\mathbf{v}_w - \mathbf{v}_c - \mathbf{v}_r|$ and $\mathbf{v}_m : \mathbf{v}_w \odot \mathbf{v}_c \odot \mathbf{v}_r$. FC means a fully connected layer.

where $\mathbf{v}_f \in \mathbb{R}^{5d_f}$. Then, logistic regression (for simplicity) is performed on $\mathbf{v}_f$ to compute the final score.

$$y = \sigma(\mathbf{W}_f\mathbf{v}_f + \mathbf{b}_f)$$

During training, the score can be directly utilized to optimize the model. At test time, on the other hand, we derive y_1 and y_2 from the trained model with the input sentences such that

$$y_1 = \text{SECOVARC}(\mathbf{c}, \mathbf{r}, \mathbf{w}_1)$$
$$y_2 = \text{SECOVARC}(\mathbf{c}, \mathbf{r}, \mathbf{w}_2)$$

where $\mathbf{c}, \mathbf{r}, \mathbf{w}_1$ and $\mathbf{w}_2$ is the claim, the reason, the first warrant, and the second warrant respectively. Then, we select the warrant whose score is greater than that of the other as a final decision.

4 Experiment and Discussion

4.1 Data Manipulation

As our model requires only one warrant at a time, data preprocessing is inevitable before training. We manipulate the original data so that the correct warrant has a score of 1 and the opposite warrant has 0. Note that this pre-processing procedure has a side effect of doubling the original training data.

4.2 Training Details

The dimension of a word vector (d_e) is fixed to 300. And hyper-parameters for other vectors are

Approach	Dev	($\pm$)	Test	($\pm$)
Human average	-	-	.798	.162
Human w/ training in reasoning	-	-	.909	.114
Random baseline	.473	.039	.491	.031
Language model	.617	-	.500	-
Attention	.488	.006	.513	.012
Attention w/ context	.502	.031	.512	.014
Intra-warrant attention	.638	.024	.556	.016
Intra-warrant attent. w/ context	.637	.040	.560	.055
SECOVARC (official record)	.731	-	.565	-
SECOVARC-last (w/o heuristics)	.701	.011	.559	.019
SECOVARC-last (w/ heuristics)	**.706**	.014	.554	.015
SECOVARC-max (w/o heuristics)	.680	.007	.591	.016
SECOVARC-max (w/ heuristics)	.684	.008	**.592**	.016

Table 1: Comparison of baselines and variants of our model on the development set and the test set.

set to $d_s = 600, d_f = 300$. We use 840B GloVe to initialize a word embedding matrix. Other model weights are randomly sampled from uniform distribution(-0.005, 0.005), except for the CoVe encoder, and biases are initialized with 0.

Our model is trained using Adam (Kingma and Ba, 2014) optimizer with a learning rate 0.001 and a batch size 64. The maximum number of training epoch is limited to 10 and we choose the best model based on development accuracy. All parameters in the model, including the word vectors, are fine-tuned during training.

For regularization, L2-norm of the parameters is added to the Cross Entropy objective with the weight of 1e-5, and Dropout (Srivastava et al., 2014) technique is also applied with $p = 0.1$.

4.3 Experimental Results

Table 1 shows the accuracies of variants of our model and baselines (Habernal et al., 2018) on the development set and the test set. Due to the instability of results caused by random initialization, we report the mean and standard deviation of 20 experimental runs (with the same hyperparameters) for each model.

The reported results show that SECOVARC-last (w/ heuristics) outperforms all the baselines on the development set, with a mean accuracy of 70.6%. However, it is SECOVARC-max (w/ heuristics) that performs best on the test set, with a mean accuracy of 59.2%. We submitted an instance obtained from SECOVARC-last (w/ heuristics) and achieved the official result of 56.5% on the leaderboard. Table 1 also demonstrates that our model benefits from the heuristics applied in the output

Approach	Dev	($\pm$)	Test	($\pm$)
BoW	.677	.006	.502	.014
Bi-LSTM-last	.678	.010	.554	.024
Bi-LSTM-max	.670	.011	.543	.027
SECOVARC-last	**.706**	.014	.554	.015
SECOVARC-max	.684	.008	**.592**	.016

Table 2: Experiment on the possibility of transfer learning in case of the argument reasoning comprehension task. Note that the heuristic methods are employed for all models.

layer, except for the test accuracy of SECOVARC-last.

4.3.1 Does transfer learning really work?

Even with the promising outcome presented by SECOVARC, an issue remains regarding how to show the effectiveness of transfer learning for the task. For this objective, we conduct additional experiments with three baselines called BoW, Bi-LSTM-last, and Bi-LSTM-max. Bi-LSTM-last and Bi-LSTM-max have the same architecture with SECOVARC, but the Bi-LSTMs in the encoding layer are randomly initialized rather than pre-trained. BoW is different from our proposed model in that it leverages the average of word vectors as a sentence representation instead of using CoVe with pooling.

Table 2 reports the comparison of the baselines and the variants of our model. The results show that our model consistently outperforms the baselines which are trained from scratch. Moreover, the smaller deviations of SECOVARCs demonstrate that transfer learning can lead to more stable and successful training of models.

5 Conclusion

In this paper, we present a novel neural architecture called SECOVARC, that utilizes a two-layered Bi-LSTM trained first on a large amount of machine translation data. And we demonstrate that the neural model for the argument reasoning comprehension task can benefit from transfer learning when it is properly designed.

As a future work, there is a way to apply contemporary works for generic sentence encoders such as Subramanian et al. (2018) and Peters et al. (2018) instead of CoVe. On the other hand, we can consider expanding the data itself directly with sophisticated rules or heuristics.

Acknowledgments

This work was supported by the National Research Foundation of Korea (NRF) grant funded by the Korea government (MSIT) (NRF-2016M3C4A7952587).

References

Samuel R Bowman, Gabor Angeli, Christopher Potts, and Christopher D Manning. 2015. A large annotated corpus for learning natural language inference. *arXiv preprint arXiv:1508.05326*.

Minmin Chen. 2017. Efficient vector representation for documents through corruption. *arXiv preprint arXiv:1707.02377*.

Junyoung Chung, Caglar Gulcehre, KyungHyun Cho, and Yoshua Bengio. 2014. Empirical evaluation of gated recurrent neural networks on sequence modeling. *arXiv preprint arXiv:1412.3555*.

Ronan Collobert, Jason Weston, Léon Bottou, Michael Karlen, Koray Kavukcuoglu, and Pavel Kuksa. 2011. Natural language processing (almost) from scratch. *Journal of Machine Learning Research*, 12(Aug):2493–2537.

Alexis Conneau, Douwe Kiela, Holger Schwenk, Loic Barrault, and Antoine Bordes. 2017. Supervised learning of universal sentence representations from natural language inference data. *arXiv preprint arXiv:1705.02364*.

Andrew M Dai and Quoc V Le. 2015. Semi-supervised sequence learning. In *Advances in Neural Information Processing Systems*, pages 3079–3087.

Zhe Gan, Yunchen Pu, Ricardo Henao, Chunyuan Li, Xiaodong He, and Lawrence Carin. 2017. Learning generic sentence representations using convolutional neural networks. In *Proceedings of the 2017 Conference on Empirical Methods in Natural Language Processing*, pages 2380–2390.

Ivan Habernal, Henning Wachsmuth, Iryna Gurevych, and Benno Stein. 2018. The argument reasoning comprehension task: Identification and reconstruction of implicit warrants. In *Proceedings of the 2018 Conference of the North American Chapter of the Association for Computational Linguistics: Human Language Technologies*, page (to appear), New Orleans, LA, USA. Association for Computational Linguistics.

Felix Hill, Kyunghyun Cho, and Anna Korhonen. 2016. Learning distributed representations of sentences from unlabelled data. *arXiv preprint arXiv:1602.03483*.

Sepp Hochreiter and Jürgen Schmidhuber. 1997. Long short-term memory. *Neural computation*, 9(8):1735–1780.

Nal Kalchbrenner, Edward Grefenstette, and Phil Blunsom. 2014. A convolutional neural network for modelling sentences. *arXiv preprint arXiv:1404.2188*.

Yoon Kim. 2014. Convolutional neural networks for sentence classification. *arXiv preprint arXiv:1408.5882*.

Diederik P Kingma and Jimmy Ba. 2014. Adam: A method for stochastic optimization. *arXiv preprint arXiv:1412.6980*.

Ryan Kiros, Yukun Zhu, Ruslan R Salakhutdinov, Richard Zemel, Raquel Urtasun, Antonio Torralba, and Sanja Fidler. 2015. Skip-thought vectors. In *Advances in neural information processing systems*, pages 3294–3302.

Quoc Le and Tomas Mikolov. 2014. Distributed representations of sentences and documents. In *International Conference on Machine Learning*, pages 1188–1196.

Zhouhan Lin, Minwei Feng, Cicero Nogueira dos Santos, Mo Yu, Bing Xiang, Bowen Zhou, and Yoshua Bengio. 2017. A structured self-attentive sentence embedding. *arXiv preprint arXiv:1703.03130*.

Yang Liu, Chengjie Sun, Lei Lin, and Xiaolong Wang. 2016. Learning natural language inference using bidirectional lstm model and inner-attention. *arXiv preprint arXiv:1605.09090*.

Bryan McCann, James Bradbury, Caiming Xiong, and Richard Socher. 2017. Learned in translation: Contextualized word vectors. In *Advances in Neural Information Processing Systems*, pages 6297–6308.

Tomas Mikolov, Kai Chen, Greg Corrado, and Jeffrey Dean. 2013. Efficient estimation of word representations in vector space. *arXiv preprint arXiv:1301.3781*.

Sewon Min, Minjoon Seo, and Hannaneh Hajishirzi. 2017. Question answering through transfer learning from large fine-grained supervision data. *arXiv preprint arXiv:1702.02171*.

Lili Mou, Rui Men, Ge Li, Yan Xu, Lu Zhang, Rui Yan, and Zhi Jin. 2015. Natural language inference by tree-based convolution and heuristic matching. *arXiv preprint arXiv:1512.08422*.

Lili Mou, Zhao Meng, Rui Yan, Ge Li, Yan Xu, Lu Zhang, and Zhi Jin. 2016. How transferable are neural networks in nlp applications? *arXiv preprint arXiv:1603.06111*.

Jeffrey Pennington, Richard Socher, and Christopher Manning. 2014. Glove: Global vectors for word representation. In *Proceedings of the 2014 conference on empirical methods in natural language processing (EMNLP)*, pages 1532–1543.

Matthew E Peters, Mark Neumann, Mohit Iyyer, Matt Gardner, Christopher Clark, Kenton Lee, and Luke Zettlemoyer. 2018. Deep contextualized word representations. *arXiv preprint arXiv:1802.05365*.

Nitish Srivastava, Geoffrey Hinton, Alex Krizhevsky, Ilya Sutskever, and Ruslan Salakhutdinov. 2014. Dropout: A simple way to prevent neural networks from overfitting. *The Journal of Machine Learning Research*, 15(1):1929–1958.

Sandeep Subramanian, Adam Trischler, Yoshua Bengio, and Christopher J Pal. 2018. Learning general purpose distributed sentence representations via large scale multi-task learning. In *International Conference on Learning Representations*.

Ilya Sutskever, Oriol Vinyals, and Quoc V Le. 2014. Sequence to sequence learning with neural networks. In *Advances in neural information processing systems*, pages 3104–3112.

ITNLP-ARC at SemEval-2018 Task 12: Argument Reasoning Comprehension with Attention

Wenjie Liu, Chengjie Sun, Lei Lin, Bingquan Liu
School of Computer Science and Technology
Harbin Institute of Technology
Harbin, China
{wjliu, cjsun, linl, liubq}@insun.hit.edu.cn

Abstract

Reasoning is a very important topic and has many important applications in the field of natural language processing. Semantic Evaluation (SemEval) 2018 Task 12 "The Argument Reasoning Comprehension" committed to research natural language reasoning. In this task, we proposed a novel argument reasoning comprehension system, ITNLP-ARC, which use Neural Networks technology to solve this problem. In our system, the LSTM model is involved to encode both the premise sentences and the warrant sentences. The attention model is used to merge the two premise sentence vectors. Through comparing the similarity between the attention vector and each of the two warrant vectors, we choose the one with higher similarity as our system's final answer.

1 Introduction

Reasoning is a very challenging, but basic part of Natural Language Inference (NLI) (Chen et al., 2017), and many relevant tasks have been proposed such as Recognizing Textual Entailment (RTE) and so on. Stanford University provided Stanford Natural Language Inference (SNLI) corpus to support Natural Language Inference task. It contained two kinds of sentences-the premise sentence and the warrant sentence.The mission is to judge whether the two sentences are inference or not. Semantic Evaluation (SemEval) 2018 Task 12-The Argument Reasoning Comprehension-give an argument consisting of the claim, the reason and two warrants. The goal is to select the correct warrant that explains reasoning with this particular argument. There are two options given and only one is correct. Compare with Stanford Natural Language Inference (SNLI) task (Bowman et al., 2015; Shen et al., 2018), it has more challenges. Because it has abundant premise in-

formation such as the reason, the claim, text information, as well as the option warrants have high semantic textual similarity (Habernal et al., 2017). In this task, we need to find an effective method to extract important information from these premise sentences.

Natural Language Reasoning can be applied to various fields such as question and answering, information retrieval and so on. With the development of Neural Networks applied in Natural Language Processing, sentence representation and reasoning have been researched and taken significant step forwards. In order to deal with the sequence problem, recurrent neural networks (RNN) (Mikolov et al., 2010, 2011) proposes the concept of hidden state, which can extract features from sequence-shaped data and then convert it to output. It can be used to encode the sentence to fixed-length vector representations. In most recent years, long short-term memory (LSTM) network (Bengio et al., 1994; Hochreiter and Schmidhuber, 1997), BiLSTM (Pennington et al., 2014a) and gated recurrent unit (GRU) (Cho et al., 2014) are widely used to get sentence representative vector, and achieved better result compared with traditional methods. Attention model also known as alignment model pays more attention to two sentences interaction (Zheng et al., 2018; Gao et al., 2018), which is usually applied in information extraction, relation extraction, text summarization and machine translation. In machine translation, the attention model can be focused on one or a few words of input to make the translation more accurate when generating each new word. (Rocktäschel et al., 2015) extend a neural word-by-word attention mechanism to encourage reasoning over entailment of pairs of words and phrases.

In our system, we use long short-term memory network to encode sentence. To make full use of

Proceedings of the 12th International Workshop on Semantic Evaluation (SemEval-2018), pages 1089–1093
New Orleans, Louisiana, June 5–6, 2018. ©2018 Association for Computational Linguistics

the information of the reason and the claim, we use attention model to get the attention sentence vector. Then, we compare the warrant sentence vector and the attention sentence vector similarity. The warrant with higher similarity is taken as an answer. In order to make the system more accurate, we use ensemble result as our final answer.

2 Method

The dataset composes with four items which are the reason, the claim, the warrant and the alternative warrant (R, C, W, AW), and two additional information: debateTitle and debateInfo. Let R be a reason for a claim C, both of which are propositions extracted from debateTitle and debateInfo. There are two warrants (AW, W) that justify the use of the reason R as support for the claim C. In this task, we choose the correct warrant by these premise information. In our system, we encode sentence with LSTM, and merge two sentences with attention. Then choose the one (AW or W) with higher similarity between the warrant vector and the attention vector as our answer. The system's neural networks model shown as Fig 1. We build the system with five parts, the following is a detailed description.

2.1 LSTM

Long short-term memory (LSTM) network is a variant of RNN, and it has been successfully applied to various kinds of NLP tasks. It can solve RNN's problem of gradient vanishing and gradient explosion and be good at dealing with sequence-shaped data. LSTM model controls the memory unit through the input gate, output gate and forget gate. The input is a sequence of sentence $X = \{x_1, x_2, \ldots, x_n\}$, where x_i is the word vector of i'th word in the sentence. The output is $H = \{h_1, h_2, \ldots, h_n\}$, where h_i is the i'th step of the LSTM's output. Here, we use the pretrained vector of global vectors (GloVe) (Pennington et al., 2014b) as the embedding layer initialization, and the word embedding dimension is 300. The formulas for LSTM include:

$$i_t = \sigma(W_i \cdot [h_{t-1}, x_t] + b_i) \qquad (1)$$

$$f_t = \sigma(W_f \cdot [h_{t-1}, x_t] + b_f) \qquad (2)$$

$$\widetilde{C_t} = tanh(W_c \cdot [h_{t-1}, x_t] + b_c) \qquad (3)$$

$$C_t = f_t * C_{t-1} + i_t * \widetilde{C_t} \qquad (4)$$

$$o_t = \sigma(W_o \cdot [h_{t-1}, x_t] + b_o) \qquad (5)$$

$$h_t = o_t * tanh(C_t) \qquad (6)$$

In our experiment,we encode the reason sentence and the claim sentence with one LSTM encoder, and encode the warrant sentence with another. We try to use the LSTM's last output, mean pooling and max pooling as the sentence vector representation.

2.2 Attention

In argument reasoning comprehension task, the claim sentence is extracted from title and information, and it supports the result. Therefore, the claim has a great impact on the reason sentence. So, we use attention model to force the reason's and the claim's similarity word, and get the better premise sentence representation. In this task, we use two kinds of attention model to merge reasons and claims vector representation. Let's $R \in \mathbb{R}^{k \times l_r}$ be a matrix consisting of the reason's LSTM output vector $R = \{r_1, r_2, \ldots, r_{l_r}\}$, and $C \in \mathbb{R}^{k \times l_c}$ be a matrix consisting of the claim's LSTM layer output vector $C = \{c_1, c_2, \ldots, c_{l_c}\}$, where l_r is the length of the reason, l_c is the length of the claim, and k is the LSTM's outputs dimension.

One of the attention model is seq-attention model. In our system, we try to represent the claim sentence vector as $c \in \mathbb{R}^k$, where c is the LSTM's last output, mean pooling or max pooling. Then, calculating the claim sentence vector c and the reason sentence vecotor's $\{r_1, r_2, \ldots, r_{l_r}\}$ similarity as the attention weight. We use the result of two vectors multiplication as the similarity weight. Finally, we can obtain the reason sentence vector with weight. The calculation process is as following:

$$e_i = c \bullet r_i \qquad (7)$$

$$\alpha_i = \frac{exp(e_i)}{\sum_{i=1}^{l} exp(e_i)} \qquad (8)$$

$$Rtt^* = \sum_{i=1}^{l} \alpha_i \bullet r_i \qquad (9)$$

where α is the attention weight. The attention vector represent as $Rtt^* \in \mathbb{R}^k$.

Another kind of attention uses matrix to calculate the weight of the claim sentence vector and the reason sentence vector. Give each sentence vector a weight matrix, and obtain the attention vector by learning the weight matrix. The formula is:

$$M = \tanh(W_y R + W_h C_{l_c} \otimes e_{l_r}) \qquad (10)$$

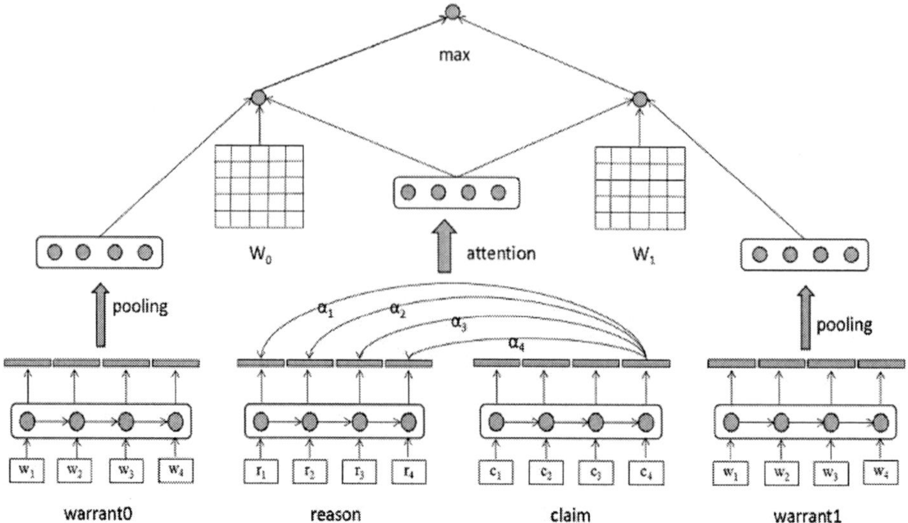

Figure 1: Our system model with attention-encoding with LSTM, merge the reason and the claim with attention, and calculating text similarity with belinear.

$$\alpha = \mathrm{softmax}(w^T M) \qquad (11)$$

$$r = R\alpha^T \qquad (12)$$

$$Rtt^* = \tanh(W_p r + W_x C_{l_c}) \qquad (13)$$

where $W_y \in \mathbb{R}^{k \times k}$, $W_h \in \mathbb{R}^{k \times k}$, $w \in \mathbb{R}^k$, $W_p \in \mathbb{R}^{k \times k}$ and $W_x \in \mathbb{R}^{k \times k}$ is a matrix with random initialization. C_n is the LSTM's last output, max pooling or mean pooling, and α is the attention weight. $Rtt^* \in \mathbb{R}^k$ is the attention vector.

2.3 Text Similarity

There are many ways to calculate the similarity of text vectors, such as cosine distance, dot product and so on. In our system, we use a Bilinear way to calculate the similarity of attention vector and warrant vector. The formula is:

$$h = Rtt^* \times W_m \times W \qquad (14)$$

where Rtt^* is the attention vector, $W_m \in \mathbb{R}^{k \times k}$ is the randomly initialized weight matrix, and W is the warrant sentence vector that using LSTM's last output, max pooling or mean pooling.

2.4 Ensemble

Since neural networks have a large number of random parameters, we try to use different random initialization or change the network layer dimensions to adjust the network structure. In order to make the prediction more accurate, we run the program many times and use the voting method to obtain the final result.

2.5 Loss Function and Evaluation

We treat this task as a classification problem, and use log-loss as our loss function. The format is:

$$log - loss = \sum_{i=1}^{n} y_i log(h_i) + (1 - y_i) log(1 - h_i)$$
$$(15)$$

where y_i is the label of i'th instance, and h_i is the probability calculated by the system.

We also treat it as a sort problem, and choosing the top 1 of sorting results as the answer. The loss function format is:

$$loss = \sum_{i=1}^{n} max(0, 1 - sim(r, wa) + sim(r, w))$$
$$(16)$$

where $sim(r, wa)$ is the true similarity of the premise and the warrant, and $sim(r, w)$ is the false similarity of the premise and the warrant.

Systems will be scored using accuracy. The format is:

$$accuracy = \frac{correct \quad predictions}{all \quad instances} \qquad (17)$$

3 Experiments and Results

Table 1 shows the parameter setting in our system. Because we use Tensorflow to build our system, the sentence needs to be set to a fixed length. The sentences with length greater than 30 words are

lstm_input_unit	lstm_output_unit	lstm_input_dropout	lstm_output_dropout	epoch
300	200	0.6	0.6	40

Table 1: parameter setting in ITNLP_ARC system.

	Train acc	Dev acc	Test acc
lstm(last-output)+seq-attention	0.7450	0.6875	0.5315
lstm(max-pooling)+seq-attention	0.7519	0.6718	0.5382
lstm(mean-pooling)+seq-attention	0.8154	0.6906	0.5427
lstm(last-output)+attention	0.7737	0.6878	0.5257
lstm(max-pooling)+attention	0.7842	0.6827	0.5372
lstm(mean-pooling)+attention	0.7860	0.6932	0.5375

Table 2: The accuracy with log-loss on Semeval 2018 data sets.

	Train acc	Dev acc	Test acc
lstm(last-output)+seq-attention	0.7926	0.6841	0.5292
lstm(max-pooling)+seq-attention	0.7838	0.6812	0.5395
lstm(mean-pooling)+seq-attention	0.8360	0.6927	0.5495
lstm(last-output)+attention	0.7871	0.6750	0.5270
lstm(max-pooling)+attention	0.7929	0.6812	0.5225
lstm(mean-pooling)+attention	0.8105	0.6906	0.5427

Table 3: The accuracy with sort loss function om Semeval 2018 data sets.

	Train acc	Dev acc	Test acc
Ensemble	0.8319	0.7246	0.5521

Table 4: The accuracy of ensembling all neural network model.

truncated from the back, with length less than 30 words are added 0 in the behind.

In our system, we build the argument reasoning comprehension task with neural networks. We try to use the LSTM's last output, max pooling or mean pooling to represent the sentence vector, and use two kinds of attention to merge the reason and the claim. Because of neural networks contains a lot number of randomly initialized parameters, we run our system ten times and average the accuracy. Table 2 shows the accuracy with log-loss function. Table 3 shows the accuracy with sort loss function. From Table 2 and Table 3, we can get conclusion that mean pooling performed better than last output and max pooling. Table 4 shows the accuracy ensemble all neural network model, and this is our system's final result.

4   Conclusion and Future Works

We propose a neural network model to solve reasoning in NLP. We use attention model and bilinear to calculate the similarity between the premise and the warrant. Our system's final result achieved 0.5521. From the experiment, we can see the train accuracy and the development accuracy is much higher than test accuracy. This may be due to over fitting. Maybe decreasing learning rate, and using batch normalization can reduce over fitting. We will try it in the future work.

Acknowledgment

This work is sponsored by the National High Technology Research and Development Program of China (2015AA015405) and National Natural Science Foundation of China (61572151 and 61602131).

References

Yoshua Bengio, Patrice Y. Simard, and Paolo Frasconi. 1994. Learning long-term dependencies with gradient descent is difficult. *IEEE Trans. Neural Networks* 5(2):157–166. https://doi.org/10.1109/72.279181.

Samuel R. Bowman, Gabor Angeli, Christopher Potts, and Christopher D. Manning. 2015. A large annotated corpus for learning natural language inference. In *Proceedings of the 2015 Conference on Empirical Methods in Natural Language Processing, EMNLP 2015, Lisbon, Portugal, September 17-21, 2015*. pages 632–642. http://aclweb.org/anthology/D/D15/D15-1075.pdf.

Qian Chen, Xiaodan Zhu, Zhen-Hua Ling, Si Wei, Hui Jiang, and Diana Inkpen. 2017. Enhanced LSTM for natural language inference. In *Proceedings of the 55th Annual Meeting of the Association for Computational Linguistics, ACL 2017, Vancouver, Canada, July 30 - August 4, Volume 1: Long Papers*. pages 1657–1668. https://doi.org/10.18653/v1/P17-1152.

Kyunghyun Cho, Bart van Merrienboer, Çaglar Gülçehre, Dzmitry Bahdanau, Fethi Bougares, Holger Schwenk, and Yoshua Bengio. 2014. Learning phrase representations using RNN encoder-decoder for statistical machine translation. In *Proceedings of the 2014 Conference on Empirical Methods in Natural Language Processing, EMNLP 2014, October 25-29, 2014, Doha, Qatar, A meeting of SIGDAT, a Special Interest Group of the ACL*. pages 1724–1734. http://aclweb.org/anthology/D/D14/D14-1179.pdf.

Xinjian Gao, Tingting Mu, John Yannis Goulermas, and Meng Wang. 2018. Attention driven multimodal similarity learning. *Inf. Sci.* 432:530–542. https://doi.org/10.1016/j.ins.2017.08.026.

Ivan Habernal, Henning Wachsmuth, Iryna Gurevych, and Benno Stein. 2017. The argument reasoning comprehension task. *CoRR* abs/1708.01425. http://arxiv.org/abs/1708.01425.

Sepp Hochreiter and Jürgen Schmidhuber. 1997. Long short-term memory. *Neural Computation* 9(8):1735–1780. https://doi.org/10.1162/neco.1997.9.8.1735.

Tomas Mikolov, Martin Karafiát, Lukás Burget, Jan Cernocký, and Sanjeev Khudanpur. 2010. Recurrent neural network based language model. In *INTERSPEECH 2010, 11th Annual Conference of the International Speech Communication Association, Makuhari, Chiba, Japan, September 26-30, 2010*. pages 1045–1048. http://www.isca-speech.org/archive/interspeech_2010/i10_1045.html.

Tomas Mikolov, Stefan Kombrink, Lukás Burget, Jan Cernocký, and Sanjeev Khudanpur. 2011. Extensions of recurrent neural network language model. In *Proceedings of the IEEE International Conference on Acoustics, Speech, and Signal Processing, ICASSP 2011, May 22-27, 2011, Prague Congress Center, Prague, Czech Republic*. pages 5528–5531. https://doi.org/10.1109/ICASSP.2011.5947611.

Jeffrey Pennington, Richard Socher, and Christopher D. Manning. 2014a. Glove: Global vectors for word representation. In *Proceedings of the 2014 Conference on Empirical Methods in Natural Language Processing, EMNLP 2014, October 25-29, 2014, Doha, Qatar, A meeting of SIGDAT, a Special Interest Group of the ACL*. pages 1532–1543. http://aclweb.org/anthology/D/D14/D14-1162.pdf.

Jeffrey Pennington, Richard Socher, and Christopher D. Manning. 2014b. Glove: Global vectors for word representation. In *Proceedings of the 2014 Conference on Empirical Methods in Natural Language Processing, EMNLP 2014, October 25-29, 2014, Doha, Qatar, A meeting of SIGDAT, a Special Interest Group of the ACL*. pages 1532–1543. http://aclweb.org/anthology/D/D14/D14-1162.pdf.

Tim Rocktäschel, Edward Grefenstette, Karl Moritz Hermann, Tomás Kociský, and Phil Blunsom. 2015. Reasoning about entailment with neural attention. *CoRR* abs/1509.06664. http://arxiv.org/abs/1509.06664.

Tao Shen, Tianyi Zhou, Guodong Long, Jing Jiang, Sen Wang, and Chengqi Zhang. 2018. Reinforced self-attention network: a hybrid of hard and soft attention for sequence modeling. *CoRR* abs/1801.10296. http://arxiv.org/abs/1801.10296.

Hai-Tao Zheng, Wei Wang, Wang Chen, and Arun Kumar Sangaiah. 2018. Automatic generation of news comments based on gated attention neural networks. *IEEE Access* 6:702–710. https://doi.org/10.1109/ACCESS.2017.2774839.

ECNU at SemEval-2018 Task 12: An End-to-End Attention-based Neural Network for the Argument Reasoning Comprehension Task

Junfeng Tian[1], Man Lan[1,2*] and **Yuanbin Wu[1,2]**

[1] School of Computer Science and Software Engineering,
East China Normal University, Shanghai, P.R.China
[2] Shanghai Key Laboratory of Multidimensional Information Processing
`51151201048@stu.ecnu.edu.cn`, `{mlan, ybwu}@cs.ecnu.edu.cn`

Abstract

This paper presents our submissions to SemEval 2018 Task 12: the Argument Reasoning Comprehension Task. We investigate an end-to-end attention-based neural network to represent the two lexically close candidate warrants. On the one hand, we extract their different parts as attention vectors to obtain distinguishable representations. On the other hand, we use their surrounds (i.e., claim, reason, debate context) as another attention vectors to get contextual representations, which work as final clues to select the correct warrant. Our model achieves 60.4% accuracy and ranks 3rd among 22 participating systems.

1 Introduction

Reasoning is a crucial part of natural language argumentation. In order to comprehend an argument, one must analyze its *warrant*, which explains why its *claim* follows form its premises (aka *reasons*) (Habernal et al., 2018a).

SemEval-2018 Task 12 provides the argument reasoning comprehension task (Habernal et al., 2018b). Given a reason and a *claim* along with the *title* and a short *description* of the debate they occur in, the goal is to identify the correct *warrant* from two candidates. Figure 1 gives an example. The abstract structure of an argument is: *reason* $\rightarrow$ (since) *warrant* $\rightarrow$ (therefore) *claim*.

The challenging factor is that both candidate warrants are plausible and lexically very close while leading to contradicting claims (Habernal et al., 2018a). Here we give three examples of the two candidate warrants:

Ex1: A huge pandemic would (not) be a great news story.

Ex2: The role of a citizen and a supreme court justice are inseparable /separable.

Ex3: The rest of the comments can be skipped easily /make the section unreadable.

Title: Have Comment Section Failed?
Description: In recent years, many media companies have disabled them because of widespread abuse and obscenity.
Reason: Many comments are thoughtful and insightful. And since {Warrant0 | Warrant1},
Claim: Comment sections have not failed.
✓ **Warrant0**: The rest of the comments can be skipped easily.
✗ **Warrant1**: The rest of the comments make the section unreadable.

Figure 1: An example of a debate in the argument reasoning comprehension task.

The differences are either negative words, or antonyms, or opposite phrases. Therefore, it is important to emphasize the different parts to obtain distinguish representations of the two warrants, which express the opposite meanings.

To address this factor, we proposed an end-to-end attention-based neural network. On the one hand, we extract the different parts of the two warrants and use them as attention vectors to obtain warrants' distinguishable representations. On the other hand, we represent their surrounds (i.e., reason, claim, debate context) as another attention vector to get the contextual representations.

2 System Architecture

Formally, given an instance containing two candidate warrants (W_0, W_1) and the context around the warrants (i.e., R, C, T, I), the goal is to choose the correct warrant $y \in \{0, 1\}$, where $y = 0$ means W_0 is the correct answer, and $y = 1$ otherwise.

2.1 Overview

The network is inspired by Siamese network (Mueller and Thyagarajan, 2016). The two candidate warrants are modeled in the same structure. Figure 2 illustrates our system architecture.

First, we first extract the different parts of war-

Proceedings of the 12th International Workshop on Semantic Evaluation (SemEval-2018), pages 1094–1098
New Orleans, Louisiana, June 5–6, 2018. ©2018 Association for Computational Linguistics

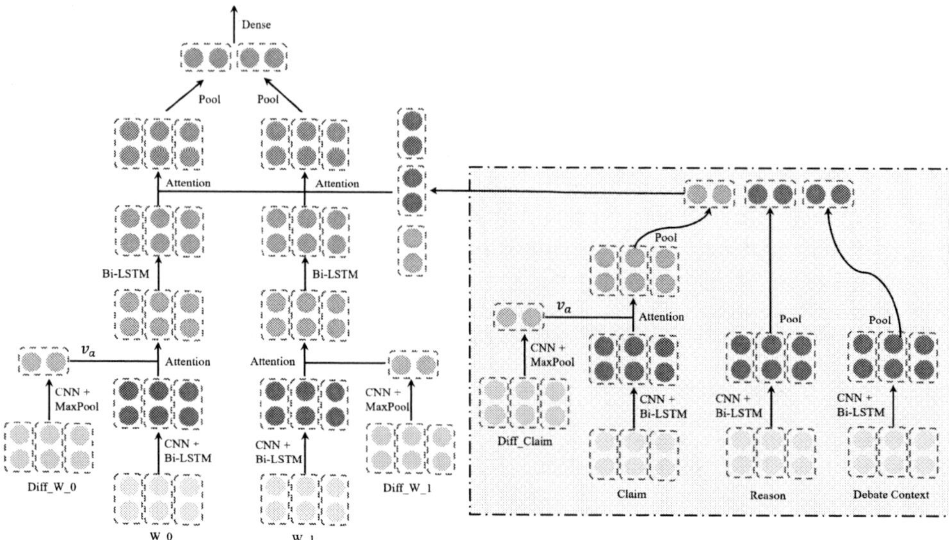

Figure 2: The system architecture

rant0, warrant1 and claim to get $Diff\_W_0$, $Diff\_W_1$ and Diff_Claim (see in Sec. 2.2).

Then, we stack a CNN and a RNN to represent each component to obtain representation of each component, because the combination of CNN and RNN can make use of the spatial and temporal context information (in Sec. 2.3).

Next, the intra-temporal attention is adopted to obtain distinguishable representations of warrants. Similarly, we apply the same strategy to the claim. The intra-temporal attention is introduced in Sec. 2.4).

After that, we concatenate the representation of surrounds (i.e., reason, claim, debate context and warrant) as another attention vector to obtain the contextual representations of the warrants.

Last, we adopt a dense layer to obtain the probability of the two candidate warrants (in Sec. 2.5). The contextual representations work as hidden clues to select the correct warrant.

2.2 Extract the Different Part

The two candidate warrants are lexically close (since they often mean the opposite), thus we extract the different part between them to serve as attention vector to guide the neural network to generate distinguishable representation for the warrants.

To do this, we remove the longest common prefix and suffix, and let the remain part as the different part, denoted as $Diff\_W_0$, $Diff\_W_1$. Take cases

mentioned in Sec. 1 as examples, it would extract "not be " as $Diff\_W_0$ and "be" as $Diff\_W_1$ in Ex1; "inseparable" as $Diff\_W_0$ and "separable" as $Diff\_W_1$ in Ex2; "can be skipped easily" as $Diff\_W_0$ and "make the section unreadable" as $Diff\_W_1$ in Ex3. Note that if the remain part is empty, we use the word after the prefix as the different part.

Similarly, we also get the different part between the claim and its opposite, denoted as Diff_Claim. There always exists the opposite claims in debates, since the reason chains $R \rightarrow W \rightarrow C$ and $R \rightarrow \neg W \rightarrow \neg C$ both exists. We collected the claims and warrants under the same debate. If the warrants express the opposite meaning, then the two claims are opposite. Besides, the organizers also provide similar dataset in "data/train-w-swap-doubled.tsv".

2.3 Context Representation

To incorporate contextual information of each components in a debate, we combine Convolutional Neural Network (CNN) and Recurrent neural network (RNN) to encode the input word vectors. CNN is good at dealing with spatially related data, such as "sometimes warranted" and "rarely warranted", while RNN is good at temporal signals. Instead of using a typical vanilla RNN, we use Long Short-Term Memory Network (Hochreiter and Schmidhuber, 1997) for eliminating the issue of long term dependencies.

Given a sentence $S = \{w_i\}_1^n$, we first map each word w_i into its vector representation $x_i \in \mathbb{R}^d$ via a look-up table of word embeddings (d is the dimension of the word embeddings).

Then, we adopt CNN on the input sequence $\{x_i\}_1^n$ to obtain the spatial representation $\{x_i'\}_1^n$:

$$
\begin{aligned}
e_i^j &= \text{ReLU}(w^j[x_i, \ldots, x_{i+k-1}]) & (1)\\
x_i' &= [e_i^1, \ldots, e_i^m](1 \le j \le m) & (2)
\end{aligned}
$$

where k is the window size, w^j is the parameter of a filter, m is the number of the filters. We also adopt padding before the convolution operation. As a result, we obtain the spatial representations $x_i' \in \mathbb{R}^m$, which has the same length as the input sequence.

After that, we utilize a bi-directional LSTM (Bi-LSTM) to obtain the temporal information. For each time step t, the LSTM unit computation corresponds to :

$$
\begin{aligned}
i_t &= \sigma(W_i x_t' + U_i h_{t-1} + b_i) & (3)\\
f_t &= \sigma(W_f x_t' + U_f h_{t-1} + b_f) & (4)\\
o_t &= \sigma(W_o x_t' + U_o h_{t-1} + b_o) & (5)\\
\tilde{c}_t &= \tanh(W_c x_t' + U_c h_{t-1} + b_c) & (6)\\
c_t &= i_t \odot \tilde{c}_t + f_t \odot c_{t-1} & (7)\\
h_t &= o_t \odot \tanh(c_t) & (8)
\end{aligned}
$$

where σ is the element-wise sigmoid function, $\odot$ is the element-wise product and i_t, f_t, o_t ,c_t demote the input gate, forget gate, output gate and memory cell respectively.

2.4 Intra-Temporal Attention

Inspired from Habernal et al. (2018a), we use an intra-temporal attention function to attend over specific parts of the input sequence. This kind of attention encourages the model to generate different representation according to the attention vector. Habernal et al. (2018a) have shown that such intra-temporal attention outperforms standard attention.

We define v_a as the attention vector, and h_t as the hidden states at time step t:

$$
\begin{aligned}
m_t &= \tanh(U_m h_t \odot v_a + b_m) & (9)\\
a_t &= \sigma(W_a m_t + b_a) & (10)\\
h_t &= h_t \odot a_t & (11)
\end{aligned}
$$

where a_t is the attention weights over the hidden states h_t, $\odot$ is element-wise multiplication.

We first apply the intra-temporal attention over W_0 and W_1, in order to obtain different warrant representations from Diff_W_0 and Diff_W_1. As a result, the model can easily distinguish the two candidate warrants. Similarly, we apply the attention over claim to make the claim representation distinguishable.

Moreover, we adopt another intra-temporal attention over W_0 and W_1, with the concatenation of {claim, reason, debate context} representations as attention vector. The candidate warrants receive the information from the claim, reason and debate context, and the model would select the correct warrant which satisfies the reasoning chain $R \rightarrow W \rightarrow C$.

Finally, we obtain two attended warrant vectors att_{W_0}, att_{W_1}.

2.5 Output

To evaluate the probability distribution of the two candidate warrants, we employ a feed-forward neural network with one dense layer, and apply the *Softmax* function to predict the probability.

$$
\begin{aligned}
h_o &= \text{ReLU}(W_o[att_{W_0}, att_{W_1}]) & (12)\\
\hat{p} &= \text{Softmax}(W_p h_o) & (13)
\end{aligned}
$$

As for the optimization, cross-entropy loss is used as the loss function since we are handling a binary classification problem:

$$
\mathcal{L} = -\Big(y_i \log \hat{p}_i + (1 - y_i) \log(1 - \hat{p}_i)\Big) \quad (14)
$$

where y_i is the gold label.

3 Experiments

3.1 Datasets

SemEval 2018 provided 1,970 instances for the argument reasoning comprehension task (Habernal et al., 2018b). The instances are divided into three sets based on the year when the debates are taken from. Table 1 lists the statistics of the datasets. We also include the number of debate topics of each set.

Dataset	# Pairs	# Topics	Source Year
Train	1,210	111	2011-2015
Dev	316	31	2016
Test	444	30	2017

Table 1: The statistics of the datasets

Being a binary task, accuracy (Acc) is adopted as the evaluation metric.

Approach	Dev
Intra-warrant attention	0.638 ($\pm$0.024)
Intra-warrant attention w/ context	0.637 ($\pm$0.040)
Our basic model	0.666 ($\pm$0.019)
$\cdot$ + Diff_$\{W_0, W_1\}$	0.678 ($\pm$0.001)
$\cdot$ + Diff_$\{W_0, W_1\}$ + CNN	0.675 ($\pm$0.010)
$\cdot$ + Diff_$\{W_0, W_1, \text{Claim}\}$ + CNN	0.676 ($\pm$0.010)
Ensemble (Vote)	0.708

Table 2: Accuracy of each approach on the developing dataset.

Approach	Test
Human average	0.798 ($\pm$0.162)
Human w/ training in reasoning	0.909 ($\pm$0.114)
Random baseline	0.508 ($\pm$0.015)
Intra-warrant attention w/ context	0.584 ($\pm$0.015)
Rank 1: GIST	0.712
Rank 2: blcu_nlp	0.606
Rank 3: ECNU	0.604

Table 3: Accuracy of each approach (humans and systems) on the test set.

3.2 Parameters Setting

The word embeddings are initialized with the 300d pre-trained word2vec (Mikolov et al., 2013), and do not fine-tune during training. The window sizes of CNN is (1,2,3) and the kernel size is 50. The dimensions of the hidden size in Bi-LSTM and Att-LSTM are set to 50. The dense layer in Output is 25. We train the model using Adam (Kingma and Ba, 2014) with gradient clipping (the max norm is set to 30, batch size is 32), The networks are regularized by dropout (the dropout ratio equals 0.8). We ran each model three times with random initializations. Our code is available at `https://github.com/rgtjf/SemEval2018-Task12`.

3.3 Results on Training Data

Table 2 shows the results of each components of our attention-based neural network. We have the following findings:

(1) Comparing with the Intra-warrant attention (w/ context) provided by the organizer, our basic model obtains 2.8% improvement through sharing parameters in Bi-LSTM. It indicates that the neural network need sufficient training data and parameters sharing could alleviate the demand.

(2) All of the three improvements achieves improved accuracy. It suggests that utilizing the different part as attention vector can obtain discriminative representation, which is beneficial for choosing the correct answer.

(3) The introduction of CNN does not seem to improve the performance of the model. The possible reason may be that RNN actually learn any computational function and capture the spatial information.

(4) The ensemble of the three networks can further improve the performance. Therefore, we configure the ensemble model as our final submission.

3.4 Results on Test Data

Table 3 lists the results of three top systems and several baselines provided by the organizer. We find that: (1) Comparing with Intra-warrant attention w/ context model, our model outperforms it by 2% in terms of accuracy, which demonstrates the efficiency of the proposed attention-based model. (2) Comparing with GIST and blcu_nlp, our result is comparable to blcu_nlp but worse than GIST. Both of them use the pre-trained ESIM model (Chen et al., 2017) trained on SNLI (Bowman et al., 2015) and MultiNLI (Nangia et al., 2017) dataset. Our model only uses the training dataset and does not require any extra resources. However, this is also the limitation of our model because this small-size dataset is insufficient to learn parameters in our model.

4 Conclusion

In this work, we propose an end-to-end neural network for the reading comprehension task. We stack a CNN and a RNN to represent each component in a debate and extract the warrants' and claim's different part as attention vector to obtain their distinguish representation. Moreover, we use another attention network to incorporate the information of reason, claim, debate context into the contextual representation of the warrants for final decisions. Our model achieves 60.4% accuracy and ranks 3rd among 22 participating systems.

Acknowledgments

The authors would like to thank Changzhi Sun for his valuable suggestions and the anonymous reviewers for their helpful comments. This work is supported by grants from Science and Technology Commission of Shanghai Municipality (15ZR1410700), the Open Project of Shanghai Key Laboratory of Trustworthy Computing (No.07dz22304201604).

References

Samuel R. Bowman, Gabor Angeli, Christopher Potts, and Christopher D. Manning. 2015. A large annotated corpus for learning natural language inference. In *Proceedings of the 2015 Conference on Empirical Methods in Natural Language Processing*, pages 632–642.

Qian Chen, Xiaodan Zhu, Zhen-Hua Ling, Si Wei, Hui Jiang, and Diana Inkpen. 2017. Enhanced lstm for natural language inference. In *Proceedings of the 55th Annual Meeting of the Association for Computational Linguistics (Volume 1: Long Papers)*.

Ivan Habernal, Henning Wachsmuth, Iryna Gurevych, and Benno Stein. 2018a. The argument reasoning comprehension task: Identification and reconstruction of implicit warrants. In *Proceedings of the 2018 Conference of the North American Chapter of the Association for Computational Linguistics: Human Language Technologies*.

Ivan Habernal, Henning Wachsmuth, Iryna Gurevych, and Benno Stein. 2018b. Semeval-2018 task 12: The argument reasoning comprehension task. In *Proceedings of the 12th International Workshop on Semantic Evaluation (SemEval-2018)*, New Orleans, LA, USA. Association for Computational Linguistics.

Sepp Hochreiter and Jürgen Schmidhuber. 1997. Long short-term memory. *Neural computation*, 9(8):1735–1780.

Diederik P. Kingma and Jimmy Ba. 2014. Adam: A method for stochastic optimization. *CoRR*, abs/1412.6980.

Tomas Mikolov, Ilya Sutskever, Kai Chen, Greg S Corrado, and Jeff Dean. 2013. Distributed representations of words and phrases and their compositionality. In *Advances in neural information processing systems*, pages 3111–3119.

Jonas Mueller and Aditya Thyagarajan. 2016. Siamese recurrent architectures for learning sentence similarity. In *Thirtieth AAAI Conference on Artificial Intelligence*.

Nikita Nangia, Adina Williams, Angeliki Lazaridou, and Samuel Bowman. 2017. The repeval 2017 shared task: Multi-genre natural language inference with sentence representations. In *Proceedings of the 2nd Workshop on Evaluating Vector Space Representations for NLP*, pages 1–10.

NLITrans at SemEval-2018 Task 12: Transfer of Semantic Knowledge for Argument Comprehension

Timothy Niven and **Hung-Yu Kao**
National Cheng Kung University
Tainan, Taiwan
tim.niven.public@gmail.com, hykao@mail.ncku.edu.tw

Abstract

The Argument Reasoning Comprehension Task requires significant language understanding and complex reasoning over world knowledge. We focus on transfer of a sentence encoder to bootstrap more complicated models given the small size of the dataset. Our best model uses a pre-trained BiLSTM to encode input sentences, learns task-specific features for the argument and warrants, then performs independent argument-warrant matching. This model achieves mean test set accuracy of 64.43%. Encoder transfer yields a significant gain to our best model over random initialization. Independent warrant matching effectively doubles the size of the dataset and provides additional regularization. We demonstrate that regularization comes from ignoring statistical correlations between warrant features and position. We also report an experiment with our best model that only matches warrants to reasons, ignoring claims. Relatively low performance degradation suggests that our model is not necessarily learning the intended task.

1 Introduction

The Argument Reasoning Comprehension Task (ARCT) (Habernal et al., 2018) addresses a significant open problem in argumentation mining: connecting reasons and claims via inferential licenses, called warrants (Toulmin, 1958). Warrants are a form of shared world knowledge and are mostly implicit in argumentation. This makes it difficult for machine learning algorithms to discover arguments, as they must acquire and use this knowledge to identify argument components and their relations. ARCT isolates the reasoning step by not requiring warrants to be discovered. A correct warrant **W** and an incorrect alternative **A** are given, and the correct one must be predicted given the corresponding claim **C** and reason **R**.

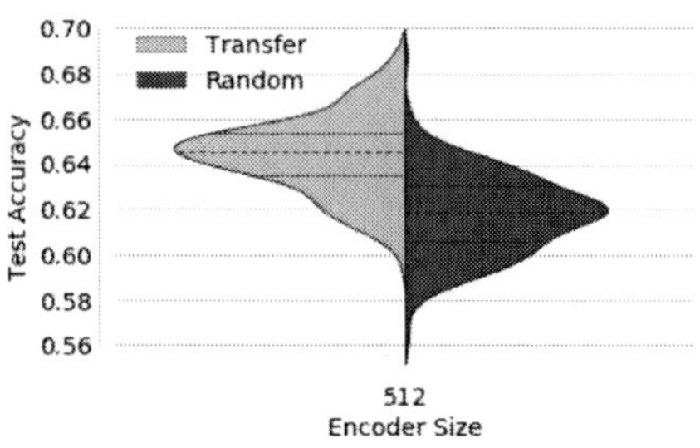

Figure 1: Benefit of transfer to our best model, COMP. Distributions come from 200 runs with different random seeds. Mean accuracy for transfer (64.43%) is higher than random (61.81%) and is significant with $p = 9.68 \times 10^{-41}$.

However, this does not eliminate the need for other forms of world knowledge. Consider the following example from the test set:

C	Google is not a harmful monopoly
R	People can choose not to use Google
W	Other search engines do not re-direct to Google
A	All other search engines re-direct to Google

It is required to know how consumer choice and web re-directs relate to the concept of monopoly in this context, and that Google is a search engine.

We do not attempt to address these other forms of world knowledge. Given the small size of the dataset we focus on transfer of semantic knowledge in the form of a sentence encoder to bootstrap inference over learned features. Following Conneau et al. (2017), we pre-train a BiLSTM encoder with max pooling on natural language inference (NLI) data (Williams et al., 2017; Bowman et al., 2015). Their results indicate transfer from the NLI domain to be useful. They hypothesized that due to the challenging nature of the

Proceedings of the 12th International Workshop on Semantic Evaluation (SemEval-2018), pages 1099–1103
New Orleans, Louisiana, June 5–6, 2018. ©2018 Association for Computational Linguistics

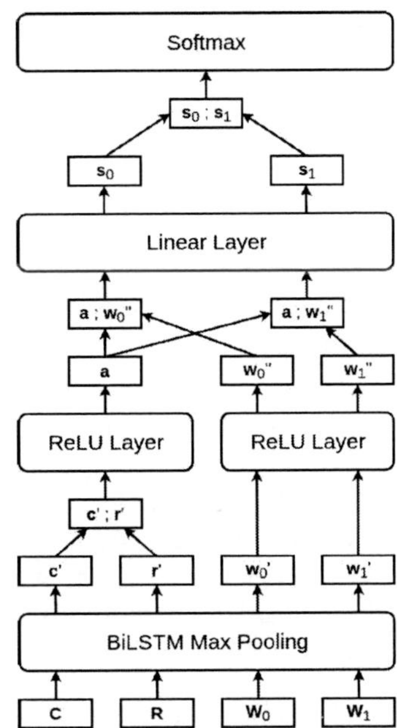

Figure 2: COMP model architecture.

task, successful encoders must necessarily learn good semantic representations. However, Nie et al. (2017) argue that due to the relatively easy nature of their out of domain generalization tasks (sentiment classification and textual similarity), they did not sufficiently demonstrate that deep semantic understanding had been learned.

In this respect our work extends the results of Conneau et al. (2017). They performed transfer by passing encoded sentence vectors to a logistic regression classifier. Our implementation of this model demonstrated very poor performance on ARCT. However, we experiment with a more complicated model (Figure 2) which significantly benefits from transfer (Figure 1). We therefore extend previous results to demonstrate the utility of this technique not only for a more semantically challenging task, but also a more complicated neural network architecture.

A key feature of our model is independent warrant classification which effectively doubles the size of the dataset. We demonstrate that it also provides regularization due to ignoring statistical correlations between warrant features and position.

Finally, we experiment with a version of our model that only matches reasons to warrants, ignoring claims. The relatively low drop in performance suggests that our model may not necessarily be learning the intended task.

2 System Description

2.1 COMP Model

A diagram of our best model which we call COMP is given in Figure 2. The key idea is to learn independent features for argument components and then perform independent warrant matching.

The inputs are word vectors for the claim $\mathbf{C}$, reason $\mathbf{R}$, and warrants $\mathbf{W}_0$ and $\mathbf{W}_1$. We use GloVe embeddings with 300 dimensions pretrained on 640B tokens (Pennington et al., 2014). First, a bi-directional LSTM (Hochreiter and Schmidhuber, 1997) with max pooling learns semantic representations of the input sentences.

$$\mathbf{c}' = \text{BiLSTM}_{\text{max}}(\mathbf{C})$$
$$\mathbf{r}' = \text{BiLSTM}_{\text{max}}(\mathbf{R})$$
$$\mathbf{w}'_0 = \text{BiLSTM}_{\text{max}}(\mathbf{W}_0)$$
$$\mathbf{w}'_1 = \text{BiLSTM}_{\text{max}}(\mathbf{W}_1)$$

Dropout (Srivastava et al., 2014) is then applied to these vectors. If d is the encoder size then each vector is of dimension $2d$ due to the concatenation of forward and backward LSTMs.

Parameter matrix $\mathbf{U} \in \mathbb{R}^{4d \times h}$ with ReLU activation (Nair and Hinton, 2010) learns argument specific feature vectors of length h from the concatenation of the claim and reason. Parameter matrix $\mathbf{V} \in \mathbb{R}^{2d \times h}$ with ReLU activation learns specific features for each warrant independently. Biases are omitted for clarity.

$$\mathbf{a} = \text{ReLU}(\mathbf{U}[\mathbf{c}'; \mathbf{r}'])$$
$$\mathbf{w}''_0 = \text{ReLU}(\mathbf{V}\mathbf{w}'_0)$$
$$\mathbf{w}''_1 = \text{ReLU}(\mathbf{V}\mathbf{w}'_1)$$

Dropout is then applied to these vectors prior to classification. Parameter vector $\mathbf{z} \in \mathbb{R}^{2h}$ is used to independently determine a matching score for each argument-warrant pair. The scores are concatenated and passed through softmax to determine a probability distribution $\hat{\mathbf{y}}$ over the two warrants. Cross entropy is then used to calculate loss with respect to the gold label y.

$$s_0 = \mathbf{z}^\top [\mathbf{a}; \mathbf{w}''_0]$$
$$s_1 = \mathbf{z}^\top [\mathbf{a}; \mathbf{w}''_1]$$
$$\hat{\mathbf{y}} = \text{softmax}([s_0; s_1])$$
$$J(\theta) = \text{CE}(\hat{\mathbf{y}}, y)$$

Encoder Size	Random	Transfer	Difference	Significance (p)
2048	0.5975	0.5942	-0.55 %	1.72×10^{-1}
1024	0.6058	0.6025	-0.54 %	1.05×10^{-1}
512	0.6181	**0.6443**	**+4.24 %**	9.68×10^{-41}
300	0.6285	0.6260	-0.40 %	1.41×10^{-1}
100	**0.6310**	0.6329	+0.30 %	2.89×10^{-1}

Table 1: Transfer results for our COMP model with different encoder sizes. Learning rates and dropout are tuned to specific encoder sizes. All other hyperparameters are the same. Results are the mean test set accuracy of 200 runs from different random seeds. "Difference" shows the percentage change of transfer relative to random.

2.2 Training Details

Pre-training BiLSTMs was done according to the specifications of Conneau et al. (2017). For all ARCT models we followed their annealing and early stopping strategy: after each epoch, if development set accuracy does not improve the learning rate is reduced by a factor of five. Training stops when the learning rate drops below 1×10^{-5}. This algorithm was found to outperform a steadily decaying learning rate. Adam (Kingma and Ba, 2014) was used for optimization.

We used grid search to find our best parameters. Best results were achieved with a batch size of 16. Dropout with $p = 0.1$ was found to be superior to $L2$-regularization. For the COMP model, a hidden representation size of 512 worked best. Tuning word embeddings was found to overfit compared to freezing them. However, tuning the transferred encoder was far superior to freezing for the COMP model.

We did not find reducing the learning rate on the encoder helped transfer. Bowman et al. (2015) also transfered AdaDelta accumulators along with an encoder on the principle that lowering the starting learning rate should help avoid blowing away transferred knowledge. Our results rather agree with Mou et al. (2016) who also found that learning rate reduction did not help transfer.

Our code is publicly available, including scripts to reproduce our results.[1]

2.3 Submission

Our submission "NLITrans" was our COMP model with a transferred encoder of dimension 2048. The principal learning rate was 0.002 and we tuned embeddings at their own rate of 0.0002. The encoder was tuned at the principal rate. Hidden representation size was 512.

Our submission test set accuracy of 59.0%

[1]https://github.com/IKMLab/arct

achieved fourth place. Following Riemers and Gurevych (2017), we consider a single run an insufficient indication of the performance of a model due to the variation resulting from random initialization. Evaluation over 20 runs with different random seeds revealed our entry was close to the mean for this configuration of 59.24%.

2.4 Best Configuration

Extended post-competition tuning on the development set revealed better hyperparameter settings that boost the generalization ability of our COMP model. Specifically, we freeze word embeddings and use an encoder of size 512. On the test set this configuration achieves a mean accuracy of 64.43% over 200 random initializations.

3 Analysis

3.1 Transfer Performance

We measure the performance of transfer by comparison with random initialization. The results in Table 1 show the performance of different encoder sizes for our best COMP model. Learning rate and dropout are re-tuned via grid search for each encoder size. More investigation is required, however these results suggest that the success of transfer depends on finding an optimal encoder size for a given model. We note that the best random performance came from the smallest encoder size, confirming that transfer is helping us bootstrap the use of more complicated models.

3.2 Independent Warrant Classification

Ablation studies showed that independent warrant classification is a significant advantage. For comparison, we built a model that considers both warrants and the argument together by replacing parameter vector $\mathbf{z}$ with a matrix $\mathbf{Z} \in \mathbb{R}^{3h \times 2}$. We call this model CORR, as it considers correlations between warrant features and position. The scores

Model	Dataset	Train	Test	Overfit
COMP	Full	0.8807	0.6443	36.69 %
	Half	0.8925	0.6332	40.95 %
	Unbal.	0.9109	0.6353	43.38 %
CORR	Full	0.8155	0.5912	37.94 %
	Half	0.8287	0.5649	46.70 %
	Unbal.	0.9368	0.5750	62.92 %

Table 2: Comparison of independent (COMP) and correlated (CORR) models on full, half, and unbalanced (Unbal.) datasets. COMP has 6,541,057 parameters and CORR has 6,543,106.

for the warrants are then calculated as

$$\mathbf{s} = \mathbf{Z}[\mathbf{a}; \mathbf{w}_0''; \mathbf{w}_1'']$$

The results in Table 2 demonstrate poorer generalization and increased overfitting relative to the independent model on the full dataset.

Independent warrant classification effectively doubles the size of the dataset. It can be seen that two separate multiplications of argument-warrant vectors with $\mathbf{z}$ lead to two backpropagated supervision signals with each data sample. To quantify this effect we evaluated the independent model trained on a randomly sampled half of the the training set. It still generalized better than CORR on twice the data (Table 2).

We hypothesized that additional regularization follows from ignoring statistical correlations between warrant features and position. To investigate this hypothesis, we picked an obvious linguistic phenomenon and looked at the statistics of its occurrence at each warrant position. We used SpaCy's dependency parser to identify tokens with the negation relation to its head. Results showed negation is ubiquitous in this dataset, covering approximately 70% of training samples - perhaps reflecting a natural way to generate pairs of conflicting warrants. Whilst the warrant with negation is correct half of the time in the training set, negation in position one is slightly more likely to be correct than position zero (26% to 25%).

To quantify model susceptibility to such correlations we created an unbalanced training set in which all correct warrants with negation occur in position one. This resulted in relabeling 300 warrants. We randomly relabeled the same amount of warrants without negation to position zero to re-balance the dataset. The results (Table 2) con-

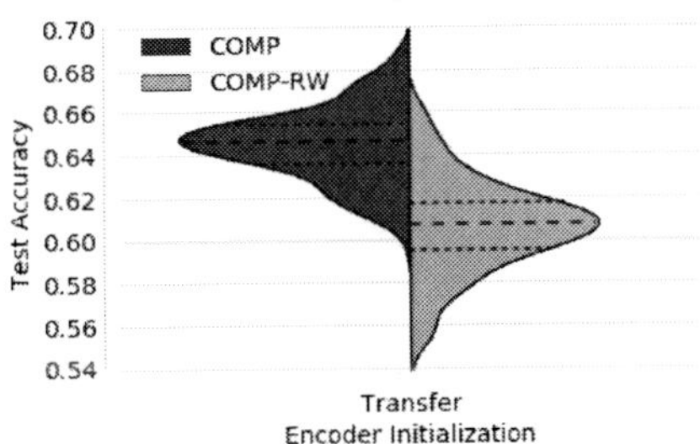

Figure 3: Results of our COMP-RW model that doesn't consider the claim, compared to our best model COMP. Distributions are calculated from 200 runs with different random seeds. The mean for COMP is 64.43%, compared to 60.60% for COMP-RW.

firm that the CORR model is more susceptible to this change, resulting in a large overfit, whilst the generalization ability of the independent model is essentially unaffected.

3.3 Matching Warrants to Reasons

In the following example a position toward the claim seems to be embedded in the reason.

C	Comment sections have not failed
R	They add a lot to the piece and I look forward to reading comments
W	Comments sections are a welcome distraction from my work
A	Comments sections always distract me from my work

Cases such as this may provide an alternative learning signal and lead our model to stray from the intended task. For example it might be possible to correctly classify this example by comparing the sentiment of the warrants to that of the reason.

To quantify this effect we experimented with a model that considers only the reasons and warrants, called COMP-RW. Since we do not input the claim we resize $\mathbf{U}$ from $\mathbb{R}^{4d \times h}$ to $\mathbb{R}^{2d \times h}$. We use an encoder of size 640 to balance this reduction which evens the parameter count for a fair comparison. Figure 3 shows the relative performance of COMP-RW versus our best COMP model. Test set accuracy deteriorates from 64.43% to 60.60%. This suggests there is enough signal coming from the reasons alone to achieve approximately two thirds of what our model is capable of above random guessing. We therefore suspect our model is not necessarily learning the intended task.

4   Conclusion

Our entry NLITrans achieved test set accuracy of 59.0% for fourth place, close to the mean for its configuration of 59.24% over 20 random initializations. Extended post-competition tuning on the development set led us to a superior configuration of our COMP model that achieved a mean of 64.43%. Transfer of an encoder pre-trained on NLI data resulted in a 4.24% boost to test set accuracy for this model. This extends previous results with this transfer technique, demonstrating its effectiveness in a more complicated neural network architecture, and for a much more semantically challenging task. An outstanding question is whether there is an optimal encoder size for transfer given a specific architecture, and how to efficiently and reliably find it. Independent argument-warrant matching proved to be beneficial, doubling the effective size of the dataset and providing additional regularization. We demonstrated that regularization comes from ignoring the correlations between warrant features and position. Adapting our model to ignore the claims resulted in a relatively low drop in performance, suggesting our model is not necessarily learning the intended task. We leave a more thorough analysis of this phenomenon for future work.

References

Samuel R. Bowman, Gabor Angeli, Christopher Potts, and Christopher D. Manning. 2015. A large annotated corpus for learning natural language inference. *CoRR*, abs/1508.05326.

Alexis Conneau, Douwe Kiela, Holger Schwenk, Loïc Barrault, and Antoine Bordes. 2017. Supervised learning of universal sentence representations from natural language inference data. *CoRR*, abs/1705.02364.

Ivan Habernal, Henning Wachsmuth, Iryna Gurevych, and Benno Stein. 2018. The argument reasoning comprehension task: Identification and reconstruction of implicit warrants. In *Proceedings of the 2018 Conference of the North American Chapter of the Association for Computational Linguistics: Human Language Technologies*, page (to appear), New Orleans, LA, USA. Association for Computational Linguistics.

Sepp Hochreiter and Jürgen Schmidhuber. 1997. Long short-term memory. *Neural computation*, 9(8):1735–1780.

Diederik P. Kingma and Jimmy Ba. 2014. Adam: A method for stochastic optimization. *CoRR*, abs/1412.6980.

Lili Mou, Zhao Meng, Rui Yan, Ge Li, Yan Xu, Lu Zhang, and Zhi Jin. 2016. How transferable are neural networks in NLP applications? *CoRR*, abs/1603.06111.

Vinod Nair and Geoffrey E. Hinton. 2010. Rectified linear units improve restricted boltzmann machines. In *ICML*.

Allen Nie, Erin D. Bennett, and Noah D. Goodman. 2017. Dissent: Sentence representation learning from explicit discourse relations. *CoRR*, abs/1710.04334.

Jeffrey Pennington, Richard Socher, and Christopher D. Manning. 2014. Glove: Global vectors for word representation. In *Empirical Methods in Natural Language Processing (EMNLP)*, pages 1532–1543.

Nils Reimers and Iryna Gurevych. 2017. Reporting score distributions makes a difference: Performance study of lstm-networks for sequence tagging. *CoRR*, abs/1707.09861.

Nitish Srivastava, Geoffrey Hinton, Alex Krizhevsky, Ilya Sutskever, and Ruslan Salakhutdinov. 2014. Dropout: A simple way to prevent neural networks from overfitting. *Journal of Machine Learning Research*, 15:1929–1958.

Stephen E. Toulmin. 1958. *The Uses of Argument.* Cambridge University Press.

Adina Williams, Nikita Nangia, and Samuel R. Bowman. 2017. A broad-coverage challenge corpus for sentence understanding through inference. *CoRR*, abs/1704.05426.

BLCU_NLP at SemEval-2018 Task 12: An Ensemble Model for Argument Reasoning Based on Hierarchical Attention

Meiqian Zhao, Chunhua Liu, Lu Liu, Yan Zhao, Dong Yu[*]
Beijing Language and Culture University
{zhaomq195, chunhualiu596, luliu.nlp, zhaoyan.nlp}@gmail.com,
yudong@blcu.edu.cn

Abstract

The argument comprehension reasoning task aims to reconstruct and analyze the argument reasoning. To comprehend an argument and fill the gap between claims and reasons, it is vital to find the implicit supporting warrants behind. In this paper, we propose a hierarchical attention model to identify the right warrant which explains why the reason stands for the claim. Our model focuses not only on the similar part between warrants and other information but also on the contradictory part between two opposing warrants. In addition, we use the ensemble method for different models. Our model achieves an accuracy of 61%, ranking second in this task. Experimental results demonstrate that our model is effective to make correct choices.

1 Introduction

The argument reasoning comprehension is a crucial part for natural language understanding and inference, since argument comprehension requires reconstruction and analysis for its reasoning. Lack of common sense makes it difficult to infer claims from corresponding reasons directly. To fill the gap between claims and reasons, several explorations have been performed on argumentative structure of a debate (Hastings, 1963; Walton et al., 2008; Walton, 1990). Argument reasoning comprehension, a new task in SemEval 2018, sheds some light on the core of reasoning in natural language argumentation: implicit warrants, which are seen as a bridge between claims and reasons. Given a reason R, a claim C and two alternative warrants W0 and W1, the goal of this task is to identify the right warrant which can justify the use of R as support for C. The difficulty of the task is the warrants are plausible and lexically close

but lead to contradicting claims (Habernal et al., 2018).

To be more specific, the reason R and the claim C are propositions extracted from a natural language argument. And warrant W is the relation between R and C which is characterized by a rule of inference (Newman and Marshall, 1992). Walton proposed that an argument refers to a claim based on reasons given in the premises (Walton, 1990). The most central part of this task is how to find the warrant for the given R and C. In the argument reasoning comprehension task, the organizer extracts the instances from Room for Debate section of the New York Times. After a complex crowd-sourcing process, 1970 valid instances are provided for the task. Two alternative warrants are provided as candidates, where one can justify the use of R as support for C and the other one can justify R as support for the opposite side of C. We need to reconstruct the reasoning and select the right warrant which stands for claim in this task. The average score for human is 79.8%, while for those with extensive formal training is 90.9% (Habernal et al., 2018).

In this paper, we not only pay attention to the similar part between each warrant and other information but also pay close attention to the contradictory part between two warrants. We propose a model for this task which consists of four components: sentence representation layer, attended warrant layer, enhanced attention layer and prediction layer. All the sentences are represented with word embeddings in the sentence representation layer. And to better understand the meaning of warrant, we incorporate the additional information to re-represent the two warrants. Then we apply an enhanced attention layer to emphasize the similar and contradictory part between the two alternative warrants W0 and W1. At last, we make prediction through a feedforward neural network layer (Fine,

---

[*]The corresponding author

Proceedings of the 12th International Workshop on Semantic Evaluation (SemEval-2018), pages 1104–1108
New Orleans, Louisiana, June 5–6, 2018. ©2018 Association for Computational Linguistics

2001). In addition to the primary model, we propose an ensemble method to achieve a stable and credible accuracy. This method is well established for obtaining highly accurate classifiers by combining less accurate ones (Dietterich, 2000). Our model improves the accuracy by 4% compared to the baseline model.

2 Model Description

Our hierarchical attention model is composed of the following major components: sentence representation, attened warrant layer, enhanced attention layer and prediction layer. Figure 1 shows a high-level view of sentence representation and attended warrant layer. And Figure 2 shows a high-level view of the enhanced attention layer and prediction layer. Our code is implemented with TensorFlow and is available on github [1].

In the attended warrant layer, we pay attention to the relevant part between each warrant and other information, and get two attended representation for the two warrants. While in the enhanced attention layer, we focus on the similarities and differences between two attended warrants. The output of our model is the predicted label for each instance, where label 0 means warrant0 stands for the claim and label 1 means warrant1 does.

2.1 Sentence Representation

We implement five BiLSTM networks with shared weights to learn each of the sentence representation. It is reasonable to use shared weights among BiLSTM networks because all the sentences are in the same vector space. The input of BiLSTM network is the sentence represented with word embeddings. For later use, we use $w0$ for the hidden states of W0 generated by the BiLSTM at time i over the input sequence. And $w1$, c, r, d for the hidden states of W1, C, R and D information at each time step.

$$w0_i = BiLSTM(W0, i), \forall i \in [1, ..., l_{W0}] \quad (1)$$

$$w1_j = BiLSTM(W1, j), \forall j \in [1, ..., l_{W1}] \quad (2)$$

$$c_k = BiLSTM(C, k), \forall k \in [1, ..., l_C] \quad (3)$$

$$r_m = BiLSTM(R, m), \forall m \in [1, ..., l_R] \quad (4)$$

$$d_n = BiLSTM(D, n), \forall n \in [1, ..., l_D] \quad (5)$$

Where l_{W0}, l_{W1}, l_C, l_R and l_D are the length of W0, W1, C, R and D respectively.

---

[1] https://github.com/blcunlp/SemEval2018–argument_reasoning_comprehension

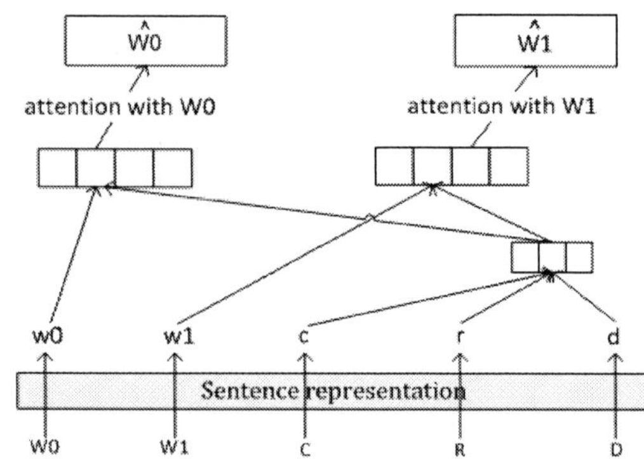

Figure 1: Sentence representation and attended warrant layer

2.2 Attended Warrant Layer

Considering the importance of the hint of reason sentence and claim sentence, we try to pay attention to the most relevant part between each warrant and these additional information. So we implement standard attention mechanism over each warrant with additional information including C, R and D, which is represented with A.

$$A = [c; r; d] \quad (6)$$

For better comprehension, we apply intra-attention over each warrant. For convenience, we combine the two processes above by concatenating the two vectors for attention. For further use, we denote attention vectors for W0 and W1 as $\overline{W0}$ and $\overline{W1}$.

$$\overline{W0} = [w0; A] \quad (7)$$

$$\overline{W1} = [w1; A] \quad (8)$$

Specifically, we apply attention over W0 and the concatenate vector for W0 as the following formulas (Tan et al., 2015). We can get $\hat{W0}_i$ to represent the vector for W0 after attention.

$$M0_i = \tanh(Uw0_i + V\overline{W0}) \quad (9)$$

$$S0_i \propto \exp(wM0_i(t)) \quad (10)$$

$$\hat{W0}_i = w0_i S0_i \quad (11)$$

Where U, V and w are attention weight parameters. In the same way, we can compute $\hat{W1}_j$ to represent the vector for W1 after attention.

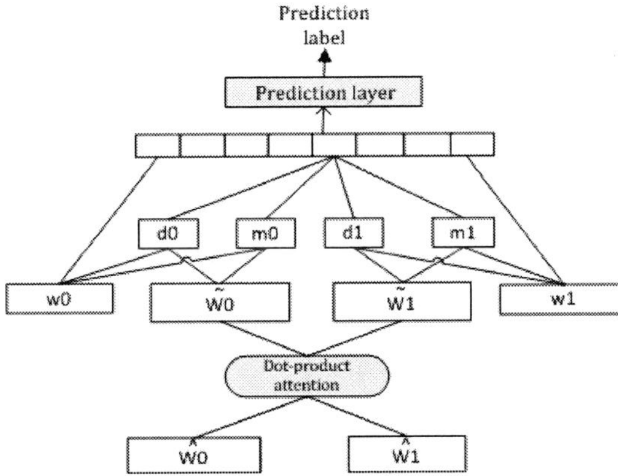

Figure 2: Enhanced attention layer and prediction layer

2.3 Enhanced Attention Layer

The similar and contradictory parts of the two warrants are the most important information for argument reasoning comprehension. In the enhanced attention layer, our model align the two warrants to focus on their similarities and differences.

$$e_{i,j} = \hat{W0_i}^T \hat{W1_j} \qquad (12)$$

$$\widetilde{W0} = \sum_{j=1}^{l_{W1}} \frac{\exp(e_{i,j})}{\sum_{k=1}^{l_{W1}} \exp(e_{i,k})} \hat{W1_j} \qquad (13)$$

$$\widetilde{W1} = \sum_{i=1}^{l_{W0}} \frac{\exp(e_{i,j})}{\sum_{k=1}^{l_{W0}} \exp(e_{k,j})} \hat{W0_i} \qquad (14)$$

Where $\widetilde{W0}$ is a weighted summation of each element in W1, the relevant element in W1 is selected and represented into $\widetilde{W0}$. We can get $\widetilde{W1}$ in the same way.

To extract the different part in W0, we let $\hat{W0_i}$ subtract $\widetilde{W0}$. To get the similar part in warrant0, we let $\hat{W0_i}$ multiply $\widetilde{W0}$ (Chen et al., 2017). In the formulas, $\odot$ is element-wise multiply of two vectors. The same is performed for W1.

$$d0 = \hat{W0} - \widetilde{W0} \qquad (15)$$

$$d1 = \hat{W1} - \widetilde{W1} \qquad (16)$$

$$m0 = \hat{W0} \odot \widetilde{W0} \qquad (17)$$

$$m1 = \hat{W1} \odot \widetilde{W1} \qquad (18)$$

2.4 Prediction Layer

To make best use of all provided information, we concatenate all the representations.

$$W0\_inf = [\hat{W0}; d0; m0] \qquad (19)$$

$$W1\_inf = [\hat{W1}; d1; m1] \qquad (20)$$

$$all\_info = [W0\_inf; W1\_inf] \qquad (21)$$

We implement a simple feedforward neural network to make the final prediction.

2.5 Model Ensemble

Ensemble learning helps improve machine learning performance by combining several models (Zhou, 2012). This approach allows the production of a better predictive performance compared to a single model. To improve and stabilize the performance of our model, we ensemble different models by majority voting strategy. We choose five models which have best performance on development data. The final result is better than every single model.

3 Experiments

3.1 Dataset

The argument reasoning comprehension task chooses the Room for Debate section of the New York Times as source data. The given reason sentences come from stance-taking comments, and the false warrant is generated by annotators. It is validated manually that the created false warrant can prove the reason which will lead to the opposite claim. And the right warrant is written by minimal modifications to the false one, which can ensure that this warrant can be inferred from the reason and stands for the claim. And also, to evaluate the performance of the models, each instance in the dataset is represented as a tuple (R;C;W0;W1) along with a label (0 or 1). If the label is 0, W0 is the correct warrant, otherwise W1. More details about dataset can be found in the work of Habernal (2018)

All the data of the argument reasoning comprehension task is provided in the GitHub by task organizers[2]. For the availability and validity, after complex manual processing, only 1955 instances are selected from 11k comments.

3.2 Experimental Setup

We use the development set to select models for testing. Training details are as follows. We use ADAM optimizer (Kingma and Ba, 2014) for training, setting the first hyperparameter to be

---

[2]the data can be found in github https://github.com/habernal/semeval2018-task12/tree/master/data

0.9 and the second 0.999. The initial learning rate is 0.001 and the batch size is 32. We use word2vec((Mikolov et al., 2013)) to pre-train the word embedding of 300 dimention and keep them from updating while training. The numbers of hidden units and layers of biLSTM networks are 64 and 1 respectively. And the dropout rate is set to be 0.1, and is applied to all biLSTM networks. For the prediction layer, we choose standard FNN with 1 layer and set the hidden cells number to 64.

3.3 Evaluation Method

We use accuracy to evaluate the performance of the models, that is, computing the ratio of the right predicted labels of all instances. A scorer and detail information are described in the task introduction website[3].The scorer can give us the expected accuracy of the model.

3.4 Results

models	dev acc	test acc
baseline model	0.632	0.548
attention model	0.653	0.585
hierarchical model	0.672	0.599
ensemble model-3	0.670	0.602
ensemble model-5	0.686	0.606
ensemble model-7	0.681	0.610

Table 1: results of different models

Table 1 shows the accuracy of different models on development dataset and test dataset. The first row is a baseline model which uses intra-warrant attention between two warrants (Habernal et al., 2018). In this model, all the representations of input sentences except warrant0 are concatenated as an attention vector for warrant0 , and all sentences except warrant1 are concatenated as an attention vector for warrant1. And the attentive representations is used for prediction .

To evaluate the performance of each part of our model, we implement experiments on different parts of our model. The attention model in Table1 includes three parts: sentence representation, attended warrant layer and prediction layer. In the prediction layer, the two attended warrant vectors are used to predict the right label. And the third model is a single hierarchical attention model, which adds the enhanced attention layer

based on the second model. The accuracy improved by 1.4% on the test data.

We use an ensemble method for different models with majority voting strategy. As we can see in Table 1, the ensemble model for 5 single models achieves the highest accuracy on development dataset.

3.5 Results Analysis

For the attended warrant layer, we use shared weights of biLSTM networks to get the representations of sentences. Also we implement intra-attention over each warrant and implement attention over each warrant and other sentences. These changes help to better understand and represent the warrant meaning itself. We introduce intra-attention to emphasize the important meaning in the warrant sentence. The alignment over warrants and the additional information provide the relativity of words in warrant and other sentences. With these attention information, we can see there is an improvement of 2%.

In the enhanced attention layer based on attended warrant layer, we emphasize the similar part and the contrary part between two warrants. The difference of attended warrant0 and warrant1 focuses on the contrary information and the multiplication of attended warrant0 and warrant1 emphasizes the similar part. So the model assigns different weights to different words of warrants according to their relativity. We can see there is about 2% points improvement for this part.

All the results mentioned above are based on the single model. And to get more stable performance, we use an ensemble method for different single models. In our experiment, the top 5 models voting result shows the best performance on development dataset, and the top 7 models voting result shows the best performance on test dataset.

4 Conclusion

In this paper, we propose a hierarchical attention model to select the supporting warrant for the argument. The model performs well in SemEval-2018 Task12: The Argument Reasoning Comprehension Task. We find that the information from both the similar part and contrary part between two alternative warrants is crucial to reconstruct the argument reasoning. Moreover, the ensemble method is of great help for the good performance and stability of our model.

---

[3]scorer can be found in https://github.com/habernal/semeval2018-task12

Acknowledgments

We would like to thank the anonymous reviewers for their helpful suggestions and comments.The research work is funded by the Natural Science Foundation of China (No.61300081), and the Fundamental Research Funds for the Central Universities in BLCU (No. 17PT05).

References

Qian Chen, Xiaodan Zhu, Zhenhua Ling, Si Wei, Hui Jiang, and Diana Inkpen. 2017. Enhanced lstm for natural language inference. pages 1657–1668.

Thomas G Dietterich. 2000. Ensemble methods in machine learning. *Proc International Workshgp on Multiple Classifier Systems*, 1857(1):1–15.

Terrence L. Fine. 2001. Feedforward neural network methodology. *Technometrics*, 42(4):432–433.

Ivan Habernal, Henning Wachsmuth, Iryna Gurevych, and Benno Stein. 2018. The argument reasoning comprehension task: Identification and reconstruction of implicit warrants. In *Proceedings of the 2018 Conference of the North American Chapter of the Association for Computational Linguistics: Human Language Technologies*, page (to appear), New Orleans, LA, USA. Association for Computational Linguistics.

Arthur Hastings. 1963. A reformulation of the modes of reasoning in argumentation.

Diederik P Kingma and Jimmy Ba. 2014. Adam: A method for stochastic optimization. *Computer Science*.

Tomas Mikolov, Kai Chen, Greg Corrado, and Jeffrey Dean. 2013. Efficient estimation of word representations in vector space. *Computer Science*.

Susan E. Newman and Catherine C. Marshall. 1992. Pushing toulmin too far: Learning from an argument representation scheme. *Xerox Parc Tech Rpt Ssl*.

Ming Tan, Bing Xiang, and Bowen Zhou. 2015. Lstm-based deep learning models for non-factoid answer selection. *CoRR*, abs/1511.04108.

Douglas Walton, Chris Reed, and Fabrizio Macagno. 2008. *Argumentation Schemes*.

Douglas N. Walton. 1990. What is reasoning? what is an argument? *Journal of Philosophy*, 87(8):399–419.

Zhi Hua Zhou. 2012. *Ensemble Methods: Foundations and Algorithms*. Taylor Francis.

YUN-HPCC at SemEval-2018 Task 12: The Argument Reasoning Comprehension Task Using a Bi-directional LSTM with Attention Model

Quanlei Liao, Xutao Yang, Jin Wang and **Xuejie Zhang**
School of Information Science and Engineering
Yunnan University
Kunming, P.R. China
Contact:xjzhang@ynu.edu.cn

Abstract

An argument is divided into two parts, the claim and the reason. To obtain a clearer conclusion, some additional explanation is required. In this task, the explanations are called warrants. This paper introduces a bi-directional long short term memory (Bi-LSTM) with an attention model to select a correct warrant from two to explain an argument. We address this question as a question-answering system. For each warrant, the model produces a probability that it is correct. Finally, the system chooses the highest correct probability as the answer. Ensemble learning is used to enhance the performance of the model. Among all of the participants, we ranked 15th on the test results.

1 Introduction

Reasoning is an important part of human logical thinking. It gives us the ability to draw fresh conclusions from some of the known points (Judea, 1988). Argument is the basis for reasoning. Except for the argument's claim and reason, usually, it needs some additional information. Therefore, what we know is the additional information and arguments reason. The claim also needs warrants for an explanation. An example is shown in Table 1.

Obviously, A is a reasonable explanation. The task is to get the reader to find a reasonable explanation for the known messages and claims in the two warrants. Due to the small number of alternative warrants, this problem can be considered to be a binary classification problem. This idea can be used as the baseline model. However, for system scalability and effectiveness, we treat this problem as the regression problem of probability prediction. The idea calculates the probability for each warrant that it is correct. Because of the diversity of natural language expression, there are

Topic	Should It Be Illegal to Declaw Your Cat?
Additional Info	With legislation pending, New York could become the first state to make removing the claws of a cat a crime.
Argument	Declawing is a crime; instead, people should be educated on proper care and training. And since ...,
Claim	It should be illegal to declaw your cat .
Warrant0	**A) owners should not have the right to be in charge of their animals.**
Warrant1	B) owners should have the right to be in charge of their animals.

Table 1: An Example of the Task.

many ways in which the same meaning can be expressed. Thus, this approach can be better to address this situation (Collobert et al., 2011).

Another benefit of addressing the problem in this way is to make the problem similar in form to the multi-choice question-answering system. The question-answering system is a classic problem of natural language processing. Many methods and models can be used for reference.

The traditional question-answering system is based on semantic and statistical methods (Alfonseca et al., 2002). This method requires an enormous background knowledge base. In addition, it is not very effective for nonstandard language expression. The state-of-the-art methods are usually based on neural networks. The trained word

Proceedings of the 12th International Workshop on Semantic Evaluation (SemEval-2018), pages 1109–1113
New Orleans, Louisiana, June 5–6, 2018. ©2018 Association for Computational Linguistics

embedding can fully express the semantics and knowledge. Therefore, the new method is usually better than the traditional statistical-based method.

In this paper, we proposed a bi-directional L-STM with an attention model. The model uses a bi-LSTM network to encode the original word embedding. Then, the semantic outputs are fed into the dense decoder with an attention mechanism. Due to the uncertainty of a single model, ensemble learning is used to enhance the performance of the model.

The remainder of the paper consists of 3 parts. The second part introduces the proposed model in detail, and the implementation is presented in the third part, while the last part presents our conclusions.

2 Model

The model contains several elements, word embeddings, the bi-directional recurrent neural network (Bi-RNN), a semantic encoder (Chen et al., 2016), the attention mechanism and dense layer decoder. Word embedding is a layer before Bi-RNN. This layer contains a map from a word index to the word embedding. This map is a pre-trained word vector look-up table. This task is dependent on semantics, and the question-answering system relies more on knowledge.Therefore, the choice of the word embedding training corpus must pay more attention to the correct grammar. Since a sentence is a whole, a single word in a semantic expression is context dependent. On the other hand, due to the variable length of the input, the Bi-RNN is the choice to complete this encoding task.

Attention mechanisms are used to remind the model of the claim's information. The final result is the probability of a fixed length. In a simple consideration, we use the full connection layer to decode under a softmax function.

2.1 Bi-directional LSTM

The RNN has a powerful ability to extract full-text features (Schuster and Paliwal, 1997), and thus, it is a good tool to obtain the word semantic information. Based on past experience, an LSTM cell is selected to avoid vanishing and exploding gradients. The LSTM is an improved RNN cell. It has two distinct improvements over traditional RNN cells. The first is the gradient problem mentioned above, and the second is the ability to carry long-

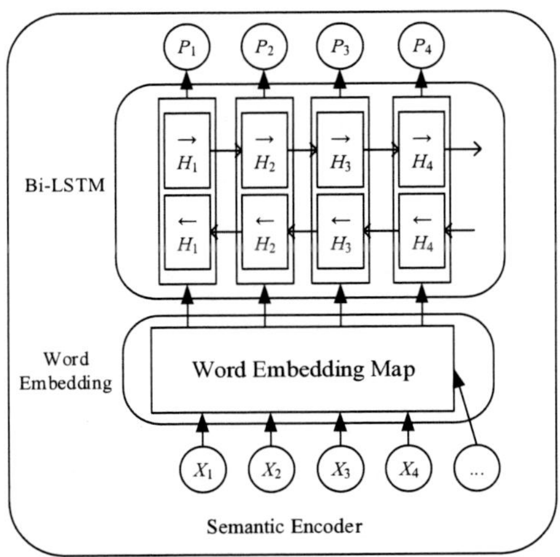

Figure 1: Semantic Encoder

term information. This arrangement is chosen because LSTM uses a gate structure to make the useful information available for long-term transmission, and the useless information can be filtered out over time. The Bi-directional network allows the forward and backward information to both be expressed.

The Bi-LSTM network is chosen to obtain semantic information over all locations in a sentence.

2.2 Semantic Encoder

Putting word embedding and Bi-LSTM together is a semantic encoder. The original text is encoded by it and has global information for each location. The structure of the semantic encoder is shown in Figure 1. The original text index sequence is fed into the encoder. Then, the word embedding layer turns it into a word embedding sequence by a pre-trained word embedding map. Bi-LSTM has forward and backward, 2 directions, to capture the global features. It outputs the combination of two directions results. The final outputs of encoder are the semantic information sequences for original text.

2.3 Attention Mechanism

Attentional mechanisms in natural language processing are usually used to provide the decoder with the source text information (Bahdanau et al., 2014). Semantic information in the original text can be fully obtained when decoding, instead of relying only on the semantic vector.

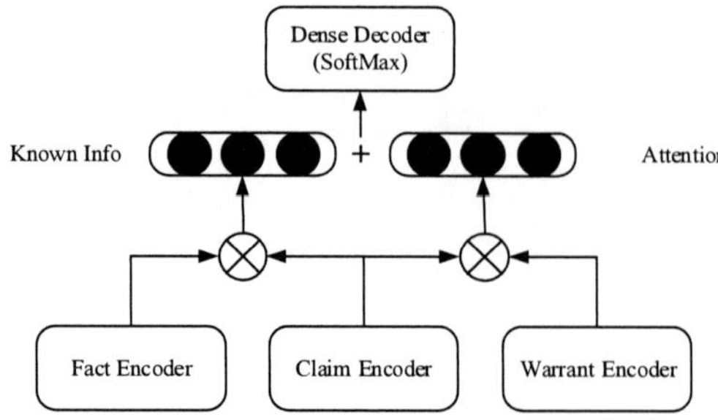

Figure 2: Model Summary

In this task, the attention mechanism is used to provide the model with the semantic information of the claim as the model is decoded.

Overall, the structure of the model is shown in Figure 2. As shown in Figure 2, the model contains 3 semantic encoders. The Fact, Claim, and Warrant are the 3 parts of the training data. Their clear definitions are presented in Part 3.1. The dot product of the two outputs of the fact encoder and claim encoder are combined with the dot product of the claim and warrants outputs. The fact and claim is referenced as known information. The result of the combination is the dense layer that is used to decode. In the decoding phase of the model, a softmax function arrives at the final prediction probability that we need. The output of the claim encoder is used twice during decoding. Its output is the attention mechanism to remind the model to focus on the valuable part of the claim.

3 Experiment

The experiment contains three parts. The first part is the selection and preprocess of experimental data. The second part is the implementation details. The third part is to show and analyze the results.

3.1 Dataset

The training corpus of the word vector, the training set of the model and the test set must be selected and processed.

As mentioned above, reading comprehension focuses more on semantic understanding (Tang et al., 2014), so GoogleNews is a good choice. Because news reports use more cautious words and more rigorous grammar. The mainstream word vector training tools are Word2Vec or GloVe. According to previous experimental results of related tasks, Word2Vec trained vector of words significantly better than GloVe (Yang et al., 2016). Thus, in this experiment, Word2vec was chosen to train the word vector.

The form of the task data is complicated. It is more difficult to obtain the data by artificial generation or online acquisition. Thus, the training data and test data are given by the official data set. Each row of the test data set is divided into several sections, including the id, topic, additional information, reason, claim, warrant0, warrant1 and label. For each row of data, it is processed into two test data of the model. Each training data contains four parts. They are fact, warrant, claim and label. Here, fact is the original topic, with additional information of reason. Warrant, claim and label are not changed. Because there are two warrants in one line, it generates two training data. This approach is similar to a question-answer system, where claim is the question, and warrant is the answer. Additionally, model is used to predict whether this answer is correct for the question.

Because English words have some special forms, such as past tense, past participle, abbreviation and so on, the lemmatisation is needed(Karr, 2006).

3.2 Implementation Detail

The model is implemented using the Keras framework with TensorFlow backend. The program based on python 3.6. The LSTM network and Bi-LSTM network are used as the baseline model.

The proposed model contains 3 semantic encoders, *i.e.*, 3 Bi-LSTM layers and 3 word embedding layers. Using the dense layer as the final decoder outputs the result. Thus, the model contains 3 hyper-parameters, including the number of units of Bi-LSTM layers (Bi-LSTM Unit Number), the dimension of the word embedding (Word Embedding Dimension) and the epochs of the training (Training Epoch).

Due to the lack of training data, when there are more parameters of the model, it is easy to cause over-fitting. There are two improvements to avoid over-fitting. The first is dropout. Dropout is a classic way to avoid over-fitting. A dropout layer is added behind each Bi-LSTM. Thus, the model has one more hyper-parameter, which is the probability of dropout (Dropout Probability).

The second method is ensemble learning. Because of the implicit relationship between claim and reason, this task is very difficult (Habernal et al., 2018). To express all of the features of the

Parameter	Pre-set Values
Bi-LSTM Unit Number	64, 96, 128
Word Embedding Dimension	200, 300
Training Epoch	5, 8
Dropout Probability	0.3, 0.4, 0.5
Ensemble Model Number	5, 7, 9, 11

Table 2: Pre-set Parameter.

Model	Acc
LSTM	0.5126
Bi-LSTM w/o ATT	0.5253
Bi-LSTM w/ ATT	0.5696

Table 3: Results of Proposed Model and Baseline Model.

input, a sufficiently complex model is required. However, too little training data is not sufficient for the model to learn all of the features. This concern is a large limitation of a single model. Ensemble learning can effectively alleviate overfitting and greatly enhance the performance of the model.

The hard voting is chosen to implement the ensemble model (Dietterich, 2000). The hard voting means training multiple models at the same time. After training, it takes all the results of the model vote. The voting results are the result of the system.

Finally, the model has a total of 5 hyperparameters, including the ensemble model number. The grid search algorithm is used as the parameter tuning method. However, because the space of the parameters are too large, a few pre-set values are used to narrow the search. The pre-set values are shown in Table 2.

3.3 Result Analysis

Because of the lack of data, the following results are the result of dev data test under official train data training unless otherwise specified. Two baseline models are used to test the performance of the proposed model. In the case of no tuning parameters, finding the average number of test results in 3 times is shown in Table 3. As seen from the results in Table 3, the attention mechanism can effectively improve the accuracy of the prediction in this task. The result is also consistent with most experimental results.

In Table 4, **Epoch** is used for the Training Epoch, **Bi-LSTM** for Bi-LSTM Unit Number, **Em-**

Ensemble Model Number	Acc
6	0.6646
7	0.6741
9	**0.6803**
11	0.6772

Table 5: Results of Ensemble Learning.

b Dim for Word Embedding Dimension, **Dropout** for Dropout Probability, and **Acc** for Accuracy, the best 3 results are shown for the parameter tuning for the single model before the ensemble learning. The time spent to tune the parameters on multiple models is very large. Hence, during the implementation of hard voting, only the number of models will be tuned. The remaining parameters are the parameters that give the best result when there is only one model. (the first line in Table 4). The results are shown in Table 5.

It can be seen that the effect on the result tends to be stable when the model is over seven. However, the improvement from ensemble learning in the results is enormous. The accuracy increased by approximately 6 percentage points.

In the official test data of the competition, we chose the hard voting with nine models. The accuracy is 0.550. We rank 15th in all 22 teams.

4 Conclusions

Due to the complexity and abstraction of the logical system of human reasoning, it is not easy for a machine to learn its laws. Thus, this task is very challenging and difficult. The attention mechanism and ensemble learning are the key points to improve the performance of the model. In the experiment, both have a very large impact on the accuracy. The final result and rankings are not very good. After analysis, there could be two reasons. The first reason is that the data cleaning was not done well. The training data is mixed with a large amount of useless information. The second point is that the model parameter tuning was very limited.

This competition has benefited us greatly. We will continue to improve our model.

Acknowledgments

This work was supported by the National Natural Science Foundation of China (NSFC) under Grant No.61702443 and No.61762091, and in part by Educational Commission of Yunnan Province of

Epoch	Bi-LSTM	Emb Dim	Dropout	Acc
8	64	300	0.3	0.6171
8	128	300	0.4	0.6107
5	64	300	0.4	0.6012

Table 4: Results of Parameter Tuning of Single Model.

China under Grant No.2017ZZX030.The authors would like to thank the anonymous reviewers and the area chairs for their constructive comments.

References

Enrique Alfonseca, Marco Boni, Jos Jara, and Suresh Manandhar. 2002. A prototype question answering system using syntactic and semantic information for answer retrieval. In *Nurs Stand*, pages 680–686.

Dzmitry Bahdanau, Kyunghyun Cho, and Yoshua Bengio. 2014. Neural machine translation by jointly learning to align and translate. *Computer Science*.

Tao Chen, Ruifeng Xu, Yulan He, and Xuan Wang. 2016. Improving sentiment analysis via sentence type classification using bilstm-crf and cnn. *Expert Systems with Applications*.

Ronan Collobert, Jason Weston, Leon Bottou, Michael Karlen, Koray Kavukcuoglu, and Pavel Kuksa. 2011. Natural language processing (almost) from scratch. *Journal of Machine Learning Research*, 12(1):2493–2537.

Thomas Dietterich. 2000. Ensemble methods in machine learning. *Proc International Workshop on Multiple Classifier Systems*, 1857(1):1–15.

Ivan Habernal, Henning Wachsmuth, Iryna Gurevych, and Benno Stein. 2018. The argument reasoning comprehension task: Identification and reconstruction of implicit warrants. In *Proceedings of the 2018 Conference of the North American Chapter of the Association for Computational Linguistics: Human Language Technologies*, page (to appear), New Orleans, LA, USA. Association for Computational Linguistics.

Pearl Judea. 1988. *Reasoning in Intelligent Systems: Networks of Plausible Inference*. Morgan Kaufmann Publishers,Inc.

Alan Karr. 2006. Exploratory data mining and data cleaning. *Proc International Workshop on Multiple Classifier Systems*, 101(473):399–399.

Mike Schuster and Kuldip Paliwal. 1997. Bidirectional recurrent neural networks. *IEEE Trans on Signal Processing*, 45(11):2673–2681.

Duyu Tang, Furu Wei, Nan Yang, Ming Zhou, Ting Liu, and Bing Qin. 2014. Learning sentiment-specific word embedding for twitter sentiment classification.

In *Meeting of the Association for Computational Linguistics*, pages 155–161.

Jinnan Yang, Bo Peng, Jin Wang, Jixian Zhang, and Xuejie Zhang. 2016. Chinese grammatical error diagnosis using single word embedding. In *Proceedings of the 3rd Workshop on Natural Language Processing Techniques for Educational Applications (NLP-TEA-16)*, pages 155–161.

HHU at SemEval-2018 Task 12: Analyzing an Ensemble-based Deep Learning Approach for the Argument Mining Task of Choosing the Correct Warrant

Matthias Liebeck, Andreas Funke, Stefan Conrad
Institute of Computer Science
Heinrich Heine University Düsseldorf
D-40225 Düsseldorf, Germany
{liebeck,conrad}@cs.uni-duesseldorf.de
andreas.funke@hhu.de

Abstract

This paper describes our participation in the SemEval-2018 Task 12 *Argument Reasoning Comprehension Task* which calls to develop systems that, given a reason and a claim, predict the correct warrant from two opposing options. We decided to use a deep learning architecture and combined 623 models with different hyperparameters into an ensemble. Our extensive analysis of our architecture and ensemble reveals that the decision to use an ensemble was suboptimal. Additionally, we benchmark a support vector machine as a baseline. Furthermore, we experimented with an alternative data split and achieved more stable results.

1 Introduction

Argument mining is a trending research domain that focuses on the extraction of arguments and their relations from text. It has been applied to multiple languages and multiple application domains, including the legal domain (Palau and Moens, 2009), persuasive essays (Stab and Gurevych, 2014), online participation (Liebeck et al., 2016), and web discourse (Habernal and Gurevych, 2017). The three most common subtasks are: argument identification, argument classification, and argument linking. These focus on the identification of argumentative text content, the extraction of argument components according to a specific argument model, and the extraction of relations between arguments components, respectively.

Currently, different argument models comprising different argument components are being used throughout the community, such as the *claim-premise family* or Toulmin's model (Toulmin, 1958). In the scope of this paper, claims, premises, and warrants are the most important argument components. Claims are often defined as controversial statements that are either true or false.

Premises are reasons that support or attack claims. In Toulmin's model, they are connected with warrants that state why the premise supports the claim.

Habernal et al. (2018b) introduced a new argument mining task called *argument reasoning comprehension* with the following definition: Given a reason and a claim, identify the correct warrant from two opposing options.

This paper describes our participation in the SemEval-2018 Task 12 *The Argument Reasoning Comprehension Task* (Habernal et al., 2018a) that uses the dataset from Habernal et al. (2018b) as a shared task. Besides a description of our machine learning systems, we evaluate additional machine learning models (we were only allowed to submit a single set of predictions for the official ranking) and we further analyze the test set.

The dataset for the challenge consists of annotated news comments from the New York Times user debate section. With Amazon Mechanical Turk as a crowdsourcing platform, 5000 randomly selected user comments were annotated in a multi-step annotation process that included three free text annotation steps (gist summarization, the creation of warrants, and of alternative warants). After the final filtering, the dataset for the Argument Reasoning Comprehesion Task comprises 1970 instances, where each instance is a tuple of (R, C, W, AW, G, T, I) comprising a reason (R), a claim (C), a warrant (W), an alternative warrant (AW), a gold label (G) indicating which of both warrants is correct, a debate title (T), and additional debate information (I) about the debate. The task organizers split the dataset into three distinct groups: training set (1,210 instances), development set (316 instances), and a test set (444 instances).

Figure 1 shows a training example of the dataset. The machine learning task of predicting the correct warrant is difficult since both warrants

Proceedings of the 12th International Workshop on Semantic Evaluation (SemEval-2018), pages 1114–1119
New Orleans, Louisiana, June 5–6, 2018. ©2018 Association for Computational Linguistics

---

Title: Do We Still Need Libraries?
Debate information: Do We Still Need Libraries? What are libraries for, and how should they evolve?
Claim: We need libraries
Reason: Libraries have lots to offer in addition to books they provide music, dvd's, magazines and more.
✓ **Warrant 1**: all these things are readily available to everyone online
✗ **Warrant 2**: none of these things are readily available to everyone online

---

Figure 1: Example of a training instance with warrant 1 as the correct gold label.

are lexically similar, and can differ in just one or two words.

In the trial phase of the challenge, the participants were given access to the training set and the dev test with gold labels. In the test phase of the challenge, the task participants were given access to the test set (with omitted gold labels) and had to submit predictions for all test instances.

2 Our Approach

For our participation in the challenge, we experimented with deep learning architectures in Keras (Chollet, 2015) with TensorFlow (Abadi et al., 2015) as the backend. We tested multiple deep learning architectures comprising different layers and input channels. For each of these models, we performed an extensive grid search for hyperparameters, such as layer sizes, embedding sizes, activation functions, optimizers, loss functions, batch sizes, dropout, number of training iterations, and different seeds for the initialization.

In our final experiments, we evaluated four different embeddings: pre-trained fastText embeddings (Bojanowski et al., 2017) on the entire Wikipedia corpus, two word embeddings with different dimensionality trained on the task's dataset with the word2vec (Mikolov et al., 2013) skip-gram model implemented in gensim (Řehůřek and Sojka, 2010), and a fourth embedding based on the task's vocabulary and corresponding Wikipedia articles.

We benchmarked each trained model on the development set. This yielded thousands of trained models. Ultimately, we selected a deep learning architecture with high accuracy scores and a low

variance, as outlined below. Our motivation was to select a model that we believed to be stable and able to generalize well on the test set.

2.1 Archictecture

We now outline our deep learning architecture, as visualized in Figure 2. We use warrants, reasons, claims, and alternative warrants as input channels of our neural network. The preprocessing for each channel consists of tokenization, padding, and word embeddings as representations for individual words, as it is common for recurrent neural networks in NLP. First, each input sequence is fed into a bidirectional LSTM (Schuster and Paliwal, 1997; Graves and Schmidhuber, 2005). In the next layer, we use two parallel LSTMs (Hochreiter and Schmidhuber, 1997). The first LSTM uses a concatenation of the warrant, the reason, and the claim as the input, whereas the concatenation of the alternative warrant, reason, and claim is used as the input of the other LSTM. The output of both LSTMs is then concatenated, dropout is applied, and finally mapped as output through two dense layers.

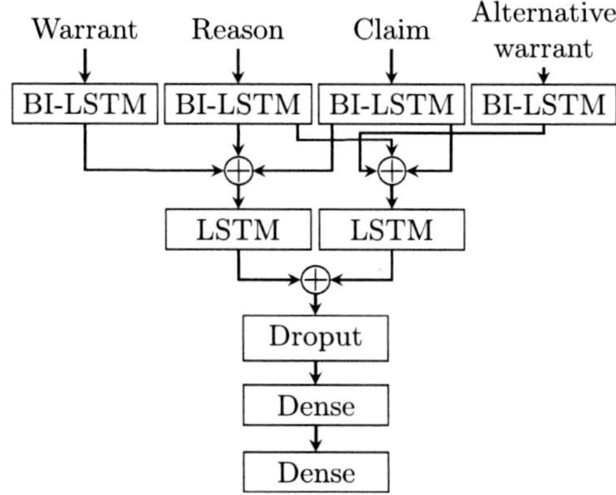

Figure 2: Illustration of our deep learning architecture.

In our experiments, we benchmarked our model with 10 different seeds and achieved an average accuracy of 67.7% ($\pm$ 2.2%) on the development set.

2.2 Ensemble

We experimented with additional ways of increasing our performance on the development set under the assumption that the test set would be very similar. By using an ensemble of multiple trained models with a majority vote as the prediction, we were able to improve our results considerably. First, we trained 2560 models of the above-described architecture with four different embeddings and various hyperparameters. Then, we combined all 623 of these models with a development set accuracy of above 67% into our final ensemble. Our ensemble yielded a promising result of 73.3% accuracy on the development set, which is a higher accuracy than all submitted and benchmarked systems in the trial phase of the challenge. Therefore, we decided to use the ensemble for our predictions instead of a single model.

3 Results

We now report the official results of our ensemble on the test set, as well as benchmarks of the single models. Additionally, we compare our deep learning approaches with a support vector machine as a classical machine learning baseline.

3.1 Deep Learning

Our ensemble achieved 17th place in the competition and yielded an accuracy score of 53.4%, which was lower than we anticipated based on our good performance on the development set.

Since we were curious to see whether the decision to use an ensemble was beneficial and in order to better understand the low results on the test set, we further analyzed all trained models on the test set after the release of the gold labels. The performance difference in terms of accuracy scores on the development set and the test set of all 2560 models that we considered for the ensemble is visualized in Figure 3. It can immediately be seen that all our models achieved better scores on the development set than on the test set and that some hyperparameters lead to models yielding bad performances. The most interesting insight from this plot is that the majority of our single models performed better than the ensemble score of 53.4%. Upon further analysis of the 623 models with a development set accuracy of above 67% that we used for our ensemble, we can observe an average accuracy score of 54.4% ($\pm$ 2.0%) on the test set. This also shows that the decision to opt for an ensemble was disadvantageous, since the ensemble was not able to generalize better than individual models.

The influence of the number of selected models from the 2560 available models is further visualized in Figure 4a, where the models were be-

ing added in descending order based on the development set performance. In our submission, we decided to use the 623 best-ranked models with a majority voting. Figure 4a shows that an ensemble with a considerably smaller number of models would have performed better on both sets, as the test scores with the majority voting began to deteriorate quickly.

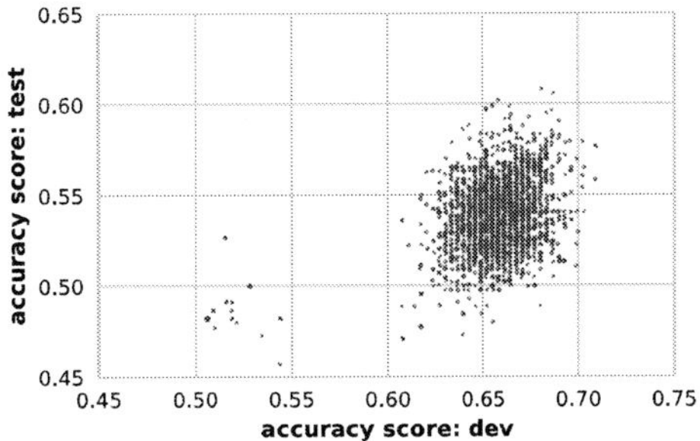

Figure 3: Performances of 2560 trained models with different hyperparameters on the development set and the test set

3.2 Support Vector Machine Baseline

Furthermore, we compared our deep learning approaches with a support vector machine (SVM). We used the same input data for the SVM as for our neural networks by using claims, reasons, warrants, and alternative warrants. All four input strings were tokenized, padded to a fixed length, represented by embedding vectors, and concatenated to achieve a fixed input length for the SVM.

In total, we trained 72 SVMs with different hyperparameters. Their performances on both sets are visualized in Figure 5. Compared with our deep learning approach, the results of the SVMs on the development set are lower, with an average score of 58.8% ($\pm$ 2.8%), but comparable for the test set, with 53.6% ($\pm$ 2.3%). Again, we observed lower accuracies for the test set than for the development set.

4 Observations of an Alternative Data Split

The performance difference on both sets motivated us repeat our experiments on an alternative data split, in which we shuffled all data points together and created three new sets (training, development, and test) with the same sizes as the original split.

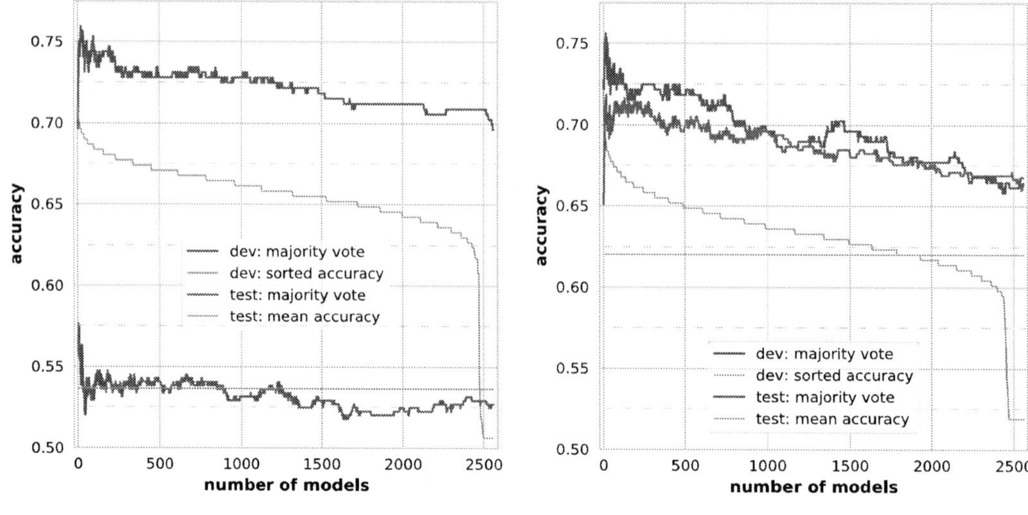

(a) Original dataset   (b) Ensemble experiment with our alternative data split

Figure 4: Influence of the number of models in our ensemble.

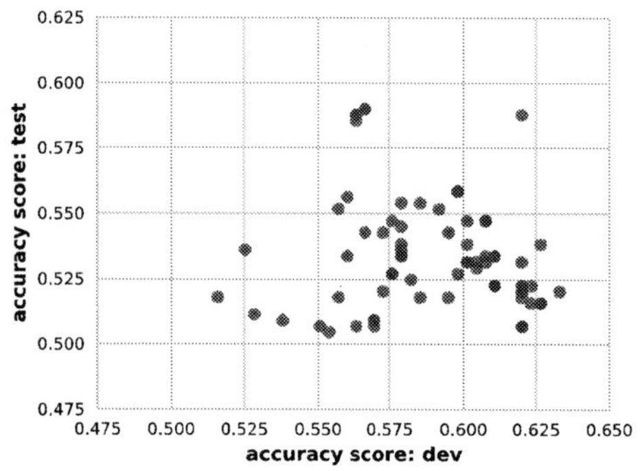

Figure 5: Performances of support vector machines on the development set and the test set.

4.1 Single Model

On the alternative split, we benchmarked our single model with 20 different seeds and achieved higher results of 63.7% ($\pm$ 1.6%) on the dev set and 62.1% ($\pm$ 2.5%) on the test set.

4.2 Ensemble

For the ensemble, we trained 2560 models with the same hyperparameters as for the original dataset. The models behaved more similarly on both the alternative development set (63% ($\pm$ 3.0%)) and the test set (62% ($\pm$ 4.1%)), as visualized in Figure 6. If we take a look at the performance of the ensemble's majority vote in Figure 4b and compare it with the original dataset in Figure 4a, we can see

that the idea of using an ensemble can be beneficial. However, this is dependent on a more evenly represented data split. In hindsight - with posterior knowledge of the test set - it would have been a better choice to decide for the ensemble's peak performance (original split dev: 76%, test: 55.6%; alternative split dev: 75.6%, test: 71.3%).

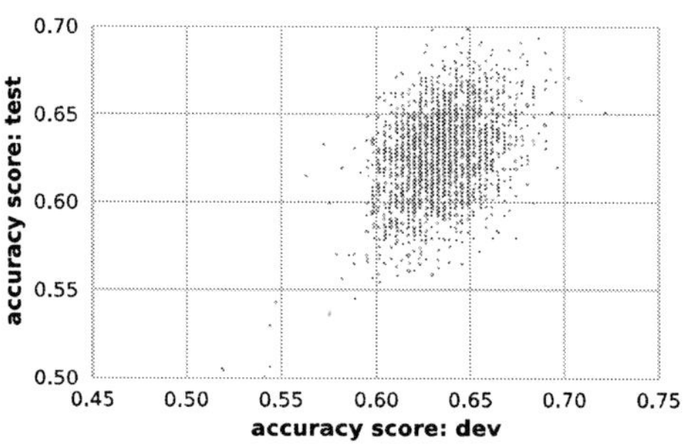

Figure 6: Performances of 2560 trained models with different hyperparameters on the alternative data split.

4.3 Support Vector Machine

We again trained 72 SVMs with different hyperparameters. With the alternative split, we achieved an average score of 55.5% ($\pm$ 2.3%) on the new dev set and 57.7% ($\pm$ 2.1%) on the new test set. Compared with our neural network, the SVM approach now performs worse.

1117

5 Conclusion

For our participation in *The Argument Reasoning Comprehension Task*, we benchmarked several deep learning approaches with different layers, embeddings, and hyperparameters. For our final submission, we decided to use an ensemble comprising 623 models with a majority voting that performed much better on the development set than a single model.

Unfortunately, our ensemble underperformed on the test set. Therefore, we extensively analyzed our ensemble approach after the release of the gold labels. We ascertained that the use of an ensemble was a suboptimal choice, and the predictions of most single models would have performed better and that the choices of hyperparameters and seeds influenced the stability of the predictions, as illustrated in Figure 3.

We compared our deep learning approach with a support vector machine as a baseline. Although our models and our ensemble performed much better on the development set, the SVM produced slightly better results on the test set.

Finally, we repeated our experiments on an alternative data split and achieved more stable results. Therefore, we conclude that the test set comprises data points with characteristics that are not present in the original training data.

Because we - and other task participants with deep learning approaches - had trouble providing a satisfying solution to the task, we also believe that additional preprocessing steps are required for a machine learning approach, since the warrants and alternative warrants are so lexically similar.

Acknowledgments

This work was funded by the PhD program *Online Participation*, supported by the North Rhine-Westphalian funding scheme *Fortschrittskollegs*. Computational support and infrastructure were provided by the "Centre for Information and Media Technology" (ZIM) at the University of Düsseldorf (Germany).

References

Martín Abadi, Ashish Agarwal, Paul Barham, Eugene Brevdo, Zhifeng Chen, Craig Citro, Greg S. Corrado, Andy Davis, Jeffrey Dean, Matthieu Devin, Sanjay Ghemawat, Ian Goodfellow, Andrew Harp, Geoffrey Irving, Michael Isard, Yangqing Jia, Rafal Jozefowicz, Lukasz Kaiser, Manjunath Kudlur, Josh Levenberg, Dandelion Mané, Rajat Monga, Sherry Moore, Derek Murray, Chris Olah, Mike Schuster, Jonathon Shlens, Benoit Steiner, Ilya Sutskever, Kunal Talwar, Paul Tucker, Vincent Vanhoucke, Vijay Vasudevan, Fernanda Viégas, Oriol Vinyals, Pete Warden, Martin Wattenberg, Martin Wicke, Yuan Yu, and Xiaoqiang Zheng. 2015. TensorFlow: Large-scale machine learning on heterogeneous systems. Software available from tensorflow.org.

Piotr Bojanowski, Edouard Grave, Armand Joulin, and Tomas Mikolov. 2017. Enriching Word Vectors with Subword Information. *Transactions of the Association for Computational Linguistics*, 5:135–146.

François Chollet. 2015. Keras. `https://github.com/fchollet/keras`.

Alex Graves and Jürgen Schmidhuber. 2005. Framewise phoneme classification with bidirectional LSTM and other neural network architectures. *Neural Networks*, 18(5-6):602–610.

Ivan Habernal and Iryna Gurevych. 2017. Argumentation Mining in User-Generated Web Discourse. *Computational Linguistics*, 43(1):125–179.

Ivan Habernal, Henning Wachsmuth, Iryna Gurevych, and Benno Stein. 2018a. SemEval-2018 Task 12: The Argument Reasoning Comprehension Task. In *Proceedings of the 12th International Workshop on Semantic Evaluation (SemEval-2018)*, page (to appear). Association for Computational Linguistics.

Ivan Habernal, Henning Wachsmuth, Iryna Gurevych, and Benno Stein. 2018b. The Argument Reasoning Comprehension Task: Identification and Reconstruction of Implicit Warrants. In *Proceedings of the 2018 Conference of the North American Chapter of the Association for Computational Linguistics: Human Language Technologies*, page (to appear). Association for Computational Linguistics.

Sepp Hochreiter and Jürgen Schmidhuber. 1997. Long Short-Term Memory. *Neural Comput.*, 9(8):1735–1780.

Matthias Liebeck, Katharina Esau, and Stefan Conrad. 2016. What to Do with an Airport? Mining Arguments in the German Online Participation Project Tempelhofer Feld. In *Proceedings of the Third Workshop on Argument Mining (ArgMining2016)*, pages 144–153. Association for Computational Linguistics.

Tomas Mikolov, Kai Chen, Greg Corrado, and Jeffrey Dean. 2013. Efficient Estimation of Word Representations in Vector Space. *CoRR*, abs/1301.3781.

Raquel Palau and Marie-Francine Moens. 2009. Argumentation Mining: The Detection, Classification and Structure of Arguments in Text. In *Proceedings of the 12th International Conference on Artificial Intelligence and Law, ICAIL '09*, pages 98–107. ACM.

Radim Řehůřek and Petr Sojka. 2010. Software Framework for Topic Modelling with Large Corpora. In *Proceedings of the LREC 2010 Workshop on New Challenges for NLP Frameworks*, pages 45–50. ELRA.

Mike Schuster and Kuldip Paliwal. 1997. Bidirectional Recurrent Neural Networks. *IEEE Trans. Signal Processing*, 45(11):2673–2681.

Christian Stab and Iryna Gurevych. 2014. Identifying Argumentative Discourse Structures in Persuasive Essays. In *Proceedings of the 2014 Conference on Empirical Methods in Natural Language Processing (EMNLP 2014)*, pages 46–56. Association for Computational Linguistics.

Stephen Toulmin. 1958. *The Uses of Argument*. Cambridge University Press.

YNU_Deep at SemEval-2018 Task 12: A BiLSTM Model with Neural Attention for Argument Reasoning Comprehension

Peng Ding, Xiaobing Zhou*

School of Information Science and Engineering

Yunnan University, Yunnan, P.R. China

*Corresponding author, `zhouxb.cn@gmail.com`

Abstract

This paper describes the system submitted to SemEval-2018 Task 12 (The Argument Reasoning Comprehension Task). Enabling a computer to understand a text so that it can answer comprehension questions is still a challenging goal of NLP. We propose a Bidirectional LSTM (BiLSTM) model that reads two sentences separated by a delimiter to determine which warrant is correct. We extend this model with a neural attention mechanism that encourages the model to make reasoning over the given claims and reasons. Officially released results show that our system ranks 6th among 22 submissions to this task.

1 Introduction

Machine comprehension of text is an important problem in natural language processing. Traditional approaches to machine comprehension are based on either hand engineered grammars (Riloff and Thelen, 2000), or information extraction methods (Poon et al., 2010).

Recently, recurrent neural networks (RNNs) with long short-term memory (LSTM) cells (Hochreiter and Schmidhuber, 1997) have been successfully applied to a wide range of NLP tasks, such as machine translation (Sutskever et al., 2014), constituency parsing (Vinyals et al., 2015), language modeling (Zaremba et al., 2014) and machine comprehension (Hermann et al., 2015). A potential issue with the LSTM models is that a neural network needs to be able to compress all the necessary information of a source sentence into a fixed-length vector (Bahdanau et al., 2014). This may make it difficult for the neural network to cope with long sentences. In order to address this issue, attention mechanisms have been successfully extended to the LSTMs. Attentive Reader (Hermann et al., 2015) used a $tanh$ layer to compute the attention between document and question embeddings. This allows a model to focus on the aspects of a document that it believes helpful to answer a question. The attention-based LSTM models have achieved state-of-the-art results in machine comprehension tasks (Kadlec et al., 2016; Chen et al., 2016; Tseng et al., 2016).

The argument reasoning comprehension task has been presented by (Habernal et al., 2018). The problem can be described as follows: Given an argument consisting of a claim and a reason, the goal is to select the correct warrant that explains reasoning of this particular argument. Compared to traditional machine comprehension task, argument reasoning comprehension requires models to possess extra reasoning abilities. Some models increase the depth of the network, continuously updating the representations of the documents and questions to realize the reasoning process (Sukhbaatar et al., 2015; Tseng et al., 2016; Dhingra et al., 2017; Sordoni et al., 2016).

In this paper, we use a BiLSTM model to encode the reason and claim pairs (reason-claim) and warrants. Then a word-to-sentence neural attention mechanism is implemented to improve the model performance.

The rest of the paper is organized as follows: Section 2 provides the details of the proposed model; Experimental settings and results are discussed in section 3. Finally, we draw conclusions in section 4.

2 System Description

Firstly, we concatenate the reason-claim and warrants with a delimiter, then we encode the reason-claim via a BiLSTM. A second BiLSTM with different parameters is used to encode the delimiter and the warrants, but its memory state is initialized with the last cell state of the previous BiLSTM. The attention mechanism is implemented by the

Proceedings of the 12th International Workshop on Semantic Evaluation (SemEval-2018), pages 1120–1123

New Orleans, Louisiana, June 5–6, 2018. ©2018 Association for Computational Linguistics

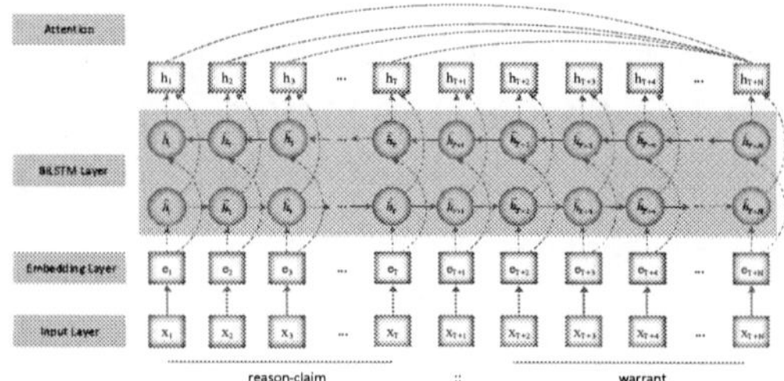

Figure 1: Our BiLSTM model with neural attention for argument reasoning comprehension, basically follows the attention model described in (Rocktäschel et al., 2015).

last output vector of the second BiLSTM and the output vector at each time step produced by the first BiLSTM. Then we use a $tanh$ activation to obtain the final representation. Finally, we predict the correct label via a fully connected layer and a $softmax$ activation.

2.1 LSTM & BiLSTM

Recurrent Neural Networks (RNNs) have been widely exploited to deal with variable-length sequence input. RNNs are networks with loops in them, allowing information to persist. A potential issue of RNNs is that they become unable to learn to connect the previous information when the length of the document grows. LSTM (Hochreiter and Schmidhuber, 1997) is one of the popular variations of RNN to mitigate the gradient vanish problem. LSTMs have three gates: input gate, forget gate and output gate. Gates are a way to optionally let information through. With these gates, LSTMs can remember information for long periods of time and avoid the long-term dependency problem. Given an input vector x_t at time step t, the previous output h_{t-1} and cell state c_{t-1}, an LSTM with hidden state size k computes the next output h_t and new cell state c_t as:

$$H = \begin{bmatrix} x_t \\ h_{t-1} \end{bmatrix} \qquad (1)$$

$$i_t = \sigma(W_i H + b_i) \qquad (2)$$

$$f_t = \sigma(W_f H + b_f) \qquad (3)$$

$$o_t = \sigma(W_o H + b_o) \qquad (4)$$

$$c_t = f_t \odot c_{t-1} + i_t \odot \tanh(W_c H + b_c) \qquad (5)$$

$$h_t = o_t \odot \tanh(c_t) \qquad (6)$$

where W_i, W_f, W_o, W_c are trained matrices, b_i, b_f, b_o, b_c are trained biases, σ and $\odot$ denote the

sigmoid function and the element-wise multiplication of two vectors, respectively.

Single direction LSTM has one drawback of not using the contextual information from the future tokens. BiLSTM exploits both the previous and future context by processing the sequence on two directions and generates two independent sequences of LSTM output vectors. One processes the input sequence in the forward direction, while the other processes the input in the backward direction. The output at each time step is the concatenation of the two output vectors from both directions, i.e. $h_t = \overrightarrow{h_t} \parallel \overleftarrow{h_t}$.

2.2 Attention

The LSTM model can alleviate the problem of gradient vanishing, but this problem persists in long range contexts. The attention mechanism is introduced to address this issue. Attention is the idea of freeing the encoder-decoder architecture from the fixed-length internal representation. This is achieved by keeping the intermediate outputs from the encoder LSTM and training the model to learn to pay selective attention to these inputs and relate them to items in the output sequence. These attention-based models have achieved state-of-the-art performance on many natural language processing tasks.

Let $C \in \mathbb{R}^{k \times T}$ be a matrix consisting of output vectors $[h_1, h_2, \dots, h_T]$ produced by the first BiLSTM when reading the T words of the reason-claim, where k is a hyperparameter denoting the hidden units of LSTM. Moreover, let h_{T+N} be the last output vector after the reason-claim and warrant are processed by the two BiLSTMs, respectively. The attention mechanism will produce a vector of attention weights and a weighted representation r of the reason-claim via:

$$M = \tanh(W_c + W_h h_{T+N} \otimes e_T) \qquad (7)$$

$$\alpha = softmax(W_m M) \qquad (8)$$

$$r = C\alpha \qquad (9)$$

where e_T is a vector of ones, $W_c, W_h \in \mathbb{R}^{k \times k}$ are trained projection matrices. $W_m \in \mathbb{R}^k$ is a trained parameter vector. The final sentence-pair representation is obtained from a non-linear combination of the attention-weighted representation r of the reason-claim and the last output vector

h_{T+N} using

$$h^* = \tanh(W_i r + W_j h_{T+N}) \qquad (10)$$

where $W_i, W_j \in \mathbb{R}^{k \times k}$ are trained projection matrices.

3 Experiments

The organizers provided training, development, and test sets, containing 1210, 316, 444 instances, respectively. We combine the reason and claim to one sentence which can determine if the warrant is correct or not. The word tokenizer we adopted is $TweetTokenizer$ in Natural Language Toolkit (NLTK[1]).

We compare two word embedding tools, Word2Vec (Mikolov et al., 2013) and GloVe (Pennington et al., 2014). Out-of-vocabulary words in the data sets are randomly initialized by sampling values uniformly from (-0.25, 0.25) and optimized during training. We set $epoch$ = 10, $batchsize$ = 256 and $LSTMUnits$ = 64. Optimization is carried out using Adaptive Moment Estimation (Adam). All models are attention-based LSTM or BiLSTM architecture.

Model	Tool	Dev Acc	Test Acc
LSTM	Word2Vec	0.626	**0.577**
LSTM	GloVe	**0.646**	0.567

Table 1: Comparison between Word2Vec and GloVe. GloVe performs better on dev data set, but Word2Vec outperforms GloVe on test data set.

We additionally try bidirectional LSTMs through experiments. Given the small scale of the data sets, we run each model 10 times, taking their average as the final result. We also use data augmentation such as shuffle the sentence order to expand the data set. Specifically, we randomize the word order of the reason-claims and the warrants to double the data set. A $randomseed$ is set to ensure our results are reproducible.

Model	Dev Acc	Test Acc
BiLSTM	**0.690**	**0.583**
BiLSTM+Shuffle	0.642	0.570

Table 2: Performance on models with or without shuffle. Both models are based on attention-based BiLSTM + GloVe architecture.

The results show that data augmentation like shuffling the sentence order does not have much

[1] http://www.nltk.org/

effect on the performance of our models. So, we use the attention-based BiLSTM model as our final system to the task. Our final result on the test set is 0.583, which ranks 6th according to the official ranking.

4 Conclusion and Future Work

In this paper, we present a BiLSTM model for argument reasoning comprehension. We adopt a word-to-sentence attention mechanism to make model perform better. In the future, we will utilize external knowledge to enhance the reasoning ability of our models. We will also pay more attention to the generalization of models on small data sets.

Acknowledgments

This work was supported by the Natural Science Foundations of China No.61463050, No.617-02443, No.61762091, the NSF of Yunnan Province No. 2015FB113, the Project of Innovative Research Team of Yunnan Province.

References

Dzmitry Bahdanau, Kyunghyun Cho, and Yoshua Bengio. 2014. Neural machine translation by jointly learning to align and translate. *arXiv preprint arXiv:1409.0473*.

Danqi Chen, Jason Bolton, and Christopher D Manning. 2016. A thorough examination of the cnn/daily mail reading comprehension task. In *Proceedings of the 54th Annual Meeting of the Association for Computational Linguistics (Volume 1: Long Papers)*, volume 1, pages 2358–2367.

Bhuwan Dhingra, Hanxiao Liu, Zhilin Yang, William Cohen, and Ruslan Salakhutdinov. 2017. Gated-attention readers for text comprehension. In *Proceedings of the 55th Annual Meeting of the Association for Computational Linguistics (Volume 1: Long Papers)*, volume 1, pages 1832–1846.

Ivan Habernal, Henning Wachsmuth, Iryna Gurevych, and Benno Stein. 2018. The Argument Reasoning Comprehension Task: Identification and Reconstruction of Implicit Warrants. In *16th Annual Conference of the North American Chapter of the Association for Computational Linguistics: Human Language Technologies*. Association for Computational Linguistics.

Karl Moritz Hermann, Tomas Kocisky, Edward Grefenstette, Lasse Espeholt, Will Kay, Mustafa Suleyman, and Phil Blunsom. 2015. Teaching machines to read and comprehend. In *Advances in Neural Information Processing Systems*, pages 1693–1701.

Sepp Hochreiter and Jürgen Schmidhuber. 1997. Long short-term memory. *Neural computation*, 9(8):1735–1780.

Rudolf Kadlec, Martin Schmid, Ondřej Bajgar, and Jan Kleindienst. 2016. Text understanding with the attention sum reader network. In *Proceedings of the 54th Annual Meeting of the Association for Computational Linguistics (Volume 1: Long Papers)*, volume 1, pages 908–918.

Tomas Mikolov, Ilya Sutskever, Kai Chen, Greg S Corrado, and Jeff Dean. 2013. Distributed representations of words and phrases and their compositionality. In *Advances in neural information processing systems*, pages 3111–3119.

Jeffrey Pennington, Richard Socher, and Christopher Manning. 2014. Glove: Global vectors for word representation. In *Proceedings of the 2014 conference on empirical methods in natural language processing (EMNLP)*, pages 1532–1543.

Hoifung Poon, Janara Christensen, Pedro Domingos, Oren Etzioni, Raphael Hoffmann, Chloe Kiddon, Thomas Lin, Xiao Ling, Alan Ritter, Stefan Schoenmackers, et al. 2010. Machine reading at the university of washington. In *Proceedings of the NAACL HLT 2010 First International Workshop on Formalisms and Methodology for Learning by Reading*, pages 87–95. Association for Computational Linguistics.

Ellen Riloff and Michael Thelen. 2000. A rule-based question answering system for reading comprehension tests. In *Proceedings of the 2000 ANLP/NAACL Workshop on Reading comprehension tests as evaluation for computer-based language understanding sytems-Volume 6*, pages 13–19. Association for Computational Linguistics.

Tim Rocktäschel, Edward Grefenstette, Karl Moritz Hermann, Tomáš Kočiský, and Phil Blunsom. 2015. Reasoning about entailment with neural attention. *arXiv preprint arXiv:1509.06664*.

Alessandro Sordoni, Philip Bachman, Adam Trischler, and Yoshua Bengio. 2016. Iterative alternating neural attention for machine reading. *arXiv preprint arXiv:1606.02245*.

Sainbayar Sukhbaatar, Jason Weston, Rob Fergus, et al. 2015. End-to-end memory networks. In *Advances in neural information processing systems*, pages 2440–2448.

Ilya Sutskever, Oriol Vinyals, and Quoc V Le. 2014. Sequence to sequence learning with neural networks. In *Advances in neural information processing systems*, pages 3104–3112.

Bo-Hsiang Tseng, Sheng-syun Shen, Hung-Yi Lee, and Lin-Shan Lee. 2016. Towards machine comprehension of spoken content: Initial toefl listening comprehension test by machine. *Interspeech 2016*, pages 2731–2735.

Oriol Vinyals, Łukasz Kaiser, Terry Koo, Slav Petrov, Ilya Sutskever, and Geoffrey Hinton. 2015. Grammar as a foreign language. In *Advances in Neural Information Processing Systems*, pages 2773–2781.

Wojciech Zaremba, Ilya Sutskever, and Oriol Vinyals. 2014. Recurrent neural network regularization. *arXiv preprint arXiv:1409.2329*.

UniMelb at SemEval-2018 Task 12: Generative Implication using LSTMs, Siamese Networks and Semantic Representations with Synonym Fuzzing

Anirudh Joshi[1,2]   **Timothy Baldwin**[1]   **Richard O. Sinnott**[1]
Cecile Paris[2]

[1] The University of Melbourne   [2] CSIRO Data61

anirudhj@student.unimelb.edu.au, tb@ldwin.net
rsinnott@unimelb.edu.au, cecile.paris@data61.csiro.au

Abstract

This paper describes a warrant classification system for SemEval 2018 Task 12, that attempts to learn semantic representations of reasons, claims and warrants. The system consists of 3 stacked LSTMs: one for the reason, one for the claim, and one shared Siamese Network for the 2 candidate warrants. Our main contribution is to force the embeddings into a shared feature space using vector operations, semantic similarity classification, Siamese networks, and multi-task learning. In doing so, we learn a form of generative implication, in encoding implication interrelationships between reasons, claims, and the associated correct and incorrect warrants. We augment the limited data in the task further by utilizing WordNet synonym "fuzzing". When applied to SemEval 2018 Task 12, our system performs well on the development data, and officially ranked 8th among 21 teams.

1 Introduction

This paper describes our system for the *Argument Reasoning Comprehension Task of SemEval 2018* (Habernal et al., 2018). The main goal of our system is to learn semantic representations of reasons, claims and warrants upon which vector operations can be applied which encode their interrelationships, whilst sharing encodings.

We train our system over the 1274 candidate reason, claim, first and second warrant examples from the edited *Room for Debate* New York Times dataset provided by the task organizers (Habernal et al., 2018), which we augment to generate a dataset that is used with a multi-task based objective function to learn semantically meaningful representations.

Our system combines these vectors to make a determination, via vector operations and semantic similarity classification, to determine which of the two warrants best fits the reason and claim representations, and best encodes the relationships between them. We replicate this for each sentence type, and mirror it for each warrant. In doing so we were able to achieve strong results on the development set, and ranked 8th overall in the competition.

2 Approach

2.1 Model Overview

As detailed in Figure 1, our system is made up of 3 stacked LSTMs, with one being essentially a Siamese network shared between the two warrants, and the other two encoding the reason and the claim. We take an average pool over the top-layer hidden representations and use them as the semantic feature vectors for each respective sentence. We take these semantic vectors and apply vector operations to them to generate embeddings for each reason, claim and warrant, which we found in practice to perform well. We then do semantic comparisons between the generated and actual encodings, marking as the same those between generated and actual encodings that include the correct warrant (i.e. correct interrelationships) and not the same for those that do not (through a logistic unit). We also do a joint loss on both warrant's logistic output with a softmax to the ground truth (same/not same), and use that as our tracking metric during training.

We tokenize each sentence using Keras (Chollet, 2018) and utilize an embedding layer based on the GloVe 300-dimensional, 840 billion token, uncased word embeddings (Pennington et al., 2014). We then push these through three stacked LSTM networks (Hochreiter and Schmidhuber, 1997) — one each for the reasons, claims and warrants —

Proceedings of the 12th International Workshop on Semantic Evaluation (SemEval-2018), pages 1124–1128
New Orleans, Louisiana, June 5–6, 2018. ©2018 Association for Computational Linguistics

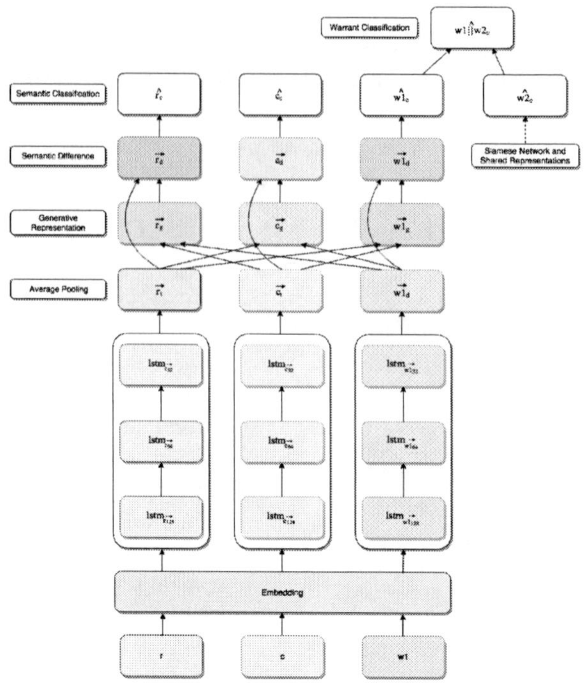

Figure 1: An overview of our model.

to generate the pooled semantic feature vectors of each phrase. Each stacked LSTM network is comprised of three layers, of 128, 64 and 32 nodes, respectively. We do this to force compression and to avoid overfitting on the dataset.

We take the final 32-dimensional embedding of each reason, claim and warrant, and apply average pooling over time to create robust compressed representations of each.

We take these representations and then perform various vector operations (addition/subtraction) between them. We use these operations as a form of implication to generate a warrant using the reason and claim representations. The generation operation does not necessarily require vector additivity (e.g. operations need not be constrained across tasks). For example the operation to learn the generative representation from a reason and a claim to a warrant can be a simple addition/subtraction, or an affine transformation, or in future scenarios it can be even more complicated dense networks.

For example given a reason and a claim, we wish to combine them together with an operation that creates a generative representation of a warrant (simple vector operations for example), and

accordingly generate a representation using the operation $\vec{r}_t - \vec{c}_t = \vec{w}_g$ (where the t subscript entails the true representation, and the g the generated one). We then set up our loss function such that we compare the absolute semantic difference between the true generative encoding (generated with the correct two representations) with that of a query encoding and compare them to determine whether or not they are the are the same (i.e. the correct or incorrect warrant vs. the true generative representation).

We additionally embed both the correct and incorrect warrant for each example, and use these representations to drive multi-task learning using a Siamese network (as each reason, claim and warrant are compared to their true generative representations with only correct triplet combinations being classified as being the same). We use Siamese networks as they have been shown to work well in settings where semantic text document comparisons are involved (Mueller and Thyagarajan, 2016).

Our objective function is intended to minimize the difference between generative and actual warrant representations, and maximize the difference between generative and incorrect warrant representations. We do this via analogy to both Deep-Face's semantic similarity classification (Taigman et al., 2014) and FaceNet's anchor representations (Schroff et al., 2015): for the similarity classification we use a logistic regression atop the absolute difference between the generative and the actual representations for the multiple tasks (same/not same), and we combine a joint softmax discriminative function that selects between the candidate warrants on that output, $\widehat{w1\|w2_c}$, as our tracking objective (for early stopping and checkpointing). In doing so we aim to push the generative and true representations closer together, and push the generative and incorrect representations further apart. In this process we should then be able to perform Generative Implication, where the semantic representations across implication tasks can be shared, but where differing operations between the representations can be used to generate each other.

Due to the small data size (~1k), we explored a variety of approaches to augment the training data. One approach is to use multiple implication tasks to generate representations. Our tasks use the two warrants and reason + conclusion to generate representations of each other. We tried multiple operations including affine transforms and dense networks, as well as vector additivity constraints across tasks (i.e. the projection operations from the shared embeddings must reconcile, cf. Mikolov et al. (2013)). However we found that they led to overfitting, and hence sought to split the implication projection from the shared representations into unconstrained operations (two of which are vector additive, $\vec{r}_g$ and $\vec{c}_g$, with $\vec{w}_g$ being split off, with the split likely acting as a regularizer):

$$\vec{r}_g = \vec{c}_t - \vec{w}_t$$
$$\vec{w}_g = \vec{r}_t - \vec{c}_t$$
$$\vec{c}_g = \vec{r}_t + \vec{w}_t$$

From this, we have a multi-task output with the generative representation of correct/incorrect warrants being compared to their semantic representations, correct with the true warrant, and incorrect with the wrong warrant.

We also augmented the data by taking random combinations of single synonym fuzzed Word-Net (Miller, 1995) sentences using their sampled closest synonyms (using the NLTK toolkit (Bird et al., 2009) and pywsd (Tan, 2014)). Through this method we generated a much larger dataset (~20×, depending on how many synonyms we could sample per sentence). We also swapped the warrants to double the size of the dataset. In doing so we ended up with ~234K examples. We did this to ensure a large enough dataset that included numerous subtleties.

2.2 Training

2.2.1 Optimization and Regularisation

We used heavy dropout (Srivastava et al., 2014), as we found overfitting to be an endemic problem, requiring heavy regularization. Along with the layers being smaller as we go up the stack, we applied progressively reduced dropout rates, from 0.8 at the 128 layer, to 0.6 (64) and 0.4 (32). We found this led to better generalization on the development set. We use Adam as our optimizer (Kingma and Ba, 2014), and checkpointing (with an accuracy max of the joint softmax with $\widehat{w1\|w2_c}$) and early stopping (Caruana et al., 2001). We trained our models using 3–10 epochs, depending on when they began to overfit.

3 Results

We ranked 8th in the competition (among 21 teams) with a test accuracy of 0.577. Amongst the teams there was a clear outlier in the GIST system (which we note used transfer learning), with the remaining systems incrementally falling from ~0.6 downwards, with the random baseline at 0.527, and the example test system at 0.56 (Habernal et al., 2018).

In terms of the different systems we trained, our top three would have ranked 4th in the competition, two of which used more aggressive dropout, and one of which used a combination of features identified above (including attention between the other two sentences). The development to test set gap was wide, indicating generalization was extremely hard (similarly with others in the competition). In terms of performance, we found early on that constrained (i.e. vector additive operations) led to lower development performance, which continued on to the test set. With the remaining systems we used the operations as defined previously (unconstrained). In general we found that regularization dominates performance measures, above and beyond operations.

System	Development	Test
Higher Starting Dropout (0.9)	0.658	0.597
Lower Dropout Reduction Between LSTM Layers (0.1)	0.658	0.592
Combination	0.668	0.592
Equal Dropout on each LSTM Layer (0.5)	0.646	0.583
Extra Layer (4 Layer, 256 Base Latent LSTM)	0.652	0.579
Test System	**0.671**	**0.577**
Attention (with Double Batch Size for speed)	0.639	0.574
Test System (Constrained)	0.665	0.568
Large Batch Size (1024 minibatch)	0.617	0.538
Noise Semantic Output Layers (Gaussian)	0.627	0.527

Table 1: Accuracy over the development and test sets for various system configuration and our official submission ("Test System"), sorted by test set accuracy. "Combination" = attention, equal dropout, 4-Layer, noise semantic layer (with double batch size for speed)

4 Discussion

A few things helped performance (specifically generalization): (1) average pooling, most likely by making the overall meaning of the sentence more stable; (2) WordNet fuzzing and the resultant data augmentation; (3) progressively reduced dropout; (4) adding layers somewhat improved performance; (5) using progressively smaller LSTM layers; (6) using uncased, larger token size GloVe vectors, likely due to the larger coverage and more specific embeddings; and (7) multi-task learning.

We did not find that using dense networks for generative semantic operations worked well, as overfitting was endemic. We tried to enforce constrained vector additivity between tasks, but found that this harmed performance, and instead we took the path of multiple unconstrained tasks projected from the shared embeddings. In future, these operations should be fully-fledged generative functions, to account for the inherent complexity of the task itself. Adding noise to the embeddings (e.g. Gaussian) as a form of data augmentation also did not aid performance. Larger batches in general did speed up training, but in general harmed overall performance. We experimented with L1/L2 regularization, but found dropout to be far more robust. We attempted shared LSTM layers (between reason, claim, warrants), but again, found it be to detrimental. We tried BiLSTMs (which did not improve performance), and GRUs (which took longer to train with comparable performance). We also tried attention (e.g. a warrant on its respective reason and claim), but this too did not improve performance.

4.1 Future Directions

There are numerous future directions from this work, mostly in the integration of transfer learning, more complicated generation functions, and low resource learning. As we found overfitting to be an endemic problem across approaches, we believe that aggressive use of transfer learning of higher-level concepts from parallel domains will likely be of use. The operations for the different tasks were originally trained to be vector additive, but we found in practice that they harmed performance. Instead, complex embedding generation will almost certainly require more complex operations than the simple ones we found to work well in this work. This opens up new directions in terms of classification and text generation within argument mining, such as the generation of implicit warrants between reasons and claims, or the detection of reasoning triplets for dataset generation. We also believe aggressive use of low resource (e.g. few-shot) learning mechanisms will be beneficial in the future.

5 Conclusion

In this paper we demonstrated a system that attempts to learn a form of generative implication from sets of reasons, claims and warrants. There was a large generalization gap between the development and test test results for both of the tested systems, as well as the competition as a whole, which highlights how large an issue overfitting is for problems based on small datasets. We demonstrated our tested models' performance on both the development and test sets, with our final submission coming in 8th (among 21).

Acknowledgments

This research is based upon work supported in part by CSIRO Data61 and the Office of the Director of National Intelligence (ODNI), Intelligence Advanced Research projects Activity (IARPA), under Contract [2017-16122000002]. The views and conclusions contained herein are those of the authors and should not be interpreted as necessarily representing the official policies, either expressed or implied, of ODNI, IARPA, or the U.S. Government. The U.S. Government is authorized to reproduce and distribute reprints for governmental purposes notwithstanding any copyright annotation therein.

References

Steven Bird, Ewan Klein, and Edward Loper. 2009. *Natural Language Processing with Python: Analyzing Text with the Natural Language Toolkit.* "O'Reilly Media, Inc.".

Rich Caruana, Steve Lawrence, and C Lee Giles. 2001. Overfitting in neural nets: Backpropagation, conjugate gradient, and early stopping. In T K Leen, T G Dietterich, and V Tresp, editors, *Advances in Neural Information Processing Systems 13*, pages 402–408. MIT Press.

François et al Chollet. 2018. keras [software]. `https://github.com/keras-team/keras`. Accessed: 2018-2-17.

Ivan Habernal, Henning Wachsmuth, Iryna Gurevych, and Benno Stein. 2018. The argument reasoning comprehension task: Identification and reconstruction of implicit warrants. In *Proceedings of the 16th Annual Conference of the North American Chapter of the Association for Computational Linguistics: Human Language Technologies*, page to appear, New Orleans, USA. Association for Computational Linguistics.

S Hochreiter and J Schmidhuber. 1997. Long short-term memory. *Neural Comput.*, 9(8):1735–1780.

Diederik P Kingma and Jimmy Ba. 2014. Adam: A method for stochastic optimization.

Tomas Mikolov, Wen-Tau Yih, and Geoffrey Zweig. 2013. Linguistic regularities in continuous space word representations. In *Proceedings of the 2013 Conference of the North American Chapter of the Association for Computational Linguistics: Human Language Technologies*, pages 746–751.

George A Miller. 1995. WordNet: a lexical database for english. *Commun. ACM*, 38(11):39–41.

Jonas Mueller and Aditya Thyagarajan. 2016. Siamese recurrent architectures for learning sentence similarity. In *AAAI*, pages 2786–2792. aaai.org.

Jeffrey Pennington, Richard Socher, and Christopher Manning. 2014. Glove: Global vectors for word representation. In *Proceedings of the 2014 conference on empirical methods in natural language processing (EMNLP)*, pages 1532–1543. aclweb.org.

Florian Schroff, Dmitry Kalenichenko, and James Philbin. 2015. Facenet: A unified embedding for face recognition and clustering. In *Proceedings of the IEEE conference on computer vision and pattern recognition*, pages 815–823.

Nitish Srivastava, Geo Rey Hinton, Alex Krizhevsky, Ilya Sutskever, and Ruslan Salakhutdinov. 2014. Dropout: A simple way to prevent neural networks from overfitting. *The Journal of Machine Learning Research*, 15(1):1929–1958.

Yaniv Taigman, Ming Yang, Marc'aurelio Ranzato, and Lior Wolf. 2014. Deepface: Closing the gap to human-level performance in face verification. In *Proceedings of the IEEE conference on computer vision and pattern recognition*, pages 1701–1708. cvfoundation.org.

Liling Tan. 2014. Pywsd: Python implementations of word sense disambiguation (WSD) technologies [software]. `https://github.com/alvations/pywsd`.

Joker at SemEval-2018 Task 12: The Argument Reasoning Comprehension with Neural Attention

[1]**Guobin Sui** , [1]**Wenhan Chao** , [2]**Zhunchen Luo**[*]
[1]School of Computer Science and Engineering / Beihang University
[2]Information Research Center of Military Science / PLA Academy of Military Science
[1]Beijing 100191, China; [2]Beijing 100142, China
`{suigb,chaowenhan}@buaa.edu.cn;zhunchenluo@gmail.com`

Abstract

This paper describes a classification system that participated in the SemEval-2018 Task 12: The Argument Reasoning Comprehension Task. Briefly the task can be described as that a natural language "argument" is what we have, with reason, claim, and correct and incorrect warrants, and we need to choose the correct warrant. In order to make fully understand of the semantic information of the sentences, we proposed a neural network architecture with attention mechanism to achieve this goal. Besides we try to introduce keywords into the model to improve accuracy. Finally the proposed system achieved 5th place among 22 participating systems.

1 Introduction

In recent years, as an extremely important part of argument mining, argument reasoning has received considerable research. The argumentation reasoning can be used in many situations such as automatic score, policy decision, stance detection, and many others (Habernal et al., 2018). The task can be described as follows in detail: Given an argument consisting of a claim and a reason, the goal is to select the correct warrant that explains reasoning of this particular argument. There are only two warrants given and only one answer is correct. The correct warrant inferred from the argument has a supported relation with the argument. However the other warrant either opposes the argument or has no correlation with the argument. Actually, this task could be treated as a binary classification(A vs. B).

The task could be regarded as an argumentative relation work. The argumentative relation mining aims at identifying relations of attack and support between natural language arguments in text, by classifying pairs of pieces of text as attack, support or neither attack nor support relations (Cocarascu and Toni, 2017). The corrected warrant means supporting the argument, while the other means attacking the argument. So we refer to some literature methods on the relationship between arguments. Cocarascu and Toni (2017) use Long Short Term Memory (LSTM) to classify the relations between arguments. Rocktäschel et al. (2016) propose neural network with attention mechanism, making neural networks interpretable. We infer to their methods and construct our model in new manner. In this paper, we use the LSTM networks with attention mechanism to construct the classification system.

The following sections are arranged as follows. In section 2, we will give an overview on the task and have an analysis of the datasets. In section 3 we describe the system used in this paper and introduce some interesting attempt in detail. Section 4 introduces the experiment and results. Finally, we get conclusions and have an outlook of the future work.

2 Task Definition

We use the corpus provided by the SemEval-2018 Task 12, which has a training corpus of 2420 samples with gold labels. The organization website also provides a corpus of 316 samples with gold labels as verification set. And finally about 444 samples without gold labels are provided by the organization website as the final test corpus. This data has a variety of contemporary issues across topics in user-generated web comments (Habernal et al., 2018).

For example:

Topic: There She Is, Miss America

Additional info: In 1968, feminists gathered in Atlantic City to protest the Miss America pageant, calling it racist and sexist. Is this beauty contest bad for women?

Argument: Miss America gives honors and education scholarships. And since ..., Miss America is good for women.

Warrant options:
a) scholarships would give women a chance to study
b) scholarships would take women from the home
Only (a) fills the gap in this argument; (b) would in fact lead to the opposite claim (such that Miss America is not good for women).

Observing the data, we find this task has some challenges. We notice that many warrants have high

Proceedings of the 12th International Workshop on Semantic Evaluation (SemEval-2018), pages 1129–1132
New Orleans, Louisiana, June 5–6, 2018. ©2018 Association for Computational Linguistics

---

[*] Corresponding author.

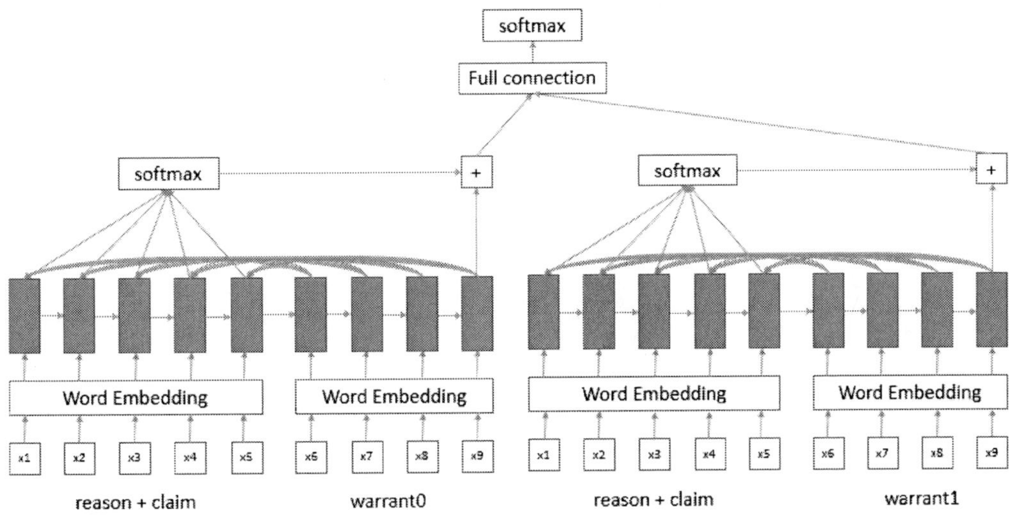

Figure 1: The system architecture - LSTM model with word-by-word attention mechanism.

semantic similarity, which makes it difficult to have a correct choice. In order to distinguish the similar sentences, the model must have the ability to model sentence semantics well. Besides, we find that many pairs of warrants' difference is the negative words. For example, consider the following warrant options from the training corpus. One warrant is "we can't have citizens being loyal to their home country", the other is "we can have citizens being loyal to their home country". The difference of them is the first one has the negative word "n't", which makes the sentences have different semantics. Every sentence has keywords which make a contribution to understand the sentence. We hope that putting the keywords extracted from the sentence into the model could enhance the comprehension of the sentences. We have a try with all these ideas.

3 System description

Our system is based on the LSTM model with word-by-word attention which could been seen as an encoder to decoder model. The encoder encodes the reason and claim and gives the initialization to the decoder. The decoder decodes the warrant and uses its output to compute the weight of tokens from the reason and claim. The higher the weight is, the more important the token is to choose the correct warrant. Besides, we introduce the keywords into the model to improve the accuracy.

3.1 Sequence model

In order to have a full understanding of the sentences, we try to use the neural network to model the sentences. The LSTM model could capture long-term dependencies (Hochreiter and Schmidhuber, 1997) so we use

that to construct the sequence model.

LSTM models, a type of RNNs, address the problem of the vanishing gradients problem while trying to capture long-term dependencies by introducing memory cells and gates into networks (Cocarascu and Toni, 2017). Although the LSTM models could solve the problem of the long-term dependencies, it usually capture the words behind the sentence, which causes a problem that the words before the sentence make a little contribution. In order to achieve full comprehension of the sentences, an attention mechanism is introduced into the model. The attention mechanism has been demonstrated success in a wide range of tasks from handwriting synthesis (Graves, 2013), machine translation (Bahdanau et al., 2015) and sentence summarization (Rush et al., 2015). In view of the effectiveness of the attention mechanism, we combine it with the LSTM model expecting a great performance.

Based on the statistics on sentence lengths in training corpus, we set the length of the reason, claim, warrant to 50, 15, 30 respectively. In this paper, we propose three deep learning methods to represent the sentences. The first is that we use BiLSTMs to parse the semantics of the sentences and then merge their output of the BiLSTMs. The concatenated vector is fed into a fully-connected neural network whose output is concatenated with the softmax function to have a prediction. The detailed computation is described in (1-5). The R_i, C_i, $W0_i$ and $W1_i$ are the embedding presentations of the reason, claim, warrant0 and warrant1 respectively and the R_o, C_o, $W0_o$ and $W1_o$ are the outputs of the BiLSTMs. V is the vector connecting them. This model is the baseline of our paper.

$$R_o = BiLSTMs(R_i) \tag{1}$$

$$C_o = BiLSTMs(C_i) \tag{2}$$

$$W0_o = BiLSTMs(W0_i) \tag{3}$$

$$W1_o = BiLSTMs(W1_i) \tag{4}$$

$$V = [R_o; C_o; W0_o; W1_o] \tag{5}$$

The second and the third method refer to the methods (Rocktäschel et al., 2016) where the author proposed LSTM with attention and word-by-word attention mechanism to solve the problem of reasoning about entailment and achieved the state-of-the-art results. We refer to their model to construct our model. The second and the third method are called LSTM model with attention and LSTM model with word-by-word attention. From the figure 1, there is the LSTM with attention and word-by-word attention mechanism. The two methods see reason and claim as the part of encoder, which gives the initial weight to the warrant and treats the warrant as decoder. The difference between them is that attention is only based on the last output vector of warrant, while the word-by-word attention is based on all output vectors of warrant.

$$Y = BiLSTMs(R_i; C_i) \tag{6}$$

$$H = BiLSTMs(W_i) \tag{7}$$

$$M_t = tanh(W^y Y + (w^h h_t + W^r r_{t-1}) \otimes e_L) \tag{8}$$

$$\alpha_t = softmax(w^T M_t) \tag{9}$$

$$r_t = Y\alpha_t^T + tanh(W^t r_{t-1}) \tag{10}$$

$$h^* = tanh(W^p r_N + W^x h_N) \tag{11}$$

Equation (6-11) provide the details about the computation on word-by-word attention. Y is the output vector of the encoder whose input is embedding representation of reason and claim. H is the output of the decoder with the embedding representation of warrant. h_t is the state of H at time t. We use h_t to compute the weight of the token from reason and claim at every time. Then we can get the weight matrix which means how important the token is for the decoder at every time. The weight matrix of attention is one dimension while the word-by-word attention has n dimensions. So the computation of the attention is simple and the same as the word-by-word attention. The two warrants with the reason and claim are used to construct the word-by-word attention respectively. Then the outputs of them are merged by concatenation and are put into a fully-connected neural network to make a prediction.

3.2 Keywords

We expect that introducing the keywords into the model could improve the accuracy. The sequence model can only express the basic meaning of the sentence and can't grab the main part. So the keywords can semantically enhance the sentence meaning. Based on that, we carry out the keywords extraction using text rank algorithm based on the graph. The specific method is described in the paper (Mihalcea and Tarau, 2004). For getting the keywords, we let G=(V,E) be a undirected graph with the set of vertices V and set of edges E where V is the token corpus and E is the weight between two tokens. The formula could be calculated according to the following equation (12) where the $S(V_i)$ is the score of the vertex V_i, the w is the edges and d is a damping factor that is usually set to 0.85. $Out(V_j)$ and $In(V_i)$ are the adjacent vertices of V_i in undirected graph. Based on the scores we could get the keywords from the sentence. The higher the score is, the more important the word is.

$$S(V_i) = (1-d)+d* \sum_{v_j \in In(V_i)} \frac{w_{ij}}{\sum_{v_k \in Out(V_j)} w_{jk}} S(V_j) \tag{12}$$

According to observing the keywords from the two warrants, we find that some pairs of warrants have the same keywords but different negative word. So we do statistics on negative words. If the number of the negative words is odd, we will add a negative word such as "not" into the keyword corpus. However, if the number of the negative words is even, we won't add any negative word into the keyword corpus. We expect to make a difference between the two warrants with the same keywords. We use the bag-of-word model to model the corpus of the keywords. Every keywords are put into the pre-trained embedding layer to get the word representation. In order to ignore the difference in the number of keywords, we adopt the average operation. The computation is introduced in equation (13-16) where r_i, c_i, $w0_i$ and $w1_i$ are the word representations of reason, claim, warrant0 and warrant1 generated from the Glove vectors (Pennington et al., 2014). The output I_i is then put into a fully-connected neural network to make a classification decision.

$$R_{ave} = \frac{1}{len(R)} \sum_{i=1}^{len(R)} r_i \tag{13}$$

$$C_{ave} = \frac{1}{len(C)} \sum_{i=1}^{len(C)} c_i \tag{14}$$

$$W0_{ave} = \frac{1}{len(W0)} \sum_{i=1}^{len(W0)} w0_i \tag{15}$$

$$W1_{ave} = \frac{1}{len(W1)} \sum_{i=1}^{len(W1)} w1_i \tag{16}$$

$$I_i = [R_{ave}; C_{ave}; W0_{ave}; W1_{ave}] \tag{17}$$

We introduce the keywords into the sequence model and combine the bag-of-word model with the word-by-word attention model. We train the bag-of-word model and incorporate it into LSTM model with word-by-word attention by averaging the predicted probabilities to get the final label to make a correct choice. We call the combination hybrid model. The details of the experiment will be introduced in next section.

Model	dev corpus	test corpus
LSTMs model	0.500	0.504
Attention	0.657	0.571
WBW attention	0.684	0.586
BOW model	0.606	0.524
hybrid model	0.654	0.585

Table 1: The results of the experiments. Attention, WBW attention, BOW model stand for LSTM model with attention, LSTM model with word-by-word attention, bag-of-word model respectively. Training on the training corpus while testing accuracy is computed on the dev corpus and test corpus.

4 Experiment and result

While training the model, the input sentences are separately embedded as 100-dimensional GloVe vectors (Pennington et al., 2014) and the embedding layer is based on the 100-dimensional GloVe vectors. We use ADAM (Kingma and Ba, 2015) for optimization and set the initial learning rate 0.001. We trained for 13 epochs or until the performance on development set stopped improving so as to avoid overfitting. Some Hyper-parameters for model: the dropout is 0.9, the embedding size is 100, the size of LSTM is 64 and the batch size is 256.

We conduct experiment on the training, dev and test corpus downloaded from the SemEval-2018 Task 12. There are five models used to make experiments are LSTM model, LSTM model with attention, LSTM model with word-by-word attention, bag-of-word model and hybrid model. The results of the experiments could be seen in Table 1. We choose the LSTM model without attention as baseline.

According to the experiment, the simple sequence model couldn't complete the semantic understanding task well. The bag-of-word model performs better than the LSTM model, which proves that the keywords could express the semantics of the sentences. As for the keywords can't express all the information of the sentences while the LSTM model with attention can not only express the whole information but also grab the important part, the bag-of-word performs worse than the attention model. LSTM model with word-by-word attention makes a great contribution to the best result. The hybrid model doesn't have an improvement in dev corpus but have a similar results with the word-by-word attention model. We guess that what causes such a result is the small data corpus and simply mechanically combining the models with each other. So we don't get a satisfactory result from the hybrid model. The LSTM model with word-by-word attention gets the accuracy of 0.586 in the final submission, achieving the fifth place in the shared task.

In the future, we will consider more reasonable combinations of the sentence model with keywords to enhance the comprehension of the sentences. Besides, we will introduce the CNN into our model to extract the word character to improve the accuracy.

5 Acknowledgments

We very appreciate the comments from reviewers which will help further improve our work. This work is supported by National Key Research and Development Program of China (Grant No. 2017YFB1402400) and National Science Foundation of China (No. 61602490).

References

Dzmitry Bahdanau, Kyunghyun Cho, and Yoshua Bengio. 2015. Neural machine translation by jointly learning to align and translate. *international conference on learning representations*.

Oana Cocarascu and Francesca Toni. 2017. Identifying attack and support argumentative relations using deep learning. *Proceedings of the 2017 Conference on Empirical Methods in Natural Language Processing*, pages 1385–1390.

Alex Graves. 2013. Generating sequences with recurrent neural networks. *arXiv: Neural and Evolutionary Computing*.

Ivan Habernal, Henning Wachsmuth, Iryna Gurevych, and Benno Stein. 2018. SemEval-2018 Task 12: The Argument Reasoning Comprehension Task. In *Proceedings of the 12th International Workshop on Semantic Evaluation (SemEval-2018)*, New Orleans, LA, USA. Association for Computational Linguistics.

Sepp Hochreiter and Jurgen Schmidhuber. 1997. Long short-term memory. *Neural Computation*, 9(8):1735–1780.

Diederik P Kingma and Jimmy Lei Ba. 2015. Adam: A method for stochastic optimization. *international conference on learning representations*.

Rada Mihalcea and Paul Tarau. 2004. Textrank: Bringing order into texts. pages 404–411.

Jeffrey Pennington, Richard Socher, and Christopher Manning. 2014. Glove: Global vectors for word representation. In *Conference on Empirical Methods in Natural Language Processing*, pages 1532–1543.

Tim Rocktäschel, Edward Grefenstette, Karl Moritz Hermann, Tomas Ko Isky, and Phil Blunsom. 2016. Reasoning about entailment with neural attention. *international conference on learning representations*.

Alexander M Rush, Sumit Chopra, and Jason Weston. 2015. A neural attention model for abstractive sentence summarization. *empirical methods in natural language processing*, pages 379–389.

TakeLab at SemEval-2018 Task12: Argument Reasoning Comprehension with Skip-Thought Vectors

Ana Brassard, Tin Kuculo, Filip Boltužić, Jan Šnajder
Text Analysis and Knowledge Engineering Lab
Faculty of Electrical Engineering and Computing, University of Zagreb
Unska 3, 10000 Zagreb, Croatia
`{name.surname}@fer.hr`

Abstract

This paper describes our system for the SemEval-2018 Task 12: Argument Reasoning Comprehension Task. We utilize skip-thought vectors, sentence-level distributional vectors inspired by the popular word embeddings and the skip-gram model. We encode preprocessed sentences from the dataset into vectors, then perform a binary supervised classification of the warrant that justifies the use of the reason as support for the claim. We explore a few variations of the model, reaching 54.1% accuracy on the test set, which placed us 16th out of 22 teams participating in the task.

1 Introduction

Reasoning is the process of thinking in a logical way to form a conclusion. Inferring conclusions using commonsense reasoning has become a popular topic in NLP. *Textual entailment* (TE) aims to determine whether a *hypothesis* can be inferred from a *premise* (Dagan et al., 2006). Approaches to solving *TE* have ranged from robust approaches based on shallow lexical and semantic features (Marelli et al., 2014) to formal computational semantics approaches based on translating sentences into logical form (Beltagy et al., 2015). The current state-of-the-art approaches to TE use deep learning for *natural logic inference* to capture human deductive reasoning (Bowman et al., 2015; Rocktäschel et al., 2015).

In online discussions, when arguing for or against a stance, people provide arguments leaving their readers to rely on common sense and non-deductive reasoning to evaluate the validity of their arguments. Human annotators can infer the reasons from claims fairly well (Boltužić and Šnajder, 2014; Hasan and Ng, 2014), even when additional (implicit) premises are required to make reasoning deductive (Boltužić and Šnajder, 2016). Habernal et al. (2018) emphasize the importance of implicit premises in argumentation by introducing the *argument reasoning comprehension* task, where one chooses between two mutually exclusive warrants to make a reason warrant the claim. They demonstrate that human experts can perform this task extremely well (up to 90% accuracy).

In this paper, we describe a system for solving the argument reasoning comprehension task, with which we participated in the SemEval-2018 Task 12. Given the reason R and claim C, debate title, debate description, and two warrants, W_1 and W_2, the task is to choose warrant W that justifies the use of R as support for C. For all warrant pairs (W_1, W_2), it holds that if warrant W_1 is W, then W_2 is $\neg W$, which justifies the use of R as support for $\neg C$ and vice versa.

Our system frames the problem as supervised classification and utilizes skip-thought vectors to represent sentences. Our system (TakeLab) ranked 16th out of 22 systems submitted to the SemEval-2018 Task 12, achieving 54.1% accuracy on the test set and 69.0% on the development set.

2 Related Work

Structuring argumentative discussions using Toulmin's argumentation model (Toulmin, 2003) is an established research area in *argumentation mining*, involving detecting claims (Levy et al., 2014; Lippi and Torroni, 2015; Rinott et al., 2015), detecting claim relations (Cabrio and Villata, 2012; Boltužić and Šnajder, 2014; Stab and Gurevych, 2014), and even reconstructing entire argumentation graphs from text (Stab and Gurevych, 2017). While systems have been proposed that tackle some of these problems, they do not as yet provide mechanisms for commonsense reasoning. The *argument comprehension problem*, warranting reasons for claim, explores the problems when the gap between the claim and reason is too wide for textual entailment.

Proceedings of the 12th International Workshop on Semantic Evaluation (SemEval-2018), pages 1133–1136
New Orleans, Louisiana, June 5–6, 2018. ©2018 Association for Computational Linguistics

3 System Description

Our system works in three steps. First, we preprocess the dataset ending up with the claim, reason, both warrant sentences, and the correct warrant sentence label per instance. Second, we utilize *skip-thought vectors* (Kiros et al., 2015) to encode sentences as vectors. Third, we use encoded sentences as features in a supervised classification setup where we predict the warrant label given the encoded sentences.

3.1 Preprocessing

We extract only the warrants, reasons, claims, and labels from the dataset, disregarding optional additional information about the debates. We clean up this data by merging multi-sentence elements in a natural way, i.e., connecting the sentences with the conjunction "and" and modifying the punctuation accordingly. For example, the two-sentence reason:

> *Biking is good for one's health and the environment. It is more expensive to maintain roads than bike lanes.*

becomes a single sentence:

> *Biking is good for one's health and the environment and it is more expensive to maintain roads than bike lanes.*

The motivation behind this is to obtain sentences that convey a single *idea* behind the reason or warrant (claims were always single-sentence). This way, we attempt to extract a *vector per thought*. This results in a consistent set of four sentences per instance.

As the warrant and alternative warrant were extremely similarly worded (68% had two or less different words), we represent warrants W_1 and W_2 as word-level relative complements:

$$W_1' = W_1 \setminus W_2 = \{w_i \in W_1 \mid w_i \notin W_2\}$$
$$W_2' = W_2 \setminus W_1 = \{w_j \in W_2 \mid w_j \notin W_1\}$$

where w_i and w_j denote words. This allowed us to boil down the warrants to their meaningful differences, e.g., just the words *"does"* and *"doesn't"* in instances where the warrants were negated, but otherwise identically worded. We experimented with other combinations, but as they did not lead to performance improvement, we omit them here.

3.2 Skip-Thought Vectors

The skip-thoughts model (Kiros et al., 2015) is a sentence-level abstraction of the skip-gram model (Mikolov et al., 2013). Instead of predicting the surrounding text from a word, it predicts sentences around the target sentence in the text. Kiros et al. (2015) chose to implement an encoder-decoder model, using an RNN encoder with GRU (Chung et al., 2014) activations and an RNN decoder with a conditional GRU. This model is nearly identical to the RNN encoder used by Cho et al. (2014) for machine translation. The encoder-decoder is trained on a large dataset of English books – *Book-Corpus* (Zhu et al., 2015), chosen for its abundance of long, context-building sentences. A trained skip-thoughts model can be used as an out-of-the-box encoder-decoder able to convert sentences to skip-thought vectors. The encoder maps words to a sentence vector and the decoder is internally used by the model to generate the surrounding sentences.

The skip-thoughts model was tested on the tasks of semantic relatedness, image-sentence ranking, and paraphrase detection. The last, when combined with basic pairwise statistics, becomes competitive with the state of the art which incorporates much more complicated features and hand-engineering. On the task of semantic relatedness, the model of Kiros et al. (2015) outperformed all previous systems from the SemEval 2014 competition despite its simplicity and the lack of feature engineering. The authors also report good results on a number of classification benchmarks for evaluating sentence representation learning methods.

The model's consistently good results on a variety of tasks motivated us to apply these vectors on our own task, which relies on the interpretation of sentences. We encode the sentences obtained from the preprocessing step into skip-thoughts using Kiros et al. (2015)'s encoder, which gives four feature vectors with 4,800 dimensions with values ranging from -0.2 to 0.2.

3.3 Classification

The final step in our system is classifying instances using an SVM classifier, whose hyperparameters were optimized with a 5-fold cross-validated grid search.[1] We also explored Gaussian Processes, Random Forests, and AdaBoost models, which were all outperformed by the SVM. Input features

---

[1] We obtained best results on the dev set with: gamma=0.3, C=3.8, degree=2, kernel ='poly'.

Classifier	Features	Dev accuracy score	Test accuracy score
AdaBoost	W_0', W_1', R, C	0.614	0.520
Random forest	W_0', W_1', R, C	0.623	0.498
Gaussian process	W_0', W_1', R, C	0.642	0.547
SVM	W_0, W_1, R, C	0.630	0.538
	W_0', W_1', R, C	0.642	0.536
	$W_0 - W_1, R$	0.661	**0.570**
	$W_0' - W_1', R, C$	0.665	0.561
	$W_0' - W_1', R$	**0.687**	0.552*

Table 1: Accuracy scores of model variants. All models have skip-thought vectors as features, where R stands for reason, C for claim, W_1 and W_2 for warrants, and, W_1' and W_2' for warrant word differences vectors. (* The official results are lower (0.541) due to an error while preparing the output)

are created by concatenating skip-thought vectors obtained in the previous step. We experimented with different variants of features by applying arithmetic operations on the vectors before concatenating them, i.e., calculating the difference between warrants. It should be noted that this difference is calculated as an element-wise subtraction of the vectors, as opposed to the word set difference in the preprocessing step. Furthermore, we experimented with two variations of skip-thought vectors – one with the original warrants intact (W_0, W_1) and one with the warrant subset differences (W_0', W_1').

4 Evaluation

4.1 Dataset Analysis

The dataset consists of 1210 training instances, 317 validation instances, and 445 test instances. Each instance is a tuple $(W_1, W_2, R, C, debateTitle, debateInfo, y)$, with y as the label of the correct warrant (0 for W_1 or 1 for W_2). Among the 1210 training instances, there are 111 different debate titles and 169 different claims, indicating the diversity of the training set. Furthermore, we found that 47.75% of the debate titles had unanimous claims (all for or all against) and 56.69% of the claims were affirmative, but only 21.62% had a balanced number of claims for both sides of the debate (a difference of 10% or less). The debate title *Do We Still Need Libraries?* was the most common debate title, and it had unanimously affirmative claims. Around 35% of the instances contained warrants worded differently, as opposed to being directly negated (by adding *not*). All of this presented a challenge in training the system, since the dataset is small, highly variable, and involves multiple domains.

4.2 Results

The official evaluation measure for this task was the accuracy of the classified instances. In the development phase, the system showed promising results – 0.690 accuracy on the validation set, after training with only the training set. Table 1 shows performances of the model variants we explored. Interestingly, the best results were obtained using the least amount of data – the difference between the modified warrants and only the reason, completely disregarding the claim. On the test set, however, the results were much lower, the official result being 0.541. The final result surprised us, since the system showed good results using various "plain" classifiers without fine-tuning the hyper-parameters (around 0.60). We hypothesize that this was due to overfitting, which was difficult to avoid completely of the small size of the dataset.

5 Conclusion

The argument reasoning comprehension task, recognizing the warrant between a claim and a supporting reason, is a challenging but important task for understanding human reasoning in argumentation. We aim to solve the task by converting sentences into skip-thought vectors and classifying justifying warrants given claims and reasons using an SVM model. This approach showed some promising results in the development stage (69% accuracy), but did not succeed to adequately generalize in order to provide competitive results in the test stage (54% accuracy). Besides using a larger sample for training, this system could be improved by applying transfer learning from other similar tasks, such as paraphrase detection or textual entailment.

Acknowledgment

This research has been partly supported by the European Regional Development Fund under the grant KK.01.1.1.01.0009 (DATACROSS).

References

Islam Beltagy, Stephen Roller, Pengxiang Cheng, Katrin Erk, and Raymond J Mooney. 2015. Representing meaning with a combination of logical form and vectors. *CoRR, abs/1505.06816.*

Filip Boltužić and Jan Šnajder. 2016. Fill the gap! Analyzing implicit premises between claims from online debates. In *Proceedings of the 3rd Workshop on Argument Mining*, pages 124–133.

Filip Boltužić and Jan Šnajder. 2014. Back up your stance: Recognizing arguments in online discussions. In *Proceedings of the First Workshop on Argumentation Mining*, pages 49–58.

Samuel R. Bowman, Gabor Angeli, Christopher Potts, and Christopher D. Manning. 2015. A large annotated corpus for learning natural language inference. *arXiv preprint arXiv:1508.05326.*

Elena Cabrio and Serena Villata. 2012. Natural language arguments: A combined approach. In *Proceedings of the 20th European Conference on Artificial Intelligence*, pages 205–210. IOS Press.

Kyunghyun Cho, Bart van Merrienboer, Çaglar Gülçehre, Fethi Bougares, Holger Schwenk, and Yoshua Bengio. 2014. Learning phrase representations using RNN encoder-decoder for statistical machine translation. *CoRR, abs/1406.1078.*

Junyoung Chung, Çaglar Gülçehre, KyungHyun Cho, and Yoshua Bengio. 2014. Empirical evaluation of gated recurrent neural networks on sequence modeling. *CoRR, abs/1412.3555.*

Ido Dagan, Oren Glickman, and Bernardo Magnini. 2006. The PASCAL recognising textual entailment challenge. In *Machine learning challenges. evaluating predictive uncertainty, visual object classification, and recognising tectual entailment*, pages 177–190. Springer.

Ivan Habernal, Henning Wachsmuth, Iryna Gurevych, and Benno Stein. 2018. SemEval-2018 Task 12: The Argument Reasoning Comprehension Task. In *Proceedings of the 12th International Workshop on Semantic Evaluation (SemEval-2018)*, page (to appear), New Orleans, LA, USA. Association for Computational Linguistics.

Kazi Saidul Hasan and Vincent Ng. 2014. Why are you taking this stance? Identifying and classifying reasons in ideological debates. In *Proceedings of the 2014 Conference on Empirical Methods in Natural Language Processing (EMNLP)*, pages 751–762.

Ryan Kiros, Yukun Zhu, Ruslan Salakhutdinov, Richard S. Zemel, Antonio Torralba, Raquel Urtasun, and Sanja Fidler. 2015. Skip-thought vectors. *CoRR*, abs/1506.06726.

Ran Levy, Yonatan Bilu, Daniel Hershcovich, Ehud Aharoni, and Noam Slonim. 2014. Context dependent claim detection. In *Proceedings of COLING 2014, the 25th International Conference on Computational Linguistics: Technical Papers*, pages 1489–1500.

Marco Lippi and Paolo Torroni. 2015. Context-independent claim detection for argument mining. In *IJCAI*, volume 15, pages 185–191.

Marco Marelli, Luisa Bentivogli, Marco Baroni, Raffaella Bernardi, Stefano Menini, and Roberto Zamparelli. 2014. SemEval-2014 Task 1: Evaluation of compositional distributional semantic models on full sentences through semantic relatedness and textual entailment. In *Proceedings of the 8th international workshop on semantic evaluation (SemEval 2014)*, pages 1–8.

Tomas Mikolov, Kai Chen, Greg Corrado, and Jeffrey Dean. 2013. Efficient estimation of word representations in vector space. *CoRR*, abs/1301.3781.

Ruty Rinott, Lena Dankin, Carlos Alzate Perez, Mitesh M. Khapra, Ehud Aharoni, and Noam Slonim. 2015. Show me your evidence-an automatic method for context dependent evidence detection. In *Proceedings of the 2015 Conference on Empirical Methods in Natural Language Processing*, pages 440–450.

Tim Rocktäschel, Edward Grefenstette, Karl Moritz Hermann, Tomáš Kočiský, and Phil Blunsom. 2015. Reasoning about entailment with neural attention. *arXiv preprint arXiv:1509.06664.*

Christian Stab and Iryna Gurevych. 2014. Identifying argumentative discourse structures in persuasive essays. In *Proceedings of the 2014 Conference on Empirical Methods in Natural Language Processing (EMNLP)*, pages 46–56.

Christian Stab and Iryna Gurevych. 2017. Parsing argumentation structures in persuasive essays. *Computational Linguistics*, 43(3):619–659.

Stephen E. Toulmin. 2003. *The uses of argument.* Cambridge University Press.

Yukun Zhu, Ryan Kiros, Richard S. Zemel, Ruslan Salakhutdinov, Raquel Urtasun, Antonio Torralba, and Sanja Fidler. 2015. Aligning books and movies: Towards story-like visual explanations by watching movies and reading books. *CoRR*, abs/1506.06724.

Lyb3b at SemEval-2018 Task 12: Ensemble-based Deep Learning Models for Argument Reasoning Comprehension Task

Yongbin Li[1,2], Xiaobing Zhou[1,*]
[1]Yunnan University, Kunming, Yunnan, P.R. China
[2]Zunyi Medical University, Zunyi, Guizhou, P.R. China
* Corresponding author, zhouxb.cn@gmail.com

Abstract

Reasoning is a crucial part of natural language argumentation. In order to comprehend an argument, we have to reconstruct and analyze its reasoning. In this task, given a natural language argument with a reason and a claim, the goal is to choose the correct implicit reasoning from two options, in order to form a reasonable structure of (Reason, Warrant, Claim). Our approach is to build distributed word embedding of reason, warrant and claim respectively, meanwhile, we use a series of frameworks such as CNN model, LSTM model, GRU with attention model and biLSTM with attention model for processing word vector. Finally, ensemble mechanism is used to integrate the results of each framework to improve the final accuracy. Experiments demonstrate superior performance of ensemble mechanism compared to each separate framework. We are the 11th in official results, the final model can reach a 0.568 accuracy rate on the test dataset.

1 Introduction

Argument reasoning comprehension is a crucial part of natural language argumentation, and the realization of argument reasoning requires the understanding of the deep meaning of the text by the computer. At the same time, argument reasoning is also an important evaluation criterion for the understanding of natural language by computer. This paper is based on the argument reasoning comprehension task proposed by (Habernal et al., 2018), which proposed a complex, yet scalable crowdsourcing process, and created a new freely licensed dataset based on authentic arguments from news comments. The dataset consists of three parts: train dataset, validation dataset and test dataset, with the quantity being 1210, 316 and 444 respectively.

The task is formally defined as follow: given an argument consisting of a reason R and a claim C along with the title and a short description of the debate they occur in, identify the correct warrant W from two candidates, the goal is to select the correct warrant W that explains reasoning of this particular argument. There are only two options given and only one answer is correct. The key point of the task is that it is difficult to find the answer through the shallow semantics, and the answer is usually implicit.

Being a binary classification task, through preliminary experiment, our approach is combining debate title and description into reason, and splitting a sample {**R (with debate title and description) ; C; W_0; W_1; correct_label**} into two quadruples, which are {**R; C; W_0; label**} and {**R; C; W_1; label**}. On the validation, we employ the same processing mode, determining the matching degree of fit between a quadruples, the highest will be chosen. The four main deep learning(DL) frameworks we employed are based on Convolutional Neural Network(CNN) model, Long Short-Term Memory(LSTM) model, GRU with attention model and Bidirectional Long Short-Term Memory (biLSTM) with attention model, which are based on utilizing word distributed representation on R and C and W respectively, on top of models, a dense layer is used to determine the matching degree.

In our paper, an ensemble mechanism is introduced into neural network (NN) models, we integrate the results of each model to improve the final accuracy. Experiments demonstrate superior performance of ensemble mechanism compared to each separate model. For confirming the effect of ensemble method, we use each separate model as a reference.

Proceedings of the 12th International Workshop on Semantic Evaluation (SemEval-2018), pages 1137–1141
New Orleans, Louisiana, June 5–6, 2018. ©2018 Association for Computational Linguistics

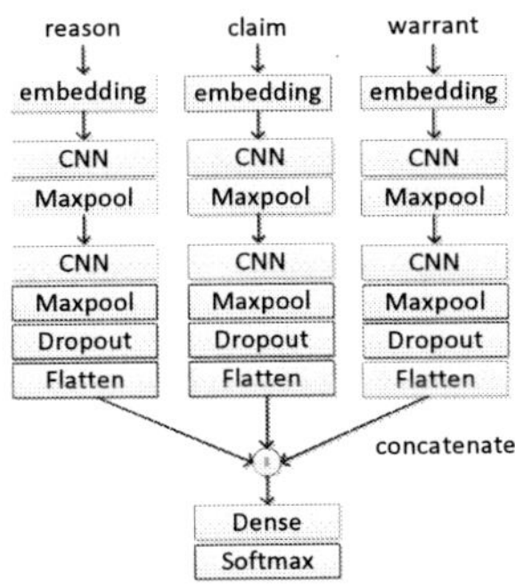

Figure 1: The architecture of CNN framework

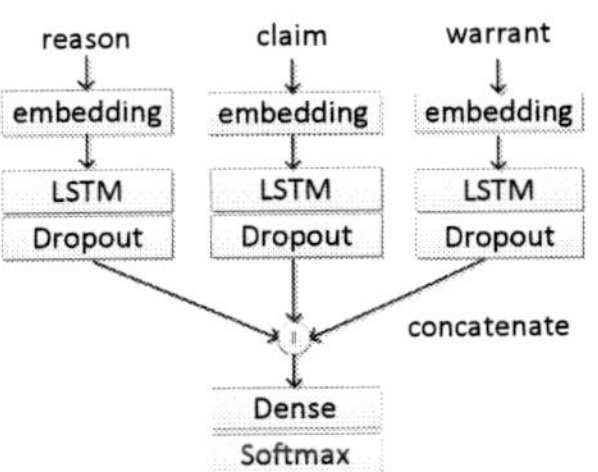

Figure 2: The architecture of LSTM framework

2 Related work

An argument consists of a claim and multiple premises was pointed out in (Damer, 2009). Toulmin elaborated on a model of argument in which the reason supports the claim on behalf of a warrant. The abstract structure of an argument then is reason → (since) warrant → (therefore) claim. But, making comprehending and analyzing arguments is hard, for claims and warrants are usually implicit (Freeman, 2011). The phenomenon is referred to as common knowledge (Macagno and Walton, 2014).

Previous, feature extraction and semantic analysis are usually used in natural language argumentation. With the development of neural networks, we adopt the method of word distributed representation from (Hinton, 1986), CNN model refers to (Kim, 2014), the LSTM model from (Hochreiter and Schmidhuber, 1997) and be improved by (Graves et al., 2013), the attention mechanism from (Hermann et al., 2015), eventually converted the task into a classification problem (Wang and Nyberg, 2015). Meanwhile, inspired by the ensemble method in statistical learning domain, we develop a very simple but efficient integrated method.

3 Model description

In this section, we describe the four main proposed deep learning frameworks, the framework architectures are shown in figure 1 to 4. The main idea of these different systems is the same: learn a distributed vector representation of given reason and claim and warrant candidates, and use a dense layer to measure the matching degree.

3.1 CNN framework

The first framework is based on CNN model. Step one is to obtain word embedding by pre-trained word2vec (Mikolov et al., 2013), the word embedding provides the distributed representation for each token in reason, claim and warrant candidates respectively. The vectors have dimensionality of 300 and were trained by 100 billion words of Google News, and was initialized from an unsupervised neural language model.

Reason, claim and warrant will be transformed to a word vector matrix and be entered into CNN layer respectively. In order to get more composite representation of semantic features, we adopted double layer CNN model. The numbers of filters are 64 and 32, and the filter size is set as 3, after each CNN layer, we resort to a MaxPooling layer of size 2.

Above the CNN layer, the output of reason, claim and warrant are merged to one and performed flatten operations, through a dense layer, the final output is passed through a two-dimensional softmax layer.

3.2 LSTM framework

LSTM is a special type of RNN that can learn to rely on long-distance history and the immediate previous hidden vector, its a remarkable variation of RNN to alleviate the gradient vanish problem.

In the same way of producing word distribution vector representation in embedding layer, the difference is that, as the LSTM model can process variable length sequences, so we employ masking method to skip (filter out) time steps whose tokens are equal to zero. Above the embedding layer, we introduced the LSTM layer with unit number of 64. Through the LSTM layer, reason, claim and warrant will be transformed to a vector respectively.

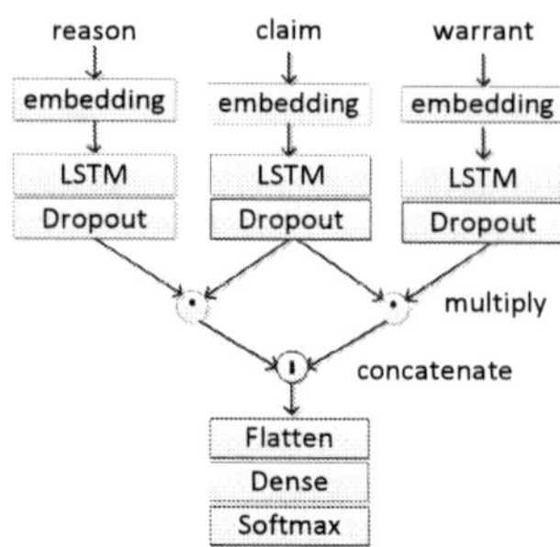
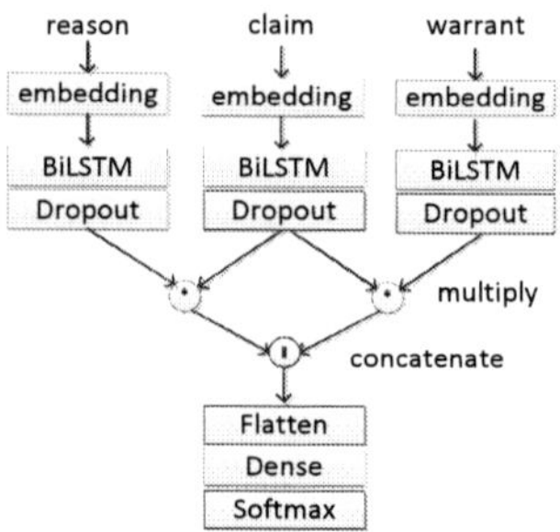

Figure 3: The architecture of GRU framework

Figure 4: The architecture of biLSTM framework

3.3 GRU with attention

Like the LSTM framework, the masking method is used in the embedding layer. Reason, claim and warrant will be transformed to a word vector matrix and be entered into GRU layer respectively. Gated recurrent unit (GRU), was proposed by (Cho et al., 2014) to make each recurrent unit to adaptively capture dependencies of different time scales. Similarly to the LSTM unit, the GRU has gating units that modulates the flow of information inside the unit, without having a separate memory cells. Unlike the LSTM framework, GRU with attention return full output sequences, instead of the final output of the model.

Through the GRU layer, reason, claim and warrant are converted into three vector matrices. Now, we investigate a state-of-the-art attention model for the warrant vector generation based on claim which is called fact matrix, and the claim vector generation based on warrant which is called attention matrix. An attention mechanism are used to alleviate weakness by dynamically aligning the more informative parts. Specifically, attention model gives more weights on certain words, just like tf-idf for each word, however, the weight is calculated by another vector. Final, we merge the two sequences to one and perform flatten operations.

3.4 biLSTM with attention

The framework is similar to the above one, just changing the GRU model into a biLSTM model, Single direction LSTMs suffers a weakness of not utilizing the contextual information from the future tokens. biLSTM utilizes both the previous and future context by processing the sequence on two directions, and generates two independent sequences of LSTM output vectors.

4 Ensemble Methods

Ensemble methods is an important method in statistical learning, which combines a number of weak models into a strong model through a certain combination. The most famous of them are the Bagging algorithm and the Boosting algorithm.

Our method is inspired by the bagging method, the differences between our method and the traditional bagging method are as follows: we use several strong classifiers for combination, and use all the data to train a single model.

Specifically, we use three ensemble methods. The first method is the soft voting based on Bagging method, that is, each framework outputs a class probability and takes the average to judge the category. The second method is hard voting, each framework predicts categories separately, and finally votes. Because four frameworks are used in the paper, the weight of the best framework is set to 2. The third method is finding the best weight which is the best accuracy on the validation dataset by the exhaustive method.

5 Experimental setup

Our approach in this task is realized by keras, we use the accuracy on validation dataset to locate the best parameters. All the results are taken three times, and the average value is taken.

In the experiment, we use the loss function of categorical cross entropy and the optimizer of adaptive moment estimation. The length of reason, claim and warrant tokens sequence all take the maximum length, if the length is not enough, then zero is added.

For comparison, we report the performance and analysis of four frameworks in Table 1. Rows (1) to (2), list accuracy of task originators models on the validation set and the test set respectively

	Framework	val	test
1	Intra-warrant attention	63.8	55.6
2	Intra-warrant attention w/context	63.7	56.0
3	CNN	63.92	52.93
4	LSTM	66.46	54.95
5	GRU with attention	67.72	56.19
6	biLSTM with attention	67.09	57.21

Table 1: Results of originator and the four main frameworks which our paper employed

	Weight	val	test
soft voting	1 1 1 1	68.35	56.85
hard voting	1 1 1 2	68.03	56.63
exhaustion weight	1 4 2 3	69.93	55.50
	0 2 1 5	69.62	56.41
	1 0 1 5	69.30	55.28

Table 2: Results of ensemble method

(Habernal et al., 2018), we take the results as the baseline to measure other frameworks. Rows (3) to (6) corresponds to our main four frameworks. Row (3) achieve acceptable results on validation set compared to the baseline. Row (4) has been greatly improved compared with CNN on the validation set and test set, especially on the validation set, reaching a 66.46% accuracy rate, proving that the LSTM model is more advantageous in processing sequence text. Row (5) has a better effect on the validation set and test set, the results have exceeded to the baseline. In these four major frameworks, the result of Row (6) is the most satisfying, improves over the baseline already, especially on the validation set, 4% higher than the baseline, on the test set, the accuracy rate of 57.21% is also reached. From the Table 1, we can perceive that the attention mechanism is beneficial to improve the capability of the model.

We report the performance of ensemble method in Table 2. As can be seen from the result, we can observe that Row (1) uses the soft voting method, which achieves a 68.35% accuracy rate on the validation set, which surpasses all the single frameworks. The performance on the test set is also good, reaching 56.85%, more than the baseline model 1%, though it is not as good as the best result of single framework, but it is also a good result. Row (2) is the hard voting method, which is slightly worse than the soft voting. The weight of Rows (3) to (5) which were found on validation set achieve the highest accuracy on the validation set, more than 69%, this is a huge improvement, but the performance on the test dataset is not the best, the reason may be the overfitting caused by this

method. **It needs to be emphasized that soft voting method is adopted in the actual tasks, that is, the Row (1). The other methods listed here are only theoretical discussions on the ensemble method from the perspective of research**.

Through these experiments, we can conclude that remarkable results can be achieved through the ensemble method. At the same time, the soft voting method is better than other methods, although the results of the validation dataset are not the best in three method, but the effect on test dataset is the best.

6 Conclusion

In this paper, we solve the Argument Reasoning Comprehension Task by employing four main frameworks and ensemble mechanism. Through a series of attempts, our experimental results demonstrate that: comparing to a single framework, ensembling a series of models can effectively improve the accuracy of the model; the results of the single framework are unstable, and the stability of the model can be improved effectively through the ensemble method, the accuracy of the integrated system on the test set is guaranteed to be above 55%; in the experiment, soft voting is a good way to integrate and achieve better results.

Acknowledgments

This work was supported by the Natural Science Foundations of China No.61463050, No.617-02443, No.61762091, the NSF of Yunnan Province No. 2015FB113, the Project of Innovative Research Team of Yunnan Province.

References

Kyunghyun Cho, Bart Van Merriënboer, Caglar Gulcehre, Dzmitry Bahdanau, Fethi Bougares, Holger Schwenk, and Yoshua Bengio. 2014. Learning phrase representations using rnn encoder-decoder for statistical machine translation. *arXiv preprint arXiv:1406.1078*.

T Edward Damer. 2009. Attacking faulty reasoning: A practical guide to fallacy-free reasoning. *Wadsworth Cengage Learning,*.

James B Freeman. 2011. Argument structure: Representation and theory. *Argumentation Library*, 121(7):1194–1206.

Alex Graves, Abdel-rahman Mohamed, and Geoffrey Hinton. 2013. Speech recognition with deep recurrent neural networks. In *Acoustics, speech and signal processing (icassp), 2013 IEEE international conference on*, pages 6645–6649. IEEE.

Ivan Habernal, Henning Wachsmuth, Iryna Gurevych, and Benno Stein. 2018. The Argument Reasoning Comprehension Task: Identification and Reconstruction of Implicit Warrants. In *16th Annual Conference of the North American Chapter of the Association for Computational Linguistics: Human Language Technologies*. Association for Computational Linguistics.

Karl Moritz Hermann, Tomas Kocisky, Edward Grefenstette, Lasse Espeholt, Will Kay, Mustafa Suleyman, and Phil Blunsom. 2015. Teaching machines to read and comprehend. In *Advances in Neural Information Processing Systems*, pages 1693–1701.

Geoffrey E Hinton. 1986. Learning distributed representations of concepts. In *Proceedings of the eighth annual conference of the cognitive science society*, volume 1, page 12. Amherst, MA.

Sepp Hochreiter and Jürgen Schmidhuber. 1997. Long short-term memory. *Neural computation*, 9(8):1735–1780.

Yoon Kim. 2014. Convolutional neural networks for sentence classification. *arXiv preprint arXiv:1408.5882*.

Fabrizio Macagno and Douglas Walton. 2014. *Emotive language in argumentation*. Cambridge University Press.

Tomas Mikolov, Ilya Sutskever, Kai Chen, Greg S Corrado, and Jeff Dean. 2013. Distributed representations of words and phrases and their compositionality. In *Advances in neural information processing systems*, pages 3111–3119.

Di Wang and Eric Nyberg. 2015. A long short-term memory model for answer sentence selection in question answering. In *Proceedings of the 53rd Annual Meeting of the Association for Computational Linguistics and the 7th International Joint Conference on Natural Language Processing (Volume 2: Short Papers)*, volume 2, pages 707–712.

TRANSRW at SemEval-2018 Task 12: Transforming Semantic Representations for Argument Reasoning Comprehension

Zhimin Chen, Wei Song,[*] Lizhen Liu
Information Engineering College
Capital Normal University
Beijing 100048, China
{zmchen, wsong, liz_liu7480}@cnu.edu.cn

Abstract

This paper describes our system in SemEval-2018 task 12: Argument Reasoning Comprehension. The task is to select the correct warrant that explains reasoning of a particular argument consisting of a claim and a reason. The main idea of our methods is based on the assumption that the semantic composition of the reason and the warrant should be close to the semantic representation of the corresponding claim. We propose two neural network models. The first one considers two warrant candidates simultaneously, while the second one processes each candidate separately and then chooses the best one. We also incorporate sentiment polarity by assuming that there are kinds of sentiment associations between the reason, the warrant and the claim. The experiments show that the first framework is more effective and sentiment polarity is useful.

1 Introduction

Argument reasoning is a key step in the process of argumentation mining and is a very challenging task in natural language processing and artificial intelligence. Maccartney and Manning (2008) suggested that the key factor in the study of natural language understanding is the mastery of natural language reasoning. When we argue for an argument, it is necessary to reconstruct the implicit reasoning (Newman and Marshall, 1992; Habernal et al., 2017) under the relevant assumption and premise to get a simple and concise explanation of the whole reasoning process.

The Argument Reasoning Comprehension task is defined as following:

Given an argument consisting of a claim C and a reason R, the goal is to select the correct warrant that explains reasoning of this particular argument. There are only two options W_0 and W_1 given and only one answer is correct.

Our solution is based on the assumption that the semantic composition of the reason and the true warrant should be close to the semantic representation of the claim. We propose two frameworks. First one is dependent on the task settings that two warrant candidates are considered simultaneously to make a decision. The second one is more general that the task is simplified as determine whether a warrant candidate can explain argument reasoning. We found that the first one performed better.

In addition, we attempt to incorporate sentiment polarity to capture the sentiment association between the reason, the warrant and the claim. The experimental results demonstrate that adding sentiment polarity can improve the performance.

The final result is produced by an ensemble approach that combines the outputs of multiple single models. Our system achieves an accuracy of 0.67 on development dataset and 0.57 on test dataset.

2 System Description

2.1 Model1: Competitive Model

The first proposed model is designed depending on the specific task setting. The architecture of Model1 is shown in Figure 1. We first get the representations of the claim C, the reason R and the two warrant candidates W_0 and W_1. Then we use a transformer to get the representation of a pseudo claim, by compositing the reason R and a warrant candidate W. Finally, the model predicts which warrant candidate is the correct one by considering the claim C and two pseudo claims.

2.1.1 Sentence Representation

Figure 2 illustrates the architecture for getting the sentence representation.

---

[*]corresponding author

Proceedings of the 12th International Workshop on Semantic Evaluation (SemEval-2018), pages 1142–1145
New Orleans, Louisiana, June 5–6, 2018. ©2018 Association for Computational Linguistics

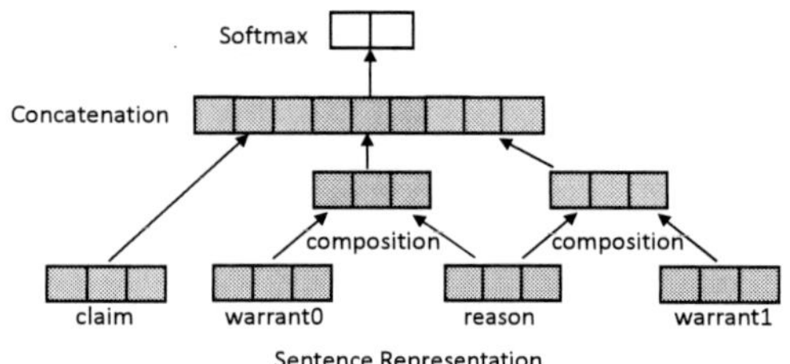

Figure 1: The architecture of Model1: Competitive Model.

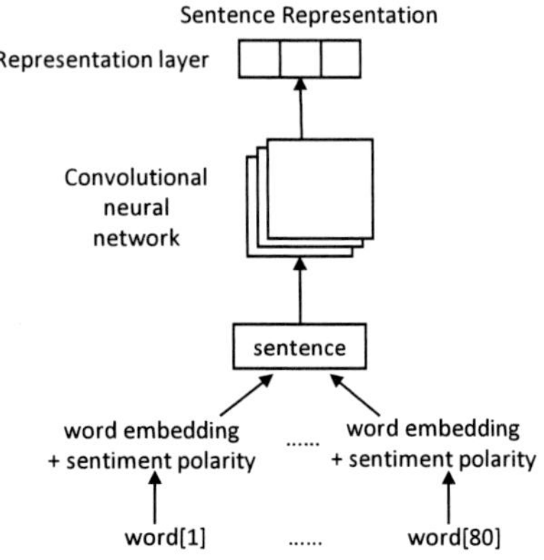

Figure 2: The representation of the sentence obtained by the convolutional neural network.

Word Embeddings. We first map each word to a word embedding, which is a dense distributed vector. Since the dataset of this task is relatively small, we hope the word embeddings can improve generalization. The word embeddings we used were pre-trained and released by Huang et al. (2012).

Sentiment Polarity of Words. We expect that there are relations between the claim, the reason and the warrant. For example, they may have the same sentiment polarity, while there may be polarity conflicts when involving a false warrant.

Therefore, we use the sentiment polarity of words as a kind of common sense knowledge. The negative words and positive words come from the dictionary provided by Hu and Liu (2004). The polarity representation of each word is a two dimensional vector. A positive word is represented as $[1, 0]$ and a negative word is represented as $[0, 1]$. The representation of out-of dictionary words is $[0, 0]$.

We concatenate the word embedding and sentiment polarity representation together as the final representation of a word.

Convolutional Neural Networks. The word embeddings are feed into a convolutional neural network (CNN) to get the representation of a sentence. We mainly follow the architecture of Kim (2014), which reports excellent performance for several sentence classification tasks. The dimension of word embeddings is k and the sentence length is fixed. A sentence s consisting of n words can be represented as the concatenation of the embeddings of the n words:

$$s = \vec{e}_1 \oplus \vec{e}_2 \oplus \cdots \oplus \vec{e}_n, \tag{1}$$

where $\vec{e}_i$ is the k-dimensional word vector of the i_{th} word. A convolution operation involves a filter $\mathbf{w} \in R^{h,k}$, which is applied to a window of h words to produce a new feature a_i:

$$a_i = f(\mathbf{w} \cdot s_{i:i+h-1} + b), \tag{2}$$

where f is a non-linear activation function, which is set to Relu (Nair and Hinton, 2010) and b is a bias term. The feature map $\mathbf{a}$ can be represented as

$$\mathbf{a} = [a_1, a_2, \cdots, a_{n-h+1}]. \tag{3}$$

Then a max-pooling operation is applied to the resulted feature map to get the sentence representation.

In experiments, $k = 52$, $h = 3$, and we used 64 filters. A dropout layer is added after the word embedding layer with a probability 0.25. The representations of the claim, reason and warrant candidates are all learned in this way.

2.1.2 Pseudo Claim Representation

We assume that the claim is a semantic composition of a reason and a warrant. Therefore, we use a composition operator to combine the representations of the reason and a warrant candidate to get the representation of a *pseudo* claim, noted as C_0 and C_1 respectively.

We have tried four composition operators: ADD, INNERPRODUCT, CONCATENATION and FULLYCONNECTEDNETWORK. In experiments, ADD performs best.

2.1.3 Prediction

Finally, we connect the representations of C, C_0 and C_1 to fully connect layers and concatenate them into one representation. And we connect the representation to the output layer through a non-linear transformation layer (Relu). The output is expected to be 1 if W_1 is right and expected to be 0 if W_0 is right. In experiments, we permuted the order of W_0 and W_1 to enlarge the training dataset.

2.2 Model2: Isolation Model

We consider a more general setting: Given the claim and reason of argument, determine whether a warrant candidate can support the argumentation. As shown in Figure 3, Model2 is just a simplification of Model1. It processes one warrant candidate individually. The output indicates whether the given warrant candidate is right.

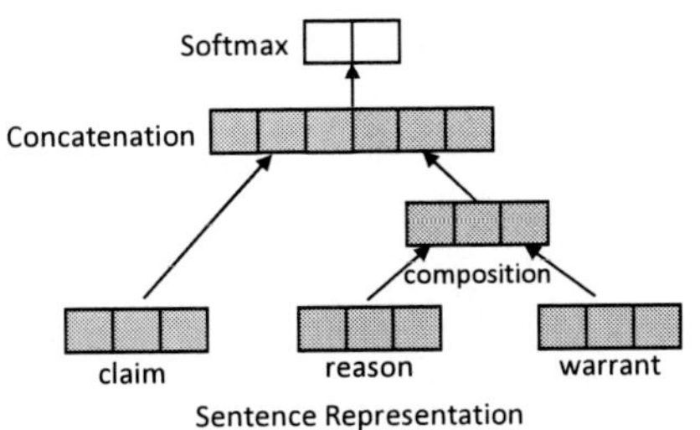

Figure 3: The architecture of Model2: Isolation Model.

For W_0 and W_1, we can get their corresponding probability $p(1|W_0)$ and $p(1|W_1)$. We choose the one with a higher probability as the predicted right warrant for the task.

2.3 Ensemble Model

We have already described the two proposed models. For each model, we trained several times with different initialization parameters. Finally, we chose 3 models from Model1 and 3 models from Model2, which performed well on the development dataset. We used the prediction probabilities of the 6 models as features and trained a random forest classifier for ensemble (Pal, 2005).

3 Evaluation

We conducted experiments on the official datasets of SemEval-2018 Task 12. The model parameters are trained using the training dataset and tuned based on the performance of development dataset. We will report the results on both development dataset and test dataset. Accuracy is the official evaluation metric. We also report precision, recall and F_1 score.

We are interested in two research questions:

- RQ1: Which proposed model is more effective?

- RQ2: Whether incorporating sentiment polarity can benefit this task?

3.1 Results on Development Dataset

Table 1 shows the results on the development dataset. The accuracy of the random baseline is 0.503. The proposed models significantly outperform the baseline.

By adding sentiment polarity representations, Model1 and Model2 both improve a lot. The accuracy of Model1 increases 3.16%, while the accuracy of Model2 increases 2.43%. The precision, recall and F_1 score all have the same trend. With the sentiment polarity added, the Model1 performs better than Model2. Without the sentiment polarity, their performance is very close.

3.2 Results on Test Dataset

Table 2 shows the results on test dataset. The random baseline submitted by task organizer is 0.527. The accuracy of the ensemble model is 0.57, which outperforms the random baseline by 4.3%. After the task organizer released the gold test dataset, we predicted it again using the ensemble model and the accuracy is 0.5811.

Similar to the results on development dataset, with the sentiment polarity added, both Model1 and Model2 achieve a better performance. We can see that on test dataset, Model1 outperforms Model2 no matter using or removing sentiment polarity representations. When using sentiment polarity, the performance difference is larger.

3.3 Discussion

From the experimental results on the development dataset and the test dataset, we can see that sentiment polarity is always useful for distinguishing the correct warrant from the false one. Model1 performs slightly better than Model2. It is reasonable since Model1 considers richer information than Model2. But Model2 actually is a more general model. With sentiment polarity added, the advantage of Model1 is amplified. This also indicates the usefulness of sentiment polarity of words.

The model performance is better on the development dataset than on the test dataset. The proposed models may still suffer the overfitting problem, since the training dataset is not very large.

4 Conclusion

In this paper we presented our system that participated in the SemEval-2018 Task 12: Argument Reasoning Comprehension. Our assumption is

Model	Precision	Recall	F_1 score	Accuracy
Random Baseline	-	-	-	0.503
Model1	0.6380 ± 0.018	0.6276 ± 0.010	0.6216 ± 0.010	0.6276 ± 0.010
w/o polarity	0.5982 ± 0.007	0.5960 ± 0.006	0.5932 ± 0.005	0.5960 ± 0.006
Model2	0.6244 ± 0.013	0.6203 ± 0.016	0.6157 ± 0.019	0.6203 ± 0.016
w/o polarity	0.5968 ± 0.018	0.5960 ± 0.017	0.5946 ± 0.017	0.5960 ± 0.017

Table 1: Results on the development dataset and w/o polarity means sentiment polarity representations of words are removed.

Model	Precision	Recall	F_1 score	Accuracy
Random Baseline	-	-	-	0.527
Model1	0.5457 ± 0.013	0.5420 ± 0.013	0.5347 ± 0.007	0.5420 ± 0.013
w/o polarity	0.5381 ± 0.009	0.5338 ± 0.011	0.5277 ± 0.010	0.5338 ± 0.011
Model2	0.5392 ± 0.019	0.5338 ± 0.021	0.5263 ± 0.028	0.5338 ± 0.021
w/o polarity	0.5340 ± 0.016	0.5285 ± 0.018	0.5227 ± 0.022	0.5285 ± 0.018
Ensemble	**0.5806**	**0.5811**	**0.5805**	**0.5811**

Table 2: Results on the test dataset and w/o polarity means sentiment polarity representations of words are removed.

that the semantic composition of the reason and the warrant should be close to the semantic representation of the corresponding claim. We proposed two neural networks based models: a competitive model that knows two warrant candidates and an isolation model that only considers one candidate for classification. In particular, we incorporated sentiment polarity of words into the models. The experimental results demonstrate that incorporating sentiment polarity of words always improves the performance. The competitive model is slightly better than the isolation model. All proposed models outperform the random baseline by a large margin.

Acknowledgements

The research work is funded by the National Natural Science Foundation of China (No.61402304), Beijing Municipal Education Commission (K-M201610028015, Connotation Development) and Beijing Advanced Innovation Center for Imaging Technology.

References

Ivan Habernal, Henning Wachsmuth, Iryna Gurevych, and Benno Stein. 2017. The argument reasoning comprehension task.

Minqing Hu and Bing Liu. 2004. Mining and summarizing customer reviews. In *Tenth ACM SIGKDD International Conference on Knowledge Discovery and Data Mining, Seattle, Washington, Usa, August,* pages 168–177.

Eric H. Huang, Richard Socher, Christopher D. Manning, and Andrew Y. Ng. 2012. Improving word representations via global context and multiple word prototypes. In *Meeting of the Association for Computational Linguistics: Long Papers,* pages 873–882.

Yoon Kim. 2014. Convolutional neural networks for sentence classification. In *Proceedings of the 2014 Conference on Empirical Methods in Natural Language Processing (EMNLP),* pages 1746–1751.

Bill Maccartney and Christopher D. Manning. 2008. Modeling semantic containment and exclusion in natural language inference. In *International Conference on Computational Linguistics,* pages 521–528.

Vinod Nair and Geoffrey E. Hinton. 2010. Rectified linear units improve restricted boltzmann machines. In *International Conference on International Conference on Machine Learning,* pages 807–814.

Susan E. Newman and Catherine C. Marshall. 1992. Pushing toulmin too far: Learning from an argument representation scheme. *Xerox Parc Tech Rpt Ssl.*

M. Pal. 2005. Random forest classifier for remote sensing classification. *International Journal of Remote Sensing,* 26(1):217–222.

Index

Association for Computational Linguistics
209 N. Eighth Street
Stroudsburg, Pennsylvania 18360

ISBN 978-1-5108-6353-8